Thorndike Century Junior Dictionary

by

E. L. Thorndike

Revised Edition

Scott, Foresman and Company

Chicago Atlanta Dallas New York

Contents

Editorial Advisory Committee

Advisory Committee on Pronunciation

To the Pupil

This book has been written for you, to help you learn the meanings, spelling, and pronunciation of words. If you find anything in it which is not helpful, I shall be glad if you will write and tell me. To make the book easier to use there are a number of simple explanations on pages xi, xii, xiii, xiv, xv, xvi, xvii, xviii, and xix.

E. L. Thorndike

To the Teacher

The ideal dictionary for a young learner is a book which will help him learn the meaning of any word that he needs to understand, the spelling of any word that he needs to write, and the pronunciation of any word that he needs to speak. It will give him the help that he needs when he needs it, with a minimum of eyestrain and fatigue. It will give him a maximum of knowledge and skill and power for reading, writing, and speaking for every minute that he spends. It will fit him in due time to make proper use of a dictionary for adults.

To make a dictionary that comes near to this ideal requires not only adequate knowledge of the English language, but also expert scientific knowledge of children's minds, and of their needs in reading, hearing, and using words. It also requires ingenuity and thoughtfulness for every detail about every word.

The Selection of Words and Meanings

The selection of words is based on counts of the actual occurrences of words in reading matter. These counts enable me to attach to each word a number showing its importance as measured by frequency and range of occurrence. The numbers 1 to 20 stand for the first twenty successive thousands. Some words within these limits are excluded because they are proper names well known to all, such as Smith or Jones, or because they are of little importance to children.

Some adverbs in *ly*, and some words derived from proper names by the addition of *n*, such as Australian, were counted in with the words from which they were derived, and so have no numbers attached to them.

The count used in the first edition was the Thorndike count of ten million words. Since then I have made a count of occurrences of all words (save 2,500 of the commonest) in each of 120 books from the Terman-Lima list of juvenile books, using only the first 40,000 words in the case of books more than 40,000 words long. Dr. Irving Lorge has made a count of over 4½ million words in current magazines. Dr. Lorge and I have also made a semantic count of nearly five million words in representative reading. This semantic count, giving the frequency of each meaning of a word, has been of great value in selecting the meanings to be defined. There is thus available now a total count of about twenty-five million instead of ten million as a guide. Various smaller counts made by others have also been studied. The selection of entries and meanings consequently has been improved in this edition.

Teaching the Meaning of Words

I have not been satisfied to abbreviate and adapt definitions made originally for adults, and for adults of much ability and knowledge. Definitions are not like clothes that can be cut down and made to fit. What has a clear and correct meaning to a well-informed adult may confuse and mislead a child. I therefore frame my definitions directly to meet the needs of children. I make great use of illustrative sentences containing the word. I use pictures when pictures can teach the child what he needs to know better than words can. The illustrative sentences and pictures are chosen or made with the same unfailing consideration of the young learner's needs as is given to the definitions.

Since the first edition appeared, I have made investigations, some of which are reported in two monographs, *Studies in the Psychology of Language* (1938) and *The Teaching of English Suffixes* (1942), which have enabled me to improve the dictionary, especially the treatment of derivatives and compounds. Every definition and every illustrative sentence or phrase has been inspected to see if it could be made to fit the learner's needs better. By sufficient labor and ingenuity many improvements of this sort have been made. The enlarged page has made possible the addition of many pictures and sentences illustrating the meanings and uses of words.

The general arrangement is in one single alphabetical list, obviously the simplest and best for a beginner.

The arrangement and spacing of the material for each word is such as will help children to find what they need to know. No uniform rigid system is followed. Arranging the different meanings of a word always in the sequence of their historical development, or according to grammatical categories, does very little good for children and may do much harm. For them the proper principles of arrangement are: literal uses before figurative, general uses before special, common uses before rare, and easily understandable uses before difficult. Each of these principles is subject to the limitation "other things being equal," and all are subject to the principle that that arrangement is best for any word which helps the learner most.

Teaching the Spelling of Words

A dictionary is a great aid in spelling if two conditions are met, namely, if the person knows the first three or four letters of the word in question and its general sound, and if the dictionary presents the word conveniently with a suitable description by definition, illustrative sentence, or picture, so that the person can easily find among the words beginning with those letters the one he wants, and can easily be sure that it is the one he wants.

The use of a dictionary in spelling makes it desirable to include and define certain derivatives whose spelling children may need to find in the dictionary, each in its proper alphabetical place, such as *brought, done,* or *knew.* It is not sufficient to tell a child who wants to know how to spell *done* that **don** is *to put on* and **done** is the *pp. of do.* For the same reason certain proper names, abbreviations, and contractions which some dictionaries omit or hide are included in regular order in our list. Each word is printed with thin spacings, which separate the syllables without unduly decreasing the resemblance of the word in the dictionary to the word as it appears in reading. As a result of these procedures, many children who have been unable to use a dictionary profitably in learning to spell, will now be able to do so.

Teaching the Pronunciation of Words

I use the system of diacritical marks and the pronunciation key devised by the committee of scholars who coöperated in the THORNDIKE-CENTURY SENIOR DICTIONARY, and who now cöoperate in this revision of the JUNIOR DICTIONARY. This system of representing English sounds is adequate, usable, and easy to learn and remember. I do not present all the permissible pronunciations of all words, but rather the one pronunciation chosen by the committee as common among educated people in the United States. This does not mean that users of the Dictionary should think that all other pronunciations are not acceptable. Some may be equally satisfactory, or even, in certain localities, preferable. For certain words, where it is helpful to pupils to have them, two pronunciations are given if both are commonly used.

The pronunciations given are for fluent speech, that is, for normal speech at a conversational rate of speed. A pupil who is slowly pronouncing a word syllable by syllable with accents on each syllable in order to learn its constituent parts or its spelling may properly replace the sound of ə by the more specific sound which the a or e or i or o or u would have if it were accented, and may replace the sound of i by that of ē in words like *detain*, *presume*, and *receive*.

Preparing Children to Use an Adult or "Big" Dictionary

The most important elements in preparation to use a regular dictionary for adults are willingness and interest. If his experiences with his first dictionary have been profitable and interesting, so that he looks upon a dictionary as a help and a saver of time and of trouble, a child will readily make the transfer to the use of the more elaborate and intricate and difficult book when the proper time comes. The dryness, the incomprehensibility, and the lack of illustrative sentences of the ordinary elementary dictionary too often prejudice children against the name and the thing in general.

Protection against Eyestrain

The hygienic aspect is important in any book for children, and especially in a dictionary. The work done by the eye in looking for a word and in reading definitions or illustrative sentences is much harder than work for the same length of time in ordinary reading, even if the type is equally large and clear. If the type or spacing is too small, the task may become absolute cruelty. The size and style of type, the spacing, and the arrangement on the page in use in the THORNDIKE-CENTURY JUNIOR DICTIONARY will be approved by all thoughtful teachers and parents. The type used in this book is especially suitable for use in narrow columns.

We have spared neither time nor trouble to make this dictionary efficient as a wordbook for boys and girls. The fundamental principles and the psychology and pedagogy by which these are applied are sound. Twenty-seven thousand words, each to be treated in the most useful way for boys and girls from 10 to 15, are, however, twenty-seven thousand separate problems, often subtle and many-sided. I cannot hope to have solved every one of them in the best possible manner. Where I have made errors by inadvertence or by insufficient ingenuity or by a failure to realize some difficulty for the young learner, or otherwise, I shall be glad to be informed.

Acknowledgments

A dictionary requires the coöperation of many people. The author is glad to acknowledge the expert assistance of Professor M. T. Whitley of Teachers College, Dr. Laura Kennon of Brooklyn College, Miss Mildred Thorndike, formerly of Evander Childs High School, and Miss Margaret V. Cobb. He also appreciates the skillful coöperation of Miss Martha Colley, Miss Nellie Starkson, Mr. Raymond E. Craig, Mr. Warner Sallman, and Mr. George White, general artists, Mr. R. J. Rice and Mr. Leon Pray, special artists for animals, and Miss Helen Snyder, special artist for plants. Thanks are due Professor George Watson, of the University of Chicago, formerly Associate Editor of the *Dictionary of American English*, for his careful reading of the manuscript. The scholarship and wisdom of the editors of the *New Century Dictionary* have been a safe guide throughout.

In this revised edition I have received valuable help from the two advisory committees, directly and through their work on the THORNDIKE-CENTURY SENIOR DICTIONARY.

E. L. Thorndike

Notes on the Use of the Dictionary

Guide Words

The words on any page are shown by the two words printed separately at the top. Thus, words from **a** to **abdication** are on page 1; words from **abdomen** to **aboriginal** are on page 2; etc.

Different Words with the Same Spelling

Sometimes there are two or more really different words which have the same spelling. Thus the word **bear** meaning to carry, and the word **bear** meaning an animal are really different words. All such words are printed and defined separately. They are marked [1] and [2]. Thus: **bear**[1], **bear**[2]. If you do not find the definition you need under **bear**[1], be sure to look through **bear**[2] for it.

bear[1] (bãr), 1. carry. It takes two men to bear that stone. That board is too thin to bear your weight. 2. endure. He cannot bear any more pain. 3. have an effect on; relate to. This story does not bear on the question. 4. bring forth; produce. This tree bears fine apples. 5. press; thrust; drive. Don't bear down so hard. *v., bore, borne* or *born, bearing. 1.*

bear[2] (bãr), 1. a large, clumsy animal with coarse hair and a very short tail. 2. gruff or surly person. 3. person who tries to lower prices in the stock market. *n.*

American black bear
(4½ ft. long; 3 ft. tall)

Pronunciation

The pronunciation of each word is shown immediately after it. Thus, **Aar on** (ãr′ən). A full key to the letters and marks which show how to pronounce the words is printed in the front and back of the book and on page xx. A short key is printed at the bottom of each right-hand page.

Regular users will very soon know the pronunciation symbols and will not need to look them up. Outside of the very frequent so-called short and long sounds (as in hat, let, it, hot, cup; āge, ēqual, īce, ōpen, ūse) there are only eight symbols for the user to learn: ã, ä, ėr, ô, ᴛʜ, ů, ü, and ə. The last symbol, ə, is called a schwa and is used to denote the neutral sound of a vowel in an unaccented syllable. It is the sound of *a* in about, *e* in taken, *i* in pencil, *o* in lemon, and *u* in circus. The use of only one symbol for this sound is the approved practice of modern phonetics.

If some meanings of a word have a pronunciation different from that of other meanings of the same word, the numbers of the definitions to which each pronunciation applies are given. Thus, in the example below, the pronunciation for definitions 1 and 2 is ab strakt′ while the pronunciation for definitions 3, 4, 5, and 6 is ab′strakt.

ab stract (ab strakt′ for 1 and 2, ab′strakt for 3, 4, 5, and 6), 1. take away. Can you abstract the watch from my pocket without my knowing it? 2. think of (a quality, such as goodness, redness, weight, beauty, or truth) apart from any real thing that has the quality. 3. thought of apart from any real thing. 4. **In the abstract** means in theory rather than in practice. In the abstract, we approve of the Golden Rule, "Do unto others as you would have them do unto you," but we do not always follow it. 5. hard to understand; difficult. 6. a brief statement of the main ideas or points in an article or a book or a case in court. *v., adj., n. 8.*

Meanings

If a word has more than one meaning, the different meanings of a word are numbered.

a bate (ə bāt′), 1. become less. The storm has abated. 2. make less. The medicine abated his pain. 3. do away with; put an end to; stop. We can abate the smoke nuisance by burning oil. *v. 6.*

Rare, archaic, or obsolete meanings, and slang uses are given only if they are important in children's literature.

gyve (jīv), 1. a fetter, especially for the leg. 2. to fetter. *n., v.* [*Old use*] *15.*

Special meanings that a word has in certain phrases are sometimes given. For example, after the five ordinary meanings of **account**, there are four special meanings:—

> **account for,** 1. tell what has been done with; answer for. The treasurer of a club has to account for the money paid to him. 2. give a reason. Late frosts accounted for the poor fruit crop.
> **of no account,** of no use or importance.
> **on no account,** under no conditions; certainly not.
> **turn to account,** make useful or helpful.
> *n., v. 1.*

If a word ends in *ed, er, est, ing, less, like, ly,* or *ness,* and is not in the dictionary, you can learn what it means by finding the word it is made from. For example, *acidless, acacialike,* and *abortiveness* are not in this dictionary, but their meanings can be learned from the meanings of *acid, acacia,* and *abortive,* by using the facts about *-less, -like,* and *-ness* given in this dictionary. See the inside cover page under WORDS MADE FROM OTHER WORDS.

Abbreviations Used

After the statement of a word's meaning there is a word or abbreviation like *adj., adv., n.* in italic type, which tells what part of speech the word is. The abbreviations used are as follows:

adj.	adjective	*ppr.*	present participle
adv.	adverb	*prep.*	preposition
conj.	conjunction	*pron.*	pronoun
interj.	interjection	*pt.*	past tense; preterit
n.	noun	*sing.*	singular
pl.	plural	*v.*	verb
pp.	past participle		

Word Frequency

Last of all there is a number which tells how widely used the word is. *1* means that the word is one of the thousand most widely used words; *2* means that the word is one of the next most widely used thousand; *3* means that the word is in the third thousand; and so on to *20* for the twentieth thousand. Words less widely used than this have no number. That is, if there is no number, the word is not one of the most widely used twenty thousand. For a word with different meanings, this number tells the importance of all the meanings together.

The meanings of the numbers 1 to 20 in terms of occurrences per million words are approximately as follows:

Successive Thousands	Number of occurrences of each word per million words
1	100 or more
2	55 to 99
3	35 to 54
4	27
5	20
6	15
7	12
8	9
9	6
10	4
11	3½
12	3+
13	2⅔
14	2⅓
15	2
16	1¾
17	1½
18	1¼
19	a little over 1 per million
20	a little under 1 per million

A word numbered 10 will thus on the average occur twice as often as one numbered 15; a word numbered 15 will on the average occur twice as often as one numbered 20. Whenever there is need to know how often a word is used in print, these numbers are the best guide now available.

Forms of Words

This dictionary gives, in italic type after the statement of a word's meaning or meanings, all information that a pupil needs about whether the word is a noun, a verb, a pronoun, etc., and about plurals, past tenses, participles, comparatives, and superlatives. For example, after the definition of **ox**, there is, in italic, *n., pl. oxen.* After the definitions of **run,** there is *v., ran, run, running, n.* After the definitions of **good**, there is *adj., better, best, n.*

If there is nothing in italic type about such forms of the word, they are formed regularly according to the following rules:—

I. Plurals of nouns. Add *s* unless the word ends in *ch, sh, s, x,* or *z.* If it ends in *ch, sh, s, x,* or *z,* add *es.*

II. Past tense and past participle of a verb. Add *ed.* If the verb itself ends in *e,* drop that *e* and add *ed.*

III. Present participle of a verb. Add *ing.* If the verb itself ends in *e,* drop that *e* and add *ing.*

IV. Present tense, third person singular of a verb. Add *s* unless the verb itself ends in *y* preceded by a consonant. If it does, use *ies* instead of *ys,* as in *He carries, She glories, It varies.*

V. Comparatives of adjectives. Add *er.* If the adjective ends in *e,* drop that *e* and add *er.* Or use *more* before the adjective.

VI. Comparatives of adverbs. Use *more* before the adverb.

VII. Superlatives of adjectives. Add *est.* If the adjective ends in *e,* drop that *e* and add *est.* Or use *most* before the adjective.

VIII. Superlatives of adverbs. Use *most* before the adverb.

Forms that follow these rules are given if it is useful for the pupil to note them. For example, *monkeys, solos, traveled, traveling, taxied, taxiing, booed,* and *booing* are given in italic type, though they follow the rules.

Restrictions of Usage

Certain words, or certain meanings of words, have phrases following them to show how, when, or where they are used.

Old use. A word or meaning not much used at the present time, though it may be found in old stories or stories about the past, is marked in this way.

> **ween** (wēn), think; suppose; believe; expect. *v. [Old use] 15.*

Not used now. A word or meaning not used at all at the present time is marked *not used now.*

> **strain**[1] (strān), ... 8. force; compel. *Not used now.* . . . . *v., n. 3.*

Used in poetry. A word or meaning used in poems but not in ordinary talking or writing is so marked.

a weary (ə wēr′i), weary; tired. *adj.* [*Used in poetry*] *20.*

Used familiarly. A word or meaning used in speaking to or about a person or thing one is well acquainted with is so marked.

dad (dad), father. *n.* [*Used familiarly*] *12.*

Used in common talk. A word or meaning used in everyday speech but not in formal talking or writing is marked in this way.

stuck-up (stuk′up′), too proud; conceited; haughty. *adj.* [*Used in common talk*]

Slang. A word, or a meaning of a word, not accepted as good English by writers and speakers at the present time, is marked *slang.*

bum (bum), 1. good-for-nothing person; drunken loafer. 2. to loaf. 3. to drink heavily. 4. a spree. 5. of poor quality; no good. *n., v., bummed, bumming, adj.* [*Slang*] *14.*

Trade name. A word or meaning that is registered by some business firm to prevent illegal use of it is so marked.

ko dak (kō′dak), 1. a kind of camera with rolls of film on which photographs are taken. *Trade name.* 2. take photographs with a kodak. *n., v. 11.*

English means used in England; *Scottish,* used in Scotland; *British,* used throughout the British Empire.

bairn (bãrn), child. *n.* [*Scottish*] *19.*

If the restriction refers to all the meanings of a word, it is put at the end after all the meanings and the grammatical material and enclosed in brackets.

boost (büst), 1. a push or shove that helps a person in rising or advancing. 2. to lift or push from below or behind. *n., v.* [*Used in common talk*] *13.*

If it refers only to one meaning of a word, it is put after the definition and examples to which it applies and is not enclosed in brackets.

grit ty (grit′i), 1. containing grit; like grit; sandy. 2. courageous; plucky. *Used in common talk. adj., grittier, grittiest.*

Cross References

Sometimes reference is made from one word to another to give additional help or information. For example, at the end of the definition of **brisket,** we find "See the diagram under **beef.**" On this diagram the part called **brisket** is labeled.

Irregular forms of words, usually verbs and nouns, have a cross reference to the word to which they belong. Under **wrote** is the reference "See **write.**" **Write** gives all of the extra help needed.

Variant Spellings

If two variant spellings whose initial spellings place them far apart are commonly used, they are fully defined under each entry and cross reference is made from one spelling to the other.

> **en close** (en klōz′), 1. shut in on all sides; surround. 2. put a wall or fence around. 3. put in an envelope along with a letter. 4. contain; as, a letter enclosing a check. *v. 3.* Also spelled **inclose.**
>
> **in close** (in klōz′), 1. shut in on all sides; surround. 2. put a wall or fence around. 3. put in an envelope along with a letter. 4. contain; as, a letter inclosing a check. *v. 4.* Also spelled **enclose.**

If one of the variants is very much less common than the other, the commoner spelling is used to define the rarer.

> **in quir y** (in kwīr′i), 1. act of inquiring; asking. 2. a search for truth, information, or knowledge. 3. a question. *n., pl. inquiries. 5.*
>
> **en quir y** (en kwīr′i), inquiry. *n., pl. enquiries. 18.*

If the spellings occur fairly close together, so that cross reference is easy, the commoner spelling is used to define the other.

> **de fense** (di fens′), 1. any thing, act, or word that defends, guards, or protects. A wall around a city was a defense against enemies. A well-built house or a warm coat is a defense against cold weather. 2. defending; being defended. *n. 3.*
>
> **de fence** (di fens′), defense. *n.*

If the spellings occur very close together with only one definition or set of definitions, the spellings are entered together.

> **adz** or **adze** (adz), tool somewhat like an ax. The blade is set across the end of the handle and curves inward. *n. 13.*

Combinations of Words

There are some combinations of words whose meanings cannot be made out from the meanings of the separate words. For example, knowledge of what *air* and *pocket* mean does not make clear that *air pocket* means "a current or condition in the air that causes an airplane to drop suddenly." Knowledge of what *turn, to,* and *account* mean does not make clear that *turn to account* means "make useful or helpful."

When any combination of words is very puzzling, though you know what each word means, look up the combination of words, to find what the words mean when taken together. For example, you will find **air pocket** between **airplane** and **airport** on page 18. You will find **bay rum** between **Bayreuth** and **bay window** on page 66. You will find **turn to account** after **account** on page 7. You will find **beat a retreat** after **beat** on page 67. If you did not find it there, you would look under **retreat.**

No school dictionary can include all the combinations of words that might puzzle some pupils. This dictionary gives those that occur in many books and might puzzle many pupils.

The Writing of Compounds

There is a great diversity in methods of writing and printing compounds. Some authors and publishers employ a system in which compound nouns are frequently hyphenated (*e.g., mountain-range, waiting-room*) while others limit the use of hyphens largely to compound adjectives (*e.g., deep-seated*) and verbs (*e.g., dry-clean*). There is no one system that is right, all others being wrong. The use of hyphens for nouns is often determined by whether the author feels the phrase to be a unit of meaning or not. This is not a satisfactory criterion, since the writing of compounds is affected by usage, by the length of the parts of a compound, etc. In this dictionary, word stress combined with certain purely formal considerations is used to decide the question of whether a word is or is not hyphenated.

The principal difference between a compound and a phrase is a difference of accentuation. The compound has only one primary word stress, the phrase more than one. A form with one primary accent (a compound) is written as one word (*gre´enhouse*), while a phrase with two or more primary accents is written as two or more words (*a gre´en ho´use*). In some cases usage demands that a phrase be written as one word, either solid or hyphenated (*aíde-de-cámp*), or that a compound be written as two words (*sítting room*). We conform to usage when it is well established. In general, compound nouns are written solid (*e.g.*, *textbook, classroom*), not hyphenated (except where usage demands a hyphen). Compound adjectives and verbs are written either solid or hyphenated. A compound adjective or verb derived from a phrase is usually hyphenated (*easy-going, cross-examine*). A compound adjective with one primary accent is usually written solid (*scátterbrained*), while one with two primary accents is usually hyphenated (*fírst-cláss*).

Full Pronunciation Key

The pronunciation of each word is shown just after the word, in this way: **ab bre vi ate** (ə brē′vi āt). The letters and signs used are pronounced as in the words below. The mark ′ is placed after a syllable with primary or strong accent, as in the example above. The mark ′ after a syllable shows a secondary or lighter accent, as in **ab bre vi a tion** (ə brē′vi ā′shən).

a	hat, cap	j	jam, enjoy	u	cup, butter
ā	age, face	k	kind, seek	u̇	full, put
ã	care, air	l	land, coal	ü	rule, move
ä	father, far	m	me, am	ū	use, music
		n	no, in		
b	bad, rob	ng	long, bring	v	very, save
ch	child, much	o	hot, rock	w	will, woman
d	did, red	ō	open, go	y	you, yet
		ô	order, all	z	zero, breeze
e	let, best	oi	oil, voice	zh	measure, seizure
ē	equal, see	ou	house, out		
ėr	term, learn				
		p	paper, cup	ə	represents:
f	fat, if	r	run, try		a in about
g	go, bag	s	say, yes		e in taken
h	he, how	sh	she, rush		i in pencil
		t	tell, it		o in lemon
i	it, pin	th	thin, both		u in circus
ī	ice, five	ᴛʜ	then, smooth		

Thorndike Century Junior Dictionary

A Child's Dictionary of the English Language

A, a (ā), the first letter of the alphabet. There are two a's in afraid. *n., pl. A's, a's.*

a (ā, *unstressed* ə), 1. Is there a pencil in the box? 2. Christmas comes once a year. This blue cloth costs ten cents a yard. *indefinite article. 1.*

a., acre; acres.

A 1 (ā′wun′), first-class.

Aar on (ãr′ən), the brother of Moses, and the first high priest of the Hebrews. *n. 9.*

a back (ə bak′), 1. toward the back; backward. 2. **Taken aback** means suddenly surprised. *adv. 15.*

a baft (ə baft′), 1. back of; behind. 2. at the stern; toward the stern. *prep., adv.*

a ban don (ə ban′dən), 1. give up entirely. 2. desert, forsake, or leave (any place, person, or thing) without intending to return. He abandoned his farm and went to sea. A good mother will not abandon her baby. 3. an unthinking, careless freedom of action; letting oneself go; carefree manner. The girls jumped up and down and waved their arms with abandon. *v., n. 4.*

a ban doned (ə ban′dənd), 1. deserted; forsaken. 2. very bad; wicked; immoral. *adj.*

a ban don ment (ə ban′dən mənt), 1. abandoning. 2. being abandoned. 3. freedom from restraint; lack of self-control; abandon. *n. 15.*

a base (ə bās′), bring down; make lower; make humble; degrade. A man who betrays a friend abases himself. *v. 12.*

a base ment (ə bās′mənt), humiliation; lowering or loss of self-respect; degradation. *n. 17.*

a bashed (ə basht′), embarrassed and confused; uneasy and somewhat ashamed. When the little boy saw the room filled with strangers, he was much abashed. *adj. 11.*

a bate (ə bāt′), 1. become less. The storm has abated. 2. make less. The medicine abated his pain. 3. do away with; put an end to; stop. We can abate the smoke nuisance by burning oil. *v. 6.*

a bate ment (ə bāt′mənt), lessening; decrease; reduction. *n. 15.*

ab bé (ab′ā), 1. a title used in France for any clergyman, especially a priest. 2. abbot. *n. 17.*

ab bess (ab′is), woman who is the head of an abbey of nuns. *n. 12.*

ab bey (ab′i), 1. the building or buildings where monks or nuns live a religious life ruled by an abbot or abbess; a monastery or convent. 2. the monks or nuns living there. 3. a church that was once an abbey or a part of it. *n., pl. abbeys. 6.*

ab bot (ab′ət), man who is the head of an abbey of monks. *n. 7.*

ab bre vi ate (ə brē′vi āt), make shorter; as, to abbreviate *hour* to *hr. v. 16.*

ab bre vi a tion (ə brē′vi ā′shən), 1. a shortened form, such as *hrs.* and *hr.* for *hours,* or *bu.* for *bushel* or *bushels.* 2. making shorter. *n. 13.*

ab di cate (ab′di kāt), give up or formally renounce; resign. The king abdicated his throne, and his brother became king. *v. 11.*

ab di ca tion (ab′di kā′shən), an abdicating; giving up an office, power, or authority; resigning. *n. 15.*

ab do men (ab′də men), 1. lower part of the human body, which contains the stomach and the intestines; belly. 2. last of the three parts of an insect's body. *n. 9.*

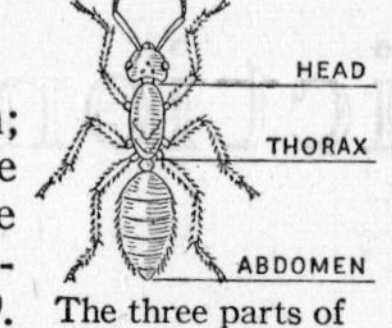

The three parts of an insect

ab dom i nal (ab dom′i-nəl), of the abdomen; in the abdomen; for the abdomen. Bending the body exercises the abdominal muscles. *adj. 9.*

ab duct (ab dukt′), kidnap; carry off (a person) by force. *v. 19.*

ab duc tion (ab duk′shən), kidnaping; carrying off a person by force; as, the abduction of a little child. *n.*

a beam (ə bēm′), 1. directly opposite a ship's side. The pirates started firing when their ship was abeam of ours. 2. straight across a ship. *adv.*

a bed (ə bed′), in bed. *adv. 11.*

A bel (ā′bəl), the second son of Adam and Eve. Abel was killed by his older brother Cain. Genesis 4:1-15. *n. 12.*

Ab er deen (ab′ər dēn′), a city in eastern Scotland. *n. 11.*

ab er ra tion (ab′ər ā′shən), 1. wandering from the right course or path. 2. abnormal behavior; wandering of the mind. 3. deviation from a standard. *n. 15.*

a bet (ə bet′), encourage or help, especially in something wrong. One man did the actual stealing, but two others abetted him. *v., abetted, abetting. 17.*

a bey ance (ə bā′əns), waiting; suspended activity. If you need more information to settle a question, you should hold the question in abeyance until you have the information. *n. 15.*

ab hor (ab hôr′), shrink away from with horror; feel disgust for; hate very, very much. *v., abhorred, abhorring. 4.*

ab hor rence (ab hor′əns), horror; disgust; very great hate. Many people show abhorrence of snakes. *n. 12.*

ab hor rent (ab hor′ənt), causing horror; disgusting; hateful. *adj. 14.*

a bide (ə bīd′), 1. stay. 2. **Abide by** means remain faithful to. He will abide by his promise. 3. dwell; continue to live (in a place). 4. wait for. He will abide my coming. 5. endure; put up with. *v., abode, abiding. 4.*

a bid ing (ə bīd′ing), permanent; lasting. *adj.*

a bil i ty (ə bil′i ti), 1. power. A horse has ability to work. 2. skill. Washington had great ability as a general. *n., pl. abilities. 4.*

ab ject (ab′jekt), 1. wretched; miserable. 2. degraded; deserving contempt. *adj. 7.*

ab jure (ab jür′), renounce; swear to give up. Some kings ordered the Jews to abjure their religion. *v. 14.*

a blaze (ə blāz′), 1. on fire. 2. blazing. The room was all ablaze with a hundred lights. *adv., adj. 17.*

a ble (ā′bəl), 1. having power. Little children are able to walk, but they are not able to earn a living. 2. having the power or skill that is needed. She is an able teacher. *adj. 1.*

-able, suffix meaning:—

1. that can be ———ed. enjoyable = that can be enjoyed.
2. adapted for or suitable to. comfortable = adapted for comfort.
3. inclined to. peaceable = inclined to peace.

ab lu tion (ab lü′shən), washing; cleansing. *n. 15.*

a bly (ā′bli), in an able manner; with skill; well. *adv. 12.*

ab ne ga tion (ab′ni gā′shən), self-denial; giving up something. *n. 20.*

ab nor mal (ab nôr′məl), not according to rule; irregular; very different from the ordinary conditions; unusual. It is abnormal for a man to have six fingers on each hand, or to be only three feet tall, or to walk in his sleep. *adj. 9.*

a board (ə bōrd′), on board; on a ship, train, etc. *adv., prep. 4.*

a bode (ə bōd′), 1. place to live in; dwelling; house. 2. See **abide.** He abode there one year. *n., pt. and pp. of abide. 4.*

a bol ish (ə bol′ish), do away with; put an end to. *v. 5.*

ab o li tion (ab′ə lish′ən), putting an end to; abolishing. The abolition of slavery in the United States occurred in 1865. *n. 8.*

ab o li tion ist (ab′ə lish′ən ist), person who wishes to abolish something. The people who wished to put an end to slavery were called abolitionists. *n. 14.*

a bom i na ble (ə bom′i nə bəl), 1. disgusting; hateful. 2. very unpleasant; very bad. *adj. 6.*

a bom i nate (ə bom′i nāt), feel disgust for; hate very much; detest; abhor; loathe. *v.*

a bom i na tion (ə bom′i nā′shən), 1. a feeling of disgust; loathing. 2. an evil or hateful thing. *n. 9.*

ab o rig i nal (ab′ə rij′i nəl), 1. existing from the beginning; first; original. 2. of the earliest known inhabitants. The use of horses was not an aboriginal custom of the American Indians, but was introduced by Europeans. *adj. 14.*

ab o rig i nes (ab′ə rij′i nēz), the earliest known inhabitants of a country. *n. pl. 17.*

a bor tion (ə bôr′shən), 1. a birth before the proper time. 2. failure to develop properly. *n. 16.*

a bor tive (ə bôr′tiv), 1. unsuccessful; fruitless. The early attempts to make airplanes were abortive. 2. born before the proper time. 3. not developed properly. *adj. 14.*

a bound (ə bound′), 1. be plentiful. Fish abound in the ocean. 2. be well supplied; be filled. The ocean abounds with fish. *v. 5.*

a bout (ə bout′), 1. This story is about horses. 2. He has about finished his work. 3. A collar goes about the neck. Look about and tell me what you see. 4. Have you a pencil about you? 5. He is about to go. 6. You are going the wrong way. Face about. 7. Turn about is fair play. *prep., adv. 1.*

a bove (ə buv′), 1. in a higher place. 2. higher than; over. Look above the tall building to see the sun. 3. more than. 4. beyond. Go to the first house above the school. 5. too high; superior to. 6. earlier in a book or article. 7. in heaven. *adv., adj., prep. 1.*

a bove board (ə buv′bōrd′), in open sight; without tricks or concealment. *adv., adj.*

a brade (ə brād′), scrape off; wear away by rubbing. The skin on Tom's knees was abraded by his fall. *v.*

A bra ham (ā′brə ham), the ancestor of the Hebrews. Genesis 12-25. *n. 4.*

a bra sion (ə brā′zhən), 1. a place that is scraped off. Abrasions of the skin are painful. 2. a scraping off. *n.*

a breast (ə brest′), 1. side by side. The soldiers marched four abreast. 2. **Abreast of** or **abreast with** means keeping up with; not behind. *adv., adj. 11.*

a bridge (ə brij′), 1. make shorter. This long story must be abridged. 2. make less. The rights of citizens must not be abridged without proper cause. *v. 10.*

a bridg ment (ə brij′mənt), 1. an abridging; making smaller; reduction in size. 2. shortened form. *n. 14.*

a broad (ə brôd′), 1. outside one's country; in foreign lands. He is going abroad this summer to travel in France and Germany. 2. widely. The news of his coming spread abroad. 3. going around; in motion. A report is abroad that the school will close. 4. outside one's house or home. He walks abroad only at night. *adv. 3.*

ab ro gate (ab′rə gāt), repeal; cancel; do away with. A law that cars may not go more than 35 miles an hour would abrogate a law that cars may not go more than 40 miles an hour. *v. 15.*

a brupt (ə brupt′), 1. sudden. He made an abrupt turn to avoid another car. 2. short, sudden, or blunt. He was very gruff and had an abrupt way of speaking. 3. very steep. The road made an abrupt rise up the hill. *adj. 7.*

Ab sa lom (ab′sə ləm), the favorite son of David, in the Bible. *n. 14.*

ab scess (ab′ses), a collection of pus in some part of the body. An abscess usually causes a painful sore. *n. 16.*

ab scond (ab skond′), go away suddenly and secretly; go off and hide. The dishonest cashier stole money from the bank and absconded with it. *v. 20.*

ab sence (ab′səns), 1. being away; time of being away. His absence from school was caused by illness. The sailor returned after an absence of two years. 2. being without; lack. Darkness is the absence of light. *n. 3.*

ab sent (ab′sənt for 1, 3, and 4, ab sent′ for 2), 1. away; not present. Three members of the class were absent. 2. keep (oneself) away. Do not absent yourself from school without reason. 3. lacking. **Be absent** sometimes means not to be or not to exist. Snow is absent in some countries. 4. paying no attention to what is going on about one. *adj., v. 3.*

ab sen tee (ab′sən tē′), person who is away. *n. 15.*

ab sent ly (ab′sənt li), without paying attention to what is going on around one. *adv.*

ab sent-mind ed (ab′sənt mīn′did), not paying attention to what is going on about one. The absent-minded man put salt in his coffee and sugar on his egg. *adj.*

ab so lute (ab′sə lüt), 1. complete; perfect. Try to tell the absolute truth. 2. unmixed; pure. 3. real; actual. 4. positive; certain. 5. not limited in any way; independent. *adj. 2.*

ab so lute ly (ab′sə lüt li), completely; wholly. *adv. 7.*

ab so lu tion (ab′sə lü′shən), absolving; freeing from guilt and punishment for sin; forgiveness. *n. 12.*

ab solve (ab solv′), 1. declare free from sin

or blame. 2. set free from a promise or duty. *v. 6.*

ab sorb (ab sôrb′), 1. take in or suck up (liquids). A sponge absorbs water. A blotter absorbs ink. 2. take in and hold. Anything black absorbs light that falls on it; that is, none of the light is sent back to the eye. 3. take up all the attention of; interest very much. The boy was absorbed in building a dam in the brook. *v. 6.*

ab sorb ent (ab sôr′bənt), 1. taking in, or ready to take in, moisture, light, or heat. 2. any substance that takes in or sucks up moisture, light, or heat. *adj., n. 12.*

ab sorb ing (ab sôr′bing), extremely interesting; as, an absorbing story of adventure. *adj. 14.*

ab sorp tion (ab sôrp′shən), 1. absorbing; as, the absorption of ink by blotting paper. 2. being absorbed; great interest. Everybody noticed the absorption of the children in their game. *n. 7.*

ab stain (ab stān′), do without something; hold oneself back; refrain. If you abstain from eating candy and rich foods, you will not be so fat. *v. 7.*

ab ste mi ous (ab stē′mi əs), temperate; moderate; sparing. Mr. Gray was very abstemious in the use of tobacco; he smoked only two cigars a week. *adj. 17.*

ab sti nence (ab′sti nəns), act of abstaining; partly or entirely giving up certain pleasures, food, drink, etc. *n. 11.*

ab stract (ab strakt′ for 1 and 2, ab′strakt for 3, 4, 5, and 6), 1. take away. Can you abstract the watch from my pocket without my knowing it? 2. think of (a quality, such as goodness, redness, weight, beauty, or truth) apart from any real thing that has the quality. 3. thought of apart from any real thing. 4. **In the abstract** means in theory rather than in practice. In the abstract, we approve of the Golden Rule, "Do unto others as you would have them do unto you," but we do not always follow it. 5. hard to understand; difficult. 6. a brief statement of the main ideas or points in an article or a book or a case in court. *v., adj., n. 8.*

ab stract ed (ab strak′tid), lost in thought; absent-minded. *adj.*

ab strac tion (ab strak′shən), 1. taking away. After the abstraction of the juice from the orange, only a tasteless pulp was left. 2. the idea of a quality apart from the real thing that has the quality. The ideas of whiteness, roundness, bravery, and length are abstractions. 3. formation of such an idea. 4. a mere idea. A line that has no width is only an abstraction. 5. being lost in thought. In a fit of abstraction he forgot to eat. *n. 10.*

ab struse (ab strüs′), hard to understand. *adj. 16.*

ab surd (ab sėrd′), plainly not true or sensible; so contrary to reason that it is laughable; foolish; ridiculous. *adj. 6.*

ab surd i ty (ab sėr′di ti), 1. folly; being absurd. You can see the absurdity of wearing shoes on your head and hats on your feet. 2. something absurd. To say that every father has a daughter is an absurdity. *n., pl. absurdities. 9.*

a bun dance (ə bun′dəns), great plenty; full supply; a quantity that is more than enough. There was such an abundance of apples that year that many were left to rot under the trees. *n. 3.*

a bun dant (ə bun′dənt), more than enough; very plentiful. *adj. 3.*

a buse (ə būz′ for 1, 3, and 6, ə būs′ for 2, 4, 5, and 7), 1. make bad use of; use wrongly. 2. bad or wrong use. 3. treat badly. 4. bad treatment. 5. a bad practice or custom. 6. scold very severely; use harsh language to. 7. a severe scolding; harsh language. *v., n. 3.*

a bu sive (ə bū′siv), 1. abusing; treating badly. 2. containing abuse; harsh. *adj. 16.*

a but (ə but′), touch at the end; border (on); end (against). The building abuts on the sidewalk; the sidewalk abuts on the street; the street abuts against the railroad. *v., abutted, abutting. 15.*

a bys mal (ə biz′məl), too deep to be measured; bottomless. *adj.*

a byss (ə bis′), a bottomless depth; a very deep crack in the earth. *n. 6.*

Ab ys sin i a (ab′i sin′i ə), a country in eastern Africa. *n.* Also called **Ethiopia.**

a ca cia (ə kā′shə), 1. a thorny tree or shrub with finely divided leaves that grows in warm regions. There are many kinds of acacia. 2. the locust tree. *n. 14.*

Acacia (def. 1)

ac a dem ic (ak′ə dem′ik), 1. having to do with schools and school studies. 2. scholarly. 3. theoretical; not practical. *adj. 8.*

ac a dem i cal (ak′ə dem′i kəl), academic. *adj. 15.*

a cad e my (ə kad′ə mi), 1. a place for instruction. 2. a private high school. 3. school where some special subject can be studied. There are academies of medicine and painting, and military or naval academies. 4. a society to encourage literature, science, or art. *n., pl. academies. 6.*

A ca di a (ə kā′di ə), a French colony in the southeastern part of Canada, including what is now Nova Scotia. *n. 17.*

ac cede (ak sēd′), 1. give in; agree. Please accede to my request. 2. attain. The prince acceded to the throne when the king died. *v. 12.*

ac cel er ate (ak sel′ər āt), 1. go or cause to go faster; increase in speed; speed up. 2. cause to happen sooner; hasten. Sunshine, fresh air, and rest often accelerate a person's recovery from sickness. *v. 14.*

ac cel er a tion (ak sel′ər ā′shən), increase in speed; hastening. *n. 17.*

ac cel er a tor (ak sel′ər ā′tər), thing or person that increases the speed of anything. *n. 19.*

ac cent (ak′sent for 1, 2, 4, and 5, ak′sent or ak sent′ for 3 and 6), 1. the greater force or stronger tone of voice given to certain syllables or words, either to direct attention to them or to give rhythm in poetry. 2. a mark (′) written or printed to show the nature and place of the spoken force of a syllable, as in yes′ter day, to day′, to mor′row. 3. pronounce or write with an accent. 4. a peculiarity of pronouncing heard in different parts of the same country, or in the speech of a person speaking a language not his own. Hans is German and speaks English with a German accent. 5. tone. She speaks to him in tender accents. 6. mark with force; emphasize. *n., v. 4.*

ac cen tu ate (ak sen′chü āt), 1. pronounce with an accent. 2. mark with an accent. 3. emphasize. Her black hair accentuated the whiteness of her skin. *v. 13.*

ac cept (ak sept′), 1. take what is offered or given to one. 2. consent to; say yes to. 3. receive with favor; approve. 4. take as true and satisfactory. We accepted her excuse. 5. sign and agree to pay. *v. 2.*

ac cept a ble (ak sep′tə bəl), worth accepting; satisfactory; agreeable; welcome. Flowers are an acceptable gift to a sick person. *adj. 9.*

ac cept ance (ak sep′təns), 1. taking what is offered or given to one. The President's acceptance of the flowers they brought delighted the children. 2. approval. 3. taking as true and satisfactory; belief. 4. a promise to pay a bill. 5. an accepted bill. *n. 6.*

ac cep ta tion (ak′sep tā′shən), the generally accepted meaning. It is more important to know the acceptation of a word than its derivation. *n. 16.*

ac cess (ak′ses), approach to places, persons, or things. Access to mountain towns is often difficult because of bad roads. Has he access to men who could help him get work? *n. 5.*

ac ces si ble (ak ses′i bəl), 1. that can be reached. 2. easy to get at; easy to reach. A public library makes good books accessible. A telephone is put where it will be accessible. *adj. 11.*

ac ces sion (ak sesh′ən), 1. attaining. His accession to the presidency pleased his friends. 2. addition. The school was increased by the accession of forty new pupils. *n. 14.*

ac ces so ry (ak ses′ə ri), 1. something added; a finishing touch. All the accessories to her costume—gloves, stockings, handkerchiefs, and purse—were perfectly matched. 2. added; helping the general effect. His tie supplied an accessory bit of color which was very pleasing. 3. person who has helped in a crime or who has helped to hide it, or who has not reported it afterwards. 4. helping; helping to commit or hide a crime. *n., pl. accessories, adj. 10.*

ac ci dent (ak′si dənt), 1. an event not wanted, intended, or planned to happen, such as dropping a dish, a shipwreck, or the killing of a dog by an automobile. 2. chance. I cut my foot by accident. We found that the front door had been left open by accident and a thief had got in. *n. 3.*

ac ci den tal (ak′si den′təl), happening by chance. Breaking Mary's doll was purely accidental; John did not mean to do it. *adj. 7.*

ac claim (ə klām′), 1. applaud; shout welcome; show approval of. The crowd acclaimed the fireman for rescuing two crippled people from the burning house. 2. announce with signs of approval; hail. The newspapers acclaimed the fireman a hero. 3. applause; welcome. *v., n. 13.*

ac cla ma tion (ak′lə mā′shən), 1. shout of welcome; show of approval; applause. 2. oral vote. All the club members said,

"Aye," and the chairman was elected by acclamation. *n. 11.*

ac cli mate (ə klī′mit), acclimatize. *v.*

ac cli ma tize (ə klī′mə tīz), accustom to a new climate, surroundings, or conditions. *v. 20.*

ac com mo date (ə kom′ə dāt), 1. hold; have room for; lodge. This big bedroom will accommodate six beds. Can you accommodate a party of five for two weeks? 2. oblige; help out. He wanted change for a quarter, but I could not accommodate him. 3. make fit; make suitable. Your eyes can accommodate themselves to seeing objects at different distances. *v. 5.*

ac com mo dat ing (ə kom′ə dāt′ing), obliging. The man was accommodating enough to lend me a quarter. *adj. 17.*

ac com mo da tion (ə kom′ə dā′shən), 1. room; lodging for a time. This hotel has accommodations for one hundred people. 2. a help; a convenience. It will be an accommodation to me if you will meet me tomorrow instead of today. 3. loan. 4. the fitting (of something) to a purpose or situation. The accommodation of our desires to a smaller income took some time. *n. 6.*

ac com pa ni ment (ə kum′pə ni mənt), anything that goes along with something else. There may be some unpleasant accompaniments to your trip, but on the whole you will like it. She sang to a piano and violin accompaniment. *n. 11.*

ac com pa nist (ə kum′pə nist), person who plays a musical accompaniment. *n.*

ac com pa ny (ə kum′pə ni), 1. go along with. He will accompany you on your walk. The rain was accompanied by a high wind. 2. make music along with. *v., accompanied, accompanying. 2.*

ac com plice (ə kom′plis), person who shares in a crime. *n. 10.*

ac com plish (ə kom′plish), do; carry out. Did you accomplish your purpose? He can accomplish more in a day than any other boy in his class. *v. 2.*

ac com plished (ə kom′plisht), 1. done; carried out; completed. 2. expert; skilled; as, an accomplished dancer. 3. skilled in social arts and graces; as, an accomplished lady. *adj. 7.*

ac com plish ment (ə kom′plish mənt), 1. accomplishing; doing. The accomplishment of his purpose took two days. 2. a completed act or undertaking. 3. something that has been done with knowledge, skill, and ability. It was a real accomplishment to finish housecleaning in two days. 4. skill in some social art or grace. She was a girl of many accomplishments. She could play, sing well, and also sew and cook. *n. 7.*

ac compt (ə kount′), account. *n., v.* [*Old use*] *17.*

ac cord (ə kôrd′), 1. agree; be in harmony. His account of the day accords with yours. 2. agreement; harmony. Their opinion of war was in accord with his. 3. **Of one's own accord** means without being asked or without suggestion from anyone else. A boy who washes his hands of his own accord is indeed unusual. 4. give; grant. The newspapers accorded the famous explorer full praise. *v., n. 4.*

ac cord ance (ə kôr′dəns), agreement; harmony. What he did was in accordance with what he said. *n. 6.*

ac cord ing ly (ə kôr′ding li), 1. in agreement with something that has been stated. These are the rules. You can act accordingly or leave the club. 2. therefore. He was too sick to stay. Accordingly, we sent him home. *adv. 3.*

according to, 1. in agreement with. He came according to his promise. You will be ranked according to the work you do. 2. on the authority of. According to this book a tiger is really a big cat. *2.*

ac cor di on (ə kôr′di ən), 1. a musical instrument with keys, metal reeds, and a bellows. An accordion is played by forcing air through the reeds by means of the bellows. 2. with folds like the bellows of an accordion; as, a skirt with accordion pleats. *n., adj. 17.*

Girl playing an accordion

ac cost (ə kôst′), speak to first; come up and speak to. A ragged beggar accosted him, asking for money. *v. 10.*

ac count (ə kount′), 1. statement of money received and spent; record of business. Jack keeps a written account of the way he spends his money. All stores, banks, factories, etc., keep accounts. 2. statement; explanation; story. The boy gave his father an account of the ball game. 3. reason. The game was put off on account of rain. George was brought up not to lie on any account. 4. sake. Don't wait on my account. 5. consider. Solomon was accounted wise. In law, a man is accounted to be innocent until he is proved guilty. 6. Some special meanings are:

account for, 1. tell what has been done with; answer for. The treasurer of a club has to account for the money paid to him. 2. give a reason. Late frosts accounted for the poor fruit crop.

of no account, of no use or importance.

on no account, under no conditions; certainly not.

turn to account, make useful or helpful. *n., v. 1.*

ac count a ble (ə koun′tə bəl), 1. responsible. Each teacher is accountable to the principal for the progress of her class. 2. explainable. His bad temper is accountable if you remember that he had a toothache all day. *adj. 12.*

ac count ant (ə koun′tənt), 1. person who examines business accounts. 2. person who manages the keeping of business accounts. Mr. Brown was promoted from bookkeeper to assistant accountant of the firm. *n. 11.*

ac cou ter or **ac cou tre** (ə kü′tər), equip; array. Knights were accoutered in armor. *v. 16.*

ac cou ter ments or **ac cou tre ments** (ə kü′tər mənts), 1. personal equipment; outfit. 2. a soldier's equipment except his gun and clothing. The belt, blanket, and knapsack are parts of a soldier's accouterments. *n. pl.*

ac cred it (ə kred′it), 1. give authority to. The president will accredit you as his assistant. 2. send with a recommendation or credentials. John was accredited to the national meeting of Boy Scouts. 3. believe; trust. They have confidence in Mary, and anything she says will be accredited. *v. 15.*

ac crue (ə krü′), come as a growth or result. Interest will accrue to you every year from money left in a savings bank. Ability to think will accrue to you from good habits of study. *v. 12.*

ac cu mu late (ə kū′mū lāt), heap up; collect; gather. He accumulated a fortune by hard work. Dust had accumulated during the weeks she was gone. *v. 8.*

ac cu mu la tion (ə kū′mū lā′shən), 1. collection. The accumulation of useful knowlege is one result of reading. 2. material collected; mass. His accumulation of old papers filled two closets. *n. 11.*

ac cu ra cy (ak′ū rə si), exactness; correctness; being without errors or mistakes. *n. 8.*

ac cu rate (ak′ū rit), precisely correct; exactly right as the result of care or pains. You must be accurate in arithmetic. *adj. 7.*

ac curs ed (ə kėr′sid or ə kėrst′), 1. under a curse. 2. damnable; detestable; hateful. *adj. 5.*

ac curst (ə kėrst′), accursed. *adj.*

ac cu sa tion (ak′ū zā′shən), a charge of having done something wrong, of being something bad, or of having broken the law. The accusation against him was that he had stolen ten dollars from the store. *n. 6.*

ac cu sa tive (ə kū′zə tiv), 1. showing the direct object; objective. *Me, us, him,* and *them* are in the accusative case, or, as we usually say for English words, the objective case. 2. the objective case. 3. word used as an object of a verb or preposition. *adj., n. 12.*

ac cuse (ə kūz′), 1. charge with having done something wrong, being something bad, or with having broken the law. The children accused Alfred of being a telltale. The man was accused of speeding. 2. find fault with; blame. *v. 3.*

ac cus er (ə kūz′ər), person who accuses another of a fault or crime. *n. 10.*

ac cus tom (ə kus′təm), make familiar by use or habit; get used. You can accustom yourself to almost any kind of food. *v. 3.*

ac cus tomed (ə kus′təmd), 1. usual. By Monday he was back in his accustomed place. 2. **Accustomed to** means used to; in the habit of. He was accustomed to hard work. *adj. 9.*

ace (ās), 1. a playing card or a side of dice having one spot. 2. **Within an ace of** means very, very near to. 3. a tiptop, first-class aviator. *n. 11.*

ac et an i lide (as′et an′i lid), a medicine used to relieve pain. *n. 20.*

ac e tate (as′i tāt), a salt of acetic acid. Cellulose acetate is used in making imitation leather, phonograph records, etc. *n. 19.*

a ce tic (ə sē′tik), of vinegar; producing vinegar. **Acetic acid** is the acid in vinegar which makes it sour. *adj. 13.*

a cet y lene (ə set′i lēn), a colorless gas that burns with a bright light and a very hot flame. *n. 15.*

ache (āk), 1. continuous pain, such as a stomach ache, headache, or toothache. 2. suffer continuous pain; be in pain. My back aches. *n., v. 3.*

a chieve (ə chēv′), 1. do; carry out. Did you achieve all that you expected to today? 2. reach (a certain end) by one's own efforts; gain by effort. George achieved distinction in mathematics and geography. *v. 4.*

a chieve ment (ə chēv′mənt), 1. achieving. 2. some plan or action carried out with courage or with unusual ability. Flying across the Atlantic for the first time was a great achievement. *n. 7.*

A chil les (ə kil′ēz), a hero of the Greeks at the siege of Troy. No weapon could injure Achilles anywhere except in the heel. *n. 8.*

ac id (as′id), 1. sour; sharp or biting to the taste. Lemons are an acid fruit. Rhubarb has an acid taste. 2. sour substance. 3. a chemical substance that unites with a base to form a salt. The sourness of vinegar is caused by the acetic acid it contains. *adj., n. 6.*

a cid i ty (ə sid′i ti), acid quality or condition; sourness. *n. 13.*

ac knowl edge (ak nol′ij), 1. admit to be true. He acknowledges his faults. 2. recognize the authority or claims of. We acknowledged him to be the best player on the baseball team. 3. express thanks for. 4. make known that one has received (a favor, gift, message, etc.). Mary acknowledged the gift with a pleasant letter. I acknowledged her letter at once. *v. 4.*

ac knowl edg ment (ak nol′ij mənt), 1. acknowledging. The accused man made acknowledgment of his guilt. 2. expression of thanks. 3. something given or done for a service, favor, message, etc. A receipt is the acknowledgment that a bill has been paid. *n. 8.*

ac me (ak′mi), highest point. A baseball player usually reaches the acme of his skill before he is thirty. The acme of the development of radio probably lies in the future. *n. 13.*

ac o lyte (ak′ō līt), 1. person who helps a priest during certain religious services. The acolyte lights the candles on the altar. 2. assistant; follower. *n.*

Aconite
(3 to 5 ft. high)

ac o nite (ak′ə nīt), 1. a poisonous plant with blue, purple, or yellow flowers, shaped like hoods. Monkshood is one kind of aconite. 2. drug used in medicine, obtained from one of these plants. *n. 13.*

a corn (ā′kôrn), the nut, or fruit, of an oak tree. See the picture below. *n. 5.*

a cous tics (ə küs′tiks), 1. qualities of a room, hall, auditorium, etc., that determine how well sounds can be heard in it. 2. science of sound. *n. pl. or sing.*

Acorns

ac quaint (ə kwānt′), 1. make familiar. Let me acquaint you with the facts. 2. **Be acquainted with** means have personal knowledge of. I have heard about your friend, but I am not acquainted with him. *v. 3.*

ac quaint ance (ə kwān′təns), 1. knowledge of persons or things gained from experience with them. I have some acquaintance with French, but I do not know it well. 2. person known to one, but not a close friend. *n. 3.*

ac qui esce (ak′wi es′), accept without making objections; agree or submit quietly. John's parents acquiesced in the principal's decision that John should not be promoted. *v. 11.*

ac qui es cence (ak′wi es′əns), consent without making objections; agreeing or submitting quietly. *n. 10.*

ac quire (ə kwīr′), gain or get as one's own; get. By the time James was thirty he had acquired a store of his own. *v. 3.*

ac quire ment (ə kwīr′mənt), 1. act of acquiring. 2. something acquired. Her musical acquirements are remarkable for a girl of her age. *n. 17.*

ac qui si tion (ak′wi zish′ən), 1. acquiring or getting as one's own. He spent hundreds of hours in the acquisition of skill with a rifle. 2. something acquired or gained. Mary's new acquisitions were two dresses, a hat, and a pair of shoes. *n. 8.*

ac quis i tive (ə kwiz′i tiv), fond of acquiring; likely to get and keep. A great scholar is acquisitive of ideas. *adj. 20.*

ac quit (ə kwit′), 1. declare not guilty. The man was acquitted of the crime. 2. **Acquit oneself** means do one's part; behave. The soldiers acquitted themselves bravely in battle. *v., acquitted, acquitting. 9.*

ac quit tal (ə kwit′əl), setting free by declaring not guilty; discharge; release. *n. 16.*

a cre (ā′kər), a measure of land, 160 square rods or 43,560 square feet. *n. 2.*

a cre age (ā′kər ij), 1. the number of acres. The acreage of this park is over 800. 2. piece of land large enough to be sold by the acre. *n. 12.*

ac rid (ak′rid), 1. sharp, bitter, or stinging to the nose, mouth, or skin. 2. sharp in manner or temper. *adj. 11.*

ac ri mo ni ous (ak′ri mō′ni əs), sharp or bitter in temper, language, or manner. *adj. 18.*

ac ri mo ny (ak′ri mō′ni), sharpness or bitterness in temper, language, or manner. *n., pl. acrimonies. 15.*

ac ro bat (ak′rə bat), person who can dance on a rope or wire, swing on trapezes, turn handsprings, etc. *n. 20.*

ac ro bat ic (ak′rə bat′ik), 1. of an acrobat. Dancing on a rope is an acrobatic feat. 2. like an acrobat's. *adj. 20.*

a crop o lis (ə krop′ə lis), 1. the high, fortified part of an ancient Greek city. 2. **The Acropolis** was a fortified hill of Athens. *n. 19.*

Acropolis

a cross (ə krôs′). The man sawed the plank across. The cat walked across the street. The woods are across the river. *adv., prep. 1.*

act (akt), 1. thing done; deed. Feeding the hungry is a kind act. 2. doing. The farmer caught the boys in the act of stealing his apples. 3. do something. The firemen acted promptly and saved the burning house. 4. have effect. Yeast acts on dough and makes it rise. 5. behave. The boy acted badly in school. 6. behave like. Most people act the fool now and then. 7. perform in a theater; play a part. The actor acts the part of the hero. He acts very well. 8. a main division in a play or opera. Most modern plays have three acts. 9. one of several performances on a program; as, the trained dog's act. 10. law; decree; as, the acts of Congress. 11. **Act as** or **act for** means do the work of; take the place of. *n., v. 1.*

act ing (ak′ting), taking another's place and doing his duties. While the principal was sick, one of the teachers was acting principal. *adj.*

ac tion (ak′shən), 1. doing something; acting. The quick action of the firemen saved the building from fire. 2. thing done; act. 3. way of working. This motor has a very easy action. 4. battle; part of a battle. 5. lawsuit. *n. 2.*

ac tive (ak′tiv), 1. acting; working; as, an active volcano, an active force. 2. showing much action; lively; moving rather quickly much of the time. 3. in grammar, showing the subject of a verb as acting. In "John broke the window," *broke* is in the active voice. 4. a verb form that does this. *adj., n. 3.*

ac tiv i ty (ak tiv′i ti), 1. being active; movement; use of power; as, mental activity. 2. action. 3. thing to do; as, outdoor activities, classroom activities. *n., pl. activities. 7.*

ac tor (ak′tər), 1. person who acts on the stage or in moving pictures. 2. person who does something. *n. 5.*

ac tress (ak′tris), woman actor. *n. 12.*

ac tu al (ak′chü əl), real; existing as a fact. What he told us was not a dream but an actual happening. *adj. 2.*

ac tu al ly (ak′chü əl i), really; in fact. *adv. 6.*

ac tu ate (ak′chü āt), 1. put into action. Our pump is actuated by a belt from an electric motor. 2. influence to act. She was actuated by love for her mother. *v. 14.*

a cu men (ə kū′men), sharpness and quickness in seeing and understanding; keen insight. Mr. Smith had the business acumen to foresee that cotton would drop in price. *n. 16.*

a cute (ə kūt′), 1. sharp-pointed. 2. sharp and severe. A toothache can cause acute pain. 3. keen. Dogs have an acute sense of smell. An acute thinker is clever and shrewd. 4. high; shrill. Some sounds are so acute we cannot hear them. 5. less than a right angle. See the diagram. 6. The *e* in *abbé* has an acute accent on it. *adj. 7.*

ACUTE ANGLE RIGHT ANGLE

a cute ness (ə kūt′nis), 1. sharpness; severeness. 2. shrillness of sound. 3. keen insight; sharpness of mind. *n. 16.*

A.D., in the year of our Lord; since Christ was born. From 200 B.C. to 500 A.D. is seven hundred years. *12.*

ad age (ad′ij), a wise saying that has been much used; a well-known proverb. "Haste makes waste" is an adage. *n. 11.*

a da gio (ə dä′jō), 1. slowly. 2. slow. 3. slow part in a piece of music. *adv., adj., n., pl. adagios.*

Ad am (ad′əm), in the Bible, the first man. *n. 5.*

ad a mant (ad′ə mant), 1. substance too hard to be cut or broken. 2. firm; unyielding. *n., adj. 10.*

ad a man tine (ad′ə man′tin), 1. very, very hard, like steel or a diamond. 2. firm; unyielding. *adj. 13.*

Ad ams (ad′əmz), 1. John Adams (1735-1826) was the second president of the United States, from 1797 to 1801. 2. His son, John Quincy Adams (1767-1848), was the sixth president, from 1825 to 1829. *n. 11.*

a dapt (ə dapt′), make fit or suitable. The farmer can adapt the barn for use as a garage. *v. 8.*

a dapt a bil i ty (ə dap′tə bil′i ti), power to change easily to fit different conditions. *n. 19.*

a dapt a ble (ə dap′tə bəl), 1. easily changed to fit different conditions. 2. changing easily to fit different conditions. *adj.*

ad ap ta tion (ad′ap tā′shən), 1. an adapting or fitting. 2. a being adapted or made to fit. 3. something made by adapting. Hawthorne's *Wonder Book* is an adaptation of old Greek myths for children. *n. 8.*

add (ad), 1. put together. When you add 4 and 2 and 3, you have 9. 2. **Add to** means put with. She added sugar to her tea. 3. **Add to** sometimes means make greater. The fine day added to our pleasure. 4. go on to say; say further. *v. 1.*

ad dend (ad′end), number to be added. *n.*

ad der (ad′ər), 1. a small poisonous snake of Europe. 2. a small harmless snake of North America. *n. 9.*

European adder (2 ft. long)

ad dict (ad′ikt), person who is addicted. A drug addict is a person so addicted to the use of drugs that he may be called a slave to drugs. *n. 16.*

ad dict ed (ə dik′tid), given up to a habit. That man is so addicted to tobacco that he smokes almost all the time. *adj. 17.*

ad di tion (ə dish′ən), 1. adding one number or quantity to another. 2+2=4 is a simple addition. 2. thing added. Workmen are building an addition to this house. 3. **In addition** or **in addition to** means besides. In addition to her work as teacher in the school, Miss Jones gives music lessons after school hours. *n. 2.*

ad di tion al (ə dish′ən əl), added; extra; more. Mother will need additional help to do the work while there is so much company. *adj. 5.*

ad di tion al ly (ə dish′ən əl i), in addition. *adv.*

ad dle (ad′əl), 1. make or become muddled. 2. muddled; confused. 3. make or become rotten. 4. rotten. *v., adj. 18.*

ad dress (ə dres′), 1. a speech, either spoken or written. The President gave an address to the nation over the radio. 2. speak to or write to. He will address you on the subject of war and peace. 3. the place to which mail is directed. Write the name and address on the letter. 4. write on (an envelope or package) where it is to be sent. Please address this letter for me. 5. manner in conversation. A salesman should be a man of pleasant address. 6. skill. He showed much address in getting people to help him. 7. apply (oneself). He addressed himself to the task of getting his lessons. *n., v. 2.*

ad duce (ə dūs′ or ə düs′), offer as a reason; give as proof or evidence; bring up as an example. *v. 16.*

ADENOIDS

ad e noids (ad′ə noidz), growths of glandular tissue in the upper part of the throat, just back of the nose. They sometimes hinder natural breathing and speaking. *n. pl. 14.*

a dept (ə dept′), 1. thoroughly skilled; expert. She is adept in music. 2. person who is adept. *adj., n. 16.*

ad e qua cy (ad′i kwə si), as much as is needed; suitableness. *n.*

ad e quate (ad′i kwit), sufficient; enough; as much as is needed. His wages are adequate to support three people. *adj. 8.*

ad here (ad hēr′), stick fast (to a substance, a party, a person, an opinion). Soft snow adheres to the branches. Most people adhere to the church of their parents. *v. 8.*

ad her ence (ad hēr′əns), attachment; act of following and supporting. *n. 18.*

ad her ent (ad hēr′ənt), 1. follower and supporter. 2. adhering; sticking fast; attached. *n., adj. 13.*

ad he sion (ad hē′zhən), adhering; sticking fast; attachment. *n. 12.*

ad he sive (ad hē′siv), sticking fast; sticky; adhering easily. *adj. 14.*

a dieu (ə dū′ or ə dü′), good-by. *interj., n., pl. adieus* or *adieux* (ə dūz′ or ə düz′). *7.*

ad i pose (ad′i pōs), fat. *adj., n. 13.*

Ad i ron dacks (ad′i ron′daks), mountains in northeastern New York State. *n. pl. 14.*

adj., adjective.

ad ja cent (ə jā′sənt), near; adjoining. The house adjacent to ours has just been sold. *adj. 7.*

ad jec tive (aj′ik tiv), the name of a quality added to the name of a person, animal, or thing to describe it more fully. Words like *green, old, short, sweet,* and *sour* are adjectives. *n. 8.*

ad join (ə join′), be next to; be close to; be side by side. His yard adjoins ours. New Jersey adjoins New York. We have adjoining desks. *v. 5.*

ad journ (ə jėrn′), 1. stop business for a time. The court adjourned from Friday until Monday. 2. put off until a later time. The president adjourned the meeting until all the members of the club could be present. *v. 9.*

ad journ ment (ə jėrn′mənt), 1. an adjourning or being adjourned. 2. time during which something is adjourned. *n. 15.*

ad judge (ə juj′), 1. decide or settle by law; decide or settle. The case was adjudged in the juvenile court. 2. condemn or sentence by law. He was adjudged to prison for two years. 3. decree; declare. He was adjudged guilty. 4. award or assign by law. The property was adjudged to the rightful owner. *v. 11.*

ad junct (aj′ungkt), something added that is less important or not necessary, but helpful. *n. 10.*

ad ju ra tion (aj′ů rā′shən), solemn command; earnest appeal. *n. 19.*

ad jure (ə jür′), 1. command or charge (a person) on oath or under some penalty (to do something). 2. ask earnestly or solemnly. I adjure you to speak the truth. *v. 12.*

ad just (ə just′), arrange; set just right; change to make fit. These desks and seats can be adjusted to the height of any child. This bill is too high and must be adjusted. *v. 6.*

ad just a ble (ə jus′tə bəl), that can be adjusted. An adjustable electric lamp can be placed in various positions. *adj. 17.*

ad just ment (ə just′mənt), settlement; changing to make fit; setting right to fit some standard or purpose. The adjustment of seats to the right height for children is necessary for their comfort. Try to make some adjustment of your differences so that you can work together without quarrels. *n. 8.*

ad ju tant (aj′ů tənt), 1. an officer in the army who assists the commanding officer by sending out orders, writing letters, giving messages, etc. 2. a large stork of Africa and India. *n. 18.*

Adjutant (5 ft. high)

ad min is ter (ad min′is tər), 1. manage. The Secretary of War administers a department of the government. A housekeeper administers a household. 2. give as medicine or treatment; apply; give (to). The nurse administers castor oil. Judges administer justice or punishment. 3. be of service; contribute; as, to administer to a person's comfort or pleasure. 4. act as administrator. *v. 7.*

ad min is tra tion (ad min′is trā′shən), 1. management. 2. management of public affairs; government. 3. giving medicine, treatment, etc. *n. 5.*

ad min is tra tive (ad min′is trā′tiv), concerning the management of affairs; executive; managing. *adj. 13.*

ad min is tra tor (ad min′is trā′tər), 1. person who administers or manages. 2. person who has authority to take charge of the estate of somebody who has died. *n. 10.*

ad mi ra ble (ad′mi rə bəl), 1. worth admiring. 2. excellent; very good. *adj. 6.*

ad mi ral (ad′mi rəl), 1. officer in command of a fleet of ships. 2. officer of the highest rank in the navy. *n. 5.*

ad mi ral ty (ad′mi rəl ti), 1. the law or court or officers dealing with affairs of the sea and ships. 2. the office or position of an admiral. *n. 14.*

ad mi ra tion (ad′mi rā′shən), 1. the feeling we have when we admire; delight or satisfaction at something fine or beautiful or well done. 2. person or thing that is admired. Helen's beautiful dress was the admiration of all her friends. *n. 4.*

ad mire (ad mīr′), regard with wonder, pleasure, and satisfaction. We admire a brave boy, a beautiful picture, or a fine piece of work. *v. 2.*

ad mir er (ad mīr′ər), person who admires. *n. 8.*

ad mis si ble (ad mis′i bəl), 1. capable or worthy of being admitted. Only adults are admissible to this club. 2. allowable. Is it admissible to smoke here? *adj.*

ad mis sion (ad mish′ən), 1. admitting. 2. being admitted. 3. the price of being admitted. Admission to the show is one dollar. 4. acknowledging. Tom's admission that he was to blame kept the other boys from being punished. *n. 5.*

ad mit (ad mit′), 1. allow to enter; let in. This ticket will admit you to the circus. He was admitted to school this year. 2. acknowledge; accept as true. Tom admits now that he was wrong. *v., admitted, admitting. 2.*

ad mit tance (ad mit′əns), the right to enter. She had admittance to all the theaters free of charge. *n. 10.*

ad mix ture (ad miks′chər), 1. mixture. 2. something added in mixing. *n. 14.*

ad mon ish (ad mon′ish), warn or advise (a person) about his faults in order that he may be guided to improve. *v. 6.*

ad mo ni tion (ad′mə nish′ən), admonishing; warning; advice concerning the faults a person has shown or may show. *n. 10.*

ad mon i to ry (ad mon′i tō′ri), admonishing; warning. *adj.*

a do (ə dü′), action; stir; fuss; trouble. There was much ado about the party by all the family. Alice made a great ado because her dress did not fit. *n. 8.*

Adobe house

a do be (ə dō′bi), 1. sun-dried brick. 2. made of sun-dried brick. Many people in southwestern United States and in Mexico live in adobe houses. *n., adj. 20.*

ad o les cence (ad′ə les′əns), 1. growth from childhood to maturity. 2. youth. *n. 17.*

ad o les cent (ad′ə les′ənt), 1. growing up to manhood or womanhood; youthful. 2. person from about 13 to 22. *adj., n. 20.*

A do nis (ə dō′nis), a beautiful youth. *n. 12.*

a dopt (ə dopt′), take for one's own; take as one's own choice. People adopt children into their families. I liked your idea and adopted it. *v. 3.*

a dop tion (ə dop′shən), 1. adopting. We are talking about the adoption of a new plan for the picnic. 2. being adopted. His adoption by the kind old man changed the boy's whole life. *n. 5.*

a dor a ble (ə dōr′ə bəl), worthy of being adored. *adj. 20.*

ad o ra tion (ad′ə rā′shən), 1. worship. 2. highest respect and love. *n. 10.*

a dore (ə dōr′), 1. worship. 2. respect and love very, very greatly. *v. 4.*

a dorn (ə dôrn′), add beauty to; ornament. *v. 4.*

a dorn ment (ə dôrn′mənt), 1. act of adorning. Mary was busy with the adornment of the church. 2. thing that adds beauty; ornament. *n. 12.*

a down (ə doun′), down. *adv., prep.* [*Used in poetry*] *16.*

A dri an o ple (ā′dri ən ō′pəl), a city in European Turkey. *n. 19.*

A dri at ic (ā′dri at′ik), the sea east of Italy. *n. 9.*

a drift (ə drift′), drifting; floating without being guided. *adv., adj. 12.*

a droit (ə droit′), skillful; ingenious. Monkeys are adroit climbers. A good teacher is adroit in asking questions. *adj. 11.*

a droit ness (ə droit′nis), skillfulness; dexterity; ingenuity. *n. 20.*

ad u la tion (aj′ů lā′shən), 1. too great praise. 2. servile flattery. *n. 14.*

a dult (ə dult′ or ad′ult), 1. full-grown; grown-up; mature; having full size and strength. 2. a grown-up person. 3. any plant or animal grown to full size and strength. *adj., n. 8.*

a dul ter ate (ə dul′tər āt), make worse by adding something of lower value. There are laws against adulterating milk with water. *v. 12.*

a dul ter a tion (ə dul′tər ā′shən), 1. act of adulterating. 2. something that has been adulterated. *n. 16.*

a dul ter er (ə dul′tər ər), person guilty of adultery. *n. 16.*

a dul ter ess (ə dul′tər is), woman guilty of adultery. *n. 17.*

a dul ter ous (ə dul′tər əs), guilty of adultery. *adj. 17.*

a dul ter y (ə dul′tər i), unfaithfulness of a husband or wife. *n., pl. adulteries. 10.*

adv., 1. adverb. 2. advertisement.

ad vance (ad vans′), 1. move forward. The angry crowd advanced toward the building. 2. put forward. The plan he advanced was not good. He advanced a large claim for damages. 3. forward movement; progress. The army's advance was very slow. 4. pay (money) before it is due. Fifty dollars was advanced to him on his salary before the work was done. 5. go up. Sugar had advanced two cents a pound. 6. put up. The grocer advanced his prices on food when he had to pay more in the market. 7. rise in price or value. 8. personal approach; approach made to gain something. Frank made the first advances toward making up his quarrel with Jack. 9. **In advance** means (1) in front. (2) ahead of time. *v., n. 2.*

ad vanced (ad vanst′), 1. in advance. 2. ahead of most others. 3. far along in life; very old. His grandfather lived to the advanced age of ninety years. *adj.*

ad vance ment (ad vans′mənt), advance; promotion. His new position means a great advancement in pay. *n. 6.*

ad van tage (ad van′tij), 1. anything that is to the good, or is a benefit; any condition, circumstance, opportunity, or means that helps in getting something which is desired. 2. help. *n., v. 2.*

ad van ta geous (ad′vən tā′jəs), helpful; profitable; favorable. This advantageous position commands three roads. *adj. 11.*

ad vent (ad′vent), coming; arrival. *n. 9.*

Ad vent (ad′vent), 1. the coming of Christ. 2. the time including the four Sundays before Christmas. *n.*

ad ven ti tious (ad′ven tish′əs), coming from without; additional; accidental. The romantic life of the author gives his book an adventitious interest. *adj. 14.*

ad ven ture (ad ven′chər), 1. a bold and difficult undertaking, usually exciting and somewhat dangerous. A hunter of tigers has many adventures. 2. an unusual experience. The trip to Mexico City was an adventure for Helen. 3. dare to do; risk. 4. venture; dare. *n., v. 3.*

ad ven tur er (ad ven′chər ər), 1. person who has or seeks adventures. 2. person who lives by his wits. 3. person who lives by his wits in ways which are not entirely honest or respectable. *n. 10.*

ad ven tur ous (ad ven′chər əs), 1. fond of adventures; ready to take risks. Stanley was a bold, adventurous explorer. 2. full of danger. The discovery of the North Pole was an adventurous undertaking. *adj. 7.*

ad verb (ad′vėrb), word that expresses time, place, manner, degree, or circumstances. Words like *soon, never, here, very,* and *gladly* are adverbs. *n. 12.*

ad ver sar y (ad′vər sãr′i), enemy; person opposing another. *n., pl. adversaries. 6.*

ad verse (ad vėrs′), 1. contrary; opposed. Adverse winds hinder ships. 2. unfavorable; harmful. Dirt and disease are adverse to the best growth of children. *adj. 6.*

ad ver si ty (ad vėr′si ti), distress; misfortune; hardship. *n., pl. adversities. 7.*

ad vert (ad vėrt′), refer (to) in speaking or writing; direct the attention. The speaker adverted to the need for more parks. *v. 16.*

ad ver tise (ad′vər tīz), 1. give public notice of; announce; call attention to. People advertise things that they wish to sell. 2. **Advertise for** means ask for by a public notice. 3. give notice. *v. 5.*

ad ver tise ment (ad′vər tīz′mənt), public announcement; printed notice. The store has an advertisement in the newspaper of a special sale. *n. 7.*

ad vice (ad vīs′), 1. opinion about what should be done. To keep well, follow the doctor's advice. 2. news; information. Advices from China show that there will be war. *n. 2.*

ad vis a ble (ad vīz′ə bəl), wise; sensible; suitable; to be advised; to be recommended. It is not advisable for him to go while he is still sick. A hot-air furnace is not advisable for a large building. *adj. 11.*

ad vise (ad vīz′), 1. give advice to. He advised me to keep my money in the bank. 2. talk over plans; consult. 3. inform. We were advised of the dangers before we began our trip. *v. 2.*

ad vise ment (ad vīz′mənt), careful consideration. The lawyer took our case under advisement and said he would give us an answer in two weeks. *n.*

ad vis er or **ad vi sor** (ad vīz′ər), person who gives advice. *n. 8.*

ad vi so ry (ad vī′zə ri), giving advice. *adj. 15.*

ad vo ca cy (ad′və kə si), speaking in favor; support. The President's advocacy of the plan got votes for it. *n. 19.*

ad vo cate (ad′və kāt), 1. speak in favor of; recommend publicly; support. He advocates building good roads. 2. person who speaks in favor; supporter. Smith is an advocate of better school buildings. 3. lawyer. *v., n. 7.*

adz or **adze** (adz), tool somewhat like an ax. The blade is set across the end of the handle and curves inward. *n. 13.*

Adz used by coopers

Ae ge an (ē jē′ən), 1. the sea east of Greece. 2. of or in this sea. *n., adj. 14.*

ae gis (ē′jis), 1. a shield or breastplate used by the Greek god Zeus and by his daughter Athena. 2. protection. *n. 16.*

hat, āge, cãre, fär; let, ēqual, tėrm; it, īce; hot, ōpen, ôrder; oil, out; cup, pu̇t, rüle, ūse; th, thin; ᴛʜ, then; ə represents *a* in about, *e* in taken, *i* in pencil, *o* in lemon, *u* in circus.

Ae ne as (ē nē′əs), a prince of Troy. He escaped from burning Troy, carrying his father and leading his little son. After years of wandering he reached Italy, where his descendants founded Rome. *n. 11.*

Ae ne id (ē nē′id), the story of the wanderings of Aeneas told in a long poem by Virgil. *n. 18.*

Ae o lus (ē′ō ləs), the Greek god of the winds. *n. 14.*

ae on (ē′on), very long time; many thousands of years. Aeons passed before life existed on the earth. *n. 16.* Also spelled **eon.**

aer ate (ãr′āt), 1. expose to air. 2. fill with air or with a gas. Water in a reservoir can be aerated by being tossed high into the air in a fine spray. *v. 19.*

aer i al (ãr′i əl), 1. of the air; in the air; consisting of air; like air. 2. thin and light as air; not real or solid. 3. a device with a radio set to receive the electric waves. 4. the wire or wires used in sending by radio. *adj., n. 7.*

aer ie or **aer y** (ãr′i or ēr′i), 1. an eagle's nest. 2. an eagle's brood. 3. lofty position. *n., pl. aeries. 16.* Also spelled **eyrie** or **eyry.**

aer o naut (ãr′ə nôt), aviator; pilot of an airplane or balloon. *n. 16.*

aer o nau tics (ãr′ə nô′tiks), science or art of aviation; navigation in the air. *n.*

aer o plane (ãr′ə plān), airplane. *n.*

Aes chy lus (es′ki ləs), famous Greek tragic poet and dramatist (525-456 B.C.). *n. 18.*

Ae sop (ē′sop), a famous Greek writer of fables who lived about 600 B.C. *n. 18.*

aes thet ic (es thet′ik), 1. of beauty; having to do with the sense of the beautiful. 2. sensitive to beauty. 3. pleasing; artistic. *adj. 12.* Also spelled **esthetic.**

ae ther (ē′thər), 1. the upper regions of space; the clear sky. 2. the fine, elastic matter supposed to fill all space and to transmit light, electric waves, etc. *n. 17.* Also spelled **ether.**

ae the re al (i thē′ri əl), 1. light; airy; delicate. 2. not of the earth; heavenly. *adj.* Also spelled **ethereal.**

Aet na (et′nə), a volcano in Sicily. *n. 15.* Also spelled **Etna.**

a far (ə fär′), far; far away; far off; from a distance. *adv. 5.*

a feard (ə fērd′), afraid. *adj. [Old use] 18.*

af fa bil i ty (af′ə bil′i ti), quality of being easy to talk to; courteous and pleasant ways. *n. 16.*

af fa ble (af′ə bəl), easy to talk to; courteous and pleasant. *adj. 10.*

af fair (ə fãr′), 1. thing to do; job; business. The President has many affairs to look after. 2. any thing or matter or happening. The party Saturday was a jolly affair. *n. 2.*

af fect[1] (ə fekt′), 1. produce a result or effect on; influence. The amount of rain affects the growth of crops. The disease affected his mind so that he could not remember what he had done. 2. touch the heart of. The stories of starving children so affected him that he sent all his spare money for relief. *v. 3.*

af fect[2] (ə fekt′), 1. be fond of and have. She affects old furniture and china. 2. pretend to have or feel. He affected ignorance of the fight, though he had seen it all. *v.*

af fec ta tion (af′ek tā′shən), behavior that is not natural. Helen's roughness is an affectation; she really is a quiet, gentle girl. *n. 9.*

af fect ed[1] (ə fek′tid), 1. acted upon; influenced. 2. injured. 3. stirred up. *adj. 14.*

af fect ed[2] (ə fek′tid), artificial; pretended. *adj.*

af fect ing (ə fek′ting), causing emotion; pathetic; moving; touching. The poor man told an affecting story of hunger and suffering. *adj.*

af fec tion (ə fek′shən), 1. friendly feeling; love. 2. disease. He is suffering from an affection of the ear. *n. 3.*

af fec tion ate (ə fek′shən it), loving; fond; showing affection. *adj. 5.*

af fer ent (af′ər ənt), bringing to a central organ or point; as, afferent nerves. *adj. 15.*

af fi ance (ə fī′əns), 1. faith; trust. 2. pledging of faith. 3. pledge; promise in marriage. *n., v. 14.*

af fi anced (ə fī′ənst), engaged to be married. *adj.*

af fi da vit (af′i dā′vit), a statement written down and sworn to be true. *n. 14.*

af fil i ate (ə fil′i āt), associate; join; connect. The two clubs did not have the same members, but they were affiliated with each other. *v. 13.*

af fil i a tion (ə fil′i ā′shən), association; connection; alliance. *n. 18.*

af fin i ty (ə fin′i ti), 1. relationship by marriage. 2. relation; connection. 3. resemblance; likeness. 4. attraction; liking. 5. person to whom one is especially attracted. *n., pl. affinities. 9.*

af firm (ə fėrm′), say firmly; declare to be

true; assert. The Bible affirms that God is love. *v. 5.*

af fir ma tion (af′ər mā′shən), declaration. *n. 15.*

af firm a tive (ə fėr′mə tiv), 1. saying yes; affirming. His answer was affirmative. 2. a word or statement that says yes or affirms. 3. the side that says yes or affirms in an argument. *adj., n. 11.*

af fix (ə fiks′ for 1, af′iks for 2), 1. stick on; fasten to. 2. a part added to a word. Affixes are either prefixes like *un-* and *re-* or suffixes like *-ly* and *-ness. v., n. 14.*

af flict (ə flikt′), cause pain to; trouble very much; distress greatly. *v. 5.*

af flic tion (ə flik′shən), 1. pain; trouble; distress. 2. misfortune. *n. 5.*

af flu ence (af′lü əns), abundant supply; wealth. *n. 16.*

af flu ent (af′lü ənt), abundant; rich. *adj. 16.*

af ford (ə fōrd′), 1. have the means; have the money, time, or strength. Can we afford to buy a new car? He cannot afford to waste so much time. 2. yield; give. His own garden affords fresh vegetables for the family. Reading this story will afford real pleasure. *v. 3.*

af fray (ə frā′), a noisy quarrel; a fight in public; a brawl. *n. 16.*

af fright (ə frīt′), 1. frighten; excite with sudden fear. 2. sudden fear; fright. *v., n.* [*Old use*] *5.*

af front (ə frunt′), 1. insult openly and purposely. The boy affronted the teacher by making a face at her. 2. offend the modesty or self-respect of. The people of the village were affronted by the superior airs of Mrs. Newrich. 3. an open insult. To be called a coward is an affront to a manly boy. *v., n. 10.*

Af ghan i stan (af gan′i stan), a country in Asia, between India and Persia. *n. 14.*

a field (ə fēld′), 1. in or on the field; to the field. 2. away; away from home. *adv. 14.*

a fire (ə fīr′), on fire. *adv., adj. 10.*

a flame (ə flām′), in flames; on fire. *adv., adj.*

a float (ə flōt′), 1. floating. John had 10 balloons afloat at one time. 2. on shipboard. On the trip around the world, we were afloat 60 days and ashore 30 days. 3. flooded. After the rain, the whole cellar was afloat. 4. going around. Rumors of a revolt were afloat. *adv., adj. 6.*

a flut ter (ə flut′ər), in a flutter. The flags were aflutter in the breeze. *adv., adj.*

a foot (ə fu̇t′), 1. on foot; walking. Did you come all the way afoot? 2. going on; in progress. Great preparations for the dinner were afoot in the kitchen. *adv., adj. 10.*

a fore (ə fōr′), before. *adv., prep., conj.* [*Old use*] *12.*

a fore said (ə fōr′sed′), said before; mentioned before. *adj. 14.*

a foul (ə foul′), in a collision; in a tangle. **Run afoul of** means get in difficulties with. *adv., adj.*

a fraid (ə frād′), frightened; feeling fear. She is afraid of snakes. *adj. 1.*

a fresh (ə fresh′), again. The child began to cry afresh. *adv. 12.*

Af ri ca (af′ri kə), the continent south of Europe. Egypt is in Africa. *n. 2.*

Af ri can (af′ri kən), 1. of Africa; having to do with Africa; from Africa. 2. a native of Africa. 3. Negro. *adj., n.*

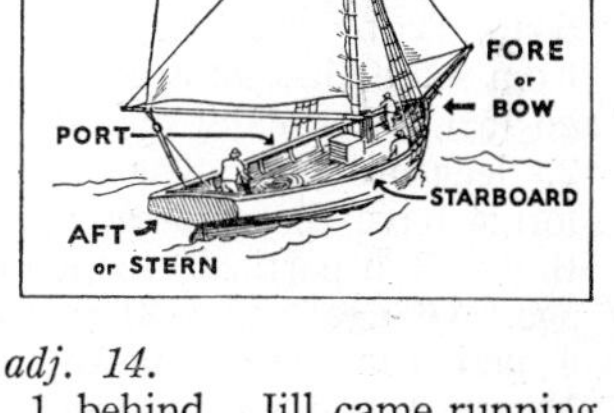

aft (aft), at the stern; toward the stern. *adv., adj. 14.*

af ter (af′tər), 1. behind. Jill came running after. 2. later than. After dinner we can go. 3. later; following. The after results of the storm were terrible. 4. in search of; in pursuit of. The dog ran after the rabbit. 5. according to. He wrote a fable after the manner of Aesop. *prep., adv., conj., adj. 1.*

af ter deck (af′tər dek′), deck toward the stern of a ship. *n.*

af ter math (af′tər math), 1. a later product or result. The aftermath of war is hunger and disease. 2. crop gathered after the first crop. *n. 19.*

af ter noon (af′tər nün′), the time from noon to evening. *n. 1.*

af ter thought (af′tər thôt′), 1. a later thought. 2. a thought that comes after the time when it could have been used. *n. 16.*

af ter ward (af′tər wərd), afterwards; later. *adv. 9.*

af ter wards (af′tər wərdz), later. The bud was small at first, but afterwards it became a large flower. *adv. 2.*

a gain (ə gen′), 1. another time; once more. 2. in return. 3. besides; moreover. 4. on the other hand. *adv. 1.*

a gainst (ə genst'), 1. in opposition to. The dogs fought against the lion. 2. upon. Rain beats against the window. 3. in preparation for. Squirrels store up nuts against the winter. *prep. 1.*

Ag a mem non (ag'ə mem'non), leader of the Greeks in the Trojan War. *n. 11.*

a gape (ə gāp'), 1. gaping; with the mouth wide open in wonder or surprise. 2. wide open. *adv., adj. 12.*

Ag as siz (ag'ə si), Louis, an American scientist of Swiss descent (1807-1873). *n. 19.*

ag ate (ag'it), 1. a stone with colored stripes or clouded colors; a kind of quartz. 2. a playing marble that looks like this. *n. 12.*

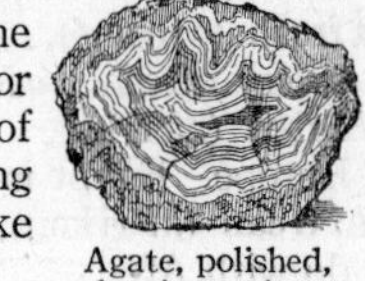
Agate, polished, showing stripes.

a ga ve (ə gā'vi), a useful plant, especially common in Mexico. Soap, alcoholic drinks, and rope are made from some kinds of agave. *n.*

age (āj), 1. time of life; as, the age of ten. 2. length of life. The great trees of California have the greatest age of any living thing. 3. a particular period of life; as, old age. **Of age** means 21 years old or over. 4. period in history; as, the Stone Age, the Middle Ages, the age of machinery. 5. a long time. 6. grow old. He is aging fast. 7. make old. *n., v. 1.*

-age, suffix meaning:—
1. act of; as in breakage.
2. collection of; group of; as in baggage.
3. condition of; rank of; as in peerage.
4. cost of; as in postage.
5. home of; as in orphanage.
Words made with -age often acquire special meanings.

a ged (ā'jid for 1, ājd for 2), 1. old; having lived a long time. The aged woman was wrinkled and bent. 2. of the age of. She was aged six when she first went to school. *adj. 6.*

a gen cy (ā'jən si), 1. the office or business of some person or company that acts for another. An agency rented my house for me. 2. means; action. Snow is drifted by the agency of the wind. Through the agency of friends he was set free. *n., pl. agencies. 5.*

a gent (ā'jənt), 1. person or company who acts for another. I made my brother my agent while I was out of the city. 2. any active power or cause that produces an effect. Heat and electricity are important agents in the life of today. *n. 4.*

ag gran dize (ag'rən dīz), make greater; make great in power, wealth, rank, etc. The king sought to aggrandize himself at the expense of his people. *v. 20.*

ag gra vate (ag'rə vāt), 1. make worse; make more severe. His bad temper was aggravated by his headache. 2. annoy; irritate; provoke. *Used in common talk. v. 7.*

ag gra va tion (ag'rə vā'shən), 1. making worse or more severe. 2. being made worse or more severe. 3. something that aggravates. *n. 17.*

ag gre gate (ag'ri gāt), 1. collect; unite. Granite is made of small particles aggregated together. 2. collection; mass of separate things joined together. 3. amount to. The money collected will aggregate $1000. 4. total. The aggregate of all the gifts was over a hundred dollars. *v., n., adj. 12.*

ag gre ga tion (ag'ri gā'shən), collection of separate things into one mass or whole. *n. 14.*

ag gres sion (ə grəsh'ən), 1. an attack. 2. the first step in an attack or quarrel. *n. 16.*

ag gres sive (ə gres'iv), 1. taking the first step in an attack or quarrel; attacking. Which was the aggressive one, John or James? 2. active; energetic. Theodore Roosevelt was aggressive. *adj. 9.*

ag gres sor (ə gres'ər), one that begins an attack or quarrel. *n. 14.*

ag grieve (ə grēv'), injure unjustly; oppress; cause grief or trouble to. He was aggrieved at the insult from his friend. *v. 11.*

a ghast (ə gast'), frightened; struck with surprise or horror; filled with terror. *adj. 11.*

ag ile (aj'il), moving quickly and easily; active; lively; nimble. An acrobat has to be agile. You need an agile mind to solve puzzles. *adj. 12.*

a gil i ty (ə jil'i ti), ability to move quickly and easily. *n. 15.*

ag i tate (aj'i tāt), 1. move or shake. The slightest wind will agitate the leaves of some trees. 2. disturb; excite. She was much agitated by the news of her brother's death. 3. keep discussing before the public; excite discussion and feeling over. Antislavery leaders agitated the question of slavery for many years. *v. 7.*

ag i ta tion (aj'i tā'shən), 1. violent moving or shaking. 2. noisy confusion; disturbance of body or mind; excitement. 3. discussion; debate; persistent urging of a cause before the public. There was much agitation for and against slavery before the Civil War. *n. 7.*

ag i ta tor (aj′i tā′tər), 1. person who tries to make people discontented with things as they are. 2. thing that agitates or stirs. *n. 11.*

a glow (ə glō′), glowing; in a glow. The baby's cheeks were aglow with health. *adv., adj. 16.*

ag nos tic (ag nos′tik), person who thinks that nothing is known or can be known about the existence of God or about things outside of human experience. *n.*

a go (ə gō′), 1. gone by; past. I met her two years ago. 2. in the past. Adam lived long ago. *adj., adv. 1.*

a gog (ə gog′), 1. eager; curious; excited. The children were all agog to see their presents. 2. with eagerness, curiosity, or excitement. *adj., adv.*

ag o nize (ag′ə nīz), 1. feel very great pain. 2. pain very much; torture. 3. struggle. *v. 12.*

ag o ny (ag′ə ni), 1. very painful suffering. 2. very great struggle of body or mind. *n., pl. agonies. 4.*

a grar i an (ə grãr′i ən), 1. having to do with land, its use, or its ownership. Most old countries have had agrarian disputes between landlords and tenants. 2. person who favors a new division of land. 3. agricultural. *adj., n. 18.*

a gree (ə grē′), 1. consent. They agreed to do the work at a low price. 2. have the same opinion. We all agree in liking the teacher. I agree with you that arithmetic is hard. 3. be in harmony. 4. **Agree with** sometimes means be good for. Bananas do not agree with everybody. 5. in grammar, have the same number, case, gender, or person. *v. 2.*

a gree a ble (ə grē′ə bəl), 1. pleasant; pleasing. 2. willing; ready to agree. 3. agreeing; suitable. *adj. 3.*

a greed (ə grēd′), 1. having the same opinion. 2. arranged by mutual consent. *adj.*

a gree ment (ə grē′mənt), 1. an agreeing; an understanding reached by two or more nations, persons, or groups of persons. Nations make treaties; certain persons make contracts. Both are agreements. 2. harmony; correspondence. *n. 5.*

ag ri cul tur al (ag′ri kul′chər əl), of agriculture; having to do with farming. *adj. 4.*

ag ri cul ture (ag′ri kul′chər), farming; cultivating the soil to make crops grow. *n. 3.*

ag ri cul tur ist (ag′ri kul′chər ist), 1. farmer. 2. an expert in farming. *n. 14.*

a ground (ə ground′), on the ground; on the shore; on the bottom in shallow water. The ship ran aground and stuck in the sand. *adv., adj. 17.*

a gue (ā′gū), 1. malarial fever with chills and sweating that occur at regular intervals. 2. a fit of shivering; a chill. *n. 12.*

ah (ä), exclamation of pain, sorrow, regret, pity, admiration, surprise, joy, dislike, contempt, etc. The meaning of *ah* varies according to the way it is spoken. *interj. 2.*

a ha (ä hä′), exclamation of triumph, satisfaction, surprise, joy, etc. *interj. 12.*

A hab (ā′hab), a king of Israel who was led into the worship of idols by his wife, Jezebel. I Kings 16-22. *n. 17.*

a head (ə hed′), 1. straight in front of one. There is danger ahead on this road. 2. forward. Go ahead with this work for another week. 3. in advance. Jim was ahead of his class in reading. *adv., adj. 3.*

a hoy (ə hoi′), a call used by sailors to attract the attention of persons at a distance. Sailors say, "Ship, ahoy!" when they call to a ship. *interj. 17.*

aid (ād), 1. help. When my arm was broken, I could not dress without aid. Mother aided me in dressing. 2. helper; assistant. Ann was my aid in the library for a time. *n., v. 2.*

aide (ād), army or navy officer who acts as an assistant to a superior officer. *n.*

aide-de-camp (ād′də kamp′), an army officer who assists a general. *n., pl. aides-de-camp. 18.*

ai grette (ā′gret), 1. a tuft or plume of the white heron's feathers used as an ornament. 2. any ornament having a similar shape. *n. 20.*

Aigrette (def. 1)

ail (āl), 1. to trouble; be the matter with. What ails the child? 2. be ill; feel sick. She has been ailing for a week. *v. 6.*

ai ler on (ā′lər on), the movable part of a wing of an airplane. It helps to keep the airplane balanced while flying. See the diagram of **airplane.** *n.*

ail ment (āl′mənt), illness; sickness. *n. 8.*

aim (ām), 1. point or direct (a gun, a blow, etc.) in order to hit. He aimed at the lion but missed. 2. act of pointing or directing at something. His aim was so poor that he missed the lion. 3. direct acts or words so as to influence a particular person or action.

His speech was aimed at the boys who had not played fair. 4. try; intend; direct one's efforts. Mary aimed to please her teachers. 5. purpose; intention. Ruth's aim was to do two years' work in one. *v., n. 2.*

aim less (ām′lis), without aim or purpose. *adj.*

ain't (ānt), 1. am not; are not; is not. 2. have not; has not. Careful speakers do not use ain't. *12.*

air (ãr), 1. Birds fly in the air. 2. It is good to air your clothes every night. 3. make known. Don't air your troubles too often. 4. melody; tune. In music, the air is the leading part. 5. way; look; manner. He had the air of a child who was afraid. 6. light wind; breeze. 7. Some special meanings are:

airs, affected or showy manners.

in the air, 1. going around. 2. uncertain; undecided.

on the air, broadcasting.

take the air, start broadcasting.

n., v. 1.

air base, airport and headquarters for military airplanes.

air castle, daydream; something that is only imagined.

air conditioning, control of the temperature and moisture in buildings, rooms, trains, etc., to make them comfortable.

air craft (ãr′kraft′), 1. airplanes, airships, or balloons. 2. any airplane, airship, or balloon. *n.*

air drome (ãr′drōm′), 1. field for aircraft; airport. 2. shed for aircraft; hangar. 3. field with sheds for aircraft. *n.*

Aire dale (ãr′dāl), a dog that has a rough brown or tan coat with black splotches on it. An Airedale is a large kind of terrier. *n. 15.*

Airedale (23 in. high)

air i ly (ãr′i li), in an airy manner; lightly. *adv.*

air ing (ãr′ing), 1. an exposure to the air for warming, drying, etc. I gave my fur coat a thorough airing. 2. a walk or drive in the open air. *n.*

air line, 1. straight line. 2. route for aircraft.

air mail, 1. mail sent by aircraft. 2. the system of sending mail by aircraft.

air man (ãr′mən), pilot of an airplane, airship, or balloon; aviator or balloonist. *n., pl. airmen.*

air plane (ãr′plān′), a flying machine that has one or more planes or wings and is driven by a motor. *n. 10.*

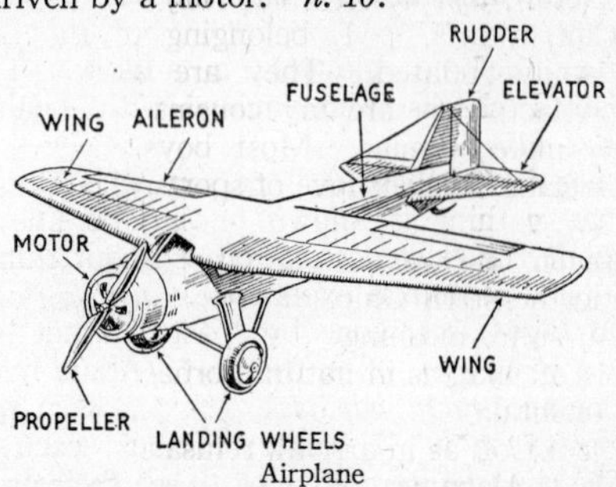

Airplane

air pocket, any current or condition in the air that causes an airplane to drop suddenly.

air port (ãr′pōrt′), place for airplanes to land at and start from. *n.*

air pump, machine for forcing air in or drawing air out of something.

air raid, attack by airplanes or airships.

air ship (ãr′ship′), a dirigible, a balloon that can be steered. *n. 17.*

air tight (ãr′tīt′), 1. so tight that no air can get in or out. 2. leaving no opening. *adj. 18.*

air way (ãr′wā′), route for airplanes. *n.*

air y (ãr′i), 1. of air; in the air. 2. breezy; with air moving through it; as, a large, airy room. 3. like air; not solid or substantial. 4. light as air; graceful; delicate. 5. gay; merry; light-hearted; as, airy laughter. *adj., airier, airiest. 5.*

aisle (īl), 1. a passage between rows of seats in a church, theater, etc. 2. long, narrow passage. A long space between trees in a forest is an aisle. 3. a part of a church at the side of the main part, separated from it by columns or piers. See also the diagram under **nave.** *n. 5.*

Aisle of a church (def. 3)

Aisne (ān), river in northern France. *n.*

a jar[1] (ə jär′), slightly open. *adv., adj. 15.*

a jar[2] (ə jär′), not in harmony. *adv., adj.*

A jax (ā′jaks), 1. a Greek hero at the siege of Troy, next to Achilles in strength and courage. 2. another Greek hero at the siege of Troy, noted for his swiftness. *n. 17.*

a kim bo (ə kim′bō), with the hand on the hip and the elbow bent outward. See the picture just below. *adv., adj. 18.*

a kin (ə kin′), 1. belonging to the same family; related. They are akin to me; in fact, they are my cousins. 2. alike; similar. Most boys are akin in their love of sports. *adj. 9.*

Boy with arms akimbo

Ak ron (ak′rən), a city in northeastern Ohio. *n. 14.*

-al, suffix meaning:—
1. of; like; as in natural, ornamental.
2. act of; as in arrival, refusal.

Ala., Alabama.

Al a bam a (al′ə bam′ə), a Southern State of the United States. *n. 7.*

al a bas ter (al′ə bas′tər), 1. a white mineral somewhat like marble. 2. white and smooth like alabaster. *n., adj. 9.*

a lack (ə lak′) alas; an exclamation of sorrow, regret, or surprise. *interj.* [*Old use*] *18.*

a lac ri ty (ə lak′ri ti), 1. brisk and eager action; liveliness. Although the man was very old, he still moved with alacrity. 2. cheerful willingness. *n. 12.*

A lad din (ə lad′in), a youth in *The Arabian Nights* who found a magic lamp and a magic ring. By rubbing either one of them he could call a powerful spirit to do whatever he asked. *n.*

Al a mo (al′ə mō), mission in San Antonio, Texas. After a siege, the Mexicans finally captured it on March 6, 1836. *n.*

a larm (ə lärm′), 1. a call to arms or action. Paul Revere gave the alarm to the towns near Boston. 2. the warning sound or signal used to give an alarm. 3. the thing that makes the sound or signal; as, a fire alarm. 4. giving an alarm; as, an alarm clock. 5. make uneasy; stir to a sense of danger; frighten. He was alarmed because his friends were so long in returning. 6. sudden fear; excitement caused by fear of danger. *n., adj., v. 2.*

a lar um (ə lar′əm), an old way of spelling **alarm.** *n. 16.*

a las (ə las′), exclamation of sorrow, grief, regret, pity, or dread. *interj. 3.*

A las ka (ə las′kə), a territory in northwestern North America belonging to the United States. *n. 9.*

alb (alb), a white linen robe with narrow sleeves, worn by priests in church. *n.*

Al ba ni a (al bā′ni ə), a former country in Europe near Greece. It is now under Italian control. *n. 17.*

Al ba ny (ôl′bə ni), the capital of New York State, on the Hudson River. *n. 5.*

al ba tross (al′bə trôs), a large, web-footed sea bird that can fly long distances. See the picture. *n. 14.*

Albatross (30 in. long)

al be it (ôl bē′it), although; even though. Albeit he has failed twice, he is not discouraged. *conj. 10.*

Al ber ta (al bėr′tə), province in southwestern Canada. *n.*

al bi no (al bī′nō) person or animal with a pale milky skin, very light hair, and pink eyes. *n., pl. albinos. 18.*

Al bi on (al′bi ən), England. *n.* [*Used in poetry*] *12.*

al bum (al′bəm), a book with blank pages for holding photographs, pictures, stamps, etc. *n. 10.*

al bu men (al bū′min), 1. the white of an egg. 2. albumin. *n. 15.*

al bu min (al bū′min), the protein in the white of an egg and in many other animal and plant tissues and juices. *n. 17.*

Al bu quer que (al′bū kėr′ki), a city in central New Mexico. *n.*

al che mist (al′ki mist), man who studied chemistry and magic in the Middle Ages. The alchemists tried to turn lead into gold. *n. 14.*

al che my (al′ki mi), 1. combination of chemistry and magic which men studied in the Middle Ages. 2. magic power or process for changing one thing into another. *n. 16.*

al co hol (al′kə hôl), 1. the colorless liquid in wine, beer, whiskey, gin, etc., which makes them intoxicating. Alcohol is used in medicines, as a fuel, and in manufacturing. Wood alcohol is a different substance. 2. any liquor containing alcohol. *n. 7.*

al co hol ic (al′kə hôl′ik), 1. of alcohol. 2. containing alcohol. *adj. 9.*

al co hol ism (al′kə hôl izm), the diseased condition caused by drinking too much alcoholic liquor. *n.*

Al cott (ôl′kət), Louisa May, an American author (1832-1888). Her most famous book is *Little Women. n.*

al cove (al′kōv), 1. a small room opening into a larger room. 2. a recess or large hollow space in a wall. *n. 11.*

Alcove

Al den (ôl′dən), John (1599-1687), one of the Pilgrims who settled at Plymouth, Massachusetts. *n. 19.*

al der (ôl′dər), 1. a tree or shrub like a birch. Alders usually grow in wet land. 2. any tree or shrub that resembles the alder; as, the black alder. *n. 10.*

al der man (ôl′dər mən), person who represents the people of a certain district on a council or board that governs a city, town, or borough. *n., pl. aldermen. 6.*

al der man ic (ôl′dər man′ik), 1. of an alderman. 2. suitable for an alderman. *adj. 16.*

Al der ney (ôl′dər ni), a British island in the English Channel. *n.*

ale (āl), a strong light-colored beer made from malt and hops. *n. 6.*

A len çon (ə len′son), 1. a city in northwestern France, famous for its lace. 2. the lace. *n. 17.*

a lert (ə lėrt′), 1. watchful; wide-awake. The dog was alert. 2. lively; nimble. A sparrow is very alert in its movements. 3. **On the alert** means watchful; ready at any instant for what is coming. *adj., n. 8.*

a lert ness (ə lėrt′nis), 1. watchfulness. 2. liveliness; nimbleness. *n. 19.*

A leu tian Is lands (ə lü′shən ī′ləndz), chain of many small islands southwest of Alaska, belonging to the United States.

Al ex an der (al′ig zan′dər). Alexander the Great (356-323 B.C.) was a king of Macedonia. He conquered most of the world known in his time. *n. 5.*

Al ex an dri a (al′ig zan′dri ə), a seaport city in northern Egypt, once famous for its library and scholars. It was founded by Alexander the Great. *n. 12.*

al fal fa (al fal′fə), a plant with deep roots, cloverlike leaves, and bluish-purple flowers. It is used as a food for horses and cattle. *n. 7.*

Alfalfa

Al fred (al′frid). Alfred the Great (849-901 A.D.) was a famous king of part of England from 871 to 901 A.D. *n. 6.*

al gae (al′jē), seaweeds and some fresh-water plants like them. *n. pl. 10.*

al ge bra (al′ji brə), a kind of mathematics that uses letters and negative numbers as well as ordinary numbers. In algebra, $-2a(3ab-a^2)$ equals $-6a^2b+2a^3$. *n. 9.*

Al ge ri a (al jēr′i ə), a country in northern Africa, belonging to France. *n. 13.*

Al giers (al jērz′), a seaport city, the capital of Algeria. *n. 13.*

Al gon quin (al gong′kwin), member of a group of tribes of American Indians. These tribes formerly lived in eastern Canada and eastern United States, but they were pushed westward across the Mississippi. *n.*

a li as (ā′li əs), 1. an assumed name; another name. The spy's real name was Harrison, but he sometimes went by the alias of Johnson. 2. otherwise; otherwise called; as, Jones alias Williams. *n., adv. 16.*

al i bi (al′i bī), 1. the plea or the fact that a person was somewhere else when a crime was committed. 2. excuse. *Used in common talk. n., pl. alibis. 16.*

al ien (āl′yən), 1. foreigner. A person who is not a citizen of the country in which he lives is an alien. 2. of another country; foreign. 3. entirely different; not harmonious; strange. Unkindness was alien to his nature. *n., adj. 7.*

al ien ate (āl′yən āt), 1. turn away in feeling or affection; make unfriendly. He was alienated from his sister by her foolish acts. 2. transfer ownership of. Enemy property was alienated during the war. *v. 11.*

al ien a tion (āl′yən ā′shən), 1. a turning away in feeling or affection. 2. transfer of ownership. *n. 16.*

al ien ist (āl′yən ist), a doctor who treats mental diseases. *n.*

a light[1] (ə līt′), 1. get down; get off; as, to alight from a horse, to alight from a train. 2. come down from the air; come down from flight. The bird alighted on our window sill. 3. come upon by chance; happen to find. *v., alighted* or *alit, alighting. 5.*

a light[2] (ə līt′), on fire; lighted up. Her face was alight with happiness. *adv., adj.*

a lign (ə līn′), put in a straight line; come into line; be in line. *v.* Also spelled **aline.**

a lign ment (ə līn′mənt), 1. arrangement in a straight line. The troops were in perfect alignment. 2. adjustment to a line. The sights of the rifle were in alignment with the target. *n. 18.* Also spelled **alinement.**

-O-O-O-O-O-O-O-O-O-O-
IN ALIGNMENT

-O-O-O-O-O-O-O-O-O-O-
OUT OF ALIGNMENT

a like (ə līk′), 1. similar; like one another. These twins are very much alike. 2. in the same way. Robert and his father walk alike. *adj., adv. 2.*

al i ment (al′i mənt), food; nourishment. *n. 19.*

al i men ta ry (al′i men′tə ri), having to do with food and nutrition. The **alimentary canal** consists of the esophagus, stomach, and intestines, or the parts of the body through which food passes. *adj. 13.*

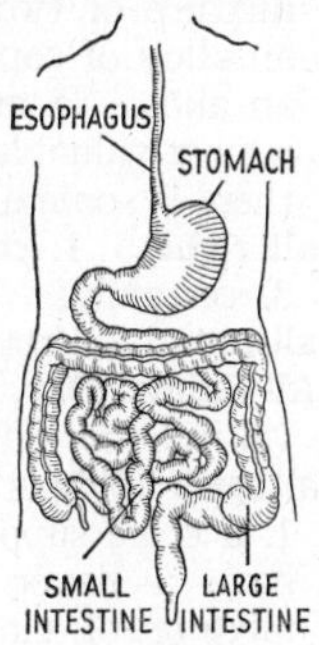

ESOPHAGUS STOMACH SMALL INTESTINE LARGE INTESTINE

Alimentary canal

a line (ə līn′), align. *v.*

a line ment (ə līn′mənt), alignment. *n.*

a live (ə līv′), 1. living. Was the snake alive or dead? 2. active; lively; brisk. **Look alive!** means "Hurry up!" 3. full of people or things in motion; swarming. The streets were alive with people. 4. **Alive to** means taking notice of; realizing. Are you alive to what is going on? *adj. 2.*

al ka li (al′kə lī), any substance like soda and potash, that neutralizes acids and forms salts. Lye and ammonia are two common alkalis. *n., pl. alkalis* or *alkalies. 10.*

al ka line (al′kə līn), 1. of or like an alkali. 2. containing an alkali. *adj. 9.*

al ka loid (al′kə loid), a substance somewhat like an alkali, found in plants. Morphine and quinine are alkaloids. *n. 12.*

all (ôl), 1. All dogs have heads. 2. The pin was all gold. 3. All is well. 4. They came after all. 5. **At all** means (1) in any way. (2) under any conditions. *adj., n., pron., adv. 1.*

Al lah (al′ə), Mohammedan name for God. *n.*

all-a round (ôl′ə round′), not limited or specialized; able to do many things; useful in many ways. *adj.*

al lay (ə lā′), make less; check; quiet; relieve. His fears were allayed by news of the safety of his family. His fever was allayed by the medicine. *v., allayed, allaying. 8.*

al le ga tion (al′i gā′shən), 1. assertion. The lawyer's allegation was proved. 2. assertion without proof. He makes so many wild allegations that no one will believe him. *n. 15.*

al lege (ə lej′), 1. assert; declare. This man alleges that his watch has been stolen. 2. assert without proof. The alleged theft really never happened. 3. give or bring forward as a reason, argument, or excuse. *v. 6.*

Al le ghe nies (al′i gā′niz), the Allegheny mountains, a range that extends from Pennsylvania to Virginia. *n. pl.*

Al le ghe ny (al′i gā′ni), river in western Pennsylvania flowing into the Ohio. *n. 12.*

al le giance (ə lē′jəns), 1. the loyalty owed by a citizen to his government or by a subject to his ruler. I pledge allegiance to the flag. 2. loyalty; faithfulness; devotion. We owe allegiance to our friends. *n. 5.*

al le gor i cal (al′i gor′i kəl), explaining or teaching something by a story; using allegory. The parables in the Bible are allegorical. *adj. 15.*

al le go ry (al′i gō′ri), a story which is told to explain or teach something. Bunyan's *Pilgrim's Progress* and the parables in the Bible are allegories. *n., pl. allegories. 12.*

al le gro (ä lā′grō), 1. in music, quick; lively. 2. a quick, lively part in a piece of music. *adv., adj., n., pl. allegros.*

al le lu ia (al′i lü′yə), 1. Praise ye the Lord! 2. a song of praise. *interj., n.* Also spelled **hallelujah** or **halleluiah.**

al ler gy (al′ər ji), unusual sensitiveness to a certain substance. Hay fever and asthma are often caused by allergies to certain pollens and dusts. *n., pl. allergies.*

al le vi ate (ə lē′vi āt), make easier to endure; relieve; lessen. Heat often alleviates pain. *v. 15.*

al le vi a tion (ə lē′vi ā′shən), 1. act of alleviating. 2. thing that alleviates. *n.*

al ley[1] (al′i), 1. a narrow back street in a city or town. 2. a path in a park or garden, bordered by trees. 3. a long, narrow, enclosed place for bowling. *n., pl. alleys. 5.*

al ley[2] (al′i), a large, white or colored marble to shoot at other marbles. *n., pl. alleys.*

All hal lows (ôl′hal′ōz), November 1, All Saints' Day. *n.*

al li ance (ə lī′əns), 1. union formed by agreement; joining of interests. An alliance may be a joining of family interests by marriage, a joining of national interests by treaty, etc. 2. the nations, persons, etc., who belong to such a union. *n. 7.*

al lied (ə līd′), 1. united by agreement; as,

allied nations, allied armies. 2. connected. His business is allied with several banks. 3. related. Allied animals, like the dog and wolf, look somewhat alike. *adj., pt. and pp. of* **ally.** *6.*

al lies (al′īz), more than one ally. The **Allies** are the United States, the British Empire, and their allies. *n. pl.*

al li ga tor (al′i gā′tər), a large crawling animal with a long body, four short legs, a thick skin, and a long tail. See the picture. Alligators live in rivers and marshes of warm parts of America. *n. 7.*

Alligator (12 ft. long)

alligator pear, avocado.

al lit er a tion (ə lit′ər ā′shən), repetition of the same first letter or sound in a group of words. *Example:* "Upon a *M*ay *m*orning when *s*oft was the *s*unshine." *n. 16.*

al lot (ə lot′), 1. divide and distribute in parts or shares. The profits have all been allotted. 2. give as a share; assign. The principal allotted each class a part in the Christmas program. *v., allotted, allotting. 8.*

al lot ment (ə lot′mənt), 1. division and distribution in parts or shares. The allotment was made on Monday. 2. share. Your allotment was four dollars. *n. 14.*

all-out (ôl′out′), complete; total. *adj.*

al low (ə lou′), 1. let; permit. Mrs. Smith allows her children to go swimming. Dogs are not allowed in this car. 2. give; let have. Grace is allowed 20 cents a day for lunch at school. 3. admit; acknowledge; concede. The judge allowed the claim. 4. add or subtract to make up for something. The trip will cost you only $20; but you ought to allow $5 more for extra expenses. 5. **Allow for** sometimes means take into consideration. In making the dress large, she allowed for its shrinking. *v. 1.*

al low a ble (ə lou′ə bəl), allowed by law; permitted by the rules of the game; not forbidden. In some parks it is allowable to walk on the grass. *adj. 12.*

al low ance (ə lou′əns), 1. a limited share set apart; a definite portion or amount given out. Mary has an allowance of 25 cents a week. Our allowance of candy is two pieces after dinner. 2. amount added or subtracted to make up for something; discount. That store makes an allowance of 2% for cash payment. 3. **Make allowance for** means take into consideration; allow for. You must make allowance for the wishes of others. *n. 7.*

al loy (al′oi for 1 and 3, ə loi′ for 2), 1. a mixture of two or more metals. Brass is an alloy of copper and zinc. 2. make into an alloy. 3. an inferior metal mixed with a more valuable one. This is not pure gold; there is some alloy in it. *n., v. 13.*

all right, 1. correct; satisfactory. 2. yes. 3. certainly.

all-round (ôl′round′), all-around. *adj.*

All Saints' Day, November 1, a church festival in honor of all the saints.

all spice (ôl′spīs′), 1. a spice supposed to have a flavor like a mixture of cinnamon, nutmeg, and clove. It is made from the dried berries of a tree that grows in the West Indies. 2. the berry it is made from. *n. 19.*

Allspice

al lude (ə lüd′), refer indirectly; mention slightly. Do not ask him about his failure; do not even allude to it. *v. 7.*

al lure (ə lür′), 1. tempt by the offer of some pleasure or reward. The circus so allured Jim that he wished to join it. 2. fascinate; attract or charm. *v. 5.*

al lure ment (ə lür′mənt), 1. temptation. 2. attractiveness; fascination; charm. 3. thing that allures. *n. 8.*

al lu sion (ə lü′zhən), indirect reference; slight mention. John was hurt by any allusion to his failure to pass. *n. 7.*

al lu vi al (ə lü′vi əl), formed by sand or mud left by flowing water. A delta is an alluvial deposit at the mouth of a river. *adj. 12.*

al ly (ə lī′ for 1, al′ī for 2), 1. unite by agreement; combine for some special purpose. One country will ally itself with another to protect its people or its interests. 2. a person or state united with another for some special purpose. England and France have been allies in some wars though they have fought against each other in others. *v., allied, allying, n., pl. allies. 8.*

al ma ma ter (al′mə mā′tər), person's school, college, or university. Alma mater means foster mother.

al ma nac (ôl′mə nak), a calendar of days, weeks, and months, often with information about the weather, the sun, moon, stars, tides, church days, and other facts. *n. 8.*

al might y (ôl mīt′i), possessing all power. God is often called **the Almighty.** *adj., n. 5.*

al mond (ä′mənd), 1. the nut or seed of a fruit growing in warm regions. 2. the tree it grows on. 3. something shaped like an almond. *n. 7.*

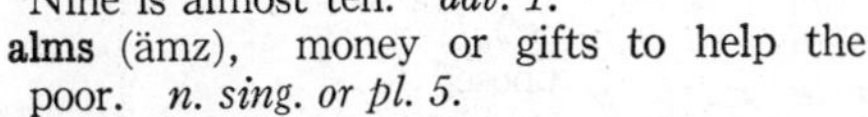
Almond with and without its shell

al mon er (al′mən ər), person who distributes alms for a king, monastery, etc. *n. 20.*

al most (ôl′mōst), nearly. Nine is almost ten. *adv. 1.*

alms (ämz), money or gifts to help the poor. *n. sing. or pl. 5.*

alms house (ämz′hous′), home for persons who have not enough money to live on. *n. 15.*

al oe (al′ō), a plant somewhat like a lily. Some aloes have erect spikes of flowers and bitter juice. *n., pl. aloes.*

al oes (al′ōz), a very bitter drug made from the juice of aloes, used as a medicine. *n. 13.*

a loft (ə lôft′), 1. far above the earth; up in the air; high up. 2. above the deck; high up among the sails and masts. *adv. 6.*

a lone (ə lōn′), 1. apart from other persons or things. One tree stood alone on the hill. 2. without anyone else. One boy alone can do this work. 3. without anything more. Meat alone is not the best food for children. 4. **Let alone** means (1) not touch; not do; not pay attention to. (2) not to mention. It would have been a hot day for July, let alone May. *adj., adv. 1.*

a long (ə lông′), 1. Trees are planted along the street. 2. March along. 3. Some special meanings are:

all along, all the time.

along with, in company with.

get along, 1. go away. 2. advance. 3. manage. 4. succeed; prosper. 5. agree.

prep., adv. 1.

a long side (ə lông′sīd′), 1. at the side; close to the side; side by side. 2. by the side of; side by side with. The boat was alongside the wharf. *adv., prep. 8.*

a loof (ə lüf′), away; apart. One boy stood aloof from the other boys. He kept aloof because he did not like them. *adv., adj. 6.*

a loud (ə loud′), 1. loud enough to be heard; not in a whisper. He spoke aloud, although he was alone. She read the story aloud to the others. 2. loudly; in a loud voice. *adv. 3.*

alp (alp), a high mountain. *n. 19.* See **Alps.**

al pac a (al pak′ə), 1. a sheeplike animal of South America having long, silky wool. 2. its wool. 3. a cloth made from this wool. 4. a glossy, wiry cloth made of wool and cotton. *n. 19.*

Alpaca (5 ft. high to top of head)

al pha (al′fə), the beginning of anything. **Alpha and omega** means the first and the last; the beginning and the end. *n. 20.*

al pha bet (al′fə bet), 1. a set of letters used in writing a language. 2. the letters of a language arranged in their usual order, not as they are in words. The English alphabet is a b c d e f g h i j k l m n o p q r s t u v w x y z. *n. 8.*

al pha bet i cal (al′fə bet′i kəl), 1. arranged by letters in the order of the alphabet. 2. of the alphabet. *adj. 13.*

al pha bet i cal ly (al′fə bet′i kəl i), according to the alphabet. *adv.*

al pha bet ize (al′fə bə tīz), arrange in alphabetical order. *v.*

al pine (al′pīn), of or like high mountains. *adj. 8.*

Al pine (al′pīn), of or like the Alps. *adj.*

Alps (alps), a mountain system in southern Europe, famous for its scenery. *n. pl. 6.*

al read y (ôl red′i), before this time; by this time; even now. You are half an hour late already. The child has already broken his new toy. *adv. 1.*

Al sace (al′sās), a former district in France. It was taken by Germany in 1871, restored in 1919, and taken again in 1940. *n. 18.*

al so (ôl′sō), too; in addition. That dress is pretty, and cheap also. *adv. 1.*

al tar (ôl′tər), 1. a stand or table in the most sacred part of a church. 2. a raised place built of earth or stone on which to make sacrifices or burn offerings to gods. *n. 3.*

al ter (ôl′tər), change; vary; make different; become different. If this coat is too large, a tailor can alter it to fit you. *v. 3.*

al ter a tion (ôl′tər ā′shən), change. Mother made some alterations in her new dress. *n. 7.*

al ter ca tion (ôl′tər kā′shən), angry dispute. The boys had an altercation over the umpire's decision. *n. 15.*

al ter nate (ôl′tər nāt for 1 and 2, ôl′tər nit for 3, 4, and 5), 1. arrange one after the other; be arranged by turns. Squares and circles alternate in this row:

□ ○ □ ○ □ ○ □ ○

2. take turns. Lucy and her sister will alternate in setting the table. 3. first one and then the other by turns. The row has alternate squares and circles. 4. every other. We buy ice on alternate days because we do not need it every day. 5. one appointed to take the place of another if it should be necessary; a substitute. *v., adj., n. 6.*

alternating current, electric current that reverses its direction at regular intervals.

al ter na tion (ôl′tər nā′shən), alternating; coming first one and then another by turns. There is an alternation of red and white stripes in the flag of the United States. *n. 12.*

al ter na tive (ôl tėr′nə tiv), 1. giving or requiring a choice between things. Father offered the alternative plans of having a picnic or taking a trip on a steamboat. 2. a choice between things. John's father gave him the alternative of staying in high school or going to work. 3. one of the things to be chosen. John chose the first alternative and stayed in school. *adj., n. 9.*

al though or **al tho** (ôl ᴛʜō′), though. *conj. 1.*

al ti tude (al′ti tūd or al′ti tüd), 1. height. What altitude did the airplane reach? 2. height above sea level. The altitude of Denver is 5300 feet. 3. a high place. In some altitudes the snow never melts. *n. 6.*

al to (al′tō), 1. part in music sung by the lowest female voice or the highest male voice. 2. a woman or man who sings alto. *n., pl. altos. 17.*

al to geth er (ôl′tə geᴛʜ′ər), 1. completely; entirely. The house was altogether destroyed by fire. 2. on the whole. Altogether, he was well pleased. *adv. 3.*

al tru is tic (al′trü is′tik), thoughtful of others; unselfish. *adj. 17.*

al um (al′əm), 1. a white mineral salt used in medicine and in dyeing. Alum is also used to stop the bleeding of a small cut. 2. colorless, crystallike salt used in baking powder. *n. 15.*

a lu mi num (ə lü′mi nəm), a silver-white, very light metal that does not tarnish easily. Aluminum is much used for making kettles and pans. *n. 10.*

a lum ni (ə lum′nī), graduates or former pupils of a school or college. *n. pl. 13.*

al ways (ôl′wāz), at all times; all the time. Night always follows day. *adv. 1.*

am (am). John said, "I am 6 years old. I am going to school." *v. 1.*

Am., 1. America. 2. American.

A.M. or **a.m.,** before noon; the time from midnight to noon. *13.*

a main (ə mān′), 1. with force or violence. 2. at full speed. *adv. 7.*

a mal gam (ə mal′gəm), 1. an alloy or mixture of mercury with another metal. Gold amalgam is a mixture of gold and mercury. 2. mixture; combination. *n. 20.*

a mal gam ate (ə mal′gə māt), combine; unite; blend. Many different races are being amalgamated in the United States. *v. 15.*

a mal gam a tion (ə mal′gə mā′shən), mixture; combination; union. Our nation is an amalgamation of many different races. *n. 17.*

a man u en sis (ə man′ū en′sis), person who writes down what another says; person who copies what another has written. *n., pl. amanuenses* (-sēz). *18.*

am a ranth (am′ə ranth), 1. an imaginary flower that never fades. *Used in poetry.* 2. plant with showy purple or crimson flowers. *n. 16.*

am a ran thine (am′ə ran′thin), 1. never fading. 2. purple; purplish-red. *adj. 15.*

am a ryl lis (am′ə ril′is), a plant with large, rose-colored flowers. *n.*

Amaryllis (2 to 4 ft. high)

a mass (ə mas′), heap together; pile up; accumulate. The miser amassed a fortune for himself. *v. 11.*

am a teur (am′ə tūr), 1. person who does something for pleasure, not for money. 2. person who does something rather poorly. 3. of amateurs. 4. being an amateur; as, an amateur musician. *n., adj. 9.*

am a teur ish (am′ə tūr ish), done as an amateur might do it; not expert; not very skillful. *adj.*

am a to ry (am′ə tō′ri), expressing love; having to do with lovemaking or lovers. *adj. 16.*

a maze (ə māz′), surprise greatly; strike with sudden wonder. The boy who had seemed so stupid amazed us all by his fine examination. She was so amazed by the surprise party that she could not think of anything to say. *v. 3.*

a maze ment (ə māz′mənt), great surprise; sudden wonder. The little girl was filled with amazement when she first saw the ocean. *n. 5.*

Am a zon (am′ə zon), 1. a river in South America, the largest river in the world. 2. one of a race of women warriors in Greek stories, supposed to live near the Black Sea. 3. a tall, strong, masculine woman. *n. 7.*

am bas sa dor (am bas′ə dər), 1. a representative of highest rank sent by one government or ruler to another. An ambassador lives in a foreign country and speaks and acts in behalf of his ruler or his government. 2. official messenger with a special errand; messenger; agent. *n. 5.*

am ber (am′bər), 1. a hard, yellow or yellowish-brown gum, used for jewelry and in making stems of pipes. Amber is the resin of pine trees that grew very long ago. 2. made of amber; as, amber beads. 3. yellow or yellowish brown. *n., adj. 5.*

am ber gris (am′bər grēs), a waxlike, grayish substance coming from the sperm whale, used in making perfumes. *n. 19.*

am bi ent (am′bi ənt), surrounding. The flowers made the ambient air fragrant. *adj. 20.*

am bi gu i ty (am′bi gū′i ti), 1. possibility of two or more meanings. 2. an expression that can have more than one meaning. *n., pl. ambiguities. 13.*

am big u ous (am big′ū əs), 1. having more than one meaning. It is ambiguous to say "After John hit Dick, he ran away," because we cannot tell which boy ran away. 2. doubtful; not clear; uncertain. He was left in an ambiguous position by his friend's failure to appear and speak for him. *adj. 12.*

am bi tion (am bish′ən), 1. strong desire for fame or honor; seeking after a high position or great power in life. 2. the thing for which one has a strong desire. Her ambition was to be a great actress. *n. 3.*

am bi tious (am bish′əs), 1. having ambition. John is ambitious to get through high school in three years. 2. showing ambition. *adj. 4.*

am ble (am′bəl), 1. the way a horse goes when it first lifts the two legs on one side and then lifts the two on the other side. 2. go in that manner. 3. an easy, gentle gait. 4. go with an easy, gentle gait. *n., v. 13.*

am bro sia (am brō′zhə), 1. the food of the gods of ancient Greece. 2. anything especially delicious. *n. 12.*

am bro sial (am brō′zhəl), like ambrosia; delicious; sweet-smelling. *adj. 14.*

am bu lance (am′bū ləns), wagon or automobile used to carry sick or wounded people. *n. 11.*

am bus cade (am′bəs kād′), ambush. *n., v. 15.*

am bush (am′bủsh), 1. soldiers hidden so that they can make a surprise attack on an approaching enemy. 2. place where the soldiers are hidden. 3. attack from an ambush. 4. act or condition of lying in wait. The Indians often trapped their enemies by ambush instead of meeting them in open battle. 5. put soldiers in some concealed place for a surprise attack. The general ambushed his troops in the heavy woods on either side of the road. *n., v. 8.*

a me ba (ə mē′bə), amoeba. *n., pl. amebas, amebae* (-bē).

a mel io rate (ə mēl′yə rāt), improve; make better; become better. *v. 20.*

a mel io ra tion (ə mēl′yə rā′shən), improvement. *n. 18.*

a men (ā′men′ or ä′men′). Amen is a word said at the end of a prayer. Perhaps it means "May it become so" or "Be it so!" *interj., n. 6.*

a me na ble (ə mē′nə bəl), 1. open to suggestion or advice; responsive; submissive. Dick is reasonable and amenable to reason or persuasion. 2. accountable; answerable. People living in a country are amenable to its laws. *adj. 15.*

a mend (ə mend′), 1. change for the better; correct. It is time you amended your ways. 2. change. Each time that they amended the law, they made it worse. *v. 5.*

a mend ment (ə mend′mənt), 1. a change for the better; correction. 2. a change. There have been many amendments to the Constitution of the United States. *n. 4.*

a mends (ə mendz′), payment for loss; satisfaction for an injury; compensation. If you took more than your share of the money, you should at once make amends by returning the extra amount. *n. sing. or pl.*

a men i ty (ə men′i ti), 1. pleasantness; agreeableness; as, the amenity of a warm climate. The amenity of his manners won him friends. 2. pleasant way; polite act. Saying "Thank you" and holding the door open for a person to pass through are amenities. *n., pl. amenities. 20.*

A mer i ca (ə mer′i kə), 1. the United States. 2. North America. 3. North America and South America. *n. 2.*

A mer i can (ə mer′i kən), 1. of the United

States; belonging to the United States. 2. citizen of the United States. 3. of America; in America. 4. person born or living in America. *adj., n. 1.*

A meri can ism (ə mer′i kən izm), 1. devotion to the United States. 2. a word or phrase originating or much used in the United States. 3. a custom or trait peculiar to the United States. *n. 20..*

A meri can i za tion (ə mer′i kən i zā′shən), act or process of Americanizing. *n. 17.*

A meri can ize (ə mer′i kən īz), make or become American in habits, customs, or character. *v.*

am e thyst (am′i thist), 1. a purple or violet quartz used for jewelry. 2. purple; violet. *n. 13.*

a mi a ble (ā′mi ə bəl), friendly; kindly; pleasing; agreeable. May is a sweet, gentle, amiable girl. *adj. 6.*

am i ca ble (am′i kə bəl), friendly; peaceable. Instead of fighting, the two nations settled their quarrel in an amicable way. *adj. 10.*

a mid (ə mid′), in the middle of; among. The little church stood unharmed amid the ruins of the bombed village. *prep. 5.*

a mid ships (ə mid′ships), in the middle of a ship. *adv. 18.*

a midst (ə midst′), amid. *prep. 9.*

a miss (ə mis′), wrong; not the way it should be; out of order; at fault. To do something amiss is to do it in the wrong way. *adv., adj. 7.*

am i ty (am′i ti), peace and friendship; friendly relations. If there were amity between nations, there would be no wars. *n., pl. amities. 12.*

Am mon (am′ən), 1. an Egyptian god represented with horns like a ram's. 2. Egyptian name for Zeus. *n. 10.*

am mo ni a (ə mō′ni ə), 1. a strong-smelling, colorless gas. 2. ammonia gas dissolved in water. Ammonia is very useful for cleaning and for many other purposes. *n. 9.*

am mon ite (am′ə nīt), a kind of coiled shell. See the picture. *n. 19.*

Ammonite

am mu ni tion (am′ū nish′ən), powder, shot, bullets, balls, bombs, and shells; military supplies. *n. 7.*

am nes ty (am′nis ti), a general pardon for offenses against a government. Order was restored and the king granted amnesty to those who had plotted against him. *n., pl. amnesties. 15.*

a moe ba (ə mē′bə), a very small and very simple water animal. *n., pl. amoebas, amoebae* (-bē). *15.* A simpler spelling is **ameba.**

Amoeba

a mok (ə muk′), amuck. *adv.*

a mong (ə mung′). His brothers were among the crowd. Divide the fruit among the boys. Was John among those present? The children quarreled among themselves. *prep. 1.*

a mongst (ə mungst′), among. *prep. 6.*

am o rous (am′ə rəs), 1. inclined to love. 2. in love. 3. showing love; loving. 4. having to do with love. *adj. 12.*

a mor phous (ə môr′fəs), 1. shapeless; formless. 2. not made of crystals. Glass is amorphous; sugar is crystalline. 3. of no particular kind or character. *adj. 18.*

A mos (ā′məs), 1. a Hebrew prophet. 2. a book of the Old Testament. *n. 12.*

a mount (ə mount′), 1. reach; be equal. The loss from the flood amounts to ten million dollars. Keeping what belongs to another amounts to stealing. 2. sum; quantity. No amount of coaxing would make the dog leave his master. 3. total sum; full value. *v., n. 1.*

a mour (ə mür′), a love affair; secret lovemaking. *n. 14.*

am pere (am′pēr), a unit for measuring the strength of an electric current. Ordinary light bulbs take from ¼ to ½ ampere. *n. 18.*

am phib i an (am fib′i ən), 1. an animal living both on land and in water. Frogs are amphibians. 2. belonging to the animals that live both on land and in water. 3. an airplane so made that it can start from or alight on either land or water. *n., adj. 13.*

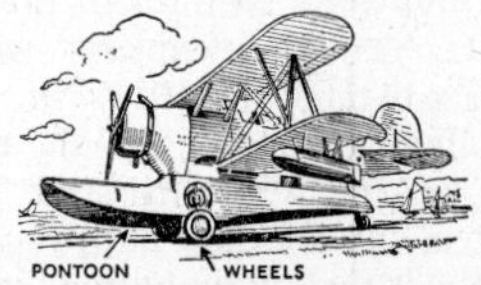

Amphibian airplane

am phib i ous (am fib′i əs), able to live both on land and in water. *adj. 16.*

am phi the a ter or **am phi the a tre** (am′fi thē′ə tər), 1. a circular or oval building with rows of seats around an open space in the center. 2. something resembling an amphitheater in form; as, an amphitheater of hills. *n. 14.*

Roman amphitheater

am ple (am′pəl), 1. large. 2. abundant; more than enough. Take an ample supply of food, for we shall be gone all day. 3. enough. The money her mother gave her was ample for carfare and lunches. *adj. 3.*

am pli fi ca tion (am′pli fi kā′shən), enlargement; extension. *n. 16.*

am pli fi er (am′pli fī′ər), 1. one that amplifies. 2. vacuum tube in a radio set for strengthening the electrical impulses. *n.*

am pli fy (am′pli fī), 1. make greater; make stronger or larger. 2. make fuller and more extensive. Amplify your description of the circus. *v., amplified, amplifying. 14.*

am pli tude (am′pli tūd or am′pli tüd), 1. largeness; great width or size. 2. abundance; more than enough. A very rich man has an amplitude of money. *n. 13.*

am ply (am′pli), in an ample manner; abundantly. *adv. 14.*

am pu tate (am′pū tāt), cut off. The doctor amputated the soldier's leg. *v.*

am pu ta tion (am′pū tā′shən), the operation of cutting off all or part of an arm or leg. *n. 18.*

Am ster dam (am′stər dam), important seaport and capital of the Netherlands. *n. 7.*

a muck (ə muk′), mad with a desire to attack. **Run amuck** means run about in a murderous frenzy. The bull ran amuck, trying to kill everyone in his way. *adv.*

am u let (am′ū lit), something worn as a magic charm against evil or harm. *n. 15.*

A mund sen (ä′mun sən), Roald (1872-1928), a Norwegian explorer who discovered the South Pole in 1911. *n.*

a muse (ə mūz′), 1. entertain; turn to pleasant thoughts and feelings; cause to feel cheerful and happy. The sailor amused the little boy by telling him a story. 2. cause to laugh or smile. *v. 4.*

a muse ment (ə mūz′mənt), 1. condition of being amused. The boy's amusement was so great that we all had to laugh with him. 2. anything that amuses; entertainment; sport. *n. 5.*

an (an, *unstressed* ən), 1. Is there an apple for me? 2. James earns ten cents an hour. *indefinite article. 1.*

-an, suffix meaning:—

1. of or having to do with; as in Mohammedan.
2. native or inhabitant of; as in Missourian.

Both meanings are shown by American, Italian, and Californian.

a nach ro nism (ə nak′rə nizm), 1. putting a person, thing, or event in some time where it does not belong. It would be an anachronism to speak of Julius Caesar telephoning or of George Washington riding in an automobile. 2. something placed or occurring out of its proper time. *n.*

an a con da (an′ə kon′də), 1. a large snake that crushes its prey. 2. a large South American snake. *n.*

Anaconda (25 ft. long)

An a con da (an′ə kon′də), city in southwestern Montana, important for its copper mines. *n.*

a nae mi a (ə nē′mi ə), anemia. *n. 20.*

an aes the sia (an′is thē′zhə), anesthesia. *n.*

an aes thet ic (an′is thet′ik), anesthetic. *n., adj. 19.*

a nal o gous (ə nal′ə gəs), similar in some ways; similar in the quality or feature that is being thought of. The heart is analogous to a pump. *adj. 13.*

a nal o gy (ə nal′ə ji), likeness in some ways with differences in others. There is an analogy between the human heart and a pump. *n., pl. analogies. 14.*

a nal y sis (ə nal′i sis), separation of anything into the parts or elements that together make it. An analysis can be made of a book, a person's character, a medicine, water, soil, etc. *n., pl. analyses* (-sēz). *8.*

an a lyt ic (an′ə lit′ik), analytical. *adj. 15.*

an a lyt i cal (an′ə lit′i kəl), separating a whole into its parts; using analysis. *adj. 14.*

an a lyze or **an a lyse** (an′ə līz), 1. separate into its parts. We can analyze water into oxygen and hydrogen. 2. examine the parts or elements of; find out the essential features of. A businessman tries to analyze the causes of success. We analyze a sentence when we explain the form and use of every word in it. *v. 7.*

an arch (an′ärk), anarchist. *n. 16.*

an ar chist (an′ər kist), person who wants to overthrow established governments and have a world without rulers and laws. *n. 11.*

an ar chy (an′ər ki), 1. absence of a system of government and law. 2. disorder; confusion. *n. 9.*

a nath e ma (ə nath′i mə), 1. a solemn curse calling down evil upon somebody or something. 2. person or thing which is accursed. *n. 13.*

a nath e ma tize (ə nath′i mə tīz), curse; utter anathemas. *v. 18.*

An a to li a (an′ə tō′li ə), Asia Minor. *n.*

an a tom i cal (an′ə tom′i kəl), of anatomy; having to do with anatomy; structural. *adj. 16.*

a nat o mist (ə nat′ə mist), person who knows much about anatomy. *n. 15.*

a nat o mize (ə nat′ə mīz), 1. dissect. 2. analyze. *v. 16.*

a nat o my (ə nat′ə mi), 1. structure of an animal or plant. The anatomy of an earthworm is much simpler than that of a man. 2. the science of the structure of animals or plants. Anatomy is a part of biology. 3. cutting apart animals or plants to study their structure. *n. 7.*

-ance, suffix meaning:—
1. act or fact of ——ing; as in avoidance, continuance.
2. quality or state of being ——ed; as in annoyance.
3. quality or state of being ——ant; as in ignorance, importance.
4. thing that ——s; as in conveyance, hindrance.
5. what is ——ed; as in contrivance, inheritance.
A word formed with -ance may have two or more of these meanings, and may acquire other meanings.

an ces tor (an′ses tər), person from whom one is descended. Your father, your mother, your grandfathers, your grandmothers, and so on back, are your ancestors. *n. 4.*

an ces tral (an ses′trəl), 1. of ancestors. The ancestral home of the Pilgrims was England. 2. inherited from ancestors. Blue eyes is an ancestral trait in that family. *adj. 8.*

an ces try (an′ses tri), 1. parents, grandparents, and other ancestors. Many of the early settlers in America had English ancestry. 2. descent from ancestors. *n., pl. ancestries. 11.*

Anchor

an chor (ang′kər), 1. shaped piece of iron attached to a chain or rope and used to hold a ship in place. The anchor grips the bottom and so keeps the ship from drifting. See the picture. 2. secure (a ship) by dropping an anchor to the bottom. 3. drop anchor. 4. fix firmly; as, to anchor a tent to the ground. 5. anything that makes a person feel sure and safe. His mother's letters were an anchor to the boy at this time. *n., v. 3.*

an chor age (ang′kər ij), 1. a place to anchor. 2. act of anchoring. 3. cost of anchoring. *n. 10.*

an cho rite (ang′kə rīt), 1. person who lives alone in a solitary place for religious meditation. 2. hermit. *n. 15.*

Anchovy

an cho vy (an′chō vi), a very small fish, somewhat like a herring. Anchovies are pickled or made into a salt paste or sauce. *n., pl. anchovies. 20.*

an cient (ān′shənt), 1. belonging to times long past. We saw the ruins of an ancient temple built six thousand years ago. **The ancients** means peoples who lived long ago, like the Greeks and Romans. 2. very old. *adj., n. 2.*

an cient ly (ān′shənt li), in ancient times. *adv.*

and (and, *unstressed* ənd or ən), 1. You can come and go on the car. 4 and 2 make 6. 2. And sometimes means to. Try and do better means try to do better. *Used in common talk. conj. 1.*

An da lu sia (an′də lü′zhə), a region in southern Spain. Andalusia has a fertile soil and is rich in minerals. *n. 13.*

an dan te (an dan′ti), 1. in music, moderately slow. 2. moderately slow movement in music; piece of music in this time. *adv., adj., n.*

An der sen (an′dər sən), Hans Christian, Danish writer of children's stories (1805-1875). *n.*

An des (an′dēz), the mountain system in western South America. *n. pl. 9.*

Andirons

and i rons (and′ī′ərnz), pair of metal supports for wood in a fireplace. See the picture. *n. pl. 15.*

an ec dote (an′ik dōt), a short account of some interesting incident or event. Many anecdotes are told about Abraham Lincoln. *n. 7.*

a ne mi a (ə nē′mi ə), lack of blood; not enough of certain parts of the blood. *n. 16.*

an e mom e ter (an′i mom′i tər), instrument for measuring the velocity or pressure of the wind. *n.*

a nem o ne (ə nem′ə ni), 1. plant with slender stems and white flowers that blossoms early in the spring. 2. the sea anemone, a flowerlike polyp. *n. 15.*

an es the sia (an′is thē′zhə), loss of feeling of pain, touch, cold, etc.; insensibility. *n.*

Sea anemone (4 in. high)

an es thet ic (an′is thet′ik), 1. thing that causes anesthesia. Chloroform is an anesthetic. 2. causing anesthesia. *n., adj. 10.*

a new (ə nū′ or ə nü′), 1. again; once more. He made so many blots on his paper that he had to begin his homework anew. 2. in a new way. The architect planned the building anew. *adv. 7.*

an gel (ān′jəl), 1. messenger from God. 2. person like an angel in goodness, innocence, loveliness, etc. 3. a spirit, good or bad. 4. an old English gold coin. *n. 2.*

an gel ic (an jel′ik), 1. of angels; heavenly. 2. like an angel; pure; innocent; good and lovely. *adj. 8.*

an gel i cal (an jel′i kəl), angelic. *adj. 17.*

An ge lus or **an ge lus** (an′jə ləs), 1. a devotional exercise in memory of Christ's assuming human form, which Roman Catholics say. 2. the bell tolled at morning, noon, and night as a signal for people to say this exercise. *n.*

an ger (ang′gər), 1. the feeling which you have when you are angry; when someone tries to hold you and you do not wish to be held; when you slap, kick, or bite at people; when someone tries to keep you from doing something which you want to do. 2. make angry. The boy's disobedience angered his father. *n., v. 2.*

an gle[1] (ang′gəl), 1. the space between two lines or surfaces that meet. 2. the figure formed by two such lines or surfaces. 3. the difference in direction between two lines. The roads lie at an angle of about 45 degrees. 4. corner. *n. 4.*

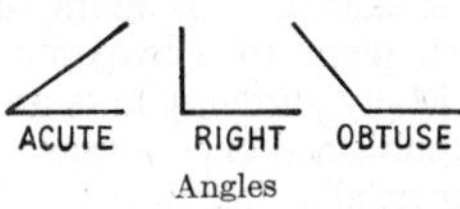

Angles

an gle[2] (ang′gəl), 1. fish with hook and line. 2. try to get something by using tricks or schemes. She angled for an invitation to his party by flattering him. *v.*

an gler (ang′glər), 1. person who fishes with hook and line. 2. a kind of fish that eats smaller fish. *n. 13.*

an gle worm (ang′gəl wėrm′), earthworm. See the picture just below. *n.*

An gli can (ang′gli kən), 1. of or having to do with the Church of England or other churches of the same faith elsewhere. 2. member of the Church of England. 3. English. *adj., n.*

Angleworm

An gli cize (ang′gli sīz), make or become English in form, habits, customs, character, etc. *Beau, belle, chauffeur,* and *garage* are French words that have been Anglicized. *v.*

an gling (ang′gling), act or art of fishing with a rod and line. *n.*

An glo-Sax on (ang′glō sak′sən), 1. one of the inhabitants of England before the Norman Conquest. 2. their language. 3. pertaining to the Anglo-Saxons or their language. 4. pertaining to the English people. 5. person of English descent. *n., adj. 15.*

An go ra (ang gō′rə), 1. a kind of long-haired cat. 2. a goat with long, silky hair. The hair of this goat is called Angora wool. 3. Ankara. *n. 17.*

an gri ly (ang′gri li), in an angry manner. *adv. 12.*

an gry (ang′gri). You are angry when someone tries to hold you and you do not wish to be held; when you slap, kick, or bite at people; when someone tries to keep you from doing something which you want to do. *adj., angrier, angriest. 2.*

an guish (ang′gwish), very great pain or grief. Fred was in anguish until the doctor set his broken leg. *n. 5.*

an gu lar (ang′gū lər), 1. having angles; sharp-cornered; as, an angular piece of rock. 2. measured by an angle; as, angular distance. *adj. 10.*

an gu lar i ty (ang′gū lar′i ti), 1. condition of having many angles; angular quality or form. 2. an angular part; an angle. *n., pl. angularities. 20.*

an i line (an′i lin), 1. poisonous, oily liquid, prepared from coal tar, used in making dyes, perfumes, etc. 2. made from aniline. *n., adj.*

an i mad ver sion (an′i mad vėr′zhən), criticism; blame; unfavorable comment. *n. 16.*

an i mad vert (an′i mad vėrt′), make criticisms; blame; comment unfavorably. *v. 19.*

an i mal (an′i məl), 1. creature that can feel and move. A dog, a bird, a fish, a snake, a fly, and a worm are all animals. All things are animals or plants or minerals. 2. If we call a person an animal, we usually mean that he is like a beast in the way he acts or thinks. 3. of animals. 4. like an animal. 5. **Animal spirits** means liveliness. *n., adj. 1.*

an i mate (an′i māt for 1, 2, and 3, an′i mit for 4), 1. give life to. 2. make lively or gay. Jim's arrival served to animate the whole party. 3. be a motive or a reason for. Love for her mother animated Alice's work. 4. living. Animate nature means all living plants and animals. *v., adj. 6.*

an i mat ed (an′i māt′id), 1. living; alive. 2. lively; gay; vigorous. *adj.*

an i ma tion (an′i mā′shən), 1. life. 2. liveliness; spirit. *n. 14.*

an i mos i ty (an′i mos′i ti), violent hatred; ill will; active dislike or enmity. *n., pl. animosities. 9.*

an i mus (an′i məs), 1. ill will; hostile spirit; active dislike or enmity. 2. spirit; temper. *n.*

an ise (an′is), 1. a plant grown for its sweet-smelling seeds. 2. the seed, used as medicine or flavoring. *n. 16.*

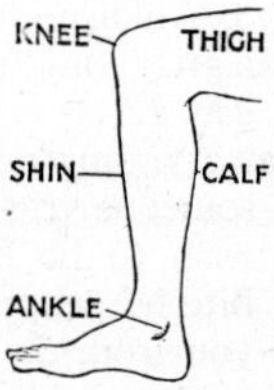

An jou (an′jü), a region in western France. *n. 14.*

An ka ra (ang′kə rə), capital of Turkey. *n.*

an kle (ang′kəl), the joint connecting the foot with the leg. *n. 4.*

an klet (ang′klit), 1. band around the ankle. An anklet may be an ornament, a brace, or a fetter. 2. short sock. *n.*

an nal ist (an′əl ist), writer of annals. *n. 17.*

an nals (an′əlz), 1. written account of events year by year. 2. historical records; history. *n. pl. 8.*

An nap o lis (ə nap′ə lis), the capital of Maryland. The United States Naval Academy is located at Annapolis. *n. 18.*

an neal (ə nēl′), toughen (glass, metals, etc.) by heating and gradually cooling; temper in this way. *v. 19.*

an nex (ə neks′ for 1, an′eks for 2), 1. join or add (a small thing) to a larger thing. The United States annexed Texas in 1845. 2. something annexed; an added part; as, an annex to a building. *v., n. 7.*

an nex a tion (an′ek sā′shən), 1. annexing; being annexed; as, the annexation of Texas to the United States. 2. thing annexed. *n. 11.*

an ni hi late (ə nī′i lāt), destroy completely; wipe out of existence. *v. 9.*

an ni hi la tion (ə nī′i lā′shən), complete destruction. *n. 15.*

an ni ver sa ry (an′i vėr′sə ri), 1. the yearly return of a date. Your birthday is one anniversary you like to have remembered. 2. a celebration of the yearly return of a date. 3. having to do with an anniversary; as, an anniversary dinner. *n., pl. anniversaries, adj. 5.*

an no tate (an′ō tāt), 1. furnish with notes. Her history is annotated. 2. make notes or comments on. *v. 20.*

an no ta tion (an′ō tā′shən), 1. a furnishing with notes. 2. note that explains or comments or criticizes. *n. 20.*

an nounce (ə nouns′), 1. make known formally. Please announce to the children that there will be no school this afternoon. 2. make known the presence or arrival of. The servant announced each guest in a loud voice. *v. 5.*

an nounce ment (ə nouns′mənt), 1. announcing. We speak of the announcement of a speaker, a meeting, a wedding, a concert, etc. 2. what is announced or made known by private or public notice of some kind. The announcement was published in the newspapers. *n. 7.*

an nounc er (ə noun′sər), 1. person or thing that announces. 2. person who makes announcements over the radio. *n.*

an noy (ə noi′), tease; vex; disturb; make angry. The baby annoys her sister by pulling her hair. *v. 5.*

an noy ance (ə noi′əns), 1. act of annoying. 2. being annoyed; vexation; feeling of dislike or trouble. 3. thing that annoys. *n. 11.*

an nu al (an′ū əl), 1. coming once a year. Your birthday is an annual event. 2. in a year; for a year. Mr. White's annual income is $2000. 3. living one year or season. 4. plant that lives for one year or season. Many garden plants are annuals. 5. a book published once a year. *adj., n. 3.*

an nu al ly (an′ū əl i), yearly; each year; year by year. *adv. 12.*

an nu i ty (ə nū′i ti or ə nü′i ti), 1. money paid every year. Mr. Smith gives his old servants annuities after they are seventy. 2. the right to receive such a yearly sum of money. *n., pl. annuities. 16.*

an nul (ə nul′), abolish; do away with; destroy the force of; cancel. The judge annulled the contract because one of the signers was too young. This law annuls all previous laws on the smoke nuisance. *v., annulled, annulling. 12.*

an num (an′əm), Latin word meaning year. *Per annum* means for each year. *n. 16.*

an nun ci a tion (ə nun′si ā′shən), 1. announcement. **The Annunciation** is the announcement by the angel Gabriel to the Virgin Mary that she was to be the mother of Christ. 2. a festival held on March 25 in memory of the Annunciation. *n. 20.*

a noint (ə noint′), 1. put oil on; smear or rub with a healing ointment; rub. Anoint sunburned places with cold cream. 2. make sacred by applying ointment or oil; apply ointment or oil to (a person) as a part of a ceremony. The bishop anointed the new king. *v. 6.*

a nom a lous (ə nom′ə ləs), departing from the common rule; irregular; abnormal. *adj. 16.*

a nom a ly (ə nom′ə li), 1. departure from the common rule; irregularity. "A lamb in school is an anomaly," said the teacher to Mary. 2. something abnormal. *n., pl. anomalies. 14.*

a non (ə non′) 1. soon; in a little while. 2. again; at another time. I won't say good-by; for I shall see you anon. *adv. 5.*

a non y mous (ə non′i məs), 1. not signed; with the author's name not known. An anonymous book is one published without the name of the author. 2. nameless; having no name. *adj. 14.*

an oth er (ə nuᴛʜ′ər), 1. one more. Drink another glass of milk. 2. a different. Show me another kind of hat. 3. a different one; someone else. *adj., pron. 1.*

ans., answer. *20.*

an swer (an′sər), 1. Who can answer the question? The boy gave a quick answer. Answer the bell by going to the door. Any response by speaking, writing, or doing something is an answer. 2. be responsible. A father must answer for his child's acts. 3. serve. A piece of paper answered for a tablecloth. 4. correspond. This boy answers to your description. *v., n. 1.*

an swer a ble (an′sər ə bəl), 1. responsible. The class treasurer is held answerable to the class for the money that is given to him. 2. that can be answered. *adj. 14.*

Small red ant. Line shows actual length.

ant (ant), a small insect. See the picture. Ants live together in large groups or communities called colonies. Ants, bees, and wasps are alike in many ways. *n. 4.*

-ant, suffix meaning:—
1. ———ing; as in buoyant, compliant, triumphant.
2. one that ———s; as in assistant, inhabitant.

an tag o nism (an tag′ə nizm), active opposition; conflict. *n. 15.*

an tag o nist (an tag′ə nist), one who fights, struggles, or contends against another in a combat or contest of any kind; opponent; adversary; rival. The knight defeated each antagonist. *n. 11.*

an tag o nis tic (an tag′ə nis′tik), acting against each other; opposing; conflicting. Cats and dogs are antagonistic. *adj. 16.*

an tag o nize (an tag′ə nīz), 1. make an enemy of. Her unkind remarks antagonized people who had been her friends. 2. oppose. *v. 18.*

ant arc tic (ant ärk′tik), 1. at or near the South Pole; of the south polar region. There is an antarctic continent. 2. the south polar region. *adj., n. 11.*

Antarctic Ocean, the ocean of the south polar region.

ante-, a prefix that means before. **Antemortem** means before death. *Ante* is used as a part of several words, such as anteroom, antedate. *18.*

ant eat er (ant′ēt′ər), an animal that eats ants. An anteater has a long tongue which can reach very far. *n.*

Anteater (3½ ft. long, including the tail)

an te ced ent (an′ti sēd′ənt), 1. going before; previous; happening before. 2. something happening before; something happening before and leading up to. 3. the noun or noun phrase to which a pronoun refers. In "The dog which killed the rat is brown," *dog* is the antecedent of *which.* 4. The **antecedents of** sometimes means the past events, circumstances, or history of. *adj., n. 11.*

an te cham ber (an′ti chām′bər), room leading into a main room or apartment. *n. 16.*

an te date (an′ti dāt′), 1. be or happen before. 2. give too early a date to. *v. 15.*

an te di lu vi an (an′ti di lü′vi ən), 1. before the Flood. 2. person who lived before the Flood. 3. very old; old-fashioned. 4. very old person; old-fashioned person; something out-of-date. *adj., n.*

an te lope (an′ti lōp), any one of certain animals somewhat like deer. See the picture. *n. 13.*

Antelope (2½ ft. high at the shoulder)

an ten na (an ten′ə), 1. feeler on the head of an insect, spider, scorpion, lobster, etc. See the picture just below. 2. long wire or wires used in radio for sending out or receiving electric waves; aerial. *n., pl. antennae* (-ē) for 1, *antennas* for 2. *13.*

an ten nae (an ten′ē), more than one antenna. *n. pl. 14.*

an te pe nult (an′ti pē′nult), the second from the last syllable in a word. In *an te ri or,* *te* is the antepenult. *n.*

Antennae of a beetle

an te ri or (an tēr′i ər), 1. front; fore; toward the front. The anterior part of a fish contains the head and gills. 2. earlier; going before. *adj. 9.*

an te room (an′ti rüm′), room leading to another; a waiting room. *n. 16.*

an them (an′thəm), 1. song of praise, devotion, or patriotism. "The Star-Spangled Banner" is the national anthem. 2. piece of sacred music usually with words from some passage in the Bible. *n. 8.*

an ther (an′thər), the part of the stamen that bears the pollen. See the diagram. *n. 8.*

Anthers

ant hill, heap of dirt piled up by ants around the entrance to their underground nest.

an thol o gy (an thol′ə ji), a collection of poems or prose selections. *n., pl. anthologies. 18.*

an thra cite (an′thrə sīt), hard coal; coal that burns with very little smoke and flame. *n. 9.*

an thrax (an′thraks), an infectious disease of cattle, sheep, etc., that human beings may get from them. *n. 17.*

an thro poid (an′thrō poid), 1. manlike; resembling man. 2. a manlike ape. Chimpanzees and gorillas are anthropoids. *adj., n. 19.*

an thro pol o gy (an′thrō pol′ə ji), science that deals with the origin, development, races, customs, and beliefs of mankind. *n. 18.*

anti-, prefix meaning against; opposed to. **Proslavery** and **antislavery** mean for slavery and against slavery; in favor of slavery and opposed to slavery. *10.*

an tic (an′tik), 1. grotesque act; silly trick. See also **antics.** 2. grotesque; odd; fantastic. *Old use.* *n., adj. 10.*

An ti christ (an′ti krīst′), the great enemy or opponent of Christ. *n. 13.*

an tic i pate (an tis′i pāt), 1. expect; look forward to. He had anticipated a good vacation in the mountains; but when the time came, he was sick. 2. do before others do; be ahead of in doing. The Chinese anticipated some modern discoveries. 3. use, take, tell, realize, or consider in advance. When mother has a headache, Mary anticipates all her wishes. *v. 7.*

an tic i pa tion (an tis′i pā′shən), act of anticipating; looking forward to; expectation. He cut more wood than usual, in anticipation of a long winter. A pleasure is sometimes greater in anticipation than in realization. *n. 8.*

an ti cli max (an′ti klī′maks), the opposite of climax; a descent from the lofty or important to the trivial. This is an anticlimax: "Alas! Alas! what shall I do? I've lost my wife and best hat, too!" *n.*

an tics (an′tiks), funny gestures and actions; silly tricks; capers. The clown amused us by his antics. *n. pl.*

an ti dote (an′ti dōt), 1. medicine that acts against a poison or a disease; a remedy. Milk is an antidote for some poisons. 2. remedy for any evil. Prosperity is a good antidote for political unrest. *n. 9.*

An tie tam (an tē′təm), small creek flowing into the Potomac River in Maryland. A battle of the Civil War was fought near it in 1862. *n.*

An til les (an til′ēz), a chain of islands in the West Indies. The Greater Antilles are Cuba, Haiti, Puerto Rico, and Jamaica; the Lesser Antilles are smaller islands near by. *n. pl. 20.*

an ti mo ny (an′ti mō′ni), a brittle, silver-white metal used in medicine and in alloys. *n. 20.*

An ti och (an′ti ok), a city in northwestern Syria. It was the capital of Syria from 300 to 64 B.C. *n. 10.*

an tip a thy (an tip′ə thi), strong or fixed dislike; a feeling against. *n., pl. antipathies. 12.*

an tip o des (an tip′ə dēz), 1. two places on opposite sides of the earth. A straight line from one of these places through the center of the earth will hit the other place. 2. two opposites or contraries; the direct opposite of anything. The spirit of Christ and the spirit of revenge are antipodes. *n. pl. 16.*

an ti quar i an (an′ti kwãr′i ən), 1. having to do with antique relics. The antiquarian section of the museum was full of old furniture. 2. antiquary. *adj., n. 14.*

an ti quar y (an′ti kwãr′i), 1. student of antique things. 2. person who collects or sells antique things. *n., pl. antiquaries. 16.*

an ti quat ed (an′ti kwāt′id), old-fashioned; out-of-date. *adj. 12.*

an tique (an tēk′), 1. of times long ago; from times long ago. This antique chair was made in 1750. 2. something made long ago. This carved chest is a real antique. 3. old-fashioned. Mother made Mary an antique costume for the fancy-dress dance. *adj., n. 6.*

an tiq ui ty (an tik′wi ti), 1. oldness; great age. That vase is of such great antiquity that nobody knows how old it is. 2. times long ago, especially those before 476 A.D. Moses and Caesar were two great men of antiquity. 3. the people of ancient times; the customs, events, things, etc., from times long ago. *n., pl. antiquities. 6.*

an ti sep tic (an′ti sep′tik), 1. preventing infection. 2. a substance that prevents infection. Alcohol, iodine, peroxide, carbolic acid, and boric acid are antiseptics. *adj., n. 11.*

an ti slav er y (an′ti slāv′ər i), opposed to slavery; against slavery. *adj. 13.*

an ti so cial (an′ti sō′shəl), opposed to the principles on which society is based. Murder, stealing, spitting in a train, and spreading diseases are antisocial acts. *adj.*

an tith e sis (an tith′i sis), 1. contrast of ideas. *Examples:* "To err is human; to forgive, divine." "Fools rush in where angels fear to tread." 2. opposition; contrast. 3. the direct opposite. Hate is the antithesis of love. *n., pl. antitheses* (-sēz). *16.*

an ti tox in (an′ti tok′sin), substance formed in the body which makes a person safe from an infection or disease; medicine used to prevent or cure an infectious disease. Diphtheria antitoxin, obtained from the blood of horses infected with diphtheria, is injected into a person to make him immune to diphtheria. *n. 8.*

ant ler (ant′lər), 1. horn of a deer. 2. branch of a deer's horn. *n. 18.*

Antlers

An toi nette (an′twä net′). Marie Antoinette (1755-1793) was the beautiful and unfortunate wife of King Louis XVI of France. She was beheaded during the French Revolution. *n. 19.*

an to nym (an′tə nim), word that means the opposite of another word. *Sharp, keen,* and *acute* are antonyms of *dull.* *n. 14.*

Ant werp (ant′wərp), a seaport city in northern Belgium. *n. 8.*

an vil (an′vil), an iron block on which metals are hammered and shaped. *n. 6.*

ANVIL

anx i e ty (ang zī′ə ti), 1. uneasy thoughts or fears about what may happen; troubled, worried, or uneasy feeling. Mothers feel anxiety when their children are sick. 2. eager desire. Nell's anxiety to succeed led her to work hard. *n., pl. anxieties. 8.*

anx ious (angk′shəs), 1. uneasy because of thoughts and fears about what may happen; troubled; worried. Mother felt anxious about the children who had been gone an hour too long. The week of the flood was an anxious time for all of us. 2. wishing very much; eager. Dick was anxious for a bicycle. Mary was anxious to please her mother. *adj. 2.*

an y (en′i), 1. one out of many. Choose any book you like. 2. some. Have you any fresh fruit? We haven't any. 3. at all. Did she cry any? *adj., pron., adv. 1.*

an y bod y (en′i bod′i), 1. any person; anyone. 2. important person. *pron., n. 3.*

an y how (en′i hou), 1. in any way whatever. It is wrong anyhow you look at it. 2. in any case; at any rate; anyway. I can see as well as you, anyhow. 3. carelessly; in ways that are not right or proper. *adv. 6.*

an y one or **any one** (en′i wun), anybody; any person. Anyone may come to the party. *pron. 3.*

an y thing (en′i thing), 1. any thing. 2. thing of any kind. 3. at all. Is your doll anything like mine? *pron., n., adv. 1.*

an y way (en′i wā), 1. in any way whatever. 2. in any case. I am coming anyway, no matter what you say. *adv. 4.*

an y where (en′i hwãr), in any place. *adv. 4.*

an y wise (en′i wīz), in any way; at all. *adv.*

a or ta (ā ôr′tə), the main artery that carries the blood from the left side of the heart to all parts of the body except the lungs. See the diagram under **auricle.** *n., pl. aortas, aortae* (-tē). *14.*

a pace (ə pās′), swiftly; fast. The summer flew by, and schooltime was coming on apace. *adv. 8.*

A pach e (ə pach′i), member of a tribe of warlike, nomadic Indians living in the southwestern United States. *n., pl. Apaches* or *Apache.*

ap a nage (ap′ə nij), appanage. *n.*

a part (ə pärt′), 1. to pieces; in pieces; in separate parts. The boy took the watch apart to see how it runs. 2. to one side; aside; off or away from others. He sets some money apart for a vacation each year. All joking apart, do you mean that? 3. away from each other. If you children quarrel, I shall have to keep you apart. *adv. 2.*

a part ment (ə pärt′mənt), 1. room or group of rooms to live in. 2. single room. *n. 5.*

apartment house, building containing many apartments.

ap a thet ic (ap′ə thet′ik), 1. lacking in feeling. 2. with little interest or desire for action; indifferent. *adj. 16.*

ap a thy (ap′ə thi), 1. lack of feeling; dullness of feeling; indifference. The stingy old miser heard the beggar's story with apathy. 2. lack of interest and activity; as, the apathy of a lazy, stupid boy. *n. 9.*

ape (āp), 1. a tailless, long-armed animal somewhat like a monkey. Apes are able to stand almost erect and to walk on two feet. Chimpanzees, gorillas, and gibbons are apes. 2. one who imitates or mimics. 3. imitate; mimic. *n., v. 6.*

Ap en nines (ap′ə nīnz), the chief mountain range in Italy. *n. pl. 14.*

ap er ture (ap′ər chər), opening; gap; hole. A window is an aperture for light and air. *n. 8.*

a pex (ā′peks), the highest point; the tip; as, the apex of a triangle. *n., pl. apexes, apices* (ap′i sēz). *12.*

a phid (ā′fid), very small insect that lives by sucking juices from plants; plant louse. *n.*

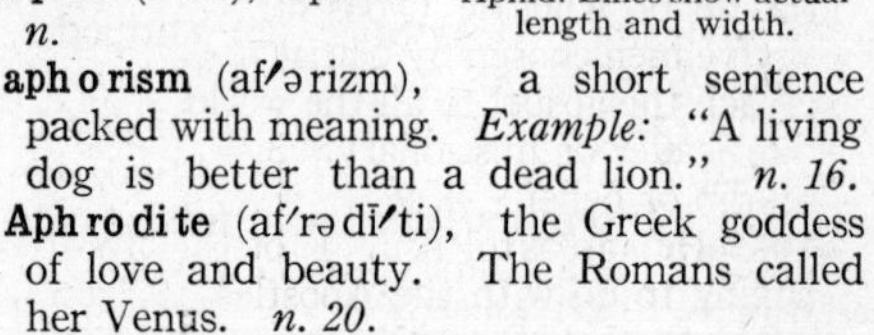
Aphid. Lines show actual length and width.

a phis (ā′fis), aphid. *n.*

aph o rism (af′ə rizm), a short sentence packed with meaning. *Example:* "A living dog is better than a dead lion." *n. 16.*

Aph ro di te (af′rə dī′ti), the Greek goddess of love and beauty. The Romans called her Venus. *n. 20.*

a piece (ə pēs′), each; for each one. These apples are five cents apiece. The boys received a dollar apiece. *adv. 5.*

a poc a lypse (ə pok′ə lips), a revelation. **The Apocalypse** is the book of Revelation, the last book of the New Testament. *n. 15.*

A poc ry pha (ə pok′ri fə), fourteen books included in the Roman Catholic Bible, but not accepted as genuine by Jews and Protestants. *n. pl.*

a poc ry phal (ə pok′ri fəl), 1. of doubtful authorship or authority; of doubtful genuineness. 2. false. *adj. 16.*

A pol lo (ə pol′ō), the Greek and Roman god of the sun, poetry, music, prophecy, and healing. Apollo was the highest type of youthful, manly beauty to the Greeks and Romans. *n. 8.*

a pol o get ic (ə pol′ə jet′ik), 1. making an apology; expressing regret; acknowledging a fault; excusing failure. 2. defending by speech or writing. *adj. 16.*

a pol o get i cal ly (ə pol′ə jet′i kəl i), in an apologetic manner. *adv.*

a pol o gist (ə pol′ə jist), person who defends an idea, argument, etc., in speech or writing. *n. 16.*

a pol o gize (ə pol′ə jīz), 1. make an apology; express regret; acknowledge a fault; offer an excuse. She apologized for hurting my feelings. 2. defend an idea, argument, etc., in speech or writing. *v. 12.*

a pol o gy (ə pol′ə ji), 1. words of regret for an offense or accident; explanation; saying one is sorry; asking pardon. Make an apology to the lady for hitting her. 2. a defense in speech or writing; explanation of the truth or justice of something; as, an apology for the Christian religion. 3. poor substitute. She thinks lamps are only an apology for sunlight. *n., pl. apologies. 7.*

ap o plex y (ap′ə plek′si), a sudden loss of the power to feel or think or move, caused by brain disease or injury. *n. 13.*

a pos ta sy (ə pos′tə si), a complete forsaking of one's religion, faith, principles, or political party. *n., pl. apostasies. 15.*

a pos tate (ə pos′tāt), person who entirely forsakes his religion, faith, principles, or political party. *n. 15.*

a pos tle or **A pos tle** (ə pos′əl), 1. one of the twelve men chosen by Christ to go forth and preach the gospel to all the world. 2. Christian leader or missionary. 3. leader of any reform or belief. *n. 9.*

ap os tol ic (ap′əs tol′ik), 1. of the Apostles; having to do with the Apostles. 2. according to the beliefs and teachings of the Apostles. 3. of the Pope; papal. *adj. 10.*

a pos tro phe[1] (ə pos′trə fi), a sign (') used (1) to show the omission of one or more letters, as in *o'er* for *over, thro'* for *through.* (2) to show the possessive forms of nouns, as in *John's* book, the *lions'* den. (3) in forming certain plurals. There are two o's in apology and four 9's in 959,990. *n. 18.*

a pos tro phe[2] (ə pos′trə fi), a speech to someone absent or dead as if he were present; a speech to a lifeless thing as if it could hear or reply. *n.*

a poth e car y (ə poth′i kãr′i), person who prepares and sells drugs and medicines; druggist. *n., pl. apothecaries. 10.*

a poth e o sis (ə poth′i ō′sis), 1. act of raising to the rank of a god; making a god. The apotheosis of the emperor became a Roman custom. 2. glorification; exaltation. *n., pl. apotheoses* (-sēz). *18.*

Appalachian Mountains, the chief mountain system in eastern North America. *9.*

Ap pa la chians (ap′ə lā′chənz), Appalachian Mountains. *n. pl.*

ap pall or **ap pal** (ə pôl′), terrify; fill with horror; dismay. She was appalled when she saw the river had risen to the doorstep. We were appalled at the thought of another war. *v., appalled, appalling. 7.*

ap pa nage (ap′ə nij), 1. land, property, or money set aside to support the younger children of kings or princes. 2. a person's assigned portion; rightful property. 3. adjunct; something that goes with. This millionaire has three houses, a yacht, and all the other appanages of wealth. *n. 16.*

ap pa ra tus (ap′ə rā′təs or ap′ə rat′əs), things necessary to carry out a purpose. Tools, special instruments, and machines are apparatus. A chemical set is apparatus; so are a grocer's scales and the equipment in a gymnasium. *n., pl. apparatus* or *apparatuses. 7.*

ap par el (ə par′əl), 1. clothing; dress. 2. clothe; dress up. The horseback riders, gaily appareled, formed part of the circus parade. *n., v., appareled, appareling. 5.*

ap par ent (ə par′ənt), 1. plain to see; so plain that one cannot help seeing it; easily understood. It is apparent that the days become shorter in October and November. 2. seeming; that appears to be. The apparent truth was really a lie. *adj. 4.*

ap par ent ly (ə par′ənt li), 1. seemingly; as far as one can judge by appearances. 2. clearly; plainly; obviously. *adv.*

ap pa ri tion (ap′ə rish′ən), 1. ghost. The apparition, clothed in white, glided through the wall. 2. appearance of something strange or unexpected. *n. 9.*

ap peal (ə pēl′), 1. an earnest request; a call to the feelings. She made one last appeal to her father to forgive her. 2. ask earnestly. The children appealed to their mother to know what they could do on a rainy day. 3. call on some person to decide some matter in one's favor. When Mother said "No," Johnnie would appeal to Father. 4. a call on some person to decide some matter in one's favor. 5. a request to have a case heard again before a higher court or judge. 6. ask that a case be taken to a higher court or judge to be heard again. 7. be interesting, attractive, or enjoyable. Blue and red appeal to me, but I don't like gray or yellow. *n., v. 3.*

ap pear (ə pēr′), 1. be seen. One by one the stars appear. 2. seem; look. The apple appeared sound, but it was rotten. 3. be published. This poet's last book appeared a year ago. 4. show or present oneself publicly or formally. A person accused of crime must appear before the court. 5. become known to the mind. Our characters appear in our acts. *v. 1.*

ap pear ance (ə pēr′əns), 1. act of coming in sight. John's appearance in the doorway was welcomed with shouts. 2. coming before the public. She made her first appearance in a concert in Boston. 3. outward look (of a person, object, animal, country, city). The appearance of the old gray house made us think it was empty. 4. thing

hat, āge, cãre, fär; let, ēqual, tėrm; it, īce; hot, ōpen, ôrder; oil, out; cup, pu̇t, rüle, ūse; th, thin; ᴛʜ, then; ə represents *a* in about, *e* in taken, *i* in pencil, *o* in lemon, *u* in circus.

that appears in sight; object seen. 5. ghost. *n. 2.*

ap pease (ə pēz′), make calm; satisfy; quiet. He tried to appease his father's anger by promising to obey. His hunger was appeased by a good dinner. *v. 6.*

ap pease ment (ə pēz′mənt), appeasing or being appeased; pacification; satisfaction. *n.*

ap pel lant (ə pel′ənt), 1. person who appeals. 2. appealing; having to do with appeals. *n., adj. 18.*

ap pel late (ə pel′it), appealed to; having to do with appeals. A person can appeal to an appellate court from the verdict of a lower court. *adj. 16.*

ap pel la tion (ap′ə lā′shən), 1. name; title. In "John the Baptist," the appellation of *John* is *the Baptist.* 2. act of calling by name. *n. 13.*

ap pend (ə pend′), add; attach. The amendments to the Constitution of the United States are appended to it. *v. 15.*

ap pend age (ə pen′dij), 1. thing attached; addition. 2. tail. *n. 9.*

ap pen di ci tis (ə pen′di sī′tis), inflammation of the vermiform appendix, which is a little outgrowth from the large intestine. *n. 12.*

ap pen dix (ə pen′diks), 1. an addition at the end of a book or document. 2. an outgrowth of some part of the body; the small saclike growth attached to the large intestine. See the diagram under **intestine.** *n., pl. appendixes, appendices* (-di sēz). *8.*

ap per tain (ap′ər tān′), pertain; belong as a part; relate. The control of traffic appertains to the police. Forestry appertains to geography, to botany, and to agriculture. *v. 10.*

ap pe tite (ap′i tīt), 1. desire for food. Mary had no appetite; so they had to coax her to eat. 2. desire. Much money is spent in satisfying the appetite for excitement and amusement. *n. 3.*

ap pe tiz ing (ap′i tīz′ing), exciting the appetite; as, appetizing food. *adj. 20.*

Ap pi an Way (ap′i ən wā′), famous Roman road extending 366 miles southeast from Rome. *18.*

ap plaud (ə plôd′), 1. express approval by clapping hands, shouting, etc. The audience applauds anything that pleases it in a play or concert. 2. approve; praise. Frank's mother applauded his decision to remain in school. *v. 6.*

ap plause (ə plôz′), 1. approval expressed by clapping hands, shouting, etc. 2. approval; praise. *n. 5.*

ap ple (ap′əl), 1. a common fruit. See the picture just below. 2. the tree it grows on. *n. 1.*

Apple

ap pli ance (ə plī′əns), 1. thing like a tool, small machine, etc., used in doing something; device. A can opener is an appliance for opening tin cans. 2. act of applying; putting into use. *n. 9.*

ap pli ca ble (ap′li kə bəl), capable of being applied; capable of being applied with good results; appropriate. The rule, "Look before you leap," is almost always applicable. *adj. 14.*

ap pli cant (ap′li kənt), person who applies (for a job, money, position, help, etc.). *n. 10.*

ap pli ca tion (ap′li kā′shən), 1. applying; putting on; as, the application of paint to a house, the application of salve to a sore. 2. act of using; use. The application of what you know will help you solve new problems. 3. the thing applied. This application is made of cold cream and ointment. 4. a request. I have put in my application to become a Boy Scout. 5. continued effort in work; close attention. By application to the study of geography, he has become a great geographer. *n. 3.*

ap plied (ə plīd′), put to practical use. Household chemistry is an applied science. *adj.*

ap ply (ə plī′), 1. put on. You can apply paint to a house, a remedy to a mosquito bite, and force to a pump. 2. use. He knows the rule but does not know how to apply it. 3. be useful or suitable; fit. When does this rule apply? 4. ask. She applied for help. 5. set to work and stick to it. He applied himself to learning French. *v., applied, applying. 2.*

ap point (ə point′), 1. decide on; set (a time or a place to be somewhere or meet someone). He appointed the schoolhouse as the place for the meeting. We shall appoint 8 o'clock as the hour to begin. 2. choose; name for an office or position. This man was appointed postmaster. 3. equip; furnish; as, a well-appointed guest room. *v. 2.*

ap point ee (ə poin′tē′), person appointed. *n.*

ap poin tive (ə poin′tiv), filled by appointment. Positions in the President's cabinet are appointive. *adj.*

ap point ment (ə point′mənt), 1. an appointing or being appointed. The appointment of Anna as secretary pleased all her friends. 2. office or position. 3. engagement to be somewhere or to meet someone. 4. equipment; furniture. *n. 4.*

Ap po mat tox (ap′ə mat′əks), village in southern Virginia. Lee surrendered to Grant there on April 9, 1865. *n.*

ap por tion (ə pōr′shən), divide and give out in fair shares; distribute according to some rule. The father's property was apportioned among his children after his death. *v. 15.*

ap por tion ment (ə pōr′shən mənt), dividing and giving out in fair shares; distribution according to some rule. *n. 14.*

ap po site (ap′ə zit), appropriate; suitable. *adj. 18.*

ap po si tion (ap′ə zish′ən), 1. placing together. 2. the relation to a noun or pronoun of another noun which is added to it as an explanation. In "Mr. Brown, our neighbor, has a new car," *Mr. Brown* and *neighbor* are in apposition. *n.*

ap prais al (ə prāz′əl), appraising; valuation; estimate. *n. 20.*

ap praise (ə prāz′), set a price on; estimate or fix the value, amount, quality, etc., of. Property is appraised for taxation. An employer should be able to appraise ability and character. *v. 10.*

ap pre ci a ble (ə prē′shi ə bəl), capable of being appreciated; enough to be felt or estimated. A slight hill makes an appreciable difference in the ease of walking. *adj. 11.*

ap pre ci a bly (ə prē′shi ə bli), to an appreciable degree. *adv.*

ap pre ci ate (ə prē′shi āt), 1. value; enjoy; think highly of. Almost everybody appreciates good food. 2. estimate; have an opinion of the value, worth, or quality of. A musician can appreciate small differences in sounds. 3. estimate correctly. 4. rise in value. This land will appreciate as soon as good roads are built. 5. raise in value. New buildings appreciate the value of land. *v. 5.*

ap pre ci a tion (ə prē′shi ā′shən), 1. appreciating; valuing. 2. valuing highly; sympathetic understanding. She has an appreciation of art and music. 3. rise in value. *n. 8.*

ap pre ci a tive (ə prē′shi ā′tiv), having appreciation; showing appreciation; recognizing the value. *adj. 14.*

ap pre hend (ap′ri hend′), 1. seize; arrest. The thief was apprehended and put into jail. 2. understand; grasp with the mind. I apprehended his meaning more from his gestures than from the queer sounds he made. 3. fear; dread. A guilty man apprehends danger in every sound. *v. 6.*

ap pre hen sion (ap′ri hen′shən), 1. seizing or arrest; as, the apprehension of a thief. 2. understanding; grasp by the mind. Tom has a clear apprehension of arithmetic. 3. fear; dread; as, the guilty man's apprehension that he would be found out. *n. 7.*

ap pre hen sive (ap′ri hen′siv), 1. afraid; anxious; worried. He felt apprehensive for their safety during the storm at sea. 2. quick to understand; able to learn. *adj. 10.*

ap pren tice (ə pren′tis), 1. person who is learning a trade, profession, or art. The apprentice had to serve his master seven years to pay for his instruction. 2. bind or take as an apprentice. 3. beginner; learner. *n., v. 9.*

ap pren tice ship (ə pren′tis ship), 1. condition of being an apprentice. 2. time during which one is an apprentice. *n. 11.*

ap prise or **ap prize** (ə prīz′), inform; notify; advise. *v. 15.*

ap proach (ə prōch′), 1. come near or nearer (in space or time). Walk softly as you approach the bed. Sunday is approaching. 2. come near to (in character, condition, or amount). The wind was approaching a gale. 3. act of coming near. 4. way by which a place or a person can be reached. The approach to the house was a narrow path. His best approach to the great man lay through a friend. *v., n. 2.*

ap pro ba tion (ap′rə bā′shən), approval; praise; favorable opinion. *n. 9.*

ap pro pri ate (ə prō′pri it for 1, ə prō′pri āt for 2 and 3), 1. suitable; proper. Plain, simple clothes are appropriate for school wear. 2. take for oneself. You should not appropriate other people's belongings without their permission. 3. set apart for some special use. The money was appropriated by the government for road building. *adj., v. 7.*

ap pro pri a tion (ə prō′pri ā′shən), 1. act of appropriating. 2. a being appropriated. The appropriation of the land made it possible to have a park. 3. thing or sum of money appropriated. The school received an appropriation of a thousand dollars for a new playground. *n. 8.*

ap prov al (ə prüv′əl), 1. approving; praise; favorable opinion. We all like others to show approval of what we do. 2. consent. The principal gave his approval to the plans for a holiday. *n. 7.*

ap prove (ə prüv′), 1. think well of; be pleased with. The teacher approved Helen's work. 2. consent to. Father approved our plans for the summer. 3. give approval. 4. show; prove to be. *v. 2.*

ap prox i mate (ə prok′si mit for 1, ə prok′si-māt for 2 and 3), 1. nearly correct. Forty is the approximate number of books needed in our class. 2. come near to; approach. This lumber approximates first-class, but it still has some defects. The crowd approximated a thousand people. 3. bring near. *adj., v. 7.*

ap prox i mate ly (ə prok′si mit li), nearly; about. *adv.*

ap prox i ma tion (ə prok′si mā′shən), an approach; nearly correct amount. An approximation for the circumference of the earth is 25,000 miles. *n. 14.*

ap pur te nance (ə pėr′ti nəns), a belonging; an addition to something more important; an accessory. *n. 16.*

a pri cot (ā′pri kot or ap′ri kot), 1. a pale orange-colored fruit, somewhat like a peach but smaller. 2. the tree it grows on. 3. pale orange-yellow. *n., adj. 9.*

A pril (ā′pril), the fourth month. It has 30 days. *n. 2.*

a pri o ri (ā pri ō′rī), 1. from cause to effect; from a general rule to a particular case. 2. based on opinion or theory rather than on actual observation or experience. *18.*

a pron (ā′prən), 1. garment worn over the front part of the body to cover or protect clothes; as, a kitchen apron. 2. something resembling an apron in use or shape. *n. 3.*

ap ro pos (ap′rə pō′), 1. fitting; to the point; relevant; as, an apropos remark. 2. **Apropos of** means concerning; with regard to; with reference to. Apropos of the party, what are you going to wear? *adj., adv. 15.*

apse (aps), a semicircular or many-sided recess in a church, usually at the east end. The roof of an apse is arched or vaulted. See the diagram under **nave.** *n. 17.*

apt (apt), 1. fitted by nature; likely. A careless person is apt to make mistakes. 2. suitable; fitting. His apt reply to the question showed that he had understood it very well. 3. quick to learn. Some pupils are more apt than others. *adj. 5.*

ap ti tude (ap′ti tūd or ap′ti tüd), 1. special fitness. 2. natural tendency; ability; capacity; as, an aptitude for a sailor's life. 3. readiness in learning; quickness to understand. *n. 14.*

apt ness (apt′nis), aptitude. *n. 17.*

aq ua plane (ak′wə plān′), 1. wide board on which a person rides for sport as he is towed by a speeding motorboat. 2. ride on such a board for sport. *n., v.*

Man riding an aquaplane

a quar i um (ə kwãr′i əm), 1. a pond, tank, or glass bowl in which living fish, water animals, and water plants are kept. 2. a building used for showing collections of living fish, water animals and water plants. *n., pl. aquariums, aquaria*(-i ə). *12.*

a quat ic (ə kwat′ik), 1. growing or living in water. Water lilies are aquatic plants. 2. taking place in or on water. Swimming and sailing are aquatic sports. *adj. 13.*

aq ue duct (ak′wi dukt), 1. artificial channel or large pipe for bringing water from a distance. 2. structure that supports such a channel or pipe. *n. 12.*

a que ous (ā′kwi əs), watery; made of water; like water. *adj. 14.*

aqueous humor, watery liquid that fills the space in the eye between the cornea and the lens. See the diagram of **eye.**

aq ui line (ak′wi līn), 1. like an eagle. 2. curved like an eagle's beak; hooked; as, an aquiline nose. *adj. 16.*

A qui nas (ə kwī′nəs), Thomas, a famous philosopher and theologian of the Roman Catholic Church (1225?-1274). *n. 20.*

Aq ui taine (ak′wi tān), a region in southwestern France. *n. 13.*

Ar ab (ar′əb), 1. a native or inhabitant of Arabia; member of the Arabic race. The Arabs are widely scattered over southwestern Asia and northern Africa. 2. of the Arabs; of Arabia. 3. swift, graceful horse belonging to a breed of horses that originally came from Arabia. *n., adj. 6.*

Arabesque

ar a besque (ar′ə besk′), 1. elaborate and fanciful design of flowers, leaves, geometrical figures. etc. 2. carved or painted in arabesque. 3. like arabesque; elaborate; fanciful. *n., adj. 18.*

A ra bi a (ə rā′bi ə), a large peninsula in southwestern Asia. *n. 4.*

A ra bi an (ə rā′bi ən), 1. of Arabia; of the Arabs. The **Arabian Nights** is a collection of Oriental stories from Arabia, Persia, and India. 2. an Arab. *adj., n.*

Ar a bic (ar′ə bik), 1. of the Arabs; belonging to Arabia; coming from the Arabs; as, Arabic architecture. The **Arabic numerals** are the figures 1, 2, 3, 4, 5, 6, 7, 8, 9, 0. 2. the language of the Arabs. *adj., n. 19.*

ar a ble (ar′ə bəl), fit for plowing. There is not much arable land on the side of a rocky mountain. *adj. 13.*

Ar a by (ar′ə bi), Arabia. *n.* [*Used in poetry*] *18.*

Ar a gon (ar′ə gon), region in northeastern Spain. It was formerly a kingdom. *n. 12.*

ar bi ter (är′bi tər), 1. person chosen to decide a dispute; judge; umpire. 2. person with full power to decide. *n. 11.*

ar bit ra ment (är bit′rə mənt), decision by an arbitrator or arbiter. *n. 17.*

ar bi trar y (är′bi trãr′i), based on one's own wishes, notions, or will; not going by any rule or law. A good judge tries to be fair and does not make arbitrary decisions. *adj. 8.*

ar bi trate (är′bi trāt), 1. give a decision in a dispute; act as arbiter. The governor offered to arbitrate between the city and the county in their dispute. 2. settle by arbitration; submit to arbitration. The two nations agreed to arbitrate their dispute and war was avoided. *v. 12.*

ar bi tra tion (är′bi trā′shən), settlement of a dispute by the decision of an arbiter. *n. 11.*

ar bi tra tor (är′bi trā′tər), 1. person chosen to decide a dispute. 2. person with full power to judge and decide. *n. 11.*

ar bi tress (är′bi tris), woman arbiter. *n. 18.*

ar bor (är′bər), 1. a naturally shaded place in the woods. 2. a shaded place formed by vines and plants growing on frames or supports. *n. 6.*

ar bo re al (är bō′ri əl), 1. of trees; like trees. 2. living in or among trees. A squirrel is an arboreal animal. *adj.*

ar bor vi tae (är′bər vī′tē), an evergreen tree often planted for hedges.

ar bu tus (är bū′təs), 1. plant that has clusters of fragrant, pink or white flowers and grows in patches on the ground. It is also called the Mayflower or trailing arbutus. 2. shrub or tree with clusters of large white or reddish flowers. *n. 16.*

arc (ärk), 1. part of a circle. 2. part of a curved line. 3. the stream of brilliant light or sparks formed as an electric current goes from one conductor to another. *n. 7.*

Arcs of circles

ar cade (är kād′), 1. a row of arches. 2. a passageway with an arched roof. 3. any covered passageway. 4. a building with a covered passageway that people can walk through. *n. 15.*

Arcade (def. 1)

Ar ca di a (är kā′di ə), 1. a mountain district in ancient Greece. It was famous for the simple, contented life of its people. 2. any region of simple, quiet contentment. *n. 9.*

Ar ca dy (är′kə di), Arcadia. *n.* [*Used in poetry*] *16.*

arch[1] (ärch), 1. a curved structure that bears the weight of the material above it. Arches often form the tops of doors, windows, and gateways. 2. a monument forming an arch or arches. 3. bend into an arch; curve. 4. furnish with an arch. The rainbow arches the heavens. 5. form an arch over. 6. something like an arch; as, the great blue arch of the sky. *n., v. 2.*

Bridge showing three arches

arch[2] (ärch), 1. chief. The arch rebel of all was Patrick Henry. 2. playfully mischievous. The little girl gave her mother an arch look and ran away. *adj.*

ar chae o log i cal (är′ki ə loj′i kəl), of or having to do with archaeology. An archaeological expedition uncovered the lost city of Troy. *adj. 16.*

ar chae ol o gy (är′ki ol′ə ji), study of the people, customs, and life of ancient times. Archaeology finds out about the remote past by studying ruins of cities, monuments, or any records that remain. *n. 20.*

ar cha ic (är kā′ik), ancient; old-fashioned; out-of-date; no longer in general use.

Archaic statues were dug up from the ruins of old Greek cities. The phrases *in sooth, I wot,* and *methinks* have become archaic. *adj. 18.*

arch an gel (ärk′ān′jəl), an angel of higher rank. *n. 16.*

Arch an gel (ärk′ān′jəl), seaport in northern Russia. *n.*

arch bish op (ärch′bish′əp), a bishop of the highest rank. *n. 8.*

arch dea con (ärch′dē′kən), assistant to a bishop in the Church of England. He superintends the work of other members of the clergy. *n. 14.*

arch duke (ärch′dūk′ or ärch′dük′), a prince of the ruling house of Austria. *n. 17.*

Archery (def. 1)

arch er (är′chər), person who shoots with bow and arrows. *n. 8.*

arch er y (är′chər i), 1. shooting with bows and arrows. 2. archers. The archery advanced, shooting steadily. *n. 14.*

ar chi e pis co pal (är′ki i pis′kə pəl), of or having to do with an archbishop. *adj. 16.*

Ar chi me des (är′ki mē′dēz), a famous Greek mathematician, scientist, and inventor (287?-212 B.C.). *n. 12.*

ar chi pel a go (är′ki pel′ə gō), 1. a sea having many islands in it. 2. a group of many islands. *n., pl. archipelagos* or *archipelagoes. 14.*

ar chi tect (är′ki tekt), person who makes plans for buildings and sees that these plans are followed by the people who actually put up the buildings. *n. 7.*

ar chi tec tur al (är′ki tek′chər əl), of architecture; having to do with architecture. *adj. 9.*

ar chi tec ture (är′ki tek′chər), 1. science or art of building. Architecture has to do with the planning of houses, churches, schools, and public and business buildings. 2. style or special manner of building. Greek architecture made much use of columns and pointed arches. 3. construction. The architecture of our school is very substantial. *n. 7.*

ar chi trave (är′ki trāv), the main beam resting on the top of a column. *n. 17.*

ar chives (är′kīvz), 1. place where public records or historical documents are kept. 2. public records or historical documents. *n. pl. 15.*

arch ly (ärch′li), playfully; mischievously; coyly. *adv.*

arch way (ärch′wā′), an entrance or passage with an arch above it; passage under an arched or curved roof. *n. 12.*

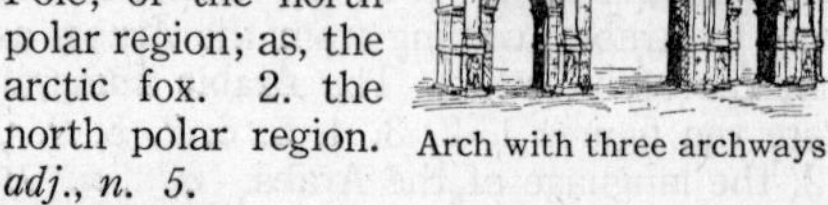

Arch with three archways

arc tic (ärk′tik), 1. near the North Pole; of the north polar region; as, the arctic fox. 2. the north polar region. *adj., n. 5.*

Arctic Ocean, ocean of the north polar region.

Arc tu rus (ärk tūr′əs or ärk tür′əs), a very bright star in the northern sky. *n. 18.*

Ar den (är′dən), 1. a district or forest in old England. 2. a land of the imagination or of romance. *n. 17.*

ar dent (är′dənt), 1. eager; full of zeal; very enthusiastic. He became an ardent worker. 2. burning; fiery hot. *adj. 8.*

ar dor (är′dər), 1. warm feeling; eagerness; zeal; enthusiasm; as, the ardor of a saint, patriotic ardor. 2. burning heat. *n. 8.*

ar du ous (är′jüəs), 1. hard to do; requiring much effort; as, an arduous lesson. 2. using up much energy; as, an arduous effort to learn the lesson. 3. steep; hard to climb; as, an arduous hill. *adj. 9.*

are (är). You are next. We are ready. They are waiting. We say: I am, you are, thou art, he is, she is, it is, we are, you are, they are. *v. 1.*

ar e a (ãr′i ə), 1. amount of surface; extent. The area of this floor is 600 square feet. 2. region. The Rocky Mountain area is the most mountainous in the United States. 3. level space. *n. 3.*

a re na (ə rē′nə), 1. a space where contests or shows take place. Men fought with lions in the arena of the great amphitheater at Rome. 2. any place of conflict and trial. *n. 14.*

aren't (ärnt), are not. *9.*

Ar es (ãr′ēz), the Greek god of war. The Romans called him Mars. *n.*

ar gent (är′jənt), 1. silver. 2. silvery; as, a knight's argent shield. *n., adj. 16.*

Ar gen ti na (är′jən tē′nə), a country in southern South America. *n. 6.*

Ar gen tine (är′jən tēn), 1. of Argentina or its people. 2. native of Argentina. *adj., n. 6.*

ar gon (är′gon), a colorless, odorless, inactive gas that forms a very small part of the air. It is used in electric-light bulbs and radio tubes. *n. 20.*

Ar gonne (är′gon), a forest in northeastern France. Battles of the first World War were fought there in 1918. *n. 18.*

ar go sy (är′gə si), 1. a large merchant ship. 2. fleet of such ships. *n., pl. argosies. 16.*

ar gue (är′gū), 1. discuss with someone who disagrees; give reasons for or against something. 2. persuade by giving reasons. He argued me into going. 3. try to prove by reasoning. Columbus argued that the world was round. 4. indicate; show; prove. Her rich clothes argue her to be wealthy. 5. raise objections. *v. 5.*

ar gu ment (är′gū mənt), 1. arguing; discussion by persons who disagree. 2. reason or reasons offered for or against something. 3. a short statement of what is in a book or poem. *n. 3.*

ar gu men ta tive (är′gū men′tə tiv), 1. fond of arguing. 2. containing argument. *adj. 19.*

Ar gus (är′gəs), 1. the son of Zeus who had a hundred eyes. 2. a watchful person. *n. 16.*

a ri a (ä′ri ə), an air or melody, usually for a single voice with accompaniment. *n. 17.*

Ari ad ne (ar′i ad′ni), the daughter of a king of Crete. She gave Theseus a ball of thread which enabled him to find his way out of the labyrinth. *n. 17.*

ar id (ar′id), dry; as, arid soil, an arid, tiresome speech. *adj. 11.*

a rid i ty (ə rid′i ti), dryness. *n.*

Ari el (ãr′i əl), the spirit who helped Prospero in Shakespeare's play *The Tempest. n. 10.*

a right (ə rīt′), correctly; rightly. *adv. 12.*

a rise (ə rīz′), 1. rise up; get up. 2. move upward. 3. come into being; come about. Trouble will arise over the ball game. *v., arose, arisen, arising. 3.*

a ris en (ə riz′ən). See **arise.** John has not yet arisen from his bed. *pp. of arise.*

ar is toc ra cy (ar′is tok′rə si), 1. a ruling body of nobles; the nobility. 2. the upper class; any class that is superior because of birth, intelligence, culture, or wealth. 3. government in which a privileged upper class rules. 4. country or state having such a government. *n., pl. aristocracies. 9.*

a ris to crat (ə ris′tə krat), 1. person who belongs to the aristocracy; a noble. 2. person who has the tastes, opinions, manners, etc., of the upper class. 3. person who favors government by an aristocracy. *n. 8.*

a ris to cra tic (ə ris′tə krat′ik), 1. belonging to the upper classes; superior in birth, intelligence, or wealth. 2. like an aristocrat in manners; proud. 3. having to do with an aristocracy. *adj. 7.*

Ar is tot le (ar′is tot′əl), a famous Greek philosopher (384-322 B.C.). *n. 11.*

a rith me tic (ə rith′mə tik), the science and art of numbers. *n. 7.*

ar ith met i cal (ar′ith met′i kəl), of arithmetic; having to do with arithmetic. *adj. 19.*

a rith me ti cian (ə rith′mə tish′ən), person skilled in arithmetic. *n.*

Ariz., Arizona.

Ar i zo na (ar′i zō′nə), a Southwestern State in the United States. *n. 9.*

ark (ärk), 1. the large boat in which Noah saved himself, his family, and a pair of each kind of animals from the Flood. 2. chest or box. The Ark of the Covenant was the wooden chest in which the Jews kept the two stone tablets containing the Ten Commandments. *n. 5.*

Ark., Arkansas.

Ar kan sas (är′kən sô), 1. Southern State of the United States. 2. river flowing from central Colorado into the Mississippi River. *n.9.*

arm[1] (ärm), 1. the part of a person's body between the shoulder and the hand. 2. something that is shaped or used like a person's arm; as, the arm of a chair, an arm of the sea. *n. 1.*

arm[2] (ärm), 1. a weapon. A gun, a sword, an ax, a stick—any of these might be arms for defense or attack. See also **arms.** 2. provide with weapons; supply with any means of defense or attack. "Arm yourselves and be ready to fight," said our leader. 3. take up arms; prepare for war. The soldiers armed for battle. *n., v.*

ar ma da (är mä′də), 1. a fleet of warships. The **Armada** usually means the fleet sent out by Spain to attack England in 1588. 2. a fleet of airplanes. *n. 9.*

ar ma dil lo (är′mə dil′ō), a small burrowing animal that has an armorlike shell. Some kinds can roll themselves up into a ball. Armadillos are found in South America and in some parts of southern North America. *n., pl. armadillos.*

Nine-banded armadillo walking; rolled up (2½ ft. long, including the tail).

ar ma ment (är′mə mənt), 1. war equipment and supplies. 2. a navy or army. *n. 12.*

ar ma ture (är′mə chər), 1. armor. 2. protective covering of an animal or plant. A turtle's shell is an armature. 3. piece of soft iron placed in contact with the poles of a magnet. 4. the part of a dynamo or generator in which the current is developed. 5. the part of a motor that receives the current and uses it up. *n. 19.*

arm chair (ärm′chãr′), a chair with sidepieces to support a person's arms or elbows. *n. 9.*

Armchair

Ar me ni a (är mē′ni ə), a former country in western Asia. Armenia has been divided between Turkey, Persia, and Russia. *n. 14.*

arm ful (ärm′fu̇l), as much as one arm can hold; as much as both arms can hold. *n., pl. armfuls. 16.*

arm hole (ärm′hōl′), a hole for the arm in a garment. *n. 10.*

ar mi stice (är′mi stis), a stop in fighting; temporary peace; truce. *n. 14.*

Armistice Day, November 11, the anniversary of the end of the first World War.

arm let (ärm′lit), ornamental band for the upper arm. *n. 19.*

ar mor (är′mər), 1. covering worn to protect the body in fighting. 2. any kind of protective covering. The steel plates of a warship and the scales of a fish are armor. *n. 3.*

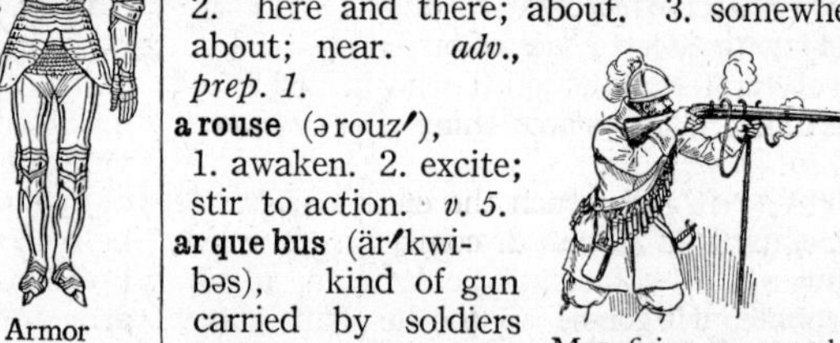

Armor

Man firing an arquebus

ar mored (är′mərd), covered or protected with armor. *adj.*

ar mor er (är′mər ər), 1. person who made or repaired armor. 2. manufacturer of firearms. 3. man in charge of firearms. The armorer of a warship takes care of the revolvers, pistols, and rifles on the ship. *n. 15.*

ar mo ri al (är mō′ri əl), having to do with coats of arms or heraldry. **Armorial bearings** means a coat of arms. See the picture. *adj. 15.*

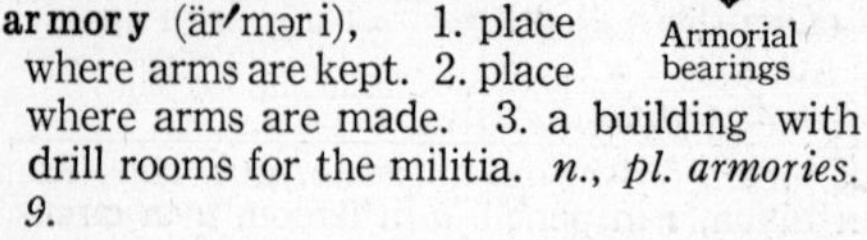

Armorial bearings

ar mor y (är′mər i), 1. place where arms are kept. 2. place where arms are made. 3. a building with drill rooms for the militia. *n., pl. armories. 9.*

arm pit (ärm′pit′), the hollow under the arm at the shoulder. *n. 13.*

arms (ärmz), 1. weapons. See also **arm**[2]. 2. fighting; war. 3. signs and devices used in heraldry or by governments. See the picture under **coat of arms.** *n. pl.*

ar my (är′mi), 1. an organized group of soldiers trained and armed for war. 2. any organized group of people. 3. multitude; very large number; as, an army of ants. *n., pl. armies. 1.*

ar ni ca (är′ni kə), 1. healing liquid used on bruises, sprains, etc., prepared from the dried flowers, leaves, or roots of a plant. 2. the plant itself. It has showy yellow flowers. *n. 19.*

Ar nold (är′nəld), 1. Benedict Arnold was an American general in the Revolution who turned traitor (1741-1801). 2. Matthew Arnold was a famous English poet and essayist (1822-1888). *n. 18.*

a ro ma (ə rō′mə), fragrance; spicy odor. *n. 15.*

ar o mat ic (ar′ə mat′ik), fragrant; spicy. The cinnamon tree has an aromatic inner bark. *adj. 8.*

a rose (ə rōz′). See **arise.** She arose from her chair. *pt. of arise. 3.*

a round (ə round′), 1. The tree measures four feet around. He walked around the house. The sun shines all around us. 2. here and there; about. 3. somewhere about; near. *adv., prep. 1.*

a rouse (ə rouz′), 1. awaken. 2. excite; stir to action. *v. 5.*

ar que bus (är′kwi bəs), kind of gun carried by soldiers before muskets were invented. *n.* Also called **harquebus.**

ar raign (ə rān′), 1. bring before a court for trial. The tramp was arraigned on a charge of stealing. 2. accuse; call in question; find fault with. *v. 11.*

ar raign ment (ə rān′mənt), 1. calling to trial; bringing before a court to answer a charge. 2. finding fault; adverse criticism. *n. 17.*

ar range (ə rānj′), 1. put in proper order. The army is arranged for battle. 2. settle. Mother arranged the dispute between Jim and Henry. 3. plan; form plans. Can you arrange to be at my house by six o'clock? 4. adapt; fit. This music for the violin is also arranged for the piano. *v. 2.*

ar range ment (ə rānj′mənt), 1. arranging. 2. the way or order in which things or persons are put. You can make six arrangements of the letters A, B, and C. 3. plan; preparation. All arrangements have been made for our trip to Chicago. 4. something arranged in a particular way; as, a musical arrangement for the piano and violin. *n. 5.*

ar rant (ar′ənt), thoroughgoing; out-and-out. He was such an arrant liar that nobody believed him. *adj. 7.*

ar ras (ar′əs), 1. a kind of tapestry. 2. a curtain or hangings of tapestry. *n. 15.*

ar ray (ə rā′), 1. order. The troops were formed in battle array. 2. put in order. The general arrayed his troops for the battle. 3. display of persons or things. The array of good players on the other team made our side lose confidence. 4. clothes; dress; as, bridal array, gorgeous array. 5. to dress; dress in fine clothes; adorn. Elsie was arrayed like a queen. *n., v. 4.*

ar rears (ə rērz′), debts due but not paid; unfinished work or other things not done on time. **In arrears** means behindhand in payments or work. *n. pl. 12.*

ar rest (ə rest′), 1. stop; check. The driver could not arrest the horses' speed. Filling a tooth arrests decay. 2. seize by legal authority; take to jail or to court. Policemen arrest thieves. 3. catch and hold. 4. stopping; seizing; arresting. *v., n. 4.*

ar riv al (ə rīv′əl), 1. act of arriving; a coming. She is waiting for the arrival of the steamboat. 2. person or thing that arrives. *n. 3.*

ar rive (ə rīv′), 1. reach the end of a journey; come to a place. 2. come. 3. be successful. *v. 1.*

ar ro gance (ar′ə gəns), too great pride; haughtiness. *n. 8.*

ar ro gant (ar′ə gənt), boastfully proud; too proud; boasting too much. *adj. 9.*

ar ro gate (ar′ō gāt), 1. claim or take without right. The king arrogated to himself power that belonged to the nobles. 2. attribute or assign without good reason. A suspicious man arrogates bad motives to other people. *v. 20.*

ar row (ar′ō), 1. a slender, pointed shaft or stick which is shot from a bow. 2. a sign (——>) used to show direction or position in maps, on road signs, and in writing. 3. anything shaped like an arrow. *n. 2.*

Arrow

ar row head (ar′ō hed′), head or tip of an arrow. The Indians made arrowheads of flint. *n.*

Indian arrowhead

ar row y (ar′ō i), 1. of arrows. 2. like an arrow in shape or speed. *adj. 16.*

ar se nal (är′si nəl), a building for storing or making weapons and ammunition for an army or navy; place for keeping guns, powder, etc. *n. 9.*

ar se nate of lead (är′si nāt əv led′), a poison used on vines, trees, etc., to kill insects. *14.*

ar se nic (är′si nik), 1. a grayish-white chemical element. 2. a compound of arsenic that is a violent poison. *n. 11.*

ar son (är′sən), the crime of setting fire to a building or other property. *n. 19.*

art[1] (ärt), 1. skill. 2. human skill. This well-kept garden owes more to art than to nature. The pupil tried to learn his master's art. 3. some kind of skill or practical application of skill. Cooking, sewing, and housekeeping are household arts. 4. a branch or division of learning. History is one of the arts; chemistry is one of the sciences. 5. a branch of learning that depends more on special practice than on general principles. Writing compositions is an art; grammar is a science. The **fine arts** include painting, drawing, sculpture, architecture, literature, music, and dancing. 6. drawing, painting, or sculpture. Nell is studying art and music. 7. principles or methods; as, the art of making friends, the art of war. 8. skillful act; cunning; trick. She deceived the youth by her arts. **Black art** means evil magic. *n. 1.*

art[2] (ärt), an old form meaning are. "Thou art" means "You are." *v.*

Ar te mis (är′ti mis), the Greek goddess of the hunt and of the moon. The Romans called her Diana. *n. 16.*

ar te ri al (är tēr′i əl), of an artery or the arteries; pertaining to the arteries; like the arteries. *adj. 17.*

ar ter y (är′tər i), 1. any of the blood vessels or tubes that carry blood from the heart to all parts of the body. 2. a main road; important channel. Main Street and Broadway are the two arteries of traffic in our city. *n., pl. arteries. 7.*

ar te sian (är tē′zhən). An **artesian well** is a deep-bored well, especially one from which water gushes up to the surface. *adj. 12.*

art ful (ärt′fəl), 1. crafty; deceitful. A swindler uses artful tricks to get people's money away from them. 2. skillful; clever. *adj. 8.*

Ar thur (är′thər), 1. a king of ancient Britain who gathered about him a famous group of knights. 2. Chester A. Arthur (1830-1886) was the 21st president of the United States, from 1881 to 1885. *n. 3.*

ar ti choke (är′ti chōk), a plant whose flowering head is cooked and eaten. *n. 13.*

Artichoke

ar ti cle (är′ti kəl), 1. a literary composition, complete in itself, but forming part of a magazine, newspaper, or book. This newspaper has a good article on gardening. 2. a separate part of anything written; as, the third article of the Constitution. 3. a particular thing. Bread is an important article of food. 4. one of the words *a*, *an*, or *the*. *A* and *an* are the indefinite articles; *the* is the definite article. *n. 1.*

ar tic u late (är tik′ū lit for 1 and 3, är tik′ū-lāt for 2, 4, and 5), 1. made up of distinct parts; distinct. A baby cries and gurgles, but does not use articulate speech. 2. speak distinctly. Articulate your words carefully. 3. jointed. 4. unite by joints. 5. fit together in a joint. After the injury the bones did not articulate so well as before. *adj., v. 8.*

ar tic u la tion (är tik′ū lā′shən), 1. way of speaking; enunciation. 2. a joint. 3. act or manner of connecting by a joint or joints; as, the articulation of the bones. *n. 15.*

ar ti fice (är′ti fis), 1. skill; craft. 2. clever device; trick. *n. 9.*

ar tif i cer (är tif′i sər), skilled workman; craftsman. *n. 14.*

ar ti fi cial (är′ti fish′əl), not natural; made by the art of man; as, artificial flowers, artificial light, artificial ice, an artificial voice or manner. *adj. 5.*

ar til ler y (är til′ər i), 1. mounted guns; cannon. 2. the part of an army that uses and manages cannon. *n. 7.*

ar ti san (är′ti zən), workman skilled in some industry or trade; craftsman. *n. 9.*

art ist (är′tist), 1. person who paints pictures. 2. person who is skilled in any of the fine arts, such as sculpture, music, or literature. 3. person who does work with skill and good taste. *n. 3.*

ar tis tic (är tis′tik), 1. of art or artists. 2. done with skill and good taste. 3. having good color and design. 4. having or showing appreciation of beauty. *adj. 5.*

ar tis ti cal ly (är tis′ti kəl i), 1. done with skill and good taste. 2. from an artistic point of view. *adv.*

art ist ry (är′tis tri), artistic work; workmanship of an artist. *n. 20.*

art less (ärt′lis), 1. natural; simple; without any trickery. Small children ask many artless questions, such as, "Mother, did you want this lady to come to see you?" 2. without art; unskilled; ignorant. *adj. 11.*

as (az, *unstressed* əz), 1. Treat others as you wish them to treat you. 2. Mary will act as teacher today. 3. As they were walking, the rain began. 4. He was well paid, as he had done the work well. 5. Mary is as tall as Nell. 6. Our dog eats such food as we give him. 7. It looks as if it would rain. 8. As for me, I will walk. 9. You may as well sit down. 10. Brave as he is, he dares not jump. 11. The house was so planned as to make the work easy. 12. Nothing has been done as yet. 13. He is careful, as his work shows. 14. Some animals, as dogs and cats, eat meat. *conj., prep., adv., pron. 1.*

as a fet i da (as′ə fet′i də), a bad-smelling substance used in medicine. Asafetida smells like garlic or onions. *n. 20.*

as bes tos (as bes′təs), a substance which will not burn and which comes in fibers that can be made into a sort of cloth or felt. Asbestos is used for mats to put under hot dishes. *n. 11.*

as cend (ə send′), go up; rise; climb. The airplane ascended higher and higher. Few people ascend high mountains. *v. 3.*

as cend an cy or **as cend en cy** (ə sen′dən si), domination; rule; controlling influence. *n. 15.*

as cend ant or **as cend ent** (əsen′dənt), 1. ascending; rising. 2. superior; dominant. 3. position of power; controlling influence. "His star is in the ascendant" means "His fortunes are improving." *adj., n.*

as cen sion (ə sen′shən), act of ascending; ascent. **The Ascension** is the bodily passing of Christ from earth to heaven. *n. 11.*

as cent (ə sent′), 1. a going up; upward movement; act of rising. 2. place or way that slopes up. *n. 8.*

as cer tain (as′ər tān′), find out. *v. 7.*

as cet ic (ə set′ik), 1. person who practices unusual self-denial and devotion, or severe discipline of self for religious reasons. 2. person who refrains from pleasures and comforts. 3. self-denying; refraining from pleasures, comfort, etc. *n., adj. 17.*

as ceti cism (ə set′i sizm), life or habits of an ascetic; extreme self-denial. *n. 20.*

as cribe (əs krīb′), assign (to a cause or a source). **Ascribe to** means think of as caused by; think of as belonging to. The discovery of America is usually ascribed to Columbus. The police ascribed the automobile accident to fast driving. *v. 7.*

as crip tion (əs krip′shən), 1. act of ascribing; as, the ascription of selfishness to a miser. 2. statement or words ascribing something. *n. 20.*

ash[1] (ash), what remains of a thing after it has been thoroughly burned. *n. 3.*

ash[2] (ash), a kind of shade tree that has a tough, straight-grained wood. *n.*

a shamed (ə shāmd′), 1. feeling shame; disturbed or uncomfortable because one has done something wrong, improper, or silly. Mary was ashamed of her dirty, ragged dress, but it was the only one she had. 2. unwilling because of shame. Tom was ashamed to tell his mother he had failed. *adj. 2.*

ash en[1] (ash′ən), 1. like ashes; pale as ashes. 2. of ashes. *adj. 16.*

ash en[2] (ash′ən), made from the wood of the ash tree. *adj.*

ash es (ash′iz), 1. what remains of a thing after it has been burned. Ashes have to be removed from fireplaces and furnaces or there would be no space for a fire. 2. a dead person or persons; as, "Peace to their ashes!" *n. pl.*

a shore (ə shōr′), 1. to the shore; to land. 2. on the shore; on land. *adv., adj. 4.*

Ash Wednesday, the first day of Lent; the seventh Wednesday before Easter.

ash y (ash′i), 1. like ashes; pale as ashes. 2. of ashes. 3. covered with ashes. *adj. 18.*

A sia (ā′zhə), the largest continent. China and India are in Asia. *n. 2.*

Asia Minor, a part of Asia between the Black Sea and the Mediterranean Sea.

A siat ic (ā′zhi at′ik), 1. of Asia; having to do with the people of Asia. 2. a native of Asia. *adj., n. 8.*

a side (ə sīd′), 1. on one side; to one side; away. Move the table aside. John spoke aside to Tom without his father's hearing him. 2. words spoken aside. *adv., n. 3.*

as i nine (as′i nīn), stupid; silly. *adj. 19.*

ask (ask), 1. Ask as many questions as you like. Ask him how old he is. 2. Ask for what you want. Ask Kate to sing. 3. Nell asked ten girls to her party. 4. She asked about our health, and asked after you, too. *v. 1.*

a skance (ə skans′), 1. with suspicion or disapproval. The students looked askance at the suggestion of having classes on Saturday. 2. sideways; to one side. *adv. 10.*

a skant (ə skant′), askance. *adv.*

a skew (ə skū′), to one side; out of the proper position; turned or twisted the wrong way. Her hat is on askew. *adv., adj. 19.*

a slant (ə slant′), 1. in a slanting direction. 2. slantingly across. *adv., prep. 14.*

a sleep (ə slēp′), 1. sleeping. The cat is asleep. 2. into a condition of sleep. The tired boy fell asleep. 3. numb. My foot is asleep. *adj., adv. 2.*

asp (asp), a kind of small poisonous snake. See the picture. *n. 14.*

Asp

as par a gus (əs par′ə gəs), 1. a plant whose shoots are used for food. 2. the shoots. *n. 8.*

as pect (as′pekt), 1. look; appearance. The judge has a sober aspect. 2. one side or part or view (of a subject). We must consider this plan in its various aspects. 3. direction anything faces. 4. side fronting in a given direction. The southern aspect of the house is the most pleasant. *n. 5.*

Asparagus shoot

as pen (as′pən), 1. a kind of poplar tree whose leaves tremble and rustle in the slightest breeze. 2. of this tree. 3. quivering; trembling. *n., adj. 19.*

as per i ty (as per′i ti), roughness; harshness; severity; as, the asperities of a very cold winter. *n., pl. asperities. 16.*

as perse (as pėrs′), spread damaging or false reports about; slander. *v.*

as per sion (as pėr′zhən), a damaging or false report; slander. *n. 16.*

as phalt (as′fôlt), 1. dark-colored substance much like tar, that is found in various parts of the world. 2. a smooth hard mixture of this substance with crushed rock. Asphalt is used for pavements, roofs, etc. *n. 8.*

as pho del (as′fə del), 1. a plant with spikes of white or yellow flowers. See the picture. 2. the flower of the Greek paradise. 3. the daffodil, a yellow spring flower. *Used in poetry. n. 15.*

Asphodel (def. 1)

as phyx i ate (as fik′si āt), suffocate. The men trapped in the coal mines were asphyxiated by the gas before help could reach them. *v.*

as phyx i a tion (as fik′si ā′shən), suffocation. *n. 15.*

as pic (as′pik), a kind of jelly made from meat, tomato juice, etc. *n. 17.*

as pir ant (əs pīr′ənt), person who aspires; person who seeks a position of honor. *n. 12.*

as pi rate (as′pi rāt for 1, as′pi rit for 2 and 3), 1. pronounce with a breathing or *h*-sound. The *h* in *hot* is aspirated. 2. pronounced with a breathing or *h*-sound. The *h* in *here* is aspirate. 3. the sound of *h;* an aspirated sound. *v., adj., n.*

as pi ra tion (as′pi rā′shən), 1. longing; desire. She had aspirations to be an actress. 2. drawing of breath. 3. aspirating; as, the aspiration of *h* in *house. n. 8.*

as pire (əs pīr′), 1. have an ambition for something; desire earnestly; seek. Tom aspired to be captain of the team. Scholars aspire after knowledge. 2. rise high. *v. 6.*

as pi rin (as′pi rin), a drug for headaches, colds, etc. *n. 18.*

ass (as), 1. donkey. 2. a fool; a stupid, silly, or stubborn person. *n. 3.*

as sa fet i da (as′ə fet′i də), asafetida. *n.*

as sail (ə sāl′), attack. *v. 5.*

as sail ant (ə sāl′ənt), person who attacks. The injured man did not know his assailant. *n. 7.*

as sas sin (ə sas′in), murderer, especially one hired to murder. *n. 10.*

as sas si nate (ə sas′i nāt), kill; murder. *v. 11.*

as sas si na tion (ə sas′i nā′shən), murder. *n. 10.*

as sault (ə sôlt′), 1. an attack; a sudden, vigorous attack. 2. to attack. *n., v. 4.*

as say (ə sā′), 1. analyze (an ore, alloy, etc.) to find out the quantity of gold, silver, or other metal in it. 2. finding out the amount of metal in an ore, alloy, etc., by measuring, weighing, or calculating. 3. to try; to test. 4. trial; test. *v., n. 9.*

as sem blage (ə sem′blij), 1. group of persons gathered together; assembly. 2. collection; group. 3. bringing together; coming together; meeting. 4. putting together; fitting together. *n. 10.*

as sem ble (ə sem′bəl), 1. gather together; bring together; come together; meet. 2. put together; fit together. *v. 3.*

as sem bly (ə sem′bli), 1. group of people gathered together for some purpose; meeting. A reception or a ball may be called an assembly. 2. a meeting of lawmakers. 3. putting together; fitting together; as, the assembly of the parts of an automobile to make an automobile. 4. signal on a bugle or drum for troops to form in ranks. *n., pl. assemblies. 3.*

as sent (ə sent′), 1. agree; express agreement. 2. agreement; acceptance of a proposal, statement, etc. *v., n. 7.*

as sert (ə sėrt′), 1. declare; state positively. 2. defend or insist on (a right, a claim, etc.). 3. put (oneself) forward. *v. 4.*

as ser tion (ə sėr′shən), 1. positive declaration; very strong statement. 2. an insisting on one's rights, a claim, etc. *n. 8.*

as ser tive (ə sėr′tiv), asserting; too confident and certain; positive. John is an assertive boy, always insisting on his own rights and opinions. *adj.*

as sess (ə ses′), 1. estimate the value of (property or income) for taxation. 2. fix the amount of (a tax, fine, etc.). 3. tax; fine (a person, property, etc.). Each member of the club will be assessed one dollar to pay for the trip. *v. 11.*

as sess ment (ə ses′mənt), 1. an assessing. 2. amount assessed. *n. 13.*

as ses sor (ə ses′ər), person who estimates the value of property or income for taxation. *n. 15.*

as set (as′et), something having value. Ability to get along with people is an asset in business. *n. 11.*

as sets (as′ets), 1. things of value; property. 2. property that can be used to pay debts. *n. pl.*

as sev er a tion (ə sev′ər ā′shən), solemn declaration; positive statement. *n. 16.*

as si du i ty (as′i dū′i ti or as′i dü′i ti), careful and steady attention; diligence. *n. 15.*

as sid u ous (ə sij′ü əs), working hard and steadily; diligent. *adj. 10.*

as sign (ə sīn′), 1. give as a share. The teacher assigned the next ten problems for today. 2. appoint. The captain assigned two soldiers to guard the gate. 3. name definitely; fix; set. The judge assigned a day for the trial. 4. transfer or hand over (property). Mr. Jones assigned his home and farm to his creditors. *v. 3.*

as sign ment (ə sīn′mənt), 1. assigning; appointment; as, the assignment of a soldier to a place of danger. 2. something assigned. Today's assignment in arithmetic is ten examples. 3. a legal transferring of property or other rights. *n. 9.*

as sim i late (ə sim′i lāt), 1. absorb; digest. Alice does so much reading that she cannot assimilate it all. The human body will not assimilate sawdust. 2. be absorbed. 3. make like. By living a long time with the Indians he was assimilated to them in his thinking and actions. 4. become like. *v. 8.*

as sim i la tion (ə sim′i lā′shən), 1. absorbing or being absorbed. Life depends on the assimilation of food. 2. making or becoming like. *n. 9.*

as sist (ə sist′), help. *v. 2.*

as sist ance (ə sis′təns), help; aid. *n. 4.*

as sist ant (ə sis′tənt), 1. helper; aid. 2. helping; assisting. *n., adj. 6.*

as siz es (ə sīz′iz), periodical sessions of court held in each county of England. *n. pl. 15.*

assn., association.

as so ci ate (ə sō′shi āt for 1, 2, and 3, ə sō′shi it for 4-7), 1. join as a companion, partner, or friend; keep company. Never associate with bad companions. 2. connect in thought. We associate giving presents with Christmas. 3. join; combine; unite. 4. companion; partner; ally. 5. thing connected with another. 6. joined in companionship, interest, action, purpose, etc. 7. admitted to some, but not all, rights, privileges, dignities, etc. Mr. Blake has been associate professor of English and will be made full professor this term. *v., n., adj. 3.*

as so ci a tion (ə sō′si ā′shən), 1. associating. 2. being associated. 3. companionship. 4. connection; relation; combination; union. 5. group of people joined together for some common purpose; a society. *n. 4.*

as sort (ə sôrt′), 1. sort out; classify; arrange in sorts. 2. furnish with various sorts. 3. group (with). 4. agree in sort or kind; fall into a class. *v. 17.*

as sort ed (ə sôr′tid), 1. selected so as to be of different kinds; various. 2. arranged by kinds; classified. 3. matched; suited, one to another. *adj.*

as sort ment (ə sôrt′mənt), 1. an assorting. 2. a collection of various sorts. 3. group; class. *n. 9.*

as suage (ə swāj′), make easier or milder; quiet; calm. *v. 11.*

as sume (ə süm′), 1. take upon oneself; undertake. 2. take on; put on. 3. pretend; as, assumed ignorance. 4. take for granted; suppose. He assumed that the train would be on time. *v. 3.*

as sump tion (ə sump′shən), 1. act of assuming. She bustled about with an assumption of authority. 2. thing assumed. John's assumption that he would win the prize proved incorrect. 3. presumption; arrogance; unpleasant boldness. Tom's assumption in always thrusting himself forward made him disliked. *n. 8.*

as sur ance (ə shür′əns), 1. making sure or certain. 2. security; certainty; confidence. 3. self-confidence. 4. impudence; too great boldness. 5. insurance. *n. 5.*

as sure (ə shür′), 1. make sure or certain. 2. tell positively. The captain of the ship assured the passengers that there was no danger. 3. make safe against loss; insure. *v. 2.*

as sured (ə shürd′), 1. sure; certain. 2. confident; bold. *adj.*

as sur ed ly (ə shür′id li), 1. surely; certainly. 2. confidently; boldly. *adv. 9.*

As syr i a (ə sir′i ə), an ancient country in southwestern Asia. Assyria was once a great empire. *n. 8.*

as ter (as′tər), a common flower with white, pink, or purple petals around a yellow center. Some asters are very small; others are large with many petals. *n. 11.*

as ter isk (as′tər isk), star (*) used in printing and writing to call attention to a footnote, indicate an omission, etc. *n.*

a stern (ə stėrn′) 1. at or toward the rear of a ship. 2. backward. 3. behind. *adv. 19.*

asth ma (az′mə), disease that causes difficulty in breathing, a feeling of suffocation, and coughing. *n. 17.*

a stig ma tism (ə stig′mə tizm), defect in an eye or a lens that makes objects look indistinct or imperfect. *n.*

a stir (ə stėr′), in motion. *adv., adj. 14.*

as ton ish (əs ton′ish), surprise greatly; amaze. The gift of ten dollars astonished me. *v. 3.*

as ton ish ing (əs ton′ish ing), very surprising; amazing. *adj. 6.*

as ton ish ment (əs ton′ish mənt), great surprise; amazement; wonder. *n. 5.*

as tound (əs tound′), surprise very greatly; amaze. *v. 8.*

a strad dle (ə strad′əl), astride. *adv., adj.*

as tra khan (as′trə kən), 1. curly furlike wool on the skin of young lambs. 2. woolen cloth that looks like this. *n.*

a stray (ə strā′), out of the right way; wandering. *adv., adj. 8.*

a stride (ə strīd′), 1. with one leg on each side. 2. with one leg on each side of. He sits astride his horse. 3. with legs far apart. *adv., adj., prep. 13.*

as trin gent (əs trin′jənt), 1. substance that shrinks tissues and checks the flow of blood by contracting blood vessels. Alum is an astringent. 2. of or like an astringent; shrinking; contracting. *n., adj. 16.*

as tro labe (as′trə lāb), an astronomical instrument formerly used for measuring the altitude of the sun or stars. *n. 19.*

as trol o ger (əs trol′ə jər), person who claims to know and interpret the influence of the stars and planets on persons, events, etc. *n. 15.*

as tro log i cal (as′trə loj′i kəl), having to do with astrology. *adj. 19.*

as trol o gy (əs trol′ə ji), a false science that claims to know and interpret the influence of the stars and planets on persons, events, etc.; study of the stars to foretell what will happen. *n. 15.*

as tron o mer (əs tron′ə mər), expert in astronomy. *n. 8.*

as tro nom i cal (as′trə nom′i kəl), of astronomy; having to do with astronomy. *adj. 12.*

as tron o my (əs tron′ə mi), the science that deals with the sun, moon, planets, stars, and other heavenly bodies. *n. 12.*

as tute (as tūt′ or as tüt′), shrewd; crafty; sagacious; clever. Many lawyers are astute. *adj. 17.*

as tute ness (as tūt′nis or as tüt′nis), shrewdness; craftiness; sagacity. *n. 19.*

A sun ción (ä sün syōn′), capital of Paraguay. *n.*

a sun der (ə sun′dər), 1. apart; separate. 2. in pieces; into separate parts. *adj., adv. 6.*

a sy lum (ə sī′ləm), 1. institution for the support and care of the insane, the blind, orphans, or other classes of unfortunate persons. 2. refuge; shelter. In olden times a church might be an asylum for a debtor or a criminal, since no one was allowed to drag a person from the altar. *n. 10.*

at (at, *unstressed* ət), 1. At is used to show where. Mary is at home. The dog ran at the cat. 2. At is sometimes used to show when. Tom goes to bed at nine o'clock. 3. England and France were at war. We were sad at hearing such bad news. *prep. 1.*

ate (āt). See **eat**. John ate his dinner. *pt. of eat. 2.*

a the ism (ā′thē izm), the belief that there is no God. *n. 17.*

a the ist (ā′thē ist), person who believes that there is no God. *n. 10.*

a the is tic (ā′thē is′tik), of atheism or atheists. *adj.*

A the na (ə thē′nə), the Greek goddess of wisdom, arts, industries, and prudent warfare. The Romans called her Minerva. *n. 18.*

A the ne (ə thē′ni), Athena. *n.*

A the ni an (ə thē′ni ən), 1. of Athens or its people. 2. a native or citizen of Athens. *adj., n. 7.*

Ath ens (ath′inz), a famous city of Greece. In ancient times Athens was famous for its art and literature. *n. 6.*

a thirst (ə thėrst′), thirsty. *adj. 15.*

ath lete (ath′lēt), person trained in exercises of strength, speed, and skill. Ballplayers, runners, boxers, and swimmers are athletes. *n. 10.*

ath let ic (ath let′ik), 1. active and strong. 2. of an athlete; like or suited to an athlete. 3. having to do with active games and sports. *adj. 5.*

ath let ics (ath let′iks), exercises of strength, speed, and skill; active games and sports. *n. sing. or pl.*

a thwart (ə thwôrt′), 1. crosswise; across from side to side. 2. across. 3. across the line or course of. The tug steamed athwart the steamer. 4. in opposition to; against. *adv., prep. 10.*

-ation, suffix meaning:—

1. act or state of ——ing; as in admiration, adoration.
2. condition or state of being ——ed; as in accusation, cancellation.
3. result of ——ing; as in civilization, preparation.

-ative, suffix meaning:—
1. tending to; as in affirmative, talkative.
2. having to do with.

At lan ta (at lan′tə), capital of Georgia. *n. 14.*

At lan tic (at lan′tik), 1. the ocean east of North and South America. 2. of the Atlantic Ocean. 3. on or near the Atlantic Ocean. *n., adj. 2.*

at las (at′ləs), a book of maps. *n. 9.*

At las (at′ləs), a giant who was supposed to hold up the heavens. *n.*

Atlas Mountains, mountain range in northwestern Africa. The highest peak is 15,000 feet.

at mos phere (at′məs fēr), 1. air. 2. the air that surrounds the earth. 3. mental and moral surroundings. *n. 5.*

at mos pher ic (at′məs fer′ik), of or having to do with the atmosphere. Atmospheric conditions often prevent observations of the stars. Atmospheric pressure is about 15 pounds to the square inch at sea level. *adj. 17.*

at oll (at′ol), ring-shaped coral island enclosing or partly enclosing a lagoon. *n.*

Atoll

at om (at′əm), 1. very small particle; tiny bit. 2. very small particle of a chemical element. A molecule of water is made of two atoms of hydrogen and one atom of oxygen. *n. 8.*

a tom ic (ə tom′ik), 1. of atoms; having to do with atoms. 2. very, very small. *adj. 11.*

at om iz er (at′əm īz′ər), apparatus used to blow a liquid in a spray of very small drops. *n. 17.*

at o my (at′ə mi), 1. very small thing; atom. 2. a tiny being; pygmy. *n., pl. atomies. 18.*

a tone (ə tōn′), make up; make amends. Tom atoned for his unkindness to Dick by taking Dick to the movies. *v. 11.*

a tone ment (ə tōn′mənt), making up for something; amends; giving satisfaction for wrong, loss, or injury. The sufferings and death of Christ are called **the Atonement.** *n. 10.*

a top (ə top′), 1. on the top; at the top. 2. on the top of. *adv., prep. 14.*

a tri um (ā′tri əm), main room of an ancient Roman house. *n. 20.*

a tro cious (ə trō′shəs), very wicked or cruel; very savage or brutal. *adj. 14.*

a troc i ty (ə tros′i ti), 1. very great wickedness or cruelty. 2. a very cruel or brutal act. *n., pl. atrocities. 9.*

at ro phy (at′rə fi), 1. wasting away. 2. waste away. *n., v., atrophied, atrophying. 15.*

at tach (ə tach′), 1. fasten (to). The boy attached a rope to his sled. 2. join. 3. assign; appoint. 4. affix. The signers attached their names to the Constitution. 5. attribute. 6. bind by affection. May is much attached to her cousin. 7. take (a person or property) by legal authority. If you owe money to a man, he may attach a part of your salary unless you pay him. 8. stick; belong; fasten itself. The blame for this accident attaches to the man who destroyed the signal. *v. 3.*

at ta ché (at′ə shā′), person belonging to the official staff of an ambassador or minister to a foreign country. *n. 20.*

at tach ment (ə tach′mənt), 1. an attaching. 2. being attached. 3. thing attached. A sewing machine has various attachments, such as a hemmer and a darner. 4. means of attaching; fastening. 5. affection. 6. legal taking of a person or property. *n. 8.*

at tack (ə tak′), 1. set upon to hurt; go against as an enemy. The dog attacked the cat. 2. go at with vigor; as, to attack a hard lesson, to attack one's dinner. 3. attacking. The attack of the enemy took us by surprise. 4. make an attack; begin fighting. *v., n. 2.*

at tain (ə tān′), 1. arrive at; reach. 2. gain; accomplish. *v. 3.*

at tain a ble (ə tān′ə bəl), capable of being attained; that can be reached or achieved. The office of President is the highest attainable in the United States. *adj. 16.*

at tain der (ə tān′dər), loss of property and civil rights as the result of being sentenced to death or being outlawed. *n. 16.*

at tain ment (ə tān′mənt), 1. act of attaining. 2. something attained. 3. accomplishment; ability. Benjamin Franklin was a man of varied attainments; he was a diplomat, statesman, writer, and inventor. *n. 12.*

at taint (ə tānt′), 1. condemn by attainder. 2. stain; disgrace; taint. *v., n. 14.*

at tar (at′ər), perfume made from flowers. *n.*

at tempt (ə tempt′), 1. try. 2. try to take or destroy. **Attempt the life of** means try to kill. 3. a trying; an effort. *v., n. 2.*

at tend (ə tend′), 1. be present at. Children must attend school. 2. give care and thought; apply oneself. Attend to your lessons. 3. wait on; go with. Noble ladies attend the queen. 4. go with as a result. Success often attends hard work. *v. 1.*

at tend ance (ə ten′dəns), 1. attending. Our class has perfect attendance today. 2. company present; persons attending. *n. 5.*

at tend ant (ə ten′dənt), 1. waiting on another to help or serve; as, an attendant nurse. 2. person who waits on another, such as a servant or a follower. 3. accompanying; going with as a result; as, attendant circumstances, weakness attendant on illness. 4. present; as, attendant hearers. 5. person who is present. *adj., n. 5.*

at ten tion (ə ten′shən), 1. act of attending. The children gave attention to the teacher. 2. power of attending. James called my attention to the cat trying to catch the mouse. 3. care; consideration. The boy shows his mother much attention. 4. courtesy. The pretty girl received many attentions, such as invitations to parties, candy, and flowers. 5. military attitude of readiness. **Come to attention** and **stand at attention** mean stand straight and still. *n. 2.*

at ten tive (ə ten′tiv), 1. giving attention; observant. 2. courteous; polite. *adj. 5.*

at ten u ate (ə ten′ū āt), 1. make thin or slender. 2. weaken; reduce. *v. 17.*

at test (ə test′), 1. bear witness; give proof of; certify. The child's good health attests his mother's care. The expert attested to the genuineness of the writing. 2. put on oath. *v. 6.*

at tic (at′ik), space just below the roof in a house. *n. 5.*

At ti ca (at′i kə), a district in ancient Greece whose chief city was Athens. *n. 18.*

At ti la (at′i lə), the barbaric leader of the Huns in their invasions of Europe in the first half of the 5th century A.D. *n. 18.*

at tire (ə tīr′), dress; array. The queen wears rich attire. She is attired in purple. *n., v. 4.*

at ti tude (at′i tūd or at′i tüd), 1. way of thinking, acting, or feeling. His attitude toward school changed from dislike to great enthusiasm. 2. position of the body. Standing, sitting, lying, and stooping are attitudes. *n. 5.*

at tor ney (ə tėr′ni), 1. person who has power to act for another. 2. lawyer. *n., pl. attorneys. 5.*

attorney general or **Attorney General,** the chief law officer of a country or State. *pl. attorneys general* or *attorney generals. 15.*

at tract (ə trakt′), 1. draw to oneself. A magnet attracts iron. 2. be pleasing to; win the attention and liking of. Bright colors attract children. *v. 4.*

Magnet attracting nails

at trac tion (ə trak′shən), 1. act or power of drawing to oneself. 2. thing that attracts. The elephants were the chief attraction at the circus. *n. 5.*

at trac tive (ə trak′tiv), 1. pleasing; winning attention and liking. 2. attracting. *adj. 4.*

at trac tive ness (ə trak′tiv nis), quality of attracting or pleasing; charm. *n. 13.*

at trib ut a ble (ə trib′ū tə bəl), that can be attributed. Some diseases are attributable to lack of cleanliness. *adj. 16.*

at trib ute (at′ri būt for 1 and 2, ə trib′ūt for 3), 1. a quality considered as belonging to a person or thing; a characteristic. Kindness is an attribute of a good teacher. 2. an object considered appropriate to a person, rank, or office; symbol. The eagle was the attribute of Jupiter. 3. assign. **Attribute to** means consider as belonging to or appropriate to; regard as an effect of; think of as caused by. We attribute Edison's success to intelligence and hard work. *n., v. 5.*

at tri bu tion (at′ri bū′shən), 1. act of attributing. 2. thing attributed; an attribute. *n. 19.*

at tune (ə tūn′ or ə tün′), tune; put in tune. *v. 12.*

au burn (ô′bərn), reddish brown. *adj., n. 9.*

auc tion (ôk′shən), 1. public sale in which each thing is sold to the person who offers the most money for it. 2. sell at an auction. *n., v. 9.*

auc tion eer (ôk′shən ēr′), 1. man whose business is conducting auctions. 2. sell at an auction. *n., v. 13.*

au da cious (ô dā′shəs), 1. bold; daring. 2. too bold; impudent. *adj. 11.*

au dac i ty (ô das′i ti), 1. boldness. 2. rude boldness; impudence. *n., pl. audacities. 8.*

au di ble (ô′di bəl), that can be heard; loud enough to be heard. *adj. 8.*

au di ence (ô′di əns), 1. people gathered in a place or building to hear or see; as, the audiences at moving-picture shows, theaters, or speeches. 2. any persons within hearing. People who hear over the radio may be called an audience. 3. a chance to be heard; hearing. He should have an audience with the committee, for his plan is good. 4. an interview with a person of high rank. The king granted an audience to the famous general. *n. 4.*

au dit (ô′dit), 1. examine and check (business accounts). 2. an examination and check of business accounts. *v., n. 14.*

au di tion (ô dish′ən), 1. hearing. 2. hearing to test the voice of a singer or speaker. *n.*

au di tor (ô′di tər), 1. hearer; listener. 2. person who audits business accounts. *n. 10.*

au di to ri um (ô′di tō′ri əm), large room for an audience in a church, a theater, a school, or the like; large hall. *n. 13.*

au di to ry (ô′di tō′ri), 1. of or having to do with hearing; as, the auditory nerve. 2. assembly of hearers; audience. 3. auditorium. *adj., n., pl. auditories. 12.*

Au du bon (ô′dü bon), John James, an American painter who made a study of birds (1785-1851). *n. 17.*

Aug., August. *6.*

au ger (ô′gər), 1. tool for boring holes in wood. 2. tool for boring holes in the earth. *n. 12.*

Auger

aught (ôt), anything. Has he done aught to help you? *n., adv. 7.*

aug ment (ôg ment′), increase; enlarge. The king augmented his power by taking over rights that had belonged to the nobles. *v. 7.*

aug men ta tion (ôg′men tā′shən), act of augmenting; enlargement; increase; addition. The power of the nobles declined with the augmentation of the power of the king. *n. 16.*

au gur (ô′gər), 1. a priest in ancient Rome who made predictions and gave advice. 2. predict; foretell. 3. be a sign. **Augur well** means be a good sign. **Augur ill** means be a bad sign. *n., v. 11.*

au gu ry (ô′gū ri), 1. foretelling the future by the flight of birds, the appearance of sacrificed animals, thunder and lightning, etc. 2. prediction; indication; sign; omen. *n., pl. auguries. 15.*

Au gust[1] (ô′gəst), the eighth month of the year. It has 31 days. *n. 2.*

au gust[2] (ô gust′), inspiring reverence and admiration; majestic; venerable. *adj. 18.*

Au gus ta (ô gus′tə), capital of Maine. *n. 12.*

Au gus tine (ô′gəs tēn), 1. Saint Augustine was one of the leaders in the early Christian church (354-430 A.D.). 2. Another Saint Augustine was sent to preach Christianity in England in 597 A.D. *n. 12.*

Au gus tus (ô gus′təs), a title given to the first emperor of Rome, who lived from 63 B.C. to 14 A.D. *n. 9.*

auk (ôk), a northern sea bird with short wings used only as paddles. *n.*

Auk (2½ ft. long)

aunt (ant), 1. sister of one's father or mother. 2. an uncle's wife. *n. 2.*

au ra (ô′rə), something supposed to come from a person or thing and surround it as an atmosphere. An aura of holiness surrounded the godly hermit. *n. 17.*

Au re li us (ô rē′li əs), Marcus, a Roman emperor famous for his high character and excellent rule (121-180 A.D.). *n. 14.*

au re ole (ô′ri ōl), halo; ring of light. See the picture under **halo.** *n. 18.*

au re voir (ō rə vwär′), a French way of saying good-by. The words mean "Till I see you again."

au ri cle (ô′ri kəl), 1. one of the two upper chambers of the heart. See the diagram. 2. the outer part of the ear. *n. 13.*

AORTA
BLOOD TO THE BODY
BLOOD FROM THE BODY
TO THE LUNGS
FROM THE LUNGS
LEFT AURICLE
RIGHT AURICLE
RIGHT VENTRICLE
LEFT VENTRICLE

Heart showing auricles

au ric u lar (ô rik′ū lər), 1. of the ear; near the ear. 2. heard by or addressed to the ear. 3. shaped like an ear. *adj. 19.*

Au ro ra (ô rō′rə), the goddess of dawn. *n. 11.*

au ro ra bo re a lis (ô rō′rə bō′ri ā′lis), northern lights; streamers or bands of light sometimes seen at night in the northern sky.

aus pic es (ôs′pi siz), 1. omens. The ancient Romans used the way birds flew as auspices to guide their actions. 2. favoring influence. The school fair was held under the auspices of the Parents' Association. *n. pl. 13.*

aus pi cious (ôs pish′əs), with signs of success; favorable; fortunate. *adj. 11.*

aus tere (ôs tēr′), 1. harsh; stern. Frank's

father was a silent, austere man, very strict with his children. 2. strict in morals. Some of the ideas of the Puritans seem to us too austere. 3. severely simple. The tall columns stood against the sky in austere beauty. *adj. 8.*

aus ter i ty (ôs ter′i ti), 1. austereness; strictness; severity. 2. **Austerities** means severe practices like going without food, or sitting up all night to pray. *n., pl. austerities. 14.*

Aus tin (ôs′tin), the capital of Texas. *n. 12.*

Aus tral a sia (ôs′trəl ā′zhə), Australia, Tasmania, New Zealand, and the nearby islands. *n. 14.*

Aus tral ia (ôs trāl′yə), 1. a continent southeast of Asia. 2. British dominion that includes this continent and Tasmania. *n. 5.*

Aus tral ian (ôs trāl′yən), 1. of Australia or its people. 2. a native or inhabitant of Australia. *adj., n.*

Aus tri a (ôs′tri ə), a country in central Europe, formerly an empire. *n. 5.*

Aus tri a-Hun ga ry (ôs′tri ə hung′gə ri), former monarchy in central Europe that included Austria and Hungary. *n. 10.*

au then tic (ô then′tik), 1. reliable. We heard an authentic report of the wreck, given by one of the ship's officers. 2. genuine; real. We saw an authentic letter by George Washington. *adj. 7.*

au then ti cate (ô then′ti kāt), 1. establish the truth of; show to be valid or genuine. 2. establish the authorship of. *v. 15.*

au then tic i ty (ô′then tis′i ti), 1. reliability. 2. genuineness. The lawyer questioned the authenticity of the signature. *n. 15.*

au thor (ô′thər), 1. person who writes books, stories, or articles. 2. person who creates or begins anything. *n. 3.*

au thor i ta tive (ô thor′i tā′tiv), 1. having authority; officially ordered. Authoritative orders came from the general. 2. commanding. In authoritative tones the policeman shouted, "Keep back!" 3. that ought to be believed or obeyed; having the authority of expert knowledge. *adj. 9.*

au thor i ty (ô thor′i ti), 1. power; control. A father has authority over his children. 2. right. A policeman has the authority to arrest fast drivers. 3. person who has power or right. 4. source of correct information or wise advice. A good dictionary is an authority on the meanings of words. *n., pl. authorities. 2.*

au thor i za tion (ô′thər i zā′shən), 1. authorizing; giving legal power to. The authorization of policemen to arrest beggars put an end to begging on the streets. 2. legal right; sanction; warrant. "What authorization have you for fishing in this brook?" asked the owner of the brook. *n. 20.*

au thor ize (ô′thər īz), 1. give power or right. The President authorized him to do this. 2. make legal. Congress authorized the spending of money for three new post-office buildings. 3. give authority for; justify. The dictionary authorizes the two spellings *traveler* and *traveller*. *v. 7.*

au thor ship (ô′thər ship), 1. occupation of an author; writing. Mary chose authorship as her work in life. 2. origin as to author. What is the authorship of that novel? *n. 19.*

au to (ô′tō), automobile. *n., pl. autos. 5.*

au to bi o graph ic (ô′tō bī′ə graf′ik), 1. having to do with the story of one's own life. 2. telling or writing the story of one's own life. *adj.*

au to bi og ra phy (ô′tō bī og′rə fi), the story of a person's life written by himself. *n., pl. autobiographies. 12.*

au toc ra cy (ô tok′rə si), absolute authority or government; rule by a monarch whose power is unlimited. Russia used to be an autocracy. *n., pl. autocracies. 16.*

au to crat (ô′tə krat), absolute ruler; monarch having unlimited power. *n. 12.*

au to crat ic (ô′tə krat′ik), of or like an autocrat; absolute in power or authority; ruling without checks or limitations. *adj. 15.*

au to gi ro (ô′tō jī′rō), airplane with a horizontal propeller that enables the airplane to go straight up or down. *n., pl. autogiros.* [*Trade name*]

au to graph (ô′tə graf), 1. a person's name written by himself. 2. write one's name on or in. 3. something written in a person's own handwriting. *n., v. 15.*

au to mat ic (ô′tə mat′ik), 1. moving or acting of itself; as, an automatic lock, an automatic pump. 2. done without thought or attention. Breathing and swallowing are usually automatic. 3. pistol that throws out the empty shell and reloads by itself when the trigger is pulled. *adj., n. 7.*

au to mat i cal ly (ô′tə mat′i kəl i), in an automatic manner. The girl ran the machine automatically, chattering with her friend all the time. *adv. 15.*

au tom a ton (ô tom′ə ton), 1. a self-moving machine. The man was selling automatons in the shapes of different animals. 2. person or animal whose actions are purely mechanical. *n. 18.*

au to mo bile (ô′tə mō bēl′), motorcar; car that carries its own engine. *n. 2.*

au ton o mous (ô ton′ə məs), self-governing; independent. *adj.*

au ton o my (ô ton′ə mi), self-government; independence. *n. 19.*

au top sy (ô′top si), medical examination of a dead body to find the cause of death. The autopsy revealed that the man had been poisoned. *n., pl. autopsies.*

au tumn (ô′təm), 1. the season of the year between summer and winter. 2. of autumn; coming in autumn; as, autumn flowers and fruits, autumn rains. *n., adj. 2.*

au tum nal (ô tum′nəl), of autumn; coming in autumn. *adj. 10.*

aux il ia ry (ôg zil′yə ri), 1. helping; assisting. 2. a helper; an aid. *adj., n., pl. auxiliaries. 10.*

a vail (ə vāl′), 1. help. Talk will not avail without work. 2. be of use or benefit to. Money will not avail you after you are dead. 3. help; use. Crying is of no avail now. 4. **Avail oneself of** means take advantage of; profit by; make use of. *v., n. 5.*

a vail a bil i ty (ə vāl′ə bil′i ti), being available; being at hand; being ready. The availability of water power helped make New England a manufacturing center. *n.*

a vail a ble (ə vāl′ə bəl), 1. that can be used. That man is not available for the job; he has other work. 2. that can be had. All available tickets were sold. *adj. 8.*

av a lanche (av′ə lanch), 1. a large mass of snow and ice, or of dirt and rocks, sliding or falling down the side of a mountain. 2. anything like an avalanche; as, an avalanche of questions. *n. 11.*

av a rice (av′ə ris), greed; greedy desire for money. *n. 6.*

av a ri cious (av′ə rish′əs), greedy; like a miser; greedy for money. *adj. 12.*

a vast (ə vast′), stop! stay! "Avast there!" shouted the sailor. *interj.*

a vaunt (ə vônt′), begone! get out! go away! *interj. [Old use] 13.*

Ave., avenue. *11.*

A ve Ma ri a (ä′vā mə rē′ə), 1. "Hail Mary!"—the first words of the Latin form of a prayer of the Roman Catholic Church. 2. the prayer.

a venge (ə venj′), get revenge for. The Indian will avenge the murder of his brother by killing the murderer. *v. 5.*

a veng er (ə ven′jər), one who avenges a wrong. *n. 12.*

av e nue (av′i nū or av′i nü), 1. wide street. 2. road or walk bordered by trees. 3. way of approach. Hard work is a good avenue to success. *n. 2.*

a ver (ə vėr′), state to be true; assert. *v., averred, averring. 10.*

av er age (av′ər ij), 1. The average of several quantities is found by dividing the sum of the quantities by the number of quantities. The average of 3 and 10 and 5 is 6. 2. find the average of. 3. obtained by averaging; as, an average price, the average temperature. 4. have as an average; be on the average. The cost of our lunches at school averaged one dollar a week. 5. usual sort or amount. His mind is about like the average. 6. usual; ordinary. *n., v., adj. 3.*

a verse (ə vėrs′), opposed; unwilling. She was averse to fighting. *adj. 9.*

a ver sion (ə vėr′zhən), 1. dislike. 2. thing or person that is disliked. *n. 9.*

a vert (ə vėrt′), 1. turn away; turn aside. She averted her eyes from the wreck. 2. prevent; avoid. The accident was averted by a quick turn of his car. *v. 8.*

a vi ar y (ā′vi ãr′i), place where many birds are kept. *n., pl. aviaries. 20.*

a vi a tion (ā′vi ā′shən), flying in airplanes. *n. 15.*

a vi a tor (ā′vi ā′tər), person who flies an airplane. *n. 14.*

av id (av′id), eager; greedy. The miser was avid for gold. *adj.*

a vid i ty (ə vid′i ti), eagerness; greediness. *n. 15.*

A vi gnon (ä vē nyōn′), a city in southeastern France. *n. 14.*

a vis (ā′vis), Latin word meaning bird. *n., pl. aves* (ā′vēz). *19.*

av o ca do (av′ō kä′dō), 1. pear-shaped tropical fruit with a dark-green skin and a very large stone. It is used in salads. 2. tree that it grows on. *n., pl. avocados.*

Avocados

av o ca tion (av′ə kā′shən), something that a person does besides his regular business; minor occupation; hobby. Mr. Brown is a lawyer, but writing stories is his avocation. *n. 18.*

a void (ə void′), 1. keep away from; keep out of the way of. We avoided driving through large cities on our trip. 2. make void. *v. 2.*

a void ance (ə void′əns), act of avoiding; keeping away from. Mary's avoidance of her old friends was noticeable. *n. 14.*

av oir du pois (av′ər də poiz′), a system of weights in which a pound containing 16 ounces is used. The avoirdupois system is used to weigh everything except gems, precious metals, and drugs. *n., adj. 16.*

A von (ā′vən), a river in central England. Stratford, the birthplace of Shakespeare, is on the Avon. *n. 10.*

a vouch (ə vouch′), 1. declare to be true. 2. guarantee. 3. acknowledge; affirm. *v. 15.*

a vow (ə vou′), declare frankly or openly; confess; admit; acknowledge. *v. 11.*

a vow al (ə vou′əl), frank or open declaration; confession; admission. *n. 14.*

a vow ed ly (ə vou′id li), admittedly; openly. *adv. 18.*

a wait (ə wāt′), 1. wait for; look forward to. He has awaited your coming for a week. 2. be ready for; be in store for. Many pleasures await you. *v. 2.*

a wake (ə wāk′), 1. wake up; arouse. 2. not asleep. *v., awoke* or *awaked, awaking, adj. 2.*

a wak en (ə wāk′ən), awake; wake up; rouse from sleep; stir up. *v. 4.*

a wak en ing (ə wāk′ən ing), a waking up; an arousing. *n. 14.*

a ward (ə wôrd′), 1. give after careful consideration; assign. The sum of $5000 was awarded to the injured man. Gold stars were awarded to the children who did well. 2. something given after careful consideration; a prize. Frank's dog won the highest award. 3. a decision by a judge. We all thought the award was fair. *v., n. 7.*

a ware (ə wãr′), knowing; realizing; conscious. I was too sleepy to be aware how cold it was. She was not aware of her danger. *adj. 5.*

a way (ə wā′), 1. not at; not near; at a distance. Go away! The sailor was far away from home. Mary stays away from the fire. My mother is away today. 2. without stopping; continuously. Fred worked away at his writing. *adv., adj. 1.*

awe (ô), 1. great fear and wonder; fear and reverence. We feel awe when we stand near vast mountains, or when we think of God's power and glory. 2. cause to feel awe; fill with awe. *n., v. 4.*

a wear y (ə wēr′i), weary; tired. *adj.* [*Used in poetry*] *20.*

awe some (ô′səm), 1. causing awe. A great fire is an awesome sight. 2. awed. *adj.*

awe-struck (ô′struk′), filled with awe. She was awe-struck by the grandeur of the mountains. *adj. 20.*

aw ful (ô′fəl), 1. dreadful; causing fear; as, an awful storm with thunder and lightning. 2. impressive; deserving great respect; as, the awful power of God. *adj. 2.*

aw ful ly (ô′fəl i), 1. terribly; dreadfully. 2. very. I'm awfully sorry that I hurt your feelings. *Used in common talk. adv. 12.*

a while (ə hwīl′), for a short time. He stayed awhile. *adv. 3.*

awk ward (ôk′wərd), 1. not graceful in movement or shape; clumsy. The seal is very awkward on land, but quite at home in the water. 2. not well suited to use. The handle of this pitcher has an awkward shape. 3. not easily managed. This is an awkward corner to turn. He asked me an awkward question. *adj. 6.*

awk ward ness (ôk′wərd nis), being awkward; clumsiness. *n. 12.*

awl (ôl), a tool used for making small holes in leather or wood. *n. 17.*

Awl

awn ing (ôn′ing), piece of canvas spread over or before a door, window, porch, etc., for protection from the sun or rain. *n. 10.*

Awnings

a woke (ə wōk′). See **awake.** He awoke at seven. John has not yet awoke. *pt. and pp. of awake. 5.*

a wry (ə rī′), 1. with a twist or turn to one side. Her hat was blown awry by the wind. 2. wrong. Our plans have gone awry. *adv., adj. 16.*

ax or **axe** (aks), tool for chopping wood. See the picture. *n., pl. axes. 2.*

Ax

ax i al (ak′si əl), of, pertaining to, or forming an axis. The wheels move on an axial rod. *adj. 19.*

ax i om (ak′si əm), a statement seen to be true without proof; a self-evident truth. It is an axiom that if equals are added to equals the results will be equal. *n. 16.*

ax i o mat ic (ak′si ə mat′ik), 1. self-evident. That a whole is greater than any of its parts is axiomatic. 2. full of axioms or maxims. *adj.*

ax is (ak′sis), 1. the straight line about which a thing turns. 2. a line around which the parts of anything are arranged regularly. The **Axis** is Germany, Italy, Japan, and their allies. *n., pl. axes* (ak′sēz). *6.*

ax le (ak′səl), 1. bar on which or with which a wheel turns. 2. crossbar on the two ends of which wheels turn. *n. 6.*

Ax min ster (aks′min stər), a velvetlike carpet. *n. 14.*

ay[1] (ā), always; ever. A mother's love lasts forever and ay. *adv. 5.* Also spelled **aye.**

ay[2] (ī), yes. *adv., n.* Also spelled **aye.**

aye[1] (ā), always; ever. *adv.*

aye[2] (ī), yes. Aye, aye, sir. The ayes won when the vote was taken. *adv., n. 7.*

Ayr shire (ãr′shir), 1. one of a breed of dairy cattle that are red and white or brown and white. 2. of or having to do with this breed. *n., adj. 12.*

a zal ea (ə zāl′yə), any one of certain plants bearing many showy flowers. *n. 20.*

Azalea

A zores (ə zōrz′), group of islands in the Atlantic Ocean west of Portugal and belonging to Portugal. *n. pl. 8.*

Az tec (az′tek), 1. a member of a highly civilized people who ruled Mexico before its conquest by the Spaniards in 1519. 2. their language. 3. of the Aztecs. *n., adj. 17.*

az ure (azh′ər), 1. blue; sky blue. 2. the blue sky. *n., adj. 6.*

B

B, b (bē), the second letter of the alphabet. There are two b's in baby. *n., pl. B's, b's.*

baa (bä), bleat. *n., v., baaed, baaing. 11.*

Ba al (bā′əl), 1. the sun god of the ancient Phoenicians. 2. a false god. *n. 10.*

bab ble (bab′əl), 1. make sounds like a baby. 2. talk that cannot be understood. 3. talk foolishly. 4. foolish talk. 5. talk too much; tell secrets. 6. murmur; as. the babble of the brook. *v., n. 4.*

babe (bāb), baby. *n. 4.*

Ba bel (bā′bəl), 1. The **Tower of Babel** was a tower built in early times intended to reach heaven. While the builders were at work, they suddenly began to speak new and different languages. Since they could not understand each other, the tower was left unfinished. Genesis 11: 1-9. 2. Noise or confusion is sometimes called **babel.** *n. 11.*

Baboon (body 2 ft. high, 2 ft. long; tail 18 in.)

ba boon (ba bün′), a kind of large, fierce monkey with a doglike face and a short tail. Baboons live in the rocky hills of Arabia and Africa. *n. 10.*

ba by (bā′bi), 1. a very young child. 2. person who acts like a baby. 3. of or for a baby. 4. young; small; as, a baby lamb. 5. treat as a baby. *n., pl. babies, adj., v., babied, babying. 1.*

ba by hood (bā′bi hůd), condition or time of being a baby. *n. 20.*

Bab y lon (bab′i lən), 1. an ancient city in southwestern Asia on the Euphrates River, which was noted for its wealth, power, magnificence, and luxury. Four thousand years ago it was the capital of the Babylonian empire. 2. any great, rich, or wicked city. *n. 6.*

Bab y lo ni a (bab′i lō′ni ə), an ancient empire in southwestern Asia, in the lower Euphrates valley. *n.*

Bab y lo ni an (bab′i lō′ni ən), 1. of or having to do with Babylon or Babylonia. 2. an inhabitant of Babylonia. 3. the language of Babylonia. 4. magnificent; luxurious. *adj., n. 11.*

bac cha nal (bak′ə nəl), 1. having to do with Bacchus or his worship. 2. worshiper of Bacchus. 3. drunken reveler. 4. a wild, noisy party; drunken revelry; orgy. *adj.,* *n. 15.*

Bac chus (bak′əs), Roman and Greek god of wine. The Greeks also called him Dionysus. *n. 13.*

Bach (bäk), a famous German composer of music (1685-1750). *n.*

bach e lor (bach′ə lər), 1. man who has not married. 2. person who has the first degree of a college or university. *n. 6.*

bach e lor's-but ton (bach′ə lərz but′ən), any of several flowers shaped like buttons, especially the cornflower. *n.*

Bachelor's-button (1 to 2 ft. high)

ba cil lus (bə sil′əs), 1. any of the rod-shaped bacteria. See the picture of **bacteria.** 2. any of the bacteria. *n., pl. bacilli* (-ī). *10.*

back (bak), 1. the part of a person's body opposite to his face or the front part of his body. In animals, the upper part from the neck to the end of the backbone is the back. 2. the side of anything away from one. 3. support or help. Many of his friends backed his plan. 4. move away from the front. He backed his car slowly. He backed away from the gun. 5. behind in space or time. Please walk back three steps. They are often back in their work. Have you read the back numbers of this paper? Some years back this land was all in farms. 6. in return. You should pay back what you borrow. *n., v., adv., adj. 1.*

back bite (bak′bīt′), speak evil of (an absent person). *v., backbit, backbitten* or *backbit, backbiting.*

back bone (bak′bōn′), 1. the main bone along the middle of the back in man, mammals, birds, reptiles, and fishes. The backbone consists of many separate bones called vertebrae. 2. the most important part. 3. strength of character. *n. 9.*

Human backbone

back er (bak′ər), person who supports another person, some plan or idea, etc. *n.*

back fire (bak′fīr′), 1. explosion of gas that takes place too soon or in the wrong place in a gasoline engine. 2. explode in this way. 3. a fire set to check a forest or prairie fire by burning off the space in front of it. *n., v.*

back gam mon (bak′gam′ən), a game for two played on a special board with 12 spaces on each side. Each player has 15 pieces, which are moved according to the throw of dice. *n. 18.*

back ground (bak′ground′), 1. the part in the back. The cottage stands in the foreground with the mountains in the background. 2. part which shows off the chief thing or person. Her dress had pink flowers on a white background. 3. **In the background** sometimes means out of sight; not in clear view. The shy boy kept in the background. 4. past experience, knowledge, and training. *n. 8.*

back hand (bak′hand′), 1. stroke made with the back of the hand turned outward. 2. handwriting in which the letters slope to the left. 3. backhanded. *n., adj.*

backhand writing

back hand ed (bak′han′did), 1. done with the back of the hand moving in front of the palm. 2. indirect. 3. insincere. *adj.*

back ing (bak′ing), 1. support; help. 2. supporters; helpers. 3. back part supporting or strengthening something. *n. 14.*

back log (bak′lôg′), 1. large log at the back of a wood fire. 2. something serving as a support. *n.*

back slide (bak′slīd′), slide back into wrong; lose one's enthusiasm for religion or the church. Mr. Brown was once active in the church, but he has backslidden. *v., backslid, backslidden* or *backslid, backsliding. 20.*

back ward (bak′wərd), 1. away from one's front. 2. with the back first; as, to tumble over backward. 3. toward the back; as, to look backward, a backward motion. 4. toward the starting point. 5. from better to worse. 6. dull; slow in development. Backward children need a special kind of schooling. 7. late; behind time. This is a backward season; spring is two weeks late. 8. shy; bashful. Shake hands with the lady; don't be backward. *adv., adj. 3.*

back ward ness (bak′wərd nis), 1. slowness. 2. lateness. 3. bashfulness; shyness. *n. 16.*

back wards (bak′wərdz), backward (definitions 1 to 5). *adv. 6.*

back wa ter (bak′wô′tər), 1. water held, pushed, or thrown back. 2. sluggish, stagnant condition. *n.*

back woods (bak′wu̇dz′), uncleared forests or wild regions far away from towns. *n. pl. 15.*

back woods man (bak′wu̇dz′mən), man who lives in the backwoods. *n., pl. backwoodsmen. 18.*

ba con (bā′kən), salted and smoked meat from the back and sides of a hog. *n. 4.*

bac te ri a (bak tēr′i ə), very, very tiny living plants, some of which cause disease. Other kinds of bacteria cause milk to sour or turn cider into vinegar. *n. pl. 7.*

Bacteria

bac te ri al (bak tēr′i əl), of bacteria; caused by bacteria. Some diseases are bacterial in origin. *adj. 17.*

bac te ri ol o gy (bak tēr′i ol′ə ji), science that deals with bacteria. *n. 18.*

bad (bad), 1. not good; not as it ought to be. 2. evil. 3. severe. 4. anything that is bad. *adj., worse, worst, n. 1.*

bad blood, unfriendly feeling; hate.

bade (bad). See **bid.** The captain bade the soldiers go on. *pt. of bid. 3.*

badge (baj), 1. something worn to show that a person belongs to a certain occupation, school, class, club, society, etc. Policemen wear badges. The Red Cross badge is a red cross on a white background. 2. a symbol or sign. Chains are a badge of slavery. *n. 6.*

DELEGATE

Badge

badg er (baj′ər), 1. a hairy, gray animal that digs holes in the ground to live in. 2. its fur. 3. question persistently; keep on teasing or annoying. An agent has been badgering me for the last two weeks to buy a new car. *n., v. 7.*

Badger (2 ft. long)

bad-tem pered (bad′tem′pərd), having a bad temper or disposition. *adj.*

baf fle (baf′əl), 1. be too hard for (a person) to understand or solve. This puzzle baffles me. 2. hinder. *v. 7.*

bag (bag), 1. paper, cloth, or other material fastened together to hold something. 2. something shaped like a bag. 3. put in a bag. 4. swell; bulge. 5. hang loosely. The man's trousers bag at the knees. 6. game killed or caught by a hunter. 7. kill or catch in hunting. *n., v., bagged, bagging. 1.*

Bag dad (bag′dad), an ancient city in southwestern Asia on the Tigris River, mentioned many times in the *Arabian Nights.* It is now the capital city of Iraq. *n. 12.*

bag gage (bag′ij), 1. the trunks, bags, suitcases, etc., that a person takes with him when he travels. 2. the equipment that an army takes with it, such as tents, blankets, dishes, etc. *n. 7.*

bag gy (bag′i), baglike; hanging loosely; as, baggy trousers. *adj.*

bag pipe (bag′pīp′), shrill-toned musical instrument made of a windbag and pipes, now used chiefly in Scotland. *n. 10.*

Scottish bagpipe

bah (bä), an exclamation of scorn or contempt. *interj. 18.*

Ba ha mas (bə hā′məz), group of British islands in the West Indies, southeast of Florida. *n. pl. 18.*

bail[1] (bāl), 1. obtain the freedom of (a person under arrest) by guaranteeing to pay a certain sum of money if he does not appear at his trial or whenever he is wanted. 2. the guarantee necessary to set a person free from arrest until he is to appear for trial. 3. the person or persons who make such a guarantee. *v., n. 8.*

bail[2] (bāl), the handle of a kettle or pail. See the picture. *n.*

BAIL

bail[3] (bāl), throw (water) out of a boat with a bucket, pail, dipper, or any kind of container. **Bail out** sometimes means to drop from an airplane with a parachute. *v.*

bail iff (bāl′if), 1. assistant to a sheriff. 2. an officer of a court who has charge of prisoners while they are in the courtroom. 3. overseer or steward of an estate. The bailiff collects rents for the owner. *n. 11.*

bairn (bãrn), child. *n.* [*Scottish*] *19.*

bait (bāt), 1. anything, especially food, used to attract fish or other animals so that they may be caught. 2. put bait on (a hook) or in (a trap). 3. thing used as a temptation or in order to get a person to begin something he would not wish to do. 4. set dogs to attack. Bulls and bears were formerly baited for sport. 5. torment by unkind or annoying remarks. 6. stop and feed. The coachman baited his horses. *n., v. 5.*

baize (bāz), a thick woolen cloth used for curtains, table covers, etc. *n. 15.*

bake (bāk), 1. cook (food) by dry heat without exposing it directly to the fire. We bake bread and cake in an oven. 2. harden by heat; as, to bake bricks or china. 3. become baked. These cakes will bake very quickly. *v. 2.*

bak er (bāk′ər), person who makes and sells bread, pies, cakes, etc. *n. 4.*

bak er y (bāk′ər i), baker's shop; place where bread, cake, etc., are made or sold. *n., pl. bakeries. 16.*

bak ing (bāk′ing), 1. cooking in dry heat. 2. amount baked at one time; batch. *n.*

baking powder, mixture of soda and cream of tartar, or of other substances, used to cause biscuits, cakes, etc., to rise.

Ba laam (bā′ləm), in the Bible, a prophet who was rebuked by the ass he rode. Numbers 22-24. *n. 11.*

bal ance (bal′əns), 1. instrument for weighing. See the picture. 2. weigh two things against each other on scales, in one's hands, or in one's mind, to see which is heavier or more important. 3. a wheel, etc., that regulates the rate of movement of a clock or watch. 4. a condition of not falling over in any direction; steadiness. 5. keep or put in a steady condition. 6. all-around development and steadiness of character. 7. difference between the debit and credit sides of an account. 8. make the debit and credit sides of (an account) equal. 9. make up for. 10. fact of balancing. 11. equality in weight, amount, etc. 12. **In the balance** sometimes means undecided. *n., v. 2.*

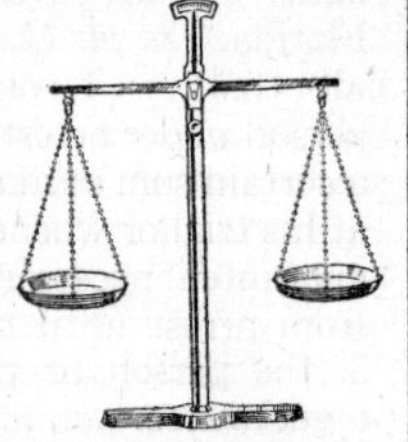

Balance or scale for weighing

Bal bo a (bal bō′ə), the Spanish adventurer (1475?-1517) who discovered the Pacific Ocean. *n. 18.*

bal co ny (bal′kə ni), 1. an outside projecting platform with an entrance from an upper floor of a building. 2. an upper floor in a theater or hall with seats for an audience. *n., pl. balconies. 10.*

Balcony

bald (bôld), 1. wholly or partly without hair on the head. 2. without its natural covering. The top of a mountain with no trees or grass on it is bald. 3. bare; plain. The bald truth is that he is a thief. 4. having white on the head; as, the bald eagle. *adj. 6.*

bal der dash (bôl′dər dash), nonsense. *n.*

bal dric (bôl′drik), belt for a sword, horn, etc., hung from one shoulder to the opposite side of the body. *n. 16.*

BALDRIC

bale (bāl), 1. a large bundle of merchandise or material securely wrapped and tied for shipping or storage; as, a bale of cotton. 2. make into bales. *n., v. 8.*

bale ful (bāl′fəl), evil; harmful. *adj. 15.*

Ba li (bä′li), island in the Dutch East Indies. *n.*

balk (bôk), 1. stop short and stubbornly refuse to go on. My horse balked at the bridge. 2. bring to a standstill; prevent from going on; hinder. The robber's plans were balked by the police. 3. hindrance. *v., n. 9.*

Bal kan (bôl′kən), of a great peninsula in southeastern Europe or the countries on it. Yugoslavia, Rumania, Bulgaria, Albania, Greece, and European Turkey are Balkan countries. The Balkans have been the scene of frequent political disputes and much warfare. *adj. 12.*

balk y (bôk′i), stopping short and stubbornly refusing to go on. *adj.*

ball[1] (bôl), 1. anything round. 2. game in which some kind of ball is thrown, hit, or kicked. 3. a bullet for firearms; a round, solid object to be shot from a gun. 4. form into a ball. *n., v. 1.*

ball[2] (bôl), large, formal party for dancing. *n.*

bal lad (bal′əd), 1. simple song. 2. poem that tells a story. Ballads are often sung. *n. 6.*

bal last (bal′əst), 1. something heavy carried in a ship to steady it. 2. gravel or crushed rock used in making the bed for a railroad track. 3. something heavy carried in a balloon or dirigible to steady it. 4. anything which makes a thing or person steady. 5. furnish with ballast. *n., v. 9.*

ball bearing, 1. bearing in which the shaft turns upon a number of loose metal balls to lessen friction. 2. one of the metal balls.

bal let (bal′ā), 1. elaborate dance by a group on a stage. 2. the dancers. *n.*

bal loon (bə lün′), 1. airtight bag filled with some gas that is lighter than air, so that it will rise and float in the air. 2. swell out like a balloon. *n., v. 8.*

Child with a toy balloon

bal lot (bal′ət), 1. piece of paper or other object used in voting. 2. the whole number of votes cast. 3. the method of secret voting. 4. to vote or decide by using ballots. *n., v. 8.*

ball room (bôl′rüm′), a large room for dancing. *n. 16.*

balm (bäm), 1. a fragrant, oily, sticky substance obtained from certain kinds of trees, used to heal or to relieve pain. 2. preparation for relieving pain or for healing. 3. anything that heals or soothes. My praise was balm to her wounded spirit. *n. 5.*

balm y (bäm′i), 1. mild; soft; gentle; as, a balmy breeze. 2. fragrant. *adj., balmier, balmiest. 7.*

bal sam (bôl′səm), 1. a kind of fir tree. Balsam firs are much used as Christmas trees. 2. balm. *n. 16.*

Bal tic (bôl′tik), 1. a sea in northern Europe, north of Germany and southeast of Sweden. 2. having to do with the Baltic Sea. *n., adj. 9.*

Bal ti more (bôl′ti mōr), a city in northern Maryland. *n. 4.*

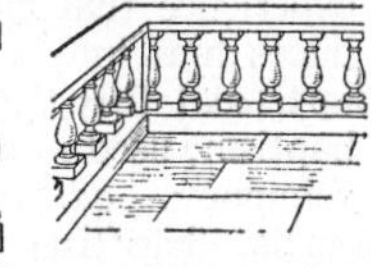

Baluster and balustrade

bal us ter (bal′əs tər), a support for a railing. See the picture. *n.*

bal us trade (bal′əs trād′), row of balusters and the railing on them. *n. 15.*

bam boo (bam bü′), a treelike plant belonging to the grass family. It is very tall, and the stiff hollow stems, which have hard thick joints, are used for making canes, furniture, and even houses. *n. 6.*

Bamboo growing

ban (ban), 1. prohibit; forbid. Swimming is banned in this lake. 2. the forbidding of an act or speech by authority of the law, the church, or public opinion. 3. curse. *v., banned, banning, n. 10.*

ba nal (bā′nəl), commonplace; trite; trivial. *adj.*

ba nan a (bə nan′ə), a slightly curved yellow or red fruit with firm, creamy flesh. Bananas are about five inches long and grow in large bunches. The plant is like a tree with great long leaves. It grows in warm countries. *n. 4.*

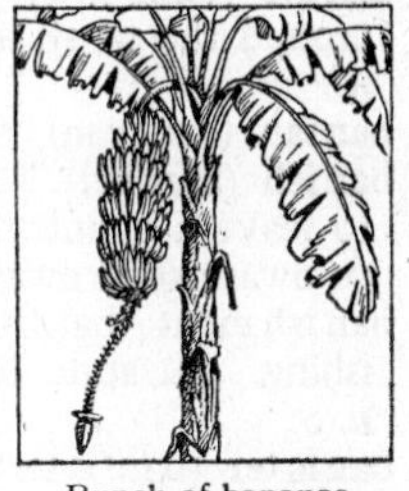

Bunch of bananas growing on the plant

band (band), 1. thin, flat strip of material for binding, trimming, or some other purpose. The oak box was strengthened with bands of iron. 2. a stripe; as, a white cup with a gold band. 3. put a band on. 4. number of persons or animals joined together; as, a band of robbers, a band of wild dogs. 5. unite in a group. 6. a company of players upon musical instruments. The band played several marches. *n., v. 1.*

band age (ban′dij), 1. a strip of cloth or other material used in dressing and binding up a wound, injured leg or arm, etc. 2. to dress or tie up with a bandage. *n., v. 8.*

Bandage on the leg

ban dan na or **ban dan a** (ban dan′ə), large, colored handkerchief. *n.*

band box (band′boks′), light cardboard box to put hats, collars, etc., in. *n.*

ban dit (ban′dit), highwayman; robber. *n. 9.*

ban dit ti (ban dit′i), bandits. *n. pl. 16.*

ban dy (ban′di), throw back and forth; hit to and fro; give and take. Do not bandy words with a foolish person. *v., bandied, bandying. 14.*

ban dy-leg ged (ban′di leg′id), having legs that curve outward; bowlegged. *adj.*

bane (bān), cause of death, ruin, or harm. Wild animals were the bane of the mountain village. *n. 9.*

bane ful (bān′fəl), deadly; harmful. *adj. 15.*

bang[1] (bang), 1. He gave the drum a bang. 2. The baby was banging on the dishpan with a tin cup. 3. Tom banged the door as he went through. 4. We heard the bang of a gun. 5. My trunk was banged in the accident. 6. Bang! went the gun. *n., v., adv., interj. 6.*

bang[2] (bang), 1. cut squarely across. She wears her hair banged. 2. a fringe of banged hair. *v., n.*

ban gle (bang′gəl), a ring worn around the wrist, arm, or ankle. *n.*

ban ian (ban′yən), banyan. *n.*

Child wearing bangs

ban ish (ban′ish), 1. condemn to leave a country. 2. force to go away; send away; drive away. *v. 3.*

ban ish ment (ban′ish mənt), 1. act of banishing. 2. state of being banished; exile. *n. 5.*

ban is ter (ban′is tər), 1. baluster. 2. **Banisters** means the balustrade of a staircase. *n. 18.* See the pictures of **baluster** and **balustrade**.

ban jo (ban′jō), stringed musical instrument played with the fingers. *n., pl. banjos* or *banjoes. 11.*

Man playing a banjo

bank[1] (bangk), 1. ridge of earth. 2. great mass of anything. There was a snowbank over ten feet deep. 3. ground bordering a river. 4. shoal; shallow place in water. 5. pile; heap. 6. slope. 7. make (an airplane) slope. 8. cover (a fire) with ashes so that it will burn slowly. *n., v. 1.*

bank[2] (bangk), 1. place for keeping, lending, exchanging, and issuing money. A savings bank is a good place to put money. 2. keep a bank. 3. keep money in a bank. 4. put (money) in a bank. *n., v.*

bank[3] (bangk), 1. bench for rowers in a galley. 2. a row or tier of oars. 3. row of keys in an organ. 4. row of things. *n.*

bank er (bangk′ər), person or company that runs a bank. *n. 5.*

bank rupt (bangk′rupt), 1. person who is declared by a court to be unable to pay his debts and whose property is distributed as far as it will go among his creditors. 2. unable to pay one's debts. 3. make bankrupt. Foolish expenditures will bankrupt him. *n., adj., v. 8.*

bank rupt cy (bangk′rupt si), bankrupt condition. *n., pl. bankruptcies. 10.*

ban ner (ban′ər), 1. flag. John carried our school banner in the parade. 2. piece of cloth with some design or words on it. 3. leading; foremost. *n., adj. 3.*

ban nock (ban′ək), a flat cake made of oatmeal or barley flour, eaten in Scotland. *n. 10.*

banns (banz), a notice given three times in church, that a certain man and woman are to be married. *n. pl.*

ban quet (bang′kwit), 1. feast. 2. formal dinner with speeches. 3. give a feast. 4. enjoy a feast. *n., v. 3.*

Ban quo (bang′kwō), man murdered by Macbeth, whose ghost causes Macbeth to reveal his guilt. *n. 18.*

ban shee or **ban shie** (ban′shē), a spirit whose wails mean that there will soon be a death in the family. *n* [*Irish and Scottish*]

Ban tam or **ban tam** (ban′təm), a small-sized kind of fowl. *n. 19.*

ban ter (ban′tər), 1. playful teasing; joking. 2. tease playfully; make fun of. 3. talk in a joking way. *n., v. 13.*

ban yan (ban′yən), a fig tree of India whose branches droop to the ground and take root. *n.*

Banyan (70 to 100 ft. high)

bap tism (bap′tizm), 1. act of baptizing; rite or sacrament of dipping a person into water or sprinkling water on him, as a sign of the washing away of sin and of admission into the Christian church. 2. an experience that cleanses a person or introduces him into a new kind of life. *n. 7.*

bap tis mal (bap tiz′məl), having to do with baptism; used in baptism; as, the baptismal ceremony. *adj. 16.*

Bap tist (bap′tist), 1. member of a Christian church that believes in baptism by dipping the whole person under water. 2. of or having to do with the Baptists. 3. person who baptizes; as, John the Baptist. *n., adj. 8.*

bap tis ter y (bap′tis tər i), place where baptism is performed. A baptistery may be a section of a church or a separate building. *n., pl. baptisteries.*

bap tis try (bap′tis tri), baptistery. *n., pl. baptistries. 20.*

bap tize (bap tīz′), 1. dip into water or sprinkle with water as a sign of the washing away of sin and of admission into the Christian church. 2. purify; cleanse. 3. give a first name to (a person) at baptism. *v. 8.*

bar (bär), 1. an evenly shaped piece of some solid, longer than it is wide or thick; as, a bar of iron, a bar of soap, a bar of chocolate. 2. a pole or rod across a door, window, etc., or across any opening. Let down the pasture bars for the cows to come in. 3. put bars across; fasten or shut off. Bar the doors. 4. anything that blocks the way or prevents progress. A bar of sand kept boats out of the harbor. A bad temper is a bar to making friends. 5. band of color; stripe. 6. mark with stripes or bands of color; as, a chicken with barred feathers. 7. a unit of rhythm in music. The regular accent falls on the first note of each bar. 8. the dividing line between two bars on the musical staff. 9. the place where a prisoner stands in a law court. Brought before the bar of conscience, his action could not be defended. 10. the whole group of practicing lawyers. After passing his law examinations, he was admitted to the bar. 11. law court. 12. anything like a law court. The bar of public opinion condemns dishonest people. 13. a counter or place where drinks are served to customers. 14. except; not including. He is the worst boy in town, bar none. 15. exclude; forbid. Rough play is barred. *n., v., barred, barring, prep. 2.*

barb (bärb), 1. a point sticking out and back from the main point. See the picture. 2. furnish with barbs. *n., v. 13.*

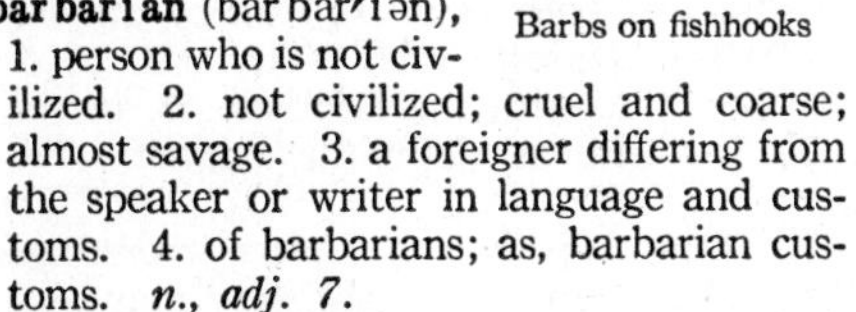

Barbs on fishhooks

Bar ba dos (bär bā′dōz), a British island in the West Indies. *n. 14.*

bar bar i an (bär bãr′i ən), 1. person who is not civilized. 2. not civilized; cruel and coarse; almost savage. 3. a foreigner differing from the speaker or writer in language and customs. 4. of barbarians; as, barbarian customs. *n., adj. 7.*

bar bar ic (bär bar′ik), like barbarians; suited to a barbarous people; rough and rude. *adj. 9.*

bar ba rism (bär′bə rizm), 1. the condition of savages or uncivilized people. People who have no alphabet live in barbarism. 2. a word or expression not in good use. *Example:* "his'n" for "his." *n. 12.*

bar bar i ty (bär bar′i ti), 1. brutal cruelty; 2. cruel act. 3. barbarous character or style. *n., pl. barbarities. 15.*

bar ba rous (bär′bə rəs), 1. not civilized. 2. savagely cruel; coarse; brutal. 3. crude; harsh. *adj. 5.*

Bar ba ry (bär′bə ri), the Mohammedan countries west of Egypt on the northern coast of Africa. *n. 18.*

bar be cue (bär′bə kū), 1. a feast at which animals are roasted whole. 2. an animal roasted whole. 3. roast (an animal) whole. 4. meat roasted before an open fire. 5. roast in this way. *n., v. 12.*

barbed (bärbd), having a barb or barbs; as, a barbed fishhook. *adj.*

bar ber (bär′bər), 1. person whose business is cutting hair, shaving men, and trimming beards. 2. cut the hair of; shave; trim the beard of. *n., v. 5.*

bar ber ry (bär′ber′i), 1. a shrub with sour red berries. 2. the berry. *n., pl. barberries. 17.*

Barberry

Bar ce lo na (bär′sə lō′nə), a seaport city in northeastern Spain. *n. 16.*

bard (bärd), 1. poet and singer of long ago. Bards sang their own poems to the music of their harps. 2. poet. *n. 5.*

bare[1] (bãr), 1. not clothed; naked; uncovered. His bare hands were blue with the cold. The top of the hill was bare, although trees grew part way up the hill. 2. empty; not furnished. The room was bare of furniture. 3. plain; unadorned. He lived in a little bare house. 4. just enough and no more; mere. He earns a bare living by his work. 5. uncover; reveal; strip. He bared his sword. 6. **Lay bare** means uncover; expose; reveal. *adj., v. 2.*

bare[2] (bãr), bore. *old pt. of* **bear**[1].

bare back (bãr′bak′), without a saddle; on a horse's bare back. *adj., adv.*

bare faced (bãr′fāst′), shameless; impudent. *adj.*

bare foot (bãr′fu̇t′), without shoes and stockings. *adj., adv. 7.*

bare head ed (bãr′hed′id), wearing nothing on the head. *adj., adv. 14.*

bare ly (bãr′li), 1. only just; scarcely. He has barely enough money to live on. 2. plainly; openly. *adv. 7.*

bare ness (bãr′nis), being bare; lack of covering; lack of furnishings and contents. *n. 18.*

bar gain (bär′gin), 1. an agreement to trade or exchange. Will you take $5 for it? Then it's a bargain. 2. something offered for sale cheap or bought cheap. 3. make a bargain; come to terms. 4. try to get good terms. She stood bargaining for ten minutes with the man for the vegetables. 5. **Bargain for** sometimes means expect or be prepared for. It is raining, and that is more than I bargained for. 6. **Into the bargain** means moreover. It is raining, into the bargain. *n., v. 3.*

barge (bärj), 1. large, flat-bottomed boat for carrying freight on rivers and canals. 2. a large boat used for excursions and special occasions. *n. 6.*

Barge used for freight

bar i tone (bar′i tōn), 1. male voice or part between tenor and bass. 2. a singer with such a voice. 3. of or for a baritone. *n., adj.*

bar i um (bãr′i əm), a soft, silvery-white metallic element. *n. 20.*

bark[1] (bärk), 1. the tough outside covering of the trunk, branches, and roots of trees. 2. strip the bark from (a tree). 3. scrape the skin from. I fell down the steps and barked my shins. *n., v. 2.*

A B C

Bark of: A, hickory; B, white oak; C, white birch.

bark[2] (bärk), 1. the short, sharp sound a dog makes; a sound like this, such as the bark of a fox, a squirrel, a gun, or a cough. 2. make this sound or one like it. 3. shout sharply. Some officers bark out their orders. *n., v.*

bark[3] (bärk), 1. a kind of ship with three masts. See the picture of **barque.** 2. boat; ship. *Used in poetry. n.* Also spelled **barque.**

bar ley (bär′li), a grasslike plant or its grain. Barley will grow in cool climates. It is used for food. *n. 4.*

Barley

Bar ley corn (bär′li kôrn′). John Barleycorn is a name for intoxicating liquor. *n. 15.*

barn (bärn), building for storing hay and grain and for sheltering cows and horses. *n. 2.*

bar na cle (bär′nə kəl), animal with a shell that attaches itself to rocks, the bottoms of ships, the timbers of wharves, etc. *n. 17.*

Barnacles (2 to 6 in. long)

barn yard (bärn′yärd′), the yard around a barn. *n. 7.*

ba rom e ter (bə rom′i tər), 1. instrument for measuring the pressure of the air and determining the height above sea level. A barometer shows probable changes in the weather. 2. something that indicates changes. Newspapers are barometers of public opinion. *n. 15.*

Barometer

bar on (bar′ən), a nobleman of the lowest rank. *n. 5.*

bar on ess (bar′ən is), 1. the wife or widow of a baron. 2. a lady whose rank is equal to a baron's. *n. 18.*

bar on et (bar′ən ıt), a person below a baron in rank, but above a knight. *n.*

ba ro ni al (bə rō′ni əl), 1. of a baron; of barons. 2. suitable for a baron. *adj. 18.*

bar on y (bar′ən i), 1. the lands of a baron. 2. the rank or title of a baron. *n., pl. baronies. 14.*

ba roque (bə rōk′), odd; fantastic; grotesque. Baroque architecture uses much ornament. *adj.*

ba rouche (bə rüsh′), a four-wheeled carriage with two seats facing each other and a folding top. *n.*

barque (bärk), 1. a kind of ship with three masts. 2. any boat or ship. *Used in poetry. n.* Also spelled **bark.**

Barque

bar racks (bar′əks), 1. building or group of buildings for soldiers to live in. 2. large plain building in which many people live. *n. pl. 11.*

bar rage (bə räzh′), a barrier of artillery fire to check the enemy or to protect one's own soldiers in advancing or retreating. *n. 16.*

bar rel (bar′əl), 1. a container with round, flat top and bottom and slightly curved sides. It is usually made of boards held together by hoops. See the picture. 2. the amount that a barrel can hold. 3. put in barrels. We plan to barrel the cider next Wednesday. 4. the metal tube of a gun. *n., v., barreled, barreling. 3.*

Barrel

bar ren (bar′ən), 1. not producing anything. A desert is barren. 2. a barren stretch of land. 3. not able to have children. 4. without interest; not attractive; dull. *adj., n. 3.*

bar ren ness (bar′ən nis), being barren; fruitlessness. *n. 13.*

bar rette (bə ret′), a pin with a clasp, used for holding the hair in place. *n. 14.*

bar ri cade (bar′i kād′), 1. a rough, hastily made barrier for defense. 2. barrier; obstruction. 3. block or obstruct with a barricade. *n., v. 15.*

bar ri er (bar′i ər), 1. something which stands in the way; something stopping progress or preventing approach. A dam is a barrier holding water back. Lack of water is a barrier to the settlement of a region. 2. something that separates or keeps apart. The Atlantic Ocean is a barrier between Europe and America. *n. 5.*

bar ring (bär′ing), excepting; leaving out of consideration. Barring accidents, the train will reach Chicago at twelve o'clock. See also def. 14 of **bar.** *prep.*

bar ris ter (bar′is tər), a lawyer in England who can plead in any court. *n. 15.*

bar room (bär′rüm′), room with a bar for the sale of liquor. *n.*

bar row[1] (bar′ō), 1. a frame with two short shafts or handles at each end, used for carrying a load. 2. wheelbarrow. 3. cart that a man pushes; handcart. *n. 11.*

bar row[2] (bar′ō), a mound of earth or stones over an ancient grave. *n.*

bar ter (bär′tər), 1. trade by exchanging goods without using money. The Indians bartered furs for beads and guns. 2. carry on trade by exchanging one kind of thing for other things. *n., v. 10.*

Bar ton (bär′tən), Clara (1821-1912), American woman who organized the American Red Cross in 1881. *n.*

bar y tone (bar′i tōn), baritone. *n., adj.*

ba sal (bā′səl), of the base; at the base; forming the base; fundamental; basic. *adj. 14.*

ba salt (bə sôlt′), a hard, dark-colored rock. *n. 18.*

base[1] (bās), 1. the part of a thing on which it rests; the bottom. The machine rests on a wide base of steel. 2. basis; foundation; groundwork. 3. a station or goal in certain games, such as baseball or hide-and-seek. 4. headquarters; starting place; place from which an army goes forth to fight and from which it is supplied. 5. a chemical substance that unites with an acid to form a salt. 6. establish; found. His large business was based on good service. *n., v. 2.*

base[2] (bās), 1. low; mean; selfish; cowardly. To betray a friend is a base action. 2. inferior. Iron and lead are base metals; gold and silver are precious metals. *adj.*

base ball (bās′bôl′), 1. a game played with bat and ball by two teams of nine players each, on a field with four bases. 2. the ball used in this game. *n. 6.*

Plan of a baseball field

base born (bās′bôrn′), 1. born of slaves, peasants, or other humble parents. 2. born of a mother who was not married; illegitimate. *adj.*

base less (bās′lis), groundless; without foundation. A rumor is baseless if it is not supported by facts. *adj. 15.*

base ment (bās′mənt), the lowest story of a building, partly or wholly below ground. *n. 11.*

base ness (bās′nis), mean, low, cowardly, and selfish character or conduct. *n. 11.*

bash ful (bash′fəl), uneasy and awkward in the company of strangers; shy. *adj. 5.*

bash ful ness (bash′fəl nis), being bashful; shyness. *n. 12.*

ba sic (bā′sik), of the base; at the base; forming the base; fundamental. Addition, subtraction, multiplication, and division are the basic processes of arithmetic. *adj. 11.*

bas il (baz′il), a sweet-smelling plant somewhat like mint, used in cooking. *n. 19.*

ba sil i ca (bə sil′i kə), an oblong hall with a row of columns at each side and a structure in the shape of a half circle at one end. *n. 19.*

bas i lisk (bas′i lisk), a fabled reptile whose breath or look was thought to be fatal. It was supposed to be somewhat like a lizard and to have a black-and-yellow skin and fiery, red eyes. 2. a tropical American lizard with a hollow crest along its back that swells up. *n. 16.*

Basilisk of tropical America (2½ ft. long)

ba sin (bā′sən), 1. a wide, shallow bowl; bowl. 2. the amount that a basin can hold. He has eaten a basin of oatmeal already. 3. a hollow place containing water. 4. all the land drained by a river and the streams that flow into it. *n. 3.*

ba sis (bā′sis), foundation; main part. The basis of this medicine is an oil. *n., pl. bases* (bā′sēz). *4.*

bask (bask), warm oneself pleasantly. The cat basks before the fire. *v. 10.*

bas ket (bas′kit), 1. container made of twigs, grasses, fibers, strips of wood, etc., woven together. 2. amount that a basket holds. We ate a basket of peaches. 3. anything that looks or is shaped like a basket. 4. the goal in the game of basketball. *n. 1.*

bas ket ball (bas′kit bôl′), 1. a game played with a large, round leather ball between two teams of five players each. The players try to toss the ball through a net shaped like a basket. 2. the ball used in this game. *n.*

bas ket ry (bas′kit ri), 1. baskets. 2. art of making baskets. *n.*

bass[1] (bās), 1. having a deep, low sound; as, a bass voice. 2. the lowest part in music; the man's voice that sings the part; any singer or instrument that has a bass voice, part, or range. *adj., n. 7.*

bass[2] (bas), a fish used for food, living in fresh water or in the ocean. *n., pl. basses* or *bass.*

bas si net (bas′i net′), a baby's basketlike cradle. *n. 19.*

bas soon (bə sün′), a deep-toned wind instrument with a doubled wooden tube and a metal mouthpiece. *n. 19.*

Man playing a bassoon

bass vi ol (bās′ vī′əl), a big violin as tall as a man.

bass wood (bas′wu̇d′), 1. an American softwood tree with large heart-shaped leaves; linden tree. 2. its wood. *n. 19.*

bast (bast), a kind of tough inner bark used in making rope, matting, etc. *n. 18.*

bas tard (bas′tərd), 1. a child whose parents are not married. 2. born of parents who are not married. *n., adj. 6.*

baste[1] (bāst), drip or pour melted fat or butter on (meat, etc.) while roasting. Meat is basted to keep it from drying out and to improve its flavor. *v. 10.*

baste[2] (bāst), sew with long, loose stitches. These stitches are usually removed after the final sewing. *v.*

Bas tille (bas tēl′), old fort in Paris that was used as a prison. *n. 14.*

bast ings (bās′tingz), the long, loose stitches used in the first sewing of a garment. They are usually removed when the garment is finished. *n. pl. 13.*

bas tion (bas′chən), 1. a projecting part of a fortification. See the picture. 2. defense. *n. 13.*

Bastion

bat[1] (bat), 1. a stout wooden stick or club, used to hit the ball in baseball, cricket, etc. 2. hit with a bat; hit. I batted the balloon over to him with my hand. He bats well. *n., v., batted, batting. 3.*

bat[2] (bat), flying animal that looks like a mouse with skin-like wings. Bats fly at night and feed on insects and fruit. *n.*

Bat

Ba ta vi a (bə tā′vi ə), seaport in northwestern Java. It is the capital of the Dutch East Indies. *n.*

batch (bach), 1. quantity of bread made at one baking. 2. quantity of anything made as one lot or set. 3. number of persons or things taken together. *n. 13.*

bate (bāt), abate; lessen; hold back. The boys listened with bated breath to the sailor's story. *v. 15.*

bath (bath), 1. a washing of the body. 2. water, etc., for a bath. Your bath is ready. 3. a tub, a room, or other place for bathing. The house had no bath, so we had one built. 4. liquid in which something is washed or dipped. 5. the container holding the liquid. *n., pl. baths* (baTHz). *3.*

bathe (bāTH), 1. take a bath. 2. give a bath to. 3. go in swimming; go into a river, lake, or ocean for sport or to get cool. 4. pour over; cover. The valley was bathed in sunlight. *v. 3.*

bath robe (bath′rōb′), long, loose garment worn to and from the bath. *n. 13.*

bath room (bath′rüm′), a room fitted up for taking baths. *n. 9.*

ba tiste (bə tēst′), a kind of fine, thin, linen or cotton cloth. *n. 13.*

ba ton (ba ton′), 1. a staff or stick used as a mark of office or authority. 2. the stick used by the leader for beating time to the music. *n. 19.*

Bat on Rouge (bat′ən rüzh′), the capital of Louisiana.

bat tal ion (bə tal′yən), 1. any large part of an army organized to act together. 2. two or more companies of a regiment of foot soldiers. *n. 9.*

bat ten[1] (bat′ən), 1. grow fat. 2. feed greedily. *v. 13.*

bat ten[2] (bat′ən), 1. a strip of wood. 2. to fasten down with strips of wood. *n., v.*

bat ter[1] (bat′ər), beat with repeated blows so as to bruise, break, or get out of shape; pound. The policeman battered down the door with a heavy ax. *v. 7.*

bat ter[2] (bat′ər), a liquid mixture of flour, milk, eggs, etc., that thickens when cooked. Cakes, pancakes, muffins, etc., are made from batter. *n.*

bat ter[3] (bat′ər), person whose turn it is to bat in baseball, cricket, etc. *n.*

battering ram, military machine used in ancient times for battering down walls, gates, etc. *16.*

Soldiers using battering ram

bat ter y (bat′ər i), 1. any set of similar or connected things. 2. a set of one or more electric cells which produce electric current. 3. a set of big guns for combined action in attack or defense. 4. the unlawful beating of another person, or any threatening touch to the person or clothes of another. He was guilty of assault and battery. *n., pl. batteries. 5.*

bat tle (bat′əl), 1. a fight between two armies; a fight; a contest. 2. struggle or fight. *n., v. 1.*

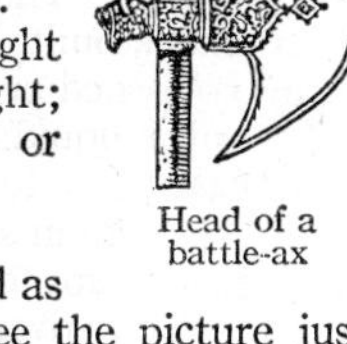

Head of a battle-ax

bat tle-ax or **bat tle-axe** (bat′əl aks′), an ax used as a weapon in battle. See the picture just above. *n., pl. battle-axes. 16.*

bat tle dore (bat′əl dōr), small racket that is used to strike a shuttlecock to and fro in play. *n. 18.*

Children playing battledore and shuttlecock

bat tle field (bat′əl fēld′), place where a battle is fought or has been fought. *n. 10.*

bat tle ground (bat′əl ground′), battlefield. *n. 20.*

bat tle ment (bat′əl mənt), 1. a wall for defense at the top of a tower or wall, lower in some places so that men could shoot through them. 2. a wall built like this for ornament. *n. 9.*

Battlement for defense

bat tle ship (bat′əl ship′), very large warship having the heaviest armor and the most powerful guns. *n. 10.*

bau ble (bô′bəl), showy trifle having no real value. Useless toys and trinkets are baubles. *n. 10.*

baux ite (bôk′sīt), claylike mineral from which aluminum is obtained. *n.*

Ba var i a (bə vãr′i ə), a district in southwestern Germany. *n. 11.*

bawd y (bôd′i), lewd; obscene. *adj. 20.*

bawl (bôl), 1. shout or cry out in a noisy way. The peddler bawled his wares in the street. 2. a loud shout or cry. *v., n. 8.*

bay[1] (bā), part of a sea or lake extending into land. See the picture under **cove.** *n. 1.*

bay[2] (bā), 1. a space or division of a wall or building between columns, pillars, buttresses, etc. 2. space with a window or set of windows in it, projecting out from a wall. See the picture of **bay window.** *n.*

bay[3] (bā), 1. long deep bark of a dog. The hunters heard the distant bay of the hounds. 2. bark; bark at. Dogs sometimes bay the moon. 3. a stand made by a hunted animal to face pursuers. The stag stood at bay on the edge of the cliff. 4. position of pursuers or foe thus kept off. The stag held the hounds at bay, but the hunters rode up and killed him. *n., v.*

bay[4] (bā), 1. small evergreen tree with smooth, shiny leaves; laurel tree. 2. **Bays** sometimes means a laurel wreath worn by poets or victors, and so also means honor or renown. *n.*

bay[5] (bā), 1. reddish-brown; as, a bay horse. 2. reddish-brown horse. *adj., n.*

bay ber ry (bā′ber′i), 1. a shrub having a waxy berry, common on the seacoast. 2. the berry. Candles are sometimes made from bayberries. *n., pl. bayberries. 20.*

bay o net (bā′ə nit), 1. a blade for piercing or stabbing, attached to a gun. 2. pierce or stab with a bayonet. *n., v. 7.*

Bayonet

bay ou (bī′ü), marshy inlet of a lake, river, or gulf in the southern United States. *n. 18.*

Bay reuth (bī roit′), city in western Germany, noted for its music festivals. *n.*

bay rum, a fragrant liquid made from the leaves of a tree growing in the West Indies.

bay window, a window or set of windows projecting out from the wall, leaving a space in a room.

Bay window

ba zaar or **ba zar** (bə zär′), 1. street or streets full of shops in Oriental countries. 2. place for the sale of many kinds of goods. 3. sale of things given for some special purpose. *n. 15.*

bbl., barrel; barrels. *13.*

bbls., barrels.

B.C., before Christ. B.C. is used for times before Christ. A.D. is used for times since Christ was born. From 20 B.C. to 50 A.D. is 70 years. *16.*

be (bē). He will be here all the year. She tries to be good. They will be punished. *v. 1.*

be-, prefix meaning:—
1. thoroughly; all around; as in bespatter.
2. at; on; to; for; about; against; as in bewail.
3. make; as in belittle.
4. provide with; as in bespangle.

beach (bēch), 1. an almost flat shore of sand or little stones over which the water washes when high. 2. run (a boat) ashore; draw up on the shore. *n., v. 2.*

bea con (bē′kən), 1. fire or light used as a signal to guide or warn. 2. radio signal for guiding aviators through fogs, storms, etc. 3. tall tower for a signal; watchtower; lighthouse. 4. give light to; guide; warn. 5. shine brightly. *n., v. 10.*

Beacon light over a rock at sea

bead (bēd), 1. small ball or bit of glass, metal, etc., with a hole through it, so that it can be strung on a thread with others like it. Beads are used for ornament or for counting prayers. 2. any small round body like a drop or bubble; as, beads of sweat. 3. a bit of metal at the front end of a gun to aim by. 4. ornament with beads. *n., v. 3.*

bead ing (bēd′ing), 1. trimming made of beads threaded into patterns. 2. narrow trimming. 3. a pattern or an edge on woodwork made of small balls. *n. 13.*

bea dle (bē′dəl), a church officer. In olden times if a boy went to sleep in church, the beadle woke him up. *n. 16.*

Beagle

bea gle (bē′gəl), a kind of a small hunting dog. *n. 15.*

beak (bēk), 1. a bird's bill, especially one that is strong and hooked and useful in striking or tearing. Eagles, hawks, and parrots have beaks. 2. anything like a beak, such as the projecting prow of an ancient warship. *n. 5.*

beak er (bēk′ər), large cup or glass. *n. 13.*

beam (bēm), 1. large, long piece of timber or metal, ready for use in building. 2. any long piece or bar; as, the beam of a plow, the beam of a balance. 3. the main horizontal support in a building or ship. 4. the widest part of a ship. 5. a ray of light. 6. send forth rays of light; shine. 7. a bright look; a smile. 8. to smile. *n., v. 2.*

bean (bēn), 1. smooth, kidney-shaped seed used as a vegetable. 2. long pod containing such seeds. The green or yellow pods are also used as a vegetable. 3. plant that beans grow on. 4. any seed shaped somewhat like a bean. Coffee beans are seeds of the coffee plant. *n. 2.*

bean stalk (bēn′stôk′), the stem of a bean plant. *n. 10.*

bear[1] (bãr), 1. carry. It takes two men to bear that stone. That board is too thin to bear your weight. 2. endure. He cannot bear any more pain. 3. have an effect on; relate to. This story does not bear on the question. 4. bring forth; produce. This tree bears fine apples. 5. press; thrust; drive. Don't bear down so hard. *v., bore, borne* or *born, bearing. 1.*

bear[2] (bãr), 1. a large, clumsy animal with coarse hair and a very short tail. 2. gruff or surly person. 3. person who tries to lower prices in the stock market. *n.*

American black bear (4½ ft. long; 3 ft. tall)

beard (bērd), 1. hair growing on a man's face. 2. something resembling or suggesting this. The chin tuft of a goat is a beard; so are the stiff hairs around the beak of a bird. 3. hairs on the heads of plants like oats, barley, and wheat. 4. face boldly; defy. *n., v. 2.*

beard ed (bēr′did), having a beard. *adj.*

beard less (bērd′lis), without a beard. *adj. 15.*

bear er (bãr′ər), 1. person or thing that carries. 2. person who presents a check or draft for payment. *n. 5.*

A B

A, bearded wheat; B, beardless wheat.

bear ing (bãr′ing), 1. way of standing, sitting, walking, etc.; manner. 2. reference; relation. His foolish question has no bearing on the problem. 3. direction; position in relation to other things. "I have lost my bearings" means "I do not know in which direction to go." 4. part of a machine on which another part turns or slides. 5. supporting part. 6. single device in a coat of arms. *n. 8.*

bear ish (bãr′ish), like a bear; rough; surly. *adj.*

beast (bēst), 1. any animal except man, especially a four-footed animal. 2. coarse, dirty, or brutal person. *n. 1.*

beast ly (bēst′li), like a beast; brutal; vile. *adj., beastlier, beastliest. 8.*

beat (bēt), 1. strike; strike again and again. The cruel man beats his horse. 2. a stroke or blow made again and again; as, a heartbeat, the beat of a drum, the beat of waves on a beach. 3. defeat; get the better of. Jack's school beat Tom's at baseball. 4. make flat. 5. make flat by much walking; tread (a path). 6. mix by stirring or striking with a fork, spoon, or other utensil; as, to beat eggs. 7. move up and down. The bird beat its wings. 8. make a sound by being struck. The drums beat loudly. 9. in music, the division of time or accent; as, three beats to a measure. A good dancer never misses a beat. 10. regular round or course made by a policeman or watchman. 11. go through in a hunt. They were beating the woods in search of the bear. 12. move against the wind by a zigzag course. The ship beat along the coast. 13. Some special meanings are:

beat a man down in price, make him set a lower price.

beat a retreat, run away.

beat time, measure off time by strokes. *v., beat, beaten, beating, n. 1.*

beat en (bēt′ən), 1. whipped; struck. The beaten dog crawled to his master's feet. 2. much walked on or traveled; as, a beaten path across the grass. 3. defeated; overcome; as, a beaten fighter. 4. shaped by blows of a hammer. This bowl is made of beaten silver. 5. See **beat.** *adj., pp. of beat. 6.*

beat er (bēt′ər), 1. person or thing that beats. 2. man hired to rouse game during a hunt. 3. a device or utensil for beating eggs, cream, etc. *n. 13.*

be a tif ic (bē′ə tif′ik), making blessed; blissful. The saint had a beatific smile. *adj. 15.*

be at i fy (bi at′i fī), 1. make blessed. 2. in the Roman Catholic Church, to declare (a dead person) to be among the blessed in heaven. *v., beatified, beatifying.*

beat ing (bēt′ing), 1. whipping. 2. defeat. *n. 7.*

be at i tude (bi at′i tūd or bi at′i tüd), 1. supreme happiness; bliss. 2. blessing. **The Beatitudes** are the verses in the Bible beginning "Blessed are the poor in spirit." Matthew 5: 3-12. *n. 16.*

beau (bō), 1. lover; young man who is courting a young woman. 2. man who pays much attention to the way he dresses and to the fashion of his clothes. *n., pl. beaus* or *beaux* (bōz). *6.*

beau te ous (bū′ti əs), beautiful. *adj. 6.*

beau ti fi er (bū′ti fī′ər), person or thing that beautifies. *n. 17.*

beau ti ful (bū′ti fəl), very pleasing to see or hear; delighting the mind or senses; as, a beautiful picture, beautiful music. *adj. 1.*

beau ti fy (bū′ti fī), 1. make beautiful; make more beautiful. Flowers beautify a garden. 2. become beautiful. *v., beautified, beautifying. 8.*

beau ty (bū′ti), 1. good looks. 2. that which pleases in flowers, music, pictures, etc. 3. something beautiful. 4. beautiful woman. *n., pl. beauties. 1.*

Beaver (3½ ft. long, including the tail)

bea ver[1] (bē′vər), 1. a soft-furred animal once common in North America. It has a broad, flat tail and feet adapted to swimming or walking. Beavers live both in water and on land and build dams across streams. 2. its soft brown fur; as, a coat trimmed with beaver. 3. man's high silk hat, formerly made of beaver fur. 4. a heavy woolen cloth. *n. 8.*

bea ver[2] (bē′vər), the movable lower part of a helmet, protecting the chin and lips. *n.*

B, beaver.

be calm (bi käm′), 1. prevent from moving by lack of wind. 2. make calm. *v. 15.*

be came (bi kām′). See **become.** The seed became a plant. *pt. of become. 2.*

be cause (bi kôz′). Boys play ball because it's fun. He cannot go to school because of sickness. *conj., adv. 1.*

beck (bek), a motion of the head or hand meant as a call or command. *n. 11.*

Beck et (bek′it), Thomas à, an archbishop of Canterbury, England, murdered in the cathedral by the order of the king (1118?-1170). *n. 13.*

beck on (bek′ən), signal (to a person) by a motion of the hand or head. He beckoned me to follow him. *v., n. 6.*

be cloud (bi kloud′), hide by a cloud or clouds; obscure. *v.*

be come (bi kum′), 1. come to be; grow to be. 2. **Become of** means happen to. What has become of the box of candy? 3. suit; look well on. A white dress becomes her. *v., became, become, becoming. 1.*

be com ing (bi kum′ing), fitting; suitable; appropriate; as, a becoming dress. *adj. 7.*

bed (bed), 1. anything to sleep or rest on. 2. any place where people or animals sleep or rest. 3. base on which anything rests. They set the pole on a bed of concrete. 4. layer. 5. the ground under a body of water; as, the bed of a stream. 6. space in a garden filled with plants. 7. provide with a bed; put to bed; put in a bed. The man bedded down his horse with straw. These plants should be bedded in rich soil. *n., v., bedded, bedding. 1.*

be dab ble (bi dab′əl), spatter all over with dirty liquid, blood, etc. *v.*

be daub (bi dôb′), smear with something dirty or sticky. *v. 20.*

Bedbug. Line shows actual length.

bed bug (bed′bug′), small, flat, bad-smelling bug. Its bite is painful. See the picture. *n.*

bed cham ber (bed′chām′bər), bedroom. *n. 10.*

bed clothes (bed′klōz′), sheets, blankets, quilts, etc. *n. pl. 20.*

bed ding (bed′ing), 1. bedclothes; blankets, sheets, quilts, mattresses, etc. 2. material for beds. Straw is used as bedding for cows and horses. *n. 13.*

be deck (bi dek′), adorn. *v. 19.*

be dew (bi dū′ or bi dü′), to wet with dew or drops like dew. *v. 15.*

bed fel low (bed′fel′ō), sharer of one's bed. *n. 20.*

Bed ford (bed′fərd), name of a county in southern England and of several towns. *n. 12.*

be dight (bi dīt′), adorned. *adj.* [*Old use*] *20.*

be dim (bi dim′), make dim; darken. *v., bedimmed, bedimming. 20.*

be di zen (bi dī′zən), dress in gaudy clothes; ornament with showy finery. *v. 20.*

bed lam (bed′ləm), 1. uproar; confusion. 2. insane asylum; madhouse. *n. 12.*

Bed ou in (bed′ü in), 1. an Arab who lives in the deserts of Arabia, Syria, or northern Africa. 2. wanderer. *n. 17.*

be drag gle (bi drag′əl), wet or soil (a garment) by dragging or trailing it. The woman's long skirt was bedraggled from the wet streets. *v.*

bed rid den (bed′rid′ən), confined to bed for a long time. *adj. 19.*

bed room (bed′rüm′), a room to sleep in. *n. 4.*

bed side (bed′sīd′), the side of a bed. The nurse sat by the sick woman's bedside. *n. 12.*

bed spread (bed′spred′), cover that is spread over the blankets on a bed to make the bed look better. *n. 13.*

bed stead (bed′sted), wooden or metal framework of a bed. *n. 13.*

bed time (bed′tīm′), time to go to bed. His regular bedtime is nine o'clock. *n. 8.*

bee (bē), 1. an insect that makes honey and wax. A bee has four wings and a sting, and usually lives with many other bees. 2. a gathering for work or amusement; as, a spelling bee, a husking bee. *n. 1.*

Worker honeybee (about ½ life size)

beech (bēch), 1. a tree with smooth, gray bark and glossy leaves. It bears a sweet nut that is good to eat. 2. its wood. *n. 6.*

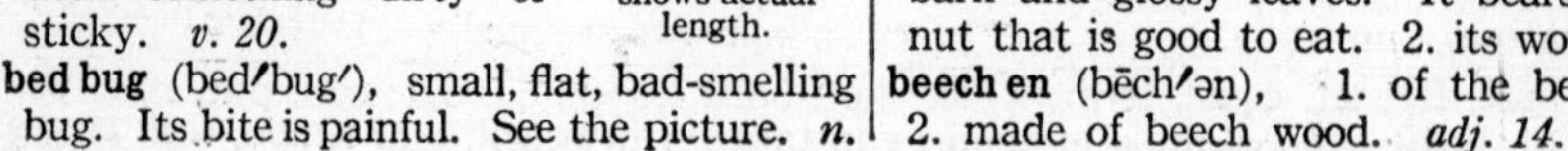

beech en (bēch′ən), 1. of the beech tree. 2. made of beech wood. *adj. 14.*

beech nut (bēch′nut′), small, triangular nut of the beech tree. *n.*

beef (bēf), 1. meat from a steer, cow, or bull, used for food. 2. a steer, cow, or bull when full-grown and fattened for food. Beeves are shipped from the farm to the city. *n., pl. beeves* (bēvz) or *beefs. 3.*

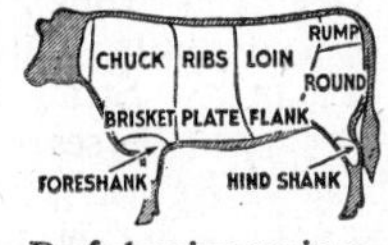

Beef showing various cuts

beef steak (bēf′stāk′), slice of beef for broiling or frying. *n. 16.*

beef y (bēf′i), fleshy; solid; heavy. *adj.*

bee hive (bē′hīv′), 1. a hive or house for bees. 2. busy, swarming place. *n. 18.*

Beehives

bee line (bē′līn′), a straight line, like the flight of a bee to its hive. *n.*

Be el ze bub (bi el′zi bub), a devil; the Devil. *n. 14.*

been (bin). See **be.** He has been here for years. This boy has been present every day. The books have been read by every girl in the room. The two boys have been friends for many years. *pp. of be. 1.*

beer (bēr), 1. an alcoholic drink made from malted barley and hops. 2. a drink made from roots or plants, such as root beer, ginger beer. *n. 5.*

Beer she ba (bēr shē′bə), town near the southern boundary of Palestine. *n. 12.*

bees wax (bēz′waks′), the wax given out by bees, from which they make their honeycomb. *n. 17.*

Beet

beet (bēt), a plant, grown for its thick, fleshy root; its root. Red beets are used as vegetables. Sugar is made from white beets. *n. 5.*

Bee tho ven (bā′tō vən), a famous German musical composer (1770-1827). *n. 15.*

bee tle¹ (bē′təl), 1. insect that has two hard, shiny cases to cover its wings when folded. 2. insect resembling a beetle. *n. 5.*

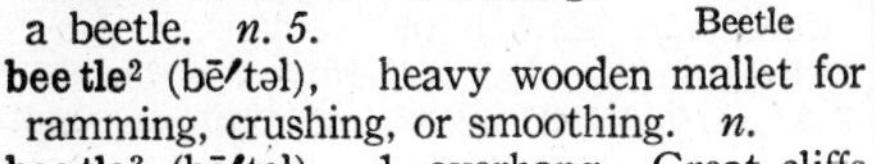
Beetle

bee tle² (bē′təl), heavy wooden mallet for ramming, crushing, or smoothing. *n.*

bee tle³ (bē′təl), 1. overhang. Great cliffs beetled above the narrow paths. 2. standing out; overhanging; as, a beetle-browed old man. *v., adj.*

bee tling (bēt′ling), overhanging; standing out; projecting. *adj. 16.*

beeves (bēvz), more than one beef. *n. pl. 14.*

be fall (bi fôl′), 1. happen to. 2. happen. *v., befell, befallen, befalling. 4.*

be fall en (bi fôl′ən). See **befall.** An accident must have befallen them. *pp. of befall.*

be fell (bi fel′). See **befall.** Evil befell the knight upon his lonely trip. *pt. of befall. 10.*

be fit (bi fit′), suit; be fit for; be proper for. *v., befitted, befitting. 8.*

be fog (bi fog′), surround with fog; obscure. *v., befogged, befogging.*

be fore (bi fōr′), 1. in front of. Before him sat a great crowd. 2. in front. He went before to see if the road was safe. 3. earlier than. Before the bell rings, you may play games. 4. earlier. Come at two o'clock, not before. 5. before now; in time past. You were never late before. 6. rather than; sooner than. *prep., adv., conj. 1.*

be fore hand (bi fōr′hand′), ahead of time. I am going to get everything ready beforehand. *adv., adj. 5.*

be foul (bi foul′), make dirty. *v.*

be friend (bi frend′), act as a friend to; help. The kind teacher befriended her pupils. *v. 8.*

be fud dle (bi fud′əl), 1. confuse. 2. make stupid with alcoholic drink. *v.*

beg (beg), 1. ask for (food, clothes, or money) as a charity. The old man said that he had no way to live but by begging. 2. ask earnestly or humbly. He begged his mother to forgive him. 3. **Beg the question** means take for granted the very thing argued about. *v., begged, begging. 2.*

be gan (bi gan′). See **begin.** Snow began to fall early in the evening. His mother began to worry when he did not come home. *pt. of begin. 1.*

be gat (bi gat′), begot. *old pt. of* **beget.** *14.*

be get (bi get′), 1. be the father of. 2. produce; cause to be. Hate begets hate and love begets love. *v., begot, begotten* or *begot, begetting. 6.*

beg gar (beg′ər), 1. person who lives by begging. 2. a very poor person. 3. bring to poverty. Your reckless spending will beggar your father. 4. make seem poor.

The beauty of the scene beggars description. *n., v. 3.*

beg gar ly (beg′ər li), fit for a beggar; poor. *adj. 13.*

beg gar y (beg′ər i), very great poverty. *n. 11.*

be gin (bi gin′). School begins at nine. We begin breakfast at seven. I begin to feel hungry. *v., began, begun, beginning. 1.*

be gin ner (bi gin′ər), person who is doing something for the first time; one who lacks skill and experience. You skate well for a beginner. *n. 9.*

be gin ning (bi gin′ing), 1. time when anything begins. 2. first part. 3. first cause; source; origin. *n. 5.*

be girt (bi gėrt′), surrounded; encircled. *adj. 16.*

be gone (bi gôn′), be gone; go away. The man bade the tramp begone. *interj., v. 10.*

be go ni a (bi gō′ni ə), a plant with handsome leaves and waxy flowers. *n.*

Begonia

be got (bi got′). See **beget.** *pt. and pp. of beget. 7.*

be grime (bi grīm′), make grimy; make dirty. *v. 16.*

be grudge (bi gruj′), grudge; envy. She is so stingy that she begrudges her dog a bone. *v. 20.*

be guile (bi gīl′), 1. deceive; cheat. He beguiled me into thinking that he was my friend. 2. charm; amuse. The old sailor beguiled the boys with stories about his life at sea. 3. while away (time) pleasantly. *v. 5.*

be gun (bi gun′). See **begin.** It has begun to rain. *pp. of begin. 2.*

be half (bi haf′), side; interest; favor. **In behalf of** means for; in the interest of. I am speaking in behalf of my friend John Smith. *n. 4.*

be have (bi hāv′), 1. act. Don't behave like a fool. 2. act well; do what is right. *v. 4.*

be hav ior (bi hāv′yər), way of acting; conduct; action; acts. His behavior showed that his feelings were hurt. The little boat's behavior was perfect on the trial trip. *n. 7.*

be head (bi hed′), cut off the head of. *v. 6.*

be held (bi held′). See **behold.** We beheld the approaching storm. You have all beheld beautiful sunsets. *pt. and pp. of behold. 3.*

be he moth (bi hē′məth), huge and powerful animal mentioned in the Bible. *n. 18.*

be hest (bi hest′), command. *n. 12.*

be hind (bi hīnd′). Stand behind me. He is behind his usual time. The men are behind in their work. *prep., adv. 1.*

be hind hand (bi hīnd′hand′), 1. behind time; late. Don't wait for Helen; she is always behindhand. They are behindhand with their rent. 2. behind others in progress; backward. Dick is behindhand in his schoolwork. *adv., adj. 20.*

be hold (bi hōld′), see; look; take notice. Behold! there is the king! *v., beheld, beholding, interj. 2.*

be hold en (bi hōl′dən), under obligations; in debt. I am much beholden to you for your help. *adj.*

be hold er (bi hōl′dər), onlooker. The man's feats of strength amazed all the beholders. *n. 14.*

be hoof (bi hüf′), use; advantage; benefit. The father's toil was for his children's behoof. *n. 15.*

be hoove (bi hüv′), 1. be necessary for. It behooves you to work hard if you want to keep this job. 2. be proper for. It does not behoove any young child to give advice to his parents. *v. 15.*

be hove (bi hüv′), behoove. *v. 19.*

be ing (bē′ing). The dog is being fed. Being hungry, he eats much. Men, women, and children are human beings. This world came into being long ago. *ppr. of* **be,** *n. 1.*

be jew el (bi jü′əl), adorn with jewels, or as if with jewels. The sky is bejeweled with stars. *v., bejeweled, bejeweling.*

be la bor (bi lā′bər), beat vigorously. The man belabored his poor donkey. *v. 19.*

be lat ed (bi lāt′id), 1. delayed; too late. The belated letter arrived at last. 2. overtaken by darkness. The belated travelers lost their way on the wild country road. *adj. 11.*

be lay (bi lā′), 1. fasten (a rope) by winding it around a pin or cleat. 2. "Belay!" is used by sailors to mean "Stop!" *v., belayed, belaying.*

Belaying pins with ropes on them

belch (belch), 1. throw out gas from the stomach through the mouth. 2. throw out with force. The volcano belched fire and smoke. 3. a belching. *v., n. 12.*

bel dam or **bel dame** (bel′dəm), 1. an old woman. 2. an ugly old woman. *n. 14.*

be lea guer (bi lē′gər), besiege. *v. 15.*

Bel fast (bel′fast), a seaport city, the capital of Northern Ireland. Belfast is noted for its manufactures, commerce, and shipbuilding industry. *n. 20.*

bel fry (bel′fri), 1. tower for a bell or bells. 2. the space for the bell in a tower. *n., pl. belfries. 12.*

Bel gian (bel′jən), 1. a native or inhabitant of Belgium. 2. of Belgium or the Belgians. *n., adj. 12.*

Bel gium (bel′jəm), a small country in western Europe, north of France. *n. 6.*

Bel grade (bel grād′), the capital of Yugoslavia. *n. 20.*

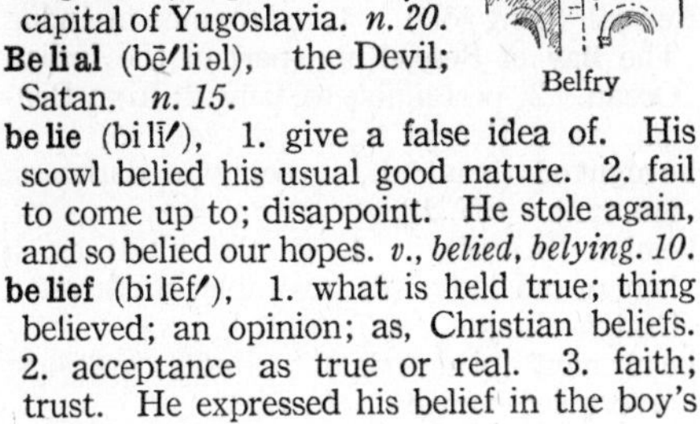

Belfry

Be li al (bē′li əl), the Devil; Satan. *n. 15.*

be lie (bi lī′), 1. give a false idea of. His scowl belied his usual good nature. 2. fail to come up to; disappoint. He stole again, and so belied our hopes. *v., belied, belying. 10.*

be lief (bi lēf′), 1. what is held true; thing believed; an opinion; as, Christian beliefs. 2. acceptance as true or real. 3. faith; trust. He expressed his belief in the boy's honesty. *n. 3.*

be lieve (bi lēv′), 1. think (something) is true or real. We all believe that the earth is round. 2. have faith; trust. Believe in God. 3. think (somebody) tells the truth. His friends believe him. *v. 1.*

be liev er (bi lēv′ər), person who believes. *n. 8.*

be like (bi līk′), very likely; perhaps. *adv. [Old use] 14.*

be lit tle (bi lit′əl), make little; make less important. *v. 20.*

bell (bel), 1. a hollow metal cup that makes a musical sound when struck by a clapper or hammer. 2. the stroke or sound of a bell. On shipboard a bell indicates a half hour of time. 3. anything shaped like a bell. 4. put a bell on. 5. swell out like a bell. *n., v. 1.*

Hand bell

bel la don na (bel′ə don′ə), 1. a poisonous plant with black berries and red flowers. 2. a drug made from this plant. *n. 20.*

belle (bel), 1. a beautiful woman or girl. 2. the prettiest or most admired woman or girl. *n. 10.*

bel li cose (bel′i kōs), warlike; fond of fighting. *adj.*

bel lig er ence (bə lij′ər əns), 1. fondness for fighting; being warlike. 2. being at war. *n.*

bel lig er ent (bə lij′ər ənt), 1. at war; engaged in war. 2. a nation or person engaged in war. 3. warlike. *adj., n. 12.*

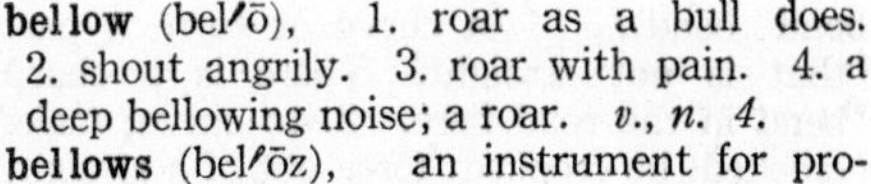

bel low (bel′ō), 1. roar as a bull does. 2. shout angrily. 3. roar with pain. 4. a deep bellowing noise; a roar. *v., n. 4.*

bel lows (bel′ōz), an instrument for producing a strong current of air, used for blowing fires or sounding an organ. *n. sing. or pl. 17.*

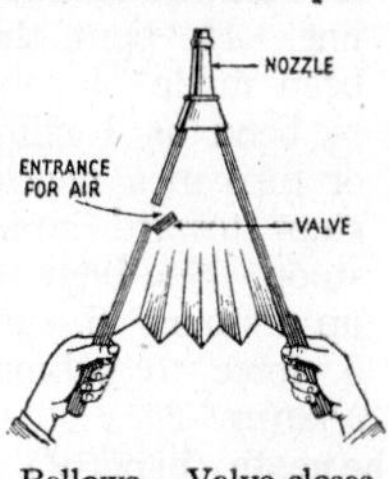

Bellows. Valve closes when sides are pushed together.

bell weth er (bel′weᴛʜ′ər), a sheep that leads the flock, wearing a bell on its neck. *n.*

bel ly (bel′i), 1. the lower part of the human body, which contains the stomach and bowels. 2. the under part of an animal's body. 3. stomach. 4. the bulging part of anything, or the hollow in it. 5. swell out; bulge. The sails bellied in the wind. *n., pl. bellies, v., bellied, bellying. 6.*

be long (bi lông′), 1. **Belong to** means be the property of. Does this cap belong to you? 2. **Belong to** also means be a part of or be a member of. Mary belongs to the Girl Scouts. 3. have one's or its proper place. That book belongs on this shelf. *v. 1.*

be long ings (bi lông′ingz), things that belong to a person; possessions. *n. pl. 20.*

be lov ed (bi luv′id or bi luvd′), 1. dearly loved; dear. 2. person who is loved; darling. *adj., n. 3.*

be low (bi lō′), 1. under; in a lower place than; not so high as. 2. beneath; lower down. *prep., adv. 2.*

belt (belt), 1. a strip of leather, cloth, etc., worn around the body to hold in or support clothes or weapons. 2. any broad strip or band. The cotton belt is the region where cotton is grown. 3. an endless band that moves the wheels and pulleys it passes over. 4. put a belt around. 5. fasten on with a belt. 6. beat with a belt. *n., v. 2.*

be moan (bi mōn′), moan about; bewail. *v. 9.*

Be na res (be nä′riz), a city in India on the Ganges River. It is a sacred city of the Hindus. *n.*

bench (bench), 1. long seat, usually of wood or stone. 2. worktable of a carpenter, or of any worker with tools and materials. 3. seat where judges sit in a law court. 4. position of a judge. 5. judge or a group of judges sitting in a law court. *n. 2.*

bend (bend), 1. a curve or turn; a part that is not straight. There is a sharp bend in the road here. 2. to curve; make crooked; be crooked; force out of a straight line. He bent the iron bar as if it had been made of rubber. The branch began to bend as I climbed along it. 3. move or turn in a new direction. He bends his steps toward home now. 4. to bow; to stoop. She bent to the ground and picked up a stone. 5. submit. I bent to his will. 6. force to submit. *n., v., bent* or *bended, bending. 2.*

be neath (bi nēth′), below; under; in a lower place. What you drop will fall upon the spot beneath. *adv., prep. 2.*

ben e dic i te (ben′i dis′i ti), 1. The **Benedicite** is a hymn of praise to God. 2. invocation of a blessing. *n. 19.*

Ben e dict (ben′i dikt). Saint Benedict (480?-543 A.D.) founded an order of monks. *n. 12.*

Ben e dic tine (ben′i dik′tēn), 1. a monk or nun following the rules of Saint Benedict. 2. having to do with the religious order following the rules of Saint Benedict. *n., adj. 13.*

ben e dic tion (ben′i dik′shən), 1. the asking of God's blessing at the end of a service in church. 2. blessing. *n. 10.*

ben e fac tion (ben′i fak′shən), 1. doing good; kind act. 2. benefit conferred; gift for charity; help given for any good purpose. *n. 18.*

ben e fac tor (ben′i fak′tər), person who has given money or kindly help. *n. 9.*

ben e fac tress (ben′i fak′tris), woman who has given money or kindly help. *n. 16.*

ben e fice (ben′i fis), a church living; an endowment, the income from which supports a clergyman. *n. 15.*

be nef i cence (bi nef′i səns), 1. kindness; doing good. 2. kindly act; gift. *n. 15.*

be nef i cent (bi nef′i sənt), kind; doing good. *adj. 11.*

ben e fi cial (ben′i fish′əl), favorable; helpful; productive of good. Sunshine is beneficial to plants. *adj. 8.*

ben e fi ci ar y (ben′i fish′i ãr′i), person who receives benefit. Mr. Day gave the city a playground, and all the children are beneficiaries. *n., pl. beneficiaries. 15.*

ben e fit (ben′i fit), 1. advantage; anything which is for the good of a person or thing. Universal peace would be of great benefit to the world. 2. do good to. The sea air will benefit you. 3. receive good; profit. He benefited by the medicine. He will benefit from the new way of doing business. 4. act of kindness; favor. 5. a performance at the theater, a game, etc., to raise money which goes to a special person or persons or to a cause. *n., v., benefited, benefiting. 2.*

be nev o lence (bi nev′ə ləns), 1. good will; kindly feeling. 2. act of kindness; something good that is done. *n. 9.*

be nev o lent (bi nev′ə lənt), kindly; charitable. *adj. 16.*

Ben gal (beng gôl′), 1. a province in India. The **Bay of Bengal** is a part of the Indian Ocean. 2. pertaining to Bengal; from Bengal; as, a Bengal tiger. *n., adj. 16.*

be night ed (bi nīt′id), being in darkness; ignorant. *adj. 12.*

be nign (bi nīn′), 1. gentle; kind; as, a benign old lady. 2. favorable; mild; as, a benign climate. *adj. 10.*

be nig nant (bi nig′nənt), kindly; gracious; favorable; benign. *adj. 15.*

be nig ni ty (bi nig′ni ti), 1. kindliness; graciousness. 2. kind act; favor. *n., pl. benignities. 16.*

ben i son (ben′i zən), blessing. *n. 15.*

Ben ja min (ben′jə min), 1. in the Bible, the youngest son of Jacob. 2. one of the twelve tribes of Israel. *n. 5.*

bent (bent), 1. See **bend.** He bent the wire. 2. determined. Tom is bent on being a sailor. 3. inclination; tendency. He has a decided bent for drawing. *pt. and pp. of bend, adj., n. 2.*

be numb (bi num′), make numb. *v. 13.*

ben zene (ben′zēn), a colorless liquid easily set on fire, obtained from coal tar. It is used for removing grease stains, in painting, and in making dyes. *n. 12.*

ben zine (ben′zēn), a colorless liquid obtained from petroleum and used in cleaning and dyeing, and as a motor fuel. *n.*

ben zol (ben′zol), benzene. *n. 19.*

be queath (bi kwēᴛʜ′), give when one dies. The father bequeathed the old home to his son. *v. 7.*

be quest (bi kwest′), something bequeathed. Mr. Hart died and left a bequest of ten thousand dollars to the church. *n. 12.*

be rate (bi rāt′), scold sharply. *v.*

be reave (bi rēv′), deprive; leave desolate. People are bereaved by the death of relatives and friends. *v., bereaved* or *bereft, bereaving. 9.*

be reave ment (bi rēv′mənt), 1. great loss. 2. loss by death. Everyone sympathized with the widow in her bereavement. *n.*

be reft (bi reft′), 1. deprived; bereaved; left desolate. Bereft of hope and friends, the old man led a wretched life. 2. See **bereave.** *adj., pt. and pp. of bereave. 7.*

be ret (be rā′), soft, round woolen cap. *n.*

Girl wearing a beret

berg (bėrg), iceberg. *n. 13.*

Ber ing (bēr′ing). 1. The **Bering Sea** is the northern portion of the Pacific Ocean. 2. **Bering Strait** is between Alaska and Asia. *n.*

Berke ley (bėrk′li), a city in California, near San Francisco. *n. 7.*

Berk shire (bėrk′shir), 1. a county in southern England. 2. a kind of hog. *n. 12.*

Ber lin (bėr lin′), the capital of Germany. *n. 8.*

Ber mu da (bər mū′də), a group of British islands off the coast of the United States in the northern Atlantic Ocean. *n. 17.*

Bern or **Berne** (bėrn), the capital of Switzerland. *n.*

Ber nard (bėr′nərd or bər närd′). Saint Bernard (923-1008) was a French monk who founded two monasteries at two mountain passes in the Alps. *n. 17.*

ber ry (ber′i), 1. a small, juicy fruit with many seeds. 2. gather berries. 3. a dry seed or kernel; as, the coffee berry. *n., pl. berries, v., berried, berrying. 2.*

berth (bėrth), 1. a place to sleep on a ship, train, or airplane. 2. a ship's place at a wharf. 3. a place for a ship to anchor conveniently or safely. 4. appointment; position; job. *n. 9.*

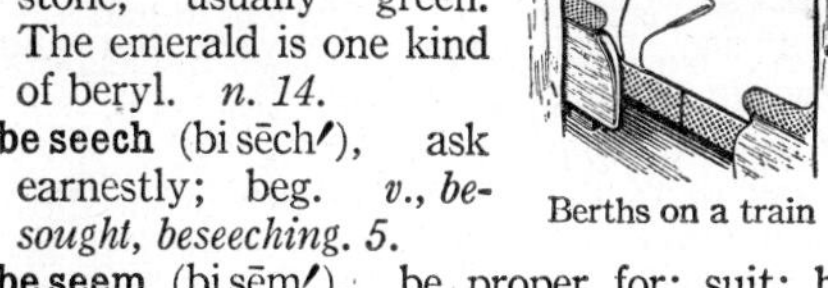

Berths on a train

ber yl (ber′il), a precious stone, usually green. The emerald is one kind of beryl. *n. 14.*

be seech (bi sēch′), ask earnestly; beg. *v., besought, beseeching. 5.*

be seem (bi sēm′), be proper for; suit; be fitting to. It does not beseem you to leave your friend without help. *v. 9.*

be set (bi set′), 1. attack; attack on all sides. 2. surround; hem in. *v., beset, besetting. 6.*

be set ting (bi set′ing), habitually attacking. Laziness is his besetting sin. *adj.*

be shrew (bi shrü′). curse. *v. [Old use] 15.*

be side (bi sīd′), 1. by the side of; near; close to. Grass grows beside the brook. 2. compared with. Nell seems dull beside her sister. 3. away from. That question was beside the mark and need not be answered. 4. **Beside oneself** means out of one's senses. *prep. 1.*

be sides (bi sīdz′), 1. also; as well; in addition; moreover. 2. in addition to; over and above. *adv., prep. 4.*

be siege (bi sēj′), 1. make a long-continued attempt to get possession of (a place) by armed force; surround and try to capture. The Greeks besieged the city of Troy for ten years. 2. crowd around. Hundreds of admirers besieged the famous aviator. 3. overwhelm with requests, questions, etc. During the flood, the Red Cross was besieged with calls for help. *v. 5.*

be sieg er (bi sēj′ər), person who besieges. *n. 13.*

be smear (bi smēr′), smear over. *v. 20.*

be smirch (bi smėrch′), make dirty; soil; sully. *v. 20.*

be som (bē′zəm), 1. broom made of twigs. 2. a broom. *n.*

Besom

be sot ted (bi sot′id), stupefied; made senseless. *adj. 12.*

be sought (bi sôt′). See **beseech.** *pt. and pp. of beseech. 8.*

be spake (bi spāk′), bespoke. *old pt. of* **bespeak.**

be span gle (bi spang′gəl), adorn with spangles. *v. 20.*

be spat ter (bi spat′ər), spatter all over; soil. *v.*

be speak (bi spēk′), 1. engage in advance; order; reserve. We have bespoken two tickets for tomorrow. 2. show; indicate. The neat appearance of this room bespeaks care. *v., bespoke, bespoken* or *bespoke, bespeaking. 13.*

be sprent (bi sprent′), strewed; sprinkled. *adj. [Used in poetry] 16.*

Bes sa ra bi a (bes′ə rā′bi ə), region in eastern and northeastern Rumania, formerly a part of Russia. *n.*

Bes se mer (bes′ə mər). The **Bessemer process** is a way of removing carbon from molten iron by means of a blast of air. *n. 18.*

best (best), 1. Mary's work is good; John's work is better; Helen's is the best. Who reads best? We want the best. 2. **Make the best of** means do as well as possible with. 3. defeat. **Get the best of** means defeat. *adj., adv., n., v. 1.*

bes tial (bes′tyəl), beastly; brutal. *adj. 13.*

be stir (bi stėr′), stir up; rouse; exert. *v., bestirred, bestirring. 14.*

be stow (bi stō′), 1. give. **Bestow on** means give to. 2. put safely; put; place. *Old use. v. 3.*

be stow al (bi stō′əl), bestowing. *n.*

be strew (bi strü′), 1. strew. The children bestrewed the path with flowers. 2. strew (things) around; scatter about. *v., bestrewed, bestrewed* or *bestrewn, bestrewing.*

be stride (bi strīd′), 1. get on or sit on (something) with one leg on each side. You can bestride a horse, a chair, or a fence. 2. stand over with one leg on each side. 3. stride across; step over. *v., bestrode* or *bestrid, bestridden* or *bestrid, bestriding. 11.*

be strode (bi strōd′). See **bestride.** *pt. of bestride. 20.*

bet (bet), 1. promise (some money or a certain thing) to another if he is right and you are wrong. I bet you two cents I won't pass this test. 2. a pledge or promise to give some money or a certain thing to another if he is right and you are wrong. I made a bet that I shouldn't pass. 3. the money or thing promised. I did pass; so I lost my bet (lost my two cents). *v., bet* or *betted, betting, n. 6.*

be take (bi tāk′). **Betake oneself** means (1) go. They betake themselves to the mountains every summer. (2) try doing; apply oneself. He betook himself to hard study. *v., betook, betaken, betaking. 12.*

Beth a ny (beth′ə ni), a village in Palestine, near Jerusalem. *n. 20.*

beth el (beth′əl). Bethel means house of God and so is used to mean any place where God is present, especially a chapel for sailors. *n. 13.*

be think (bi thingk′), think about; call to mind. **Bethink oneself** means think or remember. I bethought me that I must study. *v., bethought, bethinking. 8.*

Beth le hem (beth′li hem), 1. the birthplace of Jesus, a town in Palestine near Jerusalem. 2. a city in eastern Pennsylvania, noted for the manufacture of steel. *n. 9.*

be thought (bi thôt′). See **bethink.** *pt. and pp. of bethink. 11.*

be tide (bi tīd′), 1. happen to. Woe betide you if you hurt my dog! 2. happen. *v. 9.*

be times (bi tīmz′), early. He rose betimes in the morning. *adv. 8.*

be to ken (bi tō′kən), be a sign of; show. His smile betokens his satisfaction. *v. 14.*

be took (bi tük′). See **betake.** He betook himself home as soon as school was out. *pt. of betake. 19.*

be tray (bi trā′), 1. give away to the enemy. The traitor betrayed his country. 2. be unfaithful to. She betrayed her promises. 3. mislead; deceive. 4. show; reveal. Harry's wet shoes betrayed the fact that he had not worn his rubbers. *v. 3.*

be tray al (bi trā′əl), a betraying; a being betrayed. *n. 17.*

be troth (bi trōᴛʜ′), promise or engage to marry. Bess and Tom were now betrothed. He betrothed his daughter to a rich man. *v. 6.*

be troth al (bi trōᴛʜ′əl), engagement to be married. *n. 13.*

be trothed (bi trōᴛʜd′), person engaged to be married. His betrothed was a pretty girl named Nora. *n.*

bet ter (bet′ər), 1. We say good, better, best. Try to do better next time. 2. less sick. The sick child is better today. 3. improve. We can better that work by being more careful next time. 4. person or thing that is better. 5. Some special meanings are:

better off, in a better condition.

get the better of, defeat; be superior to.

had better, should; ought to. I had better go before it rains.

think better of, think differently about.

adj., adv., v., n. 1.

bet ter ment (bet′ər mənt), improvement. *n. 12.*

bet tor (bet′ər), person who bets. *n.*

be tween (bi twēn′). Between the two trees is a space of ten feet. The two boys shared the cake between them. There is no difference between the two dresses. We could not see the moon, for a cloud came in between. She earned between ten and twelve dollars. *prep., adv. 1.*

be twixt (bi twikst′), between. *prep., adv. 7.*

bev el (bev′əl), 1. a sloping edge. There is a bevel on the frame for a picture, on a piece of plate glass, etc. 2. cut a square edge to a sloping edge; make slope. Some mirrors have beveled edges. 3. an instrument or tool for measuring angles. *n., v., beveled, beveling. 9.*

bev er age (bev′ər ij), drink. Milk, tea, coffee, wine, and beer are beverages. *n. 7.*

bev y (bev′i), small group; as, a bevy of quail, a bevy of girls. *n., pl. bevies. 13.*

be wail (bi wāl′), mourn for; weep for; complain of. The little girl was bewailing the loss of her doll. *v. 6.*

be ware (bi wãr′), be careful; be on one's guard against. Beware! danger is here. Beware the dog! *v. 4.*

be wil der (bi wil′dər), confuse completely; puzzle; perplex. Grandma was bewildered by the crowds and noises. Some problems in arithmetic bewilder me. *v. 7.*

be wil der ment (bi wil′dər mənt), bewildered condition; confusion; perplexity. *n. 11.*

be witch (bi wich′), 1. put under a spell; use magic on. The wicked fairy bewitched the princess, so that she fell into a long sleep. 2. charm; delight very much. We were all bewitched by our pretty little cousin. *v. 7.*

be wray (bi rā′), betray; reveal; make known. *v. [Old use] 17.*

bey (bā), a Turkish governor. *n., pl. beys. 19.*

be yond (bi yond′). Your ball did not fall here; look beyond for it. The road is beyond that hill. It is an hour beyond the time you should stay. He was beyond the help of the doctor. The meaning of this story is beyond him. The price of the suit was beyond what he could pay. The day at the beach was beyond all we had hoped. **The beyond** or **the great beyond** means life after death. *adv., prep., n. 2.*

bi-, prefix meaning:—
1. twice.
2. doubly.
3. two.
4. having two.

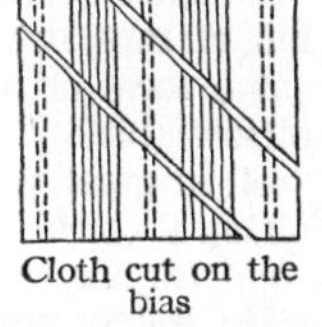
Cloth cut on the bias

bi an nu al (bī an′ū əl), occurring twice a year. *adj.*

bi as (bī′əs), 1. a slanting or oblique line. 2. slanting across the threads of cloth; oblique; diagonal. 3. opinion before there is reason for it; prejudice; a leaning of the mind. 4. to influence, usually unfairly. *n., adj., v., biased, biasing. 6.*

bi ased (bī′əst), favoring one side too much; warped; prejudiced. *adj.*

bib (bib), 1. a cloth worn under the chin by babies and small children to protect the clothing. 2. the part of an apron above the waist. See the picture. *n. 7.*

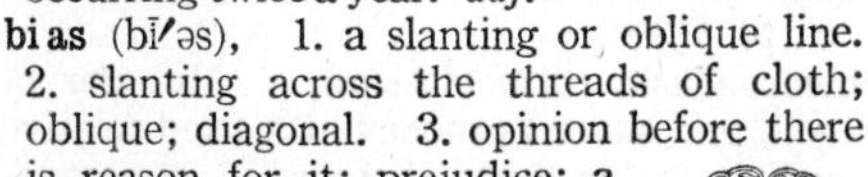
Bib for a baby

Bib of an apron

Bi ble (bī′bəl), 1. the book of sacred writings of the Christian religion; the Old Testament and the New Testament. 2. a book of the sacred writings of any religion. *n. 4.*

Bib li cal or **bib li cal** (bib′li kəl), 1. of the Bible. 2. according to the Bible. 3. in the Bible. *adj. 14.*

bib li og ra phy (bib′li og′rə fi), 1. a list of books, articles, etc., about a subject. 2. the study of the authorship, editions, classification, etc., of books. *n., pl. bibliographies. 17.*

bi car bo nate (bī kär′bə nit). **Bicarbonate of soda** is a white, alkaline powder used in cooking and medicine. *n. 17.*

bi ceps (bī′seps), the large muscle in the front part of the upper arm. If you move your fist up to your shoulder, the biceps will stick out. *n. 20.*

bick er (bik′ər), quarrel. *n., v. 11.*

bi cus pid (bī kus′pid), 1. a double-pointed tooth. A man has eight bicuspids. 2. having two points. *n., adj.*

bi cy cle (bī′si kəl), 1. See the picture. A bicycle has two wheels, one behind the other, which support a light metal frame on which there are handles and a seat for the rider. You ride a bicycle by pushing two pedals with your feet. 2. ride a bicycle. *n., v. 4.*

Boy riding a bicycle

bi cy clist (bī′si klist), bicycle rider. *n.*

bid (bid), 1. command. The captain bids his men go forward. Do as I bid you. 2. invite. Our friends gave us strawberries and bade us come again in apple time. 3. say; tell. His friends came to bid him good-by. 4. offer to pay (a certain price). First she bid $5 for the table. He then bid $6. 5. an offer; amount offered for a thing. My bid was $7. 6. state one's price for doing a certain piece of work. 7. price at which one says one can do a certain piece of work. Our bid for building the bridge was $300,000. 8. **Bid fair to** means seem likely to. The plan bids fair to succeed. *v., bade or bid, bidden or bid, bidding, n. 2.*

bid den (bid′ən). See **bid.** Twelve guests were bidden to the feast. *pp. of bid. 20.*

bid der (bid′ər), 1. person who bids. 2. person who offers to pay a certain price at an auction. *n.*

bid ding (bid′ing), 1. command. 2. invitation. 3. offering of a price at an auction. *n. 9.*

bide (bīd), 1. abide. 2. wait. **Bide one's time** means wait for a good chance. *v., bode* or *bided, bided, biding. 6.*

bi en ni al (bī en′i əl), 1. lasting two years. 2. a plant that lives two years. Carrots and onions are biennials. 3. occurring every two years. 4. something that occurs every two years. *adj., n. 12.*

bier (bēr), movable stand on which a coffin or dead body is placed. *n. 8.*

big (big), 1. large. 2. grown up. 3. important. *adj., bigger, biggest. 1.*

big a my (big′ə mi), 1. having two wives at the same time. 2. having two husbands at the same time. *n. 15.*

big horn (big′hôrn′), a wild sheep of the Rocky Mountains, having large, curving horns. *n., pl. bighorns* or *bighorn.*

Bighorn (3½ ft. high at the shoulder)

bight (bīt), 1. a long curve in a coastline. 2. a bay. 3. bend; angle; corner. 4. loop of rope. *n. 15.*

big ness (big′nis), the quality or state of being big. *n. 16.*

big ot (big′ət), bigoted person. *n. 11.*

big ot ed (big′ət id), sticking to an opinion, belief, party, etc., without reason and not tolerating other views; intolerant; prejudiced. A person may be bigoted in religion or in politics. *adj. 20.*

big ot ry (big′ət ri), conduct or state of mind of a bigot; intolerance; prejudice. *n. 15.*

bi jou (bē′zhü), jewel. *n.*

bi lat er al (bī lat′ər əl), 1. having two sides. 2. on two sides. 3. affecting or influencing two sides. *adj. 19.*

bile (bīl), 1. a bitter, yellowish liquid secreted by the liver to aid digestion. 2. ill humor; anger. *n. 12.*

bilge (bilj), 1. the lowest part of a ship's hold; the bottom of a ship's hull. 2. the widest part of a barrel. *n. 18.*

bilge water, dirty water in the bottom of a ship.

bil ious (bil′yəs), 1. suffering from some trouble with bile or the liver; as, a bilious person. 2. caused by such trouble; as, a bilious attack, a bilious headache. 3. peevish; cross. *adj. 15.*

bill[1] (bil), 1. account of money due for work done or things supplied. Pay your bills promptly. 2. send a bill to. 3. enter in a bill; charge in a bill. 4. a piece of paper money; as, a dollar bill. 5. written or printed public notice; advertisement; poster; handbill. 6. announce by bills. 7. post bills in or on. 8. written or printed statement; list of items. 9. a proposed law presented to a lawmaking body. 10. written request or complaint. *n., v. 1.*

bill[2] (bil), 1. the mouth of a bird; beak. 2. anything like a bird's bill; as, the bill of a turtle. 3. join beaks; touch bills. 4. show affection. *n., v.*

bill board (bil′bōrd′), signboard for posting advertisements or notices on. *n.*

bil let[1] (bil′it), 1. a written order to provide board and lodging for a soldier. 2. the place where a soldier is lodged. 3. assign to quarters; to place. The soldiers were billeted on the townspeople. *n., v. 12.*

bil let[2] (bil′it), 1. thick stick of wood. 2. bar of iron or steel. *n.*

bil liards (bil′yərdz), a game played with balls on a special table. A long stick called a cue is used in hitting the balls. *n. 10.*

bil lion (bil′yən), 1. in the United States and France, 1,000,000,000. 2. in England, 1,000,000,000,000. *n., adj. 13.*

bill of fare, list of the articles of food served at a meal or of those that can be ordered.

bil low (bil′ō), 1. a big wave. 2. rise or roll in great waves. *n., v. 5.*

bil low y (bil′ō i), rising in billows; surging. *adj. 17.*

bil ly (bil′i), a policeman's club or stick. *n., pl. billies.*

bi met al lism (bī met′əl izm), the use of gold and silver as money at a fixed relative value; for instance, having 16 ounces of silver equal to 1 ounce of gold. *n. 19.*

bi month ly (bī munth′li), 1. once every two months. 2. twice a month. 3. magazine published bimonthly. *adj., adv., n., pl. bimonthlies.*

bin (bin), a box or enclosed place for holding grain, coal, etc. *n. 8.*

bind (bīnd), 1. tie together; hold together; fasten. 2. stick together. 3. restrain; hold by force. 4. oblige; oblige by law. 5. put a border or edge on to strengthen or ornament. 6. bandage. 7. put a band or wreath around. 8. fasten (sheets of paper) into a cover; put a cover on (a book). *v., bound, binding. 2.*

bind er (bīn′dər), 1. person who binds.

2. anything that ties or holds together. 3. machine that cuts grain and ties it in bundles. *n. 11.*

bind ing (bīn′ding), 1. the covering of a book. 2. a strip protecting or ornamenting an edge. Binding is used on the seams of dresses. 3. that binds. *n., adj.*

bin na cle (bin′ə kəl), the box that holds a ship's compass. The binnacle is placed near the man who is steering. *n.*

bi noc u lar (bi nok′ū lər), 1. using both eyes. 2. for both eyes. *adj. 14.*

bi noc u lars (bi nok′ū lərz), field glasses or opera glasses. *n. pl.*

Binoculars

bi og ra pher (bī og′rə fər), person who writes the life of somebody. *n. 14.*

bi o graph i cal (bī′ə graf′i kəl), 1. of a person's life. 2. having to do with biography. *adj. 20.*

bi og ra phy (bī og′rə fi), 1. the written story of a person's life. 2. the part of literature which consists of biographies. *n., pl. biographies. 11.*

bi o log i cal (bī′ə loj′i kəl), 1. of plant and animal life. 2. having to do with biology; as, a biological laboratory. *adj. 9.*

bi ol o gist (bī ol′ə jist), person skilled in biology. *n. 15.*

bi ol o gy (bī ol′ə ji), the science of life or living things; study of plant and animal life. *n. 7.*

bi ped (bī′ped), animal with two feet. Birds are bipeds. *n.*

bi plane (bī′plān′), an airplane having two wings, one above the other. *n.*

Biplane

birch (bėrch), 1. a slender tree with smooth bark and close-grained wood, used in making furniture. The Indians used birch bark to cover the framework of their canoes. 2. bundle of birch twigs or a birch stick used for whipping. 3. to whip with a birch. *n., v. 4.*

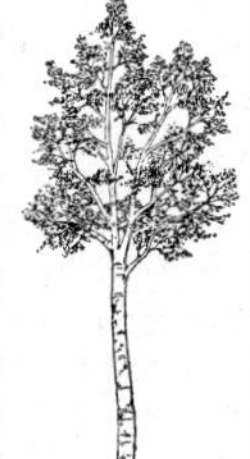

White birch

bird (bėrd), an animal that has wings and feathers. A **bird of passage** flies from one region to another as the seasons change. A **bird of prey** eats flesh. Eagles, hawks, vultures, and owls are birds of prey. *n. 1.*

bird lime (bėrd′līm′), sticky substance smeared on twigs to catch small birds that light on it. *n.*

bird of paradise, bird of New Guinea noted for its magnificent plumage.

bird's-eye (bėrdz′ī′), 1. seen from above or from a distance; general. You can get a bird's-eye view of the city from an airplane. 2. having markings somewhat like birds' eyes. Bird's-eye maple is a wood used in making furniture. *adj.*

Bir ming ham (bėr′ming əm for 1, bėr′ming-ham for 2), 1. city in western England. 2. city in central Alabama. *n. 17.*

birth (bėrth), 1. a coming into life; being born. 2. a beginning. 3. a bringing forth. 4. descent; family. He was a man of humble birth. *n. 2.*

birth day (bėrth′dā′), 1. the day on which a person was born. 2. the day on which something began. July 4th, 1776, was the birthday of a nation. 3. the yearly return of the day on which a person was born, or on which something began. Tomorrow is my birthday. *n. 2.*

birth place (bėrth′plās′), 1. the place where a person was born. 2. place of origin. *n. 7.*

birth rate, proportion of the number of births per year to the total population.

birth right (bėrth′rīt′), rights belonging to a person because he is the eldest son, or because he was born in a certain country, or because of any other fact about his birth. *n. 7.*

Bis cay (bis′kā). The **Bay of Biscay** is a part of the Atlantic Ocean north of Spain and west of France. *n. 14.*

bis cuit (bis′kit), 1. soft bread dough baked in small shapes. 2. a thin, flat, dry bread or cake; a cracker. *n., pl. biscuits* or *biscuit. 6.*

bi sect (bī sekt′), 1. divide into two parts. 2. divide into two equal parts. *v. 13.*

bish op (bish′əp), 1. a clergyman of high rank, at the head of a church district. 2. one of the pieces in the game of chess. *n. 4.*

bish op ric (bish′əp rik), 1. position, office or rank of bishop. 2. district under the charge of a bishop; diocese. *n. 14.*

Bis marck (biz′märk), 1. German statesman, the founder of the German Empire (1815-

1898). 2. capital of North Dakota. *n. 12.*

bis muth (biz′məth), a brittle, reddish-white metallic element. It is used in medicine. *n. 14.*

bi son (bī′sən), the American buffalo. See the picture. *n. 10.*

American bison (about 5½ ft. high at the shoulder)

bit (bit), 1. small piece; small amount. 2. somewhat; a little. 3. a short time. *Used in common talk.* 4. 12½ cents. A quarter is two bits. *Used in common talk.* 5. the part of a bridle that goes in the horse's mouth. 6. anything that curbs or restrains. 7. See **bite.** The strong trap bit the leg of the fox. The tramp was bit by our dog. 8. the biting or cutting part of a tool. 9. tool for boring or drilling. *n., pt. and pp. of bite. 1.*

Bit

bitch (bich), female dog. *n. 16.*

bite (bīt), 1. seize, cut into, or cut off with the teeth. 2. a cut or hold with the teeth; a nip. The dog gave a bite or two at the bone. 3. mouthful; the amount one bites off. 4. a wound made by biting or stinging. 5. cause a smarting, sharp pain to. His fingers are bitten by frost. 6. take a strong hold of. The jaws of a vise bite the wood they hold. *v., bit, bitten or bit, biting, n. 2.*

bit ing (bīt′ing), 1. sharp; cutting. 2. sarcastic; sneering. *adj.*

bit ten (bit′ən). See **bite.** The dog has bitten Jack. *pp. of bite.*

bit ter (bit′ər), 1. Grass and quinine are bitter. 2. Failure is bitter. 3. A cold wind is sometimes called bitter. 4. A bitter cry shows that a person feels pain or grief. *adj. 2.*

bit tern (bit′ərn), wading bird that has a peculiar booming cry. It is a small kind of heron living in marshes. *n. 17.*

Bittern (30 in. long)

bit ter sweet (bit′ər-swēt′), 1. climbing plant with purple flowers and poisonous, scarlet berries. 2. climbing plant with orange seed cases that open and show red seeds. 3. sweet and bitter mixed. 4. sweetness and bitterness mixed. *n., adj.*

bi tu men (bi tū′mən or bi tü′mən), mineral that will burn, such as asphalt, petroleum, naphtha, etc. *n. 17.*

bi tu mi nous (bi tū′mi nəs or bi tü′mi nəs), containing bitumen. Bituminous coal is soft coal that burns with much smoke and a yellow flame. *adj. 8.*

bi valve (bī′valv′), a water animal like an oyster or clam whose shell has two parts hinged together. *n. 14.*

biv ou ac (biv′ü ak), camp outdoors without tents. *n., v., bivouacked, bivouacking. 15.*

bi zarre (bi zär′), odd; queer; fantastic; grotesque. The frost made bizarre figures on the windowpanes. *adj. 17.*

blab (blab), tell (secrets); talk too much. *v., blabbed, blabbing. 11.*

black (blak), 1. without any light. The room was black as night. 2. the opposite of white. This print is black. 3. make black. 4. black person; Negro. 5. very dark; as, black clouds. 6. unhappy; gloomy. 7. evil; as, black magic, a black look. *adj., n., v. 1.*

black a moor (blak′ə mür), 1. a Negro. 2. a dark-skinned person. *n. 16.*

black ball (blak′bôl′), 1. a black ball put into a ballot box as a vote against a person or thing. 2. vote against. Some members of the club blackballed Jack; so he could not become a member. *n., v.*

Blackberry

black ber ry (blak′ber′i), 1. small, black or dark-purple fruit of certain bushes and vines. See the picture. 2. thorny bush or vine that it grows on. *n., pl. blackberries. 7.*

black bird (blak′bėrd′), any of several different kinds of birds. They are named blackbirds because the male birds are largely black. *n. 5.*

Red-winged blackbird (9 in. long)

black board (blak′bōrd′), dark, smooth surface for writing or drawing on with chalk. *n. 4.*

black en (blak′ən), 1. make black. 2. become black. 3. speak evil of. *v. 7.*

black guard (blag′ärd), 1. scoundrel. 2. to abuse with vile language. *n., v. 16.*

black ing (blak′ing), black polish used on shoes, stoves, etc. *n.*

black jack (blak′jak′), 1. a club with a flexible handle, used as a weapon. 2. hit with a blackjack. 3. a large drinking cup or jug. 4. the black flag of a pirate. *n., v.*

black list, list of persons who are believed to deserve punishment, blame, suspicion, etc. Some stores keep black lists of persons who do not pay their bills.

black mail (blak′māl′), 1. money obtained by threatening people. 2. get, or try to get, money from by threatening to tell something bad about a person. 3. an attempt to get money by threats. *n., v. 18.*

black ness (blak′nis), being black; black color; darkness. *n. 10.*

Black Sea, large sea between Turkey and southern Russia.

black smith (blak′smith′), man who works with iron. Blacksmiths can mend tools and shoe horses. *n. 3.*

black snake (blak′snāk′), 1. a harmless black snake of North America. 2. a heavy whip made of braided leather. *n.*

black thorn (blak′thôrn′), 1. thorny European shrub that has white flowers and dark-purple, plumlike fruit called sloes. 2. a walking stick or club made from the stem of this shrub. *n.*

blad der (blad′ər), a soft, thin bag in which liquid collects in the body. *n. 9.*

blade (blād), 1. the cutting part of anything like a knife or sword. 2. sword. 3. a smart or dashing fellow. 4. a leaf of grass. 5. the flat, wide part of a leaf. 6. the flat, wide part of anything; as, the blade of an oar or paddle. *n. 2.*

Blake (blāk), William, a famous English poet and artist (1757-1827). *n. 18.*

blam a ble (blām′ə bəl), deserving blame. *adj.*

blame (blām), 1. hold responsible. We blamed the fog for our accident. 2. responsibility. Carelessness deserves the blame for many mistakes. 3. find fault with. He will not blame us if we do our best. 4. finding fault. 5. **Be to blame** means deserve to be blamed. Each person said somebody else was to blame. *v., n. 2.*

blame less (blām′lis), that cannot be blamed; free from fault; innocent. He led a blameless life. *adj. 6.*

blanch (blanch), 1. make white. We blanch celery by keeping out the light. Almonds are blanched by soaking off their skins in boiling water. 2. turn white; become pale. The boy blanched with fear when he saw the bear coming. *v. 7.*

bland (bland), 1. smooth; mild; soft; gentle. 2. agreeable; polite. *adj. 8.*

blan dish (blan′dish), coax; flatter. *v.*

blan dish ment (blan′dish mənt), coaxing; flattery. Ulysses did not yield to Circe's blandishments. *n. 14.*

blank (blangk), 1. space left empty or to be filled in. Leave a blank after each word. 2. not written or printed on; as, blank paper. 3. a paper with spaces to be filled in. Fill out this application blank and return it at once. 4. with spaces left for filling in; as, a blank form for you to fill in. 5. empty. 6. without interest or meaning. There was a blank look on his face. *n., adj. 3.*

blan ket (blang′kit), 1. a soft, heavy covering woven from wool or cotton. Blankets are used to keep people or animals warm. 2. anything like a blanket. A blanket of snow covered the ground. 3. cover with a blanket. The snow blanketed the ground. *n., v. 4.*

blare (blãr), 1. make a loud, harsh sound. The trumpets blared, announcing the king's arrival. 2. loud, harsh sound. *v., n. 12.*

blar ney (blär′ni), 1. flattering, coaxing talk. 2. flatter. **Kiss the Blarney Stone** means get skill in flattering and cajoling. *n., v., blarneyed, blarneying. 19.*

blas pheme (blas fēm′), speak about (God or sacred things) with abuse or contempt. *v. 8.*

blas phe mous (blas′fi məs), speaking against God or sacred things with abuse or contempt. *adj. 18.*

blas phe my (blas′fi mi), abuse or contempt for God or sacred things. *n., pl. blasphemies. 7.*

blast (blast), 1. strong sudden rush of wind or air; as, the icy blasts of winter. 2. the sound made by blowing a horn or trumpet. 3. blow up (rocks, earth, etc.) by dynamite, etc. The old building was blasted. 4. explosion. We heard the blast a mile away. 5. the amount of dynamite, etc., used. 6. wither; shrivel; destroy. A disease has blasted our grapes. *n., v. 3.*

blast furnace, furnace in which ores are smelted with the aid of a blast of air.

bla tant (blā′tənt), noisy; loud-mouthed. *adj. 13.*

blaze[1] (blāz), 1. bright flame or fire. He could see the blaze of the campfire across the beach. 2. burn with a bright flame.

A fire was blazing in the fireplace. 3. show bright colors or lights. On Christmas Eve the big house blazed with lights. 4. bright display. The tulips made a blaze of color in the garden. 5. burst out in anger or excitement. 6. violent outbreak; as, a blaze of temper. *n., v. 2.*

blaze[2] (blāz), 1. a mark made on a tree by cutting off some of its bark. 2. to mark (a tree or a path) by chipping the bark of trees. 3. a white spot on the face of a horse or cow. *n., v.*

blaze[3] (blāz), make known; proclaim. *v.*

bla zon (blā′zən), 1. make known; proclaim. Big posters blazoned the wonders of the coming circus. 2. decorate with designs, names, colors, etc. 3. coat of arms. 4. describe or depict (a coat of arms). *v., n. 10.*

Blazon

bldg., building.

bleach (blēch), make white by exposing to the sun or by a chemical process. We bleach linen. Bleached bones lay on the hot sands of the desert. *v. 6.*

bleach ers (blēch′ərz), roofless seats at a baseball game or other outdoor sport. *n. pl. 20.*

Bleachers

bleak (blēk), 1. bare; swept by winds. The rocky peaks of high mountains are bleak. 2. chilly; cold. 3. dreary; dismal. *adj. 6.*

blear (blēr), 1. dim; blurred. 2. make dim. A bad cold made his nose run and bleared his eyes. *adj., v. 15.*

blear y (blēr′i), blear; dim; blurred. *adj.*

bleat (blēt), 1. cry made by a sheep, goat, or calf, or a sound like it. 2. make the cry of a sheep, goat, or calf, or a sound like it. *n., v. 5.*

bled (bled). See **bleed.** The cut bled for ten minutes. *pt. and pp. of bleed. 8.*

bleed (blēd), 1. lose blood. This cut is bleeding. 2. take blood from. Doctors used to bleed people when they were sick. 3. lose sap, juice, etc. 4. feel pity, sorrow, or grief. My heart bleeds for the poor little orphan. *v., bled, bleeding. 4.*

blem ish (blem′ish), 1. a stain; scar; injury; defect. **Without blemish** means perfect. 2. injure; mar. One bad deed can blemish a good reputation. *n., v. 7.*

blench[1] (blench), draw back; shrink away. *v. 17.*

blench[2] (blench), 1. turn pale. 2. make white. *v.*

blend (blend), 1. mix together; become mixed; mix or become mixed so thoroughly that the things mixed cannot be distinguished or separated. 2. shade into each other. Yellow and orange blend into one another. 3. thorough mixture made by blending. *v., blended or blent, blending, n. 4.*

blent (blent), blended. *pt. and pp. of* **blend.** [*Used in poetry*] *15.*

bless (bles), 1. make holy. 2. ask God's favor for. 3. wish good to. 4. make happy or successful. 5. praise. *v., blessed or blest, blessing. 1.*

bless ed (bles′id or blest), 1. holy; sacred. 2. happy; fortunate. *adj.*

bless ed ness (bles′id nis), great happiness; bliss. *n. 12.*

bless ing (bles′ing), 1. a prayer asking God to show His favor. The priest gave them his blessing. 2. a wish for happiness or success. 3. anything that makes people happy and contented. A good temper is a great blessing. *n. 2.*

blest (blest), blessed. *adj., pt. and pp. of* **bless.** *4.*

blew (blü). See **blow**[2]. All night long the wind blew. *pt. of blow*[2]. *3.*

blight (blīt), 1. any disease that causes plants to wither or decay. 2. anything that checks good fortune or withers hopes. 3. cause to wither or decay; ruin; destroy. *n., v. 7.*

blind (blīnd), 1. not able to see. 2. take away one's sight; make blind. 3. hard to see; as, a blind track. A blind stitch is one that shows only on one side. 4. without judgment or good sense. 5. take away the power to understand or judge. 6. without an opening; as, a blind wall. 7. with only one opening; as, a blind alley. 8. something that keeps out light or hinders sight. A window shade or shutter is a blind. *adj., v., n. 1.*

blind er (blīn′dər), leather flap to keep a horse from seeing sidewise. *n.*

Blinders

blind fold (blīnd′fōld′), 1. cover the eyes of. 2. with the eyes covered. *v., adj. 9.*

blind ness (blīnd′nis), lack of sight; being unable to see. *n. 5.*

blink (blingk), 1. look with the eyes opening and shutting. Mary blinked at the sudden light. 2. shut the eyes to. You cannot blink the fact that there is a war. 3. shine with an unsteady light. A lantern blinked through the darkness. *v., n. 8.*

bliss (blis), very great happiness; perfect joy. *n. 4.*

bliss ful (blis′fəl), very, very happy. *adj. 10.*

blis ter (blis′tər), 1. a little baglike place under the skin filled with watery matter. Blisters are often caused by burns or rubbing. My new shoes have made blisters on my heels. 2. a swelling on the surface of a plant, on metal, or on painted wood. 3. raise a blister on. The mustard plaster has blistered baby's chest. 4. become covered with blisters; have blisters. *n., v. 6.*

blithe (blīTH), gay; happy; cheerful. *adj. 7.*

blithe some (blīTH′səm), joyous; gay; cheerful. *adj. 20.*

blitz krieg (blits′krēg′), warfare in which the offensive is extremely rapid, violent, and hard to resist. *n.*

bliz zard (bliz′ərd), a violent, blinding snowstorm with a very strong wind and very great cold. *n. 11.*

bloat (blōt), 1. swell; puff up. 2. preserve (herring) by salting and smoking. *v. 15.*

bloc (blok), block; number of things or persons considered as a unit. *n.*

block (blok), 1. a solid piece of wood, stone, or the like. 2. fill up so as to prevent passage. The country roads were blocked with snow. The city streets are blocked with traffic. 3. put things in the way of. Her sickness blocks my plans for the party. 4. anything or any group of persons that keeps something from being done. A block in traffic keeps cars from moving on. 5. **Block out** means plan or sketch roughly without working out the details. 6. to shape. His trade is to block hats. 7. number of buildings close together; a collection of buildings side by side bounded by four streets; as, one city block. 8. the length of one side of a city square. Walk one block east. 9. a pulley on a hook. *n., v. 2.*

block ade (blok ād′), 1. control of who and what goes into or out of a place by the use of an army or navy. A blockade of all the harbors of the United States would require thousands of warships. 2. put under such control. 3. anything that blocks up or obstructs. 4. block up; obstruct. 5. **Run the blockade** means sneak into or out of a port that is being blockaded. *n., v. 7.*

block head (blok′hed′), a stupid person; dunce; fool. *n. 12.*

block house (blok′hous′), fort or building with loopholes to shoot from. *n. 19.*

Blockhouse: A, loopholes for guns.

block y (blok′i), 1. like a block; chunky. 2. having patches of light and shade. A photograph may be blocky. *adj. 20.*

blond or **blonde** (blond), 1. light-colored; as, blond hair. 2. having yellow or light-brown hair, blue or gray eyes, and a fair skin. 3. person with such hair, eyes, and skin. Such a man is a blond; such a woman is a blonde. *adj., n. 9.*

blood (blud), 1. the red liquid in the veins and the arteries; the red liquid that flows from a cut. 2. temper; state of mind. **In cold blood** means (1) cruelly or (2) on purpose. 3. family; birth; relationship; parentage; descent. 4. man of dash and spirit. *n. 1.*

blood ed (blud′id), coming from good stock; of good breed. *adj.*

blood hound (blud′hound′), a large dog with a keen scent. Bloodhounds were used to track runaway slaves. *n. 15.*

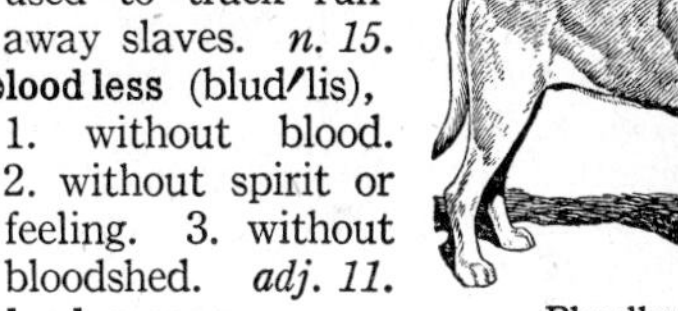

Bloodhound

blood less (blud′lis), 1. without blood. 2. without spirit or feeling. 3. without bloodshed. *adj. 11.*

blood money, 1. money paid to have somebody killed. 2. money paid to make up for killing somebody.

blood poisoning, a diseased condition of the blood caused by poisonous matter or germs.

blood root (blud′rüt′), a common wild plant with a red root, red sap, and a white flower. *n.*

blood shed (blud′shed′), the shedding of blood; slaughter. *n. 9.*

blood shot (blud′shot′), red from inflamed blood vessels. A cinder in the eye often makes it bloodshot. *adj. 18.*

blood suck er (blud′suk′ər), 1. animal that sucks blood; leech. 2. person who gets all he can from others. *n. 20.*

blood thirst y (blud′thėrs′ti), eager to shed blood; cruel; murderous. Wolves and tigers are bloodthirsty. *adj. 12.*

blood vessel, tube in the body through which the blood circulates. An artery, vein, or capillary is a blood vessel.

blood y (blud′i), 1. bleeding; covered with blood. Jack came home with a bloody nose. 2. accompanied by much killing. It was a bloody battle. 3. eager to kill. 4. to stain with blood. *adj., bloodier, bloodiest, v., bloodied, bloodying. 3.*

bloom (blüm), 1. a flower; a blossom. 2. produce flowers; to blossom. Many plants bloom in the spring. 3. to flourish. 4. blooming or flourishing condition. She was in the bloom of youth. 5. the glow of health and vigor. 6. powdery coating on some fruits and leaves. *n., v. 2.*

bloom ers (blüm′ərz), 1. loose trousers gathered at the knee, worn by women and girls. See the picture under **blouse.** 2. underwear made like these. *n. pl. 12.*

blos som (blos′əm), 1. a flower, especially of a plant which produces fruit. 2. time of blooming; early stage of growth. 3. open into flower; have flowers. My pansies are blossoming. 4. open out; develop. *n., v. 2.*

blot (blot), 1. a spot of ink; a stain of any kind. 2. to spot with ink; to stain; make blots. 3. to dry ink with paper that will soak up the extra ink. 4. **Blot out** means (1) cover up entirely; hide. (2) wipe out; destroy. *n., v., blotted, blotting. 4.*

blotch (bloch), 1. a large, irregular blot. 2. a spot on the skin. 3. to cover or mark with spots. *n., v. 14.*

blot ter (blot′ər), 1. piece of blotting paper. 2. book for recording happenings or transactions. A police station blotter keeps a record of arrests. *n. 20.*

blotting paper, soft paper used to dry writing by soaking up ink.

Girl wearing a blouse and bloomers

blouse (blous), 1. a loose upper garment worn by women and children as a part of their outer clothing. 2. a workman's loose upper garment for the protection of clothing during work. *n. 7.*

blow[1] (blō), 1. He struck the man a blow that sent him to the floor. 2. His mother's death was a great blow to him. 3. The army struck a swift blow at the enemy. *n. 1.*

blow[2] (blō), 1. send forth a strong current of air. 2. move rapidly or with power. The wind blows. 3. be carried or moved by the wind. The curtains blew in the wind. 4. force a current of air into or through. 5. break open by an explosion. 6. sound. The whistle blows at noon. 7. pant; cause to pant. 8. puff; swell. 9. a blowing. *v., blew, blown, blowing, n.*

blow er (blō′ər), 1. one that blows; as, a glass blower. 2. machine for forcing air into a building, furnace, mine, etc.; fan. *n. 17.*

blown (blōn), 1. out of breath; exhausted. 2. stale; tainted. 3. carried or driven by the wind. 4. swollen; puffed up; puffed out. *adj., pp. of* **blow**[2]**.**

blow out (blō′out′), 1. a sudden or violent escape of air, steam, or the like. 2. the bursting of an automobile tire. *n.*

blow pipe (blō′pīp′), tube for blowing air or gas into a flame to increase the heat. *n. 19.*

blub ber (blub′ər), 1. fat of whales and other sea animals. 2. weep noisily. *n., v. 11.*

bludg eon (bluj′ən), 1. a short club with a heavy end. 2. strike with a heavy club. *n., v. 18.*

blue (blü), 1. the color of the clear sky in daylight. 2. having this color. 3. sad; discouraged. I felt blue when I failed. 4. **The blue** means (1) the sky. (2) the sea. *n., adj. 1.*

blue bell (blü′bel′), a plant with blue flowers shaped like bells. The bluebell of Scotland and the wild hyacinth are two common bluebells. *n. 13.*

blue ber ry (blü′ber′i), 1. small, blue berry that is good to eat. 2. shrub that it grows on. *n., pl. blueberries. 12.*

blue bird (blü′bėrd′), a small songbird of the northern United States. The male is bright blue on the back and wings and has an orange breast. *n. 10.*

Bluebird (7 in. long)

blue bot tle (blü′bot′əl), 1. a large fly with a blue body. 2. a cornflower. *n.*

blue fish (blü′fish′), a blue-and-silver sea fish that is used for food. *n. 13.*

blue grass (blü′gras′), grass with bluish-green stems. *n.*

blue ing (blü′ing), bluing. *n.*

blue jack et (blü′jak′it), a sailor in the navy. *n.*

blue jay (blü′jā′), a noisy, chattering bird with a blue back. See the picture just below. *n.*

blue laws, very strict and puritanical laws.

blue print (blü′print′), photograph that shows white outlines on a blue background. *n.*

blu et (blü′it), small plant with blue flowers. *n.*

Bluejay (11 in. long)

bluff[1] (bluf), 1. a high, steep bank or cliff. 2. rising with a straight, broad front. 3. abrupt, frank, and hearty in manner. *n., adj. 5.*

bluff[2] (bluf), 1. confidence of action or speech put on to deceive others. We say it is a bluff when a person lets others think he knows more than he really does, or has more money or has better cards, etc., than he really has. 2. deceive by an air of confidence. 3. a threat that one knows he cannot carry out. *n., v.*

blu ing (blü′ing), blue liquid or powder put in water when rinsing clothes. It keeps white clothes from turning yellow. *n.*

blu ish (blü′ish), somewhat blue. *adj. 17.*

blun der (blun′dər), 1. stupid mistake. 2. make a stupid mistake. 3. stumble; move as if blind. *n., v. 8.*

blun der buss (blun′dər bus), a short gun with a wide muzzle, not used now. See the picture. *n. 16.*

Blunderbuss

blunt (blunt), 1. without a sharp edge or point; dull. 2. make less sharp; make less keen. 3. plain-spoken; outspoken. *adj., v. 4.*

blur (blėr), 1. make confused in form or outline. Mist blurred the hills. 2. dim. Tears blurred my sight. 3. blurred condition; dimness. 4. smear. He blurred the page with ink in two places. 5. a blot or stain. *v., blurred, blurring, n. 12.*

blurt (blėrt), say suddenly or without thinking. In his anger he blurted out the secret. *v. 16.*

blush (blush), 1. reddening of the skin caused by shame, confusion, or excitement. 2. become red from excitement, shame, or confusion. She was so shy that she blushed every time she was spoken to. 3. rosy color. 4. become or be red or rosy. 5. **At first blush** means at first thought or at first look. *n., v. 3.*

blus ter (blus′tər), 1. storm noisily. The wind blustered around the house. 2. boisterous blowing. 3. talk with noise and violence. Uncle John was very excited and angry, and blustered for a while. 4. noisy, boastful talk. *v., n. 10.*

blus ter y (blus′tər i), blustering. *adj.*

Boa for the neck

bo a (bō′ə), 1. a very large snake that is not poisonous. It kills prey by squeezing it. 2. long wrap for the neck, made of fur or feathers. *n. 19.*

boa constrictor, a very large snake that kills its prey by squeezing it.

boar (bōr), 1. a male pig or hog. 2. a wild pig or hog. See the picture. *n. 7.*

Wild boar (2½ ft. tall at the shoulder)

board (bōrd), 1. a broad, thin piece of wood. Boards are used much in building. 2. cover with boards. 3. flat piece of wood used for one special purpose; as, an ironing board. 4. table to serve food on. 5. food served on a table. 6. meals provided for pay. Mrs. Jones gives good board. 7. give food for pay. 8. get food for pay. 9. council; group of persons managing something; as, a board of health, a school board. 10. get on (a ship, train, etc.). 11. **On board** means on a ship or train. 12. **The boards** sometimes means the stage of a theater. *n., v. 1.*

board er (bōr′dər), person who pays for meals or for room and meals at another's house. *n. 11.*

board ing (bōr′ding), 1. eating away from home. A person gets tired of boarding. 2. providing room and meals; as, a boarding house, a boarding school. 3. structure made of boards. *n., adj.*

boast (bōst), 1. speak too well of oneself. 2. a statement in praise of oneself that goes far beyond the truth. 3. something that one is proud of. 4. be proud of. 5. have (something) to be proud of. Our town boasts a new school building. *v., n. 2.*

boast ful (bōst′fəl), 1. speaking too well about oneself. 2. fond of boasting. *adj. 12.*

boat (bōt), 1. a small, open vessel for water travel; as, a motorboat, a rowboat. 2. ship; as, a steamboat, a sailboat. 3. go in a boat. 4. put or carry in a boat. 5. a dish shaped somewhat like a boat for gravy or sauce. *n., v. 1.*

boat house (bōt′hous′), house or shed for boats. *n. 20.*

boat man (bōt′mən), 1. man who rows or sails boats for pay; man who rents boats. 2. man who works on a boat; man who takes care of boats. *n., pl. boatmen. 13.*

boat swain (bō′sən or bōt′swān′), an officer of a ship who has charge of the anchors, ropes, and rigging. *n. 16.*

bob (bob), 1. move up and down, or to and fro, with short, quick motions. The bird bobbed its head up and down, and its tail bobbed, too. 2. a short, quick motion up and down, or to and fro. 3. cut hair short. 4. a short haircut. 5. a weight on the end of a line. *v., bobbed, bobbing, n. 3.*

bob bin (bob′in), a reel or spool for holding thread, yarn, etc. Bobbins are used in spinning, weaving, machine sewing, lacemaking, etc. Wire is also wound on bobbins. *n. 18.*

Bobbin

bob by (bob′i), policeman. *n., pl. bobbies.* [*British slang*]

bob o link (bob′ə lingk), a common American songbird. See the picture. *n. 10.*

Bobolink (7 in. long)

bob stay (bob′stā′), a rope or chain to hold a bowsprit down. See the picture under **bowsprit.** *n.*

bob tail (bob′tāl′), 1. short tail; tail cut short. 2. animal having a bobtail. *n. 19.*

bob white (bob′hwīt′), the common American quail. The name bobwhite is given in imitation of the sound it makes. *n. 20.*

bode[1] (bōd), 1. be a sign of. The crow's cry bodes rain. 2. **Bodes well** means looks well; is a good sign; promises well. *v. 10.*

bode[2] (bōd). See **bide.** *pt. of bide.*

bod ice (bod′is), close-fitting waist of a woman's dress. *n. 14.*

bod i less (bod′i lis), without a body. *adj. 19.*

bod i ly (bod′i li), 1. of the body; in the body; as, bodily pain. 2. in person. The man whom we thought dead walked bodily into the room. 3. as one group; entirely; as a whole. The audience rose bodily. *adj., adv. 6.*

bod kin (bod′kin), 1. a large, blunt needle. 2. long hairpin. *n. 16.*

bod y (bod′i), 1. the whole material part of a man or animal. This boy has a strong, healthy body. 2. the main part of anything. 3. group of persons or things. A large body of children sang at the church. 4. mass. A lake is a body of water. The moon, the sun, and the stars are heavenly bodies. 5. person. *Used in common talk.* 6. substance. *n., pl. bodies. 1.*

bod y guard (bod′i gärd′), man or men who guard a person. A king usually has a bodyguard. *n. 19.*

Boer (bōr), a Dutch farmer in South Africa. *n. 18.*

bog (bog), 1. piece of wet, soft, spongy ground; a marsh or swamp. 2. **Be bogged** or **get bogged** means sink in or get stuck so that one cannot get out without help. *n., v., bogged, bogging. 5.*

bo gey (bō′gi), bogy. *n., pl. bogeys.*

bog gy (bog′i), swampy; like a bog. Very wet muddy ground is boggy. *adj., boggier, boggiest. 19.*

bo gus (bō′gəs), counterfeit; sham. *adj. 19.*

bo gy (bō′gi), 1. goblin; evil spirit. 2. thing or person that is feared. Arithmetic is a bogy to some children. *n., pl. bogies.*

Bo he mi a (bō hē′mi ə), 1. a district of Czecho-Slovakia, now under German control. 2. an unconventional, carefree place or sort of existence. *n. 8.*

Bo he mi an (bō hē′mi ən), 1. of Bohemia, its people, or their language. 2. a native or inhabitant of Bohemia. 3. the language of Bohemia. 4. free and easy; unconventional. 5. a gypsy. *adj., n.*

boil[1] (boil), 1. bubble up and give off steam. Water boils when heated. Liquids boil when they bubble up and turn to steam or vapor through the action of heat. 2. bring anything to the heat at which it bubbles up. 3. cook by boiling. 4. be excited; be stirred up. He boiled with anger. 5. boiling condition. *v., n. 2.*

boil[2] (boil), a red, painful swelling on the body, having a hard core with pus around it. Boils are caused by infection. *n.*

boil er (boil′ər), 1. container for heating liquids. 2. tank for making steam to heat buildings or drive engines. 3. tank for holding hot water. *n. 6.*

Boi se (boi′zi), the capital of Idaho. *n.*

bois ter ous (bois′tər əs), 1. violent; rough; as, a boisterous wind, a boisterous child. 2. noisily cheerful. *adj. 6.*

bold (bōld), 1. without fear. The bold boy stood in front of his mother, ready to protect her from danger. 2. too free in manners. The bold little boy made faces at us as we passed. 3. vigorous; free; clear. The bold outline of the mountain appeared ahead of us. 4. steep; abrupt. Bold cliffs overlooked the sea. *adj. 2.*

bold ness (bōld′nis), 1. being bold. 2. rudeness. 3. vigor; freedom; clearness. *n. 6.*

bole (bōl), the trunk of a tree. *n. 16.*

Bo liv i a (bō liv′i ə), a country in western South America. *n. 14.*

boll (bōl), the pod of cotton or flax. Seeds grow in it. *n. 18.*

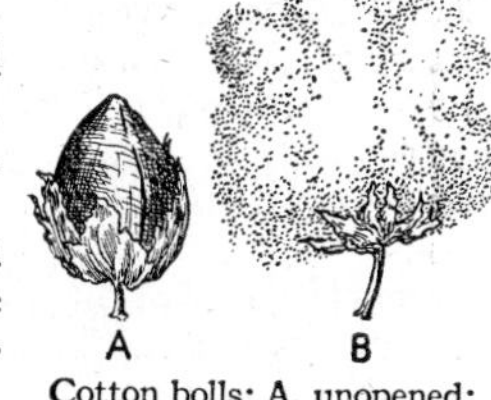

Cotton bolls: A, unopened; B, opened.

boll weevil, a kind of beetle that attacks cotton bolls.

Bo lo gna (bō lō′nyä), a city in northern Italy. *n. 14.*

bo lo gna (bə lō′nyə), large sausage made of beef, veal, and pork. *n.*

Bol she vik or **bol she vik** (bol′shə vik), 1. member of a radical party in Russia which came into power in 1917. 2. any extreme radical. *n., pl. Bolsheviks, Bolsheviki* (-vē′ki). *18.*

Bol she vism or **bol she vism** (bol′shə vizm), doctrines and practices of the Bolsheviks; extreme radicalism. *n. 18.*

bol ster (bōl′stər), 1. a long pillow for a bed. 2. cushion or pad. 3. To **bolster up** means to support; prop; keep from falling. *n., v. 10.*

bolt[1] (bōlt), 1. a strong pin of metal or wood with a head at one end and a screw thread for a nut at the other. Bolts are used to fasten things together or to hold something in place. 2. a sliding fastening for a door; the sliding piece in a lock. 3. fasten with a bolt. 4. a short arrow with a thick head. Bolts were shot from crossbows. 5. discharge of lightning. It came like a bolt from the sky. 6. sudden start; running away. 7. dash off; run away. The horse bolted. 8. break away from one's party or candidates. 9. a roll of cloth or wallpaper. 10. swallow without chewing. A dog bolts his food. 11. **Bolt upright** means stiff and straight. *n., v., adv. 3.*

Bolt with nut screwed on

Door bolt

bolt[2] (bōlt), sift through a cloth or sieve. *v.*

bomb (bom), 1. a hollow iron ball filled with gunpowder or some other explosive. A bomb is exploded by a fuse or by the force with which it strikes. 2. hurl bombs at; drop bombs on. 3. thing resembling a bomb. *n., v. 9.*

bom bard (bom bärd′), 1. attack with heavy fire of shot and shell from big guns. 2. keep attacking vigorously. She bombarded me with many questions. *v. 12.*

bom bard ment (bom bärd′mənt), an attack with heavy fire of shot and shell or with bombs. *n. 12.*

bom bast (bom′bast), high-sounding language. A little truth is better than much bombast. *n.*

bom bas tic (bom bas′tik), high-sounding; using many fine words with little thought. The politician spoke in a bombastic way of all that he would do if elected. *adj.*

Bom bay (bom bā′), large seaport in western India. *n.*

bomb er (bom′ər), airplane used for dropping bombs on the enemy. *n.*

bomb proof (bom′prüf′), strong enough to be safe from bombs and shells. *adj.*

bomb shell (bom′shel′), bomb. *n. 20.*

bo na fi de (bō′nə fī′di), in good faith; without make-believe or fraud; as, a bona fide offer.

bo nan za (bō nan′zə), 1. a rich mass of ore in a mine. 2. any rich source of profit. Mr. Smith struck a bonanza when he bought that farm, for oil has been found on it. *n. 18.*

Bo na parte (bō′nə pärt). Napoleon Bonaparte (1769-1821) was the greatest general and emperor of France. *n. 20.*

bon bon (bon′bon′), piece of candy, usually soft and often having a fancy shape. *n. 9.*

bond[1] (bond), 1. anything that ties, binds, or unites; as, a bond of affection between sisters. 2. a written agreement by which a person says he will pay a certain sum of money if he does not perform certain duties properly. 3. a certificate issued by governments or private companies which promises to pay back with interest the money borrowed from the person who owns the certificate. 4. a way of arranging bricks, stones, or boards in building. 5. bind together. 6. issue bonds on; mortgage. *n., v. 3.*

bond[2] (bond), captive; not free. *adj.* [*Old use*]

bond age (bon′dij), being held against one's own wish under the control or influence of some person or thing. *n. 6.*

bond ed (bon′did), 1. secured by bonds. 2. placed in charge of a government, under a bond. A **bonded warehouse** is a warehouse to hold bonded goods. *adj.*

bond man (bond′mən), 1. slave. 2. in the Middle Ages, a person who belonged with the land and was sold with it. *n., pl. bondmen. 9.*

bonds man (bondz′mən), 1. person who becomes responsible for another by giving a bond. 2. slave. 3. serf. *n., pl. bondsmen.*

bond wom an (bond′wu̇m′ən), woman slave. *n., pl. bondwomen. 19.*

bone (bōn), 1. the hard substance forming the framework of the body of a person or animal. 2. piece of this; as, the bones of the hand, a beef bone for soup. 3. something like a bone. Ivory and whalebone are sometimes called bone. Dice, corset steels, and two pieces of wood used to mark time are called bones. 4. take out the bones of; as, to bone fish. *n., v. 1.*

bon fire (bon′fīr′), a fire built outdoors. The boys built a bonfire at the picnic. *n. 12.*

bon net (bon′it), 1. a head covering with strings, worn by women and children. 2. a cap worn by men in Scotland. *n. 4.*

bon ny or **bon nie** (bon′i), 1. healthy-looking; fair to see; rosy and pretty. What a bonny baby! 2. gay or cheerful; excellent. *adj.* [*Scottish*] *10.*

bo nus (bō′nəs), something extra, given in addition to what is due. *n. 12.*

bon y (bōn′i), 1. of bone. 2. like bone. 3. full of bones. 4. having big bones that stick out. 5. very thin. *adj. 14.*

boo (bü), 1. a sound made to show dislike or contempt or to frighten. 2. make such a sound. *n., pl. boos, interj., v., booed, booing. 13.*

boo by (bü′bi), 1. fool; dunce. 2. a kind of sea bird. *n., pl. boobies. 15.*

book (bu̇k), 1. sheets of paper bound together. Nell read the first ten pages in her book. You can keep your accounts in this book. 2. enter in a book or list so as to engage service or get tickets. He had booked a passage from New York to London. 3. part of a book; as, the books of the Bible. 4. anything like a book. 5. **Keep books** sometimes means keep a record of business accounts. 6. **The Book** means the Bible. *n., v. 1.*

book case (bu̇k′kās′), piece of furniture with shelves for holding books. *n. 9.*

book ish (bu̇k′ish), 1. fond of reading or studying. 2. knowing books better than real life. *adj. 20.*

book keep er (bu̇k′kēp′ər), person who keeps the accounts of a business. *n. 14.*

book keep ing (bu̇k′kēp′ing), keeping the accounts of a business. *n. 17.*

book let (bu̇k′lit), little book; thin book. Booklets often have paper covers. *n. 10.*

book mark (bu̇k′märk′), something put between the pages of a book to mark a place. *n.*

book sell er (bu̇k′sel′ər), person who sells books. *n. 14.*

book worm (bu̇k′wėrm′), 1. small worm that gnaws books. 2. person who is very fond of reading. *n.*

boom[1] (büm), 1. a deep hollow sound like the roar of cannon or of big waves. 2. make a deep hollow sound like cannon or big waves. The big man's voice boomed out above the rest. 3. sudden activity and increase in business, prices, or values of property. Our town is having such a boom that it is likely to double its size in two years. 4. increase suddenly in activity; grow rapidly. 5. push or urge to rapid progress. *n., v. 8.*

boom[2] (büm), 1. a long pole or beam. A boom is used to extend the bottom of a sail or as the lifting pole of a derrick. 2. a chain or cable or line of timber that keeps logs from floating away. *n.*

boom er ang (büm′ər ang), 1. a bent piece of hard wood used as a weapon by the native Australians. It can be thrown so that it returns to the thrower. 2. something that recoils to harm the doer or user. *n. 20.*

Boomerangs

boon[1] (bün), 1. blessing. Those warm stockings were a boon to me in the cold weather. 2. something asked or granted as a favor. *Old use. n. 5.*

boon[2] (bün), pleasant; jolly. Tom and Bill were boon companions. *adj.*

boor (bür), a rude, bad-mannered person.

Boor used to mean a farm laborer or a peasant. *n. 18.*

boor ish (bür′ish), rude; having very bad manners. *adj. 17.*

boost (büst), 1. a push or shove that helps a person in rising or advancing. 2. to lift or push from below or behind. *n., v.* [*Used in common talk*] *13.*

boost er (büs′tər), one that boosts. *n.* [*Used in common talk*] *19.*

boot[1] (büt), 1. a leather or rubber covering for the foot and leg. 2. put boots on. The hunter was booted and spurred. 3. place for baggage in a coach. *n., v. 2.*

boot[2] (büt), 1. **It boots** means it benefits or it avails. It boots him little to complain. 2. **To boot** means in addition or besides. He gave me his knife for my book and a dime to boot. *v., n.*

boot black (büt′blak′), person who shines boots and shoes. *n.*

booth (büth), 1. place where goods are sold or shown at a fair, market, etc. 2. small, closed place for a telephone, moving-picture projector, etc. 3. small, closed place for voting at elections. *n. 5.*

boot leg ger (büt′leg′ər), man who sells liquor contrary to law. *n.*

boot less (büt′lis), useless. *adj. 13.*

boo ty (bü′ti), 1. things taken from the enemy in war. 2. plunder. The pirates got much booty from the raided town. 3. any valuable thing or things obtained; a prize. *n., pl. booties. 7.*

bo rax (bō′raks), substance used to destroy germs and to get dirt out of clothes. *n. 10.*

Bor deaux (bôr dō′), 1. a city in southwestern France. 2. a red or white wine made near Bordeaux. *n. 8.*

bor der (bôr′dər), 1. the side, edge, or boundary of anything, or the part near it. We pitched our tent on the border of the lake. 2. a strip on the edge of anything for strength or ornament. Her handkerchief has a blue border. 3. put a border on. 4. touch at the edge or boundary. *n., v. 2.*

bor der land (bôr′dər land′), 1. land forming a border. 2. uncertain district or space; as, the borderland between sleeping and waking. *n. 18.*

bore[1] (bōr), 1. make a hole in anything; hollow out evenly like a tube. 2. make a hole by pushing through or digging out. A mole has bored its way under my rosebed. 3. a hole made by a revolving tool. 4. the hollow space inside a pipe, a tube, or a gun barrel. He cleaned the bore of his gun. 5. the distance across the inside of a hole or a tube. The bore of this pipe is 2 inches. *v., n. 2.*

bore[2] (bōr), 1. weary by tiring talk or by being dull. This book bores me; so I shall not finish it. 2. a tiresome or dull person or thing. *v., n.*

bore[3] (bōr). See **bear**[1]. She bore her loss bravely. *pt. of bear*[1].

Bo re as (bō′ri əs), the north wind. *n. 15.*

bo ric (bō′rik), containing boron. **Boric acid** is a mild antiseptic. *adj. 11.*

born (bôrn), 1. brought forth. A baby born on Sunday is supposed to be lucky. 2. by birth; by nature; as, born rich, a born poet. *adj. 1.*

borne (bōrn). See **bear**[1]. I have borne it as long as I can. I have borne the load for two miles. She has borne three children. *pp. of bear*[1]. *3.*

Bor ne o (bôr′ni ō), large island in the East Indies. *n.*

bo ron (bō′ron), a nonmetallic element present in borax. *n.*

bor ough (bėr′ō), 1. an incorporated town in the United States, smaller than a city. 2. one of the five divisions of New York City. 3. a town in England with a municipal corporation and a charter. 4. a town in England that sends representatives to Parliament. *n. 6.*

bor row (bor′ō), 1. get (something) from another person with the understanding that it must be returned. If you lend your book to John, John has borrowed the book from you. 2. take; take and use as one's own. The word *canoe* was borrowed from the Indians. *v. 3.*

bosk y (bos′ki), 1. wooded. 2. shady. *adj. 20.*

Bos ni a (boz′ni ə), a district in western Yugoslavia. *n. 20.*

bos om (bu̇z′əm), 1. the upper front part of the human body; breast. 2. the part of a garment worn over the upper front of the body. She drew a handkerchief from her bosom. 3. the center or inmost part. He did not mention it even in the bosom of his family. 4. close; trusted. Very dear friends are bosom friends. *n., adj. 2.*

Bos po rus (bos′pə rəs), a strait near Istanbul. *n. 16.*

boss[1] (bôs), 1. person who hires workers or watches over and directs them; foreman; manager. 2. person who controls a political organization. 3. be the boss of; direct; control. Who is bossing this job? *n., v.* [*Used in common talk*] *6.*

boss[2] (bôs), 1. a raised ornament of silver, ivory, or other material on a flat surface; as, the boss on a shield. 2. decorate with ornamental nails, knobs, or studs. *n., v.*

Boss

Bos ton (bôs′tən), the capital of Massachusetts. *n. 3.*

bo tan ic (bə tan′ik), botanical. *adj.*

bo tan i cal (bə tan′i kəl), having to do with the study of plant life. *adj. 12.*

bot a nist (bot′ə nist), person who knows much about botany. *n. 12.*

bot a ny (bot′ə ni), the science of plants; the study of plants and plant life. *n. 10.*

botch (boch), 1. spoil by poor work. Careless Bill botched his model airplane. 2. poor piece of work. *v., n. 18.*

both (bōth), 1. the two. Both boys may go. 2. alike; equally. John is both ready and willing to help. *adj., pron., adv., conj. 1.*

both er (boᴛʜ′ər), 1. worry; fuss; trouble. 2. take trouble; concern oneself. Don't bother about my breakfast; I'll eat what is here. 3. person or thing that causes trouble or worry. A door that will not shut is a bother. *n., v. 4.*

both er some (boᴛʜ′ər səm), causing worry or fuss; troublesome. *adj.*

bot tle (bot′əl), 1. See the picture. We use bottles to hold milk, ink, etc. 2. He could drink a whole bottle of milk. 3. put into bottles; as, to bottle milk. **Bottle up** sometimes means hold in or control; as, to bottle up one's anger. *n., v. 2.*

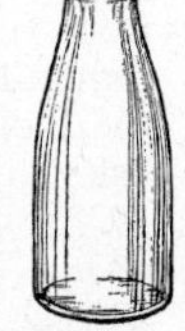

Bottle

bot tom (bot′əm), 1. the lowest part. These berries at the bottom of the basket are smaller. 2. part on which any thing rests. The bottom of that cup is wet. 3. the ground under water; as, the bottom of the sea. 4. low land along a river. 5. seat. This chair needs a new bottom. 6. basis; foundation; origin. We'll get to the bottom of the mystery. 7. the part of a ship under water; ship. 8. base; rest. 9. lowest; last. 10. underlying; fundamental. *n., v., adj. 1.*

bot tom less (bot′əm lis), 1. without a bottom. 2. very, very deep; as, sunk in the bottomless depths of the sea, a bottomless lake in the mountains. *adj. 12.*

bou doir (bü′dwär), a lady's private sitting room or dressing room. *n. 14.*

bough (bou), 1. one of the main branches of a tree. 2. branch cut from a tree. She held an apple bough in her hand. *n. 3.*

bought (bôt). See **buy**. We bought apples from the farmer. I have bought two new pencils. *pt. and pp. of buy. 2.*

bouil lon (bu̇l′yon), a clear, thin soup or broth. *n. 18.*

boul der (bōl′dər), large rock rounded or worn by the action of water and weather. *n. 11.*

Boulder Dam, large dam built on the Colorado River in southeastern Nevada.

boul e vard (bu̇l′ə värd), broad street. *n. 11.*

bounce (bouns), 1. bound like a ball. The baby likes to bounce up and down on the bed. 2. cause to bounce. 3. a bound; a spring. 4. boasting. *v., n. 7.*

bounc ing (boun′sing), 1. big; strong. 2. vigorous; healthy. *adj.*

bound[1] (bound), 1. put in covers; as, a bound book. 2. certain; sure. 3. See **bind.** The men bound their prisoners with ropes. *adj., pt. and pp. of bind. 2.*

bound[2] (bound), 1. spring back. The ball bounded from the wall. I caught the ball on the first bound. 2. leap; spring lightly along; jump. With one bound the deer went into the woods. *v., n.*

bound[3] (bound), 1. boundary; limiting line; limit; as, the farthest bounds of the earth. Keep your hopes within bounds. 2. form the boundary of; limit. The country was bounded by the sea on two sides and by the mountains on the other two. 3. name the boundaries of. *n., v.*

bound[4] (bound), going; on the way. Where are you bound? I am bound for home. *adj.*

bound a ry (boun′də ri), a limiting line; anything that limits; as, the boundary between Canada and the United States. *n., pl. boundaries. 3.*

bound en (boun′dən), required. *adj.*

bound less (bound′lis), not limited; as, the boundless ocean. *adj. 4.*

boun te ous (boun′ti əs), 1. generous. 2. given freely. 3. plentiful. *adj. 7.*

boun ti ful (boun′ti fəl), 1. generous; giving freely. 2. plentiful; abundant; more than enough. *adj. 10.*

boun ty (boun′ti), 1. whatever is given freely. 2. generosity. 3. reward; premium. The State government gives a bounty of ten cents for each skunk killed. *n., pl.* *boun-ties. 4.*

bou quet (bü kā′), 1. bunch of flowers. 2. fragrance. *n. 6.*

Bour bon (bür′bən or bėr′bən), 1. a former royal family of France and Spain. 2. an extreme conservative. 3. a kind of whiskey. *n. 11.*

bour geois (bür zhwä′), 1. person of the middle class. 2. like the middle class; ordinary. *n., adj. 12.*

bour geoi sie (bür zhwä zē′), the middle class; the people who are neither nobles nor manual workers. *n.*

bourn[1] or **bourne**[1] (bōrn), small stream. *n. 12.*

bourn[2] or **bourne**[2] (bōrn), 1. goal. 2. boundary; limit. *Old use.* *n.*

bout (bout), 1. trial of strength; contest. 2. length of time; spell. I have just had a long bout of house cleaning. *n. 8.*

bo vine (bō′vīn), 1. of an ox or cow; like an ox or cow. 2. slow; stupid. 3. stolid; without emotion. *adj.*

bow[1] (bou), 1. bend the head or body in greeting, respect, submission, etc. 2. a bending of head or body in this way. 3. express by a bow. She bowed her thanks. 4. bend. The man was bowed with old age. 5. submit; yield. We must bow to necessity. *v., n. 1.*

bow[2] (bō), 1. weapon for shooting arrows. A bow consists of a strip of elastic wood bent by a string. See the picture under **bowman.** 2. slender rod with horsehairs stretched on it for playing the violin. 3. curve; as, the bow of one's lips. 4. loop or knot; as, a bow of ribbon. *n.*

BOW

bow[3] (bou), the forward part of a ship, boat, or airplane. *n.*

bow els (bou′əlz), 1. the tube in the body into which food passes from the stomach; the intestines. 2. the inner part of anything. Miners dig for coal in the bowels of the earth. *n. pl. 4.*

bow er (bou′ər), 1. shelter of leafy branches. 2. arbor. 3. bedroom. *Used in poetry.* *n. 3.*

bow er y (bou′ər i), like a bower; shady. *adj. 18.*

bow ie knife (bō′i nīf′), a long hunting knife carried in a sheath. See the picture just below.

Bowie knife and its sheath

bowl[1] (bōl), 1. a hollow, rounded dish. 2. amount that a bowl can hold. 3. the hollow, rounded part of anything. The bowl of a pipe holds the tobacco. *n. 2.*

bowl[2] (bōl), 1. a wooden ball used in games. 2. **Bowls** is a game played with wooden balls and wooden bottle-shaped pins on grass or in a special place indoors. 3. play bowls. 4. roll or move along rapidly and smoothly. Our car bowled merrily along on that good road. 5. throw (the ball) a certain way in the game of cricket. *n., v.*

bowl der (bōl′dər), boulder. *n. 13.*

bow leg ged (bō′leg′id), having the legs curved outward. *adj.*

bowl ing (bōl′ing), 1. game of bowls; ninepins or tenpins. 2. playing the game of bowls. *n.*

bow man (bō′mən), archer; soldier armed with bow and arrows. *n., pl.* *bowmen. 16.*

Bowman

bow shot (bō′shot′), distance that a bow will shoot an arrow. *n. 19.*

bow sprit (bou′sprit), a pole or spar projecting forward from the bow of a ship. Ropes from it help to steady sails and masts. *n. 17.*

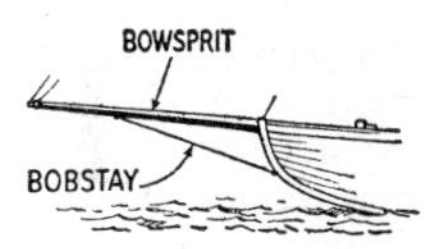

bow string (bō′string′), the string of a bow. *n. 15.*

box[1] (boks), 1. container made of wood, metal, or paper to pack or put things in. 2. the amount that a box can hold. Strawberries cost 20 cents a box. 3. pack in a box; put into a box. 4. driver's seat on a coach. 5. a small boxlike space with chairs in a theater. 6. a small shelter; as, a box for a sentry. *n., v. 1.*

box[2] (boks), 1. a blow with the open hand. A box on the ear hurts. 2. to fight with the fists. *n., v.*

box[3] (boks), a shrub or small tree which stays green all winter and is much used in gardens. *n.*

box er (bok′sər), man who fights with fists in padded gloves, according to special rules. Boxers fight for fun, for exercise, or to provide a show for others. *n. 13.*

box ing (bok′sing), fighting with fists. *n.*

box wood (boks′wu̇d′), 1. shrub or small tree that stays green all winter, much used for hedges. 2. its hard, tough wood. *n. 20.*

boy (boi), 1. male child from birth to about eighteen. 2. male servant. *n. 1.*

boy cott (boi′kot), 1. combine against and have nothing to do with. If people are boycotting a man, they will not speak to him, or buy from or sell to him, and will try to keep others from doing so. 2. refuse to buy or use. 3. a boycotting. *v., n. 16.*

boy hood (boi′hu̇d), 1. the time when one is a boy. 2. boys; as, the boyhood of the nation. *n. 7.*

boy ish (boi′ish), 1. of a boy. 2. like a boy. 3. like a boy's. 4. fit for a boy. *adj. 12.*

Boy Scouts, organization for boys to develop manliness and usefulness to others.

brace (brās), 1. thing that holds parts together or in place. An iron rod or a timber used to strengthen a building, a tight bandage for the wrist, and an iron frame to hold the ankle straight are all braces. 2. give strength or firmness to; support. 3. a pair; a couple. 4. a handle for a tool used in boring. 5. either of these signs { }, used to enclose words, figures, staves in music, etc. *n., v. 4.*

B, roof braces.

Brace and bit

brace let (brās′lit), band or chain worn for ornament around the wrist or arm. *n. 5.*

brac ing (brās′ing), giving strength and energy; refreshing. Mountain air is bracing. *adj. 17.*

brack en (brak′ən), a large fern. *n. 15.*

brack et (brak′it), 1. flat piece of stone, wood, or metal projecting from a wall as a support for a shelf, a statue, etc. 2. to support with a bracket. 3. a shelf supported by brackets. 4. either of these signs [ ], used to enclose words or figures. 5. enclose in brackets. 6. think of together; mention together; group. *n., v. 9.*

Bracket for a shelf

brack ish (brak′ish), slightly salty. A mixture of fresh water and sea water is brackish. *adj. 18.*

bract (brakt), small leaf at the base of a flower or flower stalk. *n. 19.*

brad (brad), small, thin nail. *n. 19.*

brae (brā), slope; hillside. *n.* [*Scottish*] *17.*

brag (brag), 1. boast. 2. boasting talk. *n., v., bragged, bragging. 8.*

brag gart (brag′ərt), 1. boaster. 2. boastful. *n., adj. 14.*

Brah ma (brä′mə), Hindu god of creation. *n. 19.*

Brah man or **Brah min** (brä′mən), member of the priestly caste, the highest caste or class in India. *n. 18.*

Brahms (brämz), German composer of music (1833-1897). *n.*

braid (brād), 1. a band formed by weaving together three or more strands of hair, ribbon, straw, etc. 2. to weave or twine (three or more strands of hair, ribbon, straw, etc.) together. 3. a narrow band of fabric used to trim or bind clothing. 4. trim or bind with braid. *n., v. 4.*

brain (brān), 1. the mass of nerve tissue enclosed in the skull or head of persons and animals. The brain is used in feeling and thinking. 2. dash the brains out of. 3. **Beat one's brains** means try hard to think of something. *n., v. 3.*

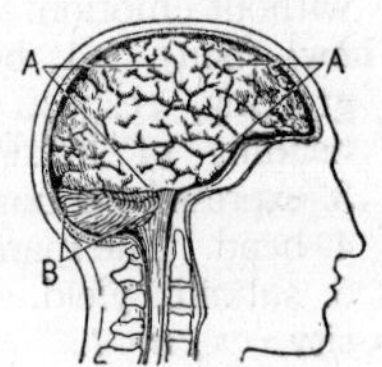

Human brain: A, cerebrum; B, cerebellum.

brain less (brān′lis), 1. without a brain. 2. stupid. *adj. 18.*

braise (brāz), cook (meat) long and slowly in a covered pan. *v.*

brake[1] (brāk), 1. anything used to check by pressing or scraping or by rubbing against. 2. slow up or stop by using a brake. *n., v. 3.*

brake[2] (brāk), thick growth of bushes. *n.*

brake[3] (brāk), any large fern. *n.*

brake man (brāk′mən), man who works brakes or helps the conductor of a railroad train. *n., pl. brakemen.*

bram ble (bram′bəl), a shrub with slender, drooping branches covered with little thorns that prick. The blackberry and the raspberry are brambles. *n. 6.*

bran (bran), the broken covering of grains like wheat and rye, which is separated from the fine-ground part called flour. *n. 6.*

branch (branch), 1. part of a tree that grows out from the trunk; any large, woody part of a tree above the ground except the trunk. A very small branch is called a twig. 2. a division; as, a branch of a river, a branch of a family, a branch of a library. Arithmetic is a branch of learning. 3. put out branches; spread in branches. 4. divide. *n., v. 1.*

brand (brand), 1. piece of wood that is burning or partly burned. 2. a mark made on the skin by a hot iron. Cattle and horses on big ranches are marked with brands to show who owns them. 3. an iron stamp for burning a mark. 4. to mark by burning with a hot iron. 5. a mark of disgrace. 6. set a mark of disgrace on. 7. a certain kind. Do you like this brand of coffee? 8. a trademark. 9. a sword. *Old and poetic use. n., v. 3.*

bran dish (bran′dish), shake or wave in a threatening manner. He brandished his sword. *v., n. 8.*

bran dy (bran′di), 1. a strong alcoholic liquor made from wine. 2. a similar alcoholic liquor made from fruit juice. *n., pl. brandies. 8.*

brant (brant), small, dark, wild goose. *n. 20.*

brass (bras), 1. a yellow metal made of two parts copper and one part zinc. 2. anything made of brass, such as band instruments, ornaments, and dishes. Mary polished all the brasses. *n. 2.*

bras sière (brə zēr′), woman's close-fitting underwaist or support for the bust. *n. 11.*

brat (brat), 1. child. 2. unpleasant child. *n. 14.*

bra va do (brə vä′dō), great show of boldness without much real courage; boastful defiance without much real desire to fight. *n., pl. bravadoes* or *bravados. 14.*

brave (brāv), 1. without fear; having courage; showing courage. 2. brave person. 3. meet without fear. Soldiers brave much danger. 4. dare; defy. He braved the king's anger. 5. a North American Indian warrior. 6. making a fine appearance. *adj., n., v. 1.*

brav er y (brāv′ər i), 1. courage; being brave. 2. fine appearance; finery. Helen came to the party in all the bravery of her new dress and pink ribbons. *n. 5.*

bra vo (brä′vō), 1. Well done! Fine! Excellent! 2. a cry of "Bravo!" *interj., n., pl. bravos. 16.*

brawl (brôl), 1. noisy quarrel. 2. quarrel noisily. *n., v. 6.*

brawn (brôn), 1. muscle; firm strong muscles. 2. muscular strength. Football requires brain as well as brawn. *n. 11.*

brawn y (brôn′i), strong; muscular. *adj., brawnier, brawniest. 14.*

bray (brā), 1. the loud harsh cry or noise of a donkey. 2. a noise like it. 3. make a loud harsh cry or noise. *n., v. 9.*

bra zen (brā′zən), 1. made of brass. 2. like brass in sound, color, or strength. 3. shameless; having no shame. 4. **Brazen a thing out** means act as if one did not feel ashamed of it. *adj., v. 6.*

bra zier (brā′zhər), pan for holding burning charcoal. In some countries, braziers are used to heat rooms. *n. 18.*

Bra zil (brə zil′), the largest country in South America. *n. 6.*

breach (brēch), 1. an opening made by breaking down something solid; gap. There is a breach in the hedge where I ran into it with my bicycle. 2. break through; make an opening in. The enemy's fierce attack finally breached the wall. 3. breaking or neglect. For me to go away today would be a breach of duty. 4. breaking of friendly relations; quarrel. There never was a breach between the two friends. *n., v. 6.*

bread (bred). We eat bread and butter. Bread is made of flour or meal. Bread sometimes means food in general. *n. 1.*

bread fruit (bred′früt′), a large, round, starchy fruit grown in the islands of the Pacific Ocean. It is baked and eaten like bread. *n.*

bread stuff (bred′stuf′), 1. grain, flour, or meal for making bread. 2. bread. *n.*

breadth (bredth), how broad a thing is; distance across; width. *n. 3.*

break (brāk), 1. The plate broke into pieces when it fell on the floor. 2. May has broken her doll. 3. fail to keep; act against. He never breaks a promise. People who break the law are punished. 4. force a way. The man broke loose from prison. A thief broke into the house. 5. dig or plow (the ground). 6. stop; put an end to; as, to break one's fast, to break off relations with a friend. 7. lessen the force of. Someone must break the news of the boy's accident to his mother. Trees break the force of the wind. 8. to tame; train to obey; as, to break a colt, to break a person's spirit. 9. come suddenly. War broke out. The storm broke within ten minutes. 10. change suddenly. 11. fail; become weak; give way. The dog's heart broke when his master died. 12. go beyond. The speed of the new train has broken all records. 13. a breaking. 14. broken place. 15. interruption. 16. Some special meanings are:

break away, 1. start before the signal. 2. go suddenly. 3. change suddenly.

break down, 1. have an accident; fail to work. 2. collapse; become weak; lose one's health. 3. begin to cry.

break in, 1. train; prepare for work or use. 2. enter by force. 3. interrupt.

break off, 1. stop suddenly. 2. stop being friends.

break out, 1. start; begin. 2. have pimples, rashes, etc., on the skin.

break up, 1. scatter. 2. stop; put an end to. 3. upset; disturb greatly. *Used in common talk.*

break with, stop being friends with.

v., broke, broken, breaking, n. 1.

break age (brāk′ij), 1. breaking; break. 2. damage or loss caused by breaking. 3. allowance made for such damage or loss. *n.*

break down (brāk′doun′), 1. failure to work. 2. collapse; weakness; loss of health; as, a nervous breakdown. *n. 14.*

break er (brāk′ər), 1. a wave which breaks into foam on the beach or on rocks. 2. person or thing that breaks. *n. 7.*

Breaker

break fast (brek′fəst), 1. the first meal of the day. 2. eat breakfast. *n., v. 1.*

break neck (brāk′nek′), likely to cause a broken neck; very dangerous. The car traveled at breakneck speed. *adj.*

break wa ter (brāk′wô′tər), a wall or barrier to break the force of waves. *n. 12.*

Breakwater

bream (brēm), any of several kinds of fish. *n. 20.*

breast (brest), 1. the upper front part of the body between the neck and the waist; the chest. 2. the heart or feelings. Pity tore his breast. **Make a clean breast of** means confess all. 3. face or oppose; struggle with. 4. a gland that gives milk. *n., v. 2.*

breast bone (brest′bōn′), thin, flat bone in the front of the chest to which the ribs are attached. *n.*

breast plate (brest′plāt′), piece of armor for the breast. *n. 12.*

Breastplate

breast work (brest′wėrk′), a low, hastily built wall for defense. *n. 17.*

breath (breth), 1. air drawn into and forced out of the lungs. 2. ability to breathe easily. Running fast makes a person lose his breath. 3. slight movement in the air. 4. **Below** or **under one's breath** means in a whisper. *n. 2.*

breathe (brēTH), 1. draw air into the lungs and force it out. 2. stop to take breath or rest after hard work or exercise. 3. whisper. Mother breathes words of love. *v. 2.*

breath less (breth′lis), 1. out of breath. Running upstairs very fast makes you breathless. 2. unable to breathe because of fear, interest, or excitement. The beauty of the scenery left her breathless. 3. without breath; dead. *adj. 7.*

bred (bred). See **breed.** He bred livestock for market. Our parents have bred us to follow in their footsteps. *pt. and pp. of breed. 4.*

breech (brēch), 1. the lower part of the back. 2. the back part of a gun or cannon. 3. clothe with breeches. *n., v. 18.*

breech es (brich′iz), short trousers fastened below the knee. *n. pl. 6.*

breed (brēd), 1. produce young. Rabbits breed rapidly. 2. raise. This farmer breeds cattle and hogs for market. 3. produce; be the cause of. Careless driving breeds accidents. 4. bring up; train. 5. race; stock. Jerseys and Guernseys are breeds of cattle. *v., bred, breeding, n. 3.*

breed er (brēd′ər), person that breeds; as, a cattle breeder, a dog breeder. *n. 10.*

breed ing (brēd′ing), 1. producing animals, especially to get improved kinds. 2. the result of training; behavior; manners. His good breeding showed in everything he did. *n. 17.*

breeze (brēz), a stirring of air; light wind. *n. 3.*

breez y (brēz′i), 1. having many breezes; with light winds blowing. 2. brisk; lively; jolly. We like his breezy, joking manner. *adj., breezier, breeziest. 11.*

Bre men (brā′mən), a city in northwestern Germany. *n. 9.*

breth ren (breтн′rin), brothers; fellow members of a church or society. *n. pl. 4.*

Bret on (bret′ən), 1. a native of Brittany. 2. the language of Brittany. 3. having to do with Brittany, its people, or their language. *n., adj. 14.*

bre vi ar y (brē′vi är′i), a book of prescribed prayers to be said daily by certain clergymen of the Roman Catholic Church. *n., pl. breviaries. 16.*

brev i ty (brev′i ti), shortness. *n. 10.*

brew (brü), 1. make (beer, ale, etc.) by soaking, boiling, and fermenting. 2. make by boiling, mixing, etc.; as, to brew tea. 3. bring about; plan; plot. Those boys are brewing some mischief. 4. be forming; gather. Dark clouds show that a storm is brewing. 5. the thing brewed. *v., n. 6.*

brew er (brü′ər), person who makes beer or ale. *n. 14.*

brew er y (brü′ər i), place where beer or ale is made. *n., pl. breweries. 14.*

bri ar[1] (brī′ər), a thorny or prickly plant or bush, especially the wild rose. *n. 4.* Also spelled **brier.**

bri ar[2] (brī′ər), a tree growing in southern Europe. Its root is used in making tobacco pipes. *n.* Also spelled **brier.**

bribe (brīb), 1. anything given or offered to get someone to do something he thinks it is wrong to do. The thief offered the policeman a bribe to let him go. 2. reward for doing something that a person does not want to do. A child should not need a bribe to obey his parents. 3. offer a bribe to; give a bribe. *n., v. 5.*

brib er y (brīb′ər i), 1. giving bribes. 2. taking bribes. *n., pl. briberies. 11.*

bric-a-brac (brik′ə brak′), interesting or curious knickknacks, used as decorations; small ornaments, such as vases, old china, or small statues. *n.*

brick (brik), 1. block of clay baked by sun or fire. Bricks are used to build houses and pave streets. 2. bricks; material bricks are made of. 3. anything shaped like a brick. Ice cream is often sold in bricks. 4. cover with bricks; build or pave with bricks. *n., v. 2.*

brick bat (brik′bat′), piece of broken brick. *n.*

brick lay er (brik′lā′ər), man who builds walls, chimneys, etc., with bricks. *n. 13.*

brick work (brik′wėrk′), work made of bricks. *n. 18.*

brid al (brīd′əl), 1. of a bride or a wedding. 2. wedding. *adj., n. 6.*

bride (brīd), woman just married or about to be married. *n. 2.*

bride groom (brīd′grüm′), man just married or about to be married. *n. 6.*

brides maid (brīdz′mād′), a young unmarried woman who attends the bride at a wedding. *n. 18.*

bridge (brij), 1. something built that carries a road, railroad, or path across a river, road, or the like. 2. make (a way) over a river or anything that hinders; make or form a bridge over. 3. the platform above the deck of a ship for the officer in command. 4. the upper bony part of the nose. 5. a mounting for false teeth fastened to real teeth nearby. 6. the movable piece over which strings of a violin, etc., are stretched. *n., v. 1.*

Bridge

bridge head (brij′hed′), a defense protecting the end of a bridge toward the enemy. *n.*

Bridge port (brij′pōrt), a city in southwestern Connecticut. *n.*

bri dle (brī′dəl), 1. the head part of a horse's harness, used to hold back and control a horse. See the picture. 2. put a bridle on. 3. anything that holds back or controls. 4. hold back; check; bring under control. 5. hold the head up high with the chin drawn back. *n., v 3.*

Bridle

brief (brēf), 1. short. 2. short statement. *adj., n. 2.*

brief case, flat container for carrying loose papers, books, drawings, etc.

bri er[1] (brī′ər), a thorny or prickly plant or bush, especially the wild rose. *n. 12.* Also spelled **briar.**

bri er[2] (brī′ər), a tree growing in southern Europe. Its root is used in making tobacco pipes. *n.* Also spelled **briar.**

brig (brig), 1. a square-rigged ship with two masts. 2. prison on a warship. *n. 16.*

Brig

bri gade (bri gād′), 1. part of an army, usually made up of two or more regiments. 2. any group of persons organized for some purpose; as, a fire brigade. *n. 11.*

brig a dier (brig′ə dēr′), officer commanding a brigade; army officer next in rank above a colonel. *n. 12.*

brigadier general, brigadier. *pl. brigadier generals.*

brig and (brig′ənd), robber; a robber who lives in the country, not in the city, and robs travelers especially. *n. 14.*

brig an tine (brig′ən tēn), a brig which has a fore-and-aft mainsail. *n. 18.*

bright (brīt), 1. Sunshine is bright. A new tin pan is bright. 2. The fire shines bright. 3. A bright girl learns quickly. 4. Everybody was bright and gay at the party. 5. Dandelions are bright yellow. *adj., adv. 1.*

bright en (brīt′ən), 1. make bright or brighter. 2. grow bright or brighter. 3. make happy or cheerful. *v. 4.*

bright ness (brīt′nis), being bright; shining quality; clearness; intelligence. *n. 5.*

bril liance (bril′yəns), great brightness; glitter; brilliant quality. *n. 14.*

bril lian cy (bril′yən si), brilliance. *n. 16.*

bril liant (bril′yənt), 1. sparkling; shining brightly; as, brilliant jewels, brilliant sunshine. 2. splendid; as, a brilliant party. 3. having great ability; as, a brilliant musician. 4. a diamond or other gem cut as shown in the picture. *adj., n. 4.*

Brilliant

brim (brim), 1. the edge of a cup or bowl; the edge of anything shaped like a cup or bowl. You have filled my glass to the brim. 2. fill to the brim; be full to the brim. 3. the projecting edge of a hat. *n., v., brimmed, brimming. 4.*

brim ful or **brim ful** (brim′fu̇l′), full to the brim; full to the very top. *adj. 11.*

brim stone (brim′stōn′), sulphur. *n. 9.*

brin dle (brin′dəl), 1. brindled. 2. brindled color. 3. brindled animal. *adj., n. 20.*

brin dled (brin′dəld), gray, tan, or tawny with darker streaks and spots. *adj.*

brine (brīn), 1. very salty water. Some pickles are kept in brine. 2. the sea. *n. 9.*

bring (bring), 1. come with (some thing or person) from another place. Bring me a clean plate and take the dirty one away. 2. cause to come. 3. influence; lead. He was brought to agree by our arguments. 4. Some special meanings are:

bring about, cause; cause to happen.

bring around, 1. restore to consciousness. 2. convince; persuade.

bring forth, 1. give birth to; bear. 2. reveal; show.

bring forward, 1. reveal; show. 2. carry over.

bring over, convince; persuade.

bring round, 1. restore to consciousness. 2. convince; persuade.

bring to, 1. restore to consciousness. 2. stop; check.

bring up, 1. care for in childhood. She brought up four children. 2. educate. He was well brought up. 3. suggest for action or discussion. Please bring your plan up at the meeting. 4. stop suddenly. *v., brought, bringing. 1.*

brink (bringk), 1. the edge at the top of a steep place. 2. the edge. **On the brink of** means very near. *n. 5.*

brin y (brīn′i), salty. *adj.*

brisk (brisk), quick and active; lively. *adj. 5.*

bris ket (bris′kit), meat from the breast of an animal. See the diagram under **beef.** *n. 16.*

brisk ness (brisk′nis), quickness; liveliness. *n. 20.*

bris tle (bris′əl), 1. one of the short, stiff, coarse hairs of hogs. Bristles are used to make brushes. 2. any short, stiff hair of an animal or plant. 3. stand up straight like bristles. The dog's hair bristled. 4. have one's hair stand up on end. The dog bristled. 5. show that one is aroused and ready to fight. 6. be thickly set. Our path bristled with difficulties. *n., v. 7.*

bris tly (bris′li), 1. rough with bristles. 2. like bristles. *adj.*

Bris tol (bris′təl), seaport in southwestern England. *n. 12.*

Brit ain (brit′ən), England, Scotland, and Wales; Great Britain. *n. 3.*

Bri tan ni a (bri tan′i ə), 1. Britain; Great Britain. 2. British Empire. *n. 18.*

Brit ish (brit′ish), 1. of Great Britain, the British Empire, or its people. 2. people of Great Britain or the British Empire. *adj., n. pl. 2.*

British Columbia, a province in western Canada, on the Pacific Ocean.

British Empire, the group of countries under British control.

Brit ish er (brit′ish ər), Englishman. *n.*

British Isles, Great Britain, Ireland, and the nearby islands.

Brit on (brit′ən), 1. native or inhabitant of Great Britain or the British Empire. 2. one of the Celtic people who lived in southern Britain long ago. *n. 6.*

Brit ta ny (brit′ə ni), a region in northwestern France. *n. 13.*

brit tle (brit′əl), very easily broken; breaking with a snap; apt to break. Thin glass and ice are brittle. *adj. 8.*

broach (brōch), 1. a tool to make and shape holes with. 2. open by making a hole. He broached a barrel of cider. 3. begin to talk about. *n., v. 10.*

broad (brôd), 1. wide; large across. Many cars can go on that broad road. 2. large; not limited or narrow; of wide range. Our minister has broad views and does not insist that everyone believe just as he does. 3. main; general. Give the broad outlines of what the speaker had to say. 4. clear; full; as, broad daylight. 5. plain; plain-spoken. 6. coarse; not refined. His jokes are too broad for nice people. *adj. 1.*

broad ax or **broad axe** (brôd′aks′), ax with a broad blade. *n., pl. broadaxes.*

broad cast (brôd′kast′), 1. send out by radio. 2. sending out by radio. 3. sent out by radio. 4. speech, music, etc., sent out by radio. 5. radio program. 6. scatter widely. 7. scattering far and wide. 8. scattered widely. 9. over a wide surface. *v., n., adj., adv. 10.*

broad cloth (brôd′klôth′), 1. a smooth-finished cotton cloth. 2. a fine woolen cloth with a smooth finish. *n. 12.*

broad en (brôd′ən), 1. make broad or broader. 2. become broad or broader. The river broadens at its mouth. *v. 13.*

broad-mind ed (brôd′mīn′did), tolerant; not prejudiced or bigoted. *adj.*

broad side (brôd′sīd′), 1. the whole side of a ship above the water line. 2. the discharge of all the guns on one side of a ship. 3. with the side turned. The ship drifted broadside to the wharf. 4. a large sheet of paper printed on one side only. Boys were giving out broadsides announcing the coming of the circus. *n., adv. 13.*

broad sword (brôd′sōrd′), sword with a broad, flat blade. *n. 18.*

Broad way (brôd′wā′), a main business street in New York City. Part of Broadway has many lights and theaters. *n. 6.*

bro cade (brō kād′), expensive cloth woven with raised designs on it; as, silk brocade, velvet brocade, or metal-cloth brocade. *n. 9.*

broc co li (brok′ə li), a variety of cauliflower with green stems and flower heads. See the picture just below. *n.*

Broccoli

bro gan (brō′gən), a coarse, strong shoe. *n.*

brogue[1] (brōg), 1. a coarse, strong shoe. 2. an ordinary shoe made for comfort and wear. *n. 20.*

brogue[2] (brōg), 1. Irish accent or pronunciation of English. 2. an accent or pronunciation peculiar to any dialect. *n.*

broi der (broi′dər), embroider. *v.* [*Old use*] *12.*

broil[1] (broil), 1. cook by holding near the fire. 2. make very hot. 3. be very hot. We broiled in the hot sun. *v. 7.*

broil[2] (broil), quarrel; fight; brawl. *n., v.*

broil er (broil′ər), 1. pan or rack for broiling. 2. young chicken for broiling. *n. 20.*

broke (brōk). See **break.** She broke her doll. *pt. and old pp. of break. 2.*

bro ken (brō′kən), 1. in pieces; violently separated into parts; as, a broken cup. 2. acted against; not kept; as, a broken promise. 3. not even; not regular. 4. imperfectly spoken. The French boy speaks broken English. 5. weakened in strength, spirit, etc.; tamed; crushed. His courage was broken by his failure. 6. See **break.** The window was broken by a ball. His sleep was broken by the noise of the party upstairs. *adj., pp. of break. 1.*

bro ken-heart ed (brō′kən här′tid), heart-broken; crushed by sorrow or grief. The broken-hearted soldiers of the defeated country wept when they read the peace terms. *adj.*

bro ker (brō′kər), person who buys and sells stocks, bonds, etc., for other people; agent. *n. 10.*

bro ker age (brō′kər ij), 1. business of a broker. 2. money charged by a broker for his services. *n. 18.*

bro mid (brō′mid), bromide. *n.*

bro mide (brō′mīd), 1. a drug used to reduce nervousness and cause sleep. 2. a compound of bromine. *n. 13.*

bro min (brō′min), bromine. *n.*

bro mine (brō′mēn), a nonmetallic element somewhat like chlorine and iodine. Bromine is a dark-brown liquid giving off a reddish vapor. *n.*

bron chi (brong′kī), the two large, main branches of the windpipe. See the picture just below. *n. pl.*

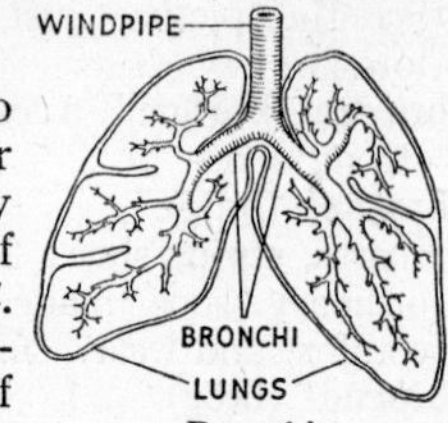

Bronchi

bron chi al (brong′ki-əl), having to do with the bronchi or with the many branching tubes of the bronchi. *adj. 14.*

bron chi tis (brong kī′-tis), inflammation of the lining of the bronchial tubes. A cough goes with it. *n. 12.*

bron co or **bron cho** (brong′kō), a pony of the western United States. Broncos are often wild or half tamed. *n., pl. broncos, bronchos. 17.*

bronze (bronz), 1. a brown alloy of copper with tin. 2. a similar alloy of copper with zinc or other metals. 3. a statue, medal, disk, etc., made of bronze. 4. made of bronze. 5. the color of bronze; yellowish brown; reddish brown. 6. make or become bronze in color. His skin is bronzed from the sun. *n., adj., v. 6.*

brooch (brōch or brüch), an ornamental pin having the point secured by a catch. *n. 8.*

Brooch

brood (brüd), 1. the young birds hatched at one time in the nest, or cared for together; as, a brood of chicks. 2. young who are cared for. 3. sit on. Hens and birds brood their eggs till the young hatch out. 4. think a long time about some one thing. *n., v. 4.*

brood er (brüd′ər), 1. closed place that can be heated, used in raising chicks, etc. 2. one that broods. *n. 18.*

brook[1] (brůk), small stream. *n. 1.*

brook[2] (brůk), put up with; endure; tolerate. We will not brook any more of your insults. *v.*

brook let (brůk′lit), little brook. *n. 12.*

Brook lyn (brůk′lin), a large city on Long Island, which is now a part of New York City. *n. 4.*

broom (brüm), 1. a brush with a long handle for sweeping floors. 2. a bush with slender branches, small leaves, and yellow flowers. *n. 3.*

broom stick (brüm′stik′), the long handle of a broom. *n. 15.*

broth (brôth), water in which meat has been boiled; soup made in this way. *n. 8.*

broth er (bruᴛʜ′ər), 1. A boy is brother to the other children of his parents. 2. close friend. 3. Members of the same church or club are often called brothers. *n., pl. brothers, brethren* (breᴛʜ′rin). *1.*

broth er hood (bruᴛʜ′ər hůd), 1. the bond between brothers; the feeling of brother for brother. 2. persons joined as brothers; an association of men with some common aim or characteristic. *n. 6.*

broth er-in-law (bruᴛʜ′ər in lô′), 1. the brother of one's husband or wife. 2. the husband of one's sister. *n., pl. brothers-in-law. 20.*

broth er ly (bruᴛʜ′ər li), 1. of a brother. 2. like a brother. 3. very friendly. He talked to me in a brotherly way. *adj. 6.*

brougham (brüm), closed carriage or automobile having an outside seat for the driver. *n. 18.*

Brougham

brought (brôt). See **bring.** He brought his gun yesterday. She was brought to school in a car. *pt. and pp. of bring. 1.*

brow (brou), 1. forehead. 2. arch of hair over the eye; eyebrow. He has heavy black brows over his eyes. 3. edge of a steep place; top of a slope. His house is on the brow of the hill. *n. 2.*

brow beat (brou′bēt′), frighten into doing something by overbearing looks or words; bully. *v., browbeat, browbeaten, browbeating. 18.*

brown (broun), 1. a dark color like that of toast, potato skins, or coffee. 2. having this color. Most Americans have brown hair. 3. make brown; become brown. *n., adj., v. 1.*

brown ie (broun′i), a good-natured, helpful elf or fairy. *n. 5.*

Brownies

Brown ing (broun′ing), Robert, a famous English poet (1812-1889). His wife, Elizabeth Barrett Browning, was also a famous poet (1806-1861). *n. 12.*

brown ish (broun′ish), somewhat brown. *adj. 20.*

brown stone (broun′stōn′), reddish-brown sandstone, used as a building material. *n.*

browse (brouz), 1. feed; graze. 2. read here and there in a book, library, etc. *v. 11.*

Bruce (brüs), Robert (1274-1329), a famous king of Scotland who defeated the English in 1314. *n. 12.*

bru in (brü′in), bear. *n. 11.*

bruise (brüz), 1. an injury to the body, caused by a fall or a blow which does not break the skin. The bruise on my arm turned black and blue. 2. an injury to the outside of a fruit, vegetable, plant, etc. 3. injure the outside of. 4. injure; hurt. His harsh words bruised her. 5. become bruised. Her flesh bruises easily. 6. pound; crush. *n., v. 4.*

bruit (brüt), 1. spread a report or rumor of. 2. report; rumor. *Old use. v., n. 16.*

bru nette or **bru net** (brü net′), 1. dark-skinned, dark-haired, and dark-eyed. 2. person having a dark skin, dark-brown or black hair, and brown or black eyes. Most Spanish women are brunettes; most Swedish and Norwegian women are blondes. *adj., n. 13.*

brunt (brunt), main force or violence; hardest part. *n. 11.*

brush[1] (brush), 1. A brush is made of bristles, hair, or wire, set in a stiff back or fastened to a handle. Brushes are used for scrubbing, cleaning, sweeping, and for putting on paint. 2. something like a brush. 3. clean, rub, paint, etc., with a brush; use a brush on. 4. a brushing; a rub with a brush. 5. remove; wipe away. The child brushed the tears from his eyes. 6. touch lightly in passing. 7. light touch in passing. 8. short, brisk fight or quarrel. 9. move quickly. *n., v. 2.*

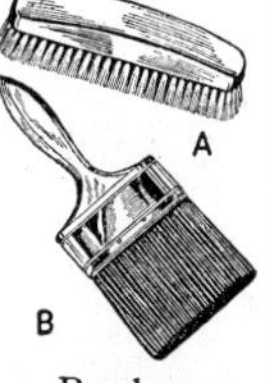

Brushes: A, clothesbrush; B, paintbrush.

brush[2] (brush), 1. shrubs, bushes, and small trees growing in the woods. 2. branches broken or cut off. *n.*

brush wood (brush′wůd′), 1. small trees or bushes growing rather thickly together. 2. branches broken or cut off. *n. 15.*

brusque (brusk), abrupt in manner or speech; blunt. *adj. 16.*

Brus sels (brus′əlz), the capital of Belgium. *n. 8.*

Brussels sprouts, 1. very small cabbages growing on a stalk. 2. the plant that bears them.

Brussels sprouts

bru tal (brü′təl), cruel; coarse and savage; like a brute. *adj. 6.*

bru tal i ty (brü tal′i ti), 1. savageness; brutal conduct. 2. a brutal act. *n., pl. brutalities. 12.*

brute (brüt), 1. an animal without power to reason. 2. like an animal. 3. a stupid or cruel person. 4. without feeling; cruel; coarse. *n., adj. 4.*

brut ish (brüt′ish), coarse, stupid; like an animal. *adj. 11.*

Bru tus (brü′təs), Marcus (85-42 B.C.), one of the men who killed Julius Caesar. *n. 9.*

Bry ant (brī′ənt), William Cullen, an American poet (1794-1878). *n. 20.*

bu., bushel; bushels. *6.*

bub ble (bub′əl), 1. A bubble is round and full of air or gas which is held in by the liquid around it. When water boils, it is full of bubbles which come to the top and break. 2. a round space filled with air. Sometimes there are bubbles in ice or in glass. 3. make sounds like water boiling; send up or rise in bubbles. Water bubbled up between the stones. 4. a plan or idea that looks bright and beautiful, but soon goes to pieces. *n., v. 3.*

bu bon ic (bū bon′ik), having inflammatory swelling of the lymphatic glands. The **bubonic plague** is a very dangerous contagious disease, with fever, chills, and swellings of the glands. *adj. 13.*

buc ca neer (buk′ə nēr′), pirate; sea robber. *n. 11.*

Bu chan an (bū kan′ən), James (1791-1868), the 15th president of the United States, from 1857 to 1861. *n.*

Bu cha rest (bü′kə rest′), capital of Rumania. *n.*

buck (buk), 1. male deer, goat, hare, or rabbit. 2. jump into the air with back curved and come down with the front legs stiff. His horse began to buck, but he managed to stay on. 3. throw by bucking. *n., v. 10.*

Bucking bronco

buck et (buk′it), 1. pail made of wood or metal. Buckets are used for carrying water, milk, coal, etc. 2. the amount that a bucket can hold. Pour on about four buckets of water. *n. 4.*

Bucket

buck eye (buk′ī′), a tree somewhat like the horse chestnut. *n.*

buck le (buk′əl), 1. a catch to hold together two loose ends of a belt, strap, or ribbon. 2. fasten together with a buckle. 3. bend; wrinkle. 4. **Buckle down to** means work hard at. *n., v. 6.*

buck ler (buk′lər), small, round shield. *n. 11.*

buck ram (buk′rəm), coarse cloth made stiff with glue or something like glue. *n. 18.*

buck saw (buk′sô′), a saw set in a light frame and held with both hands. *n. 20.*

buck shot (buk′shot′), large lead shot used for shooting deer, foxes, etc. *n.*

buck skin (buk′skin′), strong, soft leather, yellowish or grayish in color, made from the skins of deer or sheep. *n. 16.*

buck wheat (buk′hwēt′), 1. a plant with triangular seeds. The seeds of buckwheat are fed to horses and fowls, and ground into flour for pancakes. 2. the flour made from buckwheat. *n. 6.*

BRANCH
SEED
Buckwheat

bu col ic (bū kol′ik), 1. of shepherds; pastoral. 2. rustic; rural. 3. a poem about shepherds. *adj., n. 20.*

bud (bud), 1. the small beginning of a flower, leaf, or branch. 2. a flower partly opened. 3. put forth buds. 4. begin to grow. 5. graft a branch from one tree into another. *n., v., budded, budding. 2.*

Bu da pest (bü′də pest′), the capital of Hungary. *n.*

Bud dha (bůd′ə), a great religious teacher of Asia (563?-483? B.C.). *n. 18.*

Bud dhism (bůd′izm), a religion that originated long ago in northern India and spread widely over central and southern Asia. It urges self-control and right living. *n.*

Budding or grafting

Bud dhist (bůd′ist), 1. having to do with Buddha or Buddhism. 2. believer in Buddhism. *adj., n.*

budge (buj), move in the least. The stone was so heavy that the child could not budge it. *v. 10.*

budg et (buj′it), 1. an estimate of the amount of money that can be spent, and the amounts to be spent for various purposes, in a given time. Governments, schools, companies, and persons often make budgets. 2. make a plan for spending. 3. a stock or collection; as, a budget of news. *n., v. 8.*

Bue nos Ai res (bō′nəs ãr′ēz), a South American seaport city, the capital of Argentina. *14.*

buff (buf), 1. a strong, soft leather, dull-yellow in color, made from buffalo skin or oxhide. 2. made of buff. 3. dull yellow. 4. polish with a wheel covered with leather. *n., adj., v. 6.*

buf fa lo (buf′ə lō), 1. in America, the bison, a wild ox with a great, shaggy head and strong front legs. See the picture of **bison.** 2. any of several kinds of wild ox. *n., pl. buffaloes* or *buffalos* or *buffalo. 6.*

Buffalo of India (body 6 ft. long)

Buf fa lo (buf′ə lō), a city in western New York State, on Lake Erie. *n. 12.*

buff er[1] (buf′ər), 1. anything that softens the shock of a blow. Buffers are often placed at the ends of railway cars to bear the shock when the cars bump together. 2. A **buffer state** is a small country between two larger ones. *n., adj. 12.*

buff er[2] (buf′ər), 1. person who polishes. 2. thing for polishing, covered with leather. *n.*

buf fet[1] (buf′it), 1. a blow of the hand. 2. to strike with the hand. 3. a knock, stroke, or hurt. 4. to knock about, strike, or hurt. The waves buffeted him. He buffeted his way through the waves. *n., v. 5.*

buf fet[2] (bů fā′), 1. piece of dining-room furniture with a flat top, for holding dishes, silver, and table linen. 2. counter where food and drinks are served. *n.*

buf foon (bu fün′), clown; person who amuses people with tricks, pranks, and jokes. *n. 14.*

buf foon er y (bu fün′ər i), the tricks, pranks, and jokes of a clown; undignified or rude joking. *n., pl. buffooneries. 16.*

bug (bug), 1. a crawling insect. 2. any insect or insect-like animal. Ants, spiders, and flies are bugs. *n. 5.*

Bug (def. 1)

bug a boo (bug′ə bü), an object of fright, usually imaginary. The foolish nurse frightened the child with tales of witches, ghosts, and other bugaboos. *n., pl. bugaboos. 19.*

bug bear (bug′bãr′), something feared without reason; bugaboo. *n. 16.*

bug gy (bug′i), a light carriage with one seat. See the picture. *n., pl. buggies. 6.*

Buggy

bu gle (bū′gəl), 1. a musical instrument like a small trumpet, made of brass or copper. Bugles are used in the army and navy for sounding calls and orders, and in band music. 2. sound a bugle; sound on a bugle. *n., v. 4.*

Soldier blowing a bugle

bu gler (bū′glər), person who blows a bugle. *n.*

build (bild), 1. Men build houses and ships. Birds build nests. 2. An elephant has a heavy build. A giraffe has a slender build. *v., built* or (old) *builded, building, n. 1.*

build er (bil′dər), 1. person or animal that builds. 2. person whose business is building. *n. 4.*

build ing (bil′ding), 1. thing built. Barns, houses, sheds, factories, and hotels are all buildings. 2. act of one that builds. 3. art of making houses, stores, bridges, ships, etc. *n. 1.*

built (bilt). See **build.** The bird built a nest. It was built of twigs. *pt. and pp. of build. 1.*

bulb (bulb), 1. the round, underground bud or stem from which certain plants grow. Onions, tulips, and lilies grow from bulbs. 2. rounded, swelling part; as, an electric light bulb, the bulb of a thermometer. *n. 5.*

Lily bulb; bulb of thermometer; electric light bulb.

bulb ous (bul′bəs), 1. having bulbs; growing from bulbs. Daffodils are bulbous plants. 2. shaped like a bulb. The clown's mask had a big, red, bulbous nose. *adj.*

Bul gar i a (bul gãr′i ə), a country in southeastern Europe. *n. 14.*

Bul gar i an (bul gãr′i ən), 1. of or having to do with Bulgaria. 2. a native or inhabitant of Bulgaria. *adj., n.*

bulge (bulj), 1. swell outward. His pockets bulged with apples and candy. 2. outward swelling. There is a bulge on the end of this tent. *v., n. 10.*

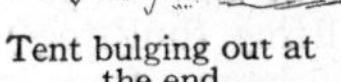
Tent bulging out at the end

bulk (bulk), 1. size; especially great size. 2. a large shape, person, or body. 3. The **bulk of** means the greater part of. The ocean forms the bulk of the earth's surface. 4. have size; be of importance. 5. mass; large mass. *n., v. 4.*

bulk head (bulk′hed′), one of the upright partitions dividing a ship into watertight compartments to prevent sinking. *n. 18.*

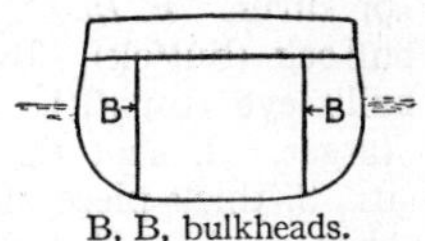

B, B, bulkheads.

bulk y (bul′ki), 1. large; taking up much space. 2. hard to handle. *adj., bulkier, bulkiest. 10.*

bull[1] (bu̇l), 1. the male of beef cattle. 2. the male of the whale, elephant, seal, and other large animals. 3. person who tries to raise prices in the stock market. *n. 3.*

bull[2] (bu̇l), a formal announcement or official order from the Pope. *n.*

bull[3] (bu̇l), an absurd and amusing mistake in language. *Example:* If you don't receive this letter, write and let me know. *n.*

bull dog (bu̇l′dôg′), 1. heavily built dog with a large head and short hair. Bulldogs are not large, but they are very muscular and courageous. 2. like that of a bulldog; as, bulldog courage, a bulldog grip. *n., adj. 17.*

Bulldog (13 to 17 in. tall)

bull doze (bu̇l′dōz′), bully; frighten by violence or threats. *v.* [*Used in common talk*]

bul let (bu̇l′it), shaped piece of lead or steel to be shot from a gun. *n. 5.*

bul le tin (bu̇l′ə tin), 1. a short statement of news. Newspapers print bulletins about a war, famine, the things the President does, and other events of public importance. Doctors issue bulletins on the progress of a sick person. 2. a magazine or newspaper appearing regularly; especially, one published by a club or society for its members. *n. 7.*

bull fight (bůl′fīt′), fight between men and a bull in an enclosed arena. It is a popular sport among Spanish people. *n.*

bull finch (bůl′finch′), a European songbird with handsome plumage and a short, stout bill. *n. 20.*

bull frog (bůl′frog′), a large frog that makes a loud, croaking noise. *n.*

Bullfrog (7 in. long)

bul lion (bůl′yən), lumps or bars of gold or silver. *n. 15.*

bull ock (bůl′ək), ox; steer. *n. 9.*

bull's-eye (bůlz′ī′), 1. the center of a target. 2. shot that hits it. 3. thick piece of glass shaped like a half-sphere in the deck or side of a ship to let in light. 4. small lantern with a lens shaped like a half-sphere to concentrate the light. *n.*

Bull's-eye lantern

bul ly (bůl′i), 1. person who teases, frightens, or injures others who are not as strong as he is. 2. frighten into doing something by noisy talk or threats. 3. very good; excellent. *Used in common talk. n., pl. bullies, v., bullied, bullying, adj. 8.*

bul rush (bůl′rush′), a tall, slender plant that grows in wet places. *n. 12.*

Bulwark for defense

bul wark (bůl′wərk), 1. person, thing, or idea that is a defense or a protection. 2. earthwork or other wall for defense against the enemy. See the picture just above. 3. breakwater for protection against the force of the waves. 4. a ship's side above the deck. *n. 7.*

Bulwark of a ship

bum (bum), 1. good-for-nothing person; drunken loafer. 2. to loaf. 3. to drink heavily. 4. a spree. 5. of poor quality; no good. *n., v., bummed, bumming, adj.* [*Slang*] *14.*

Bumblebee (about life size)

bum ble bee (bum′bəl bē′), a kind of large bee. *n. 13.*

bump (bump), 1. push, throw, or strike (against something fairly large or solid). The children all bumped against one another in their eagerness to be first. 2. move (along) with bumps. The cart bumped along the rough road. 3. hit or come against with heavy blows. 4. a heavy blow or knock. 5. a swelling caused by a bump. 6. a swelling. *v., n. 6.*

bump er (bump′ər), 1. thing that protects a car from bumps. 2. glass filled to the brim. 3. unusually large; as, a bumper crop of cotton. *Used in common talk. n., adj. 10.*

bump kin (bump′kin), awkward person from the country. *n. 19.*

bun (bun), bread or cake in small shapes. Buns are often slightly sweetened and contain spice, raisins, etc. *n. 7.*

bunch (bunch), 1. group of things of the same kind growing or fastened together, placed together, or thought of together; as, a bunch of grapes, a bunch of thieves. 2. come together in one place. 3. bring together and make into a bunch. *n., v. 3.*

bun dle (bun′dəl), 1. number of things tied together or wrapped together. 2. parcel; package. 3. tie together; make up into a bundle. 4. to wrap. 5. send or go in a hurry. *n., v. 3.*

bung (bung), 1. large stopper for closing the hole in the side of a barrel, keg, or cask. 2. hole in the side of a cask through which it is filled and emptied. 3. stop with a bung. *n., v.*

bun ga low (bung′gə-lō), a one-story house. *n. 11.*

Bungalow

bun gle (bung′gəl), 1. do or make (something) in a clumsy or unskillful way. John tried to make a rabbit house, but bungled the job. 2. a clumsy, unskillful performance. *v., n. 19.*

bun ion (bun′yən), a painful, inflamed swelling on the foot. *n. 15.*

bunk (bungk), 1. a narrow bed set against a wall like a shelf. 2. occupy a bunk. 3. sleep in rough quarters. *n., v. 13.*

bunk er (bungk′ər), 1. a place or bin for coal on a ship. 2. a mound, a sandy hollow, or a combination of both, used on a golf course as an obstacle. *n.*

Bunker Hill, hill in Boston, Massachusetts. An early battle of the American Revolution was fought near there in 1775.

bun ny (bun′i), a pet name for a rabbit. *n., pl. bunnies. 13.*

bunt (bunt), 1. strike with the head or

horns, as a goat does. 2. a push; a shove. *v., n.*

bun ting[1] (bun′ting), 1. a thin cloth used for flags. 2. flags; long pieces of cloth in flag colors and designs, used to decorate buildings and streets on holidays, etc. *n. 7.*

bun ting[2] (bun′ting), a small kind of bird, somewhat like a sparrow. *n.*

Bun yan (bun′yən), 1. John (1628-1688), the author of *Pilgrim's Progress.* 2. Paul, giant lumberjack who does marvelous deeds. *n.*

buoy (boi), 1. something kept in a certain place on the water to show what is safe and what is dangerous. 2. A life buoy is something to keep a person from sinking. 3. **Buoy up** means hold up or keep from sinking. *n., v. 8.*

Bell buoy

buoy an cy (boi′ən si), 1. power to float. Wood has more buoyancy than iron. 2. power to keep things afloat. Salt water has greater buoyancy than fresh. 3. tendency to rise. 4. light-heartedness, cheerfulness, and hopefulness. *n. 14.*

buoy ant (boi′ənt), 1. able to rise to the top of the water and float easily. Cork is buoyant. 2. able to hold things up. Salt water is more buoyant than fresh water. 3. able to recover easily; light-hearted; cheerful and hopeful. Children are more buoyant than old people. *adj. 8.*

bu pres tid bee tle (bū pres′tid bē′təl), kind of beetle whose larvae poison cattle.

bur (bėr). See **burr**[1]. *n. 20.*

Bur bank (bėr′bangk), Luther, an American who originated new fruits, flowers, plants, etc. (1849-1926). *n. 15.*

bur den[1] (bėr′dən), 1. what is carried; a load (of things, care, work, duty, or sorrow). 2. a load too heavy to carry easily. 3. to load; load too heavily; weigh down; oppress (said of things, care, work, duty, or sorrow). 4. the quantity of freight a ship can carry; the weight of a ship's cargo. *n., v. 3.*

bur den[2] (bėr′dən), 1. the main idea or message. The value of peace was the burden of her book. 2. the chorus or refrain of a song. *n.*

bur den some (bėr′dən səm), wearying; hard to bear; too heavy. *adj. 13.*

bur dock (bėr′dok′), a coarse weed with prickly heads or burrs and broad leaves. See the picture. *n. 11.*

bu reau (būr′ō), 1. a chest of drawers for clothes. It often has a mirror. 2. an office. We asked about the railroad fares at the Travel Bureau. 3. a government department. The Weather Bureau makes daily reports on weather conditions. *n., pl. bureaus. 3.*

Burdock (stem is from 2 to 5 ft. high)

bu reauc ra cy (bū rok′rə si), 1. government by groups of officials. Though the Czar was ruler in name, the government of Russia before the revolution was really a bureaucracy. 2. officials administering the government. 3. concentration of power in administrative bureaus. *n., pl. bureaucracies. 20.*

bur gess (bėr′jis), 1. member of the lower house of the colonial legislature in Virginia or Maryland. 2. a citizen or representative of an English or Scottish chartered town or borough. *n. 9.*

burgh (bėrg), borough; a chartered town in Scotland. *n. 17.*

burgh er (bėr′gər), citizen of a burgh or town; citizen. *n. 8.*

bur glar (bėr′glər), person who breaks into a house or building to steal or commit some other crime. *n. 8.*

bur glar y (bėr′glər i), act of breaking into a house or building to steal or commit some other crime. *n., pl. burglaries. 12.*

bur go mas ter (bėr′gō mas′tər), mayor of a town in the Netherlands, Flanders, or Germany. *n. 16.*

Bur gun dy (bėr′gən di), 1. a region in eastern France. 2. a red or white wine made there. *n. 10.*

bur i al (ber′i əl), 1. act of burying. 2. having to do with burial; as, a burial service. *n., adj. 4.*

bur ied (ber′id). See **bury.** The dog buried his bone. Many nuts were buried under the leaves. *pt. and pp. of bury.*

Burke (bėrk), Edmund, a famous British orator and statesman (1729-1797). *n. 18.*

bur lap (bėr′lap), coarse material used for bags, wrappings, and coverings. *n. 17.*

bur lesque (bėr lesk′), 1. comic imitation. *A Connecticut Yankee at King Arthur's Court* is a burlesque of the old legends.

2. imitate so as to make fun of. 3. comical; making people laugh. *n., v., adj. 15.*

bur ly (bėr′li), strong; sturdy; big. *adj., burlier, burliest. 14.*

Bur ma (bėr′mə), British possession east of India. *n.*

burn[1] (bėrn), 1. be on fire; be very hot. 2. set on fire; cause to burn. 3. destroy by fire. Please burn those old papers. 4. injure by fire or heat. He burned his hand on the hot iron. 5. an injury caused by fire or heat. 6. make by fire or heat. He burned a hole in the wood. 7. feel hot; give a feeling of heat. *v., burned* or *burnt, burning, n. 1.*

burn[2] (bėrn), brook. *n.* [*Scottish*]

burn er (bėr′nər), 1. man whose work is burning something; as, a charcoal burner, a brick burner. 2. thing or part that burns, or works by heat. Some stoves are oil burners; others are gas burners. *n. 8.*

bur nish (bėr′nish), polish. *v., n. 8.*

bur noose or **bur nous** (bėr nüs′), a cloak with a hood worn by Moors and Arabs. *n.*

Man wearing a burnoose

Burns (bėrnz), Robert, a famous Scottish poet (1759-1796). *n.*

burnt (bėrnt), burned. *adj., pt. and pp. of* **burn**[1]. *14.*

burr[1] (bėr), 1. prickly, clinging seed case or flower of some plants. Burrs stick to anything they touch. 2. plant or weed bearing burrs. 3. person or thing that clings like a burr. 4. rough ridge or edge left by a tool on metal, wood, etc., after cutting or drilling it. 5. tool that resembles a burr. Dentists use tiny burrs. *n. 5.* Also spelled **bur.**

burr[2] (bėr), 1. rough pronunciation; as, a Scottish burr. 2. pronounce roughly or harshly; as, to burr one's r's. 3. a rough, buzzing sound caused by the rapid motion of machines. *n., v.*

bur ro (bėr′ō), donkey. *n., pl. burros. 18.*

Burro (3 ft. high at the shoulder)

bur row (bėr′ō), 1. hole dug in the ground. Rabbits live in burrows. 2. dig a hole in the ground. 3. live in burrows. 4. hide. 5. dig. 6. search. *n., v. 7.*

burst (bėrst), 1. break open; break out suddenly; fly apart suddenly with force. The bomb burst. The trees burst into bloom. 2. go, come, do, etc., by force or suddenly. He burst into the room. 3. be full. The barns were bursting with grain. 4. a bursting; an outbreak; as, a burst of feeling. *v., burst, bursting, n. 2.*

bur then (bėr′ᴛʜən), burden. *n., v.* [*Old use*] *11.*

bur y (ber′i), 1. place in the earth, in a tomb, or in the sea. A dead body is usually buried. 2. put away; cover up; forget. Many nuts were buried under the dead leaves. *v., buried, burying. 2.*

bus (bus), a large vehicle with seats inside and sometimes also on the roof. A bus is used to carry passengers between fixed stations along a route. *n., pl. busses* or *buses. 9.*

Bus

bush (bu̇sh), 1. a woody plant smaller than a tree, often with many separate stems starting near the ground. 2. open forest or wild land. 3. **Beat about the bush** means avoid coming to the point of a matter. *n. 2.*

bush el (bu̇sh′əl), a measure for grain, fruit, vegetables, and other dry things, containing 4 pecks or 32 quarts. *n. 3.*

bush ing (bu̇sh′ing), a metal lining which can be taken out, used to protect parts of machinery from wear. *n. 14.*

bush y (bu̇sh′i), 1. growing thickly. 2. overgrown with bushes. *adj., bushier, bushiest. 11.*

bus i ly (biz′i li), actively. *adv. 6.*

busi ness (biz′nis), 1. thing one is busy at; work; occupation. Business comes before pleasure. A carpenter's business is building. 2. matter; affair. Mind your own business. Taking chances is bad business. 3. trade; buying and selling. This store does a big business. 4. a commercial enterprise; industrial establishment. They sold their business for ten million dollars. *n. 1.*

busi ness like (biz′nis līk′), having system and method; well-managed. *adj. 17.*

bus kin (bus′kin), 1. a boot reaching to the calf or knee, worn in olden times. 2. Tragic actors in Greece and Rome wore buskins with very thick soles to make them look more impressive. So the buskin has become a symbol of tragedy. *n. 13.*

Ancient buskins

buss (bus), kiss. *n., v.* [*Old use*]

bust (bust), 1. statue of a person's head, shoulders, and chest. 2. the upper front part of the body, especially of a woman. *n. 5.*

bus tle[1] (bus′əl), 1. be noisily busy and in a hurry. 2. make (others) hurry or work hard. 3. noisy or excited activity. *v., n. 7.*

bus tle[2] (bus′əl), a pad used to puff out the upper back part of women's skirts. *n.*

Bustle

bus y (biz′i), 1. working; active; having plenty to do. 2. full of work or activity; as, a busy day, a busy street. 3. make busy; keep busy. *adj., busier, busiest, v., busied, busying. 1.*

bus y bod y (biz′i bod′i), meddler; person who interferes in the affairs of others. *n., pl. busybodies.*

but (but), 1. on the other hand. You may go, but you must come home at six o'clock. 2. except. Father works every day in the week but Sunday. 3. only. We can but try. Jack is but a small boy. 4. who not; which not. None come to his doors but are fed. *conj., prep., adv. 1.*

butch er (bu̇ch′ər), 1. man whose work is killing animals for food. 2. man who sells meat. 3. kill (animals) for food. 4. kill (people, wild animals, or birds) wholesale, needlessly, or cruelly. 5. cut up roughly, without attending to details, so that the thing is spoiled. 6. spoil. Don't butcher that song! *n., v. 3.*

butch er y (bu̇ch′ər i), 1. murder. 2. great slaughter. *n., pl. butcheries.*

but ler (but′lər), manservant in charge of pantry and table service in a household; head servant. *n. 8.*

butt[1] (but), 1. thicker end of a tool or weapon. 2. end that is left; stub or stump. 3. object, aim, or target. That queer boy was the butt of our jokes. *n. 6.*

butt[2] (but), 1. strike, push, or fight by pushing or knocking hard with the head. A goat butts. 2. a push or blow with the head. *v., n.*

butt[3] (but), a large barrel or cask for wine or beer. *n.*

Butte

butte (būt), a steep hill standing alone. *n. 14.*

Butte (būt), a city in southwestern Montana. *n.*

but ter (but′ər), 1. the yellowish fat obtained from cream by churning. 2. put butter on. 3. something like butter in looks or use. *n., v. 1.*

but ter cup (but′ər kup′), a common plant with bright-yellow flowers shaped like cups. *n. 9.*

Butterfly (about ½ life size)

but ter fat (but′ər fat′), fat in milk. It can be made into butter. *n.*

but ter fly (but′ər flī′), an insect with a slender body and four large, usually bright-colored, wings. *n., pl. butterflies. 3.*

but ter milk (but′ər milk′), the sour liquid left after butter has been separated from milk. Milk can also be changed to buttermilk artificially. *n. 15.*

but ter nut (but′ər nut′), 1. oily kind of walnut that is good to eat. 2. tree that bears butternuts. *n.*

but tocks (but′əks), rump. *n. pl. 15.*

but ton (but′ən), 1. a knob, or a round flat piece of any material, fastened on clothing, shoes, and other things, to hold them closed or to decorate them. 2. a knob used as a handle or catch, either to take hold of, or push, or to turn so that it holds or closes something. 3. fasten the buttons of. Please button my dress for me. 4. enclose by fastening buttons. *n., v. 2.*

but ton hole (but′ən hōl′), 1. the hole or slit through which a button is passed. 2. make buttonholes in. 3. detain in conversation, as if we held a man by the buttonhole of his coat and made him listen. *n., v. 20.*

Buttresses: A, ordinary; B, flying.

but ton wood (but′ən wu̇d′), 1. a tall plane tree yielding a useful wood; the sycamore tree of America. 2. its wood. *n.*

but tress (but′ris), 1. a support built against a wall or building to steady it; a support like this. See the picture. 2. to support and strengthen. *n., v. 13.*

bux om (buk′səm), plump and good to look at; healthy and cheerful. *adj. 20.*

buy (bī), get by paying a price. You can buy a pencil for five cents. *v., bought, buying. 1.*

buy er (bī′ər), person who buys. *n. 6.*

buzz (buz), 1. the humming sound made by flies, mosquitoes, or bees. 2. the low confused sound of many people talking quietly. 3. make a steady humming sound; hum loudly. 4. to sound in a low confused way. 5. talk excitedly. 6. **Buzz about** means move about busily. *n., v. 3.*

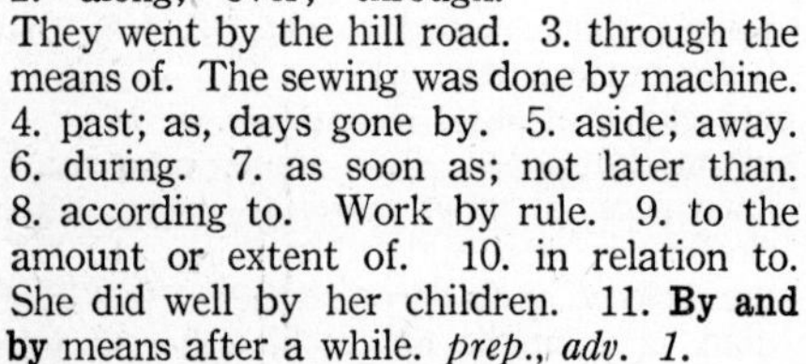
Buzzard (def. 1) (2½ ft. long)

buz zard (buz′ərd), 1. kind of heavy hawk. 2. kind of vulture. *n. 11.*

buzz er (buz′ər), 1. thing that buzzes. 2. electrical device that makes a buzzing sound as a signal. *n.*

by[1] (bī), 1. near. Stand by me. He lives close by. 2. along; over; through. They went by the hill road. 3. through the means of. The sewing was done by machine. 4. past; as, days gone by. 5. aside; away. 6. during. 7. as soon as; not later than. 8. according to. Work by rule. 9. to the amount or extent of. 10. in relation to. She did well by her children. 11. **By and by** means after a while. *prep., adv. 1.*

by-and-by (bī′ənd bī′), future. *n.*

bye or **by**[2] (bī), 1. **By the bye** means by the way. 2. aside; out of the main way. By in this meaning is usually a part of a compound word; as, by-path, by-product, byword. *n., adj. 5.*

by gone (bī′gôn′), 1. past; former; departed. 2. something in the past. *adj., n. 10.*

by law (bī′lô′), 1. law made by a city, company, etc., for the control of its own affairs. 2. secondary law or rule, not one of the main rules. Our club has a constitution and bylaws. *n. 11.*

by-pass (bī′pas′), road, channel, pipe, etc., providing a secondary passage to be used instead of the main passage. *n.*

by-path (bī′path′), side path; byway. *n.*

by-prod uct (bī′prod′əkt), something produced in making or doing something else; not the main product. *n. 16.*

by-road (bī′rōd′), side road. *n.*

By ron (bī′rən), a famous English poet (1788-1824). *n. 11.*

by stand er (bī′stan′dər), person who stands near or looks on but does not take part. *n.*

by way (bī′wā′), side path; way that is little used. *n. 13.*

by word (bī′wėrd′), 1. object of contempt; thing people scorn. His cowardice made him a byword to all who knew him. 2. common saying; proverb. *n. 12.*

Byz an tine (biz′ən tēn), having to do with the Eastern Roman Empire or a style of architecture developed there. Byzantine architecture uses the round arch, the cross, the circle, the dome, and mosaics. *adj. 20.*

Example of Byzantine architecture

By zan ti um (bi zan′shi əm), ancient city where Istanbul (Constantinople) now is. It became the capital of the Roman Empire in 330 A.D. *n. 17.*

C

C, c (sē), the third letter of the alphabet. There are two c's in cocoa. *n., pl. C's, c's.*

C, Roman numeral for 100.

c., cent; cents. *6.*

cab (kab), 1. automobile that can be hired; taxicab. 2. carriage that can be hired, pulled by one horse. 3. covered part of a locomotive where the engineer sits. *n. 6.*

ca bal (kə bal′), 1. small group of persons working or planning in secret. 2. secret schemes of such a group. *n. 15.*

cab a ret (kab′ə rā′), 1. restaurant where an entertainment of singing and dancing is provided. 2. the entertainment. *n.*

cab bage (kab′ij), a vegetable whose thick leaves are closely folded into a round head. *n. 4.*

Cabbage

cab in (kab′in), 1. a small, roughly built house; hut. See the picture on the next page. 2. room in a ship. 3. place for passengers in an airplane or airship. *n. 3.*

cab i net (kab′i nit), 1. piece of furniture with shelves or drawers, used to contain articles for display or use, such as jewels, dishes, letters. A kitchen cabinet is used for storing food supplies and dishes. 2. a group of men chosen by the president or head of a nation to help him in the government; council of advisers. 3. room. *n. 4.*

cab i net mak er (kab′i nit māk′ər), man whose work is making fine woodwork and furniture. *n. 20.*

ca ble (kā′bəl), 1. a strong, thick rope, often made of wires twisted together. 2. a protected bundle of wires, used for sending telegraph messages under the ground or under the ocean. 3. message sent across the sea by cable. 4. send a message across the sea by cable. *n., v. 4.*

ca ble gram (kā′bəl gram), message sent under the ocean by cable. *n. 18.*

ca boose (kə büs′), 1. small car on a freight train in which the trainmen can rest and sleep. 2. kitchen on the deck of a ship. *n.*

Cab ot (kab′ət), John (1450?-1498), explorer who discovered North America in 1497. *n.*

ca ca o (kə kä′ō), 1. a small tree from whose seeds cocoa and chocolate are made. 2. the seeds of the tree. *n., pl. cacaos. 20.*

cache (kash), 1. hiding place for food or other things. 2. hidden store of food or supplies. 3. put in a cache; hide. *n., v. 19.*

cack le (kak′əl), 1. the shrill, broken sound that a hen makes after laying an egg. 2. make this sound. 3. broken or harsh laughter. 4. laugh brokenly or harshly, like a hen cackling. 5. noisy chatter; silly talk. *n., v. 8.*

Common cactus

cac tus (kak′təs), a plant with a fleshy stem, usually having spines but no leaves. Cactuses grow in dry, hot regions. *n., pl. cactuses, cacti* (-tī). *10.*

cad (kad), boy or man who claims to be a gentleman, but does not act like one. *n. 19.*

ca dav er ous (kə dav′ər əs), so pale and ghastly as to look like a dead person. *adj. 20.*

Cactus with a watery pulp

cad die or **cad dy** (kad′i), person who helps a golf player by carrying golf clubs. *n., pl. caddies.*

ca dence (kā′dəns), 1. rhythm. 2. a fall of the voice. 3. a changing of the voice. 4. a series of chords that bring part of a piece of music to an end. *n. 7.*

ca det (kə det′), 1. young man who is training to be an officer in the army or navy. 2. younger son or brother. *n. 20.*

Cad mus (kad′məs), Greek prince who killed a dragon and sowed its teeth. From these teeth, armed men sprang up who fought until only five were left. Cadmus and these men founded the Greek city of Thebes. *n. 14.*

Cae sar (sē′zər), 1. Julius Caesar (102?-44 B.C.) was a Roman general, statesman, and historian. 2. title of the Roman emperors. 3. emperor; dictator. *n. 3.*

cae su ra (si zhür′ə), a pause in a line of poetry. *n. 19.*

ca fé (ka fā′), restaurant. *n. 13.*

caf e te ri a (kaf′ə tēr′i ə), restaurant where people wait on themselves. *n. 15.*

caf fein or **caf feine** (kaf′ēn), a stimulating drug found in coffee and tea. *n. 14.*

cage (kāj), 1. prison for animals or birds, made of wire, strong iron bars, or wood. 2. anything shaped or used like a cage; as, the cage or car of an elevator. 3. put or keep in a cage. *n., v. 3.*

Cain (kān), the oldest son of Adam and Eve. Cain killed his brother Abel. *n. 6.*

Log cabin

cairn (kãrn), a pile of stones heaped up by somebody as a memorial, tomb, or landmark. *n. 18.*

Cai ro (kī′rō), the capital of Egypt. *n. 15.*

cais son (kā′sən), 1. box for ammunition. 2. wagon to carry ammunition. 3. a watertight box or chamber in which men can work under water. *n.*

cai tiff (kā′tif), 1. a mean, bad person; coward. 2. vile; cowardly; mean. *n., adj. 13.*

WATER
MUD
ROCK

Caisson (def. 3)

ca jole (kə jōl′), coax; persuade by pleasant words, flattery, or false promises. *v. 16.*

ca jol er y (kə jōl′ər i), coaxing; flattery; persuasion by smooth, deceitful words. *n., pl. cajoleries.*

cake (kāk), 1. a baked mixture of flour, sugar, eggs, and other things; as, a layer cake, a sponge cake, a fruit cake. 2. a flat, thin mass of dough baked or fried; as, a pancake, an oatcake. 3. a shaped, flat mass of food or other substance; as, a fish cake, a cake of soap, a cake of ice. 4. form into a compact mass. Mud cakes as it dries. *n., v. 1.*

cal a bash (kal′ə bash), 1. gourd whose dried shell is used to make bottles, bowls, etc. 2. bottle, bowl, etc., made from such a dried shell. *n.*

Decorated calabashes

Cal ais (kal′ā), the French seaport nearest England. *n. 7.*

ca lam i tous (kə lam′i təs), causing calamity; accompanied by calamity; disastrous. *adj. 15.*

ca lam i ty (kə lam′i ti), a great misfortune such as a flood, a fire, the loss of one's sight or hearing, or of much money or property. *n., pl. calamities. 6.*

cal ci fy (kal′si fī), make or become bony or chalky; harden by the deposit of lime. An injured cartilage sometimes calcifies. *v., calcified, calcifying.*

cal ci mine (kal′si mīn), 1. a white or tinted wash for walls, ceilings, etc. 2. cover with calcimine. *n., v. 20.*

cal cine (kal′sīn), 1. change to lime by heating. 2. burn to ashes; roast. *v. 20.*

cal ci um (kal′si əm), a substance which is part of lime, chalk, milk, bone, and many other things. *n. 8.*

cal cu late (kal′kū lāt), 1. reckon; add, subtract, multiply, divide, etc., in order to find out something; as, to calculate the cost of furnishing a house. 2. find out beforehand by any process of reasoning; as, to calculate the day of the week on which Christmas will fall. 3. plan; intend. That remark was calculated to hurt someone's feelings. 4. rely; count. You can calculate on earning $20 a week. *v. 7.*

cal cu la tion (kal′kū lā′shən), 1. adding, subtracting, multiplying, or dividing to find a result. 2. the result found by calculating. 3. careful thinking; deliberate planning. *n. 10.*

cal cu la tor (kal′kū lā′tər), person or machine that calculates. *n. 16.*

cal cu lus (kal′kū ləs), a part of mathematics which can be learned after algebra is learned. *n. 17.*

Cal cut ta (kal kut′ə), large city in eastern India. *n. 17.*

cal dron (kôl′drən), large kettle or boiler. *n. 12.*

Cal e do ni a (kal′i dō′ni ə), Scotland. *n. 17.*

cal en dar (kal′ən dər), a table showing the months, weeks, and days of the year. A calendar shows the day of the week on which each day of the month falls. *n. 5.*

DECEMBER						
S	M	T	W	T	F	S
..	..	..	..	..	..	1
2	3	4	5	6	7	8
9	10	11	12	13	14	15
16	17	18	19	20	21	22
23	24	25	26	27	28	29
30	31	..	..	..	..	..

Page of calendar

cal en der (kal′ən dər), 1. a machine in which cloth or paper is smoothed and glazed by pressing between rollers. 2. press or finish in a calender. *n., v. 20.*

calf[1] (kaf), 1. a young cow or bull. 2. a young elephant, whale, deer, etc. 3. leather made of the skin of a calf. *n., pl. calves. 4.*

calf[2] (kaf), the thick, fleshy part of the back of the leg below the knee. *n., pl. calves.*

calf skin (kaf′skin′), 1. skin of a calf. 2. leather made from it. *n.*

Cal i ban (kal′i ban), a beastlike slave in Shakespeare's play *The Tempest.* *n. 20.*

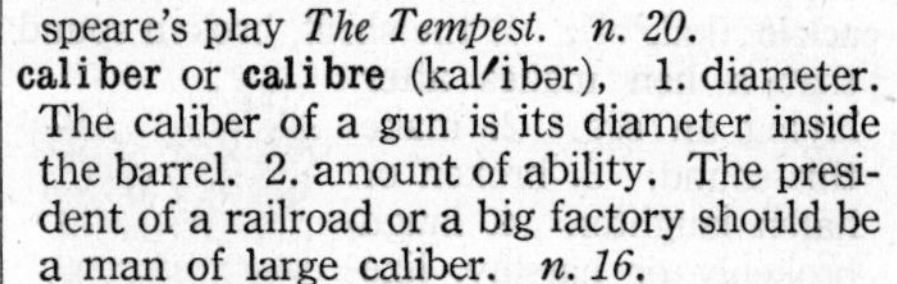

cal i ber or **cal i bre** (kal′i bər), 1. diameter. The caliber of a gun is its diameter inside the barrel. 2. amount of ability. The president of a railroad or a big factory should be a man of large caliber. *n. 16.*

cal i co (kal′i kō), cotton cloth printed with colored patterns; plain white cotton cloth. *n., pl. calicoes* or *calicos. 8.*

Calif., California.

Cal i for ni a (kal′i fôr′ni ə), 1. a Western State of the United States, on the Pacific coast. 2. **Gulf of California,** arm of the Pacific Ocean. *n. 3.*

cal i pers (kal′i pərz), instrument used to measure the diameter or thickness of something. *n. pl. 19.*

Calipers

ca liph or **ca lif** (kā′lif), the head of a Moslem state. *n. 14.*

cal is then ics (kal′is then′iks), exercises to develop a strong and graceful body. *n. pl.*

calk[1] (kôk), fill up (a seam or crack or joint) so that it will not leak; make tight. Sailors calk boats with tar. Plumbers calk joints in pipe with lead. *v. 16.* Also spelled **caulk.**

calk[2] (kôk), projecting piece on a horseshoe that catches in the ground or ice and prevents slipping. *n.*

call (kôl), 1. cry; shout; speak loudly. Hear them calling. 2. a shout; a cry. 3. speak to; give a signal to; arouse. Call me at seven o'clock. 4. command or ask to come. He called his dog away from the fight. 5. a command; an invitation. 6. to name. That boy is called John. 7. make a short visit. Our pastor called yesterday. 8. short visit. 9. demand payment of. 10. **Call for** means order; demand; need; go and get. 11. **Call on** means appeal to. 12. **Call up** means (1) bring to mind. (2) telephone to. *v., n. 1.*

call er (kôl′ər), 1. person who makes a short visit. 2. person who calls out names, etc., in a loud voice. *n. 10.*

call ing (kôl′ing), 1. profession, occupation, or trade. 2. summons; invitation. *n. 17.*

cal li o pe (kə lī′ə pi or kal′i ōp), a musical instrument sounded by steam. *n.*

cal lis then ics (kal′is then′iks), calisthenics. *n. pl.*

cal lous (kal′əs), 1. hard; hardened. Going barefoot makes the bottoms of your feet callous. 2. unfeeling. Only a callous person can see suffering without trying to relieve it. *adj. 13.*

cal low (kal′ō), 1. without experience. 2. not fully grown. 3. without feathers. *adj. 18.*

cal lus (kal′əs), hard, thickened place on the skin. *n., pl. calluses.*

calm (käm), 1. quiet; still; not stormy or windy; not stirred up; peaceful. 2. quietness; stillness; absence of wind or motion. 3. make calm; become calm. She soon calmed the baby. The baby calmed down. *adj., n., v. 2.*

calm ness (käm′nis), peace; quiet; calm. *n. 13.*

cal o mel (kal′ə mel), white, tasteless compound of mercury, used as a medicine. *n. 13.*

cal o rie or **cal o ry** (kal′ə ri), 1. the unit of heat. 2. a unit of the energy supplied by food. An ounce of sugar will produce about a hundred calories. *n., pl. calories. 9.*

ca lum ni ate (kə lum′ni āt), slander; say false and injurious things about. *v. 16.*

ca lum ni ous (kə lum′ni əs), slanderous. The old gossip said calumnious things about her neighbors. *adj. 20.*

cal um ny (kal′əm ni), slander; false statement made on purpose to do harm to someone. *n., pl. calumnies. 13.*

Cal va ry (kal′və ri), the place where Jesus died on the cross. *n. 20.*

calves (kavz), more than one calf. *n. pl. 6.*

Cal vin (kal′vin), John, a famous French Protestant (1509-1564). *n. 15.*

ca lyx (kā′liks), a part of a flower. See the picture. The calyx is made of the sepals and is a sort of holder for the petals. *n. 10.*

PETAL
SEPAL
Calyx of a rose

cam (kam), a projection on a wheel or shaft that changes a regular rotary motion to an irregular motion. Cams cause the up-and-down movements of the valves in an automobile. *n. 18.*

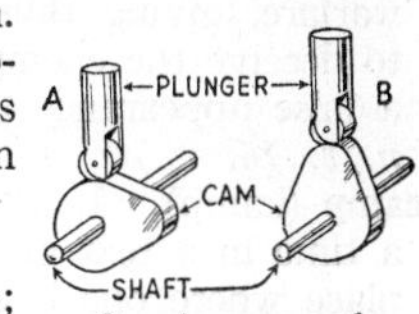

Cam in open and closed positions

ca ma ra de rie (kä′mə rä′də rē), comradeship; friendliness and loyalty among comrades. *n.*

cam bi um (kam′bi əm), a layer of soft tissue between the bark and the wood of trees and shrubs. New bark and new wood grow from it. *n. 12.*

cam bric (kām′brik), a fine, thin linen or cotton cloth. *n. 9.*

Cam bridge (kām′brij), 1. a university in England. 2. the city near Boston, Massachusetts, where Harvard University is located. *n. 8.*

Cam den (kam′dən), city in New Jersey. *n. 14.*

came (kām). See **come.** He came to school late this morning. *pt. of come. 1.*

Camel

cam el (kam′əl), a large, four-footed animal with one or two humps on its back. Camels are used in the deserts of Africa and Arabia because they can go a long time without drinking water. *n. 4.*

ca mel lia (kə mēl′yə), a plant with glossy evergreen leaves and white or red waxy flowers like roses. *n.*

Cam e lot (kam′ə lot), the place in England where King Arthur had his palace and court. *n. 20.*

cam e o (kam′i ō), a precious stone carved so that there is a raised part on a background. *n., pl. cameos. 16.*

Cameo

cam er a (kam′ər ə), a machine for taking photographs. See the picture just below. *n. 8.*

Camera

cam o mile (kam′ə mīl), plant with daisylike flowers. Its flowers and leaves are sometimes dried and used in medicine. *n.*

cam ou flage (kam′ə fläzh), 1. disguise; deception. The white fur of a polar bear is a natural camouflage, for it prevents its being easily seen against the snow. 2. in warfare, giving things a false appearance to deceive the enemy. 3. to disguise; give a false appearance to in order to conceal. *n., v. 16.*

camp (kamp), 1. live away from home for a time in a tent or hut or outdoors. 2. a place where one lives in a tent or hut or outdoors. 3. persons living in a camp. 4. pitch tents and stay for a time. The Boy Scout troop camped at the foot of the mountain for two weeks. 5. the camping ground where an army is camping. 6. live simply, as one does in a tent. *v., n. 2.*

cam paign (kam pān′), 1. a number of related military operations in a war which are aimed at some special purpose, such as taking a city. The summer campaign of our army resulted in opening a way into the enemy's country. 2. series of connected activities to do or get something; planned course of action for some special purpose; as, a campaign to raise money for a college, a campaign to advertise some article, a campaign to elect someone to political office. 3. take part or serve in a campaign. *n., v. 4.*

cam paign er (kam pān′ər), person who campaigns or has campaigned. *n. 20.*

cam pa ni le (kam′pə nē′li), bell tower. *n.*

Campanile

camp er (kamp′ər), one who camps. *n. 14.*

camp fire (kamp′fīr′), 1. fire in a camp for warmth or cooking. 2. social gathering of soldiers, scouts, etc. *n.*

cam phor (kam′fər), a white substance with a strong odor and a bitter taste. *n. 9.*

cam pus (kam′pəs), the grounds of a college, university, or school. *n. 13.*

can[1] (kan), 1. be able to. 2. know how to. He can read rapidly. 3. have the right to. Anyone can cross the street here. 4. may. You can go at 4 o'clock. *v., pl. could. 1.*

can[2] (kan), 1. a container of metal or glass in various forms; as, an oil can, a milk can, a can of fruit. 2. to preserve by putting up in airtight containers. Mother cans fruit. *n., v., canned, canning.*

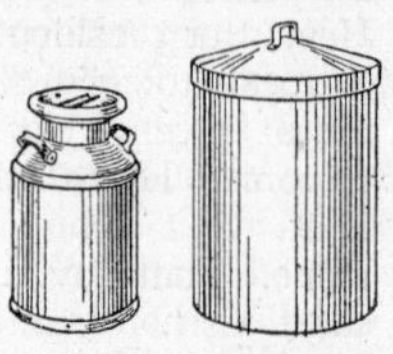
Milk can and ash can

Ca naan (kā′nən), 1. the region in Palestine lying between the river Jordan and the Mediterranean Sea. God promised Canaan to Abraham and his descendants. 2. land of promise. *n. 11.*

Ca naan ite (kā′nən īt), inhabitant of Canaan before its conquest by the Hebrews. *n. 13.*

Can a da (kan′ə də), the country north of the United States. *n. 3.*

Ca na di an (kə nā′di ən), 1. of Canada or its people. 2. a native or inhabitant of Canada. *adj., n. 8.*

ca nal (kə nal′), 1. waterway dug across land for ships or small boats to go through, or to carry water to places that need it. 2. tube in a plant or animal that carries food, liquid, or air. *n. 3.*

Canal Zone, Panama Canal and the land five miles on each side, governed by the United States.

ca nard (kə närd′), false rumor. *n.*

ca nar y (kə nãr′i), 1. a songbird with pretty yellow feathers, originally from the Canary Islands. 2. light yellow. *n., pl. canaries, adj. 8.*

Canary Islands, a group of islands off the northwest coast of Africa.

can cel (kan′səl), 1. cross out; mark so that it cannot be used; as, a canceled stamp. 2. wipe out; abolish; do away with. He canceled his order for the books. This will cancel your debt to me. *v., canceled, canceling. 8.*

can cel la tion (kan′sə lā′shən), 1. a canceling or being canceled. 2. something canceled. *n. 14.*

can cer (kan′sər), a very harmful growth in the body. *n. 7.*

Can cer (kan′sər), 1. the tropic of Cancer, a circle around the world 23.45 degrees north of the equator. 2. a certain group of stars shaped somewhat like a crab. *n.*

can de la brum (kan′də lä′brəm), an ornamental, branched candlestick. *n., pl. candelabra (-brə) or candelabrums. 20.*

can did (kan′did), frank; sincere. *adj. 12.*

can di da cy (kan′di də si), being a candidate. Three boys spoke in favor of John's candidacy for president of the club. *n. 13.*

can di date (kan′di dāt), person who is proposed for some office or honor. There are three candidates for president of the club. *n. 4.*

can died (kan′did), 1. turned into sugar. Candied honey is sugary, not smooth. 2. cooked in sugar. *adj.*

can dle (kan′dəl), a stick of tallow or wax with a wick in it, burned to give light. Long ago, before there was gas or electric light, people burned candles to see by. *n. 2.*

Birthday cake with candles

can dle light (kan′dəl līt′), 1. light of a candle. 2. time when candles are lighted. *n. 15.*

candle power, the light given by a standard candle, used as a unit of measurement of light.

can dle stick (kan′dəl-stik′), holder for a candle, to make it stand up straight. *n. 7.*

Candlesticks with candles

can dor (kan′dər), 1. speaking openly what one really thinks; honesty in giving one's view or opinion. 2. fairness. *n. 12.*

can dy (kan′di), 1. sugar or syrup boiled with water and flavoring, cooled, and made into small pieces for eating. 2. form into sugar. This honey has candied. 3. cook in sugar; preserve by boiling with sugar. *n., pl. candies, v., candied, candying. 2.*

can dy tuft (kan′di tuft′), a plant with white, purple, or pink flowers. *n.*

cane (kān), 1. a long, jointed stem. The stems of bamboo, sugar cane, and rattan are canes. 2. a stick made from a cane stem; any slender stick used as an aid in walking. 3. beat with a cane. *n., v. 3.*

ca nine (kā′nīn), 1. dog. 2. of a dog; like a dog. The four pointed teeth are called canine teeth. *n., adj. 10.*

can is ter (kan′is tər), 1. small box or can. 2. can filled with bullets that is shot from a cannon. *n. 19.*

can ker (kang′kər), 1. a sore in the mouth. 2. anything that causes rot or decay or destroys by a gradual eating away. 3. spoil with disease; eat away. *n., v. 8.*

can ker worm (kang′kər wėrm′), a caterpillar that eats away the leaves of trees and plants. *n. 17.*

can na (kan′ə), a plant with large leaves and large, showy flowers. *n.*

canned (kand), preserved in airtight containers of glass, tin, etc. *adj. 13.*

can ner y (kan′ər i), factory where meat, fish, fruit, vegetables, etc., are canned. *n., pl. canneries.*

can ni bal (kan′i bəl), 1. person who eats human flesh. 2. animal that eats others of its own kind. *n. 9.*

can ni bal ism (kan′i bəl izm), practice of eating the flesh of one's own kind. *n.*

can non (kan′ən), big mounted gun or guns. *n., pl. cannons or cannon. 3.*

Cannon

can non ade (kan′ən ād′), 1. a continued firing of cannons. 2. attack with cannons. *n., v. 11.*

can not (kan′not), can not. *1.*

can ny (kan′i), shrewd; cautious. *adj., cannier, canniest. 16.*

ca noe (kə nü′), 1. a light boat moved with paddles. 2. paddle a canoe; go in a canoe. *n., pl. canoes, v., canoed, canoeing. 4.*

Indian paddling a canoe

can on (kan′ən), 1. law of a church. 2. standard; rule by which a thing is judged. 3. official list of the books contained in the Bible; books of the Bible accepted by the Christian church. 4. list of saints. 5. member of a group of clergymen living according to a certain rule. *n. 9.*

ca ñon (kan′yən), canyon. *n. 16.*

ca non i cal (kə non′i kəl), according to church laws. *adj. 15.*

can on ize (kan′ən īz), declare formally to be a saint. Joan of Arc was canonized in 1920. *v. 16.*

can o py (kan′ə pi), 1. a covering fixed over a bed or a throne; a covering carried on poles over a person. 2. covering; shelter; shade. 3. to cover with a canopy. *n., pl. canopies, v., canopied, canopying. 9.*

Canopy over a bed

canst (kanst), an old form meaning **can.** "Thou canst" means "you can." *v. 3.*

cant[1] (kant), 1. talk that is not sincere; moral and religious statements that many people make, but few really believe or act upon. 2. the peculiar language of a special group, using many strange words; as, college cant, thieves' cant. *n. 11.*

cant[2] (kant), 1. slant; slope. 2. tip; tilt. *n., v.*

can't (kant), cannot. *2.*

can ta loupe or **can ta loup** (kan′tə lōp), a kind of sweet, juicy melon. It is also called a muskmelon. *n.*

can tan ker ous (kan tang′kər əs), hard to get on with because ready to make trouble and oppose anything suggested. A mule is a cantankerous animal. *adj.*

can ta ta (kən tä′tə), music to be sung by a chorus, telling a story or drama. *n. 19.*

can teen (kan tēn′), 1. small container to carry water or other drinks in. 2. place where food and drink are sold to soldiers and sailors. *n. 16.*

can ter (kan′tər), 1. gallop gently. 2. an easy gallop. *v., n. 12.*

Can ter bur y (kan′tər ber′i), a city in southeastern England. Many pilgrims traveled there during the Middle Ages to visit the shrine of Saint Thomas à Becket. *n. 10.*

can ti cle (kan′ti kəl), a short song, hymn, or chant used in church services. *n. 16.*

can ti lev er (kan′ti lev′ər), a large bracket. A **cantilever bridge** is made by two big brackets or cantilevers. *n., adj.*

Cantilever bridge

can to (kan′tō), one of the main divisions of a long poem. A canto of a poem is like a chapter of a story. *n., pl. cantos. 14.*

can ton[1] (kan′tən), a small part or division of a country. Switzerland is made up of 22 cantons. *n. 8.*

Can ton[2] (kan ton′ for 1, kan′tən for 2), 1. a city in southern China. 2. a city in northeastern Ohio. *n.*

can ton ment (kan ton′mənt), place where soldiers live. *n. 18.*

can vas (kan′vəs), 1. strong cloth with a rather coarse, even weave. Canvas is used for sails and tents, and for painting on. 2. made of canvas. 3. anything made of canvas. 4. a picture painted on canvas. *n., adj. 3.*

can vass (kan′vəs), 1. examine the parts of. John canvassed the papers carefully, hunting for notices of jobs. 2. ask persons of; go about asking for subscriptions, votes, orders, etc. Mary canvassed the village for subscriptions to the weekly paper. 3. an asking for subscriptions, votes, orders, etc. 4. discuss. 5. discussion. 6. an investigation by inquiry. *v., n. 12.*

can yon (kan′yən), narrow valley with high, steep sides, usually with a stream at the bottom. *n. 10.* Another spelling is **cañon.**

caout chouc (kou′chük), the gum from which rubber is made; rubber. *n. 18.*

cap (kap), 1. a soft, close-fitting covering for the head with little or no brim. 2. a special headdress showing rank, occupation, etc.; as, a nurse's cap, a student's cap and gown, a fool's cap. 3. anything like a cap. The top of a mushroom is called a cap; 4. highest part; top. 5. put a cap on. cover. 6. do or follow up with something as good or better. Each of the two clowns capped the last joke of the other. 7. small quantity of explosive in a wrapper of some kind. *n., v., capped, capping. 1.*

ca pa bil i ty (kā′pə bil′i ti), ability; power; fitness; capacity. *n., pl. capabilities. 11.*

ca pa ble (kā′pə bəl), able; having fitness or ability. Capable of improvement means able to improve or to be improved. *adj. 3.*

ca pa cious (kə pā′shəs), roomy; able to hold much. *adj. 6.*

ca pac i ty (kə pas′i ti), 1. the amount of room or space in a dish, a basket, a room, or a container of any kind. This can has a capacity of 4 quarts. This room has a seating capacity of 100 people.

Caparison

2. ability to learn or do; power; fitness. 3. position or relation. He is here in the capacity of a teacher. *n., pl. capacities. 4.*

ca par i son (kə par′i sən), 1. an ornamental covering for a horse. See the picture just above. 2. dress; equipment. 3. to dress richly. *n., v. 14.*

cape[1] (kāp), an outer garment, or a part of one, without sleeves, worn falling loosely from the shoulders. *n. 3.*

Soldier wearing a cape

cape[2] (kāp), a point of land extending into the water. *n.*

Cape of Good Hope, a cape near the southern tip of Africa.

ca per (kā′pər), 1. to leap or skip in a playful way. 2. a playful leap or skip. *v., n. 7.*

Cape Town or **Cape town** (kāp′toun′), a city near the southern tip of Africa. *n.*

cap il lar y (kap′i lãr′i), 1. like a hair; very slender. 2. tube with a very slender, hair-like opening or bore. Capillaries join the end of an artery to the beginning of a vein. *adj., n., pl. capillaries. 8.*

cap i tal (kap′i təl), 1. the city where the government of a country or State is located. Washington is the capital of the United States. Each State of the United States has a capital. 2. A **capital** or **capital letter** is used to begin a sentence or the name of a person or place. 3. the amount of money or property that a company or a person uses in carrying on a business. The Smith Company has a capital of $30,000. 4. resources; source of power or advantage. He made capital out of his father's fame. 5. important; leading. 6. of the best kind; excellent. A maple tree gives capital shade. 7. **Make capital of** means take advantage of; use to one's own advantage. 8. involving death; punishable by death. Murder is a capital crime. 9. the top part of a column. *n., adj. 2.*

Capital

cap i tal ism (kap′i təl izm), 1. an economic system based on private property and competition. 2. the concentration of wealth with its power and influence in the hands of a few. *n. 20.*

cap i tal ist (kap′i təl ist), 1. person who has much wealth employed in business. 2. wealthy person. *n. 9.*

cap i tal is tic (kap′i təl is′tik), 1. having to do with capitalism; of capitalists. 2. favoring or supporting capitalism. *adj. 18.*

cap i tal i za tion (kap′i təl i zā′shən), 1. a capitalizing or being capitalized. 2. the amount realized from capitalizing; the capital stock of a company. *n. 18.*

cap i tal ize (kap′i təl īz), 1. write or print in capital letters. 2. turn into capital; use as capital. *v. 19.*

Cap i tol (kap′i təl), 1. the building at Washington in which Congress meets. 2. the building in which a State legislature meets. *n. 7.*

ca pit u late (kə pich′ů lāt), surrender on certain terms or conditions. The men in the fort capitulated, on the condition that they should be allowed to go away unharmed. *v. 14.*

ca pit u la tion (kə pich′ů lā′shən), act of capitulating. *n. 15.*

ca pon (kā′pən), rooster specially raised to be eaten. *n. 20.*

ca price (kə prēs′), a sudden change of mind without reason; notion; fancy. If you decided that all your clothes must be blue, and would wear nothing else, that would be called a caprice. *n. 11.*

ca pri cious (kə prish′əs), guided by one's fancy; changeable. A spoiled child is often capricious. *adj. 10.*

Cap ri corn (kap′ri kôrn), the tropic of Capricorn, a circle around the world 23.45 degrees south of the equator. *n. 17.*

cap size (kap sīz′), upset; overturn; turn bottom side up. *v. 13.*

Sailors turning a capstan

cap stan (kap′stən), a machine for lifting or pulling that stands upright. Sailors hoist the anchor by turning the capstan. *n. 19.*

cap sule (kap′səl), small case or covering. Medicine is often given in capsules made of gelatin. The seeds of some plants grow in capsules. *n. 10.*

Capsule for medicine

Capt., Captain.

cap tain (kap′tin), 1. leader; chief. 2. army officer in command of a company. 3. navy officer in command of a warship. 4. commander of a ship. 5. leader of a team in sports. 6. lead or command as captain. Tom will captain the team. *n., v. 1.*

cap tion (kap′shən), title; heading. Pictures in newspapers and magazines often have captions explaining them. *n.*

cap tious (kap′shəs), hard to please; finding fault. *adj. 16.*

cap ti vate (kap′ti vāt), charm; fascinate; hold captive by beauty or interest. The beautiful music captivated him. The children were captivated by the animal story. *v. 12.*

cap tive (kap′tiv), 1. prisoner. The army brought back a thousand captives. 2. held as prisoner; made a prisoner. The captive soldiers were shut up in a pen. *n., adj. 4.*

cap tiv i ty (kap tiv′i ti), 1. being in prison.

2. being held against one's will. *n., pl. captivities. 5.*

cap tor (kap′tər), man who takes or holds a prisoner. *n. 17.*

cap ture (kap′chər), 1. make a prisoner of; take by force or trick. We capture butterflies with a net. 2. the thing or person captured. 3. act of capturing; fact of capturing or being captured. *v., n. 3.*

car (kär), 1. vehicle moving on wheels. 2. automobile. 3. a railroad car, a streetcar, etc. 4. chariot. *Used in poetry.* 5. part of a balloon, elevator, etc., for carrying passengers. *n. 1.*

ca ra ba o (kä′rə bä′ō), water buffalo of the Philippine Islands. *n., pl. carabaos.*

car a cul (kar′ə kəl), fur made from the skin of lambs. Caracul has flat, loose curls. *n.* Also spelled **karakul.**

car a mel (kar′ə məl or kär′məl), 1. burnt sugar used for coloring and flavoring. 2. a kind of candy. *n. 9.*

car at (kar′ət), 1. one 24th part. Gold in watches is often 18 carats fine or pure and 6 parts alloy. 2. a unit of weight for precious stones equaling about 3 grains or $\frac{1}{150}$ ounce troy. *n. 15.*

car a van (kar′ə van), 1. a group of merchants, pilgrims, tourists, etc., traveling together for safety through a desert or a dangerous country. 2. a large covered wagon for people or goods; a house on wheels; a van. *n. 6.*

car a van sa ry (kar′ə van′sə ri), 1. an inn or hotel where caravans rest. 2. any large inn or hotel. *n., pl. caravansaries. 20.*

car a vel (kar′ə vel), small, fast ship of former times. *n. 20.*

Caravel

car a way (kar′ə wā), a plant whose seeds are used in cooking and medicine. *n. 20.*

car bine (kär′bīn), short rifle or musket. *n. 18.*

car bo hy drate (kär′bō hī′drāt), a substance, like sugar and starch, which is made of carbon, hydrogen, and oxygen. *n. 7.*

car bol ic ac id (kär bol′ik as′id), a poison used for killing germs. *9.*

car bon (kär′bən), the substance that coal, charcoal, and graphite are made of. Carbon united with other substances is found in most animals and plants. *n. 8.*

car bon ate (kär′bən āt), 1. a salt of carbonic acid. 2. form into a carbonate. 3. charge with carbon dioxide. Soda water is carbonated to make it bubble and fizz. *n., v. 12.*

car bon di ox ide (kär′bən dī ok′sīd), heavy, colorless, odorless gas.

car bon ic (kär bon′ik), containing carbon; of carbon. **Carbonic acid** breaks up into water and carbon dioxide very easily. *adj. 18.*

car bon if er ous (kär′bən if′ər əs), coal-bearing. *adj. 15.*

car bon ize (kär′bən īz), 1. turn into carbon. 2. cover with carbon. *v.*

car bon mon ox ide (kär′bən mon ok′sīd), a colorless, odorless, very poisonous gas.

car bun cle (kär′bung kəl), 1. very painful, inflamed swelling on the skin, somewhat like a boil, but worse. 2. pimple. 3. round-shaped garnet or other deep-red jewel. *n. 11.*

car bu re tor (kär′bə rā′tər), device for mixing air with gas. The engine of an automobile is supplied with a mixture of gasoline and air by the carburetor. *n. 9.*

car case (kär′kəs), carcass. *n. 11.*

car cass (kär′kəs), 1. dead body of an animal. 2. body. *n. 8.*

card[1] (kärd), 1. flat piece of stiff paper or thin cardboard. Cards are used for various purposes. There are post cards, visiting cards, cards of admission, and notice cards. 2. one of a pack of cards used in playing games. *n. 2.*

card[2] (kärd), 1. a toothed tool or wire brush. 2. clean or comb with such a tool; as, to card wool for spinning. *n., v.*

card board (kärd′bōrd′), a stiff material made of paper and used for making cards, boxes, etc. *n. 11.*

car di gan (kär′di gən), a knitted woolen jacket. *n. 14.*

Cardigan

car di nal (kär′di nəl), 1. of first importance; chief; principal. The **cardinal numbers** are one, two, three, four, five, etc. The **cardinal points** of the compass are north, south, east, and west. 2. one of the seventy princes or high officials in the Roman Catholic Church, appointed by the Pope. Cardinals wear red robes and red hats. 3. bright, rich red. 4. an American songbird whose feathers are red, black, and white. *adj., n. 6.*

Cardinal
(8 to 9 in. long)

care (kãr), 1. thought. A mother has care for her baby's health. 2. worry. I wish I could be free from care. 3. attention. A good cook does her work with care. 4. charge. Mary was left in her sister's care. 5. food, shelter, and protection. Your child will have the best of care. 6. something that requires care. 7. feel interest. He cares about music. 8. wish; like. A cat does not care to be washed. 9. **Care for** means (1) like. (2) take charge of. The nurse will care for him now. *n., v. 1.*

ca reen (kə rēn′), 1. lean to one side. 2. cause to lean over or keel over. The strong wind careened the ship. *v. 19.*

ca reer (kə rēr′), 1. a run at full speed; going with force. We were in full career when we struck the post. 2. general course of action through life. It is interesting to read of the careers of great men and women. 3. occupation; profession. 4. rush along wildly. The runaway horse careered through the streets, banging the carriage behind him. *n., v. 4.*

care free (kãr′frē′), without worry; happy; gay. *adj.*

care ful (kãr′fəl), 1. full of care for something; taking pains; watchful; cautious. 2. done with care; showing care. *adj. 1.*

care ful ness (kãr′fəl nis), being careful. *n. 18.*

care less (kãr′lis), 1. not thinking or watching what one says or does. One careless step may cost a life. 2. not exact in doing work; not exactly done; as, a careless worker, careless work. 3. not caring or troubling. *adj. 3.*

care less ness (kãr′lis nis), being without care; thoughtlessness; indifference. *n. 8.*

ca ress (kə res′), 1. a touch showing affection; tender embrace or kiss. 2. to touch or stroke tenderly; kiss. *n., v. 6.*

car et (kar′ət), a mark (∧) to show where something should be put in in writing or printing. *n. 20.*

care tak er (kãr′tāk′ər), one who takes care of a person, place, or thing. *n. 19.*

care worn (kãr′wōrn′), showing signs of worry; tired; weary. *adj. 16.*

car go (kär′gō), freight carried by a ship; load. *n., pl. cargoes* or *cargos. 4.*

Car ib be an (kar′i bē′ən or kə rib′i ən), the sea between Central America, the West Indies, and South America. *n.*

car i bou (kar′i bü), the name of several kinds of North American reindeer. *n., pl. caribous* or *caribou. 18.*

Caribou (4 ft. high at the shoulder)

car i ca ture (kar′i kə chər), 1. a picture or description that exaggerates the peculiarities or defects of a person or thing. 2. the art of making such pictures or descriptions. 3. make a caricature of. *n.,v. 12.*

car il lon (kar′i lon), set of bells arranged for playing melodies. *n.*

car load (kär′lōd′), as much as a car can hold or carry. *n. 20.*

Car lyle (kär līl′), Thomas, famous Scottish prose writer and philosopher (1795-1881). *n. 13.*

car mine (kär′min), 1. deep red with a tinge of purple. 2. light crimson. *n., adj. 18.*

Carnation

car nage (kär′nij), slaughter of a great number of people. *n. 14.*

car nal (kär′nəl), 1. worldly; not spiritual. 2. bodily. *adj. 10.*

car na tion (kär nā′shən), 1. a highly cultivated garden flower with a spicy fragrance. 2. rosy pink. *n., adj. 11.*

car ni val (kär′ni vəl), 1. place of amusement having merry-go-rounds, games, etc. 2. feasting and merrymaking; noisy and unrestrained revels. 3. time of feasting and merrymaking just before Lent. *n. 11.*

car niv o rous (kär niv′ə rəs), flesh-eating. Cats, dogs, lions, tigers, and bears are carnivorous animals. *adj. 11.*

car ol (kar′əl), 1. song of joy. 2. Christmas hymn. 3. sing; sing joyously; praise with carols. *n., v., caroled, caroling. 7.*

Car o li na (kar′ə lī′nə), either North Carolina or South Carolina. *n. 5.*

ca rous al (kə rouz′əl), a drinking party; a carouse. *n. 17.*

ca rouse (kə rouz′), 1. a noisy feast or drinking party. 2. drink heavily; take part in noisy revels. *n., v. 12.*

carp[1] (kärp), find fault. *v. 11.*

carp[2] (kärp), a fresh-water fish that lives in ponds and sluggish streams. *n.*

Car pa thi ans (kär pā′thi ənz), a mountain system in central Europe. *n. pl. 16.*

car pel (kär′pəl), modified leaf from which a pistil of a flower is formed. *n. 14.*

CARPEL

car pen ter (kär′pən tər), worker who builds the wooden parts of houses, barns, ships, etc. *n. 3.*

car pen try (kär′pən tri), the work of a carpenter. *n.*

car pet (kär′pit), 1. heavy, woven fabric used for covering floors and stairs. 2. a smooth, soft, or bright stretch of grass, flowers, etc.; as, a carpet of leaves. 3. to cover with a carpet. In the spring, the ground was carpeted with violets. *n., v. 3.*

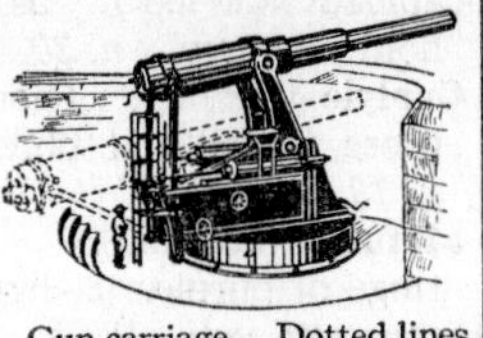

Gun carriage. Dotted lines show position of gun before it is raised for firing.

car riage (kar′ij), 1. taking persons or goods from one place to another. 2. the cost of taking anything from one place to another. 3. manner of holding the head and body; bearing. She has a queenly carriage. 4. a vehicle having wheels. Carriages are usually drawn by horses and are used to carry people. 5. the support of a gun. 6. a sliding part of machinery. *n. 2.*

car ri er (kar′i ər), 1. person or thing that takes goods, packages, and messages from one place to another. The mail carriers deliver mail twice a day in our town. Railroad and steamship lines are called common carriers. 2. anything that carries something. Water and milk are often carriers of disease germs. *n. 5.*

car ri on (kar′i ən), 1. dead and decaying flesh. 2. dead and decaying. *n., adj. 11.*

car rot (kar′ət), a vegetable which is the long, tapering, orange-colored root of a plant. Rabbits like to eat carrots. *n. 8.*

Carrot

car ry (kar′i), 1. take (a thing or person) from one place to another. Railroads carry coal from the mines to your town. The man carried the child home. This story will carry your thoughts back to the first of the year. 2. cover the distance. His voice will carry to the back of the room. This gun will carry a mile. 3. win. Our side carried the election for club president. 4. hold or bear. This boy carries himself well. 5. Some special meanings are:

carry away, arouse strong feeling in; influence beyond reason.

carry on, 1. do; manage; conduct. 2. go ahead with; go on with after being stopped. 3. keep going; not stop; continue.

carry out, do; get done; complete.

v., carried, carrying. 1.

Car son Cit y (kär′sən sit′i), the capital of Nevada.

cart (kärt), 1. strong vehicle with two wheels, used in farming and for carrying heavy loads. 2. light wagon used for delivering goods or for general business. 3. small vehicle on wheels, moved by hand. 4. carry in a cart. Cart away this rubbish. *n., v. 3.*

Cart (def. 1)

car tel (kär tel′), 1. a large combination of industries for some purpose. 2. a written agreement between nations at war, for the exchange of prisoners or for some other purpose. 3. written challenge to a duel. *n.*

cart er (kär′tər), man whose work is driving a cart. *n. 7.*

Car thage (kär′thij), a famous, powerful city in northern Africa, founded by the Phoenicians. Carthage fought against Rome and was finally destroyed. *n. 12.*

Car tha gin i an (kär′thə jin′i ən), 1. of Carthage. 2. a native or inhabitant of Carthage. *adj., n. 14.*

car ti lage (kär′ti lij), gristle; a firm, elastic, flexible substance forming parts of a skeleton. *n. 11.*

car ton (kär′tən), box made of pasteboard. *n.*

car toon (kär tün′), a sketch or drawing which interests or amuses us by showing public persons or events in an exaggerated way. *n. 11.*

car tridge (kär′trij), 1. a case made of metal or cardboard for holding gunpowder. 2. a roll of camera film. *n. 12.*

Cartridge: A, metal case; B, bullet; C, powder.

carve (kärv), 1. cut. To carve a statue is to cut it out of stone or wood, etc. A picture may be carved on the surface of wood or stone. 2. ornament with cut figures and designs; as, a carved box. 3. cut into slices or pieces. Father carves the meat at the table. *v. 3.*

carv er (kär′vər), 1. person who carves. 2. knife for carving meat. *n. 13.*

carv ing (kär′ving), carved work; as, wood carving, stone carving, carvings in ivory. *n.*

car y at id (kar′i at′id), a statue of a woman used as a column. *n. 18.*

cas cade (kas kād′), small waterfall. *n. 6.*

Cascade

Cascade Range, mountain range in northwestern United States.

cas car a (kas kãr′ə), a medicine prepared from the bark of a shrub or tree. It is used to move the bowels. *n. 19.*

case[1] (kās), 1. A case of measles keeps a child away from school. The children agreed that every case of cheating should be punished. The man told of the sad case of starving children in India. Any special condition of a person or thing can be called a case. In case of fire walk quietly to the nearest door. 2. a matter for a law court to decide. 3. a certain form or relation of nouns, pronouns, or adjectives in grammar. *I* is in the subjective case. *Me* is in the objective case. 4. **In any case** means anyhow or no matter what happens. *n. 1.*

case[2] (kās), 1. covering. Put the knife back in its case. 2. box. There is a big case full of books in the hall. 3. quantity in a box. 4. frame. *n.*

ca se in (kā′si in), protein present in milk. Cheese is mostly casein. Casein is used in certain kinds of paints. *n. 14.*

case ment (kās′mənt), a window opening on hinges like a door. *n. 6.*

Casement

cash (kash), 1. ready money; coins and bills. 2. change into cash; give cash for. The bank will cash your five-dollar check. 3. get cash for. *n., v. 3.*

cash ew (kash′ü), a tree that grows in tropical America. The cashew nut is soft and good to eat. *n.*

cash ier[1] (kash ēr′), person in charge of money in a bank, or in any business. *n. 6.*

cash ier[2] (kash ēr′), dismiss from service; discharge in disgrace. A dishonest army or navy officer is deprived of his rank and cashiered. *v.*

cash mere (kash′mēr), 1. a fine, soft wool. 2. a costly kind of shawl made of this wool. 3. a fine, soft woolen cloth. *n. 20.*

cas ing (kās′ing), 1. thing put around something; covering; case. 2. frame. Windows fit in a casing. *n. 13.*

ca si no (kə sē′nō), 1. a building for meetings, parties, or games. 2. a card game. *n., pl. casinos. 18.*

cask (kask), 1. barrel. A cask may be large or small, and is usually made to hold liquids. 2. the amount a cask holds. *n. 7.*

cas ket (kas′kit), 1. a small box, often fine and beautiful, used to hold jewels and letters. 2. coffin. *n. 8.*

Cas pi an Sea (kas′pi ən sē′), an inland salt sea between Europe and Asia. *11.*

casque (kask), helmet. *n. 11.*

Cas san dra (kə san′drə), a daughter of King Priam of Troy. Apollo gave her the gift of prophecy, but later in anger decreed that no one should believe her. *n. 17.*

cas sa va (kə sä′və), 1. tropical plant with starchy roots. 2. starch from its roots. Tapioca is made from cassava. *n.*

cas se role (kas′ə rōl), 1. a covered baking dish, in which food can be both cooked and served. 2. a mold of boiled rice, mashed potatoes, etc., filled with meat or vegetables. *n. 13.*

cas sia (kash′ə), 1. an inferior kind of cinnamon. 2. the tree that produces it. 3. a plant yielding leaves that are used as a laxative. *n. 19.*

cas sock (kas′ək), a long garment, usually black, worn by a clergyman. *n. 14.*

cast (kast), 1. throw; throw off; let fall off. 2. a throw; the distance a thing is thrown. 3. let harden in a mold. 4. thing that is molded. 5. select to take a part in a play. 6. the actors in a play. 7. form; appearance. 8. sort; kind. 9. hue; a slight amount of some color. 10. Some special meanings are:

cast a ballot, vote.

cast about, 1. search; look. 2. make plans.

cast down, 1. turn downward; lower. 2. make sad or discouraged.

cast up, 1. turn upward; raise. 2. add up; find the sum of.

v., cast, casting, n. 2.

cas ta nets (kas′tə nets′), instruments of hard wood or ivory held in the palm of the hand and struck together to beat time for dancing and music. *n. pl.*

cast a way (kast′ə wā′), 1. thrown away; cast adrift. 2. a shipwrecked person. 3. outcast. *adj., n. 16.*

caste (kast), 1. one of the social classes into which Hindus are divided. A Hindu cannot rise from the caste of his forefathers. 2. any social class like this. 3. a social system having set classes separated by differences of rank, wealth, position, etc. 4. **Lose caste** means lose social rank or position. Many European nobles felt that they would lose caste by working. *n. 9.*

cas tel lat ed (kas′tə lāt′id), built like a castle with turrets and battlements. *adj. 16.*

cast er (kas′tər), 1. person or thing that casts. 2. castor. *n. 13.*

cas ti gate (kas′ti gāt), punish; criticize severely. *v. 19.*

cas ti ga tion (kas′ti gā′shən), punishment; severe criticism. *n. 20.*

Cas tile (kas tēl′), 1. a region in north central Spain. 2. **Castile soap** is a pure, hard soap made from olive oil. *n., adj. 7.*

Cas til ian (kas til′yən), 1. of Castile, its people, or their language. Castilian Spanish is the accepted standard form of the language. 2. Castilian Spanish. 3. a native or inhabitant of Castile. *adj., n. 11.*

cast ing (kas′ting), 1. something cast in a mold. 2. A **casting vote** is a vote cast by the presiding officer to decide a question when the votes are evenly divided. *n., adj. 20.*

cast iron, hard, brittle form of iron made by casting. *18.*

cast-i ron (kast′ī′ərn), 1. made of cast iron. 2. hard; not yielding. 3. hardy; strong. *adj.*

cas tle (kas′əl), 1. a large building or group of buildings with thick walls, towers, and other defenses against attack. 2. a palace that once had defenses against attack. 3. large and stately residence. 4. one of the pieces with which the game of chess is played. *n. 2.*

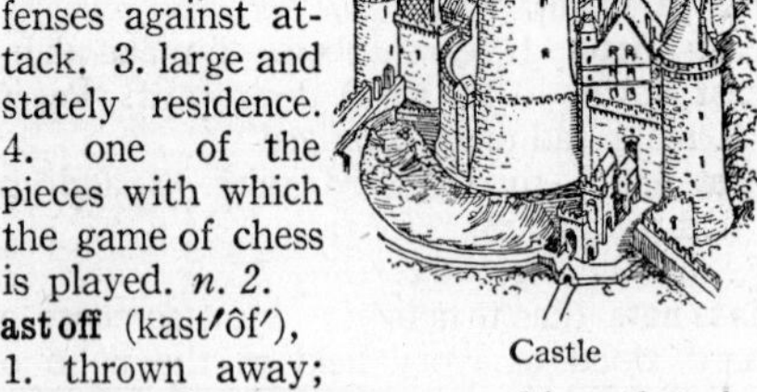

Castle

cast off (kast′ôf′), 1. thrown away; abandoned. 2. person or thing that has been cast off. *adj., n.*

cas tor (kas′tər), 1. a small wheel on a piece of furniture to make it easy to move. 2. bottle containing salt, mustard, vinegar, or other seasoning for table use. 3. holder for a set of cruets, saltcellars, etc. *n. 11.* Also spelled **caster.**

Castor (def. 1)

castor oil, a medicine used to move the bowels thoroughly, made from the beans of the castor-oil plant.

cas trate (kas′trāt), remove the male glands of. An ox is a castrated bull. *v.*

cas u al (kazh′ü əl), 1. happening by chance. 2. careless; not planned. I gave a casual glance in his direction. 3. irregular. A casual laborer is one who has no steady job. *adj. 6.*

cas u al ty (kazh′ü əl ti), 1. accident. 2. mishap; unfortunate accident. 3. soldier or sailor who has been wounded, killed, or lost. 4. person injured or killed in an accident. *n., pl. casualties. 13.*

cas u ist (kazh′ü ist), 1. person who studies and decides questions of conscience or conduct. 2. person who reasons and argues cleverly but falsely. *n. 14.*

cat (kat), 1. small animal often kept as a pet or for catching mice. Cats, lions, tigers, and leopards all belong to the same group of animals. 2. any animal belonging to this group. 3. a whip made of rope. *n. 2.*

cat a clysm (kat′ə klizm), 1. flood or earthquake or any sudden violent change in the earth. 2. any violent change. The World War was a cataclysm for all of Europe. *n. 16.*

cat a comb (kat′ə kōm), underground gallery forming a burial place. *n. 16.*

cat a logue or **cat a log** (kat′ə lôg), 1. a list. A library usually has a catalogue of its books. Some business companies print catalogues showing pictures and prices of what they have to sell. 2. make a list of; enter in the proper place in a list. *n., v. 5.*

Cat a lo ni a (kat′ə lō′ni ə), region in northeastern Spain. *n.*

ca tal pa (kə tal′pə), a tree with large, heart-shaped leaves, clusters of bell-shaped flowers, and long pods. *n. 17.*

Catalpa: A, pod; B, branch with flowers.

cat a mount (kat′ə mount), wild cat, such as a puma or lynx. *n.*

cat a pult (kat′ə pult), 1. ancient weapon for shooting stones, arrows, etc. 2. slingshot. 3. device for launching an airplane from the deck of a ship. 4. shoot from a catapult; throw; hurl. *n., v. 14.*

cat a ract (kat′ə rakt), 1. a large, steep waterfall. 2. a violent rush or downpour of water. 3. a disease of the eye that makes a person partly or entirely blind. *n. 6.*

Cataract

ca tarrh (kə tär′), an inflamed condition, usually in the nose or throat, causing a discharge. *n. 10.*

ca tas tro phe (kə tas′trə fi), a sudden, widespread, or extraordinary disaster; great calamity or misfortune. A big earthquake or flood is a catastrophe; so is a big fire. *n. 8.*

cat bird (kat′bėrd′), a North American songbird that can make a noise like a cat mewing. *n.*

cat boat (kat′bōt′), sailboat with one mast set far forward. A catboat has no bowsprit or jib. *n.*

cat call (kat′kôl′), shrill cry or whistle to express disapproval. *n.*

catch (kach), 1. take and hold (something moving); seize; capture. Catch the ball with both hands. The cat catches mice. The policeman caught the thief. The rat was caught in the trap. We were caught in the storm. Bright colors catch a baby's eye. 2. take; get. Paper catches fire easily. Put a warm coat on, or you will catch cold. He spoke so rapidly that I didn't catch the meaning of what he said. The soldiers suddenly caught sight of the enemy behind a wall. You have just five minutes to catch your train. 3. come upon suddenly; surprise. Mother caught me just as I was hiding her present. "Don't catch me up on every little mistake," said Dick to his big sister. 4. **Catch up with** means come up to while going the same way. Our dog ran as hard as he could to catch up with our car. 5. to act as catcher. John catches for our school team. 6. act of catching. Dick made a fine catch with one hand. 7. thing that catches. The catch on that door is broken. There is a catch to that question. 8. thing that is caught. A catch of fish is the amount caught. 9. a kind of song; a round. "Three Blind Mice" is a catch. *v., caught, catching, n. 1.*

catch er (kach′ər), 1. person or thing that catches. 2. baseball player who stands behind the batter to catch the ball thrown by the pitcher. *n. 12.*

catch ing (kach′ing), 1. causing infection; liable to spread from one person to another. Colds are catching. 2. attractive; fascinating. *adj.*

catch y (kach′i), 1. attractive; easy to remember; as, a catchy tune. 2. that catches; deceptive; as, a catchy question in an examination. *adj., catchier, catchiest.*

cat e chism (kat′i kizm), 1. book of questions and answers about religion. 2. set of questions and answers about any subject. 3. set of questions. *n. 10.*

cat e chize or **cat e chise** (kat′i kīz), 1. teach by questions and answers. 2. question closely. *v.*

cat e gor i cal (kat′i gor′i kəl), positive; without conditions or qualifications. *adj.*

cat e go ry (kat′i gō′ri), a general division in classification; a class. Helen groups all people into two categories: those she likes and those she dislikes. *n., pl. categories. 13.*

ca ter (kā′tər), 1. provide food or supplies. He runs a restaurant and also caters for weddings and parties. 2. supply means of enjoyment. Some magazines cater to boys. *v. 11.*

cat er pil lar (kat′ər pil′ər), the larva or wormlike form in which insects such as the butterfly and the moth hatch from the egg. *n. 6.*

Caterpillar on a twig (about ½ life size)

caterpillar tractor, a kind of tractor for pulling heavy loads over rough or soft ground.

cat er waul (kat′ər wôl), howl; screech. *n., v.*

cat fish (kat′fish′), any of several scaleless fishes which have long, slender feelers about the mouth. *n., pl. catfishes or catfish. 20.*

ca thar tic (kə thär′tik), strong laxative. Epsom salts and castor oil are cathartics. *n. 17.*

Ca thay (ka thā′), old name for China. *n.*

ca the dral (kə thē′drəl), 1. official church of a bishop. The bishop of the district or diocese has a throne in the ca-

Cathedral

thedral. 2. large or important church. See the picture on page 117. *n. 4.*

cath o lic (kath′ə lik), 1. universal; including all; of interest or use to all people. 2. having sympathies with all; broad-minded; liberal. 3. of the whole Christian church. *adj.*

Cath o lic (kath′ə lik), 1. of the Christian church governed by the Pope; Roman Catholic. 2. a member of this church. *adj., n. 4.*

cath o lic i ty (kath′ə lis′i ti), 1. universality; wide prevalence. 2. broad-mindedness. *n.*

cat kin (kat′kin), soft, downy spike of flowers of the willow or birch. *n.*

Catkin

cat nip (kat′nip), a common plant somewhat like mint. *n. 14.*

Ca to (kā′tō), either of two Romans, both famous as soldiers and statesmen. *n. 10.*

cat-o'-nine-tails (kat′ə nīn′tālz′), whip consisting of nine pieces of knotted cord fastened to a handle. The cat-o'-nine-tails used to be a means of punishment in the navy. *n., pl. cat-o'-nine-tails.*

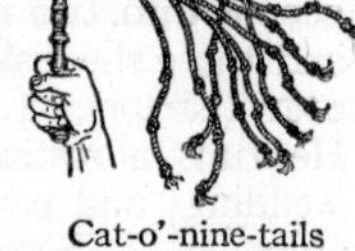

Cat-o'-nine-tails

Cats kills (kats′kilz), low mountains in New York State. *n. pl. 12.*

cat's-paw or **cats paw** (kats′pô′), person used by another to do something unpleasant or dangerous. *n.*

cat sup (kat′səp or kech′əp), a sauce to use with meat, fish, etc. Tomato catsup is made of tomatoes, onions, salt, sugar, and spices. *n. 19.*

cat tail (kat′tāl′), tall marsh plant with flowers in long, round, furry, brown spikes. *n.*

cat tle (kat′əl), farm animals; livestock; oxen, bulls, cows, calves, etc. *n. 2.*

cat tle man (kat′əl mən), man who raises or takes care of cattle. *n., pl. cattlemen.*

Cau ca sian (kô kā′zhən), 1. a member of the white race. Frenchmen, Germans, and Swedes are Caucasians. 2. of or having to do with the white race. *n., adj. 15.*

Cattails (4 to 8 ft. high)

Cau ca sus (kô′kə səs), a mountain range between Europe and Asia, extending from the Black Sea to the Caspian Sea. *n. 10.*

cau cus (kô′kəs), a meeting of members or leaders of a political party to make plans or choose candidates. *n. 13.*

cau dal (kô′dəl), 1. of, at, or near the tail. 2. like a tail. *adj. 18.*

caught (kôt). See **catch.** He caught the ball. *pt. and pp. of catch. 2.*

caul dron (kôl′drən), caldron. *n. 16.*

cau li flow er (kô′li flou′ər), a vegetable having a solid, white head with a few leaves around it. *n. 12.*

Cauliflower

caulk (kôk), fill up (a seam or crack or joint) so that it will not leak; make tight. *v.* Also spelled **calk.**

cause (kôz), 1. person or thing or event that makes something happen. One little mistake was the cause of all her trouble. 2. make happen; make do; bring about. A fever caused her death. A loud noise caused me to jump back. 3. reason or occasion for action. You have no cause to complain. 4. subject or movement in which many people take an interest. World peace is the cause she works for. *n., v. 1.*

cause less (kôz′lis), 1. without any known cause. 2. without good reason. *adj. 13.*

cause way (kôz′wā′), 1. a raised road or path over wet ground, shallow water, etc. 2. main road; highway. *n. 14.*

caus tic (kôs′tik), 1. substance that burns or destroys flesh. My warts were burned away by the caustic put on them. 2. that burns or destroys flesh. Lye is caustic soda or caustic potash. 3. very critical; sarcastic. *n., adj. 14.*

cau ter ize (kô′tər īz), burn with a hot iron or a caustic substance. Doctors cauterize snake bites to prevent the poison from spreading. *v. 20.*

cau tion (kô′shən), 1. being very careful; taking care to be safe; never taking chances. Use caution in crossing streets. 2. a warning. A sign with "Danger!" on it is a caution. 3. warn. *n., v. 6.*

cau tious (kô′shəs), very careful; never taking chances. *adj. 6.*

cav al cade (kav′əl kād′), procession of persons riding on horses or drawn by horses. *n. 17.*

cav a lier (kav′ə lēr′), 1. horseman; knight. 2. courteous gentleman. 3. a courteous escort for a lady. 4. offhand. 5. haughty. *n., adj. 6.*

cav al ry (kav′əl ri), soldiers who fight on horseback. *n., pl. cavalries. 10.*

cav al ry man (kav′əl ri mən), soldier who fights on horseback. *n., pl. cavalrymen. 18.*

cave (kāv), 1. hollow space underground. 2. **Cave in** means fall in. *n., v. 2.*

cave man, 1. man who lived in caves. 2. rough, crude man.

cav ern (kav′ərn), large cave. *n. 6.*

cav ern ous (kav′ər nəs), 1. like a cavern; large and hollow. 2. full of caverns. *adj. 16.*

caviar or **caviare** (kav′iär), a salty relish made from the eggs of fish. *n. 18.*

cav il (kav′il), 1. find fault unnecessarily. 2. petty objection or criticism. *v., caviled, caviling, n. 14.*

cav i ty (kav′i ti), hole; hollow place. Most cavities in teeth are caused by decay. *n., pl. cavities. 7.*

ca vort (kə vôrt′), prance about. A horse cavorts when he feels excited. *v.*

caw (kô), 1. harsh cry made by a crow or raven. 2. make this cry. *n., v. 6.*

cay enne (kī en′), red pepper; a hot, biting powder made from the seeds or fruit of a pepper plant. *n. 20.*

cay use (kī ūs′), an Indian pony of the western United States. *n.*

cease (sēs), stop. *v., n. 2.*

cease less (sēs′lis), never stopping; going on all the time. *adj. 9.*

ce dar (sē′dər), an evergreen tree with hard, reddish, fragrant wood which is used for posts, clothes closets, cedar chests, pencils, and cigar boxes. *n. 3.*

Cedar

cede (sēd), give up; surrender; hand over to another. Spain ceded the Philippine Islands to the United States. *v. 10.*

ceil ing (sēl′ing), 1. the inside top covering of a room. 2. greatest height to which an airplane or airship can go under certain conditions. 3. top limit. *n. 4.*

cel an dine (sel′ən dīn), a plant with yellow flowers. *n.*

cel e brate (sel′i brāt), 1. observe (a special time or day) with activities of a proper kind. We celebrated Christmas with a tree and presents. 2. perform with the proper rites and ceremonies. The priest celebrates Mass. 3. praise and honor in public. *v. 2.*

cel e brat ed (sel′i brāt′id), famous; well-known; much talked about. *adj.*

cel e bra tion (sel′i brā′shən), 1. special services or activities in honor of a particular man, act, time, or day. A Fourth of July celebration often includes fireworks. 2. act of celebrating. *n. 5.*

ce leb ri ty (si leb′ri ti), 1. famous person. 2. being talked about or praised; fame. *n., pl. celebrities. 11.*

ce ler i ty (si ler′i ti), swiftness; speed. *n. 15.*

cel er y (sel′ər i), vegetable whose long stalks are whitened by keeping the stalks covered while they grow. Celery is eaten raw or cooked. *n. 6.*

ce les tial (si les′chəl), 1. of the sky; having to do with the sky. The sun and moon are celestial bodies. 2. heavenly; divine; very good or beautiful. *adj. 4.*

cel i ba cy (sel′i bə si), unmarried state; single life. *n. 15.*

cel i bate (sel′i bāt), 1. person who does not get married. 2. unmarried. *n., adj.*

cell (sel), 1. a small room in a prison, convent, or monastery. 2. any small, hollow space. Bees store honey in the cells of a honeycomb. 3. a container holding materials for producing electricity by chemical action. 4. All animals and plants are made of small units called cells, which are formed of a small amount of living matter called protoplasm. *n. 3.*

cel lar (sel′ər), underground room or rooms, usually under a building, used for storing fuel and food. *n. 3.*

cel list or **'cel list** (chel′ist), person who plays the cello. *n.*

cel lo or **'cel lo** (chel′ō), violoncello, a musical instrument like a violin, but much larger; a bass violin. A cello is held between the knees while being played. *n., pl. cellos, 'cellos.*

Man playing a cello

cel lo phane (sel′ə fān), transparent substance made from cellulose. It is used as a wrapping for food, candy, tobacco, and many other things. *n.* [*Trade name*]

cel lu lar (sel′ū lər), 1. having to do with cells. 2. consisting of cells. All animal and plant tissue is cellular. *adj. 14.*

cel lu loid (sel′ū loid), a hard substance made from camphor and cotton soaked in special acids. It catches fire easily. Combs, toilet articles, and small boxes are often made of white or colored celluloid. *n.* [*Trade name*] *13.*

cel lu lose (sel′ū lōs), the woody part of all plants and trees. Wood, cotton, hemp, and flax are made of cellulose. *n. 9.*

Celt (selt), a member of a people to which the Irish, Highland Scotch, Welsh, and Bretons belong. *n. 13.*

Celt ic (sel′tik), 1. of the Celts or their languages. 2. the languages spoken by the Celts. *adj., n. 10.*

ce ment (si ment′), 1. a substance made by burning clay and limestone. Cement is mixed with sand and water and used for holding stones and bricks together in the walls of buildings and for making hard walls, floors, and walks. Cement becomes hard like stone. 2. anything applied soft, which hardens to make things stick together. 3. fasten together with cement. A broken vase can be cemented. 4. spread cement over. *n., v. 4.*

cem e ter y (sem′i ter′i), place for burying the dead; graveyard. *n., pl. cemeteries. 5.*

cen ser (sen′sər), container in which incense is burned. *n. 9.*

cen sor (sen′sər), 1. person who tells people how they ought to behave. 2. person who changes books, plays, magazines, moving pictures, etc., so as to make them satisfactory to the government or to the organization that employs him. 3. act as censor; make changes in; take out part of. 4. person who likes to find fault. 5. a Roman magistrate who took the census and told people how to behave. *n., v. 13.*

cen so ri ous (sen sō′ri əs), too ready to find fault; severely critical. *adj. 16.*

cen sor ship (sen′sər ship), 1. act or system of censoring. New York State has a censorship for moving pictures. 2. position or work of a censor. *n. 18.*

cen sure (sen′shər), 1. expression of unfavorable opinion; blame. Censure is sometimes harder to bear than punishment. 2. to blame; find fault with. *n., v. 5.*

cen sus (sen′səs), an official count of the people of a country taken to find out the number of people, their ages, sex, what they do to make a living, and many other facts about them. *n. 10.*

cent (sent), a copper coin of the United States and Canada. 100 cents make one dollar. *n. 1.*

cen taur (sen′tôr), a monster in Greek myths having the head, arms, and chest of a man, and the body and legs of a horse. *n. 14.*

Centaur

cen ten ni al (sen ten′i əl), 1. having to do with 100 years or the 100th anniversary. 2. 100 years old. 3. 100th anniversary. The town is celebrating its centennial. 4. the celebration of the 100th anniversary. *adj., n. 16.*

cen ter (sen′tər), 1. a point within a circle or sphere equally distant from all points of the circumference or surface. 2. middle point; as, the center of a room. 3. person, thing, or group in a middle position. 4. principal point or place. New York City is a center of trade. 5. place in or at a center. 6. collect at a center. 7. be at a center. *n., v. 1.*

cen ti grade (sen′ti grād), divided into 100 degrees. The centigrade thermometer has 0 degrees for the temperature at which ice melts and 100 degrees for the temperature at which water boils. *adj. 13.*

cen ti gram or **cen ti gramme** (sen′ti gram), in the metric system, the unit of weight equal to $\frac{1}{100}$ of a gram. *n. 18.*

cen time (sän′tēm), in French money, $\frac{1}{100}$ of a franc. *n. 20.*

cen ti me ter or **cen ti me tre** (sen′ti mē′tər), a measure of length equal to $\frac{1}{100}$ of a meter; .3937 inch. *n. 9.*

cen ti pede (sen′ti pēd), a small wormlike animal with many pairs of legs. *n. 16.*

Centipede (1 in. long)

cen tral (sen′trəl), 1. of the center; being the center. 2. at the center; near the center. 3. from the center. 4. equally distant from all points; easy to get to or from. 5. main; chief; leading; principal. 6. telephone exchange. *adj., n. 2.*

Central America, the part of North America between Mexico and South America. Guatemala, El Salvador, Honduras, British Honduras, Nicaragua, Costa Rica, and Panama are in Central America.

cen tral i za tion (sen′trəl i zā′shən), 1. the coming or bringing to a center. 2. concentration at a center. 3. the concentration of administrative power in a central government. *n. 18.*

cen tral ize (sen′trəl īz), 1. collect at a center; gather together. 2. bring under one control. *v. 15.*

cen tral ly (sen′trəl i), at the center; near the center. *adv.*

cen tre (sen′tər), center. *n., v.*

cen trif u gal (sen trif′ū gəl), moving away from the center. *adj. 13.*

cen trip e tal (sen trip′i təl), moving toward the center. Centripetal force is a force directed toward the center. *adj.*

cen tu ri on (sen tūr′i ən or sen tür′i ən), the commander of a group of about 100 soldiers in the ancient Roman army. *n. 15.*

cen tu ry (sen′chə ri), 1. each 100 years, counting from some special time like the birth of Christ. The first century is 1 to 100; the nineteenth century is 1801 to 1900; the twentieth century is 1901 to 2000. 2. a period of 100 years. From 1824 to 1924 is a century. 3. a group of 100 men or 100 things. *n., pl. centuries. 2.*

Century plant (sometimes 30 ft. high)

century plant, a Mexican plant, so named because it was wrongly supposed to bloom only once in every hundred years.

Cer ber us (sėr′bər əs), 1. dog with three heads that guarded the entrance to Hades. 2. a surly, watchful guard. *n. 16.*

Cerberus

ce re al (sēr′i əl), 1. any grass producing grain which is used as a food. Wheat, rice, corn, oats, and barley are cereals. 2. grain. 3. food made from grain. Oatmeal, corn meal, and rice are cereals. 4. of or having to do with grain or the grasses producing it. *n., adj. 8.*

cer e bel lum (ser′i bel′əm), a part of the brain. See the picture. *n. 17.*

cer e bral (ser′i brəl), of the brain. Thought goes with cerebral action. *adj. 16.*

cer e brum (ser′i brəm), a part of the brain. See the picture. *n. 14.*

Human brain: A, cerebrum; B, cerebellum.

cere ment (sēr′mənt), cloth in which a dead body is wrapped for burial. *n. 19.*

cer e mo ni al (ser′i mō′ni əl), 1. formal. 2. of or having to do with ceremony. 3. the formal actions proper to an occasion. Bowing the head and kneeling are ceremonials of religion. *adj., n. 11.*

cer e mo ni ous (ser′i mō′ni əs), very formal; extremely polite. *adj. 17.*

cer e mo ny (ser′i mō′ni), 1. a special form or set of acts to be done on special occasions such as weddings, funerals, graduations, Christmas, or Easter. The marriage ceremony was performed in the church. 2. very polite conduct; a way of conducting oneself that follows all the rules of polite social behavior. The old gentleman showed us to the door with a great deal of ceremony. *n., pl. ceremonies. 4.*

Ce res (sēr′ēz), the Roman goddess of agriculture. The Greeks called her Demeter. *n. 13.*

ce rise (sə rēz′), bright, pinkish red. *n., adj.*

cer tain (sėr′tən), 1. sure. It is certain that 3 and 2 do not make 6. 2. some. Certain plants will not grow in this country. 3. A certain person or thing means a person or thing that one could name, but does not need to name. *adj. 1.*

cer tain ly (sėr′tən li), surely; without doubt. *adv. 5.*

cer tain ty (sėr′tən ti), 1. a fact that one is sure of. 2. freedom from doubt; being certain. The man's certainty was amusing, for we could all see that he was wrong. *n., pl. certainties. 8.*

cer tes (sėr′tēz), certainly. *adv.* [*Old use*] *15.*

cer tif i cate (sər tif′i kit), written or printed statement that may be used as proof of some fact. This certificate shows that John Williams has completed the schoolwork of the eighth grade. *n. 5.*

cer ti fy (sėr′ti fī), 1. declare (something) true or correct by a spoken, written, or printed statement. 2. guarantee. **Certified milk** is guaranteed to be up to certain standards. *v., certified, certifying. 10.*

ce ru le an (si rü′li ən), sky-blue. *adj. 18.*

ces sa tion (se sā′shən), ceasing; pause; stop. During the summer there is a cessation of schoolwork. *n. 11.*

ces sion (sesh′ən), a ceding; a giving up; a handing over. *n. 14.*

cess pool (ses′pül′), a pool or pit for house drains to empty into. *n. 13.*

Cey lon (si lon′), a British island in the Indian Ocean. *n. 10.*

chafe (chāf), 1. rub. The mother chafes her child's cold hands to warm them. 2. make sore or become sore by rubbing. This stiff collar chafes my neck. 3. make angry. His big brother's teasing chafed him. 4. get angry. He chafed under his brother's teasing. *v. 6.*

chaff[1] (chaf), 1. stiff, strawlike bits around the grains of wheat, rye, or oats. Chaff is separated from the grain by threshing. 2. hay or straw cut fine for feeding cattle. 3. worthless stuff; rubbish. *n. 5.*

chaff[2] (chaf), 1. make fun of in a good-natured way before one's face. The boys chaffed the French boy a good deal about his mistakes in speaking English. 2. good-natured joking about a person to his face. *v., n.*

Chaffinch (6 in. long)

chaf finch (chaf′inch), a European songbird. *n. 18.*

cha grin (shə grin′), 1. a feeling of disappointment, failure, or humiliation. John felt chagrin because he did not get a prize. 2. cause to feel chagrin. *n., v. 13.*

chain (chān), 1. row of links joined together. The dog is fastened to a post by a chain. 2. series of things linked together; as, a chain of mountains, a chain of happenings. 3. fasten with a chain. 4. anything that binds or restrains. 5. bind; restrain. 6. keep in prison; make a slave of. 7. **Chains** sometimes means imprisonment or bondage. 8. a measure (66 feet in surveying, 100 feet in engineering). *n., v. 1.*

Chain with eleven links

chair (chãr), 1. single seat with a back. 2. seat of position, dignity, or authority. 3. chairman. *n. 1.*

chair man (chãr′mən), 1. person who is in charge of a meeting. 2. person at the head of a committee. *n., pl. chairmen. 5.*

chair man ship (chãr′mən ship), position of chairman. *n. 20.*

Chaise

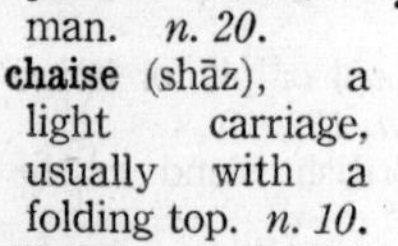

chaise (shāz), a light carriage, usually with a folding top. *n. 10.*

Chal de a (kal dē′ə), an ancient region in southwestern Asia, on the Tigris and Euphrates rivers. *n. 13.*

cha let (sha lā′), 1. Swiss cottage with wide eaves. 2. cottage like a Swiss cottage. *n. 19.*

chal ice (chal′is), 1. cup. 2. the cup used at the Communion service. 3. a flower shaped like a cup. *n. 14.*

Chalice used at Communion service

chalk (chôk), 1. a soft, white or gray limestone, made up mostly of very small sea shells. Chalk is used for writing and for making lime. 2. material like chalk used to make white and colored crayons for writing or drawing on a blackboard. 3. to mark with chalk. *n., v. 4.*

chalk y (chôk′i), 1. of chalk; containing chalk. 2. like chalk; white as chalk. The clown's face was chalky. *adj. 13.*

chal lenge (chal′inj), 1. a sudden questioning or calling to answer. "Who goes there?" is the challenge of a soldier on guard. 2. stop a person and question his right to do what he is doing or to be where he is. When I tried to enter the building, the guard at the door challenged me. 3. doubt; demand proof of before one will accept. The teacher challenged my statement that rice grows in Oregon. 4. a demand for proof of the truth of a statement; a doubting or questioning of the truth of a statement. 5. invitation to a game or contest of any kind. Giving a challenge often means that one undertakes to beat everybody else. 6. invite to a contest. The champion swimmer challenged anyone in the world to beat him. *n., v. 6.*

chal leng er (chal′in jər), person who challenges. *n. 15.*

chal lis or **chal lie** (shal′i), a lightweight material, used for dresses. *n. 13.*

cham ber (chām′bər), 1. a room, especially a bedroom. 2. **Chambers** sometimes means a set of rooms in a building arranged for living or for offices. 3. hall where a legislature or a governing body meets. 4. group of lawmakers. The United States Congress has two chambers, the Senate and the House of Representatives. 5. group of people organized for some business purpose. There is a Chamber of Commerce in many American cities. 6. any enclosed space in the body of animals or plants, or in some kinds of machinery. The part of a gun or a cannon that holds the charge is called the chamber. The heart has four chambers. *n. 2.*

cham ber lain (chām′bər lin), person who manages the household of a king or of a great noble. *n. 7.*

cham ber maid (chām′bər mād′), maid who takes care of bedrooms. *n. 12.*

cham bray (sham′brā), cotton cloth woven from white and colored threads, used for dresses and men's shirts. It is a kind of gingham. *n. 9.*

cha me le on (kə mē′li ən), 1. a lizard with the power of changing its color. 2. a changeable or fickle person. *n. 13.*

Chameleon (6 in. long)

cham ois (sham′i), 1. a small, goatlike antelope, which lives in the high mountains of Europe and southwestern Asia. 2. a soft leather made from the skin of sheep, goats, deer, etc. *n., pl. chamois. 14.*

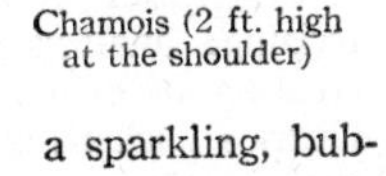
Chamois (2 ft. high at the shoulder)

champ (champ), 1. bite and chew noisily. 2. bite impatiently. The race horse champed at its bit. *v. 13.*

cham pagne (sham pān′), a sparkling, bubbling wine. *n. 18.*

cham paign (sham pān′), wide plain; level, open country. *n. 7.*

cham pi on (cham′pi ən), 1. one that comes out ahead of all rivals for first place; as, the swimming champion of the world. 2. first; ahead of all others; as, a champion runner, a champion rose or tomato. 3. person who fights or speaks for another person; person who defends a cause; as, a great champion of peace. 4. fight for; defend. John championed his friend. *n., adj., v. 4.*

cham pi on ship (cham′pi ən ship′), the position of champion; first place. *n. 13.*

Cham plain (sham plān′), 1. long, narrow lake between New York State and Vermont. 2. French explorer and colonizer (1567-1635). *n. 10.*

chance (chans), 1. opportunity; as, a chance to make some money. 2. possibility; probability. There is a chance that the sick child will get well. 3. fate; luck. 4. a happening. Chance led to the finding of the diamond mine. 5. happen. 6. risk. 7. not expected; accidental; as, a chance visit. *n., v., adj. 1.*

chan cel (chan′səl), the space around the altar of a church, used by the clergy and the choir. *n. 16.*

chan cel lor (chan′sə lər), a very high official. Chancellor is the title used for the chief man in the government of some countries, for the chief judge in some courts, and for the president in some universities. *n. 6.*

chan cer y (chan′sər i), a court of equity. *n., pl. chanceries. 13.*

chan de lier (shan′də lēr′), fixture with branches for lights, usually hanging from the ceiling. *n. 13.*

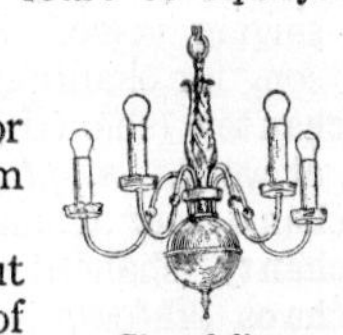
Chandelier

change (chānj), 1. put (something) in place of another; take in place of. You change your soiled clothes for clean ones. You can change a dollar bill for ten dimes. 2. make different; become different. She changed the room by painting the walls green. The wind changed from east to south. 3. passing from one form or place to a different one. The change from flower to fruit is interesting to watch. A change from the city to the country in the summer is good for children. 4. money returned to a person when he has given a larger amount than the price of what he buys. 5. small coins. Please give me change for this fifty-cent piece. *v., n. 1.*

change a ble (chān′jə bəl), that can change; that does change; likely to change; variable; varying; fickle. April weather is changeable. Do not trust her love; she is changeable. Silk is called changeable when it looks different in different lights. *adj. 11.*

change ful (chānj′fəl), full of changes; likely to change; changing. We watched the changeful color of the ocean. *adj. 13.*

change less (chānj′lis), not changing. *adj. 15.*

change ling (chānj′ling), 1. a child secretly substituted for another. 2. a strange, stupid, or ugly child left by fairies in place of a child carried off by them. *n. 16.*

chan nel (chan′əl), 1. the bed of a stream, river, etc. 2. body of water joining two larger bodies of water. The English Channel lies between two seas. 3. the deeper part of a waterway. There is shallow water on both sides of the channel in this river. 4. passage for liquids; a groove. 5. the means by which something is carried. The information came through secret channels. 6. form a channel in; cut out as one does a channel. The river had channeled its way through the rocks. *n., v., channeled, channeling. 3.*

Channel Islands, Jersey, Guernsey, Alderney, and other British islands near the northwestern coast of France.

chant (chant), 1. song. 2. to sing. 3. a kind of tune used as part of a church service. 4. say a psalm or a prayer in a singing voice. 5. psalm, prayer, or other song for chanting. *n., v. 5.*

chan tey (shan′ti), song sung by sailors at work. *n., pl. chanteys.*

chan ti cleer (chan′ti klēr), rooster. *n. 7.*

chan ty (shan′ti), chantey. *n., pl. chanties.*

cha os (kā′os), very great confusion; complete disorder. The whirlwind left chaos behind it. *n. 6.*

cha ot ic (kā ot′ik), like chaos; very confused or disordered. John's room was a chaotic mess of clothes, books, and toys. *adj. 15.*

chap[1] (chap), crack open; become or make rough. The skin often chaps in cold weather. Cold weather chaps the skin. *v., chapped, chapping. 7.*

chap[2] (chap), fellow; man; boy. Hello, old chap! *n.* [*Used in common talk*]

chap el (chap′əl), 1. a building for Christian worship, not so large as a church. 2. a small place for worship in a larger building. 3. in England, a place of worship for Christians who do not belong to the Church of England. *n. 3.*

chap er on or **chap er one** (shap′ər ōn), 1. a married woman or older woman who accompanies a young girl or unmarried woman in public for the sake of good form. 2. act as chaperon to. *n., v. 10.*

chap lain (chap′lin), clergyman officially on duty with a family, court, society, public institution, regiment, or warship. *n. 11.*

chap let (chap′lit), 1. wreath for the head. 2. string of beads. *n. 12.*

chap man (chap′mən), peddler. *n., pl. chapmen. 18.*

chaps (chaps), strong leather trousers worn by cowboys. *n. pl.*

chap ter (chap′tər), 1. a main division of a book, written about a particular part of the subject or story. 2. local division of an organization, which holds its own meetings. *n. 4.*

char (chär), 1. burn to charcoal. 2. scorch; burn slightly. *v., charred, charring. 13.*

char ac ter (kar′ik tər), 1. nature. What is the character of the plan you suggest? The trees on those islands are of a peculiar character. 2. moral nature; moral strength or weakness. The special ways in which any person feels, thinks, and acts, considered as good or bad, make up his character. 3. a special thing or quality which makes one person, one animal or thing, or a group of any kind, different from others. The trunk is a character found only in elephants. 4. a letter, figure, or sign used in writing or printing. 5. a person in a play or book. 6. person who attracts attention because he is different or odd. The old captain was a character in the village. *n. 2.*

char ac ter is tic (kar′ik tər is′tik), 1. marking off or distinguishing a certain person or thing from others; as, the characteristic smell of bananas. 2. special quality or feature. The characteristic I like best in him is his cheerfulness. *adj., n. 5.*

char ac ter is ti cal ly (kar′ik tər is′ti kəl i), typically; in a way that shows the peculiar quality or character. *adv. 20.*

char ac ter i za tion (kar′ik tər i zā′shən), 1. description of characteristics; a characterizing; analysis by portraying. 2. the creation of characters in a play or book. Charles Dickens is famous for characterization. *n. 19.*

char ac ter ize (kar′ik tər īz), 1. describe the special qualities or features of (a person or thing). 2. distinguish; mark out. The camel is characterized by the humps on its back and an ability to go without water for days. *v. 9.*

cha rade (shə rād′), a game of guessing a word from the descriptive or dramatic representation of each syllable or part, and of the whole. An example of descriptive representation is:—

"My first begins with bee,
My second rules the sea,
My whole I would spend with thee."

Honeymoon is the answer. *n.*

char coal (chär′kōl′), a black substance made by partly burning wood or bones in a place from which the air is shut out. Charcoal is used chiefly as fuel. *n. 8.*

charge (chärj), 1. load; fill. He charged the gun with powder and shot. 2. a load. A gun is fired by exploding the charge of powder. 3. order; give a task or duty to. Mother charged Alice to take good care of the baby. 4. duty; responsibility. 5. care. Dr. Brown is in charge of the case. 6. an order; direction; as, the charge of a judge to a jury. 7. blame; accuse. The driver was charged with speeding. 8. an accusing. He admitted the charge and paid the fine. 9. ask as a price; put a price on. The grocer charged 40 cents a dozen for eggs. 10. price; expense. 11. put down as a debt. The store will charge things bought and send a bill at the end of the month. 12. rush at; attack. The soldiers charged the enemy. 13. an attack. The charge drove the enemy back. *v., n. 1.*

charge a ble (chär′jə bəl), that can be charged. If you take money that belongs to somebody else, you are chargeable with theft. *adj. 13.*

charg er[1] (chär′jər), war horse. *n. 7.*

charg er[2] (chär′jər), large, flat dish; platter. *n.*

char i ot (char′i ət), a two-wheeled car pulled by horses. The chariot was used in ancient times for fighting, for racing, and in processions. *n. 3.*

Roman chariot

char i ot eer (char′i ət ēr′), person who drives a chariot. *n. 14.*

char i ta ble (char′i tə bəl), 1. generous in giving to the poor. 2. of charity; for charity. 3. kindly in judging people and their actions. *adj. 7.*

char i ty (char′i ti), 1. generous giving to the poor, or to institutions which look after the sick, the poor, and the helpless. 2. institution for helping the sick, the poor, and the helpless. 3. kindness in judging people's faults. 4. Christian love of one's fellow men. *n., pl. charities. 3.*

char la tan (shär′lə tən), person who pretends to have more knowledge or skill than he really has; quack. *n. 18.*

Char le magne (shär′lə mān), Charles the Great (742?-814 A.D.). He was king of the Franks and champion against the invading Moors. *n. 10.*

Charles ton (chärlz′tən), 1. the capital of West Virginia. 2. a seaport city in southeastern South Carolina. *n. 7.*

charm (chärm), 1. a word, verse, act, or thing supposed to have magic power to help or harm people. 2. to act on as if by magic. His grandchildren's laughter charmed away the old man's troubles. 3. give magic power to; protect as by a charm. He bears a charmed life. 4. a quality or feature in persons, in books, or in conduct which delights or fascinates; the power of delighting. Our grandmother did not lose her charm for us as she grew old. 5. please greatly; delight. The boys were charmed by the sailor's tales of adventure. *n., v. 2.*

charm er (chär′mər), one who charms, delights, or fascinates. *n. 11.*

charm ing (chär′ming), highly pleasing; delightful; fascinating. *adj.*

char nel house (chär′nəl hous′), place where dead bodies or bones are laid. *15.*

Char on (kãr′on), in Greek mythology, the boatman who ferried the spirits of the dead across the river Styx to Hades. *n. 16.*

chart (chärt), 1. a sailor's map of the sea which shows the coasts, rocks, and shallow places. 2. map. 3. a sheet of information arranged in pictures, diagrams, etc. 4. make a map or chart of. *n., v. 5.*

char ter (chär′tər), 1. a written grant of certain rights by a ruler to his subjects, or by a legislature to citizens or to companies formed to do special kinds of business. 2. a written order from the authorities of a society, giving to a group of persons the right to organize a new chapter, branch, or lodge. 3. give a charter to. 4. hire. He chartered a sailboat for a month. *n., v. 4.*

char wom an (chär′wu̇m′ən), woman hired to clean or do odd jobs by the day. *n., pl. charwomen.*

char y (chãr′i), 1. careful. A cat is chary of wetting its paws. 2. shy. A bashful person is chary of strangers. 3. sparing; stingy. Mrs. Smith is chary of praise. *adj., charier, chariest. 16.*

Cha ryb dis (kə rib′dis), a whirlpool, opposite the rock Scylla, that sucked down ships. **Between Scylla and Charybdis** means between two dangers, one of which must be met. *n. 12.*

chase (chās), 1. run after to catch or kill. 2. act of running after to catch or kill. We watched the chase. 3. act of hunting wild animals. 4. a hunted animal. The chase escaped the hunter. 5. drive; drive away. *v., n. 2.*

chasm (kazm), 1. a deep opening or crack in the earth. 2. wide difference of feeling or interests be-

Chasm

tween two persons, two groups, or two parties. The chasm between England and the American colonies grew wider and wider until it finally resulted in the Revolutionary War. *n. 8.*

chas sis (shas′i), 1. the frame, wheels, and machinery of an automobile. The chassis supports the body. 2. frame that supports the body of an airplane. *n., pl. chassis* (shas′iz). *15.*

chaste (chāst), 1. pure. 2. pure in taste or style; simple; not ornamented. *adj. 5.*

chas ten (chās′ən), 1. punish to improve. God chastened Moses. 2. restrain from excess or crudeness. *v. 9.*

chas tise (chas tīz′), punish; beat. *v. 8.*

chas tise ment (chas′tiz mənt), punishment. *n. 9.*

chas ti ty (chas′ti ti), 1. being chaste. 2. simplicity of style or taste. *n. 9.*

chat (chat), 1. easy, familiar talk. 2. to talk in an easy, familiar way. 3. bird with a chattering cry. *n., v., chatted, chatting. 5.*

châ teau (sha tō′), 1. castle. 2. country residence. *n., pl. châteaux* (sha tōz′). *11.*

chat e laine (shat′ə lān), 1. mistress of a castle. 2. clasp or chain worn at a woman's waist to which keys, purse, etc., are fastened. *n. 16.*

Chat ta noo ga (chat′ə nü′gə), a city in southeastern Tennessee. *n. 12.*

chat tel (chat′əl), movable possession. Furniture, horses, and automobiles are chattels. *n. 11.*

chat ter (chat′ər), 1. talk constantly in a quick, foolish way. 2. quick, foolish talk. 3. make quick, indistinct sounds. The monkey chattered in anger. 4. quick, indistinct sounds. The chatter of sparrows annoyed her. 5. rattle together. Cold makes your teeth chatter. *v., n. 4.*

chat ty (chat′i), fond of friendly, familiar talk. *adj., chattier, chattiest. 20.*

Chau cer (chô′sər), Geoffrey, the first great English poet (1340?-1400). *n. 11.*

chauf feur (shō′fər or shō fėr′), man who drives an automobile for a living. *n. 8.*

chaunt (chônt), an old way of spelling **chant.** *n., v. 15.*

chau tau qua or **Chau tau qua** (shə tô′kwə), an assembly for education and entertainment by lectures, concerts, etc., held for several days. *n. 11.*

cheap (chēp), 1. costing little. 2. costing less than it is worth. 3. easily obtained. 4. common; of low value. **Feel cheap** means feel inferior and ashamed. *adj. 2.*

cheap en (chēp′ən), make cheap; lower the value of. *v. 15.*

cheat (chēt), 1. deceive or trick; play or do business in a way that is not honest. 2. person who is not honest and does things to deceive and trick others. 3. fraud; trick. *v., n. 4.*

check (chek), 1. stop suddenly. They checked their steps. 2. sudden stop. The message gave a check to our plans. 3. hold back; control; as, to check one's anger. 4. any person or thing that controls or holds back action; as, the check on a furnace. 5. proving or proof by comparing. My work will be a check on yours. 6. prove true or right by comparing. Check your answers with mine. 7. a mark showing that something has been examined or compared. 8. a written order directing a bank to pay money to the person named. 9. a ticket or metal piece given in return for baggage or a package, to show ownership or the right to claim again later. Show your trunk check when you want your trunk. 10. a pattern made of squares. Do you want a check or a stripe for your new dress? 11. a single one of these squares. The checks are small in this pattern. 12. in chess, a word meaning that the king is in danger and must be moved. *v., n., interj. 2.*

check er (chek′ər), 1. mark in a pattern of squares of different colors. 2. a pattern made of squares. 3. mark off with patches different from one another. The ground under the trees was checkered with sunlight and shade. 4. change; vary; have ups and downs. 5. one of the pieces used in the game of checkers. *v., n.*

check ered (chek′ərd), 1. marked with squares; as, a checkered apron. 2. marked by frequent changes; as, a checkered career. *adj. 16.*

check ers (chek′ərz), a game played by two people, each with 12 flat, round pieces of wood, ivory, etc., on a board marked off into 64 squares of two alternating colors. *n. 7.*

check mate (chek′māt′), 1. make a move in chess that wins the game. 2. the move that ends the game by putting the opponent's king in check. 3. defeat completely. 4. a complete defeat or check. *v., n.*

check rein (chek′rān′), short rein to keep a horse from lowering its head. *n.*

cheek (chēk), 1. side of the face below either eye. 2. bold talk or action, especially from a child or an inferior; impudence. *Used in common talk. n. 2.*

cheep (chēp), 1. make a noise like a young bird; chirp; peep. 2. a young bird's cry. *v., n. 18.*

cheer (chēr), 1. good spirits; hope; gladness. The warmth of the campfire and a good meal brought cheer to our hearts again. 2. to comfort; make glad. It cheered the old woman to have us visit her. 3. "**Cheer up!**" means "Don't be sad; be glad!" 4. a shout of sympathy and support or praise. Give three cheers for the boys who won the game for us. 5. urge on by cheers or other means. 6. show praise and approval by cheers. 7. food. *n., v. 2.*

cheer ful (chēr′fəl), 1. full of cheer; joyful; glad. 2. pleasant; bringing cheer. 3. willing; as, a cheerful helper. *adj. 2.*

cheer ful ness (chēr′fəl nis), 1. good spirits. 2. pleasantness. 3. willingness. *n. 10.*

cheer i ly (chēr′i li), in a cheerful or cheery manner; in a way suggesting or bringing cheer. *adv. 9.*

cheer less (chēr′lis), without comfort or happiness; gloomy; dreary. *adj. 13.*

cheer y (chēr′i), cheerful; pleasant; bright; gay. Sunshine and the singing of birds are cheery. *adj., cheerier, cheeriest. 6.*

cheese (chēz), a solid food made from the thick part of milk. *n. 2.*

cheese cloth (chēz′klôth′), a thin, loosely woven cotton cloth. *n. 19.*

chee tah (chē′tə), an animal somewhat like a leopard, found in southern Asia and Africa. Cheetahs can be trained to hunt deer and antelope. *n.*

Cheetah (2 ft. high at the shoulder)

chef (shef), head cook. *n. 18.*

chem i cal (kem′i kəl), 1. of chemistry. 2. made by chemistry; used in chemistry. 3. any substance such as sulphuric acid, bicarbonate of soda, borax, etc. *adj., n. 8.*

che mise (shə mēz′), loose, shirtlike undergarment, worn by women and girls. *n. 8.*

chem ist (kem′ist), 1. person who makes chemistry his occupation or who knows a great deal about it. 2. in England, a druggist. *n. 8.*

chem is try (kem′is tri), 1. science that deals with the characteristics of elements or simple substances, the changes that take place when they combine to form other substances, and the laws of their combination and behavior under various conditions. 2. the application of this knowledge to any particular subject; as, the chemistry of foods. *n. 9.*

cheque (chek), a check; a written order directing a bank to pay money to the person named. *n. [In British use] 12.*

cher ish (cher′ish), 1. hold dear; treat with tenderness; aid or protect. A mother cherishes her baby. 2. keep in mind; cling to. She cherished the hope of her son's return. *v. 5.*

Cher o kee (cher′ə kē′), 1. member of a tribe of American Indians, now living mostly in Oklahoma. 2. their language. *n., pl. Cherokees* or *Cherokee.*

cher ry (cher′i), 1. a small, round fruit with a stone in the middle. 2. the tree it grows on. 3. bright red; as, cherry ribbons. *n., pl. cherries, adj. 2.*

cher ub (cher′əb), 1. angel. 2. child with wings. 3. beautiful or innocent child. *n., pl. cherubs, cherubim* for 1 or 2, *cherubs* for 3. *7.*

Cherub

cher u bim (cher′ə bim), cherubs. *n. pl. 7.*

Ches a peake (ches′ə pēk), a bay in Maryland and Virginia. *n. 12.*

chess (ches), a game played by two persons, each with 16 pieces which can make various moves, on a board marked off into 64 squares. *n. 10.*

chest (chest), 1. part of a person's or an animal's body enclosed by ribs. 2. large box with a lid, used for holding things; as, a linen chest, a medicine chest, a tool chest. *n. 2.*

chest nut (ches′nut), 1. a nut that is good to eat. 2. the tree it grows on. 3. the wood of this tree. 4. deep, reddish brown. *n., adj. 3.*

che tah (chē′tə), cheetah. *n.*

chev a lier (shev′ə lēr′), 1. knight. *Old use.* 2. member of an order of merit; as, a chevalier of the French Legion of Honor. *n. 18.*

chev i ot (shev′i ət), 1. a rough woolen cloth. 2. cotton cloth like it. *n. 10.*

C, chevrons.

chev ron (shev′rən), a decoration shaped like a V upside down, used on a coat of arms or worn on the sleeve of a noncommissioned officer, policeman, or soldier. *n.*

chew (chü), 1. crush or grind with the teeth. 2. a bite. *v., n. 6.*

che wink (chi wingk′), bird of North America whose cry sounds somewhat like its name. *n.*

Chewink (8 in. long)

Chey enne (shī en′), the capital of Wyoming. *n.*

chic (shēk), 1. style. 2. stylish. *n., adj.*

Chi ca go (shi kô′gō or shi kä′gō), a city in Illinois, on Lake Michigan. Chicago is the second largest city in America. *n. 3.*

chi can er y (shi kān′ər i), trickery; unfair practice; a puzzling and perplexing quibble. By legal chicanery the lawyer managed to obtain a new trial for the thief. *n., pl. chicaneries.*

chick (chik), 1. young chicken. 2. young bird. 3. child. *n. 3.*

chick a dee (chik′ə dē), a small bird. See the picture. *n.*

Chickadee (5 in. long)

chick en (chik′in), 1. young hen or rooster. 2. any hen or rooster. 3. any young bird. 4. the flesh of a chicken. *n. 2.*

chicken pox, a mild contagious disease of children, with an eruption of the skin.

chick weed (chik′wēd′), a common weed whose leaves and seeds are eaten by birds. *n. 20.*

chic o ry (chik′ə ri), 1. a plant with bright-blue flowers. Its leaves are used for salad; its roots are roasted and used as a substitute for coffee. 2. the root of this plant. *n., pl. chicories. 17.*

chid (chid). See **chide.** Only yesterday the teacher chid Tom for being late. *pt. and pp. of chide. 12.*

chide (chīd), reproach; blame; scold. She chid the little girl for soiling her dress. *v., chid* or *chided, chiding. 7.*

chief (chēf), 1. head of a tribe or group; leader; person in authority. 2. **In chief** means at the head or in the highest position. 3. highest in rank or authority; at the head; most important. *n., adj. 1.*

chief ly (chēf′li), 1. mainly; mostly. We visited Washington chiefly to see the Capitol. 2. first of all; above all. *adv. 6.*

chief tain (chēf′tən), 1. the chief of a tribe or clan. 2. leader. *n. 10.*

chif fon (shi fon′), a very thin, silk cloth, used for dresses. *n. 10.*

chif fo nier (shif′ə nēr′), high bureau, sometimes with a mirror, used as bedroom furniture. *n. 10.*

chil blain (chil′blān′), itching sore or redness on the hands or feet caused by cold. *n. 18.*

child (chīld), 1. baby. 2. young boy or girl. 3. son or daughter. 4. **Child's play** sometimes means something very easy to do. *n., pl. children. 1.*

child birth (chīld′bėrth′), giving birth to a child. *n. 20.*

child hood (chīld′hu̇d), 1. being a child. 2. time during which one is a child. *n. 4.*

child ish (chīl′dish), 1. of a child. 2. like a child. 3. not proper for a grown person; silly; weak; babyish. Crying for things you can't have is childish. *adj. 6.*

child ish ness (chīl′dish nis), 1. being like a child. 2. weakness; silliness. *n. 16.*

child less (chīld′lis), having no child. *adj. 10.*

child like (chīld′līk′), such as a child should have or be. *adj. 10.*

chil dren (chil′drən), 1. young boys and girls. 2. sons and daughters. *n. pl. of* **child.** *1.*

Chil e (chil′i), country in southwestern South America. *n. 7.*

Chil e an (chil′i ən), 1. of or having to do with Chile or its people. 2. a native or inhabitant of Chile. *adj., n. 14.*

chil i or **chil li** (chil′i), hot-tasting red pepper. Chilies are eaten for seasoning. *n., pl. chilies, chillies.*

chill (chil), 1. unpleasant coldness. 2. unpleasantly cold. 3. make cold. 4. become cold; feel cold. 5. a sudden coldness of the body with shivering. 6. harden (metal) by sudden cooling. *n., adj., v. 3.*

chill y (chil′i), 1. cold; unpleasantly cool. 2. not kind. *adj., chillier, chilliest. 8.*

chime (chīm), 1. a set of bells tuned to the musical scale and played usually by hammers or simple machinery. 2. the music made by a set of tuned bells. 3. ring out musically. 4. be in harmony or agreement. His ideas chimed in beautifully with mine. *n., v. 4.*

chi me ra or **chi mae ra** (ki mēr′ə), 1. a monster with a lion's head, a goat's body, and a serpent's tail. A chimera was supposed to breathe fire. 2. a horrible creature of the

Chimera

imagination. 3. absurd idea; wild fancy. The hope of changing dirt to gold was a chimera. *n. 16.*

chi mer i cal (ki mer′i kəl), unreal; imaginary; impossible. The crazy man had many chimerical schemes for getting rich. *adj. 16.*

chim ney (chim′ni), 1. an upright structure to make a draft and carry away smoke. 2. a glass tube placed around the flame of a lamp. *n., pl. chimneys. 2.*

Chimney

chimney sweep, person whose work is cleaning out chimneys.

chim pan zee (chim-pan′zi or chim′pan-zē′), an African ape as big as a large dog. Chimpanzees are very intelligent. *n. 17.*

Chimpanzee (4½ ft. tall when standing)

chin (chin), the front of the lower jaw below the mouth. *n. 4.*

Chi na (chī′nə), a large country in eastern Asia. *n. 2.*

chi na (chī′nə), 1. a fine, white ware made of clay baked by a special process, first used in China. Colored designs can be baked into china. 2. dishes, vases, ornaments, etc., made of china. *n.*

Chi na man (chī′nə mən), man belonging to the Chinese race. *n., pl. Chinamen. 13.*

chi na ware (chī′nə wãr′), dishes, vases, ornaments, etc., made of China. *n.*

chinch (chinch), 1. bedbug. 2. chinch bug. *n. 19.*

chinch bug, small, black-and-white bug that does much damage to grain in dry weather.

Chinch bug. Line shows actual length.

chin chil la (chin chil′ə), 1. a small, ratlike South American animal with soft, light-gray fur which is valuable. 2. its fur. 3. a thick, woolen material woven in small, closely set tufts, used for warm coats, etc. *n. 14.*

Chinchilla (15 in. long with tail)

Chi nese (chī nēz′), 1. of China, its people, or their language. 2. a member of the native race of China. 3. language of China. *adj., n., pl. Chinese. 5.*

chink[1] (chingk), 1. narrow opening; crack. The chinks in the cabin let in wind and snow. 2. fill up (narrow openings). The cracks in the log wall were chinked with plaster. *n., v. 7.*

chink[2] (chingk), 1. a sound like glasses or coins striking against one another. 2. make such a sound. I could hear the spoons chink in the glasses. 3. cause to make such a sound. He chinked the coins in his pocket. *n., v.*

chi nook (chi nük′), warm wind blowing from the sea to land in winter and spring in northwestern United States. *n.*

chintz (chints), cotton cloth printed in patterns of various colors and often glazed. *n. 15.*

chip (chip), 1. a small, thin piece cut from wood or broken from stone or china. 2. a place in china or stone from which a small piece has been broken. 3. cut or break (small pieces) from wood, stone, or dishes. 4. become chipped easily. These cups chip if they are not handled carefully. 5. shape by cutting at the surface or edge with an ax or chisel. 6. a flat piece for counting, used in games. *n., v., chipped, chipping. 4.*

chip munk (chip′-mungk), small, striped American squirrel. *n. 18.*

Chipmunk (10 in. long with tail)

chi ro prac tor (kī′rō prak′tər), person who treats disease by manipulating the spine. *n.*

chirp (chėrp), 1. the short, sharp sound made by some small birds and insects. 2. make a chirp. Crickets chirp. Sparrows chirp. *n., v. 5.*

chir rup (chir′əp or chėr′əp), chirp. *n., v. 16.*

chis el (chiz′əl), 1. a tool with a steel cutting edge at the end of a strong blade. Chisels are used for shaping wood, stone, or metal. 2. cut or shape with a chisel. *n., v., chiseled, chiseling. 6.*

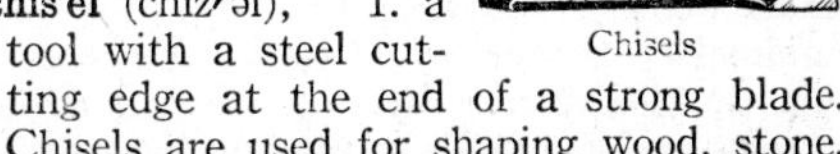
Chisels

chiv al ric (shiv′əl rik or shi val′rik), knightly; chivalrous. *adj.*

chiv al rous (shiv′əl rəs), 1. knightly; having the virtues of an ideal knight; gallant, courteous, helpful and honorable. 2. having to do with chivalry. *adj. 9.*

chiv al ry (shiv′əl ri), 1. the qualities of an ideal knight in the Middle Ages; skill in fighting with arms, bravery, honor, protection of the weak, devotion to women, and fairness to an enemy. 2. the rules, customs, and beliefs of knights in the Middle Ages. *n. 6.*

chive (chīv), a plant like an onion. Its long, slender leaves are used as a seasoning. *n.*

chlo ral (klō′rəl). a drug that causes sleep. *n. 15.*

chlo rid (klō′rid), chloride. *n.*

chlo ride (klō′rīd), compound of chlorine. *n. 13.*

chlo rin (klō′rin), chlorine. *n.*

chlo rine (klō′rēn), a greenish-yellow, bad-smelling gas, very irritating to the nose and throat. *n. 15.*

chlo ro form (klō′rə fôrm), 1. a colorless liquid which, when inhaled, makes a person unable to feel pain. 2. make unable to feel pain by giving chloroform. 3. kill with chloroform. *n., v. 11.*

chlo ro phyll or **chlo ro phyl** (klō′rə fil), the green coloring matter of plants. *n. 9.*

choc o late (chôk′ə lit), 1. a substance made from the roasted seeds of the cacao tree. 2. a drink made from chocolate with sugar and hot water or milk. 3. candy made of chocolate. 4. dark brown. *n., adj. 4.*

choice (chois), 1. act of choosing. Use careful choice in buying dress goods. 2. person or thing chosen. This is my choice 3. power or chance to choose. 4. quantity and variety to choose from. You haven't much choice now. 5. excellent; of fine quality. The choicest fruit has the highest price. *n., adj. 2.*

choir (kwīr), 1. the group of singers used in a church service. 2. the part of the church set apart for the singers. 3. any group of singers. *n. 4.*

choke (chōk), 1. stop the breath of (an animal or person) by squeezing the throat or by blocking it up. 2. be unable to breathe. 3. check or put out by cutting off air; smother; as, to choke a fire. 4. hold; control. He choked down his anger and choked back a sharp reply. 5. fill up or block. Sand is choking the river. 6. act or sound of choking. The man gave a few chokes and then got his breath. *v., n, 4.*

chol er (kol′ər), anger. *n. 17.*

chol er a (kol′ər ə), 1. an acute disease of the digestive tract that is not infectious. 2. a more dangerous disease that is infectious. Both kinds of cholera are marked by diarrhea, vomiting, and cramps. *n. 8.*

chol er ic (kol′ər ik), easily made angry; often angry. *adj. 12.*

choose (chüz), 1. pick out; select from a number. Choose the cake you like best. He chose wisely. 2. prefer and decide; think fit. She did not choose to accept my present. *v., chose, chosen, choosing. 1.*

chop[1] (chop), 1. cut by blows; as, to chop wood with an ax. 2. cut into small pieces; as, to chop up cabbage. 3. cutting blow. 4. slice of meat, especially of lamb, veal, or pork with a piece of rib. 5. move in small, jerky waves. *v., chopped, chopping, n. 3.*

chop[2] (chop), jaw. The dog licked his chops. *n.*

chop[3] (chop), shift suddenly; veer. *v., chopped, chopping.*

Cho pin (shō pan′), Polish pianist and composer who lived in France (1809-1849). *n.*

chop per (chop′ər), person, tool, or machine that chops; as, a wood chopper, a meat chopper. *n. 12.*

chop py[1] (chop′i), 1. jerky. 2. forming short, irregular, broken waves. *adj.*

chop py[2] (chop′i), changing suddenly. *adj.*

chop sticks (chop′stiks′), small sticks used by the Chinese to raise food to the mouth. *n. pl.*

Chopsticks

cho ral (kō′rəl), 1. of a choir or chorus. 2. sung by a choir or chorus. *adj. 11.*

chord[1] (kôrd), a combination of three or more notes of music sounded at the same time in harmony. *n. 7.*

chord[2] (kôrd), 1. a straight line connecting two points of a circumference. 2. a structure in an animal body that looks like a string. 3. the string of a harp. *n.*

AB, CD, and EF are chords.

chore (chōr), odd job; small task. Feeding the chickens and milking cows are chores on the farm. *n. 13.*

chor is ter (kor′is tər), 1. singer in a choir. 2. boy who sings in a choir. 3. leader of a choir. *n. 16.*

cho roid coat (kō′roid kōt′), delicate membrane in the eye, just back of the retina.

chor tle (chôr′təl), chuckle loudly. *v.*

cho rus (kō′rəs), 1. group of singers who sing together, such as a choir. 2. song sung by many singers together. 3. a musical composition to be sung by all singers together. 4. a repeated part of a song coming after each stanza. 5. sing or speak all at the same time. The birds were chorusing around me. 6. a saying by many at the same time. My question was answered by a chorus of No!'s. 7. group of singers and dancers. *n., v. 7.*

chose (chōz). See **choose.** Mary chose the pink dress. *pt. of choose. 2.*

cho sen (chō′zən), 1. See **choose.** Have you chosen a book from the library? 2. picked out; selected from a group. *pp. of choose, adj.*

chow (chou), 1. a dog of medium size, with a thick, even coat of brown or black hair and a black tongue. 2. food. *Slang. n.*

Chow

chow der (chou′dər), a thick soup or stew made of clams or fish with potatoes, onions, etc. *n. 20.*

Christ (krīst), Jesus, the founder of the Christian religion. *n. 3.*

chris ten (kris′ən), 1. baptize as a Christian. 2. give a first name to (a person) at baptism. The child was christened James. 3. give a name to. *v. 10.*

Chris ten dom (kris′ən dəm), 1. Christian countries; Christian part of the world. 2. all Christians. *n. 10.*

chris ten ing (kris′ən ing), baptism; act or ceremony of baptizing and naming. *n.*

Chris tian (kris′chən), 1. person who believes in Christ. 2. person whose life follows the teachings of Christ. 3. believing in or belonging to the religion of Christ; as, the Christian church, Christian countries. 4. showing a gentle, humble, helpful spirit; as, Christian charity. 5. of Christ, His teachings, or His followers. 6. Your **Christian name** is your first name or names, not your family name. John is the Christian name of John Smith. *n., adj. 2.*

Chris ti an i ty (kris′chi an′i ti), 1. the religion taught by Christ and His followers. 2. Christian beliefs or faith; Christian spirit or character. *n. 11.*

Chris tian ize (kris′chən īz), make Christian. *v. 15.*

Christian Science, religion and system of healing founded by Mary Baker Eddy in 1866. It treats disease by mental and spiritual means.

Christ mas (kris′məs), the yearly celebration of the birth of Christ on December 25. A **Christmas tree** is an evergreen tree hung with decorations. *n., adj. 1.*

chro mat ic (krō mat′ik), 1. of color or colors. 2. in music, progressing by half tones instead of by the regular intervals of the scale. *adj. 18.*

chrome (krōm), chromium. *n. 17.*

chro mi um (krō′mi əm), a lustrous, hard, brittle metal. The element chromium occurs in compounds that are used for making dyes and paints, in photography, etc. *n.*

chron ic (kron′ik), continuing a long time; constant; habitual. Rheumatism is often a chronic disease. *adj. 10.*

chron i cle (kron′i kəl), 1. history; story; an account of events in the order that they took place. 2. write the history of; tell the story of. *n., v. 5.*

chron i cler (kron′i klər), recorder; person who writes a chronicle; historian. *n. 11.*

Chron i cles (kron′i kəlz), two books of the Old Testament, called I and II Chronicles. *n.*

chron o log i cal (kron′ə loj′i kəl), arranged in the order in which the events happened. In telling a story you naturally follow the chronological order. *adj. 16.*

chro nol o gy (krə nol′ə ji), 1. the science of time and dates. 2. an order of past events. *n., pl. chronologies. 15.*

chrys a lis (kris′ə lis), 1. a stage in the life of an insect when it is in a case. It comes between the larva (caterpillar) and the winged adult stage (butterfly). 2. the case. *n. 11.*

Chrysalis

chry san the mum (kri san′thi məm), a round flower with many petals, which blossoms in the fall. *n. 16.*

Chrysanthemum

chrys o lite (kris′ō līt), a green or yellow gem. *n. 13.*

chub by (chub′i), round and plump; as, a chubby child. *adj., chubbier, chubbiest. 19.*

chuck[1] (chuk), 1. pat; tap;

as, a chuck under the chin. 2. throw; toss. *n., v. 6.*

chuck[2] (chuk), 1. clamp. 2. the cut of beef between the neck and the shoulder. See the diagram of **beef.** *n.*

chuck le (chuk′əl), 1. laugh to oneself. 2. a soft laugh; quiet laughter. *v., n. 6.*

chug (chug), 1. the sound made by an engine. 2. make such a sound. *n., v., chugged, chugging. 19.*

chum (chum), 1. very close friend. 2. be on very friendly terms. 3. roommate. *n., v., chummed, chumming. 11.*

chum my (chum′i), like a chum; very friendly; intimate. *adj.* [*Used in common talk*] *20.*

chunk (chungk), a thick piece or lump; as, a chunk of wood, bread, etc. *n. 20.*

church (chėrch), 1. a building for public Christian worship. 2. public worship of God in a church. 3. all Christians. 4. group of Christians with the same beliefs and under the same authority; as, the Methodist church, the Presbyterian church. *n. 1.*

church man (chėrch′mən), 1. clergyman. 2. member of a church. *n., pl. churchmen. 8.*

Church of England, Christian church in England that is recognized as a national institution by the government. Its head is the king.

church ward en (chėrch′wôr′dən), a lay officer in the Episcopal Church who manages the church property and finances. *n. 16.*

church yard (chėrch′yärd′), the ground around a church. A churchyard is sometimes used for a burial ground. *n. 6.*

churl (chėrl), 1. a rude, surly person. 2. peasant; person of low birth. *n. 11.*

churl ish (chėr′lish), rude; surly; bad-tempered. *adj. 13.*

churn (chėrn), 1. container or machine in which butter is made from cream by beating and shaking. 2. beat and shake (cream, etc.) in a churn. 3. move as if beaten and shaken. *n., v. 12.*

chute (shüt), a steep slide. There are chutes for carrying mail, soiled clothes, coal, etc., to a lower level. A toboggan slide is called a chute. A chute in a river is a waterfall or rapid. *n.*

Cicada (about ⅓ life size)

ci ca da (si kā′də), a large insect with transparent wings. The male makes a shrill sound in hot, dry weather. *n. 17.*

Cic e ro (sis′ə rō), a famous Roman orator, writer, and statesman (106-43 B.C.). *n. 10.*

ci der (sī′dər), the juice of apples, used as a drink and in making vinegar. *n. 7.*

ci gar (si gär′), tight roll of tobacco leaves for smoking. *n. 5.*

cig a rette (sig′ə ret′), small roll of finely cut tobacco enclosed in a thin sheet of paper for smoking. *n. 10.*

cil i a (sil′i ə), 1. eyelashes. 2. hairlike parts of leaves, wings, or insects, and in very tiny animals. *n. pl. 10.*

Cim me ri an (si mēr′i ən), 1. one of a people said to live in perpetual darkness. 2. dark; gloomy. *n., adj. 13.*

cinch (sinch), 1. a strong girth for a saddle or pack. 2. put on with a cinch; bind firmly. 3. a firm hold or grip. *Used in common talk.* 4. something sure and easy. *Slang. n., v. 18.*

cin cho na (sin kō′nə), 1. small tree that grows in South America, the East Indies, India, and Java. 2. its bitter bark. Quinine and other drugs are obtained from this bark. *n. 18.*

Cin cin nat i (sin′si nat′i), a city in southwestern Ohio. *n. 8.*

cinc ture (singk′chər), belt; girdle. The knight was cinctured with a sword belt. *n., v. 16.*

cin der (sin′dər), 1. wood or coal partly burned and no longer flaming. 2. burned-up wood or coal; ash. Cinders are made up of larger and coarser pieces than ashes are. *n. 7.*

Cin der el la (sin′dər el′ə), the girl in the story who was forced to work very hard, but was rescued by her fairy godmother and married to a prince. *n. 5.*

cin e ma (sin′i mə), moving picture. *n. 18.*

cin na mon (sin′ə mən), 1. the inner bark of a tree, used as a spice and in medicine. 2. spice made from this bark. 3. the tree itself. 4. light, reddish brown; as, a cinnamon bear. *n., adj. 10.*

ci pher (sī′fər), 1. zero; 0. 2. person or thing of no importance. 3. do arithmetic. Mary can read, write, and cipher. 4. work by arithmetic. 5. secret writing. He sent me a telegram in cipher. 6. something in secret writing. 7. the key to secret writing. *n., v. 13.*

Cir ce (sėr′si), an enchantress who changed men into animals. Ulysses withstood her spell and forced her to set free his companions, whom she had changed to swine. *n. 8.*

cir cle (sėr′kəl), 1. a line every point of which is equally distant from a point within called the center. 2. a plane figure bounded by such a line. 3. something flat and round or roundish. 4. a ring. The girls danced in a circle. 5. move in a circle. An airplane circles before it lands. 6. enclose in a circle; surround. 7. complete series; as, the circle of the months. 8. a group of people bound by the same interests; as, the family circle, a circle of friends. *n., v. 1.*

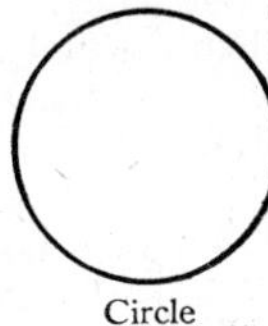

Circle

cir clet (sėr′klit), 1. a small circle. 2. a circular ornament worn on the head, neck, arm, or finger. *n. 14.*

cir cuit (sėr′kit), 1. a going around; a moving around. 2. the distance around any space; the line enclosing an area. 3. a way over which a person or a group makes repeated journeys at certain times; the part of the country through which such journeys are made. A judge's journey to hold court in certain districts is a circuit. Theater companies travel over regular circuits. 4. the complete path over which an electric current flows. *n. 4.*

cir cu i tous (sər kū′i təs), roundabout; not direct. We took a circuitous route home to avoid poor roads. *adj. 14.*

cir cu lar (sėr′kū lər), 1. round like a circle. 2. moving in a circle; as, a circular trip. 3. having to do with a circle. 4. sent to each of a number of people; as, a circular letter. 5. a notice or advertisement sent around to a number of people. *adj., n. 4.*

cir cu lar ize (sėr′kū lər īz), send circulars to. *v.*

cir cu late (sėr′kū lāt), 1. go around. A newspaper circulates among people who read it. Water circulates in the pipes of a building. Money circulates as it goes from person to person. 2. send around from person to person or place to place. He circulated the news of the holiday. This book has been widely circulated among boys. *v. 8.*

cir cu la tion (sėr′kū lā′shən), 1. a going round; circulating. Open windows increase the circulation of air in a room. 2. the movement of the blood from the heart through the body and back to the heart. 3. sending around books, papers, news, etc., from person to person or place to place. 4. the number of copies of a book, newspaper, magazine, etc., that are sent out during a certain time. *n. 7.*

cir cu la to ry (sėr′kū lə tō′ri), having to do with circulation. Arteries and veins are parts of the circulatory system of the human body. *adj. 16.*

cir cum cise (sėr′kəm sīz), cut off the foreskin of. *v. 12.*

cir cum ci sion (sėr′kəm sizh′ən), circumcising. *n. 15.*

cir cum fer ence (sər kum′fər əns), 1. boundary line of a circle or of certain other surfaces. Every point in the circumference of a circle is at the same distance from the center. 2. the distance around. The circumference of the circle shown here is a little over two inches. That of the circle in column 1 is about 2½ inches. *n. 8.*

cir cum lo cu tion (sėr′kəm lō kū′shən), a roundabout way of speaking. "The wife of your father's brother" is a circumlocution for "Your aunt." *n. 20.*

cir cum nav i gate (sėr′kəm nav′i gāt), sail around. Magellan's ship circumnavigated the earth. *v. 13.*

cir cum scribe (sėr′kəm skrīb′), 1. draw a line around; mark the boundaries of. 2. surround. 3. limit; restrict. A prisoner's activities are circumscribed. *v. 12.*

cir cum spect (sėr′kəm spekt), careful; cautious; prudent. *adj. 13.*

cir cum spec tion (sėr′kəm spek′shən), care; caution; prudence. *n. 15.*

cir cum stance (sėr′kəm stans), 1. condition of an act or event. The place, the weather, and the other circumstances made the picnic a great success. 2. fact or event. It was a lucky circumstance that she found her money. **Circumstances** sometimes means condition or state of affairs. A rich man is in good circumstances; a poor man is in bad circumstances. 3. ceremony; display. *n. 3.*

cir cum stan tial (sėr′kəm stan′shəl), 1. depending on circumstances. If stolen jewels were found in a man's possession, it would be circumstantial evidence that he had stolen them. 2. incidental; not essential. 3. giving full and exact details; complete; as, a circumstantial report. *adj. 13.*

cir cum vent (sėr′kəm vent′), 1. get the better of. 2. go around. 3. catch in a trap. *v. 15.*

cir cus (sėr′kəs), 1. a traveling show of acrobats, clowns, horses, riders, and wild animals. The performers who give the show and the show that they give are both called the circus. 2. a round or oval space with seats around it in rows, each row higher than the one in front of it. *n. 5.*

cirque (sėrk), 1. circular space. 2. natural amphitheater. 3. circlet; ring. *Used in poetry. n. 15.*

cir rus (sir′əs), thin, fleecy cloud very high in the air. *n.*

cis tern (sis′tərn), reservoir or tank for storing water. *n. 6.*

cit a del (sit′ə dəl), fortress, especially one in a city. *n. 10.*

ci ta tion (sī tā′shən), 1. quotation; reference. 2. honorable mention for bravery in war. 3. a summons to appear before a law court. *n. 13.*

cite (sīt), 1. quote. He cited the Bible and Shakespeare to prove his statement. 2. refer to; mention; bring up as an example. Can you cite another case like this one? 3. summon to appear before a law court. *v. 6.*

cit i zen (sit′i zən), 1. person who by birth or by choice is a member of a state or nation which gives him certain rights and which claims his loyalty. Many foreigners have become citizens of the United States. 2. inhabitant of a city or town. *n. 2.*

cit i zen ry (sit′i zən ri), citizens as a group. *n.*

cit i zen ship (sit′i zən ship′), the duties, rights, and privileges of a citizen. *n. 10.*

cit ric (sit′rik), of lemons; pertaining to or derived from lemons, limes, and similar fruits. *adj.*

cit ron (sit′rən), 1. a pale-yellow fruit somewhat like a lemon but larger, less acid, and with a thicker rind. 2. the shrub or small tree it grows on. 3. the rind of citron candied for use in fruit cake, plum pudding, etc. *n. 10.*

cit rous (sit′rəs), pertaining to fruits such as lemons, limes, and oranges. *adj.*

cit rus (sit′rəs), any tree bearing lemons, limes, oranges, or similar fruit. *n.*

cit y (sit′i), 1. a large, important town that manages its own affairs. 2. the people living in a city. The city was alarmed by the great fire. 3. division of local government in the United States having a charter from the State that fixes its boundaries and powers. A city is usually governed by a mayor and a board of aldermen or councilmen. 4. division of local government in Canada of the highest class. 5. of a city. 6. in a city. *n., pl. cities, adj. 1.*

civ et (siv′it), 1. a small animal somewhat like a skunk. 2. a strong, musklike perfume obtained from the civet. *n. 17.*

civ ic (siv′ik), 1. of a city. 2. of or having to do with citizenship. Every person has some civic duties, such as obeying the laws, voting, or paying taxes. 3. of citizens. *adj. 9.*

civ ics (siv′iks), study of the duties, rights, and privileges of citizens. *n.*

civ il (siv′il), 1. of a citizen or citizens; having to do with citizens. Every citizen has civil rights and civil duties. Civil war is war between two groups of citizens in the same country. 2. not naval, military, or connected with the church. Post offices are part of the civil service of the government. 3. polite; courteous. The boy pointed out our road in a civil way. *adj. 3.*

ci vil ian (si vil′yən), 1. person who is not a soldier or sailor. All men not in the army or navy are civilians. 2. of civilians; not military or naval. *n., adj. 16.*

ci vil i ty (si vil′i ti), politeness; courtesy. *n., pl. civilities. 9.*

civ i li za tion (siv′i li zā′shən), 1. civilized condition; an advanced stage in social development. 2. the nations that have reached advanced stages in social development. All civilization ought to be aroused against war. 3. the culture or ways of living of a race. There are differences between Chinese civilization and our own. *n. 7.*

civ i lize (siv′i līz), bring out of a savage condition; train in science, art, and other features of culture. Schools will help to civilize the wild tribes of Africa. *v. 6.*

civil service, public service concerned with affairs not military, naval, legislative, or judicial. The post office and the mint belong to the civil service.

Civil War, the war between the Northern and the Southern States of the United States of America from 1861 to 1865.

clack (klak), 1. make a short, sharp sound. The old lady's needles clacked as she knitted. 2. short, sharp sound. We heard the clack of her heels on the sidewalk. 3. chatter. *v., n. 20.*

clad (klad), clothed. *pt. and pp. of* **clothe.** *4.*

claim (klām), 1. demand as one's own or one's right. Does anyone claim this pencil? 2. such a demand. Mary makes a claim to the pencil. 3. a right or title to a thing; a right to demand something. She has a claim on us because she is my mother's cousin. 4. piece of land which someone claims; as, a miner's claim. 5. When things claim your attention, they deserve or require it. The care of the baby claims half my time. 6. **Claim to be** means maintain that one is. He claims to be the best speller in the school. *v., n. 2.*

claim ant (klām′ənt), person who makes a claim. *n. 15.*

clair voy ant (klãr voi′ənt), 1. having the power of seeing things that are out of sight. 2. person having or claiming such power. The clairvoyant claimed to be able to locate lost articles, and to give news of faraway people. *adj., n.*

clam (klam), 1. an animal somewhat like an oyster, with a soft body and hinged double shell, living in sand along the seashore, or in the edges of rivers, lakes, etc. Many kinds are good to eat. 2. go out after clams; dig for clams. *n., v., clammed, clamming. 6.*

Shell of a clam

clam ber (klam′bər), climb, using both hands and feet; scramble. *v. 10.*

clam my (klam′i), cold and damp. *adj., clammier, clammiest.*

clam or (klam′ər), 1. loud noise, especially of voices; confused shouting. 2. make a loud noise. 3. noisy demand. 4. **Clamor for** means demand noisily. The children were clamoring for candy. *n., v. 4.*

clam or ous (klam′ər əs), loud and noisy. *adj. 8.*

clamp (klamp), 1. an iron brace or band for giving strength to other materials or for holding two things together. 2. tool with its opposite sides connected by a screw, for holding things tightly together. 3. fasten together with a clamp; fix in a clamp; strengthen with clamps. *n., v. 9.*

Clamp (def. 2)

clan (klan), 1. group of related families that claim to be descended from a common ancestor. 2. group of people closely joined together by some common interest. *n. 9.*

clan des tine (klan des′tin), secret; concealed; underhand. *adj. 15.*

clang (klang), 1. a loud, harsh, ringing sound like metal being hit; as, the clang of the dinner gong. 2. make a loud, harsh, resounding sound. *n., v. 5.*

clan gor (klang′gər), a clang; a continued clanging. *n. 17.*

clank (klangk), 1. a sound like the rattle of a heavy chain. 2. make such a sound. The swords clashed and clanked as the men fought together. *n., v. 15.*

clan nish (klan′ish), 1. pertaining to a clan. 2. closely united; not liking outsiders. The old families of a town are likely to be clannish. *adj.*

clans man (klanz′mən), member of a clan. *n., pl. clansmen. 17.*

clap (klap), 1. a sudden noise, such as a single burst of thunder, the sound of the hands struck together, or the sound of a loud slap. 2. make such a noise, especially with the hands. When the show was over, we all clapped. 3. strike with a quick blow. He clapped his friend on the back. *n., v., clapped, clapping. 3.*

clap board (klab′ərd or klap′bōrd), 1. a thin board, thicker along one edge than along the other. Clapboards are used in covering the outer walls of wooden buildings. 2. to cover with clapboards. *n., v. 15.*

clap per (klap′ər), 1. person or thing that claps. 2. part that strikes a bell. 3. device for making noise. *n. 15.*

clar et (klar′ət), 1. a kind of red wine. 2. dark, purplish red. *n., adj. 15.*

clar i fi ca tion (klar′i fi kā′shən), making clear; freeing from defects or impurities. *n.*

clar i fy (klar′i fī), make clear. The explanation in the note clarified the difficult sentence. *v., clarified, clarifying. 20.*

clar i net (klar′i net′), a wooden wind instrument played by means of holes and keys. See the picture. *n. 20.*

Man playing a clarinet

clar i on (klar′i ən), 1. clear and shrill. 2. a trumpet with clear, shrill tones. 3. the sound made by this trumpet or a sound like it. *adj., n. 13.*

clar i ty (klar′i ti), clearness. *n. 20.*

clash (klash), 1. a loud, harsh sound like that of two things running into each other, of striking metal, or of bells rung together but not in tune. 2. hit with a clash. In her haste, she clashed the saucepans against the stove. 3. a strong disagreement; a conflict. There are many clashes of opinion in that family, for no two of them think alike. 4. disagree strongly; conflict; go badly together. Your feelings and your judgment sometimes clash. *n., v. 5.*

clasp (klasp), 1. a fastening somewhat like a buckle or a hook. 2. fasten together with a clasp. 3. hold closely with the hand or the arms. The mother clasped her baby to her breast. He clasped a knife in his hand. 4. a grasp of the hand. He gave my hand a warm clasp. 5. a close hold. I could not escape from the bear's clasp. *n., v. 3.*

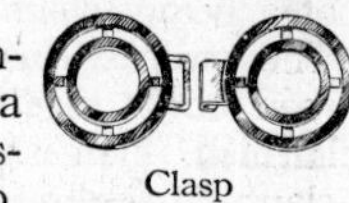

Clasp

class (klas), 1. group of persons or things of the same kind. 2. group of pupils taught together. 3. their time of meeting. 4. rank of society; as, upper class, middle class, working class. 5. system of dividing society in this manner. 6. high rank in society. 7. put in a class. *n., v. 1.*

clas sic (klas′ik), 1. an author or an artist of acknowledged excellence. Shakespeare is a classic. 2. a fine book or painting produced by such a man. *Robinson Crusoe* is a classic. 3. of the first class; excellent; as, a classic author. 4. simple; well thought out; finished in fine form; as, the classic style of Bach's music. 5. relating to the best ancient Greek and Latin writers, their art and culture. 6. **The classics** often means the literature of ancient Greece and Rome. *n., adj. 4.*

clas si cal (klas′i kəl), 1. first-class. She likes classical literature and music. 2. having to do with the culture of the ancient Greeks and Romans. *adj. 7.*

clas si fi ca tion (klas′i fi kā′shən), arrangement in classes or groups; grouping according to some system. *n. 7.*

clas si fy (klas′i fī), arrange in groups or classes. Children in school are classified into grades, according to how much they know. Mother classifies the clean clothes, and Mary puts them away. In the post office mail is classified according to the places where it is to go. *v., classified, classifying. 10.*

class mate (klas′māt′), member of the same class in school. *n. 14.*

class room (klas′rüm′), room in which classes are held; schoolroom. *n. 16.*

clat ter (klat′ər), 1. confused noise like many plates being struck together. The clatter in the big dining room was so great that we could hardly hear one another speak. 2. move or fall with confused noise; make a confused noise. 3. noisy talk. 4. talk fast and noisily. *n., v. 5.*

clause (klôz), 1. part of a sentence, with a subject and verb. In "He came before we left," "He came" is a main clause, and "before we left" is a subordinate clause. 2. a single provision of a law, a treaty, or any other written agreement; short sentence. There is a clause in our contract that says we may not keep a dog in this building. *n. 5.*

claw (klô), 1. a sharp, hooked nail on a bird's or animal's foot. 2. a foot provided with these sharp, hooked nails. 3. thing like a claw. The pincers of lobsters or crabs are claws. The part of a hammer used for pulling nails is the claw. 4. to scratch, tear, seize, or pull with claws or hands. The kitten was clawing the screen door. *n., v. 5.*

Claws of a bird

clay (klā), 1. a sticky kind of earth which hardens when it is baked. Bricks and dishes are made from various kinds of clay. 2. in the Bible, the human body. *n. 2.*

clay ey (klā′i), 1. of, like, or containing clay. 2. covered or smeared with clay. *adj.*

clean (klēn), 1. Soap and water make us clean. 2. The saint had a clean heart. 3. The cat is a clean animal. 4. Washing cleans clothes. Clean up the yard. Clean out your desk. 5. Anything well shaped and neat is called clean. 6. Anything well done may be called clean. 7. The new owner of the newspaper made a clean sweep by dismissing all the workers and hiring new ones. 8. The horse jumped clean over the brook. Boards of the bridge were cut clean through. *adj., v., adv. 1.*

clean er (klēn′ər), 1. person whose work is keeping buildings, windows, or other objects clean. 2. anything that removes dirt, grease, or stains. *n. 8.*

clean li ness (klen′li nis), cleanness; being habitually clean. *n. 7.*

clean ly[1] (klen′li), clean; habitually clean. A cat is a cleanly animal. *adj., cleanlier, cleanliest. 19.*

clean ly[2] (klēn′li), in a clean manner. The butcher's knife cut cleanly through the meat. *adv.*

clean ness (klēn′nis), being clean. The cleanness of the rooms pleased the good housekeeper. *n. 18.*

cleanse (klenz), 1. make clean. 2. make pure. *v. 4.*

clear (klēr), 1. A clear sky is free from clouds. Healthy children have clear skins. There is a clear view of the sea from that hill. He told a clear story. 2. He will clear the land of trees. 3. It rained and then it cleared. **Clear up** sometimes means explain. 4. The bullet went clear through the door. *adj., v., adv. 1.*

clear ance (klēr′əns), 1. act of making clear. 2. clear space. 3. the meeting of requirements to get a ship or cargo free on entering or leaving a port. *n. 14.*

clear-cut (klēr′kut′), 1. having clear, sharp outlines. 2. clear; definite; distinct. *adj.*

clear ing (klēr′ing), open space of cleared land in a forest. *n. 14.*

clear ness (klēr′nis), being clear. *n. 11.*

cleat (klēt), 1. strip of wood or iron fastened across anything for support or for sure footing. A gangway has cleats to keep people from slipping. 2. small, wedge-shaped block fastened to a spar, etc., as a support, check, etc. 3. piece of wood or iron used for securing ropes or lines. *n. 18.*

Cleat securing a rope

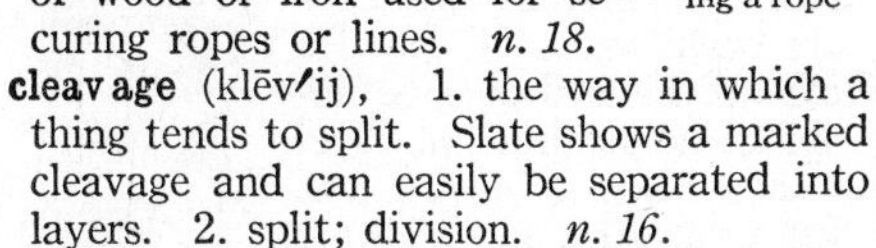

cleav age (klēv′ij), 1. the way in which a thing tends to split. Slate shows a marked cleavage and can easily be separated into layers. 2. split; division. *n. 16.*

cleave[1] (klēv), cut or split open. A blow of the whale's tail cleaved our boat in two. *v., cleaved* or *cleft* or *clove, cleaved* or *cleft* or *cloven, cleaving. 4.*

cleave[2] (klēv), hold fast (to); cling; be faithful. *v., cleaved, cleaving.*

cleav er (klēv′ər), a butcher's tool with a heavy blade and a short handle, used for cutting through meat or bone. *n. 13.*

clef (klef), symbol in music indicating the pitch of the notes on a staff. *n. 18.*

G clef F clef

cleft (kleft), 1. See **cleave**[1]. His blow had cleft the bear's head in two. 2. split; divided. 3. space or opening made by splitting; crack. *pt. and pp. of cleave*[1], *adj., n. 6.*

clem a tis (klem′ə tis), vine with clusters of fragrant white or purple flowers. *n. 17.*

clem en cy (klem′ən si), 1. mercy. The judge showed clemency to the prisoner. 2. mildness. The clemency of the weather allowed them to live outdoors. *n. 12.*

Clem ens (klem′ənz), Samuel Langhorne, the real name of Mark Twain. *n.*

clem ent (klem′ənt), 1. merciful. 2. mild; gentle. *adj. 11.*

clench (klench), 1. close tightly together; as, to clench one's teeth, to clench one's hand, a clenched fist. 2. grasp firmly. He clenched my arm. 3. tight grip. I felt the clench of his hand on my arm. 4. clinch. *v., n. 9.*

Cle o pa tra (klē′ō pā′trə), queen of Egypt, famous for her charm (69?-30 B.C.). *n. 11.*

cler gy (klėr′ji), persons ordained for religious work; ministers, pastors, and priests. *n., pl. clergies. 8.*

cler gy man (klėr′ji mən), minister; pastor; priest. We have clergymen to help us in religion just as we have doctors to help us in health or teachers to help us in education. *n., pl. clergymen. 7.*

cler ic (kler′ik), 1. clergyman. 2. of a clergyman or the clergy. *n., adj. 20.*

cler i cal (kler′i kəl), 1. of a clerk; of clerks; for clerks. A big bank employs many persons for clerical work. 2. of a clergyman or the clergy. *adj. 11.*

clerk (klėrk), 1. man or woman employed to sell goods in a store or shop. 2. person employed in an office to file records, copy letters, keep accounts, etc. 3. public official in charge of files or records. 4. work as a clerk. *n., v. 2.*

Cleve land (klēv′lənd), 1. a city in northeastern Ohio, on Lake Erie. 2. Grover Cleveland (1837-1908) was twice president of the United States. *n. 5.*

clev er (klev′ər), 1. bright; intelligent; having a ready mind. 2. skillful in doing some particular thing. Mr. Jones is a clever carpenter. 3. showing skill or intelligence; as, a clever trick, a clever answer. *adj. 4.*

clev er ness (klev′ər nis), being clever; quickness of mind; skill; ability. *n. 15.*

clew (klü), 1. a guide to the solving of a mystery or problem. 2. a ball of thread or yarn. The old legend is that a clew was used as a guide out of a maze. *n. 11.* Also spelled **clue.**

click (klik), 1. a short, sharp sound like that of a key turning in a lock. We heard the click as he cocked his pistol. 2. make such a sound. *n., v. 10.*

cli ent (klī′ənt), 1. person for whom a lawyer acts. 2. customer. *n. 7.*

cliff (klif), a high, steep rock. *n. 3.*

cli mate (klī′mit), 1. the kind of weather a place has. Climate includes conditions of heat and cold, moisture and dryness, clearness and cloudiness, wind and calm. 2. a region with certain conditions of heat and cold, rainfall, wind, sunlight, etc. The doctor ordered him to go to a drier climate. *n. 3.*

cli mat ic (klī mat′ik), of climate; connected with climate. *adj. 13.*

cli max (klī′maks), 1. the arrangement of ideas in a rising scale of force and interest. 2. the highest point of interest; the most exciting part. We had had two punctures and a blowout, but the climax came when both front wheels fell off. *n. 8.*

climb (klīm), 1. go up; as, to climb a hill, to climb a ladder. 2. grow up. A vine climbs by twining about a support of some kind. 3. the act of going up. Our climb took two hours. 4. go in any direction, especially with the help of the hands. He climbed down the rope. *v., n. 2.*

climb er (klīm′ər), 1. person or thing that climbs. 2. a climbing plant; vine. *n. 16.*

clime (klīm), country; region; climate. *n.* [*Used in poetry*] *5.*

clinch (klinch), 1. fasten (a driven nail) by bending down the point. 2. fasten firmly; settle decisively. A deposit of five dollars clinched the bargain. 3. hold on tight in fighting or wrestling. 4. act of clinching. *v., n. 17.*

cling (kling), stick or hold fast. A vine clings to its support. Wet clothes cling to the body. The child clung to his mother's skirt. We cling to the beliefs of our fathers. *v., clung, clinging. 5.*

clin ic (klin′ik), 1. a place connected with a medical school or hospital where poor people may receive treatment free. 2. instruction of medical students by examining or treating patients in their presence. 3. a place for practical instruction and treatment. *n. 11.*

clin i cal (klin′i kəl), of or having to do with a clinic. *adj. 15.*

clink (klingk), 1. a light, sharp, ringing sound, like that of glasses hitting together. 2. make a sharp, ringing sound. The spoons and glasses clinked. 3. cause to clink. *n., v. 9.*

clink er (klingk′ər), large, rough cinder. *n.*

clip[1] (klip), 1. cut; cut short; trim with shears or scissors; as, to clip the hair, to clip the fleece of sheep. 2. cut a person's hair; cut the hair of a horse or dog; cut the fleece of a sheep. The dog has been clipped too short. 3. shearing; cutting hair. 4. the amount of wool clipped from a sheep or flock of sheep. 5. a rapid motion. *v., clipped, clipping, n. 4.*

clip[2] (klip), 1. hold or grip tightly; as, to clip papers together. 2. thing used for clipping. A clip for papers is often made of a piece of bent wire. *v., clipped, clipping, n.*

Clippers for bushes

clip per (klip′ər), 1. an instrument for clipping; as, hair clippers, a nail clipper. 2. a fast sailing ship. New England used to be famous for her clipper ships. *n. 14.*

clip ping (klip′ing), 1. piece cut out of a newspaper, magazine, etc. 2. thing cut out or off of something else. *n.*

clique (klēk), small, exclusive group of people. *n.*

cloak (klōk), 1. loose outer garment with or without sleeves. 2. to cover with a cloak. 3. anything that covers or hides. 4. hide. He cloaked his evil purpose under friendly words. *n., v. 2.*

Man wearing a cloak

clock[1] (klok), instrument for measuring and showing time. A clock is not made to be carried about as a watch is. *n. 1.*

clock[2] (klok), ornament on each side of a stocking, extending from the ankle up. *n.*

clock wise (klok′wīz′), in the direction in which the hands of a clock move. *adv., adj.*

clock work (klok′wėrk′), machinery of a clock or like that of a clock. *n. 17.*

clod (klod), 1. lump of earth. 2. stupid person. *n. 7.*

clog (klog), 1. fill up or choke up with waste matter. 2. become filled or choked up. 3. hinder; interfere. 4. anything that hinders or interferes. 5. any weight, such as a block of wood, fastened to the leg of an animal or person to hinder motion. 6. a shoe with a wooden sole. *v., clogged, clogging, n. 11.*

Cloister

clois ter (klois′tər), 1. a covered walk having one side walled and the other with windows or rows of pillars, built in a part of a church, college, or convent.

2. convent or monastery. 3. a quiet place shut away from the world. 4. shut away in a quiet place. *n., v. 9.*

clomb (klōm), climbed. *old pt. and old pp. of* **climb.** *14.*

close[1] (klōz), 1. shut. 2. bring together. 3. come together. 4. bring to an end. 5. an end. *v., n. 1.*

close[2] (klōs), 1. with little space. 2. with little fresh air. 3. near. 4. nearly equal. 5. stingy. 6. an enclosed place. *adj., n.*

close ly (klōs′li), 1. with little difference; narrowly; almost the same. 2. snugly; tightly. Her coat fits closely. *adv.*

close ness (klōs′nis), 1. being close. 2. narrowness. 3. lack of fresh air. 4. nearness. 5. stinginess. *n. 10.*

clos et (kloz′it), 1. a small room used for storing clothes or household supplies, such as canned fruits, china, or linen. 2. a small, private room for prayer, study, or interviews with people. 3. shut up in a room for a secret talk. He was closeted with the lawyer for over an hour. 4. water closet; toilet. *n., v. 3.*

clo sure (klō′zhər), 1. a closing. 2. closed condition. 3. conclusion. *n. 17.*

clot (klot), 1. half-solid mass; as, a clot of blood. 2. form into clots. Milk clots when it becomes sour. *n., v., clotted, clotting. 12.*

cloth (klôth), 1. Cloth is made in sheets or webs from wool, silk, linen, cotton, or other fiber. Cloth is used for clothing, curtains, bedding, and many other purposes. 2. piece of cloth used for a special purpose; as, a cloth for the table, a dishcloth, a washcloth. 3. profession of a clergyman; clergy. *n., pl. cloths* (klôᴛʜz or klôths). *1.*

clothe (klōᴛʜ), 1. put clothes on; cover with clothes; dress. 2. provide with clothes. 3. cover. The trees are clothed in green leaves. We clothe our thoughts in words. 4. provide; furnish; equip. A judge is clothed with the authority of the government. *v., clothed* or *clad, clothing. 1.*

clothes (klōz or klōᴛʜz), 1. coverings for the body. Lucy has pretty clothes. 2. coverings for a bed. *n. pl. 1.*

clothes pin (klōz′pin′), wooden clip to hold clothes on a line. *n.*

cloth ier (klōᴛʜ′yər), 1. dealer in clothes. 2. seller of cloth. *n. 16.*

cloth ing (klōᴛʜ′ing), clothes, *n. 6.*

cloud (kloud), 1. a white or gray or almost black mass in the sky, made up of tiny drops of water. 2. a mass of smoke or dust. 3. cover with a cloud or clouds. 4. grow cloudy. The sky clouded over. 5. anything like a cloud; as, a cloud of arrows, a cloud of birds in flight. The dark veins in marble are sometimes called clouds. We may speak of a person as being under a cloud of disgrace or suspicion. 6. make dark; become gloomy. His face clouded with anger. 7. put under suspicion, disgrace, etc. *n., v. 1.*

cloud less (kloud′lis), clear; bright; sunny; without a cloud. *adj. 10.*

cloud y (kloud′i), 1. covered with clouds; having clouds in it; as, a cloudy sky. 2. not clear; as, a cloudy liquid, cloudy ideas. *adj., cloudier, cloudiest. 3.*

clout (klout), 1. cloth; rag. *Old use.* 2. the mark shot at in archery. 3. a shot that hits this. 4. a rap or knock. *Used in common talk.* 5. hit. *Used in common talk. n., v. 12.*

clove[1] (klōv), 1. strong, fragrant spice, made from the dried flower buds of a tree grown in the tropics. 2. the flavor of clove. *n. 5.*

clove[2] (klōv), cleft. *pt. and poetic pp. of* **cleave**[1], *old pt. of cleave*[3].

clo ven (klō′vən), 1. split; divided into two parts. Cows have cloven hoofs. 2. cleaved. *adj., pp. of* **cleave**[1]. *15.*

clo ver (klō′vər), a plant with leaves of three small leaflets and sweet-smelling rounded heads of red or white flowers. Clover is grown as food for horses and cattle and to improve the soil. *n. 4.*

Clover

clown (kloun), 1. man who makes a business of making people laugh by tricks and jokes. 2. act like a clown; play tricks and jokes; act silly. 3. bad-mannered, awkward person. *n., v. 7.*

clown ish (kloun′ish), like a clown. *adj. 15.*

cloy (kloi), 1. weary by too much, too sweet, or too rich food. My appetite was cloyed by all the candy I had eaten. 2. weary by too much of anything pleasant. *v. 9.*

club (klub), 1. a heavy stick of wood, thicker at one end, used as a weapon. 2. a stick or bat used in some games played with a ball; as, golf clubs. 3. beat with a club or something similar. 4. group of people joined together for some special purpose; as, a social club, tennis club, yacht club, nature-study club. 5. the building or rooms used by a club. 6. combine for some purpose. The children clubbed together to buy their mother a plant for her birthday. *n., v., clubbed, clubbing. 2.*

cluck (kluk), 1. the sound that a hen makes when calling to her chickens. 2. make such a sound. *n., v. 4.*

clue (klü), 1. a guide to the solving of a mystery or problem. 2. a ball of thread or yarn. The old legend is that a clue was used as a guide out of a maze. *n. 17.* Also spelled **clew.**

clump (klump), 1. a lump; as, a clump of earth. 2. a cluster; as, a clump of trees. 3. walk heavily and clumsily. The lame man clumps along. *n., v. 9.*

clum si ly (klum′zi li), in a clumsy manner; awkwardly. *adv.*

clum si ness (klum′zi nis), being clumsy; awkwardness. *n.*

clum sy (klum′zi), 1. awkward in moving. 2. not well-shaped or well-made. Jack's rowboat was a clumsy affair, for he had made it himself. *adj., clumsier, clumsiest. 8.*

clung (klung). See **cling.** The child clung to her mother. *pt. and pp. of cling. 6.*

clus ter (klus′tər), 1. a number of things of the same kind growing or grouped together; as, a cluster of grapes, a cluster of curls, a little cluster of houses. 2. be in a bunch; gather in a group. The girls clustered around their teacher. *n., v. 3.*

clutch (kluch), 1. a tight grasp. 2. grasp tightly; snatch; seize eagerly. A drowning man will clutch at a straw. 3. an arrangement in a machine for connecting or disconnecting its parts. 4. **Clutches** sometimes means grasping hands or claws. The lion almost had me in his clutches. *n., v. 5.*

clut ter (klut′ər), 1. litter; confusion; disorder. 2. to litter with things. Her desk was all cluttered with old papers, strings, and trash. *n., v. 18.*

Clyde (klīd), a river and inlet in Scotland. *n. 18.*

cm., centimeter; centimeters. *20.*

co-, prefix meaning:—

1. with; together. Coöperate means act with or together.
2. joint; fellow. Coauthor means joint or fellow author.
3. equally. Coextensive means equally extensive.

Co., company. Jones and Co. means Jones and Company. *12.*

coach (kōch), 1. a large, old-fashioned, closed carriage with seats inside. Those which carried passengers along a regular run, with stops for meals and fresh horses,

Coach

often had seats on top too. 2. a passenger car of a railroad train. 3. a teacher. The football coach and the baseball coach are brothers. 4. train or teach. 5. make ready for a special test. *n., v. 2.*

coach man (kōch′mən), man who drives a coach or carriage for a living. *n., pl. coachmen. 7.*

co ad ju tor (kō′ə jü′tər), assistant. *n. 15.*

co ag u late (kō ag′ū lāt), change from a liquid to a thickened mass; thicken. Cooking coagulates the white of egg. *v. 11.*

co ag u la tion (kō ag′ū lā′shən), 1. act of coagulating. If coagulation did not take place after a cut or wound, the injured person might bleed to death. 2. a coagulated mass. *n. 20.*

coal (kōl), 1. black mineral that burns and gives off heat. We use hard coal and soft coal. 2. a piece of this. 3. a piece of glowing, partly burned, or burned-out material. The big log had burned down to a few red coals. 4. supply with coal. 5. take in a supply of coal. *n., v. 1.*

co a lesce (kō′ə les′), 1. grow together. 2. unite into one body, mass, party, etc.; combine. The thirteen colonies coalesced to form a nation. *v. 16.*

co a les cence (kō′ə les′əns), 1. a growing together. 2. union; combination. *n. 20.*

co a li tion (kō′ə lish′ən), union into one body; combination; alliance. *n. 15.*

coal oil, 1. kerosene. 2. petroleum.

coal scuttle, bucket for holding or carrying coal.

coal tar, black, sticky substance formed when gas is made from coal. Coal tar, when distilled, yields certain medicines, dyes, flavorings, and perfumes. The waste matter left is used in making pavements.

coarse (kōrs), 1. not fine; made up of fairly large parts; as, coarse sand. 2. rough; as, coarse cloth. 3. common; poor; inferior; as, coarse food. 4. not delicate; crude; vulgar; as, coarse manners. *adj. 3.*

coars en (kōr′sən), make coarse; become coarse. *v.*

coarse ness (kōrs′nis), coarse condition; vulgarity. *n. 11.*

coast (kōst), 1. land along the sea; seashore. Many ships were wrecked on that rocky coast. 2. go along or near the shore of. We coasted South America on our trip last winter. 3. sail from port to port of a coast. 4. ride down a hill without using effort or power. 5. slide downhill on a sled. 6. slide. The icy hill made a good coast for sleds. *n., v. 1.*

coast al (kōs′təl), at the coast; along a coast; near a coast. *adj. 12.*

coast er (kōs′tər), 1. person or thing that coasts. 2. ship trading along a coast. *n. 19.*

coast guard, 1. group of men whose work is saving lives and preventing smuggling along the coast of a country. 2. member of this group.

coast wise (kōst′wīz′), along the coast. *adv., adj.*

coat (kōt), 1. outer garment with sleeves. 2. any outer covering; as, a dog's coat, a coat of bark on a tree. 3. thin layer; as, a coat of paint. 4. cover or provide with a coat. 5. cover with a thin layer. The floor is coated with varnish. The pill is coated with sugar. *n., v. 1.*

coat ing (kōt′ing), layer of any substance spread over a surface; as, a coating of paint. *n.*

Coat of arms

coat of arms, a shield with pictures and designs on it. Each knight or lord had his own coat of arms.

coat of mail, garment made of metal rings or plates, worn as armor. *pl. coats of mail.*

coax (kōks), persuade by soft words; influence by pleasant ways. She coaxed her father to let her go to the dance. I coaxed a smile from the baby. We coaxed the squirrel into his cage with peanuts. *v. 8.*

Coat of mail

cob (kob), 1. the central part of an ear of corn, on which the grains grow. 2. a strong horse with short legs. *n. 9.*

co balt (kō′bôlt), 1. a silver-white metallic element with a pinkish tint. 2. a dark-blue coloring matter made from it. *n. 16.*

cob ble[1] (kob′əl), 1. mend; repair; patch. 2. put together clumsily. *v. 14.*

cob ble[2] (kob′əl), cobblestone. *n.*

cob bler (kob′lər), 1. man whose work is mending shoes. 2. clumsy workman. 3. a fruit pie baked in a deep dish. *n. 5.*

Cobblestones in a street

cob ble stone (kob′əl stōn′), a rounded stone that was formerly much used in paving. *n. 20.*

co bra (kō′brə), a very poisonous snake, found most often in India. *n. 18.*

cob web (kob′web′), 1. a spider's web, or the stuff it is made of. 2. anything thin and slight or entangling like a spider's web. *n. 8.*

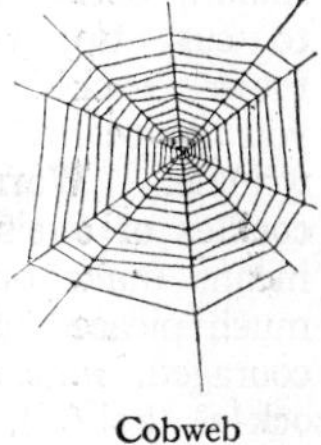
Cobweb

co caine (kō kān′), a drug used to deaden pain and as a stimulant. *n. 18.*

Co chin (kō′chin), large breed of domestic fowl that has many feathers on its legs. *n. 19.*

Cochin China, French colony in Indo-China.

coch i neal (koch′i nēl′), a bright-red dye made from the dried bodies of certain insects found in Mexico and Central America. *n. 17.*

cock[1] (kok), 1. a male chicken; a rooster. 2. a male bird; as, a turkey cock. 3. a faucet used to turn the flow of a liquid or gas on or off. 4. the hammer of a gun. 5. the position the hammer is in when it is pulled back ready to fire. 6. pull back the hammer of (a gun), ready to fire. *n., v. 2.*

Cock (def. 3)

cock[2] (kok), 1. turn or stick up, especially as if to defy. The little bird cocked his eye at me. 2. an upward turn or bend of the nose or eye. 3. the turn of the brim of a hat. *v., n.*

cock[3] (kok), 1. a small, round pile of hay that rises to a point at the top. 2. pile in cocks. *n., v.*

cock ade (kok ād′), knot of ribbon or a rosette worn on the hat as a badge. *n. 18.*

cock a too (kok′ə tü′), a large crested parrot. See the picture. *n., pl. cockatoos. 18.*

cock a trice (kok′ə tris), a serpent whose look was supposed to cause death. A cockatrice is usually represented as part cock and part serpent. The cockatrice does not really exist. *n. 16.*

Cockatoo (about 18 in. long)

cock er el (kok′ər əl), young rooster, not more than one year old. *n. 19.*

cock er span iel (kok′ər span′yəl), any of a breed of small dogs with long, silky hair and drooping ears. See the picture just below.

cock le[1] (kok′əl), 1. a shellfish that is good to eat. 2. its shell. 3. a small, light, shallow boat. 4. tend to curl up; wrinkle. Paper cockles when you paste it. 5. a wrinkle. **Warm the cockles of one's heart** means make one feel much pleased and encouraged. *n., v. 10.*

Cocker spaniel (1 ft. tall at the shoulder)

cock le[2] (kok′əl), a kind of weed growing in grain fields. *n.*

cock ney (kok′ni), 1. a native of London; an inhabitant of a poorer section of London who speaks a peculiar English. 2. pertaining to cockneys or to their way of speaking. *n., pl. cockneys, adj.*

cock pit (kok′pit′), small, open place in an airplane, boat, etc., where the pilot or passengers sit. *n.*

cock roach (kok′rōch′), an insect often found in kitchens, around water pipes, etc. Cockroaches come out at night. *n. 13.*

Cockroach (about ½ life size)

cocks comb (koks′kōm′), 1. fleshy, red part on the head of a rooster. 2. pointed cap somewhat like this, worn by a jester or clown. 3. plant with crested or feathery clusters of red or yellow flowers. 4. coxcomb. *Old use. n.*

cock sure (kok′shür′), 1. perfectly sure. 2. too sure. *adj.*

cock tail (kok′tāl′), 1. an alcoholic mixed drink. 2. any appetizing drink served just before a meal. 3. shellfish served in a small glass with a highly seasoned sauce. 4. mixed fruits served in a glass. *n. 18.*

co co or **co coa**[1] (kō′kō), a tall palm tree on which coconuts grow. *n., pl. cocos, cocoas.*

co coa[2] (kō′kō), 1. a powder made from the seeds of the cacao tree. 2. a drink made from this powder with milk or water and sugar. *n. 7.*

Coco palm

co co nut or **co coa nut** (kō′kə nut′), the large, round, brown, hard-shelled fruit of the coco palm. Coconuts have a white lining that is good to eat and a white liquid called coconut milk. The white lining is cut up into shreds and used for cakes, puddings, and pies. *n. 6.*

Half of a coconut

co coon (kə kün′), silky case or shell made by worms and caterpillars to live in while they are turning into moths or butterflies. See the picture just below. *n. 10.*

cod (kod), an important food fish found in the cold parts of the northern Atlantic Ocean. *n., pl. cod* or *cods. 4.*

Cod (kod). **Cape Cod** is a hook-shaped peninsula in southeastern Massachusetts. *n.*

Cocoons of: B, butterfly; S, silkworm.

C.O.D., cash or collect on delivery.

cod dle (kod′əl), 1. treat tenderly; pamper. Sick children are often coddled. 2. cook in hot water without boiling; as, a coddled egg. *v. 18.*

code (kōd), 1. a collection of the laws of a country arranged in a clear way so that they can be understood and used. 2. any set of rules. 3. A moral code is made up of the notions of right and wrong conduct held by a person, a group of persons, or a society. 4. a system of military or naval signals. 5. an arrangement of words or figures to keep a message short and secret. 6. The alphabet used in telegraphing is called the Morse code. 7. translate into a code. *n., v. 8.*

co dex (kō′deks), manuscript volume. *n. 18.*

cod fish (kod′fish′), cod. *n., pl. codfishes* or *codfish. 12.*

cod i fy (kod′i fī), arrange according to some system. Napoleon had French laws codified. *v., codified, codifying.*

cod ling (kod′ling), 1. small, inferior apple. 2. unripe apple. 3. The **codling moth** is a small moth whose larvae destroy apples, pears, etc. *n., adj. 18.*

co ef fi cient (kō′i fish′ənt), in algebra, a number multiplying another. In *3x, 3* is the coefficient of *x*. *n. 19.*

co erce (kō ėrs′), compel; force. *v. 11.*

co er cion (kō ėr′shən), compulsion; constraint; government by force. England tried coercion upon the American colonies and provoked open rebellion. *n. 16.*

co er cive (kō ėr′siv), compelling. *adj. 17.*

co e val (kō ē′vəl), 1. of the same age, date, or duration. 2. a contemporary. *adj., n. 15.*

co ex ist (kō′eg zist′), exist together or at the same time. Orange trees have coexisting fruit and flowers. *v. 16.*

cof fee (kôf′i), 1. a common drink. 2. the seeds from which the drink is made. Coffee is roasted and ground. 3. the tree or shrub whose seeds are used to make coffee. *n. 2.*

Coffee: A, branch; B, seed.

cof fer (kôf′ər), 1. a box, chest, or trunk, especially one used to hold money or other valuable things. 2. **Coffers** often means treasury or funds. *n. 9.*

cof fin (kôf′in), a box in which a dead person is put to be buried. *n. 5.*

cog (kog), one of a series of teeth on the edge of a wheel that transfers motion by locking into the teeth of another wheel of the same kind. *n. 13.*

co gen cy (kō′jən si), force; power of convincing. *n. 20.*

co gent (kō′jənt), forcible; convincing; as, a cogent argument. *adj. 14.*

cog i tate (koj′i tāt), think over; consider with care; meditate; ponder. Mr. Smith cogitated a long time about changing his occupation. *v. 19.*

cog i ta tion (koj′i tā′shən), deep thought; careful consideration; meditation. *n. 13.*

co gnac (kō′nyak), a kind of French brandy. *n. 20.*

cog nate (kog′nāt), related by family, origin, nature, or quality. *adj. 20.*

cog ni tion (kog nish′ən), knowledge; the act of knowing. *n. 18.*

cog ni zance (kog′ni zəns), awareness; notice; knowledge. The king had cognizance of plots against him. *n. 15.*

cog ni zant (kog′ni zənt), aware. The general was cognizant of the movements of the enemy. *adj. 20.*

cog no men (kog nō′men), 1. surname; family name; last name. 2. name. 3. nickname. *n.*

cog wheel (kog′hwēl′), wheel with teeth cut in the rim for transmitting or receiving motion. *n.*

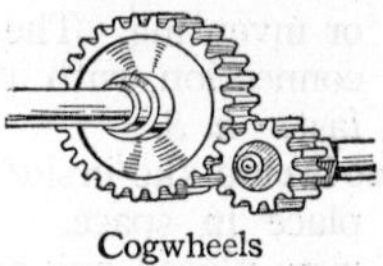
Cogwheels

co here (kō hēr′), 1. stick together; hold together. Brick and mortar cohere. 2. be well connected. *v. 20.*

co her ence (kō hēr′əns), 1. a sticking together. 2. being consistent; logical connection. *n. 18.*

co her ent (kō hēr′ənt), 1. sticking together. 2. connected; consistent. Our geography gives a coherent account of the climate of the United States. *adj. 14.*

co he sion (kō hē′zhən), a sticking together; tendency to hold together. Wet sand has more cohesion than dry sand. *n. 16.*

co he sive (kō hē′siv), sticking together; tending to hold together. *adj.*

co hort (kō′hôrt), 1. a division of troops. An ancient Roman legion was divided into ten cohorts, each containing from 300 to 600 men. 2. a group; a band or company; as, a cohort of angels. *n. 12.*

coif (koif), 1. cap or hood that fits closely around the head. 2. cover with a coif or something like a coif. *n., v.*

Coif (def. 1)

coif fure (kwä fūr′), 1. style of arranging the hair. 2. covering for the hair; headdress. *n.*

coil (koil), 1. wind round and round into a pile, a tube, or a curl. A snake can coil itself up or coil around a branch. A wire spring is evenly coiled. 2. anything that is coiled; as, a coil of rope. One wind or turn of a coil is a single coil. 3. a series of connected pipes arranged in a coil or row as in a radiator. 4. a spiral wire for carrying electric current. *v., n. 5.*

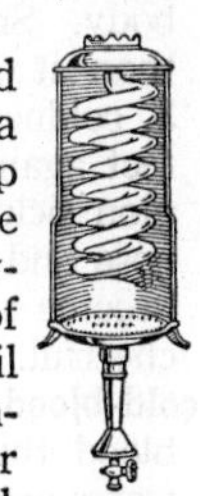
Coil of pipe in a heater

coin (koin), 1. piece of metal stamped by the government for use as money. Pennies, nickels, dimes, and quarters are coins. 2. metal money. 3. make (money) by stamping metal. 4. make (metal) into money. 5. make up; invent; as, to coin a new word or phrase. *n., v. 2.*

coin age (koin′ij), 1. the making of coins. 2. coins. 3. system of coins. The United States has a decimal coinage. 4. making or inventing. The coinage of new words in connection with radio has gone on very fast. *n. 8.*

co in cide (kō′in sīd′), 1. occupy the same place in space. If these triangles △△ were placed one on top of the other, they would coincide. 2. occupy the same time. The working hours of Mr. Adams and Mr. Black coincide. 3. correspond exactly; agree. Her opinion coincides with mine. *v. 11.*

co in ci dence (kō in′si dəns), 1. exact correspondence; agreement; especially, the chance occurrence of two things at such a time as to seem remarkable, fitting, etc. My cousin was born on the very same day that I was. Isn't that a coincidence? 2. a coinciding; occupying the same time or place. *n. 9.*

co in ci dent (kō in′si dənt), 1. coinciding; happening at the same time. 2. occupying the same place or position. *adj. 13.*

coke (kōk), the black substance that is left after coal has been heated in an oven from which most of the air has been shut out. *n. 14.*

Col., 1. Colonel. 2. Colorado. A better abbreviation is **Colo.** *18.*

col an der (kul′ən dər), a vessel or dish full of small holes for draining off liquids. *n. 19.*

Colander

cold (kōld), 1. much less warm than the body. Snow and ice are cold. 2. less warm than it usually is. This coffee is cold. 3. coldness; being cold. Warm clothes protect against the cold of winter. 4. a common sickness that causes a running at the nose and a sore throat. **Catch cold** means become sick with a cold. 5. not kind and cheerful. *adj., n. 1.*

cold-blood ed (kōld′blud′id), 1. having blood that is about as cold as the air or water around the animal. Turtles are cold-blooded; dogs are warm-blooded. 2. lacking in feeling; cruel. *adj.*

cold ness (kōld′nis), condition of being cold. *n. 11.*

cole (kōl), a plant somewhat like cabbage. *n. 17.*

Cole ridge (kōl′rij), Samuel Taylor, an English poet, philosopher, and literary critic (1772-1834). *n. 14.*

col ic (kol′ik), severe pains in the stomach and bowels. *n. 14.*

col i se um (kol′i sē′əm), large building or stadium for games, contests, etc. *n. 18.*

Col i se um (kol′i sē′əm), Colosseum. *n.*

col lab o rate (kə lab′ə rāt), work together. Two authors collaborated on this novel. *v.*

col lapse (kə laps′), 1. fall in; shrink together suddenly. The little chair collapsed when my uncle sat down on it. 2. falling in. Six people were killed by the collapse of the building. 3. break down; fail suddenly. Both his health and his business collapsed within a year. 4. breakdown; failure. *v., n. 8.*

Collar of a shirt

col lar (kol′ər), 1. the straight or turned-over neckband of a coat, a dress, or a shirt. 2. a separate band of linen, lace, or other material worn around the neck. 3. a leather or metal band for a dog's neck. 4. a leather roll for a horse's neck to bear the weight of the loads he pulls. 5. any of the various kinds of rings, bands, or pipes in machinery. 6. put a collar on. 7. seize by the collar; capture. *n., v. 2.*

Collar for machinery

col lar bone (kol′ər bōn′), bone connecting the breastbone and the shoulder blade. *n.*

COLLARBONE

BREASTBONE

col lat er al (kə lat′ər əl), 1. side by side. 2. aside from the main thing; secondary. 3. descended from the same ancestors, but in a different line. 4. additional. 5. stocks, bonds, etc., pledged as security for a loan. *adj., n. 12.*

col league (kol′ēg), associate; fellow worker. Professor Brown is a colleague of Professor Allen. *n. 8.*

col lect (kə lekt′), 1. bring together; come together. Do you collect stamps? Dust collects under beds. A crowd collects when there is an accident. 2. ask and receive pay for (debts, bills, dues, or taxes). *v. 2.*

col lec tion (kə lek′shən), 1. bringing together; coming together. The collection of these stamps took ten years. The collection of a crowd there was unexpected. 2. a group of things gathered from many places and belonging together. The library has a large collection of books. 3. money gathered from people; as, to take up a collection in church. 4. mass; heap. There is a collection of dust in an unused room. *n. 3.*

col lec tive (kə lek′tiv), 1. of a group; as a group; taken all together. 2. singular in form, but plural in meaning. *Crowd, people, troop,* and *herd* are collective nouns. 3. collective noun. 4. formed by collecting. *adj., n. 14.*

col lec tive ly (kə lek′tiv li), 1. as a group; all together. 2. in a singular form, but with a plural meaning. *adv.*

col lec tor (kə lek′tər), person or thing that collects. Mr. Gray is a tax collector. These curtains are dust collectors. *n. 9.*

col lege (kol′ij), 1. a school that gives degrees. 2. school. 3. the buildings and grounds of a college. 4. group of persons with the same duties and privileges. *n. 2.*

col le gi an (kə lē′ji ən), college student. *n.*

col le gi ate (kə lē′ji it), 1. of or like a college. 2. of or like college students. *adj. 13.*

col lide (kə līd′), 1. rush against; hit or strike violently together. In running around the corner, John collided with another boy. 2. clash; conflict. *v. 15.*

col lie (kol′i), an intelligent kind of dog used for tending sheep and as a pet. *n. 17.*

Collie (about 2 ft. high at the shoulder)

col lier (kol′yər), 1. ship for carrying coal. 2. coal miner. *n. 14.*

col lier y (kol′yər i), a coal mine and its buildings. *n., pl. collieries. 14.*

col li sion (kə lizh′ən), 1. violent rushing against; hitting or striking violently together. Eight people were killed in the automobile collision. 2. clash; conflict. *n. 9.*

col lo ca tion (kol′ō kā′shən), act of placing together; arrangement; putting in place; as, the collocation of words in a sentence. *n. 16.*

col lo qui al (kə lō′kwi əl), used in common talk; belonging to everyday, familiar talk, but not used in formal speech or writing. Such expressions as *pants* for *trousers, I guess* for *I think,* etc., are colloquial. *adj. 14.*

col lo qui al ism (kə lō′kwi əl izm), colloquial word or phrase. *n.*

col lo quy (kol′ə kwi), a talking together; conversation. After a brief colloquy with the hotel clerk, Mr. Smith went to his room. *n., pl. colloquies. 14.*

col lu sion (kə lü′zhən), a secret agreement for some wrong purpose. *n. 12.*

Colo., Colorado.

co logne (kə lōn′), fragrant liquid, not so strong as perfume. *n. 6.*

Co logne (kə lōn′), a city in Germany on the river Rhine. *n.*

Co lom bi a (kə lum′bi ə), a country in northwestern South America. *n. 20.*

co lon[1] (kō′lən), a mark (:) of punctuation. Colons are used before explanations, lists, long quotations, etc., to set them off from the rest of the sentence. *n. 9.*

co lon[2] (kō′lən), the lower part of the large intestine. *n.*

colo nel (kėr′nəl), officer who commands a regiment of soldiers. *n. 7.*

co lo ni al (kə lō′ni əl), 1. of a colony; having to do with colonies. 2. having to do with the thirteen British colonies which became the United States of America. 3. person who lives in a colony. *adj., n. 5.*

col o nist (kol′ə nist), 1. person who helped to found a colony. 2. person who lives in a colony; settler. *n. 4.*

col o ni za tion (kol′ə ni zā′shən), the establishment of a colony or colonies. The English, French, and Spanish took part in the colonization of North America. *n. 14.*

col o nize (kol′ə nīz), 1. establish a colony in. The English colonized New England. 2. establish (persons) in a colony. *v. 17.*

col on nade (kol′ə nād′), a series of columns set the same distance apart. *n. 12.*

Colonnade

col o ny (kol′ə ni), 1. a group of people who leave their own country and go to settle in another land, but who still remain citizens of their own country. 2. the settlement made by such a group of people. 3. territory distant from the country that governs it. 4. group of people of one country or occupation living in their own part of a city; as, the Italian colony in Boston, a colony of artists. 5. group of animals or plants of the same kind, living or growing together.

We found a colony of ants under the steps. *n., pl. colonies. 2.*

col or (kul′ər), 1. Red, yellow, blue, green, purple, etc., are colors. 2. give color to; put color on; change the color of. 3. paint; stain; dye. 4. outward appearance. His story has some color of truth. 5. change to give a wrong idea. The dishonest general colored his report of the battle. 6. **The colors** often means the flag. *n., v. 1.*

Col o rad o (kol′ə rad′ō), 1. a Western State of the United States. 2. a river flowing from this State into the Gulf of California. *n. 5.*

col or a tion (kul′ər ā′shən), way in which something is colored. The coloration of animals is often like that of their surroundings. *n. 15.*

col or-blind (kul′ər blīnd′), unable to tell certain colors apart; unable to see certain colors. *adj.*

col ored (kul′ərd), 1. having color. 2. belonging to some other race than the white. 3. of the Negro race. *adj. 4.* See also **color.**

col or ful (kul′ər fəl), 1. full of color. 2. picturesque; vivid. *adj.*

col or ing (kul′ər ing), 1. way in which something is colored. 2. substance used to color. 3. false appearance. He lies with a coloring of truth. *n.*

col or less (kul′ər lis), 1. without color. 2. without vividness; dull; as, a colorless person. *adj. 10.*

co los sal (kə los′əl), huge; gigantic; vast. *adj. 7.*

Colosseum as it is now

Col os se um (kol′ə-sē′əm), a large stadium at Rome built about 80 A.D. The Colosseum was used for games, contests, and shows. *n. 14.*

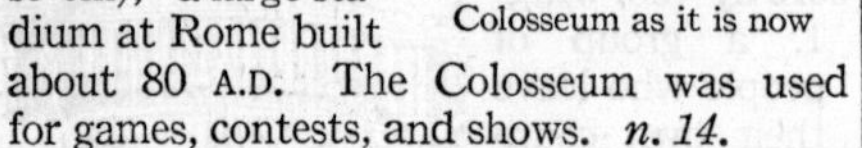

co los sus (kə los′əs), 1. a huge statue. The **Colossus of Rhodes** was a statue of Apollo at Rhodes, made about 280 B.C. It was one of the Seven Wonders of the World. 2. anything huge and gigantic. *n., pl. colossi* (-ī) or *colossuses. 17.*

Two colossi of ancient Egypt

colt (kōlt), young horse, donkey, etc. *n. 3.*

Co lum bi a (kə lum′bi ə), 1. the capital of South Carolina. 2. a river flowing between Washington and Oregon into the Pacific Ocean. 3. a name for the United States. 4. a university in New York City. *n. 4.*

col um bine (kol′əm bīn), plant whose flowers have petals shaped like hollow spurs. Wild columbines have red-and-yellow or blue-and-white flowers. *n. 18.*

Co lum bus (kə lum′bəs), 1. Christopher Columbus (1446?-1506) was the discoverer of America in 1492. 2. the capital of Ohio. *n. 3.*

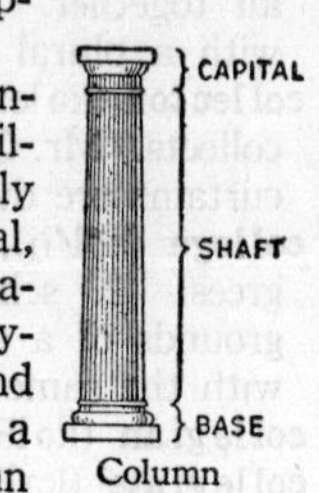

Column

col umn (kol′əm), 1. a slender, upright structure; a pillar. Columns are usually made of stone, wood, or metal, and used as supports or ornaments to a building. 2. anything that seems slender and upright like a column; as, a column of smoke, a column of figures. The spinal column is the backbone. 3. soldiers or ships following one another in a single line. 4. slender part of a page reading from top to bottom, separated by lines or by blank spaces. Some newspapers have eight columns to a page. 5. part of a newspaper used for a special subject or written by a special writer; as, the children's column. *n. 3.*

com-, prefix meaning:—with; together. commingle = mingle with one another. compress = press together.

co ma (kō′mə), stupor; prolonged unconsciousness caused by disease, injury, or poison. *n. 20.*

Comb for hair

comb (kōm), 1. a narrow, short piece of metal, rubber, celluloid, etc., with teeth, used to arrange or clean the hair or to hold it in place. 2. anything shaped or used like a comb, especially an instrument for combing wool. 3. clean; take out tangles in; arrange with a comb. 4. search through. We had to comb the whole city before we found our lost dog. 5. the thick, red, fleshy piece on top of the head of chickens and some other fowls. 6. the system of cells made by bees, in which they store honey. 7. the top of a wave. 8. roll over or break at the top; as, combing waves. *n., v. 4.*

Comb of rooster

Honeycomb

com bat (kom′bat), fight; struggle; battle. *n., v., combated, combating. 4.*

com bat ant (kom′bə tənt), 1. a fighter.

The two combatants let loose of one another to take breath. 2. fighting. *n., adj. 10.*

com ba tive (kom′bə tiv), ready to fight; fond of fighting. *adj. 18.*

combe (küm), narrow valley; deep hollow among hills. *n. 19.*

com bi na tion (kom′bi nā′shən), 1. combining or being combined; union. 2. one whole made by combining two or more different things. 3. a united set of things or persons. The farmers are forming a combination to market their goods at better prices. *n. 3.*

com bine (kəm bīn′), join together. *v. 3.*

com bus ti ble (kəm bus′ti bəl), 1. capable of taking fire and burning. Gasoline is highly combustible. 2. a combustible substance. Wood and coal are combustibles. 3. easily excited; fiery. *adj., n. 14.*

com bus tion (kəm bus′chən), act or process of burning. We heat houses by the combustion of coal. The body does work by the slow combustion of food. *n. 7.*

come (kum). One boy came; the other went. The train comes at noon. Snow comes in winter. Are you coming home? **Come out** means (1) be revealed or shown. (2) be offered to the public. (3) do one's part. (4) be introduced to society; make a debut. *v., came, come, coming. 1.*

co me di an (kə mē′di ən), 1. an actor in comedies. 2. person who amuses an audience with funny talk or actions. *n. 13.*

com e dy (kom′ə di), 1. a light, amusing play or show having a happy ending. 2. an amusing happening. *n., pl. comedies. 5.*

come li ness (kum′li nis), 1. pleasant appearance. 2. fitness; suitable behavior; propriety. *n. 8.*

come ly (kum′li), 1. pleasant to look at. 2. fitting; suitable; proper. *adj., comelier, comeliest. 6.*

com er (kum′ər), one who comes. First comers will be served first. *n. 11.*

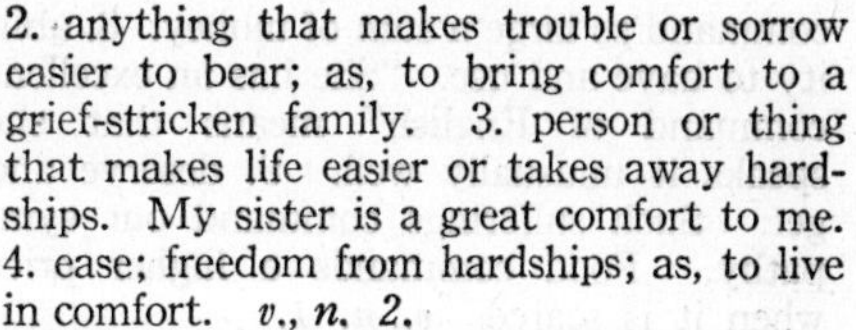
Comet

com et (kom′it), a heavenly body with a starlike point and often with a tail of light. Comets move around the sun like planets, but in a long oval course. *n. 7.*

com fit (kum′fit), piece of candy; sweetmeat. *n. 19.*

com fort (kum′fərt), 1. ease the grief or sorrow of. Her mother's words of love and help comforted the sobbing child. 2. anything that makes trouble or sorrow easier to bear; as, to bring comfort to a grief-stricken family. 3. person or thing that makes life easier or takes away hardships. My sister is a great comfort to me. 4. ease; freedom from hardships; as, to live in comfort. *v., n. 2.*

com fort a ble (kum′fər tə bəl), 1. giving comfort; as, a comfortable chair or room. 2. in comfort; at ease; free from pain or hardship. A warm fire makes you feel comfortable after a cold day outdoors. 3. a padded covering for a bed. *adj., n. 2.*

com fort a bly (kum′fər tə bli), in a comfortable manner; easily. *adv.*

com fort er (kum′fər tər), 1. person who makes pain and sorrow easier to bear; person who brings help and cheer in time of trouble. 2. a padded covering for a bed. 3. a long woolen scarf. *n. 5.*

com fort less (kum′fərt lis), 1. bringing no comfort or ease of mind; as, comfortless words. 2. having none of the comforts of life; as, a comfortless room. *adj. 10.*

com ic (kom′ik), 1. of comedy. 2. amusing; funny. 3. funny story told by pictures. 4. any story told by pictures. *Used in common talk. adj., n. 12.*

com i cal (kom′i kəl), amusing; funny. A story or an action which makes you laugh is comical. *adj. 10.*

com ing (kum′ing), 1. approach; arrival. 2. approaching; next. *n., adj. 1.*

com i ty (kom′i ti), courtesy; civility. The comity of nations is the respect shown by them for one another's laws and customs. *n., pl. comities. 17.*

com ma (kom′ə), a mark (,) of punctuation. Commas are used to show interruptions in the thought or in the grammatical structure of a sentence. *n. 14.*

com mand (kə mand′), 1. order; bid; direct. The captain commanded the men to fire. 2. an order; a bidding. "Halt!" was the sentry's command. 3. be in authority over; have power over; be master of. The captain commands his ship. The general commands the army. 4. possession of authority; power; control. The general is in command of the army. 5. body of troops or district under a commander. 6. control by position; overlook. The fortress commanded the plain beneath. The house stood on a hill commanding the sea. 7. be able to have and use. He cannot command so large a sum of money. 8. ability to have and use. "She has an excellent command of English" means that she speaks it unusually well. 9. deserve and get. Such sufferings command our sympathy. Food commands a higher price when it is scarce. *v., n. 1.*

com man dant (kom′ən dant′), 1. commander. 2. the commanding officer of a fort, navy yard, etc. *n. 15.*

com man deer (kom′ən dēr′), 1. seize (private property) for public use. All automobiles in the town were commandeered by the army. 2. force (men) into military service. *v.*

com mand er (kə man′dər), 1. person who commands. Anyone who has people or supplies under his control is the commander of them. 2. officer in charge of an army or a part of an army. 3. in the navy, officer ranking next below a captain. *n. 4.*

commander in chief, commander of a whole army or fleet. *pl. commanders in chief. 18.*

com mand ment (kə mand′mənt), a law; especially, one of the ten laws of Moses in the Old Testament. "Thou shalt not kill" is one of the Ten Commandments. *n. 6.*

com mem o rate (kə mem′ə rāt), 1. preserve the memory of. Roman emperors built arches to commemorate their victories. 2. honor the memory of. Christmas commemorates Christ's birth. *v. 9.*

com mem o ra tion (kə mem′ə rā′shən), 1. act of commemorating. 2. a service, celebration, etc., in memory of some person or event. The Holy Communion is a commemoration of Christ's Last Supper and of His death. **In commemoration of** means to honor the memory of. *n. 14.*

com mence (kə mens′), begin. *v. 3.*

com mence ment (kə mens′mənt), 1. beginning; start. 2. the day or the ceremonies during which degrees and diplomas are given by colleges and schools to persons who have completed certain work. *n. 10.*

com mend (kə mend′), 1. praise. 2. hand over for safekeeping. She commended the child to her aunt's care. *v. 3.*

com mend a ble (kə men′də bəl), worthy of praise. *adj.*

com men da tion (kom′ən dā′shən), 1. praise. 2. giving over (a person) to somebody's good will or care. *n. 8.*

com men su rate (kə men′shů rit), 1. having the same measure. 2. proportionate. The pay should be commensurate with the work. 3. having a common measure. An ant and an elephant are commensurate, but love and a turnip are not. *adj. 16.*

com ment (kom′ent), 1. a note or remark that explains, praises, or finds fault with a book, a person, or a thing. 2. write notes or remarks that explain, praise, or find fault (with a book, a play, a concert, etc.). 3. make remarks (about persons or things). We all noticed the cut on Jack's face, but no one dared to comment on it. *n., v. 6.*

com men tar y (kom′ən tãr′i), 1. series of notes for explaining the hard parts of a book; explanation. Some Bibles have commentaries at the back that give much information and help. 2. comment. *n., pl. commentaries. 9.*

com men ta tor (kom′ən tā′tər), person who makes comments explaining or criticizing books, concerts, recent events, etc. *n. 12.*

com merce (kom′ərs), trade; business; buying and selling in large amounts between different places. *n. 2.*

com mer cial (kə mėr′shəl), 1. having to do with trade or business. 2. made to be sold. *adj. 3.*

com mer cial ize (kə mėr′shəl īz), make a matter of business or trade. To charge admission to church services would be to commercialize religion. *v.*

com min gle (kə ming′gəl), mingle together; blend. *v. 16.*

com mis er a tion (kə miz′ər ā′shən), pity; sorrow for another's suffering or trouble; sympathy. *n. 12.*

com mis sar i at (kom′i sãr′i at), the department of an army that supplies food, etc. *n. 20.*

com mis sar y (kom′i sãr′i), 1. store handling food and supplies in a mining camp, lumber camp, army camp, etc. 2. an army officer in charge of food and daily supplies for soldiers. 3. deputy; representative. *n., pl. commissaries. 15.*

com mis sion (kə mish′ən), 1. a written paper giving certain powers, privileges, and duties. My brother has just received his commission as lieutenant in the army. 2. give (a person) the right, the power, or the duty (of doing something). A man may commission his bankers to do business for him. The club commissions one of its members to buy supplies. 3. the thing trusted to a person to do; errand. 4. a group of persons appointed or elected with authority to do certain things. The President can appoint a commission to find out why food costs so much. 5. a percentage of the amount of business done, paid to the agent who does it. Some salesmen receive a commission of 10 per cent on all sales made, in addition to their salaries. 6. committing; as, the commission of a crime. 7. put into active service; make ready for use; as, to commission a warship. 8. **In commission** means in working order. I must get my broken bicycle in commission again. **Out of commission** means not in working order. *n., v. 3.*

com mis sion er (kə mish′ən ər), 1. member of a commission. 2. person in charge of some public department; as, a police commissioner. Some counties have road commissioners. *n. 4.*

com mit (kə mit′), 1. hand over for safekeeping. Commit yourself to the doctor's care; commit a poem to memory; commit a thought to writing; commit a body to the earth, or to flames; commit a thief to prison. 2. refer for consideration. 3. perform; do (something wrong); as, to commit a crime. 4. bind or involve (oneself) in any course of action; pledge. I have committed myself now and cannot draw back. *v., committed, committing. 3.*

com mit ment (kə mit′mənt), 1. committing. 2. being committed. 3. sending to prison or to an asylum. 4. pledge; promise. *n.*

com mit tee (kə mit′i), group of persons appointed or elected to do some special thing. Our club has a committee on entertainments. *n. 3.*

com mode (kə mōd′), 1. chest of drawers. 2. a stand in a bedroom, to hold a washbasin, pitcher of water, etc.; washstand. *n. 19.*

com mo di ous (kə mō′di əs), roomy. *adj. 10.*

com mod i ty (kə mod′i ti), 1. any thing that is bought and sold. Groceries are commodities. 2. any useful thing. *n., pl. commodities. 7.*

com mo dore (kom′ə dōr), 1. in the United States navy, a retired officer next above a captain. 2. captain in the British navy in temporary command of a squadron. 3. title given as an honor to the president of a yacht club, or to a captain. *n. 12.*

com mon (kom′ən), 1. belonging equally to all. The house is the common property of the three brothers. 2. general; of all; from all; by all. By common consent of the class, Dick was chosen for president. 3. public; generally known; as, a common nuisance. 4. often met with; usual. Snow is common in cold countries. 5. without rank. A common soldier is a private. 6. below ordinary; mean; low. 7. land owned or used by all the people of a village, etc. 8. **In common** means equally with another or others; owned, used, done, etc., by both or all. *adj., n. 1.*

com mon er (kom′ən ər), one of the common people; person who is not a noble. *n. 14.*

com mon ly (kom′ən li), usually; generally. Arithmetic is commonly taught in schools. *adv. 7.*

common noun, name for any one of a class. *Boy, city,* and *dog* are common nouns. *John, Boston,* and *Rover* are proper nouns.

com mon place (kom′ən plās′), 1. everyday thing. The commonplaces of our civilization, from watches to automobiles, are objects of wonder to savages. 2. ordinary remark. 3. ordinary; not new or interesting. *n., adj. 11.*

com mons (kom′ənz), 1. the common people; those who do not belong to the nobility or ruling class. 2. **The House of Commons,** or **the Commons,** is the main lawmaking body in England. 3. food provided at a common table. 4. food. The orphans were kept on short commons. 5. place where food is provided. *n. pl.*

com mon weal (kom′ən wēl′), 1. the common welfare; the public good. 2. a commonwealth. *Old use. n. 20.*

com mon wealth (kom′ən welth′), 1. the people who make up a state; the citizens of a state. 2. a state in which the people make the laws; a republic. The United States is a commonwealth. 3. one of the 48 States of the United States. *n. 5.*

com mo tion (kə mō′shən), violent movement; confusion; tumult; noisy moving about; disturbance. *n. 7.*

com mu nal (kom′ū nəl), of a community; public. *adj. 16.*

com mune[1] (kə mūn′), 1. talk in an intimate way. 2. receive Holy Communion. *v. 6.*

com mune[2] (kom′ūn), the smallest division for local government in France, Belgium, and several other European countries. *n.*

com mu ni ca ble (kə mū′ni kə bəl), that can be communicated. Ideas are communicable by words. Scarlet fever is communicable. *adj. 13.*

com mu ni cate (kə mū′ni kāt), 1. pass or transfer. A stove communicates heat to a room. 2. give (information or news) by speaking or writing. I asked your sister to communicate my wishes to you. 3. be connected. The dining room communicates with the kitchen. 4. receive Holy Communion. *v. 6.*

com mu ni ca tion (kə mū′ni kā′shən), 1. giving information or news by speaking or writing. Communication with people who are deaf is difficult. 2. the information or news given; letter, message, etc., which gives information or news. Your communication came in time to change all my plans. 3. passage; means of going from one to the other. There is no communication between these two rooms. *n. 4.*

com mun ion (kə mūn′yən), 1. sharing; having in common. 2. exchange of thoughts and feelings; fellowship. 3. quiet talk between persons who are dear to one another or are devoted to the same purpose; spiritual conversation. 4. a group of people having the same religious beliefs. 5. **The Communion** means (1) sharing in the Lord's Supper as a part of church worship. (2) the celebration of the Lord's Supper. *n. 7.*

com mu nism (kom′ū nizm), a plan by which most or all property is owned by the state and shared by all citizens. *n. 16.*

com mu nist or **Com mu nist** (kom′ū nist), person who advocates communism. *n. 15.*

com mu ni ty (kə mū′ni ti), 1. the people of any district or town. 2. a group of people living together; as, a community of monks. 3. the public; as, the approval of the community. 4. ownership together; sharing together; as, community of food supplies, community of ideas. *n., pl. communities. 4.*

com mu ta tion (kom′ū tā′shən), 1. exchange; substitution. 2. reduction to a less severe payment or penalty. The prisoner obtained a commutation of his sentence from death to life imprisonment. *n.*

com mu ta tor (kom′ū tā′tər), a device for reversing the direction of an electric current. *n. 15.*

com mute (kə mūt′), 1. exchange; substitute. 2. change (an obligation, penalty, etc.) for an easier one. The governor commuted the prisoner's sentence of death to one of life imprisonment. *v. 17.*

com pact[1] (kəm pakt′), 1. closely and firmly packed together. The leaves of a cabbage are folded into a compact head. 2. pack firmly together. 3. using few words; brief. *adj., v. 5.*

com pact[2] (kom′pakt), agreement. *n.*

com pan ion (kəm pan′yən), 1. one who goes along with or accompanies another; one who shares in what another is doing. 2. anything that matches or goes with another in kind, size, and color. 3. go along with; be a companion to. *n., v. 2.*

com pan ion a ble (kəm pan′yən ə bəl), fitted to be a companion; sociable; pleasant as a companion. *adj. 18.*

com pan ion ship (kəm pan′yən ship), being a companion; fellowship. *n. 8.*

com pa ny (kum′pə ni), 1. group of people. A great company came to church. 2. group of people joined together for some purpose, such as carrying on a business or acting plays. 3. companions. You are known by the company that you keep. 4. companionship. 5. guest or guests; visitor or visitors. *Used in common talk.* 6. the part of an army commanded by a captain. 7. a ship's crew. 8. **Keep company** means (1) go (with). (2) go together. *n., pl. companies. 1.*

com pa ra ble (kom′pə rə bəl), 1. able to be compared. A fire is comparable with the sun; both give light and heat. 2. fit to be compared. A cave is not comparable to a house for comfort. *adj. 12.*

com par a tive (kəm par′ə tiv), 1. that compares; as, the comparative method of studying. 2. measured by comparison with something else. Screens give us comparative freedom from flies. 3. the second degree of comparison of an adjective or adverb. *Fairer, faster,* and *better* are the comparatives of *fair, fast,* and *good. adj., n. 5.*

com par a tive ly (kəm par′ə tiv li), by comparison; relatively; somewhat. Mountains are comparatively free from mosquitoes. *adv.*

com pare (kəm pãr′), 1. find out or point out how persons or things are alike and how they differ. We compare one teacher with another. She compared several samples of silk for a dress. 2. liken; say (something) is like (something else). The fins of a fish may be compared to the legs of a dog. 3. **Cannot compare with** means cannot appear well when compared with. No artificial light can compare with daylight for general use. 4. **Beyond compare** means without an equal; most excellent. 5. In grammar, to compare an adjective or adverb is to form the comparative and superlative degrees of it. *v., n. 2.*

com par i son (kəm par′i sən), 1. act of comparing; finding out the likenesses and the differences. The teacher's comparison of the heart to a pump helped the children to understand its action. 2. **In comparison with** means compared with. 3. **There is no comparison between them** means that one is plainly better than the other. 4. In grammar, the degrees of comparison of adjectives are positive, comparative, and superlative. The comparison of *good* is: *good, better, best.* *n. 4.*

com part ment (kəm pärt′mənt), a separate division set off in any enclosed space. Your pencil box has several compartments for holding different things. *n. 10.*

com pass (kum′pəs), 1. an instrument for showing directions, consisting of a needle that points to the magnetic north. 2. boundary; circumference. A prison is within the compass of its walls. 3. space within limits; area; extent; range. The old sailor had many adventures within the compass of his lifetime. 4. in music, the range of a voice or an instrument. 5. **Compasses** are an instrument for drawing circles and measuring distances. 6. go around; move around. 7. hem in; surround. 8. grasp with the mind. 9. accomplish; obtain. *n., v. 2.*

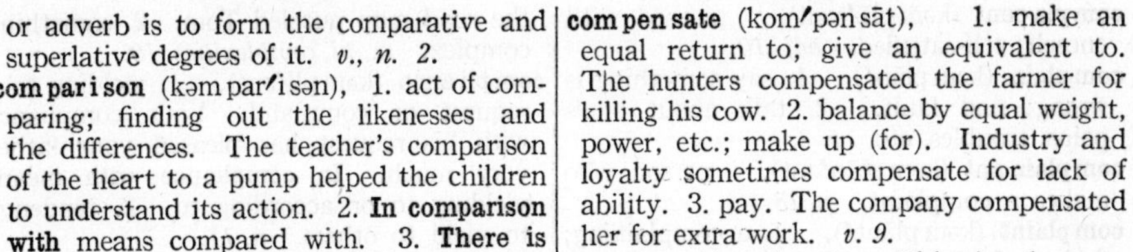

Compass for showing directions

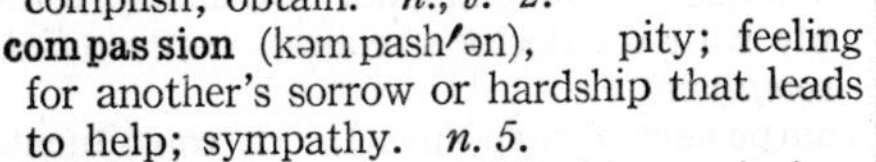

Compasses for drawing

com pas sion (kəm pash′ən), pity; feeling for another's sorrow or hardship that leads to help; sympathy. *n. 5.*

com pas sion ate (kəm pash′ən it), pitying; wishing to help those that suffer. *adj. 8.*

com pat i ble (kəm pat′i bəl), able to exist together; that can get on well together; agreeing; in harmony. *adj. 15.*

com pa tri ot (kəm pā′tri ət), fellow countryman. *n. 13.*

com peer (kom pēr′), 1. an equal; a peer. 2. comrade. *n. 13.*

com pel (kəm pel′), 1. force. The rain compelled us to stop our ball game. 2. bring about by force. A policeman can compel obedience. *v., compelled, compelling. 3.*

com pen sate (kom′pən sāt), 1. make an equal return to; give an equivalent to. The hunters compensated the farmer for killing his cow. 2. balance by equal weight, power, etc.; make up (for). Industry and loyalty sometimes compensate for lack of ability. 3. pay. The company compensated her for extra work. *v. 9.*

com pen sa tion (kom′pən sā′shən), 1. something given to make up for something else; something which does make up for something else. Tom gave me a new knife as compensation for the one of mine he lost. 2. pay. He said that equal compensation should be given to men and women for equal work. *n. 8.*

com pete (kəm pēt′), 1. try to win. John was competing against James for the prize in arithmetic. 2. take part (in a contest). Shall you compete in the race? *v. 8.*

com pe tence (kom′pi təns), 1. ability. A chef has special competence in cooking. 2. enough money or property to provide a comfortable living. *n. 10.*

com pe ten cy (kom′pi tən si), 1. enough money or property to provide a comfortable living. The widow has a small competency. 2. capacity; ability. *n. 14.*

com pe tent (kom′pi tənt), able; fitted. A doctor should be competent to treat many diseases. *adj. 9.*

com pe ti tion (kom′pi tish′ən), contest; competing; trying to win or gain something for which others are trying at the same time. There is competition in a class for first place. *n. 6.*

com pet i tive (kəm pet′i tiv), decided by competition; involving competition; pertaining to competition. The insurance business is competitive. A competitive examination for the job of postal clerk will be held January 10. *adj. 9.*

com pet i tor (kəm pet′i tər), person who tries to win something for which others are trying at the same time; rival. *n. 8.*

com pile (kəm pīl′), 1. collect and bring together in one list or account. 2. make (a book, report, etc.) out of various materials. *v. 11.*

com pla cence (kəm plā′səns), 1. self-satisfaction. 2. contentment. *n. 20.*

com pla cen cy (kəm plā′sən si), 1. self-satisfaction. The criminal's complacency during the trial angered the jury. 2. contentment. *n. 12.*

com pla cent (kəm plā′sənt), pleased with oneself; self-satisfied. *adj. 10.*

com plain (kəm plān′), 1. say something is wrong; find fault. 2. talk about one's pains, troubles, etc. *v. 2.*

com plain ant (kəm plān′ənt), person who makes a complaint. *n. 18.*

com plaint (kəm plānt′), 1. a complaining; finding fault. 2. accusation. 3. illness; disease. A cold is a very common complaint. *n. 4.*

com plai sance (kəm plā′zəns), obligingness; agreeableness. *n. 16.*

com plai sant (kəm plā′zənt), obliging; agreeable; inclined to do what is asked. *adj. 17.*

com ple ment (kom′pli mənt for 1 and 2, kom′pli ment for 3), 1. something that completes or makes perfect. 2. number required to fill. The ship now had its full complement of men, and no more could be taken on. 3. supply a lack of any kind; complete. My furniture just complemented my sister's, so that together we had what we needed. *n., v. 7.*

com ple men ta ry (kom′pli men′tə ri), completing; forming a complement. Two complementary colors mixed make white. *adj. 14.*

com plete (kəm plēt′), 1. with all the parts; whole; entire; as, a complete set of Dickens's novels. 2. make whole or perfect; make up the full number or amount of. She completed her set of dishes by buying the cups and saucers. 3. perfect; thorough; as, a complete surprise. 4. finish. 5. finished. *adj., v. 1.*

com plete ly (kəm plēt′li), 1. entirely; wholly. 2. thoroughly; perfectly. *adv. 6.*

com ple tion (kəm plē′shən), 1. finishing; act of completing. 2. condition of being completed. The work is near completion. *n. 10.*

com plex (kom′pleks), 1. made up of a number of parts. A complex sentence has one or more clauses besides the main clause. 2. complicated. The directions for reaching the house were so complex that we could not understand them. 3. strong prejudice; an unreasonable bias. Mr. Pierce has a complex against foreigners. *adj., n. 7.*

com plex ion (kəm plek′shən), 1. the color, quality, and general appearance of the skin, particularly of the face. 2. general appearance; nature; character. The complexion of the war was changed by two great victories. *n. 5.*

com plex i ty (kəm plek′si ti), 1. complex quality or condition. The complexity of the road map puzzled Tom. 2. something complex. *n., pl. complexities. 10.*

com pli ance (kəm plī′əns), 1. yielding to a request or command. Your compliance with his request has pleased your father very much. **In compliance with** means yielding to or according to. 2. tendency to yield to others. *n. 11.*

com pli ant (kəm plī′ənt), complying; yielding; obliging. A compliant person gives in to other people. *adj. 19.*

com pli cate (kom′pli kāt), 1. mix up; make hard to understand or to settle. The fact that no two of us have the same hours free complicates the arrangement of a meeting of all five of us. 2. make worse or more mixed up; as, a headache complicated by eye trouble. *v. 8.*

com pli ca tion (kom′pli kā′shən), 1. confused state of affairs hard to understand or settle. Such a complication of little rules and restrictions you never saw. 2. something that makes matters harder to untangle or settle. *n. 10.*

com plic i ty (kəm plis′i ti), partnership in wrongdoing. Knowingly receiving stolen goods is complicity in theft. *n.*

com pli ment (kom′pli mənt for 1 and 3, kom′pli ment for 2), 1. something good said about one; something said in praise of one's work. 2. pay a compliment to. He complimented my mother on the way she had trained her children. 3. **Compliments** sometimes means greetings. *n., v. 5.*

com pli men ta ry (kom′pli men′tə ri), 1. expressing a compliment; praising. 2. given free. *adj. 12.*

com ply (kəm plī′), act in agreement with a request or a command. We should comply with the doctor's request. *v., complied, complying. 5.*

com po nent (kəm pō′nənt), 1. constituent. Blade and handle are the component parts of a knife. 2. part; necessary or essential part. A chemist can separate a medicine into its components. *adj., n. 10.*

com port (kəm pōrt′), 1. behave. The judge comports himself with dignity. 2. agree; suit. Silliness does not comport with the position of judge. *v. 16.*

com pose (kəm pōz′), 1. make up. The ocean is composed of salt water. Our party was composed of three grown-ups and four children. 2. put together. To compose a story or poem is to construct it from words. To compose a piece of music is to invent the tune and write down the notes. To compose in a printing office is to set up type to form words and sentences. To compose a picture is to get an artistic arrangement of the things in it. 3. get (oneself) ready; make up one's mind; as, to compose oneself to read a book. 4. make calm (oneself or one's features). Try to compose yourself before the doctor gets here. 5. settle; arrange; as, to compose a dispute. *v. 4.*

com posed (kəm pōzd′), calm; quiet; tranquil. *adj. 15.*

com pos er (kəm pōz′ər), 1. person who composes. 2. writer of music. *n. 15.*

com pos ite (kəm poz′it), made up of various parts; compound. Daisies and dandelions are composite flowers. *adj. 13.*

com po si tion (kom′pə zish′ən), 1. the make-up of anything; what is in it. The composition of this candy includes sugar, chocolate, and milk. There is no meanness in his composition. 2. the putting together of a whole. Writing sentences, making pictures, and setting type in printing are all forms of composition. 3. thing composed, such as a piece of music, writing, etc. 4. a mixture of substances. The dentist filled my teeth with some composition which had silver in it. 5. agreement; settlement. *n. 4.*

com post (kom′pōst), 1. mixture. 2. mixture of leaves, manure, etc., for fertilizing land. *n. 16.*

com po sure (kəm pō′zhər), calmness; quiet; self-control. *n. 8.*

com pound (kom′pound for 1, 2, and 3, kom pound′ for 4 and 5), 1. having more than one part. A palm leaf is a compound leaf. "John bought a hat, and Philip bought a coat" is a compound sentence. Steamship is a compound word. 2. a mixture. A medicine is usually a compound. 3. a substance formed by chemical combination of two or more substances. Water is a compound of hydrogen and oxygen. 4. mix; combine. The man in the drug store compounds medicines and drinks. 5. settle (a quarrel or a debt) by a yielding on both sides. *adj., n., v. 5.*

com pre hend (kom′pri hend′), 1. understand. 2. include; contain. *v. 4.*

com pre hen si ble (kom′pri hen′si bəl), understandable. *adj.*

com pre hen sion (kom′pri hen′shən), act or power of understanding. Algebra is beyond the comprehension of fourth-grade pupils. *n. 11.*

com pre hen sive (kom′pri hen′siv), 1. including; including much. The term's work ended with a comprehensive review. 2. comprehending. *adj. 8.*

com press (kəm pres′ for 1, kom′pres for 2), 1. squeeze together; make smaller by pressure. Cotton is compressed into bales. 2. pad of wet cloth applied to the throat or other parts of the body in sickness; as, a cold compress, a hot compress. *v., n. 8.*

com pres sion (kəm presh′ən), 1. compressing. 2. being compressed. *n. 14.*

com prise or **com prize** (kəm prīz′), consist of; include. The United States comprises 48 States. *v. 7.*

com pro mise (kom′prə mīz), 1. settle (a quarrel or difference of opinion) by agreeing that each will give up part of what he demands. 2. settlement of a quarrel or a difference of opinion by a partial yielding on both sides. George and Tom both wanted the apple; their compromise was to share it. 3. put under suspicion. You will compromise your good name if you go around with thieves and liars. *v., n. 7.*

comp trol ler (kən trōl′ər), person employed to look after expenditures; controller. *n. 13.*

com pul sion (kəm pul′shən), act of compelling; use of force; force. John can be made to take his medicine only by compulsion. An agreement signed under compulsion is not legal. *n. 11.*

com pul so ry (kəm pul′sə ri), 1. compelled; required. Attendance at school is compulsory. 2. compelling; using force. *adj. 8.*

com punc tion (kəm pungk′shən), remorse; the pricking of conscience; regret. *n. 12.*

com pu ta tion (kom′pū tā′shən), reckoning; calculation. Addition and subtraction are forms of computation. *n. 12.*

com pute (kəm pūt′), do by arithmetical work; reckon; calculate. Mother computed the cost of our trip. *v. 8.*

com rade (kom′rad or kom′rid), 1. companion and friend. 2. person who shares in what another is doing; partner; fellow worker. **Comrades at arms** means fellow soldiers. *n. 4.*

con[1] (kon), 1. against. 2. a reason against. The pros and cons of a question are the arguments for and against it. *adv., n. 11.*

con[2] (kon), study; learn well enough to remember. *v., conned, conning.*

con cat e na tion (kon kat′i nā′shən), 1. linking together. 2. a connected series of things or events. *n. 18.*

con cave (kon′kāv), hollow and curved, like the inside of a circle or sphere. The palm of one's hand is slightly concave. *adj. 7.*

Concave lenses

con cav i ty (kon kav′i ti), 1. concave condition or quality. 2. concave surface or thing. *n., pl. concavities. 20.*

con ceal (kən sēl′), hide. *v. 3.*

con ceal ment (kən sēl′mənt), 1. hiding. 2. means or place for hiding. *n. 10.*

con cede (kən sēd′), 1. admit; admit as true. Everyone concedes that 2 and 2 make 4. 2. allow (a person) to have; grant. He conceded us the right to walk through his land. *v. 9.*

con ceit (kən sēt′), 1. too much pride in oneself or one's ability to do things. 2. a pleasing fancy; a witty thought or expression. *n. 5.*

con ceit ed (kən sēt′id), having too high an opinion of oneself; vain. *adj. 9.*

con ceiv a ble (kən sēv′ə bəl), imaginable. We take every conceivable precaution against fire. *adj. 13.*

con ceive (kən sēv′), 1. form in the mind; think up; imagine. 2. have an idea or feeling; think. 3. become pregnant. *v. 3.*

con cen trate (kon′sən trāt), 1. bring together to one place. 2. make stronger. A concentrated solution of acid is one which has very much acid in it. 3. pay close attention. He concentrated upon the problem. *v. 7.*

con cen tra tion (kon′sən trā′shən), 1. concentrating. 2. being concentrated. 3. close attention. *n. 8.*

con cen tric (kon sen′trik), having the same center. *adj. 12.*

Concentric circles

con cept (kon′sept), a thought; a general notion or idea. *n. 15.*

con cep tion (kən sep′shən), 1. conceiving; being conceived. 2. thought; notion; idea. *n. 7.*

con cern (kən sėrn′), 1. have to do with; belong to. This letter concerns nobody but me. 2. Anything that touches or has to do with one's work or one's interests is one's concern. 3. interest. We are all concerned about the school play. 4. troubled interest; anxiety. The mother's concern over her sick child kept her awake all night. 5. make anxious. 6. business company; firm. *v., n. 2.*

con cerned (kən sėrnd′), 1. interested. 2. troubled; anxious. *adj. 9.*

con cern ing (kən sėr′ning), about. *prep. 4.*

con cert (kon′sėrt for 1, 2, and 4, kən sėrt′ for 3), 1. musical entertainment. 2. agreement; harmony. 3. arrange. The rebels concerted a plan for seizing the government. 4. **In concert** means all together. *n., v. 4.*

con cert ed (kən sėr′tid), 1. arranged by agreement. 2. combined. The ants made a concerted attack upon the injured wasp. *adj.*

con cer ti na (kon′sər tē′nə), a small musical instrument somewhat like an accordion. *n.*

Man playing a concertina

con cer to (kon cher′tō), a piece of music to be played by one or more principal instruments, such as a violin, piano, etc., with the accompaniment of an orchestra. *n., pl. concertos. 18.*

con ces sion (kən sesh′ən), 1. a conceding; a yielding. As a concession, mother let Nell stay up an hour longer. 2. anything conceded or yielded. Lands, mines, etc., given by a government to a business company are usually called grants or concessions. *n. 9.*

conch (kongk), a large, spiral sea shell. *n. 20.*

Conch

con cil i ate (kən sil′i āt), 1. win over; soothe. Mrs. Lee conciliated her cook with a present. 2. reconcile; bring into harmony. *v. 12.*

con cil i a tion (kən sil′i ā′shən), 1. winning over or soothing; reconciling. 2. being won over or soothed; being reconciled. *n. 11.*

con cil i a to ry (kən sil′i ə tō′ri), tending to win over, soothe, or reconcile. *adj. 15.*

con cise (kən sīs′), expressing much in few words; brief but full of meaning. *adj. 11.*

con clave (kon′klāv), 1. a private meeting. 2. meeting of the cardinals for the election of a pope. *n. 14.*

con clude (kən klüd′), 1. end. The book concluded happily. 2. reach (certain facts or opinions) by reasoning. We concluded that the animal must have been a deer. 3. settle; arrange. The two nations concluded a treaty of peace. 4. decide; resolve. I concluded not to go. *v. 3.*

con clu sion (kən klü′zhən), 1. end; as, the conclusion of the story. A book or article often has a conclusion summing up all of the important points. 2. decision reached by reasoning. Jack came to the conclusion that he must work harder to succeed. 3. settlement; arrangement; as, the conclusion of a peace between two countries. 4. **Try conclusions with** means take part in a trial of skill with. *n. 5.*

con clu sive (kən klü′siv), decisive; convincing; final. *adj. 11.*

con coct (kon kokt′), prepare; make up. The children concocted some queer messes in the kitchen. *v. 13.*

con coc tion (kon kok′shən), 1. act of concocting. 2. thing concocted. *n. 17.*

con com i tant (kon kom′i tənt), 1. accompanying. 2. an accompaniment. *adj., n. 16.*

con cord (kong′kôrd), agreement; peace; harmony. *n. 7.*

Con cord (kong′kərd), 1. a town in eastern Massachusetts. The second battle of the Revolutionary War was fought there, April 19, 1775. 2. the capital of New Hampshire. *n. 11.*

con cord ance (kon kôr′dəns), 1. agreement; harmony. 2. an alphabetical list of the principal words of a book with references to the passages in which they occur. *n. 16.*

con course (kong′kōrs), 1. running or coming together. The fort was built at the concourse of two rivers. 2. a crowd. 3. a place where crowds come. *n. 12.*

con crete (kon′krēt or kon krēt′), 1. real; existing of itself in the material world, not merely in idea or as a quality. All actual objects are concrete. 2. a mixture of cement, sand or gravel, and water that hardens as it dries. Concrete is used for foundations, whole buildings, sidewalks, roads, dams, and bridges. 3. made of this mixture; as, a concrete sidewalk. *adj., n. 6.*

con cu bine (kong′kū bīn), 1. In countries where one man can have many wives, some of the wives may be called concubines. 2. woman who lives with a man without being married to him. *n. 14.*

con cur (kən kėr′), 1. agree; be of the same opinion. The judges all concurred in giving John the prize. 2. work together. The events of the boy's life concurred to make him what he was. 3. come together. *v., concurred, concurring. 13.*

con cur rence (kən kėr′əns), 1. agreement. 2. a happening at the same time. 3. a coming together; as, the concurrence of many lines of railroad track. *n. 13.*

con cur rent (kən kėr′ənt), 1. concurring; happening together; existing together. 2. coöperating; agreeing; acting together. 3. a concurrent thing or event. *adj., n. 20.*

con cus sion (kən kush′ən), 1. shaking; shock. 2. an injury to the brain or spine from a blow or fall or other shock. *n. 13.*

con demn (kən dem′), 1. express strong disapproval of. We condemn cruelty and cruel people. 2. pronounce guilty of crime or wrong. The prisoner is sure to be condemned. 3. to doom; as, condemned to death. 4. declare not sound or suitable for use. This bridge has been condemned because it is no longer safe. 5. take for public use under special provision of the law. These four blocks have been condemned to make a park. *v. 3.*

con dem na tion (kon′dem nā′shən), condemning; being condemned; as, the condemnation of a prisoner by a judge, the condemnation of an unsafe bridge. *n. 8.*

con den sa tion (kon′den sā′shən), 1. condensing; as, the condensation of milk by removing most of the water from it. 2. being condensed; as, the condensation of steam into water. 3. a condensed mass. A cloud is a condensation of water vapor in the atmosphere. *n. 9.*

con dense (kən dens′), 1. make denser; become more compact. 2. increase the strength of. Light is condensed by means of lenses. 3. change from a gas or a vapor to a liquid. If steam touches cold surfaces, it condenses or is condensed into water. 4. put into fewer words. A long story can sometimes be condensed into a few sentences. *v. 6.*

con dens er (kən den′sər), 1. person or thing that condenses something. 2. device for receiving and holding a charge of electricity. *n. 7.*

con de scend (kon′di send′), come down willingly or graciously to the level of one's inferiors in rank. The king condescended to eat with the beggars. *v. 9.*

con de scen sion (kon′di sen′shən), 1. pleasantness to inferiors. 2. a patronizing attitude. *n. 12.*

con di ment (kon′di mənt), something used to give flavor and relish to food, such as pepper and spices. *n. 16.*

con di tion (kən dish′ən), 1. state in which a person or thing is. The condition of John's health kept him from going to camp. 2. put in good condition. This man conditions dogs for dog shows. 3. rank in society. Lincoln's parents were people of humble condition. 4. thing on which something else depends; that without which something else cannot be. Ability is one of the conditions of success. 5. to subject to a condition. The gift to the boy was conditioned on his good behavior. 6. make conditions; make it a condition. 7. **On condition that** means if. *n., v. 1.*

con di tion al (kən dish′ən əl), 1. depending on something else. "You may go if the sun shines" is a conditional promise. 2. expressing or containing a condition. "If the sun shines" is a conditional clause. *adj. 11.*

con di tion al ly (kən dish′ən əl i), under a condition or conditions. He accepted conditionally. *adv.*

con dole (kən dōl′), express sympathy; grieve. The widow's friends condoled with her at the funeral. *v. 12.*

con do lence (kən dō′ləns), act of condoling; expression of sympathy. *n. 16.*

con done (kən dōn′), forgive; overlook. Friends condone each other's faults. *v. 20.*

Condor (4 ft. long; wingspread 9 ft.)

con dor (kon′dər), large vulture with a bare neck and head. Condors live on high mountains in South America and California. *n. 18.*

con duce (kən dūs′ or kən düs′), lead; contribute; be favorable. Darkness and quiet conduce to sleep. *v. 11.*

con du cive (kən dū′siv or kən dü′siv), helpful; favorable. Exercise is conducive to health. *adj. 12.*

con duct (kon′dukt for 1, kən dukt′ for 2-5), 1. action; way of acting or guiding oneself; behavior thought of as good or bad. 2. **Conduct oneself** means behave or act. 3. guide or lead. Conduct me to your teacher. 4. manage; direct. He conducts an orchestra of fifty instruments. 5. be a channel for; as, to conduct heat or electricity. *n., v. 2.*

con duc tion (kən duk′shən), 1. transmission; as, the conduction of electricity along a wire. 2. conducting; as, the conduction of water through a pipe. *n. 18.*

con duc tiv i ty (kon′duk tiv′i ti), power of conducting heat, electricity, etc. *n. 20.*

con duc tor (kən duk′tər), 1. guide or leader; one who is conducting. The conductor of an orchestra or chorus trains the performers to work together, selects the music to be used, and beats time for the orchestra. 2. person in charge of passengers on a train, a streetcar, or a bus. 3. thing that transmits heat, sound, or electricity. Copper wire is used as a conductor of electricity. *n. 5.*

con duit (kon′dit), 1. a channel or pipe for carrying liquids long distances. 2. a specially made tube or underground passage for electric wires. *n. 9.*

Cone

cone (kōn), 1. a solid that has a flat, round base and narrows to a point at the top. 2. anything shaped like a cone; as, an ice-cream cone, the cone of a volcano. 3. part that bears the seeds on pine, cedar, fir, and other evergreen trees. *n. 6.*

Cone of fir Cone of pine

co ney (kō′ni), cony. *n., pl. coneys.*

con fec tion (kən fek′shən), 1. piece of candy, candied fruit, sugared nut, etc. 2. elaborate hat or dress. 3. any fancy compound or compounding. *n. 13.*

con fec tion er (kən fek′shən ər), person who makes or sells candies, ice cream, and cakes. *n. 13.*

con fec tion er y (kən fek′shən er′i), 1. confections; candies. 2. candy shop. *n. 13.*

con fed er a cy (kən fed′ər ə si), a union of countries or states; a group of people joined together for a special purpose. **The Confederacy** usually means the Confederate States of America which seceded from the United States in 1860-1861. *n., pl. confederacies. 6.*

con fed er ate (kən fed′ər it for 1, 2, and 3, kən fed′ər āt for 4), 1. joined together for a special purpose. The Southern Confederacy was called the **Confederate States of America.** 2. A person who fought for this government was called a **Confederate.** 3. person or state joined with another for a special purpose, usually a bad one. The thief and his confederates escaped to another city. 4. join together. *adj., n., v. 7.*

con fed er a tion (kən fed′ər ā′shən), 1. federation. 2. league; alliance. *n. 9.*

con fer (kən fėr′), 1. consult; talk the matter over; take counsel. The teacher conferred with the principal about Dick's promotion. 2. give. The school confers a medal on any student who is not absent a single day. *v., conferred, conferring. 4.*

con fer ence (kon′fər əns), 1. a meeting of interested persons to discuss a particular subject. A conference was called to discuss getting a playground for the school. 2. taking counsel; talking something over; consulting with a person or a group of persons. You cannot see Mr. Smith just now; he is in conference. *n. 4.*

con fess (kən fes′), 1. acknowledge; admit; own up. I confess you are right on one point. 2. admit one's guilt. 3. tell one's mistakes and sins, especially to a priest. 4. hear (a person) tell his mistakes and sins, as a priest does. *v. 3.*

con fes sion (kən fesh′ən), 1. owning up; confessing; telling one's mistakes or sins. 2. thing confessed. *n. 5.*

con fes sion al (kən fesh′ən əl), the stall or box in which a priest hears confessions. *n. 16.*

con fes sor (kən fes′ər), 1. person who confesses. 2. priest who has the authority to hear confessions. *n. 9.*

con fet ti (kən fet′i), bits of colored paper thrown about at carnivals, weddings, etc. *n. pl.*

con fi dant (kon′fi dant′), person trusted with secrets or private affairs. *n. 9.*

con fide (kən fīd′), 1. tell as a secret. 2. give to another for safekeeping; hand over. She confides her baby to the day nursery while she is at work. 3. put trust. Confide in God. *v. 9.*

con fi dence (kon′fi dəns), 1. firm belief or trust. We have no confidence in a liar. 2. boldness. The little boy's confidence in the water startled his parents. 3. thing told as a secret. I listened to her confidences for half an hour. *n. 3.*

con fi dent (kon′fi dənt), fully trusting; certain. I feel confident that our team will win. *adj. 5.*

con fi den tial (kon′fi den′shəl), 1. spoken or written as a secret matter. The detective made a confidential report. 2. trusted with secret matters. A confidential secretary should be discreet. *adj. 9.*

con fid ing (kən fīd′ing), trustful; trusting. *adj.*

con fig u ra tion (kən fig′ū rā′shən), manner of arrangement; shape; outline. Geography describes the configuration of the surface of the earth. *n. 18.*

con fine (kən fīn′ for 1, kon′fīn for 2), 1. keep in; hold in. He was confined in prison for two years. A cold confined him to the house. 2. boundary; limit. These people have never been beyond the confines of their own valley. *v., n. 4.*

con fine ment (kən fīn′mənt), 1. confining; being confined; as, confinement within doors on account of a cold. 2. imprisonment. *n. 13.*

con firm (kən fėrm′), 1. make certain; make more certain by putting in writing, by consent, or by encouragement. The written order confirmed his telephone message. The treaty was confirmed by the king. He was confirmed in his opinions by all his friends. 2. **Be confirmed** sometimes means be admitted to full membership in a church. *v. 4.*

con fir ma tion (kon′fər mā′shən), 1. making sure by more evidence. 2. a religious ceremony of various Christian churches. A baby is baptized, and when he grows old enough to understand, his confirmation allows him to share in all the privileges of the church. *n. 6.*

con firmed (kən fėrmd′), settled; firmly established; habitual; as, a confirmed invalid. *adj.*

con fis cate (kon′fis kāt), 1. seize for the public treasury. The traitor's property was confiscated. 2. seize by authority; take and keep. The policeman confiscated the robber's pistol. *v. 8.*

con fis ca tion (kon′fis kā′shən), a confiscating or being confiscated; as, the confiscation of wealth. *n. 15.*

con fla gra tion (kon′flə grā′shən), a big fire, especially one which destroys buildings or forests. *n. 11.*

con flict (kon′flikt for 1 and 2, kən flikt′ for 3), 1. a fight; a struggle. 2. active opposition of persons or ideas. A conflict of opinion arose over what food was best for our rabbit. 3. be actively opposed; clash; differ in thought and action. *n. v. 4.*

con flu ence (kon′flü əns), 1. a flowing together; as, the confluence of two rivers. 2. a coming together of people or things; a throng. *n. 14.*

con flu ent (kon′flü ənt), flowing or running together; blending into one. *adj. 18.*

con flux (kon′fluks), flowing together. *n. 15.*

con form (kən fôrm′), 1. make like. 2. act according to law or rule; be in agreement with generally accepted standards of business, law, conduct, or worship. *v. 8.*

con form a ble (kən fôr′mə bəl), 1. similar. 2. in agreement; agreeable. 3. submissive. The boy was conformable to his father's wishes. *adj. 16.*

con for ma tion (kon′fôr mā′shən), 1. manner in which a thing is formed; structure; form. 2. a conforming. *n. 15.*

con form i ty (kən fôr′mi ti), 1. likeness. 2. action in agreement with generally accepted standards of business, law, conduct, or worship; fitting oneself and one's actions to the ideas of others. *n., pl. conformities. 8.*

con found (kon found′), 1. confuse; perplex. To confound two things means not to be able to tell them apart. 2. defeat. *Old use. v. 4.*

con front (kən frunt′), 1. meet face to face; stand facing. 2. face boldly; oppose. 3. bring face to face; place before. The lawyer confronted the prisoner with the forged check. *v. 10.*

Con fu cius (kən fū′shəs), a famous Chinese philosopher and moral teacher (551?-478 B.C.). *n.*

con fuse (kən fūz′), 1. mix up; throw into disorder. So many people talking to me at once confused me. 2. mistake (one thing for another). People often confuse Mary with her twin sister. *v. 5.*

con fus ed ly (kən fūz′id li), in a confused manner. *adv. 18.*

con fu sion (kən fū′zhən), 1. a mixed-up condition of things or of the mind. The confusion in the room showed that he had packed in a hurry. 2. mistaking one thing for another. Words like *believe* and *receive* are a source of confusion in spelling. 3. tumult; as, the confusion in a busy street. *n. 3.*

con fu ta tion (kon′fū tā′shən), 1. confuting; disproving. 2. the thing that confutes or disproves. *n. 16.*

con fute (kən fūt′), 1. prove (an argument, etc.) to be false or weak. Two witnesses confuted the testimony of Mr. Brown. 2. prove (a person) to be wrong. *v. 14.*

con geal (kən jēl′), freeze; thicken as if frozen. *v. 10.*

con gen ial (kən jēn′yəl), 1. having similar tastes and interests; getting on well together. Congenial companions made the trip pleasant. 2. agreeable; pleasing. He seeks more congenial work. *adj. 7.*

con gen i tal (kən jen′i təl), inborn; present at birth. *adj. 20.*

con gen i tal ly (kən jen′i təl i), from the time of birth. *adv.*

con ger (kong′gər), a large ocean eel, sometimes 10 feet long, which is caught for food along the coasts of Europe. *n. 14.*

Conger

con gest (kən jest′), 1. fill too full; overcrowd. The streets of cities are often congested. 2. cause too much blood to gather in one part of the body. 3. become too full of blood. The lungs are congested in pneumonia. *v. 12.*

con ges tion (kən jes′chən), 1. an overcrowded or congested condition. Sunday's congestion of traffic made him half an hour late. 2. too much blood in one part of the body. *n. 10.*

con glom er ate (kən glom′ər āt for 1, kən-glom′ər it for 2, 3, and 4), 1. gather in a rounded mass; collect together. 2. gathered into a rounded mass; clustered. 3. a mass formed of fragments. 4. a rock made up of pebbles and gravel with a cementing material. *v., adj., n. 19.*

Conglomerate (def. 4)

Con go (kong′gō), 1. a river in central Africa. 2. a section of Africa. *n. 17.*

con grat u late (kən grach′ů lāt), express one's pleasure at the happiness or good fortune of. I congratulated my friend on her birthday. *v. 5.*

con grat u la tion (kən grach′ů lā′shən), congratulating; wishing a person joy; expression of pleasure at the happiness or good fortune of another. *n. 7.*

con grat u la to ry (kən grach′ů lə tō′ri), expressing pleasure at another's happiness or good fortune. *adj.*

con gre gate (kong′gri gāt), come together in a crowd or mass. Bits of steel congregate around the end of a magnet. Many children congregated around the Christmas tree. *v. 8.*

con gre ga tion (kong′gri gā′shən), 1. coming together into a crowd or mass. 2. a gathering of people. 3. a gathering of people for worship. *n. 5.*

con gre ga tion al (kong′gri gā′shən əl), 1. of a congregation; as, congregational singing.

2. A **Congregational Church** acts as an independent, self-governing body, while keeping up fellowship with other churches having the same belief. *adj. 17.*

con gress (kong′gris), 1. coming together; meeting. 2. a meeting of representatives for the discussion of some subject. 3. the national lawmaking body of the United States, composed of the Senate and the House of Representatives, with members elected from every state. The Capitol at Washington is the place where Congress meets. *n. 2.*

con gres sion al (kən gresh′ən əl), of Congress; having to do with Congress. *adj. 11.*

con gress man (kong′gris mən), member of the United States Congress, especially of the House of Representatives. *n., pl. congressmen. 13.*

con gru ent (kong′grü ənt), agreeing; harmonious; suitable. *adj. 20.*

con gru ous (kong′grü əs), 1. agreeing; harmonious. 2. fitting; proper; appropriate. *adj.*

con i cal (kon′i kəl), cone-shaped. *adj. 15.*

co ni fer (kō′ni fər), a cone-bearing tree. The pine, fir, spruce, hemlock, and larch are conifers. *n. 14.*

conj., conjunction.

con jec tur al (kən jek′chər əl), 1. involving a guess. His opinion was merely conjectural, not proved. 2. inclined to guessing. *adj.*

con jec ture (kən jek′chər), guess. *n., v. 7.*

con join (kən join′), join together; unite; combine. *v. 18.*

con joint (kən joint′), 1. united; combined. 2. joint. *adj. 19.*

con joint ly (kən joint′li), together; in combination. Three clubs gave a party conjointly. *adv. 19.*

con ju gal (kon′jü gəl), 1. of marriage. 2. of husband or wife. *adj. 15.*

con ju gate (kon′jü gāt), 1. give a systematic arrangement of the forms of (a verb). 2. joined together; coupled. *v., adj. 10.*

con ju ga tion (kon′jü gā′shən), 1. a systematic arrangement of the forms of a verb. 2. joining together. *n. 9.*

con junc tion (kən jungk′shən), 1. union; connection. A severe illness in conjunction with the hot weather has left the baby very weak. 2. a word that connects sentences, clauses, phrases, or words. *And, or, but, though,* and *if* are conjunctions. *n. 8.*

con junc tive (kən jungk′tiv), 1. connective; joining together. 2. joined; united; joint. 3. like a conjunction. *adj. 20.*

con ju ra tion (kon′jü rā′shən), 1. invoking by a sacred name. 2. the practice of magic. The princess had been changed to a toad by conjuration. 3. magic form of words used in conjuring; magic spell. *n. 17.*

con jure (kən jür′ for 1, kun′jər for 2 and 3), 1. make a solemn appeal to. By all that is holy, I conjure you not to betray your country. 2. compel to appear or disappear by a set form of words. Nowadays we do not try to conjure up spirits or devils. 3. perform tricks by very quick deceiving movements of the hands; juggle. *v. 7.*

con jur er (kun′jər ər), 1. magician. 2. person who performs tricks with quick deceiving movements of the hands; juggler. *n. 18.*

con jur or (kun′jər ər), conjurer. *n. 17.*

Conn., Connecticut.

con nect (kə nekt′), 1. join one thing to another. 2. think of one thing with another. 3. join with others in some business or interest; have any kind of practical relation with. *v. 2.*

Con nect i cut (kə net′i kət), a New England State of the United States. *n. 5.*

con nec tion (kə nek′shən), 1. act of connecting. 2. being joined together or connected; union. 3. thing that connects; connecting part; bond; tie. 4. any kind of practical relation with another thing. I have no connection with my brother's firm. 5. group of people associated in some way. 6. thinking of persons or things together; linking together of words or ideas in proper order. 7. meeting of trains, ships, etc., so that passengers can change from one to the other without delay. 8. related person; relative. She is a connection of ours by marriage. *n. 3.*

con nec tive (kə nek′tiv), 1. connecting. 2. anything that connects. Conjunctions and relative pronouns are connectives. *adj., n. 13.*

conn ing tow er (kon′ing tou′ər), small tower on the back of a submarine, used as an entrance and as a place for observation.

con niv ance (kə nīv′əns), conniving; pretended ignorance or secret encouragement of wrongdoing. *n. 14.*

con nive (kə nīv′), 1. shut one's eyes to anything wrong. 2. avoid noticing what one might have to condemn. 3. give aid to wrongdoing by not telling of it, or by helping it secretly. Some dishonest policemen connive at gambling. *v. 15.*

con nois seur (kon′i sėr′), an expert; a critical judge. Mr. Blake is a connoisseur of antique furniture. *n. 14.*

con no ta tion (kon′ō tā′shən), what is suggested in addition to the simple meaning. When Elaine is described as "the lily maid," the connotation is that she was pale blonde in coloring, delicate, sweet, and pure. *n.*

con note (kə nōt′), mean besides; add to the simple meaning; imply. A chubby face means a plump face, and connotes ideas of youth, roundness, and pleasant looks. *v.*

con nu bi al (kə nū′bi əl or kə nü′bi əl), having to do with marriage. *adj. 16.*

con quer (kong′kər), overcome by force; get the better of; take in war. We can conquer an enemy, a bad habit, or a country. *v. 2.*

con quer or (kong′kər ər), person who conquers. *n. 4.*

con quest (kong′kwest), 1. conquering. 2. thing conquered. 3. person whose love or favor has been won. *n. 3.*

con san guin i ty (kon′sang gwin′i ti), relationship by blood. Brothers and cousins are united by ties of consanguinity. *n. 15.*

con science (kon′shəns), sense of right and wrong. Your conscience is the ideas and feelings within you which tell you what is wrong and keep you from doing it, and which tell you what is right and lead you to do it. *n. 3.*

con sci en tious (kon′shi en′shəs), 1. careful to do what one knows is right; controlled by conscience. 2. done with care to make it right. Conscientious work is careful and exact. *adj. 9.*

con scious (kon′shəs), 1. knowing; having experience; aware. She was not conscious of his presence in the room. 2. able to feel. After an hour he became conscious again. 3. known to oneself. Talking is more often conscious than breathing is. *adj. 4.*

con scious ness (kon′shəs nis), 1. being conscious; awareness. Consciousness did not return to the injured man for two hours. 2. all the thoughts and feelings of a person. Everything of which you are conscious makes up your consciousness. *n. 7.*

con script (kon′skript for 1 and 3, kən skript′ for 2 and 4), 1. person compelled to serve in the army or navy. 2. compel to serve in the army or navy; draft. 3. enrolled; enrolled by being drafted. 4. take for government use. The government proposed to conscript both capital and labor. *n., v., adj. 13.*

con scrip tion (kən skrip′shən), 1. compulsory enrollment of men as soldiers or sailors; draft. 2. act or system of forcing contributions of money, labor, or other services to the government or as the government directs. *n. 18.*

con se crate (kon′si krāt), 1. set apart as sacred; make holy. A church is consecrated to worship. 2. devote to a purpose. A doctor's life is consecrated to keeping people well. *v. 5.*

con se cra tion (kon′si krā′shən), 1. making holy; devoting to God; consecrating. 2. devoting to a purpose. *n. 7.*

con sec u tive (kən sek′ū tiv), following without interruption. Monday, Tuesday, and Wednesday are consecutive days. *adj. 10.*

con sen sus (kən sen′səs), general agreement. *n.*

con sent (kən sent′), 1. agree. My father would not consent to my leaving school. 2. agreement; permission. We have mother's consent to go swimming. *v., n. 2.*

con se quence (kon′si kwens), 1. result. The consequence of his fall was a broken leg. 2. importance. The loss of that old hat is a matter of no consequence. *n. 3.*

con se quent (kon′si kwent), 1. resulting; following as an effect. His long illness and consequent absence put him far behind in his work. 2. an event, a part, or a number that follows another. *adj., n. 5.*

con se quen tial (kon′si kwen′shəl), 1. following as a result or effect. 2. self-important. *adj. 20.*

con se quent ly (kon′si kwent li), as a result; therefore. *adv.*

con ser va tion (kon′sər vā′shən), preservation; avoidance of waste. The conservation of forests is very important. *n. 7.*

con serv a tism (kən sėr′və tizm), the disposition to keep things as they are; opposition to change. *n. 16.*

con serv a tive (kən sėr′və tiv), 1. inclined to keep things as they are. A conservative person distrusts and opposes change and too many new ideas. 2. cautious. 3. a political party which opposes change in national institutions. Great Britain has three parties—the Conservative, the Liberal, and the Labor party. 4. member of a conservative party. 5. person opposed to change. 6. conserving; preserving. 7. means of preserving. *adj., n. 7.*

con serv a to ry (kən sėr′və tō′ri), 1. greenhouse for display of plants and flowers. 2. a school for instruction in music. *n., pl. conservatories. 11.*

con serve (kən sėrv′), 1. keep from harm or decay; keep from loss or from being used up; preserve. 2. fruit preserved in sugar; jam. *v., n. 8.*

con sid er (kən sid′ər), 1. think about in order to decide. Take till tomorrow to consider this offer. 2. think to be; regard as. I consider him a very able man. 3. allow for; take into account. This watch runs very well, if you consider how old it is. 4. take thought for (the feelings of others). *v. 2.*

con sid er a ble (kən sid′ər ə bəl), 1. worth thinking about; important; as, a considerable sum of money. 2. not a little; much. *adj. 4.*

con sid er a bly (kən sid′ər ə bli), much; a good deal. The boy was considerably older than he looked. *adv. 8.*

con sid er ate (kən sid′ər it), thoughtful of others and their feelings. *adj. 11.*

con sid er a tion (kən sid′ər ā′shən), 1. thinking about things in order to decide them. Please give careful consideration to this question. 2. something thought of as a reason. Price and quality are two considerations in buying anything. 3. **Take into consideration** means take into account; consider; make allowance for. 4. **In consideration of** means (1) in return for. (2) on account of. 5. money paid; any payment. Dishonest people will do anything for a consideration. 6. thoughtfulness for others and their feelings. *n. 4.*

con sid er ing (kən sid′ər ing), taking into account; making allowance for. Considering his age, the little boy reads very well. *prep.*

con sign (kən sīn′), 1. hand over; deliver. The man was consigned to prison. The father consigned the child to his sister's care. 2. transmit; send. We will consign the goods to Mr. Clark by express. *v. 7.*

con sign ment (kən sīn′mənt), 1. act of consigning. 2. the thing consigned. *n. 18.*

con sist (kən sist′), 1. be made up. A week consists of seven days. 2. agree; be in harmony. 3. **Consist in** means be contained in; be made up of. *v. 2.*

con sist ence (kən sis′təns), degree of firmness; consistency. *n. 19.*

con sist en cy (kən sis′tən si), 1. degree of firmness. Frosting for a cake must be of the right consistency to spread easily without dripping. 2. agreement. 3. keeping to the same principles, course, etc. *n., pl. consistencies. 9.*

con sist ent (kən sis′tənt), 1. thinking or acting today in agreement with what one thought yesterday; keeping to the same principles, course, etc. 2. harmonious; agreeing. So much noise is not consistent with comfort. *adj. 8.*

con sis to ry (kən sis′tə ri), a court of clergymen to decide church matters. *n., pl. consistories. 13.*

con so la tion (kon′sə lā′shən), 1. comfort. 2. comforting person, thing, or event. *n. 6.*

con sol a to ry (kən sol′ə tō′ri), consoling; comforting. *adj. 14.*

con sole[1] (kən sōl′), comfort. *v. 8.*

con sole[2] (kon′sōl), 1. the keyboard, stops, and pedals of an organ. 2. radio cabinet made to stand on the floor. 3. bracket. 4. table made with brackets. *n.*

Console of an organ

con sol i date (kən sol′i dāt), 1. unite; combine. The three banks in this town will consolidate and form a single large bank. 2. make solid or firm. The army spent a day in consolidating its gains by digging trenches. *v. 9.*

con sol i da tion (kən sol′i dā′shən), consolidating; being consolidated; strengthening; combination. *n. 15.*

con som mé (kon′sə mā′), clear soup made by boiling meat in water. *n. 20.*

con so nance (kon′sə nəns), 1. agreement. 2. harmony of sounds. *n. 20.*

con so nant (kon′sə nənt), 1. any letter of the alphabet that is not a vowel. B, c, d, and f are consonants. 2. agreeing. His action is consonant with his beliefs. *n., adj. 8.*

con sort (kon′sôrt for 1 and 3, kən sôrt′ for 2), 1. a husband or wife. 2. associate. Do not consort with thieves. 3. a ship accompanying another. *n., v. 6.*

con spic u ous (kən spik′ū əs), 1. easily seen. A traffic sign should be conspicuous. 2. remarkable; attracting notice. Lincoln is a conspicuous example of a poor boy who succeeded. *adj. 6.*

con spir a cy (kən spir′ə si), secret planning with others to do something wrong; plot. *n., pl. conspiracies. 5.*

con spir a tor (kən spir′ə tər), person who conspires; plotter. Conspirators planned to kill the king. *n. 9.*

con spire (kən spīr′), 1. plan secretly with others to do something wrong; plot. 2. act together. All things conspired to make her birthday a happy one. *v. 6.*

con sta ble (kon′stə bəl or kun′stə bəl), police officer. *n. 6.*

con stab u lar y (kən stab′ū lãr′i), police force organized like an army; state police. *n., pl. constabularies.*

con stan cy (kon′stən si), faithfulness; firmness in belief or feeling. We admire the constancy of Columbus in looking for a way around the earth. *n. 8.*

con stant (kon′stənt), 1. always the same; not changing. 2. a thing that is always the same; number or quantity that does not change. 3. continually happening; as, the constant ticking of the clock. 4. faithful. A constant friend helps you when you need help. *adj., n. 2.*

Con stan ti no ple (kon′stan ti nō′pəl), a large city in southeastern Europe. Constantinople was the capital of the Eastern Roman Empire and later the capital of Turkey. It is now called Istanbul. *n. 8.*

con stant ly (kon′stənt li), 1. always; without change. 2. without stopping. 3. often; again and again. *adv.*

con stel la tion (kon′stə lā′shən), a group of stars. The Big Dipper is the easiest constellation to locate. *n. 8.*

con ster na tion (kon′stər nā′shən), dismay; paralyzing terror. To our consternation the train rushed on toward the burning bridge. *n. 12.*

con sti pa tion (kon′sti pā′shən), a sluggish condition of the bowels. *n. 12.*

con stit u en cy (kən stich′ü ən si), 1. the voters in a district. The congressman carried out the wishes of his constituency. 2. the district itself. 3. group of supporters, customers, etc. *n., pl. constituencies. 15.*

con stit u ent (kən stich′ü ənt), 1. forming a necessary part; making up. Flour, liquid, salt, and yeast are constituent parts of bread. 2. a part of a whole; a necessary part. Sugar is the main constituent of candy. 3. appointing; electing. 4. voter. *adj., n. 9.*

con sti tute (kon′sti tūt or kon′sti tüt), 1. make up; form. Seven days constitute a week. 2. appoint. We constituted him our captain. 3. set up; establish. Courts are constituted by law to give justice. *v. 5.*

con sti tu tion (kon′sti tū′shən or kon′sti tü′shən), 1. the way in which anything is organized; nature; make-up. John has a very healthy constitution. 2. the fundamental principles according to which a country, a state, or a society is governed. The **Constitution** is the written constitution by which the United States is governed. *n. 3.*

con sti tu tion al (kon′sti tū′shən əl or kon′sti tü′shən əl), 1. of or in a person's constitution or nature. A constitutional weakness makes George subject to colds. 2. of or pertaining to the constitution; as, a constitutional amendment. 3. walk taken for the health. *adj., n. 8.*

con sti tu tion al i ty (kon′sti tū′shən al′i ti or kon′sti tü′shən al′i ti), accordance with the constitution of a nation, state, or group. The constitutionality of the new law was disputed. *n. 18.*

con strain (kən strān′), control by force; compel. *v. 6.*

con straint (kən strānt′), 1. compelling; being compelled. 2. holding back of natural feelings. *n. 11.*

con strict (kən strikt′), draw together; contract; compress. *v. 18.*

con stric tion (kən strik′shən), 1. a constricting. 2. feeling of tightness. He coughed and complained of a constriction in his chest. 3. something that constricts. *n. 18.*

con stric tive (kən strik′tiv), drawing together; contracting; compressing. *adj. 16.*

con struct (kən strukt′), put together; fit together; build. *v. 3.*

con struc tion (kən struk′shən), 1. act of constructing; building; putting together. 2. way in which a thing is constructed. 3. thing built or put together. 4. arrangement of words in a sentence. 5. meaning; interpretation. She unfairly puts a bad construction upon everything I say or do. *n. 4.*

con struc tive (kən struk′tiv), 1. tending to construct; building up; helpful; as, a constructive suggestion. 2. having to do with construction. *adj. 16.*

con strue (kən strü′), 1. show the meaning of; explain; interpret. Different lawyers may construe the same law differently. 2. analyze the grammatical construction of (a sentence, etc.). *v. 9.*

con sul (kon′səl), 1. an officer appointed by a government to live in some foreign city. A consul looks after the business interests of his own country and protects citizens of his country who are traveling or living there. 2. either of the two chief magistrates of the ancient Roman republic; a similar official. *n. 6.*

con su lar (kon′sə lər), 1. of a consul. 2. serving as a consul. Mr. Adams is the consular representative of the United States at Liverpool. *adj. 14.*

con su late (kon′sə lit), official residence or offices of a consul. *n.*

con sul ship (kon′səl ship), 1. duties, authority, and position of a consul. 2. consul's term of office. *n. 15.*

con sult (kən sult′), 1. seek information or advice from. You can consult persons, books, or maps to find out what you wish to know. 2. take into consideration; have regard for. A good teacher consults the interests of her class. *v. 3.*

con sul ta tion (kon′səl tā′shən), 1. seeking information or advice. 2. a meeting for talking over something. The three doctors held a consultation to decide what was the best way to cure the child. *n. 7.*

con sume (kən süm′), 1. use up. A student consumes much of his time in studying. 2. eat or drink up. 3. destroy; burn up. 4. waste away; be destroyed. 5. spend; waste (time, money, etc.). *v. 4.*

con sum er (kən süm′ər), 1. person who uses food, clothing, or any article which a producer makes. A low price for wheat should reduce the price of flour to the consumer. 2. person or thing which uses up, makes away with, or destroys. *n. 9.*

con sum mate (kon′sə māt for 1, kən sum′it for 2), 1. to complete; fulfill. John's happiness was consummated when his father let him drive the new car. 2. complete; perfect; in the highest degree. The airmail pilot showed consummate skill in flying through the fog and landing on time. *v., adj. 8.*

con sum ma tion (kon′sə mā′shən), completion; fulfillment; perfection. *n. 12.*

con sump tion (kən sump′shən), 1. using up; use. This food is for our consumption on the trip. 2. amount used up. The consumption of coal in that factory is five tons a day. 3. a wasting disease of the lungs; tuberculosis. *n. 6.*

con sump tive (kən sump′tiv), 1. having or likely to have tuberculosis. 2. person suffering from tuberculosis of the lungs. 3. consuming; destructive; wasteful. *adj., n. 17.*

con tact (kon′takt), 1. touch. 2. place where things touch; connection. *n. 7.*

con ta gion (kən tā′jən), 1. spreading disease by touching. 2. a disease spread in this way. 3. communication of any influence from one to another. A contagion of fear swept through the audience and caused a panic. *n. 10.*

con ta gious (kən tā′jəs), 1. spreading by touch. Scarlet fever is contagious. 2. easily spreading from one to another. Yawning is often contagious. *adj. 8.*

con tain (kən tān′), 1. have within itself; hold as contents. My purse contains money. Books contain information. 2. be capable of holding. That pitcher will contain a quart of milk. 3. be equal to. A pound contains 16 ounces. 4. include. 5. control; hold back; restrain (one's feelings). He contained his anger. She could hardly contain herself when the boy kicked her dog. 6. be divisible by (a number) without a remainder. 12 will contain 2, 3, 4, and 6. *v. 1.*

con tain er (kən tān′ər), box, can, jar, etc., used to hold or contain something. *n. 12.*

con tam i nate (kən tam′i nāt), defile; pollute; taint; corrupt. Flies contaminate food. *v. 8.*

con tam i na tion (kən tam′i nā′shən), 1. contaminating. 2. being contaminated. Milk should be kept very clean to avoid contamination. 3. thing that contaminates. *n. 13.*

con temn (kən tem′), treat with scorn; disdain; despise. The foolish girl contemned the advice of her mother. *v. 10.*

con tem plate (kon′təm plāt), 1. look at or think about for a long time. 2. have in mind; expect; intend. She is contemplating a change of work. *v. 6.*

con tem pla tion (kon′təm plā′shən), 1. looking at or thinking about something for a long time; deep thought. He was sunk in contemplation. 2. expectation; intention. *n. 6.*

con tem pla tive (kon′təm plā′tiv), thoughtful; meditative; caring for contemplation rather than action. *adj. 12.*

con tem po ra ne ous (kən tem′pə rā′ni əs), belonging to the same period of time; contemporary. The lives of Lincoln and Lee were contemporaneous. *adj. 18.*

con tem po rar y (kən tem′pə rãr′i), 1. belonging to the same period of time. 2. person who belongs to the same period of time. Lincoln and Lee were contemporaries. *adj., n., pl. contemporaries. 7.*

con tempt (kən tempt′), 1. despising; scorn; feeling that a person or act is mean and low. We feel contempt for a sneak. 2. condition of being despised; disgrace. A cowardly traitor is held in contempt. 3. in law, open disobedience to the order of a court. A person can be put in jail for contempt of court. *n. 4.*

con tempt i ble (kən temp′ti bəl), deserving contempt; mean; that is scorned. *adj. 7.*

con temp tu ous (kən temp′chü əs), showing contempt; scornful. *adj. 7.*

con tend (kən tend′), 1. fight; struggle. The first settlers in America had to contend with the Indians, sickness, and lack of food. Five runners were contending in the first race. 2. argue. Columbus contended that the earth was round. *v. 4.*

con tent[1] (kon′tent), 1. what is contained in anything; as, the contents of the room, the contents of a container or holder of any kind. 2. what is written in a book; what is said in a speech. Did you agree with the content of the speech? 3. amount contained. *n. 2.*

con tent[2] (kən tent′), 1. satisfy. Will it content you if I let you have the candy tomorrow? 2. satisfied; contented. Will you be content to wait till tomorrow? 3. contented state; satisfaction. *v., adj., n.*

con tent ed (kən ten′tid), satisfied. *adj. 7.*

con ten tion (kən ten′shən), 1. quarreling; disputing. Contention has no place in the schoolroom. 2. a statement or point which one has argued for. Columbus's contention that the earth was round turned out to be correct. *n. 6.*

con ten tious (kən ten′shəs), quarrelsome. A contentious person argues and disputes about trifles. *adj. 10.*

con tent ment (kən tent′mənt), satisfaction; being pleased; happiness. *n. 8.*

con test (kən test′ for *v.*, kon′test for *n.*), 1. dispute; struggle; fight. 2. a trial of skill. A game or race is a contest. *v., n. 3.*

con test ant (kən tes′tənt), person who contests; person who takes part in a contest. *n.*

con text (kon′tekst), the parts directly before or after a word or sentence that influence its meaning. You can often tell the meaning of a word from its context. *n. 15.*

con ti gu i ty (kon′ti gū′i ti), nearness; contact. *n. 13.*

con tig u ous (kən tig′ū əs), 1. touching; being in contact. 2. adjoining; near. *adj. 13.*

con ti nence (kon′ti nəns), self-restraint. *n. 18.*

con ti nent[1] (kon′ti nənt), 1. one of the six great masses of land on the earth. The continents are Europe, Asia, Africa, North America, South America, and Australia. 2. The mainland of Europe is called **the Continent.** *n. 3.*

con ti nent[2] (kon′ti nənt), temperate; having control of one's actions. *adj.*

con ti nen tal (kon′ti nen′təl), of a continent; like a continent. *adj. 8.*

Con ti nen tal (kon′ti nen′təl), 1. belonging to or characteristic of the mainland of Europe. Continental customs differ from those of England. 2. a European. 3. of or having to do with the American colonies during and immediately after the Revolutionary War. 4. a soldier of the American army in the Revolutionary War. *adj., n.*

con tin gen cy (kən tin′jən si), 1. uncertainty of occurrence; dependence on chance. 2. chance; accident. 3. possibility; a thing dependent on something uncertain. The explorer carried supplies for every conceivable contingency. *n., pl. contingencies. 13.*

con tin gent (kən tin′jənt), 1. happening by chance; accidental. 2. liable to happen or not to happen; uncertain; possible. 3. dependent on something not certain; conditional. Our plans for a picnic tomorrow are contingent upon pleasant weather. 4. something contingent. 5. share of troops, laborers, etc., to be furnished. 6. group that is part of a larger group. The New York contingent had seats together at the Democratic convention. *adj., n. 14.*

con tin u al (kən tin′ū əl), 1. never stopping; as, the continual flow of the river. 2. repeated many times; very frequent. *adj. 3.*

con tin u al ly (kən tin′ū əl i), 1. always; without stopping. 2. again and again; very frequently. *adv.*

con tin u ance (kən tin′ū əns), 1. going on; lasting; as, during the continuance of the war. 2. remaining; stay. His continuance in school depends on his health. 3. adjournment or postponement to a future day. *n. 7.*

con tin u a tion (kən tin′ū ā′shən), 1. act of going on with a thing after stopping; a beginning again. Continuation of my work was hard after I had been ill for a month. 2. anything by which a thing is continued; added part. The continuation of the story will appear in next month's magazine. *n. 8.*

con tin ue (kən tin′ū), 1. keep up; keep on; not stop; last; cause to last. The rain continued all day. 2. maintain; retain. Mr. Wilson was continued in office for two terms. 3. stay. The children must continue at school till July. Jack continues sullen. 4. take up; carry on. The story will be continued next month. 5. put off until a later time; postpone; adjourn. *v. 1.*

con ti nu i ty (kon′ti nū′i ti or kon′ti nü′i ti), 1. state or quality of being continuous. 2. a continuous or connected whole; unbroken series. 3. detailed plan of a moving picture. 4. connecting comments or announcements between the parts of a radio program. *n., pl. continuities. 13.*

con tin u ous (kən tin′ū əs), connected; unbroken; without a stop; as, a continuous line, a continuous sound, continuous work, a continuous line of cars. *adj. 4.*

con tort (kən tôrt′), twist; bend; draw out of shape. The clown contorted his face. *v.*

con tor tion (kən tôr′shən), 1. twisting. 2. twisted condition. The acrobat went through various contortions. *n. 12.*

con tour (kon′tür), outline. The contour of the Atlantic coast of America is very irregular. *n. 9.*

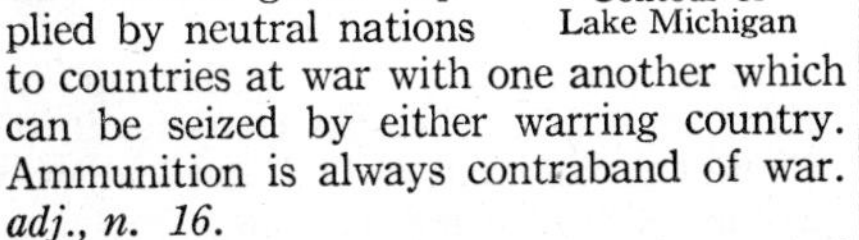

Contour of Lake Michigan

con tra band (kon′trə band), 1. against the law; prohibited. The sale of stolen goods is contraband in the United States. 2. trading contrary to law; smuggling. 3. smuggled goods. 4. **Contraband of war** means goods supplied by neutral nations to countries at war with one another which can be seized by either warring country. Ammunition is always contraband of war. *adj., n. 16.*

con tract (kon′trakt for 1 and 2, kən trakt′ for 3-6), 1. an agreement. In a contract two or more people agree to do or not to do certain things. 2. a written agreement that can be enforced by law. 3. make a contract. A builder contracts to build a new

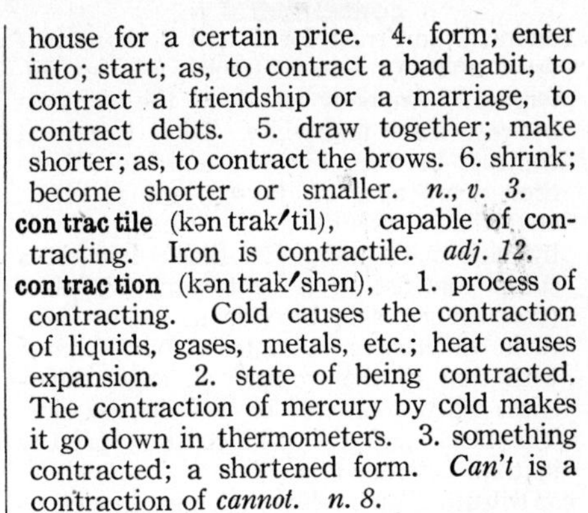

house for a certain price. 4. form; enter into; start; as, to contract a bad habit, to contract a friendship or a marriage, to contract debts. 5. draw together; make shorter; as, to contract the brows. 6. shrink; become shorter or smaller. *n., v. 3.*

con trac tile (kən trak′til), capable of contracting. Iron is contractile. *adj. 12.*

con trac tion (kən trak′shən), 1. process of contracting. Cold causes the contraction of liquids, gases, metals, etc.; heat causes expansion. 2. state of being contracted. The contraction of mercury by cold makes it go down in thermometers. 3. something contracted; a shortened form. *Can't* is a contraction of *cannot*. *n. 8.*

con trac tor (kon′trak tər or kən trak′tər), person who agrees to furnish materials or to do a piece of work for a certain price. *n. 10.*

con tra dict (kon′trə dikt′), 1. deny; deny a statement. To contradict a statement is to say that it is not true. To contradict a person is to say the opposite of what he has said, or to say that his statement is not true. 2. be contrary to. Your story and your brother's story contradict each other. *v. 8.*

con tra dic tion (kon′trə dik′shən), 1. denying what has been said. 2. a statement that contradicts. 3. disagreement. *n. 8.*

con tra dic to ry (kon′trə dik′tə ri), contradicting; saying the opposite. Reports of the result of the battle were contradictory. *adj. 16.*

con tra dis tinc tion (kon′trə dis tingk′shən), distinction by opposition or contrast. Today we cross the continent in fast airplanes in contradistinction to the slow covered wagons of our ancestors. *n. 16.*

con tral to (kən tral′tō), 1. lowest woman's voice. 2. part to be sung by the lowest woman's voice. 3. person who sings this part. 4. of or for a contralto. *n., pl. contraltos, adj. 20.*

con tra ri wise (kon′trãr i wīz′), 1. in the opposite way. 2. on the contrary. 3. perversely. *adv. 19.*

con tra ry (kon′trãr i), 1. opposed; opposite; completely different. My sister's taste in dresses is just contrary to my own. 2. the opposite. **On the contrary** sometimes means "No, the contrary is true." 3. opposing. A contrary boy is one who often opposes what is suggested. *adj., n. 3.*

con trast (kon′trast for 1 and 2, kən trast′ for 3 and 4), 1. difference; a great difference. Anybody can see the contrast between black and white. There is a great contrast between life now and life a hundred years ago. 2. person, thing, event, etc., that shows differences when put side by side with another. Black hair is a sharp contrast to a light skin. 3. place (two things) side by side so as to show their differences. Contrast our climate with that of the tropics. 4. show differences when compared or put side by side. The black and the gold contrast prettily in that design. *n., v. 4.*

con trib ute (kən trib′ūt), 1. give money or help. Will you contribute to the Red Cross? 2. write (articles, stories, etc.) for a newspaper or magazine. 3. **Contribute to** means help bring about. Poor food contributed to the child's illness. *v. 5.*

con tri bu tion (kon′tri bū′shən), 1. act of contributing; giving money or help. She felt that contribution to the church was a duty and a pleasure. 2. money or help contributed; gift. Small contributions will be gratefully received. 3. something written for a newspaper or magazine. *n. 7.*

con trib u tor (kən trib′ū tər), person or thing that contributes. *n. 12.*

con trib u to ry (kən trib′ū tō′ri), contributing; helping to bring about. The workman's own carelessness was contributory to the accident. *adj.*

con trite (kon′trīt), 1. broken in spirit by a sense of guilt; penitent. 2. showing deep regret. He wrote an apology in contrite words. *adj. 9.*

con tri tion (kən trish′ən), 1. sorrow for one's sins or guilt; being contrite; repentance. 2. deep regret. *n. 15.*

con triv ance (kən trīv′əns), 1. thing invented; mechanical device. 2. act or manner of contriving. 3. power or ability of contriving. 4. plan; scheme. *n. 8.*

con trive (kən trīv′), 1. invent; design. He contrived a new kind of engine. 2. plan; scheme; plot. 3. manage. I will contrive to be there by ten o'clock. *v. 6.*

con trol (kən trōl′), 1. command; have in one's power. A captain controls his boat. 2. power; authority. My oldest son is no longer under my control. 3. hold back. It is hard to control one's anger. 4. holding back; keeping down; restraint. He lost control of his temper. 5. means of restraint; check. The President's power to veto is a control over the legislation passed by Congress. 6. device that controls a machine. *v., controlled, controlling, n. 2.*

con trol ler (kən trōl′ər), 1. person employed to look after expenditures; as, the controller of the city of New York. 2. person who controls, directs, or restrains. *n. 14.*

control stick, lever that controls the direction of an airplane's movement.

con tro ver sial (kon′trə vėr′shəl), 1. having to do with controversy. 2. disputed. 3. fond of disputing. *adj. 16.*

con tro ver sy (kon′trə vėr′si), a dispute; a long dispute; argument. *n., pl. controversies. 6.*

con tro vert (kon′trə vėrt), 1. dispute; deny; oppose. The statement of the last witness controverts the evidence of the first two. 2. dispute about; discuss; debate. *v. 16.*

con tu ma cious (kon′tū mā′shəs or kon′tü mā′shəs), stubbornly rebellious; obstinately disobedient. *adj. 16.*

con tu ma cy (kon′tū mə si or kon′tü mə si), obstinate resistance; disobedience to authority. *n., pl. contumacies. 18.*

con tu me ly (kon′tū mi li or kon′tü mi li), 1. insolent contempt; insulting words or actions; humiliating treatment. The nobles treated the peasants with contumely. 2. humiliating insult. *n., pl. contumelies. 14.*

co nun drum (kə nun′drəm), a riddle; puzzling problem. "When is a door not a door?" is a conundrum. *n. 18.*

con va lesce (kon′və les′), recover health and strength after illness. *v.*

con va les cence (kon′və les′əns), the gradual recovery of health and strength after illness. *n. 17.*

con va les cent (kon′və les′ənt), 1. recovering health and strength after illness. 2. person recovering after illness. *adj., n. 13.*

con vec tion (kən vek′shən), 1. conveying. 2. the movement of heat in a liquid or gas from hotter to colder bodies. *n.*

con vene (kən vēn′), 1. gather in one place; assemble. Congress convenes in the Capitol at Washington, D. C., at least once a year. 2. call together. *v. 9.*

con ven ience (kən vēn′yəns), 1. any thing or arrangement that is convenient. We find our folding table a great convenience. It will be a convenience if you can come to my house this time. 2. **At your convenience** means so as to suit you as to time, place, or other conditions. 3. comfort; advantage. Many towns have camping places for the convenience of travelers by automobile. *n. 5.*

con ven ient (kən vēn′yənt), 1. handy; suitable; saving trouble; well arranged; easy to reach or use. You can use a convenient tool, take a convenient bus, live in a convenient house, or meet at a convenient place. 2. easily done; done with advantage. Will it be convenient for you to bring your lunch to school? *adj. 3.*

con vent (kon′vent), 1. a group of women living together, who devote their lives to religion. 2. the building or buildings in which they live. *n. 5.*

con ven ti cle (kən ven′ti kəl), 1. a secret religious meeting of Protestants who dissented from the doctrines and forms of the Church of England. 2. the place of such a meeting. *n. 15.*

con ven tion (kən ven′shən), 1. a meeting arranged for some particular purpose. A political party holds a convention to choose candidates for public offices. 2. an agreement. 3. general consent; custom. Convention now permits short hair for women, but it used to be thought queer. 4. a custom or practice approved by convention. Using the right hand to shake hands is a convention. *n. 4.*

con ven tion al (kən ven′shən əl), 1. depending on conventions; customary. "Good morning" is a conventional greeting. 2. formal; not natural; not original. 3. in art, following custom rather than nature. Flowers and leaves are used in a conventional design without any idea of making them look real. *adj. 9.*

con ven tion al i ty (kən ven′shən al′i ti), 1. conventional quality or character. 2. adherence to custom. Conventionality requires men to wear coats even in hot weather. 3. conventional practice, rule, form, etc. The girls at boarding school were required to observe the conventionalities very strictly. *n., pl. conventionalities. 20.*

con verge (kən vėrj′), 1. tend to meet in a point. 2. turn toward each other. If you look at the end of your nose, your eyes converge. 3. come together. The interest of all the students converged upon the celebration. *v. 12.*

con ver gence (kən vėr′jəns), converging; a tendency toward one point. *n. 20.*

con ver sant (kon′vər sənt), familiar by use or study; acquainted. Mr. Taylor is thoroughly conversant with modern music. *adj. 10.*

con ver sa tion (kon′vər sā′shən), talk. *n. 3.*

con ver sa tion al (kon′vər sā′shən əl), 1. having to do with conversation. 2. fond of conversation; good at conversation. *adj.*

con verse[1] (kən vėrs′ for 1, kon′vėrs for 2), 1. to talk. 2. conversation. *v., n. 5.*

con verse[2] (kon′vėrs), 1. opposite; contrary. 2. reversed in order; turned about. 3. something that is turned about, opposite, or contrary to something else. *adj., n.*

con verse ly (kon′vėrs li or kon vėrs′li), if turned the other way around. Gray is lighter than black; conversely, black is darker than gray. *adv.*

con ver sion (kən vėr′zhən), 1. a change. Heat causes the conversion of water into steam. 2. a change from unbelief to faith. *n. 8.*

con vert (kən vėrt′ for 1 and 2, kon′vėrt for 3), 1. change; turn. These machines convert cotton into cloth. One last effort converted defeat into victory. 2. cause to change from unbelief to faith. This missionary converted many Indians to the Christian religion. 3. person who has been converted. *v., n. 4.*

con vert i ble (kən vėr′ti bəl), capable of being converted. Wood is convertible into paper. *adj. 18.*

con vex (kon′veks or kon veks′), curved out, like the outside of a sphere or circle. The crystal of a watch is slightly convex. *adj. 8.*

Convex lenses

con vey (kən vā′), 1. carry. A bus conveys passengers from the train to the boat. 2. communicate. Do my words convey any meaning to you? 3. hand over; make over; transfer. The old farmer conveyed his farm to his son. *v. 4.*

con vey ance (kən vā′əns), 1. carrying; transmission; communication. Books are for the conveyance of ideas. 2. thing which conveys; vehicle; carriage. 3. transfer of property from one person to another. *n. 7.*

con vict (kən vikt′ for 1 and 2, kon′vikt for 3), 1. prove guilty. 2. declare guilty. The prisoner was convicted of murder. 3. person serving a prison sentence for some crime. *v., n. 6.*

con vic tion (kən vik′shən), 1. proving or declaring guilty. 2. being proved or declared guilty. 3. firm belief. *n. 9.*

con vince (kən vins′), make (a person) feel sure; persuade firmly. The mistakes Nan made convinced me that she had not studied her lesson. *v. 3.*

con viv i al (kən viv′i əl), 1. fond of eating and drinking with friends. 2. belonging to a feast; festive; gay. *adj. 18.*

con vo ca tion (kon′vō kā′shən), 1. calling together. 2. an assembly. *n. 9.*

con voke (kən vōk′), call together; summon to assemble. *v. 18.*

con vo lu tion (kon′və ül′shən), 1. a coiling, winding, or twisting together; as, the convolutions of a snake. 2. a coil; a winding; a twist. *n. 14.*

con voy (kon voi′ for 1, kon′voi for 2, 3, and 4), 1. accompany; escort and protect. Warships convoy merchant ships during time of war. 2. act of convoying; protection. The gold was sent under convoy of troops. 3. thing that convoys. 4. thing that is convoyed. *v., n. 10.*

con vulse (kən vuls′), 1. shake violently. 2. cause violent disturbance in. His face was convulsed with rage. 3. throw into convulsions. The sick child was convulsed before the doctor came. 4. throw into fits of laughter. The clown convulsed the audience with his funny acts. *v. 14.*

con vul sion (kən vul′shən), 1. a violent contraction of the muscles; a fit. The sick child's convulsions frightened its mother. 2. a fit of laughter. 3. violent disturbance. The country was undergoing a political convulsion. *n. 9.*

con vul sive (kən vul′siv), 1. violently disturbing. 2. having convulsions. 3. producing convulsions. *adj. 11.*

co ny (kō′ni), 1. rabbit. 2. rabbit fur. *n., pl. conies. 18.*

coo (kü), 1. the soft, murmuring sound made by doves or pigeons. 2. make this sound. 3. murmur softly; speak in a soft, loving manner. *n., pl. coos, v., cooed, cooing. 7.*

cook (kůk), 1. prepare (food) by using heat. We use coal, wood, gas, oil, and electricity for cooking. 2. undergo cooking; be cooked. Let the meat cook slowly. 3. person who cooks. 4. **Cook up** sometimes means prepare, or prepare falsely. *Used in common talk. v., n. 1.*

cook er (kůk′ər), an apparatus for cooking; as, a steam cooker. *n. 17.*

cook er y (kůk′ər i), cooking. *n. 12.*

cook y or **cook ie** (kůk′i), a small, flat, sweet cake. *n., pl. cookies. 7.*

cool (kül), 1. somewhat cold; more cold than hot. 2. allowing or giving a cool feeling; as, a cool dress. 3. not excited; calm. 4. having little enthusiasm or interest; not cordial. 5. something cool. 6. become cool. 7. make cool. 8. bold or impudent in a calm way. *adj., n., v. 1.*

cool er (kül′ər), a container that cools foods or drinks or keeps them cold. *n. 17.*

Cool idge (kül′ij), Calvin (1872-1933), president of the United States from 1923 to 1929. *n.*

coo lie or **coo ly** (kü′li), an unskilled laborer in China or India. *n., pl. coolies. 17.*

coon (kün), raccoon. *n. 12.*

coop (küp), 1. a small cage or pen for chickens, rabbits, etc. 2. keep in a coop; confine. The children were cooped up indoors by the rain. *n., v. 18.*

Chicken coop

coop er (küp′ər), man who makes or repairs barrels, tubs, casks, etc. *n. 14.*

Coo per (kü′pər), James Fenimore, famous American novelist (1789-1851). He wrote stories of Indian and frontier life. *n. 16.*

co öp er ate (kō op′ər āt), work together. The children coöperated with their teachers in keeping their rooms neat. *v. 9.*

co öp er a tion (kō op′ər ā′shən), working together; united effort or labor. Coöperation can accomplish many things which no individual could do alone. *n. 8.*

co öp er a tive (kō op′ər ā′tiv), 1. wanting or willing to work together with others. John was sulky and not coöperative. 2. an organization in which the profits and losses are shared by all members. *adj., n. 9.*

co ör di nate (kō ôr′di nit for 1 and 2, kō-ôr′di nāt for 3), 1. equal in importance. 2. an equal. 3. arrange in proper order. A swimmer should coördinate the movements of his arms and legs. *adj., n., v. 9.*

co ör di na tion (kō ôr′di nā′shən), 1. putting or being put into the same order or rank. 2. proper order or proper relation. *n. 15.*

coot (küt), a swimming and diving bird. *n. 14.*

European coot (18 in. long)

cope[1] (kōp), fight with some chance of success; struggle evenly; get on successfully. She was unable to cope with the duties of her new position. *v. 7.*

cope² (kōp), 1. a long cape worn by priests during certain religious rites. 2. a cloak-like covering; a canopy. Sometimes the sky is called a cope. *n.*

C, cope.

Co pen ha gen (kō′pən hā′gən), capital of Denmark and its largest city. *n. 13.*

Co per ni cus (kō pėr′ni kəs), the Polish astronomer who demonstrated that the earth and the planets move around the sun (1473-1543). *n.*

cop ing (kōp′ing), the top layer of a wall of brick or stone. Copings are usually built with a slope so that they shed water. See the picture just below. *n. 11.*

COPING

co pi ous (kō′pi əs), plentiful; abundant. *adj. 7.*

cop per (kop′ər), 1. a reddish metal, easy to work with and hard to rust. Pennies are made of copper. 2. thing made of copper. 3. cover with copper. 4. of copper; as, a copper kettle. 5. reddish brown. *n., v., adj. 2.*

cop per as (kop′ər əs), a green sulphate of iron, used in making ink and in dyeing materials black. *n. 12.*

cop per head (kop′ər hed′), 1. a poisonous snake of the United States. It has a copper-colored head, and grows to be about three feet long. 2. Northern sympathizers with the South during the Civil War were called **Copperheads.** *n.*

Copperhead

cop pice (kop′is), a wood or thicket of small trees or bushes. *n. 14.*

cop ra (kop′rə), the dried meat of coconuts. *n.*

copse (kops), a number of small trees or bushes growing together; a thicket or grove of small trees. *n. 8.*

cop y (kop′i), 1. thing made to be just like another; thing made on the model of another. A written page, a picture, a dress, or a piece of furniture can be an exact copy of another. 2. make a copy of. Copy this page. She copied my hat. 3. be a copy of; be like; imitate. 4. something set or used as a pattern or model. 5. one of a number of books, of magazines, of pictures, etc., made at the same printing. 6. written material ready to be set in print in newspapers, magazines, or books. *n., pl. copies, v., copied, copying. 2.*

cop y right (kop′i rīt′), 1. the exclusive right to make and sell a book, picture, etc., given by law. 2. protect by copyright. Books, pieces of music, plays, etc., are usually copyrighted. *n., v. 12.*

co quet ry (kō′kə tri), 1. flirting. 2. trifling. *n., pl. coquetries. 15.*

co quette (kō ket′), a flirt; woman who tries to attract men just to please her vanity. *n. 13.*

co quet tish (kō ket′ish), like a coquette; of a coquette. The pretty girl winked and gave him a coquettish smile. *adj.*

Fisherman with coracle

cor a cle (kor′ə kəl), a small, light boat made by covering a wooden frame with waterproof material. *n. 17.*

cor al (kor′əl), 1. a hard red, pink, or white substance. Coral is made out of the skeletons of tiny sea animals. 2. the coral polyp, or little animal which makes coral. 3. deep pink or red. *n., adj. 5.*

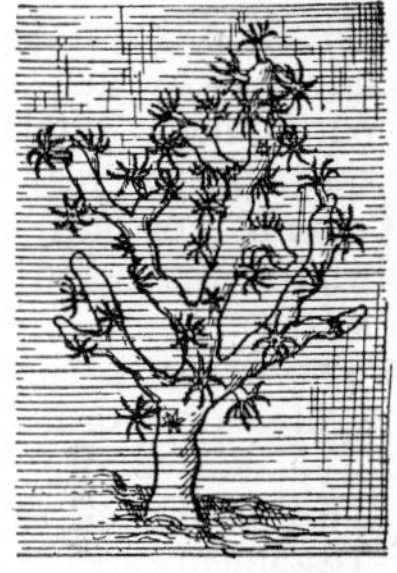
Red coral under water with some polyps

cord (kôrd), 1. thick, well-made string; very thin rope. 2. fasten or tie up with a cord. 3. a structure in an animal body that is like a cord. The spinal cord is in the backbone. 4. anything resembling a cord. A pair of covered wires with fittings to connect an electric iron or lamp with a socket is a cord. 5. a measure of cut wood. A pile of wood 8 by 4 by 4 feet is a cord. 6. pile (wood) in cords. *n., v. 3.*

cord age (kôr′dij), 1. cords; ropes. The cordage of a ship is its rigging. 2. quantity of wood measured in cords. *n. 15.*

cor dial (kôr′jəl), 1. sincere; hearty; warm; friendly. 2. reviving; cheering. 3. any food, drink, or medicine which makes the heart beat faster. *adj., n. 3.*

cor dial i ty (kôr jal′i ti), cordial quality; cordial feeling; heartiness; warm friendliness. The cordiality of his welcome made Tom feel at home. *n., pl. cordialities. 14.*

cor dil le ra (kôr dil′ər ə), a long mountain range; a chain of mountains. *n. 19.*

cor don (kôr′dən), 1. a line of sentinels, policemen, soldiers, forts, military posts, or the like, enclosing or guarding a place. 2. a cord, braid, or ribbon worn as an ornament or as a badge of honor. *n.*

Cor do van (kôr′dō vən), 1. kind of soft, fine-grained leather. 2. of or having to do with this leather. *n., adj. 19.*

cor du roy (kôr′də roi), 1. thick cotton cloth with close, velvetlike ridges. 2. **Corduroys** is a name for corduroy trousers. 3. A **corduroy road** is one made of logs laid crosswise, often across low, wet land. *n., adj. 12.*

cord wood (kôrd′wu̇d′), 1. wood sold by the cord; firewood piled in cords. 2. wood cut in 4-foot lengths. *n. 19.*

core (kōr), 1. the hard, central part containing the seeds of fruits like apples and pears. 2. the central or most important part. The core of an electromagnet is a soft iron bar. The core of the doctor's advice was that we should take care of our bodies. 3. take out the core of; as, to core apples. *n., v. 7.*

Cor inth (kor′inth), city in ancient Greece which was noted for its art and luxury. *n. 12.*

Co rin thi an (kə rin′thi ən), 1. of Corinth or its people. 2. a native of Corinth. Two books of the New Testament are letters of the Apostle Paul to the Corinthians. 3. pertaining to one of the three kinds of Greek architecture. See the picture. *adj., n. 10.*

Corinthian capital

cork (kôrk), 1. the light, thick, outer bark of a tree called the cork oak. Cork is used for bottle stoppers, floats for fishing lines, filling for some kinds of life preservers, and some floor coverings. 2. a shaped piece of cork; as, the cork of a bottle. 3. a stopper made of glass, rubber, etc. 4. stop up with a cork. 5. confine; restrain; check. *n., v. 5.*

Corkscrew

cork screw (kôrk′skrü′), 1. tool used to pull corks out of bottles. 2. shaped like a corkscrew; spiral. *n., adj. 13.*

cor mo rant (kôr′mə rənt), a large, greedy sea bird with a long neck and a pouch under the beak for holding captured fish. *n. 9.*

Cormorant (3 ft. long)

corn[1] (kôrn), 1. a grain or seed. 2. wheat, barley, rye, or oats. 3. a grain that grows on large ears; the plant it grows on. See the picture just below. Also called **maize** or **Indian corn.** 4. preserve (meat) with strong salt water or with dry salt. *n., v. 1.*

corn[2] (kôrn), a hardening of the skin with a tender sore spot. Shoes that do not fit properly often cause corns on the toes. *n.*

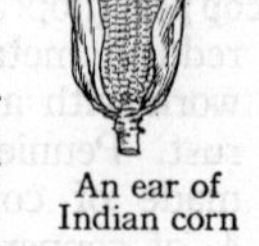

An ear of Indian corn

corn bread, bread made from corn meal instead of flour.

corn cob (kôrn′kob′), central, woody part of an ear of corn, on which the kernels grow. *n.*

corn crib (kôrn′krib′), bin or building for storing unshelled corn. *n.*

cor ne a (kôr′ni ə), the transparent outside coat of the eyeball. *n. 13.*

corned (kôrnd), preserved with strong salt water or dry salt; as, corned beef. *adj.*

cor ner (kôr′nər), 1. place where two lines or surfaces meet; as, the corner of a room. 2. place where two streets meet. 3. at a corner. 4. for a corner. 5. put in a corner; drive into a corner. 6. piece to protect a corner. The leather pocketbook has gold corners. 7. secret place; place away from crowds. The money was hidden in odd corners all over the house. 8. region; quarter; place that is far away; as, all the corners of the earth. 9. difficult place. His enemies had driven him into a corner. **Turn the corner** sometimes means pass the danger point in illness. 10. force into a difficult position. 11. buying up a large amount of some stock or article to raise its price; as, a corner in wheat. 12. buy up (something) to raise its price. *n., adj., v. 1.*

cor ner stone (kôr′nər stōn′), 1. a stone at the corner of two walls that holds them together. 2. such a stone built into the corner of a building as its formal beginning. The laying of a cornerstone is often accompanied with ceremonies. 3. something of fundamental importance. The cornerstone of religion is faith in God. *n. 19.*

cor net (kôr net′ for 1, kôr′net for 2 and 3), 1. a musical wind instrument like a trumpet, usually made of brass. 2. a little cone of paper twisted at one end, to hold candy, etc. 3. The officer in a troop of cavalry who carried the flag used to be called a cornet. *n. 13.*

Boy playing a cornet

corn field (kôrn′fēld′), field in which corn is grown. *n. 11.*

corn flow er (kôrn′flou′ər), a plant with blue, pink, white, or purple flowers; bachelor's-button. *n. 19.*

cor nice (kôr′nis), molding along the top of a wall, pillar, or side of a building. *n. 10.*

Cor nish (kôr′nish), 1. of or having to do with Cornwall, its people, or the language formerly spoken by them. 2. the ancient Celtic language of Cornwall. *adj., n. 12.*

corn starch (kôrn′stärch′), a starchy flour made from corn, used to thicken puddings, custard, etc. *n.*

cor nu co pi a (kôr′nū kō′pi ə or kôr′nü kō′pi ə), 1. horn-shaped container or ornament. Cornucopias are hung on Christmas trees. 2. the horn of plenty, represented overflowing with fruits and flowers. *n.*

Cornucopia, or horn of plenty

Corn wall (kôrn′wôl), a county in southwestern England. *n. 11.*

co rol la (kə rol′ə), petals. See the picture just below. *n. 11.*

cor ol lar y (kor′ə lãr′i), 1. something proved incidentally in proving something else. 2. something inferred. 3. natural consequence or result. Good health is a corollary of having good habits. *n., pl. corollaries. 16.*

PETALS
Corolla

co ro na (kə rō′nə), 1. ring of light seen around the sun or moon. 2. crown. *n. 19.*

cor o nal (kor′ə nəl), 1. crown or coronet. 2. garland. *n. 16.*

cor o na tion (kor′ə nā′shən), crowning (of a king or a queen). *n. 8.*

cor o ner (kor′ə nər), the officer who, with a jury, investigates any death not clearly due to natural causes. *n. 17.*

cor o net (kor′ə net), 1. small crown worn as a mark of high rank. The king wears a crown; the prince, a coronet. 2. a circle of gold, jewels, or flowers worn around the head as an ornament. *n. 7.*

Coronet of the Prince of Wales

cor po ral[1] (kôr′pə rəl), of the body; as, corporal punishment. *adj. 6.*

cor po ral[2] (kôr′pə rəl), the lowest noncommissioned officer in the army. A corporal is higher than a private and lower than a sergeant. *n.*

cor po rate (kôr′pə rit), 1. forming a corporation. 2. of a corporation. 3. united in one body. *adj. 11.*

cor po ra tion (kôr′pə rā′shən), a group of persons who obtain a charter giving them as a group certain rights and privileges. A corporation can buy and sell, own property, manufacture goods, and ship products, as if its members were a single person. *n. 5.*

cor po re al (kôr pō′ri əl), 1. of or for the body; bodily. Food and water are corporeal nourishment. 2. material; tangible. Land, trees, and money are corporeal things. *adj. 15.*

corps (kōr), 1. a division of an army; as, the Marine Corps, the Signal Corps. 2. group of people with special training, organized under a director. A large hospital has a corps of nurses. *n., pl. corps* (kōrz). *9.*

corpse (kôrps), a dead human body. *n. 6.*

cor pu lence (kôr′pū ləns), fatness. *n. 17.*

cor pu lent (kôr′pū lənt), fat. *adj. 16.*

cor pus (kôr′pəs), 1. dead body of a person or animal. 2. collection of writings or laws. *n. 15.*

cor pus cle (kôr′pus əl), 1. a very small particle. 2. any of the cells that form a large part of blood. Red corpuscles carry oxygen from the lungs to various parts of the body; some white corpuscles destroy disease germs. *n. 9.*

cor ral (kə ral′), 1. pen for horses, cattle, etc. 2. drive into or keep in a corral. 3. hem in; surround;

Corral

capture. 4. circular camp formed by wagons for defense against attack. 5. form (wagons) into such a camp. *n., v., corralled, corralling. 14.*

cor rect (kə rekt′), 1. true; right; as, the correct answer. 2. agreeing with a good standard of taste; proper; as, correct manners. 3. set right; mark the mistakes in; change to what is right. Our teacher corrects our speech. 4. punish; set right by punishing; find fault with to improve. *adj., v. 2.*

cor rec tion (kə rek′shən), 1. act of correcting; setting right. 2. what is put in place of a mistake or an error. Write in your corrections neatly. 3. punishment. A prison is sometimes called a house of correction. *n. 6.*

cor rec tive (kə rek′tiv), 1. tending to correct; making better. Corrective exercises will make weak muscles strong. 2. something that corrects. *adj., n. 20.*

cor re late (kor′ə lāt), 1. be related one to the other. The diameter and circumference of a circle correlate. 2. put into relation. Try to correlate your knowledge of history with your knowledge of geography. *v. 16.*

cor re la tion (kor′ə lā′shən), mutual relation of two or more things, parts, etc. There is a close correlation between climate and crops. *n. 19.*

cor rel a tive (kə rel′ə tiv), 1. having a mutual relation. 2. either of two things which have a mutual relation. Pairs of words like *either* and *or, parent* and *child* are called correlatives. *adj., n. 18.*

cor re spond (kor′i spond′), 1. agree; be in harmony. Her white hat, shoes, and stockings correspond with her white dress. 2. agree in amount or position; be similar. Double doors usually correspond. 3. exchange letters; write letters to one another. Will you correspond with me while I am away? *v. 4.*

cor re spond ence (kor′i spon′dəns), 1. agreement. Your account of the accident has little correspondence with the story John told. 2. exchange of letters; friendly letter writing. 3. letters. Bring me the correspondence concerning that order. *n. 4.*

cor re spond ent (kor′i spon′dənt), 1. person who exchanges letters with another. Mabel and I have been regular correspondents for over two years; we write weekly. 2. person employed by a newspaper to send news from a distant place. The *New York Times* has correspondents in Great Britain, France, Germany, Russia, China, and other countries. 3. person or business that has regular business with another, usually in a distant city. 4. in agreement. *n., adj. 8.*

cor ri dor (kor′i dər), long hallway; passage in a large building into which rooms open; as, the corridor in a school. *n. 7.*

Corridor

cor rob o rate (kə rob′ə rāt), make more certain; confirm. Witnesses corroborated the policeman's statement. *v. 10.*

cor rob o ra tion (kə rob′ə rā′shən), confirmation; additional proof. Tom's sticky face and hands were corroboration of his mother's suspicion that he had been eating jam. *n. 16.*

cor rode (kə rōd′), eat away gradually. Rust corrodes iron. *v. 9.*

cor ro sive (kə rō′siv), 1. eating away gradually; tending to corrode. Most acids are corrosive. 2. something that corrodes. *adj., n. 11.*

cor ru gate (kor′ə gāt), wrinkle. *v. 14.*

cor rupt (kə rupt′), 1. rotten. 2. start decay in. 3. wicked; as, a corrupt man, corrupt desires. 4. make evil. 5. influenced by bribes; dishonest; as, a corrupt judge. 6. bribe. 7. changed for the worse by mistakes. These Indians speak a corrupt Spanish. *adj., v. 4.*

cor rupt i ble (kə rup′ti bəl), that can be corrupted. *adj. 19.*

cor rup tion (kə rup′shən), 1. decay. 2. evil conduct. 3. bribery; dishonesty. 4. becoming less correct; as, the corruption of a language. *n. 6.*

cor sage (kôr säzh′), 1. bouquet to be worn on the waist or shoulder of a woman's dress. 2. the waist of a woman's dress. *n. 18.*

cor sair (kôr′sãr), 1. pirate. 2. pirate ship. 3. privateer. *n. 15.*

corse (kôrs), corpse; a dead human body. *n.* [*Now used only in poetry*] *9.*

corse let or **cors let** (kôrs′lit), armor for the body. *n. 16.*

C, corselet.

cor set (kôr′sit), a close-fitting undergarment worn about the waist and hips to support the body, or to shape it to the prevailing style. *n. 7.*

Cor si ca (kôr′si kə), an island in the northwestern Mediterranean Sea, belonging to France. *n. 14.*

Cor tes or **Cor tez** (kôr′tez), Spanish soldier who conquered Mexico (1485-1547). *n.*

cor tex (kôr′teks), 1. bark. 2. the layer of gray matter which covers most of the surface of the brain. *n., pl. cortices* (-ti sēz). *12.*

cor ti cal (kôr′ti kəl), of or pertaining to a cortex. *adj. 16.*

co sine (kō′sīn), the ratio of the side adjacent to the hypotenuse in a right triangle. *n. 19.*

cos met ic (koz met′ik), 1. preparation for beautifying the skin or hair. Powder, rouge, and face creams are cosmetics. 2. beautifying. *n., adj. 19.*

cos mic (koz′mik), 1. of the cosmos; having to do with the whole universe. Cosmic forces produce stars and meteors. 2. vast. *adj. 18.*

cosmic ray, extremely powerful ray somewhat like an X ray.

cos mog o ny (koz mog′ə ni), theory of the origin of the universe. *n., pl. cosmogonies. 15.*

cos mo pol i tan (koz′mə pol′i tən), 1. belonging to all parts of the world. A big oil company may have cosmopolitan interests. 2. free from the prejudices of any nation. 3. cosmopolitan person; person who feels at home in all parts of the world. *adj., n. 9.*

cos mos (koz′mos), 1. the universe as an ordered whole; the opposite of chaos. 2. a complete, harmonious system. 3. plant with white, pink, or purple flowers that blooms in the fall. *n. 13.*

Cos sack (kos′ak), one of a people living in southern Russia, noted as horsemen. *n. 12.*

cost (kôst), 1. price paid. The cost of this hat was $10. 2. loss; sacrifice. The poor fox escaped from the trap at the cost of a leg. 3. be obtained at the price of; require. This hat costs $10. The school play cost much time and effort. Courtesy costs little and means much. 4. expense in a lawsuit. Mr. Brown had to pay a $1000 fine and $50 costs. *n., v., cost, costing. 1.*

Cos ta Ri ca (kos′tə rē′kə), a country in Central America. *18.*

cos ter mon ger (kos′tər mung′gər), person who sells fruit, vegetables, fish, etc., in the street. *n.*

cos tive (kos′tiv), constipated. *adj.*

cost li ness (kôst′li nis), great cost; expensiveness. *n. 18.*

cost ly (kôst′li), 1. of great value. 2. costing much. *adj., costlier, costliest. 3.*

cos tume (kos′tūm or kos′tüm for 1 and 2, kos tūm′ or kos tüm′ for 3), 1. dress; outer clothing; style of dress, including the way the hair is worn. In our play the characters wore Colonial costumes. 2. complete set of outer garments; as, a street costume, a hunting costume. 3. provide a costume for. *n., v. 5.*

cos tum er (kos tūm′ər or kos tüm′ər), person who makes, sells, or rents costumes. *n. 19.*

co sy (kō′zi), cozy. *adj., cosier, cosiest, n., pl. cosies.*

Cot

cot[1] (kot), a small, light bed. *n. 4.*

cot[2] (kot), 1. cottage. 2. small building for shelter. *n.*

cote (kōt), a shelter for animals or birds. *n. 14.*

co te rie (kō′tə ri), a set or circle of acquaintances. Alice and her coterie gave a party to which we were not invited. *n. 15.*

co til lion (kə til′yən), a dance with complicated steps and much changing of partners. It is led by one couple. *n.*

cot tage (kot′ij), 1. small house. 2. house at a summer resort. *n. 2.*

cot tag er (kot′ij ər), person who lives in a cottage. *n. 16.*

cot ter[1] (kot′ər), pin, wedge, etc., to hold parts together. *n. 15.*

cot ter[2] or **cot tar** (kot′ər), Scottish peasant who works for a farmer and lives in a cottage on the farm. *n.*

Cotton plant

cot ton (kot′ən), 1. the cotton plant. See the picture. 2. the soft, white fibers surrounding the seed of the cotton plant. 3. thread of cloth made from these white fibers. 4. made of cotton. *n., adj. 2.*

cot ton mouth (kot′ən mouth′), water moccasin, a large poisonous American snake. *n.*

cot ton seed (kot′ən sēd′), the seed of the cotton plant. It is used for making cottonseed oil, fertilizer, cattle food, etc. *n. 13.*

cot ton tail (kot′ən tāl′), the common American rabbit. See the picture in the next column. *n.*

cot ton wood (kot′ən wu̇d′), a kind of American poplar with cottonlike tufts on the seeds. *n. 17.*

cot y le don (kot′i lē′dən), the first leaf, or one of the first pair of leaves, growing from a seed. *n. 9.*

C, cotyledon.

couch (kouch), 1. a bed or sofa for sleep or rest. 2. any place for sleep or rest. The deer got up from its grassy couch. 3. put (oneself or another) in a bed or any resting place. 4. put in a position ready to attack; as, to couch a spear. 5. lie hidden ready to attack. 6. put in words; express. His thoughts were couched in beautiful language. *n., v. 3.*

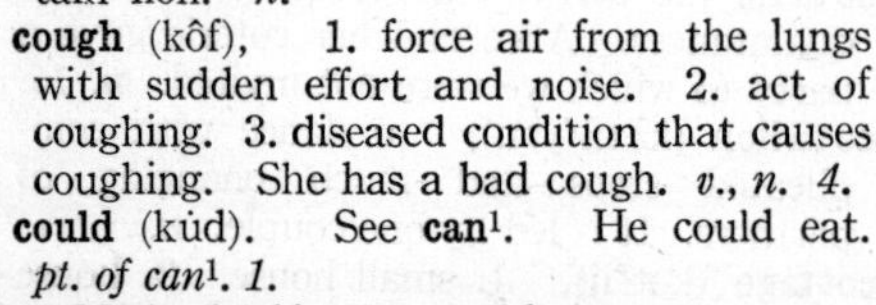

Lion couchant

couch ant (kouch′ənt), lying down with the head raised. *adj. 15.*

cou gar (kü′gər), puma; mountain lion. *n.*

cough (kôf), 1. force air from the lungs with sudden effort and noise. 2. act of coughing. 3. diseased condition that causes coughing. She has a bad cough. *v., n. 4.*

could (ku̇d). See **can**[1]. He could eat. *pt. of can*[1]. *1.*

could n't (ku̇d′ənt), could not. *3.*

couldst (ku̇dst), old form meaning **could.** "Thou couldst" means "you could." *v. 3.*

coun cil (koun′səl), 1. a group of persons called together to give advice, and discuss or settle questions. 2. a small group of persons elected by the people to make laws for and manage a town or city. *n. 2.*

coun ci lor or **coun cil lor** (koun′sə lər), member of a council. *n. 13.*

coun sel (koun′səl), 1. act of exchanging ideas; act of talking things over. 2. advice. A wise person gives good counsel. 3. person or group that gives advice about the law; lawyer or group of lawyers. Each side of a case in court has its own counsel. 4. give advice to; advise. 5. recommend. He counseled acting at once. 6. **Take counsel** means exchange ideas; talk things over; consult together. *n., v., counseled, counseling. 3.*

coun se lor or **coun sel lor** (koun′sə lər), 1. person who advises. 2. lawyer. *n. 8.*

count[1] (kount), 1. name numbers in order. The child can count up to ten. 2. add up; find the number of. He counted the books and found there were fifty. 3. adding up; finding out how many. The count showed that 5000 votes had been cast. 4. total number; amount. 5. use in reckoning; take account of. Let's not count that game. 6. consider. He counts himself fortunate in having good health. 7. depend. We count on your help. 8. be counted; be included in reckoning or consideration. 9. have an influence; be of account or value. Everything we do counts. *v., n. 1.*

Cottontail (17 in. long)

count[2] (kount), nobleman; a title or rank. A French count was about equal to an English earl. *n.*

coun te nance (koun′ti nəns), 1. expression of the face. His angry countenance showed how he felt. **Keep one's countenance** means (1) be calm; not show feeling. (2) keep from smiling or laughing. 2. face. 3. approve or encourage (a person, an action, or a person in doing something). Mother countenanced the boys' friendship. 4. approval. *n., v. 4.*

count er[1] (koun′tər), 1. small piece of metal, etc., usually round, used to keep count in games of cards, etc.; imitation coin. 2. long table in a store or bank on which money is counted out, and across which goods are given to customers. 3. one who counts. *n. 5.*

coun ter[2] (koun′tər), 1. contrary; opposed. He acted counter to his promise. 2. oppose. He countered my proposal with one of his own. 3. blow given in boxing or fighting in return for another. 4. give such a blow. 5. stiff piece inside the back of a shoe around the heel. *adv., adj., v., n.*

counter-, prefix meaning:—
1. against; in opposition to; as in counteract.
2. in return; as in counterattack.
3. so as to correspond; as in counterpart.

coun ter act (koun′tər akt′), act against; hinder; neutralize. *v. 8.*

coun ter at tack (koun′tər ə tak′), 1. attack made to counteract an attack. 2. attack in return. *n., v.*

coun ter bal ance (koun′tər bal′əns for 1 and 2, koun′tər bal′əns for 3), 1. weight balancing another weight. 2. influence or power acting in opposition. 3. act as a counterbalance to. The boy's earnest effort counterbalanced his slowness at learning. *n., v. 14.*

coun ter check (koun′tər chek′), 1. a check; a check controlling another check. 2. to check; check by a second check. *n., v. 20.*

coun ter claim (koun′tər klām′), opposing claim. *n.*

coun ter feit (koun′tər fit), 1. copy (money, pictures, handwriting, etc.) in order to deceive. He was sent to prison for counterfeiting five-dollar bills. 2. something copied and passed as genuine. 3. not genuine; as, a counterfeit stamp. 4. pretend. *v., n., adj. 8.*

coun ter mand (koun′tər mand), 1. withdraw or cancel (a command or order). 2. recall or stop by a contrary order. *v. 18.*

coun ter pane (koun′tər pān′), outer covering for a bed; bedspread. *n. 16.*

coun ter part (koun′tər pärt′), 1. a copy or duplicate. 2. person or thing closely resembling another. This twin is her sister's counterpart. 3. thing that complements another. Night is the counterpart of day. *n. 11.*

coun ter point (koun′tər point′), 1. in music, a melody added to another as accompaniment. 2. the art of adding melodies to a given melody according to fixed rules. *n. 19.*

coun ter poise (koun′tər poiz′), 1. weight balancing another weight. 2. any equal and opposing power or force. 3. the condition of being in balance. 4. balance by an opposing weight. *n., v. 15.*

coun ter rev o lu tion (koun′tər rev′ə lü′shən), revolution against a revolution. *n. 20.*

coun ter sign (koun′tər sīn′), 1. secret signal; watchword; password. The soldier had to give the countersign before he could pass the sentry. 2. signature added to another signature to confirm it. 3. sign (something) already signed by another. *n., v. 18.*

coun ter sink (koun′tər singk′). 1. enlarge the upper part of (a hole) to make room for the head of a screw or bolt. 2. sink (the head of a screw or bolt) into such a hole. *v., countersunk, countersinking. 17.*

count ess (koun′tis), 1. wife or widow of a count or an earl. 2. lady equal in rank to a count or earl in her own right. *n. 11.*

counting house, a building or office used for keeping accounts and doing business. *18.*

count less (kount′lis), too many to count; as, the countless sands of the seashore. *adj. 6.*

coun try (kun′tri), 1. land; region. The country around the mining town was rough and mountainous. 2. all the land of a nation. He came from France, a country across the sea. 3. A person's country is the land where he was born or where he is a citizen. 4. the people of a country. All the country hated the king. 5. land without many houses. Bob likes the country better than the city. 6. of the country; in the country. 7. like the country. *n., pl. countries, adj. 1.*

coun try man (kun′tri mən), 1. man of one's own country. We will protect our countrymen. 2. man who lives in the country. *n., pl. countrymen. 7.*

coun try side (kun′tri sīd′), 1. rural district; country. 2. certain section of a country. 3. its people. *n. 17.*

coun try wom an (kun′tri wu̇m′ən), 1. woman of one's own country. 2. woman who lives in the country. *n., pl. countrywomen. 17.*

coun ty (koun′ti), a division for purposes of government next smaller than a country or State. The county officers conduct local business, collect taxes, hold court, keep roads in repair, and maintain county schools. County may mean the land, the people, or the officers of the county. *n., pl. counties. 3.*

coup (kü), sudden, brilliant action; unexpected, clever move; master stroke. A **coup d'é tat** (kü′ dā tä′) is a sudden, decisive act in politics, usually bringing about a change of government. *n. 13.*

cou pé (kü pā′), a closed carriage or automobile. *n. 15.*

cou ple (kup′əl), 1. two things of the same kind that go together; a pair. 2. man and woman who are married, engaged, or partners in a dance. 3. partners in a dance. 4. join together; as, to couple two freight cars. *n., v. 2.*

cou plet (kup′lit), two lines of poetry that belong together. *Example:*

Those who in quarrels interpose
Must often wipe a bloody nose. *n. 17.*

cou pling (kup′ling), 1. joining together. 2. device for joining together parts of machinery. 3. device used to join together two railroad cars. *n. 9.*

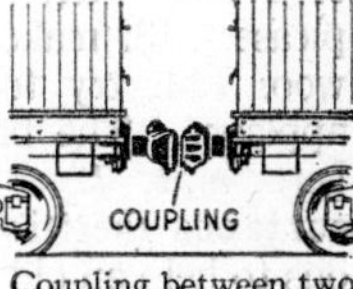

Coupling between two railroad cars

cou pon (kü′pon), 1. printed statement of interest due on a bond, which can be cut from the bond and presented for payment. 2. part of a ticket, etc., that gives the person who holds it certain rights. She saved the coupons that came with each box of soap. *n. 11.*

cour age (kėr′ij), bravery; meeting danger without fear. *n. 2.*

cou ra geous (kə rā′jəs), fearless; brave; full of courage. *adj. 6.*

cour i er (kėr′i ər or kür′i ər), 1. messenger sent in haste. 2. man hired by travelers to go with them and be in charge of the arrangements of the journey. *n. 11.*

course (kōrs), 1. an onward movement. 2. direction taken. 3. line of action. 4. track. 5. channel. 6. number of like things arranged in some regular order. 7. regular order. **Of course** means (1) surely; certainly. (2) naturally; as should be expected. 8. part of a meal served at one time. 9. row of bricks or stones in a wall. 10. hunt. 11. run. *n., v. 1.*

cours er (kōr′sər), a swift horse. *n.* [*Used in poetry*] *12.*

court (kōrt), 1. space partly or wholly enclosed by walls or buildings. The apartment house is built around a court. 2. short street. 3. place marked off for a game; as, a tennis court, a handball court. 4. place where a king or other sovereign lives. 5. establishment and followers of a king, emperor, etc. The court of King Solomon was noted for its splendor. 6. a sovereign and his advisers as a ruling body or power. By order of the Court of St. James is by order of the British government. 7. assembly held by a sovereign. 8. place where justice is administered. The prisoner was brought to court for trial. 9. persons who are chosen to administer justice; judge or judges. The court found him guilty. 10. assembly of such persons to administer justice. Several cases await trial at the next court. 11. effort to please; as, to pay court to a king, a high official, or a lady. 12. seek the favor of; try to please. 13. make love to; seek to marry; woo. 14. try to get; seek; as, to court applause. The brave soldier courted danger. *n., v. 1.*

cour te ous (kėr′ti əs), polite. It is courteous to help an old lady. *adj. 5.*

cour te sy (kėr′ti si), 1. polite behavior; kind conduct. 2. a kindness; act of consideration; polite act. 3. curtsy. *n., pl. courtesies. 5.*

cour te san or **cour te zan** (kėr′ti zən), prostitute. *n. 18.*

court house (kōrt′hous′), 1. a building in which courts of law are held. 2. a building used for the government of a county. *n. 14.*

cour ti er (kōr′ti ər), 1. person often present at the court of a prince, king, emperor, etc.; court attendant. 2. person who tries to win the favor of another. *n. 4.*

court li ness (kōrt′li nis), politeness; elegance; polish. *n.*

court ly (kōrt′li), 1. having manners fit for a king's court; polite; elegant. 2. flattering; trying hard to please one's superior. *adj., courtlier, courtliest. 13.*

court-mar tial (kōrt′mär′shəl), 1. a court of army or navy officers for judging offenders against military or naval laws. 2. try by such a court. *n., pl. courts-martial, v., court-martialed, court-martialing. 19.*

court ship (kōrt′ship), making love; wooing. *n. 10.*

court yard (kōrt′yärd′), space enclosed by walls, in or near a large building. *n. 11.*

cous in (kuz′ən), 1. the son or daughter of one's uncle or aunt. Your first cousins are other grandchildren of your grandparents. Your second cousins are the other great-grandchildren of your great-grandparents, and so for third cousins, fourth, etc. 2. Distant relatives or related nations are sometimes called cousins. *n. 2.*

BAY
COVE

cove (kōv), small bay; mouth of a creek; inlet on the shore. *n. 9.*

cov e nant (kuv′ə nənt), 1. a solemn agreement between two or more persons or groups. 2. agree solemnly (to do certain things). *n., v. 6.*

Cov en try (kuv′ən tri), 1. a city in England. 2. **Send to Coventry** means refuse to associate with. *n. 14.*

cov er (kuv′ər), 1. Cover this box with a wide board. Cover this sleeping child with your coat. Do not try to cover a mistake. 2. Anything that protects or hides is a cover. Books have covers. Under cover of the dark night, the dog was stolen. 3. His clothes were covered with dirt. 4. The cars cover 200 miles a day. 5. This book covers all of the year's work in arithmetic. 6. A cover sometimes means a place at the table set for one person. *v., n. 1.*

cov er ing (kuv′ər ing), anything that covers; as, bed coverings. *n.*

cov er let (kuv′ər lit), an outer covering of a bed; bedspread. *n. 10.*

cov ert (kuv′ərt), 1. secret; hidden; disguised; as, covert glances at one's neighbors. 2. a shelter; a hiding place; a thicket in which animals hide. *adj., n. 20.*

cov et (kuv′it), desire eagerly (something that belongs to another). The boys coveted John's new bat. *v. 5.*

cov et ous (kuv′i təs), desiring things that belong to others. *adj. 8.*

cov et ous ness (kuv′i təs nis), eager desire for another person's property; avarice. *n. 13.*

cov ey (kuv′i), 1. small flock of partridges. 2. small flock; group. *n., pl. coveys. 18.*

cow[1] (kou), 1. common dairy animal that furnishes milk. 2. female of various other large animals; as, a buffalo cow, an elephant cow. *n. 1.*

Cow (def. 1)

cow[2] (kou), make afraid; frighten. *v.*

cow ard (kou′ərd), person who lacks courage or is afraid; one who runs from danger. *n. 3.*

cow ard ice (kou′ər dis), lack of courage; being easily made afraid. *n. 7.*

cow ard ly (kou′ərd li), without courage; like a coward. *adj. 6.*

cow boy (kou′boi′), a man, usually on horseback, who looks after cattle on a ranch. *n. 9.*

cow er (kou′ər), crouch in fear or shame. The whipped dog cowered under the table. *v. 12.*

cow herd (kou′hėrd′), person whose work is looking after cattle while they are at pasture. *n.*

cow hide (kou′hīd′), 1. the hide of a cow. 2. leather made from it. 3. a strong, heavy whip made of rawhide or braided leather. 4. to whip with a cowhide. *n., v. 17.*

Cowl (def. 2)

cowl (koul), 1. monk's cloak with a hood. 2. the hood itself. *n. 7.*

cow slip (kou′slip), a wild plant with yellow flowers. *n. 8.*

cox comb (koks′kōm′), vain, empty-headed man. *n. 10.*

cox swain (kok′sən or kok′swān), the man who steers a boat. *n. 20.*

coy (koi), 1. shy; modest; bashful. 2. seeming more shy than one really is. *adj. 9.*

Coyote (4 ft. long, including tail)

coy o te (kī ō′ti or kī′ōt), prairie wolf of western North America. *n., pl. coyotes* or *coyote. 13.*

coz en (kuz′ən), cheat; deceive; beguile. *v. 15.*

coz en age (kuz′ən ij), the practice of cozening; fraud; deception. *n. 16.*

co zy (kō′zi), 1. warm and comfortable; snug. 2. padded cloth cover to keep a teapot warm. *adj., cozier, coziest, n., pl. cozies. 9.*

crab[1] (krab), 1. water animal with eight legs, two claws, and a broad, flat, shell covering. Many kinds of crabs are good to eat. 2. find fault; criticize. *Used in common talk.* 3. a sour, cross person. *n., v., crabbed, crabbing. 4.*

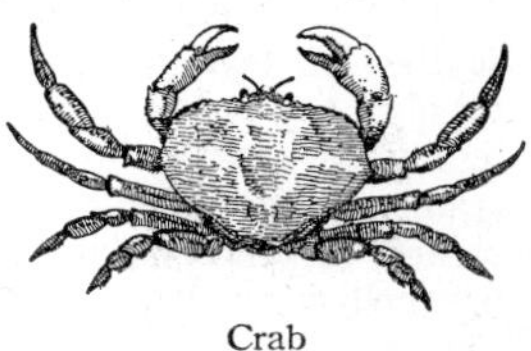
Crab

crab[2] (krab), crab apple. *n.*

crab apple, 1. very small, sour apple used to make jelly. 2. tree on which it grows.

crab bed (krab′id), 1. peevish; ill-natured; cross. 2. perplexing; hard to make out. 3. hard to read. *adj. 18.*

crack (krak), 1. a sudden, sharp noise like that made by loud thunder, by a whip, or by something breaking. 2. make or cause to make a sudden, sharp noise; as, to crack a whip, the whip cracked. 3. break with a sharp noise. The tree cracked loudly and fell. We cracked the nuts. 4. a hard, sharp blow. *Used in common talk.* 5. a split made by breaking without separating into parts. There is a crack in this cup. 6. break without separating into parts. You have cracked the window. 7. **Crack a joke** means tell a joke; say something funny. 8. excellent; first-rate. *Used in common talk. n., v., adj. 2.*

crack er (krak′ər), 1. a thin, crisp biscuit. 2. an instrument for breaking things into parts; as, a nutcracker. 3. firework that bursts with a sharp noise. *n. 6.*

crack le (krak′əl), 1. make slight, sharp sounds. The papers crackled in the waste basket. A fire crackled on the hearth. 2. a slight, sharp sound, such as paper makes when crushed. 3. very small cracks covering the surface of china or glass. *v., n. 5.*

cra dle (krā′dəl), 1. a baby's little bed on rockers. 2. the place where anything begins its growth. 3. any kind of framework looking like or used as a cradle. The framework upon which a ship rests during building or repairs is a cradle. The rocking machine or trough in which gold-bearing earth is shaken in water is also a cradle. 4. a frame fastened to a scythe for laying grain evenly as it is cut. 5. lay or rock as in a cradle. She cradled the child in her arms. 6. shelter or train in early youth. *n., v. 3.*

Miner's cradle (def. 3)

Man using a cradle (def. 4)

craft (kraft), 1. skill. He shaped the bits of wood and fitted them together with loving craft. 2. a trade or art requiring skilled work; as, needlecraft. 3. members of a skilled trade. He belongs to the craft of masons. 4. skill in deceiving others; slyness; trickiness. By craft he got all their money from them. 5. boat or boats; ship or ships. *n. 5.*

craft i ness (kraf′ti nis), skill in deceiving others; being crafty; cunning. *n. 18.*

crafts man (krafts′mən), skilled workman. *n., pl. craftsmen. 10.*

craft y (kraf′ti), skillful in deceiving others; as, the crafty fox, a crafty villain. *adj., craftier, craftiest. 8.*

crag (krag), a steep, rugged rock rising above others. *n. 6.*

crag gy (krag′i), with many crags; rugged; rough. *adj. 13.*

cram (kram), 1. force into; force down; stuff. He crammed all his clothes quickly into the bag. 2. fill too full. 3. eat too fast or too much. 4. learn hurriedly; stuff with knowledge. *Used in common talk. v., crammed, cramming. 6.*

cramp (kramp), 1. metal bar bent at both ends, used for holding things together. 2. shut into a small space; limit. His work was cramped by the very short time he could spend on it. 3. sudden, painful contracting or pulling together of muscles from chill or strain. The swimmer was seized with cramps and had to be taken into the boat. 4. cause to have a cramp. *n., v. 8.*

Cranberry

cran ber ry (kran′ber′i), a firm, sour, dark-red berry that grows on low shrubs in marshes. Jelly, sauce, etc., are made from cranberries. *n., pl. cranberries. 10.*

crane (krān), 1. machine with a long, swinging arm, for lifting and moving heavy weights. 2. a large wading bird with long legs, neck, and bill. 3. stretch (the neck) as a crane does, in order to see better. *n., v. 7.*

Crane for lifting

cra ni al (krā′ni əl), of the skull; having to do with the skull. *adj. 19.*

cra ni um (krā′ni əm), 1. skull. 2. part of the skull enclosing the brain. *n. 14.*

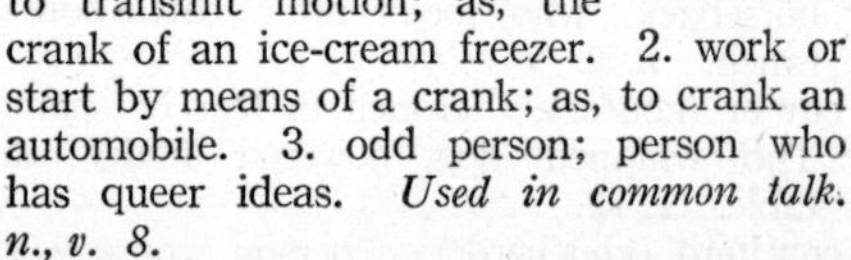

White crane

crank (krangk), 1. part or handle of a machine connected at right angles to another part to transmit motion; as, the crank of an ice-cream freezer. 2. work or start by means of a crank; as, to crank an automobile. 3. odd person; person who has queer ideas. *Used in common talk. n., v. 8.*

cran ny (kran′i), crack; chink; crevice. *n., pl. crannies. 10.*

crape (krāp), a thin, light fabric with a finely crinkled surface. Black crape is used as a sign of mourning. *n. 10.*

crash[1] (krash), 1. a sudden, loud noise like many dishes falling and breaking, or like sudden, loud band music. 2. make a crash. The dishes crashed to the floor. 3. the violent striking of one solid thing against another. 4. strike violently and shatter. 5. sudden ruin; business failure. 6. fall to the earth in an airplane; make a very bad landing. 7. such a fall or landing. *n., v. 4.*

crash[2] (krash), coarse linen cloth, used for towels, clothing, etc. *n.*

crass (kras), 1. gross; stupid; as, crass ignorance. 2. thick; coarse. *adj.*

crate (krāt), 1. a large frame, box, or basket made of wicker or of strips of wood, for shipping glass, china, fruit, household goods, or furniture. 2. pack in a crate for shipping. *n., v. 7.*

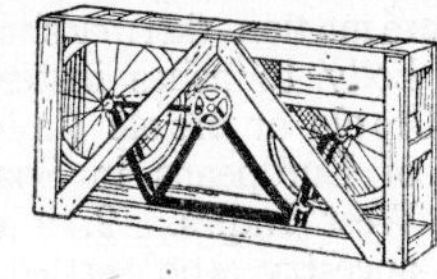

Crate containing a bicycle

cra ter (krā′tər), 1. the opening of a volcano. 2. a bowl-shaped hole. The battlefield was full of craters made by exploding shells. *n. 13.*

cra vat (krə vat′), 1. necktie. 2. neckcloth; scarf. *n. 7.*

crave (krāv), 1. long for; desire very much. A thirsty man craves water. 2. ask earnestly for. He craved a favor of the king. *v. 4.*

cra ven (krā′vən), 1. cowardly. 2. coward. 3. **Cry craven** means surrender. *adj., n. 9.*

crav ing (krāv′ing), longing; yearning. A hungry man has a craving for food. *n. 12.*

craw (krô), 1. crop of a bird or insect. 2. stomach of any animal. *n.*

craw fish (krô′fish′), crayfish. *n., pl. crawfishes* or *crawfish. 16.*

crawl (krôl), 1. move slowly, pulling the body along the ground. A worm or snake crawls. 2. move slowly on hands and knees. The boys crawled through a hole in the wall. 3. swarm with crawling things. The ground was crawling with ants. 4. feel creepy. My flesh crawled at the thought of the huge black snakes. 5. slow movement along the ground; any slow movement. *v., n. 3.*

cray fish (krā′fish′), a fresh-water animal looking like a small lobster; a similar but larger salt-water shellfish. *n., pl. crayfishes* or *crayfish. 13.*

Crayfish (3 to 6 in. long)

cray on (krā′ən), 1. a stick or pencil of chalk, charcoal, etc., for drawing or writing. 2. draw with crayons. 3. drawing made with crayons. *n., v. 13.*

craze (krāz), 1. a short-lived, eager interest in doing some one thing. 2. make diseased or injured in mind; make crazy. *n., v. 5.*

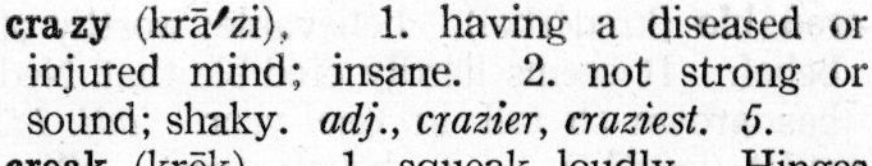

cra zy (krā′zi), 1. having a diseased or injured mind; insane. 2. not strong or sound; shaky. *adj., crazier, craziest. 5.*

creak (krēk), 1. squeak loudly. Hinges creak when they need oiling. 2. creaking noise. *v., n. 7.*

cream (krēm), 1. the oily, yellowish part of milk which rises slowly to the top. Butter is made from cream. 2. take the cream from. 3. form a thick layer like cream on the top; foam. 4. a fancy sweet food made of cream or like cream; as, ice cream. 5. make into a mixture like cream. The cook creamed butter and sugar together for a cake. 6. oily preparation put on the skin to make it smooth and soft. 7. yellowish white. 8. best part of anything. *n., v., adj. 2.*

cream er y (krēm′ər i), 1. place where butter and cheese are made. 2. place where cream, milk, and butter are bought and sold. *n., pl. creameries. 10.*

cream y (krēm′i), 1. like cream. 2. having much cream in it. *adj., creamier, creamiest. 9.*

crease (krēs), 1. a line or mark produced by folding; fold; ridge; wrinkle. 2. make creases in; fall into creases. *n., v. 11.*

cre ate (krē āt′), 1. make a thing which has not been made before; bring into being. She created this garden in the desert. 2. be the cause of. Do not create a disturbance. *v. 2.*

cre a tion (krē ā′shən), 1. creating; the act of making a thing which has not been made before. 2. all things that have been brought into being; the world; the universe. Let all creation praise the Lord. 3. a thing produced by intelligence or skill, usually an important or original one. *n. 4.*

cre a tive (krē ā′tiv), having the power to create; inventive; productive. *adj. 11.*

cre a tor (krē ā′tər), person who creates. **The Creator** is another name for God. *n. 6.*

crea ture (krē′chər), 1. any living person or animal. 2. person who is merely a tool, carrying out the will of another. *n. 2.*

cre dence (krē′dəns), belief. Don't give credence to all the gossip you hear. *n. 15.*

cre den tials (kri den′shəlz), letters of introduction; references. The man's credentials were so favorable that he was given a job in the bank. *n. pl. 13.*

cred i bil i ty (kred′i bil′i ti), quality of being believable. *n. 19.*

cred i ble (kred′i bəl), believable; worthy of belief. It seems hardly credible that Ned has grown so tall in one year. *adj. 14.*

cred it (kred′it), 1. belief; trust. **Give credit to** a story means believe it. 2. believe in. I can credit all that you are telling me. 3. trust in a person's ability and intention to pay. Buy **on credit** means buy without paying until later. 4. make a record of payment or goods received. I will credit you with $4 on our books. 5. acknowledgment by putting down a record in one's accounts. 6. one's reputation in money matters. If you pay your bills, your credit will be good. 7. **Credit a person with** means think that he has. I credit him with some sense. 8. praise; honor. "It is to your credit" or "It does you credit" means that you may rightly be proud of it. *n., v. 3.*

cred it a ble (kred′it ə bəl), bringing credit or honor. Alice's record of perfect attendance is very creditable to her. *adj. 12.*

cred i tor (kred′i tər), person to whom money or goods are due; one to whom a debt is owed. *n. 6.*

cre du li ty (kri dū′li ti or kri dü′li ti), too great readiness to believe. Nan's credulity led her to believe improbable stories. *n. 7.*

cred u lous (krej′ù ləs), too ready to believe; easily deceived. *adj. 8.*

creed (krēd), 1. a brief statement of the essential points of Christian belief as approved by some church. 2. any statement of faith or of cherished opinions. *n. 8.*

creek (krēk), 1. small stream. 2. narrow bay running inland for some distance. *n. 4.*

creel (krēl), 1. basket for holding fish. See the picture. 2. basketlike trap to catch fish or lobsters. *n. 18.*

Creel to hold fish

creep (krēp), 1. move slowly with the body lying close to the ground or floor; crawl. A baby learns to creep before it learns to walk. 2. move in a slow or sly way. When we were playing Indians, we crept silently through the bushes. 3. move timidly. 4. grow along the ground or over a wall by means of clinging stems; as, a creeping plant. Ivy creeps. 5. feel as if things were creeping over the skin. It made my flesh creep to hear her moan. 6. creeping; slow movement. *v., crept, creeping, n. 2.*

creep er (krēp′ər), 1. person or thing that creeps. 2. a creeping plant. *n. 12.*

creep y (krēp′i), having or causing a creeping sensation of the skin. Ghost stories make some children creepy. *adj., creepier, creepiest. 19.*

cre mate (krē′māt), 1. burn (a dead body) to ashes. 2. burn. *v.*

cre ma tion (kri mā′shən), burning of a dead body to ashes instead of burying it. *n.*

Cre ole or **cre ole** (krē′ōl), 1. a descendant of Europeans in Spanish America or the West Indies. 2. a descendant of French ancestry who settled in Louisiana. Half-breed Negroes are incorrectly called creoles. 3. the French language as spoken in Louisiana. 4. having to do with Creoles; as, Creole customs. *n., adj. 17.*

cre o sote (krē′ə sōt), an oily liquid with a burning taste and a penetrating odor, obtained from wood tar. Shingles are often dipped in creosote. *n. 13.*

crepe or **crêpe** (krāp), 1. a thin cloth with a wavy surface. 2. tissue paper that looks like crepe. *n. 6.*

crept (krept). See **creep.** We had crept up on the enemy without their seeing us. *pt. and pp. of creep. 3.*

cre scen do (krə shen′dō), 1. gradually increasing in force or loudness. 2. gradual increase in force or loudness. *adj., adv., n., pl. crescendos.*

Crescent moon

cres cent (kres′ənt), 1. shape of the moon in its first or last quarter. 2. anything that curves in a similar way, such as a street or a row of houses. 3. shaped like the moon in its first or last quarter. 4. increasing. *n., adj. 7.*

cress (kres), a plant whose leaves are used as a garnish or a salad. *n. 14.*

cres set (kres′it), metal container holding grease or oil which is burned for light, mounted on a pole or hung from above. *n. 16.*

Cresset

Cres si da (kres′i də), the daughter of a Trojan priest, loved by Troilus. *n. 16.*

crest (krest), 1. a tuft or mane on the head of an animal; a rooster's comb. 2. a decoration of plumes or feathers worn on a helmet. 3. decoration at the top of a coat of arms. 4. top of a hill or a wave. *n. 4.*

Crest on a coat of arms

crest ed (kres′tid), having a crest. *adj.*

crest fall en (krest′fôl′ən), with bowed head;

dejected; discouraged. Nell came home crestfallen because she had a poor report card. *adj. 17.*

Cre tan (krē′tən), 1. of or having to do with Crete or its inhabitants. 2. a native or inhabitant of Crete. *adj., n. 17.*

Crete (krēt), island southeast of Greece. *n. 12.*

cre tonne (kri ton′ or krē′ton), a strong cotton cloth with designs printed on one or both sides. Cretonne is used for curtains and furniture covers. *n. 10.*

cre vasse (krə vas′), 1. deep crack or crevice in the ice of a glacier. 2. a break in a dam or dike or levee. *n.*

Crevasse

crev ice (krev′is), a narrow split or crack. *n. 8.*

crew[1] (krü), 1. the men needed to do the work on a ship, or to row a boat. 2. group of people working or acting together; as, a repairing crew on the railroad. 3. gang; mob. The boys on that street are a rough crew. *n. 2.*

crew[2] (krü), crowed. The cock crew. *pt. of* **crow**[1].

crib (krib), 1. small bed with high barred sides so that a baby cannot fall out. 2. barred manger for feeding animals. 3. a building or box for storing grain, salt, etc. 4. framework of logs or timbers used in building. 5. use the words or ideas of another without giving credit to their author. 6. notes or helps in a student's work which it is not fair to use. 7. make use of notes or helps which it is not fair to use in preparing schoolwork. *n., v., cribbed, cribbing.* [5, 6, *and* 7 *are used in common talk*] *6.*

Crib for a baby

crib bage (krib′ij), a card game played with a board and pegs. *n. 17.*

crick et[1] (krik′it), a black insect of the grasshopper family. On a summer evening you can hear the crickets chirping. *n. 4.*

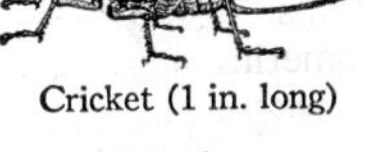
Cricket (1 in. long)

crick et[2] (krik′it), an English outdoor game played by two teams of eleven players each, with ball, bats, and wickets. *n.*

crick et[3] (krik′it), a small, low stool. *n.*

cried (krīd). See **cry.** The baby cried for its mother. *pt. and pp. of cry. 1.*

cri er (krī′ər), 1. person who cries or shouts. 2. officer who shouts out public announcements. *n. 14.*

cries (krīz). See **cry.** *v., n. pl. 4.*

crime (krīm), 1. very wrong deed that is against the law. 2. evil act; sin. *n. 3.*

Cri me a (krī mē′ə), large peninsula extending into the Black Sea from the north. *n. 20.*

crim i nal (krim′i nəl), 1. person who has committed a crime. 2. guilty of wrongdoing. 3. having to do with crime; of crime. *n., adj. 5.*

crimp (krimp), 1. press into small and regular folds; make wavy. The children crimped tissue paper to trim May baskets. The girl crimps her hair by braiding it very tightly. 2. a fold; a wave. 3. act of crimping. *v., n. 12.*

crim son (krim′zən), 1. deep red. 2. turn deep red in color. *n., adj., v. 4.*

cringe (krinj), 1. shrink; crouch in fear; bend down from lack of spirit. The dog cringed at the sight of the whip. 2. act of cringing. *v., n. 14.*

crin kle (kring′kəl), 1. wrinkle; ripple. Crepe paper is crinkled. 2. rustle. Paper crinkles when it is crushed. *v., n. 18.*

crin o line (krin′ə lin), 1. a material used for stiffening garments. A coat collar is usually lined inside with crinoline. 2. petticoat of stiff material to make a dress stand out. 3. hoop skirt. *n. 20.*

Crinoline or hoop skirt

crip ple (krip′əl), 1. person who cannot use his body properly, because of injury or lack; lame person. 2. make a cripple of. 3. damage; weaken. The ship was crippled by the storm. *n., v. 4.*

cri sis (krī′sis), 1. turning point in a disease, toward life or death. 2. deciding event in history. 3. time of danger or anxious waiting. *n., pl. crises* (krī′sēz). *8.*

crisp (krisp), 1. hard and thin; breaking easily when bitten. Dry toast is crisp. Fresh celery is crisp. 2. make crisp; become crisp. 3. fresh; sharp and clear; bracing. The air was cool and crisp. 4. short and decided; as, a crisp manner. 5. curly and wiry; as, crisp hair. *adj., v. 5.*

cri te ri on (krī tēr′i ən), standard of judgment; rule; test. Money is only one criterion of success. *n., pl. criteria* (-tēr′i ə) or *criterions. 15.*

crit ic (krit′ik), 1. person who makes a judgment, especially one concerning books, music, pictures, plays, acting, etc. 2. one who is a critic by profession, who writes his judgments for publication and is paid for it. 3. person who disapproves or finds fault. *n. 5.*

crit i cal (krit′i kəl), 1. inclined to find fault or disapprove; as, a critical disposition. 2. skilled as a critic. 3. coming from one who is skilled as a critic; as, a critical judgment. 4. belonging to the work of a critic; as, critical essays. 5. of a crisis; being important at a time of danger and difficulty; as, the critical moment. His delay was critical. *adj. 8.*

crit i cism (krit′i sizm), 1. making judgments; approving or disapproving. 2. the work of a critic. 3. unfavorable remarks or judgments; finding fault. *n. 7.*

crit i cize or **crit i cise** (krit′i sīz), 1. judge or speak as a critic. 2. blame; find fault with. Do not criticize him until you know all the circumstances. *v. 8.*

cri tique (kri tēk′), 1. a critical essay or review. Some newspapers have critiques of new books. 2. the art of criticism. *n. 16.*

croak (krōk), 1. the deep, hoarse sound made by a frog, a crow, or a raven. 2. make croaks. 3. be always prophesying evil. 4. be dissatisfied; grumble. *n., v. 5.*

Cro a tia (krō ā′shə), district in Yugoslavia. *n.*

cro chet (krō shā′), 1. make wool or cotton thread into sweaters, shawls, and other things in a way somewhat like knitting, but using only one needle, with a hooked end, called a crochet hook. 2. garments, lace, or trimmings which have been crocheted. *v., n. 7.*

Crocheting

crock (krok), a pot or jar made of baked clay. *n. 11.*

crock er y (krok′ər i), earthenware. *n. 11.*

croc o dile (krok′ə dīl), 1. a large animal with a long body, four short legs, a thick skin, and a long tail. See the picture. Crocodiles live in the rivers and marshes of the warm parts of Africa, Asia, Australia, and America. 2. **Crocodile tears** means false or insincere tears because of the story that crocodiles shed tears while eating their victims. *n., adj. 7.*

Crocodile (14 ft. long)

cro cus (krō′kəs), 1. small plant that blooms very early in the spring and has white, yellow, or purple flowers. 2. the flower. *n., pl. crocuses. 10.*

Crocuses

Croe sus (krē′səs), 1. a king in Asia Minor in the 6th century B.C., famous for his riches. 2. very rich man. *n. 17.*

croft (krôft), 1. small enclosed field. 2. very small farm. *n. 16.*

Crom well (krom′wəl), Oliver (1599-1658), an English general, statesman, and Puritan leader. *n. 6.*

crone (krōn), old woman. *n. 16.*

cro ny (krō′ni), very close friend; chum. *n., pl. cronies. 13.*

crook (kru̇k), 1. hook; bend; curve. There is a crook in the stream around the cliff. He crooked his arm. 2. the curved or bent part of anything. 3. a shepherd's hooked staff. 4. person who is not honest in his dealings. *Used in common talk. n., v. 9.*

crook ed (kru̇k′id), 1. not straight; bent; twisted. 2. not honest. *adj. 4.*

crook neck (kru̇k′nek′), kind of squash with a long, curved neck. *n.*

croon (krün), hum, sing, or murmur in a low tone. The mother was crooning to her baby. *v. 14.*

crop (krop), 1. food plants grown or gathered by people for their use. 2. the whole amount (of wheat, corn, or the produce of any plant or tree) which is borne in one season. The potato crop was very small this year. 3. cut or bite off the top of. Sheep crop grass very short. 4. clip or cut short (the tail, ear, hair, edge of book). 5. act or result of cropping; short hair. 6. a baglike swelling of a bird's food passage where food is prepared for digestion. 7. a short whip with a loop instead of a lash. 8. **Crop out** means appear; come to the surface. 9. **Crop up** means turn up unexpectedly. *n., v., cropped, cropping. 2.*

crop per (krop′ər), 1. person or thing that crops. 2. a heavy fall. **Come a cropper** sometimes means suffer a calamity. *Used in common talk. n. 14.*

cro quet (krō kā′), an outdoor game played by knocking balls through arches with mallets. *n. 13.*

cro quette (krō ket′), small mass of meat, fish, vegetables, etc., coated with crumbs and fried. *n.*

Girl playing croquet

cro sier (krō′zhər), the staff carried by or before a bishop or abbot. *n. 16.*

cross (krôs), 1. a stick or post with another across it like a T or an X. Jesus died on the cross. 2. mark with a ×. 3. draw a line across. 4. move from one side to another; go across. 5. lying or going across; crossing. 6. make the sign of a cross. 7. mix breeds of (animals). 8. a mixing of breeds. 9. hinder; oppose. 10. in a bad temper. 11. burden of duty or suffering. *n., v., adj. 1.*

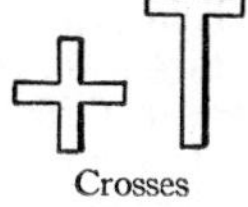
Crosses

cross bar (krôs′bär′), a bar, line, or stripe going crosswise. *n. 15.*

cross bones (krôs′bōnz′), two bones placed crosswise, usually below a skull, to mean death. *n. pl.*

cross bow (krôs′bō′), an old-time weapon for shooting arrows, stones, etc., consisting of a bow fixed across a wooden stock to direct the arrows. *n. 15.*

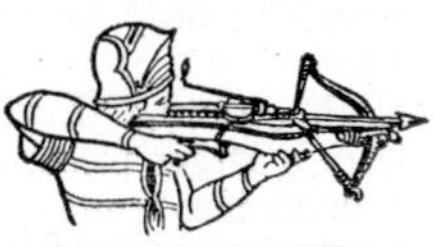
Man using a crossbow

cross bun, a bun marked with a cross, often eaten on Good Friday.

cross cut (krôs′kut′), 1. a cut, course, or path, going across. We took a crosscut through the fields. 2. made for crosswise cutting; as, a crosscut saw. *n., adj. 17.*

cross-ex am ine (krôs′eg zam′in), examine very closely to check a previous examination. A lawyer cross-examines the witnesses of the opposing side to test the truth of their evidence. *v.*

cross-eyed (krôs′īd′), having both eyes turned toward the nose. *adj.*

cross ing (krôs′ing), 1. place where lines, tracks, etc., cross. "Railroad crossing! Stop! Look! Listen!" 2. place at which a street, river, etc., may be crossed. *n.*

cross piece (krôs′pēs′), piece of wood, metal, etc., that goes across. *n.*

cross-pur pose (krôs′pėr′pəs), an opposing or contrary purpose. **Be at cross-purposes** means misunderstand each other's purpose. *n.*

cross-ques tion (krôs′kwes′chən), question closely or severely; cross-examine. *v.*

cross reference, reference from one part of a book, etc., to another part. "See **cry**" under **cried** is a cross reference from **cried** to **cry.**

cross road (krôs′rōd′), 1. road that crosses another. 2. road that connects main roads. 3. A **crossroads** is a place where roads cross. *n. 16.*

cross section, 1. act of cutting anything across. Bananas and tomatoes are sliced by making a series of cross sections. 2. piece cut in this way. 3. sample; small selection of people, things, etc., with the same qualities as the entire group. *19.*

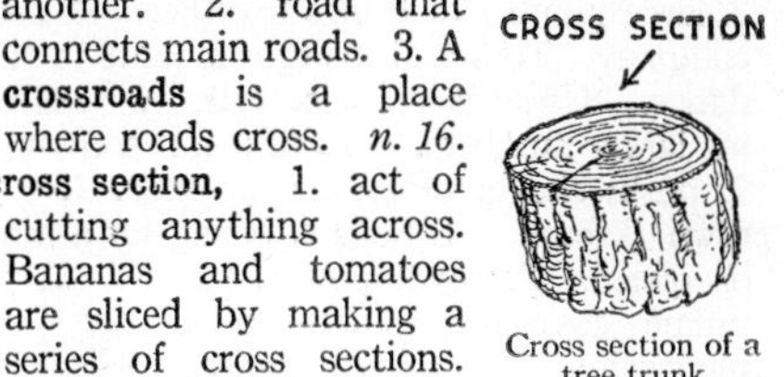

Cross section of a tree trunk

cross trees (krôs′trēz′), two horizontal bars of wood near the top of a mast. *n. pl.*

cross way (krôs′wā′), crossroad. *n. 19.*

cross ways (krôs′wāz′), crosswise. *adv.*

cross wise (krôs′wīz′), 1. across. 2. in the form of a cross. *adv. 12.*

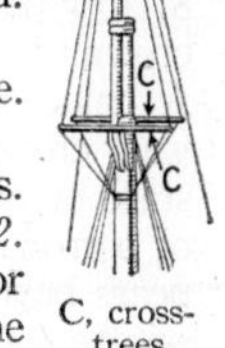

C, crosstrees.

crotch (kroch), forked piece or part. The nest was in the crotch of a tree. *n. 18.*

crotch et (kroch′it), 1. odd fancy; whim. The old man had many crotchets. 2. small hook or hooklike part. *n. 15.*

crouch (krouch), 1. stoop low with bent legs like an animal ready to spring, or a person hiding. 2. shrink down in fear. 3. act of crouching. 4. crouching position. *v., n. 5.*

croup¹ (krüp), a children's disease of the windpipe that causes a cough and difficult breathing. *n. 13.*

croup² (krüp), the rump of a horse. *n.*

crow¹ (krō), 1. the loud cry of a rooster. 2. make this cry. 3. happy sound made by a baby. 4. make this sound. 5. boast; show one's happiness and pride; as, to crow over one's victory, to crow over one's defeated enemy. *n., v., crowed* or *crew* for 2, *crowed, crowing. 2.*

crow[2] (krō), a kind of large black bird with a harsh cry. See the picture just below. *n.*

Crow
(18 to 20 in. long)

crow bar (krō′bär′), a bar of iron used to lift things or pry them apart. *n. 12.*

crowd (kroud), 1. large number of people together. 2. people in general; the masses. 3. large number of things together. 4. set; company. Tom and his crowd went to the dance. *Used in common talk.* 5. collect in large numbers. 6. fill; fill too full. 7. push; shove; press; cram. *n., v. 1.*

crown (kroun), 1. head covering for a king or queen. 2. royal power; supreme governing power in a monarchy. **The Crown** granted lands in America to certain men. 3. of a crown; having to do with a crown; as, crown jewels. 4. wreath for the head. The winner of the race received a crown. 5. sign of victory; reward. 6. to honor; reward. 7. head. 8. top part; as, the crown of a hat, the crown of a mountain. 9. top with a crown. A palace crowns the hill. His hard work was crowned with success. 10. highest state or quality of anything; as, the crown of sorrow. 11. part of a tooth which appears beyond the gum, or an artificial substitute for it. 12. put a crown on. 13. a British coin worth 5 shillings, or about $1.24. *n., adj., v. 1.*

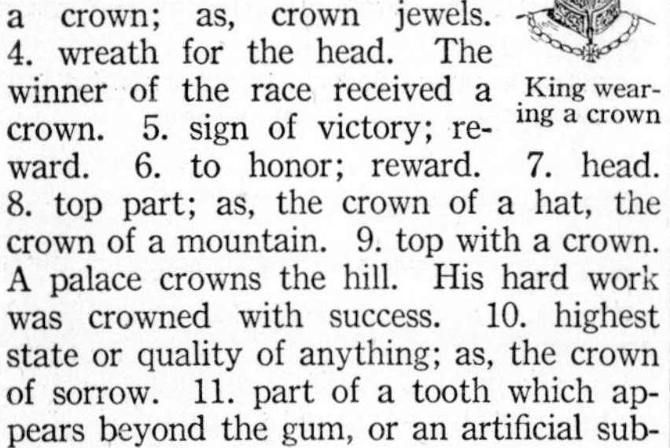

King wearing a crown

crow's-nest (krōz′nest′), a box or barrel for the lookout man on a ship, fastened near the top of a mast. *n.*

cru cial (krü′shəl), very important; critical; decisive. It was a crucial act for Caesar to cross the Rubicon. *adj. 16.*

cru ci ble (krü′si bəl), pot to melt metals in. *n. 13.*

cru ci fix (krü′si fiks), cross with the figure of Christ crucified on it. *n. 10.*

cru ci fix ion (krü′si fik′shən), 1. crucifying. 2. **The Crucifixion** means the putting to death of Christ on the cross. *n. 20.*

cru ci fy (krü′si fī), 1. put to death by nailing the hands and feet to a cross 2. treat severely; torture. *v., crucified, crucifying. 9.*

crude (krüd), 1. in a natural or raw state. Oil, ore, sugar, etc., before being refined and prepared for use are crude. 2. in the rough; lacking finish, grace, taste, or refinement; as, a crude log cabin, a crude chair made out of a box, the crude manners of a boor. *adj. 6.*

cru el (krü′əl), 1. ready to give pain to others or to delight in their suffering; hardhearted; as, a cruel master. 2. showing a cruel nature; as, cruel acts. 3. causing pain or suffering; as, a cruel war, a cruel disease. *adj. 2.*

cru el ty (krü′əl ti), 1. readiness to give pain to others or to delight in their suffering; having a cruel nature. 2. cruel act or acts. *n., pl. cruelties. 4.*

cru et (krü′it), glass bottle to hold vinegar, oil, etc., for the table. *n. 18.*

Cruet

cruise (krüz), 1. sail about from place to place. 2. a voyage for pleasure with no special destination in view; a voyage in search of something whose position is not known exactly. *v., n. 11.*

cruis er (krüz′ər), 1. person or thing that cruises. 2. armed warship of fair speed. An armored cruiser has less armor and greater speed than a battleship. *n. 10.*

crul ler (krul′ər), rich, sweet dough fried brown in deep fat; twisted doughnut. *n. 15.*

crumb (krum), 1. very small piece broken from a larger piece; as, a crumb of bread. 2. break into crumbs. 3. cover with crumbs, for frying or baking. 4. little bit; as, a crumb of comfort. 5. the soft inside part of bread. *n., v. 4.*

crum ble (krum′bəl), break into small pieces or crumbs; fall to bits. *v. 5.*

crum ple (krum′pəl), crush together; wrinkle. He crumpled the letter into a ball. *v. 10.*

crunch (krunch), 1. crush noisily with the teeth. 2. make such a sound. The hard snow crunched under our feet. 3. act or sound of crunching. *v., n 20.*

crup per (krup′ər), 1. a strap attached to the back of a harness and passing under a horse's tail. See the picture of **harness.** 2. the rump of a horse. *n. 17.*

cru sade (krü sād′), 1. any one of the Christian military expeditions between the years 1096 and 1272 to recover the Holy Land from the Mohammedans. 2. war begun by the Church in the name of religion. 3. vigorous movement against a public evil or in favor of some new idea. 4. take part in a crusade. *n., v. 8.*

cru sad er (krü sād′ər), person who takes part in a crusade. The Crusaders of the Middle Ages tried to win back Jerusalem from the Turks. *n. 10.*

cruse (krüz), a jug, pot, or bottle of earthenware. *n.* [*Old use*] *17.*

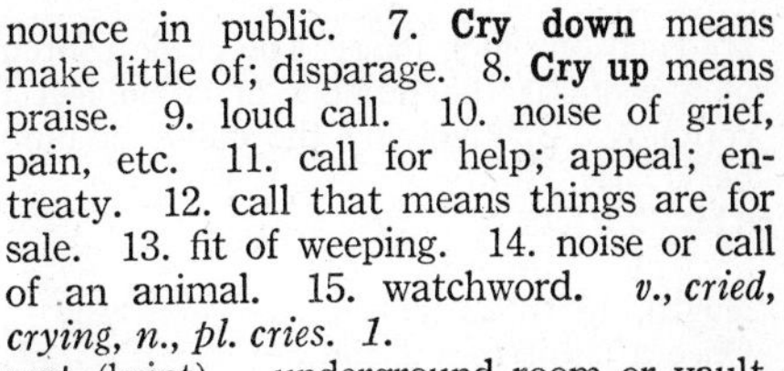
Cruse

crush (krush), 1. squeeze together violently so as to break or bruise. 2. wrinkle or crease by wear or rough handling. 3. break into fine pieces by grinding, pounding, or pressing. 4. violent pressure like grinding or pounding. 5. mass of people crowded close together. 6. subdue; conquer. *v., n. 2.*

Cru soe (krü′sō). Robinson Crusoe was the shipwrecked hero in a book of the same name by Daniel Defoe. *n. 6.*

crust (krust), 1. the hard surface of bread. 2. piece of the crust; any hard, dry piece of bread. 3. rich dough rolled out thin and baked for pies. 4. any hard outside covering; as, the crust of the earth. 5. cover with a crust; form into a crust; become covered with a crust. By the next day the snow had crusted over. *n., v. 4.*

crus ta cean (krus tā′shən), 1. belonging to a numerous class of animals with hard shells, mostly living in water. 2. one of these animals. Crabs, lobsters, and shrimps are crustaceans. *adj., n. 12.*

crust y (krus′ti), 1. of or like a crust; having a crust; as, crusty bread. 2. harsh in manner, speech, etc. *adj., crustier, crustiest.*

crutch (kruch), 1. a support to help a lame person walk. It is a stick with a padded piece at the top to fit under the arm, and often a handhold lower down, so that a person can swing along on the crutches without having to touch the lame foot to the ground. 2. a support; prop; anything like a crutch in shape or use. *n. 5.*

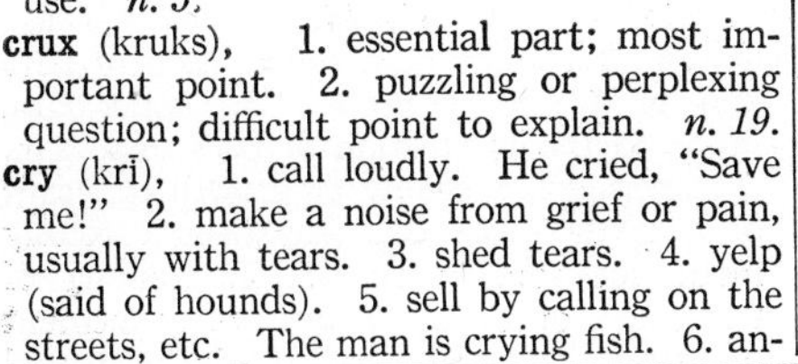
Two kinds of crutches

crux (kruks), 1. essential part; most important point. 2. puzzling or perplexing question; difficult point to explain. *n. 19.*

cry (krī), 1. call loudly. He cried, "Save me!" 2. make a noise from grief or pain, usually with tears. 3. shed tears. 4. yelp (said of hounds). 5. sell by calling on the streets, etc. The man is crying fish. 6. announce in public. 7. **Cry down** means make little of; disparage. 8. **Cry up** means praise. 9. loud call. 10. noise of grief, pain, etc. 11. call for help; appeal; entreaty. 12. call that means things are for sale. 13. fit of weeping. 14. noise or call of an animal. 15. watchword. *v., cried, crying, n., pl. cries. 1.*

crypt (kript), underground room or vault. The crypt beneath a church formerly was used as a burial place. *n. 13.*

cryp tic (krip′tik), hidden; secret; puzzling. The oracle gave the cryptic reply, "You will win if you fight with all your might." *adj.*

crys tal (kris′təl), 1. a clear, transparent mineral that looks like ice. 2. piece of glass cut into form for use or ornament; as, crystals hung around the lights in a great hall. 3. very transparent glass. 4. the glass over the face of a watch. 5. made of crystal; as, crystal ornaments. 6. clear as crystal; as, crystal water. 7. the regularly shaped pieces with angles and flat surfaces into which many substances solidify. *n., adj. 4.*

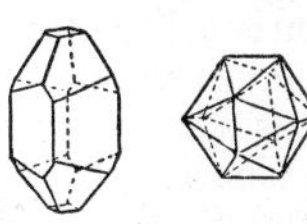
Crystal shapes

crys tal line (kris′təl in), 1. made of crystals. 2. as clear as crystal. *adj. 12.*

crys tal lize (kris′təl īz), 1. form into crystals. Honey crystallizes if kept too long. 2. form into definite shape. His vague ideas crystallized into a clear plan. *v. 11.*

ct., cent.

cu., cubic. *10.*

cub (kub), a young bear, fox, lion, etc. *n. 12.*

Cu ba (kū′bə), the largest island in the West Indies. *n. 4.*

Cu ban (kū′bən), 1. of or pertaining to Cuba. 2. a native or inhabitant of Cuba. *adj., n.*

cube (kūb), 1. a solid with six square faces or sides, all equal. 2. the product when a number is used three times as a factor. 125 is the cube of 5, for 5×5×5=125. 3. use a number three times as a factor. To cube 4 is to get 64: 4×4×4=64. If you cube 10, the result is 1000. 4. make or form into the shape of a cube. *n., v. 5.*

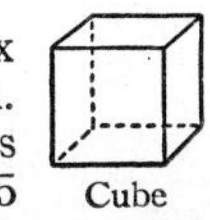
Cube

cu bic (kū′bik), 1. cube-shaped. 2. having length, breadth, and thickness. A cubic inch is the volume of a cube whose edges are each one inch long. The cubic content of a room is the number of cubic feet it contains. 3. involving the cubes of numbers. *adj. 7.*

cu bit (kū′bit), an ancient measure of length, 18 to 22 inches. Once a cubit meant the length of the forearm, from the elbow down. *n. 9.*

cuck oo (ku̇k′ü), 1. a bird which lays its eggs in the nests of other birds, one egg in each nest, instead of building a nest for itself. 2. the call of the cuckoo. *n., pl. cuckoos. 4.*

European cuckoo (about 14 in. long)

cu cum ber (kū′kum bər), 1. a long, fleshy, green vegetable eaten usually in thin slices as a salad, or used to make pickles. 2. the vine it grows on. *n. 8.*

cud (kud), food brought back from the first stomach of cattle or similar animals for a slow second chewing in the mouth. *n. 13.*

cud dle (kud′əl), 1. hold close and lovingly in one's arms or lap. Mary was cuddling the little kittens. 2. lie close and comfortably. *v. 7.*

cudg el (kuj′əl), 1. short, thick stick used as a weapon; a club. 2. beat with a cudgel. 3. **Cudgel one's brains** means try very hard to think. *n., v., cudgeled, cudgeling. 11.*

cue[1] (kū), 1. the last words of an actor's speech in a play which serve as the signal for another actor to come on the stage or to speak. 2. a signal like this to a singer or musician. 3. a hint as to what one should do. *n. 12.*

cue[2] (kū), 1. queue. 2. long stick used for striking the ball in the game of billiards. *n.*

cuff[1] (kuf), 1. a band of some material worn around the wrist. 2. the turned-up fold around the bottom of a sleeve or of a leg of a pair of trousers. *n. 4.*

cuff[2] (kuf), hit with the hand; slap. *v., n.*

cui rass (kwi ras′), 1. piece of armor for the body made of a breastplate and a plate for the back fastened together. 2. the breastplate alone. *n. 15.*

Cuirass (def. 1)

cui ras sier (kwē′rə sēr′), a cavalry soldier wearing a cuirass. *n. 15.*

cui sine (kwi zēn′), 1. style of cooking; cooking; cookery. 2. kitchen. *n.*

cu li nar y (kū′li nãr′i), 1. having to do with cooking. 2. used in cooking. *adj. 15.*

cull (kul), 1. pick out; select. 2. something inferior picked out. Poor fruit, stale vegetables, and animals not up to standard are called culls. *v., n. 8.*

cul mi nate (kul′mi nāt), reach its highest point. The Christmas party at school culminated in the distribution of the presents. *v. 10.*

cul pa ble (kul′pə bəl), deserving blame. The policeman was dismissed for culpable neglect of duty. *adj. 15.*

cul prit (kul′prit), 1. offender; person guilty of a fault or crime. 2. prisoner in court accused of a crime. *n. 11.*

cult (kult), 1. system of religious worship. Buddhism includes many cults. 2. great admiration for a person or thing; worship. *n. 13.*

cul ti vate (kul′ti vāt), 1. prepare and use (land) to raise crops by plowing it, planting seeds, and taking care of the growing plants. 2. help (plants) grow by labor and care. 3. loosen the ground around (growing plants) to kill weeds, etc. 4. improve; develop. It takes time, thought, and effort to cultivate your mind. 5. give time, thought, and effort to; seek better acquaintance with. An artist cultivates art. She cultivated people who could help her. *v. 3.*

cul ti va tion (kul′ti vā′shən), 1. preparing land and growing crops by plowing, planting, and necessary care. 2. giving time and thought to improving and developing (the body, mind, or manners). 3. culture; the result of improvement or growth through education and experience. *n. 7.*

cul ti va tor (kul′ti vā′tər), 1. person or thing that cultivates. 2. an implement or tool for loosening the ground and destroying weeds. A cultivator is pulled between rows of growing plants. *n. 8.*

cul tur al (kul′chər əl), having to do with culture. Literature, art, and music are cultural studies. *adj. 14.*

cul ture (kul′chər), 1. preparation of land and producing of crops. 2. proper care given to the production of bees, fish, silk, or germs. 3. a colony or growth of germs of a given kind, that has been carefully made for some purpose. 4. training of the mind or of the body. 5. refinement of taste; the result of good education and surroundings. 6. The civilization of a given race or nation at a given time, its customs, its arts, and its conveniences, may be called its culture. *n. 6.*

cul tured (kul′chərd), cultivated; refined. *adj.*

cul vert (kul′vərt), a drain crossing under a road or railroad. *n. 18.*

Culvert

cum ber (kum′bər), hinder; burden. The lumberman's heavy boots cumbered him in walking. Household cares cumber the busy mother. *v. 15.*

cum ber some (kum′bər səm), hard to manage; unwieldy; clumsy; burdensome; troublesome. Old-time armor was cumbersome. *adj. 15.*

Cumulus cloud

cum brous (kum′brəs), cumbersome. *adj. 12.*

cu mu la tive (kū′mū lā′tiv), increasing by additions. *adj. 16.*

cu mu lus (kū′mū ləs), 1. cloud made up of rounded heaps with a flat bottom. See the picture. 2. heap. *n.*

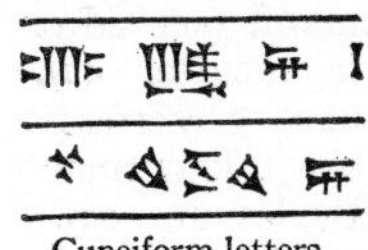
Cuneiform letters

cu ne i form (kū nē′i fôrm), 1. wedge-shaped. 2. wedge-shaped letters used in writing in ancient Babylonia, Assyria, Persia, etc. *adj., n. 19.*

cun ning (kun′ing), 1. skillful; clever in doing. With cunning hand he shaped the little pieces. 2. clever in deceit; sly; as, a cunning fox, a cunning villain. 3. skillful or sly ways of getting what one needs or wants, or of escaping one's enemies. Some animals have a great deal of cunning. 4. skill. *Old use.* 5. pretty and dear; attractive. Kittens and babies are cunning. *adj., n. 3.*

cup (kup), 1. dish to drink from. Most cups have handles. 2. as much as a cup holds. She drank a cup of milk. 3. something shaped like a cup; as, the cup of a flower. 4. shape like a cup; as, to cup one's hands to catch a ball. 5. something to endure or experience. 6. **In one's cups** means partly or wholly drunk. *n., v., cupped, cupping. 1.*

cup bear er (kup′bãr′ər), person who fills and passes around the cups in which drinks are served. *n. 15.*

cup board (kub′ərd), closet or cabinet with shelves for dishes and food supplies. *n. 5.*

Cu pid (kū′pid), 1. the Roman god of love, son of Venus. Cupid is usually represented as a winged boy with bow and arrows. 2. A **cupid** is a winged baby used as a symbol of love; as, cupids on a valentine. *n. 6.*

cu pid i ty (kū pid′i ti), greed. *n. 20.*

cu po la (kū′pə lə), 1. rounded dome on a roof. 2. a small dome or tower on a roof. *n. 16.*

CUPOLA

cur (kėr), 1. worthless dog of mixed breed. 2. an ill-bred, cowardly fellow. *n. 10.*

cu rate (kūr′it), an assistant clergyman; helper of a pastor, rector, or vicar. *n. 11.*

cu ra tor (kū rā′tər), person in charge. The curator of an art museum knows much about pictures. *n. 16.*

curb (kėrb), 1. a chain or a strap attached to a horse's bit and passing under the lower jaw, used as a check. 2. a check or restraint. 3. hold in check; restrain. 4. enclosing border of wood or stone along the edge of a pavement, or around the top of a well. *n., v. 4.*

curd (kėrd), 1. the thick part of milk that separates from the watery part when the milk sours. Cheese is made from curds. 2. form into curds. *n., v. 9.*

cur dle (kėr′dəl), 1. form into curds. Milk curdles when kept too long. 2. **Curdle the blood** means horrify; terrify. The horrors of war curdle one's blood. *v. 10.*

cure (kūr), 1. bring back to health; make well; as, to cure a child of a cold. 2. get rid of; as, to cure a cold, to cure a bad habit. 3. remedy; means of removing or relieving disease or any bad condition; as, a cure for sore eyes, a cure for laziness. 4. a medicine or treatment that cures; as, a rest cure. 5. preserve (bacon or other meat) by drying or salting. 6. spiritual charge; religious oversight. *v., n. 2.*

cu ré (kū rā′), a French word meaning parish priest. *n.*

cur few (kėr′fū), 1. the ringing of a bell at a fixed hour in the evening as a signal to put out fires and lights. 2. the ringing of a bell at a fixed hour in the evening as a signal for children to leave the streets. 3. the time of ringing. 4. the bell rung. *n. 16.*

cu ri o (kūr′i ō), article valued as a curiosity. The traveler brought back curios from many lands. *n., pl. curios. 14.*

cu ri os i ty (kūr′i os′i ti), 1. eager desire to know. Her curiosity made her open the forbidden door. 2. a strange, rare object. *n., pl. curiosities. 5.*

cu ri ous (kūr′i əs), 1. eager to know. Small children are very curious, and ask many questions. 2. strange; odd; unusual. *adj. 3.*

curl (kėrl), 1. twist into rings. Mother curls Mary's hair. Helen's hair curls naturally. 2. curve or twist out of shape. Paper curls up when it burns. You can curl up in a big chair. 3. rise in rings. Smoke curls slowly from the chimney. 4. a curled lock of hair. 5. anything curled or bent into a curve. A carpenter's shavings are curls. *v., n. 2.*

cur lew (kėr′lü), a wading bird with a long, thin bill. *n., pl. curlews* or *curlew. 18.*

Curlew (from 1 to 2 ft. long)

curl y (kėr′li), 1. curling; as, curly hair. 2. having curls or curly hair; as, a curly head. *adj., curlier, curliest. 11.*

cur rant (kėr′ənt), 1. a small raisin without seeds made from grapes grown along the eastern shores of the Mediterranean Sea. Currants are much used in puddings, cakes, and buns. 2. a sour red, white, or black berry, which is used for jelly and preserves; the bush it grows on. *n. 6.*

Currants (def. 2)

cur ren cy (kėr′ən si), 1. money in actual use in a country; as, paper currency, gold currency. 2. circulation; passing from person to person; as, the currency of a rumor. 3. general acceptance; prevalence. *n., pl. currencies. 7.*

cur rent (kėr′ənt), 1. flow of water, air, or any liquid; running stream; draft. 2. flow of electricity through a wire, etc. 3. the course or movement (of events or of opinions). Newspapers influence the current of thought. 4. of the present time. The current issue of a magazine is the latest one issued. 5. in general use; passing from person to person; as, current money, current jokes, current opinion. *n., adj. 2.*

cur rent ly (kėr′ənt li), 1. at the present time; now. 2. generally; commonly. *adv.*

cur ric u lum (kə rik′ū ləm), a course of study. The curriculum in Grade 6 includes arithmetic, geography, history, reading, and spelling. *n. 14.*

cur ry[1] (kėr′i), 1. rub and clean (a horse) with a brush or scraper. 2. prepare (tanned leather) for use by soaking, scraping, beating, coloring, etc. 3. **Curry favor** means seek favor in ways that a self-respecting person would not use. *v., curried, currying. 18.*

cur ry[2] (kėr′i), 1. a peppery sauce or powder. 2. food flavored with it. 3. prepare (food) with curry. *n., pl. curries, v., curried, currying.*

curse (kėrs), 1. ask God to bring evil or harm on. He cursed his enemy solemnly. 2. the words that a person says when he asks God to curse someone or something. 3. bring evil or harm on; torment; as, cursed with blindness. He is cursed with a bad temper. 4. trouble; harm. My quick temper has been a curse to me all my life. 5. swear; say bad words. 6. words used in swearing. *v., n. 2.*

curs ed (kėr′sid or kėrst), damned; deserving a curse. *adj.*

cur so ry (kėr′sə ri), hasty; superficial. Joe spent four minutes in a cursory study of the lesson. *adj. 16.*

curt (kėrt), short; rudely brief; abrupt. Mr. Smith's curt way of speaking makes him seem impolite. *adj. 13.*

cur tail (kėr tāl′), cut short; cut off part of. John's father curtailed his allowance. *v. 9.*

cur tain (kėr′tən), 1. cloth hung at windows or in doors for protection or ornament. 2. a hanging screen which separates the stage of a theater from the part where the audience is. 3. provide with a curtain; hide by a curtain. *n., v. 2.*

Lady curtsying

curt sey (kėrt′si), curtsy. *n., pl. curtseys, v., curtseyed, curtseying.*

curt sy (kėrt′si), 1. bow of respect or greeting made by bending the knees and lowering the body slightly. 2. make a curtsy. *n., pl. curtsies, v., curtsied, curtsying. 16.*

cur va ture (kėr′və chər), curving. *n. 11.*

curve (kėrv), 1. line that has no straight

part. 2. bend so as to form a line that has no straight part. *n., v. 3.*

cur vet (kėr′vet for 1, kėr vet′ for 2 and 3), 1. a leap of a horse in which the forelegs are first raised and then the hind legs, so that, for a second, all legs are off the ground at once. 2. to leap in this way. 3. make (a horse) do this. *n., v., curvetted, curvetting. 15.*

cush ion (ku̇sh′ən), 1. a soft pillow or pad for a couch, chair, etc. 2. anything that makes a soft place; as, a cushion of moss. 3. supply with a cushion. *n., v. 3.*

cusp (kusp), point; pointed end. *n. 20.*

cus pi dor (kus′pi dôr), container to spit into. *n. 20.*

cus tard (kus′tərd), a baked or boiled mixture of eggs, milk, and sugar. Custard is used as a dessert or as a food for sick persons. *n. 9.*

cus to di an (kus tō′di ən), guardian; keeper. *n. 14.*

cus to dy (kus′tə di), 1. keeping; care. Parents have the custody of their young children. 2. **In custody** means in prison or in the care of the police. *n. 7.*

cus tom (kus′təm), 1. any usual action. It was his custom to rise early. 2. a long-established habit having the force of law. The social customs of many countries differ from ours. 3. business support by being a customer. That store would like to have your custom. 4. made to order; making to order; as, custom clothes, a custom tailor. 5. **Customs** are taxes paid to the government on goods brought in from foreign countries. *n., adj. 2.*

cus tom ar y (kus′təm ãr′i), usual. *adj. 6.*

cus tom er (kus′təm ər), one who buys. *n. 3.*

custom house, a government building, usually at a seaport, where customs are collected. *12.*

cut (kut), 1. a stroke or blow with a knife or any tool that has a sharp edge. 2. sharp stroke or blow. 3. opening made by a knife or sharp-edged tool. 4. make such an opening in; divide or wound with a sharp-edged tool. 5. strike sharply; hurt. 6. refuse to recognize socially. *Used in common talk.* 7. an action or speech that hurts the feelings. 8. make by cutting. 9. piece that has been cut off or cut out; as, a cut of meat. 10. place that has been made by cutting. The train went through a deep cut. 11. reduce. You must cut expenses this month. 12. reduction. 13. A **short cut** is a quicker way. 14. go by a short cut; go. 15. cross; divide by crossing. 16. be cut. Cheese cuts easily. 17. an engraved block or plate used for printing; picture made from such a block. 18. the style or fashion of anything; as, the cut of a coat. 19. **Cut teeth** means have teeth grow through the gums. *n., v., cut, cutting. 1.*

cute (kūt), 1. pretty and dear. 2. clever; shrewd; cunning. *adj.* [*Used in common talk*] *9.*

cu ti cle (kū′ti kəl), outer skin. The cuticle about the fingernails tends to become hard. *n. 11.*

cut lass (kut′ləs), a short, heavy, slightly curved sword. *n. 12.*

Cutlass

cut ler (kut′lər), person who makes, sells, or repairs knives and other cutting instruments. *n. 13.*

cut ler y (kut′lər i), 1. knives, scissors, and other cutting instruments. 2. knives, forks, spoons, etc., for table use. 3. the business of a cutler. *n. 10.*

cut let (kut′lit), 1. slice of meat for broiling or frying, especially of veal or mutton. 2. chopped meat shaped in flat cakes and fried. *n. 19.*

Cutter (def. 3)

cut ter (kut′ər), 1. person who cuts; as, a garment cutter, a wood cutter. 2. machine made to cut; as, a meat cutter, a bread cutter. 3. small sleigh. 4. small sailboat with one mast. 5. boat belonging to a warship, used for carrying supplies and passengers to and from shore. 6. a small, armed ship used by the coast guard. *n. 5.*

cut throat (kut′thrōt′), 1. murderer. 2. murderous. *n., adj. 16.*

cut ting (kut′ing), 1. a small shoot cut from a plant to grow a new plant. 2. a newspaper clipping. 3. an excavation through high ground. 4. that cuts. 5. hurting the feelings. *n., adj.*

cut tle fish (kut′əl fish′), an animal that has ten sucker-bearing arms and squirts out a black fluid. *n., pl. cuttlefishes* or *cuttlefish.*

Cuttlefish

cut worm (kut′wėrm′), caterpillar that

cuts off the stalks of young plants near or below the ground. *n.*

cwt., hundredweight.

-cy, suffix meaning:—
1. office, position, or rank of; as in captaincy.
2. quality, state, condition, or fact of being; as in bankruptcy.

cy cle (sī′kəl), 1. any period of time or complete process of growth or action which repeats itself in the same order. The seasons of the year—spring, summer, autumn, and winter—make a cycle. 2. complete set or series. 3. all the stories or legends told about a certain hero or event. There is a cycle of stories about the adventures of King Arthur and his knights. 4. a long period of time. 5. ride a bicycle or tricycle. *n., v. 9.*

cy clic (sī′klik), 1. of a cycle. 2. moving in cycles; coming in cycles. *adj. 17.*

cy clist (sī′klist), rider of a bicycle or tricycle. *n. 19.*

cy clone (sī′klōn), 1. very violent windstorm. 2. a storm moving around and toward a center of low pressure, which also moves. *n. 14.*

cy clon ic (sī klon′ik), 1. of a cyclone. 2. like a cyclone. *adj. 20.*

cy clo pe di a or **cy clo pae di a** (sī′klō pē′di ə), a book or books with articles about many branches of knowledge; encyclopedia. *n. 17.*

Cy clops (sī′klops), one-eyed giant. *n., pl. Cyclopes* (sī klō′pēz). *14.*

cyg net (sig′nit), a young swan. *n. 17.*

cyl in der (sil′in dər), a hollow or solid body shaped like a roller. *n. 5.*

Cylinder

cy lin dri cal (si lin′dri kəl), shaped like a cylinder. Silos, candles, and water pipes are usually cylindrical. *adj. 13.*

cym bal (sim′bəl), one of a pair of brass plates which are struck together to make a ringing sound. *n. 8.*

Cymbals

cyn ic (sin′ik), 1. person inclined to doubt the goodness of human motives and to display this doubt by sneers and sarcasm. 2. cynical. *n., adj. 10.*

cyn i cal (sin′i kəl), 1. doubting the worth of life. 2. sneering or sarcastic. *adj. 9.*

cyn i cism (sin′i sizm), 1. cynical disposition. 2. cynical remark. *n. 13.*

cy no sure (sī′nə shür), 1. the group of stars called the Little Dipper. Because the North Star is in the cynosure, it was formerly used as a guide by sailors. 2. something used for guidance or direction. 3. a center of attraction, interest, or attention. *n. 20.*

cy press (sī′prəs), 1. an evergreen tree with hard wood and dark leaves. 2. the wood of this tree. Cypress is much used for doors. *n. 6.*

Cy prus (sī′prəs), an island in the Mediterranean, south of Turkey. *n. 11.*

Cy rus (sī′rəs). Cyrus the Great (died 529 B.C.) was king of Persia and founder of its empire. *n. 8.*

cyst (sist), a small sac in the body containing diseased matter. *n. 14.*

czar (zär), emperor. When Russia had an emperor, his title was czar. *n. 6.*

cza ri na (zä rē′nə), the wife of a czar; Russian empress. *n.*

Czech (chek), 1. a member of a branch of the Slavs, including Bohemians, Moravians, and Slovaks. 2. Bohemian. *n., adj. 17.*

Czech o-Slo va ki a or **Czech o slo va ki a** (chek′ō slō vä′ki ə), a former country in central Europe, now under German control. *n. 20.*

D

D, d (dē), 1. fourth letter of the alphabet. There are two d's in dead. 2. Roman numeral for 500. *n., pl. D's, d's.*

d., English penny; pence. 2d = 4 cents.

dab (dab), 1. touch lightly; pat with something soft or moist; tap; peck. The girl dabbed at her face with a powder puff. 2. a quick, light blow; a pat; a tap; a peck. 3. a small soft or moist mass. The maid scraped the little dabs of butter from the plates. *v., dabbed, dabbing, n. 13.*

dab ble (dab′əl), 1. wet by dabs; put in and out of water or mud; splash. 2. play. 3. **Dabble at** means do superficially, not thoroughly; as, to dabble at painting, to dabble in stocks. *v. 9.*

dace (dās), a small fresh-water fish. *n., pl. daces* or *dace. 17.*

dachs hund (däks′hůnt′), a small hound with a long body and very short legs. See the picture. *n.*

Dachshund (about 8 in. high at the shoulder)

dad (dad), father. *n.* [*Used familiarly*] *12.*

dad dy (dad′i), father. *n., pl. daddies.* [*Used familiarly*] *9.*

dad dy-long legs (dad′i lông′legz′), animal that looks much like a spider, but does not bite. It has a small body and long, thin legs. *n., pl. daddy-longlegs.*

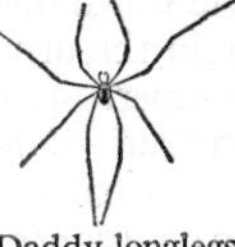
Daddy-longlegs

daf fo dil (daf′ə dil), a yellow spring flower with long, slender leaves. See the picture in the next column. *n. 9.*

daft (daft), 1. silly; foolish. 2. crazy; insane. *adj. 19.*

dag ger (dag′ər), a weapon for stabbing, with a short, pointed blade. *n. 6.*

Dagger

Da gon (dā′gon), chief god of the Philistines, half man and half fish. Judges 16:23. *n. 13.*

dahl ia (dal′yə), a plant with showy flowers of many colors and varieties. *n. 10.*

Dahlia

dai ly (dā′li), 1. done, happening, or appearing every day; as, a daily paper, a daily visit. 2. newspaper printed every day. 3. every day; day by day. *adj., n., pl. dailies, adv. 2.*

dain ti ness (dān′ti nis), being fresh, delicate, and pretty; fineness of taste. *n.*

dain ty (dān′ti), 1. fresh, delicate, and pretty. The violet is a dainty spring flower. 2. delicate in tastes and feeling. She is dainty about her eating. 3. good to eat. 4. choice bit of food; something very pleasing to eat. *adj., daintier, daintiest, n., pl. dainties. 4.*

dair y (dãr′i), 1. a room or building where milk and cream are kept and made into butter and cheese. 2. farm where milk and cream are produced and butter and cheese made. 3. store or company that sells milk, cream, butter, and cheese. *n., pl. dairies. 3.*

dair y maid (dãr′i mād′), girl or woman who works in a dairy. *n.*

dair y man (dãr′i mən), 1. owner or manager of a dairy. 2. man who works in a dairy. *n., pl. dairymen. 17.*

da is (dā′is), raised platform at the end of a hall or large room, for a throne, seats of honor, a lecture desk, etc. *n. 20.*

Dais for a throne

dai sy (dā′zi), a wild flower having a yellow center from which grow rays of white, pink, or yellow. See the picture just below. *n., pl. daisies. 3.*

Daisy

Da kar (dä kär′), French seaport in western Africa. *n.*

Da ko ta (də kō′tə), North Dakota or South Dakota. *n. 8.*

dale (dāl), valley. *n. 5.*

Dal las (dal′əs), a city in northeastern Texas. *n. 18.*

dal li ance (dal′i əns), dallying; trifling; caressing play. *n. 16.*

dally (dal′i), 1. act in a playful manner. The soft breeze dallies with the flowers. 2. flirt with danger, temptation, etc.; to trifle. He dallied with the offer for days but finally refused it. 3. be idle; loiter. *v., dallied, dallying. 10.*

dam[1] (dam), 1. wall built to hold back the water of a stream or any flowing water. 2. provide with a dam; hold back or block up with anything; as. to dam a stream. *n., v., dammed, damming. 4.*

Dam

dam[2] (dam), a mother animal in sheep, cattle, horses, and other four-footed animals. *n.*

Daffodil (12 to 18 in. high)

dam age (dam′ij), 1. a harm or injury that lessens value or usefulness. The accident did very little damage to either car. 2. to harm or injure so as to lessen value or usefulness. I damaged my sweater in football practice today. 3. **Damages** means money claimed by law, or paid to make up for harm done to a person or to his property. The man who was run over asked for $5000 damages. *n., v. 3.*

Da mas cus (də mas′kəs), an ancient city in southern Syria. Damascus was famous for its metalwork and its fabrics. *n. 10.*

dam ask (dam′əsk), 1. of or named from the city of Damascus; as, damask steel, damask silk or linen. 2. silk woven with an elaborate pattern; as, hangings of damask. 3. linen with woven designs. Spotless damask covered the table. 4. rose color; as, damask cheeks. 5. steel with a wavy pattern or markings. *adj., n. 11.*

dame (dām), 1. lady, especially in titles; as, Dame Fortune. 2. old woman. *n. 3.*

damn (dam), 1. declare (something) to be bad; condemn. 2. doom to hell. 3. say "damn"; swear. 4. a curse. *v., n. 5.*

dam na ble (dam′nə bəl), detestable; abominable; outrageous. *adj. 13.*

dam na tion (dam nā′shən), 1. damning; being damned. 2. a curse. *n. 10.*

Da mon (dā′mən), one of a famous pair of friends. Pythias was the other. *n. 20.*

damp (damp), 1. slightly wet; moist. 2. moisture. 3. make slightly wet. 4. to dull; check; put out. 5. a chill; a check. Mary's illness cast a damp over the party. 6. gas that gathers in mines. *adj., n., v. 3.*

damp en (dam′pən), 1. make damp; become damp. 2. depress; cast a chill over. The bad news dampened our spirits. *v. 20.*

damp er (dam′pər), 1. person or thing that discourages or checks. 2. a movable plate to control the draft in a stove or furnace. *n. 14.*

dam sel (dam′zəl), maiden. *n. 5.*

dam son (dam′zən), 1. a small, dark-purple plum. 2. the tree it grows on. *n. 19.*

Dan (dan), 1. a boy's name. 2. city in northern Palestine. 3. **From Dan to Beersheba** means from one end of a place to the other. *n. 3.*

dance (dans), 1. move in time with music. Helen can dance very well. 2. movement in time with music. 3. a party where people dance. 4. one round of dancing. 5. piece of music for dancing. 6. jump up and down; move in a lively way. See that boat dancing on the water. 7. do; perform. They danced a waltz. **Dance attendance** means attend often and with much care. *v., n. 1.*

Children dancing

danc er (dan′sər), 1. person who dances. 2. person who dances for pay. *n. 7.*

dan de li on (dan′di lī′ən), a common weed with deeply notched leaves and bright-yellow flowers that bloom in the spring. *n. 7.*

Dandelion

dan dle (dan′dəl), 1. move (a child) up and down on the knees or in the arms. 2. pet; pamper. *v. 10.*

dan druff (dan′drəf), small scales that form on the scalp. *n. 14.*

dan dy (dan′di), 1. man very careful of his dress and appearance. 2. excellent or first-rate thing. *Slang.* 3. excellent; first-rate. *Slang. n., pl. dandies, adj. 9.*

Dane (dān), 1. person living in Denmark; person born in Denmark. 2. A **Great Dane** is a large, strong, short-haired dog. *n. 8.*

dan ger (dān′jər), 1. chance of harm; nearness to harm; risk; peril. A soldier's life is full of danger. 2. thing that may cause harm. *n. 2.*

dan ger ous (dān′jər əs), likely to cause harm; not safe. *adj. 2.*

dan gle (dang′gəl), 1. hang loosely and sway. The curtain cord dangles. 2. hold or carry (a thing) so that it sways loosely. The nurse dangled the toys in front of the baby. 3. hang about; follow. Several dogs dangled near the butcher's truck. *v. 6.*

Dan iel (dan′yəl), 1. a man in the Bible who showed great faith in God. 2. the book in the Old Testament that tells about him. *n. 4.*

Dan ish (dān′ish), 1. of or having to do with the Danes, their country, or their language. 2. language of the Danes. *adj., n. 8.*

dank (dangk), moist; wet; unpleasantly damp. The cave was dark, dank, and chilly. *adj. 12.*

Dan te (dan′ti), Italy's greatest poet (1265-1321). *n. 8.*

Dan ube (dan′ūb), river flowing from southwestern Germany into the Black Sea. *n. 8.*

Dan zig (dant′sig), seaport on the Baltic Sea. It was formerly a free city, but is now under German control. *n. 20.*

Daph ne (daf′ni), a nymph pursued by Apollo, whom she escaped by being changed into a laurel tree. *n. 16.*

dap per (dap′ər), 1. neat; trim. 2. small and active. *adj. 15.*

dap ple (dap′əl), 1. spotted; as, a dapple horse. 2. mark or become marked with spots. *adj., v. 10.*

Dar da nelles (där′də nelz′), a strait connecting the Sea of Marmara with the Aegean Sea. In ancient times it was called the Hellespont. *n.*

dare (dãr), 1. be bold; be bold enough. He does not dare to jump from that wall. 2. have courage to try; be bold enough for. 3. challenge. I dare you to jump. 4. a challenge. 5. **I dare say** sometimes means probably or maybe. *v., dared* or *durst, dared, daring, n. 1.*

dare dev il (dãr′dev′əl), 1. reckless person. 2. recklessly daring. *n., adj.*

Dar i en (dãr′i en), an old name for the Isthmus of Panama. *n. 19.*

dar ing (dãr′ing), 1. boldness; courage to take risks. 2. bold; fearless. *n., adj. 6.*

Da ri us I (də rī′əs), a famous king of Persia (558?-486? B.C.). *n. 10.*

dark (därk). A night without a moon is dark. She has dark-brown eyes. Rain and clouds make a dark day. Do not be afraid of the dark. It was a dark secret. I am in the dark about his plan. *adj., n. 1.*

dark en (där′kən), make dark; become dark. *v. 4.*

dark ling (därk′ling), 1. in the dark. 2. dark. *adv., adj. 15.*

dark ly (därk′li), 1. in a dark manner. 2. not clearly. *adv.*

dark ness (därk′nis), being dark; lack of light. *n. 2.*

dark some (därk′səm), 1. dark. 2. gloomy. *adj. 13.*

dark y or **dark ey** (där′ki), a Negro. *n., pl. darkies, darkeys.* [*Used in common talk*]

dar ling (där′ling), 1. person very dear to another; person much loved. 2. very dear; much loved. *n., adj. 3.*

darn (därn), 1. mend with rows of stitches back and forth. 2. act of darning. 3. place so mended. *v., n. 6.*

dar nel (där′nəl), weed with poisonous seeds that looks somewhat like rye. Darnel often grows in grainfields. *n. 20.*

dart (därt), 1. a slender, pointed weapon, thrown by the hand. 2. throw suddenly and rapidly. The savages darted spears at the lion. 3. a sudden, swift movement. 4. move swiftly. The deer saw us and darted away. 5. send suddenly. Ella darted an angry glance at her sister. *n., v. 3.*

Dart

Dar win (där′win), Charles, a famous English scientist (1809-1882). *n. 9.*

dash (dash), 1. throw. We dashed water over him. 2. splash. She dashed some paint on it. 3. rush. They dashed by in a car. 4. throw and break. He dashed the bowl to bits on a rock. 5. **Dash off** sometimes means do quickly. 6. ruin. Our hopes were dashed. 7. a short race; as, the 100-yard dash. 8. energy; spirit. 9. a mark (—) used in writing or printing. 10. small amount. Put in just a dash of pepper. *v., n. 2.*

dash ing (dash′ing), 1. full of energy; lively. 2. showy. *adj. 17.*

das tard (das′tərd), 1. a mean coward; sneak. 2. cowardly and mean. *n., adj. 12.*

das tard ly (das′tərd li), cowardly. *adj.*

da ta (dā′tə or dat′ə), facts; facts known or granted; information. Names, ages, and other data about the class are written in the teacher's classbook. *n. pl. of* **datum.** *10.*

date[1] (dāt), 1. time; a statement of a time. 1492 is the date of the discovery of America by Columbus. 2. mark the time of; put a date on. Please date your letter. 3. find out the date of; give a date to. 4. be dated; have a date on it. 5. period of time. At that date there were no airplanes. **Out of date** means out of fashion. **Up to date** means (1) in fashion. (2) up to the present time. 6. belong to a certain period of time; have its origin. The oldest house in town dates from the 18th century. *n., v. 1.*

date[2] (dāt), 1. the sweet fruit of a kind of palm tree. 2. the tree that bears it. *n.*

Date palm (40 to 80 ft. high)

date less (dāt′lis), 1. without a date; not dated. 2. endless. *adj. 19.*

da tive (dā′tiv), 1. showing the indirect object of a verb. In "Give me the book," *me* is in the dative case. 2. the dative case. 3. word in this case. *adj., n. 18.*

da tum (dā′təm or dat′əm), fact; thing known or admitted; fact from which conclusions may be drawn. *n., pl. data* (dā′tə or dat′ə). *14.*

daub (dôb), 1. coat or cover with plaster, clay, mud, etc.; apply (greasy or sticky stuff). 2. anything daubed on. 3. to soil; make dirty; stain. You have daubed your skirt with mud. 4. paint unskillfully. 5. a picture badly painted. *v., n. 11.*

daugh ter (dô′tər), 1. A girl is the daughter of her father and mother. 2. female descendant; as, daughter of Eve. 3. girl or woman attached to a country, cause, etc., as a child is to its parents. *n. 1.*

daugh ter-in-law (dô′tər in lô′), the wife of one's son. *n., pl. daughters-in-law. 20.*

daugh ter ly (dô′tər li), 1. of a daughter. 2. like that of a daughter. 3. proper for a daughter. *adj.*

daunt (dônt), frighten; discourage. Danger did not daunt the hero. *v. 8.*

daunt less (dônt′lis), brave; not to be frightened or discouraged; as, a dauntless aviator. *adj. 8.*

dau phin (dô′fin), the title of the oldest son of the king of France, from 1349 to 1830. *n. 12.*

dav en port (dav′ən pōrt), a long couch with back and ends. Some davenports can be made into beds. *n. 12.*

Davenport

Da vid (dā′vid), the second king of Israel, famous as an organizer and as a poet. David wrote many of the Psalms in the Bible. *n. 3.*

Da vis (dā′vis), Jefferson (1808-1889), the president of the Confederate States of America at the time of the Civil War. *n. 9.*

dav it (dav′it), 1. one of a pair of arms for lowering a small boat. See the picture. 2. a crane for raising or lowering the anchor of a boat. *n. 20.*

Davits

Da vy Jones (dā′vi jōnz′), the spirit of the sea; the sailor's devil. **Go to Davy Jones's locker** means perish in the ocean.

daw (dô), jackdaw, a bird like a crow. *n. 16.*

daw dle (dô′dəl), waste time; idle; loiter. *v. 15.*

dawn (dôn), 1. the break of day; the first light in the east. 2. beginning; as, before the dawn of history. 3. grow bright or clear. Day dawns in the east. 4. grow clear to the eye or mind. The ocean dawned on our view. 5. begin; appear. A new era is dawning. *n., v. 2.*

day (dā), 1. the time of light between sunrise and sunset. 2. Sometimes the 24 hours of day and night is called a day. 3. the hours given to work; the working day. An eight-hour day is common. 4. time; period; as, the present day. 5. **Win the day** means win the game, battle, or contest. *n. 1.*

day break (dā′brāk′), dawn; the first light of day. *n. 8.*

day dream (dā′drēm′), 1. dreamy thinking of pleasant things; reverie. 2. to think dreamily of pleasant things. *n., v.*

day light (dā′līt′), 1. the light of day. Lamplight is not so good for the eyes as daylight. 2. dawn; daybreak. He was up at daylight. 3. In **daylight-saving time** clocks are set forward one hour in the spring and back one hour in the fall. *n. 3.*

day spring (dā′spring′), dawn; the first light of day. *n. 14.*

day time (dā′tīm′), the time when it is day and not night. Baby sleeps even in the daytime. *n. 5.*

Day ton (dā′tən), a city in southwestern Ohio. *n. 18.*

daze (dāz), 1. confuse; deaden in the mind; cause to feel stupid. A blow on the head dazed him so that he could not find his way home. The child was dazed by the sudden noise and bright lights. 2. dazed condition. He was in a daze and could not understand what was happening. *v., n. 8.*

daz zle (daz′əl), 1. hurt (the eyes) with too bright light, or quick-moving lights. To look straight at the sun dazzles the eyes. 2. overcome the sight or the mind of with anything very bright. The poor little girl was dazzled by the richness of her new home. 3. a dazzling, bewildering brightness; as, the dazzle of powerful electric lights. *v., n. 5.*

D.C., District of Columbia.

de or **De** (də), a French word meaning of or from. *prep. 13.*

de-, prefix meaning:—

1. do the opposite of; as in decamp, deforest, demobilize.
2. down; as in depress, descend.
3. In some words de- has special meanings.

dea con (dē′kən), 1. an officer of a church who helps the minister in church duties not connected with preaching. 2. member of the clergy next below a priest in rank. *n. 10.*

dead (ded), 1. with life gone from it. **The dead** means all who no longer have life. 2. without life. 3. dull; not active. 4. without force, power, spirit, feeling, activity, etc. 5. the time when there is the least life stirring; as, the dead of night. 6. sure; as, a dead shot, a dead certainty. 7. complete; as, a dead loss. 8. completely. You are dead right. 9. directly. Walk dead ahead two miles. *adj., n., adv. 1.*

dead en (ded′ən), make weak. Some medicines are given to deaden pain. Thick walls deaden the noises from the street. The force of the blow was deadened by his heavy clothing. *v. 12.*

dead letter, 1. law that is no longer kept. 2. letter unclaimed at the post office, which cannot be delivered because of faulty address, etc.

dead lock (ded′lok′), 1. a complete standstill. The employers and the strikers are at a deadlock. 2. bring or come to a complete standstill. *n., v. 9.*

dead ly (ded′li), 1. causing or likely to cause death; fatal; as, a deadly disease, deadly hatred, the deadly berries of a poisonous bush. 2. like that of death; as, deadly paleness, a deadly faintness. 3. extremely. *adj., deadlier, deadliest, adv. 4.*

Dead Sea, a salt lake in Palestine. It is 1293 ft. below sea level.

deaf (def), 1. not able to hear. 2. not able to hear well. 3. not willing to hear. A miser is deaf to all requests for money. *adj. 3.*

deaf en (def′ən), 1. make deaf. 2. stun with noise. *v. 12.*

deaf-mute (def′mūt′), person who is deaf and dumb. *n.*

deaf ness (def′nis), being deaf. *n. 17.*

deal (dēl), 1. have to do (with). Arithmetic deals with numbers. 2. act. Teachers should deal fairly with their pupils. 3. carry on business. This garage deals in gasoline, oil, tires, etc. 4. a bargain. *Used in common talk.* 5. give. One fighter dealt the other a hard blow. 6. give out among several. Deal the cards. 7. a giving out; arrangement; plan; as, a new deal, a square deal. 8. part; portion; amount. A great deal of her money is spent for doctor's bills. *v., dealt, dealing, n. 1.*

deal er (dēl′ər), 1. man who trades; any person engaged in buying and selling. 2. the person who distributes the cards to the players. *n. 4.*

deal ing (dēl′ing), 1. way of doing business. 2. conduct toward others. Mr. Just is honored for his fair dealing. 3. **Dealings** sometimes means (1) business relations. (2) friendly relations. *n. 5.*

dealt (delt). See **deal.** The knight dealt his enemy a blow. The cards are dealt. *pt. and pp. of deal. 13.*

dean (dēn), 1. a member of the faculty of a college or university who has charge of the behavior or studies of the students. 2. the head of a group of teachers in a college or university. 3. a high officer in the church. A dean is often in charge of a cathedral. 4. member who has belonged to a group longest. *n. 6.*

dear (dēr), 1. His sister was very dear to him. "Come, my dear," said mother. 2. Fruit is still too dear to can. Tom's mistake cost him dear. 3. alas. Oh, dear! My head aches. *adj., n., adv., interj. 1.*

dear ly (dēr′li), 1. fondly. 2. at a high price. *adv.*

dear ness (dēr′nis), 1. being dear. 2. great cost. *n. 20.*

dearth (dėrth), scarceness; lack; too small a supply. *n. 8.*

dear y or **dear ie** (dēr′i), dear; darling. *n., pl. dearies.* [*Used familiarly*] *20.*

death (deth), 1. dying; the ending of any form of life in people, animals, or plants. 2. any ending that is like dying. 3. being dead. 4. any condition like being dead. 5. power that destroys life. *n. 1.*

death bed (deth′bed′), 1. bed on which a person dies. 2. during the last hours of life. The murderer made a deathbed confession. *n., adj. 10.*

death less (deth′lis), never dying; living forever; immortal; eternal. *adj. 13.*

death like (deth′līk′), like that of death; as, a deathlike silence. *adj. 19.*

death ly (deth′li), 1. like that of death. 2. causing death. *adj., adv. 19.*

death rate, the proportion of the number of deaths per year to the total population.

death's-head (deths′hed′), human skull. *n.*

Death Valley, valley in eastern California that is below sea level.

de bar (di bär′), bar out; shut out; prevent. John was debarred from playing on the school team because his work had been so poor. *v., debarred, debarring. 11.*

de base (di bās′), make low or lower; lessen the value of. You can debase yourself or your character by evil actions. Paper money is debased when the government that issued it can no longer give the full amount of gold or silver for it. *v. 9.*

de base ment (di bās′mənt), act of debasing; being debased. Debasement of coinage is brought about by increasing the alloy in coins. *n. 15.*

de bat a ble (di bāt′ə bəl), 1. capable of being debated. To be debatable, a topic must have at least two sides. 2. not decided; in dispute. *adj. 18.*

de bate (di bāt′), 1. consider; discuss; talk about reasons for and against. I am debating buying a car. 2. discussion of reasons for and against. There has been much debate about the best boy to choose for captain. 3. a public argument for and against a question in a meeting. 4. hold a debate about. *v., n. 3.*

de bat er (di bāt′ər), person who debates. *n. 14.*

de bauch (di bôch′), 1. lead away from duty, virtue, or morality; corrupt; seduce. Bad companions had debauched the boy. 2. a period of sensual indulgence; as, a drunken debauch. *v., n. 11.*

de bauch er y (di bôch′ər i), 1. indulgence in intemperance and impurity. 2. departure from duty, virtue, or morality. *n., pl. debaucheries. 14.*

de bil i tate (di bil′i tāt), weaken. A hot, wet climate is debilitating to white men. *v. 15.*

de bil i ty (di bil′i ti), weakness; feebleness. Long illness may cause general debility. *n. 16.*

deb it (deb′it), 1. an entry of something owed in an account. 2. charge with a debt. Debit Mr. Brown's account $500. *n., v. 18.*

deb o nair or **deb o naire** (deb′ə nãr′), pleasant; courteous; gay. *adj. 13.*

de bris or **dé bris** (dā brē′), scattered fragments; ruins; rubbish. The street was covered with debris from the explosion. *n. 11.*

debt (det), 1. something owed to another. 2. **In debt** means owing. *n. 2.*

debt or (det′ər), person who owes something to another. If I borrow 10 cents from you, I am your debtor. *n. 7.*

de but or **dé but** (dā bū′), a first appearance in society or before the public; as, a girl's debut in society, an actor's debut on the stage. *n. 18.*

deb u tante or **dé bu tante** (deb′ū tänt′), 1. woman making a debut. 2. girl during her first year in society. *n. 17.*

Dec., December. *12.*

dec ade (dek′ād), ten years. From 1900 to 1910 was a decade. Two decades ago means twenty years ago. *n. 7.*

de ca dence (di kā′dəns or dek′ə dəns), falling off; decline; decay. The decadence of morals was one of the causes of the fall of Rome. *n. 16.*

de ca dent (di kā′dənt or dek′ə dənt), 1. falling off; declining; growing worse. 2. decadent person. *adj., n.*

dec a logue or **Dec a logue** (dek′ə lôg), the Ten Commandments. Exodus 20: 2-17. *n. 16.*

de camp (di kamp′), 1. depart quickly, secretly, or without ceremony. 2. leave a camp. *v. 20.*

de cant (di kant′), 1. pour off (liquor or a solution) gently without disturbing the sediment. 2. pour from one container to another. *v. 20.*

de cant er (di kan′tər), a glass bottle with a stopper, used for serving wine or liquor. *n. 16.*

Decanter

de cap i tate (di kap′i tāt), cut off the head of. *v.*

de cay (di kā′), 1. rot. Old fruits and vegetables decay. Your teeth decay if they are not cared for. The decay had not proceeded very far. 2. grow less in power, strength, wealth, or beauty. The power of the Roman Empire was decaying at the time of Nero. 3. growing less in power, strength, wealth, or beauty. The decay of her beauty was very gradual. *v., n. 3.*

de cease (di sēs′), 1. death. 2. die. *n., v. 5.*

de ceit (di sēt′), 1. deceiving; lying; making a person believe as true something that is false. 2. dishonest trick; a lie spoken or acted. 3. the quality in a person that makes him tell lies. *n. 5.*

de ceit ful (di sēt′fəl), 1. ready or willing to deceive or lie. 2. deceiving; misleading. 3. meant to deceive. *adj. 7.*

de ceive (di sēv′), 1. make (a person) believe as true something that is false; mislead. The boy tried to deceive his mother, but she knew what he had done. 2. lie; use deceit. *v. 2.*

de ceiv er (di sēv′ər), person who deceives. *n. 10.*

De cem ber (di sem′bər), the 12th and last month of the year. December 25 is Christmas. *n. 2.*

de cen cy (dē′sən si), 1. being decent; propriety of behavior. 2. proper regard for modesty or delicacy; respectability. 3. something decent or proper. *n., pl. decencies. 10.*

de cent (dē′sənt), 1. respectable; modest; fit and proper. It is not decent to laugh at a funeral. 2. good enough; not wonderful and not very bad. I get decent marks at school. 3. not severe; rather kind. *adj. 6.*

de cep tion (di sep′shən), 1. deceiving. 2. being deceived. 3. trick; fraud; sham. *n. 9.*

de cep tive (di sep′tiv), deceiving. *adj. 19.*

de cide (di sīd′), 1. settle. Let us decide it by tossing a penny. 2. give judgment. Mother decided in favor of the blue dress. 3. resolve; make up one's mind. John decided to be a sailor. *v. 1.*

de cid ed (di sīd′id), 1. definite; unquestionable. 2. resolute; determined. Bill was very decided in his determination to go to college. *adj. 14.*

de cid ed ly (di sīd′id li), more than a little; distinctly; without question. John's work is decidedly better than Frank's. It was a decidedly warm morning. *adv. 8.*

de cid u ous (di sij′ü əs), 1. falling off at a particular season or stage of growth. 2. shedding leaves annually. Maples, oaks, and elms are deciduous trees. *adj. 12.*

dec i mal (des′i məl), 1. a fraction like $\frac{4}{100}$ or .04, .2 or $\frac{2}{10}$. 2. a number like 75.24, 3.062, .7, or .091. 3. of tens; proceeding by tens. United States money has a decimal system. *n., adj. 12.*

dec i mate (des′i māt), 1. destroy much of; kill a large part of. A plague had decimated the population. 2. destroy one tenth of. *v. 16.*

de ci pher (di sī′fər), 1. make out the meaning of (bad writing, an unknown language, or anything puzzling). 2. change (something in cipher) into ordinary writing; interpret by using a key. *v. 10.*

de ci sion (di sizh′ən), 1. deciding; judgment; making up one's mind. The judge gives a decision in a lawsuit. 2. firmness; being decided. **With decision** means without any wavering or doubt, promptly and with force. *n. 4.*

de ci sive (di sī′siv), 1. having a clear result; settling something beyond question; as, a decisive victory. 2. having or showing decision; as, a decisive answer. *adj. 8.*

deck (dek), 1. one of the floors or platforms extending from side to side and often from end to end of a ship. The upper, main, middle, and lower decks of a ship are somewhat like the stories of a house. Often the upper deck has no roof over it. 2. cover; dress; adorn. 3. a pack of playing cards. *n., v. 2.*

de claim (di klām′), speak like an orator; recite in public; make a formal speech. *v. 20.*

dec la ma tion (dek′lə mā′shən), 1. act of declaiming; making formal speeches. 2. a formal speech. 3. a noisy speech. 4. the art of oratory. *n. 15.*

dec la ra tion (dek′lə rā′shən), a statement; an open or public statement; a very strong statement. The **Declaration of Independence** was a public statement adopted by the American colonies on July 4, 1776 declaring that they were free and independent of Great Britain. **Make a declaration** means declare. *n. 7.*

de clar a tive (di klar′ə tiv), making a statement; explaining. "I eat" and "The dog has four legs" are declarative sentences. *adj.*

de clare (di klãr′), say; make known; say openly or strongly. The boy declared that he would never go back to school again. Congress has the power to declare war. Travelers returning to the United States must declare the things which they bought abroad. Peace was declared at last. The boys declared themselves against cheating. *v. 2.*

de clen sion (di klen′shən), 1. giving different endings to nouns, pronouns, and adjectives according to their case or their relation to other words in the sentence. The declension of *who* is: *who, whose, whom.* 2. a group of words whose endings for the different cases are alike. *n. 10.*

dec li na tion (dek′li nā′shən), 1. downward bend. 2. deviation of the needle of a compass from true north and south. 3. polite refusal. *n. 15.*

de cline (di klīn′), 1. refuse; turn away from doing. The man declined my offer. The boy declined to do what he was told. 2. bend or slope down. The high hill declines to a fertile valley. 3. grow less in strength and power; grow worse. A man's power declines as he grows old. Great nations have risen and declined. 4. falling to a lower level; losing strength; growing worse; as, the decline of the Roman Empire, the decline of the sun to the horizon, a decline in prices. 5. the last part of anything; as, the decline of the day, the decline of a person's life. 6. give the case endings of (a noun, pronoun, or adjective). *v., n. 3.*

de cliv i ty (di kliv′i ti), a downward slope. A precipice is a very, very steep declivity. *n., pl. declivities. 15.*

dé col le té (dā′kol tā′), 1. low-necked; as, a décolleté gown. 2. wearing a low-necked gown. *adj. 20.*

de com pose (dē′kəm pōz′), 1. decay; rot. 2. separate (a substance) into what it is made of. A prism decomposes sunlight. *v. 8.*

de com po si tion (dē′kom pə zish′ən), 1. act or process of decomposing. 2. decay. *n. 13.*

dec o rate (dek′ə rāt), 1. make beautiful; trim; adorn. We decorated the Christmas tree with shining balls. 2. give a badge, ribbon, or medal to. The king decorated the soldier for his brave act. *v. 6.*

dec o ra tion (dek′ə rā′shən), 1. decorating. 2. ornament. 3. a badge, ribbon, or medal given as an honor. *n. 5.*

Decoration Day, Memorial Day. In most States it falls on May 30.

dec o ra tive (dek′ə rā′tiv), ornamental; helping to make beautiful. *adj. 12.*

dec o ra tor (dek′ə rā′tər), person who decorates. An interior decorator plans the woodwork, wallpaper, and furnishings for a house. *n. 19.*

dec o rous (dek′ə rəs or di kō′rəs), well-behaved; acting properly; suitable; dignified. *adj. 16.*

de co rum (di kō′rəm), 1. propriety of action, speech, dress, etc. You behave with decorum when you do what is fit and proper. 2. an observance or requirement of polite society. Mary's mother had taught her to observe all the little decorums that mark a lady. *n. 11.*

de coy (di koi′), 1. lead (wild birds, animals, etc.) into a trap or within gunshot. 2. a wooden bird used to entice birds into a trap or within gunshot. 3. a trained bird or other animal used for the same purpose. 4. entice; lead or tempt into danger. 5. any person or thing used to entice; a lure. *v., n. 10.*

Wooden decoy for ducks

de crease (di krēs′ for 1 and 2, dē′krēs for 3 and 4), 1. grow or become less. Hunger decreases as one eats. 2. make less. Decrease the dose of medicine as you feel better. 3. growing less. Toward night there was a decrease of heat. 4. the amount by which a thing is made less. *v., n. 4.*

de cree (di krē′), 1. something ordered or settled by authority; a decision; a law. By the king's decree all thieves were hanged. The court granted Mrs. Smith a decree of divorce. 2. order or settle by authority. Fate decreed that Ulysses should travel long and far. *n., v. 4.*

de crep it (di krep′it), broken down or weakened by old age; old and feeble. *adj. 11.*

de crep i tude (di krep′i tūd or di krep′i tüd), weakness or feebleness of old age. The decrepitude of the house was shown in shaky floors, a broken chimney, and cracks in the walls. *n. 16.*

de cry (di krī′), 1. condemn. The minister decried gambling in all its forms. 2. make little of; try to lower the value of. The lumber dealer decried the use of concrete for houses. *v., decried, decrying. 14.*

ded i cate (ded′i kāt), 1. set apart for a purpose. A minister or priest is dedicated to the service of God. The land on which the battle of Gettysburg was fought was dedicated to the memory of the soldiers who had died there. 2. address (a book or other work) to a friend or patron. *v. 5.*

ded i ca tion (ded′i kā′shən), 1. setting apart for a purpose; being set apart for a purpose; as, the dedication of a church. 2. words dedicating a book, poem, etc., to a friend or patron. *n. 10.*

de duce (di dūs′ or di düs′), infer from a general rule or principle; reach (a conclusion) by reasoning. *v. 11.*

de duct (di dukt′), take away; subtract. *v. 10.*

de duc tion (di duk′shən), 1. act of taking away; subtraction. No deduction in pay is made for absence due to illness. 2. amount deducted. 3. inference from a general rule or principle. A person using deduction reasons from general laws to particular cases. 4. thing deduced; a conclusion. Sherlock Holmes made brilliant deductions. *n. 13.*

de duc tive (di duk′tiv), of deduction; using deduction; reasoning by deduction. *adj.*

deed (dēd), 1. something done; an act; an action. To feed the hungry is a good deed. Deeds, not words, are needed. 2. a written or printed agreement. The buyer of land receives a deed to the property from the former owner. *n. 2.*

deem (dēm), think; believe; consider. The general deemed it wise to retreat. *v. 3.*

deep (dēp). The ocean is deep here. The men dug a deep well to get pure water. The lot on which the house stands is 100 feet deep. She heard the low tones of the deep voice. A deep subject is one that is hard to understand. Deep feeling is hard to put into words. A deep sleep is one that is hard to be wakened from. The men dug deep before they found water. The color was a deep red. **The deep** sometimes means the sea. *adj., adv., n. 1.*

deep en (dēp′ən), make deeper; become deeper. *v. 5.*

deep-root ed (dēp′rüt′id), 1. deeply rooted. 2. firmly fixed. Many people have a deep-rooted dislike for snakes. *adj. 20.*

deep-seat ed (dēp′sēt′id), 1. far below the surface. 2. firmly fixed. The disease was so deep-seated that it could not be cured. *adj.*

deer (dēr), a graceful animal that chews the cud. The male deer has horns. See the picture. *n., pl. deer. 3.*

Virginia deer (3½ ft. high at the shoulder)

deer skin (dēr′skin′), 1. skin of a deer. 2. leather made from it. *n. 18.*

def., definition.

de face (di fās′), spoil the appearance of; mar. Thoughtless boys have defaced the desks by marking on them. *v. 9.*

de fal ca tion (dē′fal kā′shən), 1. a misuse or theft of money trusted to one. The cashier's defalcation was discovered. 2. amount misused or stolen; as, a defalcation of $5000. *n.*

def a ma tion (def′ə mā′shən), slander; libel. *n.*

de fame (di fām′), attack the good name of; harm the reputation of; speak evil of; slander. Men in public life are sometimes defamed by opponents. *v. 13.*

de fault (di fôlt′), 1. failure to do something or to appear somewhere when due; neglect. If, in any contest, one side does not appear, it loses by default. 2. fail to do something or to appear somewhere when due. They defaulted in the tennis tournament. *n., v. 10.*

de feat (di fēt′), 1. overcome; gain the victory over; as, to defeat the enemy in battle, to defeat another school in basketball. 2. make useless; undo. Tom's effort to toughen himself by going without an overcoat defeated itself, for he caught a bad cold. 3. defeating. 4. being defeated. *v., n. 3.*

de fect (di fekt′ or dē′fekt), 1. fault. A piece of cloth often shows defects in weaving. 2. the lack of something essential to completeness; falling short. A bad temper was the defect in Henry's kind and generous nature. *n. 5.*

de fec tion (di fek′shən), falling away from loyalty, duty, etc.; desertion. Mr. Ward was blamed for defection from his political party. *n. 15.*

de fec tive (di fek′tiv), not complete; not perfect; faulty. This pump is defective and will not work. *adj. 7.*

de fence (di fens′), defense. *n.*

de fence less (di fens′lis), defenseless. *adj.*

de fend (di fend′), 1. keep safe; protect. 2. act, speak, or write in favor of. The newspapers defended the governor's action. 3. fight or contest (a claim or suit at law). *v. 2.*

de fend ant (di fen′dənt), person against whom a legal action is brought. This defendant is accused of theft. *n. 12.*

de fend er (di fen′dər), person who defends; guardian. *n. 11.*

de fense (di fens′), 1. any thing, act, or word that defends, guards, or protects. A wall around a city was a defense against enemies. A well-built house or a warm coat is a defense against cold weather. 2. defending; being defended. *n. 3.*

de fense less (di fens′lis), having no defense; helpless against attack. A baby is defenseless; he cannot prevent what is done to him. A city without guns or water is defenseless before an army. *adj. 11.*

de fen si ble (di fen′si bəl), that can be defended or justified. *adj. 20.*

de fen sive (di fen′siv), 1. on the defense; defending; ready to defend; intended to defend. 2. thing that defends. 3. defensive position or attitude. *adj., n. 10.*

de fer[1] (di fėr′), put off; delay. Let us defer our departure until tomorrow. *v., deferred, deferring. 8.*

de fer[2] (di fėr′), yield in judgment or opinion. **Defer to** another person means put his opinion ahead of one's own; show respect to him. Children should defer to their parents' wishes. *v., deferred, deferring.*

def er ence (def′ər əns), 1. yielding to the judgment, opinion, wishes, etc., of another. 2. great respect. Wisdom deserves deference. 3. **In deference to** means out of respect for the wishes or authority of. *n. 11.*

def er en tial (def′ər en′shəl), showing deference; respectful. *adj. 15.*

de fi ance (di fī′əns), defying; standing up against authority and refusing to recognize or obey it; open resistance to power. He shouted defiance at the enemy. He goes without a hat all winter in defiance of the cold weather. *n. 5.*

de fi ant (di fī′ənt), showing defiance; disobedient. The boy said, "I won't," in a defiant manner. *adj. 9.*

de fi cien cy (di fish′ən si), 1. a lack or absence of something needed. There is a deficiency of salt in this stew; put more in. 2. the amount by which a thing falls short or is too small. If a bill to be paid is $10 and you have only $6, the deficiency is $4. *n., pl. deficiencies. 7.*

de fi cient (di fish′ənt), lacking; incomplete; not enough. *adj. 8.*

def i cit (def′i sit), the amount by which a sum of money falls short. Since the club owed $15 and had only $10 in the treasury, there was a deficit of $5. *n. 16.*

de file[1] (di fīl′), 1. make dirty, bad-smelling, or in any way disgusting. 2. destroy the pureness or cleanness of (anything sacred). The barbarians defiled the church by using it as a stable. *v. 6.*

de file[2] (di fīl′), 1. to march in a line. 2. a narrow way through which troops can march only in narrow columns; a steep and narrow valley. *v., n.*

de file ment (di fīl′mənt), pollution; defiling; being defiled. *n. 16.*

de fine (di fīn′), 1. explain the nature of; make clear the meaning of. A dictionary defines words. 2. settle the limits of. The powers of the courts are defined by law. The boundary between the United States and Canada is defined. *v. 7.*

def i nite (def′i nit), 1. clear; precise; not vague. 2. having settled limits. 3. The definite article is *the. adj. 6.*

def i ni tion (def′i nish′ən), 1. explaining the nature of a thing; making clear the meaning of a word. 2. a statement in which the nature of a thing is explained or the meaning of a word is made clear. *n. 8.*

de fin i tive (di fin′i tiv), conclusive; final. *adj. 13.*

de flate (di flāt′), 1. let air or gas out of (a tire, balloon, football, etc.). 2. reduce (currency, prices, etc.) from an inflated condition. *v.*

de fla tion (di flā′shən), 1. letting the air out; as, the deflation of a tire. 2. reduction of currency, prices, etc., from an inflated condition. *n.*

de flect (di flekt′), bend or turn aside; change the direction of. The wind deflected the arrow's flight. *v. 14.*

De foe or **De Foe** (di fō′), Daniel (1661?-1731), English author who wrote *Robinson Crusoe. n. 17.*

de for est (dē for′ist), remove the trees from; clear of trees. Some land has to be deforested before settlers can farm it. *v.*

de form (di fôrm′), 1. spoil the form or shape of. Shoes which do not fit deform the feet. A hunchback or a cripple is deformed. 2. make ugly. Anger deforms the face. *v. 6.*

de for ma tion (dē′fôr mā′shən), act or result of deforming; disfigurement. *n.*

de form i ty (di fôr′mi ti), 1. something in the shape of a body that is not as it should be, such as a hump on the back or a stump instead of a foot. 2. an ugliness of mind or body. 3. the state or fact of being deformed. *n., pl. deformities. 9.*

de fraud (di frôd′), cheat; take away from by fraud. *v. 9.*

de fray (di frā′), pay (costs or expenses). The expenses of national parks are defrayed by the taxpayers. *v. 12.*

deft (deft), skillful; nimble; clever. The fingers of a violinist are deft. *adj. 11.*

deft ness (deft′nis), skillfulness; nimbleness; cleverness. *n. 20.*

de funct (di fungkt′), dead; extinct. *adj. 16.*

de fy (di fī′), 1. challenge (a person) to do or prove something. We defy you to show that our game is not fair. 2. set oneself openly against (authority). Now that the boy was earning his own living he could defy his father's strict rules. 3. withstand; resist. This strong fort defies capture. *v., defied, defying. 3.*

de gen er a cy (di jen′ər ə si), degenerate condition. *n. 14.*

de gen er ate (di jen′ər āt for 1 and 2, di jen′ər it for 3 and 4), 1. grow worse; decline in physical, mental, or moral qualities. 2. sink to a lower type; lose the normal or more highly developed characteristics of its race or kind. 3. that has degenerated; showing a decline in physical, mental, or moral qualities. The thief was a degenerate member of a fine family. 4. person having an evil and unwholesome character. Only a degenerate could have committed such a horrible crime. *v., adj., n. 7.*

de gen er a tion (di jen′ər ā′shən), growing worse; degenerate condition. *n. 16.*

deg ra da tion (deg′rə dā′shən), 1. degrading. 2. being degraded. The family was living in degradation with no regard for cleanliness or morals. Degradation from rank is a military punishment. *n. 8.*

de grade (di grād′), 1. reduce to a lower rank, often as a punishment; take away a position or an honor from. The captain was degraded for disobeying orders. 2. make worse; lower. You degrade yourself when you tell a lie. *v. 6.*

de gree (di grē′), 1. a step in a scale; a stage in a process. By degrees the lake gets warm enough to swim in. 2. amount; extent. To what degree are you interested in reading? 3. rank. A princess is a lady of high degree. 4. a rank or title given by a college to a student whose work fulfills requirements, or to a noted person as an honor. 5. In grammar, the positive, comparative, and superlative degrees are the forms an adjective or adverb may take, such as *fast, faster, fastest,* or *quickly, more quickly, most quickly.* 6. a unit for measuring temperature. The freezing point of water is 32 degrees (32°) Fahrenheit. A degree on the centigrade scale is 1.8 times a degree on the Fahrenheit scale. 7. a unit for measuring the opening of an angle or an arc of a circle. A degree is $\frac{1}{90}$ of a right angle or $\frac{1}{360}$ of the circumference of a circle. *n. 2.*

Degrees (def. 7)

de i fi ca tion (dē′i fi kā′shən), 1. making a god (of). The deification of the emperor was customary in ancient Rome. 2. being made a god. After his deification, altars were erected to him. *n.*

de i fy (dē′i fī), 1. make a god of. 2. regard or worship as a god. Some people deify wealth. *v., deified, deifying. 10.*

deign (dān), condescend; think fit. So great a man would never deign to notice us. *v. 6.*

de ist (dē′ist), person who believes in God. *n. 15.*

de i ty (dē′i ti), 1. a god or goddess. Neptune was a deity of the sea. 2. divine nature; being a god. His deity was not questioned. 3. **The Deity** means God. *n., pl. deities. 6.*

de ject ed (di jek′tid), in low spirits; sad; discouraged. *adj. 7.*

de jec tion (di jek′shən), lowness of spirits; sadness. Ruth's face showed her dejection at missing the party. *n. 11.*

Del., Delaware.

Del a ware (del′ə wãr), 1. an Eastern State of the United States. 2. a river flowing from southern New York between New Jersey and Pennsylvania into the Atlantic Ocean. *n. 6.*

de lay (di lā′), 1. put off till a later time. We will delay the party for a week. 2. putting off till a later time. The delay upset our plans. 3. make late; keep waiting; hinder the progress of. The accident delayed the train for two hours. Ignorance delays progress. 4. be late; go slowly; stop along the way. Do not delay on this errand. 5. a wait; making late; hindering; stopping along the way. We were so late that we could afford no further delay. *v., n. 2.*

de lec ta ble (di lek′tə bəl), delightful; very pleasing. *adj. 12.*

de lec ta tion (dē′lek tā′shən), delight; pleasure; entertainment. The magician did many tricks for the delectation of the children. *n.*

del e gate (del′i gāt), 1. person who acts for others; a representative. We sent two delegates to the meeting. 2. appoint or send (a person) as a representative. The children delegated Mary to buy the flowers. 3. give over (one's power or authority) to another so that he may act for one. The States delegated some of their rights to the nation. *n., v. 5.*

del e ga tion (del′i gā′shən), 1. delegating; being delegated. 2. a group of delegates. Each club sent a delegation to the convention. *n. 11.*

de lete (di lēt′), strike out or take out (anything written or printed); remove; omit; cross out. References to places of battles were deleted from soldiers' letters during the war. *v.*

del e te ri ous (del′i tēr′i əs), harmful; injurious. *adj. 17.*

delft (delft), a kind of glazed earthenware, usually decorated in blue. *n. 18.*

Delft

Del hi (del′i), the capital of India. *n.*

de lib er ate (di lib′ər it for 1, 2, and 3, di lib′ər āt for 4 and 5), 1. intended; done on purpose;

thought over beforehand. His excuse was a deliberate lie. 2. slow and careful in deciding what to do. Judges are more deliberate than gamblers, as a rule. 3. slow; not hurried. The old man walked with deliberate steps. 4. think over; think over carefully. I was deliberating where to put up my new picture. 5. talk over reasons for and against; debate. Congress was deliberating over the question of taxes. *adj., v. 6.*

de lib er ate ly (di lib′ər it li), 1. on purpose. 2. slowly. *adv.*

de lib er a tion (di lib′ər ā′shən), 1. careful thought. After long deliberation, he decided not to go. 2. talking about reasons for or against an action; as, the deliberations of Congress. 3. slowness. He aimed his gun with great deliberation. *n. 8.*

del i ca cy (del′i kə si), 1. fineness of weave, quality, or make; slightness and grace; as, delicacy of silks or colors, the delicacy of a baby's skin. 2. fineness of feeling for small differences; as, delicacy of hearing or touch. 3. need of care, skill, or tact. A matter of great delicacy is one that requires careful handling. 4. thought for the feelings of others. 5. shrinking from what is offensive or not modest. 6. weakness; being easily hurt or made ill. The child's delicacy was a constant worry to his mother. 7. a dainty; a choice kind of food. *n., pl. delicacies. 7.*

del i cate (del′i kit), 1. pleasing to the taste; lightly flavored; mild; soft; as, delicate foods, delicate colors, delicate fragrance. 2. of fine weave, quality, or make; thin; easily torn. A spider's web is very delicate. 3. requiring careful handling; as, delicate flowers, a delicate situation, a delicate question. 4. very quickly responding to slight changes of condition; finely sensitive; as, delicate instruments, a delicate sense of touch. 5. easily hurt or made ill; as, a delicate child. *adj. 3.*

del i ca tes sen (del′i kə tes′ən), 1. prepared foods, such as cooked meats, smoked fish, cheese, salads, pickles, etc. 2. a shop selling such foods. *n.*

de li cious (di lish′əs), very pleasing or satisfying; delightful, especially to taste or smell. *adj. 4.*

de light (di līt′), 1. great pleasure; joy. 2. something which gives great pleasure. Dancing is her delight. 3. please greatly. The circus delighted the children. 4. have great pleasure. Children delight in surprises. *n., v. 1.*

de light ful (di līt′fəl), giving joy; very pleasing; as, a delightful ride, a delightful person. *adj. 3.*

de lin e ate (di lin′i āt), to sketch; portray; describe. *v. 15.*

de lin e a tion (di lin′i ā′shən), drawing or describing; a diagram, sketch, portrait, or description. *n. 15.*

de lin quen cy (di ling′kwən si), 1. failure in a duty; neglect of an obligation. 2. fault; guilt; shortcoming; offense. *n., pl. delinquencies. 17.*

de lin quent (di ling′kwənt), 1. failing in a duty; neglecting an obligation. 2. guilty of an offense. 3. an offender. *adj., n. 15.*

del i ques cent (del′i kwes′ənt), becoming liquid by absorbing moisture from the air. *adj. 20.*

de lir i ous (di lir′i əs), 1. out of one's senses; wandering in mind; raving. 2. wildly excited. *adj. 11.*

de lir i um (di lir′i əm), 1. a disorder of the mind that occurs during fevers, insanity, drunkenness, etc. Delirium is characterized by restlessness, excitement, strange ideas, and wild talk. 2. wild excitement. *n. 12.*

de liv er (di liv′ər), 1. carry and give out. The postman delivers letters. 2. give up; hand over. Dick delivered his mother's message to Mrs. Brown. 3. strike; throw; as, to deliver a blow. 4. give forth in words. The traveler delivered a course of talks on his travels. The jury delivered its verdict. 5. set free; save from evil or trouble. "Deliver us from evil." *v. 2.*

de liv er ance (di liv′ər əns), 1. release; freedom. The soldiers rejoiced in their deliverance from prison. 2. utterance; formal opinion or judgment. *n. 5.*

de liv er er (di liv′ər ər), 1. rescuer; savior. 2. person who delivers. *n. 8.*

de liv er y (di liv′ər i), 1. carrying and giving out letters, goods, etc.; as, parcel-post delivery. 2. giving over; handing over. The captive was released upon the delivery of his ransom. 3. manner of speaking. Our minister has an excellent delivery. 4. giving birth to a child. 5. any act of delivering. *n., pl. deliveries. 4.*

dell (del), a small, sheltered glen or valley, usually with trees in it. *n. 6.*

Del phi (del′fī), the town in ancient Greece where the famous oracle of Apollo was located. *n. 12.*

Del phic (del′fik), 1. having to do with the oracle of Apollo at Delphi. 2. obscure; with double meaning. *adj. 13.*

del ta (del′tə), the deposit of earth and sand that collects at the mouth of some rivers and is usually three-sided. See the picture. *n. 6.*

Delta of the Mississippi River

de lude (di lüd′), mislead; deceive. *v. 9.*

del uge (del′ūj), 1. a great flood. The **Deluge** was the great flood in the days of Noah. Genesis 7. 2. heavy fall of rain. 3. to flood; overflow. *n., v. 9.*

de lu sion (di lü′zhən), a false belief or opinion. The crazy man had a delusion that he was George Washington. *n. 8.*

de lu sive (di lü′siv), misleading; deceptive; false; unreal. *adj. 12.*

de luxe (di lu̇ks′ or di luks′), of exceptionally good quality; elegant.

delve (delv), dig. That professor is always delving for knowledge in old books and manuscripts. *v. 12.*

de mag net ize (dē mag′ni tīz), deprive of magnetism. *v.*

dem a gogue or **dem a gog** (dem′ə gog), a popular leader who stirs up the people in order to get something for himself. A demagogue usually appeals to the emotions and prejudices of the people. *n. 10.*

de mand (di mand′), 1. ask for as a right. The prisoner demanded a trial. 2. ask for with authority. The policeman demanded the boys' names. 3. call for; require; need. Training a puppy demands patience. 4. a claim. A mother has many demands upon her time. 5. a call; a request. Taxicabs are in great demand on rainy days. The supply of apples exceeds the demand this year. *v., n. 1.*

de mar ca tion (dē′mär kā′shən), 1. act of setting and marking the limits. 2. separation; distinction. *n.*

de mean[1] (di mēn′), to lower in dignity or standing. The duke's son would not demean himself by working. *v.*

de mean[2] (di mēn′), behave; conduct (oneself). *v.*

de mean or (di mēn′ər), behavior; manner; the way one acts and looks; as, a quiet, modest demeanor. *n. 7.*

de ment ed (di men′tid), insane; crazy. *adj.*

de mer it (dē mer′it), 1. fault; defect. 2. a mark against a person for bad behavior or poor work. *n. 16.*

de mesne (di mān′), 1. possession and actual use of land. 2. house and land reserved for the owner's use. 3. domain; district; region. *n. 14.*

De me ter (di mē′tər), Greek goddess of agriculture. The Romans called her Ceres. *n.*

dem i god (dem′i god′), a god; one who is partly divine and partly human. Hercules was a demigod. *n. 11.*

dem i john (dem′i jon), a large bottle of glass or earthenware, often enclosed in wicker. *n.*

Demijohn

de mise (di mīz′), death. *n.*

de mo bi lize (dē mō′bi līz), disband. When a war is over, the armies are demobilized. *v.*

de moc ra cy (di mok′rə si), 1. a government that is run by the people who live under it. In a democracy the people rule either directly through meetings which all may attend, such as a town meeting in New England towns, or indirectly through the election of certain representatives to attend to the business. 2. a country or town in which the government is a democracy. The United States is a democracy. 3. treating other people as one's equals. The old gentleman's democracy made him liked by all classes. *n., pl. democracies. 7.*

dem o crat (dem′ə krat), 1. person who believes that a government should be run by the people who live under it. 2. person who holds or acts on the belief that all people are his equals. 3. A **Democrat** is a member of the Democratic Party. *n. 6.*

dem o crat ic (dem′ə krat′ik), 1. of a democracy; like a democracy. 2. treating all classes of people as one's equals. The queen's democratic ways made her dear to her people. 3. The **Democratic Party** is one of the two main political parties in the United States. 4. of the Democratic Party. *adj. 8.*

de mol ish (di mol′ish), pull or tear down; destroy. *v. 10.*

dem o li tion (dem′ə lish′ən), destruction. *n. 16.*

de mon (dē′mən), 1. devil; evil spirit; fiend. 2. a very wicked or cruel person. 3. person who has great energy and vigor. 4. an inferior god. *n. 7.*

de mo ni ac (di mō′ni ak), 1. of demons. 2. devilish; fiendish. Burning people is a demoniac torture. 3. raging; frantic. 4. possessed by an evil spirit. 5. person supposed to be possessed by an evil spirit. *adj., n. 16.*

de mo ni a cal (dē′mə nī′ə kəl), demoniac. *adj.*

de mon stra ble (di mon′strə bəl), that can be shown or proved. *adj. 20.*

dem on strate (dem′ən strāt), 1. show clearly; prove. 2. teach by carrying out experiments, or by showing and explaining samples or specimens. 3. show, advertise, or make publicly known, by carrying out a process in public. He demonstrated his washing machine to us by washing some clothes with it. 4. show (feeling) openly. 5. show feeling by a parade, meeting, etc. 6. display military strength to frighten or deceive an enemy. *v. 6.*

dem on stra tion (dem′ən strā′shən), 1. clear proof; as, a demonstration that the earth is round. 2. teaching by carrying out experiments, or by showing and explaining samples or specimens. 3. showing some new product or process in a public place; as, the demonstration of a washing machine. 4. open show or expression of feeling. He greeted them with every demonstration of joy. 5. a showing of feeling by a meeting, a procession, or the like. 6. a showing of military force planned to rouse fear, to hide other activities going on, or to show preparedness for war. *n. 7.*

de mon stra tive (di mon′strə tiv), 1. expressing one's feelings freely and openly. 2. showing or pointing out. *This* and *that* are demonstrative pronouns. *adj. 9.*

dem on stra tor (dem′ən strā′tər), 1. person who demonstrates. 2. person who takes part in a public demonstration. *n.*

de mor al i za tion (di mor′əl i zā′shən), 1. demoralizing. 2. being demoralized. *n. 16.*

de mor al ize (di mor′əl īz), 1. corrupt the morals of (people). The drug habit demoralizes people. 2. weaken or spoil the spirit, courage, or discipline of (an army, a school, a team, etc.). Lack of food and ammunition demoralized the besieged soldiers. *v. 16.*

De mos the nes (di mos′thə nēz), the most famous of ancient Greek orators (384?-322 B.C.). *n. 12.*

de mote (di mōt′), reduce to a lower grade. Jack was demoted from Grade 4 to Grade 3. *v.*

de mur (di mėr′), 1. to object. The clerk demurred at working overtime without extra pay. 2. objection. *v., demurred, demurring, n. 9.*

de mure (di mūr′), 1. sober; serious; sedate. The Puritan maiden was demure. 2. falsely sedate or modest; as, the demure smile of a flirt. *adj. 9.*

den (den), 1. a wild animal's home. The bear's den was in a cave. 2. place where thieves have their headquarters. 3. a small, dirty room. 4. one's private room for reading and work, usually small and cozy. *n. 3.*

de na ture (dē nā′chər), 1. change the nature of. 2. make unfit for eating or drinking without destroying usefulness for other purposes; as, denatured alcohol. *v.*

de ni al (di nī′əl), 1. saying (a thing) is not so; as, a denial of the truth of a statement, a denial of the existence of fairies. 2. saying that one does not hold or accept a belief. He made a public denial of socialism. 3. refusing. His denial of our request seemed very impolite. 4. disowning. *n. 9.*

den im (den′im), a heavy, twilled cotton cloth, commonly dyed in plain colors and used for overalls, upholstery, etc. *n. 20.*

den i zen (den′i zən), 1. inhabitant; occupant. Fish are denizens of the sea. 2. a foreigner who is given certain rights. 3. a foreign word, plant, or animal that has been adopted. Plants from all over the world are denizens of the New York Botanical Gardens. *n. 15.*

Den mark (den′märk), a small country in northern Europe. *n. 6.*

de nom i nate (di nom′i nāt for 1, di nom′i nit for 2), 1. give a name to. 2. called by a specified name. 6. ft., 4 oz., 10 in., and 9 lb. are denominate numbers. *v., adj. 15.*

de nom i na tion (di nom′i nā′shən), 1. a name, especially a name for a class of things. 2. a religious group; sect. Some of the Protestant denominations are the Episcopalians, Methodists, Presbyterians, and Baptists. 3. a class or kind of units. Reducing $\frac{5}{12}$, $\frac{1}{3}$, and $\frac{1}{6}$ to the same denomination gives $\frac{5}{12}$, $\frac{4}{12}$, and $\frac{2}{12}$. The United States coin of lowest denomination is a cent. *n. 11.*

de nom i na tion al (di nom′i nā′shən əl), having to do with some religious denomination. *adj.*

de nom i na tor (di nom′i nā′tər), the number below the line in a fraction, which states the size of the parts. In $\frac{3}{4}$, *4* is the denominator, and *3* is the numerator. *n. 20.*

de note (di nōt′), 1. indicate; be the sign of. A fever usually denotes sickness. If I write "Excellent" on your paper, it denotes very good work. 2. be a name for; mean:

say or mean exactly. The word *stool* denotes a small chair without a back. *v. 7.*

de nounce (di nouns′), 1. speak against. The preacher denounced sin. 2. announce or report as something bad; give information against. He denounced his own brother as a thief. *v. 6.*

dense (dens), 1. closely packed together; thick; as, a dense forest, a dense fog. 2. stupid. *adj. 4.*

den si ty (den′si ti), 1. closeness; compactness. The density of the woods prevented us from seeing more than a little way ahead. 2. in physics, the amount of matter to a unit of bulk. The density of lead is greater than the density of wood. 3. stupidity. *n., pl. densities. 9.*

dent (dent), 1. a hollow made by a blow or pressure. The desk showed the dents of many years' use. 2. make a dent in. That table was dented in moving. 3. become dented. *n., v. 13.*

den tal (den′təl), 1. of or for the teeth. 2. of or for a dentist's work. *adj. 11.*

den ti frice (den′ti fris), paste, powder, or liquid for cleaning the teeth. *n.*

den tin (den′tin), dentine. *n.*

DENTINE

den tine (den′tēn), hard, bony material beneath the enamel of teeth. It forms the main part of a tooth. *n.*

den tist (den′tist), person who makes a business of filling, cleaning, and taking out teeth. *n. 8.*

den tist ry (den′tis tri), the work of a dentist. *n.*

de nude (di nūd′ or di nüd′), make bare; strip of clothing or covering. Most trees are denuded of their leaves in winter. *v. 16.*

de nun ci a tion (di nun′si ā′shən), 1. denouncing; condemnation; as, a teacher's denunciation of cheating. 2. an accusation before a public prosecutor. *n. 13.*

Den ver (den′vər), capital of Colorado. *n. 9.*

de ny (di nī′), 1. say (something) is not true. The prisoner denied the charges against him. They denied the existence of disease in the town. 2. say that one does not hold or accept. 3. refuse. I could not deny her the favor. 4. disown; refuse to acknowledge. He denied his signature. *v., denied, denying. 2.*

de part (di pärt′), 1. go away; leave. We arrived in the village in the morning, and departed that night. 2. turn away (from); change. He departed from his usual way of working. 3. die. *v. 2.*

de part ment (di pärt′mənt), 1. a separate part of some whole; as, the fire department of a city government. 2. A **department store** sells many different kinds of things in separate departments under one management. *n., adj. 3.*

de par ture (di pär′chər), 1. act of going away. His departure was very sudden. 2. turning away; change; as, a departure from our old custom. 3. starting on a new course of action or thought. This dancing class will be a new departure for me, for I have never done anything like it. *n. 5.*

de pend (di pend′), 1. rely; trust. You can depend on the timetable to tell you when trains leave. 2. **Depend on** means (1) be a result of. Health depends on good food, fresh air, and enough sleep. (2) have as a support; get help from. Children depend on their parents for food and clothing. 3. depend on something. *v. 2.*

de pend a ble (di pen′də bəl), reliable; trustworthy. Newspapers ought to be dependable. *adj. 14.*

de pend ant (di pen′dənt), dependent. *adj., n. 8.*

de pend ence (di pen′dəns), 1. the fact or condition of being dependent; as, the dependence of crops on the weather. 2. trust. Do not put your dependence in him, for he sometimes fails us. 3. living at the cost of another. The boy wished to go to work so that he could end his dependence on his uncle. *n. 8.*

de pend en cy (di pen′dən si), something trusting to or depending on another person or thing for support, especially a country under the control of another. The Hawaiian Islands are a dependency of the United States. *n., pl. dependencies. 10.*

de pend ent (di pen′dənt), 1. trusting to or depending on another person or thing for support. A child is dependent on its parents. 2. a person who is supported by another. 3. One happening is dependent on another when it is possible only if something else takes place. Being promoted is dependent on doing good enough work in school. A farmer's success is dependent on having the right kind of weather for his crops. *adj., n. 7.*

de pict (di pikt′), represent by drawing, painting, or describing; portray. The artist and the author both tried to depict the splendor of the sunset. *v. 8.*

de plete (di plēt′), empty; exhaust. Because his funds were depleted, the traveler went back home. *v. 16.*

de ple tion (di plē′shən), emptying; exhausting. *n. 18.*

de plor a ble (di plōr′ə bəl), that is to be deplored; lamentable; regrettable. *adj. 13.*

de plore (di plōr′), be very sorry about; express great sorrow for. We deplore the accident. *v. 7.*

de pop u late (dē pop′ū lāt), deprive of inhabitants, wholly or in part. The conquerors depopulated sections of the enemy's country, driving the inhabitants away or killing them. *v. 15.*

de pop u la tion (dē pop′ū lā′shən), 1. depopulating. 2. being depopulated. *n. 16.*

de port (di pōrt′), 1. carry off; remove; banish. When an alien is deported, he is sent out of the country, usually back to his native land. 2. behave (oneself) in a particular manner. Deport yourself like a gentleman. *v. 19.*

de por ta tion (dē′pōr tā′shən), removal from a country by banishment or expulsion. Deportation of criminals from England to Australia was once common. *n. 15.*

de port ment (di pōrt′mənt), behavior; conduct; way a person acts. *n. 8.*

de pose (di pōz′), 1. put out of office or position, especially a high one like that of king. 2. declare under oath. He deposed that he had seen the prisoner on the day of the murder. *v. 7.*

de pos it (di poz′it), 1. put down. He deposited his bundles on the table. 2. leave lying. The flood deposited a layer of mud in the streets. 3. laying down material by natural means; the material laid down; as, deposits of tin. 4. put in a place for safekeeping. Deposit your money in the bank. 5. something put in a certain place for safekeeping. Money put in the bank is a deposit. 6. pay down as a pledge for carrying out a promise to do something or to pay more later. If you will deposit $5, we will hold the coat for you. 7. the money paid down as a pledge of this sort. *v., n. 3.*

dep o si tion (dep′ə zish′ən), 1. act of deposing or putting down; removal from office, position, or power. 2. the giving of testimony under oath. 3. statement or testimony. The deposition of the last witness convicted the accused man. 4. depositing; putting in place or position; as, the deposition of funds in a bank, the deposition of sediment in a liquid. 5. thing deposited; a deposit. *n. 12.*

de pos i tor (di poz′i tər), person who deposits. Depositors in savings banks may receive interest on the money deposited. *n.*

de pos i to ry (di poz′i tō′ri), place where anything is stored for safekeeping; storehouse. *n., pl. depositories. 15.*

de pot (dē′pō), 1. railroad station. 2. storehouse. 3. place for storing military supplies. *n. 5.*

de prave (di prāv′), make bad; corrupt; injure morally. Drinking too much alcoholic liquor often depraves a person's character. *v.*

de praved (di prāvd′), vicious; having very bad morals. That murderer is so depraved that he has no regard for human life. *adj. 13.*

de prav i ty (di prav′i ti), wickedness; corruption; viciousness. *n., pl. depravities. 15.*

dep re cate (dep′ri kāt), express strong disapproval of. Peace lovers deprecate war. *v. 10.*

dep re ca tion (dep′ri kā′shən), strong expression of disapproval; a pleading or protesting against something. *n.*

de pre ci ate (di prē′shi āt), 1. lessen the value or price of. 2. lessen in value. Rubber goods depreciate if they are kept very long. 3. speak slightingly of; belittle. Mr. Brown depreciates the value of exercise. *v. 10.*

de pre ci a tion (di prē′shi ā′shən), a lowering or being lowered in price, value, or estimation. *n. 11.*

dep re da tion (dep′ri dā′shən), act of plundering; robbery; a ravaging. *n. 14.*

de press (di pres′), 1. press down; lower. When you play the piano, you depress the keys. 2. make less active; weaken. Some medicines depress the action of the heart. 3. make sad. Rainy weather always depresses me. She was depressed by the death of her son. *v. 7.*

de pres sion (di presh′ən), 1. pressing down; a lowering or sinking. 2. a hollow. Water filled the depressions in the ground. 3. low spirits; sadness. In a fit of depression the sick man killed himself. 4. dullness; inactivity. Many men lost their jobs during the business depression. *n. 7.*

dep ri va tion (dep′ri vā′shən), 1. depriving. 2. being deprived; loss. *n. 12.*

de prive (di prīv′). **Deprive of** means (1) take away from by force. The people deprived the cruel dictator of his power. (2) keep from having. His troubles deprived him of sleep. *v. 5.*

dept., department. *18.*

depth (depth), 1. distance from the top to the bottom; as, the depth of a hole, the depth of a lake. 2. the deepest or most central part of anything; as, in the depths of the earth, in the depths of one's heart, in the depth of winter. 3. distance from front to back. The depth of our house lot is 125 feet. 4. deepness. *n. 3.*

dep u ta tion (dep′ū tā′shən), 1. act of deputing. 2. group of persons sent to represent others. A deputation of workingmen called upon the owner of the factory to ask for higher pay. *n. 12.*

de pute (di pūt′), 1. appoint to do one's work or act in one's place. The teacher deputed John to take charge of the room while she was out of it. 2. give (one's work, power, etc.) to another. *v. 10.*

dep u tize (dep′ū tīz), 1. appoint as deputy. 2. act as deputy. *v.*

dep u ty (dep′ū ti), person appointed to do the work or take the place of another. John was the teacher's deputy for half an hour. *n., pl. deputies. 5.*

de rail (dē rāl′), 1. cause (a train, etc.) to run off the rails. 2. run off the rails. *v.*

de range (di rānj′), 1. disturb the arrangement of; throw into confusion. Sudden illness in the family deranged our plans for a trip. 2. make insane. *v. 14.*

de range ment (di rānj′mənt), 1. deranging. 2. being deranged. 3. mental disorder or insanity. *n. 18.*

der by (dėr′bi), a stiff hat with rounded crown and narrow brim. *n., pl. derbies. 12.*

Derby

Der by (dėr′bi), a famous horse race in England, founded by the Earl of Derby in 1780 and run every year near London. *n.*

der e lict (der′i likt), 1. abandoned; as, a derelict ship. 2. something abandoned; an abandoned ship. *adj., n.*

der e lic tion (der′i lik′shən), 1. neglect of duty; failure in duty. Because of the watchman's dereliction, thieves managed to enter the bank. 2. abandoning. 3. being abandoned. *n. 15.*

de ride (di rīd′), make fun of; laugh at in scorn. The boys derided Percy because of his curls. *v. 8.*

de ri sion (di rizh′ən), scornful laughter; ridicule. Children dread the derision of their playmates. *n. 7.*

de ri sive (di rī′siv), mocking; ridiculing. *adj. 13.*

der i va tion (der′i vā′shən), 1. deriving; obtaining from a source. 2. origin; descent. The celebration of Halloween is of Scottish derivation. 3. a theory of the formation of a word. *n. 13.*

de riv a tive (di riv′ə tiv), 1. derived. 2. something derived. Words formed by adding prefixes and suffixes to other words are called derivatives. *adj., n. 17.*

de rive (di rīv′), 1. get; obtain. He derives much pleasure from his books. From *deep* you can derive *deeper, deeply,* and *deepen.* 2. originate. *v. 4.*

der mis (dėr′mis), 1. the sensitive layer of skin beneath the outer skin. 2. skin. *n. 19.*

der o gate (der′ə gāt), 1. take away; detract. 2. grow worse in value or character. *v. 16.*

der o ga tion (der′ə gā′shən), 1. a lessening of authority, estimation, etc. 2. deterioration; debasement. *n. 19.*

de rog a to ry (di rog′ə tō′ri), lessening the value of; belittling; disparaging; unfavorable. *adj. 18.*

der rick (der′ik), 1. a machine for lifting and moving heavy objects. A derrick has a long arm that swings at an angle from the base of an upright post or frame. 2. towerlike framework over an oil well, gas well, etc., that holds the drilling and hoisting machinery. *n. 14.*

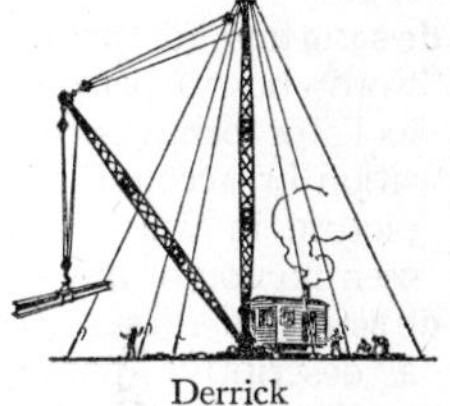
Derrick

der vish (dėr′vish), a member of any of various Mohammedan orders of religious enthusiasts. Dancing dervishes dance and spin about violently. Howling dervishes chant and shout loudly. *n. 17.*

des cant (des kant′), talk at great length. Helen descanted upon the wonders of her trip to California. *v. 14.*

de scend (di send′), 1. go or come down from a higher to a lower place. We descend the stairs, a mountain, a river. The river descends to the sea. 2. go from earlier to later time. 3. go from greater to less numbers; go from higher to lower on any scale. 75-50-25 form a descending series. 4. be handed down from parent to child. This land has belonged to our family for 150 years, descending from father to son. 5. make a sudden attack. The wolves descended on the sheep and killed them. *v. 2.*

de scend ant (di sen′dənt), 1. person born of a certain family or group; as, a descendant of the Pilgrims. 2. offspring; child, grandchild, great-grandchild, etc. You are a direct descendant of your parents, grandparents, great-grandparents, etc. *n. 7.*

de scent (di sent′), 1. coming or going down from a higher to a lower place. The descent of the balloon was more rapid than its rise had been. 2. downward slope. 3. handing down from parent to child. We can trace the descent of this shape of lip through five generations. 4. family line. I can trace my descent back to a family in Kent, England, in the 16th century. 5. sudden attack. *n. 5.*

de scribe (di skrīb′), 1. tell in words how a person looks, feels, or acts, or how a place, a thing, or an event looks; tell about in words. 2. trace or form; draw the outline of. The spinning top described a figure 8. *v. 2.*

de scrip tion (di skrip′shən), 1. a telling in words how a person, place, thing, or event looks or behaves; a describing. 2. composition or account that describes or gives a picture in words. 3. kind; sort. I have seen no dog of any description today. *n. 3.*

de scrip tive (di skrip′tiv), describing. Write a descriptive paragraph about a flower garden. *adj. 10.*

de scry (di skrī′), catch sight of; be able to see; make out; see at a distance; see with difficulty. We descried the little boat. *v., descried, descrying. 6.*

des e crate (des′i krāt), treat or use without respect; disregard the sacredness of. The enemy desecrated the church by using it as a stable. *v. 16.*

des e cra tion (des′i krā′shən), 1. desecrating. The Puritans felt that work or amusement on the Sabbath was a desecration. 2. being desecrated. *n. 19.*

des ert[1] (dez′ərt), 1. a region without water and trees; as, the Sahara Desert. 2. not inhabited or cultivated; barren and desolate. Robinson Crusoe was shipwrecked on a desert island. *n., adj. 2.*

de sert[2] (di zėrt′), forsake; go away and leave a person or a place, especially one which should not be left. A soldier who deserts is punished. The deserted house fell into ruins. *v.*

de sert[3] (di zėrt′), what one deserves; due reward or punishment. The thief was punished according to his deserts. The thief got his just deserts. *n.*

de sert er (di zėr′tər), 1. person who deserts. 2. a soldier or sailor who runs away from duty. *n. 16.*

de ser tion (di zėr′shən), 1. a deserting. 2. a being deserted. 3. act of running away from duty or leaving military service without permission. *n. 10.*

de serve (di zėrv′), have a right to; have a claim to; be worthy of. Good work deserves good pay. Bad acts deserve punishment. *v. 2.*

de serv ed ly (di zėr′vid li), according to what is deserved; properly; as was right. The criminal was deservedly punished. *adv. 18.*

des ic cate (des′i kāt), 1. dry thoroughly. The soil in a desert is desiccated. 2. preserve by drying; as, desiccated fruit. *v. 18.*

de sid er a tum (di sid′ər ā′təm), something desired or needed. Health, security and affection are desiderata. *n., pl. desiderata* (-tə). *17.*

de sign (di zīn′), 1. a drawing, plan, or sketch made to serve as a pattern from which to work. She is working now from my designs. 2. arrangement of details, form, and color in painting, weaving, building, etc.; as, a wallpaper design in tan and brown. 3. make a first sketch of; plan out; arrange form and color of. 4. draw a plan to be carried out by others; make drawings, plans, or sketches for manufacturers; as, to design a dress. He designs for our dress department. 5. a plan in mind to be carried out; a purpose. The thief was not able to carry out his designs because of the dog. 6. have in mind to do; to purpose. Did you design this result? 7. set apart; intend; plan. The nursery was designed for the baby's use. His parents designed him for the ministry. *n., v. 3.*

Design for a calendar

des ig nate (dez′ig nāt), 1. mark out; point out; show. Will you designate the flowers you wish? 2. name. The ruler of a kingdom is designated a king. *v. 8.*

des ig na tion (dez′ig nā′shən), 1. act of marking out; act of pointing out. The designation of places on a map should be clear. 2. appointment to an office or position. The designation of Mr. Mann as principal pleased the teachers. 3. name; description; title. *n. 13.*

de sign ed ly (di zīn′id li), purposely; intentionally. *adv. 20.*

de sign er (di zīn′ər), person who designs; as, a designer of wallpaper, a designer of dresses, a designer of machinery. *n. 10.*

de sign ing (di zīn′ing), 1. scheming; plotting. 2. showing plan or forethought. 3. art of making designs, patterns, sketches, etc. *adj., n. 17.*

de sir a bil i ty (di zīr′ə bil′i ti), desirable quality; condition to be wished for. *n.*

de sir a ble (di zīr′ə bəl), 1. worth wishing for. 2. pleasant; satisfying; good. *adj. 5.*

de sire (di zīr′), 1. wish. 2. wish earnestly for. 3. ask for. 4. a long, earnest wish. 5. thing wished for. *v., n. 1.*

de sir ous (di zīr′əs), desiring; wishing; eager; as, desirous of going to Mexico. *adj. 6.*

de sist (di zist′), stop; cease. *v. 10.*

desk (desk), piece of furniture with a flat or sloping top on which to write or to rest books for reading. *n. 2.*

Des Moines (də moin′), capital of Iowa.

des o late (des′ə lāt for 1 and 5, des′ə lit for 2, 3, 4, 6, and 7), 1. make unfit to live in. 2. not lived in; as, a desolate house. 3. left alone. 4. barren. 5. make unhappy. We are desolated to hear that you are going away. 6. unhappy; forlorn. The child looked desolate. 7. gloomy; dark; as, a desolate life. *v., adj. 4.*

des o la tion (des′ə lā′shən), 1. making desolate. 2. a ruined, lonely, or deserted condition. 3. desolate place. 4. sadness; lonely sorrow. *n. 5.*

De So to (di sō′tō), Spanish explorer who discovered the Mississippi (1500?-1542). *18.*

de spair (di spãr′), 1. loss of hope; a being without hope; a dreadful feeling that nothing good can happen. Despair seized us as we felt the boat sinking under us. 2. lose hope; be without hope. The doctors despaired of saving the child's life. 3. something that causes loss of hope. *n., v. 3.*

des patch (dis pach′), dispatch. *v., n. 6.*

des per a do (des′pər ā′dō), a reckless man ready for desperate deeds or crimes. *n., pl. desperadoes* or *desperados. 14.*

des per ate (des′pər it), 1. not caring what happens because hope is gone. 2. having little chance for hope or cure; very dangerous; as, a desperate illness. 3. ready to run any risk; as, a desperate robber. *adj. 4.*

des per a tion (des′pər ā′shən), 1. recklessness; readiness to try anything. In desperation he decided on a dash through the flames. 2. despair. *n. 10.*

des pi ca ble (des′pi kə bəl), contemptible. It is despicable to go away and leave a cat behind to starve. *adj. 15.*

de spise (di spīz′), look down upon; scorn; think of as beneath one's notice, or as too mean or low for one to do. Honest boys despise lies and liars. *v. 3.*

de spite (di spīt′), 1. in spite of. The boys went for a walk despite the rain. 2. contempt; scorn. The selfish lord turned from the beggar in despite. *Old use.* 3. insult; injury. The hero avenged the despite done to his brother. 4. spite; malice. *prep., n. 4.*

de spite ful (di spīt′fəl), spiteful; malicious. *adj.* [*Old use*] *17.*

de spoil (di spoil′), rob; plunder. *v. 12.*

de spond (di spond′), lose heart, courage, or hope. Though very ill, he did not despond. *v. 18.*

de spond ence (di spon′dəns), loss of spirits; dejection. *n. 17.*

de spond en cy (di spon′dən si), very low spirits; discouraged state; loss of hope. *n. 11.*

de spond ent (di spon′dənt), having lost heart, courage, or hope; depressed; dejected. *adj. 17.*

des pot (des′pot), an absolute ruler; tyrant; person who does just as he likes. In ancient times many rulers were despots. *n. 8.*

des pot ic (des pot′ik), tyrannical; arbitrary. *adj. 9.*

des pot ism (des′pət izm), the rule of a despot; absolute power; tyranny. *n. 10.*

des sert (di zėrt′), a course of sweets or fruit at the end of a meal. In America we call pie, cake, puddings, and ice cream, desserts. In England dessert means fruit and nuts. *n. 7.*

des ti na tion (des′ti nā′shən), the place to which a person or thing is going. *n. 7.*

des tine (des′tin), 1. intend; set apart for a purpose or use. The boy was destined from his birth to enter the church. 2. cause by fate. My letter was destined never to reach him. 3. **Destined for** means (1) intended to go to; bound for; as, ships destined for England. (2) intended for; as, destined for the ministry. *v. 4.*

des ti ny (des′ti ni), 1. what becomes of a person or thing in the end. 2. fate; what is determined beforehand to happen. *n., pl. destinies. 5.*

des ti tute (des′ti tūt or des′ti tüt), 1. needing necessary things such as food, clothing, and shelter. A destitute family needs help from charity. 2. **Destitute of** means having no; empty of. *Destitute of* usually implies that the thing might have been there but isn't. A bald head is destitute of hair. *adj. 7.*

des ti tu tion (des′ti tū′shən or des′ti tü′shən), lack of the means of living; utter poverty. *n. 20.*

de stroy (di stroi′), pull down; break to pieces; spoil; ruin; put an end to; kill. Fire destroys many trees every year. A heavy rain destroyed all hope of a picnic. *v. 1.*

de stroy er (di stroi′ər), 1. person or thing that destroys. 2. small, fast warship with guns, torpedoes, and other weapons. *n. 10.*

de struc tion (di struk′shən), 1. destroying. 2. ruin. The storm left destruction behind it. *n. 3.*

de struc tive (di struk′tiv), destroying; causing destruction. Fires and earthquakes are destructive. Destructive criticism shows things to be wrong, but does not show how to correct them. *adj. 10.*

des ue tude (des′wi tūd or des′wi tüd), disuse. Many words once commonly employed have fallen into desuetude. *n. 15.*

des ul to ry (des′əl tō′ri), jumping from one thing to another; disconnected; without aim or method. The careful study of a few books is better than the desultory reading of many. *adj. 11.*

de tach (di tach′), 1. unfasten; loosen and remove; separate. He detached his watch from the chain. 2. in the army or navy, to send away on special duty. One squad of soldiers was detached to guard the road. *v. 9.*

de tach a ble (di tach′ə bəl), that can be detached; as, a notebook with detachable leaves. *adj. 17.*

de tach ment (di tach′mənt), 1. separation. 2. aloofness. 3. freedom from prejudice; impartial attitude. 4. troops or ships sent away on special duty. *n. 8.*

de tail (di tāl′ for 1, 2, 3, 4, and 5, or dē′tāl for 1, 2, and 4), 1. a small or unimportant part. All the details of her costume carried out the brown color scheme. 2. dealing with small things one by one. She does not enjoy the details of housekeeping. 3. tell fully; give the particulars of. The new boy detailed to us all the wonders he had seen in his travels. 4. in the army, a small group of men or officers sent on some special duty. The captain sent a detail of ten men to guard the bridge. 5. send on special duty. The captain detailed three soldiers to watch the road. *n., v. 4.*

de tain (di tān′), keep back; delay; keep from going ahead; keep from going away. The police detained the suspected thief for further questioning. *v. 4.*

de tect (di tekt′), find out; make out; discover; catch. Could you detect any odor in the room? Tom was detected stealing cookies in the pantry. *v. 6.*

de tec tion (di tek′shən), discovery; finding out. *n. 15.*

de tec tive (di tek′tiv), 1. a policeman or private person whose business is to get information secretly. 2. having to do with detectives and their work. 3. used in discovering or finding out; as, detective methods. *n., adj. 11.*

de tec tor (di tek′tər), 1. person or thing that detects. 2. vacuum tube or crystal in a radio. *n. 12.*

de ten tion (di ten′shən), 1. act of detaining. 2. state of being detained. Detention after hours used to be a common punishment in school. 3. confinement. A **house of detention** is a kind of jail. *n. 15.*

de ter (di tėr′), discourage; keep back; hinder. The extreme heat deterred us from going downtown. *v., deterred, deterring. 11.*

de te ri o rate (di tēr′i ə rāt), 1. make worse. A hot, damp climate deteriorates leather. 2. become worse. Machinery deteriorates rapidly if it is not taken care of. *v. 13.*

de te ri o ra tion (di tēr′i ə rā′shən), making or becoming worse. The Smiths moved away because of the deterioration of the neighborhood. *n. 15.*

de ter mi nant (di tėr′mi nənt), 1. determining; deciding. The longer vacation offered was the determinant factor in Mr. Brown's change of position. 2. thing that determines. *adj., n. 17.*

de ter mi nate (di tėr′mi nit), with exact limits; fixed; definite. *adj. 10.*

de ter mi na tion (di tėr′mi nā′shən), 1. deciding; settling beforehand. The determination of the list of things to prepare for that important dinner took a long time. 2. finding out the exact amount or kind by weighing, measuring, or calculating; as, the determination of the gold in a sample of rock. 3. fixed purpose; great firmness in carrying out a purpose. The boy's determination was not weakened by the difficulties he met. *n. 7.*

de ter mine (di tėr′min), 1. make up one's mind very firmly. He determined to become the best Scout in his troop. 2. fix or settle beforehand. Can we now determine the date for our party? 3. be the deciding fact in reaching a certain result. The number of examples you get right determines your mark on this test. Tomorrow's events will determine whether we are to go or stay. 4. settle; decide. 5. give an aim to; direct. 6. limit; define. The meaning of a word is partly determined by its use in the particular sentence. 7. bring to an end; come to an end. *v. 2.*

de ter mined (di tėr′mind), 1. with one's mind firmly made up; resolved. The determined explorer kept on his way in spite of the storm. 2. firm; resolute. His determined look showed that he had made up his mind. *adj.*

de test (di test′), dislike very much; hate. *v. 7.*

de test a ble (di tes′tə bəl), deserving to be detested; hateful. Murder is a detestable crime. *adj. 11.*

de tes ta tion (dē′tes tā′shən), 1. great hatred. 2. the object of hatred. Snakes are her detestation. *n. 15.*

de throne (di thrōn′), put off a throne; remove from ruling power; depose. *v. 10.*

de throne ment (di thrōn′mənt), removal from the throne. *n. 17.*

det o nate (det′ō nāt), explode with a loud noise. The men detonated the dynamite. *v.*

det o na tion (det′ō nā′shən), 1. explosion with a loud noise. 2. loud noise. *n.*

de tour (dē′tür), 1. road that is used when the main or direct road cannot be traveled. 2. roundabout way. 3. use a detour. *n., v. 14.*

de tract (di trakt′), take away. The ugly frame detracts from the beauty of the picture. *v. 18.*

de trac tion (di trak′shən), taking away; speaking evil of; belittling. *n. 12.*

de trac tor (di trak′tər), person who speaks evil of or belittles another. *n.*

det ri ment (det′ri mənt), loss; damage; injury. John worked his way through college without detriment to his studies. *n. 10.*

det ri men tal (det′ri men′təl), harmful; injurious. Lack of sleep is detrimental to one's health. *adj. 15.*

de tri tus (di trī′təs), particles of rock or other material worn away from a mass. *n. 19.*

De troit (di troit′), the largest city in Michigan, and the fourth city in the United States for size. *n. 8.*

deuce (dūs or düs), 1. the two spot at cards or dice. 2. in tennis, an even score of 40 each, or five games each. 3. an exclamation of annoyance meaning bad luck, the mischief, the devil. *n., interj. 17.*

Deu ter on o my (dū′tər on′ə mi or dü′tər on′ə mi), the fifth book of the Old Testament. *n. 18.*

dev as tate (dev′əs tāt), destroy; ravage; lay waste; make desolate. A long war devastated Europe. *v. 10.*

dev as ta tion (dev′əs tā′shən), destruction; ravage; desolation; laying waste or being laid waste. *n. 14.*

de vel op (di vel′əp), 1. grow; bring or come into being or activity. Plants develop from seeds. The seeds develop into plants. A boy may develop an interest in stamps. An interest in cooking developed in Mary when she was ten. 2. work out in greater and greater detail. Gradually we developed our plans for the Boys' Club. Day by day the story was developed in the author's mind. 3. treat (a photographic plate or film) with chemicals so that the picture shows. *v. 3.*

de vel op ment (di vel′əp mənt), 1. developing; gradual unfolding; growth; bringing or coming to light. 2. outcome; result; news. A newspaper gives news about the latest developments. 3. working out in greater and greater detail. *n. 4.*

de vi ate (dē′vi āt), turn aside (from a way, course, rule, truth, etc.). The teacher deviated from her custom and gave out no homework. *v. 13.*

de vi a tion (dē′vi ā′shən), turning aside. No deviation from the rules will be allowed. *n. 13.*

de vice (di vīs′), 1. a mechanical invention used for a special purpose; machine; apparatus; as, a device for lighting a gas stove. 2. a plan; a scheme; sometimes, a trick.

By some device or other the thief got the boy to let him into the house. 3. a drawing or figure used in a pattern or as an ornament. 4. **Left to one's own devices** means left to do as one thinks best. *n. 4.*

dev il (dev′əl), 1. **The Devil** means the evil spirit, the enemy of goodness, or Satan. 2. any evil spirit. 3. person who is especially wicked, reckless, clever, active, etc. 4. person who has to work for others and stand their abuse. A printer's devil is the errand boy in a printing office. 5. bother; tease; torment. *n., v., deviled, deviling. 2.*

dev iled (dev′əld), highly seasoned; as, deviled ham. *adj.*

dev il fish (dev′əl fish′), 1. a large, odd-shaped sea animal. 2. octopus. *n.*

Devilfish (def. 1) (about 20 ft. across)

dev il ish (dev′əl ish), 1. very evil; worthy of the devil; like a devil. 2. very; extremely; very great. *adj., adv. 8.*

dev il ment (dev′əl mənt), devilish action or behavior; mischief. *n.*

dev il try (dev′əl tri), 1. evil action; wicked behavior. 2. great cruelty or wickedness. 3. mischief; daring behavior. *n., pl. deviltries.*

de vi ous (dē′vi əs), 1. out of the direct way; winding. We took the devious route home to avoid the crowds in the main roads. 2. wandering; straying. *adj. 12.*

de vise (di vīz′), 1. think out; plan; contrive; invent. The boys are trying to devise some scheme of earning money. 2. give; assign. *v. 8.*

de void (di void′), empty. **Devoid of** means having no; without. A well devoid of water is useless. *adj. 12.*

de voir (də vwär′), 1. act of courtesy or respect. 2. duty. *n. 16.*

de volve (di volv′), 1. transfer (duty, work, etc.) to someone else. 2. be transferred; be handed down. If the President is unable to attend to his duties, they devolve upon the Vice-President. *v. 13.*

Dev on (dev′ən), a county in southwestern England. *n. 12.*

de vote (di vōt′), give up (oneself, one's money, time, or efforts) to some person, purpose, or service. A mother devotes herself to her children. Mary devotes too much time to eating. He devoted his efforts to the improvement of the parks in his city. *v. 3.*

de vot ed (di vōt′id), very loyal; as, a devoted friend. *adj.*

dev o tee (dev′ə tē′), person who gives himself up to something with great zeal. *n. 11.*

de vo tion (di vō′shən), 1. deep, steady affection; as, the devotion of a mother to her child. 2. a giving up or being given up to some person, purpose, or service. 3. **Devotions** means worship, prayers, or praying. *n. 5.*

de vo tion al (di vō′shən əl), pertaining to devotion; used in worship. *adj. 20.*

de vour (di vour′), 1. eat (said of animals). The lion devoured the sheep. 2. eat like an animal; eat very hungrily. The hungry boy was devouring his dinner. 3. consume, waste, or destroy; as, a devouring disease. 4. take in with eyes or ears in a hungry, greedy way; as, to devour a new book. *v. 4.*

de vout (di vout′), 1. religious; active in worship and prayer. 2. earnest; sincere; hearty; as, devout thanks. *adj. 6.*

dew (dū or dü), 1. moisture condensed from the air. In the morning there are drops of dew on the grass and flowers. 2. something fresh or refreshing like dew; as, the dew of youth, the dew of sleep. 3. to wet with dew; moisten. *n., v. 2.*

dew ber ry (dū′ber′i or dü′ber′i), a kind of blackberry. *n., pl. dewberries. 20.*

dew drop (dū′drop′ or dü′drop′), drop of dew. *n. 10.*

dew lap (dū′lap′ or dü′lap′), the loose fold of skin under the throat of cattle and some other animals. *n.*

DEWLAP

dew y (dū′i or dü′i), 1. wet with dew. 2. looking as if wet with dew. *adj., dewier, dewiest. 7.*

dex ter i ty (deks ter′i ti), skill in using the hands or mind; cleverness. A good surgeon works with dexterity. *n. 8.*

dex ter ous (deks′tər əs), 1. having skill with the hands. A typist, a dressmaker, an artist, and a pianist need to be dexterous. 2. quick and skillful in bodily movement. 3. having skill with the mind; clever. A manager should be dexterous in handling men. *adj. 11.*

dex trous (deks′trəs), dexterous. *adj.*

di a be tes (dī′ə bē′tis), a disease in which a person's system cannot properly absorb sugar or starchy food. *n. 13.*

di a bol ic (dī′ə bol′ik), devilish; like the devil; very cruel or wicked. *adj. 15.*

di a bol i cal (dī′ə bol′i kəl), diabolic. *adj.*

di a crit ic (dī′ə krit′ik), 1. a diacritical mark. 2. diacritical. *n., adj.*

di a crit i cal (dī′ə krit′i kəl), used to distinguish. **Diacritical marks** are marks like ¨ ^ ¯ ′, put on letters to indicate pronunciation, accent, etc. *adj.*

di a dem (dī′ə dem), crown; headband worn by kings or queens. *n. 8.*

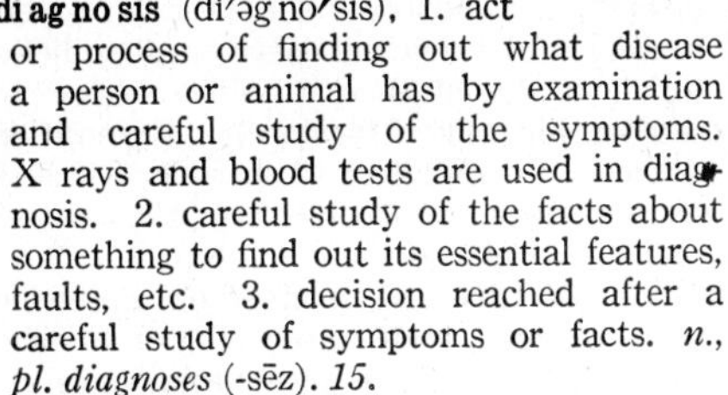

Diadem

di ag nose (dī′əg nōs′), make a diagnosis of; find out the nature of by an examination. *v. 16.*

di ag no sis (dī′əg nō′sis), 1. act or process of finding out what disease a person or animal has by examination and careful study of the symptoms. X rays and blood tests are used in diagnosis. 2. careful study of the facts about something to find out its essential features, faults, etc. 3. decision reached after a careful study of symptoms or facts. *n., pl. diagnoses* (-sēz). *15.*

di ag o nal (dī ag′ə nəl), 1. a straight line that cuts across in a slanting direction, often from corner to corner. 2. taking the direction of a diagonal; slanting; as, a ship sailing on a diagonal course, a diagonal ridge in cloth. *n., adj. 9.*

A B

Line AB is a diagonal.

di ag o nal ly (dī ag′ə nəl i), in a diagonal direction. *adv.*

di a gram (dī′ə gram), 1. a drawing or sketch showing important parts of a thing. A diagram may be an outline, a plan, a drawing, a figure, a chart, or a combination of any of these, made to show clearly what a thing is or how it works. Tom drew a diagram to show us how to get to his house. The engineer drew a diagram of the bridge. A plan of a house or a steamship is a diagram. 2. put on paper in the form of a drawing or sketch; make a diagram of. *n., v., diagramed, diagraming. 8.*

di a gram mat ic (dī′ə grə mat′ik), 1. in the form of a diagram. 2. in outline only; sketchy. *adj.*

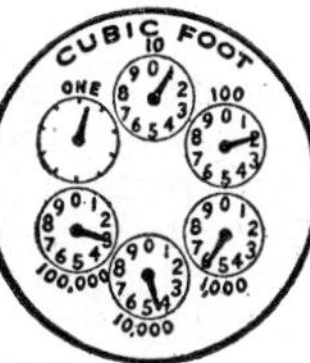

Dials on a gas meter

di al (dī′əl), 1. a marked surface on which a moving pointer shows how much there is of something. The face of a clock or of a compass is a dial. A dial may show the amount of water in a tank or the amount of steam pressure in a boiler. 2. plate, disk, etc., of a radio with numbers, letters, etc., on it for tuning in to a radio station. 3. the part of an automatic telephone used in making telephone calls. 4. show on a telephone dial. 5. call by means of a telephone dial. Martha dialed Main 2590 to call her father's office. 6. sundial. *n., v., dialed, dialing. 6.*

di a lect (dī′ə lekt), a form of speech peculiar to a district or class; as, the Scottish dialect, the Negro dialect, the dialect spoken in southern Louisiana. *n. 7.*

di a lec tal (dī′ə lek′təl), of a dialect; like that of a dialect. *adj.*

di a logue or **di a log** (dī′ə lôg), 1. conversation. Two actors had a dialogue in the middle of the stage. 2. a conversation written out. *n. 7.*

di am e ter (dī am′i tər), 1. a straight line passing through the center from one side of a circle, or other object, to the other side. 2. the length of such a line; measurement through the center. *n. 8.*

A B

Line AB is a diameter.

di a met ri cal ly (dī′ə met′ri kəl i), 1. as a diameter. 2. **Diametrically opposed** means directly opposite; exactly contrary. *adv.*

di a mond (dī′ə mənd), 1. a colorless or tinted precious stone, formed of pure carbon in crystals. It is the hardest substance known. 2. a figure shaped like this ◊. 3. the space inside the lines that connect the bases in baseball. *n. 2.*

Diamond

Di an (dī′an), Diana. *n.* [*Used in poetry*] *18.*

Di an a (dī an′ə), the Roman goddess of the hunt and of the moon, and the protectress of women. The Greeks called her Artemis. *n. 6.*

di a pa son (dī′ə pā′zən), 1. harmony. 2. melody; strain. 3. a swelling musical sound. 4. the range of a voice or instrument. 5. a fixed standard of musical pitch. 6. either of two principal stops in an organ. *n. 15.*

di a per (dī′ə pər), 1. small piece of cloth used as a part of a baby's underclothing. 2. pattern of small, constantly repeated geometric figures. 3. white cotton or linen cloth woven with such a pattern. 4. ornament with such a pattern. *n., v. 11.*

di a phragm (dī′ə fram), 1. a partition of muscles and tendons separating the cavity of the chest from the cavity of the abdomen. 2. a dividing partition. 3. vibrating disk in a telephone. *n. 10.*

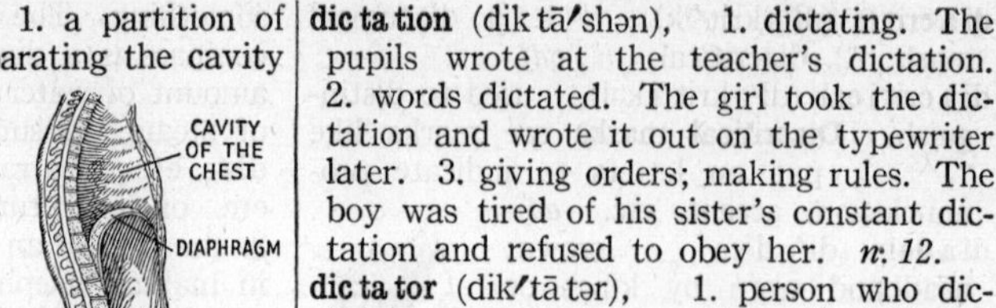

di ar rhe a or **di ar rhoe a** (dī′ə rē′ə), too many and too loose movements of the bowels. *n. 13.*

di a ry (dī′ə ri), 1. an account, written down each day, of what has happened to one, or what one has done or thought, during that day. 2. a blank book with a space for each day in which to keep a daily record. *n., pl. diaries. 8.*

di a tribe (dī′ə trīb), a speech or discussion bitterly and violently denouncing some person or thing. *n.*

dib ble (dib′əl), pointed tool for making holes in the ground for seeds, young plants, etc. *n. 20.*

Dibble

dice (dīs), 1. small cubes with a different number of spots (one to six) on each side. Dice are used in playing games of chance. 2. play dice, tossing them to see how many spots there will be on the sides turned up. 3. cut into small cubes. Carrots are sometimes diced before being cooked. *n. pl. of* **die**[2], *v. 7.*

Dice

Dick ens (dik′inz), Charles, a famous English novelist (1812-1870). *n. 10.*

dick er (dik′ər), 1. to trade by barter or by petty bargaining. 2. a petty bargain. Mr. Smith made a dicker with his neighbor to take care of his hens during his absence in return for the eggs the hens laid. *v., n. 20.*

dic tate (dik′tāt), 1. say or read aloud to another person or other persons who are to write what is said or read. The teacher dictated a spelling list. A businessman often dictates to his secretary. 2. speak with authority; make others do what one says. The country that wins a war dictates the terms of peace to the country that loses. No one shall dictate to me. 3. a direction or order that is to be carried out or obeyed; as, the dictates of a ruler or of the teacher. *v., n. 5.*

dic ta tion (dik tā′shən), 1. dictating. The pupils wrote at the teacher's dictation. 2. words dictated. The girl took the dictation and wrote it out on the typewriter later. 3. giving orders; making rules. The boy was tired of his sister's constant dictation and refused to obey her. *n. 12.*

dic ta tor (dik′tā tər), 1. person who dictates. 2. person exercising absolute authority. The dictator of a country has complete power over its people. *n. 11.*

dic ta to ri al (dik′tə tō′ri əl), 1. of or like that of a dictator; as, dictatorial government. 2. imperious; domineering; overbearing. The soldiers disliked the dictatorial manner of their officers. *adj.*

dic ta tor ship (dik′tā tər ship′), 1. position or rank of a dictator. 2. period of time a dictator rules. 3. absolute authority; power to give orders that must be obeyed. *n.*

dic tion (dik′shən), manner of expressing ideas in words; style of speaking or writing. Good diction implies grammatical correctness, a wide vocabulary, and skill in the choice and arrangement of words. *n. 14.*

dic tion ar y (dik′shən ãr′i), a book that explains the words of a language, or some special kind of words. *n., pl. dictionaries. 7.*

dic tum (dik′təm), a saying; an utterance of authority. *n., pl. dictums, dicta* (-tə). *17.*

did (did). See **do**[1]. Did he go to school yesterday? Yes, he did. *pt. of do*[1]. *1.*

di dac tic (dī dak′tik), 1. meant to instruct; as, a didactic story. 2. teacherlike. Mary has a didactic manner toward her younger brothers and sisters. *adj. 15.*

did n't (did′ənt), did not. *3.*

didst (didst), an old form meaning **did.** "Thou didst" means "you did." *v.*

die[1] (dī), 1. stop living. 2. lose force or strength; come to an end. The music died away. 3. want very much. I am just dying to go with you. *v., died, dying. 1.*

die[2] (dī), 1. a carved metal block or plate. Different kinds of dies are used for coining money, for raising printing up from the surface of paper, and for giving a certain shape to articles made by forging and cutting. 2. a small cube used in games of chance. Dice is a game played with these cubes. **The die is cast** means the decision is made and cannot be changed. *n., pl. dies* for 1, *dice* for 2.

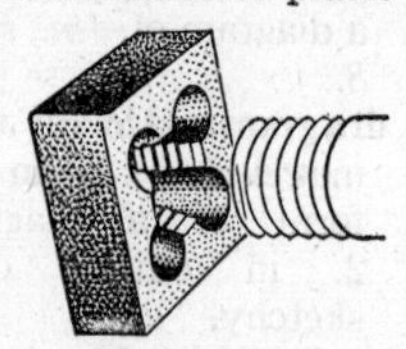
Die for cutting threads of bolts

Die sel en gine (dē′zəl en′jən), internal-combustion engine that burns oil with heat caused by the compression of air.

di et[1] (dī′ət), 1. the usual food for a person or an animal. A rich diet is not wholesome. The diet of the giraffe consists of young leaves and shoots. 2. any special selection of food eaten in sickness, or to make oneself fat, thin, etc. 3. eat special food as a part of a doctor's treatment, or in order to gain or lose weight. *n., v. 5.*

di et[2] (dī′ət), a formal assembly for discussion. *n.*

di e tar y (dī′ə tãr′i), pertaining to diet. Dietary rules tell what food to eat and how to prepare it. *adj. 17.*

di e tet ic (dī′ə tet′ik), of diet. *adj. 18.*

di e tet ics (dī′ə tet′iks), science that deals with the amount and kinds of food needed by the body. *n.*

di e ti tian or **di e ti cian** (dī′ə tish′ən), person trained to plan meals with a proper proportion of various kinds of food. Many hospitals and schools employ dietitians. *n.*

dif fer (dif′ər), 1. be unlike; be different. 2. hold or express a different opinion; disagree. *v. 3.*

dif fer ence (dif′ər əns), 1. being different; as, the difference of night and day. 2. the amount or manner of being different. The difference between 6 and 15 is 9. 3. a dispute. 4. **Make a difference** means (1) give or show different treatment. (2) matter; be important. *n. 1.*

dif fer ent (dif′ər ənt), 1. not alike; not like. People have different names. An automobile is different from a cart. 2. not the same; separate; distinct. We called three different times, but never found Alice at home. *adj. 1.*

dif fer en tial (dif′ər en′shəl), 1. of a difference; showing a difference; depending on a difference. Differential duties, rates, charges, etc., are those which differ according to circumstances. 2. arrangement of gears in an automobile that allows one of the rear wheels to turn faster than the other in going round a corner or curve. *adj., n. 13.*

dif fer en ti ate (dif′ər en′shi āt), 1. make different. Consideration of others differentiates good manners from mere politeness. 2. become different. One genus of plants often differentiates into many species. 3. perceive the difference in; make a distinction between. A botanist can differentiate varieties of plants. *v. 14.*

dif fer en ti a tion (dif′ər en′shi ā′shən), differentiating; alteration; modification; distinction. *n. 18.*

dif fi cult (dif′i kult), 1. hard to do or understand. The higher mathematics is difficult. 2. hard to manage; hard to please. The prima donna was difficult. *adj. 2.*

dif fi cul ty (dif′i kul ti), 1. a thing that is hard to do or understand. 2. something which stands in the way of getting things done, such as lack of money, lack of people to help, lack of understanding, or objections to plans. 3. the degree to which a thing is difficult. The difficulty of the job was not suspected at first. 4. hard work. Some children have a great deal of difficulty in learning how to spell. 5. trouble. *n., pl.* ***difficulties****. 3.*

dif fi dence (dif′i dəns), shyness; lack of self-confidence. *n. 11.*

dif fi dent (dif′i dənt), shy; lacking in self-confidence. *adj. 11.*

dif fuse (di fūz′ for 1 and 3, di fūs′ for 2 and 4), 1. spread out so as to cover a larger space or surface. Light, heat, kindness, good humor, and knowledge can be diffused. 2. spread out; not drawn together at a single point; as, diffuse light. 3. mix together by spreading into one another, as gases and liquids do. 4. using many words where a few would do; as, a diffuse writer. *v., adj. 5.*

dif fu sion (di fū′zhən), 1. spreading; being scattered; distribution. The invention of printing was a great aid to the diffusion of knowledge. 2. mixing together by spreading into one another; as, the diffusion of gases or liquids. *n. 11.*

dig (dig), 1. use hands, spade, claws, or snout in making a hole or in turning over the ground. 2. make by digging. They dug a cellar. 3. make a way by digging; as, to dig through or under a mountain. 4. get by digging; as, to dig potatoes or clams. 5. thrust; poke. 6. work hard. *v., dug* or *digged, digging, n. 2.*

di gest (di jest′ for 1, 2, and 4, dī′jest for 3), 1. change (food) in the stomach and intestines, so that the body can use it. We digest our food; the food digests or is digested. 2. think over until one understands (it) clearly, or until it becomes a part of one's own thought. 3. a brief statement of what is in a longer book or article. 4. make a brief statement of. *v., n. 7.*

di gest i ble (di jes′ti bəl), capable of being digested; easily digested. *adj. 13.*

di ges tion (di jes′chən), 1. the digesting of food. 2. the power of digesting. *n. 7.*

di ges tive (di jes′tiv), having to do with digestion; as, digestive trouble, digestive tablets. *adj. 8.*

dig ger (dig′ər), 1. person or thing that digs. 2. the part of a machine that turns up the ground. *n. 7.*

dight (dīt), clothed; decked; adorned. *adj.* [*Old use*] *20.*

dig it (dij′it), 1. finger or toe. 2. any of the figures 0, 1, 2, 3, 4, 5, 6, 7, 8, 9. Sometimes 0 is not called a digit. *n. 16.*

dig ni fied (dig′ni fīd), having dignity; noble; stately; of great worth. *adj. 12.*

dig ni fy (dig′ni fī), give dignity to; make noble, worth while, or worthy. The low farmhouse was dignified by the great elms around it. *v., dignified, dignifying. 5.*

dig ni tar y (dig′ni tãr′i), person who has a position of honor. A bishop is a church dignitary. *n., pl. dignitaries. 13.*

dig ni ty (dig′ni ti), 1. quality of character or ability that wins the respect and high opinion of others; worth; being noble, worthy, or stately. A judge should maintain the dignity of his position. 2. high office, rank, or title; position of honor. Any native-born citizen of the United States may attain the dignity of the presidency. 3. proud and self-respecting character or manner; stateliness. Milton's poetry has dignity. *n., pl. dignities. 4.*

di gress (di gres′), turn aside; get off the main subject in talking or writing. *v. 18.*

di gres sion (di gresh′ən), digressing; turning aside from the main subject. *n. 12.*

dike (dīk), 1. a bank of earth or a dam built as a defense against flooding by a river or the sea. 2. a ditch. 3. provide with dikes. *n., v. 12.*

di lap i dat ed (di lap′i dāt′id), falling to pieces; partly ruined or decayed through neglect; as, a dilapidated house. *adj. 12.*

di lap i da tion (di lap′i dā′shən), a falling to pieces; decay; ruin; tumble-down condition. The house was in the last stage of dilapidation. *n. 20.*

di late (dī lāt′), 1. make or become larger or wider. The pupil of the eye dilates when the light gets dim. 2. speak or write at length. Mother was dilating on Johnnie's success. *v. 6.*

di la tion (dī lā′shən), dilating; being dilated; widening; expansion; enlargement. *n. 19.*

dil a to ry (dil′ə tō′ri), tending to delay; not prompt. Many people are dilatory in paying their bills. *adj. 16.*

di lem ma (di lem′ə), a position requiring a choice between two evils; embarrassing or perplexing situation; difficult choice. Mary's dilemma was whether to go to the party in her old dress or to stay at home. *n. 13.*

dil et tan te (dil′ə tan′ti), 1. lover of the fine arts. 2. person who follows some art or science as an amusement or in a trifling way. 3. trifler. *n., pl. dilettantes, dilettanti* (-ti). *17.*

dil i gence (dil′i jəns), working hard; being diligent; ability to work steadily. *n. 7.*

dil i gent (dil′i jənt), hard-working; industrious; not lazy. *adj. 5.*

dill (dil), seed used in flavoring pickles. *n. 18.*

dil ly-dal ly (dil′i dal′i), loiter; waste time; trifle. *v., dilly-dallied, dilly-dallying.*

di lute (di lüt′), 1. make weaker or thinner by adding water or some other liquid. 2. weakened or thinned by water or some other liquid. *v., adj. 11.*

di lu tion (di lü′shən), 1. diluting. 2. being diluted. 3. something diluted. *n. 19.*

dim (dim), 1. not bright; not clear; not distinct. 2. not clearly seen, heard, or understood. 3. not seeing, hearing, or understanding clearly. My eyesight is getting dim. 4. make or become dim. *adj., dimmer, dimmest, v., dimmed, dimming. 3.*

dime (dīm), silver coin of the United States and of Canada, worth 10 cents. Ten dimes make one dollar. *n. 4.*

di men sion (di men′shən), 1. measurement of length, breadth, or thickness. If a room is 10 feet wide, 16 feet long, and 12 feet high, those are its dimensions. 2. **Dimensions** sometimes means size or extent. *n. 7.*

di min ish (di min′ish), make or become smaller in size, amount, or importance. The heat diminished as the sun went down. Our diminishing supply of food had to be given out very carefully. *v. 5.*

dim i nu tion (dim′i nū′shən or dim′i nü′shən), lessening; reduction; decrease. *n. 10.*

di min u tive (di min′ū tiv), 1. small; tiny. 2. a small person or thing. 3. expressing smallness. Such words as *droplet* and *lambkin* have diminutive endings. 4. a suffix expressing smallness, such as *-let* and *-kin.* *adj., n. 8.*

dim i ty (dim′i ti), 1. a thin cotton cloth woven with heavy threads at intervals in striped or crossbarred arrangement, used for dresses, curtains, etc. 2. a strong cotton cloth with raised stripes, used for hangings and for covering furniture. *n., pl. dimities. 15.*

dim ple (dim′pəl), 1. small hollow, usually in the cheek or chin. 2. any small, hollow place. 3. form dimples. Alice dimples whenever she smiles. 4. make or show dimples in. *n., v. 6.*

din (din), 1. a loud, confused noise that lasts. 2. make a din. 3. say (one thing) over and over. He was always dinning into our ears the importance of hard work. *n., v., dinned, dinning. 5.*

dine (dīn), 1. eat dinner. 2. give dinner to; give a dinner for. The Chamber of Commerce dined the famous traveler. *v. 2.*

din er (dīn′ər), 1. person who is eating dinner. 2. railroad car in which meals are served. *n.*

ding (ding), 1. make the sound of a bell. 2. this sound. *v., n. 20.*

din gey (ding′gi), dinghy. *n., pl. dingeys.*

din ghy (ding′gi), 1. small rowboat. 2. small boat. *n., pl. dinghies.*

Dinghy

din gi ness (din′ji nis), dirtiness; lack of cleanness and freshness. *n. 20.*

din gle (ding′gəl), a small, deep, shady valley. *n. 15.*

din gy (din′ji), dirty-looking; lacking brightness or freshness. *adj., dingier, dingiest. 9.*

din ner (din′ər), 1. the main meal of the day. In the city we have dinner at night, but in the country we have dinner at noon. 2. a formal meal in honor of some person or occasion. *n. 1.*

di no saur (dī′nə sôr), one of a group of extinct reptiles. Some dinosaurs were bigger than elephants. Some were smaller than cats. *n. 18.*

Dinosaur

dint (dint), 1. force. By dint of hard work the man became successful. 2. a dent. 3. make a dent in. *n., v. 9.*

di oc e san (dī os′i sən), 1. of or having to do with a diocese. 2. bishop in charge of a diocese. *adj., n. 18.*

di o cese (dī′ə sēs), the district over which a bishop has authority. *n. 13.*

Di og e nes (dī oj′i nēz), a Greek cynic philosopher who lived in a tub to show his indifference to comfort (412?-323 B.C.). *n. 14.*

Di o ny sus (dī′ə nī′səs), the Greek god of wine; Bacchus. *n.*

di ox ide (dī ok′sīd), an oxide containing two atoms of oxygen and one atom of a metal or other element. *n. 9.*

dip (dip), 1. put under water or any liquid and lift quickly out again. Mary dipped her head into the clear pool. 2. go under water and come quickly out again. 3. a dipping of any kind, especially, a plunge into and out of a tub of water, the sea, etc. 4. dye by dipping in a liquid. 5. wash or clean by dipping in a liquid. 6. mixture in which to dip something. 7. make (a candle) by putting a wick into hot tallow or wax. *v., dipped, dipping, n. 3.*

diph the ri a (dif thēr′i ə), a dangerous infectious disease of the throat. Antitoxin cures diphtheria. *n. 9.*

diph thong (dif′thông), a union of two vowels pronounced in one syllable, such as *oi* in *noise* or *ou* in *out. n. 18.*

di plo ma (di plō′mə), a written or printed paper given by a school or college, which says that a person has completed a certain course of study, or has been graduated after a certain amount of work. *n. 9.*

di plo ma cy (di plō′mə si), 1. the management of relations between nations. The making of treaties, international agreements, etc., is an important part of diplomacy. 2. skill in managing such relations. 3. skill in dealing with people; tact. Tom showed diplomacy in being very helpful at home the day he wanted to use the car. *n., pl. diplomacies. 13.*

dip lo mat (dip′lə mat), 1. person whose work is to handle the relations of his country with other nations; statesman. 2. person who is skillful in dealing with people. *n. 10.*

dip lo mat ic (dip′lə mat′ik), 1. of or having to do with diplomacy. Ministers and consuls to foreign countries are in the diplomatic service. 2. skillful in dealing with people; tactful. *adj. 13.*

dip per (dip′ər), 1. person or thing that dips. 2. a long-handled cup or larger container for lifting water or liquids. 3. The **Big Dipper** and the **Little Dipper** are two groups of stars in the northern sky. See the picture just below. *n. 6.*

Dipper for water

dire (dīr), dreadful; causing great fear or suffering. *adj. 6.*

di rect (di rekt′), 1. manage; control. The teacher directs the work of the pupils. 2. order; command. The captain directed his men to advance slowly. 3. tell or show the way. Can you direct me to the railroad station? Signposts direct travelers. 4. point (to); aim (at). We should direct our effort to a useful end. 5. address (a letter, package, etc.) to a person or place. 6. straight. Our house is in direct line with the school. A bee makes a direct flight home to the hive. 7. in an unbroken line. That man is a direct descendant of John Adams. 8. frank; truthful; plain. The boy gave direct answers. He made a direct denial of the charge of cheating. 9. directly. *v., adj., adv. 1.*

Big Dipper and Little Dipper

direct current, electric current that flows in one direction.

di rec tion (di rek′shən), 1. guiding; managing; control. The school is under the direction of a good teacher. 2. order; command. 3. knowing or telling what to do, how to do, where to go, etc.; instruction. Can you give me directions how to reach Chicago? 4. the address on a letter or package. 5. the course taken by a moving body, such as a ball or a bullet. 6. any way in which one may face or point. North, south, east, etc., are directions. Our school is in one direction and the post office is in another. 7. line of action; tendency, etc. The town shows improvement in many directions. *n. 2.*

di rect ly (di rekt′li), 1. in a direct line or manner; straight. This road runs directly north. 2. exactly; absolutely; as, directly opposite. 3. immediately; at once. Come home directly. *adv.*

di rect ness (di rekt′nis), straightness; tendency to act without delay. *n. 17.*

di rec tor (di rek′tər), 1. manager; person who directs. 2. one of the persons elected or appointed by the owners of a company to direct its business. *n. 4.*

di rec to ry (di rek′tə ri), a book of names and addresses. A telephone book is a directory. *n., pl. directories. 13.*

dire ful (dīr′fəl), dire; terrible. *adj. 12.*

dirge (dėrj), funeral song or tune. *n. 8.*

dir i gi ble (dir′i ji bəl), 1. a balloon that can be steered. See the picture. 2. capable of being directed. *n., adj. 15.*

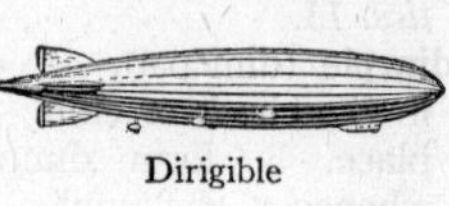
Dirigible

dirk (dėrk), dagger. *n. 15.*

dirt (dėrt), 1. mud, dust, earth, or anything like them which soils skin, clothing, houses, or furniture. 2. loose earth or soil. 3. an unclean thing, action, or speech. *n. 3.*

dirt i ness (dėr′ti nis), being dirty. *n.*

dirt y (dėr′ti), 1. not clean; soiled by mud, dust, earth, or anything like them. 2. not clean or pure in language or action; low; base. 3. not clear or pure in color; as, a dirty red. 4. stormy; rough; as, dirty weather. 5. make dirty; soil. *adj., dirtier, dirtiest, v., dirtied, dirtying. 3.*

dis-, prefix meaning:—
1. opposite of; as in discontent.
2. reverse of; as in disentangle.

dis a bil i ty (dis′ə bil′i ti), 1. lack of ability or power. His disability was due to illness. 2. something that disqualifies. Relationship to an accused man is a disability which disqualifies a person for service on the jury at his trial. *n., pl. disabilities. 11.*

dis a ble (dis ā′bəl), deprive of ability or power; make useless; cripple. A war kills and disables many men. *v. 9.*

dis a buse (dis′ə būz′), free from deception or error. Education should disabuse people of foolish prejudices. *v.*

dis ad van tage (dis′əd van′tij), 1. lack of advantage; unfavorable condition. Mary's shyness puts her at a disadvantage in company. 2. loss; injury. Gossip to Mr. Brown's disadvantage was spread abroad by his enemies. *n. 7.*

dis ad van ta geous (dis ad′vən tā′jəs), unfavorable. *adj. 18.*

dis af fect ed (dis′ə fek′tid), unfriendly; disloyal; discontented. *adj. 16.*

dis af fec tion (dis′ə fek′shən), unfriendliness; disloyalty; discontent. Lack of food and supplies caused disaffection among the soldiers. *n. 14.*

dis a gree (dis′ə grē′), 1. fail to agree; be different. Your story disagrees with his.

2. have unlike opinions; differ. Doctors sometimes disagree. 3. quarrel. 4. have a bad effect. Some foods disagree with him. *v. 9.*

dis a gree a ble (dis'ə grē'ə bəl), 1. not to one's liking; not pleasant. A headache is disagreeable. 2. not friendly; unkind; bad-tempered; cross. Mary is sometimes disagreeable until she has her breakfast. *adj. 6.*

dis a gree ment (dis'ə grē'mənt), 1. the state or fact of disagreeing; difference of opinion; dissent. 2. difference; unlikeness. 3. dissension; quarrel. *n. 12.*

dis al low (dis'ə lou'), refuse to allow; deny the truth or value of; reject. The request for a new trial was disallowed. *v. 13.*

dis ap pear (dis'ə pēr'), pass from sight or from existence; be lost. The little dog disappeared down the road. When spring comes, the snow disappears. *v. 2.*

dis ap pear ance (dis'ə pēr'əns), act of disappearing. *n. 11.*

dis ap point (dis'ə point'), 1. fail to satisfy one's desire, wish, or hope; leave (one) wanting something. The circus disappointed him, for there was no elephant. We were disappointed that our cousin could not come. 2. fail to keep a promise to. You promised to come; do not disappoint me. *v. 3.*

dis ap point ment (dis'ə point'mənt), 1. being disappointed; the feeling one has when one's expectation or hope is not fulfilled. When she did not find her mother, the disappointment seemed too great to bear. 2. person or thing that causes disappointment. Her lazy son was a disappointment to her. 3. act of disappointing. *n. 4.*

dis ap pro ba tion (dis'ap rə bā'shən), disapproval. *n. 16.*

dis ap prov al (dis'ə prüv'əl), having an opinion or feeling against; expressing an opinion against. *n. 8.*

dis ap prove (dis'ə prüv'), consider not good or not suitable; express disapproval. Some girls disapprove of rough games. *v. 9.*

dis arm (dis ärm'), 1. take weapons away from. The police captured the bandits and disarmed them. 2. stop having an army or navy; reduce the size of an army or navy. 3. remove unfriendliness or suspicion. The little boy's smile could always disarm those who were about to scold or punish him. 4. make harmless. *v. 7.*

dis ar ma ment (dis är'mə mənt), 1. disarming. 2. reduction of armies, navies, and their equipment. *n.*

dis ar range (dis'ə rānj'), disturb the arrangement of; put out of order. The wind disarranged her hair. *v. 18.*

dis ar ray (dis'ə rā'), 1. disorder; confusion. 2. put into disorder or confusion. 3. disorder of clothing. 4. undress; strip. *n., v. 16.*

dis as ter (di zas'tər), an event such as a flood, fire, shipwreck, earthquake, or great loss of money, which brings distress to many people; a great misfortune. *n. 5.*

dis as trous (di zas'trəs), bringing disaster; causing danger, suffering, loss, pain, or sorrow to many people. *adj. 7.*

dis a vow (dis'ə vou'), deny that one knows about, approves of, or is responsible for; disclaim. The prisoner disavowed any share in the plot against the king. *v. 16.*

dis band (dis band'), break up; dismiss. When peace is declared, armies are disbanded. *v. 9.*

dis be lief (dis'bi lēf'), lack of belief. *n. 20.*

dis be lieve (dis'bi lēv'), have no belief in; lack belief. *v. 16.*

dis bur den (dis bėr'dən), relieve of a burden. The boy disburdened his mind to his mother. *v.*

dis burse (dis bėrs'), pay out. Our city treasurer disburses thousands of dollars each week. *v. 17.*

dis burse ment (dis bėrs'mənt), 1. paying out. 2. money paid out. *n. 17.*

disc (disk), disk. *n. 9.*

dis card (dis kärd' for 1 and 4, dis'kärd for 2, 3, and 5), 1. throw aside; give up as useless or worn out. You can discard clothes, ways of doing things, or beliefs. 2. act of throwing aside as useless. 3. thing or things thrown aside. That old book can go into the discard now; I don't want it. 4. in playing cards, to throw aside from one's hand (the cards not wanted). 5. the cards thrown aside as not wanted. *v., n. 9.*

dis cern (di zėrn'), perceive; distinguish; see clearly; recognize. I looked where he pointed, but could discern nothing. When there is so much propaganda, it is hard to discern the truth. *v. 4.*

dis cern i ble (di zėr'ni bəl), capable of being discerned. *adj. 18.*

dis cern ing (di zėr'ning), shrewd; acute; discriminating. *adj.*

dis cern ment (di zėrn′mənt), 1. keenness in perceiving and understanding; good judgment. 2. act of discerning. *n. 12.*

dis charge (dis chärj′), 1. unload (a ship); unload (cargo) from a ship. 2. unloading. The discharge of this cargo will not take long. 3. fire off; as, to discharge a gun. 4. firing off a gun, a blast, etc. The discharge could be heard for three miles. 5. release; let go; dismiss; as, to discharge a patient from a hospital, to discharge a committee, to discharge a servant. 6. release; letting go; dismissing; as, the discharge of a prisoner from jail. 7. give off; let out. The wound discharges pus. 8. giving off; letting out. In a thunderstorm there is a discharge of electricity from the clouds. 9. thing given off or let out; as, the watery discharge from a sore. 10. pay (a debt). 11. payment of a debt. 12. perform (a duty). 13. performing of a duty. *v., n. 3.*

dis ci ple (di sī′pəl), 1. a believer in the thought and teaching of any leader; a follower. 2. in the New Testament, one of the followers of Jesus. *n. 8.*

dis ci pline (dis′i plin), 1. training; especially, training of the mind or character. 2. a trained condition of order and obedience; order kept among school pupils, soldiers, or members of any group. When the fire broke out, the pupils showed good discipline. 3. train; bring to a condition of order and obedience; bring under control. 4. punishment. A little discipline would do him a world of good. 5. punish. You ought to discipline that rude boy for his bad behavior. *n., v. 5.*

dis claim (dis klām′), 1. refuse to recognize as one's own; cast off; deny connection with. He disclaimed the ownership of the dog. 2. give up all claim to. She disclaimed any share in the invention. *v. 11.*

dis close (dis klōz′), 1. uncover. The lifting of the curtain disclosed a beautiful Christmas tree. 2. make known. This letter discloses a secret. *v. 5.*

dis clo sure (dis klō′zhər), 1. disclosing. 2. thing disclosed; revelation. *n. 10.*

dis col or (dis kul′ər), 1. change or spoil the color of. Smoke had discolored the building. 2. become changed in color. Many materials discolor if exposed to bright sunshine. *v. 12.*

dis col or a tion (dis kul′ər ā′shən), 1. discoloring. 2. being discolored. 3. a stain. *n. 16.*

dis com fit (dis kum′fit), 1. defeat; overthrow completely; rout. 2. defeat the plans or hopes of; frustrate. 3. confuse; embarrass greatly; disconcert. *v. 12.*

dis com fi ture (dis kum′fi chər), 1. defeat; complete overthrow; rout. 2. defeat of plans or hopes; frustration. 3. confusion. *n. 12.*

dis com fort (dis kum′fərt), 1. uneasiness; lack of comfort. 2. thing that causes discomfort. *n. 10.*

dis com pose (dis′kəm pōz′), disturb the composure of; bring into disorder. The grins of his friends discomposed Jack when he tried to make his speech before the school. *v. 15.*

dis con cert (dis′kən sėrt′), 1. disturb the self-possession of; confuse. Henry was disconcerted to find that he had come to school without combing his hair. 2. throw into confusion; disorder. The late arrival of the speaker of the evening disconcerted the plans of the committee. *v. 14.*

dis con nect (dis′kə nekt′), separate; unfasten; undo or break the connection of. He disconnected the electric fan by pulling out the plug. *v. 13.*

dis con so late (dis kon′sə lit), without hope; forlorn; unhappy; cheerless. Mary was disconsolate because her kitten died. *adj. 9.*

dis con tent (dis′kən tent′), 1. uneasy feeling; dissatisfaction; a dislike of what one has and a desire for something different. 2. dissatisfy; displease. *n., v. 4.*

dis con tent ed (dis′kən ten′tid), not contented; not satisfied; displeased and restless; disliking what one has and wanting something different. *adj.*

dis con tin ue (dis′kən tin′ū), stop; give up. That train has been discontinued. After the patient got well, the doctor discontinued his visits. *v. 9.*

dis con tin u ous (dis′kən tin′ū əs), not continuous; broken; interrupted. *adj.*

dis cord (dis′kôrd), 1. harsh, clashing sounds. 2. in music, a lack of harmony in notes sounded at the same time. 3. difference of opinion; disputing. *n. 6.*

dis cord ant (dis kôr′dənt), 1. harsh; clashing. Many automobile horns are discordant. 2. not in harmony; as, a discordant note in music. 3. not in agreement; not fitting together. Many discordant views were expressed. *adj. 10.*

dis count (dis′kount), 1. take off a certain amount from (a price). The store discounts 3 per cent on all bills paid when due. 2. the amount taken off from a price. During the sale the dealer allowed a 10 per cent discount on all cash purchases. 3. take off from (a statement); allow for exaggeration in. You must discount what Jack tells you, for he is too fond of a good story. 4. allow for. In his plans he discounted the future. *v., n. 10.*

dis coun te nance (dis koun′ti nəns), 1. refuse to approve; discourage. This school discountenances secret societies. 2. put to shame. *v. 16.*

dis cour age (dis kėr′ij), 1. take away the courage of; destroy the hopes of. Repeated failure discourages anyone. 2. try to prevent. All Nell's friends discouraged her from such a dangerous step. 3. frown on; make seem not worth while. The chill of coming winter soon discouraged our picnics. *v. 4.*

dis cour age ment (dis kėr′ij mənt), 1. act of discouraging. 2. state of being or feeling discouraged. 3. something that discourages. *n. 16.*

dis course (dis′kōrs for 1 and 2, dis kōrs′ for 3), 1. talk; conversation. 2. a long written or spoken discussion of some subject. Sermons and lectures are discourses. 3. to talk; converse. *n., v. 5.*

dis cour te ous (dis kėr′ti əs), not courteous; not polite; rude. *adj. 14.*

dis cour te sy (dis kėr′ti si), impoliteness; rudeness. *n., pl. discourtesies. 18.*

dis cov er (dis kuv′ər), 1. find out; see or learn of for the first time. Columbus discovered America. No one has discovered a way to turn copper into gold. 2. make known; reveal. The knight would not discover his name to the prince. *Old use. v. 1.*

dis cov er y (dis kuv′ər i), 1. finding out; seeing or learning of something for the first time. 2. the thing found out. Franklin's discovery was that lightning was electricity. *n., pl. discoveries. 3.*

dis cred it (dis kred′it), 1. cast doubt on; destroy belief in (a person, something thought to be true, a story told, or evidence offered). 2. doubt. This throws discredit on your account of the matter. 3. refuse to believe. 4. the loss of good name or standing. 5. thing that causes loss of good name or standing. *v., n. 10.*

dis cred it a ble (dis kred′it ə bəl), bringing discredit; disgraceful. *adj.*

dis creet (dis krēt′), prudent and careful in speech and action. *adj. 6.*

dis crep an cy (dis krep′ən si), difference; lack of consistency. There was a discrepancy in the two reports of the accident. *n., pl. discrepancies. 14.*

dis cre tion (dis kresh′ən), 1. freedom to judge or choose. It is within the principal's discretion to punish a pupil. 2. good judgment; care in speech and action; caution. My brother rushed in front of the car, but I showed more discretion. *n. 7.*

dis cre tion ar y (dis kresh′ən ãr′i), with freedom to decide or choose; left to one's own judgment. The law gave the mayor certain discretionary powers. *adj. 17.*

dis crim i nate (dis krim′i nāt), 1. make or see a difference between; distinguish. The study of English makes a person able to discriminate between good books and worthless ones. 2. make a distinction. The law does not discriminate against any race, creed, or color. *v. 9.*

dis crim i na tion (dis krim′i nā′shən), 1. making or recognizing differences and distinctions. Do not buy things without discrimination. 2. the ability to make fine distinctions. 3. making a difference in favor of or against. There is discrimination against Jews in Germany. *n. 14.*

dis cur sive (dis kėr′siv), wandering from one subject to another; rambling. A carefully planned speech will not be discursive, but will develop one topic. *adj. 16.*

dis cus (dis′kəs), a circular plate of stone or metal for throwing, used by athletes. *n.*

DISCUS

Man throwing a discus

dis cuss (dis kus′), talk over; consider from various points of view. The class discussed several problems. Congress is discussing tax rates. *v. 4.*

dis cus sion (dis kush′ən), talk; going over the reasons for and against; discussing things. His arrival caused much discussion in the village. After two hours' discussion, we seemed no nearer a decision. *n. 5.*

dis dain (dis dān′), 1. to scorn; look down on; consider beneath one. He disdained our friendly offers. She disdains to speak to us. 2. scorn; looking down on a person or an act as beneath one. Dick treated his younger brothers and sisters with disdain. *v., n. 4.*

dis dain ful (dis dān′fəl), proud and scornful. *adj. 9.*

dis ease (di zēz′), 1. sickness; illness. 2. any particular sickness, such as grippe, measles, scarlet fever, whooping cough, or tuberculosis. A disease is killing all the chestnut trees. *n. 2.*

dis eased (di zēzd′), 1. having a disease. 2. disordered; as, a diseased mind. *adj.*

dis em bark (dis′em bärk′), go or put on shore from a ship; land from a ship. *v. 13.*

dis em bod y (dis′em bod′i), separate (a soul) from its body. A disembodied spirit is said to haunt this house. *v., disembodied, disembodying. 16.*

dis en chant (dis′en chant′), free from enchantment or illusion. *v. 20.*

dis en cum ber (dis′en kum′bər), free from a burden, annoyance, or trouble. *v. 17.*

dis en gage (dis′en gāj′), 1. free from an engagement, pledge, obligation, etc. 2. detach; loosen. The mother gently disengaged her hand from that of the sleeping child. *v. 11.*

dis en tan gle (dis′en tang′gəl), free from tangles or complications. *v. 15.*

dis es teem (dis′es tēm′), scorn; dislike. *v., n. 19.*

dis fa vor (dis fā′vər), 1. dislike; disapproval. The workers looked with disfavor on any attempt to lower their wages. 2. to dislike; disapprove. *n., v. 18.*

dis fig ure (dis fig′yər), spoil the appearance of; hurt the beauty of. Huge advertising signs disfigure the countryside. A scar disfigured his face. *v. 8.*

dis fran chise (dis fran′chīz), 1. take the rights of citizenship away from. A disfranchised person cannot vote. 2. take a privilege or right away from. *v. 17.*

dis gorge (dis gôrj′), 1. throw out from the throat. 2. pour forth; discharge. Swollen streams disgorge their waters into the river. 3. give up unwillingly. The robbers were forced to disgorge their plunder. *v. 12.*

dis grace (dis grās′), 1. loss of favor; a lowering in position or esteem; loss of respect or honor. To be put in prison is usually a disgrace. 2. cause disgrace to; lower the worldly position of; bring shame upon. 3. anything that causes dishonor or shame. *n., v. 3.*

dis grace ful (dis grās′fəl), shameful; causing dishonor or loss of respect; deserving disgrace. *adj. 11.*

dis grun tled (dis grun′təld), discontented; in bad humor. *adj.*

dis guise (dis gīz′), 1. hide what one is by appearing as something else. In his Santa Claus costume my uncle was quite disguised. 2. the use of a changed or unusual dress and appearance in order not to be known. You will have to try disguise in order to succeed with that plan. 3. the clothes or actions used to hide or deceive. His disguise was perfect. 4. hide or cover up (purpose or thought) by seeming to have some other purpose or thought. For a time he disguised his hatred by a false show of friendly interest. 5. a deceiving manner; a trick. His seeming friendliness was a disguise. *v., n. 3.*

dis gust (dis gust′), 1. strong dislike; sickening dislike. We feel disgust for bad odors or tastes. 2. arouse disgust in. *n., v. 5.*

dish (dish), 1. We eat from dishes. Cups, saucers, plates, bowls, and platters are dishes. 2. put (food) into a dish for serving at the table. You may dish the dinner now. 3. food served. Sliced peaches with cream is the dish I like best. 4. amount served in a dish. *n., v. 2.*

dis heart en (dis här′tən), discourage. Long illness is disheartening. *v. 10.*

di shev eled (di shev′əld), hanging loosely or in disorder; disordered. *adj. 10.*

dis hon est (dis on′ist), 1. not fair play. Lying, cheating, and stealing are dishonest. 2. not honest; ready to cheat; not upright. A man who lies or steals is dishonest. *adj. 9.*

dis hon es ty (dis on′is ti), 1. lying, cheating, or stealing; disposition to lie, cheat, or steal. 2. dishonest act. *n., pl. dishonesties. 10.*

dis hon or (dis on′ər), 1. disgrace; shame; loss of reputation or standing in the world. 2. thing that causes dishonor. A lazy man is a dishonor to his family. 3. bring reproach or shame upon. 4. refuse to pay money on (a check or bill); refuse to recognize as worth money. A bank will dishonor your checks if you do not have money in the bank to pay them. *n., v. 5.*

dis hon or a ble (dis on′ər ə bəl), without honor; disgraceful; shameful. *adj. 9.*

dis il lu sion (dis′i lü′zhən), 1. free from illusion. People are apt to become disillusioned as they grow old. 2. freeing or being freed from illusion. *n., v. 18.*

dis in cli na tion (dis in′kli nā′shən), unwillingness. *n. 18.*

dis in cline (dis′in klīn′), 1. make unwilling. 2. be unwilling. *v. 12.*

dis in fect (dis′in fekt′), destroy the disease germs in. If you nurse someone who has scarlet fever, you should disinfect yourself and your clothes every time you leave the room where the sick person is. *v. 12.*

dis in fect ant (dis′in fek′tənt), a means for destroying disease germs. Alcohol, iodine, and carbolic acid are disinfectants. *n. 13.*

dis in fec tion (dis′in fek′shən), the process of destroying disease germs. *n. 18.*

dis in her it (dis′in her′it), prevent from inheriting. A father disinherits his son if he leaves none of his property to the son. *v. 11.*

dis in te grate (dis in′ti grāt), break up; separate into small parts or bits. The papers had disintegrated into a pile of fragments and dust. *v. 11.*

dis in te gra tion (dis in′ti grā′shən), breaking up; reduction to small bits. Rain and frost cause the gradual disintegration of rock. *n. 17.*

dis in ter (dis′in tėr′), dig up from its grave; take out of a tomb. *v., disinterred, disinterring. 20.*

dis in ter est ed (dis in′tər es tid), free from selfish motives; as, disinterested kindness. *adj. 9.*

dis in ter est ed ness (dis in′tər es tid nis), freedom from selfish motives. *n. 15.*

dis join (dis join′), separate; prevent from being joined. *v. 16.*

dis joint (dis joint′), 1. take apart at the joints; as, to disjoint a chicken. 2. break up; put out of order. The boy's speech was stumbling and disjointed. 3. put out of joint; as, a disjointed wrist. *v. 14.*

disk (disk), 1. a flat, thin, round plate shaped like a coin. 2. a round flat surface, or a surface that seems so. *n. 9.* Also spelled **disc.**

Disk

dis like (dis līk′), 1. a feeling of not liking; a feeling against. I have a dislike of rain and fog. 2. not like; object to. Mice dislike cats. *n., v. 5.*

dis lo cate (dis′lō kāt), 1. put out of joint; as, a dislocated collarbone. 2. put out of place; disorder. *v. 14.*

dis lo ca tion (dis′lō kā′shən), 1. dislocating. 2. being dislocated. *n. 15.*

dis lodge (dis loj′), drive or force out of a place, position, etc. The workman used a crowbar to dislodge a heavy stone from the wall. Heavy gunfire dislodged the enemy from the fort. *v. 10.*

dis loy al (dis loi′əl), not loyal; faithless. A disloyal servant let robbers into the house. *adj. 10.*

dis loy al ty (dis loi′əl ti), unfaithfulness. The traitor was shot for disloyalty to his country. *n., pl. disloyalties. 13.*

dis mal (diz′məl), 1. dark; gloomy. A rainy day is dismal. 2. dreary; miserable. Sickness or bad luck often makes a person feel dismal. *adj. 4.*

dis man tle (dis man′təl), 1. strip of furniture, defenses, or equipment; as, to dismantle a house, a fort, or a ship. 2. pull down; take apart. We had to dismantle the bookcases in order to move them. *v. 14.*

dis may (dis mā′), 1. a loss of courage because of dislike or fear of what is about to happen. 2. trouble greatly; make afraid. The thought that she might fail dismayed her. *n., v. 4.*

dis mem ber (dis mem′bər), 1. divide limb from limb; as, to dismember a human body. 2. separate (a kingdom, country, etc.) into parts; divide. *v. 16.*

dis miss (dis mis′), 1. send away; allow to go. At noon the teacher dismissed the class. 2. remove from office or service; not allow to keep a job. We dismissed the cook because her cooking was so poor. 3. put away; stop thinking about. Let us dismiss our troubles. *v. 3.*

dis miss al (dis mis′əl), 1. act of dismissing. 2. state or fact of being dismissed. 3. written or spoken order dismissing someone. *n. 10.*

dis mis sion (dis mish′ən), dismissal. *n. 20.*

dis mount (dis mount′), 1. get off a horse. The cavalry dismounted near the woods. 2. throw from one's horse. The first knight dismounted the second. 3. take (a thing) from its setting or support. The cannons were dismounted for shipping. *v. 7.*

dis o be di ence (dis′ə bē′di əns), refusal to obey; failure to obey. Disobedience cannot be allowed in the army. *n. 10.*

dis o be di ent (dis′ə bē′di ənt), failing to follow orders or rules; refusing or forgetting to obey. *adj. 11.*

dis o bey (dis′ə bā′), refuse to obey; fail to obey. *v. 5.*

dis o blige (dis′ə blīj′), 1. neglect to oblige; not oblige. We had to disoblige them, for we could not do what they asked. 2. refuse to oblige; refuse to do a favor for. *v.*

dis or der (dis ôr′dər), 1. lack of order; confusion. 2. disturb or confuse the regular order or working of. A series of accidents disordered the shop. 3. tumult; riot. 4. sickness; disease. 5. cause sickness or disease in. Anxiety may disorder the heart or stomach. *n., v. 5.*

dis or der ly (dis ôr′dər li), 1. not orderly; untidy; confused. A messy room is disorderly. 2. causing disorder; making a disturbance; breaking rules; unruly. *adj. 10.*

dis or gan ize (dis ôr′gən īz), throw into confusion or disorder. Heavy snowstorms disorganized the train service. *v. 12.*

dis own (dis ōn′), refuse to recognize as one's own; cast off. Mr. Jones disowned his wicked son. *v. 9.*

dis par age (dis par′ij), 1. speak slightingly of; say (something) is of less value or importance than it might be, or than it actually is. The coward disparaged the hero's brave rescue. 2. bring discredit on; lower. *v. 10.*

dis par age ment (dis par′ij mənt), 1. disparaging. 2. something that lowers a thing or person in worth or importance. 3. a lessening in esteem or standing. Say nothing that will be to his disparagement with his new employer. *n. 12.*

dis par i ty (dis par′i ti), inequality; difference. There will be a disparity in the accounts of the same event given by several people. *n., pl. disparities. 15.*

dis part (dis pärt′), separate. *v. 16.*

dis pas sion ate (dis pash′ən it), free from emotion or prejudice; calm; impartial. Judges are more dispassionate than agitators. *adj. 14.*

dis patch (dis pach′), 1. send off to some place or for some purpose. He dispatched a messenger to tell the king what had happened. 2. sending off a letter, a messenger, etc. Hurry up the dispatch of this telegram. 3. a written message, such as special news or government business. This dispatch has been two days on the way. 4. get (something) done promptly. 5. prompt doing of anything. This boy works with neatness and dispatch. 6. kill. He dispatched the deer at his first shot. 7. finish off; eat up. The hungry boy quickly dispatched the meal. *Used in common talk. v., n. 7.*

dis pel (dis pel′), disperse; drive away and scatter. The captain's cheerful laugh dispelled our fears. *v., dispelled, dispelling. 9.*

dis pen sa ry (dis pen′sə ri), a place where medicine and medical advice are given free or very cheaply. *n., pl. dispensaries. 12.*

dis pen sa tion (dis′pen sā′shən), 1. dealing out; distribution; as, the dispensation of charity to the poor. 2. rule; management; as, England under the dispensation of Queen Elizabeth. 3. ruling or ordering of the affairs of the world. 4. a religious system; as, the Christian dispensation, the Jewish dispensation. 5. official permission to disregard a rule. *n. 9.*

dis pense (dis pens′), 1. give out; distribute. 2. apply; carry out; put in force. Judges and law courts dispense justice. 3. prepare and give out. A druggist dispenses medicines for sick people. 4. **Dispense with** means (1) do away with. (2) do without. *v. 5.*

dis pens er (dis pen′sər), person who deals out or distributes. *n. 15.*

dis per sal (dis pėr′səl), dispersion; a scattering or being scattered; as, the dispersal of a crowd. *n. 14.*

dis perse (dis pėrs′), 1. scatter; send in different directions. 2. go in different directions. The crowd dispersed when the policeman came. *v. 4.*

dis per sion (dis pėr′zhən), 1. dispersing. 2. being dispersed. *n. 13.*

di spir it (di spir′it), depress; discourage; dishearten. A week of rain dispirited us all. *v. 11.*

dis place (dis plās′), 1. take the place of; put something else in the place of. The automobile has practically displaced the horse and buggy. 2. remove from a position of authority. 3. put out of place; move from its usual place or position. *v. 8.*

dis place ment (dis plās′mənt), 1. displacing. 2. being displaced. His laziness has caused his displacement from office. 3. the weight of the volume of water displaced by a ship or by any floating object. *n. 20.*

dis play (dis plā′), 1. show. He displayed his good nature by answering all our questions. The flag is displayed on the Fourth of July. He did not like the boy's display of bad temper. 2. show in a special way, so as to attract attention. The boys' suits were displayed in the big window of the store. 3. a planned showing of a thing, for some special purpose. *v., n. 3.*

dis please (dis plēz′), offend; annoy; not please. By failing to obey your mother you displeased her. *v. 4.*

dis pleas ure (dis plezh′ər), annoyance; dislike; slight anger; dissatisfaction. We feel displeasure at something we dislike. *n. 7.*
dis port (dis pōrt′), sport; play; amuse oneself. People laughed at the clumsy bears disporting themselves in the water. *v. 15.*
dis pos al (dis pōz′əl), 1. placing in a certain order or position. Do you approve of my disposal of these folds in the curtain? 2. sale. The disposal of the property will bring him in several thousand dollars. 3. dealing with; settling. His disposal of the difficulty pleased everybody. 4. act of getting rid (of something); as, the disposal of garbage. 5. **At one's disposal** means ready for one's use or service at any time. I will put my room and my books at your disposal. *n. 6.*
dis pose (dis pōz′), 1. put in a certain order or position. The ships were disposed in a straight line. 2. make ready or willing; influence. The good pay and short hours disposed him to take the new job. 3. **Be disposed** means be willing; be favorable toward. He is disposed to grant your request for a transfer to this new job. 4. **Dispose of** means (1) get rid of. Dispose of that rubbish. (2) give or sell. The agent disposed of all their property for $5000. (3) arrange; settle. *v. 3.*
dis po si tion (dis′pə zish′ən), 1. natural way of acting toward others; as, a cheerful disposition, a selfish disposition, a changeable disposition. 2. a tending or natural bent; as, a disposition to argue. 3. a putting in order; arrangement. The disposition of the papers on my desk had been changed. 4. disposing; settlement. What disposition did you make of Johnny's case? 5. giving or selling; as, the disposition of goods. *n. 5.*
dis pos sess (dis′pə zes′), 1. put (a person) out of possession. The sheriff dispossessed the man who owed rent by taking all his furniture away. 2. deprive of something. Fear dispossessed him of his senses. *v. 12.*
dis praise (dis prāz′), 1. speak against; to blame. 2. blame. *v., n. 12.*
dis proof (dis prüf′), 1. a disproving. 2. proof to the contrary. *n.*
dis pro por tion (dis′prə pōr′shən), 1. lack of proportion. 2. make disproportionate. *n., v. 13.*
dis pro por tion ate (dis′prə pōr′shən it), not well proportioned; out of relation in size, number, etc. (to something else). A penny would be disproportionate pay for a week's work. *adj. 16.*
dis prove (dis prüv′), prove false. John disproved Tom's statement that he had less candy by weighing both boxes. *v. 12.*
dis pu ta ble (dis′pū tə bəl), questionable; liable to be disputed. *adj. 19.*
dis pu tant (dis′pū tənt), person who disputes or debates. *n. 15.*
dis pu ta tion (dis′pū tā′shən), debate; controversy. *n. 10.*
dis pute (dis pūt′), 1. argue; debate; 2. an argument; a debate. 3. quarrel because of a difference of opinion. 4. disagree with (a statement); declare not true; call in question. 5. fight against; oppose; resist. Our soldiers disputed every inch of ground when the enemy attacked. 6. try to win. Our team disputed the victory up to the last minute of play. *v., n. 3.*
dis qual i fi ca tion (dis kwol′i fi kā′shən), 1. disqualifying. 2. being disqualified. 3. something that disqualifies. *n. 16.*
dis qual i fy (dis kwol′i fī), 1. make unfit for service; make unable to do something. His lame foot disqualified him for active work. 2. deprive of the right to do a certain thing. Fred and Will cannot play on the football team because their low marks disqualify them. *v., disqualified, disqualifying. 10.*
dis qui et (dis kwī′ət), 1. make uneasy; trouble; disturb; worry. Will's strange actions disquieted mother. 2. uneasy feelings; anxiety. Her disquiet made the rest of us uneasy, too. *v., n. 11.*
dis qui e tude (dis kwī′ə tūd or dis kwī′ə-tüd), uneasiness; worry; anxiety. *n. 15.*
dis qui si tion (dis′kwi zish′ən), a long or formal speech or writing about a subject. *n. 16.*
dis re gard (dis′ri gärd′), 1. pay no attention to; take no notice of. Disregarding the child's screams, the doctor cleaned and bandaged the cut. 2. neglect; lack of attention. The boy's failure was due to continued disregard of his studies. *v., n. 9.*
dis rel ish (dis rel′ish), dislike. *v., n. 16.*
dis rep u ta ble (dis rep′ū tə bəl), 1. having a bad reputation; as, a disreputable dance hall. 2. not respectable; as, a disreputable old hat. *adj. 20.*
dis re pute (dis′ri pūt′), loss of good name. **Be in disrepute** means have a bad reputation; be discredited. *n. 17.*

dis re spect (dis′ri spekt′), rudeness; lack of respect. I am sure he meant no disrespect by his remark. *n. 14.*

dis re spect ful (dis′ri spekt′fəl), rude; showing no respect; lacking in courtesy to elders or superiors. The disrespectful boy laughed at his father. *adj. 15.*

dis robe (dis rōb′), undress. *v. 18.*

dis rupt (dis rupt′), break up; split. Slavery seemed likely to disrupt the Union. *v. 20.*

dis rup tion (dis rup′shən), 1. a breaking up; a splitting. 2. a being broken up; a being split; forcible separation. *n. 18.*

dis sat is fac tion (dis′sat is fak′shən), the opposite of satisfaction; discontent; displeasure. *n. 12.*

dis sat is fy (dis sat′is fī), make discontented or displeased. Envy may dissatisfy us with our lot. *v., dissatisfied, dissatisfying. 10.*

dis sect (di sekt′), 1. cut up. 2. cut apart (an animal, plant, etc.) so as to examine. 3. examine part by part; analyze. One pupil dissected the other's composition. *v. 9.*

dis sec tion (di sek′shən), act of cutting up; analysis. *n. 13.*

dis sem ble (di sem′bəl), 1. disguise; hide (a feeling, thought, purpose, etc.). She dissembled her anger with a smile. 2. put on the appearance of; feign; give a false impression. The bored listener dissembled an interest he didn't feel. 3. pretend not to see or notice; ignore. *v. 12.*

dis sem i nate (di sem′i nāt), scatter like seed; spread abroad. Missionaries disseminate Christian doctrines all over the world. *v. 14.*

dis sem i na tion (di sem′i nā′shən), scattering like seed; spreading abroad; diffusion; being scattered or spread abroad. *n. 18.*

dis sen sion (di sen′shən), disputing; quarreling; hard feeling caused by a difference in opinion. Differences in religion do not need to cause dissension between people. *n. 7.*

dis sent (di sent′), 1. disagree; think differently; express a different opinion from others. The Puritans dissented from the doctrines of the established or state church in England. 2. disagreement; difference of opinion; expressing such a difference. *v., n. 9.*

dis sent er (di sen′tər), one who dissents. *n. 11.*

dis ser ta tion (dis′ər tā′shən), formal discussion of a subject. *n. 14.*

dis sev er (di sev′ər), cut in parts; sever; separate. *v. 15.*

dis sim i lar (di sim′i lər), unlike; different. *adj. 16.*

dis sim i lar i ty (di sim′i lar′i ti), lack of similarity; unlikeness. *n., pl. dissimilarities.*

dis sim u late (di sim′ū lāt), disguise or hide under a pretense; hide the truth; dissemble. *v.*

dis sim u la tion (di sim′ū lā′shən), deceit; pretense; hypocrisy. *n. 14.*

dis si pate (dis′i pāt), 1. scatter; spread in different directions. 2. disappear or cause to disappear; dispel. 3. spend foolishly; waste on things of little value. The extravagant son soon dissipated his father's fortune. 4. indulge too much in evil or foolish pleasures. *v. 9.*

dis si pat ed (dis′i pāt′id), indulging too much in vicious or unwise pleasures. A youth who spends his time in drinking and gambling is dissipated. *adj. 17.*

dis si pa tion (dis′i pā′shən), 1. scattering in different directions. 2. wasting by misuse. 3. amusement. 4. intemperance; loose living. *n. 12.*

dis so ci ate (di sō′shi āt), separate; break the connection or association with. John learned that his companions were thieves and dissociated himself from them. *v.*

dis so lute (dis′ə lüt), living an evil life; very wicked; vicious. *adj. 13.*

dis so lu tion (dis′ə lü′shən), 1. a breaking up; an ending. The partners arranged for the dissolution of their partnership. 2. a dissolving; decomposing. 3. death. *n. 8.*

dis solve (di zolv′), 1. make liquid; become liquid, especially by putting or being put into a liquid. You can dissolve sugar in water. Sugar dissolves in water. 2. put an end to; as, to dissolve an agreement or a partnership. 3. fade away. *v. 3.*

dis so nance (dis′ə nəns), discord; a combination of sounds that is not harmonious. *n. 16.*

dis so nant (dis′ə nənt), 1. harsh in sound; clashing; not harmonious. 2. disagreeing; out of harmony with other views or persons. *adj. 15.*

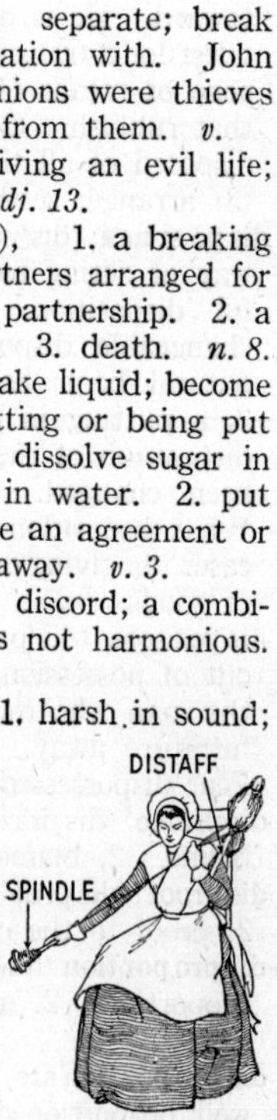

dis suade (di swād′), persuade not to do something. The father finally dissuaded his son from leaving school. *v. 10.*

DISTAFF
SPINDLE

dis taff (dis′taf), 1. a split stick about a yard long that held the wool or flax for spinning into thread when this was done by hand.

2. the part of a spinning wheel that holds the wool or flax. *n. 10.*

dis tance (dis′tәns), 1. space in between. The distance from the farm to the town is five miles. 2. being far away. The farm is at a distance from any railroad. 3. a place far away. The sailors saw a light in the distance. 4. coldness of manner. Seeming distance is often caused by shyness. 5. leave far behind; do much better than. The big black horse distanced the others. *n., v. 1.*

dis tant (dis′tәnt), 1. far away in space. The moon is distant from the earth. 2. away. The town is three miles distant. 3. far apart in time, relationship, likeness, etc.; not close. A third cousin is a distant relative. 4. not friendly. She gave him only a distant nod. *adj. 2.*

dis taste (dis tāst′), dislike. *n. 11.*

dis taste ful (dis tāst′fәl), unpleasant; displeasing; offensive; as, a distasteful medicine, a distasteful task. *adj. 10.*

dis tem per (dis tem′pәr), 1. sickness of body or mind. 2. a disease of dogs and other animals marked by a cough and weakness. *n. 7.*

dis tend (dis tend′), stretch out; expand; swell out. The balloon was distended almost to the bursting point. *v. 11.*

dis till or **dis til** (dis til′), 1. give off in drops. These flowers distill a sweet nectar. 2. make (a liquid) pure by turning it into a vapor by heat and then cooling it into liquid form again; as, distilled water. 3. make by distilling. Gasoline is distilled from crude oil. 4. get out the essential principle. A jury must distill the truth from the testimony of witnesses. *v., distilled, distilling. 6.*

dis til la tion (dis′ti lā′shәn), 1. a distilling; as, the distillation of water to purify it, the distillation of alcohol. 2. something distilled. *n. 12.*

dis till er (dis til′әr), 1. person or thing that distills. 2. person who makes whiskey, rum, brandy, etc. *n. 16.*

dis till er y (dis til′әr i), place where alcoholic liquor is distilled. *n., pl. distilleries. 13.*

dis tinct (dis tingkt′), 1. separate; not the same. 2. different in quality or kind. Mice are distinct from rats. 3. clear; easily seen, heard, or understood. Your speech and writing should be distinct. 4. unmistakable; definite; decided. *adj. 3.*

dis tinc tion (dis tingk′shәn), 1. making a difference. He gave every servant ten dollars without distinction. 2. difference. What is the distinction between ducks and geese? 3. a quality or mark that distinguishes. 4. a mark or sign of honor. He won many distinctions for bravery. 5. excellence; superiority. A governor of any of our States should be a man of character and distinction. *n. 5.*

dis tinc tive (dis tingk′tiv), distinguishing; characteristic. Boy Scouts wear a distinctive uniform. *adj. 9.*

dis tinct ness (dis tingkt′nis), being distinct; clearness. *n. 17.*

dis tin guish (dis ting′gwish), 1. see the differences in; tell apart. Can you distinguish cotton cloth from linen? 2. see or hear clearly; make out plainly. It is too dark for me to distinguish anything clearly. 3. make different; be a special quality or feature of. A trunk distinguishes the elephant. 4. make famous or well known. Tom distinguished himself by winning three prizes. *v. 3.*

dis tin guish a ble (dis ting′gwish ә bәl), capable of being distinguished. *adj. 14.*

dis tin guished (dis ting′gwisht), 1. great; well-known; as, a distinguished artist. 2. having the appearance of a great person. *adj. 11.*

dis tort (dis tôrt′), 1. pull or twist out of shape; make crooked or ugly. Crying distorts the face. 2. change from the truth. The man distorted the facts of the accident to escape blame. *v. 9.*

dis tor tion (dis tôr′shәn), 1. a distorting; twisting out of shape. A lie is a distortion of the truth. 2. being distorted. 3. anything distorted. *n. 14.*

dis tract (dis trakt′), 1. draw away (the mind or attention). The talking of the other children distracts me from my studying. 2. confuse; disturb. 3. **Distracted** sometimes means made almost insane. *v. 5.*

dis trac tion (dis trak′shәn), 1. drawing away the mind or attention. 2. thing that draws away the mind or the attention. Noise is a distraction when you are trying to study. 3. confusion of mind; wildness. The mother of the lost children scarcely knew what she was doing in her distraction. 4. amusement; relief from continued thought, grief, or effort. *n. 10.*

dis train (dis trān′), seize for unpaid rent or other debts. The landlord distrained his tenants' trunks. *v. 20.*

dis traught (dis trôt′), distracted; very much excited; crazed. The poor woman was wandering about distraught. *adj.*

dis tress (dis tres′), 1. great pain or sorrow; anxiety; trouble. 2. cause pain or sorrow to; make unhappy. 3. something that causes suffering; misfortune. 4. dangerous condition; difficult situation. A sinking ship at sea is in distress. *n., v. 3.*

dis tress ful (dis tres′fəl), painful; causing distress. *adj. 16.*

dis trib ute (dis trib′ūt), 1. give some to each; deal out. I distributed the spelling papers for our teacher. 2. spread; scatter. Distribute your paint evenly over the wall. 3. divide into parts. 4. arrange. A mail clerk distributes mail when he puts each letter into the proper bag. *v. 5.*

dis tri bu tion (dis′tri bū′shən), 1. act of distributing. After the contest the distribution of prizes to the winners took place. 2. way of being distributed. If some get more than others, there is an uneven distribution. 3. thing distributed. *n. 5.*

dis trib u tive (dis trib′ū tiv), 1. having to do with distribution. 2. referring to each individual. *Each, every,* and *either* are distributive pronouns. *adj.*

dis trib u tor (dis trib′ū tər), person or thing that distributes. This firm is a distributor of French perfumes. *n. 12.*

dis trict (dis′trikt), 1. portion of a country; region. 2. portion of a country, a state, or a city, marked off for a special purpose, such as providing schools or law courts, electing certain government officers, or supporting a church. 3. divide into districts. *n., v. 2.*

District of Columbia, district in eastern United States belonging to the Federal government. It is entirely occupied by the capital, Washington.

dis trust (dis trust′), 1. have no trust in; not trust; not depend on; doubt. 2. lack of trust; lack of belief in the goodness of; doubt. *v., n. 8.*

dis trust ful (dis trust′fəl), not trusting; suspicious. *adj. 16.*

dis turb (dis tėrb′), 1. break in upon with noise or change. Do not disturb the baby; he is asleep. 2. put out of order. Someone has disturbed all my papers. 3. make uneasy; trouble. He was disturbed to hear of her illness. *v. 3.*

dis turb ance (dis tėr′bəns), 1. a disturbing or being disturbed. 2. thing that disturbs. 3. confusion; disorder. 4. uneasiness; trouble; worry. *n. 6.*

dis un ion (dis ūn′yən), 1. separation; division. 2. lack of unity; disagreement; unfriendliness. *n.*

dis u nite (dis′ū nīt′), 1. separate; divide. 2. destroy the unity of; cause to disagree or to become unfriendly. *v. 16.*

dis use (dis ūs′ for 1, dis ūz′ for 2), 1. lack of use; not being used. The old tools were rusted from disuse. Many words common in Shakespeare's time have fallen into disuse. 2. stop using. *n., v. 10.*

ditch (dich), 1. a long, narrow place dug in the earth. Ditches are usually to carry off water. 2. dig a ditch in. 3. run (into a ditch); throw into a ditch. The careless driver ditched his automobile. *n., v. 3.*

dit to (dit′ō), 1. the same. 2. a mark (") that means the same. *Example:*

6 lb. butter at 54c.......$3.24
4 "   "   "   " 2.16

3. likewise; as said before. *n., pl. dittos, adv.*

dit ty (dit′i), a short, simple song or poem. *n., pl. ditties. 10.*

di ur nal (dī ėr′nəl), 1. daily. 2. belonging to the daytime. 3. lasting a day. *adj. 13.*

di van (dī′van), long, low, soft couch or sofa. *n. 11.*

dive (dīv), 1. plunge head first into water. 2. act of diving. 3. downward plunge of an airplane. 4. plunge (the body, the hand, or the mind) suddenly into anything. He dived into his pockets and fished out a dollar. 5. a low, cheap place for drinking and gambling. *Used in common talk. v., dived* or *dove, dived, diving, n. 4.*

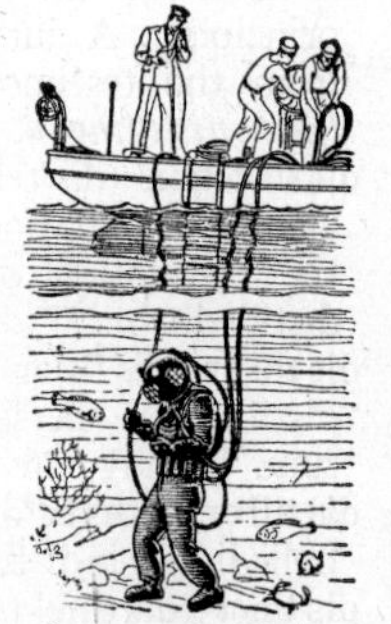
A diver at work in a diving suit

div er (dīv′ər), 1. one that dives. 2. person whose occupation is to work under water. 3. a diving bird. *n. 9.*

di verge (di vėrj′), 1. move or lie in different directions from the same point. Our paths diverge here; you go north and I go south. 2. differ. *v. 9*

di ver gence (di vėr′jəns), diverging; difference. The committee couldn't come to an agreement because of the wide divergence of opinion among its members. *n. 12.*

di ver gent (di vėr′jənt), diverging; different. *adj.*

di vers (dī′vərz), various; several different. *adj. 7.*

di verse (di vėrs′ or dī′vėrs), different. *adj. 8.*

di ver si fy (di vėr′si fī), make diverse; give variety to. Some people diversify their investments by investing in many different companies. *v., diversified, diversifying. 15.*

di ver sion (di vėr′zhən), 1. a turning aside. A magician's talk creates a diversion of attention so that people do not see how he does his tricks. 2. distraction from work, care, etc.; amusement; entertainment; pastime. Golf is a popular diversion. *n. 9.*

di ver si ty (di vėr′si ti), 1. being different; difference. Their diversity did not prevent them from being friends. 2. variety. The diversity of food on the table made it hard for him to choose. *n., pl. diversities. 8.*

di vert (di vėrt′), 1. turn aside. A ditch diverted water from the stream into the fields. He diverted trade to his own store when he could. The rattle diverted the baby's attention from the knife. 2. amuse; entertain. We were diverted by the clown's tricks. *v. 7.*

di vest (di vest′), 1. strip; rid; free. The sailor divested himself of his clothes and dived in the water. 2. deprive; force to give up. Citizens were divested of their right to vote. *v. 12.*

di vide (di vīd′), 1. separate into parts. A brook divides the field. The river divides and forms two streams. 2. separate into equal parts. When you divide 8 by 2, you get 4. 3. to share. The children divided the candy. 4. to separate in feeling, opinion, etc. The school divided on the choice of a motto. 5. a ridge between the regions drained by two different river systems. The Rocky Mountains are called the Great Divide. *v., n. 1.*

div i dend (div′i dend), 1. a number or quantity to be divided. In 728÷16, 728 is the dividend. 2. money earned by a company and divided among the owners of the company. *n. 7.*

di vid er (di vīd′ər), 1. thing or person that divides. 2. Measuring compasses are called dividers. *n. 11.*

Dividers

div i na tion (div′i nā′shən), 1. foreseeing the future or foretelling the unknown. 2. a skillful guess or prediction. *n. 11.*

di vine (di vīn′), 1. of God or a god. 2. by or from God. 3. to or for God; sacred; holy. 4. like God or a god; heavenly. 5. very excellent; unusually good or great. 6. clergyman who knows much about theology; minister; priest. 7. find out or foretell by inspiration, by magic, or by guessing; predict. *adj., n., v. 2.*

di vin er (di vīn′ər), person who discovers or foretells things; prophet. *n. 14.*

di vin i ty (di vin′i ti), 1. divine being; a god. **The Divinity** means God. 2. divine nature or quality. 3. study of God, religion, and divine things; theology. *n., pl. divinities. 6.*

di vis i ble (di viz′i bəl), 1. capable of being divided. 2. capable of being divided without leaving a remainder. Any even number is divisible by 2. *adj. 13.*

di vi sion (di vizh′ən), 1. dividing; being divided. 2. giving some to each; sharing; as, division of labor. 3. the process of dividing one number by another. 26÷2=13 is a simple division. 4. dividing line; boundary. 5. one of the parts into which a thing is divided. Some divisions of the army are mechanized. 6. a difference of opinion, thought, or feeling; disagreement. *n. 3.*

di vi sor (di vī′zər), 1. a number or quantity by which another is divided. In 728÷16, 16 is the divisor. 2. a number that divides another number without a remainder. *n. 11.*

di vorce (di vōrs′), 1. legal ending of a marriage. 2. end legally a marriage between. The judge divorced Mr. and Mrs. Jones. 3. get rid of by divorce. Mrs. Bush tried to divorce her husband. 4. separation. In this country there is a complete divorce of government and religion. 5. separate. In sports, exercise and play are not divorced. *n., v. 4.*

di vulge (di vulj′), tell; reveal; make known. The traitor divulged secret plans to the enemy. *v. 13.*

Dix ie (dik′si), 1. the Southern States of the United States. 2. a song to a lively tune with the refrain "Away down south in Dixie." *n.*

diz zi ness (diz′i nis), dizzy condition. *n.*

diz zy (diz′i), 1. disposed to fall, stagger,

or spin around. When you spin round and round, and stop suddenly, you feel dizzy. 2. confused; not steady. 3. make dizzy. 4. likely to make dizzy; causing dizziness. The airplane climbed to a dizzy height. *adj., dizzier, dizziest, v., dizzied, dizzying. 6.*

Dnie per (nē′pər), river flowing from western Russia into the Black Sea. *n.*

do[1] (dü), 1. When you carry through to an end any action or piece of work, you do it. Do your work well. 2. act; behave. He did very well today. 3. Do is used (1) to make what one says stronger. I do want to go. Do come, please. (2) to ask questions. Do you like milk? (3) to stand for another word. My dog goes where I do. Nell's sister walks just as Nell does. 4. **Do up** means wrap up. 5. be satisfactory. That knife will do. *v., did, done, doing. 1.*

do[2] (dō), in music, the first and last tone of the scale. Do, re, mi, fa, sol, la, ti, do are the names of the tones of the scale. *n.*

doat (dōt), dote. *v. 17.*

dob bin (dob′in), slow, gentle horse. *n.*

doc ile (dos′il), 1. easily managed; obedient. 2. easily taught; willing to learn. *adj. 12.*

do cil i ty (dō sil′i ti), docile quality. *n. 16.*

dock[1] (dok), 1. platform built on the shore or out from the shore; wharf; pier. 2. place where a ship may be repaired, often built watertight so that the water may be kept high or pumped out. See the picture of **dry dock.** 3. bring (a ship) to dock. The sailors docked the ship and began to unload it. *n., v. 4.*

Ship loading at a dock

dock[2] (dok), 1. the solid, fleshy part of an animal's tail. 2. cut short; cut off the end of. 3. cut some off of. The company docked the men's wages if they came late to work. *n., v.*

dock[3] (dok), the place where an accused person stands in a law court to be tried. *n.*

dock[4] (dok), large weed with sour or bitter leaves. *n.*

dock et (dok′it), 1. a list of lawsuits to be tried by a court. 2. any list of matters to be considered by some person or group. 3. enter on a docket. 4. a label or ticket giving information as to contents, to be attached to a package, etc. *n., v.*

dock yard (dok′yärd′), an enclosure containing docks, shops, warehouses, etc., where ships are repaired, fitted out, and built. *n. 18.*

doc tor (dok′tər), 1. person who knows how to treat diseases. 2. treat disease in. A mother doctors her children for colds and stomach aches. 3. person who has received one of the highest degrees given by a university; as, a Doctor of Laws. *n., v. 1.*

doc tri nal (dok′tri nəl), of or having to do with doctrine. We heard a doctrinal sermon about baptism. *adj. 19.*

doc trine (dok′trin), 1. what is taught; teachings. 2. what is taught as the belief of a church, a nation, or a group of persons; a belief. *n. 4.*

doc u ment (dok′ū mənt), something written or printed that gives information and can be used as evidence of some fact; any object used as evidence. Letters, maps, and pictures are documents. *n. 6.*

doc u men ta ry (dok′ū men′tə ri), consisting of documents; in writing, print, etc. The man's own letters were documentary evidence of his guilt. *adj. 19.*

dod der (dod′ər), shake; tremble; totter. He dodders about as if he were ninety years old. *v.*

Dodo (4 ft. long)

dodge (doj), 1. move quickly to one side. 2. move quickly in order to get away from (a person, a blow, or something thrown). 3. a sudden movement to one side. 4. get away from by some trick. 5. a trick to cheat. *v., n. 7.*

do do (dō′dō), a large clumsy bird not able to fly. Dodos are now extinct. See the picture just above. *n., pl. dodos or dodoes.*

doe (dō), a female deer, rabbit, or hare. *n. 8.*

Doe of the Virginia deer (about 2¾ ft. high at the shoulder)

do er (dü′ər), person who does or accomplishes. John is a dreamer, and his brother is a doer. *n. 9.*

does (duz). See **do**[1]. He does all his work. Does she sing well? *v. 1.*

doe skin (dō′skin′), 1. the skin of a doe. 2. leather made from it. 3. smooth, soft, woolen cloth, sometimes used for men's suits. *n.*

does n't (duz′ənt), does not. *3.*

doff (dof), take off (hat, clothes, etc.). A man doffs his hat when he enters a house. *v. 12.*

dog (dôg), 1. My dog guards the house. Tom's dog hunts rats. 2. something made to hold or grip like a dog's teeth. 3. hunt or follow like a dog. The police dogged the suspected thief. *n., v., dogged, dogging. 1.*

Dog for gripping

dog days, period of very hot and uncomfortable weather during July and August.

doge (dōj), the chief magistrate of the old republics of Venice and Genoa. *n.*

dog-ear (dôg′ēr′), 1. folded-down corner of a page in a book. A dog-ear is often made to mark the page where the reader has stopped. 2. fold down the corner of (a page or pages in a book). *n., v.*

dog fish (dôg′fish′), a small kind of shark. *n. 13.*

dog ged (dôg′id), obstinate; persistent. Dick's dogged determination helped him to win the prize. *adj. 8.*

dog ger el (dôg′ər əl), 1. worthless poetry. 2. irregular; crude; poor. Doggerel verses are often used in advertisements. *n., adj. 16.*

do gie (dō′gi), motherless calf on a ranch. *n.*

dog ma (dôg′mə), 1. a belief taught as true, especially by authority of a church. 2. doctrine; belief. *n. 11.*

dog mat ic (dôg mat′ik), 1. having to do with dogma; doctrinal. 2. asserting opinions as if one were the highest authority; positive; overbearing. 3. asserted without proof. *adj. 15.*

dog ma tism (dôg′mə tizm), 1. dogmatic nature. 2. being dogmatic; positive assertion of opinion. Dogmatism is likely to arouse opposition. *n. 18.*

dog trot (dôg′trot′), gentle, easy trot. *n.*

dog wood (dôg′wu̇d′), a tree with large white or pinkish flowers in the spring and red berries in the fall. *n. 20.*

doi ly (doi′li), a small piece of linen, lace, or paper, used on the table at meals. Ornamental doilies are often placed under vases or other art objects in other parts of the house. *n., pl. doilies. 12.*

do ings (dü′ingz), actions; conduct; proceedings. *n. pl. 3.*

doit (doit), 1. a small copper coin formerly used by the Dutch. 2. trifle; bit. No one cares a doit what Tom thinks. *n. 14.*

dol drums (dol′drəmz), 1. certain parts of the ocean near the equator having calms and light winds. The ship was in the doldrums and could make no headway. 2. dullness; low spirits. *n. pl.*

dole[1] (dōl), 1. a portion of money, food, etc., given in charity. 2. deal out in portions to the poor. 3. small portion. 4. give in small quantities. *n., v. 8.*

dole[2] (dōl), grief; sorrow. *n.* [*Old use*]

dole ful (dōl′fəl), sad; dreary; dismal. *adj. 8.*

doll (dol). A doll looks like a baby, a child, or a grown person. *n. 2.*

Doll wearing doll's clothes

dol lar (dol′ər), 1. the unit of United States money; one hundred cents. $1.00 means one dollar. 2. a silver coin or a paper note equal to 100 cents. 3. a large silver coin of Canada, Mexico, and some other countries. *n. 2.*

doll y (dol′i), child's name for a doll. *n., pl. dollies. 5.*

do lor (dō′lər), sorrow; grief. *n. 15.*

dol or ous (dol′ər əs), 1. mournful; sorrowful. She uttered a little dolorous cry. 2. grievous; painful. The dolorous day was ending. *adj. 19.*

dol phin (dol′fin), 1. small whale that has a beaklike snout. 2. a large sea fish that changes color when it is taken out of the water. *n. 8.*

Dolphin (def. 1) (6 to 10 ft. long)

dolt (dōlt), a dull, stupid person; blockhead. *n. 13.*

-dom, suffix meaning:—
1. position, rank, or realm of ——. kingdom = realm of a king.
2. condition of being ——. martyrdom = condition of being a martyr.
3. all those who are ——. heathendom = all those who are heathen.

do main (dō mān′), 1. the lands belonging to a ruler, a nobleman, or a government, and under his or its rule. 2. a field of thought and action. Edison was a leader in the domain of invention. *n. 8.*

dome (dōm), 1. a large, rounded roof on a circular or many-sided base. 2. thing shaped like a dome; as, the rounded dome of a hill. *n. 4.*

Dome of a church

do mes tic (də mes′tik), 1. of the home, the household, or family affairs; as, domestic cares, a domestic scene. 2. fond of home. 3. household servant. 4. tame. Horses, dogs, cats, cows, and pigs are domestic animals. 5. of one's country; not foreign. A good newspaper usually publishes both domestic and foreign news. *adj., n. 3.*

do mes ti cate (də mes′ti kāt), 1. to tame; make over (animals and plants) from a wild to a tame state. 2. cause to be or feel at home. 3. make fond of home. *v. 12.*

do mes ti ca tion (də mes′ti kā′shən), 1. domesticating. 2. being domesticated. *n. 15.*

do mes tic i ty (dō′mes tis′i ti), 1. home and family life. 2. fondness for home and family life. *n.*

dom i cile (dom′i sil), 1. house; home; dwelling place. 2. place of permanent residence. 3. establish in a domicile. 4. dwell. *n., v. 17.*

dom i nance (dom′i nəns), rule; control; being dominant. *n. 18.*

dom i nant (dom′i nənt), 1. ruling; governing; controlling; most influential. The white race is dominant in the world today. 2. rising high above its surroundings; occupying a commanding position. A dominant cliff rose at the bend of the river. 3. the fifth note in a musical scale. G is the dominant in the key of C. *adj., n. 7.*

dom i nate (dom′i nāt), 1. control or rule by strength or power; have or exercise control. The boy dominates his smaller friend. 2. hold a commanding position over. The town in the valley is dominated by a high mountain. *v. 10.*

dom i na tion (dom′i nā′shən), control; rule; dominating. *n. 10.*

dom i neer (dom′i nēr′), rule over at one's own will; tyrannize; be overbearing in asserting one's authority. Dick domineers over his little sisters. *v. 15.*

Dom i nic (dom′i nik). Saint Dominic (1170-1221) founded an order of preaching friars. *n. 19.*

Do min i can (dō min′i kən), 1. of Saint Dominic or the order of preaching friars founded by him. 2. Dominican friar. 3. of or having to do with the Dominican Republic. 4. a native or inhabitant of the Dominican Republic. *adj., n. 17.*

Dominican Republic, republic in the eastern part of the island of Haiti, in the West Indies. Also called **Santo Domingo.**

dom i nie (dom′i ni), 1. schoolmaster. 2. clergyman. *n.*

do min ion (də min′yən), 1. rule; control. Englishmen have dominion over a large part of the world. 2. lands under the control of one ruler or government. 3. a self-governing territory; as, the Dominion of Canada. *n. 4.*

dom i no (dom′i nō), 1. a loose cloak with a face mask worn as a disguise, especially at masquerades. 2. one of a set of small pieces of bone or wood marked with spots. **Dominoes** is the name of the game played with them. *n., pl. dominoes* or *dominos. 9.*

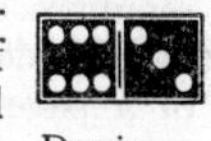
Dominoes

don[1] (don), 1. in Spain, Don is a title meaning Mr. or Sir. 2. In England, a don is the head of a college, or a tutor. *n. 7.*

don[2] (don), put on (clothing, etc.). *v., donned, donning.*

do nate (dō′nāt), give; contribute. *v. 16.*

do na tion (dō nā′shən), 1. act of giving. 2. gift; contribution. All business men were called upon to make donations to the Red Cross. *n. 12.*

done (dun), 1. finished; completed. 2. cooked. 3. worn out. 4. See **do**[1]. *adj., pp.* of *do*[1]. *1.*

don jon (dun′jən), large, strongly fortified tower of a castle. *n.*

don key (dong′ki), 1. a small animal somewhat like a horse but with longer ears, a shorter mane, and a tuft of hair at the end of its tail. 2. stubborn person; silly or stupid person. *n., pl. donkeys. 4.*

Donkey (3 ft. high at the shoulder)

do nor (dō′nər), giver. *n. 11.*

Don Quix ote (don kwik′sət), a famous character in a book who was chivalrous and idealistic, but extremely impractical.

don't (dōnt), do not. *1.*

doom (düm), 1. fate. 2. terrible fate; ruin; death. The soldiers marched to their doom. 3. condemn to some fate. The prisoner was doomed to death. 4. judgment; sentence. The judge pronounced the guilty man's doom. *n., v. 3.*

dooms day (dümz′dā′), end of the world; day of God's final judgment of mankind. *n. 14.*

door (dōr), 1. a door closes the entrance of a house, a room, or a building. 2. place where a door is. *n. 1.*

door keep er (dōr′kēp′ər), person who guards an entrance. *n. 15.*

door step (dōr′step′), step leading from an outside door to the ground. *n. 11.*

door way (dōr′wā′), an opening in the wall where a door is. *n. 7.*

door yard (dōr′yärd′), yard about the door of a house; yard around a house. *n. 18.*

dope (dōp), 1. drug. 2. information; forecast. *n., v.* [*Slang*] *13.*

Dor ic (dor′ik), of or having to do with the oldest and simplest of the Greek kinds of architecture. *adj. 17.*

Doric capital

dor mant (dôr′mənt), 1. sleeping. 2. quiet as if asleep. Bears are dormant during the winter. 3. inactive. Plant bulbs stay dormant during the cold of winter. *adj. 11.*

Dormer and window

dor mer (dôr′mər), 1. upright window that projects from a sloping roof. 2. projecting part of a roof that contains such a window. *n. 19.*

dor mi to ry (dôr′mi tō′ri), 1. a building containing a large number of sleeping rooms. 2. a sleeping room large enough for a number of beds. *n., pl. dormitories. 12.*

dor mouse (dôr′mous′), a small animal somewhat like a mouse and somewhat like a squirrel. It sleeps during cold weather. *n., pl. dormice. 15.*

Dormouse (about 5 in. long including the tail)

dor sal (dôr′səl), of, on, or near the back. A shark has a dorsal fin. *adj. 10.*

Dor set (dôr′sit), a county in southern England. *n. 18.*

do ry (dō′ri), a rowboat with a narrow, flat bottom and high sides, used for fishing, etc. *n., pl. dories.*

Dory

dose (dōs), 1. the amount of a medicine to be taken at one time; as, a dose of cod-liver oil. 2. give medicine to. *n., v. 7.*

dost (dust), an old form meaning **do.** "Thou dost" means "you do." *v. 4.*

dot (dot), 1. small spot or point. There is a dot over each *i* in this line. 2. mark with a dot or dots. *n., v., dotted, dotting. 2.*

dot age (dōt′ij), the foolish or childish condition caused by old age. *n. 10.*

do tard (dō′tərd), person who is weak-minded from old age. *n. 14.*

dote (dōt), 1. be weak-minded and childish because of old age. 2. **Dote on** means be foolishly fond of; be too fond of. *v. 7.*

doth (duth), an old form meaning **does.** *v. 3.*

dou ble (dub′əl), 1. twice as great, as large, as strong, etc. The man was given double pay for working overtime. 2. twice. 3. a number or amount twice as large. Four is the double of two. 4. make twice as much; make twice as many. Mr. Smith doubled his money in ten years by investing it wisely. 5. become twice as much. Money left in a savings bank will double in about twenty years. 6. made of two like parts; in a pair; as, double doors. 7. having two meanings, characters, etc. The word *fast* has a double meaning. 8. person or thing just like another. Here is the double of your lost glove. 9. fold over. Jack doubled his slice of bread to make a sandwich. The boy doubled his fists. 10. bend or turn sharply backward. The fox doubled on his track and escaped the dogs. 11. a sharp turn. 12. go around. The ship doubled Cape Horn. 13. having more than one set of petals. Some roses are double, others single. *adj., adv., n., v. 1.*

dou ble-deal ing (dub′əl dēl′ing), deceiving; pretending to do one thing and then doing another. *n., adj.*

dou ble-joint ed (dub′əl join′tid), having joints that let fingers, arms, legs, etc., bend in unusual ways. *adj.*

dou ble-quick (dub′əl kwik′), 1. next quickest step to a run in marching. 2. very quick. 3. in double-quick time. 4. march in double-quick step. *n., adj., adv., v.*

dou blet (dub′lit), a man's close-fitting jacket. See the picture. Men wore doublet and hose in Europe from 1400 to 1600. *n. 11.*

Doublet

dou bloon (dub lün′), a former Spanish gold coin of varying value, usually worth about $5. *n. 20.*

dou bly (dub′li), in a double manner, measure, or degree. Doubly careful means twice as careful. *adv. 13.*

doubt (dout), 1. not believe; not be sure; feel uncertain. The captain doubted whether the sinking ship would reach land. 2. difficulty in believing; an uncertain state of mind. The men were in doubt as to the right road. 3. uncertainty. **No doubt** means certainly. *v., n. 1.*

doubt ful (dout′fəl), full of doubt; undecided; not certain. We are doubtful about the weather for tomorrow. *adj. 4.*

doubt less (dout′lis), 1. without doubt; surely. 2. probably. *adv. 4.*

dough (dō), the mixture of flour, milk, fat, and other materials from which bread, biscuits, pie, etc., are made. *n. 6.*

dough boy (dō′boi′), a private soldier in the United States infantry. *n.* [*Used in common talk*] *20.*

dough nut (dō′nut′), piece of sweetened dough cooked in deep fat. A doughnut is usually made in the shape of a ring. *n. 11.*

dough ty (dou′ti), strong; stout; hardy. All King Arthur's doughty knights fought gallantly. *adj., doughtier, doughtiest. 14.*

dour (dür), severe; stern; gloomy; as, a dour nature, a dour look, dour silence. *adj.*

Dove (about 1 ft. long)

douse (dous), 1. plunge into water. 2. throw water over. *v. 20.*

dove[1] (duv), pigeon. Tame doves are often kept near a house. See the picture. *n. 3.*

dove[2] (dōv), dived. *a pl. of* **dive.**

dove cot (duv′kot′), dovecote. *n. 19.*

dove cote (duv′kōt′), small house or shelter for doves or pigeons. *n.*

Dovecote

Do ver (dō′vər), 1. English seaport nearest France. 2. strait between France and England. 3. capital of Delaware. *n. 10.*

dove tail (duv′tāl′), 1. fasten (two boards) together by cutting them so that projections on one fit into openings of the other. 2. the parts so shaped. 3. fit together exactly. The evidence dovetailed completely. *v., n.*

Dovetails

dow a ger (dou′ə jər), 1. woman who holds some title or property from her dead husband. The queen and her mother-in-law, the queen dowager, were both present. 2. a dignified elderly lady. *Used in common talk. n. 13.*

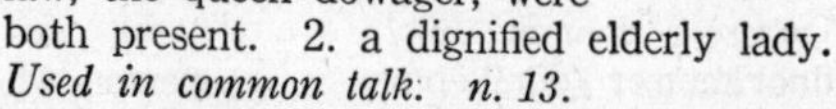

dow dy (dou′di), 1. poorly dressed; shabby; not stylish. 2. a poorly dressed woman. *adj., dowdier, dowdiest, n., pl. dowdies. 20.*

dow el (dou′əl), peg on a piece of wood, metal, etc., to fit into a corresponding hole on another piece, and so form a joint fastening the two pieces together. *n.*

DOWEL

dow er (dou′ər), 1. the wife's share for life of her dead husband's property. 2. a gift of nature, such as ability, beauty, or any good or great quality. 3. provide with a dower. *n., v. 10.*

down[1] (doun), 1. to a lower place; in a lower place. They ran down from the top of the hill. The stone step was worn down by many feet. 2. from an earlier time to a later time. The story has come down through many years. 3. down along. He went down the hill. 4. put down. *adv., adj., prep., v. 1.*

down[2] (doun), soft feathers; soft hair or fluff. *n.*

down[3] (doun), rolling, green land. *n.*

down cast (doun′kast′), 1. turned downward. She stood before us with downcast eyes. 2. dejected; sad; discouraged. He was downcast because of his failure. *adj. 11.*

down fall (doun′fôl′), 1. ruin; as, the downfall of an empire, the moral downfall of a person. 2. a heavy rain or snow. *n. 8.*

down heart ed (doun′här′tid), discouraged; dejected; depressed. *adj.*

down hill (doun′hil′), down the slope of a hill; downward. *adv., adj.*

down pour (doun′pōr′), heavy rain. *n.*

down right (doun′rīt′), 1. thorough; complete; as, a downright thief, a downright lie. 2. thoroughly; completely. He was downright rude to me. 3. plain; positive. His downright answer left no doubt as to what he thought. *adj., adv. 9.*

down stairs (doun′stãrz′), 1. down the

stairs. 2. on a lower floor. 3. lower floor or floors. *adv., adj., n. 7.*

down stream (doun′strēm′), with the current of a stream; down a stream. *adv., adj. 12.*

down town (doun′toun′), 1. to or in the lower part of a town. 2. to or in the main part or business part of a town. *adv., adj. 18.*

down trod den (doun′trod′ən), 1. oppressed. 2. trodden down. *adj.*

down ward (doun′wərd), 1. toward a lower place. 2. toward a later time. *adv., adj. 3.*

down wards (doun′wərdz), downward. *adv.*

down y (doun′i), 1. of soft feathers or fluff. 2. covered with down. 3. soft as down. A kitten's fur is downy. *adj., downier, downiest. 10.*

dow ry (dou′ri), 1. the money or property that a woman brings to her husband when she marries him. 2. a gift of nature; a natural talent. Good health and intelligence are a useful dowry. *n., pl. dowries. 10.*

dox ol o gy (doks ol′ə ji), a hymn or statement praising God. Two familiar doxologies begin: "Glory be to the Father, and to the Son, and to the Holy Ghost," and "Praise God from whom all blessings flow." *n., pl. doxologies. 18.*

doz., dozen. *7.*

doze (dōz), 1. sleep lightly; be half asleep. 2. light sleep; a nap. *v., n. 9.*

doz en (duz′ən), 12; group of 12. *n., pl. dozens* or (after a number) *dozen. 2.*

Dr. or **Dr,** Doctor; as, Dr. W. H. Smith. *5.*

drab (drab), 1. dull; monotonous; unattractive; as, the drab houses of the mining town. 2. dull, brownish gray. *adj., drabber, drabbest, n. 11.*

drachm (dram), dram. *n. 16.*

draft (draft), 1. a current of air. 2. device for controlling a current of air. Opening the draft of a furnace makes the fire burn faster. 3. a plan; a sketch. 4. make a plan or sketch of. 5. rough copy. He made three different drafts of his speech before he had it in final form. 6. write out a rough copy of. 7. a selection of persons for some special purpose. In time of war men are often supplied to the army and navy by draft. 8. the persons chosen for special service. 9. select for some special purpose. 10. act of pulling loads. 11. for pulling loads. A draft horse is used for pulling wagons and plows. 12. pulling of a net to catch fish. 13. all the fish caught in one drawing of a net. 14. a written order from one person or bank to another, requiring the payment of a stated amount of money. 15. a heavy demand or drain on anything. 16. the depth of water a ship requires to float it, or the depth it sinks into the water, especially when loaded. 17. a single act of drinking. 18. amount drunk at a single drink. *n., v., adj. 3.* Also spelled **draught.**

drafts man (drafts′mən), 1. person who draws sketches, plans, designs, or diagrams. 2. person who prepares documents. *n., pl. draftsmen. 18.* Also spelled **draughtsman.**

drag (drag), 1. pull or move along heavily or slowly; pull or draw along the ground. A team of horses dragged the big log out of the forest. 2. go too slowly. A piece of music played too slowly drags. Time drags when you have nothing to do. 3. pull a net, hook, harrow, etc., over or along for some purpose. People drag a lake for fish or for a drowned person's body. 4. Anything that holds back or is pulled may be called a drag. Some old ideas and ways are a drag on progress. *v., dragged, dragging, n. 2.*

Dragnet for fish

drag gle (drag′əl), 1. make or become wet or dirty by dragging through mud, water, dust, etc. 2. follow slowly; lag behind; straggle. *v.*

drag net (drag′net′), a net pulled over the bottom of a river, pond, etc., or along the ground. Dragnets are used to catch fish and small birds. *n.*

Dragon with three heads

drag on (drag′ən), in old stories, a terrible creature like a huge winged snake with scales and claws, which often breathed fire. *n. 3.*

drag on fly (drag′ən flī′), a large, harmless insect with a long, slender body and two pairs of gauzy wings. *n., pl. dragonflies. 18.*

Dragonfly (½ to 4 in. long)

dra goon (drə gün′), 1. soldier who fights on horseback. Dragoons formerly rode horses to the battlefield, but sometimes fought on foot. 2. oppress or persecute by dragoons. 3. compel by oppression or persecution. *n., v. 13.*

drain (drān), 1. draw off (water or any

liquid); draw liquid from; empty of liquid; as, to drain swamps, drain a cup. 2. dry by the flowing off of water. Set the dishes here to drain. 3. a channel or pipe for carrying off water or waste of any kind. 4. take away from slowly; use up little by little; deprive. War drains a country of its people and money. 5. a slow taking away; a using up little by little. Working or playing too hard is a drain on your strength. *v., n. 2.*

drain age (drān′ij), 1. draining; drawing off water. The drainage of swamps improves a town. 2. a system of channels or pipes for carrying off water or waste of any kind. 3. what is drained off. *n. 8.*

drake[1] (drāk), male duck. *n. 7.*

Drake[2] (drāk), Sir Francis, an English pirate and admiral (1540?-1596). *n.*

dram (dram), 1. a small weight. In apothecaries' weight, 8 drams make 1 ounce; in avoirdupois weight, 16 drams make 1 ounce. 2. small drink of intoxicating liquor. *n. 10.* Also spelled **drachm.**

dra ma (drä′mə or dram′ə), 1. a play such as one sees in a theater; a story acted out by actors on the stage. 2. the art of writing and producing plays. 3. part of real life that seems to have been planned like a story. The history of America is a great and thrilling drama. *n. 5.*

dra mat ic (drə mat′ik), 1. of drama; having to do with plays. 2. sudden; exciting; full of action or feeling. *adj. 8.*

dra mat i cal ly (drə mat′i kəl i), in a dramatic manner; emotionally. *adv.*

dra mat ics (drə mat′iks), art of acting or producing plays. *n.*

dram a tist (dram′ə tist), writer of plays. *n. 11.*

dram a tize (dram′ə tīz), 1. make a drama of; as, to dramatize a novel. 2. represent dramatically. The children dramatized the story of Rip Van Winkle. *v. 10.*

drank (drangk). See **drink.** She drank her milk. *pt. of drink. 4.*

drape (drāp), 1. cover or hang with cloth of any kind, especially as a decoration. The buildings were draped with red, white, and blue. 2. arrange to hang loosely in folds. Can you drape this skirt? 3. cloth hung in folds. Some curtains are drapes. *v., n. 8.*

dra per y (drā′pər i), 1. cloths or fabrics, especially those used for hangings and garments. 2. clothing or hangings arranged in folds. *n., pl. draperies. 7.*

dras tic (dras′tik), acting with force or violence. The police took drastic measures to put a stop to the crime wave. *adj. 13.*

draught (draft), draft. *n., v., adj. 4.*

draughts (drafts), the game of checkers. *n. pl. [In British use]*

draughts man (drafts′mən), draftsman. *n., pl. draughtsmen. 19.*

drave (drāv), drove. *old pt. of* **drive.** *13.*

draw (drô), 1. pull; drag; haul. The horses draw the wagon. 2. attract. Accidents in the streets always draw crowds. 3. pull out; pull up; cause to come out; take out; get. Draw a pail of water from this well. She drew ten dollars from the bank. Draw no conclusions now. 4. make a picture or likeness of anything with pen, pencil, or chalk. 5. tie. A game is a draw when neither side wins. 6. part of a drawbridge. Draw also has special meanings in special cases, as follows: 7. inhale; as, draw a breath. 8. make longer; stretch. The battle was long drawn out. 9. write. The lawyer drew up documents. 10. need for floating. The big ship draws 28 feet of water. 11. move. The car drew near. 12. make a draft of air to carry off smoke. The chimney does not draw well. 13. a kind of valley. *v., drew, drawn, drawing, n. 1.*

draw back (drô′bak′), a condition that is not favorable; a disadvantage; anything which makes a situation or experience less complete or satisfying. Our trip was interesting, but the rainy weather was a drawback. *n. 10.*

draw bridge (drô′brij′), bridge that can be entirely or partly lifted, lowered, or moved to one side. *n. 13.*

Two drawbridges on a castle

draw er (drô′ər for 1, drôr for 2 and 3), 1. person who draws. 2. a box with handles built to slide in and out of a table, desk, or bureau. 3. **Drawers** are a two-legged undergarment fastened about the waist. *n. 4.*

draw ing (drô′ing), 1. a sketch, plan, or design done with pen, pencil, or crayon. 2. representing objects by lines. *n. 19.*

drawing room, room for receiving or entertaining guests; parlor.

drawl (drôl), 1. talk in a slow, lazy way. 2. slow, lazy way of talking. *v., n. 12.*

drawn (drôn). See **draw.** That old horse has drawn many loads. *pp. of draw. 4.*
dray (drā), a low, strong cart for carrying heavy loads. *n. 15.*
dray man (drā′mən), man who drives a dray. *n., pl. draymen. 19.*
dread (dred), 1. look forward to with fear; dislike to experience; fear greatly. Tom dreaded his visits to the dentist. Cats dread water. 2. fear, especially fear of something that will happen, or may happen. 3. dreaded; dreadful. 4. awe-inspiring; solemn. *v., n., adj. 2.*
dread ful (dred′fəl), 1. terrible; awful; fearful. 2. very bad; very unpleasant. *Used in common talk. adj. 2.*
dread ful ly (dred′fəl i), in a dreadful manner; to a dreadful degree; terribly. *adv. 11.*
dread nought (dred′nôt′), big, powerful battleship with heavy armor and large guns. *n. 19.*
dream (drēm), 1. something thought, felt, or seen in sleep. 2. something as unreal as the fancies of sleep. The boy had dreams of being a hero. 3. think, feel, hear, or see in sleep. 4. form fancies; imagine. The girl dreamed of being in the movies. 5. suppose in a vague way. The day seemed so bright that we never dreamed there would be rain. *n., v., dreamed* or *dreamt, dreaming. 1.*
dream er (drēm′ər), 1. person who dreams. 2. person who does not fit his ideas to real conditions. *n. 15.*
dream land (drēm′land′), the land of dreams; place where one seems to be when one is dreaming. *n. 12.*
dreamt (dremt), dreamed. *pt. and pp. of* **dream.**
dream y (drēm′i), 1. full of dreams; as, a dreamy sleep. 2. fond of daydreaming; fanciful; not practical; as, a dreamy person. 3. like a dream; vague; dim; as, a dreamy recollection. *adj., dreamier, dreamiest. 17.*

Dredge (def. 1)

drear (drēr), dreary. *adj. 14.*
drear y (drēr′i), dull; without cheer; gloomy. *adj., drearier, dreariest. 5.*
dredge (drej), 1. machine for cleaning out or deepening a harbor or channel. 2. clean out or deepen with a dredge. 3. machine used for gathering oysters, etc., from the bottom of a river. 4. gather with a dredge. *n., v. 12.*
dregs (dregz), 1. solid bits of matter that settle to the bottom of a liquid. After pouring the tea she rinsed the dregs out of the teapot. 2. most worthless part. Thieves and murderers are the dregs of humanity. 3. **Not a dreg** means not a bit; not any. He left not a dreg in the cup. *n. pl. 9.*
drench (drench), 1. wet thoroughly; soak. 2. a soaking. *v., n. 8.*
Dres den (drez′dən), a city in central Germany, noted for the manufacture of china. *n. 10.*
dress (dres), 1. the usual outer garment worn by women, girls, and babies. 2. clothing, especially outer clothing. Boys think less about dress than girls do. 3. put clothes on. 4. make ready to use; care for. The butcher will dress the chickens for you. To dress hair is to comb and brush and arrange it. To dress a cut or sore is to treat it with medicine and bandages. 5. form in a straight line. The captain ordered the soldiers to dress their ranks. 6. smooth; finish; as, to dress leather. *n., v., dressed* or *drest, dressing. 1.*
dress er[1] (dres′ər), 1. person who dresses (himself, another person, a shop window, or a wound). 2. tool or machine to prepare things for use. *n. 6.*
dress er[2] (dres′ər), 1. piece of furniture with shelves for dishes. 2. a chest or set of drawers with a mirror, properly called a bureau. *n.*
dress ing (dres′ing), 1. medicine, bandage, etc., put on a wound or sore. 2. sauce for salads, fish, meat, etc. 3. a stuffing of bread crumbs, seasoning, etc., for chicken, turkey, etc. *n.*
dressing gown, loose robe worn while dressing or resting.
dress mak er (dres′māk′ər), person, usually a woman, whose work is making women's or children's dresses. *n. 11.*
dress mak ing (dres′māk′ing), making dresses, coats, etc. *n. 17.*
drest (drest), dressed. *a pt. and a pp. of* **dress.** *20.*
drew (drü). See **draw.** He drew a picture of his mother. *pt. of draw. 2.*
drib ble (drib′əl), 1. flow or let flow in

drops or small amounts; trickle. That faucet dribbles. 2. drip from the mouth. The baby dribbles on his bib. 3. a dropping; a dripping. 4. very light rain. 5. move (a ball) along by bouncing it or giving it short kicks. *v., n. 18.*

drib let (drib′lit), small amount. *n.*

dried (drīd). See **dry.** I dried my hands. This bread has been dried in the oven. *pt. and pp. of dry. 4.*

dri er (drī′ər), 1. thing or person that dries. 2. machine or person that removes water. 3. a substance mixed with paint or varnish to make it dry more quickly. *n. 9.*

drift (drift), 1. be carried along by currents of air or water. A raft drifts if it is not steered. 2. carry along. The current was drifting us along. 3. go along or live without a goal or without knowing where one will come out. Some people just drift through life. 4. being driven; the motion of being carried along by wind or water. 5. direction. The drift of this current is to the south. 6. meaning; direction of thought. I caught the drift of his words. 7. anything carried along by wind, water, or ice. 8. pile or be piled into heaps, like snow blown by the wind. 9. snow, sand, etc., heaped up by the wind. *v., n. 4.*

drift wood (drift′wu̇d′), wood carried along by water; wood washed ashore from the water. *n. 13.*

drill[1] (dril), 1. tool for boring holes; machine for using such a tool. 2. make (a hole) with a drill; use a drill. 3. teach by having the pupil do a thing over and over. 4. doing a thing over and over for practice. 5. group instruction and training in physical exercises or in marching, handling a gun, and other duties of soldiers. 6. do military or physical exercises. 7. cause to do such exercises. The sergeant drilled the new soldiers. *n., v. 2.*

Drill

drill[2] (dril), machine for planting seeds in rows. It makes a small furrow, drops the seed, and then covers the furrow. *n.*

drink (dringk), 1. swallow anything liquid, such as water or milk. 2. anything liquid swallowed to make one less thirsty. 3. suck up; absorb. The soil drank water like a sponge. 4. take. Our ears had drunk in the music. 5. alcoholic liquor. 6. drink alcoholic liquor. *v., drank, drunk, drinking, n. 1.*

drink er (dringk′ər), 1. person who drinks. 2. person who drinks alcoholic liquor often or too much. *n. 14.*

drip (drip), 1. fall or let fall in drops. Rain drips from an umbrella. 2. falling in drops. 3. be wet enough to shed drops. His forehead was dripping. 4. a liquid which falls in drops. *v., dripped* or *dript, dripping, n. 4.*

drive (drīv), 1. make go. Drive the dog away. Drive the nail in. 2. make go where one wishes. Can you drive a car? 3. make go ahead; make succeed. He drove a good bargain at the store. 4. go in a car or carriage; carry in a car, etc. 5. a trip in a car or carriage. 6. road. He built a drive to his house. 7. go fast or violently. The ship drove on the rocks. 8. strike; aim. **Let drive** means strike or aim. 9. work hard. 10. pressure; impelling force. Hunger is a drive to action. 11. special effort. Our church made a drive to get $10,000. 12. act of driving. 13. the thing or things driven. *v., drove, driven, driving, n. 1.*

driv el (driv′əl), 1. have saliva running out of the mouth or liquid running down from the nose. 2. a flow from the mouth or nose. 3. talk like a child or an idiot. 4. silly talk; nonsense. *v., driveled, driveling, n. 16.*

driv el er (driv′əl ər), person who drivels. *n. 18.*

driv en (driv′ən). See **drive.** Mr. Jones has just driven past. *pp. of drive. 13.*

driv er (drīv′ər), 1. person who drives; especially, a driver of horses, of an automobile, or of an engine. 2. person who makes the people under him work very hard. *n. 4.*

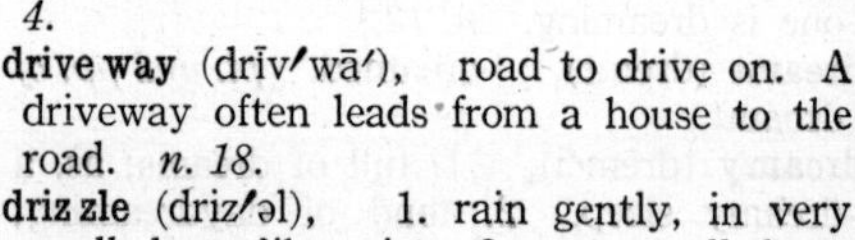

drive way (drīv′wā′), road to drive on. A driveway often leads from a house to the road. *n. 18.*

driz zle (driz′əl), 1. rain gently, in very small drops like mist. 2. very small drops of rain like mist. *v., n. 10.*

driz zly (driz′li), drizzling. *adj.*

droll (drōl), odd and amusing; quaint and laughable. We smiled at the monkey's droll tricks. *adj. 11.*

droll er y (drōl′ər i), 1. something odd and amusing; laughable trick. 2. quaint humor. 3. jesting. *n., pl. drolleries.*

drom e dar y (drom′ə dãr′i), a swift camel for riding, usually the one-humped camel of Arabia. *n., pl. dromedaries. 16.*

Dromedary (6 ft. high at the shoulder)

drone (drōn), 1. male honeybee. Drones do no work. 2. person not willing to work; idler; loafer. 3. spend time idly; loaf. 4. make a deep, continuous, humming sound. Bees droned among the flowers. 5. such a sound. Soldiers listened for the drone of the airplane motors. 6. talk or say in a monotonous voice. The weary beggar droned a prayer. *n., v. 7.*

Drone (about life size)

droop (drüp), 1. hang down; bend down. These flowers will soon droop if they are not put in water. 2. hanging down; bending position. The droop of the branches brought them within our reach. 3. become weak; lose strength and energy. 4. become discouraged; be sad and gloomy. *v., n. 3.*

drop (drop), 1. a small amount of liquid in a round shape; as, a drop of rain, a drop of blood. 2. fall in drops. 3. very small amount of liquid. Drink a drop of this. 4. sudden fall. 5. the distance down; a sudden fall in level; as, a drop of thirty feet. 6. take a sudden fall. The man dropped from the top of the building. The price of sugar will drop soon. 7. let fall. Drop that package. 8. cause to fall. 9. fall dead, wounded, or tired out. 10. cause to fall dead; kill. 11. go lower; sink. 12. make lower. Drop your voice. 13. let go; dismiss. The boss dropped six men Saturday. 14. leave out; omit. 15. stop; end; cease. We let the quarrel drop. 16. come. Drop in and see me some day. 17. go with the current or tide. The raft dropped down the river. *n., v., dropped* or *dropt, dropping. 1.*

drop let (drop′lit), tiny drop. *n. 17.*

drop si cal (drop′si kəl), 1. of or like dropsy. 2. having the dropsy. *adj. 20.*

drop sy (drop′si), a disease in which a liquid collects in the body. *n. 15.*

dross (drôs), 1. the waste that comes to the surface of melting metals. 2. rubbish; waste material. *n. 9.*

drought (drout), 1. long period of dry weather; lack of rain. 2. lack of water; dryness. *n. 8.*

drouth (drouth), drought. *n. 14.*

drove (drōv), 1. group of cattle, sheep, hogs, etc., moving or driven along together; herd; flock. We sent a drove of cattle to market. 2. many people moving along together; crowd. 3. See **drive.** We drove twenty miles today. *n., v., pt. of drive. 2.*

dro ver (drō′vər), 1. man who drives cattle, sheep, etc., to market. 2. a dealer in cattle. *n. 15.*

drown (droun), 1. die under water or other liquid because of lack of air to breathe. 2. kill by keeping under water. 3. be stronger than; keep from being heard. His loud voice drowned what the girl was trying to tell us. *v. 2.*

drowse (drouz), 1. be dull and sleepy; be half asleep. She drowsed, but did not quite fall asleep. 2. a light sleep. *v., n. 12.*

drow si ness (drou′zi nis), sleepiness; being drowsy. *n. 12.*

drow sy (drou′zi), 1. sleepy; half asleep. 2. making one sleepy. *adj., drowsier, drowsiest. 4.*

drub (drub), beat with a stick or the like; thrash. *v., drubbed, drubbing.*

drudge (druj), 1. person who does hard, disagreeable work; a slave; an overworked servant. 2. do tiresome or disagreeable work. *n., v. 11.*

drudg er y (druj′ər i), hard or uninteresting work. *n., pl. drudgeries. 12.*

drug (drug), 1. a substance (other than food) that, when taken into the body, produces a change in it. If the change helps the body, the drug is a medicine; if the change harms the body, the drug is a poison. 2. give harmful drugs to, particularly drugs that cause sleep. 3. mix harmful drugs with (food or drink). 4. affect or overcome (the body or the senses) in a way not natural. The wine had drugged him. 5. An article that is too abundant, or is no longer in demand, or is of too slow sale, is called a **drug on the market.** *n., v., drugged, drugging. 3.*

drug gist (drug′ist), person who sells drugs, medicines, toilet articles, etc. *n. 8.*

Dru id or **dru id** (drü′id), one of an order of priests among the ancient Celts of Britain, Ireland, and France. The Druids worshiped in groves and sometimes offered sacrifices. *n. 9.*

drum (drum), 1. a musical instrument that makes a sound when it is beaten. A drum is hollow with a covering stretched tightly over the ends. 2. the sound made by beating a drum; any noise like this. 3. play the drum; make a sound by beating a drum. 4. beat, tap, or strike again and again. He drummed on the table. 5. teach or drive into one's head by repeating over and over. Tom's lessons had to be drummed into him because he did not like school. 6. thing shaped like a drum. 7. a thick bar or cylinder in a machine on which something is wound. 8. a drum-shaped container for packing dried fruits or holding oil. 9. **Drum up** means call together. We could not drum up enough children for our game. 10. **Drum out of** means drive out of. *n., v., drummed, drumming. 2.*

drum major, leader of a marching band.

drum mer (drum′ər), person who plays a drum. *n. 12.*

drum stick (drum′stik′), 1. a stick for beating a drum. 2. the lower half of the leg of a cooked chicken, turkey, etc. *n.*

drunk (drungk), 1. overcome by alcoholic liquor. He was so drunk he could not stand up. 2. See **drink.** *adj., pp. and old pt. of drink. 4.*

drunk ard (drungk′ərd), person who is often drunk; person who drinks too much alcoholic liquor. *n. 7.*

drunk en (drungk′ən), 1. drunk. 2. caused by being drunk; as, a drunken act, drunken words. *adj. 5.*

drunk en ness (drungk′ən nis), 1. condition caused by drinking too much alcoholic liquor. 2. habit of drinking so much alcoholic liquor as to become drunk. *n. 9.*

dry (drī), 1. not wet; not moist. Dust is dry. 2. make dry by wiping, draining, or heating. 3. not giving water or milk. The cow is dry. 4. make or become dry; stop giving water. 5. having little or no rain; as, a dry climate. 6. thirsty; wanting a drink. 7. solid; not liquid; as, on dry land. 8. showing no feeling. 9. not interesting; dull. 10. forbidding the sale of alcoholic drinks. Some States in the United States are dry. *Used in common talk. adj., drier, driest, v., dried, drying. 1.*

dry ad or **Dry ad** (drī′ad), a nymph that lives in a tree; wood nymph. *n. 14.*

Dry den (drī′dən), John, a noted English poet, dramatist, and prose writer (1631-1700). *n. 9.*

dry dock, a dock from which the water can be pumped.

Ship in dry dock

dry er (drī′ər), drier. *n.*

dry goods, cloth, ribbons, laces, and the like.

dry ly (drī′li), in a dry manner. President Coolidge spoke little and dryly. *adv.*

dry ness (drī′nis), being dry; dry quality. *n. 19.*

dry-shod (drī′shod′), having dry shoes; without getting the feet wet. *adj.*

D. S. T., Daylight Saving Time.

du al (dū′əl or dü′əl), 1. of two; showing two. 2. consisting of two parts; double; twofold. The airplane had dual controls, one set for the learner and one for the teacher. *adj. 10.*

dub (dub), 1. make (a man) a knight by striking his shoulder lightly with a sword. 2. give a title to; name or call. The boys dubbed Tom "Fatty." 3. make (a timber) smooth. *v., dubbed, dubbing. 12.*

du bi ous (dū′bi əs or dü′bi əs), 1. doubtful; uncertain; as, a dubious compliment, of dubious authorship, a dubious manner. 2. of questionable character; probably bad; as, a dubious scheme for making money. *adj. 9.*

Dub lin (dub′lin), the capital of Eire. *n. 18.*

du cal (dū′kəl or dü′kəl), of a duke; having the title of duke. *adj. 14.*

duc at (duk′ət), any of various gold coins once used in Europe, usually worth about $2.30. *n. 15.*

Du ce (dü′chā), title given to Mussolini. Duce means "leader." *n.*

duch ess (duch′is), 1. the wife or widow of a duke. 2. a woman with a rank equal to a duke's. *n. 7.*

duch y (duch′i), the territory ruled by a duke or a duchess; dukedom. *n., pl. duchies. 17.*

Duck

duck[1] (duk), a wild or tame swimming bird with a flat bill and short neck and legs. See the picture. Ducks are very often kept to use as food and for their eggs. *n. 2.*

duck[2] (duk), 1. plunge or dip the head or the whole body under water and come up quickly, as a duck does; put under water for a short time. 2. a quick plunge below the water. 3. lower the head or bend the body quickly to keep off a blow. 4. a sudden lowering of the head or bending of the body. *v., n.*

duck[3] (duk), a strong cotton or linen fabric, lighter and finer in weave than canvas. Duck is used for small sails, and for outer clothing by sailors and by persons living in hot climates. *n.*

duck bill (duk′bil′), small water mammal that lays eggs. It has webbed feet and a beak like a duck's. See the picture. *n.*

Duckbill
(about 1½ ft. long)

duck ling (duk′ling), young duck. *n.*

duct (dukt), 1. tube, pipe, or channel for carrying liquid, air, wires, etc. 2. tube in the body for carrying a bodily fluid; as, tear ducts. *n. 11.*

duc tile (duk′til), 1. capable of being hammered out thin or drawn out into wire. Gold and copper are ductile metals. 2. capable of being molded or shaped. Wax is ductile. 3. easily managed or directed. *adj. 16.*

duct less (dukt′lis), having no duct. A **ductless gland** gives up its products directly to the blood or the lymph. The thyroid, the spleen, and the thymus are ductless glands. *adj. 17.*

dudg eon (duj′ən), anger; resentment. *n.*

due (dū or dü), 1. owed as a debt; owing; to be paid. The money due him for his work was paid today. 2. a person's right; what is owed or due to a person. Courtesy is his due while he is your guest. 3. proper; rightful; fitting. He has his due reward for good work. 4. what a person owes. **Dues** sometimes means a fee or tax for some purpose; as, club dues. 5. **Due to** means caused by. The accident was due to his careless use of the gun. 6. looked for; expected; set by agreement; promised to come or to do. The train is due at noon. He is due to speak twice tomorrow. 7. exactly; directly. The ship sailed due west. *adj., n., adv. 2.*

du el (dū′əl or dü′əl), 1. a formal fight to settle a quarrel. Duels are fought with guns, swords, etc., between two persons in the presence of two others called seconds. 2. any contest between two opposing parties, whether persons, animals, or political parties. 3. fight a duel. *n., v., dueled, dueling. 8.*

du el ist (dū′əl ist or dü′əl ist), man who fights duels. *n. 18.*

du en na (dū en′ə or dü en′ə), 1. an elderly woman acting as governess and companion in a Spanish family. 2. governess; chaperon. *n.*

du et (dū et′ or dü et′), 1. piece of music for two voices or instruments. 2. two singers or players. *n. 17.*

dug (dug). See **dig.** The potatoes have all been dug. *pt. and pp. of dig. 3.*

dug out (dug′out′), 1. rough shelter or dwelling formed by digging. 2. boat made by hollowing out a large log. *n.*

duke (dūk or dük), 1. in Great Britain and some other countries, a nobleman of the highest title that passes from father to son, outside the royal family. 2. in some parts of Europe, a prince who rules a small, independent state called a duchy. *n. 3.*

duke dom (dūk′dəm or dük′dəm), 1. the territory ruled by a duke. 2. the title or rank of a duke. *n. 9.*

dul cet (dul′sit), sweet; pleasing; soothing, especially to the ear. *adj. 15.*

dul ci mer (dul′si mər), a musical instrument with strings, played by striking with two hammers. *n. 15.*

Man playing
a dulcimer

dull (dul), 1. not sharp or pointed; as, a dull knife, a dull joke. 2. not bright or clear; as, dull eyes, a dull color, a dull day, a dull sound. 3. slow in understanding; stupid; as, a dull mind, a dull boy. 4. not interesting or pleasant; boring. 5. not active. 6. make dull. 7. grow dull. *adj., v. 3.*

dull ard (dul′ərd), dull, stupid person. *n.*

dull ness (dul′nis), being dull; slowness of understanding; lack of sharpness, brightness, clearness, or interest. *n. 9.*

dul ly (dul′li), in a dull manner. *adv*

Du luth (dů lüth′), a city in Minnesota, on Lake Superior. *n. 17.*

du ly (dū′li or dü′li), as due; according to what is due; rightly; suitably. *adv. 6.*

dumb (dum), 1. not able to speak. 2. silent; not speaking. 3. stupid; dull. *Used in common talk. adj. 3.*

dumb bell (dum′bel′), short bar of wood or iron with large, heavy, round ends. It is lifted or swung around to exercise the muscles of the arms, back, etc. *n.*

Dumbbell

dumb wait er (dum′wāt′ər), 1. a box with shelves that can be pulled up or down a shaft. A dumbwaiter is used to carry food, rubbish, etc., from one floor to another, 2. a stand to hold food, dishes, etc., placed near a dining table. *n.*

dum found or **dumb found** (dum′found′), amaze and make unable to speak; bewilder; confuse. The watchers were dumfounded to see the supposed dead man rise from his coffin. *v.*

dum my (dum′i), 1. figure of a person, used to display clothing in store windows, to shoot at in rifle practice, to tackle in football, etc. 2. stupid person with no more sense than such a figure. 3. an imitation, counterfeit, or copy of something; sham. The boys played soldier with dummy swords made of wood. 4. person acting for another, who seems to be acting for himself. 5. in cardplaying, the player whose hand is turned up and played by his partner. *n., pl. dummies, adj. 19.*

dump (dump), 1. empty out; throw down. The truck backed up to the curb and dumped the coal on the sidewalk. 2. place for throwing rubbish. 3. heap of rubbish. *v., n. 8.*

dump ling (dump′ling), 1. a rounded mass of boiled or steamed dough served with stew. 2. a pudding consisting of dough wrapped around an apple or other fruit. *n.*

dumps (dumps), low spirits; gloomy feelings. *n. pl.*

dump y (dump′i), short and fat. *adj., dumpier, dumpiest.*

dun[1] (dun), 1. demand payment of a debt from, again and again. 2. a demand for payment. 3. person who keeps demanding payment. *v., dunned, dunning, n. 11.*

dun[2] (dun), dull, grayish brown. *n., adj.*

dunce (duns), 1. child slow at learning his lessons in school. 2. stupid person. *n. 6.*

dune (dūn or dün), a mound or ridge of loose sand heaped up by the wind. *n. 9.*

Dunes

dung (dung), waste matter from the bowels of animals; manure. *n. 9.*

dun geon (dun′jən), a strong underground room for prisoners. *n. 4.*

dung hill (dung′hil′), a heap of dung or refuse in the farmyard. *n. 11.*

dupe (dūp or düp), 1. person easily deceived or tricked. 2. deceive; trick. *n., v. 12.*

du plex (dū′pleks or dü′pleks), twofold; double. *adj. 18.*

du pli cate (dū′pli kit or dü′pli kit for 1, 2, 4, and 5, dū′pli kāt or dü′pli kāt for 3), 1. exactly like something else; corresponding to something else. We have duplicate keys for the front door. 2. one of two things exactly alike; exact copy. He mailed the letter, but kept a duplicate. 3. make an exact copy of; repeat exactly. 4. double. 5. having two corresponding parts; twofold. A person's lungs are duplicate, but he has only one heart. *adj., n., v. 8.*

du pli ca tion (dū′pli kā′shən or dü′pli kā′shən), 1. duplicating. 2. being duplicated. 3. a copy. *n.*

du plic i ty (dū plis′i ti or dü plis′i ti), deceitfulness; treachery; secretly acting in one way and publicly acting in another in order to deceive. *n., pl. duplicities. 17.*

du ra bil i ty (dūr′ə bil′i ti or dür′ə bil′i ti), lasting quality; ability to stand wear. *n. 15.*

du ra ble (dūr′ə bəl or dür′ə bəl), lasting a long time; not soon injured or worn out. *adj. 7.*

du rance (dūr′əns or dür′əns), imprisonment. *n. 15.*

du ra tion (dū rā′shən or dü rā′shən), length of time; the time during which anything continues. He enlisted for the duration of the war. *n. 9.*

du ress (dūr′es or dür′es), 1. compulsion. The law will not require a person to fulfill a contract signed under duress. 2. restraint by force; imprisonment. *n. 19.*

dur ing (dūr′ing or dür′ing). The boys played during the afternoon. Sometime during the day come to see me. During recess means while recess lasts. *prep. 1.*

durst (dėrst), dared. *pt. of* **dare.** *7.*

dusk (dusk), 1. the time just before dark. 2. shade; gloom. 3. dark-colored; dim. *n., adj. 6.*

dusk y (dus′ki), 1. somewhat dark; dark-colored. 2. dim; obscure. 3. sad; gloomy. *adj., duskier, duskiest. 6.*

dust (dust), 1. fine, dry earth; any fine powder. Dust lay thick in the street. The old papers had turned to dust. The tomb contains the dust of kings. The bee is covered with yellow dust from the flowers. 2. get dust off; brush or wipe the dust from. The maid dusts the furniture after sweeping. 3. get dust on; soil with dust. 4. sprinkle with (dust or powder). The nurse dusted powder over the baby. 5. earth; ground. 6. low or humble condition. The king raised his general from the dust. 7. Some special meanings are:

bite the dust, fall dead or wounded.

lick the dust, 1. fall dead or wounded. 2. humble oneself slavishly.

shake the dust off one's feet, go away feeling angry or scornful.

throw dust in one's eyes, deceive or mislead a person.

n., v. 1.

dust er (dus′tər), 1. a cloth or brush for removing dust. 2. person who dusts clothes or furniture. 3. a long, light garment to protect clothing from dust. *n. 10.*

dust y (dus′ti), 1. covered with dust; filled with dust. 2. like dust; dry and powdery. 3. having the color of dust; grayish. *adj., dustier, dustiest. 4.*

Dutch (duch), 1. of or having to do with the Netherlands, its people, or their language. 2. the people of the Netherlands. 3. their language. 4. **High Dutch** means central or southern German; **Low Dutch** means northern German. 5. Dutch sometimes means German. The Pennsylvania Dutch came from Germany, not from the Netherlands. 6. A **Dutch treat** is an entertainment or meal in which each person pays for himself. *Used in common talk.* 7. **Beat the Dutch** means surpass anything before known or heard of. *Used in common talk. adj., n. 3.*

Dutch East Indies, islands and colonies in the East Indies belonging to the Netherlands.

Dutch man (duch′mən), 1. person born or living in the Netherlands. 2. a German. *Slang. n., pl. Dutchmen. 10.*

du te ous (dū′ti əs or dü′ti əs), dutiful; obedient. *adj. 12.*

du ti a ble (dū′ti ə bəl or dü′ti ə bəl), on which a duty or tax must be paid. *adj. 18.*

du ti ful (dū′ti fəl or dü′ti fəl), performing the duties required of one; obedient; submissive; as, a dutiful daughter. *adj. 13.*

du ty (dū′ti or dü′ti), 1. the thing that is right to do; what a person ought to do. 2. the binding force of what is right. A sense of duty makes a person do what he thinks is right. 3. the things a person has to do in filling his position. The mailman said his duties were to sort and deliver the letters. 4. the behavior that is due or owing. 5. a tax on the manufacture or sale of articles; a tax on taking articles out of, or bringing them into, a country. *n., pl. duties. 1.*

dwarf (dwôrf), 1. a person, an animal, or a plant much below the usual size for its kind. 2. in fairy tales, an ugly little man with magic power. 3. below the usual size for its kind; stopped in growth. 4. keep from growing large. 5. cause to seem small by comparison or by distance. That tall building dwarfs all those around it. *n., adj., v. 4.*

dwarf ish (dwôr′fish), like a dwarf. *adj. 18.*

dwell (dwel), 1. live; make one's home. They dwell in the country. 2. **Dwell on** a thought or a subject means think, speak, or write about it for a long time. *v., dwelt or dwelled, dwelling. 2.*

dwell er (dwel′ər), one who dwells or lives. A city dweller lives in cities. A cliff dweller lives on cliffs. *n. 9.*

dwell ing (dwel′ing), house; place in which one lives. *n. 3.*

dwelling place, a dwelling. *12.*

dwelt (dwelt). See **dwell.** We dwelt in the country for years. *pt. and pp. of dwell. 4.*

dwin dle (dwin′dəl), become smaller and smaller; shrink. Our supply of crayons has dwindled. *v. 6.*

dye (dī), 1. to color or stain by dipping into water containing coloring matter; as, to have a dress dyed. 2. a color used for dyeing materials. 3. a color produced by dipping into water containing dye. 4. to color or stain. His blood dyed the ground. *v., dyed, dyeing, n. 4.*

dye ing (dī′ing), coloring fabrics with dye. *n.*

dy er (dī′ər), one who dyes cloth, etc. *n. 12.*

dye stuff (dī′stuf′), substance yielding a dye or used as a dye. Indigo and cochineal are dyestuffs. *n.*

dy ing (dī′ing), 1. about to die; ceasing to live; as, a dying man. 2. coming to an end; as, the dying year. *adj. 3*

dyke (dīk), dike. *n., v. 14.*

dy nam ic (dī nam′ik), 1. having to do with energy or force in motion. 2. active; energetic; forceful. *adj. 18.*

dy na mite (dī′nə mīt), 1. the material most commonly used in blasting rocks. Dynamite is made of nitroglycerin. 2. blow up with dynamite. *n., v. 10.*

dy na mo (dī′nə mō), a machine for changing mechanical energy into electric energy. You can see dynamos at the powerhouse of any electric-light company. *n., pl. dynamos. 11.*

dy nas tic (dī nas′tik), having to do with a dynasty. *adj. 20.*

dy nas ty (dī′nəs ti), 1. series of rulers who belong to the same family. The Bourbon dynasty ruled France for about 240 years. 2. period of time during which a dynasty rules. *n., pl. dynasties. 9.*

dys en ter y (dis′ən ter′i), a disease of the intestines, producing diarrhea with mucus and blood. *n. 11.*

dys pep si a (dis pep′si ə), indigestion; poor digestion. *n. 12.*

dys pep tic (dis pep′tik), 1. pertaining to dyspepsia. 2. suffering from dyspepsia. 3. person who has dyspepsia. 4. gloomy. *adj., n. 18.*

E

E, e (ē), the fifth letter of the alphabet. There are two e's in see. *n., pl. E's, e's.*

E or **E.**, 1. east. 2. eastern.

each (ēch). Each of the six boys had a dog. We gave one bone to each dog. Each cup has a saucer. *pron., adj. 1.*

ea ger (ē′gər), wanting very much. The child is eager to have the candy. *adj. 2.*

ea ger ness (ē′gər nis), keen desire. *n. 8.*

ea gle (ē′gəl), 1. a large bird that can see far and fly strongly. 2. like that of an eagle. The eagle eye of the guide was watching every move. 3. a design or picture shaped like an eagle often used on a flag, a stamp, or a coat of arms. 4. a former gold coin of the United States, worth $10. *n., adj. 2.*

Eagle (3 ft. from head to tail)

ea glet (ē′glit), young eagle. *n. 20.*

ear[1] (ēr), 1. the part of the body by which men and animals hear. 2. something like an ear. 3. the sense of hearing. She has a good ear for music. 4. **Give ear** means listen or attend. *n. 1.*

ear[2] (ēr), 1. the part of certain plants that contains the grains. The grains of corn, wheat, oats, barley, and rye are formed on ears. 2. grow ears. Soon the corn will ear. *n., v.*

Ear of corn

ear ache (ēr′āk′), pain in the ear. *n.*

ear drum (ēr′drum′), thin membrane across the middle ear that vibrates when sound waves strike it. *n.*

earl (ėrl), an English noble, below a marquis but above a viscount. *n. 4.*

earl dom (ėrl′dəm), 1. lands of an earl. 2. rank or title of an earl. *n. 10.*

ear ly (ėr′li), 1. In his early years he liked ships. 2. The sun is not hot early in the day. Please come early before the others come. *adj., earlier, earliest, adv. 1.*

ear mark (ēr′märk′), 1. a mark made on the ear of a sheep or other animal to show who owns it. 2. special mark, quality, or feature that gives information about a thing or person; sign. 3. mark with an earmark. 4. set aside for some special purpose. One hundred dollars is earmarked to buy books for the library. *n., v. 18.*

earn (ėrn), 1. get in return for work or service; be paid. Mary gives her mother half of what she earns. 2. do enough work for; do good enough work for. Donald is paid more than he really earns. *v. 2.*

ear nest[1] (ėr′nist), 1. putting one's whole self into it. An earnest pupil has his mind on his work. 2. **In earnest** means determined or sincere. *adj., n. 2.*

ear nest[2] (ėr′nist), a part given or done in advance as a pledge for the rest. *n.*

ear nest ness (ėr′nist nis), seriousness of purpose; being earnest. *n. 10.*

earn ings (ėr′ningz), money earned; wages; profits. *n. pl. 9.*

ear phone (ēr′fōn′), receiver for a telephone, telegraph, or radio that is fastened over the ear. *n.*

ear ring (ēr′ring′), ornament for the ear. *n.*

ear shot (ēr′shot′), range of hearing. We shouted, but he was out of earshot. *n.*

earth (ėrth), 1. the globe on which we live. China is on the other side of the earth. 2. ground. The earth in his garden is good soft soil. *n. 1.*

earth en (ėr′thən), 1. made of earth. 2. made of baked clay. *adj. 8.*

earth en ware (ėr′thən wār′), dishes or containers made of baked clay; crockery or pottery of the coarser kinds. *n. 9.*

earth ly (ėrth′li), 1. having to do with the

earth, not with heaven. 2. **No earthly use** means no use at all. *adj. 3.*

earth quake (ėrth′kwāk′), a shaking or sliding of the ground, caused by changes far beneath the surface. Earthquakes sometimes destroy whole cities. *n. 4.*

earth work (ėrth′wėrk′), a bank of earth piled up for a fortification. *n. 17.*

earth worm (ėrth′wėrm′), the commonest worm that lives in the earth. It helps in loosening the soil. *n. 8.*

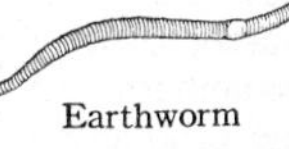
Earthworm

earth y (ėr′thi), 1. of earth or soil. 2. like earth or soil. 3. worldly; not spiritual. 4. coarse; not refined. *adj.*

ease (ēz), 1. freedom from pain or trouble. 2. make free from pain or trouble. 3. freedom from trying hard. **With ease** means without trying hard. 4. make less; lighten. Some medicines ease pain. 5. make easy; loosen. The belt is too tight; ease it a little. 6. move slowly and carefully. He eased the big box through the narrow door. *n., v. 2.*

ea sel (ē′zəl), a support for a picture, blackboard, etc. See the picture. *n.*

Easel

eas i er (ēz′i ər), not so hard; less difficult; more easy. *adj. 4.*

eas i ly (ēz′i li), 1. in an easy manner. 2. without trying hard; with little effort. 3. without pain or trouble; comfortably. 4. smoothly; freely. 5. beyond question. She is easily the best singer in the choir. 6. probably. A war may easily happen. *adv. 2.*

east (ēst), 1. the direction of the sunrise. 2. toward the east; farther toward the east. Walk east to find the road. 3. **East of** means further east than. 4. from the east; as, an east wind. 5. in the east; living in the east. 6. the part of any country toward the east. *n., adj., adv. 1.*

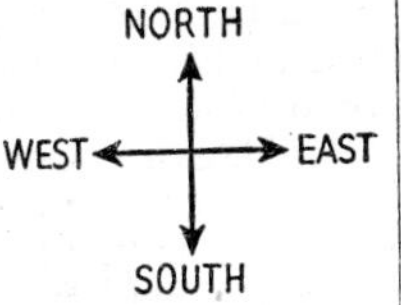

East (ēst), 1. eastern part of the United States; region from Maine through Maryland. 2. the countries in Asia; Orient. *n.*

East er (ēs′tər), 1. the day for celebrating Christ's rising from the dead; a yearly church holiday that comes on a Sunday between March 21 and April 26. 2. of Easter; as, Easter music. *n., adj. 4.*

east er ly (ēs′tər li), 1. toward the east. 2. from the east. *adv., adj. 17.*

east ern (ēs′tərn), 1. toward the east. 2. from the east. 3. of the east; in the east. *adj. 3.*

East ern (ēs′tərn), 1. of or in the eastern part of the United States. 2. of or in the countries in Asia; Oriental. *adj.*

Eastern Hemisphere, the half of the world that includes Europe, Asia, Africa, and Australia.

east ern most (ēs′tərn mōst), farthest east. *adj.*

East Indies, islands between Australia and Asia. Java and the Philippine Islands are in the East Indies.

East St. Louis, a city in Illinois, across the Mississippi River from St. Louis, Missouri.

east ward (ēst′wərd), toward the east; east. He walked eastward. The orchard is on the eastward slope of the hill. *adv., adj. 6.*

east wards (ēst′wərdz), eastward. *adv.*

eas y (ēz′i), 1. not hard to do or get. 2. not hard to bear; as, easy terms, an easy life. 3. giving comfort or rest; as, an easy chair. 4. not strict or harsh; not hard to get on with; kindly. 5. smooth and pleasant; as, easy manners, an easy way of speaking. *adj., easier, easiest. 1.*

eas y-go ing (ēz′i gō′ing), taking matters easily; not worrying. *adj.*

eat (ēt), 1. chew and swallow (food). Cows eat grass and grain. 2. have a meal. Where shall we eat? 3. destroy as if by eating. The flames ate up the wood. Acid eats metal. *v., ate, eaten, eating. 1.*

eat a ble (ēt′ə bəl), 1. fit to eat. 2. **Eatables** means food. *adj., n. 20.*

eat en (ēt′ən). See **eat.** Have you eaten your dinner? *pp. of eat.*

eat er (ēt′ər), one that eats. *n. 12.*

eaves (ēvz), the lower edge of a roof that stands out a little from the building. *n. pl. 6.*

EAVES

eaves drop (ēvz′drop′), listen to what one is not supposed to hear. *v., eavesdropped, eavesdropping.*

eaves drop per (ēvz′drop′ər), person who overhears talk that he is not supposed to hear. *n.*

ebb (eb), 1. a flowing of the tide away from the shore; fall of the tide. 2. flow out; fall. We waded farther out as the tide ebbed. 3. a growing less or weaker; decline. His fortunes were at an ebb. 4. grow less or weaker; decline. His courage began to ebb as he neared the haunted house. *n., v. 6.*

ebb tide, flowing back of the tide. Ebb tide occurs once in about thirteen hours.

eb on (eb′ən), 1. made of ebony. 2. black. *adj. [Used in poetry] 12.*

eb on y (eb′ən i), a hard, black wood, used for the black keys of a piano, brushes, and ornamental woodwork. *n., pl. ebonies. 8.*

eb ul li tion (eb′ə lish′ən), 1. boiling or bubbling up. 2. outburst (of feeling, etc.). *n. 16.*

ec cen tric (ek sen′trik), 1. out of the ordinary; not usual; peculiar; odd. It would be eccentric for you to turn around after every ten steps. 2. not having the same center. These circles ◎ are eccentric. 3. not moving in a circle. The orbit of an eccentric planet is not circular. 4. a device for changing circular motion into back-and-forth motion. *adj., n. 8.*

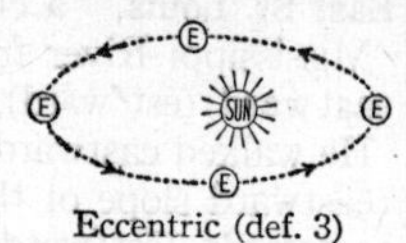

Eccentric (def. 3)

ec cen tric i ty (ek′sen tris′i ti), 1. queerness of behavior; peculiarity. 2. eccentric condition. One of Dr. Johnson's eccentricities was the habit of touching every lamppost he passed. *n., pl. eccentricities. 18.*

Ec cle si as tes (i klē′zi as′tēz), a book of the Old Testament. *n. 18.*

ec cle si as tic (i klē′zi as′tik), 1. clergyman. 2. ecclesiastical. *n., adj. 12.*

ec cle si as ti cal (i klē′zi as′ti kəl), of the church or the clergy. *adj. 13.*

ech o (ek′ō), 1. sounding again. We say there is an echo when sound waves are sent back by a cliff or a hillside, so that shouted words are heard again as if from a distance. 2. repeat; be heard again. 3. say always what another says. *n., pl. echoes, v. 2.*

é clair (ā klãr′), pastry filled with whipped cream or custard and covered with icing. *n.*

é clat (ā klä′), 1. brilliant success. 2. glory; renown. *n. 20.*

e clipse (i klips′), 1. passing from sight because light is cut off. In an eclipse of the sun, the moon is between us and the sun, so that from any point within the moon's shadow on the earth the sun is invisible. 2. cut off the light from, and so make invisible; darken. 3. outshine; cast into the shade. In sports he quite eclipsed his older brother. *n., v. 6.*

Sun showing almost entire eclipse

e clip tic (i klip′tik), the great circle in which the sun apparently moves. *n. 17.*

e co nom ic (ē′kə nom′ik), 1. having to do with economics. Economic problems have to do with the production, distribution, and consumption of wealth. 2. having to do with economy. *adj. 9.*

e co nom i cal (ē′kə nom′i kəl), avoiding waste; thrifty; saving. *adj. 8.*

e co nom ics (ē′kə nom′iks), the science of the production, distribution, and consumption of wealth. Economics deals with the material welfare of mankind and studies the problems of capital, labor, wages, prices, tariffs, taxes, etc. *n.*

e con o mist (i kon′ə mist), person who knows much about economics. *n. 8.*

e con o mize (i kon′ə mīz), 1. use little of; use to the best advantage. 2. cut down expenses. *v. 13.*

e con o my (i kon′ə mi), 1. making the most of what one has; thrift; freedom from waste in the use of anything. 2. management of the affairs and resources of a group. *n., pl. economies. 7.*

ec ru (ek′rü), pale brown; light tan. *n., adj.*

ec sta sy (ek′stə si), rapture; a state of very great joy; strong feeling that thrills the heart. She was in ecstasies over her first Christmas tree. *n., pl. ecstasies. 6.*

ec stat ic (ek stat′ik), 1. very joyful; thrilling. 2. caused by ecstasy. *adj. 10.*

ec stat i cal ly (ek stat′i kəl i), in an ecstatic manner. *adv.*

Ec ua dor (ek′wə dôr), a country in northwestern South America. *n. 14.*

ec ze ma (ek′si mə or eg zē′mə), an itching skin disease. *n.*

-ed, 1. suffix forming the past tense. 2. suffix forming the past participle. 3. suffix meaning:—having; supplied with; as in bearded, long-legged, tender-hearted. 4. suffix meaning:—having the characteristics of; as in honeyed.

ed dy[1] (ed′i), 1. a small whirlpool or whirlwind; water, air, or smoke whirling around. 2. whirl. *n., pl. eddies, v., eddied, eddying. 7.*

Ed dy[2] (ed′i), Mary Baker, founder of the Christian Science Church (1821-1910). *n.*

E den (ē′dən), 1. the garden where Adam and Eve lived. 2. delightful spot; a paradise. *n. 5.*

edge (ej), 1. the part that is farthest from the middle; the side; as, the edge of the paper. 2. the thin side that cuts. The knife had a very sharp edge. 3. move side first. She edged her way through the crowd. 4. move little by little. He edged his chair nearer to the fire. *n., v. 1.*

edge ways (ej′wāz′), with the edge forward; in the direction of the edge. *adv.*

edge wise (ej′wīz′), edgeways. *adv.*

edg ing (ej′ing), thing forming an edge or put on along an edge; border or trimming for an edge. *n. 12.*

ed i ble (ed′i bəl), 1. fit to eat. 2. thing fit to eat. *adj., n. 8.*

e dict (ē′dikt), a decree; an order by some authority. *n. 11.*

ed i fi ca tion (ed′i fi kā′shən), moral improvement or benefit. Good books give edification. *n. 15.*

ed i fice (ed′i fis), a building, especially a large or imposing one. *n. 5.*

ed i fy (ed′i fī), instruct and uplift, especially morally, spiritually, or religiously. *v., edified, edifying. 8.*

Ed in burgh (ed′in bə rə), the capital of Scotland. *n. 12.*

Ed i son (ed′i sən), Thomas A., the greatest American inventor (1847-1931). *n. 14.*

ed it (ed′it), 1. prepare (another person's writings) for publication. The teacher is editing famous speeches for use in schoolbooks. 2. have charge of (a newspaper, magazine, etc.) and decide what shall be printed in it. *v. 13.*

e di tion (i dish′ən), 1. all the copies of a book, newspaper, etc., printed just alike and at or near the same time. The first edition of *Robinson Crusoe* was printed in 1719. 2. the form in which a book is printed. The new edition of *Mother Goose* has better pictures than the older editions. *n. 6.*

ed i tor (ed′i tər), 1. person who edits. 2. person who writes editorials. *n. 8.*

ed i to ri al (ed′i tō′ri əl), 1. of an editor; as, editorial work. 2. an article in a newspaper or magazine written by the editor or under his direction, giving the opinion or attitude of the paper upon some subject. *adj., n. 8.*

ed i tor ship (ed′i tər ship′), position, duties, or authority of an editor. *n. 20.*

ed u cate (ej′ů kāt), teach; send to school. *v. 6.*

ed u ca tion (ej′ů kā′shən), 1. schooling; teaching; changing a person's nature. In the United States, public schools offer an education to all children. 2. the knowledge and abilities gained through training. *n. 3.*

ed u ca tion al (ej′ů kā′shən əl), 1. giving education; as, an educational moving picture. 2. having to do with education; as, an educational association. *adj. 8.*

ed u ca tor (ej′ů kā′tər), person who educates. *n. 19.*

e duce (i dūs′ or i düs′), bring out; develop. The teacher's questions educed many facts about home gardens. *v. 16.*

-ee, suffix meaning:—
1. person who is ——; as in absentee.
2. person who is ——ed; as in appointee.
3. person to whom something is ——ed; as in mortgagee.

eel (ēl), a long, slippery fish shaped like a snake. An eel is hard to hold; so we say "as slippery as an eel." *n. 10.*

Eel (2½ ft. long)

e'en (ēn), even. *adv.*

e'er (ãr), ever. *adv. 4.*

ee rie or **ee ry** (ēr′i), strange; weird; causing fear. *adj., eerier, eeriest. 17.*

ef face (i fās′), 1. rub out; blot out; do away with; destroy; wipe out. It takes many years to efface the unpleasant memories of a war. 2. keep (oneself) from being noticed. The shy boy effaced himself by staying in the background. *v. 10.*

ef face ment (i fās′mənt), 1. an effacing. 2. a being effaced. *n.*

ef fect (i fekt′), 1. bring about; make happen. 2. result; what is caused. The effect of the gale was to overturn several boats. 3. the result intended. 4. Some special meanings are:
effects, goods; personal property.
for effect, for show; to impress others.
give effect to, put in operation.
in effect, 1. in result; in fact; really. 2. in operation; active.
take effect, operate; become active.
to the effect, with the meaning or purpose.
v., n. 2.

ef fec tive (i fek′tiv), 1. producing an effect. 2. producing the desired effect. 3. in operation; active. A federal law is effective as soon as the President signs the act. *adj. 7.*

ef fec tu al (i fek′chü əl), producing the effect desired; capable of producing the effect desired. Quinine is an effectual preventive of malaria. *adj. 7.*

ef fec tu al ly (i fek′chü əl i), with a desired effect; thoroughly. *adv.*

ef fem i na cy (i fem′i nə si), unmanly softness or weakness. *n. 15.*

ef fem i nate (i fem′i nit), womanish; lacking in manly qualities. *adj. 8.*

ef fer ent (ef′ər ənt), conveying outward from a central organ or point. Efferent nerves carry impulses from the brain to the muscles. *adj. 19.*

ef fer vesce (ef′ər ves′), 1. give off bubbles of gas; bubble. Ginger ale effervesces. 2. be lively and gay; be excited. *v.*

ef fer ves cence (ef′ər ves′əns), 1. a bubbling. 2. liveliness; gaiety. *n. 16.*

ef fer ves cent (ef′ər ves′ənt), 1. bubbling. 2. lively; gay. *adj.*

ef fete (i fēt′), worn out; exhausted; no longer able to produce. *adj. 19.*

ef fi ca cious (ef′i kā′shəs), effective; producing results. Vaccination for smallpox is efficacious. *adj. 15.*

ef fi ca cy (ef′i kə si), power to produce a desired result. *n., pl. efficacies. 8.*

ef fi cien cy (i fish′ən si), ability to do things without waste; activity that counts toward a purpose. *n., pl. efficiencies. 9.*

ef fi cient (i fish′ənt), capable; doing things without waste. An efficient cook receives good pay. *adj. 8.*

ef fi gy (ef′i ji), an image, usually of a person. The dead man's monument bore his effigy. The king was burned in effigy by the angry mob. *n., pl. effigies. 11.*

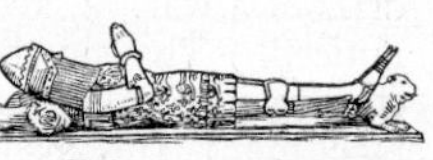

Effigy on a tomb

ef fort (ef′ərt), 1. use of energy and strength to do something; trying hard. Climbing a steep hill takes effort. 2. hard try; strong attempt. 3. result of effort; thing done with effort. Works of art are artistic efforts. *n. 2.*

ef fron ter y (i frun′tər i), shameless boldness; boldness; impudence. *n. 15.*

ef ful gence (i ful′jəns), radiance; splendor; as, the effulgence of the queen's jewels. *n. 15.*

ef ful gent (i ful′jənt), shining brightly; radiant. *adj.*

ef fu sion (i fū′zhən), 1. pouring out; as, the effusion of blood. 2. unrestrained expression of feeling, etc., in talking or writing. *n. 13.*

ef fu sive (i fū′siv), showing too much feeling; too demonstrative and emotional. *adj.*

eft (eft), a small newt or lizard. *n. 17.*

eft soon (eft sün′), soon afterward. *adv.* [*Old use*] *20.*

e.g., for example.

egg[1] (eg). Birds' eggs have shells. We eat hens' eggs. Fishes come from eggs. Birds, chickens, snakes, and alligators also come from eggs. *n. 1.*

egg[2] (eg), urge. The other boys egged John on to fight. *v.*

egg nog (eg′nog′), drink made of eggs beaten up with milk and sugar, often containing whiskey, brandy, or wine. *n.*

egg plant (eg′plant′), a plant with large purple fruit shaped somewhat like an egg, used as a vegetable. *n. 16.*

Eggplant

egg shell (eg′shel′), 1. shell covering an egg. 2. like an eggshell; very thin and delicate. *n., adj.*

eg lan tine (eg′lən tīn), a rose with a tall, prickly stem and single pink flowers; sweetbrier. *n. 11.*

Eglantine

e go tism (ē′gō tizm), 1. the excessive use of *I*, *my*, and *me;* the habit of thinking, talking, or writing too much of oneself. 2. self-conceit. 3. selfishness. *n. 14.*

e go tist (ē′gō tist), 1. person who thinks and talks about himself a great deal; conceited, boastful person. 2. selfish person. *n.*

e go tis tic (ē′gō tis′tik), 1. characterized by egotism; conceited. 2. selfish. *adj.*

e gre gious (i grē′jəs), remarkable; extraordinary; very great; as, an egregious lie, an egregious blunder. *adj. 16.*

e gress (ē′gres), 1. a going out. The enemy blocked the narrow pass so that no egress was possible for our soldiers. 2. way out; exit. *n. 15.*

e gret (ē′gret), 1. large heron with tufts of beautiful long plumes. 2. one of its plumes. *n.*

Great white egret of America

E gypt (ē′jipt), a country in the northeastern part of Africa. The river Nile flows through Egypt. *n. 3.*

E gyp tian (i jip′shən), 1. of Egypt. 2. a native of Egypt. 3. language of the ancient Egyptians. *adj., n. 5.*

eh (ā), an exclamation expressing surprise

or doubt, or suggesting "Yes" for an answer. Wasn't it lucky, eh? *interj. 13.*

ei der (ī′dər), a large sea duck, generally black and white. The soft breast feathers of eiders make a valuable down. *n.*

Eider (2 ft. long)

eider down, 1. soft feathers from the breasts of eiders, used as trimming and to fill bed coverings. 2. quilt stuffed with these feathers. *20.*

eight (āt), one more than seven; 8. Four and four make eight. *n., adj. 1.*

eight een (ā′tēn′), eight more than ten; 18. *n., adj. 2.*

eight eenth (ā′tēnth′), 1. next after the 17th. 2. one of 18 equal parts. *adj., n. 6.*

eighth (ātth), 1. next after the 7th. 2. one of 8 equal parts. *adj., n. 3.*

Eighth note

eighth note, in music, a very short note, one eighth of a whole note.

eight i eth (ā′ti ith), 1. next after the 79th. 2. one of 80 equal parts. *adj., n. 17.*

eight y (ā′ti), eight times ten; 80. *n., pl. eighties, adj. 3.*

Ein stein (īn′stīn), scientist who developed the theory of relativity (born 1879). *n.*

Eir e (ãr′ə), country in central and southern Ireland, formerly called the Irish Free State. *n.*

ei ther (ē′ᴛʜər or ī′ᴛʜər), 1. one or the other of two. A door must be either shut or open. Either come in or go out. 2. each of two. On either side of the river lie cornfields. 3. any more than another. If you do not go, I shall not go either. *conj., pron., adj., adv. 1.*

e jac u late (i jak′ū lāt), say suddenly and briefly; exclaim. *v. 18.*

e jac u la tion (i jak′ū lā′shən), something said suddenly and briefly; exclamation. *n. 15.*

e ject (i jekt′), throw out; turn out; drive out. *v. 10.*

e jec tion (i jek′shən), 1. ejecting. 2. being ejected. 3. something ejected. Lava is an ejection from a volcano. *n.*

eke (ēk), also. *adv., conj.* [*Old use*] *11.*

eke out, add to; increase; help. She eked out her income by working in the evenings.

e lab o rate (i lab′ə rit for 1, i lab′ə rāt for 2 and 3), 1. worked out with great care; having many details; complicated. 2. work out with great care; add details to. The inventor spent months in elaborating his plans for a new engine. 3. talk, write, etc., in great detail; give added details. The witness was asked to elaborate upon one of his statements. *adj., v. 7.*

e lab o ra tion (i lab′ə rā′shən), 1. an elaborating. 2. a being elaborated. 3. something elaborated. *n. 20.*

e lapse (i laps′), pass; slip away; glide by. Hours elapsed while he slept like a log. *v. 8.*

e las tic (i las′tik), 1. that can be stretched or pressed together and then return to its own shape. Toy balloons, sponges, and steel springs are elastic. 2. springing back. 3. recovering easily. His elastic spirits never let him be discouraged for long. 4. tape woven partly of rubber. 5. a rubber band. *adj., n. 5.*

e las tic i ty (i las′tis′i ti or ē′las tis′i ti), elastic quality. Rubber has great elasticity. *n. 12.*

e late (i lāt′), raise the spirits of; make proud. **Elated** means in high spirits. *v. 20.*

e la tion (i lā′shən), high spirits; joyous pride; exultant gladness. Ruth was filled with elation at having won the prize. *n.*

El ba (el′bə), island between Italy and Corsica. Napoleon was in exile there from 1814 to 1815. *n.*

El be (el′bə), a river in Germany, flowing into the North Sea. *n. 12.*

Elbow of a stovepipe

el bow (el′bō), 1. the joint between the upper and lower arm. 2. any bend or corner having the same shape as a bent arm. 3. push with the elbow; make (one's way) by pushing. *n., v. 3.*

eld (eld), 1. old age. 2. old times. *n.* [*Old use*] *15.*

eld er[1] (el′dər), 1. older. 2. an older person. Children should respect their elders. 3. an officer in a church. *adj., n. 3.*

el der[2] (el′dər), elderberry. *n.*

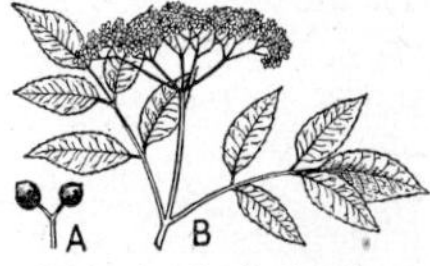
Elder bush: A, berries; B, branch.

el der ber ry (el′dər ber′i), 1. shrub or tree with flat clusters of white flowers and black or red berries, sometimes used in making wine. 2. berry of this plant. *n., pl. elderberries. 18.*

eld er ly (el′dər li), somewhat old. *adj. 9.*

eld est (el′dist), oldest. *adj. 4.*

El Do ra do (el də rä′dō), 1. a city supposed to be full of gold and treasure, sought in South America by early explorers. 2. any place said to be wealthy. *pl. El Dorados. 20.*

e lect (i lekt′), 1. choose. 2. choose by vote. Washington was elected president. 3. chosen; selected. *v., adj. 2.*

e lec tion (i lek′shən), 1. choice. 2. choosing by vote. *n. 3.*

e lec tion eer (i lek′shən ēr′), work for the success of a candidate or party in an election. *v. 20.*

e lec tive (i lek′tiv), 1. chosen by an election. Senators are elective officials. 2. filled by an election. The office of president of the United States is elective. 3. open to choice; not required. In high school, pupils must take certain subjects, but others are elective. 4. a study or course which a student may select from several. I am taking two electives. *adj., n. 15.*

e lec tor (i lek′tər), 1. person who has the right to vote in an election. 2. one of the persons chosen to elect the president and vice-president of the United States. *n. 8.*

e lec tor al (i lek′tər əl), 1. of electors. The electoral college elects the president of the United States. 2. of an election. *adj. 11.*

e lec tor ate (i lek′tər it), the persons having a right to vote in an election. *n. 20.*

e lec tric (i lek′trik), 1. of electricity; having to do with electricity. 2. charged with electricity; as, an electric battery. 3. giving an electric shock; as, an electric eel. 4. run by electricity. 5. exciting; thrilling. *adj. 3.*

e lec tri cal (i lek′tri kəl), electric. *adj. 6.*

e lec tri cal ly (i lek′tri kəl i), by electricity. *adv.*

e lec tri cian (i lek′trish′ən), person who repairs or installs electric wiring, lights, motors, etc. *n. 11.*

e lec tric i ty (i lek′tris′i ti), 1. form of energy which can give certain metals the power to pull together or push apart from one another, and which can produce light and heat. 2. electric current. Electric refrigerators are run by electricity. *n. 7.*

e lec tri fi ca tion (i lek′tri fi kā′shən), 1. electrifying. 2. being electrified. *n.*

e lec tri fy (i lek′tri fī), 1. charge with electricity. 2. equip for the use of electric power. 3. give an electric shock to. 4. excite; thrill. The speaker electrified his audience. *v., electrified, electrifying. 10.*

electro-, a form used to represent *electric* or *electricity* in compound words. *17.*

e lec tro cute (i lek′trə kūt), kill by electricity. The murderer was electrocuted. *v.*

e lec trode (i lek′trōd), either of the two poles, or terminals, of a battery or any other source of electricity. *n. 14.*

e lec trol y sis (i lek′trol′i sis), the use of an electric current to break up a chemical compound into its elements. *n.*

e lec tro lyte (i lek′trō līt), a compound that is broken up by an electric current. *n. 20.*

e lec tro mag net (i lek′trō mag′nit), piece of iron that becomes a strong magnet when an electric current is passing through wire coiled around it. *n. 18.*

Electro-magnet

e lec tro mo tive (i lek′trō mō′tiv), producing a flow of electricity. *adj. 19.*

e lec tron (i lek′tron), a tiny particle containing one unit of negative electricity. All atoms are built up of electrons and protons. *n. 20.*

e lec tro plate (i lek′trō plāt′), cover with a coating of metal by the use of electricity. Old silver spoons can be electroplated. *v.*

e lec tro type (i lek′trə tīp), 1. a copy of a page of type, an engraving, or the like, consisting of a shell of metal deposited by electrolysis in a wax mold of the original. 2. a print made from such a copy. *n. 18.*

el e gance (el′i gəns), refined grace and richness; luxury free from coarseness. *n. 12.*

el e gant (el′i gənt), showing good taste; refined; superior. *adj. 4.*

el e gy (el′i ji), a mournful or melancholy poem; lament for the dead. *n., pl. elegies. 12.*

el e ment (el′i mənt), 1. a simple substance, one of 92 that cannot yet be separated into simpler parts. Gold, iron, oxygen, carbon, and tin are elements. In ancient times, people thought that there were four elements: earth, water, air, and fire. 2. one of the parts of which anything is made up. Honesty, industry, and kindness are elements of a good life. 3. a simple or necessary part. We learn the elements of arithmetic before the seventh grade. 4. **The elements** means the forces of the air, especially in bad weather. 5. **Be in one's element** means be where one can succeed. *n. 3.*

el e men tal (el′i men′təl), 1. of the four elements—earth, water, air, and fire. 2. of the forces of the air or the weather; as, the elemental fury of the storm. 3. fundamental; unaltered; as found in nature. Hunger is an elemental feeling. 4. simple; not a compound. *adj. 10.*

el e men ta ry (el′i men′tə ri), 1. dealing with first principles; introductory; as, elementary arithmetic. 2. consisting of one element. Silver is an elementary substance. *adj. 7.*

African elephant (10 ft. tall; body 8 ft. long; ears 5 ft. across)

el e phant (el′i-fənt), the largest four-footed animal now living. See the pictures. *n. 4.*

Indian elephant (9 ft. tall; body 7 ft. long; ears 2 ft. across)

el e phan tine (el′i fan′tīn), 1. like an elephant; huge and clumsy. 2. of elephants. *adj.*

el e vate (el′i vāt), raise; lift up. He spoke from an elevated platform. The soldier was elevated to knighthood for bravery. Reading good books elevates the mind. *v. 4.*

el e va tion (el′i vā′shən), 1. raised place; high place. A hill is an elevation. 2. height above the earth's surface. The airplane fell from an elevation of 2000 feet. 3. height above sea level. The elevation of Denver is 5300 feet. 4. elevating; being elevated; as, the elevation of Caesar to be the ruler of Rome. *n. 6.*

el e va tor (el′i vā′tər), 1. something that lifts. 2. machine for carrying people up and down in a building or for lifting things. 3. a building for storing grain. 4. adjustable, flat piece that causes an airplane or airship to go up or down. *n. 7.*

e lev en (i lev′ən), 1. one more than ten; 11. 2. a football or cricket team. *n., adj. 2.*

e lev enth (i lev′ənth), 1. next after the 10th. 2. one of 11 equal parts. *adj., n. 6.*

elf (elf), a tiny being that is full of mischief; a fairy. *n., pl. elves. 5.*

Elf

elf in (el′fin), 1. of elves; like an elf's; as, an elfin dance, an elfin smile. 2. elf. *adj., n. 13.*

elf ish (el′fish), like an elf; like an elf's. *adj. 20.*

e lic it (i lis′it), draw forth; as, to elicit a reply, to elicit applause, to elicit the truth. *v. 10.*

el i gi bil i ty (el′i ji bil′i ti), fitness. *n. 18.*

el i gi ble (el′i ji bəl), fit to be chosen; desirable; qualified. Pupils must pass in all subjects to be eligible for the team. *adj. 13.*

E li jah (i lī′jə), in the Bible, a famous prophet. *n. 10.*

e lim i nate (i lim′i nāt), 1. remove; get rid of. Bridges over railroad tracks eliminate danger in crossing. 2. leave out; omit. Eliminate slang in a dignified speech. *v. 7.*

e lim i na tion (i lim′i nā′shən), eliminating; removing; removal. *n. 13.*

E li sha (i lī′shə), in the Bible, a prophet who was taught by Elijah. *n. 14.*

é lite or **e lite** (ā lēt′), the choice part; the best people. The élite of the city were present at the reception for the governor. *n.*

e lix ir (i lik′sər), 1. substance supposed to have the power of changing lead, iron, etc., into gold or of lengthening life, sought for by the experimenters of the Middle Ages. 2. universal remedy; cure-all. 3. medicine made of drugs or herbs mixed with alcohol and syrup. *n. 15.*

E liz a beth (i liz′ə bəth), 1. famous queen of England who lived from 1533 to 1603 and reigned from 1558 to 1603. 2. city in northeastern New Jersey. *n. 4.*

E liz a be than (i liz′ə bē′thən), 1. of the time of Queen Elizabeth. 2. person or writer of the time of Queen Elizabeth. Shakespeare is the most famous Elizabethan. *adj., n. 15.*

American elk (def. 2) (5 ft. high at the shoulder)

elk (elk), 1. large deer of Europe and Asia. It has antlers like a moose. 2. large, red deer of North America; wapiti. *n., pl. elks* or *elk. 14.*

ell (el), an old-time measure of length, in England just 45 inches. Give him an inch (a little) and he'll take an ell (much). *n. 12.*

el lipse (i lips′), oval having both ends alike. See the diagrams. *n. 15.*

Ellipses

el lip tic (i lip′tik), elliptical. *adj.*

el lip ti cal (i lip′ti kəl), shaped like an ellipse. *adj. 20.*

elm (elm), 1. a tall, graceful, shade tree. 2. its hard, heavy wood. *n. 3.*

el o cu tion (el′ə kū′shən), the art of public speaking or reading; correct use of the voice. *n. 13.*

el o cu tion ist (el′ə kū′shən ist), person skilled in elocution. *n.*

e lon gate (i lông′gāt), 1. lengthen; extend. A rubber band will elongate easily. 2. lengthened. 3. long and thin; as, the elongate leaf of the willow. *v., adj. 13.*

e lon ga tion (ē′lông gā′shən), lengthening; extension. *n. 19.*

e lope (i lōp′), 1. run away with a lover. 2. run away; escape. *v. 12.*

el o quence (el′ə kwəns), 1. a flow of speech that has grace and force. The eloquence of the President moved all hearts. 2. power to win by speaking; the art of speaking so as to stir the feelings. *n. 5.*

el o quent (el′ə kwənt), 1. having eloquence. 2. very expressive. *adj. 7.*

El Pas o (el pas′ō), a city in western Texas, on the Rio Grande.

El Sal va dor (el sal′və dôr), country in western Central America.

else (els), 1. other; not that one; instead. Will somebody else speak? What else could I say? 2. differently. How else can he act? 3. otherwise; if not. Hurry, else you will be late. *adj., adv. 1.*

else where (els′hwãr), somewhere else; in or to some other place. *adv. 4.*

e lu ci date (i lü′si dāt), make clear; explain. *v. 16.*

e lu ci da tion (i lü′si dā′shən), making clear; explanation. *n. 16.*

e lude (i lüd′), avoid or escape by quickness or cleverness; slip away from. The fox eluded the dogs. *v. 9.*

e lu sive (i lü′siv), tending to elude or escape; evasive; baffling; hard to express or define; as, an elusive enemy. *adj. 17.*

elves (elvz), more than one elf. *n. pl. 7.*

E ly sian (i lizh′ən), 1. heavenly; happy; delightful. 2. The ancient Greeks believed that after death the blessed lived in the **Elysian Fields.** *adj. 12.*

E ly sium (i lizh′əm), 1. in Greek mythology, the place where the blessed lived after death. 2. a place or condition of perfect happiness. *n. 12.*

em or **'em** (əm), them. *pron. pl.* [*Used in common talk*] *6.*

e ma ci ate (i mā′shi āt), make thin from loss of flesh. *v. 15.*

e ma ci at ed (i mā′shi āt′id), thin from losing flesh. *adj.*

e ma ci a tion (i mā′shi ā′shən), thinness from loss of flesh. *n. 18.*

em a nate (em′ə nāt), go out (from); issue (from); proceed (from). Light and heat emanate from the sun. *v. 15.*

em a na tion (em′ə nā′shən), 1. a coming forth. 2. anything that comes forth from a source. Light and heat are emanations from the sun. *n. 13.*

e man ci pate (i man′si pāt), set free from slavery of any kind; release. Women have been emancipated from many old restrictions. *v. 11.*

e man ci pa tion (i man′si pā′shən), release; setting free from slavery of any kind; as, emancipation of slaves, emancipation from a father's authority. *n. 9.*

e man ci pa tor (i man′si pā′tər), person who emancipates. *n.*

e mas cu late (i mas′kū lāt), 1. deprive of manhood. 2. weaken. *v. 19.*

em balm (em bäm′), 1. preserve (a dead body) with spices or drugs. 2. keep in memory. 3. fill with sweet scent. Roses embalmed the June air. *v. 10.*

em bank ment (em bangk′mənt), a raised bank of earth, stone, etc., used to hold back water, support a roadway, etc. *n. 14.*

em bar go (em bär′gō), 1. an order of a government forbidding ships to enter or leave its ports. During the War of 1812, Congress laid an embargo on commerce with Great Britain. 2. a restriction put on commerce by law. 3. a restraint or hindrance. 4. lay an embargo on; forbid to enter or leave port. *n., pl. embargoes, v., embargoed, embargoing. 16.*

em bark (em bärk′), 1. go on board ship. The troops embarked for France. 2. put on board ship. 3. set out; start. **Embark on** means begin; enter upon. *v. 7.*

em bar ka tion (em′bär kā′shən), embarking. *n. 19.*

em bar rass (em bar′əs), 1. disturb (a person); make self-conscious. She embarrassed me by asking me if I really liked her. 2. hinder. His business was embarrassed for a time by lack of ready money. 3. burden with debt. *v. 6.*

em bar rass ment (em bar′əs mənt), 1. embarrassing. 2. being embarrassed. 3. thing that embarrasses. *n. 9.*

em bas sy (em′bə si), 1. one or more persons sent, usually to the ruler or government of a country, with authority to make some arrangement. 2. the errand on which an embassy is sent. 3. the headquarters of an ambassador. *n., pl. embassies. 7.*

em bat tled (em bat′əld), 1. drawn up ready for battle; prepared for battle. 2. fortified. *adj. 9.*

em bed (em bed′), 1. put in a bed. He embedded the bulbs in a box of sand. 2. fix or enclose in a surrounding mass. Precious stones are found embedded in rock. *v., embedded, embedding. 13.* Also spelled **imbed.**

em bel lish (em bel′ish), 1. decorate; ornament; adorn. We embellished our room with new rugs, lamps, and pictures. 2. touch up or improve (an account, a story, etc.) by additions. He embellished the old stories, so that they sounded new. *v. 10.*

em bel lish ment (em bel′ish mənt), 1. ornament; decoration; adornment. 2. something added to touch up or improve an account, a story, etc. *n. 11.*

em ber (em′bər), piece of wood or coal from a fire, still burning a little. **Embers** often means ashes in which there is still some fire. *n. 8.*

em bez zle (em bez′əl), steal (money entrusted to one's care). The cashier embezzled $50,000 from the bank and ran away. *v. 18.*

em bez zle ment (em bez′əl mənt), theft of money entrusted to one's care. *n.*

em bit ter (em bit′ər), make bitter. The unhappy old man was embittered by the loss of his money. *v. 10.*

em bla zon (em blā′zən), 1. display conspicuously; picture in bright colors. 2. decorate; adorn. The knight's shield was emblazoned with his coat of arms. 3. praise highly; make known the fame of. King Arthur's exploits were emblazoned in song and story. *v. 17.*

em blem (em′bləm), symbol; sign of an idea; token. The dove is an emblem of peace. The white flag is the emblem of surrender. *n. 9.*

em blem at ic (em′blə mat′ik), serving as an emblem; symbolical. The lion is emblematic of courage. *adj. 16.*

em bod i ment (em bod′i mənt), 1. act of embodying. 2. condition of being embodied. 3. person or thing symbolizing some idea or quality. Lincoln was an embodiment of democracy. 4. thing embodied. *n. 14.*

em bod y (em bod′i), 1. give a body to; give a concrete form to. A building embodies the idea of the architect. 2. form into a body; include. The Boy Scouts' *Handbook for Boys* embodies the information a boy needs to become a good Scout. 3. make part of an organized book, law, system, etc. The new engineer's suggestions were embodied in the revised plan of the bridge. *v., embodied, embodying. 7.*

em bold en (em bōl′dən), make bold; encourage. *v. 11.*

em bos om (em bu̇z′əm), 1. envelop; enclose; as, trees embosoming a house. 2. embrace; cherish. *v. 16.*

em boss (em bôs′), 1. raise the surface of into a pattern; ornament with a raised pattern. The silver cup is embossed with a design of flowers. 2. cause to stand out on the surface of. *v. 10.*

em bow er (em bou′ər), enclose in a shelter of leafy branches. *v. 12.*

em brace (em brās′), 1. fold in the arms to show love; hold in the arms. A mother embraces her baby. 2. include; contain. The cat family embraces lions and tigers. 3. take up; accept. He eagerly embraced the offer of a trip to Mexico. 4. surround; enclose. 5. clasping in the arms; a hug. *v., n. 3.*

em bra sure (em brā′zhər), 1. opening in a wall for a gun, with sides that spread outward. 2. slanting off of the wall at an oblique angle on the inner sides of a door or window. *n. 15.*

Embrasure for a gun

em broi der (em broi′dər), 1. ornament with stitches; sew at embroidery. 2. add imaginary details to; exaggerate. *v. 5.*

em broi der y (em broi′dər i), art needlework; ornamental figures sewn with solid or open stitches. *n., pl. embroideries. 5.*

em broil (em broil′), 1. involve in a quarrel. A wise person does not become embroiled in other people's disputes. 2. throw into a state of confusion. *v. 16.*

em bry o (em′bri ō), 1. an animal or plant in the earlier stages of its development, or before birth. A chicken within an egg is an embryo. The plant contained within a seed is an embryo. 2. a beginning or undeveloped stage; as, a plan in embryo. 3. undeveloped; as, an embryo idea. *n., pl. embryos, adj. 7.*

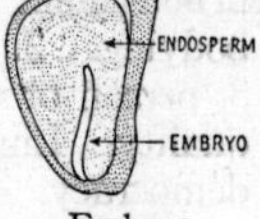

ENDOSPERM
EMBRYO
Embryo (def. 1)

em bry on ic (em′bri on′ik), 1. of the embryo. 2. undeveloped. *adj. 19.*

e mend (i mend′), to free from faults or errors; correct. *v.*

e men da tion (ē′men dā′shən), emending; correction. *n. 18.*

em er ald (em′ər əld), 1. a bright-green precious stone or jewel. 2. bright green. *n., adj. 7.*

e merge (i mėrj′), come out; come up; come into view. The sun emerged from behind a cloud. Many facts emerged as a result of the investigation. *v. 6.*

e mer gence (i mėr′jəns), an emerging. *n. 18.*

e mer gen cy (i mėr′jən si), sudden need for immediate action. I keep a fire extinguisher in my car for use in an emergency. *n., pl. emergencies. 7.*

e mer i tus (i mer′i təs), retired or honorably discharged from service. *adj.*

Em er son (em′ər sən), Ralph Waldo, a famous American author (1803-1882). *n. 9.*

em er y (em′ər i), a hard dark mineral which is used for grinding, smoothing, and polishing metals, stones, etc. *n. 10.*

e met ic (i met′ik), 1. causing vomiting. 2. a medicine that causes vomiting. *adj., n. 14.*

em i grant (em′i grənt), one who leaves his own country to settle in another. *n. 9.*

em i grate (em′i grāt), leave one's own country to settle in another. *v. 9.*

em i gra tion (em′i grā′shən), 1. leaving one's own country to settle in another. There has been much emigration from Italy. 2. body of emigrants. The largest emigration to the United States in a single year was that of 1907. *n. 10.*

em i nence (em′i nəns), 1. a high place; a high point of land. 2. high position in affairs; greatness; fame. Edison won eminence as an inventor. 3. A cardinal in the Roman Catholic Church has the title **Eminence.** *n. 8.*

em i nent (em′i nənt), high; above all others. Washington, Grant, and Lee were eminent generals. *adj. 6.*

em i nent ly (em′i nənt li), so as to be conspicuous and distinguished from others; specially. *adv.*

e mir (ə mēr′), 1. an Arabian chieftain or prince. 2. a title of honor of the descendants of Mohammed. 3. the title of certain Turkish officials. *n. 15.*

em is sar y (em′i sãr′i), 1. person sent on a mission or errand. 2. spy; secret agent. *n., pl. emissaries. 12.*

e mis sion (i mish′ən), 1. act or fact of emitting; a sending out; as, the emission of light from the sun. 2. the thing emitted. *n. 19.*

e mit (i mit′), send out; give off. A volcano emits smoke. The sun emits light. He emitted a roar of rage. *v., emitted, emitting. 9.*

Em man u el (i man′ū əl), Christ. *n. 12.* Also spelled **Immanuel.**

e mol u ment (i mol′ū mənt), profit from a job; salary; fees. *n. 14.*

e mo tion (i mō′shən), strong feeling of any kind. Joy, grief, fear, hate, love, rage, and excitement are emotions. *n. 5.*

e mo tion al (i mō′shən əl), 1. of the emotions. 2. appealing to the emotions. The speaker made an emotional plea for money to help crippled children. 3. easily excited. Emotional people are likely to cry if they hear sad music or read sad stories. *adj. 12.*

em per or (em′pər ər), the ruler of an empire. Japan has an emperor. *n. 3.*

em pha sis (em′fə sis), 1. special force of voice put on particular words or syllables. In reading, put emphasis upon the most important words. 2. stress; importance. That school puts emphasis on arithmetic and reading. *n., pl. emphases* (-sēz). *7.*

em pha size (em′fə sīz), 1. make emphatic. He emphasized that word by saying it very loudly. 2. call attention to. The great number of automobile accidents emphasizes the need for careful driving. *v. 8.*

em phat ic (em fat′ik), said or done with force; meant to stand out; clear; positive;

striking; emphasized. Her answer was an emphatic "No." *adj. 10.*

em phat i cal ly (em fat′i kəl i), in an emphatic manner; to an emphatic degree. *adv.*

em pire (em′pīr), 1. a group of nations or states under one head or government; as, the British Empire. 2. a country ruled by an emperor; as, the Japanese Empire. 3. power; rule. *n. 2.*

em pir ic (em pir′ik), 1. person without regular or proper training; a quack. 2. empirical. *n., adj. 16.*

em pir i cal (em pir′i kəl), 1. based on observation and experiment. Chemistry is largely an empirical science. 2. based on or guided by practical experience without regard to science or theory. Empirical knowledge is likely to be weak and faulty. *adj.*

em ploy (em ploi′), 1. use. You should employ your time wisely. 2. give work and pay to. She employs a cook. *v. 2.*

em ploy ee (em ploi′ē), person who works for some person or firm for pay. *n. 4.*

em ploy er (em ploi′ər), person who employs others. *n. 7.*

em ploy ment (em ploi′mənt), 1. work; what one is doing. 2. use. *n. 5.*

em po ri um (em pō′ri əm), 1. center of trade; market place. 2. large store selling many different things. *n. 19.*

em pow er (em pou′ər), 1. give power or authority to. The secretary was empowered to sign certain contracts. 2. enable; permit. Man's erect position empowers him to use his hands freely. *v. 8.*

em press (em′pris), 1. woman who rules over an empire. 2. wife of an emperor. *n. 6.*

em prise (em prīz′), 1. adventurous undertaking. 2. knightly daring. *n.* [*Old use*] *19.*

emp ti ness (emp′ti nis), being empty; lack of contents. *n. 10.*

emp ty (emp′ti), 1. with nothing in it. The birds had gone, and their nest was left empty. 2. pour out or take out all that is in (a thing). Billy emptied his glass quickly. 3. flow out. The Mississippi River empties into the Gulf of Mexico. *adj., emptier, emptiest, v., emptied, emptying. 2.*

em pur pled (em pėr′pəld), made purple; colored with purple. *adj. 15.*

em pyr e al (em pir′i əl or em′pi rē′əl), celestial; heavenly. *adj. 16.*

em py re an (em′pi rē′ən), 1. the highest heaven. 2. the visible heavens; the sky. 3. celestial; heavenly. *n., adj. 15.*

e mu (ē′mū), a large, three-toed Australian bird like an ostrich, but smaller. An emu cannot fly. *n.*

Emu (6 ft. tall)

em u late (em′ū lāt), try to equal or excel. The proverb tells us to emulate the industry of the ant. *v. 12.*

em u la tion (em′ū lā′shən), imitation in order to equal or excel; desire to equal or excel. *n. 8.*

em u lous (em′ū ləs), wishing to equal or excel. *adj. 15.*

e mul sion (i mul′shən), a milklike liquid, containing very tiny drops of fat or of some other substance. *n. 9.*

en a ble (en ā′bəl), make able; give ability, power, or means to. Airplanes enable people to travel through the air. *v. 4.*

en act (en akt′), 1. make into law. 2. act out; play. He enacted the part of an Indian very well. *v. 7.*

en act ment (en akt′mənt), 1. enacting. 2. being enacted. 3. a law. *n. 14.*

en am el (en am′əl), 1. glasslike substance melted and then cooled to make a smooth, hard surface. Different colors of enamel are used to cover or decorate metal, pottery, etc. 2. paint or varnish used to make a smooth, hard, glossy surface. 3. smooth, hard, glossy, outer layer of the teeth. 4. any smooth, hard coating or surface that shines. 5. cover or decorate with enamel. *n., v., enameled, enameling. 6.*

en am or (en am′ər), arouse to love; charm. Her beauty enamored the prince. **Enamored of** means in love with. *v. 9.*

en camp (en kamp′), make camp; settle in tents for a time. *v. 6.*

en camp ment (en kamp′mənt), 1. forming a camp. 2. a camp of soldiers. *n. 13.*

en case (en kās′), 1. put into a case. 2. enclose; cover completely. Armor encased the knight's body. *v. 17.* Also spelled **incase.**

-ence, suffix meaning:—

1. act, fact, quality, or state of——ing; as in abhorrence, dependence.
2. quality or state of being——ent; as in absence, confidence, prudence.

en chain (en chān′), 1. fasten with a chain. 2. hold fast. The speaker's earnestness enchained the attention of his audience. *v. 15.*

en chant (en chant′), 1. use magic on; put under a spell. The witch had enchanted the princess. 2. delight greatly; charm. The dance music was enchanting. *v. 5.*

en chant er (en chan′tər), person who enchants; magician. *n. 10.*

en chant ment (en chant′mənt), 1. the use of magic spells; a spell or charm. In the Greek story, Circe turned men into pigs by her enchantments. 2. something that gives rapture or delight. We felt the enchantment of the moonlight on the lake. *n. 7.*

en chan tress (en chan′tris), 1. woman who enchants; witch. 2. very delightful, charming woman. *n. 9.*

en cir cle (en sėr′kəl), 1. form a circle around; surround. Trees encircled the pond. 2. go in a circle around. The moon encircles the earth. *v. 8.*

en close (en klōz′), 1. shut in on all sides; surround. 2. put a wall or fence around. 3. put in an envelope along with a letter. 4. contain; as, a letter enclosing a check. *v. 3.* Also spelled **inclose.**

en clo sure (en klō′zhər), 1. act of enclosing. 2. state of being enclosed. 3. an enclosed place. A pen is an enclosure for animals. 4. thing that encloses. A wall or fence is an enclosure. 5. thing enclosed. The envelope contained a letter and $5 as an enclosure. *n. 9.* Also spelled **inclosure.**

en co mi um (en kō′mi əm), formal praise; very high praise. The singer received many encomiums from those who heard her. *n. 15.*

en com pass (en kum′pəs), go or reach all the way around; encircle. The atmosphere encompasses the earth. *v. 9.*

en core (äng′kōr), 1. again; once more. 2. a demand by the audience for the repetition of a song, etc. 3. call for the repetition of. 4. the repetition by the performer. 5. an extra song or the like given by the performer. *interj., n., v. 16.*

en coun ter (en koun′tər), 1. meet unexpectedly. What if we should encounter a bear? 2. meet as an enemy. 3. a battle. 4. unexpected meeting. *v., n. 3.*

en cour age (en kėr′ij), 1. give hope, courage, or confidence to; urge on. The cheers of his schoolmates encouraged him. 2. give help to; make favoring conditions for. High prices for corn and wheat will encourage farming. *v. 3.*

en cour age ment (en kėr′ij mənt), 1. urging on toward success; act of encouraging. 2. something that gives hope, courage, or confidence. *n. 8.*

en croach (en krōch′), 1. go beyond proper or usual limits. The sea encroached upon the shore and submerged the beach. 2. trespass upon the property or rights of another; intrude. A good salesman will not encroach upon his customer's time. *v. 9.*

en croach ment (en krōch′mənt), 1. an advance beyond proper limits. The cliff is being worn back by the encroachments of the sea. 2. trespassing on the property or rights of another. *n. 11.*

en crust (en krust′), 1. cover with a crust or hard coating. The inside of the kettle is encrusted with lime. 2. form a crust; form into a crust. Overnight the snow had encrusted so that the next morning it would bear our weight. 3. decorate (a surface) with a layer of costly material. The gold crown was encrusted with precious gems. *v. 16.* Also spelled **incrust.**

en cum ber (en kum′bər), 1. burden with weight, difficulties, cares, debt, etc. Mother is encumbered with household cares. Do not encumber your farm with a mortgage. 2. fill; block up. His yard was encumbered with old carts and other rubbish. *v. 9.* Also spelled **incumber.**

en cum brance (en kum′brəns), burden; something useless or in the way; annoyance; trouble. *n. 16.* Also spelled **incumbrance.**

-ency, suffix meaning:—

1. act, fact, quality, or state of———ing; as in dependency.
2. quality or state of being———ent; as in frequency.

ency. or **encyc.,** encyclopedia.

en cyc li cal (en sik′li kəl), 1. a letter about the general welfare of the church from the Pope to his clergy. 2. intended for wide circulation. *n., adj.*

en cy clo pe di a or **en cy clo pae di a** (en sī′klō pē′di ə), 1. a book giving information arranged alphabetically on all branches of knowledge. 2. a book treating one subject very thoroughly, with its articles arranged alphabetically. *n. 8.*

en cy clo pe dic or **en cy clo pae dic** (en sī′klō pē′dik), 1. covering a wide range of subjects; possessing wide and varied information. 2. having to do with an encyclopedia. *adj. 17.*

en cyst (en sist′), enclose or become enclosed in a cyst or sac. *v. 20.*

end (end), 1. last part. He read to the end of the book. 2. the part where a thing begins or where it stops. Every stick has two ends. 3. bring or come to its last part; finish. Let us end this fight. 4. purpose; what is aimed at in doing any piece of work. He had this end in mind—to do his work without a mistake. *n., v. 1.*

en dan ger (en dān′jər), cause danger to. A war endangers millions of lives. *v. 12.*

en dear (en dēr′), make dear. Her kindness endeared her to all of us. *v. 8.*

en dear ment (en dēr′mənt), 1. an endearing. 2. thing that endears. 3. act or word showing love or affection; caress. *n. 12.*

en deav or (en dev′ər), 1. try; make an effort; strive. A runner endeavors to win a race. 2. an effort; an attempt. *v., n. 4.*

end ing (en′ding), end; last part. *n. 5.*

en dive (en′dīv), kind of chicory used for salad. *n.*

end less (end′lis), 1. having no end; never stopping; lasting or going on forever. 2. joined in a circle; without ends; as, an endless chain. *adj. 4.*

en dorse (en dôrs′), 1. write one's name, a comment, etc., on the back of (a check, note, or other document). He had to endorse the check before the bank would cash it. 2. approve; support. Parents heartily endorsed the plan for a school playground. *v. 11.* Also spelled **indorse**.

en dorse ment (en dôrs′mənt), 1. the writing on the back of a document, check, note, bill, etc. 2. approval; support. *n.* Also spelled **indorsement.**

en do sperm (en′dō spėrm), nourishment for the embryo enclosed with it in the seed of a plant. See the picture under **embryo.** *n. 13.*

en dow (en dou′), 1. give money or property to provide an income for. The rich man endowed a college. 2. give from birth. Nature endowed her with both beauty and brains. *v. 5.*

en dow ment (en dou′mənt), 1. endowing. 2. the money or property given to a person or institution to provide income. 3. gift; talent. A good sense of rhythm is a natural endowment. *n. 9.*

en due (en dū′ or en dü′), 1. put on (a garment, etc.). 2. clothe (a person) as with a garment. 3. furnish; supply; endow (with qualities, powers, etc.). *v. 6.* Also spelled **indue.**

en dur a ble (en dūr′ə bəl or en dür′ə bəl), 1. bearable; that can be endured. 2. likely to last a long time. *adj. 18.*

en dur ance (en dūr′əns or en dür′əns), 1. ability to last and to withstand hard wear. A man must have great endurance to run 30 miles in a day. Cheap silk has not much endurance. 2. power to stand something without giving out; holding out; bearing up. His endurance of the pain was remarkable. *n. 8.*

en dure (en dūr′ or en dür′), 1. last; keep on. A gold ring will endure for a thousand years. 2. undergo; bear; stand. The Indians endured much pain. *v. 3.*

end ways (end′wāz′), 1. on end. 2. with the end forward. 3. lengthwise. 4. end to end. *adv.*

end wise (end′wīz′), endways. *adv.*

En dym i on (en dim′i ən), a beautiful youth beloved by Artemis (Diana). *n. 20.*

en e my (en′i mi), 1. one who is on the other side or against; not a friend. Two countries fighting against each other are enemies. 2. anything that will harm. Frost is an enemy of flowers. *n., pl. enemies. 1.*

en er get ic (en′ər jet′ik), full of energy; active; eager to work; full of force. Cool autumn days make us feel energetic. *adj. 8.*

en er get i cal ly (en′ər jet′i kəl i), with energy; vigorously. *adv.*

en er gize (en′ər jīz), give energy to. Ambition energizes men. *v. 18.*

en er gy (en′ər ji), 1. vigor; will to work. He is so full of energy that he cannot keep still. 2. power to work or act; force. *n., pl. energies. 4.*

en er vate (en′ər vāt), weaken; lessen the vigor or strength of. A hot climate enervates people who are not used to it. *v. 14.*

en fee ble (en fē′bəl), make feeble. *v. 10.*

en fold (en fōld′), 1. fold in; wrap up. The old lady was enfolded in a shawl. 2. embrace; clasp. The mother enfolded her baby in her arms. *v. 13.* Also spelled **infold.**

en force (en fōrs′), force obedience to; cause to be carried out. The teacher will enforce the rules of the school. *v. 5.*

en force a ble (en fōr′sə bəl), that can be enforced. *adj. 20.*

en force ment (en fōrs′mənt), putting into force. Strict enforcement of the laws against speeding will reduce automobile accidents. *n. 12.*

en fran chise (en fran′chīz), 1. set free. 2. admit to citizenship; give the right to vote. The 19th amendment to the Constitution enfranchised American women. *v. 10.*

en fran chise ment (en fran′chiz mənt), 1. release from slavery. 2. admission to citizenship; giving the right to vote. *n. 15.*

Eng., 1. England. 2. English. *19.*

en gage (en gāj′), 1. promise; bind oneself. I will engage to be there on time. 2. promise to marry. John and Mary are engaged. John is engaged to Mary. 3. keep busy; be active. They engaged in conversation. I cannot call Mr. Smith; he is engaged just now. 4. hire. They engaged a cook for the summer. 5. attract. Bright objects engage a baby's attention. 6. fit into; lock together. The teeth in one gear engage in another. 7. start a battle against; attack. Our soldiers engaged the enemy. *v. 2.*

Cog wheels engaged

en gaged (en gājd′), 1. pledged to marry. 2. busy; occupied. *adj.*

en gage ment (en gāj′mənt), 1. promise; pledge. 2. a promise to marry. 3. a meeting with someone at a certain time; an appointment. 4. a battle. *n. 5.*

en gag ing (en gāj′ing), attractive; pleasing; as, an engaging smile. *adj. 17.*

en gen der (en jen′dər), bring into being; cause; produce. Filth engenders disease. *v. 9.*

en gine (en′jən), 1. machine for turning power on to some work, especially a machine that can start others moving. 2. the machine that pulls a railroad train. 3. anything used to bring about a result; machine; instrument. Cannons are engines of war. *n. 2.*

Steam engine for providing power

en gi neer (en′jə nēr′), 1. man who makes, takes care of, or runs engines. 2. man who plans and builds machines, roads, bridges, canals, forts, and the like. 3. do the work of an engineer. 4. guide; manage. Mary engineered the whole job from start to finish. *n., v. 4.*

en gi neer ing (en′jə nēr′ing), the science, work, or profession of an engineer. James is studying engineering. The Hudson River bridge is a triumph of engineering. *n. 16.*

en gine ry (en′jən ri), 1. engines; machines. 2. the work of engineers. 3. crafty schemes. *n. 16.*

Eng land (ing′glənd), the largest division of Great Britain. *n. 1.*

Eng land er (ing′glən dər), Englishman. *n. 4.*

Eng lish (ing′glish), 1. of or having to do with England, its people, or their language. 2. the people of England. 3. the language of England. English is spoken also in Canada, the United States, South Africa, and Australia. *adj., n. 1.*

English Channel, the part of the Atlantic Ocean between England and France.

English horn, wooden musical instrument resembling an oboe, but larger and having a lower tone.

Eng lish man (ing′glish mən), a man born in England, living there, or having English parents. *n., pl. Englishmen. 4.*

Eng lish wom an (ing′glish wům′ən), woman born in England, living there, or having English parents. *n., pl. Englishwomen. 17.*

en graft (en graft′), 1. put (a shoot of one tree) into another. Peach trees can be engrafted upon plum trees. 2. fix in; implant. Honesty and thrift are engrafted in his character. *v. 17.* Also spelled **ingraft.**

en grave (en grāv′), 1. carve; cut (a mark) deeply in; as, a name engraved on a tombstone. 2. fix in the memory. 3. cut in lines on wood, stone, metal, or glass plates for printing. *v. 7.*

en grav er (en grāv′ər), person who does engraving. *n. 13.*

en grav ing (en grāv′ing), 1. the art or act of a person who engraves. 2. a copy of a picture made from an engraved plate; a print. *n. 17.*

en gross (en grōs′), 1. occupy wholly; fill the mind of. She was engrossed in an interesting story. 2. copy or write in large letters; write a beautiful copy of. *v. 9.*

en gulf (en gulf′), swallow up. The waves engulfed the boat. *v. 13.*

en hance (en hans′), add to; make greater. Health enhances beauty. The growth of a city often enhances the value of land close to it. *v. 9.*

e nig ma (i nig′mə), a riddle; anything puzzling. The girl's habit of eating paper was an enigma to her parents. *n. 12.*

e nig mat ic (ē′nig mat′ik), enigmatical. *adj. 20.*

e nig mat i cal (ē′nig mat′i kəl), containing an enigma; puzzling; perplexing; mysterious. *adj. 14.*

en join (en join′), 1. order; direct; urge. The father enjoined good conduct on his son. 2. forbid. *v. 6.*

en joy (en joi′), 1. have or use with joy; be happy with; take pleasure in. 2. have as an advantage or benefit. He enjoyed good health. 3. **Enjoy oneself** means be happy; have a good time. *v. 1.*

en joy a ble (en joi′ə bəl), giving joy; pleasant. *adj. 18.*

en joy ment (en joi′mənt), 1. pleasure; joy; delight. 2. possession or use. The son now has the enjoyment of his father's wide lands. *n. 7.*

en kin dle (en kin′dəl), kindle into flames; excite; rouse into action. *v. 16.*

en large (en lärj′), 1. make larger. 2. grow larger. 3. **Enlarge upon a subject** means talk or write more about it. *v. 4.*

en large ment (en lärj′mənt), 1. making larger. 2. amount that is added. 3. a photograph or other thing that has been made larger. *n. 12.*

en light en (en līt′ən), make clear; give the light of truth and knowledge to; inform; instruct. *v. 7.*

en light en ment (en līt′ən mənt), illumination of the mind; information. *n.*

en list (en list′), 1. join. 2. join the army or navy. 3. induce to join. 4. get the support of. The Red Cross seeks to enlist the interest of all citizens. *v. 6.*

en list ment (en list′mənt), 1. enlisting. 2. being enlisted. *n.*

en liv en (en līv′ən), make lively, active, gay, or bright. Spring enlivens all nature. Bright curtains enliven a dull room. *v. 9.*

en mi ty (en′mi ti), the feeling that enemies have for each other; hate. *n., pl. enmities. 6.*

en no ble (en nō′bəl), 1. raise to noble rank; make (a man) a nobleman. 2. make noble; raise. A good deed ennobles the person who does it. *v. 6.*

en nui (än′wē), a feeling of weariness and discontent from lack of occupation or interest. *n. 16.*

e nor mi ty (i nôr′mi ti), 1. monstrous wickedness. The enormity of his offense made it probable that the man was not sane. 2. extremely wicked crime. *n., pl. enormities. 15.*

e nor mous (i nôr′məs), very, very large. Long ago there were enormous beasts in the world. *adj. 3.*

e nor mous ly (i nôr′məs li), to an enormous degree; extremely; vastly. *adv.*

e nough (i nuf′), 1. as many as needed. 2. as much as needed. 3. sufficiently; until no more is needed or desired. Have you played enough? *adj., n., adv. 1.*

en quire (en kwīr′), inquire. *v. 6.*

en quir y (en kwīr′i), inquiry. *n., pl. enquiries. 18.*

en rage (en rāj′), make very angry; make furious; madden. *v. 6.*

en rap ture (en rap′chər), move to rapture; delight beyond measure. The singer held his audience enraptured. *v. 16.*

en rich (en rich′), make rich or richer. An education enriches your mind. You can enrich a food by adding cream or butter. Fertilizer enriches the soil. *v. 5.*

en rich ment (en rich′mənt), 1. an enriching. 2. a being enriched. 3. thing that enriches. *n.*

en roll or **en rol** (en rōl′), 1. write in a list. 2. have one's name written in a list. 3. make a member. 4. become a member. 5. enlist. *v., enrolled, enrolling. 6.*

en roll ment or **en rol ment** (en rōl′mənt), 1. an enrolling. 2. number enrolled. The school has an enrollment of 200 students. *n. 11.*

en route (än rüt′), on the way. We shall stop at Philadelphia en route from New York to Washington.

en sam ple (en sam′pəl), example. *n. [Old use] 19.*

en san guine (en sang′gwin), stain with blood. The pirate waved an ensanguined sword. *v. 16.*

en sconce (en skons′), establish in a safe, secret, or comfortable place. The troops were ensconced in strongly fortified trenches. The cat ensconced itself in the armchair. *v. 17.*

en sem ble (än säm′bəl), 1. all the parts of a thing taken together; general effect. 2. a woman's complete costume; a dress and coat to be worn together. *n.*

en shrine (en shrīn′), 1. enclose in a shrine. A fragment of the Cross is enshrined in the cathedral. 2. keep sacred; as, memories enshrined in one's heart. *v. 13.*

en shroud (en shroud′), cover; hide; veil. Fog enshrouded the ship. *v. 17.*

en sign (en′sīn, also en′sən for 2), 1. a flag or banner. 2. the lowest commissioned officer in the navy. 3. army officer whose duty it was to carry the flag. 4. a symbol or sign of some office or society. *n. 6.*

en si lage (en′si lij), green fodder preserved and stored in a silo or pit. Ensilage is used to feed cattle in winter. *n. 14.*

en slave (en slāv′), make a slave of; take away freedom from. *v. 10.*

en snare (en snãr′), trap; catch in a snare. *v. 11.* Also spelled **insnare.**

en sue (en sü′), 1. follow. The ensuing year means the year following this. 2. happen as a result. In his anger he hit the man, and a fight ensued. *v. 5.*

en sure (en shür′), 1. make sure or certain. Careful planning and hard work ensured the success of the party. 2. make sure of getting; secure. A letter of introduction will ensure you an interview. 3. make safe; protect. Proper clothing ensured us against suffering from the cold. *v. 17.* Also spelled **insure.**

-ent, suffix meaning:—
1. ——ing; as in absorbent, indulgent.
2. one that ——s; as in correspondent, president, superintendent.
3. other meanings; as in competent, confident.

en tail (en tāl′), 1. impose; require; put (a burden, work, etc.) on somebody. Owning an automobile entailed greater expense than he had expected. 2. limit the inheritance of (property) to a specified line of heirs, so that it cannot be willed to anyone else. An entailed estate usually passes to the eldest son. 3. entailing. 4. something entailed. 5. the order of inheritance settled for an estate. Though Lord Bland had quarreled with his heir, he could not break the entail and leave the estate to someone else. *v., n. 11.*

en tan gle (en tang′gəl), 1. get mixed and caught. Threads are easily entangled. 2. involve; get into difficulty. Do not entangle him with your schemes. *v. 6.*

en tan gle ment (en tang′gəl mənt), 1. entangling. 2. being entangled. George Washington warned against entanglements with foreign countries. 3. thing that entangles; snare; something hard to get out of or to get through. The trenches were protected by barbed wire entanglements. *n. 15.*

en tente (än tänt′), 1. an understanding. 2. the parties to an understanding. *n. 18.*

en ter (en′tər), 1. go into; come into. He entered the house. 2. go in; come in. Let them enter. 3. join; become a part or member of. Soldiers enter the army. 4. cause to join or enter. Parents enter their children in school. 5. begin; start. 6. write or print in a book, list, etc. A dictionary enters words in alphabetical order. *v. 1.*

en ter prise (en′tər prīz), 1. an important, difficult, or dangerous undertaking. 2. an undertaking; project; as, a business enterprise. 3. readiness to start projects. Benjamin Franklin showed great enterprise. *n. 5.*

en ter pris ing (en′tər prīz′ing), likely to start projects; ready to face difficulties. *adj. 13.*

en ter tain (en′tər tān′), 1. interest; please; make fun for. A circus entertains children. 2. have as a guest. She entertained ten people at dinner. 3. have guests; provide entertainment for guests. She entertains a great deal. 4. take into the mind; consider. I refuse to entertain such a foolish idea. *v. 3.*

en ter tain er (en′tər tān′ər), 1. person who entertains. 2. a singer, reciter, musician, etc., who takes part in public entertainment. *n.*

en ter tain ing (en′tər tān′ing), interesting; pleasing; amusing. *adj.*

en ter tain ment (en′tər tān′mənt), 1. something that interests, pleases, or amuses, such as a show or a circus; an amusement. 2. food and lodging; a supplying of wants. That hotel is famous for its good entertainment. 3. entertaining; being entertained. *n. 5.*

en thrall or **en thral** (en thrôl′), 1. captivate; fascinate; charm. *Treasure Island* is an enthralling story of adventure. 2. make a slave of. *v., enthralled, enthralling. 14.*

en throne (en thrōn′), 1. set on a throne. 2. place highest of all; exalt. Washington is enthroned in the hearts of his countrymen. *v. 9.*

en thuse (en thüz′), 1. show enthusiasm. 2. fill with enthusiasm. *v.* [*Used in common talk*]

en thu si asm (en thü′zi azm), eager interest; zeal. Hunting and fishing arouse enthusiasm in many boys. *n. 5.*

en thu si ast (en thü′zi ast), 1. person who is filled with enthusiasm. 2. person who is carried away by his feelings for a cause. *n. 11.*

en thu si as tic (en thü′zi as′tik), full of enthusiasm; eagerly interested. *adj. 6.*

en thu si as ti cal ly (en thü′zi as′ti kəl i), with enthusiasm. *adv. 18.*

en tice (en tīs′), attract; lead into something by raising hopes or desires; tempt. The smell of food enticed the hungry children into the hut. *v. 5.*

en tice ment (en tīs′mənt), 1. enticing; being enticed. 2. something that entices. Enticements of milk and meat induced the frightened cat to come down from the tree. *n. 17.*

en tire (en tīr′), 1. whole; complete; having all the parts. 2. not broken; in one piece. *adj. 1.*

en tire ly (en tīr′li), wholly; fully. *adv. 7.*

en tire ty (en tīr′ti), completeness; the whole. *n., pl. entireties. 17.*

en ti tle (en tī′təl), 1. give a claim or right. The one who guesses the answer is entitled to ask the next question. 2. give the title of. The King of England is also entitled Emperor of India. *v. 4.*

en ti ty (en′ti ti), 1. something that has a real existence. Persons and animals are entities. 2. existence; being. *n., pl. entities. 14.*

en tomb (en tüm′), place in a tomb; bury. *v. 12.*

en to mol o gist (en′tə mol′ə jist), person skilled in entomology. *n. 18.*

en to mol o gy (en′tə mol′ə ji), the study of insects. *n. 16.*

en trails (en′trālz), 1. the inner parts of the bodies of animals. Before a chicken can be cooked, the entrails must be removed. 2. intestines; bowels. *n. pl. 9.*

en train (en trān′), 1. get on a train. 2. put on a train. *v.*

en trance[1] (en′trəns), 1. act of entering. 2. place by which to enter. 3. freedom or right of entering. *n. 2.*

en trance[2] (en trans′), 1. put into a trance. 2. delight; carry away with joy. *v.*

en trant (en′trənt), person who enters. *n.*

en trap (en trap′), 1. catch in a trap. 2. bring into difficulty or danger. The lawyer entrapped the witness into contradicting himself. *v., entrapped, entrapping. 12.*

en treat (en trēt′), keep asking earnestly; beg and pray. The savage entreated Robinson Crusoe not to kill him. *v. 5.* Also spelled **intreat.**

en treat y (en trēt′i), a prayer; an earnest request. *n., pl. entreaties. 8.*

en trench (en trench′), 1. surround with a trench; fortify with trenches, etc. Our soldiers were entrenched opposite the enemy. 2. establish firmly. Exchanging gifts at Christmas is a custom entrenched by long tradition. 3. trespass; encroach; infringe. Do not entrench upon the rights of another. *v. 17.* Also spelled **intrench.**

en trench ment (en trench′mənt), 1. an entrenching. 2. an entrenched position. 3. a defense consisting of a trench and a rampart of earth or stone. *n. 15.* Also spelled **intrenchment.**

en trust (en trust′), 1. trust; charge with a trust. We entrusted Joe with all the money to pay the fares. 2. give (something or somebody) in trust; as, to entrust children to the care of a nurse, to entrust one's life to a surgeon. *v. 9.* Also spelled **intrust.**

en try (en′tri), 1. act of entering. 2. place by which to enter; way to enter. An entrance hall is an entry. 3. thing written or printed in a book, list, etc. Each word explained in a dictionary is an entry. 4. person or thing that takes part in a contest. *n., pl. entries. 4.*

en twine (en twīn′), 1. twine together. 2. twine about. Roses and honeysuckle entwine the little cottage. *v. 13.*

e nu mer ate (i nū′mər āt or i nü′mər āt), 1. name one by one; give a list of. He enumerated the 48 States. 2. count. *v. 8.*

e nu mer a tion (i nū′mər ā′shən or i nü′mər-ā′shən), 1. act of enumerating; counting. 2. a list. *n. 15.*

e nun ci ate (i nun′si āt), 1. speak or pronounce words. The trained actor enunciates very distinctly. 2. announce; state definitely. The philosopher enunciated a new theory. *v. 16.*

e nun ci a tion (i nun′si ā′shən), 1. manner of pronouncing words. 2. announcement; statement. *n.*

en vel op (en vel′əp), to wrap, cover, or hide. The baby was so enveloped in blankets that we could hardly see its face. *v. 11.*

en ve lope (en′və lōp), 1. a folded and gummed paper cover in which a letter or anything flat may be mailed. 2. a wrapper; a covering. *n. 4.*

en vel op ment (en vel′əp mənt), 1. an enveloping. 2. a being enveloped. 3. thing that envelops; wrapping; covering. *n.*

en ven om (en ven′əm), 1. make poisonous. 2. fill with bitterness, hate, etc. The wicked boy envenomed his father's mind against his half brother. *v. 15.*

en vi a ble (en′vi ə bəl), to be envied; desirable. Susan has an enviable school record. *adj. 18.*

en vi ous (en′vi əs), 1. wishing to have something which someone else has. 2. disliking someone who has more than oneself. The weak are often envious of the strong. *adj. 5.*

en vi ron (en vī′rən), surround; enclose; hem in. *v. 10.*

en vi ron ment (en vī′rən mənt), 1. surrounding. 2. being surrounded. 3. surrounding things, conditions, or influences. A child's character is greatly influenced by his home environment. *n. 7.*

en vi rons (en vī′rənz), districts surrounding a place; suburbs. We visited Boston and its environs. *n. pl.*

en voy (en′voi), 1. messenger. 2. a diplomatic agent next to an ambassador in rank. *n. 11.*

en vy (en′vi), 1. discontent or ill will at another's good fortune because one wishes it had been his; dislike for a person who has what one wants. All the boys were filled with envy when they saw Tom's new bicycle. 2. feel envy toward. Some people envy the rich. 3. feel envy because of. James envied his friend's success. 4. the object of such feeling; person who is envied. She was the envy of the younger girls in the school. *n., pl. envies, v., envied, envying. 3.*

en wrap (en rap′), wrap. *v., enwrapped, enwrapping. 16.*

en zyme (en′zīm), chemical substance produced in living cells, that can cause changes in other substances without being changed itself. Pepsin is an enzyme. *n. 20.*

e on (ē′on), very long time; many thousands of years. Eons passed before life existed on the earth. *n.* Also spelled **aeon.**

ep au let or **ep au lette** (ep′ə let), ornament worn on the shoulders of a uniform. See the picture. *n. 18.*

Epaulet

e phem er al (i fem′ər əl), lasting but a day or a very short time; very short-lived. *adj. 16.*

E phe sian (i fē′zhən), 1. of Ephesus or its people. 2. native or inhabitant of Ephesus. *adj., n. 12.*

E phe sians (i fē′zhənz), book of the New Testament written in the name of the Apostle Paul to the Christians at Ephesus. *n.*

Eph e sus (ef′i səs), ancient Greek city in Asia Minor. Its ruins are near Smyrna. *n. 10.*

eph od (ef′od), vestment worn by Hebrew priests, especially that worn by the high priest. *n. 17.*

ep ic (ep′ik), 1. long poem that tells rather grandly of the adventures of one or more great heroes. Homer's *Iliad* and Milton's *Paradise Lost* are epics. 2. grand in style. *n., adj. 10.*

ep i cure (ep′i kūr), person who cares much about foods and drinks. *n. 18.*

ep i cu re an (ep′i kū rē′ən), 1. pleasure-loving; luxurious; as, an epicurean banquet. 2. person devoted to pleasure and luxury. *adj., n. 10.*

ep i dem ic (ep′i dem′ik), 1. rapid spreading of a disease so that many people have it at the same time. All the schools in the city were closed during the epidemic of scarlet fever. 2. widespread. *n., adj. 8.*

ep i der mis (ep′i dėr′mis), the outer layer of the skin. *n. 9.*

ep i glot tis (ep′i glot′is), a valve that covers the top of the windpipe during swallowing, so that food does not get into the lungs. *n. 20.*

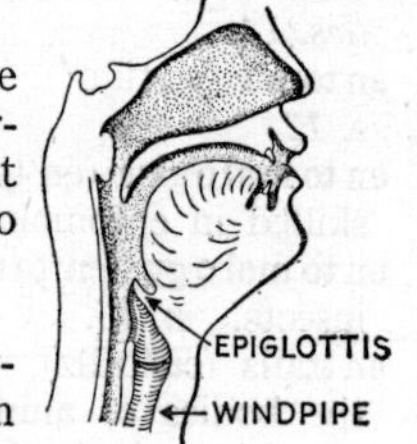

ep i gram (ep′i gram), 1. a short, pointed saying. *Example:* "Speech is silver, but silence is golden." 2. a short poem ending in a witty or clever turn of thought. *Example:*
"Here lies our Sovereign Lord the King,
Whose word no man relies on.
He never said a foolish thing,
And never did a wise one." *n. 11.*

ep i gram mat ic (ep′i grə mat′ik), short and pointed in expression. *adj.*

ep i lep sy (ep′i lep′si), a nervous disease characterized by fits, in which the patient may fall down unconscious and foam at the mouth. *n. 15.*

ep i lep tic (ep′i lep′tik), 1. of epilepsy. 2. having epilepsy. 3. person who has epilepsy. *adj., n. 18.*

ep i logue or **ep i log** (ep′i lôg), 1. concluding part of a novel, poem, etc. 2. a speech or poem addressed to the audience by one of the actors at the end of a play. *n. 17.*

E piph a ny (i pif′ə ni), January 6, the anniversary of the coming of the Wise Men to Christ at Bethlehem. *n.*

E pis co pal (i pis′kə pəl), having to do with the Church of England or certain Protestant churches in the United States. *adj. 9.*

e pis co pal (i pis′kə pəl), 1. of or having to do with bishops. 2. governed by bishops. *adj.*

E pis co pa lian (i pis′kə pāl′yən), 1. member of an Episcopal church. 2. Episcopal. *n., adj. 20.*

ep i sode (ep′i sōd), a single happening or group of happenings in real life or a story. *n. 9.*

e pis tle (i pis′əl), a letter. In the Bible, the **Epistles** were letters written by the Apostles to various churches and individuals. *n. 8.*

e pis to lar y (i pis′tə lãr′i), 1. carried on by letters. 2. of letters. *adj. 18.*

ep i taph (ep′i taf), what is written on a gravestone or tomb; words about the person buried there. *n. 7.*

ep i thet (ep′i thet), a descriptive expression; an adjective or noun expressing some quality or attribute; such as *crafty* Ulysses, Richard *the Lion-Hearted, Honest* Abe. *n. 11.*

e pit o me (i pit′ə mi), 1. a condensed account; a summary. 2. condensed representation of something. Solomon is often spoken of as the epitome of wisdom. *n. 14.*

ep och (ep′ək), 1. a period of time; an era. 2. a period of time in which striking things happened. 3. the starting point of such a period. *n. 9.*

ep och-mak ing (ep′ək māk′ing), beginning an epoch; causing important changes. *adj.*

Ep som salts (ep′səm sôltz′), a white crystalline powder used to purge the bowels. *13.*

eq ua ble (ek′wə bəl), changing little; uniform; even; tranquil; as, equable temperature, equable laws, an equable disposition. *adj. 12.*

e qual (ē′kwəl), 1. the same in amount, size, number, or value. Ten dimes are equal to one dollar. 2. be the same as. Four times five equals twenty. 3. person or thing that is equal. In spelling she had no equal. 4. make or do something equal to. Our team equaled the other team's score, and the game ended in a tie. 5. **Equal to** sometimes means strong enough for. One horse is not equal to pulling a load of five tons. *adj., n., v., equaled, equaling. 1.*

e qual i ty (ē kwol′i ti), sameness in size, number, value, rank, etc. *n., pl. equalities. 6.*

e qual i za tion (ē′kwəl i zā′shən), 1. making equal. 2. being made equal. *n. 20.*

e qual ize (ē′kwəl īz), make equal. *v. 12.*

e qual iz er (ē′kwəl īz′ər), 1. one that equalizes. 2. device for equalizing strains, pressure, etc. *n. 20.*

e qual ly (ē′kwəl i), in equal shares; in equal manner; to an equal degree. The sun shines equally on all. The two sisters are equally pretty. *adv.*

e qua nim i ty (ē′kwə nim′i ti), evenness of mind or temper; calmness; composure. A wise man bears misfortune with equanimity. *n. 16.*

e quate (ē kwāt′), 1. state to be equal; put into the form of an equation. 2. make equal; treat as equal. *v.*

e qua tion (ē kwā′zhən), 1. an expression of the equality of two quantities. $(4\times9)+8=44$ and $C=2\pi r$ are equations. 2. making equal. 3. an equally balanced state. *n. 8.*

e qua tor (ē kwā′tər), an imaginary circle around the middle of the earth, halfway between the North Pole and the South Pole. The United States is north of the equator. *n. 6.*

e qua to ri al (ē′kwə tō′ri əl), 1. of or near the equator. 2. like conditions at or near the equator. The heat this week was almost equatorial. *adj. 10.*

eq uer ry (ek′wər i or i kwer′i), an officer of a royal or noble household who has charge of the horses, or who accompanies his master's carriage. *n., pl. equerries.*

e ques tri an (i kwes′tri ən), 1. of horseback riding. The riding master has equestrian skill. 2. on horseback. An equestrian statue shows a person riding a horse. 3. a rider or performer on horseback. *adj., n. 14.*

e qui dis tant (ē′kwi dis′tənt), equally distant. All points of the circumference of a circle are equidistant from the center. *adj. 17.*

e qui lat er al (ē′kwi lat′ər əl), having all sides equal. *adj.*

Equilateral triangle

e qui lib ri um (ē′kwi lib′ri əm), balance. The acrobat in the circus maintained equilibrium on a tightrope. Scales are in equilibrium when weights on each side are equal. *n. 13.*

e quine (ē′kwīn), of horses; like a horse; like that of a horse. *adj.*

e qui noc tial (ē′kwi nok′shəl), pertaining to an equinox or to equal day and night. An equinoctial storm occurs at an equinox. *adj. 15.*

e qui nox (ē′kwi noks), the time when the sun crosses the equator and day and night are equal, occurring about March 21 and September 22. *n. 14.*

e quip (i kwip′), fit out; provide; furnish with all that is needed. The soldiers equipped the fort with guns, powder, and food. Is the ship fully equipped for its voyage? *v., equipped, equipping. 5.*

eq ui page (ek′wi pij), 1. carriage. 2. carriage with its horses, driver, and servants. 3. equipment; outfit. *n. 11.*

e quip ment (i kwip′mənt), 1. fitting out; providing. 2. outfit; what one is equipped with; furnishings; supplies. *n. 6.*

e qui poise (ē′kwi poiz), 1. equal distribution of weight or force; even balance. 2. balancing force; counterbalance. *n. 18.*

eq ui ta ble (ek′wi tə bəl), fair; just. *adj. 13.*

eq ui ty (ek′wi ti), fairness; justice. *n., pl. equities. 6.*

e quiv a lent (i kwiv′ə lənt), 1. equal. 2. something equivalent. *adj., n. 7.*

e quiv o cal (i kwiv′ə kəl), 1. having two or more meanings; ambiguous. His equivocal answer left us uncertain as to his real opinion. 2. undecided; uncertain. The result of the experiment was equivocal and proved nothing. 3. questionable; suspicious. There was something equivocal about his long and secret trips. *adj. 13.*

e quiv o cate (i kwiv′ə kāt), use expressions of double meaning in order to mislead. When asked if he had finished his arithmetic, Jack equivocated by saying, "Why, I was working on that an hour ago." *v. 16.*

e quiv o ca tion (i kwiv′ə kā′shən), 1. the use of expressions of double meaning to mislead. 2. equivocal expression. *n. 15.*

-er, suffix meaning:—
1. person or thing that ——s; as in admirer, burner.
2. more; as in longer, stronger.
3. other meanings; as in villager and officer.

e ra (ēr′ə), 1. an age in history; historical period. The years from 1817 to 1824 in United States history are often called the Era of Good Feeling. 2. period of time starting from some important or significant happening, date, etc. We live in the 20th century of the Christian era. *n. 8.*

e rad i cate (i rad′i kāt), 1. get entirely rid of; destroy completely. Yellow fever has been eradicated in the United States but it still exists in some other countries. 2. pull out by the roots. *v. 9.*

e rad i ca tion (i rad′i kā′shən), uprooting; complete destruction. *n.*

e rase (i rās′), rub out; scrape out. *v. 10.*

e ras er (i rās′ər), thing used to rub out or erase. *n. 10.*

E ras mus (i raz′məs), Dutch scholar and religious teacher (1466?-1536). *n. 18.*

ere (ãr), before. He will come ere long. *prep., conj. 2.*

Er e bus (er′i bəs), in Greek mythology, the dark, gloomy place through which the dead passed on their way to Hades. *n.*

e rect (i rekt′), 1. straight up; not tipping; not bending. A flagpole stands erect. 2. set up; build. That building was erected fifty years ago. *adj., v. 2.*

e rec tion (i rek′shən), 1. setting up; raising. 2. thing erected; building. *n. 10.*

er e mite (er′i mīt), hermit. *n. 19.*

ere while (ãr′hwīl′), a while before; a short time ago. *adv.* [*Old use*] *15.*

er go (ėr′gō), therefore. *adv., conj. 18.*

E rie (ēr′i), 1. one of the five Great Lakes, between the United States and Canada. 2. a canal in New York State that connects Lake Erie with the Hudson River. 3. a railroad that goes from New York City to Chicago. 4. a city in northwestern Pennsylvania. *n. 7.*

Er in (ãr′in), Ireland. *n.* [*Used in poetry*] *13.*

er mine (ėr′min), 1. a weasel that is brown in summer, but white in winter, except for a black tip on its tail. 2. its soft, white fur, used on the robes of English judges and for women's garments. 3. the position, rank, or duties of a judge. *n., pl. ermine or ermines. 13.*

Ermine (length with tail 15 in.)

e rode (i rōd′), eat out; eat away; wear away. Acid erodes metal. Water erodes soil and rock. *v.*

e ro sion (i rō′zhən), eating away; being worn away. In geography, we study the erosion of the earth by water. *n. 10.*

err (ėr), 1. go wrong; make a mistake. 2. be wrong. 3. do wrong; sin. *v. 3.*

er rand (er′ənd), 1. a trip to do something. She is gone on an errand. 2. what one is sent to do. She did ten errands in one trip. *n. 4.*

er rant (er′ənt), 1. wandering; roving. He was a knight-errant seeking adventures. 2. wrong; mistaken. *adj. 13.*

er rat ic (i rat′ik), 1. uncertain; irregular; as, an erratic clock. 2. queer; as, erratic ideas. 3. wandering; as, the erratic moon. *adj. 18.*

er rat i cal ly (i rat′i kəl i), in an erratic manner. *adv.*

er ro ne ous (i rō′ni əs), mistaken; incorrect; wrong. *adj. 8.*

er ror (er′ər), mistake; something done that is wrong; something that is not the way it ought to be. *n. 2.*

erst (ėrst), formerly; long ago. *adv.* [*Old use*] *13.*

erst while (ėrst′hwīl′), 1. formerly; in time past. *Old use.* 2. former; past. *adv., adj.*

er u dite (er′ü dīt), scholarly; learned. *adj. 19.*

er u di tion (er′ü dish′ən), learning; scholarship; acquired knowledge. *n. 13.*

e rupt (i rupt′), burst forth. Lava and ashes erupted from the volcano. Teeth are said to erupt when they break through the gums. *v.*

e rup tion (i rup′shən), 1. bursting forth. There was an eruption of glowing melted rock from the mountain top. 2. a rash; red spots on the skin. In scarlet fever, there is an eruption on the body. *n. 9.*

e rup tive (i rup′tiv), 1. bursting forth. 2. breaking out in a rash. Measles is an eruptive disease. *adj. 20.*

-ery, suffix meaning:—
1. place for ———ing; as in cannery.
2. place for ———s; as in nunnery.
3. occupation or business of a ———; as in cookery.
4. state or condition of a ———; as in slavery.
5. qualities, actions, etc., of a ———; as in knavery.
6. ———s as a group; as in machinery.

er y sip e las (er′i sip′ə ləs), an acute infectious disease that causes fever and a deep-red inflammation of the skin. *n. 14.*

E sau (ē′sô), in the Bible, Isaac's older son, who sold his birthright to his brother Jacob. *n. 11.*

es ca la tor (es′kə lā′tər), a moving stairway. *n.*

es ca pade (es′kə pād′), a breaking loose from rules or restraint; wild prank. *n. 15.*

es cape (es kāp′), 1. get free; get out and away. The soldier escaped from the enemy's prison. 2. keep free or safe from. We all escaped the measles. 3. act of escaping. 4. way of escaping. *v., n. 1.*

es cape ment (es kāp′mənt), device in a timepiece by which the motions of the wheels and of the pendulum or balance wheel are accommodated to each other. One tooth of the wheel escapes at each swing of the pendulum. *n.*

Escapement of a clock

es carp ment (es kärp′mənt), 1. a steep slope. 2. ground made into a steep slope as a part of a fortification. *n. 19.*

es chew (es chü′), avoid; shun; keep away from. A wise person eschews bad company. *v. 11.*

es cort (es′kôrt for 1, es kôrt′ for 2), 1. one or more persons going with other persons, or with valuable goods, to see that they keep safe, or to honor them. Her escort to the party was a tall young man. An escort of ten airplanes greeted the famous aviator. 2. go with in order to keep safe or to honor. Warships escorted the steamer. *n., v. 6.*

es cu lent (es′kū lənt), suitable for food; edible. *adj.*

es cutch eon (es kuch′ən), 1. a shield on which a coat of arms is put. 2. **A blot on the escutcheon** means a disgrace to honor or reputation. *n. 9.*

Escutcheon

-ese, suffix meaning:—
1. of or pertaining to. She admires Chinese art.
2. native or inhabitant of. The Portuguese colonized Brazil.
3. language of. Can you read Chinese?

Es ki mo (es′ki mō), 1. member of a race that lives on the Arctic shores of North America. Eskimos are short and stocky, and have broad, flat faces, yellowish skin, and black hair. 2. such as Eskimos have; as, Eskimo dog, Es-

Eskimos

kimo house. *n., pl. Eskimos* or *Eskimo, adj. 10.*

e soph a gus (ē sof′ə gəs), passage for food from the mouth to the stomach; the gullet. See the diagram under **alimentary.** *n. 18.*

es o ter ic (es′ō ter′ik), 1. understood only by the select few; intended for an inner circle of disciples, scholars, etc. 2. private; secret. *adj. 20.*

esp., especially.

es pe cial (es pesh′əl), special; chief; more than others. *adj. 2.*

es pe cial ly (es pesh′əl i), particularly; principally; chiefly. *adv.*

es pi o nage (es′pi ə nij), spying; the use of spies. *n. 18.*

es pous al (es pouz′əl), 1. the ceremony of becoming engaged or married. 2. espousing; adoption (of a cause, etc.). *n. 18.*

es pouse (es pouz′), 1. marry. 2. take up or make one's own. Late in life he espoused a new religion. *v. 7.*

es prit (es prē′), a French word meaning spirit; lively wit. *n. 19.*

es prit de corps (es prē′ də kôr′). French words meaning a sense of union and of common interests and responsibilities. The regiment had a strong *esprit de corps*.

es py (es pī′), see; spy. We usually say espy only if the thing is hard to see because it is far away, or small, or hidden. *v., espied, espying. 8.*

Esq., Esquire. *20.*

es quire (es kwīr′), 1. a knight's attendant; a squire. 2. man ranking next below a knight. *n.*

Es quire (es kwīr′), title of respect placed after a man's last name, instead of *Mr.* before the name. John Jones, Esquire = Mr. John Jones. *n.*

-ess, suffix meaning female; as in heiress, hostess, lioness.

es say (es′ā for *n.*, e sā′ for *v.*), 1. a short composition on a particular subject. 2. try; attempt. *n., v. 6.*

es say ist (es′ā ist), writer of essays. *n. 15.*

es sence (es′əns), 1. that which makes a thing what it is. Kindness of heart is the essence of politeness. 2. a concentrated preparation; as, essence of peppermint. 3. perfume. *n. 6.*

es sen tial (e sen′shəl), 1. needed to make a thing what it is; necessary; very important. Good food and enough rest are essential to good health. 2. absolutely necessary element or quality. Learn the essentials first; then learn the details. *adj., n. 5.*

es sen tial ly (e sen′shəl i), in essence; in essentials; in an essential manner. *adv.*

-est, suffix meaning most; as in warmest, nearest.

es tab lish (es tab′lish), 1. set up permanently; as, to establish a government or a business. 2. settle in a position; set up in business. A new doctor has established himself on this street. 3. bring about permanently; make accepted; as, to establish a custom. 4. show beyond dispute; prove; as, to establish a fact. *v. 2.*

es tab lish ment (es tab′lish mənt), 1. establishing. 2. being established. 3. something established. A household, a large store, a church, or an army can be called an establishment. *n. 5.*

es tate (es tāt′), 1. that which a person owns. When the rich man died, he left an estate of two million dollars. Land and buildings are called real estate. 2. a large piece of land. He has a beautiful estate 40 miles from New York with a country house and a swimming pool on it. 3. a class or condition in life. A boy attains man's estate at 21. *n. 3.*

es teem (es tēm′), 1. think highly of. We esteem courage. 2. high regard. Courage is held in esteem. 3. think; consider. *v., n. 3.*

Es ther (es′tər), 1. a Jewish queen who saved her race from massacre. 2. the book of the Old Testament that tells her story. *n. 12.*

es thet ic (es thet′ik), 1. of beauty; having to do with the sense of the beautiful. 2. sensitive to beauty. 3. pleasing; artistic. *adj.* Also spelled **aesthetic.**

es ti ma ble (es′ti mə bəl), worthy of esteem; deserving high regard. *adj. 15.*

es ti mate (es′ti māt, also es′ti mit for 1), 1. a judgment or opinion as to how much, how many, how good, etc. His estimate of the length of the fish was 15 inches. 2. form a judgment or an opinion. Father estimated that the rug was 9 feet long and 6 feet wide. *n., v. 4.*

es ti ma tion (es′ti mā′shən), 1. opinion; judgment. In my estimation, your plan will not work. 2. esteem; respect. *n. 8.*

Es to ni a (es tō′ni ə), country in northern Europe, on the Baltic Sea. *n.*

es trange (es trānj′), make unfriendly; keep apart. A quarrel has estranged John from his brother. *v. 10.*

es trange ment (es trānj′mənt), a turning away in feeling; becoming distant or unfriendly. *n. 17.*

es tu ar y (es′chü ãr′i), 1. broad mouth of a river into which the tide flows. 2. inlet of the sea. *n., pl. estuaries. 13.*

etc., et cetera. *4.*

et cet er a (et set′ər ə), Latin words meaning: and so forth; and so on; and the rest; and the like.

etch (ech), 1. engrave (a design) on a metal plate by acid that eats the lines. Filled with ink, the lines of the design will reproduce a copy on paper. 2. use this method of producing designs and pictures. *v. 14.*

etch ing (ech′ing), 1. picture or design printed from an etched plate. 2. etched plate; etched drawing or design. 3. process of engraving a drawing or design on metal, glass, etc., by means of acid. *n. 19.*

e ter nal (i tėr′nəl), 1. without beginning or ending; lasting throughout all time. 2. always and forever the same. 3. seeming to go on forever. *adj. 3.*

e ter nal ly (i tėr′nəl i), 1. without beginning or ending; throughout all time. 2. always and forever. 3. constantly. *adv.*

e ter ni ty (i tėr′ni ti), all time; going back or on forever; endlessness. *n., pl. eternities. 5.*

e ther (ē′thər), 1. a drug which produces unconsciousness when it is inhaled. 2. the upper regions of space; the clear sky. 3. the fine, elastic matter supposed to fill all space and to transmit light, electric waves, etc. *n. 7.* When *ether* has meanings 2 and 3 it is also spelled **aether.**

e the re al (i thēr′i əl), 1. light; airy; delicate. 2. not of the earth; heavenly. *adj. 7.* Also spelled **aethereal.**

eth i cal (eth′i kəl), 1. of morals; moral. 2. in accordance with rules of right and wrong. It is not considered ethical for a doctor to tell facts about his patients. *adj. 12.*

eth ics (eth′iks), 1. the principles or science of right conduct. 2. rules of right and wrong. It is against medical ethics for doctors to advertise. *n. sing. or pl. 11.*

E thi o pi a (ē′thi ō′pi ə), 1. an ancient region of Africa, south of Egypt. 2. the official name for modern Abyssinia. *n. 9.*

E thi o pi an (ē′thi ō′pi ən), 1. of or having to do with Ethiopia or its people. 2. native of Ethiopia. 3. Negro. *adj., n.*

eth nol o gy (eth nol′ə ji), the science that deals with the various races of people, their origin and distribution, distinctive characteristics, customs, institutions, and culture. *n. 19.*

et i quette (et′i ket), 1. conventional rules for behavior in polite society. Etiquette requires a man to rise when a woman enters the room. 2. rules for behavior in a profession or special group; as, medical etiquette. *n. 11.*

Et na (et′nə), a volcano in Sicily. *n. 14.* Also spelled **Aetna.**

E ton (ē′tən), a famous English school for boys. *n. 14.*

E tru ri a (i trür′i ə), ancient country in western Italy. *n. 14.*

E trus can (i trus′kən), 1. of or having to do with Etruria, its people, their language, art, or customs. 2. native or inhabitant of Etruria. 3. language of Etruria. *adj., n. 15.*

-ette, suffix meaning:—
1. little; as in kitchenette, statuette.
2. female; as in farmerette, suffragette.
3. substitute for; as in leatherette.

é tude (ā tūd′), piece of music intended to develop skill in technique. *n. 18.*

et y mol o gy (et′i mol′ə ji), 1. an account of the origin and history of a word. 2. a study dealing with the origin and history of words. *n., pl. etymologies. 15.*

Eucalyptus leaves

eu ca lyp tus (ū′kə lip′təs), very tall tree that is very common in Australia. It is valued for its timber and for a medicinal oil made from its leaves. *n.*

Eu cha rist (ū′kə rist), 1. sacrament of the Lord's Supper; Holy Communion. 2. consecrated bread and wine used in this sacrament. *n. 16.*

Eu clid (ū′klid), a famous Greek mathematician who wrote a book on geometry about 300 B.C. *n. 12.*

eu gen ics (ū jen′iks), the science of improving the human race. Eugenics would apply the same principles to human beings that have long been applied to animals and plants, and develop healthier, more intelligent, and better children. *n. sing. or pl.*

eu lo gize (ū′lə jīz), praise very highly. *v.*

eu lo gy (ū′lə ji), speech or writing in praise of a person or thing; high praise. The orator pronounced a eulogy over the grave of the dead hero. *n., pl. eulogies. 13.*

eu nuch (ū′nək), man in charge of the part of an Oriental palace in which the ruler's wives live; a castrated male. *n. 7.*

eu phe mism (ū′fi mizm), 1. use of a mild or indirect expression instead of one that is harsh or unpleasantly direct. 2. a word or expression used in this way. "Pass away" is a euphemism for "die"; "not very bright" is a euphemism for "feeble-minded." *n.*

eu phe mis tic (ū′fi mis′tik), using mild or indirect words instead of harsh or unpleasant ones. *adj.*

eu pho ny (ū′fə ni), agreeable sound; pleasing effect to the ear. *n., pl. euphonies. 19.*

Eu phra tes (ū frā′tēz), a river in southwestern Asia that joins the river Tigris before flowing into the sea. *n. 9.*

Eur a sia (ūr ā′zhə), Europe and Asia. *n. 20.*

eu re ka (ū rē′kə), I have found it! *interj.*

Eu rip i des (ū rip′i dēz), great Greek tragic poet (480?-406? B.C.). *n. 15.*

Eu rope (ūr′əp), a continent east of the Atlantic Ocean. France, Germany, and Spain are countries in Europe. *n. 2.*

Eu ro pe an (ūr′ə pē′ən), 1. of or having to do with Europe or its people. 2. person who was born in or lives in Europe. *adj., n. 4.*

Eu sta chi an tube (ū stā′ki ən tūb′), slender canal that equalizes the air pressure on the two sides of the ear drum. *18.*

e vac u ate (i vak′ū āt), 1. leave empty; withdraw from. The soldiers will evacuate the town today. 2. make empty; as, to evacuate the stomach. *v. 14.*

e vac u a tion (i vak′ū ā′shən), 1. leaving empty; withdrawal. 2. making empty. 3. discharge. *n. 14.*

e vade (i vād′), get away from by trickery; avoid by cleverness. Criminals evade the law. When Father asked who broke the window, Dick tried to evade the question. *v. 11.*

e val u ate (i val′ū āt), find the value or the amount of; fix the value of. An expert will evaluate the old furniture. *v.*

ev a nes cent (ev′ə nes′ənt), vanishing; soon passing away. *adj. 15.*

e van gel i cal (ē′van jel′i kəl), 1. of or according to the gospels of the Christian religion. 2. of or having to do with the Protestant churches that emphasize Christ's atonement and salvation by faith as the most important part of Christianity. Methodists and Baptists are evangelical; Unitarians and Universalists are not. *adj. 13.*

e van gel ism (i van′jə lizm), the work of an evangelist. *n.*

e van gel ist (i van′jə list), 1. preacher of the gospel. 2. traveling preacher who stirs up religious feeling. *n. 13.*

E van gel ist (i van′jə list), writer of one of the four Gospels; Matthew, Mark, Luke, or John. *n.*

e vap o rate (i vap′ə rāt), 1. turn into vapor. Boiling water evaporates rapidly. 2. remove water from. Evaporated milk comes in cans. 3. give off moisture. 4. vanish; die. His good resolutions evaporated soon after New Year's. *v. 8.*

e vap o ra tion (i vap′ə rā′shən), evaporating. Wet clothes on a line become dry by evaporation. *n. 8.*

e vap o ra tor (i vap′ə rā′tər), apparatus for driving off moisture; as, an evaporator for drying paints. *n. 19.*

e va sion (i vā′zhən), getting away from something by trickery; avoiding by cleverness; an attempt to escape an argument, a charge, a question, etc.; as, evasion of responsibility. *n. 11.*

e va sive (i vā′siv), tending or trying to evade. "Perhaps I may go" is an evasive answer. *adj. 18.*

eve[1] (ēv), 1. the evening or day before some special day; as, Christmas Eve. 2. the time just before; as, on the eve of battle. 3. evening. *Used in poetry. n. 3.*

Eve[2] (ēv), in the Bible, the first woman, the wife of Adam. A **daughter of Eve** means a woman. *n.*

e ven[1] (ē′vən), 1. level; flat; smooth. The country is even, with no high hills. 2. at the same level. The snow is even with the window. 3. keeping about the same; uniform. The car goes with an even motion. This boy has an even temper. 4. equal; no more or less than. They had even shares of the money. 5. make equal or level; as, to even off edges. 6. that can be divided by 2 without a remainder. 2, 4, 6, 8, and 10 are even numbers. 7. in an even manner. 8. just. He went away even as you came. 9. indeed. He is ready, even eager, to fight. 10. Even often gives the idea of something that would not be expected. Some of the expressions are: He wants even more than that. Even young children can understand it. Even the last man arrived on time. I will come even if I am tired. 11. still; yet. You can read even better if you try. *adj., v., adv. 1.*

e ven[2] (ē′vən), evening. *n.* [*Used in poetry*]

eve ning (ēv′ning), the time between day and night; the time between sunset and bedtime. *n. 1.*

evening star, bright planet seen in the western sky after sunset. Venus is often the evening star.

e vent (i vent′), 1. happening; important happening. The discovery of America was a great event. 2. result; outcome. We made careful plans and awaited the event. 3. **In the event of** means in the case of. In the event of her being sick, she will not be able to go to the party. 4. item or contest in a program of sports. *n. 2.*

e vent ful (i vent′fəl), 1. full of events; having many unusual events. The World War was an eventful period in history. 2. having important results; important. *adj. 10.*

e ven tide (ē′vən tīd′), evening. *n.* [*Used in poetry*] *12.*

e ven tu al (i ven′chü əl), 1. coming in the end. 2. depending on uncertain events; possible. *adj. 8.*

e ven tu al ly (i ven′chü əl i), finally; in the end. *adv.*

ev er (ev′ər), 1. at any time. Is he ever at home? 2. at all times; always. A mother is ever ready to help her children. 3. by any chance; at all. What did you ever do to make him so angry? 4. **Ever so** means very. The ocean is ever so deep. *adv. 1.*

ev er glade (ev′ər glād), large swamp or marsh. *n.*

ev er green (ev′ər grēn′), 1. having green leaves all the year. 2. evergreen plant. Pine, spruce, cedar, ivy, box, rhododendrons, etc., are evergreens. 3. **Evergreens** sometimes means evergreen twigs or branches used for decoration. *adj., n. 7.*

A large evergreen tree, the spruce.

ev er last ing (ev′ər las′ting), 1. lasting forever; never stopping. 2. lasting a long time. 3. lasting too long; tiresome. 4. eternity. *adj., n. 4.*

ev er more (ev′ər mōr′), always; forever. I shall evermore remember this narrow escape from death. *adv., n. 5.*

eve ry (ev′ri). Every word is made of letters. Every boy has a head. **Every now and then** means from time to time. **Every other** means every second. *adj. 1.*

eve ry bod y (ev′ri bod′i), every person. *pron. 2.*

eve ry day (ev′ri dā′), 1. of every day; daily. Accidents are everyday occurrences. 2. for every ordinary day; not for Sundays or holidays. A person wears everyday clothes to work. 3. usual; not exciting. *adj. 7.*

eve ry one or **every one** (ev′ri wun), each one; everybody. *n. 4.*

eve ry thing (ev′ri thing), every thing; all things. *n. 1.*

eve ry where (ev′ri hwãr), in every place; in all places or lands. *adv. 3.*

e vict (i vikt′), expel (a tenant) from land or from a building by lawful methods. *v.*

ev i dence (ev′i dəns), 1. facts; proof; anything that shows or makes clear. The evidence showed that he had not been near the place. His first day's work gave evidence of his speed. 2. show clearly. His smiles evidenced his pleasure. 3. **In evidence** means easily seen or noticed. A crying baby is much in evidence. *n., v. 4.*

ev i dent (ev′i dənt), easy to see or understand; clear; plain. It is evident that children grow up. He has brought Betty a kitten to her evident joy. *adj. 3.*

e vil (ē′vəl), 1. bad; wrong; that does harm. 2. something bad; evil quality or act. 3. thing causing harm. *adj., n. 2.*

e vil do er (ē′vəl dü′ər), person who does wrong. *n. 13.*

e vil-mind ed (ē′vəl mīn′did), wicked; malicious. *adj.*

e vince (i vins′), show clearly. The cat evinced fear of the big dog. *v. 9.*

e voke (i vōk′), call forth; bring out. A good joke evokes a laugh. *v. 16.*

ev o lu tion (ev′ə lü′shən), 1. a gradual development; as, the evolution of the flower from the bud, the evolution of one kind of animal or plant from a simpler kind. 2. the theory of the development of all living things from a few simple forms of life, or from a single form. 3. a movement or pattern developed in a dance. 4. a movement of ships or of soldiers, planned beforehand. 5. a releasing or giving off; as, the evolution of heat from burning coal. *n. 9.*

ev o lu tion ar y (ev′ə lü′shən ãr′i), 1. having to do with evolution or development. 2. developing. *adj. 16.*

e volve (i volv′), unfold; develop gradually. The boys evolved a plan for earning money during their summer vacation. *v. 14.*

ewe (ū), a female sheep. *n. 4.*

ew er (ū′ər), wide-mouthed water pitcher. A ewer and bowl are on the washstand. *n. 19.*

Ewer and bowl

ex-, prefix meaning:—
1. former; formerly; as in ex-president.
2. out of; from; out; as in exclude.
3. thoroughly; as in exasperate.

ex act (eg zakt′), 1. without any error; correct; as, an exact measurement, the exact amount. 2. demand and get. If he does the work, he can exact payment for it. *adj., v. 2.*

ex act ing (eg zak′ting), 1. requiring much; hard to please. 2. requiring effort, care, or attention. Flying an airplane is exacting work. *adj.*

ex ac tion (eg zak′shən), 1. requirement. 2. wrong or excessive requirement. *n. 14.*

ex act i tude (eg zak′ti tūd or eg zak′ti tüd), exactness. *n. 17.*

ex act ly (eg zakt′li), 1. accurately; precisely. 2. just so; quite right. *adv.*

ex act ness (eg zakt′nis), being exact. *n. 19.*

ex ag ger ate (eg zaj′ər āt), 1. make too large; say or think something is greater than it is; go beyond the truth. The little boy exaggerated when he said there were a million cats in the back yard. 2. increase beyond what is normal. *v. 7.*

ex ag ger a tion (eg zaj′ər ā′shən), 1. exaggerating. 2. being exaggerated. 3. an exaggerated statement. It is an exaggeration to say that you would rather die than touch a snake. *n. 11.*

ex alt (eg zôlt′), 1. make high in rank, honor, power, character, or quality. We exalt a man when we elect him President of our country. 2. fill with pride or joy or noble feeling. An exalted mood is one in which we think noble thoughts. 3. praise; honor. God shall be exalted. *v. 4.*

ex al ta tion (eg′zôl tā′shən), 1. raising up in rank, honor, power, etc.; elevation. 2. high emotion; rapture. *n. 12.*

ex am i na tion (eg zam′i nā′shən), examining; test. The doctor made a careful examination of my eyes. The teacher gave us an examination in arithmetic. *n. 3.*

ex am ine (eg zam′in), 1. look at closely and carefully. 2. test; test the knowledge or ability of; ask questions of. *v. 2.*

ex am in er (eg zam′in ər), person who examines. *n. 9.*

ex am ple (eg zam′pəl), 1. a sample; one thing taken to show what the others are like. New York is an example of a busy seaport. 2. a model; a pattern. Lincoln is a good example for boys to follow. **Set an example** means give, show, or be an example. 3. a problem in arithmetic. 4. warning to others. The captain made an example of the soldiers who shirked by making them clean up the camp. *n. 2.*

ex as per ate (eg zas′pər āt), irritate; annoy greatly; make angry. The little boy's noise exasperated his father. *v. 10.*

ex as per a tion (eg zas′pər ā′shən), extreme annoyance; anger; irritation. *n. 17.*

Ex cal i bur (eks kal′i bər), magic sword of King Arthur. *n.*

ex ca vate (eks′kə vāt), 1. make hollow; hollow out. 2. make by digging; dig. The tunnel was excavated through solid rock. 3. dig out; scoop out. Steam shovels excavated the dirt and loaded it into trucks. 4. uncover by digging. They excavated an ancient buried city. *v. 11.*

ex ca va tion (eks′kə vā′shən), 1. digging out; digging. 2. hole made by digging. *n. 9.*

ex ca va tor (eks′kə vā′tər), person or thing that excavates. *n. 19.*

Excavator

ex ceed (ek sēd′), go beyond; be more or greater than. The sum of 5 and 7 exceeds 10. To lift a heavy trunk exceeds a girl's strength. *v. 3.*

ex ceed ing (ek sēd′ing), 1. very great. Helen is a girl of exceeding beauty. 2. exceedingly. *Old use. adj., adv. 5.*

ex ceed ing ly (ek sēd′ing li), very greatly; to an unusual degree; very. *adv.*

ex cel (ek sel′), 1. be better than; do better than. John excelled his class in spelling. 2. be better than others; do better than others. Solomon excelled in wisdom. *v., excelled, excelling. 4.*

ex cel lence (ek′sə ləns), high quality; being better than others. California is famous for the excellence of its climate. *n. 7.*

ex cel len cy (ek′sə lən si), 1. excellence. 2. a title of honor. A governor is formally spoken of as His Excellency. *n., pl. excellencies. 10.*

ex cel lent (ek′sə lənt), very, very good; better than others. *adj. 2.*

ex cel si or (ek sel′si ôr for 1, ek sel′si ər for 2), 1. a Latin word meaning higher. The motto of New York State is "Excelsior." 2. fine wood shavings used for packing dishes, glassware, and other breakable articles. *adj., n. 20.*

ex cept (ek sept′), 1. leaving out; other than. He works every day except Sunday. 2. leave out. The teacher excepted John from the examination list. 3. unless. *Old use. prep., v., conj. 1.*

ex cept ing (ek sep′ting), leaving out; except. *prep. 13.*

ex cep tion (ek sep′shən), 1. leaving out. She likes all her teachers with the exception of Miss Smith. 2. thing left out. She praised them all, with two exceptions. 3. thing that is different from the rule. 4. objection. **Take exception** means (1) object. (2) be offended. *n. 4.*

ex cep tion al (ek sep′shən əl), unusual; out of the ordinary. This warm weather is exceptional for January. *adj. 6.*

ex cerpt (ek′sėrpt for 1, ek sėrpt′ for 2), 1. a passage taken out of a book, etc.; an extract. Mr. Jones read aloud excerpts from the newspapers. 2. quote; take out (a passage) from a book, etc. *n., v.*

ex cess (ek ses′, also ek′ses for 4), 1. the part that is too much. Pour off the excess. 2. **To excess** means too much. He eats to excess. 3. amount by which one thing is greater than another. The excess of 7 over 5 is 2. **In excess of** means more than. 4. extra. We pay excess fare on some very fast trains. *n., adj. 4.*

ex ces sive (ek ses′iv), too much; too great; extreme; as, an excessive price. *adj. 5.*

ex ces sive ly (ek ses′iv li), too much; too greatly. *adv.*

ex change (eks chānj′), 1. change; give and take. You two boys exchange places. 2. giving and taking. Ten pennies for a dime is a fair exchange. 3. central telephone office. 4. a place where men trade. *v., n. 2.*

ex cheq uer (eks chek′ər), 1. treasury of a state or nation. **The Exchequer** is the department of the British government in charge of its finances and the public revenues. 2. treasury. 3. finances; funds. *n. 9.*

ex cise[1] (ek sīz′ or ek′sīz), a tax on the manufacture, sale, or use of certain articles made and used within a country. There is an excise on tobacco. *n. 12.*

ex cise[2] (ek sīz′), cut out; remove. The editor excised passages from the book. *v.*

ex cit a ble (ek sīt′ə bəl), easily excited. *adj. 16.*

ex cite (ek sīt′), 1. stir up the feelings of. The news of war excited everybody. 2. arouse. Her new dress excited envy. 3. stir to action. Do not excite the dog; let him keep still. *v. 3.*

ex cite ment (ek sīt′mənt), 1. excited state. The baby's first step caused great excitement in the family. 2. a cause of being excited. *n. 5.*

ex claim (eks klām′), cry out; speak suddenly in surprise, strong feeling, etc. "Here you are at last!" exclaimed Jack's mother. *v. 3.*

ex cla ma tion (eks′klə mā′shən), something said suddenly as the result of feeling. A mark (!) after a printed word that means that the word was exclaimed. Oh! Hurrah! Well! Look! Listen! are common exclamations. *n. 7.*

ex clam a to ry (eks klam′ə tō′ri), using, containing, or expressing exclamation. *adj. 20.*

ex clude (eks klüd′), 1. shut out; keep out. Curtains exclude light. The government excludes certain immigrants. 2. drive out and keep out. Perfect faith excludes doubt. *v. 7.*

ex clu sion (eks klü′zhən), 1. an excluding. **To the exclusion of** means so as to shut out or keep out. 2. a being excluded. *n. 9.*

ex clu sive (eks klü′siv), 1. shutting out all others. Plant and animal are exclusive terms; a thing cannot be both a plant and an animal. **Exclusive of** means leaving out. There are 26 days in that month, exclusive of Sundays. 2. shutting out all or most. This school is exclusive; only very bright children can go to it. 3. single; sole; not divided or shared with others. An inventor has an exclusive right for a certain number of years to make what he has invented. 4. very particular about choosing friends, members, patrons, etc. It is hard to get admitted to an exclusive club. *adj. 4.*

ex clu sive ly (eks klü′siv li), with the exclusion of all others. That selfish girl looks out for herself exclusively. *adv.*

ex com mun i cate (eks′kə mū′ni kāt), cut off from membership in the church; shut out from communion with the church. *v. 8.*

ex com mu ni ca tion (eks′kə mū′ni kā′shən), 1. expulsion from membership in the church and from any part in its ceremonies. 2. the official statement announcing this. *n. 12.*

ex cre ment (eks′kri mənt), the waste matter discharged from the body. *n. 9.*

ex cres cence (eks kres′əns), an unnatural growth. A corn or a wart is an excrescence. *n. 17.*

ex crete (eks krēt′), separate and expel (waste matter). The skin excretes sweat. *v. 19.*

ex cre tion (eks krē′shən), 1. separation and discharge of waste matter. 2. the waste matter that is separated and discharged. Sweat is an excretion. *n. 11.*

ex cre to ry (eks′kri tō′ri), excreting; having the task of excreting. The kidneys are excretory organs. *adj. 14.*

ex cru ci at ing (eks krü′shi āt′ing), torturing; very, very painful. *adj.*

ex cur sion (eks kėr′zhən), 1. a short journey. 2. a trip taken for interest or pleasure, often by a number of people together; as, an excursion to the seashore. *n. 6.*

ex cur sive (eks kėr′siv), wandering; rambling; off the point. *adj. 16.*

ex cus a ble (eks kūz′ə bəl), that can be excused; deserving pardon. *adj.*

ex cuse (eks kūz′ for 1-4, eks kūs′ for 5 and 6), 1. offer an apology for; try to remove the blame of. **Excuse oneself** means ask to be pardoned. 2. be a reason or explanation for. Sickness excuses absence from school. 3. pardon; forgive. Excuse me; I have to go now. 4. let off. You are excused from spelling today. 5. a reason, real or pretended, that is given. He had many excuses for coming late. 6. act of excusing. *v., n. 2.*

ex e cra ble (ek′si krə bəl), abominable; detestable. *adj. 16.*

ex e crate (ek′si krāt), 1. abhor; detest. 2. curse. *v. 16.*

ex e cra tion (ek′si krā′shən), 1. act of execrating. 2. a curse. 3. the thing execrated. *n. 11.*

ex e cute (ek′si kūt), 1. carry out; do. The nurse executed the doctor's orders. 2. put into effect; enforce. Congress makes the laws; the President executes them. 3. put to death according to law. The murderer was executed. 4. make according to a plan or design. An artist executes a painting or statue. 5. make (a deed, lease, contract, will, etc.) legal by signing, sealing, or doing whatever is necessary. *v. 4.*

ex e cu tion (ek′si kū′shən), 1. a carrying out; a doing. 2. a putting into effect. 3. way of carrying out or doing; skill. 4. a putting to death according to law. 5. a making according to a plan or design. 6. a making legal by signing, sealing, or doing anything else that is necessary. *n. 5.*

ex e cu tion er (ek′si kū′shən ər), person who kills criminals who are sentenced to death. *n. 10.*

ex ec u tive (eg zek′ū tiv), 1. having to do with management. An executive job is a job at managing something. The President is the executive head of the nation. 2. manager; person who carries out what he (or another) has decided should be done. A good executive usually gets on well with people. 3. the branch of a government that carries out the laws. *adj., n. 5.*

ex ec u tor (eg zek′ū tər), person chosen to carry out what a person has said shall be done with his money and other belongings after his death. *n. 8.*

ex em pla ry (eg zem′plə ri), 1. worthy of imitation; as, exemplary conduct. 2. serving as a warning; as, exemplary punishment. 3. illustrative; typical. *adj. 13.*

ex em pli fi ca tion (eg zem′pli fi kā′shən), 1. illustration by example. 2. an example. *n. 20.*

ex em pli fy (eg zem′pli fī), show by example; be an example of. Knights exemplified courage and courtesy. *v., exemplified, exemplifying.*

ex empt (eg zempt′), 1. make free (from). The school exempts good pupils from examinations. 2. freed (from). School property is exempt from all taxes. *v., adj. 6.*

ex emp tion (eg zemp′shən), 1. act of exempting. 2. freedom from a duty, obligation, rule, etc.; release. Exemption from taxation is given to schools and churches. *n. 13.*

ex er cise (ek′sər sīz), 1. use; practice. It is wise to exercise caution in crossing the street. Exercise of the body is good for the health. 2. something that gives practice. Do the exercises on page 50. 3. procedure; activity; performance. The opening exercises in our Sunday school are a song and a prayer. *v., n. 1.*

ex ert (eg zėrt′), use; put into use; use fully. A fighter exerts strength. A ruler exerts authority. **Exert oneself** means make an effort; try hard; strive. *v. 8.*

ex er tion (eg zėr′shən), 1. effort. The exertions of the firemen kept the fire from spreading. 2. use; active use; putting into action. Unwise exertion of authority may cause rebellion. *n. 8.*

ex ha la tion (eks′hə lā′shən), 1. an exhaling. Breathing out is an exhalation of air. 2. something exhaled; air, vapor, smoke, odor, etc. *n. 11.*

ex hale (eks hāl′), 1. breathe out. We exhale air from our lungs. 2. give off (air, vapor, smoke, odor, etc.). 3. pass off as vapor; rise like vapor. Sweet odors exhale from the flowers. *v. 8.*

ex haust (eg zôst′), 1. to empty; as, to exhaust a well. 2. to use up; as, to exhaust the supply of water, to exhaust one's strength or money. To **exhaust a subject** is to find out or say everything important about it. 3. tire out; as, to exhaust oneself by hard work. 4. escape of used steam, gasoline, etc., from a machine. 5. means or way for used steam, gasoline, etc., to escape from an engine. 6. used steam, gasoline, etc., that escapes. *v., n. 4.*

ex haust ed (eg zôs′tid), 1. used up. 2. worn out; very tired. *adj.*

ex haus tion (eg zôs′chən), 1. act of exhausting. 2. being exhausted. 3. extreme fatigue. *n. 7.*

ex haus tive (eg zôs′tiv), tending to exhaust or use up (resources, strength, or a subject); thorough. We were given an exhaustive examination that lasted two hours. *adj. 14.*

ex hib it (eg zib′it), 1. show. The child exhibited a bad temper at an early age. He exhibits interest whenever you talk about dogs. 2. show publicly. You should exhibit your roses in the Flower Show. 3. something shown to the public. Their exhibit of corn products won the prize. *v., n. 4.*

ex hi bi tion (ek′si bish′ən), 1. showing. Such an exhibition of bad manners I never saw before. 2. public show. The art school held an exhibition. 3. thing or things shown publicly; exhibit. *n. 6.*

ex hib i tor or **ex hib it er** (eg zib′i tər), one that exhibits. *n. 17.*

ex hil a rate (eg zil′ə rāt), cheer; make merry; make lively. The joy of Christmas exhilarates us all. *v. 11.*

ex hil a ra tion (eg zil′ə rā′shən), high spirits; lively joy. *n. 18.*

ex hort (eg zôrt′), urge strongly; advise earnestly. The preacher exhorted his hearers to live a better life. *v. 9.*

ex hor ta tion (eg′zôr tā′shən or ek′sôr tā′shən), 1. strong urging; earnest advice or warning. 2. speech, sermon, etc., that exhorts. *n. 8.*

ex hume (eks hūm′), dig (a dead body) out of the earth. *v.*

ex i gen cy (ek′si jən si), a case demanding prompt action or remedy; emergency; need. The lamp upset, but Mrs. Smith proved equal to the exigency and put out the flames with a heavy rug. *n., pl. exigencies. 14.*

ex i gent (ek′si jənt), 1. urgent; pressing; as, the exigent pangs of hunger. 2. demanding a great deal; exacting. A busy doctor has an exigent occupation. *adj. 18.*

ex ile (eg′zīl or ek′sīl), 1. make (a person) go from home or country, often by law as a punishment; banish. Napoleon was exiled from France for life. 2. person who is banished. He has been an exile for ten years. 3. banishment. He was sent into exile for life. *v., n. 4.*

ex ist (eg zist′), 1. be. The world has existed a long time. 2. be real. Do fairies exist or not? 3. live. A man cannot exist without air. 4. occur. Cases exist of persons who cannot smell anything. *v. 4.*

ex ist ence (eg zis′təns), 1. being; as, come into existence. 2. being real. People do not now believe in the existence of ghosts. 3. life. Many aviators lead a dangerous existence. *n. 4.*

ex ist ent (eg zis′tənt), 1. existing. 2. now existing; present-day. *adj.*

ex it (eg′zit or ek′sit), 1. way out. The theater had six exits. 2. the departure of a player from the stage. 3. act of going out. *n. 8.*

ex o dus (ek′sə dəs), going out; departure. Every summer there is an exodus from the city. *n. 13.*

Ex o dus (ek′sə dəs), 1. the departure of the Israelites from Egypt under Moses. 2. the second book of the Old Testament, containing an account of this departure. *n.*

ex of fi ci o (eks ə fish′i ō), because of his, her, or their office. The vice-president is, ex officio, the presiding officer of the Senate.

ex on er ate (eg zon′ər āt), free from blame; prove or declare innocent. Witnesses of the accident completely exonerated the driver of the truck. *v.*

ex or bi tant (eg zôr′bi tənt), very excessive; much too high. Two dollars is an exorbitant price to pay for a dozen eggs. *adj. 16.*

ex or bi tant ly (eg zôr′bi tənt li), 1. extravagantly. 2. in an excessive degree or amount; beyond reasonable limits. *adv.*

ex or cise or **ex or cize** (ek′sôr sīz), 1. expel (an evil spirit) by ceremonies, prayers, etc. 2. free (a person or place) from an evil spirit. *v.*

ex ot ic (eg zot′ik or eks ot′ik), 1. from a foreign country. We saw many exotic plants at the Flower Show. 2. anything exotic. *adj., n. 14.*

ex pand (eks pand′), spread out; open out; unfold; swell; make or grow larger. A balloon expands when it is blown up. Our country has expanded many times. A man may expand his business, his umbrella, or a speech. *v. 6.*

ex panse (eks pans′), open or unbroken stretch; a wide, spreading surface. The Pacific Ocean is a vast expanse of water. *n. 9.*

ex pan sion (eks pan′shən), 1. an expanding. Heat causes the expansion of gas. 2. a being expanded; increase in size, volume, etc. The expansion of the factory made room for more machines. *n. 7.*

ex pan sive (eks pan′siv), 1. capable of expanding; tending to expand. 2. wide; spreading. 3. broad; extensive; taking in much or many things. 4. showing one's feelings freely and openly; unrestrained; effusive; demonstrative. *adj. 13.*

ex pa ti ate (eks pā′shi āt), write or talk much. Mary expatiated upon the thrills of her trip out west. *v. 14.*

ex pa tri ate (eks pā′tri āt for 1 and 2, eks pā′tri it for 3), 1. banish. 2. withdraw from one's country or citizenship. Some Americans expatriate themselves and live in Europe. 3. expatriated person. *v., n.*

ex pa tri a tion (eks pā′tri ā′shən), 1. exile. 2. withdrawal from one's country. *n.*

ex pect (eks pekt′), look for; think something will come or happen. We expect hot days in summer. *v. 1.*

ex pect an cy (eks pek′tən si), expectation. *n., pl. expectancies. 12.*

ex pect ant (eks pek′tənt), expecting; looking for; thinking something will come or happen. Mary was expectant of a doll on her birthday. *adj. 8.*

ex pec ta tion (eks′pek tā′shən), 1. an expecting or being expected; anticipation. 2. thing expected. 3. good reason for expecting something; prospect. He has expectations from a rich uncle. *n. 5.*

ex pec to rate (eks pek′tə rāt), spit; expel (a discharge) from the throat or lungs by coughing or by clearing the throat and spitting. *v. 20.*

ex pe di ence (eks pē′di əns), expediency. *n. 17.*

ex pe di en cy (eks pē′di ən si), 1. usefulness; suitability for bringing about a desired result; fitness under the circumstances. Consider expediency as well as truth in what you say. 2. personal advantage; self-interest. The crafty lawyer was influenced more by expediency than by the love of justice. *n., pl. expediencies. 16.*

ex pe di ent (eks pē′di ənt), 1. useful; helping to attain some end. It is expedient to make friends if you wish to be elected president of your class. 2. a means to an end. If you wish a fire and have no matches, you can try such expedients as using flint, steel, and tinder. *adj., n. 7.*

ex pe dite (eks′pi dīt), make easy; hurry along. Railroads expedite travel. The telephone expedites business. *v. 17.*

ex pe di tion (eks′pi dish′ən), 1. a journey for a special purpose, such as war, discovery, or collecting new plants. 2. the people, ships, etc., making such a journey. 3. speed. *n. 4.*

ex pe di tion ar y (eks′pi dish′ən ãr′i), of, concerning, or making up an expedition. The **American Expeditionary Force** was the army sent to Europe by the United States in the first World War. *adj. 20.*

ex pe di tious (eks′pi dish′əs), quick; speedy; efficient and prompt. *adj. 15.*

ex pel (eks pel′), 1. drive out with much force. A bullet is expelled from the barrel of a gun. 2. put out. A bad boy may be expelled from a school. *v., expelled, expelling. 5.*

ex pend (eks pend′), spend; use up. *v. 8.*

ex pen di ture (eks pen′di chər), 1. a spending; a using up. A large piece of work requires the expenditure of much money, time, and effort. 2. amount of money, etc., spent; expense. Limit your expenditures to what is necessary. *n. 8.*

ex pense (eks pens′), 1. paying out money; cost; laying out of money. One expense followed another until Emma's money was all gone. 2. **Expenses** often means (1) charges incurred in doing something. (2) money to repay such charges. A salesman often receives a salary plus expenses. *n. 2.*

ex pen sive (eks pen′siv), costly; high-priced. He had a very expensive knife which cost $6. *adj. 4.*

ex pe ri ence (eks pēr′i əns), 1. what happens to a person; as, a pleasant or sad experience, to know by experience. 2. practice; knowledge gained by doing or seeing things. Have you had any experience in this kind of work? 3. feel; have happen to one; as, to experience very great pain. *n., v. 2.*

ex pe ri enced (eks pēr′i ənst), 1. taught by experience. 2. skillful or wise through experience; as, an experienced teacher, an experienced nurse. *adj.*

ex per i ment (eks per′i ment for 1, eks per′i mənt for 2), 1. try in order to find out; make trials or tests. A baby experiments with his hands. That man is experimenting with dyes to get the color he wants. 2. a trial or test to find out something; as, a cooking experiment. Science tests out theories by experiment. *v., n. 5.*

ex per i men tal (eks per′i men′təl), 1. based on experiments. Chemistry is an experimental science. 2. used for experiments. We worked in the experimental room. 3. based on experience, not on theory or authority. 4. testing; trying out. This trip will be only experimental. *adj. 9.*

ex per i men ta tion (eks per′i men tā′shən), experimenting. Cures for disease are found by experimentation on animals. *n. 18.*

ex pert (eks′pėrt, also eks pėrt′ for 2), 1. person who has skill or who knows a great deal about some special thing. Alice is an expert at fancy skating. 2. having skill; knowing a great deal about some special thing. His father is an expert painter. *n., adj. 4.*

ex pi ate (eks′pi āt), atone for (sin); pay the penalty of. The thief expiated his theft by giving back twice as much as he stole. *v. 12.*

ex pi a tion (eks′pi ā′shən), 1. an expiating; atonement. 2. the means of atonement. *n. 15.*

ex pi ra tion (ek′spi rā′shən), 1. a coming to an end. We shall move at the expiration of our lease. 2. a breathing out; as, the expiration of air from the lungs. *n. 10.*

ex pire (ek spīr′), 1. come to an end. You must obtain a new license when your old one expires. 2. die. 3. breathe out. Used air is expired from the lungs. *v. 4.*

ex plain (eks plān′), make plain; tell the meaning of; tell how to do. Can you explain the working of an air pump? *v. 2.*

ex pla na tion (eks′plə nā′shən), 1. an explaining; clearing up a difficulty or mistake. He did not understand the teacher's explanation of long division. 2. something that explains. We had an explanation and agreed to quarrel no more. *n. 5.*

ex plan a to ry (eks plan′ə tō′ri), that explains; helping to make clear. Read the explanatory part of the lesson before you try to do the problems. *adj. 15.*

ex ple tive (eks′pli tiv), 1. completing; filling out a sentence or a line. 2. something that fills out. In the sentence "There is a book on the table," *there* is an expletive. 3. an oath. "Damn" is an expletive. 4. exclamation. "My goodness" is an expletive. *adj., n. 16.*

ex pli ca ble (eks′pli kə bəl), capable of being explained. *adj.*

ex plic it (eks plis′it), 1. clearly expressed; distinctly stated; definite. He gave such explicit directions that everyone understood them. 2. frank; not reserved; outspoken. *adj. 15.*

ex plode (eks plōd′), 1. blow up; burst with a loud noise. The building was destroyed when the defective boiler exploded. 2. cause to explode. Many boys explode firecrackers on the Fourth of July. 3. burst forth noisily. The speaker's mistake was so funny the audience exploded with laughter. 4. cause to be rejected. Columbus and other navigators helped to explode the theory that the earth is flat. *v. 8.*

ex ploit (eks ploit′, also eks′ploit for 1), 1. bold, unusual act; daring deed. Old stories tell about the exploits of famous heroes. 2. make use of; turn to practical account. A mine is exploited for its minerals. 3. make unfair use of; use selfishly for one's own advantage. Nations used to exploit their colonies, taking as much wealth out of them as they could. *n., v. 5.*

ex ploi ta tion (eks′ploi tā′shən), 1. exploiting. 2. selfish use. *n. 17.*

ex plo ra tion (eks′plə rā′shən), 1. a traveling in little known lands or seas for the purpose of discovery. 2. a going over carefully; a looking into closely; examining. *n. 5.*

ex plore (eks plōr′), 1. travel over little known lands or seas for the sake of discovery. Byrd explored around the South Pole. 2. go over carefully; examine. The children explored the new house from attic to cellar. *v. 4.*

ex plor er (eks plōr′ər), person who explores. *n. 7.*

ex plo sion (eks plō′zhən), 1. a blowing up; a bursting with a loud noise. The explosion of the bomb shook the whole neighborhood. 2. loud noise caused by this. People five miles away heard the explosion. 3. noisy bursting forth; outbreak; as, explosions of anger, an explosion of laughter. *n. 8.*

ex plo sive (eks plō′siv), 1. of or for explosion; tending to explode. Gunpowder is explosive. 2. explosive substance. Explosives are used in making fireworks. 3. tending to burst forth noisily. The irritable old man had an explosive temper. *adj., n. 8.*

ex po nent (eks pō′nənt), 1. person or thing that explains. 2. person or thing that stands as a representative or type of something. Lincoln was an exponent of self-education. *n. 13.*

ex port (eks′pōrt, also eks pōrt′ for 1), 1. send out of one country for sale in another. The United States exports many kinds of machinery. 2. exporting; exportation. 3. article exported. Cotton is the important export of the Southern States of the United States. *v., n. 5.*

ex por ta tion (eks′pōr tā′shən), 1. sending goods out of a country to be sold in another. 2. thing so sent. *n. 13.*

ex port er (eks pōr′tər), person or company whose business is exporting goods. *n.*

ex pose (eks pōz′), 1. lay open; uncover; leave unprotected. Soldiers in an open field are exposed to the enemy's gunfire. Foolish actions expose a person to ridicule. 2. show openly; display. Goods are exposed for sale in a store. 3. make known; reveal; show up. He exposed the plot to the police. 4. abandon; put out without shelter. The ancient Spartans used to expose babies that they did not want. 5. allow light to reach and act on (a photographic film or plate). *v. 3.*

ex po si tion (eks′pə zish′ən), 1. public show or exhibition. A world's fair is an exposition. 2. explanation. 3. speech or writing explaining a process, thing, or idea. *n. 8.*

ex pos i tor (eks poz′i tər), person who explains. *n. 19.*

ex pos i to ry (eks poz′i tō′ri), explanatory. *adj.*

ex pos tu late (eks pos′chů lāt), reason earnestly with a person against something he means to do or has done; remonstrate. The teacher expostulated with the janitor about the coldness of the schoolroom. *v. 13.*

ex pos tu la tion (eks pos′chů lā′shən), a protest; remonstrance. When his expostulations failed the leader used threats. *n. 14.*

ex po sure (eks pō′zhər), 1. exposing; laying open; making known. The exposure of the real criminal cleared the innocent man. Anyone would dread public exposure of all his faults. 2. being exposed. Exposure to the weather has spoiled this chair. 3. "This house has a southern exposure" means that the house is exposed to sun and wind from the south. 4. time during which light reaches and acts on a photographic film or plate. 5. part of a photographic film for one picture. 6. abandoning; putting out without shelter. *n. 8.*

ex pound (eks pound′), 1. make clear; explain. The teacher expounds each new principle in arithmetic to the class. 2. set forth in detail. *v. 9.*

ex-pres i dent (eks′prez′i dənt), former president; person who once was president, but no longer is. *n. 19.*

ex press (eks pres′), 1. put into words. Try to express your idea clearly. **Express oneself** means say what one thinks. 2. show by look, voice, or action. A smile expresses joy. 3. clear and definite. It was his express wish that we should go without him. 4. a company that carries packages, money, etc. 5. a quick means of sending; as, to send it by express. 6. send by some quick means; as, to express a package. 7. by express; specially. Send your trunk express to Boston. 8. quick; as, an express train. 9. press out. Wine is made by expressing the juice from grapes. *v., adj., n., adv. 1.*

ex pres sion (eks presh′ən), 1. putting into words; as, the expression of an idea. 2. a word or words used as a unit. "Swell guy" is a slang expression. 3. showing by look, voice, or action; as, the expression of a feeling. 4. a look that shows feeling; as, a hurt expression. 5. bringing out the meaning or beauty of something read, spoken, sung, or played. Try to read with more expression. 6. pressing out. *n. 5.*

ex pres sive (eks pres′iv), 1. expressing. Alas! is a word expressive of sadness. 2. carrying much feeling. "His skin hung on his bones" is a more expressive sentence than "He was very emaciated." *adj. 9.*

ex press ly (eks pres′li), 1. plainly. You are expressly forbidden to touch it. 2. on purpose. I came expressly to bring it to you. *adv. 12.*

ex pul sion (eks pul′shən), 1. a forcing out; as, expulsion of air from the lungs. 2. being forced out. Expulsion from school is a punishment for bad behavior. *n. 12.*

ex punge (eks punj′), erase; blot out; remove completely. The secretary was directed to expunge certain remarks from the record. *v. 15.*

ex pur gate (eks′pər gāt), remove objectionable passages or words from (a book, letter, etc.); purify. *v.*

ex qui site (eks′kwi zit), 1. very lovely; delicate; beautifully made. The violet is an exquisite flower. 2. sharp; as, exquisite pain. 3. of highest excellence; most admirable. She has exquisite taste and manners. *adj. 5.*

ex tant (eks′tənt or ek stant′), still existing. Some of Washington's letters are extant. *adj. 10.*

ex tem po ra ne ous (eks tem′pə rā′ni əs), spoken or done without preparation; offhand; as, an extemporaneous speech. *adj.*

ex tem po re (eks tem′pə ri), on the spur of the moment; without preparation; offhand. Each pupil will be called on to speak extempore. *adv. 16.*

ex tend (eks tend′), 1. stretch out; as, to extend your hand, to extend help to the poor, an extended visit, a road that extends to New York. 2. give; grant. Charity extends help to poor people. *v. 1.*

ex ten sion (eks ten′shən), 1. stretching out; as, the extension of a road. 2. addition; as, a new extension built on the old school. *n. 5.*

ex ten sive (eks ten′siv), far-reaching; large; as, extensive changes, an extensive park. *adj. 5.*

ex tent (eks tent′), 1. size, space, length, amount, or degree to which a thing extends. Railroads carry people and goods through the whole extent of the country. The extent of a judge's power is limited by law. 2. something extended; extended space; as, a vast extent of prairie. *n. 4.*

ex ten u ate (eks ten′ū āt), make (guilt, a fault or offense) seem less; excuse in part. His foreign bringing-up extenuates his faulty pronunciation. *v. 10.*

ex ten u a tion (eks ten′ū ā′shən), 1. an extenuating. The lawyer pleaded his client's youth in extenuation of the crime. 2. something that lessens the seriousness of guilt, a fault, an offense, etc.; partial excuse. *n. 20.*

ex te ri or (eks tēr′i ər), 1. outside. I saw only the exterior of the house, not the interior. The man has a harsh exterior, but a kind heart. 2. outer. Skin is the exterior covering of our bodies. 3. coming from without; happening outside; as, exterior influences. *n., adj. 7.*

ex ter mi nate (eks tėr′mi nāt), destroy completely. This poison will exterminate rats. *v. 11.*

ex ter mi na tion (eks tėr′mi nā′shən), complete destruction. Poison and traps are useful for the extermination of rats. *n. 11.*

ex ter nal (eks tėr′nəl), 1. outer; outside; outside ourselves. 2. outside part. 3. easily seen but not essential. Going to church is an external act of worship. 4. to be used on the outside of the body. This alcohol is for external use only; it must not be used internally. *adj., n. 8.*

ex ter nal ly (eks tėr′nəl i), on the outside. *adv.*

ex tinct (eks tingkt′), 1. no longer existing. The dodo is an extinct bird. 2. gone out; not burning; as, an extinct volcano. *adj. 7.*

ex tinc tion (eks tingk′shən), 1. act of extinguishing. 2. extinct condition. 3. suppression; wiping out; destruction. Physicians are working for the extinction of diseases. *n. 12.*

ex tin guish (eks ting′gwish), 1. put out. 2. wipe out; bring to an end. We can extinguish a fire with water. *v. 6.*

ex tin guish er (eks ting′gwish ər), thing or person that extinguishes. There are many kinds of fire extinguishers. *n. 17.*

ex tir pate (eks′tər pāt), 1. remove completely; destroy totally. Kidnaping must be extirpated. 2. tear up by the roots. *v. 15.*

ex tir pa tion (eks′tər pā′shən), 1. complete removal; total destruction. 2. tearing up by the roots. *n. 15.*

ex tol or **ex toll** (eks tōl′), praise highly. *v., extolled, extolling. 6.*

ex tort (eks tôrt′), obtain (money, a promise, etc.) from a person by force, threat, wrong use of authority, etc. *v. 11.*

ex tor tion (eks tôr′shən), 1. extorting. 2. something extorted. Very high interest on loans is considered extortion and is forbidden by law. *n. 12.*

ex tor tion ate (eks tôr′shən it), 1. characterized by extortion; as, extortionate demands. 2. much too great; as, an extortionate price. *adj.*

ex tra (eks′trə), 1. beyond what is usual, expected, or needed; as, extra pay, extra fine quality, extra fare. 2. anything that is extra. Her bill for extras was $30. 3. special edition of a newspaper. *adj., adv., n. 4.*

ex tract (eks trakt′ for 1, eks′trakt for 2), 1. draw out, usually with some effort; take out; as, to extract oil from olives or iron from the earth, to extract a tooth, to extract pleasure from a situation. 2. something drawn out or taken out. He read several extracts from the poem. Vanilla extract is made from vanilla beans. *v., n. 5.*

ex trac tion (eks trak′shən), 1. extracting; being extracted; as, the extraction of a tooth. 2. descent; origin. Miss Del Rio is of Spanish extraction. *n. 15.*

ex trac tor (eks trak′tər), one that extracts. *n. 20.*

ex tra dite (eks′trə dīt), 1. give up (a fugitive or prisoner) to another nation or authority. If an escaped prisoner of the State of Ohio is caught in Indiana, he can be extradited from Indiana to Ohio. 2. obtain the surrender of (such a person). *v. 20.*

ex tra di tion (eks′trə dish′ən), the surrender of a fugitive or prisoner by one nation or authority to another. *n. 16.*

ex tra ne ous (eks trā′ni əs), from outside; not belonging; foreign. A gritty feeling showed that some extraneous matter had got into the butter. *adj. 20.*

ex traor di nar i ly (eks trôr′di nãr′i li), most unusually. *adv. 12.*

ex traor di nar y (eks trôr′di nãr′i), 1. beyond what is ordinary; very unusual; remarkable; special. Seven feet is an extraordinary height for a man. 2. special. An envoy extraordinary is one sent on a special mission. *adj. 4.*

ex trav a gance (eks trav′ə gəns), 1. careless and lavish spending; waste. His extravagance kept him always in debt. 2. going beyond the bounds of reason. The extravagance of his story made us doubt him. *n. 11.*

ex trav a gant (eks trav′ə gənt), 1. spending carelessly and lavishly; wasteful. An extravagant man has extravagant tastes and habits. 2. beyond the bounds of reason; as, extravagant language, extravagant actions. *adj. 7.*

ex treme (eks trēm′), 1. very great; very strong; as, extreme love for one's country. 2. at the very end; the farthest possible; last. 3. something extreme. Love and hate are two extremes of feeling. **Go to extremes** means to do or say too much. *adj., n. 2.*

ex treme ly (eks trēm′li), much more than usual; very. *adv. 3.*

ex trem ist (eks trēm′ist), person who goes to extremes; supporter of extreme doctrines or practices. *n. 16.*

ex trem i ty (eks trem′i ti), 1. the very end; the tip. 2. **The extremities** are the hands and feet. 3. extreme degree. Perfect bliss is the extremity of happiness. 4. an extreme measure. The soldiers were forced to the extremity of firing to scatter the mob. 5. **In extremity** means in very great danger or need. People on a sinking ship are in extremity. *n., pl. extremities. 6.*

ex tri cate (eks′tri kāt), release; free from entanglements, difficulties, embarrassing situations, etc. Tom extricated the kitten from the net. *v. 13.*

ex trin sic (eks trin′sik), 1. not essential. 2. caused by external circumstances. 3. external; coming from without. *adj.*

ex u ber ance (eg zü′bər əns), 1. luxuriant growth; as, exuberance of shrubbery. 2. very great abundance. *n. 15.*

ex u ber ant (eg zü′bər ənt), very abundant; luxuriant; overflowing; lavish. *adj. 14.*

ex ude (eg züd′ or eks ūd′), 1. come or send out in drops; ooze. Sweat exudes from the pores in the skin. 2. give forth. Some successful men exude self-confidence. *v. 18.*

ex ult (eg zult′), be very glad; rejoice greatly. The winners exulted in their victory. *v. 7.*

ex ult ant (eg zul′tənt), exulting; rejoicing greatly; triumphant. *adj. 13.*

ex ul ta tion (eg′zul tā′shən), great joy; triumph. There was exultation over the army's victory. *n. 8.*

-ey, suffix meaning:—full of; containing; like; as in clayey, skyey.

eye (ī), 1. the part of the body by which men and animals see. 2. action of the eye; seeing. 3. power of seeing. An artist should have an eye for color. 4. look; glance. 5. to watch; observe. The children eyed the stranger.

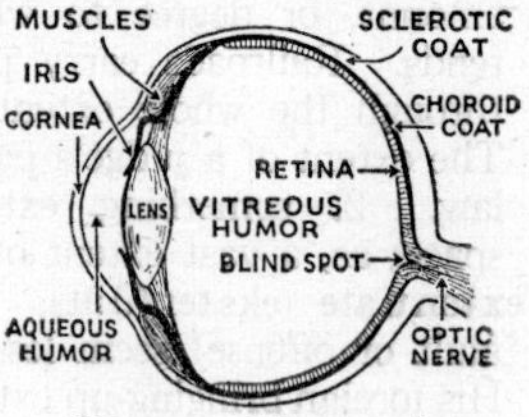

MUSCLES
SCLEROTIC COAT
IRIS
CORNEA
CHOROID COAT
RETINA
LENS
VITREOUS HUMOR
BLIND SPOT
AQUEOUS HUMOR
OPTIC NERVE

Diagram of the eye of a human being

6. way of looking. Taking stolen goods is a crime in the eye of the law. 7. regard; view; aim. 8. something like an eye or that suggests an eye. The little spots on potatoes, the hole in a needle, and the loop into which a hook fastens are all called eyes. 9. Some special meanings are:

an eye for an eye, punishment as severe as the injury.

catch one's eye, attract one's attention.

have an eye to, look out for; pay attention to. Almost everyone has an eye to his own advantage.

in the public eye, 1. often seen in public. 2. widely known.

keep an eye on, look after; watch carefully. Keep an eye on the baby.

make eyes at, look at with liking or love.

open a person's eyes, make him see what is really happening.

see eye to eye, agree entirely.

set eyes on, see; look at.

n., v., eyed, eying or *eyeing. 1.*

eye ball (ī′bôl′), the eye without the surrounding lids and bony socket. It is shaped like a ball. *n. 10.*

eye brow (ī′brou′), 1. arch of hair above the eye. 2. bony ridge that it grows on. *n. 6.*

eye glass (ī′glas′), 1. a lens to aid poor vision. 2. **Eyeglasses** means a pair of glass lenses to help vision. *n.*

eye lash (ī′lash′), 1. one of the hairs on the edge of the eyelid. 2. fringe of such hairs. *n. 18.*

eye less (ī′lis), without eyes. *adj. 17.*

eye let (ī′lit), 1. small, round hole for a lace or cord to go through. 2. metal ring around such a hole to strengthen it. *n. 11.*

eye lid (ī′lid′), the cover of skin, upper or lower, by means of which we can shut and open our eyes. *n. 6.*

eye piece (ī′pēs′), the lens or lenses in a telescope, microscope, etc., that are nearest the eye of the user. *n.*

eye sight (ī′sīt′), sight; power to see. *n. 9.*

eye sore (ī′sōr′), something offensive to the eye. A garbage heap is an eyesore. *n.*

eye strain (ī′strān′), tired or weak condition of the eyes caused by using them too much, reading in a dim light, etc. *n.*

eye wit ness (ī′wit′nis), person who sees some act or happening. *n.*

ey rie or **ey ry** (ãr′i), 1. an eagle's nest. 2. an eagle's brood. 3. lofty position. *n., pl. eyries. 17.* Also spelled **aerie** or **aery.**

E zek iel (i zēk′yəl), 1. Hebrew prophet. 2. book of the Old Testament. *n.*

Ez ra (ez′rə), a book of the Old Testament. *n. 20.*

F

F, f (ef), the sixth letter of the alphabet. There are two f's in offer. *n., pl. F's, f's.*

F., Fahrenheit.

fa (fä), in music, the fourth tone of the scale. Do, re, mi, fa, sol, la, ti, do are the names of the tones of the scale. *n.*

Fa bi an (fā′bi ən), using stratagem and delay to wear out an enemy or opposition; cautious. *adj. 18.*

fa ble (fā′bəl), 1. story that is made up to teach a lesson. Fables are often about animals who can talk, such as *The Hare and the Tortoise* and *The Fox and the Crow.* 2. story that is not true. 3. tell or write fables. *n., v. 4.*

Fa bre (fä′brə), Jean Henri, French student of insects and author of interesting books about them (1823-1915). *n.*

fab ric (fab′rik), 1. cloth; woven or knitted material. Velvet, canvas, linen, and flannel are fabrics. 2. thing that is put together. 3. frame or structure; way in which a thing is put together. *n. 6.*

fab ri cate (fab′ri kāt), 1. build; construct; manufacture. Automobiles are fabricated from parts made in different factories. 2. make up; invent (a story, lie, excuse, etc.). *v. 14.*

fab ri ca tion (fab′ri kā′shən), 1. fabricating; manufacture. 2. something fabricated; story, lie, excuse, etc. *n. 16.*

fab u lous (fab′ū ləs), 1. like a fable. 2. not believable; amazing. That antique shop asks fabulous prices. 3. of or belonging to a fable; imaginary. The phoenix is a fabulous bird. *adj. 8.*

fa çade (fə säd′), the front of a building. *n. 12.*

face (fās), 1. the front part of the head. Your eyes, nose, and mouth are parts of your face. 2. look; expression. His face was sad. 3. the front part; the right side; surface; as, the face of a clock, the whole face of the earth. 4. outward appearance. This action, on the face of it, looks bad. 5. to front toward. The house faces the street. The picture faces page 60 in my book. 6. meet bravely or boldly. 7. boldness; impudence. 8. dignity; self-respect. Face is very important to Oriental peoples. 9. stated value. The face of the note was $100, but $73 was all that anybody would pay for it. 10. cover with a different material. She faced the sleeves with silk. A wooden house is sometimes faced with brick. 11. **In the face of** means (1) in the presence of. (2) in spite of. *n., v. 1.*

fac et (fas′it), one of the polished surfaces of a cut gem. *n. 18.*

Cut gem showing facets

fa ce tious (fə sē′shəs), 1. having the habit of joking. 2. said in fun; not to be taken seriously. Facetious remarks are out of place at a funeral. *adj. 15.*

fa cial (fā′shəl), 1. of the face; as, a facial massage. 2. for the face. *adj. 10.*

fac ile (fas′il), 1. easily done, used, etc.; as, a facile task, facile methods. 2. moving, acting, working, etc., with ease; as, a facile hand, a facile tongue, a facile pen. 3. of easy manners or temper; agreeable; yielding. Alice's facile nature readily adapted itself to any company. *adj. 10.*

fa cil i tate (fə sil′i tāt), make easy; lessen the labor of; help forward; assist. A vacuum cleaner facilitates housework. *v. 10.*

fa cil i ty (fə sil′i ti), 1. ease; absence of difficulty. The boy ran and dodged with such facility that no one could catch him. 2. power to do anything easily, quickly, and smoothly. 3. aid; convenience; something which makes an action easy. Ropes, swings, and sand piles are facilities for play. *n., pl. facilities. 7.*

fac ing (fās′ing), 1. a covering of different material for ornament, protection, etc. A wooden house sometimes has a brick facing. 2. material put around the inside or outside edge of cloth to protect or trim it; as, a blue coat with red facings on the collar and cuffs. *n. 20.*

fac sim i le (fak sim′i li), an exact copy or likeness. *n.*

fact (fakt), 1. thing known to be true; thing known to have happened. 2. what is real; truth. 3. thing said or supposed to be true or to have really happened. We doubted his facts. *n. 1.*

fac tion (fak′shən), 1. group of persons who stand up for their side against the rest of a larger group. 2. selfish or unscrupulous group. A faction in our church tried to make the pastor resign. 3. strife among the members of a political party, club, or neighborhood. *n. 6.*

fac tious (fak′shəs), 1. fond of party strife; stirring up disputes. 2. of or caused by faction. *adj. 13.*

fac ti tious (fak tish′əs), forced; developed by effort; not natural; artificial. Extensive advertising can cause a factitious demand for an article. *adj. 15.*

fac tor (fak′tər), 1. any one of the causes of a result; one element in a situation. Ability, industry, and health are factors of success in school. 2. any of the numbers or expressions which, when multiplied together, form a product. 2 and 5 are factors of 10. 3. separate into factors. 4. person who does business for another; agent. *n., v. 7.*

fac to ry (fak′tə ri), 1. a building or group of buildings where things are manufactured. A factory usually has machines in it. 2. a trading post in a foreign country. *n., pl. factories. 3.*

fac to tum (fak tō′təm), person employed to do all kinds of work. Tony is our factotum; he takes care of the furnace and the garden, washes the windows and the dog, and does many odd jobs besides. *n. 20.*

fac tu al (fak′chü əl), concerned with fact; consisting of facts. *adj.*

fac ul ty (fak′əl ti), 1. power to do some special thing, especially a power of the mind. Nell has a great faculty for arithmetic. Old people sometimes lose their faculties. 2. the teachers of a school, college, or university. 3. a department of learning in a university; as, the faculty of theology, of law, or of medicine. *n., pl. faculties. 5.*

fad (fad), 1. a fashion or craze; something everybody is doing for a time. This new game is only a fad. 2. hobby. Collecting stamps is a fad. *n. 13.*

fade (fād), 1. become less bright; lose color. Daylight fades when the sun sets. Colored cloth often fades when it is washed. 2. become weak; die slowly. The sound fades after a train goes by. Flowers fade. 3. cause to fade. Sunlight will fade some dresses. *v. 2.*

faer ie (făr′i), 1. fairyland. *Old use.* 2. fairy. *n., adj. 13.*

faer y (făr′i), faerie. *n., pl. faeries, adj.*

fag (fag), 1. work hard or until wearied. Tom fagged away at his arithmetic. 2. tire by work. The horse was fagged. 3. hard, uninteresting work. 4. in English schools, a boy who waits on an older boy. 5. be a fag; make a fag of. 6. a drudge. *v., fagged, fagging, n. 19.*

fag end, 1. the last and poorest part of anything; remnant. 2. the unfinished end of a piece of cloth. 3. the untwisted end of a rope.

Fagot of twigs

fag got (fag′ət), fagot. *n., v. 11.*

fag ot (fag′ət), 1. a bundle of sticks or twigs tied together for fuel. 2. sew with an ornamental stitch. *n., v. 15.*

Fahr en heit (far′ən hīt). On the Fahrenheit thermometer, 32 degrees is the temperature at which water freezes, and 212 degrees is the temperature at which water boils. *adj. 9.*

Fagoting (def. 2)

fail (fāl), 1. not succeed; come to nothing; not be able to do. He tried hard to learn to sing, but he failed. 2. not do; neglect. He failed to follow our advice. 3. be of no use to when needed. When I wanted his help, he failed me. 4. be missing; be not enough. The wind failed us, so that we could not sail home. 5. grow weak; die away. The sick man's heart was failing. 6. not be able to pay what one owes; as, to fail in business. 7. **Without fail** means surely. *v., n. 2.*

fail ing (fāl′ing), 1. failure. 2. fault; weakness; defect. 3. lacking; in the absence of. Failing good weather, the game will be played indoors. *n., prep.*

fail ure (fāl′yər), 1. failing; lack of success. 2. falling short; as, failure of crops. 3. losing strength; becoming weak; as, failure of eyesight. 4. being unable to pay what one owes. 5. person or thing that has failed. The picnic was a failure because it rained. *n. 5.*

fain (fān), 1. gladly; willingly; by choice. 2. willing, but far from eager. 3. glad; willing. 4. eager; desirous. *adv., adj.* [*Used now only in poetry*] *6.*

faint (fānt), 1. a condition in which one lies as if dead and does not know what is going on around him. 2. fall into a faint. 3. **Feel faint** means feel ready to faint. 4. weak; dim; not plain; as, a faint voice, faint colors, a faint idea. *n., v., adj. 2.*

faint-heart ed (fānt′här′tid), lacking courage; cowardly; timid. *adj. 17.*

fair[1] (făr), 1. just; honest; as, fair play. 2. average; not bad. There is a fair crop of wheat this year. 3. light; not dark. She had fair hair and skin. 4. clear; sunny; not stormy. The weather will be fair today. 5. beautiful. The fair maiden smiled at him. 6. gentle; civil; courteous; as, fair words. 7. clean. Make a fair copy and throw that dirty one away. 8. plain; easily read; as, fair handwriting. 9. in a fair manner; honestly; as, fair-spoken, to play fair. 10. **Fair game** means game that it is right to hunt. 11. **Bid fair** means seem likely; have a good chance. *adj., adv. 1.*

fair[2] (făr), 1. a showing of products and manufactured goods for the purpose of helping people see what has been done and urging them to buy better seeds, stock, and machinery. 2. a gathering of people for the buying and selling of goods, often held at regular times during the year. 3. an entertainment and sale of articles. The church held a fair to raise money for charity. *n.*

fair ly (făr′li), 1. in a fair manner; justly. 2. moderately; rather. A fairly good pupil is neither bad nor very good. 3. actually; really. *adv. 7.*

fair ness (făr′nis), being fair. *n. 17.*

fair y (făr′i), 1. a tiny being, very lovely and delicate, who could help or harm human beings. 2. of fairies. 3. like a fairy; lovely; delicate. *n., pl. fairies, adj. 2.*

Fairy

fair y land (făr′i land′), 1. the place where the fairies live. 2. an enchanting and pleasant place. *n. 5.*

fairy tale, 1. a story about fairies. 2. something said that is not true.

faith (fāth), 1. trust; believing without proof. 2. believing in God or in God's promises. 3. what a person believes. 4. religion. 5. being loyal. 6. **Keep faith** means keep one's promise. 7. **In good faith** means honestly; sincerely. *n. 2.*

faith ful (fāth′fəl), 1. loyal; worthy of trust;

as, a faithful friend, a faithful servant. 2. true to fact; accurate; as, a faithful account of what happened. 3. **The faithful** means (1) true believers. (2) loyal followers or supporters. *adj., n. 2.*

faith ful ness (fāth′fəl nis), being faithful; being loyal; truth. *n. 9.*

faith less (fāth′lis), 1. not true to duty or to one's promises. A traitor is faithless. 2. without faith. He was a faithless unbeliever. *adj. 6.*

fake (fāk), 1. make up to seem satisfactory; hide defects. Jack faked an answer. 2. fraud. The beggar's limp was a fake. 3. false; intended to deceive; as, a fake telegram. *v., n., adj.* [*Used in common talk*] *18.*

fa kir (fə kēr′ or fā′kər), a Mohammedan or Hindu beggar. Fakirs sometimes do extraordinary tricks, such as lying upon sharp knives. *n.*

Falchion

fal chion (fôl′chən), a broad, short sword with an edge curving sharply to the point. *n. 16.*

fal con (fô′kən), 1. a hawk trained to hunt and kill birds and small game. In the Middle Ages, hunting with falcons was a popular sport. 2. swift-flying hawk having a short, curved bill and long claws and wings. *n. 6.*

fal con er (fô′kən ər), 1. man who hunts with falcons. 2. man who breeds and trains falcons. *n. 17.*

Falcon (17 in. long)

fal con ry (fô′kən ri), 1. the sport of hunting with falcons. 2. the training of falcons to hunt. *n. 17.*

fall (fôl), 1. drop or come down from a higher place. Snow is falling fast. His hat fell off. Leaves fall from the trees. 2. dropping from a higher place. The fall from his horse hurt him. 3. amount that comes down; as, the fall of rain for a year. 4. distance anything drops or comes down. The fall of the river here is two feet. 5. fall of water. 6. come down suddenly from a standing position. A baby often falls when learning how to walk. 7. coming down suddenly from a standing position. 8. become bad or worse. He was tempted and fell. 9. becoming bad or worse; ruin; destruction; as, Adam's fall. 10. be taken by any evil. The city fell into the power of its enemies. Rome fell. 11. die. Many men fell in battle. 12. pass into some condition, position, etc. He fell sick. The baby fell asleep. They fell in love. We fell to work. The honest country boy fell among thieves. The interest on the money falls due in May. 13. come by lot or chance. The choice falls on you. 14. happen. When night falls, it grows dark. 15. have proper place or position. The money fell to John as the only son. The accent of *farmer* falls on the first syllable. 16. proper place or position; as, the fall of an accent. 17. become lower or less. Prices are falling. The water in the river has fallen two feet. 18. becoming lower or less; as, a fall in prices, the fall of the tide. 19. be divided. His story falls into five parts. 20. to slope. The land falls away here. 21. a slope. 22. season of the year between summer and winter; autumn. 23. way of throwing or being thrown; as, falls in wrestling. 24. Some special meanings are:

fall back, retreat; go toward the rear.

fall back on, 1. go back to for safety. 2. turn to for help or support.

fall behind, be late in paying.

fall in, 1. take a place in line. "Fall in!" said the officer to the soldiers. 2. meet. On our trip we fell in with some interesting people. 3. agree. They fell in with our plans.

fall off, drop; become less.

fall on, attack.

fall out, 1. leave a place in line. "Fall out!" said the officer to the soldiers. 2. quarrel; stop being friends.

falls, waterfall; as, Niagara Falls.

fall through, fail.

fall to, begin.

fall under, come under.

fall upon, attack.

v., fell, fallen, falling, n. 1.

fal la cious (fə lā′shəs), 1. deceptive; misleading. 2. not logical. Faulty reasoning causes fallacious conclusions. *adj. 14.*

fal la cy (fal′ə si), 1. misleading argument; flaw in reasoning. 2. anything deceptive or false; delusion; error. It is a fallacy to suppose that riches always bring happiness. *n., pl. fallacies. 13.*

fall en (fôl′ən), 1. dropped. 2. face down; down on the ground; down flat. 3. degraded. 4. overthrown; ruined. 5. dead. 6. See **fall.** Much rain has fallen. *adj., pp. of fall. 3.*

fal li ble (fal′i bəl), liable to err; liable to be mistaken or deceived. *adj. 17.*

fal low (fal′ō), 1. plowed and left unseeded for a season or more; uncultivated. 2. land left unseeded for a season or more. 3. plowing of land without seeding it for a season in order to destroy weeds, improve the soil, etc. *adj., n. 9.*

fallow deer, small, European deer with a yellowish coat that is spotted with white in the summer.

Fallow deer (3 ft. high at the shoulder)

Fall River, a seaport city in Massachusetts.

false (fôls), 1. not true; not correct; wrong. A false note is wrong in pitch. A false step is a stumble or a mistake. 2. lying; as, a false witness. 3. disloyal; deceitful; as, a false friend, a man false to his promise. 4. used to deceive; as, false weights, false signals. A ship sails under **false colors** when she raises the flag of another country than her own. A **false bottom** in a trunk or drawer is used to form a secret compartment. 5. not real; artificial; as, false teeth, false diamonds. 6. based on wrong notions; ill-founded. False pride kept the poor man from accepting money from his rich brothers. 7. improperly so called. One name for the locust tree is "false acacia." 8. in a false manner. *adj., adv. 2.*

false hood (fôls′hu̇d), 1. a lie. 2. a being false; falsity. *n. 4.*

false ness (fôls′nis), being false; falsity. *n. 20.*

fal set to (fôl set′ō), 1. an unnaturally high-pitched voice, especially in a man. 2. person who sings with such a voice. 3. of or for such a voice. *n., pl. falsettos, adj.*

fal si fi ca tion (fôl′si fi kā′shən), making false; alteration made to deceive. The falsification of the will was not detected for three months. *n.*

fal si fy (fôl′si fī), 1. make false or incorrect; change in order to deceive; misrepresent. The cheat falsified his score. 2. lie. 3. prove to be false; disprove. Investigations falsified the pretender's claims. *v., falsified, falsifying. 16.*

fal si ty (fôl′si ti), 1. being false; incorrectness. Education shows us the falsity of superstitions. 2. untruthfulness; deceitfulness; treachery. *n., pl. falsities. 18.*

Fal staff (fôl′staf). Sir John Falstaff is a fat, boastful, brazen, jolly character in some of Shakespeare's plays. *n. 18.*

fal ter (fôl′tər), 1. not go straight on; hesitate; waver; lose courage. The soldiers faltered for a moment as their captain fell. 2. become unsteady in movement; stumble; stagger. 3. speak in hesitating and broken words. Greatly embarrassed, he faltered out his thanks. 4. faltering. *v., n. 6.*

fame (fām), 1. having a good deal said about one; fact, state, or condition of being well known; as, the fame of George Washington. 2. what is said about one. *n. 2.*

famed (fāmd), made famous; celebrated; well known. *adj.*

fa mil iar (fə mil′yər), 1. known to all. A knife is a familiar tool. 2. well known. French was as familiar to him as English. 3. well acquainted. He is familiar with French. 4. close; personal; intimate. Familiar friends know each other very well. 5. like home; friendly; not stiff or formal. 6. too friendly; forward. His manner is too familiar. 7. a spirit or demon supposed to serve a person. A black cat was thought to be a witch's familiar. *adj., n. 2.*

fa mil i ar i ty (fə mil′i ar′i ti), 1. close acquaintance. 2. freedom of behavior suitable only to friends; lack of formality or ceremony. 3. an instance of such behavior. She dislikes such familiarities as the use of her first name by people that she has just met. *n., pl. familiarities. 10.*

fa mil iar ize (fə mil′yər īz), 1. make (a person) well acquainted with something. Before playing the new game familiarize yourself with the rules. 2. make well known. Radio has familiarized the word *broadcast*. *v. 15.*

fam i ly (fam′i li), 1. father, mother, and their children. 2. children; offspring. She brought up a family. 3. group of people living in the same house. 4. all of a person's relatives. 5. tribe; race; group of related people. 6. group of related animals or plants. Lions, tigers, and leopards belong to the cat family. 7. any group of related or similar things. *n., pl. families. 1.*

fam ine (fam′in), 1. lack of food in a place; a time of starving. Many people died during the famine in India. 2. a very great lack of anything; as, a coal famine. 3. starvation. *n. 3.*

fam ish (fam′ish), be very hungry; starve; starve to death. *v. 8.*

fa mous (fā′məs), very well known; noted. A great crowd of people greeted the famous hero. *adj. 1.*

fa mous ly (fā′məs li), 1. in a famous manner. 2. excellently. *adv.*

Lady's fan

Electric fan

fan[1] (fan), 1. thing with which to stir the air in order to cool a room or one's face, or to blow dust away. 2. thing that is flat and spread out. 3. stir (the air); blow on; stir up. *n., v., fanned, fanning. 2.*

fan[2] (fan), person extremely interested (in baseball, movies, radio, etc.). *n.* [*Slang*]

fa nat ic (fə nat′ik), 1. person who is carried away beyond reason by his feelings or beliefs. My friend was such a fanatic about fresh air that he would not stay in any room with the windows closed. 2. enthusiastic or zealous beyond reason. *n., adj. 9.*

fa nat i cal (fə nat′i kəl), enthusiastic or zealous beyond reason, especially in religion. *adj. 15.*

fa nat i cism (fə nat′i sizm), unreasoning enthusiasm or zeal. *n. 15.*

fan ci er (fan′si ər), person who is especially interested in something. A dog fancier is interested in breeding and raising dogs. *n. 14.*

fan ci ful (fan′si fəl), 1. showing fancy; quaint; odd; fantastic; as, a fanciful decoration. 2. led by fancy; using fancies. Hans Christian Andersen is a fanciful writer. 3. imaginary; unreal. A story about a trip to the moon is fanciful. *adj. 12.*

fan cy (fan′si). All the meanings of fancy have something to do with the imagination or play of the mind. 1. picture to oneself; imagine. Can you fancy yourself in fairyland? 2. power to imagine. Dragons, fairies, and giants are creatures of fancy. 3. something imagined. Is it a fancy, or do I hear a sound? 4. like. I fancy the idea of having a picnic. 5. liking. He has a fancy for bright ties. 6. arranged especially to please; as, fancy dress, fancy dancing, fancywork. 7. costing extra to please the mind; as, fancy fruits, a fancy price. *v., fancied, fancying, n., pl. fancies, adj., fancier, fanciest. 2.*

fane (fān), temple; church. *n.* [*Used now only in poetry*] *12.*

fan fare (fan′fãr), 1. a short tune played on trumpets, bugles, or the like. 2. a showy parade. *n.*

fang (fang), 1. a long, pointed tooth of a dog or wolf or snake. 2. something like it. The root of a tooth is called a fang. *n. 9.*

Fangs of a snake

fan tail (fan′tāl′), 1. tail, end, or part spread out like an open fan. 2. pigeon whose tail spreads out like an open fan. See the picture just below. *n.*

fan tas tic (fan tas′tik), odd; due to fancy; unreal; strange and wild in shape or manner. Many dreams are fantastic. *adj. 6.*

fan tas ti cal (fan tas′ti kəl), fantastic. *adj. 14.*

Fantail

fan ta sy (fan′tə si), 1. imagination; play of the mind. 2. a picture in the mind. 3. a wild, strange fancy. *n., pl. fantasies. 9.*

far (fär), 1. a long way; a long way off. 2. more distant. He lives on the far side of the hill. 3. much. It is far better to go by train. 4. Some special meanings are:

by far, very much.

far and away, very much.

far and near, everywhere.

far and wide, everywhere; even in distant parts.

far cry, long way.

how far, how much; to what distance.

in so far as, to the extent that.

so far, 1. to this or that point. 2. until now or then.

adj., farther, farthest, adv., farther, farthest. 1.

far a way (fär′ə wā′), 1. distant; far away. 2. dreamy. She had a faraway look in her eyes. *adj. 14.*

farce (färs), 1. a play full of ridiculous or absurd happenings, meant to be very funny. 2. a show of doing something so easily seen through that it is absurd or ridiculous. *n. 7.*

far ci cal (fär′si kəl), ridiculous; absurd; improbable. *adj.*

fare (fãr), 1. the money that one pays to ride in a train, car, bus, etc. 2. passenger. 3. food. 4. **Fare well** or **ill** means have good or have poor food. 5. do; get on. He is faring well in school. 6. go; as, to fare forth on a journey. *n., v. 2.*

Far East, China, Japan, and other parts of eastern Asia.

fare well (fãr′wel′), 1. good luck; good-by.

2. good wishes at parting. 3. parting; as, a farewell kiss. *interj., n., adj. 2.*

far-fetched (fär′fecht′), not closely related to the topic; forced; strained. *adj.*

far-flung (fär′flung′), widely spread. *adj.*

farm (färm), 1. the land which a person uses to raise crops or animals. 2. raise crops or animals either to eat or to sell. 3. cultivate (land). 4. let for hire. Mr. Bond farms out the right to pick berries on his land. *n., v. 1.*

farm er (fär′mər), man who owns or works a farm. *n. 1.*

farm house (färm′hous′), the dwelling house on a farm. *n. 8.*

farm ing (fär′ming), business of raising crops or animals on a farm; agriculture. *n.*

farm stead (färm′sted), farm with its buildings. *n. 16.*

farm yard (färm′yärd′), the yard connected with the farm buildings or enclosed by them. *n. 7.*

far-off (fär′ôf′), distant; far away. *adj. 6.*

far-reach ing (fär′rēch′ing), having a wide influence or effect. *adj. 14.*

far ri er (far′i ər), 1. blacksmith who shoes horses. 2. veterinary; horse doctor. *n. 12.*

far row (far′ō), 1. litter of pigs. 2. give birth to pigs. *n., v. 20.*

far-see ing (fär′sē′ing), 1. able to see far. 2. planning wisely for the future. *adj.*

far-sight ed (fär′sīt′id), 1. seeing distant things more clearly than near ones. 2. seeing to a great distance. 3. looking ahead; shrewd; prudent. A far-sighted man saves money when wages are high. *adj.*

far-sight ed ness (fär′sīt′id nis), 1. the ability to see distant objects more clearly than near ones. 2. the ability to see at a great distance. 3. the power of looking ahead; shrewdness. *n. 20.*

far ther (fär′ᴛʜər), 1. more far. Three miles is farther than two. We walked farther than we meant to. 2. more; to a greater degree. Do you need farther help? 3. also; in addition. *adj., adv. 2.*

far ther most (fär′ᴛʜər mōst), most distant; farthest. *adj.*

far thest (fär′ᴛʜist), 1. most distant. 2. to or at the greatest distance. 3. most. 4. longest. *adj., adv. 5.*

far thing (fär′ᴛʜing), an English coin, a fourth of a penny, worth about half a cent in United States money. *n. 9.*

fas ci nate (fas′i nāt), 1. charm. Alice is a fascinating girl. 2. hold motionless by strange power or by terror. Snakes are said to fascinate small birds. *v. 7.*

fas ci na tion (fas′i nā′shən), 1. a fascinating. 2. powerful attraction; charm. *n. 11.*

Fas cism (fash′izm), principles or methods of the members of a national society in Italy, formed in 1919 to oppose socialism and communism. *n.*

Fas cist (fash′ist), 1. person who favors and supports Fascism. 2. of or having to do with Fascism or Fascists. *n., adj.*

fash ion (fash′ən), 1. to make, shape, or form. He fashioned a whistle out of a piece of wood. 2. the way a thing is shaped or made or done. He walks in a peculiar fashion. 3. style. She likes to read about the latest fashions. **Set the fashion** means fix the fashion, method, etc., for others to follow. *v., n. 2.*

fash ion a ble (fash′ən ə bəl), 1. following the fashion; in fashion; stylish. 2. of, like, or used by people who set the styles. *adj. 6.*

fash ion a bly (fash′ən ə bli), in a fashionable manner. *adv.*

fast[1] (fast), 1. Airplanes go fast. A fast runner can beat a slow one. The car made a fast trip. 2. When a watch is fast, it shows time ahead of what it really is. 3. Fast sometimes means too gay or wild. He led a fast life, drinking and gambling. 4. firmly fixed. This is a fast color which will not wash out. He held fast as the car went on down the hill. The fox was caught fast in the trap. 5. firm. They were fast friends. 6. thoroughly. The baby is fast asleep. *adv., adj. 1.*

fast[2] (fast), 1. go without food; eat very little. Members of some churches fast on certain days. 2. fasting. 3. a day or time of fasting. *v., n.*

fas ten (fas′ən), tie, lock, or make hold together in any way; as, to fasten a dress, to fasten a door, to fasten two cars together, to fasten one's eyes on something. *v. 2.*

fas ten er (fas′ən ər), person or thing that fastens. *n. 20.*

fas ten ing (fas′ən ing), thing used to fasten something. Locks, bolts, clasps, hooks, buttons, etc., are all fastenings. *n.*

fas tid i ous (fas tid′i əs), hard to please; dainty in taste; easily disgusted. *adj. 13.*

fast ness (fast′nis), 1. strong, safe place; stronghold. The bandits hid in their mountain fastness. 2. firmness. *n. 12.*

fat (fat), 1. a white or yellow oily substance formed in the body of animals. 2. having much of this; as, fat meat. 3. having much flesh; well fed; as, a fat boy, a fat pig. 4. Live on **the fat of the land** means have the best of everything. 5. plentiful; full of good things. A fat job pays well. 6. make or become fat. 7. dull; stupid. *n., adj., fatter, fattest, v., fatted, fatting. 1.*

fa tal (fā′təl), 1. causing death; as, fatal accidents. 2. causing destruction or ruin. The loss of all our money was fatal to our plans. 3. important; fateful. At last the fatal day for the contest arrived. *adj. 3.*

fa tal i ty (fā tal′i ti), 1. fatal accident or happening; death. Automobiles cause thousands of fatalities every year. 2. fatal influence or effect; deadliness. Doctors are trying to reduce the fatality of diseases. 3. liability to disaster. 4. inevitable necessity. *n., pl. fatalities. 15.*

fa tal ly (fā′təl i), 1. in a manner leading to death or disaster. This man was fatally wounded. 2. according to fate. *adv.*

fate (fāt), 1. a power that is believed to fix what is to happen. He does not believe in fate. **The Fates** were three Greek goddesses who determined human life. 2. what is fixed to happen. 3. one's lot or fortune. In every game it was Mary's fate to get caught. *n. 2.*

fat ed (fāt′id), 1. controlled by fate. 2. destined. *adj.*

fate ful (fāt′fəl), 1. controlled by fate. 2. determining what is to happen; important; decisive. 3. showing what fate decrees; prophetic. 4. causing death, destruction, or ruin; disastrous. *adj. 20.*

fa ther (fä′ᴛʜər), 1. male parent. The father of a family tries to take good care of his children. 2. take care of as a father does. 3. person who helps to make something. 4. man who led in the early life of a country or a church. George Washington is called the father of his country. 5. be the cause of; originate. He fathered many inventions. 6. priest. 7. God is called **Our Father.** *n., v. 1.*

fa ther hood (fä′ᴛʜər hu̇d), condition of being a father. *n. 18.*

fa ther-in-law (fä′ᴛʜər in lô′), father of one's husband or wife. *n., pl. fathers-in-law. 18.*

fa ther land (fä′ᴛʜər land′), one's native country. *n. 13.*

fa ther less (fä′ᴛʜər lis), 1. without a father living. 2. without a known father. *adj. 10.*

fa ther ly (fä′ᴛʜər li), 1. of a father. 2. like a father; like a father's. The old gentleman gave the little boy a fatherly smile. *adj. 12.*

fath om (faᴛʜ′əm), 1. a measure of 6 feet, used mostly in speaking of the depth of water. The ship sank in 10 fathoms. 2. find the depth of. 3. get to the bottom of; understand. *n., v. 6.*

fath om less (faᴛʜ′əm lis), 1. too deep to be measured. 2. that cannot be comprehended; as, the fathomless purposes of God. *adj. 12.*

fa tigue (fə tēg′), 1. make weary or tired. 2. weariness. *v., fatigued, fatiguing, n. 6.*

fat ness (fat′nis), amount of fat; state of being fat. *n. 13.*

fat ten (fat′ən), 1. make fat. 2. become fat. *v. 8.*

fat ty (fat′i), 1. of fat; containing fat. 2. like fat; oily; greasy. *adj., fattier, fattiest. 19.*

fat u ous (fach′ü əs), foolish; silly; stupid but self-satisfied. *adj. 20.*

fau cet (fô′sit), a device for controlling the flow of water or other liquid from a pipe or container holding it. See the picture. *n. 10.*

Faucet

fault (fôlt), 1. something that is not as it should be. Her dog has two faults; it eats too much, and it howls at night. 2. mistake. **Find fault** means find mistakes; complain. **Find fault with** means object to or criticize. *n. 2.*

fault find er (fôlt′fīn′dər), person who finds fault; person who complains. *n.*

fault find ing (fôlt′fīn′ding), complaining; finding fault. *n., adj.*

fault less (fôlt′lis), without a single fault or defect; perfect. *adj. 9.*

fault y (fôl′ti), having faults; imperfect; defective. *adj., faultier, faultiest. 9.*

faun (fôn), a Roman god that helped farmers and shepherds. A faun looked like a man, but had the ears, horns, tail, and sometimes the legs of a goat. *n. 11.*

Faun

fau na (fô′nə), the animals of a given region or time; as, the fauna of Australia, the fauna of the period before the glaciers. *n. 16.*

Faust (foust), in German legend, a man who sold his soul to the devil in return for having everything that he wanted on earth. *n. 16.*

fa vor (fā′vər), 1. kindness. Do me a favor. 2. show kindness to; oblige. Favor us with a song. 3. liking. The king looked on Joseph with favor. 4. prefer. We favor John's plan. 5. give more than is fair to. The teacher favors you. 6. aid; help. **In his favor** means for him; to his benefit. 7. a gift to show fondness. The knight wore his lady's favor on his sleeve. 8. look like. She favors her mother. 9. **In favor of** means (1) on the side of. (2) to the advantage of. *n., v. 1.*

fa vor a ble (fā′vər ə bəl), 1. favoring; approving; as, a favorable answer. 2. being to one's advantage; helping; as, a favorable wind. *adj. 3.*

fa vor a bly (fā′vər ə bli), with consent or approval; hopefully; kindly. *adv.*

fa vor ite (fā′vər it), 1. the one liked very much. Bob is a favorite with everybody. 2. liked best. What is your favorite flower? *n., adj. 2.*

fa vor it ism (fā′vər it izm), favoring a certain one more than others; having favorites. *n. 18.*

fawn[1] (fôn), 1. deer less than a year old. 2. light yellowish brown. *n., adj. 7.*

Fawn of the Virginia deer

fawn[2] (fôn), crouch and lick as a dog does; try to get favor or notice by slavish acts. Many flattering relatives fawned on the rich old man. *v.*

fay (fā), fairy. *n. 12.*

fe al ty (fē′əl ti), 1. loyalty and duty owed by a vassal to his feudal lord. The nobles swore fealty to the king. 2. loyalty; faithfulness; allegiance. *n. 10.*

fear (fēr), 1. a feeling which makes you turn away or run from something, or cover your eyes, or scream, or jump away. 2. have fear. 3. be afraid of. Cats fear big dogs. Monkeys fear big snakes. Babies fear loud noises. 4. have an uneasy feeling or idea. He fears that the children will be sick. I fear that I am late. *n., v. 1.*

fear ful (fēr′fəl), 1. causing fear; terrible; dreadful. 2. feeling fear; frightened. 3. showing fear. 4. easily frightened; timid. *adj. 3.*

fear less (fēr′lis), afraid of nothing; brave. *adj. 5.*

fea si bil i ty (fē′zi bil′i ti), feasible quality. *n.*

fea si ble (fē′zi bəl), that can be done; possible without difficulty or damage. The committee selected the plan that seemed most feasible. *adj. 12.*

feast (fēst), 1. a rich meal prepared for some special occasion, usually a rejoicing. 2. eat many good things. 3. provide a rich meal for. The king feasted his friends. 4. take delight in; delight. We feasted our eyes on the beautiful picture. 5. celebration. Christmas and Easter are the most important Christian feasts. *n., v. 2.*

feat (fēt), great deed; act requiring great skill, strength, or daring. *n. 5.*

feath er (feᴛʜ′ər), 1. Birds are covered with feathers which grow out from the skin. Feathers are very light, so that we say "as light as a feather." 2. supply or cover with feathers. 3. **A feather in one's cap** means something to be proud of. *n., v. 2.*

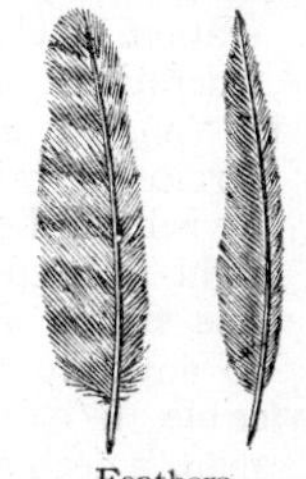
Feathers

feath er y (feᴛʜ′ər i), 1. having feathers; covered with feathers. 2. like feathers; as, feathery snow. 3. light; flimsy. *adj. 10.*

fea ture (fē′chər), 1. part of the face. Your features are your forehead, eyes, nose, mouth, chin, etc. 2. a distinct part or quality. Your plan for the picnic has many good features and some bad ones. 3. whatever makes a thing different from others. The main features of southern California are the climate and the scenery. 4. to outline; show the features of. 5. be or make a feature of. *Used in common talk. n., v. 2.*

Feb., February. *13.*

Feb ru ar y (feb′rü ãr′i), the second month of the year. It has 28 days except in leap years, when it has 29. *n. 2.*

fe cund (fē′kənd), fruitful; productive; fertile. Edison had a fecund mind. *adj.*

fe cun di ty (fi kun′di ti), fruitfulness; fertility; productiveness. *n. 14.*

fed (fed). See **feed.** We fed the birds yesterday. *pt. and pp. of feed. 2.*

fed er al (fed′ər əl), 1. of the central government of the United States, not of any State or city alone. The federal courts are managed by the national government. Congress makes the federal laws. Coining money is a federal power. 2. formed by an agreement of states. The League of Nations is a federal union. 3. favoring federal union or power. After the Revolutionary War the Federal Party wanted a strong central government. 4. person favoring federal union or power. The Federals supported the United States government during the Civil War. *adj., n. 5.*

fed er al ist (fed′ər əl ist), a supporter of federal union or power. *n. 14.*

fed er ate (fed′ər āt), form into a federation. *v.*

fed er a tion (fed′ər ā′shən), league; union by agreement, often a union of states or nations; as, a federation of students, a federation of clubs. The United States is a federation. *n. 8.*

fee (fē), 1. a charge; money paid for some service or privilege. The doctor's fee for a visit will be $3. 2. give a fee to. 3. the right to keep and use land. 4. ownership. **Fee simple** is ownership with right to sell to anybody. *n., v., feed, feeing. 4.*

fee ble (fē′bəl), weak; as, a feeble old man, a feeble mind, a feeble cry, a feeble attempt. *adj. 3.*

fee ble-mind ed (fē′bəl mīn′did), weak in mind; lacking normal intelligence. *adj. 19.*

fee ble ness (fē′bəl nis), weakness. *n. 16.*

fee bly (fē′bli), weakly. *adv.*

feed (fēd), 1. We feed a baby who cannot feed himself. We put cows to feed in the meadow. Feed this grain to the chickens. Feed the fire. 2. Corn is used as chicken feed. *v., fed, feeding, n. 1.*

feed er (fēd′ər), 1. person who feeds. 2. thing that supplies or feeds into something else. These brooks are feeders of the big river. A branch railroad or canal that brings traffic to the main line is a feeder. 3. eater. *n. 6.*

feel (fēl), 1. touch. Feel the cloth. 2. try to touch; try to find by touching. He felt in his pocket for a match. 3. find out by touching. Feel how cold my hands are. 4. be aware of. He felt the cool breeze. She felt the heat. 5. be. She feels glad. He feels angry. 6. have the feeling of being. We felt hot. She felt sure. 7. give the feeling of being. The air feels cold. Your dress feels wet. 8. have in one's mind; experience. They feel pity. I felt pain. He felt fear of the thunder. 9. have a feeling. I felt for the poor, lonesome dog. Try to feel more kindly toward her. I feel that Jack will come. 10. feeling. Wet soap has a greasy feel. *v., felt, feeling, n. 1.*

feel er (fēl′ər), 1. something that feels. A cat's whiskers are its feelers. The long feelers on the heads of insects help them find their way. 2. a suggestion, remark, hint, or question meant to bring out the plans, opinions, or purposes of others. *n. 9.*

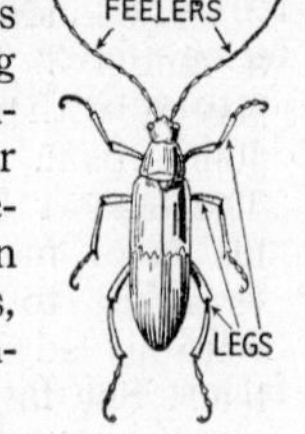

feel ing (fēl′ing), 1. the sense of touch. By feeling we tell what is hard from what is soft. 2. awareness. 3. emotion. The loss of the ball game stirred up much feeling. 4. opinion. What is your feeling about this idea? 5. that feels; sensitive; as, a feeling heart. *n., adj. 2.*

feet (fēt), more than one foot. *n. pl. 1.*

feign (fān), 1. pretend. Some animals feign death when in danger. 2. make up to deceive; as, to feign an excuse. *v. 4.*

feint (fānt), 1. pretense. Jack made a feint of being absorbed in his lessons, but he was listening to the radio. 2. a movement made with the purpose of deceiving; a sham attack or blow. The fighter made a feint at his opponent with his right hand and struck with his left. 3. make a feint. *n., v. 16.*

feld spar (feld′spär′), a crystalline mineral, white or red in color. The feldspars are silicates of aluminum. *n.*

fe lic i tate (fi lis′i tāt), congratulate. The young man's friends felicitated him upon his engagement. *v.*

fe lic i tous (fi lis′i təs), appropriate; apt; well-worded; as, a felicitous speech of thanks. *adj. 18.*

fe lic i ty (fi lis′i ti), 1. happiness; bliss. 2. good fortune; blessing. 3. pleasing ability in expression; grace or appropriateness; as, the felicity of an author's style. 4. happy turn of thought; well-chosen phrase. *n., pl. felicities. 12.*

fe line (fē′līn), 1. belonging to the cat family. 2. an animal of the cat family. Tigers, lions, and leopards are felines. 3. catlike. The Indian stalked the deer with noiseless, feline movements. *adj., n.*

fell[1] (fel). See **fall.** Snow fell last night. *pt. of fall. 1.*

fell[2] (fel), 1. cause to fall; knock down. One blow felled him to the ground. 2. cut down (a tree). 3. turn down and stitch one edge of (a seam) over the other. *v*

fell[3] (fel), heavy; terrible; cruel; as, a fell blow, a fell disease, the murderer's fell plans. *adj.*

fell[4] (fel), the skin or hide of an animal. *n.*

fel loe (fel′ō), the circular rim of a wheel into which the outer ends of the spokes are inserted. See the picture. *n., pl. fel-loes. 16.* Also spelled **felly.**

fel low (fel′ō), 1. one; a man, boy, dog, etc. Never mind, old fellow. Poor fellow! 2. I or me. Have pity on a fellow. 3. companion; one of the same class; equal. He was cut off from his fellows. 4. the other one of a pair; a match. I have the fellow of your glove. 5. being in the same or a like condition; as, fellow citizens, fellow sufferers, fellow workers. 6. an honored member of a learned society. 7. person who has a fellowship from a university or college. *n., adj. 1.*

fel low ship (fel′ō ship), 1 companionship; friendliness. 2. being one of a group; membership; sharing. I have enjoyed my fellowship with you in this club. 3. a group. 4. money or position given by a university or college to a student to enable him to continue his studies. *n. 5.*

fel ly (fel′i), felloe. *n., pl. fellies.*

fel on[1] (fel′ən), 1. criminal. Murderers and thieves are felons. 2. wicked; cruel. *n., adj. 9.*

fel on[2] (fel′ən), very painful inflammation of a finger or toe near the nail. *n.*

fe lo ni ous (fi lō′ni əs), having to do with a felony; criminal; wicked. *adj. 20.*

fel on y (fel′ən i), a serious crime, such as murder or burglary. *n., pl. felonies. 14.*

felt[1] (felt). See **feel.** He felt the soft fur of the cat. Things are felt with the hands. *pt. and pp. of feel. 1.*

felt[2] (felt), 1. cloth not woven, but made by rolling and pressing wool, hair, or fur together. 2. made of felt; as, a felt hat. *n., adj.*

fe male (fē′māl), 1. woman or girl. 2. of or pertaining to women or girls. 3. belonging to the sex that brings forth young. Mares and cows are female animals. 4. animal belonging to this sex. *n., adj. 3.*

fem i nine (fem′i nin), 1. of women or girls. Jewelry and lace are mostly feminine belongings. 2. like a woman; womanly; weak; gentle. 3. in grammar, of the gender to which names of females belong. *Actress* and *tigress* are the feminine nouns for *actor* and *tiger*. *adj. 6.*

fe mur (fē′mər), thighbone. *n. 20.*

fen (fen), marsh; swamp; marshland. *n. 8.*

fence (fens), 1. something put around a yard, garden, field, farm, etc., to show where it ends or to keep out people or animals. Most fences are made of wood, wire, or metal. A stone fence is a wall. A fence of growing bushes is a hedge. 2. put a fence around. 3. **On the fence** means not having made up one's mind which side to take. 4. fight with long slender swords or foils. 5. person who buys stolen goods; his place of business. *n., v. 2.*

Girls fencing

fenc er (fen′sər), person who knows how to fight with a sword or foil. *n.*

fenc ing (fen′sing), 1. the art of attack and defense with swords or foils. 2. material for fences. 3. fences. *n.*

fend (fend), 1. ward off; as, to fend off blows with one's arm. 2. make defense. 3. **Fend for oneself** means provide for oneself; get along by one's own efforts. Some animals let their young fend for themselves at an early age. *v.*

fend er (fen′dər), 1. thing that protects by being between and keeping something off; as, the fender of an automobile, the fender of a streetcar or a locomotive. 2. the bar, frame, or screen before a fireplace to keep hot coals and sparks from the room. 3. the rope or log put between a boat and the landing. *n. 12.*

Fennel

fen nel (fen′əl), a tall plant with yellow flowers, whose seeds are used in medicine and cookery. *n. 16.*

fer ment (fər ment′ for 1 and 4, fėr′ment for 2 and 3), 1. undergo or produce a gradual chemical change, becoming sour or alcoholic and giving off bubbles of gas. Vinegar is formed when cider ferments. 2. substance that causes others to ferment. Yeast is a ferment. 3. tumult; excitement. The school was in a ferment. 4. excite; be excited. *v., n. 8.*

fer men ta tion (fėr′men tā′shən), 1. the change brought about by fermenting. The fermentation of milk is necessary in the making of cheese. 2. excitement; unrest. *n. 8.*

fern (fėrn), a kind of plant that does not have flowers. The feathery leaves are usually pretty. The tiny seeds (called spores) grow in the little brown dots on the backs of the leaves. *n. 4.*

Fern

fe ro cious (fi rō′shəs), fierce; savage; very cruel. *adj. 11.*

fe roc i ty (fi ros′i ti), fierceness; savageness; great cruelty. *n. 10.*

Fer ra ra (fe rä′rə), a city in northeastern Italy. *n. 17.*

fer ret (fer′it), 1. a kind of weasel used for killing rats, driving rabbits from their holes, etc. 2. to hunt with ferrets. 3. hunt; search. The detectives ferreted out the criminal. *n., v. 11.*

Ferret (about 1½ ft. long, including tail)

fer rule (fer′ül), a metal ring or cap put round the end of a cane, umbrella, etc., for strength or protection. *n. 14.* Also spelled **ferule.**

fer ry (fer′i), 1. carry (people and goods) back and forth across a river or narrow stretch of water. 2. the boat that makes the trip. 3. a place where boats carry people and goods across a river or narrow stretch of water. 4. go across in a ferryboat. *v., ferried, ferrying, n., pl. ferries. 5.*

fer ry boat (fer′i bōt′), boat that carries people, animals, and things across a river or narrow stretch of water. *n.*

Ferryboat leaving ferry

fer tile (fėr′til), 1. bearing seeds; bearing many seeds. 2. producing fruit; producing much fruit. 3. bringing forth; bringing forth many young ones. 4. able to bear seeds, fruit, or young. Chicks hatch from fertile eggs. 5. producing crops easily; as, fertile soil. 6. producing much of anything. *adj. 4.*

fer til i ty (fər til′i ti), 1. bearing, or abundant bearing, of seeds, fruits, crops, or young. 2. power to produce. Fertility of the mind means power to produce many ideas. *n. 8.*

fer ti li za tion (fėr′ti li zā′shən), 1. fertilizing. 2. being fertilized. *n. 9.*

fer ti lize (fėr′ti līz), 1. make fertile. 2. make (a thing) start to grow. 3. make (the soil) richer by adding manure or other fertilizer. *v. 6.*

fer ti liz er (fėr′ti līz′ər), manure or any substance spread over the soil to make it richer in plant foods. *n. 6.*

fer ule[1] (fer′ül), 1. stick or ruler for punishing children by striking them on the hand. 2. punish with a stick or ruler. *n., v. 14.*

fer ule[2] (fer′ül), ferrule. *n.*

fer vent (fėr′vənt), 1. showing warmth of feeling; very earnest. 2. hot; glowing. *adj. 8.*

fer vid (fėr′vid), burning; ardent; spirited; as, a fervid orator. *adj. 13.*

fer vor (fėr′vər), great warmth of feeling; earnestness. *n. 8.*

fes tal (fes′təl), of a feast or holiday; gay; festive. A wedding or a birthday is a festal occasion. *adj. 10.*

fes ter (fes′tər), 1. form pus. The neglected wound festered and became very painful. 2. a sore that forms pus; small ulcer. 3. cause pus to form. 4. cause soreness or pain; rankle. Resentment festered in his mind. 5. decay; rot. *v., n. 10.*

fes ti val (fes′ti vəl), 1. a day or special time of rejoicing or feasting, often in memory of some great happening. Christmas and Easter are two festivals of the Christian church. 2. celebration; entertainment. Every year the city has a music festival during the first week in May. 3. merrymaking. *n. 4.*

fes tive (fes′tiv), of or suitable for a feast or holiday; gay; merry. Helen's birthday was a festive occasion. *adj. 9.*

fes tiv i ty (fes tiv′i ti), rejoicing and feasting; being merry. The wedding festivities were very gay. *n., pl. festivities. 10.*

fes toon (fes tün′), 1. flowers, leaves, ribbons, etc., hanging in a curve. 2. form into festoons; adorn with festoons. The house was festooned with Christmas decorations. *n., v. 13.*

Festoon

fetch (fech), go and get; bring. Please

fetch me my glasses. These eggs will fetch a good price. *v. 2.*

fetch ing (fech′ing), charming; attractive. She wore a fetching hat. *adj.*

fete or **fête** (fāt), 1. festival; party. Mrs. Rich is holding a great fete for the benefit of the hospital. 2. entertain. The bride-to-be was feted by her friends. *n., v.*

fet id (fet′id), smelling very bad; stinking. *adj. 20.*

fe tish (fē′tish), 1. thing supposed to have magic powers. 2. any object of unreasoning reverence or blind devotion. Some people make a fetish of stylish clothes. *n. 17.*

Fetish from Africa

fet lock (fet′lok), 1. the tuft of hair above a horse's hoof on the back part of his leg. 2. the part of a horse's leg where this tuft grows. *n. 14.*

FETLOCK

fet ter (fet′ər), 1. chain or shackle for the feet. Fetters prevent escape. 2. bind with fetters; chain the feet of. 3. anything that shackles or binds. 4. bind; restrain. *n., v. 5.*

fet tle (fet′əl), condition; state. The horse is in fine fettle and will surely win the race. *n. 20.*

fe tus (fē′təs), embryo; young animal in the womb or in the egg. *n.* Also spelled **foetus.**

feud (fūd), 1. a deadly quarrel between families, often passed down from generation to generation. 2. bitter hatred between two persons or groups. *n. 8.*

feu dal (fū′dəl), of or having to do with feudalism. *adj. 8.*

feu dal ism (fū′dəl izm), the social and political system of Europe in the Middle Ages, by which men gave military or other service to their lord in return for protection and the use of land. *n. 18.*

feudal system, feudalism.

feu da to ry (fū′də tō′ri), 1. owing feudal services to a lord. Paying ransom for the lord if he were captured was a feudatory obligation. 2. feudal vassal. The duke summoned his feudatories to aid him in war. 3. feudal estate; fief. *adj., n., pl. feudatories. 20.*

fe ver (fē′vər), 1. body temperature that is greater than usual. A sick person may have a fever. 2. any sickness that heats the body and makes the heart beat fast; as, scarlet fever. 3. an excited, restless condition. When gold was discovered the miners were in a fever of excitement. *n. 2.*

fe vered (fē′vərd), 1. having fever. 2. excited; restless. *adj.*

fe ver ish (fē′vər ish), 1. having fever. 2. having a slight degree of fever. 3. excited; restless. 4. infested with fever; as, a feverish swamp. *adj. 8.*

few (fū), not many. There are few men more than six feet tall. Winter has not many warm days, only a few. *adj., n. 1.*

few ness (fū′nis), small number. *n. 20.*

fez (fez), a felt cap, usually red and ornamented with a long black tassel, formerly worn by Turkish men. *n., pl. fezzes.*

Fez

ff., and the following; and what follows.

fi an cé (fē′än sā′), man engaged to be married. *n. 17.*

fi an cée (fē′än sā′), girl or woman engaged to be married. *n.*

fi as co (fi as′kō), failure; breakdown. *n., pl. fiascos* or *fiascoes.*

fi at (fī′at), decree; order. *n. 15.*

fib (fib), 1. a lie about some small matter. 2. tell such a lie. *n., v., fibbed, fibbing. 13.*

fi ber (fī′bər), 1. thread; threadlike part. A muscle is made up of many fibers. 2. substance made up of threads or threadlike parts. Hemp fiber can be spun into rope or woven into a coarse cloth. 3. texture; as, cloth of coarse fiber. 4. character; nature. A person of strong moral fiber can resist temptation. *n. 5.*

fi bre (fī′bər), fiber. *n. 19.*

fi brin (fī′brin), a white, tough, elastic substance found in clotted blood and in some plants. *n. 17.*

fi brous (fī′brəs), stringy; made of fibers. *adj. 11.*

fick le (fik′əl), changing; not constant; likely to change without reason; as, fickle fortune, a fickle lover. *adj. 6.*

fic tion (fik′shən), something made up; a story that is not fact. Short stories and novels are fiction. *n. 6.*

fic ti tious (fik tish′əs), made-up; not real. *adj. 12.*

fid dle (fid′əl), 1. violin. 2. play the fiddle. *n., v.* [*Used in common talk*] *6.*

fid dler (fid′lər), person who plays the violin. *n. 13.*

fid dle stick (fid′əl stik′), 1. the bow with which a violin is played. 2. **Fiddlesticks!** means Nonsense! Rubbish! *n., interj.*

fi del i ty (fī del′i ti), 1. loyalty; being faithful. 2. accuracy; exactness. *n. 7.*

fidg et (fij′it), 1. move about restlessly; be uneasy. A child fidgets if he has to sit still a long time. 2. make uneasy. 3. condition of being restless or uneasy. The long, tiresome speech gave Bob the fidgets. *v., n. 14.*

fidg et y (fij′i ti), restless; uneasy. That fidgety girl keeps twisting her fingers and jerking her head and getting up out of her seat. *adj. 19.*

fie (fī), for shame; shame. Fie upon you! *interj. 11.*

fief (fēf), 1. piece of land held on condition of giving military and other services to the lord owning it in return for protection and the use of the land. 2. the land so held. *n. 15.*

field (fēld), 1. land with few or no trees. They rode through forest and field. 2. piece of land used for crops or for pasture. 3. piece of land used for some special purpose; as, a baseball field. 4. a battlefield. 5. land yielding some product; as, the coal fields of Pennsylvania, the gold fields of South Africa. 6. flat space. A field of ice surrounds the North Pole. 7. a space; region. There is a field of force at the end of a magnet. 8. a range or sphere of activity; as, the field of politics, the field of art, the field of science. 9. in baseball, to stop (a batted ball) and throw it in. 10. **Take the field** means begin a battle, campaign, game, etc. *n., v. 1.*

Field (fēld), Eugene, an American journalist and poet (1850-1895). *n.*

field day, 1. day for athletic contests and outdoor sports. 2. day when soldiers perform drills, mock fights, etc.

field er (fēl′dər), 1. a baseball player who is stationed outside the diamond to stop the ball and throw it in. 2. a similar player in the game of cricket. *n. 17.*

field glass, small telescope.

field gun, cannon mounted on a carriage for use in the field.

Field glasses

field marshal, army officer ranking next to the commander in chief in the British, German, and some other armies.

field mouse, mouse that lives in fields.

field piece (fēld′pēs′), field gun. *n.*

fiend (fēnd), 1. devil; an evil spirit. 2. very wicked or cruel person. *n. 5.*

fiend ish (fēn′dish), devilish; very cruel. *adj. 18.*

fierce (fērs), savage; raging; wild; violent; as, a fierce lion, fierce anger, a fierce wind. *adj. 2.*

fierce ness (fērs′nis), wildness and rage; cruelty. *n. 9.*

fi er y (fī′ri), 1. containing fire; burning; flaming. 2. like fire; very hot. 3. full of feeling or spirit; as, a fiery speech. 4. easily aroused or excited; as, a fiery temper. *adj., fierier, fieriest. 3.*

fies ta (fyes′tä), 1. religious festival; saint's day. 2. holiday; festivity. *n.*

fife (fīf), 1. a small, shrill musical instrument like a flute, played by blowing. Fifes are used with drums in warlike music. 2. play on a fife. *n., v. 6.*

Man playing a fife

fif teen (fif′tēn′), five more than ten; 15. *n., adj. 2.*

fif teenth (fif′tēnth′), 1. next after the 14th. 2. one of 15 equal parts. *adj., n. 5.*

fifth (fifth), 1. next after the 4th. 2. one of 5 equal parts. Twenty cents is a fifth of a dollar. *adj., n. 2.*

fif ti eth (fif′ti ith), 1. next after the 49th. 2. one of 50 equal parts. *adj., n. 12.*

fif ty (fif′ti), five times ten; 50. *n., pl. fifties, adj. 2.*

fig (fig), 1. a small, soft, sweet fruit that grows in warm regions. Figs are sometimes eaten fresh or canned, but usually are dried like dates and raisins. 2. the tree it grows on. 3. a very small amount. I don't care a fig for your opinion. *n. 4.*

Figs

Fig. or **fig.,** figure.

fight (fīt). When boys fight, they hit one another. Soldiers fight by shooting with guns. Countries fight with armies and ships. A fight ends when one side gives up. We speak of fighting disease and other bad conditions. We may fight against our own feelings and desires. **Fight shy of** means keep away from. *v., fought, fighting, n. 1.*

fight er (fīt′ər), one that fights. *n. 6.*

fig ment (fig′mənt), something imagined; made-up story. *n.*

fig ur a tive (fig′yər ə tiv), 1. representing by a likeness or symbol. Baptism is a figurative ceremony; it represents cleansing by religion. 2. full of figures of speech; using words out of their ordinary meaning. Much poetry is figurative. *adj. 14.*

fig ure (fig′yər), 1. symbol for a number. 1, 2, 3, 4, etc., are figures. 2. use numbers to find out the answer to some problem. 3. price. His figure for that house is very high. 4. Squares, triangles, cubes, and other shapes are called figures. 5. form or shape. I could see the figure of a woman against the window. 6. Figure is used in telling how a person looks. She was a figure of distress. He cut a poor figure. 7. person; character. George Washington is the best-known figure in American history. 8. be conspicuous; appear. 9. a design or pattern; as, the figures in the wallpaper or of a dance. 10. a form of speech in which the meaning is pictured, or in which words have not their usual meanings. "Heaven-kissing hills" is a figure of speech. 11. picture; drawing; diagram; illustration. This book has many figures to help explain words. 12. **Figure out** means think out; understand. *n., v. 1.*

Artist painting a design for a figured glass window

fig ured (fig′yərd), 1. decorated with a design or pattern; not plain. 2. formed; shaped. *adj.*

fig ure head (fig′yər hed′), 1. a figure placed for ornament on the front of a ship. 2. person who is head in name only, without real authority. *n. 19.*

Figurehead

figure of speech, expression in which words are used out of their literal meaning or out of their ordinary use to add beauty or force. Similes and metaphors are figures of speech.

Fi ji (fē′jē), islands in the southern Pacific Ocean. *n. 20.*

fil a ment (fil′ə mənt), very fine thread; very slender, threadlike part. The wire that gives off light in a bulb is a filament. *n. 8.*

FILAMENT

fil bert (fil′bərt), a kind of cultivated hazelnut. *n. 16.*

filch (filch), steal in small quantities. He filched apples from the pantry. *v. 14.*

file[1] (fīl), 1. place for keeping papers in order. 2. set of papers kept in order. 3. put away in order. 4. a row of persons or things one behind another; as, a file of soldiers, or ships sailing in file. 5. march or move in file. *n., v. 3.*

File for papers

file[2] (fīl), 1. steel tool with many small ridges or teeth on it. Its rough surface is used to smooth or wear away hard substances. See the picture just below. 2. smooth or wear away with a file. *n., v.*

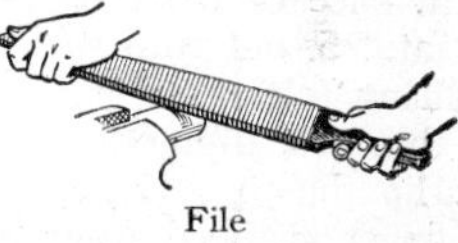

File

fi let (fi lā′), 1. net or net lace. 2. a slice of fish or meat without bones or fat; fillet. *n. 17.*

fil i al (fil′i əl), due from a son or daughter toward a mother or father; as, filial affection. *adj. 8.*

fil i bus ter (fil′i bus′tər), 1. a pirate. 2. person who without authority fights against a foreign state with which his own country may be at peace. 3. a member of a legislature who hinders the passage of a bill by long speeches or other tricks. 4. to act as a filibuster. *n., v.*

fil i gree (fil′i grē), 1. ornamented lacelike work of gold or silver wire. 2. anything very delicate or fanciful; as, frost filigree on window panes. *n. 17.*

Filigree around a gem

fil ings (fīl′ingz), small pieces removed by a file. *n. pl. 19.*

Fil i pi no (fil′i pē′nō), 1. a native of the Philippine Islands. 2. Philippine. *n., pl. Filipinos, adj. 20.*

fill (fil), 1. put into until there is room for nothing more; make full. Fill this bottle with water. Fill this hole with something. 2. become full. The well filled with water. 3. take up all the space in. Children filled the room. 4. that which fills. 5. as much

as there is room for. He ate his fill. 6. supply what is needed for. The druggist filled the doctor's prescription. Can John fill the office of class president? 7. Some special meanings are:
fill in, put in or insert.
fill out, 1. grow larger. 2. supply what is needed in.
fill up, fill; fill completely.
v., n. 1.

fill er (fil′ər), 1. person or thing that fills. 2. thing put in to fill something. A pad of paper for a notebook, a preparation put on wood before painting it, and the tobacco inside of cigars are all fillers. *n. 11.*

fil let (fil′it for 1, 2, and 3, fil′ā or fil′it for 4 and 5), 1. a band around the head to hold the hair in place, often ornamental. 2. a narrow band or strip of material. 3. bind with a fillet. 4. slice of meat or fish without bones or fat. 5. cut into such slices. *n., v. 9.*

Woman wearing a fillet

fill ing (fil′ing), thing put in to fill something; a filling in a tooth. *n.*

fil lip (fil′ip), 1. strike with the nail of a finger snapped from the end of a thumb. 2. tap or strike quickly. 3. the quick slight stroke thus given. 4. thing that rouses, excites, or revives. Relishes serve as a fillip to the appetite. *v., n. 17.*

Fill more (fil′mōr), Millard (1800-1874), the 13th president of the United States, from 1850 to 1853. *n.*

fil ly (fil′i), female colt; young mare. *n., pl. fillies. 17.*

film (film), 1. a very thin surface or coating, often of liquid; as, a film of oil over water. 2. cover or become covered with a film. Tears filmed her eyes. 3. a roll or sheet covered with a coating that is changed by light, used to take pictures. 4. a moving picture. 5. make a moving picture of. They filmed the scene three times. 6. photograph or be photographed for moving pictures. *n., v. 5.*

film y (fil′mi), 1. like film; very thin. 2. covered with a film. *adj., filmier, filmiest. 14.*

fil ter (fil′tər), 1. a device for passing water or other liquids, or air, through felt, paper, sand, or charcoal, in order to remove impurities. 2. the material through which the liquid or gas passes in a filter. 3. pass or flow slowly through a filter. The water filters slowly through the sand. 4. put through a filter. 5. act as a filter for. The charcoal filters the water. 6. remove by a filter. *n., v. 7.*

filth (filth), 1. foul dirt. 2. dirty words or thoughts. *n. 7.*

filth i ness (fil′thi nis), a filthy state or condition. *n. 17.*

filth y (fil′thi), very dirty; foul. *adj., filthier, filthiest. 6.*

fil tra tion (fil trā′shən), 1. filtering. 2. being filtered. *n. 15.*

fin (fin), 1. one of the movable winglike or fanlike parts at the sides and tail of a fish with which it moves the water in swimming and in balancing itself. The large fins of a flying fish unfold like a fan and can carry it a little way through the air. 2. thing shaped or used like a fin. *n. 7.*

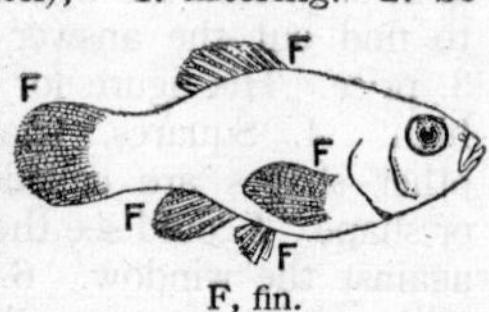

F, fin.

fi nal (fī′nəl), coming last; deciding; closing the question. **Finals** means the last or deciding set in a series of games or examinations. *adj., n. 2.*

fi na le (fi nä′li), 1. the concluding part of a piece of music or a play. 2. the end. *n. 18.*

fi nal i ty (fī nal′i ti), 1. being final, finished, or settled. John recognized the finality of his father's decision. 2. final act, speech, etc. *n., pl. finalities. 18.*

fi nal ly (fī′nəl i), 1. at the end; at last. 2. in such a way as to decide or close the question. *adv. 2.*

fi nance (fi nans′), 1. money matters. The millionaire boasted of his skill in finance. 2. provide money for. His father financed Dick's way through college. 3. **Finances** means money; funds; revenues; financial condition. *n., v. 7.*

fi nan cial (fi nan′shəl), 1. having to do with money matters. 2. having to do with the management of large sums of public or private money. *adj. 5.*

fi nan cial ly (fi nan′shəl i), in relation to finances; in respect to money matters. *adv.*

fin an cier (fin′ən sēr′), person occupied or skilled in money matters. Bankers are financiers. *n. 10.*

House finch (6 in. long)

finch (finch), a small songbird. See the picture. Sparrows, buntings, and canaries are finches. *n. 13.*

find (fīnd), 1. meet with; come upon. He found a dollar in the road. They found trouble everywhere. 2. look for and get. Please find my hat for me. 3. get; get the use of. 4. reach; arrive at. 5. learn; discover. We found that he could not swim. **Find out** means discover. 6. decide and declare. The jury found the thief guilty. 7. provide; supply. 8. finding. 9. something found. 10. **Find oneself** sometimes means learn one's abilities and how to make good use of them. *v., found, finding, n. 1.*

find er (fīn′dər), 1. person or thing that finds. 2. small extra lens on the outside of a camera that shows what is being photographed. *n.*

find ing (fīn′ding), 1. discovery. 2. thing found. 3. decision reached after an examination or inquiry. The verdict of a jury is its finding. *n.*

fine[1] (fīn), 1. Thread is finer than rope. Sand is finer than gravel. A spider web is fine. 2. Everybody praised her fine singing. Lee was a fine general. 3. without impurities. Fine gold is not mixed with any other metal. 4. delicate; refined. 5. clear; as, fine weather. *adj. 1.*

fine[2] (fīn), 1. a sum of money paid as a punishment for not doing the right thing. 2. make pay such a sum. *n., v.*

fine arts, arts appealing to the sense of beauty; painting, drawing, sculpture, architecture. Literature, music, dancing, and acting are also often included in the fine arts.

fine ness (fīn′nis), 1. thinness; as, the fineness of a line, thread, needle, or wire. 2. sharpness; as, the fineness of an edge or point. 3. degree of purity; as, the fineness of a metal. 4. clearness; as, the fineness of the weather. 5. fine quality; perfection; as, the fineness of goods. *n. 9.*

fin er y (fīn′ər i), showy clothes, ornaments, etc. *n., pl. fineries.*

fi nesse (fi nes′), 1. skill; delicacy of execution. Some artists show wonderful finesse. 2. skillful handling of a delicate situation to one's advantage. A shrewd diplomat must be a master of finesse. 3. use finesse. 4. in card games, playing a low card on the chance that it will take the trick. 5. make a finesse with a card. *n., v. 18.*

fin ger (fing′gər), 1. Each hand has one thumb and four fingers. 2. anything shaped or used like a finger. 3. touch or handle with the fingers; use the fingers on. *n., v. 1.*

fin ger print (fing′gər print′), 1. impression of the markings on the inner surface of the last joint of the thumb or a finger. A person's fingerprints can be used to identify him. 2. take the fingerprints of. *n., v.*

fin i cal (fin′i kəl), too dainty or particular; too precise; fussy. *adj.*

fi nis (fī′nis), the end. *n.*

fin ish (fin′ish), 1. end; as, to fight to a finish. 2. complete; bring to an end; reach the end of; as, to finish a dress, to finish one's dinner, to finish a race. 3. the way in which the surface is prepared; as, a smooth finish on furniture. 4. prepare the surface of in some way. 5. perfection; polish; as, the finish of a person's manners. 6. to perfect; to polish. *n., v. 1.*

fin ished (fin′isht), 1. ended. 2. completed. 3. brought to the highest degree of excellence. *adj.*

fi nite (fī′nīt), having bounds or limits. Human understanding is finite. *adj. 11.*

Fin land (fin′lənd), a country in northern Europe. *n. 11.*

Finn (fin), a native or inhabitant of Finland. *n. 18.*

fin nan had die (fin′ən had′i), smoked haddock.

Finn ish (fin′ish), 1. of or having to do with Finland, its people, or their language. 2. the language of Finland. *adj., n. 18.*

fin ny (fin′i), 1. abounding with fish. The sea is sometimes called the finny deep. 2. having fins. 3. like a fin. *adj. 20.*

Fiord

fiord (fyōrd), a long, narrow bay bordered by steep cliffs. *n. 13.*

fir (fėr), a tree somewhat like a pine. Small firs are often used for Christmas trees. The leaves have a pleasant smell. *n. 4.*

Branch of fir with cones

fire (fīr), 1. something burning. 2. a

flame. 3. make burn; set on fire. 4. to discharge. He fired his gun four times. 5. the discharge of guns. 6. arouse; excite; inflame. 7. heat of feeling; readiness to act; excitement. Their hearts and minds were full of fire. 8. Some special meanings are:
between two fires, attacked from both sides.
catch fire, begin to burn.
fire up, start a fire in a furnace, boiler, etc.
lay a fire, build a fire ready to be lit.
miss fire, 1. fail to go off. 2. fail to do what was attempted.
on fire, 1. burning. 2. full of feeling or spirit like fire.
under fire, 1. exposed to shooting from the enemy's guns. Soldiers are under fire in a battle. 2. attacked; blamed.
n., v. 1.

fire arms (fīr′ärmz′), guns, pistols, and other weapons to shoot with, usually such as a man can carry. *n. pl. 11.*

fire brand (fīr′brand′), 1. piece of burning wood. 2. person who arouses angry feelings in others. *n. 9.*

fire crack er (fīr′krak′ər), a paper roll containing gunpowder and a fuse. Firecrackers explode with a loud noise. *n.*

fire damp (fīr′damp′), a gas formed in coal mines, dangerously explosive when mixed with certain proportions of air. *n.*

fire engine, an engine for throwing water to put out fires.

Fire engine

fire escape, a stairway or ladder to use when a building is on fire.

fire fly (fīr′flī′), a small insect flying at night, which shines with a little light. See the picture under **lightning bug.** *n., pl. fireflies. 12.*

fire less (fīr′lis), without a fire. *adj. 14.*

fire light (fīr′līt′), the light from a fire. *n. 18.*

fire man (fīr′mən), 1. man who belongs to a fire company, trained to help put out fires. 2. man who looks after fires in engines, furnaces, etc., *n., pl. firemen. 7.*

Fireplace in a room

fire place (fīr′plās′), place built to hold a fire. Fireplaces are sometimes made of stones out of doors, but usually of brick or stone in a room, with a chimney leading up from them. Cooking used to be done over the fire in a big fireplace. *n. 6.*

fire proof (fīr′prüf′), 1. that will not burn, or will not burn easily; as, a fireproof building. 2. make so that it will not burn, or not burn easily; as, to fireproof a roof, to fireproof a theater curtain. *adj., v. 12.*

fire side (fīr′sīd′), 1. space around the fireplace. 2. beside the fire; as, fireside comfort. 3. hearth. 4. home. *n., adj. 7.*

fire wa ter (fīr′wô′tər), a word used by the American Indians for whiskey, gin, rum, or other strong liquors. *n.*

fire wood (fīr′wu̇d′), wood to make a fire. *n. 10.*

fire works (fīr′wėrks′), rockets, pinwheels, bombs, and other things that make a beautiful fiery display at night. *n. pl. 14.*

firm (fėrm), 1. not yielding when pressed; as, firm flesh, firm ground. 2. solid; fixed in place; not easily shaken or moved; as, a tree firm in the earth. We speak also of a firm voice, character, or belief. 3. a company of two or more persons in business together. *adj., n. 1.*

fir ma ment (fėr′mə mənt), the sky; the arch of the heavens. *n. 5.*

fir man (fėr′mən), order issued by an oriental ruler. *n. 20.*

firm ness (fėrm′nis), firm state; steadiness. *n. 8.*

first (fėrst), 1. coming before all others. John is first in his class. 2. what is first; the beginning. At first, John did not like school. 3. before all others; before anything else. We eat first and then feed the cat. 4. rather; sooner. The soldiers said they would never give up their flag, but would die first. 5. for the first time. When first I met her, she was a child. 6. in music, highest in pitch; playing or singing the part highest in pitch; as, first soprano, first violin. *adj., n., adv. 1.*

first aid, emergency treatment given to an injured person before a doctor comes.

first-aid (fėrst′ād′), of or for first aid. *adj.*

first-born (fėrst′bôrn′), 1. born first; oldest. 2. first-born child. *adj., n. 7.*

first-class (fėrst′klas′), 1. of the highest class or best quality; excellent. 2. on a first-class ship, train, etc. *adj., adv. 17.*

first fruits, 1. earliest fruits of the season. 2. first products or results of anything. *14.*

first-hand (fėrst′hand′), direct; from the original source; as, first-hand information. *adj., adv.*

first ling (fėrst′ling), the first of its kind; the first product or result; the first offspring of an animal. *n. 13.*

first-rate (fėrst′rāt′), 1. of the highest class. 2. excellent; very good. 3. excellently; very well. *Not used as an adverb in formal writing. adj., adv. 15.*

firth (fėrth), narrow arm of the sea. *n. 14.*

fis cal (fis′kəl), 1. financial. 2. having to do with public finance. *adj. 12.*

fish (fish), 1. an animal that lives in the water, is covered with scales, has gills to breathe with, and has a long backbone for support. 2. catch fish; try to catch fish. 3. try for something as if with a hook. Tom fished with a stick for his watch which had fallen through a grating. 4. find and pull. Jim fished the old map out of a box. *n., pl. fishes* or *fish, v. 1.*

fish er (fish′ər), 1. man who fishes; anything that fishes. 2. a kind of marten. See the picture. *n. 6.*

Fisher (about 2 ft. long, without the tail)

fish er man (fish′ər mən), man who fishes, especially one who makes his living by catching fish. *n., pl. fishermen. 4.*

fish er y (fish′ər i), 1. the occupation of catching fish. 2. place for catching fish. *n., pl. fisheries. 11.*

fish hawk, a large bird that feeds on fish; osprey.

fish hook (fish′hůk′), hook used for catching fish. *n. 15.*

fish ing (fish′ing), catching fish for a living or for pleasure. *n.*

fish mon ger (fish′mung′gər), dealer in fish. *n.*

fish wife (fish′wīf′), woman who sells fish. Fishwives are said to use coarse and abusive language. *n., pl. fishwives.*

fish y (fish′i), 1. fishlike in shape, smell, or taste. 2. abounding in fish. 3. doubtful; not probable; as, a fishy story. *Used in common talk. adj., fishier, fishiest.*

fis sure (fish′ər), a split; a crack; long, narrow opening. Water dripped from a fissure in the rock. *n. 9.*

fist (fist), the hand closed tightly. He shook his fist at me. *n. 3.*

fist i cuffs (fis′ti kufs′), a fight with the fists. *n. pl.*

fis tu la (fis′chů lə), 1. a tube or a pipe. 2. a long, tubelike sore. *n., pl. fistulas, fistulae* (-lē). *20.*

fit[1] (fit), 1. He is now well and fit for work. Grass is a fit food for cows; it is not fit for men. A lace dress is fit for parties. 2. be right, proper, or suitable to. 3. make right, proper, or suitable. 4. try to make fit; adjust. 5. to suit; as, to fit the action to the word. 6. the way something fits. The coat was not a very good fit. 7. **Fit out** means supply with everything needed. 8. **See fit** or **think fit** means decide. *adj., fitter, fittest, v., fitted, fitting, n. 1.*

fit[2] (fit), 1. a sudden, sharp attack of disease. 2. any sudden, sharp attack; as, a fit of anger. 3. a short period of doing some one thing; as, a fit of laughing. 4. **By fits and starts** means irregularly; starting, stopping, beginning again, and so on. *n.*

Fitch (about 17 in. long, without the tail)

fitch (fich), 1. a European animal like a weasel. 2. its fur. Fitch is yellowish with brown markings. *n. 17.*

fit ful (fit′fəl), irregular; going on and then stopping for a while; as, a fitful sleep, a fitful conversation. *adj. 13.*

fit ly (fit′li), 1. in a suitable manner. 2. at a proper time. *adv.*

fit ness (fit′nis), being fit; being right or suitable. *n. 8.*

fit ter (fit′ər), 1. person who fits dresses, suits, etc., on people. 2. man who supplies and fixes anything necessary for some purpose. A gas fitter fixes gas fixtures, stoves, etc. *n.*

fit ting (fit′ing), proper; suitable; fit. *adj.*

fit tings (fit′ingz), furnishings; fixtures. Desks, chairs, and files are office fittings. *n. pl.*

five (fīv), one more than four; 5. *n., adj. 1.*

five fold (fīv′fōld′), 1. five times as many or as much. 2. having five parts. *adj., adv.*

fix (fiks), 1. make firm; become firm. The man fixed the post in the ground. The boy fixed the spelling lesson in his mind. 2. settle; set; as, to fix a price, to fix an amount to be raised, to fix on a day for a picnic. 3. direct or hold steadily (eyes, attention, etc.); be directed. 4. put or place definitely; as, to fix the blame on someone. 5. make or become stiff or rigid; as, eyes fixed in death. 6. treat to prevent fading or otherwise changing; as, to fix a dye. 7. set right; put in order; as, to fix one's hair. 8. mend; repair; as, to fix a watch. 9. position hard to get out of. The boy who cried "Wolf" got himself into a bad fix. *v., n. 1.*

fix a tion (fiks ā′shən), 1. fixing; keeping fixed. 2. putting into a solid or lasting form; as, the fixation of a photographic film. *n. 14.*

fixed (fikst), made firm; set; definitely assigned; as, fixed charges for taxicabs. A **fixed idea** is a persistent idea, sometimes becoming an insane delusion. *adj.*

fix ed ly (fik′sid li), in a fixed manner; without change. She stared fixedly at the ring. *adv.*

fixed star, star whose position in relation to other stars appears not to change.

fix ture (fiks′chər), something put in place to stay; as, bathroom fixtures. *n. 7.*

fizz or **fiz** (fiz), 1. make a hissing sound. 2. hissing sound; bubbling. *v., fizzed, fizzing, n.*

fiz zle (fiz′əl), 1. make a hissing sound that dies out weakly. The firecracker did not go off with a bang, but just fizzled. 2. fizzling or hissing. 3. come to a poor end; fail. The plans for the picnic fizzled out. *Used in common talk.* 4. failure. *Used in common talk. v., n. 19.*

fjord (fyōrd), fiord. *n.*

Fla., Florida.

flab bi ness (flab′i nis), flabby quality or condition; being flabby in substance, purpose, or character. *n.*

flab by (flab′i), lacking firmness or force; soft; weak; as, flabby flesh, a flabby nature, a flabby will. *adj., flabbier, flabbiest. 15.*

flac cid (flak′sid), limp; weak; as, flaccid muscles, a flaccid will. *adj. 16.*

flag[1] (flag), 1. piece of cloth, usually with square corners, on which is the picture or pattern that stands for some country; as, the flag of the United States, the British flag. Flags are hung on poles over buildings, ships, army camps, etc. 2. Other flags mean other things. The white flag of truce means "Stop fighting." Pirate ships carried black flags. Weather flags are flown to let people know what kind of weather is coming. 3. to signal or stop (a person, train, etc.) by waving a flag. *n., v., flagged, flagging. 2.*

flag[2] (flag), a blue, white, purple, or yellow flower with sword-shaped leaves. *n.*

flag[3] (flag), droop; get tired; grow weak. My horse was flagging, but I urged him on. *v., flagged, flagging.*

Flag Day, June 14, the anniversary of the day in 1777 when the Stars and Stripes became the flag of the United States.

flag el la tion (flaj′ə lā′shən), whipping; scourging; lashing. *n.*

fla gi tious (flə jish′əs), shamefully bad or wicked. *adj. 19.*

flag on (flag′ən), 1. a container for liquids, with a handle, spout, and cover. 2. large bottle. *n. 14.*

Flagon

flag pole (flag′pōl′), pole from which a flag is flown. *n.*

fla grant (flā′grənt), glaring; notorious; scandalous. *adj. 15.*

flag ship (flag′ship′), the ship that carries the officer in command of a fleet and displays his flag. *n. 17.*

flag staff (flag′staf′), pole from which a flag is flown. *n.*

flag stone (flag′stōn′), a large, flat stone, used for paving paths, etc. *n.*

Flagstone path

flail (flāl), an instrument for threshing grain by hand. A flail consists of a wooden handle with a short, heavy stick fastened at one end by a thong. *n. 13.*

Farmer using a flail

flair (flãr), 1. natural talent. The poet had a flair for making clever rhymes. 2. keen perception. That trader had a flair for bargains. *n.*

flake (flāk), 1. a flat, thin piece, usually not very large, and sometimes rather loosely held together; as, a flake of snow, flakes of rust. 2. come off in flakes; separate into flakes. *n., v. 5.*

flak y (flāk′i), 1. consisting of flakes. 2. coming off in flakes. 3. like flakes. *adj., flakier, flakiest. 18.*

flam boy ant (flam boi′ənt), 1. flaming; gorgeous; showily striking. 2. marked in wavy, flamelike lines; as, flamboyant designs. *adj. 20.*

flame (flām), 1. one of the glowing tongues of light, usually red or yellow, that come when a fire blazes up. 2. blaze; rise up in flames. 3. be or act like a flame. 4. something like flame. *n., v. 2.*

fla min go (flə ming′gō), tropical wading bird with very long legs and neck, and feathers that vary from pink to scarlet. *n., pl. flamingos* or *flamingoes. 16.*

Red flamingo (about 4½ ft. tall from head to toe)

Flan ders (flan′dərz), a district in Europe, north of France. It is now part of France, Belgium, and the Netherlands. *n. 10.*

flange (flanj), an edge, collar, or rim, that stands out or is raised. It is used to keep an object in place, fasten it to another, strengthen it, etc. Railroad cars have wheels with flanges to keep them on the track. *n. 12.*

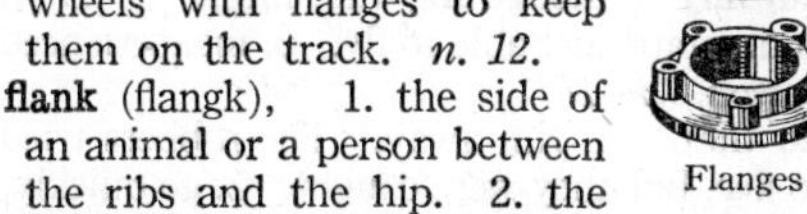
Flanges

flank (flangk), 1. the side of an animal or a person between the ribs and the hip. 2. the side of a mountain, building, etc. 3. be at the side of. 4. the far right or the far left side of an army, fort, or fleet. 5. get around the side of (an enemy's army). 6. attack from the side. *n., v. 5.*

flan nel (flan′əl), 1. a soft, warm material made of wool. 2. **Flannels** are clothes made of this. 3. made of flannel. *n., adj. 6.*

flan nel ette (flan′əl et′), a soft, warm, cotton material like flannel. *n. 12.*

flap (flap), 1. strike noisily with something broad and loose. The sail flapped. 2. a blow from something broad and loose; as, a flap from a whale's tail. 3. move (wings) up and down; fly by flapping the wings. 4. flapping motion; flapping noise. 5. piece hanging or fastened at one edge only; as, the flap of cloth over the opening to a pocket. *v., flapped, flapping, n. 5.*

flap jack (flap′jak′), a thin, flat batter cake fried in a pan; pancake. *n.*

flap per (flap′ər), 1. something broad and flat to strike with. 2. a broad fin. 3. a young bird just able to fly. 4. a half-grown girl. *Used in common talk. n. 18.*

flare (flãr), 1. flame up briefly or unsteadily, sometimes with smoke. A lamp flares when it is turned too high. 2. a blaze; a bright, brief, unsteady flame. The match gave a last flare. 3. spread out in the shape of a bell. This skirt flares at the bottom. 4. spreading out; a bell shape; as, the flare of a skirt. See the picture just below. 5. burst into sudden action or feeling. **Flare up** or **out** means burst out into anger, violence, etc. *v., n. 8.*

Dress with a flared skirt

flash (flash), 1. a sudden, brief light or flame; as, a flash of lightning. 2. give out such a light or flame. The lighthouse flashes signals twice a minute. 3. come suddenly; pass quickly. A bird flashed across the road. 4. a sudden, short feeling; as, a flash of hope. 5. a very short time. It all happened in a flash. 6. give out or send out like a flash. 7. send by telegraph, radio, etc. *n., v. 2.*

flash light (flash′līt′), 1. a light that flashes, used in a lighthouse or for signaling. 2. a portable electric light. 3. a preparation that gives out a brilliant flash of light, used when taking photographs indoors or at night. *n.*

flash y (flash′i), 1. flashing; brilliant for a short time. 2. showy; gaudy. *adj., flashier, flashiest. 18.*

flask (flask), a bottle or can. *n. 9.*

Flask

flat[1] (flat), 1. smooth and level; even. A floor is flat. 2. horizontal; at full length; as, lying flat on the ground. 3. thing that is flat. 4. the flat part; as, with the flat of the sword. 5. flat land. 6. not very deep or thick; as, a flat dish, flat bone. 7. positive; not to be changed. A flat rate has no extra charges. 8. without much flavor; dull; as, to taste flat. 9. below the true pitch; as, to sing flat. 10. a tone one half step below natural pitch; as, music written in B flat. 11. the sign in music (♭) that shows this. 12. flatly. 13. make flat; become flat. 14. **Fall flat** means fail entirely. *adj., flatter, flattest, adv., n., v., flatted, flatting. 2.*

flat[2] (flat), an apartment or set of rooms on one floor. *n.*

flat boat (flat′bōt′), a large, flat-bottomed boat used especially for floating goods down a river. *n. 19.*

flat-bot tomed (flat′bot′əmd), having a flat bottom; as, a flat-bottomed boat. *adj. 18.*

flat car (flat′kär′), railroad freight car without a roof or sides. *n.*

flat fish (flat′fish′), any of a group of fishes having a flat body and swimming on one side. Halibut, flounder, and sole are flatfishes. *n., pl. flatfishes* or *flatfish.*

Flatfish

flat i ron (flat′ī′ərn), an iron with a flat surface for smoothing cloth. See the picture just below. *n.*

flat ten (flat′ən), make flat; become flat. The silk has been wrinkled, but it will flatten out again if you iron it. *v. 11.*

Flatirons: P, plain; E, electric.

flat ter (flat′ər), 1. praise beyond the truth. 2. show as more beautiful or better looking than is the truth. This picture flatters him. 3. win over or please by praising words, often not true. *v. 3.*

flat ter y (flat′ər i), act of flattering; words of praise, usually untrue or overstated. Some people use flattery to get favors. *n., pl. flatteries. 5.*

flaunt (flônt), 1. wave proudly; as, banners flaunting in the breeze. 2. show off. She flaunts her riches in public. *v. 9.*

fla vor (flā′vər), 1. taste; as, the flavor of peppermint. 2. add salt, pepper, or herbs to; to season; give taste to. The onion flavors the whole stew. *n., v. 4.*

fla vor ing (flā′vər ing), something used to give a particular taste to food or drink; as, chocolate flavoring. *n.*

flaw (flô), 1. a crack; slight defect; fault. His nasty temper is the only flaw in his character. 2. to damage; become defective. *n., v. 7.*

flaw less (flô′lis), perfect. *adj.*

flax (flaks), 1. a slender, upright plant from whose stems linen is made. Flax has small narrow leaves and blue flowers. Linseed oil is made from its seeds. 2. the threadlike parts into which the stems of this plant separate, prepared ready for spinning. *n. 4.*

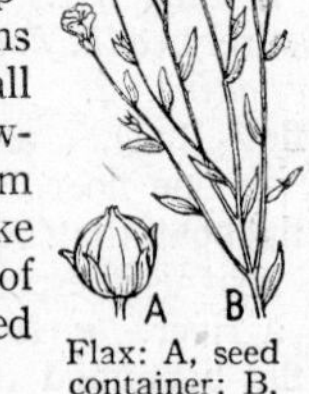

Flax: A, seed container; B, branch.

flax en (flak′sən), 1. made of flax. 2. like flax; pale-yellow; as, flaxen hair. *adj. 13.*

flax seed (flaks′sēd′), seeds of flax; linseed. Flaxseed is used to make linseed oil and in medicine. *n.*

flay (flā), 1. take the skin off of. 2. scold severely and painfully. *v. 11.*

flea (flē), a small, jumping insect without wings. Fleas live in the fur of dogs, cats, and monkeys or under the clothing of human beings, and feed on their blood. *n. 9.*

Flea. Line shows actual length.

fleck (flek), 1. spot; mark; speck; spot of color or light. Freckles are brown flecks on the skin. 2. to spot; mark with spots of color or light. The bird's breast is flecked with brown. *n., v. 13.*

fled (fled). See **flee.** The clouds fled before the wind. *pt. and pp. of flee. 3.*

fledge (flej), 1. grow the feathers needed for flying. 2. furnish with wings or feathers. *v. 11.*

fledg ling or **fledge ling** (flej′ling), 1. a young bird just able to fly. 2. inexperienced person. *n. 17.*

flee (flē), 1. run away. The robbers tried to flee, but they were caught. 2. go quickly. The clouds are fleeing before the wind. *v., fled, fleeing. 3.*

fleece (flēs), 1. the wool that covers a sheep. The coat of wool cut off or shorn from one sheep is called a fleece. 2. cut the fleece from. 3. rob; cheat; strip of money or belongings. *n., v. 4.*

fleec y (flēs′i), like a fleece; soft and white. Fleecy clouds floated in the blue sky. *adj., fleecier, fleeciest. 7.*

fleet[1] (flēt), 1. ships under one command; ships sailing together; as, the American fleet, a fleet of fishing boats. 2. airplanes, automobiles, or the like, moving or working together. *n. 2.*

fleet[2] (flēt), swiftly moving; rapid; as, a fleet horse. *adj.*

fleet ing (flēt′ing), passing swiftly; soon gone. *adj. 18.*

fleet ness (flēt′nis), swiftness. *n. 18.*

Flem ing (flem′ing), 1. a native of Flanders. 2. a Belgian who speaks Flemish. *n. 12.*

Flem ish (flem′ish), 1. of or pertaining to Flanders, its people, or their language. 2. the people of Flanders. 3. their language. *adj., n. 11.*

flesh (flesh), 1. the softer substance of the body that covers the bones. A fat person has a great deal of flesh. 2. meat. 3. the body, not the soul. 4. the human race; all living creatures. All flesh must die. 5. one's family; as, one's own flesh and blood. 6. the soft part of fruits or vegetables; the part of fruits that can be eaten. The flesh of the peach is yellow and white. 7. **In the flesh** means (1) alive. (2) really present, not merely thought of. *n. 2.*

flesh ly (flesh′li), 1. of the flesh; bodily. 2. sensual. *adj., fleshlier, fleshliest. 17.*

flesh y (flesh′i), having much flesh; plump; fat. *adj., fleshier, fleshiest. 12.*

fleur-de-lis (flėr′də lē′), 1. the iris flower or plant. 2. a design, perhaps taken from the iris, used as part of the royal arms of France. *n., pl. fleurs-de-lis* (flėr′də lēz′).

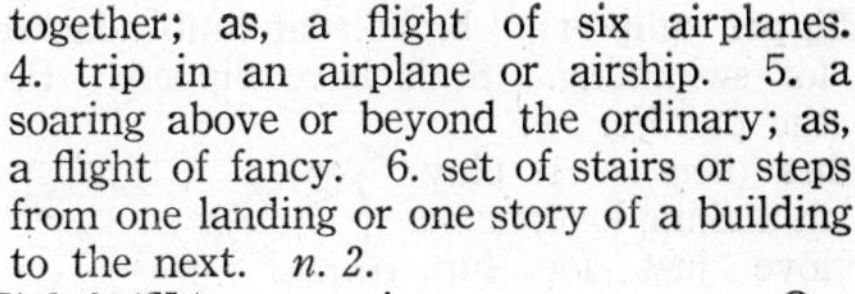

Fleur-de-lis design

flew (flü). See **fly**². The bird flew high in the air. *pt. of fly*². *2.*

flex (fleks), bend. *v.*

flex i bil i ty (flek′si bil′i ti), flexible quality. The flexibility of a man's muscles lessens as he becomes old. *n. 14.*

flex i ble (flek′si bəl), 1. that can be bent without breaking; not stiff; easily bent in all directions. Leather, rubber, and wire are flexible. 2. easily managed. *adj. 7.*

flick (flik), 1. a sudden light blow or stroke. The farmer drove the fly from his horse's head by a flick of his whip. 2. strike lightly with whip or finger. He flicked the dust from his coat sleeve. 3. move with a jerk. The boys flicked wet towels at each other. *n., v.*

flick er¹ (flik′ər), 1. shine with a wavering, unsteady light. The firelight flickered on the walls. 2. a wavering, unsteady flame or light. 3. move lightly and quickly in and out, or back and forth. The tongue of a snake flickers. 4. a flickering movement; as, the flicker of an eyelash. *v., n. 8.*

flick er² (flik′ər), a bird common in eastern North America, the golden-winged woodpecker or yellowhammer. *n.*

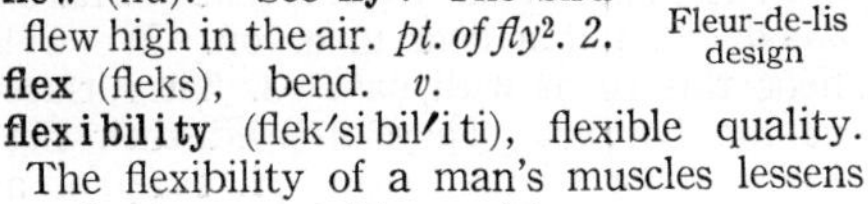

Flicker (about 12 in. long)

fli er (flī′ər), 1. something that flies, such as a bird or insect. The eagle is a high flier. 2. an aviator. 3. very fast train, ship, bus, etc. *n. 17.*

flies (flīz), 1. A bird flies. He flies. 2. There are many flies on the window. *v., n. pl. 3.*

flight¹ (flīt), 1. act or manner of flying; as, the flight of a bird through the air. 2. distance a bird, bullet, airplane, etc., can fly. 3. group of things flying through the air together; as, a flight of six airplanes. 4. trip in an airplane or airship. 5. a soaring above or beyond the ordinary; as, a flight of fancy. 6. set of stairs or steps from one landing or one story of a building to the next. *n. 2.*

flight² (flīt), running away; escape. Our soldiers put the enemy to flight. *n.*

flight y (flīt′i), 1. likely to have sudden fancies; frivolous. 2. light-headed; a little crazy. *adj., flightier, flightiest. 17.*

flim sy (flim′zi), light and thin; slight; frail; without strength; easily broken. Thin muslin is too flimsy to be used for sails. His excuse was so flimsy that everybody laughed at him. *adj., flimsier, flimsiest. 10.*

flinch (flinch), 1. draw back from difficulty, danger, or pain; shrink. The baby flinched when he touched the hot radiator. 2. drawing back. *v., n. 11.*

fling (fling), 1. throw; throw with force. 2. rush. 3. a throw. 4. move violently; plunge; kick. 5. a time of doing as one pleases. She had her fling when she was young. 6. a lively Scottish dance. *v., flung, flinging, n. 4.*

flint (flint), 1. a very hard stone, which makes a spark when struck against steel. 2. anything very hard. *n. 5.*

Flint (flint), a city in southeastern Michigan. *n.*

FLINT STEEL TRIGGER PRIMING CUP

Gun showing flintlock

flint lock (flint′lok′), 1. gunlock in which a piece of flint striking against steel makes sparks that set fire to the gunpowder. 2. old-fashioned gun with such a lock. *n.*

flint y (flin′ti), 1. made of flint; containing flint. 2. like flint; very, very hard. *adj., flintier, flintiest. 11.*

flip (flip), 1. put into motion by the snap of a finger and thumb; move with a jerk or toss. The man flipped a coin on the counter. The driver flipped at a fly with his whip. The twig flipped back and scratched his face. 2. a snap; smart tap; sudden jerk. The cat gave the kitten a flip on the ear. *v., flipped, flipping, n. 19.*

flip pan cy (flip′ən si), flippant quality; flippant behavior. *n.*

flip pant (flip′ənt), smart or pert in speech; not respectful. She gave him a flippant answer. *adj. 12.*

flip per (flip′ər), broad, flat limb adapted for swimming. Seals have flippers. See the picture. *n.*

FLIPPERS

flirt (flėrt), 1. play at making love; make love just for fun. 2. person who makes love without meaning it. 3. move quickly. She flirted her fan. 4. a quick movement. *v., n. 6.*

flir ta tion (flėr tā′shən), 1. flirting. 2. love affair that is not serious. *n. 18.*

flir ta tious (flėr tā′shəs), 1. inclined to flirting. 2. having to do with flirtation. *adj.*

flit (flit), 1. fly lightly and quickly. A hummingbird flitted by. 2. move lightly and quickly. 3. a light, quick movement. *v., flitted, flitting, n. 5.*

flitch (flich), the side of a hog salted and cured; side of bacon. *n. 20.*

fliv ver (fliv′ər), small, cheap automobile. *n.* [*Slang*]

float (flōt), 1. stay on top of or be held up by air, water, or other liquid. A cork will float, but a stone sinks. 2. anything that stays up or holds up something else in water. A raft is a float. A cork on a fish line is a float. 3. move along without trying; be moved along by the movement of what one is in or on. The boat floated out to sea. 4. a low, flat-topped car that carries something to be shown in a parade. 5. set going (a company, scheme, etc.); be set going. *v., n. 2.*

flock (flok), 1. a group of animals of one kind keeping, feeding, or herded together; as, a flock of sheep, a flock of geese. 2. people of the same church group. 3. a large number; multitude. 4. go in a flock; keep in groups. Snowbirds usually flock together. 5. come crowding. The children flocked around the Christmas tree. *n., v. 2.*

floe (flō), a field or sheet of floating ice. *n.*

Floe

flog (flog), beat or whip hard. *v., flogged, flogging. 11.*

flood (flud), 1. fill to overflowing. A wave flooded the holes I had dug in the sand. 2. flow over. The river flooded our fields. 3. a flow of water over what is usually dry land. 4. **The Flood** means the water that covered the earth in the time of Noah. Genesis 7. 5. a large amount of water. 6. a great outpouring of anything; as, a flood of light, a flood of words. 7. fill, cover, or overcome, as if with a flood. The room was flooded with moonlight. The governor was flooded with applications for positions. *v., n. 2.*

flood gate (flud′gāt′), 1. gate in a canal, river, stream, etc., to control the flow of water. 2. thing that controls any flow or passage. *n.*

flood light (flud′līt′), 1. lamp that gives a broad beam of light. 2. broad beam of light from such a lamp. 3. illuminate by such a lamp. *n., v.*

floor (flōr), 1. the part of a room to walk on. The floor of this room is made of hardwood. 2. put a floor in or on. We will floor this room with oak. 3. flat surface at the bottom. They dropped their net to the floor of the ocean. 4. story of a building. Five families live on the fourth floor. 5. knock down. 6. to defeat. *Used in common talk. n., v. 1.*

floor ing (flōr′ing), 1. floor. 2. floors. 3. material for making floors. *n. 13.*

floor walk er (flōr′wôk′ər), person employed in a large store to oversee sales, direct customers, etc. *n.*

flop (flop), 1. move loosely or heavily; flap around clumsily. The fish flopped helplessly on the deck. 2. fall, drop, throw, or move heavily or clumsily. He flopped down into a chair. 3. a flopping. 4. sound made by flopping. 5. change or turn suddenly. 6. failure. *v., flopped, flopping, n.* [*Used in common talk*] *12.*

flo ra (flō′rə), the plants of a particular region or time. The desert of Sahara has a scanty flora. *n. 9.*

flo ral (flō′rəl), of flowers; as, floral decorations. *adj. 16.*

Flor ence (flor′əns), 1. city in central Italy. 2. a girl's name. *n. 5.*

Flor en tine (flor′ən tēn), 1. of Florence. 2. a native or inhabitant of Florence. *adj., n. 13.*

flor id (flor′id), 1. ruddy; highly colored; as, a florid complexion. 2. flowery; much ornamented; showy; as, florid language, florid architecture. *adj. 14.*

Flori da (flor′i də), a State at the southeast corner of the United States. *n. 5.*

flor in (flor′in), 1. a gold or silver coin of varying value current at various times in different countries of Europe. 2. an English silver coin worth 2 shillings. 3. an old English gold coin worth about 6 shillings. *n. 16.*

flo rist (flō′rist), person who raises or sells flowers. *n. 10.*

floss (flôs), 1. silky fiber like that in milkweed pods. 2. shiny, untwisted silk thread for embroidery. Waxed floss is used for cleaning between the teeth. *n. 8.*

flo til la (flō til′ə), 1. small fleet. 2. fleet of small ships. *n. 20.*

flot sam (flot′səm), parts of a wreck found floating on the water. *n.*

flounce[1] (flouns), 1. fling the body angrily or proudly. 2. a sudden angry or proud fling of the body. *v., n. 10.*

flounce[2] (flouns), 1. wide strip of cloth, gathered along the top edge and sewed to a dress, skirt, etc., for trimming; wide ruffle. 2. trim with a flounce or flounces. *n., v.*

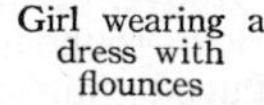
Girl wearing a dress with flounces

floun der[1] (floun′dər), 1. plunge about; struggle without making much progress. Men and horses were floundering in the deep snow beside the road. 2. be clumsy and make mistakes. The girl was frightened by the audience and floundered through her song. 3. a floundering movement or action. *v., n. 7.*

floun der[2] (floun′dər), flatfish that has a large mouth. *n.*

Flounder

flour (flour), 1. the fine meal made by grinding grain, especially wheat. 2. cover with flour. *n., v. 2.*

flour ish (flėr′ish), 1. grow in vigor; thrive; be prosperous. His newspaper business grew and flourished. 2. wave in the air. John flourished the letter when he saw us. 3. waving about. The donkey gave a flourish of his heels. 4. a display or show. The agent showed us about the house with much flourish. 5. a showy trill or passage in music. 6. an extra ornament or curve in handwriting. *v., n. 3.*

Flourishes in handwriting

flour y (flour′i), 1. of or like flour. 2. covered or white with flour. *adj.*

flout (flout), 1. mock; scoff at; treat with disdain or contempt. The foolish boy flouted his mother's advice. 2. a mockery; sneer; insult. *v., n. 12.*

flow (flō), 1. run like water. A stream flows past the house. 2. current; stream. There is a constant flow of water from the spring. 3. glide; move easily; as, a flowing movement in a dance, flowing verse. 4. hang loosely; as, flowing robes, a flowing tie. 5. any smooth, steady movement; as, a flow of words. 6. pouring out; as, a flow of blood. 7. the rise of the tide. 8. rate of flowing. *v., n. 1.*

flow er (flou′ər), 1. blossom. The flower is the part of a plant or tree which produces the seed. Flowers are often beautifully colored or shaped. 2. a plant grown for its blossoms. 3. produce flowers; bloom; cover with flowers. 4. the finest part of a thing. The flower of the land would be killed by a war. 5. the time when a thing is at its best. 6. be at its best. *n., v. 1.*

flow er et (flou′ər et), small flower. *n. 10.*

flow er ing (flou′ər ing), having flowers. *adj.*

flow er pot (flou′ər pot′), pot to hold dirt for a plant to grow in. *n. 17.*

flow er y (flou′ər i), 1. having many flowers. 2. full of fine words and fanciful expressions. *adj. 4.*

flown (flōn). See **fly**[2]. The bird has flown. The flag is flown on all national holidays. *pp. of fly*[2]. *11.*

fluc tu ate (fluk′chü āt), move like waves; rise and fall; change continually; waver. Prices fluctuate from year to year. The temperature fluctuates. *v. 12.*

fluc tu a tion (fluk′chü ā′shən), wavelike motion; continual change; going up and down; wavering. *n. 9.*

flue (flü), a passage for smoke or hot air, such as there is in a chimney. *n. 12.*

flu en cy (flü′ən si), 1. smooth, easy flow. The orator had great fluency of speech. 2. easy, rapid speaking or writing. *n. 19.*

flu ent (flü′ənt), 1. flowing smoothly or easily. Long practice enabled the American to speak fluent French. 2. speaking or writing easily and rapidly; as, a fluent speaker. *adj. 9.*

fluff (fluf), 1. soft, light, downy particles, such as come from cotton or from new blankets. 2. a soft, light, downy mass of fur or feathers. 3. make into fluff; shake or puff out (hair, feathers, etc.) into a fluffy mass. The maid fluffed the pillows when she made the beds. *n., v. 12.*

fluff i ness (fluf′i nis), softness and lightness. *n.*

fluff y (fluf′i), 1. soft and light like fluff. Whipped cream is fluffy. 2. covered with fluff; as, fluffy baby chicks. *adj., fluffier, fluffiest. 14.*

flu id (flü′id), 1. any liquid or gas; something that will flow. Water, mercury, air, and oxygen are fluids. 2. like a liquid or a gas; flowing. She poured the fluid mass of hot candy into a dish to harden. *n., adj. 4.*

fluke[1] (flük), 1. the flat, three-cornered piece at the end of each arm of an anchor, which catches in the ground and holds it fast. 2. the barbed head of an arrow or harpoon. 3. either of the two halves of a whale's tail. *n. 16.*

Anchor showing flukes

fluke[2] (flük), a lucky stroke in games, business, or life. *n.* [*Used in common talk*]

flume (flüm), 1. a deep and very narrow valley containing a mountain torrent. 2. large, inclined trough or chute for carrying water. Flumes are used to transport logs or to furnish water for power. *n.*

Flume (def. 2)

flung (flung). See **fling.** The boy flung the ball. The paper was flung away. *pt. and pp. of fling. 4.*

flunk (flungk), 1. fail in schoolwork. 2. cause to fail. 3. mark as failing. 4. failure. *v., n.* [*Used in common talk*]

flunk ey (flungk′i), flunky. *n., pl. flunkeys.*

flunk y (flungk′i), 1. a male servant dressed in livery; footman. 2. a flattering, fawning person. *n., pl. flunkies.*

flur ry (flėr′i), 1. sudden gust of wind. 2. light fall of rain or snow. 3. sudden commotion. 4. fluster; excite; agitate. Noise in the audience flurried the actor so that he forgot his lines. *n., pl. flurries, v., flurried, flurrying. 12.*

flush (flush), 1. blush. The girl flushed when they laughed at her. 2. cause to blush. 3. a rosy glow or blush. The flush of sunrise was on the clouds. 4. rush suddenly. 5. a sudden rush; rapid flow. 6. send a sudden rush of water over or through. 7. start up suddenly; cause to start up suddenly. Our dog flushed a partridge in the woods. 8. even; level. Make that shelf just flush with this one. Their edges should be flush. 9. full; full to overflowing. 10. having plenty of money. *v., n., adj., adv. 8.*

flus ter (flus′tər), 1. excite; confuse. Mary was flustered by her surprise party. 2. confusion. *v., n. 16.*

flute (flüt), 1. a long, slender, pipelike musical instrument. A flute is played by blowing across a hole on the side near one end. Different notes are made by covering the different holes along the side with the fingers or with keys. 2. play on a flute. 3. sing or whistle so as to sound like a flute. 4. long, round groove. Some pillars have flutes. 5. make long, round grooves in. *n., v. 5.*

Man playing a flute

flut ed (flüt′id), grooved; furrowed; as, fluted columns. *adj. 19.*

Fluted wood

flut ter (flut′ər), 1. wave back and forth quickly and lightly. A flag flutters in the breeze. 2. flap the wings; flap. 3. come or go with a trembling or wavy motion. 4. move restlessly. 5. tremble. 6. a fluttering. 7. excitement. *v., n. 3.*

flux (fluks), 1. a flowing; a flow. 2. a flowing in of the tide. 3. continuous change. New words and meanings keep the English language in a state of flux. 4. an unnatural discharge of blood or other liquid from the body. 5. a substance used to help metals to melt together. Borax is used as a flux. *n. 12.*

fly[1] (flī), 1. an insect with two wings. 2. a fishhook with silk, tinsel, etc., on it to suggest a fly. *n., pl. flies. 1.*

House fly. Line shows actual length.

fly[2] (flī), 1. move through the air with wings. Birds fly long distances. 2. travel through the air in an airplane or airship. 3. float or wave in the air. Our flag flies every day. 4. cause to fly. We fly kites. 5. move swiftly. The ship flies before the wind. 6. run away. 7. a batted ball going high in the air. 8. a flap to cover buttons on a garment. *v.,* ***flew, flown, flying,*** *n., pl. flies.*

fly catch er (flī′kach′ər), bird that catches insects while flying. See the picture just below. *n.*

fly er (flī′ər), flier. *n.*

fly ing (flī′ing), 1. that flies; moving through the air. 2. floating or waving in the air. 3. swift. 4. short and quick; hasty. *adj.*

Flycatcher (about 7½ in. long)

flying boat, airplane that can float on water; seaplane.

flying fish, tropical sea fish that has winglike fins and can leap through the air. See the picture.

flying machine, 1. airplane. 2. airship.

fly leaf (flī′lēf′), a blank leaf at the beginning or end of a book. *n., pl. flyleaves.*

Flying fish of the Atlantic coast (about 8 in. long)

fly speck (flī′spek′), spot left by a fly. *n.*

fly wheel (flī′hwēl′), a heavy wheel attached to machinery to keep the speed even. *n. 20.*

foal (fōl), 1. young horse or donkey. 2. give birth to (a foal). *n., v. 18.*

foam (fōm), 1. a mass of very small bubbles. 2. form foam. 3. break into foam. *n., v. 3.*

foam y (fōm′i), 1. foaming; covered with foam. 2. made of foam. 3. like foam. *adj., foamier, foamiest. 14.*

fob (fob), 1. watch pocket. 2. short watch chain, ribbon, etc., that hangs out of the watch pocket. 3. ornament worn at the end of such a chain, ribbon, etc. *n. 14.*

Fob

f.o.b. or **F.O.B.,** free on board. The price $850, f.o.b. Detroit, means that the $850 does not pay for freight or other expenses after the article has been put on board a freight car at Detroit.

fo cal (fō′kəl), of a focus; having to do with a focus. The focal distance or the focal length of a lens is the distance from its center to its principal focus. *adj. 17.*

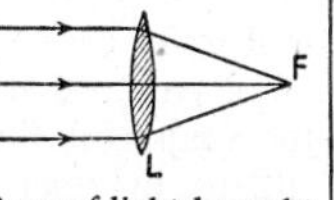

Rays of light brought to a focus at F by the lens, L.

fo cus (fō′kəs), 1. a point at which rays of light, heat, etc., meet after being reflected or refracted; a point from which rays appear to come. 2. bring (rays of light, etc.) to a focus. 3. the distance from a lens or mirror to the point where rays from it meet. A near-sighted eye has a shorter focus than a normal eye. 4. the position of an object necessary to produce a clear image. You cannot take a good photograph unless the object is in focus. 5. adjust (a lens, the eye, etc.) to a focus. A defect of vision prevented him from focusing accurately. 6. bring (an image, etc.) into focus. 7. a central point of attraction, attention, activity, etc. The collision was for a few moments the focus of attention. 8. concentrate. When studying, he focused his mind on his lessons. *n., pl. focuses, foci* (fō′sī), *v., focused, focusing. 7.*

fod der (fod′ər), coarse food for horses, cattle, etc. Hay and cornstalks with their leaves are fodder. *n. 6.*

foe (fō), enemy. *n. 2.*

foe man (fō′mən), enemy; foe. *n., pl. foemen. 19.*

foe tus (fē′təs), embryo; young animal in the womb or in the egg. *n. 19.* Also spelled **fetus.**

fog (fog), 1. thick mist. 2. to cover with fog. 3. make misty or cloudy. *n., v., fogged, fogging. 4.*

fog gy (fog′i), having much fog; misty; not clear. *adj., foggier, foggiest. 8.*

fog horn (fog′hôrn′), horn that warns ships in foggy weather. *n.*

fo gy (fō′gi), old-fashioned person; person who is behind the times. *n., pl. fogies. 19.*

foi ble (foi′bəl), weak point. *n. 13.*

foil[1] (foil), outwit; prevent from carrying out (plans). The hero foiled the villain. *v. 5.*

foil[2] (foil), 1. metal beaten, hammered, or rolled into a very thin sheet. Candy is sometimes wrapped in tin foil to keep it fresh. 2. something which, when placed near a thing, makes it look better by contrast. The green pillow was a foil for Mary's red hair. *n.*

foil[3] (foil), long, narrow sword with a knob or button on the point to prevent injury, used in fencing. *n.*

Foil

foist (foist), palm off; bring in secretly; impose by fraud. The dishonest shopkeeper foisted inferior goods on his customers. *v.*

fold[1] (fōld), 1. bend or double over on itself.

You fold a letter or your napkin. 2. bend till close to the body. You fold your arms. A bird folds its wings. 3. put the arms around and hold tenderly. A mother folds her child to her breast. 4. wrap. He folded the pills in a blue paper. 5. a layer of something folded. *v., n. 2.*

fold[2] (fōld), 1. pen for sheep. 2. a church. *n.*

-fold, suffix meaning:—
1. times as many; times as great; as in tenfold.
2. formed or divided into —— parts; as in manifold.

fold er (fōl′dər), 1. a holder for papers made of stiff paper doubled once. 2. a pamphlet made of one or more folded sheets. 3. person or thing that folds. *n. 11.*

fo li age (fō′li ij), the leaves of a plant. *n. 6.*

fo li o (fō′li ō), 1. a sheet of paper folded once. 2. a volume consisting of sheets folded once (that is, with four pages to each sheet); a volume having pages of the largest size. 3. pertaining to or having the form of a folio. 4. the page number of a printed book. 5. a sheet of paper, parchment, etc., of a manuscript or book, numbered on the front side only. *n., pl. folios, adj. 9.*

folk (fōk), 1. people. 2. tribe; nation. 3. **Folks** often means (1) people. (2) relatives. How are all your folks? *n., pl. folk* or *folks. 2.*

folk dance, 1. dance popular among the common people of a country. 2. music for it.

folk lore (fōk′lōr′), the beliefs, legends, customs, etc., of a people or tribe. *n.*

folk song, 1. song originating and handed down among the common people. 2. song imitating a real folk song. "Swanee River" and "Old Black Joe" are folk songs.

fol li cle (fol′i kəl), a small cavity, bag, or gland. Hairs grow from follicles. *n. 14.*

fol low (fol′ō), 1. go or come after. Night follows day. He leads; we follow. 2. result from; result. Misery follows war. If you eat too much candy, a stomach ache will follow. 3. go along (a road, etc.). Follow this road to the corner. 4. use; obey; act according to; take as a guide. Follow her advice. 5. keep the eyes on. I could not follow that bird's flight. 6. keep the mind on. Try to follow the President's speech. 7. take part in; be concerned with. Harry expects to follow the profession of lawyer. 8. **Follow up** means pursue closely; act upon with energy. *v. 1.*

fol low er (fol′ō ər), 1. person or thing that follows. 2. person who follows the ideas or beliefs of another. 3. member of the household of a king or nobleman. *n. 4.*

fol low ing (fol′ō ing), 1. group of followers. 2. that follows; next after. If that was Sunday, then the following day must have been Monday. *n., adj. 1.*

fol ly (fol′i), 1. being foolish; lack of sense; unwise conduct. It is folly to eat too much. 2. foolish act, practice, or idea; something silly. *n., pl. follies. 3.*

fo ment (fō ment′), promote; foster (trouble, rebellion, etc.). Three sailors were fomenting a mutiny on the ship. *v. 14.*

fond (fond), 1. loving; liking; as, a fond look. 2. loving foolishly or too much. 3. cherished. *adj. 2.*

fon dle (fon′dəl), pet; caress. *v. 16.*

fond ness (fond′nis), affection; liking. *n. 12.*

font (font), 1. basin holding water for baptism. 2. basin for holy water. 3. fountain; source. *n. 12.*

Font (def. 1)

food (füd). Plants, animals, and people eat or drink food to make them live and grow. *n. 1.*

food stuff (füd′stuf′), material for food. Grain and meat are foodstuffs. *n. 9.*

fool (fül), 1. person without sense; person who acts unwisely. 2. a clown formerly kept in a nobleman's house to amuse people. 3. act like a fool for fun; play; joke. 4. make a fool of; deceive; trick. *n., v. 2.*

fool er y (fül′ər i), foolish action. *n., pl. fooleries. 15.*

fool har di ness (fül′här′di nis), foolish boldness; rashness. *n.*

fool har dy (fül′här′di), foolishly bold; rash. The man made a foolhardy attempt to go over Niagara Falls in a barrel. *adj. 16.*

fool ish (fül′ish), without sense; unwise; like a fool. *adj. 2.*

fool ish ness (fül′ish nis), foolish behavior; lack of sense. *n. 9.*

fool proof (fül′prüf′), so safe that even a fool can use it. *adj.*

fools cap (fülz′kap′), paper in sheets from 12 to 13½ inches wide and 15 to 17 inches long. *n. 20.*

foot (fu̇t), 1. the part that a person or animal stands on. 2. soldiers that go on foot; infantry. 3. the lowest part; the base; as, the foot of a column, the foot of a hill, the foot of a page. 4. walk. The boys footed the whole ten miles. 5. make the foot of; as, to foot a stocking. 6. add. Foot this column of numbers. 7. pay. We foot the bill. *Used in common talk.* 8. 12 inches. 9. one of the parts into which a line of poetry is divided. This line has four feet: "The boy | stood on | the burn | ing deck. |" *n., pl. feet, v. 1.*

foot ball (fu̇t′bôl′), 1. a leather ball used in games where the ball is kicked. 2. a game played with a football which is to be kicked or carried past the goal line at the end of the field. *n. 5.*

foot board (fu̇t′bōrd′), 1. a board or small platform on which to support the feet. 2. an upright piece across the foot of a bed. *n.*

foot fall (fu̇t′fôl′), sound of steps coming or going; footstep. *n. 12.*

foot hill (fu̇t′hil′), low hill at the base of a mountain or mountain range. *n.*

foot hold (fu̇t′hōld′), place to put a foot; support for the feet; footing. The man climbed the steep cliff by getting footholds in cracks. *n. 12.*

foot ing (fu̇t′ing), 1. a firm placing or position of the feet. Jim lost his footing and fell down on the ice. 2. a place or support for the feet. The steep cliff gave us no footing. 3. a secure position. 4. condition; position; relationship. We are on a friendly footing with the Smiths. 5. adding up a column of figures. 6. the total sum of a column of figures. *n. 9.*

foot lights (fu̇t′līts′), the row of lights at the front of a stage. *n. pl.*

foot man (fu̇t′mən), 1. a man servant dressed in a special suit, who answers the bell, waits on table, goes with the carriage or car to open the door, etc. 2. foot soldier. *n., pl. footmen. 6.*

foot note (fu̇t′nōt′), a note at the bottom of a page about something on the page. *n.*

foot pad (fu̇t′pad′), a highway robber who goes on foot. *n.*

foot path (fu̇t′path′), path for people on foot only. *n. 13.*

foot print (fu̇t′print′), the mark made by a foot. *n. 13.*

foot rest (fu̇t′rest′), support on which to rest the feet. *n.*

foot rule, ruler; wood or metal measure one foot long.

foot soldier, soldier who fights on foot.

foot sore (fu̇t′sōr′), having sore feet from much walking. *adj. 15.*

foot step (fu̇t′step′), 1. a person's step. 2. distance covered in one step. 3. the sound of steps coming or going. 4. the mark made by a foot. **Follow in one's footsteps** means do as another has done. *n. 4.*

foot stool (fu̇t′stül′), footrest; low stool on which to place the feet when seated. *n. 10.*

Footstool

foot work (fu̇t′wėrk′), way of using the feet. Footwork is important in boxing and dancing. *n.*

fop (fop), man very fond of clothes; dandy. *n. 14.*

fop per y (fop′ər i), the behavior or dress of a fop. *n., pl. fopperies. 16.*

fop pish (fop′ish), like a fop; empty-headed and fond of clothes. *adj. 18.*

for (fôr). For shows very many relations between things. Some are: 1. in place of. He gave me a new book for the old one. 2. in support of. He stands for honest government. 3. in honor of. A party was given for him. 4. in return; in consideration of. These apples are twelve for a dollar. We thanked him for his kindness. 5. with the object or purpose of; as, to go for a walk, to act for advantage, a suit for damages, to seek for happiness. 6. used with; suited to; as, a box for gloves, books for children. 7. with a feeling toward; as, an eye for beauty, to long for home, love for friends. 8. with regard or respect to; as, warm for April, bad for one's health. 9. because of; by reason of; as, to shout for joy, to punish for stealing. 10. as far as. We walked for a mile. 11. as long as. We worked for an hour. 12. as being. They know it for a fact. 13. because. His story of the fight is true, for I saw it myself. 14. **For** (a person) **to** sometimes means that (the person) should. 15. **O! for** means I wish I might have. *prep., conj. 1.*

for age (for′ij), 1. food for horses, cattle, etc. 2. hunt or search for food. 3. get by hunting or searching about. 4. hunt; search about. 5. get or take food from. The soldiers foraged the villages near their camp. *n., v. 8.*

for ag er (for′ij ər), person who hunts for food. *n. 14.*

for as much as (fôr′əz much′ az), because; seeing that; since. *18.*

for ay (for′ā), 1. raid for plunder. Armed bandits made forays on unprotected villages. 2. plunder; lay waste; pillage. *n., v. 14.*

for bade or **for bad** (fôr bad′). See **forbid.** The doctor forbade the sick boy to leave his bed. *pt. of forbid. 8.*

for bear[1] (fôr bãr′), 1. hold back; keep from doing, saying, using, etc. The boy forbore to hit back because the other boy was smaller. 2. be patient; control oneself. *v., forbore, forborne, forbearing. 5.*

for bear[2] (fôr′bãr), forebear; ancestor. *n.*

for bear ance (fôr bãr′əns), patience; control; not acting against someone when you have a right to do so. *n. 9.*

for bid (fôr bid′), not allow; say one must not do; make a rule against. The teacher forbade us to leave our seats. If my father had known that I was going, he would have forbidden it. *v., forbade* or *forbad, forbidden, forbidding. 2.*

for bid den (fôr bid′ən), 1. not allowed; against the law or the rules. Eve ate the forbidden fruit. 2. See **forbid.** My father has forbidden me to go swimming after breakfast. *adj., pp. of forbid. 4.*

for bid ding (fôr bid′ing), causing fear or dislike; looking dangerous or unpleasant. The coast was rocky and forbidding. *adj.*

for bore (fôr bōr′). See **forbear**[1]. He forbore from showing his anger. *pt. of forbear*[1]. *13.*

for borne (fôr bōrn′). See **forbear**[1]. We have forborne from vengeance. *pp. of forbear*[1].

force (fōrs), 1. power; strength. 2. strength used against a person or thing; violence. 3. make (a person) act against his will; make do by force. Give it to me at once, or I will force you to. 4. take by force. 5. break through; as, to force a door. 6. press or urge to violent effort. 7. hurry the growth of (flowers, fruits, or a child's mind). 8. group of people who work together; as, an office force. **Forces** sometimes means the army or navy. 9. any cause that produces, changes, or stops motion in a body; as, the force of gravitation, electric force. *n., v. 1.*

forced (fōrst), 1. made, compelled, or driven by force. The work of slaves is forced labor. 2. done by unusual effort. The soldiers made a forced march of three days. 3. strained; not natural. She hid her dislike with a forced smile. *adj.*

force ful (fōrs′fəl), full of force; forcible; effective; vigorous. *adj. 11.*

for ceps (fôr′seps), small pincers or tongs used by surgeons, dentists, etc., for seizing and holding. Dentists use forceps for pulling teeth. *n., pl. forceps. 15.*

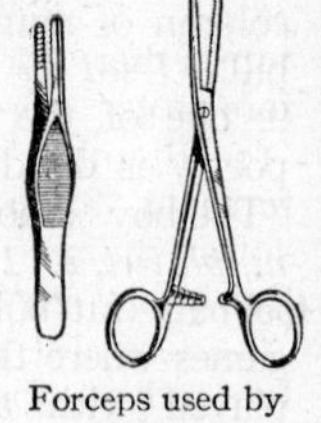
Forceps used by surgeons

for ci ble (fōr′si bəl), 1. made or done by force; using force; as, a forcible entrance into a house. 2. having or showing force; strong; powerful; as, a forcible speaker. *adj. 7.*

ford (fōrd), 1. place where a river, stream, or other body of water is not too deep to cross by walking through the water. 2. cross (a river, etc.) by walking or driving through the water. *n., v. 4.*

fore (fōr), 1. at the front; toward the beginning or front; forward. 2. the front part. 3. a cry of warning used in golf. *adj., adv., n., interj. 5.*

fore-and-aft (fōr′ənd aft′), lengthwise on a ship; from bow to stern. Fore-and-aft sails are set lengthwise. *adj.*

fore arm[1] (fōr′ärm′), the part of the arm between the elbow and the wrist. *n. 13.*

fore arm[2] (fōr ärm′), prepare for trouble ahead of time; arm beforehand. *v.*

fore bear (fōr′bãr), ancestor; forefather. *n.*

fore bode (fōr bōd′), 1. predict; give warning of. Black clouds forebode a storm. 2. have a feeling that something bad is going to happen. *v. 11.*

fore bod ing (fōr bōd′ing), 1. prediction. 2. a feeling that something bad is going to happen. *n.*

fore cast (fōr′kast′), 1. prophecy; a statement of what is coming. What is the forecast about the weather for today? 2. prophesy; tell what is coming. *n., v., forecast* or *forecasted, forecasting. 10.*

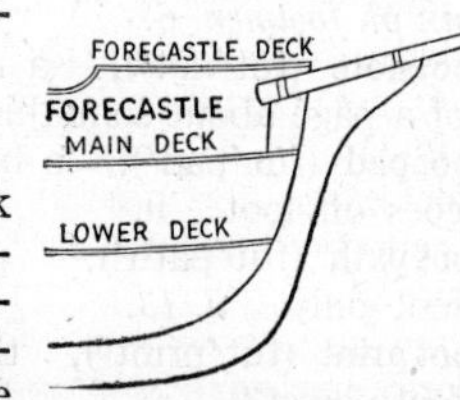

fore cas tle (fōk′səl or fōr′kas′əl), 1. the upper deck in front of the foremast. See the diagram. 2. the sailors' rooms in the forward part of a merchant ship. *n. 11.*

fore close (fōr klōz′), 1. shut out; prevent. 2. take away the right to redeem (a mortgage). Since neither the interest nor principal was paid, the holder of the mortgage foreclosed and took possession of the house. *v. 20.*

fore clo sure (fōr klō′zhər), act of foreclosing a mortgage. *n.*

fore doom (fōr düm′), doom beforehand. *v. 18.*

fore fa ther (fōr′fä′ᴛʜər), ancestor. *n. 6.*

fore fin ger (fōr′fing′gər), the finger next to the thumb. *n. 11.*

fore foot (fōr′fu̇t′), one of the front feet of an animal. *n., pl. forefeet. 11.*

fore front (fōr′frunt′), the extreme front; the foremost part or place. *n. 12.*

fore gath er (fōr gaᴛʜ′ər), forgather. *v.*

fore go (fōr gō′), do without; give up. Alice decided to forego the movies and do her lessons. *v., forewent, foregone, foregoing. 7.*

fore go ing (fōr′gō′ing), preceding; going before. There have been many pictures in the foregoing pages. *adj.*

fore gone (fōr′gôn), previous; that has gone before. A **foregone conclusion** is a fact that was almost surely known beforehand. *adj. 11.*

fore ground (fōr′ground′), the part of a picture or scene nearest the observer; the part in the front. The cottage stands in the foreground with the mountains in the background. *n. 11.*

fore hand (fōr′hand′), made with the palm turned forward; as, a forehand stroke in tennis. *adj. 18.*

Forehand stroke

fore hand ed (fōr′-han′did), providing for the future; prudent; thrifty. *adj.*

fore head (for′id), 1. the part of the face above the eyes. 2. front part. *n. 2.*

for eign (for′in), 1. outside one's own country. She has traveled much in foreign countries. 2. coming from outside one's own country; as, a foreign ship, a foreign language, foreign money. 3. having to do with other countries; as, foreign trade. 4. not belonging. Sitting still all day is foreign to a healthy boy's nature. *adj. 2.*

for eign er (for′in ər), person from another country; an outsider. *n. 4.*

fore know (fōr nō′), know beforehand. *v., foreknew, foreknown, foreknowing. 16.*

fore knowl edge (fōr′nol′ij), knowledge of a thing before it happens. *n. 13.*

fore land (fōr′land′), cape; headland; promontory. *n. 18.*

fore leg (fōr′leg′), one of the front legs of an animal. *n. 20.*

fore lock (fōr′lok′), the lock of hair that grows just above the forehead. **Take time by the forelock** means plan ahead; do things in plenty of time. *n. 11.*

fore man (fōr′mən), 1. man in charge of a group of workmen; man in charge of the work in some part of a factory. 2. chairman of a jury. *n., pl. foremen. 9.*

fore mast (fōr′məst or fōr′mast′), the mast nearest the bow of a ship. *n.*

fore most (fōr′mōst), 1. first. He stumbled and fell head foremost. 2. chief; leading. *adj., adv. 4.*

fore noon (fōr′nün′), the time from about eight o'clock to noon; the part of the day from sunrise to noon. *n. 4.*

fo ren sic (fə ren′sik), oratorical; like that used in a law court or a public debate. *adj. 20.*

fore or dain (fōr′ôr dān′), determine beforehand; appoint beforehand. *v.*

fore part (fōr′pärt′), front part; early part. *n. 18.*

fore paw (fōr′pô′), front paw. *n.*

fore run ner (fōr′run′ər), 1. one that goes before or is sent before and shows something more is coming. 2. a sign that something is coming. Black clouds are forerunners of a storm. 3. predecessor; ancestor. *n. 12.*

fore sail (fōr′səl or fōr′sāl′), 1. the principal sail on the foremast of a schooner. 2. the lowest sail on the foremast of a square-rigged ship. *n.*

fore saw (fōr sô′). See **foresee.** *pt. of foresee. 11.*

fore see (fōr sē′), see or know beforehand. Mother put up a big picnic lunch, because she foresaw how hungry we would be. *v., foresaw, foreseen, foreseeing. 5.*

fore shad ow (fōr shad′ō), indicate before hand; be a warning of. Dark clouds foreshadow a storm. *v. 13.*

fore short en (fōr shôr′tən), represent (lines, etc.) in a drawing as of less than true length in order to give the proper impression to the eye. *v. 18.*

Foreshortening of lines in a cube

fore sight (fōr′sīt′), 1. power to see or know beforehand. 2. careful thought for the future; prudence. 3. looking ahead; view into the future. *n. 8.*

fore skin (fōr′skin′), the fold of skin that covers the end of the male sex organ. *n. 18.*

for est (fôr′ist), 1. thick woods; woodland, often covering many miles. 2. of the forest; as, forest fires. 3. plant with forest trees. *n., adj., v. 1.*

fore stall (fōr stôl′), get ahead of; act sooner than and so get the better of. By settling the deal by telegraph, Mr. Field had forestalled all his competitors. *v. 15.*

for est er (fôr′is tər), 1. officer in charge of a forest to guard against fires, look after timber, etc. 2. person who lives in a forest. *n. 9.*

forest preserve, forest protected by the government from wasteful cutting, fires, etc.

for est ry (fôr′is tri), the science and art of taking care of forests. *n. 10.*

fore taste (fōr′tāst′ for *n.*, fōr tāst′ for *v.*), taste beforehand. The boy got a foretaste of business life by working during his vacation from school. *n., v. 12.*

fore tell (fōr tel′), tell beforehand; predict; prophesy. Who can foretell what a baby will do next? *v., foretold, foretelling. 10.*

fore thought (fōr′thôt′), 1. previous thought or consideration; planning. A little forethought will often save you much trouble afterwards. 2. careful thought for the future; prudence; foresight. *n. 17.*

fore told (fōr tōld′). See **foretell.** He foretold the World War. The Weather Bureau had foretold the cold wave. *pt. and pp. of foretell. 6.*

fore top (fōr′təp or fōr′top′), platform at the head of a foremast. *n.*

for ev er (fôr ev′ər), 1. for ever; for always; without ever coming to an end. 2. always; all the time. *adv. 3.*

for ev er more (fôr ev′ər mōr′), forever. *adv.*

fore warn (fōr wôrn′), tell beforehand, especially of the coming of something that must be prepared for. *v. 12.*

fore word (fōr′wėrd′), introduction; preface. *n.*

for feit (fôr′fit), 1. lose or have to give up by one's own act, neglect, or fault. He forfeited his life by his careless driving. 2. thing lost or given up because of some act, neglect, or fault. His health was the forfeit he paid for carelessness. 3. lost or given up. *v., n., adj. 5.*

for fei ture (fôr′fi chər), forfeit; loss by forfeiting. *n. 10.*

for fend (fôr fend′), avert; prevent. "God forfend that the good knight should perish!" cried the lady. *v.* [*Old use*]

for gath er (fôr gaᴛʜ′ər), 1. gather together; assemble; meet. 2. meet by accident. 3. associate (with); be friendly. *v.*

for gave (fôr gāv′). See **forgive.** She forgave my mistake. *pt. of forgive. 9.*

forge[1] (fōrj), 1. place with fire where metal is heated very hot and then hammered into shape. A blacksmith uses a forge. 2. blacksmith's shop; smithy. 3. heat (metal) very hot and then hammer into shape. 4. place where iron or other metal is melted and refined. 5. make; shape; form. 6. make or write (something false). 7. sign (a name that is not one's own) falsely to deceive. *n., v. 4.*

Blacksmith's forge

forge[2] (fōrj), move forward slowly but steadily. One runner forged ahead of the others and won the race. *v.*

forg er (fōr′jər), 1. man who forges metals. 2. person who forges another person's name or makes any fraudulent imitation. *n. 18.*

for ger y (fōr′jər i), 1. act of forging something that is false. 2. a paper written falsely; name signed falsely in order to deceive. The signature on the check was not my own but a forgery. *n., pl. forgeries. 11.*

for get (fôr get′), 1. let go out of the mind; fail to remember. 2. fail to think of; fail to do, take notice, etc. *v., forgot, forgotten* or *forgot, forgetting. 1.*

for get ful (fôr get′fəl), 1. apt to forget; having a poor memory. 2. heedless. *adj. 15.*

for get ful ness (fôr get′fəl nis), forgetting; poor memory. *n. 7.*

for get-me-not (fôr get′mē-not′), a small blue flower, or the plant bearing it. *n.*

Forget-me-not

for giv a ble (fôr giv′ə bəl), that can be forgiven. *adj.*

for give (fôr giv′), pardon; give up the wish to punish; not have hard feelings at or toward. She forgave her brother for breaking her doll. Please forgive my mistake. *v., forgave, forgiven, forgiving. 3.*

for giv en (fôr giv′ən). See **forgive.** Your mistakes are forgiven. *pp. of forgive.*

for give ness (fôr giv′nis), 1. act of forgiving; pardon. 2. willingness to forgive. *n. 5.*

for go (fôr gō′), forego. *v., forwent, forgone, forgoing. 16.*

for got (fôr got′). See **forget.** Tom was so busy that he forgot to eat his lunch. *pt. and sometimes pp. of forget. 2.*

for got ten (fôr got′ən). See **forget.** He has forgotten much of what he learned. *pp. of forget. 2.*

fork (fôrk), 1. a handle with two or more long points, with which to lift food. 2. a much larger kind with which to lift hay; a pitchfork. 3. lift with a fork. 4. any branching; as, the fork of a tree, the fork of a road or stream. 5. one of the branches of a fork. 6. have forks; divide into forks. *n., v. 2.*

A B

Forks: A, table fork; B, pitchfork.

forked (fôrkt), 1. having a fork; as, a forked stick. 2. zigzag; as, forked lightning. *adj.*

for lorn (fôr lôrn′), left alone; neglected; miserable; hopeless. The lost kitten, a forlorn little animal, was wet and dirty. *adj. 5.*

form (fôrm), 1. a shape. Circles and triangles are forms. 2. to shape; make. 3. take shape. Ice formed in the pail. 4. become. Water forms ice when it freezes. 5. develop. Form good habits while you are young. 6. a kind; a sort. Ice, snow, and steam are forms of water. 7. manner; method. Her form in swimming is excellent. There are good and bad forms of speech and action. 8. formality; ceremony. Many forms have no meaning. He said "Good morning" as a matter of form, although he hardly noticed me. 9. arrangement. In what form did he put the list of words? 10. mold; pattern. Ice cream is often made in forms. A **form letter** is one copied from a pattern. 11. a class in school. Fred is now in the fifth form. 12. long seat; bench. *n., v., adj. 1.*

for mal (fôr′məl), 1. stiff; not familiar and homelike; as, a formal call, a formal manner. 2. according to set customs or rules. 3. done with the proper forms; clear and definite. A written contract is a formal agreement to do something. 4. having to do with the form, not the content of a thing. *adj. 6.*

form al de hyde (fôr mal′di hīd), a gas used to disinfect and to preserve. *n. 12.*

for mal ism (fôr′məl izm), strict observance of outward forms. *n. 20.*

for mal i ty (fôr mal′i ti), 1. an outward form; a ceremony; something required by custom; as, the formalities of a wedding or a funeral. 2. attention to forms and customs. Visitors at the court of a king are received with formality. 3. stiffness of manner, behavior, or arrangement. *n., pl. formalities. 9.*

for ma tion (fôr mā′shən), 1. the forming, making, or shaping (of something); as, the formation of a crust on bread as it bakes. 2. the way in which something is arranged; arrangement; order; as, troops in battle formation. 3. thing formed. Clouds are formations of tiny drops of water in the sky. *n. 6.*

for mer (fôr′mər), 1. the first of two. Both the pink and the blue dresses are pretty, but I like the former better. 2. earlier; past; long past. In former times, cooking was done in fireplaces instead of stoves. *adj. 1.*

for mer ly (fôr′mər li), in time past; some time ago. *adv. 4.*

for mi da ble (fôr′mi də bəl), hard to overcome; hard to deal with; to be dreaded. *adj. 7.*

form less (fôrm′lis), without form; shapeless. *adj. 18.*

For mo sa (fôr mō′sə), an island near China, belonging to Japan. Formosa is famous for its tea. *n. 18.*

for mu la (fôr′mū lə), 1. a set form of words, especially one which by much use has partly lost its meaning. "How do you do?" is a polite formula. 2. a statement of religious belief or doctrine. 3. a rule for doing something, especially as used by those who do not know the reason back of it. 4. a recipe or prescription; as, a formula for making soap. 5. an expression showing by chemical symbols the composition of a compound. The formula for water is H_2O. 6. a rule or principle expressed in algebraic symbols. $(a+b)^2=a^2+2ab+b^2$ is a formula. *n., pl. formulas, formulae* (-lē). *8.*

for mu lar y (fôr′mū lãr′i), 1. a collection of formulas. 2. a set form of words. *n. 17.*

for mu late (fôr′mū lāt), express in a formula; state definitely or systematically. A church may formulate its doctrines in a creed. *v. 9.*

for mu la tion (fôr′mū lā′shən), expression in a formula; definite expression or statement. *n. 15.*

for sake (fôr sāk′), give up; leave; leave alone. *v., forsook, forsaken, forsaking. 3.*

for sak en (fôr sāk′ən), 1. deserted; abandoned; forlorn. 2. See **forsake.** Mary has forsaken her old friends. *adj., pp. of forsake.*

for sook (fôr sůk′). See **forsake.** He forsook his family. *pt. of forsake. 7.*

for sooth (fôr süth′), in truth; indeed. *adv. 16.*

for swear (fôr swãr′), 1. reject or renounce upon oath or with earnestness. His mother asked him to forswear smoking. 2. be untrue to one's sworn word or promise; perjure (oneself). *v., forswore, forsworn, forswearing.*

for sworn (fôr swōrn′), 1. perjured; untrue to one's sworn word or promise. 2. See **forswear.** Harry has forsworn his bad habits. *adj., pp. of forswear. 13.*

for syth i a (fôr sith′i ə), shrub having many bell-shaped, yellow flowers in early spring before the leaves come out. *n.*

fort (fōrt), a strong building or castle that can be defended against an enemy. *n. 2.*

forte[1] (fōrt), something one does very well; strong point. Her forte is playing the piano. *n. 18.*

for te[2] (fôr′tā), in music, loud. *adj., adv.*

forth (fōrth), 1. forward. 2. out; into view. The sun came forth from behind the clouds. 3. away. *adv. 1.*

forth com ing (fōrth′kum′ing), coming forth; about to appear; approaching; ready when wanted. The forthcoming week will be busy. *adj. 11.*

forth right (fōrth′rīt′), 1. straightforward; direct; frank and outspoken. Mr. Jones made forthright objections to the proposal. 2. directly; straight. The soldiers marched forthright to battle. *adj., adv.*

forth with (fōrth′wiᴛʜ′), at once; immediately. *adv. 5.*

for ti eth (fôr′ti ith), 1. next after the 39th. 2. one of 40 equal parts. *adj., n. 13.*

for ti fi ca tion (fôr′ti fi kā′shən), 1. making strong; adding strength to. 2. place made strong by building walls and forts. 3. a wall or a fort built to make a place strong. *n. 9.*

for ti fy (fôr′ti fī), 1. make strong; add strength to. 2. protect a place against attack; strengthen with forts, walls, etc. 3. build forts, walls, etc. *v., fortified, fortifying. 6.*

for tis si mo (fôr tis′i mō), in music, very loud. *adj., adv.*

for ti tude (fôr′ti tūd or fôr′ti tüd), courage in pain, danger, or trouble; firmness of spirit. *n. 8.*

fort night (fôrt′nīt), two weeks. *n. 7.*

for tress (fôr′tris), fort; a place built with walls and defenses. *n. 4.*

for tu i tous (fôr tū′i təs or fôr tü′i təs), happening by chance; accidental; as, a fortuitous meeting, fortuitous acquaintance. *adj. 14.*

for tu nate (fôr′chə nit), 1. lucky; having good luck. 2. bringing good luck; having favorable results. *adj. 3.*

for tune (fôr′chən), 1. great deal of money or property; riches; wealth. 2. luck; chance; what happens. Fortune was against us; we lost. 3. good luck; success; prosperity. 4. **Tell a person's fortune** means tell what is going to happen to him. *n. 2.*

for tune tell er (fôr′chən tel′ər), person who claims to be able to foretell what is going to happen to people. *n.*

Fort Wayne (fōrt′ wān′), a city in northeastern Indiana.

Fort Worth, a city in northern Texas.

for ty (fôr′ti), four times ten; 40. *n., pl. forties, adj. 2.*

fo rum (fō′rəm), 1. the public square of an ancient Roman city where business was done and courts and public assemblies were held. 2. an assembly for the discussion of questions of public interest. An open forum is held in the community house every Tuesday evening. 3. law court; tribunal. *n. 10.*

for ward (fôr′wərd), 1. onward; ahead. Forward, march! 2. to the front. He brought forward several new ideas. 3. advanced; as, a child forward for his years. 4. help on; as, to forward your friends' plans. 5. send on farther; as, to forward a letter. 6. ready; eager. 7. pert; bold. *adv., adj., v. 1.*

for ward ness (fôr′wərd nis), 1. readiness; eagerness. 2. pertness; boldness. *n. 16.*

for wards (fôr′wərdz), onward; ahead; to the front. *adv.*

fos sil (fos′il), 1. the hardened remains or trace of an animal or plant. Fossils of ferns are found in coal. 2. very old-fashioned person who is set in his ways. 3. belonging to the outworn past; as, fossil ideas. *n., adj. 7.*

fos ter (fos′tər), 1. bring up; rear; make grow. 2. care for as one's own child. 3. help the growth or development of; encourage. 4. in the same family, but not related by birth. A **foster child** is a child brought up by a person not his parent. A **foster father, foster mother,** and **foster parent** are persons who bring up the child of another. *v., adj. 5.*

foster brother, boy brought up with another though not related to him or to her.

foster sister, girl brought up with another though not related to him or to her.

fought (fôt). See **fight.** He fought bravely yesterday. A battle was fought. *pt. and pp. of fight. 2.*

foul (foul), 1. very dirty; nasty; smelly. We opened the windows to let out the foul air. 2. make dirty; become dirty. 3. very wicked; vile. Murder is a foul crime. 4. unfair. 5. in football, basketball, etc., an unfair play. 6. in baseball, a batted ball that does not count because the ball lands outside the base lines. 7. hit against. 8. hitting against. One boat went foul of the other. 9. get tangled up with. The rope they threw fouled our anchor chain. 10. tangled; caught; as, a foul rope. 11. clogged up. The fire will not burn because the chimney is foul. 12. clog up. Grease has fouled this drain. 13. unfavorable; stormy; as, foul weather. *adj., v., n. 3.*

fou lard (fü lärd′), a soft, thin silk, usually with a printed pattern, used for dresses, neckties, etc. *n. 19.*

found[1] (found). See **find.** We found the treasure. The lost child was found. *pt. and pp. of find. 1.*

found[2] (found), establish. The Pilgrims founded a colony in the new country. John Wesley founded the Methodist Church. *v.*

foun da tion (foun dā′shən), 1. the part on which the rest stands or depends; base. The foundation of a house is built first. 2. founding; establishing. 3. being founded or established. *n. 3.*

found er[1] (foun′dər), person who founds or establishes. *n. 4.*

foun der[2] (foun′dər), 1. fall down. 2. stumble; break down. 3. fill with water and sink. The ship foundered in the storm. *v.*

found ling (found′ling), a baby or little child found deserted. *n.*

found ry (foun′dri), 1. place where metal is melted and molded; place where things are made of molten metal. 2. melting and molding metal; making things of molten metal. *n., pl. foundries. 13.*

fount (fount), 1. fountain. 2. source. *n. 7.*

foun tain (foun′tən), 1. water flowing or rising into the air in a spray; the pipes through which water is forced and the basin built to receive it. 2. spring of water. 3. place to get a drink; as, a drinking fountain, a soda fountain. 4. source. John found that his father was a fountain of information. *n. 2.*

Fountain

foun tain head (foun′tən hed′), 1. source of a stream. 2. original source. God is the fountainhead of all goodness. *n. 18.*

fountain pen, a pen for writing which has a reservoir to give a continuous supply of ink.

four (fōr), one more than three; 4. A dog has four legs. *n., adj. 1.*

four fold (fōr′fōld′), 1. four times as much or as many. 2. having four parts. *adj., adv. 13.*

four-foot ed (fōr′fu̇t′id), having four feet. *adj.*

four score (fōr′skōr′), four twenties; 80. *adj. 7.*

four some (fōr′səm), game played by four persons together. *n.*

four square (fōr′skwãr′), 1. having its four sides and angles equal; square. 2. frank; outspoken. 3. firm; not yielding. *adj. 14.*

four teen (fōr′tēn′), four more than ten; 14. *n., adj. 3.*

four teenth (fōr′tēnth′), 1. next after the 13th. 2. one of 14 equal parts. *adj., n. 9.*

fourth (fōrth), 1. next after the 3rd. 2. a quarter; one of four equal parts. Twenty-five cents is one fourth of a dollar. *adj., n. 1.*

four-wheeled (fōr′hwēld′), having four wheels; running on four wheels. *adj.*

fowl (foul), 1. any bird; as, a waterfowl. 2. a common rooster or hen. 3. the flesh of a fowl used for food. *n., pl. fowls or fowl. 3.*

Fowl (def. 2)

fowl er (foul′ər), person who hunts or traps wild birds. *n. 12.*

fowling piece, a light gun for shooting wild birds.

fox (foks), 1. a small animal somewhat like a dog. See the picture. In many stories the fox gets the better of other animals by his cunning. 2. its fur. 3. a cunning or crafty person. *n. 2.*

Red fox (about 3½ ft. long, including the tail)

fox glove (foks′gluv′), plant with tall stalks having many bell-shaped flowers. *n. 8.*

fox hound (foks′hound′), hound with a keen sense of smell, trained to hunt foxes. *n.*

fox terrier, a small active dog kept as a pet.

Fox terrier (15 in. high at the shoulder)

fox trot, 1. a modern dance having short, quick steps; music for it. 2. pace of a horse between a walk and a trot.

fox y (fok′si), crafty; like a fox. *adj., foxier, foxiest.*

foy er (foi′ər), 1. lounging room in a theater or hotel. 2. entrance hall. *n. 19.*

fra cas (frā′kəs), disorderly noise; noisy quarrel or fight. *n. 20.*

frac tion (frak′shən), 1. one or more of the equal parts of a whole. $\frac{1}{2}$, $\frac{1}{4}$, $\frac{3}{4}$, $\frac{1}{3}$, and $\frac{2}{3}$ are fractions. 2. a part broken off; not all of a thing. *n. 5.*

frac tion al (frak′shən əl), 1. having to do with fractions. 2. forming a fraction. 440 yards are a fractional part of a mile. 3. small by comparison; insignificant. *adj. 15.*

frac ture (frak′chər), 1. break; crack. The boy fell from a tree and fractured his arm. 2. a breaking. 3. a being broken. 4. the breaking of a bone or cartilage. *v., n. 9.*

frag ile (fraj′il), easily broken; delicate; frail. Thin glass is fragile. *adj. 8.*

frag ment (frag′mənt), a part broken off; piece of something broken. When Ann broke the dish, she tried to put the fragments back together. *n. 5.*

frag men tar y (frag′mən tãr′i), incomplete; made up of fragments; disconnected; as, fragmentary remains of a temple, a fragmentary account of the accident. *adj. 17.*

fra grance (frā′grəns), sweet smell; pleasing odor. *n. 5.*

fra grant (frā′grənt), sweet-smelling. A rose is fragrant. *adj. 4.*

frail (frāl), 1. weak; slender and not very strong; as, a frail child. 2. easily broken or giving way. Be careful; those branches are a very frail support. 3. morally weak. *adj. 3.*

frail ty (frāl′ti), 1. weakness. 2. moral weakness. *n., pl. frailties. 6.*

frame (frām), 1. support over which something is stretched or built; as, the frame of a house. 2. body; as, a man of heavy frame. 3. the way in which a thing is put together. 4. make; put together; plan. 5. the border in which a thing is set; as, a window frame, a picture frame. 6. put a border around; as, to frame a picture. 7. **Frame of mind** means way one is thinking or feeling; disposition; mood. *n., v. 2.*

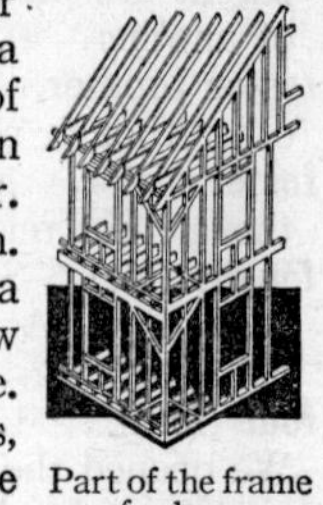
Part of the frame of a house

Picture frame

frame work (frām′wėrk′), support or skeleton; the stiff part which gives shape. The bridge had a steel framework. *n. 9.*

franc (frangk), the unit of money in France and Switzerland. A franc used to be equal to 19.3 cents of United States money. Since the first World War the value of the French franc has varied greatly. *n. 10.*

France (frans), a country in western Europe. *n. 1.*

fran chise (fran′chīz), 1. privilege or right granted by a government. The city granted the company a franchise to operate its busses on the city streets. 2. right to vote. The United States granted the franchise to women in 1920. *n. 11.*

Fran cis (fran′sis). Saint Francis (1181?-1226) founded an order of friars. *n. 4.*

Fran cis can (fran sis′kən), 1. of the religious order founded by Saint Francis. 2. member of the religious order founded by Saint Francis in 1209. *adj., n. 17.*

frank (frangk), 1. free to express one's real thoughts and feelings; open; not hiding one's mind; not afraid to say what one thinks. 2. send (a letter or package) without charge. 3. a mark to show that a letter or package is to be sent without charge. *adj., v., n. 2.*

Frank (frangk), member of the German tribes that conquered Gaul in the sixth century A.D. *n.*

Frank fort (frangk′fərt), 1. the capital of Kentucky. 2. a city in western Germany. *n. 7.*

frank furt er (frangk′fər tər), reddish sausage made of beef and pork. *n.*

frank in cense (frangk′in sens), fragrant resin from certain Asiatic or African trees. It gives off a sweet, spicy odor when burned. *n. 10.*

Frank ish (frangk′ish), of or having to do with the Franks. *adj. 19.*

Frank lin (frangk′lin), Benjamin (1706-1790), an American who helped very much in the Revolutionary War. *n. 5.*

frank ness (frangk′nis), being frank; plainness of speech; saying just what one thinks. *n. 9.*

fran tic (fran′tik), very much excited; wild with rage, pain, or grief. *adj. 8.*

fran ti cal ly (fran′ti kəl i), in a frantic manner; with wild excitement. *adv.*

fra ter nal (frə tėr′nəl), brotherly. *adj. 7.*

fra ter ni ty (frə tėr′ni ti), 1. brotherhood. 2. group of men or boys joined together for fellowship or for some other purpose. There are student fraternities in many American colleges. 3. group of men having the same interests, kind of work, etc. *n., pl. fraternities. 8.*

frat er nize (frat′ər nīz), associate in a brotherly way; be friendly. *v. 18.*

Frau (frou), German word meaning (1) wife. (2) Mrs. *n. 16.*

fraud (frôd), 1. dishonest dealing; cheating; trickery. 2. something which is not what it seems to be. 3. person who cheats. *Used in common talk. n. 5.*

fraud u lent (frôj′ů lənt), 1. cheating; dishonest. 2. done by fraud; obtained by trickery. *adj. 12.*

fraught (frôt), loaded; filled. A battlefield is fraught with horror. *adj. 7.*

Fräu lein (froi′līn), German word meaning (1) Miss. (2) unmarried woman; young lady. *n.*

fray[1] (frā), a fight; noisy quarrel. *n. 6.*

fray[2] (frā), 1. separate into threads; make or become ragged or worn along the edge. Long wear had frayed the collar and cuffs of his old shirt. 2. wear away; rub. *v.*

fraz zle (fraz′əl), 1. ravel; fray; wear to shreds. 2. remnant; shred. *v., n.* [*Used in common talk*]

freak (frēk), 1. something very queer or unusual. A green leaf growing in the middle of a rose would be called a freak of nature. 2. sudden change of mind without reason; odd notion or fancy. *n. 9.*

freak ish (frēk′ish), full of freaks; very queer or unusual. *adj. 16.*

freck le (frek′əl), 1. one of the small light-brown spots that some people have on the skin. 2. make freckles on. 3. become marked with freckles. *n., v. 7.*

free (frē), 1. loose; not fastened or shut up. 2. not held back from action or thought by law or by persons. 3. not bound to any country, person, or thing. 4. having no tax or duty; as, free trade. 5. without anything to pay. These tickets are free. 6. not strict. 7. let go; let loose. 8. make free; relieve from any kind of burden, bondage, or slavery. 9. to clear. He will have to free himself of this charge of stealing. 10. **Free from** or **free of** means without; lacking; as, free from fear, air free of dust. 11. easy; not hindered; as, a free step. 12. open to all; as, a free port. *adj., freer, freest, adv., v., freed, freeing. 1.*

free boot er (frē′büt′ər), pirate; buccaneer. *n. 18.*

freed man (frēd′mən), man freed from slavery. *n., pl. freedmen. 19.*

free dom (frē′dəm), 1. being free. 2. liberty; power of choosing what one will do. 3. free use. We give a guest the freedom of the house. 4. too great liberty. We did not like the freedom of his manner. 5. ease of movement or action. *n. 2.*

free hand (frē′hand′), done by the hand without the aid of instruments. *adj.*

free hand ed (frē′han′did), generous; liberal. *adj.*

free man (frē′mən), man not a slave nor a serf; man who could own land. *n., pl. freemen. 5.*

Free ma son (frē′mā′sən), a member of a world-wide secret order. The society of Freemasons has as its purpose mutual aid and fellowship. *n. 18.*

free stone (frē′stōn′), 1. any stone which can be easily worked or quarried without splitting, such as sandstone. 2. having a stone from which the pulp is easily separated; as, a freestone peach. *n., adj.*

free think er (frē′thingk′ər), person who forms his religious opinions independently of authority or tradition. *n.*

free will (frē′wil′), of one's own accord; as, a freewill offering to the Red Cross. *adj. 16.*

freeze (frēz), 1. turn into ice; harden by cold. 2. make very cold. 3. become very cold. 4. kill or injure by frost. 5. cover or become covered with ice. 6. a freezing. 7. being frozen. 8. make or become stiff and unfriendly. 9. chill or be chilled with fear, etc. 10. become motionless. *v., froze, frozen, freezing, n. 2.*

freight (frāt), 1. the goods that a ship or a train carries. 2. the price paid for carrying. 3. a freight train or ship. He sent the box by freight. 4. load freight into. They freighted the boat with bananas. 5. send as freight. 6. carry as freight. *n., v. 3.*

freight er (frāt′ər), ship that carries mainly freight. *n.*

French (french), 1. of or having to do with France, its people, or their language. 2. the people of France. 3. the language of France. *adj., n. pl. or sing. 1.*

French horn, brass wind instrument that has a mellow tone.

Man playing a French horn

French Indo-China, group of French possessions in southeastern Asia, south of China.

French man (french′mən), man born in France, living there, or having French parents. *n., pl. Frenchmen. 6.*

French Revolution, revolution in France from 1789 to 1799, which changed France from a monarchy to a republic.

fren zied (fren′zid), frantic; wild; very much excited. *adj.*

fren zy (fren′zi), brief fury; almost madness; very great excitement. *n., pl. frenzies. 6.*

fre quen cy (frē′kwən si), 1. frequent occurrence. 2. rate of occurrence. *n., pl. frequencies. 12.*

fre quent (frē′kwənt for 1, fri kwent′ for 2), 1. happening often, near together, or every little while. Storms are frequent in March. 2. be often in; go to often. Frogs frequent ponds, streams, and marshes. *adj., v. 2.*

fre quent ly (frē′kwənt li), often. *adv.*

fres co (fres′kō), 1. painting with water colors on damp, fresh plaster. 2. picture or design so painted. Beautiful frescoes covered the walls and ceiling of the cathedral. 3. paint in fresco. *n., pl. frescoes* or *frescos, v. 14.*

fresh (fresh), 1. newly made, grown, or gathered. These are fresh vegetables. 2. new. Is there any fresh news from home? 3. not salty. Rivers are usually fresh water. 4. not spoiled. 5. not tired out. Put in fresh horses. 6. healthy-looking. 7. pure; cool; as, a fresh breeze. *adj. 1.*

fresh en (fresh′ən), 1. make fresh. 2. become fresh. *v. 13.*

fresh et (fresh′it), 1. a flood caused by heavy rains or melted snow. 2. a rush of fresh water flowing into the sea. *n. 16.*

fresh man (fresh′mən), 1. student in the first year of a high-school or college course. 2. of these students; as, the freshman team. *n., pl. freshmen, adj. 12.*

fresh ness (fresh′nis), being fresh. *n. 7.*

fresh-wa ter (fresh′wô′tər), of or living in water that is not salty. The catfish is a fresh-water fish. *adj. 20.*

fret (fret), 1. to worry; be peevish; be discontented. Don't fret over your mistakes. Baby frets in hot weather. 2. make peevish; make discontented. 3. condition of worry or discontent. She is in a fret about her examinations. *v., fretted, fretting, n. 3.*

fret ful (fret′fəl), peevish; discontented; ready to fret. Babies are fretful when cutting their teeth. *adj. 6.*

fret work (fret′wėrk′), ornamental openwork or carving. *n. 15.*

Fretwork

Fri., Friday.

fri a ble (frī′ə bəl), easily crumbled. Dry soil is friable. *adj. 20.*

fri ar (frī′ər), man who belongs to one of certain religious brotherhoods of the Roman Catholic Church. *n. 5.*

fric as see (frik′ə sē′), 1. meat cut up, stewed, and served in its own gravy. 2. prepare (meat) in this way. She will fricassee the chicken for dinner. *n., v. 20.*

fric tion (frik′shən), 1. the rubbing of one thing against another, such as skates on ice, hand against hand, a brush on shoes. Matches are lighted by friction. 2. resistance to motion of surfaces in contact. Oil reduces friction. 3. clash; conflict; as, friction between England and Germany. *n. 7.*

Fri day (frī′di), the sixth day of the week. *n. 2.*

fried (frīd), 1. cooked in hot fat. 2. See **fry**[1]. I fried the ham. Are the potatoes fried? *adj., pt. and pp. of fry*[1]. *7.*

friend (frend), 1. person who knows and likes another. 2. person who favors and supports. Our church has many friends. 3. person who belongs to the same side or group. *n. 1.*

Friend (frend), Quaker. *n.*

friend less (frend′lis), without friends. *adj. 12.*

friend li ness (frend′li nis), friendly nature; friendly action. *n. 13.*

friend ly (frend′li), 1. of a friend. 2. like a friend; like a friend's. 3. on good terms; as, friendly relations between countries. 4. wanting to be a friend; as, a friendly dog. 5. as a friend. *adj., friendlier, friendliest, adv. 2.*

friend ship (frend′ship), 1. state of being friends. 2. a liking between friends. 3. friendly feeling or behavior. *n. 3.*

Fries land (frēz′lənd), a district in the Netherlands. *n. 19.*

frieze (frēz), a band or ornament on a wall. *n. 9.*

Frieze

frig ate (frig′it), fast, three-masted sailing warship of medium size. Frigates were much used from 1750 to 1850. *n. 11.*

Frigate

fright (frīt), 1. sudden fear; sudden terror. 2. person or thing that is ugly, shocking, or ridiculous. *Used in common talk.* 3. frighten. *n., v. 2.*

fright en (frīt′ən), make afraid. *v. 2.*

fright ful (frīt′fəl), that would frighten; dreadful. *adj. 6.*

frig id (frij′id), 1. very cold; as, a frigid climate, the north frigid zone. 2. cold in feeling or manner; stiff; chilling; as, a frigid bow, frigid conversation. *adj. 9.*

frill (fril), 1. a ruffle. 2. put a ruffle on. 3. thing added merely for show; useless ornament. *n., v. 11.*

fringe (frinj), 1. border or trimming made of threads, cords, etc., either loose or tied together in small bunches. 2. anything like this; a border. A fringe of hair hung over her forehead. 3. make a fringe for. 4. be a fringe for. Bushes fringed the road. *n., v. 4.*

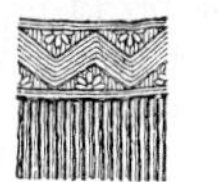

Fringes

frip per y (frip′ər i), 1. showy, cheap clothes or ornaments. 2. foolish display. *n., pl. fripperies. 9.*

frisk (frisk), frolic about joyously; dance and skip in play. A lively puppy frisks all over the house. *v. 9.*

frisk y (fris′ki), playful; lively. *adj., friskier, friskiest. 14.*

frith (frith), narrow arm of the sea; firth. *n. 16.*

frit ter[1] (frit′ər), 1. waste little by little; as, to fritter away time, money, or energy. 2. small piece; fragment. *v., n. 16.*

frit ter[2] (frit′ər), a small cake of batter, sometimes containing fruit or other food, fried in fat; as, corn fritters. *n.*

fri vol i ty (fri vol′i ti), 1. being frivolous; trifling; silly behavior. 2. a silly thing; a frivolous act. *n., pl. frivolities. 14.*

friv o lous (friv′ə ləs), 1. lacking in seriousness or sense; silly. Frivolous behavior is out of place in church. 2. of little worth or importance. He wasted his time on frivolous matters. *adj. 8.*

friz zle[1] (friz′əl), curl (hair) in small crisp curls. *v. 14.*

friz zle[2] (friz′əl), 1. make a hissing, sputtering noise when cooking; sizzle. The ham frizzled in the frying pan. 2. hissing, sputtering noise; sizzle. *v., n.*

fro (frō). **To and fro** means first one way and then back again; back and forth. *adv. 4.*

frock (frok), 1. gown; dress. 2. loose outer garment. 3. robe worn by a clergyman. *n. 5.*

frog (frog), 1. a small, leaping animal that lives in or near water. Some frogs live in trees. 2. a long, covered button and the fancy loop that goes over it, used to fasten cloaks, etc. *n. 3.*

Frog

frol ic (frol′ik), 1. a joyous game or party; play; fun. 2. play about joyously; have fun together. *n., v., frolicked, frolicking. 5.*

F, frogs on a cloak.

frol ic some (frol′ik səm), playful; merry. *adj. 15.*

from (from, *unstressed* frəm). This book came from New York. Five miles from here is another school. Three weeks from today is a holiday. Steel is made from iron. He took a book from the table. Dick is suffering from a cold which he caught from his brother. Anyone can tell apples from oranges. A child can count from 1 to 10. *prep. 1.*

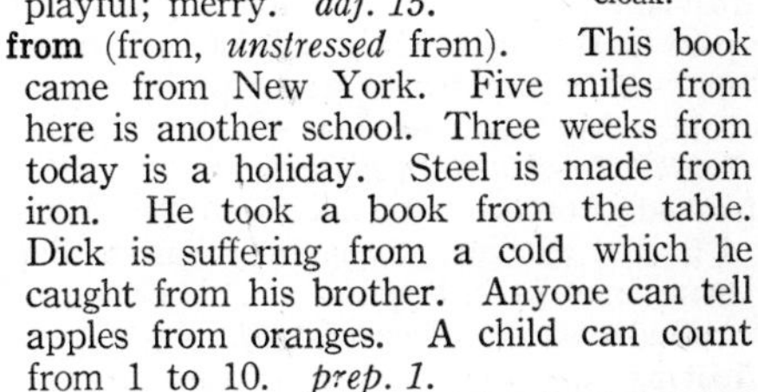

frond (frond), the leaf of a fern or of a palm tree. See the picture just below. *n. 17.*

front (frunt), 1. first part. 2. part that faces forward. 3. thing fastened or worn on the front. 4. place where fighting is going on. 5. land facing a street, river, etc. 6. on the front; at the front. 7. have the front toward; face. 8. be in front of. 9. meet face to face; meet as an enemy. 10. forehead. 11. face. *n., adj., v. 1.*

Fronds of maidenhair fern

front age (frun′tij), 1. the front of a building or lot. 2. land facing a street, river, etc. 3. the land between a building and the street. *n. 18.*

fron tal (frun′təl), 1. of or on the front; as, a frontal attack. 2. of the forehead; as, frontal bones. *adj. 13.*

fron tier (frun tēr′), 1. the last edge of settled country, where the wilds begin. 2. part of one country that touches the edge of another; boundary line between two countries. *n. 6.*

fron tiers man (frun tērz′mən), man who lives on the frontier. *n., pl. frontiersmen. 19.*

fron tis piece (frun′tis pēs), picture facing the title page of a book or of a division of a book. *n.*

front let (frunt′lit), 1. a band or ornament worn on the forehead. 2. the forehead. *n. 19.*

frost (frôst), 1. freezing. 2. cold weather. 3. moisture frozen on or in a solid surface. 4. frozen dew or vapor. On cold fall mornings there is frost on the grass. 5. kill by freezing. 6. cover with frost. 7. cover with anything that suggests frost; as, to frost a cake with sugar and white of egg mixed together. *n., v. 2.*

frost bite (frôst′bīt′), 1. freezing of some part of the body; the result of such freezing. 2. injure by frost; harm by severe cold. My ears were frostbitten. *n., v., frostbit, frostbitten, frostbiting.*

frost ed (frôs′tid), 1. covered with frost; as, a frosted window. 2. having a surface like frost; as, frosted glass. 3. iced; as, a frosted cake. 4. frozen. *adj.*

frost ing (frôs′ting), 1. a mixture of sugar and some liquid for covering cake. 2. a dull finish of glass or metal. *n.*

frost y (frôs′ti), 1. cold enough for frost; as, a frosty morning. 2. covered with frost. The glass is frosty. 3. cold and unfriendly with no warmth of feeling; as, a frosty manner. *adj., frostier, frostiest. 5.*

froth (frôth), 1. foam. There was froth on the mad dog's lips. 2. to foam; cover with foam. 3. cause to foam by beating, pouring, etc. 4. something light and trifling; unimportant talk. *n., v. 11.*

froth y (frôth′i), 1. of, like, or having froth; as, frothy soapsuds. 2. light; trifling; not substantial; as, frothy conversation. *adj., frothier, frothiest.*

fro ward (frō′wərd), willful; contrary; not easily managed. The mule is a froward animal. *adj. 7.*

frown (froun), 1. a drawing together of the brows, usually in deep thought or in strong feeling. 2. draw the brows together; look with disapproval. You may frown when you are angry or not pleased. 3. look displeased or angry. *n., v. 3.*

frowz y (frouz′i), 1. dirty; untidy. 2. smelling bad. *adj., frowzier, frowziest.*

froze (frōz). See **freeze.** The water in the pond froze. *pt. of freeze. 7.*

fro zen (frō′zən), 1. hardened with cold; turned into ice; as, a river frozen over, frozen pudding. 2. killed with cold; as, frozen to death. 3. cold and unfeeling; as, a frozen heart. 4. too frightened or stiff to move; as, frozen to the spot in horror. 5. See **freeze.** The water has frozen to ice. *adj., pp. of freeze. 2.*

fru gal (frü′gəl), 1. without waste; not wasteful; saving; using things well. A frugal housekeeper buys and uses food carefully. 2. costing little. He ate a frugal supper of bread and milk. *adj. 8.*

fru gal i ty (frü gal′i ti), being frugal; thrift. *n., pl. frugalities. 15.*

fruit (früt), 1. Apples, pears, oranges, bananas, peaches, and plums are fruit. 2. the part of the plant in which the seeds are. 3. useful product of plant growth; as, fruits of the earth. 4. the result of anything. His invention was the fruit of much effort. 5. produce fruit. *n., v. 1.*

fruit age (früt′ij), 1. a having or producing fruit. 2. fruit; crop of fruit. 3. product; result. *n. 15.*

fruit er er (früt′ər ər), dealer in fruit. *n.*

fruit ful (früt′fəl), 1. producing much fruit. 2. producing much of anything. 3. having good results; bringing benefit or profit. A successful plan is fruitful. *adj. 4.*

fruit ful ness (früt′fəl nis), 1. abundant production of fruit. 2. abundant production of any sort. *n. 15.*

fru i tion (frü ish′ən), 1. condition of having results; fulfillment; attainment. After years of hard work his plans came to fruition. 2. pleasure that comes from possession or use. 3. condition of producing fruit. *n. 14.*

fruit less (früt′lis), 1. having no results; useless; unsuccessful. 2. producing no fruit. *adj. 7.*

fruit y (früt′i), tasting or smelling like fruit. *adj.*

frus trate (frus′trāt), foil; bring to nothing; defeat; baffle. *v. 7.*

frus tra tion (frus trā′shən), check; defeat. *n. 19.*

fry[1] (frī), 1. cook in fat, in a deep or shallow pan. 2. something fried. *v., fried, frying, n., pl. fries. 5.*

fry[2] (frī), young fishes. *n. pl.*

ft., 1. foot. 2. feet. 3. fort. *4.*

fuch sia (fū′shə), a plant with handsome drooping flowers. *n. 20.*

Fuchsia

fud dle (fud′əl), make or become stupid with drink; confuse. *v. 18.*

fudge (fuj), 1. a kind of soft candy. 2. nonsense. *n. 16.*

Fueh rer (fū′rər), Führer. *n.*

fu el (fū′əl), 1. anything that can be burned to make a useful fire. Coal, wood, and oil are fuels. 2. anything that keeps up or increases a feeling. Her insults were fuel to his hatred. *n. 3.*

fu gi tive (fū′ji tiv), 1. person who is running away. The murderer became a fugitive from justice. 2. running away; as, a fugitive slave. 3. lasting a very short time; passing swiftly. *n., adj. 5.*

fugue (fūg), a musical composition in which different parts or instruments repeat the same melody with variations. *n. 18.*

Füh rer (fū′rər), German word meaning leader. *n.*

-ful, suffix meaning:—
1. full of; as in cheerful.
2. having; characterized by; as in careful, thoughtful.
3. having a tendency to; as in harmful, mournful.
4. enough to fill a; as in cupful, handful.
5. other meanings; as in manful, useful.

ful crum (ful′krəm), support on which a lever turns or is supported in moving or lifting something. *n. 13.*

LEVER
FULCRUM
Man lifting a stone with a lever

ful fill or **ful fil** (fu̇l fil′), 1. carry out (a promise, prophecy, etc.). 2. perform or do (a duty, command, etc.). 3. satisfy (requirements, etc.); answer (a purpose). 4. finish or complete (a period of time, work, etc.). *v., fulfilled, fulfilling. 4.*

ful fill ment or **ful fil ment** (fu̇l fil′mənt), fulfilling; accomplishment. *n. 11.*

full (fu̇l), 1. that can hold no more. **Full of** means filled with. 2. complete; entire; as, a full supply of clothes. 3. completely. 4. completeness; greatest degree. He satisfied his ambition to the full. 5. plump; well filled out; as, a full face. 6. having wide folds; as, a full skirt. *adj., adv., n. 1.*

full er (fu̇l′ər), person who cleanses and thickens cloth. *n. 18.*

full-fledged (fu̇l′flejd′), 1. fully developed. 2. of full rank or standing. John is now a full-fledged Boy Scout. *adj.*

full-grown (fu̇l′grōn′), fully grown; mature. *adj.*

full ness or **ful ness** (fu̇l′nis), being full. *n. 5.*

ful ly (fu̇l′i), 1. completely; entirely. 2. abundantly. 3. quite. *adv. 3.*

ful mi nate (ful′mi nāt), 1. thunder forth. Church and press fulminated against the crime wave. 2. explode with a loud noise. 3. an explosive. *v., n. 17.*

ful some (fu̇l′səm), so much as to be disgusting. *adj. 12.*

Ful ton (fu̇l′tən), Robert (1765-1815), an American who built the first steamboat in 1803, and took one up the Hudson River in 1807. *n. 5.*

fum ble (fum′bəl), 1. grope awkwardly. He fumbled in the darkness for the doorknob. 2. handle awkwardly; let drop instead of catching and holding. The first baseman fumbled the ball, and two runs were scored. 3. an awkward attempt to find or handle something. *v., n. 10.*

fume (fūm), 1. vapor, gas, or smoke. 2. give off vapor, gas, or smoke. The candle fumed, sputtered, and went out. 3. pass off in fumes. 4. treat with fumes. 5. let off one's rage in angry complaints.

He fumed about the slowness of the train. *n., v. 6.*

fu mi gate (fū′mi gāt), disinfect with fumes; expose to fumes. They fumigated the building to kill the vermin. *v. 16.*

fu mi ga tion (fū′mi gā′shən), a fumigating or being fumigated. *n.*

fun (fun), 1. playfulness; merry play; amusement; joking. 2. **Make fun of** means laugh at; ridicule. *n. 2.*

func tion (fungk′shən), 1. proper work; purpose; use. The function of the stomach is to help digest food. 2. to work; be used; act. Mary functioned as teacher. This patent pencil does not function very well. 3. a formal public or social gathering for some purpose, such as a wedding. *n., v. 5.*

func tion al (fungk′shən əl), 1. of a function. 2. acting; operating. *adj. 18.*

func tion ar y (fungk′shən ãr′i), an official. *n., pl. functionaries.*

fund (fund), 1. a stock or store ready for use. There is a fund of knowledge in a dictionary. 2. a sum of money set aside for a special purpose. Our school has a fund of $1000 to buy books with. 3. put in a fund. 4. **Funds** sometimes means (1) money ready to use. (2) money. 5. change from short-term to long-term (debt). *n., v. 4.*

fun da men tal (fun′də men′təl), of or forming a basis; essential. *adj. 7.*

Fun dy (fun′di), **Bay of,** deep inlet of the Atlantic, in southeastern Canada. *n.*

fu ner al (fū′nər əl), 1. things that are done at the burial or burning of a dead body. A funeral includes a religious service and taking the body from the church or house to the graveyard. 2. of a funeral; suitable for a funeral. A funeral march is very slow. *n., adj. 3.*

fu ne re al (fū nēr′i əl), of or like a funeral; gloomy; dismal. *adj. 14.*

fun gi (fun′jī), more than one fungus. *n. pl. 14.*

fun gous (fung′gəs), 1. of or like a fungus; spongy. 2. springing up suddenly, but not lasting. *adj. 16.*

fun gus (fung′gəs), plant without flowers, leaves, or green coloring matter. Mushrooms, toadstools, molds, smuts, and mildews are fungi. *n., pl. fungi* (fun′jī) or *funguses. 8.*

Fungi growing on a tree

funk (fungk), 1. fear; panic. 2. be afraid of. 3. frighten. 4. shrink from; shirk. *n., v.* [*Used in common talk*] *20.*

fun nel (fun′əl), 1. an open vessel ending at the bottom in a tube. If a funnel is used, anything such as a liquid, powder, or grain, may be poured into a small opening without spilling. 2. anything that is shaped like a funnel. 3. the smokestack or chimney on a steamship or steam engine. *n. 12.*

A, Funnel for pouring; B, Funnel for smoke.

fun ny (fun′i), 1. causing laughter. 2. strange; queer; odd. *Used in common talk. adj., funnier, funniest. 3.*

fur (fėr), 1. the soft coat of hair that covers many animals. 2. clothes made of fur. Furs keep you warm. 3. line or trim with fur; clothe with fur. 4. make furry; coat with foul or waste matter. Your tongue may become furred when you have a fever. *n., v., furred, furring. 2.*

fur be low (fėr′bə lō), 1. a bit of elaborate trimming. There were many frills and furbelows on her dress. 2. trim in a fussy, elaborate way. *n., v. 20.*

fur bish (fėr′bish), 1. polish. 2. restore to freshness of appearance or condition. Since she is going to France, Mary must furbish up her half-forgotten French. *v. 15.*

fu ri ous (fūr′i əs), 1. raging; violent. 2. full of wild, fierce anger. *adj. 3.*

furl (fėrl), roll up; fold up; as, to furl a sail, to furl a flag. Birds furl their wings. In the morning, the boys broke up camp and furled the tent. *v. 14.*

fur long (fėr′lông), a measure of distance, ⅛ of a mile. *n. 12.*

fur lough (fėr′lō), 1. leave of absence. The soldier has two weeks' furlough. 2. give leave of absence to. *n., v. 18.*

fur nace (fėr′nis), something to make a hot fire in, in order to melt iron, make glass, or heat a building. A furnace has an enclosed chamber or box for the fire. *n. 3.*

fur nish (fėr′nish), 1. supply; provide; as, to furnish an army with blankets. 2. supply with beds, chairs, tables, etc.; as, to furnish a bedroom. *v. 2.*

fur nish ings (fėr′nish ingz), 1. furniture or equipment for a house. 2. accessories of dress; as, a store for men's furnishings. *n. pl.*

fur ni ture (fėr′ni chər), 1. articles needed. 2. articles needed in a house or room, such as chairs, tables, beds, desks, etc. *n. 2.*

fu ror (fūr′ôr), 1. wild enthusiasm or excitement. The aviator who first flew over the ocean was received with furor. 2. mania; craze. 3. rage; fury. *n.*

furred (fėrd), 1. having fur. 2. made, covered, trimmed, or lined with fur. *adj.*

fur ri er (fėr′i ər), 1. a dealer in furs. 2. person who dresses furs or makes and repairs fur coats, etc. *n. 18.*

fur row (fėr′ō), 1. the long, narrow track in the earth cut by a plow. 2. cut furrows in. 3. a wrinkle. 4. make wrinkles in. *n., v. 5.*

F, furrow; P, plow.

fur ry (fėr′i), covered with fur; soft like fur. *adj., furrier, furriest. 12.*

fur ther (fėr′ᴛʜər), 1. farther. 2. more. 3. help forward. *adv., adj., v. 2.*

fur ther ance (fėr′ᴛʜər əns), furthering; promotion; advancement. *n. 13.*

fur ther more (fėr′ᴛʜər mōr), moreover; also; besides. *adv. 6.*

fur ther most (fėr′ᴛʜər mōst), furthest. *adj.*

fur thest (fėr′ᴛʜist), 1. farthest. 2. most. *adv., adj. 19.*

fur tive (fėr′tiv), done by stealth; secret; sly; stealthy; as, a furtive snatch at the candy, a furtive glance into the forbidden room, a furtive manner. *adj. 10.*

fu ry (fūr′i), 1. rage; a storm of anger. 2. violence. 3. a raging or violent person. 4. **The Furies** were avenging spirits. *n., pl. furies. 3.*

furze (fėrz), a low, prickly shrub with yellow flowers, common on waste lands in Europe. *n. 15.*

Furze

fuse[1] (fūz), 1. part of an electric circuit that melts and breaks the circuit if the current becomes dangerously strong. 2. the wick in a firecracker; a longer wick used to set off a bomb or a blast of gunpowder, so that one may have time to get away after lighting it. *n. 9.* Also spelled **fuze.**

fuse[2] (fūz), 1. melt; join together by melting. 2. blend; unite. *v.*

fu se lage (fū′zə lij or fū′zə läzh′), body of an airplane. The wings and tail are fastened to it. The fuselage holds the passengers, cargo, etc. See the picture of **airplane.** *n.*

fu si ble (fū′zi bəl), that can be fused or melted. *adj.*

fu sil ier or **fu sil eer** (fū′zi lēr′), 1. a soldier armed with a light musket. 2. man of certain British regiments. *n.*

fu sil lade (fū′zi lād′), 1. a discharge of many firearms. 2. attack or shoot down by a fusillade. 3. something that resembles a fusillade. The reporters greeted the mayor with a fusillade of questions. *n., v. 20.*

fu sion (fū′zhən), 1. fusing; melting; melting together. Bronze is made by the fusion of copper and tin. 2. blending; union. There was a fusion of independent Republicans and Democrats in a third party. 3. a fused mass. *n. 9.*

fuss (fus), 1. much bother about small matters; useless talk and worry; attention given to something not worth it. 2. make a fuss. Nervously she fussed about with her work. *n., v. 7.*

fuss y (fus′i), 1. inclined to fuss; never satisfied. A sick child is often fussy; nothing suits him. 2. much trimmed; elaborately made. The cheaper dress was too fussy. *adj., fussier, fussiest. 19.*

fus tian (fus′chən), 1. a coarse, strong cloth. 2. made of such cloth. 3. pompous, high-sounding language; would-be eloquence. 4. pompous and high-sounding, but cheap. *n., adj. 16.*

fust y (fus′ti), 1. having a stale smell; moldy; stuffy. 2. too old-fashioned; out of date. *adj., fustier, fustiest.*

fu tile (fū′til), 1. useless; not successful. 2. trifling; not important. *adj. 10.*

fu til i ty (fū til′i ti), 1. uselessness. 2. unimportance. *n., pl. futilities. 17.*

fu ture (fū′chər), 1. the time not yet come; what is to come. 2. coming; that will be. We hope your future years will all be happy. 3. the verb form with *shall* or *will* that expresses occurrence in time to come. "I shall go" is the future of "I go." *n., adj. 2.*

fu tu ri ty (fū tūr′i ti or fū tür′i ti), the future; time to come. *n., pl. futurities. 10.*

fuze (fūz). See **fuse**[1]. *n.*

fuzz (fuz), fine down; loose light fibers or hairs; as, the fuzz on a caterpillar. *n. 19.*

fuzz y (fuz′i), 1. of fuzz. 2. like fuzz. 3. covered with fuzz. *adj., fuzzier, fuzziest. 14.*

-fy, suffix meaning:—

1. make; cause to be; change into; as in simplify, intensify.
2. become; as in solidify.

G

G, g (jē), seventh letter of the alphabet. There are two g's in egg. *n., pl. G's, g's.*

Ga., Georgia.

gab (gab), 1. talk too much; chatter. 2. chatter; idle talk. *v., gabbed, gabbing, n.* [*Used in common talk*]

gab ar dine or **gab er dine** (gab′ər-dēn), 1. long, loose cloak or frock. 2. kind of closely woven cloth, used for raincoats, suits, etc. *n. 7.*

Gabardine (def. 1)

gab ble (gab′əl), 1. talk rapidly with little or no meaning. 2. rapid talk with little or no meaning. *v., n. 10.*

ga ble (gā′bəl), end of a ridged roof, with the three-cornered piece of wall that it covers. *n. 13.*

ga bled (gā′bəld), built with a gable or gables; having or forming gables. *adj.*

Ga bri el (gā′bri əl), an angel that brings comfort or news. *n. 10.*

gad[1] (gad), move about restlessly; go about looking for pleasure or excitement. *v., gadded, gadding. 7.*

gad[2] (gad), goad. *n.*

gad a bout (gad′ə bout′), person who moves about restlessly or goes about looking for pleasure or excitement. *n.*

gad fly (gad′flī′), a fly that stings cattle and other animals. *n., pl. gadflies. 20.*

gadg et (gaj′it), small mechanical device or contrivance; any ingenious device. *n* [*Used in common talk*]

Gael (gāl), 1. a Scottish Highlander. 2. an Irish Celt. *n.*

Gael ic (gāl′ik), 1. of or having to do with the Gaels or their language. 2. language of the Gaels. *adj., n.*

gaff (gaf), 1. a strong hook or spear used for pulling in large fish. 2. hook or pull (a fish) out of water with a gaff. 3. a spar or pole extending along the upper edge of a sail set lengthwise of a ship. *n., v. 18.*

gag (gag), 1. something put in the mouth to silence a person. 2. stop up the mouth of with a gag. 3. to strain in an effort to vomit. *n., v., gagged, gagging. 13.*

gage[1] (gāj), 1. a glove thrown down as a challenge to combat; a challenge. 2. pledge; security. The knight left a diamond as gage for the horse and armor. 3. to pledge; wager. He gaged a costly ring upon the speed of his greyhound. *Old use. n., v. 15.*

gage[2] (gāj), gauge. *n., v.*

gai e ty (gā′i ti), 1. being gay; joyousness. 2. bright appearance. *n., pl. gaieties. 9.* Also spelled **gayety.**

gai ly (gā′li), 1. as if gay; merrily; happily. 2. brightly; showily. *adv. 7.* Also spelled **gayly.**

gain (gān), 1. get; obtain; secure. The king gained possession of more lands. 2. profit. How much did I gain by that? 3. win. We will gain the battle. 4. arrive at. The swimmer gained the shore. 5. make progress. The sick child is gaining. 6. advance. One boat is gaining on another. 7. advantage; what one gains. 8. **Gains** sometimes means profits; earnings; winnings. *v., n. 1.*

gain ful (gān′fəl), bringing in money or advantage; profitable. *adj. 18.*

gain say (gān′sā′), deny; contradict; dispute. *v., gainsaid* or *gainsayed, gainsaying. 12.*

gainst or **'gainst** (genst), against. *prep.* [*Used in poetry*] *10.*

gait (gāt), the kind of steps used in going along; manner of walking; as, a slow gait, a lame gait. *n. 5.*

gai ter (gā′tər), 1. an outer covering of cloth or leather for the leg below the knee or for the ankle, for outdoor wear. 2. cloth or leather shoe with an elastic strip in each side. *n. 10.*

Gaiters (def. 1)

gal., gallon; gallons. *7.*

ga la (gā′lə), 1. festival. 2. festive; as, a gala day. *n., adj. 16.*

Gal a had (gal′ə had), the noblest and purest knight of the Round Table, who found the Holy Grail. *n. 12.*

Ga la tia (gə lā′shə), ancient country in central Asia Minor. It later became a Roman province. *n. 17.*

Ga la tians (gə lā′shənz), a book of the New Testament written by the Apostle Paul. *n. 14.*

gal ax y (gal′ək si), brilliant or splendid group. The queen was followed by a galaxy of brave knights and fair ladies. *n., pl. galaxies. 15.*

Gal ax y (gal′ək si), Milky Way, the faintly luminous band of countless stars that stretches across the sky. *n.*

gale (gāl), 1. very strong wind. 2. noisy outburst; as, gales of laughter. *n. 4.*

ga le na (gə lē′nə), a valuable lead ore. *n. 20.*

Ga li cia (gə lish′ə), a former part of Austria-Hungary. *n.*

Gal i le an (gal′i lē′ən), 1. of or having to do with Galilee or its people. 2. native or inhabitant of Galilee. *adj., n. 19.*

Gal i lee (gal′i lē), 1. the northern part of Palestine. 2. The **Sea of Galilee** is a small fresh-water lake in northeastern Palestine. *n. 9.*

Gal i le o (gal′i lē′ō), a famous Italian astronomer (1564-1642). Galileo was the first person to use the telescope and to prove that the earth goes round the sun. *n. 18.*

gall[1] (gôl), 1. a bitter liquid made in the liver. 2. anything very bitter. 3. bitterness; hate. *n. 5.*

gall[2] (gôl), 1. a sore spot on the skin caused by rubbing. 2. make sore by rubbing. The rough strap galled the horse's skin. 3. annoy; irritate. *n., v.*

gall[3] (gôl), a lump or ball that swells up on the leaves, stems, or roots of plants where they have been injured by insects. Ink is made from the galls of oak trees. *n.*

Galls on a leaf

gal lant (gal′ənt), 1. noble in spirit or in looks; brave. King Arthur was a gallant knight. 2. grand; fine; stately. A ship with all of its sails spread is a gallant sight. 3. looking dressed up and gay. The garden made a gallant show. 4. a man of fashion; a fine gentleman. 5. showing respect and courtesy to women. 6. a man who is very polite and attentive to women. *adj., n. 4.*

gal lant ry (gal′ən tri), 1. bravery; dashing courage. 2. respect and courtesy to women. 3. gallant act or speech. *n., pl. gallantries. 9.*

gall bladder, sac attached to the liver, in which excess gall or bile is stored until needed.

gal le on (gal′i ən), a kind of large ship, usually with several decks. See the picture just below. *n. 14.*

Galleon

gal ler y (gal′ər i), 1. a hall or long narrow passage. 2. a balcony looking down into a large hall or room. 3. the highest balcony of a theater. 4. people who sit there. 5. a building or room used to show collections of pictures and statues. *n., pl. galleries. 4.*

gal ley (gal′i), 1. long, narrow ship of former times having oars and sails. Galleys were often rowed by slaves or convicts. 2. a large rowboat. 3. the kitchen of a ship. *n., pl. galleys. 8.*

Galley (def. 1)

gall fly (gôl′flī′), insect that causes galls on plants. *n., pl. gallflies.*

Gal lic (gal′ik), 1. of or having to do with Gaul or its people; as, Caesar's Gallic Wars. 2. French; as, Gallic wit. *adj. 12.*

gal lon (gal′ən), the amount of 4 quarts of liquid. *n. 5.*

gal lop (gal′əp), 1. the fastest gait of a horse or other four-footed animal. In a gallop, all four feet are off the ground together at each leap. 2. ride at a gallop. 3. go at a gallop. 4. cause to go at a gallop. 5. go very fast; hurry. *n., v. 3.*

gal lows (gal′ōz), 1. wooden frame made of a crossbar on two upright posts, used for hanging criminals. 2. hanging as a punishment. *n., pl. gallowses or gallows. 5.*

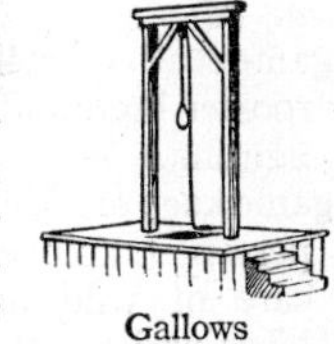

Gallows

ga lore (gə lōr′), in abundance. Every town has automobiles galore. *adv. 20.*

ga losh (gə losh′), rubber overshoe. We wear galoshes in wet weather. *n.*

gal van ic (gal van′ik), 1. producing an electric current by chemical action. 2. of or caused by an electric current. 3. startling. *adj. 17.*

gal va nism (gal′və nizm), 1. electricity produced by chemical action. 2. the science dealing with this. 3. use of such electricity for medical purposes. *n. 18.*

gal va nize (gal′və nīz), 1. apply an electric current to. 2. startle; arouse suddenly. 3. cover (iron or steel) with a thin coating of zinc to prevent rust. *v. 13.*

Gal ves ton (gal′vəs tən), seaport city in southeastern Texas. *n. 19.*

gam ble (gam′bəl), 1. play games of chance for money. 2. take great risks in business or speculation. 3. bet; wager. 4. **Gamble away** means lose by gambling. *v. 8.*

gam bler (gam′blər), 1. person who gambles. 2. person who gambles a great deal. *n. 19.*

gam bol (gam′bəl), 1. a frolic; running and jumping about in play. 2. to frolic; run and jump about; play. Lambs gamboled in the meadow. *n., v., gamboled, gamboling. 9.*

gam brel roof (gam′brəl rüf′), roof having two slopes on each side. The lower slope is usually steeper than the upper one.

Gambrel roof

game (gām), 1. a way of playing; as, a game with bat and ball, a game of tag. 2. the things needed for a game. This store sells games. 3. contest with certain rules. One person or side tries to win it. 4. the score in a game. 5. scheme; plan. 6. animals and birds that are hunted. 7. the flesh of wild animals and birds when used for food. 8. having to do with game and hunting; as, game laws. 9. brave; plucky; daring to do a thing. 10. gamble. 11. **Make game of** means make fun of; laugh at. *n., adj., v. 1.*

game cock (gām′kok′), rooster bred and trained for fighting. *n.*

game keep er (gām′kēp′ər), person employed to take care of wild animals and birds and see that they are not stolen. *n. 17.*

Gamecock (about 1½ ft. from head to toe)

game some (gām′səm), full of play; sportive; ready to play. *adj. 15.*

game ster (gām′stər), gambler. *n. 14.*

gam in (gam′in), neglected boy left to run about the streets. *n.*

gam ing (gām′ing), gambling. *n.*

gam mon[1] (gam′ən), nonsense; humbug. *n.* [*Rarely used in formal writing*] *13.*

gam mon[2] (gam′ən), 1. the lower end of a side of bacon. 2. a smoked or cured ham. *n.*

gam ut (gam′ət), 1. the whole series of recognized musical notes. 2. the major scale. 3. the whole range of anything. In one minute I ran the gamut of feeling from hope to despair. *n. 12.*

gam y (gām′i), 1. having the flavor of game; slightly tainted. 2. brave; plucky. *adj., gamier, gamiest.*

gan (gan), began. *v.* [*Old use*] *15.*

gan der (gan′dər), male goose. *n. 11.*

Gan dhi (gän′di), Hindu political, social, and religious leader, born in 1869. *n.*

gang (gang), 1. group of people acting or going around together. Criminals often form gangs. 2. group of people working together under one foreman. Two gangs of workmen were mending the road. 3. set of similar tools or machines arranged to work together. *n. 5.*

Gan ges (gan′jēz), a famous sacred river in northern India. *n. 13.*

gan gli on (gang′gli ən), 1. a group of nerve cells forming a nerve center. 2. a center of force, activity, etc. *n., pl. ganglia* (gang′gli ə) or *ganglions. 13.*

gang plank (gang′plangk′), a movable bridge used in passing on and off a ship. *n.*

Gangplank

gan grene (gang′grēn), 1. the decay of a part of a living person or animal. 2. cause gangrene in; have gangrene in; decay. The wounded leg gangrened and had to be cut off. *n., v. 14.*

gang ster (gang′stər), member of a bad gang. *n.*

gang way (gang′wā′), 1. a passageway. 2. a passageway on a ship. This ship has a gangway between the rail and the cabins. 3. gangplank. 4. Get out of the way! Stand aside and make room! *n., interj. 19.*

gan net (gan′it), large swimming bird. *n.*

gant let (gänt′lit), gauntlet. *n.*

Gan y mede (gan′i mēd), a beautiful boy carried off by Zeus in the form of an eagle. Ganymede became cupbearer to the gods of Olympus. *n. 14.*

gaol (jāl), jail. *n. 13.*

gaol er (jāl′ər), jailer. *n. 16.*

gap (gap), 1. break or opening; as, a gap in a fence or wall. 2. unfilled space; a blank. The record is not complete; there are several gaps in it. 3. a pass through mountains. *n. 4.*

gape (gāp), 1. open wide. A deep hole in the earth gaped before us. 2. wide opening.

3. open the mouth wide; yawn. 4. act of opening the mouth wide; a yawning. 5. stare with the mouth open. The savages gaped when they saw an airplane for the first time. *v., n. 6.*

ga rage (gə räzh′), place for keeping automobiles; shop for repairing automobiles. *n. 6.*

garb (gärb), 1. the way one is dressed. 2. clothing. 3. clothe. *n., v. 8.*

gar bage (gär′bij), waste food from the kitchen or dining room; scraps of food to be thrown away. *n. 9.*

gar ble (gär′bəl), make unfair or misleading selections from (facts, statements, writings, etc.); omit parts in order to misrepresent. Foreign newspapers gave a garbled account of the President's speech. *v. 20.*

gar den (gär′dən), 1. ground used for growing vegetables, flowers, or fruits. 2. take care of a garden. He liked to garden, for it kept him out of doors. *n., v. 1.*

gar den er (gärd′nər), 1. person hired to take care of a garden. 2. person who makes a garden or works in a garden. *n. 4.*

gar de ni a (gär dē′ni ə), fragrant, white flower with waxy petals. *n.*

Gar field (gär′fēld), James A. (1831-1881), 20th president of the United States. He was assassinated in 1881. *n. 18.*

gar gle (gär′gəl), 1. wash (the throat or mouth) with a liquid kept in motion by the breath. 2. liquid used for gargling. *v., n. 18.*

gar goyle (gär′goil), a spout ending in a grotesque head, for carrying off rain water. *n.*

Gargoyle

Gar i bal di (gar′i bôl′di), Italian patriot and general (1807-1882). *n.*

gar ish (gãr′ish), glaring; unpleasantly bright; showy. *adj. 15.*

gar land (gär′lənd), 1. wreath of flowers, leaves, etc. 2. decorate with garlands. *n., v. 4.*

gar lic (gär′lik), a plant like an onion, used in cooking. Its flavor is stronger than that of an onion. *n. 13.*

gar ment (gär′mənt), any article of clothing. *n. 2.*

gar ner (gär′nər), 1. gather and store away. Wheat is cut and garnered at harvest time. 2. storehouse for grain. 3. a store of anything. *v., n. 12.*

gar net (gär′nit), 1. a deep-red precious stone. 2. deep red. *n. 17.*

gar nish (gär′nish), 1. something laid on or around a dish as a decoration. The turkey was served with a garnish of cranberries and parsley. 2. decorate (food). 3. decoration; trimming. 4. decorate; trim. *n., v. 7.*

gar ni ture (gär′ni chər), a garnish; decoration; trimming. *n. 18.*

gar ret (gar′it), space in a house just below a sloping roof; attic. *n. 8.*

gar ri son (gar′i sən), 1. the soldiers stationed in a fort, town, etc., to defend it. 2. place that has a garrison. 3. station soldiers in (a fort, town, etc.) to defend it. 4. occupy (a fort, town, etc.) as a garrison. *n., v. 6.*

gar ru lous (gar′ů ləs), talking too much about trifles. *adj. 13.*

gar ter (gär′tər), 1. band or strap to hold up a stocking or sock. It is usually elastic. 2. fasten with a garter. *n., v. 6.*

garter snake, a harmless snake, brown or green with long yellow stripes.

Gar y (gãr′i), a city in northwestern Indiana, noted for making steel. *n.*

gas (gas), 1. vapor; not a solid or liquid; any substance when it is like air in form. 2. a gas obtained from coal and other substances. Gas was once much used for lighting and is now used for cooking and heating. 3. gasoline. 4. kill or injure by poisonous gas. *n., pl. gases, v., gassed, gassing. 3.*

gas e ous (gas′i əs), in the form of gas; of gas; like gas. Steam is water in a gaseous condition. *adj. 8.*

gash (gash), 1. a long, deep cut or wound. 2. make a long, deep cut or wound in. *n., v. 7.*

gas mask, tight covering that fits over the mouth and nose to prevent breathing poisonous gas.

gas o line or **gas o lene** (gas′ə lēn), a colorless liquid made from petroleum. It evaporates and burns very easily. Gasoline is used to run automobiles. *n. 5.*

gasp (gasp), 1. a catching of the breath with open mouth. 2. catch the breath with open mouth; breathe with gasps. 3. utter with gasps. *n., v. 6.*

gas tric (gas′trik), of the stomach. **Gastric juice** is the digestive liquid formed in the stomach. *adj. 9.*

gat (gat), got. *old pt. of* **get.** *17.*

gate (gāt), 1. an opening in a wall or fence,

hat, āge, cãre, fär; let, ēqual, tėrm; it, īce; hot, ōpen, ôrder; oil, out; cup, pu̇t, rüle, ūse; th, thin; ᴛʜ, then; ə represents *a* in about, *e* in taken, *i* in pencil, *o* in lemon, *u* in circus.

usually fitted with a door. 2. a door in a wall or fence. 3. door, valve, etc., to stop or control the flow of water in a pipe, dam, lock, etc. *n. 1.*

gate way (gāt′wā′), 1. an opening in a wall or fence where a gate is. 2. way to go in or out; way to get to something. *n. 6.*

gath er (gaᴛʜ′ər), 1. collect; bring into one place. 2. come together. 3. pick; glean or pluck. Farmers gather their crops. 4. put together in the mind. I gathered from his words that he was really much upset. 5. pull together in folds. The sewing woman gathers a skirt at the top. 6. one of the little folds between the stitches when cloth is gathered. 7. draw together. Some sores gather to a head. *v., n. 1.*

gath er ing (gaᴛʜ′ər ing), 1. an assembly; a meeting. 2. a swelling that comes to a head. A boil is a painful gathering. *n.*

gaud (gôd), showy ornament. Savages like beads, mirrors, and such gauds. *n. 16.*

gaud y (gôd′i), too bright and gay to be in good taste; cheap and showy. *adj., gaudier, gaudiest. 9.*

gauge (gāj), 1. standard measure; measure. There are gauges of the capacity of a barrel, the thickness of sheet iron, the diameter of a shotgun bore, wire, etc. 2. instrument for measuring. A steam gauge measures the pressure of steam. 3. measure accurately. 4. estimate; judge. It is difficult to gauge the character of a stranger. 5. distance between the rails of a railroad. *n., v. 9.*

Gauge for measuring wire

Gaul (gôl), 1. an ancient country in western Europe including France, Belgium, and parts of the Netherlands, Switzerland, Germany, and Italy. 2. one of the Celtic inhabitants of ancient Gaul. 3. a Frenchman. *n. 9.*

gaunt (gônt), 1. thin and bony; hollow-eyed and starved-looking. 2. looking bare and gloomy; desolate. *adj. 6.*

gaunt let¹ (gônt′lit), 1. an iron glove which was part of a knight's armor. 2. a stout, heavy glove with a deep, flaring cuff. 3. **Throw down the gauntlet** means give a challenge. *n. 10.* Also spelled **gantlet.**

Iron gauntlet

gaunt let² (gônt′lit). **Run the gauntlet** means pass between two rows of men each of whom strikes the victim as he passes. *n.* Also spelled **gantlet.**

gauze (gôz), a very thin, light cloth, easily seen through. *n. 8.*

gauz y (gôz′i), like gauze; thin as gauze. *adj., gauzier, gauziest.*

gave (gāv). See **give.** He gave me some of his candy. *pt. of give. 1.*

gav el (gav′əl), a small mallet used by a presiding officer to signal for attention or order. The chairman rapped on the table twice with his gavel. *n.*

Ga wain (gä′win), one of the knights of King Arthur's Round Table. *n. 17.*

gawk (gôk), 1. awkward person; clumsy fool. 2. stare rudely or stupidly. *Used in common talk. n., v.*

gawk y (gôk′i), awkward; clownish; clumsy. *adj., gawkier, gawkiest.*

gay (gā), 1. happy and full of fun; merry. 2. bright-colored. *adj. 2.*

gay e ty (gā′i ti), gaiety. *n., pl. gayeties. 13.*

gay ly (gā′li), gaily. *adv.*

gaze (gāz), 1. look long and steadily. 2. a long, steady look. *v., n. 2.*

ga zelle (gə zel′), small, graceful kind of antelope with large, soft eyes. *n. 18.*

gaz er (gāz′ər), one who gazes; as, a stargazer. *n. 15.*

Gazelle (about 2 ft. high at the shoulder)

ga zette (gə zet′), 1. a newspaper; as, the *Emporia Gazette.* 2. an official government journal containing lists of appointments, promotions, etc. 3. publish, list, or announce in a gazette. *n., v. 14.*

gaz et teer (gaz′ə tēr′), 1. dictionary of geographical words. Names of places, seas, mountains, etc., are arranged alphabetically in a gazetteer. 2. journalist. *n. 15.*

gear (gēr), 1. an arrangement of parts for some purpose, such as harness, tools, machinery, clothing, or household goods. 2. a wheel having teeth that fit into teeth in another wheel; wheels turning one another by teeth. 3. **In gear** means connected with the motor. **Out of gear** means not connected with the motor. An automobile in low gear moves slowly, but strongly. 4. provide with gear. 5. come into gear or be in gear. *n., v. 7.*

Wheels in gear

gear ing (gēr′ing), the parts of machinery by which motion is transferred, often a series of toothed wheels. *n.*

geck o (gek′ō), small, harmless, insect-eating lizard with suction pads on its feet so that it can walk on ceilings, walls, etc. *n., pl. geckos* or *geckoes.*

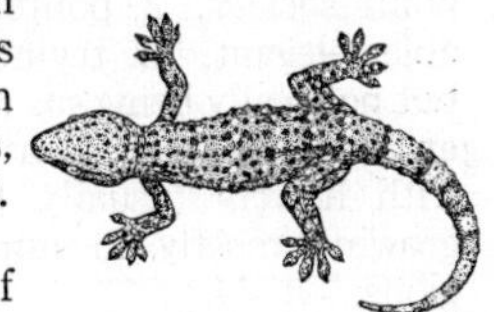
Gecko (about 1 ft. long)

gee (jē), a word of command to oxen or horses directing them to turn to the right. *interj. 13.*

geese (gēs), more than one goose. *n. pl. 4.*

gei sha (gā′shə), a Japanese singing and dancing girl. *n., pl. geisha* or *geishas.*

gel a tin or **gel a tine** (jel′ə tin), a substance like glue or jelly obtained by boiling the bones, hoofs, and other waste parts of animals. Gelatin is used in making glue and desserts. *n. 10.*

ge lat i nous (ji lat′i nəs), 1. of or like jelly. 2. of or like gelatin. *adj. 17.*

gem (jem), 1. a precious stone; jewel. Diamonds and rubies are gems. 2. anything that is very beautiful. 3. the most precious thing. The gem of his collection was a rare Persian stamp. 4. set with gems. Stars gem the sky. 5. muffin. *n., v., gemmed, gemming. 2.*

Gen., 1. General. 2. Genesis.

gen darme (zhän′därm), a French soldier who has the duties of a policeman. *n. 20.*

gen der (jen′dər), grouping of words as masculine, feminine, or neuter. *n. 10.*

gen e a log i cal (jen′i ə loj′i kəl), having to do with genealogy. A genealogical table or chart shows the descent of a person or family from an ancestor. *adj. 18.*

gen e al o gy (jen′i al′ə ji), 1. account of the descent of a person or family from an ancestor or ancestors. 2. descent of a person or family from an ancestor; pedigree; lineage. 3. study of pedigrees. *n., pl. genealogies. 15.*

gen er a (jen′ər ə), more than one genus. *n. pl. 18.*

gen er al (jen′ər əl), 1. of all; for all; from all. 2. widespread; not limited to a few, but for or from many. There is a general interest in radio. 3. not detailed. He made only a general plan. 4. not special; as, a general store, a general magazine. 5. chief; as, attorney general, postmaster general. 6. a high officer in command of many men in an army. 7. **In general** means usually; commonly. *adj., n. 1.*

gen er al i ty (jen′ər al′i ti), 1. a general or vague statement not definite enough to be useful. The candidate spoke only in generalities; not once did he say what he would do if elected. 2. general quality. A rule of great generality is one that has very few exceptions. 3. a general principle or rule. "Nothing happens without a cause" is a generality. 4. the common run; the mass; the main body. The generality of people must work for a living. *n., pl. generalities. 15.*

gen er al i za tion (jen′ər əl i zā′shən), 1. working out and stating a general rule, law, or principle. Don't be hasty in generalization. 2. a general rule or principle. *n. 15.*

gen er al ize (jen′ər əl īz), 1. make into one general statement; bring under a common heading, class, or law. 2. infer a general rule from particular facts. If you have seen cats, lions, leopards, and tigers eat meat, you can generalize and say, "The cat family eats meat." 3. make vague; represent vaguely; use generalities. Since I do not know the details, I can only generalize about the matter. 4. bring into general use. *v. 13.*

gen er al ly (jen′ər əl i), 1. for the most part; usually. 2. in a general way; not specially. Speaking generally, our coldest weather comes in January. *adv. 6.*

gen er al ship (jen′ər əl ship′), 1. ability as a general; skill in commanding an army. 2. skillful management; leadership. 3. rank, commission, authority, or term of office of a general. *n.*

gen er ate (jen′ər āt), produce; cause to be. Burning coal can generate steam. The steam can generate electricity by turning an electric generator. *v. 8.*

gen er a tion (jen′ər ā′shən), 1. the people born in the same period; as, our grandmother's generation, the coming generation. 2. about thirty years, or the time from the birth of one generation to the birth of the next generation. 3. one step or degree in a family. The picture showed four generations—great-grandmother, grandmother, mother, and baby. 4. bringing into being; as, the generation of steam in a boiler. *n. 3.*

gen er a tive (jen′ər ā′tiv), 1. having to do with the production of offspring. 2. having the power of producing. *adj. 17.*

gen er a tor (jen′ər ā′tər), 1. person or thing that generates. 2. apparatus for producing electricity, gas, or steam. *n. 15.*

ge ner ic (ji ner′ik), 1. characteristic of a genus, kind, or class. Cats and lions show generic differences. 2. general; not specific or special. Liquid is a generic term. *adj. 20.*

gen er os i ty (jen′ər os′i ti), 1. being generous; unselfishness; willingness to share with others. 2. nobleness of heart; freedom from meanness. 3. generous behavior; generous act. *n., pl. generosities. 7.*

gen er ous (jen′ər əs), 1. unselfish; willing to share with others. 2. noble-minded; forgiving; not mean. 3. large; plentiful. A quarter of a pie is a generous piece. *adj. 3.*

Gen e sis (jen′i sis), the first book of the Old Testament. Genesis gives an account of the creation of the world. *n. 17.*

gen e sis (jen′i sis), origin; creation; coming into being. *n.*

ge net ic (ji net′ik), of or concerning origin and growth. *adj. 20.*

Ge ne va (ji nē′və), 1. a city in Switzerland. 2. a lake in Switzerland. *n. 12.*

gen ial (jēn′yəl), 1. smiling and pleasant; cheerful and friendly; kindly; as, a genial welcome. 2. helping growth; pleasantly warming; comforting; as, genial sunshine. *adj. 4.*

ge ni al i ty (jē′ni al′i ti), genial quality; genial behavior. *n.*

ge nie (jē′ni), a spirit or jinni. When Aladdin rubbed his lamp, the genie came and did what Aladdin asked. *n.*

ge ni i (jē′ni ī), 1. guardian spirits of a person, place, institution, etc. 2. the two spirits, one good and one evil, supposed to influence a person's fate. *n. pl. 16.*

gen i tive (jen′i tiv), a form of nouns and pronouns showing possession, source, or origin. *n. 20.*

gen ius (jēn′yəs), 1. very great natural power of mind. 2. a person having such power. Shakespeare was a genius. 3. great natural ability. A great actor has a genius for acting. 4. special character or spirit of a person, nation, age, language, etc. 5. guardian spirit of a person, place, institution, etc. 6. either of two spirits, one good and one evil, supposed to influence a person's fate. 7. person who powerfully influences another. *n., pl. geniuses* for 1, 2, 3, 4, and 7, *genii* (jē′ni ī) for 5 and 6. *4.*

Gen o a (jen′ō ə), a famous seaport city in northwestern Italy. *n. 9.*

Gen o ese (jen′ō ēz′), 1. of Genoa or its people. 2. native or inhabitant of Genoa. *adj., n., pl. Genoese.*

gen teel (jen tēl′), 1. belonging or suited to polite society. 2. polite; well-bred; fashionable; elegant. 3. trying to be aristocratic, but not really being so. *adj. 8.*

gen tian (jen′shən), a plant with flowers (usually blue), growing mostly in hilly regions. *n. 14.*

Gentian

gen tile or **Gen tile** (jen′tīl), 1. person who is not a Jew. 2. not Jewish. *n., adj. 8.*

gen til i ty (jen til′i ti), 1. gentle birth; membership in the aristocracy or upper class. 2. good manners. 3. refinement. *n., pl. gentilities. 12.*

gen tle (jen′təl), 1. mild; not rough; as, a gentle tap. 2. soft; low; as, a gentle sound. 3. moderate; as, gentle heat, a gentle slope. 4. kindly; friendly; as, a gentle disposition. 5. easy to manage; as, a gentle dog. 6. of good family and social position; wellborn. 7. refined; polite. *adj. 1.*

gen tle folk (jen′təl fōk′), people of good family and social position. *n. pl. 19.*

gen tle man (jen′təl mən), 1. man of good family and social position. 2. man who is honorable and well-bred. 3. polite term for any man. *n., pl. gentlemen. 1.*

gen tle man ly (jen′təl mən li), like a gentleman; well-bred; polite. *adj.*

gen tle ness (jen′təl nis), being gentle; softness in voice, touch, and manner. *n. 6.*

gen tle wom an (jen′təl wu̇m′ən), 1. woman of good family and social position. 2. well-bred woman; lady. 3. woman attendant of a lady of rank. *n., pl. gentlewomen. 12.*

gen tly (jen′tli), 1. in a gentle way; tenderly; softly. 2. gradually; as, a gently sloping hillside. *adv. 3.*

gen try (jen′tri), 1. the class of wellborn and well-bred people. 2. in England, the class next below the nobility. 3. people of any particular class. *n. 8.*

gen u ine (jen′ū in), 1. real; true; as, genuine leather, a genuine diamond. 2. frank; free from pretense; sincere; as, genuine sorrow. *adj. 5.*

ge nus (jē′nəs), kind; sort; class. One genus of animals usually includes several species. *n., pl. genera* (jen′ər ə) or *genuses. 11.*

ge og ra pher (ji og′rə fər), person who knows much about geography. *n. 11.*

ge o graph ic (jē′ə graf′ik), of geography. *adj. 15.*

ge o graph i cal (jē′ə graf′i kəl), of or pertaining to geography. *adj. 8.*

ge o graph i cal ly (jē′ə graf′i kəl i), 1. in geographical respects. 2. according to geography. *adv.*

ge og ra phy (ji og′rə fi), 1. study of the earth's surface, climate, continents, countries, peoples, industries, and products. 2. surface features of a place or region. 3. book about geography. *n., pl. geographies. 4.*

ge o log i cal (jē′ə loj′i kəl), of geology; having to do with geology. *adj. 15.*

ge o log i cal ly (jē′ə loj′i kəl i), 1. in geological respects. 2. according to geology. *adv.*

ge ol o gist (ji ol′ə jist), person skilled in geology. *n. 16.*

ge ol o gy (ji ol′ə ji), the science that deals with the earth's crust, the layers of which it is composed, and their history. *n., pl. geologies. 10.*

ge o met ric (jē′ə met′rik), 1. of geometry; according to the principles of geometry; as, geometric proof. 2. consisting of straight lines, circles, triangles, etc.; regular and symmetrical; as, a geometric design. *adj. 13.*

Geometric design

ge o met ri cal (jē′ə met′ri kəl), geometric. *adj. 16.*

ge om e try (ji om′i tri), the study that measures and compares lines, angles, surfaces, and solids; the mathematics of space. *n., pl. geometries. 9.*

George (jôrj), 1. George III (1738-1820) was king of Great Britain when the American colonies revolted. 2. **Saint George** is the patron saint of England. *n. 2.*

geor gette (jôr jet′), a very thin silk crepe. *n. 9.*

Geor gia (jôr′jə), a Southern State of the United States. *n. 5.*

ge ra ni um (ji rā′ni əm), 1. a popular garden plant with showy flowers of scarlet, pink, or white. 2. a wild plant with pink or purple flowers. *n. 8.*

Garden geranium

germ (jėrm), 1. a simple animal or plant, too small to be seen, which causes disease; as, the germ of scarlet fever. 2. a seed or bud. 3. the beginning of anything. *n. 6.*

Ger man (jėr′mən), 1. of Germany, its people, or their language. 2. person born in Germany, living there, or having German parents. 3. the language of Germany. *adj., n. 2.*

Ger man ic (jėr man′ik), 1. German. 2. Teutonic. *adj. 17.*

Ger ma ny (jėr′mə ni), a country in central Europe. *n. 3.*

ger mi cide (jėr′mi sīd), something that kills germs. Carbolic acid is a part of many germicides. *n.*

ger mi nate (jėr′mi nāt), 1. begin to grow; develop; sprout. Seeds germinate in the spring. 2. cause to grow. You can germinate beans by soaking them in water and planting them in damp sawdust. *v. 9.*

ger mi na tion (jėr′mi nā′shən), a starting to grow or develop; a sprouting. Germination takes place when seeds are warm and moist. *n. 11.*

ger und (jer′ənd), a form of a verb which is used as a noun, but keeps verbal qualities and powers. In the sentence "Studying Latin for four years has improved Jim's English," *studying* is a gerund. *n. 19.*

ges tic u late (jes tik′ū lāt), make motions to show ideas or feelings. The speaker gesticulated by raising his arms, pounding the desk, and stamping his foot. *v. 20.*

ges tic u la tion (jes tik′ū lā′shən), 1. making lively or excited gestures. 2. a lively or excited gesture. *n. 15.*

ges ture (jes′chər), 1. a motion of the body used instead of words or with words to help express an idea or a feeling. 2. any action for effect or to impress others. Her refusal was merely a gesture; she really wanted to go. 3. make gestures; use gestures. *n., v. 6.*

get (get), 1. obtain. 2. become. 3. persuade; influence. Try to get Jack to come, too. 4. cause to be or do. Get the windows open. Mary got her work done. 5. Some special meanings are:

get away, 1. go away. 2. escape.

get in, 1. go in. 2. put in. 3. arrive. 4. become friendly or familiar.

get off, 1. come down from or out of. 2. take off. 3. escape. 4. help to escape. 5. start.

get on, 1. go up on or into. 2. put on. 3. advance. 4. manage. 5. succeed. 6. agree.

get out, 1. go out. 2. take out. 3. go away. 4. escape. 5. help to escape. 6. become known. 7. publish. 8. find out.

get over, 1. recover from. 2. overcome.
get together, 1. bring together; meet. 2. come to an agreement. *Used in common talk.*
get up, 1. arise. He got up at six o'clock. 2. stand up. 3. prepare.
v., got, got or *gotten, getting. 1.*

Geth sem a ne (geth sem′ə ni), the garden near Jerusalem which was the scene of Jesus's agony, betrayal, and arrest. *n.*

Get tys burg (get′iz bėrg), a town in southern Pennsylvania. One of the important battles of the Civil War was fought there July 1, 2, and 3, 1863. *n. 20.*

get-up (get′up′), 1. arrangement; way a thing is put together; style. 2. dress; costume. *n.* [*Used in common talk*]

gew gaw (gū′gô), 1. showy trifle; a gaudy, useless ornament or toy; bauble. The shops are filled with gewgaws for the dressing table, like fancy boxes, trays, pincushions, etc. 2. showy, but trifling. *n., adj. 15.*

gey ser (gī′zər), a hot spring that sends up at frequent intervals a fountain or jet of hot water or steam. *n. 12.*

Geyser

ghast ly (gast′li), 1. horrible. Murder is a ghastly crime. 2. like a dead person or ghost; deathly pale. A very sick person looks ghastly. 3. in a ghastly manner. *adj., ghastlier, ghastliest, adv. 6.*

Ghent (gent), a city in northwestern Belgium. *n. 18.*

gher kin (gėr′kin), a small cucumber made into pickles. *n.*

ghet to (get′ō), a part of a city in which the Jews live; Jewish quarter. *n., pl. ghettos.*

ghost (gōst), the spirit of one who is dead appearing to the living. The ghost of the murdered man haunted the house. *n. 2.*

ghost ly (gōst′li), 1. like a ghost. A ghostly form walked across the stage. 2. spiritual. His ghostly adviser means his spiritual or religious adviser. *adj., ghostlier, ghostliest. 9.*

ghoul (gül), 1. in Oriental stories, a horrible demon that feeds on corpses. 2. grave robber. 3. person who enjoys what is revolting to decent people. *n. 18.*

gi ant (jī′ənt), 1. a man of great size or very great power. 2. huge; as, a giant potato. *n., adj. 2.*

gib ber (jib′ər), 1. chatter senselessly like a monkey or an idiot; talk nonsense. 2. senseless chattering. *v., n. 15.*

gib ber ish (jib′ər ish or gib′ər ish), meaningless chatter; rapid, unintelligible talk. *n.*

gib bet (jib′it), 1. an upright post with a projecting arm at the top, from which the bodies of criminals were hung after execution. 2. hang on a gibbet. 3. hold up to public scorn or ridicule. 4. gallows. 5. put to death by hanging. *n., v. 10.*

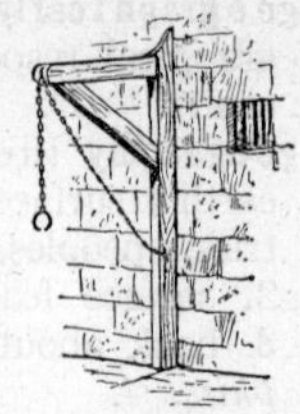
Gibbet

gib bon (gib′ən), a small, long-armed ape of southeastern Asia and the East Indies, that lives in trees. See the picture just below. *n. 19.*

gibe (jīb), jeer; scoff; sneer. *v., n. 14.* Also spelled **jibe.**

gib let (jib′lit), the heart, liver, or gizzard of a fowl. *n. 20.*

Gi bral tar (ji brôl′tər), a British fortress on a high rock on the Mediterranean coast of Spain. *n. 15.*

Gibbon (about 30 in. tall)

gid di ness (gid′i nis), 1. a confused, whirling sensation; a dizzy or giddy feeling. 2. lightness of mind; lack of steadiness and seriousness. *n. 17.*

gid dy (gid′i), 1. dizzy; having a whirling in the head. It makes me giddy to go on a merry-go-round. 2. making dizzy; as, a giddy dance. 3. never serious; living for the pleasure of the moment; in a whirl. Nobody can tell what that giddy girl will do next. *adj., giddier, giddiest. 7.*

gift (gift), 1. something given; a present; as, the gift of a million dollars to a university. 2. giving. The house came to him by gift from an uncle. 3. natural talent; special ability; as, a gift for painting. *n. 1.*

gift ed (gif′tid), very able; having special ability. Beethoven was gifted in music. *adj.*

gig[1] (gig), 1. a light, two-wheeled carriage drawn by one horse. 2. a long, light ship's boat moved by oars or by sails. *n. 8.*

Gig

gig[2] (gig), 1. a fish spear. 2. to fish with a gig. *n., v., gigged, gigging.*

gi gan tic (jī gan′tik), big like a giant; huge. *adj. 7.*

gig gle (gig′əl), 1. laugh in a silly or undignified way. 2. a silly or undignified laugh. *v., n. 14.*

Gi la mon ster (hē′lə mon′stər), a large, orange-and-black poisonous lizard of New Mexico, Arizona, and Mexico.

Gila monster (1½ ft. long)

gild[1] (gild), 1. cover with a thin layer of gold. 2. make (a thing) look bright and pleasing. *v., gilded* or *gilt, gilding. 4.*

gild[2] (gild), guild. *n.*

Gil e ad (gil′i əd), 1. a district in ancient Palestine, east of the river Jordan. 2. a mountain there. *n. 19.*

gill[1] (gil), a part of the body arranged for breathing in water. Fish, tadpoles, and crabs have gills. *n. 7.*

gill[2] (jil), a small liquid measure, one quarter of a pint. A gill is about half a cup. *n.*

gilt (gilt), 1. gilded. 2. material with which a surface is gilded. The gilt is coming off from this frame. *pt. and pp. of* **gild**[1], *adj., n. 8.*

gim crack (jim′krak′), 1. a showy, useless trifle; a toy. 2. showy but useless. *n., adj.*

gim let (gim′lit), a small tool with a screw point for boring holes. *n. 16.*

Gimlet

gin[1] (jin), strong alcoholic drink, usually flavored with juniper berries. *n. 6.*

gin[2] (jin), 1. a machine for separating cotton from its seeds. 2. separate (cotton) from its seeds. *n., v., ginned, ginning.*

gin ger (jin′jər), 1. spice made from the root of a tropical plant. It is used for flavoring and in medicine. 2. the root. Ginger is often preserved in syrup or candied. 3. the plant. 4. liveliness; energy. *Used in common talk. n. 5.*

ginger ale, bubbling drink flavored with ginger. It contains no alcohol.

gin ger bread (jin′jər bred′), 1. a kind of cake flavored with ginger. Gingerbread is often made in fancy shapes to please children. 2. showy; gaudy. Gingerbread work on a house is fussy ornament. *n., adj. 6.*

gin ger ly (jin′jər li), with extreme care or caution. *adv., adj.*

gin ger snap (jin′jər snap′), a thin, crisp cookie flavored with ginger. *n.*

ging ham (ging′əm), a cotton cloth made from colored threads. The patterns are usually in stripes, plaids, and checks. *n. 6.*

gin seng (jin′seng), a plant whose root is much used in medicine by the Chinese. *n.*

gip sy (jip′si), gypsy. *n., pl. gipsies, adj. 9.*

Giraffe (about 18 ft. tall)

gi raffe (ji raf′), a large African animal with a very long neck and legs and a spotted skin. Giraffes are the tallest living animals. *n. 15.*

gird (gėrd), 1. put a belt around. 2. fasten with a belt or girdle; as, to gird up one's clothes. 3. surround. 4. get ready. The soldiers girded themselves for battle. *v., girt* or *girded, girding. 5.*

gird er (gėr′dər), main supporting beam. The weight of a floor is usually supported by girders. A tall building or big bridge often has steel girders for its frame. *n. 20.*

GIRDER

gir dle (gėr′dəl), 1. belt. 2. a kind of elastic corset. 3. anything that surrounds; as, a girdle of trees around a pond. 4. put a girdle on or around. *n., v. 4.*

girl (gėrl), 1. female child. 2. young, unmarried woman. 3. female servant. 4. sweetheart. *Used in common talk. n. 1.*

girl hood (gėrl′hůd), 1. the time of being a girl. 2. girls; as, the girlhood of the nation. *n.*

girl ish (gėr′lish), 1. of a girl. 2. like that of a girl. 3. proper for girls. *adj. 14.*

Girl Scouts, organization for girls that seeks to develop health, character, and a knowledge of homemaking.

girt (gėrt), 1. girded. The knight girt himself for battle. We visited a seagirt island. 2. gird; put a belt, girdle, or girth around. 3. fasten with a belt, girdle, or girth. *v., pt. and pp. of* **gird.** *6.*

girth (gėrth), 1. the measure around anything; as, a man of large girth, the girth of a tree. 2. to measure in girth. 3. the strap or band that keeps the saddle in place on a horse. 4. fasten with a girth. 5. girdle. *n., v. 9.*

gist (jist), essential part; real point; main

idea; the substance of a longer statement. The gist of his long speech was that we should build a new school. *n.*

give (giv), 1. hand over as a present without pay. He likes to give books to his friends. 2. pay. He can give as much as three dollars for the wagon. 3. cause by some action of the body. Some boys give hard blows, even in play. 4. produce. This farm gives large crops. Reading gives knowledge. 5. present; offer. This newspaper gives a full story of the game. 6. put forth; utter. He gave a cry of pain. 7. cause; make. Don't give the teacher any trouble. 8. yield to force. The lock gives under hard pushing. 9. a yielding to force. 10. Some special meanings are:

give away, 1. give as a present. 2. hand over (a bride) to a bridegroom. 3. cause to be known; reveal; betray. *Used in common talk.*

give back, return.

give in, 1. stop fighting and admit defeat; yield. 2. hand in.

give off, send out; put forth.

give out, 1. send out; put forth. 2. distribute. 3. make known. 4. become used up or worn out.

give up, 1. hand over; surrender. 2. stop having or doing. 3. stop trying. 4. have no more hope for. 5. devote entirely.

v., gave, given, giving, n. 1.

giv en (giv′ən), 1. stated. At the given time she arrived. 2. inclined; disposed; addicted; as, given to boasting. 3. See **give.** That book was given to me. *adj., pp. of give. 1.*

given name, name given to a person in addition to his family name. *John* is the given name of John Smith.

giv er (giv′ər), person who gives. *n. 6.*

giz zard (giz′ərd), a bird's second stomach, where the food from the first stomach is ground up fine. *n. 13.*

gla cial (glā′shəl), icy; of ice; having much ice. During the glacial period, much of the northern hemisphere was covered with great ice sheets. *adj. 15.*

gla cier (glā′shər), a large mass of ice formed from the snow on high ground and moving very slowly down a mountain side or along a valley. *n. 6.*

glad (glad). She is glad to be well again. The glad news made her happy. *adj., gladder, gladdest. 1.*

glad den (glad′ən), make glad; become glad. *v. 11.*

glade (glād), a little open space in a wood or forest. *n. 6.*

glad i a tor (glad′i ā′tər), a slave, captive, or paid fighter who fought at the public shows in ancient Rome. *n. 11.*

glad i o lus (glad′i ō′ləs), a plant with spikes of large, handsome flowers in various colors. *n., pl. gladioluses, gladioli* (glad′i ō′lī). *18.*

Gladiolus

glad ness (glad′nis), glad feeling; happiness; joy. *n. 6.*

glad some (glad′səm), 1. glad; joyful; cheerful. 2. causing gladness; pleasant; delightful. *adj. 18.*

glam or ous (glam′ər əs), fascinating; charming. *adj.*

glam our or **glam or** (glam′ər), magic; charm. The moon cast a glamour over the garden. *n. 15.*

glance (glans), 1. a quick look. 2. look quickly. 3. a flash of light; gleam. 4. hit and go off at a slant. The spear glanced against the wall and missed him by a few inches. *n., v. 2.*

gland (gland), an organ in the body which makes and gives out some substance. Glands make the liquid which moistens the mouth. A cow has glands which make milk. The liver, the kidneys, the pancreas, and the thyroid are glands. *n. 10.*

glan du lar (glan′jü lər), of or like a gland; having glands; made up of glands. *adj. 13.*

glare (glãr), 1. a strong, unpleasant light; a light that shines so brightly that it hurts the eyes. 2. shine strongly or unpleasantly; shine so as to hurt the eyes. 3. a fierce, angry stare. 4. stare fiercely and with anger. *n., v. 4.*

glar ing (glãr′ing), 1. very bright; shining so brightly that it hurts the eyes; dazzling. 2. staring fiercely and angrily. 3. too bright and showy. 4. very easily seen; conspicuous. *adj.*

Glas gow (glas′gō), the largest city and chief seaport in Scotland. *n. 13.*

glass (glas), 1. a hard substance that breaks easily and can usually be seen through. Windows are made of glass. 2. thing or things made of glass. 3. something to drink from made of glass. 4. the amount a glass can hold; as, to drink a glass of water. 5. mirror. Look at yourself in the glass. 6. **Glasses** often means eyeglasses. 7. made of glass; as, a glass dish. 8. cover or protect with glass. *n., adj., v. 1.*

glass ful (glas′fu̇l), as much as a glass holds. *n., pl. glassfuls. 13.*
glass ware (glas′wãr′), articles made of glass. *n. 11.*
glass y (glas′i), 1. like glass; smooth; easily seen through. 2. having a fixed, stupid stare. *adj., glassier, glassiest. 11.*
glaze (glāz), 1. put glass in; cover with glass; as, to glaze a window or a picture. 2. a smooth, glossy surface or coating; as, the glaze on a china cup, a glaze of ice on the walk. 3. make a glossy or glassy surface on (vases, dishes, foods, etc.). 4. become glossy or glassy. The man's eyes were glazed in death. *v., n. 7.*
gla zier (glā′zhər), person whose work is putting glass in windows, picture frames, etc. *n.*
gleam (glēm), 1. a flash or beam of light. 2. send forth a gleam; shine. 3. short appearance. After one gleam of hope, all was discouraging and dark. *n., v. 4.*
glean (glēn), 1. gather stalks of grain left on the field by reapers. 2. gather little by little. *v. 6.*
glebe (glēb), 1. the soil; earth; field. *Used in poetry.* 2. a portion of land assigned to a clergyman. *n. 14.*
glee (glē), 1. joy; delight; mirth. 2. a song for three or more voices carrying different parts. *n. 5.*
glee ful (glē′fəl), merry; joyous. *adj.*
glen (glen), a small, narrow valley. *n. 5.*
glib (glib), 1. speaking or spoken smoothly and easily. A glib salesman sold her a set of dishes that she did not want. 2. speaking or spoken too smoothly and easily to be sincere. No one believed his glib excuses. *adj., glibber, glibbest. 13.*
glide (glīd), 1. move along smoothly, evenly, and easily. Birds, ships, dancers, and skaters glide. 2. smooth, even, easy movement. *v., n. 3.*
glid er (glīd′ər), airplane without a motor. Rising air currents keep it up in the air. *n.*

Glider

glim mer (glim′ər), 1. faint, unsteady light. 2. shine with a faint, unsteady light. The match glimmered and went out. 3. vague idea; faint glimpse. *n., v. 6.*
glimpse (glimps), 1. a very brief view; a short look. I got a glimpse of the falls as our train went by. 2. catch a brief view of. *n., v. 5.*
glint (glint), gleam; flash. *v., n. 11.*
glis ten (glis′ən), sparkle; glitter; shine. *v., n. 5.*
glis ter (glis′tər), glisten; glitter; sparkle. *v., n. [Old use] 16.*
glit ter (glit′ər), 1. sparkle; seem to have shining bits in it. 2. shine with a bright, sparkling light. Jewels and new coins glitter. 3. bright, sparkling light. 4. be bright and showy. 5. brightness; showiness. *v., n. 3.*
gloam ing (glōm′ing), evening twilight; dusk. *n.*
gloat (glōt), gaze or think about intently and with satisfaction. The miser gloated over his gold. *v. 19.*
globe (glōb), 1. anything that is round like a ball. 2. the earth; world. 3. a sphere with a map of the earth on it. *n. 3.*
glob u lar (glob′ū lər), 1. shaped like a globe; round. 2. composed of little spheres. *adj. 19.*

Globe (def. 3)

glob ule (glob′ūl), a very small sphere or ball. Globules of sweat stood on the worker's forehead. *n. 12.*
gloom (glüm), 1. darkness; deep shadow; dim light. 2. become dark. 3. dark thoughts and feelings; low spirits; sadness. *n., v. 4.*
gloom y (glüm′i), 1. dark; dim. 2. sad; melancholy. 3. dismal; causing gloom. *adj., gloomier, gloomiest. 5.*
Glo ri a or **glo ri a** (glō′ri ə), a song of praise to God; the music for it. *n. 20.*
glo ri fi ca tion (glō′ri fi kā′shən), glorifying; being glorified. *n. 20.*
glo ri fy (glō′ri fī), 1 give glory to; make glorious. 2. to worship; to praise. 3. make more beautiful or splendid. *v., glorified, glorifying. 5.*
glo ri ous (glō′ri əs), 1. having or deserving glory. 2. giving glory. 3. magnificent; splendid. *adj. 2.*
glo ry (glō′ri), 1. great praise and honor; fame. 2. something that brings praise and honor. 3. be proud; rejoice. 4. brightness; splendor. 5. condition of magnificence, splendor, or greatest prosperity.

6. heaven. *n., pl. glories, v., gloried, glorying.* *2.*

gloss (glôs), 1. a smooth, shiny surface on anything. Varnished furniture has a gloss. 2. put a smooth, shiny surface on. 3. a surface that covers wrong underneath. 4. **Gloss** (a thing) **over** means smooth it over or make it seem right even though it is really wrong. *n., v. 8.*

glos sa ry (glos′ə ri), a list of hard words with explanations. Some schoolbooks have glossaries at the end. *n., pl. glossaries. 19.*

gloss y (glôs′i), smooth and shiny. *adj., glossier, glossiest. 8.*

Glouces ter (glos′tər), 1. a city in southwestern England. 2. a fishing seaport in northeastern Massachusetts. *n. 17.*

glove (gluv), 1. a covering for the hand with separate places for each finger. 2. cover with a glove; provide with gloves. *n., v. 2.*

glov er (gluv′ər), person who makes or sells gloves. *n.*

glow (glō), 1. the shine from something that is red-hot or white-hot; a similar shine. 2. shine as if red-hot or white-hot. 3. a bright, warm color; as, the glow of sunset. 4. the warm feeling or color of the body; as, the glow of health on his cheeks. 5. show a warm color; look warm. 6. an eager look on the face; as, a glow of interest or excitement. 7. look eager. His face glowed at the idea. *n., v. 2.*

glow er (glou′ər), stare; scowl. The sullen boy glowered at his father. *v., n. 13.*

glow worm (glō′wėrm′), insect larva or insect that glows in the dark. Fireflies develop from glowworms. *n. 11.*

gloze (glōz), smooth over; explain away. Kate tried to gloze over her mistakes. *v. 15.*

glu cose (glü′kōs), 1. a kind of sugar occurring in fruits. 2. a syrup made from starch. *n. 16.*

glue (glü), 1. substance made from the hoofs of animals and used to stick pieces of wood together. 2. any similar substance. Glues are stronger than pastes. 3. stick together with glue. 4. fasten tightly. He glued his eyes to the windows. *n., v. 5.*

glum (glum), gloomy; dismal; sullen. *adj., glummer, glummest. 15.*

glut (glut), 1. feed as much as can be eaten, or more. The boys glutted themselves with cake. 2. fill; choke up. 3. a full supply. 4. fill too full; provide too much for. 5. too great a supply. *v., glutted, glutting, n. 14.*

glu ten (glü′tən), the tough, sticky substance that remains in flour when the starch is taken out. *n. 12.*

glu ti nous (glü′ti nəs), sticky. *adj. 16.*

glut ton (glut′ən), 1. greedy eater. 2. wolverene, a thickset animal living in northern regions. *n. 12.*

Glutton (about 3½ ft. long, including the tail)

glut ton ous (glut′ən əs), inclined to eat too much; greedy. *adj. 18.*

glut ton y (glut′ən i), excess in eating. *n., pl. gluttonies. 14.*

glyc er in or **glyc er ine** (glis′ər in), a colorless, sweet, syrupy liquid obtained from fats and oils. Glycerin is used in ointments, lotions, and explosives. *n. 10.*

gnarl (närl), a knot in wood; hard, rough lump. *n. 14.*

gnarled (närld), containing gnarls; knotted; twisted; rugged. The farmer's gnarled hands grasped the plow firmly. *adj.*

gnash (nash), strike together. Angry animals often gnash their teeth. *v. 10.*

gnat (nat), a small, two-winged insect or fly. Most gnats make bites that itch. *n. 7.*

Gnat. Line shows actual length.

gnaw (nô), bite at and wear away. A mouse has gnawed right through the cover of this box. *v., gnawed, gnawed* or *gnawn, gnawing. 5.*

gneiss (nīs), a rock much like granite. *n. 20.*

gnome (nōm), a dwarf supposed to live in the earth and to guard treasures of precious metals and stones. *n. 15.*

gnu (nü), large, African antelope with an oxlike head and a long tail; wildebeest. *n., pl. gnus* or *gnu.*

Gnu (about 4 ft. high at the shoulder)

go (gō). Cars go on the road. The wheels go round. Does your watch go well? His work is going well. Summer had gone. All my money is gone. Some special meanings are:

go by, 1. pass. 2. be guided by; follow. 3. be known by.

go into, 1. be contained in. 2. investigate.

go off, 1. leave; depart. 2. explode; be fired. 3. happen; take place.

go on, 1. go ahead; go forward. 2. manage. 3. behave.
go out, 1. stop being; end. 2. go to parties, etc. 3. give sympathy. 4. go on strike.
go over, 1. look at carefully. 2. do again. 3. read again. 4. succeed. *Used in common talk.*
go up, 1. ascend; rise. 2. increase.
let go, 1. allow to escape. 2. give up one's hold. 3. give up.
let oneself go, give way to one's feelings or desires.
v., went, gone, going. 1.

goad (gōd), 1. sharp-pointed stick for driving cattle. 2. anything that drives or urges one on. 3. drive or urge on; act as a goad to. Hunger goaded him to steal a loaf of bread. *n., v. 9.*

goal (gōl), 1. place reached at the end of a race. 2. something desired. The goal of his ambition was to be captain of the ball team. 3. place which players try to reach in games. 4. points won by reaching this place. *n. 4.*

goat (gōt), a small lively animal with horns. Goats are stronger, less timid, and more active than sheep. *n., pl. goats* or *goat. 2.*

Goat

goat herd (gōt′hėrd′), person who tends goats. *n.*

goat skin (gōt′skin′), 1. the skin of a goat. 2. leather made from it. *n. 16.*

gob ble[1] (gob′əl), eat fast and greedily. *v. 6.*

gob ble[2] (gob′əl), 1. the noise a turkey makes. 2. make this noise or one like it. *n., v.*

gob bler (gob′lər), a male turkey. *n. 14.*

go-be tween (gō′bi twēn′), person who goes back and forth between others with messages, proposals, suggestions, etc. *n.*

gob let (gob′lit), a drinking glass that stands high above its base on a stem, and has no handle. *n. 6.*

Goblet

gob lin (gob′lin), a mischievous spirit or elf in the form of an ugly-looking little man. *n. 9.*

go cart (gō′kärt′), a wheeled seat for taking a small child about; a light cart or carriage, often pulled by hand. *n. 17.*

God (god), the maker and ruler of the world; a being that loves and helps man. *n. 1.*

god (god), a being with greater powers than any man has. *n.*

god child (god′chīld′), the child for whom a grown-up person takes vows at its baptism. *n., pl. godchildren.*

god dess (god′is), 1. a female god. 2. a very beautiful or wonderful woman. *n. 4.*

god fa ther (god′fä′ᴛʜər), man who takes vows for a child when it is baptized. *n. 12.*

god head or **God head** (god′hed), divine nature; God. *n. 11.*

god less (god′lis), 1. not believing in God. 2. ungodly; wicked; evil. *adj. 17.*

god like (god′līk′), 1. like God or a god. 2. suitable for God or a god. *adj. 7.*

god li ness (god′li nis), piety; righteousness. *n. 10.*

god ly (god′li), religious; pious; obeying, loving, and fearing God. *adj., godlier, godliest. 10.*

god moth er (god′muᴛʜ′ər), woman who takes vows for a child when it is baptized. *n. 6.*

god par ent (god′pãr′ənt), godfather or godmother. *n.*

god send (god′send′), something unexpected but very welcome, as if sent from God. The chance to go to a warm climate was a godsend to the sick man. *n.*

God speed (god′spēd′), a wish of success to a person setting out on a journey or undertaking. *n.*

goes (gōz). See **go.** He goes to school. *v. 2.*

Goe the (gā′tə), a famous German poet and prose writer (1749-1832). *n. 13.*

gog gle (gog′əl), 1. roll the eyes; stare with bulging eyes. 2. roll or bulge and stare. The boy's eyes goggled as the pirates treasure lay revealed before him. 3. **Goggles** are large spectacles to protect the eyes from light or dust. *v., n. 20.*

go ing (gō′ing), 1. leaving. His going was very sudden. 2. moving; in action. Set the clock going. 3. condition of the roads. The going is bad through this muddy road. 4. that goes; that can or will go. *n., adj. 1.*

goi ter or **goi tre** (goi′tər), 1. disease of the thyroid gland that often causes a large swelling in the neck. 2. the swelling. *n.*

gold (gōld), 1. a heavy, bright-yellow, precious metal. Gold is used in making coins, watches, and rings. 2. money in large sums. 3. made of gold. 4. like gold. 5. bright yellow. *n., adj. 1.*

gold en (gōl′dən), 1. made of gold; as, golden dishes. 2. containing gold. 3. shining like gold; bright-yellow; as, golden hair. 4. very good; as, a golden age, golden deeds. 5. very happy; flourishing. *adj. 1.*

Golden Fleece, fleece of gold that was guarded by a dragon until Jason and his companions carried it away with the help of Medea.

Golden Gate, entrance to San Francisco Bay.

Golden Gates, entrance to heaven.

gold en rod (gōl′dən-rod′), a common fall plant with tall stalks of small yellow flowers. *n. 13.*

Goldenrod

golden rule, the rule that Jesus asked us to follow: "Do unto others as you would have them do unto you." Matthew 7:12.

gold finch (gōld′finch′), a small yellow songbird marked with black. *n. 20.*

gold fish (gōld′fish′), a small fish of golden color kept in garden pools or in glass bowls indoors. *n., pl. goldfish* or *goldfishes. 19.*

American gold-finch (5 in. long)

gold leaf, gold beaten into a very thin sheet.

gold smith (gōld′smith′), man who makes articles of gold. *n. 8.*

Gold smith (gōld′smith′), Oliver, a British poet, novelist, and dramatist (1728-1774). *n.*

golf (golf), 1. an outdoor game played with a small, hard rubber ball and club-headed sticks. The player tries to drive the ball into a number of holes with as few strokes as possible. 2. play this game. See the picture. *n., v. 8.*

Man playing golf

Gol go tha (gol′gə thə), 1. place of Christ's crucifixion. 2. place of burial. *n. 20.*

Go li ath (gō lī′əth), in the Bible, a giant whom David killed with a stone from a sling. *n. 14.*

Go mor rah or **Go mor rha** (gə mor′ə), in the Bible, a wicked city destroyed by fire from heaven. *n. 14.*

gon do la (gon′də lə), 1. a long, narrow boat with a high peak at each end, used on the canals of Venice. 2. freight car that has low sides and no top. 3. car that hangs under a dirigible and holds the motors, passengers, etc. *n. 15.*

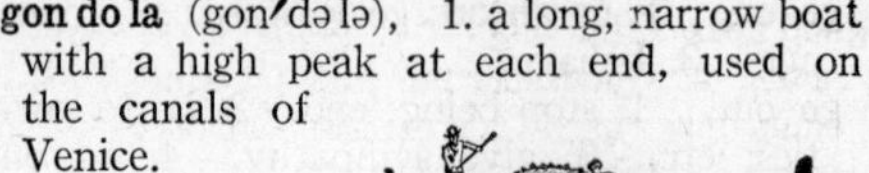

Gondola

gon do lier (gon′də lēr′), man who rows or poles a gondola. *n. 16.*

gone (gôn), 1. moved away; left. 2. lost 3. dead. 4. used up. 5. failed. 6. weak; faint. 7. See **go.** He has gone far away. *adj., pp. of go. 1.*

gong (gông), piece of metal shaped like a bowl or a saucer which makes a loud noise when struck. A gong is a kind of bell. *n. 13.*

good (gu̇d), 1. excellent. 2. well-behaved 3. right; as it ought to be. 4. desirable 5. satisfying. 6. pleasant. 7. kind friendly. Say a good word for me. 8. real; genuine. 9. that which is good. 10. benefit. 11. Some special meanings are:

as good as, almost; practically.

for good, forever; finally; permanently.

make good, 1. make up for; pay for. 2. fulfill; carry out. 3. succeed in doing 4. succeed. 5. prove.

to the good, on the side of profit or advantage; in one's favor.

adj., better, best, n. 1.

good-by or **good-bye** (gu̇d′bī′), farewell. We say "Good-by" to a friend when he goes away. *interj., n., pl. good-bys, good-byes. 3.*

good day, form of greeting or farewell.

Good Friday, the anniversary of Christ's crucifixion, the Friday before Easter.

Good Hope. The **Cape of Good Hope** is a cape near the southwestern tip of Africa.

good-hu mored (gu̇d′hū′mərd), having good humor; pleasant; amiable. *adj.*

good li ness (gu̇d′li nis), 1. handsomeness. 2. excellence. *n. 12.*

good-look ing (gu̇d′lu̇k′ing), handsome; making a good appearance. *adj.*

good ly (gu̇d′li), 1. pleasant; as, a goodly land. 2. good-looking; as, a goodly youth. 3. considerable; as, a goodly quantity. *adj., goodlier, goodliest. 3.*

good man (gu̇d′mən), master of a household. *n., pl. goodmen.* [*Old use*] *8.*

good-na tured (gu̇d′nā′chərd), pleasant; kindly; obliging; cheerful. *adj. 17.*

good ness (gu̇d′nis), 1. being good; kindness. 2. **Goodness me** and **Goodness gracious** are used to express surprise. *n., interj. 3.*

goods (gu̇dz), 1. personal property; belongings. He gave half of his goods to the poor. 2. wares; thing or things for sale. *n. pl.*

Good Samaritan, traveler who rescued another traveler who had been beaten and robbed by thieves. Luke 10: 30-37.

good-sized (gu̇d′sīzd′), large; somewhat large. *adj.*

good-tem pered (gu̇d′tem′pərd), easy to get along with; cheerful; agreeable. *adj.*

good wife (gu̇d′wīf′), mistress of a household. *n., pl. goodwives. [Old use] 17.*

good will, 1. kindly feeling; friendly attitude. 2. the standing a business has with its customers. *7.*

good y (gu̇d′i), 1. something very good to eat; a piece of candy or cake. 2. an exclamation of pleasure. Are we going? Oh, goody! *n., pl. goodies, interj.* [*Used in common talk*] *6.*

Wild goose

goose (güs), 1. a tame or wild bird like a duck, but larger and with a longer neck. 2. female goose. 3. flesh of a goose used for food. 4 silly person. *n., pl. geese. 2.*

goose ber ry (güz′ber′i), 1. small, sour berry somewhat like a currant but larger. Gooseberries are used to make pies, tarts, jam, etc. 2. a thorny bush that it grows on. *n., pl. gooseberries. 10.*

Gooseberries

goose flesh, a rough condition of the skin, like that of a plucked goose, caused by cold or fear.

goose step, a marching step in which the leg is swung high with straight, stiff knee.

go pher (gō′fər), 1. a ratlike animal of North America with large cheek pouches. Gophers dig holes in the ground. 2. a ground squirrel. *n. 15.*

Gopher (about 9 in. long, including the tail)

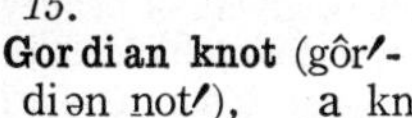

Gor di an knot (gôr′diən not′), a knot tied by an ancient king to be undone only by one who should rule Asia. Alexander the Great cut it. **Cut the Gordian knot** means find and use a quick, easy way out of a difficulty. *16.*

gore[1] (gōr), blood that is spilled; thick blood. The battlefield was covered with gore. *n. 5.*

gore[2] (gōr), wound with a horn or tusk. The savage bull gored the farmer to death. *v.*

gore[3] (gōr), 1. a long, three-sided piece in a skirt, sail, etc. 2. piece that tapers. 3. put or make a gore in. *n., v.*

gorge (gôrj), 1. a deep, narrow valley, usually steep and rocky. 2. eat greedily until full. Don't gorge yourself. 3. throat. *Old use. n., v. 6.*

Gorge

gor geous (gôr′jəs), richly colored; splendid. The peacock spread his gorgeous tail. The gorgeous sunset thrilled us all. *adj. 4.*

Gor gon (gôr′gən), one of three horrible sisters who had snakes for hair, and whose look turned the beholder to stone. *n. 14.*

go ril la (gəril′ə), a very large, manlike ape found in Africa. *n. 15.*

Gorilla (standing height of male 6 ft.)

gorse (gôrs), a low, prickly shrub with yellow flowers and many branches, common on waste lands in many parts of Europe. *n. 16.*

gor y (gōr′i), bloody. *adj., gorier, goriest. 15.*

gos hawk (gos′hôk′), a powerful, short-winged hawk. *n.*

Go shen (gō′shən), 1. in the Bible, a part of Egypt where the Israelites were permitted to live free from plagues. 2. a land of plenty and comfort. *n. 15.*

Gorse

gos ling (goz′ling), a young goose. *n. 19.*

gos pel (gos′pəl), 1. teachings of Jesus and the apostles. 2. anything earnestly believed. Drink plenty of water; that is my gospel. 3. absolute truth. They take her words for gospel. *n. 4.*

hat, āge, cãre, fär; let, ēqual, tėrm; it, īce; hot, ōpen, ôrder; oil, out; cup, pu̇t, rüle, ūse; th, thin; ᴛʜ, then; ə represents *a* in about, *e* in taken, *i* in pencil, *o* in lemon, *u* in circus

Gos pel (gos′pəl), 1. any one of the first four books of the New Testament by Matthew, Mark, Luke, and John. 2. part of one of these books read during a religious service. *n.*

gos sa mer (gos′ə mər), 1. film or thread of cobweb. 2. any very thin, light cloth or substance. 3. thin and light. *n., adj. 15.*

gos sip (gos′ip), 1. idle talk, not always true, about other people and their affairs. 2. repeat what one knows or hears about other people and their affairs. 3. person who gossips a good deal. *n., v. 6.*

got (got). See **get.** We got the letter yesterday. *pt. and pp. of get. 1.*

Goth (goth), member of a tribe which conquered Rome long ago and settled in southern Europe. *n. 12.*

Goth am (goth′əm), New York City. *n.*

Goth ic (goth′ik), 1. style of architecture using pointed arches and high, steep roofs,

Cathedral in the Gothic style

developed in western Europe from about 1150 to 1550. 2. of this kind of architecture. 3. of the Goths or their language. 4. language of the Goths. *n., adj. 6.*

got ten (got′ən). See **get.** It has gotten to be quite late. *pp. of get. 12.*

gouge (gouj), 1. chisel with a curved blade. 2. cut with a gouge; dig out. 3. groove or hole made by gouging. *n., v. 16.*

Gouge

gou lash (gü′läsh), a stew of meat and vegetables with seasoning. *n.*

gourd (gōrd), 1. the fruit of a plant whose dried shell is used for bottles, bowls, etc. 2. the plant itself. 3. a bottle, bowl, etc., made from such a dried shell. *n. 10.*

Gourds

gour mand (gür′mənd), person who is fond of good eating. *n.*

gout (gout), 1. a painful disease of the joints, especially of the big toe. 2. drop; splash; as, gouts of blood. *n. 10.*

gout y (gout′i), 1. diseased or swollen with gout. 2. of gout; caused by gout. 3. causing gout. *adj. 15.*

Gov., Governor.

gov ern (guv′ərn), rule; control; manage. *v. 3.*

gov ern a ble (guv′ər nə bəl), capable of being governed. *adj.*

gov ern ance (guv′ər nəns), government; rule; control. *n. 15.*

gov ern ess (guv′ər nis), woman who teaches children in a private house. *n. 10.*

gov ern ment (guv′ərn mənt), 1. the ruling of a country. 2. the person or persons ruling a country at any time. 3. a country ruled. 4. system of ruling. 5. rule; control. *n. 1.*

gov ern men tal (guv′ərn men′təl), of government. *adj. 12.*

gov er nor (guv′ər nər), 1. man who rules. 2. ruler of a State or province. 3. the executive head of a State. 4. a device arranged to keep a machine going at an even speed. *n. 2.*

gov er nor ship (guv′ər nər ship′), position or term of office of governor. *n.*

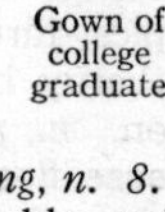

Gown of college graduate

gown (goun), 1. woman's dress. 2. a loose outer robe worn by college graduates, lawyers, and others. 3. nightgown. *n. 2.*

gr., 1. gram; grams. 2. grain; grains.

Gr., 1. Greek. 2. Grecian. 3. Greece.

grab (grab), 1. snatch; seize suddenly. The dog grabbed the meat and ran. 2. a snatching; a sudden seizing. *v., grabbed, grabbing, n. 8.*

grace (grās), 1. pleasing or agreeable quality; beauty of form or movement. 2. willingness; as, to obey with good grace or bad grace. 3. favor; as, to be in a person's good graces or bad graces. 4. favor shown by granting a delay. 5. the time of the delay; as, a three days' grace allowed after a bill is due. 6. favor and love of God. 7. a short prayer of thanks given before or after a meal. 8. behavior put on to seem attractive. Mary came home from boarding school with little airs and graces. 9. **The Graces** were three sister goddesses, givers of beauty and charm. 10. a title of a duke, duchess, or archbishop. May I assist **Your Grace?** 11. give grace or honor to. Will you grace our party with your presence? *n., v. 1.*

grace ful (grās′fəl), beautiful in form or movement; pleasing; agreeable; as, a graceful dance, a graceful speech of thanks. *adj. 4.*

grace less (grās′lis), 1. without grace. 2. not caring for what is right or proper. That boy is a graceless rascal. *adj. 11.*

gra cious (grā′shəs), 1. pleasant and kindly. Mrs. Brown received her guests in a gracious manner which made them feel at ease. 2. pleasant and kindly to people of lower social position. The queen greeted her with a gracious smile. *adj. 3.*

grack le (grak′əl), a kind of blackbird. *n.*

Grackle (1 ft. long)

gra da tion (grā dā′shən), 1. a change by steps or stages; a gradual change. Our acts show gradation between right and wrong. 2. one of the steps in a series. There are many gradations between poverty and wealth. The rainbow shows gradations of color besides the six main colors. *n. 9.*

grade (grād), 1. a class in school; as, the fifth grade. 2. **The grades** means elementary school or grammar school. 3. a degree in rank, quality, or value; as, Grade B milk. 4. group of persons or things having the same rank, quality, value, etc. 5. place in classes; arrange in grades; sort. These apples are graded by size. 6. number or letter that shows how well one has done. 7. give a grade to. 8. the slope of a road; as, a steep grade, up grade. 9. make more nearly level; as, to grade a road. 10. change gradually. Red grades into orange. *n., v. 2.*

grade crossing, place where a railroad crosses a street or another railroad on the same level.

grad u al (graj′ü əl), by degrees too small to be separately noticed; little by little. *adj. 3.*

grad u al ly (graj′ü əl i), by degrees; little by little. *adv.*

grad u ate (graj′ü āt), 1. finish the course of a school or college and be given a diploma or paper saying so. 2. person who has graduated and has a diploma. 3. that has graduated; as, a graduate student. 4. of or for graduates; as, a graduate school. 5. mark out in equal spaces. A ruler is graduated in inches. *v., n., adj. 4.*

grad u a tion (graj′ü ā′shən), 1. graduating from a school or college. 2. graduating exercises. 3. division into spaces. 4. one of the spaces into which a vessel or instrument is divided. *n. 11.*

graft[1] (graft), 1. a shoot from one tree or plant fixed in a slit in another tree or plant, to grow there as a part of it. A graft from a fine apple tree may be put on a worthless one to improve it. 2. make a graft; put (a shoot) from one plant into another. *n., v. 8.*

Grafting

graft[2] (graft), 1. taking money wrongfully in connection with government or city business. 2. make dishonest money through one's job, especially in political positions. *n., v.* [*Used in common talk*]

gra ham (grā′əm), made from wheat flour that has not been sifted; as, graham crackers. *adj. 12.*

Grail (grāl), the Holy Grail, the cup supposed to be used by Christ at the Last Supper, in which was received the last drop of blood from Christ's body on the cross. *n. 9.*

grain (grān), 1. the seed of plants like wheat, oats, and corn. 2. one of the tiny bits of which sand, sugar, salt, etc., are made up. 3. a very small weight. A pound equals 7000 grains. 4. the little lines and markings in wood, marble, etc.; the arrangement of the particles of anything. Mahogany has a fine grain. 5. to paint in imitation of the grain of wood. 6. temper; natural character. Bad luck goes against the grain. *n., v. 1.*

gram or **gramme** (gram), a unit of weight in the metric system. Twenty-eight grams weigh about one ounce. *n. 12.*

gra mer cy (grə mėr′si), 1. many thanks! 2. an exclamation of surprise. *interj.* [*Old use*] *18.*

gram mar (gram′ər), 1. the study of the forms and uses of words. 2. the rules about the use of words. 3. the use of words according to these rules. *n. 5.*

gram mar i an (grə mãr′i ən), person who is skilled in grammar. *n. 15.*

grammar school, 1. in the United States, a public school having the grades between primary and high school. 2. in England, a secondary school where Latin and Greek are important subjects. *14.*

gram mat i cal (grə mat′i kəl), 1. according

to the correct use of words. Our French teacher speaks grammatical English but has a French accent. 2. of grammar. "He ain't" is a grammatical mistake. *adj. 13.*

gram mat i cal ly (grə mat′i kəl i), according to the principles and rules of grammar; as regards grammar. *adv.*

gram pus (gram′pəs), 1. large fierce dolphin; killer whale. 2. sea animal somewhat like a whale. *n.*

Grampus (def. 1) (15 to 20 ft. long)

Gra na da (grə nä′də), a city in southern Spain, the stronghold of the Moors till they were driven out of Spain. *n. 17.*

gran a ry (gran′ə ri), place or building where grain is stored. *n., pl. granaries. 11.*

grand (grand), 1. large and of fine appearance; as, grand mountains. 2. fine; noble; dignified; as, a very grand palace, grand music, a grand old man. 3. highest or very high in rank; chief; as, grand jury, grand duke. 4. great; important; main; as, the grand staircase. 5. complete; comprehensive; as, grand total. 6. very satisfactory. *Used in common talk. adj. 2.*

gran dam or **gran dame** (gran′dam), grandmother. *n. 15.*

Grand Canyon, deep gorge of the Colorado River, in northern Arizona. 217 mi. long; over 1 mi. deep.

grand child (grand′chīld′), child of one's son or daughter. *n., pl. grandchildren. 13.*

grand chil dren (grand′chil′drən), more than one grandchild. *n. pl. 14.*

grand daugh ter (grand′dô′tər), daughter of one's son or daughter. *n. 13.*

gran dee (gran dē′), 1. a Spanish or Portuguese nobleman of the highest rank. 2. person of high rank or great importance. *n. 15.*

gran deur (gran′jər), greatness; majesty; nobility; dignity; splendor. *n. 8.*

grand fa ther (grand′fä′ᴛʜər), 1. father of one's father or mother. 2. any forefather. *n. 3.*

gran dil o quent (gran dil′ə kwənt), using lofty or pompous words. *adj.*

gran di ose (gran′di ōs), 1. magnificent; grand in an imposing or impressive way. 2. grand in an affected or pompous way; not really magnificent, but trying to seem so. *adj. 14.*

grand jury, jury of from 12 to 23 persons chosen to investigate accusations and decide whether there is enough evidence for a trial in court before an ordinary jury.

grand ma (grand′mä′), grandmother. *n. 4.*

grand moth er (grand′muᴛʜ′ər), mother of one's mother or father. *n. 2.*

grand neph ew (grand′nef′ū), son of a nephew or a niece. *n. 20.*

grand niece (grand′nēs′), daughter of one's nephew or niece. *n.*

grand pa (grand′pä′), grandfather. *n. 4.*

grand par ent (grand′pãr′ənt), grandfather or grandmother. *n. 16.*

Grand Rapids, a city in southwestern Michigan.

grand sire (grand′sīr′), 1. grandfather. 2. any forefather. 3. an old man. *n. [Old use] 7.*

grand son (grand′sun′), son of one's son or daughter. *n. 7.*

grand stand (grand′stand′), the principal seating place for people at an athletic field, race track, etc. *n.*

Grandstand

grange (grānj), 1. farm with its buildings. 2. an association of farmers. *n. 6.*

gran ite (gran′it), a very hard rock, used for buildings, monuments, etc. Granite is usually gray. *n. 5.*

gran ny (gran′i), 1. grandmother. 2. old woman. *n., pl. grannies. [Used in common talk]*

grant (grant), 1. allow; give what is asked; as, to grant a request. 2. admit. I grant that you are right so far. 3. **Take for granted** means use as proved or agreed to. 4. a gift; especially, land or rights given by the government. *v., n. 1.*

Grant (grant), Ulysses S. (1822-1885), an American general, who was the 18th president of the United States, from 1869 to 1877. *n.*

gran u lar (gran′ū lər), 1. consisting of grains; containing granules. 2. like grains or granules. *adj.*

gran u late (gran′ū lāt), 1. make into grains; form grains; as, granulated sugar. 2. roughen the surface of. *v. 11.*

gran ule (gran′ūl), 1. a little grain. 2. a small bit or spot like a grain. *n. 13.*

Grapes

grape (grāp), 1. a small, round fruit, red, purple, or pale-green, that grows in bunches on a vine. Grapes are eaten, or made into raisins or wine. 2. grapevine. *n. 2.*

grape fruit (grāp′früt′), a pale-yellow fruit like an orange, but larger and sourer. *n. 18.*

grape shot (grāp′shot′), cluster of small iron balls used as a charge for cannon. *n.*

grape vine (grāp′vīn′), vine that bears grapes. *n.*

graph (graf), 1. a line or diagram showing how one quantity depends on or changes with another. You could draw a graph to show how your weight has changed each year with your change in age. 2. any line or lines representing a series of relations. *n. 18.*

Graph of the temperature on a winter day for 12 hours

graph ic (graf′ik), 1. lifelike; vivid; as, a graphic account of a battle. 2. of or about diagrams and their use; as, a graphic record of school attendance for a month. 3. of or about drawing, painting, engraving, or etching; as, the graphic arts. 4. of handwriting. *adj. 15.*

graph i cal ly (graf′i kəl i), by a diagram or pictures; vividly. *adv.*

graph ite (graf′īt), a soft, black form of carbon used for lead in pencils and for greasing machinery. *n. 10.*

grap nel (grap′nəl), 1. an instrument with one or more hooks for seizing and holding something. Grapnels thrown by ropes were used to catch on an enemy's ship. 2. a small anchor with three or more hooks. *n. 20.*

Grappling iron

grap ple (grap′əl), 1. seize and hold fast; grip or hold firmly. 2. a seizing and holding fast; firm grip or hold. 3. struggle; fight. 4. A **grappling iron** is an iron bar with hooks at one end for seizing and holding something. *v., n. 9.*

grasp (grasp), 1. seize; hold fast by closing the fingers around. 2. seizing and holding tightly; clasp of the hand. 3. **Grasp at** means try to grasp; try to take hold of. 4. power of seizing and holding; reach. 5. control; possession. 6. understand. 7. understanding. She has a good grasp of arithmetic. *v., n. 4.*

grasp ing (gras′ping), greedy; eager to get all that one can. *adj.*

grass (gras), 1. the green blades that cover fields and lawns. 2. land covered with grass; pasture. 3. a plant that has jointed stems and long, narrow leaves. Wheat, corn, and sugar cane are grasses. *n. 1.*

grass hop per (gras′hop′ər), an insect with strong legs and wings for jumping. *n. 4.*

Grasshopper (2 to 3 in. long)

grass land (gras′land′), land with grass on it, used for pasture. *n.*

grass y (gras′i), 1. covered with grass; having much grass. 2. of grass. 3. like grass. *adj. 7.*

grate[1] (grāt), 1. a framework of iron to hold a fire. 2. iron bars, such as those over a prison window. 3. furnish with iron bars. *n., v. 4.*

Grate for an open fire

grate[2] (grāt), 1. have an annoying or unpleasant effect. Her manners grate on me. 2. rub with a harsh sound. The door grated on its old rusty hinges. 3. wear down or grind off in small pieces; as, to grate cheese. *v.*

grate ful (grāt′fəl), 1. feeling gratitude; thankful. 2. pleasing; welcome. A breeze is grateful on a hot day, a fire on a cold one. *adj. 3.*

grat er (grāt′ər), 1. person or thing that grates. 2. instrument with a rough surface for rubbing off small particles; as, a nutmeg grater. *n.*

grat i fi ca tion (grat′i fi kā′shən), 1. gratifying. 2. being gratified. 3. something that pleases or satisfies. *n. 9.*

grat i fy (grat′i fī), 1. please; give pleasure to. Praise gratifies most people. 2. give satisfaction to. A drunkard gratifies his craving for liquor. *v., gratified, gratifying. 7.*

Grating

grat ing[1] (grāt′ing), grate; a framework of parallel or crossed bars. *n.*

grat ing[2] (grāt′ing), 1. irritating; unpleasant. 2. harsh or jarring in sound. *adj.*

gra tis (grā′tis), for nothing; free of charge. *adv., adj. 9.*

grat i tude (grat′i tūd or grat′i tüd), thankfulness; kindly feeling because of a favor received; desire to do a favor in return. *n. 4.*

gra tu i tous (grə tū′i təs or grə tü′i təs), 1. freely given or obtained; free. 2. without reason or cause; uncalled-for. *adj. 15.*

gra tu i ty (grə tū′i ti or grə tü′i ti), 1. a present of money in return for service; a tip. A person gives gratuities to waiters, porters, servants, etc. 2. a present; gift. *n., pl. gratuities. 19.*

grave[1] (grāv), 1. hole dug in the ground where a dead body is to be buried. 2. any place of burial; as, a watery grave. 3. death. *n. 2.*

grave[2] (grāv), 1. earnest; thoughtful; serious; as, grave words, a grave situation. 2. dignified; slow-moving; not gay; as, grave music. 3. important. 4. The first *a* in the French phrase *à la mode* has a grave accent on it. *adj.*

grave[3] (grāv), engrave; carve. *v., graved, graven* or *graved, graving.*

grav el (grav′əl), 1. pebbles and rock fragments coarser than sand. Gravel is much used for roads and walks. 2. cover with gravel. *n., v., graveled, graveling. 5.*

grav en (grāv′ən), engraved; carved; as, graven images. *adj., pp. of* **grave**[3]. *10.*

grave ness (grāv′nis), importance; seriousness; being grave. *n. 20.*

grave stone (grāv′stōn′), stone that marks a grave. *n.*

grave yard (grāv′yärd′), place for burying the dead; cemetery; burial ground. *n.*

grav i tate (grav′i tāt), 1. move or tend to move toward a body by the force of gravity; tend toward the lowest level. 2. settle. If you shake a pail of pebbles, the largest ones will gravitate to the bottom. 3. be strongly attracted. The attention of the crowd gravitated to the airplane as it rose. *v.*

grav i ta tion (grav′i tā′shən), 1. the fact that the earth pulls any object toward it and that the sun, moon, stars, and other such bodies in the universe do the same; the force or pull that makes bodies in the universe tend to move toward one another. 2. a moving or tendency to move caused by this force. 3. a settling down; a sinking; a falling. 4. a natural tendency toward some point or object of influence; as, the gravitation of population to cities. *n. 9.*

grav i ty (grav′i ti), 1. natural force that causes objects to move or tend to move toward the center of the earth. Gravity causes objects to have weight. 2. natural force that makes objects move or tend to move toward each other; gravitation. 3. heaviness; weight. He balanced the long pole at its center of gravity. 4. seriousness. The gravity of the child playing nurse was amusing in one so small. 5. importance. The gravity of the situation was greatly increased by threats of war. *n., pl. gravities. 7.*

gra vy (grā′vi), 1. the juice that comes out of meat in cooking. 2. a sauce for meat, potatoes, etc., made from this juice. *n., pl. gravies. 6.*

gray (grā), 1. any shade obtained by mixing black and white. 2. having a shade between black and white. Ashes, lead, and hair getting white with age are gray. 3. become gray; make gray. *n., adj., v. 1.*

gray beard (grā′bērd′), old man. *n. 20.*

gray-head ed (grā′hed′id), having gray hair. *adj. 13.*

gray ling (grā′ling), a fresh-water fish, somewhat like a trout. *n. 17.*

Alaska grayling

graze[1] (grāz), 1. feed on growing grass. Cattle were grazing in the field. 2. put (cattle, sheep, etc.) to feed on growing grass. *v. 3.*

graze[2] (grāz), 1. touch lightly in passing; rub lightly against. 2. scrape the skin from. The bullet grazed his shoulder. 3. a grazing. *v., n.*

grease (grēs), 1. soft animal fat. 2. any thick, oily substance. 3. rub grease on. 4. put grease or oil on. Indians greased their bodies. *n., v. 5.*

greas y (grēs′i), 1. containing much grease; oily. 2. having grease on it. 3. like grease; smooth; slippery. *adj., greasier, greasiest. 13.*

great (grāt), 1. big; large. 2. much; more than is usual; as, great pain, great kindness. 3. important; high in rank; remarkable; as, a great singer, a great event, a great picture. *adj. 1.*

great-aunt (grāt′ant′), aunt of one's father or mother. *n.*

Great Bear, a constellation containing the seven bright stars forming the Big Dipper.

Great Britain, England, Scotland, and Wales. It is the largest island of Europe. *17.*

Great Dane (2½ to 3 ft. high at the shoulder)

great coat (grāt′kōt′), heavy overcoat. *n.*

Great Dane, one of a breed of large, powerful, short-haired dogs. See the picture.

great-grand child (grāt′grand′chīld′), child of one's grandchild. *n.*

great-grand fa ther (grāt′grand′fä′THər), father of a grandparent. *n. 17.*

great-grand moth er (grāt′grand′muTH′ər), mother of a grandparent. *n.*

great-heart ed (grāt′här′tid), 1. noble; generous. 2. brave; fearless. *adj.*

Great Lakes, lakes Ontario, Erie, Huron, Michigan, and Superior.

great ly (grāt′li), 1. in a great manner. Solomon ruled greatly and wisely. 2. much; as, greatly feared; desiring greatly to be rich. *adv.*

great ness (grāt′nis), 1. being great; bigness. 2. high place or power. 3. great mind or character. *n. 4.*

greave (grēv), armor for the leg below the knee. *n.*

grebe (grēb), 1. a diving bird. 2. its breast feathers, used to trim hats, etc. *n.*

Grebe (about 19 in. long)

Gre cian (grē′shən), Greek. *adj., n. 7.*

Greece (grēs), a small country in southeastern Europe. *n. 5.*

greed (grēd), wanting more than one's share; as, a miser's greed for money. *n. 16.*

greed i ly (grēd′ili), in a greedy manner; piggishly. *adv.*

greed i ness (grēd′inis), greed; greedy nature; greedy behavior. *n. 12.*

greed y (grēd′i), 1. wanting to get more than one's share. 2. wanting to get a great deal. 3. piggish; wanting to eat a great deal in a hurry. *adj., greedier, greediest. 4.*

Greek (grēk), 1. person born in Greece, living there, or having Greek parents. 2. the language of Greece. 3. of Greece, its people, or their language. *n., adj. 3.*

green (grēn), 1. the color of most growing plants, grass, and the leaves of trees in summer. 2. having this color; of this color. 3. not ripe; not fully grown. Green fruit is not good to eat. 4. not trained. He was a green boy in business. 5. ground covered with grass. 6. **Greens** means (1) green leaves and branches used for decoration. (2) leaves and stems of plants used for food. *n., adj. 1.*

green back (grēn′bak′), a piece of United States paper money having the back printed in green. *n. 15.*

green horn (grēn′hôrn′), 1. person without experience. 2. person easy to trick or cheat. *n.*

green house (grēn′hous′), building with a glass roof and glass sides kept warm for growing plants; hothouse. *n. 13.*

green ish (grēn′ish), somewhat green. *adj. 12.*

Green land (grēn′lənd), a very cold country northeast of North America. Greenland belongs to Denmark. *n. 10.*

green ness (grēn′nis), 1. amount of green; being green. 2. freshness. 3. unripeness. *n. 16.*

green sward (grēn′swôrd′), green grass; turf. *n. 14.*

Green wich (grin′ij), a place in London. Longitude is measured east and west of Greenwich. *n. 12.*

green wood (grēn′wu̇d′), forest in spring and summer when the trees are green with leaves. *n. 11.*

greet (grēt), 1. say "Hello," "How do you do," "Welcome," etc., to; address in welcome; hail. 2. respond to. His speech was greeted with cheers. 3. meet; present itself to. When she opened the door, a strange sight greeted her eyes. *v. 2.*

greet ing (grēt′ing), the act or words of a person who greets somebody; welcome. *n. 4.*

gre gar i ous (gri gãr′i əs), 1. living in flocks or groups. Sheep are gregarious; lions are not. 2. fond of being with others. Man is a gregarious animal. *adj. 19.*

Gre go ri an (gri gō′ri ən), 1. of or pertaining to Gregory I; as, a Gregorian chant. 2. of Gregory XIII. The Gregorian calendar is the one we use today. *adj. 20.*

Greg o ry (greg′ə ri), 1. Gregory I was pope from 590 to 604 A.D. 2. Gregory XIII was pope from 1572 to 1585. *n.*

gre nade (gri nād′), 1. a small bomb. The soldiers threw grenades into the enemy's trenches. 2. a round glass bottle filled with chemicals which scatter as the glass breaks. Fire grenades are thrown on fires to put them out. *n.*

Grenadier of the 18th century blowing fuse to light a grenade

gren a dier (gren′ə dēr′), 1. a soldier who threw grenades. 2. a very tall foot soldier. 3. a

hat, āge, cãre, fär; let, ēqual, tėrm; it, īce; hot, ōpen, ôrder; oil, out; cup, pu̇t, rüle, ūse; **th,** thin; TH, then; ə represents *a* in about, *e* in taken, *i* in pencil, *o* in lemon, *u* in circus.

member of a certain regiment of the British army. *n. 15.*

Gret na Green (gret′nə grēn′), a village in Scotland where many runaway couples from England were married. *17.*

grew (grü). See **grow.** It grew cold. *pt. of grow. 1.*

grey (grā), gray. *n., adj., v. 3.*

grey beard (grā′bērd′), graybeard. *n. 18.*

grey-head ed (grā′hed′id), gray-headed. *adj.*

grey hound (grā′hound′), a tall, slender hunting dog with a long nose. Greyhounds can run very fast. *n. 7.*

Greyhound (about 28 in. high at the shoulder)

grid (grid), grate; a frame of bars with spaces between them. See the picture under **gridiron.** *n. 16.*

grid dle (grid′əl), a heavy, flat plate on which to cook griddlecakes. *n. 10.*

grid dle cake (grid′əl kāk′), a thin, flat cake of batter cooked on a griddle. *n.*

grid i ron (grid′ī′ərn), 1. a utensil with parallel bars for broiling. 2. a frame or structure like this; a frame for supporting scenery in a theater. 3. a football field. *n.*

Gridiron for broiling

grief (grēf), heavy sorrow; deep sorrow; that which causes sorrow. **Come to grief** means have trouble; fail. *n. 2.*

griev ance (grēv′əns), a real or imagined wrong; reason for being annoyed or angry. *n. 7.*

grieve (grēv), 1. feel grief; be very sad. 2. cause to feel grief; make sad. *v. 3.*

griev ous (grēv′əs), 1. hard to bear; causing great pain or suffering; severe; as, grievous cruelty. 2. outrageous. Wasting food when people are starving is a grievous wrong. 3. causing grief. 4. full of grief; showing grief; as, a grievous cry. *adj. 5.*

grif fin (grif′in), imaginary creature with the head, wings, and forelegs of an eagle, and the body, hind legs, and tail of a lion. *n.*

Griffin

grill (gril), 1. gridiron. 2. to broil; cook by holding near the fire. 3. a dish of broiled meat, fish, etc. 4. a dining room in a hotel or restaurant, especially one specializing in serving broiled meat, fish, etc. 5. to torture with heat. 6. question severely and persistently. The detectives grilled the prisoner until he finally confessed. *n., v. 12.*

grim (grim), 1. stern; harsh; fierce; without mercy. 2. not yielding; not relenting. 3. looking stern, fierce, or harsh. 4. horrible; frightful; ghastly. He made grim jokes about death and ghosts. *adj., grimmer, grimmest. 5.*

gri mace (gri mās′), 1. a twisting of the face; an ugly or funny smile. 2. make faces. *n., v. 11.*

grime (grīm), 1. dirt rubbed deeply and firmly into a surface; as, the grime on a coal miner's hands. 2. make very dirty. *n., v. 13.*

Grimm (grim), Jakob and Wilhelm, brothers famous as collectors of fairy tales. *n.*

grim y (grīm′i), covered with grime; very dirty. *adj., grimier, grimiest. 17.*

grin (grin), 1. smile broadly. 2. broad smile. 3. draw back the lips and show the teeth. *v., grinned, grinning, n. 4.*

grind (grīnd), 1. crush into bits, into meal, or into powder. A mill grinds corn. Our teeth grind meat. 2. crush by harsh rule. The slaves were ground down by their masters. 3. sharpen or smooth by rubbing on something rough. He grinds the ax on the grindstone. 4. work by turning a handle. He grinds out music from a street organ. 5. rub harshly together; as, to grind one's heel into the earth, to grind one's teeth. 6. long, hard work. *Used in common talk.* 7. work or study hard. *Used in common talk. v., ground, grinding, n. 2.*

grind er (grīn′dər), 1. person or thing that grinds. 2. man or machine that sharpens tools. 3. back tooth for grinding food; molar. *n. 12.*

Man using a grindstone

grind stone (grīnd′stōn′), flat, round stone set in a frame and turned by a crank, treadle, etc. It is used to sharpen tools, or to smooth and polish things. *n. 9.*

grip (grip), 1. seizing and holding tight; a tight grasp; a firm hold. 2. seize and hold tight; take a firm hold on. 3. a certain way of gripping the hand as a sign of belonging to some secret society. 4. a handle. 5. a small suitcase or handbag. 6. control. 7. understanding. 8. grippe. *n., v., gripped, gripping. 4.*

gripe (grīp), 1. clutch; pinch. 2. cause pain in the bowels; cause distress. 3. colic. *v., n. 9.*

grippe (grip), a severe cold with fever, also called influenza. *n. 17.*

gris ly (griz′li), frightful; horrible; ghastly. *adj., grislier, grisliest. 10.*

grist (grist), 1. grain to be ground. 2. grain that has been ground; meal or flour. *n. 12.*

gris tle (gris′əl), hard elastic tissue such as is found in meat. Babies have gristle instead of bone in some parts of the skull. *n. 18.*

gris tly (gris′li), of gristle; like gristle. *adj.*

grist mill, mill for grinding grain. *20.*

grit (grit), 1. very fine gravel or sand. 2. coarse sandstone. 3. pluck; endurance; courage. 4. grind; make a grating sound by holding closed and rubbing. He grits his teeth. *n., v., gritted, gritting. 11.*

grits (grits), oats, wheat, etc., husked and coarsely ground. *n. pl.*

grit ty (grit′i), 1. containing grit; like grit; sandy. 2. courageous; plucky. *Used in common talk. adj., grittier, grittiest.*

griz zled (griz′əld), grayish; gray. *adj. 14.*

griz zly (griz′li), 1. grayish. 2. a large, fierce bear of western North America. *adj., grizzlier, grizzliest, n., pl. grizzlies. 12.*

Grizzly bear (about 8 ft. long)

groan (grōn), 1. a deep-throated sound expressing grief, pain, or disapproval; a deep, short moan. 2. give a groan or groans. 3. be loaded or overburdened. The table groaned with food. *n., v. 3.*

groat (grōt), an old English silver coin worth four pence. *n. 20.*

gro cer (grō′sər), person who sells tea, coffee, sugar, flour, fruits, spices, and other articles of food. *n. 4.*

gro cer y (grō′sər i), 1. grocer's shop. 2. **Groceries** sometimes means articles of food sold by a grocer. *n., pl. groceries. 6.*

grog (grog), 1. rum and water; whiskey and water. 2. any strong, alcoholic drink. *n. 16.*

grog gy (grog′i), 1. shaky; unsteady. 2. drunk; intoxicated. *adj., groggier, groggiest.* [*Used in common talk*]

groin (groin), 1. the hollow on either side of the body where the thigh joins the abdomen. 2. the curved line where two vaults of a roof cross. 3. form or build with groins. *n., v. 14.*

A, groin.

groom (grüm), 1. manservant; man or boy who has charge of horses. 2. feed and take care of (horses); rub down and brush. 3. take care of the appearance of; make neat and tidy; as, a well-groomed person. 4. bridegroom; man just married or about to be married. *n., v. 5.*

groove (grüv), 1. a long, narrow channel or furrow cut by a tool. The plate rests in a groove on the rack. 2. any similar channel; a rut. Wheels leave grooves in a dirt road. 3. make a groove in. The sink shelf is grooved so that the water will run off. 4. fixed way of doing things. It is hard to get out of a groove. *n., v. 6.*

grope (grōp), 1. feel about with the hands. He groped for a flashlight when the lights went out. 2. search blindly and uncertainly. The detectives groped for some clue to the murder. 3. find by feeling about with the hands; feel (one's way) slowly. The blind man groped his way to the door. *v. 6.*

gros beak (grōs′bēk′), a bird with a large, stout bill. *n.*

Red-breasted grosbeak (about 8 in. long)

gross (grōs), 1. whole; entire; with nothing taken out; total. Gross receipts are all the money taken in. 2. the total amount. 3. twelve dozen; 144. 4. very bad; easy to see. She makes gross errors in pronouncing words. 5. coarse; vulgar. Her manners are too gross for a lady. 6. too big; overfed; too fat. 7. thick; heavy; dense; as, the gross growth of a jungle. *adj., n., pl. grosses* for 2, *gross* for 3. *4.*

gross ness (grōs′nis), being gross. *n. 12.*

grot (grot), grotto. *n.* [*Used in poetry*] *12.*

gro tesque (grō tesk′), 1. fantastic; queer; odd or unnatural in shape, appearance, manner, etc. The book had pictures of hideous dragons and other grotesque monsters. 2. ridiculous; absurd. The monkey's grotesque antics made the children laugh. 3. painting, sculpture, etc., combining designs, ornaments, figures of persons or animals, etc., in a fantastic or unnatural way. *adj., n. 8.*

grot to (grot′ō), 1. cave. 2. an artificial cave made for coolness or pleasure. *n., pl. grottoes* or *grottos. 15.*

grouch (grouch), 1. be sulky or ill-tempered; complain. 2. sulky person. 3. a sulky, discontented feeling. *v., n.* [*Used in common talk*]

grouch y (grouch′i), sulky; sullen; discontented. *adj., grouchier, grouchiest.* [*Used in common talk*] *19.*

ground[1] (ground), 1. the surface of the earth; soil. 2. any piece of land or region used for some purpose. The West was his favorite hunting ground. 3. of the ground; on the ground; as, the ground floor of a building. 4. put on the ground; cause to touch the ground. 5. run aground. The ship was grounded in shallow water. 6. foundation for what is said or done; basis; reason. There is no ground for complaining of his conduct. On what ground do you say that is true? 7. fix firmly; establish. This class is well grounded in arithmetic. 8. background. The pattern was red on a gray ground. 9. connect (an electric wire) with the ground. 10. Some special meanings are:

break ground, 1. dig; plow. 2. begin building.

gain ground, 1. go forward; advance; progress. 2. become more common or widespread.

give ground, retreat; yield.

grounds, 1. land, lawns, and gardens around a house. 2. small bits that sink to the bottom of a drink such as coffee or tea; dregs; sediment.

lose ground, 1. go backward; retreat; yield. 2. become less common or widespread.

n., adj., v. 1.

ground[2] (ground). See **grind.** Wheat is ground to make flour. *pt. and pp. of grind.*

ground hog, a woodchuck. Ground hogs grow fat in summer and sleep in their holes in the ground all winter. The ground hog is supposed to come out of his hole on February 2. If the sun is shining and he sees his shadow, he goes back in his hole for six more weeks of winter.

Ground hog (about 2 ft. long, including the tail)

ground less (ground′lis), without foundation or reason. *adj. 14.*

ground ling (ground′ling), 1. plant or animal that keeps close to the ground. 2. spectator or reader who has inferior taste. *n. 20.*

ground plan, 1. plan of a floor of a building. 2. first or fundamental plan.

ground squirrel, 1. gopher. 2. chipmunk.

ground swell, broad, deep waves of the sea caused by a distant storm.

ground work (ground′wėrk′), foundation; basis. *n. 16.*

group (grüp), 1. a number of persons or things together. A group of children were playing tag. The statue will be a group of three figures. 2. number of persons or things belonging or classed together. Wheat, rye, and oats belong to the grain group. 3. form into a group. 4. put in a group. *n., v. 2.*

grouse (grous), game bird with feathered legs. The prairie chicken, sage hen, and ruffed grouse of the United States are different kinds. *n., pl. grouse. 15.*

Ruffed grouse (about 1½ ft. long)

grove (grōv), group of trees standing together. An orange grove is an orchard of orange trees. *n. 2.*

grov el (gruv′əl), lie face downward, crawl at someone's feet; humble oneself. The dog groveled before his master when he saw the whip. *v., groveled, groveling. 11.*

grow (grō), 1. become bigger; increase. Plants and animals grow by taking in food. His business has grown fast. 2. become. It grew cold. 3. cause to develop; raise. We grow cotton in Texas. *v., grew, grown, growing. 1.*

grow er (grō′ər), 1. person who grows something; as, a fruit grower. 2. plant that grows in a certain way; as, a quick grower. *n. 13.*

growl (groul), 1. sound like that made by a fierce dog; a deep, warning snarl. 2. make such a sound. The dog growled at the tramp. 3. grumble; complain about things. *n., v. 5.*

grown (grōn), 1. arrived at full growth. A grown man is an adult. 2. See **grow.** This flower has grown very tall. *adj., pp. of grow.*

grown-up (grōn′up′), 1. arrived at full growth. 2. adult. *adj., n.*

growth (grōth), 1. growing; development. 2. amount grown; increase; progress; as, one year's growth. 3. what has grown or is growing; as, a thick growth of bushes. *n. 3.*

grub (grub), 1. dig; dig up; root out of the ground. Pigs grub for roots. 2. a smooth, thick, wormlike larva of an insect, especially that of a beetle. 3. to toil. 4. food. *Slang. v., grubbed, grubbing, n. 8.*

grudge (gruj), 1. ill will; a sullen feeling against; a dislike of long standing. 2. feel ill will at. Bill grudged Dick his prize even though he had won a better prize himself. 3. give unwillingly. The mean man grudged the food his horse ate. *n., v. 5.*

grudg ing ly (gruj′ing li), unwillingly. *adv.*

gru el (grü′əl), a thin, almost liquid food made by boiling oatmeal, etc., in water or milk. Gruel is often made for persons who are sick or old. *n. 10.*

gru el ing (grü′əl ing), exhausting; very tiring; as, a grueling contest. *adj.* [*Used in common talk*]

grue some (grü′səm), horrible; revolting. *adj.*

gruff (gruf), rough or harsh in voice or manner; rude. *adj. 5.*

grum ble (grum′bəl), 1. complain rather sullenly; mutter in discontent; find fault. 2. a mutter of discontent; bad-tempered complaint. 3. make a low, heavy sound like far-off thunder. *v., n. 5.*

grump y (grump′i), surly; ill-humored; gruff. The grumpy old man found fault with everything. *adj., grumpier, grumpiest.*

grunt (grunt), 1. deep, hoarse sound that a hog makes. 2. a sound like this. The old man got out of his chair with a grunt. 3. make this sound. 4. say with this sound. The sullen boy grunted his apology. *n., v. 8.*

Guam (gwäm), an island in the Pacific Ocean east of the Philippines. Guam belongs to the United States. *n.*

gua no (gwä′nō), manure of sea birds, found especially on islands near Peru. Guano is an excellent fertilizer. *n.*

guar an tee (gar′ən tē′), 1. a backing; promise to pay or do something if another fails to do it; pledge to replace goods if they are not as represented. 2. person who so promises. 3. stand back of; give a guarantee for. This company guarantees its clocks for a year. 4. undertake to secure for another. He will guarantee us possession of the house by May. 5. secure (against or from). His insurance guarantees him against money loss in case of fire. 6. pledge to do (something); promise (that) something has been or will be. I will guarantee to prove every statement I made. *n., v., guaranteed, guaranteeing. 5.*

guar an tor (gar′ən tôr), person who makes or gives a guarantee. *n.*

guar an ty (gar′ən ti), 1. giving security. 2. a guarantee. *n., pl. guaranties. 20.*

guard (gärd), 1. watch over; take care of; keep safe; defend. 2. keep from escaping. 3. that which guards; person who guards; any arrangement to give safety. 4. a position in which one is ready to defend in fencing, boxing, and in some games. 5. careful watch; as, keep guard. **On guard** means ready to defend or protect; watchful. 6. a picked body of soldiers. 7. man who opens and closes the gates or doors on a train. 8. player at either side of the center in football. 9. either of two players defending the goal in basketball. *v., n. 1.*

guard ed (gär′did), 1. kept safe; carefully watched over; defended; protected. 2. careful; cautious. "Maybe" is a guarded answer to a question. *adj.*

guard house (gärd′hous′), 1. a building used by soldiers on guard. 2. a prison. *n.*

guard i an (gär′di ən), 1. person who takes care of another or of some special thing. 2. person appointed by law to take care of the affairs of someone who is young or cannot take care of them himself. 3. protecting. My guardian angel must have looked after me then. *n., adj. 5.*

guard i an ship (gär′di ən ship′), the position or care of a guardian. *n. 15.*

guard room (gärd′rüm′), 1. room used by soldiers on guard. 2. room used as a jail for soldiers. *n.*

guards man (gärdz′mən), 1. a guard. 2. a member of the militia or any other body of troops called guards. *n., pl. guardsmen. 18.*

Gua te ma la (gwä′ti mä′lə), a country in Central America. *n. 16.*

gu ber na to ri al (gū′bər nə tō′ri əl), of a governor; having to do with a governor. *adj.*

gudg eon (guj′ən), 1. a small, European, fresh-water fish that is easy to catch. 2. person easily fooled or cheated. *n. 16.*

guer don (gėr′dən), reward. *n., v. 13.*

Guern sey (gėrn′zi), 1. an island in the English Channel. 2. one of a breed of dairy cattle like the Jersey, but somewhat larger. *n. 13.*

guer ril la or **gue ril la** (gə ril′ə), fighter in an irregular war carried on by independent bands. Guerrillas harass the enemy by sudden raids, ambushes, plundering supply trains, etc. *n.*

guess (ges), 1. an opinion formed without really knowing. My guess is that it will rain tomorrow. 2. form an opinion when one does not know exactly. Let us guess at the height of the tree. 3. get right by guessing; as, to guess a riddle. 4. think; believe; suppose. I guess he is really sick after all. *n., v. 1.*

guess work (ges′wėrk′), guessing; work, action, or results based on guessing. *n.*

guest (gest), 1. visitor; person who is received and entertained at another's house or table. 2. person who is living at a hotel, etc. *n. 2.*

guf faw (gu fô′), 1. a loud, coarse burst of laughter. 2. laugh loudly and coarsely. *n., v.*

Gui a na (gi ä′nə), a region in northern South America. It is divided into British, French, and Dutch colonies. *n. 17.*

guid ance (gīd′əns), 1. guiding; direction; leadership. Under her mother's guidance, Nan learned how to cook. 2. thing that guides. *n. 9.*

guide (gīd), 1. show the way; lead; direct. 2. person or thing that shows the way. Tourists and hunters sometimes hire guides. Your feelings are often a poor guide for actions and beliefs. 3. guidebook. *v., n. 1.*

guide book (gīd′bu̇k′), book of directions and information for travelers. *n.*

guide post (gīd′pōst′), a post where roads meet that tells what places each road leads to and how far they are. *n. 13.*

Guidepost

guild (gild), 1. society for mutual aid or for some common purpose; as, the Ladies' Auxiliary Guild of a church. 2. In the Middle Ages, a guild was a union of the men in one trade to keep standards high, and to look out for the interests of their trade. *n. 9.*

guil der (gil′dər), a Dutch silver coin, worth about 68 cents in 1940. *n. 14.*

guild hall (gild′hôl′), hall in which a guild meets. *n.*

guile (gīl), crafty deceit; cunning; craftiness; sly tricks. By guile the fox got the cheese from the crow. *n. 7.*

guile less (gīl′lis), without guile; straightforward. *adj. 17.*

guil lo tine (gil′ə tēn for 1, gil′ə tēn′ for 2), 1. machine for cutting off people's heads by a heavy blade sliding in two grooved posts. The guillotine was used during the French Revolution. 2. behead with this machine. *n., v. 15.*

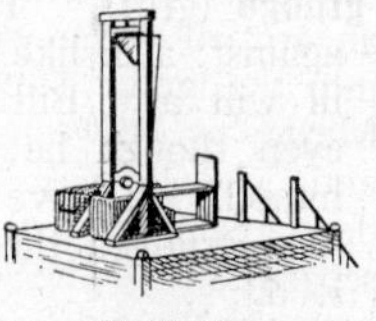
Guillotine

guilt (gilt), 1. fact or state of having done wrong; being guilty; being to blame. 2. guilty action or conduct; crime; offense. *n. 4.*

guilt i ness (gil′ti nis), guilt. *n. 20.*

guilt less (gilt′lis), not guilty; free from guilt; innocent. *adj. 5.*

guilt y (gil′ti), 1. having done wrong; deserving to be blamed and punished. The jury pronounced the prisoner guilty of murder. 2. knowing or showing that one has done wrong. The one who did the crime had a guilty conscience and a guilty look. *adj., guiltier, guiltiest. 3.*

guin ea (gin′i), 1. a British gold coin, not made since 1813, worth 21 shillings. 2. the amount of 21 shillings, used in stating prices, fees, etc. This hat is worth two guineas. *n. 6.*

Guin ea (gin′i), region along the coast of western Africa, divided into French, Portuguese, and Spanish colonies. *n.*

Guinea hen (about 1½ ft. long, from bill to tip of tail)

guinea hen, a fowl having dark-gray feathers with small white spots. Its flesh and its eggs are eaten. A guinea hen can fly better than an ordinary hen.

guinea pig, a short-eared, short-tailed animal like a big, fat, harmless rat.

Guin e vere (gwin′ə vēr), King Arthur's queen. *n. 14.*

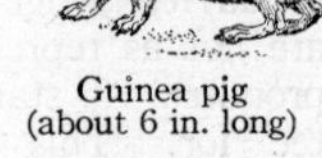
Guinea pig (about 6 in. long)

guise (gīz), 1. style of dress; garb. The soldier went in the guise of a monk and was not recognized. 2. appearance; assumed appearance. He deceived them all by his guise of simplicity. *n. 8.*

gui tar (gi tär′), a musical instrument with six strings, played with the fingers. *n. 10.*

Man playing a guitar

gulch (gulch), a very deep, narrow valley. *n.*

gul den (gu̇l′dən), guilder. *n.*

gules (gūlz), red. *n., adj. 18.*

gulf (gulf), 1. a large bay; an arm of water extending into the land. The Gulf of Mexico is between Florida and Mexico. 2. a very deep break or cut in the earth. 3. wide separation. The quarrel created a gulf between the old friends. *n. 2.*

Gulf Stream, a warm ocean current coming from the Gulf of Mexico. It flows northward along the United States coast, and then in a northeasterly direction toward the British Isles.

gull[1] (gul), graceful gray-and-white bird living on or near large bodies of water. A gull has long wings, webbed feet, and a thick, strong beak. *n. 9.*

Gull (about 18 in. long)

gull[2] (gul), 1. deceive; cheat. 2. person who is easily deceived or cheated. *v., n.*

gul let (gul′it), 1. the passage for food from the mouth to the stomach. 2. throat. *n. 11.*

gull i ble (gul′i bəl), easily deceived or cheated. *adj.*

gul ly (gul′i), narrow gorge; little steep valley; ditch made by heavy rains. *n., pl. gullies. 12.*

gulp (gulp), 1. swallow eagerly or greedily. 2. act of swallowing. 3. amount swallowed at one time; mouthful. 4. keep in; choke back; repress. The disappointed boy gulped down a sob. 5. gasp; choke. *v., n. 10.*

gum[1] (gum), 1. the sticky juice of trees which is used for sticking paper and other things together. 2. a gum tree. 3. chewing gum. 4. stick together with gum. 5. become sticky. Jack's pocket is all gummed up with candy. *n., v., gummed, gumming. 5.*

gum[2] (gum), the flesh around the teeth. *n.*

gum bo (gum′bō), 1. the okra plant. 2. its sticky pods. 3. a soup thickened with these pods. 4. a kind of very sticky soil. *n.*

gum my (gum′i), 1. sticky. 2. covered with gum. 3. giving off gum. *adj., gummier, gummiest. 20.*

gum tree, any of several trees yielding gum. The eucalyptus is one kind of gum tree.

gun (gun), 1. weapon with a metal tube for shooting bullets, shot, etc. A rifle or cannon is a gun. Pistols and revolvers are called guns in ordinary talk. 2. anything resembling a gun in use or shape. 3. shooting of a gun as a signal or salute. The President gets twenty-one guns as a salute. 4. shoot with a gun; hunt with a gun. *n., v., gunned, gunning. 2.*

gun boat (gun′bōt′), small warship that can be used in shallow water. *n. 20.*

gun cot ton (gun′kot′ən), an explosive made by treating cotton with nitric and sulphuric acids. *n.*

gun lock (gun′lok′), the part of a gun that controls the hammer and fires the charge. *n.*

gun man (gun′mən), man who uses a gun to rob or kill. *n., pl. gunmen. 20.*

gun metal, 1. a dark-gray alloy used for watches, chains, umbrella handles, etc. 2. dark gray. 3. an alloy of copper and tin or zinc, formerly used for guns.

gun ner (gun′ər), 1. man trained to fire artillery; soldier who handles and fires cannon. 2. navy officer in charge of a ship's guns. 3. person who hunts with a gun. *n. 10.*

gun ner y (gun′ər i), 1. the construction and management of large guns. 2. the use of guns. *n. 18.*

gun ny (gun′i), 1. a strong, coarse material used for sacks, bags, etc. 2. a bag or sack made of this material. *n., pl. gunnies.*

gun pow der (gun′pou′dər), a powder that goes off with noise and force when touched with fire. Gunpowder is used in firearms, blasting, and fireworks. *n. 6.*

gun shot (gun′shot′), 1. the shooting of a gun; a shot. We heard gunshots. 2. the distance that a gun will shoot. The deer was within gunshot. *n.*

gun stock (gun′stok′), the wooden support in which the barrel of a gun is fixed. *n.*

gun wale (gun′əl), the upper edge of a ship's or boat's side. *n. 16.*

gur gle (gėr′gəl), 1. flow or run with a bubbling sound. Water gurgles when it is poured out of a bottle or flows among stones. 2. a bubbling sound. 3. make a bubbling sound. The baby gurgled happily. *v., n. 13.*

gush (gush), 1. a rush of water or other liquid from an enclosed space. If you get a deep cut, there usually is a gush of blood. 2. rush out suddenly; pour out. 3. give out a rush of soft or silly talk about one's affections or enthusiasms. 4. silly emotional talk. *Used in common talk. n., v. 5.*

gush er (gush′ər), oil well that gives oil in great quantities without pumping. *n.*

gus set (gus′it), triangular piece of material inserted to give greater strength or more room. *n.*

gust (gust), 1. a sudden rush of wind, often whirling. 2. an outburst of anger or other feeling. *n. 7.*

gus to (gus′tō), keen relish; hearty enjoyment. The hungry boy ate his dinner with gusto. *n.*

gust y (gus′ti), windy; stormy; coming in gusts. *adj., gustier, gustiest. 10.*

gut (gut), 1. intestine. 2. catgut; string made from the intestines of animals. Gut is used for violin strings and for tennis rackets. 3. plunder; destroy the inside of. Fire gutted the building and left only the brick walls standing. *n., v., gutted, gutting. 11.*

Gu ten berg (gü′tən bėrg), a German who is supposed to have invented printing (1398?-1468). *n. 20.*

gut ta-per cha (gut′ə pėr′chə), substance like rubber, made from the thick, milky juice of certain tropical trees. *n.*

gut ter (gut′ər), 1. channel or ditch along the side of a street or road to carry off water; low part of a street beside the sidewalk. 2. channel or trough along the lower edge of a roof to carry off rain water. 3. channel; groove. 4. form gutters in. 5. flow or melt in streams. A candle gutters when the melted wax runs down its sides. *n., v. 5.*

gut tur al (gut′ər əl), 1. of the throat. 2. formed in the throat; harsh. The German spoke in a deep guttural voice. 3. a sound formed between the tongue and the soft palate. The letters *k* and hard *g*, as in *go* and *give*, are gutturals. *adj., n. 12.*

guy[1] (gī), 1. a rope or chain attached to something to steady it. 2. to guide, steady, or secure with a guy or guys. *n., v. 11.*

guy[2] (gī), 1. a queer-looking person. 2. a fellow. *Slang.* 3. make fun of; tease. *Used in common talk. n., v.*

guz zle (guz′əl), drink greedily; drink too much. *v. 17.*

gym (jim), gymnasium. *n.*

gym na si um (jim nā′zi əm), room, building, etc., fitted up for physical exercise or training and for indoor athletic sports. *n. 6.*

gym nast (jim′nast), person skilled in gymnastics; acrobat. *n.*

gym nas tic (jim nas′tik), having to do with bodily exercise or activities. *adj.*

gym nas tics (jim nas′tiks), exercises for developing the muscles, such as are done in a gymnasium. *n. pl. 9.*

gyp (jip), 1. cheat; swindle. 2. a cheat; swindler. *v., gypped, gypping, n.* [*Slang*]

gyp sum (jip′səm), mineral used as fertilizer and to make plaster of Paris. *n. 20.*

gyp sy (jip′si), 1. person belonging to a wandering race of dark-skinned, dark-eyed people who probably came from India long ago. 2. person who looks or lives like a gypsy. 3. of the gypsies; as, a gypsy girl. *n., pl. gypsies, adj. 8.* Also spelled **gipsy.**

gypsy moth, a moth whose larva is very destructive to trees.

gy rate (jī′rāt), go in a circle or spiral; whirl; rotate. A top gyrates. *v.*

gy ra tion (jī rā′shən), circular or spiral motion; whirling; rotation. *n.*

gy ro scope (jī′rə skōp), an instrument consisting of a wheel so mounted that its axis can turn freely in several or in all directions. A gyroscope can be used to keep a ship steady. *n.*

Gyroscope

gyve (jīv), 1. a fetter, especially for the leg. 2. to fetter. *n., v.* [*Old use*] *15.*

H

H, h (āch), eighth letter of the alphabet. There are two h's in high. *n., pl. H's, h's.*

ha (hä), 1. an exclamation of surprise, joy, or triumph. "Ha! I've caught you!" cried the giant to Jack. 2. sound of a laugh. "Ha! ha! ha!" laughed the boys. *interj. 3.*

hab er dash er y (hab′ər dash′ər i), 1. place

where men's shirts, collars, neckties, gloves, etc., are sold. 2. articles sold in a haberdashery. *n., pl. haberdasheries.*

hab er geon (hab′ər jən), short coat of mail. *n. 20.*

ha bil i ment (hə bil′i mənt), an article of clothing, such as a hat, coat, or shoes. **Habiliments** means clothing. *n. 17.*

hab it (hab′it), 1. custom; practice. Form the habit of brushing your teeth twice a day. 2. condition of body or mind. The runner was of lean habit. 3. the dress of a religious order; as, a nun's habit. 4. a woman's riding dress. The lady on the white horse wore a black habit. *n. 3.*

hab it a ble (hab′i tə bəl), fit to live in. *adj. 10.*

hab i tat (hab′i tat), 1. place where an animal or plant naturally lives or grows. The jungle is the habitat of tigers. 2. dwelling place. *n. 15.*

hab i ta tion (hab′i tā′shən), 1. a place or building to live in. 2. living in. Is the house fit for habitation? *n. 6.*

ha bit u al (hə bich′ü əl), 1. done by habit; caused by habit; as, a habitual smile, habitual courtesy. 2. being or doing something by habit; regular; steady. A habitual reader reads a great deal. 3. usual; customary; often done, seen, or used. Ice and snow are a habitual sight in arctic regions. *adj. 8.*

ha bit u al ly (hə bich′ü əl i), as a habit; regularly; commonly. *adv.*

ha bit u ate (hə bich′ü āt), accustom; make used (to). Lumbermen are habituated to hard work. *v. 15.*

Habs burg (häps′bürk), Hapsburg. *n. 19.*

ha ci en da (hä′si en′də), a Spanish American word meaning a landed estate; any country establishment for farming, stock raising, mining, or manufacturing. *n.*

hack[1] (hak), 1. cut roughly. Tom hacked the box apart with the dull ax. 2. a rough cut. 3. give short, dry coughs. *v., n. 6.*

hack[2] (hak), 1. a carriage for hire. Hacks were waiting at the railroad station. 2. a horse for hire. 3. a riding horse for common use. 4. a drudge. 5. drudging. Hack work is work done just for money. *n., adj.*

hack ney (hak′ni), 1. a riding horse for common use. 2. a carriage for hire. 3. hired; as, a hackney coach. 4. use too often; make commonplace. *n., pl. hackneys, adj., v., hackneyed, hackneying. 10.*

hack neyed (hak′nid), used too often; made commonplace. "White as snow" is a hackneyed comparison. *adj.*

had (had). See **have.** She had a party. A fine time was had by all who came. *pt. and pp. of have. 1.*

had dock (had′ək), food fish of the northern Atlantic, somewhat like a cod, but smaller. *n., pl. haddocks or haddock. 12.*

Haddock (about 20 in. long)

Ha des (hā′dēz), 1. the Greek home of the dead, below the earth. 2. hell. *Used in common talk. n. 18.*

had n't (had′ənt), had not. *12.*

hadst (hadst), an old form meaning **had.** "Thou hadst" means "you had." *v. 4.*

haft (haft), handle of a knife, sword, etc. *n. 14.*

hag (hag), 1. a very ugly old woman. 2. witch. *n. 12.*

Ha gar (hā′gär), in the Bible, a slave of Abraham's wife Sarah. She and her son were driven into the desert because of Sarah's jealousy. Genesis 16. *n. 9.*

Hag ga i (hag′ā ī), 1. a Hebrew prophet. 2. a book of the Old Testament. *n. 18.*

hag gard (hag′ərd), wild-looking from pain, fatigue, worry, hunger, etc.; careworn. *adj. 8.*

hag gle (hag′əl), dispute, especially about a price. The cook and the grocer haggled over the price of eggs. *v.*

Hague (hāg). **The Hague** is one of the two capitals of the Netherlands. *n. 13.*

hail[1] (hāl), 1. frozen rain. Hail fell with such violence that it broke windows. 2. fall in hail. Sometimes it hails during a summer thundershower. 3. shower like hail. A hail of bullets met the soldiers. 4. pour down in a shower like hail. The angry mob hailed blows on the thief. *n., v. 2.*

hail[2] (hāl), 1. greet; cheer. The crowd hailed the victor. 2. a greeting. Hail to the chief! 3. Greetings! Welcome! Hail to the winner! 4. call loudly to; shout. The boys hailed passing cars to beg a ride. 5. loud call; shout. The ship moved on without heeding our hails. 6. **Hail from** means come from. The ship hails from Boston. *v., n., interj.*

hail stone (hāl′stōn′), frozen drop of rain. Hailstones are usually very small, but sometimes they are as big as marbles. *n. 12.*

hair (hãr). The hair on her head was yellow and silky. The hairs on a plant are fine like threads. *n. 1.*

hair breadth (hãr′bredth′), very narrow; extremely close; as, a hairbreadth escape. *adj.*

hair cloth (hãr′klôth′), fabric made of hair for covering furniture, etc. The hermit wore haircloth shirts as a penance. *n.*

hair i ness (hãr′i nis), hairy condition. *n.*

hair less (hãr′lis), without hair. *adj. 15.*

hair's-breadth or **hairs breadth** (hãrz′-bredth′), 1. very narrow space; very small distance. 2. very narrow; extremely close. *n., adj.*

hair split ting (hãr′split′ing), making too fine distinctions. *n., adj.*

hair spring (hãr′spring′), a fine, hairlike spring in a watch or clock, for regulating the motion of the balance wheel. *n.*

hair y (hãr′i), 1. covered with hair; having much hair; as, hairy hands, a hairy ape. 2. like hair. *adj., hairier, hairiest. 8.*

Hai ti (hā′ti), 1. the former name of Hispaniola, the second largest island in the West Indies. 2. a Negro republic on the western end of this island. *n. 9.*

hal berd (hal′bərd), a weapon that is both a spear and a battle-ax. *n.*

Halberd

hal bert (hal′bərt), halberd. *n. 20.*

hal cy on (hal′si ən), happy; calm; peaceful. *adj. 16.*

hale[1] (hāl), strong and well. *adj. 6.*

hale[2] (hāl), drag by force. *v.*

half (haf), 1. one of two equal parts. A half of 4 is 2. 2. making a half of; needing as much more to make a whole; as, a half pound, a half barrel. 3. to a half of the full amount or degree; as, half cooked. 4. partly. She spoke half aloud. 5. **Not half bad** means fairly good. *n., pl. halves* (havz), *adj., adv. 1.*

half-breed (haf′brēd′), child whose parents are of different races. *n.*

half brother, brother by one parent only.

half-caste (haf′kast′), 1. child of one European parent and one Asiatic parent. 2. half-breed. *n.*

half-heart ed (haf′här′tid), lacking courage, interest, or enthusiasm. *adj.*

half-hour (haf′our′), 1. 30 minutes. 2. halfway point in an hour. 3. of or lasting a half-hour. *n., adj.*

half-mast (haf′mast′), position halfway or part way down from the top of a mast, staff, etc. A flag is lowered to half-mast as a mark of respect for someone who has died, or as a signal of distress. *n.*

half note, half the time of a full note in music.

half pen ny (hā′pən i), a British bronze coin equal in value to a United States cent. *n., pl. halfpence* (hā′pəns) or *halfpennies.*

half sister, sister by one parent only.

half way (haf′wā′), 1. half over the way; as, a rope reaching only halfway. **Meet** (someone) **halfway** means do one's share to agree or be friendly with. 2. one half. The lesson is halfway finished. 3. midway; as, a halfway house between two towns. 4. incomplete; not going far enough; as, halfway prevention of fires. *adv., adj. 11.*

half-wit ted (haf′wit′id), 1. feeble-minded. 2. very stupid; foolish. *adj.*

hal i but (hal′i bət), very large flatfish, much used for food. Halibuts sometimes weigh several hundred pounds. *n., pl. halibuts* or *halibut. 14.*

Halibut

Hal i fax (hal′i faks), the capital of Nova Scotia, Canada. *n. 17.*

hall (hôl), 1. a way to go through a building; passageway. A hall ran the length of the upper floor of the house. 2. a passage or room at the entrance of a building. Leave your umbrella in the hall. 3. a large room for holding meetings, parties, banquets, etc. No hall in town was large enough for the crowd gathered to hear the famous singer. 4. a building for public business, assemblies, etc. The town hall contains several offices and a big assembly room. 5. the house of an English landowner. 6. a building of a school or college. *n. 1.*

hal le lu jah or **hal le lu iah** (hal′i lü′yə), 1. Praise ye the Lord! 2. a song of praise. *interj., n. 18.* Also spelled **alleluia.**

hall mark (hôl′märk′), 1. a mark indicating standard of purity, put on gold or silver articles. 2. a mark or sign of genuineness or good quality. Courtesy and self-control are the hallmarks of a gentleman. 3. put a hallmark on. *n., v.*

hal lo (hə lō′), hello. *interj., n., pl. hallos, v., halloed, halloing.*

hal loa (hə lō′), hallo. *interj., n., pl. halloas, v., halloaed, halloaing. 19.*

hal loo (hə lü′), hallo. *interj., n., pl. halloos, v., hallooed, hallooing. 6.*

hal low (hal′ō), make holy or sacred. *v. 5.*

Hal low een or **Hal low e'en** (hal'ō ēn′), the evening of October 31. *n. 13.*

hal lu ci na tion (hə lü'si nā′shən), 1. a seeing or hearing things that have no basis outside of a person's brain. A person alone in a perfectly quiet room suffers from hallucination if he sees people around him or hears voices. 2. thing seen or heard when there is no external cause for it. *n. 15.*

Halo about the head of Joan of Arc

hall way (hôl′wā'), hall; a passage in a building. *n. 19.*

ha lo (hā′lō), 1. ring of light around the sun, moon, or other shining body. 2. golden circle or disk of light represented about the head of a saint, etc., in pictures, etc. 3. glory; glamour. A halo of romance surrounds King Arthur and his knights. *n., pl. halos* or *haloes. 15.*

halt[1] (hôlt), stop. The soldiers halted for a short rest. *v., n. 4.*

halt[2] (hôlt), 1. hesitate. Shyness made the boy speak in a halting manner. 2. limp. 3. lame; crippled. *v., adj.*

hal ter (hôl′tər), 1. a rope or strap for leading or tying an animal. 2. a rope for hanging a person. *n. 7.*

Halter

halve (hav), 1. divide into two equal parts; share equally. The knight halved his bread with the beggar. 2. reduce to half. The new machine halves the time of doing the work. *v. 11.*

halves (havz), more than one half. *n. pl.*

hal yard (hal′yərd), a rope used to raise or lower a sail, yard, or flag. *n.*

ham (ham), 1. salted and smoked meat from the upper part of a hog's hind leg. See the diagram under **pork.** 2. the back of the thigh; the thigh and buttock. *n. 4.*

Ha man (hā′mən), in the Bible, an enemy of the Jews who was hanged on a gallows about 75 feet high. Esther 7. *n. 18.*

Ham burg (ham′bėrg), a city in northwestern Germany. *n. 14.*

ham burg er (ham′bėr gər), 1. Hamburg steak. 2. sandwich made with Hamburg steak. *Used in common talk. n.*

Hamburg steak, ground beef, usually shaped into round flat cakes and fried or broiled.

Ham il ton (ham′il tən), Alexander, a famous American statesman (1757-1804). He was the first secretary of the treasury. *n.*

ham let[1] (ham′lit), small village; little group of houses in the country. *n. 4.*

Ham let[2] (ham′lit), 1. a famous play by Shakespeare. 2. the principal character in the play. *n.*

ham mer (ham′ər), 1. a tool with a metal head and a handle, used for driving nails, etc. 2. something shaped or used like a hammer. The hammer of a gun explodes the charge. 3. drive, hit, or work with a hammer. 4. beat into shape with a hammer. Metal is hammered into ornaments. 5. fasten by using a hammer. 6. force by many efforts. Arithmetic has to be hammered into that dull boy's head. 7. work out with much effort. *n., v. 2.*

Hammer (def. 1)

ham mer head (ham′ər hed'), a fierce shark whose wide head looks somewhat like a double-headed hammer. *n.*

Hammerhead (about 14 ft. long)

ham mer less (ham′ər lis), having no hammer or no visible hammer. A hammerless pistol has its hammer covered. *adj. 12.*

ham mock (ham′ək), hanging bed or couch made of canvas, netted cord, etc. *n. 8.*

Hammock

ham per[1] (ham′pər), get in the way of; hinder. Poor health hampers him. *v. 8.*

ham per[2] (ham′pər), a large basket with a cover. *n.*

Hamp shire (hamp′shir), 1. a county in southern England. 2. New Hampshire is one of the New England States. *n. 10.*

ham string (ham′string'), 1. in man, one of the tendons behind the knee; in four-legged animals, the great tendon behind the hock. 2. cut the hamstring of, and so cripple. *n., v., hamstrung, hamstringing.*

Han cock (han′kok), John, an American statesman, the first signer of the Declaration of Independence (1737-1793). *n.*

hand (hand), 1. the end part of the arm, which takes and holds objects. Each hand has four fingers and a thumb. 2. thing like a hand; as, the hands of a watch. 3. a hired worker who uses his hands; as, a farm hand, a factory hand. 4. give with the hand. Please hand me a spoon. 5. help with the hand. He handed the lady into her car. 6. possession; control. This property is no longer in my hands. 7. part or share in doing something. He had no hand in the matter. 8. side. At her left hand stood two men. On the other hand, it costs more than I wish to pay. 9. source. She heard the story at second hand. 10. style of handwriting. He writes in a clear hand. 11. skill; ability. The artist's work showed a master's hand. 12. promise of marriage. 13. the breadth of a hand, 4 inches. This horse is 18 hands high. 14. the cards held by a player. 15. a single round in a card game. 16. a player in a card game. 17. Some special meanings are:

at hand, 1. within reach; near. 2. ready.

change hands, pass from one person to another.

from hand to mouth, without providing for the future.

hand and glove, in close relations.

hand down, pass along. The story was handed down from father to son.

hand in glove, in close relations.

hand in hand, 1. holding hands. 2. together.

hand to hand, close together; as, to fight hand to hand.

have one's hands full, have all one can do; be very busy.

in hand, under control.

lay hands on, 1. seize; take; get. 2. arrest. 3. attack; harm.

on hand, 1. within reach; near. 2. ready. 3. present.

turn one's hand to, work at.

n., v. 1.

hand bag (hand′bag′), 1. a woman's small bag for money, toilet articles, etc. 2. a small traveling bag to hold clothes, etc. *n.*

hand ball (hand′bôl′), 1. a game in which a small ball is batted against a wall with the hand. 2. the ball used in this game. *n.*

hand bill (hand′bil′), printed announcement to be handed out to people. *n. 20.*

hand book (hand′bu̇k′), small book of directions. *n.*

hand cuff (hand′kuf′), 1. a device to keep a person from using his hands, usually one of two bracelets joined by a short chain. 2. put handcuffs on. *n., v.*

Handcuffs and key

Han del (han′dəl), a famous German musical composer (1685-1759). *n. 14.*

hand ful (hand′fu̇l), 1. as much or as many as the hand can hold; as, a handful of candy. 2. a small number. A handful of men could defend this mountain pass against hundreds. *n., pl. handfuls. 4.*

hand i cap (han′di kap), 1. a race, contest, or game in which some are given special advantages and some are given special disadvantages. 2. the advantage or disadvantage given in such a race, contest, or game. If a runner has a handicap of 5 yards in a 100-yard dash, it means that he has to run either 95 yards or 105 yards. 3. give a handicap to. 4. an extra burden or task; hindrance. A sore throat is a handicap to a singer. 5. hinder; give an extra burden to. A lame arm handicapped the baseball player. *n., v., handicapped, handicapping. 8.*

hand i craft (han′di kraft), 1. skill with the hands. 2. a trade or art requiring skill with the hands. *n. 15.*

hand i ly (han′di li), in a handy manner. *adv.*

hand i ness (han′di nis), skill with the hands; being handy. *n.*

hand i work (han′di wėrk′), 1. work done by a person's hands. 2. work which one has done himself. *n. 11.*

hand ker chief (hang′kər chif), a soft square of cloth used for wiping the nose, face, hands, etc. Large handkerchiefs are sometimes worn about the neck. *n. 2.*

han dle (han′dəl), 1. a part of a thing made to be grasped by the hand. Spoons, pitchers, hammers, and pails have handles. 2. to touch; feel or use with the hand. Don't handle that book until you wash your hands. 3. manage; direct. The captain handles his men well. 4. behave or act when handled. This car handles easily. 5. treat. The poor cat had been roughly handled by the cruel boys. 6. deal in. This shop handles meat and groceries. 7. chance; opportunity. Don't let your conduct give any handle for gossip. *n., v. 2.*

hand made (hand′mād′), made by hand, not by machine. *adj. 11.*

hand maid (hand′mād′), female servant. *n. 10.*

hand maid en (hand′mād′ən), female servant. *n. 18.*

hand organ, a large music box which is made to play tunes by turning a crank.

Man playing a hand organ

hand shake (hand′shāk′), act of clasping and shaking of hands. *n.*

hand some (han′səm), 1. good-looking;

pleasing in appearance. We usually say that a man is handsome, but that a woman is pretty or beautiful. 2. fairly large; considerable. Ten thousand dollars is a handsome sum of money. 3. generous. Each year he gave each servant a handsome gift of one hundred dollars. *adj. 2.*

hand spike (hand′spīk′), a bar of wood used as a lever, especially on a ship. *n.*

hand spring (hand′spring′), a spring or leap in which a person turns his heels over his head while balancing on one or both hands. *n.*

hand-to-hand (hand′tü hand′), close together; at close quarters; as, a hand-to-hand fight. *adj.*

hand work (hand′wėrk′), work done by hand, not by machinery. *n.*

hand writ ing (hand′rīt′ing), 1. writing by hand; writing with pen, pencil, etc. 2. manner or style of writing. He recognized his mother's handwriting on the envelope. *n. 13.*

hand y (han′di), 1. easy to reach or use; saving work; useful. Handy shelves were near the kitchen sink. 2. skillful with the hands. *adj., handier, handiest. 7.*

hang (hang), 1. fasten or be fastened to something above. Hang your cap on the hook. The swing hangs from a tree. 2. fasten so as to leave swinging freely; as, to hang a door on its hinges. 3. put to death by hanging with a rope around the neck. 4. droop; bend down; as, to hang the head in shame. 5. to cover or decorate with things that are fastened to something above. All the walls were hung with pictures. 6. the way in which a thing hangs; as, the hang of a skirt. 7. meaning; way of using or doing. I can't get the hang of this problem. *v., hung* (or, usually, *hanged* for 3), *hanging, n. 1.*

han gar (hang′ər), a shed for airships or airplanes. *n. 10.*

hang dog (hang′dôg′), ashamed; sneaking; degraded. *adj.*

hang er (hang′ər), 1. person who hangs things. A paper hanger puts on wallpaper. 2. tool or machine that hangs things. 3. thing on which something else is hung. 4. kind of short sword. *n.*

hang er-on (hang′ər on′), 1. follower; dependent. 2. undesirable follower. *n., pl. hangers-on.*

hang ing (hang′ing), 1. death by hanging with a rope around the neck. 2. thing that hangs from a wall, bed, etc. Curtains and draperies are hangings. 3. that hangs. *n., adj.*

hang man (hang′mən), man who puts criminals to death. *n., pl. hangmen. 11.*

hang nail (hang′nāl′), a bit of skin that hangs partly loose near a fingernail. *n.*

hank (hangk), coil; skein. *n. 19.*

han ker (hang′kər), wish; crave. *v. 20.*

Han ni bal (han′i bəl), a great general (247-183? B.C.) of Carthage who fought against Rome and invaded Italy. *n. 18.*

Han o ver (han′ō vər), 1. a district in northwestern Germany. 2. The royal family of England was called the House of Hanover because they came from Hanover. *n. 8.*

han som (han′səm), a two-wheeled cab for two passengers. The driver sits on a seat high up behind. *n.*

Hansom

hap (hap), 1. chance; luck. 2. happen. *n., v., happed, happing.* [*Old use*] *7.*

hap haz ard (hap′haz′ərd), 1. chance. 2. random; not planned. Haphazard answers are usually wrong. 3. by chance; at random. *n., adj., adv. 13.*

hap less (hap′lis), unlucky; unfortunate. *adj. 7.*

hap ly (hap′li), perhaps; by chance. *adv. 6.*

hap pen (hap′ən), 1. take place; occur. Nothing happened while we were there. 2. be or take place by chance. Accidents will happen. 3. have the fortune (to). I happened to sit beside Mary. 4. be done (to). Something has happened to this lock; the key won't turn. 5. **Happen on** means (1) meet. (2) find. *v. 1.*

hap pen ing (hap′ən ing), 1. event. 2. thing that happens. *n.*

hap pi ly (hap′i li), 1. in a happy manner. She lives happily. 2. by luck; with good fortune. Happily I saved you from falling. *adv. 4.*

hap pi ness (hap′i nis), 1. being happy; gladness. 2. good luck. *n. 2.*

hap py (hap′i), 1. feeling as you do when you are well and are having a good time; contented. 2. showing that one is glad; as, a happy smile, a happy look. 3. lucky. By a happy chance we found the watch just where I left it. 4. fit; successful; fortunate; as, a happy way of expressing an idea. *adj., happier, happiest. 1.*

hap py-go-luck y (hap′i gō luk′i), 1. taking things easily as they come; trusting to luck. Some people are happy-go-lucky. 2. by mere chance. *adj., adv.*

Haps burg (haps′bėrg), a German princely family prominent since about 1100. Many of the rulers of the Holy Roman Empire, Austria, Hungary, and Spain were Hapsburgs. *n. 16.*

ha rangue (hə rang′), 1. a noisy speech. 2. a long, pompous speech. 3. to address in a harangue. 4. deliver a harangue. *n., v., harangued, haranguing. 10.*

har ass (har′əs or hə ras′), 1. trouble by repeated attacks. The pirates harassed the villages along the coast. 2. disturb; worry. *v. 8.*

har bin ger (här′bin jər), 1. one that goes ahead to announce another's coming; a forerunner. The robin is a harbinger of spring. 2. announce. *n., v. 10.*

har bor (här′bər), 1. place of shelter for ships. 2. any place of shelter. 3. give shelter to. The shaggy dog harbors fleas. Don't harbor unkind thoughts. *n., v. 2.*

har bor age (här′bər ij), shelter; a place of shelter. The ship rests in a quiet harborage. *n. 20.*

hard (härd), 1. like steel, glass, and rock; not soft; not yielding to touch. 2. firm; solid. 3. firmly; solidly. 4. not yielding to influence; stern. He was a hard father. 5. needing much ability, effort, or time; as, a hard job, a hard lesson, a hard man to get on with. 6. with effort; with vigor. Try hard to lift this log. It is raining hard. 7. severe; causing much pain, trouble, care, etc. Last winter was a hard winter. When our father was out of work, we had a hard time. 8. severely; badly. It will go hard with him if he is caught. 9. not pleasant; harsh; ugly. That man has a hard face. 10. near. The house stands hard by the bridge. 11. not too much moved by the feelings; as, a hard head. 12. **Hard of hearing** means somewhat deaf. 13. Sounds are called hard when they are made with a puff of breath. The letter *c* is hard in *cat* but soft in *cell.* 14. containing much alcohol; as, hard liquor. 15. **Hard water** contains substances that hinder the action of soap. *adj., adv. 1.*

hard coal, coal that burns with very little smoke or flame.

hard en (här′dən), make hard; become hard. *v. 4.*

hard-head ed (härd′hed′id), not easily excited or deceived; practical; shrewd. *adj.*

hard-heart ed (härd′här′tid), without pity; cruel. *adj. 13.*

har di hood (här′di hu̇d), boldness; daring. *n. 12.*

har di ly (här′di li), boldly. *adv.*

har di ness (här′di nis), 1. strength; endurance. 2. hardihood. *n. 17.*

Har ding (här′ding), Warren G. (1865-1923), the 29th president of the United States, from 1921 to 1923. *n. 19.*

hard ly (härd′li), 1. barely; only just. We hardly had time to eat breakfast. 2. not quite. His story is hardly true. 3. probably not. They will hardly come in all this rain. 4. with trouble or effort; as, a hardly fought game. 5. in a hard manner; harshly; severely. *adv. 2.*

hard ness (härd′nis), being hard. *n. 8.*

hard ship (härd′ship), something hard to bear. Hunger, cold, and sickness are hardships. *n. 5.*

hard tack (härd′tak′), very hard biscuit, eaten by sailors. *n.*

hard ware (härd′wãr′), articles made from metal. Locks, hinges, nails, screws, knives, etc., are hardware. *n. 5.*

hard wood (härd′wu̇d′), hard, compact wood. Oak, cherry, maple, ebony, and mahogany are hardwoods. *n. 14.*

har dy (här′di), 1. able to bear hard treatment. Cold weather does not kill hardy plants. 2. bold; daring. *adj., hardier, hardiest. 4.*

hare (hãr), an animal with long ears, a divided upper lip, a short tail, and long hind legs. A hare is very much like a rabbit, but larger. *n. 3.*

Hare (about 2 ft. long)

hare bell (hãr′bel′), a slender plant with blue, bell-shaped flowers; the bluebell. *n. 15.*

hare brained (hãr′brānd′), giddy; heedless; reckless. *adj.*

hare lip (hãr′lip′), a deformity in which the upper lip is divided. *n.*

har em (hãr′əm), 1. part of a Mohammedan house where the women live. 2. its occupants; the wives, female relatives, female servants, etc., of a Mohammedan household. *n. 12.*

hark (härk), listen. *v. 3.*

hark en (här′kən), hearken; listen. *v.*

Har lem (här′ləm), a part of New York City where many Negroes live. *n. 11.*

Har le quin (här′lə kwin), character in comedy and pantomime who is usually masked, has a costume of varied colors, and carries a wooden sword. *n.*

har le quin (här′lə kwin), 1. mischievous person; buffoon. 2. varied in color; many-colored. *n., adj. 15.*

Harlequin

har lot (här′lət), a bad woman; prostitute. *n. 6.*

harm (härm), hurt; damage. *n., v. 2.*

harm ful (härm′fəl), injurious; hurtful. *adj. 9.*

harm less (härm′lis), doing no harm; not harmful; such as would not harm anyone or anything. *adj. 5.*

har mon ic (här mon′ik), 1. having to do with harmony in music. 2. fainter and higher tone heard along with the main tone; overtone. 3. having to do with such tones. 4. musical. *adj., n. 13.*

har mon i ca (här mon′i kə), a small musical instrument played by the mouth; mouth organ. See the picture. *n.*

Harmonica

har mo ni ous (här mō′ni əs), 1. getting on well together; not disturbed by disagreement. The children played in a harmonious group. 2. going well together. 3. sweet-sounding; musical. *adj. 7.*

har mo nize (här′mə nīz), be in or bring into harmony, accord, or agreement. The colors used in the room harmonize. The musician harmonized the old air for part singing. *v. 10.*

har mo ny (här′mə ni), 1. getting on well together. There was perfect harmony between the two brothers. 2. going well together. His plans are in harmony with mine. 3. sweet or musical sound. 4. the sounding together of musical notes in a chord. 5. the study of chords, or of the chord structure in music. *n., pl. harmonies. 3.*

har ness (här′nis), 1. leather fittings for a horse, which connect him to a carriage, plow, etc., or are used in riding. Reins, collar, and bridle are parts of a horse's harness. 2. put harness on. Harness the horse. 3. control and put to work. We harness streams by dams and machinery. 4. **In harness** means in one's regular work. I was glad to get back in harness again after my long vacation. 5. the armor of a knight or warrior. *Old use.* 6. put armor on. *Old use. n., v. 3.*

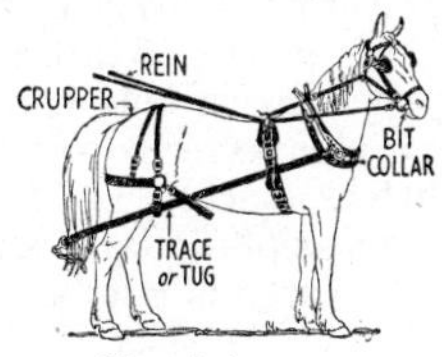

Horse's harness

harp (härp), 1. a large stringed musical instrument played with the fingers. 2. **Harp on** a subject means talk about it very much or too much. 3. play on the harp. *n., v. 4.*

Woman playing a harp

harp er (här′pər), person who plays a harp. *n. 13.*

harp ist (här′pist), harper. *n.*

har poon (här pün′), 1. a spear with a rope tied to it. It is used for catching whales and other sea animals. 2. strike, catch, or kill with a harpoon. *n., v. 17.*

harp si chord (härp′si kôrd), an instrument like a piano, used from about 1550 to 1750. It had a weak and tinkling sound because the strings were plucked by leather or quill points instead of being struck by hammers. *n. 15.*

Harpsichord

har py (här′pi), a cruel, greedy person. The ancient Greeks believed that there were monsters with a woman's head and a bird's body, wings, tail, legs, and claws called **Harpies.** *n., pl. harpies. 12.*

har que bus (här′kwi bəs), an old form of portable gun used before muskets were invented. See the picture under the other spelling, **arquebus.** *n.*

har ri er (har′i ər), 1. a small hound trained to hunt hares. 2. a cross-country runner. *n.*

Har ris burg (har′is bėrg), the capital of Pennsylvania. *n.*

Har ri son (har′i sən), 1. William Henry Harrison (1773-1841) was the 9th president of the United States, in 1841. 2. Benjamin Harrison (1833-1901), his grandson, was the 23rd president of the United States, from 1889 to 1893. *n. 7.*

har row (har′ō), 1. a heavy frame with iron teeth or upright disks. Harrows are used by farmers to break up plowed ground into finer pieces, or to cover seed with earth. 2. draw a harrow over. 3. to hurt; wound. 4. arouse uncomfortable feelings in. He told a harrowing tale of ghosts. *n., v. 6.*

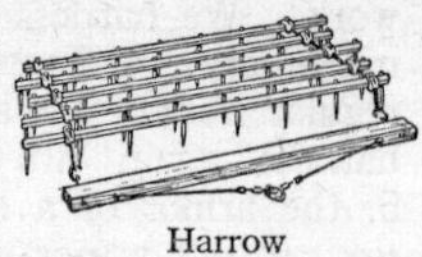
Harrow

har ry (har′i), 1. raid and rob with violence. The pirates harried the towns along the coast. 2. keep troubling; worry; torment. Fear of losing his job harried the clerk. *v., harried, harrying. 2.*

harsh (härsh), 1. rough to the touch, taste, eye, or ear; as, a harsh voice, a harsh climate. 2. cruel; unfeeling; as, a harsh man. *adj. 4.*

harsh ness (härsh′nis), being harsh; roughness; cruelty. *n. 10.*

hart (härt), a male deer, especially of the red deer after its fifth year. *n. 5.*

Hart ford (härt′fərd), the capital of Connecticut. *n. 10.*

harts horn (härts′hôrn′), a form of ammonia used as smelling salts. *n.*

har um-scar um (hãr′əm skãr′əm), 1. reckless; rash. 2. recklessly; rashly. 3. reckless person. *adj., adv., n.*

Har vard (här′vərd), a university for men, in Cambridge, Mass. It is the oldest one in the United States. *n. 9.*

har vest (här′vist), 1. reaping and gathering in grain and other food crops, usually in the fall. 2. the time or season of the harvest. 3. gather in and bring home for use; as, to harvest wheat. 4. one season's yield of any natural product; crop. The oyster harvest was small this year. 5. result; consequences. He is reaping the harvest of his mistakes. *n., v. 2.*

har vest er (här′vis tər), 1. person who works in a harvest field; reaper. 2. machine for harvesting crops, especially grain. *n. 17.*

Har vey (här′vi), William (1578-1657), an English physician who discovered that blood circulates through the body. *n. 18.*

has (haz). See **have.** Who has my book? Dick has been sick. *v. 1.*

hash (hash), 1. mixture of cooked meat, potatoes, etc., chopped into small pieces and fried or baked. 2. chop into small pieces. 3. mixture. 4. a mess; muddle. *n., v. 19.*

hash ish or **hash eesh** (hash′ēsh), dried flowers, top leaves, and tender parts of Indian hemp prepared for use as a narcotic. In the Orient, hashish is smoked or chewed for its intoxicating effect. *n.*

has n't (haz′ənt), has not. *6.*

hasp (hasp), a fastening for a door, window, box, etc. *n. 19.*

Hasp on a door

has sock (has′ək), 1. a thick cushion to sit or kneel on; footstool. 2. bunch of coarse grass. *n. 18.*

hast (hast), an old form meaning **have.** "Thou hast" means "you have." *v. 3.*

Hassock

haste (hāst), 1. a hurry; trying to be quick. Bring the doctor in haste. All his haste was of no use. **Make haste** means hurry; be quick. 2. hasten. *n., v. 2.*

has ten (hās′ən), 1. hurry; cause to be quick; speed. 2. be quick; go fast. *v. 2.*

hast i ly (hās′ti li), 1. in a hurried way; quickly and not very carefully. 2. rashly. 3. in a quick-tempered way. *adv. 5.*

hast i ness (hās′ti nis), 1. quickness of motion. 2. rashness. 3. quick temper. *n.*

Has tings (hās′tingz), a battle in 1066 which made William the Conqueror king of England. *n. 18.*

hast y (hās′ti), 1. quick; hurried; as, a hasty glance, a hasty trip to town. 2. rash; not well thought out; as, a hasty decision. 3. easily angered; quick-tempered; as, a hasty old gentleman. *adj., hastier, hastiest. 4.*

hasty pudding, 1. corn-meal mush. 2. oatmeal or flour mush.

hat (hat), 1. a covering for the head when outdoors. A hat usually has a crown and brim. 2. provide with a hat; put a hat on. 3. **Pass the hat** means ask for contributions. *n., v., hatted, hatting. 1.*

hatch[1] (hach), 1. bring forth (young) from an egg or eggs. A hen hatches chickens. 2. keep (an egg or eggs) warm until the young come out. It takes three weeks to hatch hens' eggs. 3. come out from the egg. Three of the chickens hatched today. 4. grow to be young animals. Will these eggs hatch? 5. a brood. There are twelve chickens in this hatch. 6. arrange; plan. 7. plan secretly; plot. *v., n. 5.*

hatch[2] (hach), 1. an opening in a ship's deck through which the cargo is put in. 2. opening in the floor or roof of a building, etc. 3. the trap door covering this opening. 4. the lower half of a divided door. *n.*

Hatch (def. 1)

hatch er y (hach′ər i), place for hatching eggs, especially fish eggs. *n., pl. hatcheries. 17.*

hatch et (hach′it), 1. a small ax with a handle about a foot long. 2. **Bury the hatchet** means make peace. **Dig up the hatchet** means make war. *n. 5.*

Hatchet

hatch way (hach′wā′), 1. an opening in a ship's deck to a lower part. 2. a similar opening in a floor, roof, etc. *n.*

hate (hāt). Cats usually hate dogs. God hates sin. She felt a very strong dislike or hate of snakes. Her hate for lies would not let her be friends to any girl who lied. *v., n. 2.*

hate ful (hāt′fəl), 1. causing hate. 2. feeling hate; showing hate. *adj. 5.*

hat er (hāt′ər), one who hates. *n. 13.*

hath (hath), an old form meaning **has.** *v. 4.*

ha tred (hā′trid), very strong dislike; hate. *n. 4.*

hat ter (hat′ər), person who makes or sells hats. *n.*

Hat ter as (hat′ər əs). **Cape Hatteras** is a cape on an island off North Carolina. *n.*

hau berk (hô′bėrk), a long coat of mail. *n. 20.*

Hauberk

haugh ti ness (hô′ti nis), being haughty; disdainful pride; arrogant looking down on other people. *n. 16.*

haugh ty (hô′ti), 1. too proud of oneself and too scornful of others. 2. showing too great pride of oneself and scorn for others. *adj., haughtier, haughtiest. 4.*

haul (hôl), 1. pull or drag with force. The logs were hauled to the mill by horses. 2. act of hauling; hard pull. 3. load hauled. Powerful trucks are used for heavy hauls. 4. distance that a load is hauled. 5. amount won, taken, etc., at one time; catch. The fishing boats made a good haul today. 6. change the course of (a ship). *v., n. 5.*

haunch (hônch), 1. the part of the body around the hips. A dog sits on his haunches. 2. the leg and loin of an animal, used for food; as, a haunch of venison. *n. 10.*

haunt (hônt), 1. go often to; visit frequently. People say ghosts haunt that old house. 2. place visited often. The swimming pool was a favorite haunt of the boys in the summer. 3. be often with. Memories of his youth haunted the old man. *v., n. 3.*

haunt ed (hôn′tid), visited by ghosts. *adj.*

haut boy (hō′boi), oboe. *n.*

hau teur (hō tėr′), haughtiness; haughty manner or spirit. *n.*

Ha van a (hə van′ə), capital of Cuba. *n. 7.*

have (hav), 1. hold. I have a club in my hand. 2. possess; own. He has a big house and farm. A house has windows. She has no news of her brother. 3. know; understand. She has your idea. 4. be forced; be compelled. All animals have to sleep. He will have to go now because his work begins. 5. cause (somebody to do something or something to be done). Please have the boy bring my mail. She will have the car washed for me. 6. get; take. You need to have a rest. 7. experience. Have a pleasant time. They had trouble with this engine. 8. allow; permit. Ann won't have any noise while she is reading. 9. Have is used with words like *asked, been, broken, done,* or *called* to express completed action. He has eaten. She had gone before. I have called her. They will have seen her by Sunday. *v., had, having. 1.*

ha ven (hā′vən), 1. harbor, especially one for shelter from a storm. 2. place of shelter and safety. The old cabin was a haven from the storm. *n. 5.*

have n't (hav′ənt), have not.

hav er sack (hav′ər sak), a bag used by soldiers and hikers for carrying food when on a march or hike. *n. 20.*

Hiker carrying a haversack

hav oc (hav′ək), very great destruction or injury. Tornadoes, severe earthquakes, and plagues create widespread havoc. *n. 7.*

Ha vre (hä′vər), a seaport city in northwestern France. *n. 18.*

haw[1] (hô), 1. the red berry of the hawthorn. 2. the hawthorn. *n. 18.*

haw[2] (hô), 1. the sound "haw." 2. make such a sound; stammer. *interj., n., v.*

haw[3] (hô), a word of command to horses or oxen directing them to turn to the left. *interj.*

Ha wai i (hə wī′ē), 1. Hawaiian Islands. 2. largest of the Hawaiian Islands. *n. 13.*

Ha wai ian (hə wī′yən), 1. of or having to do with Hawaii, its people, or their language. 2. native or inhabitant of Hawaii. 3. language of Hawaii. *adj., n.*

Hawaiian Islands, island group in the North Pacific Ocean, a Territory of the United States.

hawk[1] (hôk), 1. a bird of prey with a strong, hooked beak, and large curved claws. Long ago hawks were trained to hunt and kill other birds. 2. to hunt with trained hawks. *n., v. 3.*

Red-tailed hawk (about 2 ft. long)

hawk[2] (hôk), carry (goods) about for sale, as a street hawker or peddler does. *v.*

hawk er[1] (hôk′ər), person who carries goods about for sale; peddler. *n. 15.*

hawk er[2] (hôk′ər), person who hunts with a hawk. *n.*

haw ser (hô′zər), large rope or small cable. Hawsers are used for mooring or towing ships. *n. 16.*

haw thorn (hô′thôrn), a shrub or small tree with many thorns and clusters of fragrant flowers and red berries. *n. 8.*

Haw thorne (hô′thôrn), Nathaniel, an American author of novels and short stories (1804-1864). *n.*

hay (hā), 1. grass cut and dried as food for cattle and horses. 2. cut and dry grass for hay. 3. supply with hay. *n., v. 2.*

hay cock (hā′kok′), a small pile of hay in a field. *n. 11.*

Haycock

Hay dn (hī′dən), Franz Joseph, Austrian composer of symphonies and other music (1732-1809). *n.*

Hayes (hāz), Rutherford B. (1822-1893), the 19th president of the United States, from 1877 to 1881. *n.*

hay fever, a disease like a cold, caused by the pollen of ragweed and other plants.

hay field (hā′fēld′), a field in which grass is grown or cut for hay. *n. 17.*

hay loft (hā′lôft′), place in a stable or barn where hay is stored. *n.*

hay mow (hā′mou′), 1. place in a barn for storing hay. 2. hay stored in a barn. *n.*

hay rick (hā′rik′), haystack. *n.*

hay stack (hā′stak′), a large pile of hay outdoors. *n. 20.*

haz ard (haz′ərd), 1. risk; danger. The life of an aviator is full of hazards. 2. chance. 3. to risk; take a chance with. I would hazard my life on his honesty. 4. an obstruction on a golf course. 5. a dice game. *n., v. 7.*

haz ard ous (haz′ər dəs), dangerous; risky; perilous. *adj. 11.*

haze[1] (hāz), 1. a small amount of mist or smoke in the air. A thin haze veiled the distant hills. 2. vagueness of the mind; slight confusion. *n. 9.*

haze[2] (hāz), force to do unnecessary or ridiculous tasks; bully. The freshmen resented being hazed by the sophomores. *v.*

ha zel (hā′zəl), 1. a shrub or small tree whose light-brown nuts are good to eat. 2. light brown. *n., adj. 6.*

Hazel leaves and nuts

ha zy (hā′zi), 1. misty; smoky; dim; as, a hazy sky. 2. not distinct; obscure; as, a hazy idea. *adj., hazier, haziest. 15.*

he (hē), 1. the boy, man, or male animal spoken about. He works hard, but his work pays him well. 2. male. *pron., pl. they, n., pl. hes. 1.*

head (hed), 1. the top part of the human body where the eyes and mouth are. 2. the front of an animal where the eyes and mouth are. 3. the top part of anything; as, the head of a pin, a cabbage, a crane, a drum, or a barrel. 4. the front or face part of anything; as, the head of a procession, or the head of a street. 5. at the front or top. 6. be at the front or the top of. 7. coming from in front; as, a head wind, a head sea. 8. move toward; face toward. 9. chief person; leader. 10. chief; leading. 11. be the head or chief of; lead. 12. one or ones; an individual. Ten cows are ten head of cattle. 13. the striking part of a tool or implement; as, the head of a hammer, the head of a golf club. 14. mind; understanding; intelligence. He has a good head for figures. 15. topic. He arranged his speech under four heads. 16. crisis; conclusion. His sudden refusal brought matters to a head. 17. pressure; as, a head of steam. 18. source; as, the head of a brook. 19. Some special meanings are:

head off, get in front of; check.

keep one's head, not get excited; stay calm.

lay heads together, plan or plot together.

out of one's head, crazy.

over one's head, 1. too hard for one to understand. 2. passing over a person without giving him a chance to act.

n., adj., v. 1.

head ache (hed′āk′), a pain in the head. *n. 6.*

head dress (hed′dres′), a covering or decoration for the head. *n.*

Headdress worn about 1395

head er (hed′ər), 1. person or instrument that puts on or takes off heads of grain, barrels, pins, nails, etc. 2. a plunge head foremost. *Used in common talk. n. 20.*

head first (hed′fėrst′), 1. with the head first. 2. hastily; rashly. *adv.*

head fore most (hed′fōr′mōst), headfirst. *adv.*

head gear (hed′gēr′), 1. covering for the head; hat, cap, etc. 2. harness for an animal's head. *n.*

head ing (hed′ing), 1. something used as a head, top, or front. 2. something written or printed at the top of a page. 3. title of a page, chapter, etc.; topic. *n. 17.*

head land (hed′lənd), cape; point of land running out into water. *n. 9.*

head less (hed′lis), 1. having no head. 2. without a leader. 3. without brains; foolish; stupid. *adj. 11.*

head light (hed′līt′), a bright light at the front of an automobile, a streetcar, a train, etc. *n. 13.*

head line (hed′līn′), 1. a title line over an article in a newspaper. 2. the line at the top of a page containing the title, etc. 3. furnish with a headline. *n., v. 18.*

head long (hed′lông), 1. headfirst; as, to plunge headlong into the sea. 2. with great haste and force; as, to rush headlong into the crowd. 3. in too great a rush; without stopping to think. *adv., adj. 5.*

head man (hed′man′), chief; leader. *n., pl. headmen.*

head mas ter (hed′mas′tər), person in charge of a school; principal. *n.*

head-on (hed′on′), with the head or front first. *adj.*

head piece (hed′pēs′), 1. piece of armor for the head. 2. any covering for the head. 3. the head. 4. decoration at the head of a page or chapter. *n. 19.*

head quar ters (hed′kwôr′tərz), 1. in an army, the place where the commander in chief or the officer in charge lives or has his office; the place from which orders are sent out. 2. the main office; the center of operations or of authority. *n. pl. or sing. 5.*

head ship (hed′ship), position as head; chief authority; leadership; command; direction. *n.*

heads man (hedz′mən), man who cuts off the heads of prisoners condemned to death. *n., pl. headsmen. 19.*

head stone (hed′stōn′), 1. a stone set at the head of a grave. 2. the principal stone in a foundation. *n. 17.*

head strong (hed′strông′), rashly or foolishly determined to have one's own way; hard to control or manage; obstinate. *adj. 12.*

head wa ters (hed′wô′tərz), the sources or upper parts of a river. *n. pl.*

head way (hed′wā′), 1. motion forward. The ship could make no headway against the strong wind and tide. 2. progress with work, etc. 3. clear space, such as in a doorway or under an arch. *n. 15.*

head y (hed′i), 1. headlong; rash. 2. apt to affect the head; intoxicating. *adj., headier, headiest. 16.*

heal (hēl), 1. cure; make well; bring back to health. 2. grow well; become well. *v. 3.*

health (helth), 1. being well or not sick, freedom from illness of any kind. 2. condition of the body; as, good health, poor health. 3. **Drink a health** to (someone) means drink in honor of (someone) and wish (him) well. *n. 1.*

health ful (helth′fəl), giving health; good for the health; as, healthful exercise, a healthful diet. *adj. 6.*

health i ness (hel′thi nis), being healthy; good health. *n.*

health y (hel′thi), 1. having good health; as, a healthy baby. 2. giving health; good for the health. *adj., healthier, healthiest. 4.*

heap (hēp), 1. pile of many things thrown or lying together; as, a heap of stones, a sand heap. 2. form into a heap; gather in heaps. 3. large amount. *Used in common talk.* 4. give generously or in large amounts. 5. fill full or more than full; as, to heap a plate with food. *n., v. 2.*

hear (hēr). We hear with our ears. You must hear what he has to say. Have you heard from your friends in China? *v., heard, hearing. 1.*

heard (hėrd). See **hear.** I heard the noise. The gun was heard a mile away. *pt. and pp. of hear. 1.*

hear er (hēr′ər), person who hears or listens. *n. 6.*

hear ing (hēr′ing), 1. the sense by which sound is perceived. The old man's hearing is poor. 2. act or process of perceiving sound. Hearing the good news made him happy. 3. chance to be heard. The judge gave both sides a hearing. 4. the distance that a sound can be heard; as, to be within hearing of the baby, to talk freely in the hearing of others. *n.*

heark en (här′kən), listen. *v. 5.*

hear say (hēr′sā′), common talk; gossip. *n. 18.*

hearse (hėrs), a carriage or car to carry a dead person to his grave. *n. 16.*

heart (härt), 1. the part of the body that pumps the blood. 2. feelings; mind; soul. She has a kind heart. 3. the part that feels, loves, hates, and desires; as, to give one's heart. 4. person loved or praised. 5. kindness; sympathy. 6. courage; enthusiasm. 7. middle; center; as, the heart of the forest. 8. main part; most important part. 9. figure shaped somewhat like the picture. 10. Some special meanings are:

after one's heart, just as one likes it.

at heart, in one's deepest thoughts or feelings.

lay to heart, 1. keep in mind; remember. 2. think seriously about.

learn by heart, memorize.

take heart, be encouraged.

take to heart, think seriously about.

with all one's heart, 1. sincerely. 2. gladly. *n. 1.*

heart ache (härt′āk′), great sorrow or grief; deep pain. *n.*

heart bro ken (härt′brō′kən), crushed by sorrow or grief. *adj.*

heart burn (härt′bėrn′), 1. a burning feeling in the stomach, often rising to the chest and throat. 2. envy; jealousy. *n.*

heart ed (här′tid), having a heart of the kind mentioned; as, good-hearted, sad-hearted. *adj. 6.*

heart en (här′tən), cheer; cheer up; encourage. Good news heartens you. *v. 11.*

heart felt (härt′felt′), sincere; genuine; as, heartfelt sympathy. *adj. 10.*

hearth (härth), 1. the floor of a fireplace. 2. fireside; home. The soldiers longed for their own hearths. *n. 3.*

hearth side (härth′sīd′), 1. the side of a hearth. 2. home. *n.*

hearth stone (härth′stōn′), 1. a stone forming a hearth. 2. the fireside; the home. *n. 18.*

heart i ly (här′ti li), 1. sincerely; warmly; as, to express good wishes very heartily. 2. with a good will; in good spirits for what one is doing; as, to set to work heartily. 3. with a good appetite; as, to eat heartily. 4. very completely. My mother was heartily tired of so much housework. *adv. 6.*

heart i ness (här′ti nis), 1. sincerity. 2. warmth. 3. vigor. *n. 20.*

heart less (härt′lis), without a heart; unfeeling; cruel. *adj. 13.*

heart-rend ing (härt′ren′ding), causing mental anguish. To be in a shipwreck is a heart-rending experience. *adj.*

heart sick (härt′sik′), sick at heart; very depressed; very unhappy. *adj. 20.*

heart strings (härt′stringz′), feelings; deepest feelings. *n. pl.*

heart y (här′ti), 1. cheerful; friendly; eager; full of feeling; sincere; as, a hearty manner, a hearty greeting, hearty wishes for a happy birthday. We bade them a hearty good-by. 2. strong and well; vigorous; as, to be hale and hearty at sixty. 3. abundant; heavy; as, a hearty meal. *adj., heartier, heartiest. 4.*

heat (hēt), 1. hotness; warmth; as, the heat of a fire. 2. make warm or hot. The stove heats the room. 3. hot weather. 4. hottest point; most violent stage. In the heat of the fight he lost his temper. 5. one trial in a race. He won the first heat, but lost the final race. *n., v. 1.*

heat er (hēt′ər), something that gives heat or warmth, such as a stove, furnace, or radiator. *n. 9.*

heath (hēth), 1. open, waste land with heather or low bushes growing on it; moor. It has few or no trees. 2. low bush growing on such land. Heather is a kind of heath. *n. 5.*

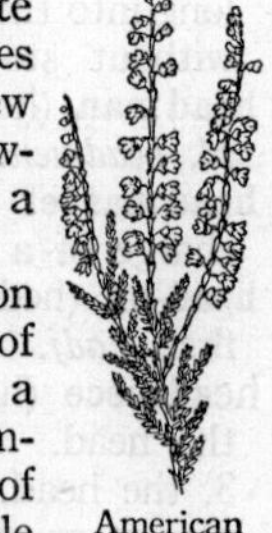
American heath

hea then (hē′ᴛʜən), 1. person who does not accept the God of the Bible; person who is not a Christian, Jew, or Mohammedan. The wild savages of Africa are heathens. 2. people who are heathen. 3. of or having to do with the heathen. *n., pl. heathens* or *heathen, adj. 4.*

hea then ish (hē′ᴛʜən ish), 1. having to do with the heathen. 2. like the heathen. *adj. 19.*

heath er (heᴛʜ′ər), a low shrub which covers waste lands in Scotland and northern England. *n. 10.*

heave (hēv), 1. lift with force or effort. He heaved the heavy box into the wagon. 2. lift and throw. The sailors heaved the anchor overboard. 3. pull with force or effort; haul. They heaved on the rope. 4. give (a sigh, groan, etc.) with a deep, heavy breath. 5. rise and fall alternately. Waves heave in a storm. 6. breathe hard; pant. 7. rise; swell; bulge; as, heaving waves. 8. heaving; throw. 9. Some special meanings are:

Scotch heather

heave ho! sailors' cry when pulling up the anchor, etc.

heave in sight, come into view.

heave to, stop a ship; stop.

v., heaved or *hove, heaving, n. 3.*

heav en (hev′ən), 1. place where God and His angels live. 2. God; Providence. It was the will of Heaven. 3. place or condition of greatest happiness. 4. upper air in which clouds float, winds blow, and birds fly; the sky. We usually say heavens. 5. **For heaven's sake** and **Good heavens** are exclamations expressing surprise or a protest. *n., interj. 1.*

heav en ly (hev′ən li), 1. of or in heaven. God is our heavenly Father. 2. like heaven; suited to heaven; as, a heavenly spot, heavenly peace. 3. very, very excellent. 4. of or in the heavens. The sun, moon, and the stars are heavenly bodies. *adj. 4.*

heav en ward (hev′ən wərd), toward heaven. *adv., adj. 11.*

heav i ly (hev′i li), in a heavy way or manner. *adv. 4.*

heav i ness (hev′i nis), 1. being heavy; great weight. 2. sadness. *n. 7.*

heav y (hev′i), 1. hard to lift or carry; having much weight. Iron is heavy and feathers are light. 2. of more than usual weight for its kind; as, heavy silk, heavy bread. 3. large; greater than usual; as, a heavy rain, a heavy crop, a heavy meal, a heavy vote, a heavy sea, a heavy sleep. 4. weighted down; laden; as, air heavy with moisture, eyes heavy with sleep. A heavy heart is full of sorrow. 5. hard to bear or endure. 6. hard to deal with, manage, etc. A heavy road is muddy or sandy, so that a load is hard to draw. Heavy food is hard to digest. 7. gloomy; as, a heavy sky. 8. heavily. *adj., heavier, heaviest, adv. 1.*

heav y weight (hev′i wāt′), 1. person or thing of much more than average weight. 2. boxer or wrestler who weighs 175 pounds or more. *n.*

He be (hē′bi), the Greek goddess of youth. *n. 18.*

He brew (hē′brü), 1. a Jew; a descendant of one of the desert tribes led by Moses who settled in Palestine. 2. Jewish. 3. the ancient language of the Jews. *n., adj. 7.*

He brews (hē′brüz), book of the New Testament. *n.*

Heb ri des (heb′ri dēz), group of islands northwest of Scotland. *n. pl. 17.*

He bron (hē′brən), town in Palestine. *n. 13.*

Hec a te (hek′ə ti), a Greek goddess of ghosts, the earth, and infernal regions. She was also thought to be associated with magic and witchcraft. *n. 19.*

hec a tomb (hek′ə tom), 1. a sacrifice of 100 oxen. 2. a great slaughter. *n. 16.*

heck le (hek′əl), ask many bothersome questions in order to annoy (a speaker). *v.*

hec tic (hek′tik), 1. very exciting; feverish. 2. consumptive; showing the signs of tuberculosis; having flushed cheeks, hot skin, and loss of flesh. *adj. 14.*

Hec tor (hek′tər), a great Trojan fighter in Homer's *Iliad.* *n. 8.*

hec tor (hek′tər), 1. a bragging, bullying fellow. 2. bluster; bully. *n., v.*

he'd (hēd), 1. he had. 2. he would. *7.*

hedge (hej), 1. a thick row of bushes or low trees planted as a fence or boundary. 2. a barrier of any kind. 3. put a hedge around; as, to hedge a garden. 4. **Hedge in** means hem in; surround on all sides. 5. bet on both sides in order to reduce one's possible losses. 6. avoid giving a direct answer; evade questions. *n., v. 3.*

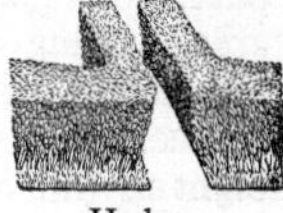
Hedge

hedge hog (hej′hog′), 1. a small animal of the Old World with spines on its back. When attacked, hedgehogs roll up into a bristling ball. 2. the porcupine of North America. *n. 6.*

European hedgehog (about 10 in. long)

hedge row (hej′rō′), a thick row of bushes or small trees forming a hedge. *n. 11.*

heed (hēd), 1. give careful attention to; take notice of. Now heed what I say. 2. careful attention. She pays heed to her clothes. *v., n. 3.*

heed ful (hēd′fəl), careful; attentive; mindful. *adj.*

heed less (hēd′lis), careless; thoughtless. *adj. 8.*

heed less ness (hēd′lis nis), carelessness; thoughtlessness. *n. 17.*

heel[1] (hēl), 1. the back part of the human foot, below the ankle. 2. the part of a stocking or shoe that covers the heel. 3. the part of a shoe or boot that is under the heel or raises the heel. 4. touch the ground with the heel. 5. put a heel or heels on; as, to heel a pair of shoes. 6. anything shaped or used like a heel. *n., v. 2.*

heel[2] (hēl), 1. lean over to one side. 2. act of heeling. *v., n.*

heft (heft), 1. weight. 2. heave; lift. 3. judge (weight) by lifting. *n., v.* [*Used in common talk*]

Hei del berg (hī′dəl bėrg), a city in western Germany, where there is a famous university. *n. 17.*

heif er (hef′ər), a young cow that has not had a calf. *n. 5.*

heigh-ho (hī′hō′), a sound made to express surprise, joy, sadness, or weariness. *interj.*

height (hīt), 1. how tall a person is; how high anything is; how far up a thing goes; as, the height of a mountain. 2. a rather great distance up; as, rising at a height above the valley. 3. a high point or place; as, on the mountain heights. 4. highest part; top. 5. highest point; greatest degree. Being reckless in an automobile is the height of folly. 6. high rank; high degree. *n. 1.*

height en (hīt′ən), 1. make or become higher. 2. increase; make stronger. *v. 8.*

hei nous (hā′nəs), very wicked; hateful; offensive. *adj. 10.*

heir (ãr), person who has the right to somebody's property after that one dies. The rich man adopted the boy and made him his heir. *n. 3.*

heir apparent, person who will be heir if he lives longer than the one holding the property or title. The king's oldest son was heir apparent to the throne. *pl. heirs apparent.*

heir ess (ãr′is), 1. heir who is a woman or girl. 2. woman or girl inheriting great wealth. *n. 14.*

heir loom (ãr′lüm′), a possession handed down from generation to generation. This clock is a family heirloom. *n. 12.*

held (held). See **hold**[1]. Mary held the baby. The swing is held by strong ropes. *pt. and pp. of hold*[1]. *1.*

Hel en (hel′ən). **Helen of Troy** was a very beautiful Greek woman. Her kidnaping by Paris caused the Trojan War. *n. 4.*

Hel e na (hel′i nə), the capital of Montana. *n.*

Hel i con (hel′i kon), a mountain in ancient Greece, sacred to the Muses. *n. 19.*

he li o graph (hē′li ō graf′), 1. device for signaling by means of a movable mirror that flashes beams of light to a distance. 2. signal by heliograph. *n., v.*

Heliograph

He li os (hē′li os), Greek god of the sun. *n.*

he li o trope (hē′li ə trōp), 1. a plant with small, sweet-smelling, purple or white flowers. 2. light purple. *n., adj. 19.*

he li um (hē′li əm), a very light gas. Helium is used in balloons and dirigibles because it will not burn. *n. 19.*

hell (hel), 1. the place where wicked persons are punished after death. 2. any very bad place or condition. *n. 3.*

he'll (hēl), 1. he will. 2. he shall. *10.*

Hel las (hel′əs), Greece. *n. 20.*

hel le bore (hel′i bōr), a poisonous plant whose roots are used in medicine or as a powder to kill insects. *n. 16.*

Hellebore

Hel lene (hel′ēn), Greek. *n.*

Hel len ic (he len′ik), Greek. *adj. 20.*

Hel les pont (hel′is pont), the Dardanelles, a strait connecting the Sea of Marmara with the Aegean Sea. *n.*

hell ish (hel′ish), devilish; fit to have come from hell; as, hellish shrieks, a hellish thing to do. *adj. 13.*

hel lo (he lō′), 1. a call of greeting or surprise. Tom said, "Hello! Bill." 2. a call or shout. The girl gave a loud hello to let us know where she was. 3. to shout. He asked us to hello until somebody came. *interj., n., pl. hellos, v., helloed, helloing.*

helm[1] (helm), 1. the handle or wheel by which a ship is steered. 2. position of control or guidance. *n. 5.*

helm[2] (helm), helmet. *n.* [*Old use*]

hel met (hel′mit), a covering to protect the head. Knights wore helmets as part of their armor. Soldiers wear steel helmets; firemen wear leather helmets. *n. 4.*

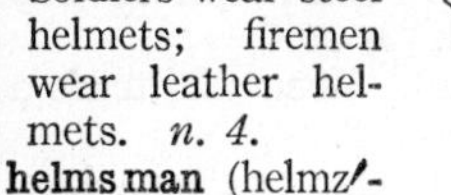

Modern Medieval
Soldiers' helmets

helms man (helmz′mən), man who steers a ship. *n., pl. helmsmen. 13.*

hel ot (hel′ət), slave; serf. *n. 17.*

help (help), 1. Please give me some help. A sewing machine is a help in making clothes. Mother helps us. 2. means of making better. The medicine was a help. 3. make better. The doctor helped my sore throat. 4. give food to; serve with food. 5. avoid; keep from. He cannot help going to sleep. 6. a helping. *n., v. 1.*

help er (hel′pər), person that helps. *n. 5.*

help ful (help′fəl), useful. *adj. 5.*

help ing (hel′ping), a portion of food served to a person at one time. *n.*

help less (help′lis), 1. not able to help oneself. A little baby is helpless. 2. without help. *adj. 4.*

help less ness (help′lis nis), being helpless; as, the helplessness of a little baby. *n. 13.*

help mate (help′māt′), companion and helper; wife or husband. *n. 19.*

help meet (help′mēt′), helpmate; wife. *n.*

Hel sing fors (hel′sing fôrs), seaport and capital of Finland. *n.*

hel ter-skel ter (hel′tər skel′tər), with headlong, disorderly haste. The children ran helter-skelter when the dog rushed at them. *adv. 14.*

helve (helv), handle of an ax, hammer, etc. *n.*

hem[1] (hem), 1. a border or edge on a garment; the edge made by folding over the cloth and sewing it down. 2. fold over and sew down the edge of (cloth). 3. **Hem in, around,** or **about** means close in, or surround, and not let out. *n., v., hemmed, hemming. 4.*

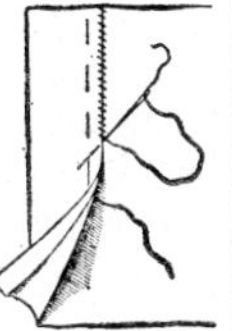
Hemming

hem[2] (hem), 1. a sound like clearing the throat, used to attract attention or show doubt or hesitation. 2. make this sound. *interj., n., v., hemmed, hemming.*

hem i sphere (hem′i sfēr), 1. half of a sphere or globe. 2. half of the earth's surface. North and South America are in the Western Hemisphere; Europe, Asia, and Africa are in the Eastern Hemisphere. All the countries north of the equator are in the Northern Hemisphere. *n. 6.*

hem lock (hem′lok), 1. a poisonous plant with spotted stems, finely divided leaves, and small white flowers. 2. a poisonous drink made of hemlock. 3. an evergreen tree, a kind of spruce. Hemlock bark is used in tanning. 4. its wood. *n. 8.*

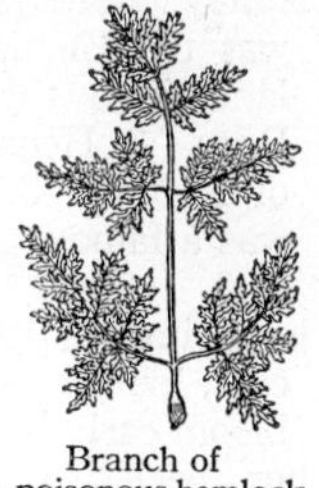
Branch of poisonous hemlock

he mo glo bin (hē′mō glō′bin), the red substance in the blood. *n. 14.*

Branch of ordinary hemlock

hem or rhage (hem′ə rij), a discharge of blood. Consumptives have hemorrhages from the lungs. A nosebleed is a mild hemorrhage. *n. 18.*

hemp (hemp), a tall plant whose tough fibers are made into string, rope, and coarse cloth. *n. 9.*

hemp en (hem′pən), 1. made of hemp. 2. like hemp. *adj. 16.*

hem stitch (hem′stich′), 1. to hem along a line from which threads have been drawn out, gathering the cross threads into a series of little groups. 2. the stitch used. These towels are trimmed with hemstitches. 3. ornamental needlework made by hemstitching. *v., n. 14.*

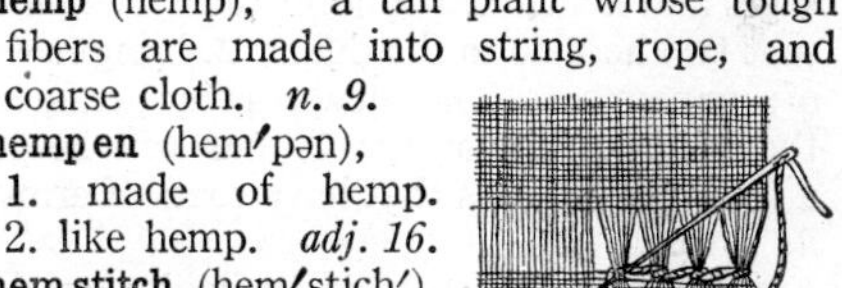
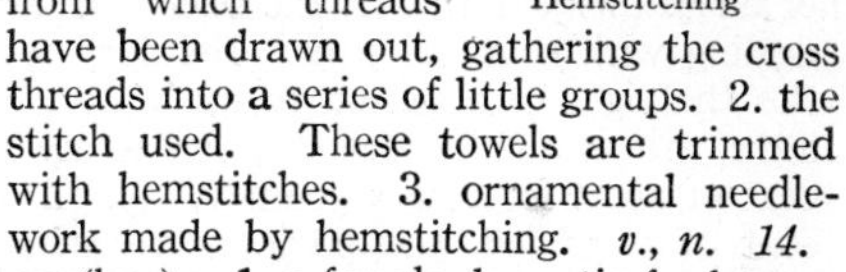
Hemstitching

hen (hen), **1.** a female domestic fowl; as, a hen and her chickens. **2.** the female of other birds; as, a hen sparrow. *n. 2.*

hence (hens), 1. from here; from now. 2. from this; as a result of this; therefore. 3. **Hence!** means go away. 4. **Hence with him!** means away with him; take him away. *adv., interj. 2.*

hence forth (hens′fōrth′), from this time on; from now on. *adv. 3.*

hence for ward (hens′fôr′wərd), from this time on; from now on. *adv. 12.*

hench man (hench′mən), 1. trusty attendant or follower. 2. an obedient, unscrupulous follower. *n., pl. henchmen. 16.*

hen coop (hen′küp′), coop for hens. *n.*

hen na (hen′ə), 1. a dark, reddish-orange dye. 2. reddish brown. *n., adj. 18.*

hen peck (hen′pek′), domineer over. He was henpecked by his wife. *v. 18.*

Hen ry (hen′ri), 1. Henry VIII (1491-1547) was the English king who withdrew England from the religious authority of the Pope. 2. Henry IV (1553-1610) was a king of France. 3. Patrick Henry (1736-1799) was a famous American patriot and orator. *n. 2.*

he pat i ca (hi pat′i kə), low plant with delicate, purple, pink, or white flowers that bloom early in the spring. *n.*

her (hėr), 1. She is not here. Have you seen her? Find her. She and her mean the girl or woman or female animal spoken about. 2. of her; belonging to her. She has left her book. The cat won't let you touch her kittens. *pron., adj. 1.*

He ra (hēr′ə), a Greek goddess, wife of Zeus. She was the queen of gods and men and the goddess of marriage. The Romans called her Juno. *n.*

her ald (her′əld), 1. person who carries messages and makes announcements. The king sent two heralds to the duke. 2. bring news of; announce. The newspapers heralded the arrival of the army. 3. man who keeps a record of families that have coats of arms. *n., v. 5.*

he ral dic (he ral′dik), of or having to do with heraldry or heralds. *adj. 18.*

her ald ry (her′əld ri), 1. the science or art dealing with coats of arms. Heraldry settles the right of a person to use a coat of arms, traces family descent, makes up a coat of arms for a new country, etc. 2. a coat of arms. 3. the pomp or ceremony connected with the life of noble families. *n., pl. heraldries. 11.*

herb (ėrb or hėrb), 1. a plant with leaves that are used for medicine, seasoning, or food. Sage, mint, and lavender are herbs. 2. flowering plant whose stems live only one season. *n. 4.*

herb age (ėr′bij or hėr′bij), herbs; grass. *n. 11.*

her cu le an or **Her cu le an** (hėr kū′li ən), 1. of great strength, courage, or size. 2. very hard to do. *adj. 12.*

Her cu les (hėr′kū lēz), a hero of Greek mythology famous for his great strength and for the twelve tasks he performed. *n. 7.*

herd (hėrd), 1. a number of animals together; as, a herd of cows, a herd of horses, a herd of elephants. 2. keeper of a herd; as, a cowherd, a goatherd. 3. a large number of people. 4. common people. 5. join together; flock together. 6. form into a flock, herd, or group. 7. tend or take care of (cattle or sheep). *n., v. 2.*

herd er (hėr′dər), herdsman; person who takes care of a herd. *n. 20.*

herds man (hėrdz′mən), man who tends a herd. *n., pl. herdsmen. 8.*

here (hēr), 1. in this place; at this place. We live here in the summer. We will stop here. 2. to this place. Bring the children here for their lesson. 3. this place. 4. now; at this time. 5. in this life. 6. this life. 7. In answering a roll call, **Here!** means "I am present!" 8. Here is sometimes used in calling attention to a person or thing. My friend here can help you. 9. **Here's to you!** means "I wish you health or success." *adv., n., interj. 1.*

here a bout (hēr′ə bout′), about this place; around here; near here. *adv. 14.*

here a bouts (hēr′ə bouts′), hereabout. *adv.*

here af ter (hēr af′tər), 1. after this; after now. 2. **The hereafter** means the life or time after death. *adv., n. 4.*

here by (hēr bī′), by this; by this means. The license said, "You are hereby given the right to hunt and fish in Dover County." *adv. 7.*

he red i tar y (hi red′i tãr′i), 1. coming by inheritance. *Prince* is a hereditary title. 2. holding a position by inheritance. The king of England is a hereditary ruler. 3. caused by heredity. Color blindness is hereditary. 4. coming from one's parents; as, a hereditary belief. 5. having to do with inheritance or heredity. *adj. 8.*

he red i ty (hi red′i ti), 1. the fact that one generation of plants and animals produces the next. 2. the qualities of body and mind that have come to a child from its parents. 3. the tendency of children to be like their parents. *n. 10.*

here in (hēr in′), in this. *adv. 6.*

here of (hēr ov′), of this; about this. We will speak further hereof. *adv. 16.*

here on (hēr on′), 1. on this. 2. immediately after this. *adv.*

here's (hērz), here is. *10.*

her e sy (her′ə si), 1. a belief different from the accepted belief of a church, school, or profession. 2. the holding of such a belief. *n., pl. heresies. 8.*

her e tic (her′ə tik), person who holds a belief that is different from the accepted belief of his church, school, or profession. *n. 8.*

he ret i cal (hi ret′i kəl), 1. of heresy. 2. containing heresy; characterized by heresy. *adj. 18.*

here to fore (hēr′tů fōr′), before this time; until now. *adv. 6.*

here un to (hēr′un tü′), to this. *adv. 20.*

here up on (hēr′ə pon′), 1. upon this. 2. immediately after this. *adv. 18.*

here with (hēr wiTH′), with this. I am sending ten cents in stamps herewith. *adv. 7.*

her it a ble (her′i tə bəl), 1. capable of being inherited. 2. capable of inheriting. *adj.*

her it age (her′i tij), what is or may be handed on to a person from his ancestors; inheritance. *n. 7.*

Her mes (hėr′mēz), the messenger of the gods. Hermes was the Greek god of boundaries and roads, of commerce, invention, eloquence, luck, and cunning, and the patron of thieves. The Romans called him Mercury. *n. 15.*

her met i cal (hėr met′i kəl), closed tightly so that air cannot get in. *adj. 17.*

her mit (hėr′mit), person who goes away from other people and lives by himself. A hermit often lives a religious life. *n. 5.*

her mit age (hėr′mi tij), the home of a hermit. *n. 13.*

he ro (hēr′ō), 1. very brave boy or man. 2. the most important male person in a story or play. *n., pl. heroes. 2.*

Her od (her′əd), the king of the Jews at the time Jesus Christ was born. *n. 9.*

He rod o tus (hi rod′ə təs), a famous Greek historian (484?-425? B.C.). *n.*

he ro ic (hi rō′ik), 1. like a hero; very brave; noble. 2. of or about heroes. 3. bold; daring. The doctor used a heroic treatment. *adj. 4.*

he ro i cal (hi rō′i kəl), heroic. *adj. 14.*

he ro ics (hi rō′iks), language that sounds too grand and noble. *n. pl.*

her o in (her′ō in), a powerful drug made from morphine. *n. 20.*

her o ine (her′ō in), 1. very brave girl or woman. 2. the most important female person in a story or play. *n. 7.*

her o ism (her′ō izm), 1. great courage. 2. doing something noble at great cost to oneself. *n. 9.*

her on (her′ən), a wading bird with long legs, a long neck, and a long bill. *n. 11.*

Great blue heron (about 5 ft. tall)

Herr (her), a German word meaning (1) Mr.; Sir. (2) a gentleman. *n., pl. Herren* (her′ən). *14.*

her ring (her′ing), a food fish of the northern Atlantic Ocean. *n., pl. herrings* or *herring. 8.*

Herring (about 7 in. long)

hers (hėrz), 1. of her; belonging to her. This money is hers. 2. the one or ones belonging to her. Your problems are wrong; hers are right. *pron. 5.*

her self (hėr self′), 1. Herself is used to make a statement stronger. Mary herself brought the book. 2. Herself is used instead of she or her in cases like: She hurt herself. Mary did it by herself. 3. her self. The cat saw herself in the glass. 4. her real or true self. In those fits she is not herself. *pron. 1.*

he's (hēz), he is. *6.*

hes i tan cy (hez′i tən si), tendency to hesitate. *n.*

hes i tant (hez′i tənt), hesitating; undecided. *adj.*

hes i tate (hez′i tāt), 1. hold back; feel doubtful; be undecided; show that one has not yet made up one's mind. 2. to stop an instant; pause. 3. speak in a hesitating way. 4. feel that perhaps one shouldn't; not wish to. She hesitated to hurt the child's feelings. *v. 5.*

hes i ta tion (hez′i tā′shən), 1. act of hesitating; doubt. 2. a slight stopping; as, a hesitation in one's speech. *n. 9.*

Hes per i des (hes per′i dēz), the four nymphs who guarded the golden apples of Hera. *n. pl. 15.*

Hes per us (hes′pər əs), the evening star. *n. 17.*

Hes sian (hesh′ən), German soldier hired by England to fight against the Americans during the Revolutionary War. *n. 19.*

het er o dox (het′ər ə doks), the opposite of orthodox; rejecting the regularly accepted beliefs or doctrines. *adj. 20.*

het er o dox y (het′ər ə dok′si), 1. the opposite of orthodoxy; turning away from regularly accepted beliefs or doctrines. 2. a belief or doctrine not in agreement with what is regularly accepted. *n., pl. heterodoxies. 19.*

het er o ge ne ous (het′ər ə jē′ni əs), not alike; varied; miscellaneous; of different kinds. *adj. 10.*

hew (hū), cut; chop. They hewed the logs

into beams. *v., hewed, hewed* or *hewn, hewing. 4.*

hew er (hū′ər), person or thing that hews. *n. 16.*

hewn (hūn), hewed. *pp. of* **hew.** *17.*

hex a gon (hek′sə gon), a figure having six angles and six sides. *n. 11.*

Hexagons

hex ag o nal (heks ag′ə nəl), having the form of a hexagon. *adj.*

hex am e ter (heks am′i tər), 1. consisting of six feet or measures. 2. poetry having six feet or measures in each line. Example: "This′ is the | for′est pri | me′val. The | mur′muring | pine′ and the | hem′locks." *adj., n. 15.*

hey (hā), a sound made to attract attention, express surprise or other feeling, or ask a question. Hey! stop! Hey! here's Charles. Hey? what did you say? *interj. 11.*

hey day (hā′dā′), period of greatest strength, vigor, spirits, prosperity, etc. *n. 15.*

Hez e ki ah (hez′i kī′ə), a king of Judah. *n. 13.*

hi a tus (hī ā′təs), gap; empty space; space that needs to be filled. *n., pl. hiatuses. 20.*

Hi a wath a (hī′ə woth′ə), the young Indian brave who is the hero of Longfellow's poem *Hiawatha. n. 6.*

hi ber nate (hī′bər nāt), 1. spend the winter in sleep, as bears and some other wild animals do. 2. spend the winter. *v. 13.*

hic cup or **hic cough** (hik′up), 1. an involuntary catching of the breath. 2. do this; have the hiccups. *n., v.*

hick o ry (hik′ə ri), 1. a tree whose nuts are good to eat. 2. its tough, hard wood. *n., pl. hickories. 10.*

BRANCH
NUT
Hickory

hid (hid). See **hide**[1]. The dog hid his bone. The money was hid in a safe place. *pt. and pp. of hide*[1]. *2.*

hi dal go (hi dal′gō), a Spanish nobleman of the second class, not so high in rank as a grandee. *n., pl. hidalgos. 19.*

hid den (hid′ən), 1. put or kept out of sight; secret; not clear. The story is about hidden treasure. 2. See **hide**[1]. The moon was hidden behind a dark cloud. *adj., pp. of hide*[1]. *4.*

hide[1] (hīd), 1. put out of sight; keep out of sight. Hide it where no one else will know of it or know where it is. 2. shut off from sight; be in front of. Clouds hide the sun. 3. keep secret. 4. hide oneself. I'll hide, and you find me. *v., hid, hidden* or *hid, hiding. 1.*

hide[2] (hīd), 1. an animal's skin, raw or tanned. 2. one's own skin. He tried to save his own hide. I'll tan your hide if you touch that. 3. beat; thrash. *Used in common talk. n., v., hided, hiding.*

hide bound (hīd′bound′), 1. with the skin sticking close to the bones. 2. narrow-minded and stubborn. He was too hidebound to accept new ideas even when they were good. *adj.*

hid e ous (hid′i əs), ugly; frightful; horrible. *adj. 6.*

hid e ous ness (hid′i əs nis), hideous nature or quality. *n. 17.*

hie (hī), go quickly. *v., hied, hieing* or *hying. 10.*

hi er ar chy (hī′ər är′ki), 1. government by priests. 2. group of church officials of different ranks. The church hierarchy is composed of archbishops, bishops, priests, etc. 3. organization of persons or things that has higher and lower ranks. *n., pl. hierarchies. 15.*

hi er o glyph ic (hī′ər ə glif′ik), 1. a picture of an object standing for a word, idea, or sound; a character or symbol standing for a word, idea, or sound. The ancient Egyptians used hieroglyphics instead of an alphabet like ours. 2. writing that uses hieroglyphics. 3. a secret symbol. 4. writing that is hard to read. *n. 12.*

Hieroglyphics for "weeping" and "forest"

Egyptian hieroglyphics

hig gle dy-pig gle dy (hig′əl di pig′əl di), 1. in jumbled confusion. 2. confused; jumbled. *adv., adj.*

high (hī), 1. up above the ground; as, a high jump. 2. up above others. A general has high rank. Washington was a man of high character. 3. great; greater or stronger than others; as, a high price, a high wind. 4. chief; main; as, the high altar. 5. at or to a high point, place, rank, amount, degree, price, etc. The eagle flies high. Strawberries come high in winter. Gamblers play high. 6. shrill; sharp. 7. Some special meanings are:

high and dry, 1. up out of water. 2. all alone; without help.

high seas, the open ocean. The high seas are outside the authority of any country.
high spirits, cheerfulness; gaiety.
high tide, the time when the ocean comes up highest on the shore.
high time, the time just before it is too late.
high words, angry words.
adj., adv. 1.

high born (hī′bôrn′), of noble birth. *adj. 19.*

high brow (hī′brou′), person who claims to care a great deal for knowledge and culture; person who cares for learning. *n.* [*Slang*]

high-flown (hī′flōn′), 1. aspiring; extravagant. 2. attempting to be elegant or eloquent; as, high-flown compliments. *adj.*

high-grade (hī′grād′), of fine quality; superior. *adj.*

high-hand ed (hī′han′did), acting or done in a bold, arbitrary way; arbitrary; overbearing. *adj.*

high land (hī′lənd), 1. country that is mostly hills and mountains; land high above sea level. 2. The **Highlands** of Scotland are in the northern and western part of Great Britain. *n. 4.*

High land er (hī′lən dər), 1. inhabitant of the hills of Scotland. 2. soldier of a regiment from the Highlands of Scotland. *n. 15.*

high ly (hī′li), 1. in a high degree; very; very much; as, highly amusing, highly recommended. 2. very favorably; as, to speak highly of your best friend. 3. at a high price; as, highly paid. *adv.*

high-mind ed (hī′mīn′did), 1. having or showing high principles and feelings. 2. proud. *adj.*

high ness (hī′nis), being high; height. *n. 6.*

High ness (hī′nis), title of honor given to members of royal families. The Prince of Wales is addressed as "Your Highness" and spoken of as "His Royal Highness." *n.*

high road (hī′rōd′), 1. main road. 2. direct and easy way. *n. 16.*

high school, a school attended after the elementary school. *18.*

high-spir it ed (hī′spir′i tid), 1. proud. 2. courageous. 3. spirited; fiery. *adj. 17.*

high-strung (hī′strung′), very sensitive; very nervous. *adj.*

hight (hīt), named; called. The knight was hight Gawain. *adj.* [*Old use*] *17.*

high way (hī′wā′), 1. public road. 2. a main road or route. *n. 4.*

high way man (hī′wā′mən), man who robs travelers on the public road. *n., pl. highwaymen. 16.*

hike (hīk), 1. take a long walk; march. 2. a tramp or march. *v., n.* [*Not used in formal writing*] *17.*

hi lar i ous (hi lãr′i əs), very merry; noisily gay. *adj.*

hi lar i ty (hi lar′i ti), great mirth; noisy gaiety. *n. 17.*

hill (hil), 1. a raised part of the earth's surface, not so big as a mountain. 2. a heap of any kind; as, an ant hill. 3. plant with a little heap of soil over and around its roots; as, a hill of corn. *n. 1.*

hill ock (hil′ək), little hill. *n. 10.*

hill side (hil′sīd′), side of a hill. *n. 4.*

hill top (hil′top′), the top of a hill. *n. 11.*

hill y (hil′i), 1. having many hills; as, hilly country. 2. like a hill; steep; as, a hilly slope. *adj., hillier, hilliest. 11.*

hilt (hilt), handle of a sword or dagger. *n. 10.*

HILT
Hilt of a sword

him (him). Don't hit him hard. Give him a drink. Go to him. He and him mean the boy or man or male animal spoken about. *pron. 1.*

Hi ma la yas (hi mä′lə yəz), mountain range extending for 1600 miles along the northern border of India. *n. pl.*

him self (him self′), 1. Himself is used to make a statement stronger. Did you see John himself? 2. Himself is used instead of he or him in cases like: He cut himself. John asked himself what he really wanted. He kept the toy for himself. 3. He cared more for himself than for anything else. 4. his real self. He feels like himself again. *pron. 1.*

hind[1] (hīnd), back; rear. *adj. 3.*

hind[2] (hīnd), a female deer, especially of the red deer after its third year. *n., pl. hinds* or *hind.*

hind[3] (hīnd), farm worker. *n.*

Hin den burg (hin′dən bėrg), Paul von (1847-1934), German general, president of Germany from 1925 to 1934. *n.*

hin der[1] (hin′dər), hold back; be in the way of; stop; make hard to do. Deep mud hindered travel. *v. 4.*

hind er[2] (hīn′dər), hind; back; rear. *adj.*

hind er most (hīn′dər mōst), hindmost. *adj.*

hind most (hīnd′mōst), farthest behind; nearest the rear; last. *adj. 12.*

hin drance (hin′drəns), 1. person or thing that hinders; obstacle. Noise is a hindrance to studying. 2. a hindering. *n. 9.*

Hin du or **Hin doo** (hin′dü), 1. member of a native race of India. 2. having to do with this race, its language, or its religion. *n., pl. Hindus, Hindoos, adj. 13.*

Hin du stan (hin′dů stän′), India. *n. 18.*

hinge (hinj), 1. a joint on which a door, gate, cover, lid, etc., moves back and forth. See the picture. 2. furnish with hinges; attach by hinges. 3. hang or turn on a hinge. 4. depend. The success of the picnic hinges on the kind of weather we will have. *n., v. 5.*

Hinge on a door

hint (hint), 1. slight sign; indirect suggestion. A small black cloud gave a hint of a coming storm. 2. suggest slightly; show in an indirect way. Nell hinted that she wanted to go to bed by saying, "Do you often stay up this late?" *n., v. 4.*

hin ter land (hin′tər land′), land or district behind a coast; back country. *n.*

hip (hip), 1. the part that sticks out on each side of the body below a person's waist. 2. a similar part in animals, where the hind leg joins the body. *n. 4.*

hip po drome (hip′ə drōm), 1. in ancient Greece and Rome, an oval track for horse races and chariot races, surrounded by tiers of seats for spectators. 2. an arena or building for a circus, etc. *n. 17.*

hip po pot a mus (hip′ə pot′ə məs), a huge animal found near the rivers of Africa. It lives on plants and can stay under water for a considerable time. *n., pl. hippopotamuses, hippopotami* (-mī). *12.*

Hippopotamus (about 13 ft. long)

hire (hīr), 1. pay for the use of. He hired a car and a man to drive it. 2. employ. The storekeeper hired ten girls for the Christmas rush. 3. wages. Some men fight for glory; some fight for hire. *v., n. 2.*

hire ling (hīr′ling), person who works for money. Men who care only for their pay, and not about doing their work well are hirelings. *n. 10.*

his (hiz), 1. of him; belonging to him. His name is Bill. 2. the one or ones belonging to him. My books are new; his are old. *pron., adj. 1.*

His pan io la (his′pən yō′lə), the second largest island in the West Indies. *n.*

hiss (his), 1. make a sound like *ss*, or like a drop of water on a hot stove. Geese and snakes hiss. 2. a sound like *ss*. Hisses were heard from many who disliked what the speaker was saying. *v., n. 4.*

hist (hist), be still! listen! The guide said, "Hist! You can hear the deer coming." *interj. 14.*

his to ri an (his tō′ri ən), person who writes about history. *n. 7.*

his tor ic (his tor′ik), 1. famous in history. Plymouth Rock and Bunker Hill are historic spots. 2. historical. *adj. 5.*

his tor i cal (his tor′i kəl), 1. of history; having to do with history. 2. according to history; based on history. 3. known to be real or true; in history, not in legend. *adj. 7.*

his tor i cal ly (his tor′i kəl i), according to history; as history. *adv.*

his to ry (his′tə ri), 1. a statement of what has happened. 2. the story of a man or a nation. 3. a known past. This knife has a history. *n., pl. histories. 2.*

hit (hit), 1. When boys fight, they hit each other. He hit the ball with a bat. He hit his head against the shelf. The man hit out at the thieves who attacked him. 2. come upon; meet with; find. We hit the right road in the dark. The boys hit upon a plan for making money. 3. have a painful effect on; affect severely. The stockbroker was hard hit by the fall in stocks. 4. a blow; a stroke. 5. stroke of sarcasm, blame, etc. 6. successful attempt or performance. The new play is the hit of the season. 7. stroke of luck. 8. **Hit it off** means agree; get on well with. 9. **Hit off** means imitate; represent. *v., hit, hitting, n. 2.*

hitch (hich), 1. move or pull with a jerk. He hitched his chair nearer to the fire. 2. short, sudden pull or jerk. The sailor gave his trousers a hitch. 3. fasten with a hook, ring, rope, strap, etc. He hitched his horse to a post. 4. fasten; catch; become fastened or caught. A knot made the rope hitch. 5. obstacle; stopping. A hitch in their plans made them miss the train. 6. kind of knot used for temporary fastening. *v., n. 8.*

hith er (hiᴛʜ′ər), 1. here; to this place. 2. on this side; nearer. 3. **Hither and thither** means here and there. *adv. 3.*

hith er to (hiᴛʜ′ər tü′), up to this time; until now. *adv. 5.*

hith er ward (hiᴛʜ′ər wərd) toward this place; hither. *adv.*

Hit ler (hit′lər), Adolf (born 1889), German dictator, born in Austria, chancellor of Germany since 1934. He is called "Der Führer," which means "The Leader." *n.*

hit ter (hit′ər), one that hits. *n.*

Hit tite (hit′īt), member of an ancient people in Asia Minor and Syria. Their civilization existed from about 2000 B.C. until about 1200 B.C. *n. 17.*

Beehives

hive (hīv), 1. a house for bees to live in. 2. a large number of bees living together. The whole hive was busy. 3. put (bees) in a hive. 4. enter a hive. 5. live close together as bees do. 6. a busy place full of people or animals. *n., v. 4.*

hives (hīvz), a disease in which the skin itches and shows patches of red. *n.*

ho (hō), 1. an exclamation of surprise, joy, or scornful laughter. 2. an exclamation to get attention. *interj. 4.*

hoar (hōr), hoary. *adj. 7.*

hoard (hōrd), 1. save and store up. The squirrel hoards nuts for the winter. A miser hoards money. 2. things stored. The squirrel keeps his hoard in a tree. *v., n. 6.*

hoar frost (hōr′frôst′), white frost. *n. 16.*

hoar hound (hōr′hound′), horehound, a plant used to make candy for coughs. *n.*

hoarse (hōrs), 1. sounding rough and deep; as, the hoarse sound of the bullfrog. 2. having a rough voice. A bad cold often makes a person hoarse. *adj. 7.*

hoar y (hōr′i), 1. white or gray. 2. white or gray with age; as, hoary hair. 3. old; as, hoary ruins. *adj., hoarier, hoariest. 6.*

hoax (hōks), trick. The rich old man was deceived by the hoax of his new-found friends. *n., v. 18.*

hob[1] (hob), 1. a shelf at the back or side of a fireplace. 2. a peg used as a target. *n.*

hob[2] (hob), hobgoblin; elf. **Play hob** or **raise hob** means cause trouble. *n.*

hob ble (hob′əl), 1. walk awkwardly; limp. The wounded man hobbled away. 2. a limping walk. 3. tie the legs of (a horse, etc.) together. 4. a rope or strap used to hobble an animal. 5. hinder. *v., n. 12.*

hob by (hob′i), something a person especially likes to work at or to study which is not his main business. Growing roses is her hobby. *n., pl. hobbies. 7.*

hob by horse (hob′i hôrs′), 1. stick with a horse's head used as a child's plaything. 2. rocking horse. *n.*

hob gob lin (hob′gob′lin), 1. goblin; elf. 2. ghost; bogy. *n. 12.*

hob nail (hob′nāl′), short nail with a large head to protect the soles of heavy shoes. *n. 18.*

Hobnails

hob nob (hob′nob′), 1. talk together. 2. drink together. *v., hobnobbed, hobnobbing.*

ho bo (hō′bō), tramp. *n., pl. hobos* or *hoboes.*

HOCK

hock (hok), a joint on the hind leg of an animal. See the picture. *n. 14.*

hock ey (hok′i), game played by two teams on ice or on a field. The players hit a rubber disk or ball with curved sticks to drive it across a goal. *n. 14.*

ho cus-po cus (hō′kəs pō′kəs), 1. a form of words used in conjuring. 2. trickery; deception. *n. 20.*

hod (hod), 1. a trough at the top of a long straight handle, used by builders for carrying bricks, mortar, etc., on the shoulder. 2. a pail for carrying coal. *n. 11.*

Hod for mortar

hodge podge (hoj′poj′), disorderly mixture; mess; jumble. *n.*

hoe (hō), 1. a tool with a small blade at the end of a long handle, used for loosening soil, cutting small weeds, etc. 2. loosen, dig, or cut with a hoe. 3. use a hoe. *n., pl. hoes, v., hoed, hoeing. 4.*

hoe cake (hō′kāk′), kind of bread made of corn meal. *n.*

hog (hog), 1. pig. See the picture below. 2. full-grown pig. 3. a selfish, greedy, or dirty person. *Used in common talk. n. 3.*

Hoe

hog gish (hog′ish), 1. like a hog; greedy; very selfish. 2. dirty; filthy. *adj.*

hogs head (hogz′hed), 1. a large barrel containing from 100 to 140 gallons. 2. a liquid measure equal to 63 gallons. *n. 14.*

Hog

Hoh en zol lern (hō′ən zol′ərn), the royal family of Prussia, the family of German emperors from 1871 to 1918. *n. 17.*

hoist (hoist), 1. raise on high; lift up, often with ropes and pulleys; as, to hoist a flag, to hoist sails, to hoist blocks of stone in building. 2. a hoisting; a lift. He gave me a hoist up the wall. 3. elevator. *v., n. 7.*

hold[1] (hōld), 1. grasp and keep. Please hold my hat. Hold my watch while I play this game. 2. a grasp or grip. Take a good hold of this rope. 3. thing to hold by. 4. keep in some place or position. Hold the dish level. He will hold the paper steady while you draw. 5. keep. Hold the fort. 6. place to be kept; fort; stronghold. *Old use.* 7. contain. This cup will hold water. How much will it hold? This theater will hold a thousand people. 8. have. Shall we hold a meeting of the club? He holds much property in the city. That man holds two offices in our town. He holds a high opinion of you. 9. be true. Will this rule hold in all cases? 10. be faithful. He held to his promise. 11. consider; think. People once held that the world was flat. 12. keep the same; continue. Will the weather hold warm? 13. keep from acting; keep back; as, to hold one's tongue, to hold one's breath. 14. Some special meanings are:

hold forth, 1. talk; preach. 2. offer.

hold in, 1. keep in; keep back. 2. restrain oneself.

hold off, keep at a distance.

hold on, 1. keep one's hold. 2. keep on; continue. 3. stop! *Used in common talk.*

hold out, 1. continue; last. 2. keep resisting; not give in.

hold over, 1. postpone. 2. stay in office beyond the regular term.

hold up, 1. keep from falling. 2. show; display. 3. continue; last; endure. 4. stop. 5. stop by force and rob. *Used in common talk.*

hold with, 1. side with. 2. agree with. 3. approve of.

lay hold of, 1. seize; grasp. 2. get control of.

v., held, holding, n. 1.

hold[2] (hōld), the lowest part of a ship's interior. A ship's cargo is carried in its hold. *n.*

hold back (hōld′bak′), thing that holds back; restraint; hindrance. *n.*

hold er (hōl′dər), 1. person who holds something. An owner or possessor of property is a holder. 2. thing to hold something else with. Pads of cloth are used as holders for lifting hot dishes. *n. 4.*

hold ing (hōl′ding), 1. land; piece of land. 2. property in stocks or bonds. Mr. Adams has large holdings in a new company. *n. 19.*

hole (hōl), 1. open place; as, a hole in a stocking. 2. a hollow place in something solid. Swiss cheese has holes in it. 3. place which is lower than the parts around it; as, a hole in the road. 4. a small, dark, mean place. 5. make holes in. 6. put in a hole. *n., v. 1.*

holi day (hol′i dā), 1. a day when one does not work; a day of enjoyment. Christmas is a holiday for everyone. 2. vacation. *n. 2.*

ho li ness (hō′li nis), 1. being holy or sacred. 2. **His Holiness** is a title of the Pope. *n. 6.*

Hol land (hol′ənd), the Netherlands, a small country in Europe, west of Germany and north of Belgium. *n. 4.*

Hol land er (hol′ən dər), a native or inhabitant of Holland. *n. 18.*

hol lo (hə lō′), hello. *interj., n., pl. hollos, v., holloed, holloing.*

hol loa (hə lō′), hello. *interj., n., pl. holloas, v., holloaed, holloaing.*

hol low (hol′ō), 1. having nothing, or only air, inside; empty; with a hole inside; not solid. A tube or pipe is hollow. Most rubber balls are hollow. 2. bowl-shaped; cup-shaped; as, a hollow dish for vegetables. 3. a hollow place; a hole; as, a hollow in the road. 4. bend or dig out to a hollow shape. He hollowed a whistle out of the piece of wood. 5. a valley; as, Sleepy Hollow. 6. dull; as if coming from something hollow; as, a hollow voice or groan, the hollow boom of a foghorn. 7. not real or sincere; false; as, hollow promises, hollow joys. 8. hungry. *adj., n., v. 2.*

hol low ness (hol′ō nis), being hollow. *n.*

hol ly (hol′i), an evergreen shrub with shiny, sharp-pointed leaves and bright red berries, used especially as Christmas decorations. *n., pl. hollies. 6.*

Holly

hol ly hock (hol′i hok), a tall plant with clusters of large, showy flowers of various colors. *n. 16.*

Hol ly wood (hol′i wu̇d′), section of Los Angeles where many moving pictures are made. *n.*

holm (hōm), an evergreen oak with leaves like those of the holly. *n. 20.*

Holmes (hōmz), Oliver Wendell, a famous American author and humorist (1809-1894). *n. 14.*

hol o caust (hol′ə kôst), 1. complete destruction by fire, especially of animals or human beings. 2. great or wholesale destruction. *n. 20.*

Hol stein (hōl′stīn), one of a breed of black-and-white dairy cattle. *n. 9.*

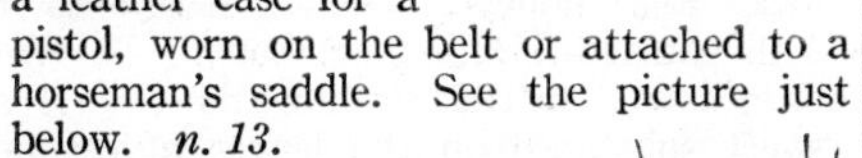

Holstein cow (about 4¼ ft. high at the shoulder)

hol ster (hōl′stər), a leather case for a pistol, worn on the belt or attached to a horseman's saddle. See the picture just below. *n. 13.*

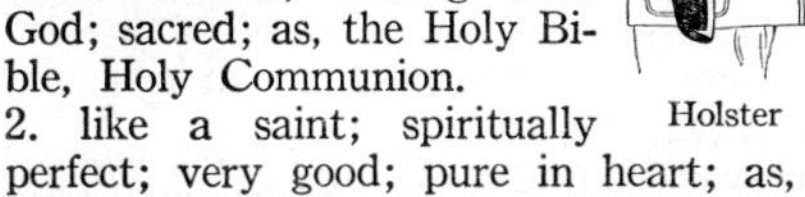

Holster

ho ly (hō′li), 1. given or belonging to God; set apart for God's service; coming from God; sacred; as, the Holy Bible, Holy Communion. 2. like a saint; spiritually perfect; very good; pure in heart; as, a holy man. 3. worthy of reverence. The grave of the unknown soldier is a holy place. 4. The **holy of holies** means the most sacred place. *adj., holier, holiest, n., pl. holies. 2.*

Holy Communion, 1. sharing in the Lord's Supper as a part of the church worship. 2. the celebration of the Lord's Supper.

holy day, religious festival. Christmas and Easter are holy days.

Holy Ghost, the spirit of God.

Holy Grail, cup or dish supposed to have been used by Christ at the Last Supper, and by one of his followers to catch the last drops of Christ's blood at the cross.

Holy Land, Palestine.

Holy Roman Empire, the empire in western and central Europe from 962 to 1806.

Holy See, the office or jurisdiction of the Pope; the Pope's court.

ho ly stone (hō′li stōn′), 1. piece of soft sandstone used for scrubbing the decks of ships. 2. scrub with a holystone. *n., v.*

Holy Week, the week before Easter.

Holy Writ, the Bible.

hom age (hom′ij), 1. respect; reverence; honor. 2. formal acknowledgment by a vassal that he owed faith and service to his lord. *n. 6.*

home (hōm), 1. the place where one lives. Her home is at 25 South Street. 2. the town or country where one was born. His home is New York. 3. place where one can rest and be safe. 4. place where people who are homeless, poor, old, sick, blind, etc., may live. 5. place where a thing is specially common. Alaska is the home of the fur seal. 6. having to do with one's home or country. Write me all the home events. 7. at or to one's home or country. I want to go home. 8. the goal in many games. 9. to its goal; to the place where it belongs. The spear struck home to the tiger's heart. 10. to the heart or center; deep in. 11. go home. 12. have a home. *n., adj., adv., v. 1.*

home land (hōm′land′), country that is one's home; native land. *n.*

home less (hōm′lis), without a home. *adj. 12.*

home like (hōm′līk′), like home; friendly; familiar; comfortable. *adj. 18.*

home li ness (hōm′li nis), 1. familiarity; comfort. 2. plain looks; being homely. *n.*

home ly (hōm′li), 1. suited to home life; simple; everyday; as, homely pleasures, homely food. 2. of plain manners; unpretending; as, a simple, homely man. 3. ugly; plain; not good-looking. *adj., homelier, homeliest. 5.*

home made (hōm′mād′), made at home. *adj. 18.*

Ho mer (hō′mər), great epic poet of ancient Greece. According to legend, Homer lived about the ninth century B.C. and was the author of the *Iliad* and the *Odyssey. n. 6.*

Ho mer ic (hō mer′ik), 1. by Homer. The *Iliad* and the *Odyssey* are the Homeric poems. 2. of Homer. 3. in the style of Homer. Homeric laughter is loud, hearty laughter, such as Homer describes. *adj. 18.*

home sick (hōm′sik′), overcome by sadness because home is far away; ill with longing for home. *adj. 7.*

home sick ness (hōm′sik′nis), longing for home. *n. 19.*

home spun (hōm′spun′), 1. spun or made at home. 2. cloth made of homespun yarn. 3. cloth of similar appearance, loose in texture, but strong. 4. plain; simple; not polished; as, homespun manners. *adj., n. 10.*

home stead (hōm′sted), 1. a house with its buildings and grounds; a farm with its buildings. 2. land granted to a settler under certain conditions by the United States government. *n. 7.*

home ward (hōm′wərd), toward home. We turned homeward. The ship is on her homeward course. *adv., adj. 5.*

home wards (hōm′wərdz), homeward. *adv.*

home work (hōm′wėrk′), 1. work done at home. 2. lesson to be studied or prepared outside the classroom. *n.*

home y or **hom y** (hōm′i), homelike. *adj.* [*Not used in formal writing*]

hom i cide (hom′i sīd), 1. the killing of one human being by another. Intentional homicide is murder. 2. person who kills a human being. *n. 14.*

hom i ly (hom′i li), 1. sermon, usually on some part of the Bible. 2. serious moral talk or writing. *n., pl. homilies. 14.*

hom ing pi geon (hōm′ing pij′ən), pigeon trained to fly home from great distances carrying written messages.

Homing pigeon

hom i ny (hom′i ni), corn hulled and crushed or coarsely ground. Hominy is eaten boiled. *n. 14.*

ho mo (hō′mō), a Latin word meaning man. *n. 20.*

ho mo ge ne ous (hō′mō jē′ni əs), 1. of the same kind; similar. 2. composed of similar parts. *adj. 14.*

hom o nym (hom′ə nim), a word having the same pronunciation as another word but a different meaning. *Meat* and *meet* are homonyms. *n.*

Hon., Honorable (used as a title). *18.*

Hon du ras (hon dür′əs), a country in Central America. Honduras is independent. **British Honduras** is a British colony. *n. 19.*

hone (hōn), 1. stone on which to sharpen tools, especially razors. 2. sharpen on a hone. *n., v. 13.*

hon est (on′ist), 1. fair and upright; truthful; not lying, cheating, or stealing. Job was an honest man. 2. without lying, cheating, or stealing. He lived an honest life. 3. frank; open; not hiding one's real nature. 4. genuine; pure; not mixed with something of less value. Stores should sell honest goods. *adj. 2.*

hon es ty (on′is ti), honest behavior; honest nature; honest quality. *n. 7.*

hon ey (hun′i), 1. a thick, sweet, yellow liquid, good to eat, that bees make out of the drops they collect from flowers. 2. the drop of sweet liquid found in many flowers, that draws bees to them. 3. sweetness. 4. darling. *n., pl. honeys. 2.*

hon ey bee (hun′i bē′), a bee that makes honey. See the picture below. *n. 18.*

hon ey comb (hun′i kōm′), 1. a structure of wax containing rows of six-sided cells formed by bees to hold honey and their eggs. 2. thing like this. 3. like a honeycomb; as, a honeycomb weave of cloth, a honeycomb pattern in knitting. 4. make like a honeycomb. 5. pierce with many holes. The rock was honeycombed with passages. *n., adj., v. 6.*

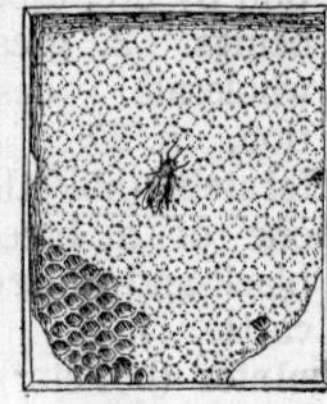
Honeycomb

hon ey dew (hun′i dū′ or hun′i dü′), 1. a sweet substance on the leaves of certain plants in hot weather. 2. a sweet substance on leaves and stems, secreted by tiny insects called aphids. 3. a kind of melon. *n. 19.*

Honeybee (about life size)

hon eyed (hun′id), 1. sweetened with honey; as, honeyed drinks. 2. laden with honey. 3. sweet as honey; as, honeyed words. *adj.*

hon ey moon (hun′i mün′), 1. the holiday spent together by a newly married couple. 2. spend or have a honeymoon. *n., v. 12.*

hon ey suck le (hun′i suk′əl), a climbing shrub with fragrant flowers. *n. 8.*

Trumpet honeysuckle

Hong Kong or **Hong kong** (hong′ kong′), a seaport city in southeastern China. *18.*

honk (hongk), 1. the cry of a wild goose. 2. any similar sound; as, the honk of an auto horn. 3. make such a sound. *n., v.*

Hon o lu lu (hon′ə lü′lü), the capital of the Hawaiian Islands. *n. 19.*

hon or (on′ər), 1. glory; fame; renown. 2. good name; credit for acting well. It was greatly to his honor that he refused the reward. 3. **Honors** at school consist in special mention for having done work much above the average. 4. a source of credit; person or thing that reflects honor; as, to be an honor to one's family or one's school. 5. nobleness of mind; a nice sense of what is right or proper. 6. great respect; high regard. George Washington is held in honor. 7. an act that shows respect or high regard; as, funeral honors, military honors. The **honors of war** means favors shown to brave foes, such as keeping their flag flying. 8. respect highly; think highly of. 9. show respect to. 10. be an honor to. 11. accept (a check, note, etc.) as good and pay it. *n., v. 1.*

Hon or (on′ər), title used in speaking to or of a judge, mayor, etc. *n.*

hon or a ble (on′ər ə bəl), 1. honest; upright; in keeping with honor. It is not honorable to steal. 2. bringing honor to the one who has it; as, honorable wounds. 3. noble; worthy of honor; as, an honorable name, to perform honorable deeds. 4. having a title, rank, or position of honor. *adj. 3.*

Hon or a ble (on′ər ə bəl), title of respect before the names of certain officials and others. *adj.*

hon or ar y (on′ər ãr′i), 1. given or done as an honor. 2. as an honor only, without pay or regular duties. Some associations have honorary secretaries as well as regular paid secretaries. *adj. 13.*

hood (hu̇d), 1. a soft covering for the head and neck, either separate or as part of a cloak. My raincoat has a hood. 2. anything like a hood in shape or use. 3. the metal covering over the engine of an automobile. 4. to cover with a hood. 5. a fold of cloth, banded with distinguishing colors to show what degrees are held, that hangs down over the black gown worn by graduates of universities and colleges. *n., v. 3.*

-hood, suffix meaning:—
1. state or condition of being; as in boyhood, likelihood.
2. character or nature of; as in manhood, sainthood.
3. group; body of; as in priesthood, a sisterhood of noble women.

hood ed (hu̇d′id), 1. having a hood. 2. shaped like a hood. *adj.*

hood lum (hüd′ləm), rowdy; street ruffian. *n.* [*Used in common talk*]

hoo doo (hü′dü), 1. Negro magic; voodoo. 2. person or thing that brings bad luck. 3. bad luck. 4. bring or cause bad luck to. *n., pl. hoodoos, v., hoodooed, hoodooing* [2, 3, *and* 4 *are used in common talk*].

hood wink (hu̇d′wingk), 1. mislead by a trick; deceive. 2. blindfold. *v. 18.*

hoof (hüf), 1. the hard, horny covering of the foot of a horse, cow, sheep, pig, and some other animals. 2. the whole foot of such animals. 3. The human foot is sometimes called a hoof in fun. *n., pl. hoofs. 3.*

hoofed (hüft), having hoofs. *adj.*

hook (hu̇k), 1. piece of metal, wood, or other stiff material, curved or having a sharp angle, for catching hold of something or for hanging things on. 2. catch hold of with a hook. 3. fasten with hooks. Will you hook my dress for me? 4. bent piece of wire, usually with a backward bend at the end, for catching fish. 5. catch (fish) with a hook. 6. A reaping hook is a large curved knife for cutting down grass or grain. 7. a sharp bend; as, a hook in a river. 8. a point of land. 9. **By hook or by crook** means by fair means or foul. 10. **On one's own hook** means independently; without being told. *Used in common talk. n., v. 2.*

Coat-hook

hooked (hu̇kt), 1. curved or bent like a hook. 2. having hooks. 3. made with a hook. A **hooked rug** is made by drawing yarn or strips of cloth through a foundation of canvas, burlap, etc. *adj.*

hook up (hu̇k′up′), arrangement and connection of the parts of a radio set, telephone, etc. *n.*

hook worm (hu̇k′wėrm′), 1. a worm that gets into the intestines and causes a disease with weakness and apparent laziness. 2. this disease. *n. 13.*

hoop (hüp), 1. a ring or a flat band in the form of a circle; as, a hoop for holding together the staves of a barrel. 2. fasten together with hoops. 3. a large wooden or iron circle to be rolled along the ground by a child. 4. a circular frame formerly used to hold out a woman's skirt. See the picture. 5. an iron arch used in the game of croquet. *n., v. 5.*

Hoop skirt

hoot (hüt), 1. sound that an owl makes. 2. make this sound or one like it. 3. shout to show disapproval or scorn. 4. make such a shout. 5. show disapproval of, or scorn for, by hooting. The audience hooted the speaker's plan. 6. force or drive by hooting. They hooted him off the platform. *n., v. 6.*

Hoo ver (hü′vər), Herbert C. (born 1874), the 31st president of the United States, from 1929 to 1933. *n.*

hop[1] (hop), 1. spring, or move by springing, on one foot. How far can you hop on your right foot? 2. spring, or move by springing, with all feet at once. Many birds hop. A kangaroo hops. 3. hop over; as, to hop a ditch. *v., hopped, hopping, n. 3.*

hop[2] (hop), 1. vine having flower clusters that look like small, yellow pine cones. 2. **Hops** are the dried, ripe, flower clusters of the hop vine, used to flavor beer and other malt drinks. 3. pick hops. 4. flavor with hops. *n., v., hopped, hopping.*

Hops

hope (hōp), 1. a feeling that what you desire will happen. His words gave me hope. 2. wish and expect. You hope to do well in school this year. 3. thing hoped for. 4. a cause of hope. He is the hope of the family. *n., v. 1.*

hope ful (hōp′fəl), 1. feeling hope. 2. giving hope; likely to succeed. 3. A **young hopeful** is a boy or girl thought likely to succeed. *adj., n. 6.*

hope less (hōp′lis), 1. feeling no hope. 2. giving no hope; as, a hopeless illness. *adj. 4.*

hop per (hop′ər), 1. one that hops. 2. a grasshopper or other hopping insect. 3. the receiver of grain in a mill; the receiver in various machines, larger at the top than at the bottom, which feeds material into the machine. *n. 13.*

Hopper (def. 3)

hop scotch (hop′skoch′), children's game in which the players hop over the lines of a figure drawn on the ground. *n.*

Hor ace (hor′is), a Latin poet who lived near Rome (65-8 B.C.). *n. 6.*

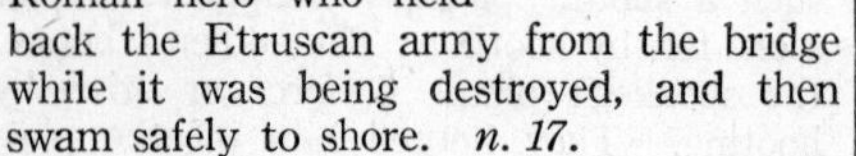

Girl playing hopscotch

Ho ra tius (hō rā′shəs), a Roman hero who held back the Etruscan army from the bridge while it was being destroyed, and then swam safely to shore. *n. 17.*

horde (hōrd), 1. multitude; crowd; swarm; as, hordes of grasshoppers. 2. wandering tribe or troop. Hordes of Tartars invaded Europe in the Middle Ages. *n. 9.*

hore hound (hōr′hound′), a plant used to make candy for coughs. *n.*

ho ri zon (hə rī′zən), 1. the line where earth and sky appear to meet. You cannot see beyond the horizon. 2. the limit of one's thinking, experience, or interest. *n. 4.*

hor i zon tal (hor′i zon′təl), 1. parallel to the horizon; at right angles to a vertical line. 2. flat; level. 3. of or at the horizon. 4. horizontal line, plane, direction, position, etc. *adj., n. 7.*

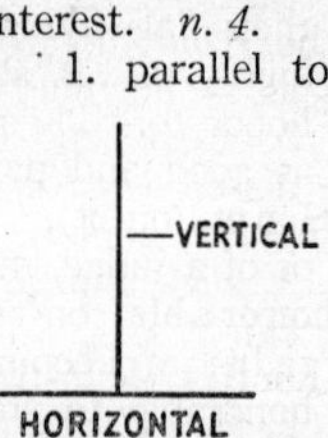

horn (hôrn), 1. a hard growth, often curved and pointed, on the heads of cattle, sheep, goats, and some other animals. 2. one of a pair of branching growths on the head of deer, which fall off and grow afresh each year. 3. anything that sticks up on the head of an animal; as, a snail's horns, an insect's horns. 4. the substance or material of horns. 5. a container made by hollowing out a horn; as, a drinking horn, a powder horn. 6. a musical instrument sounded by blowing; as, a hunting horn, a French horn, an English horn. 7. the tip of the new moon, or of some crescent. 8. A **horn of plenty** is a horn-shaped container filled with fruit, vegetables, and flowers. *n. 2.*

Powder horn

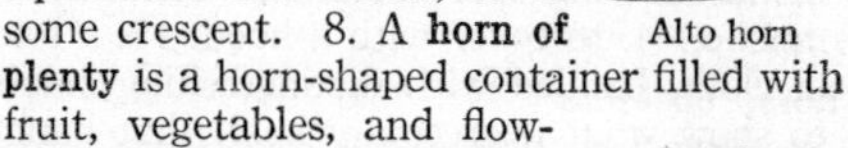

Alto horn

Horn (hôrn). **Cape Horn** is a cape on an island at the southern tip of South America. *n.*

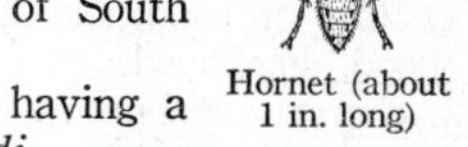

Hornet (about 1 in. long)

horned (hôrnd), having a horn or horns. *adj.*

horned toad, small lizard with a broad, flat body, short tail, and many spines.

hor net (hôr′nit), a large insect like a wasp, that can give a very painful sting. *n. 12.*

horn less (hôrn′lis), without horns. *adj. 20.*

horn pipe (hôrn′pīp′), 1. lively dance done by one person. It is popular among sailors. 2. music for it. 3. wind instrument of olden times, consisting of a wooden pipe with a bell-shaped end. *n. 20.*

horn y (hôr′ni), 1. made of horn or a substance like it. 2. hard like horn. A farmer's hands are horny from work. 3. having a horn or horns. *adj., hornier, horniest. 19.*

hor o scope (hor′ə skōp), 1. the appearance of the heavens with the relative position of the planets at the hour of a person's birth, regarded as influencing his life. 2. a diagram of the heavens used in telling fortunes by the planets and the stars. *n. 19.*

hor ri ble (hor′i bəl), 1. frightful; shocking; as, a horrible murder, a horrible disease. 2. extremely unpleasant; as, a horrible noise. *Used in common talk. adj. 3.*

hor rid (hor′id), 1. terrible; frightful. 2. very unpleasant. *Used in common talk. adj. 5.*

hor ri fy (hor′i fī), 1. cause to feel horror. 2. shock very much. *v., horrified, horrifying. 12.*

hor ror (hor′ər), 1. a shivering, shaking terror. 2. very strong dislike. Little girls sometimes have a horror of snakes or spiders. 3. thing that causes great fear. *n. 4.*

horse (hôrs), 1. See the picture. Horses are used for riding and for carrying and pulling loads. 2. soldiers on horses; cavalry. 3. provide with a horse or horses. 4. put on horseback. 5. a supporting frame. *n., v. 1.*

Horse

horse back (hôrs′bak′), 1. the back of a horse. 2. on the back of a horse; as, to ride horseback. *n., adv. 4.*

horse chestnut, 1. a shade tree with spreading branches, large leaves, clusters of showy white flowers, and glossy brown nuts. 2. the nut.

horse fly (hôrs′flī′), fly that bites horses. *n., pl. horseflies.*

Horsefly (somewhat over life size)

horse hair (hôrs′hãr′), 1. hair from the mane or tail of a horse. 2. made of horsehair; stuffed with horsehair. *n., adj. 13.*

horse man (hôrs′mən), 1. man who rides on horseback. 2. man who is skilled in managing horses. *n., pl. horsemen. 3.*

horse man ship (hôrs′mən ship), the management of horses; skill in riding horses. A good rider is proud of his horsemanship. *n. 11.*

horse play (hôrs′plā′), rough, boisterous fun. *n.*

horse pow er (hôrs′pou′ər), a unit or measure of power used in estimating the power of steam engines, automobiles, machinery, etc. One horsepower equals 550 foot-pounds per second. A foot-pound equals the work of raising one pound to the height of one foot. *n. 12.*

horse rad ish (hôrs′rad′ish), 1. a plant with a hot-tasting root which is ground and used as a relish with meat. See the picture below. 2. this relish. *n. 18.*

horse shoe (hôrs′shü′), 1. a U-shaped metal plate nailed to a horse's hoof to protect it. 2. put a horseshoe or horseshoes on. 3. thing shaped like a horseshoe. *n., v. 9.*

Horseshoe

horse sho er (hôrs′shü′ər), man who puts horseshoes on horses. *n. 18.*

horse whip (hôrs′hwip′), 1. a whip for controlling horses. 2. beat with a horsewhip. *n., v., horsewhipped, horsewhipping.*

horse wom an (hôrs′wům′ən), 1. woman who rides on horseback. 2. woman skilled in managing horses. *n., pl. horsewomen.*

hors y (hôr′si), 1. having to do with horses. 2. fond of horses or horse racing. 3. dressing or talking like people who spend much time with horses. *adj.*

hor ti cul tur al (hôr′ti kul′chər əl), having to do with the growing of flowers, fruits, and vegetables. Florists sometimes give a horticultural exhibit in the spring or fall. *adj. 15.*

Horseradish

hor ti cul ture (hôr′ti kul′chər), 1. the growing of flowers, fruits, and vegetables. 2. the cultivation of a garden. *n. 20.*

ho san na (hō zan′ə), a shout of praise to God. *interj., n. 13.*

hose (hōz), 1. stockings. 2. a tube of rubber or something else that will bend, for carrying any liquid for short distances. A hose is used in pumping gasoline into automobiles. 3. tights or breeches worn by men in olden times. *n., pl. hose. 4.*

Rubber hose for sprinkling

Ho se a (hō zē′ə), 1. book of the Old Testament. 2. its author, a Hebrew prophet who lived in the eighth century B.C. *n.*

ho sier y (hō′zhər i), stockings. *n. 9.*

hos pice (hos′pis), a house of rest for travelers; as, the hospice of the monks of Saint Bernard in the Alps. *n. 18.*

hos pi ta ble (hos′pi tə bəl), 1. giving or liking to give a welcome, food and shelter, and friendly treatment to guests or strangers; as, a hospitable family. 2. willing and ready to entertain; as, a person hospitable to new ideas. *adj. 6.*

hos pi ta bly (hos′pi tə bli), in a hospitable manner. *adv.*

hos pi tal (hos′pi təl), a place for the care of the sick or wounded. The doctor removed my tonsils at the hospital. *n. 3.*

hos pi tal i ty (hos′pi tal′i ti), friendly reception; generous treatment of guests or strangers. *n., pl. hospitalities. 7.*

host[1] (hōst), 1. one who receives another person at his house as his guest. 2. the keeper of an inn or hotel. 3. **Reckon without one's host** means overlook the chances of one's plans going wrong. 4. the plant or animal in or on which a parasite lives. The oak tree is the host of the mistletoe that grows on it. *n. 2.*

host[2] (hōst), a large number. As it grew dark, a few stars appeared, then a host. *n.*

Host[3] (hōst), the bread or wafer used in the Mass of the Roman Catholic Church. *n.*

hos tage (hos′tij), 1. person given to another or to an enemy as a pledge. The hostage will be kept safe and will be returned when the promises or agreements have been carried out. 2. pledge; security. *n. 10.*

hos tel (hos′təl), inn; hotel. *n. 16.*

hos tel ry (hos′təl ri), inn; hotel. *n., pl. hostelries. 15.*

host ess (hōs′tis), 1. woman who receives another person as her guest. 2. woman who keeps an inn or hotel, or helps her husband to do so. *n. 8.*

hos tile (hos′til), 1. of an enemy or enemies; as, the hostile army. 2. unfriendly; unfavorable; as, a hostile look. *adj. 5.*

hos til i ty (hos til′i ti), 1. unfriendliness; feeling as an enemy does; being an enemy. He showed signs of hostility to our plan. 2. being at war. 3. **Hostilities** means acts of war; warfare; fighting. *n., pl. hostilities. 8.*

hos tler (hos′lər or os′lər), person who takes care of horses at an inn or stable. *n.* Also called **ostler.**

hot (hot), 1. having much heat. Fire is hot. The sun is hot. That long run has made me hot. 2. tasting sharp, as pepper and mustard do. 3. fiery; eager. 4. new; fresh; as, a hot scent or trail. 5. with much heat. *adj., hotter, hottest, adv. 1.*

hot bed (hot′bed′), 1. a bed of earth covered with glass and kept warm for growing plants. 2. place favorable to rapid growth. *n. 19.*

ho tel (hō tel′), house or large building that supplies rooms and food to travelers and others. *n. 3.*

hot-head ed (hot′hed′id), 1. having a fiery temper; easily angered. 2. impetuous; rash. *adj.*

hot house (hot′hous′), a building with a glass roof and sides, kept warm for growing plants. *n. 16.*

Hothouse

Hot ten tot (hot′ən-tot), 1. member of a South African race having a dark, yellowish-brown complexion. 2. their language. *n. 19.*

hough (hok), a joint on the hind leg of an animal. See the picture under the other spelling, **hock.** *n. 20.*

hound (hound), 1. dog of any of various breeds, most of which hunt by scent and have large, drooping ears and short hair. 2. any dog. 3. hunt; chase. 4. urge (on). *n., v. 4.*

hour (our), 1. 60 minutes make an hour. 24 hours make a day. It is 12 hours from noon to midnight. 2. the time of day. This clock strikes the hours and the half hours. 3. the time for anything. Our breakfast hour is at eight. Our school hours are 9 to 12 and 1 to 4. *n. 1.*

hour glass (our′glas′), a device for measuring time. See the picture. It takes just an hour for the sand to pass from the top part to the bottom. *n.*

Hourglass

hou ri (hü′ri), one of the beautiful girls of the Mohammedan paradise. *n., pl. houris. 15.*

hour ly (our′li), 1. every hour. Give two doses hourly. 2. done, happening, or counted every hour; as, to give hourly doses of a medicine. 3. very often; frequently. Messages were coming from the front hourly. 4. frequent; as, hourly messages from the front. *adv., adj. 10.*

house (hous for 1, 2, 3, 5, 6, and 7, houz for 4), 1. a building in which people live. 2. building for any purpose; as, a storehouse, a henhouse, a schoolhouse. 3. a family; especially, a noble family. 4. take or put into a house; shelter. Where can we house all these children? 5. business firm. 6. an assembly for making laws and considering questions of government. In the United States, a **House of Representatives** is the lower branch of Congress or of a State legislature. 7. audience. A large house heard him. *n., pl. houses* (houz′iz), *v. 1.*

house boat (hous′bōt′), boat fitted up for use as a place to live in. *n.*

house break ing (hous′brāk′ing), entering a house to steal or commit some other crime. *n.*

house fly (hous′flī′), two-winged fly that lives around and in houses, feeding on food, garbage, and filth. *n., pl. houseflies.*

Housefly. Line shows actual length.

house hold (hous′hōld), 1. all the people living in a house; family; family and servants. 2. a home and its affairs. 3. of a household; having to do with a household; domestic; as, household expenses, household cares. *n., adj. 3.*

house hold er (hous′hōl′dər), 1. person who owns or lives in a house. 2. head of a family. *n. 18.*

house keep er (hous′kēp′ər), 1. woman who manages a home and its affairs and does the housework. 2. woman who directs the servants that do the housework. *n. 6.*

house keep ing (hous′kēp′ing), 1. management of a home and its affairs. 2. housework. *n. 13.*

house maid (hous′mād′), woman servant who does housework. *n. 18.*

house top (hous′top′), top of a house; roof. *n. 6.*

house warm ing (hous′wôr′ming), party given when a family moves into a house for the first time. *n.*

house wife (hous′wīf′), 1. woman who manages a home and its affairs. A housewife plans the housework and does the buying for the family. 2. woman who is the head of a household. *n., pl. housewives. 6.*

house wif er y (hous′wīf′ər i), work of a housewife. *n. 18.*

house work (hous′wėrk′), washing, ironing, cleaning, sweeping, cooking, etc. *n. 11.*

hous ing[1] (houz′ing), 1. sheltering; providing shelter. 2. houses. The housing of that city is not enough for the people who will be there next year. *n. 15.*

hous ing[2] (houz′ing), an ornamental covering on an animal's back. Under the saddle was a housing of red velvet. *n.*

Hous ton (hūs′tən), 1. Samuel (1793-1863), an American general who was twice president of Texas before it became a State in 1845. 2. a city in southeastern Texas. *n. 5.*

hove (hōv), heaved. The sailors hove at the ropes. *pt. and pp. of* **heave.**

hov el (huv′əl), 1. a house that is small, mean, and unpleasant to live in. 2. open shed for sheltering cattle, tools, etc. *n. 15.*

hov er (huv′ər), 1. stay in or near one place in the air. The two birds hovered over their nest. 2. stay in or near one place. The dogs hovered around the meat truck. 3. be in an uncertain condition; waver. The sick man hovered between life and death. *v. 5.*

how (hou), 1. in what way. I wonder how you go there? How can it be done? How did it happen? 2. to what degree or amount. How tall are you? How hot is it? How much shall I bring you? 3. in what condition. How is your health? Tell me how Mrs. Jones is. How do I look? 4. for what reason; why. How is it you don't like candy? *adv. 1.*

how be it (hou bē′it), nevertheless. *adv. 12.*

how dah (hou′də), a seat for persons riding on the back of an elephant. *n.*

Howdah

how e'er (hou ãr′), however. *conj., adv. 6.*

how ev er (hou ev′ər), 1. nevertheless. 2. to whatever degree or amount. 3. in whatever way; by whatever means. *conj., adv. 1.*

how itz er (hou′it sər), a short cannon for firing shells in a high curve. *n. 19.*

Howitzer

howl (houl), 1. give a long, loud, mournful cry. Dogs often howl at night. 2. a long, loud, mournful cry; as, the howl of a wolf. 3. give a long, loud cry of pain or rage. 4. a loud cry of pain or rage. 5. yell; shout. It was so funny that we howled with laughter. 6. force or drive by howling. The angry mob howled the speaker off the platform. *v., n. 3.*

how so ev er (hou′sō ev′ər), 1. in whatever way; by whatever means. 2. to whatever extent. *adv. 12.*

hoy den (hoi′dən), boisterous, romping girl; tomboy. *n.*

hr., hour; hours. *7.*

H.R.H., 1. His Royal Highness. 2. Her Royal Highness.

hrs., hours.

hub (hub), 1. the central part of a wheel. 2. center of activity, etc. London is the hub of English life. *n. 13.*

SPOKE
HUB
AXLE
FELLOE
Hub

hub bub (hub′ub), loud, confused noise; uproar. The roomful of boys was in a hubbub. *n. 17.*

huck le ber ry (huk′əl ber′i), 1. a small berry like a blueberry, but darker in color. 2. the shrub it grows on. *n., pl. huckleberries. 18.*

Huckleberry

huck ster (huk′stər), 1. peddler. 2. person who sells small articles. 3. a mean and unfair trader. *n. 20.*

hud dle (hud′əl), 1. to crowd close. The sheep huddled together in a corner. 2. put close together. She huddled all four boys into one bed. 3. a confused heap, mass, or crowd. Your books and papers are in a huddle; put them in better order at once. *v., n. 7.*

Hud son (hud′sən), 1. a river in New York State. New York City is at its mouth. 2. a very large bay in central Canada. *n. 3.*

hue (hū), color; tint. The girls' dresses showed almost all the hues of the rainbow. *n. 5.*

hue and cry, shouts of alarm or protest.

huff (huf), 1. a fit of anger. She has such a bad temper that she gets into a huff about nothing. 2. make angry; offend. *n., v. 12.*

huff y (huf′i), 1. offended. 2. easily offended; touchy. *adj., huffier, huffiest.*

hug (hug), 1. put the arms around and hold close. The girl hugs her big doll. 2. a tight clasp with the arms. Give mother a hug. 3. cling firmly or fondly to; as, to hug an opinion. 4. keep close to. The boat hugged the shore. *v., hugged, hugging. n. 5.*

huge (hūj), very, very large. A whale or an elephant is a huge animal. *adj. 2.*

Hu go (hū′gō), Victor, a famous French author (1802-1885). *n. 11.*

Hu gue not (hū′gə not), a French Protestant of the 16th and 17th centuries. *n. 10.*

hulk (hulk), 1. the body of an old or worn-out ship. 2. ship used as a prison. 3. a big, clumsy person. 4. anything large and hard to manage. *n. 9.*

hulk ing (hul′king), big and clumsy. *adj.*

Strawberry

hull (hul), 1. body or frame of a ship. Masts, sails, and rigging are not part of the hull. 2. main body or frame of a seaplane, airship, etc. 3. outer covering of a seed. 4. calyx of some fruits. We call the green frill of a strawberry its hull. 5. remove the hull or hulls from. 6. any outer covering. *n., v. 8.*

hul la ba loo (hul′ə bə lü′), loud noise or disturbance; uproar. *n., pl. hullabaloos.*

hum (hum), 1. make a continuous murmuring sound like that of a bee or of a spinning top. The sewing machine hums busily. 2. a continuous, murmuring sound; as, the hum of bees, the hum of the city streets. 3. make a low sound like the letter *m*, in hesitation, embarrassment, dissatisfaction, etc. 4. a low sound like the letter *m*. Hum, I don't know what to do. 5. sing with closed lips, not sounding words; as, to hum a tune. 6. a singing in this way. 7. put or bring by humming. The mother hummed her baby to sleep. 8. be busy and active. The new president made things hum. *Used in common talk. v., hummed, humming, n., interj. 3.*

hu man (hū′mən), 1. of man; like a man. Men, women, and children are human beings. Some monkeys look almost human. 2. belonging to mankind. The history of America has great human interest. *adj. 2.*

hu mane (hū mān′), kind; not cruel or brutal. *adj. 7.*

hu man ist (hū′mən ist), 1. student of human nature or affairs. 2. student of Latin and Greek culture. *n. 19.*

hu man i tar i an (hū man′i tãr′i ən), 1. person who is devoted to the welfare of all human beings. 2. helpful to humanity; philanthropic. *n., adj.*

hu man i ty (hū man′i ti), 1. people. All humanity will be helped by advances in medical sciences. 2. the nature of man. History teaches us about humanity. 3. kindness. Treat animals with humanity. 4. The **humanities** means the Latin and Greek classics. *n., pl. humanities. 5.*

hu man ize (hū′mən īz), 1. make human; become human. 2. make kind; become kind. *v. 16.*

hu man kind (hū′mən kīnd′), people; mankind. *n. 14.*

hu man ly (hū′mən li), 1. in a human manner. 2. by human means. We will do all that is humanly possible. 3. according to the feelings, knowledge, or experience of men. *adv.*

hum ble (hum′bəl), 1. low in position or condition; not important; not grand. He held a humble position with a very small salary. We live in a humble cottage of one room. 2. modest; not proud. 3. make humble; make lower in position, condition, or pride. *adj., v. 3.*

hum ble ness (hum′bəl nis), 1. being humble; freedom from pride. 2. lowly state or condition. *n. 12.*

hum bly (hum′bli), in a humble manner. *adv.*

hum bug (hum′bug′), 1. a cheat; a sham. 2. to cheat; deceive with a sham. *n., v., humbugged, humbugging. 15.*

hum drum (hum′drum′), dull; without variety; commonplace. *adj. 14.*

hu mid (hū′mid), moist; damp. The air is very humid near the sea. *adj. 14.*

hu mid i ty (hū mid′i ti), 1. moistness; dampness. The humidity today is worse than the heat. 2. amount of moisture in the air. *n. 9.*

hu mil i ate (hū mil′i āt), lower the pride, dignity, or self-respect of. John felt humiliated by his failure. A child who behaves badly when guests are present humiliates his parents. *v. 9.*

hu mil i a tion (hū mil′i ā′shən), a lowering of pride, dignity, or self-respect. *n. 10.*

hu mil i ty (hū mil′i ti), humbleness of mind; lack of pride; meekness. *n. 5.*

hum ming bird (hum′ing bėrd′), a very small, brightly colored American bird with a long, narrow bill and narrow wings that make a humming sound. *n.*

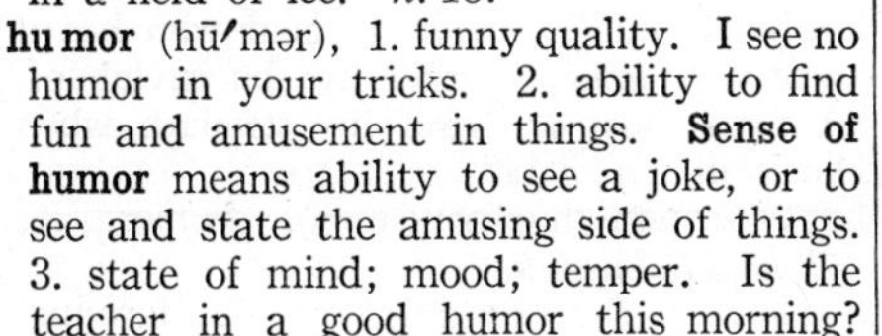

Hummingbird (about 3¾ in. long)

hum mock (hum′ək), 1. a very small, rounded hill; knoll; hillock. 2. a bump or ridge in a field of ice. *n. 18.*

hu mor (hū′mər), 1. funny quality. I see no humor in your tricks. 2. ability to find fun and amusement in things. **Sense of humor** means ability to see a joke, or to see and state the amusing side of things. 3. state of mind; mood; temper. Is the teacher in a good humor this morning? I feel in the humor for working. **Out of humor** means cross; in a bad mood. 4. fancy; whim. 5. give in to (a person); agree with. A sick child has to be humored. *n., v. 3.*

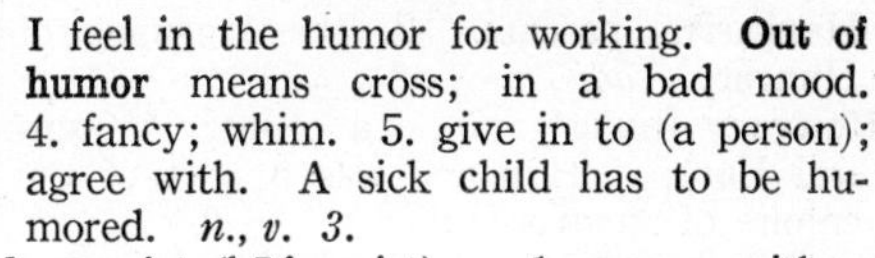

hu mor ist (hū′mər ist), 1. person with a strong sense of humor. 2. humorous talker; writer of jokes and funny stories. *n. 15.*

hu mor ous (hū′mər əs), full of humor; funny; amusing. Mark Twain was a humorous writer. *adj. 7.*

hump (hump), 1. a rounded lump that sticks out. Some camels have two humps on their backs. 2. raise or bend up into a lump. The cat humped her back when she saw the dog. *n., v. 12.*

hump back (hump′bak′), 1. a back having a hump on it. 2. person or animal with a hump on its back. *n. 17.*

humph (həm), an exclamation expressing doubt, disgust, contempt, etc. *interj., n. 20.*

hu mus (hū′məs), soil made from dead leaves and other vegetable matter. *n. 14.*

Hun (hun), 1. member of a warlike, brutal Asiatic race. Led by their king Attila, the Huns overran Europe in the fifth century A.D. 2. a barbarous, destructive person. *n. 14.*

hunch (hunch), 1. hump. 2. draw, bend, or form into a hump. He sat hunched up with his chin on his knees. 3. move, push, or shove by jerks. 4. expectation without conscious reasoning. *Used in common talk. n., v. 9.*

hunch back (hunch′bak′), person with a hump on his back; humpback. *n.*

hunch backed (hunch′bakt′), humpbacked. *adj.*

hun dred (hun′drəd), ten times ten; 100. There are one hundred cents in a dollar. *n., adj. 1.*

hun dred fold (hun′drəd fōld′), a hundred times as much or as many. *adj., adv., n.*

hun dredth (hun′drədth), 1. next after the 99th. 2. one of 100 equal parts. *adj., n. 8.*

hun dred weight (hun′drəd wāt′), 1. in the United States, 100 pounds. 2. in England, 112 pounds. *n., pl. hundredweights* or (as after a numeral) *hundredweight. 20.*

hung (hung). See **hang.** He hung up his cap. Your dress has hung here all day. *pt. and pp. of hang. 2.*

Hun gar i an (hung gãr′i ən), 1. of Hungary, its people, or their language. 2. person born in Hungary, living there, or having

Hungarian parents. 3. the language of Hungary. *adj., n. 8.*

Hun ga ry (hung′gəri), a country in central Europe. Hungary was a part of the empire of Austria-Hungary. *n. 9.*

hun ger (hung′gər), 1. painful feeling caused by having nothing to eat. The little boy who ran away from home soon felt hunger. 2. desire or need for food. 3. feel hunger; be hungry. 4. strong desire; as, a hunger for books. 5. have a strong desire. The lonely girl hungered for friends. *n., v. 3.*

hun gri ly (hung′gri li), in a hungry manner. *adv.*

hun gry (hung′gri), 1. feeling a desire or need for food. 2. showing hunger. The cook saw a hungry look on the beggar's face. 3. eager; as, hungry for books. *adj., hungrier, hungriest. 2.*

hunk (hungk), a big lump or piece. *n.* [*Used in common talk*] *20.*

hunt (hunt), 1. chase (game and other wild animals) for food or for fun. 2. hunting. 3. a group of people hunting together. 4. search; seek; look; as, to hunt for a lost book. 5. a search; an attempt to find something. 6. drive; chase; as, to hunt a neighbor's chickens out of our yard. *v., n. 1.*

hunt er (hun′tər), 1. person who hunts. 2. a horse or dog for hunting. *n. 2.*

hunt ress (hun′tris), woman who hunts. *n. 16.*

hunts man (hunts′mən), 1. hunter. 2. manager of a hunt. *n., pl. huntsmen. 8.*

Hurdles for racing

hur dle (hėr′dəl), 1. barrier for people or horses to jump over in a race. **Hurdles** is a race in which the runners jump over hurdles. 2. jump over. 3. obstacle, difficulty, etc. 4. overcome (an obstacle, difficulty, etc.). 5. frame made of sticks and used as a fence. 6. enclose with such frames. *n., v. 15.*

Man playing a hurdy-gurdy

hur dy-gur dy (hėr′di gėr′di), a hand organ or street piano played by turning a handle. *n., pl. hurdy-gurdies.*

hurl (hėrl), throw with much force. The man hurled his spear at one bear, and the dogs hurled themselves at the other. *v., n. 4.*

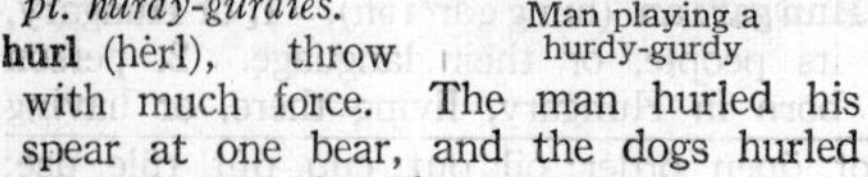

hur ly-bur ly (hėr′li bėr′li), disorder and noise; tumult. *n. 16.*

Hu ron (hūr′ən), second largest of the five Great Lakes, between the United States and Canada. *n. 17.*

hur rah (hů rä′). Give a hurrah for the hero! We hurrah when we see the soldiers go by. *interj., n., v. 5.*

hur ray (hů rā′), hurrah. *interj., n., v. 17.*

hur ri cane (hėr′i kān), 1. tropical cyclone; storm with violent wind and, usually, very heavy rain. The wind in a hurricane blows from 70 to 100 miles per hour. 2. sudden, violent outburst. *n. 8.*

hur ried (hėr′id), 1. forced to hurry. 2. done or made in a hurry; hasty. *adj.*

hur ried ly (hėr′id li), in a hurry; hastily. She packed her bags hurriedly so as to catch the train. *adv. 15.*

hur ry (hėr′i), 1. to drive, carry, send, or move quickly. They hurried the sick child to the doctor. He hurried his book out of sight when the teacher appeared. 2. move or act with more than an easy or natural speed. If you hurry, your work may be poor. He hurried to get the doctor. 3. hurried movement or action. In her hurry she dropped the eggs. 4. eagerness to have quickly or do quickly. She was in a hurry to see her father. 5. urge to act soon or too soon. 6. urge to great speed or to too great speed. 7. hasten; make go on or occur more quickly. Please hurry dinner. *v., hurried, hurrying, n., pl. hurries. 1.*

hurt (hėrt), 1. cause pain or injury to. The stone hurt his foot badly. 2. a cut or bruise; the breaking of a bone; any wound or injury. 3. suffer pain. My hand hurts. 4. have a bad effect on; do damage or harm to. Will it hurt this hat if it gets wet? 5. harm; wrong. It would do no hurt to get the house painted this summer. *v., hurt, hurting, n. 1.*

hurt ful (hėrt′fəl), causing hurt, harm, or damage. *adj. 12.*

hur tle (hėr′təl), 1. dash violently; rush violently. Spears hurtled against shields. 2. hurtling; a clash. *v., n. 19.*

hus band (huz′bənd), 1. man who has a wife. 2. manage carefully; be saving of. A man must husband his strength when he is ill. *n., v. 1.*

hus band man (huz′bənd mən), farmer. *n., pl. husbandmen. 9.*

hus band ry (huz′bənd ri), 1. farming. 2. management of one's affairs. 3. careful management; thrift. *n. 7.*

hush (hush), 1. stop making a noise. Hush! Hush! The wind has hushed. 2. stillness. *interj., v., n. 3.*

husk (husk), 1. the dry outer covering of certain seeds or fruits. An ear of corn has a husk. 2. dry or worthless outer covering of anything. 3. remove the husk from. Husk the corn. *n., v. 6.*

Husk on an ear of corn

husk i ness (hus′ki nis), hoarseness or roughness of voice. *n.*

husking bee, a gathering of neighbors and friends to husk corn.

husk y[1] (hus′ki), 1. dry in the throat; hoarse; rough of voice; as, a husky cough. 2. of, like, or having husks; as, a husky covering. 3. big and strong. *Used in common talk.* 4. person who is big and strong. *Used in common talk. adj., huskier, huskiest, n., pl. huskies. 10.*

Husk y or **husk y**[2] (hus′ki), Eskimo dog. *n., pl. Huskies, huskies.*

hus sar (hu̇ zär′), a European light-armed cavalry soldier. *n. 16.*

hus sy (huz′i), 1. a bad-mannered or pert girl. 2. a worthless woman. *n., pl. hussies. 20.*

hus tle (hus′əl), 1. hurry. Mother hustled baby to bed. 2. rush roughly; push one's way; as, to hustle along through the crowd. 3. push or shove roughly. The other boys hustled Ned along the street. 4. go or work quickly or with energy. 5. hustling. It was done with much hustle and bustle. *v., n. 7.*

hut (hut), a small, roughly made house; a small cabin. The boys built a hut in the woods. *n. 3.*

hutch (huch), 1. a pen for rabbits. 2. hut. 3. box. *n. 16.*

huz za (hu zä′), a loud shout of joy or applause; hurrah. *interj., n. 16.*

hy a cinth (hī′ə sinth), a spring plant that grows from a bulb and has a spike of small, fragrant, bell-shaped flowers. *n. 9.*

Hyacinth

hy brid (hī′brid), 1. the offspring of two animals or plants of different races, varieties, or species. The loganberry is a hybrid because it is a cross between the raspberry and the blackberry. 2. bred from two different races, varieties, or species. A mule is a hybrid animal. 3. thing of mixed origin. The English language is a hybrid of Anglo-Saxon and French. 4. of mixed origin. *n., adj. 8.*

hy brid i za tion (hī′brid i zā′shən), production of hybrids. *n. 19.*

hy brid ize (hī′brid īz), 1. cause to produce hybrids. Botanists hybridize different kinds of plants in order to get new varieties. 2. produce hybrids. *v.*

hy dra (hī′drə), 1. in Greek mythology, a monstrous serpent with nine heads, each of which was replaced by two after being cut off, unless the wound was burned. Hercules killed the Hydra. 2. evil that is hard to overcome. *n. 12.*

hy dran gea (hī drān′jə), a shrub with large, showy flower clusters, white, pink, or bluish in color. *n. 20.*

hy drant (hī′drənt), a large pipe with a valve for drawing water; a hose connection. Hydrants are used to get water to put out fires and to wash the streets. *n. 17.*

Hydrant

hy drau lic (hī drô′lik), 1. having to do with water in motion. 2. operated by water; as, a hydraulic press. 3. hardening under water; as, hydraulic cement. *adj. 10.*

hy dro car bon (hī′drō kär′bən), any compound containing only hydrogen and carbon. Gasoline is a mixture of hydrocarbons. *n.*

hy dro chlo ric (hī′drə klō′rik), containing hydrogen and chlorine. **Hydrochloric acid** is used in cleaning metals. *adj. 13.*

hy dro e lec tric (hī′drō i lek′trik), developing electricity from water power. *adj.*

hy dro gen (hī′drə jən), a colorless gas that burns easily. Hydrogen weighs less than any other known substance. It combines with oxygen to form water. *n. 7.*

hy drom e ter (hī drom′i tər), an instrument for finding the specific gravities or densities of liquids. A hydrometer is used to test the battery of an automobile. *n. 11.*

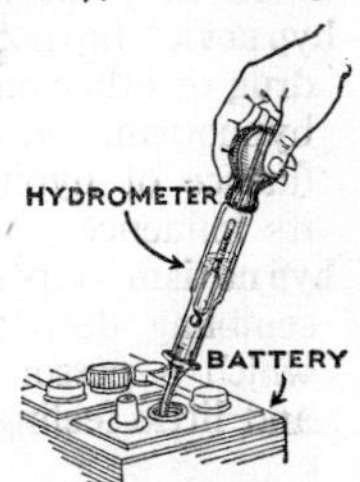

Hydrometer

hy dro pho bi a (hī′drə fō′bi ə), the disease a mad dog has. If bitten by a mad dog, a person may get the disease. *n. 15.*

hy dro plane (hī′drə plān), 1. motorboat that glides on the surface of water. 2. seaplane; airplane provided with floats or with a boatlike underpart, enabling it to alight upon and ascend from water. *n.*

hy e na (hī ē′nə), a wild animal much like a large dog in shape and size. Most hyenas are cowardly, but utter bloodcurdling yells. *n. 16.*

Striped hyena (about 2 ft. high at the shoulder)

hy giene (hī′jēn), the rules of health; the science of keeping well. *n. 8.*

hy gi en ic (hī′ji en′ik), 1. healthful; sanitary. 2. having to do with health or hygiene. *adj. 15.*

Hy men (hī′mən), the Greek god of marriage. *n. 10.*

hy me ne al (hī′mə nē′əl), having to do with marriage. *adj. 15.*

hymn (him), 1. song in praise or honor of God. 2. any song of praise. *n. 4.*

hym nal (him′nəl), a book of hymns. *n.*

hy per bo le (hī pėr′bə li), exaggeration for effect. *Example:* Waves mountain-high broke over the reef. *n. 15.*

hy per crit i cal (hī′pər krit′i kəl), too critical. *adj.*

hy phen (hī′fən), a mark (-) used to connect the parts of a compound word, or the parts of a word divided at the end of a line. *n. 18.*

hy phen ate (hī′fən āt), join by a hyphen; write or print with a hyphen. *v.*

hyp not ic (hip not′ik), 1. causing sleep. 2. a drug or other means of causing sleep. 3. of hypnotism. 4. one who is under the influence of hypnotism or easily put under its influence. *adj., n. 18.*

hyp no tism (hip′nə tizm), a condition resembling deep sleep, but more active, in which a person has little will of his own and little feeling, and acts according to the suggestions of the person who has brought about the condition. *n.*

hyp no tize (hip′nə tīz), put into a hypnotic state. *v. 11.*

hy po chon dri ac (hī′pə kon′dri ak), 1. person who is depressed without reason. 2. one who imagines that he is ill when he is not. *n. 20.*

hy poc ri sy (hi pok′ri si), 1. putting on a false appearance of goodness or religion. 2. pretending to be what one is not; pretense. *n., pl. hypocrisies. 7.*

hyp o crite (hip′ə krit), 1. person who puts on a false appearance of goodness or religion. 2. person who pretends to be what he is not; pretender. *n. 6.*

hyp o crit i cal (hip′ə krit′i kəl), of or like a hypocrite; insincere. *adj. 15.*

hy pot e nuse (hī pot′i nūs or hī pot′i nüs), the side of a right-angled triangle opposite the right angle. *n. 19.*

AB is the hypotenuse.

hy poth e sis (hī poth′i sis), something assumed because it seems likely to be a true explanation; theory. Let us act on the hypothesis that he is honest. *n., pl. hypotheses* (-sēz). *11.*

hy po thet i cal (hī′pə thet′i kəl), of or involving an hypothesis; supposed; assumed. *adj.*

hys sop (his′əp), 1. a very fragrant, bushy plant, used for medicine, flavoring, etc. 2. in the Bible, a plant whose twigs were used in Jewish ceremonies. *n. 11.*

hys te ri a (his tēr′i ə), 1. a nervous disorder that causes violent fits of laughing and crying, imaginary illnesses, or general lack of self-control. 2. senseless excitement. *n. 19.*

hys ter ic (his ter′ik), hysterical. *adj.*

hys ter i cal (his ter′i kəl), unnaturally excited; showing an unnatural lack of control; unable to stop laughing, crying, etc.; suffering from hysteria. *adj. 11.*

hys ter ics (his ter′iks), a fit of hysterical laughing and crying. *n. pl. 11.*

I

I[1], **i** (ī), the ninth letter of the alphabet. There are two i's in Indian. *n., pl. I's, i's.*

I[2] (ī), the person speaking. John said, "I am ten years old." I like my dog, and he likes me. *pron., pl. we. 1.*

Ia., Iowa.

i am bic (ī am′bik), 1. a measure in poetry consisting of two syllables, an unaccented followed by an accented. 2. of or containing such measures. Much English poetry is iambic. *Example:*

"The sun′ | that brief′ | Decem′ | ber day′
Rose cheer′ | less o′ | ver hills′ | of gray′."

n., adj. 15.

-ian, form of **-an** used in Bostonian, Episcopalian, etc.

i bis (ī′bis), a long-legged, wading bird with white and black feathers, living in warm regions. The ancient Egyptians regarded the ibis as sacred. *n., pl. ibises* or *ibis. 19.*

Ibis (about 3½ ft. tall)

-ible, suffix meaning:—that can be ———ed; as in perfectible, reducible.

-ic, suffix meaning:—
1. of or pertaining to; as in atmospheric, Icelandic.
2. having the nature of; as in artistic, heroic.
3. constituting or being; as in bombastic, monolithic.
4. characterized by; containing; made up of; as in alcoholic.
5. made by; caused by; as in volcanic.
6. like; like that of; characteristic of; as in meteoric, antagonistic, idyllic, sophomoric.

Many words in *-ic* have two or more of these meanings.

-ically, ic+ly. Instead of artistic-ly we say artistically; instead of alphabetic-ly we say alphabetically. *suffix.*

ice (īs), 1. water made solid by cold. 2. of ice; having to do with ice. 3. make cool with ice; put ice in or around. 4. a sugary covering for a cake; icing. 5. cover (cake) with icing. 6. a frozen dessert, usually one made of sweetened fruit juice. *n., adj., v. 1.*

Iceberg

ice berg (īs′bėrg′), a large mass of ice floating in the sea. A ship may be wrecked on an iceberg. See the picture above. *n. 9.*

ice boat (īs′bōt′), 1. a triangular frame on runners, fitted with sails for sailing on ice. 2. a strong boat used to break a channel through ice. *n.*

ice box (īs′boks′), box in which to keep food, liquids, etc., cool with ice, etc. *n.*

ice cream, a dessert made of cream or custard sweetened, flavored, and frozen.

Iceboat for sailing

Ice land (īs′lənd), a large island in the Atlantic Ocean between Greenland and Europe. *n. 10.*

Ice lan dic (īs lan′dik), 1. of or having to do with Iceland, its people, or their language. 2. the language of Iceland. *adj., n. 19.*

Ichneumon (about 3 ft. long, including the tail)

ich neu mon (ik nū′mən or ik nü′mən), a small brown animal of Egypt, like a weasel. *n. 18.*

i ci cle (ī′si kəl), a pointed, hanging stick of ice formed by the freezing of dripping water. *n. 11.*

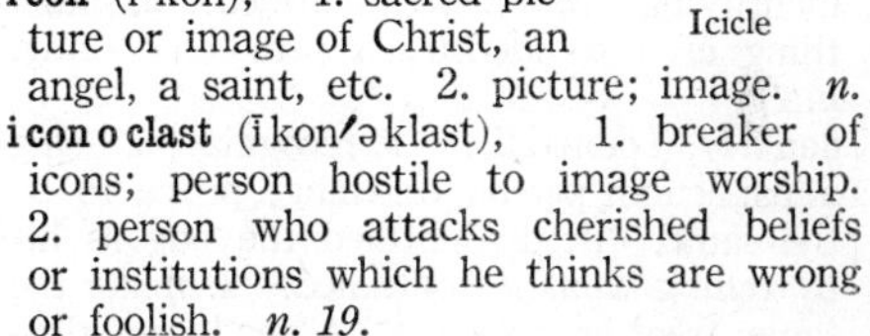

Icicle

i ci ly (ī′si li), very coldly. *adv.*

ic ing (īs′ing), a mixture of sugar with white of egg or other things, used to cover cakes. *n. 20.*

i con (ī′kon), 1. sacred picture or image of Christ, an angel, a saint, etc. 2. picture; image. *n.*

i con o clast (ī kon′ə klast), 1. breaker of icons; person hostile to image worship. 2. person who attacks cherished beliefs or institutions which he thinks are wrong or foolish. *n. 19.*

i cy (ī′si), 1. like ice; very cold; slippery. 2. having much ice; covered with ice. 3. of ice. 4. without warm feeling; cold and unfriendly. *adj., icier, iciest. 4.*

I'd (īd), 1. I should; I would. 2. I had. *4.*

Id. or **Ida.,** Idaho.

I da ho (ī′də hō), a Western State of the United States. *n. 10.*

i de a (ī dē′ə), 1. a plan, picture, or belief of the mind. Candy and toys are a child's ideas of happiness. 2. thought; fancy; opinion. John had no idea that work at school was so hard. *n. 2.*

i de al (ī dē′əl), 1. a perfect type; a model to be imitated. Ruth's mother is her ideal. The Christian religion holds up high ideals. 2. perfect; just as one would wish. A clear, warm day is ideal for a picnic. 3. existing only in thought. A point without length, breadth, or thickness is an ideal object. *n., adj. 4.*

i de al ism (ī dē′əl izm), 1. an acting according to one's ideals of what ought to be, regardless of circumstances or of the approval or disapproval of others. 2. a cherishing of fine ideals. *n. 12.*

i de al ist (ī dē′əl ist), 1. person who acts

according to his ideals; person who has fine ideals. 2. person who neglects practical matters in following ideals. *n. 18.*

i de al is tic (ī dē′əl is′tik), 1. having high ideals and acting according to them. 2. forgetting or neglecting practical matters in trying to follow out one's ideals; not practical. 3. of idealism or idealists. *adj.*

i de al ize (ī dē′əl īz), make ideal; think of or represent as perfect rather than as is actually the case. Mary idealized her sister and thought everything she did was right. *v. 16.*

i de al ly (ī dē′əl i), 1. according to an ideal; perfectly. 2. in idea or theory. *adv.*

i den ti cal (ī den′ti kəl), 1. the same. That is the identical pen I lost. 2. exactly alike. The two boys took identical trips last summer. *adj. 7.*

i den ti fi ca tion (ī den′ti fi kā′shən), 1. an identifying. 2. a being identified. 3. something used to identify a person or thing. *n. 12.*

i den ti fy (ī den′ti fī), 1. recognize as being a particular person or thing; prove to be the same. Fred identified the bag as his by telling what it contained. 2. make the same; treat as the same. A good king identifies the interest of his people with his own prosperity. 3. connect; link; associate. *v., identified, identifying. 8.*

i den ti ty (ī den′ti ti), 1. individuality; who a person is; what a thing is. The writer concealed his identity under a false name. 2. sameness; exact likeness. The identity of the crimes led the police to think that the same person committed them. *n., pl. identities. 12.*

ides (īdz), in the ancient Roman calendar, the 15th day of March, May, July, and October, and the 13th day of the other months. *n. pl. 19.*

id i o cy (id′i ə si), 1. being an idiot. 2. acting like an idiot. 3. very great stupidity. *n., pl. idiocies. 19.*

id i om (id′i əm), 1. a phrase or expression whose meaning cannot be understood from the ordinary meanings of the words in it. "How do you do?" and "I have caught cold" are English idioms. 2. a language; a dialect. He spoke in the idiom of the New England countryside. 3. a people's way of expressing itself; as, the French idiom. *n. 17.*

id i o mat ic (id′i ə mat′ik), 1. using an idiom or idioms. 2. of idioms; concerning idioms. 3. showing the individual character of a language; characteristic of a particular language. *adj. 20.*

id i o mat i cal ly (id′i ə mat′i kəl i), in an idiomatic manner. *adv.*

id i o syn cra sy (id′i ō sing′krə si), personal peculiarity. *n., pl. idiosyncrasies. 16.*

id i ot (id′i ət), 1. person so stupid that he can never learn to read or to count; a born fool. 2. very stupid or foolish person. *n. 5.*

id i ot ic (id′i ot′ik), very stupid or foolish. *adj. 19.*

id i ot i cal ly (id′i ot′i kəl i), in an idiotic manner. *adv.*

i dle (ī′dəl), 1. not doing anything; not busy; as, idle hours of a holiday. 2. lazy; not willing to do things. The idle boy would not study. 3. useless. It is idle for a girl to wish to be a boy. 4. without any good reason or cause; as, idle fears, idle rumors. 5. be idle; do nothing. 6. waste (time); spend. Jane idled away many hours lying in the hammock. 7. run slowly without transmitting power. A motor idles when it is out of gear and running slowly. *adj., v. 2.*

i dle ness (ī′dəl nis), 1. having nothing to do. The closing of the large factory made many workers live in idleness. 2. being lazy. Idleness may be caused by poor health. 3. uselessness. *n. 5.*

i dler (ī′dlər), a lazy person. *n. 10.*

i dly (ī′dli), in an idle manner; doing nothing. *adv.*

i dol (ī′dəl), 1. a thing, usually an image, that is worshiped. 2. person or thing that is loved very, very much. Little Mary was the idol of her family. *n. 4.*

Idol

i dol a ter (ī dol′ə tər), person who worships idols. *n. 17.*

i dol a tress (ī dol′ə tris), woman who worships idols. *n.*

i dol a trous (ī dol′ə trəs), 1. worshiping idols. 2. having to do with the worship of idols. *adj. 16.*

i dol a try (ī dol′ə tri), 1. the worship of idols. 2. worship of any person or thing; extreme devotion. The queen was adored to the point of idolatry. *n., pl. idolatries. 8.*

i dol ize (ī′dəl īz), 1. worship as an idol; make an idol of. 2. love very, very much. *v. 16.*

i dyl or **i dyll** (ī′dəl), 1. a short description in poetry or prose of a simple and charming scene or event, especially one connected with country life. 2. a scene or event which is simple and charming, so that a poem could be written about it. *n. 14.*

i dyl lic (ī dil′ik), suitable for an idyl; simple and charming. *adj.*

i.e., that is; namely.

if (if). Come if you can. If it rains tomorrow, we shall stay at home. I do not know if he is rich or poor. *conj. 1.*

ig loo (ig′lü), an Eskimo hut that is often shaped like a dome, and built of blocks of hard snow. *n., pl. igloos.*

Igloo

ig ne ous (ig′ni əs), 1. of fire; pertaining to fire. 2. produced by fire, intense heat, or volcanic action. Granite is an igneous rock. *adj.*

ig nite (ig nīt′), 1. set on fire. You ignite a match by scratching it. 2. take fire; begin to burn. *v. 11.*

ig ni tion (ig nish′ən), 1. a setting on fire. 2. a catching on fire. 3. in a gasoline engine, the switch and apparatus controlling the sparks that set the gasoline on fire in the cylinders. *n. 13.*

ig no ble (ig nō′bəl), 1. mean; base; without honor. To betray a friend is ignoble. 2. of low birth. Some very great men have come from ignoble families. *adj. 6.*

ig no bly (ig nō′bli), meanly; basely. *adv.*

ig no min i ous (ig′nə min′i əs), shameful; disgraceful; humiliating. *adj. 12.*

ig no min y (ig′nə min i), loss of one's good name; public shame and disgrace. *n., pl. ignominies. 13.*

ig no ra mus (ig′nə rā′məs), person who knows little. *n.*

ig no rance (ig′nə rəns), lack of knowledge; being ignorant. *n. 4.*

ig no rant (ig′nə rənt), knowing little or nothing. Nell is ignorant of farm life. This boy is not stupid, but he has never been to school or had much chance to learn; so he is very ignorant. *adj. 3.*

ig nore (ig nōr′), pay no attention to; disregard. When you bump your head, it is better to ignore the pain than to cry. *v. 11.*

I graine (i grān′), mother of King Arthur. *n.*

i gua na (i gwä′nə), a large climbing lizard found in tropical countries. See the picture just below. *n.*

Iguana (about 5 ft. long)

il-, prefix meaning:— not; as in illegal, illegible. *in-* becomes *il-* before *l.*

Il i ad (il′i əd), a long Greek epic poem about the siege of Troy. Homer is supposed to be the author of *The Iliad. n. 10.*

Il i um (il′i əm), ancient Troy. *n.*

ilk (ilk), 1. same. *Old use.* **Of that ilk** means (1) of that same name or place. (2) of that kind or sort. 2. family; class; kind. *Used in common talk. adj., n.*

ill (il), 1. not well; having some disease; as, ill with a fever. 2. sickness; disease. 3. bad; evil; as, to do a person an ill turn. 4. badly; as, work ill done. 5. an evil; a harm. Poverty is an ill. *adj., worse, worst, n., adv. 1.*

I'll (īl), 1. I shall. 2. I will. *2.*

Ill., Illinois.

ill-bred (il′bred′), badly brought up; impolite; rude. *adj.*

il le gal (i lē′gəl), not lawful; against the law. *adj. 9.*

il leg i ble (i lej′i bəl), not plain enough; very hard to read. The ink had faded so that many words were illegible. *adj.*

il le git i mate (il′i jit′i mit), 1. not according to the law or the rules. 2. An illegitimate child is one born of parents who are not married. *adj. 16.*

ill-fa vored (il′fā′vərd), 1. not pleasant to look at; ugly. 2. offensive. *adj.*

il lib er al (i lib′ər əl), 1. not liberal; narrow-minded. 2. mean; stingy. *adj. 16.*

il lic it (i lis′it), not permitted by law; forbidden; improper. *adj. 15.*

il lim it a ble (i lim′it ə bəl), limitless; boundless. *adj. 14.*

Il li nois (il′i noi′ or il′i noiz′), a Middle Western State of the United States. *n. 5.*

il lit er a cy (i lit′ər ə si), inability to read or write. *n. 17.*

il lit er ate (i lit′ər it), 1. unable to read or write. 2. person who is unable to read or write. 3. not cultured. He writes in a very illiterate way. *adj., n. 10.*

ill-man nered (il′man′ərd), having or showing bad manners; impolite; rude. *adj.*

ill-na tured (il′nā′chərd), cross; disagreeable. *adj.*

ill ness (il′nis), sickness; poor health. Scarlet fever is a serious illness. *n. 5.*

il log i cal (i loj′i kəl), 1. not logical. 2. not reasonable. *adj. 17.*

ill-tem pered (il′tem′pərd), having or showing an ill temper; cross. *adj.*

ill-treat (il′trēt′), treat cruelly; treat badly; do harm to. *v. 19.*

ill treatment, bad treatment. *18.*

il lume (i lüm′), illuminate. *v.* [*Used in poetry*] *14.*

il lu mi nate (i lü′mi nāt), 1. light up; make bright. The room was illuminated by four large lamps. 2. throw a strong light on. The big searchlight illuminates a spot a mile away. 3. make clear; explain. Our interesting teacher could illuminate almost any subject we studied. 4. When letters in books are ornamented in gold and colors, they are said to be illuminated. *v. 7.*

il lu mi na tion (i lü′mi nā′shən), 1. lighting; lights. 2. the light supplied. 3. making clear. 4. decoration of letters in books with gold or color. *n. 9.*

il lu mine (i lü′min), light up; make bright. Electric lights illumine our houses. A smile often illumines a homely face. *v. 9.*

ill-use (il′ūz′), treat badly. *v.*

il lu sion (i lü′zhən), 1. an appearance which is not real. That slender snow-covered bush at the gate gave me an illusion of a woman waiting there. 2. a false idea. *n. 7.*

il lu sive (i lü′siv), due to an illusion; unreal; misleading; deceptive. *adj. 16*

il lu so ry (i lü′sə ri), illusive. *adj. 17.*

il lus trate (il′əs trāt or i lus′trāt), 1. make clear or explain by stories, examples, comparisons, etc. The way that a pump works is used to illustrate how the heart sends blood around the body. 2. provide with pictures, diagrams, maps, etc., that explain or decorate. This book is well illustrated. *v. 5.*

il lus tra tion (il′əs trā′shən), 1. picture, diagram, map, etc., used to explain or decorate something. 2. story, example, comparison, etc., used to make clear or explain something. The teacher cut an apple into four equal pieces as an illustration of what ¼ means. 3. act or process of illustrating. Illustration is used in teaching children. *n. 6.*

il lus tra tive (i lus′trə tiv), illustrating; used to illustrate; helping to explain. A good teacher uses many illustrative examples. *adj. 13.*

il lus tra tor (il′əs trā′tər), 1. artist who makes pictures for books. 2. person who illustrates. *n.*

il lus tri ous (i lus′tri əs), very famous. Washington and Lincoln are illustrious Americans. *adj. 5.*

ill will, unfriendly feeling.

I'm (īm), I am. *2.*

im-, prefix meaning:—not; the opposite of; the absence of; as in immoral, impatient. *in-* becomes *im-* before *b, m,* and *p.*

im age (im′ij), 1. a likeness or representation. You see your image in the mirror. She is almost the exact image of her mother. I can shut my eyes and see images of things and persons. 2. a likeness made of stone, wood, or some other material; statue. The shelf was full of little images of all sorts of animals. 3. make an image of. 4. reflect as a mirror does. The clouds were imaged in the still waters of the lake. 5. imagine; picture in one's mind. He could image what each one was doing at home. 6. a comparison used to add force or beauty. Some poems contain many images. *n., v. 3.*

im age ry (im′ij ri), 1. images; statues. 2. pictures formed by the mind. 3. descriptions and figures of speech that help the mind to form pictures. Poetry contains imagery. *n., pl. imageries. 11.*

i mag i na ble (i maj′i nə bəl), that can be imagined. Cinderella was dressed with the greatest splendor imaginable. *adj. 11.*

i mag i nar y (i maj′i nãr′i), existing only in the imagination; not real. Fairies are imaginary. The equator is an imaginary line. *adj. 7.*

i mag i na tion (i maj′i nā′shən), 1. imagining; the power of forming pictures in the mind of things not present to the senses. The child's imagination filled the woods with strange animals and fairies. 2. ability to create new things or ideas or to combine old ones in new forms. Poets, artists, and inventors need imagination. 3. a creation of the mind; a fancy. *n. 3.*

i mag i na tive (i maj′i nā′tiv), 1. able to imagine well. The imaginative child made up fairy stories. 2. of imagination. 3. showing imagination. *adj. 9.*

i mag ine (i maj′in), form a picture of in the mind; have an idea. Charles likes to imagine himself a knight. We can hardly imagine life without gas and electricity. *v. 2.*

im be cile (im′bi sil), 1. weak in mind; very stupid. 2. person who has a very weak mind. An imbecile is almost an idiot. *adj., n. 13.*

im be cil i ty (im′bi sil′i ti), 1. feebleness of mind; mental weakness. 2. very great stupidity. 3. very stupid or foolish action, remark, etc. *n., pl. imbecilities. 15.*

im bed (im bed′), 1. put in a bed. He imbedded the bulbs in a box of sand. 2. fix or enclose in a surrounding mass. Precious stones are found imbedded in rock. *v., imbedded, imbedding. 15.* Also spelled **embed.**

im bibe (im bīb′), 1. drink; drink in. 2. absorb. The roots of a plant imbibe moisture from the earth. 3. take into one's mind. Children often imbibe superstitions that last through life. *v. 10.*

im bro glio (im brōl′yō), 1. a complicated or difficult situation. 2. a complicated misunderstanding or disagreement. *n., pl. imbroglios. 19.*

im bue (im bū′), 1. fill; inspire. He imbued his son's mind with an ambition to succeed. 2. fill with moisture or color; as, garments imbued with red. *v. 14.*

im i tate (im′i tāt), 1. try to be like; follow the example of. The boy imitates his older brother. 2. make or do something like; copy. The parrot imitates the sounds he hears. 3. act like. John amused the class by imitating a baby, an old man, and a bear. 4. be like; look like. Wood is sometimes painted to imitate stone. *v. 4.*

im i ta tion (im′i tā′shən), 1. imitating. We learn many things by imitation. 2. copy. Give as good an imitation as you can of a rooster crowing. 3. not real. You can buy imitation pearls in the ten-cent stores. *n., adj. 8.*

im i ta tive (im′i tā′tiv), imitating; copying. Monkeys are imitative. *Whiz* and *bang* are imitative words. *adj. 11.*

im i ta tor (im′i tā′tər), one who imitates. *n. 15.*

im mac u late (i mak′ū lit), 1. without a spot or stain. 2. pure; without sin. *adj. 9.*

Im man u el (i man′ū əl), Christ. *n. 16.* Also spelled **Emmanuel.**

im ma te ri al (im′ə tēr′i əl), 1. not important. 2. not material; spiritual. *adj. 12.*

im ma ture (im′ə tūr′ or im′ə tür′), not mature; not ripe; not full-grown. *adj. 11.*

im meas ur a ble (i mezh′ər ə bəl), 1. that cannot be measured. 2. very great; as, immeasurable faith. *adj. 9.*

im meas ur a bly (i mezh′ər ə bli), to an extent too great to be measured. *adv.*

im me di ate (i mē′di it), 1. coming at once; without delay. 2. nearest; with nothing between. My immediate neighbor is Mrs. Jones. 3. near. *adj. 2.*

im me di ate ly (i mē′di it li), 1. at once; without delay. I answered his letter immediately. 2. next; with nothing between. *adv.*

im me mo ri al (im′i mō′ri əl), extending back beyond the bounds of memory; very, very old. *adj. 9.*

im mense (i mens′), very, very large; huge; vast. *adj. 3.*

im mense ly (i mens′li), very greatly. *adv.*

im men si ty (i men′si ti), vastness; boundless or vast extent; as, the ocean's immensity. *n., pl. immensities. 12.*

im merse (i mėrs′), 1. plunge into (a liquid). 2. baptize by dipping (a person) under water. 3. absorb; involve deeply; as, immersed in thought, immersed in debts. *v. 10.*

im mer sion (i mėr′shən or i mėr′zhən), 1. immersing. 2. baptism by dipping a person under water. 3. absorption. *n. 15.*

im mi grant (im′i grənt), person who comes into a country or region to live. Canada has many immigrants from Europe. California has many immigrants from other States. *n. 7.*

im mi grate (im′i grāt), come into a country or region to live there. *v.*

im mi gra tion (im′i grā′shən), 1. coming into a country or region to live. There was immigration to America from all the countries of Europe. 2. the persons who immigrate. The immigration of 1910 included many Italians. *n. 11.*

im mi nence (im′i nəns), being imminent; hanging over; nearness. Dark clouds and thunder showed the imminence of a storm. *n. 18.*

im mi nent (im′i nənt), likely to happen soon; about to occur. Black clouds, thunder, and lightning show that a storm is imminent. *adj. 8.*

im mod er ate (i mod′ər it), too much; going too far; extreme; more than is proper. *adj. 15.*

im mod est (i mod′ist), 1. not modest. 2. indecent; improper. *adj. 18.*

im mod es ty (i mod′is ti), 1. lack of modesty. 2. lack of decency; improper behavior. *n.*

im mo la tion (im′ō lā′shən), sacrifice. *n. 20.*

im mor al (i mor′əl), 1. morally wrong; wicked. Lying and stealing are immoral. 2. lewd; unchaste. *adj. 20.*

im mo ral i ty (im′ə ral′i ti), wickedness; wrongdoing; vice. *n., pl. immoralities. 18.*

im mor tal (i môr′təl), 1. living forever; never dying; everlasting. A man's body dies, but his soul may be immortal. The fame of Homer should be immortal. 2. an immortal being. The **immortals** often means the gods, especially the gods of ancient Greece and Rome. 3. person remembered or famous forever. Shakespeare is one of the immortals. *adj., n. 3.*

im mor tal i ty (im′ôr tal′i ti), 1. endless life; living forever. 2. fame that lasts forever. *n. 6.*

im mor tal ize (i môr′təl īz), 1. make immortal. 2. give everlasting fame to. Great authors are immortalized by their works. *v. 12.*

im mov a ble (i müv′ə bəl), that cannot be moved; fixed; firm; steadfast; as, immovable mountains, an immovable purpose. *adj. 9.*

im mune (i mūn′), exempt; not susceptible; resistant; having immunity; protected by inoculation. *adj. 16.*

im mu ni ty (i mū′ni ti), 1. resistance to disease, poison, etc. One attack of measles usually gives a person immunity to that disease for a number of years. 2. freedom. The law gives immunity from taxation to schools and churches. *n., pl. immunities. 10.*

im mu nize (im′ū nīz), give immunity to. Vaccination immunizes people against smallpox. *v.*

im mure (i mūr′), shut up within walls; put in prison; confine. *v. 13.*

im mu ta ble (i mū′tə bəl), never changing; unchangeable. *adj. 12.*

imp (imp), 1. a child of the devil; little devil. 2. mischievous child. *n. 11.*

Imp

im pact (im′pakt), striking of one thing against another. The impact of the two swords broke both of them. *n. 13.*

im pair (im pãr′), make worse; damage; harm; weaken. Poor food impaired his health. *v. 7.*

im pale (im pāl′), 1. pierce through with a stake; pierce with anything. The butterflies are impaled on small pins stuck in a sheet of cork. 2. torture or punish by thrusting upon a pointed stake. *v. 14.*

im pal pa ble (im pal′pə bəl), 1. that cannot be perceived by the sense of touch. Sunbeams are impalpable. A thread of a spider's web is so thin as to be almost impalpable. 2. that cannot be grasped by the mind; as, impalpable distinctions. *adj. 19.*

im pan el (im pan′əl), 1. put on a list for duty on a jury. 2. select (a jury) from the list. *v., impaneled, impaneling.*

im part (im pärt′), give a share in; give; communicate; tell. A teacher imparts knowledge to her pupils. I will impart a secret to you. *v. 4.*

im par tial (im pär′shəl), fair; just; showing no more favor to one side than to the other. *adj. 7.*

im par ti al i ty (im′pär shi al′i ti), fairness; justice. *n. 15.*

im pass a ble (im pas′ə bəl), not passable; so that one cannot go through. The muddy road was impassable. *adj. 16.*

im pas si ble (im pas′i bəl), incapable of suffering; without feeling. *adj. 15.*

im pas sioned (im pash′ənd), emotional; full of strong feeling; ardent. The general gave an impassioned speech to his soldiers. *adj. 9.*

im pas sive (im pas′iv), 1. without feeling or emotion; unmoved. He listened with an impassive face. 2. not feeling pain or injury; insensible. The soldier lay as impassive as if he were dead. *adj. 15.*

im pa tience (im pā′shəns), 1. lack of patience; being impatient. 2. uneasiness and eagerness. *n. 8.*

im pa tient (im pā′shənt), 1. not patient; not willing to bear delay, pain, bother, etc. Jim is impatient with his little sister. 2. restless. The horses were impatient to start in the race. 3. showing lack of patience; as, an impatient answer. *adj. 5.*

im peach (im pēch′), 1. call in question; as, to impeach a person's honor or accuracy. 2. accuse; charge with wrongdoing. 3. accuse (a public officer) of wrong conduct during office before a competent tribunal. A judge may be impeached for taking a bribe. *v. 8.*

im peach ment (im pēch′mənt), impeaching; being impeached. The most famous impeachment in the United States was that of President Andrew Johnson. He was not found guilty. *n. 11.*

im pec ca ble (im pek′ə bəl), faultless. *adj.*

im pe cu ni ous (im′pi kū′ni əs), having no money; poor. *adj.*

im pede (im pēd′), hinder; obstruct. *v. 9.*

im ped i ment (im ped′i mənt), 1. hindrance; obstacle. 2. defect in speech. *n. 7.*

im pel (im pel′), 1. drive; force; cause. Hunger impelled me to eat. 2. push forward; drive on. A strong tide impels the boat toward the island. *v., impelled, impelling. 7.*

im pend (im pend′), 1. be ready to happen; be near. Black clouds are signs that a storm impends. 2. hang over. Above him were impending cliffs. *v. 8.*

im pen e tra ble (im pen′i trə bəl), 1. that cannot be entered, pierced, or passed. The thorny branches made a thick, impenetrable hedge. A thick sheet of steel is impenetrable by an ordinary bullet. 2. that cannot be seen into or understood. *adj. 12.*

im pen i tent (im pen′i tənt), not penitent; not repenting; not sorry for wrongdoing. *adj. 16.*

im per a tive (im per′ə tiv), 1. urgent; not to be avoided; necessary. It is imperative that a very sick child should stay in bed. 2. command. The great imperative is "Love thy neighbor as thyself." 3. expressing a command. "Go!" and "Stop, look, listen!" are in the imperative mood. 4. a form of a verb expressing a command. *adj., n. 7.*

im per cep ti ble (im′pər sep′ti bəl), that cannot be perceived or felt; very slight. *adj. 10.*

im per fect (im pėr′fikt), 1. not perfect; having some defect or fault. A crack in the cup made it imperfect. 2. not complete. *adj. 5.*

im per fec tion (im′pər fek′shən), 1. lack of perfection; imperfect condition or character. 2. fault; defect. *n. 11.*

im pe ri al (im pēr′i əl), 1. of or pertaining to an empire or its ruler. 2. having the rank of an emperor. 3. supreme; majestic; magnificent. 4. a very small beard left growing beneath the lower lip. *adj., n. 4.*

Man wearing an imperial

im pe ri al ism (im pēr′i əl izm), 1. the policy of extending the rule or authority of a nation over other countries. 2. an imperial system of government. *n. 13.*

im pe ri al ist (im pēr′i əl ist), person who favors imperialism. *n. 16.*

im pe ri al is tic (im pēr′i əl is′tik), 1. of imperialism or imperialists. 2. favoring imperialism. *adj.*

im per il (im per′il), put in danger. *v., imperiled, imperiling. 13.*

im pe ri ous (im pēr′i əs), 1. haughty; arrogant; domineering; overbearing. 2. not to be avoided; urgent; necessary. *adj. 8.*

im per ish a ble (im per′ish ə bəl), everlasting; not perishable; indestructible. *adj. 17.*

im per son al (im pėr′sən əl), 1. referring to all or any persons, not to any special one. "First come, first served" is an impersonal remark. 2. having no existence as a person. Electricity is an impersonal force. 3. An impersonal verb has *it* as its subject and does not refer to some special thing. *Example:* It seems likely that it will rain. *adj. 11.*

im per son al ly (im pėr′sən əl i), in an impersonal manner; without personal reference or connection. *adv.*

im per son ate (im pėr′sən āt), 1. play a part. Alice impersonated Little Red Ridinghood. 2. represent in personal form; typify; personify. Washington to me impersonates the ideal American. *v. 15.*

im per son a tion (im pėr′sən ā′shən), 1. playing the part of. 2. a representation; a type. *n.*

im per ti nence (im pėr′ti nəns), 1. impertinent quality; impudence; insolence. 2. impertinent act or speech. *n. 13.*

im per ti nent (im pėr′ti nənt), saucy; impudent; insolent; rude. *adj. 10.*

im per turb a ble (im′pər tėr′bə bəl), not easily excited; calm. *adj. 17.*

im per vi ous (im pėr′vi əs), 1. not letting a thing pass through; not allowing passage. Rubber cloth is impervious to moisture. 2. not open to argument, suggestions, etc. She is impervious to all the gossip about her. *adj. 9.*

im pet u os i ty (im pech′ü os′i ti), sudden or rash energy; violence; ardor. The impetuosity of the flood swept all before it. The impetuosity of the speaker stirred the audience. *n., pl. impetuosities. 15.*

im pet u ous (im pech′ü əs), 1. moving with great force; as, the impetuous rush of water over Niagara Falls. 2. acting hastily, rashly, or with sudden feeling. Boys are more impetuous than old men. *adj. 8.*

im pe tus (im′pi təs), 1. the force with which an object moves. Anything that you can stop easily has little impetus. 2. driving force. Ambition is an impetus to work. *n. 11.*

im pi e ty (im pī′ə ti), 1. lack of reverence for God; wickedness. 2. lack of dutifulness or respect. 3. impious act. *n., pl. impieties. 10.*

im pinge (im pinj′), 1. hit; strike. Rays of light impinge on the eye. 2. encroach; infringe. *v. 20.*

im pi ous (im′pi əs), not pious; not having reverence for God; wicked. *adj. 6.*

imp ish (imp′ish), 1. of an imp; like an imp. 2. mischievous. *adj.*

im pla ca ble (im plā′kə bəl), that cannot be placated, soothed, or appeased; unyielding. *adj. 10.*

im plant (im plant′), 1. plant. 2. insert. 3. instill; fix deeply. A good teacher implants high ideals in children. *v. 17.*

im ple ment (im′pli mənt for 1, im′pli ment for 2 and 3), 1. useful article of equipment; tool; instrument; utensil. 2. provide with implements or other means. Do not undertake a project unless you can implement it. 3. carry out; get done. *n., v. 5.*

im pli cate (im′pli kāt), 1. show to have a part or to be connected; involve. The thief's confession implicated two other men. 2. imply. *v. 15.*

im pli ca tion (im′pli kā′shən), 1. an implying or being implied. 2. something implied; indirect suggestion; hint. There was no implication of dishonesty in his failure in business. 3. an implicating or being implicated. *n. 14.*

im plic it (im plis′it), 1. implied but not plainly expressed. He gave us implicit consent to take the apples, for he smiled when he saw us do it. 2. absolute; without doubting, hesitating, or asking questions. A soldier must give implicit obedience to his officers. *adj. 14.*

im plic it ly (im plis′it li), 1. unquestioningly. 2. by implication. *adv.*

im plore (im plōr′), 1. beg earnestly for. The prisoner implored pardon. 2. beg (a person) to do something. He implored the judge to spare his life. *v. 5.*

im ply (im plī′), mean (a thing) without saying it outright; express indirectly. Silence often implies consent. The teacher's smile implied that she had forgiven us. *v., implied, implying. 8.*

im po lite (im′pə līt′), not polite; having or showing bad manners; rude. *adj.*

im pol i tic (im pol′i tik), not politic; not expedient; not judicious; unwise. It is impolitic to offend people who can help you. *adj. 15.*

im port (im pōrt′ for 1 and 3, im′pōrt for 2, 4, and 5), 1. bring in from a foreign country. The United States imports sugar from Cuba. 2. an article brought into a country. Rubber is a useful import. 3. mean; make known. What does this message import? 4. meaning. 5. importance. *v., n. 3.*

im por tance (im pôr′təns), being important; consequence; value. Anybody can see the importance of good health. *n. 3.*

im por tant (im pôr′tənt), 1. meaning much; having value or influence; as, important business, an important occasion. 2. acting as if important; seeming to have influence. An important little man rushed around giving orders. *adj. 1.*

im por ta tion (im′pōr tā′shən), 1. bringing in merchandise from foreign countries. 2. something brought in. Her shawl is a recent importation from Mexico. *n. 10.*

im port er (im pōr′tər), a merchant or company that imports goods from foreign countries. *n. 12.*

im por tu nate (im pôr′chù nit), asking repeatedly; urgent; persistent. *adj. 14.*

im por tune (im′pôr tūn′ or im′pôr tün′), ask urgently or repeatedly; trouble with demands. The boy importuned the teacher to raise his mark. *v. 14.*

im por tu ni ty (im′pôr tū′ni ti or im′pôr tü′ni ti), urgent or repeated asking; demanding again and again. *n., pl. importunities. 12.*

im pose (im pōz′), 1. put (a burden, tax, or punishment) on. The judge imposed a fine of $500 on the guilty man. Do not let the children impose on you. 2. **Impose on** or **upon** sometimes means (1) take advantage of. (2) deceive. *v. 4.*

im pos ing (im pōz′ing), impressive because of size, appearance, dignity, etc. The Capitol at Washington, D. C., is an imposing building. *adj.*

im po si tion (im′pə zish′ən), 1. putting a burden, tax, or punishment on. 2. a burden, tax, or punishment. Would it be an imposition to ask you to mail this parcel? 3. deceit; fraud; trick. *n. 10.*

im pos si bil i ty (im pos′i bil′i ti), 1. being impossible. 2. something impossible. *n., pl. impossibilities. 11.*

im pos si ble (im pos′i bəl), 1. that cannot be or happen. 2. not possible to use; not to be done; not possible to endure. *adj. 2.*

im post (im′pōst), tax. There are imposts

on wool and woolen cloth imported from other countries. *n. 17.*

im pos tor (im pos′tər), 1. person who assumes a false name or character. 2. deceiver; cheat. *n. 9.*

im pos ture (im pos′chər), deception; fraud. *n. 16.*

im po tence (im′pə təns), lack of power; helplessness. *n. 12.*

im po tent (im′pə tənt), not having power; helpless. Without guns and ammunition the soldiers were impotent. The cripple fell back in an impotent rage. *adj. 9.*

im pound (im pound′), 1. shut up in a pen or pound. The town impounds stray animals. 2. shut up; enclose; confine. A dam impounds water. 3. put in the custody of a law court. *v.*

im pov er ish (im pov′ər ish), 1. make very poor. 2. exhaust the strength or richness of; as, to impoverish the soil, the blood, or the mind. *v. 10.*

im prac ti ca ble (im prak′ti kə bəl), not working well in practice; that cannot be used. *adj. 9.*

im prac ti cal (im prak′ti kəl), not practical; not useful. *adj.*

im pre ca tion (im′pri kā′shən), 1. act of calling down evil on a person; cursing. 2. a curse. The beggar shouted imprecations after the traveler. *n. 15.*

im preg na ble (im preg′nə bəl), not to be taken by force; able to resist attack; as, an impregnable fortress, an impregnable argument. *adj. 12.*

im preg nate (im preg′nāt), 1. make pregnant; fertilize. 2. fill (with). Sea water is impregnated with salt. *v. 13.*

im preg na tion (im′preg nā′shən), 1. impregnating. 2. being impregnated. *n. 17.*

im pre sa ri o (im′pre sä′ri ō), the organizer or manager of an opera or concert company. *n., pl. impressarios. 19.*

im press[1] (im pres′ for 1, 2, 4, and 5, im′pres for 3 and 6), 1. make marks on by pressing or stamping. We can impress wax with a seal. 2. to imprint; to stamp. 3. impression; mark; a stamp. An author leaves the impress of his personality on what he writes. 4. have a strong effect on the mind or feelings of. A hero impresses us with his courage. 5. fix in the mind. She repeated the words to impress them in her memory. 6. act of impressing. *v., n. 5.*

im press[2] (im pres′), seize by force for public use. The police impressed Mr. Smith's automobile in order to pursue the robbers. *v.*

im pres sion (im presh′ən), 1. effect produced on a person. Punishment seemed to make little impression on the child. 2. idea; notion. I have a vague impression that I left the house unlocked. 3. something made by pressure, such as a mark, stamp, or print. The thief had left an impression of his foot in the garden. 4. impressing; being impressed. *n. 4.*

im pres sion a ble (im presh′ən ə bəl), sensitive to impressions; easily impressed or influenced. Children are more impressionable than grown-ups. *adj.*

im pres sive (im pres′iv), able to impress the mind, feelings, conscience, etc.; as, an impressive sermon, an impressive storm, an impressive ceremony. *adj. 8.*

im print (im′print for 1, 2, and 3, im print′ for 4 and 5), 1. mark made by pressure; print; as, the imprint of a foot in the sand. 2. impression; mark; as, the imprint of suffering on her face. 3. the printer's or publisher's name with the place, date, etc., on the title page or at the end of a book. 4. to stamp; as, to imprint a postmark on a letter, to imprint a letter with a postmark. 5. press or impress; as, to imprint a kiss on someone's cheek, a scene imprinted on my memory. *n., v. 12.*

im pris on (im priz′ən), 1. put in prison; keep in prison. 2. confine closely. *v. 5.*

im pris on ment (im priz′ən mənt), 1. an imprisoning. 2. a being imprisoned. *n. 6.*

im prob a bil i ty (im prob′ə bil′i ti), 1. being improbable. 2. something improbable. *n., pl. improbabilities.*

im prob a ble (im prob′ə bəl), not probable; not likely to happen; not likely to be true. *adj. 12.*

im promp tu (im promp′tū or im promp′tü), 1. without previous thought or preparation; offhand; as, a speech made impromptu. 2. made or done without previous thought or preparation; as, an impromptu speech, party, or costume. 3. something so made or done. *adv., adj., n. 13.*

im prop er (im prop′ər), 1. wrong; not correct. "We ain't" is an improper usage. 2. not suitable. A bright dress is improper for a funeral. 3. not decent. 4. An **improper fraction** is a fraction greater than 1.

$\frac{3}{2}$, $\frac{5}{3}$, $\frac{7}{4}$, $\frac{21}{12}$, and $\frac{8}{5}$ are improper fractions. *adj. 8.*

im pro pri e ty (im′prə prī′ə ti), 1. being improper. 2. an improper act, expression, etc. *n., pl. improprieties. 15.*

im prove (im prüv′), 1. make better. You could improve your handwriting if you tried. 2. become better; as, to improve in health. 3. use well. We had two hours to wait and improved the time by seeing the city. *v. 2.*

im prove ment (im prüv′mənt), 1. making better; becoming better. Will's schoolwork shows much improvement since last term. 2. anything that adds value. The improvements in his house cost over a thousand dollars. 3. better condition; a gain; advance. Automobiles are an improvement over horses. *n. 4.*

im prov i dence (im prov′i dəns), lack of foresight; lack of thrift. *n. 19.*

im prov i dent (im prov′i dənt), not looking ahead; not thrifty. *adj. 16.*

im pro vi sa tion (im′prə vī zā′shən), 1. an improvising. 2. something improvised. *n.*

im pro vise (im′prə vīz), 1. compose or utter (verse, music, etc.) without preparation. John improvised a new verse for the school song at the football game. 2. prepare or provide offhand; extemporize. A packing box served the boys as an improvised boat. *v. 13.*

im pru dence (im prü′dəns), lack of prudence; imprudent behavior. *n. 15.*

im pru dent (im prü′dənt), not prudent; rash; not discreet. *adj. 16.*

im pu dence (im′pū dəns), lack of shame or modesty; rude boldness. *n. 12.*

im pu dent (im′pū dənt), without shame or modesty; forward; rudely bold. The impudent boy made faces at the teacher. *adj. 9.*

im pugn (im pūn′), call in question; attack by words or arguments. *v. 15.*

im pulse (im′puls), 1. driving on; thrust; push; as, the impulse of a wave, the impulse of pity, of hunger, of curiosity. 2. a sudden inclination or tendency to act. A mob is influenced more by impulse than by reason. *n. 7.*

im pul sion (im pul′shən), 1. impelling; driving force. The impulsion of hunger drove the man to steal. 2. impulse. *n. 18.*

im pul sive (im pul′siv), 1. pushing; driving onward; impelling. 2. acting upon impulse; easily moved. The impulsive child gave all his money to the beggar. *adj. 14.*

im pu ni ty (im pū′ni ti), freedom from punishment or bad consequences. You cannot pull a tiger's tail with impunity. *n. 7.*

im pure (im pūr′), 1. not pure; dirty. The air in cities is often impure. 2. mixed with foreign matter. The salt we use is slightly impure. 3. bad; corrupt. Avoid impure talk, thoughts, acts, and people. *adj. 11.*

im pu ri ty (im pūr′i ti), 1. lack of purity; being impure. 2. impure thing or element; thing that makes something else impure. Filtering the water removed some of its impurities. *n., pl. impurities. 9.*

im pu ta tion (im′pū tā′shən), 1. imputing. 2. a charge or hint of wrongdoing. No imputation has ever been made against his good name. *n. 14.*

im pute (im pūt′), consider as belonging; attribute; charge (a fault, etc.) to a person; blame. I impute John's failure to his laziness. *v. 6.*

in (in). We live in the country in the summer. You can do this in an hour. He is in business for himself. She is dressed in white. The child was in tears. The party is in honor of Mary's birthday. The board broke in two. Come in. Lock the dog in. Mrs. Smith is in. A sheepskin coat has the woolly side in. In has many special meanings in connection with other words. Most of them are well known. The **ins** means those that are in office. **Ins and outs** means the different parts; the twists and turns. **In with** means (1) friendly with. (2) partners with. *prep., adv., adj., n. 1.*

in-, prefix meaning:—not; the opposite of; the absence of; as in inattention, inconvenient, inexpensive.

in., inch; inches. *6.*

in a bil i ty (in′ə bil′i ti), lack of ability, means, or power. *n. 12.*

in ac ces si ble (in′ak ses′i bəl), 1. that cannot be reached easily. A fort on top of a steep hill is inaccessible. 2. that cannot be reached at all. *adj. 10.*

in ac cu ra cy (in ak′ū rə si), 1. lack of accuracy. 2. mistake. *n., pl. inaccuracies. 20.*

in ac cu rate (in ak′ū rit), not accurate; not exact; containing mistakes. *adj. 16.*

in ac tion (in ak′shən), absence of action; idleness. *n. 15.*

in ac tive (in ak′tiv), not active; idle; sluggish. *adj. 9.*

in ac tiv i ty (in′ak tiv′i ti), absence of action; idleness; sluggishness. *n. 16.*

in ad e qua cy (in ad′i kwə si), being inadequate or insufficient. *n. 20.*

in ad e quate (in ad′i kwit), not adequate; not enough; not so much as is required. *adj. 9.*

in ad mis si ble (in′əd mis′i bəl), 1. not allowable. 2. not to be admitted. *adj. 16.*

in ad vert ence (in′əd vėr′təns), 1. lack of attention; carelessness. 2. an inadvertent act. *n.*

in ad vert ent (in′əd vėr′tənt), 1. not attentive; careless; negligent. 2. not done on purpose. *adj. 15.*

in ad vis a ble (in′əd vīz′ə bəl), not advisable; unwise; not prudent. *adj. 20.*

in al ien a ble (in āl′yən ə bəl), that cannot be given away or taken away. Life, liberty, and the pursuit of happiness have been called the inalienable rights of man. *adj. 16.*

in ane (in ān′), 1. silly. 2. empty. *adj.*

in an i mate (in an′i mit), 1. lifeless; as, inanimate stones. 2. dull; as, an inanimate face. *adj. 9.*

in a ni tion (in′ə nish′ən), 1. emptiness. 2. weakness from lack of food. *n. 20.*

in an i ty (in an′i ti), 1. silliness; lack of sense. 2. a silly act, practice, remark, etc. 3. emptiness. *n., pl. inanities.*

in ap pli ca ble (in ap′li kə bəl), not to be applied; not suitable. The name Tiny is inapplicable to a big dog. *adj. 18.*

in ap pre ci a ble (in′ə prē′shi ə bəl), too small to be noticed or felt; very slight. *adj.*

in ap pro pri ate (in′ə prō′pri it), not appropriate; not suitable; not fitting. *adj. 19.*

in apt (in apt′), 1. not apt; not suitable. 2. unskillful; awkward. *adj.*

in ap ti tude (in ap′ti tūd or in ap′ti tüd), 1. unfitness. 2. lack of skill. *n.*

in ar tic u late (in′är tik′ū lit), 1. not distinct; not like regular speech; as, an inarticulate mutter or groan. 2. dumb; unable to speak. Cats and dogs, though inarticulate, express affection. The stroke rendered the man inarticulate. 3. not jointed. A jellyfish's body is inarticulate. *adj. 14.*

in ar tis tic (in′är tis′tik), not artistic; lacking taste. *adj.*

in as much (in′əz much′). **Inasmuch as** means (1) in so far as. (2) because. Bob was given a start in the race, inasmuch as he was smaller than the others. *adv. 8.*

in at ten tion (in′ə ten′shən), lack of attention; negligence; carelessness. John lost his job through inattention. *n. 16.*

in at ten tive (in′ə ten′tiv), not attentive; negligent; careless. *adj. 18.*

in au di ble (in ô′di bəl), that cannot be heard. *adj. 13.*

in au gu ral (in ô′gū rəl), 1. of or for an inauguration. The President gives an inaugural address or speech when he takes office. 2. the address or speech made by a person when formally admitted to office. *adj., n. 19.*

in au gu rate (in ô′gū rāt), 1. install in office with a ceremony. A President of the United States is inaugurated every four years. 2. make a formal beginning of; begin. The invention of the airplane inaugurated a new era in transportation. 3. begin public use of with a ceremony or celebration. *v. 9.*

in au gu ra tion (in ô′gū rā′shən), 1. act or ceremony of installing a person in office. The inauguration of a President of the United States takes place on January 20. 2. formal beginning; beginning. 3. opening for public use with a ceremony or celebration. *n. 11.*

in aus pi cious (in′ôs pish′əs), unfavorable; unlucky. *adj. 16.*

in born (in′bôrn′), instinctive; born in a person; as, an inborn love of rhythm, inborn talent for art. *adj. 16.*

in bred (in′bred′), 1. inborn; natural. The man, though poor, showed an inbred courtesy. 2. bred for generations from ancestors closely related; as, an inbred strain of horses or cattle. *adj. 20.*

in breed (in′brēd′), breed from closely related animals. *v., inbred, inbreeding.*

inc., incorporated. *17.*

In ca (ing′kə), 1. member of a tribe of Indians who ruled Peru before the Spanish conquered it. 2. the ruler of this tribe. *n.*

in cal cu la ble (in kal′kū lə bəl), 1. beyond counting; too great to be calculated. The sands of the sea are incalculable in number. 2. not to be reckoned beforehand. A flood in that valley would cause incalculable losses. 3. not to be relied on; uncertain; as, a person with an incalculable disposition. *adj. 10.*

in can des cence (in′kən des′əns), red-hot or white-hot condition. *n.*

FILAMENT

Incandescent lamp

in can des cent (in′kən des′ənt), 1. glowing with heat; red-hot or white-hot. The light of an electric lamp comes from an incandescent filament. 2. intensely bright; brilliant. *adj. 15.*

in can ta tion (in′kan tā′shən), 1. set of words spoken as a magic charm. "Double, double, toil and trouble, Fire burn and caldron bubble," is an incantation. 2. use of such words. *n. 13.*

in ca pa ble (in kā′pə bəl), 1. not capable. A foreigner is incapable of becoming President of the United States. 2. not able; having very little ability. An idiot is very incapable. *adj. 8.*

in ca pac i tate (in′kə pas′i tāt), make incapable or unfit. The man's injury incapacitated him for working. *v. 16.*

in ca pac i ty (in′kə pas′i ti), lack of ability, power, or fitness; disability. *n., pl. incapacities. 12.*

in car cer ate (in kär′sər āt), imprison. *v.*

in car cer a tion (in kär′sər ā′shən), imprisonment. *n.*

in car nate (in kär′nit or in kär′nāt for 1, in kär′nāt for 2 and 3), 1. embodied in flesh, especially in human form. The villain was a fiend incarnate. 2. make incarnate; embody. 3. put into an actual form. He incarnated his vision in a beautiful statue. *adj., v. 11.*

in car na tion (in′kär nā′shən), 1. a taking on of human form by a divine being. 2. person or thing that represents some quality or idea. A miser is an incarnation of greed. *n. 13.*

in case (in kās′), 1. put into a case. 2. enclose; cover completely. Armor incased the knight's body. *v.* Also spelled **encase.**

in cau tious (in kô′shəs), not cautious; reckless; rash. *adj. 18.*

in cen di ar y (in sen′di ãr′i), 1. having to do with the setting of property on fire maliciously. 2. person who maliciously sets fire to property. 3. causing fires; used to start a fire. The enemy town was set on fire with incendiary shells and bombs. 4. deliberately stirring up strife or rebellion. A man can be arrested for making incendiary speeches. *adj., n., pl. incendiaries. 16.*

in cense[1] (in′sens), 1. a substance giving off a sweet smell when burned. 2. the perfume or smoke from it. 3. something sweet like incense; as, the incense of flowers, the incense of flattery, the incense of praise, etc. *n. 4.*

in cense[2] (in sens′), make very angry. Cruelty incenses kind people. *v.*

in cen tive (in sen′tiv), 1. motive; stimulus. The fun of playing the game was a greater incentive than the prize. 2. inciting; encouraging. *n., adj. 9.*

in cep tion (in sep′shən), beginning. *n.*

in ces sant (in ses′ənt), never stopping; continual. The roar of Niagara Falls is incessant. The incessant noise of whistles kept me awake all night. *adj. 7.*

in cest (in′sest), marriage or sexual relationship between brother and sister or parent and child. *n. 15.*

inch (inch), 1. a measure of length, $\frac{1}{12}$ of a foot. An inch of rainfall is the amount of water that would cover a surface to the depth of one inch. 2. move by inches or little by little. The worm inched along. 3. Some special meanings are:

by inches, by slow degrees or gradually.

every inch, completely. Elizabeth was every inch a queen.

within an inch of, very near. The man was within an inch of death.

n., v. 1.

in ci dence (in′si dəns), 1. range of occurrence or influence; the way in which (a tax, disease, etc.) falls or distributes itself. In an epidemic the incidence of disease is widespread. The incidence of the income tax was widened in 1941. 2. a falling on. *n. 15.*

in ci dent (in′si dənt), 1. a happening; an event. 2. an unimportant event. 3. liable to happen; belonging. Hardships are incident to the life of an explorer. *n., adj. 5.*

in ci den tal (in′si den′təl), 1. happening or likely to happen in connection with something else. Certain discomforts are incidental to camping out. 2. occurring by chance. 3. something incidental. On our trip we spent $52 for meals, room, and railroad fare, and $1.50 for incidentals, such as candy, magazines, and stamps. *adj., n. 9.*

in ci den tal ly (in′si den′təl i), as an incident along with something else; accidentally. *adv.*

in cin er ate (in sin′ər āt), burn to ashes. *v.*

in cin er a tion (in sin′ər ā′shən), a burning or being burned to ashes. *n.*

in cin er a tor (in sin′ər ā′tər), a furnace or other arrangement for burning things. *n.*

in cip i ent (in sip′i ənt), just beginning; in an early stage. *adj. 16.*

in cise (in sīz′), 1. cut into. 2. engrave. *v.*

in ci sion (in sizh′ən), 1. a cut made in something; gash. The doctor made an incision to take out the splinter in my hand. 2. act of incising. *n. 14.*

in ci sive (in sī′siv), cutting; sharp; penetrating; as, an incisive criticism. *adj. 20.*

in ci sor (in sī′zər), a tooth adapted for cutting; one of the front teeth. We have eight incisors in all. *n. 14.*

in cite (in sīt′), urge on; stir up; rouse. Their captain's example incited the men to bravery. *v. 10.*

Incisor

in cite ment (in sīt′mənt), 1. thing that urges, stirs up, or rouses. Interest is an incitement to study. 2. act of urging on, stirring up, or rousing. *n. 16.*

in ci vil i ty (in′si vil′i ti), 1. rudeness; lack of courtesy; impoliteness. 2. rude or impolite act. *n., pl. incivilities. 19.*

in clem en cy (in klem′ən si), severity; harshness. The inclemency of the weather kept us from school. *n., pl. inclemencies. 16.*

in clem ent (in klem′ənt), 1. rough; stormy. 2. severe; harsh; as, an inclement ruler. *adj. 16.*

in cli na tion (in′kli nā′shən), 1. tendency. 2. preference; liking. Most boys have a strong inclination for sports. 3. a leaning; a bending; a bowing. A nod is an inclination of the head. 4. slope; slant; as, the inclination of a roof. *n. 7.*

in cline (in klīn′ for 1, 2, 3, and 5, in′klīn or in klīn′ for 4), 1. be favorable; be willing; tend. Dogs incline to eat meat as a food. 2. make favorable; make willing; influence. Incline your hearts to obey God's laws. 3. slope; slant. 4. sloping surface. The side of a hill is an incline. 5. lean; bend; bow. *v., n. 3.*

Man pushing a wheelbarrow up an inclined plank

in clined (in klīnd′), 1. favorable; willing; tending. 2. sloping; slanting. *adj.*

in close (in klōz′), 1. shut in on all sides; surround. 2. put a wall or fence around. 3. put in an envelope along with a letter. 4. contain; as, a letter inclosing a check. *v. 4.* Also spelled **enclose.**

in clo sure (in klō′zhər), 1. act of enclosing. 2. state of being enclosed. 3. an enclosed place. A pen is an inclosure for animals. 4. thing that encloses. A wall or fence is an inclosure. 5. thing enclosed. The envelope contained a letter and $5 as an inclosure. *n.* Also spelled **enclosure.**

in clude (in klüd′), hold or enclose within limits; contain. The price includes both house and furniture. Their farm includes 160 acres. *v. 2.*

in clu sion (in klü′zhən), 1. including; being included. 2. the thing included. *n. 20.*

in clu sive (in klü′siv), including. "Read pages 10 to 20 inclusive" means begin with page 10 and read through page 20. *adj. 12.*

in cog ni to (in kog′ni tō), 1. unknown; with one's name, character, rank, etc., concealed. The prince traveled incognito to avoid crowds and ceremonies. 2. disguised state or condition. *adj., adv., n., pl. incognitos. 19.*

in co her ence (in′kō hēr′əns), 1. failure to stick together; looseness. 2. lack of logical connection. 3. disconnected thought or speech; as, the incoherence of a madman. *n.*

in co her ent (in′kō hēr′ənt), 1. not sticking together. 2. disconnected; confused. *adj. 17.*

in com bus ti ble (in′kəm bus′ti bəl), not capable of being burned; fireproof. *adj. 20.*

in come (in′kum), what comes in from property, business, labor, etc.; money that comes in; receipts; returns. The grocer's store brings in an income of $5000. The **income tax** is a government tax on a person's income above a certain amount. *n., adj. 5.*

in com ing (in′kum′ing), 1. coming in. The incoming tenant will pay a higher rent. 2. a coming in; as, the incoming of the tide. *adj., n.*

in com men su rate (in′kə men′shu̇ rit), 1. not in proportion; not adequate; as, strength incommensurate to a task. 2. having no common measure; that cannot be compared. *adj.*

in com mode (in′kə mōd′), inconvenience; trouble. Will it incommode you if we open the window? *v.*

in com mu ni ca ble (in′kə mū′ni kə bəl), not capable of being communicated or told. *adj. 17.*

in com pa ra ble (in kom′pə rə bəl), 1. without equal; matchless. Helen of Troy had incomparable beauty. 2. not comparable; not to be compared. *adj. 10.*

in com pat i ble (in′kəm pat′i bəl), 1. not able to live or act together peaceably; opposed in character. Cats and dogs are often incompatible. 2. inconsistent. Late hours are incompatible with health. *adj. 15.*

in com pe tence (in kom′pi təns), lack of ability, power, or fitness. The workman was discharged for incompetence. *n. 19.*

in com pe tent (in kom′pi tənt), 1. not competent; without ability or qualifications. 2. person who is without ability. 3. not legally qualified. *adj., n. 14.*

in com plete (in′kəm plēt′), not complete; lacking some part; unfinished. *adj. 10.*

in com pre hen si ble (in′kom pri hen′si bəl), impossible to understand. *adj. 12.*

in com press i ble (in′kəm pres′i bəl), not capable of being squeezed into a smaller size. *adj. 14.*

in con ceiv a ble (in′kən sēv′ə bəl), impossible to imagine; unthinkable. A circle without a center is inconceivable. *adj. 16.*

in con clu sive (in′kən klü′siv), not decisive; not effective. The jury found the evidence against the prisoner inconclusive and acquitted him. *adj.*

in con gru i ty (in′kən grü′i ti), incongruous thing, quality, or condition. *n., pl. incongruities. 15.*

in con gru ous (in kong′grü əs), 1. out of keeping; not appropriate; out of place. 2. lacking in agreement or harmony; not consistent. *adj. 14.*

in con se quent (in kon′si kwent), not logical; not to the point; off the subject; as, an inconsequent argument, an inconsequent remark. *adj.*

in con se quen tial (in kon′si kwen′shəl), 1. unimportant. 2. inconsequent. *adj.*

in con sid er a ble (in′kən sid′ər ə bəl), not worth consideration; not important; insignificant. *adj. 15.*

in con sid er ate (in′kən sid′ər it), not thoughtful of others; thoughtless. *adj. 15.*

in con sist en cy (in′kən sis′tən si), 1. lack of agreement or harmony. 2. failure to keep to the same principles, course of action, etc. 3. thing, act, etc., that is inconsistent. *n., pl. inconsistencies. 12.*

in con sist ent (in′kən sis′tənt), not consistent; not in agreement with itself or with something else. The policeman's failure to arrest the thief was inconsistent with his duty. *adj. 9.*

in con sol a ble (in′kən sōl′ə bəl), not to be comforted; broken-hearted. The child was inconsolable at the loss of her kitten. *adj. 18.*

in con spic u ous (in′kən spik′ū əs), not conspicuous; attracting little or no attention. *adj. 14.*

in con stan cy (in kon′stən si), lack of constancy; changeableness; fickleness. *n. 15.*

in con stant (in kon′stənt), not constant; changeable; fickle. *adj. 11.*

in con test a ble (in′kən tes′tə bəl), not to be disputed; unquestionable. *adj.*

in con ti nence (in kon′ti nəns), lack of self-restraint. *n. 15.*

in con tro vert i ble (in′kon trə vėr′ti bəl), that cannot be disputed; unquestionable. *adj. 19.*

in con ven ience (in′kən vēn′yəns), 1. trouble; bother; lack of convenience or ease. 2. cause of trouble, difficulty, or bother. 3. to cause trouble, difficulty, or bother to. Will it inconvenience you to carry this package to your mother? *n., v. 6.*

in con ven ient (in′kən vēn′yənt), not convenient; troublesome; causing bother, difficulty, or discomfort. *adj. 9.*

in cor po rate (in kôr′pə rāt for 1, 2, and 3, in kôr′pə rit for 4), 1. make (something) a part of something else; join or unite (something) with something else. We will incorporate your suggestion in this new plan. 2. form into a corporation. When Mr. Smith's business became large, he incorporated it. 3. become a corporation. 4. united; combined; incorporated. *v., adj. 8.*

in cor po ra tion (in kôr′pə rā′shən), 1. an incorporating. The incorporation of air bubbles in the glass spoiled it. 2. a being incorporated. Incorporation gives a company the power to act as one person. *n. 16.*

in cor po re al (in′kôr pō′ri əl), spiritual; not made of any material substance. *adj.*

in cor rect (in′kə rekt′), 1. not correct; wrong; faulty. 2. not proper. *adj. 9.*

in cor ri gi ble (in kor′i ji bəl), 1. so firmly fixed (in bad ways, a bad habit, etc.,) that nothing else can be expected; as, an incorrigible liar. 2. so fixed that it cannot be changed or cured; as, an incorrigible habit of wrinkling one's nose. 3. an incorrigible person. *adj., n. 14.*

in cor rupt i ble (in′kə rup′ti bəl), 1. honest; not to be corrupted. The incorruptible man could not be bribed. 2. not capable of decay. Diamonds are incorruptible. *adj. 19.*

in crease (in krēs′ for 1, 2, and 3, in′krēs for 4 and 5), 1. make greater, more numerous, richer, more powerful, etc. The driver increased the speed of the car. 2. become greater; grow in numbers. His weight has increased ten pounds. These flowers will increase every year. 3. gain in size, numbers, etc.; growth. 4. addition; the amount added; the result of increasing. 5. **On the increase** means increasing. *v., n. 1.*

in creas ing ly (in krēs′ing li), more and more; to a greater degree. *adv. 19.*

in cred i ble (in kred′i bəl), beyond belief; seeming too extraordinary to be possible. The hero fought with incredible bravery. Old superstitions seem incredible to educated people. *adj. 7.*

in cred i bly (in kred′i bli), beyond belief; so as to be incredible; as, an incredibly swift flight. *adv.*

in cre du li ty (in′kri dū′li ti or in′kri dü′li ti), lack of belief; doubt. *n. 12.*

in cred u lous (in krej′ů ləs), 1. not ready to believe. People nowadays are incredulous about ghosts and witches. 2. showing a lack of belief. *adj. 9.*

in cre ment (in′kri mənt), 1. increase; growth. 2. the amount by which something increases. The wages are $20 a week with an increment of $2 for each year of service. *n. 17.*

in crim i nate (in krim′i nāt), accuse of a crime; show to be guilty. In his confession the thief incriminated two others who helped him steal. *v.*

in crust (in krust′), 1. cover with a crust or hard coating. The inside of the kettle is incrusted with lime. 2. form a crust; form into a crust. Overnight the snow had incrusted so that next morning it would bear our weight. 3. decorate (a surface) with a layer of costly material. The gold crown was incrusted with precious gems. *v.* Also spelled **encrust.**

in cu bate (in′kū bāt), 1. sit on (eggs) to hatch them. 2. hatch (eggs) by artificial heat. 3. brood. *v.*

in cu ba tion (in′kū bā′shən), hatching of eggs, of a plot, etc. *n.*

in cu ba tor (in′kū bā′tər), 1. an apparatus for hatching eggs artificially. An incubator consists of a box or chamber that can be kept at a certain temperature. 2. any similar apparatus. Very small babies are sometimes kept for a time in incubators. *n. 11.*

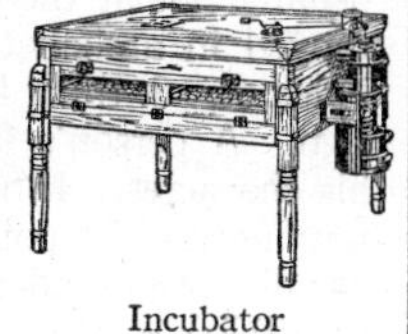
Incubator

in cu bus (in′kū bəs), 1. nightmare. 2. something that oppresses a person like a nightmare. This debt will be an incubus until I have paid it all. *n. 16.*

in cul cate (in kul′kāt), impress by repetition; teach persistently. Week after week she inculcated good manners in her pupils. *v. 14.*

in cum bent (in kum′bənt), 1. lying, leaning, or pressing on something. 2. resting (on a person) as a duty. She felt it incumbent on her to answer the letter at once. 3. the holder of an office, especially a clergyman. The former incumbent had been much liked in the parish. *adj., n. 14.*

in cum ber (in kum′bər), 1. burden with weight, difficulties, cares, debt, etc. Mother is incumbered with household cares. Do not incumber your farm with a mortgage. 2. fill; block up. His yard was incumbered with old boxes and other rubbish. *v.* Also spelled **encumber.**

in cum brance (in kum′brəns), burden; something useless or in the way; annoyance; trouble. *n. 16.* Also spelled **encumbrance.**

in cur (in kėr′), run or fall into (something unpleasant); bring (blame, punishment, etc.) on oneself. The hunter incurred great danger in killing the tiger. *v., incurred, incurring. 5.*

in cur a ble (in kūr′ə bəl), 1. not capable of being cured; that cannot be cured; as, an incurable invalid, an incurable disease. 2. person suffering from an incurable disease. That building is a home for incurables. *adj., n. 8.*

in cur sion (in kėr′zhən), invasion; raid; sudden attack. The pirates made incursions along the coast. *n. 15.*

Ind., Indiana. *8.*

in debt ed (in det′id), owing money or gratitude; in debt; obliged. We are indebted to science for many of our comforts. *adj. 6.*

in debt ed ness (in det′id nis), 1. the condition of being in debt. 2. amount owed; debts. *n. 16.*

in de cen cy (in dē′sən si), 1. indecent behavior. 2. indecent quality. *n., pl. indecencies.*

in de cent (in dē′sənt), 1. not decent; in very bad taste; improper. He showed an indecent lack of gratitude to the man who saved his life. 2. not modest; morally bad; disgusting; obscene. *adj. 13.*

in de ci sion (in′di sizh′ən), lack of decision; tendency to delay or to hesitate; tendency to put off deciding, or to change one's mind. *n. 19.*

in de ci sive (in′di sī′siv), 1. having the habit of hesitating and putting off decisions. 2. not deciding or settling the matter; as, an indecisive battle, an indecisive answer. *adj. 16.*

in de clin a ble (in′di klīn′ə bəl), not changing its spelling for changes in grammatical use. *None* is an indeclinable pronoun. *adj.*

in dec o rous (in dek′ə rəs), not suitable; improper; unseemly. *adj. 19.*

in deed (in dēd′), 1. in fact; in truth; really. She is hungry; indeed, she is almost starving. War is indeed terrible. 2. expression of surprise or contempt. Indeed! I never would have thought it. *adv., interj. 1.*

in de fat i ga ble (in′di fat′i gə bəl), tireless; untiring. *adj. 15.*

in de fea si ble (in′di fē′zi bəl), not to be annulled or made void. Kings used to think they had an indefeasible right to rule. *adj. 16.*

in de fen si ble (in′di fen′si bəl), that cannot be defended; as, an indefensible island, an indefensible lie. *adj.*

in de fin a ble (in′di fīn′ə bəl), that cannot be defined. *adj.*

in def i nite (in def′i nit), 1. not clearly defined; not precise; vague. "Maybe" is a very indefinite answer. 2. not limited. We have an indefinite time to finish this work. 3. The **indefinite articles** are *a* and *an*. *adj. 8.*

in del i ble (in del′i bəl), 1. that cannot be erased or removed; permanent; as, indelible ink, an indelible disgrace. 2. making an indelible mark; as, an indelible pencil. *adj. 14.*

in del i ca cy (in del′i kə si), lack of delicacy; being indelicate. *n., pl. indelicacies.*

in del i cate (in del′i kit), 1. not delicate; coarse; crude. 2. improper; immodest. *adj.*

in dem ni fi ca tion (in dem′ni fi kā′shən), 1. indemnifying; being indemnified. 2. compensation; recompense. *n.*

in dem ni fy (in dem′ni fī), 1. repay; make good; compensate for damage, loss, or expense incurred. He promised to indemnify me. 2. secure against damage or loss; insure. *v., indemnified, indemnifying. 15.*

in dem ni ty (in dem′ni ti), 1. payment for damage, loss, or expense incurred. Money demanded by a victorious nation at the end of a war as a condition of peace is an indemnity. 2. security against damage or loss; insurance. *n., pl. indemnities. 11.*

Indented molding

in dent[1] (in dent′), 1. form notches or deep bays in. 2. begin (a line) farther from the edge than the other lines. The first line of a paragraph is usually indented. *v. 8.*

in dent[2] (in dent′), 1. make a dent in; mark with a dent. 2. press in; stamp. *v.*

in den ta tion (in′den tā′shən), 1. an indenting or being indented. 2. dent; notch; cut. *n. 12.*

in den ture (in den′chər), 1. written agreement. 2. a contract by which a person is bound to serve someone else. 3. bind by a contract to serve someone else. Many persons came to the colonies indentured for several years. *n., v. 14.*

in de pend ence (in′di pen′dəns), freedom from the control, support, or influence of others. The American colonies won independence from England. *n. 4.*

in de pend ent (in′di pen′dənt), 1. needing, wishing, or getting no help from others; as, independent work, independent thinking. 2. acting, working, or, especially, voting by one's own ideas, not as the crowd does. 3. guiding, ruling, or governing one's self; not under another's rule. The American colonies became independent of England. 4. not depending on others. Miss Jones has an independent fortune. 5. person who votes without regard to party. *adj., n. 3.*

in de scrib a ble (in′di skrīb′ə bəl), that cannot be described; beyond description. *adj. 9.*

in de struct i ble (in′di struk′ti bəl), that cannot be destroyed. *adj. 17.*

in de ter mi nate (in′di tėr′mi nit), not determined; not fixed; indefinite; vague. *adj. 10.*

in dex (in′deks), 1. list of what is in a book, telling on what pages to find each thing, usually put at the end of the book and arranged in alphabetical order. 2. make an index of. 3. thing that points out or shows; sign. A person's face is often an index of his character. 4. finger next to the thumb; forefinger. 5. pointer. A dial or scale usually has an index. *n., pl. indexes, indices* (in′di sēz), *v. 6.*

In di a (in′di ə), 1. a country in southern Asia. Most of it is under British control. 2. **India ink** is a black paint or ink. 3. **India paper** is a thin tough printing paper. *n., adj. 3.*

In di an (in′di ən), 1. one of the so-called red people living in America before the white people came; an American Indian. 2. of or having to do with American Indians; as, an Indian camp, Indian blankets, an Indian language. 3. any one of the languages of the American Indians. 4. made of Indian corn or maize; as, Indian pudding. 5. of, living in, or belonging to India; as, Indian elephants, Indian temples, Indian costumes. 6. a native of India or the East Indies. *n., adj. 1.*

In di an a (in′di an′ə), a Middle Western State of the United States. *n. 5.*

In di an ap o lis (in′di ən ap′ə lis), the capital of Indiana. *n. 13.*

Indian club, bottle-shaped, wooden club swung for exercise.

Indian club

Indian corn, 1. a plant whose grain grows on large ears. Also called **corn** or **maize.** See the picture just below. 2. the grain.

Indian Ocean, an ocean south of Asia, east of Africa, and west of Australia.

Indian summer, a time of mild, dry, hazy weather in late autumn.

Indian Territory, former territory of the United States, now part of Oklahoma.

India rubber or **india rubber,** rubber.

in di cate (in′di kāt), 1. point out; show; make known. The arrow on a sign indicates the way to go. 2. be a sign of. Fever indicates illness. *v. 2.*

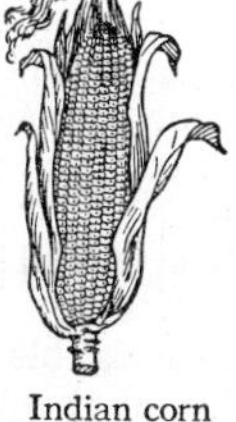
Indian corn (Ears are from 1 in. to 20 in. long.)

in di ca tion (in′di kā′shən), 1. an indicating. 2. thing that indicates; sign. *n. 9.*

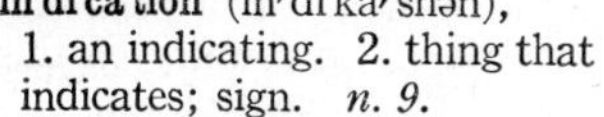

in dic a tive (in dik′ə tiv), 1. pointing out; showing; being a sign (of); suggesting. A frown is often indicative of eyestrain. 2. expressing or denoting a state, act, or happening as actual; asking a question of simple fact. In "I go" and "Did I go?" the verbs are in the indicative mood. 3. indicative mood or verb form. *adj., n. 8.*

in di ca tor (in′di kā′tər), 1. person or thing that indicates. 2. a pointer on a dial that shows the amount of heat, pressure, speed, etc. 3. any recording apparatus. *n. 12.*

in di ces (in′di sēz), indexes. *n. pl. of* **index.**

in dict (in dīt′), 1. charge with an offense or crime. 2. find enough evidence against (an accused person) so that a trial is necessary. *v. 13.*

in dict ment (in dīt′mənt), accusation; formal accusation; as, an indictment for murder. *n. 9.*

In dies (in′dēz), 1. the East Indies, islands between Australia and Asia. 2. the West Indies, islands in the Atlantic Ocean between Florida and South America. *n. pl. 5.*

in dif fer ence (in dif′ər əns), 1. not caring; lack of interest or attention. The boy's indifference to his schoolwork worried his parents. 2. lack of importance. It was a matter of indifference to Tom whether his family stayed in town or went to the country. *n. 7.*

in dif fer ent (in dif′ər ənt), 1. not caring one way or the other. 2. unimportant; not mattering much. The time for starting is indifferent to me. 3. having or showing no interest. Mary enjoyed the trip, but Ann was indifferent. 4. neither good nor bad; just fair; as, an indifferent ballplayer. *adj. 7.*

in dif fer ent ly (in dif′ər ənt li), 1. with indifference. 2. without distinction; equally. 3. moderately. 4. poorly; badly. *adv.*

in di gence (in′di jəns), poverty. *n. 15.*

in dig e nous (in dij′i nəs), native; originating in the region or country where found. Lions are indigenous to Africa. *adj. 14.*

in di gent (in′di jənt), poor; needy. *adj. 14.*

in di gest i ble (in′di jes′ti bəl), that cannot be digested; hard to digest. *adj. 9.*

in di ges tion (in′di jes′chən), inability to digest food; difficulty in digesting food. *n. 9.*

in dig nant (in dig′nənt), angry at something unworthy, unjust, or mean. She was indignant at the man who beat his horse. *adj. 6.*

in dig na tion (in′dig nā′shən), anger at something unworthy, unjust, or mean; anger mixed with scorn; righteous anger. Cruelty to animals should arouse indignation. *n. 4.*

in dig ni ty (in dig′ni ti), an injury to dignity; an insult. Bill felt that being called "Willie, dear" was an indignity. *n., pl. indignities. 10.*

in di go (in′di gō), 1. a blue dye obtained from various plants. 2. a plant yielding it. 3. deep violet-blue. *n., pl. indigos* or *indigoes, adj. 6.*

A branch of indigo

in di rect (in′di rekt′), 1. not direct; not straight. 2. not directly connected. Happiness is an indirect result of doing one's work well. 3. not straightforward and to the point. She would not answer yes or no but gave an indirect answer to my question. *adj. 7.*

in di rec tion (in′di rek′shən), 1. a roundabout act, course, or method. 2. deceitful or crooked dealing. *n.*

indirect object, person or thing that is indirectly affected by the action of the verb. The indirect object comes before the direct object and shows to whom or for whom something is done. In "I gave John a book," *John* is the indirect object and *book* is the direct object.

in dis creet (in′dis krēt′), not discreet; not wise and judicious. The indiscreet girl often talked with strangers. *adj. 11.*

in dis cre tion (in′dis kresh′ən), 1. imprudence; lack of good judgment. 2. indiscreet act. *n. 13.*

in dis crim i nate (in′dis krim′i nit), 1. confused. He tipped everything out of his suitcase in an indiscriminate pile. 2. not discriminating; with no feeling for differences. He is an indiscriminate reader and likes both good books and bad ones. *adj. 10.*

in dis pens a ble (in′dis pen′sə bəl), absolutely necessary. Air is indispensable to life. *adj. 8.*

in dis pose (in′dis pōz′), 1. make unwilling; make not inclined. You are indisposed to make friends with someone who has been unkind to you. 2. make slightly ill. 3. make unfit or unable. *v. 11.*

in dis posed (in′dis pōzd′), 1. slightly ill. 2. unwilling. *adj.*

in dis po si tion (in′dis pə zish′ən), 1. slight illness. 2. unwillingness. *n. 15.*

in dis pu ta ble (in dis′pū tə bəl), that cannot be disputed; as, an indisputable fact. *adj. 16.*

in dis sol u ble (in′di sol′ū bəl), not capable of being dissolved, undone, or destroyed; lasting; firm. *adj. 15.*

in dis tinct (in′dis tingkt′), not distinct; not clear to the eye, ear, or mind; confused; as, an indistinct picture, an indistinct roar from the distant ocean. *adj. 11.*

in dis tin guish a ble (in′dis ting′gwish ə bəl), that cannot be distinguished. *adj. 17.*

in dite (in dīt′), put in words; compose; write. *v. 13.*

in di vid u al (in′di vij′ü əl), 1. a person. Robert is a tall individual. 2. a single person, animal, or thing. 3. single; separate; for one only. Benches are for several people; chairs are individual seats. Washbowls are for general use; toothbrushes are for individual use. 4. belonging to or marking off one person or thing specially. Alice has an individual style of arranging her hair. *n., adj. 3.*

in di vid u al ism (in′di vij′ü əl izm), 1. a theory that individual freedom is as important as the welfare of the community or group as a whole. 2. each for himself; absence of coöperation; wanting a separate existence for oneself. *n. 18.*

in di vid u al ist (in′di vij′ü əl ist), 1. person who lives his own life for himself, and does not try to coöperate with others. 2. a supporter of individualism. *n.*

in di vid u al i ty (in′di vij′ü al′i ti), 1. the character or sum of the qualities which distinguish one person or thing from another. 2. being individual; existence as an individual. 3. an individual person or thing. *n., pl. individualities. 9.*

in di vid u al ize (in′di vij′ü əl īz), 1. make different for each individual. This school individualizes its course of study. 2. consider one by one; list one by one; specify. *v.*

in di vid u al ly (in′di vij′ü əl i), 1. personally; one at a time; as individuals. Sometimes our teacher helps us individually. 2. each from the others. People differ individually. *adv.*

in di vis i bil i ty (in′di viz′i bil′i ti), not being divisible. *n. 8.*

in di vis i ble (in′di viz′i bəl), not capable of being divided. *adj. 13.*

In do-Chi na (in′dō chī′nə), 1. a peninsula in southeastern Asia. 2. a country on this peninsula, under French control. *n.*

in do lence (in′də ləns), laziness; dislike of work; idleness. *n. 12.*

in do lent (in′də lənt), lazy; disliking work. *adj. 9.*

in dom i ta ble (in dom′i tə bəl), unconquerable; unyielding. *adj. 10.*

in door (in′dōr′), in a house or building. *adj.*

in doors (in′dōrz′), in or into a house or building. *adv. 6.*

in dorse (in dôrs′), 1. write one's name, a comment, etc., on the back of (a check, note, or other document). He had to indorse the check before the bank would cash it. 2. approve; support. Parents heartily indorse the plan for a school playground. *v. 10.* Also spelled **endorse.**

in dorse ment (in dôrs′mənt), 1. the writing on the back of a document, check, note, bill, etc. 2. approval; support. *n. 19.* Also spelled **endorsement.**

in du bi ta ble (in dū′bi tə bəl or in dü′bi tə bəl), not to be doubted; certain. Laziness and stupidity are two indubitable causes of failure. *adj. 16.*

in duce (in dūs′ or in düs′), 1. lead on; influence; persuade. Advertising induces people to buy. 2. cause; bring about. The label says that this medicine will induce sleep. 3. produce (an electric current, etc.) without contact. 4. infer by reasoning from particular facts to a general rule or principle. *v. 4.*

in duce ment (in dūs′mənt or in düs′mənt), something that influences or persuades; incentive. Prizes are inducements to work. *n. 9.*

in duct (in dukt′), 1. bring in; introduce (into a place, seat, position, etc.). 2. put formally in possession of (an office, etc.). Mr. Gage was inducted into the office of governor. *v.*

in duc tion (in duk′shən), 1. reasoning from particular facts to general truths or principles. 2. a conclusion so reached. 3. bringing forward facts, evidence, etc. 4. introduction; installing. 5. process by which an object having electrical or magnetic properties produces similar properties in a nearby object, usually without direct contact. *n. 13.*

in duc tive (in duk′tiv), 1. of or having to do with induction. 2. using induction. *adj. 19.*

in due (in dū′ or in dü′), 1. put on (a garment, etc.). 2. clothe (a person) as with a garment. 3. furnish; supply; endow (with qualities, powers, etc.). *v. 16.* Also spelled **endue.**

in dulge (in dulj′), 1. yield to the wishes of; humor; as, to indulge a child, to indulge the fancies of a sick person. 2. give way to one's pleasure; give oneself up to; allow oneself something desired; as, to indulge in tobacco, to indulge in a fit of temper, to indulge in a new hat. *v. 6.*

in dul gence (in dul′jəns), 1. an indulging. 2. thing indulged in. 3. favor; privilege. 4. in the Roman Catholic Church, remission of the punishment still due to sin after the guilt has been forgiven. *n. 7.*

in dul gent (in dul′jənt), 1. indulging; kind; almost too kind. The indulgent mother bought her boy everything he wanted. 2. lenient; making allowances; not critical. *adj. 10.*

In dus (in′dəs), a river in northwestern India. *n. 17.*

in dus tri al (in dus′tri əl), 1. of or having to do with industry. Industrial workers work at trades or in factories. An industrial school teaches trades. 2. of or having to do with the workers in industries; as, industrial insurance. *adj. 9.*

in dus tri ous (in dus′tri əs), hard-working. *adj. 4.*

in dus try (in′dəs tri), 1. steady effort; busy application. Industry and thrift bring success. 2. systematic work. 3. any branch of business, trade, or manufacture. The steel industry and the automobile industry employ hundreds of thousands of men. ***n.***, *pl. industries. 2.*

in e bri ate (in ē′bri āt for 1, in ē′bri it for 2), 1. make drunk; intoxicate. 2. drunken person. *v., n. 15.*

in ed i ble (in ed′i bəl), not fit to eat. *adj.*

in ef fa ble (in ef′ə bəl), not to be expressed in words; too great to be described in words; as, the ineffable beauty of a sunset. *adj. 13.*

in ef fec tive (in′i fek′tiv), not effective; of little use. *adj. 12.*

in ef fec tu al (in′i fek′chü əl), 1. without effect; useless. 2. not able to produce the effect wanted. *adj. 11.*

in ef fi cien cy (in′i fish′ən si), inability to get things done. *n. 12.*

in ef fi cient (in′i fish′ənt), 1. not efficient; not able to produce an effect without waste of time, energy, etc. A machine that uses too much power is inefficient. 2. incapable; not able to get things done. *adj. 15.*

in el e gant (in el′i gənt), not elegant; not in good taste; crude; vulgar. *adj.*

in el i gi ble (in el′i ji bəl), 1. not suitable; not qualified. A foreign-born citizen of the United States is ineligible for the Presidency. 2. person who is not suitable or not qualified. *adj., n.*

in ept (in ept′), 1. not suitable; out of place. 2. absurd; foolish. *adj.*

in e qual i ty (in′ē kwol′i ti), 1. lack of equality; a being unequal in amount, size, value, rank, etc. 2. lack of evenness, regularity, or uniformity. ***n.***, *pl. inequalities. 11.*

in eq ui ta ble (in ek′wi tə bəl), not fair; not just. *adj.*

in ert (in ėrt′), 1. lifeless; having no power to move or act. A stone is an inert mass of matter. 2. inactive; slow; sluggish. 3. with few or no active properties. Helium and neon are inert gases. *adj. 8.*

in er tia (in ėr′shə), 1. tendency to remain in the state one is in, and not start changes. 2. tendency of all objects and matter in the universe to stay still if still, or, if moving, to go on moving in the same direction, unless acted on by some outside force. *n. 15.*

in es ti ma ble (in es′ti mə bəl), of too great worth or value to be measured. Freedom is an inestimable privilege. *adj. 10.*

in ev i ta ble (in ev′i tə bəl), not to be avoided; sure to happen. Death is inevitable. *adj. 5.*

in ex act (in′eg zakt′), not exact; not accurate. *adj.*

in ex cus a ble (in′eks kūz′ə bəl), that ought not to be excused; that cannot be justified. *adj. 15.*

in ex haust i ble (in′eg zôs′ti bəl), 1. that cannot be exhausted; very abundant. 2. tireless. *adj. 14.*

in ex o ra ble (in ek′sə rə bəl), relentless; unyielding; not influenced by prayers or entreaties. *adj. 8.*

in ex pe di ent (in′eks pē′di ənt), not expedient; not practical, suitable, or wise. *adj.*

in ex pen sive (in′eks pen′siv), not expensive; cheap. *adj. 17.*

in ex pe ri ence (in′eks pēr′i əns), lack of experience; lack of practice; lack of skill or wisdom gained by experience. *n. 19.*

in ex pe ri enced (in′eks pēr′i ənst), not experienced; without practice; lacking the skill and the wisdom gained by experience. *adj. 9.*

in ex pert (in′eks pėrt′), not expert; unskilled. *adj. 20.*

in ex pi a ble (in eks′pi ə bəl), that cannot be atoned for; as, an inexpiable crime. *adj. 17.*

in ex pli ca ble (in eks′pli kə bəl), mysterious; that cannot be explained. *adj. 12.*

in ex press i ble (in′eks pres′i bəl), that cannot be expressed; beyond expression. *adj. 13.*

in ex tin guish a ble (in′eks ting′gwish ə bəl), that cannot be put out or stopped. *adj. 16.*

in ex tri ca ble (in eks′tri kə bəl), 1. that one cannot get out of. 2. that cannot be disentangled or solved. *adj. 15.*

in fal li bil i ty (in fal′i bil′i ti), absolute freedom from error. *n. 15.*

in fal li ble (in fal′i bəl), 1. free from error; that cannot be mistaken; as, an infallible rule. 2. absolutely reliable; sure; as, infallible obedience. *adj. 9.*

in fa mous (in′fə məs), 1. shamefully bad; very wicked. 2. having a very bad reputation; in public disgrace. A traitor's name is infamous. *adj. 7.*

in fa my (in′fə mi), 1. very bad reputation; public disgrace. Traitors are held up to infamy. 2. extreme wickedness. *n., pl. infamies. 9.*

in fan cy (in′fən si), 1. babyhood; early childhood. 2. an early stage of anything. Television is still in its infancy. *n., pl. infancies. 6.*

in fant (in′fənt), 1. baby; very young child. 2. of or for an infant; as, an infant class, infant food. 3. in an early stage; just beginning to develop. *n., adj. 3.*

in fan tile (in′fən tīl), 1. of an infant or infants; having to do with infants. 2. like an infant; babyish; childish. 3. in an early stage; just beginning to develop. *adj. 19.*

infantile paralysis, acute infectious disease that causes paralysis of various muscles, and often death. It attacks children especially, often leaving them crippled.

in fan tine (in′fən tīn), of infants; babyish; childish. *adj. 17.*

in fan try (in′fən tri), soldiers who fight on foot. *n., pl. infantries. 10.*

in fan try man (in′fən tri mən), soldier who fights on foot. *n., pl. infantrymen.*

in fat u at ed (in fach′ü āt′id), extremely adoring; foolishly in love. *adj. 15.*

in fat u a tion (in fach′ü ā′shən), 1. infatuating. 2. being infatuated. 3. foolish love; unreasoning fondness. *n. 19.*

in fect (in fekt′), 1. cause disease in by introducing germs. Anyone with a bad cold may infect the people around him. 2. influence in a bad way. One bad boy may infect a whole class. 3. influence by spreading. The captain's courage infected his men. *v. 7.*

in fec tion (in fek′shən), 1. a causing of disease in people, animals, and plants by the introduction of germs. Air, water, clothing, and insects are all means of infection. 2. disease caused in this way. Measles is an infection that spreads from one person to another. 3. influence, feeling, or idea spreading from one to another. *n. 8.*

in fec tious (in fek′shəs), 1. spread by infection. Measles is an infectious disease. 2. causing infection. 3. apt to spread. He has a jolly, infectious laugh. *adj. 9.*

in fer (in fėr′), 1. conclude; find out by reasoning. People inferred that so able a governor would make a good president. 2. indicate; imply. Ragged clothing infers poverty. *v., inferred, inferring. 8.*

in fer ence (in′fər əns), 1. the process of inferring. 2. that which is inferred; conclusion. When they saw the pile of paper on the teacher's desk, the class made the inference that they would have written work. *n. 9.*

in fe ri or (in fēr′i ər), 1. lower in position or rank. A lieutenant is inferior to a captain. 2. lower in quality; not so good; worse. A wolf is inferior to a lion. 3. below the average; as, an inferior mind, an inferior grade of coffee. 4. person who is lower in rank or station. A good leader gets on well with inferiors. 5. thing that is below average. *adj., n. 4.*

in fe ri or i ty (in fēr′i or′i ti), inferior nature or condition; quality of being inferior. *n. 14.*

in fer nal (in fėr′nəl), 1. of the lower world; of hell. 2. hellish. The heartless conqueror showed infernal cruelty. An **infernal machine** is an apparatus for producing an explosion to destroy life or property. *adj. 7.*

in fer no (in fėr′nō), 1. hell. 2. place of torment. Firemen fought their way through a roaring inferno of flames. *n., pl. infernos. 18.*

in fest (in fest′), trouble or disturb in large numbers. Mosquitoes infest swamps. The mountains were infested by robbers. *v. 8.*

in fi del (in′fi dəl), 1. person who does not believe in religion. 2. not believing in religion. 3. person who does not accept a particular faith. Mohammedans call Christians infidels. 4. person who does not accept Christianity. *n., adj. 9.*

in fi del i ty (in′fi del′i ti), 1. unbelief in religion, especially in Christianity. 2. lack of faithfulness, especially to husband or wife. *n., pl. infidelities. 15.*

in field (in′fēld′), 1. baseball diamond. 2. first, second, and third basemen and shortstop of a baseball team. *n.*

in fil trate (in fil′trāt), 1. pass into or through by filtering. 2. filter into or through. *v.*

in fil tra tion (in′fil trā′shən), 1. an infiltrating or being infiltrated. 2. thing that infiltrates. 3. method of attack in which small groups of men penetrate the enemy's lines at various weak points. *n.*

in fi nite (in′fi nit), 1. without limits or bounds. 2. very, very great. 3. that which is infinite. 4. **The Infinite** is a name for God. *adj., n. 4.*

in fi nite ly (in′fi nit li), to an infinite degree. "I am infinitely pleased to see you," said the flatterer. *adv.*

in fi ni tes i mal (in′fi ni tes′i məl), so small as to be almost nothing. *adj. 16.*

in fin i tive (in fin′i tiv), a form of a verb not limited by person and number. *Examples:* Let him *go*. We want *to go* now. *n. 11.*

in fin i tude (in fin′i tūd or in fin′i tüd), 1. being infinite. 2. an infinite extent, amount, or number. *n. 20.*

in fin i ty (in fin′i ti), 1. being infinite. 2. infinite space, time, or quantity. 3. infinite extent, amount, or number; as, the infinity of God's mercy. *n., pl. infinities. 14.*

in firm (in fėrm′), 1. weak; feeble. She was old and infirm. 2. not steadfast; faltering. The boy was infirm in his ambitions. *adj. 11.*

in fir ma ry (in fėr′mə ri), place for the care of the sick or injured; a hospital in a school or institution. *n., pl. infirmaries. 18.*

in fir mi ty (in fėr′mi ti), weakness; feebleness. *n., pl. infirmities. 6.*

in flame (in flām′), 1. excite; make more violent. His stirring speech inflamed the crowd. 2. become excited with strong feeling. 3. make unnaturally hot, red, sore, or swollen. The smoke had inflamed the fireman's eyes. 4. become red or hot from disease, etc. *v. 5.*

in flam ma ble (in flam′ə bəl), 1. easily set on fire. Paper is inflammable. 2. easily excited or aroused; excitable. *adj. 13.*

in flam ma tion (in′flə mā′shən), 1. a diseased condition of some part of the body, causing heat, redness, swelling, and pain. 2. inflaming; being inflamed. *n. 10.*

in flam ma to ry (in flam′ə tō′ri), 1. tending to excite or arouse. The leader of the mob made an inflammatory speech. 2. of, causing, or accompanied by inflammation; as, an inflammatory condition of the tonsils. *adj. 15.*

in flate (in flāt′), 1. blow out or swell with air or gas; as, to inflate a balloon. 2. swell or puff out; as, to inflate with pride. 3. increase (prices or currency) beyond the normal amount. *v. 10.*

in fla tion (in flā′shən), 1. a swelling (with air, gas, pride, etc.). 2. a swollen state; too great expansion. 3. the increase of the currency of a country by issuing too much paper money. *n. 18.*

in flect (in flekt′), 1. change the tone or pitch of (the voice). 2. vary the form of (a word) to show case, number, gender, person, tense, mood, or comparison. By inflecting *who* we have *whose* and *whom.* 3. bend; curve. *v.*

in flec tion (in flek′shən), 1. change in the tone or pitch of the voice. We usually end questions with a rising inflection. 2. variation in the form of a word to show case, number, gender, person, tense, mood, or comparison. 3. bending; curving. 4. bend; curve. *n. 9.*

in flex i ble (in flek′si bəl), 1. stiff; rigid. 2. firm; unyielding. *adj. 13.*

in flict (in flikt′), 1. give or cause (a stroke, blow, or wound). 2. impose (suffering, punishment, something unwelcome, etc.). Only cruel people like to inflict pain. Disagreeable Mrs. Jones has inflicted herself upon her relatives for a long visit. *v. 5.*

in flic tion (in flik′shən), 1. act of inflicting; The cruel emperor delighted in the infliction of pain. 2. something inflicted; punishment; burden; suffering. The poor old man endured many inflictions with patience. *n. 12.*

in flow (in′flō′), 1. a flowing in. The discovery of gold in Alaska caused an inflow of people. 2. that which flows in. *n.*

in flu ence (in′flü əns), 1. power of persons or things to act on others. Use your influence to persuade your friends to join the club. 2. use such power on; have power over. The moon influences the tides. What we read influences our thinking. 3. person or thing that has power. *n., v. 2.*

in flu en tial (in′flü en′shəl), 1. having much influence; having influence. Influential friends helped John to get a good job. 2. using influence; producing results. *adj. 12.*

in flu en za (in′flü en′zə), an acute, contagious disease like a bad cold in its symptoms, but much more dangerous and exhausting. *n. 8.*

in flux (in′fluks), a flowing in; steady flow; as, the influx of immigrants into a country. *n. 14.*

in fold (in fōld′), 1. fold in; wrap up. The old lady was infolded in a shawl. 2. embrace; clasp. The mother infolded her baby in her arms. *v. 10.* Also spelled **enfold.**

in form (in fôrm′), 1. tell; supply with knowledge. Please inform us how to find Dr. Brown's house. 2. tell tales about; accuse. The thief who was caught informed on the others. 3. inspire. God informed their hearts with pity. *v. 2.*

in for mal (in fôr′məl), not formal; without ceremony. *adj. 8.*

in for mal i ty (in′fôr mal′i ti), 1. absence of form or ceremony. 2. informal act or behavior. *n., pl. informalities.*

in form ant (in fôr′mənt), person who gives information. My informant saw the thing with his own eyes. *n.*

in for ma tion (in′fər mā′shən), 1. knowledge; facts; news. A dictionary contains much information. The general sent the people information of his victory. 2. informing. This guidebook is for the information of travelers. 3. accusation or complaint against a person. *n. 3.*

in form er (in fôr′mər), 1. person who informs. 2. person who tells the authorities of violations of the law. An informer told the police that the store was selling stolen furs. *n. 15.*

in frac tion (in frak′shən), breaking of a law or obligation. Reckless driving is an infraction of the law. *n. 16.*

in fre quent (in frē′kwənt), rare; scarce. *adj. 16.*

in fringe (in frinj′), 1. violate. A false label infringes the food and drug law. 2. trespass. Do not infringe upon the rights of others. *v. 10.*

in fringe ment (in frinj′mənt), 1. violation. 2. trespassing. *n. 14.*

in fu ri ate (in fūr′i āt), make furious; enrage. *v. 13.*

in fuse (in fūz′), 1. pour in; put in. The captain infused his own courage into his soldiers. 2. inspire. The soldiers were infused with his courage. 3. steep or soak in a liquid to get something out. Tea leaves are infused in hot water to make tea. *v. 10.*

in fu sion (in fū′zhən), 1. an infusing. 2. a liquid extract obtained by steeping or soaking. *n. 12.*

-ing[1], suffix meaning:—

1. action, result, product, material; as in the art of painting, a beautiful drawing, a blue lining, white shirting.

2. of one that ——s; of those that ——; as in smoking habit, printing trade, drinking song.

-ing[2], 1. suffix that forms the present participle.

2. suffix meaning:—that ——s; as in seeing eye, lasting happiness, growing child.

in gen ious (in jēn′yəs), 1. clever; skillful in making; good at inventing. The ingenious boy made a radio set for himself. 2. cleverly planned and made. This mousetrap is an ingenious device. *adj. 6.*

in ge nu i ty (in′ji nū′i ti or in′ji nü′i ti), cleverness; skill in planning, inventing, etc. The boy showed ingenuity in making toys. *n., pl. ingenuities. 7.*

in gen u ous (in jen′ū əs), 1. frank; open; sincere. 2. simple; natural; innocent. *adj. 14.*

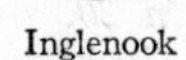
Inglenook

in gle nook (ing′gəl nůk′), a corner by the fire. *n.*

in glo ri ous (in glō′ri əs), 1. bringing no glory; shameful; disgraceful. 2. having no glory; not famous. *adj. 11.*

in got (ing′gət), a mass of gold, silver, or steel cast in a mold. *n. 16.*

in graft (in graft′), 1. put (a shoot of one tree) into another. The gardener ingrafted a choice variety of apple upon the ordinary apple tree. 2. fix in; implant. Honesty and thrift are ingrafted in his character. *v.* Also spelled **engraft.**

in grain (in grān′ for 1 and 2, in′grān′ for 3 and 4), 1. to dye in the fiber before manufacture. 2. fix deeply and firmly; as, beliefs ingrained in the mind, an ingrained habit. 3. dyed before manufacture. 4. yarn, wool, etc., dyed before manufacture. *v., adj., n. 17.*

in grate (in′grāt), ungrateful person. *n. 18.*

in gra ti ate (in grā′shi āt), bring (oneself) into favor. Alfred tried to ingratiate himself with the teacher by giving her presents. *v. 20.*

in grat i tude (in grat′i tūd or in grat′i tüd), lack of thankfulness; being ungrateful. *n. 8.*

in gre di ent (in grē′di ənt), one of the parts of a mixture. The ingredients of sponge cake are eggs, sugar, flour, and flavoring. *n. 6.*

in gress (in′gres), 1. going in. A high fence prevented ingress to the field. 2. a way of going in; entrance. 3. the right to go in. *n. 14.*

in hab it (in hab′it), live in. Fish inhabit the sea. Thoughts inhabit the mind. *v. 4.*

in hab it a ble (in hab′i tə bəl), capable of being inhabited. *adj.*

in hab it ant (in hab′i tənt), a person or animal that lives in a place. *n. 5.*

in hab it ed (in hab′i tid), lived in; as, an inhabited house. *adj.*

in ha la tion (in′hə lā′shən), 1. breathing in. 2. medicine to be inhaled. *n. 17.*

in hale (in hāl′), draw into the lungs: breathe in (air, gas, fragrance, tobacco smoke, etc.). *v. 10.*

in har mo ni ous (in′här mō′ni əs), not harmonious; discordant. *adj. 17.*

in her ent (in hēr′ənt), existing; abiding; belonging to a person or thing as a quality or attribute. In spite of flattery, she kept her inherent modesty. *adj. 10.*

in her ent ly (in hēr′ənt li), by its own nature; essentially. *adv.*

in her it (in her′it), 1. receive as an heir. Mr. Jones's widow inherited his farm. 2. get or possess from one's ancestors. Mary inherits her father's blue eyes. *v. 4.*

in her it ance (in her′i təns), 1. inheriting. Mr. Jones received his house by inheritance from an aunt. 2. thing inherited. Good health is a fine inheritance. *n. 5.*

in her i tor (in her′i tər), heir; person who inherits. *n. 12.*

in hib it (in hib′it), 1. check; restrain; hinder. The soldier's sense of duty inhibited his impulse to run away. 2. forbid. *v. 14.*

in hi bi tion (in′hi bish′ən), 1. act of inhibiting. 2. state of being inhibited. 3. idea, emotion, attitude, habit, or other inner force that restrains natural impulses. *n. 15.*

in hos pi ta ble (in hos′pi tə bəl), not hospitable; not making visitors comfortable. The Pilgrims encountered a rocky, inhospitable shore. *adj. 11.*

in hos pi tal i ty (in hos′pi tal′i ti), lack of hospitality. *n.*

in hu man (in hū′mən), unfeeling; brutal; cruel. *adj. 11.*

in hu man i ty (in′hū man′i ti), lack of feeling; cruelty; brutality. *n., pl. inhumanities. 16.*

in im i cal (in im′i kəl), 1. unfriendly; hostile. 2. unfavorable; harmful. Lack of ambition is inimical to success. *adj.*

in im i ta ble (in im′i tə bəl), that cannot be imitated or copied; matchless. *adj. 13.*

in iq ui tous (in ik′wi təs), very unjust; wicked. *adj. 20.*

in iq ui ty (in ik′wi ti), 1. very great injustice. 2. a wicked and unjust act. *n., pl. iniquities. 7.*

i ni tial (i nish′əl), 1. first; earliest; occurring at the beginning. Tom's initial effort at skating was a failure. 2. the first letter of a word. The initials U. S. stand for United States. 3. to mark or sign with initials. Mr. John A. Smith initialed the note J. A. S. *adj., n., v., initialed, initialing. 7.*

i ni tial ly (i nish′əl i), at the beginning. *adv.*

i ni ti ate (i nish′i āt), 1. begin; be the one to start; set going. This year we shall initiate a series of free concerts. 2. admit (a person) with formal ceremonies into a group or society. 3. introduce into the knowledge of some art or subject; as, to initiate a person into business methods. 4. person who is initiated. *v., n. 11.*

i ni ti a tion (i nish′i ā′shən), 1. initiating. 2. being initiated. 3. formal admission into a group or society. 4. ceremonies by which one is admitted to a group or society. *n. 14.*

i ni ti a tive (i nish′i ə tiv), 1. active part in taking the first steps in any undertaking; the lead. Charles is shy and does not take the initiative in making acquaintances. 2. readiness and ability to be the one to start a thing. A leader must have initiative. 3. the right of citizens outside the legislature to introduce a new law by vote. *n. 8.*

in ject (in jekt′), 1. force (liquid, medicine, etc.) into (a cavity, passage, or tissue); as, to inject a drug into the body. 2. fill (a cavity, etc.) with liquid forced in. 3. throw in; as, to inject a remark into the conversation. *v. 8.*

in jec tion (in jek′shən), 1. act or process of injecting. Drugs are given by injection as well as through the mouth. 2. liquid injected. *n. 13.*

in ju di cious (in′jü dish′əs), showing bad judgment; unwise; not prudent. *adj. 15.*

in junc tion (in jungk′shən), 1. command; order. John obeyed his mother's injunction to hurry straight home. 2. a formal order from a court of law requiring somebody to do or not to do something. Mr. Jones got an injunction preventing people from lighting fires on the vacant lot next to his house. *n. 8.*

in jure (in′jər), 1. do damage to; harm; hurt. Do not break or injure the bushes in the park. 2. do wrong to. *v. 3.*

in ju ri ous (in jür′i əs), doing injury; wrongful; hurtful. *adj. 6.*

in ju ry (in′jər i), 1. harm; hurt; damage. Mr. Smith escaped from the train wreck without injury. His trunks received many injuries. The accident will be an injury to the reputation of the railroad. 2. wrong. *n., pl. injuries. 4.*

in jus tice (in jus′tis), 1. lack of justice. 2. an unjust act. *n. 6.*

ink (ingk), 1. a liquid used for writing or printing. 2. put ink on; mark or stain with ink. *n., v. 3.*

ink horn (ingk′hôrn′), a small container of horn formerly used to hold ink. *n. 19.*

Inkhorn and quill pens

ink ling (ingk′ling), a hint; a slight suggestion; a vague notion. *n. 20.*

ink stand (ingk′stand′), 1. a stand to hold ink and pens. 2. container used to hold ink. *n. 20.*

ink well (ingk′wel′), container used to hold ink on a desk or table. *n. 12.*

ink y (ingk′i), 1. like ink; dark; black. 2. covered with ink. 3. of ink. *adj., inkier, inkiest. 15.*

in laid (in′lād′ or in lād′), 1. set in the surface as a decoration or design. The desk had an inlaid design of light wood in dark. 2. decorated with a design or material set in the surface. The box had an inlaid cover. 3. pt. and pp. of **inlay.** *adj., v. 9.*

in land (in′lənd), 1. away from the coast or the border; situated in the interior; as, an inland sea. 2. the interior of a country; land away from the border or the coast. 3. in or toward the interior. 4. domestic, not foreign; as, inland trade. *adj., n., adv. 5.*

Design made by inlaying black in white

in lay (in lā′ or in′lā′ for 1 and 2, in′lā′ for 3), 1. set in the surface of a thing as a decoration or design; as, to inlay ivory or metal in wood. 2. decorate with a design set in the surface; as, to inlay a wooden box with silver. 3. something inlaid. *v., inlaid, inlaying, n. 15.*

in let (in′let), 1. a narrow strip of water running from a larger body of water into the land or between islands. The fishing village was on a small inlet of the sea. 2. entrance. *n. 9.*

in mate (in′māt), 1. occupant; inhabitant. 2. person confined in a prison, asylum, hospital, etc. *n. 10.*

in most (in′mōst), 1. farthest in; deepest. We went to the inmost depths of the mine. 2. most secret. Her inmost desire was to be an actress. *adj. 9.*

inn (in), a public house for lodging and

caring for travelers. Hotels have taken the place of the old inns. *n. 3.*

in nate (in′āt or i nāt′), natural; inborn; as, an innate talent for drawing, innate wit. *adj. 15.*

in ner (in′ər), 1. farther in; inside; as, an inner room. 2. more private; more secret. She kept her inner thoughts to herself. 3. of the mind or soul. *adj. 4.*

in ner most (in′ər mōst), farthest in; inmost. *adj. 10.*

in ning (in′ing), 1. the turn of one side in a game; chance to play. 2. the time a person or party is in power; chance for action. When our party lost the election, the others had their inning. *n. 14.*

inn keep er (in′kēp′ər), person who keeps an inn. *n. 9.*

in no cence (in′ə səns), 1. freedom from sin, wrong, or guilt. The accused man proved his innocence of the crime. 2. simplicity; lack of cunning; as, the innocence of a little child. *n. 4.*

in no cent (in′ə sənt), 1. doing no wrong or evil; free from sin or wrong; not guilty. An innocent boy was hurt in the quarrel. 2. without knowledge of evil. A baby is innocent. 3. doing no harm; as, innocent amusements. 4. an innocent person. *adj., n. 3.*

in noc u ous (i nok′ū əs), harmless. *adj. 15.*

in no vate (in′ō vāt), make changes. *v.*

in no va tion (in′ō vā′shən), 1. change made in the established way of doing things. The new teacher made many innovations. 2. making changes; bringing in new things or new ways of doing things. *n. 10.*

in no va tor (in′ō vā′tər), person who makes changes or introduces new methods. *n. 17.*

in nu en do (in′ū en′dō), 1. an indirect hint or reference. 2. an indirect suggestion against somebody. The gossipy old woman spread much scandal by innuendoes. *n., pl. innuendoes. 16.*

in nu mer a ble (i nū′mər ə bəl or i nü′mər ə-bəl), too many to count; very, very many. *adj. 6.*

in oc u late (in ok′ū lāt), 1. infect (a person or an animal) with germs that will cause a mild form of a disease, so that the individual will not take the regular disease. Doctors inoculate against smallpox, diphtheria, typhoid fever, and other diseases. 2. use disease germs to prevent or cure diseases. 3. put bacteria, serums, etc., into. Farmers inoculate the soil with bacteria that will take nitrogen from the air and change it so it can be used by plants. 4. fill (a person's mind). *v. 13.*

in oc u la tion (in ok′ū lā′shən), 1. inoculating; the introduction of a mild form of a disease into a person or animal to prevent his taking the regular disease. 2. filling the mind; as, a thorough inoculation with patriotism. *n. 18.*

in of fen sive (in′ə fen′siv), not offensive; harmless; not arousing objections. *adj. 13.*

in op er a tive (in op′ər ā′tiv), not working; without effect. *adj. 20.*

in op por tune (in op′ər tūn′ or in op′ər tün′), coming at a bad time; not appropriate. An inopportune visitor delayed us. *adj. 18.*

in or di nate (in ôr′di nit), much too great; excessive. *adj. 11.*

in or di nate ly (in ôr′di nit li), excessively. *adv.*

in or gan ic (in′ôr gan′ik), 1. not having the organized physical structure of plants and animals. Minerals are inorganic. 2. in chemistry, not produced by animal or plant activities. *adj. 12.*

in quest (in′kwest), a legal inquiry before a jury. An inquest is held to determine the cause of a death that may have been the result of a crime. *n. 16.*

in quire (in kwīr′), 1. ask; try to find out by questions; as, to inquire a person's name or business, to inquire about a room. 2. search for information, knowledge, or truth. *v. 3.*

in quir er (in kwīr′ər), person who inquires. *n. 14.*

in quir y (in kwīr′i), 1. act of inquiring; asking. 2. a search for truth, information, or knowledge. 3. a question. *n., pl. inquiries. 5.*

in qui si tion (in′kwi zish′ən), 1. questioning; inquiry; search; investigation. 2. a judicial or official inquiry or investigation. 3. **The Inquisition** was a body of men appointed by the Roman Catholic Church to suppress heresy. *n. 9.*

in quis i tive (in kwiz′i tiv), 1. curious; asking many questions. 2. too curious; prying into other people's affairs. *adj. 8.*

in quis i tor (in kwiz′i tər), person who makes an inquisition; official investigator. *n. 14.*

in road (in′rōd′), raid; attack. The expenses of her illness made inroads upon the money she had saved. *n. 11.*

in rush (in′rush′), a rushing in; inflow. *n.*

in sane (in sān′), 1. not sane; crazy. Insane people are kept in asylums. 2. for insane people. 3. extremely foolish; completely lacking in common sense. *adj. 8.*

in san i tar y (in san′i tãr′i), not sanitary; not healthful. *adj.*

in san i ty (in san′i ti), 1. state of being insane; madness; mental disease. 2. extreme folly. *n., pl. insanities. 11.*

in sa tia ble (in sā′shə bəl), that cannot be satisfied; very greedy. *adj. 15.*

in sa ti ate (in sā′shi it), never satisfied; as, an insatiate desire for praise. *adj. 14.*

in scribe (in skrīb′), 1. write, engrave, or mark (words, letters, etc.) on paper, metal, stone, etc. 2. mark or engrave (with words, letters, etc.). His tombstone was inscribed with his name and the date of his death. 3. address or dedicate (a book, etc.) informally to a person. 4. impress deeply. My father's words are inscribed on my memory. 5. put in a list; enroll. *v. 8.*

in scrip tion (in skrip′shən), something inscribed; as, the inscription on a monument, on a coin, or on an old temple. *n. 7.*

Inscription on a coin

in scru ta ble (in skrü′tə bəl), that cannot be understood; so mysterious or obscure that one cannot make out its meaning; incomprehensible. *adj. 10.*

in sect (in′sekt), a small creature with body divided into three parts and with three pairs of legs. Flies, mosquitoes, gnats, and bees are insects. Bugs and spiders are often called insects. *n. 3.*

FEELERS
HEAD
THORAX
WINGS
LEG
ABDOMEN
Parts of an insect

in sec ti cide (in sek′ti sīd), a substance for killing insects. *n.*

in se cure (in′si kūr′), 1. unsafe. 2. liable to give way; as, an insecure support, lock, or hold. *adj. 16.*

in se cu ri ty (in′si kūr′i ti), 1. unsafe condition. 2. danger of giving way. 3. something insecure. *n., pl. insecurities. 19.*

in sen sate (in sen′sāt), 1. without sensation. 2. unfeeling; as, insensate cruelty. 3. senseless; stupid. *adj. 17.*

in sen si bil i ty (in sen′si bil′i ti), 1. lack of feeling. 2. lack of consciousness. *n. 14.*

in sen si ble (in sen′si bəl), 1. not able to feel. A blind man is insensible to colors. 2. not aware. The boys in the boat were insensible of the danger. 3. not able to feel anything; unconscious. He was hit by a truck and was insensible for four hours. 4. not easily felt. The room grew cold by insensible degrees. *adj. 7.*

in sen si tive (in sen′si tiv), not sensitive; without feeling. *adj.*

in sep a ra ble (in sep′ə rə bəl), that cannot be separated. *adj. 7.*

in sert (in sėrt′ for 1, in′sėrt for 2), 1. put in; set in; as, to insert a key into a lock, to insert a letter into a word, to insert an advertisement into a newspaper. 2. something put in or set in. The book contained an insert of several pages of pictures. *v., n. 5.*

in ser tion (in sėr′shən), 1. an inserting. 2. something inserted. *n. 9.*

LACE INSERTION

in set (in set′ for 1, in′set′ for 2), 1. set in; insert. 2. something inserted. *v., inset, insetting, n.*

in shore (in′shōr′), 1. near the shore. 2. in toward the shore. *adj., adv.*

in side (in′sīd′ for 1, 2, and 3, in′sīd′ for 4 and 5), 1. the part within; the inner surface. The inside of the box was lined with colored paper. 2. the contents. The inside of the book was more interesting than the cover. 3. being on the inside; covered up; secret. I have inside information of their plans. 4. within; in the inner part. Please step inside. 5. in. The nut is inside the shell. *n., adj., adv., prep. 2.*

in sid er (in′sīd′ər), 1. person who is inside some place, society, organization, etc. 2. person who is so situated as to understand the actual conditions or facts of a case. *n.*

in sid i ous (in sid′i əs), 1. wily; crafty; sly; tricky. 2. working secretly or subtly; as, an insidious disease. *adj. 11.*

in sight (in′sīt′), 1. a view of the inside with understanding. Take the machine apart and get an insight into how it works. 2. wisdom and understanding in dealing with people or with facts. We study science to gain insight into natural laws. *n. 10.*

in sig ni a (in sig′ni ə), medals; badges; distinguishing marks of office or of honor. The crown and the scepter are the insignia of kings. *n. pl. 13.*

Naval aviation corps insignia

in sig nif i cance (in′sig nif′i kəns), 1. unimportance. 2. meaninglessness. *n.*

in sig nif i cant (in′sig nif′i kənt), having little meaning, use, or importance; as, insignificant chatter, an insignificant-looking person. A tenth of a cent is an insignificant amount of money. *adj. 6.*

in sin cere (in′sin sēr′), not sincere; not honest or candid; deceitful. *adj. 19.*

in sin cer i ty (in′sin ser′i ti), lack of sincerity; hypocrisy. *n., pl. insincerities. 20.*

in sin u ate (in sin′ū āt), 1. push in or get in by an indirect, twisting way. The stray cat insinuated herself into our kitchen. Laura insinuated herself into Ann's friendship. 2. hint; suggest indirectly. To say "Fred can't do it; no coward can" is to insinuate that Fred is a coward. *v. 9.*

in sin u a tion (in sin′ū ā′shən), 1. insinuating. 2. an indirect suggestion against someone. 3. hint; suggestion. 4. an act or speech to gain favor. *n. 14.*

in sip id (in sip′id), 1. without taste or flavor. Milk and water is an insipid drink. 2. dull; uninteresting; colorless; weak. *adj. 11.*

in sist (in sist′), keep firmly to some demand, statement, or position. John insists that he had a right to use his brother's tools. Mother insists that we wash our hands before eating. *v. 3.*

in sist ence (in sis′təns), 1. act of insisting. 2. being insistent. *n. 11.*

in sist ent (in sis′tənt), 1. insisting. In spite of the rain he was insistent on going out. 2. compelling attention or notice; pressing; urgent. *adj. 12.*

in snare (in snãr′), trap; catch in a snare. *v.* Also spelled **ensnare.**

in sole (in′sōl′), 1. inner sole of a shoe or boot. 2. thickness of warm or waterproof material laid on the sole inside a shoe or boot. *n. 14.*

in so lence (in′sə ləns), bold rudeness; insulting behavior or speech. *n. 9.*

in so lent (in′sə lənt), boldly rude; insulting. "Shut up!" the insolent boy said to his father. *adj. 8.*

in sol u ble (in sol′ū bəl), 1. that cannot be dissolved. A diamond is insoluble. 2. that cannot be solved; as, an insoluble mystery. *adj. 9.*

in sol ven cy (in sol′vən si), condition of not being able to pay one's debts; bankruptcy. *n., pl. insolvencies. 18.*

in sol vent (in sol′vənt), not able to pay one's debts; bankrupt. *adj. 16.*

in som ni a (in som′ni ə), inability to sleep. *n. 13.*

in so much (in′sō much′), to such an extent or degree; so. *adv. 9.*

in spect (in spekt′), 1. look at carefully; examine. A dentist inspects the pupils' teeth twice a year. 2. examine formally or officially. All factories and mines are inspected by government officials. *v. 7.*

in spec tion (in spek′shən), 1. an inspecting. An inspection of the roof showed no leaks. 2. formal or official examination. The soldiers lined up for their daily inspection by their officers. *n. 7.*

in spec tor (in spek′tər), 1. person who inspects. 2. an officer appointed to inspect; as, a milk inspector. 3. a police officer ranking next below a superintendent. *n. 6.*

in spi ra tion (in′spi rā′shən), 1. influence of thought and strong feelings on actions, especially on good actions. Some people get inspiration from sermons; some, from nature. 2. any influence that arouses effort to do well. A brave leader is an inspiration to his followers. 3. influence from God which helped men to write the Bible. 4. idea that is inspired. 5. breathing in; drawing air into the lungs. *n. 5.*

in spi ra tion al (in′spi rā′shən əl), 1. inspiring. The sermon was both instructive and inspirational. 2. inspired. 3. of or pertaining to inspiration. *adj.*

in spire (in spīr′), 1. put thought, feeling, life, force, etc., into. The speaker inspired the crowd. 2. cause (thought or feeling). The leader's courage inspired confidence in others. 3. influence with a thought or feeling. His sly ways inspire me with distrust. 4. arouse or influence by a divine force. 5. suggest; cause to be told or written. His enemies inspired false stories about him. 6. breathe in; breathe in air. *v. 4.*

in spir it (in spir′it), put spirit into; encourage; hearten; cheer. *v. 14.*

inst., instant. The 10th inst. means the tenth day of the present month. *15.*

in sta bil i ty (in′stə bil′i ti), lack of firmness; liability to fall, give way, or change. *n. 15.*

in stall (in stôl′), 1. place (a person) in office with ceremonies. The new judge was installed without pomp. 2. establish in a place. The cat installed itself in the easy chair. 3. put in position for use. The new owner of the house had electric lights installed at once. *v. 5.*

in stal la tion (in′stə lā′shən), 1. installing; being installed. 2. machinery placed in position for use. *n. 13.*

in stall ment or **in stal ment** (in stôl′mənt), 1. a part of a sum of money or a debt that is to be paid at stated times. Julia has to pay an installment of $10 each month on her coat till she has paid $100. 2. one of several parts issued at different times; as, a serial story in six installments. 3. installing; as, the installment of electric lights in a house. 4. being installed; as, our installment in our new home. *n. 8.*

in stance (in′stəns), 1. example; case. Lincoln is an instance of a poor boy who became famous. 2. refer to as an example. He instanced the fly as a dirty insect. 3. occasion. I went in the first instance because I was asked to go. 4. request; suggestion; urging. At the instance of the losing team we agreed to play them again next week. *n., v. 3.*

in stant (in′stənt), 1. a moment of time. Stop talking this instant! 2. immediate. The medicine gave instant relief. 3. pressing; urgent; as, instant need for action. 4. present; of the present month. The 10th instant means the tenth day of the present month. *n., adj. 2.*

in stan ta ne ous (in′stən tā′ni əs), occurring, done, or made in an instant; as, an instantaneous photograph, an instantaneous flash of lightning. *adj. 14.*

in stant ly (in′stənt li), in an instant; at once. *adv. 8.*

in stead (in sted′), 1. in place (of). Instead of studying, Grace read a story. 2. in (my, your, her, etc.) place. Ruth stayed home, and her sister went riding instead. *adv. 1.*

in step (in′step), 1. the upper surface of the human foot between the toes and the ankle. 2. the part of a shoe, stocking, etc., over the instep. *n.*

in sti gate (in′sti gāt), urge on; stir up. Tom instigated a quarrel between Jim and Joe. *v. 11.*

in sti ga tion (in′sti gā′shən), urging on; stirring up. *n. 12.*

in still or **in stil** (in stil′), 1. put in little by little. Reading good books instills a feeling for really fine literature. 2. put in drop by drop. *v., instilled, instilling. 14.*

in stinct (in′stingkt for 1 and 2, in stingkt′ for 3), 1. a natural feeling, knowledge, or power, such as that which guides animals; an unlearned tendency. An instinct leads birds to fly. 2. a natural bent, tendency, or gift. Dorothy has such an instinct for color that she will study art. 3. charged or filled with something. The picture is instinct with life and beauty. *n., adj. 5.*

in stinc tive (in stingk′tiv), of or having to do with instinct; caused or done by instinct; born in an animal or person, not learned. Climbing is instinctive in monkeys. *adj. 7.*

in sti tute (in′sti tūt or in′sti tüt), 1. set up; establish; begin. The Pilgrims instituted Thanksgiving. After the accident the police instituted an inquiry into its causes. 2. established principle, law, custom, organization, or society; institution. 3. organization or society for some special purpose. An art institute teaches or displays art. A technical school is often called an institute. 4. building used by such an organization or society. *v., n. 4.*

in sti tu tion (in′sti tū′shən or in′sti tü′shən), 1. something established, such as a law, custom, society, club, college, or any organization. A church, school, college, hospital, asylum, or prison is an institution. Giving presents on Christmas is an institution. 2. a building used for the work of an institution. 3. beginning; starting; establishing; providing for. We hope for the institution of a hot lunch at school this winter. *n. 4.*

in sti tu tion al (in′sti tū′shən əl or in′sti tü′shən əl), of or like an institution. *adj.*

in struct (in strukt′), 1. teach. 2. direct. The owner instructed his agent to sell the property. 3. inform. My lawyer instructs me that your last payment on the house is due March first. *v. 3.*

in struc tion (in struk′shən), 1. teaching; education; knowledge. 2. **Instructions** often means directions or orders. *n. 3.*

in struc tive (in struk′tiv), instructing; useful for instruction; giving information. A trip around the world is an instructive experience. *adj. 10.*

in struc tor (in struk′tər), 1. teacher. 2. a teacher below the rank of professor in American colleges. *n. 8.*

in stru ment (in′strů mənt), 1. thing with or by which something is done; person made use of by another; means. The master criminal used many men and women as instruments in his crimes. 2. tool; mechanical device; as, a dentist's instruments. 3. device for producing musical sounds; as, wind instruments, stringed instruments.

4. a formal legal document, such as a contract, deed, or grant. *n. 3.*

in stru men tal (in′strü menʹtəl), 1. acting as an instrument; useful; helpful. Mr. Beal was instrumental in finding a job for George. 2. played on or written for musical instruments. An orchestra provided instrumental music to accompany the singing. *adj. 10.*

in stru men tal i ty (in′strü men talʹi ti), helpfulness; agency; means. *n., pl. instrumentalities. 18.*

in sub or di nate (in′sə bôrʹdi nit), not submitting to authority; disobedient. *adj. 20.*

in sub or di na tion (in′sə bôr′di nāʹshən), disobedience; rebellion. *n.*

in sub stan tial (in′səb stanʹshəl), 1. frail; flimsy. A cobweb is very insubstantial. 2. unreal; imaginary. Dreams and ghosts are insubstantial. *adj. 16.*

in suf fer a ble (in sufʹər ə bəl), unbearable. His insufferable insolence cost him many friends. *adj. 15.*

in suf fi cien cy (in′sə fishʹən si), lack; deficiency; too small an amount. *n. 15.*

in suf fi cient (in′sə fishʹənt), not enough. *adj. 10.*

in su lar (inʹsə lər), 1. of or having to do with islands. 2. dwelling or situated on an island. 3. of or like people living on an island. 4. narrow-minded; as, insular prejudices. *adj. 16.*

in su late (inʹsə lāt), 1. protect from losing heat or electricity. Telephone wires are insulated by a covering of rubber or paper. 2. set apart; separate from other things. *v. 11.*

in su la tion (in′sə lāʹshən), 1. insulating. 2. being insulated. 3. material used in insulating. *n. 14.*

in su la tor (inʹsə lā′tər), that which insulates; something that prevents the passage of electricity or heat; nonconductor. *n. 13.*

Glass insulator for electric wires

in su lin (inʹsə lin), drug used for persons who have diabetes. *n.*

in sult (in sultʹ for 1, inʹsult for 2), 1. treat with scorn, abuse, or great rudeness. They insulted the flag by throwing mud on it. 2. an insulting speech or action. *v., n. 4.*

in su per a ble (in süʹpər ə bəl), that cannot be passed over or overcome. The deep river was an insuperable barrier to those who could not swim. *adj. 15.*

in sup port a ble (in′sə pōrʹtə bəl), not endurable; intolerable. *adj. 15.*

in sur ance (in shürʹəns), 1. an insuring of property, person, or life. Fire insurance, burglary insurance, accident insurance, life insurance, and health insurance are some of the many kinds. 2. the business of insuring property, life, etc. 3. amount of money for which a person or thing is insured. He has $10,000 insurance, which his wife will receive when he dies. 4. amount of money paid for insurance; premium. His insurance is $300 a year. *n. 5.*

in sure (in shürʹ), 1. make sure or certain. Check your work to insure its accuracy. 2. make safe; protect. More care will insure you against making so many mistakes. 3. arrange for money payment in case of loss, accident, or death. An insurance company will insure your house against fire. 4. make safe against loss by paying money to an insurance company. He insured his car against theft. *v. 7.*

in sur gent (in sėrʹjənt), 1. rising in revolt. 2. rebel. *adj., n. 12.*

in sur mount a ble (in′sėr mounʹtə bəl), that cannot be overcome. *adj. 16.*

in sur rec tion (in′sə rekʹshən), rising against established authority; revolt; rebellion. *n. 7.*

in tact (in taktʹ), untouched; uninjured; whole; with no part missing. The money was returned intact by its finder. *adj. 11.*

in take (inʹtāk′), 1. place where water, air, gas, etc., enters a channel, pipe, or other narrow opening. 2. act or process of taking in. 3. amount or thing taken in. *n. 14.*

in tan gi ble (in tanʹji bəl), 1. not capable of being touched. Sound and light are intangible. 2. not easily grasped by the mind. She had that intangible something called charm. *adj. 15.*

in te ger (inʹti jər), 1. a whole number. 1, 2, 3, 4, 15, 26, etc., are integers. 2. thing complete in itself. *n. 19.*

in te gral (inʹti grəl), 1. necessary to the completeness of the whole; essential. Steel is an integral part of a modern skyscraper. 2. entire; complete. 3. of an integer or whole number. *adj. 14.*

in te grate (inʹti grāt), 1. make into a whole. 2. bring together into a whole. *v. 16.*

in te gra tion (in′ti grāʹshən), integrating. *n. 18.*

in teg ri ty (in teg′ri ti), 1. honesty; sincerity; uprightness. A man of integrity is respected. 2. wholeness; completeness. France lost its integrity in 1940. 3. perfect condition; soundness. *n. 7.*

in teg u ment (in teg′ū mənt), covering. The skin or shell of an animal or vegetable is its integument. *n. 17.*

in tel lect (in′tə lekt), 1. the power of knowing; the understanding. Our actions are influenced by our intellect, will, and feelings. 2. intelligence; high mental ability; as, a man of intellect. 3. person of high mental ability; as, the great intellects of the age. *n. 8.*

in tel lec tu al (in′tə lek′chü əl), 1. of the intellect. 2. needing or using intelligence. Teaching is a more intellectual occupation than sweeping. 3. showing intelligence; as, an intellectual book, an intellectual face. 4. person who is well informed and intelligent. *adj., n. 7.*

in tel lec tu al ly (in′tə lek′chü əl i), 1. in an intellectual way. 2. so far as intellect is concerned. *adv.*

in tel li gence (in tel′i jəns), 1. ability to learn and know; understanding; mind. A dog has more intelligence than a worm. Intelligence tests are given in many schools. 2. knowledge; news; information. The general had secret intelligence of the plans of the enemy. The **intelligence department** of a government collects and studies information that will help its army and navy. *n., adj. 4.*

in tel li gent (in tel′i jənt), having or showing understanding; able to learn and know; quick at learning. Elephants are intelligent animals. *adj. 5.*

in tel li gi ble (in tel′i ji bəl), capable of being understood. *adj. 11.*

in tel li gi bly (in tel′i ji bli), so as to be understood. *adv.*

in tem per ance (in tem′pər əns), 1. lack of temperance; excess. 2. drinking too much intoxicating liquor. *n. 12.*

in tem per ate (in tem′pər it), 1. not moderate; lacking in self-control; excessive. 2. drinking too much intoxicating liquor. 3. not temperate; severe; as, an intemperate winter. *adj. 13.*

in tend (in tend′), mean; plan. We intend to go home soon. Mr. Smith intends that his sons shall go to college. He was intended for the ministry. *v. 2.*

in tend ed (in ten′did), 1. meant; planned. The medicine did not have the intended effect. 2. prospective; as, a woman's intended husband. 3. an intended husband or wife. *Used in common talk. adj., n.*

in tense (in tens′), 1. very much; very great; very strong; as, intense happiness, intense pain, intense light. 2. An intense person is one who feels things very deeply and is likely to be extreme in action. *adj. 6.*

in tense ly (in tens′li), 1. in an intense manner. 2. exceedingly; extremely. *adv.*

in ten si fi ca tion (in ten′si fi kā′shən), making or becoming more intense. *n.*

in ten si fy (in ten′si fī), 1. make more intense. Blowing on a fire intensifies the heat. 2. become more intense. *v., intensified, intensifying. 12.*

in ten si ty (in ten′si ti), 1. quality of being intense. 2. extreme degree; great vigor; violence; as, intensity of thought, intensity of feeling. 3. amount or degree of strength of electricity, heat, light, sound, etc., per unit of area, volume, etc. *n., pl. intensities. 7.*

in ten sive (in ten′siv), 1. deep and thorough. An intensive study of a few books is more valuable than much careless reading. 2. in grammar, giving force or emphasis. In "He himself said it," *himself* is an intensive pronoun. *adj. 16.*

in tent (in tent′), 1. purpose; intention. The thief shot with intent to kill. 2. meaning. What is the intent of that sentence? **To all intents and purposes** means in almost every way; almost; practically. 3. very attentive; having the eyes or thoughts earnestly fixed on something; earnest; as, an intent look, intent on a task. 4. earnestly engaged; much interested. She is intent on doing her best. *n., adj. 3.*

in ten tion (in ten′shən), 1. intending; purpose; design. Tom hurt his sister's feelings without intention. Our intention is to travel next summer. 2. meaning. *n. 4.*

in ten tion al (in ten′shən əl), done on purpose; intended. His insult was intentional; he wanted to hurt your feelings. *adj. 16.*

in ten tion al ly (in ten′shən əl i), with intention; on purpose. *adv.*

in ter (in tėr′), put (a dead body) into a grave or tomb. *v., interred, interring. 8.*

inter-, prefix meaning:—

1. together; one with the other; as in intercommunicate, intermixture.
2. between; as in interpose, interlay, interlude.
3. among a group; as in interscholastic, interchange.

in ter act (in′tər akt′), act on each other. *v.*

in ter ac tion (in′tər ak′shən), action on each other. *n.*

in ter breed (in′tər brēd′), breed by using different varieties or species of animals or plants; breed by the mating of different kinds. *v., interbred, interbreeding.*

in ter cede (in′tər sēd′), plead for another; ask a favor from one person for another. Dan did not dare ask the teacher himself; so Will interceded with her for Dan. *v. 14.*

in ter cept (in′tər sept′), 1. take or seize on the way from one place to another; as, to intercept a letter, to intercept a messenger. 2. cut off (light, water, etc.). 3. check; stop; as, to intercept the flight of a criminal. 4. mark off between two points or lines. *v. 8.*

The line intercepts the circle at A and B.

in ter ces sion (in′tər sesh′ən), interceding; pleading for another. Only the President's intercession could save the spy's life. *n. 9.*

in ter ces sor (in′tər ses′ər), person who pleads for another. *n. 17.*

in ter change (in′tər chānj′ for 1 and 3, in′tər chānj′ for 2 and 4), 1. put each of (two persons or things) in the place of the other. 2. putting each of two persons or things in the other's place. The word *team* becomes *meat* by the interchange of the end letters. 3. make an exchange. Tom and Dick interchange things when Tom trades his knife for Dick's ball. 4. giving and taking; exchange. *v., n. 7.*

in ter change a ble (in′tər chān′jə bəl), 1. capable of being used in place of each other. 2. able to change places. *adj. 16.*

in ter col le gi ate (in′tər kə lē′ji it), between colleges; as, intercollegiate football games. *adj.*

in ter co lo ni al (in′tər kə lō′ni əl), between colonies; as, intercolonial trade. *adj. 19.*

in ter com mu ni cate (in′tər kə mū′ni kāt), communicate with each other. *v.*

in ter com mu ni ca tion (in′tər kə mū′ni kā′shən), communication with each other. *n.*

in ter course (in′tər kōrs), communication; dealings between people; exchange of thoughts, services, and feelings. Roads, railroads, and telephones make intercourse easier. *n. 7.*

in ter de pend ence (in′tər di pen′dəns), mutual dependence; dependence upon each other. *n. 20.*

in ter de pend ent (in′tər di pen′dənt), mutually dependent; dependent upon each other. *adj. 19.*

in ter dict (in′tər dikt′ for 1 and 2, in′tər dikt for 3 and 4), 1. forbid; prohibit; restrain. 2. cut off from certain church privileges. 3. a prohibition based on authority. 4. cutting off from certain church privileges. *v., n. 12.*

in ter dic tion (in′tər dik′shən), forbidding; prohibition. *n. 19.*

in ter est (in′tər est), 1. a feeling of wanting to know, do, own, or share in. Bob has an interest in reading and in collecting stamps. 2. stir up such a feeling in. A good story interests us. 3. the power to excite such feelings. Your plan has no interest for the others. 4. advantage; profit; benefit. Mother looks after the interests of the family. 5. a share in property and actions. Father has a half interest in that farm. 6. cause to take a share in; engage or excite the concern, curiosity, attention, etc., of. The agent tried to interest us in buying a car. We were interested in the results of the election. 7. group of people concerned in one sort of thing; as, the business interests of the town. 8. money paid for the use of money. This bank pays 3% interest. *n., v. 1.*

in ter est ed (in′tər es tid), 1. feeling or showing interest. 2. having a share. 3. influenced by personal considerations; prejudiced. The manufacturers were interested in maintaining a high tariff. *adj.*

in ter est ing (in′tər es ting), arousing interest; holding one's attention. *Black Beauty* is an interesting book for children. *adj. 5.*

in ter fere (in′tər fēr′), 1. clash; come into opposition with. The two plans interfered. He will come Saturday if nothing interferes. 2. meddle. That woman is always interfering in other people's affairs. 3. **Interfere with** means hinder. *v. 6.*

in ter fer ence (in′tər fēr′əns), interfering. *n. 7.*

in ter fuse (in′tər fūz′), mix; blend; permeate. *v.*

in ter im (in′tər im), the meantime; the time between. *n. 12.*

in te ri or (in tēr′i ər), 1. inside; inner surface or part. The interior of the house was beautifully decorated. 2. inner; on the inside. 3. part of a region or country away from the coast or border. 4. away from the coast or border. 5. affairs within a country. The United States has a Department of the Interior. 6. having to do with such affairs; domestic. *n., adj. 4.*

interj., interjection.

in ter ject (in′tər jekt′), throw in between other things; insert. Every now and then the speaker interjected a joke or story. *v.*

in ter jec tion (in′tər jek′shən), 1. an exclamation regarded as a part of speech. *Oh! ah! alas!* and *hurrah!* are interjections. 2. interjecting. 3. remark; exclamation. *n. 15.*

in ter lace (in′tər lās′), 1. arrange (threads, strips, branches, etc.) so that they go over and under each other. We interlace reeds or fibers to make a basket. 2. cross each other over and under; mingle together. The branches of the trees interlaced above the path. *v. 10.*

in ter lard (in′tər lärd′), mix; intersperse; give variety to. The speaker interlarded his long speech with amusing stories. *v.*

in ter line[1] (in′tər līn′), provide (a garment) with an inner lining put between the outer fabric and the ordinary lining. *v.*

in ter line[2] (in′tər līn′), write between the lines of (a book, document, etc.). *v.*

in ter lock (in′tər lok′), lock or join with one another. The two stags were fighting with their horns interlocked. The puzzle consisted of interlocking rings. *v. 13.*

in ter lop er (in′tər lōp′ər), intruder. *n. 16.*

in ter lude (in′tər lüd), 1. anything that is thought of as filling the time between two things. There was an interlude of sunshine between two showers. 2. piece of music played between the parts of a song, church service, or drama. 3. an entertainment between the acts of a play. *n. 15.*

in ter mar riage (in′tər mar′ij), marriage between two families, tribes, castes, etc. *n. 16.*

in ter mar ry (in′tər mar′i), become connected by marriage (said of families, tribes, castes, etc.). The people of this old town have intermarried for generations. *v., intermarried, intermarrying. 18.*

in ter med dle (in′tər med′əl), meddle; interfere. *v. 19.*

in ter me di ar y (in′tər mē′di ãr′i), 1. go-between; person who acts for one person with another. John Alden acted as intermediary between Miles Standish and Priscilla. 2. acting between. 3. being between. A cocoon is an intermediary stage between caterpillar and butterfly. *n., pl. intermediaries, adj. 19.*

in ter me di ate (in′tər mē′di it), 1. being or occurring between. The intermediate department of the Sunday School is between the primary and the adult departments. Gray is intermediate between black and white. 2. something between. *adj., n. 9.*

in ter ment (in tėr′mənt), burial; putting a dead body in a grave or tomb. *n. 12.*

in ter mi na ble (in tėr′mi nə bəl), endless; so long as to seem endless. *adj. 10.*

in ter min gle (in′tər ming′gəl), mix together; mingle. *v. 10.*

in ter mis sion (in′tər mish′ən), 1. pause; time between periods of activity. The band played from eight to twelve with a short intermission at ten. 2. stopping for a time; interruption. The rain continued all day without intermission. *n. 9.*

in ter mit (in′tər mit′), stop for a time. *v., intermitted, intermitting. 14.*

in ter mit tent (in′tər mit′ənt), stopping and beginning again. The intermittent noise of the railroad trains kept me awake. *adj. 9.*

in ter mix (in′tər miks′), mix one with another. Oil and water do not intermix. *v. 14.*

in ter mix ture (in′tər miks′chər), mixing together; mixture. *n. 16.*

in tern (in tėrn′ for 1, in′tėrn for 2), 1. confine within a country or place. In war, soldiers who flee to a neutral country are interned there. 2. a doctor acting as an assistant in a hospital. *v., n.*

in ter nal (in tėr′nəl), 1. inner; inside; as, the internal organs of the body, medicine for internal use. Internal evidence of the date of a book is obtained from statements made in the book itself. 2. existing within a country; domestic; as, internal disturbances. *adj. 5.*

in ter nal ly (in tėr′nəl i), 1. inside. 2. inside the body. This ointment must not be taken internally. *adv.*

in ter na tion al (in′tər nash′ən əl), 1. between or among nations. A treaty is an international agreement. 2. having to do with the relations between nations; as, international law. *adj. 8.*

in ter na tion al ize (in′tər nash′ən əl īz), make international; bring (territory) under the control of several nations. *v. 12.*

in ter na tion al ly (in′tər nash′ən əl i), between nations; among nations; so as to influence many nations. *adv.*

in terne (in′tėrn), a doctor acting as an assistant in a hospital. *n.*

in ter ne cine (in′tər nē′sin), 1. destructive to both sides. 2. deadly; destructive. *adj.*

in ter play (in′tər plā′), action or influence on each other; as, the interplay of light and shadow. *n.*

in ter po late (in tėr′pə lāt), 1. alter (a book, passage, etc.) by putting in new words or groups of words. 2. put in (new words or passages). *v. 18.*

in ter po la tion (in tėr′pə lā′shən), 1. interpolating. 2. something interpolated. The old manuscript contained many interpolations of later date. *n. 20.*

in ter pose (in′tər pōz′), 1. put between. 2. come between. 3. put in. He interposed an objection at this point. 4. interfere in order to help. Mother interposed in the dispute. *v. 7.*

in ter po si tion (in′tər pə zish′ən), 1. an interposing. 2. thing interposed. *n. 15.*

in ter pret (in tėr′prit), 1. explain the meaning of; as, to interpret a hard passage in a book, to interpret a dream. 2. bring out the meaning of (a dramatic work, a character, music, etc.). The actor interpreted the part of the soldier wonderfully. 3. understand. We interpret your silence as consent. 4. translate. *v. 5.*

in ter pre ta tion (in tėr′pri tā′shən), 1. interpreting; explanation. What is your interpretation of Jack's queer behavior? 2. bringing out the meaning of a dramatic part, music, etc. The actor's interpretation of Hamlet was praised by most of the newspapers. *n. 7.*

in ter pre ta tive (in tėr′pri tā′tiv), used for interpreting; explanatory. *adj.*

in ter pret er (in tėr′pri tər), 1. person who interprets. 2. person whose business it is to translate words spoken in a foreign language. *n. 7.*

in ter reg num (in′tər reg′nəm), 1. time between the end of a king's reign and the coming to the throne of his successor. 2. any similar period between rulers or activities. 3. pause. *n. 16.*

in ter re lat ed (in′tər ri lāt′id), related; related back and forth among a group. *adj.*

in ter ro gate (in ter′ə gāt), ask questions of; examine by questions. The principal interrogated the boy about the work he had done in his former school. *v. 16.*

in ter ro ga tion (in ter′ə gā′shən), 1. questioning. 2. question. *n. 18.*

interrogation mark or **point,** question mark (?).

in ter rog a tive (in′tə rog′ə tiv), 1. asking a question; having the form of a question; as, an interrogative sentence, an interrogative look or tone of voice. 2. in grammar, a word used in asking a question. *Who, why,* and *what* are interrogatives. *adj., n. 12.*

in ter rupt (in′tə rupt′), break in on; hinder; stop. A fire drill interrupted the lesson. It is not polite to interrupt a speaker. *v. 3.*

in ter rup tion (in′tə rup′shən), breaking in on; break; stopping. The rain continued without interruption all day. *n. 9.*

in ter sect (in′tər sekt′), 1. cut or divide by passing through or crossing. A path intersects the field. 2. cross each other. Streets usually intersect at right angles. *v. 12.*

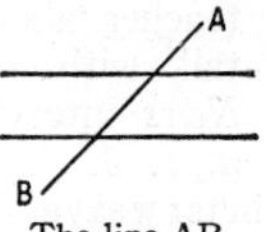

The line AB intersects the parallel lines.

in ter sec tion (in′tər sek′shən), 1. intersecting. 2. the place where one thing crosses another. In the diagram above, there are two intersections where the line AB crosses the parallel lines. *n. 15.*

in ter sperse (in′tər spėrs′), 1. scatter here and there among other things. Bushes were interspersed among the trees. 2. vary with something put here and there. The grass is interspersed with beds of flowers. *v. 11.*

in ter state (in′tər stāt′), between persons or organizations in different states. The federal government regulates interstate commerce. *adj. 11.*

in ter stice (in tėr′stis), a small or narrow space between things or parts; chink; crevice. *n. 20.*

in ter twine (in′tər twīn′), twine, one with another. Two vines intertwined on the wall. *v. 12.*

in ter twist (in′tər twist′), twist, one with another. *v. 19.*

in ter ur ban (in′tər ėr′bən), between cities; as, an interurban railway. *adj. 16.*

in ter val (in′tər vəl), 1. time or space between. There is an interval of a week between Christmas and New Year's Day. She has intervals of freedom from pain. There are trees at intervals of twenty feet. 2. in music, the difference in pitch between two tones. 3. **At intervals** means (1) now and then. (2) here and there. *n. 5.*

in ter vene (in′tər vēn′), 1. come between; be between. A week intervenes between Christmas and New Year's Day. 2. come in to help settle a dispute. The President was asked to intervene in the coal strike. *v. 8.*

in ter ven tion (in′tər ven′shən), 1. intervening. The strike was settled by the intervention of the President. 2. interference by one nation in the affairs of another; interference. *n. 12.*

in ter view (in′tər vū), 1. a meeting, generally of two people, to talk over something special. Father had an interview with the teacher about John's work. 2. visit and talk with. The reporters from *The Daily News* interviewed the returning explorers. *n., v. 5.*

in ter weave (in′tər wēv′), 1. weave together. 2. mix together; mingle. *v., interwove* or *interweaved, interwoven* or *interwove* or *interweaved, interweaving.*

in ter wo ven (in′tər wō′vən), 1. woven together. 2. mixed together; mingled. *adj., pp. of* **interweave.** *12.*

in tes tate (in tes′tāt), having made no will; as, to die intestate. *adj. 19.*

in tes ti nal (in tes′ti nəl), of the intestines; in the intestines. *adj. 11.*

in tes tine (in tes′tin), 1. a part of the bowels. **The intestines** means the bowels. 2. internal; inward. Civil war is intestine strife. *n., adj. 9.*

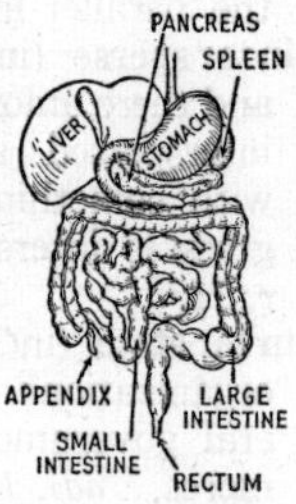

Human intestines

in ti ma cy (in′ti mə si), a being intimate; closeness; close acquaintance. *n., pl. intimacies. 8.*

in ti mate[1] (in′ti mit), 1. very familiar; known very well; closely acquainted. 2. a close friend. 3. far within; inmost. *adj., n. 5.*

in ti mate[2] (in′ti māt), 1. hint; suggest. 2. make known. *v.*

in ti ma tion (in′ti mā′shən), 1. hint; suggestion. 2. announcement. *n. 12.*

in tim i date (in tim′i dāt), frighten; make afraid; influence by fear. *v. 15.*

in tim i da tion (in tim′i dā′shən), making afraid; being made afraid. *n. 17.*

in to (in′tü), 1. Into shows motion or direction to or toward a place within a thing. Come into the house. Look into the matter of his mistakes. 2. Into also shows a change. Divide the apple into three parts. Cold weather turns water into ice. *prep. 1.*

in tol er a ble (in tol′ər ə bəl), unbearable; too hard to be endured. The pain from the toothache was intolerable. *adj. 8.*

in tol er ance (in tol′ər əns), 1. unwillingness to let others think as they choose, especially in matters of religion. The Pilgrims came to this country because of intolerance and persecution. 2. lack of tolerance; inability to tolerate. *n. 13.*

in tol er ant (in tol′ər ənt), 1. not tolerant; not willing to let others think as they choose, especially in matters of religion. 2. **Intolerant of** means not able to endure; unwilling to endure. *adj. 14.*

in to na tion (in′tō nā′shən), 1. reciting in a singing voice; as, the intonation of a psalm. 2. the production of musical tones. 3. the manner of sounding words or speaking. *n. 15.*

in tone (in tōn′), 1. read or recite in a singing voice; chant. A priest intones part of the service. 2. utter with a particular tone. *v. 17.*

in tox i cant (in tok′si kənt), 1. alcoholic liquor. 2. any drug that intoxicates. *n. 19.*

in tox i cate (in tok′si kāt), 1. make drunk. Alcohol intoxicates people. 2. excite beyond self-control. The joy of victory so intoxicated him that he jumped and sang and behaved like a crazy man. *v. 7.*

in tox i cat ed (in tok′si kāt′id), 1. drunk. An intoxicated man loses control of himself. 2. very much excited. *adj.*

in tox i cat ing (in tok′si kāt′ing), 1. making drunk. Whiskey is an intoxicating liquor. 2. very exciting. *adj.*

in tox i ca tion (in tok′si kā′shən), 1. drunkenness. 2. great excitement. 3. in medicine, poisoning. *n. 13.*

in trac ta ble (in trak′tə bəl), hard to manage; stubborn. *adj. 18.*

in tra mu ral (in′trə mūr′əl), within the walls; inside. Intramural games are games played between students of the same school. *adj.*

in tran si tive (in tran′si tiv), not taking a direct object. The verbs *belong, go,* and *seem* are intransitive. *adj.*

in treat (in trēt′), keep asking earnestly; beg and pray. *v. 19.* Also spelled **entreat.**

in trench (in trench′), 1. surround with a trench; fortify with trenches; etc. Our soldiers were intrenched opposite the enemy. 2. establish firmly. Exchanging gifts at Christmas is a custom intrenched by long tradition. 3. trespass; encroach; infringe. Do not intrench upon the rights of another. *v. 13.* Also spelled **entrench.**

in trench ment (in trench′mənt), 1. an intrenching. 2. an intrenched position. 3. a defense consisting of a trench and a rampart of earth or stone. *n. 18.* Also spelled **entrenchment.**

Intrenchment

in trep id (in trep′id), fearless; dauntless; very brave. A policeman or soldier must be intrepid. *adj. 14.*

in tre pid i ty (in′tri pid′i ti), fearlessness; great courage. *n. 16.*

in tri ca cy (in′tri kə si), 1. intricate nature or condition. The intricacy of the plan made it hard to understand. 2. an intricate thing or event. The law is full of intricacies. *n., pl. intricacies. 16.*

in tri cate (in′tri kit), 1. with many twists and turns; perplexing; entangled; complicated; as, an intricate knot, an intricate maze, an intricate plot. 2. very hard to understand; as, an intricate design, intricate directions. *adj. 9.*

in trigue (in trēg′), 1. underhand plotting; crafty dealings. The royal palace was filled with intrigue. 2. form and carry out plans, plots, love affairs, etc., in a secret or underhand way. He will fight openly, but he will not intrigue against you. 3. a secret love affair. 4. excite the curiosity and interest of. *n., v. 9.*

in trin sic (in trin′sik), belonging in a thing by its very nature; essential. The intrinsic value of a dollar bill is only that of a piece of paper. *adj. 12.*

in trin si cal ly (in trin′si kəl i), essentially; by itself alone. *adv.*

in tro duce (in′trə dūs′ or in′trə düs′), 1. bring in; as, to introduce a story into the conversation. 2. put in; insert. The doctor introduced a tube down the sick man's throat. 3. bring into use, notice, knowledge, etc.; as, to introduce a new fashion, a new food, or a reform. 4. make known; bring into acquaintance with. Mrs. Brown, may I introduce Mr. Smith? The principal introduced the speaker to the students. I introduced a country cousin to the city. 5. bring forward; as, to introduce a question for debate. 6. begin. *v. 3.*

in tro duc tion (in′trə duk′shən), 1. an introducing. The introduction of steel made tall buildings easy to build. 2. the beginning of a speech, a piece of music, or a book. 3. a first book for beginners. 4. being introduced. Mary was shy at her introduction to the company. 5. thing made known; the thing brought into use. Radios are a later introduction than telephones. *n. 6.*

in tro duc to ry (in′trə duk′tə ri), used for introducing; preliminary. *adj. 18.*

in tro spec tion (in′trə spek′shən), the examination of one's own thoughts and feelings. *n.*

in tro vert (in′trə vėrt′), person more interested in his own thoughts and feelings than in what is going on around him; person tending to think rather than act. *n. 15.*

in trude (in trüd′), 1. thrust in; force in. Do not intrude your opinions on others. 2. thrust oneself in; come unasked and unwanted. *v. 7.*

in trud er (in trüd′ər), one that intrudes. *n. 8.*

in tru sion (in trü′zhən), act of intruding; coming unasked and unwanted. *n. 8.*

in tru sive (in trü′siv), intruding; coming unasked and unwanted. *adj. 14.*

in trust (in trust′), 1. trust; charge with a trust. We intrusted Joe with all the money to pay the fares. 2. give (something or somebody) in trust; as, to intrust children to the care of a nurse, to intrust one's life to a surgeon. *v. 8.* Also spelled **entrust.**

in tu i tion (in′tū ish′ən or in′tü ish′ən), 1. perception of truths, facts, etc., without reasoning. By experience with many people Mr. Jones had developed great powers of intuition. 2. something so perceived. *n. 13.*

in tu i tive (in tū′i tiv or in tü′i tiv), 1. perceiving by intuition; as, intuitive power. 2. acquired by intuition; as, intuitive knowledge. *adj. 11.*

in un date (in′un dāt), overflow; flood. *v. 15.*

in un da tion (in′un dā′shən), overflowing; a flood. *n. 14.*

in ure (in ūr′), 1. accustom. Poverty had inured the beggar to hardship. 2. be useful. The agreement inures to the special benefit of the employees. *v. 14.*

in vade (in vād′), 1. enter with force or as an enemy; attack. Grasshoppers invade fields and eat the crops. Disease invades the body. 2. enter as if to take possession.

Tourists invaded the city. Night invades the sky. 3. interfere with; encroach upon; violate. The law punishes people who invade the rights of others. *v. 4.*

in vad er (in vād′ər), person or thing that invades. *n. 8.*

in va lid[1] (in′və lid), 1. a sick, weak person not able to get about and do things. 2. not well; weak and sick. 3. for the use of invalids; as, an invalid chair. 4. make weak or sick; disable. 5. remove from active service because of sickness or injury. The wounded soldier was invalided and sent home. *n., adj., v. 7.*

in val id[2] (in val′id), without force; without value. Unless a will or check is signed, it is invalid. *adj.*

in val i date (in val′i dāt), make valueless; deprive of all force. A contract is invalidated if only one person signs it. *v.*

in val u a ble (in val′ū ə bəl), priceless; valuable beyond measure. *adj. 9.*

in var i a ble (in vãr′i ə bəl), not changing; always the same. *adj. 7.*

in var i a bly (in vãr′i ə bli), 1. without change. 2. without exception. *adv.*

in va sion (in vā′zhən), invading; entering by force. *n. 7.*

in vec tive (in vek′tiv), a violent attack in words; strong language. *n. 15.*

in veigh (in vā′), make a violent attack in words. *v. 20.*

in vei gle (in vā′gəl or in vē′gəl), entice; allure; mislead by trickery. The saleswoman inveigled Dora into buying two hats. *v. 16.*

in vent (in vent′), 1. make or think out (something new); as, to invent a method, a machine, or a name. 2. make up; as, to invent an excuse. *v. 3.*

in ven tion (in ven′shən), 1. making something new; as, the invention of gunpowder. 2. the thing invented. The radio was a wonderful invention. 3. the power of inventing. To be a good writer of stories a person needs invention. 4. made-up story; false statement. *n. 3.*

in ven tive (in ven′tiv), 1. good at inventing. An inventive person thinks up ways to save time, money, and work. 2. showing power of inventing. *adj. 15.*

in ven tor (in ven′tər), person who invents. Edison was a great inventor. *n. 6.*

in ven to ry (in′vən tō′ri), 1. detailed list of articles. 2. collection of articles that are or may be so listed; stock. A storekeeper had a sale to reduce his inventory. 3. make a detailed list of; enter in a list. Some stores inventory their stock once a month. *n., pl. inventories, v., inventoried, inventorying. 11.*

in verse (in vėrs′ or in′vėrs), 1. inverted; reversed in position, direction, or tendency. 2. something reversed. DCBA is the inverse of ABCD. $\frac{4}{3}$ is the inverse of $\frac{3}{4}$. *adj., n. 15.*

in ver sion (in vėr′zhən), 1. inverting. 2. being inverted. 3. something inverted. *n. 16.*

in vert (in vėrt′), 1. turn upside down; as, to invert a glass. 2. turn around or reverse in position, direction, or order. If you invert "I can," you have "Can I?" *v. 6.*

in ver te brate (in vėr′ti brāt), 1. without a backbone. 2. an animal without a backbone. All animals except fishes, amphibians, reptiles, birds, and mammals are invertebrates. *adj., n. 13.*

in vest (in vest′), 1. use money to buy something which will produce a profit or an income or both. If I had any money to invest, I would invest it in that land. 2. clothe. The castle was invested with mystery and romance. 3. give power, authority, or right to. He invested his lawyer with complete power to act for him. 4. surround with troops; besiege. The enemy invested the city and cut it off from our army. *v. 5.*

in ves ti gate (in ves′ti gāt), search into; examine closely. Detectives investigate crimes. Scientists investigate nature. *v. 6.*

in ves ti ga tion (in ves′ti gā′shən), a careful search; a detailed or careful examination. *n. 6.*

in ves ti ga tor (in ves′ti gā′tər), person who investigates. *n. 11.*

in ves ti ture (in ves′ti chər), the formal enduing of a person with an office, dignity, power, right, etc. *n. 16.*

in vest ment (in vest′mənt), 1. investing. 2. a laying out of money. Getting an education was a wise investment of time and money. 3. something bought which is expected to yield money as interest or profit or both. Mr. Smith has a good income from wise investments. He considers United States bonds the safest investment. 4. money invested. His investments amount to thousands of dollars. *n. 7.*

in ves tor (in ves′tər), person who invests money. *n. 14.*

in vet er ate (in vet′ər it), 1. long and firmly established. Cats have an inveterate dislike of dogs. 2. fixed; confirmed in a habit, practice, feeling, etc. General Grant was an inveterate smoker. *adj. 12.*

in vid i ous (in vid′i əs), likely to arouse ill will or resentment; giving offense because unfair or unjust. *adj. 15.*

in vig or ate (in vig′ər āt), give vigor to; fill with life and energy. *v. 12.*

in vin ci ble (in vin′si bəl), unconquerable; not to be overcome. *adj. 9.*

in vi o la ble (in vī′ə lə bəl), 1. that must not be violated or injured; sacred; as, an inviolable vow. 2. that cannot be violated or injured. The gods are inviolable. *adj. 15.*

in vi o late (in vī′ə lāt), not violated; unbroken; uninjured; not profaned. *adj. 15.*

in vis i ble (in viz′i bəl), not visible; not capable of being seen. Thought is invisible. The queen kept herself invisible in her palace. Germs are invisible to the naked eye. *adj. 4.*

in vis i bly (in viz′i bli), without being seen; so as not to be seen. *adv.*

in vi ta tion (in′vi tā′shən), 1. a request to come to some place or to do something. The children received invitations to the party. 2. act of inviting. *n. 3.*

in vite (in vīt′), 1. ask (someone) politely to come to some place or to do something. We invited Helen to join our club. 2. make a polite request for. Alice invited our opinion of her story. 3. give occasion for. The letter invites some questions. 4. attract; tempt. The calm water invited us to swim. *v. 2.*

in vit ing (in vīt′ing), attractive; tempting. *adj.*

in vo ca tion (in′və kā′shən), 1. act of calling upon God or another divine being in prayer; appealing for aid or protection. 2. calling forth spirits by magic. *n. 13.*

in voice (in′vois), 1. list of goods sent to a purchaser showing prices, amounts, shipping charges, etc. 2. make an invoice of; enter on an invoice. 3. shipment of invoiced goods. *n., v. 12.*

in voke (in vōk′), 1. call on (God or another divine being) in prayer; appeal to for aid or protection. 2. ask earnestly for. The condemned murderer invoked the judge's mercy. 3. call forth by magic. *v. 9.*

in vol un tar i ly (in vol′ən tãr′i li), without intention; unwillingly. *adv.*

in vol un tar y (in vol′ən tãr′i), 1. not done of one's own free will; unwilling. 2. not intended; not done on purpose; as, an involuntary injury. 3. not controlled by the will. Breathing is mainly involuntary. *adj. 7.*

in volve (in volv′), 1. have as a necessary part; take in; include. Housework involves cooking, washing dishes, sweeping, and cleaning. 2. bring (into difficulty, danger, etc.). One foolish mistake can involve you in a good deal of trouble. 3. entangle; complicate. Long involved sentences are hard to understand. 4. take up the attention of; occupy. She was involved in working out a puzzle. 5. wrap; enfold. Clouds involved the mountain top. The outcome of the contest is involved in doubt. *v. 4.*

in vul ner a ble (in vul′nər ə bəl), that cannot be wounded or hurt; proof against attack. Achilles was invulnerable except for his heel. *adj. 15.*

in ward (in′wərd), 1. toward the inside; as, a passage leading inward. 2. placed within; as, the inward parts of the body. 3. directed toward the inside; as, the inward slant of the eyes. 4. into the mind or soul. Turn your thoughts inward. 5. in the mind or soul; as, inward peace. *adv., adj. 4.*

in ward ly (in′wərd li), 1. on the inside; within. 2. toward the inside. 3. in the mind or soul. 4. not aloud or openly. *adv.*

in wards (in′wərdz), 1. inward. 2. the stomach and intestines. *adv., n. pl.*

in wrought (in′rôt′), 1. having a decoration worked in. 2. worked in. *adj. 16.*

i o din (ī′ə din), iodine. *n.*

i o dine (ī′ə dīn), a substance used in medicine, in photography, and in making dyes. Iodine is put on cuts and wounds to kill disease germs and prevent infection. *n. 11.*

-ion, suffix meaning:—

1. act of ———ing; as in attraction, calculation.
2. condition or state of being ———ed; as in adoption, fascination.
3. result of ———ing; as in abbreviation, collection, connection.

I o ni a (ī ō′ni ə), a region on the western coast of Asia Minor, with the islands near it. The Greeks colonized Ionia in very early times. *n. 12.*

Ionic capital

I on ic (ī on′ik), 1. noting or pertaining to the order of Greek architecture having scrolls in the capitals of the columns. 2. of Ionia or its people. *adj. 20.*

i o ta (ī ō′tə), a very small part or quantity; a jot. *n. 20.*

I.O.U. or **I O U** (ī′ō ū′), 1. I owe you. 2. informal note showing a debt. Write me your I.O.U. for ten dollars.

I o wa (ī′ə wə), a Middle Western State of the United States. *n. 7.*

ir-, prefix meaning:—not; the opposite of; the absence of; as in irregular, irresistible. *in-* becomes *ir-* before *r.*

I ran (i rän′), official name of Persia. *n.*

I raq (i räk′), a country between Persia and Arabia. *n.*

i ras ci ble (i ras′i bəl), irritable; easily made angry. *adj. 17.*

i rate (ī′rāt or ī rāt′), angry. *adj.*

ire (īr), anger. *n. 11.*

ire ful (īr′fəl), wrathful; angry. *adj. 20.*

Ire land (īr′lənd), one of the British Isles. Ireland is divided into Eire and Northern Ireland. *n. 5.*

ir i des cent (ir′i des′ənt), 1. displaying colors like those of the rainbow. 2. changing colors. *adj. 20.*

Iris

i ris (ī′ris), 1. a plant with beautiful flowers and sword-shaped leaves. 2. the flower. 3. the colored part of the eye around the pupil. 4. the rainbow. *n. 6.*

I rish (ī′rish), 1. of or having to do with Ireland, its people, or their language. 2. the people of Ireland. 3. their language; Gaelic. 4. English as spoken by the Irish. *adj., n. 4.*

Irish Free State, former name of Eire, a British dominion in central and southern Ireland.

I rish man (ī′rish mən), a man of Irish birth or descent. *n., pl. Irishmen. 10.*

Irish potato, the common white potato.

irk (ėrk), weary; disgust; annoy; trouble; bore. It irks us to wait for people who are late. *v. 18.*

irk some (ėrk′səm), tiresome; tedious. Hoeing corn all day is an irksome task. *adj. 10.*

i ron (ī′ərn), 1. the strong, cheap metal from which steel is made. 2. something made of iron. 3. made of iron; as, an iron fence. 4. like iron; hard; strong; as, an iron constitution. 5. furnish or cover with iron. 6. **Irons** means chains or bands of iron; handcuffs; shackles. 7. to fetter or fasten with irons. 8. an implement to press clothing. 9. to press with an iron. *n., adj., v. 1.*

i ron clad (ī′ərn klad′), 1. protected with steel plates. 2. warship protected with steel plates. 3. very hard to change or get out of. An ironclad agreement must be kept. *adj., n.*

i ron ic (ī ron′ik), ironical. *adj.*

i ron i cal (ī ron′i kəl), 1. expressing one thing and meaning the opposite. "Speedy" was the ironical name the children gave their lazy little donkey. 2. of irony; suggesting irony. It was ironical that the man was run over by his own automobile. *adj. 12.*

i ron sides (ī′ərn sīdz′), a name given in praise of strength. Cromwell's soldiers were called **Ironsides.** The old United States frigate *Constitution* is called **Old Ironsides.** *n. 19.*

i ron work (ī′ərn wėrk′), things made of iron; work in iron. *n.*

i ron works (ī′ərn wėrks′), place where iron is made or worked into iron articles. *n. pl.*

i ro ny (ī′rə ni), 1. a method of expression in which the ordinary meaning of the words is the opposite of the thought in the speaker's mind. The boys called the very thin boy "Fatty" in irony. 2. a tendency to turn what would normally have been good into harm. By the irony of fate the farmers had rain when they needed sun, and sun when they needed rain. 3. an event contrary to what would naturally be expected. *n., pl. ironies. 12.*

Ir o quois (ir′ə kwoi), member of a group of North American Indian tribes once living in what is now the northeastern United States. *n., pl. Iroquois. 14.*

ir ra di ate (i rā′di āt), 1. shine upon; make bright; illuminate. 2. shine. 3. radiate; give out. 4. treat with ultraviolet rays, etc. *v. 15.*

ir ra tion al (i rash′ən əl), 1. not rational; unreasonable. To be afraid of the number 13 is irrational. 2. unable to think and reason clearly. *adj. 11.*

ir re claim a ble (ir′i klām′ə bəl), that cannot be reclaimed. *adj.*

ir rec on cil a ble (i rek′ən sīl′ə bəl), that cannot be reconciled; that cannot be made to agree; opposed; as, irreconcilable enemies. *adj. 13.*

ir re cov er a ble (ir′i kuv′ər ə bəl), that cannot be got back, regained, or remedied. Lost youth is irrecoverable. *adj. 15.*

ir re deem a ble (ir′i dēm′ə bəl), 1. that cannot be brought back. 2. that cannot be turned into coin; as, irredeemable paper money. 3. beyond remedy; hopeless; as, an irredeemable misfortune. *adj.*

ir re duc i ble (ir′i dūs′i bəl or ir′i düs′i bəl), that cannot be reduced. *adj.*

ir ref u ta ble (i ref′ū tə bəl), that cannot be refuted or disproved; as, irrefutable arguments. *adj.*

ir reg u lar (i reg′ū lər), 1. not regular; not according to rule. 2. not even; not smooth; not straight. *adj. 4.*

ir reg u lar i ty (i reg′ū lar′i ti), 1. lack of regularity; being irregular. 2. something irregular. *n., pl. irregularities. 14.*

ir rel e vant (i rel′i vənt), not to the point; off the subject. Questions about arithmetic would be irrelevant in a spelling lesson. *adj. 15.*

ir re li gious (ir′i lij′əs), not religious. *adj. 14.*

ir re me di a ble (ir′i mē′di ə bəl), that cannot be remedied; incurable. *adj. 19.*

ir rep a ra ble (i rep′ə rə bəl), that cannot be repaired or made good. Losing a leg is an irreparable injury. *adj. 15.*

ir re press i ble (ir′i pres′i bəl), that cannot be held back. *adj. 15.*

ir re proach a ble (ir′i prōch′ə bəl), free from blame; faultless. *adj. 16.*

ir re sist i ble (ir′i zis′ti bəl), that cannot be resisted; too great to be withstood. *adj. 8.*

ir res o lute (i rez′ə lüt), not resolute; unable to make up one's mind; not sure of what one wants; hesitating. Irresolute persons make poor leaders. *adj. 10.*

ir res o lu tion (i rez′ə lü′shən), lack of firm decision; hesitation. *n. 19.*

ir re spec tive (ir′i spek′tiv), regardless. All pupils, irrespective of age, are invited to join the club. *adj. 17.*

ir re spon si ble (ir′i spon′si bəl), 1. not responsible; that cannot be called to account. A dictator is an irresponsible ruler. 2. without a sense of responsibility. *adj. 13.*

ir re triev a ble (ir′i trēv′ə bəl), that cannot be recovered. *adj. 14.*

ir rev er ence (i rev′ər əns), lack of reverence; disrespect. *n. 19.*

ir rev er ent (i rev′ər ənt), not reverent; disrespectful. *adj. 15.*

ir re vers i ble (ir′i vėr′si bəl), not capable of being reversed. *adj.*

ir rev o ca ble (i rev′ə kə bəl), not to be recalled, withdrawn, or annulled; as, an irrevocable decision. *adj. 14.*

ir ri gate (ir′i gāt), 1. supply (land) with water by means of ditches. 2. supply (a wound, etc.) with a constant flow of some liquid. *v. 8.*

ir ri ga tion (ir′i gā′shən), supplying land with water from ditches; irrigating. See the picture just below. *n. 7.*

ir ri ta bil i ty (ir′i tə bil′i ti), 1. impatience; being irritable. 2. unnatural sensitiveness (of an organ or part of the body). *n., pl. irritabilities. 16.*

Irrigation of an orchard

ir ri ta ble (ir′i tə bəl), 1. easily made angry; impatient. 2. unnaturally sensitive. *adj. 9.*

ir ri tant (ir′i tənt), 1. thing that irritates. A mustard plaster is an irritant. 2. causing irritation. *n., adj.*

ir ri tate (ir′i tāt), 1. annoy; provoke; vex; arouse to impatience or anger. Flies irritate horses. The boy's foolish questions irritated his mother. 2. bring (a part of the body) to an unnaturally sensitive condition. Sunburn irritates the skin. *v. 7.*

ir ri ta tion (ir′i tā′shən), annoyance; vexation; irritating; being irritated. *n. 9.*

ir rup tion (i rup′shən), breaking in; bursting in. The irruption of barbarians was one cause of the downfall of the Roman Empire. *n. 15.*

Ir ving (ėr′ving), Washington, a famous American author (1783-1859). *n. 12.*

is (iz). See **be.** The earth is round. He is in China. A child is loved by its mother. *v. 1.*

I saac (ī′zək), son of Abraham and Sarah, and father of Jacob and Esau. Genesis 21: 3. *n. 7.*

I sa iah (ī zā′ə), 1. the greatest of the Hebrew prophets. 2. a book of the Old Testament. *n. 13.*

Is car i ot (is kar′i ət), Judas, who betrayed Christ. *n. 14.*

-ish, suffix meaning:—
1. somewhat; as in oldish, sweetish.
2. resembling; like; as in a childish man.
3. like that of; having the characteristics of; as in a childish idea.
4. of or pertaining to; belonging to; as in British, Spanish, Turkish.
5. tending to; inclined to; as in bookish, thievish.

Ish ma el (ish′mi əl), 1. the son of Abraham and Hagar, driven into the wilderness by Sarah. Genesis 16. 2. an outcast. *n. 14*

i sin glass (ī′zing glas′), 1. a kind of gelatin obtained from certain fishes. 2. mica, a mineral that divides into thin, semitransparent layers. *n. 14.*

I sis (ī′sis), a goddess of the ancient Egyptians. *n. 13.*

Is lam (is′ləm), 1. Mohammedan religion. 2. Mohammedans as a group. 3. the countries under Mohammedan rule. *n. 20.*

is land (ī′lənd), 1. a body of land surrounded by water. The hermit lived alone on an island. 2. something that suggests a piece of land surrounded by water. Platforms in the middle of crowded streets are safety islands. *n. 1.*

is land er (ī′lən dər), 1. one born on an island. 2. one living on an island. *n. 12.*

isle (īl), island; small island. *n. 3.*

is let (ī′lit), little island. *n. 13.*

-ism, suffix meaning:—
1. action; practice; as in baptism, criticism.
2. doctrine; system; principle; as in communism, socialism.
3. quality; characteristic; state; condition; as in heroism, paganism, Americanism.
4. illustration; case; instance; as in colloquialism, witticism.
5. unhealthy condition caused by; as in alcoholism.

is n't (iz′ənt), is not. *6.*

i so late (ī′sə lāt or is′ə lāt), place apart; separate from others. People with contagious diseases should be isolated. *v. 7.*

i so la tion (ī′sə lā′shən or is′ə lā′shən), 1. setting apart. 2. being set apart. 3. complete separation. *n. 10.*

i sos ce les (ī sos′ə lēz), having two sides equal. *adj. 20.*

Isosceles triangles

i so therm (ī′sō thėrm), a line connecting places which have the same average temperature. *n. 20.*

Is ra el (iz′ri əl), 1. name given to Jacob after he had wrestled with the angel. Genesis 32:28. 2. name given to his descendants; the Jews; the Hebrews. 3. their kingdom in northern Palestine. *n. 4.*

Is ra el ite (iz′ri əl īt), Jew or Hebrew; a descendant of Israel. *n. 11.*

is sue (ish′ü), 1. send out; put forth. This magazine is issued every week. 2. something sent out. Did you read the last issue of our weekly paper? 3. sending out. 4. come out; go out; proceed. Smoke issues from the chimney. 5. coming forth; flowing out; discharge. Nosebleed is an issue of blood from the nose. 6. way out; outlet. 7. result; as, the issue of the battle. 8. to result. The game issued in a tie. 9. point to be debated. 10. problem. 11. **At issue** means in question. 12. **Take issue** means disagree. 13. children. **Without issue** means without children. *v., n. 2.*

-ist, suffix meaning:—
1. a person who does or makes; as in theorist, tourist.
2. one who knows about or has skill with; as in biologist, pianist.
3. one engaged in or busy with; as in agriculturist, machinist.
4. one who believes in; as in abolitionist, idealist.

Is tan bul (is′tän bül′), Constantinople. *n.*

isth mus (is′məs), a narrow strip of land, with water on both sides of it, connecting two larger bodies of land; as, the Isthmus of Panama. *n. 3.*

Isthmus of Panama

it (it), the thing, part, animal, or person spoken about. Here is your paper; read it. Look at it carefully. He said, "It is I. What is it you want?" It snows in winter. It is now my turn. *pron., pl. they or them. 1.*

I tal ian (i tal′yən), 1. of Italy, its people, or their language. 2. a native or inhabitant of Italy. 3. the language of Italy. *adj., n. 3.*

i tal ic (i tal′ik), 1. of or in type whose letters slant to the right. *These words are in italic type.* 2. **Italics** means type whose letters slant to the right. *adj., n. 18.*

i tal i cize (i tal′i sīz), 1. print in type in which the letters slope to the right. Example: *italicize.* 2. underline (written words, etc.) with a single line. We italicize expressions which we wish to distinguish or emphasize. *v.*

It a ly (it′ə li), a country in southern Europe. Sicily and Sardinia are parts of Italy. *n. 3.*

itch (ich), 1. a tickly, prickling feeling in the skin that makes one restless, and want to scratch. 2. a disease causing this feeling. 3. cause this feeling. Mosquito bites itch. 4. feel this way in the skin. 5. a restless, uneasy longing or desire for anything; as, an itch to get away and explore. 6. be restless with any desire. John itched to find out their secret. *n., v. 6.*

i tem (ī′təm), 1. separate thing or article. The list contained twelve items. 2. piece of news. 3. also. *n., adv. 4.*

i tem ize (ī′təm īz), state each item of; list by items. The storekepeer itemized the bill to show each article bought and its price. *v.*

it er ate (it′ər āt), repeat. *v. 19.*

it er a tion (it′ər ā′shən), repetition. *n. 17.*

it er a tive (it′ər ā′tiv), repeating; full of repetitions. *adj.*

Ith a ca (ith′ə kə), a small island west of Greece, the home of Odysseus. *n. 14.*

i tin er ant (ī tin′ər ənt), 1. traveling from place to place. 2. person who travels from place to place. *adj., n. 18.*

i tin er ar y (ī tin′ər ãr′i), 1. route; plan of travel. 2. a record of travel. 3. a guidebook for travelers. 4. of traveling or routes of travel. *n., pl. itineraries, adj. 17.*

its (its), of it; belonging to it. The cat chased its tail. This chair has lost one of its legs. *pron., adj. 1.*

it's (its), it is. *4.*

it self (it self′), 1. *Itself* is used to make a statement stronger. The land itself is worth the money, without the house. 2. *Itself* is used instead of it, him, or her in cases like: The baby hurt itself. 3. its self. The dog saw itself in the glass. *pron. 2.*

-ity, suffix meaning:—condition or quality of being; as in absurdity, brutality, cordiality, activity, hostility, sincerity.

I've (īv), I have. *3.*

i vied (ī′vid), covered or overgrown with ivy. *adj.*

i vo ry (ī′və ri), 1. the hard, white substance composing the tusks of elephants, walruses, etc. Ivory is used for piano keys and ornaments. 2. substance like ivory. 3. made of ivory. 4. of or like ivory. 5. creamy white. *n., pl. ivories, adj. 3.*

Ivy: A, English ivy; B, poison ivy.

i vy (ī′vi), a climbing plant with evergreen leaves. *n., pl ivies. 5.*

-ize, suffix meaning:—
1. make; as in legalize, centralize.
2. become; as in crystallize, materialize.
3. engage in; be busy with; use; as in apologize, theorize.
4. treat with; as in circularize, macadamize.
5. other meanings; as in alphabetize, colonize, criticize, memorize.

J

J, j (jā), the tenth letter of the alphabet. Few English words have two j's. *n., pl. J's, j's.*

jab (jab), poke; thrust with something pointed. He jabbed his fork into the potato. *v., jabbed, jabbing, n.*

jab ber (jab′ər), 1. talk very fast in a confused, senseless way; chatter. 2. very fast, confused, or senseless talk; chatter. *v., n. 18.*

ja bot (zha bō′ or zhab′ō), a ruffle or frill of lace, etc., worn for ornament at the throat or on the breast. *n. 20.*

jack (jak), 1. a man or fellow. A **jack of all trades** is a person who can do many different kinds of work. **Every man jack** means every one. 2. A **Jack** or **Jack Tar** means a sailor. 3. tool or machine for lifting or pushing up heavy weights small distances. We raise or lift the axle off the ground with a jack to change a tire. 4. To **jack** or to **jack up** means to lift or push up with a jack. 5. a device for turning meat roasting before the fire. 6. a ship's flag, smaller than usual, especially one used to show nationality or as a signal. *n., v. 2.*

Jack for lifting

jack al (jak′ôl), a wild dog of Asia and Africa, about as big as a fox. It was supposed to hunt prey for the lion and eat what the lion left. *n. 10.*

Jackal (about 15 in. high at the shoulder)

jack a napes (jak′ə nāps), pert, presuming fellow. *n.*

jack ass (jak′as′), 1. male donkey. 2. a very stupid or foolish person. *n. 17.*

jack boot (jak′büt′), a large strong boot reaching above the knee. *n.*

jack daw (jak′dô′), European crow. *n. 18.*

jack et (jak′it), 1. short coat. 2. outer covering, such as the paper cover for protecting a book, a casing around a steam pipe, or the skin of a potato. *n. 5.*

jack knife (jak′nīf′), a large, strong pocketknife. *n., pl. jackknives.*

jack-o'-lan tern (jak′ə lan′tərn), 1. a pumpkin hollowed out and cut to look like a face, used as a lantern at Halloween. 2. a will-o'-the-wisp, a flitting light appearing at night over marshy places. *n.*

jack rabbit, large hare of western North America, having very long legs and ears.

Jack rabbit (about 2 ft. long)

Jack son (jak′sən), 1. Andrew Jackson (1767-1845) was an American general who became the seventh president of the United States, from 1829 to 1837. 2. Stonewall Jackson (1824-1863) was a Confederate general. 3. the capital of Mississippi. *n. 5.*

Jack son ville (jak′sən vil), a city in northeastern Florida. *n.*

jack straws (jak′strôz′), a game, consisting of strips of wood thrown in a confused pile which are to be picked up singly without disturbing the rest of the pile. *n.*

Ja cob (jā′kəb), the son of Isaac, and the younger brother of Esau. From Jacob's 12 sons the 12 tribes of Israel traced their descent. *n. 4.*

jade[1] (jād), a hard green stone used for jewelry. *n. 9.*

jade[2] (jād), 1. inferior or worn-out horse. 2. a woman. 3. to tire; to weary; as, a jaded horse. *n., v.*

Jaf fa (jaf′ə), a seaport of Palestine. *n.*

jag (jag), 1. a point sticking out; as, a jag of rock. 2. cut or tear unevenly; as, a jagged rent in cloth. 3. make notches in. *n., v., jagged, jagging. 13.*

jag ged (jag′id), with points sticking out; notched. We cut our bare feet on the jagged rocks. *adj. 17.*

jag uar (jag′wär), fierce animal much like a leopard, but larger. It lives in forests in the warmer parts of America. *n.*

Jaguar (about 6 ft. long, including the tail)

jail (jāl), 1. a prison, especially one for persons awaiting trial or being punished for offenses that are not very serious. 2. put in jail; keep in jail. *n., v. 5.*

jail er or **jail or** (jāl′ər), the keeper of a jail. *n. 11.*

jam[1] (jam), 1. press or squeeze tightly between surfaces. The ship was jammed between two rocks. 2. bruise or crush by squeezing; as, to jam your fingers in the door. 3. press or squeeze (things or people) tightly together. A crowd jammed into the streetcar. 4. push or thrust (a thing) hard (into a place); as, to jam a fist into a fellow's face. 5. cause (part of a machine) to become caught so that it cannot work; stick fast. 6. fill or block up (the way, etc.) by crowding. The river was jammed with logs. 7. a crush or squeeze; stoppage of a machine due to jamming; crowded mass. She was delayed by the traffic jam. *v., jammed, jamming, n. 8.*

jam[2] (jam), a preserve of fruit boiled thick with sugar. *n.*

Ja mai ca (jə mā′kə), an island in the West Indies owned by Great Britain. *n. 12.*

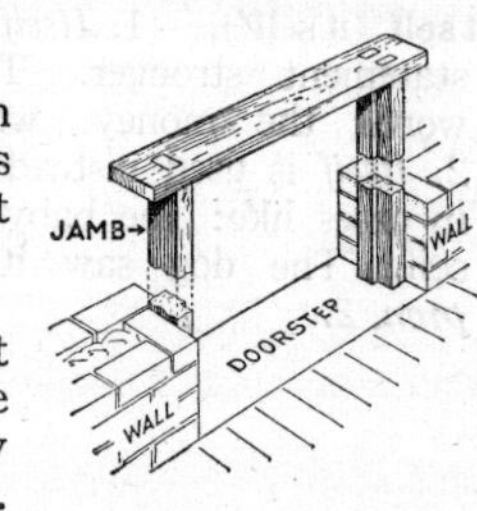

jamb or **jambe** (jam), an upright piece forming the side of a doorway or window. *n. 19.*

James (jāmz), 1. name of two of Christ's disciples. 2. book of the New Testament. *n. 2.*

James town (jāmz′toun′), the first successful English settlement in the United States (1607), in Virginia. *n. 6.*

Jan., January. *5.*

jan gle (jang′gəl), 1. sound harshly. 2. cause to sound harshly. 3. a harsh sound. 4. speak angrily; quarrel. 5. a quarrel; a dispute. *v., n. 10.*

jan i tor (jan′i tər), 1. person hired to take care of a building, offices, etc. 2. doorkeeper. *n. 9.*

Jan u ar y (jan′ū ãr′i), the first month of the year. It has 31 days. *n. 2.*

Ja nus (jā′nəs), the Roman god of gates and doors, and of beginnings and endings. He is represented with two faces, one looking forward, one back. January was named for Janus. *n. 14.*

Ja pan (jə pan′), an island empire east of Asia. *n. 4.*

ja pan (jə pan′), 1. a hard, glossy black varnish. 2. put japan on. 3. articles varnished and ornamented in the Japanese manner. *n., v., japanned, japanning.*

Jap a nese (jap′ə nēz′), 1. of Japan, its people, or their language; as, Japanese art, writings, customs, etc. 2. a native of Japan. 3. the language of Japan. *adj., n., pl. Japanese. 5.*

Japanese beetle, small green and brown beetle that eats fruits, leaves, and grasses. It causes much damage to crops in the United States.

jar[1] (jär), deep container made of earthenware, stone, or glass, with a wide mouth. *n. 3.*

Glass jar

jar[2] (jär), 1. shake; rattle. Your heavy footsteps jar my table. 2. make a harsh, grating noise. 3. a harsh, grating noise. 4. have a harsh, unpleasant effect on; send a shock through (one's ears, nerves, feelings, etc.). The children's screams jar my nerves. 5. a slight shock to the ears, nerves, feelings, etc. 6. clash; quarrel. We did not get on well together, for our opinions always jarred. *v., jarred, jarring, n.*

jar di niere (jär′di nēr′), ornamental pot or stand for flowers or plants. *n.*

jar gon (jär′gən), 1. confused, meaningless talk. 2. talk that is not understood; as, the jargon of foreigners. 3. talk containing a mixture of languages. *n. 14.*

jas mine (jas′min), shrub or vine with clusters of fragrant flowers. There are yellow, white, and red jasmines. *n. 15.*

Flowering branch of yellow jasmine

Ja son (jā′sən), the Greek hero who secured the Golden Fleece. *n. 14.*

jas per (jas′pər), 1. a colored quartz, usually red or brown. 2. among the ancients, a more valuable stone, green in color. *n. 11.*

jaun dice (jôn′dis), 1. disease that causes yellowness of the skin, eyes, and body fluids, and disturbed vision. 2. cause jaundice in. 3. a disturbed or unnaturally sour mental outlook, due to envy, jealousy, etc. 4. prejudice the mind and judgment of, by envy or discontent or jealousy; sour the temper of. *n., v. 13.*

jaunt (jônt), 1. a short journey or excursion, especially for pleasure. 2. take such a trip. *n., v. 18.*

jaun ti ly (jôn′ti li), in an easy, lively manner; smartly. *adv.*

jaun ty (jôn′ti), easy and lively; sprightly. When you are well and happy, you usually feel jaunty. He walks with a jaunty step. *adj., jauntier, jauntiest. 11.*

Ja va (jä′və), 1. the most important island of the Dutch East Indies. 2. a kind of coffee obtained from Java and nearby islands. *n. 10.*

jave lin (jav′lin), light spear to be thrown. *n. 9.*

jaw (jô), 1. the lower part of the face. 2. The upper and lower **jaws** are two bones or sets of bones that form the framework of the mouth. 3. The **jaws** may mean the mouth of a narrow valley, a pass, or a channel. 4. The **jaws** of a tool or machine are the parts that bite or grasp. 5. go on talking at great length, in a boring way. *Slang.* 6. scold. *Slang. n., v. 3.*

jaw bone (jô′bōn′), one of the bones in which the teeth are set, especially the lower jaw. *n. 20.*

jay (jā), 1. noisy American bird with blue feathers; bluejay. 2. noisy European bird with a crest. *n. 6.*

jazz (jaz), 1. noisy dance music with the accents falling at unusual places. 2. of or like jazz; as, a jazz band, jazz music. 3. play such music or dance to such music. 4. liveliness; dash; energy. *Slang.* 5. put energy into. *Slang. n., adj., v. 13.*

European jay (about 1 ft. long)

jeal ous (jel′əs), 1. feeling as one does when people who usually pay attention to him neglect him and pay much attention to somebody else; fearful that one you love may love someone else better, or may prefer someone else to you. When Tommy sees his mother pet Baby, he becomes jealous. 2. envious; full of envy; as, to be jealous of John's marks, or of Amy's new dress. 3. requiring complete loyalty or faithfulness. "The Lord thy God is a jealous God." 4. watchful in keeping or guarding something. Our city is jealous of its rights within the State. 5. close; watchful; suspicious. The dog was such a jealous guardian of the child that he would not let him cross the street. *adj. 3.*

jeal ous y (jel′əs i), being jealous; dislike or fear of rivals; envy; anxious or suspicious watchfulness. *n., pl. jealousies. 4.*

jean (jēn), a stout, twilled cotton fabric used for overalls, etc. **Jeans** often means overalls. *n. 5.*

Jeanne d'Arc (zhän′ därk′), Joan of Arc.

jeer (jēr), 1. make fun rudely or unkindly; scoff. Do not jeer at the mistakes or misfortunes of others. 2. a mocking or insulting remark. *v., n. 8.*

Jef fer son (jef′ər sən), Thomas (1743-1826), a famous statesman, the third president of the United States, from 1801 to 1809. He drafted the Declaration of Independence. *n. 8.*

Jefferson City, the capital of Missouri.

Je ho vah (ji hō′və), one of the names of God in the Old Testament. *n. 10.*

Je hu (jē′hū), 1. a famous driver in the Bible. II Kings 9:20. 2. fast driver. 3. coachman. *n. 12.*

je june (ji jün′), lacking nourishing or satisfying qualities. *adj. 20.*

jel ly (jel′i), 1. a food, soft when hot, but firm and partly transparent when cold. Jelly can be made by boiling fruit juice and sugar together, or by cooking meat juice, or by using some stiffening preparation like gelatin. 2. a jellylike substance. 3. become jelly; turn into jelly. Strong soup will jelly as it cools. *n., pl. jellies, v., jellied, jellying. 4.*

jel ly fish (jel′i fish′), a sea animal like a lump of jelly. *n., pl. jellyfishes* or *jellyfish. 13.*

Jellyfish

jen net (jen′it), a small Spanish horse. *n. 17.*

jen ny (jen′i), 1. a machine for spinning. 2. a name for the female of certain animals; as, jenny wren. *n., pl. jennies.*

jeop ard ize (jep′ər dīz), risk; imperil; endanger. Soldiers jeopardize their lives in war. *v. 18.*

jeop ard y (jep′ər di), danger. The man's life was in jeopardy as the tree fell. *n. 10.*

Jeph thah (jef′thə), a man in the Bible who sacrificed his daughter to fulfill a rash vow. Judges 11:30-40. *n. 13.*

Jer e mi ah (jer′i mī′ə), 1. a Hebrew prophet who denounced and lamented the evils of his time. 2. a book of the Old Testament. *n. 12.*

Jer i cho (jer′i kō), an ancient city in Palestine. Its walls fell down at the noise made by Joshua's attacking army. *n. 11.*

jerk[1] (jėrk), 1. a sudden, sharp pull, twist, or start. His old car started with a jerk. 2. pull or twist suddenly. If the water is unexpectedly hot, you jerk your hand out. 3. throw with a movement that stops suddenly. 4. move with a jerk. The old wagon jerked along. 5. a pull or twist of the muscles that one cannot control. *n., v. 7.*

jerk[2] (jėrk), dry (meat) by cutting it in slices and exposing it to the sun. *v.*

jer kin (jėr′kin), short coat or jacket, with or without sleeves. Men wore tight leather jerkins in the 16th and 17th centuries. *n. 14.*

jerk y (jėr′ki), starting suddenly; with jerks. *adj., jerkier, jerkiest.*

Jerkin

Je rome (jə rōm′). Saint Jerome was a monk and scholar (340?-420 A.D.). *n. 20.*

Jer sey (jėr′zi), 1. one of a group of British islands near the coast of France. 2. a breed of cattle that came from the island of Jersey. Jerseys give very rich milk. 3. New Jersey, a State on the Atlantic coast. *n., pl. Jerseys. 4.*

jer sey (jėr′zi), 1. close-fitting sweater that is pulled on over the head. 2. woman's close-fitting knitted undergarment. 3. machine-knitted cloth. *n., pl. jerseys.*

Jersey City, a seaport city in New Jersey, across the Hudson River from New York City.

Je ru sa lem (ji rü′sə ləm), a famous city of eastern Palestine. *n. 5.*

jes sa mine (jes′ə min), jasmine. *n. 15.*

jest (jest), 1. joke. 2. fun. **Spoken in jest** means spoken in fun, not seriously. 3. poke fun; as, to jest at another person's ideals. 4. act of poking fun at; mockery. 5. thing to be mocked or laughed at. *n., v. 4.*

jest er (jes′tər), person who jests; joker. Princes and nobles in the Middle Ages often kept jesters to amuse them. *n. 11.*

Je su (jē′zū or jē′zü), Jesus. *n.* [*Used in poetry*] *12.*

Jes u it (jezh′ü it), a member of a Roman Catholic religious order, called the Society of Jesus, founded in 1534 by Ignatius Loyola. Some of the first explorers of North America were Jesuits. *n. 12.*

Je sus (jē′zəs), the founder of the Christian religion. The name means "God is salvation." *n. 5.*

Jesus Christ, Jesus.

jet[1] (jet), 1. a stream of water, steam, gas, or any liquid, sent with force, especially from a small opening. A fountain sends up a jet of water. 2. a spout or nozzle for sending out a jet. 3. shoot forth in a jet or forceful stream; gush out. *n., v., jetted, jetting. 5.*

Gas jet

jet[2] (jet), 1. a hard black mineral, shining when polished, used for beads and other ornaments. 2. made of jet. 3. deep, shining black; as, hair of jet. *n., adj.*

jet sam (jet′səm), goods which are thrown overboard to lighten a ship in distress and are often washed ashore. *n.*

jet ty (jet′i), 1. a structure of stones, timbers, etc., projecting out from the shore to break the force of current or waves; breakwater. 2. landing place; pier. *n., pl. jetties. 15.*

Jetty or breakwater

Jew (jü), Hebrew; member of a race that once lived in Palestine, but now lives in many countries. *n. 4.*

jew el (jü′əl), 1. precious stone; gem. Jewels are used in the works of watches, as well as worn in pins and other ornaments. 2. a valuable ornament to be worn, set with precious stones. 3. person or thing that is very precious. 4. set or adorn with jewels; as, a jeweled comb, a sky jeweled with stars. *n., v., jeweled, jeweling* or *jewelled, jewelling. 3.*

jew el er or **jew el ler** (jü′əl ər), person who makes or sells jewels. *n. 11.*

jew el ry or **jew el ler y** (jü′əl ri), jewels. *n. 4.*

Jew ess (jü′is), Jewish woman or girl. *n. 19.*

Jew ish (jü′ish), of the Jews; belonging to the Jews; characteristic of the Jews; as, Jewish customs. *adj. 10.*

Jew ry (jü′ri), 1. the Jews. 2. a district inhabited by Jews. *n., pl. Jewries. 19.*

jews'-harp or **jew's-harp** (jüz′härp′), simple musical instrument, held between the teeth and played by striking the free end of a piece of metal with a finger. *n.*

Jews'-harp

Jez e bel (jez′ə bəl), 1. the wicked wife of Ahab, king of Israel. 2. a shameless, immoral woman. *n. 14.*

jib (jib), a triangular sail set in front of the foremast. *n. 14.*

jibe[1] (jīb), 1. shift (a sail) from one side of a boat to the other when sailing before the wind. 2. shift itself in this way. Be careful or your mainsail will jibe. 3. change the course of a boat so that the sails shift in this way. *v.*

jibe[2] (jīb), jeer; scoff; sneer. *v., n.* Also spelled **gibe.**

jibe[3] (jīb), agree; be in harmony. *v. [Used in common talk]*

jif fy (jif′i), a second; a very short time. *n., pl. jiffies. [Used in common talk] 16.*

jig (jig), 1. a lively dance. 2. music for it. 3. dance a jig. 4. a device used in fishing. *n., v., jigged, jigging. 7.*

jilt (jilt), 1. cast off (a lover or sweetheart) after giving encouragement. 2. woman who casts off a lover after encouraging him. *v., n. 18.*

jim my (jim′i), 1. a short crowbar used by burglars to force windows, doors, or other things open. 2. force open with a jimmy. *n., pl. jimmies, v., jimmied, jimmying.*

jin gle (jing′gəl), 1. a sound like that of little bells, or of coins or keys striking together. 2. make such a sound. Sleigh bells jingle. 3. cause (something) to jingle; as, to jingle one's money. 4. a verse that has a jingling sound. Mother Goose rhymes are jingles. 5. make jingling verses. 6. be full of simple rhymes and repetitions. *n., v. 8.*

jin go (jing′gō), person who urges a warlike policy. *n., pl. jingoes. 20.*

jinn (jin), spirits or spirit that can appear in human or animal form and do good or harm to people. The jinn turned the stone into gold. *n. pl., often used as singular.*

jin ni or **jin nee** (ji nē′), one of the jinn. *n., pl. jinn.*

jin rik i sha or **jin rick sha** (jin rik′shə), a small, two-wheeled, hooded carriage, pulled by one or more men, used in Japan. *n.*

Jinrikisha

jit ney (jit′ni), 1. automobile that carries passengers for a small fare. It usually travels along a regular route. 2. five-cent piece; nickel. *n., pl. jitneys.* [*Slang*]

jiu jit su or **jiu jut su** (jü jit′sü), jujitsu. *n.*

Joan of Arc (jōn′ əv ärk′), a French heroine who led armies against the invading English and saved the city of Orléans. She was condemned as a witch and burned to death in 1431. In 1920 she was made a saint. (The same as **Jeanne d'Arc.**)

job[1] (job), piece of work; a definite piece of work done regularly for pay. Washing dishes is Mary's job. This carpenter is out of a job. *n. 3.*

Job[2] (jōb), 1. a very patient man in the Bible. 2. the book of the Old Testament which tells about him. *n.*

job ber (job′ər), wholesale dealer; one who buys goods from manufacturers and sells to retail dealers. *n. 17.*

jock ey (jok′i), 1. boy or man who rides horses in races as an occupation. 2. to trick; cheat. Mr. Smith was jockeyed into putting his money into oil stock. 3. maneuver so as to get advantage. The crews were jockeying their boats to get into the best position for the race. *n., pl. jockeys, v., jockeyed, jockeying. 11.*

jo cose (jō kōs′), jesting; humorous; playful. *adj. 20.*

joc u lar (jok′ū lər), funny; joking. *adj. 16.*

joc u lar i ty (jok′ū lar′i ti), 1. jocular quality. 2. jocular talk or behavior. 3. jocular remark or act. *n., pl. jocularities. 16.*

joc und (jok′ənd), cheerful; merry; gay. *adj. 6.*

Jo el (jō′əl), 1. a Hebrew prophet. 2. a book of the Old Testament. *n. 14.*

jog[1] (jog), 1. shake with a push or jerk. You may jog a person's elbow to get his attention. 2. a shake, push, or nudge. 3. stir up (one's own or another person's memory). 4. an urge; a hint or reminder; as, to give one's memory a jog. 5. move up or down with a jerk or a shaking motion. The old horse jogged along, and jogged me up and down on his back. 6. go forward heavily and slowly. 7. slow walk or trot. *v., jogged, jogging, n. 10.*

jog[2] (jog), part that sticks out or in; unevenness in a line or a surface. *n.*

jog gle (jog′əl), 1. shake slightly. 2. slight shake. *v., n.*

John (jon), 1. the disciple "whom Jesus loved." 2. any one of four books in the New Testament called by this name. 3. King John (1167?-1216) was king of England from 1199 to 1216. He signed the Magna Charta in 1215. *n. 1.*

John Bull, 1. a typical Englishman. 2. the English nation.

john ny cake (jon′i kāk′), a kind of corn bread. *n.*

John son (jon′sən), 1. Andrew Johnson (1808-1875) was the 17th president of the United States, from 1865 to 1869. 2. Samuel Johnson (1709-1784) was a famous English author, dictionary maker, and literary leader. *n. 6.*

John the Baptist, man in the Bible who foretold the coming of Christ and baptized him. Matthew 3.

join (join), 1. bring or put together; connect, fasten, or clasp together; as, to join hands, to join an island to the mainland by a bridge, to join two points. 2. unite; make one; become one; as, to join in marriage. 3. take part with others; as, to join in a song. 4. unite with; as, to join a church. The stream joins the river just below the mill. 5. take or return to one's place in; as, to join one's ship or one's regiment. 6. **Join battle** means begin to fight. 7. come into the company of. My friend joined me at the corner. 8. joining; a point or line where things are joined. *v., n. 1.*

join er (join′ər), 1. one that joins. 2. carpenter who makes doors and windows and does other light work. *n. 15.*

joint (joint), 1. the place at which two things are joined together. 2. the way parts are joined. 3. connect by a joint or joints. 4. in an animal, the parts where two bones move on one another, and the way those parts are put together. **Out of joint** means moved out of place at the joint. 5. one of the parts of which a jointed thing is made up; as, the middle joint of the finger. 6. the part of the stem from which a leaf or branch grows. 7. piece of meat cut for cooking. 8. divide at the joints. Please joint this chicken before sending it. 9. owned together; owned by, held by, or done by two or more persons. By our joint efforts we managed to push the car back on the road. 10. sharing. My brother and I are joint owners of this dog. *n., v., adj. 3.*

Finger joints: J, joints; K, knuckles and their joints.

joint ly (joint′li), together; in common. The two boys owned the newsstand jointly. *adv.*

joist (joist), one of the parallel pieces of timber to which the boards of a floor or of a ceiling are fastened. *n. 19.*

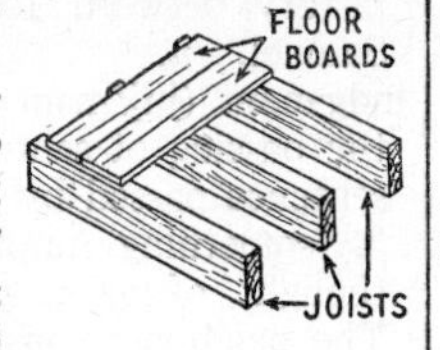

joke (jōk), 1. something said or done to make somebody laugh; a remark that is clever and funny; a happening that makes us laugh; something funny. 2. make jokes. 3. person or thing laughed at. 4. laugh at; tease in a laughing or joking way. *n., v. 3.*

jok er (jōk′ər), 1. person who jokes. 2. trick for getting the better of someone; especially, a phrase or sentence put into a bill in order to defeat its purpose if it becomes a law. 3. an extra playing card used in some games. *n.*

jol li ty (jol′i ti), fun; merriment. *n., pl. jollities. 13.*

jol ly (jol′i), 1. merry; full of fun. 2. pleasant. *Used in common talk.* 3. extremely; very. *Used in common talk. adj., jollier, jolliest, adv. 4.*

Jol ly Rog er (jol′i roj′ər), pirates' black flag with a skull and crossbones on it.

jolt (jōlt), 1. to jar; shake up; move with a shock or jerk. The wagon jolted us when it went over the rocks. 2. a jar; a shock; a jerk. He put his brakes on suddenly, and the car stopped with a jolt. *v., n. 9.*

Jo nah (jō′nə), 1. in the Bible a man who was thrown overboard, swallowed by a large fish, and later cast up on land. 2. person whose presence is supposed to bring bad luck. *n. 12.*

Jon a than (jon′ə thən), the son of Saul, a close friend of David. *n. 9.*

Jones (jōnz), John Paul, a famous American sea captain (1747-1792). *n. 6.*

jon quil (jong′kwil), a yellow flower much like a daffodil; a kind of narcissus. *n. 18.*

Jonquil

Jop pa (jop′ə), former name of Jaffa, a seaport of Palestine. *n. 19.*

Jor dan (jôr′dən), a river in Palestine, flowing into the Dead Sea. *n. 7.*

Jo seph (jō′zəf), 1. the favorite son of Jacob, sold by his jealous brothers into slavery in Egypt, where he became governor. 2. the husband of Mary, the mother of Jesus. *n. 3.*

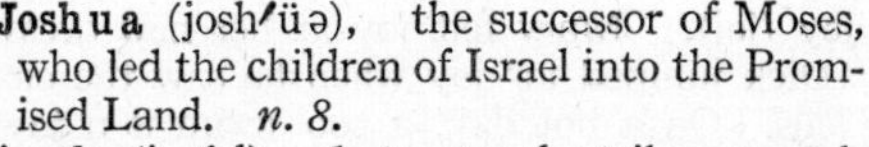

Josh u a (josh′ü ə), the successor of Moses, who led the children of Israel into the Promised Land. *n. 8.*

jos tle (jos′əl), 1. to crowd, strike, or push against; elbow roughly. We were jostled by the big crowd at the entrance to the circus. 2. a jostling; a push; a knock. *v., n. 7.*

jot (jot), 1. little bit; very small amount. I do not care a jot. 2. write briefly or in haste. The clerk jotted down the order. *n., v., jotted, jotting. 10.*

jounce (jouns), bounce; bump; jolt. *v., n.*

jour nal (jėr′nəl), 1. a daily record. 2. an account of what happens, or of what one thinks, feels, or notices, such as a diary, a ship's log, the written account of what happens at each meeting of a society or a town meeting. 3. a newspaper or magazine. 4. in bookkeeping, a book in which is written down every bit of business done, so that it can be entered under the proper account. *n. 5.*

jour nal ism (jėr′nəl izm), the occupation of writing for, editing, or conducting a newspaper. *n. 19.*

jour nal ist (jėr′nəl ist), person engaged in newspaper work. Editors and reporters are journalists. *n. 17.*

jour nal is tic (jėr′nəl is′tik), of or like journalism or journalists. *adj.*

jour ney (jėr′ni), 1. a trip; as, a journey around the world. 2. to travel; take a trip. *n., pl. journeys, v., journeyed, journeying. 1.*

jour ney man (jėr′ni mən), qualified workman who works for another person. *n., pl. journeymen. 18.*

joust (just), 1. a combat between two knights on horseback, armed with lances. 2. fight with lances on horseback. Knights used to joust with each other for sport. *n., v. 15.*

Joust

Jove (jōv), the Roman god Jupiter, king of gods and men. *n. 5.*

jo vi al (jō′vi əl), good-hearted and full of fun; good-humored and merry. *adj. 10.*

jo vi al i ty (jō′vi al′i ti), jollity. *n.*

Jo vi an (jō′vi ən), of or like the god Jove. *adj.*

jowl (joul), 1. the jaw, especially the under jaw. 2. the cheek. *n. 15.*

joy (joi). Mary felt joy at her new dress. Dick jumped for joy when he saw the circus. On a hot day, a cool swim is a joy. Sometimes joy means be glad or make glad. *n., v. 1.*

joy ance (joi′əns), joy; gladness; gaiety. *n.* [*Old use*] *16.*

joy ful (joi′fəl), 1. glad; happy; as, a joyful heart. 2. causing joy; as, joyful news. *adj. 2.*

joy less (joi′lis), without joy; sad. *adj. 12.*

joy ous (joi′əs), joyful; glad; gay. *adj. 5.*

Jr., Junior.

ju bi lant (jü′bi lənt), rejoicing; exulting. *adj. 14.*

ju bi la tion (jü′bi lā′shən), rejoicing. *n.*

ju bi lee (jü′bi lē), 1. time of rejoicing; as, to hold a jubilee over a victory. 2. great joy; as, a day of jubilee. 3. an anniversary thought of as a time of rejoicing; as, a twenty-fifth or fiftieth wedding jubilee. Once every fifty years, the Jews used to hold a year of jubilee. 4. in the Roman Catholic Church, a year in which church punishment for sin is remitted, after repentance and the performance of certain acts. *n. 6.*

Ju daea (jü dē′ə), Judea. *n. 11.*

Ju dah (jü′də), 1. a son of Jacob and ancestor of the tribe of Judah. 2. the most powerful of the twelve tribes of Israel. 3. the kingdom made up of the tribes of Judah and Benjamin. *n. 7.*

Ju da ism (jü′dā izm), 1. the religion of the Jews. 2. the following of Jewish rules and customs. *n. 17.*

Ju das (jü′dəs), 1. in the Bible, Judas Iscariot, the disciple who betrayed Christ for money. 2. an utter traitor. 3. one of the apostles, not Iscariot. *n. 10.*

Ju de a (jü dē′ə), part of Palestine. *n. 17.*

judge (juj), 1. a public officer appointed or elected to hear and decide cases in a law court. 2. act as a judge; hear and decide (cases) and pass sentence on (the prisoner). 3. person chosen to settle a dispute or to decide who wins a race, etc. 4. settle (a dispute); decide on the winner in a race, a debate, etc. 5. person who can decide on how good a thing is; as, a good (or poor) judge of dogs, of marbles, of character. 6. form an opinion (about). 7. consider and blame. "Judge not, that ye be not judged." 8. think; suppose; conclude. I judged that you had forgotten to come. 9. in ancient Israel, the name given to the ruling officer before they had kings. *n., v. 1.*

Judg es (juj′iz), book of the Old Testament dealing with the period in Hebrew history between Joshua and the birth of Samuel. *n.*

judg ment (juj′mənt), 1. act of judging; the passing of sentence on a person. 2. a sentence passed by a judge in a law court. 3. something unpleasant that happens, thought of as a punishment from God. The neighbors considered his broken leg a judgment on him for staying away from church. 4. weighing and blaming. Do not pass judgment on your neighbors. 5. opinion; estimate; as, in my judgment. 6. power to judge well; good sense. Since she has judgment in such matters, we will ask her. *n. 2.*

ju di cial (jü dish′əl), 1. of judges; having to do with a court of law or the administration of justice. 2. ordered, permitted, or enforced by a judge of a court. Mrs. Barnes got a judicial separation from her husband. 3. of or suited to a judge. A judicial mind looks fairly at both sides of a dispute. *adj. 14.*

ju di ci ar y (jü dish′i ãr′i), 1. the branch of government that administers justice. 2. the judges of a county, State, or city. 3. of or having to do with courts, judges, or the administration of justice. *n., pl. judiciaries, adj. 16.*

ju di cious (jü dish′əs), wise; sensible; having, using, or showing good judgment. A judicious parent encourages his children to make their own decisions. *adj. 8.*

Ju dith (jü′dith), a Jewish widow who saved her countrymen by killing an Assyrian general. *n.*

jug (jug), a container for holding liquids. A jug usually has a spout or a narrow neck and a handle. *n. 7.*

Jug

jug gle (jug′əl), 1. perform tricks by the skill of hand or eye. He juggled with knives by balancing them on his nose. 2. perform tricks. 3. perform tricks with. The dishonest cashier juggled the accounts to hide his theft. 4. deceive. 5. trick; fraud. *v., n. 8.*

jug gler (jug′lər), one who juggles. *n. 14.*

Ju go slav or **Ju go-Slav** (ū′gō släv′), 1. a native or inhabitant of Jugoslavia. 2. of or having to do with Jugoslavia or its people. *n., adj. 20.* Also spelled **Yugoslav.**

Ju go sla vi a or **Ju go-Sla vi a** (ū′gō slä′vi ə), a country in southeastern Europe. *n.* Also spelled **Yugoslavia.**

jug u lar (jug′ū lər), of the neck or throat. The jugular veins are in the neck. *adj.*

juice (jüs), the liquid part of fruits and vegetables, or of animal bodies; as, the juice of a lemon, meat juice, the juices of the body. *n. 4.*

juic i ness (jüs′i nis), being juicy. *n.*

juic y (jüs′i), full of juice; having much juice. *adj., juicier, juiciest. 8.*

ju jit su (jü jit′sü), a Japanese way of wrestling or fighting that uses the strength and weight of an opponent to his disadvantage. *n.*

ju lep (jü′lip), a drink made of whiskey or brandy, sugar, crushed ice, and fresh mint. *n.*

Ju li et (jü′li et), the heroine of Shakespeare's play *Romeo and Juliet. n. 8.*

Jul ius (jül′yəs). Julius Caesar was the great Roman general, statesman, and historian (102?-44 B.C.). *n. 8.*

Ju ly (jü lī′), the seventh month of the year. It has 31 days. *n. 2.*

jum ble (jum′bəl), 1. mix or confuse. It is easy to jumble up everything in your drawer when you are hunting for something. 2. a muddle; mixed-up mess; state of confusion. *v., n. 9.*

jump (jump), 1. to spring from the ground; to leap; to bound. Our cat can jump to the table, off the table, across the path, etc. 2. a spring from the ground; a leap; a bound. 3. cause to jump; as, to jump a horse over a fence, to jump a child up and down. 4. give a sudden start or jerk. We often jump when a sudden sight, noise, or touch startles us. 5. a sudden, nervous start. 6. Some special meanings are:

jump a mining claim, seize a mining claim after the owner has left it or lost claim to it.

jump at (a chance, an offer, a bargain), accept it eagerly and at once.

jump the track, leave the rails suddenly.

take a jump, rise suddenly in price.

v., n. 2.

jump er[1] (jump′ər), one that jumps. *n. 17.*

jump er[2] (jump′ər), 1. loose jacket. Workmen and sailors often wear jumpers to protect their clothes. 2. loose blouse reaching to the hips. *n.*

jump y (jump′i), 1. moving by jumps; making sudden, sharp jerks. 2. nervous; easily excited or frightened. *adj., jumpier, jumpiest.*

jun co (jung′kō), snowbird; any of several small North American finches often seen in flocks during the winter. *n., pl. juncos.*

Junco (about 6 in. long)

junc tion (jungk′shən), 1. joining or being joined; as, the junction of two rivers. 2. place of joining or meeting; station where railroad lines meet or cross. *n. 9.*

junc ture (jungk′chər), 1. joining. 2. being joined. 3. a point or line where two things join; joint. 4. **At this juncture** means when affairs were in this state; at this moment. *n. 15.*

June (jün), the sixth month of the year. It has 30 days. *n. 2.*

Ju neau (jü′nō), the capital of Alaska. *n.*

June bug, 1. large brown beetle of the northern United States that appears in June. 2. large green beetle of the southern United States, very destructive to fruit.

NORTHERN SOUTHERN
June bugs

jun gle (jung′gəl), wild land thickly overgrown with bushes, vines, trees, etc. They cut a path through the jungle. *n. 9.*

jun ior (jün′yər), 1. the younger (used of a son having the same name as his father). John Parker, Junior, is the son of John Parker, Senior. 2. younger person. Tom is his brother's junior by two years. 3. of lower position; of less standing than some others; as, the junior partner, a junior officer. 4. person of lower standing. 5. student during the third year of a high-school or college course. 6. of or having to do with the third-year students. *adj., n. 5.*

Branch of juniper

ju ni per (jü′ni pər), an evergreen shrub with purple berries. See the picture just above. *n. 10.*

junk[1] (jungk), rubbish; trash. *n. 9.*

junk[2] (jungk), Chinese sailing ship. *n.*

Junk

hat, āge, cãre, fär; let, ēqual, tėrm; it, īce; hot, ōpen, ôrder; oil, out; cup, pu̇t, rüle, ūse; th, thin; ᴛʜ, then; ə represents *a* in about, *e* in taken, *i* in pencil, *o* in lemon, *u* in circus.

jun ket (jung′kit), 1. milk curdled, sweetened, and flavored. 2. feast; picnic. 3. pleasure trip. 4. go on a pleasure trip. *n., v. 15.*

Ju no (jü′nō), Roman goddess, wife of Jupiter and queen of gods and men. Juno was the goddess of marriage. The Greeks called her Hera. *n. 9.*

jun to (jun′tō), political faction; group of plotters or partisans. *n., pl. juntos.*

Ju pi ter (jü′pi tər), 1. a Roman god, the ruler of gods and men. The Greeks called him Zeus. 2. the largest planet. *n. 8.*

ju ris dic tion (jür′is dik′shən), 1. the right or power to give out justice; the giving out of justice. 2. authority; power; control. 3. the things over which authority extends. It does not lie within my jurisdiction to set you free. 4. the territory over which jurisdiction extends. *n. 9.*

ju ris pru dence (jür′is prü′dəns), 1. the science or philosophy of law. 2. a system of laws. 3. a department of law; as, medical jurisprudence. *n. 15.*

ju rist (jür′ist), person expert in law; writer on law. *n. 18.*

ju ror (jür′ər), member of a jury. *n.*

ju ry (jür′i), 1. a group of persons sworn to give a true answer to the question put before them in a law court, that is, "Is the prisoner guilty or not?" 2. any group of persons chosen to give a judgment or to decide who is the winner. 3. See also **grand jury.** *n., pl. juries. 6.*

ju ry man (jür′i mən), a member of a jury. *n., pl. jurymen. 19.*

just[1] (just), 1. right; fair; as, a just reward, a just opinion, a just price. 2. righteous; as, a just person, a just life. 3. exact; as, a just scale. 4. exactly. That is just right. 5. only; merely. He is just an ordinary man. 6. a very little while ago. He just left me. 7. barely. I just caught the train. *adj., adv. 1.*

just[2] (just), joust. *n., v. 15.*

jus tice (jus′tis), 1. fairness; rightness; being just; as, the justice of a claim. Justice consists in giving every man what he deserves. 2. just conduct; fair dealing. 3. trial and judgment by process of law; court proceedings; as, a court of justice. 4. judge. The Supreme Court of the United States consists of nine justices. 5. **Do justice to** means (1) treat fairly. (2) see the good points of; show proper appreciation for. 6. **Not do oneself justice** means not do so well as one really can do. *n. 2.*

jus ti fi a ble (jus′ti fī′ə bəl), capable of being justified; proper. An act is justifiable if it can be shown to be just or right. *adj. 14.*

jus ti fi ca tion (jus′ti fi kā′shən), 1. justifying. 2. being justified. 3. a fact or circumstance that justifies; a good reason or excuse. What is your justification for being so late? *n. 9.*

jus ti fy (jus′ti fī), 1. give a good reason for. The fine quality of this cloth justifies its high cost. 2. show to be just or right. Can you justify your act? 3. clear from blame. *v., justified, justifying. 4.*

jus tle (jus′əl), jostle. *v., n. 18.*

jut (jut), 1. stick out; project; stand out. The pier juts out from the shore into the water. 2. a part that sticks out or projects. *v., jutted, jutting, n. 6.*

jute (jüt), a strong fiber used for making coarse fabrics, rope, etc. Jute is obtained from two tropical plants. *n. 11.*

ju ve nile (jü′və nil or jü′və nīl), 1. young; youthful. 2. young person. 3. of or for boys and girls; as, juvenile books. 4. book for boys and girls. 5. actor who plays youthful parts. *adj., n. 13.*

jux ta po si tion (juks′tə pə zish′ən), 1. a putting close together; a placing side by side. 2. position close together or side by side. *n. 16.*

K

K, k (kā), the 11th letter of the alphabet. There are two k's in kick. *n., pl. K's, k's.*

Kaf fir or **Kaf ir** (kaf′ər), 1. member of a Negro race of South Africa. 2. the language spoken by them. *n. 16.*

kai ak (kī′ak), kayak. *n.*

Kai ser (kī′zər), 1. the German word for emperor. 2. the title of former rulers of Germany and Austria. *n. 12.*

kale or **kail** (kāl), a kind of cabbage with curled leaves not forming a head. Kale looks somewhat like spinach. *n. 14.*

ka lei do scope (kə lī′də skōp), tube containing bits of colored glass and two mirrors.

As it is turned, it reflects continually changing patterns. *n. 17.*

ka lei do scop ic (kə lī′də skop′ik), of or like a kaleidoscope; continually changing. *adj.*

Kan. or **Kans.,** Kansas.

kan ga roo (kang′-gə rü′), an animal that lives in Australia. It has small forelegs and very strong hind legs, which give it great leaping power. The mother kangaroo has a pouch in front in which she carries her young. *n., pl. kangaroos* or *kangaroo. 13.*

Kangaroo (about 8 ft. long, including the tail)

Kan sas (kan′zəs), a Middle Western State of the United States. *n. 6.*

Kansas City, 1. a city in western Missouri. 2. a city in northeastern Kansas that adjoins it. *18.*

Kant (kant), Immanuel, a German philosopher (1724-1804). *n. 18.*

kar a kul (kar′ə kəl), fur made from the skin of lambs. Karakul has flat, loose curls. *n.* Also spelled **caracul.**

ka ty did (kā′ti did), a large green insect that makes a shrill noise like "Katy did, Katy didn't." *n. 18.*

Katydid (about ⅓ life size)

kay ak (kī′ak), an Eskimo canoe made of skins stretched over a light frame of wood or bone with an opening in the middle for a person. *n.*

Kayak

Keats (kēts), John, a famous English poet (1795-1821). *n. 17.*

keel (kēl), 1. the main timber or steel piece that extends the whole length of the bottom of a ship or boat. The whole ship is built up on the keel. 2. part in an airplane or airship resembling a ship's keel. 3. **Keel** or **keel over** means turn or become turned keel up; turn upside down; upset. *n., v. 8.*

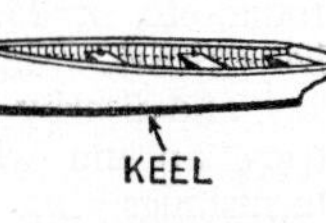

keel son (kel′sən or kēl′sən), beam or line of timbers or iron plates fastened along the top of a ship's keel to strengthen it. *n.*

keen (kēn), 1. so shaped as to cut well; sharp; cutting; as, a keen blade, keen wit, keen pain. 2. eager; as, a keen player. 3. able to do its work quickly and accurately; as, a keen mind, a keen sense of smell. *adj. 3.*

keen ness (kēn′nis), keen or cutting quality; sharpness. *n. 14.*

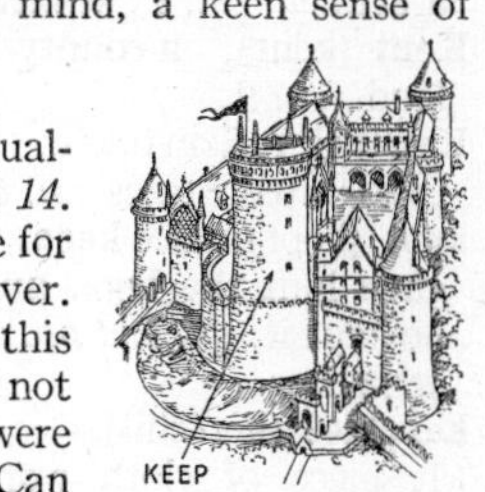

keep (kēp), 1. have for a long while or forever. You may keep this book. 2. have and not let go. They were kept in prison. Can she keep a secret? 3. have and take care of. She keeps chickens. My aunt keeps two boarders. 4. take care of and protect. The bank keeps money for people. 5. have; hold. Keep this in mind. 6. continue; stay as one is. Keep along this road for two miles. This milk kept sweet for five days. 7. do the right thing with; observe. Good Christians keep the Sabbath. 8. food and a place to sleep. The money he earns would not pay for his keep. 9. the main part of a fortress; a stronghold. See the picture. 10. Some special meanings are:

keep in with, keep acquaintance or friendship with. *Used in common talk.*

keep on, continue; go on.

keep silence, remain silent.

keep time, go correctly (said of a watch or clock); move at just the right rate.

keep up with, go or move as fast as.

v., kept, keeping, n. 1.

keep er (kēp′ər), one that watches, guards, or takes care of persons or things. *n. 4.*

keep ing (kēp′ing), 1. care; charge; as, money in safekeeping. 2. observance; as, the keeping of Christmas. 3. agreement; harmony. His actions are in keeping with his promises. *n.*

keep sake (kēp′sāk′), thing kept in memory of the giver. My friend gave me his picture as a keepsake before going away. *n.*

keg (keg), small barrel, usually holding less than ten gallons. *n. 14.*

kelp (kelp), 1. a large, tough, brown seaweed. 2. ashes of seaweed. Kelp contains iodine. *n.*

ken (ken), 1. range of sight. 2. range of knowledge. What happens on the moon is beyond our ken. 3. know. *Scottish.* 4. recognize. *Old use. n., v., kenned, kenning. 10.*

ken nel (ken′əl), 1. house for a dog or dogs. 2. place where dogs are bred. 3. put into or keep in a kennel. 4. take shelter or lodge in a kennel. *n., v., kenneled, kenneling. 8.*

Kent (kent), a county in southeastern England. *n. 9.*

Ken tuck y (kən tuk′i), a Southern State of the United States. *n. 8.*

kept (kept). See **keep.** I gave him the book and he kept it. *pt. and pp. of keep. 1.*

Kerchief

ker chief (kėr′chif), 1. piece of cloth worn over the head or around the neck. 2. handkerchief. *n. 10.*

kern or **kerne** (kėrn), 1. an Irish foot soldier carrying light weapons. *Old use.* 2. an Irish peasant. *n. 19.*

ker nel (kėr′nəl), 1. the softer part inside the hard shell of a nut or inside the stone of a fruit. 2. a grain or seed like that of wheat or corn. 3. the central or important part of anything around which it is formed or built up. *n. 7.*

Kernel and shell of a nut

ker o sene (ker′ə sēn), a thin oil made from petroleum, used in lamps and stoves. *n. 6.*

ketch (kech), a small, strongly built sailing ship with two masts, and with fore-and-aft rig. *n.*

ketch up (kech′əp), catsup, a sauce made from tomatoes and other things. *n.*

ket tle (ket′əl), 1. any metal container for boiling liquids, cooking fruit, etc. 2. a metal container with a handle and spout for heating water. *n. 3.*

ket tle drum (ket′əl drum′), a drum consisting of a hollow hemisphere of brass or copper with a top of parchment. *n. 17.*

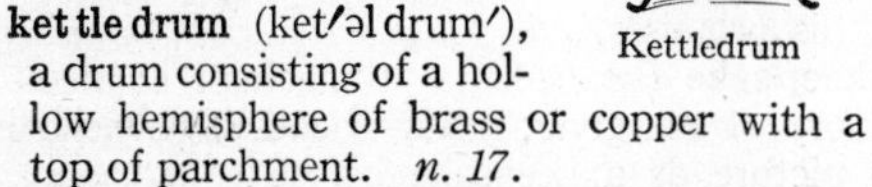

Kettledrum

key[1] (kē), 1. a small metal instrument for locking and unlocking the lock of a door, a padlock, or any other thing. 2. a place that commands or gives control of a sea, a district, etc., because of its position. Gibraltar is the key to the Mediterranean Sea. 3. the answer to a puzzle or problem. The key to this puzzle will be published next week. 4. a sheet or book of answers. 5. in studying languages, a book that gives the translation one is working out. 6. one of a set of parts pressed in playing a piano, in typewriting, and in operating other instruments. 7. a scale or system of notes in music related to one another in a special way and based on a particular note; as, a song written in the key of B flat. 8. tone of voice; style of thought or expression. He writes in a melancholy key. 9. regulate the pitch of; as, to key a piano up to concert pitch. 10. **Key** (a person) **up** means raise his courage or nerve (to the point of doing something). I keyed myself up to ask for a higher salary. *n., pl. keys, v., keyed, keying. 2.*

Door key

key[2] (kē), a low island or reef. There are keys near the coast of Florida. *n., pl. keys.*

key board (kē′bōrd′), the set of keys in a piano, organ, typewriter, etc. *n. 15.*

C D E F G A B C D E F G A B C
←DOWN UP→
Part of the keyboard of a piano

key hole (kē′hōl′), small opening in a lock through which a key is put in to turn the lock. *n. 14.*

key note (kē′nōt′), 1. in music, the note on which a scale or system of tones is based. 2. main idea; guiding principle. World peace was the keynote of his speech. *n. 12.*

KEYSTONE

key stone (kē′stōn′), middle stone at the top of an arch, holding the other pieces in place. See the picture. *n. 12.*

kha ki (kä′ki), 1. the color of dust; dull yellowish-brown. 2. heavy cloth of this color, much used for uniforms of soldiers. *n., pl. khakis, adj. 14.*

Khan

khan[1] (kän), a title of a ruler among Tartar tribes; a title of dignity in Persia, Afghanistan, India, etc. *n. 16.*

khan[2] (kän), in Turkey and nearby countries, an inn without furnishings. *n.*

khe dive (kə dēv′), title of the Turkish viceroys who ruled Egypt between 1867 and 1914. *n.*

kibe (kīb), a sore on the heel. *n. 19.*

kick (kik). The bad man kicked my dog.

This horse kicks. One of his kicks knocked a boy down. The boy kicked the football. Kick off your shoes. Don't kick up so much dust. The blow given to a person's shoulder by a gun when it is fired is called a kick. This old gun kicks. Kick is used in slang to mean (1) grumble or find fault. (2) excitement or thrill. *v., n. 2.*

kid (kid), 1. a baby goat. 2. the leather made from the skin of a young goat, used for gloves and shoes. 3. child. *Used in common talk. n. 2.*

kid nap (kid′nap), steal (a child); carry off (anyone) by force. *v., kidnaped, kidnaping* or *kidnapped, kidnapping. 12.*

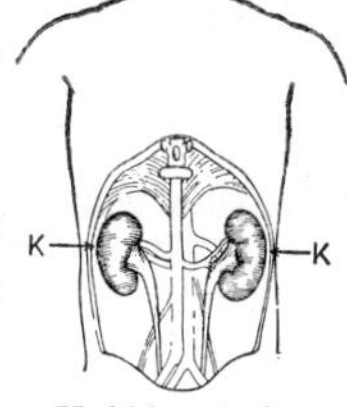

K, kidneys of a human being.

kid ney (kid′ni), 1. one of the pair of organs that separate waste matter and water from the blood and pass it off through the bladder in liquid form. 2. kidney or kidneys of an animal, cooked for food. 3. nature; disposition. 4. kind; sort. *n., pl. kidneys. 7.*

Kiel (kēl), seaport in northwestern Germany, on the Baltic Sea. *n.*

Kiel Canal, ship canal from the North Sea to the Baltic Sea.

Ki ev (kē′ef), city in southwestern Russia. *n.*

kill (kil), 1. put to death. 2. put an end to; get rid of. 3. act of killing. 4. animal killed. *v., n. 1.*

kill deer (kil′dēr′), small wading bird that has a loud, shrill cry, the commonest plover of North America. *n., pl. killdeers* or *killdeer.*

Killdeer (about 10 in. long)

kill er (kil′ər), person, animal, or thing that kills. *n. 17.*

kiln (kil or kiln), furnace or oven for burning, baking, or drying something. Limestone is burned in a kiln to make lime. Bricks are baked in a kiln. *n. 13.*

ki lo (kē′lō), kilogram. *n., pl. kilos. 13.*

kil o cy cle (kil′ə sī′kəl), 1. 1000 cycles. 2. 1000 cycles per second. The kilocycle is used especially in radio for measuring the frequency of electric waves. *n.*

kil o gram or **kil o gramme** (kil′ə gram), a weight equal to 1000 grams or 2.2046 pounds. *n. 10.*

kil o me ter or **kil o me tre** (kil′ə mē′tər), distance equal to 1000 meters or 3280.8 feet. *n. 7.*

kil o watt (kil′ə wot′), a unit of electric power equal to 1000 watts. *n. 19.*

Man wearing a kilt

kilt (kilt), pleated skirt, reaching to the knees, worn by men in the Scottish Highlands. *n. 19.*

kil ter (kil′tər), good condition; order. Our old radio is so out of kilter that we cannot tune in most stations. *n.* [*Used in common talk*]

ki mo no (ki mō′nə), 1. the loose, outer garment worn by both men and women in Japan. 2. a woman's loose dressing gown. *n., pl. kimonos. 12.*

Japanese kimono

kin (kin), 1. family or relatives. All our kin came to the family reunion. 2. family relationship. What kin is she to you? **Near of kin** means closely related. 3. related. My cousin Ann is kin to me. *n., adj. 6.*

kind[1] (kīnd). A kind girl tries to help people and make them happy. Taking a blind man across a street is a kind act. *adj. 1.*

kind[2] (kīnd). All kinds of animals were in the ark. What kind of cake do you like best? *n.*

kin der gar ten (kin′dər gär′tən), a school for children from 3 to 6 years old that educates them by games, toys, and pleasant occupations. *n. 10.*

kind-heart ed (kīnd′här′tid), having or showing a kind heart; kindly; sympathetic. *adj.*

kin dle (kin′dəl), 1. set on fire. Light the paper with a match to kindle the wood. 2. catch fire. This damp wood will never kindle. 3. stir up; arouse. His cruelty kindled our anger. 4. become bright or excited. The boy's face kindled as he told about the circus. *v. 4.*

kind li ness (kīnd′li nis), 1. kindly feeling or quality. 2. a kindly act. *n. 18.*

kin dling (kin′dling), small pieces of wood for starting a fire. *n.*

kind ly (kīnd′li), 1. kind; friendly. 2. pleasant; agreeable. 3. in a kind or friendly way. 4. with pleasure. The cat took kindly to her warm bed. *adj., kindlier, kindliest, adv. 2.*

kind ness (kīnd′nis), 1. kind nature; being kind. We admire his kindness. 2. kind treatment. Thank you for your kindness. 3. a kind act. He showed me many kindnesses. *n. 2.*

kin dred (kin′drid), 1. a person's family or relatives. 2. family relationship. Does he claim kindred with you? 3. related; as, kindred tribes. 4. being alike; resemblance. 5. like; similar; connected. She learned about dew, frost, and kindred facts of nature. *n., adj. 4.*

kine (kīn), cows; cattle. *n. pl.* [*Old use*] *10.*

ki net ic (ki net′ik), 1. of motion. 2. caused by motion. *adj. 17.*

king (king), 1. the man who rules a country and its people. Richard the Lion-Hearted was king of England. 2. a man with the title of ruler, but with limited power to rule. 3. person who has power such as kings used to have. 4. an important piece in the game of chess or checkers. *n. 1.*

king bird (king′bėrd′), quarrelsome bird that catches and eats insects as it flies. *n.*

king dom (king′dəm), 1. a country that is governed by a king or a queen; the land or territory ruled by one king. 2. a realm, domain, or province. The mind is the kingdom of thought. 3. one of the three divisions of the natural world: the animal kingdom, the vegetable kingdom, and the mineral kingdom. *n. 2.*

king fish er (king′fish′ər), a bright-colored bird. One kind of kingfisher eats fish; the other eats insects. *n. 17.*

Belted kingfisher (about 1 ft. long)

king ly (king′li), 1. of a king or kings; of royal rank. 2. fit for a king; as, a kingly crown. 3. like a king; royal; noble. 4. as a king does. *adj., kinglier, kingliest, adv. 5.*

Kings (kingz), 1. in the Protestant Old Testament, either of two books (I Kings or II Kings) containing the history of the reigns of the Hebrew kings after David. 2. in the Roman Catholic Old Testament, one of four books. *n.*

king ship (king′ship), 1. position, rank, or dignity of a king. 2. rule of a king; government by a king. *n. 13.*

kink (kingk), 1. a twist or curl in thread, rope, hair, etc. 2. form a kink; make kinks in. 3. mental twist; queer idea. *n., v. 19.*

kins folk (kinz′fōk′), family or relatives. *n. pl. 15.*

kin ship (kin′ship), 1. being kin; family relationship. 2. resemblance. *n. 14.*

kins man (kinz′mən), male relative. *n., pl. kinsmen. 6.*

kins wom an (kinz′wu̇m′ən), female relative. *n., pl. kinswomen.*

ki osk (ki osk′), 1. small building with one or more sides open, used as a newsstand, a bandstand, or an opening to a subway. 2. summerhouse in Turkey or Persia. *n.*

Kip ling (kip′ling), Rudyard, an English writer of stories, novels, and poems (1865-1936). He was born in India. *n.*

kip per (kip′ər), 1. to salt and dry or smoke (herring, salmon, etc.). 2. herring or other fish that has been salted and dried or smoked. *v., n.*

kirk (kėrk), Scottish word meaning church. *n. 14.*

kir tle (kėr′təl), 1. skirt. 2. man's short coat. *n.* [*Old use*] *15.*

kiss (kis), 1. to touch with the lips as a sign of love, greeting, or respect. 2. a touch with the lips as a sign of love, greeting, or respect. 3. touch gently. A soft wind kisses the tree tops. 4. gentle touch. 5. a kind of candy. 6. a fancy cake made of sugar and white of egg. *v., n. 1.*

Boy flying a kite

kit (kit), 1. the equipment that a soldier carries with him. 2. any person's equipment packed for traveling. 3. workman's outfit of tools; as, a shoemaker's kit. 4. small wooden tub, pail, etc. *n. 9.*

kitch en (kich′ən), room where food is cooked. *n. 2.*

kitch en ette (kich′ə net′), 1. very small kitchen. 2. part of a room fitted up as a kitchen. *n.*

kitch en ware (kich′ən wãr′), kitchen utensils. Pots, kettles, and pans are kitchenware. *n.*

kite (kīt), 1. a light wooden frame covered with paper or cloth. Kites are flown in the air on the end of a long string. See the picture above. 2. a hawk with long, pointed wings. *n. 4.*

Swallow-tailed kite (about 2 ft. long)

kith (kith), friends; acquaintances. **Kith and kin** means friends and relatives. *n. 16.*

kit ten (kit′ən), a young cat. *n. 3.*

kit ty (kit′i), a pet name for a kitten. *n., pl. kitties. 4.*

Klon dike (klon′dīk), region in northwestern Canada, along the Yukon River, famous for its gold fields. *n.*

km., kilometer; kilometers.

knack (nak), special skill; power to do something easily. A clown has a knack of saying very funny things. *n. 9.*

knap sack (nap′sak′), a soldier's leather or canvas bag for clothes, etc., carried on the back; any similar bag or sack. *n. 16.*

Knapsack

knave (nāv), 1. a tricky or dishonest man. 2. male servant; man of humble birth or position. *Old use. n. 4.*

knav er y (nāv′ər i), 1. trickery; dishonesty; the behavior of a knave or rascal. 2. a knavish act. *n., pl. knaveries. 16.*

knav ish (nāv′ish), tricky; dishonest. *adj. 16.*

knead (nēd), 1. work over or work up (moist flour or clay) with the hands into dough or paste. Machines have been invented to knead bread dough. 2. make or shape by kneading. 3. work over with the hands as if kneading; massage. The trainer kneaded the lame muscles of the runner. *v. 8.*

knee (nē), 1. the joint between the thigh and the lower leg. 2. anything like a bent knee in shape or position. *n. 1.*

knee cap (nē′kap′), 1. the flat, movable bone at the front of the knee. 2. a covering to protect the knee. *n.*

kneel (nēl), 1. go down on one's knee or knees. She knelt down to pull a weed from the flower bed. 2. remain on the knees. They knelt in prayer for half an hour. *v., knelt* or *kneeled, kneeling. 4.*

knell (nel), 1. the sound of a bell rung slowly after a death or at a funeral. 2. ring slowly. 3. something regarded as a sign of death or as telling of a death. Their refusal rung the knell of our hopes. 4. sound sadly; give a warning sound. *n., v. 4.*

knelt (nelt). See **kneel.** She knelt and prayed. *pt. and pp. of kneel. 9.*

knew (nū or nü). See **know.** Jane knew the right answer. *pt. of know. 1.*

Knick er bock er (nik′ər bok′ər), 1. person descended from the old Dutch settlers of New York. 2. person living in New York. *n. 9.*

knick er bock ers (nik′ər bok′ərz), short, loose trousers gathered in at or just below the knee. *n. pl.*

knick ers (nik′ərz), knickerbockers. *n. pl.*

knick knack (nik′nak′), a pleasing trifle; ornament; trinket. *n.*

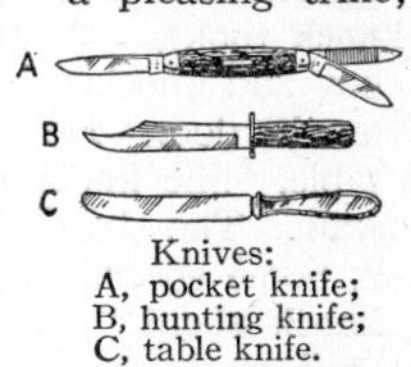

Knives: A, pocket knife; B, hunting knife; C, table knife.

knife (nīf), 1. a flat piece of steel, silver, etc., with a sharp edge, fastened in a handle so that it can be used to cut. A table knife is stiff, with no joint; a pocket knife has a joint so that the sharp edge can be folded inside the handle. 2. a sharp blade forming part of a tool or machine; as, the knives of a lawn mower. 3. cut or stab with a knife. *n., pl. knives* (nīvz), *v. 2.*

knight (nīt), 1. in the Middle Ages, a man raised to an honorable military rank and bound to do good deeds. After serving as a page and squire, a man was made a knight by the king or a lord. 2. in modern times, a man raised to an honorable rank because of personal greatness. A knight has the title *Sir* before his name. 3. raise to the rank of knight. He was knighted by the king. 4. a piece in the game of chess. *n., v. 2.*

knight-er rant (nīt′er′ənt), knight traveling in search of adventure. *n., pl. knights-errant.*

knight-er rant ry (nīt′er′ən tri), 1. conduct or action characteristic of a knight-errant. 2. quixotic conduct or action. *n., pl. knight-errantries.*

knight hood (nīt′hůd), 1. the rank of a knight. 2. the profession or occupation of a knight. 3. the character or qualities of a knight. 4. knights; as, all the knighthood of France. *n. 9.*

knight ly (nīt′li), 1. of a knight; brave; generous; courteous. 2. bravely; generously; as a knight should do. *adj., adv. 13.*

Knitting

knit (nit), 1. make with long needles out of wool yarn, or out of silk or cotton thread. Lucy is knitting a sweater. Jersey is knitted cloth. 2. join closely and firmly together. The man has a well-knit frame. 3. grow together. A broken bone knits. 4. draw (the brows) together in wrinkles. *v., knitted* or *knit, knitting. 3.*

knit ter (nit′ər), person or thing that knits. *n. 19.*

knives (nīvz), more than one knife. *n. pl. 6.*

knob (nob), 1. a rounded lump. 2. the handle of a door or of a drawer. *n. 7.*

knock (nok), 1. Bill ran against another boy and knocked him down. She knocked on the door. He knocked the dish off the table. She knocked her head against the wall. The hard knock made her cry. 2. Some special meanings are:

knock about, wander. *Used in common talk.*

knock down, 1. sell (an article) to the highest bidder at an auction. 2. take apart.

knock off, 1. take off; as, to knock off 10 cents from the price. 2. stop work.

knock out, hit so hard as to make helpless or unconscious.

knock together, make or put together hastily.

v., n. 2.

knock er (nok′ər), 1. one that knocks. 2. a hinged knob, ring, or the like, fastened on a door for use in knocking. *n. 11.*

knock-kneed (nok′nēd′), having legs bent inward at the knee. *adj.*

knoll (nōl), a small hill; a mound. *n. 6.*

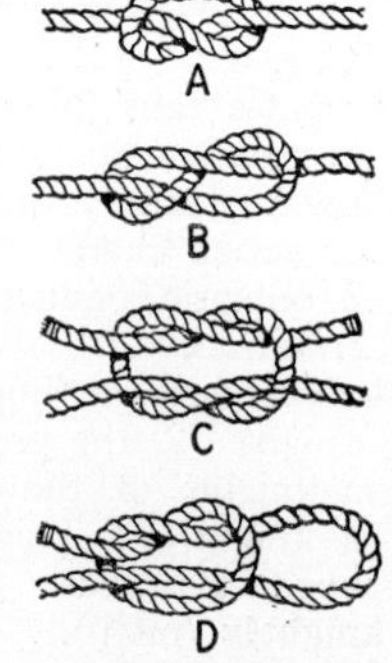

Knots: A, overhand; B, figure-ot-eight; C, square; D, slip.

knot (not), 1. a tying or twining together of parts of one or more ropes, strings, etc., to fasten them together; as, a square knot, a slip knot. 2. to tie in a knot. 3. a bow (of ribbon); ribbon made up into an ornament to be put on a dress, etc.; as, a shoulder knot. 4. make knots for fringes. 5. make (fringes). 6. unit of speed used on ships; one nautical mile (6080.27 ft.) per hour. This ship's usual speed is about 18 knots. 7. the hard mass formed in a tree where a branch grows out, which shows as a round, cross-grained piece in a board. 8. a joint where leaves grow out on the stem of a plant. 9. a group or cluster of persons or things. 10. a difficulty or problem. 11. unite closely in a way that is hard to undo. 12. tangle. *n., v., knotted, knotting. 3.*

knot hole (not′hōl′), a hole in a board formed where a knot has fallen out. *n.*

knot ty (not′i), 1. full of knots; as, knotty wood. 2. difficult; puzzling. *adj., knottier, knottiest. 20.*

know (nō). We know that 2 and 2 make 4. Doctor Jones does not guess; he knows. Do you know that girl? Do you know where she lives? How many kinds of birds do you know? *v., knew, known, knowing. 1.*

know ing (nō′ing), 1. having knowledge. 2. clever; shrewd. 3. suggesting shrewd or secret understanding of matters; as, a knowing glance. *adj.*

know ing ly (nō′ing li), 1. in a knowing way. 2. to one's own knowledge. He would not knowingly hurt any living thing. *adv.*

knowl edge (nol′ij), 1. what one knows. 2. all that is known or can be learned. 3. the fact of knowing. The knowledge of our victory caused great joy. 4. the act of knowing. *n. 2.*

known (nōn). See **know.** Washington is known as a general. *pp. of know. 1.*

Knox (noks), John, a famous Scottish preacher (1505?-1572). *n. 18.*

Knox ville (noks′vil), a city in eastern Tennessee. *n.*

knuck le (nuk′əl), 1. a joint in a finger, especially one of the joints at the roots of the fingers. 2. the knee or hock joint of an animal used as meat; as, pigs' knuckles. 3. **Knuckle down** means (1) submit. (2) work hard. 4. **Knuckle under** means submit. *n., v. 10.*

ko dak (kō′dak), 1. a kind of camera with rolls of film on which photographs are taken. *Trade name.* 2. take photographs with a kodak. *n., v. 11.*

kohl ra bi (kōl′rä′bi), a vegetable that looks somewhat like a turnip. *n., pl. kohlrabies. 20.*

Kohlrabi

ko peck or **ko pek** (kō′pek), a Russian copper coin. A kopeck was equal to about one-half cent in United States money. *n.*

Ko ran (kō rän′), the sacred book of the Mohammedans. *n. 14.*

Ko re a (kō rē′ə), a country in eastern Asia, belonging to Japan. *n. 18.*

Ko re an (kō rē′ən), 1. of Korea, its people, or their language. 2. native or inhabitant of Korea. 3. language of Korea. *adj., n.*

ko sher (kō′shər), right or clean according to Jewish law; as, kosher meat. *adj.*

Kos suth (ko süth′), Louis, Hungarian patriot (1802-1894). *n.*

kow tow (kou′tou′), 1. kneel and touch the ground with the forehead to show deep respect, submission, or worship. 2. show slavish respect or obedience. *v.*

Kreis ler (krīs′lər), Fritz, Austrian violinist and composer (born 1875). *n.*

Krem lin (krem′lin), citadel of Moscow. The chief offices of the Russian government are in the Kremlin. *n.*

Kriss Krin gle (kris′ kring′gəl), Santa Claus.

kum quat (kum′kwot), 1. yellow fruit somewhat like a small orange. It has a sour pulp and a sweet rind, and is used in preserves and candy. 2. tree that it grows on. *n.*

Ky., Kentucky.

Kyo to (kyō′tō), city in central Japan. It was formerly the capital. *n.*

L

L, l (el), 1. the 12th letter of the alphabet. There are two l's in ball. 2. Roman numeral for 50. *n., pl. L's, l's.*

la[1] (lä), in music, the sixth tone of the scale. Do, re, mi, fa, sol, la, ti, do are the names of the tones of the scale. *n. 11.*

la[2] (lä), an exclamation of surprise. *interj.*

La., Louisiana.

la bel (lā′bəl), 1. a slip of paper or other material attached to anything and marked to show what or whose it is, or where it is to go. Can you read the label on the box? 2. put or write a label on. The bottle is labeled "Poison." 3. put in a class; call; name; as, to label a man a liar. *n., v., labeled, labeling. 5.*

la bi al (lā′bi əl), 1. of the lips. 2. pronounced with the lips closed or nearly closed. 3. a sound made with the lips closed or nearly closed. *B, p,* and *m* are labials. *adj., n. 17.*

la bor (lā′bər), 1. work; toil. 2. workers. 3. move slowly and heavily. The ship labored in the heavy seas. *n., v. 1.*

lab o ra to ry (lab′ə rə tō′ri), place where scientific work is done; as, a chemical laboratory. *n., pl. laboratories. 8.*

Labor Day, the first Monday in September, a legal holiday in honor of labor and laborers.

la bored (lā′bərd), done with difficulty; not easy or natural. *adj.*

la bor er (lā′bər ər), 1. worker. 2. person who does work that requires strength rather than skill and training. *n. 5.*

la bo ri ous (lə bō′ri əs), 1. requiring much work; requiring hard work. Climbing a mountain is laborious. 2. hard-working. Ants and bees are laborious insects. 3. showing signs of effort; not easy. *adj. 10.*

labor union, an association of workers to protect and promote their interests.

Lab ra dor (lab′rə dôr), peninsula of North America between Hudson Bay and the Atlantic Ocean. *n. 7.*

la bur num (lə bėr′nəm), a small tree with hanging clusters of yellow flowers. *n. 18.*

lab y rinth (lab′i rinth), maze; place through which it is hard to find one's way. *n. 8.*

lab y rin thine (lab′i rin′thin), of a labyrinth; forming a labyrinth. *adj. 15.*

Lace (def. 1)

lace (lās), 1. an open weaving or net of fine thread in an ornamental pattern. 2. trim with lace. 3. a cord, string, or leather strip for pulling or holding together; as, a shoelace. 4. put laces through; pull or hold together with a lace or laces; as, to lace up your shoes. 5. gold or silver braid used for trimming. Some uniforms have lace on them. 6. adorn or trim with narrow braid; as, cloth laced with gold, a white flower laced with red. 7. lash, beat, or thrash. *n., v. 2.*

Lac e dae mo ni an (las′ə di mō′ni ən), Spartan. *adj., n. 17.*

lac er ate (las′ər āt), tear roughly; mangle. The bear's claws lacerated the hunter's flesh. Your sharp words lacerated my feelings. *v. 16.*

lac er ation (las′ər ā′shən), 1. tearing; mangling. 2. result of rough tearing; tear. A torn, jagged wound is a laceration. *n.*

lach ry mal (lak′ri məl), of tears or weeping; for tears. *adj. 19.*

lack (lak), 1. being without. Lack of food made him hungry; lack of fire made him cold. 2. have no; be without. Guinea pigs lack tails. A coward lacks courage. 3. be absent or wanting. *n., v. 2.*

lack a dai si cal (lak′ə dā′zi kəl), languid; languishing; pretending to be tired; weakly sentimental. *adj.*

lack ey (lak′i), 1. male servant; footman. 2. a completely obedient servant. 3. wait on; attend. *n., pl. lackeys, v., lackeyed, lackeying. 16.*

lack ing (lak′ing), 1. absent; not here. Water is lacking because the pipe is broken. 2. without; not having. Lacking anything better, we must use what we have. *adj., prep.*

lack lus ter or **lack lus tre** (lak′lus′tər), dull; not shining. *adj. 19.*

la con ic (lə kon′ik), using few words; brief in speech or expression; concise. *adj. 16.*

lac quer (lak′ər), 1. a varnish consisting of shellac dissolved in alcohol, used for coating brass, etc. 2. a natural varnish obtained from the resin of a sumac tree of southeastern Asia. It is used for producing a highly polished surface on wood. 3. to coat with lacquer. 4. articles coated with lacquer. *n., v. 15.*

la crosse (lə krôs′), game played with a ball and long-handled rackets by two sides of 12 players each. The players try to send the ball through a goal. *n.*

lac te al (lak′ti əl), 1. of milk; like milk. 2. carrying a milky fluid formed of digested food. 3. any of the tiny vessels that carry this fluid to be mixed with the blood. *adj., n. 17.*

lac tic (lak′tik), of milk; obtained from milk. **Lactic acid** is formed in sour milk. *adj. 17.*

lac y (lās′i), 1. of lace. 2. like lace. *adj., lacier, laciest.*

lad (lad), boy. *n. 2.*

lad der (lad′ər), 1. a set of rungs or steps fastened into two long sidepieces of wood, metal, or rope, for use in climbing up and down. 2. a means of climbing higher. *n. 3.*

Wooden ladder

lade (lād), load; put a burden on. *v., laded, laden* or *laded, lading. 4.*

lad en (lād′ən), loaded; burdened. The camels were laden with bundles of silk. *adj., pp. of* **lade.**

la dies (lā′diz), more than one lady. *n. pl. 2.*

lad ing (lād′ing), load; freight; cargo; what a thing is loaded with. A **bill of lading** is a written receipt given by a railroad, express company, etc., for goods delivered to it for transportation. *n. 10.*

la dle (lā′dəl), 1. deep, cup-shaped spoon with a long handle, for dipping out liquids. 2. dip out. *n., v. 10.*

Ladle

la dy (lā′di), 1. the mistress of a house. 2. gentlewoman; well-bred woman. 3. woman of high social standing. 4. in Great Britain, **Lady** is a title given to women of certain ranks. 5. **Our Lady** is a title of the Virgin Mary. 6. A **lady in waiting** is an attendant of a queen or princess. *n., pl. ladies. 1.*

la dy bird (lā′di bėrd′), ladybug. *n.*

la dy bug (lā′di bug′), a small, roundish beetle, reddish with black spots. *n.*

la dy like (lā′di līk′), 1. like a lady. 2. suitable for a lady. *adj. 18.*

la dy ship (lā′di ship). **Your** or **her Ladyship** is a title used in speaking of or to one having the rank of lady. *n. 12.*

la dy-slip per (lā′di slip′ər), lady's-slipper. *n.*

la dy's-slip per (lā′diz slip′ər), wild orchid whose flower looks somewhat like a slipper. *n.*

Lady's-slipper

La fay ette (lä′fā et′), a French general (1757-1834) who came to help the Americans during the Revolution. *n. 9.*

lag (lag), 1. move too slowly; fall behind. The child lagged because he was tired. 2. falling behind. *v., lagged, lagging, n. 5.*

lag gard (lag′ərd), 1. person who lags or is backward; loiterer. 2. lagging; slow; falling behind. *n., adj. 12.*

la goon (lə gün′), 1. small pond connected with a larger body of water. 2. shallow water separated from the sea by low sandbanks. 3. the water within a ring-shaped coral island. *n. 13.*

laid (lād). See **lay**[1]. He laid down the heavy bundle. Those eggs were laid this morning. *pt. and pp. of lay*[1]*. 1.*

lain (lān). See **lie**[2]. The snow has lain on the ground a week. *pp. of lie*[2]*. 6.*

lair (lãr), the den or resting place of a wild animal. *n. 8.*

laird (lãrd), a Scottish word meaning an owner of land. *n. 18.*

la i ty (lā′i ti), laymen; the people as distinguished from the clergy or from a professional class. Doctors use many words that the laity do not understand. *n. 14.*

lake (lāk), body of water surrounded by land. A lake is larger than a pond. *n. 1.*

Lamb

lamb (lam), 1. a baby sheep. 2. meat from a lamb; as, roast lamb. 3. give birth to a lamb or lambs. 4. a young, innocent, or dear person. *n., v. 2.*

Lamb (lam), Charles, an English writer, chiefly of essays (1775-1834). *n.*

lam bent (lam′bənt), 1. moving lightly over a surface without burning it; as, a lambent flame. 2. playing lightly and brilliantly over a subject; as, lambent wit. 3. softly bright; as, lambent eyes, the lambent moon. *adj. 16.*

lamb kin (lam′kin), little lamb. *n. 10.*

lame (lām), 1. stiff and sore. His arm is lame from playing ball. 2. not able to walk properly; having a hurt leg. 3. make lame; cripple. The accident lamed him for life. 4. poor; not very good. Stopping to play is a lame excuse for being late to school. *adj., v. 3.*

lame ness (lām′nis), being lame. *n. 12.*

la ment (lə ment′), 1. sorrow for; mourn. 2. weep; sorrow. 3. a wail; an expression of grief or sorrow. 4. a poem, song, or tune that expresses grief. *v., n. 4.*

lam en ta ble (lam′ən tə bəl), 1. to be regretted or pitied; as, a lamentable accident, a lamentable failure. 2. sorrowful; mournful. *adj. 8.*

lam en ta tion (lam′ən tā′shən), loud grief; mourning; wailing; cries of sorrow. *n. 5.*

lamp (lamp), 1. a vessel for giving light. Oil lamps hold oil and a wick by which the oil is burned. 2. a gas or electric light, especially when covered with a glass globe or other shade. 3. anything that gives light. *n. 2.*

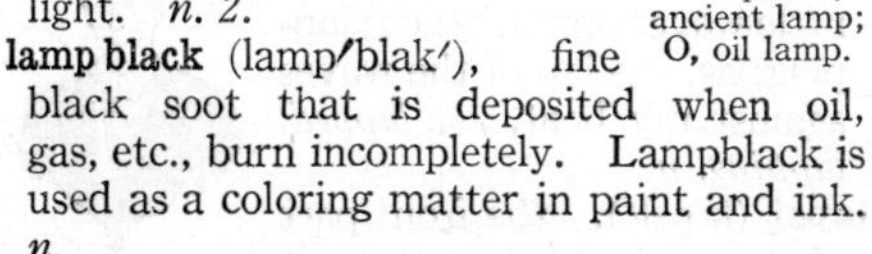

Lamps: A, ancient lamp; O, oil lamp.

lamp black (lamp′blak′), fine black soot that is deposited when oil, gas, etc., burn incompletely. Lampblack is used as a coloring matter in paint and ink. *n.*

lam poon (lam pün′), 1. piece of malicious or abusive writing that attacks and ridicules a person. 2. attack in a lampoon. *n., v. 16.*

lam prey (lam′pri), water animal having a body like an eel, gill slits like a fish, no jaws, and a large, round mouth. *n., pl. lampreys.*

Lan ca shire (lang′kə shir), a county in northwestern England. *n. 18.*

Lan cas ter (lang′kəs tər), 1. the English royal house from 1399 to 1461. 2. Lancashire. *n. 12.*

lance (lans), 1. a long wooden spear with a sharp iron or steel head. Knights carried lances. 2. soldier who carries a lance. 3. pierce with a lance. 4. cut open with a lancet or surgeon's knife; as, to lance the gum where a new tooth has difficulty in coming through. 5. hurl. *Used in poetry. n., v. 4.*

Lan ce lot (lan′sə lot), the bravest of King Arthur's knights of the Round Table. *n. 12.*

lanc er (lan′sər), a mounted soldier armed with a lance. *n.*

lan cet (lan′sit), small, sharp knife used by doctors or surgeons in opening boils, sores, etc. *n. 12.*

land (land), 1. the solid part of the earth's surface. 2. ground; soil. This is good land for a garden. 3. a country and its people. 4. come to land; bring to land. The ship landed at the pier. The pilot landed the airplane in a field. 5. put on shore from a ship or boat. The ship landed its passengers. 6. go on shore from a ship or boat. The passengers landed. 7. arrive. The thief landed in jail. 8. catch; get. *Not used in formal writing. n., v. 1.*

land ed (lan′did), 1. owning land. 2. consisting of land. *adj.*

land hold er (land′hōl′dər), person who owns or occupies land. *n.*

land ing (lan′ding), 1. coming to land; as, the landing of the Pilgrims at Plymouth. 2. place where persons or goods are landed from a ship; as, the steamboat landing. 3. platform between flights of stairs. *n.*

land la dy (land′lā′di), 1. woman who owns buildings or lands that she rents to others. 2. mistress of an inn, lodging house, or boarding house. *n., pl. landladies. 12.*

land locked (land′lokt′), 1. shut in, or nearly shut in, by land. 2. living in waters shut off from the sea. *adj.*

land lord (land′lôrd′), 1. person who owns buildings or lands that he rents to others.

2. the keeper of an inn, lodging house, or boarding house. *n. 8.*

land lub ber (land′lub′ər), person not used to being on ships; person clumsy on ships. Sailors call landsmen landlubbers in scorn. *n.*

land mark (land′märk′), 1. something familiar or easily seen, used as a guide. 2. any important fact or event; any happening that stands out above others. The printing press, the telegraph, the telephone, and the radio are landmarks in the progress of communication. 3. stone or other object that marks the boundary of a piece of land. *n. 8.*

land own er (land′ōn′ər), person who owns land. *n. 19.*

land scape (land′skāp), 1. land scene; a view of scenery on land. The two hills with the valley formed a beautiful landscape. 2. picture showing a land scene. 3. make (land) more pleasant to look at by arranging trees, shrubs, flowers, etc. A park is landscaped. *n., v. 5.*

land slide (land′slīd′), 1. a sliding down of a mass of soil or rock on a steep slope. 2. the mass that slides down. 3. an overwhelming majority of votes for one party or candidate. *n.*

lands man (landz′mən), man who lives or works on land. *n., pl. landsmen. 18.*

land ward (land′wərd), toward the land or shore. *adv., adj. 14.*

land wards (land′wərdz), landward. *adv.*

lane (lān), 1. path between hedges, walls, or fences; a narrow or short grassy road in the country. 2. an alley between buildings. 3. the course or route used by ships or airplanes going in the same direction. 4. any narrow way. The six generals walked down a lane formed by two lines of soldiers and sailors. *n. 3.*

lan guage (lang′gwij), 1. human speech, spoken or written. 2. the speech of one nation or race; as, the French language. 3. form, style, or kind of language; as, Shakespeare's language, the language of chemistry. 4. wording; words; as, in the language of the Lord's Prayer. 5. any means of expressing thoughts or feelings; as, a dog's language, the language of the eyes. *n. 2.*

lan guid (lang′gwid), feeling weak; without energy; drooping. A hot, sticky day makes a person feel languid. *adj. 8.*

lan guish (lang′gwish), 1. grow weak; droop. The flowers languish from lack of water. 2. droop with longing. She languished for home. 3. put on a longing, tender look for effect. *v. 5.*

lan guor (lang′gər), 1. weakness; faintness; lack of energy. Disease and fatigue produce languor. 2. lack of mental energy; listless condition. 3. softness or tenderness of mood. 4. quietness; stillness; as, the languor of a summer afternoon. *n. 11.*

lan guor ous (lang′gər əs), languid; listless. *adj.*

lank (langk), 1. long and thin; lean; as, a lank boy. 2. long and slender; as, lank grasses. 3. straight and flat; as, lank locks of hair. *adj. 9.*

lank y (langk′i), lank; awkwardly long and thin. *adj., lankier, lankiest.*

Lan sing (lan′sing), the capital of Michigan. *n.*

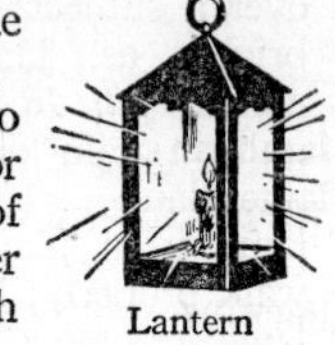
Lantern

lan tern (lan′tərn), a case to protect a light from wind or rain. A lantern has sides of glass, paper, or some other material through which light can shine. *n. 4.*

lap[1] (lap), 1. the part from the waist to the knees of a person sitting down, with the clothing. Mother holds the baby on her lap. 2. place where anything rests or is cared for. 3. flap; the loosely hanging edge of a garment; the front part of a skirt. *n. 2.*

lap[2] (lap), 1. to wind or wrap round; fold over or about something. Lap this edge over that. 2. enfold or wrap in; surround. 3. extend out beyond something. 4. lie together, one partly over or beside another. The pieces lap over each other. 5. act of lapping. 6. the part that laps over. 7. one time around a race track; as, the first lap of the race. *v., lapped, lapping, n.*

lap[3] (lap), 1. drink as a dog does, by lifting up with the tongue; lick. 2. move or beat gently with a lapping sound. The waves lapping against the shore put me to sleep. 3. act of lapping; as, one lap of the tongue. 4. the sound of little waves on the beach; lapping; as, the lap of the waves against my boat. *v., lapped, lapping, n.*

Lapels

la pel (lə pel′), the front part of a coat folded back just below the collar. *n. 18.*

lap i dar y (lap′i dãr′i), person who cuts, polishes, or engraves precious stones. *n., pl. lapidaries.*

lap is laz u li (lap′is laz′ū lī), 1. deep-blue, opaque semiprecious stone. 2. deep blue. *adj., n. 1.*

Lap land (lap′land), a region in northern Norway, Sweden, Finland, and northwestern Russia. *n. 12.*

Lapp (lap), 1. member of the people living in Lapland. 2. the language of this people. *n.*

lap pet (lap′it), a small flap or fold. *n. 19.*

L, lappet.

lapse (laps), 1. a moment's forgetfulness; a slip of the tongue or pen; a slip away from right conduct. 2. slip back; sink down. The house lapsed into ruin. He sometimes lapses from good behavior. 3. the slipping by of time. 4. slip by; pass away. The boy's interest soon lapsed. 5. the ending of a right, privilege, etc., because not renewed, not used, or not attended to. 6. to end. A claim lapses after a certain time. *n., v. 7.*

lap wing (lap′wing′), a bird that has a slow, irregular flight and a peculiar wailing cry. *n. 14.*

Lapwing (about 1 ft. long)

lar board (lär′bərd), 1. the left or port side of a ship. See the picture under **aft.** 2. on the left side of a ship. *n., adj. 15.*

lar ce ny (lär′sə ni), theft. *n., pl. larcenies. 16.*

larch (lärch), 1. a tree with small cones and needles that fall off in the autumn. 2. the wood of this tree. *n. 9.*

Branch of larch

lard (lärd), 1. the fat of pigs or hogs, melted down and made clear for use in cooking. 2. put strips of bacon or pork in (meat) before cooking. 3. enrich by inserts; trim. *n., v. 4.*

lar der (lär′dər), 1. pantry; place where food is kept. 2. stock of food. *n. 11.*

lar es and pe na tes (lãr′ēz ənd pe nā′tēz), 1. household gods of the ancient Romans. 2. cherished possessions of a family or household.

large (lärj). A horse is a large animal. America is larger than England. A very large man is called a giant. **At large** means (1) free. Is the prisoner still at large? (2) in general. The people at large wanted peace. (3) not elected by a special district. Vote for two members at large. *adj., n. 1.*

large ly (lärj′li), much; to a great extent. *adv. 9.*

large ness (lärj′nis), bigness; great size or extent. *n. 13.*

lar gess or **lar gesse** (lär′jes), 1. generous giving. 2. a generous gift or gifts. *n. 14.*

lar i at (lar′i ət), 1. lasso; a long rope with a noose for catching horses, cattle, etc. A cowboy throws a lariat at horses or cattle to catch them. 2. a rope for fastening horses, mules, etc., while they graze. *n.*

lark[1] (lärk), 1. a small songbird of Europe that soars and sings while in the air. 2. a similar bird in America; as, the meadow lark. *n. 3.*

lark[2] (lärk), 1. something that is good fun; joke. 2. have fun; play tricks. *n., v.* [*Used in common talk*]

lark spur (lärk′spėr), a plant with tall spikes of beautiful blue flowers. *n. 16.*

lar va (lär′və), early form of an insect from the time it leaves the egg until it becomes a pupa. A caterpillar is the larva of a butterfly or moth. A grub is the larva of a beetle. Maggots are the larvae of flies. *n., pl. larvae* (-vē). *7.*

Larva of a butterfly

lar val (lär′vəl), 1. of a larva; having to do with larvae. 2. in the form of a larva. *adj. 16.*

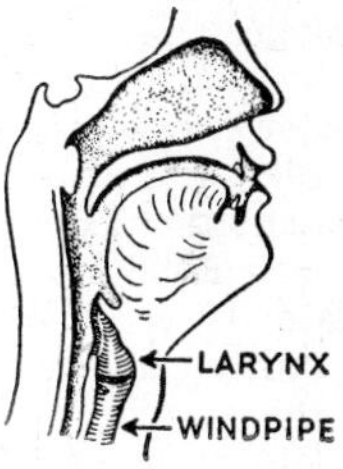

lar ynx (lar′ingks), the upper end of the windpipe, where the vocal cords are. See the picture. *n. 13.*

La Salle (lə sal′), a Frenchman (1643-1687) who explored the Mississippi Valley. *13.*

las civ i ous (lə siv′i əs), 1. feeling lust. 2. causing lust. *adj. 10.*

lash (lash), 1. the part of a whip that is not the handle. 2. a stroke or blow with a whip, etc. 3. strike with a whip. 4. beat back and forth. A lion lashes his tail. The wind lashes the sails. 5. hurt severely by words. 6. hit. 7. tie or fasten with a rope or cord; as, a body lashed to a mast. 8. one of the little hairs on the edge of the eyelid. *n., v. 5.*

lass (las), girl; young girl. *n. 5.*

las sie (las′i), girl. *n. 20.*

las si tude (las′i tūd or las′i tüd), weariness of body or mind; a feeling of weakness; lack of energy. *n. 15.*

Cowboy using a lasso

las so (las′ō), 1. long rope with a running noose at the end, used for catching horses and cattle. 2. to catch with a lasso. *n., pl. lassos* or *lassoes, v., lassoed, lassoing.*

last[1] (last). *Z* is the last letter; *A* is the first. Ned came last in the line. It rained last night. When did you see him last? **At last** means finally. *adj., adv., n. 1.*

last[2] (last), hold out; continue; continue in good condition. How long will our money last? I hope these shoes last a year. *v.*

last[3] (last), block shaped like the human foot, on which shoes and boots are formed or mended. *n.*

last ing (las′ting), that lasts; that will last; that will last a long time. *adj. 14.*

last ly (last′li), finally; in the last place. *adv. 14.*

Last Supper, Jesus's last meal with His disciples before His Crucifixion.

Latch on a door

latch (lach), 1. a catch for fastening a door, gate, or window, often one not needing a key. 2. fasten with a latch. *n., v. 5.*

latch et (lach′it), strap or lace for fastening a shoe or sandal. *n.* [*Old use*] *20.*

latch key (lach′kē′), a key used to unfasten the latch of a door. *n.*

latch string (lach′string′), string used to unfasten the latch of a door. *n.*

late (lāt), 1. We had a late supper because father came home late. 2. It was late in the evening. You should not sit up too late at night. 3. recent. The late storm did much harm. 4. recently dead or gone out of office. The late Mr. Smith was a good citizen. The late president is still working actively. 5. **Of late** means lately; a short time ago. *adj., later* or *latter, latest* or *last, adv., later, latest* or *last, n. 1.*

Lateen sails

la teen sail (la tēn′ sāl′), triangular sail held up by a long yard on a short mast. See the picture.

late ly (lāt′li), a little while ago; not long ago. *adv. 7.*

la tent (lā′tənt), hidden; concealed; present but not active. The power of a grain of wheat to grow into a plant remains latent if it is not planted. *adj. 8.*

lat er al (lat′ər əl), of the side; at the side; from the side; toward the side. *adj. 8.*

lath (lath), 1. a thin, narrow strip of wood, used with others like it to form a support for plaster or to make a lattice. 2. cover or line with laths. *n., pl. laths* (laᴛʜz), *v. 14.*

lathe (lāᴛʜ), a machine for holding articles of wood, metal, etc., and turning them rapidly against a tool used to shape them. *n. 10.*

lath er (laᴛʜ′ər), 1. foam made from soap and water. 2. put lather on. He lathers his face before shaving. 3. form a lather. 4. foam formed in sweating. 5. become covered with lather. The horse lathered from his hard gallop. *n., v. 15.*

Lat in (lat′in), 1. the language of the ancient Romans. 2. of Latin; in Latin; as, Latin poetry, Latin grammar, a Latin scholar. 3. of Latium or its people. 4. a native or inhabitant of Latium. The Romans were Latins. 5. of the peoples (Italians, French, Spanish, and Portuguese) whose languages have come from Latin. *n., adj. 3.*

lat i tude (lat′i tūd or lat′i tüd), 1. distance north or south of the equator, measured in degrees. 2. place or region having a certain latitude. 3. room to act; freedom from narrow rules. You are allowed much latitude in this work. *n. 7.*

La ti um (lā′shi əm), an ancient country in southern Italy. *n. 19.*

lat ter (lat′ər), 1. the second of two. Canada and the United States are in North America; the former lies north of the latter. 2. more recent; later; toward the end; as, the latter part of the week, the old man's latter days. *adj. 2.*

Latter-day Saint, Mormon.

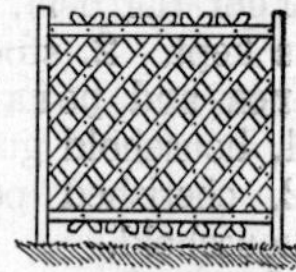
Lattice

lat ter ly (lat′ər li), lately; of late. *adv.*

lat tice (lat′is), 1. wooden or metal strips crossed with open spaces between them. 2. form into a lattice. 3. furnish with a lattice. *n., v. 10.*

lat tice work (lat′is wėrk′), 1. lattice. 2. lattices. *n.*

Lat vi a (lat′vi ə), a small country in northern Europe, on the Baltic Sea. *n.*

laud (lôd), praise; extol. *v. 10.*

laud a ble (lôd′ə bəl), worthy of praise. Unselfishness is laudable. *adj. 12.*

lau da num (lô′də nəm), a solution of opium in alcohol, used as a medicine and as a poison. *n. 16.*

lau da tion (lô dā′shən), praise. *n. 20.*

laud a to ry (lôd′ə tō′ri), expressing praise. *adj.*

laugh (laf), 1. You laugh when you hear a good joke. 2. the sound made when a person laughs. 3. be gay or lively. The little brook laughed. 4. **Laugh at** means make fun of. 5. **Laugh on the other side of one's mouth** means be sorry. *v., n. 1.*

laugh a ble (laf′ə bəl), amusing; funny. *adj. 12.*

laugh ing stock (laf′ing stok′), person or thing that is made fun of. *n.*

laugh ter (laf′tər), 1. the action of laughing. 2. the sound of laughing. *n. 3.*

launch[1] (lônch), 1. the largest boat carried by a warship. 2. a rather small open motorboat for pleasure trips. *n. 5.*

launch[2] (lônch), 1. cause to slide into the water; set afloat. A new ship is launched from the supports on which it was built. 2. start; set going; set out. His friends launched him in business by lending him money. He used the money to launch into a new business. 3. throw; hurl; send out. A bow launches arrows into the air. An angry person launches threats against his enemies. *v.*

laun der (lôn′dər), wash and iron clothes. *v. 13.*

laun dress (lôn′dris), woman who washes and irons clothes. *n. 18.*

laun dry (lôn′dri), 1. a room or building where clothes are washed and ironed. 2. clothes that are washed. *n., pl. laundries. 5.*

laun dry man (lôn′dri mən), man who works in a laundry. *n., pl. laundrymen. 18.*

lau re ate (lô′ri it), 1. crowned with laurel as a mark of honor or greatness; honored; distinguished. Alfred Tennyson became poet laureate of England. 2. the chosen poet of a nation or court. *adj., n. 10.*

lau rel (lô′rəl), 1. a small evergreen tree with smooth, shiny leaves. The ancient Greeks and Romans made wreaths of laurel to put on the heads of persons whom they wished to honor. 2. any tree or shrub like this. The mountain laurel has beautiful pale-pink clusters of blossoms. 3. **Laurels** means (1) victory. (2) high honor. *n. 4.*

Laurel (def. 1)

la va (lä′və), 1. molten rock flowing from a volcano. 2. rock formed by the cooling of this molten rock. Some lavas are hard and glassy; others are light and porous. *n. 9.*

lav a to ry (lav′ə tō′ri), 1. room where a person can wash his hands and face. 2. bowl or basin to wash in. *n., pl. lavatories. 14.*

lave (lāv), wash; bathe. The lady laves her hands. The stream laves its banks. *v. [Used in poetry] 13.*

lav en der (lav′ən dər), 1. pale purple. 2. a small shrub with spikes of fragrant, pale-purple flowers, yielding an oil much used in perfumes. 3. its dried flowers, leaves, and stalks used to scent or preserve linen. *adj., n. 8.*

la ver (lā′vər), a bowl or basin to wash in. *n. [Old use] 16.*

lav ish (lav′ish), 1. very abundant; too abundant; more than is needed; as, a lavish helping of pudding. 2. liberal; too free; as, lavish with his money. 3. pour out wastefully; as, to lavish affection on a naughty, cruel child. *adj., v. 5.*

Lavender

law (lô), 1. a rule made by a country, state, king, etc. Good citizens obey the laws. There is a law against spitting in streetcars. 2. any rule. A law of nature states how things act. The laws of a game tell how to play it. 3. a system of rules formed to protect society. English law is not like French law. 4. the study of such a system of rules; the profession of a lawyer. This young man is studying law. 5. **Go to law** means appeal to law courts. *n. 1.*

law break er (lô′brāk′ər), person who breaks the law. *n.*

law ful (lô′fəl), according to law; done as the law directs; allowed by law; rightful. *adj. 5.*

law giv er (lô′giv′ər), lawmaker; man who has given a system of laws to a people. *n. 14.*

law less (lô′lis), 1. paying no attention to the law; breaking the law. 2. hard to control; disorderly. 3. having no laws. *adj. 6.*

law mak er (lô′māk′ər), person who helps make the laws of a country; member of a legislature, congress, or parliament. *n. 11.*

lawn[1] (lôn), piece of land covered with grass kept closely cut. *n. 2.*

lawn[2] (lôn), a kind of thin linen or cotton cloth. *n.*

Law rence (lô′rəns), a city in northeastern Massachusetts. *n. 6.*

law suit (lô′süt′), a case in a law court; an application to a court for justice. *n. 13.*

law yer (lô′yər), person who knows the laws and gives advice about matters of law or acts for another person in court. *n. 3.*

lax (laks), 1. loose; slack; not firm; as, a lax cord. 2. not strict; careless; loose in morals. People sometimes become lax when they go away from home. 3. not exact; vague. *adj. 13.*

lax a tive (lak′sə tiv), 1. medicine that makes the bowels move. 2. making the bowels move. *n., adj. 13.*

lax i ty (lak′si ti), lax condition or quality; looseness; slackness. *n. 16.*

lay[1] (lā), 1. beat down; as, crops laid low by a storm. 2. put down; keep down. Lay your hat on the table. This shower has laid the dust. 3. make quiet or make disappear; as, to lay a ghost. 4. place in a lying-down position. Lay the baby down gently. 5. place or set; as, to lay one's hand on one's heart, to lay a tax on tea. The scene of the story is laid in New York. 6. put. Lay aside that book for me. The horse laid his ears back. 7. put in place; as, to lay bricks. They laid the carpet on the floor. 8. put into a certain state; as, to lay a wound open. 9. put down as a bet; offer as a bet. I lay $5 he will not come. 10. Of a hen, to lay means to give an egg or eggs. 11. way, position, or direction in which something lies. 12. Some special meanings are:

lay about, hit out on all sides.

lay away or **lay by** (money), save.

lay off, 1. put aside. 2. put out of work. 3. mark off.

lay of the land, the nature of the place; the position of hills, water, woods, etc.

lay oneself out, take great pains.

lay out (a body), get it ready for burial.

lay out (a garden), plan and plant it.

lay (something) **to one** or **at one's door,** give one the blame or credit for it.

lay up, 1. save. 2. cause to stay in bed because of illness.

v., laid, laying, n. 1.

lay[2] (lā). See **lie**[2]. After a long walk I lay down for a rest. *pt. of lie*[2].

lay[3] (lā), 1. of ordinary people; not of the clergy. 2. of ordinary people; not of lawyers, doctors, or those learned in the profession in question. The lay mind understands little of the causes of diseases. *adj.*

lay[4] (lā), 1. a short poem meant to be sung. 2. any song or poem. The blackbird whistles his merry lay. *n.*

lay er (lā′ər), 1. person or thing that lays; as, a bricklayer. 2. one thickness or fold; as, the layer of clothing next the skin, a layer of clay between two layers of sand. A layer cake is one made of two or more layers put together. *n. 5.*

lay ette (lā et′), a set of clothes and bedding ready for a newborn baby. *n. 13.*

lay man (lā′mən), person outside of any particular profession, especially one not belonging to the clergy. It is hard for a layman to understand a medical journal. *n., pl. laymen. 8.*

lay out (lā′out′), 1. act of laying out. 2. arrangement; plan. This map shows the layout of the camp. 3. something laid out; a display. *n. 20.*

Laz a rus (laz′ə rəs), 1. the brother of Mary and Martha, whom Jesus raised from the dead. 2. the beggar in the parable who suffered on earth but went to heaven. *n. 11.*

la zi ly (lā′zi li), in a lazy manner. *adv.*

la zi ness (lā′zi nis), dislike of work; unwillingness to work or be active; being lazy. *n. 16.*

la zy (lā′zi), 1. not willing to work or be active. 2. moving slowly; not very active. *adj., lazier, laziest. 2.*

lb., pound; pounds. *4.*

lea (lē), meadow; grassy field; pasture. *n. 6.*

leach (lēch), 1. run water through slowly. 2. dissolve out by running water through slowly. Potash is leached from wood ashes and used to make soap. 3. lose soluble parts when water passes through. *v. 16.*

lead[1] (lēd), 1. show the way by going along with or in front of. He leads the horses to water. 2. be first among. She leads the class in spelling. 3. be a way or road. Hard work leads to success. 4. pass or spend (time) in some special way. He leads a quiet life in the country. 5. go first; begin a game. You may lead this time.

6. place of leader; place in front. He always takes the lead when we plan to do anything. 7. right to play first. It is your lead this time. 8. amount that one is ahead. He had a lead of 3 yards in the race. *v., led, leading, n. 1.*

lead[2] (led), 1. a heavy, easily melted, bluish-gray metal, used to make pipe, etc. 2. made of lead. 3. a long thin piece of a soft black substance used in pencils. 4. a weight on a line used to find out the depth of water. *n., adj.*

lead en (led′ən), 1. made of lead; as, a leaden coffin. 2. heavy; hard to lift or move; as, leaden arms tired from working. 3. bluish-gray; as, leaden clouds. *adj. 11.*

lead er (lēd′ər), one who leads, or is well fitted to lead. *n. 2.*

lead er ship (lēd′ər ship), 1. being a leader. 2. ability to lead. *n. 7.*

OAK ELM
Leaves (def. 1)

leaf (lēf), 1. one of the thin, flat, green parts of a tree or other plant that grow on the stem or grow up from the roots. 2. a petal of a flower; as, a rose leaf. 3. put forth leaves. The trees leaf out in spring. 4. a thin sheet or piece; as, a leaf of a book, gold leaf. 5. a flat movable piece in the top of a table. *n., pl. leaves, v. 5.*

leaf less (lēf′lis), having no leaves. *adj. 9.*

leaf let (lēf′lit), 1. a small or young leaf. 2. a small flat or folded sheet of printed matter; as, leaflets containing the Sunday-school lessons, advertising leaflets. *n. 9.*

leaf y (lēf′i), having many leaves; covered with leaves. *adj., leafier, leafiest. 8.*

league[1] (lēg), 1. a union of persons, parties, or nations to help one another. 2. unite in a league; form a union. *n., v. 2.*

league[2] (lēg), a measure of distance, usually about 3 miles. *n.*

League of Nations, an organization intended to promote helpfulness and good feeling among nations and to maintain peace. It was formed in 1919.

Le ah (lē′ə), the older sister of Rachel, and the first wife of Jacob. Genesis 29:16. *n. 18.*

leak (lēk), 1. a hole or crack not meant to be there that lets something in or out; as, a leak in a paper bag which lets the sugar run out, a leak in the roof. 2. let something in or out which is meant to stay where it is. My boat leaks and lets water in. That pipe leaks gas. 3. go in or out through a hole or crack, or in ways suggesting a hole or crack. Spies leaked into the city. The gas leaked out. The news leaked out. *n., v. 6.*

leak age (lēk′ij), 1. leaking; entrance or escape by a leak. 2. that which leaks in or out. *n. 15.*

leak y (lēk′i), leaking; having a leak. *adj., leakier, leakiest. 14.*

leal (lēl), loyal. *adj.* [*Old or Scottish use*] *20.*

lean[1] (lēn), 1. bend; stand slanting, not upright. A small tree leans over in the wind. 2. rest sloping or slanting. Lean against me. 3. set or put in a leaning position. Lean the picture against the wall till I am ready for it. 4. depend; as, to lean on a friend's advice. 5. bend or turn a little; as, to lean toward mercy. *v., leaned* or *leant, leaning. 2.*

lean[2] (lēn), 1. not fat; thin. 2. meat having little fat. 3. producing little; as, a lean harvest. *adj., n.*

lean ness (lēn′nis), thinness; being lean. *n. 19.*

leant (lent), leaned. *pt. and pp. of* **lean**[1]. *19.*

lean-to (lēn′tü′), 1. a building attached to another, with its supports leaning on the adjoining wall or building. 2. having supports so arranged; as, a lean-to roof. *n., pl. lean-tos, adj.*

leap (lēp), 1. a jump or spring. 2. to jump. A frog leaps. 3. to jump over. Jack leaped the wall. *n., v., leaped* or *leapt, leaping. 2.*

leap frog (lēp′frog′), game in which one player leaps over another who is bending over. *n.*

Boys playing leapfrog

leapt (lept or lēpt), leaped. *pt. and pp. of* **leap.**

leap year, year having 366 days. The extra day is February 29. A year is a leap year if its number can be divided exactly by four, except years at the end of a century, which must be exactly divisible by 400. The years 1944 and 2000 are leap years; 1943 and 1900 are not.

Lear (lēr), a king in Shakespeare's play *King Lear,* who had two very ungrateful daughters. *n. 18.*

learn (lėrn). In school we learn to read. He learned that $\frac{1}{4}+\frac{1}{4}=\frac{1}{2}$. She is learning history and geography. Some children learn slowly. *v., learned* or *learnt, learning. 1.*

learn ed (lėr′nid), scholarly; showing or requiring knowledge. *adj.*

learn er (lėr′nər), 1. person who is learning. 2. beginner. *n. 20.*

learn ing (lėr′ning), 1. gaining knowledge or skill. 2. possession of knowledge gained by study; scholarship. *n.*

lease (lēs), 1. the right to use property for a certain length of time by paying rent for it. 2. a written statement saying for how long a certain property is rented and how much money shall be paid for it. 3. to rent. We have leased an apartment for one year. *n., v. 7.*

leash (lēsh), 1. a strap or line for holding an animal in check. The boy leads the dog on a leash. **Hold in leash** means control. 2. hold in with a leash; control. 3. among sportsmen, three. *n., v. 12.*

least (lēst). A dime is a little money; five cents is less; one cent is least. The least bit of dirt in a watch may make it stop. The least you can do is to thank him. *adj., n., adv. 1.*

leath er (leтн′ər), 1. a material made from the skin of animals by removing the hair and then tanning it. Shoes are made of leather. 2. made of leather; as, leather gloves. *n., adj. 2.*

leath er ette (leтн′ər et′), imitation leather. *n.*

leath ern (leтн′ərn), made of leather. *adj. 10.*

leath er y (leтн′ər i), like leather; tough. *adj.*

leave[1] (lēv), 1. go away. We leave tonight. 2. go away from. They left the room. He has left his home and friends and gone to sea. 3. stop living in, belonging to, or working at or for; as, to leave the country, to leave the Boy Scouts, to leave one's job. 4. go without taking; let stay behind; as, to leave a book on the table. 5. let stay (in a certain condition); as, to leave unsaid or undone. I was left alone as before. The story left him unmoved. 6. let alone. Then the potatoes must be left to boil for half an hour. 7. give (to family, friends, charity) when one dies. He left a large fortune to his two sons. 8. give or hand over (to someone else) to do. I left the cooking to my sister. 9. not attend to. I shall leave my homework till tomorrow. 10. **Leave off** means stop. He left off smoking. 11. **Leave out** means not say, do, or put in; as, to leave out a word when reading. *v., left, leaving. 1.*

leave[2] (lēv), 1. consent; permission. Have I your leave to go? 2. **Leave of absence** means permission to stay away (from the army, navy, one's work, or school). 3. length of time for which one has leave of absence. Our annual leave is thirty days. 4. **Take leave of** means say good-by to. *n.*

leave[3] (lēv), put forth leaves. Trees leave in the spring. *v., leaved, leaving.*

leav en (lev′ən), 1. any substance, such as yeast, that will cause fermentation and raise dough. 2. raise with a leaven; make (dough) light or lighter. 3. an influence which, spreading silently and strongly, changes conditions or opinions. 4. spread through and transform. *n., v. 7.*

leaves (lēvz), more than one leaf. *n. pl. 11.*

leave-tak ing (lēv′tāk′ing), act of taking leave; saying good-by. *n.*

leav ings (lēv′ingz), remnants; things left. *n. pl.*

Leb a non (leb′ə nən), 1. country in southwestern Syria, under the control of France. 2. a mountain range in Syria. *n. 7.*

lec ture (lek′chər), 1. speech; a planned talk on a chosen subject; such a talk written down or printed. 2. give a lecture. 3. a scolding. My mother gives me a lecture when I come home late. 4. scold. *n., v. 4.*

lec tur er (lek′chər ər), person who gives a lecture. *n. 10.*

led (led). See **lead**[1]. The policeman led the children across the street. That blind man is led by his dog. *pt. and pp. of lead*[1]. *1.*

ledge (lej), 1. narrow shelf; as, a window ledge. 2. a shelf or ridge of rock. *n. 5.*

ledg er (lej′ər), book of accounts in which a business keeps a record of all money transactions. *n. 12.*

lee[1] (lē), 1. side or part sheltered from the wind. The wind was so fierce that we ran to the lee of the house. 2. sheltered from the wind; as, the lee side of a ship. 3. A **lee shore** means a shore toward which the wind is blowing. *n., adj. 4.*

Lee[2] (lē), Robert E., a great Confederate general (1807-1870). *n.*

leech (lēch), 1. worm living in ponds and streams that sucks the blood of animals. Doctors used to use leeches to suck blood from sick people. 2. person who tries persistently to get what he can out of others. 3. doctor. *Old use. n. 8.*

Leeds (lēdz), city in northern England. *n.*

leek (lēk), a vegetable somewhat like an onion. See the picture just below. *n. 13.*

leer (lēr), 1. a sly, nasty look to the side; evil glance. 2. give a sly, evil glance. *n., v. 11.*

lees (lēz), dregs; sediment. *n. pl. 16.*

lee ward (lü′ərd), 1. on the side away from the wind. 2. the side away from the wind. 3. in the direction toward which the wind is blowing. *adv., adj., n. 13.*

Leek

Lee ward Is lands (lē′wərd ī′ləndz), northern part of the Lesser Antilles in the West Indies.

lee way (lē′wā′), 1. the sidewise movement of a ship to leeward, out of its course. 2. extra space at the side; time, money, etc., more than needed; margin of safety. If you have $10 more than you need on a trip, you are allowing yourself a leeway of $10. *n. 20.*

left¹ (left). A man has a right hand and a left hand. Your left side is toward the west when you face north. Take the left road. He sat at my left. *adj., n. 1.*

left² (left). See **leave**¹. He left his hat in the hall. *pt. and pp. of leave*¹.

left-hand (left′hand′), 1. on or to the left. 2. of, for, or with the left hand. *adj.*

left-hand ed (left′han′did), 1. using the left hand more easily and readily than the right. 2. done with the left hand. 3. made to be used with the left hand. 4. turning from right to left; as, a left-handed screw. 5. A **left-handed compliment** is either one so awkward as to be rather rude or one intentionally insincere. *Example:* "You must have made that dress yourself." *adj.*

leg (leg), 1. Dogs stand on their four legs. A man uses his two legs in walking and running. 2. anything shaped or used like a leg; any support that is much longer than it is wide; as, a table leg, a leg of a pair of compasses. *n. 1.*

leg a cy (leg′ə si), 1. money or other property left to a person by the will of someone who has died. 2. something that has come down from an ancestor. *n., pl. legacies. 8.*

le gal (lē′gəl), 1. of law; as, legal knowledge. 2. of lawyers. 3. lawful. *adj. 5.*

le gal i ty (lē gal′i ti), accordance with law; lawfulness. The legality of the act could not be disputed. *n., pl. legalities. 19.*

le gal ize (lē′gəl īz), make legal. *v. 17.*

le gal ly (lē′gəl i), 1. in a legal manner. 2. according to law. He is legally responsible for his wife's debts. *adv.*

leg ate (leg′it), ambassador; representative; messenger; especially, a representative of the Pope. *n. 10.*

leg a tee (leg′ə tē′), person to whom a legacy is left. *n. 19.*

le ga tion (li gā′shən), 1. the diplomatic representative of a country and his staff of assistants. A legation ranks next below an embassy. 2. official residence, offices, etc., of such a representative in a foreign country. 3. office, position, or dignity of a legate. *n. 18.*

leg end (lej′ənd), 1. a story coming down from the past, which many people have believed. The stories about King Arthur and his knights are legends. 2. such stories as a group. 3. what is written on a coin or medal or below a picture. *n. 5.*

leg en dar y (lej′ən dãr′i), of legend or legends; like a legend; not historical. Robin Hood is a legendary person. *adj. 9.*

leg er de main (lej′ər di mān′), 1. sleight of hand; conjuring tricks; jugglery. A common trick of legerdemain is to take rabbits from an apparently empty hat. 2. trickery. *n.*

leg gings (leg′ingz), extra outer coverings of cloth or leather for the legs, for use out of doors. *n. pl. 7.*

Child wearing leggings

leg horn (leg′hôrn), 1. a hat made of a fine, smooth plaited straw. 2. a rather small domestic fowl. *n. 13.*

leg i bil i ty (lej′i bil′i ti), legible condition or quality; clearness of print or writing. *n.*

leg i ble (lej′i bəl), 1. that can be read. 2. easy to read; plain and clear. Her handwriting is beautiful and legible. *adj. 14.*

leg i bly (lej′i bli), clearly. *adv.*

le gion (lē′jən), 1. a division in the ancient Roman army containing several thousand foot soldiers and several hundred horsemen. 2. a body of soldiers; army. 3. a great many; a very large number. *n. 4.*

le gion ar y (lē′jən ãr′i), 1. of or belonging to a legion. 2. member of a legion. *adj., n., pl. legionaries. 16.*

leg is late (lej′is lāt), make laws. Congress legislates for the United States. *v. 14.*

leg is la tion (lej′is lā′shən), 1. making laws. Congress has the power of legislation. 2. the laws made. *n. 7.*

leg is la tive (lej′is lā′tiv), 1. having to do with lawmaking; as, legislative reforms. 2. having the duty and power of making laws. Congress is a legislative body. 3. ordered by law; made to be as it is by law. *adj. 9.*

leg is la tor (lej′is lā′tər), a lawmaker; member of a legislative body. Senators and Representatives are legislators. *n. 9.*

leg is la ture (lej′is lā′chər), group of persons that has the duty and power of making laws for a State or country. Each State of the United States has a legislature. *n. 5.*

le git i ma cy (li jit′i mə si), being legitimate or lawful; being recognized as lawful or proper. *n. 20.*

le git i mate (li jit′i mit), 1. rightful; lawful; allowed. Sickness is a legitimate reason for a child's being absent from school. 2. A legitimate child is one born of parents who are married. *adj. 8.*

leg ume (leg′ūm), 1. a vegetable that is the seed of a plant having pods. Beans and peas are legumes. 2. a pod opening in two parts with seed inside. A peanut is really a legume, not a nut. *n. 12.*

le gu mi nous (li gū′mi nəs), 1. of legumes. 2. bearing legumes. 3. of or belonging to the same group of plants as beans and peas. *adj. 19.*

Leices ter (les′tər), a name of persons and places. *n. 11.*

Leip zig or **Leip sic** (līp′sik), a city in central Germany. *n. 14.*

lei sure (lē′zhər), 1. time free from required work in which a person may rest, amuse himself, and do the things he likes to do. A busy man hasn't much leisure to read. 2. free; not busy; as, leisure hours. *n., adj. 5.*

lei sure ly (lē′zhər li), without hurry; taking plenty of time. A person, a movement, a performance, or one's manner may be leisurely. He walked leisurely across the street. *adj., adv. 14.*

lem on (lem′ən), 1. sour, light-yellow fruit that grows in warm climates. The juice of lemons is much used for flavoring and for making lemonade. 2. the tree it grows on. 3. pale yellow. 4. flavored with lemon. *n., adj. 4.*

Lemons

lem on ade (lem′ən ād′), a drink made of lemon juice, sugar, and water. *n. 5.*

le mur (lē′mər), animal somewhat like a monkey but having a foxlike face and woolly fur, found mainly in Madagascar. *n.*

Lemur (about 3 ft. long, including the tail)

lend (lend), 1. let another have or use for a time. Will you lend me your bicycle for an hour? 2. make a loan or loans. 3. give; give (help, etc.) for a time. A becoming dress lends charm to a girl. *v., lent, lending. 3.*

lend er (len′dər), one who lends. *n. 12.*

length (length), 1. The length of your arm is how long it is. The length of this stick is 8 inches. The length of a room is the longest way it can be measured. The length of a speech is how long it lasts. The length of a race is the distance run. 2. In poetry, the length of a syllable or vowel is the force with which it is spoken, or the way it is pronounced. 3. long stretch or extent. 4. piece of cloth, etc., of a given length; as, a dress length of silk. 5. Some special meanings are:

at full length, with the body stretched out flat.

at length, 1. at last. 2. with all the details; in full.

go to any length (in doing something), do everything possible.

keep a person at arm's length, not let him become friendly.

n. 1.

length en (leng′thən), 1. make longer. 2. become or grow longer. *v. 6.*

length ways (length′wāz), lengthwise. *adv., adj.*

length wise (length′wīz), in the direction of the length. He cut the cloth lengthwise. *adv., adj. 10.*

length y (leng′thi), long; too long. *adj., lengthier, lengthiest. 19.*

le ni ence (lē′ni əns), leniency. *n.*

le ni en cy (lē′ni ən si), mildness; gentleness; mercy. *n. 16.*

le ni ent (lē′ni ənt), mild; gentle; merciful. *adj. 11.*

Len in (len′in), the founder of the Soviet government in Russia (1870-1924). *n.*

Len in grad (len′in grad), a city in northwestern Russia. It was formerly called St. Petersburg or Petrograd and was the capital of Russia. *n.*

len i ty (len′i ti), mildness; gentleness; mercifulness. *n. 15.*

lens (lenz), piece of glass, or something like glass, that will bring closer together or send wider apart the rays of light passing through it. The lens of the eye and the lens of a camera make pictures. The lenses of a telescope make things look larger and nearer. *n. 10.*

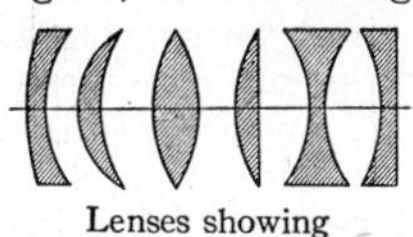
Lenses showing different shapes

lent[1] (lent). See **lend.** I lent you my pencils. He had lent me his eraser. *pt. and pp. of lend. 4.*

Lent[2] (lent), the forty weekdays before Easter, kept as a time for fasting and repenting of sins. *n.*

Lent en or **lent en** (len′tən), of Lent; during Lent; suitable for Lent. *adj.*

len til (len′təl), a vegetable much like a bean. *n. 16.*

Le o nar do da Vin ci (lā′ō när′dō dä vin′chi), an Italian painter, sculptor, architect, engineer, and scholar (1452-1519).

le o nine (lē′ə nīn), of a lion; like a lion. *adj. 19.*

leop ard (lep′ərd), 1. a fierce animal of Africa and Asia, having a dull-yellowish skin spotted with black. 2. The jaguar is sometimes called the American leopard. *n. 8.*

Leopard (length about 7 ft. to tip of tail)

lep er (lep′ər), person who has leprosy. *n. 9.*

lep ro sy (lep′rə si), a loathsome infectious disease that causes ulcers and white scaly scabs, and eats away the body. *n. 10.*

lep rous (lep′rəs), 1. having leprosy; as, a leprous person. 2. of or like leprosy; as, white leprous scales. *adj. 13.*

lese-maj es ty (lēz′maj′is ti), a crime or offense against the sovereign power in a state; treason. *n.*

less (les), 1. smaller; as, of less width, less importance. 2. not so much; not so much of; as, to have less rain, to put on less butter, to eat less meat. 3. smaller amount; as, could do no less, weigh less than before, refuse to take less than $5. 4. with (something) taken away; without; as, five less two, a coat less one sleeve. 5. not so; not so much; not so well; as, less bright, less important, less known, less talked of. *adj., adv., n., prep. 1.*

-less, suffix meaning:—
1. without; that has no; as in doubtless, homeless.
2. that does not; as in tireless.
3. that cannot be ——ed; as in countless.

les see (les ē′), person to whom a lease is granted. *n. 19.*

less en (les′ən), 1. grow less. 2. make less; decrease. *v. 5.*

less er (les′ər), 1. less; smaller. 2. the less important of two. *adj. 6.*

les son (les′ən), 1. something to be learned or taught; something that has been learned or taught. Children study many different lessons in school. 2. unit of teaching or learning; what is to be studied at one time. Tomorrow we take the tenth lesson. 3. a selection from the Bible, read as part of a church service. 4. to rebuke or lecture. *n., v. 1.*

lest (lest), 1. for fear that; that . . . not; in order that . . . not. Be careful lest you fall from that tree. 2. After words meaning fear, danger, etc., lest means that. I was afraid lest he should come too late to save us. *conj. 3.*

let[1] (let), 1. allow; permit. Let the dog have a bone. 2. allow to run out. Doctors used to let some of the blood of their fever patients. 3. rent; hire out. Mrs. Bacon lets rooms to students. 4. Let is used in giving suggestions and commands. "Let's go fishing" means "I suggest that we go fishing." Let every man do his duty. 5. suppose. Let the two lines be parallel. 6. Some special meanings are:
let be, not touch; not disturb.
let down, 1. lower. He let the box down from the roof. 2. slow up. 3. disappoint.
let in, admit; permit to enter.
let know, tell; inform.
let off, let go free.
let out, 1. let go out. 2. make larger. 3. rent.
v., let, letting. 1.

let[2] (let), 1. prevent. *Old use.* 2. prevention. *Old use.* **Without let or hindrance** means with nothing to prevent, hinder, or obstruct. *n., v., letted* or *let, letting.*

-let, suffix meaning:—little; as in booklet, streamlet.

le thal (lē′thəl), causing death; as, lethal weapons, a lethal dose of a drug. *adj.*

le thar gic (li thär′jik), 1. unnaturally drowsy; sluggish; dull. A hot humid day produces a lethargic condition. 2. producing lethargy. *adj. 15.*

leth ar gy (leth′ər ji), 1. drowsy dullness; lack of energy; sluggish inactivity. 2. an unnatural sleep. *n., pl. lethargies. 13.*

Le the (lē′thi), 1. a river in Hades. Drinking its water caused forgetfulness of the past. 2. oblivion; forgetfulness. *n. 14.*

let's (lets), let us. *6.*

let ter (let′ər), 1. a mark or sign that stands for any one of the sounds that make up words. There are 26 letters in our alphabet. 2. a block of type bearing a letter, used in printing. 3. mark with letters. 4. make letters (on). 5. **To the letter** means very exactly; just as one has been told. I carried out your orders to the letter. **Letter-perfect** means knowing one's part or lesson perfectly. 6. a written message. Put a stamp on that letter before you mail it. 7. **Letters** sometimes means literature. *n., v. 1.*

let ter head (let′ər hed′), 1. words printed at the top of a sheet of letter paper, usually a name and address. 2. a sheet of paper so printed. *n. 15.*

let ter ing (let′ər ing), letters drawn, painted, or stamped. *n.*

let tuce (let′is), a garden plant with large, crisp, green leaves that are used for salad. *n. 6.*

leu co cyte (lü′kō sīt), a white blood corpuscle; one of the tiny white cells of the blood that destroy disease germs. *n. 20.*

Le vant (li vant′), the region about the eastern Mediterranean; the coasts of Asia Minor, Syria, and Egypt. *n. 20.*

lev ee[1] (lev′i), 1. a bank built to keep a river from overflowing. There are levees along the lower Mississippi River. 2. landing place for ships. *n. 13.*

lev ee[2] (lev′i), reception. French kings used to hold levees in the morning while they were getting up and dressing. *n.*

lev el (lev′əl), 1. flat; even; having just the same height everywhere; as, a level floor. 2. something that is level. 3. an instrument for showing whether a surface is level. 4. height. The flood rose to a level of 60 feet. 5. make level or the same level. 6. raise and hold level for shooting; aim. 7. well-balanced; sensible. *Used in common talk. adj., n., v., leveled, leveling. 2.*

lev el er or **lev el ler** (lev′əl ər), one that levels. *n. 19.*

lev er (lev′ər), 1. a bar for raising or moving a weight at one end by pushing down at the other end. It must be supported at a point in between. 2. any bar working on an axis or support. *n. 9.*

LEVER
FULCRUM
Man lifting a stone with a lever

lev er age (lev′ər ij), 1. action of a lever. 2. advantage or power gained by using a lever. 3. increased power. *n. 16.*

Le vi (lē′vī), in the Bible, a son of Jacob, ancestor of the Levites. *n. 10.*

le vi a than (li vī′ə thən), 1. a huge sea animal. 2. a huge ship. 3. anything very great and powerful. *n. 13.*

Le vite (lē′vīt), member of the tribe of Levi, from which assistants to the Jewish priests were taken. *n. 10.*

lev i ty (lev′i ti), lightness of mind, character, or behavior; lack of proper seriousness or earnestness. Giggling in church shows levity. *n., pl. levities. 10.*

lev y (lev′i), 1. order to be paid. The government levies taxes for national expenses. 2. collect (men) for an army. Troops are levied in time of war. 3. men collected. 4. **Levy war on** means make war on. 5. seize by law for unpaid debts. One can levy on a person's property for unpaid rent. 6. act of levying. 7. money collected. *v., levied, levying, n., pl. levies. 6.*

lewd (lüd), not decent; lustful. *adj. 7.*

lewd ness (lüd′nis), being lewd. *n. 11.*

lex i cog ra pher (lek′si kog′rə fər), writer of a dictionary. *n. 20.*

lex i con (lek′si kən), dictionary, especially of Greek, Latin, or Hebrew. *n. 16.*

Lex ing ton (lek′sing tən), 1. a town in eastern Massachusetts where the first battle of the Revolutionary War was fought on April 19, 1775. 2. a city in northern Kentucky. *n. 13.*

Ley den (lī′dən), city in the Netherlands. *n. 16.*

li a bil i ty (lī′ə bil′i ti), 1. being liable or under obligation; as, liability to disease, liability for debt. 2. debt. 3. thing to one's disadvantage. John's poor writing is a liability in getting a new job. *n., pl. liabilities. 11.*

li a ble (lī′ə bəl), 1. likely; unpleasantly likely. Glass is liable to break. You are liable to slip on ice. 2. in danger of having, doing, etc. We are all liable to diseases. 3. responsible; under obligation; bound by law to pay. The Post Office Department is not liable for damage to a parcel sent by mail unless it is insured. *adj. 6.*

li ai son (lē ā zōn′), 1. connection between parts of an army to secure proper coöperation. 2. unlawful relationship between a man and a woman. *n. 15.*

li ar (lī′ər), person who tells lies; one who says what is not true. *n. 5.*

li ba tion (lī bā′shən), 1. pouring out wine, etc., as an offering to a god. 2. the wine offered in this way. *n. 12.*

li bel (lī′bəl), 1. a statement that is likely to harm the reputation of the person about whom it is made. 2. write or publish a libel. *n., v., libeled, libeling. 10.*

li bel ous or **li bel lous** (lī′bəl əs), 1. containing injurious statements about a person. 2. making injurious statements about a person on purpose. *adj.*

lib er al (lib′ər əl), 1. generous. A liberal giver gives freely. 2. plentiful; abundant. He put in a liberal supply of coal for the winter. 3. broad-minded; not narrow in one's ideas. 4. person favorable to progress and reforms. 5. The Liberal party of Great Britain is a political party that favors progress and reforms. 6. A **liberal education** develops the mind broadly. *adj., n. 4.*

lib er al ism (lib′ər əl izm), liberal views or opinions; belief in progress and reforms. *n. 18.*

lib er al i ty (lib′ər al′i ti), 1. generosity; generous act or behavior. 2. broad-mindedness. *n., pl. liberalities. 9.*

lib er ate (lib′ər āt), set free. Lincoln liberated the slaves. *v. 8.*

lib er a tion (lib′ər ā′shən), 1. setting free. 2. being set free. *n. 12.*

lib er a tor (lib′ər ā′tər), person who sets free; deliverer. *n. 16.*

Li be ri a (lī bēr′i ə), country on the western coast of Africa, colonized with freed American Negro slaves. *n. 17.*

lib er tine (lib′ər tēn), 1. person without moral restraints; man who does not respect women. 2. without moral restraints; unrestrained in regard to sex. *n., adj. 15.*

lib er ty (lib′ər ti), 1. freedom. 2. right or power to do as one pleases; power or opportunity to do something. 3. leave granted to a sailor to go ashore. 4. too great freedom; as, to take liberties with mother's sewing basket. 5. **At liberty** means (1) free. (2) permitted. You are at liberty to make any choice you please. (3) not busy. *n., pl. liberties. 2.*

li brar i an (lī brãr′i ən), person in charge of a library. *n. 12.*

li brar y (lī′brãr′i), 1. a collection of books. 2. room or building in which a collection of books is kept. *n., pl. libraries. 2.*

li bret to (li bret′ō), 1. the words of an opera or other long musical composition. 2. a book containing the words. *n., pl. librettos. 20.*

Lib y a (lib′i ə), the ancient Greek and Roman name for northern Africa, west of Egypt. *n. 12.*

lice (līs), more than one louse. *n. pl. 11.*

li cense or **li cence** (lī′səns), 1. being allowed to do something. 2. permission given by law to do something; as, a license to run an automobile. 3. the paper, card, plate, etc., that gives such permission. 4. permit by law. A doctor is licensed to practice medicine. 5. **Poetic license** is the freedom from rules that is permitted in poetry and other arts. 6. too much liberty of action; lack of proper control; abuse of freedom. *n., v. 4.*

li cen tious (lī sen′shəs), 1. disregarding commonly accepted rules or principles. 2. not restrained by law or morality. 3. not restrained in sex activities; lewd. *adj. 14.*

li chen (lī′kən), a dry-looking, flowerless plant that grows like a patch of skin on rocks, trees, and other surfaces. Lichens are gray, yellow, brown, black, or greenish in color. *n. 9.*

Lichens growing on a tree

lick (lik), 1. lap up with the tongue. 2. pass about or play over like a tongue. The flames were licking our house. 3. a stroke of the tongue over something. 4. small quantity. 5. a brief stroke of activity or effort. 6. a blow. Jim gave his horse a few gentle licks with his hand. 7. beat or thrash. *v., n. (Defs. 5, 6, and 7 are used in common talk.) 4.*

lic o rice (lik′ə ris), 1. the sweet-tasting, dried root of a plant. 2. black substance obtained from it, used in medicine and candy. *n.*

lic tor (lik′tər), one of the group of attendants on a magistrate in ancient Rome, who punished offenders at his orders. *n. 16.*

lid (lid), 1. movable cover; top; as, the

lid of a box, a stove lid. 2. the cover of skin that is moved in opening and shutting the eye; eyelid. *n. 4.*

lie[1] (lī), 1. something said that is not true; something that is not true said to deceive. 2. speak falsely; tell a lie. *n., v., lied, lying. 1.*

lie[2] (lī), 1. have one's body in a flat position along the ground or other surface; as, to lie on the grass, to lie in bed. 2. be in the grave. His body lies in Plymouth. 3. be kept or stay in a given state; as, to lie idle, to lie hidden, to lie unused. 4. rest (on a surface). The book was lying on the table. 5. be; be placed; as, land that lies high, a lake that lies to the south of us, a road that lies among trees, a ship lying at anchor. 6. exist; be found to be. The cure lies in education. 7. Some special meanings are:

lie back, get into a lying position.

lie down, get into a lying position.

lie off. If a ship lies off shore, it stays some way off.

lie of the land, the nature of the place; the position of hills, water, woods, etc.

lie over, be left waiting (till another time). That matter can just as well lie over till fall.

lie to. If a ship lies to, it comes almost to a stop, facing the wind.

take a thing lying down, yield to it; not to stand up before it.

v., lay, lain, lying, n.

lied (līd). See **lie**[1]. He lied about his tardiness. He says that he has never lied. *pt. and pp. of lie*[1].

lief (lēf), willingly. I would as lief go hungry as eat that nasty mess. *adv. 10.*

liege (lēj), the relation between a lord and his vassals in the Middle Ages. He was their liege lord, or liege, and had a right to their loyal service; they were his lieges, or liegemen, whom he protected. *n., adj. 7.*

Li ége (li āzh′), a city in eastern Belgium. *n. 18.*

liege man (lēj′mən), vassal; faithful follower. *n., pl. liegemen. 19.*

lien (lēn), in law, a claim on the property of another for payment of a debt. The garage owner has a lien upon Mr. Smith's automobile until he pays for having it painted. *n. 18.*

lieu (lü). **In lieu of** means in place of or instead of. *n. 10.*

Lieut., Lieutenant.

lieu ten an cy (lü ten′ən si), rank, commission, or authority of a lieutenant. *n., pl. lieutenancies.*

lieu ten ant (lü ten′ənt), 1. one who acts in the place of someone above him. 2. in the army, an officer next below a captain. 3. in the navy, an officer ranking much below a captain. In the navy the order is captain, commander, lieutenant commander, lieutenant, ensign. *n. 4.*

lieutenant general, army officer ranking next above a major general.

life (līf), 1. People, animals, and plants have life; rocks and metals do not. Life or being alive is shown by growing and producing. 2. Each person has his own life or existence. 3. a living being; person. Five lives were lost. 4. living beings. The desert island had almost no animal or vegetable life. 5. period of existence. The life of that government was very short. 6. way of living; as, a country life, a dull life. 7. account of a person's life; as, a life of Lincoln. 8. spirit; vigor. Put more life into your work. *n., pl. lives* (līvz). *1.*

life belt, life preserver made like a belt. *n.*

life blood (līf′blud′), 1. blood necessary to life. 2. source of strength and energy. *n. 18.*

life boat (līf′bōt′), a strong boat specially built for saving lives at sea or along a coast. *n. 16.*

life buoy, life preserver.

life guard (līf′gärd′), man employed on a bathing beach to help in case of accident or danger to bathers. *n.*

life insurance, 1. a system by which a person pays a small sum yearly to have a large sum paid to his family if he dies. 2. the sum paid by the insurance company at death. 3. the payments made to the insurance company.

life less (līf′lis), 1. not living. My doll, poor lifeless thing, was no comfort. 2. dead. The lifeless body floated ashore. 3. dull. It was a lifeless party until Marion came. *adj. 9.*

life like (līf′līk′), like life; looking as if alive; like the real thing. *adj. 14.*

life long (līf′lông′), lasting all one's life. *adj. 11.*

life preserver, a wide belt, usually made of cloth and cork, to keep a person afloat in the water; something to keep a person afloat until rescued.

Boy wearing a life preserver

life sav ing (līf′sāv′ing), 1. saving people's lives; keeping people from drowning. 2. designed or used to save people's lives. *adj., n.*

life size, the same size as the living thing. The picture of a bumblebee on page 100 is about life size.

life time (līf′tīm′), the time over which a life lasts. Grandfather has seen many changes during his lifetime. *n. 7.*

life work (līf′wėrk′), work that takes or lasts a whole lifetime; main work in life. *n.*

lift (lift), 1. raise; raise up higher; raise into the air; take up; pick up. Mother lifts the baby from the bed. 2. go up; be raised. This window will not lift. 3. go. The darkness lifts. 4. act of lifting. 5. the distance through which a thing is lifted. 6. helping hand. Give me a lift with this job. 7. free ride. 8. elevator. *In British use.* 9. steal. *Used in common talk. v., n. 1.*

lift er (lif′tər), 1. one that lifts. 2. thing with which to lift. *n. 15.*

lig a ment (lig′ə mənt), a band of strong tissue which connects bones or holds parts of the body in place. *n. 14.*

lig a ture (lig′ə chər), 1. anything used to bind or tie up. 2. a band, bandage, or cord, especially one used to tie up a bleeding artery. *n. 19.*

light[1] (līt), 1. that by which we see. The sun gives light to the earth. 2. thing that gives light. We saw the lights of the city. Bring a light quickly. 3. bright; clear. It was light as day. 4. brightness; clearness. 5. daytime. The workman gets up before light. 6. knowledge; information. We need more light on this subject. 7. open view. The reformer brought to light graft in the city government. 8. aspect. Look at the matter in the right light. 9. means of letting in light; window or part of a window. 10. model; example; famous person. George Washington is one of the lights of history. 11. bright part; as, light and shade in a painting. 12. pale in color; approaching white; as, light hair, light blue. 13. give light to; fill with light. The room is lighted by six windows. 14. set fire to; as, to light the fire, to light the candles. 15. take fire. 16. make bright or clear; as, a face lighted by a smile. 17. become light. The sky lights up at sunset. *n., adj., v., lighted* or *lit, lighting. 1.*

light[2] (līt), 1. easy to carry; not heavy; as, a light load. 2. not looking heavy; graceful; delicate; as, a light bridge, light carving. 3. of little weight for its size. Feathers are light. 4. of less than usual weight; as, light clothing. 5. not hard to bear or do; as, light punishment, a light task. 6. moving easily; as, a light step. 7. lightly armed or equipped. 8. less than usual in amount, force, etc.; as, a light rain, a light sleep, a light meal, a light wine. 9. not important. **Make light of** (a thing) means treat it as of little importance. 10. happy; gay. 11. cheerfully careless. 12. not serious enough; as, a light mind, light of purpose. 13. sandy; as, light soil. 14. **Light in the head** means (1) dizzy. (2) silly; foolish. *adj.*

light[3] (līt), 1. come down to the ground; alight. 2. come down from flight. A bird lighted on the branch. 3. come by chance. His eye lighted upon a sentence. 4. fall suddenly. The blow lit on his head. *v., lighted* or *lit, lighting.*

light en[1] (līt′ən), 1. brighten; become brighter. The sky lightens before the dawn. 2. flash with lightning. It thundered and lightened outside. *v. 4.*

light en[2] (līt′ən), 1. reduce the load of; make or become lighter. 2. make or become more cheerful. *v.*

light er[1] (līt′ər), thing or person that lights; as, a cigar lighter, a lamplighter. *n.*

light er[2] (līt′ər), 1. flat-bottomed barge used for loading and unloading ships. 2. carry (goods) in such a barge. *n., v.*

light-foot ed (līt′fu̇t′id), stepping lightly. *adj.*

light-head ed (līt′hed′id), 1. empty-headed; thoughtless. 2. dizzy; giddy; out of one's head; as, to be light-headed from fever. *adj.*

light-heart ed (līt′här′tid), carefree; cheerful; gay. *adj.*

light house (līt′hous′), tower or framework built to hold a bright light which shines over the sea to warn and guide ships. *n. 6.*

Lighthouse

light-mind ed (līt′mīn′did), empty-headed; thoughtless; frivolous. *adj.*

light ness[1] (līt′nis), 1. brightness; clearness. 2. paleness; whitishness. 3. the amount of light. The lightness of the sky showed that the rain was really over. *n. 13.*

light ness[2] (līt′nis), 1. being light; not being heavy. The lightness of this load is a relief after the heavy one I was carrying. 2. being gay or cheerful; as, lightness of spirits. 3. lack of proper seriousness. Such lightness of conduct is not to be permitted in church. *n.*

light ning (līt′ning), a flash of electricity in the sky. The sound that it makes is thunder. *n. 3.*

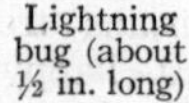
Lightning bug (about ½ in. long)

lightning bug, firefly.

lightning rod, a metal rod fixed on a building or ship to conduct lightning into the earth or water.

light ship (līt′ship′), ship with a bright light anchored at a dangerous place to warn ships away. *n. 17.*

Lightship

light some (līt′səm), 1. bright; light; as, a lightsome face. 2. nimble; as, lightsome feet. 3. gay; as, a lightsome heart. *adj. 18.*

lig nite (lig′nīt), a dark-brown kind of coal, often having a woody texture. *n. 15.*

lik a ble (līk′ə bəl), pleasing; popular. *adj.*

like[1] (līk), 1. Mary is like her sister. She can sing like a bird. **Something like** $100 means about $100. **Nothing like as good** means not nearly so good. We shall not see his like again. John's uncle promised him $10 if he could earn a like sum. 2. such as one would expect of. Isn't that just like a boy! 3. in the right condition for. He feels like working. 4. **And the like** means (1) and so forth. He studied painting, music, arithmetic, and the like. (2) and other like things. We went to the zoo and saw elephants, tigers, lions, bears, and the like. 5. likely. The king is sick and like to die. *Used in common talk. prep., adj., adv., n. 1.*

like[2] (līk). Boys like to play. Baby likes milk. Mother knows all my likes and dislikes. *v., n.*

-like, suffix meaning:—
1. like; as in wolflike.
2. like that of; as in childlike.
3. suited to; proper for; as in businesslike.

like li hood (līk′li hu̇d), probability. Is there any great likelihood of rain this afternoon? *n. 10.*

like ly (līk′li), 1. probable. One likely result of this heavy rain is the rising of the river. 2. probably. I shall very likely be at home all day. 3. to be expected. It is likely to be hot in August. 4. promising; suitable. Is this a likely place to fish? *adj., likelier, likeliest, adv. 3.*

lik en (līk′ən), compare; represent as like. *v. 7.*

like ness (līk′nis), 1. resembling; being like; as, a boy's likeness to his father. 2. something that is like; picture; as, to have one's likeness painted. 3. appearance; shape. His fairy godmother came to him in the likeness of a bird. *n. 5.*

like wise (līk′wīz′), 1. the same. See what I do. Now you do likewise. 2. also; moreover; too. Mary must go home now, and Nell likewise. *adv. 4.*

lik ing (līk′ing), preference; kindly feeling; fondness; as, a liking for apples, a liking for children. *n.*

li lac (lī′lək), 1. a shrub with clusters of fragrant, pale pinkish-purple or white blossoms. 2. pale pinkish-purple. She wore a lilac gown. *n., adj. 10.*

Lilac

Lille (lēl), city in northern France. *n. 13.*

lilt (lilt), 1. sing or play (a tune) in a light, tripping manner. 2. a lively song or tune with a swing. 3. a lively, springing movement. *v., n. 16.*

lil y (lil′i), 1. a plant that grows from a bulb. Its flowers are usually large, bell-shaped, and beautiful, and are often divided into six parts as shown in the picture. 2. like a white lily; pure and lovely. *n., pl. lilies, adj. 3.*

Tiger lily

lily of the valley, a plant having tiny, sweet-smelling, bell-shaped white flowers arranged up and down a single flower stem. *pl. lilies of the valley.*

Li ma (lē′mä), the capital of Peru. *n. 19.*

limb (lim), 1. Legs, arms, and wings are limbs. 2. large branch; as, the limb of a tree. *n. 2.*

lim ber (lim′bər), 1. bending easily; flexible. Willow is a limber wood. Mary has limber fingers. 2. make or become limber. Tom is stiff when he begins to skate, but limbers up quickly. *adj., v. 14.*

lim bo (lim′bō), 1. a region on the border of hell for unbaptized infants and righteous people who died before the coming of Christ. 2. place for persons and things forgotten or cast aside or out of date. The belief that the earth is flat belongs to the limbo of outworn ideas. 3. prison; jail; confinement. *n., pl. limbos. 15.*

Lim burg er (lim′bėr gər), a soft cheese having a strong smell. *n.*

lime[1] (līm), 1. a white substance obtained by burning limestone, shells, bone, etc. Lime is used in making mortar and on fields to improve the soil. 2. put lime on. He drained the land and limed it. *n., v. 4.*

lime[2] (līm), 1. juicy fruit much like a lemon. A lime is smaller, greener, and sourer than a lemon; its juice is used for flavoring and in medicine. 2. the tree it grows on. *n.*

lime[3] (līm), the linden tree, often used for shade and ornament. *n.*

lime light (līm′līt′), 1. strong light thrown upon the stage of a theater to light up certain persons or objects. 2. the glare of public observation. Some people are never happy unless they are in the limelight showing off. *n.*

lim er ick (lim′ər ik), a nonsense verse of five lines. *Example:*

"There was a young lady from Lynn
Who was so exceedingly thin
That when she essayed
To drink lemonade
She slid down the straw and fell in."

n. 20.

lime stone (līm′stōn′), a rock made mostly of calcium carbonate, used for building and for making lime. Marble is a kind of limestone. *n. 7.*

lime wa ter (līm′wô′tər), a solution of lime and water. *n. 20.*

lim it (lim′it), 1. the farthest edge or boundary; where something ends or must end. Keep within the limits of the school grounds. 2. set a limit to; restrict. We must limit the expense to $10. Her food was limited to bread and water. *n., v. 2.*

lim i ta tion (lim′i tā′shən), 1. limiting; being limited. 2. that which limits; boundary; limiting rule or circumstance. Mary's weak ankle was a limitation on her walks. *n. 8.*

lim it ed (lim′i tid), kept within limits. A limited train is limited in the number of stops, the class of passengers, the time taken, etc. *adj.*

lim it less (lim′it lis), without limits; boundless. *adj. 11.*

limn (lim), 1. paint (a picture). 2. portray in words. *v. 15.*

lim ou sine (lim′ů zēn′), a closed automobile, seating from three to five passengers inside, with a driver's seat outside covered by the same roof. *n. 18.*

limp[1] (limp), 1. a lame step or walk. 2. to walk with a limp. *n., v. 5.*

limp[2] (limp), lacking stiffness. This starched collar soon gets limp in hot weather. I feel as limp as a rag. *adj.*

lim pet (lim′pit), a small shellfish that sticks to rocks. *n. 19.*

lim pid (lim′pid), clear; transparent; as, a spring of limpid water, limpid eyes. *adj. 14.*

Lin coln (ling′kən), 1. Abraham Lincoln (1809-1865) was president of the United States during the Civil War. 2. the capital of Nebraska. *n. 3.*

lin den (lin′dən), a shade tree with heart-shaped leaves and clusters of small, sweet-smelling, greenish-yellow flowers. *n. 7.*

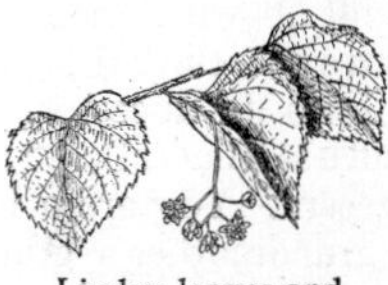

Linden leaves and flowers

line[1] (līn), 1. piece of rope, cord, or wire; as, a clothesline, a fish line, a telegraph line. Reins are sometimes called lines. 2. a cord for measuring, making level, etc. 3. a long narrow mark. Draw two lines here. 4. the use of such lines in drawing; as, a picture in line, clearness of line in an artist's work. 5. mark with lines. 6. cover with lines. 7. anything that is like a long narrow mark; as, the lines in your face. 8. an edge or boundary. 9. straight line. The lower edges of the two pictures are about on a line. 10. the equator. 11. a row of persons or things; as, a line of chairs. 12. arrange in line. Cars were lined up along the road for a mile. 13. a row of words on a page or in a newspaper column. 14. a single verse of poetry. 15. a connected set or series of persons or things; as, to trace back one's family line. 16. a double row (front and rear rank) of soldiers. 17. a certain way of doing. I shall proceed on these lines till further notice. 18. a course, track, or direction; as, the line of march of an army, a railroad line. 19. a branch of business; a kind of activity; as, the dry-goods line. That is not in my line. 20. a kind or branch of goods. He carries the best line of shoes in town.

21. $\frac{1}{12}$ of an inch. 22. Some special meanings are:

actor's lines, the words he speaks.

all along the line, at every point.

in line with, in agreement with.

lines, one's fate; one's lot in life.

line up, form a line; form into a line.

read between the lines, get from what one is reading more than the words themselves say.

the lines, the rows of trenches or other defenses used in war.

n., v. 1.

line[2] (līn), 1. put a layer of paper, cloth, padding, etc., inside of (a dress, hat, box, bag, etc.). 2. serve the purpose of lining. This piece of silk would line your coat very nicely. 3. **Line one's purse or pocket** means fill it with money, often dishonestly. *v.*

lin e age (lin′i ij), 1. descent in a direct line from an ancestor. 2. family; race. *n. 11.*

lin e al (lin′i əl), 1. in the direct line of descent. You are a lineal descendant of your grandmother's grandfather. 2. of or like a line. *adj. 12.*

lin e a ment (lin′i ə mənt), part or feature; part or feature of a face with attention to its outline. *n. 10.*

lin e ar (lin′i ər), 1. of a line or lines; in a line or lines; as, linear design, a linear series. 2. of length; as, linear measure. 3. like a line; long and narrow. A pine tree has linear leaves. *adj. 18.*

line man (līn′mən), 1. man who sets up or repairs telegraph and telephone wires. 2. man who inspects railroad tracks. 3. man who carries the line in surveying. *n., pl. linemen. 20.*

lin en (lin′in), 1. cloth or thread made from flax. 2. articles made of linen. Tablecloths, napkins, sheets, towels, shirts, and collars may be called linen even when they are made of some substitute. 3. made of linen. *n., adj. 2.*

lin er (līn′ər), 1. ship or airplane belonging to a transportation system. 2. person or thing that makes lines. *n. 15.*

lin ger (ling′gər), stay on; go slowly, as if unwilling to leave. Daylight lingers long in the summertime. *v. 4.*

lin ge rie (lan′zhə rē), fine underclothes for women. *n. 12.*

lin go (ling′gō), 1. language. 2. any speech regarded as outlandish or queer. Writers about baseball use a strange lingo. *n., pl. lingoes.* [*Used humorously or in contempt*]

lin guist (ling′gwist), one skilled in a number of languages besides his own. *n. 17.*

lin i ment (lin′i mənt), a healing liquid for rubbing on the skin. Liniment is used to relieve lameness, sprains, and bruises. *n. 13.*

lin ing (līn′ing), inside layer; as, the lining of a coat, the lining of a stove. *n. 5.*

link (lingk), 1. one ring or loop of a chain. 2. anything that joins as a link joins. 3. a fact or thought that connects others; as, a link in a chain of evidence. 4. join as a link does; unite or connect. *n., v. 3.*

links (lingks), golf course. *n. pl.*

Linnet (about 6 in. long)

lin net (lin′it), a small songbird of Europe, Asia, and Africa. *n. 10.*

li no le um (li nō′li əm), a floor covering made by putting a hard surface of ground cork mixed with linseed oil on a canvas back. *n. 10.*

lin seed (lin′sēd′), the seed of flax. *n. 8.*

linseed oil, the oil obtained by pressing linseed. It is used in making paints, printing inks, and linoleum.

lin sey (lin′zi), linsey-woolsey. *n. 19.*

lin sey-wool sey (lin′zi wu̇l′zi), strong coarse fabric made of linen and wool or of cotton and wool. *n.*

lint (lint), 1. the soft down or fleecy material obtained by scraping linen. Lint was formerly much used for putting on wounds. 2. tiny bits of thread. *n. 12.*

LINTEL
SILL

lin tel (lin′təl), a horizontal beam or stone above a door or window. *n. 13.*

li on (lī′ən), 1. a large, strong animal of Africa and southern Asia that has a dull-yellowish skin. 2. person who is very brave and strong. 3. famous man. *n. 1.*

li on ess (lī′ən is), female lion. *n. 12.*

Lion and lioness (about 3 ft. high at the shoulder)

lip (lip), 1. either one of the two fleshy, movable edges of the mouth. 2. the folding or bent-out edge of any opening; as, the lip of a pitcher. 3. not heartfelt or deep, but just on the surface. *n., adj. 1.*

liq ue fac tion (lik′wi fak′shən), 1. process of changing into a liquid. 2. liquefied condition. *n. 19.*

liq ue fy (lik′wi fī), make liquid; become liquid. Liquefied air is extremely cold. *v., liquefied, liquefying. 20.*

li queur (li kėr′), a strong, sweet, highly flavored alcoholic liquor. *n.*

liq uid (lik′wid), 1. a substance that is not a solid or a gas; a substance that flows freely like water. 2. in the form of a liquid; melted; as, liquid soap, butter heated until it is liquid. 3. clear and bright like water. 4. clear and smooth-flowing in sound; as, the liquid notes of a bird. 5. the sound of *l* or *r*. 6. easily turned into cash. United States bonds are a liquid investment. *n., adj. 3.*

liq ui date (lik′wi dāt), 1. pay (a debt). 2. settle the accounts of (a business); clear up the affairs of (a bankrupt). 3. get rid of. The French Revolution liquidated the nobility. *v.*

liq ui da tion (lik′wi dā′shən), 1. a liquidating. 2. a being liquidated. *n. 18.*

liq uor (lik′ər), 1. a drink, such as brandy or whiskey, that can make a person drunk. 2. anything liquid. *n. 4.*

li ra (lēr′ə), the unit of money in Italy. One lira equals 5¼ cents. It used to equal 19.3 cents. *n., pl. liras, lire* (lēr′ā). *19.*

Lis bon (liz′bən), capital of Portugal. *n. 10.*

lisle (līl), 1. a fine, hard-twisted cotton or linen thread. 2. made of lisle; as, lisle stockings. *n., adj. 14.*

lisp (lisp), 1. say *th* instead of *s* or *z* in speaking. She lisped and said, "Thing a thong" for "Sing a song." 2. speak imperfectly. 3. saying a *th* sound for *s* and *z*. *v., n. 6.*

lis some or **lis som** (lis′əm), lithe; supple; bending easily. *adj.*

list[1] (list), 1. series of names, numbers, words, or phrases. 2. make a list of. I shall list my errands on a card. *n., v. 1.*

list[2] (list), the edge of cloth, where the material is a little different; such edges torn off and used as material. *n.*

list[3] (list), 1. tipping a ship to one side; a tilt. 2. of ships, to tip to one side; to tilt. *n., v.*

list[4] (list), please. The enemy plundered where they listed. *v.* [*Old use*]

list[5] (list), listen; listen to. *v.* [*Used in poetry*]

lis ten (lis′ən), 1. try to hear; attend with the ears so as to hear. The mother listens for her baby's cry. I like to listen to music. 2. **Listen in** means (1) listen to others talking on a telephone. (2) listen to the radio. *v. 1.*

lis ten er (lis′nər), person listening. *n. 9.*

list less (list′lis), seeming too tired to care about anything; not interested in things; not caring to be active. *adj. 10.*

list less ness (list′lis nis), indifference; lack of interest. *n. 16.*

lists (lists), field where knights fought in tournaments. *n. pl.*

lit (lit), lighted. *pt. and pp. of* **light**[1] *and* **light**[3]. *6.*

lit a ny (lit′ə ni), 1. an arranged prayer consisting of a series of supplications said by the minister and responses said by the people. 2. any similar series. *n., pl. litanies. 14.*

li ter (lē′tər), the common measure of capacity in France, Germany, and other countries which use the metric system. One liter equals 1.0567 quarts liquid measure, or .908 quart dry measure. *n. 14.*

lit er a cy (lit′ər ə si), ability to read and write. *n. 19.*

lit er al (lit′ər əl), 1. following the exact words of the original; as, a literal translation. 2. taking words in their usual meaning, without exaggeration or imagination; matter-of-fact; as, the literal meaning of a phrase, a literal type of mind. 3. of the letters of the alphabet; expressed by letters. *adj. 7.*

lit er al ly (lit′ər əl i), word for word; without exaggeration; without imagination. *adv.*

lit er ar y (lit′ər ãr′i), 1. having to do with literature. 2. knowing much about literature. 3. engaged in literature as a profession. *adj. 5.*

lit er ate (lit′ər it), 1. able to read and write. 2. person who can read and write. 3. educated; acquainted with literature. *adj., n.*

lit er a ture (lit′ər ə chər), 1. writings of a period or of a country, especially those kept alive by their beauty of style or thought. Shakespeare is the greatest name in English literature. 2. all the books on a subject; as, the literature of stamp collecting. 3. writing books as a profession. 4. the study of literature. I shall take literature and mathematics this spring. *n. 4.*

lithe (līᴛʜ), bending easily; supple. *adj. 10.*

lith o graph (lith′ə graf), 1. picture, print, etc., made from a flat, specially prepared, stone or metal plate. 2. make from such a plate. *n., v.*

Lith u a ni a (lith′ü ā′ni ə), a small country in northern Europe, on the Baltic Sea. *n.*

lit i gant (lit′i gənt), person engaged in a lawsuit. *n. 19.*

lit i ga tion (lit′i gā′shən), 1. going to law. 2. carrying on a lawsuit. *n. 14.*

lit mus (lit′məs), a blue coloring matter. **Litmus paper** will turn red if put into acid. *n., adj. 17.*

li tre (lē′tər), liter. *n.*

lit ter (lit′ər), 1. little bits left about in disorder; things scattered about. Children must pick up their own litter. 2. scatter things about; leave odds and ends lying around; make untidy. You have littered the room with your papers. 3. the young animals produced at one time; as, a litter of puppies. 4. give birth to (young animals). 5. straw, hay, etc., used as bedding for animals. 6. make a bed for (an animal) with straw. 7. a stretcher for carrying a sick or wounded person. 8. a framework to be carried on men's shoulders, or by beasts of burden, with a couch usually enclosed by curtains. *n., v. 5.*

Litter (def. 8)

lit tle (lit′əl), 1. A grain of sand or the head of a pin is little. 2. Wait a little while, and I'll go a little way with you. 3. A very sick child has little strength and eats little food. 4. Mr. Skinflint has a mean little soul. 5. George had a big box of candy but gave his sister only a little. 6. Rest a little. After a little you will feel better. 7. They live in a little known town called Dracut. 8. A coward is little liked. 9. **Not a little** means a great deal; much. 10. **Make little of** means treat as of little importance. *adj., less* or *lesser* or *littler, least* or *littlest, adv., less, least, n. 1.*

lit tle ness (lit′əl nis), smallness; meanness. *n. 17.*

Little Rock, the capital of Arkansas.

lit ur gy (lit′ər ji), a form of public worship. The Book of Common Prayer is called the liturgy of the Episcopal Church. *n., pl. liturgies. 15.*

liv a ble (liv′ə bəl), 1. fit to live in; as, a livable house. 2. easy to live with; as, a livable person. 3. worth living. *adj.*

live[1] (liv), 1. have life. 2. remain alive. 3. last; endure. 4. keep up life. Most men live by working. 5. feed. Lions live upon other animals. 6. pass life; as, to live well, to live in peace. 7. dwell. Who lives in this house? 8. keep up (life); as, to live a life of ease. 9. carry out in life; as, to live one's ideals. 10. **Live down** means live so well that (some fault or sin of the past) is overlooked or forgotten. *v. 1.*

live[2] (līv), 1. having life; as, a live dog. 2. burning or glowing; as, live coals. 3. loaded; as, a live cartridge. 4. carrying an electric current; as, a live wire. 5. full of energy or activity; up-to-date; as, a live person, a live question. *adj.*

live li hood (līv′li hůd), means of living. John earned his livelihood by working for a farmer. *n. 8.*

live li ness (līv′li nis), vigor; activity; vividness; gaiety. *n.*

live long (liv′lông′), the whole length of. *adj. 9.*

live ly (līv′li), 1. full of life and spirit; active. 2. exciting. 3. full of cheer; bright. 4. in a lively manner. *adj., livelier, liveliest, adv. 3.*

liv en (līv′ən), 1. put life into; cheer up. 2. become more lively; brighten. *v.*

liv er[1] (liv′ər), the large, reddish-brown organ in people and animals that makes bile and aids in the absorption of food. Calf's liver is used as a food. *n. 4.*

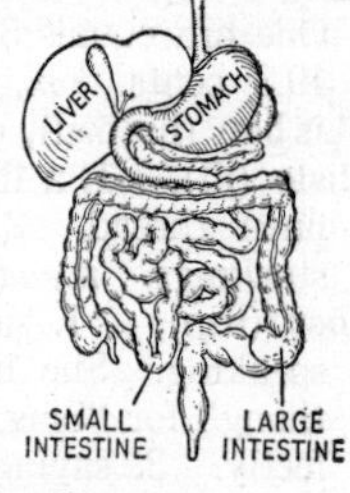

liv er[2] (liv′ər), person who lives. *n.*

liv er ied (liv′ər id), clothed in livery. *adj.*

Liv er pool (liv′ər pül), seaport city in western England. It is the English city next in importance to London. *n. 11.*

liv er wort (liv′ər wėrt′), 1. a plant somewhat like moss. 2. a delicate flower growing wild in the woods in spring. *n. 19.*

liv er y (liv′ər i), 1. any special uniform provided for the servants of a household, or adopted by any other group or profession. 2. the feeding, stabling, and care of horses for pay; the hiring out of horses and carriages. 3. stable where horses are cared for or hired out for pay. *n., pl. liveries. 5.*

lives (līvz), more than one life. *n. pl.*

live stock (līv′stok′), farm animals. Cows, horses, sheep, and pigs are livestock. *n. 15.*

liv id (liv′id), 1. having a dull-bluish or leaden color; as, the livid face of a dead man. 2. discolored by a bruise; as, the livid marks of blows on his arm. *adj. 14.*

liv ing (liv′ing), 1. being alive. The sick man is tired of living. 2. a means of keeping alive; livelihood. Mr. Meyer earned his living as a grocer. 3. manner of life. The preacher urged the importance of right living. 4. vigorous; strong; active; as, a living faith. 5. in actual existence; still in use; alive; as, living languages. 6. true to life; vivid; as, a picture which is the living image of a person. 7. of life; for living in; as, living conditions, a living room. 8. sufficient to live on; as, a living wage. 9. a position in the church with the income attached. *n., adj.*

Liv ing stone (liv′ing stən), David, a noted Scottish missionary and explorer in Africa (1813-1873). *n. 19.*

Liv y (liv′i), a Roman historian (59 B.C.-17 A.D.). *n. 15.*

liz ard (liz′ərd), a small animal somewhat like a snake, but having four legs. *n. 9.*

European green lizard (about 11 in. long)

lla ma (lä′mə), a South American animal somewhat like a camel, but smaller and without a hump. *n., pl. llamas* or *llama. 15.*

lla no (lä′nō), a large treeless plain. *n., pl. llanos. 19.*

lo (lō), look! see! behold! *interj. 4.*

load (lōd), 1. what one is carrying. The cart has a load of hay. The nurse bears a load of anxiety. 2. put in or put on whatever is to be carried; as, to load a ship. 3. one charge of powder and shot for a gun. 4. put a charge in (a gun). *n., v. 1.*

Llama (about 3 ft. high at the shoulder)

load stone (lōd′stōn′), 1. stone that attracts iron as a magnet does. 2. something that attracts. Gold was the loadstone that drew men to Alaska. *n.*

loaf[1] (lōf), 1. bread baked as one piece. A loaf comes apart easily from the loaves it is baked with. 2. A loaf of cake is a rather large cake, often baked in the shape of a loaf of bread. 3. food shaped like a loaf of bread. Veal loaf is veal chopped and mixed with egg and then baked. *n., pl. loaves* (lōvz). *4.*

loaf[2] (lōf), spend time idly; do nothing. Now that vacation has come, I shall loaf for a few days. *v.*

loaf er (lōf′ər), person who loafs; lazy idler. *n.*

loam (lōm), rich, fertile earth such as may be obtained in the woods; earth in which decaying leaves, etc., are mixed with clay and sand. *n. 11.*

loan (lōn), 1. a lending. 2. anything that is lent, especially money. 3. make a loan; lend. *n., v. 7.*

loath (lōth), unwilling. The little girl was loath to leave her mother. *adj. 8.* Also spelled **loth.**

loathe (lōᴛʜ), feel disgust for; abhor; hate. We loathe rotten food or a nasty smell. *v. 6.*

loath ing (lōᴛʜ′ing), strong dislike and disgust; intense aversion. *n.*

loath some (lōᴛʜ′səm), disgusting; making one feel sick. A dead cat's decaying body is loathsome. *adj. 7.*

loaves (lōvz), more than one loaf. *n. pl. 11.*

lob by (lob′i), 1. entrance hall; passageway; as, the lobby of a theater, the lobby of a hotel. 2. person or persons that try to influence members of a legislative body. 3. try to influence the members of a legislative body. *n., pl. lobbies, v., lobbied, lobbying. 8.*

lobe (lōb), a rounded projecting part. The lobe of the ear is the lower rounded end. *n. 11.*

lo be li a (lō bē′li ə), plant with blue, red, yellow, or white flowers. *n.*

lob lol ly (lob′lol′i), 1. pine tree of the southern United States that has thick bark and long needles. 2. its coarse, inferior wood. 3. thick mud; swamp. *n., pl. loblollies.*

Lobster (about 1 ft. long, including claws)

lob ster (lob′stər), a sea animal about a foot long with two big claws in front and eight legs. Lobsters are used for food. Their shells turn a light bright red when boiled. *n. 10.*

lo cal (lō′kəl), 1. of place; having to do with a certain place or places; as, the local doctor, local self-government, local news.

2. of just one part of the body; as, a local pain, local disease, local application of a remedy. 3. making all, or almost all, stops; as, a local train. *adj. 3.*

lo cal i ty (lō kal′i ti), place; region; one place and the places near it. *n., pl. localities. 7.*

lo cal ize (lō′kəl īz), make local; fix in, assign, or limit to a particular place or locality. The infection seemed to be localized in the foot. *v. 11.*

lo cal ly (lō′kəl i), in a local manner; with regard to place; in one place; in a number of places, but not widely. Outbreaks of the disease occurred locally. *adv.*

lo cate (lō′kāt), 1. establish in a place. He located his new store on Main Street. 2. establish oneself in a place. 3. find out the exact position of. The general tried to locate the enemy's camp. 4. state or show the position of. Can you locate Paris and Berlin on the map? 5. **Be located** means lie or be situated. Albany is located on the Hudson. *v. 3.*

lo ca tion (lō kā′shən), 1. a locating. 2. a being located. 3. position or place. 4. lot; plot of ground marked out by boundaries. *n. 4.*

loch (lok), 1. lake; as, Loch Lomond. 2. an arm of the sea partly shut in by land. *n.* [*Scottish*] *16.*

Loch in var (lok′in vär′), the hero in Scott's poem, who boldly carries off his sweetheart as she is about to be married to another man. *n. 18.*

lock[1] (lok), 1. a means of fastening (doors, boxes, etc.), usually needing a key of special shape to open it. 2. fasten with a lock. 3. shut (something in or out or up). We lock up jewels in a safe. 4. join, fit, jam, or link together. They lock arms. Two cars locked together in passing.

Locks in a canal

5. the part of a canal or dock in which the level of the water can be changed by letting water in or out, to raise or lower ships. 6. the part of a gun by means of which it is fired. *n., v. 2.*

lock[2] (lok), 1. curl of hair. 2. portion of hair, wool, etc. *n.*

lock er (lok′ər), a chest, small closet, or cupboard. *n. 17.*

lock et (lok′it), a little ornamental case of gold, silver, etc., for holding a picture of someone or a lock of hair. A locket is usually worn around the neck on a necklace. *n. 12.*

Locket

lock jaw (lok′jô′), a form of blood poisoning in which the jaws become firmly closed. Tetanus is another name for lockjaw. *n. 15.*

lock out (lok′out′), the refusal of an employer to furnish work to employees, used as a means of making them accept his terms. *n. 19.*

lock smith (lok′smith′), man who makes or repairs locks and keys. *n.*

lock up (lok′up′), jail. *n.*

lo co mo tion (lō′kə mō′shən), act or power of moving from place to place. Walking, swimming, and flying are common forms of locomotion. *n. 12.*

lo co mo tive (lō′kə mō′tiv), 1. railroad engine. 2. any engine that goes from place

Railroad locomotive

to place on its own power. 3. moving from place to place. 4. having to do with the power to move from place to place. *n., adj. 5.*

lo cust (lō′kəst), 1. a kind of grasshopper. Sometimes locusts come in great swarms destroying the crops.

Locust (1¼ to 3 in. long)

2. a tree with small rounded leaflets and clusters of sweet-smelling white flowers. *n. 6.*

lode (lōd), a vein of metal ore. The miners struck a rich lode of copper. *n. 19.*

lode star (lōd′stär′), 1. star that shows the way. 2. polestar; North Star. 3. guide. *n. 16.*

lode stone (lōd′stōn′), loadstone. *n.*

lodge (loj), 1. live in a place for a time. 2. supply with a place to sleep or live in for a time. 3. a place to live in; a house, especially a small or temporary house. 4. live in a rented room in another's house. We are merely lodging at present. 5. get caught or stay in a place without falling or going farther. The boy's kite lodged in the branches of a big tree. 6. fix; put into a particular place. The hunter lodged a bullet in the lion's heart. 7. lay before some authority. We lodged a complaint with the police. 8. one of the branches of certain secret societies. 9. the place where it meets. 10. the den of an animal, such as a beaver or an otter. *v., n. 2.*

lodg er (loj′ər), person who lives in a rented room in another's house. *n. 11.*

lodg ing (loj′ing), place where one is living only for a time. **Lodgings** means a rented room or rooms in a house, not in a hotel. *n. 6.*

lodg ment (loj′mənt), 1. act of lodging. 2. being lodged; as, the lodgment of a claim against a company. 3. something lodged or deposited; as, a lodgment of earth on a ledge of rock. *n. 19.*

loft (lôft), 1. attic. 2. the room under the roof of a barn; as, a hayloft. 3. a gallery in a church or hall. 4. upper floor of a business building or storehouse. *n. 8.*

loft i ness (lôf′ti nis), 1. height. 2. pride. 3. elevated or exalted condition, character, etc. *n. 15.*

loft y (lôf′ti), 1. very high. 2. proud; haughty. 3. exalted; dignified; grand. *adj., loftier, loftiest. 3.*

log (lôg), 1. a length of wood just as it comes from the tree. 2. made of logs; as, a log house. 3. cut down trees, cut them into logs, and get them out of the forest. 4. the daily record of a ship's voyage. 5. a float for measuring the speed of a ship. *n., adj., v., logged, logging. 2.*

Log cabin

lo gan ber ry (lō′gən ber′i), a large purplish-red berry. The loganberry is a cross between the blackberry and the red raspberry. *n., pl. loganberries.*

log a rithm (lôg′ə riтнm), 1. the power to which a fixed number (usually 10) must be raised in order to produce a given number. If the fixed number is 10, the logarithm of 1000 is 3; the logarithm of 10,000 is 4; the logarithm of 100,000 is 5. 2. one of a system of such numbers used to shorten calculation in mathematics. *n. 18.*

log book (lôg′bu̇k′), 1. a book in which a daily record of a ship's voyage is kept. 2. a book for records of an airplane's trips. 3. a journal of travel. *n.*

log ger head (lôg′ər hed′), 1. stupid person. 2. **At loggerheads** means disputing or at enmity. 3. a large-headed sea turtle. *n.*

log ging (lôg′ing), the work of cutting trees down, sawing them into logs, and moving the logs out from the forest. *n.*

log ic (loj′ik), 1. the science of proof. 2. science of reasoning. 3. reasoning; use of argument. 4. reason; sound sense. *n. 7.*

log i cal (loj′i kəl), 1. having to do with logic. 2. reasonable. 3. reasoning correctly. *adj. 12.*

lo gi cian (lō jish′ən), person skilled in logic. *n. 16.*

loin (loin), 1. the part of the body of an animal or man between the ribs and the hipbones. The loins are on both sides of the backbone and nearer to it than the flanks. 2. a piece of meat from this part. See the diagrams under **beef** and **pork.** *n. 4.*

Loire (lwär), longest river in France. *n. 13.*

loi ter (loi′tər), 1. linger idly; stop and play along the way. Mary loitered along the street, looking into all the shopwindows. 2. spend idly; as, to loiter the hours away. *v. 6.*

loi ter er (loi′tər ər), person who lingers idly or delays on his way. *n. 16.*

Lo ki (lō′ki), Norse god of destruction. *n.*

loll (lol), 1. recline or lean in a lazy manner; as, to loll on a sofa. 2. hang loosely or droop. A dog's tongue lolls out. 3. allow to hang or droop. A dog lolls out his tongue. *v. 13.*

lol li pop (lol′i pop), piece of hard candy, often on the end of a small stick. *n.*

Lom bard (lom′bärd), 1. member of a German tribe which in the sixth century A.D. conquered the part of northern Italy since known as Lombardy. 2. native or inhabitant of Lombardy. 3. having to do with the Lombards or Lombardy. *n., adj. 14.*

Lom bard y (lom′bər di), a plain in northern Italy. *n. 16.*

Lo mond (lō′mənd). **Loch Lomond** is a lake in western Scotland. *n.*

Lon don (lun′dən), the capital of Great Britain in southern England, on the Thames River. London and New York are the largest cities in the world. *n. 2.*

lone (lōn), alone; single; lonely. The lone traveler was cheered by the news that a friend would travel with him. *adj. 3.*

lone li ness (lōn′li nis), being lonely; solitude. *n. 9.*

lone ly (lōn′li), 1. alone. 2. without many

people; as, a lonely road. 3. feeling oneself alone and longing for company. *adj., lonelier, loneliest. 4.*

lone some (lōn′səm), 1. feeling lonely. 2. making one feel lonely. *adj. 5.*

long[1] (lông), 1. An inch is short; a mile is long. A year is a long time. He told a long story. We call anything long if it has a large measure from end to end. 2. in length. My table is three feet long. 3. having a long, narrow shape; as, a long board. 4. a long time. Summer will come before long. 5. Some special meanings are:
all day long, through all the day.
as long as, since; if only.
long vowel, vowel like *a* in *late*, *e* in *be*, or *o* in *note*.
adj., adv., n. 1.

long[2] (lông), wish very much; desire greatly. He longed for his mother. She longed to see him. *v.*

Long Beach, a city south of Los Angeles, California.

lon gev i ty (lon jev′i ti), long life. Good habits promote longevity. *n. 14.*

Long fel low (lông′fel′ō), Henry Wadsworth, a poet who lived in New England (1807-1882). *n. 7.*

long hand (lông′hand′), ordinary writing, not shorthand or typewriting. *n.*

long ing (lông′ing), 1. earnest desire; as, a longing for home. 2. having or showing earnest desire; as, a child's longing look at a window full of toys. *n., adj.*

Long Island, large island south of Connecticut. It is a part of New York State.

lon gi tude (lon′ji tūd or lon′ji tüd), distance east or west on the earth's surface, measured in degrees from a certain meridian (line from the North to the South Pole), usually the meridian through Greenwich, England. *n. 7.*

lon gi tu di nal (lon′ji tū′di nəl or lon′ji tü′di nəl), 1. of length; in length. 2. running lengthwise. Our flag has longitudinal stripes. 3. of longitude. The longitudinal difference between New York and San Francisco is about 50 degrees. *adj. 13.*

long shore man (lông′shōr′mən), man whose work is loading and unloading ships. *n., pl. longshoremen.*

long-suf fer ing (lông′suf′ər ing), 1. suffering or enduring for a long time. 2. patient under trouble, pain, or injury. 3. long and patient endurance. *adj., n. 16.*

long-wind ed (lông′win′did), 1. capable of long effort without getting out of breath. A long-distance runner must be long-winded. 2. talking or writing at great length; tiresome; as, a long-winded speaker or sermon. *adj.*

look (lu̇k), 1. see; try to see; turn the eyes. Look at the pictures. 2. look hard; stare. 3. search. 4. a glance; seeing. 5. to face. The house looks to the south. 6. seem; appear. Flowers look pretty. 7. show how one feels by one's appearance. 8. appearance. Good looks means a good appearance. 9. Some special meanings are:
look after, attend to; take care of.
look alive, hurry.
look down on, despise.
look for, expect.
look forward to, expect with pleasure.
look in, make a short visit.
look into, examine; investigate.
look on, 1. watch without taking part. 2. regard; consider.
look oneself, seem like oneself; seem well.
look out, be careful; watch out.
look over, examine; inspect.
look to, 1. attend to; take care of. 2. turn to for help.
look up, hunt up.
look up to, respect.
v., n. 1.

Loon (about 32 in. long)

look er-on (lu̇k′ər on′), onlooker. *n., pl. lookers-on.*

looking glass, mirror.

look out (lu̇k′out′), 1. a sharp watch for someone to come or for something to happen. Keep a good lookout for Mother. 2. place from which to watch. 3. the person who has the duty of watching. 4. what one sees ahead. See those clouds! A poor lookout for our picnic! *n. 9.*

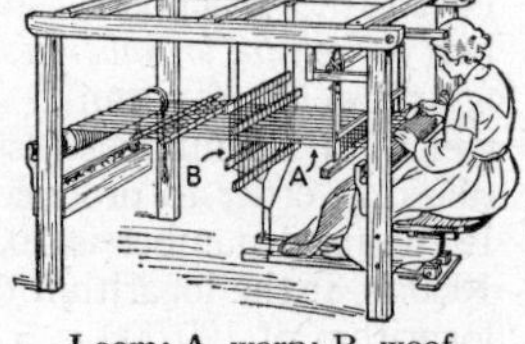

Loom: A, warp; B, woof.

loom[1] (lüm), machine for weaving cloth. *n. 5.*

loom[2] (lüm), appear indistinctly. A large iceberg loomed through the thick gray fog. *v.*

loon[1] (lün), a large diving bird. Loons have a loud, wild cry. See the picture above. *n. 11.*

loon[2] (lün), worthless, stupid person. *n.*

loop (lüp), 1. the shape of a curved string, ribbon, bent wire, etc., that crosses itself.

In writing, *b* and *g* and *h* and *l* have loops. See the picture just below. 2. a fastening or ornament formed of cord, etc., bent and crossed. 3. make a loop of. 4. make loops in. 5. fasten with a loop. 6. form a loop or loops. *n., v. 4.*

Loops (def. 1)

loop hole (lüp′hōl′), 1. a small opening in a wall for looking through, for letting in air, or for firing through at an enemy outside. 2. a means of escape. A clever lawyer often finds a loophole in the law to save his client even if he is guilty. *n. 8.*

Loophole

loose (lüs), 1. not fastened; as, a loose thread. 2. not tight; as, loose clothing. 3. not firmly set or fastened in; as, a loose tooth. 4. not bound together; as, loose papers. 5. not put up in a box, can, etc.; as, loose coffee. 6. free; not shut in or up. We leave the dog loose at night. 7. not pressed close together; as, loose earth, cloth with a loose weave. 8. not strict, close, or exact; as, a loose translation from another language. 9. careless about morals or conduct; as, a loose character. 10. set free; let go; unbind; make loose. *adj., v., adv. 2.*

loos en (lüs′ən), 1. make loose or looser; untie; unfasten. 2. become loose or looser. *v. 6.*

loot (lüt), 1. spoils; plunder; booty; as, loot taken by soldiers from a captured town, burglar's loot. 2. to plunder; rob. *n., v. 13.*

lop[1] (lop), 1. cut; cut off. 2. cut branches from. *v., lopped, lopping. 10.*

lop[2] (lop), 1. hang loosely; droop. 2. flop. *v., lopped, lopping.*

lope (lōp), 1. to run with a long, easy stride. 2. a long, easy stride. *v., n. 18.*

lop sid ed (lop′sīd′id), larger or heavier on one side than the other. *adj. 20.*

lo qua cious (lō kwā′shəs), talking much; fond of talking. *adj. 15.*

lord (lôrd), 1. owner, ruler, or master; person who has the power. 2. in Great Britain, a man of high rank. 3. rule proudly or absolutely. Philip was the oldest and lorded it over the rest of us. *n., v. 1.*

Lord (lôrd), 1. God. 2. Christ. 3. a title given to men of certain ranks in Great Britain; as, Lord Mayor of London. 4. **The Lords** is the upper house of the British Parliament. *n.*

lord ly (lôrd′li), 1. like a lord; suitable for a lord; grand; magnificent. 2. haughty; insolent; scornful. The spoiled child treated his friends with lordly contempt. *adj., lordlier, lordliest. 9.*

lord ship (lôrd′ship), 1. the title given to a lord. Yes, Your Lordship. 2. rule; ownership. Your lordship over these lands is not questioned. *n. 6.*

Lord's Prayer, the prayer given by Jesus to His disciples. Matthew 6:9-13.

Lord's Supper, 1. Jesus's last meal with His disciples before His crucifixion. 2. church service in memory of this; Holy Communion.

lore (lōr), 1. the facts and tales about a certain subject; as, fairy lore, bird lore, Irish lore. 2. learning; knowledge. *n. 10.*

lor gnette (lôr nyet′), 1. eyeglasses mounted on a handle. 2. opera glass. *n. 20.*

Woman using a lorgnette

lorn (lôrn), forsaken; forlorn. *adj. 16.*

Lor raine (lo rān′), a region in France. Most of it was taken by Germany in 1870, returned in 1919, but is now again under German control. *n. 13.*

lor ry (lor′i), 1. automobile truck. *British.* 2. long, flat wagon without sides. *n., pl. lorries.*

Lorry (def. 2)

Los An ge les (los an′jə lēz), the principal city in southern California. *12.*

lose (lüz), 1. not have any longer; have taken away from one by accident, carelessness, parting, death, etc.; as, to lose a dollar, lose one's life, lose a limb, a father, a friend. 2. fail to keep; as, to lose your patience or your temper. 3. be or become worse off in money, in numbers, etc. The army lost heavily in yesterday's battle. 4. become unable to find; as, to lose a book. 5. waste; spend or let go by without any result; as, to lose time waiting, to lose one's trouble, to lose a chance. 6. miss; fail to get, catch, see, or hear; as, to lose a train, to lose a few words of what was said. 7. not to win; be defeated; as, to lose a bet or a game. 8. cause one to lose. That one act lost him his job. 9. Some special meanings are:

be lost, have lost one's way.

be lost in (something), be so taken up with it that one fails to notice anything else.

lose (one's) **road,** fail to keep it in sight; fail to follow it.

lose (one's) **way,** not to know any longer where one is.

v., lost, losing. 1.

los er (lüz′ər), 1. one who loses something. 2. one who is beaten in a game or battle. *n. 10.*

los ing (lüz′ing), that cannot win. You are playing a losing game if you are not careful crossing streets. *adj.*

loss (lôs), 1. losing or having lost something. The loss of health is serious, but the loss of a pencil is not. 2. that which is lost. The loss was $10,000. 3. defeat. Our team had two losses and one tie out of ten games played. 4. **At a loss** means puzzled; not sure. *n. 1.*

lost (lôst), 1. See **lose.** I lost my new pencil. My ruler is lost, too. 2. destroyed; ruined; as, a lost soul. 3. no longer possessed; as, a lost friend. 4. missing; not found. 5. not won; as, a lost battle, a lost prize. 6. A **lost cause** is one defeated already or sure to be defeated. 7. insensible. The deserting soldier was lost to all sense of duty to his country. *pt. and pp. of lose, adj. 1.*

lot[1] (lot), 1. one of a set of objects, such as bits of paper, wood, etc., used to decide something by chance. We drew lots to see who should be captain. 2. such a method of deciding. It was settled by lot. 3. choice made by lot. The lot fell to me. 4. what one gets by lot; one's share. 5. one's fate or fortune. It was his lot later to become president. 6. a plot of ground. 7. a portion or part. He divided the fruit into ten lots. 8. a number of persons or things considered as a group; collection. This lot of oranges was not so good as the last. 9. great many. I have a lot of marbles. *Used in common talk. n. 1.*

Lot[2] (lot), a righteous man who was allowed to escape from Sodom before God destroyed it. His wife looked back and was changed into a pillar of salt. *n.*

loth (lōth), unwilling. The little girl was loth to leave her mother. *adj.* Also spelled **loath.**

lo tion (lō′shən), a liquid containing medicine. Lotions are applied to the skin to relieve pain, to heal, to cleanse, or to benefit the skin. Soda and water is a soothing lotion for insect bites. *n. 19.*

lot ter y (lot′ər i), a scheme for distributing prizes by lot or chance. In a lottery a large number of tickets are sold, some of which draw prizes. *n., pl. lotteries. 14.*

lo tus (lō′təs), 1. a kind of water lily that grows in Egypt and Asia. 2. a plant with red, pink, or white flowers. 3. a plant supposed by the ancient Greeks to cause a happy, dreamy state of mind in which one forgets his real life. *n. 9.*

Egyptian lotus

loud (loud), 1. not quiet or soft; making a great sound. A gun goes off with a loud noise. 2. in a loud manner. 3. showy in dress or manner; too bright; as, loud clothes. *adj., adv. 1.*

loud-speak er (loud′spēk′ər), a device for increasing sound. With a loud-speaker, speech or music received by radio can be heard throughout a room and farther. *n.*

Lou is (lü′i). Louis XVI was king of France from 1774 to 1793. He and his wife, Marie Antoinette, were beheaded during the French Revolution. *n.*

Lou i si an a (lü ē′zi an′ə), a Southern State of the United States. *n. 10.*

Lou is ville (lü′i vil), city in northern Kentucky, on the Ohio River. *n. 18.*

lounge (lounj), 1. stand, stroll, sit, or lie at ease and lazily. 2. a comfortable and informal room in which one can lounge and be at ease. 3. a couch. *v., n. 9.*

lour (lour), 1. look dark and threatening. 2. dark and threatening look. 3. frown; scowl. *v., n. 18.* Also spelled **lower.**

louse (lous), 1. small, wingless insect that infests the hair or the bodies of people. 2. any of similar insects that infest animals or plants. *n., pl. lice* (līs). *19.*

Louse (def. 1)

lous y (louz′i), 1. infested with lice. 2. dirty. *Slang. adj., lousier, lousiest.*

lout (lout), awkward, stupid fellow. *n. 17.*

Lou vre (lü′vrə), famous museum in Paris, formerly a palace of the kings of France. *n. 16.*

lov a ble (luv′ə bəl), worthy of being loved; endearing. She was a most lovable person, always kind and thoughtful. *adj. 12.*

love (luv), 1. a fond, deep, tender feeling. 2. have such a feeling for. She loves her mother. 3. person who is loved. 4. warm liking. 5. like very much. He loves music. 6. something that is lovely. What

a love of a bracelet! 7. a score of zero in some games. 8. Some special meanings are:
fall in love, begin to love; come to feel love.
for the love of, for the sake of.
make love to, woo; court.
not for love or money, not for any reason; not at all.
There is no love lost between them. They dislike each other.
n., v. 1.

love knot, knot of ribbons as a symbol or token of love.

love less (luv′lis), without love; unloved; unloving. *adj. 17.*

love li ness (luv′li nis), beauty. *n. 10.*

love lorn (luv′lôrn′), suffering because of love; forsaken by the person whom one loves. *adj.*

love ly (luv′li), beautiful; beautiful in mind or character; lovable. *adj., lovelier, loveliest. 2.*

lov er (luv′ər), person who loves; man who is in love. *n. 2.*

lov ing (luv′ing), affectionate; fond. *adj.*

lov ing-kind ness (luv′ing kīnd′nis), kindness coming from love. *n.*

lov ing ly (luv′ing li), in a loving or affectionate manner. *adv. 20.*

low[1] (lō), 1. not high or tall. A footstool is low. 2. in a low place; near the ground. 3. of a humble rank. 4. mean; coarse; vulgar. 5. poor; poorly. 6. small; less than usual; at a small price. 7. nearly used up. 8. not high in the musical scale. 9. not loud; not loudly. 10. feeble; weak. 11. **Low spirits** means a condition with little energy or joy. 12. **Low tide** is the time when the ocean is lowest on the shore. *adj., adv. 1.*

low[2] (lō), 1. make the sound of a cow; moo. 2. sound a cow makes; mooing. *v., n.*

Low ell (lō′əl), 1. James Russell Lowell was an American poet (1819-1891). 2. a city in northeastern Massachusetts. *n. 9.*

low er[1] (lō′ər), 1. let down or haul down; as, to lower a flag. 2. make lower. 3. sink or become lower. 4. more low. Prices were lower last year than this. *v., adj., adv. 1.*

low er[2] (lou′ər), lour. *v., n.*

low er most (lō′ər mōst), lowest. *adj.*

lower world, 1. hell; Hades. 2. earth.

low land (lō′lənd), 1. land that is lower and flatter than the neighboring country. 2. of the lowlands; in the lowlands. *n., adj. 5.*

low li ness (lō′li nis), humbleness of feeling or behavior; humble station in life. *n. 12.*

low ly (lō′li), 1. low in rank, station, position, or development. 2. humble; meek; modest in feeling, behavior, or condition. 3. humbly; meekly. *adj., lowlier, lowliest, adv. 6.*

low-spir it ed (lō′spir′i tid), sad; depressed. *adj.*

loy al (loi′əl), 1. true and faithful to love, promise, or duty. 2. faithful to one's king, one's government, or one's country. *adj. 4.*

loy al ist (loi′əl ist), person who supports his king or the existing government, especially in time of revolt. *n. 17.*

loy al ty (loi′əl ti), loyal feeling or behavior; faithfulness. *n., pl. loyalties. 5.*

Loy o la (loi ō′lə), Ignatius (1491-1556), Spanish soldier, priest, and saint, founder of the Jesuit Order. *n.*

loz enge (loz′inj), 1. a figure having a shape like this ◊. 2. a small tablet of any shape used as medicine or candy; as, cough lozenges. *n. 16.*

Lt., Lieutenant.

Ltd. or **ltd.,** limited. *19.*

lub ber (lub′ər), 1. a big, clumsy, stupid fellow. 2. a clumsy sailor. *n. 13.*

lu bri cant (lü′bri kənt), oil, grease, etc., for putting on parts of machines that slide or move against one another, to make them smooth and slippery so that they will work easily. *n. 11.*

lu bri cate (lü′bri kāt), make machinery smooth, slippery, and easy to work by putting on oil or grease. *v. 12.*

lu bri ca tion (lü′bri kā′shən), 1. lubricating or oiling. 2. being lubricated or oiled. *n. 15.*

lu bri ca tor (lü′bri kā′tər), 1. person or thing that makes things smooth and easy-running. 2. a device for oiling machinery. *n. 14.*

lu cent (lü′sənt), 1. shining; bright; luminous. 2. clear; letting the light through. *adj. 17.*

lu cid (lü′sid), 1. shining; bright. 2. clear; easy to follow or understand. A good explanation is lucid. 3. sane. An insane person sometimes has lucid intervals. *adj. 10.*

lu cid i ty (lü sid′i ti), clearness, especially of thought, expression, perception, understanding, etc. *n. 19.*

Lu ci fer (lü′si fər), the chief rebel angel,

who was cast out of heaven; Satan; the Devil. *n. 12.*

luck (luk), 1. that which seems to happen or come to one by chance; fortune; chance. Luck favored me, and I won. 2. good luck. I am in luck. She gave me a penny for luck. *n. 3.*

luck i ly (luk′i li), by good luck; fortunately. *adv.*

luck less (luk′lis), having or bringing bad luck. That Friday was a luckless day for me. *adj. 9.*

Luck now (luk′nou), a city in central India. *n.*

luck y (luk′i), having or bringing good luck. *adj., luckier, luckiest. 4.*

lu cra tive (lü′krə tiv), bringing in money; profitable. *adj. 14.*

lu cre (lü′kər), money considered as bad or degrading. *n. 11.*

Lu cre tius (lü krē′shəs), a Roman poet (99?-55 B.C.). *n. 14.*

lu cu bra tion (lü′kū brā′shən), 1. laborious study. 2. a scholarly or carefully written production. *n. 16.*

lu di crous (lü′di krəs), ridiculous; amusingly absurd; as, the ludicrous acts of a clown. *adj. 10.*

luff (luf), 1. **Luff, luff the ship,** and **luff the helm** all mean turn the bow of the ship nearer to the wind. 2. act of luffing. 3. part of the fore-and-aft sail nearest the mast or stay. *v., n. 18.*

lug[1] (lug), pull along or carry with effort; drag. The children lugged home a big Christmas tree. *v., lugged, lugging. 15.*

lug[2] (lug), projecting piece by which something is supported. *n.*

lug gage (lug′ij), baggage. *n. 6.*

lug ger (lug′ər), boat with lugsails. *n.*

Lugger

lug sail (lug′səl or lug′sāl′), four-cornered sail held by a yard that slants across the mast. *n.*

lu gu bri ous (lü gū′bri əs), sad; mournful; as, the lugubrious howl of a dog. *adj. 19.*

Luke (lük), 1. in the Bible, a physician who was the companion of the Apostle Paul. 2. the third book of the New Testament. It tells the story of the life of Christ. *n.10.*

luke warm (lük′wôrm′), 1. neither hot nor cold. 2. half-hearted; showing little enthusiasm. *adj. 11.*

lull (lul), 1. to hush to sleep. The mother lulled the crying baby. 2. to quiet; become calm or more nearly calm. The captain lulled our fears. The wind lulled. 3. period of less noise or violence; brief calm. We ran home during a lull in the storm. *v., n. 4.*

lul la by (lul′ə bī′), song for singing to a child in a cradle; soft song to put a baby to sleep. *n., pl. lullabies. 8.*

lum ba go (lum bā′gō), pain in the muscles of the small of the back and loins. *n.*

lum bar (lum′bər), of the loin or loins; as, the lumbar region. *adj. 20.*

lum ber[1] (lum′bər), 1. timber, logs, beams, boards, etc., roughly cut and prepared for use. 2. cut and prepare lumber. 3. household articles no longer in use, old furniture, etc., that take up room. 4. fill up or obstruct by taking space which is wanted for something else. Do not lumber up my shelf with your collection of stones and insects. *n., v. 2.*

lum ber[2] (lum′bər), move along heavily and noisily; roll along with difficulty. The old-time coaches were lumbering means of travel. *v.*

lum ber jack (lum′bər jak′), man whose work is cutting down trees and getting out the logs. *n.*

lum ber man (lum′bər mən), 1. man who works at cutting down trees and getting out the logs. 2. person who prepares lumber or buys and sells lumber. *n., pl. lumbermen. 12.*

lu mi nar y (lü′mi nãr′i), 1. the sun or moon or other light-giving body. 2. famous person. *n., pl. luminaries. 15.*

lu mi nous (lü′mi nəs), 1. bright; shining by its own light; full of light. The sun and stars are luminous bodies. 2. clear; easily understood. *adj. 7.*

lump (lump), 1. a small mass of no particular shape. 2. a swelling; a bump. There is a lump on my head where I bumped it. 3. put together. We will lump all our expenses. 4. form into a lump or lumps. Cornstarch will lump if cooked too fast. 5. in lumps; in a lump; including a number of items. *n., v., adj. 4.*

lump ish (lump′ish), like a lump; heavy; dull; stupid. *adj. 19.*

Lu na (lü′nə), 1. the Roman goddess of the moon. 2. the moon. *n. 17.*

lu na cy (lü′nə si), 1. insanity. 2. great folly. *n., pl. lunacies. 15.*

lu nar (lü′nər), 1. of the moon; as, a lunar eclipse. A **lunar month** is the interval between one new moon and the next, about 29½ days. 2. like the moon. *adj. 14.*

lu na tic (lü′nə tik), 1. crazy person. 2. insane. 3. extremely foolish. *n., adj. 8.*

lunch (lunch), 1. light meal. 2. a light meal between breakfast and dinner. 3. eat a light meal. *n., v. 3.*

lunch eon (lun′chən), 1. lunch. 2. a formal lunch. *n., v. 6.*

lung (lung), either one of the pair of breathing organs found in the chest of man and of other animals with backbones. *n. 4.*

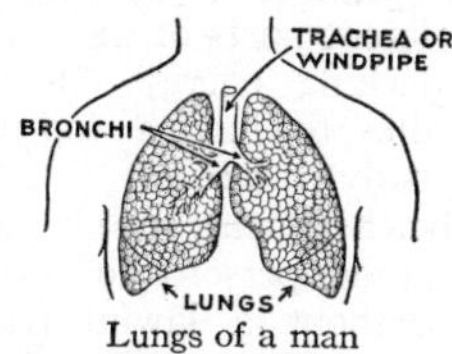

Lungs of a man

lunge (lunj), 1. a thrust; any sudden forward movement. 2. to thrust; make a lunge. *n., v.*

lu pine (lü′pin), plant with long spikes of flowers, clusters of hairy leaflets, and flat pods with bean-shaped seeds. *n.*

Lupine
(1 to 2 ft. high)

lurch[1] (lėrch), 1. a sudden leaning or roll to one side, like that of a ship, a car, or a staggering person. The car gave a lurch and upset. 2. make a lurch; stagger. The wounded man lurched forward. *n., v. 11.*

lurch[2] (lėrch). **Leave in the lurch** means leave in a helpless condition or difficult situation. *n.*

lure (lür), 1. lead (away or into something) by arousing desire. 2. attraction. Many people feel the lure of the sea. 3. attract with a bait. We lured the fox into a trap. 4. a decoy; bait. *v., n. 5.*

lu rid (lür′id), 1. lighted up with a red or fiery glare. The sky was lurid with the flames and smoke of the burning city. 2. terrible; sensational; startling. *adj. 15.*

lurk (lėrk), stay about without arousing attention; wait out of sight; be hidden. A tiger was lurking in the jungle outside the village. *v. 4.*

lus cious (lush′əs), 1. delicious; richly sweet; as, a luscious peach. 2. very pleasing to taste, smell, hear, see, or feel. *adj. 9.*

lush (lush), 1. tender and juicy; growing thick and green. Lush grass grows along the river banks. 2. abundant. *adj.*

lust (lust), 1. strong desire. 2. have a strong desire. A miser lusts after gold. 3. a bad desire or appetite. 4. desire for indulgence of sex. *n., v. 4.*

lus ter or **lus tre** (lus′tər), 1. a bright shine on the surface; as, the luster of pearls. 2. a kind of china that has a lustrous surface; as, pink luster teacups. 3. a thin fabric of cotton and wool that has a lustrous surface. 4. brightness. Her eyes lost their luster. 5. fame; glory; brilliance. The deeds of heroes add luster to a nation's history. *n. 4.*

lust ful (lust′fəl), full of lust or desire; sensual; lewd. *adj. 19.*

lust i ly (lus′ti li), vigorously; heartily. The boys cheered lustily. *adv.*

lus trous (lus′trəs), having luster; shining; glossy; as, lustrous pearls. *adj. 11.*

lust y (lus′ti), strong and healthy; full of vigor; as, a lusty boy. *adj., lustier, lustiest. 5.*

lute (lüt), an old-time stringed instrument somewhat like a banjo. *n. 6.*

Woman playing a lute

Lu ther (lü′thər), Martin, the German reformer who was the leader in the separation of many people from the Roman Catholic Church (1483-1546). *n. 8.*

Lu ther an (lü′thər ən), 1. having to do with Luther or the church that was named for him. 2. member of the Lutheran Church. *adj., n. 12.*

Lux em burg (luk′səm bėrg), a small country between Germany, France, and Belgium. *n.*

lux u ri ance (lug zhür′i əns), luxuriant growth or productiveness; rich abundance. *n. 16.*

lux u ri ant (lug zhür′i ənt), 1. growing thick and green. 2. producing abundantly. 3. rich in ornament. *adj. 8.*

lux u ri ate (lug zhür′i āt), 1. indulge in luxury. 2. take great delight. The explorer planned to luxuriate in hot baths, clean clothes, and good food when he came home. *v.*

lux u ri ous (lug zhür′i əs), 1. fond of luxury; tending toward luxury; self-indulgent. 2. giving luxury; very comfortable and beautiful. *adj. 7.*

lux u ry (luk′shə ri), 1. the comforts and

beauties of life beyond what are really necessary. 2. use of the best and most costly food, clothes, houses, furniture, and amusements. 3. thing that one enjoys, usually something choice and costly. A new car every year is a luxury that few people can afford. 4. thing pleasant but not necessary. *n., pl. luxuries. 3.*

Lu zón or **Lu zon** (lü zon′), chief island of the Philippines. *n.*

-ly, suffix forming adverbs having the following patterns of meaning:—

1. in a —— manner; as, cheerfully.
2. in —— ways or respects; as, financially, medically, physically.
3. to a —— degree or extent; as, greatly, slightly, moderately.
4. in, to, or from a —— direction; as, northwardly.
5. in a —— place; as, inwardly, thirdly.
6. at a —— time; as, recently.

-ly also forms adjectives having the following patterns of meaning:—

7. like a ——; as, a ghostly form.
8. like that of a ——; as, a brotherly kiss.
9. suited to a ——; proper for a ——; as, a manly fight, womanly kindness.
10. of each or every ——; occurring once per ——; as, hourly, daily, monthly.
11. being a ——; that is a ——; as, our heavenly home.

ly ce um (lī sē′əm), 1. lecture hall; place where popular lectures are given. 2. an association for instruction and entertainment through lectures, debates, and concerts. *n. 15.*

Lyd i a (lid′i ə), an ancient country in western Asia Minor. *n. 9.*

lye (lī), any strong alkaline solution. Lye is used in cleaning and in making soap. *n. 15.*

ly ing[1] (lī′ing), 1. telling a lie; habit of telling lies. 2. false; untruthful. *n., adj. 2.*

ly ing[2] (lī′ing). See **lie**[2]. *ppr. of lie*[2].

lymph (limf), a nearly colorless liquid from the tissues of the body, somewhat like blood without the red corpuscles. *n. 9.*

lym phat ic (lim fat′ik), 1. of lymph. A **lymphatic vessel** carries the lymph to different parts of the body. 2. sluggish; pale; lacking energy (thought formerly to be due to having too much lymph in the body). *adj. 13.*

lynch (linch), put (an accused person) to death without a lawful trial. *v. 14.*

Lynx (about 3 ft. long, including the tail)

Lynn (lin), a city in Massachusetts. *n. 10.*

lynx (lingks), a wildcat common in the northern United States and Canada. *n., pl. lynxes* or *lynx. 13.*

lynx-eyed (lingks′īd′), having sharp eyes or keen sight. *adj.*

Ly ons (lī′ənz), a large city on the Rhone River in eastern France. *n. 11.*

lyre (līr), ancient stringed musical instrument somewhat like a small harp. See the picture. *n. 6.*

Lyre

lyr ic (lir′ik), 1. a short poem expressing personal emotion. A love poem, a lament, and a hymn might all be lyrics. 2. having to do with such poems. 3. of, expressed in, or suitable for song. *n., adj. 9.*

lyr i cal (lir′i kel), lyric; emotional. *adj. 13.*

M

M, m (em), 1. the 13th letter of the alphabet. M comes after j, k, l in the alphabet. There are three m's in mammoth. 2. Roman numeral for 1000. *n., pl. M's, m's.*

ma (mä), mamma; mother. *n.* [*Used in common talk*] *6.*

ma'am (mam), madam. *n. 16.*

mac ad am (mə kad′əm), 1. small broken stones. Layers of macadam are rolled until solid and smooth to make roads. 2. roads made of this. *n. 17.*

mac ad am ize (mə kad′əm īz), make or cover (a road) with macadam. *v. 17.*

mac a ro ni (mak′ə rō′ni), flour paste dried in the form of long, hollow tubes to be cooked for food. *n. 15.*

mac a roon (mak′ə rün′), a small, very sweet cake, made of ground almonds, white of egg, and sugar. *n. 13.*

Ma cau lay (mə kô′li), Thomas Babington, a noted English essayist, historian, poet, and statesman (1800-1859). *n. 18.*

ma caw (mə kô′), a large, long-tailed parrot with brilliant plumes and a harsh voice. *n.*

Mac beth (mək beth′), 1. a play by Shakespeare. 2. the principal character in the play, who kills his king and becomes king himself. His wife, Lady Macbeth, helps him do this. *n. 14.*

mace[1] (mās), 1. a war club used as a weapon in the Middle Ages. 2. a staff, usually with a crown at the top, carried as a sign of authority. *n. 8.*

Mace (def. 1)

mace[2] (mās), a spice made from the dried outer covering of nutmegs. *n.*

Mac e don (mas′i don), Macedonia. *n. 16.*

Mac e do ni a (mas′i dō′ni ə), an ancient country in Europe, north of Greece. Macedonia now forms parts of Yugoslavia, Bulgaria, and Greece. *n. 9.*

ma che te (mä chā′tā), large heavy knife, used as a tool and weapon in South America, Central America, and the West Indies. *n.*

Machete

Mach i a vel li (mak′i ə vel′i), Italian statesman and writer who placed advantage above fairness in politics and advised the use of craft and deceit by rulers (1469-1527). *n. 17.*

Mach i a vel li an (mak′i ə vel′i ən), 1. of Machiavelli; like his political policy. 2. crafty; cunning. *adj.*

mach i na tion (mak′i nā′shən), 1. evil or artful plotting; scheming against authority. 2. evil plot; a secret or cunning scheme. He could not have been elected without the machinations of his gang. *n. 13.*

ma chine (mə shēn′), 1. an arrangement of parts, usually metal parts, for doing work, each part having some special thing to do. Sewing machines and washing machines make housework easier. 2. a device for applying force. Levers and pulleys are, in effect, machines. 3. an automobile. 4. airplane. 5. person or group that acts without thinking. 6. The persons controlling an organization are often called a machine; as, the Democratic or Republican machine. *n. 2.*

machine gun, gun for keeping up a rapid fire of bullets.

Machine gun

ma chin er y (mə shēn′ər i), 1. machines. A factory contains much machinery. 2. the parts or works of a machine. Machinery is oiled to keep it running smoothly. 3. any combination of things or persons by which something is kept going or something is done. Policemen, judges, courts, and prisons are legal machinery. *n., pl. machineries. 3.*

ma chin ist (mə shēn′ist), 1. skilled worker with machine tools. 2. person who runs a machine. 3. man who makes and repairs machinery. *n. 13.*

Mac ken zie (mə ken′zi), a river in northwestern Canada, flowing into the Arctic Ocean. *n. 17.*

mack er el (mak′ər əl), a salt-water fish, much used for food. *n., pl. mackerel* or *mackerels. 11.*

Mackerel (about 1 ft. long)

Mack i nac (mak′i nak), a strait between lakes Michigan and Huron. *n.*

mack i naw (mak′i nô), 1. a kind of thick blanket, often woven with bars of color, used in the northern and western United States by Indians, lumbermen, etc. 2. a short jacket of thick plaid wool. *n.*

mack in tosh (mak′in tosh), 1. waterproof coat; raincoat. 2. waterproof cloth. *n.*

ma cron (mā′kron), straight horizontal line (¯) placed over a vowel to show its sound. *Examples:* cāme, bē. *n.*

mad (mad), 1. out of one's head; crazy; insane. A man must be mad to do a mad thing like cutting himself on purpose. 2. much excited; foolish; wild. The dog made mad efforts to catch up with the automobile. 3. blindly and unreasonably fond. Some girls are mad about going to dances. 4. **Like mad** means furiously; very hard. I ran like mad to catch the train. 5. very angry. Don't be mad at me. *Used in common talk.* 6. having rabies or hydrophobia. A mad dog foams at the mouth and may bite people. *adj., madder, maddest. 2.*

Mad a gas car (mad′ə gas′kər), a large island east of southern Africa. *n. 14.*

mad am or **mad ame** (mad′əm), a polite title used in speaking of a lady or to a lady. Madam, will you take my seat? *n. 3.*

mad cap (mad′kap′), 1. person who goes ahead and carries out wild ideas without stopping to think first. 2. wild; hasty. *n., adj. 14.*

mad den (mad′ən), make mad; drive mad; become mad. *v. 10.*

made (mād), 1. built; constructed; formed; prepared. 2. See **make.** The cook made the cake. It was made of flour, milk, butter, eggs, and sugar. *adj., pt. and pp. of make. 1.*

Ma dei ra (mə dēr′ə), 1. a group of five Portuguese islands in the Atlantic Ocean, west of northern Africa. 2. a wine made in Madeira. *n. 10.*

mad e moi selle (mad′ə mə zel′), a French word meaning Miss. *n. 17.*

mad house (mad′hous′), 1. an asylum for the insane. 2. place of uproar and confusion. *n.*

Mad i son (mad′i sən), 1. James Madison (1751-1836) was one of the men who helped to make the Constitution of the United States. He was president of the United States from 1809 to 1817. 2. the capital of Wisconsin. *n. 4.*

mad ly (mad′li), 1. insanely. 2. furiously. 3. foolishly. *adv.*

mad man (mad′man′), man who is crazy. *n., pl. madmen. 6.*

mad ness (mad′nis), 1. being crazy; loss of one's mind. 2. great rage; fury. In his madness he tried to kill his best friend. 3. folly. It would be madness to try to sail a boat in this storm. *n. 4.*

Ma don na (mə don′ə), 1. Mary, the mother of Jesus. 2. picture or statue of her. *n. 12.*

mad ras (mad′rəs), closely woven cotton cloth, used for shirts. *n. 9.*

Ma drid (mə drid′), capital of Spain. *n. 10.*

mad ri gal (mad′ri gəl), 1. a short poem that can be set to music. 2. a song with parts for several voices. 3. any song. *n. 11.*

mael strom (māl′strəm), 1. any great or violent whirlpool, not only of water or air, but of affairs, feelings, or thoughts. 2. The **Maelstrom** is a dangerous whirlpool off the northwestern coast of Norway. *n.*

mag a zine (mag′ə zēn′), 1. a publication appearing weekly or monthly, containing stories and articles by different writers. 2. room in a fort or warship for keeping gunpowder and other dangerous substances that might explode. 3. building for storing gunpowder, guns, food, and other supplies in time of war. 4. place for cartridges in a repeating gun. 5. place for film in a camera. *n. 4.*

Magazine of a gun

mag da len (mag′də len), magdalene. *n.*

mag da lene (mag′də lēn), a woman reformed from a life of sin. In the Bible, Mary Magdalene was a repentant sinner forgiven by Jesus. Luke 7:37-50. *n. 10.*

Ma gel lan (mə jel′ən), a Portuguese navigator (1480?-1521) who discovered the Philippine Islands. The **Strait of Magellan** at the southern end of South America was named for him. *n. 13.*

ma gen ta (mə jen′tə), 1. purplish-red dye. 2. purplish red. *n., adj.*

mag got (mag′ət), an insect in the earliest, legless stage just after leaving the egg. Maggots usually live in decaying matter. *n. 8.*

MAGGOT ADULT

Fly. Lines show actual length.

Ma gi (mā′jī), 1. priests of ancient Media and Persia. 2. the Three Wise Men who came to honor the infant Jesus. Matthew 2:1, 2, 7-13. *n. pl. 19.*

mag ic (maj′ik), 1. the art of making things happen by secret charms and sayings. The fairy's magic changed the brothers into swans. 2. something that produces results as if by magic. 3. done by magic or as if by magic. A magic palace stood in place of their hut. *n., adj. 3.*

mag i cal (maj′i kəl), magic. The waving of the fairy's wand produced a magical effect upon Cinderella. *adj. 10.*

ma gi cian (mə jish′ən), person who can use magic. The wicked magician cast a spell over the princess. *n. 8.*

magic lantern, device with a lamp and lenses that throws a magnified image of a picture on a screen. The picture is on a glass slide.

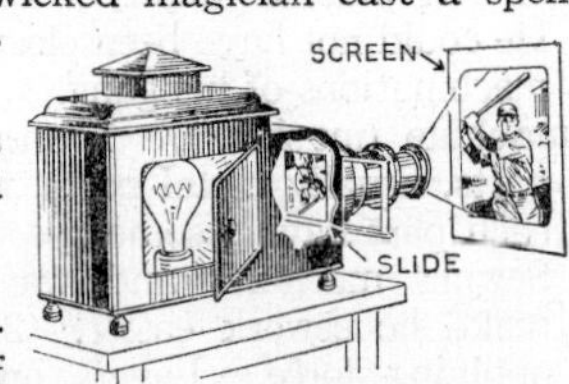

Magic lantern

mag is te ri al (maj′is tēr′i əl), 1. of or suited to a magistrate or judge. 2. showing authority. The colonel spoke with a magisterial voice. 3. imperious; overbearing. *adj. 15.*

mag is tra cy (maj′is trə si), 1. the position, rank, or duties of a magistrate or judge. 2. magistrates or judges as a group. *n., pl. magistracies. 15.*

mag is trate (maj′is trāt), 1. an officer of the government who has power to apply the law and put it in force. The President is the chief magistrate of the United States.

2. a judge. A justice of the peace is a magistrate. *n. 4.*

Mag na Char ta or **Mag na Car ta** (mag′nə kär′tə), 1. the great charter of the personal and political liberties of the people of England, demanded and obtained from King John in 1215. 2. any fundamental constitution guaranteeing rights.

mag na nim i ty (mag′nə nim′i ti), magnanimous nature or quality; nobility of soul or mind. The soldiers showed magnanimity by treating their prisoners well. *n., pl. magnanimities. 11.*

mag nan i mous (mag nan′i məs), noble in soul or mind; generous in forgiving; above small meannesses. *adj. 10.*

mag nate (mag′nāt), great man; important man. *n. 14.*

mag ne sia (mag nē′shə), a white, tasteless powder used as a medicine. *n. 15.*

mag ne si um (mag nē′shi əm), a light, silver-white metal that burns with a dazzling white light. *n. 16.*

mag net (mag′nit), 1. a stone or piece of iron or steel that attracts or draws to it bits of iron or steel. 2. anything that attracts. The kittens and rabbits in our back yard were a magnet which attracted all the children. *n. 7.*

Magnet attracting nails

mag net ic (mag net′ik), 1. having the properties of a magnet; as, the magnetic needle of a compass. 2. having to do with magnetism. 3. capable of being magnetized. 4. very attractive; as, a magnetic personality. *adj. 8.*

mag net ism (mag′ni tizm), 1. the properties or qualities of a magnet; the showing of magnetic properties. 2. the science dealing with magnetism. 3. power to attract or charm. If John had magnetism, he would be a leader among his schoolmates. *n. 12.*

mag net ize (mag′ni tīz), 1. give the properties or qualities of a magnet to. You can magnetize a needle by rubbing it with a magnet. 2. attract or influence (a person). Her beautiful voice magnetized the audience. *v. 19.*

mag ne to (mag nē′tō), a small machine for producing electricity. In some gasoline engines, a magneto supplies an electric spark to explode the vapor. *n., pl. magnetos. 12.*

mag nif i cence (mag nif′i səns), splendor; grand beauty; richness of material, color, and ornament. We may speak of the magnificence of mountain scenery, of kings, or of furnishings. *n. 6.*

mag nif i cent (mag nif′i sənt), grand; stately; splendid; richly ornamented; as, the magnificent palace of a king, the magnificent jewels of a queen. *adj. 3.*

mag ni fi er (mag′ni fī′ər), one that magnifies; a lens that makes things look larger. *n. 20.*

mag ni fy (mag′ni fī), 1. cause to look larger than it really is. A microscope is a magnifying glass. 2. make too much of; go beyond the truth in telling. Do not magnify the faults of your friends. *v., magnified, magnifying. 5.*

mag nil o quent (mag nil′ə kwənt), 1. speaking in a lofty style with big words; expressed in high-flown language. 2. boastful. *adj.*

mag ni tude (mag′ni tūd or mag′ni tüd), 1. size. 2. importance. The voters were impressed by the magnitude of the nation's problems. *n. 9.*

mag no li a (mag nō′li ə), a North American tree with large white, pink, or purplish flowers. There are several kinds. *n. 16.*

Magnolia flower

mag pie (mag′pī), 1. a black-and-white bird that chatters a great deal. 2. person who chatters. *n. 10.*

Mag yar (mag′yär), 1. member of the chief race of Hungary. 2. their language; Hungarian. 3. of the Magyars or their language. *n., adj. 12.*

ma ha ra ja or **ma ha ra jah** (mä′hə rä′jə), great ruler; the title of certain great ruling princes in India. *n. 20.*

American magpie (15 to 20 in. long)

ma hog a ny (mə hog′ə ni), 1. a tree that grows in tropical America. 2. the dark reddish-brown wood of this tree, which is very hard and takes a high polish. It is much used for furniture. 3. dark reddish brown. *n., pl. mahoganies, adj. 6.*

Ma hom et (mə hom′it), Mohammed. *n. 13.*

Ma hom et an (mə hom′i tən), Mohammedan. *adj., n.*

maid (mād), 1. girl; young unmarried woman. 2. unmarried woman. 3. female servant. 4. A **maid of honor** is (1) an unmarried woman who is the chief attendant of the bride at a wedding. (2) an unmarried lady who attends a queen or a princess. *n. 2.*

maid en (mād′ən), 1. girl; young unmarried woman; maid. 2. of a maiden; as, maiden grace. 3. virgin; unmarried; pure. 4. new; fresh; untried; unused. 5. first. It was the ship's maiden voyage. *n., adj. 2.*

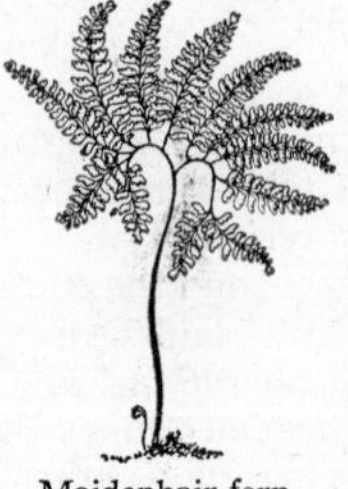
Maidenhair fern (8 to 20 in. high)

maid en hair (mād′ən hãr′), delicate fern with very slender stalks. *n.*

maid en hood (mād′ən hůd), time or condition of being a maiden. *n. 14.*

maid en ly (mād′ən li), 1. of a maiden. 2. like a maiden; gentle; modest. 3. suited to a maiden. *adj. 18.*

maid serv ant (mād′sėr′vənt), servant girl. *n.*

mail[1] (māl), 1. letters to be sent by post. 2. the system by which letters are sent, run by the Post Office Department. 3. all that comes by one post or delivery. 4. train, boat, etc., that carries mail. 5. send by mail; put in a mailbox. *n., v. 2.*

Coat of mail

mail[2] (māl), 1. armor; metal garments made of rings, small loops of chain linked together, or plates, for protecting the body against the enemy's arrows, spears, etc. 2. clothe with armor or as if with armor. The **mailed fist** means armed force. *n., v.*

mail box (māl′boks′), 1. box from which mail is collected. 2. box to which mail is delivered. *n.*

maim (mām), cut off or hurt an arm, leg, ear, etc.; cripple or disable. He lost two toes by the accident, but we were glad that he was not more seriously maimed. *v. 7.*

main (mān), 1. most important; largest; as, the main dish at dinner, the main line of a railway. 2. a large pipe for water, gas, etc. 3. the open sea. *Used in poetry.* 4. **In the main** means for the most part. 5. **By main strength** means by using full strength. 6. **With might and main** means with all one's force. *adj., n. 2.*

Maine (mān), a New England State in the extreme northeast of the United States. *n. 6.*

main land (mān′land′), land that is not a small island; the main part of a continent. *n. 8.*

main ly (mān′li), chiefly; mostly; for the most part. Jim is interested mainly in sports and neglects his school work. *adv. 12.*

main mast (mān′məst or mān′mast′), the principal mast in a ship. In a three-masted ship, the middle mast is the mainmast. *n. 20.*

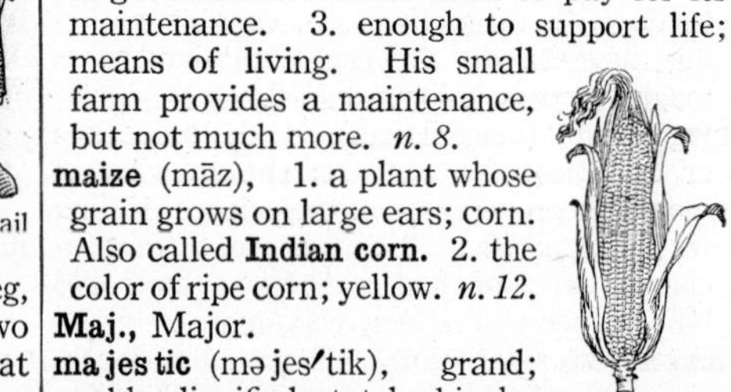

main sail (mān′səl or mān′sāl′), largest sail of a ship. *n. 17.*

main sheet (mān′shēt′), rope that controls the angle at which the mainsail is set. *n.*

main spring (mān′spring′), 1. the principal spring in a clock, watch, etc. 2. the chief force. *n. 19.*

main stay (mān′stā′), 1. rope supporting the mainmast. 2. main support. Loyal friends are a person's mainstay in time of trouble. *n. 19.*

main tain (mān tān′), keep; keep up; carry on; uphold. One may maintain one's hold on a rope, maintain a family or a household, maintain war, or maintain an opinion. *v. 2.*

main te nance (mān′ti nəns), 1. a maintaining. Maintenance of quiet is necessary in a hospital. 2. a being maintained; support. A government collects taxes to pay for its maintenance. 3. enough to support life; means of living. His small farm provides a maintenance, but not much more. *n. 8.*

Maize

maize (māz), 1. a plant whose grain grows on large ears; corn. Also called **Indian corn.** 2. the color of ripe corn; yellow. *n. 12.*

Maj., Major.

ma jes tic (mə jes′tik), grand; noble; dignified; stately; kingly. *adj. 4.*

ma jes ti cal (mə jes′ti kəl), majestic; stately. *adj. 16.*

maj es ty (maj′is ti), 1. stateliness; royal dignity; nobility. 2. **Your Majesty** or **His Majesty** is a title given to kings and queens, emperors, and the like. *n., pl. majesties. 3.*

ma jol i ca (mə jol′i kə), kind of enameled Italian pottery richly decorated in colors. *n.*

ma jor (mā′jər), 1. an officer in the army, ranking next above a captain. 2. greater. The major part of a little baby's life is spent in sleeping. *n., adj. 4.*

ma jor-do mo (mā′jər dō′mō), 1. man in charge of a great household. 2. steward; butler. *n., pl. major-domos. 19.*

major general, army officer ranking next below a lieutenant general and next above a brigadier general.

ma jor i ty (mə jor′i ti), 1. the greater number or part; more than half. A majority of the children chose red covers for the books they made. 2. the number by which the votes on one side are more than those on the other. John had 18 votes, and James had 12; so John had a majority of 6. 3. legal age for voting; usual legal age for managing one's property, etc. Fred is twenty and will reach his majority next year and can manage his own affairs after that. *n., pl. majorities. 3.*

make (māk), 1. bring into being; build; form or shape; as, to make a rag rug, a poem, a boat, a medicine. 2. style; build; character. Do you like the make of that coat? 3. kind; brand. What make of car is this? 4. put into condition for use; arrange; as, to make the beds. 5. get (a thing) started; as, to make a fire. 6. cause; bring about; as, to make a noise, to make peace. 7. give; as, make room for me. 8. pass (a law); decide that there shall be (such a law, rule, etc.). 9. come to have; as, to make a new friend. 10. cause to be or become; as, to make a room warm, make a fool of oneself. 11. become; turn out to be. She will make a good teacher. 12. come to; amount to. 2 and 3 make 5. That makes 40 cents you owe me. 13. count as; be counted as. This makes twice I have been in New York. I made it 47. 14. be; be the whole of. Bread and milk will make a supper for us. 15. earn; gain; as, to make good marks, to make one's living. 16. cause the success of. One big deal made the young businessman. 17. force to. Make brother stop hitting me. 18. do; perform; as, to make a journey, make an attempt, make a mistake. 19. reach; arrive at. Will the ship make harbor? 20. reach or keep up a speed of. Some airplanes can make more than 200 miles an hour. 21. Some special meanings are:

make away with, 1. get rid of. 2. kill. 3. steal.

make believe, pretend.

make out, 1. write out. 2. prove; try to prove. 3. understand. 4. see with difficulty. I can barely make out what these letters are. 5. complete; fill out. We need two more eggs to make out a dozen. 6. get along; manage.

make over, 1. alter; make different; as, to make over a dress. 2. hand over possession of legally. The king made over his kingdom to his little son.

make time, go with speed.

make up, 1. put together; as, to make up cloth into a dress. 2. arrange; set up; as, to make up a page of type. 3. invent; as, to make up a story. 4. put paint, powder, etc., on the face. 5. become friends again after a quarrel. 6. give or do in place of; as, to make up for lost time. 7. decide; as, to make up one's mind.

v., made, making, n. 1.

make-be lieve (māk′bi lēv′), 1. pretended. Children often have make-believe playmates. 2. pretense. Fairies live in the land of make-believe. *adj., n.*

mak er (māk′ər), person or thing that makes. *n. 3.*

make shift (māk′shift′), something made to use for a time instead of the right thing. Spools, bottles, and buttons were the child's makeshifts for toys. *n. 17.*

make-up (māk′up′), the manner of being made up or put together; composition; nature; constitution. People of a nervous make-up are excitable. The make-up of an actor is the way he is dressed and painted in order to look his part. The make-up of a paper or magazine is the arrangement of type, illustrations, etc., or the kind of articles, stories, etc., used. *n. 19.*

mal a dy (mal′ə di), sickness; illness; disease. *n., pl. maladies. 8.*

Mal a ga (mal′ə gə), 1. a province in southern Spain. 2. a kind of large, oval, firm white grape. 3. a white wine. *n.*

mal a pert (mal′ə pėrt), too bold; pert; saucy. *adj.* [*Old use*] *20.*

ma lar i a (mə lãr′i ə), a disease characterized by chills, fever, and sweating. Malaria is transmitted by the bite of certain mosquitoes. *n. 8.*

ma lar i al (mə lãr′i əl), 1. having malaria. 2. of or like malaria. *adj. 14.*

Ma lay (mā′lā), 1. member of the brown race living in a peninsula of southeastern Asia and nearby islands. 2. their language. 3. of the Malays, their country, or their language. *n., adj. 13.*

Malay Archipelago, group of islands between southeastern Asia and Australia; East Indies.

Malay Peninsula, peninsula in southeastern Asia, north of Sumatra.

Malay Archipelago

mal con tent (mal′kən tent′), 1. discontented; dissatisfied. 2. discontented person. 3. inclined to rebel. 4. person inclined to rebel. *adj., n. 14.*

male (māl). Boys and men are males. A bull, a rooster, and a he-goat are all males. *n., adj. 3.*

mal e dic tion (mal′i dik′shən), curse. *n. 17.*

mal e fac tor (mal′i fak′tər), evildoer; criminal. *n. 15.*

ma lev o lence (mə lev′ə ləns), spite; extreme ill will; the wish to have evil come to others. *n. 15.*

ma lev o lent (mə lev′ə lənt), spiteful; showing ill will; wishing evil to come to others. *adj. 15.*

mal fea sance (mal fē′zəns), official misconduct; violation of a public trust or obligation. A judge is guilty of malfeasance if he accepts a bribe. *n.*

mal for ma tion (mal′fôr mā′shən), bad shape; faulty structure. A hunchback has a malformation of the spine. *n.*

mal ice (mal′is), active ill will; spite; a wish to hurt or make suffer. Lincoln asked the people of the North to act "with malice toward none, with charity for all." *n. 5.*

ma li cious (mə lish′əs), spiteful; showing ill will; wishing to hurt or make suffer. No one likes a malicious telltale. *adj. 7.*

ma lign (mə līn′), 1. speak evil of; slander. You malign Mr. Jones when you call him stingy, for he gives all he can afford to give. 2. evil; injurious. Gambling often has a malign influence. 3. hateful; malicious. *v., adj. 10.*

ma lig nant (mə lig′nənt), 1. very evil; very hateful; very malicious. 2. very harmful; causing death. Cancer is a malignant disease. *adj. 9.*

ma lig ni ty (mə lig′ni ti), 1. very great malice or ill will. 2. very great harmfulness; deadliness. *n., pl. malignities. 12.*

mall (môl), a shaded walk; a public walk or promenade. *n. 14.*

mal lard (mal′ərd), kind of wild duck. The male has a green head and a white band around his neck. *n., pl. mallards* or *mallard. 19.*

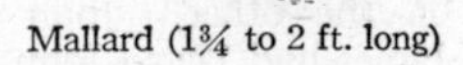
Mallard (1¾ to 2 ft. long)

mal le a ble (mal′i ə bəl), 1. that can be hammered or pressed into various shapes without breaking. Gold, silver, copper, and tin are malleable and can be beaten into thin sheets. 2. adaptable; yielding. *adj. 17.*

mal let (mal′it), wooden hammer. Specially shaped mallets are used to play croquet and polo. *n. 10.*

Mallet for pounding

mal low (mal′ō), a plant with purple, pink, or white flowers, and downy leaves and stems. *n. 13.*

malm sey (mäm′zi), kind of strong sweet wine. *n.*

mal nu tri tion (mal′nū trish′ən or mal′nü-trish′ən), poorly nourished condition. Children suffer from malnutrition because of wrong food as well as from lack of food. *n. 20.*

mal prac tice (mal prak′tis), 1. neglect or wrong treatment of a patient by a physician. 2. wrong practice or conduct in any official or professional position. *n.*

malt (môlt), 1. grain, usually barley, soaked in water until it has sprouted and tastes sweet. Malt is used in making beer and ale. 2. make into malt. 3. prepare with malt. Malted milk is a food. 4. change into malt. *n., v. 10.*

Mal ta (môl′tə), an island in the Mediterranean Sea, south of Sicily, belonging to Great Britain. *n. 13.*

Mal tese (môl tēz′), 1. of Malta or its people. 2. a kind of bluish-gray cat. *adj., n.*

Maltese cross, kind of cross. See the picture.

Maltese cross

mal treat (mal trēt′), treat roughly or cruelly; abuse. Only very mean children maltreat animals. *v. 17.*

mal treat ment (mal trēt′mənt), rough or cruel treatment; abuse. *n.*

ma ma (mä′mə), mother. *n. 10.*

mam ma (mä′mə), mother. *n. 3.*

mam mal (mam′əl), an animal that gives milk to its young. Human beings, horses, cattle, dogs, and cats are mammals. *n. 8.*

mam ma li an (ma mā′li ən), of mammals. *adj.*

Mam mon or **mam mon** (mam′ən), riches thought of as an evil influence. *n. 10.*

mam moth (mam′əth), 1. a very large extinct kind of elephant with a hairy skin and long curved tusks. 2. huge; gigantic. Digging the Panama Canal was a mammoth undertaking. *n., adj. 10.*

Mammoth (about 9 ft. tall)

mam my (mam′i), 1. a childish word for mother. 2. a colored woman in charge of white children; an old Negro woman. *n., pl. mammies. 17.*

man (man), 1. A man is a boy grown up. 2. human being; person. 3. the human race. Man likes company. Man has existed for thousands of years. 4. a male follower, servant, or employee; as, Robin Hood and his merry men. 5. supply with men. We can man ten ships. 6. make strong for action. The captive manned himself to endure torture. 7. **To a man** means every one of them. 8. **Be one's own man** means (1) be free to do as one pleases. (2) have complete control of oneself. *n., pl. men, v., manned, manning. 1.*

man a cle (man′ə kəl), 1. a handcuff; a fetter for the hands. 2. to fetter the hands of. The pirates manacled their prisoner. 3. to chain; restrain; hamper. *n., v. 16.*

man age (man′ij), 1. control; conduct; handle. A good rider manages his horse well. They hired a man to manage the business. 2. succeed in doing something. I shall manage to keep warm. 3. make use of. *v. 2.*

man age a ble (man′ij ə bəl), that can be managed. *adj. 20.*

man age ment (man′ij mənt), 1. handling; control. Bad management caused the failure. 2. the persons that manage a business or an institution. The management of the store decided to use red wrapping paper at Christmas time. *n. 5.*

man ag er (man′ij ər), person who manages. *n. 6.*

man a ge ri al (man′ə jēr′i əl), of a manager; having to do with management. *adj.*

Ma nas seh (mə nas′ə), 1. one of the twelve tribes of the Hebrews. 2. king of Judah from 692? to 638? B.C. *n. 12.*

man-at-arms (man′ət ärmz′), 1. soldier. 2. heavily armed soldier on horseback. *n., pl. men-at-arms.*

man a tee (man′ə tē′), sea cow, a large sea mammal with flippers and a flat, oval tail. Manatees live in warm shallow water near coasts. *n.*

Manatee (7 to 13 ft. long)

Man ches ter (man′chis tər), a large city in western England. *n. 12.*

Man chu (man chü′), 1. member of a Mongolian people inhabiting Manchuria. The Manchus conquered China in the 17th century. 2. their language. 3. of the Manchus, their country, or their language. *n., adj.*

Man chu kuo or **Man chou kuo** (man′chü′kwō′), a country in eastern Asia, now controlled by Japan. *n.*

Man chu ri a (man chür′i ə), a region north of China, now a part of Manchukuo. *n. 19.*

man da rin (man′də rin), a Chinese official of high rank. *n. 16.*

man date (man′dāt), 1. a command, especially a legal order from a source superior to oneself. 2. the expressed will of voters to their representative. 3. a commission given to one nation by a group of nations to administer the government and affairs of a territory, etc. 4. put (a territory, etc.) in the charge of a nation. 5. the territory. *n., v. 11.*

man da to ry (man′də tō′ri), commanded; of or containing a command. *adj.*

man di ble (man′di bəl), 1. a jaw, especially the lower jaw. 2. either part of a bird's beak. 3. an organ in insects for seizing and biting. The ant seized the dead fly with his mandibles. *n. 12.*

man do lin (man′də lin), a stringed musical instrument. *n. 18.*

Man playing a mandolin

man drake (man′drāk), a plant with a very short stem and a thick root which is often forked, used in medicine. *n. 16.*

man drill (man′dril), a large fierce baboon of western Africa. The face of the male mandrill is marked with blue and scarlet. *n.*

Mandrill (about 3 ft. long)

mane (mān), the long heavy hair on the neck of a horse, a lion, etc. *n. 5.*

ma neu ver (mə nü′vər), 1. a planned movement of troops or warships. Every year the army and navy hold maneuvers for practice. 2. perform maneuvers; cause troops to perform maneuvers. 3. a movement that is hard to follow, or deceives the eye or the mind. 4. carry out such a movement or maneuver; to manipulate skillfully. 5. a skillful plan; a clever series of moves. He forced us to support him by a series of maneuvers. 6. to scheme; use methods that the other fellow cannot follow. That schemer is maneuvering for some advantage. 7. to force or drive (a person or thing) by some scheme. She maneuvered her mother out of the kitchen. *n., v. 11.*

man ful (man′fəl), manly; brave. *adj. 11.*

man ga nese (mang′gə nēs), a hard, brittle, grayish-white metal. *n. 19.*

mange (mānj), skin disease of animals that forms scabs and causes loss of hair. *n.*

Two stalls with mangers

man ger (mān′jər), box in a barn or stable built against the wall at the right height for horses and cows to eat from. *n. 5.*

man gle[1] (mang′gəl), 1. cut or tear roughly. The two cats bit and clawed until both were much mangled. 2. spoil. The music was too difficult for little Edith to play and she mangled it badly. *v. 8.*

man gle[2] (mang′gəl), 1. machine with rollers for ironing sheets, towels, etc. 2. to press or smooth in a mangle. *n., v.*

Mango fruit

man go (man′gō), 1. the oblong, slightly sour fruit of a tropical tree. Mangoes are eaten ripe or pickled when green. 2. the tree itself. *n., pl. mangoes* or *mangos. 15.*

man grove (mang′grōv), a tree that sends down branches which take root and become new trunks. Mangroves grow in the tropics near water. *n.*

Mangroves (10 to 20 ft. high)

man gy (mān′ji), 1. having the mange; with the hair falling out. 2. shabby and dirty. *adj., mangier, mangiest.*

man han dle (man′han′dəl), handle roughly. *v.*

Man hat tan (man hat′ən), island on which part of New York City is. *n. 5.*

man hole (man′hōl′), hole through which a man can enter a sewer, steam boiler, etc., to inspect or repair it. *n.*

man hood (man′hůd), 1. condition or time of being a man. 2. courage; manliness. 3. men; as, the manhood of the United States. *n. 5.*

ma ni a (mā′ni ə), 1. a kind of insanity characterized by great excitement. 2. a craze; a rage; an unreasonable desire. She has a mania for dancing and going to parties. He has a mania for collecting old bottles. *n. 16.*

ma ni ac (mā′ni ak), 1. madman; raving lunatic. 2. insane; raving. *n., adj. 15.*

ma ni a cal (mə nī′ə kəl), insane; raving. *adj.*

man i cure (man′i kūr), 1. to care for (the hands and fingernails). 2. the care of the hands and fingernails. 3. manicurist. *v., n. 15.*

man i cur ist (man′i kūr′ist), person whose work is manicuring. *n.*

man i fest (man′i fest), 1. clear; apparent to the eye or to the mind; plain. 2. show plainly. 3. show; prove. 4. a list of a ship's cargo. *adj., v., n. 4.*

man i fes ta tion (man′i fes tā′shən), a showing; a making manifest; an act that shows or proves. Entering a burning building is a manifestation of courage. *n. 10.*

man i fes to (man′i fes′tō), a public declaration by a ruler, government, or body of persons; a proclamation. *n., pl. manifestoes. 16.*

man i fold (man′i fōld), 1. having many parts or forms. 2. appearing in many ways. 3. doing many different things. 4. many and various. *adj. 5.*

man i kin or **man ni kin** (man′i kin), 1. a model or figure of a person used by tailors, by artists, in store windows, etc. Also spelled **mannequin.** 2. a little man; dwarf.

3. a model of the human body used in studying anatomy. *n. 14.*

Ma nil a (mə nil′ə), 1. capital and largest city of the Philippine Islands. 2. **Manila Bay** is the bay on which it is situated. *n. 10.*

ma nil a or **ma nil la** (mə nil′ə), 1. a strong fiber made from the leaves of a Philippine banana plant, used for making ropes, fabrics, etc. 2. **Manila paper** is brownish-yellow wrapping paper made from this fiber or from other material. *n., adj.*

ma nip u late (mə nip′ū lāt), 1. handle or treat, especially with skill. She watched him manipulate all the handles and gears in his automobile until she thought she could run it herself. 2. manage by clever use of influence, especially unfair influence. He so manipulated the ball team that he was elected captain, although they really thought John would be a better leader. 3. treat unfairly; change for one's own purpose or advantage. The bookkeeper manipulated the accounts to conceal his theft. *v. 14.*

ma nip u la tion (mə nip′ū lā′shən), 1. skillful treatment or handling. 2. clever use of influence. 3. a change for one's own purpose or advantage. *n. 15.*

ma nip u la tor (mə nip′ū lā′tər), one that manipulates. *n. 20.*

man i to (man′i tō), among certain American Indians, a good or evil spirit; a being or object having supernatural powers. **The Manito** is the Great Spirit. *n.*

Man i to ba (man′i tō′bə), a province in southern Canada. *n.*

man i tou (man′i tü), manito. *n.*

man kind (man′kīnd′ for 1, man′kīnd′ for 2), 1. the human race; all human beings. 2. men; the male sex. Mankind and womankind both like praise. *n. 3.*

man like (man′līk′), 1. like a man. 2. suitable for a man. *adj. 14.*

man li ness (man′li nis), manly quality; manly behavior. *n. 15.*

man ly (man′li), 1. like a man; as a man should be; strong, frank, brave, noble, independent, and honorable. On his father's death, the boy set to work in a very manly way. 2. suitable for a man. *adj., manlier, manliest. 5.*

man na (man′ə), 1. in the Bible, the food God supplied to the Israelites in the desert. Exodus 16:14-36. 2. something that nourishes or refreshes the soul or spirit. *n. 11.*

man ne quin (man′i kin), 1. woman in a shop who puts on clothes to show the customers. 2. a model or figure of a person used by tailors, by artists, in store windows, etc. Also spelled **manikin** or **mannikin.** *n.*

man ner (man′ər), 1. way; way of doing or happening; person's way of acting or behaving; style; fashion. 2. **Manners** means ways or customs. 3. **Manners** sometimes means good manners. 4. kind or kinds. We saw all manner of birds in the forest. *n. 1.*

man ner ism (man′ər izm), 1. too much use of a particular manner of speaking, writing, or behaving. 2. an odd little trick, habit, gesture, or way of acting. *n. 15.*

man ner ly (man′ər li), 1. having or showing good manners; polite. 2. politely. *adj., adv.*

man nish (man′ish), 1. characteristic of a man; as, a mannish way of holding a baby. 2. like a man, not a woman; imitating a man; as, a mannish style of dress. *adj. 18.*

ma noeu vre (mə nü′vər), maneuver. *n., v., manoeuvred, manoeuvring. 20.*

man-of-war (man′əv wôr′), warship. *n., pl. men-of-war.*

man or (man′ər), landed estate, part of which was set aside for the lord and the rest divided among his peasants, who paid the owner rent in goods, services, or money. In the Middle Ages, if the lord sold his manor, the peasants or serfs were sold with it. *n. 10.*

ma no ri al (mə nō′ri əl), 1. of a manor. 2. forming a manor. *adj. 19.*

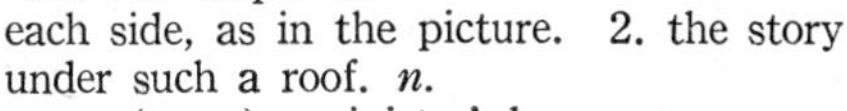
Mansard roof

man sard (man′särd), 1. roof with two slopes on each side, as in the picture. 2. the story under such a roof. *n.*

manse (mans), minister's house; parsonage. *n. 17.*

man sion (man′shən), large house; stately residence. *n. 4.*

man slaugh ter (man′slô′tər), 1. act of killing a human being. 2. killing a person unlawfully but not intentionally. *n. 17.*

Mantel

man tel (man′təl), shelf above a fireplace with its supports. *n. 13.*

man tel piece (man′təl pēs′), 1. a shelf above a fireplace. 2. mantel. *n. 18.*

man tle (man′təl), 1. a loose cloak without sleeves. 2. anything that covers like a mantle. The ground had a mantle of snow. 3. clothe with a mantle. 4. flush; glow with a blush. Her cheek mantled. 5. a light, lacelike tube fixed around a flame, which gets so hot that it glows and gives light. *n., v. 3.*

Mantle

Man tu a (man′chü ə), a city in northern Italy. *n. 12.*

man u al (man′ū əl), 1. a handbook; a small book that is easy to understand and use. A cookbook is a manual. 2. a small book that explains how to use another book. 3. of the hands; done with the hands; as, manual labor. *n., adj. 8.*

manual training, hand training for school children by practice in various arts and crafts, especially in making things out of wood.

man u fac tor y (man′ū fak′tər i), a building in which things are made; a factory. *n., pl. manufactories. 14.*

man u fac ture (man′ū fak′chər), 1. making of articles by hand or by machine, especially in large quantities. 2. make, especially with division of the labor among different persons and with machines. 3. the thing manufactured. 4. make into useful articles. 5. invent; make up. The dishonest lawyer manufactured evidence. *n., v. 2.*

man u fac tur er (man′ū fak′chər ər), 1. person who manufactures. 2. person who employs a number of people in making things. *n. 5.*

man u mis sion (man′ū mish′ən), 1. freeing from slavery. 2. release from slavery. *n. 20.*

ma nure (mə nūr′ or mə nür′), 1. any substance put in or on the soil to make it rich. 2. put manure in or on. *n., v. 6.*

man u script (man′ū skript), a book or paper written by hand or typewritten. *n. 7.*

man y (men′i). There are many children in the city. Do you know many? He counted how many days it was until Christmas. *adj., more, most, n., pron. 1.*

Ma o ri (mä′ō ri), 1. member of the native brown race of New Zealand. 2. their language. *n., pl. Maoris.*

map (map), 1. a flat drawing of the earth's surface or of part of it, showing countries, towns, rivers, seas, mountains, etc. 2. a flat drawing of the sky, showing the positions of the stars, etc. 3. make a map of. 4. plan; arrange in detail; as, to map out the week's work. *n., v., mapped, mapping. 2.*

ma ple (mā′pəl), 1. a tree grown for shade, ornament, wood, or sugar. There are many kinds of maples. 2. the wood of the maple. *n. 4.*

Maple leaf

mar (mär), injure; spoil the beauty of; ruin. The nails in my father's shoes have marred our newly finished floors. *v., marred, marring. 5.*

Mar., March.

Mar a thon (mar′ə thon), the place about 20 miles northeast of Athens, where the Athenians defeated the Persians in a famous battle in 490 B.C. A runner ran with the news of victory all the way to Athens. *n. 17.*

mar a thon (mar′ə thon), 1. a foot race of 26⅕ miles, named after Marathon. 2. any long race or contest. *n.*

ma raud er (mə rôd′ər), person or animal that goes about in search of plunder; as, the night marauders of the jungle. *n. 11.*

ma raud ing (mə rôd′ing), going about in search of plunder; making raids for booty. The marauding Indians stole many horses. *adj. 17.*

mar ble (mär′bəl), 1. hard limestone, white or colored, that will take a beautiful polish. Marble is much used for statues and in buildings. 2. made of marble. 3. like marble; hard; unfeeling. 4. to color in imitation of the patterns in marble. Some books have marbled edges. 5. a small ball of marble, clay, glass, etc., used in games. 6. **Marbles** means any game played with marbles. *n., adj., v. 2.*

mar cel (mär sel′), 1. to wave (the hair) in regular, continuous waves. 2. such a wave. *v., marcelled, marcelling, n. 17.*

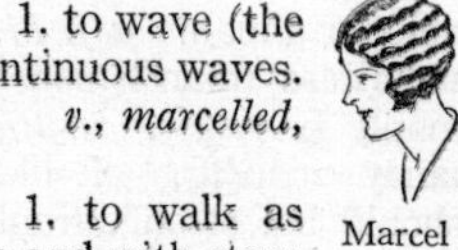
Marcel

march[1] (märch), 1. to walk as soldiers do, in time and with steps of the same length. 2. marching. The news of the enemy's march made whole villages flee. 3. music meant for marching. 4. to walk or go on steadily. The spy marched bravely to his death. 5. distance marched; a long, hard walk. 6. progress; as, the march of events. 7. to cause to march. His mother marched him right off home with her. 8. **Steal a march** means gain an advantage without being noticed. *v., n. 1.*

march[2] (märch), land along the border of a country; a border. *n.*

March[3] (märch), the third month of the year. It has 31 days. *n.*

mar chion ess (mär′shən is), in England, the wife or widow of a marquis, or a lady equal in rank to a marquis. *n. 15.*

Mar co ni (mär kō′ni), an Italian inventor (1874-1937) who perfected the wireless telegraph. *n.*

Mar co Po lo (mär′kō pō′lō), an Italian traveler (1254?-1324?) in Asia who wrote of his travels.

Mar di gras (mär′di grä′), the last day before Lent. Mardi gras is celebrated in New Orleans and other cities with parades and festivities.

mare (mãr), a female horse, donkey, etc. *n. 4.*

mar ga rin (mär′jə rin), margarine. *n.*

mar ga rine (mär′jə rēn), substitute for butter, made from vegetable oils and animal fats; oleomargarine. *n.*

marge (märj), margin. *n.* [*Used in poetry*] *13.*

mar gin (mär′jin), 1. edge; border; as, the margin of the lake. 2. the space around a page that has no writing or printing on it. 3. extra amount; amount beyond what is necessary; difference. We allow a margin of 15 minutes in catching a train. *n. 5.*

mar gin al (mär′ji nəl), 1. written in a margin. 2. of a margin. 3. on or near the margin. **Marginal land** is barely fit for farming. *adj. 13.*

mar grave (mär′grāv), a title of certain German princes. *n. 18.*

mar gue rite (mär′gə rēt′), a kind of daisy with white petals and a yellow center. *n.*

Marigold

mar i gold (mar′i gōld), a plant with yellow, orange, or red flowers. *n. 8.*

ma rine (mə rēn′), 1. of the sea; found in the sea; produced by the sea. Seals and whales are marine animals. 2. shipping; fleet; as, our merchant marine. 3. of shipping; of the navy; for use at sea; as, marine supplies. 4. a soldier serving at sea. *adj., n. 6.*

mar i ner (mar′i nər), sailor; seaman. *n. 5.*

mar i o nette (mar′i ə net′), a doll or puppet moved by strings or by the hands, often on a little stage. *n.*

Marionettes

mar ish (mar′ish), 1. marsh. 2. marshy. *n., adj.* [*Old use*] *20.*

mar i tal (mar′i təl), 1. of marriage; having to do with marriage. A man and a woman take marital vows when they marry. 2. of a husband. Providing for one's wife is a marital obligation. *adj. 19.*

mar i time (mar′i tīm), 1. on the sea; near the sea. Boston is a maritime city. 2. living near the sea. Many maritime peoples are fishermen. 3. of the sea; having to do with shipping and sailing. Ships and sailors are governed by maritime law. *adj. 8.*

mark[1] (märk), 1. something to be aimed at. Standing there, the lion was an easy mark. 2. target for scorn, etc. 3. sign; something that shows what a thing is. Courtesy is a mark of good breeding. 4. make a mark on or put one's name on to show whose a thing is. 5. tag with a mark on it. Take the price mark off from your new suit. 6. put a price mark on; tag. 7. a cross or sign made by a person who cannot write, instead of signing his name. Make your mark here. 8. written stroke or sign. She took up her pen and made a few marks on the paper. 9. make a mark on by stamping, cutting, writing, etc. 10. a grade; a letter or number to show how well one has done. My mark in arithmetic was B. 11. a line to show position. This mark shows how far you jumped. 12. put in a pin, make a line, etc., to show where a place is. Mark all the large cities on this map. 13. a standard; what is usual or proper or expected. Helen does not feel up to the mark. 14. a spot, stain, or scar; as, the mark of an old wound. 15. importance; fame; as, a man of mark. 16. see; notice; give attention to. Mark how carefully he moves. Mark well my words. 17. record (the score of a game). 18. Some special meanings are:

be marked, have marks.

beside the mark, not hitting it, hitting far to one side, above or below.

hit one's mark, succeed in something one tried to do.

make one's mark, become well known.

marked difference, a difference that is very plain. There is a marked difference between a giant and a dwarf.

mark off or **mark out,** make lines, etc., to show the position of or to separate. We marked out a tennis court. The hedge marks off one yard from another.

mark out for, set aside for, select for. He seemed marked out for trouble.

mark time, move the feet as in marching, but without going forward.

miss one's mark, fail in something one tried to do.

n., v. 1.

mark² (märk), German unit of money, worth about 24 cents in 1940. *n.*

Mark³ (märk), 1. the second book of the New Testament. It tells the story of the life of Christ. 2. the Apostle who wrote it. *n.*

marked (märkt), 1. having a mark or marks on it. 2. very noticeable; very plain. There are marked differences between apples and oranges. *adj.*

mark ed ly (mär′kid li), in a marked manner or degree; conspicuously; noticeably; plainly. *adv.*

mark er (mär′kər), 1. person or thing that marks; especially, one who keeps the score in a game. 2. bookmark. *n. 13.*

mar ket (mär′kit), 1. a meeting of people for buying and selling. 2. the people at such a meeting. 3. an open space or covered building where food, cattle, etc., are shown for sale. 4. a store for the sale of food; as, a meat market. 5. the demand for something; price offered. 6. chance to buy or sell. 7. region in which goods may be sold. South America is a market for American automobiles. 8. buy or sell in a market. 9. sell. *n., v. 1.*

mar ket a ble (mär′kit ə bəl), that can be sold; salable. *adj. 18.*

market place, the place where a market is held. *10.*

marks man (märks′mən), person who shoots well. *n., pl. marksmen. 17.*

marks man ship (märks′mən ship), skill in shooting. *n.*

Mark Twain, author of *Tom Sawyer* and *Huckleberry Finn.* His real name was Clemens (1835-1910).

marl (märl), soil containing clay and calcium carbonate, used as a fertilizer and in making cement. *n. 16.*

mar line spike or **mar lin spike** (mär′lin spīk′), pointed iron implement used by sailors to separate strands of rope in splicing, etc. *n.*

Mar lowe (mär′lō), Christopher, an English dramatist and poet (1564-1593). *n. 18.*

mar ma lade (mär′mə lād), a preserve similar to jam, made of oranges or of other fruit. The peel is usually sliced up and boiled with the fruit. *n. 13.*

Marmoset (length, including the tail, 16 in.)

Mar ma ra (mär′mə rə). The **Sea of Marmara** is a small sea between Europe and Asia. *n.*

mar mo set (mär′mə zet), a very small monkey in South and Central America with soft thick fur. See the picture just above. *n.*

mar mot (mär′mət), a bushy-tailed thickset animal, somewhat like rats and rabbits. Woodchucks and prairie dogs are marmots. *n.*

Marmot (length, including the tail, 2½ ft.)

Marne (märn), river in northern France. *n. 19.*

ma roon¹ (mə rün′), 1. put (a person) ashore and leave (him) on a desert island or in a desolate place. Pirates used to maroon people on desert islands. 2. leave in a lonely, helpless position. *v. 15.*

ma roon² (mə rün′), very dark red. *n., adj.*

marque (märk), permission from a government to capture the merchant ships of an enemy. Governments used to issue **letters of marque** to individuals authorizing them to plunder an enemy's shipping. *n. 20.*

mar quess (mär′kwis), marquis. *n. 17.*

Mar quette (mär ket′), a French Jesuit missionary and explorer of the Mississippi River (1637-1675). *n. 19.*

mar quis (mär′kwis), nobleman ranking below a duke and above an earl or count. *n. 9.*

mar quise (mär kēz′), 1. wife or widow of a marquis. 2. woman equal in rank to a marquis. *n.*

mar qui sette (mär′ki zet′), a thin silk or cotton fabric resembling voile. *n. 20.*

mar riage (mar′ij), 1. act of marrying. 2. the ceremony of being married; a wedding. 3. living together as husband and wife; married life. 4. a close union. *n. 3.*

mar riage a ble (mar′ij ə bəl), fit for marriage; as, of marriageable age. *adj. 19.*

mar ried (mar′id), 1. having to do with marriage. Married life has many duties. 2. having a husband or wife. *adj. 2.*

mar row (mar′ō), 1. a soft substance that fills the hollow central part of most bones. 2. the inmost or important part. *n. 7.*

mar ry[1] (mar′i), 1. join as husband and wife. The minister married them. 2. take as husband or wife. John married Grace. 3. become married. She married late in life. 4. give in marriage. She has married all her daughters. 5. bring together in any close union. *v., married, marrying. 2.*

mar ry[2] (mar′i), exclamation showing surprise, indignation, etc. *interj.* [*Old use*]

Mars (märz), 1. the Roman god of war. The Greeks called him Ares. 2. the planet nearest the earth. Some people think Mars is inhabited. *n. 8.*

Mar seil laise (mär′sə lāz′), the French national song, written in 1792 during the French Revolution. *n.*

Mar seilles (mär sālz′), a seaport city in southeastern France. *n. 11.*

marsh (märsh), swamp; soft wet land; lowland covered at times by water. *n. 5.*

mar shal (mär′shəl), 1. officer of various kinds, especially a police officer. A United States marshal is an officer of a Federal court whose duties are like those of a sheriff. 2. a high officer in an army. A Marshal of France is a general of the highest rank in the French Army. 3. person arranging the order of march in a parade. 4. person in charge of events. 5. arrange in proper order. He won the argument because he marshaled his facts well. 6. conduct with ceremony; as, to marshal a foreign visitor into the presence of the king. *n., v., marshaled, marshaling. 5.*

Mar shall (mär′shəl), John (1755-1835), a chief justice of the United States Supreme Court. *n. 18.*

marsh mal low (märsh′mal′ō), a soft, white, spongy candy, covered with powdered sugar. *n. 20.*

marsh mallow, a kind of mallow, a plant with pink flowers that grows in marshy places.

Marsh mallow

marsh y (mär′shi), soft and wet like a marsh. *adj., marshier, marshiest. 11.*

mart (märt), market; center of trade. New York and London are the great marts of the world. *n. 9.*

mar ten (mär′tən), 1. a slender animal like a weasel, valued for its fur. 2. the fur. *n., pl. martens* or *marten.*

Marten (length, including the tail, about 2½ ft.)

Mar tha (mär′thə), in the Bible, the sister of Lazarus and Mary. Jesus often visited her home in Bethany. *n. 5.*

mar tial (mär′shəl), 1. of war; warlike; as, martial music. 2. brave; fond of fighting; as, a boy of martial spirit. *adj. 6.*

martial law, rule by the army in a time of trouble or of war instead of by the ordinary civil authorities.

Mar tian (mär′shən), 1. of Mars. 2. an inhabitant of Mars. *adj., n.*

mar tin (mär′tin), a bird somewhat like a swallow. See the picture. There are several kinds. *n. 5.*

Purple martin (about 8 in. long)

mar ti net (mär′ti net′), person who upholds and enforces strict discipline on those under him. *n.*

Mar ti nique (mär′ti nēk′), French island in the West Indies. *n.*

mar tyr (mär′tər), 1. person who is put to death or is made to suffer greatly because of his religion or other beliefs. 2. put (a person) to death because of his beliefs. 3. person who suffers greatly. 4. cause to suffer greatly; torture. *n., v. 5.*

mar tyr dom (mär′tər dəm), 1. the suffering or death of a martyr. 2. torment; suffering. *n. 8.*

mar vel (mär′vəl), 1. wonderful thing. The airplane and the radio are among the marvels of science. 2. to wonder. *n., v., marveled, marveling. 4.*

mar vel ous or **mar vel lous** (mär′vəl əs), 1. wonderful; extraordinary. 2. improbable. Children like tales of marvelous things, like that of Aladdin and his lamp. *adj. 3.*

Mar y (mãr′i), 1. the mother of Jesus. Matthew 1:18-25. 2. a sister of Lazarus and Martha. 3. **Mary, Queen of Scots** (1542-1587), had a romantic and tragic life and was finally killed by order of her cousin, Queen Elizabeth of England. *n. 2.*

Mar y land (mer′i lənd), an Eastern State of the United States. *n. 5.*

mas cot (mas′kot), an animal, person, or thing supposed to bring good luck. The mascot of the West Point cadets is a mule. *n.*

mas cu line (mas′kū lin), 1. of men; male. 2. like a man; manly; strong; vigorous. 3. having qualities suited to a man; mannish. 4. in grammar, of the gender of male names. *Actor, king, ram,* and *bull* are masculine nouns. *adj. 5.*

mash (mash), 1. a soft mixture; a soft mass. 2. beat into a soft mass; crush to a uniform mass. 3. a warm mixture of bran, meal, and water for horses and other animals. 4. crushed malt or meal soaked in hot water for making beer. 5. mix (malt) with hot water in brewing. *n., v. 7.*

mask (mask), 1. a covering to hide or protect the face. 2. to cover the face with a mask. 3. a clay or wax likeness of a person's face. 4. a disguise. He hid his evil plans under a mask of friendship. 5. to hide or disguise. At a masked ball the guests wear masks. 6. a masked person. *n., v. 4.*

Mask to hide the face

Mask for disguise

masked ball, dance at which masks are worn.

mask er (mas′kər), person who masks or masquerades. *n.*

ma son (mā′sən), man whose work is building with stone or brick. *n. 5.*

Ma son (mā′sən), member of the world-wide secret society of Freemasons. *n.*

Mason and Dixon's line, the boundary between Pennsylvania and Maryland, formerly thought of as separating the North and the South of the United States.

Ma son ic or **ma son ic** (mə son′ik), of Masons; having to do with the society of Freemasons. *adj. 14.*

ma son ry (mā′sən ri), 1. work built by a mason; stonework; brickwork. 2. the trade or skill of a mason. *n., pl. masonries. 9.*

masque (mask), 1. an amateur dramatic entertainment, with fine costumes and scenery. Masques were much given in England in the 16th and 17th centuries, at court and at the homes of nobles. 2. masked ball; masquerade. *n. 12.*

mas quer ade (mas′kər ād′), 1. party or dance at which masks and fancy costumes are worn. 2. take part in a masquerade. 3. a disguise; a false pretense. 4. disguise oneself; go about under false pretenses. In *The Prince and the Pauper,* the poor boy masquerades as the prince, and the prince masquerades as the boy with whom he has changed clothes. *n., v. 7.*

mass[1] (mas), 1. a lump; as, a mass of dough. 2. a large quantity together; as, a mass of treasure. 3. form or collect into a mass. It would look better to mass the peonies behind the roses than to mix them. 4. majority; greater part. The great mass of men consider themselves healthy. 5. bulk; size. 6. **The masses** sometimes means the common people; the working people; lower classes of society. 7. the quantity of matter a body contains. The mass of a piece of lead is not changed by melting it. *n., v. 2.*

Mass or **mass**[2] (mas), 1. central service of worship in the Roman Catholic Church; Holy Eucharist as a sacrifice. The ritual of the Mass consists of various prayers and ceremonies. 2. music written for certain parts of it. *n.*

Mass., Massachusetts. *20.*

Mas sa chu setts (mas′ə chü′sits), a New England State of the United States. *n. 4.*

mas sa cre (mas′ə kər), 1. a wholesale, pitiless slaughter of people or animals. 2. kill (the helpless) in large numbers. *n., v. 8.*

mas sage (mə säzh′), 1. rubbing and kneading the muscles and joints to stimulate their circulation and to make them work better. A thorough massage feels good when you are tired. 2. give a massage to. Let me massage your back for you. *n., v. 12.*

mas sive (mas′iv), large and heavy; large and solid. *adj. 7.*

mass meeting, large assembly to hear or discuss some matter of common interest. The school held a mass meeting to plan for a field day.

mass y (mas′i), massive. *adj., massier, massiest. 6.*

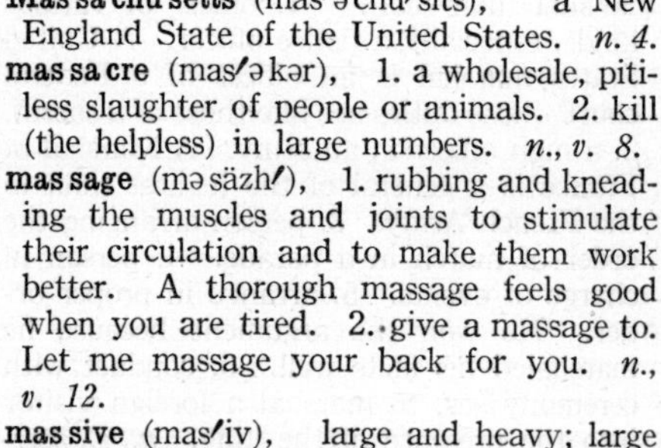

mast (mast), 1. long pole of wood or steel set up on a ship to hold the sails and rigging. 2. any tall upright pole. 3. **Before the mast** sometimes means as a common sailor, because the sailors slept in the forward part of the ship. *n. 3.*

mas ter (mas′tər), 1. person who rules

or commands people or things; director; employer; head of a household, a school, a ship, etc.; the one in control; the owner. 2. male teacher. 3. title of respect for a boy; as, Master Henry Adams. 4. an expert, such as a great artist or skilled workman; person who knows all there is to know about his work. 5. picture by a great artist. 6. being master; of a master; principal; controlling. 7. become the master of; conquer; control. She learned to master her anger. 8. become master of; become skillful at. He has mastered long division. *n., adj., v. 1.*

mas ter ful (mas′tər fəl), 1. fond of power or authority; domineering. 2. masterly; showing mastery. *adj. 12.*

mas ter ly (mas′tər li), 1. expert; skillful. 2. expertly; skillfully. *adj., adv.*

mas ter piece (mas′tər pēs′), 1. anything done or made with wonderful skill; perfect piece of workmanship. 2. a person's greatest piece of work. *n. 7.*

mas ter ship (mas′tər ship), 1. the office, duties, or position of a master, especially the office of master of a school. 2. rule; control. 3. unusual skill or knowledge. *n. 18.*

mas ter y (mas′tər i), 1. power such as a master has; rule; control. 2. the upper hand; victory. 3. very great skill or knowledge. *n., pl. masteries. 10.*

mas tic (mas′tik), yellowish resin used in making varnish, chewing gum, incense, and as an astringent. *n.*

mas ti cate (mas′ti kāt), chew. *v.*

mas ti ca tion (mas′ti kā′shən), chewing. *n. 17.*

Mastiff (about 28 in. high at the shoulder)

mas tiff (mas′tif), a large, strong dog with drooping ears and hanging lips. *n. 13.*

mas to don (mas′tə don), a very large animal much like an elephant. There are no mastodons living now. *n. 17.*

Mastodon (about 9 ft. high at the shoulder)

mat[1] (mat), 1. piece of fabric made of woven rushes, straw, rope, fiber, etc., used for floor covering, for wiping mud from the shoes, etc. A mat is like a small rug. 2. piece of material to put under a dish, vase, lamp, etc.; something to put under a hot dish when it is brought to the table. 3. anything growing thickly packed or twisted together; as, a mat of weeds. 4. twist or pack together like a mat. The swimmer's wet hair was all matted together. *n., v., matted, matting. 3.*

mat[2] (mat), a border or background for a picture, between it and the frame. *n.*

mat[3] (mat), dull; not shiny; as, a mat finish. *adj.*

match[1] (mach), 1. a short, slender piece of wood, pasteboard, etc., tipped with a mixture that takes fire when rubbed on a rough or specially prepared surface. 2. a wick or cord prepared to burn at a uniform rate, for firing guns and cannon. *n. 2.*

match[2] (mach), 1. person or thing equal to another or much like another; an equal; a mate. A boy is not a match for a man. 2. a pair that fit. Those two horses make a good match. 3. find the equal of or one exactly like; as, to match a vase so as to have a pair. 4. be similar; go well together. The rugs and the wallpaper match. 5. the coming together of two sides for a contest, game, etc.; as, a baseball match. 6. be equal to in a contest. No one could match the unknown archer. 7. try (one's skill against). Tom matched his strength against Bob's. 8. marriage. Paul and Ellen made a match of it. 9. person considered as a possible husband or wife. That young man is a good match. 10. marry. The duke matched his daughter with the king's son. *n., v.*

match less (mach′lis), so great or wonderful that it cannot be equaled. *adj. 7.*

match lock (mach′lok′), an old form of gun fired by lighting the charge of powder with a wick or cord. *n. 19.*

Soldier using a matchlock

mate (māt), 1. one of a pair. The eagle mourned his dead mate. Where is the mate to this glove? 2. join in a pair. Birds mate in the spring. 3. husband or wife. 4. marry. 5. companion or fellow worker. Hand me that hammer, mate. 6. officer of a ship next under the captain. 7. assistant; as, cook's mate. *n., v. 2.*

ma te ri al (mə tēr′i əl), 1. what a thing is made from or done with; as, dress material, building materials, writing materials, the material of which history is made. 2. of matter or things; as, the material world. 3. of the body. Food and shelter are material comforts. 4. leaving out or forgetting the spiritual side of things; worldly; as, a material point of view. 5. that matters; important. The baking is a material factor in making cake. Hard work is a material factor in success. *n., adj. 2.*

ma te ri al ism (mə tēr′i əl izm), 1. the belief that nothing exists except matter and its movement and changes, and that all action, including thought and feeling, is a part of the material world. 2. a tendency to emphasize and to care too much for material things or for the things of this world. *n. 17.*

ma te ri al ist (mə tēr′i əl ist), 1. believer in materialism. 2. person who cares too much for the things of this world and neglects spiritual needs. *n.*

ma te ri al is tic (mə tēr′i əl is′tik), of materialists; of materialism. *adj. 19.*

ma te ri al ize (mə tēr′i əl īz), 1. give material form to. An inventor materializes his ideas by building a model. 2. appear or cause to appear in material or bodily form. A spirit materialized from the smoke of the magician's fire. 3. become an actual fact; be realized. Our plans for the party did not materialize. *v. 18.*

ma te ri al ly (mə tēr′i əl i), 1. physically. He improved materially and spiritually. 2. considerably; substantially. The tide helped the progress of the boat materially. *adv. 14.*

ma ter nal (mə tėr′nəl), 1. motherly; of or like a mother. 2. related on the mother's side of the family. Everyone has two paternal grandparents and two maternal grandparents. *adj. 8.*

ma ter ni ty (mə tėr′ni ti), motherhood; being a mother. *n. 15.*

math., mathematics.

math e mat i cal (math′i mat′i kəl), 1. of mathematics; having to do with mathematics; as, mathematical problems. 2. exact; accurate. *adj. 11.*

math e mat i cal ly (math′i mat′i kəl i), 1. according to mathematics. 2. exactly; accurately. *adv.*

math e ma ti cian (math′i mə tish′ən), person skilled in mathematics. *n. 15.*

math e mat ics (math′i mat′iks), the study of number, measurement, and space. Mathematics includes arithmetic, algebra, and geometry. *n. 6.*

mat i née or **mat i nee** (mat′i nā′), a dramatic or musical performance held in the afternoon. *n. 14.*

mat ins (mat′inz), 1. in the Roman Catholic Church, the first of the seven canonical hours in the breviary. 2. in the Church of England, morning prayers. 3. morning song. *Used in poetry. n. pl. 11.*

ma tri ces (mā′tri sēz), more than one matrix. *n. pl.*

ma tric u late (mə trik′ū lāt), 1. enroll as a student; admit to membership and privileges in a college or university by enrolling. 2. enroll or be enrolled as a candidate for a degree. *v.*

mat ri mo ni al (mat′ri mō′ni əl), of marriage; having to do with marriage. *adj. 11.*

mat ri mo ny (mat′ri mō′ni), marriage. *n. 11.*

ma trix (mā′triks), that which gives origin or form to something enclosed within it. A mold for a casting or the rock in which gems are imbedded is called a matrix. *n., pl. matrices* (mā′tri sēz) or *matrixes. 17.*

ma tron (mā′trən), 1. wife or widow, especially an older married woman. 2. woman who manages the household matters of a school, hospital, dormitory, or other institution. A police matron has charge of the women in a jail. *n. 6.*

ma tron ly (mā′trən li), like a matron; suitable for a matron; dignified; grave. *adj.*

mat ted (mat′id), 1. formed into a mat; roughly tangled; as, a dog's matted hair. 2. covered with mats or matting. *adj.*

mat ter (mat′ər), 1. what things are made of; material; substance. Matter occupies space. 2. the substance of the material world; the opposite of mind or spirit. 3. what is said or written, thought of apart from the way in which it is said or written. 4. grounds; cause; basis. You have no matter for complaint in that. 5. thing; things; as, a matter of fact, a matter of record, a matter of accident. 6. things written or printed; as, printed matter. 7. amount; quantity; as, a matter of two days, a matter of ten minutes. 8. importance. Let it go since it is of no matter. 9. be important. Nothing seems to matter when you are very sick. 10. affair; as, business matters, a matter of life and death. 11. pus; to form or discharge pus. 12. Some special meanings are:

as a matter of fact, in truth; in reality.

for that matter, so far as that is concerned.

matter of course, something that is to be expected.

"What is the matter?" means "What is wrong?"

n., v. 1.

mat ter-of-fact (mat′ər əv fakt′), sticking to facts; not imaginative or fanciful. *adj.*

Mat thew (math′ū), 1. the first book of the New Testament. It tells the story of the life of Christ. 2. its author. *n. 8.*

mat ting (mat′ing), a fabric of grass, straw, hemp, or other fiber, for covering floors, for mats, for wrapping material, etc. *n. 17.*

mat tock (mat′ək), a large tool with a steel head having a flat blade on one side. A pickax having one of its ends flat is a mattock. *n. 11.*

Mattock

mat tress (mat′ris), 1. covering of strong cloth stuffed with hair, cotton, straw, etc. It is used on a bed or as a bed. 2. A spring mattress is made of wire spring stretched on a frame. It is used as a support for a mattress and bedding. *n. 7.*

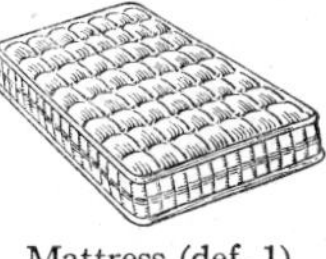

Mattress (def. 1)

ma ture (mə tūr′ or mə tür′), 1. ripen; come to full growth. These apples are maturing fast. 2. ripe; full-grown. Fifty is a mature age. 3. work out carefully. He matured his plans for the long trip. 4. fully worked out; carefully thought out; fully developed; as, mature plans. 5. fall due. This note to the bank matured yesterday. 6. due; payable. *v., adj. 4.*

ma tu ri ty (mə tūr′i ti or mə tür′i ti), 1. ripeness; full development. He reached maturity at twenty years. 2. being completed or ready. 3. falling due; the time a note or debt is payable. *n. 9.*

maud lin (môd′lin), 1. sentimental in a weak, silly way; as, maudlin sympathy for criminals. 2. tearfully silly because of drunkenness or excitement. *adj. 16.*

mau gre (mô′gər), in spite of; notwithstanding. *prep.* [*Old use*] *18.*

maul (môl), 1. a very heavy hammer or mallet. 2. beat and pull about; handle roughly. Don't maul the cat. *n., v. 9.*

maun der (môn′dər), 1. talk in a rambling, foolish way. Mrs. Poor maunders on by the hour and never says anything worth while. 2. move or act in an aimless, confused manner. The drunken man maundered along the street. *v.*

mau so le um (mô′sə lē′əm), a large, magnificent tomb. *n. 14.*

mauve (mōv), delicate, pale purple. *n., adj. 19.*

mav er ick (mav′ər ik), calf or other animal not marked with an owner's brand. *n.*

ma vis (mā′vis), the European song thrush. *n. 18.*

maw (mô), 1. mouth. 2. throat. 3. stomach. *n. 11.*

mawk ish (môk′ish), 1. sickening. 2. sickly sentimental. *adj. 17.*

max im (mak′sim), rule of conduct; proverb. "A stitch in time saves nine" and "Look before you leap" are maxims. *n. 7.*

max i mum (mak′si məm), 1. greatest amount; greatest possible amount. Sixteen miles in a day was the maximum that any of our campers walked last summer. 2. greatest; greatest possible. The maximum score is 100. *n., pl. maximums, maxima* (-mə), *adj. 9.*

may[1] (mā), 1. May I have an apple? May I go now? 2. It may rain tomorrow. The train may be late. 3. Good luck! May you be very happy. 4. *May* is sometimes used instead of *can*. *v., pt. might. 1.*

May[2] (mā), the fifth month of the year. It has 31 days. *n.*

May apple, 1. a plant about two feet high with white waxy blossoms and a yellowish, egg-shaped fruit. 2. the fruit of this plant, sometimes used as a food.

may be (mā′bi), possibly; perhaps; it may be. *adv. 4.*

May Day, the first day of May, celebrated by hanging May baskets, crowning the queen of the May, dancing around the Maypole, etc.

may flow er (mā′flou′ər), a plant whose flowers blossom in May. Mayflower usually means the trailing arbutus in the United States; in England, it means the hawthorn or cowslip. *n. 10.*

May flow er (mā′flou′ər), the ship on which the Pilgrims came to America in 1620.

may hap (mā′hap′), perhaps. *adv.* [*Old use*]

may on naise (mā′ə nāz′), a salad dressing made of olive oil, vinegar, egg yolks, and seasoning, beaten together until thick. *n. 17.*

may or (mā′ər), the man at the head of a city government. *n. 3.*

may or al ty (mā′ər əl ti), 1. position of a

mayor. 2. the term of office of a mayor. *n., pl. mayoralties. 20.*

May pole or **may pole** (mā′pōl′), a high pole decorated with flowers or ribbons, around which merrymakers dance on May Day. *n. 17.*

mayst (māst), an old form meaning **may.** "Thou mayst" means "you may." *v. 6.*

maze (māz), 1. a network of paths through which it is difficult to find one's way. 2. confusion of thought. He was in such a maze that he couldn't speak. *n. 6.*

maz y (māz′i), like a maze; intricate. *adj. 14.*

Mc Kin ley (mə kin′li), 1. William McKinley (1843-1901) was the 25th president of the United States, from 1897 to 1901. 2. **Mount McKinley** in Alaska is the highest peak in North America. *n. 13.*

Md., Maryland.

M.D., doctor of medicine. *19.*

mdse., merchandise.

me (mē). *I* and *me* mean the person speaking. Mary said, "Give the dog to me. I like it and it likes me." *pron. 1.*

Me., Maine.

mead[1] (mēd), meadow. *n.* [*Used in poetry*] *5.*

mead[2] (mēd), an intoxicating drink made from honey and water. *n.*

mead ow (med′ō), 1. piece of grassland, especially one used for raising hay. 2. low grassy land by the bank of a stream. *n. 2.*

meadow lark, a North American bird about as big as a robin, having a yellow breast marked with black.

Meadow lark (about 10 in. long)

mea ger or **mea gre** (mē′gər), 1. poor; scanty; as, a meager meal. 2. thin; lean; as, a meager face. *adj. 7.*

meal[1] (mēl), 1. breakfast, lunch, dinner, or supper. 2. the food eaten or served at any one time. *n. 2.*

meal[2] (mēl), 1. grain ground up; as, corn meal. 2. anything ground to a powderlike meal. *n.*

meal time (mēl′tīm′), the usual time for eating a meal. *n. 20.*

meal y (mēl′i), 1. like meal; dry and powdery; as, mealy potatoes. 2. of meal. 3. covered with meal; as, the miller's mealy hands. 4. pale; as, a mealy complexion. *adj., mealier, mealiest. 19.*

mean[1] (mēn), 1. intend; have as a purpose; have in mind. Do you think they mean to fight us? Do you mean to use the chops for dinner? He was meant for a soldier. **Mean well by** means have kindly feelings toward. 2. have as its thought; intend to say. Can you make out what this sentence means? *v., meant, meaning. 1.*

mean[2] (mēn), 1. of low quality or grade. "He is no mean scholar" means "he is a good scholar." 2. low in social position or rank; humble. A peasant is of mean birth; a king is of noble birth. 3. of poor appearance; shabby. 4. not noble; small-minded. It is mean to spread gossip about your friends. 5. stingy; selfish. *adj.*

mean[3] (mēn), 1. halfway between two extremes; average. 6 is the mean number between 3 and 9. 2. a condition, quality, or course of action part way between two opposites. Eight hours is a happy mean between too much sleep and too little. 3. A **means** is that or those by which something is brought about. We win trade by fair means. That was the means of saving his life. 4. **By means of** means by the use of; through. I found my dog by means of a notice in the paper. 5. **By all means** means certainly; in any possible way; at any cost. 6. **By no means** means certainly not; in no way. 7. **Means** sometimes means wealth; as, a man of means. *adj., n.*

me an der (mi an′dər), 1. to wind about; as, a river which meanders. 2. a winding path or course; as, the meanders of a brook. 3. to wander aimlessly. We were meandering through the park. 4. an aimless wandering. *v., n. 12.*

mean ing (mēn′ing), 1. that which is meant or intended. 2. that means something; expressive; as, a meaning look. *n., adj. 6.*

mean ing less (mēn′ing lis), without meaning; not making sense; not significant. *adj. 20.*

mean ly (mēn′li), in a mean manner; stingily; poorly. *adv.*

mean ness (mēn′nis), 1. being selfish in small things; stinginess. 2. being mean in grade or quality; poorness. *n. 15.*

meant (ment). See **mean**[1]. He explained what he meant. That sign was meant as a warning. *pt. and pp. of mean*[1]. *2.*

mean time (mēn′tīm′), 1. time between. 2. in the time between. 3. at the same time. *n., adv. 4.*

mean while (mēn′hwīl′), meantime. *n., adv. 4.*

mea sles (mē′zəlz), 1. an infectious disease

characterized by a bad cold, fever, and a breaking out of small red spots on the skin. Measles is a disease which children have much more commonly than grown-ups do. 2. **German measles** is a less severe disease with a similar breaking out. *n. 10.*

meas ur a ble (mezh′ər ə bəl), that can be measured. *adj. 16.*

meas ur a bly (mezh′ər ə bli), to an amount or degree that can be measured. The sick man has improved measurably since yesterday. *adv.*

meas ure (mezh′ər), 1. find the size or amount of (anything); find how long, wide, deep, large, much, etc., (a thing) is. We measured the room and found it was 20 feet long and 15 feet wide. We measured the pail by finding out how many quarts of water it would hold. 2. mark off or out (in inches, feet, quarts, etc.). Measure off 2 yards of this silk. 3. compare with a standard or with some other person or thing by estimating, judging, or acting. The soldier measured his strength with that of his enemy in a hand-to-hand fight. 4. be of a certain size or amount. Buy some paper that measures 8 by 10 inches. The party did not measure up to her expectations. 5. find out size or amount. Can he measure accurately? 6. size or amount; as, one's waist measure. **Short measure** means less than it should be; **full measure** means all it should be. 7. something with which to measure. A foot rule, a yardstick, and a quart dipper are common measures. 8. a unit or standard of measure, such as an inch, mile, acre, peck, quart, gallon, etc. 9. system of measurement; as, liquid measure, dry measure, square measure. 10. limit; bound. "Her joy knew no measure" or "was beyond measure" means it was very, very great. 11. quantity, degree, or proportion. Drunkenness and carelessness are in large measure responsible for automobile accidents. 12. particular movement or arrangement in poetry or music; as, the measure in which a poem or song is written. 13. a bar of music. 14. a dance movement. 15. action meant as means to an end. What measures shall we take to find out the thief? 16. a proposed law; a law. This measure has passed the Senate. *v., n. 1.*

Measure (def. 13)

meas ured (mezh′ərd), 1. regular; uniform; as, the measured march of soldiers. 2. rhythmical; written in poetry, not in prose. 3. deliberate; restrained; as, measured speech. *adj.*

meas ure less (mezh′ər lis), without measure; not limited; vast; as, the measureless ocean, the measureless prairie. *adj. 19.*

meas ure ment (mezh′ər mənt), 1. way of measuring; way of finding the size, quantity, or amount. Clocks give us a measurement of time. 2. measuring; finding the size, quantity, or amount. The measurement of length by a yardstick is easy. 3. size, quantity, or amount as measured. The measurements of the room are 10 by 15 feet. 4. system of measuring or of measures. *n. 5.*

meat (mēt), 1. animal flesh used for food. Fish and poultry are usually not called meat. 2. food; as, meat and drink. 3. part that can be eaten; as, the meat of a nut. *n. 1.*

meat y (mēt′i), 1. of meat. 2. like meat. 3. full of meat. 4. full of substance; solid and nourishing. It was a meaty lesson containing many valuable ideas. *adj., meatier, meatiest.*

Mec ca (mek′ə), 1. city in Arabia, where Mohammed was born. Mohammedans turn toward Mecca when praying and go there on pilgrimages. 2. place that a person longs to visit. 3. the goal of one's desires or ambitions. *n. 11.*

me chan ic (mi kan′ik), workman skilled with tools, especially one who makes, repairs, and uses machines. *n. 4.*

me chan i cal (mi kan′i kəl), 1. having to do with machinery. 2. made by machinery. 3. without expression. Her reading is very mechanical. 4. pertaining to mechanics. *adj. 7.*

me chan i cal ly (mi kan′i kəl i), 1. in a mechanical manner. He greeted us mechanically. 2. in mechanical respects. That new engine is mechanically perfect. 3. toward mechanics. Boys are more mechanically inclined than girls are. *adv.*

me chan ics (mi kan′iks), 1. the science dealing with force and motion. 2. the science of machinery. *n.*

mech a nism (mek′ə nizm), 1. machine; machinery; means or way by which something is done. 2. a system of parts working together as the parts of a machine do. The bones and muscles are parts of the mechanism of the body. *n. 8.*

mech a nize (mek′ə nīz), 1. make mechanical. 2. do by machinery, rather than by hand. Much housework can be mechanized. 3. replace men or animals by machinery in (a business, army, etc.). *v. 20.*

med al (med′əl), piece of metal like a coin, with a figure or inscription stamped on it. A medal is often given as an honor to somebody who has done something great. Sometimes medals are given to celebrate some event or to reward someone for doing something well. *n. 5.*

Medal

me dal lion (mi dal′yən), 1. large medal. 2. design, ornament, etc., shaped like a medal. *n. 15.*

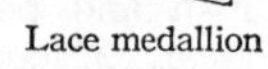

Lace medallion

med dle (med′əl), busy oneself with or in other people's things or affairs. Don't meddle with my books or my toys. *v. 5.*

med dler (med′lər), person who interferes or meddles. *n.*

med dle some (med′əl səm), meddling; interfering; likely to meddle in other people's affairs. *adj.*

Mede (mēd), a native or an inhabitant of Media. **The law of the Medes and the Persians** is law that does not change. *n. 11.*

Me de a (mi dē′ə), a witch or enchantress who helped Jason win the Golden Fleece and returned to Greece with him. Later he forsook her. *n. 12.*

me di a[1] (mē′di ə), more than one medium. Newspapers, magazines, and billboards are important media for advertising. *n. pl. 11.*

Me di a[2] (mē′di ə), an ancient kingdom of Asia, south of the Caspian Sea. *n.*

me di ae val (mē′di ē′vəl), medieval. *adj.*

me di al (mē′di əl), 1. in the middle. 2. average; ordinary. *adj. 17.*

me di an (mē′di ən), 1. in the middle; as, the median vein of a leaf. 2. the middle number of a series. 4 is the median of 1, 3, 4, 8, 9. *adj., n. 13.*

me di ate (mē′di āt for 1 and 2, mē′di it for 3), 1. be a connecting link between. 2. be a go-between; act in order to bring about an agreement between persons or sides. 3. connected, but not directly; connected through some other person or thing. A vassal's relation to his king was mediate through the lord on whose estate he lived. *v., adj. 19.*

me di a tion (mē′di ā′shən), mediating: effecting an agreement; friendly interference. *n. 14.*

me di a tor (mē′di ā′tər), one who tries to make two persons or nations friendly by helping to settle their quarrels. Mother acts as a mediator when John and Jim quarrel. *n. 10.*

med i cal (med′i kəl), having to do with healing or with the science and art of medicine; as, medical advice, medical schools, medical treatment. *adj. 5.*

med i cal ly (med′i kəl i), in medical ways or respects; for medical purposes. *adv.*

me dic a ment (me dik′ə mənt), a medicine; a substance used to cure or heal. *n.*

med i cat ed (med′i kāt′id), containing medicine; as, medicated gauze. *adj.*

Med i ci (med′i chē), rich, famous, and powerful family of Florence, Italy, during the 15th and 16th centuries. *n.*

me dic i nal (me dis′i nəl), having value as medicine; healing; helping; relieving. *adj. 12.*

med i cine (med′i sin), 1. substance, drug, or means used to cure disease or improve health. 2. science of curing disease or improving health; skill in healing; doctor's art; treatment of diseases. 3. magic power that savages believe certain men have over disease, evil spirits, and other things. *n. 2.*

medicine man, man supposed by his tribe to have magic power over disease and other things.

me di e val (mē′di ē′vəl), belonging to or having to do with the Middle Ages (the years from about 500 A.D. to about 1450 A.D.). *adj. 11.*

Me di na (mā dē′nə), a city in western Arabia. Mohammed's tomb is there. *n.*

me di o cre (mē′di ō′kər), of average quality; neither good nor bad; ordinary. *adj. 16.*

me di oc ri ty (mē′di ok′ri ti), 1. an average quality that is neither good nor bad; mediocre ability or accomplishment. 2. a mediocre person. *n., pl. mediocrities. 16.*

med i tate (med′i tāt), 1. think quietly; reflect. Monks and nuns meditate on God for hours at a time. 2. think about; consider; plan. *v. 5.*

med i ta tion (med′i tā′shən), quiet thought. *n. 6.*

med i ta tive (med′i tā′tiv), thoughtful; fond of meditating. *adj. 9.*

Med i ter ra ne an (med′i tə rā′ni ən), 1. the sea between Europe and Africa. 2. of this sea or the lands around it. *n., adj. 6.*

me di um (mē′di əm), 1. having a middle position, quality, or condition. Eggs can be cooked hard, soft, or medium. 2. that which is in the middle; neither one extreme nor the other; middle condition. 3. a substance or agent through which anything acts; a means. Radio is a medium of communication. 4. a substance in which something can live. Water is the only medium in which fish can live. 5. person through whom supposed messages from the world of spirits are sent. *adj., n., pl. mediums, media* (-ə). *4.*

med ley (med′li), 1. a mixture of things that do not belong together. 2. piece of music made up of parts of other pieces. *n., pl. medleys. 12.*

Me du sa (mi dū′sə or mi dū′sə), one of the three Gorgons or horrible monsters with snakes for hair. *n. 19.*

meed (mēd), reward; what one deserves. *n.* [*Used in poetry*] *10.*

meek (mēk), 1. mild; patient; not easily angered. 2. submitting tamely when ordered about or injured by others. The boy was as meek as a lamb when the other boys made fun of him. *adj. 4.*

meek ness (mēk′nis), patience under injury or trouble; submitting easily to another's will. *n. 6.*

meer schaum (mēr′shôm), 1. very soft, light stone used to make tobacco pipes. 2. tobacco pipe made of this material. *n.*

meet[1] (mēt), 1. come face to face with (something or someone coming from the other direction). Our car met another car on a narrow road. 2. come together; join. 3. receive and welcome on arrival. I must go to the station to meet my mother. 4. be introduced to. Have you met my sister? 5. pay (a bill, one's debts, etc.) when due. 6. a meeting; as, an athletic meet. 7. Some special meanings are:

meet in battle, duel, etc., battle with, duel with, etc.

meet needs, wishes, demands, etc., satisfy them.

meet the eye or **the ear,** be seen or heard.

meet with, come across, have, or get. We met with rough weather.

v., met, meeting, n. 1.

meet[2] (mēt), fit; proper; suitable. It is meet that you should help your friends. *adj.*

meet ing (mēt′ing), 1. coming together. 2. an assembly of persons for worship; as, a Quaker meeting, a prayer meeting. 3. any assembly. *n. 6.*

meeting house, building used for worship; church.

meg a phone (meg′ə fōn), a large horn used to increase the sound of the voice. The cheerleader at the football game yelled through a megaphone. *n. 20.*

Cheer leader using a megaphone

mel an chol y (mel′ən kol i), 1. sadness; low spirits; tendency to be sad. 2. sad; gloomy. A melancholy man is not good company. 3. causing sadness; as, a melancholy scene. *n., pl. melancholies, adj. 5.*

Mel bourne (mel′bərn), seaport city in southeastern Australia. *n. 20.*

me lee or **mê lée** (mā′lā), confused fight among a number; hand-to-hand fight among a number of fighters. *n. 16.*

mel lif lu ous (me lif′lü əs), sweetly or smoothly flowing. We enjoyed the mellifluous speech of the orator. *adj. 16.*

mel low (mel′ō), 1. soft and full-flavored from ripeness; sweet and juicy; as, a mellow apple. 2. soft and rich; as, a violin with a mellow tone, a mellow light in a picture, a mellow color. 3. softened and made wise by age and experience. 4. make or become mellow. Apples mellow after they have been picked. *adj., v. 5.*

me lo di ous (mi lō′di əs), 1. sweet-sounding; musical. 2. producing melody. *adj. 9.*

mel o dra ma (mel′ə drä′mə or mel′ə dram′ə), 1. a sensational drama with exaggerated appeal to the emotions and a happy ending. Shakespeare's play *The Merchant of Venice* is really a melodrama. 2. any writing, speech, or action that suggests a stage melodrama. *n. 17.*

mel o dra mat ic (mel′ə drə mat′ik), of, like, or suitable to melodrama; sensational and exaggerated. *adj.*

mel o dy (mel′ə di), 1. sweet music; any sweet sound. 2. tune; a succession of single tones in music. Music has melody, harmony, and rhythm. 3. the chief part in harmony; the air. *n., pl. melodies. 4.*

Watermelon

mel on (mel′ən), a large juicy fruit of a vinelike

plant much like the pumpkin, squash, and cucumber. The common melons in the United States are the watermelon, the cantaloupe or muskmelon, and the honeydew melon. *n. 6.*

melt (melt), 1. change from solid to liquid. The ice melts in the warmth of spring. Great heat melts iron. 2. dissolve. Sugar melts in water. 3. disappear gradually. The clouds melted away, and the sun came out. 4. change very gradually. In the rainbow, the green melts into blue, the blue into violet. 5. soften. Pity melted her heart. *v. 2.*

mem ber (mem′bər), 1. one who belongs to a group. Every member of the family came home for Christmas. Our church has over five hundred members. 2. part of an animal, especially a leg or an arm. *n. 1.*

mem ber ship (mem′bər ship), 1. being a member. Do you enjoy your membership in the Boy Scouts? 2. the members. The whole membership of the class was present. *n. 7.*

mem brane (mem′brān), a thin soft skin, sheet, or layer of animal tissue, lining or covering some part of the body; a similar layer of vegetable tissue. *n. 7.*

mem bra nous (mem′brə nəs), 1. of or like membrane. 2. characterized by the formation of a membrane. In membranous croup, a membrane forms in the throat and hinders breathing. *adj. 17.*

me men to (mi men′tō), thing serving as a reminder, warning, or remembrance. This ring is a memento of an old friend. These postcards are mementos of our trip abroad. *n., pl. mementos* or *mementoes. 16.*

mem oir (mem′wär), 1. a record of facts or events written from personal knowledge or from special information. The retired general wrote his memoirs of army life. 2. a record of one's own life and experiences. 3. a biography. *n. 14.*

mem o ra ble (mem′ə rə bəl), worth remembering; not to be forgotten; notable. *adj. 8.*

mem o ran da (mem′ə ran′də), memorandums. *n. pl.*

mem o ran dum (mem′ə ran′dəm), 1. short written statement for future use; note to aid one's memory. The cook made a memorandum of the groceries needed. 2. informal letter, note, or report. *n., pl. memorandums, memoranda* (-də). *13.*

me mo ri al (mi mō′ri əl), 1. something that is a reminder of some event or person, such as a statue, an arch or column, a book, or a holiday. 2. helping one remember. **Memorial Day** is a day for decorating the graves of soldiers and sailors (in most States, May 30). 3. a statement, sent to a government, a society, etc., giving facts, and usually asking to have some public wrong set right. *n., adj. 4.*

mem o rize (mem′ə rīz), commit to memory; learn by heart. *v. 7.*

mem o ry (mem′ə ri), 1. ability to remember or keep in the mind. Some children have better memories than others. 2. something that is remembered. His mother died when he was small; she is only a memory to him now. 3. **In memory of** means to help in remembering; as a reminder of. I send you this card in memory of our happy summer together. *n., pl. memories. 2.*

Mem phis (mem′fis), 1. a city in Tennessee, on the Mississippi River. 2. a city in ancient Egypt. *n. 17.*

men (men), 1. Boys grow up to be men. 2. persons in general. Men and animals have some things in common. *n. pl. 1.*

men ace (men′is), 1. threat. In dry weather forest fires are a menace. 2. threaten. Floods menaced the valley towns with destruction. *n., v. 8.*

me nag er ie (mə naj′ər i), 1. a collection of wild animals kept in cages for exhibition. 2. place where such animals are kept. *n. 13.*

mend (mend), 1. repair; set right; improve; as, to mend a road, to mend a broken doll, to mend stockings. 2. place that has been mended. The mend in your dress scarcely shows. 3. get back one's health. The child will soon mend if she drinks plenty of milk. *v., n. 3.*

men da cious (men dā′shəs), 1. lying; as, a mendacious person. 2. false; not true; as, a mendacious report. *adj.*

Men dels sohn (men′dəl sōn), German composer of music (1809-1847). *n.*

mend er (men′dər), person or thing that mends. *n. 16.*

men di cant (men′di kənt), 1. begging. Mendicant friars ask alms for charity. 2. beggar. We were surrounded by mendicants asking for money. *adj., n. 14.*

Men e la us (men′ə lā′əs), a Greek king, husband of Helen and brother of Agamemnon. *n.*

men folk (men′fōk′), men. *n. pl.*

me ni al (mē′ni əl), 1. belonging to or suited to a servant. 2. a servant who does the humblest and most unpleasant tasks. *adj., n. 12.*

men in gi tis (men′in jī′tis), very serious disease caused by inflammation of the membranes of the brain or spinal cord. *n. 13.*

Men non ite (men′ən īt), member of a Christian sect opposed to infant baptism, taking oaths, holding public office, and military service. The Mennonites wear very plain clothes. *n. 19.*

men su ra tion (men′shů rā′shən), 1. the act, art, or process of measuring. 2. the branch of mathematics that deals with length, area, and volume. *n. 20.*

-ment, suffix meaning:—

1. act or state or fact of ———ing; as in enjoyment, management.
2. state or condition or fact of being ———ed; as in amazement, astonishment.
3. product or result of ———ing; as in pavement.
4. means or instrument for ———ing; as in inducement.
5. two or more of these meanings; as in improvement, measurement, settlement.

men tal (men′təl), 1. of the mind; as, a mental test. 2. for the mind; done by the mind; as, mental arithmetic. *adj. 7.*

men tal i ty (men tal′i ti), mind; mental capacity. Persons of very low mentality are called idiots. *n., pl. mentalities. 16.*

men tal ly (men′təl i), with the mind; in the mind. He is strong physically, but weak mentally. *adv.*

men thol (men′thol), a white crystalline substance obtained from oil of peppermint, used in medicine. *n. 17.*

men tion (men′shən), 1. speak about. Do not mention the accident before the children. 2. a short statement. **Make mention of** means mention. He made mention of a tiger he had shot. *v., n. 2.*

men tor (men′tər), wise and trusted adviser. *n.*

Men tor (men′tər), a faithful friend of Ulysses. When Ulysses went to fight the Trojans, he left his son with Mentor to be taught and advised. *n.*

men u (men′ū), 1. list of the food served at a meal. 2. the food served. *n. 13.*

me ow (mi ou′), 1. the sound made by a cat or kitten. 2. to make this sound. *n., v. 13.*

mer can tile (mėr′kən til), of merchants or trade; commercial; as, a mercantile firm, mercantile law. *adj. 12.*

mer ce nar y (mėr′sə nãr′i), 1. working for money only; acting with money as the motive. 2. a soldier serving for pay in a foreign army. *adj., n., pl. mercenaries. 8.*

mer cer (mėr′sər), a dealer in cloth, especially silks. *n.* [*In British use*] *16.*

mer cer ize (mėr′sər īz), treat (cotton goods) with a substance which makes the cloth stronger and makes it hold dyes better. Mercerizing cotton gives it a silky shine or luster. *v. 13.*

mer chan dise (mėr′chən dīz), goods for sale; wares; articles bought and sold. *n. 4.*

mer chant (mėr′chənt), 1. person who buys and sells. 2. person who buys and sells wholesale or on a large scale. 3. a trader whose business is especially with foreign countries. 4. trading; pertaining to trade; as, merchant ships. *n., adj. 2.*

mer chant man (mėr′chənt mən), ship used in commerce. *n., pl. merchantmen. 18.*

merchant marine, ships used in trade, not in war.

mer ci ful (mėr′si fəl), having mercy; showing or feeling mercy; full of mercy. *adj. 6.*

mer ci less (mėr′si lis), without pity; having no mercy; showing no mercy. *adj. 6.*

mer cu ri al (mėr kūr′i əl), 1. sprightly; quick. 2. changeable; fickle. 3. caused by the use of mercury; as, mercurial poisoning. 4. containing mercury; as, a mercurial ointment. *adj. 15.*

mer cu ry (mėr′kū ri), a heavy, silver-white metal that is liquid at ordinary temperatures. Mercury is used in thermometers. *n. 5.*

Mer cu ry (mėr′kū ri), 1. the messenger of the gods, and the Roman god of commerce, skill of hands, quickness of wit, and eloquence. The Greeks called him Hermes. 2. the planet nearest the sun. *n.*

mer cy (mėr′si), 1. more kindness than justice requires; kindness beyond what can be claimed. 2. a blessing; something to be thankful for. 3. **At the mercy of** means in the power of. *n., pl. mercies. 2.*

mere[1] (mēr), nothing else than; only. The cut was a mere scratch. The mere sight of a dog makes him afraid. *adj. 2.*

mere[2] (mēr), lake; pond. *n.* [*Used in poetry*]

mere ly (mēr′li), simply; only; and nothing more; and that is all. *adv.*

mer e tri cious (mer′i trish′əs), attractive in a showy way; alluring by false charms. A wooden building painted to look like marble is meretricious. *adj. 20.*

merge (mėrj), 1. swallow up; absorb; combine and absorb; combine. The steel trusts merged various small businesses. 2. become swallowed up or absorbed in something else. The twilight merges into darkness. *v. 9.*

merg er (mėr′jər), act of merging; combination. One big company was formed by the merger of four small ones. *n. 20.*

me rid i an (mərid′iən), 1. a circle passing through any place on the earth's surface and through the North and South poles. All the places on the same meridian have the same longitude. 2. the highest point which the sun or any star reaches in the sky. 3. the highest point. *n. 6.*

me ringue (mərang′), a mixture of white of egg and sugar, beaten stiff. Meringue is often spread on puddings and pies or made into small cakes. *n.*

me ri no (mərē′nō), 1. a kind of sheep with fine wool. 2. the wool of this sheep. 3. a fine woolen yarn made from it. 4. a thin soft woolen cloth made from this or some substitute. *n., pl. merinos. 11.*

mer it (mer′it), 1. goodness; worth; value; that which deserves reward or praise. Each child will get a mark according to the merit of his work. 2. deserve. A hard-working boy merits praise. 3. real fact or quality, good or bad. I will consider your case on its merits. *n., v. 3.*

mer i to ri ous (mer′itō′riəs), worthy; deserving reward or praise. John's work was meritorious, but not brilliant. *adj. 15.*

Merle
(about 10 in. long)

merle or **merl** (mėrl), the common European blackbird. *n.* [*Used in poetry*] *17.*

Mer lin (mėr′lin), the magician who helped King Arthur. *n. 7.*

mer maid (mėr′mād′), a sea maiden in fairy tales, who is a fish from the waist down. *n. 9.*

Mermaid

mer man (mėr′man′), a man in fairy tales, who is a fish from the waist down. *n., pl. mermen. 16.*

mer ri ly (mer′ili), in a merry manner; laughing and gay. *adv.*

Mer ri mac (mer′imak), United States frigate rebuilt with iron armor by the Confederates and renamed the Virginia. The Merrimac was the first armored warship. *n. 17.*

mer ri ment (mer′imənt), laughter; fun; mirth; merry enjoyment; gaiety. *n. 9.*

mer ry (mer′i), joyous; fun-loving; full of fun; laughing and gay; as, a merry Christmas, a merry laugh. *adj., merrier, merriest. 2.*

mer ry-go-round (mer′igōround′), 1. a set of animals, etc., that go round and round by machinery. Children ride on them for fun. 2. any whirl or rapid round. The holidays were a merry-go-round of fun. *n.*

mer ry mak er (mer′imāk′ər), person who is being merry; person engaged in merrymaking. *n. 18.*

mer ry mak ing (mer′imāk′ing), 1. laughter and gaiety; fun. 2. gay festival; merry entertainment. 3. gay and full of fun; engaged in merrymaking. *n., adj.*

Mesa

me sa (mā′sə), a small high plateau with steep sides. *n.*

mes dames (mādäm′), ladies. *n. pl.* of **madam** or **madame.**

me seem eth (misēm′ith), it seems to me. *v.* [*Old use*]

me seems (misēmz′), it seems to me. *v.* [*Old use*]

mesh (mesh), 1. an open space of a net, sieve, or screen. This net has half-inch meshes. 2. **Meshes** sometimes means network. A fish was entangled in the meshes. 3. catch in a net. 4. engage or become engaged. The teeth of the small gear mesh with the teeth of a larger one. 5. **In mesh** means in gear; fitted together. *n., v. 8.*

Gear teeth in mesh

mes mer ism (mes′mərizm), hypnotism. *n. 20.*

mes mer ize (mes′mərīz), hypnotize. *v.*

Mes o po ta mi a (mes′əpətā′miə), a part of Asia between the Tigris and Euphrates rivers. *n. 10.*

mes quite (meskēt′), a tree or shrub common in the southwestern United States and Mexico. Cattle eat mesquite pods. *n.*

mess (mes), 1. a dirty or untidy mass or group of things; a dirty or untidy condition. Look what a mess you have made of your dress, playing in that dirt. 2. **Mess** or **mess up** means make dirty; spoil; make a failure of. 3. confusion; difficulty. 4. an unpleasant or unsuccessful affair or state of affairs. 5. **Mess about** or **mess around** means busy oneself without seeming to accomplish anything. 6. a group of people who take meals together regularly; especially, such a group in the army or navy. 7. a meal of such a group. He is at mess now. 8. take one's meals (with). 9. a portion of food; a portion of soft food. He caught a mess of fish. *n., v. 5.*

mes sage (mes′ij), words sent from one person to another. *n. 2.*

mes sa line (mes′ə lēn′), a thin silk with a surface like satin. *n. 13.*

mes sen ger (mes′ən jər), 1. person who carries a message or goes on an errand. 2. any animal or thing thought of as carrying a message. Each bullet was a messenger of death. 3. a herald. *n. 3.*

Mes si ah (mə sī′ə), 1. the expected deliverer of the Jewish people. 2. in Christian use, Jesus. 3. any savior. *n. 12.*

mes sieurs (mes′ərz), gentlemen. *n. pl. of* **monsieur.**

mess mate (mes′māt′), one of a group of people who eat together regularly. *n. 19.*

Messrs. (mes′ərz), messieurs, used before names as the plural of Mr.; as, Messrs. Smith and Jones. *11.*

mess y (mes′i), in a mess; like a mess; untidy; in disorder; dirty. *adj., messier, messiest.*

met (met). See **meet**[1]. My father met us this morning at ten o'clock. *pt. and pp. of meet*[1]. *1.*

me tab o lism (me tab′ə lizm), the processes of (1) building food up into living matter and (2) using living matter until it is broken down into simpler substances or waste matter. Growth and action depend on metabolism. *n. 15.*

met al (met′əl), 1. a substance such as iron, gold, silver, copper, lead, and tin. Aluminum, steel, and brass are also metals. 2. made of a metal, or of a mixture of metals. 3. broken stone used for roads. 4. material; substance. Cowards are not made of the same metal as heroes. *n., adj. 2.*

me tal lic (mi tal′ik), 1. of metal; as, a metallic compound. 2. like metal; characteristic of metal; as, the metallic luster of a beetle. *adj. 8.*

met al lur gy (met′əl ėr′ji), science or art of separating metals from their ores and refining them for use. *n.*

met a mor phose (met′ə môr′fōz), change in form; transform. The witch metamorphosed men into animals. *v. 14.*

met a mor pho sis (met′ə môr′fə sis), 1. change of form. Tadpoles become frogs by metamorphosis; they lose their tails and grow legs. 2. the changed form. 3. change of character or condition. *n., pl. metamorphoses* (-fə sēz). *8.*

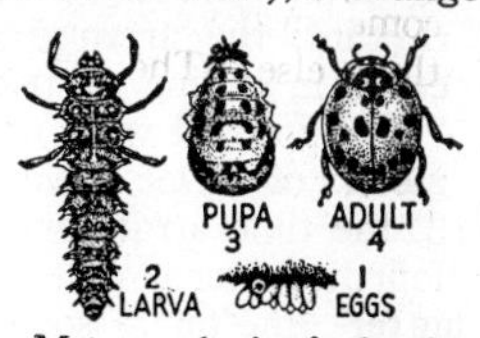

Metamorphosis of a beetle

met a phor (met′ə fôr), an implied comparison between two different things; a figure of speech in which a word or phrase that ordinarily means one thing is used of another thing in order to suggest a likeness between the two. "A copper sky" and "a heart of stone" are metaphors. *n. 10.*

met a phor i cal (met′ə for′i kəl), using metaphors; figurative. *adj. 20.*

met a phys i cal (met′ə fiz′i kəl), 1. of metaphysics; about the real nature of things. 2. highly abstract; very hard to understand. *adj. 15.*

met a phys ics (met′ə fiz′iks), a branch of philosophy that tries to explain reality and knowledge; the study of the real nature of things. *n. 12.*

mete (mēt), give to each his share or what is due him. The judges will mete out praise and blame. *v. 11.*

me te or (mē′ti ər), shooting star; mass of stone or metal that comes toward the earth from outer space with enormous speed. Meteors become so hot from rushing through the air that they glow and often burn up. *n. 6.*

me te or ic (mē′ti or′ik), 1. of meteors; as, a meteoric shower. 2. flashing like a meteor; swift; brilliant and soon ended; as, a man's meteoric rise to fame. 3. of the atmosphere; dependent on the weather. *adj. 20.*

me te or ite (mē′ti ər īt), a mass of stone or metal that has reached the earth from outer space. *n.*

me te or o log i cal (mē′ti ər ə loj′i kəl), having to do with the atmosphere and weather; pertaining to meteorology. *adj. 16.*

me te or ol o gy (mē′ti ər ol′ə ji), the science dealing with the atmosphere and weather—winds, moisture, temperature, etc. Forecasts of the weather depend on meteorology. *n.*

me ter[1] (mē′tər), 1. a measure of length used in many countries. A meter is equal to 39.37 inches. 2. any kind of poetic rhythm; the arrangement of beats or accents in a line of poetry. The meter of "Jack and Jill went up the hill" is not the meter of "One, two, buckle my shoe." 3. the time arrangement in music. Three-fourths meter is waltz time. *n. 4.*

me ter[2] (mē′tər), something that measures, or measures and records; as, a gas meter, a water meter. *n.*

me thinks (mi thingks′), it seems to me. *v. [Old use] 5.*

meth od (meth′əd), 1. way of doing something; as, a method of teaching music. Roasting is one method of cooking meat. 2. order or system in getting things done or in thinking. If you used more method, you wouldn't waste so much time. *n. 3.*

me thod i cal (mi thod′i kəl), done according to a method; arranged or acting according to a method. *adj. 13.*

Meth od ism (meth′əd izm), the doctrine, organization, and manner of worship of the Methodist Episcopal Church. *n.*

Meth od ist (meth′əd ist), 1. member of a church which had its origin in the work of John Wesley. 2. of the Methodists or Methodism. *n., adj. 12.*

me thought (mi thôt′), it seemed to me. *pt. of* **methinks.** *[Old use] 6.*

Me thu se lah (mi thü′zə lə), 1. in the Bible, a man who lived 969 years. 2. a very old man. *n. 18.*

me tic u lous (mi tik′ū ləs), very careful or too particular about small details. *adj.*

me tre (mē′tər). See **meter**[1]. *n.*

met ric (met′rik), 1. The **metric system** is a decimal system of weights and measures, or one which counts by tens. It is based on the meter (about 39½ inches long), and uses tenths and hundredths of the meter, and ten-meter and hundred-meter lengths. A cubic centimeter of water weighs one gram, the metric unit of weight. 2. of or about the meter or the metric system. 3. metrical. *adj. 12.*

met ri cal (met′ri kəl), 1. of or written in meter, not in prose; as, a metrical translation of Homer. 2. of or pertaining to measurement. *adj. 17.*

Metronome

met ro nome (met′rə nōm), clocklike device that can be adjusted to tick at different speeds. Children practicing music sometimes use a metronome to help them keep time. *n.*

me trop o lis (mi trop′ə lis), 1. the most important city of a country or region. New York is the metropolis of North America. 2. large city; important center. Chicago is a busy metropolis. *n. 7.*

met ro pol i tan (met′rə pol′i tən), 1. of large cities; as, metropolitan newspapers. 2. person who lives in large cities and knows their ways. *adj., n. 10.*

met tle (met′əl), disposition; spirit; courage. **On one's mettle** means ready to do one's best. *n. 10.*

met tle some (met′əl səm), full of mettle; spirited. *adj.*

mew[1] (mū), 1. the sound made by a cat or kitten. 2. cry like a cat; say meow. Our kitten mews when it gets hungry. *n., v. 4.*

mew[2] (mū), a sea gull; a gull. *n.*

mew[3] (mū), 1. a cage. 2. to shut up as if in a cage; conceal; confine. *n., v.*

mewl (mūl), cry like a baby; whimper. *v.*

Mex i can (mek′si kən), 1. of Mexico or its people. 2. native or inhabitant of Mexico. *adj., n. 6.*

Mex i co (mek′si kō), 1. a country in North America, south of the United States. 2. The **Gulf of Mexico** is a gulf of the Atlantic, south of the United States and east of Mexico. *n. 4.*

Mexico City, the capital of Mexico.

mez za nine (mez′ə nēn), a low story between two higher stories of a building. It is usually just above the ground floor. Sometimes it extends only part way over the floor below it, forming a balcony. *n.*

mfg., manufacturing. *20.*

mi (mē), in music, the third tone of the scale. Do, re, mi, fa, sol, la, ti, do are the names of the tones of the scale. *n.*

mi., mile; miles. *7.*

Mi am i (mī am′i), a city in southeastern Florida. *n.*

mi ca (mī′kə), isinglass, a mineral that divides into thin, partly transparent layers. Mica is used in lanterns and stove doors, where the heat might break glass. *n. 11.*

Mi cah (mī′kə), 1. a Hebrew prophet. 2. a book of the Old Testament. *n. 17.*

mice (mīs), more than one mouse. *n. pl. 4.*

Mich., Michigan.

Mi chael (mī′kəl), archangel who led the loyal angels in defeating the revolt of the angel Lucifer. *n.*

Mich ael mas (mik′əl məs), feast of the archangel Michael, September 29. *n. 14.*

Mi chel an ge lo (mī′kəl an′jə lō), an Italian sculptor, painter, architect, and poet (1475-1564). *n.*

Mich i gan (mish′i gən), 1. a Middle Western State of the United States. 2. one of the Great Lakes. *n. 6.*

mick le (mik′əl), much. *adj., adv., n.* [*In Scottish use*] *18.*

mi crobe (mī′krōb), a germ. Some microbes cause diseases. *n. 12.*

mi crom e ter (mī krom′i tər), a device for measuring very small distances, angles, etc. *n. 15.*

Micrometer

mi cro ör gan ism (mī′ krō ôr′gən izm), an animal or vegetable organism too small to be seen except with a microscope. *n.*

mi cro phone (mī′krə fōn), 1. a device for increasing small sounds. 2. a radio device for transmitting sounds. *n.*

mi cro scope (mī′krə skōp), an instrument with a lens or combination of lenses for magnifying objects so that one can see clearly things not visible to, or not clearly visible to, the naked eye. *n. 7.*

Microscope: 1, screws to adjust eyepiece; 2, eyepiece; 3, screw to adjust focus; 4, platform to hold objects; 5, mirror.

mi cro scop ic (mī′krə-skop′ik), 1. that cannot be seen without using a microscope; tiny; as, microscopic germs. 2. like a microscope; suggesting a microscope; as, microscopic exactness, a microscopic eye for mistakes. 3. of a microscope; with a microscope. *adj. 8.*

mi cro scop i cal ly (mī′krə skop′i kəl i), 1. by the use of a microscope. 2. as if with a microscope; in great detail. *adv.*

mid[1] or **'mid** (mid), amid. *prep.* [*Used in poetry*] *4.*

mid[2] (mid), middle. *adj.*

mid-, prefix meaning:—
1. the middle point or part of.
2. of, in, or near the middle of.

Mi das (mī′dəs), in Greek legend, a king whose touch was supposed to turn everything to gold. *n. 12.*

mid day (mid′dā′), noon. *n. 8.*

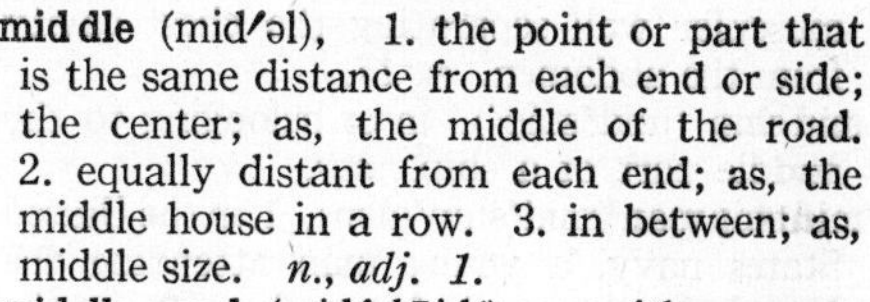

mid dle (mid′əl), 1. the point or part that is the same distance from each end or side; the center; as, the middle of the road. 2. equally distant from each end; as, the middle house in a row. 3. in between; as, middle size. *n., adj. 1.*

mid dle-aged (mid′əl ājd′), neither young nor old; from about 40 to about 60 years of age. *adj.*

Middle Ages, the period between ancient and modern times (from about 500 A.D. to about 1450 A.D.).

middle class, people between the aristocracy or the very wealthy and the working class.

mid dle man (mid′əl man′), trader or merchant who buys goods from the producer and sells them to a retailer or directly to the consumer. *n., pl. middlemen. 18.*

Mid dle sex (mid′əl seks), a county in southeastern England. *n. 17.*

Middle West, part of the United States west of the Appalachian Mountains, east of the Rocky Mountains, and north of the Ohio River and the southern boundaries of Missouri and Kansas.

mid dling (mid′ling), 1. medium in size, quality, grade, etc. 2. moderately; fairly. *Used in common talk. adj., adv. 15.*

mid dlings (mid′lingz), 1. products of medium size, quality, grade, or price. 2. coarse particles of ground wheat mixed with bran. *n. pl.*

mid dy (mid′i), 1. a midshipman. *Used in common talk.* 2. a blouse like a sailor's. *n., pl. middies. 12.*

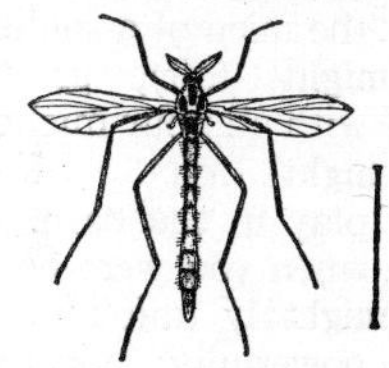

Midge. Line shows actual length.

midge (mij), a kind of small insect. *n. 16.*

midg et (mij′it), very small person; dwarf. *n. 20.*

mid land (mid′lənd), 1. the middle part of a country; the interior. 2. in or of the midland. *n., adj. 16.*

mid most (mid′mōst), in the very middle; middle. *adj. 19.*

mid night (mid′nīt′), 1. twelve o'clock at night; the middle of the night. 2. of or like midnight. *n., adj. 2.*

MIDRIB

mid rib (mid′rib′), central vein of a leaf. *n.*

mid riff (mid′rif), diaphragm;

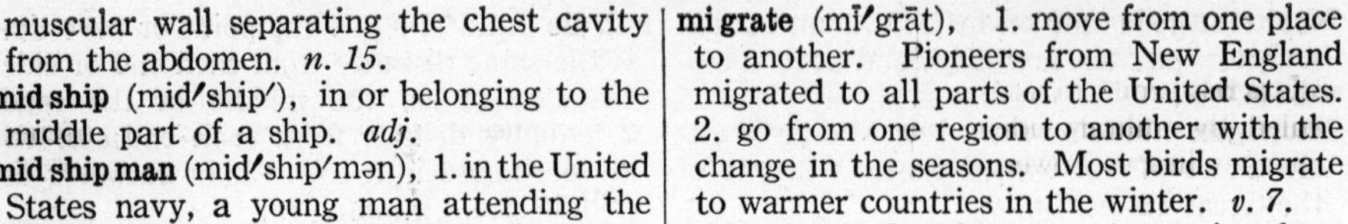

muscular wall separating the chest cavity from the abdomen. *n. 15.*

mid ship (mid′ship′), in or belonging to the middle part of a ship. *adj.*

mid ship man (mid′ship′mən), 1. in the United States navy, a young man attending the Naval Academy at Annapolis. 2. in the British navy, a young graduate of the governmental naval schools, or an officer of the same rank. 3. formerly, a boy or young man who assisted the officers of a ship. *n., pl. midshipmen. 20.*

midst[1] (midst), middle. **In the midst of** sometimes means among. **In our midst** means among us. *n. 3.*

midst[2] or **'midst** (midst), amidst. *prep.*

mid stream (mid′strēm′), the middle of the stream. *n.*

mid sum mer (mid′sum′ər), 1. the middle of summer. 2. in the middle of summer. 3. the time near June 21. *n., adj. 7.*

mid way (mid′wā′), halfway; in the middle. *adj., adv. 7.*

Mid west ern (mid′wes′tərn), of or in the Middle West. *adj.*

mid wife (mid′wīf′), woman who helps women in childbirth. *n., pl. midwives. 11.*

mid win ter (mid′win′tər), 1. the middle of winter. 2. in the middle of winter. 3. December 22, or the time just before or after. *n., adj. 12.*

mien (mēn), how one bears oneself; one's air, appearance, look, manner, or aspect; as, the mien of a soldier. *n. 7.*

might[1] (mīt), great power; strength. Work with all your might. *n. 1.*

might[2] (mīt). Mother said that we might play in the barn. He might have done it when you were not looking. *pt. of* **may.**

might i ly (mīt′i li), 1. in a mighty manner; powerfully; vigorously. Samson strove mightily. 2. very much; greatly. We were mightily pleased at winning. *adv.*

might y (mīt′i), 1. powerful; strong. 2. very great. 3. very. *Used in common talk. adj., mightier, mightiest, adv. 2.*

mi gnon ette (min′yən et′), a plant with spikes of small, very fragrant, greenish-white flowers. *n. 11.*

Mignonette

mi graine (mī′grān), a severe headache, usually on one side only. *n.*

mi grant (mī′grənt), 1. migrating; roving. 2. person, animal, bird, or plant that migrates. *adj., n. 19.*

mi grate (mī′grāt), 1. move from one place to another. Pioneers from New England migrated to all parts of the United States. 2. go from one region to another with the change in the seasons. Most birds migrate to warmer countries in the winter. *v. 7.*

mi gra tion (mī grā′shən), 1. moving from one place to another. 2. a number of people or animals migrating together. *n. 9.*

mi gra to ry (mī′grə tō′ri), moving from one place to another; as, migratory laborers, a migratory pain, migratory birds. *adj. 11.*

mi ka do or **Mi ka do** (mi kä′dō), a title of the emperor of Japan. The Japanese seldom use this title except in poetry. *n., pl. mikados or Mikados.*

Mi lan (mi lan′), city in northern Italy. *n. 9.*

milch (milch), giving milk; kept for the milk it gives; as, a milch cow. *adj. 14.*

mild (mīld), 1. gentle; kind; as, a mild old gentleman. 2. calm; warm; temperate; not severe; as, mild weather. 3. soft or sweet to the senses; not sharp, sour, bitter, or strong in taste; as, mild cheese, a mild cigar. *adj. 2.*

mil dew (mil′dū or mil′dü), 1. a kind of fungus that appears on plants or on paper, clothes, leather, etc., during damp weather. Mildew killed the rosebuds in our garden. Damp clothes left in a pile will show mildew in a few days. 2. become covered with mildew. *n., v. 8.*

mild ness (mīld′nis), being mild; gentleness; as, the mildness of the weather in spring. *n. 11.*

mile (mīl), a distance equal to 5280 feet. A nautical or geographical mile is about 6080 feet. *n. 1.*

mile age (mīl′ij), 1. miles covered or traveled; as, the track mileage of a railroad, the mileage of our car this summer. 2. an allowance for traveling expenses at so much per mile. Congressmen are allowed mileage from their homes to Washington, D. C. *n. 12.*

mile post (mīl′pōst′), a post set up to show distance in miles to a certain place. A milepost showed that we were 38 miles from Chicago. *n.*

mile stone (mīl′stōn′), 1. a stone set up on a road to show distance in miles to a certain place. 2. some event which marks a stage in the journey of life. *n. 16.*

Milestone

mil i tant (mil′i tənt), 1. fighting; warlike. 2. militant person. *adj., n. 14.*

mil i ta rism (mil′i tə rizm), 1. policy of making military organization and power very strong. 2. military spirit and ideals. *n.*

mil i ta rist (mil′i tə rist), 1. person who is ruled by military ideas; one who believes that military power is very important. 2. one skilled in warfare. *n.*

mil i tar y (mil′i tãr′i), 1. of soldiers or war. 2. done by soldiers. 3. fit for soldiers; suitable for war. 4. warlike. 5. the army; soldiers. *adj., n. 3.*

mil i tate (mil′i tāt), fight (in a figurative sense); act; operate. Bad weather militated against the success of our picnic. *v. 16.*

mi li tia (mi lish′ə), a military force; army of citizens partly trained for war. Every State has a militia called the National Guard. *n. 7.*

milk (milk), 1. the white liquid from cows, which we drink and use in cooking. 2. Many other animals produce milk for their young ones. 3. draw milk from (a cow, goat, etc.). 4. the white juice of a plant, tree, nut, etc. *n., v. 1.*

milk maid (milk′mād′), woman who milks cows or works in a dairy. *n. 9.*

milk man (milk′man′), man who sells milk or delivers it to customers. *n., pl. milkmen. 16.*

milk sop (milk′sop′), soft, unmanly, cowardly fellow. *n.*

milk weed (milk′wēd′), a weed with white juice that looks like milk. *n. 13.*

milk-white (milk′hwīt′), white as milk. *adj. 14.*

milk y (mil′ki), 1. like milk; white as milk. 2. of milk; containing milk. *adj., milkier, milkiest. 6.*

POD

Milkweed

Milky Way, broad band of faint light that stretches across the sky at night. It is made up of countless stars, too far away to be seen separately without a telescope.

mill¹ (mil), 1. a machine for grinding corn, wheat, or other substances. 2. the building where such a machine is housed. 3. grind very fine. 4. a building where manufacturing is done. A cotton mill makes thread from cotton. 5. make grooves such as there are around the edges of coins; groove or stamp. 6. move about in a circle in a confused way. Cattle sometimes mill when they are frightened. *n., v. 1.*

A small mill (def. 2)

mill² (mil), one tenth of a cent in United States money. *n.*

mil len ni al (mi len′i əl), 1. of a thousand years. 2. like Christ's millennium; fit for the millennium; to be expected only when the millennium comes. *adj.*

mil len ni um (mi len′i əm), 1. a period of a thousand years. The world is many millenniums old. 2. the period of a thousand years during which Christ is to reign on earth. 3. a period of righteousness and happiness. *n. 15.*

mill er (mil′ər), 1. one who owns or runs a mill, especially a flour mill. 2. an insect whose wings look as if they were powdered with flour. *n. 4.*

Miller (def. 2)

mil let (mil′it), a grain used for food in Asia and in southern Europe. In the United States, millet is grown chiefly for hay. *n. 11.*

mil li me ter or **mil li me tre** (mil′i mē′tər), one thousandth of a meter, or .03937 inch. *n. 19.*

mil li ner (mil′i nər), person who makes or sells women's hats. *n. 16.*

mil li ner y (mil′i ner′i), 1. women's hats. 2. the business of making, trimming, and selling women's hats. *n. 10.*

mil lion (mil′yən), one thousand thousand; 1,000,000. *n., adj. 2.*

mil lion aire (mil′yən ãr′), 1. person who has a million dollars. 2. very wealthy person. *n. 6.*

mil lionth (mil′yənth), 1. last in a series of a million. 2. one of a million equal parts. *adj., n.*

mill race (mil′rās′), 1. the current of water that drives a mill wheel. 2. the channel in which it flows to the mill. *n.*

mill stone (mil′stōn′), 1. one of a pair of round flat stones for grinding corn, wheat, etc. 2. heavy burden. 3. anything that grinds or crushes. *n. 7.*

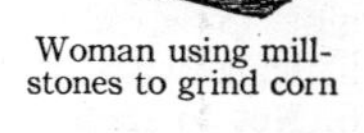

Woman using millstones to grind corn

mill wheel, a wheel that supplies power for a mill.

mill work (mil′wėrk′), 1. doors, windows,

moldings, and other things made in a wood mill. 2. work in a mill. *n.*

Mil ton (mil′tən), John, a great English poet (1608-1674). *n. 6.*

Mil wau kee (mil wô′ki), a city in south-eastern Wisconsin. *n. 12.*

mime (mīm), 1. jester; clown. 2. imitate; mimic. 3. a coarse farce among the ancient Greeks and Romans, using funny actions and gestures. 4. an actor. *n., v. 19.*

mim e o graph (mim′i ə graf′), 1. a machine for making copies of written or typewritten material. *Trade name.* 2. make (copies) with a mimeograph. *n., v. 17.*

mim ic (mim′ik), 1. make fun of by imitating. We like to get John to mimic our old music teacher. 2. person or thing that imitates. 3. copy closely. A parrot can mimic a person's voice. 4. resemble closely. There are insects which mimic leaves. 5. not real, but imitated or pretended for some purpose. The soldiers staged a mimic battle for the visiting general. *v., mimicked, mimicking, n., adj. 9.*

mim ic ry (mim′ik ri), 1. mimicking. 2. **Protective mimicry** means the close resemblance of an animal to its surroundings or to some different animal, which prevents its enemies from attacking it. *n., pl. mimicries. 15.*

Protective mimicry: a butterfly that mimics dead leaves.

mi mo sa (mi mō′sə), a tree, shrub, or plant growing in warm regions. There are many kinds. *n. 19.*

min., minute; minutes. *12.*

min a ret (min′ə ret′), a slender, high tower attached to a Mohammedan mosque, from which a crier calls the people to prayer. *n. 15.*

mince (mins), 1. chop up into very small pieces. 2. meat cut up into very small pieces. 3. mincemeat. 4. put on fine airs in speaking or walking. 5. walk with little short steps. 6. **Not to mince matters** means to speak plainly and frankly. *v., n. 6.*

Minaret

mince meat (mins′mēt′), a mixture of chopped meat, apples, suet, raisins, currants, spices, etc., used as a filling for pies. *n.*

minc ing (min′sing), putting on an elegant and refined way of speaking, walking, or behaving. *adj.*

mind (mīnd), 1. the part of a person that knows and thinks and feels and wishes and chooses. 2. intelligence; mental ability; intellect. To learn arithmetic easily you must have a good mind. 3. what one thinks or feels. Speak your mind freely. 4. notice; observe. 5. take care. 6. attend to; take care of. 7. obey. 8. remember. 9. feel bad about; object to. Some people don't mind cold weather. 10. Some special meanings are:

be of one mind, have the same opinion.

have a mind to, intend to; think of doing.

have in one's mind, remember; think of; consider.

know one's own mind, know what one wants and stick to it.

make up one's mind, decide.

on one's mind, in one's mind; in one's thoughts.

pass out of mind, be forgotten.

put in mind, remind.

set one's mind on, want very much.

the mind's eye, imagination.

to my mind, to my way of thinking; in my opinion.

n., v. 1.

mind ed (mīn′did), 1. having a certain kind of mind; as, high-minded. 2. inclined; disposed. Elizabeth was minded to argue with the teacher about her mark. *adj.*

mind ful (mīnd′fəl), 1. thinking; being aware. Mindful of your advice, I went slowly. 2. taking thought; careful. We had to be mindful of every step we took on the slippery sidewalk. *adj. 7.*

mind less (mīnd′lis), 1. without mind; senseless. 2. thoughtless; careless. *adj. 18.*

mine[1] (mīn), 1. of me; belonging to me. This book is mine. 2. the one or ones belonging to me. Your shoes are black; mine are brown. 3. my (used only before a vowel or *h*); as, mine eyes, mine heart. *Old use. pron., adj. 1.*

mine[2] (mīn), 1. a large hole or space dug in the earth in order to get out something valuable; as, a coal mine, a gold mine. 2. dig a mine; make a hole or space underground. 3. get from a mine; as, to mine coal, gold, etc. 4. dig in for coal, gold, etc.; as, to mine the earth. 5. a rich or plentiful source. The book proved to be a regular mine of information about radio. 6. an underground passage in which gunpowder is placed to blow up an enemy's forts, etc. 7. make underground passages below. 8. a bomb to be placed just under the surface of the sea, at the entrance to harbors, etc., to blow up an enemy's ships if they should come there. 9. lay mines under; as, to mine the mouth of a harbor. *n., v.*

min er (mīn′ər), man who works in a mine. *n. 6.*

min er al (min′ər əl), 1. a substance obtained by mining or digging in the earth. Coal is a mineral. 2. any substance that is neither plant nor animal. 3. like a mineral. 4. containing minerals; as, mineral water. *n., adj. 4.*

min er al o gy (min′ər al′ə ji), the science of minerals. *n. 17.*

Mi ner va (mi nėr′və), the Roman goddess of wisdom, the arts, and war. The Greeks called her Athena. *n. 11.*

min gle (ming′gəl), mix. Two rivers which join mingle their waters. He is very shy and does not mingle much with the children at school. *v. 3.*

min i a ture (min′i ə chər), 1. anything represented on a small scale. In the museum there is a miniature of the ship *Mayflower.* 2. done on a very small scale; tiny. Mary had miniature furniture for her little doll. 3. a very small painting, usually a portrait. *n., adj. 8.*

min i mize (min′i mīz), 1. reduce to the least possible amount or degree. The polar explorers took every precaution to minimize the dangers of their trip. 2. state at the lowest possible estimate; make the least of. An ungrateful person minimizes the help others have given him. *v. 15.*

min i mum (min′i məm), 1. least possible amount; lowest amount. Each of the children had to drink some milk at breakfast; half a glass was the minimum. 2. least possible; lowest. The minimum weight is 10 pounds. *n., pl. minimums, minima* (-mə), *adj. 8.*

min ing (mīn′ing), 1. working mines for ores, coal, etc. 2. laying explosive mines. *n.*

min ion (min′yən), 1. servant or follower ready to do bad deeds for his master. 2. a darling; a favorite. *n. 9.*

min is ter (min′is tər), 1. clergyman serving a church; spiritual guide; pastor. 2. serve as the minister of a church. 3. act as a servant or nurse; be of service or aid; be helpful; as, to minister to a sick man's wants. 4. person who is given charge of a department of the government; as, the Minister of War. 5. person sent to a foreign country to represent his own government; as, the United States Minister to Persia. *n., v. 2.*

min is te ri al (min′is tēr′i əl), 1. of a minister; having to do with a minister. 2. suited to a clergyman; as, a ministerial manner. *adj. 15.*

min is trant (min′is trənt), 1. ministering. 2. one who ministers. *adj., n. 16.*

min is tra tion (min′is trā′shən), 1. service as a minister of a church. 2. help; aid. *n. 11.*

min is try (min′is tri), 1. the office, duties, or time of service of a minister. 2. the ministers of a church. 3. the ministers of a government. 4. ministering or serving. *n., pl. ministries. 6.*

mink (mingk), 1. a weasellike animal that lives in water part of the time. 2. its valuable brown fur. *n. 12.*

Mink (length, including the tail, about 2 ft.)

Minn., Minnesota.

Min ne ap o lis (min′i ap′ə lis), a city in southeastern Minnesota, on the Mississippi River. *n. 12.*

Min ne so ta (min′i sō′tə), a Middle Western State of the United States. *n. 7.*

min now (min′ō), 1. a very small freshwater fish. 2. any fish when it is very small. *n. 9.*

mi nor (mī′nər), 1. smaller; lesser. Correct the important errors in your paper, but do not bother with the minor ones. 2. person under the legal age of responsibility. You cannot vote while you are a minor. 3. Minor is used in music for certain sets of intervals, chords, scales, and keys. *adj., n. 8.*

mi nor i ty (mi nor′i ti), 1. the smaller number or part; less than half. A minority of the children wanted a party, but the majority chose a picnic. 2. the condition or time of being under the legal age of responsibility. *n., pl. minorities. 8.*

Min o taur (min′ə tôr), in Greek mythology, a monster, half man and half bull, kept in the labyrinth at Crete and fed with human flesh. *n. 19.*

min ster (min′stər), 1. the church of a

monastery. 2. a large or important church; a cathedral. *n. 9.*

min strel (min′strəl), 1. a singer or musician in the household of a lord in the Middle Ages. 2. a singer or musician who went about and sang or recited poems, often of his own making. 3. member of a company of actors, usually white men made up as Negroes, giving songs, music, and jokes supposed to have come from the Negroes. *n. 6.*

min strel sy (min′strəl si), 1. the art or practice of a minstrel. 2. songs, ballads, etc. 3. a company of minstrels. *n., pl. minstrelsies. 12.*

mint[1] (mint), 1. a sweet-smelling plant used for flavoring. Peppermint and spearmint are kinds of mint. 2. piece of candy flavored with mint. *n. 6.*

mint[2] (mint), 1. place where money is coined. 2. to coin (money). 3. a large amount. A million dollars is a mint of money. *n., v.*

min u end (min′ū end), a number or quantity from which another is to be subtracted. In 100−23=77, the minuend is 100. *n. 20.*

min u et (min′ū et′), 1. a slow, stately dance. 2. music for it. *n. 11.*

Dancing the minuet

mi nus (mī′nəs), 1. the sign (−) meaning that the quantity following it is to be subtracted. 2. less; lacking; decreased by. 12 minus 3 leaves 9. 3. less than zero. If you have no money, and owe someone 3 cents, you have —3c. *n., prep., adj. 10.*

min ute[1] (min′it), 1. 60 minutes of time make one hour. 2. 60 minutes of angle make 1 degree or $\frac{1}{360}$ of a circumference. 3. a short time; an instant. I'll be there in a minute. 4. an exact point of time. The minute you see him coming, please tell me. 5. The **minutes of a meeting** means the account of what happened at the meeting, kept by the secretary. *n. 1.*

mi nute[2] (mī nūt′ or mī nüt′), 1. very small; tiny. 2. going into small details. He gave me minute instructions about my work. *adj.*

min ute man (min′it man′), member of the American militia just before and during the Revolution, who held themselves ready for military service at a minute's notice. *n., pl. minutemen.*

mi nute ness (mī nūt′nis or mī nüt′nis), 1. extreme smallness; being tiny. 2. attention to very small details. *n. 17.*

mi nu ti ae (mi nū′shi ē or mi nü′shi ē), very small matters; exact details; trifling details. *n. pl. 20.*

minx (mingks), a pert girl. *n. 19.*

mir a cle (mir′ə kəl), 1. a wonderful happening that is above, against, or independent of the known laws of nature. It would be a miracle if the sun should stand still in the heavens for an hour. 2. something marvelous; a wonder. 3. remarkable example. She must be a miracle of patience to do all that fine hemming. *n. 4.*

mi rac u lous (mi rak′ū ləs), 1. going against the known laws of nature. 2. wonderful; marvelous. *adj. 8.*

mi rage (mi räzh′), an appearance of scenes or objects which are really somewhere else, due to conditions of the air which make it reflect images of distant objects, often upside down. Travelers on the desert may see a mirage of palm trees and water. *n. 16.*

mire (mīr), 1. soft deep mud; slush. 2. get stuck in mire. He mired his horses and had to go for help. 3. to soil with mud or mire. *n., v. 5.*

mir ror (mir′ər), 1. a glass in which you can see yourself; a looking glass; a surface that reflects light. 2. whatever reflects or gives a true description. This book is a mirror of the times. 3. reflect as a mirror does. The water was so still that it mirrored the trees along the bank. *n., v. 3.*

mirth (mėrth), merry fun; being joyous or gay; laughter. *n. 3.*

mirth ful (mėrth′fəl), merry; jolly; gay; laughing. *adj. 9.*

mir y (mīr′i), muddy; swampy. *adj. 14.*

mis-, prefix meaning:—bad or badly; wrong or wrongly; as in misconduct, misprint, and misrule.

mis ad ven ture (mis′əd ven′chər), bad luck; mishap; unfortunate accident. *n. 16.*

mis an thrope (mis′ən thrōp), hater of mankind; person who dislikes or distrusts human beings. *n. 20.*

mis ap plied (mis′ə plīd′), put to a wrong use; applied wrongly. *adj. 16.*

mis ap ply (mis′ə plī′), apply wrongly. *v., misapplied, misapplying.*

mis ap pre hend (mis′ap ri hend′), misunderstand. *v.*

mis ap pre hen sion (mis′ap ri hen′shən), misunderstanding; wrong idea. *n. 14.*

mis ap pro pri ate (mis′ə prō′pri āt), 1. put to a wrong use. 2. use dishonestly as one's own. The treasurer had misappropriated the club funds. *v.*

mis ap pro pri a tion (mis′ə prō′pri ā′shən), 1. dishonest use as one's own. 2. any act of putting to a wrong use. *n.*

mis be have (mis′bi hāv′), behave badly. *v. 18.*

mis be hav ior (mis′bi hāv′yər), bad behavior. *n.*

misc., miscellaneous.

mis cal cu late (mis kal′kū lāt), calculate wrongly. *v. 19.*

mis cal cu la tion (mis′kal kū lā′shən), wrong calculation. *n.*

mis call (mis kôl′), call by a wrong name. *v. 16.*

mis car riage (mis kar′ij), 1. failure. Because the judge was unfair, that trial resulted in a miscarriage of justice. 2. the birth of a baby before it is able to live. *n. 14.*

mis car ry (mis kar′i), 1. go wrong. John expected to meet us; but his plans miscarried, and he could not come. My letter to mother must have miscarried, for she did not receive it. 2. have a miscarriage. *v., miscarried, miscarrying. 15.*

mis cel la ne ous (mis′ə lā′ni əs), not all of one kind or nature. Fred had a miscellaneous collection of stones, butterflies, marbles, stamps, birds' nests, and many other things. *adj. 9.*

mis cel la ny (mis′ə lā′ni), 1. mixture. 2. a collection of miscellaneous articles in one book. *n., pl. miscellanies. 12.*

mis chance (mis chans′), misfortune; bad luck. By some mischance he didn't receive my telegram. *n. 10.*

mis chief (mis′chif), 1. harm; injury, usually done by some person. Go away, or I'll do you a mischief. 2. conduct that causes harm or trouble, often without meaning it. Children's mischief may cause serious harm. 3. one who does harm, often just in fun. You little mischief! You have untied my apron. 4. merry teasing. Her eyes were full of mischief. *n. 3.*

mis chie vous (mis′chi vəs), 1. harmful; as, a mischievous belief. 2. full of mischief; naughty. 3. full of pranks and teasing fun; as, mischievous children. *adj. 7.*

mis con ceive (mis′kən sēv′), misunderstand; have wrong ideas about. *v. 18.*

mis con cep tion (mis′kən sep′shən), mistaken idea or notion; wrong conception. *n. 17.*

mis con duct (mis kon′dukt for 1 and 3, mis′kən dukt′ for 2 and 4), 1. bad behavior. The misconduct of the city treasurer resulted in his being put in prison. 2. behave badly. 3. bad management. The misconduct of that business resulted in a loss of 10,000 dollars. 4. manage badly. *n., v. 14.*

mis con struc tion (mis′kən struk′shən), wrong meaning; mistaken meaning; misunderstanding. What you said was open to misconstruction. *n.*

mis con strue (mis′kən strü′), take in a wrong sense; misunderstand. Ethel's shyness was sometimes misconstrued as rudeness. *v. 19.*

mis count (mis kount′), 1. count wrongly. 2. wrong count. *v., n.*

mis cre ant (mis′kri ənt), 1. having very bad morals; base. 2. a villain. *adj., n. 13.*

mis deal (mis dēl′), 1. deal wrongly at cards. 2. a wrong deal. *v., misdealt, misdealing, n.*

mis deed (mis dēd′), bad act; wicked deed. *n. 14.*

mis de mean or (mis′di mēn′ər), 1. a breaking of the law, not so serious as a crime. Disturbing the peace and breaking traffic laws are misdemeanors. 2. wrong deed. *n. 12.*

mis di rect (mis′di rekt′), direct wrongly; give wrong directions to. *v.*

mis do ing (mis dü′ing), wrongdoing; wrong deed. *n.*

mi ser (mī′zər), person who loves money for its own sake; one who lives poorly in order to save money and keep it. A miser dislikes to spend money for anything, except to gain more money. *n. 6.*

mis er a ble (miz′ər ə bəl), 1. unhappy. A sick child is often miserable. 2. causing trouble or unhappiness. I have a miserable cold. 3. poor; mean; wretched. The ragged child lives in a miserable tenement. *adj. 4.*

mis er a bly (miz′ər ə bli), in a miserable manner. *adv.*

mi ser ly (mī′zər li), of, like, or suited to a miser; stingy. *adj.*

mis er y (miz′ər i), 1. a miserable, unhappy state of mind. Think of the misery of having no home or friends. 2. poor, mean, miserable circumstances. The very poor live in misery, without beauty or comfort around them. *n., pl. miseries. 3.*

mis fit (mis fit′ for 1, mis′fit′ for 2), 1. fit badly. 2. bad fit. Do not buy shoes which are misfits. *v., misfitted, misfitting, n.*

mis for tune (mis fôr′chən), bad luck. *n. 5.*

mis gave (mis gāv′). See **misgive.** *pt. of misgive. 20.*

mis give (mis giv′), cause to feel doubt, suspicion, or anxiety. *v., misgave, misgiven, misgiving.*

mis giv ing (mis giv′ing), a feeling of doubt, suspicion, or anxiety. We started off through the storm with some misgivings. *n. 9.*

mis gov ern (mis guv′ərn), govern or manage badly. *v.*

mis gov ern ment (mis guv′ərn mənt), bad government. *n. 17.*

mis guide (mis gīd′), mislead; lead into mistakes or wrongdoing. The misguided youth had joined a gang of thieves. *v. 15.*

mis hap (mis hap′), an unlucky accident. *n. 6.*

mis in form (mis′in fôrm′), give wrong or misleading information to. *v. 19.*

mis in for ma tion (mis′in fər mā′shən), wrong or misleading information; incorrect information. *n.*

mis in ter pret (mis′in tėr′prit), interpret wrongly; explain wrongly; misunderstand. *v.*

mis in ter pre ta tion (mis′in tėr′pri tā′shən), wrong interpretation; wrong explanation; misunderstanding. *n.*

mis judge (mis juj′), judge wrongly or unjustly. *v.*

mis lay (mis lā′), 1. put in the wrong place. 2. put in a place and then forget where the place is. *v., mislaid, mislaying.*

mis lead (mis lēd′), 1. lead astray; cause to go in the wrong direction. Our guide misled us in the woods, and we got lost. 2. cause to do wrong; lead into wrongdoing. He is a good boy, but bad companions misled him. 3. lead to think what is not so; deceive. His lies misled me. *v., misled, misleading. 8.*

mis lead ing (mis lēd′ing), causing error or wrongdoing. *adj.*

mis led (mis led′). See **mislead.** The boy was misled by bad companions. *pt. and pp. of mislead. 11.*

mis like (mis līk′), dislike. *v. 16.*

mis man age (mis man′ij), manage badly. If you mismanage the business, you will lose money. *v. 19.*

mis man age ment (mis man′ij mənt), bad management. *n. 17.*

mis name (mis nām′), call by a wrong name. That lazy, careless boy is misnamed Ernest. *v. 19.*

mis no mer (mis nō′mər), 1. a name that describes wrongly. "Lightning" is a misnomer for a slow, old horse. 2. wrong name. *n. 16.*

mis place (mis plās′), 1. put in the wrong place. 2. give (one's love or trust) to the wrong person. *v. 14.*

mis play (mis plā′), 1. wrong play. 2. play wrongly. *n., v.*

mis print (mis′print′), mistake in printing. *n.*

mis pro nounce (mis′prə nouns′), pronounce wrongly. *v.*

mis pro nun ci a tion (mis′prə nun′si ā′shən), wrong pronunciation. *n.*

mis quote (mis kwōt′), quote wrongly. *v.*

mis read (mis rēd′), 1. read wrongly. 2. misunderstand; interpret wrongly. *v., misread (mis red′), misreading. 20.*

mis rep re sent (mis′rep ri zent′), represent falsely; give a wrong idea of. He misrepresented this automobile when he said it was in good running order. *v.*

mis rep re sen ta tion (mis′rep ri zen tā′shən), 1. false representation. He obtained the position by misrepresentation. 2. an incorrect story or explanation. *n. 15.*

mis rule (mis rül′), 1. bad or unwise rule. 2. rule badly. 3. disorder. *n., v. 15.*

miss[1] (mis), 1. fail to hit. Johnny hammers away, but half the time he misses the nail. He fired twice, but both shots missed. 2. a failure to hit or reach; as, to make more misses than hits. **A miss is as good as a mile** means (1) that a miss that is almost a hit is as good for the persons aimed at as a miss of a mile. (2) that a little failure or error is no better than a big one. 3. fail to find, get, or meet. I set out to meet my father, but in the dark I missed him. 4. let slip by; not seize. I missed the chance of a ride to town. 5. fail to catch; as, to miss the train. 6. leave out; as, to miss a word in reading. 7. fail to hear or understand. What did you say? I missed a word or two. 8. fail to keep, do, or be present at. I missed my music lesson today. 9. notice the absence of; feel keenly the absence of. I did not miss my purse till I got home. I miss my mother when she goes away. *v., n. 1.*

Miss[2] (mis), 1. a title given to a girl or to a woman who is not married; as, Miss Brown, the Misses Brown, the Miss Browns. 2. A **miss** is a girl. *n.*

Miss., Mississippi.

mis sal (mis′əl), a book containing the prayers, etc., for celebrating Mass throughout the year. *n. 16.*

mis shap en (mis shāp′ən), badly shaped; deformed. *adj. 11.*

mis sile (mis′il), 1. an object that is thrown, hurled, or shot, such as a stone, a bullet, an arrow, or a lance. 2. capable of being thrown, hurled, or shot. *n., adj. 14.*

miss ing (mis′ing), lacking; wanting; absent; not found; gone. One book is missing. *adj. 9.*

mis sion (mish′ən), 1. errand; sending or being sent on some special work. 2. persons sent out on some special business. He was one of a mission sent by our government to France. A mission was sent to Africa by the Baptist Church. 3. the station or headquarters of a religious mission. 4. the business on which a mission is sent. 5. one's business or purpose in life; one's calling. It seemed to be her mission to care for her brother's children. 6. The organized effort to spread the Christian religion in foreign lands is called foreign missions. *n. 5.*

mis sion ar y (mish′ən ãr′i), 1. person who goes on the work of a religious mission. The missionary went to India to convert people to Christianity. 2. of religious missions or missionaries. *n., pl. missionaries, adj. 6.*

Mis sis sip pi (mis′i sip′i), 1. the largest river in North America. It flows south through the United States to the Gulf of Mexico. 2. a Southern State of the United States. *n. 3.*

mis sive (mis′iv), a written message; a letter. *n. 14.*

Mis sou ri (mi zür′i or mi zür′ə), 1. large river in the northern part of the United States, flowing into the Mississippi River. 2. a Middle Western State of the United States. *n. 5.*

Mis sou ri an (mi zür′i ən), 1. of Missouri or its people. 2. native or inhabitant of Missouri. *adj., n.*

mis spell (mis spel′), spell wrongly. *v., misspelled* or *misspelt, misspelling. 17.*

mis spell ing (mis spel′ing), wrong spelling. *n.*

mis spend (mis spend′), spend foolishly or wrongly; waste. *v., misspent, misspending.*

mis spent (mis spent′), spent foolishly or wrongly; wasted. *adj., pt. and pp. of* **misspend.** *20.*

mis state (mis stāt′), state wrongly. *v.*

mis state ment (mis stāt′mənt), wrong statement. *n.*

mis step (mis step′), 1. wrong step. 2. error. *n.*

mist (mist), 1. a cloud of very fine drops of water in the air; fog. 2. come down in mist; rain in very fine drops. It is misting. 3. a haze or cloud that dims, blurs, or obscures. 4. cover with a mist; put a mist before; make dim. Tears misted her eyes. *n., v. 3.*

mis take (mis tāk′), 1. error; blunder; misunderstanding of a thing's meaning. I used your towel by mistake. 2. make a mistake; misunderstand what is seen or heard; take wrongly. I mistook that stick for a snake. *n., v., mistook, mistaken, mistaking. 2.*

mis tak en (mis tāk′ən), 1. wrong in opinion; having made a mistake. A mistaken person should admit his error. 2. wrong; wrongly judged; misplaced. It was a mistaken kindness to give that boy more candy, for it will make him sick. 3. See **mistake.** *adj., pp. of mistake. 18.*

mis tak en ly (mis tāk′ən li), by mistake; wrongly. *adv.*

Mis ter (mis′tər), Mr., a title put before a man's name or the name of his office; as, Mr. Smith, Mr. President. Dr. Henry Jones did not like to be called "mister." *n. 6.*

mist i ly (mis′ti li), in a misty or cloudy manner. *adv.*

mist i ness (mis′ti nis), misty condition; cloudy quality. *n.*

mis tle toe (mis′əl tō), plant with small, waxy white berries, that grows high up in trees. It is used as a Christmas decoration. *n. 14.*

Mistletoe growing on a branch of a tree

mis took (mis tu̇k′). See **mistake.** I mistook you for your sister yesterday. *pt. of mistake. 14.*

mis treat (mis trēt′), treat badly. *v.*

mis tress (mis′tris), 1. the woman who is at the head of the household. 2. a woman or country who is in control or can rule. Great Britain is mistress of the seas. 3. a woman who has a thorough knowledge or mastery. She is complete mistress of the arts of cookery. 4. a woman teaching in a school, or at the head of a school, or giving lessons in a special subject; as, the dancing mistress. 5. a woman loved and courted by a man. *Used in poetry.* 6. a woman who improperly occupies the place of a wife. 7. **Mistress** may mean Mrs., Madam, or Miss. *Old use. n. 2.*

mis tri al (mis trī′əl), a trial in which the jury fails to come to a decision; a trial of no effect in law because of some error in the proceedings. *n.*

mis trust (mis trust′), 1. feel no confidence in; doubt. She mistrusted her ability to learn to swim. 2. lack of trust or confidence. *v., n. 6.*

mis trust ful (mis trust′fəl), lacking trust; distrustful; doubting; suspicious. *adj. 16.*

mist y (mis′ti), 1. of mist. 2. covered with mist. 3. not clearly seen or outlined. 4. as if seen through a mist. *adj., mistier, mistiest. 6.*

mis un der stand (mis′un dər stand′), understand wrongly; take in a wrong sense; give the wrong meaning to. *v., misunderstood, misunderstanding. 7.*

mis un der stand ing (mis′un dər stan′ding), 1. understanding wrongly; failure to understand; mistake as to meaning. 2. disagreement. *n.*

mis un der stood (mis′un dər stůd′). See **misunderstand.** *pt. and pp. of misunderstand. 20.*

mis use (mis ūz′ for 1 and 2, mis ūs′ for 3), 1. to abuse; to treat badly. He misuses his horses by giving them loads that are too heavy. 2. to use for the wrong purpose. He misuses his knife at the table by lifting food with it. 3. wrong use. I notice a misuse of the word *who* in your letter. *v., n. 8.*

Mite (about 10 times actual length)

mite (mīt), 1. anything very small; little bit. Though poor, she gave her mite to charity. 2. very small child. What a little mite Dorothy is! 3. a very tiny animal that lives in cheese or on plants or on other animals. *n. 10.*

mi ter or **mi tre** (mī′tər), 1. a folded cap worn by bishops during sacred ceremonies. 2. a kind of joint or corner where two pieces of wood are fitted together at right angles, with the ends cut slanting, as at corners of a picture frame. 3. join thus; prepare (ends of wood) for such joining. *n., v. 6.*

Miter

Mith ri da tes (mith′ri dā′tēz), a king who is said to have become immune to poisons by taking gradually increasing doses of them. *n. 12.*

mit i gate (mit′i gāt), make mild; make milder; soften. We may mitigate a person's anger, grief, or pain, mitigate a punishment, or mitigate great heat or cold. *v. 9.*

mit i ga tion (mit′i gā′shən), 1. mitigating; being mitigated. 2. something that mitigates. The cool breeze was a welcome mitigation of the heat of the afternoon. *n. 17.*

mitt (mit), 1. a kind of long glove without fingers, or with very short fingers. 2. a baseball glove. 3. mitten. *n. 16.*

mit ten (mit′ən), a kind of winter glove, covering the four fingers together and the thumb separately. *n. 5.*

Mitten

mix (miks), 1. put together; stir well together. We mix butter, sugar, milk, and flour for a cake. 2. prepare by putting different things together; as, to mix a cake. 3. join; be mixed. Oil and water will not mix. 4. associate together. Some people do not mix well with a group like ours. 5. **Mix up** sometimes means confuse. I was so mixed up that I used the wrong method in that problem. *v. 2.*

mixed (mikst), 1. formed of different kinds; as, mixed candy, mixed tea. A **mixed number** is a whole number and a fraction; as, $3\frac{5}{8}$ and $28\frac{3}{4}$. A **mixed chorus** has both men and women singers. 2. confused. *adj.*

mix er (mik′sər), 1. a thing that mixes; as, a bread mixer. 2. one who mixes. A person who gets along well with others is called a good mixer. *n. 14.*

mix ture (miks′chər), 1. mixing. 2. what has been mixed. *n. 4.*

Miz pah (miz′pə), a word used to recall these words: "The Lord watch between me and thee, when we are absent one from another." Genesis 31: 49. *n. 19.*

miz zen (miz′ən), 1. the mast nearest the stern in a three-masted ship. 2. the sail set on the aft side of this mast. 3. the mast or sail nearest the stern in a two-masted ship (yawl or ketch). *n.*

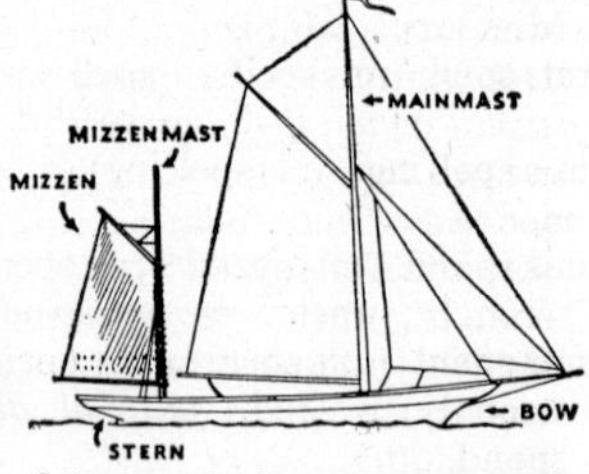

Mizzen and mizzenmast on a yawl

miz zen mast (miz′ən məst or miz′ən mast′), the mast nearest the stern in a three-masted or two-masted ship. *n.*

Mlle., Mademoiselle. *pl. Mlles.*

mm., millimeter; millimeters.

Mme., Madame. *pl. Mmes.*

Mo., Missouri.

mo., month; months. **mos.** is also used for months.

Mo ab (mō′ab), an ancient kingdom in Palestine, east of the Dead Sea and the river Jordan. *n. 13.*

Mo ab ite (mō′əb īt), member of a warlike tribe in ancient Palestine. *n. 17.*

moan (mōn), 1. a long low sound of suffering. 2. any similar sound; as, the moan of the wind. 3. make moans. 4. complain about; grieve for. *n., v. 4.*

moat (mōt), a deep, wide ditch dug around a castle or town as a protection against enemies. Moats were usually kept filled with water. *n. 8.*

mob (mob), 1. a large number of people or animals, usually crowded closely together. 2. the common mass of people. 3. a lawless crowd, easily moved to act without thinking. 4. to crowd around in curiosity, anger, etc. The eager children mobbed the candy man the moment he appeared. 5. to attack with violence as a mob does. *n., v., mobbed, mobbing. 5.*

mo bile[1] (mō′bil), movable; moving easily; easy to move. The tongue is mobile. A mobile mind is one that is easily moved by ideas or feelings. *adj. 15.*

Mo bile[2] (mō bēl′), seaport city in Alabama, on the Gulf of Mexico. *n.*

mo bil i ty (mō bil′i ti), being mobile; ability or readiness to move or be moved. *n. 15.*

mo bi li za tion (mō′bi li zā′shən), 1. a mobilizing; calling troops or ships into active military service. 2. a being mobilized. *n.*

mo bi lize (mō′bi līz), 1. call (troops, ships) into active military service; organize for war. 2. assemble and prepare for war. The troops mobilized quickly. 3. put into active use; as, to mobilize the wealth of a country. *v. 18.*

Moccasin

moc ca sin (mok′ə sin), 1. a soft shoe or sandal of deerskin or other leather worn by North American Indians. 2. a poisonous snake found in the southern part of the United States. *n. 7.*

Mo cha (mō′kə), 1. a seaport city in southwestern Arabia, near the mouth of the Red Sea. 2. a choice variety of coffee originally coming from Arabia. *n. 20.*

mock (mok), 1. laugh at; make fun of. 2. make fun of by copying or imitating. The thoughtless children mocked the queer speech of the new boy. 3. imitate; copy; as, a mockingbird. 4. not real; copying; imitation; as, a mock king, a mock battle, mock modesty. 5. make light of; pay no attention to. 6. deceive; disappoint. 7. mockery. *v., adj., n. 2.*

mock er (mok′ər), 1. one that mocks. 2. mockingbird. *n. 11.*

mock er y (mok′ər i), 1. making fun of. Their mockery of John hurt his feelings. 2. something to be made fun of. Through his foolishness he became a mockery in the village. 3. a bad copy or imitation. The children's housekeeping was a mockery of their elders'. 4. disregarding; setting at naught. This unfair trial was a mockery of justice. *n., pl. mockeries. 6.*

Mockingbird (about 10 in. long)

mock ing bird (mok′ing bėrd′), a songbird that imitates the notes of other birds. *n.*

mode (mōd), 1. the manner or way in which a thing is done. The mode of his coming was quite unusual. 2. the style, fashion, or custom that prevails; the way most people are doing. Bobbed hair became the mode about 1920. 3. the form of a verb which shows whether the act or state is thought of as a fact, a command, etc.; as, the indicative, subjunctive, or imperative mode. *n. 3.*

mod el (mod′əl), 1. a small copy; as, a model of a ship or an engine, a model of an island. 2. a figure in clay or wax that is to be copied in marble, bronze, etc.; as, a model for a statue. 3. make, shape, or fashion; design or plan. Model a bird's nest in clay. 4. the way in which a thing is made; the style. I want a dress like yours, for that model is becoming to me. 5. thing or person to be copied or imitated. Make your father

Water moccasin (about 3½ ft. long)

your model, and you will become a fine man. 6. follow as a model. Model yourself on your father. 7. just right or perfect, especially in conduct. Lucy is a model child. 8. person who poses for artists. 9. girl in a clothing store who puts on garments in order to show customers how they look. *n., v., modeled, modeling, adj. 2.*

mod er ate (mod′ər it for 1-4, mod′ər āt for 5), 1. kept or keeping within proper bounds; not extreme; as, moderate expenses, moderate styles. 2. calm; not violent; as, moderate in speech or opinion. 3. fair; medium; not very large or good; as, to make a moderate profit. 4. person who holds moderate opinions. 5. make less violent; become less extreme. The wind is moderating. *adj., n., v. 3.*

mod er a tion (mod′ər ā′shən), 1. act of moderating. 2. proper restraint; freedom from excess; temperance. *n. 7.*

mod er a tor (mod′ər ā′tər), presiding officer; chairman; as, the moderator of a town meeting, the moderator of a church assembly. *n. 16.*

mod ern (mod′ərn), 1. of the present time; of times not long past. The radio is a modern invention. 2. person of modern times. 3. person who has modern ideas and tastes. *adj., n. 2.*

mod ern ize (mod′ər nīz), 1. make modern; bring up to present ways or standards. 2. become modern. *v. 15.*

mod est (mod′ist), 1. not thinking too highly of oneself; not vain; humble. 2. bashful; not bold; shy; held back by a sense of what is fit and proper. 3. decent; not calling attention to one's body. 4. not too great; not asking too much; as, a modest request. 5. quiet; not gaudy; humble in appearance; as, a modest little house. *adj. 3.*

mod es ty (mod′is ti), 1. freedom from vanity; being modest or humble. 2. being shy or bashful. 3. being decent; not calling attention to one's body. *n., pl. modesties. 6.*

mod i cum (mod′i kəm), a small or moderate quantity. John is so bright that even with a modicum of effort he does excellent work. *n. 19.*

mod i fi ca tion (mod′i fi kā′shən), 1. modifying or being modified; toning down. With the modification of his anger he could think clearly again. 2. limitation of meaning; qualification. 3. partial alteration or change. With some modification your composition will do for the school paper. 4. modified form; variety. *n. 12.*

mod i fi er (mod′i fī′ər), one that modifies. In "a very tight coat," the adjective *tight* is a modifier of *coat*, and the adverb *very* is a modifier of *tight*. *n.*

mod i fy (mod′i fī), 1. change somewhat; as, to modify the terms of a lease. 2. make less; tone down; make less severe or strong; as, to modify one's demands. 3. qualify; limit the meaning of. Adverbs modify verbs. *v., modified, modifying. 9.*

mod ish (mōd′ish), fashionable; stylish. *adj. 17.*

mod u late (moj′ů lāt), 1. regulate; adjust; vary; soften; tone down. 2. alter (the voice) for expression. 3. change from one musical key or note to another. 4. change (a radio current) by adding sound waves to it. *v. 12.*

mod u la tion (moj′ů lā′shən), 1. modulating; being modulated. 2. the change from one key to another in the course of a piece of music. *n. 16.*

Mo gul (mō gul′), 1. a Mongolian. 2. one of the Mongol conquerors of India in the 16th century or one of their descendants. **The Great Mogul** was the emperor of most of India. *n. 13.*

mo gul (mō gul′), a great personage. The football captain was the mogul of the school. *n.*

mo hair (mō′hãr), 1. cloth made from the long silky hair of the Angora goat. 2. a similar cloth made of wool and cotton. *n. 11.*

Mo ham med (mō ham′id), the founder and prophet of Islam (570?-632 A.D.), a religion widely accepted in Asia and Africa. *n. 16.*

Mo ham med an (mō ham′i dən), 1. of Mohammed or the religion founded by him. 2. a follower of Mohammed; a believer in his religion. *adj., n. 11.*

Mo ham med an ism (mō ham′i dən izm), Mohammedan religion. *n.*

Mo hawk (mō′hôk), 1. member of a tribe of American Indians, formerly living in central New York State. 2. a river in New York State, flowing into the Hudson. *n. 17.*

Mo hi can (mō hē′kən), member of a tribe of American Indians, formerly living in Connecticut and New York State. *n.*

moi e ty (moi′ə ti), 1. half. 2. part. Only a small moiety of the graduates of high school go to college. *n., pl. moieties. 14.*

moil (moil), 1. work hard; drudge. 2. hard work; drudgery. 3. trouble; confusion. *v., n.* [*Old use*] *17.*

moist (moist), slightly wet; damp. *adj. 4.*

moist en (moi′sən), make moist; become moist. *v. 6.*

mois ture (mois′chər), slight wetness; water or other liquid spread in very small drops in the air or on a surface. Dew is moisture that collects at night on the grass. *n. 4.*

mo lar (mō′lər), 1. adapted for grinding. 2. a tooth with a broad surface for grinding. A person's back teeth are molars. *adj., n. 14.*

Molar

mo las ses (mə las′iz), a sweet syrup. Molasses is obtained in the process of making sugar from sugar cane. *n. 8.*

mold[1] (mōld), 1. a hollow shape in which anything is formed or cast; as, the mold into which melted metal is poured to harden into shape, the mold in which jelly is left to stiffen. 2. the shape or form which is given by a mold. 3. the model according to which anything is shaped. 4. make or form into shape; as, to mold dough into loaves to be baked, on a molding board. Children mold figures out of clay. Her character was molded by the trials she went through. *n., v. 8.*

mold[2] (mōld), 1. a woolly or furry growth, often greenish in color, which appears on food and other animal or vegetable substances when they are left too long in a warm moist place. 2. become covered with mold. *n., v.*

mold[3] (mōld), loose earth; fine, soft, rich soil. Many wild flowers grow in the forest mold. *n.*

mold er (mōl′dər), crumble away; break up gradually into dust. *v. 9.*

mold ing (mōl′ding), 1. act of shaping; as, the molding of dishes from clay. 2. something molded; a decorative outline used in architecture. 3. a strip, usually of wood, around the upper walls of a room, used to support pictures, to cover electric wires, etc. *n.*

mold y (mōl′di), 1. covered with a woolly or furry, often greenish, growth of mold; as, a moldy crust of bread, moldy cheese. 2. musty; stale; as, a moldy smell. *adj., moldier, moldiest. 9.*

mole[1] (mōl), a spot on the skin, usually brown. *n. 5.*

Mole (about 7 in. long, including the tail)

mole[2] (mōl), small animal that lives underground most of the time. Moles have velvety fur and very small eyes that cannot see well. *n.*

mole[3] (mōl), barrier built of stone to break the force of the waves; a breakwater. *n.*

mol e cule (mol′i kūl), 1. the smallest particle into which a substance can be divided without chemical change. A molecule consists of two or more atoms. 2. very small particle. *n. 12.*

mole hill (mōl′hil′), 1. small mound or ridge of earth raised up by moles burrowing under the ground. 2. something insignificant. *n.*

mo lest (mō lest′), meddle with and injure; interfere with and trouble; disturb. We did not molest the big dog, because we were afraid of him. *v. 7.*

mo les ta tion (mō′les tā′shən), a molesting or being molested; annoying or hostile interference. *n. 14.*

mol li fy (mol′i fī), soften; appease; mitigate. He tried to mollify his father's anger by apologizing. *v., mollified, mollifying. 14.*

mol lusk or **mol lusc** (mol′əsk), an animal with a soft body usually protected with a shell. Snails, mussels, oysters, and clams are mollusks. *n. 19.*

mol ly cod dle (mol′i kod′əl), 1. a milksop; a boy or a man accustomed to being fussed over and pampered. 2. coddle; pamper. *n., v.*

Mo loch (mō′lok), 1. a fire god of ancient times. Parents sacrificed their children to Moloch. 2. anything requiring frightful sacrifice. War is a Moloch. *n.*

molt (mōlt), 1. shed the feathers, skin, etc., before a new growth. Birds and snakes molt. 2. act or time of doing this. *v., n. 19.*

molt en (mōl′tən), 1. melted. 2. made by melting and casting; as, a molten image. *pp. of* **melt,** *adj. 6.*

Mo luc cas (mō luk′əz), group of Dutch islands in the East Indies. *n. pl.*

mo ment (mō′mənt), 1. a very short space of time; an instant. I started the very moment I got your message. 2. importance. The President is busy on a matter of moment. *n. 1.*

mo men tar i ly (mō′mən tãr′i li), 1. for a moment. 2. at every moment; from moment to moment. The danger was increasing momentarily. 3. at any moment. *adv.*

mo men tar y (mō′mən tãr′i), lasting only a moment. *adj. 7.*

mo men tous (mō men′təs), very important.

Choosing between peace and war is a momentous decision. *adj. 12.*

mo men tum (mō men′təm), 1. the force with which a body moves, the product of its weight and its speed. A falling object gains momentum as it falls. 2. impetus resulting from movement. *n.*

Mon., Monday.

Mon a co (mon′ə kō), a tiny country in southeastern France. *n.*

mon arch (mon′ərk), king, queen, emperor, etc.; ruler. *n. 3.*

mo nar chi cal (mə när′ki kəl), 1. of a monarch or monarchy. 2. favoring a monarchy. *adj. 19.*

mon ar chist (mon′ər kist), a believer in monarchy. *n.*

mon ar chy (mon′ər ki), 1. government by a monarch. 2. a nation governed by a monarch. *n., pl. monarchies. 7.*

mon as ter y (mon′əs ter′i), a building where monks or nuns live in seclusion. *n., pl. monasteries. 9.*

mo nas tic (mə nas′tik), 1. of monks or nuns; as, the monastic vows of poverty, chastity, and obedience. 2. of monasteries; as, monastic architecture. 3. a monk. *adj., n. 9.*

mo nas ti cism (mə nas′ti sizm), the system or condition of living according to fixed rules, in groups shut off from the world and devoted to religion. *n. 20.*

Mon day (mun′di), the second day of the week, the day after Sunday. *n. 2.*

mon e tar y (mon′i tãr′i), 1. of the money of a country. The monetary unit in the United States is the dollar. 2. of money; as, a monetary reward. *adj. 17.*

mon ey (mun′i), 1. gold, silver, and copper made into coins for use in buying and selling; paper notes which represent gold or silver. 2. wealth. *n., pl. moneys. 1.*

mon eyed (mun′id), 1. having money; wealthy. 2. consisting of or representing money; as, moneyed resources. *adj.*

money order, order for the payment of money. You can buy a money order at the post office and send it to a person in another city, who can get the money at the post office there.

mon ger (mung′gər), a dealer in some sort of article; as, a cheesemonger, a fishmonger, a scandalmonger. *n. 16.*

Mon gol (mong′gol), 1. member of an Asiatic race now inhabiting Mongolia and nearby parts of China and Siberia. 2. Mongolian. *n., adj. 20.*

Mon go li a (mong gō′li ə), a vast region in Asia, north of China and south of Siberia. *n.*

Mon go li an (mong gō′li ən), 1. of or pertaining to the yellow race, which has a yellowish skin, prominent cheekbones, slanting eyes, short broad nose, and straight black hair. Chinese, Japanese, Tartars, and Eskimos are Mongolian peoples. 2. of or pertaining to a member of an Asiatic race living in Mongolia. 3. member of the Mongolian race. 4. a Mongolian language. *adj., n. 14.*

mon goose or **mon goos** (mong′güs), a slender, ferretlike animal of India, used for destroying rats and noted for its ability to kill poisonous snakes without being harmed. *n., pl. mongooses.*

Mongoose (length, including the tail, about 2 ft.)

mon grel (mung′grəl), 1. an animal or plant of mixed breed, especially a dog. 2. of mixed breed, race, origin, nature, etc.; as, a mongrel speech which is half Spanish and half Indian. *n., adj. 14.*

mon i tor (mon′i tər), 1. pupil in school with special duties, such as helping to keep order and taking attendance. 2. person who gives advice or warning. 3. a low armored warship having one or more turrets for guns. *n. 12.*

Mon i tor (mon′i tər), Union ironclad warship with a low hull topped by a revolving turret for the guns. *n.*

mon i to ry (mon′i tō′ri), 1. warning; reminding. 2. a warning; a reminder, especially in a letter from a bishop. *adj., n.*

monk (mungk), man who gives up everything else for religion and enters a monastery to live. *n. 5.*

mon key (mung′ki), 1. an animal of the group most like man. 2. one of the smaller animals in this group, not a chimpanzee, gorilla, or other large ape. 3. person, especially a child, who is full of mischief. 4. play; fool; trifle. *n., pl. monkeys, v. 4.*

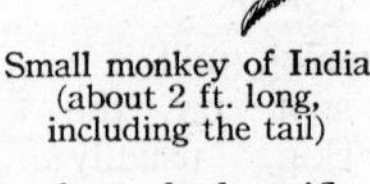
Small monkey of India (about 2 ft. long, including the tail)

monkey wrench, wrench with a movable jaw that can be adjusted to fit different sizes of nuts.

monk ish (mungk′ish), 1. of a monk or

monks; like a monk. 2. characteristic of a monk or of their way of life. *adj.* [*Often used in an unfriendly way*] *13.*

monks hood (mungks′hu̇d′), a kind of plant with hooded flowers. See the picture in the next column. *n.*

mon o cle (mon′ə kəl), an eyeglass for one eye. *n.*

Monocle

mon o gram (mon′ə gram), a person's initials combined in one design. Monograms are used on note paper, table linen, clothing, jewelry, etc. *n. 14.*

Monogram

mon o lith (mon′ə lith), 1. a single large block of stone. 2. a monument, column, statue, etc., formed of a single large block of stone. *n. 20.*

mon o logue (mon′ə lôg), 1. long speech by one person in a group. 2. entertainment by a single speaker. 3. a play for a single actor. 4. part of a play in which a single actor speaks alone. *n. 17.*

mon o ma ni a (mon′ə mā′ni ə), 1. insanity in which the person is insane on one subject only. 2. an interest or tendency so strong as to seem almost insane. *n.*

mon o plane (mon′ə plān), airplane with a single plane. *n.*

Monoplane

mo nop o list (mə-nop′ə list), 1. person who has a monopoly. 2. person who favors monopoly. *n. 18.*

mo nop o lize (mə nop′ə līz), have or get exclusive possession or control of. This firm practically monopolizes the production of linen thread. *v. 19.*

mo nop o ly (mə nop′ə li), 1. the exclusive control of a commodity or service. The gas company in our city has a monopoly. 2. such a control granted by a government. An inventor has a monopoly of his invention for a certain number of years. 3. the exclusive possession or control of something. No one country has a monopoly of virtue. 4. control which, though not exclusive, enables a person or corporation to fix prices. 5. person or corporation which has a monopoly of some commodity or service. *n., pl. monopolies. 7.*

mon o syl lab ic (mon′ə si lab′ik), 1. having only one syllable. 2. consisting of a word or words of one syllable. "No, not now," is a monosyllabic reply. *adj.*

mon o syl la ble (mon′ə sil′ə bəl), word of one syllable. *Yes, no,* and *grand* are monosyllables. *n. 16.*

mon o the ism (mon′ə thē′izm), belief that there is only one God. *n.*

Monkshood

mon o tone (mon′ə tōn), 1. sameness of tone, of style of writing, of color, etc. Don't read in a monotone; use expression. 2. continuing on one tone; of one tone, style, or color. *n., adj. 16.*

mo not o nous (mə not′ə nəs), 1. continuing in the same tone. 2. not varying; without change. 3. wearying because of its sameness; as, monotonous work. *adj. 8.*

mo not o ny (mə not′ə ni), 1. sameness of tone or pitch. 2. lack of variety. 3. wearisome sameness. *n. 10.*

mon ox ide (mon ok′sīd), an oxide containing one oxygen atom in each molecule. *n. 17.*

Mon roe (mən rō′), James (1758-1831), the fifth president of the United States, from 1817 to 1825. He was famous for first stating the Monroe Doctrine. *n. 7.*

Monroe Doctrine, the doctrine that European nations should not interfere with American nations or try to acquire more territory in America.

Mon sei gneur or **mon sei gneur** (mon senyėr′), a French word meaning my lord, used of princes, bishops, and the like. *n.*

mon sieur (mə syė′), a French word for Mr. or sir. *n., pl. messieurs* (mes′ərz). *9.*

Mon si gnor or **mon si gnor** (mon sē′nyər), 1. title given to certain dignitaries in the Roman Catholic Church. 2. person having this title. *n.*

mon soon (mon sün′), 1. a seasonal wind of the Indian Ocean and southern Asia. It blows from the southwest from April to October and from the northeast during the rest of the year. 2. the season during which this wind blows from the southwest, usually having heavy rains. *n. 18.*

mon ster (mon′stər), 1. any animal or plant that is out of the usual course of nature. A huge sea animal or a cow with two heads is a monster. Imaginary animals having parts of different animals, such as a centaur, sphinx, or griffin, are monsters. 2. person too wicked to be human. He is a monster of cruelty. 3. huge creature or thing. 4. huge. *n., adj. 4.*

mon stros i ty (mon stros′i ti), 1. state or character of being monstrous. 2. a monster. *n., pl. monstrosities. 16.*

mon strous (mon′strəs), 1. huge. 2. wrongly formed or shaped; like a monster. 3. so wrong or absurd as to be almost unheard of. 4. shocking; horrible; dreadful. *adj. 4.*

Mont., Montana.

Mon taigne (mon tān′), a French essayist (1533-1592). *n. 17.*

Mon tan a (mon tan′ə), a Western State of the United States. *n. 9.*

Mont Blanc (mōn blän′), the highest mountain in the Alps, between France and Italy. It is 15,781 ft. high.

Mon te ne gro (mon′ti nē′grō), former country in southern Europe, on the Adriatic Sea. After the first World War it became a part of Yugoslavia. *n. 16.*

Mon te vi de o (mon′ti vi dā′ō), the capital of Uruguay. *n.*

Mont gom er y (mənt gum′ər i), the capital of Alabama. *n.*

month (munth). The year is divided into 12 months. The months I like best are June and October. *n. 1.*

month ly (munth′li), 1. of a month; for a month; lasting a month; as, a monthly supply, a monthly salary. 2. done, happening, payable, etc., once a month; as, a monthly meeting, a monthly examination. 3. once a month; every month. Some magazines come monthly. 4. a magazine published once a month. *adj., adv., n., pl. monthlies. 6.*

Mont pel ier (mont pēl′yər), the capital of Vermont. *n.*

Mont re al (mont′ri ôl′), a large city in southeastern Canada on the St. Lawrence River. *n. 9.*

mon u ment (mon′ū mənt), 1. something set up to keep a person or an event from being forgotten; anything that keeps alive the memory of a person or an event. A monument may be a building, pillar, arch, statue, tomb, or stone. 2. an enduring or prominent instance. The professor's researches were monuments of learning. *n. 3.*

mon u men tal (mon′ū men′təl), 1. of a monument. 2. serving as a monument. 3. like a monument. 4. weighty and lasting; important. The Constitution of the United States is a monumental document. A great encyclopedia is a monumental production. 5. very great; as, monumental ignorance. *adj. 8.*

moo (mü), 1. the sound made by a cow. 2. make this sound. *n., pl. moos, v., mooed, mooing.*

mood[1] (müd), state of mind or feeling. I am in the mood to play just now; I don't want to study. *n. 4.*

mood[2] (müd), the form of a verb which shows whether the act or state is thought of as a fact, a command, etc.; as, the indicative, subjunctive, or imperative mood. *n.* Also called **mode.**

mood y (müd′i), 1. likely to have changes of mood. 2. often having gloomy moods. She has been moody ever since she lost her job. 3. gloomy; sullen; sunk in sadness. *adj., moodier, moodiest. 10.*

moon (mün), 1. The moon shines in the sky at night. It is a body which revolves around the earth once in 28 days, and looks bright because it reflects the sun's light. 2. A **moon** is about a month or 28 days. The Indians counted time by moons. 3. anything round like the moon. 4. wander about or gaze idly or dreamily. *n., v. 1.*

OLD MOON

Phases of the moon

moon beam (mün′bēm′), a ray of moonlight. *n. 11.*

moon light (mün′līt′), 1. the light of the moon. 2. having the light of the moon; as, a moonlight night. *n., adj. 4.*

moon lit (mün′lit′), lighted by the moon. *adj. 12.*

moon shine (mün′shīn′), 1. moonlight. 2. empty talk; foolish talk or ideas; nonsense. 3. intoxicating liquor made unlawfully, or unlawfully brought into the country. *Used in common talk. n. 10.*

moon stone (mün′stōn′), whitish gem with a pearly luster. Moonstone is a variety of feldspar. *n.*

moon struck (mün′struk′), dazed; crazed. *adj.*

moor[1] (mür), open waste land, especially if heather grows on it. *n. 4.*

moor[2] (mür), put or keep (a ship, etc.) in place by means of ropes or chains fastened to the shore or to anchors. *v.*

Moor[3] (mür), person of a race related to the Arabs, living in northwestern Africa. In the 8th century the Moors invaded and conquered Spain. They were finally driven out in 1492. *n.*

Moore (mōr), Thomas, a famous Irish poet (1779-1852). *n. 12.*

moor ings (mür′ingz), 1. ropes or cables by which a ship is fastened. 2. place where a ship is moored. *n. pl.*

Moor ish (mür′ish), of the Moors. *adj. 12.*

moor land (mür′land′), moor; land covered with heather. *n. 11.*

moose (müs), an animal like a large deer, living in Canada and the northern part of the United States. *n., pl. moose. 10.*

Moose (about 6 ft. high at the shoulder)

moot (müt), 1. argue. 2. bring forward (a point, subject, case, etc.) for discussion. 3. debatable; doubtful; as, a moot point. *v., adj. 11.*

mop (mop), 1. a bundle of coarse yarn, rags, or cloth fastened at the end of a stick, for cleaning floors, etc. 2. wash or wipe up; clean with a mop; as, to mop up the floor. 3. wipe tears or sweat from; as, to mop one's brow with one's handkerchief. 4. thick head of hair like a mop. *n., v., mopped, mopping. 10.*

Mop

mope (mōp), 1. give oneself up to being dull, silent, and out of spirits. 2. person who mopes and allows himself to be dull and out of spirits. *v., n. 11.*

mo raine (mə rān′), a mass of rocks, dirt, etc., deposited at the side or end of a glacier. *n. 19.*

mor al (mor′əl), 1. the lesson, inner meaning, or teaching of a fable, a story, or an event. The moral of the story was "Look before you leap." 2. **Morals** means character; principles in regard to conduct; behavior. George Washington's morals were excellent. 3. having to do with character, or with the difference between right and wrong; as, a moral question. 4. good in character or conduct; right; just; virtuous according to civilized standards of right and wrong; as, a moral act, a moral man. 5. capable of understanding right and wrong. A little baby is not a moral being. 6. teaching a good lesson; having a good influence. 7. A **moral victory** is a defeat that has the effect on the mind that a victory would have. 8. A **moral certainty** is a probability so great that it might just as well be a certainty. *n., adj. 3.*

mo rale (mə ral′), moral or mental condition as regards courage, confidence, enthusiasm, etc.; as, the morale of troops, the morale of a school. *n. 18.*

mor al ist (mor′əl ist), 1. person who thinks much about moral duties, sees the moral side of things, and leads a moral life. 2. person who teaches, studies, or writes about morals. *n. 12.*

mo ral i ty (mə ral′i ti), 1. the right or wrong of an action; as, to question the morality of dancing on Sunday. 2. doing right; virtue. 3. a system of morals; a set of rules or principles of conduct. *n., pl. moralities. 8.*

mor al ize (mor′əl īz), 1. think, talk, or write about questions of right and wrong. 2. point out the lesson or inner meaning of. 3. improve the morals of. *v. 11.*

mor al ly (mor′əl i), 1. in a moral manner. 2. in morals; as to morals. The king was a good man morally but too stupid for a position of importance. 3. from a moral point of view; ethically. 4. practically. I am morally sure that I locked the door. *adv.*

mo rass (mə ras′), piece of low, soft, wet ground; swamp. *n. 11.*

mor a to ri um (mor′ə tō′ri əm), 1. legal authorization to delay payment of money due. 2. period during which such authorization is in effect. *n.*

Mo ra vi a (mō rā′vi ə), district in central Europe under the control of Germany. It was a part of Czecho-Slovakia from 1919 to 1938. *n. 17.*

Mo ra vi an (mō rā′vi ən), 1. of or pertaining to Moravia or its people. 2. a native or inhabitant of Moravia. *adj., n.*

mor bid (môr′bid), 1. unhealthy; not wholesome; sickly; as, morbid fancies, a morbid book, a morbid liking for horrors. 2. caused by disease; characteristic of disease; diseased. Cancer is a morbid growth. *adj. 10.*

mor dant (môr′dənt), 1. biting; cutting; sarcastic. The mordant criticism hurt his feelings. 2. a substance that fixes colors in dyeing. 3. an acid that eats into metal. *adj., n.*

Mor de cai (môr′di kī), the foster father of Esther, who helped her save the Jews from being destroyed by Haman. Esther 3-8. *n. 14.*

more (mōr), 1. A foot is more than an inch. This plant needs more water. Take one step more. A burn hurts more than a scratch does. The storm grew more and more severe. A horse eats more than a dog does. Tell me more about your farm. 2. More helps to make the comparative form of most adverbs, and of most adjectives longer than one syllable; as, more easily, more truly, more careful, more common. "More common" means commoner. 3. **More or less** means (1) somewhat. Most people are more or less selfish. (2) about. My horse weighs 900 pounds more or less. *adj., adv., n. 1.*

more o ver (mōr ō′vər), also; besides; in addition to that. I don't want to go skating. Moreover, the ice is too thin. *adv. 3.*

mor ga nat ic (môr′gə nat′ik). A morganatic marriage is a marriage between a person of high rank, like a king or duke, and a woman of lower rank. The person of high rank arranges that the wife and children shall have no right to his rank or property. *adj.*

morgue (môrg), place in which the bodies of unknown persons found dead are kept until they can be identified and taken away by their family or friends. *n. 17.*

Mor mon (môr′mən), 1. member of a church founded in 1830 by Joseph Smith. 2. The sacred book of this church is called the **Book of Mormon.** *n. 10.*

morn (môrn), morning. *n.* [*Used in poetry*] *4.*

morn ing (môr′ning), the early part of the day, ending at noon. *n. 1.*

morn ing-glo ry (môr′ning glō′ri), a climbing vine with heart-shaped leaves and funnel-shaped flowers of blue, lavender, pink, or white. *n., pl. morning-glories.*

Morning-glory

morning star, planet, especially Venus, seen in the eastern sky before sunrise.

Mo roc co (mə rok′ō), a country in northwestern Africa, mostly under French and Spanish control. *n. 12.*

mo roc co (mə rok′ō), a fine leather made from goatskins, used in binding fine books. It was first made in Morocco. *n.*

mo ron (mō′ron), person whose intellect as an adult is only that of an ordinary child from 8 to 12 years of age. *n.*

mo rose (mə rōs′), gloomy; sullen; ill-humored. *adj. 14.*

Mor pheus (môr′fūs), god of dreams. *n. 20.*

mor phine (môr′fēn), a drug made from opium, used to dull pain and to cause sleep. *n. 13.*

mor ris chair (mor′is chãr′), armchair with an adjustable back.

Morris chair

morris dance, an old English dance performed by persons in fancy costumes.

mor row (mor′ō), 1. the following day or time. 2. morning. *Old use. n. 4.*

Morse (môrs), Samuel F. B., an American, made the first telegraph instrument (1791-1872). The Morse telegraphic alphabet or code is named after him. *n. 11.*

mor sel (môr′səl), 1. a mouthful; a small bite. 2. piece; fragment. *n. 6.*

mor tal (môr′təl), 1. sure to die sometime. 2. a being that is sure to die sometime. All living creatures are mortals. 3. of man; of mortals. 4. man; human being. 5. of death. 6. causing death of the soul; as, mortal sin. 7. causing death; as, a mortal wound, a mortal illness. 8. to the death; as, a mortal enemy, a mortal battle. 9. very great; deadly; as, mortal terror. *adj., n. 2.*

mor tal i ty (môr tal′i ti), 1. mortal nature; being sure to die sometime. 2. loss of life on a large scale. The mortality from automobile accidents is dreadful. 3. death rate; number of deaths per thousand cases of a disease, or per thousand persons in the population. The mortality from typhoid fever is decreasing. *n. 7.*

mor tal ly (môr′təl i), 1. fatally; so as to cause death; as, mortally wounded. 2. very greatly; bitterly; grievously; as, mortally offended. *adv.*

mor tar (môr′tər), 1. a mixture of lime, sand, and water, for holding bricks or stones together. 2. a very short cannon for shooting shells or fireworks high into the air. 3. a bowl of very hard material, in which substances may be pounded to a powder. *n. 8.*

Mortar and pestle

mort gage (môr′gij), 1. a claim on property, given to a person who has loaned money in case the money is not repaid when due. 2. a document that gives such a claim. 3. give a lender a claim to (one's property) in case a debt is not paid when due. 4. pledge. *n., v. 6.*

mor ti fi ca tion (môr′ti fi kā′shən), 1. mortifying or being mortified; as, the mortification of the body by fasting. 2. humiliating; cause of humiliating; as, mortification at having spilled food on the table. 3. the death of one part of the body while the rest is alive. The soldier's leg had to be cut off because mortification had set in. *n. 10.*

mor ti fy (môr′ti fī), 1. to wound (a person's feelings); make (a person) feel humbled or ashamed. A mother is mortified when her child behaves badly. 2. overcome (bodily desires and feelings) by pain and going without things. The saint mortified his body. 3. die; decay. The injured foot has mortified and must be cut off. *v., mortified, mortifying. 8.*

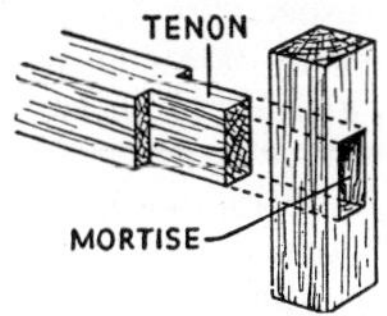

Mortise and tenon joint

mor tise or **mor tice** (môr′tis), 1. a hole in one piece of wood cut to receive a projection on another piece (called the tenon), so as to form a joint. See the picture. 2. fasten by a mortise. Good furniture is mortised together, not nailed. *n., v. 16.*

mor tu a ry (môr′chü ãr′i), 1. a building where dead bodies are kept for a while. 2. having to do with death or burial. *n., pl. mortuaries, adj.*

mos., months.

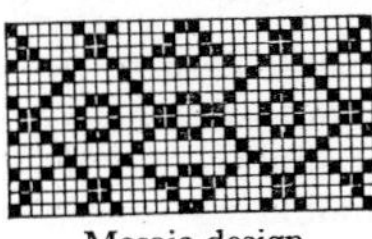
Mosaic design

mo sa ic[1] (mō zā′ik), 1. small pieces of stone, glass, wood, etc., of different colors inlaid to form a design. 2. formed by, pertaining to, or resembling such work. 3. such a picture or design. Mosaics are used in the floors, walls, or ceilings of some fine buildings. 4. anything like a mosaic. *n., adj. 9.*

Mo sa ic[2] (mō zā′ik), of Moses; as, the Mosaic law. *adj.*

Mos cow (mos′kou or mos′kō), capital of the Soviet Union, in the central part of European Russia. *n. 10.*

Mo ses (mō′ziz), the great leader and lawgiver of the Israelites who led them out of Egypt. *n. 5.*

Mos lem (moz′ləm), 1. a follower of Mohammed. 2. Mohammedan. *n., pl. Moslems* or *Moslem, adj. 12.*

Mosque

mosque (mosk), a Mohammedan place of worship. *n. 14.*

mos qui to (məs kē′tō), a small slender insect. The female gives a bite or sting that itches. There are many kinds of mosquitoes; some kinds transmit malaria; some transmit yellow fever. *n., pl. mosquitoes* or *mosquitos. 8.*

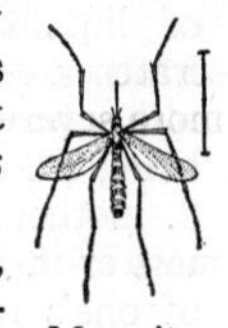
Mosquito. Line shows actual length.

moss (môs), very small, soft, green plants that grow close together like a carpet on the ground, on rocks, on trees, etc. See the picture below. *n. 3.*

moss y (môs′i), 1. covered with moss; as, a mossy bank. 2. like moss; as, mossy green. *adj., mossier, mossiest. 7.*

Moss growing on a rock

most (mōst), 1. You have the most fun on Saturday. April is the most rainy month. The person wins who has most votes. This burn hurts most. That is the most I can do. Most people like ice cream. Most of the toys are broken. 2. *Most* helps to make the superlative form of most adverbs, and of most adjectives longer than one syllable; as, most easily, most truly, most careful, most common. "Most common" means commonest. 3. **For the most part** means mainly; usually. **At most** means not more than. *adj., adv., n. 1.*

-most, suffix forming superlatives; as in foremost, inmost, topmost, uttermost.

most ly (mōst′li), mainly; chiefly; almost all; for the most part. *adv.*

mote (mōt), a speck of dust. *n. 11.*

moth (môth), 1. small winged insect that lays eggs in cloth, fur, etc. Its larvae eat holes in the material. 2. broad-winged insect very much like a butterfly, but flying mostly at night. *n., pl. moths* (môᴛʜz or môths). *5.*

moth-eat en (môth′ēt′ən), 1. eaten by moths; having holes made by moths. 2. worn-out; out-of-date. *adj.*

moth er[1] (muᴛʜ′ər), 1. Mother and father are parents. 2. take care of. 3. the cause or source of anything. 4. the head of a large community of religious women. *n., v. 1.*

hat, āge, cãre, fär; let, ēqual, tėrm; it, īce; hot, ōpen, ôrder; oil, out; cup, pu̇t, rüle, ūse; th, thin; ᴛʜ, then; ə represents *a* in about, *e* in taken, *i* in pencil, *o* in lemon, *u* in circus.

moth er² (muTH′ər), stringy, sticky substance formed in vinegar or on the surface of liquids that are turning to vinegar. Mother consists of bacteria. *n.*

moth er hood (muTH′ər hůd), 1. state of being a mother. 2. qualities of a mother. 3. mothers. *n. 19.*

moth er-in-law (muTH′ər in lô′), the mother of one's husband or wife. *n., pl. mothers-in-law.*

moth er land (muTH′ər land′), 1. native country. 2. land of one's ancestors. *n.*

moth er less (muTH′ər lis), having no mother. *adj.*

moth er ly (muTH′ər li), like a mother; like a mother's; kindly. *adj. 12.*

moth er-of-pearl (muTH′ər əv pėrl′), the hard rainbow-colored lining of the shell of the pearl oyster and certain other shells. It is used to make buttons and ornaments. *n.*

mo tif (mō tēf′), 1. a subject for development or treatment in art, literature, or music; a principal idea or feature. This opera contains a love motif. 2. a distinctive figure in a design. *n. 15.*

mo tion (mō′shən), 1. movement; moving; change of position or place; as, the motion of a ship, the motion of one's hand in writing. Anything is in motion which is not at rest. 2. make a movement, as of the hand or head, to show one's meaning; show (a person) what to do by such a motion. He motioned me out. 3. formal suggestion made in a meeting, to be voted on. The motion to adjourn was carried. *n., v. 2.*

mo tion less (mō′shən lis), not moving. *adj. 7.*

motion picture, moving picture.

mo ti vate (mō′ti vāt), provide with a motive. *v.*

mo tive (mō′tiv), 1. the thought or feeling that makes one act. His motive in going was his wish to please his mother. 2. that makes something move; as, motive power of steam or electricity. 3. motif. *n., adj. 3.*

Clown wearing a motley costume

mot ley (mot′li), 1. suit of more than one color worn by clowns. 2. of different colors like a clown's suit. 3. a mixture of things that are different. 4. made up of units not alike; as, a motley collection. *n., pl. motleys, adj. 9.*

mo tor (mō′tər), 1. engine which makes a thing go; as, an electric motor, a gasoline motor. 2. run by a motor; as, a motor bicycle. 3. an automobile. 4. travel by automobile. 5. having to do with motion. Motor nerves arouse muscles to action. *n., adj., v. 4.*

mo tor boat (mō′tər bōt′), boat that is run by a motor. *n. 15.*

mo tor car (mō′tər kär′), automobile. *n. 20.*

mo tor cy cle (mō′tər sī′kəl), bicycle run by a motor. *n. 11.*

Motorcycle

mo tor ist (mō′tər ist), person who travels by automobile, especially one who does it a great deal. *n. 14.*

mo tor man (mō′tər mən), 1. man who runs an electric streetcar or train. 2. man who runs a motor. *n., pl. motormen. 14.*

mot tle (mot′əl), 1. mark with spots or streaks of different colors. 2. a mottled coloring or pattern. *v., n. 12.*

mot tled (mot′əld), spotted or streaked with different colors. *adj.*

mot to (mot′ō), 1. a brief sentence adopted as a rule of conduct. "Think before you speak" is a good motto. 2. a sentence, word, or a phrase written or engraved on some object. *n., pl. mottoes or mottos. 7.*

mould (mōld), mold. *n., v. 4.*

mould er (mōl′dər), molder. *v.*

mould ing (mōl′ding), molding. *n.*

mould y (mōl′di), moldy. *adj., mouldier, mouldiest.*

moult (mōlt), molt. *v., n. 17.*

mound (mound), a bank or heap of earth or stones. *n. 4.*

mount¹ (mount), 1. go up; ascend; as, to mount a hill or a ladder. 2. get up on; as, to mount a horse, to mount a platform. 3. get on a horse. Paul Revere mounted in haste. 4. put on a horse; furnish with a horse; as, the mounted police. 5. horse for riding. The general had an excellent mount. 6. rise; increase. The cost of living mounts steadily. 7. put in proper position or order for use. 8. have or carry (guns). The ship mounts eight guns. 9. fix in proper setting, backing, support, etc.; as, to mount photographs on cards, to mount gems in gold. 10. that on which anything is mounted, fixed, supported, or placed; as, the mount for a picture. 11. provide (a play) with scenery and costumes. *v., n. 1.*

mount² (mount), mountain; high hill. *n.*

moun tain (moun′tən), 1. a very high hill. 2. of or pertaining to mountains; as, mountain air, mountain plants. 3. a very large heap or pile of anything; as, a mountain of rubbish. *n., adj. 1.*

moun tain eer (moun′tə nēr′), 1. person who lives in the mountains. 2. person skilled in mountain climbing. *n. 8.*

mountain goat, white antelope of the Rocky Mountains.

Mountain goat (about 3 ft. high at the shoulder)

mountain lion, a large American wildcat.

moun tain ous (moun′tə nəs), 1. covered with mountain ranges; as, mountainous country. 2. huge; as, a mountainous wave. *adj. 5.*

mountain range, a row of mountains; a series of mountains.

moun te bank (moun′ti bangk), 1. person who sells quack medicines in public, appealing to his audience by tricks, stories, jokes, etc. 2. anybody who tries to deceive people by tricks, stories, and jokes. *n. 14.*

mount ing (moun′ting), support, setting, etc. Her photograph is on a heavy cardboard mounting. *n.*

Mount Ver non (mount′ vėr′nən), the home of George Washington in Virginia, on the Potomac River near Washington, D. C.

mourn (mōrn), 1. grieve. 2. feel or show sorrow over. Mary mourned her lost doll. *v. 2.*

mourn er (mōr′nər), person who mourns, especially at a funeral. *n. 7.*

mourn ful (mōrn′fəl), sad; sorrowful; full of grief. *adj. 5.*

mourn ing (mōr′ning), 1. wearing of black or some other color to show that a relative has died. 2. draping of buildings, hanging flags at half-mast, etc., as outward signs of sorrow for death. 3. clothes or decorations to show sorrow. 4. of mourning; used in mourning. *n., adj.*

mouse (mous for 1, mouz for 2 and 3), 1. a small, gray, gnawing animal. See the picture. The kind that lives in houses is about three or four inches long. Field mice live in the grass. 2. hunt for mice; catch mice for food, as cats and owls do. 3. search as a cat does; move about as if searching. *n., pl. mice, v. 2.*

Mouse

mouse trap (mous′trap′), trap for catching mice. *n.*

mousse (müs), a fancy food made with whipped cream, either frozen or stiffened with gelatine; as, chocolate mousse, tomato mousse. *n.*

mous tache (məs tash′), mustache. *n.*

mouth (mouth for *n.*, mouᴛʜ for *v.*), 1. an opening through which an animal takes in food; a space containing tongue and teeth. 2. an opening suggesting a mouth; as, the mouth of a cave, of a river, or of a bottle. 3. utter (words) in an affected, pompous way. 4. seize or rub with the mouth. 5. grimace. *n., pl. mouths* (mouᴛʜz), *v. 1.*

mouth ful (mouth′fu̇l), 1. the amount the mouth can easily hold. 2. what is taken in one bite. 3. small amount. *n., pl. mouthfuls. 12.*

mouth piece (mouth′pēs′), 1. the part of a pipe, horn, etc., that is placed in or at the mouth. 2. person, newspaper, etc., that speaks for others. *n. 15.*

mov a ble (müv′ə bəl), 1. that can be moved. Our fingers are movable. 2. that can be carried from place to place as personal possessions can. 3. changing from one date to another in different years. Easter is a movable holy day. 4. piece of furniture that is not a fixture but can be moved to another house. 5. **Movables** means personal property. *adj., n. 6.*

move (müv), 1. put in a different place. Move your chair to the other side of the table. 2. go to another place. 3. change the position of. Do not move your hand. 4. change position. The child moved in his sleep. 5. change one's place of living. We have moved from 96th Street to 110th Street. 6. **Move in** sometimes means to move oneself, one's family, one's belongings, etc., into a new place to live. 7. put or keep in motion; shake; stir. The wind moves the leaves. **Move heaven and earth** to do something means try every possible way of doing it. 8. go. The train moves out slowly. 9. impel; arouse (a person to laughter, anger, pity, etc.). 10. take action (in some matter); act. 11. action taken to bring about some result. 12. in games, to change to a different square according to rules; as, to move a pawn in chess. 13. the moving of a piece in chess and other games. That was a good move. 14. a player's turn to move. It is your move now. 15. make a move in chess or other games. 16. in a meeting, to bring forward or propose. Mr. President, I move that we have the picnic Friday. *v., n. 1.*

move a ble (müv′ə bəl), movable. *adj., n.*

move ment (müv′mənt), 1. moving. We run by movements of the legs. 2. change in the placing of troops or ships. 3. the moving parts (of a machine); a special group of parts that move on each other. The movement of a watch consists of many little wheels. 4. in music, the kind of rhythm a piece has, its speed, etc. 5. one division of a long musical selection; as, the second movement of Beethoven's Fifth Symphony. 6. the efforts and results of a group of people working together to bring about some one thing; as, the movement for a safe and sane Fourth of July. *n. 3.*

mov er (müv′ər), one that moves. *n. 12.*

mov ie (müv′i), moving picture. *n.* [*Used in common talk*] *15.*

mov ing (müv′ing), 1. that moves; as, moving pictures. 2. causing action. John was the moving spirit of the undertaking. 3. touching; pathetic; as, a moving story. *adj.*

moving picture, picture shown on a screen in which persons or things move.

mow[1] (mō), 1. cut down with a machine or a scythe; as, to mow grass. The men are mowing today. 2. mow the grass or grain from; as, to mow a field. 3. destroy at a sweep or in large numbers, as if by mowing. The firing of the enemy mowed down our men like grass. *v., mowed, mowed* or *mown, mowing. 7.*

mow[2] (mou), 1. the place in the barn where hay, grain, etc., is piled or stored. 2. a pile or stack of hay, grain, etc., in a barn. *n.*

mow er (mō′ər), person or thing that mows; as, a lawn mower. *n. 6.*

mown (mōn), mowed. New-mown hay is hay that has just been cut. *pp. of* **mow**[1].

Mo zam bique (mō′zəm bēk′), Portuguese colony in southeastern Africa. *n.*

Mo zart (mō′zärt), a great Austrian musical composer (1756-1791). *n.*

M.P. or **MP,** Member of Parliament.

Mr. or **Mr** (mis′tər), a title put in front of a man's name or the name of his position; as, Mr. Jackson, Mr. Speaker. *1.*

Mrs. or **Mrs** (mis′iz), a title put in front of a married woman's name. *1.*

Ms. or **MS.** or **ms.,** manuscript.

Mt., mount; mountain; as, Mt. Whitney.

much (much), 1. There is much water in the sea. A million dollars is much money. Don't eat too much of the cake. How much do you want? 2. We are much pleased when we win. A long rest made her feel much better. 3. Some special meanings are:

make much of, pay much attention to or do much for.

much of a size, height, etc., nearly the same size, height, etc.

not much of a, not a very good. That is not much of a hat.

too much for, more than a match for.

adj., more, most, adv., more, most, n. 1.

mu ci lage (mū′si lij), a sticky, gummy substance used to make things stick together. *n. 17.*

muck (muk), 1. moist farmyard manure. 2. dirt; filth. 3. a mess; an untidy condition. *Used in common talk. n. 6.*

muck-rake (muk′rāk′), hunt for and expose corruption. *v.*

mu cous (mū′kəs), 1. of or like mucus. 2. containing mucus. The mucous membrane is the lining of the nose, throat, and other cavities of the body that are open to the air. *adj. 10.*

mu cus (mū′kəs), a slimy substance that moistens the linings of the body. A cold in the head causes a discharge of mucus. *n.*

mud (mud), earth so wet that it is soft and sticky; as, mud on the ground after rain, mud at the bottom of a pond. *n. 2.*

mud dle (mud′əl), 1. mix up; bring (things) into a mess; as, to muddle a piece of work. 2. think or act in a confused, blundering way; as, to muddle over a problem, to muddle through a difficulty. 3. make confused or stupid. 4. a mess; disorder; confusion. When Mother came home, she found the house in a muddle. *v., n. 11.*

mud dy (mud′i), 1. of or like mud; as, muddy footprints on the floor. 2. having much mud; covered with mud; as, a muddy road, muddy shoes. 3. clouded with mud; dull; not pure; as, muddy water, a muddy color. 4. confused; not clear. 5. make muddy; become muddy. *adj., muddier, muddiest, v., muddied, muddying. 6.*

Muff

muff (muf), 1. a covering, usually of fur, into which a woman puts both hands, one at each end, to keep them warm. 2. fail to catch (a ball) when it comes into one's hands. 3. clumsy failure to catch a ball that comes into one's hands. The catcher's muff allowed the runner to score. 4. handle awkwardly; bungle. *n., v. 6.*

muf fin (muf′in), a small, round cake made of wheat flour, corn meal, or the like, eaten with butter, and usually served hot. *n. 9.*

muf fle (muf′əl), 1. wrap or cover up in order to keep warm and dry. She muffled her throat in a warm scarf. 2. wrap up the head of (a person) in order to keep him from speaking. 3. wrap in something in order to soften or stop the sound. A bell can be muffled with cloth. 4. to dull or deaden (a sound). 5. muffled sound. *v., n. 8.*

muf fler (muf′lər), 1. a wrap or scarf worn for warmth. 2. thing used to deaden sound. An automobile engine has a muffler attached to the exhaust. *n. 11.*

muf ti (muf′ti), ordinary clothes, not a uniform. The retired general appeared in mufti. *n. 19.*

mug[1] (mug), 1. a heavy china or metal drinking cup with a handle. 2. amount a mug holds; as, to drink a mug of milk. *n. 6.*

Mug

mug[2] (mug), face; mouth. *n.* [*Slang*]

mug gy (mug′i), warm, damp, and close. The weather was muggy. *adj., muggier, muggiest. 18.*

mu lat to (mū lat′ō), person having one white parent and one Negro parent. *n., pl. mulattoes.*

mul ber ry (mul′ber′i), 1. a tree whose leaves are used for feeding silkworms; any of several similar trees. 2. the sweet berry that is the fruit of the mulberry tree. 3. dark purplish red. *n., pl. mulberries, adj. 7.*

Mulberry leaves and berries

mulch (mulch), 1. straw, leaves, loose earth, etc., spread on the ground around trees or plants. Mulch is used to protect the roots from cold or heat, to prevent evaporation of moisture from the soil, or to keep the fruit clean. 2. to cover with straw, leaves, etc. *n., v. 13.*

mulct (mulkt), 1. deprive of something; deprive. He was mulcted of his money by a shrewd trick. 2. punish by a fine. 3. fine; penalty. *v., n.*

mule (mūl), 1. an animal which is half donkey and half horse. 2. a stupid or stubborn person. 3. a kind of spinning machine. *n. 4.*

Mule (about 5 ft. high at the shoulder)

mu le teer (mū′lə tēr′), a driver of mules. *n. 20.*

mul ish (mūl′ish), like a mule; stubborn. *adj.*

mull[1] (mul), ponder; think without making much progress. *v.* [*Used in common talk*] *12.*

mull[2] (mul), make (wine, beer, etc.) into a warm drink, with sugar, spices, etc. *v.*

mul lein or **mul len** (mul′in), a weed with coarse woolly leaves and spikes of yellow flowers. *n. 19.*

Mullein

mul let (mul′it), a kind of edible fish. There are red mullets and gray mullets. *n. 18.*

mul ti far i ous (mul′ti fãr′i əs), 1. having many different parts, elements, forms, etc. 2. many and varied. *adj.*

mul ti form (mul′ti fôrm), having many different shapes, forms, or kinds. *adj. 16.*

mul ti mil lion aire (mul′ti mil′yən ãr′), person who owns property worth several millions (of dollars, pounds, francs, etc.). *n.*

mul ti ple (mul′ti pəl), 1. of, having, or involving many parts, elements, relations, etc.; as, a man of multiple interests. 2. a number that contains another number a certain number of times without a remainder. 12 is a multiple of 3. The **least common multiple** is the least quantity that contains two or more given quantities exactly. 12 is the least common multiple of 3 and 4 and 6. *adj., n. 10.*

mul ti pli cand (mul′ti pli kand′), number or quantity to be multiplied by another. In 5 times 497, the multiplicand is 497. *n.*

mul ti pli ca tion (mul′ti pli kā′shən), multiplying; being multiplied. *n. 6.*

mul ti plic i ty (mul′ti plis′i ti), manifold variety; a great many. Theodore Roosevelt had a multiplicity of interests. *n. 15.*

mul ti pli er (mul′ti plī′ər), 1. a thing that multiplies. 2. the number by which another number is to be multiplied. In 5 times 8, 5 is the multiplier. *n. 19.*

mul ti ply (mul′ti plī), 1. take (a number or quantity) a given number of times. To multiply 6 by 3 means to take 6 three times, making 18. 2. increase in number. As we climbed up the mountain the dangers and difficulties multiplied. *v., multiplied, multiplying. 3.*

mul ti tude (mul′ti tūd or mul′ti tüd), a great number; a crowd. *n. 3.*

mul ti tu di nous (mul′ti tū′di nəs or mul′ti-tü′di nəs), forming a multitude; very numerous. *adj. 13.*

mum (mum), silent; saying nothing. Keep mum about this; tell no one. *adj., interj. 13.*

mum ble (mum′bəl), 1. speak indistinctly, as a person does when his lips are partly closed. 2. chew as a person does who has no teeth. The old dog mumbled the crust. 3. mumbling. *v., n. 8.*

mum mer (mum′ər), 1. person who wears a mask, fancy costume, or disguise for fun. Six mummers acted in a play at Christmas. 2. actor. *n. 17.*

mum mer y (mum′ər i), 1. the performance of mummers. 2. a useless or silly show or ceremony. *n., pl. mummeries. 16.*

mum mi fy (mum′i fī), 1. make into a mummy. 2. shrivel; dry up. *v., mummified, mummifying.*

mum my (mum′i), a dead body preserved from decay. Egyptian mummies have lasted more than 3000 years. *n., pl. mummies. 9.*

Egyptian mummy and mummy case

mumps (mumps), a contagious disease marked by swelling of the neck and face and difficulty in swallowing. *n. 16.*

munch (munch), chew vigorously and steadily; chew noisily. A horse munches its oats. *v. 10.*

mun dane (mun′dān), 1. of this world, not of heaven; earthly. 2. of the universe, the world, or the earth. *adj. 15.*

Mu nich (mū′nik), a large city in southwestern Germany. *n. 9.*

mu nic i pal (mū nis′i pəl), having to do with the affairs of a city, town, or other municipality. *adj. 10.*

mu nic i pal i ty (mū nis′i pal′i ti), city, town, or other district having local self-government. *n., pl. municipalities. 16.*

mu nif i cence (mū nif′i səns), very great generosity. *n. 15.*

mu nif i cent (mū nif′i sənt), extremely generous. *adj. 14.*

mu ni tion (mū nish′ən), 1. material used in war. Munitions are military supplies such as guns, powder, bombs, etc. 2. pertaining to military supplies. A munition plant is a factory for making munitions. 3. provided with military supplies; as, to munition a fort. *n., adj., v. 10.*

mu ral (mūr′əl), 1. on a wall. A mural painting is painted on a wall of a building. 2. picture painted on a wall. 3. of a wall; having to do with walls; like a wall. *adj., n. 9.*

mur der (mėr′dər), 1. the unlawful killing of a human being when it is planned beforehand. 2. kill thus. 3. To murder a song or a poem is to give it very badly. *n., v. 3.*

mur der er (mėr′dər ər), one who murders somebody. *n. 5.*

mur der ess (mėr′dər is), woman who murders somebody. *n.*

mur der ous (mėr′dər əs), 1. able to kill; as, a murderous blow. 2. ready to murder; as, a murderous villain. 3. causing murder. *adj. 8.*

murk (mėrk), darkness; gloom. *n. 18.*

murk y (mėr′ki), dark; gloomy; as, a murky prison. *adj., murkier, murkiest. 15.*

mur mur (mėr′mər), 1. a soft, low, indistinct sound that rises and falls a little and goes on without breaks; as, the murmur of a stream or of voices in another room. 2. make such a sound. 3. a softly spoken word or speech. 4. say in a murmur. 5. a complaint made under the breath, not aloud. 6. complain in this way; grumble. *n., v. 2.*

mur rain (mėr′in), 1. plague. A murrain on you! *Old use.* 2. an infectious disease of cattle. *n.*

mus cle (mus′əl), 1. the tissue in the bodies of people and animals which can be tightened or let loose and thus make the body move. 2. a special bundle of such tissue which moves some particular bone or part. The biceps muscle bends the arm. 3. strength. *n. 6.*

Frog's legs showing muscles: R, relaxed; C, contracted.

mus cu lar (mus′kū lər), 1. of the muscles; influencing the muscles; as, a muscular strain. 2. having well-developed muscles; strong; as, a muscular arm. *adj. 7.*

muse[1] (mūz), think; think in a dreamy way. *v. 3.*

Muse[2] (mūz), 1. one of the nine goddesses of the fine arts and sciences. 2. A **muse**

or **Muse** is the spirit that gives a poet or composer his ideas. *n.*

mu se um (mū zē′əm), the building or rooms in which a collection of objects illustrating science, ancient life, art, or other subjects is kept. *n. 4.*

mush (mush), 1. corn meal boiled in water. 2. a soft thick mass. *n. 14.*

Mushrooms (stalk 2 to 5 in. high)

mush room (mush′rüm), 1. a small fungus shaped like an umbrella, that grows very fast. Some mushrooms are good to eat; some are poisonous. 2. of or like a mushroom. 3. of very rapid growth. *n., adj. 8.*

mu sic (mū′zik), 1. the art of making sounds that are beautiful, and putting them together into beautiful arrangements. 2. sounds and compositions made to be beautiful and pleasing to the ear. 3. written or printed signs for tones. Can you read music? **Set to music** means provide (the words of a song) with music. 4. any pleasant sound; as, the music of streams, the music of the wind. *n. 1.*

mu si cal (mū′zi kəl), 1. of music; as, musical instruments. 2. sounding beautiful; like music. 3. set to music or accompanied by music; as, a musical comedy. 4. fond of music. 5. skilled in music. *adj. 3.*

musical instrument, piano, violin, or other instrument for producing music.

mu si cal ly (mū′zi kəl i), 1. in a musical manner. 2. in music. She is well educated musically. *adv.*

mu si cian (mū zish′ən), 1. person skilled in music. 2. person who sings or plays on a musical instrument, especially as a profession or business. *n. 4.*

mus ing (mūz′ing), absorbed in thought; dreamy; meditative. *adj.*

musk (musk), 1. substance with a strong and lasting odor, used in making perfumes. Musk is found in a special gland in the male musk deer. 2. the odor of musk. *n. 9.*

musk deer, a small hornless deer, the male of which has a gland containing musk.

mus kel lunge (mus′kə lunj), large American pike. It is a very hard fish to catch. *n., pl. muskellunge.*

mus ket (mus′kit), gun used by soldiers before rifles were invented. *n. 8.*

Musket

mus ket eer (mus′ki tēr′), soldier armed with a musket. *n.*

mus ket ry (mus′kit ri), 1. muskets. 2. the fire of muskets. *n. 15.*

Musk ox (about 5 ft. high at the shoulder)

musk mel on (musk′mel′ən), a kind of sweet, juicy melon. It is also called cantaloupe. *n.*

musk ox, arctic animal, somewhat like an ox and even more like a sheep, that has a musky smell.

musk rat (musk′rat′), 1. a water animal of North America, like a rat, but larger. 2. its fur. Muskrat is valu able for garments. *n., pl. muskrats* or *muskrat. 12.*

Muskrat (length, including the tail, about 20 in.)

musk y (mus′ki), of musk; like musk; like that of musk; as, a musky odor. *adj.*

mus lin (muz′lin), 1. a thin, fine, cotton cloth, used for dresses, curtains, etc. 2. a heavier cotton cloth, used for sheets, undergarments, etc. 3. made of muslin; as, white muslin curtains. *n., adj. 6.*

muss (mus), 1. put into disorder; rumple. The child's dress was mussed. 2. disorder; a mess. *v., n.* [*Used in common talk*]

mus sel (mus′əl), a shellfish having two parts to its shell, living in either salt water or fresh water. *n. 15.*

Mussel

Mus so li ni (mu̇s′ə lē′ni), Benito (born 1883), leader of the Italian Fascists and prime minister of Italy since 1922. The Italians call him "Il Duce," which means "the Leader." *n.*

Mus sul man (mus′əl mən), a Mohammedan; a Moslem. *n., pl. Mussulmans. 13.*

must (must), 1. be obliged to; be forced to. All men must die. 2. ought to; should. I must keep my promise. You must read this story. 3. be certain to be, do, etc. The man must be crazy to talk so. *v. 1.*

mus tache (məs tash′), 1. hair growing on a man's upper lip. 2. hairs or bristles growing near the mouth of an animal. *n. 10.*

mus ta chio (məs tä′shō), mustache. *n., pl. mustachios.*

mus tang (mus′tang), the small wild or half-wild horse of the American plains. *n.*

mus tard (mus′tərd), 1. a plant whose seeds have a sharp hot taste. 2. a powder or paste used for flavoring meats, etc., made from its seeds. *n. 7.*

Mustard

mus ter (mus′tər), 1. assemble; gather together; collect. 2. assembly; collection. 3. summon; as, to muster up courage. 4. bringing together of men or troops for review or service. 5. list of those mustered. 6. the number mustered. *v., n. 6.*

must n't (mus′ənt), must not.

mus ty (mus′ti), 1. moldy; having a smell or taste suggesting mold or damp; as, a musty room, musty crackers. 2. stale; out-of-date; as, musty laws. *adj., mustier, mustiest. 11.*

mu ta bil i ty (mū′tə bil′i ti), 1. tendency to change. 2. fickleness. *n. 15.*

mu ta ble (mū′tə bəl), 1. liable to change; as, mutable customs. 2. fickle; as, a mutable person. *adj. 14.*

mu ta tion (mū tā′shən), change; alteration. *n. 10.*

mute (mūt), 1. silent; not making any sound. The little girl stood mute. 2. dumb; unable to speak. 3. person who cannot speak. 4. a clip or pad put on a musical instrument to soften the sound. 5. put such a clip or pad on. He played the violin with muted strings. *adj., n., v. 4.*

mu ti late (mū′ti lāt), cut, tear, or break off a part of; injure seriously by cutting, tearing, or breaking off some part. The victims of the accident were badly mutilated; some lost arms, some lost legs. *v. 9.*

mu ti la tion (mū′ti lā′shən), 1. mutilating. 2. being mutilated; the loss of an arm, leg, ear, or any other important part of the body. *n. 16.*

mu ti neer (mū′ti nēr′), person who takes part in a mutiny. *n. 13.*

mu ti nous (mū′ti nəs), rebellious. *adj. 10.*

mu ti ny (mū′ti ni), 1. open rebellion against lawful authority, especially by sailors or soldiers against their officers. 2. to rebel; take part in a mutiny. *n., pl. mutinies, v., mutinied, mutinying. 7.*

mut ter (mut′ər), 1. speak or utter low and indistinctly, with lips partly closed. 2. complain; grumble. 3. muttering. 4. muttered words. *v., n. 4.*

mut ton (mut′ən), meat from a sheep. We had roast mutton for dinner. *n. 5.*

mutton chop, 1. small piece of mutton from the ribs or loin for broiling or frying. 2. patch of whiskers on the side of the face, shaped somewhat like a chop.

Mutton chop whiskers

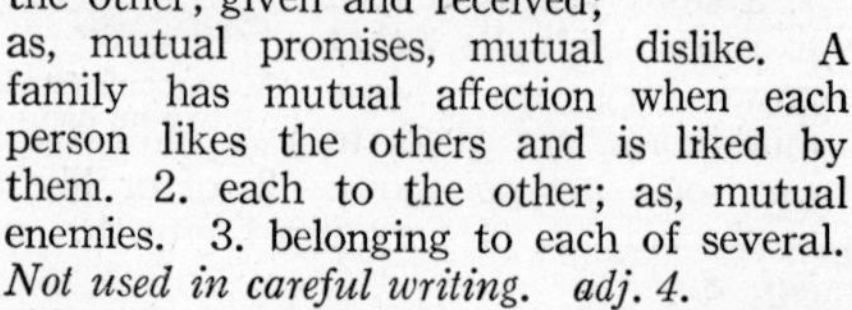

mu tu al (mū′chü əl), 1. done, said, felt, etc., by each toward the other; given and received; as, mutual promises, mutual dislike. A family has mutual affection when each person likes the others and is liked by them. 2. each to the other; as, mutual enemies. 3. belonging to each of several. *Not used in careful writing. adj. 4.*

mu tu al ly (mū′chü əl i), each toward the other. *adv.*

mu zhik or **mu zjik** (mü zhik′), Russian peasant. *n.*

muz zle (muz′əl), 1. the nose, mouth, and jaws of a four-footed animal. 2. a cover or cage of straps or wires to put over an animal's head to keep it from biting or eating. 3. put such a muzzle on. 4. compel (a person) to keep silent about something. 5. the open end of a gun, pistol, etc. *n., v. 5.*

Muzzle on a dog's head

my (mī), of me; belonging to me. I learned my lesson. *pron. 1.*

My ce nae (mī sē′ni), very ancient city in Greece. *n.*

myr i ad (mir′i əd), a very great number. There are myriads of stars. *n. 6.*

myr mi don (mėr′mi don), 1. an obedient and unquestioning follower. The term is ordinarily used with the added idea of cruelty, or with contempt. 2. The **Myrmidons** were a warlike people of ancient Thessaly who accompanied Achilles, their king, to the Trojan War. *n. 16.*

myrrh (mėr), a fragrant, gummy substance with a bitter taste, obtained from a shrub that grows in Arabia and eastern Africa. Myrrh is used in medicines, in perfumes, and in incense. *n. 11.*

myr tle (mėr′təl), 1. an evergreen shrub with shiny leaves and fragrant white flowers. 2. a low, creeping evergreen plant with blue flowers; the periwinkle. *n. 6.*

Myrtle (def. 1)

my self (mī self′), 1. Myself is used to

make a statement stronger. I did it myself. 2. Myself is used instead of I or me in cases like: I can cook for myself. I hurt myself. 3. I don't think much of myself for doing that. *pron. 1.*

mys te ri ous (mis tēr′i əs), 1. full of mystery; hard to explain. 2. suggesting mystery. *adj. 4.*

mys ter y (mis′tər i), 1. a secret; something that is hidden or unknown. 2. secrecy; obscurity. 3. something that is not explained or understood; as, the mystery of God's love. 4. religious rite to which only initiated persons are admitted. 5. a kind of play based on the Bible. *n., pl. mysteries. 3.*

mys tic (mis′tik), 1. mystical. 2. person who believes that his soul can commune directly with God. *adj., n. 8.*

mys ti cal (mis′ti kəl), 1. mysterious; having some secret meaning; beyond human understanding. 2. spiritually symbolic. The lamb and the dove are mystical symbols of the Christian religion. 3. of or concerned with mystics or mysticism. 4. of or having to do with secret rites open only to the initiated. *adj. 10.*

mys ti cism (mis′ti sizm), 1. the beliefs or mode of thought of mystics. 2. the doctrine that truth or God may be known through spiritual insight, independent of the mind. *n. 16.*

mys ti fi ca tion (mis′ti fi kā′shən), 1. mystifying. 2. bewilderment; perplexity. 3. something meant to mystify. *n.*

mys ti fy (mis′ti fī), 1. bewilder purposely; puzzle; perplex. The magician's tricks mystified the audience. 2. make mysterious. *v., mystified, mystifying. 16.*

myth (mith), 1. a legend or story, usually one that attempts to account for something in nature. The myth of Proserpina is the ancient Greek explanation of summer and winter. 2. any invented story. 3. a made-up person or thing. Amy's wealthy uncle was a myth invented to impress the other girls. *n. 12.*

myth i cal (mith′i kəl), 1. of a myth; like a myth; in myths; as, a mythical interpretation of nature, mythical monsters, mythical heroes, mythical places. 2. not real; made-up. The Smiths' wealth is merely mythical. *adj. 19.*

myth o log i cal (mith′ə loj′i kəl), of mythology. The phoenix is a mythological bird. *adj. 15.*

my thol o gy (mi thol′ə ji), 1. myths; as, Greek mythology. 2. the study of myths. *n., pl. mythologies. 10.*

N

N, n (en), the 14th letter of the alphabet. N comes after j, k, l, m. There are two n's in cannot. *n., pl. N's, n's.*

N or **N.,** 1. North. 2. Northern.

n., 1. noun. 2. north. 3. northern.

nab (nab), grab; catch or seize suddenly. *v., nabbed, nabbing.* [*Slang*]

na dir (nā′dər), 1. the point in the heavens directly beneath the place where one stands; the point opposite the zenith. 2. the lowest point. *n.*

nag[1] (nag), find fault with (a person) all the time; scold; irritate or annoy by peevish complaints. *v., nagged, nagging. 13.*

nag[2] (nag), 1. horse. 2. inferior horse. *n.*

Na hum (nā′həm), 1. Hebrew prophet. 2. book of the Old Testament containing his prophecies. *n.*

nai ad or **Nai ad** (nā′ad), nymph guarding a stream or spring. *n. 12.*

nail (nāl), 1. a small, slender piece of metal to be hammered in to hold things together, or to be used as a peg. 2. fasten with a nail or nails. 3. hold or keep fixed; make secure. 4. catch; seize. *Used in common talk.* 5. the hard layer at the end of a finger or toe. *n., v. 2.*

nain sook (nān′su̇k), a very soft, fine cotton cloth. *n. 17.*

na ïve or **na ive** (nä ēv′), simple in nature; like a child; artless. *adj. 17.*

na ïve té (nä ēv tā′), quality of being naïve; unspoiled freshness; artlessness. *n.*

na ked (nā′kid), 1. with no clothes on; bare. A barefoot boy has naked feet. 2. not covered. The **naked truth** is the plain truth without ornament. The **naked eye** is the bare eye not helped by any glass, telescope, or microscope. *adj. 3.*

na ked ness (nā′kid nis), bareness; naked condition. *n. 7.*

name (nām), 1. word or words by which a

person, animal, place, or thing is spoken of or to. Our dog's name is Jack. Mary knows all her chickens by name. 2. give a name to. They named the baby Mary. 3. call by name; mention by name. 4. give the right name for. Can you name these flowers? 5. **Know only by name** means know only by hearing about. 6. a word that means any object, or any one of a group of objects. 7. **Call a person names** means call him bad names. 8. reputation; as, to get a bad name, to have a name for honest dealing, to win oneself a name. 9. **In the name of** means (1) acting for. I bought it in my sister's name. (2) for the sake of. 10. mention; give as an instance. She named several cases. 11. appoint; nominate; as, to name Smith for president. 12. choose; settle on. *n., v. 1.*

name less (nām′lis), 1. having no name; as, a nameless grave. 2. not named; as, a book by a nameless writer. 3. that cannot be named or described; as, a strange, nameless longing. 4. not fit to be mentioned. *adj. 6.*

name ly (nām′li), that is to say. Only two pupils got 100 in the test—namely, Arthur and Blanche. *adv. 5.*

name sake (nām′sāk′), one having the same name as another; especially, one named after another; as, Theodore, namesake of President Theodore Roosevelt. *n. 12.*

nan keen or **nan kin** (nan kēn′), a firm, yellow or buff cloth. *n.*

Nan king (nan′king′), city in eastern China. *n.*

nap[1] (nap), 1. a short sleep. Baby takes a nap after his dinner. 2. take a short sleep. Grandfather naps in his armchair. *n., v., napped, napping. 4.*

nap[2] (nap), the soft, short, woolly threads or hairs on the surface of cloth; as, the nap on velvet or flannelette. *n.*

nape (nāp), the back of the neck. *n. 15.*

naph tha (naf′thə), a liquid made from petroleum, coal tar, etc., used as fuel and to take spots from clothing. *n. 14.*

nap kin (nap′kin), 1. piece of cloth used at meals for protecting the clothing or for wiping the lips or fingers. 2. any similar piece, such as a baby's diaper or a small towel. *n. 3.*

Na ples (nā′pəlz), seaport on the southwestern coast of Italy, famous for its beautiful bay. *n. 10.*

Na po le on (nə pō′li ən). Napoleon Bonaparte (1769-1821) was one of the greatest generals of the world, who made himself emperor of France. Napoleon III (1808-1873), his nephew, tried to imitate his famous uncle and became emperor of France. *n. 8.*

Na po le on ic (nə pō′li on′ik), of, having to do with, or resembling, Napoleon. *adj. 15.*

nar cis sus (när sis′əs), a spring flower that grows from a bulb. Jonquils and daffodils are narcissuses. *n. 12.*

Narcissus

Nar cis sus (när sis′əs), beautiful youth in Greek mythology who fell in love with his reflection in a spring. He pined away and was changed into the flower narcissus. *n.*

nar cot ic (när kot′ik), 1. drug that produces drowsiness, sleep, dullness, or an insensible condition, and lessens pain by dulling the nerves. Opium is a powerful narcotic. 2. having the properties and effects of a narcotic. *n., adj. 8.*

nard (närd), 1. a fragrant plant. 2. an ointment prepared from this plant. *n. 17.*

Nar ra gan sett (nar′ə gan′sit), bay in Rhode Island. *n.*

nar rate (na rāt′), tell the story of. *v. 12.*

nar ra tion (na rā′shən), 1. telling; that form of composition which relates an event or a story. Novels, short stories, histories, and biographies are forms of narration. 2. story; account. *n. 20.*

nar ra tive (nar′ə tiv), 1. story. 2. narration; storytelling. 3. that narrates. *Evangeline* is a narrative poem. *n., adj. 7.*

nar ra tor (na rā′tər), person who tells a story. *n. 17.*

nar row (nar′ō), 1. not wide; having little width. A path a foot wide is narrow. 2. less wide than usual for its kind; as, narrow ribbon. 3. **Narrows** means a narrow part of a river, strait, sound, valley, pass, etc. 4. limited; small. He had only a narrow circle of friends. 5. make narrow; become narrow; decrease in width. 6. not going far from a narrow track; not seeing much beyond a narrow space; as, a narrow mind. 7. close; with a small margin; as, a narrow escape. *adj., n., v. 1.*

nar row-mind ed (nar′ō mīn′did), lacking breadth of view or sympathy; prejudiced. *adj.*

nar whal (när′wəl), kind of small whale. *n.*

na sal (nā′zəl), 1. of the nose; as, nasal catarrh, a nasal discharge. 2. spoken through the nose. *M*, *n*, and *ng* are nasal sounds or nasals. *adj., n. 9.*

Nash ville (nash′vil), the capital of Tennessee. *n. 17.*

Nas sau (nas′ô), capital of the Bahamas. *n. 14.*

nas ti ness (nas′ti nis), 1. disgusting dirtiness; filth. 2. moral filth; vileness. 3. extreme unpleasantness. *n.*

na stur tium (nə stėr′shəm), a garden plant with yellow, orange, and red flowers and sharp-tasting seeds and leaves. *n. 13.*

Nasturtium

nas ty (nas′ti), 1. disgustingly dirty; filthy; as, a nasty room, a nasty person. 2. morally filthy; vile; as, a nasty word or story, a nasty mind. 3. very unpleasant; as, nasty weather, nasty medicines, a nasty cut or fall, a nasty temper. *adj., nastier, nastiest. 10.*

na tal (nā′təl), of one's birth. Your natal day is your birthday. *adj. 11.*

Na tal (nə tal′), an eastern province of the Union of South Africa. *n.*

nathe less (nāth′les), 1. nevertheless. 2. notwithstanding. *adv., prep.* [*Old use*]

na tion (nā′shən), 1. a group of people occupying the same country, united under the same independent government, and mostly speaking the same language. Great Britain, the United States, and China are great nations. 2. a people, race, or tribe; those having the same descent, language, and history; as, the Chinese nation. *n. 1.*

na tion al (nash′ən əl), 1. of a nation; belonging to a whole nation; as, national laws, a national disaster. 2. citizen of a nation. *adj., n. 2.*

National Guard, militia of the individual States of the United States. It may be called upon at any time to serve the Federal government.

na tion al ism (nash′ən əl izm), 1. patriotic feelings or efforts. 2. desire and plans for national independence. *n. 19.*

na tion al ist (nash′ən əl ist), 1. upholder of nationalism; person who believes in nationalism. 2. nationalistic. *n., adj.*

na tion al is tic (nash′ən əl is′tik), of nationalism or nationalists. *adj.*

na tion al i ty (nash′ən al′i ti), 1. nation. 2. condition of belonging to a nation. Citizens of the same country have the same nationality. 3. condition of being a nation. After the Revolutionary War the colonies attained nationality. *n., pl. nationalities. 8.*

na tion al ize (nash′ən əl īz), 1. make national. 2. bring (land, industries, railroads, etc.) under the control or ownership of a nation. 3. make into a nation. *v.*

na tion al ly (nash′ən əl i), as a nation; throughout the nation. *adv.*

na tive (nā′tiv), 1. person born in a certain country. The natives are the people living in a place, not visitors or foreigners. 2. born in a certain place or country. People born in New York are native sons and daughters of New York. 3. belonging to one because of his birth; as, one's native land. 4. belonging to one because of his country or race; as, one's native language. 5. born in a person; natural; as, native ability, native courtesy. 6. member of an uncivilized race, usually not white. 7. of or having to do with the natives, especially those not white; as, native customs, native huts. 8. animal or plant that originated in a place. 9. originating, grown, or produced in a certain place. Tobacco is native to America. 10. found in nature; not produced. Native salt is refined for use. *n., adj. 2.*

na tive-born (nā′tiv bôrn′), born in the place or country indicated; as, a native-born American. *adj.*

na tiv i ty (nə tiv′i ti), birth. **The Nativity** means the birth of Christ. *n., pl. nativities. 8.*

natl., national.

nat ty (nat′i), trim and tidy; neatly smart in dress or appearance; as, a natty uniform, a natty young officer. *adj., nattier, nattiest.*

nat u ral (nach′ə rəl), 1. produced by nature; coming in the ordinary course of events. We speak of natural feelings and actions, a natural complexion, natural curls, a natural death, a natural result. 2. inborn; belonging to the nature one has. It is natural for ducks to swim. 3. in accordance with the facts of some special case; as, a natural conclusion. 4. like nature; as, a natural portrait or natural acting. 5. of or about nature; as, natural history, the natural sciences. 6. in music, not changed in pitch by a sharp or a flat. *adj. 1.*

nat u ral ist (nach′ə rəl ist), person who makes a study of animals and plants. *n. 8.*

nat u ral i za tion (nach′ə rəl i zā′shən), 1. naturalizing. 2. being naturalized. *n. 16.*

nat u ral ize (nach′ə rəl īz), 1. admit (a foreigner) to citizenship. After living in the United States for a certain number of years, an immigrant can be naturalized if he passes a test. 2. adopt (a foreign word or custom). *Chauffeur* is a French word that has been naturalized in English. 3. introduce and make at home in another country. The English oak has become naturalized in parts of Massachusetts. *v. 12.*

nat u ral ly (nach′ə rəl i), 1. in a natural way. Speak naturally; don't try to imitate some actress. 2. by nature; as, a naturally obedient child. 3. as might be expected; of course. She offered me some candy; naturally, I took it. *adv.*

na ture (nā′chər), 1. the world; all things except those made by man. 2. the regular ways in which things are and act. 3. life without artificial things. 4. quality; character; what a thing really is. It is the nature of robins to fly and to build nests. Women have kinder natures than men. 5. sort; kind. Books of that nature do not interest her. *n. 1.*

naught (nôt), 1. nothing. 2. zero; 0. *n. 6.*

naugh ti ness (nô′ti nis), badness; disobedience; mischief. *n.*

naugh ty (nô′ti), bad; not obedient. The naughty child hit his baby sister. *adj., naughtier, naughtiest. 4.*

nau se a (nô′shi ə), 1. seasickness. 2. the feeling that one is about to vomit. 3. sick disgust; loathing. *n. 15.*

nau se ate (nô′shi āt), 1. cause nausea in; make sick. 2. feel nausea; become sick. 3. cause to feel loathing. *v. 19.*

nau se ous (nô′shi əs), 1. causing nausea; sickening. 2. disgusting; loathsome. Bloody entrails are nauseous. *adj. 19.*

nau ti cal (nô′ti kəl), having to do with ships, sailors, or navigation. *adj. 12.*

nautical mile, about 6080 feet.

nau ti lus (nô′ti ləs), a small sea animal having a shell. The pearly nautilus has a spiral shell, pearly inside. The paper nautilus has saillike arms and a very thin shell. *n. 10.*

Pearly nautilus

Nav a ho (nav′ə hō), member of a tribe of American Indians living in New Mexico, Arizona, and Utah. The Navahos are noted for their skill in weaving blankets and rugs with bright patterns. *n., pl. Navahos.*

Nav a jo (nav′ə hō), Navaho. *n., pl. Navajos.*

na val (nā′vəl), 1. of or for warships or the navy; as, naval supplies, a naval officer. 2. having a navy; as, the naval powers. *adj. 7.*

nave (nāv), the main part of a church or cathedral between the side aisles. The nave extends from the main entrance to the transepts. *n. 10.*

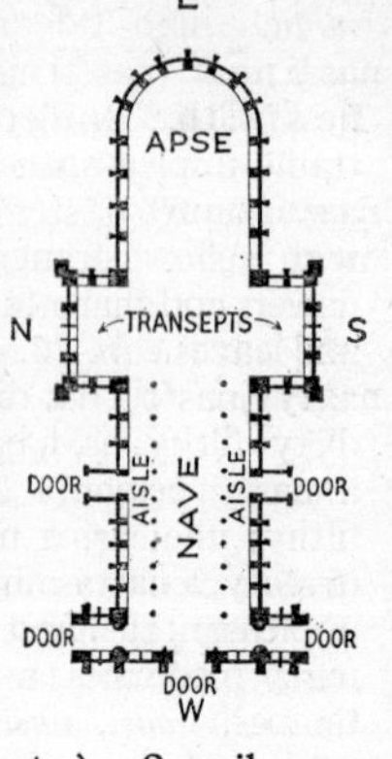

na vel (nā′vəl), the mark in the middle of the surface of the belly. *n. 17.*

nav i ga ble (nav′i gə bəl), 1. that ships can travel on. The Mississippi River is deep enough to be navigable. 2. that can be sailed; seaworthy. 3. that can be steered. *adj. 6.*

nav i gate (nav′i gāt), 1. sail, manage, or steer (a ship, airplane, etc.). 2. sail on or over (a sea or river). 3. sail the seas. *v. 10.*

nav i ga tion (nav′i gā′shən), 1. navigating. 2. the art or science of finding a ship's position and course. *n. 7.*

nav i ga tor (nav′i gā′tər), 1. one who sails the seas. 2. one who has charge of the navigating of a ship or who is skilled in navigating. 3. an explorer of the seas. The navigator set out on his long voyage. 4. one who finds the position and course of an airship. *n. 8.*

na vy (nā′vi), 1. all the ships of war of a country, with their men and the department that manages them. 2. the officers and men of the navy. 3. a fleet of ships. *n., pl. navies. 3.*

nay (nā), 1. no. 2. not only that, but also. We are willing, nay, eager to go. 3. negative vote or voter. *adv., n. 4.*

Naz a rene (naz′ə rēn′), 1. person born in Nazareth, or living in Nazareth. Jesus is often called "the Nazarene." 2. The early Christians were sometimes called Nazarenes. *n.*

Naz a reth (naz′ə reth), town in Palestine where Jesus lived in childhood. *n. 11.*

Naz a rite (naz′ə rīt), 1. in the Old Testament, a Jew who had taken certain vows to live a strict life. 2. a native of Nazareth. *n. 13.*

Na zi (nä′tsi), 1. member or supporter of the party in Germany organized under the leadership of Adolf Hitler. 2. of or having to do with that party. *n., pl. Nazis, adj.*

N.B. or **n.b.,** note well; observe carefully.

N.C., North Carolina.

N. Dak. or **N.D.,** North Dakota.

NE or **N. E.** or **n. e.,** 1. northeast. 2. northeastern.

neap (nēp). A neap tide or neap is one in which high tide is the lowest it ever is. *adj., n.*

Ne a pol i tan (nē′ə pol′i tən), 1. of or pertaining to Naples. 2. a native of Naples. *adj., n. 20.*

near (nēr), 1. at or to a short distance; close; not far; not distant. They searched far and near. Christmas is drawing near. 2. close to; not far from. We live near New York. My birthday is near Christmas. 3. come or draw near to. The vacation was nearing its end. 4. close. It was five o'clock as near as he could guess. 5. **Near at hand** means (1) within easy reach. (2) not far in the future. 6. close in feeling; as, a near friend. 7. **It lies near his heart** means he cares a great deal about it. 8. short; direct. Take the nearest route. 9. almost; nearly. 10. **Come near doing** means almost do. I came near forgetting. 11. stingy. 12. on the left-hand side; as, the near horse of a pair. *adv., adj., prep., v. 1.*

near by (nēr′bī′), near; close at hand. *adj. 11.*

Near East, Asia Minor, Syria, and Palestine. Sometimes the term includes the Balkans.

near ly (nēr′li), 1. almost. It is nearly bedtime. 2. closely. This matter concerns you very nearly. *adv. 3.*

near ness (nēr′nis), being near. *n. 11.*

near-sight ed (nēr′sīt′id), not able to see far. *adj.*

neat (nēt), 1. clean and in order; as, a neat desk, a neat room, a neat dress. 2. able and willing to keep things in order; as, a neat child. 3. well-formed; in proportion; as, a neat design. 4. skillful; clever; as, a neat trick. 5. without anything mixed in it. He took a drink of brandy neat. *adj. 3.*

neat ness (nēt′nis), being neat. *n. 14.*

Ne bo (nē′bō), the mountain where Moses looked down upon the Promised Land. Deuteronomy 34:1-4. *n. 15.*

Nebr. or **Neb.,** Nebraska.

Ne bras ka (ni bras′kə), a Middle Western State of the United States. *n. 12.*

Neb u chad nez zar (neb′ū kəd nez′ər), a king of Babylon who captured Jerusalem. Later he became crazy and ate grass as cattle do. Daniel 1-4. *n. 13.*

neb u la (neb′ū lə), a bright spot like a small bright cloud, visible in the sky at night. A nebula may be either a mass of luminous gas or a cluster of stars very, very far away from our sun and its planets. *n., pl. nebulae* (-lē) or *nebulas. 16.*

neb u lous (neb′ū ləs), 1. hazy; vague; indistinct; confused. 2. cloudlike. 3. of or like a nebula or nebulae. *adj. 16.*

nec es sar i ly (nes′i sãr′i li), 1. because of necessity. Leaves are not necessarily green. 2. as a necessary result. War necessarily causes misery and waste. *adv. 13.*

nec es sar y (nes′i sãr′i), 1. that must be. 2. that must be had; that must be done; required. 3. something necessary. Food, clothing, and shelter are necessaries of life. *adj., n., pl. necessaries. 1.*

ne ces si tate (ni ses′i tāt), 1. make necessary. Tom's broken leg necessitated an operation. 2. compel; force. *v. 8.*

ne ces si ty (ni ses′i ti), 1. need. We understand the necessity of eating. 2. thing which cannot be done without; necessary thing. Water is a necessity. 3. that which forces one to act in a certain way. Necessity often drives people to do disagreeable things. 4. poverty. This poor family is in great necessity. *n., pl. necessities. 3.*

neck (nek), 1. the part of the body that connects the head with the shoulders. 2. the part of a garment that fits the neck; as, the neck of a shirt. 3. narrow part like a neck; as, a neck of land. *n. 1.*

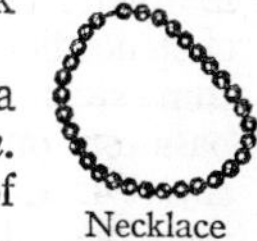
Necklace

neck er chief (nek′ər chif), a cloth worn round the neck. *n.*

neck lace (nek′lis), string of jewels, gold, silver, beads, etc., worn around the neck as an ornament. *n. 6.*

neck tie (nek′tī′), a band or tie worn around the neck and tied in front. *n. 7.*

neck wear (nek′wãr′), collars, ties, and other articles that are worn around the neck. *n. 14.*

Neckties

nec ro man cer (nek′rō-man′sər), magician; wizard; person who is supposed to foretell the future by communicating with the dead. *n. 16.*

nec ro man cy (nek′rō man′si), magic; foretelling the future by communicating with the dead. *n.*

nec tar (nek′tər), 1. in Greek stories, the

drink of the gods. 2. any delicious drink. 3. a sweet liquid found in many flowers. Bees gather nectar and make it into honey. *n. 13.*

nec tar ine (nek′tər ēn′), a kind of peach having no down on its skin. *n. 19.*

née or **nee** (nā), born. **Née** is placed after the name of a married woman to show her maiden name, as in Mrs. Smith, *née* Adams. *adj.*

need (nēd), 1. something that has to be. **If need be** means if it has to be. **There is no need for it** means it does not have to be. 2. **Have need to** or **need** means must, should, have to, or ought to. I have need to go to town. You need not bother. Why need you go today? Do not stay longer than you need. 3. want; lack. For need of a nail the shoe was lost. 4. be in want of; ought to have; be unable to do without. I need a new hat. 5. thing wanted or lacking; that for which a want is felt. 6. time or condition of need; as, a friend in need, to fail someone in his need. 7. being poor. This family's need was so great the children did not have shoes. *n., v. 1.*

need ful (nēd′fəl), needed; necessary. *adj. 5.*

nee dle (nē′dəl), 1. a very slender tool, sharp at one end, and with a hole or eye to pass a thread through, used in sewing. 2. Knitting needles and crochet needles have no eyes. 3. a thin steel pointer on a compass or on electrical machinery. 4. the end of a syringe, used for injecting something below the skin. 5. the needle-shaped leaf of a fir tree or pine tree. *n. 2.*

A B C

Needles for A, sewing; B, crocheting; C, knitting.

need less (nēd′lis), not needed; unnecessary. *adj. 5.*

nee dle wom an (nē′dəl wům′ən), 1. user of the needle. My sister is a very good needlewoman. 2. woman who earns her living by sewing. *n., pl. needlewomen. 12.*

nee dle work (nē′dəl wėrk′), work done with a needle; sewing; embroidery. *n. 8.*

need n't (nēd′ənt), need not. *20.*

needs (nēdz), because of necessity. A soldier needs must go where duty calls. *adv.*

need y (nēd′i), very poor; not having enough to live on; as, a needy family. *adj., needier, neediest. 8.*

ne'er (nãr), never. *adv.* [*Used in poetry*] *5.*

ne'er-do-well (nãr′dü wel′), worthless fellow; good-for-nothing person. *n.*

ne far i ous (ni fãr′i əs), very wicked. *adj. 18.*

ne gate (ni gāt′), deny. *v. 14.*

ne ga tion (ni gā′shən), 1. denying; denial. Shaking the head is a sign of negation. 2. the absence or opposite of some positive thing or quality. Darkness is the negation of light. *n. 11.*

neg a tive (neg′ə tiv), 1. saying no. His answer was negative. 2. word or statement that says no or denies. 3. say no to; deny; vote against. 4. the side that says no or denies in an argument. 5. not positive; consisting in the lack of the opposite. Negative kindness means not being unkind. 6. minus; counting down from zero. Three below zero is a negative quantity. 7. the kind of electricity produced on resin when it is rubbed with silk. 8. showing the lights and shadows reversed; as, the negative image on a photographic plate. 9. a photographic image in which the lights and shadows are reversed. Prints are made from it. *adj., n., v. 6.*

neg lect (neg lekt′), 1. give too little care or attention to. 2. leave undone. The maid neglected her work. 3. omit; fail. Don't neglect to water the plants. 4. neglecting. 5. want of attention to what should be done. 6. being neglected. *v., n. 2.*

neg lect ful (neg lekt′fəl), careless. A man who does not vote is neglectful of his duty. *adj.*

neg li gee (neg′li zhā′), 1. a woman's loose house gown. 2. easy, informal dress. *n.*

neg li gence (neg′li jəns), 1. neglect; lack of proper care or attention. Negligence was the cause of the child's illness. 2. carelessness; indifference. *n. 9.*

neg li gent (neg′li jənt), 1. neglectful; showing neglect. 2. careless; indifferent. *adj. 11.*

neg li gi ble (neg′li ji bəl), that can be disregarded. In buying a suit, a difference of ten cents in prices is negligible. *adj. 17.*

ne go ti a ble (ni gō′shi ə bəl), capable of being negotiated or sold; whose ownership can be transferred. *adj.*

ne go ti ate (ni gō′shi āt), 1. talk over and arrange terms. The colonists negotiated for peace with the Indians. 2. arrange for. They finally negotiated a peace treaty. 3. sell. 4. get past or over. The car negotiated the sharp curve by slowing down. *Used in common talk. v. 8.*

ne go ti a tion (ni gō′shi ā′shən), negotiating; arrangement. Negotiations for the new school are nearly finished. *n. 7.*

ne go ti a tor (ni gō′shi ā′tər), person who negotiates. *n.*

ne gress (nē′gris), Negro woman or girl. *n. 17.*

Ne gro or **ne gro** (nē′grō), 1. person belonging to any of the black races of Africa. 2. a colored person having some black ancestors. 3. of or pertaining to Negroes. *n., pl. Negroes* or *negroes, adj. 3.*

ne gus (nē′gəs), a drink made of wine, hot water, sugar, lemon, and nutmeg. *n. 19.*

Ne he mi ah (nē′i mī′ə), 1. a famous Hebrew leader. 2. a book of the Old Testament. *n. 19.*

neigh (nā), 1. the sound that a horse makes. 2. make such a sound. *n., v. 5.*

neigh bor (nā′bər), 1. someone who lives in the next house or near by. 2. person or thing near or next to another. The big tree brought down several of its smaller neighbors as it fell. 3. near; neighboring. 4. be near or next too. 5. fellow human being. *n., adj., v. 1.*

neigh bor hood (nā′bər hůd), 1. region near some place or thing. She lives in the neighborhood of the mill. 2. place; district. Is North Street in a good neighborhood? 3. people living near one another; people of a place. The whole neighborhood came to the big party. 4. neighborly feeling or conduct. 5. nearness. *n. 3.*

neigh bor ing (nā′bər ing), living or being near; bordering; adjoining; near. The bird calls from the neighboring woods. *adj.*

neigh bor ly (nā′bər li), kindly; friendly. *adj.*

nei ther (nē′ꟻHər or nī′ꟻHər) 1. not either. 2. nor yet; nor. "They toil not, neither do they spin." *conj., adj., pron. 1.*

Nem e sis (nem′i sis), 1. the goddess of vengeance. 2. A just punishment for evil deeds is often called a **nemesis.** *n. 15.*

ne on (nē′on), a rare gas. Tubes containing neon are used in television sets and for display signs. *n.*

ne o phyte (nē′ō fīt), 1. new convert; one recently admitted to a religious body. 2. beginner; novice. *n. 16.*

neph ew (nef′ū), son of one's brother or sister; son of one's brother-in-law or sister-in-law. *n. 4.*

nep o tism (nep′ə tizm), the showing of too much favor by one in power to his relatives, especially by giving them desirable appointments. *n.*

Nep tune (nep′tūn or nep′tün), 1. the Roman god of the sea. The Greeks called him Poseidon. 2. a large planet so far from the earth and the sun that it cannot be seen with the naked eye. *n. 11.*

Ne re id or **ne re id** (nēr′i id), a sea nymph. *n. 19.*

Ne ro (nēr′ō), a Roman emperor noted for his vices, cruelty, and tyranny (37-68 A.D.). *n. 12.*

Human nerves

nerve (nėrv), 1. a fiber or bundle of fibers connecting the brain or spinal cord with the eyes, ears, muscles, glands, etc. 2. mental strength; courage; vigor. 3. arouse strength or courage in. She nerved herself for the struggle. 4. rude boldness; impudence. *Slang.* 5. a vein of a leaf. 6. **Strain every nerve** means exert oneself to the utmost. 7. **Nerves** sometimes means an attack of nervousness. *n., v. 4.*

Leaf nerves

nerve less (nėrv′lis), 1. without strength or vigor; feeble; weak. The gun dropped from his nerveless hand. 2. without nerves. *adj.*

nerv ous (nėr′vəs), 1. of the nerves. The brain is a part of the nervous system of the human body. 2. having nerves that are weak or out of order; restless or uneasy; easily excited or upset. A person who has been overworking is likely to become nervous. 3. strong; vigorous. *adj. 4.*

nerv ous ness (nėr′vəs nis), being nervous; being easily upset. Nellie had to overcome her nervousness before she could recite well in school. Nervousness made Bob stutter. *n. 12.*

-ness, suffix meaning:—
1. quality, state, or condition of being ——; as in blackness, goodness, preparedness.
2. —— action; —— behavior; as in some uses of carefulness, kindness, meanness.

nest (nest), 1. Birds build or choose nests in which to lay eggs and protect their young ones. Some animals and insects make nests in which to

Bird's nest

live or lay their eggs. Squirrels and wasps have nests. 2. the birds, animals, etc., living in a nest. 3. warm, cozy place; place to sleep. The little girl cuddled down in a nest among the sofa cushions. 4. something suggesting a nest; as, a nest or series of boxes, baskets, or bowls, the smaller fitting within the larger. 5. place that swarms, usually with something bad; as, a nest of thieves. 6. make and use a nest. The bluebirds are nesting here now. 7. place in a nest. *n., v. 1.*

Wasp's nest

nest egg, 1. egg left in a nest to induce a bird to lay eggs there. 2. money saved.

nes tle (nes′əl), 1. settle oneself or be settled comfortably and cozily; as, to nestle down in a big chair, to nestle close to one's mother, a house nestling among trees. 2. hold closely and comfortably. A mother nestles her baby in her arms. *v. 6.*

nest ling (nest′ling), a bird too young to leave the nest. *n. 16.*

Nes tor (nes′tər), 1. the oldest and wisest of the Greeks at the siege of Troy. 2. a wise old man. *n. 13.*

net[1] (net), 1. string, cord, thread, or hair, knotted together into an open fabric, leaving large or small holes regularly arranged. 2. A fish net is used for catching fish. A mosquito net keeps off mosquitoes. A hair net holds the hair in place. A tennis net is used in the game of tennis. 3. a lacelike cloth. 4. a trap or snare. The guilty boy was caught in the net of his own lies. 5. catch in a net; as, to net fish. 6. cover, confine, or protect with a net. *n., v., netted, netting. 2.*

Tennis net

net[2] (net), 1. remaining after deductions; free from deductions. A net gain or profit is the actual gain after all working expenses have been paid. The net weight of a glass jar of candy is the weight of the candy itself. The net price of a book is the real price, from which no discount can be made. 2. to gain. The sale netted me a good profit. *adj., v., netted, netting.*

neth er (neᴛʜ′ər), lower. *adj. 6.*

Neth er lands (neᴛʜ′ərləndz), Holland, a small country in Europe, west of Germany and north of Belgium. *n. 5.*

Netherlands Indies, Dutch East Indies.

neth er most (neᴛʜ′ər mōst), lowest. *adj.*

net ting (net′ing), a netted or meshed material; as, mosquito netting, wire netting for window screens. *n.*

net tle (net′əl), 1. a kind of plant having sharp leaf hairs that sting the skin when touched. 2. sting the mind; irritate; make angry; vex. *n., v. 8.*

Nettle

net work (net′wėrk′), 1. netting; net. 2. any system of lines that cross; as, a network of vines, a network of railroads. 3. group of connected radio stations. *n. 8.*

neu ral gia (nū ral′jə or nü ral′jə), pain, usually sharp, along the course of a nerve. *n. 20.*

neu ri tis (nū rī′tis or nü rī′tis), inflammation of a nerve or nerves. *n.*

neu rot ic (nū rot′ik or nü rot′ik), 1. suffering from a nervous disease. 2. too nervous. 3. person who is too nervous. *adj., n. 20.*

neu ter (nū′tər or nü′tər), 1. in grammar, neither masculine nor feminine. *It* is a neuter pronoun. 2. the neuter gender. 3. not developed in sex. Worker bees are neuter. 4. an animal or plant without sex. 5. being on neither side; neutral. *adj., n. 12.*

neu tral (nū′trəl or nü′trəl), 1. neither one thing nor the other. 2. on neither side in a quarrel or war. 3. a neutral person or country; one not taking part in a war. 4. having little or no color; grayish. 5. neither acid nor alkaline. *adj., n. 8.*

neu tral i ty (nū tral′i ti or nü tral′i ti), being neutral. *n. 11.*

neu tral ize (nū′trəl īz or nü′trəl īz), 1. make neutral; keep war out of. There was talk of neutralizing Belgium. 2. make of no effect by some opposite force; counterbalance. Jane neutralized the bright colors in her room by using a tan rug. *v. 8.*

neutral vowel, unstressed vowel sound such as the sound of *a* in *about, u* in *circus,* etc.

Nev., Nevada.

Ne vad a (nə vad′ə), a Western State of the United States. *n. 11.*

nev er (nev′ər), 1. not ever; at no time. 2. not at all. *adv. 1.*

nev er more (nev′ər mōr′), never again. *adv. 18.*

nev er the less (nev′ər ᴛʜə les′), however; none the less; for all that; in spite of it. She was very tired; nevertheless she kept on working. *adv., conj. 4.*

new (nū or nü), 1. never having been before; now first made, thought out, known or heard of, felt or discovered; as, a new school, a new house, a new idea. 2. lately grown, come, or made; not old; now first used; not worn or used up; as, new potatoes, new cheese, new furniture, new dresses. 3. as if new; fresh; as, to go on with new courage. 4. different; changed; as, to have a new teacher; to feel like a new person. 5. later; modern; recent; as, the new dances, the new woman. 6. not yet used (to). She is still new to the work. 7. beginning again. The new moon is the moon when seen as a thin crescent. 8. newly; as, a newborn babe, new-fallen snow, a new-found friend, new-laid eggs, new-mown hay. 9. anew; again. *adj., adv. 1.*

New ark (nū′ərk or nü′ərk), city in New Jersey, near New York City. *n. 9.*

New Bedford, city in southeastern Massachusetts, formerly an important whaling port.

new born (nū′bôrn′ or nü′bôrn′), 1. just born; as, a newborn baby. 2. ready to start a new life; born again. *adj. 10.*

New Brunswick, province in southeastern Canada.

new com er (nū′kum′ər or nü′kum′ər), person who has just come or who came not long ago. *n. 8.*

new el (nū′əl or nü′əl), post that supports the railing of a stairway. *n.*

Newel

New England, the northeastern part of the United States. Maine, New Hampshire, Vermont, Massachusetts, Rhode Island, and Connecticut are the New England States. *16.*

new fan gled (nū′fang′gəld or nü′fang′gəld), 1. lately come into fashion; of a new kind. 2. fond of novelty. *adj. 16.*

New found land (nū′fənd land′ or nü′fənd-land′ for 1, nū found′lənd or nü found′-lənd for 2), 1. a large island east of Canada. 2. dog like a spaniel, but much larger. *n. 7.*

Newfoundland (about 27 in. high)

New Guinea, large island north of Australia. Also called **Papua.**

New Hampshire, a New England State of the United States.

New Haven, city in southern Connecticut. Yale University is located at New Haven. *20.*

New Jersey, an Eastern State of the United States. *13.*

new ly (nū′li or nü′li), lately; recently; as, newly discovered, newly painted. *adv.*

New Mexico, a Southwestern State of the United States. *18.*

New Or le ans (nū ôr′li ənz or nü ôr′li ənz), large city in southeastern Louisiana, near the mouth of the Mississippi River. *18.*

New port (nū′pōrt or nü′pōrt), city in Rhode Island, on Narragansett Bay. Newport is a very fashionable summer resort. *n. 10.*

news (nūz or nüz), something told as having just happened; information about something which has just happened or will soon happen. The news that our teacher was leaving made us sad. *n. 2.*

news boy (nūz′boi′ or nüz′boi′), boy who sells or delivers newspapers. *n. 20.*

New South Wales, a State in southeastern Australia.

news pa per (nūz′pā′pər or nüz′pā′pər), sheets of paper printed every day or week, telling the news, carrying advertisements, and having stories, poems, jokes, and useful information. *n. 2.*

news reel (nūz′rēl′ or nüz′rēl′), moving picture showing current events. *n.*

newt (nūt or nüt), small animal like a salamander that lives in water part of the time. *n. 14.*

Newt (3 to 6 in. long)

New Testament, the part of the Bible which contains the life and teachings of Christ recorded by His followers, together with their own experiences and teachings.

New ton (nū′tən or nü′tən), Isaac, an English scientist and mathematician (1642-1727). Newton discovered the law of gravitation. *n. 12.*

New World, North and South America.

New Year or **New Year's,** January 1, the first day or days of the year.

New York, 1. an Eastern State of the United States. 2. seaport in southeastern New York State, at the mouth of the Hudson River. It is the largest city in the United States. *1.*

New Zea land (nū zē′lənd or nü zē′lənd), a British dominion in the southern Pacific Ocean. New Zealand consists of two main islands and various small ones. *18.*

next (nekst), 1. nearest. Who is the girl next to Alice? 2. having nothing of the same kind coming in between. The next day after Sunday is Monday. 3. nearest to. We live in the house next the church. 4. in the next place. I am going to do my arithmetic problems next. *adj., prep., adv. 1.*

next door, very close. Cheating is an act next door to a crime.

next-door (nekst′dōr′), in or at the next house; as, my next-door neighbor. *adj.*

N.H., New Hampshire.

Ni ag a ra (nī ag′ə rə), a short river and a great waterfall, on the boundary between the United States and Canada, between Lake Erie and Lake Ontario. **Niagara Falls** is one of the great sights of the world. *n., adj. 7.*

nib (nib), 1. pen point. 2. the point of anything. 3. bird's bill. *n.*

nib ble (nib′əl), 1. eat away with quick small bites, as a rabbit or a mouse does. 2. bite gently or lightly. A fish nibbles at the bait. 3. a nibbling; small bite. *v., n. 6.*

Nic a ra gua (nik′ə rä′gwə), country in Central America. *n. 17.*

nice[1] (nīs), 1. pleasing; agreeable; satisfactory; as, a nice day, a nice ride, a nice child. 2. very particular; dainty; having a refined or critical taste; as, to be nice in one's habits or dress. 3. very fine; minute; subtle; as, a nice distinction, a nice point or shade of meaning. 4. precise; exact; making very fine distinctions; as, weighed in the nicest scales. *adj. 1.*

Nice[2] (nēs), a famous seaside resort in southeastern France. *n.*

ni ce ty (nī′sə ti), 1. exactness; accuracy; delicacy. A radio set requires some nicety of adjustment to give the clearest tone. 2. fine point; small distinction; detail. I can make my car go, but I have not yet learned all the little niceties of driving. 3. quality of being very particular. 4. something dainty or refined. 5. **To a nicety** means just right; as, cakes browned to a nicety. *n., pl. niceties. 14.*

Vase in a niche

niche (nich), 1. a recess or hollow in a wall for a statue, vase, etc. 2. suitable place or position; place into which a person fits. *n. 12.*

Nich o las (nik′ə ləs), **Saint,** 1. patron saint of young people, sailors, travelers, and Russians. 2. Santa Claus. *n. 6.*

nick (nik), 1. a place where a small bit has been cut or broken out. She hit a saucer and made a nick in the edge of it. 2. make a nick or nicks in. 3. **In the nick of time** means just at the right moment. *n., v. 7.*

nick el (nik′əl), 1. a metal that looks like silver and is somewhat like iron. Nickel is much used in mixtures with other metals. 2. cover or coat with nickel. 3. a coin made of nickel; a United States five-cent piece. *n., v., nickeled, nickeling. 4.*

nick name (nik′nām′), 1. a name added to a person's real name, or used instead of it. Ed is a nickname for Edward. 2. give a nickname to. They nicknamed the tall boy "Shorty" as a joke. *n., v. 11.*

nic o tine (nik′ə tēn), a poison contained in the leaves of tobacco. *n. 13.*

niece (nēs), daughter of one's brother or sister; daughter of one's brother-in-law or sister-in-law. *n. 6.*

Ni ger (nī′jər), river in western Africa. *n. 11.*

Ni ge ri a (nī jēr′i ə), British colony and protectorate in western Africa. *n.*

nig gard (nig′ərd), 1. a stingy person. 2. stingy. *n., adj. 10.*

nig gard li ness (nig′ərd li nis), stinginess. *n.*

nig gard ly (nig′ərd li), 1. stingy. 2. stingily. 3. meanly small or scanty; as, a niggardly gift. *adj., adv.*

nigh (nī), 1. near. 2. nearly. *adv., adj., prep.* [*Old use*] *4.*

Nighthawk
(9 to 10 in. long)

night (nīt), 1. the time between evening and morning; the time from sunset to sunrise, especially when it is dark. 2. evening. *n. 1.*

night cap (nīt′kap′), 1. a cap to be worn in bed. 2. a drink taken just before going to bed. *n. 13.*

night fall (nīt′fôl′), the coming of night. *n. 14.*

night gown (nīt′goun′), the garment a woman or child wears in bed. *n. 12.*

night hawk (nīt′hôk′), 1. a bird that flies mostly by night. See the picture above. 2. person who stays up late at night. *n.*

Nightingale
(6 to 7 in. long)

night in gale (nīt′ən gāl), a small reddish-brown bird of Europe. The male sings sweetly at night as well as in the daytime. *n. 4.*

Night in gale (nīt′ən gāl), Florence, an Englishwoman who brought about great improvements in nursing (1820-1910). *n.*

night ly (nīt′li), 1. happening every night. 2. every night. Performances are given nightly except on Sunday. 3. happening at night. 4. at night. *adj., adv. 6.*

night mare (nīt′mãr′), 1. very distressing dream. 2. very distressing experience. 3. horrible fear or dread. *n. 10.*

night shade (nīt′shād′), any of various plants somewhat like the potato and the tomato. The black nightshade has white flowers and black poisonous berries. The deadly nightshade has red berries. *n. 15.*

night shirt (nīt′shėrt′), a boy's or man's long shirt to wear in bed. *n. 16.*

nil (nil), nothing. *n.*

Nile (nīl), great river in Africa, flowing north through Egypt into the Mediterranean Sea. *n. 7.*

nim ble (nim′bəl), 1. quick-moving; active and sure-footed; light and quick. Goats are nimble in climbing among the rocks. 2. clever; quick to understand and to reply. The boy had a nimble mind, and could think up excuses as quickly as his mother or teacher could ask for them. *adj. 5.*

nim bly (nim′bli), quickly and lightly. *adv.*

Nim rod (nim′rod), 1. great hunter. Genesis 10:8 and 9. 2. hunter. *n. 15.*

nine (nīn), 1. one more than eight; 9. Six and three make nine. 2. set of nine persons or things. *n., adj. 1.*

nine fold (nīn′fōld′), nine times as great or as much. *adj., adv.*

nine pins (nīn′pinz′), a game in which nine large wooden pins are set up, to be bowled down with a ball. *n. 18.*

Ninepins

nine teen (nīn′tēn′), nine more than ten; 19. *n., adj. 4.*

nine teenth (nīn′tēnth′), 1. next after the 18th. 2. one of 19 equal parts. *adj., n. 8.*

nine ti eth (nīn′ti ith), 1. next after the eighty-ninth. 2. one of 90 equal parts. *adj., n. 18.*

nine ty (nīn′ti), nine times ten; 90. *n., pl. nineties, adj. 3.*

Nin e veh (nin′ə və), an ancient city of Assyria. *n. 10.*

nin ny (nin′i), fool. *n., pl. ninnies.*

ninth (nīnth), 1. next after the 8th. 2. one of 9 equal parts. *adj., n. 3.*

Ni o be (nī′ō bi), a mother whose fourteen beautiful children were slain because she boasted about them. Turned by Zeus into a stone fountain, she weeps forever for her children. *n. 13.*

nip[1] (nip), 1. squeeze tight and suddenly; pinch; bite. The crab nipped my toe. 2. tight squeeze; pinch; sudden bite. 3. injure; hurt at the tips; spoil; as, plants nipped by frost. Mother said, "No!" and nipped my plans in the bud. 4. injury caused by frost. *v., nipped, nipping, n. 6.*

nip[2] (nip), a small drink. *n.*

Nippers (def. 3)

nip per (nip′ər), 1. one that nips. 2. a big claw of a lobster or crab. 3. **Nippers** means pincers, forceps, pliers, or any tool that nips. *n. 14.*

nip ple (nip′əl), 1. the small projection through which the baby animal gets its mother's milk; as, the nipples of a mother dog or cat. 2. the rubber cap or mouthpiece of a baby's bottle, through which the baby gets its milk. *n. 12.*

Nip pon (ni pon′), Japan. *n.*

nir va na or **Nir va na** (nir vä′nə), the Buddhist idea of heavenly peace; perfect happiness reached by complete absorption of oneself into the supreme universal spirit. *n.*

ni ter or **ni tre** (nī′tər), 1. a salt (potassium nitrate) obtained from potash, used in making gunpowder; saltpeter. 2. nitrate of sodium, or Chile saltpeter, used as a fertilizer. *n. 14.*

ni trate (nī′trāt), 1. a salt of nitric acid. 2. potassium nitrate or sodium nitrate, used as a fertilizer. *n. 10.*

ni tric (nī′trik), of or containing nitrogen. **Nitric acid** is a clear, colorless liquid that eats into flesh, clothing, metal, and other substances. *adj. 15.*

ni tro gen (nī′trə jən), a gas without color, taste, or odor which forms about four-fifths of the air. *n. 7.*

ni trog e nous (nī troj′i nəs), containing nitrogen. *adj. 12.*

ni tro glyc er in or **ni tro glyc er ine** (nī′trō-glis′ər in), an oily, explosive liquid made by treating glycerin with nitric and sulphuric acids. Dynamite is made of nitroglycerin. *n.*

ni trous (nī′trəs), 1. of nitrogen. 2. of

niter. **Nitrous oxide** is a gas which dulls pain. *adj. 17.*

nix ie (nik′si), water fairy. *n.*

N.J., New Jersey. *18.*

N.M. or **N. Mex.,** New Mexico.

no (nō), 1. No means the same as shaking your head. Can a cow fly? No. 2. not any. Dogs have no wings. Eat no more. 3. a vote against. The noes won. *adv., adj., n., pl. noes. 1.*

no., number. *12.*

No ah (nō′ə). Noah made an ark to save himself, his family, and a pair of each kind of animal from the Flood. *n. 6.*

nob (nob), the head. *n.* [*Slang*] *14.*

no bil i ty (nō bil′i ti), 1. people of noble rank. Earls, counts, princes, and kings belong to the nobility. 2. noble birth; noble rank. 3. noble character. *n., pl. nobilities. 5.*

no ble (nō′bəl), 1. high and great by birth, rank, or title. 2. person high and great by birth, rank, or title. 3. high and great in character; showing greatness of mind; good; as, a noble knight, a noble deed. 4. excellent; fine; splendid; magnificent. Niagara Falls is a noble sight. *adj., n. 2.*

no ble man (nō′bəl mən), man of noble rank, title, or birth. *n., pl. noblemen. 6.*

no ble ness (nō′bəl nis), noble character; noble birth; noble rank. *n. 12.*

no bly (nō′bli), in a noble manner; splendidly; as a noble person would do. *adv. 15.*

no bod y (nō′bod i), 1. no one; no person. 2. person of no importance. *pron., n., pl. nobodies. 2.*

noc tur nal (nok tėr′nəl), 1. of the night. 2. in the night. 3. active in the night. The owl is a nocturnal bird. 4. closed by day, open by night; as, a nocturnal flower. *adj. 12.*

noc tur nal ly (nok tėr′nəl i), 1. at night. 2. every night. *adv.*

nod (nod), 1. bow (the head) slightly and raise it again quickly. 2. say yes by nodding. 3. a nodding of the head. He gave us a nod as he passed. 4. let the head fall forward and bob about when sleepy or falling asleep. 5. be sleepy; become careless and dull. 6. droop, bend, or sway back and forth; as, nodding plumes. *v., nodded, nodding, n. 2.*

NODE
NODE

node (nōd), 1. knot; knob; swelling. 2. a joint on a stem where leaves grow out. *n. 13.*

nod ule (nod′ūl), 1. a small knot, knob, or swelling. 2. a small, rounded mass or lump; as, nodules of pure gold. *n. 15.*

No ël (nō el′), 1. Christmas. 2. A **noël** is a Christmas song. *n.*

nog gin (nog′in), 1. a small cup or mug. 2. a small drink; one fourth of a pint. *n.*

noise (noiz), 1. a sound that is not musical or pleasant. 2. a sound. 3. tell; spread the news of. It was noised abroad that the king was dying. *n., v. 2.*

noise less (noiz′lis), making no noise; making little noise; as, a noiseless typewriter. *adj. 6.*

nois i ly (noiz′i li), in a noisy manner. *adv.*

nois i ness (noiz′i nis), being noisy; making a noise. *n.*

noi some (noi′səm), 1. offensive; disgusting; bad-smelling; as, a noisome dungeon, a noisome sewer. 2. harmful; injurious; as, a noisome pestilence. *adj. 13.*

nois y (noiz′i), 1. making much noise; as, a noisy crowd, a noisy boy, a noisy little clock. 2. full of noise; as, a noisy house, a noisy street, the noisy city. 3. having much noise with it; as, a noisy game, a noisy quarrel. *adj., noisier, noisiest. 6.*

no mad (nō′mad), 1. member of a tribe which moves from place to place to have food or pasture for its cattle. 2. wandering from place to place to find pasture. 3. wanderer. 4. wandering. *n., adj. 9.*

no mad ic (nō mad′ik), wandering; roving; of nomads or their life. *adj. 13.*

no men cla ture (nō′mən klā′chər), a set or system of names or terms; as, the nomenclature of music. *n. 15.*

nom i nal (nom′i nəl), 1. existing in name only; not real. Miss Brown is our nominal teacher, but she is so busy that her assistant really teaches us most of the time. 2. too small to be considered. We paid our friend a merely nominal rent for the cottage each summer—$5 a month. *adj. 9.*

nom i nal ly (nom′i nəl i), in name; as a matter of form; in a nominal way only. *adv.*

nom i nate (nom′i nāt), 1. name as candidate for an office. Three times Bryan was nominated for President, but he was never elected. 2. appoint for an office. The President nominated him for Secretary of State. *v. 8.*

nom i na tion (nom′i nā′shən), 1. naming as candidate for office. 2. selection for office; appointment to office. 3. being nominated. *n. 6.*

nom i na tive (nom′i nə tiv), 1. showing the subject of a verb and words agreeing with the subject. *I*, *he*, *she*, *we*, and *they* are in the nominative case. 2. the nominative case. 3. word in that case. *Who* and *I* are nominatives. *adj., n. 20.*

nom i nee (nom′i nē′), person nominated for an office or to be a candidate for election to an office. *n. 17.*

non-, prefix meaning:—not; opposite of; lack of; as in nonbreakable, nonconductor, nonessential, nonpartisan.

non ag gres sion (non′ə gresh′ən), lack of aggression. *n.*

nonce (nons). **For the nonce** means for the present time or occasion. *n. 18.*

non cha lance (non′shə ləns), cool unconcern; indifference. Eleanor received the prize with pretended nonchalance. *n. 20.*

non cha lant (non′shə lənt), without enthusiasm; coolly unconcerned; indifferent. *adj. 19.*

non com bat ant (non kom′bə tənt), 1. person who is not a fighter in the army or navy in time of war. Surgeons, nurses, chaplains, etc., are noncombatants even though with the army. 2. not fighting. *n., adj.*

non com mis sioned (non′kə mish′ənd), without a commission; not commissioned. Corporals and sergeants are noncommissioned officers. *adj.*

non com mit tal (non′kə mit′əl), not committing oneself; not saying yes or no. "I will think it over" is a noncommittal answer. *adj.*

non con duc tor (non′kən duk′tər), a substance which does not readily conduct heat, electricity, etc. Rubber is a nonconductor of electricity. *n.*

non con form ist (non′kən fôr′mist), 1. person who refuses to conform to an established church. 2. In England, all Protestants not members of the Church of England were called Nonconformists. *n. 14.*

non de script (non′di skript), 1. not easily classified; not of any one particular kind; as, eyes of nondescript shade, neither brown, blue, nor gray. 2. a nondescript person or thing. *adj., n. 16.*

none (nun), 1. not any. 2. no one; not one. 3. no persons. 4. not at all. *pron., adv. 1.*

non en ti ty (non en′ti ti), 1. person or thing of little or no importance. 2. something which does not exist. *n., pl. nonentities. 16.*

non es sen tial (non′e sen′shəl), 1. not essential; not necessary. 2. person or thing not essential. *adj., n.*

non me tal lic (non′mi tal′ik), not like a metal. Carbon, oxygen, sulphur, and nitrogen are nonmetallic chemical elements. *adj.*

non pa reil (non′pə rel′), 1. having no equal. 2. a beautifully colored bird of the southern United States. *adj., n. 17.*

non par ti san or **non par ti zan** (non pär′ti zən), not partisan; not supporting any of the regular political parties. *adj. 18.*

non plussed (non′plust), puzzled; at a loss; not knowing what to say or do. We were nonplussed when we saw two roads leading off to the left where we had expected only one. *adj.*

non res i dent (non rez′i dənt), 1. living elsewhere; not living in a particular place. 2. not living where duty requires. 3. nonresident person. *adj., n.*

non sense (non′sens), words, ideas, or acts without meaning; foolish talk or doings; a plan or suggestion that is foolish. Father says "Nonsense!" when he hears something that cannot be true or is very foolish. *n. 5.*

non sen si cal (non sen′si kəl), foolish; absurd. *adj.*

non stop (non′stop′), without stopping. *adj., adv.*

non un ion (non ūn′yən), 1. not belonging to a trade union. 2. not following trade-union rules. 3. not recognizing or favoring trade unions. *adj.*

noo dle (nü′dəl), a mixture of flour and water, or flour and eggs, like macaroni, but made in flat strips. *n.*

nook (nu̇k), 1. cozy little corner. 2. hidden spot; sheltered place. *n. 5.*

noon (nün), 12 o'clock in the daytime; the middle of the day. *n. 1.*

noon day (nün′dā′), noon. *n., adj. 5.*

noon tide (nün′tīd′), noon. *n. 7.*

noose (nüs), 1. loop with a slip knot that tightens as the string or rope is pulled. Nooses are used especially in lassos and snares. 2. a snare or bond; as, the noose of marriage. 3. catch with a noose; snare. *n., v. 11.*

Noose

nor (nôr), 1. and no. There was neither river nor stream in that desert. He had neither food nor drink left. 2. neither. Nor silver nor gold can buy it. *Used in poetry.*

3. and not. I have not gone there, nor will I ever go. *conj. 1.*

Nor dic (nôr′dik), 1. belonging to or characteristic of the people of northern Europe. 2. a northern European. Scandinavians are Nordics. *adj., n.*

Nor folk (nôr′fək), 1. city on the coast of Virginia, near the mouth of the Potomac River. 2. county in eastern England. *n. 10.*

Norfolk jacket, a loose coat with a belt, worn by men and boys.

norm (nôrm), standard; type; model; pattern. In spelling, the class is above the norm for the fifth grade. *n.*

nor mal (nôr′məl), 1. of the usual standard; regular; usual. The normal temperature of the human body is 98.6 degrees. 2. the usual state or level; as, two pounds above normal. *adj., n. 5.*

nor mal ly (nôr′məl i), in the normal way; regularly; if things are normal. A child normally begins to lose his first teeth at six years. *adv.*

normal school, a school where people are trained to be teachers.

Nor man (nôr′mən), 1. native or inhabitant of Normandy in France. 2. member of the mixed race descended from the Scandinavians who settled in Normandy and the French. 3. of the Normans or Normandy. *n., adj. 8.*

Norman Conquest, conquest of England by the Normans in 1066, under the leadership of William the Conqueror.

Nor man dy (nôr′mən di), district in northwestern France. *n. 10.*

Norse (nôrs), 1. of or having to do with ancient Scandinavia, its people, or their language. 2. people of ancient Scandinavia; Norsemen; Northmen. 3. language of these people. It is often called Old Norse. 4. of or having to do with Norway or its people. 5. Norwegians. 6. language of Norway. *adj., n. pl. or sing.*

Norse man (nôrs′mən), Northman; ancient Scandinavian. The Vikings were Norsemen. *n., pl. Norsemen. 12.*

north (nôrth), 1. the direction to which a compass needle points; the direction to your right as you face the setting sun. See the diagram. 2. toward the north; farther toward the north. Drive north for the next mile. 3. **North of** means farther north than. Boston is north of New York. 4. from the north; as, a north wind. 5. in the north; living in the north. 6. the part of any country toward the north. In the United States, **the North** means the States north of Maryland, the Ohio River, and Missouri. *n., adv., adj. 1.*

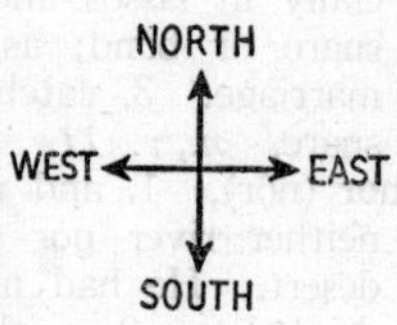

North America, the northern continent of the Western Hemisphere. The United States, Mexico, and Canada are countries in North America.

North Carolina, a Southern State of the United States. *18.*

North Da ko ta (nôrth′ də kō′tə), a Middle Western State of the United States.

north east (nôrth′ēst′), 1. halfway between north and east. 2. a northeast direction. 3. a place that is in the northeast part or direction. 4. toward, from, or in the northeast. *adj., n., adv. 7.*

north east er (nôrth′ēs′tər), a wind or storm from the northeast. *n.*

north east er ly (nôrth′ēs′tər li), 1. toward the northeast. 2. from the northeast. *adj., adv. 20.*

north east ern (nôrth′ēs′tərn), 1. toward the northeast. 2. from the northeast. 3. of or pertaining to the northeast. *adj. 9.*

north er ly (nôr′ᴛʜər li), 1. toward the north. The windows face northerly. 2. from the north. 3. of the north. *adj., adv. 11.*

north ern (nôr′ᴛʜərn), 1. toward the north; as, the northern side of a building. 2. from the north. 3. of the north. He has traveled in northern countries. 4. of the North of the United States; as, a Northern city. *adj. 2.*

North ern er (nôr′ᴛʜər nər), person born or living in the North. *n. 20.*

Northern Hemisphere, the half of the earth that is north of the equator.

Northern Ireland, self-governing district in Ireland that refused to join the Irish Free State and is still politically united with Great Britain.

northern lights, streamers and bands of light appearing in the sky in northern regions.

north ern most (nôr′ᴛʜərn mōst), farthest north. *adj.*

North man (nôrth′mən), member of a tall, fair race which used to live in the north of Europe, where Norway, Sweden, and Denmark now are. The Northmen were great sailors and sea fighters. *n., pl. Northmen. 17.*

North Pole, northern end of the earth's axis.

North Sea, the sea between Great Britain and western Europe.

North Star, bright star almost directly above the North Pole.

North um ber land (nôr thum′bər lənd), a county in northeastern England. *n. 14.*

North um bri a (nôr thum′bri ə), an ancient kingdom in northern England. *n. 13.*

north ward (nôrth′wərd), 1. toward the north; north. He walked northward. The orchard is on the northward slope of the hill. Rocks lay northward of the ship's course. 2. northward part, direction, or point. *adv., adj., n. 11.*

north wards (nôrth′wərdz), northward. *adv.*

north west (nôrth′west′), 1. halfway between north and west. 2. a northwest direction. 3. a place that is the northwest part or direction. 4. toward, from, or in the northwest. *adj., n., adv. 5.*

north west er (nôrth′wes′tər), a wind or storm from the northwest. *n.*

north west er ly (nôrth′wes′tər li), 1. toward the northwest. 2. from the northwest. *adj., adv.*

north west ern (nôrth′wes′tərn), 1. toward the northwest. 2. from the northwest. 3. of the northwest; pertaining to the northwest. *adj. 8.*

Nor way (nôr′wā), a mountainous country in northern Europe, west and north of Sweden. *n. 5.*

Nor we gian (nôr wē′jən), 1. of Norway, its people, or their language; as, Norwegian villages, a Norwegian costume. 2. person who lives in Norway, was born in Norway, or comes of Norwegian parents. 3. the language of Norway. *adj., n. 9.*

nose (nōz), 1. the part of the face or head just above the mouth. The nose has openings for breathing and smelling. 2. sense of smell. Most dogs have a good nose. A mouse has a good nose for cheese. 3. to smell; discover by smell; smell out. 4. rub with the nose. 5. sniff (at). 6. part that stands out, especially the bow of a ship or boat. At last we saw the little steamer's nose poking around the cliff. 7. push (its way) with the nose. The little boat nosed carefully between the rocks. 8. search (for); pry (into). *n., v. 1.*

nose bleed (nōz′blēd′), flow of blood from the nose. *n.*

nose dive, a swift plunge downward by an airplane.

nose-dive (nōz′dīv′), take a nose dive. *v., nose-dived, nose-diving.*

nose gay (nōz′gā), a bunch of flowers; bouquet. *n. 14.*

nos tril (nos′tril), either of the two openings in the nose. Air is breathed into the lungs, and smells come into the sensitive parts of the nose, through the nostrils. *n. 4.*

nos trum (nos′trəm), 1. a medicine made by the person who is selling it; patent medicine; quack remedy. 2. pet scheme for producing wonderful results; cure-all. *n. 15.*

not (not). Not says "no." Cold is not hot. Six and two do not make ten. *adv. 1.*

no ta ble (nō′tə bəl), 1. worthy of notice; striking; remarkable; as, a notable event, a notable man. 2. person who is notable. Many notables came to the President's reception. *adj., n. 5.*

no ta bly (nō′tə bli), in a notable manner; to a notable degree. *adv.*

no ta ry (nō′tə ri), a public officer, usually called a **notary public,** authorized to certify deeds and contracts, to record the fact that a certain person swears that something is true, and to attend to other legal matters. *n., pl. notaries. 9.*

no ta tion (nō tā′shən), 1. a set of signs or symbols used to represent numbers, quantities, or other values. In arithmetic we use the Arabic notation (1, 2, 3, 4, etc.), and sometimes the Roman notation (I, II, III, IV, etc.). 2. the representing of numbers, quantities, or other values by symbols or signs. Music has a special system of notation, and so has chemistry. 3. record; note to assist memory; jotting. He made a notation on the margin of the paper. *n. 13.*

notch (noch), 1. a V-shaped nick or cut made in an edge or on a curving surface. The Indians cut notches on a stick to keep count of numbers. 2. make a notch or notches in. 3. deep, narrow pass or gap between mountains. *n., v. 8.*

Notches on a stick

note (nōt), 1. a short sentence, phrase, or single word, written down to remind one of what was in a book, a speech, an agreement, etc.; as, to take notes of a lecture. I must make a note of that. 2. write down as a thing to be remembered. 3. a comment, remark, or piece of information added concerning a word or a passage in a book, often to help pupils in studying the book. Her copy of *Evangeline* has many helpful notes at the back. 4. very short letter. 5. letter from one government to another. 6. a written promise to pay a certain amount of money at a certain time. 7. greatness; fame. Washington is a person of note. 8. observe; notice; give attention to. Now note what I do next. 9. in music, the written sign to show the pitch and the length of a sound. 10. a single musical sound. Sing this note for me. 11. any one of the black or white keys of a piano. 12. a song or call of a bird. 13. significant sound or way of expression. There was a note of anxiety in her voice. 14. Some special meanings are: **compare notes,** exchange ideas or opinions. **take note of,** give attention to; observe. *n., v. 1.*

Notes in music: A, whole note; B, half note; C, quarter note; D, eighth note.

note book (nōt′bu̇k′), a book in which to write notes of things to be learned or remembered. *n. 12.*

not ed (nōt′id), well-known; specially noticed; conspicuous; celebrated; famous. Samson was noted for his strength. *adj.*

note wor thy (nōt′wėr′ᴛʜi), worthy of notice; remarkable. The first flight across the Atlantic was a noteworthy achievement. *adj. 11.*

noth ing (nuth′ing), 1. not anything. 2. thing of no value or importance. 3. zero. 4. not at all. He was nothing wiser than he was before. *pron., n., adv. 1.*

noth ing ness (nuth′ing nis), 1. being nothing; condition of not existing. 2. being of no value; worthlessness. *n. 17.*

no tice (nō′tis), 1. heed; attention. Take no notice of her. A sudden movement or sound catches one's notice. 2. see; take notice of; give attention to. I noticed a hole in my stocking. 3. warning. The driver sounded his horn to give notice that he was going to turn the corner. 4. a written or printed sign; a paper posted in a public place; a large sheet of paper giving information or directions. We saw a notice of today's moving picture outside the theater. 5. telling that one is leaving a rented house or leaving a person's employ, or that one must leave the house one is living in or the position one is filling, at a given time. A month's notice is required from whichever party wishes to end the agreement. 6. a written or printed account in a newspaper. There is a notice in the paper describing Mary's birthday party. 7. speak of; refer to; mention. *n., v. 1.*

no tice a ble (nō′tis ə bəl), 1. easily seen or noticed. This kitten was noticeable because it was the only one of the five which was yellow. 2. worth noticing. *adj. 8.*

no tice a bly (nō′tis ə bli), to a noticeable degree. Oranges are noticeably less sour than lemons. It is noticeably cooler in the shade. *adv.*

no ti fi ca tion (nō′ti fi kā′shən), 1. notifying. 2. notice. Have you received a notification of the meeting? *n. 16.*

no ti fy (nō′ti fī), let know; inform; give notice to; announce to. Our teacher notified us that there would be a test on Monday. My uncle in Canada notified us that he was coming here on a visit. *v., notified, notifying. 5.*

no tion (nō′shən), 1. idea. He has no notion of what I mean. 2. opinion; view; belief. One common notion is that red hair means a quick temper. 3. foolish idea or opinion. That silly girl has too many notions. 4. **Notions** sometimes means small useful articles, such as pins, thread, tape, etc. *n. 3.*

no to ri e ty (nō′tə rī′i ti), 1. being famous for something bad; ill fame. A crime or scandal brings much notoriety to those involved in it. 2. being widely known. *n., pl. notorieties. 14.*

no to ri ous (nō tō′ri əs), well-known or commonly known, especially because of something bad. That notorious criminal has been sent to prison. Philip is a notorious crybaby. *adj. 7.*

Not ting ham (not′ing əm), 1. county in central England. 2. city in this county. *n. 10.*

not with stand ing (not′wiᴛʜ stan′ding), 1. in spite of. Notwithstanding her naughtiness, I love my little girl. 2. in spite of the fact that. 3. in spite of it; nevertheless. It is raining; but I shall go, notwithstanding. *prep., conj., adv. 5.*

nought (nôt), 1. nothing; naught. All my work came to nought. 2. zero; 0. Put two noughts after a six to make six hundred. *n. 5.*

noun (noun), a word used as the name of a person, thing, quality, or event. Words like *John, table, school, kindness, skill,* and *party* are nouns. *n. 10.*

nour ish (nėr′ish), 1. feed; make grow, or keep alive and well, with food. Milk is all we need to nourish a small baby. 2. maintain; foster: as, to nourish a hope. *v. 5.*

nour ish ment (nėr′ish mənt), food. *n. 6.*

Nov., November. *8.*

No va Sco tia (nō′və skō′shə), province in southeastern Canada consisting chiefly of a peninsula extending into the Atlantic. *12.*

nov el (nov′əl), 1. new; strange; of a new kind or nature. Flying gives people a novel sensation. Red snow is a novel idea to us. 2. a story with characters and a plot, long enough to fill one or more volumes. Novels are usually about people, scenes, and happenings such as might be met in real life. *adj., n. 5.*

nov el ist (nov′əl ist), writer of novels. *n. 10.*

nov el ty (nov′əl ti), 1. newness. The novelty of washing dishes soon wore off, and then Mary did not want to do it any more. 2. new or unusual thing. Staying up late was a novelty to the children, and they enjoyed it. **Novelties** are small, unusual articles, toys, cheap jewelry, etc. *n., pl. novelties. 4.*

No vem ber (nō vem′bər), the 11th month of the year; the month just before December. *n. 2.*

nov ice (nov′is), 1. beginner; one who is new to what he is doing. 2. person who is not yet a monk or a nun, but is on trial. *n. 8.*

no vi ti ate or **no vi ci ate** (nō vish′i it), 1. the period of trial and preparation in a religious order. 2. the state or period of being a beginner in anything. *n. 16.*

now (nou), 1. at this time. We do not believe in ghosts now. 2. by this time. She must have reached the city now. 3. this time; as, by now, until now, from now on. 4. since; now that. Now I am older, I have changed my mind. Now you mention it, I do remember. 5. as things are; as it is. Now I can never believe you again. 6. then; next. 7. Now is used in many sentences where it makes very little difference in the meaning. Now what do you mean? Oh, come now! Now you knew that was wrong. 8. Some special meanings are:

just now, only a few moments ago.

now and then or **now and again** means from time to time; once in a while.

adv., n., conj. 1.

now a days (nou′ə dāz′), 1. at the present day; in these times. Nowadays people travel in automobiles. 2. the present day; these times. *adv., n. 8.*

no way (nō′wā), in no way; not at all. *adv.*

no ways (nō′wāz), nowise. *adv.*

no where (nō′hwãr), in no place; at no place; to no place. *adv. 6.*

no wise (nō′wīz), in no way; not at all. *adv. 18.*

nox ious (nok′shəs), very harmful; poisonous. *adj. 11.*

noz zle (noz′əl), a tip put on a hose, etc., forming an outlet. *n. 11.*

Nu bi a (nū′bi ə or nü′bi ə), region in northeastern Africa south of Egypt and bordering on the Red Sea. *n. 17.*

nu cle ar (nū′kli ər or nü′kli ər), forming a nucleus; having to do with nuclei. *adj. 17.*

nu cle us (nū′kli əs or nü′kli əs), 1. a central part or thing around which other parts or things are collected. 2. a beginning, to which additions are to be made. John's five-dollar bill became the nucleus of a flourishing bank account. 3. in biology, an active body lying within the substance of a cell of an animal or a plant, without which the cell cannot grow and divide. 4. the dense, central part of a comet's head. *n., pl. nuclei* (nū′kli ī or nü′kli ī) or *nucleuses. 7.*

nude (nūd or nüd), 1. naked; unclothed; bare. 2. a naked figure in painting or sculpture. *adj., n. 19.*

nudge (nuj), 1. push slightly; jog with the elbow to attract attention, etc. 2. a slight push or jog. *v., n. 13.*

nug get (nug′it), lump; valuable lump; as, nuggets of gold, nuggets of wisdom. *n. 17.*

nui sance (nū′səns or nü′səns), thing or person that annoys, troubles, offends, or is disagreeable. Flies are a nuisance. *n. 8.*

null (nul), 1. not binding; of no effect; as if not existing. A promise obtained by force is legally null. **Null and void** means without force or effect; worthless. 2. empty; valueless. 3. not any; zero. *adj. 11.*

nul li fi ca tion (nul′i fi kā′shən), 1. nullifying. 2. being nullified; as, the nullification of a treaty. *n. 13.*

nul li fy (nul′i fī), 1. make not binding or not the law; render void; as, to nullify a law. 2. make of no effect; wipe out. The difficulties of the plan nullify its advantages. *v., nullified, nullifying. 16.*

nul li ty (nul′i ti), 1. the state or fact of being null; nothingness. 2. a mere nothing. The king's power in Italy is practically a nullity. 3. something that is null, such as a law or agreement. *n., pl. nullities. 19.*

numb (num), 1. having lost the power of

feeling or moving. My fingers are numb with cold. 2. make numb. 3. dull the feelings of; as, numbed with grief. *adj., v. 10.*

num ber (num′bər), 1. A number tells how many. Two, thirteen, twenty-one, fifty, and one hundred are numbers. Number means the count or sum of a group of things or persons. The number of boys in our class is twenty. 2. a figure or mark that stands for a number. 2, 7, and 9 are numbers. 3. count; find out the number of. 4. give a number to. The pages of this book are numbered. 5. be or amount to a given number. The States in the Union number forty-eight. 6. a large or small quantity. We saw a number of birds. There were numbers who stayed out of school that day. 7. reckon as one of a class or collection. 8. amount to; reach the number of. 9. being more; as, to win a battle by force of numbers. 10. an issue of a magazine. The May number of *Boys' Life* is unusually good. 11. limit; fix the number of. 12. in grammar, a word form or ending which shows whether one or more than one is meant. *Boy, ox,* and *this* are in the singular number; *boys, oxen,* and *these* are in the plural number. 13. Some special meanings are:

number one, oneself.

speak in numbers, speak in verse, or with rhythm, as in music.

without number, too many to be counted; as, stars without number.

n., v. 1.

num ber less (num′bər lis), very numerous; too many to count. There are numberless fish in the sea. *adj. 8.*

Num bers (num′bərz), the fourth book of the Old Testament. *n.*

numb ness (num′nis), lack of feeling or movement; numb condition; lack of sensation. *n. 16.*

nu mer al (nū′mər əl or nü′mər əl), 1. a figure or group of figures standing for a number. 7, 25, 463, III, and XIX are numerals. 2. of numbers; standing for a number. 3. **Numerals** sometimes means big cloth numbers given by a school for excellence in some sport. They state the year in which the person who wins them will graduate. *n., adj. 8.*

nu mer ate (nū′mər āt or nü′mər āt), number; count. *v.*

nu mer a tor (nū′mər ā′tər or nü′mər ā′tər), the number above the line in a fraction, which shows how many parts are taken. In $\frac{3}{8}$, *3* is the numerator. *n.*

nu mer i cal (nū mer′i kəl or nü mer′i kəl), having to do with number or numbers; in numbers; by numbers. *adj. 12.*

nu mer i cal ly (nū mer′i kəl i or nü mer′i-kəl i), by numbers; in a numerical manner; in numerical respects. *adv.*

nu mer ous (nū′mər əs or nü′mər əs), 1. very many. The child asked numerous questions. 2. in great numbers. He has a numerous acquaintance among politicians. *adj. 3.*

nu mis mat ics (nū′miz mat′iks or nü′miz-mat′iks), study of coins and medals. *n.*

num skull (num′skul′), stupid person; blockhead. *n.*

nun (nun), woman who gives up everything else for religion, and with other religious women lives a life of prayer and worship. Some nuns teach; others care for the sick. *n. 5.*

nun ci o (nun′shi ō), an official representative of the Pope. *n., pl. nuncios. 17.*

nun ner y (nun′ər i), building or buildings where nuns live; convent. *n., pl. nunneries. 10.*

nup tial (nup′shəl), 1. of marriage or weddings. 2. **Nuptials** means a wedding or the wedding ceremony. *adj., n. 7.*

Nu rem berg (nūr′əm bėrg or nür′əm bėrg), city in western Germany, noted for the manufacture of toys. *n. 17.*

nurse (nėrs), 1. person who takes care of the sick or the old, or is trained to do this. Hospitals employ nurses. 2. be or act as a nurse for sick people; wait on or try to cure the sick. 3. woman who cares for and brings up the young children or babies of another person. 4. act as a nurse; have charge of or bring up (children). 5. one who feeds and protects. 6. nourish; make grow; protect; treat with special care; as, to nurse a hatred in the heart, to nurse a plant, to nurse a sore arm. 7. hold closely; clasp fondly. 8. give milk to (a baby). 9. suck milk from a mother. *n., v. 2.*

nurse maid (nėrs′mād′), girl or woman employed to care for children. *n.*

nurs er y (nėr′sər i), 1. a room set apart for the use of the children of the household. 2. A **day nursery** is a place where babies and small children are cared for during the day. 3. a piece of ground or place where young plants are raised for transplanting or sale. *n., pl. nurseries. 6.*

nurs er y man (nėr′sər i mən), man who grows or sells young trees and plants. *n., pl. nurserymen. 17.*

nurs ling or **nurse ling** (nėrs′ling), 1. a baby that is being nursed. 2. any person or thing that is having tender care. *n. 15.*

nur ture (nėr′chər), 1. rear; bring up; care for; foster; train. She nurtured the child as if he had been her own. 2. rearing; bringing up; training; education. The two sisters had received very different nurture, one at home and the other at a convent. 3. nourish. 4. nourishment. *v., n. 9.*

nut (nut), 1. a dry fruit or seed with a hard woody or leathery shell and a kernel inside which is good to eat. 2. the kernel of a nut. 3. a small block, usually of metal, which screws on to a bolt to hold the bolt in place. *n. 2.*

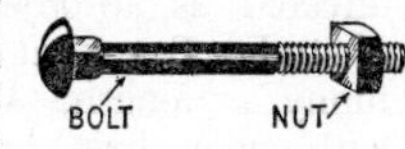

Bolt with nut screwed on

nut crack er (nut′krak′ər), 1. an instrument for cracking the shells of nuts. 2. a bird of the crow family which feeds on nuts. *n.*

Nutcracker

nut hatch (nut′hach′), small sharp-beaked bird that feeds on small nuts, seeds, and insects. *n.*

nut meg (nut′meg), a hard spicy seed about as big as a marble, obtained from the fruit of an East Indian tree. The seed is grated and used for flavoring food. *n. 9.*

nu tri ent (nū′tri ənt or nü′tri ənt), 1. nourishing. 2. a food. *adj., n. 9.*

nu tri ment (nū′tri mənt or nü′tri mənt), nourishment; food. *n. 15.*

nu tri tion (nū trish′ən or nü trish′ən), 1. food; nourishment. 2. process by which food is changed to living tissues. *n. 8.*

nu tri tious (nū trish′əs or nü trish′əs), nourishing; valuable as food. *adj. 13.*

nu tri tive (nū′tri tiv or nü′tri tiv), 1. nutritious. 2. having to do with foods and the use of foods. Digestion is part of the nutritive process. *adj. 12.*

nut shell (nut′shel′), 1. the shell of a nut. 2. **In a nutshell** means in a few words. *n.*

nut ting (nut′ing), gathering nuts. *n. 13.*

nut ty (nut′i), 1. containing many nuts; as, nutty cake. 2. like nuts; tasting like nuts. *adj., nuttier, nuttiest.*

nuz zle (nuz′əl), 1. poke or rub with the nose; press the nose against. 2. nestle; snuggle; cuddle. *v.*

NW or **N.W.,** northwest.

N.Y., New York State. *16.*

N.Y.C., New York City.

ny lon (nī′lon), an extremely strong, elastic, and durable substance, used to make stockings, bristles, etc. *n.* [*Trade name*]

nymph (nimf), a lesser goddess of nature, who lived in seas, rivers, fountains, hills, woods, or trees. *n. 5.*

O

O, o (ō), the 15th letter of the alphabet. There are two o's in Ohio. *n., pl. O's, o's. 1.*

O (ō), 1. O is used before a person's name or title in beginning to speak; as, O King, hear my prayer! 2. O is the same word as **Oh.** O dear me! O joy! *interj.*

O., Ohio.

o' (ə or ō), 1. of; as in man-o'-war. 2. on. *prep.*

oaf (ōf), 1. a very stupid child or man. 2. deformed child. *n.*

A B
Oak: leaf and acorn of A, European; B, American.

oak (ōk), 1. any of several kinds of trees found in all parts of the world, having leaves like those in the picture and nuts which are called acorns. The wood is very hard and very useful. 2. of an oak; as, oak leaves. 3. the wood of the oak tree. 4. made of oak wood. *n., adj. 1.*

oak en (ōk′ən), made of oak wood; as, an oaken chest. *adj. 8.*

Oak land (ōk′lənd), a large city across the bay from San Francisco. *n. 13.*

oa kum (ō′kəm), loose fiber obtained by untwisting and picking apart old ropes. Oakum is used for stopping up the seams or cracks in ships. *n. 14.*

oar (ōr), 1. a long pole with a flat end, used in rowing. Sometimes an oar is used to steer a boat. 2. use an oar; row. 3. person who rows. Dick is the best oar in the crew. *n., v. 4.*

Oar

oar lock (ōr′lok′), notch in which the oar

rests in rowing; rowlock. See the picture under **rowlock.** *n.*

oars man (ōrz′mən), 1. man who rows. 2. man who rows well. *n., pl. oarsmen.*

o a sis (ō ā′sis), fertile spot in the desert where there is water. *n., pl. oases* (ō ā′sēz). *7.*

oat (ōt), a plant whose grain is used for food. **Oats** means the grain of the oat plant. *n. 3.*

oat en (ōt′ən), 1. made of oats or oatmeal. 2. made of oat straw. *adj. 15.*

oath (ōth), 1. a solemn promise or statement that something is true, which God is called on to witness. 2. the name of God used as an exclamation to add force or to express anger. 3. a curse; word used in swearing. *n., pl. oaths* (ōᴛʜz). *7.*

oat meal (ōt′mēl′), 1. oats made into meal; ground oats; rolled oats. 2. porridge made from oatmeal. *n. 7.*

ob du ra cy (ob′dū rə si or ob′dů rə si), hardness of heart; stubbornness. *n. 16.*

ob du rate (ob′dū rit or ob′dů rit), 1. stubborn; unyielding; as, an obdurate refusal. 2. hardened in feelings or heart; not repentant; as, an obdurate criminal. *adj. 14.*

o be di ence (ō bē′di əns), doing what one is told; submitting to authority or law. Parents demand obedience from their children. Soldiers act in obedience to the orders of their officers. *n. 4.*

o be di ent (ō bē′di ənt), doing what one is told; willing to obey. The obedient dog came at his master's whistle. *adj. 5.*

o bei sance (ō bā′səns), 1. a movement of the body expressing deep respect; deep bow. The men made obeisance to the king. 2. deference; homage. *n. 11.*

ob e lisk (ob′ə lisk), a tapering, four-sided shaft of stone with a top shaped like a pyramid. *n. 12.*

Obelisk

O ber on (ō′bər on), the king of the fairies. *n. 14.*

o bese (ō bēs′), extremely fat. *adj. 19.*

o bes i ty (ō bēs′i ti), extreme fatness. *n. 13.*

o bey (ō bā′), 1. do what one is told. The dog obeyed and went home. 2. follow the orders of. We obey our father. 3. yield to the control of. A car obeys the driver. A horse obeys the rein. *v. 2.*

o bit u ar y (ō bich′ü ãr′i), 1. a notice of death, often with a brief account of the person's life. 2. of a death; recording a death; as, the obituary notices in the newspaper. *n., pl. obituaries, adj. 18.*

ob ject (ob′jikt for 1-5, əb jekt′ for 6 and 7), 1. thing; something that can be seen or touched. What is that object by the fence? A dark object moved between me and the door. A baby is likely to put any small object into its mouth. 2. person or thing toward which feeling, thought, or action is directed; as, an object of charity, an object of study. 3. person or thing that is absurd, funny, or foolish. What an object you are with your hair pulled back that way. 4. thing aimed at; end; purpose. My object in coming here was to get Mary's address. 5. a word or group of words toward which the action of the verb is directed or to which a preposition expresses some relation. In "John threw the ball to his brother," *ball* is the object of *threw,* and *brother* is the object of *to.* 6. make objections; be opposed; feel dislike. Many people object to loud noise. 7. give as a reason against something. Mother objected that the weather was too wet to play outdoors. *n., v. 1.*

ob jec tion (əb jek′shən), 1. something said in objecting; a reason or argument against something. 2. a feeling of disapproval or dislike. *n. 5.*

ob jec tion a ble (əb jek′shən ə bəl), 1. likely to be objected to. 2. unpleasant; disagreeable. *adj. 15.*

ob jec tive (əb jek′tiv), 1. something aimed at. My objective this summer will be learning to drive a car. 2. real; existing outside the mind as an actual object, and not merely in the mind as an idea. 3. about outward things, not about the thoughts and feelings of the speaker, writer, painter, etc.; giving facts as they are, without a bias toward either side; impersonal. 4. showing the direct object of a verb or the object of a preposition. In "John hit me," *me* is in the objective case. 5. the objective case. 6. word in that case. *n., adj. 14.*

ob la tion (ob lā′shən), 1. act of offering to God or a god. 2. the offering of bread and wine in the Communion service. 3. something offered to a god; sacrifice; victim. 4. gift for religious uses. *n. 13.*

ob li gate (ob′li gāt), bind morally or legally; pledge. A witness in court is obligated to tell the truth. *v. 16.*

ob li ga tion (ob′li gā′shən), 1. duty under the law; duty due to a promise or contract; duty on account of social relationship or kindness received. Taxes are an obligation which may fall on everybody. The man is really under obligation to paint our house first. A wife's first obligation is to her husband and children. 2. binding power (of a law, promise, sense of duty, etc.). The one who did the damage is under obligation to pay for it. *n. 5.*

ob lig a to ry (əb lig′ə tō′ri), binding morally or legally; required. Attendance at school is obligatory. *adj.*

o blige (ə blīj′), 1. bind by a promise, contract, duty, etc.; compel; force. The law obliges parents to send their children to school. I am obliged to leave early to catch my train. 2. bind by a favor or service; do a favor to. Kindly oblige me by closing the door. Grace obliged the company with a song. *v. 2.*

o blig ing (ə blīj′ing), willing to do favors; helpful. *adj. 12.*

ob lique (əb lēk′), slanting; not straight up and down; not straight across. AB, CD, EF, and GH are oblique lines. An oblique angle is any angle that is not a right angle. Ann gave an oblique glance to one side. *adj. 9.*

B D F H A C E G

ob liq ui ty (əb lik′wi ti), 1. indirectness or crookedness of thought or behavior, especially conduct which is not upright and moral. 2. being oblique. *n., pl. obliquities. 14.*

ob lit er ate (əb lit′ər āt), blot out; remove all traces of; destroy. The heavy rain obliterated all footprints. *v. 10.*

ob liv i on (əb liv′i ən), 1. condition of being entirely forgotten. Many ancient cities have long since passed into oblivion. 2. forgetfulness. *n. 8.*

ob liv i ous (əb liv′i əs), 1. forgetful; not mindful. The book was so interesting that I was oblivious of my surroundings. 2. bringing forgetfulness; as, an oblivious slumber. *adj. 10.*

ob long (ob′lông), 1. longer than broad; as, an oblong loaf of bread. 2. a rectangle that is not a square. *adj., n. 15.*

Oblong

ob lo quy (ob′lə kwi), 1. abuse; blame; public reproach. 2. disgrace; shame. *n., pl. obloquies. 15.*

ob nox ious (əb nok′shəs), offensive; very disagreeable; hateful. His disgusting table manners made him obnoxious to us. *adj. 10.*

o boe (ō′bō), a wooden wind instrument in which the tone is produced by a double reed. *n.*

Man playing an oboe

ob scene (ob sēn′), offending modesty or decency; impure; filthy; vile. *adj. 9.*

ob scen i ty (ob sen′i ti or ob sēn′i ti), obscene words or actions. *n., pl. obscenities. 17.*

ob scure (əb skūr′), 1. not distinct; not clear; as, an obscure form, obscure sounds. I had only an obscure view of it. 2. hidden; not easily discovered; as, an obscure meaning. 3. not well known; attracting no notice; as, an obscure little village, an obscure poet, an obscure position. 4. dark; dim. 5. make obscure; dim; darken; hide from view. Clouds obscure the sun. His difficult style obscures his meaning. *adj., v. 5.*

ob scu ri ty (əb skūr′i ti), 1. dimness; lack of light. The dog hid in the obscurity of the thick bushes. 2. lack of clearness; difficulty in being understood. The obscurity of the passage makes several interpretations possible. 3. being unknown. Lincoln rose from obscurity to fame. *n., pl. obscurities. 7.*

ob se quies (ob′si kwiz), funeral rites or ceremonies; a stately funeral. *n. pl. 12.*

ob se qui ous (əb sē′kwi əs), servile; fawning; polite or obedient from hope of gain or from fear. Obsequious courtiers greeted the king. *adj. 10.*

ob serv a ble (əb zėr′və bəl), 1. noticeable; easily seen. 2. that can be observed; that should be observed. *adj. 18.*

ob serv ance (əb zėr′vəns), 1. act of observing or keeping laws or customs; as, the observance of the Sabbath. 2. act performed as a sign of worship or respect; religious ceremony. 3. respectful attention or service. *Old use. n. 7.*

ob serv ant (əb zėr′vənt), 1. observing; quick to notice; watchful. If you are observant in the fields and woods, you will find many flowers that others fail to notice. 2. careful in observing a law, rule, custom, etc.; as, observant of the traffic rules. *adj. 12.*

ob ser va tion (ob′zər vā′shən), 1. the act, habit, or power of seeing and noting. By his trained observation the doctor knew that the man was not really dead. 2. the fact of being seen; notice; being seen. The tramp avoided observation. 3. something seen and noted. The student of bird life kept a record of his observations. 4. remark. "Haste makes waste," was father's observation as Harry spilled the ice cream. *n. 4.*

ob serv a to ry (əb zėr′və tō′ri), 1. a building fitted up for observing the stars and other heavenly bodies, or sometimes for observing other facts and happenings of nature. 2. high place or building giving a wide view. *n., pl. observatories. 12.*

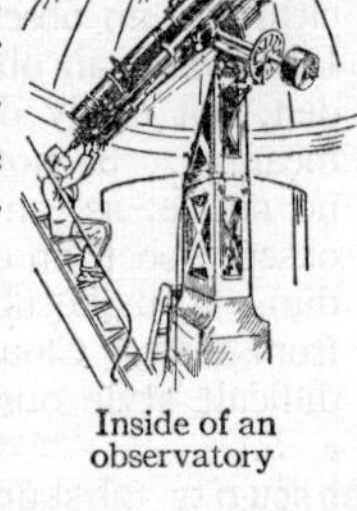
Inside of an observatory

ob serve (əb zėrv′), 1. see and note; notice. Did you observe anything strange in the man's conduct? 2. examine closely; study. An astronomer observes the stars. 3. remark. "Bad weather," the captain observed. 4. keep; follow in practice; as, to observe silence, to observe a rule. 5. show regard for; celebrate; as, to observe Christmas. *v. 2.*

ob serv er (əb zėr′vər), person who observes. *n. 8.*

ob serv ing (əb zėr′ving), that observes; quick to notice. *adj.*

ob sess (əb ses′), haunt; fill the mind of; keep the attention of. Fear that someone might steal his money obsessed the old miser. *v. 14.*

ob ses sion (əb sesh′ən), 1. an obsessing or being obsessed; the influence of a feeling, idea, etc., which a person cannot escape. 2. the feeling or idea itself. *n. 15.*

ob sid i an (ob sid′i ən), hard, dark, glassy rock that is formed when lava cools. *n. 18.*

ob so les cent (ob′sə les′ənt), passing out of use; tending to become out of date. Horse carriages are obsolescent. *adj.*

ob so lete (ob′sə lēt), no longer in use; out of date. Wooden warships are obsolete. *adj. 11.*

ob sta cle (ob′stə kəl), something that stands in the way or stops progress. A tree fallen across the road was an obstacle to our car. Blindness is an obstacle in most occupations. *n. 5.*

ob sti na cy (ob′sti nə si), 1. stubbornness; being obstinate. Obstinacy sometimes drives us to stick to a thing we have once said, even after we begin to realize that we were mistaken. 2. obstinate act. *n., pl. obstinacies. 8.*

ob sti nate (ob′sti nit), 1. stubborn; not giving in. The obstinate girl would go her own way, in spite of all warnings. 2. hard to control or treat; as, an obstinate cough. *adj. 5.*

ob strep er ous (əb strep′ər əs), 1. noisy; boisterous. 2. unruly; disorderly. *adj. 17.*

ob struct (əb strukt′), 1. block up; make hard to pass through. Fallen trees obstruct the road. 2. be in the way of; hinder. Trees obstruct our view of the ocean. A strike obstructed the work of the factory. *v. 8.*

ob struc tion (əb struk′shən), 1. thing that obstructs; something in the way. The soldiers had to get over such obstructions as ditches and barbed wire. Ignorance is an obstruction to progress. 2. blocking; hindering; as, the obstruction of progress by prejudices. *n. 9.*

ob struc tive (əb struk′tiv), obstructing; blocking; hindering. *adj.*

ob tain (əb tān′), 1. get. One may obtain a position one applies for, obtain a prize one has been working for, obtain possession of a house one has leased, obtain knowledge through study, etc. 2. be in use; be customary; prevail. Different rules obtain in different schools. *v. 2.*

ob tain a ble (əb tān′ə bəl), that can be obtained. *adj. 10.*

ob trude (əb trüd′), thrust forward unwanted; intrude. Do not obtrude your opinions upon others. *v. 14.*

ob tru sive (əb trü′siv), inclined to obtrude; putting oneself forward; intrusive. *adj. 19.*

ob tuse (əb tūs′ or əb tüs′), 1. not sharp or acute; blunt. An obtuse angle is larger than a right angle. 2. dull; slow in understanding; stupid. Jacob was too obtuse to take the hint. *adj. 14.*

OBTUSE ANGLE RIGHT ANGLE

ob verse (ob′vėrs), the side of a coin, medal, etc., that has the principal design on it. *n.*

ob vi ate (ob′vi āt), meet and dispose of; clear out of the way; remove; as, to obviate a difficulty, to obviate danger, to obviate objections. *v. 14.*

ob vi ous (ob′vi əs), plain; easily seen or understood; clear to the eye or mind; not to be doubted. It is obvious that two and two make four. That a blind man ought not to drive an automobile is too obvious to need proof. *adj. 7.*

oc ca sion (ə kā′zhən), 1. a particular time. We have met Mr. Smith on several occasions. 2. special event. The jewels were worn only on great occasions. 3. a good chance; opportunity. 4. a cause; a reason. The dog which was the occasion of the quarrel had run away. 5. to cause; bring about. *n., v. 2.*

oc ca sion al (ə kā′zhən əl), 1. happening or coming now and then, or once in a while. We had fine weather all through July except for an occasional thunderstorm. 2. rising out of, or used for, some special time or event. A war calls forth much occasional poetry. *adj. 4.*

oc ca sion al ly (ə kā′zhən əl i), now and then; once in a while. *adv.*

Oc ci dent or **oc ci dent** (ok′si dənt), countries in Europe and America; the West. The Occident and the Orient have different ideals and customs. *n. 20.*

Oc ci den tal or **oc ci den tal** (ok′si den′təl), 1. western; of the Occident. 2. a native of the West. Europeans are Occidentals. *adj., n. 13.*

oc cult (o kult′), 1. mysterious; beyond the bounds of ordinary knowledge. 2. outside the laws of the natural world; magical. Astrology and alchemy are occult sciences. *adj. 17.*

oc cu pan cy (ok′ū pən si), occupying; holding (land, houses, a pew, etc.) by being in possession. *n. 19.*

oc cu pant (ok′ū pənt), 1. person who occupies. The occupant of the shack stepped out as I approached. 2. person in actual possession of a house, estate, office, etc. *n. 8.*

oc cu pa tion (ok′ū pā′shən), 1. business; employment; trade. Teaching is Miss Day's occupation. 2. possession; occupying; being occupied; as, the occupation of a town by the enemy, the occupation of a house by a family. *n. 3.*

oc cu py (ok′ū pī), 1. take up; fill. The building occupies an entire block. The lessons occupy the morning. 2. keep busy; engage; employ. Sports occupy Jim's attention. 3. take possession of. The enemy occupied our fort. 4. hold; have in use; live in. A judge occupies an important position. The robins are occupying their former nest. *v., occupied, occupying. 2.*

oc cur (ə kėr′), 1. happen; take place. Storms often occur in winter. 2. be found; exist. *E* occurs in print more often than any other letter. 3. come to mind; suggest itself. Did it occur to you to close the windows? *v., occurred, occurring. 2.*

oc cur rence (ə kėr′əns), 1. an occurring. The occurrence of storms delayed our trip. 2. a happening; an event. *n. 7.*

o cean (ō′shən), 1. the great body of salt water that covers almost three fourths of the earth's surface; the sea. 2. any of its five main divisions—the Atlantic, Pacific, Indian, Arctic, or Antarctic oceans. *n. 1.*

o ce an ic (ō′shi an′ik), 1. of the ocean; as, oceanic islands. 2. living in the ocean; as, oceanic fish. 3. like the ocean; wide; vast. *adj. 20.*

o ce lot (ō′sə lot or os′ə lot), a spotted wildcat somewhat like a leopard, which is found from Texas through South America. *n.*

Ocelot (about 4 ft. long, including the tail)

o cher or **o chre** (ō′kər), 1. a yellow earth used to make paint. 2. yellow. *n.*

o'clock (ə klok′), of the clock; by the clock. What o'clock is it? It is one o'clock. *2.*

Oct., October. *7.*

oc ta gon (ok′tə gon), a plane figure having eight angles and eight sides. *n. 17.*

Octagon

oc tave (ok′tiv or ok′tāv), 1. in music, the interval between a note and another note having twice (or half) as many vibrations. From middle C to the C above it is an octave. 2. the eighth note above (or below) a given tone, having twice (or half) as many vibrations per second. 3. the series of notes or of keys of an instrument filling the interval between a note and its octave. 4. the sounding together of a note and its octave. *n. 15.*

Two octaves on the piano (def. 3)

oc ta vo (ok tā′vō), 1. the page size of a book in which each leaf is one eighth of a whole sheet of paper. 2. having this size. 3. a book having this size, usually about 6 by 9½ inches. *n., pl. octavos, adj. 15.*

Oc to ber (ok tō′bər), the tenth month of the year. It has 31 days. *n. 2.*

oc to pus (ok′tə-pəs), 1. a sea animal having a soft body and eight arms with suckers on them. 2. anything like an octopus; powerful, grasping organization with far-reaching influence. *n. 15.*

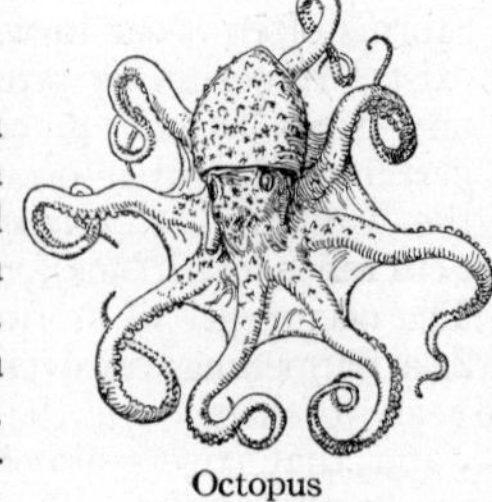
Octopus

oc u lar (ok′ū lər), 1. of or having to do with the eye; as, an ocular muscle. 2. seen; received by actual sight; as, ocular proof. *adj. 16.*

oc u list (ok′ū list), doctor who treats defects and diseases of the eye. *n. 15.*

odd (od), 1. left over; extra. Here are seven plums for three of you; John may have the odd one. Pay the bill with this money and keep the odd change. We speak of odd jobs, odd moments, and odd numbers or volumes of a magazine. 2. being one of a pair or set of which the rest is missing. There seems to be an odd stocking in the wash. 3. with some extra; as, six hundred odd children in school, thirty odd dollars. 4. leaving a remainder of one when divided by two. Seven is an odd number. 5. strange; peculiar; queer. A corncob makes an odd doll. It seems odd that summer should come in December in South Africa. *adj. 2.*

odd i ty (od′i ti), 1. strangeness; queerness; peculiarity. 2. strange, queer, or peculiar person or thing. *n., pl. oddities. 15.*

odd ly (od′li), queerly; strangely. *adv. 17.*

odds (odz), 1. difference in favor of one and against another; advantage. The odds are in our favor and we should win. 2. In betting, odds of 3 to 1 means that 3 will be paid if the bet is lost for every 1 that will be received if it is won. 3. In games, odds is an extra allowance given to the weaker side. 4. Some special meanings are:

at odds, quarreling or disagreeing.

odds and ends, remnants; stray bits left over.

the odds are, the chances are.

n. pl. or sing.

ode (ōd), a poem full of noble feeling expressed with dignity. *n. 8.*

O des sa (ō des′ə), a seaport city in Russia on the Black Sea. *n.*

O din (ō′din), the most important god in Norse mythology. Odin was the god of wisdom, culture, and war. *n.*

o di ous (ō′di əs), hateful; very displeasing; offensive. *adj. 6.*

o di um (ō′di əm), 1. hatred; dislike. 2. reproach; blame. *n. 20.*

o dor (ō′dər), 1. smell; as, the odor of roses, the odor of garbage. 2. reputation. Those hoodlums were in bad odor because they were suspected of stealing. *n. 3.*

o dor if er ous (ō′dər if′ər əs), giving out an odor. The rose is an odoriferous flower. *adj. 15.*

o dor ous (ō′dər əs), having an odor; giving out an odor; sweet-smelling; fragrant. *adj. 10.*

O dys seus (ō dis′ūs), Ulysses, king of Ithaca and shrewdest of the Greek leaders against Troy. *n. 20.*

Od ys sey (od′i si), 1. a long Greek epic poem, describing the ten years of wandering of Odysseus and his final return home. 2. any long series of wanderings and adventures. *n., pl. Odysseys. 11.*

Oed i pus (ed′i pəs), a king of Thebes. Without intention he killed his father and married his mother. His misery made him a famous character in tragedy. *n.*

o'er (ōr), over. *prep., adv.* [*Used in poetry*] *3.*

of (ov, *unstressed* əv), 1. Of may mean about the same as belonging to; as, the children of the family, a student of the Washington School, a friend of his boyhood, the news of the day, the teacher of our class, the captain of the ship, the mother of the boy who was hurt, the cause of the quarrel, the result of his act. 2. Of may mean about the same as from or away from; as, to be north of Boston, to shoot wide of the mark, to cure of a sickness, to be bare of leaves, to take leave of a friend, to be independent of one's parents. 3. Of may mean about the same as made from, which (who) has, which (who) is, or which (who) is the same as; as, castles of sand, built of brick, a house of six rooms, the name of Mary, that group of trees, the city of New York, to make a fool of me. 4. Of may mean about the same as out of or owing to; as, to come of a good family, to expect much of a new medicine, to wish one joy of a new possession, to be sick of or die of a disease, to be tired of, glad of, proud of, etc. 5. Of may mean about the same as which (who) has as a quality; as, a look of pity, a word of encouragement, an hour of prayer, a person of importance, a woman of good judgment. 6. Of may mean the same as concerning or in regard to; as, to think well of someone, to have heard of it, to take care of, to think of, to feel sure of, to be fond of, to be hard of heart, to be fifteen years of age. 7. Of may mean about the same as among; as, a friend of mine, of late years. His mind is of the quickest. Two of us went, and two of us stayed at home. The whole five of us went. 8. Of connects nouns or adjectives having verbal sense with the noun which would be the object of the verb. When we speak of the eating of fruit, fruit is that which is eaten. So we say the love of truth, the drinking of wine, the speaking of pieces, in search of a ball, a hall smelling of onions, a man sparing of words, a boy desirous of good marks. *prep. 1.*

off (ôf), 1. away; at a distance; to a distance. He went off in his car. 2. from; away from; far from. He pushed me off my seat. You are off the road. 3. not on; not connected; loose. 4. In some phrases which mean to stop, off is added to the verb. He broke off in the middle of a sentence. 5. wholly; in full. She cleared off her desk. 6. Be **well off, badly off,** or **comfortably off** means be so situated, especially in regard to money or worldly goods. 7. **Off and on** means from time to time; occasionally. 8. straight out from. The boat anchored off the fort. 9. on the right-hand side; as, the off horse of a pair. 10. possible, not very likely. I came on the off chance that I would find you. 11. Be off! *adv., prep., adj., interj. 1.*

of fal (of′əl), 1. the waste parts of an animal killed for food. 2. garbage; refuse. *n. 10.*

of fence (ə fens′), offense. *n.*

of fend (ə fend′), 1. pain; displease; hurt the feelings of; make angry. My friend was offended by my laughter. 2. sin; do wrong. In what have I offended? *v. 3.*

of fend er (ə fen′dər), 1. person who offends. 2. person who does wrong or breaks a law. No smoking here; offenders will be fined $5. *n. 6.*

of fense (ə fens′), 1. sin; breaking the law; as, an offense against God and man. The punishment for that offense is two years in prison. 2. cause of wrongdoing. 3. condition of being offended; hurt feelings; anger. He tried not to cause offense. 4. offending; hurting someone's feelings. No offense was meant. 5. attacking; being the one to attack rather than defend. A gun is a weapon of offense. *n. 3.*

of fen sive (ə fen′siv), 1. giving offense; unpleasant; disagreeable; disgusting. "Shut up" is an offensive remark. Bad eggs have an offensive odor. 2. used for attack; having to do with attack; as, offensive weapons, an offensive war for conquest. 3. attitude of attack; attack. The army took the offensive. *adj., n. 7.*

of fer (ôf′ər), 1. hold out; present; as, to offer one's hand, to offer a gift, to offer help. 2. propose; as, to offer a price, to offer to cure, to offer to go. 3. present in worship; as, to offer sacrifices, to offer prayers. 4. try; attempt. The dog did not offer to hurt Jack, but stopped him if he offered to move. 5. present itself; occur. I will come if opportunity offers. 6. act of offering; as, an offer of money, an offer to sing, an offer of marriage, an offer of $10,000 for a house. *v., n. 1.*

of fer ing (ôf′ər ing), 1. giving something as an act of worship. 2. contribution. *n.*

of fer to ry (ôf′ər tō′ri), 1. collection at a religious service. 2. verses said or the music sung or played while the offering is received. *n., pl. offertories.*

off hand (ôf′hand′), 1. at once; without previous thought or preparation. The carpenter could not tell offhand how much the work would cost. 2. done or made offhand. His offhand remarks were sometimes very wise. 3. careless; informal. *adv., adj. 12.*

of fice (ôf′is), 1. position, especially a public position; as, to accept or resign an office. The President holds the highest public office in the United States. 2. the duty of one's position; task; job; work. It is my office to open the mail. His office is to decide on applications for aid. 3. the place in which the work of a position is done. His office is on the second floor. The post office is on Main Street. 4. an attention; an act of kindness or unkindness; a service or an injury. Through the good offices of a friend, I was able to get a ticket. 5. a religious ceremony or prayer. *n. 1.*

of fi cer (ôf′i sər), 1. person who commands others in the army or navy, such as a major, a general, a captain, or an admiral. 2. person who holds a public, church, or government office; as, a health officer, a police officer. 3. the president, vice-president, secretary, treasurer, etc., of a society or club. 4. furnish with officers. 5. be an officer to; direct; manage. The army was officered by brave men. *n., v. 1.*

of fi cial (ə fish′əl), 1. person who holds a public position or who is in charge of some public work or duty. Postmasters are government officials. 2. officer; person holding office; as, bank officials. 3. of or pertaining to an office. Policemen wear an official uniform. 4. having authority. An official record is kept of the proceedings of Congress. 5. suitable for a person in office; as, the official dignity of a judge. *n., adj. 3.*

of fi cial ly (ə fish′əl i), in an official manner; as an official. *adv. 14.*

of fi ci ate (ə fish′i āt), 1. perform the duties of any office or position. The president officiates as chairman at all club meetings. 2. perform the duties of a priest or minister. The bishop officiated at the cathedral. *v. 12.*

of fi cious (ə fish′əs), too ready to offer services or advice; meddling; minding other people's business. *adj. 10.*

off ing (ôf′ing), 1. the more distant part of the sea as seen from the shore. 2. position at a distance from the shore. *n.*

off ish (ôf′ish), inclined to keep aloof; distant and reserved in manner. *adj.* [*Used in common talk*]

off scour ings (ôf′skour′ingz), filth; refuse. *n. pl.*

off set (ôf′set′ for 1 and 2, ôf′set′ for 3, 4, and 5), 1. make up for; balance. The better roads offset the greater distance. We offset the greater distance by the better roads. 2. set off or balance; as, to offset the better roads against the greater distance. 3. something which makes up for something else; a compensation. The better roads on this route are an offset for the greater distance. 4. a short side shoot from a main stem or root which starts a new plant. 5. any offshoot. *v., offset, offsetting, n. 9.*

off shoot (ôf′shüt′), a shoot from a main stem; a branch; as, an offshoot of a plant, of a mountain range, of a railroad, of a family, etc. *n. 17.*

off shore (ôf′shōr′), off or away from the shore; as, a wind blowing offshore, offshore fisheries. *adv., adj.*

off spring (ôf′spring′), what is born from or grows out of something; child or children; descendants. Every one of his offspring had red hair just like his own. *n. 5.*

oft (ôft), often. *adv.* [*Used in poetry*] *3.*

of ten (ôf′ən), many times. *adv. 1.*

of ten times (ôf′ən tīmz′), often. *adv. 9.*

oft times (ôft′tīmz′), often. *adv.* [*Used in poetry*] *11.*

o gle (ō′gəl), 1. make eyes at; look at with desire. 2. an ogling look. *v., n. 13.*

o gre (ō′gər), giant or monster that eats people. *n. 10.*

oh or **Oh** (ō), 1. Oh is used before a person's name in beginning to speak. Oh, Mary, have you seen this? 2. Oh is the same word as **O**. Oh, dear me! Oh! joy! Oh, what a pity! *interj. 1.*

O hi o (ō hī′ō), 1. a Middle Western State of the United States. 2. a river flowing from Pittsburgh, Pennsylvania, into the Mississippi River. *n. 4.*

ohm (ōm), the unit of electrical resistance. A wire in which one volt produces a current of one ampere has a resistance of one ohm. *n. 16.*

oil (oil), 1. any of several kinds of thick fatty or greasy liquids lighter than water, which will burn easily, and will not mix or dissolve in water but will dissolve in alcohol. Mineral oils are used for fuel; animal and vegetable oils are used in cooking and medicine, and in many other ways. 2. put oil on or in. 3. become oil. Butter oils when heated. 4. paint made by grinding coloring matter in oil. *n., v. 2.*

oil cloth (oil′klôth′), 1. cloth made waterproof by coating it with paint. It is used to cover floors, tables, etc. 2. cloth made waterproof by treating it with oil; oilskin. *n. 10.*

oil skin (oil′skin′), 1. cloth made waterproof by treating it with oil. 2. **Oilskins** are garments made of it. *n. 20.*

oil y (oil′i), 1. of oil. 2. containing oil. 3. covered or soaked with oil; as, oily rags. 4. like oil; slippery. 5. too smooth; suspiciously or disagreeably smooth. Mr. Heep has an oily manner. *adj., oilier, oiliest. 9.*

oint ment (oint′mənt), a substance made from oil or fat, often containing medicine, used on the skin to heal or to make soft and white. Cold cream and salve are ointments. *n. 6.*

O.K. (ō′kā′), 1. all right; correct; approved. 2. endorse; approve. 3. approval. *adj., adv., v., O.K.'d, O.K.'ing, n., pl. O.K.'s.* [*Used in common talk*]

Okla., Oklahoma.

O kla ho ma (ō′klə hō′mə), a Southern State of the United States. *n. 8.*

Oklahoma City, the capital of Oklahoma.

o kra (ō′krə), 1. a plant with sticky pods used as a vegetable and in soups. 2. the pods. *n.*

Okra pods

old (ōld), 1. not young; having been for some time; aged. **The old** often means old people. **Old age** means the last part of one's life when one is very old. 2. that seems old; that is like an old one; like an old person in wisdom, feebleness, etc. That child has an old face. 3. much worn by age; worn; as, an old coat, old clothes. 4. of age; in age; as, to be ten months old, a four-year-old child. 5. having much experience; as, to be old in wrongdoing, to be an old hand at it. 6. belonging to the past; dating far back; ancient; as, old countries. The **old country** means the country an emigrant comes from (often Great Britain or Ireland). 7. not new; not recent; as, an old debt, an old family. 8. former. An old pupil came back to visit his teacher. 9. long known or familiar or dear. Old Rover, I'm glad to see you. 10. the time of long ago; the past; as, the heroes of old. *adj., older, oldest* or *elder, eldest, n. 1.*

old en (ōl′dən), old; of old; ancient. *adj. 10.*

old-fash ioned (ōld′fash′ənd), 1. of an old fashion; as, an old-fashioned dress. 2. keeping to old ways, ideas, etc. *adj. 9.*

Old Glory, the flag of the United States; the Stars and Stripes.

oldish (ōld′ish), somewhat old. *adj.*

Old Testament, the earlier part of the Bible, which contains the religious and social laws of the Hebrews, a record of their history, their important literature, and writings of their prophets.

old-time (ōld′tīm′), of former times; like old times. *adj.*

old-world (ōld′wėrld′), 1. of or pertaining to the old or ancient world. The mammoth was an old-world elephant. 2. belonging to or characteristic of a former period; as, old-world courtesy. 3. of or pertaining to the Eastern Hemisphere; as, old-world folk songs. *adj.*

Old World, 1. Europe, Asia, and Africa. 2. of the Old World.

o le an der (ō′li an′dər), a poisonous evergreen shrub with fragrant red or white flowers. *n.*

o le o mar ga rin (ō′li ō mär′jə rin), oleomargarine. *n.*

o le o mar ga rine (ō′li ō mär′jə rēn), a substitute for butter made from animal fat and vegetable oils. *n. 16.*

ol fac to ry (ol fak′tə ri), 1. having to do with smelling; of smell. The nose is our olfactory organ. 2. an olfactory organ. *adj., n., pl. olfactories. 11.*

ol i garch (ol′i gärk), one of a small number of persons holding the ruling power in a state. *n.*

ol i gar chy (ol′i gär′ki), 1. a form of government in which a few people have the power. 2. a country or state having such a government. Ancient Sparta was really an oligarchy, though it had two kings. 3. the ruling few. *n., pl. oligarchies. 19.*

ol ive (ol′iv), 1. a kind of evergreen tree with gray-green leaves. The olive tree grows in southern Europe and similar climates. 2. the fruit of this tree, with a hard stone and bitter pulp. Olives are eaten as a relish and used to make olive oil. 3. a wreath of olive leaves; olive branch. 4. yellowish green. 5. yellowish brown. *n., adj. 3.*

Olives

olive branch, a branch of the olive tree as an emblem of peace.

olive oil, oil from olives.

O lym pi a (ō lim′pi ə), 1. a plain in ancient Greece, where games were held every four years in honor of Zeus. 2. the capital of Washington. *n. 9.*

O lym pi an (ō lim′pi ən), 1. pertaining to Olympia in Greece or to Mount Olympus. 2. like a god; heavenly. 3. one of the major Greek gods. *adj., n.*

O lym pic (ō lim′pik), 1. pertaining to Olympia in Greece. The **Olympic games** were held every four years in honor of Zeus. In modern times, these games have been revived and are held every four years in a different country. 2. pertaining to Mount Olympus. *adj. 17.*

O lym pus (ō lim′pəs), a mountain in Greece where the Greek gods were supposed to live. *n. 11.*

O ma ha (ō′mə hô), a city in eastern Nebraska. *n. 16.*

o meg a (ō meg′ə or ō mē′gə), the last of any series; the end. *n. 17.*

om e let or **om e lette** (om′ə let), eggs beaten up with milk or water, fried or baked, and then folded over. *n. 18.*

o men (ō′mən), a sign of what is to happen; an object or event that is believed to mean good or bad fortune. Spilling salt is said to be an omen of misfortune. *n. 8.*

om i nous (om′i nəs), of bad omen; unfavorable; threatening. Those clouds look ominous for our picnic. *adj. 8.*

o mis sion (ō mish′ən), 1. an omitting. 2. a being omitted. 3. thing omitted. *n. 7.*

o mit (ō mit′), 1. leave out; as, to omit a letter in a word. 2. fail to do; neglect. Mary omitted making her bed. *v., omitted, omitting. 4.*

om ni bus (om′ni bus), 1. bus; a large vehicle with seats inside and sometimes also on the roof. An omnibus is used for carrying passengers between fixed stations along a route. 2. covering many things at once; as, an omnibus law. *n., pl. omnibuses, adj. 12.*

om nip o tence (om nip′ə təns), complete power; unlimited power; as, the omnipotence of God. *n. 20.*

om nip o tent (om nip′ə tənt), having all power; almighty. *adj. 10.*

om ni pres ence (om′ni prez′əns), presence everywhere at the same time; as, God's omnipresence. *n.*

om ni pres ent (om′ni prez′ənt), present everywhere at the same time. *adj. 16.*

om nis cience (om nish′əns), knowledge of everything; complete or infinite knowledge. *n. 19.*

om nis cient (om nish′ənt), knowing everything. *adj. 16.*

om niv o rous (om niv′ə rəs), 1. eating every kind of food. 2. eating both animal and vegetable food. Man is an omnivorous animal. 3. taking in everything; fond of all kinds. Betty is an omnivorous reader. *adj. 17.*

on (on), 1. On helps to answer the question where. Then it means supported by, covering, round about, etc. The book is on the table. His ship is on the ocean. Drop it on the ground. Put the ring on her finger. It hangs on the wall. We put our stockings on. In telling where, on also means close to, touching, in the direction of; as, a house on the shore, to march on Boston, to turn one's back on one's home, to smile on a child, to make an attack on the city. 2. On helps to answer the question how, in what way, or by what means; as, to turn on one's heel, to have a thing on good authority, to be on half pay, a story founded on fact, to do it on purpose, to play a piece on the violin, to be on fire, on sale, on the move, on duty, on the watch, or on one's best behavior, to speak on, to turn the gas on. 3. On helps to answer the question when; as, on Tuesday, on time, on the hour, on arriving, on my return, on looking closely, later on, from that day on. 4. On helps to answer the question which one, about or concerning what. Then it means about or concerning; as, a tax on tea, interest on one's money, a profit on sales, a book on animals, to have an opinion on the weather. 5. On helps to answer the question why, for what purpose; as, to go on an errand. He drew his knife on me. 6. **On us,** etc., may mean so far as we, etc., are concerned. That is hard on us. His work is telling on him. 7. **Be on a committee, a board,** etc., means be a member of it. 8. **on and on** means without stopping. *prep., adv. 1.*

once (wuns), 1. one time. Read it once more. 2. at some one time in the past; formerly. That big man was once a little baby. 3. if ever. Most boys like to swim, once they have learned how. 4. **At once** means (1) immediately. You must come at once. (2) at the same time. All three boys spoke at once. *adv., n., conj. 1.*

on com ing (on′kum′ing), 1. approaching; as, oncoming winter. 2. approach; as, the oncoming of the storm. *adj., n.*

one (wun), 1. the number 1. 2. a single. A man has one head and one neck. 3. a single person or thing. I like the ones in that box. 4. some. One day he will get run over. 5. some person or thing. 6. any person, standing for people in general. One does not like to be left out. 7. the same. All face one way. 8. united. The class was one in its approval. 9. a certain. 10. Some special meanings are:

be at one, agree.

It is all one. It makes no difference.
make one, join.
one by one, one after another.
one or two, a few.
one too many, one more than is needed or desired; too much.
n., adj., pron. 1.

one ness (wun′nis), 1. singleness. 2. sameness. 3. unity. 4. agreement. *n.*

on er ous (on′ər əs), burdensome; oppressive. Overtime work is well paid, but it is often onerous. *adj. 15.*

one self (wun′self′), one's own self. At the age of seven one ought to dress oneself. **Be oneself** means (1) have full control of one's mind or body. (2) act naturally. *pron. 12.*

one-sid ed (wun′sīd′id), 1. having but one side. 2. having one side larger or more developed than the other. 3. partial; unfair; prejudiced; seeing only one side of a question. The umpire seemed one-sided in his decisions. *adj. 19.*

on ion (un′yən), a vegetable with a bulblike root, eaten raw and used in cooking. Onions have a sharp, strong smell and taste. *n. 4.*

Onion bulb

on look er (on′lu̇k′ər), spectator; person who watches without taking part. *n.*

on ly (ōn′li), 1. by itself; one and no more. Water is his only drink. Mary and John are their only children. This was her one and only hope. This is the only road along the shore. 2. just; merely; and no one else; and nothing more; and that is all. It was only the wind. **If only** often means I wish. If only the sun would shine! **Only too glad** means very glad. 3. but then; it must be added that. We had camped right beside a stream, only the water was not fit to drink. 4. except that; if it had not. I could do it, only it would be wrong. He would have started, only it rained. 5. best; finest. *adj., adv., conj. 1.*

on rush (on′rush′), violent forward rush. *n.*

on set (on′set′), 1. attack. The onset of the enemy took us by surprise. 2. beginning. The onset of this disease is gradual. *n. 9.*

on slaught (on′slôt′), vigorous attack. The Indians made an onslaught on the settlers' fort. *n. 15.*

On tar i o (on tãr′i ō), 1. the smallest of the Great Lakes. 2. a province of Canada, north of the Great Lakes. *n. 11.*

on to (on′tü), on to; to a position on; as, to throw a ball onto the roof, to get onto a horse, a boat driven onto the rocks. *prep. 17.*

on ward (on′wərd), on; further on; toward the front; forward. The crowd around the store window began to move onward. An onward movement began. *adv., adj. 3.*

on wards (on′wərdz), onward. *adv.*

on yx (on′iks), a semiprecious stone with layers of different colors, especially black. Mrs. Jones has a clock and a set of jewelry made of onyx. *n. 16.*

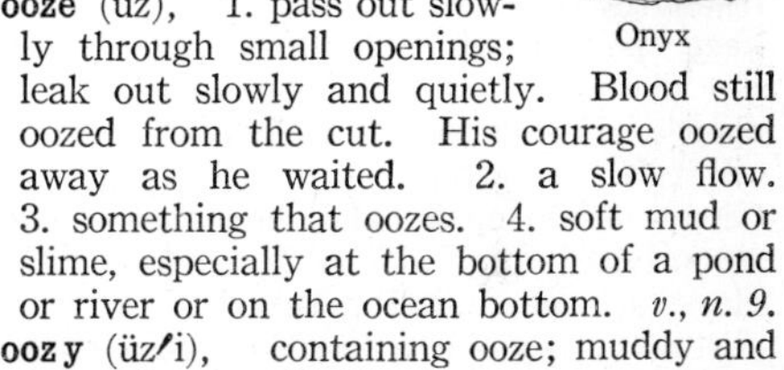

Onyx

ooze (üz), 1. pass out slowly through small openings; leak out slowly and quietly. Blood still oozed from the cut. His courage oozed away as he waited. 2. a slow flow. 3. something that oozes. 4. soft mud or slime, especially at the bottom of a pond or river or on the ocean bottom. *v., n. 9.*

ooz y (üz′i), containing ooze; muddy and soft; slimy. *adj. 16.*

o pal (ō′pəl), a gem that shows beautiful changes of color. The common opal is milky white with colored lights. *n. 11.*

o pal es cent (ō′pəl es′ənt), having a play of colors like that of an opal. *adj.*

o paque (ō pāk′), 1. not letting light through; not transparent. 2. not shining; dark; dull. 3. obscure; hard to understand. *adj. 9.*

ope (ōp), open. *v., adj.* [*Used now only in poetry*] *15.*

o pen (ō′pən), 1. not shut; not closed; letting (anything or anyone) in or out. Open windows let in the fresh air. 2. not having its gate, door, lid, etc., closed; not shut up; as, an open box, drawer, house, etc. 3. not covered; as, an open fire, an open jar. 4. not closed in; as, the open sea, an open field, an open car. **The open** means open or clear space, open country, open air. 5. not hidden or secret; as, open war. Come **out into the open** with one's plans, etc., means to tell them, not keep them hidden. 6. that may be entered, used, shared, etc., by all, or by a person or persons mentioned; as, an open meeting, an open market. The race is open to boys under 15. 7. free from hindrance; especially, free from ice; as, open water, a river or harbor now open. An **open winter** is one so warm and free from snow that getting about is easy. 8. unfolded; spread out; as, an open flower, letter, or book. 9. frank and sincere; as, an open heart. Please be open with me. 10. make or become open; as, to open a path through the woods. 11. begin; as, to open a debate. School opens in September. To **open fire** means to begin shooting. 12. start or set up; as, to open a new store, an office, an account. 13. spread out or unfold; as, to open a fan, a book, or a letter. 14. come apart or burst open; as, a crack where the earth had opened. The clouds opened, and the sun shone through. 15. Some special meanings are:

keep open house, offer food and shelter to all visitors or to all one's friends.

open a person's eyes, make him see what is really going on.

Give with an **open hand** means give generously.

Have an **open mind** means be ready to listen to new ideas, and to judge them fairly; not to be prejudiced.

open ranks, separate, so that there is more space between man and man.

open to conviction, offers, etc., means ready to receive them.

open to, into, or **onto,** have an opening or passage. This door opens into the dining room. My window opens to the south.

open up, open a way to; uncover; bring to notice.

adj., n., v. 1.

open air, outdoors.

o pen er (ō′pən ər), person or thing that opens. *n. 12.*

o pen ing (ō′pən ing), 1. gap; hole; open or clear space; as, an opening in a wall, an opening in the forest. 2. place or position that is open or vacant; as, an opening in a bank, store, or school. 3. favorable chance or opportunity. In talking with your mother, I made an opening to ask her about sending you to camp. As soon as I saw an opening, I landed a blow on his head. 4. the first part; the beginning; as, the opening of his lecture. 5. first; beginning; as, the opening words of his speech. 6. a formal beginning. The opening will be at three o'clock tomorrow afternoon. 7. act of making open. 8. fact of becoming open. *n., adj.*

o pen ly (ō′pən li), without secrecy; frankly. *adv.*

o pen ness (ō′pən nis), 1. being open. 2. frankness; lack of secrecy. *n. 18.*

open question, something that is not yet decided.

open shop, shop which employs members of labor unions and nonmembers on equal terms.

op er a (op′ər ə), a play that is mostly sung, with costumes, scenery, acting, and music to go with the singing. *Lohengrin, Faust,* and *Carmen* are well-known operas. *n. 4.*

opera glasses or **opera glass,** a small binocular telescope for use in theaters. Opera glasses are like field glasses, but smaller.

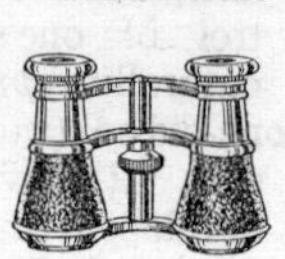
Opera glasses

op er ate (op′ər āt), 1. run; keep working; manage. The machinery operates night and day. The boy operates the elevator. The company operates three factories. 2. work; act; produce an effect. Several causes operated to bring on the war. 3. produce a desired effect. The medicine operated quickly. 4. perform an operation. The doctor operated on the injured man. *v. 5.*

op er at ic (op′ər at′ik), of or like the opera; as, operatic music. *adj. 13.*

op er a tion (op′ər ā′shən), 1. working; action; the way a thing works. The operation of this machine is simple. **In operation** means in action or in use. 2. doing; activity; as, the operation of brushing one's teeth. 3. something done to the body, usually with instruments, to improve health. Taking out the tonsils is a common operation. 4. movement of troops, ships, etc.; as, military and naval operations. 5. addition, subtraction, multiplication, division, and other work in arithmetic. *n. 2.*

op er a tive (op′ər ā′tiv), 1. operating; effective; as, the laws operative in a community. 2. worker; laborer. Mr. Smith is a skilled machine operative. 3. having to do with work or productiveness; as, operative departments of a manufacturing establishment. *adj., n. 14.*

op er a tor (op′ər ā′tər), person who operates; as, a telegraph or telephone operator, the operators of a mine or railroad, a surgical operator. *n. 8.*

op er et ta (op′ər et′ə), a short, amusing opera. *n.*

oph thal mi a (of thal′mi ə), inflammation of the eye. *n. 18.*

o pi ate (ō′pi it), 1. a drug that contains opium and so dulls pain or brings sleep. 2. containing opium. 3. anything that quiets. 4. bringing sleep or ease. *n., adj. 13.*

o pine (ō pīn′), think; hold or express an opinion. Mr. Jones opined that the weather would get better by night. *v. 16.*

o pin ion (ə pin′yən), 1. what one thinks; belief not so strong as knowledge; judgment. 2. impression; estimate. Everyone has a poor opinion of a coward. 3. formal judgment by an expert; professional advice. Mother wanted the doctor's opinion about the cause of my headache. *n. 2.*

o pin ion at ed (ə pin′yən āt′id), obstinate or conceited with regard to one's opinions; dogmatic. He is too opinionated to listen to anybody else. *adj.*

o pi um (ō′pi əm), a powerful drug that causes sleep and eases pain. Opium is made from a kind of poppy. *n. 7.*

Opossum

o pos sum (ə pos′əm), a small American animal that lives in trees. When it is caught, it pretends to be dead. The opossum is common in the southern United States. An opossum is often called a **possum.** *n. 17.*

op po nent (ə pō′nənt), 1. person who is on the other side in a fight or game or discussion; person fighting, struggling, or speaking against (one). Our opponents won the game because they were quicker than we. 2. opposing. *n., adj. 7.*

op por tune (op′ər tūn′ or op′ər tün′), fortunate; well-chosen; favorable; suitable. You have come at a most opportune moment, for I need your advice. *adj. 9.*

op por tun ist (op′ər tūn′ist or op′ər tün′ist), person who is influenced more by particular circumstances than by general principles. *n.*

op por tu ni ty (op′ər tū′ni ti or op′ər tü′ni ti), good chance; favorable time; convenient occasion. I had an opportunity to earn some money picking blueberries. I have had no opportunity to give John your message, because I have not seen him. *n., pl. opportunities. 2.*

op pose (ə pōz′), 1. be against; be in the way of; act, fight, or struggle against; try to hinder; resist. A swamp opposed the advance of the army. 2. set up against; place in the way of. Let us oppose good nature to anger, and smiles to cross words. 3. put in contrast. Night is opposed to day. Love is opposed to hate. *v. 3.*

op po site (op′ə zit), 1. placed against; as different in direction as can be; face to face; back to back. 2. as different as can be; just contrary. North and south are opposite directions. **Sour** is opposite to **sweet.** 3. a thing or person as different as can be. **Black** is the opposite of **white.** A brave boy is the opposite of a coward. *adj., n. 2.*

op po si tion (op′ə zish′ən), 1. action against; resistance. The mob offered opposition to the police. 2. contrast. 3. political party opposed to the party which is in power. 4. a placing opposite. *n. 5.*

op press (ə pres′), 1. govern harshly; keep down unjustly or by cruelty. A good ruler will not oppress the poor. 2. burden; weigh down; lie heavily on. A sense of trouble ahead oppressed my spirits. *v. 4.*

op pres sion (ə presh′ən), 1. oppressing; burdening. The oppression of the people by the nobles caused the war. 2. a being oppressed or burdened. 3. cruel or unjust treatment. 4. a heavy, weary feeling. *n. 5.*

op pres sive (ə pres′iv), 1. hard to bear; burdensome. Great heat is oppressive. 2. harsh; severe; unjust. *adj. 10.*

op pres sor (ə pres′ər), person who is cruel or unjust to people under him. *n. 8.*

op pro bri ous (ə prō′bri əs), expressing scorn, reproach, or abuse. **Coward, liar,** and **thief** are opprobrious names. *adj. 15.*

op pro bri um (ə prō′bri əm), the disgrace or reproach caused by shameful conduct; infamy; scorn; abuse. *n. 20.*

op tic (op′tik), of the eye; of the sense of sight. The optic nerves go from the eyes to the brain. *adj. 9.*

op ti cal (op′ti kəl), 1. visual; of the eye. Being short-sighted is an optical defect. 2. made to assist sight. Telescopes and microscopes are optical instruments. 3. of vision and light in relation to each other. *adj. 11.*

op ti cian (op tish′ən), a maker or seller of eyeglasses and other optical instruments. *n. 19.*

op ti mism (op′ti mizm), 1. tendency to look on the bright side of things. 2. belief that everything will turn out for the best. 3. doctrine that the existing world is the best of all possible worlds. *n. 14.*

op ti mist (op′ti mist), 1. person who looks on the bright side of things. 2. person who believes that everything in life will turn out for the best. *n. 18.*

op ti mis tic (op′ti mis′tik), 1. inclined to look on the bright side of things. 2. hoping for the best. 3. pertaining to optimism. *adj. 17.*

op tion (op′shən), 1. right or freedom of choice. Each state has local option about daylight-saving time. 2. choosing; a choice. Pupils have the option of taking French, Spanish, or German. 3. the right to buy something at a certain price within a certain time. The man paid $500 for an option on the land. *n. 13.*

op tion al (op′shən əl), left to one's choice; not required. Our attendance at graduation is optional. *adj. 20.*

op u lence (op′ū ləns), 1. wealth; riches. 2. abundance; plenty. *n. 12.*

op u lent (op′ū lənt), 1. wealthy; rich. 2. abundant; plentiful. *adj. 13.*

o pus (ō′pəs), work; composition. The violinist played his own opus, No. 16. *n., pl. opera* (op′ər ə).

or (ôr), 1. Or suggests a choice, or a difference, or connects words or groups of words of equal importance in the sentence. Is it sweet or sour? Shall you walk or ride? 2. Or may state the only choice left. Either eat this or go hungry. 3. Or may state what will happen if the first does not happen. Hurry, or you will be late. 4. Or may explain what goes before; as, an igloo or rounded snow house. *conj. 1.*

-or, suffix meaning:—
1. person or thing that ———s; as in actor, accelerator, elevator, orator, survivor.
2. act, state, condition, quality, characteristic, etc.; as in error, horror.

or a cle (or′ə kəl), 1. the answer of a god to a question. 2. the place where the god gives answers. A famous oracle was at Delphi. 3. the priest, priestess, or other means by which the god's answer was given. 4. a high authority; a very wise person. *n. 5.*

o rac u lar (ō rak′ū lər), 1. of an oracle; like an oracle. 2. with a hidden meaning which is difficult to make out. 3. very wise. *adj. 12.*

o ral (ō′rəl), 1. spoken; using speech. An oral agreement is not enough; we must have a written promise. 2. of the mouth. The oral opening in an earthworm is small. *adj. 8.*

o ral ly (ō′rəl i), 1. by spoken words. 2. by the mouth. *adv.*

or ange (or′inj), 1. a round, reddish-yellow, juicy fruit. Oranges grow in warm climates. 2. the tree it grows on. 3. reddish yellow. *n., adj. 2.*

or ange ade (or′inj ād′), a drink made of orange juice, sugar, and water. *n.*

o rang-ou tang (ō rang′ü tang′), orang-utan. *n.*

o rang-u tan (ō rang′ü-tan′), large ape of the forests of Borneo and Sumatra, that has very long arms and long, reddish-brown hair. It lives mostly in trees and eats fruits and leaves. *n.*

Orang-utan (4 to 4½ ft. tall)

o ra tion (ō rā′shən), a formal public speech delivered on a special occasion. *n. 6.*

or a tor (or′ə tər), 1. person who makes an oration. 2. person who can speak very well in public. *n. 6.*

or a tor i cal (or′ə tor′i kəl), of oratory; having to do with orators or oratory; as, an oratorical contest. *adj. 16.*

or a to ri o (or′ə tō′ri ō), a religious musical composition for solo voices, chorus, and orchestra, dramatic in character but performed without action, costumes, or scenery. *n., pl. oratorios. 17.*

or a to ry[1] (or′ə tō′ri), 1. skill in public speaking; fine speaking. 2. the art of public speaking. *n. 11.*

or a to ry[2] (or′ə tō′ri), a small chapel; a room set apart for prayer. *n., pl. oratories.*

orb (ôrb), 1. sphere; globe. 2. sun, moon, planet, or star. 3. the eyeball or eye. *Used in poetry.* 4. form into a circle or sphere. *n., v. 5.*

or bit (ôr′bit), 1. the path of the earth or any one of the planets about the sun. 2. the path of any heavenly body about another heavenly body. 3. the socket in which the eye is placed. *n. 8.*

Orbit of the earth (E) around the sun. Arrows show direction.

or chard (ôr′chərd), 1. piece of ground on which fruit trees are grown. 2. the trees in an orchard. The orchard is bearing well this year. *n. 2.*

or ches tra (ôr′kis trə), 1. the musicians playing at a concert, an opera, or a play. 2. the violins, cellos, clarinets, and other instruments played by the musicians together in an orchestra. 3. the part of a theater just in front of the stage, where the musicians sit to play. 4. the main floor of a theater, especially the part near the front. Buy two seats in the orchestra. *n. 5.*

or ches tral (ôr kes′trəl), of an orchestra; composed for or performed by an orchestra. *adj. 18.*

or chid (ôr′kid), 1. any of a large group of plants with beautiful, queerly shaped flowers. 2. the flower. 3. light purple. *n., adj. 11.*

or dain (ôr dān′), 1. order; fix; decide; appoint; pass as a law. The law ordains that the murderers shall be hanged. 2. officially appoint or consecrate as a minister in a Christian church. *v. 4.*

or deal (ôr dēl′), 1. severe test or experience. Jack dreaded the ordeal of a visit to the dentist. 2. in early times, an effort to decide the guilt or innocence of an accused person by making him do something dangerous like holding fire or taking poison. The idea was that God would not let an innocent person be harmed by such danger. *n. 12.*

or der (ôr′dər), 1. the way one thing follows another; as, in order of size, in alphabetical order, to copy them in order. 2. a condition in which every part or piece is in its right place; as, to put a room in order. 3. put in order; arrange; as, to order one's affairs. 4. condition; state. 5. the way the world works; the way things happen; as, the order of nature. 6. state or condition of things in which the law is obeyed and there is no trouble; as, to keep order. Order was established. Perfect order reigned throughout the country after the revolution. 7. the principles and rules by which a meeting is run. 8. a command; telling what to do. The orders of the captain must be obeyed. 9. tell what to do; command; bid; give an order. 10. a paper saying that money is to be given or paid, or something handed over; as, a postal money order. 11. a statement or list of things telling a store or tradesman what you wish sent. I gave the grocer an order for two dozen eggs. 12. give (a store, etc.) an order for. A factory orders many tons of coal during the winter. 13. decide; will. The gods ordered it otherwise. 14. kind or sort; as, to have ability of a high order. 15. in biology, a group in the classifying of plants and animals which is below or smaller than a class, but larger than a family. The rose family, the bean family, and several others belong to one order. 16. social rank, grade, or class; as, all orders of society. 17. a rank or position in the church; as, the order of bishops. 18. a brotherhood of monks, friars, or knights; as, the Franciscan order. 19. a society to which one is admitted as an honor; as, the Order of the Golden Fleece. 20. the badge worn by those belonging to an honorary order. 21. a style or kind of architecture. 22. a regular form of worship for a given occasion. 23. Some special meanings are:

Greek orders of architecture

by order, according to an order given by the proper person; as, by order of the governor.

in order, 1. in the right arrangement or condition. 2. working right. 3. allowed by the rules of a meeting, etc.

in order that, so that; with the aim that.

in order to, as a means to; with a view to; for the purpose of. She worked hard in order to win the prize.

made to order, made to fit a certain person or place.

order about or **around,** send here and there; tell to do this and that.

order a (**the**) **dinner,** tell what to have for dinner.

order of the day, the way things are; the way people are doing; the style.

out of order, 1. not working rightly. 2. against the rules (of a meeting).

take orders, become a clergyman.

n., v. 1.

or der li ness (ôr′dər li nis), orderly condition; orderly behavior. *n.*

or der ly (ôr′dər li), 1. in order; with regular arrangement, method, or system; as, an orderly arrangement of dishes on shelves, an orderly mind. 2. keeping order; well-behaved or regulated; as, an orderly class. 3. a noncommissioned officer or private soldier who attends a superior officer to carry orders, etc. 4. a hospital attendant who keeps things clean and in order. *adj., n., pl. orderlies. 13.*

or di nal (ôr′di nəl), 1. showing order or position in a series. First, second, third, etc., are ordinal numbers; one, two, three, etc., are cardinal numbers. 2. ordinal number. *adj., n.*

or di nance (ôr′di nəns), a rule or law made by authority; decree. Some cities have ordinances forbidding Sunday amusements. *n. 4.*

or di nar i ly (ôr′di nãr′i li), commonly; usually; normally. *adv.*

or di nar y (ôr′di nãr′i), 1. common; usual; normal. Jack's ordinary supper consists of bread and milk. 2. somewhat below the average. The speaker was ordinary and tiresome. *adj. 3.*

or di na tion (ôr′di nā′shən), 1. the ceremony of admitting to the Christian ministry. 2. admission to a Christian church as minister. His ordination gives him the right to conduct a marriage or a funeral. *n. 15.*

ord nance (ôrd′nəns), 1. cannon or artillery. 2. military weapons of all kinds. *n. 12.*

or dure (ôr′dūr), filth; dung; excrement. *n. 20.*

ore (ōr), rock, sand, or dirt, containing some metal. *n. 10.*

Ore. or **Oreg.,** Oregon.

Or e gon (or′i gən or or′i gon), a Northwestern State of the United States, on the Pacific Coast. *n. 6.*

or gan (ôr′gən), 1. a musical instrument made of pipes of different lengths, which are sounded by air blown by a bellows and played by keys. Organs are used especially in churches. 2. part of an animal or plant fitted to do certain things in life. The eyes, stomach, heart, and lungs are organs of the body. Stamens and pistils are organs of flowers. 3. a means of action; instrument. A court is an organ of government. 4. a newspaper or magazine which speaks for and gives the views of a political party. *n. 2.*

or gan dy or **or gan die** (ôr′gən di), a fine, thin, stiff muslin, used for dresses. *n., pl. organdies. 11.*

or gan ic (ôr gan′ik), 1. of the bodily organs; vital; affecting the structure of an organ; as, organic disease. 2. having organs, or an organized physical structure as plants and animals have; not of the mineral kingdom. 3. in chemistry, produced by animal or plant activities. Starch is an organic compound. 4. made up of related parts, but being a unit; coördinated. 5. fundamental; part of the structure or constitution of a person or thing. *adj. 7.*

or gan i cal ly (ôr gan′ikəl i), 1. in an organic manner. 2. in organization. 3. as part of an organization. *adv.*

or gan ism (ôr′gən izm), 1. an organized body; one made up of organs; an individual animal or plant. 2. a whole made up of related parts that work together. Human society, or any community, may be spoken of as a social organism. *n. 7.*

or gan ist (ôr′gən ist), person who plays an organ. *n. 9.*

or gan i za tion (ôr′gən i zā′shən), 1. grouping and arranging parts to form a whole. The organization of a big picnic takes time and thought. 2. the way in which a thing's parts are arranged to work together. The organization of the human body is very complicated. 3. thing made up of related parts, each having a special duty. A tree is an organization of roots, trunk, branches, leaves, and fruit. 4. group of persons united for some purpose. Churches, clubs, and political parties are organizations. *n. 5.*

or gan ize (ôr′gən īz), 1. put into working order; get together and arrange. The explorer organized an expedition to the North Pole. 2. furnish with organs. A rose is a highly organized plant. *v. 4.*

or gy (ôr′ji), 1. a wild drunken revel. 2. **Orgies** were secret rites or ceremonies in the worship of certain Greek and Roman gods, especially the god of wine, celebrated with drinking, wild dancing, and singing. *n., pl. orgies. 9.*

o ri el (ō′ri əl), a bay window projecting from the outer face of a wall. *n. 17.*

Oriel

o ri ent or **O ri ent** (ō′ri ənt for 1, 2, 5, and 6, ō′ri ent for 3 and 4), 1. the East; eastern countries. China and Japan are important nations of the Orient. **The Orient** usually includes Asia and countries east and southeast of the Mediterranean. 2. eastern. *Used in poetry.* 3. to place so as to face the east. 4. to place in the right position.

Orient oneself means get in the right relations to the things or persons about one. 5. bright; shining; as, an orient pearl. 6. rising; as, the orient sun. *n., adj., v. 5.*

o ri en tal or **O ri en tal** (ō′ri en′təl), 1. eastern; of the Orient. 2. a native of the East. Turks, Arabs, Persians, Hindus, and Chinese are Orientals. *adj., n. 6.*

O ri en tal ist or **o ri en tal ist** (ō′ri en′təl ist), person who knows Oriental languages, literature, history, etc., well. *n.*

o ri en tate (ō′ri en tāt), 1. to place facing the east; face toward the east. 2. to orient; place exactly; find the exact position of, with regard to north, south, east, and west; as to orientate oneself on coming to a new city. 3. bring into clearly understood relations; as, to orientate oneself in the group of people one is to work with. *v.*

o ri en ta tion (ō′ri en tā′shən), 1. orienting. 2. being oriented. *n. 20.*

or i fice (or′i fis), mouth; opening; hole; as, the orifice of a tube or pipe. *n. 10.*

or i gin (or′i jin), 1. beginning; starting point; that from which anything comes; as, the origin of the quarrel, the origin of a disease. 2. parentage; ancestry; birth. *n. 5.*

o rig i nal (ə rij′i nəl), 1. first; earliest; belonging to the beginning. The hat has been marked down from its original price. 2. new; fresh; novel. It is hard to plan original games for a party. 3. inventive; able to do, make, or think something new. 4. not copied; not translated. 5. thing from which another is copied, imitated, or translated. The original of this picture is in Rome. 6. the language in which a book was first written. Our minister can read the New Testament in the original. 7. an unusual person. *adj., n. 3.*

o rig i nal i ty (ə rij′i nal′i ti), 1. ability to do, make, or think up something new. 2. freshness; novelty. 3. being original. *n. 10.*

o rig i nal ly (ə rij′i nəl i), 1. by origin; as, a plant originally African. 2. at first; in the first place; as, a house originally small. 3. in an original manner. We want this room decorated originally. *adv.*

o rig i nate (ə rij′i nāt), 1. cause to be; invent. 2. come into being; begin; arise. *v. 8.*

o rig i na tion (ə rij′i nā′shən), an originating; origin. *n.*

o rig i na tor (ə rij′i nā′tər), one that originates; inventor. *n. 14.*

O ri no co (ō′ri nō′kō), a large river in South America, flowing through Venezuela into the Atlantic Ocean. *n. 14.*

o ri ole (ō′ri ōl), 1. any of several American birds having yellow-and-black or orange-and-black coloring. 2. any of several European birds having yellow or black coloring. *n. 10.*

Baltimore oriole (about 7 in. long)

O ri on (ō rī′ən), group of stars near the equator of the heavens. To the ancients they suggested a man with a belt around his waist and a sword by his side. *n. 10.*

or i son (or′i zən), prayer. *n.* [*Old use*] *14.*

Ork ney (ôrk′ni), a group of islands northeast of Scotland. *n. 14.*

Or lé ans (ôr lēnz′), city in central France. *n. 6.*

or na ment (ôr′nə mənt for 1 and 2, ôr′nə ment for 3), 1. something pretty; something to add beauty. Lace, jewels, vases, and statues are ornaments. 2. person or act that adds beauty, grace, or honor. Charming Miss Fair would be an ornament to any society. 3. add beauty to; make more pleasing or attractive; decorate. *n., v. 3.*

or na men tal (ôr′nə men′təl), 1. of or having to do with ornament. 2. for ornament; used as an ornament. 3. decorative. *adj. 8.*

or na men ta tion (ôr′nə men tā′shən), 1. an ornamenting. 2. a being ornamented. 3. decorations; ornaments. The Quaker chapel has no ornamentation. *n. 19.*

or nate (ôr nāt′), much adorned; much ornamented. *adj. 12.*

or ni thol o gist (ôr′ni thol′ə jist), person who studies birds or who knows much about birds. *n.*

or ni thol o gy (ôr′ni thol′ə ji), the study of birds. *n.*

o ro tund (ō′rō tund), 1. strong, full, rich, and clear in voice or speech. 2. pompous; bombastic. *adj.*

or phan (ôr′fən), 1. a child whose parents are dead. 2. of or for such children; as, an orphan asylum. 3. without a father or mother or both. 4. make an orphan of. The war orphaned me when I was five years old. *n., adj., v. 4.*

or phan age (ôr′fən ij), home for orphans. *n. 20.*

Or pheus (ôr′fūs), a musician who played his lyre so sweetly that animals and even trees and rocks followed him. *n. 13.*

or tho dox (ôr′thə doks), 1. generally accepted, especially in religion. 2. having orthodox views or opinions, especially in religion. 3. approved by convention; usual; customary; as, the orthodox Christmas dinner of turkey and plum pudding. *adj. 9.*

Orthodox Church, group of Christian churches in eastern Europe and western Asia that do not recognize the Pope as the supreme head of the Church.

or tho dox y (ôr′thə dok′si), holding of correct or generally accepted beliefs; orthodox practice, especially in religion; being orthodox. *n., pl. orthodoxies. 15.*

or thog ra phy (ôr thog′rə fi), 1. correct spelling; spelling considered as right or wrong. 2. the art of spelling; the study of spelling. *n. 15.*

-ory, suffix meaning:
1. ———ing; as in contradictory.
2. of or pertaining to ———; as in advisory.
3. characterized by ———ion; as in adulatory.
4. serving to ———; as in preparatory.
5. tending to ———; inclined to ———; as in conciliatory.
6. place or establishment for ———ing; as in depository.
7. other meanings; as in conservatory, desultory, directory.

o ryx (ō′riks), African antelope with long, nearly straight horns. *n., pl. oryxes* or *oryx.*

Oryx (about 4 ft. high at the shoulder)

O sa ka (ō sä′kə), a large city in Japan. *n.*

os cil late (os′i lāt), 1. swing to and fro like a pendulum; move to and fro between two points. 2. vary between opinions, purposes, etc. *v. 15.*

os cil la tion (os′i lā′shən), oscillating; vibrating; as, the oscillation of an electric current. *n. 17.*

os cu late (os′kū lāt), kiss. *v.*

o sier (ō′zhər), a willow whose branches are used in making baskets, etc. *n. 10.*

Os lo (os′lō), the capital of Norway. *n.*

os mo sis (os mō′sis), 1. the tendency of two fluids which are separated by something porous to go through it and become mixed. 2. the diffusion or spreading of fluids through a membrane or partition till they are mixed. *n. 10.*

os prey (os′pri), a large hawk that feeds on fish. *n., pl. ospreys. 16.*

Osprey (about 2 ft. long)

Os sa (os′ə), a mountain in eastern Greece. The Greek story says that when the giants made war on the gods, they piled Mount Ossa on Mount Olympus and Mount Pelion upon Mount Ossa in an attempt to reach heaven. *n. 18.*

os si fi ca tion (os′i fi kā′shən), 1. changing into bone. 2. being changed into bone. 3. a part which is ossified. *n.*

os si fy (os′i fī), 1. change into bone; become bone. The soft parts of a baby's skull ossify as it grows older. 2. harden like bone; become fixed, hard-hearted, or very conservative. *v., ossified, ossifying. 20.*

os ten si ble (os ten′si bəl), apparent; pretended; professed. Mrs. Brown's ostensible purpose was borrowing some sugar, but she really wanted to see the new furniture. *adj. 11.*

os ten si bly (os ten′si bli), apparently; on the face of it; as openly stated or shown. Though ostensibly studying his geography, Tom was really eating an apple behind the big book. *adv.*

os ten ta tion (os′ten tā′shən), showing off; display intended to impress others; as, the ostentation of a rich, vain man. *n. 12.*

os ten ta tious (os′ten tā′shəs), 1. done for display; intended to attract notice. Tom rode his new bicycle up and down in front of Dick's house in an ostentatious way. 2. showing off; liking to attract notice. *adj. 10.*

os te o path (os′ti ə path), person who treats disease by manipulating the bones and muscles. *n.*

os te op a thy (os′ti op′ə thi), treatment of diseases by manipulating the bones and muscles. *n.*

ost ler (os′lər), hostler; person who takes care of horses. *n. 19.*

os tra cism (os′trə sizm), 1. banishment from one's native country. 2. being shut out from society, from favor, from privileges, or from association with one's fellows. *n. 17.*

os tra cize (os′trə sīz), 1. banish. The ancient Greeks ostracized a dangerous or unpopular citizen by public vote. 2. shut out from society, from favor, from privileges, etc. The newly-rich family were ostracized by the exclusive neighborhood into which they had moved. *v.*

os trich (os′trich), a large African and Arabian bird. Ostriches run swiftly but cannot fly. They have large feathers or plumes which were much used as ornaments. *n. 6.*

Ostrich
(6 to 8 ft. tall)

O thel lo (ō thel′ō), a brave but jealous Moor, the hero of Shakespeare's play *Othello.* He is made to believe his wife Desdemona is not true to him and kills her. *n. 14.*

oth er (uᴛʜ′ər), 1. not the same; different. Come some other day. 2. remaining. John is here, but the other boys are at school. 3. additional. I have no other place to go. 4. other person or thing. 5. in any different way. I could not do other than I did. 6. **Every other** sometimes means every second. We have spelling every other day. 7. The **other world** sometimes means the life to come. We may see angels in the other world. *adj., pron., adv. 1.*

oth er wise (uᴛʜ′ər wīz′), 1. differently; in a different way. I could not do otherwise. 2. different; in a different condition. It might have been otherwise. 3. in other ways. He is noisy, but otherwise a nice boy. 4. or else; if not. Come at once; otherwise you will be too late. *adv., adj., conj. 3.*

Ot ta wa (ot′ə wə), the capital of Canada. *n. 17.*

ot ter (ot′ər), 1. a water animal that eats fish. The otter is hunted for its fur. 2. its fur. *n. 10.*

Otter (3 to 4 ft. long, including the tail)

Ot to man (ot′ə-mən), 1. Turk. 2. Turkish. *n., pl. Ottomans, adj. 12.*

ot to man (ot′ə mən), a low cushioned seat without back or arms. *n., pl. ottomans.*

ouch (ouch), an exclamation expressing sudden pain. *interj.*

ought (ôt). Ought is put before another verb to express the idea of being bound or required by: 1. duty. You ought to obey your parents. 2. rightness. It ought not to be allowed. 3. fitness. You ought to know better. 4. wisdom. I ought to have gone yesterday. 5. very strong likelihood. It ought to be a fine day tomorrow. *v. 1.*

ounce (ouns), 1. a unit of weight, $\frac{1}{16}$ of a pound in avoirdupois, and $\frac{1}{12}$ of a pound in troy weight. 2. a little bit; a very small amount. *n. 3.*

our (our), of us; belonging to us. We need our coats now. *pron. 1.*

ours (ourz), 1. of us; belonging to us. This garden is ours. 2. the one or ones belonging to us. Ours is a large family. I like ours better than yours. *pron. 3.*

our self (our self′). Ourself is used by an author, king, judge, etc., meaning myself. "We will ourself reward the victor," said the queen. *pron. 3.*

our selves (our selvz′), 1. Ourselves is used to make a statement stronger. We ourselves will do the work. 2. Ourselves is used instead of we or us in cases like: We cook for ourselves. We help ourselves. 3. us. We cannot see ourselves as others see us. *pron. pl. 3.*

-ous, suffix meaning:—
1. having; having much; full of; as in joyous and perilous.
2. like; as in thunderous.

oust (oust), push out; drive out. The sparrows have ousted the bluebirds from our birdhouse. *v. 15.*

out (out), 1. away; not in or at a place; forth. The water will rush out. Spread the rug out. 2. not at home; away from one's office, work, etc. My mother is out just now. 3. not having power; not in possession; in baseball, not batting. 4. not burning; no longer lighted. The fire (light, etc.) is out. 5. not correct. He was out in his figuring. 6. **Out with him!** means put him out. 7. into the open; made public; make known; into being; so as to be seen. The secret is out now. His new book is out. Many flowers were coming out. A rash broke out on his chest. 8. aloud; plainly. Speak out so that all can hear. 9. **Speak out** also means speak frankly. 10. go out; come out. Murder will out. 11. to or at an end; completely. Let them fight it out. 12. to others; as, to let out

rooms, to give out books. 13. from among others. Pick out an apple for me. 14. not friendly. 15. Some special meanings are:
out and away, by far.
out and out, thoroughly.
out of, 1. from within. He came out of the house. 2. not within. He is out of town. 3. away from; as, 40 miles out of New York. 4. beyond the reach of. She was out of sight. 5. without. He is out of work. 6. from. It is made out of tin. 7. because of. He did it out of love.
adv., adj., interj., v. 1.

out-, prefix meaning:—
1. outward; forth; away; as in outburst and outgoing.
2. outside; at a distance; as in outbuilding, outfield, outlying.
3. more than or longer than; as in outbid, outlive, outnumber.
4. better than; as in outdo, outrun.

out-and-out (out′ənd out′), thorough; complete; as, an out-and-out refusal. *adj.*

out bid (out bid′), bid higher than (someone else). *v., outbid, outbid* or *outbidden, outbidding.*

outboard motor, small motor attached to the stern of a boat or canoe.

out bound (out′bound′), outward bound. *adj.*

out brave (out brāv′), 1. face bravely. 2. be braver than. *v. 20.*

out break (out′brāk′), 1. a breaking out; as, outbreaks of anger. 2. a riot; a public disturbance. *n. 8.*

out build ing (out′bil′ding), a shed or building built against or near a main building. *n. 19.*

out burst (out′bėrst′), bursting forth; as, an outburst of laughter, anger, smoke, etc. *n. 13.*

out cast (out′kast′), 1. cast out from home and friends; homeless; friendless. 2. an outcast person or animal. That kitten was just a little outcast when Tom found it and brought it home. *adj., n. 9.*

out class (out klas′), be of a higher class than; be much better than. *v.*

out come (out′kum′), result; consequence. *n. 10.*

out crop (out′krop′), 1. a coming to the surface of the earth; as, the outcrop of a vein of coal. 2. part that comes to the surface. The outcrop that we found proved to be very rich in gold. *n.*

out cry (out′krī′), 1. a crying out; sudden cry or scream. 2. a great noise or clamor. *n., pl. outcries. 8.*

out did (out did′). See **outdo.** *pt. of outdo. 18.*

out dis tance (out dis′təns), leave behind. *v.*

out do (out dü′), do more or better than; surpass. Men will outdo boys in most things. *v., outdid, outdone, outdoing. 17.*

out done (out dun′). See **outdo.** *pp. of outdo. 20.*

out door (out′dōr′), done, used, or living outdoors; as, outdoor games. *adj. 14.*

out doors (out′dōrz′), 1. out in the open air; not indoors or in the house. 2. the world outside of houses; the open air. *adv., n. 6.*

out er (out′ər), on the outside; farther out. *adj. 6.*

out er most (out′ər mōst), farthest out. *adj. 13.*

out field (out′fēld′), 1. in baseball, the part of the field beyond the diamond or infield. 2. the three players in the outfield. *n.*

out fit (out′fit), 1. all the articles necessary for any undertaking or purpose; as, a sailor's outfit, the outfit for a camping trip, a bride's outfit. 2. furnish with everything necessary for any purpose; equip. 3. group working together. *n., v., outfitted, outfitting. 6.*

out flank (out flangk′), 1. go or extend beyond the flank of (an opposing army, etc.); turn the flank of. 2. get the better of. *v.*

out gen er al (out jen′ər əl), be a better general than; get the better of by superior strategy. *v., outgeneraled, outgeneraling.*

out go (out′gō′), what goes out; what is paid out; amount that is spent. *n., pl. outgoes. 10.*

out go ing (out′gō′ing), 1. a going out. 2. that which goes out. 3. departing; outward bound; as, outgoing steamships. *n., adj.*

out grow (out grō′), 1. grow too large for; as, to outgrow one's clothes. 2. grow beyond or away from; get rid of by growing older; as, to outgrow early friends, to outgrow a babyish habit, opinion, fault, etc. 3. grow faster or taller than. This variety of pole bean will outgrow the dwarf kind. By the time he was ten, Tom had outgrown his older brother. *v., outgrew, outgrown, outgrowing. 12.*

out growth (out′grōth′), 1. a natural development, product, or result. This big store is an outgrowth of the little shop James started ten years ago. 2. offshoot; something that has grown out. A corn is an outgrowth on a toe. 3. growing out or forth; as, the outgrowth of new leaves in spring. *n. 18.*

out house (out′hous′), a separate building used in connection with a main building. Near the farmhouse were sheds and outhouses. *n. 20.*

out ing (out′ing), a short pleasure trip; a walk or airing; holiday spent outdoors away from home. *n. 9.*

out land ish (out lan′dish), 1. not familiar; queer; strange or ridiculous. 2. looking or sounding as if it belonged to a foreign country. *adj. 12.*

out last (out last′), last longer than. *v. 16.*

out law (out′lô′), 1. person put outside the protection of the law; an exile; an outcast. 2. a lawless person; a criminal. 3. make or declare (a person) an outlaw. 4. make or declare unlawful. A group of nations agreed to outlaw war. 5. deprive of legal force. An outlawed debt is one that cannot be collected because it has been due too long. *n., v. 10.*

out law ry (out′lô′ri), 1. being condemned as an outlaw; being outlawed. Outlawry was formerly used as a punishment in England. 2. condition of being an outlaw. *n., pl. outlawries. 20.*

out lay (out′lā′), 1. expense; laying out money; spending. 2. the amount spent. 3. expend; as, to outlay money in improvements. *n., v., outlaid, outlaying. 16.*

out let (out′let), a means or place of letting out or getting out; a way out; as, the outlet of a lake, an outlet for one's energies. *n. 4.*

out line (out′līn′), 1. the line that shows the shape of an object; the line that bounds a figure. This diagram is the outline of an egg: The outline of Italy suggests a boot. 2. a drawing or style of drawing that gives only outer lines. This is an outline of a house. 3. draw the outer line of anything. Outline a map of America. 4. a plan; rough draft. Make an outline before trying to write a composition. The teacher gave a brief outline of the work planned for the term. 5. give a plan of; sketch; as, to outline a trip abroad. *n., v. 5.*

out live (out liv′), live longer than; last longer than. She outlived her older sister. The idea was good once, but it has outlived its usefulness. *v. 8.*

out look (out′lu̇k′), 1. what one sees on looking out; view. The room has a pleasant outlook. 2. what seems likely to happen; prospect. The outlook for our picnic is not very good; it looks as if it would rain. 3. way of thinking about things; attitude of mind; point of view. 4. lookout; tower to watch from. *n. 11.*

out ly ing (out′lī′ing), lying outside the boundary; far from the center; remote. *adj. 12.*

out num ber (out num′bər), be more than; exceed in number. They outnumbered us three to one. *v. 12.*

out-of-date (out′əv dāt′), old-fashioned; not in present use. *adj.*

out-of-door (out′əv dōr′), outdoor. *adj.*

out-of-doors (out′əv dōrz′), 1. outdoor. 2. outdoors. *adj., adv., n.*

out-of-the-way (out′əv ŦHə wā′), 1. remote; unfrequented; secluded; as, an out-of-the-way cottage. 2. seldom met with; unusual; as, out-of-the-way bits of information. *adj.*

out post (out′pōst′), 1. a guard, or small number of soldiers, placed at some distance from an army or camp, to prevent surprise. 2. place where they are stationed. *n. 12.*

out pour (out pōr′ for 1, out′pōr′ for 2 and 3), 1. pour out. 2. that which is poured out. 3. a pouring out. *v., n. 20.*

out put (out′pu̇t′), 1. the amount produced; the product or yield; as, the daily output of automobiles, of lumber, of shoes. 2. putting forth; as, a sudden output of effort. *n. 8.*

out rage (out′rāj), 1. an overturning of the rights of others by force; an act showing no regard for the feelings of others; an act of violence; an offense; an insult. 2. offend greatly; insult; do violence to. 3. break (the law, a rule of morality, etc.) openly; treat as nothing at all. *n., v. 6.*

out ra geous (out rā′jəs), shocking; very bad or insulting. *adj. 8.*

out ran (out ran′). See **outrun.** *pt. of outrun. 10.*

out rank (out-rangk′), rank higher than. A captain outranks a lieutenant. *v.*

out rig ger (out′-rig′ər), frame-work ending in a

Outrigger

float, extending outward from the side of a canoe to prevent upsetting. *n.*

out right (out′rīt′), 1. altogether; entirely; not gradually. 2. complete; thorough. He would have to be an outright thief to do that. 3. downright; straightforward; direct. *adv., adj. 10.*

out run (out run′), 1. run faster than. Dick can outrun his older sister. 2. leave behind; run beyond; pass the limits of. I am afraid your story outruns the facts. *v., outran, outrun, outrunning. 6.*

out set (out′set′), a setting out; a start; a beginning. *n. 14.*

out shine (out shīn′), shine more brightly than. *v., outshone, outshining.*

out side (out′sīd′), 1. the side or surface that is out; the outer part; as, to ride on the outside of a bus. 2. on the outside; of or nearer the outside; as, the outside leaves. 3. on or to the outside; outdoors. I feel clean outside and in. Run outside and play. 4. space that is beyond or not inside. 5. out of; beyond the limits of. Stay outside the house. That is outside my plans. 6. the most. I can do it in a week, at the outside. 7. highest; largest; as, an outside estimate, to quote outside prices. *Used in common talk. n., adj., adv., prep. 1.*

out sid er (out′sīd′ər), person not belonging to a particular group, set, company, party, etc. *n. 18.*

out skirts (out′skėrts′), outer parts or edges of a town, district, etc., or of a subject of discussion; outlying parts. *n. pl. 11.*

out spo ken (out′spō′kən), frank; not reserved; as, an outspoken person, an outspoken criticism. Your own family is likely to be outspoken in its remarks about you. *adj.*

out spread (out′spred′ for *adj.*, out spred′ for *v.*), spread out; as, an eagle with outspread wings. *adj., v., outspread, outspreading. 10.*

out stand ing (out stan′ding), 1. well-known; important. 2. unpaid; as, outstanding debts. 3. standing out. *adj. 14.*

out stretched (out′strecht′), stretched out; extended. He welcomed his old friend with outstretched arms. *adj. 6.*

out strip (out strip′). 1. go faster than; leave behind in a race. A horse can outstrip a man. 2. do better than; excel. Frank can outstrip John both in sports and in studies. *v., outstripped, outstripping. 11.*

out ward (out′wərd), 1. going toward the outside; turned toward the outside; as, an outward motion. She gave one outward glance. 2. toward the outside; away. 3. outer; as, to all outward appearances. 4. on the outside. 5. that can be seen; plain to see; seeming; on the surface; as, the outward man. *adj., adv. 4.*

out ward ly (out′wərd li), on the outside; in appearance. Though frightened, the boy remained outwardly calm. *adv.*

out wards (out′wərdz), outward. *adv.*

out wear (out wãr′), 1. wear longer than. 2. wear out; as, to outwear someone's patience. 3. outgrow. *v., outwore, outworn, outwearing.*

out weigh (out wā′), 1. weigh more than. 2. exceed in value, importance, influence, etc. The advantages of the plan outweigh its disadvantages. *v. 10.*

out wit (out wit′), get the better of; be too clever for. The prisoner outwitted his guards and escaped. *v., outwitted, outwitting. 15.*

out work (out′wėrk′ for 1, out wėrk′ for 2), 1. a part of the fortifications of a place lying outside the main ones; a less important defense; as, the outworks of a castle. 2. work harder or faster than. *n., v. 17.*

out worn (out′wōrn′), 1. worn out; as, outworn clothes. 2. outgrown; out of date; as, outworn opinions, outworn habits, outworn customs. *adj. 17.*

o val (ō′vəl), 1. egg-shaped. 2. shaped like an ellipse. 3. something having an oval shape. *adj., n. 10.*

Ovals

o va ry (ō′və ri), 1. the organ of a female in which eggs are produced. 2. the part of a plant enclosing the young seeds. *n., pl. ovaries. 8.*

o va tion (ō vā′shən), an enthusiastic public welcome; burst of loud clapping or cheering. The crowd welcomed the famous orator with an ovation. *n. 16.*

ov en (uv′ən), 1. a space in a stove or near a fireplace, for baking food. 2. a small furnace for heating or drying. *n. 3.*

o ver (ō′vər), 1. above; as, the sky over our heads, a window right over the water. 2. across; so as to get beyond or above; on or to the other side of; as, to jump over the brook, to cross over the road, spoke over her shoulder, payments lasting over several years. 3. moving above; so as to get past. Can you climb over that hill? 4. across a space or distance. Go over to the store for me. 5. out and down (from an edge or from an upright position). If you go too near the edge, you may fall over. 6. out and down from; down from the edge of; as, to lean over the edge. 7. about or upon, so as to cover. Cover the tar over with sand until it has hardened. 8. on; at all or various places on. A smile came over her face. The water ran over the floor. Farms were scattered over the valley. 9. to and fro upon; round about; all through; as, to travel over the United States. He went over everything in his pocket, looking for the letter. 10. from beginning to end; at some length; again. Do that three times over. 11. at an end; done with; settled. The fight is over. 12. about; concerning; in connection with. He is troubled over his health. Don't go to sleep over your work. 13. more than. It cost over ten dollars. 14. too; more: besides; as, to be over careful, not to feel over well, whatever is left over. 15. the other side up; upside down. Turn it over. Roll over and over. 16. higher up; extra; too great. 17. yonder; in the distance; as, over the hill. 18. **Over against** means (1) opposite to; in front of. (2) so placed as to bring out a difference. *prep., adv., adj. 1.*

over-, prefix meaning:—
1. too; too much; too long, etc.; as in overcrowd, overbold, overburden, overcharge, oversleep.
2. extra; as in overdose, overtime.
3. over; as in overflow and overthrow.

o ver alls (ō′vər ôlz′), loose trousers worn over clothes to keep them clean. Overalls usually have a part that covers the chest. *n. pl. 9.*

o ver arch (ō′vər ärch′), arch over; curve like an arch. The street was overarched by elm trees. *v. 15.*

o ver awe (ō′vər ô′), overcome or restrain with awe. Seeing an airplane overawed the savages. *v. 14.*

o ver bal ance (ō′vər bal′əns), 1. be greater than in weight, importance, value, etc. The gains overbalanced the losses. 2. cause to lose balance. Tom's weight as he leaned over the side overbalanced the canoe and it upset. *v. 17.*

o ver bear (ō′vər bãr′), 1. oppress; master; overcome by weight or force. My father overbore all my objections. 2. bear down by weight or force; overthrow; upset. *v., overbore, overborne, overbearing. 12.*

o ver bear ing (ō′vər bãr′ing), inclined to dictate; masterful; domineering; forcing others to one's own will. *adj.*

o ver board (ō′vər bōrd′), from a ship into the water. Throw that box overboard. *adv. 10.*

o ver bold (ō′vər bōld′), too bold. *adj. 18.*

o ver bur den (ō′vər bėr′dən), load with too great a burden. *v. 20.*

o ver came (ō′vər kām′). See **overcome.** *pt. of overcome. 7.*

o ver cap i tal ize (ō′vər kap′i təl īz), fix the capital of (a corporation, business, etc.) at too high an amount. *v.*

o ver cast (ō′vər kast′), 1. cloudy; dark; gloomy. The sky was overcast before the storm. 2. cover (the sky, sun, etc.) with clouds or darkness. 3. fasten by stitching roughly through and over the edges of a seam. *adj., v., overcast, overcasting. 10.*

Overcasting

o ver charge (ō′vər chärj′ for 1 and 3, ō′vər chärj′ for 2), 1. charge too high a price. The grocer overcharged you for the eggs. 2. a charge that is too great. 3. charge or load too heavily. The overcharged old musket burst. *v., n. 11.*

o ver cloud (ō′vər kloud′), cloud over; become clouded over; darken; make gloomy. *v.*

o ver coat (ō′vər kōt′), heavy coat worn over the regular coat. *n. 4.*

o ver come (ō′vər kum′), 1. get the better of; conquer; win the victory over; defeat; as, to overcome an enemy, one's faults, all difficulties. Rage overcame her and she tore her hair. 2. made weak or helpless. The child was overcome by weariness and slept. *v., overcame, overcome, overcoming. 3.*

o ver crowd (ō′vər kroud′), crowd too much; put in too much or too many. *v. 9.*

o ver do (ō′vər dü′), 1. do too much. She overdid and became tired. 2. exaggerate. The funny scenes in the play were overdone. 3. cook too much; as, overdone beef. *v., overdid, overdone, overdoing.*

o ver done (ō′vər dun′). See **overdo.** *pp. of overdo.*

o ver dose (ō′vər dōs′ for 1, ō′vər dōs′ for 2), 1. too big a dose. 2. give too big a dose to. *n., v.*

o ver draw (ō′vər drô′), 1. draw from (a bank account, an allowance, etc.) more than one has a right to. 2. exaggerate. The characters in the book were greatly overdrawn. *v., overdrew, overdrawn, overdrawing.*

o ver dress (ō′vər dres′ for 1, ō′vər dres′ for 2), 1. dress too richly. 2. a dress worn over the main dress. Her overdress was made of lace. *v., n.*

o ver due (ō′vər dū′ or ō′vər dü′), more than due; due some time ago but not yet arrived, paid, etc. The train is overdue. This bill is overdue. *adj. 20.*

o ver eat (ō′vər ēt′), eat too much. *v., overate, overeaten, overeating. 16.*

o ver es ti mate (ō′vər es′ti māt for 1, ō′vər es′ti mit for 2), 1. to estimate at too high a value, amount, rate, etc. 2. an estimate that is too high. *v., n. 16.*

o ver feed (ō′vər fēd′), feed too much. *v., overfed, overfeeding.*

o ver flow (ō′vər flō′ for 1-5, ō′vər flō′ for 6), 1. flow over (the top). Stop! The milk is overflowing. 2. have the contents flowing over. My cup is overflowing. 3. cover; flood. The river overflowed my garden. 4. extend out beyond; be too many for. The crowd overflowed my little parlor and filled the hall. 5. be very abundant; as, an overflowing harvest, overflowing kindness. 6. overflowing; excess. *v., n. 4.*

o ver grow (ō′vər grō′), 1. grow over. The wall is overgrown with vines. 2. grow too fast; become too big; as, an overgrown boy. *v., overgrew, overgrown, overgrowing. 10.*

o ver hand (ō′vər hand′), 1. with the hand raised above the shoulder; as, an overhand throw, to pitch overhand. 2. with the knuckles upward. *adj., adv. 20.*

o ver hang (ō′vər hang′ for 1, ō′vər hang′ for 2 and 3), 1. hang over; project over. Overhanging branches of trees formed an arch across the street. 2. hanging over. 3. something that projects. The overhang of the roof shaded the flower bed beneath. *v., overhung, overhanging, n. 11.*

o ver haul (ō′vər hôl′), 1. examine thoroughly so as to make any repairs or changes that are needed. 2. gain upon; overtake. *v. 12.*

o ver head (ō′vər hed′ for 1, ō′vər hed′ for 2, 3, and 4), 1. above; on high; in the sky; on the floor above; as, the flag overhead, the stars overhead, the family overhead. 2. placed above; placed high up. 3. general expenses or charges, such as rent, lighting, heating, taxes, repairs. 4. general; applying to one and all. *adv., adj., n. 4.*

o ver hear (ō′vər hēr′), hear when one is not meant to hear. They spoke so loud that I could not help overhearing what they said. *v., overheard, overhearing. 7.*

o ver heat (ō′vər hēt′), heat too much. *v.*

o ver hung (ō′vər hung′ for 1, ō′vər hung′ for 2), 1. hung from above; as, an overhung door. 2. See **overhang.** *adj., pt. and pp. of overhang. 19.*

o ver joy (ō′vər joi′), make very, very joyful. *v. 14.*

o ver joyed (ō′vər joid′), very joyful; filled with joy; delighted. *adj.*

o ver laid (ō′vər lād′), See **overlay.** The workmen overlaid the dome with gold. The iron had become overlaid with rust. *pt. and pp. of overlay. 12.*

o ver land (ō′vər land′), on land; by land. We traveled overland from New York to Florida. *adv., adj. 8.*

o ver lap (ō′vər lap′), lap over; cover and extend beyond. Shingles are laid to overlap each other. *v., overlapped, overlapping. 12.*

o ver lay (ō′vər lā′ for 1, ō′vər lā′ for 2), 1. put a coating over the surface of. The dome is overlaid with gold. 2. something laid over something else; covering; ornamental layer. *v., overlaid, overlaying, n. 13.*

o ver leap (ō′vər lēp′), leap over; pass beyond. Her joy overleaped all bounds. *v. 13.*

o ver lie (ō′vər lī′), lie over or upon. *v., overlay, overlain, overlying.*

o ver load (ō′vər lōd′ for 1, ō′vər lōd′ for 2), 1. load too heavily. 2. too great a load. *v., n. 11.*

o ver look (ō′vər lůk′), 1. have a view of from above; be higher than. This high window overlooks half of New York City. 2. fail to see. Here are some letters which you overlooked. 3. excuse; pay no attention to. I will overlook your behavior this time. *v. 4.*

o ver lord (ō′vər lôrd′), person who is lord over another. The duke was the overlord of barons and knights who held land from him. *n.*

o ver mas ter (ō′vər mas′tər), overcome; overpower. *v.*

o ver much (ō′vər much′), too much. *adj., adv., n. 12.*

o ver night (ō′vər nīt′ for *adv.*, ō′vər nīt′ for *adj.*), 1. during the night; as, to stay overnight with a friend; an overnight stop. 2. for the night. An overnight bag contains articles needed for one night's stay. 3. on the night before. Preparations were made overnight for an early start. *adv., adj. 10.*

o ver pass (ō′vər pas′ for 1, 2, and 3, ō′vər pas′ for 4), 1. pass over (a region, bounds, etc.). 2. go beyond; exceed. 3. pass without notice; overlook. 4. bridge over a road, railroad, canal, etc. *v., overpassed* or *overpast, overpassing, n. 18.*

o ver plus (ō′vər plus), surplus; too great an amount. *n. 20.*

o ver pow er (ō′vər pou′ər), 1. overcome; master; overwhelm. He overpowered all his enemies. I was overpowered by the heat. 2. be much greater or stronger than. The wind brought a horrible smell which overpowered all others. Sudden anger overpowered every other feeling. *v. 7.*

o ver pro duc tion (ō′vər prə duk′shən), production of more than is needed or more than can be sold. *n.*

o ver ran (o′vər ran′). See **overrun.** *pt. of overrun.*

o ver rate (ō′vər rāt′), to rate or estimate too highly. *v. 16.*

o ver reach (ō′vər rēch′), 1. reach over or beyond. 2. reach too far. 3. get the better of by cunning; as, to overreach a man in a bargain. 4. **Overreach oneself** means (1) fail or miss by trying for too much. (2) fail by being too tricky. *v. 16.*

o ver ride (ō′vər rīd′), 1. ride over; trample on. 2. ride over (a region, place, etc.). 3. act in spite of; as, to override advice or objections. 4. prevail over; as, a new rule overriding all previous ones. 5. tire out by riding; ride too much; as, to override a horse. *v., overrode, overridden, overriding. 16.*

o ver rule (ō′vər rül′), 1. rule or decide against (a plea, argument, objection, etc.); set aside. 2. rule over. 3. prevail over. I was overruled by the majority. *v. 9.*

o ver run (ō′vər run′), 1. spread over and spoil or harm in some way. Weeds had overrun the old garden. 2. spread over. Vines overran the wall. 3. run or go beyond; exceed. The speaker overran the time set for him. *v., overran, overrun, overrunning. 9.*

o ver sea (ō′vər sē′ for *adv.*, ō′vər sē′ for *adj.*), overseas. *adv., adj.*

o ver seas (ō′vər sēz′ for 1, ō′vər sēz′ for 2 and 3), 1. across the sea; beyond the sea; abroad. 2. done, used, or serving overseas. 3. of countries across the sea; foreign. *adv., adj. 10.*

o ver see (ō′vər sē′), look after and direct (work or workers); superintend; manage. *v., oversaw, overseen, overseeing. 17.*

o ver se er (ō′vər sē′ər), one who oversees, superintends, or looks after the work of others. *n. 13.*

o ver set (ō′vər set′ for *v.*, ō′vər set′ for *n.*), upset; overturn. *v., overset, oversetting, n. 14.*

o ver shad ow (ō′vər shad′ō), 1. be more important than. 2. cast a shadow over. *v. 10.*

o ver shoe (ō′vər shü′), a rubber shoe or a felt shoe with a rubber sole, worn over another shoe to keep the foot dry. *n. 10.*

o ver shoot (ō′vər shüt′), 1. shoot over or beyond. 2. go too far. *v., overshot, overshooting. 18.*

o ver shot (ō′vər shot′ for 1 and 2, ō′vər-shot′ for 3), 1. having the upper jaw projecting beyond the lower. 2. driven by water flowing above; as, an overshot water wheel. 3. See **overshoot.** *adj., pt. and pp. of overshoot.*

Overshot water wheel

o ver sight (ō′vər sīt′), 1. failure to notice or think of something. Through an oversight, the kitten got no supper last night. 2. watchful care. While children are at school they are under their teacher's oversight and direction. *n. 9.*

o ver sleep (ō′vər slēp′), sleep beyond (a certain hour); sleep too long. *v., overslept, oversleeping.*

o ver spread (ō′vər spred′), spread over. A smile overspread his broad face. *v., overspread, overspreading. 9.*

o ver state (ō′vər stāt′), state too strongly; exaggerate. *v.*

o ver state ment (ō′vər stāt′mənt), too strong a statement; exaggeration. *n.*

o ver step (ō′vər step′), go beyond; exceed. *v., overstepped, overstepping. 16.*

o ver stock (ō′vər stok′ for 1, ō′vər stok′ for 2), 1. supply with more than is needed. 2. too great a stock or supply. *v., n.*

o ver strain (ō′vər strān′ for 1, ō′vər strān′ for 2), 1. strain too much. 2. too great strain. *v., n. 18.*

o vert (ō′vėrt), open; evident; not hidden. *adj. 15.*

o ver take (ō′vər tāk′), 1. come up with. The blue car overtook ours. 2. come upon suddenly. A storm overtook the children. *v., overtook, overtaken, overtaking. 4.*

o ver tak en (ō′vər tāk′ən). See **overtake.** *pp. of overtake.*

o ver tax (ō′vər taks′), 1. tax too heavily. 2. put too heavy burdens on. *v. 14.*

o ver threw (ō′vər thrü′). See **overthrow.** *pt. of overthrow. 9.*

o ver throw (ō′vər thrō′ for 1, 2, and 3, ō′vər thrō′ for 4), 1. overturn; upset; knock down. 2. destroy; put an end to. 3. take away the power of; defeat; as, to overthrow a king. 4. a defeat; an upset. The overthrow of his plans left him much discouraged. *v., overthrew, overthrown, overthrowing, n. 4.*

o ver thrown (ō′vər thrōn′). See **overthrow.** *pp. of overthrow.*

o ver time (ō′vər tīm′), 1. extra time; time beyond the regular hours. 2. beyond the regular hours. *n., adv. 17.*

o ver tone (ō′vər tōn′), a fainter and higher tone heard along with the main or fundamental tone; harmonic. *n. 20.*

o ver took (ō′vər tu̇k′). See **overtake.** *pt. of overtake. 6.*

o ver top (ō′vər top′), 1. rise above; be higher than. The new building will overtop all the others. 2. surpass; excel. *v., overtopped, overtopping. 14.*

o ver ture (ō′vər chər), 1. proposal; offer. The enemy is making overtures for peace. 2. a musical composition played by the orchestra as an introduction to an opera, oratorio, etc. *n. 10.*

o ver turn (ō′vər tėrn′ for 1, 2, and 3, ō′vər-tėrn′ for 4), 1. turn upside down. 2. upset; fall down; fall over. The boat overturned. 3. make fall down; overthrow; defeat; destroy the power of. 4. an overturning. *v., n. 5.*

o ver watch (ō′vər woch′), 1. watch over. 2. make weary by watching. *v. 17.*

o ver ween ing (ō′vər wēn′ing), thinking too much of oneself; conceited; self-confident; presumptuous. *adj. 17.*

o ver weight (ō′vər wāt′ for 1, 2, and 3, ō′vər wāt′ for 4), 1. having too much weight; as, a boy overweight for his age. 2. too much weight. 3. extra weight. The butcher gave us overweight on this roast. 4. overburden; as, a small child overweighted with heavy schoolbooks. *adj., n., v. 13.*

o ver whelm (ō′vər hwelm′), 1. crush; overcome completely. She was overwhelmed with grief. 2. cover completely as a flood would. A great wave overwhelmed the boat. *v. 5.*

o ver work (ō′vər wėrk′ for 1 and 3, ō′vər wėrk′ for 2), 1. too much work. 2. to work too hard or too long. 3. extra work. *n., v., overworked* or *overwrought, overworking. 11.*

o ver wrought (ō′vər rôt′), 1. wearied or exhausted by too much work or excitement; greatly excited. 2. decorated all over. The shield was overwrought with a design of flowers and leaves. 3. too elaborate. 4. overworked. *adj., pt. and pp. of* **overwork.** *11.*

o vule (ō′vūl), 1. a little ovum. 2. the part of a plant that develops into a seed. *n. 10.*

o vum (ō′vəm), an egg; the female germ cell. *n., pl. ova* (ō′və). *15.*

owe (ō), 1. have to pay; be in debt. William owes his cousin a dollar. He is always owing for something. 2. be obliged or indebted for. We owe a great deal to our parents. *v. 2.*

ow ing (ō′ing), 1. that owes; as, a man owing money. 2. due; as, to pay what is owing. 3. **Owing to** sometimes means on account of; because of. *adj.*

owl (oul), a bird having a big head, big eyes, and a short, hooked beak. See the picture. Owls hunt mice and small birds at night. You can tell an owl by the noise or hoot it makes. *n. 2.*

American great horned owl (about 2 ft. long, from ears to tip of tail)

owl et (oul′et), 1. a young owl. 2. a small owl. *n. 10.*

own (ōn), 1. have; possess. I own many books. 2. of one's self. This is my own book. Nell makes her own dresses. 3. admit that one owns or is the father of. His father will not own him. 4. admit. I own you are right. 5. Some special meanings are:

come into one's own, 1. get what belongs to one. 2. get the success or credit that one deserves.

hold one's own, keep one's position; not be forced back.

of one's own, belonging to one.

on one's own, not ruled or directed by someone else.

own brother, full brother, not a half-brother, having the same parents.

own cousin, first cousin, a grandchild of your grandparents.
own to, confess. I own to being afraid.
own up, confess. The prisoner owned up. *v., adj., n. 1.*
own er (ōn′ər), one who owns. *n. 2.*
own er ship (ōn′ər ship), being an owner; the possessing (of something); right of possession. *n. 9.*
ox (oks), 1. the full-grown male of domestic cattle when fitted and trained for farm work. 2. any of the group of animals to which cattle, buffaloes, and bison belong. *n., pl. oxen. 2.*
ox en (ok′sən), more than one ox. *n. pl.*
Ox ford (oks′fərd), 1. a city in southern England. 2. a great English university located in that city. *n. 5.*
ox ford (oks′fərd), a kind of low shoe. *n.*
Oxford gray, very dark gray.
ox i da tion (ok′si dā′shən), 1. oxidizing. Burning is one kind of oxidation. 2. being oxidized. *n. 9.*
ox ide (ok′sīd), a compound of oxygen with another element. *n. 13.*
ox i dize (ok′si dīz), combine with oxygen. When a substance burns or rusts, it is oxidized. *v. 9.*
ox y gen (ok′si jən), a gas without color or odor that forms about one fifth of the air. Oxygen is present in a combined form in water and many other substances. Animals and plants cannot live without oxygen. Fire will not burn without oxygen. *n. 8.*
oys ter (ois′tər), a kind of shellfish much used as food, having a rough irregular shell in two halves. Oysters live in shallow water along seacoasts. *n. 4.*

Oyster

oz., ounce; ounces. *4.*
O zark Moun tains (ō′zärk moun′tənz), low mountain range in southern Missouri, northern Arkansas, and eastern Oklahoma.
O zarks (ō′zärks), the Ozark Mountains. *n. pl.*
o zone (ō′zōn), 1. a form of oxygen with a peculiar odor, produced by electricity and present in the air, especially after a thunderstorm. 2. pure air that is refreshing. *Used in common talk. n.*

P

P, p (pē), the 16th letter of the alphabet. There are two p's in papa. **Mind your P's and Q's** means be careful about what you say or do. *n., pl. P's, p's.*
p., 1. page. 2. participle. *19.*
pa (pä), papa; father. *n.* [*Used in common talk*] *6.*
Pa., Pennsylvania.
p.a., participial adjective.
pace (pās), 1. a step. 2. to walk with regular steps. The tiger paced up and down his cage. 3. the length of a step in walking; about 2½ feet. There were perhaps ten paces between me and the bear. 4. to measure by paces. We paced off the distance and found it to be 69 paces. 5. way of going along. The walk, trot, and gallop are some of the paces of the horse. 6. a particular pace of some horses in which the feet on the same side are lifted and put down together. 7. move thus. Some horses are trained to pace. 8. rate; speed. John sets a fast pace in walking. *n., v. 2.*
Pa cif ic (pə sif′ik), the great ocean between Asia and America. *n. 3.*
pa cif ic (pə sif′ik), making peace; loving peace; peaceful. *adj.*
pac i fi ca tion (pas′i fi kā′shən), pacifying; making peaceful; being in a state of peace. *n.*
pac i fism (pas′i fizm), opposition to war; the principle or policy of universal peace; settlement of all differences between nations by peaceful means. *n.*
pac i fist (pas′i fist), person who is opposed to war and favors settling all disputes between nations by peaceful means. *n.*
pac i fy (pas′i fī), make calm; quiet down; give peace to. Can't you pacify that screaming baby? We tried to pacify the man we ran into. *v., pacified, pacifying. 11.*
pack[1] (pak), 1. bundle of things wrapped up or tied together for carrying. The soldier carried a pack on his back. 2. put together in a bundle, box, etc. Pack your books in this box. Peaches are often packed in cans for the market. 3. fill with things; put one's things into. Pack your trunk. 4. press or crowd closely together. A hundred men were packed into one small room. 5. set; lot; a number together; as,

a pack of thieves, a pack of nonsense, a pack of lies. 6. a number of animals hunting together; a number of dogs kept together for hunting. Lions do not hunt in packs, but alone. 7. a complete set of playing cards, usually 52. 8. a large area of floating pieces of ice pushed together. The ship forced its way through the pack. 9. **Pack** (a person) **off** means send him away. **Send** (a person) **packing** means send him away in a hurry. 10. make tight with something that water, steam, air, etc., cannot leak through. *n., v. 2.*

pack[2] (pak), arrange unfairly. To pack a jury or a convention is to fill it unfairly with those who will favor one side. *v.*

pack age (pak′ij), bundle of things packed together; parcel; box with things packed in it. *n. 3.*

pack animal, animal used for carrying loads or packs.

Pack animal

pack er (pak′ər), person or thing that packs; especially, one who packs meat, fruit, vegetables, etc., to be sold. *n. 12.*

pack et (pak′it) 1. small package; parcel; as, a packet of letters. 2. A **packet boat** is a mail boat and is sometimes called simply a packet. *n., adj. 7.*

pack horse, horse used to carry packs of goods.

pact (pakt), agreement; compact. *n.*

pad (pad), 1. cushion; soft mass used for comfort, protection, or stuffing. The baby's carriage has a pad made to fit it. 2. fill with something soft; stuff; as, a padded chair, a padded suit for football. 3. use words just to fill space. 4. number of sheets of paper fastened tightly together; a tablet. 5. one of the cushionlike parts on the bottom side of the feet of dogs, foxes, and some other animals. 6. foot of a dog, fox, etc. 7. large floating leaf of the water lily. *n., v., padded, padding. 5.*

pad ding (pad′ing), 1. material used to pad with, such as hair, cotton, or straw. 2. words used just to fill space in making a written paper or a speech longer. *n.*

Paddle

pad dle[1] (pad′əl), 1. short oar with a broad blade at one end or both ends, used without resting it against the boat. 2. move (a boat or a canoe) with a paddle or paddles. 3. act of paddling; a turn at the paddle. 4. one of the broad boards fixed around a water wheel or a paddle wheel to push, or be pushed by, the water. 5. a paddle-shaped piece of wood used for stirring, for mixing, for beating clothes, etc. 6. beat with a paddle. *n., v. 6.*

pad dle[2] (pad′əl), move the hands or feet about in water. *v.*

paddle wheel, wheel with paddles fixed around it for propelling a ship over the water.

pad dock (pad′ək), 1. small field near a stable or house used as a pasture. 2. a pen for horses at a race track. *n. 19.*

Pa de rew ski (pä′dəref′ski), Polish pianist, composer, and statesman (1860-1941). *n.*

pad lock (pad′lok′), 1. a lock that can be put on and removed. It hangs by a curved bar, hinged at one end and snapped shut at the other. See the picture. 2. fasten with a padlock. *n., v. 13.*

Padlock

pa dre (pä′drā), a Spanish, Portuguese, or Italian word meaning father, used as a name for a priest. *n. 20.*

Pad u a (pad′ū ə), a city in northeastern Italy. *n. 12.*

pae an (pē′ən), song of praise, joy, or triumph. *n. 18.*

pa gan (pā′gən), heathen; not Christian; one who worships false gods. The ancient Greeks were pagans. *n., adj. 8.*

pa gan ism (pā′gən izm), 1. a pagan attitude toward religion or morality. 2. the beliefs and practices of pagans. 3. being a pagan. *n. 15.*

page[1] (pāj), 1. one side of a leaf of paper; as, a page in this book. 2. a record; as, the pages of history. 3. number the pages of. *n., v. 1.*

page[2] (pāj), 1. boy servant; errand boy. The pages at hotels usually wear uniforms. 2. try to find (a person) at a hotel, club, etc., by sending someone to call his name. 3. a youth who attends a person of rank. 4. a youth who was preparing to be a knight. *n., v.*

pag eant (paj′ənt), 1. a show; an elaborate spectacle; a procession in costume; pomp; display. The coronation of the new king was a splendid pageant. 2. a public entertainment that represents scenes from history, legend, or the like. Our school gave a pageant of the coming of the Pilgrims to America. *n. 7.*

pag eant ry (paj′ənt ri), 1. splendid show; gorgeous display or pomp. 2. mere show; empty display. *n. 12.*

pa go da (pə gō′də), temple having many stories forming a tower. Pagodas are built in India, Japan, and China. *n. 16.*

Pagoda

paid (pād). See **pay.** I have paid my bills. These bills are all paid. *pt. and pp. of pay. 2.*

pail (pāl), 1. a round container for carrying liquids, etc.; bucket. 2. the amount a pail holds. *n. 3.*

pail ful (pāl′fu̇l), amount that fills a pail. *n., pl. pailfuls.*

Pail

pain (pān), 1. A cut gives pain; a toothache is a pain. The death of one we love causes us pain. Does your tooth pain you? 2. **Take pains** means be careful. 3. **On pain of death** means with a risk of being killed if something is not done. *n., v. 1.*

pain ful (pān′fəl), hurting; causing pain; unpleasant; as, a painful illness, a painful duty. *adj. 5.*

pain less (pān′lis), without pain; causing no pain. *adj. 17.*

pains tak ing (pānz′tāk′ing), very careful. *adj. 11.*

paint (pānt), 1. solid coloring matter mixed with a liquid, used to color anything. 2. cover or decorate with paint; as, to paint a house. 3. use paint. 4. represent in colors. The artist painted fairies and angels. 5. make pictures. 6. to picture vividly in words. *n., v. 1.*

paint er[1] (pān′tər), 1. person who paints pictures; an artist. 2. person who paints houses, woodwork, etc. *n. 3.*

paint er[2] (pān′tər), a rope fastened to the bow of a boat, for tying it to a ship, pier, etc. *n.*

paint er[3] (pān′tər), mountain lion. *n.*

paint ing (pān′ting), picture; something painted. *n. 6.*

pair (pãr), 1. a set of two; two that go together; as, a pair of shoes or a pair of horses. 2. arrange or be arranged in pairs. 3. a single thing consisting of two parts that cannot be used separately; as, a pair of scissors, a pair of trousers. 4. two people who are married or are engaged to be married. 5. join in love and marriage. 6. two animals which are mated. 7. to mate. 8. two members on opposite sides who agree not to vote on a certain question. 9. the arrangement thus made. *n., v. 1.*

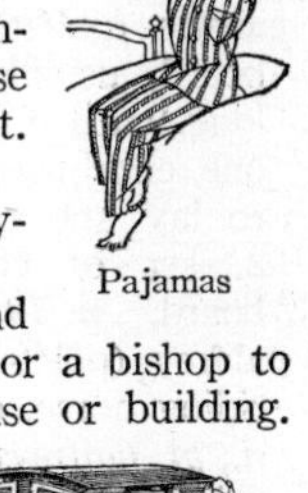
Pajamas

pa ja mas (pə jä′məz), garments to sleep in, etc., consisting of a coat and loose trousers fastened at the waist. *n. pl. 10.*

pal (pal), comrade; playmate. *n.* [*Slang*] *12.*

pal ace (pal′is), 1. a grand house for a king, a queen, or a bishop to live in. 2. a very fine house or building. *n. 2.*

pal an quin (pal′ən-kēn′), covered couch carried by poles resting on men's shoulders. *n.*

Palanquin

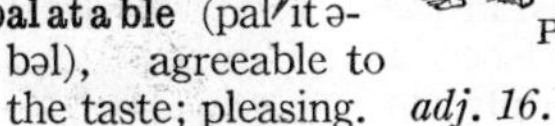

pal at a ble (pal′it ə-bəl), agreeable to the taste; pleasing. *adj. 16.*

pal ate (pal′it), 1. the roof of the mouth. The bony part in front is the hard palate, and the fleshy part in back is the soft palate. 2. the sense of taste. The new flavor pleased his palate. 3. liking. *n. 10.*

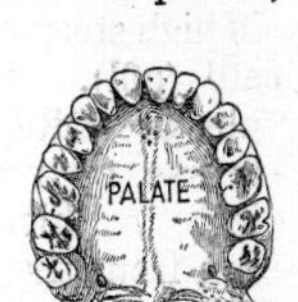

pa la tial (pə lā′shəl), like a palace; fit for a palace; magnificent. *adj. 17.*

pal a tine (pal′ə tīn), having royal rights in his own territory. A count palatine was subject only to the emperor or king. *adj. 15.*

pa lav er (pə lav′ər), 1. a parley or conference, especially between travelers and uncivilized natives. 2. flowing talk; smooth, persuading talk. 3. to talk fluently and flatteringly. *n., v. 19.*

pale[1] (pāl), 1. without much color; whitish. When you have been ill, your face is sometimes pale. 2. not bright; dim. 3. turn pale. *adj., v. 2.*

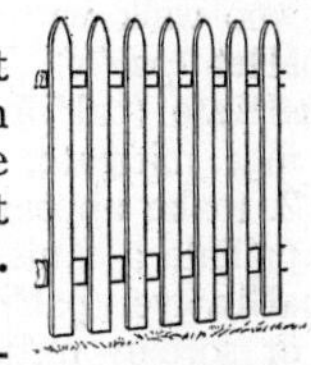
Fence made of pales

pale[2] (pāl), 1. a long, narrow board, pointed at the top, used for fences. 2. a boundary; as, outside the pale of civilized society. 3. enclose with pales. *n., v.*

pale face (pāl′fās′), white person. The North American Indians are said to have called white people palefaces. *n. 13.*

pale ness (pāl′nis), being pale. *n. 10.*

Pal es tine (pal′is tīn), Canaan; the Holy Land; the home of the Jewish people, in southwestern Asia. *n. 7.*

pal ette (pal′it), 1. a thin board, usually oval or oblong, with a thumb hole at one end, used by painters to lay and mix colors on. 2. set of colors on this board. *n. 19.*

Artist's palette

pal frey (pôl′fri), a gentle riding horse, especially one used by ladies. *n., pl. palfreys. 11.*

pal ing (pāl′ing), 1. fence of pales. 2. long, narrow board, pointed at the top, used for fences. *n.*

pal i sade (pal′i sād′), 1. a long, strong, wooden stake pointed at the top end. 2. a fence of stakes set firmly in the ground to enclose or defend. 3. a line of high steep cliffs. *n. 9.*

Palisades

pall[1] (pôl), 1. a heavy cloth of black, purple, or white velvet spread over a coffin, a hearse, or a tomb. 2. dark, gloomy covering. A thick pall of smoke shut out the sun from the city. *n. 9.*

pall[2] (pôl), become distasteful or very tiresome because there has been too much of it. Fireworks pall on grown-up people after an hour or so. *v.*

pal la di um (pə lā′di əm), anything regarded as an important safeguard. *n. 17.*

Pal las (pal′əs), a name of Athena, the Greek goddess oı wisdom. *n. 11.*

pall bear er (pôl′bãr′ər), one of the men who walk with the coffin at a funeral. *n.*

pal let (pal′it), bed of straw; poor bed. *n. 13.*

pal li ate (pal′i āt), 1. lessen without curing; mitigate; as, to palliate a disease. 2. make appear less serious; excuse; as, to palliate a fault. *v. 15.*

pal li a tive (pal′i ā′tiv), 1. useful to lessen or soften; mitigating; excusing. 2. something that lessens, softens, mitigates, or excuses. *adj., n. 20.*

pal lid (pal′id), pale; lacking color; as, a pallid complexion. *adj. 11.*

pal lor (pal′ər), paleness; lack of color from fear, illness, death, etc. *n. 16.*

palm[1] (päm), 1. the inside of the hand between the wrist and the fingers. 2. the width of a hand; 3 to 4 inches. 3. conceal in the hand. 4. to pass or get accepted (something not good). *n., v. 3.*

palm[2] (päm), 1. any of many kinds of trees growing in warm climates. Most palms are tall and have a bunch of large leaves at the top. 2. a branch or leaf of a palm tree as a symbol of victory or triumph. 3. victory; triumph. He bore off the palm both in tennis and in swimming. *n.*

Sentinel palm

palm er (päm′ər), 1. pilgrim returning from the Holy Land bringing a palm branch as a token. 2. pilgrim. *n. 8.*

pal met to (pal met′ō), a kind of palm with fan-shaped leaves, abundant on the southeastern coast of the United States. *n., pl. palmettos* or *palmettoes. 20.*

Palm Sunday, the Sunday before Easter Sunday.

palm y (päm′i), 1. abounding in palms; shaded by palms. 2. flourishing; prosperous; glorious. *adj., palmier, palmiest. 11.*

pal pa ble (pal′pə bəl), 1. readily seen or heard and recognized; obvious; as, a palpable error. 2. that can be touched or felt. *adj. 11.*

pal pa bly (pal′pə bli), 1. plainly; obviously. 2. to the touch. *adv.*

pal pi tate (pal′pi tāt), 1. beat very rapidly. Your heart palpitates when you are excited. 2. quiver; tremble. His body palpitated with terror. *v. 18.*

pal pi ta tion (pal′pi tā′shən), 1. very rapid beating of the heart. 2. quivering; trembling. *n. 17.*

pal sied (pôl′zid), 1. having the palsy; paralyzed. 2. shaking; trembling. *adj.*

pal sy (pôl′zi), 1. paralysis; loss of power to feel, to move, or to control motion in any part of the body. The man had palsy in his arm. 2. paralyze; afflict with palsy. *n., pl. palsies, v., palsied, palsying. 9.*

pal ter (pôl′tər), 1. talk or act insincerely; trifle deceitfully. Do not palter with the truth. 2. trifle; act carelessly. No one should palter with a decision involving life and death. 3. deal crookedly; use tricks and dodges in bargaining. *v. 16.*

pal tri ness (pôl′tri nis), meanness; very slight value. *n.*

pal try (pôl′tri), trifling; almost worthless; petty; mean. *adj., paltrier, paltriest. 9.*

pam pas (pam′pəz), the vast treeless plains of South America, especially in Argentina. *n. pl. 17.*

pam per (pam′pər), indulge too much; allow too many privileges; as, to pamper a child or a sick person, to pamper one's appetite. *v. 10.*

pam phlet (pam′flit), a booklet in paper covers. *n. 8.*

pam phlet eer (pam′flit ēr′), writer of pamphlets. *n. 18.*

pan[1] (pan), 1. a dish for cooking and other household uses, usually broad, shallow, and with no cover. 2. anything like this. Gold and other metals are sometimes obtained by washing ore in pans. The dishes on a pair of scales are called pans. 3. wash (gravel) in a pan to separate the gold. 4. cook in a pan. 5. **Pan out** means turn out or work out. His scheme panned out well. 6. in old-fashioned guns, the hollow part of the lock that held a little gunpowder to set the gun off. *n., v., panned, panning. 2.*

Pan[2] (pan), the Greek god of forests, pastures, flocks, and shepherds. Pan had legs like a goat and played on musical pipes. *n.*

pan a ce a (pan′ə sē′ə), cure-all; remedy for all diseases or ills. *n. 17.*

Pan a ma (pan′ə mä), 1. the isthmus or narrow neck of land which connects North and South America. 2. The **Panama Canal** is a canal cut across the Isthmus of Panama to connect the Atlantic and Pacific oceans. It was built and is owned by the United States. 3. a country in Central America, on either side of the Panama Canal. 4. the capital of Panama. *n., adj. 4.*

pan a ma (pan′ə mä), a fine hat plaited from the young leaves of a palmlike plant of Central and South America. *n.*

Pan-A mer i can (pan′ə mer′i kən), of all the people or countries of North and South America. *adj.*

pan cake (pan′kāk′), a thin, flat cake made of batter and fried in a pan or on a griddle. *n. 6.*

pan cre as (pan′kri əs), a gland near the stomach that helps digestion. See the diagram under **intestine**. The pancreas of animals when used for food is called the sweetbread. *n. 10.*

pan cre at ic (pan′kri at′ik), of the pancreas. The pancreatic juice aids digestion. *adj. 14.*

pan da (pan′də), 1. giant panda; bearlike mammal of Tibet, mostly white with black legs. 2. reddish-brown mammal somewhat like a raccoon, that lives in the Himalayas. *n.*

Giant panda (about 6 ft. long)

pan de mo ni um (pan′di mō′ni əm), 1. the abode of all the demons. 2. place of wild disorder or lawless confusion. 3. wild uproar or lawlessness. *n.*

pan der (pan′dər), 1. person who helps other people indulge base passions. 2. to act as a pander; supply material or opportunity for vices. Some newspapers pander to people's liking for sensational stories. *n., v. 16.*

Pan do ra (pan dō′rə), a beautiful woman who opened a box and let out all sorts of ills on mankind. Only Hope remained in the bottom. *n. 12.*

pane (pān), single sheet of glass in a division of a window, a door, or a sash. Hailstones as big as eggs broke several panes of glass. *n. 4.*

pan e gyr ic (pan′i jir′ik), 1. speech or writing in praise of a person or thing. 2. enthusiastic or extravagant praise. *n. 10.*

pan el (pan′əl), 1. a strip or surface that is different in some way from what is around it. A panel is often sunk below or raised above the rest, and used for a decoration. Panels may be in a door or other woodwork, on large pieces of furniture, or made as parts of a dress. 2. arrange in panels; furnish or decorate with panels. 3. a picture, photograph, or design much longer than wide. 4. a list of persons called as jurors; the members of a jury. *n., v., paneled, paneling. 8.*

Panels

pang (pang), a sudden, short, sharp pain or feeling; as, the pangs of a toothache, a pang of pity. *n. 4.*

pan ic (pan′ik), 1. unreasoning fear; a fear spreading through a multitude of people so that they lose control of themselves. When the theater caught fire, there was a panic. When four banks failed in one day, there was a panic among businessmen. 2. caused by panic; showing panic; unreasoning; as, panic terror, panic fear. *n., adj. 7.*

pan ick y (pan′ik i), 1. caused by panic. 2. showing panic. 3. like panic. 4. liable to lose self-control and have a panic. *adj.*

pan ic-strick en (pan′ik strik′ən), frightened out of one's wits; demoralized by fear. *adj.*

Panniers

pan ni er (pan′i ər), a basket, especially one of a pair of considerable size to be slung across the shoulders, or across the back of a beast of burden. *n. 15.*

pan o plied (pan′ə plid), completely armed, equipped, covered, or arrayed. *adj.*

pan o ply (pan′ə pli), 1. a complete suit of armor. 2. complete equipment or covering; as, an Indian in panoply of war paint and feathers. *n., pl. panoplies. 13.*

pan o ram a (pan′ə ram′ə), 1. a picture of a landscape or other scene often shown as if seen from a central point; a picture unrolled a part at a time and made to pass continuously before the spectators. 2. a continuously passing or changing scene; as, the panorama of city life. 3. a wide, unbroken view of a surrounding region; as, a panorama of beach and sea. 4. complete survey of some subject. *n. 12.*

pan sy (pan′zi), a flower somewhat like a violet but much larger and often having several colors. *n., pl. pansies. 5.*

pant (pant), 1. breathe hard and quickly. 2. a short, quick breath. 3. speak with short, quick breaths. 4. long eagerly. I am just panting for my turn. *v., n. 3.*

pan ta lets or **pan ta lettes** (pan′tə lets′), long drawers extending to the ankles, formerly worn by women and girls. *n. pl.*

Pantalets

pan ta loon (pan′tə lün′), 1. clown. 2. **Pantaloons** are trousers. *n. 9.*

pan the ism (pan′thē izm), the belief that the universe is God. *n.*

Pan the on (pan′thi on), a temple for all the gods, built at Rome about 27 B.C., now used as a Christian church. *n. 15.*

pan ther (pan′thər), 1. a puma or mountain lion. 2. a leopard. 3. the jaguar. *n. 10.*

Panther (about 5 ft. long, without the tail)

pan to mime (pan′tə mīm), 1. a play without words in which the actors express themselves by gestures. 2. gestures without words. *n. 13.*

pan try (pan′tri), small room in which food, dishes, silver, or table linen is kept. *n., pl. pantries. 5.*

pants (pants), trousers. *n.pl.* [*In common talk*]

pap (pap), soft food for infants or invalids. *n. 15.*

pa pa (pä′pə), father; daddy. *n. 3.*

pa pa cy (pā′pə si), 1. the position, rank, or authority of the Pope. 2. popes. 3. government by a pope. *n., pl. papacies. 15.*

pa pal (pā′pəl), 1. of the Pope; as, a papal letter. 2. of the Roman Catholic Church; as, papal ritual. *adj. 9.*

pa paw (pô′pô), 1. small North American tree bearing oblong fruit with many beanlike seeds. 2. this fruit. *n.*

pa per (pā′pər), 1. a material used for writing, printing, drawing, wrapping packages, and covering walls. This book is made of paper. Paper is made in thin sheets from wood pulp, rags, etc. 2. piece or sheet of paper. 3. document. Important papers were stolen. 4. a newspaper. 5. an article; an essay. Professor Wise read a paper on how to teach English. 6. written promise to pay money; note. 7. made of paper; as, paper dolls, paper money. 8. thin; as, almonds with paper shells. 9. existing only on paper. When he tried to sell, his paper profits disappeared. 10. wallpaper. 11. to cover with paper. *n., adj., v. 1.*

pa pil la (pə pil′ə), small nipplelike projection; as, the papillae on the tongue. *n., pl. papillae (-ē). 14.*

pa pist (pā′pist), a Roman Catholic. *n.* [*Used in an unfriendly sense*] *14.*

Papoose on its mother's back

pa poose or **pap poose** (pa püs′), a North American Indian baby. *n. 18.*

pap ri ka (pap rē′kə or pap′ri kə), a kind of red pepper not so strong as the ordinary kind. *n. 17.*

Pap u a (pap′ū ə), a large island north of Australia. *n.* Also called **New Guinea.**

pa py rus (pə pī′rəs), 1. tall water plant

from which the ancient Egyptians, Greeks, and Romans made a kind of paper to write on. 2. writing material made from the pith of the papyrus plants. 3. an ancient record written on papyrus. *n., pl. papyri* (-rī). *17.*

par (pär), 1. equality; an equal level. The gains and losses are about on a par. He is quite on a par with his brother in intelligence. 2. an average or normal amount, degree, or condition. Tom has been feeling below par lately. 3. average; normal. 4. the value of a bond, a note, a share of stock, etc., that is printed on it; face value. That stock is selling above par. 5. a score in golf made by perfect playing. *n., adj. 17.*

par a ble (par′ə bəl), a short story used to teach some truth or moral lesson. Jesus taught in parables. *n. 9.*

pa rab o la (pə rab′ə lə), a plane curve formed by the intersection of a cone with a plane parallel to a side of the cone. *n. 15.*

Parabola

par a chute (par′ə shüt), an umbrellalike apparatus used in descending safely through the air from a great height. *n. 12.*

Man descending with parachute

pa rade (pə rād′), 1. a procession; a march for display. The circus had a parade. 2. to march in procession; to walk proudly as if in a parade. 3. group of people walking for display or pleasure. 4. place where people walk for pleasure. 5. great show or display. A modest man will not make a parade of his wealth. 6. make a great show of. 7. a military display or review of troops. 8. come together in military order for review or inspection. 9. the place used for the regular parade of troops. *n., v. 5.*

par a dise (par′ə dīs), 1. heaven. 2. place or condition of great happiness. 3. the garden of Eden. *n. 3.*

par a dox (par′ə doks), 1. a statement that may be true but seems to say two opposite things. "More haste, less speed" and "The child is father to the man" are paradoxes. 2. a statement that is false because it says two opposite things. *n. 12.*

par a dox i cal (par′ə dok′si kəl), 1. of paradoxes; involving a paradox. 2. having the habit of using paradoxes. *adj. 15.*

par af fin (par′ə fin), white tasteless substance like wax, used for making candles and for sealing jars. *n. 10.*

par a gon (par′ə gon), model of excellence or perfection. *n. 10.*

par a graph (par′ə graf), 1. group of sentences which belong together; a distinct part of a chapter, letter, or composition. 2. to divide into paragraphs. 3. a separate note or item of news in a newspaper. 4. to write paragraphs about. *n., v. 6.*

Par a guay (par′ə gwā), 1. a country in South America, between Brazil and Argentina. 2. a river in South America. *n.*

par a keet (par′ə kēt), any of various small parrots, most of which have slender bodies and long tails. *n.*

par al lax (par′ə laks), the change or amount of change in the direction in which a star or other heavenly body is seen, caused by a change in the position of the observer. Seen from A, star S is in direction AS. Seen from B, it is in direction BS. The parallax is the difference between these two directions, or the angle ASB. *n. 17.*

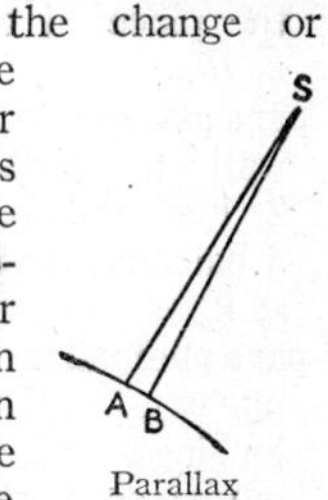

Parallax

par al lel (par′ə lel), 1. at or being the same distance apart everywhere, like the two rails of a railroad track. 2. be at the same distance from. The street parallels the railroad. 3. a parallel line or surface. 4. The parallel circles around the earth, marking degrees of latitude, are called parallels. 5. a comparison to show likeness; as, to draw a parallel between this winter and last winter. 6. compare in order to show likeness. 7. find a case which is similar or parallel to. Can you parallel that for friendliness? 8. **Parallel cases** or **happenings** are similar or corresponding ones. *adj., v., paralleled, paralleling, n. 4.*

Three sets of parallel lines

par al lel ism (par′ə lel izm), 1. being parallel. 2. likeness; correspondence; agreement. *n. 16.*

par al lel o gram (par′ə lel′ə-gram), a four-sided figure whose opposite sides are parallel. *n. 16.*

Parallelograms

pa ral y sis (pə ral′i sis), 1. a lessening or loss of the power of motion or sensation in any part of the body. 2. crippling; condition of powerlessness or helpless inactivity. The war caused a paralysis of trade. *n., pl. paralyses* (-sēz). *11.*

par a lyt ic (par′ə lit′ik), 1. of paralysis; having paralysis. 2. person who has paralysis. *adj., n. 16.*

par a lyze or **par a lyse** (par′ə līz), 1. affect with a lessening or loss of the power of motion or feeling. His left arm was paralyzed. 2. cripple; make powerless or helplessly inactive. Fear paralyzed my mind. *v. 8.*

par a mount (par′ə mount), above others; chief in importance; supreme. Truth is of paramount importance. *adj. 10.*

par a mour (par′ə mür), person who takes the place of a husband or wife illegally. *n. 10.*

par a pet (par′ə pet), 1. low wall to protect soldiers. 2. low wall at the edge of a balcony, roof, bridge, etc. *n. 9.*

Parapet of a fort

par a pher nal ia (par′ə fər nāl′yə), 1. personal belongings. 2. equipment; outfit; as, camp paraphernalia, military paraphernalia. *n. pl. 19.*

par a phrase (par′ə frāz), 1. state the meaning of (a passage) in other words. 2. an expression of the meaning of a passage in other words. *v., n. 16.*

par a site (par′ə sīt), 1. an animal or plant that lives on another. Lice and tapeworms are parasites. Mistletoe is a parasite on oak trees. 2. person who lives on others without making any useful and fitting return; a hanger-on. Beggars and tramps are parasites. *n. 7.*

par a sit ic (par′ə sit′ik), of or like a parasite; living on others. *adj. 11.*

par a sol (par′ə sôl), a light umbrella used as a protection from the sun. *n. 16.*

par boil (pär′boil′), boil till partly cooked. People sometimes parboil beans before baking them. *v.*

par cel (pär′səl), 1. a bundle of things wrapped or packed together; a box with things packed in it. 2. piece; as, a parcel of land. 3. **Parcel out** means divide into or distribute in portions. *n., v., parceled, parceling. 3.*

parcel post, branch of the postal service which carries parcels.

parch (pärch), 1. dry by heating; roast slightly; as, parched corn. 2. make or become hot and dry or thirsty. I am parched with the heat. *v. 6.*

parch ment (pärch′mənt), 1. the skin of sheep or goats, prepared for use as a writing material. 2. manuscript or document written on parchment. 3. paper that looks like parchment. *n. 7.*

pard (pärd), leopard. *n. [Old use] 16.*

par don (pär′dən), 1. forgiveness. **I beg your pardon** means please excuse me. 2. forgive. 3. excuse. 4. set free from punishment. The governor pardoned the thief. 5. setting free from punishment. *n., v. 2.*

par don a ble (pär′dən ə bəl), that can be pardoned; excusable. *adj. 18.*

par don er (pär′dən ər), person who pardons. *n. 17.*

pare (pãr), 1. cut, trim, or shave off the outer part of; peel; as, to pare an apple. 2. cut away little by little; as, to pare down expenses. *v. 6.*

par ent (pãr′ənt), 1. father or mother. 2. source; cause. *n. 2.*

par ent age (pãr′ən tij), descent from parents; family line; ancestry. *n. 9.*

pa ren tal (pə ren′təl), of or having to do with a parent. *adj. 14.*

pa ren the sis (pə ren′thi sis), 1. a word, phrase, sentence, etc., inserted within a sentence, to explain or qualify something. 2. either or both of two curved lines ( ) used to set off such an expression. *n., pl. parentheses* (-sēz). *20.*

par en thet ic (par′ən thet′ik), 1. qualifying; explanatory. 2. put in parentheses. 3. using parentheses. *adj.*

par en thet i cal (par′ən thet′i kəl), parenthetic. *adj.*

pa ri ah (pə rī′ə), outcast. *n. 19.*

par ing (pãr′ing), the part pared off; skin; rind; as, apple parings. *n.*

Par is (par′is), 1. a large city on the Seine River, the capital of France until 1940. 2. son of Priam, king of Troy. The kidnaping of Helen by Paris was the cause of the Trojan War. *n. 3.*

par ish (par′ish), 1. a district that has its own church and clergyman. 2. people of a parish. 3. county in Louisiana. *n. 6.*

pa rish ion er (pə rish′ən ər), member of a parish. *n. 15.*

Pa ri sian (pə rizh′ən), 1. of Paris or its people. 2. person born in Paris, living in Paris, or born of a family that lives in Paris. *adj., n. 9.*

par i ty (par′i ti), equality. *n. 20.*

park (pärk), 1. land set apart for the

pleasure of the public. Chicago has many beautiful parks. 2. land set apart for wild animals. 3. grounds around a fine house. 4. leave (an automobile, etc.) for a time in a certain place. Park your car here. 5. place to leave an automobile, etc., for a time. 6. space where army wagons and mules, supplies, and big guns are put when an army camps. 7. arrange (army wagons, guns, etc.) in a park. *n., v. 2.*

par lance (pär′ləns), talk; language; way of speaking. *n. 16.*

par ley (pär′li), 1. a conference or informal talk to discuss terms or matters in dispute. The general held a parley with the enemy about exchanging prisoners. 2. discuss terms with an enemy. *n., pl. parleys, v., parleyed, parleying. 10.*

par lia ment (pär′li mənt), a council or congress that is the highest lawmaking body of a country. The British Parliament consists of the House of Lords and the House of Commons. *n. 4.*

par lia men ta ry (pär′li men′tə ri), 1. of a parliament. 2. done by a parliament. 3. according to the rules and customs of a parliament. *adj. 12.*

par lor (pär′lər), 1. room for receiving or entertaining guests; sitting room. 2. a decorated room used as a shop; a shop; as, a beauty parlor. *n. 3.*

parlor car, railroad passenger car for day travel, more luxurious than ordinary cars.

par lous (pär′ləs), 1. perilous. 2. very clever; shrewd. 3. extremely. *adj., adv.* [*Old use*] *20.*

Par nas sus (pär nas′əs), a mountain in Greece sacred to Apollo and the Muses. *n.*

pa ro chi al (pə rō′ki əl), 1. of or in a parish; as, parochial calls, a parochial school. 2. narrow; limited. His viewpoint was too parochial. *adj. 15.*

par o dy (par′ə di), 1. a humorous imitation of a serious writing. A parody follows the form of the original, but changes its sense to nonsense, thus making fun of the writer's characteristics. 2. make fun of by imitating; make a parody on. *n., pl. parodies, v., parodied, parodying. 16.*

pa role (pə rōl′), 1. word of honor. The prisoner of war gave his parole not to try to escape. 2. put on parole. The judge paroled the boys on condition that they report to him every three months. *n., v. 19.*

par ox ysm (par′ək sizm), 1. a severe, sudden attack; as, a paroxysm of coughing. 2. fit; convulsion; as, a paroxysm of rage. *n. 16.*

par quet (pär kā′), inlaid wooden flooring. *n.*

par ra keet (par′ə kēt), parakeet. *n.*

par ri cide (par′i sīd), 1. the crime of killing one's parent. 2. person who kills his parent. *n. 14.*

Parquet

par rot (par′ət), 1. bird with a stout hooked bill and often with bright-colored feathers. Some parrots can imitate sounds and repeat words and sentences. 2. person who repeats words or acts without understanding them. 3. repeat without understanding. *n., v. 5.*

Gray parrot (about 1 ft. tall)

par ry (par′i), 1. ward off; turn aside; evade (a thrust, stroke, weapon, question, etc.). 2. act of parrying; avoiding. *v., parried, parrying, n., pl. parries. 17.*

parse (pärs), 1. tell the part of speech of a word, its form, and its use in a sentence. 2. analyze (a sentence). *v.*

Par see or **Par si** (pär′sē), member of a sect of fire worshipers in India, descended from the Persians who settled there in the eighth century A.D. *n. 20.*

par si mo ni ous (pär′si mō′ni əs), too economical; stingy. *adj. 16.*

par si mo ny (pär′si mō′ni), extreme economy; stinginess. *n. 15.*

Parsley

pars ley (pärs′li), a garden plant with finely divided fragrant leaves. Parsley is used to flavor food and to trim platters of meat. *n. 10.*

pars nip (pärs′nip), 1. vegetable that is the long, tapering whitish root of a plant belonging to the same family as the carrot. 2. the plant. *n. 10.*

Parsnip

par son (pär′sən), 1. a minister in charge of a parish. 2. any clergyman; minister. *n. 4.*

par son age (pär′sən ij), the house provided for a minister by a church. *n. 14.*

part (pärt), 1. something less than the whole; fraction. Jack ate part of an apple. A dime is a tenth part of a dollar. 2. thing that helps to make up a whole. A radio has many parts. 3. share. Tom had no part in the mischief. 4. side in a dispute or contest. John always takes his brother's part. 5. character in a play; the words spoken by a character. Jane spoke the part of the fairy in our play. 6. divide into two or more pieces. 7. force apart; divide. The policeman on horseback parted the crowd. 8. go apart; separate. The friends parted in anger. 9. ability; talent. Mr. Bright is a man of parts. 10. one of the voices or instruments in music. The four parts in singing are soprano, alto, tenor, and bass. 11. the music for it. 12. region; district; place. He has traveled much in foreign parts. 13. a dividing line left in combing one's hair. 14. less than the whole; as, part time. 15. partly; in some measure or degree. 16. **Part with** means give up. 17. **Part of speech** means one of the divisions or groups of words, such as noun, verb, or adjective. *n., v., adj., adv. 1.*

par take (pär tāk′), take a share; eat or drink some. Will you partake of our breakfast with us? *v., partook, partaken, partaking. 5.*

par tak er (pär tāk′ər), one who takes some; one who shares. *n. 10.*

Par the non (pär′thi non), the temple of Athena on the Acropolis in Athens, regarded as the finest example of Doric architecture. *n. 14.*

Parthenon

par tial (pär′shəl), 1. not complete; not total; as, a partial loss. 2. inclined to favor one side more than another; favoring unfairly. Our teacher sometimes seems partial to the girls. 3. having a liking for; favorably inclined. She is partial to tomatoes. *adj. 5.*

par ti al i ty (pär′shi al′i ti), 1. the favoring of one more than another or others; favorable prejudice; being partial. 2. a particular liking; fondness; as, a partiality for chocolate cake. *n., pl. partialities. 14.*

par tial ly (pär′shəl i), partly. *adv. 14.*

par tic i pant (pär tis′i pənt), one who shares or participates. *n. 16.*

par tic i pate (pär tis′i pāt), have a share; take part. The teacher participated in the children's games. *v. 7.*

par tic i pa tion (pär tis′i pā′shən), participating; taking part. *n. 9.*

par ti cip i al (pär′ti sip′i əl), of or having to do with a participle; as, a participial adjective (a *masked* man, a *becoming* dress), or a participial noun (in *cutting* ice, the fatigue of *marching*). *adj.*

par ti ci ple (pär′ti si pəl), a form of a verb that is much like an adjective in its use. A participle retains all the attributes of a verb, such as tense, voice, power to take an object, and modification by adverbs. *Examples:* the girl *writing* sentences at the blackboard, the man *waiting* for a train, the silver *stolen* recently, John *having missed* the boat. In these phrases, *writing* and *waiting* are present participles; *stolen* and *having missed* are past participles. *n. 15.*

par ti cle (pär′ti kəl), 1. a very little bit. I got a particle of dust in my eye. 2. a prefix, a suffix, a preposition, a conjunction, an article, or an interjection. *Un-*, *-ment, in, if, an,* and *ah* are particles. *n. 6.*

par ti-col ored (pär′ti kul′ərd), colored differently in different parts. *adj.*

par tic u lar (pər tik′ū lər), 1. belonging to some one person, thing, group, occasion, etc. Jack's particular task is to care for the dog. A particular characteristic of a skunk is his smell. 2. apart from others; single; considered separately. That particular chair is already sold. 3. different from others; unusual. This vacation was of particular importance to Mary, for she was going to Brazil. Harry is a particular friend of Dick. 4. hard to please; wanting everything to be just right; very careful. Mrs. Brown is so particular about her housework that servants will not work for her. 5. an individual part; item; point. The work is complete in every particular. All the particulars of the accident are now known. 6. **In particular** means especially. We played around, going nowhere in particular. *adj., n. 2.*

par tic u lar i ty (pər tik′ū lar′i ti), 1. detailed quality; minuteness. 2. attentiveness to details. 3. being hard to please or easily disgusted. 4. special carefulness. 5. a particular feature or trait. 6. the fact of being particular. *n., pl. particularities. 17.*

par tic u lar ize (pər tik′ū lər īz), 1. mention particularly; treat in detail. 2. mention individually; state or discuss in detail. *v. 17.*

par tic u lar ly (pər tik′ū lər li), 1. in a high degree; especially. She mentioned that point particularly. 2. in a particular manner; in detail; minutely. *adv.*

part ing (pär′ting), 1. departure; going away; taking leave; separation. 2. given, taken, done, etc., at parting; as, a parting request, a parting shot. 3. departing. 4. place of division or separation. *n., adj. 6.*

par ti san or **par ti zan** (pär′ti zən), 1. strong supporter of a person, party, or cause; one whose support is based on feeling rather than on reasoning. 2. of or like a partisan. *n., adj. 8.*

par ti san ship or **par ti zan ship** (pär′ti zən-ship′), 1. strong loyalty to a party or cause. 2. taking sides. *n.*

par ti tion (pär tish′ən), 1. division into parts; as, the partition of a man's wealth when he dies. 2. divide into parts; as, to partition an empire among three brothers, to partition a house into rooms. 3. a wall between rooms. *n., v. 7.*

part ly (pärt′li), in part; in some measure or degree. *adv. 2.*

part ner (pärt′nər), 1. one who shares. My sister was the partner of my walks. 2. member of a company or firm, sharing the risks and profits of the business. 3. wife or husband. 4. companion in a dance. 5. player on the same side in a game. *n. 3.*

part ner ship (pärt′nər ship), being a partner; association; joint interest; as, a business partnership, the partnership of marriage. *n. 9.*

par took (pär tu̇k′). See **partake.** He partook of food and drink. *pt. of partake. 17.*

par tridge (pär′trij), 1. any of several kinds of game birds belonging to the same group as the quail, pheasant, and grouse. 2. in the United States, the ruffed grouse or the quail. *n., pl. partridges* or *partridge. 6.*

Common gray partridge of Europe (1 ft. from beak to tip of tail)

par ty (pär′ti), 1. group of people doing something together; as, a sewing party, a dinner party, a scouting party of three soldiers. Jean had a party on her birthday. 2. group of people thinking alike and wanting the same kind of government or action; as, the Democratic party. 3. of or pertaining to a party; as, party feeling. 4. one who takes part in, aids, or knows about. He was a party to our plot. 5. each of the persons or sides in a contract, lawsuit, etc. 6. person. *Used in common talk. n., pl. parties, adj. 1.*

par ve nu (pär′və nū or pär′və nü), 1. person who has risen above his class. 2. one who has risen to a higher place than he is fit for; upstart. *n. 20.*

Pas a de na (pas′ə dē′nə), a city in California, near Los Angeles. *n.*

pa sha (pə shä′), a Turkish title of rank; a civil or military official of high rank in Turkey. *n. 17.*

pass (pas), 1. go by; move past. The parade passed. Many people pass our house every day. 2. move on. The days pass quickly. 3. come to an end; die. King Arthur passed in peace. 4. take place; happen. Mrs. Brown can tell you all that has passed. **Bring to pass** means accomplish. 5. get through or by. The ship passed the channel. Tom passed the examination. The bill passed Congress. 6. go from person to person. Property passes from father to son. Hot words pass when men quarrel. 7. hand around; hand from one to another. Please pass the butter. Dick passed the football quickly. 8. change. Water passes from a liquid to a solid state when it freezes. 9. give a judgment or opinion. Please pass upon this question. A judge passes sentence upon a guilty person. 10. promise; as, to pass one's word. 11. go without notice. Bill was rude, but let that pass. 12. be taken. Ann could pass for twenty. Mr. Crook moved to another city where he passed by the name of Smith. 13. use or spend; as, to pass the days pleasantly. 14. go beyond. Your story passes belief. 15. move. Pass your hand over the velvet and feel how soft it is. 16. in cardplaying, to give up a chance or to refuse to play a hand. 17. in fencing, to thrust. 18. a thrust in fencing. 19. narrow road; path. A pass crosses the mountains. 20. written permission; as, a pass to visit the battle front. 21. a free ticket. 22. state; condition. Things have come to a strange pass when children give orders to their parents. 23. motion of the hands. The magician made passes in the air while doing his tricks. 24. be successful in (an examination). 25. act of passing; success in an examination. *v., passed, passed* or *past, passing, n. 1.*

pass a ble (pas′ə bəl), 1. that can be passed; as, a passable road, river, etc. 2. fairly good; moderate; as, a passable knowledge of geography. *adj. 16.*

pas sage (pas′ij), 1. a hall or way through a building; passageway. 2. a means of passing; a way through; as, to ask for passage through a crowd. 3. passing; as, the passage of time. 4. piece from a speech or writing; as, a passage from the Bible. 5. going across; voyage. We had a stormy passage across the Atlantic. 6. making into law by a favoring vote of a legislature; as, the passage of a bill. 7. what passes between persons. 8. an exchange of blows; as, a passage of arms. *n. 3.*

pas sage way (pas′ij wā′), a way along which one can pass; passage. Halls and alleys are passageways. *n. 19.*

pas sé (pa sā′), past; past its usefulness; out of date. *adj.*

pas sen ger (pas′ən jər), traveler in a train, bus, boat, etc., usually one that pays a fare. *n. 3.*

pass er (pas′ər), person who passes. *n. 18.*

pass er-by (pas′ər bī′), one that passes by. *n., pl. passers-by. 18.*

pass ing (pas′ing), 1. going by. 2. done or given in passing. 3. allowing one to pass an examination or test. 75 will be a passing mark. 4. surpassingly; very. *Old use. n., adj., adv.*

pas sion (pash′ən), 1. very strong feeling. Hate and fear are passions. 2. rage; violent anger. He flew into a passion. 3. love between man and woman. 4. very strong liking. She has a passion for music. 5. object of a passion. Music is her passion. 6. suffering. *Old use.* **The Passion** means the sufferings of Jesus on the cross or after the Last Supper. *n. 3.*

pas sion ate (pash′ən it), 1. having or showing strong feelings. A tiger is a passionate animal. 2. easily moved by strong feelings. 3. resulting from strong feeling. He made a passionate speech. *adj. 6.*

Passion Play or **passion play,** a play representing the sufferings and death of Christ.

pas sive (pas′iv), 1. not acting in return; being acted on without itself acting; as, a passive mind or disposition. 2. not resisting; yielding or submitting to the will of another. The slaves gave passive obedience to their master. 3. in grammar, showing the subject as acted on; a verb form that does this. In "The window was broken by John," *was broken* is in the passive voice. *adj., n. 8.*

pass key (pas′kē′), 1. a key for opening several locks. 2. a private key. *n.*

Pass o ver (pas′ō′vər), an annual feast of the Jews in memory of the sparing of the Hebrews in Egypt, when God killed the first-born children of the Egyptians. *n. 12.*

pass port (pas′pōrt), 1. a paper or book giving one official permission to travel in a foreign country, under the protection of one's own government. 2. anything that gives one admission or acceptance. An interest in gardening was a passport to my aunt's favor. *n. 10.*

pass word (pas′wėrd′), secret word that allows a person who says it to pass a guard. *n. 17.*

past (past), 1. passed. Summer is past. The past year was full of trouble. For some time past I have known that. 2. past time; what has happened in past time; one's past life. We cannot change the past. 3. the verb form that expresses occurrence in past time. The past tense of *do* is *did.* 4. beyond; as, half past two, a boy past twelve, to run past the house, hurt past bearing. 5. passing by; by. The cars go past once an hour. *pp. of* **pass,** *adj., n., prep., adv. 1.*

paste (pāst), 1. a mixture of flour and water, usually boiled, that will stick paper together. 2. to stick with paste. 3. a soft mixture. Pottery is made from a paste of clay and water. 4. pie dough. 5. a hard glassy material used in making imitations of precious stones. *n., v. 5.*

paste board (pāst′bōrd′), a stiff material made of sheets of paper pasted together or of paper pulp pressed and dried. *n.*

pas tel (pas tel′), 1. a kind of crayon used in drawing. 2. a drawing made with such crayons. 3. soft and pale; as, pastel pink, pastel shades. *n., adj. 20.*

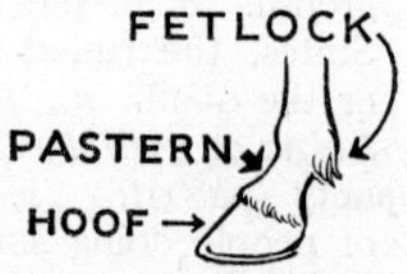

pas tern (pas′tərn), the part of a horse's foot between the fetlock and the hoof. *n. 16.*

FETLOCK
PASTERN
HOOF

Pas teur (päs tėr′), Louis, a French chemist who invented a way of preventing hydrophobia and of keeping milk from spoiling (1822-1895). *n. 12.*

pas teur ize (pas′tər īz), heat hot enough and long enough to kill certain germs. The milk sold in many cities is pasteurized. *v. 14.*

pas time (pas′tīm′), pleasant way of passing time. Games and sports are pastimes. *n. 4.*

pas tor (pas′tər), minister in charge of a church; spiritual guide. *n. 5.*

pas tor al (pas′tər əl), 1. of shepherds or country life. 2. a pastoral play, poem, or picture. 3. simple or naturally beautiful like the country. 4. of a pastor or his duties. *adj., n. 7.*

past participle, participle that indicates time gone by, or a former action or state. *Played* and *thrown* are past participles in "She has played all day." "The ball should have been thrown to me."

pas try (pās′tri), 1. food made of baked flour paste, made rich with lard or butter. 2. pies, tarts, and other foods wholly or partly made of rich flour paste. *n., pl. pastries. 8.*

past tense, 1. tense expressing time gone by, or a former action or state. 2. verb form in the past tense.

pas tur age (pas′chər ij), 1. growing grass and other plants for cattle, sheep, or horses to feed on. 2. pasture land. 3. pasturing. *n. 12.*

pas ture (pas′chər), 1. grassy field or hillside; grasslands on which cattle, sheep, or horses can feed. 2. grass and other growing plants. These lands afford good pasture. 3. put (cattle, sheep, etc.) out to pasture. 4. feed on growing grass, etc. *n., v. 2.*

past y[1] (pās′ti), 1. like paste. 2. pale. 3. flabby. *adj., pastier, pastiest. 20.*

pas ty[2] (pas′ti), a pie filled with game, fish, etc.; as, a venison pasty. *n., pl. pasties.*

pat (pat), 1. strike or tap lightly with something flat. He patted the dog with his hand. 2. to tap with the hand as a sign of sympathy, approval, or affection; as, to pat a dog. 3. a light stroke or tap with something flat. 4. the sound made by patting. 5. a small mass, especially of butter. 6. apt; suitable; to the point; as, a pat reply. 7. aptly; exactly; suitably. 8. **Stand pat** means hold to things as they are and refuse to change. *Used in common talk. v., patted, patting, n., adj., adv. 3.*

Pat a go ni a (pat′ə gō′ni ə), region in Argentina and Chile, at the extreme south of South America. *n.*

patch (pach), 1. piece put on to mend a hole or a tear. 2. piece of cloth, etc., put over a wound or a sore. 3. pad over a hurt eye to protect it. 4. a small bit of black cloth that ladies used to wear on their faces to show off their fair skin. 5. put patches on; mend; protect or adorn with a patch or patches. 6. to piece together; make hastily; as, to patch up a costume for a play. 7. make right; as, to patch up a quarrel. 8. a small, uneven spot; as, a patch of brown on the skin. 9. piece of ground; as, a garden patch. 10. a scrap or bit of cloth left over. *n., v. 3.*

patch work (pach′wėrk′), 1. pieces of cloth of various colors or shapes sewed together. She made a cover of patchwork for the cushion. 2. anything like this. From the airship, we saw a patchwork of fields and woods. *n. 11.*

pate (pāt), the head; the top of the head; as, a bald pate. *n. 10.*

pat ent (pat′ənt for 1-5, pā′tənt for 6), 1. a government grant to a person by which he is the only one allowed to make or sell a new invention for a certain number of years. 2. given or protected by a patent. 3. get a patent for. 4. an invention that is patented. 5. an official document from a government giving a right or privilege. 6. open; evident; plain. It is patent that cats dislike dogs. *n., adj., v. 5.*

pat ent ee (pat′ən tē′), person to whom a patent is granted. *n. 16.*

pat ent leath er (pat′ənt leᴛʜ′ər), leather with a very glossy, smooth surface, usually black.

patent medicine, 1. a medicine that is patented. 2. a medicine that some company owns and sells.

pa ter nal (pə tėr′nəl), 1. fatherly; of or like a father. 2. related on the father's side of the family. Everyone has two paternal grandparents and two maternal grandparents. *adj. 7.*

pa ter nal ism (pə tėr′nəl izm), managing the affairs of a country or group of people as a father manages the affairs of his children. *n.*

pa ter ni ty (pə tėr′ni ti), 1. fatherhood; being a father. 2. paternal origin. King Arthur's paternity was unknown. *n. 19.*

pa ter nos ter (pā′tər nos′tər), the Lord's Prayer, especially in Latin. *n.*

Pat er son (pat′ər sən), a city in northeastern New Jersey. *n.*

path (path), 1. a way made by people or animals walking. 2. road too narrow for a wagon or automobile. 3. line along which a person or thing moves; as, the path of the moon through the heavens. 4. way of behaving. *n., pl. paths* (paᴛʜz). *1.*

pa thet ic (pə thet′ik), pitiful; arousing pity. A lost child is pathetic. *adj. 8.*

pa thet i cal ly (pə thet′i kəl i), so as to arouse pity. She was pathetically ignorant and helpless. *adv.*

path less (path′lis), without paths. *adj. 12.*

path o log i cal (path′ə loj′i kəl), 1. of pathology; dealing with diseases or concerned with diseases; as, pathological studies. 2. due to disease or accompanying disease; as, a pathological condition of the blood cells. *adj. 16.*

pa thol o gy (pə thol′ə ji), 1. the science of diseases. 2. unhealthy conditions and processes. *n., pl. pathologies. 17.*

pa thos (pā′thos), the quality in speech, writing, music, events, or a scene that arouses a feeling of pity or sadness. *n. 12.*

path way (path′wā′), path. *n. 16.*

pa tience (pā′shəns), 1. calm bearing of pain, of waiting, or of anything that annoys, troubles, or hurts. A cat shows patience by watching a mousehole. You need patience when you are having your teeth filled. 2. sticking to a piece of work. 3. a card game. *n. 3.*

pa tient (pā′shənt), 1. having patience; showing patience. 2. person who is being treated by a doctor. *adj., n. 2.*

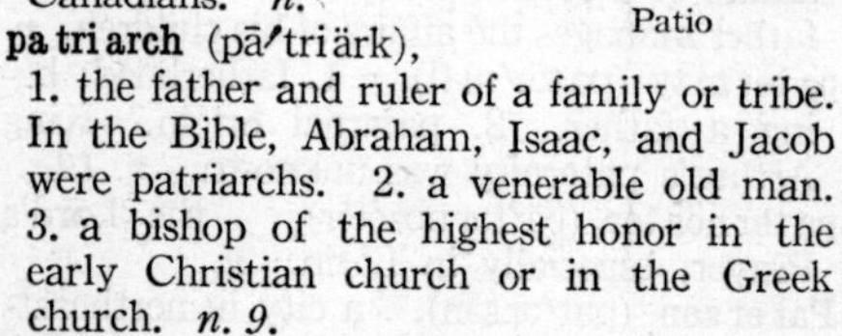
Patio

pa ti o (pä′ti ō), an inner court or yard open to the sky. Houses in Spanish countries are often built around patios. *n., pl. patios.*

pa tois (pa twä′), a dialect spoken by the common people of a district; as, the patois of the French Canadians. *n.*

pa tri arch (pā′tri ärk), 1. the father and ruler of a family or tribe. In the Bible, Abraham, Isaac, and Jacob were patriarchs. 2. a venerable old man. 3. a bishop of the highest honor in the early Christian church or in the Greek church. *n. 9.*

pa tri ar chal (pā′tri är′kəl), 1. suitable to a patriarch; pertaining to a patriarch. 2. under the rule of a patriarch; as, patriarchal life, patriarchal customs, a patriarchal church. *adj. 15.*

pa tri cian (pə trish′ən), 1. member of the nobility of ancient Rome. 2. a noble; aristocrat. 3. aristocratic; of high social rank. 4. suitable for an aristocrat. *n., adj. 14.*

Pat rick (pat′rik). Saint Patrick (389?-461? A.D.) was a British missionary and bishop who converted Ireland to Christianity. He is the patron saint of Ireland. *n. 10.*

pat ri mo ni al (pat′ri mō′ni əl), pertaining to a patrimony; inherited from one's father or ancestors. *adj. 15.*

pat ri mo ny (pat′ri mō′ni), 1. property inherited from one's father or ancestors. 2. property belonging to a church, monastery, or convent. *n., pl. patrimonies. 12.*

pa tri ot (pā′tri ət), person who loves and loyally supports his country. *n. 5.*

pa tri ot ic (pā′tri ot′ik), 1. loving one's country. 2. showing love and loyal support of one's own country. *adj. 6.*

pa tri ot ism (pā′tri ət izm), love and loyal support of one's country. *n. 7.*

pa trol (pə trōl′), 1. go the rounds as a watchman or a policeman does. The camp was carefully patrolled. 2. going the rounds to watch or guard. 3. the men who patrol. The patrol was changed at midnight. 4. group of soldiers, ships, or airplanes, sent out to find out all they can about the enemy. 5. unit of eight boy or girl scouts. *v., patrolled, patrolling, n. 12.*

pa trol man (pə trōl′mən), 1. man who patrols. 2. policeman who patrols a certain district. *n., pl. patrolmen.*

pa tron (pā′trən), 1. person who stands back of the work of another, perhaps helps it with money, and gives it the advantage of his approval and his name. 2. person who buys regularly at a given store. 3. guarding; protecting; as, the patron saint of travelers. *n., adj. 4.*

pa tron age (pā′trən ij), 1. the favor, encouragement, or support given by a patron. 2. regular business given to a store, hotel, etc., by customers. 3. condescending favor; as, an air of patronage. 4. power to give jobs or favors; as, the patronage of a congressman. *n. 8.*

pa tron ess (pā′trən is), 1. female patron. 2. woman who helps some entertainment with her name, money, or presence. *n. 11.*

pa tron ize (pā′trən īz), 1. act as a patron toward; support or protect. People are urged to patronize their neighborhood stores. 2. treat in a condescending way. We dislike to have anybody patronize us. *v. 14.*

pa troon (pə trün′), landowner under the old Dutch governments of New York and New Jersey who had certain privileges. A patroon usually owned a large amount of land. *n. 18.*

pat ter[1] (pat′ər), 1. make rapid taps. The

rain patters on a windowpane. Bare feet pattered along the hard floor. 2. a series of quick taps or the sound they make; as, the patter of rain, the patter of little feet. *v., n. 7.*

pat ter[2] (pat′ər), 1. talk or say rapidly and easily, without much thought. 2. rapid and easy talk. *v., n.*

pat tern (pat′ərn), 1. a fine example; a model to be followed. Washington was a pattern of manliness. Mary used a paper pattern in cutting out her new dress. 2. make according to a pattern. She patterned herself after her mother. 3. a design; arrangement of forms and colors; as, the patterns of wallpaper, rugs, cloth, jewelry, etc. *n., v. 2.*

pat ty (pat′i), a hollow form of pastry filled with chicken, oysters, etc. *n., pl. patties. 10.*

Paul (pôl). Saint Paul was a follower of Jesus' teachings who started Christian groups in many countries. He wrote many of the books of the New Testament. *n. 3.*

paunch (pônch), belly; stomach. *n. 14.*

pau per (pô′pər), very poor person; person supported by charity. *n. 13.*

pau per ism (pô′pər izm), 1. being very poor. 2. paupers. *n. 17.*

pau per ize (pô′pər īz), make a pauper of. *v.*

pause (pôz), 1. stop for a time; wait. He made a short pause and then went on reading. The dog paused when he heard me. 2. in music, a sign (◡ or ◠) above or below a note, meaning that it is to be held for a longer time. *n., v. 3.*

pave (pāv), 1. cover (a street, sidewalk, etc.) with a pavement. 2. prepare; make smooth or easy. He paved the way for me by doing careful work. *v. 4.*

pave ment (pāv′mənt), covering or surface for streets, sidewalks, etc., made of stones, bricks, wood, asphalt, etc. *n. 4.*

pa vil ion (pə vil′yən), 1. a light building, usually one somewhat open, used for shelter, pleasure, etc.; as, a bathing pavilion. 2. tent; a large tent raised on posts. 3. part of a building higher and more decorated than the rest. 4. one of a group of buildings forming a hospital. *n. 6.*

Pavilion for dancing

pav ing (pāv′ing), 1. material for pavement. 2. pavement. *n.*

paw (pô), 1. the foot of an animal having claws; as, a cat's paw, a dog's paw. 2. strike or scrape with the paws or feet. The cat pawed the mouse she had caught. The horse was pawing the ground, eager to be going again. 3. handle awkwardly or roughly. The big man pawed over the baby's clothes helplessly. *Not used in formal writing. n., v. 3.*

pawl (pôl), a short iron bar acting as a catch to prevent a windlass or capstan from turning back; a pivoted bar arranged to catch in the teeth of a ratchet wheel or the like so as to prevent movement backward or to impart motion. *n.*

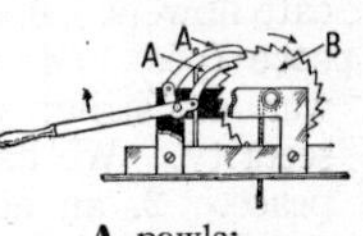

A, pawls;
B, ratchet wheel.

pawn[1] (pôn), 1. leave (something) with another person as security that borrowed money will be returned; pledge. She pawned her watch to buy food. 2. something left as security. 3. **In pawn** means being in another's possession as security. Her watch is in pawn. *v., n. 10.*

pawn[2] (pôn), in chess, one of the 16 pieces of lowest value. *n.*

pawn bro ker (pôn′brō′kər), man who lends money on articles that are left with him as security for the loan. *n. 19.*

pawn shop (pôn′shop′), a pawnbroker's shop. *n.*

paw paw (pô′pô), papaw. *n.*

pay (pā), 1. give money for things or work. 2. give money to or for. A good lawyer is highly paid. His uncle paid John's way through college. 3. money given for things or work. Tom gets his pay every Saturday. 4. give what is due. 5. return for favors or hurts. Kate got her pay for being mean. 6. give; offer; as, to pay attention, to pay a compliment. 7. give a profit; be worth while. It pays to be polite. *v., paid, paying, n. 1.*

pay a ble (pā′ə bəl), 1. due; required to be paid. He must spend $100 soon on bills payable. 2. that may be paid. *adj. 9.*

pay mas ter (pā′mas′tər), person whose job is to pay wages. *n.*

pay ment (pā′mənt), 1. paying. 2. amount paid; as, a monthly payment of $10. 3. pay. Baby's good health is payment enough for me. *n. 3.*

pay roll, 1. a list of persons to be paid and the amounts that each one is to receive. 2. the total amount to be paid to them. *18.*

pd., paid.

pea (pē), 1. a round seed in the pod of a plant, used as a vegetable; the plant itself. 2. The **sweet pea** is a climbing plant with many-colored delicate flowers. *n. 3.*

Pod opened to show peas

peace (pēs), 1. freedom from war or strife; public quiet, order, and security. We had been working for world peace. 2. an agreement to end war; as, the Peace of Paris. 3. quiet; calm; stillness. We enjoy the peace of the country. 4. **Hold one's peace** means keep still. *n. 1.*

peace a ble (pēs′ə bəl), 1. liking peace; keeping peace. 2. peaceful. *adj. 6.*

peace ful (pēs′fəl), 1. quiet; calm; full of peace. 2. liking peace; keeping peace. 3. of or having to do with peace. *adj. 3.*

peace mak er (pēs′māk′ər), person who makes peace. *n. 17.*

peach (pēch), 1. the juicy, nearly round fruit of a tree, having a rough stone or pit in it. 2. the tree it grows on. 3. yellowish pink. *n., adj. 3.*

pea cock (pē′kok′), 1. large bird with beautiful green, blue, and gold feathers, and a splendid tail. The tail feathers have spots like eyes on them and can be spread out and held upright like a fan. 2. strut like a peacock. *n., v. 5.*

Peacock with tail spread out

peak (pēk), 1. the pointed top of a mountain or hill. 2. a mountain that stands alone; as, Pike's Peak. 3. any pointed end or top; as, the peak of a beard, the peak of a roof. 4. the highest point. 5. the front part or the brim of a cap, that stands out. 6. the narrow part of a ship's hold, at either end. *n. 4.*

Mountain peak

peaked[1] (pēkt), pointed; as, a peaked cap. *adj.*

peak ed[2] (pēk′id), thin. *adj.*

peal (pēl), 1. a loud, long sound; as, a peal of thunder. 2. loud ringing of bells. 3. a chime; a set of bells. 4. sound out in a peal; ring. The bells pealed forth their message of Christmas joy. *n., v. 4.*

pea nut (pē′nut′), 1. a seed like a nut used for food. 2. the plant it grows on. *n. 7.*

pear (pãr), 1. a sweet juicy fruit rounded at one end and smaller toward the stem end. 2. the tree it grows on. *n. 3.*

Pear

pearl (pėrl), 1. a white or nearly white gem that has a soft shine like satin. Pearls are found inside the shell of a kind of oyster, or in other similar shellfish. 2. a very fine one of its kind. She is a pearl among women. 3. thing that looks like a pearl, such as a dewdrop, or a tear. 4. very pale, clear, bluish gray. *n., adj. 2.*

pearl y (pėr′li), like a pearl in color or luster; as, pearly teeth. *adj. 9.*

peas ant (pez′ənt), 1. a farmer of the working class in Europe. 2. of peasants; as, peasant labor. *n., adj. 4.*

peas ant ry (pez′ənt ri), peasants. *n. 11.*

pease (pēz), peas. *n. pl.* [*Old use*] *18.*

peat (pēt), a kind of turf, used as fuel after being dried. Peat is made of partly rotted moss and plants. *n. 19.*

peb ble (peb′əl), a small stone, usually worn and rounded by being rolled about by water. *n. 5.*

peb bly (peb′li), having many pebbles; covered with pebbles. *adj. 17.*

pe can (pi kan′), 1. an olive-shaped nut with a smooth shell. 2. the tree it grows on. Pecans grow in the southern United States. *n. 13.*

A B

Pecan: A, branch; B, nuts.

pec ca dil lo (pek′ə dil′ō), a slight sin or fault. *n., pl. peccadilloes* or *peccadillos.*

pec ca ry (pek′ə ri), kind of wild pig found in South America and as far north as Texas. *n., pl. peccaries.*

Peccary (about 3 ft. long)

peck[1] (pek), 1. strike at and pick up with the beak. A hen pecks corn. 2. make by striking with the beak. Woodpeckers peck holes in trees. 3. a hole or mark made by pecking. 4. make a pecking motion. 5. a stroke with the beak. The hen gave me a peck. 6. eat only a little, bit by bit. Because she is not feeling well today, she just pecks at her food. *Used in common talk.* 7. a stiff, unwilling kiss. *v., n. 3.*

peck[2] (pek), 1. a unit of dry measure, eight quarts or one fourth of a bushel; as, a peck of beans, a peck of potatoes. 2. a container holding just a peck, to measure with. 3. great deal; as, a peck of trouble. *n.*

pec to ral (pek′tə rəl), of, in, or on the breast or chest. *adj. 16.*

pec u la tion (pek′ū lā′shən), stealing money or goods intrusted to one. *n. 20.*

pe cul iar (pi kūl′yər), 1. strange; odd; unusual. It is peculiar that he has not come today, for he usually appears every Tuesday. A woman's hat on a man's head looks peculiar. What a peculiar thing to say! 2. special; belonging to one person or thing and not to another. This book has a peculiar value. The Quakers wore a dress peculiar to themselves. *adj. 3.*

pe cu li ar i ty (pi kū′li ar′i ti), 1. being peculiar; strangeness; oddness; unusualness. We noticed the peculiarity of his manner at once. 2. some little thing that is strange or odd. One of his peculiarities is that his two eyes are not the same color. *n., pl. peculiarities. 8.*

pe cu ni ar y (pi kū′ni ãr′i), of or pertaining to money; in the form of money. *adj. 14.*

ped a gogue or **ped a gog** (ped′ə gog), 1. teacher of children. 2. a narrow-minded teacher. *n. 11.*

ped a go gy (ped′ə gō′ji), 1. teaching. 2. the science or art of teaching. *n.*

ped al (ped′əl), 1. a lever worked by the foot; the part on which the foot is placed to move any kind of machinery. Organs and pianos have pedals for changing the tone. The two pedals of a bicycle, pushed down one after the other, make it go. 2. work or use the pedals; move by pedals. He pedaled his bicycle slowly up the hill. 3. of or having to do with the foot or feet. *n., v., pedaled, pedaling, adj. 11.*

ped ant (ped′ənt), one who overrates his book learning or knowledge. A pedant may make a show of knowledge without knowing how to use it well. *n. 14.*

pe dan tic (pi dan′tik), 1. displaying one's knowledge more than is necessary. 2. tediously learned; scholarly in a dull and narrow way. *adj. 15.*

ped ant ry (ped′ənt ri), 1. tiresome display of knowledge. 2. overemphasis on book learning. *n., pl. pedantries. 15.*

ped dle (ped′əl), 1. carry from place to place and sell. 2. sell or deal out in small quantities; as, to peddle candy, to peddle gossip. 3. travel about with things to sell. *v. 19.*

ped dler (ped′lər), man who travels about selling things which he carries in a pack or in a cart. *n. 7.*

ped es tal (ped′is təl), 1. the base on which a column or a statue stands. 2. the base of a tall vase, lamp, etc. *n. 8.*

Pedestal for a statue

pe des tri an (pi des′tri ən), 1. going on foot; walking. 2. person who goes on foot. *adj., n. 12.*

ped i gree (ped′i grē), 1. list of ancestors; family tree. 2. ancestry; line of descent. *n. 9.*

ped i greed (ped′i grēd), having a pedigree. Horses, cows, dogs, and other animals of known and recorded ancestry are called pedigreed stock. *adj.*

ped i ment (ped′i mənt), 1. a low triangular part on the front of buildings in the Greek style. A pediment is like a gable. See the picture. 2. any similar decorative part in any building. *n. 20.*

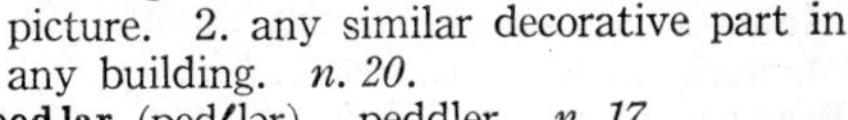

Pediment

ped lar (ped′lər), peddler. *n. 17.*

peek (pēk), 1. look quickly and slyly; peep. You must not peek while you are counting in such games as hide-and-seek. 2. a quick, sly look. *v., n. 13.*

peel (pēl), 1. the rind or outer covering of fruit, etc. 2. strip the skin, rind, or bark from; as, to peel an orange, to peel a potato. 3. strip. The Indians peeled the bark from trees to make canoes. 4. come off. When I was sunburnt, my skin peeled. The paint is peeling. *n., v. 5.*

peep[1] (pēp), 1. to look through a small or narrow hole or crack. 2. such a look; a little look; as, to take a peep into the pantry. 3. to look when no one knows it. 4. a secret look. 5. look out, as if peeping; come partly out. 6. the first looking or coming out; as, at the peep of day. *v., n. 2.*

peep[2] (pēp), 1. the cry of a young bird or chicken; a sound like a chirp or a squeak. 2. make such a sound; chirp. *n., v.*

peer[1] (pēr), 1. equal. He is so fine a man

that it would be hard to find his peer. 2. man who has a title; man who is high and great by birth or rank. A duke, marquis, earl, count, viscount, or baron is a peer. *n. 2.*

peer[2] (pēr), 1. look closely to see clearly, as a near-sighted person does. She peered at the tag to read the price. 2. come out slightly; peep out. The sun was peering from behind a cloud. *v.*

peer age (pēr′ij), 1. the rank or dignity of a peer. 2. the peers of a country. 3. a book giving a list of the peers of a country. *n. 13.*

peer ess (pēr′is), 1. the wife or widow of a peer. 2. woman having the rank of peer in her own right. *n. 16.*

peer less (pēr′lis), without an equal; matchless. Washington was the peerless leader of our country in his day. *adj. 9.*

pee vish (pē′vish), cross; fretful; complaining. A peevish child is unhappy and makes others unhappy. *adj. 12.*

pee vish ness (pē′vish nis), crossness; fretting. *n. 17.*

peg (peg), 1. a pin or small bolt of wood, metal, etc., used to fasten parts together, to hang things on, to stop a hole, to make fast a rope or string on, to mark the score in a game, etc. 2. fasten or hold with pegs; as, to peg down a tent. 3. **Take a person down a peg or two** means humble him. 4. work hard. *n., v., pegged, pegging. 5.*

Peg a sus (peg′ə səs), 1. a horse with wings, the steed of the Muses. 2. poetic genius; the means by which men soar in the realms of poetry. *n. 15.*

Pei ping (pā′ping′), Peking. *n.*

Pe kin (pē′kin′), Peking. *n. 20.*

Pe king (pē′king′), a large city in the northeastern part of China, the capital of China for many years. It is now called Peiping. *n. 16.*

Pe king ese (pē′king ēz′), small dog with long hair and a pug nose. *n., pl. Pekingese.*

pe koe (pē′kō), a kind of black tea. *n.*

pelf (pelf), money or riches, thought of as bad or degrading. *n. 13.*

Pelican

peli can (pel′i kən), a very large, fish-eating water bird with a huge bill and a pouch for storing food. *n. 11.*

Pe li on (pē′li ən), a mountain in eastern Greece. The Greek story says that when the giants made war on the gods, they piled Mount Ossa on Mount Olympus, and Mount Pelion upon Mount Ossa in an attempt to reach their foes in heaven. *n. 16.*

pe lisse (pə lēs′), 1. a coat lined or trimmed with fur. 2. a woman's long cloak. *n. 18.*

pel let (pel′it), little ball of mud, paper, food, medicine, etc.; a pill. *n. 12.*

pell-mell (pel′mel′), 1. in a rushing, tumbling mass or crowd. The children dashed pell-mell down the beach and into the waves. 2. in headlong haste. 3. headlong; tumultuous. 4. violent disorder or confusion. *adv., adj., n. 13.*

pel lu cid (pə lü′sid), transparent; clear; as, a pellucid stream, pellucid language. Mark Twain's pellucid style is easy to understand. *adj. 15.*

pelt[1] (pelt), 1. throw things at; attack; assail. The boys were pelting the dog with stones. 2. beat heavily. The rain came pelting down. 3. speed. The horse is coming at full pelt. *v., n. 8.*

pelt[2] (pelt), the skin of a sheep, goat, or small fur-bearing animal, before it is tanned. *n.*

pel vic (pel′vik), of or pertaining to the pelvis. *adj. 18.*

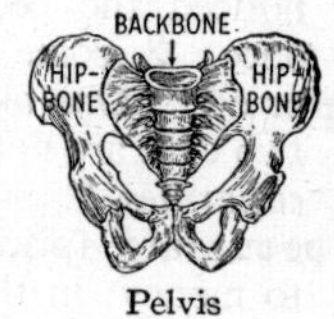

Pelvis

pel vis (pel′vis), 1. the basin-shaped cavity formed by the backbone and hipbones. 2. the bones forming the cavity. *n. 17.*

pem mi can (pem′i kən), dried meat pounded into a paste with melted fat. *n.*

pen[1] (pen), 1. small yard for cows, sheep, pigs, chickens, etc. 2. shut up in a pen. 3. shut. John had me penned in a corner where I could not escape. *n., v., penned or pent, penning. 1.*

pen[2] (pen), 1. a tool used in writing with ink. 2. write. I penned a few words to father today. *n., v., penned, penning.*

pe nal (pē′nəl), of, having to do with, or given as punishment; as, penal laws, a penal offense, penal labor. *adj. 12.*

pe nal ize (pē′nəl īz), 1. declare punishable by law or by rule; set a penalty for. Speeding on city streets is penalized. Fouls are penalized in many games. 2. punish; inflict a penalty on. Our team was penalized five yards. *v. 17.*

pen al ty (pen′əl ti), punishment. The penalty for speeding is a fine of ten dollars. *n., pl. penalties. 7.*

pen ance (pen′əns), punishment borne to

show sorrow for sin, to make up for a wrong done, and to obtain pardon from the church for sin. *n. 7.*

pence (pens), pennies. *n. pl. 7.*

pen chant (pen′chənt), inclination; strong taste or liking; as, a penchant for taking long walks. *n.*

pen cil (pen′səl), 1. a pointed tool to write or draw with. 2. mark or write with a pencil. *n., v., penciled, penciling. 2.*

pend ant (pen′dənt), 1. a hanging ornament, such as a locket. 2. pendent. *n., adj. 7.*

Pendant

pend ent (pen′dənt), 1. hanging; as, the pendent branches of willow which touch the water. 2. pending. 3. pendant. *adj., n. 9.*

pend ing (pen′ding), 1. waiting to be decided or settled; as, while the agreement was pending. 2. until; while waiting for. Pending his return, let us get the car all ready. 3. during; as, pending the investigation. *adj., prep. 11.*

pen du lous (pen′jù ləs), 1. hanging loosely. The oriole builds a pendulous nest. 2. swinging. *adj. 12.*

pen du lum (pen′jù ləm), a weight so hung from a fixed point that it is free to swing to and fro. The movement of the works of a tall clock is often timed by a pendulum. *n. 9.*

Pendulum. Dotted lines show motion.

Pe nel o pe (pi nel′ə pi), the faithful wife of Odysseus. She waited twenty years for his return in spite of the entreaties of her many suitors. *n. 16.*

pen e tra ble (pen′i trə bəl), that can be penetrated. *adj. 19.*

pen e trate (pen′i trāt), 1. get into or through. A bullet can penetrate a wall, or two inches into a wall. 2. pierce through. Our eyes could not penetrate the darkness. Even where the trees were thickest, the sunshine penetrated. 3. soak through; spread through. The rain penetrated all our clothes. The odor penetrated the whole house. 4. see into; understand. I could not penetrate the mystery. *v. 13.*

pen e tra tion (pen′i trā′shən), 1. penetrating. 2. sharpness of intellect; insight. *n. 13.*

pen e tra tive (pen′i trā′tiv), penetrating; piercing; acute; keen. *adj. 19.*

pen guin (peng′gwin), a sea bird with flippers for diving and swimming in place of wings for flying. *n.*

pen in su la (pən in′sə lə), piece of land almost surrounded by water, or extending far out into the water. Florida is a big peninsula. *n. 5.*

pen in su lar (pən in′sə lər), 1. like a peninsula. 2. in or of a peninsula. *adj.*

King penguin (about 3 ft. tall)

pen i tence (pen′i təns), sorrow for doing wrong; repentance. *n. 12.*

pen i tent (pen′i tənt), 1. sorry for doing wrong. 2. one who is sorry for sin, especially one who is doing penance under the direction of the church. *adj., n. 7.*

pen i ten tial (pen′i ten′shəl), 1. of, showing, or pertaining to penitence. The penitential psalms express remorse for sin. 2. of or pertaining to penance. *adj. 14.*

pen i ten tia ry (pen′i ten′shə ri), 1. a prison for criminals. 2. making one liable to punishment in a prison; as, a penitentiary offense. 3. used for punishment, discipline, and reformation; as, penitentiary houses, penitentiary measures. 4. of penance; penitential. *n., pl. penitentiaries, adj. 15.*

pen knife (pen′nīf′), small pocketknife. *n., pl. penknives. 18.*

pen man (pen′mən), 1. writer. 2. person who has good handwriting. *n., pl. penmen.*

pen man ship (pen′mən ship), handwriting; writing with pen, pencil, etc. *n. 18.*

Penn (pen), William (1644-1718), a Quaker, the leader of the first settlement in Pennsylvania, at Philadelphia. *n.*

Penn. or **Penna.**, Pennsylvania. *9.*

pen name, name used by a writer instead of his real name.

pen nant (pen′ənt), a flag, usually long and narrow, used on ships, in signaling, as a school banner, etc. *n. 18.*

Pennant

pen ni less (pen′i lis), without a cent of money; very poor. *adj. 14.*

pen non (pen′ən), 1. a long triangular flag, originally carried on the lance of a knight. 2. any flag or banner. *n. 15.*

Penn syl va ni a (pen′sil vā′ni ə), an Eastern State of the United States. *n. 3.*

pen ny (pen′i), 1. cent; copper coin of the U. S. and Canada. 100 pennies = 1 dollar.

2. an English bronze coin equal to one twelfth of a shilling, or about two cents. 3. sum of money. It will cost you a **pretty penny** means that it will cost you a large sum of money. *n., pl. pennies* or *pence. 2.*

pen ny weight (pen′i wāt′), 24 grains or one twentieth of an ounce in troy weight. *n.*

pen ny-wise (pen′i wīz′), saving in regard to small sums. **Penny-wise and pound-foolish** means saving in small expenses and wasteful in big ones. *adj.*

pen ny worth (pen′i wėrth′), 1. as much as can be bought for a penny. 2. small amount. Give me a pennyworth of advice. *n.*

pen sion (pen′shən), 1. a regular payment to a person which is not wages. Pensions are often paid because of long service, special merit, or injuries received. 2. give a pension to. *n., v. 6.*

pen sion er (pen′shən ər), person who receives a pension. *n. 9.*

pen sive (pen′siv), thoughtful in a serious or sad way. *adj. 5.*

pent (pent), penned; closely confined; shut; as, pent in the house all winter, her pent-up feelings. *adj. 7.*

pen ta gon (pen′tə gon), a figure having five sides and five angles. *n. 14.*

Pentagon

Pen ta teuch (pen′tə tūk or pen′tə tük), the first five books of the Old Testament. *n. 19.*

Pen te cost (pen′ti kost), 1. the seventh Sunday after Easter. Pentecost is a Christian festival in memory of the descent of the Holy Ghost upon the Apostles. Also called **Whitsunday.** 2. a Jewish harvest festival. *n. 15.*

pent house (pent′hous′), 1. a sloping roof projecting from a building. 2. a shed with a sloping roof attached to a building. 3. a shed or house built on the top of a building. *n. 16.*

pe nu ri ous (pi nūr′i əs or pi nür′i əs), mean about spending or giving money; stingy. *adj. 16.*

pen u ry (pen′ū ri), very great poverty. *n. 9.*

pe on (pē′on), 1. person doing work that requires little skill. 2. worker held as a slave to work off a debt. *n.*

pe o ny (pē′ə ni), 1. a garden plant with large showy flowers. 2. the flower. *n., pl. peonies. 16.*

Peony

peo ple (pē′pəl), 1. men, women, and children; persons. There were ten people present. 2. race; nation; as, the peoples of Asia, the American people. 3. persons in general; the public. 4. persons of a place, class, or group; as, city people, Southern people, the people here. 5. persons in relation to a superior; as, the king and his people, a pastor and his people. 6. the lower classes. The French nobles oppressed the people. 7. fill with people. Europe very largely peopled America. 8. family. John spends his holidays with his people. *n., v. 1.*

Pe o ri a (pi ō′ri ə), a city in central Illinois. *n. 19.*

pep per (pep′ər), 1. a seasoning with a hot taste, used for soups, meats, vegetables, etc. Pepper is made by grinding the ripe or unripe berries of black pepper. 2. a hollow red or green vegetable that is baked or fried, and used in pickles. 3. season with pepper; sprinkle with pepper. 4. hit with small objects sent thick and fast. We peppered the enemy's lines with our shot. *n., v. 4.*

pep per corn (pep′ər kôrn′), one of the dried berries that make black pepper when they are ground up. *n. 12.*

pep per mint (pep′ər mint), 1. an herb grown for its oil, used in medicine and in candy. 2. this oil. 3. candy flavored with peppermint oil. *n. 16.*

Peppermint

pep per y (pep′ər i), 1. like pepper; full of pepper. 2. hot; sharp. 3. having a hot temper; easily made angry. *adj.*

pep sin (pep′sin), 1. a substance in the gastric juice of the stomach that helps to digest meats, eggs, cheese, and similar foods. 2. medicine containing this substance. *n. 14.*

per (pėr), 1. for each; as, a pound of candy per child, ten cents per pound. 2. through; by; by means of. I send this per my son. *prep. 2.*

per ad ven ture (pėr′əd ven′chər), 1. perhaps. Peradventure he will come today. *Old use.* 2. chance. Beyond peradventure he will come. *adv., n. 7.*

per am bu late (pər am′bū lāt), 1. walk through. 2. walk about. 3. walk through and examine. *v. 17.*

per am bu la tor (pər am′bū lā′tər), 1. a small carriage in which a baby is pushed about. 2. person who perambulates. *n. 19.*

per an num (pər an′əm), per year; yearly; for each year. Her salary was $1800 per annum.

per cale (pər kāl′), a closely woven cotton cloth with a smooth finish. *n. 13.*

per cap i ta (pər kap′i tə), for each person. $40 for eight men is $5 per capita. *17.*

per ceive (pər sēv′), 1. be aware of through the senses; see, hear, taste, smell, or feel. Did you perceive a red color or a blue one? 2. take in with the mind; observe. I perceived that I could not make him change his mind. *v. 3.*

per cent (pər sent′), 1. hundredths. Five per cent of 40 is 2. 2. for each hundred; in each hundred. Seven per cent of the children failed. **Per cent.** and **percent** are other spellings. *7.*

per cent age (pər sen′tij), 1. rate or proportion of each hundred; part of each hundred. What percentage of children were absent? 2. part or proportion. A large percentage of schoolbooks now have pictures. 3. the part of arithmetic that deals with numbers expressed in per cents. *n. 9.*

per cep ti ble (pər sep′ti bəl), that can be perceived. The other ship was barely perceptible in the fog. *adj. 9.*

per cep ti bly (pər sep′ti bli), in a perceptible way or amount. *adv.*

per cep tion (pər sep′shən), 1. act of perceiving. His perception of the change came in a flash. 2. power of perceiving; as, a keen perception. 3. the understanding that is the result of perceiving. Did you have time to get a clear perception of the accident? *n. 8.*

perch[1] (pėrch), 1. a bar, branch, or anything else on which a bird can come to rest. 2. alight and rest; sit. A robin perched on our porch railing. 3. high seat. 4. sit rather high. He perched on a stool. 5. to place high up; as, a village perched on a high hill. 6. a measure of length, 5½ yards. A square perch is 30¼ square yards. *n., v. 3.*

perch[2] (pėrch), a small fresh-water fish, used for food. *n.*

Perch
(about 10 in. long)

per chance (pər chans′), perhaps. *adv. 5.*

per co late (pėr′kə lāt), 1. drip or drain through small holes or spaces. Let the coffee percolate for seven minutes. 2. filter through; permeate. Water percolates sand. *v. 15.*

per co la tor (pėr′kə lā′tər), a kind of coffee pot in which boiling water drains through ground coffee. *n. 20.*

per cus sion (pər kush′ən), 1. the striking of one body against another with force; a stroke or blow. 2. the shock made by the striking of one body against another with force. *n.*

per di tion (pər dish′ən), 1. loss of one's soul and the joys of heaven. 2. hell. 3. utter loss. *n. 9.*

per e gri na tion (per′i gri nā′shən), journey; travel. *n. 17.*

per emp to ry (pər emp′tə ri), 1. decisive; final; absolute; leaving no choice; as, a peremptory decree. 2. allowing no denial or refusal; as, a peremptory command. 3. imperious; positive. *adj. 9.*

per en ni al (pər en′i əl), 1. lasting through the whole year; as, a perennial stream. 2. lasting for a long time; as, the perennial beauty of the hills. 3. living more than two years; as, perennial garden plants. 4. a perennial plant. Roses are perennials. *adj., n. 11.*

per fect (pėr′fikt for 1, 3, 6, and 7, pər fekt′ for 2, 4, and 5), 1. having no faults; not spoiled at any point; as, a perfect spelling paper, a perfect apple, a perfect life. 2. remove all faults from; make perfect; add the finishing touches to. The artist was perfecting his picture. 3. whole; having all its parts there. The set was perfect; nothing was missing or broken. 4. carry through; complete; as, to perfect a plan or an invention. 5. raise to the highest point; as, to perfect one's skill. 6. entire; utter; as, a perfect stranger to us. 7. verb form that shows an event completed at the time of speaking. In "I have eaten already," *have eaten* is in the perfect tense. *adj., v., n. 1.*

per fect i ble (pər fek′ti bəl), capable of becoming, or being made, perfect. *adj.*

per fec tion (pər fek′shən), 1. faultlessness; the highest excellence. 2. perfect person or thing. His work is always perfection. 3. making complete or perfect. Perfection of our plans will take another week. *n. 4.*

per fect ly (pėr′fikt li), in a perfect manner; completely; thoroughly; exactly; entirely. *adv.*

per fect ness (pėr′fikt nis), completeness; being without a single fault or defect. *n. 20.*

per fid i ous (pər fid′i əs), deliberately faithless; treacherous. *adj. 12.*

per fi dy (pėr′fi di), breaking faith; base treachery; being false to a trust. *n., pl. perfidies. 13.*

per fo rate (pėr′fə rāt), 1. make a hole or holes through. The target was perforated by bullets. 2. make rows of holes through. Sheets of postage stamps are perforated. *v. 11.*

per fo ra tion (pėr′fə rā′shən), 1. perforating. 2. being perforated. 3. a hole bored or punched through something; as, the perforations in the top of a salt shaker. *n. 16.*

per force (pər fōrs′), by necessity; necessarily. *adv. 15.*

per form (pər fôrm′), 1. do. Perform your duty. 2. put into effect; carry out. Perform your promise. 3. act, play, sing, or do tricks in public. *v. 2.*

per form ance (pər fôr′məns), 1. carrying out; doing; as, in the performance of one's regular duties. 2. act; deed. The child's kicks and screams made a disgraceful performance. 3. the giving of a play, circus, or other show. The evening performance is at 8 o'clock. *n. 5.*

per form er (pər fôr′mər), person who performs; player. *n. 12.*

per fume (pėr′fūm for 1 and 2, pər fūm′ for 3), 1. sweet smell; as, the perfume of flowers. 2. liquid having the sweet smell of flowers. 3. fill with sweet odor. Flowers perfumed the air. *n., v. 4.*

per fum er y (pər fūm′ər i), 1. perfume; perfumes. 2. the business of making or selling perfumes. *n., pl. perfumeries. 17.*

per func to ry (pər fungk′tə ri), 1. done merely for the sake of getting rid of the duty; done from force of habit; mechanical; indifferent. The little boy gave his face a perfunctory washing. 2. acting in a perfunctory way. The new nurse was perfunctory; she did not really care about her work. *adj.*

per haps (pər haps′), it may be. Perhaps a letter will come to you today. *adv. 1.*

Per i cles (per′i klēz), a famous Athenian statesman (490?-429 B.C.). *n.*

per il (per′əl), 1. chance of harm; danger. 2. put in danger. *n., v., periled, periling. 4.*

per il ous (per′i ləs), dangerous. *adj. 5.*

pe rim e ter (pə rim′i tər), 1. the outer boundary of a surface or figure. 2. the distance around such a boundary. The perimeter of a square equals four times the length of one side. *n. 20.*

pe ri od (pēr′i əd), 1. a portion of time marked off by events that happen again and again; a time after which the same things begin to happen again. A month, from new moon to new moon, is a period. 2. a certain series of years; as, the period of the Civil War. 3. portion of time. He visited us for a short period. 4. the time needed for a disease to run its course. 5. end. 6. complete sentence. The orator spoke in stately periods. 7. pause at the end of a sentence. 8. dot (.) marking the end of most sentences or showing an abbreviation, as in Mr. or Dec. *n. 2.*

pe ri od ic (pēr′i od′ik), 1. occurring, appearing, or done again and again at regular intervals; as, periodic attacks of malaria. 2. happening every now and then; as, a periodic fit of clearing up one's desk. 3. having to do with a period. The coming of the new moon is a periodic occurrence. 4. expressed in formal sentences whose meanings are not complete without the final words. *adj. 16.*

pe ri od i cal (pēr′i od′i kəl), 1. See definitions 1, 2, and 3 of **periodic.** 2. published at regular intervals less often than daily. 3. a magazine that appears regularly. *adj., n. 6.*

pe ri od i cal ly (pēr′i od′i kəl i), 1. at regular intervals. 2. every now and then. *adv.*

per i pa tet ic (per′i pə tet′ik), walking about; traveling from place to place; as, a peripatetic umbrella mender. *adj. 20.*

pe riph er y (pə rif′ər i), outside boundary. The periphery of a circle is called the circumference. *n., pl. peripheries. 19.*

per i scope (per′i skōp), an instrument that allows those in a submarine or trench to see a view of the surface. It is a tube with an arrangement of prisms or mirrors that reflect light rays down the tube. *n.*

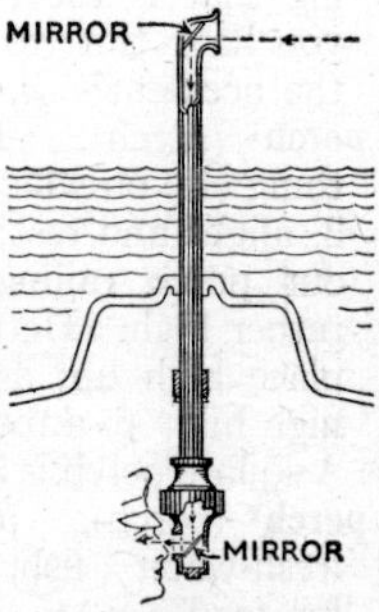

MIRROR

MIRROR

Periscope on a submarine

per ish (per′ish), die; be destroyed. Flowers perish when frost comes. *v. 3.*

per ish a ble (per′ish ə bəl), liable to spoil or decay. Fruit is perishable. *adj. 14.*

per i wig (per′i wig), wig. *n. 15.*

per i win kle[1] (per′i wing′kəl), a low trailing evergreen plant with blue flowers. The American periwinkle is called myrtle. *n. 16.*

per i win kle[2] (per′i wing′kəl), a sea snail used for food in Europe. See the picture just below. *n.*

Periwinkle (about ¾ in. long)

per jure (pėr′jər). **Perjure oneself** means (1) swear falsely. The witness perjured himself by lying about what he saw on the night of the murder. (2) break a solemn promise. *v. 12.*

per ju ry (pėr′jər i), 1. act of swearing that something is true which one knows to be false. 2. breaking a solemn promise. *n., pl. perjuries. 12.*

perk (pėrk), 1. move, lift the head, or act briskly or saucily. 2. raise smartly or briskly. 3. put oneself forward briskly or assertively. 4. **Perk up** means brighten up; become lively and vigorous. *v. 12.*

perk y (pėr′ki), smart; brisk; saucy; pert; as, a perky squirrel. *adj., perkier, perkiest.*

per ma nence (pėr′mə nəns), being permanent; lasting quality or condition. *n. 12.*

per ma nen cy (pėr′mə nən si), 1. permanence. 2. a permanent person, thing, or position. *n.*

per ma nent (pėr′mə nənt), lasting; intended to last; not for a short time only; as, a permanent filling in a tooth. After doing odd jobs for a week, he got a permanent position as office boy. *adj. 4.*

per me a ble (pėr′mi ə bəl), that can be permeated. A sponge is permeable by water. *adj. 20.*

per me ate (pėr′mi āt), 1. spread through the whole of; pass through; soak through. The smoke permeated the house. 2. penetrate. Water will easily permeate through a cotton dress. *v. 12.*

per mis si ble (pər mis′i bəl), allowable; that may be permitted. *adj. 18.*

per mis sion (pər mish′ən), consent; leave; permitting. He asked the teacher's permission to go early. Father gave me permission to use his car. *n. 4.*

per mis sive (pər mis′iv), 1. permitting. 2. permitted; allowed. *adj. 20.*

per mit (pər mit′ for 1, pėr′mit for 2), 1. let; allow. My mother will not permit me to stay up late. 2. a formal written order giving permission to do something. Have you a permit to fish in this lake? *v., permitted, permitting, n. 2.*

Per nam bu co (pėr′nam bū′kō), a seaport city in eastern Brazil. *n.*

per ni cious (pər nish′əs), 1. that will destroy or ruin; causing great harm or damage. Gambling is a pernicious habit. 2. fatal. *adj. 8.*

per o ra tion (per′ə rā′shən), 1. the last part of an oration or discussion. 2. the summing up of an argument. *n. 16.*

per ox ide (pər ok′sīd), a compound having much oxygen in it. Hydrogen peroxide is often used on cuts to kill germs. *n. 13.*

per pen dic u lar (pėr′pən dik′ū lər), 1. upright; standing straight up; as, a perpendicular cliff. 2. at right angles. One line is perpendicular to another when it makes a square corner with another. See the diagrams. The floor of a room is perpendicular to the side walls and parallel to the ceiling. 3. a perpendicular line or plane. *adj., n. 8.*

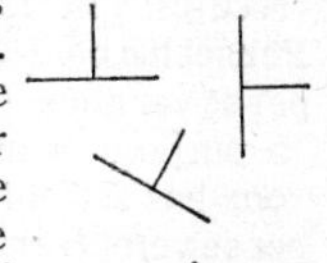

per pe trate (pėr′pi trāt), do or commit (a crime, fraud, trick, or anything bad or foolish). The king's brother perpetrated the cruel murder of the prince. *v. 13.*

per pe tra tor (pėr′pi trā′tər), doer; person who does something bad or foolish. *n. 17.*

per pet u al (pər pech′ü əl), 1. eternal; lasting forever; lasting throughout life; as, the perpetual hills, a perpetual income. 2. continuous; never ceasing; as, a disease that puts a person in perpetual pain. *adj. 4.*

per pet u al ly (pər pech′ü əl i), forever. *adv.*

per pet u ate (pər pech′ü āt), make perpetual; keep from being forgotten. The Washington Monument was built to perpetuate the memory of a great man. *v. 10.*

per pet u a tion (pər pech′ü ā′shən), carrying on; making perpetual; being made perpetual. *n.*

per pe tu i ty (pėr′pi tū′i ti or pėr′pi tü′i ti), being perpetual; existence forever. **In perpetuity** means forever. *n. 15.*

per plex (pər pleks′), 1. puzzle. This problem is hard enough to perplex even the teacher. 2. trouble with doubt. 3. make difficult to understand or settle. *v. 4.*

per plex i ty (pər plek′si ti), 1. perplexed condition; confusion; being puzzled; not knowing what to do or how to act. 2. something that perplexes. *n., pl. perplexities. 8.*

per qui site (pėr′kwi zit), anything received for work besides the regular pay. The maid had the old dresses of her mistress as a perquisite. *n. 17.*

per se cute (pėr′si kūt), 1. pursue to injure; treat badly; do harm to again and again; oppress. The cruel boy persecuted the kitten by throwing stones at it whenever it came near. 2. punish for religious reasons. *v. 5.*

per se cu tion (pėr′si kū′shən), 1. persecuting; as, the boy's persecution of the kitten. 2. being persecuted; as, the kitten's persecution by the boy. *n. 6.*

per se cu tor (pėr′si kū′tər), one who persecutes. *n. 13.*

Per seph o ne (pər sef′ə ni), Proserpina. *n.*

per se ver ance (pėr′si vēr′əns), sticking to a purpose or an aim; never giving up what one has set out to do. *n. 7.*

per se vere (pėr′si vēr′), persist; continue steadily in doing something hard. To try, try, try again is to persevere. *v. 7.*

Per sia (pėr′zhə), a country in southwestern Asia. The official name is now Iran. *n. 5.*

Per sian (pėr′zhən), 1. person born in Persia, living there, or having Persian parents. 2. the language of Persia. 3. of or pertaining to Persia, its people, or their language. *n., adj.*

per si flage (pėr′si fläzh), light, joking talk. *n. 20.*

per sim mon (pər sim′ən), 1. a North American tree with a plumlike fruit. 2. the fruit of this tree, very bitter when green, but sweet and good to eat when very ripe. *n. 19.*

Persimmon

per sist (pər sist′), 1. continue firmly; refuse to stop or be changed. Johnny persists in reading in bed. 2. last; stay; endure. On the tops of some mountains snow persists throughout the year. 3. say again and again; maintain. He persisted that he was innocent of the crime. *v. 6.*

per sist ence (pər sis′təns), 1. being persistent; as, the persistence of a fly buzzing around one's head. 2. continuing existence; as, the persistence of a cough. *n. 10.*

per sist en cy (pər sis′tən si), persistence. *n. 16.*

per sist ent (pər sis′tənt), 1. persisting; having staying qualities, especially in the face of dislike or disapproval; as, a persistent worker, a persistent beggar. 2. lasting; going on; continuing; as, a persistent headache that lasted for three days. *adj. 8.*

per son (pėr′sən), 1. man, woman, or child. 2. the body; bodily appearance. The person of the king was sacred. 3. in grammar, a form of pronouns or verbs used to show the speaker, the person spoken to, or the person spoken of. *I* and *we* are used for the first person; *thou* and *you,* for the second person; *he, she, it,* and *they,* for the third person. *n. 1.*

per son a ble (pėr′sən ə bəl), having a pleasing appearance; pleasant to look at. *adj.*

per son age (pėr′sən ij), 1. person of importance. 2. person. 3. a character in a book or a play. *n. 7.*

per son al (pėr′sən əl), 1. individual; private; as, a personal letter. 2. done in person; directly by oneself, not through others or by letter; as, a personal call. 3. of the body or bodily appearance; as, personal beauty or charms. 4. about or against a person or persons; as, personal remarks, personal abuse. 5. in grammar, showing person. *I, we, thou, you, he, she, it,* and *they* are the personal pronouns. 6. **Personal property** means possessions that can be moved, not land, or mines, or forests. 7. a short paragraph in a newspaper about a particular person or persons. *adj., n. 3.*

per son al i ty (pėr′sə nal′i ti), 1. the personal or individual quality that makes one person be different or act differently from another. A baby two weeks old does not have much personality. 2. the qualities of a person. The boy is developing a fine personality. 3. a remark made about or against one particular person. Personalities are not in good taste in general conversation. 4. person; personage. *n., pl. personalities. 7.*

per son al ly (pėr′sən əl i), 1. in person; not by the aid of others. The hostess saw to the comfort of her guests personally. 2. as a person. We like Mr. Hart personally, but we dislike his way of living. 3. as far as oneself is concerned. *adv.*

per son ate (pėr′sən āt), 1. act the part of (a character in a play, etc.). 2. pretend to be. *v. 16.*

per son i fi ca tion (pər son′i fi kā′shən), 1. type; striking example. Elsie is the very personification of selfishness. 2. representing as a person, such as speaking of the sun as *he* and the *moon* as *she.* 3. a figure of speech in which a lifeless thing or quality is spoken of as if alive. *Examples:* The music sobbed. Duty calls us. *n. 14.*

per son i fy (pər son′i fī), 1. embody; be a type of. Satan is evil personified. 2. regard or represent as a person. We often personify the sun and moon, calling the sun *he* and the moon *she.* *v., personified, personifying. 15.*

per son nel (pėr′sə nel′), persons employed in any work, business, or service. *n. 14.*

per spec tive (pər spek′tiv), 1. the art of picturing objects on a flat surface so as to give the appearance of distance. 2. drawn so as to show the proper perspective; as, a perspective drawing. 3. the effect of distance on the appearance of objects. 4. the effect of the distance of events upon the mind. Many happenings of last year seem less important when viewed in perspective. 5. a view of things or facts in which they are in the right relations. 6. the view in front; distant view. *n., adj. 9.*

per spi ca cious (pėr′spi kā′shəs), keen in observing and understanding; discerning. *adj.*

per spi cac i ty (pėr′spi kas′i ti), keen perception; discernment; wisdom and understanding in dealing with people or with facts. *n.*

per spi cu i ty (pėr′spi kū′i ti), clearness in expression; ease in being understood. *n. 19.*

per spic u ous (pər spik′ū əs), clear; easily understood. *adj. 16.*

per spi ra tion (pėr′spi rā′shən), 1. sweat. 2. sweating. *n. 11.*

per spire (pər spīr′), sweat. *v. 14.*

per suade (pər swād′), win over to do or believe; make willing. He persuaded me to go. We persuaded Harry that he was wrong. *v. 3.*

per sua sion (pər swā′zhən), 1. persuading. All our persuasion was of no use; she would not come. 2. power of persuading. 3. firm belief. 4. religious belief. All Christians are not of the same persuasion. *n. 7.*

per sua sive (pər swā′siv), able to persuade; fitted to persuade. The salesman had a very persuasive way of talking. *adj. 8.*

pert (pėrt), saucy; bold; too forward or free in speech; as, a pert girl, a pert reply. *adj. 10.*

per tain (pər tān′), 1. belong. We own the house and the land pertaining to it. 2. refer; be related. "Pertaining to school" means "having to do with school." 3. be appropriate. We had turkey and everything else that pertains to Thanksgiving Day. *v. 6.*

per ti na cious (pėr′ti nā′shəs), holding firmly to a purpose, action, or opinion; very persistent. A bulldog is a pertinacious fighter. *adj. 15.*

per ti nac i ty (pėr′ti nas′i ti), great persistence; holding firmly to a purpose, action, or opinion. *n. 16.*

per ti nence (pėr′ti nəns), fitness; being to the point. The pertinence of the boy's replies showed that he was not stupid. *n.*

per ti nent (pėr′ti nənt), having to do with what is being considered; relating to the matter in hand; to the point. If your question is pertinent, I will answer it. *adj. 12.*

per turb (pər tėrb′), disturb greatly; make uneasy or troubled. Mrs. Smith was much perturbed by her son's illness. *v. 11.*

per tur ba tion (pėr′tər bā′shən), perturbing; being perturbed; disturbance. *n. 14.*

Pe ru (pə rü′), a mountainous country on the west coast of South America. *n. 6.*

pe ruke (pə rük′), wig. Men in the 17th and 18th centuries wore perukes. *n.*

Peruke

pe rus al (pə rüz′əl), perusing; reading. I have just finished the perusal of your letter. *n. 14.*

pe ruse (pə rüz′), 1. read thoroughly and carefully. 2. read. *v. 7.*

Pe ru vi an (pə rü′vi ən), 1. of or pertaining to Peru or its people. 2. native or inhabitant of Peru. *adj., n. 14.*

Peruvian bark, bark from which quinine is obtained.

per vade (pər vād′), go or spread throughout; be throughout. The odor of pines pervades the air. He worked so hard that weariness pervaded his whole body. *v. 8.*

per va sive (pər vā′siv), 1. tending to pervade. 2. having power to pervade. *adj.*

per verse (pər vėrs′), 1. contrary. The perverse child did just what we told him not to do. 2. persistent in wrong. 3. wicked. 4. not correct; wrong; as, perverse reasoning. *adj. 7.*

per verse ness (pər vėrs′nis), being perverse. The child's perverseness led him to do everything he was told not to do. *n. 13.*

per ver sion (pər vėr′zhən), turning or being turned to what is wrong; a change to what is unnatural, abnormal, or wrong. A tendency to eat sand is a perversion of appetite. *n. 16.*

per ver si ty (pər vėr′si ti), 1. quality of being perverse. 2. perverse character or conduct. *n., pl. perversities.*

per vert (pər vėrt′ for 1 and 2, pėr′vėrt for

3), 1. lead or turn from the right way or from the truth. Reading silly stories perverts our taste. To pervert what a person has said is to give a wrong meaning to it. His enemies perverted his friendly remark and made it into an insult. 2. use for wrong purposes or in a wrong way. A clever criminal perverts his talents. 3. perverted person. *v., n. 8.*

pe so (pā′sō), any of various coins used in Spanish-speaking countries. The Mexican peso was worth about 50 cents in 1940. *n., pl. pesos.*

pes si mism (pes′i mizm), 1. tendency to look on the dark side of things or to see difficulties and disadvantages. 2. belief that things naturally tend to evil, or that life is not worth while. *n. 15.*

pes si mist (pes′i mist), 1. person inclined to see all the difficulties and disadvantages or to look on the dark side of things. 2. person who thinks that life holds more evil than good, and so is not worth living. *n. 16.*

pes si mis tic (pes′i mis′tik), favoring pessimism. *adj.*

pest (pest), 1. thing or person that causes trouble, injuries, or destruction; nuisance. Flies and mosquitoes are pests. 2. pestilence. *n. 9.*

pes ter (pes′tər), annoy; trouble; vex. Flies pester us. *v. 15.*

pest house (pest′hous′), hospital for persons ill with very infectious diseases. *n.*

pes tif er ous (pes tif′ər əs), 1. bringing disease or infection. Rats are pestiferous. 2. bringing moral evil; as, the pestiferous influence of a bad example. 3. troublesome; annoying. *adj. 20.*

pes ti lence (pes′ti ləns), a disease that spreads rapidly, causing many deaths. Smallpox, yellow fever, and the plague are pestilences. *n. 6.*

pes ti lent (pes′ti lənt), 1. often causing death. Smallpox is a pestilent disease. 2. harmful to morals; destroying peace; as, a pestilent den of vice, the pestilent effects of war. 3. troublesome; annoying. *adj. 13.*

pes ti len tial (pes′ti len′shəl), 1. like a pestilence; having to do with pestilences. 2. carrying infection. *adj. 15.*

pes tle (pes′əl), 1. a tool for pounding something to a powder. 2. pound or crush with a pestle. *n., v. 15.*

Pestle in a bowl

pet¹ (pet), 1. an animal kept as a favorite and treated with affection. 2. a darling or favorite; as, teacher's pet. 3. treat as a pet; yield to the wishes of; stroke or pat; touch lovingly and gently. 4. treated as a pet. *n., v., petted, petting, adj. 4.*

pet² (pet), fit of peevishness; fretful discontent. *n.*

pet al (pet′əl), one of the parts of a flower that are usually colored. A rose has many petals. *n. 6.*

pet cock (pet′kok′), small faucet. *n.*

Petcock

Pe ter (pē′tər), 1. Saint Peter was one of the twelve Apostles of Jesus. Two books of the New Testament bear his name. 2. **Peter the Great** (1672-1725) was a famous czar of Russia. *n. 2.*

pet i ole (pet′i ōl), slender stalk by which a leaf is attached to the stem. *n.*

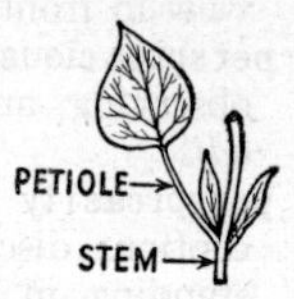

pe tite (pə tēt′), small. *adj.*

pe ti tion (pi tish′ən), 1. formal request. The people on our street signed a petition asking the city council for a new sidewalk. 2. ask earnestly; make a petition to. They petitioned the mayor to use his influence with the city council. 3. prayer. 4. pray. *n., v. 5.*

pe ti tion er (pi tish′ən ər), person who petitions. *n. 19.*

Pe trarch (pē′trärk), an Italian poet, famous for his sonnets (1304-1374). *n. 11.*

pet rel (pet′rəl), a small black-and-white sea bird with long, pointed wings. *n.*

pet ri fy (pet′ri fī), 1. turn into stone. There is a petrified forest in Arizona. 2. paralyze with fear, horror, or surprise. The bird seemed petrified as the snake came near. *v., petrified, petrifying. 10.*

Stormy petrel (about 5½ in. long)

Pet ro grad (pet′rō grad), the former capital of Russia, now called Leningrad. *n. 14.*

pet rol (pet′rəl), gasoline. [*British*] *n.*

pe tro le um (pi trō′li əm), an oily, dark-colored liquid found in the earth. Gasoline, kerosene, and paraffin are made from petroleum. *n. 6.*

pet ti coat (pet′i kōt), 1. a skirt that hangs from the waist or from the shoulders, worn beneath the dress by women, girls, and babies. 2. skirt. 3. female or feminine; as, petticoat government. *n., adj. 5.*

pet ti fog ger (pet′i fog′ər), 1. an inferior lawyer who uses petty, mean, cheating methods. 2. any inferior person who uses petty, mean, cheating methods. *n.*

pet ti ness (pet′i nis), smallness; meanness; petty nature or behavior. *n.*

pet tish (pet′ish), peevish; cross. *adj. 17.*

pet ty (pet′i), 1. small; having little importance or value. She insisted on telling me all her petty troubles. 2. mean; narrow-minded. 3. lower; subordinate. A **petty officer** is a noncommissioned officer in the navy. *adj., pettier, pettiest. 5.*

pet u lance (pech′ů ləns), being peevish; bad humor; being irritated by trifles. *n. 15.*

pet u lant (pech′ů lənt), peevish; subject to little fits of bad temper; irritable over trifles. *adj. 15.*

pe tu ni a (pi tū′ni ə or pi tü′ni ə), a common garden plant with funnel-shaped flowers of white, pink, and various shades of purple. *n. 19.*

Petunia

pew (pū), 1. a fixed bench with a back, in a church. 2. place in a church set apart for the use of a certain family or group of people. *n. 8.*

Pews

pe wee (pē′wē), small American bird with an olive-colored or gray back. *n.*

pew ter (pū′tər), 1. alloy of tin with lead, copper, or other metals. 2. dishes or other utensils made of this. 3. made of pewter; as, a pewter mug. *n., adj. 12.*

pha e ton or **pha ë ton** (fā′i tən), 1. light four-wheeled carriage with or without a top. 2. open automobile of the touring car type. *n. 19.*

Phaeton

pha lanx (fā′langks), 1. a special battle formation of infantry fighting in close ranks with their shields joined and long spears overlapping each other. 2. a compact or closely massed body of persons, animals, or things. 3. a number of persons united for a common purpose. *n. 11.*

phan tasm (fan′tazm), 1. an unreal fancy; thing seen only in one's imagination; as, the phantasms of a dream or fever. 2. a deceiving likeness (of something). 3. a supposed appearance of an absent person, living or dead. *n. 15.*

phan ta sy (fan′tə si), fantasy. *n., pl. phantasies. 15.*

phan tom (fan′təm), 1. ghost; an image in the mind which seems to be real; a vague, dim, or shadowy appearance. His fevered brain filled the room with phantoms from the past. 2. like a ghost; unreal; as, a phantom ship. *n., adj. 6.*

Phar aoh (fãr′ō), a title given to the kings of ancient Egypt. *n. 8.*

Phar i see (far′i sē), 1. member of a Jewish sect or group at the time of Christ, very strict in keeping to tradition and the laws of their religion, who thought themselves very holy. 2. A **pharisee** is a person who makes a show of religion rather than follows its spirit, and thinks he is much better than other men. *n. 11.*

phar ma cist (fär′mə sist), druggist; a chemist who prepares medicines. *n.*

phar ma cy (fär′mə si), 1. the preparation and dispensing of drugs and medicines; the occupation of a druggist. 2. drug store. *n., pl. pharmacies. 19.*

phar ynx (far′ingks), the cavity at the back of the mouth where the passages to the nose, lungs, and stomach begin. *n., pl. pharynxes, pharynges* (fə rin′jēz). *12.*

PHARYNX

phase (fāz), 1. one of the changing states or stages of development of a thing. At present Dick's voice is changing; that is a phase all boys go through. 2. one side, part, or view (of a subject). What phase of arithmetic are you studying now? 3. the apparent shape of the moon or of a planet at a given time. The new moon, first quarter, full moon, and last quarter are four phases of the moon. *n. 10.*

pheas ant (fez′ənt), a game bird with a long tail and brilliant feathers. Wild pheasants live in many parts of Europe and America. *n., pl. pheasants* or *pheasant. 10.*

English pheasant (about 2½ ft. long, including the tail)

phe nix (fē′niks), phoenix. *n.*

phe nom e na (fi nom′i nə), more than one phenomenon. *n. pl. 16.*

phe nom e nal (fi nom′i nəl), 1. of or pertaining to a phenomenon or phenomena. 2. having the nature of a phenomenon. 3. extraordinary; as, a phenomenal memory. *adj. 13.*

phe nom e non (fi nom′i non), 1. fact, event, or circumstance that can be observed. Lightning is an electrical phenomenon. Fever and inflammation are phenomena of disease. 2. something extraordinary or remarkable. An eclipse is an interesting phenomenon. The fond parents think their child is a phenomenon. *n., pl. phenomena* (-nə) or (especially for def. 2) *phenomenons. 7.*

phi al (fī′əl), vial; small bottle. *n. 17.*

Phid i as (fid′i əs), a famous Greek sculptor (500?-432? B.C.). *n. 15.*

Phila., Philadelphia.

Phil a del phi a (fil′ə del′fi ə), the largest city in Pennsylvania and one of the largest cities in the United States. *n. 3.*

phil an throp ic (fil′ən throp′ik), 1. pertaining to or characterized by philanthropy. 2. charitable; benevolent; kindly. *adj. 18.*

phi lan thro pist (fi lan′thrə pist), person who loves mankind and works for its welfare. *n. 11.*

phi lan thro py (fi lan′thrə pi), 1. love of mankind shown by practical kindness and helpfulness to humanity. The Red Cross appeals to philanthropy. 2. thing that benefits humanity. A hospital is a useful philanthropy. *n., pl. philanthropies. 12.*

phi lat e ly (fi lat′ə li), the collecting, arranging, and study of postage stamps, stamped envelopes, post cards, etc. *n.*

Phil ip (fil′ip), one of the twelve disciples chosen by Jesus as his apostles. *n.*

Phil ip pine (fil′i pēn), of or having to do with the Philippine Islands or their inhabitants. *adj. 6.*

Philippine Islands, group of 7083 islands in the West Pacific Ocean, southeast of Asia and north of Australia. The Philippine Islands are under the guardianship of the United States until 1945, when they will receive their independence.

Phil ip pines (fil′i pēnz), Philippine Islands. *n. pl.*

Phi lis tine (fi lis′tēn), 1. in the Bible, one of the warlike people in southwestern Palestine who attacked the Israelites many times. 2. person who is commonplace in ideas and tastes. 3. of the Philistines. 4. lacking culture; commonplace. *n., adj. 6.*

phi lol o gy (fi lol′ə ji), the science of language; the study of language and literature. *n. 18.*

phi los o pher (fi los′ə fər), 1. lover of wisdom; person who studies philosophy much. 2. person who has a system of philosophy. 3. person who shows the calmness of philosophy under hard conditions, accepting life and making the best of it. *n. 4.*

phil o soph ic (fil′ə sof′ik), 1. of philosophy. 2. knowing much about philosophy. 3. devoted to philosophy. 4. wise; calm; reasonable. *adj. 10.*

phil o soph i cal (fil′ə sof′i kəl), philosophic; like a philosopher. *adj. 9.*

phi los o phize (fi los′ə fīz), think or reason as a philosopher does; try to understand and explain things; as, to philosophize about life, death, mind, matter, God, etc. *v. 20.*

phi los o phy (fi los′ə fi), 1. the study of the truth or principles underlying all knowledge; the study of the most general causes and principles of the universe. 2. an explanation of the world. 3. a system for guiding life. 4. calmness; reasonable attitude; accepting things as they are and making the best of them. *n., pl. philosophies. 4.*

phil ter or **phil tre** (fil′tər), a drug or potion used to make a person fall in love; a magic drink. *n.*

phlegm (flem), 1. the thick discharge from the throat that accompanies a cold. 2. sluggish disposition or temperament; indifference. 3. coolness; calmness. *n. 16.*

phleg mat ic (fleg mat′ik), 1. sluggish; indifferent. 2. cool; calm. John is phlegmatic; he never seems to get excited about anything. *adj. 13.*

Phlox

phlox (floks), a common garden plant with showy flower clusters of various colors. *n.*

Phoe be[1] (fē′bi), 1. the goddess of the moon. Phoebe is also called Artemis or Diana. 2. the moon. *Used in poetry. n. 10.*

phoe be[2] (fē′bi), a small American bird. See the picture. *n.*

Phoebe (about 7 in. long)

Phoe bus (fē′bəs), 1. Apollo, the god of the sun. 2. the sun. *Used in poetry. n. 7.*

Phoe ni cia (fi nish′ə), an ancient country on the coast west of Palestine, famous for its traders. *n.*

Phoe ni cian (fi nish′ən), 1. having to do with Phoenicia, its people, or their language. 2. one of the people of Phoenicia. 3. the language of Phoenicia. *adj., n. 14.*

phoe nix (fē′niks), a bird, the only one of its kind, said to live 500 or 600 years, to burn itself on a funeral pile, and rise again from the ashes, fresh and beautiful, for another long life. *n. 13.*

Phoe nix (fē′niks), the capital of Arizona. *n.*

phone (fōn), telephone. *n., v. 5.*

pho net ic (fō net′ik), representing sounds made with the voice. Systems of phonetic spelling spell words as they are pronounced, and represent the same sound by the same letter. Phonetic symbols are marks used to show pronunciation. We use ᴛʜ as the phonetic symbol for the sound of *th* in *the* or *then.* Phonetic exercises are drills in pronunciation. *adj. 17.*

pho net ics (fō net′iks), the science of sounds made in speech. *n.*

phon ics (fon′iks), 1. the science of sound. 2. the science of the sounds made in speech; phonetics. 3. simplified phonetics for teaching reading. *n.*

pho no graph (fō′nə graf), an instrument that records and reproduces sounds. *n. 9.*

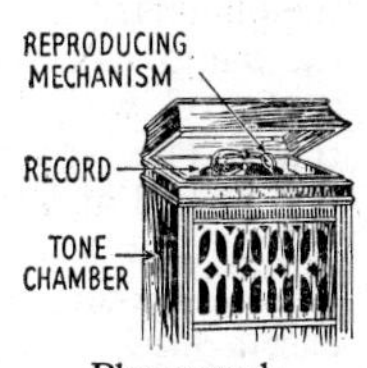

Phonograph

phos phate (fos′fāt), 1. a salt of an acid containing phosphorus. Bread contains phosphates. 2. a fertilizer containing such salts. *n. 7.*

Phos phor (fos′fər), the morning star. *n.* [*Used in poetry*] *18.*

phos pho res cence (fos′fə res′əns), 1. act or process of giving out light without burning or by very slow burning that seems not to give out heat; as, the phosphorescence of fireflies. 2. light given out in this way. *n.*

phos pho res cent (fos′fə res′ənt), showing phosphorescence. *adj. 17.*

phos phor ic (fos for′ik), pertaining to or containing phosphorus. *adj. 8.*

phos pho rous (fos′fə rəs), pertaining to or containing phosphorus. *adj.*

phos pho rus (fos′fə rəs), a nonmetallic element that looks like yellow wax. Phosphorus burns slowly at ordinary temperatures and shines in the dark. *n.*

pho to (fō′tō), photograph. *n., pl. photos. 10.*

pho to graph (fō′tə graf), 1. a picture made with a camera. A photograph is made by the action of the light rays from the thing pictured that pass through the lens of the camera to a film spread over the surface of glass, paper, celluloid, or metal. 2. take a photograph of. *n., v. 6.*

pho tog ra pher (fə tog′rə fər), person who takes photographs. *n. 13.*

pho to graph ic (fō′tə graf′ik), 1. of or like photography; as, photographic accuracy. 2. used in or produced by photography; as, photographic plates, a photographic record of a trip. *adj. 11.*

pho tog ra phy (fə tog′rə fi), the taking of photographs. *n. 16.*

pho to play (fō′tō plā′), moving-picture play. *n.*

phrase (frāz), 1. a combination of words. He spoke in simple phrases, so that the children understood him. 2. an expression often used. "Call up" is the common phrase for "get a telephone connection with." 3. a group of words not containing a subject and predicate and used as a single word. *In the house, coming by the church,* and *to eat too fast* are phrases. 4. express in a particular way. She phrased her excuse politely. *n., v. 4.*

phra se ol o gy (frā′zi ol′ə ji), selection and arrangement of words; the particular way in which a person expresses himself in language; as, scientific phraseology, the phraseology of the Bible, the phraseology of the sports page in a newspaper. *n., pl. phraseologies. 14.*

Phryg i a (frij′i ə), an ancient country in Asia Minor. *n. 14.*

phys ic (fiz′ik), 1. a medicine, especially one that moves the bowels. 2. give medicine to. 3. move the bowels of. 4. the art of healing; the science and practice of medicine. *n., v., physicked, physicking. 8.*

phys i cal (fiz′i kəl), 1. of the body; as, physical exercise, physical strength, physical education. 2. of matter; material. His physical force was weak, but his mental and moral force was very great. 3. according to the laws of nature. It is a physical impossibility for the sun to rise in the west. 4. dealing with the natural features of the earth. **Physical geography** teaches about the earth's formation, climate, clouds, and tides. *adj. 5.*

phys i cal ly (fiz′i kəl i), in a physical manner; in physical respects; as regards the body. After his vacation he was in fine condition both physically and mentally. *adv.*

phy si cian (fi zish′ən), doctor of medicine. *n. 3.*

phys i cist (fiz′i sist), person who knows much about physics. *n. 17.*

phys ics (fiz′iks), the science that deals with matter and energy, or the action of different forms of energy on matter. Physics studies mechanics, heat, light, sound, and electricity. *n. 13.*

phys i og no my (fiz′i og′nə mi), 1. kind of features or type of face one has; one's face. Can you read his physiognomy? 2. art of estimating character from the features of the face or the form of the body. 3. general aspect or looks of a countryside, a situation, etc. *n., pl. physiognomies. 13.*

phys i o log i cal (fiz′i ə loj′i kəl), pertaining to physiology. Digestion is a physiological process. *adj. 17.*

phys i ol o gist (fiz′i ol′ə jist), one who knows much about physiology. *n. 17.*

phys i ol o gy (fiz′i ol′ə ji), the science dealing with the normal functions of living things or their organs; as, animal physiology, human physiology, vegetable physiology, the physiology of the blood. *n. 10.*

phy sique (fi zēk′), body; bodily structure, organization, or development; as, a man of strong physique. *n. 14.*

pi (pī), the ratio of the circumference of any circle to its diameter, usually written as π. $\pi = 3.14159$. *n.*

P.I., Philippine Islands.

pi a nis si mo (pē′ə nis′i mō), in music: 1. very soft. 2. very softly. *adj., adv.*

pi an ist (pi an′ist), person who plays the piano. *n. 13.*

pi an o (pi an′ō), large musical instrument whose tones come from many wires. The wires are sounded by hammers which are worked by pressing keys on a keyboard. *n., pl. pianos. 4.*

Piazza or porch

pi an o for te (pi an′ō-fôr′ti), piano. *n. 19.*

pi az za (pi az′ə), 1. a large porch along one or more sides of a house. 2. an open public square in Italian towns. *n. 9.*

Piazza or public square

pi broch (pē′brok), a kind of musical piece performed on the bagpipe. It is usually warlike or sad. *n.*

Pic ar dy (pik′ər di), region in northern France. *n. 18.*

pic a yune (pik′ə ūn′), 1. small coin. 2. insignificant person or thing; trifle. 3. small; petty; mean. *n., adj.*

pic co lo (pik′ə lō), small shrill flute, sounding an octave higher than an ordinary flute. *n., pl. piccolos.*

pick (pik), 1. choose; select. Mr. Sport thinks he can pick a winning horse at a race. 2. choice or selection. 3. the best part. 4. pull away with the fingers; gather; as, to pick fruit or flowers. 5. the amount of a crop picked at one time. 6. a heavy tool with a sharp point for breaking up earth or rock. 7. a sharp-pointed instrument. Ice is broken into pieces with a pick. 8. pierce, dig into, or break up with some pointed tool. 9. use something pointed to remove things from; as, to pick one's teeth, to pick a bone. 10. prepare for use by removing waste parts. 11. pull apart. The hair in the pillow needs to be picked, as it has matted. 12. use the fingers with a plucking motion. The sick man picked at the blankets. 13. pluck at. The boy picked the banjo. 14. seek and find. Carl picked a quarrel with Dick. 15. eat a bit at a time. The bird picks at the bread. Alice just picked at her food because she did not like it. 16. Some special meanings are:

pick a chicken, pull out its feathers.

pick a lock, open it with a pointed instrument, wire, etc.

pick a pocket, steal from a person's pocket.

pick flaws, find fault.

pick off, shoot one by one.

pick out, choose; select.

pick over, look over; prepare for use.

pick up, 1. take up. The boy picked up a stone. 2. get. The woman picks up a bargain. 3. learn without teaching. Jack picks up games easily.

v., n. 1.

Pickax

pick a nin ny (pik′ə nin′i), a Negro child. *n., pl. pickaninnies. 19.*

pick ax or **pick axe** (pik′aks′), heavy tool with a sharp point for breaking up dirt, rocks, etc.; pick. *n. 13.*

pick er (pik′ər), 1. person who gathers, picks, or collects. 2. tool for picking anything. *n. 16.*

Pickerel

pick er el (pik′ər əl), kind of large fresh-water fish with a long, narrow, pointed head. *n., pl. pickerel* or *pickerels. 14.*

pick et (pik′it), 1. a pointed stake or peg

driven into the ground to make a fence, to tie a horse to, etc. 2. enclose with pickets. 3. tie to a picket. Picket your horse here. 4. a small body of troops, or a single man, posted at some place to watch for the enemy and guard against surprise. 5. person stationed by a labor union near a place of work to keep workers from working. 6. station as pickets. 7. station pickets at or near; as, to picket a factory. *n., v. 14.*

pick le (pik′əl), 1. salt water, vinegar, or other liquid in which meat and vegetables can be preserved. 2. a cucumber preserved in pickle. 3. any other vegetable preserved in pickle. 4. preserve in pickle; as, pickled beets. 5. trouble; difficulty. I got in a bad pickle today. *Used in common talk. n., v. 5.*

pick pock et (pik′pok′it), person who steals from people's pockets. *n. 17.*

pic nic (pik′nik), 1. a trip or pleasure party, with a meal in the open air. 2. go on such a trip. 3. eat in picnic style. *n., v., picnicked, picnicking. 4.*

pic nick er (pik′nik ər), one who picnics. *n.*

pi cot (pē′kō), one of a number of fancy loops in embroidery, tatting, etc., or along the edge of lace, ribbon, etc. *n. 18.*

Pict (pikt), member of a race of people formerly living in Scotland, especially northern Scotland. *n. 20.*

pic to ri al (pik tō′ri əl), 1. pertaining to pictures; expressed in pictures. 2. making a picture for the mind; vivid. 3. illustrated by pictures; as, a pictorial history, a pictorial magazine. 4. having to do with painters or painting; as, pictorial skill. *adj. 15.*

pic ture (pik′chər), 1. a drawing, painting, or photograph; a printed copy of any of these. That book contains a good picture of him. 2. scene. The trees and brook make a lovely picture. 3. something beautiful. 4. likeness; image. Mary is the picture of her mother. 5. draw, paint, etc. The artist pictured the saints. 6. form a picture of; imagine. It is hard to picture life a hundred years ago. 7. a vivid description. 8. show by words; describe vividly. The soldier pictured the battle. The speaker pictured the suffering of the poor. 9. moving picture. *n., v. 1.*

pic tur esque (pik′chər esk′), 1. quaint or interesting enough to be used as the subject of a picture; as, a picturesque old mill. 2. making a picture for the mind; vivid. *adj. 5.*

pic tur esque ness (pik′chər esk′nis), being picturesque; picturesque quality. *n. 17.*

pie[1] (pī), fruit, meat, etc., enclosed in pastry and baked, such as an apple pie, a chicken pie. *n. 2.*

pie[2] (pī), magpie, a black-and-white bird that chatters a great deal. *n.*

pie bald (pī′bôld′), 1. spotted in two colors, especially black and white; as, a piebald horse. 2. a spotted horse. *adj., n.*

piece (pēs), 1. bit; scrap; one of the parts into which a thing is divided. The cup broke in pieces. 2. limited part; as, a piece of land containing two acres. **Give a person a piece of one's mind** means scold him. 3. small quantity; as, a piece of bread, a piece of wood. 4. single thing of a set or class. Some pieces of the dinner set have been broken. 5. single composition in an art; as, a piece of poetry, a piece of music. 6. coin. A nickel is a five-cent piece. 7. **Pieces of eight** were dollars used by the Spanish in Spain and America. 8. example; instance. Sleeping with a light in the room is a piece of nonsense. 9. quantity in which goods are put up for the market. The piece of cloth contains ten yards. 10. the amount of work done; as, paid by the piece. 11. gun; cannon. 12. make or repair by adding or joining pieces. Mother pieced a quilt yesterday. 13. join the pieces of. *n., v. 1.*

piece meal (pēs′mēl′), 1. piece by piece; a little at a time; as, work done piecemeal. 2. piece from piece; to pieces; into fragments. The lamb was torn piecemeal by the wolves. *adv. 15.*

piece work (pēs′wėrk′), work done and paid for by the piece. *n. 19.*

pied (pīd), having patches of two or more colors; many colored. *adj. 11.*

Pied mont (pēd′mont), 1. a plateau in Virginia, North Carolina, South Carolina, Georgia, and Alabama. 2. district of northwestern Italy. *n. 10.*

pier (pēr), 1. a structure supported on columns extending into the water, and used as a walk or a landing place. 2. breakwater. 3. pillar; one of the solid supports

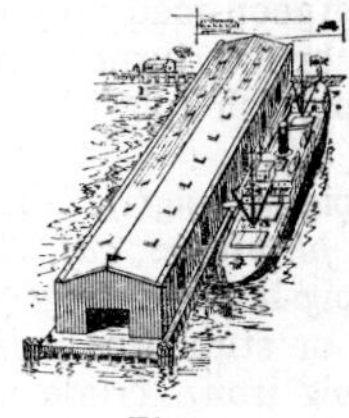

Pier

on which the arches of a bridge rest. 4. solid part of a wall between windows, doors, etc. *n. 6.*

pierce[1] (pērs), 1. go into; go through. A tunnel pierces the mountain. 2. make a hole in; bore into or through. A nail pierced the tire of our car. 3. force a way through or into. The cold wind pierced our clothes. A sharp cry pierced the air. 4. make a way through with the eye or mind; as, to pierce a disguise, to pierce a mystery. 5. affect sharply with some feeling. Her heart was pierced with grief. *v. 3.*

Pierce[2] (pērs), Franklin (1804-1869), the 14th president of the United States, from 1853 to 1857. *n.*

Pierre (pēr), the capital of South Dakota. *n. 18.*

pi e ty (pī′ə ti), 1. being pious; religious character or conduct; holiness; goodness. 2. dutiful regard for one's parents. 3. pious act. *n., pl. pieties. 6.*

Pigs

pig (pig), 1. a domestic animal raised for its meat. 2. a young hog. 3. person who seems or acts like a pig; one who is greedy, dirty, dull, sullen, or stubborn. *n. 2.*

pi geon (pij′ən), a bird with a stout body and short legs; dove. See the picture. *n. 4.*

Pigeon

pi geon hole (pij′ən hōl′), 1. a small place built, usually as one of a series, for a pigeon to nest in. 2. one of a set of square boxlike compartments for holding papers and other articles in a desk, a cabinet, etc. 3. put in a pigeonhole; put away. 4. classify and lay aside in memory where one can refer to it. 5. put aside with the idea of dismissing, forgetting, or neglecting. The city council pigeonholed the people's request for a new park. *n., v. 17.*

pi geon-toed (pij′ən tōd′), having the toes or feet turned inward. *adj.*

pig gish (pig′ish), like a pig; greedy; filthy. *adj.*

pig gy (pig′i), 1. little pig. 2. greedy. *n., pl. piggies, adj. 12.*

pig-head ed (pig′hed′id), stupidly obstinate or stubborn. *adj.*

pig iron, crude iron as it first comes from the blast furnace or smelter. It is usually in the form of oblong masses called pigs.

pig ment (pig′mənt), a coloring matter. Paint and dyes are made by mixing pigments with liquid. The color of a person's hair, skin, and eyes is due to pigment in the cells of the body. *n. 8.*

pig my (pig′mi), 1. a dwarf. The pigmies living in Africa and Asia are less than five feet high. 2. very small; as, a pigmy mind. *n., pl. pigmies, adj. 13.* Also spelled **pygmy.**

pig skin (pig′skin′), 1. the skin of a pig. 2. leather made from it. 3. a saddle or a football. *Used in common talk. n.*

pig sty (pig′stī′), pen for pigs. *n., pl. pigsties.*

pig tail (pig′tāl′), a braid of hair hanging from the back of the head. *n.*

pike[1] (pīk), 1. spear; a long wooden handle with a spearhead, which foot soldiers used to carry. 2. point; spike. *n. 7.*

Soldier holding a pike

pike[2] (pīk), a large fresh-water fish with a long, narrow, pointed head. *n.*

pike[3] (pīk), turnpike; a road that has, or used to have, a gate where toll is, or was, paid. *n.*

Pike's Peak (pīks′ pēk′), mountain of the Rocky Mountains, in central Colorado.

pike staff (pīk′staf′), staff or shaft of a pike or spear. *n., pl. pikestaves* (-stāvz′). *19.*

pi las ter (pi las′tər), a rectangular pillar, especially when not standing alone, but supporting a part of a wall from which it projects somewhat. *n. 17.*

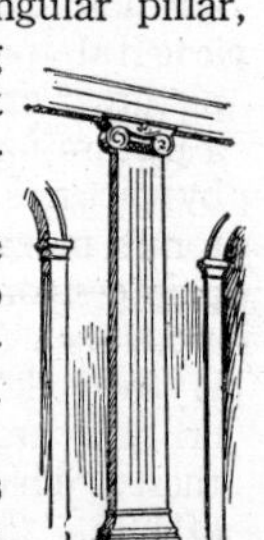
Pilaster

Pi late (pī′lət). Pontius Pilate was the Roman governor who was ruling over Judea in Palestine when Jesus was crucified. *n. 12.*

pile[1] (pīl), 1. many things lying one upon another in a more or less orderly way; as, a pile of wood. 2. a mass like a hill or mound; as, a pile of dirt. 3. make into a pile; heap evenly; heap up. 4. gather or rise in piles. Snow piled against the fences. 5. large amount. *Used in common talk. n., v. 2.*

pile[2] (pīl), heavy beam driven upright into the ground or the bed of a river to help support a bridge, wharf, etc. *n.*

pile[3] (pīl), 1. a soft, thick nap on velvet, plush, and many carpets. 2. soft, fine hair or down; wool. *n.*

pile driver, machine for driving down piles or stakes, usually a tall framework in which a heavy weight is raised to a height and then allowed to fall upon the pile.

pil fer (pil′fər), steal in small quantities. *v. 11.*

Pil grim (pil′grim), one of the English settlers who founded Plymouth, Massachusetts, in 1620. *n.*

pil grim (pil′grim), 1. person who goes on a journey to a sacred or holy place as an act of religious devotion. In the Middle Ages, many people went as pilgrims to Jerusalem and to holy places in Europe. 2. traveler. *n. 4.*

pil grim age (pil′gri mij), 1. a pilgrim's journey; a journey to some sacred place. 2. a long journey. *n. 6.*

pill (pil), 1. medicine made up into a tiny ball to be swallowed whole. 2. a very small ball of anything. *n. 5.*

pil lage (pil′ij), 1. to plunder; rob with violence. Pirates pillaged the towns along the coast. 2. plunder; robbery. *v., n. 9.*

pil lar (pil′ər), 1. a slender upright support; a column. Pillars are usually made of stone, wood, or metal and used as supports or ornaments for a building. Sometimes a pillar stands alone as a monument. 2. anything slender and upright like a pillar. 3. an important support. A person of strong character or important position is a pillar of society. *n. 4.*

Pillars around a building

pil lion (pil′yən), a pad attached behind a saddle for a person to sit on. *n.*

pil lo ry (pil′ə ri), 1. a frame of wood with holes through which a person's head and hands were put. The pillory was formerly used as a punishment, being set up in a public place where the crowd could make fun of the offender. 2. put in the pillory. 3. expose to public ridicule, contempt, or abuse. *n., pl. pillories, v., pilloried, pillorying. 9.*

Pillory

pil low (pil′ō), 1. a bag or case filled with feathers, down, or other soft material. 2. rest on a pillow. *n., v. 3.*

pil low case (pil′ō kās′), cotton or linen cover pulled over a pillow. *n.*

pi lot (pī′lət), 1. man who steers a ship. 2. man whose business is to steer ships in or out of a harbor or through dangerous waters. A steamer takes on a pilot before coming into a strange harbor. 3. person who steers an airplane, balloon, or airship. 4. act as a pilot of; steer. The aviator pilots his airplane. 5. guide; leader. 6. guide; lead. The manager piloted us through the large factory and explained each process. *n., v. 6.*

pi men to (pi men′tō), 1. a kind of sweet pepper, used as a vegetable, relish, and stuffing for green olives. 2. allspice. *n., pl. pimentos. 20.*

pi mien to (pi myen′tō), sweet pepper. *n., pl. pimientos.*

pim per nel (pim′pər nel), a small scarlet, purple, or white flower that closes in bad weather. *n. 19.*

pim ple (pim′pəl), a small, inflamed swelling of the skin. *n. 14.*

pin (pin), 1. a short slender piece of wire with a point at one end and a head at the other, for fastening things together. 2. a badge with a pin or clasp to fasten it to the clothing. She wore her class pin. 3. an ornament which has a pin or clasp; brooch. 4. a peg made of wood or metal, used to fasten things together, hold something, or hang things on. 5. fasten with a pin or pins; put a pin through. 6. hold fast in one position. When the tree fell, it pinned his shoulder to the ground. 7. a bottle-shaped piece of wood used in ninepins, tenpins, etc *n., v., pinned, pinning. 2.*

pin a fore (pin′ə fōr′), a child's apron that covers most of the dress. *n. 15.*

pin cers (pin′sərz), 1. a tool for gripping and holding tight, made like scissors but with jaws instead of blades. 2. the large claw of crabs and lobsters which can be used to pinch or nip; pair of claws. *n. pl. or sing. 11.*

pinch (pinch), 1. squeeze between two hard edges; press on so as to hurt; squeeze with thumb and forefinger. He pinched his finger in the door. My new shoes pinch. 2. a squeeze; sharp pressure that hurts; as, the pinch of tight shoes, the pinch of cold, the pinch of hunger. 3. cause to shrink or become thin; as, a face pinched by hunger. 4. as much as can be taken up with the tips of finger and thumb; as, a pinch of salt. 5. be stingy. *v., n. 4.*

pin cush ion (pin′ku̇sh′ən), small cushion to stick pins in until needed. *n. 19.*

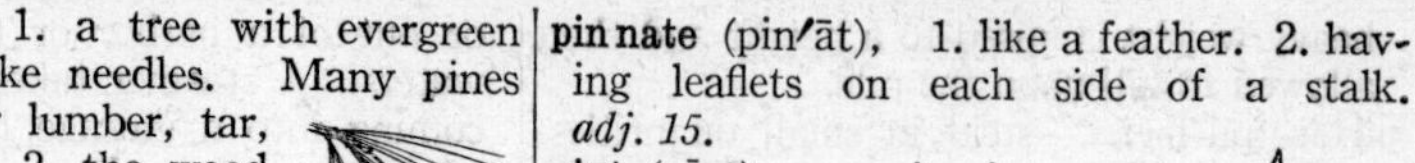

pine[1] (pīn), 1. a tree with evergreen leaves shaped like needles. Many pines are of value for lumber, tar, turpentine, etc. 2. the wood of the pine. *n. 2.*

Pine leaves and cone

pine[2] (pīn), 1. long eagerly; yearn. 2. waste away with pain, hunger, grief, or desire. *v.*

pine ap ple (pīn′ap′əl), 1. a large juicy fruit growing in hot climates, that looks somewhat like a big pine cone. 2. the plant with slender stiff leaves on which the pineapple is grown. *n. 9.*

pin feath er (pin′feᴛʜ′ər), the small stub that is a developing feather. Remove all the pinfeathers from the chicken before cooking it. *n.*

Pineapple

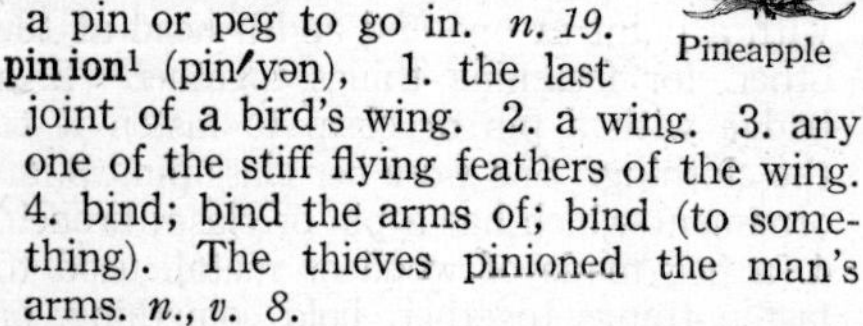

pin hole (pin′hōl′), 1. a hole made by a pin. 2. a hole for a pin or peg to go in. *n. 19.*

pin ion[1] (pin′yən), 1. the last joint of a bird's wing. 2. a wing. 3. any one of the stiff flying feathers of the wing. 4. bind; bind the arms of; bind (to something). The thieves pinioned the man's arms. *n., v. 8.*

pin ion[2] (pin′yən), small gear. Its teeth fit into those of a larger gear or rack. *n.*

pink[1] (pingk), 1. the color obtained by mixing red with white; light or pale red. 2. a garden plant with spicy-smelling flowers of various colors, mostly white, pink, and red. A carnation is one kind of pink. 3. the highest degree or condition. By exercising every day John kept himself in the pink of health. *n., adj. 2.*

pink[2] (pingk), 1. prick or pierce with a sword. 2. ornament with small round holes. 3. cut the edge of (cloth) in small scallops. *v.*

pink ish (pingk′ish), somewhat pink. *adj.*

pin money, an allowance of money made by a husband to his wife for her private use; such an allowance made to a daughter, etc.

pin nace (pin′is), 1. a ship's boat. 2. a very small schooner. *n. 11.*

pin na cle (pin′ə kəl), 1. a high peak or point of rock. 2. the highest point; as, at the pinnacle of his fame. 3. a slender turret or spire. *n. 8.*

Pinnacle

pin nate (pin′āt), 1. like a feather. 2. having leaflets on each side of a stalk. *adj. 15.*

Pinnate leaf

pint (pīnt), a unit of measure equal to half a quart. *n. 4.*

pin to (pin′tō), 1. spotted in two colors; piebald. 2. a pinto horse. *adj., n., pl. pintos.*

pi o neer (pī′ə nēr′), 1. person who settles in a part of the country that has not been occupied before, except by savage tribes. 2. person who goes first, or does something first, and so prepares a way for others. 3. prepare or open up (a way); take the lead. *n., v. 5.*

pi ous (pī′əs), 1. religious; devoted to a religious life. 2. done under pretense of religion; as, a pious fraud. *adj. 4.*

pip[1] (pip), the seed of an apple, orange, etc. *n. 17.*

pip[2] (pip), a disease of birds. *n.*

pipe (pīp), 1. a tube through which a liquid or gas flows. 2. supply with pipes. Our street is being piped for gas. 3. carry by means of pipes. 4. a musical instrument with a single tube into which the player blows. **Pipes** sometimes means a bagpipe. 5. play music on a pipe. 6. any one of the tubes in an organ. 7. voice, song, or note; as, the pipe of the lark. 8. make a shrill noise; sing in a shrill voice. 9. a tube of clay, wood, etc., with a bowl at one end, for smoking. *n., v. 2.*

pip er (pīp′ər), person who plays on a pipe, especially one who goes about the country playing at different places. *n. 6.*

pip ing (pīp′ing), 1. shrill sound; as, the piping of frogs in the spring. 2. shrill. 3. pipes; as, lead piping. 4. material for pipes. 5. the music of pipes. 6. a narrow band of material, sometimes containing a cord, used for trimming along edges and seams. 7. **Piping hot** means boiling hot. *n., adj., adv.*

pip pin (pip′in), any of several kinds of apple; as, a yellow pippin. *n. 12.*

pi quan cy (pē′kən si), 1. quality of exciting the appetite, being odd to the taste, or pleasantly sharp. 2. quality of exciting the mind pleasantly. *n. 20.*

pi quant (pē′kənt), 1. pleasantly sharp; stimulating to the taste; as, piquant pickles, a piquant sauce. 2. stimulating to the mind, interest, etc.; as, a piquant bit of news, a piquant face. *adj. 20.*

pique (pēk), 1. a little feeling of anger at being slighted; wounded pride. In a pique, she left the party. 2. wound the pride of. It piqued Mary that they should have a secret she did not share. 3. arouse; stir up. The curiosity of the boys was piqued by the locked trunk. 4. **Pique oneself** means feel pride. She piqued herself on her skill in making pies. *n., v. 8.*

pi qué (pi kā'), a cotton fabric with narrow ribs or raised stripes. *n.*

pi ra cy (pī'rə si), robbery on the sea. *n., pl. piracies. 16.*

pi rate (pī'rit), 1. one who attacks and robs ships unlawfully; robber on the sea. 2. be a pirate; plunder; rob. *n., v. 6.*

pi rat i cal (pī rat'i kəl), of pirates; like pirates; like piracy. *adj. 14.*

pir ou ette (pir'ü et'), 1. a whirling about on one foot or on the toes, as in dancing. 2. to whirl in this way. *n., v.*

Pi sa (pē'zə), a city in northwestern Italy famous for its leaning tower. *n. 13.*

pis ta chi o (pis tä'shi ō), 1. a greenish nut having a flavor that suggests almond. 2. its flavor. 3. light green. *n., pl. pistachios.*

pis til (pis'til), the seed-bearing part of a flower. *n. 8.*

pis til late (pis'ti lāt), 1. having a pistil or pistils. 2. having a pistil or pistils but no stamens. *adj. 19.*

pis tol (pis'təl), a small short gun held and fired with one hand. *n. 4.*

Pistol

pis ton (pis'tən), a short cylinder, or a flat round piece of wood or metal, fitting closely inside a tube or hollow cylinder in which it is moved back and forth by some force (often the pressure of steam). A piston receives or transmits motion by means of a rod that is attached to it. *n. 11.*

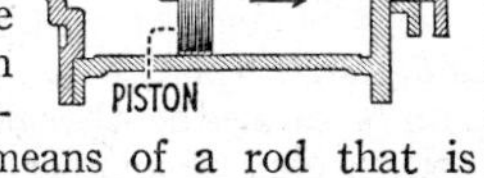

pit[1] (pit), 1. hole in the ground. 2. hole dug deep into the earth. 3. a hollow on the surface of anything; hole; as, the armpit. 4. a little hole or scar such as is left by smallpox. 5. to mark with small pits or scars. 6. **Pit one thing against another** means set them to fight one against another. 7. hell, or part of it. *n., v., pitted, pitting. 3.*

pit[2] (pit), the stone of a cherry, peach, plum, date, etc. *n.*

pitch[1] (pich), 1. throw; fling; hurl; toss. The men were pitching horseshoes. 2. in baseball, to throw (a ball) to the man batting. 3. fix firmly in the ground; set up; as, to pitch a tent. 4. fall or plunge forward. The man lost his balance and pitched down the cliff. 5. plunge with the bow rising and then falling. The ship pitched about in the storm. 6. set at a certain point, degree, or level. 7. determine the key of (a tune, etc.). 8. act or manner of pitching. 9. point; position; degree. The poor man has reached the lowest pitch of bad fortune. 10. degree of highness or lowness of a sound. 11. height; as, the pitch of an arch. 12. amount of slope. 13. **Pitch into** means attack. 14. **Pitch in** means work vigorously. *v., n. 3.*

pitch[2] (pich), 1. a black sticky substance made from tar or turpentine, used to cover the seams of ships, to cover roofs, to make pavements, etc. 2. to cover with pitch. *n., v.*

pitch er[1] (pich'ər), 1. a container made of china, glass, silver, etc., with a lip at one side and a handle at the other. Pitchers are used for holding and pouring out water, milk, etc. 2. amount that a pitcher holds. *n. 4.*

Pitcher

pitch er[2] (pich'ər), the player on a baseball team who throws the ball for the batter to hit. *n.*

pitch fork (pich'fôrk'), a large fork with a long handle for lifting and throwing hay, etc. *n. 15.*

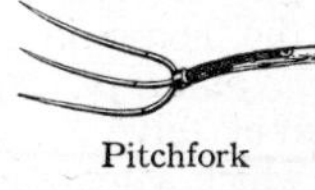
Pitchfork

pitch y (pich'i), 1. full of pitch. 2. like pitch; sticky. 3. black. *adj. 18.*

pit e ous (pit'i əs), to be pitied; moving the heart; deserving pity. The starving children are a piteous sight. *adj. 7.*

pit fall (pit'fôl'), 1. hidden pit to catch animals in. 2. any trap or hidden danger. *n. 17.*

pith (pith), 1. the central spongy tissue of plant stems. 2. similar soft tissue; as, the pith of an orange. 3. the important or essential part; as, the pith of a speech. 4. strength; energy. *n. 8.*

pith i ly (pith'i li), in a pithy manner; forcibly; concisely. *adv.*

pith y (pith'i), 1. having much pith; as, a pithy orange. 2. of or like pith. 3. full of substance, meaning, force, or vigor; as, pithy phrases, a pithy speaker. *adj., pithier, pithiest. 14.*

pit i a ble (pit′i ə bəl), 1. to be pitied; moving the heart; deserving pity. 2. deserving contempt; mean; to be scorned. *adj. 12.*

pit i ful (pit′i fəl), 1. to be pitied; moving the heart; deserving pity. The starving children are a pitiful sight. 2. feeling pity; feeling sorrow for the trouble of others. 3. deserving contempt; mean; to be scorned. *adj. 6.*

pit i less (pit′i lis), without pity or mercy. *adj. 6.*

Pitt (pit). William Pitt was the first Earl of Chatham (1708-1778). He and his son William (1759-1806) were famous English statesmen. *n. 13.*

pit tance (pit′əns), 1. small amount or share. 2. a small allowance of money or food. *n. 15.*

Pitts burgh (pits′bėrg), a large city in southwestern Pennsylvania, a center of the iron industry. *n. 6.*

pi tu i tar y (pi tū′i tãr′i or pi tü′i tãr′i), 1. of, pertaining to, or secreting mucus. 2. The **pituitary gland** or **pituitary body** is a small oval gland situated beneath the brain. It secretes important hormones. 3. pertaining to the pituitary gland. *adj. 17.*

pit y (pit′i), 1. sympathy; sorrow for another's suffering; a feeling for the sorrows of others. 2. feel pity for. I pity those who are out in the cold tonight. 3. cause for pity or regret. It is a pity to be kept in the house in fine weather. *n., pl. pities, v., pitied, pitying. 2.*

piv ot (piv′ət), 1. a shaft, pin, or point on which something turns. 2. mount on, attach by, or provide with a pivot. 3. to turn on a pivot; as, to pivot on one's heel. 4. that on which something turns, hinges, or depends; central point. Ed's pitching was the pivot of our hopes. *n., v. 8.*

pix y or **pix ie** (pik′si), fairy. *n., pl. pixies.*

Pixy sitting on a mushroom

pk., peck. *7.*

pkg., package.

pl., plural.

plac ard (plak′ärd, also plə kärd′ for 2), 1. a notice to be posted in a public place; poster. 2. put placards on or in. The circus placarded the city with advertisements. *n., v. 13.*

pla cate (plā′kāt), soothe or satisfy the anger of; make peaceful; as, to placate a person one has offended. *v.*

place (plās), 1. the part of space occupied by a person or thing. 2. a city, town, village, district, island, etc. What place do you come from? 3. house; dwelling. The Smiths have a beautiful place in the country. 4. a building or spot used for some particular purpose. A church is a place of worship. A store or office is a place of business. 5. a part or spot in a body or surface; as, a decayed place in a tooth, a sore place on one's foot. 6. rank; position; way of life. John won first place in the contest. The servant filled his place well. 7. position in time; part of time occupied by an event. The performance went too slowly in several places. 8. right position; usual position. There is a time and place for everything. Each book is in its place on the shelf. 9. a space or seat for a person. We took our places at the table. 10. put in a particular spot, position, or condition. Place the books on the table. The child was placed in a home. We placed an order for hats with this store. The people placed confidence in their leader. 11. duty; business. It is not my place to find fault. 12. work; job; employment. 13. **In place of** means instead of. *n., v. 1.*

plac er (plas′ər), place where gold or other minerals can be washed out of loose sand or gravel. *n.*

plac id (plas′id), calm; peaceful; quiet; as, a placid lake. *adj. 7.*

pla cid i ty (plə sid′i ti), calmness; peace; tranquility. *n.*

plack et (plak′it), the opening or slit at the top of a skirt which makes it easy to put on. *n.*

pla gi a rism (plā′ji ə rizm), taking and using as one's own the idea, writing, invention, etc., of another; especially, the taking and using of a passage, plot, etc., from the work of another writer. *n. 19.*

pla gi a rize (plā′ji ə rīz), take and use as one's own (the thoughts, writings, inventions, etc., of another); especially, to take and use (a passage, plot, etc., from the work of another writer). *v.*

plague (plāg), 1. a very dangerous disease that spreads rapidly and often causes death. 2. a punishment thought to be sent by God. 3. thing or person that torments, vexes, annoys, troubles, offends, or is disagreeable. 4. vex; annoy; bother. *n., v. 3.*

plaid (plad), 1. a long piece of woolen cloth, usually having a pattern of checks or stripes in many colors, worn about the shoulders by the Scottish Highlanders. See the picture just below. 2. any cloth with a pattern of checks or stripes. 3. having a pattern of checks or stripes; as, a plaid dress. *n., adj. 7.*

Scottish Highlander's plaid

plain (plān), 1. clear; easy to understand; easily seen or heard. 2. clearly; in a plain manner. 3. without ornament; as, a plain dress. 4. all of one color; as, a plain blue dress. 5. not rich; as, plain food. 6. common; ordinary; simple in manner; as, a plain man of the people. 7. not pretty; as, a plain girl. 8. frank; honest; sincere; as, plain speech. 9. flat; level; smooth. 10. a flat stretch of land. Cattle wandered over the plains. *adj., adv., n. 1.*

plain ness (plān′nis), being plain. *n. 9.*

plains man (plānz′mən), man who lives on the plains. *n., pl. plainsmen.*

plain-spo ken (plān′spō′kən), plain or frank in speech. *adj.*

plaint (plānt), 1. complaint. 2. lament. *Old use. n. 13.*

plain tiff (plān′tif), person who begins a lawsuit. The plaintiff accused the defendant of injuring him. *n. 13.*

plain tive (plān′tiv), mournful; sad. *adj. 8.*

plait (plat), 1. a braid. She wore her hair in a plait. 2. to braid. She plaits her hair. 3. a flat, usually narrow, fold made in cloth by doubling it on itself; a pleat. 4. fold or arrange in plaits; pleat; as, a plaited skirt. *n., v. 9.*

plan (plan), 1. think out beforehand how something is to be made or done; decide on methods and materials. I plan to reach New York by train on Tuesday, and stay two days. 2. a way of making or doing something that has been worked out beforehand. Our summer plans were upset by my mother's illness. 3. make a plan of. Have you planned your trip? 4. a drawing or diagram to show how a garden, a floor of a house, a park, etc., is arranged. *v., planned, planning, n. 1.*

Plan of a house

plane[1] (plān), 1. a flat or level surface. 2. flat or level. 3. a level. Keep your work at a high plane. 4. a thin, flat or curved supporting surface of an airplane. 5. airplane. *n., adj. 4.*

plane[2] (plān), 1. a carpenter's tool with a blade for smoothing wood. 2. a machine for smoothing metal. 3. to smooth (wood or metal) with a plane. *n., v.*

Plane for wood

plan et (plan′it), one of the heavenly bodies that move around the sun. Mercury, Venus, the earth, Mars, Jupiter, Saturn, Uranus, Neptune, and Pluto are planets. *n. 4.*

plan e tar y (plan′i tãr′i), of a planet; having to do with planets. *adj. 13.*

plane tree, a tall, spreading tree with broad leaves and bare patches on the trunk. The American plane tree is also called the buttonwood or sycamore.

plank (plangk), 1. a long, flat piece of sawed timber thicker than a board. 2. to cover with planks. 3. cook on a board; as, planked steak. 4. **Plank down** means put down or pay then and there. *Used in common talk.* 5. A plank in the platform of a political party is any one of the ideas for which the party stands. 6. **Walk the plank** means be put to death by walking along and off a plank extending from a ship's side over the water. *n., v. 5.*

plant (plant), 1. Trees, bushes, vines, grass, vegetables, and seaweed are all plants. 2. A plant often means a small growth; as, a tomato plant, a house plant. 3. a young growth ready to be set out in another place. The farmer set out 100 cabbage plants. 4. put in the ground to grow. Farmers plant seeds. 5. set firmly; put; place. Columbus planted the flag of Spain in the ground. The boy planted his feet far apart. 6. establish (a colony, city, etc.); settle. 7. put in (ideas, feelings, etc.). Missionaries planted civilization among the savages. 8. the building, machinery, tools, etc., used in manufacturing some article. *n., v. 1.*

Plan tag e net (plan taj′i nit), the family name of the kings of England from 1154 to 1485. *n. 12.*

plan tain[1] (plan′tin), 1. a kind of large banana. 2. plant that it grows on. *n. 10.*

plan tain[2] (plan′tin), a common weed with large spreading leaves close to the ground and long slender spikes carrying flowers and seeds. *n.*

plan ta tion (plan tā′shən), 1. a large farm or estate on which cotton, tobacco, sugar, etc., are grown. The work on a plantation is done by laborers who live there. 2. a large group of trees or other plants that have been planted; as, a rubber plantation. 3. colony. *n. 5.*

plant er (plan′tər), 1. man who owns or runs a plantation; as, a cotton planter. 2. a machine for planting; as, a corn planter. 3. person who plants. *n. 6.*

plaque (plak), 1. an ornamental tablet of metal, porcelain, etc. 2. a platelike ornament or badge. *n.*

plash (plash), splash. *v., n. 16.*

plash y (plash′i), marshy; wet. *adj. 16.*

plas ma (plaz′mə), blood or lymph without the corpuscles. *n. 10.*

plas ter (plas′tər), 1. a soft mixture of lime, sand, and water that hardens in drying, used for covering walls or ceilings. 2. cover (a wall) with plaster. 3. spread with anything thickly. 4. a medical preparation consisting of some substance spread on cloth, that will stick to the body and protect cuts, relieve pain, etc. 5. apply a plaster to. *n., v. 5.*

plas ter ing (plas′tər ing), covering of plaster on walls, etc. *n.*

plas tic (plas′tik), 1. molding or giving shape to material. Sculpture is a plastic art. 2. easily molded or shaped. Clay, wax, and plaster are plastic substances. *adj. 10.*

plat (plat), 1. a plan; a map. 2. to map. 3. a small piece of ground; plot. *n., v., platted, platting. 16.*

plate (plāt), 1. a dish, usually round, that is almost flat. Our food is served on plates. 2. something having a similar shape. 3. food served to one person at a meal. 4. dishes or utensils of silver or gold. The family plate included a silver pitcher, candlesticks, and the usual knives, forks, and spoons. 5. dishes or utensils coated with gold or silver. 6. cover with a thin layer of gold, silver, or some other metal. 7. a thin, flat sheet or piece of metal. The warship was covered with steel plates. 8. to cover with metal plates for protection. 9. a thin, flat piece of metal on which something is engraved. Plates are used for printing pictures. 10. something printed from such a piece of metal. 11. a metal copy of a page of type. 12. a thin sheet of glass coated with chemicals that are sensitive to light. Plates are used in taking some photographs. 13. in baseball, the home base. 14. a thin cut of beef from the lower end of the ribs. See the diagram of **beef.** *n., v. 2.*

pla teau (pla-tō′), a plain in the mountains, or at a height above the sea. *n. 5.*

plate glass, thick and very clear glass used for large windowpanes, mirrors, etc.

plat form (plat′fôrm), 1. a raised level surface. There usually is a platform beside the track at a railroad station. A hall usually has a platform for speakers. 2. a plan of action or statement of beliefs of a group. The platform of the new political party demands lower taxes. *n. 4.*

plat i num (plat′i nəm), a heavy metal that looks like silver or white gold, but costs much more. Platinum does not tarnish or melt easily. Some watches and rings are made of platinum. *n. 10.*

plat i tude (plat′i tūd or plat′i tüd), 1. a dull or commonplace remark, especially one given out solemnly, as if it were fresh and important. "Better late than never" is a platitude. 2. flatness; triteness; dullness. *n. 19.*

Pla to (plā′tō), a famous Greek philosopher (427?-347? B.C.). Plato was the pupil of Socrates and the teacher of Aristotle. *n. 8.*

Pla ton ic (plə ton′ik), 1. of or pertaining to Plato or his philosophy. 2. idealistic; not practical. The League of Nations seemed a Platonic scheme to many people. 3. friendly but not loverlike. *adj. 17.*

pla toon (plə tün′), 1. a group of soldiers acting as a unit. A platoon is smaller than a company and larger than a squad. 2. small group. *n. 16.*

Platte (plat), a river flowing through Nebraska into the Missouri River. *n.*

plat ter (plat′ər), a flat dish longer than it is wide. *n. 6.*

Platter

plau dit (plô′dit), enthusiastic expression of approval or praise. The actress bowed in response to the plaudits of the audience. *n. 17.*

plau si bil i ty (plô′zi bil′i ti), the appearance of being true or reasonable. *n. 15.*

plau si ble (plô′zi bəl), 1. appearing true, reasonable, or fair. 2. apparently worthy of confidence but often not really so; as, a plausible liar. *adj. 11.*

play (plā), 1. fun; sport; action to amuse oneself. All work and no play makes Jack a dull boy. The children are happy at play. 2. have fun; do something in sport; perform. The kitten plays with its tail. Jack played a joke on his sister. 3. take part in (a game). Children play tag and ball. 4. play against. Our team played the sixth-grade team. 5. cause to play. 6. a turn, move, or act in a game. It is your play next. Tom made a good play at checkers. 7. action; as, fair play, foul play. He brought all his strength into play to move the rock. 8. act; as, to play the fool, to play fair. 9. a light, quick movement; as, the play of sunlight on leaves. 10. move lightly. A breeze played on the waters. The poet's fancy played over the old legend and gave it a new form. 11. cause to act or to move. The ship played its light along the coast. 12. freedom for action, motion, etc. The boy gave his fancy full play in telling what he could do with a million dollars. 13. make music on an instrument; make give forth music; produce as music. 14. a story acted on the stage. *Peter Pan* is a charming play. 15. act a part; act the part of. Maude Adams played Peter Pan. 16. make believe; pretend in fun. Let's play the hammock is a boat. 17. act carelessly; do foolish things. Don't play with your pencil. 18. gamble. 19. gambling. The man lost money at play. 20. Some special meanings are:

a play on words, a pun, the humorous use of a word where it can have two different meanings.

play into the hands of (a person), act so as to give him the advantage.

play off (one person) **against** (another), set one person against another.

n., v. 1.

play er (plā′ər), 1. person who plays; as, a ballplayer, a cardplayer. 2. an actor in a theater. 3. thing or device that plays. *n. 5.*

play fel low (plā′fel′ō), playmate. *n. 11.*

play ful (plā′fəl), 1. full of fun; fond of playing. 2. joking; not serious. *adj. 9.*

play ground (plā′ground′), piece of ground for play. *n. 6.*

play house (plā′hous′), 1. small house for a child to play in. 2. toy house. 3. theater. *n. 12.*

playing card, one of a set of cards to play games with.

play mate (plā′māt′), person who plays with another. *n. 4.*

play thing (plā′thing′), thing to play with; toy. *n. 5.*

play wright (plā′rīt′), writer of plays; dramatist. *n. 11.*

pla za (plä′zə), a public square in a city or town. *n.*

plea (plē), 1. request; asking; as, a plea for pity. The giant laughed at Jack's plea for pity. 2. excuse; defense. The man's plea was that he did not see the signal. 3. answer made by a defendant to a charge against him in a law court. *n. 6.*

plead (plēd), 1. offer reasons for or against something; argue. 2. ask earnestly. When the rent was due, the poor man pleaded for more time. 3. offer as an excuse. The woman who stole pleaded poverty. 4. speak for or against in a law court. He had a good lawyer to plead his case. *v., pleaded* or *plead* (pled), *pleading. 3.*

plead er (plēd′ər), person who pleads, especially in a law court. *n. 16.*

pleas ance (plez′əns), 1. pleasure. *Old use.* 2. a pleasant place, usually with trees, fountains, and flowers. *n. 17.*

pleas ant (plez′ənt), 1. that pleases; giving pleasure; as, a pleasant swim on a hot day. 2. easy to get along with; friendly. 3. fair; not stormy. *adj. 1.*

pleas ant ness (plez′ənt nis), pleasing quality; as, the pleasantness of sunshine. *n. 13.*

pleas ant ry (plez′ənt ri), 1. good-natured joke; witty remark. 2. joking. *n., pl. pleasantries. 12.*

please (plēz), 1. Toys please children. Sunshine and flowers please most people. 2. Do what you please. 3. Please is a polite way of asking. Come here, please. 4. Mary is a sweet child and tries to please. 5. **Please God** means if it is God's will. *v. 1.*

pleas ing (plēz′ing), giving pleasure; pleasant. *adj. 7.*

pleas ur a ble (plezh′ər ə bəl), pleasant; agreeable. *adj. 15.*

pleas ure (plezh′ər), 1. the feeling of being pleased; delight; joy. The boy's pleasure in the gift was good to see. 2. something that pleases; a joy; a delight. It would be a pleasure to see you again. 3. anything that amuses; sport; play. He takes his pleasure in riding and hunting. 4. desire; choice. Is it your pleasure to go now? *n. 1.*

Girl wearing a dress with a pleated skirt

pleat (plēt), 1. a flat, usually narrow, fold made in cloth by doubling it on itself. 2. fold or arrange in pleats; as, a pleated skirt. *n., v. 20.*

ple be ian (pli bē′ən), 1. belonging or pertaining to the common people; common; vulgar. 2. one of the common people. 3. belonging or pertaining to the lower class of citizens in ancient Rome. 4. member of this class. *adj., n. 8.*

pleb i scite (pleb′i sīt), a direct vote by the qualified voters of a state. *n. 17.*

pledge (plej), 1. a promise. The drunkard signed the pledge never to drink again. 2. to promise. 3. security; something that secures or makes safe. The knight left a jewel as pledge of his return. 4. give as security. 5. drink a health to; drink in honor of (someone) and wish (him) well. The knights rose from the banquet table to pledge the king. 6. the drinking of a health. 7. something given to show favor or love. *n., v. 3.*

Plei a des (plē′ə dēz), a famous group of six bright stars and one very faint star. *n. pl. 10.*

ple na ry (plē′nə ri), full; complete; entire; absolute. *adj. 20.*

plen i po ten ti ar y (plen′i pə ten′shi ãr′i), 1. having full power; absolute. The United States usually has a minister plenipotentiary in every important foreign country. 2. a diplomatic agent having full power or authority. *adj., n., pl. plenipotentiaries. 17.*

plen i tude (plen′i tūd or plen′i tüd), fullness; completeness; abundance. *n. 15.*

plen te ous (plen′ti əs), plentiful. *adj. 7.*

plen ti ful (plen′ti fəl), more than enough; ample; abundant. Ten gallons of gasoline is a plentiful supply for a seventy-mile trip. Apples are cheap now because they are plentiful. *adj. 5.*

plen ty (plen′ti), full supply; all that one needs; a large enough number or amount. You have plenty of time to catch the train. *n. 2.*

pleu ri sy (plür′i si), inflammation of the thin membrane covering the lungs and lining the thorax. *n. 19.*

plex us (plek′səs), a network of nerves, blood vessels, or fibers. The **solar plexus** is a collection of nerves behind the stomach. *n. 20.*

pli a ble (plī′ə bəl), 1. easily bent; flexible; supple. Willow twigs are pliable. 2. easily influenced; yielding. He is too pliable to be a good captain. *adj. 16.*

pli an cy (plī′ən si), being easily bent or influenced. *n. 19.*

pli ant (plī′ənt), 1. bending easily; pliable. 2. easily influenced; yielding. *adj. 12.*

pli ers (plī′ərz), a tool used to hold or turn or bend things. *n. pl. or sing. 12.*

Pliers

plight[1] (plīt), condition or state, usually bad. He was in a sad plight when he became ill and had no money. *n. 5.*

plight[2] (plīt), pledge; promise. **I plight my troth** means I promise to be faithful. *v., n.*

plinth (plinth), 1. the lower square part of the base of a column. 2. a square base of a pedestal. *n. 18.*

PLINTH

plod (plod), 1. walk heavily; trudge. The old man plods wearily along the road. 2. proceed in a slow or dull way; work patiently with effort. That boy plods away at his lessons until he learns them. *v., plodded, plodding. 9.*

plod der (plod′ər), 1. person who plods. 2. person who works hard but slowly. *n. 19.*

plot (plot), 1. secret plan. Two men formed a plot to rob the bank. 2. to plan; plan secretly with others to do something wrong. The traitors plotted against the government. 3. the plan or main story of a play, novel, poem, etc. Boys like plots dealing with adventure and mystery. 4. a small piece of ground; as, a garden plot. 5. divide (land) into plots. The old farm was plotted out into house lots. 6. a map or diagram. 7. make a map or diagram of. 8. mark the position of something on a map or diagram. *n., v., plotted, plotting. 3.*

plough (plou), plow. *n., v. 4.*

plough boy (plou′boi′), plowboy. *n.*

plough man (plou′mən), plowman. *n., pl. ploughmen. 13.*

Golden plover (about 11 in. long)

plough share (plou′shãr′), plowshare. *n. 14.*

plov er (pluv′ər), a bird with a short tail and a bill like that of a pigeon. See the picture just above. *n. 14.*

Plow

plow (plou), 1. a big heavy instrument for cutting the soil and turning it over. 2. turn up (the soil) with a plow. 3. a machine for removing snow, usually called a snowplow.

4. use a plow. 5. move through anything as a plow does. The ship plowed through the waves. *n., v. 3.*

plow boy (plou′boi′), boy who guides a plow. *n.*

plow man (plou′mən), 1. man who guides a plow. 2. a farm worker. *n., pl. plowmen. 13.*

plow share (plou′shãr′), the blade of a plow, the part that cuts the soil. See the picture of **plow**. *n.*

pluck (pluk), 1. pick; pull off. She plucked flowers in the garden. 2. pull; pull at. 3. **Pluck up** means (1) pull up. Pluck up the dandelions. (2) gather up courage. Pluck up! you aren't hurt badly. 4. courage. The cat showed pluck in fighting the dog. 5. rob. *Slang. v., n. 2.*

pluck y (pluk′i), having or showing courage; as, a plucky dog. *adj., pluckier, pluckiest. 12.*

plug (plug), 1. piece of wood, etc., used to stop up a hole. 2. stop up or fill with a plug. 3. an electrical connecting device. 4. put in as a plug. 5. a place where a hose can be attached. 6. to plod; work steadily. 7. a cake of pressed tobacco. *n., v., plugged, plugging. 7.*

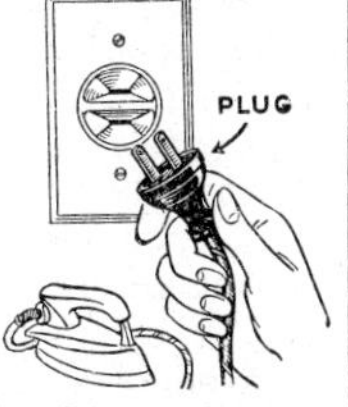

Plug (def. 3.)

plum (plum), 1. a fruit with a smooth skin. See the picture. Plums are red, green, purple, or yellow. 2. the tree it grows on. 3. raisin. 4. made of raisins. A plum cake has raisins in it. 5. something good. This new job is a fine plum for Mr. Jones. *n., adj. 3.*

Plums

plum age (plüm′ij), the feathers of a bird. A parrot has bright plumage. *n. 9.*

plumb (plum), 1. a small weight used on the end of a line to find the depth of water or to see if a wall is vertical. 2. test by a plumb line. Our line was not long enough to plumb the depths of the lake. 3. vertical. **Out of plumb** or **off plumb** means not vertical. *n., v., adj., adv. 10.*

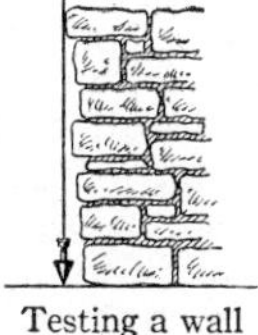
Testing a wall with a plumb

plumb er (plum′ər), man whose work is putting in and repairing water pipes and fixtures in buildings. When the water pipe froze, we sent for a plumber. *n. 11.*

plumb ing (plum′ing), 1. the work or trade of a plumber. 2. the system of pipes for carrying water, etc., in a building; as, bathroom plumbing. *n.*

plumb line, a line with a plumb at the end, used to find the depth of water, or to see if a wall is vertical.

plume (plüm), 1. feather; a large, long feather; a feather ornament. 2. smooth or arrange the feathers of. The eagle plumed its wing. 3. show pride in (oneself). Mary plumed herself on her skill in dancing. 4. furnish with plumes. *n., v. 4.*

Plumes

plum met (plum′it), a weight fastened to a line; plumb. *n. 12.*

plump[1] (plump), 1. rounded out; attractively fat. A healthy baby has plump cheeks. 2. make plump; become plump. *adj., v. 5.*

plump[2] (plump), 1. fall or drop heavily or suddenly. All out of breath, she plumped down on a chair. 2. a sudden plunge; a heavy fall. 3. heavily or suddenly. The lunch basket fell plump into the pond. He ran plump into me. 4. direct; positive; blunt; as, a plump denial. *v., n., adv., adj.*

plum pudding, a rich boiled pudding containing raisins, currants, spices, etc.

plu mule (plü′mūl), small soft feather. *n. 14.*

plum y (plüm′i), 1. having feathers. 2. adorned with plumes. 3. feathery. *adj. 20.*

plun der (plun′dər), 1. rob; rob by force. The pirates entered the harbor and began to plunder the town. 2. act of robbing by force. During the plunder soldiers came. 3. things stolen. The pirates buried their plunder in a secret place. *v., n. 5.*

plun der er (plun′dər ər), robber. *n. 17.*

plunge (plunj), 1. throw or thrust with force into a liquid or into a place. Plunge your hand into the water. The soldier plunged his sword into the heart of his enemy. 2. throw oneself (into water, danger, a fight, etc.). 3. rush; dash. 4. a jump or thrust; a dive. 5. pitch suddenly and violently. The ship plunged about in the storm. *v., n. 3.*

plung er (plun′jər), 1. one that plunges. 2. a part of a machine that acts with a plunging motion. See the picture under **piston,** which is a kind of plunger. *n. 18.*

plu per fect (plü′pėr′fikt), the verb form showing that an event was completed before a given past time. In "He had learned to read before he went to school," *had learned* is the pluperfect tense of *learn.* Pluperfect and past perfect mean the same. *n., adj. 13.*

plu ral (plür′əl), 1. more than one. 2. the form of a word which shows that it means more than one. *Books* is the plural of *book; men,* of *man; are,* of *is; we,* of *I; these,* of *this.* *adj., n. 10.*

plu ral i ty (plü ral′i ti), 1. the state or fact of being plural. 2. a large number; multitude. 3. the greater number; the majority. 4. the difference between the number of votes received by the highest candidate and the number received by the next highest candidate. *n., pl. pluralities. 14.*

plus (plus), 1. added to. 3 plus 2 equals 5. 2. and also. The work of an engineer requires intelligence plus experience. 3. and more. His mark was B plus. 4. showing addition; as, the plus sign (+). *prep., adj. 8.*

plush (plush), a fabric like velvet but thicker and softer. *n. 12.*

Plu tarch (plü′tärk), a Greek who wrote lives of famous Greeks and Romans (46?-120? A.D.). *n. 11.*

Plu to (plü′tō), 1. Greek and Roman god of the lower world. 2. the planet that is farthest from the sun. *n. 10.*

plu to crat (plü′tə krat), person who has power or influence because of his wealth. *n. 20.*

ply (plī), 1. work with; use. The dressmaker plies her needle. 2. keep up work on; work at or on. The enemy plied our messenger with questions to make him tell his errand. 3. go back and forth regularly between certain places. The bus plies from the station to the hotel. 4. thickness, fold, or twist. Three-ply rope is made up of three twists. *v., plied, plying, n., pl. plies. 5.*

Plym outh (plim′əth), 1. a seaport in southwestern England. 2. a town in southeastern Massachusetts founded by the Pilgrims in 1620. **Plymouth Rock** is the rock on which the Pilgrims are said to have landed. *n. 8.*

P.M. or **p.m.,** 1. afternoon. 2. the time from noon to midnight. *13.*

pneu mat ic (nū mat′ik or nü mat′ik), 1. filled with air; containing air; as, a pneumatic tire. 2. worked by air; as, a pneumatic drill. 3. having to do with air and gases. *adj. 12.*

pneu mo ni a (nū mō′ni ə or nü mō′ni ə), a disease in which the lungs are inflamed. *n. 9.*

Po (pō), a river in northern Italy, flowing into the Adriatic Sea. *n. 9.*

P.O., post office.

poach[1] (pōch), 1. trespass on another's land, especially to hunt or fish. 2. take (game or fish) without any right. *v. 13.*

poach[2] (pōch), cook (an egg) by breaking it into boiling water. *v.*

poach er (pōch′ər), person who hunts or fishes on another's land without any right. *n. 19.*

Po ca hon tas (pō′kə hon′təs), Indian girl who is said to have saved the life of Captain John Smith (1595?-1617). *n. 20.*

pock (pok), a mark or pit left on the skin by smallpox and certain other diseases. *n.*

pock et (pok′it), 1. a small bag sewed into clothing. 2. put in one's pocket. 3. meant to be carried in a pocket; as, a pocket handkerchief. 4. small enough to go in a pocket; as, a pocket camera. 5. **Be out of pocket** means (1) spend or lose money. (2) be a loser. 6. a small bag or pouch. 7. a hollow place. 8. a hole in the earth containing gold or other ore. The miner struck a pocket of silver. 9. shut in; hem in. 10. hold back; suppress; hide. He pocketed his pride and said nothing. 11. take and endure, without doing anything about it. He pocketed the insult. 12. take secretly or dishonestly. 13. any current or condition in the air which causes an airplane to drop suddenly. *n., v., adj. 2.*

pock et book (pok′it bu̇k′), 1. a case for carrying money, papers, etc., in the pocket. 2. woman's purse. *n. 13.*

pock et knife (pok′it nīf′), a small knife with one or more blades that fold into the handle. *n., pl. pocketknives.*

pod (pod), the shell or case in which plants like beans and peas grow their seeds. *n. 10.*

Pod of peas

Poe (pō), Edgar Allan, an American poet and writer of tales (1809-1849). *n.*

po em (pō′im), 1. a composition in verse; an arrangement of words in lines with a regularly repeated accent. 2. a composition showing great beauty of language or thought. *n. 3.*

po e sy (pō′i si), poetry. *n., pl. poesies.* [*Old use*] *13.*

po et (pō′it), person who makes poems. Longfellow and Scott were poets. *n. 2.*

po et ess (pō′it is), woman poet. *n. 15.*

po et ic (pō et′ik), 1. having to do with poems or poets. 2. suitable for poems or poets. *Alas, o'er, plenteous,* and *blithe* are poetic words. 3. showing imagination. Alice has such poetic fancies as calling the clouds sheep and the new moon a boat. *adj. 6.*

po et i cal (pō et′i kəl), poetic. *adj. 9.*

po et ry (pō′it ri), 1. the art of writing poems. Shakespeare and Milton are masters of English poetry. 2. poems. Hymns are sometimes poetry. *n. 4.*

poign an cy (poin′ən si), being poignant; sharpness; piercing quality; as, poignancy of flavor, poignancy of suffering or delight. *n.*

poign ant (poin′ənt), 1. very painful; piercing; as, poignant suffering. 2. keen; intense; as, a subject of poignant interest, a poignant delight. 3. sharp in taste or smell; as, poignant sauces, poignant perfumes. *adj. 14.*

poin set ti a (poin set′i ə), a plant with large scarlet leaves that look like flower petals. Poinsettias are much used as Christmas decorations. *n.*

Poinsettia

point (point), 1. a sharp end; as, the point of a needle. 2. a dot; a punctuation mark. A period is a point. 3. item; small part. The speaker replied to the argument point by point. 4. the main idea or purpose. Your answer is not to the point. I did not get the point of his argument. 5. special quality or feature. Courage and endurance were his good points. 6. piece of land with a sharp end sticking out into the water; cape. 7. place; spot. At this point the cars stopped. 8. a position without length or width. 9. direction. North, northeast, and north-northeast are points of the compass. 10. give a point to; sharpen. The preacher told a story to point his advice. 11. to aim. Don't point your gun at me. 12. show position or direction. 13. **Point out** means show or call attention to. Please point out my mistakes. 14. degree; stage; as, freezing point, boiling point. 15. a unit of scoring. Four points make a game in tennis. 16. **Point of view** means place from which one looks at something; attitude of mind. *n., v. 1.*

point-blank (point′blangk′), 1. aimed straight at the mark; direct; plain and blunt; as, a point-blank question. 2. directly; straight. Tom refused point-blank to go. *adj., adv. 17.*

point ed (poin′tid), 1. having a point or points; as, a pointed roof. 2. sharp; piercing; as, a pointed wit. 3. directed; aimed. 4. emphatic. He showed her pointed attention. *adj.*

Pointer (about 26 in. high at the shoulder)

point er (poin′tər), 1. one that points. 2. a long, tapering stick used in pointing things out on a map, blackboard, etc. 3. a short-haired hunting dog. A pointer is trained to show where game is by standing still with his head and body pointing toward it. *n. 16.*

point less (point′lis), 1. without a point. 2. without force or meaning. *adj.*

poise (poiz), balance. She has perfect poise both of mind and body and never seems embarrassed. The athlete poised the weight in the air before throwing it. Poise yourself on your toes. *n., v. 6.*

poi son (poi′zən), 1. a drug or other substance very dangerous to life and health. Strychnine, gas, arsenic, and opium are poisons. 2. kill or harm by poison. 3. put poison in or on. *n., v. 3.*

poison ivy, a climbing plant that looks like ivy, and causes a painful rash on most people if they touch it.

Poison ivy

poi son ous (poi′zən əs), containing poison; very harmful to life and health. The rattlesnake's bite is poisonous. *adj. 7.*

poke[1] (pōk), 1. push against with something pointed; thrust into; thrust; push. You can poke a person in the ribs with your elbow, or poke a fire. A gossip pokes her nose into other people's business. 2. a poking; a thrust; a push. 3. go lazily; loiter. 4. a bonnet or hat with a large brim in front. *v., n. 8.*

poke[2] (pōk), bag; sack. *n.*

pok er[1] (pōk′ər), a metal rod for stirring a fire. *n. 12.*

pok er[2] (pōk′ər), a card game. *n.*

pok y or **pok ey** (pōk′i), slow; dull. *adj., pokier, pokiest.*

Poke bonnet

hat, āge, cãre, fär; let, ēqual, tėrm; it, īce; hot, ōpen, ôrder; oil, out; cup, pu̇t, rüle, ūse; th, thin; ᴛʜ, then; ə represents *a* in about, *e* in taken, *i* in pencil, *o* in lemon, *u* in circus.

Po land (pō′lənd), country in central Europe. It is now divided between Germany and Russia. *n. 6.*

po lar (pō′lər), 1. near the North or South Pole. It is very cold in the polar regions. 2. having to do with a pole or poles. *adj. 6.*

polar bear, a large white bear of the arctic regions.

Polar bear (about 4 ft. high at the shoulder; about 8 ft. long)

Po lar is (pō lãr′is), the North Star; the polestar. *n.*

pole[1] (pōl), 1. long, slender piece of wood, etc.; as, a telephone pole, a flag pole. 2. make (a boat) go with a pole. *n., v. 2.*

pole[2] (pōl), 1. The North Pole and the South Pole are the ends of the earth's axis. 2. The parts of a magnet, battery, etc., where the two opposite forces are strongest are called the positive pole and the negative pole. *n.*

Pole[3] (pōl), native or inhabitant of Poland. *n.*

pole cat (pōl′kat′), 1. small, dark-brown European animal with a very disagreeable odor. 2. a skunk. *n. 19.*

Polecat (about 17 in. long; tail about 8 in. long)

po lem ic (pō lem′ik), 1. an argument or dispute; a disputing discussion. 2. of dispute; of controversy or disagreement. *n., adj. 16.*

po lem i cal (pō lem′i kəl), of dispute; of controversy or disagreement. *adj. 20.*

pole star (pōl′stär′), 1. the North Star, formerly much used as a guide by sailors. 2. a guide; a guiding principle. *n.*

po lice (pə lēs′), 1. the department of government that keeps order and arrests persons who break the law. 2. the men who do this for a city or state. 3. keep in order; as, to police the camp. *n., v. 4.*

po lice man (pə lēs′mən), member of the police force; police officer. *n., pl. policemen. 5.*

pol i cy[1] (pol′i si), 1. plan of action; way of management. It is a poor policy to promise more than you can do. 2. prudence; practical wisdom. *n., pl. policies. 3.*

pol i cy[2] (pol′i si), a written agreement about insurance. My fire insurance policy states that I shall receive $5000 if my house burns down. *n., pl. policies.*

pol ish[1] (pol′ish), 1. make smooth and shiny; as, to polish shoes. 2. smoothness; polished condition. The polish of the furniture reflected our faces like a mirror. Travel with polite people gives polish to a girl's manners. 3. substance used to give smoothness or shine; as, silver polish. 4. become smooth and shiny; take on a polish. *v., n. 3.*

Pol ish[2] (pōl′ish), 1. of or pertaining to Poland, its people, or their language. 2. the language of Poland. *adj., n.*

po lite (pə līt′), 1. behaving properly; having or showing good manners. 2. refined; elegant. *adj. 3.*

po lite ness (pə līt′nis), polite nature or behavior. The French and Japanese are noted for their politeness. *n. 9.*

pol i tic (pol′i tik), 1. wise in looking out for one's own interests; prudent. A politic person tries not to offend people. 2. political. The state is a body politic. *adj. 4.*

po lit i cal (pə lit′i kəl), 1. having to do with citizens or the government. Treason is a political offense. Who shall have the right to vote is a political question. 2. of politicians or their methods. *adj. 4.*

political science, science of the principles and conduct of government.

pol i ti cian (pol′i tish′ən), one who gives much time to political affairs. Politicians are busy near election time. *n. 8.*

pol i tics (pol′i tiks), 1. the management of political affairs; the science and art of government. Theodore Roosevelt was engaged in politics for many years. 2. political principles or opinions. *n. 9.*

pol i ty (pol′i ti), 1. government. 2. an organized society; a community with a government. *n., pl. polities. 16.*

Polk (pōk), James Knox (1795-1849), the 11th president of the United States, from 1845 to 1849. *n.*

pol ka (pōl′kə), 1. a kind of lively dance. 2. music for it. *n. 20.*

poll (pōl), 1. the voting at an election. 2. the number of votes cast at an election. 3. list of persons, especially a list of voters. 4. receive at an election. 5. vote; cast (a vote at an election). 6. take the votes of. 7. the head. 8. cut off; cut short. *n., v. 4.*

pol len (pol′ən), the fine yellowish powder on flowers. Grains of pollen carried to the pistils of flowers fertilize them. *n. 10.*

pol li nate (pol′i nāt), carry pollen from stamens to (pistils); shed pollen on. Flowers are pollinated by bees. *v. 19.*

pol li na tion (pol′i nā′shən), carrying pollen to the pistils of flowers. *n. 17.*

pol li wog or **pol ly wog** (pol′i wog), tadpole. *n.*

polls (pōlz), voting place or places. *n. pl.*

poll tax, a tax on every person, or on every person of a specified class.

pol lute (pə lüt′), make dirty; defile. The water at the bathing beach was polluted by garbage from the city. *v. 7.*

pol lu tion (pə lü′shən), polluting; defiling; uncleanness. *n. 8.*

po lo[1] (pō′lō), a game like hockey played by men on horseback with long-handled mallets and a wooden ball. *n. 9.*

Man playing polo

Po lo[2] (pō′lō), Marco (1254?-1324?), an Italian traveler in Asia who wrote of his travels. *n.*

pol troon (pol trün′), mean coward. *n. 16.*

po lyg a mous (pə lig′ə məs), having more than one wife at the same time. *adj.*

po lyg a my (pə lig′ə mi), the practice or condition of having more than one wife at the same time. The Mohammedan religion permits polygamy. *n. 15.*

pol y glot (pol′i glot), 1. written in several languages. 2. person who knows several languages. *adj., n. 20.*

pol y gon (pol′i gon), a plane figure having more than four angles and four sides. *n. 19.*

Polygons

Pol y ne sia (pol′i nē′zhə), group of many small islands in the Pacific Ocean, east of Australia and the Philippines. The Hawaiian Islands are in Polynesia. *n.*

Pol y ne sian (pol′i nē′zhən), 1. member of any of the brown races that live in Polynesia. 2. any of the languages spoken in Polynesia. 3. of or pertaining to Polynesia, its people, or their languages. *n., adj.*

pol yp (pol′ip), a rather simple form of water animal, not much more than a saclike stomach with fingerlike tentacles around the edge to gather in food. Polyps often grow in colonies, with their bases connected. Corals and sea anemones are polyps. *n. 15.*

pol y syl la ble (pol′i sil′ə bəl), word of more than three syllables. *n. 19.*

pol y tech nic (pol′i tek′nik), pertaining to or dealing with many arts or sciences; as, a polytechnic school. *adj. 19.*

pol y the ism (pol′i thē′izm), the belief in more gods than one. The religion of the Greeks was polytheism. *n. 16.*

po made (pə mād′), perfumed ointment for the scalp and hair. *n.*

Pomegranate: A, fruit; B, fruit cut to show seeds.

pome gran ate (pom′gran′it), 1. a reddish-yellow fruit with a thick skin, red pulp, and many seeds. The pulp and seeds have a pleasant, slightly sour taste. 2. the tree it grows on. *n. 9.*

pom mel (pum′əl), 1. the part of a saddle that sticks up at the front. 2. a rounded knob on the hilt of a sword. 3. strike or beat; beat with the fists. *n., v., pommeled, pommeling. 14.*

pomp (pomp), splendid show or display; magnificence. The king was crowned with great pomp. *n. 4.*

pom pa dour (pom′pə dōr), 1. an arrangement of a woman's hair in which it is puffed high over the forehead. 2. an arrangement of a man's hair in which it is brushed straight up and back from the forehead. *n.*

Pompadour

Pom peii (pom pā′), city in ancient Italy, which was buried by an eruption of Mount Vesuvius in 79 A.D. Its ruins have been partly laid bare by excavation. *n.*

Pom pey (pom′pi), Roman general and statesman (106-48 B.C.). *n. 7.*

pom pon (pom′pon), an ornamental tuft or ball of feathers, silk, or the like, worn on a hat or dress, on the shoes, etc. *n.*

Pompon on a clown's hat

pom pous (pom′pəs), fond of display; acting proudly; self-important; trying to seem magnificent. The leader of the band bowed in a pompous manner. *adj. 9.*

Ponce de Le ón (pons′ də lē′ən), Juan (1460?-1521), Spanish soldier who discovered Florida. He sought the fountain of youth.

pon cho (pon′chō), a large piece of cloth, often waterproof, with a slit in the middle for the head to go through. Ponchos are worn in South America as cloaks. *n., pl. ponchos.*

pond (pond), a body of still water, smaller than a lake. *n. 2.*

pon der (pon′dər), consider carefully; as, to ponder a problem. *v. 6.*

pon der ous (pon′dər əs), 1. very heavy. 2. heavy and clumsy. A hippopotamus is ponderous. 3. dull; tiresome. The speaker talked in a ponderous way. *adj. 7.*

pon gee (pon jē′), a kind of soft silk, usually left in natural brownish-yellow color. *n. 13.*

pon iard (pon′yərd), dagger. *n. 14.*

Poniard

pon tiff (pon′tif), 1. a high priest; chief priest. 2. a bishop. 3. the Pope. *n. 15.*

pon tif i cal (pon tif′i kəl), 1. of or pertaining to a bishop. 2. of or pertaining to the Pope; papal. *adj. 16.*

pon tif i cate (pon tif′i kāt), the office or term of office of a pontiff. *n. 17.*

pon toon (pon tün′), 1. a low flat-bottomed boat. 2. such a boat, or some other floating structure, used as one of the supports of a temporary bridge. 3. either of the two boat-shaped parts of an airplane, for landing on or taking off from water. See the picture of **amphibian airplane.** *n.*

Bridge supported by pontoons

po ny (pō′ni), a kind of small horse. *n., pl. ponies. 3.*

poo dle (pü′dəl), an intelligent pet dog with thick curly hair. *n. 16.*

Poodle (12 to 15 in. high at the shoulder)

pooh (pü), an exclamation of contempt. Pooh! You don't dare jump. *interj., n. 13.*

pooh-pooh (pü′pü′), express contempt for. *v.*

pool[1] (pül), small pond; small body of still water. Our school has a swimming pool. *n. 3.*

pool[2] (pül), 1. a game like billiards, played with balls on a special table. 2. put (things or money) together for common advantage. The three boys pooled their savings for a year to buy a boat. 3. the things or money put together by different persons. 4. the persons who form a pool. *n., v.*

poop (püp), 1. a deck at the stern above the ordinary deck, often forming the roof of a cabin. 2. the stern of a ship. *n. 16.*

POOP

poor (pür), 1. having few things or nothing. **The poor** are those who have little or nothing. 2. not good in quality; lacking something needed; as, poor soil, a poor crop, poor milk, a poor cook, a poor story, a poor head for figures, poor health. 3. needing pity. This poor child has hurt himself. *adj., n. 1.*

poor house (pür′hous′), a house in which paupers live at public expense. *n. 19.*

poor ly (pür′li), 1. not sufficiently. A desert is poorly supplied with water. 2. badly; not well. Tom did poorly in the test. *adv.*

pop (pop), 1. make a short, quick, explosive sound. The firecrackers popped in bunches. 2. a short, quick, explosive sound. We heard the pop of a cork. 3. burst open; cause to burst open. When you pop corn, the heat makes the kernels burst open. 4. move, go, or come suddenly or unexpectedly. Our neighbor popped in for a short call. 5. thrust or put suddenly. She popped her head out through the window. 6. shoot; fire a gun or pistol. 7. a soft, bubbling drink; as, strawberry pop. *v., popped, popping, n. 5.*

pop corn (pop′kôrn′), 1. a kind of corn, the kernels of which burst open and puff out when heated. 2. the white puffed-out kernels. *n.*

Pope or **pope** (pōp), the head of the Roman Catholic Church; as, the Pope, the last three popes. *n. 3.*

pop gun (pop′gun′), a toy gun. *n.*

pop in jay (pop′in jā), vain, overtalkative person; conceited, silly person. *n. 19.*

pop ish (pōp′ish), pertaining to the Roman Catholic Church. The word popish is used by opponents of that church in an unfriendly way. *adj. 13.*

Lombardy poplar

pop lar (pop′lər), 1. tree that grows rapidly. The cottonwood is one kind of poplar. 2. its soft wood. *n. 7.*

pop lin (pop′lin), a ribbed dress fabric often made of silk and wool. *n. 11.*

pop o ver (pop′ō′vər), a very light and hollow muffin. *n.*

pop py (pop′i), a plant with showy flowers; one of its flowers. Opium is made from one kind of poppy. *n., pl. poppies. 6.*

Poppy

pop u lace (pop′ū lis), the common people. *n. 9.*

pop u lar (pop′ū lər), 1. of the people; by the people; representing the people. The United States has a popular government. 2. suited to the people; as, popular prices, books on popular science. 3. liked by most people; as, a popular song. 4. liked by acquaintances or associates. Fred's good nature makes him the most popular boy in the school. *adj. 3.*

pop u lar i ty (pop′ū lar′i ti), being liked generally. *n. 8.*

pop u lar ize (pop′ū lər īz), make popular. *v. 16.*

pop u lar ly (pop′ū lər li), 1. in a popular manner. 2. by the people; in general. *adv.*

pop u late (pop′ū lāt), 1. inhabit; as, a densely populated city. 2. furnish with inhabitants. Europeans populated America. *v. 13.*

pop u la tion (pop′ū lā′shən), 1. the people of a city, country, or district. 2. the number of people. 3. furnishing with inhabitants. *n. 3.*

pop u lous (pop′ū ləs), full of people; having many people per square mile. Rhode Island is the most populous State of the United States. *adj. 8.*

por ce lain (pôr′sə lin), very fine earthenware; china. Teacups are often made of porcelain. *n. 7.*

Porch

porch (pōrch), 1. covered entrance to a building. 2. veranda. *n. 2.*

por cu pine (pôr′kū pīn), an animal covered with spines or quills. *n. 9.*

pore[1] (pōr), 1. gaze earnestly or steadily. 2. study long and steadily. He would rather pore over a book than play. *v. 6.*

Porcupine (about 3 ft. long, including the tail)

pore[2] (pōr), a very small opening. Sweat comes through the pores in the skin. *n.*

pork (pōrk), the meat of a pig or hog used for food. See the picture just below. *n. 4.*

Cuts of pork

pork er (pōr′kər), pig, especially one fattened to eat. *n.*

po rous (pō′rəs), full of pores or tiny holes. Cloth, blotting paper, and ordinary flowerpots are porous. *adj. 10.*

por phy ry (pôr′fi ri), 1. a hard rock found in Egypt. It is purplish red in color and has small white crystals. 2. any of several similar rocks. *n., pl. porphyries. 15.*

por poise (pôr′pəs), a sea animal from five to eight feet long that looks like a small whale. Porpoises eat fish. *n. 12.*

por ridge (por′ij), cereal cooked in water or milk. *n. 10.*

por rin ger (por′in jər), a small dish from which soup, porridge, bread and milk, etc., can be eaten. *n.*

port[1] (pōrt), 1. harbor; place where ships and boats can be sheltered from storms. 2. the town or city by a harbor. *n. 2.*

port[2] (pōrt), 1. opening in the side of a ship to let in light and air. 2. opening in a ship through which to shoot. *n.*

port[3] (pōrt), 1. the left side of a ship. See the picture under **aft.** 2. on the left side of a ship. 3. turn (the helm) to the left side. *n., adj., v.*

port[4] (pōrt), way of carrying oneself; bearing. *n.*

port[5] (pōrt), a strong sweet wine. *n.*

port a ble (pōr′tə bəl), capable of being carried or moved. A portable garage can be moved to a new place. *adj. 9.*

por tage (pōr′tij), 1. carrying boats, provisions, etc., overland from one river, lake, etc., to another. 2. a place over which this is done. 3. the cost of carriage. *n. 14.*

por tal (pōr′təl), gate; door. *n. 6.*

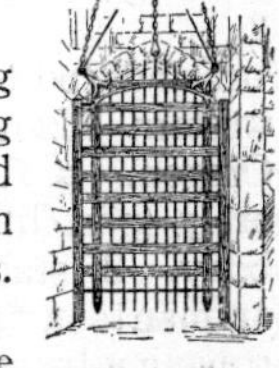

Portcullis

port cul lis (pōrt kul′is), strong gate or grating of iron sliding up or down in grooves, used to close the gateway of an ancient castle or fortress. *n. 17.*

por tend (pōr tend′), indicate beforehand; give warning of. Black clouds portend a storm. *v. 10.*

por tent (pōr′tent), sign; omen; a warning of coming evil. *n. 11.*

hat, āge, cãre, fär; let, ēqual, tėrm; it, īce; hot, ōpen, ôrder; oil, out; cup, pu̇t, rüle, ūse; th, thin; ᴛʜ, then; ə represents *a* in about, *e* in taken, *i* in pencil, *o* in lemon, *u* in circus.

por ten tous (pōr ten′təs), 1. indicating evil to come; ominous; threatening. 2. amazing; extraordinary. *adj. 10.*

por ter[1] (pōr′tər), 1. man employed to carry burdens or baggage. Give your bags to the porter. 2. attendant in a parlor car or sleeping car. *n. 4.*

por ter[2] (pōr′tər), doorkeeper. The porter let them in. *n.*

por ter[3] (pōr′tər), a dark-brown beer. *n.*

por ter house (pōr′tər hous′), a choice cut of beef containing sirloin and tenderloin. *n. 20.*

port fo li o (pōrt fō′li ō), 1. brief case; portable case for loose papers, drawings, etc. 2. the office of a minister of state or member of a cabinet. The Secretary of War resigned his portfolio. *n., pl. portfolios. 11.*

Portfolio

port hole (pōrt′hōl′), 1. an opening in a ship's side to let in light and air. 2. an opening in a ship, wall, etc., through which to shoot. *n. 19.*

Por ti a (pōr′shi ə), the beautiful and clever heroine in Shakespeare's play *The Merchant of Venice* who acts as a lawyer. *n. 19.*

por ti co (pōr′ti kō), a roof supported by columns, forming a porch or a covered walk. *n., pl. porticoes* or *porticos. 14.*

Portico

por tiere or **por tière** (pōr tyãr′), a curtain hung at a doorway. *n. 9.*

por tion (pōr′shən), 1. a part or share. Each child had his portion of meat. A portion of each school day is devoted to arithmetic. 2. divide into parts or shares. After the rich man's death his money was portioned out among his children. *n., v. 2.*

Port land (pōrt′lənd), 1. city in southwestern Maine. 2. city in northwestern Oregon. *n. 7.*

port ly (pōrt′li), 1. stout; having a large body. 2. stately; dignified. *adj. 13.*

port man teau (pōrt man′tō), a stiff, oblong traveling bag with two compartments opening like a book. *n. 16.*

Por to Ri co (pōr′tō rē′kō), island in the West Indies belonging to the United States. The official name is **Puerto Rico.** *7.*

por trait (pōr′trāt), picture of a person. *n. 9.*

por trai ture (pōr′tri chər), 1. act of portraying. 2. a portrait. *n. 15.*

por tray (pōr trā′), 1. make a likeness of in a drawing or painting. 2. picture in words; describe. The book *Black Beauty* portrays the life of a horse. 3. represent on the stage. *v. 9.*

por tray al (pōr trā′əl), 1. portraying by drawing or in words. 2. picture; description. *n.*

Por tu gal (pōr′chu̇ gəl), a small country in Europe, west of Spain. *n. 6.*

Por tu guese (pōr′chu̇ gēz), 1. a native or inhabitant of Portugal. 2. the language of Portugal. 3. of or pertaining to Portugal, its people, or their language. *n., pl. Portuguese, adj. 6.*

pose (pōz), 1. position of the body; way of holding the body. 2. hold a position. He posed an hour for his portrait. 3. put in a certain position; put. The photographer posed him before taking his picture. 4. an attitude assumed for effect; pretense; affectation. She takes the silly pose of being an invalid when really she is well and strong. 5. take a false position for effect. He posed as a rich man though he owed more than he owned. *n., v. 9.*

Po sei don (pō sī′dən), the Greek god of the sea. The Romans called him Neptune. *n.*

po si tion (pə zish′ən), 1. place where a thing or person is. The flowers grew in a sheltered position behind the house. 2. way of being placed. Put the baby in a comfortable position. 3. proper place. 4. job. He lost his position because he was not honest. 5. rank; standing; high standing. He was raised to the position of captain. 6. way of thinking; a set of opinions. What is your position on this question? *n. 3.*

pos i tive (poz′i tiv), 1. admitting of no question; sure. We have positive knowledge that the earth moves around the sun. 2. too sure. Her positive manner annoys people. 3. definite; emphatic. "No. I will not," is a positive refusal. 4. the simple form of an adjective or adverb as distinct from the comparative and superlative. *Fast* is the positive; *faster* is the comparative; *fastest* is the superlative. 5. that surely does something or adds something; practical. Don't just make a negative criticism; give us some positive help. 6. that may be thought of as real and present. Light is a positive thing; darkness is only the absence of light. 7. the kind of electricity produced on glass when it is rubbed with silk. 8. plus; counting up from zero. Five above zero is a positive quantity. 9. in photography, having the lights and shadows in the same position as in the original. *adj., n. 5.*

pos se (pos′i), a group of men summoned by a sheriff to help him. The posse pursued the thief. *n.*

pos sess (pə zes′), 1. own; have. Washington possessed great force and wisdom. 2. hold; occupy. 3. control. 4. control by an evil spirit. He fought like one possessed. *v. 2.*

pos ses sion (pə zesh′ən), 1. a possessing; a holding. 2. ownership. At his father's death he came into possession of a million dollars. 3. thing possessed; property. Please move your possessions from my room. 4. self-control. *n. 2.*

pos ses sive (pə zes′iv), 1. showing possession. *My, your, his,* and *our* are called possessive pronouns because they indicate who possesses or owns. 2. the possessive case. 3. word in that case. In "the boy's book," *boy's* is a possessive. *adj., n. 11.*

pos ses sor (pə zes′ər), 1. owner. 2. holder. *n. 10.*

pos si bil i ty (pos′i bil′i ti), 1. being possible. There is a possibility that the train may be late. 2. a possible thing or event. A whole week of rain is a possibility. *n., pl. possibilities. 5.*

pos si ble (pos′i bəl), 1. that can be; that can be done; that can happen. 2. that can be true or a fact. *adj. 1.*

pos si bly (pos′i bli), 1. by any possibility; no matter what happens. I cannot possibly go. 2. perhaps. Possibly you are right. *adv. 6.*

pos sum (pos′əm), opossum. *n.* [*Used in common talk*]

post[1] (pōst), 1. piece of timber, iron, etc., firmly set up, usually to support something else; as, a signpost, a doorpost, a gatepost, the posts of a bed. 2. fasten (a notice) up in a place where it can easily be seen. 3. make public; make known by means of a posted notice. 4. put (a name) in a list that is to be posted up. The steamer *George Washington* is posted as late. 5. to cover. The wall is posted over with notices. *n., v. 1.*

post[2] (pōst), 1. place where a soldier, policeman, etc., is stationed; place where one is supposed to be when one is on duty. When the fire alarm sounds, each man rushes to his post. 2. place where soldiers are stationed; fort. 3. the soldiers in a post. 4. a trading station, especially in uncivilized or unsettled country; as, a post of a fur company. 5. to station at a post; place. 6. job or position. *n., v.*

post[3] (pōst), 1. mail; a single delivery of mail. I shall send the package by post. The post has come. 2. send by mail; put into the mailbox; mail; as, to post a letter. 3. travel with haste; hurry. *n., v.*

post age (pōs′tij), amount paid on anything sent by mail. *n. 4.*

postage stamp, official stamp placed on mail to show that postage has been paid.

post al (pōs′təl), 1. having to do with mail and post offices. 2. post card; a post card with a postage stamp printed on it. *adj., n. 5.*

postal card, post card.

post card, card about 3½ by 5½ inches for sending a message by mail. *12.*

post chaise, hired carriage used for traveling in the days before there were railroads. *18.*

post er (pōs′tər), 1. large printed sheet put up in some public place. 2. person who posts notices, etc. *n. 8.*

pos te ri or (pos tēr′i ər), 1. back; rear; hind; situated behind. 2. later; coming after. *adj. 10.*

pos ter i ty (pos ter′i ti), 1. anyone's children, and their children, and their children, and so on and on. 2. the generations of the future. If we burn up all the coal in the world, what will posterity do? *n. 5.*

pos tern (pōs′tərn), 1. a back door or gate. 2. any small door or gate. 3. rear; lesser. The castle had a postern door. *n., adj. 13.*

post grad u ate (pōst graj′ü it), student who continues studying in college or at school after graduation. *n.*

post haste (pōst′hāst′), in great haste; very speedily. *adv.*

post hu mous (pos′tū məs or pos′chủ məs), 1. born after the death of the father; as, a posthumous child. 2. published after the death of the author. 3. happening after death; as, posthumous fame. *adj. 15.*

pos til ion or **pos til lion** (pōs til′yən), man who rides one of the horses drawing a carriage. *n. 17.*

post man (pōst′mən), man who carries and

delivers mail for the government. *n., pl. postmen. 7.*

post mark (pōst′märk′), 1. an official mark stamped on mail to cancel the postage stamp and record the place and date of mailing. 2. to stamp with a postmark. *n., v.*

post mas ter (pōst′mas′tər), person in charge of a post office. *n. 12.*

post mis tress (pōst′mis′tris), woman in charge of a post office. *n.*

post-mor tem (pōst′môr′təm), 1. after death. A post-mortem examination showed that the man had been poisoned. 2. examination made after death. *adj., n.*

post office, 1. place where mail is handled and postage stamps are sold. 2. the government department that takes charge of mail. *5.*

post paid (pōst′pād′), with the postage paid for. *adj.*

post pone (pōst pōn′), put off till later; put off to a later time; delay. The ball game was postponed because of rain. *v. 9.*

post pone ment (pōst pōn′mənt), putting off till later; delay. The postponement of the game disappointed many people. *n.*

post road, 1. road or route over which mail is or was carried. 2. road with stations which furnish horses.

post script (pōst′skript), an addition to a letter, written after the writer's name has been signed. *n. 6.*

pos tu late (pos′chu̇ lāt for 1 and 2, pos′chu̇ lit for 3), 1. require; demand; claim. 2. assume without proof; take for granted. Geometry postulates certain things as a basis for its reasoning. 3. something taken for granted or assumed as a basis for reasoning; a fundamental principle; a necessary condition. One postulate of geometry is that a straight line may be drawn between any two points. *v., n. 14.*

pos ture (pos′chər), 1. position of the body; way of holding the body. Good posture is important to health. 2. take a position. The dancer postured before a mirror. 3. to place in a particular posture. *n., v. 8.*

po sy (pō′zi), 1. flower. 2. a bunch of flowers; bouquet. 3. a motto or a line of poetry engraved within a ring. *n., pl. posies. 11.*

pot (pot), 1. a kind of vessel or dish. There are many different kinds and shapes of pots. They are made of iron, tin, earthenware, and other substances. A pot may hold food or drink or contain earth for flowers to grow in. 2. a pot and what is in it; the amount a pot will hold. He had a pot of beans. 3. put into a pot. 4. to shoot. *n., v., potted, potting. 2.*

pot ash (pot′ash′), 1. any of several substances made from wood ashes and used in soap, fertilizers, etc. 2. potassium. *n. 12.*

po tas si um (pə tas′i əm), a soft silver-white metallic element, occurring in nature only in compounds. *n. 9.*

po ta tion (pō tā′shən), 1. act of drinking. 2. a drink, especially of alcoholic liquor. *n. 17.*

po ta to (pə tā′tō), a vegetable growing underground. We eat sweet potatoes and white potatoes. *n., pl. potatoes. 2.*

po ten cy (pō′tən si), power; strength; as, the potency of an argument, the potency of a drug. *n., pl. potencies. 11.*

po tent (pō′tənt), powerful; having great power; strong; as, a potent remedy. *adj. 6.*

po ten tate (pō′tən tāt), 1. person having great power. 2. ruler. Kings, queens, and emperors were potentates. *n. 7.*

po ten tial (pə ten′shəl), 1. possible as opposed to actual; capable of coming into being or action. 2. in grammar, expressing possibility by the use of *may, might, can, could,* etc.; as, the potential mood of a verb. 3. electromotive force expressed in volts. A current of high potential is used in transmitting electric power over long distances. *adj., n. 9.*

po ten ti al i ty (pə ten′shi al′i ti), 1. possible power. 2. possibility; something potential. *n., pl. potentialities. 14.*

po ten tial ly (pə ten′shəl i), possibly, but not yet actually. *adv.*

poth er (poᴛʜ′ər), 1. confusion; disturbance; fuss. The children are making a great pother about the picnic. 2. to bother; to fuss. *n., v. 18.*

pot hook (pot′hu̇k′), 1. hook for hanging a pot or kettle over an open fire. 2. a rod with a hook for lifting hot pots. 3. an S-shaped stroke in writing, especially one made by children in learning to write. *n.*

po tion (pō′shən), a drink, especially one that is used as a medicine or poison, or in magic. *n. 10.*

pot luck (pot′luk′), whatever food that happens to be ready for a meal. Come into the house and take potluck with me. *n.*

Po to mac (pə tō′mək), river between Maryland and Virginia, flowing into Chesapeake Bay. Washington, **D. C.,** is on the Potomac River. *n. 10.*

pot pie (pot′pī′), 1. baked meat pie. 2. a stew with dumplings. *n.*

pot pour ri (pō pü rē′ or pot pür′i), 1. a fragrant mixture of dried flower petals with spices. 2. a medley or mixture. *n.*

pot shot, 1. a shot fired at game to get food, with little regard to skill or the rules of sport. 2. a shot at an animal or person within easy reach.

pot tage (pot′ij), a thick soup. *n. 14.*

pot ter[1] (pot′ər), person who makes pots and dishes out of clay. *n. 8.*

pot ter[2] (pot′ər), keep busy in a rather useless way. She potters about the house all day, but gets very little done. *v.*

potter's field, piece of ground used for burying people who have no friends or money.

pot ter y (pot′ər i), 1. pots, dishes, vases, etc., made from clay and hardened by heat. 2. the art or business of making them. 3. a place where such pots, dishes, vases, etc., are made. *n., pl. potteries. 11.*

Piece of Indian pottery

pouch (pouch), 1. bag or sack; as, a postman's pouch. 2. a baglike fold of skin. Old people often have pouches under their eyes. A kangaroo carries its young in a pouch. 3. put into a pouch. 4. form a pouch. *n., v. 6.*

poul tice (pōl′tis), 1. a soft moist mass of mustard, herbs, etc., applied to the body as a medicine. 2. put a poultice on. *n., v. 15.*

poul try (pōl′tri), chickens, turkeys, geese, ducks, etc. *n. 4.*

pounce (pouns), 1. jump suddenly and seize; a sudden swoop or pouncing. The cat pounced upon the mouse. 2. dash suddenly; come suddenly. *v., n. 9.*

pound[1] (pound), 1. a measure of weight; 16 ounces. Two cupfuls of water weigh about a pound. 2. a unit of troy weight; 12 ounces. 3. a sum of British money worth 20 shillings. In ordinary times a pound is worth about $4.86. *n. 1.*

pound[2] (pound), 1. strike or beat heavily again and again. He pounded the door with his fist. After a hard run your heart pounds. 2. crush to powder by beating. 3. a heavy blow, or its sound. *v., n.*

pound[3] (pound), an enclosed place to put stray animals in. *n.*

pour (pōr), 1. cause to flow in a steady stream. I poured the milk from the bottle into the cups. 2. flow in a steady stream. The crowd poured out of the church. The rain poured down. 3. a pouring. 4. a heavy rain. *v., n. 2.*

pout (pout), 1. thrust or push out the lips, as a displeased or sulky child does. 2. a pushing out of the lips when displeased or sulky. *v., n. 10.*

pov er ty (pov′ər ti), 1. condition of being poor. Being out of work causes poverty. 2. poorness. The poverty of the soil makes the crops small. 3. small amount. The dull child's talk shows poverty of ideas. *n. 3.*

pov er ty-strick en (pov′ər ti strik′ən), very, very poor. *adj.*

pow der (pou′dər), 1. a solid reduced to dust by pounding, crushing, or grinding. 2. some special kind of powder. The doctor gave her powders to take after meals. 3. make into powder; become powder. 4. sprinkle or cover with powder. 5. sprinkle. The ground was lightly powdered with snow. 6. gunpowder. *n., v. 3.*

powder flask, a bottle or can for carrying gunpowder.

powder horn, a powder flask made of the horn of an animal. See the picture.

Powder horn

pow der y (pou′dər i), 1. of powder. 2. like powder; in the form of powder. 3. covered with powder. *adj. 19.*

pow er (pou′ər), 1. strength; force; might. 2. ability to do or act. I will give you all the help in my power. The fairy had power to change into different shapes. 3. authority; right; control; influence. Congress has power to declare war. Jack was in the power of the giant. 4. person or thing who has authority or influence; an important nation. Five powers held a peace conference. 5. the product obtained by multiplying a number by itself one or more times. 16 is the fourth power of 2. 6. energy or force that can do work. A fifty candle power electric-light bulb gives as much light as fifty candles. 7. the capacity of an instrument to magnify. The higher the power of a telescope or microscope the more details you can see. *n. 1.*

pow er ful (pou′ər fəl), strong; having great power or force; mighty; as, a powerful man, a powerful medicine, a powerful sermon, a powerful nation. *adj. 3.*

pow er ful ly (pou′ər fəl i), strongly; with power. *adv.*

pow er house (pou′ər hous′), building containing boilers, engines, dynamos, etc., for generating power. *n.*

pow er less (pou′ər lis), without power; helpless. The mouse was powerless in the cat's claws. *adj. 9.*

pow wow (pou′wou′), a North American Indian word meaning: 1. priest or medicine man. 2. ceremony. 3. council or conference. 4. hold a powwow. *n., v.*

pox (poks), any disease that covers the body or parts of the body with sores, such as chicken pox or smallpox. *n. 20.*

pp., 1. past participle. 2. pages.

ppr., present participle.

prac ti ca ble (prak′ti kə bəl), 1. that can be done; capable of being put into practice; as, a practicable idea. 2. that can be used; as, a practicable road. *adj. 10.*

prac ti cal (prak′ti kəl), 1. having to do with action or practice rather than thought or theory. Earning a living is a practical matter. 2. engaged in actual practice or work. 3. fit for actual practice. 4. useful. 5. having good sense. 6. A **practical joke** is a trick played on someone in order to have a laugh on him. 7. virtual; being such in effect. *adj. 3.*

prac ti cal ly (prak′ti kəl i), 1. really; in effect. 2. almost; nearly. 3. in a practical way; in a useful way. 4. by actual practice. *adv.*

prac tice (prak′tis), 1. action done many times over for skill. Practice makes perfect. 2. the skill gained by experience or exercise. He was out of practice at batting. 3. do (some act) again and again to learn to do it well. You can practice pitching a ball, adding, or playing music. Mary practices on the piano every day. 4. do usually; make a custom of. Practice what you preach. 5. follow, observe, or use day after day; as, to practice moderation. 6. the usual way; the custom. It is the practice in our town to blow the whistles at noon. 7. follow as a profession; as, to practice medicine. 8. do something as a habit or profession. That young man is just beginning to practice as a lawyer. 9. the business of a doctor or a lawyer. Dr. Adams sold his practice. 10. to work (on or upon) in order to deceive or persuade. *n., v. 1.*

prac ticed or **prac tised** (prak′tist), skilled; expert; as, a practiced musician. *adj.*

prac tise (prak′tis), practice (*when used as a verb.* See definitions 3, 4, 5, 7, 8, 10). *v.*

prac ti tion er (prak tish′ən ər), person engaged in the practice of a profession. He was a medical practitioner for ten years; later he taught medicine. *n. 14.*

prae tor (prē′tər), a magistrate or judge in ancient Rome. A praetor ranked next below a consul. *n. 16.*

prae to ri an (prē tō′ri ən), 1. of or pertaining to a praetor. 2. pertaining to the bodyguard of a Roman commander or emperor. 3. a soldier of this bodyguard. *adj., n. 17.*

Prague (präg), the capital of Czecho-Slovakia. It is now under German control. *n. 11.*

Prairie chicken (about 1½ ft. from bill to end of tail)

prai rie (prãr′i), a large piece of level or rolling land with grass but no trees. *n. 5.*

prairie chicken, any of several grouse of the prairies of North America.

prairie dog, an animal like a woodchuck but smaller. See the picture.

prairie schooner, large covered wagon used in crossing the plains of North America before the railroads were built. See the picture below.

Prairie dog

praise (prāz), 1. speak well of. 2. saying that a thing or person is good; words which tell the worth or value of a thing or person. 3. worship. *v., n. 2.*

Prairie schooner

praise wor thy (prāz′wėr′ᴛʜi), worthy of praise; deserving approval. *adj. 13.*

prance (prans), 1. spring about on the hind legs. Horses prance when they feel lively. 2. move gaily or proudly. *v., n. 7.*

prank (prangk), playful trick; piece of mischief. The fairy Puck liked to play pranks on people. *n. 6.*

prate (prāt), 1. talk a great deal in a foolish way. 2. empty or foolish talk. *v., n. 7.*

prat tle (prat′əl), 1. talk as a child does; tell freely and carelessly. 2. talk in a foolish way; babble. 3. simple, artless talk.

4. baby talk. 5. sounds like baby talk; babble; as, the prattle of the brook. *v., n. 10.*

prawn (prôn), any of several shellfish much like shrimps. *n. 20.*

Prawn

pray (prā), 1. ask from God; speak to God in worship. 2. ask earnestly. 3. bring or get by praying. 4. please. Pray come with me. *v. 2.*

prayer (prãr), 1. act of praying. 2. thing prayed for. 3. a form of worship. 4. a form of words to be used in praying; as, the Lord's Prayer. 5. an earnest request. *n. 2.*

prayer book, a book of prayers.

prayer ful (prãr′fəl), having the habit of praying often; devout. *adj.*

pre-, a prefix that means before. *Pre* is used to form certain words, such as prepay, precede, prewar. *19.*

preach (prēch), 1. speak on a religious subject; deliver (a sermon). 2. give earnest advice. 3. urge; recommend strongly. He was always preaching exercise and fresh air. *v. 2.*

preach er (prēch′ər), person who preaches; clergyman; minister. *n. 5.*

preach ment (prēch′mənt), 1. preaching. 2. sermon, especially a tiresome one. *n. 17.*

pre am ble (prē′am′bəl), an introduction to a speech or a writing. The reasons for a law and its general purpose are often stated in a preamble. *n. 14.*

pre car i ous (pri kãr′i əs), uncertain; not safe; not secure. A soldier leads a precarious life. A prospector for gold makes a precarious living. *adj. 8.*

pre cau tion (pri kô′shən), 1. care taken beforehand. Locking doors is a precaution. 2. taking care beforehand. *n. 8.*

pre cau tion ar y (pri kô′shən ãr′i), of or using precaution; as, precautionary measures against catching a cold. *adj. 18.*

pre cede (prē sēd′), 1. go before; come before. Mr. Hoover preceded Mr. Roosevelt as President. 2. be higher in rank or importance. A major precedes a captain. *v. 6.*

pre ced ence (prē sēd′əns), 1. coming before in time or order. 2. higher position or rank; greater importance; as, to take precedence over all others. 3. the right to precede others in ceremonies or social affairs; social superiority. A Senator takes precedence over a Representative. *n. 11.*

pre ced en cy (prē sēd′ən si), precedence. *n. 18.*

prec e dent (pres′i dənt for 1, prē sēd′ənt for 2), 1. action that may serve as an example for later action. There is no precedent for electing the same man President of the United States four times. 2. preceding. *n., adj. 7.*

pre ced ing (prē sēd′ing), going before; coming before; previous. *adj.*

pre cept (prē′sept), rule or direction. "If at first you don't succeed, try, try again" is a familiar precept. *n. 6.*

pre cep tor (pri sep′tər), instructor; teacher. *n. 15.*

pre cinct (prē′singkt), 1. the space within a boundary. Do not leave the school precincts during school hours. 2. a part or district of a city. There are over 300 election precincts in that city. 3. boundary; limit. *n. 7.*

pre cious (presh′əs), 1. having great value. Gold and silver are often called the precious metals. Diamonds and rubies are precious stones. 2. dear; much loved. *adj. 2.*

prec i pice (pres′i pis), very steep place. *n. 7.*

pre cip i tant (pri sip′i tənt), 1. falling or rushing headlong; acting in a hasty or rash manner; very sudden or abrupt. Our men put the enemy to precipitant flight. 2. a substance that causes another substance in solution in a liquid to be deposited in solid form. *adj., n.*

pre cip i tate (pri sip′i tāt for 1, 2, 4, and 6, pri sip′i tit for 3 and 5), 1. throw down, fling, hurl, send, or plunge in a violent, sudden, or headlong manner; as, to precipitate a rock down a cliff, to precipitate oneself into a struggle. 2. hasten the beginning of; bring about suddenly; as, to precipitate a war. 3. with great haste and force; plunging or rushing; hasty; rash. 4. separate (a substance) out in solid form from a solution. 5. a substance precipitated from a solution. 6. condense (moisture) from vapor in the form of rain, dew, etc. *v., adj., n. 7.*

pre cip i ta tion (pri sip′i tā′shən), 1. act or state of precipitating; throwing down or falling headlong. 2. hastening or hurrying. 3. sudden haste; unwise or rash rapidity. 4. the sudden bringing on; as, the precipitation of a war or a quarrel. 5. the separating of a substance from a solution. 6. the depositing of moisture in the form of rain or dew. 7. something that is precipitated, such as rain, dew, and snow. *n. 11.*

pre cip i tous (pri sip′i təs), like a precipice; very steep; as, precipitous cliffs. *adj. 10.*

pre cise (pri sīs′), 1. exact; accurate; definite. The precise sum was 34½ cents. 2. careful. 3. strict. *adj. 6.*

pre cise ly (pri sīs′li), in a precise manner; exactly. Do precisely as the directions say. *adv.*

pre ci sion (pri sizh′ən), accuracy; exactness; as, the precision of a machine. *n. 8.*

pre clude (pri klüd′), shut out; prevent; make impossible. *v. 14.*

pre co cious (pri kō′shəs), 1. developed earlier than usual. This very precocious child could read well at the age of four. 2. developed too early. She had a precocious knowledge of diseases. *adj. 10.*

pre coc i ty (pri kos′i ti), precocious development; early maturity. Macaulay's precocity was extraordinary. When a child of four, he began to write a history of the world. *n. 17.*

pre con ceive (prē′kən sēv′), form an idea of beforehand. The beauty of the scenery surpassed all our preconceived notions. *v. 15.*

pre con cep tion (prē′kən sep′shən), an idea or opinion formed beforehand. *n.*

pre con cert (prē′kən sėrt′), arrange beforehand. At a preconcerted signal the policemen rushed in. *v.*

pre cur sor (prē kėr′sər), forerunner. A severe cold may be the precursor of pneumonia. *n. 17.*

pred a to ry (pred′ə tō′ri), 1. of or inclined to plundering or robbery; as, predatory border warfare, predatory bands infesting the highways. 2. preying upon other animals. Lions and tigers are predatory animals; hawks and owls are predatory birds. *adj. 15.*

pred e ces sor (pred′i ses′ər), person holding a position or office before another. John Adams was Jefferson's predecessor as President. *n. 7.*

pre des ti na tion (prē des′ti nā′shən), 1. fate; destiny; ordaining beforehand. 2. the action of God in deciding beforehand whatever comes to pass; the decree of God by which men are fated to everlasting happiness or misery. *n. 15.*

pre des tine (prē des′tin), determine or settle beforehand; foreordain. *v. 16.*

pre de ter mine (prē′di tėr′min), determine or decide beforehand. We met at the predetermined time. *v. 16.*

pre dic a ment (pri dik′ə mənt), 1. an unpleasant, trying, or dangerous situation. Having missed the last train home, Mary was in a predicament. 2. thing declared to be true. *n. 10.*

pred i cate (pred′i kit for 1 and 2, pred′i kāt for 3 and 4), 1. in grammar, the word or words expressing what is said about the subject. *Examples:* Men *work.* The men *dug wells.* The men *are soldiers.* 2. in grammar, belonging to the predicate. In "Horses are strong," *strong* is a predicate adjective. 3. found or base (a statement, action, etc.) on something. 4. declare, assert, or affirm to be real or true. The Christian religion predicates life after death. *n., adj., v. 14.*

pre dict (pri dikt′), tell beforehand; prophesy. The weather bureau predicts rain for tomorrow. *v. 7.*

pre dic tion (pri dik′shən), a prophecy. His predictions seldom come true. *n. 8.*

pre di gest (prē′di jest′), 1. digest beforehand. 2. treat (food) by an artificial process similar to digestion in order to make it more digestible. *v.*

pre di lec tion (prē′di lek′shən), liking; preference. *n. 15.*

pre dis pose (prē′dis pōz′), incline beforehand; make subject or liable. A cold predisposes a person to other diseases. *v. 16.*

pre dis po si tion (prē′dis pə zish′ən), inclination; tendency; condition of being predisposed. She has a predisposition toward seeing the dark side of things. *n. 15.*

pre dom i nance (pri dom′i nəns), a being predominant; as, the predominance of weeds in the deserted garden. *n. 15.*

pre dom i nant (pri dom′i nənt), 1. having most power; superior. 2. prevailing; most noticeable. *adj. 10.*

pre dom i nate (pri dom′i nāt), be greater in power, strength, influence, or numbers. *v. 11.*

pre ëm i nence (prē em′i nəns), excellence; being at the top; as, the preëminence of Edison among inventors. *n. 10.*

pre ëm i nent (prē em′i nənt), standing out above all others; superior to others. *adj. 12.*

pre ëmpt (prē empt′), 1. secure before someone else can. He preëmpted the land by occupying it. 2. acquire or take possession of beforehand. The cat had preëmpted the comfortable chair. *v.*

preen (prēn), 1. smooth or arrange (the

feathers) with the beak, as a bird does. 2. dress (oneself) carefully. *v. 19.*

pre ëx ist (prē′eg zist′), exist beforehand, or before something else. *v. 17.*

pre ëx ist ent (prē′eg zis′tənt), existing previously. *adj. 20.*

pref ace (pref′is), 1. an introduction to a book, writing, or a speech. Has your history book a preface? 2. introduce by written or spoken remarks; give a preface to. *n., v. 8.*

pref a to ry (pref′ə tō′ri), introductory; preliminary; made as a preface. *adj. 20.*

pre fect (prē′fekt), 1. a title of various military and civil officers in ancient Rome and elsewhere. 2. the chief administrative official of a department of France. *n. 20.*

pre fec ture (prē′fek chər), the office, jurisdiction, territory, or official residence of a prefect. *n. 20.*

pre fer (pri fėr′), 1. like better; choose rather. I will come later, if you prefer. She prefers reading. 2. put forward; present. In a few words John preferred his claim to the office of captain. 3. promote; advance. He was preferred to be a bishop. *v., preferred, preferring. 2.*

pref er a ble (pref′ər ə bəl), more desirable. *adj. 10.*

pref er a bly (pref′ər ə bli), by choice. He wants a new secretary, preferably one who is a college graduate. *adv.*

pref er ence (pref′ər əns), 1. act of liking better. My preference is for beef rather than lamb. 2. thing preferred; first choice. Helen's preference in reading is a fairy story. 3. the favoring of one above another. A teacher should not show preference for any one of her pupils. *n. 7.*

pref er en tial (pref′ər en′shəl), of, giving, or receiving preference. *adj.*

pre fer ment (pri fėr′mənt), advancement; promotion. *n. 10.*

pre fig ure (prē fig′yər), 1. represent beforehand by a figure or type. In one painting of Christ, His shadow is that of a cross, prefiguring the Crucifixion. 2. imagine to oneself beforehand. *v. 13.*

pre fix (prē′fiks for 1, prē fiks′ for 2), 1. a syllable or syllables put at the beginning of a word to make another word, as in *pre*paid, *un*like. 2. put before. We prefix *Mr.* to a man's name. *n., v. 11.*

preg nan cy (preg′nən si), pregnant quality or condition. *n. 16.*

preg nant (preg′nənt), 1. soon to have a baby. 2. filled; loaded. 3. fertile; rich; abounding. 4. filled with meaning; very significant. Most proverbs are pregnant sayings. *adj. 7.*

pre his tor ic (prē′his tor′ik), of or belonging to periods before recorded history. We find arrowheads made by prehistoric men. *adj. 12.*

pre judge (prē juj′), judge beforehand; judge without knowing all the facts. *v. 17.*

prej u dice (prej′ủ dis), 1. an opinion formed without taking time and care to judge fairly; as, a prejudice against doctors. 2. cause a prejudice in; fill with prejudice. That one happening has prejudiced me against all lawyers. 3. harm or injury. I will do nothing to the prejudice of my cousin in this matter. 4. to harm or injure. *n., v. 6.*

prej u diced (prej′ủ dist), having an emphatic opinion without good reasons. She is so prejudiced in favor of living in the country that she will not even try the city. *adj.*

prej u di cial (prej′ủ dish′əl), causing prejudice or disadvantage; hurtful. *adj. 14.*

prel a cy (prel′ə si), 1. the position or rank of a prelate. 2. prelates. 3. church government by prelates. *n., pl. prelacies. 20.*

prel ate (prel′it), clergyman of high rank, such as a bishop. *n. 7.*

pre lim i nar y (pri lim′i nãr′i), 1. coming before the main business; leading to something more important. After the preliminary exercises of prayer and song, the speaker of the day gave an address. 2. a preliminary step; something preparatory. A physical examination is a preliminary to joining the army. *adj., n., pl. preliminaries. 6.*

prel ude (prel′ūd), 1. anything serving as an introduction; a preliminary performance; as, the organ prelude to a church service. 2. be a prelude or introduction to. 3. introduce with a prelude. *n., v. 12.*

pre ma ture (prē′mə tūr′ or prē′mə tür′), before the proper time; too soon. *adj. 9.*

pre med i tate (prē med′i tāt), consider or plan beforehand. It was a deliberate, premeditated murder. *v. 15.*

pre med i ta tion (prē′med i tā′shən), previous deliberation or planning. *n. 19.*

pre mi er (prē′mi ər for 1 and 3, pri mēr′ for 2), 1. first in rank; chief. 2. a chief officer; the prime minister. 3. first in time; earliest. *adj., n. 11.*

prem ise (prem′is for 1, 2, and 3, pri mīz′ for 4), 1. in logic, a statement assumed to be true from which a conclusion is drawn. Major premise: Children should go to school. Minor premise: Jack is a child. Conclusion: Jack should go to school. 2. In law, **premises** mean (1) things mentioned previously, such as the names of the parties concerned, a description of the property, the price, etc. (2) the property forming the subject of the document. 3. **Premises** also means a house or building with its grounds. 4. set forth as an introduction. *n., v. 9.*

pre mi um (prē′mi əm), 1. reward; prize. Some magazines give premiums for obtaining new subscriptions. 2. something more than the ordinary price or wages. Mr. Brown has to pay six per cent interest on his loan and also a premium of two hundred dollars. 3. money paid for insurance. Father pays premiums on his life insurance four times a year. 4. an unusual, unfair value. Giving money to beggars may put a premium on idleness. *n. 7.*

pre mo ni tion (prē′mə nish′ən), a forewarning. *n.*

pre mon i to ry (prē mon′i tō′ri), giving warning beforehand. *adj.*

pre oc cu pa tion (prē ok′ū pā′shən), 1. preoccupying. 2. absorption; being preoccupied. *n.*

pre oc cu pied (prē ok′ū pīd), absorbed; engrossed. *adj.*

pre oc cu py (prē ok′ū pī), 1. take up all the attention of. The question of getting to New York preoccupied her mind. 2. occupy beforehand; take possession of before others. Our favorite seats had been preoccupied. *v., preoccupied, preoccupying. 12.*

pre or dain (prē′ôr dān′), ordain beforehand; foreordain; determine or appoint beforehand. *v. 20.*

prep., preposition.

pre paid (prē pād′), paid in advance; paid for beforehand. Send this shipment prepaid. *pt. and pp. of* **prepay.** *10.*

prep a ra tion (prep′ə rā′shən), 1. making ready. 2. being ready. 3. thing done to get ready. 4. a specially made medicine or food or mixture of any kind. *n. 3.*

pre par a to ry (pri par′ə tō′ri), 1. making ready. Preparatory schools fit pupils for colleges. 2. as an introduction; preliminary. *adj. 9.*

pre pare (pri pãr′), 1. make ready; get ready. Bob prepares his lessons while his mother prepares supper. 2. make by a special process. *v. 1.*

pre par ed ness (pri pãr′id nis), being prepared; readiness. *n.*

pre pay (prē pā′), 1. pay in advance. 2. pay for in advance. *v., prepaid, prepaying.*

pre pon der ance (pri pon′dər əns), 1. greater number; greater weight; greater power or influence. In the summer hot days have the preponderance. 2. being the chief or most important element; as, the preponderance of oaks in these woods. *n. 14.*

pre pon der ant (pri pon′dər ənt), 1. weighing more; being stronger or more numerous; having more power or influence. 2. chief; most important. Greed for gold is the miser's preponderant characteristic. *adj. 17.*

pre pon der ate (pri pon′dər āt), 1. be greater than (something else) in weight, power, force, influence, number, amount, etc. In November cloudy weather preponderates over sunshine. 2. be chief; be most important. Oaks and maples preponderate in our woods. *v. 16.*

prep o si tion (prep′ə zish′ən), a word that shows certain relations between other words. *With, for, by,* and *in* are prepositions in the sentence "A man *with* rugs *for* sale walked *by* our house *in* the morning." *n. 10.*

pre pos sess (prē′pə zes′), 1. fill with a favorable feeling or opinion. I was prepossessed by the boy's frank face and modest behavior from the moment he entered. 2. fill (a person) with a feeling. *v. 16.*

pre pos sess ing (prē′pə zes′ing), making a favorable first impression; attractive; pleasing. Clean clothes and good manners are prepossessing. *adj.*

pre pos ses sion (prē′pə zesh′ən), a bias; a prejudice; a favorable feeling or opinion formed beforehand. A well-written letter applying for a position will create a prepossession in the writer's favor. *n. 16.*

pre pos ter ous (pri pos′tər əs), contrary to nature, reason, or common sense; absurd; senseless; ridiculous; foolish. It would be preposterous to shovel coal with a teaspoon. That the moon is made of green cheese is a preposterous notion. *adj. 9.*

pre req ui site (prē rek′wi zit), 1. thing required beforehand. A high-school course is the usual prerequisite to college work. 2. required beforehand. *n., adj.*

pre rog a tive (pri rog′ə tiv), a right or

privilege that nobody else has. The government has the prerogative of coining money. *n. 8.*

pres age (pres′ij for 1 and 2, pri sāj′ for 3 and 4), 1. a feeling that something is about to happen. 2. a sign felt as a warning; omen. 3. predict; give warning of. Some people think that a circle around the moon presages a storm. 4. have or give a prophetic impression of. *n., v. 9.*

pres by ter (prez′bi tər), 1. an elder in the early Christian church. 2. in the Presbyterian Church, a minister or a lay elder. 3. in the Episcopal Church, a minister or a priest. *n. 15.*

Pres by te ri an (prez′bi tēr′i ən), 1. being or naming a Protestant denomination or church governed by elected presbyters or elders all of equal rank. 2. of the Presbyterian Church. 3. member of the Presbyterian Church. *adj., n. 9.*

pres by ter y (prez′bi ter′i), 1. in the Presbyterian church, a meeting or court of all the ministers and certain of the elders within a district. 2. the district under the jurisdiction of a presbytery. 3. the part of a church set aside for the clergy. *n., pl. presbyteries. 18.*

pre sci ence (prē′shi əns), knowledge of things before they exist or happen; foreknowledge; foresight. People used to believe that animals have an instinctive prescience of the approach of danger. *n. 15.*

pre sci ent (prē′shi ənt), knowing beforehand; foreseeing. *adj. 19.*

pre scribe (pri skrīb′), 1. order. Good citizens do what the laws prescribe. 2. order as medicine. The doctor prescribed a complete rest for Ann. 3. give medical advice. *v. 4.*

pre scrip tion (pri skrip′shən), 1. an order; a direction. 2. a written direction or order for medicine; as, a prescription for a cough. 3. the possession or use of a thing long enough to give a right or title to it. *n. 9.*

pre scrip tive (pri skrip′tiv), 1. prescribing. 2. established by law or custom. *adj. 18.*

pres ence (prez′əns), 1. being present in a place. I knew of his presence in the other room. 2. place where a person is. The messenger was admitted to my presence. 3. **In the presence of** means in the sight or company of. He signed his name in the presence of two witnesses. 4. appearance; bearing; as, man of noble presence. 5. something present, especially a ghost, spirit, or the like. 6. **Presence of mind** means ability to think calmly and quickly when taken by surprise. *n. 2.*

pres ent[1] (prez′ənt), 1. at hand; not absent. Every member of the class was present. 2. **Be present** sometimes means be or exist. Oxygen is present in the air. 3. at this time; being or occurring now; as, the present ruler, present prices. 4. now; the time being. That is enough for the present. **At present** means now. 5. the verb form that expresses an event as occurring now. *Sings* is in the present tense. *adj., n. 1.*

pre sent[2] (pri zent′ for 1, 3-6, prez′ənt for 2), 1. give. They presented flowers to their teacher. **Present with** sometimes means give to. Our class presented the school with a picture. 2. gift; something given; as, a Christmas present. 3. introduce; make acquainted; bring (a person, etc.) before somebody. Miss Smith, may I present Mr. Brown? 4. offer; set forth in words. The speaker presented arguments for his side. 5. hand in; send in. The grocer presented his bill. 6. point or turn. The soldier presented his face to his enemy. *v., n.*

pre sent a ble (pri zen′tə bəl), 1. fit to be seen. 2. suitable in appearance, dress, manners, etc., for being introduced into society or company. 3. suitable to be offered or given. *adj. 17.*

pres en ta tion (prez′ən tā′shən), 1. introduction; as, the presentation of a lady to the queen. 2. exhibition; showing; as, the presentation of a play or motion picture. 3. act of giving; delivering; as, the presentation of a gift. 4. the gift that is presented. *n. 8.*

pre sen ti ment (pri zen′ti mənt), a feeling or impression that something is about to happen; a vague sense of approaching misfortune; a foreboding. *n. 13.*

pres ent ly (prez′ənt li), soon. The clock will strike presently. *adv. 7.*

pre sent ment (pri zent′mənt), 1. a presenting; a being presented. 2. the statement by a grand jury of an offense from their own knowledge. 3. representation on the stage or by a portrait. *n. 16.*

present participle, participle that expresses time that is now. In "Singing merrily, we turn our steps toward home," *singing* is a present participle.

pres er va tion (prez′ər vā′shən), 1. preserving; keeping safe. 2. being preserved; being kept safe. *n. 8.*

pre serv a tive (pri zėr′və tiv), 1. any substance that will prevent decay or injury. Paint is a preservative for wood surfaces. Salt is a preservative for meat. 2. that preserves. *n., adj. 12.*

pre serve (pri zėrv′), 1. keep from harm or change; keep safe; protect. 2. keep up; maintain. 3. keep from spoiling. Ice helps to preserve food. 4. prepare (food) to keep it from spoiling. Boiling with sugar, salting, smoking, and pickling are different ways of preserving food. 5. fruit cooked with sugar and sealed from the air. Mother made some plum preserves. 6. place where wild animals or fish are protected. People are not allowed to hunt on the preserves. *v., n. 2.*

pre serv er (pri zėr′vər), person or thing that saves and protects from danger. Life preservers made like cork vests help to save people from drowning. *n. 10.*

pre side (pri zīd′), 1. hold the place of authority; have charge of a meeting. Our principal will preside at our election of school officers. 2. have authority; have control. The manager presides over the business of the store. *v. 5.*

pres i den cy (prez′i dən si), 1. office of president. Lucy was elected to the presidency of the Junior Club. 2. time during which a president is in office. The United States entered the first World War during the Presidency of Woodrow Wilson. *n., pl. presidencies. 9.*

pres i dent (prez′i dənt), chief officer of a company, college, society, club, etc. The highest officer of a modern republic is usually called the President. *n. 2.*

pres i den tial (prez′i den′shəl), of or belonging to a president or presidency; having to do with a president or presidency; as, a presidential election, a presidential candidate. *adj. 8.*

press[1] (pres), 1. use force or weight steadily in pushing; push; force. Press the button to ring the bell. You press clothes with an iron. Press the orange juice out. 2. hug. Mother pressed the baby to her. 3. urge; keep asking (somebody) earnestly. Because it was so stormy, we pressed our guest to stay all night. 4. keep on pushing one's way; push ahead with eagerness or haste. The boys pressed on in spite of the wind. 5. a push; force; pressure. The press of many duties keeps her busy. 6. crowd. The little boy was lost in the press. 7. a machine for pressing; as, a printing press, an ironing press. 8. the business of printing newspapers and magazines. 9. the newspapers and the people who write for them. Our school picnic was reported by the press. *v., n. 1.*

press[2] (pres), 1. force into service, usually naval or military. Navy officers used to visit towns and merchant ships to press men for the fleet. 2. forcing into service. *v., n.*

press ing (pres′ing), requiring immediate action or attention; persistent. *adj.*

pres sure (presh′ər), 1. the continued action of a weight or force. The small box was flattened by the pressure of the heavy book on it. The pressure of the wind filled the sails of the boat. 2. force per unit of area. There is a pressure of 20 pounds to the inch on this tire. 3. a state of trouble or strain; as, the pressure of poverty, working under pressure. 4. a compelling influence. Pressure was brought to bear on John to make him change his mind about not doing his work. *n. 5.*

pres tige (pres tēzh′), reputation, influence, or distinction, based on what is known of one's abilities, achievements, opportunities, associations, etc. Tom's prestige rose when the boys learned that his father was a captain. *n. 12.*

pres to (pres′tō), 1. quickly. 2. quick. 3. a quick part of a piece of music. *adv., adj., n. 14.*

pre sum a ble (pri züm′ə bəl), that can be taken for granted; probable; likely; as, the presumable time of their arrival. *adj. 10.*

pre sum a bly (pri züm′ə bli), probably. *adv.*

pre sume (pri züm′), 1. suppose; take for granted without proving. You'll play out of doors, I presume, if there is sunshine. 2. take upon one's self; venture; dare. May I presume to tell you you are wrong? 3. take an unfair advantage. Don't presume on a person's good nature by borrowing from him every week. *v. 4.*

pre sum ing (pri züm′ing), bold; forward. It would be presuming to camp in a man's yard without permission. *adj.*

pre sump tion (pri zump′shən), 1. thing taken for granted. As his mouth was sticky, the presumption was that he had eaten the cake. 2. unpleasant boldness. It is presumption to go to a party when one has not been invited. 3. cause or reason for presuming. 4. act of presuming. *n. 8.*

pre sump tive (pri zump′tiv), 1. presumed; based on likelihood. An heir presumptive is one who will inherit if no nearer heir is born in the meantime. 2. giving ground for presumption or belief. The man's running away was regarded as presumptive evidence of his guilt. *adj. 16.*

pre sump tu ous (pri zump′chü əs), forward; too bold; daring too much. *adj. 6.*

pre sup pose (prē′sə pōz′), 1. take for granted in advance; assume beforehand. Let us presuppose that he wants more money. 2. require as a condition; imply. A fight presupposes fighters. *v. 18.*

pre sup po si tion (prē′sup ə zish′ən), 1. a presupposing. 2. something assumed beforehand; a supposition. The detective acted upon the presupposition that the thief knew the value of the jewels. *n.*

pre tence (prē′tens), pretense. *n.*

pre tend (pri tend′), 1. make believe. 2. claim. I don't pretend to be a musician. 3. claim falsely. She pretends to like you, but talks about you behind your back. 4. lay claim. James Stuart pretended to the English throne. *v. 3.*

pre tend er (pri ten′dər), 1. person who pretends. 2. person who makes claims to a throne without just right. *n. 15.*

pre tense or **pre tence** (pri tens′), 1. a make-believe; pretending. My anger was all pretense. 2. false appearance. Under pretense of picking up the handkerchief, she took the money. 3. false claim. The girls made a pretense of knowing the boys' secret. 4. claim. 5. display; showing off. Her manner is modest and free from pretense. *n. 5.*

pre ten sion (pri ten′shən), 1. a claim. The young prince has pretensions to the throne. 2. a putting forward of a claim; laying claim to. 3. doing things for show or to make a fine appearance; showy display. *n. 10.*

pre ten tious (pri ten′shəs), 1. making claims to excellence or importance; as, a pretentious person, book, or speech. 2. doing things for show or to make a fine appearance; as, a pretentious style of entertaining guests. *adj. 16.*

pret er it or **pret er ite** (pret′ər it), 1. the verb form that expresses occurrence in the past; the past tense. *Obeyed* is the preterit of *obey; spoke,* of *speak;* and *saw,* of *see.* 2. expressing past time. *n., adj. 20.*

pre ter nat u ral (prē′tər nach′ə rəl), 1. out of the ordinary course of nature; abnormal. 2. supernatural; due to something above or beyond nature. *adj. 15.*

pre text (prē′tekst), a misleading excuse; a false reason concealing the real reason; a pretense. He used his sore finger as a pretext for not going to school. *n. 10.*

pret ti ly (prit′i li), in a pretty manner: pleasingly. *adv.*

pret ti ness (prit′i nis), quality or state of being pretty; pleasing appearance. *n.*

pret ty (prit′i), 1. pleasing; as, a pretty face, a pretty dress, a pretty tune, a pretty story, pretty manners. Pretty is used to describe people and things that are dainty, sweet, charming, etc., but not stately, grand, elegant, or very important. 2. fairly; rather. It is pretty late. 3. brave; bold; strong; as, a pretty fellow. *Old use. adj., prettier, prettiest, adv. 1.*

pret zel (pret′səl), a hard biscuit in the form of a knot, salted on the outside. *n.*

pre vail (pri vāl′), 1. be the stronger; gain the victory. The knights prevailed against their foe. 2. be the most usual or strongest. Yellow is the prevailing color in her room. Sadness prevailed in our minds. 3. exist in many places; be in general use. The custom still prevails of hanging up stockings the night before Christmas. 4. **Prevail on** or **prevail upon** means persuade. Can't I prevail upon you to stay to dinner? *v. 3.*

pre vail ing (pri vāl′ing), 1. that prevails; having superior force or influence. 2. in general use; common; as, a prevailing style. The prevailing summer winds here are from the west. *adj.*

prev a lence (prev′ə ləns), widespread occurrence; general use; as, the prevalence of complaints about the weather, the prevalence of automobiles. *n. 9.*

prev a lent (prev′ə lənt), widespread; in general use; common. Colds are prevalent in winter. *adj. 7.*

pre var i cate (pri var′i kāt), lie; turn aside from the truth in speech or act. *v. 20.*

pre var i ca tion (pri var′i kā′shən), act of prevaricating; departure from the truth. *n. 20.*

pre var i ca tor (pri var′i kā′tər), person who turns aside from the truth in speech or action. *n.*

pre vent (pri vent′), 1. keep (from). Illness prevented him from doing his work. 2. keep from happening. Rain prevented the game.

3. hinder. I'll meet you at six if nothing prevents. *v. 2.*

pre vent a ble (pri ven′tə bəl), that can be prevented. *adj. 17.*

pre vent i ble (pri ven′ti bəl), preventable. *adj.*

pre ven tion (pri ven′shən), 1. preventing; hindering; as, the prevention of fire. 2. something that prevents. *n. 8.*

pre ven tive (pri ven′tiv), 1. that prevents or hinders; as, preventive measures against disease. 2. something that prevents. Vaccination is a preventive against smallpox. *adj., n. 9.*

pre vi ous (prē′vi əs), 1. coming before; that came before. She did better in the previous lesson. 2. **Previous to** means before. Previous to her departure she gave a big party. *adj., adv. 4.*

pre vi ous ly (prē′vi əs li), at a previous time; before. *adv.*

pre war (prē′wôr′), before the war. *adj. 14.*

prey (prā), 1. animal hunted or seized for food. Mice and birds are the prey of cats. 2. person or thing injured; victim; as, to be a prey to fear or disease. 3. take plunder; seize prey; hunt. Cats prey upon mice. 4. do harm. Worry preys on her mind. 5. the habit of hunting. Hawks are birds of prey. *n., v. 3.*

Pri am (prī′am), the king of Troy at the time of the Trojan War. *n. 15.*

price (prīs), 1. the amount for which a thing is sold or can be bought; the cost to the buyer. The price of this hat is $2.98. 2. amount paid for any result. We paid a heavy price for victory, for we lost ten thousand men. 3. find out the price of. Mother is pricing rugs. 4. put a price on; set the price of. 5. **Beyond price** or **without price** means so valuable that it cannot be bought. *n., v. 1.*

price less (prīs′lis), beyond price; very, very valuable. *adj. 13.*

prick (prik), 1. sharp point. 2. the little hole or mark a sharp point makes. 3. make a mark on with a sharp point. I pricked the map with a pin to show our route. 4. a pain like that made by a sharp point. 5. cause such a pain. Thorns prick. The cat pricked me with its claws. 6. act of pricking. 7. state of being pricked. 8. **Prick up the ears** means (1) point the ears upward. (2) to give sudden attention. 9. to spur; urge; ride fast. *Old use. n., v. 3.*

prick le (prik′əl), 1. a small sharp point. 2. feel a prickly or smarting sensation. Her skin prickled when she saw the big snake. 3. cause such a sensation in. *n., v. 18.*

prick ly (prik′li), 1. having many sharp points like thorns; as, a prickly rosebush. 2. smarting. Heat sometimes causes a prickly rash on the skin. *adj. 11.*

pride (prīd), 1. high opinion of one's own worth or possessions. Pride in our city should make us help to keep it clean. 2. too high an opinion of oneself. Pride goes before a fall. 3. something that one is proud of. Her youngest child is her great pride. 4. **Pride oneself on** means be proud of. We pride ourselves on our clean streets. *n., v. 2.*

pride ful (prīd′fəl), proud. *adj.*

priest (prēst), 1. special servant of a god; as, priests of Apollo. 2. clergyman or minister of a Christian church. *n. 3.*

priest ess (prēs′tis), woman who serves at an altar or in sacred rites; as, a priestess of Diana. *n. 15.*

priest hood (prēst′hůd), 1. position or rank of priest. He was admitted to the priesthood. 2. priests as a group. The priesthood had great power in Spain. *n. 9.*

priest ly (prēst′li), 1. of or pertaining to a priest. 2. like a priest; suitable for a priest. *adj. 13.*

prig (prig), person who is too particular about speech and manners, and prides himself on being better than others. *n. 19.*

prig gish (prig′ish), too particular about doing right in things that show outwardly; priding oneself on being better than others. *adj.*

prim (prim), stiffly precise, neat, proper, or formal. *adj., primmer, primmest. 12.*

pri ma cy (prī′mə si), 1. being first in order, rank, importance, etc. 2. the position of a bishop of highest rank. 3. in the Roman Catholic Church, the supreme power of the Pope. *n., pl. primacies. 15.*

pri ma don na (prē′mə don′ə), the principal woman singer in an opera. *pl. prima donnas.*

pri mal (prī′məl), 1. first; of early times; primeval. 2. chief; fundamental. *adj. 13.*

pri ma ri ly (prī′mãr i li), 1. chiefly; principally. She likes books primarily. 2. at first; originally. *adv. 11.*

pri ma ry (prī′mãr i), 1. first in time; first in order. Little children go to the primary school. 2. original; from which others are made. The primary colors are red, blue, and yellow. 3. chief; first in importance. Good health and character are primary.

4. a meeting of the voters of a political party to choose candidates for office. *adj., n., pl. primaries. 5.*

pri mate (prī′māt), 1. an archbishop or bishop ranking first among the bishops of a province or country. 2. any of the highest order of animals, including the monkeys, the apes, and man. *n. 13.*

prime[1] (prīm), 1. first in rank; chief. The prime minister of England is the head of the government. His prime object was to lower the tax rate. 2. first in quality; first-rate; excellent; as, prime ribs of beef. 3. first part. 4. best part; best time; best condition. Rome was in its prime in the age of Augustus. A man of forty is in the prime of life. 5. that cannot be divided without a remainder by any whole number except itself and 1. 7, 11, and 13 are prime numbers. *adj., n. 4.*

prime[2] (prīm), load; prepare by putting something in or on. *v.*

prim er (prim′ər), 1. first book in reading. 2. first book; beginner's book. *n. 9.*

pri me val (prī mē′vəl), 1. of or pertaining to the first age or ages. In its primeval state the earth was a fiery glowing ball. 2. ancient; as, primeval forests untouched by the ax. *adj. 14.*

prim i tive (prim′i tiv), 1. first of the kind; as, primitive Christians. 2. very early; living long ago. Primitive men lived in caves. 3. very simple; such as people had early in human history. A primitive way of making fire is by rubbing two sticks together. *adj. 7.*

pri mo gen i ture (prī′mō jen′i chər), 1. the fact of being the first-born among the children of the same parents. 2. the right or rule by which the eldest son inherits his father's land and buildings; inheritance by the first-born. *n. 16.*

pri mor di al (prī môr′di əl), 1. existing at the very beginning; primitive. 2. original; elementary. *adj. 20.*

prim rose (prim′rōz′), 1. a little plant with pale-yellow flowers. 2. a plant like this; as, the evening primrose. 3. pale yellow. 4. **The primrose path** means the pleasant way. *n., adj. 8.*

Primrose (def. 1)

prince (prins), 1. son of a king; son of a king's son. 2. a ruler of a small state or country. 3. man of highest rank; the best; the chief; as, a merchant prince, a prince of artists. *n. 1.*

Prince Edward Island, province of Canada on an island in the Gulf of St. Lawrence, just north of Nova Scotia.

prince ly (prins′li), 1. of a prince or his rank. 2. like a prince; noble. 3. fit for a prince. *adj., princelier, princeliest. 8.*

Prince of Wales, title of the oldest son, or heir apparent, of the British sovereign.

prin cess (prin′sis), 1. daughter of a king; daughter of a king's son. 2. wife of a prince. 3. woman having the rank of a prince. *n. 3.*

Prince ton (prins′tən), a university in Princeton, New Jersey. *n. 14.*

prin ci pal (prin′si pəl), 1. most important; chief; main. Chicago is the principal city of Illinois. 2. chief person; one who gives orders; as, the principal of a school. 3. person who hires another person to act for him. Smith does the business of renting the houses for Mr. Jones, his principal. 4. a sum of money on which interest is paid. *adj., n. 2.*

prin ci pal i ty (prin′si pal′i ti), 1. a small state or country ruled by a prince. 2. the country from which a prince gets his title. 3. supreme power. *n., pl. principalities. 8.*

prin ci pal ly (prin′si pəl i), chiefly; above all; mainly; for the most part. *adv. 10.*

prin ci ple (prin′si pəl), 1. a rule of science explaining how things act; as, the principle by which a machine works. 2. a truth that is a foundation for other truths; as, the principles of democratic government. 3. a rule of action or conduct. I make it a principle to save some money every month. 4. a fundamental belief; as, religious principles. 5. uprightness; honor. Washington was a man of principle. *n. 3.*

print (print), 1. a mark made by pressing or stamping, such as a footprint. 2. words in ink stamped by type. This book has clear print. 3. use type to stamp words on (paper, etc.). Who prints this newspaper? 4. cause to be printed; publish; as, to print books. Most newspapers are printed daily. 5. A book is **out of print** when no more printed copies can be bought from the publisher. 6. make letters the way they look in print instead of writing them. 7. to mark (cloth, paper, etc.) with patterns or designs. Machines print wallpaper. 8. cloth with a pattern pressed on it. 9. a picture made in a special way; a printed picture or design. *n., v. 2.*

print er (prin′tər), person whose business or work is printing or setting type. *n. 9.*

print ing (prin′ting), 1. the producing of books, newspapers, etc., by impression from movable types, plates, etc. 2. printed words, etc. 3. letters made like those in print. *n.*

printing press, machine for printing on paper, etc., from types, plates, etc.

pri or (prī′ər), 1. earlier. I have a prior engagement and so can't go with you. **Prior to** means earlier than or before. 2. the superior officer in a monastery for men. The monks had to obey their prior. *adj., adv., n. 7.*

pri or ess (prī′ər is), woman at the head of a monastery for women. *n. 18.*

pri or i ty (prī or′i ti), 1. being earlier in time. The priority of the visit of the Norsemen to America to that of Columbus has been established. 2. coming before in order or importance. Fire engines and ambulances have priority over other traffic. *n., pl. priorities. 14.*

pri o ry (prī′əri), religious house governed by a prior or prioress. *n., pl. priories. 17.*

Pris cil la (pri sil′ə), the heroine of Longfellow's poem *The Courtship of Miles Standish. n.*

prism (prizm), 1. a solid whose bases or ends have the same size and shape and are parallel to one another, and each of whose sides has two pairs of parallel edges. A six-sided pencil before it is sharpened has the shape of one kind of prism. 2. a transparent solid, often of glass, having the shape of a prism, usually with three-sided ends, which will separate white light passing through it into the colors of the rainbow. *n. 7.*

Prisms: A, def. 1; B, def. 2.

pris mat ic (priz mat′ik), 1. of or like a prism. 2. formed by a transparent prism; varied in color; brilliant. 3. The **prismatic colors,** formed when white light is passed through a prism, are red, orange, yellow, green, blue, indigo, and violet. These are the colors of the rainbow. *adj. 12.*

pris on (priz′ən), 1. place where one is shut up against his will. Lawbreakers are put in prison. The small apartment was a prison to the big dog and he longed to be back on the farm. 2. imprison; put in a prison; keep shut up. *n., v. 2.*

pris on er (priz′ən ər), 1. person who is kept shut up against his will, or who is not free to move. 2. person taken by the enemy in war. *n. 2.*

pris tine (pris′tēn), as it was in its earliest time or state; original; primitive; ancient. The colors of the paintings inside the pyramid had kept their pristine freshness. *adj. 15.*

prith ee (priтн′i). I pray thee; I ask you. Prithee, who art thou? *interj.* [*Used now only in poetry, old stories, etc.*] *12.*

pri va cy (prī′və si), 1. condition of being private; being away from others. 2. secrecy. He told me his reasons in strict privacy. *n., pl. privacies. 9.*

pri vate (prī′vit), 1. not for the public; for just a few special people or for one; as, a private car, a private house, a private letter. 2. having no public office; as, a private citizen. 3. a common soldier, not an officer. 4. secret. **In private** means secretly. *adj., n. 2.*

pri va teer (prī′və tēr′), 1. an armed ship owned by private persons, holding a government commission to attack and capture enemy ships. 2. commander of a privateer; one of its crew. 3. to cruise as a privateer. *n., v. 14.*

pri vate ly (prī′vit li), in a private manner; not publicly; secretly. *adv.*

pri va tion (prī vā′shən), 1. lack of the comforts or of the necessities of life. Many children died because of privation during the war. 2. loss; absence; being deprived. Privation of the company of all other human beings is a serious hardship. *n. 11.*

priv et (priv′it), any of several shrubs with small leaves much used for hedges. Some are evergreen. *n.*

Privet

priv i lege (priv′i lij), 1. a special right, advantage, or favor. Mr. Hope has given us the privilege of using his radio. 2. give a privilege to. *n., v. 3.*

priv i leged (priv′i lijd), having a special advantage or advantages. The nobility in Europe was a privileged class. *adj.*

priv i ly (priv′i li), secretly. *adv.*

priv y (priv′i), 1. private. A **privy council** is a body of personal advisers to a ruler. 2. secret. **Privy to** means having secret or private knowledge of. *adj. 6.*

prize[1] (prīz), 1. a reward worth working for. 2. a reward won after trying against other people. Prizes will be given for the three best stories. 3. something captured from the enemy in war. 4. worthy of a prize; given as a prize. *n., adj. 2.*

prize[2] (prīz), value highly. Mother prizes her best china. *v.*

prize fight, a fight with fists which people pay money to see.

pro (prō), 1. in favor of; for. 2. a reason in favor. The pros and cons of a question are the arguments for and against it. *adv., n., pl. pros. 13.*

prob a bil i ty (prob′ə bil′i ti), 1. quality of being likely or probable; chance. There is a probability that school will close a week earlier than usual. 2. something likely to happen. A storm is one of the probabilities for tomorrow. *n., pl. probabilities. 8.*

prob a ble (prob′ə bəl), 1. likely to happen. Cooler weather is probable after this shower. 2. likely to be true. Something he ate is the probable cause of his pain. *adj. 2.*

prob a bly (prob′ə bli), more likely than not. *adv.*

pro bate (prō′bāt), 1. in law, the official proving of a will as genuine. 2. a true copy of a will with a certificate that it has been proved genuine. 3. prove by legal process the genuineness of (a will). 4. of or concerned with the probating of wills; as, a probate court. *n., v., adj. 18.*

pro ba tion (prō bā′shən), 1. trial or testing of conduct, character, qualifications, etc. John was admitted to the sixth grade on probation. After a period of probation a novice becomes a nun. 2. the system of letting young offenders against the law, or first offenders, go free without receiving the punishment which they are sentenced to unless there is a further offense. *n. 11.*

pro ba tion er (prō bā′shən ər), person who is on probation. *n.*

probe (prōb), 1. search into; examine thoroughly; as, to probe into the causes of a crime, to probe one's thoughts or feelings to find out why one acted as one did. 2. a slender instrument with a rounded end for exploring the depth or direction of a wound, a cavity in the body, etc. 3. examine with a probe. *v., n. 10.*

pro bi ty (prō′bi ti), uprightness; honesty; high principle. *n. 17.*

prob lem (prob′ləm), 1. question; difficult question. 2. a matter of doubt or difficulty. *n. 3.*

prob lem at ic (prob′ləm at′ik), having the nature of a problem; doubtful; uncertain; questionable. Whether any medicine can ever be found to cure cancer is problematic. What the weather will be is often problematic. *adj.*

prob lem at i cal (prob′ləm at′i kəl), problematic. *adj. 17.*

pro bos cis (prō bos′is), 1. an elephant's trunk 2. a long flexible snout, like that of the tapir. 3. the mouth parts of some insects, developed to great length for sucking; as, the proboscis of a fly or a mosquito. *n. 12.*

Head of a tapir showing a proboscis

pro ce dure (prō sē′jər), 1. way of proceeding; method of doing things. What is your procedure in making bread? 2. manner or way of conducting business; as, parliamentary procedure, legal procedure. *n. 9.*

pro ceed (prō sēd′), 1. go on after having stopped; move forward. Please proceed with your story. The train proceeded at the same speed as before. 2. carry on any activity. He proceeded to light his pipe. 3. come forth; issue; go out. Heat proceeds from fire. *v. 2.*

pro ceed ing (prō sēd′ing), 1. action; conduct; what is done. 2. **Start proceedings against** (a person) means sue him in a court of law. 3. The **proceedings** of a society club, etc., are the records of its doings, especially as published each year. *n. 13.*

pro ceeds (prō′sēdz), 1. results. 2. money obtained from a sale, etc. The proceeds from the school play will be used to buy a new curtain for the stage. *n. pl.*

proc ess (pros′es), 1. going on; moving forward. In process of time the house will be finished. 2. a set of actions or changes in a special order. By what processes is cloth made from wool? 3. treat or prepare by some special method. 4. a written command or summons to appear in a court of law. 5. a part that grows out or sticks out; as, the process of a bone. *n., v. 3.*

pro ces sion (prō sesh′ən), 1. something that moves forward; persons marching. A funeral procession filled the street. 2. an orderly moving forward. We formed lines to march in procession onto the platform. *n. 4.*

pro ces sion al (prō sesh′ən əl), 1. of a procession. 2. used or sung in a procession;

as, a processional hymn. 3. processional music. The choir and clergy march into church singing the processional. 4. a book containing hymns, etc., for use in religious processions. *adj., n. 17.*

pro claim (prō klām′), make known publicly and officially; declare publicly. War was proclaimed. The people proclaimed him king. *v. 3.*

proc la ma tion (prok′lə mā′shən), proclaiming; a public and official announcement. Every year the President issues a Thanksgiving proclamation. *n. 7.*

pro con sul (prō kon′səl), a governor or military commander of an ancient Roman province with duties and powers like a consul's. *n. 15.*

pro cras ti nate (prō kras′ti nāt), put things off until later; delay. *v. 16.*

pro cras ti na tion (prō kras′ti nā′shən), the act or habit of putting things off till later; delay. *n. 20.*

proc tor (prok′tər), 1. an officer in a university or school who keeps good order. 2. person employed to manage another's cause in a court of law. *n. 19.*

pro cur a ble (prō kūr′ə bəl), that may be procured; obtainable. *adj.*

proc u ra tor (prok′ū rā′tər), 1. person employed to manage the affairs of another, or to act for another; agent. 2. among the ancient Romans, a financial agent or administrator in an imperial province. *n. 16.*

pro cure (prō kūr′), 1. obtain by care or effort; get. A friend procured a position in the bank for my big brother. It is hard to procure water in a desert. 2. bring about; cause. *v. 4.*

prod (prod), 1. poke with something pointed; as, to prod an animal with a stick. 2. stir up; urge on; goad; as, to prod a lazy boy to action by threats and entreaties. 3. a poke; a thrust. 4. a sharp-pointed stick; a goad. *v., prodded, prodding, n. 19.*

prod i gal (prod′i gəl), 1. spending too much; wasting money or other things; wasteful. America has been prodigal of its forests. 2. abundant; lavish. 3. person who wastes. The father welcomed the prodigal back home. *adj., n. 8.*

prod i gal i ty (prod′i gal′i ti), 1. wasteful or reckless extravagance. 2. rich abundance; profuseness. *n., pl. prodigalities. 12.*

prod i gal ly (prod′i gəl i), 1. wastefully; extravagantly. 2. lavishly; profusely. *adv.*

pro di gious (prō dij′əs), 1. huge; vast. 2. wonderful; marvelous. *adj. 7.*

prod i gy (prod′i ji), 1. a marvel; a wonder. An infant prodigy is a child remarkably brilliant in some respect. 2. a wonderful sign or omen. An eclipse of the sun seemed a prodigy to early man. *Rare. n., pl. prodigies. 11.*

pro duce (prō dūs′ or prō düs′ for 1, 2, and 3, prod′ūs or prod′üs for 4), 1. bring forward; show. Produce your proof. Our class produced a play. 2. to supply; bring forth. Hens produce eggs. 3. make. This factory produces stoves. Hard work produces success. 4. the yield. Vegetables are a garden's produce. *v., n. 2.*

pro duc er (prō dūs′ər or prō düs′ər), 1. one that produces; as, the producer of a play. 2. person who grows or manufactures things that are to be used or consumed by others. *n. 10.*

prod uct (prod′əkt), 1. that which is produced; a result of work or of growth; as, factory products, farm products. 2. a number or quantity resulting from multiplying two or more numbers or quantities together. 40 is the product of 5 and 8. *n. 2.*

pro duc tion (prō duk′shən), 1. act of producing; creation; manufacture. His business is the production of automobiles. 2. something which is produced. That worthless book is the production of an ignorant author. *n. 5.*

pro duc tive (prō duk′tiv), 1. producing; bringing forth; as, fields now productive only of weeds, the hasty words that are productive of quarrels. 2. producing food or other articles of commerce. Farming is productive labor. 3. fertile; producing abundantly; as, a productive farm, a productive writer. *adj. 8.*

pro duc tive ness (prō duk′tiv nis), being productive; fertility; abundant production. *n. 17.*

pro duc tiv i ty (prō′duk tiv′i ti), power to produce; productiveness. *n. 17.*

pro em (prō′em), introduction; preface. *n. 20.*

Prof., professor. *10.*

prof a na tion (prof′ə nā′shən), showing contempt or disregard toward something holy; treatment of something sacred as it should not be treated. *n. 15.*

pro fane (prō fān′), 1. not sacred. 2. with contempt or disregard for God or holy things; as, a profane man using profane language. 3. treat (holy things) with contempt or disregard. Soldiers profaned the church when they stabled their horses in it. *adj., v. 5.*

pro fane ness (prō fān′nis), profane state or quality. *n. 18.*

pro fan i ty (prō fan′i ti), 1. swearing; use of profane language. 2. being profane; lack of reverence. *n., pl. profanities. 15.*

pro fess (prō fes′), 1. declare openly. He professed his loyalty to the United States. 2. lay claim to; claim. He professed the greatest respect for the law. I don't profess to be an expert. 3. declare one's belief in. Christians profess Christ and the Christian religion. 4. have as one's profession or business; as, to profess law. *v. 5.*

pro fes sion (prō fesh′ən), 1. an occupation requiring an education; especially, law, medicine, teaching, or the ministry. 2. the people engaged in such an occupation. The medical profession favors this law. 3. act of professing. I don't believe her profession of friendship for us. *n. 5.*

pro fes sion al (prō fesh′ən əl), 1. of or pertaining to a profession. Dr. Smith has a professional gravity very unlike his ordinary joking manner. 2. engaged in a profession. A lawyer or a doctor is a professional man. 3. making a business or trade of something which others do for pleasure; as, professional ballplayers, professional musicians. 4. person who does this. *adj., n. 7.*

pro fes sion al ly (prō fesh′ən əl i), in a professional manner; in a professional capacity. *adv.*

pro fes sor (prō fes′ər), 1. a teacher of the highest rank in a college or university. 2. teacher. 3. person who professes; as, a professor of religion. *n. 3.*

pro res so ri al (prō′fe sō′ri əl), of, pertaining to, or characteristic of a professor. *adj.*

pro fes sor ship (prō fes′ər ship), the position or rank of a professor. *n. 19.*

prof fer (prof′ər), offer. We proffered regrets at having to leave so early. His proffer of advice was accepted. *v., n. 8.*

pro fi cien cy (prō fish′ən si), being proficient; knowledge; skill; an advanced state of expertness. *n. 18.*

pro fi cient (prō fish′ənt), advanced in any art, science, or subject; skilled; expert. She was very proficient in music. *adj. 11.*

pro file (prō′fīl), 1. side view. 2. outline. *n. 12.*

Profile of Lincoln

prof it (prof′it), 1. the gain from a business; what is left when the cost of goods and of carrying on the business is subtracted from the amount of money taken in. The profits in this business are not large. 2. advantage; benefit. What profit is there in worrying? 3. get advantage; gain; benefit. A wise person profits from his mistakes. *n., v. 2.*

prof it a ble (prof′it ə bəl), bringing gain; useful; yielding profit. We spent a profitable afternoon in the library. The sale held by the Girl Scouts was very profitable. *adj. 5.*

prof it a bly (prof′it ə bli), with profit. *adv.*

prof it eer (prof′i tēr′), 1. person who makes an unfair profit by taking advantage of public necessity. Profiteers made much money during the World War. 2. seek or make such excessive profits. *n., v. 15.*

prof it less (prof′it lis), without profit. *adj. 15.*

prof li ga cy (prof′li gə si), 1. great wickedness; vice. 2. reckless extravagance. *n. 20.*

prof li gate (prof′li git), 1. very wicked; shamelessly bad. 2. recklessly extravagant. 3. person who is very wicked. *adj., n. 15.*

pro found (prō found′), 1. very deep; as, a profound sigh, a profound sleep. 2. deeply felt; very great. 3. going far deeper than what is easily understood; having or showing great knowledge or understanding; as, a profound book, a profound thinker, a profound thought. *adj. 5.*

pro fun di ty (prō fun′di ti), 1. depth. 2. a very deep thing or place. *n., pl. profundities. 16.*

pro fuse (prō fūs′), 1. very abundant; as, profuse thanks. 2. spending or giving freely. He was so profuse with his money that he is now poor. *adj. 8.*

pro fu sion (prō fū′zhən), 1. great abundance. 2. extravagance; lavishness. *n. 13.*

pro gen i tor (prō jen′i tər), forefather; ancestor. *n. 9.*

prog e ny (proj′i ni), children; offspring; descendants. A cat's kittens are her progeny. *n. 8.*

prog nos tic (prog nos′tik), 1. indicating something in the future. 2. indication; sign. 3. a forecast; prediction. *adj., n. 16.*

prog nos ti cate (prog nos′ti kāt), forecast; predict from facts. *v. 17.*

prog nos ti ca tion (prog nos′ti kā′shən), a forecast; prediction. *n. 15.*

pro gram or **pro gramme** (prō′gram), 1. list of items or events. There are concert programs, theater programs, and programs of a meeting. 2. plan of what is to be done; as, a school program, a business program, a government program. *n. 5.*

pro gress (prō gres′ for 1 and 3, prog′res for 2 and 4), 1. move forward; go ahead. 2. moving forward; going ahead. 3. advance; develop; get better. 4. an advance; growth; development; improvement. *v., n. 3.*

pro gres sion (prō gresh′ən), 1. progressing or progress. Creeping is a slow method of progression. 2. in mathematics, a series in which there is always the same relation between a number and the one after it. *2, 4, 6, 8, 10* are in arithmetical progression. *2, 4, 8, 16* are in geometrical progression. *n. 18.*

pro gres sive (prō gres′iv), 1. making progress; advancing to something better; improving; as, a progressive nation. 2. favoring progress. 3. person who favors improvement and reform in government, religion, or business. He is a progressive in his beliefs. *adj., n. 6.*

pro hib it (prō hib′it), 1. forbid by law or authority. Picking flowers in the park is prohibited. 2. prevent. *v. 5.*

pro hi bi tion (prō′i bish′ən), 1. act of prohibiting or forbidding. 2. a law or laws against making or selling alcoholic liquors. *n. 7.*

pro hi bi tion ist (prō′i bish′ən ist), person who favors laws against the manufacture and sale of alcoholic liquors. *n. 19.*

pro hib i tive (prō hib′i tiv), prohibiting; preventing. Gold would make excellent roofs, if the price were not prohibitive. *adj. 18.*

pro hib i to ry (prō hib′i tō′ri), prohibitive. *adj.*

proj ect (proj′ekt for 1, prō jekt′ for 2, 3, and 4), 1. a plan. Flying in a heavy machine was once thought an impossible project. 2. to plan; scheme. 3. throw or cast forward; cause to fall on a surface. Moving pictures are projected on the screen. The tree projects a shadow on the grass. 4. stick out. The rocky point projects far into the water. *n., v. 5.*

pro jec tile (prō jek′til), 1. an object that can be thrown, hurled, or shot, such as a stone or bullet. 2. impelling; forcing forward; as, a projectile force. 3. capable of bring thrown, hurled, or shot. Bullets and arrows are projectile weapons. *n., adj. 14.*

pro jec tion (prō jek′shən), 1. part that projects or sticks out; as, rocky projections on the face of a cliff. 2. a sticking out. 3. a throwing or casting; as, the projection of a cannon ball from a cannon. *n. 8.*

pro jec tor (prō jek′tər), 1. apparatus for projecting a picture on a screen. 2. person who forms projects; schemer. *n. 16.*

pro le tari an (prō′li tãr′i ən), 1. of or belonging to the proletariat. 2. person belonging to the proletariat. *adj., n. 20.*

pro le tari at (prō′li tãr′i ət), 1. lowest class in economic and social status. The proletariat includes unskilled laborers, casual laborers, and tramps. 2. in Europe, the laboring class. *n. 16.*

pro lif ic (prō lif′ik), 1. producing offspring abundantly. Rabbits are prolific. 2. producing much; as, a prolific tree, garden, imagination, or writer. *adj. 8.*

pro lix (prō′liks), too long; tedious; using too many words. *adj. 16.*

pro lix i ty (prō lik′si ti), too great length; tedious length of speech or writing. *n. 19.*

pro logue or **pro log** (prō′lôg), 1. a speech or poem addressed to the audience by one of the actors at the beginning of a play. 2. an introduction to a novel, poem, or other literary work. *n. 9.*

pro long (prō lông′), make longer; extend. Good care may prolong a sick person's life. The dog uttered prolonged howls whenever the family left the house. *v. 4.*

pro lon ga tion (prō′lông gā′shən), 1. extension; lengthening in time or space; as, the prolongation of one's school days by a year of graduate study. 2. an added part. The summer kitchen was a prolongation of the shed. *n. 17.*

prom e nade (prom′i nād′), 1. walk for pleasure or for show. The Easter promenade is well known as a fashion show. He promenaded back and forth on the ship's deck. 2. a public place for such a walk. The boardwalk at Atlantic City is a famous promenade. *n., v. 7.*

Pro me theus (prō mē′thūs), a demigod who stole fire from heaven and taught men its use. Zeus punished him by chaining him to a rock. *n. 17.*

prom i nence (prom′i nəns), 1. something that juts out or projects, especially upward. A hill is a prominence. 2. being prominent, distinguished, or conspicuous; as, the prominence of athletics in some schools. *n. 13.*

prom i nent (prom′i nənt), 1. standing out; projecting. Some insects have prominent eyes. 2. easy to see. A single tree in a field is prominent. 3. well-known; important; as, a prominent citizen. *adj. 4.*

pro mis cu ous (prō mis′kū əs), 1. mixed and in disorder; as, a promiscuous heap of clothing on your closet floor. 2. making no distinctions; not discriminating; as, promiscuous friendships. *adj. 12.*

prom ise (prom′is), 1. words said, binding a person to do or not to do something. A man of honor always keeps his promise. 2. give one's word; give a promise. He promised to stay till we came. 3. make a promise of; as, to promise help. 4. that which gives hope of success; as, a pupil of promise in music. 5. give hope; give hope of. The rainbow promises fair weather. *n., v. 1.*

Promised Land, 1. the land promised by God to Abraham; Canaan. 2. heaven. 3. a place or condition of expected happiness. America has been a promised land for many immigrants.

prom is ing (prom′is ing), likely to turn out well; hopeful. *adj.*

prom is so ry (prom′i sō′ri), containing a promise. A **promissory note** is a written promise to pay a stated sum of money. *adj. 16.*

prom on to ry (prom′ən tō′ri), a high point of land extending from the coast into the water; headland. *n., pl. promontories. 11.*

Promontory

pro mote (prə mōt′), 1. raise in rank or importance. Pupils who pass this test will be promoted to the next grade. 2. help to grow or develop; help to success. A kindly feeling toward other countries will promote peace. 3. help to organize; start. Several bankers promoted the new company. *v. 6.*

pro mot er (prə mōt′ər), 1. person or thing that promotes. Good humor is a promoter of friendship. 2. person who organizes new companies and secures capital for them. *n. 13.*

pro mo tion (prə mō′shən), 1. advance in rank or importance. The clerk was given a promotion and an increase in salary. 2. helping along to success. The doctors were busy in the promotion of a health campaign. 3. helping to organize; starting. *n. 6.*

prompt (prompt), 1. quick; on time; done at once. Be prompt to obey. 2. cause (someone) to do something. His curiosity prompted him to ask questions. 3. remind of the words or actions needed. Do you know your part in the play or shall I prompt you? *adj., v. 2.*

prompt er (promp′tər), person who tells actors, speakers, etc., what to say when they forget. *n. 20.*

promp ti tude (promp′ti tūd or promp′ti-tüd), promptness; readiness in acting or deciding. *n. 16.*

pro mul gate (prō mul′gāt), 1. proclaim formally; announce officially. The king promulgated a decree. 2. spread far and wide. Schools try to promulgate knowledge and good habits. *v. 11.*

pro mul ga tion (prō′mul gā′shən), promulgating; publication. *n. 17.*

pron., 1. pronoun. 2. pronunciation.

prone (prōn), 1. inclined; liable. We are prone to think evil of people we don't like. 2. lying face down. *adj. 7.*

prong (prông), one of the pointed ends of a fork, antler, etc. *n. 17.*

prong horn (prông′hôrn′), animal like an antelope, found on the plains of western North America. *n., pl. pronghorns or pronghorn.*

Pronghorn (about 3 ft. high at the shoulder)

pro noun (prō′noun), a word used to indicate without naming, such as *you, it, they, him, we, your, whose, this,* or *whoever;* a word used instead of a noun. *n. 7.*

pro nounce (prə nouns′), 1. speak; make the sounds of. Pronounce your words clearly. 2. declare solemnly or positively. The judge pronounced sentence on the prisoner. *v. 2.*

pro nounced (prə nounst′), strongly marked; decided. She held pronounced opinions on many questions. *adj.*

pro nounce ment (prə nouns′mənt), formal statement; declaration. *n.*

pro nun ci a tion (prə nun′si ā′shən), speaking; making the sounds of words; way of sounding words. *n. 7.*

proof (prüf), 1. way or means of showing beyond doubt the truth of something. Is what you say a guess or have you proof? 2. act of testing. That box looks big enough;

but let us put it to the proof. 3. of tested value against something; as, proof against being taken by surprise. *n., adj. 2.*

-proof, suffix meaning:—protected against; safe from; as in fireproof, waterproof, bombproof, rainproof.

prop (prop), 1. hold up by placing a support under or against. Prop the clothesline with a stick. He was propped up in bed with pillows. 2. thing or person used to support another. A son is the prop of his father's old age. *v., propped, propping, n. 6.*

prop a gan da (prop′ə gan′də), 1. systematic efforts to spread opinions or beliefs; any plan or method for spreading an opinion or belief. Life insurance companies engage in health propaganda. 2. the opinions or beliefs thus spread. *n. 11.*

prop a gan dist (prop′ə gan′dist), person who gives time or effort to spreading of some opinion, belief, or principle. *n.*

prop a gate (prop′ə gāt), 1. produce young. 2. increase in number. Trees propagate themselves by seeds. 3. cause to increase in number by the production of young. 4. pass on; send further. 5. spread (news or knowledge). Don't propagate unkind reports. *v. 6.*

prop a ga tion (prop′ə gā′shən), 1. the breeding of plants or animals. Our propagation of poppies is by seed, and of roses by cuttings. 2. the handing down of qualities, etc., in a family line. 3. spreading; getting more widely believed; making more widely known; as, the propagation of the principles of science. 4. passing on; sending further; spreading or extending; as, the propagation of sound waves, the propagation of the shock of an earthquake. *n. 10.*

pro pel (prō pel′), drive forward; as, a boat propelled by oars, a person propelled by ambition. *v., propelled, propelling. 9.*

pro pel ler (prō pel′ər), 1. a device consisting of a revolving hub with blades for propelling boats, airships, and airplanes. 2. person or thing that propels. *n. 18.*

pro pen si ty (prō pen′si ti), leaning the mind toward; a natural inclination or bent. Most boys have a propensity for playing with machinery. *n., pl. propensities. 11.*

prop er (prop′ər), 1. correct; right; fitting. Night is the proper time to sleep, and bed the proper place. 2. belonging to one or a few; not common to all. *John Adams* is a proper name. 3. A **proper noun** names a particular person or thing. *John, Chicago,* and *Monday* are proper nouns. *Boy, city,* and *day* are common nouns. 4. A **proper fraction** is a fraction less than 1. $\frac{2}{3}$, $\frac{1}{8}$, $\frac{3}{4}$, and $\frac{133}{200}$ are proper fractions. *adj. 1.*

prop er ly (prop′ər li), 1. in a proper, correct, or fitting manner; as, to eat properly. 2. rightly; justly; as, to be properly indignant at the offer of a bribe. 3. strictly. Properly speaking, a whale is not a fish. *adv.*

prop er ty (prop′ər ti), 1. thing or things owned; possessions. This farmhouse is the property of Mr. Jones. Ask for your purse at the lost-property office. 2. ownership. 3. a quality or power belonging specially to something. Soap has the property of removing dirt. *n., pl. properties. 2.*

proph e cy (prof′i si), 1. telling what will happen; foretelling future events. 2. thing told about the future. The Greeks had much faith in the prophecies made by the priestess at Delphi. 3. divinely inspired utterance, revelation, writing, etc. *n., pl. prophecies. 5.*

proph e sy (prof′i sī), 1. tell what will happen; foretell; predict. The sailor prophesied a severe storm. 2. speak when or as if inspired by God. *v., prophesied, prophesying. 5.*

proph et (prof′it), 1. person who tells what will happen. Don't be a bad-luck prophet. 2. person who preaches what he thinks has been revealed to him. Every religion has its prophets. *n. 3.*

proph et ess (prof′it is), woman who prophesies. *n. 10.*

pro phet ic (prō fet′ik), 1. belonging to a prophet; such as a prophet has; as, prophetic power. 2. containing prophecy; as, a prophetic saying. 3. giving warning of what is to happen. *adj. 7.*

pro phy lac tic (prō′fi lak′tik), 1. protecting from disease. 2. a medicine or measure that protects against disease. He took cold baths as a prophylactic against colds. *adj., n.*

pro pin qui ty (prō ping′kwi ti), nearness. *n. 18.*

pro pi ti ate (prō pish′i āt), prevent the anger of; win the favor of; appease or conciliate. *v. 15.*

pro pi ti a tion (prō pish′i ā′shən), act of propitiating. *n. 16.*

pro pi tious (prō pish′əs), 1. favorable; as, propitious weather for our trip. 2. favorably inclined; gracious. *adj. 9.*

pro por tion (prə pōr′shən), 1. relation of two things in magnitude; a size, number, or amount compared to another. This door is narrow in proportion to its height. Mix water and orange juice in the proportions of three to one by taking three measures of water to every measure of orange juice. 2. proper relation between parts. His short legs were not in proportion to his long body. 3. fit (one thing to another) so that they go together. The designs in that rug are well proportioned. 4. part; share. A large proportion of Nevada is desert. 5. an equality of ratios. *Example:* 4 is to 2 as 10 is to 5. *n., v. 3.*

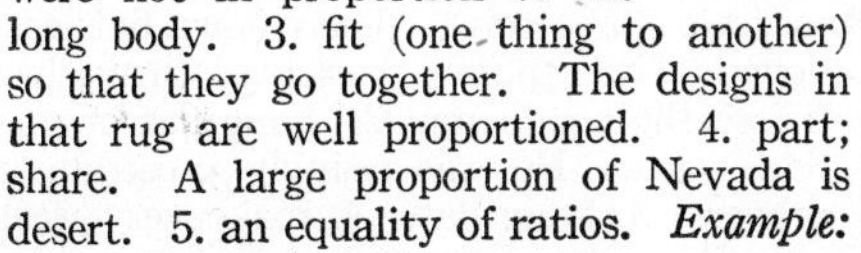

pro por tion al (prə pōr′shən əl), 1. in the proper proportion; corresponding. The increase in price is proportional to the improvement in the car. The pay will be proportional to the amount of time put in. The dwarf's long arms were not proportional to his height. 2. one of the terms of a proportion in mathematics. *adj., n. 16.*

pro por tion al ly (prə pōr′shən əl i), in proportion. *adv.*

pro por tion ate (prə pōr′shən it), proportioned; proportional; in the proper proportion. The money obtained by the fair was really not proportionate to the effort we put into it. *adj. 14.*

pro por tion ate ly (prə pōr′shən it li), in proportion. The money the boys earned was divided proportionately to the time each worked. *adv.*

pro pos al (prə pōz′əl), 1. plan; scheme; suggestion. The club will now hear this member's proposal. 2. an offer of marriage. 3. act of proposing. Proposal is easier than performance. *n. 7.*

pro pose (prə pōz′), 1. put forward; suggest; as, to propose that we take turns at the swing. 2. make an offer of marriage. 3. present (the name of someone) for an office. I propose John for president. 4. intend; plan. She proposes to save half of all she earns. *v. 3.*

prop o si tion (prop′ə zish′ən), 1. what is offered to be considered; proposal. The tailor made a proposition to buy out his rival's business. 2. a statement; a statement that is to be proved true. 3. a problem to be solved. *n. 5.*

pro pound (prə pound′), put forward; propose; as, to propound a theory, a question, or a riddle. *v.*

pro pri e tar y (prə prī′ə tãr′i), 1. owned by a private person; belonging to or controlled by a private person as property. A proprietary medicine is a patented medicine, that is, one which may be made and sold only by some one person or certain persons. 2. belonging to a proprietor. 3. holding property. 4. owner. 5. group of owners. 6. ownership; the holding of property. *adj., n., pl. proprietaries. 17.*

pro pri e tor (prə prī′ə tər), owner. *n. 7.*

pro pri e tor ship (prə prī′ə tər ship′), ownership. *n. 19.*

pro pri e tress (prə prī′ə tris), female owner or manager. *n.*

pro pri e ty (prə prī′ə ti), 1. fitness. 2. proper behavior. She acted with propriety. Propriety demands that a boy tip his hat to a lady whom he knows. *n., pl. proprieties. 9.*

pro pul sion (prō pul′shən), 1. a driving forward or onward. 2. a propelling force or impulse. *n. 20.*

pro sa ic (prō zā′ik), like prose; matter-of-fact; ordinary; not exciting. *adj. 16.*

pro scribe (prō skrīb′), 1. put outside of the protection of the law; outlaw. In olden times, a proscribed person's property belonged to the state and anyone might kill him. 2. banish; forbid to come into a certain place. 3. talk against; prohibit as wrong or dangerous. In earlier days, the church proscribed dancing and cardplaying. *v. 14.*

pro scrip tion (prō skrip′shən), 1. a proscribing. 2. a being proscribed; banishment; outlawry. *n. 15.*

prose (prōz), 1. the ordinary form of spoken or written language; plain language not arranged in verses. 2. matter-of-fact; commonplace. 3. write or talk in a dull way. *n., adj., v. 6.*

pros e cute (pros′i kūt), 1. bring before a court of law. People failing to shovel the snow from their sidewalks will be prosecuted. 2. carry out; follow up. He prosecuted an inquiry into reasons for the company's failure. *v. 9.*

pros e cu tion (pros′i kū′shən), 1. the carrying on of a lawsuit. The prosecution will be abandoned if the stolen money is returned. 2. side that starts action against another in a law court. The prosecution makes certain charges against the defense. 3. carrying out; following up. In prosecution of his plan, he stored away a supply of food. *n. 9.*

pros e cu tor (pros′i kū′tər), 1. person who starts legal proceedings against another person. Who is the prosecutor in this case? 2. the lawyer who takes charge of the State's side or city's side of a case against an accused person. *n. 18.*

pros e lyte (pros′ə līt), 1. person who has changed from one opinion, religious belief, etc., to another. 2. to convert from one opinion, religious belief, etc., to another. *n., v. 15.*

Pro ser pi na (prō sėr′pi nə), the daughter of Jupiter and Ceres. She was carried off by Pluto and made queen of the lower world, but she was allowed to spend part of the year on earth with her mother. At that time the earth blooms, but while Proserpina is in the lower world we have winter. *n. 11.*

Pro ser pi ne (prō sėr′pi nē), Proserpina. *n.*

pros o dy (pros′ə di), the science of poetic meters and verses. *n. 19.*

pros pect (pros′pekt), 1. view; scene. The prospect from the mountain was grand. 2. looking forward; expectation. The prospect of a vacation is pleasant. 3. things expected or looked forward to; as, good prospects in business. 4. to search or look; as, to prospect for gold. *n., v. 3.*

pro spec tive (prə spek′tiv), 1. probable; expected. 2. looking forward in time; future. *adj. 9.*

pro spec tive ly (prə spek′tiv li), in prospect; in expectation; in the future. *adv.*

pros pec tor (pros′pek tər), one who explores or examines a region, searching for gold, silver, oil, etc., or estimating the value of some other product of the region. *n. 15.*

pro spec tus (prə spek′təs), a printed statement describing and advertising something. *n.*

pros per (pros′pər), 1. be successful; flourish; have good fortune. 2. make successful. *v. 4.*

pros per i ty (pros per′i ti), success; good fortune; prosperous condition. Peace brings prosperity. *n., pl. prosperities. 4.*

Pros per o (pros′pər ō), the exiled duke of Milan in Shakespeare's play *The Tempest,* who, by magic, restores himself and his daughter Miranda to their proper rank and wealth. *n. 20.*

pros per ous (pros′pər əs), 1. successful; thriving; doing well; fortunate. A prosperous person is one who is happy, healthy, paying his way, and getting on well in his work. 2. favorable; helpful; as, prosperous weather for growing wheat. *adj. 3.*

pros ti tute (pros′ti tūt or pros′ti tüt), 1. woman who gets money for immoral behavior with men. 2. person who does base things for money. 3. put to an unworthy or base use. *n., v. 11.*

pros ti tu tion (pros′ti tū′shən or pros′ti tü′shən), the use of one's body, honor, talents, etc., in a base way. *n. 15.*

pros trate (pros′trāt), 1. lay down flat; cast down. The captives prostrated themselves before the conqueror. 2. lying flat or face downward. He was humbly prostrate in prayer. 3. lying flat. 4. make very weak or helpless; exhaust. Sickness often prostrates people. 5. overcome; helpless. She is prostrate with her great grief. *v., adj. 6.*

pros tra tion (pros trā′shən), 1. prostrating; bowing down low or lying face down before a king, before idols, or before God. Prostration is an act of submission, or of respect, or of worship. 2. exhaustion; dejection; being very much worn out or used up in body or mind. *n. 19.*

pros y (prōz′i), like prose; commonplace; dull; tiresome. *adj., prosier, prosiest.*

pro te an (prō′ti ən), readily assuming different forms; exceedingly variable. *adj.*

pro tect (prə tekt′), shield from harm or danger; shelter; defend; guard. Protect yourself from danger. Protect the baby's eyes from the sun. *v. 2.*

pro tec tion (prə tek′shən), 1. act of protecting; condition of being kept from harm; defense. We have policemen for our protection. 2. thing or person that prevents damage. An apron is a protection when doing dirty work. 3. a system of taxing foreign goods so that people are more likely to buy goods made in their own country; the opposite of free trade. *n. 3.*

pro tec tive (prə tek′tiv), 1. protecting; being a defense; as, the hard protective covering of a turtle. 2. preventing injury to those around; as, a protective device on a machine. 3. guarding against foreign-made goods by a high tax or duty on them. *adj. 11.*

pro tec tor (prə tek′tər), one that protects; defender. *n. 6.*

pro tec tor ate (prə tek′tər it), 1. When a strong country steps in to keep others out of a weaker one, especially one inhabited by native tribes, it is said to hold a protectorate over this weaker country. 2. a country thus taken charge of. *n. 14.*

pro té gé (prō′tə zhā), person who has been taken under the protection or kindly care of a friend or patron. *n. 17.*

pro te in (prō′tē in), one of the substances containing nitrogen which is a necessary part of the cells of animals and plants. Meat, milk, cheese, eggs, and beans contain protein. *n. 7.*

pro test (prō′test for 1 and 2, prō test′ for 3, 4, and 5), 1. statement that denies or objects strongly. They yielded only after protest. 2. a statement that a check, note, etc., has not been paid. 3. declare solemnly; assert. The accused man protested his innocence. 4. to object. The boys protested against having girls in the game. 5. object to. John protested the umpire's decision. *n., v. 4.*

Prot es tant (prot′is tənt), 1. member of any of most Christian churches except the Roman Catholic and Greek Catholic. Baptists, Presbyterians, Methodists, Quakers, and many others are all Protestants. 2. of Protestants or their religion. *n., adj. 7.*

Prot es tant ism (prot′is tənt izm), 1. the religion of Protestants. 2. their principles and beliefs. 3. Protestants as a group. *n. 16.*

prot es ta tion (prot′es tā′shən), 1. protesting; solemn declaration; as, to make a protestation of one's innocence. 2. a protest. *n. 10.*

Pro teus (prō′tūs), a Greek sea god who had the power of assuming different forms. *n. 11.*

pro ton (prō′ton), tiny particle carrying one unit of positive electricity. All atoms are built up of electrons and protons. *n.*

pro to plasm (prō′tə plazm), living matter; the substance that is the physical basis of life; the living substance of all plant and animal cells. Protoplasm is a colorless substance something like a soft jelly or white of egg. *n. 8.*

pro to type (prō′tə tīp), the first or primary type of anything; the original or model. A modern ship has its prototype in the hollowed log used by savages. *n. 16.*

pro tract (prō trakt′), 1. draw out; lengthen in time; as, a protracted visit. 2. slide out; thrust out; extend. *v. 11.*

pro trac tion (prō trak′shən), drawing out; extension. *n.*

pro trac tor (prō trak′tər), 1. instrument for measuring angles. 2. person or thing that protracts. *n.*

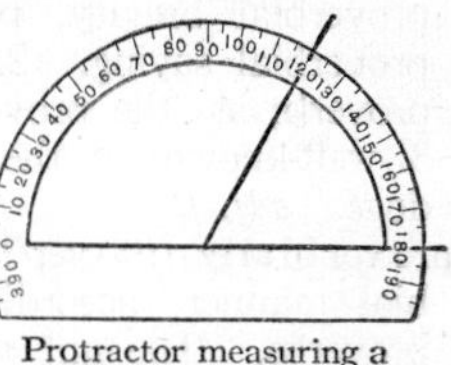
Protractor measuring a 120-degree angle

pro trude (prō trüd′), 1. thrust forth; stick out. The saucy child protruded her tongue. 2. be thrust forth; project. Helen's teeth protrude too far. *v. 9.*

pro tru sion (prō trü′zhən), 1. sticking out. Starvation caused the protrusion of the poor cat's bones. 2. projection; something that sticks out. A protrusion of rock gave us shelter from the storm. *n.*

pro tu ber ance (prō tū′bər əns or prō tü′bər əns), part that sticks out; bulge; swelling. From the protuberance in their father's coat pocket, the children guessed that he had brought them candy. *n. 15.*

pro tu ber ant (prō tū′bər ənt or prō tü′bər ənt), bulging out; prominent. *adj.*

proud (proud), 1. thinking well of oneself. 2. thinking too well of oneself. 3. **Proud of** means thinking well of or being well satisfied with. 4. very pleasing to the feelings or self-esteem. It was a proud moment for Tom when he shook hands with the President. 5. grand; magnificent. The big ship was a proud sight. *adj. 1.*

proud ly (proud′li), with pride. *adv.*

prove (prüv), 1. show that (a thing) is true and right. Prove this row of answers. 2. turn out; be found to be. The book proved interesting. 3. try; test; as, to prove a new tool. 4. know because of having tested. We have proved John's good temper. *v., proved, proved* or (sometimes) *proven, proving. 1.*

prov en (prüv′ən), proved. *v., a pp. of* **prove.**

Pro ven çal (prō′vän säl′), 1. of or pertaining to Provence, its people, or their language. 2. native or inhabitant of Provence. 3. language of Provence. *adj., n. 19.*

Pro vence (prō väns′), a part of southeastern France, a province of ancient Rome, famous during the Middle Ages for chivalry and poetry. *n. 14.*

prov en der (prov′ən dər), food; dry food for animals, such as hay or corn. *n. 12.*

prov erb (prov′ərb), a short wise saying used for a long time by many people. "Haste makes waste" is a proverb. *n. 6.*

pro ver bi al (prō vėr′bi əl), 1. of proverbs; expressed in a proverb; like a proverb; as, proverbial brevity, proverbial wisdom, a proverbial saying. 2. that has become a proverb; as, the proverbial stitch in time. 3. well-known; as, the proverbial loyalty of dogs. *adj. 15.*

pro ver bi al ly (prō vėr′bi əl i), in a proverbial manner; according to a proverb or proverbs. The ant is proverbially industrious. *adv.*

Prov erbs (prov′ərbz), book of the Old Testament supposed to contain the wise sayings of Solomon. *n.*

pro vide (prə vīd′), 1. take care for the future; as, to provide against accident, to provide for old age. 2. get ready; prepare. Mother provides a good dinner. 3. supply; furnish. Sheep provide us with wool. 4. state as a condition beforehand. Our club's rules provide that dues must be paid monthly. *v. 2.*

pro vid ed (prə vīd′id), on the condition that. She will go provided her friends can go also. *conj.*

prov i dence (prov′i dəns), 1. God's care; God. Trusting in Providence, the Pilgrims sailed for the unknown world. 2. care for the future. Greater providence on the father's part would have kept the children from poverty. *n. 4.*

Prov i dence (prov′i dəns), the capital of Rhode Island. *n. 18.*

prov i dent (prov′i dənt), careful in providing for the future; having or showing foresight. Provident men lay aside money for their families. *adj. 15.*

prov i den tial (prov′i den′shəl), 1. of or proceeding from God's care; as, providential help. 2. fortunate. Our delay seemed providential, for the train we had planned to take was wrecked. *adj. 16.*

prov ince (prov′ins), 1. a part of a country at a distance from the capital. 2. a big division of a country. Canada is divided into provinces instead of into States. 3. a division; a department; as, the province of science, the province of literature. 4. proper work or activity. Teaching spelling is not within the province of a college. *n. 2.*

pro vin cial (prə vin′shəl), 1. of a province; as, provincial government. 2. person born or living in a province. 3. having the manners, speech, dress, point of view, etc., of people living in a province. 4. of the country; like that of the country; local; as, provincial English. 5. narrow; as, a provincial point of view. 6. a provincial person. *adj., n. 10.*

pro vin cial ism (prə vin′shəl izm), 1. provincial manners, habit of thought, etc. 2. narrow-mindedness. 3. a word, expression, or way of pronunciation peculiar to a district of a country. *Reckon* for *think*, and *get to go* for *go* are provincialisms. *n.*

pro vi sion (prə vizh′ən), 1. that which is made ready; a supply; a stock, especially of food; food. **Provisions** means a supply of food and drinks. They took plenty of provisions on their trip. 2. to supply with provisions. 3. act of providing; preparation. Mr. Arch made provision for his children's education. 4. statement making a condition. Our library has a provision that hands must be clean before books are taken out. *n., v. 3.*

pro vi sion al (prə vizh′ən əl), for the time being; temporary; as, a provisional agreement, a provisional governor. *adj. 19.*

pro vi so (prə vī′zō), a condition; a sentence or part of a sentence in a contract or other agreement, that states a condition. Tom was admitted to the eighth grade with the proviso that he was to be put back if he failed in any subject. *n., pl. provisos* or *provisoes. 10.*

prov o ca tion (prov′ə kā′shən), 1. something that stirs one up; cause of anger. Though the other boys' remarks were a provocation, John kept his temper. 2. act of provoking. *n. 7.*

pro voc a tive (prə vok′ə tiv), 1. tending or serving to call forth action, thought, laughter, anger, etc.; as, a remark provocative of mirth. 2. irritating. *adj. 17.*

pro voke (prə vōk′), 1. make angry; vex. She provoked him by her teasing. 2. stir up; excite. An insult provokes a person to anger. 3. call forth; bring about; cause; start into action. *v. 3.*

prov ost (prov′əst), person appointed to superintend or preside, such as the head of certain colleges or churches, or the chief magistrate in a Scottish town. *n. 12.*

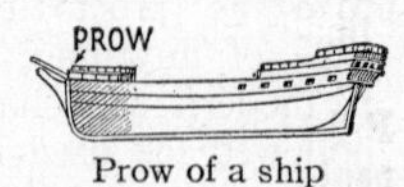

Prow of a ship

prow (prou), 1. the bow or forward pointed part of a ship or boat. 2. something like it; as, the prow of an airship. *n. 10.*

prow ess (prou′is), 1. bravery; daring. 2. brave or daring acts. 3. unusual skill or ability. The knights of old were famous for their prowess with the spear. *n. 6.*

prowl (proul), 1. go about slowly and secretly hunting for something to eat or steal. Many wild animals prowl at night. 2. wander. *v. 9.*

prox im i ty (proks im′i ti), nearness. I rested in close proximity to the fire. *n. 11.*

prox y (prok′si), 1. the action of a deputy or substitute. In marriage by proxy, someone is substituted for the absent bridegroom at the marriage service. 2. agent; deputy; substitute. 3. a writing authorizing a proxy to act or vote for a person. 4. a vote so given. *n., pl. proxies. 14.*

prude (prüd), person who is too proper or too modest; person who puts on extremely proper or modest airs. *n. 17.*

pru dence (prü′dəns), wise thought before acting; good judgment. *n. 6.*

pru dent (prü′dənt), planning carefully ahead of time; sensible; discreet. A prudent man saves part of his wages. *adj. 5.*

pru den tial (prü den′shəl), of, marked by, or showing prudence; as, prudential reasons for an act. *adj. 16.*

prud er y (prüd′ər i), 1. extreme modesty or propriety, especially when not genuine. 2. prudish act or remark. *n., pl. pruderies. 19.*

prud ish (prüd′ish), like a prude; extremely proper or modest; too modest. *adj.*

prune[1] (prün), a kind of plum that is dried. We had stewed prunes for breakfast. *n. 4.*

prune[2] (prün), 1. cut out useless parts from. 2. cut off; cut. *v.*

Prus sia (prush′ə), the most powerful division of Germany. *n. 8.*

Prus sian (prush′ən), 1. of or having to do with Prussia or its people. 2. a native or inhabitant of Prussia. *adj., n.*

prus sic ac id (prus′ik as′id), a deadly poison that smells like bitter almonds.

pry[1] (prī), look with curiosity; peep. She is always prying into other people's affairs. *v., pried, prying. 8.*

pry[2] (prī), 1. raise or move by force. Pry up that stone with your pickax. 2. a lever for prying. 3. get with much effort. We finally pried the secret out of him. *v., pried, prying, n., pl. pries.*

P.S., postscript.

psalm (säm), a sacred song or poem, especially one of the Psalms of the Old Testament. *n. 5.*

psalm ist (säm′ist), author of a psalm. David is **the Psalmist.** *n. 12.*

Psalms (sämz), a book of the Old Testament containing psalms. *n. pl.*

Psal ter (sôl′tər), the Book of Psalms, in the Old Testament. Each pew contained several hymn books and psalters. *n. 16.*

psal ter y (sôl′tər i), an ancient musical instrument played by plucking the strings. *n., pl. psalteries. 12.*

Man playing a psaltery

pseu do (sü′dō), false; sham; pretended; as, pseudo religion. *adj.*

pseu do nym (sü′də nim), a name used by an author instead of his real name. Mark Twain is a pseudonym for Samuel Clemens. *n. 19.*

pshaw (shô), an exclamation expressing impatience, contempt, etc. *interj., n. 17.*

Psy che (sī′ki), in Greek and Roman myths, the soul, mind, or spirit, in the form of a maiden, often with butterfly wings. *n. 11.*

psy chic (sī′kik), 1. of the soul or mind; mental; as, illness due to psychic causes, a psychic influence. 2. **Psychic force** is a spiritual force which is taken for granted by spiritualists to explain second sight, telepathy, table moving, tappings, etc. *adj. 15.*

psy chi cal (sī′ki kəl), psychic. *adj. 17.*

psy cho log i cal (sī′kə loj′i kəl), 1. of the mind. Memories and dreams are psychological facts. 2. of psychology; as, a psychological problem, a psychological explanation. 3. The **psychological moment** means (1) the very moment to get the desired effect in the mind. (2) the critical moment. *adj. 13.*

psy chol o gy (sī kol′ə ji), the science of mind. Psychology tries to explain why people act and think and feel as they do. *n., pl. psychologies. 11.*

pt., 1. pint. 2. past tense; preterit. *6.*

ptar mi gan (tär′mi gən), any of several kinds of grouse found in mountainous and cold regions. *n., pl. ptarmigans or ptarmigan.*

Ptarmigan (15 in. from bill to tail)

Ptol e my (tol′i mi), a Greek mathematician, astronomer, and geographer at Alexandria in the second century A.D. *n. 19.*

pto maine or **pto main** (tō′mān), a substance, often poisonous, produced in decaying matter. Improperly canned foods may contain ptomaines. *n. 19.*

pu ber ty (pū′bər ti), the physical beginning of manhood and womanhood. Puberty comes at about 14 in boys and about 12 in girls. *n. 15.*

pub lic (pub′lik), 1. of the people; as, public opinion. 2. belonging to the people; as, public buildings. 3. by the people; as, public help for the poor. 4. for the people; serving the people; as, public meetings, public libraries, public schools. 5. known to many or all; not private; as, a matter of public knowledge. 6. all the people. *adj., n. 1.*

pub li can (pub′li kən), 1. a tax collector of ancient Rome. 2. the keeper of a saloon, called a public house, where alcoholic drinks are sold. *British. n. 10.*

pub li ca tion (pub′li kā′shən), 1. book, newspaper, or magazine; anything that is published. *Boys' Life* is a publication of the Boy Scouts. 2. the printing and selling of books, newspapers, magazines, etc. 3. act of making known; fact or state of being made known; public announcement. *n. 6.*

public house, 1. in England, a place where alcoholic liquor is sold to be drunk; tavern. 2. inn; hotel.

pub li cist (pub′li sist), 1. person skilled or trained in law or in public affairs. 2. writer on law, politics, or public affairs. *n. 17.*

pub lic i ty (pub lis′i ti), 1. being public; being seen by or known to everybody; as, in the publicity of the street. 2. being brought to public notice by special effort, through newspapers, signs, radio, etc. 3. public notice; as, the publicity which actors desire. 4. the measures used for getting, or the process of getting, public notice; as, a campaign of publicity for a new automobile. *n. 9.*

pub lic ly (pub′lik li), 1. in a public manner; openly. 2. by the public. *adv.*

pub lic-spir it ed (pub′lik spir′i tid), having or showing an unselfish desire for the public good. *adj.*

pub lish (pub′lish), 1. prepare and offer (a book, paper, map, piece of music, etc.) for sale or distribution. 2. make publicly or generally known. Don't publish the faults of your friends. *v. 3.*

pub lish er (pub′lish ər), person or company whose business is to print and sell books, magazines, etc. Look at the bottom of the title page of a book for the publisher's name. *n. 7.*

puck (puk), 1. a mischievous spirit; a goblin. 2. a rubber disk used in place of a ball in hockey. *n. 20.*

Puck

puck er (puk′ər), 1. draw into wrinkles or irregular folds; as, to pucker one's brow, to pucker cloth in sewing. A baby puckers his lips before crying. 2. a wrinkle; an irregular fold. There are puckers at the shoulders of this ill-fitting coat. *v., n. 10.*

pud ding (pu̇d′ing), a soft cooked food, usually sweet, such as rice pudding. *n. 3.*

pud dle (pud′əl), 1. a small dirty pool; as, a puddle of rain water, a puddle of ink. 2. wet clay and sand stirred into a paste. 3. use such a mixture to stop water from running through. Puddle up this hole in the wall. 4. stir (melted iron) with other things to make wrought iron. *n., v. 10.*

pudg y (puj′i), short and fat; as, a child's pudgy hand, a pudgy little man. *adj., pudgier, pudgiest.*

pueb lo (pweb′lō), 1. an Indian village built of adobe and stone. There were many pueblos in the southwestern United States. 2. A **Pueblo** is an Indian living in such a village. *n., pl. pueblos. 13.*

pu er ile (pū′ər il), childish; foolish for a grown person to say or do. *adj. 16.*

Puer to Ri co (pwer′tō rē′kō), island in the eastern part of the West Indies. Puerto Rico belongs to the United States.

puff (puf), 1. blow with short, quick blasts. The engine puffed. 2. a little, short, quick blast. A puff of wind blew away the letter. 3. breathe quick and hard. She puffed as she climbed the stairs. 4. swell with air or pride. He puffed out his cheeks. 5. act of puffing. 6. light pastry filled with whipped cream, jam, etc.; as, a cream puff. 7. praise in exaggerated language. They puffed him to the skies. 8. soft round mass. She wore her hair in three puffs. 9. arrange in puffs; arrange softly and loosely. 10. a small pad for putting powder on the skin, etc. *v., n. 3.*

Puffin (about 13 in. from bill to tip of tail)

puf fin (puf′in), sea bird of the northern Atlantic that has a high, narrow, furrowed, parti-colored bill. *n.*

puff i ness (puf′i nis), puffy condition. *n.*

puff y (puf′i), 1. puffed out; swollen. Her eyes are puffy from crying. 2. puffed up; vain. 3. coming in puffs. *adj., puffier, puffiest. 19.*

pug (pug), a small, tan-colored dog with a curly tail and a short, turned-up nose. *n. 12.*

Pug (about 12 in. high at the shoulder)

Pu get Sound (pū′jit sound′), a long narrow bay or fiord between Vancouver Island and Washington.

pu gi list (pū′ji list), person who fights with the fists; a boxer. *n. 17.*

pug na cious (pug nā′shəs), having the habit of fighting; fond of fighting; quarrelsome. English sparrows are pugnacious birds. *adj. 16.*

pug nac i ty (pug nas′i ti), fondness for fighting. *n.*

pug nose, a short, turned-up nose.

pu is sance (pū′i səns), power; might; force. *n. 14.*

pu is sant (pū′i sənt), powerful; mighty. *adj. 14.*

pule (pūl), cry in a thin voice, as a sick child does; whimper; whine. *v.*

pull (pu̇l), 1. She pulled Nell's hair. Pull the trigger of the gun. He pulled my tooth out. We will pull the sled. Baby pulled the flower to pieces. Pull toward the shore, sailor. The train pulled out from the station. **Pull through** means get through a difficult or dangerous situation. **Pull oneself together** means get control of one's mind, energies, etc. 2. act of pulling. The boy gave a pull at the rope. 3. force exerted in pulling; effort. It was a hard pull to get up the hill. 4. a handle to pull by. 5. influence. *Slang. v., n. 1.*

pull er (pu̇l′ər), person or machine that pulls. *n. 7.*

pul let (pu̇l′it), young hen, usually one less than a year old. *n. 17.*

pul ley (pu̇l′i), a wheel with a hollowed rim in which a rope can run, and so lift weights, or change the direction of the pull. The flag is raised to the top of a pole by a rope which goes over a small pulley. See the picture of a pulley in use in the next column. *n., pl. pulleys. 11.*

Pull man (pu̇l′mən), 1. a railroad sleeping car. 2. a railroad car with specially comfortable single seats. *n. 13.*

pul mo nar y (pul′mə nãr′i), of or pertaining to the lungs. Tuberculosis and pneumonia are pulmonary diseases. *adj. 11.*

pul mo tor (pul′mō′tər), a device for producing artificial breathing. A pulmotor is used on a person who has almost drowned or smothered. *n.* [*Trade name*]

pulp (pulp), 1. the soft fleshy part of any fruit. 2. the soft inner part of a tooth. 3. any soft wet mass. Paper is made from wood ground to a pulp. *n. 7.*

pul pit (pu̇l′pit), 1. a platform in a church from which the minister preaches. 2. preachers or preaching; as, the influence of the pulpit. *n. 6.*

Pulpit

pulp y (pul′pi), of pulp; like pulp; fleshy; soft. *adj.*

pul sate (pul′sāt), 1. beat; throb. 2. vibrate; quiver. *v. 16.*

pul sa tion (pul sā′shən), 1. vibration; beating; throbbing. 2. a beat; a throb. *n. 15.*

pulse[1] (puls), 1. the beating of the heart; the changing flow of blood in the arteries caused by the beating of the heart. 2. any regular, measured beat; as, the pulse in music, the pulse of an engine. 3. beat; throb; vibrate. His heart pulsed with excitement. *n., v. 4.*

pulse[2] (puls), peas, beans, and lentils used as food. *n.*

pul ver ize (pul′vər īz), grind to powder; become dust. *v. 11.*

pu ma (pū′mə), a large American wildcat. The mountain lion is also a common name for it. *n. 18.*

Puma (4 or 5 ft. long, not including the tail)

pum ice (pum′is), light spongy stone thrown up from volcanoes, used for cleaning and polishing. Rub your hands with pumice to remove ink. *n. 13.*

pum mel (pum′əl), strike or beat; beat with the fists; pommel. *v., pummeled, pummeling. 19.*

pump[1] (pump), 1. a machine for forcing liquids, air, or gas into or out of things; as, a water pump, an oil pump. 2. move (liquids, air, etc.) by a pump. Pump water from the well into the pail. Pump up the car's tires. 3. get information out of. Don't let him pump you. *n., v. 3.*

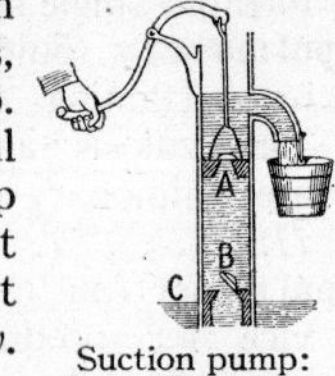

Suction pump: A and B, valves; C, water.

pump[2] (pump), a low shoe with a thin sole and no fasteners. *n.*

pump kin (pump′kin or pung′kin), a large orange-yellow fruit of a trailing vine, much like a squash; the vine itself. Some pumpkins weigh over 100 pounds. *n. 4.*

Pumpkin

pun (pun), 1. the humorous use of a word where it can have different meanings; a play on words. "We must all hang together or we shall all hang separately," said Benjamin Franklin to the Revolutionary leaders. This is a famous pun. 2. make puns. *n., v., punned, punning. 13.*

punch[1] (punch), 1. hit with the fists. Boys punch; girls often slap. 2. a quick thrust or blow. 3. a tool for making holes. 4. pierce a hole in. The train conductor punches the tickets. *v., n. 5.*

Punch

punch[2] (punch), a drink made of different liquids mixed together. *n.*

Punch[3] (punch), the chief character in the puppet show *Punch and Judy. n.*

pun cheon (pun′chən), a large cask for liquor. *n. 16.*

punc til i o (pungk til′i ō), 1. a little point of honor, conduct, ceremony, etc. The knight observed every punctilio. 2. care in attending to such little points. *n., pl. punctilios. 20.*

punc til i ous (pungk til′i əs), 1. very careful and exact. A nurse should be punctilious in obeying the doctor's orders. 2. paying strict attention to details of conduct and ceremony. May is unconventional, but Helen is very punctilious. *adj. 17.*

punc tu al (pungk′chü əl), prompt; on time. He is punctual to the minute. *adj. 6.*

punc tu al i ty (pungk′chü al′i ti), promptness; being on time. Our schoolteacher insists on punctuality. *n. 19.*

punc tu ate (pungk′chü āt), 1. use periods, commas, and other marks to help make the meaning clear. 2. put punctuation marks in. 3. interrupt now and then; as, a speech punctuated with cheers. *v. 18.*

punc tu a tion (pungk′chü ā′shən), use of periods, commas, and other marks to help make the meaning clear. Punctuation does for writing or printing what pauses and change of voice do for speech. *n. 19.*

punctuation mark, mark used in writing or printing to help make the meaning clear. Periods, commas, question marks, colons, etc., are punctuation marks.

punc ture (pungk′chər), 1. hole made by something pointed. 2. make such a hole in. 3. have or get a puncture. 4. act or process of puncturing. *n., v. 15.*

pun gen cy (pun′jən si), sharpness (of taste, smell, feeling, etc.); as, the pungency of pepper, ammonia, incense, remarks, wit. *n.*

pun gent (pun′jənt), 1. sharply affecting the organs of taste and smell; as, a pungent pickle, the pungent smell of burning leaves. 2. sharp; biting; as, pungent criticism. 3. keen; lively; stimulating to the mind; as, a pungent wit. *adj. 14.*

pun ish (pun′ish), cause pain, loss, or discomfort to. *v. 2.*

pun ish a ble (pun′ish ə bəl), 1. liable to punishment. 2. deserving punishment. *adj. 19.*

pun ish ment (pun′ish mənt), 1. punishing; being punished. 2. pain, suffering, or loss. Her punishment for stealing was a year in prison. *n. 3.*

pu ni tive (pū′ni tiv), 1. concerned with punishment; as, punitive laws. 2. inflicting punishment; as, a punitive military expedition. *adj.*

Pun jab (pun jäb′), a province of northern India. *n. 19.*

punk (pungk), 1. a preparation that burns very slowly. A stick of punk is used to light fireworks. 2. decayed wood used as tinder. *n. 17.*

punt (punt), 1. shallow, flat-bottomed boat having square ends. 2. propel (a boat) by thrusting with a pole against the bottom of the river or pond. 3. kick (a football) before it touches the ground after dropping it from the hands. 4. such a kick. *n., v.*

Man pushing a punt

pu ny (pū′ni), 1. weak; of less than usual size and strength. 2. petty; not important. *adj., punier, puniest. 10.*

pup (pup), a young dog; puppy. The young of foxes, wolves, and other animals are also called pups. *n. 11.*

pu pa (pū′pə), a stage in the life of an insect when it is in a case. It comes between the larva (caterpillar) and the winged adult stage. Pupae often live in cocoons. *n., pl. pupae* (pū′pē). *8.*

pu pil (pū′pəl), 1. one who is learning in school or being taught by someone. The music teacher takes private pupils. 2. the black center of the eye. *n. 2.*

Puppet show

pup pet (pup′it), 1. small doll. In a puppet show the puppets are often moved by wires. 2. anybody who is not independent, waits to be told how to act, and does what somebody else says. *n. 13.*

pup py (pup′i), 1. a young dog. 2. a silly, conceited young man. *n., pl. puppies. 5.*

pur blind (pėr′blīnd′), nearly blind. *adj. 15.*

pur chas a ble (pėr′chəs ə bəl), that can be bought. *adj.*

pur chase (pėr′chəs), 1. buy; get by paying a price. 2. get in return for something; as, to purchase safety at the cost of happiness. 3. act of buying. 4. thing bought. That hat was a good purchase. 5. a firm hold to help move something, or to keep from slipping. Wind the rope twice around that tree for a better purchase. *v., n. 2.*

pur chas er (pėr′chəs ər), buyer. *n. 10.*

pure (pūr), 1. clean; clear; genuine; without defects. 2. not mixed with anything else; as, pure fun, pure gold. 3. with no evil; without sin; as, a pure mind. *adj. 1.*

pu rée (pū rā′ or pūr′ā), thick soup; as, purée of peas. *n. 20.*

pure ly (pūr′li), 1. in a pure manner. 2. exclusively; entirely. 3. merely. 4. innocently; chastely. *adv.*

pure ness (pūr′nis), cleanness; innocence; purity. *n. 13.*

pur ga tive (pėr′gə tiv), 1. a medicine that causes movements of the bowels. Castor oil is a purgative. 2. purging; cleansing. *n., adj. 19.*

pur ga to ry (pėr′gə tō′ri), 1. in the belief of the Roman Catholics, a temporary condition or place in which the souls of those dying penitent are purified from sin by punishment. 2. any condition or place of temporary suffering or punishment. *n., pl. purgatories. 10.*

purge (pėrj), 1. wash away all that is not clean; make clean. King Arthur tried to purge his land from sin. 2. to empty (the bowels). 3. a medicine that does this. A large dose of castor oil makes a good purge. *v., n. 5.*

pu ri fi ca tion (pūr′i fi kā′shən), purifying. *n. 10.*

pu ri fy (pūr′i fī), make pure. Filters are used to purify water. Gold is purified by fire. *v., purified, purifying. 6.*

pur ist (pūr′ist), person who cares much or too much for purity in language. A purist dislikes slang and all expressions that are not absolutely correct. *n.*

Pu ri tan (pūr′i tən), person belonging to a division of the Protestant Church which wanted simpler forms of worship and stricter morals than others did (in the 16th and 17th centuries). *n. 6.*

pu ri tan (pūr′i tən), person who is strict in morals and religion. *n.*

pu ri tan i cal (pūr′i tan′i kəl), like a Puritan; very, very strict; too strict. *adj.*

pu ri ty (pūr′i ti), 1. freedom from dirt or mixture; clearness; cleanness. 2. freedom from evil; innocence. No one doubts the purity of Joan of Arc's motives. 3. careful correctness; as, purity of language. *n. 5.*

purl[1] (pėrl), 1. to flow with rippling motions and a murmuring sound. A shallow brook purls. 2. the motion and sound of a purling brook. *v., n. 14.*

Purling

purl[2] (pėrl), knit with inverted stitches. *v.*

pur lieu (pėr′lü), 1. piece of land on the border of a forest. 2. **Purlieus** means any bordering, neighboring, or outlying regions. *n. 14.*

pur loin (pėr loin′), steal. *v. 15.*

pur ple (pėr′pəl), 1. a dark color made by mixing red and blue. 2. Because purple cloth was worn by persons of high rank, purple has come to mean royal, imperial, or splendid, and also imperial or lofty rank or power. A prince is born to the purple. 3. Purple used to mean red. *n., adj. 2.*

pur plish (pėr′plish), somewhat purple. *adj.*

pur port (pėr′pōrt for 1, pėr pōrt′ for 2 and 3), 1. meaning. The purport of her letter was that she would not pay. 2. to mean; have as its main idea. 3. to claim. The letter purported to be from the governor. *n., v. 9.*

pur pose (pėr′pəs), 1. plan; aim; intention; something one has in mind to get or do. 2. to plan; to aim; to intend. 3. **On purpose** means with a purpose; not by accident. *n., v. 1.*

pur pose ful (pėr′pəs fəl), having a purpose. *adj.*

pur pose less (pėr′pəs lis), lacking a purpose. *adj.*

pur pose ly (pėr′pəs li), on purpose; intentionally. *adv. 14.*

purr or **pur** (pėr), 1. low murmuring sound such as a cat makes when pleased. 2. make this sound. *n., v., purred, purring. 9.*

purse (pėrs), 1. little bag or case for carrying money around with one. 2. a sum of money. A purse was made up for the victims of the fire. 3. draw together; press into folds or wrinkles. *n., v. 2.*

Pocket purse

purs er (pėr′sər), officer on a ship who buys provisions, keeps the accounts, checks the tickets of the passengers, etc. *n.*

purs lane (pėrs′lān), 1. a common plant, sometimes used for salad or for flavoring. It has yellow flowers. 2. any of several plants like it. *n.*

Purslane (def. 1)

pur su ance (pər sü′əns), following; carrying out; pursuit. In pursuance of his custom, Mr. Smith sent his nieces checks at Christmas. *n. 16.*

pur su ant (pər sü′ənt), following; carrying out. **Pursuant to** means following; acting according to; in accordance with. *adj., adv.*

pur sue (pər sü′), 1. follow to catch or kill; chase. The policeman pursued the robbers. 2. follow closely and annoy; as, to pursue with questions. 3. strive for; try to get. 4. carry on; keep on with. She pursued the study of French for four years. *v. 2.*

pur su er (pər sü′ər), one who pursues. *n. 9.*

pur suit (pər süt′), 1. act of pursuing; chase. The dog is in pursuit of the cat. 2. occupation. Fishing is his favorite pursuit; reading is mine. *n. 4.*

pur sui vant (pėr′swi vənt), 1. an assistant to a herald; officer below a herald in rank. 2. follower; attendant. *n. 16.*

pur vey (pėr vā′), provide; furnish; supply (food or provisions); as, to purvey meat for the army, to purvey for a royal household. *v. 15.*

pur vey ance (pėr vā′əns), 1. purveying. 2. provisions; supplies. 3. formerly in England, the right of the king or queen to supplies, use of horses, and personal service. *n.*

pur vey or (pėr vā′ər), person who supplies provisions; person who supplies anything. *n. 14.*

pur view (pėr′vū), range of operation, activity, concern, etc.; scope; extent. *n.*

pus (pus), a thick yellowish-white fluid found in sores. *n. 17.*

push (pu̇sh), 1. move (something) away by pressing against it. Push the door; don't pull. 2. press hard. We pushed with all our strength. 3. go forward by force. We pushed through the crowd. 4. urge; make go forward. He pushed his plans cleverly. Please push this job and get it done this week. 5. act of pushing. Give the door a push. 6. force; power to succeed. She has plenty of push. *Used in common talk. v., n. 2.*

pu sil la nim i ty (pū′si lə nim′i ti), cowardice; meanness of spirit. *n. 17.*

pu sil lan i mous (pū′si lan′i məs), cowardly; mean-spirited; faint-hearted. The pusillanimous man would not defend his own family. *adj. 14.*

puss (pu̇s), 1. cat. 2. hare. *n. 6.*

puss y (pu̇s′i), 1. cat. 2. catkin. *n., pl. pussies. 3.*

pussy willow, a small willow with silky catkins.

Pussy willow

put (pu̇t), 1. place; lay; set; cause to be in some place or position. I put sugar in my tea. Put away your toys. Put on your hat. 2.cause to be in some condition or relation. Put your room in order. Put the question in writing. The murderer was put to death. 3. express. The teacher puts things plainly. 4. Some special meanings are:

A ship **puts out** to sea, **puts in** to port, **puts about** to change its direction.

put by, save for future use.

put forth, grow; sprout; issue.

put off, 1. lay aside; make wait. 2. go away; start out.

put on, 1. take upon oneself. 2. pretend.

put out, 1. extinguish; make an end to; destroy; as, to put out a fire, to put out one's eye. 2. provoked or offended.

put through, carry out successfully.
put to it, force to a course; put in difficulty.
put up, 1. lay aside (work). 2. pack up or preserve (fruit). 3. build. 4. offer; offer for sale. 5. give lodging or food to. 6. get (a person) to do.
put up with, bear with patience; endure.
v., put, putting. 1.

Pylon

pu tre fac tion (pū′trifak′shən), decay; rotting. *n. 16.*
pu tre fy (pū′tri fī), rot; decay. Putrefying meat has a bad smell. *v., putrefied, putrefying. 13.*
pu trid (pū′trid), rotten; foul. *adj. 16.*
putt (put), 1. strike (a golf ball) gently and carefully in an effort to make it roll into the hole. 2. the stroke itself. *v., n.*
put tee (pə tē′ or put′i), 1. long narrow strip of cloth wound round the leg from ankle to knee, worn by sportsmen, soldiers, etc. 2. gaiter of cloth or leather reaching from ankle to knee worn by soldiers, riders, etc. *n.*

A B
Puttees: A, cloth; B, leather.

put ter[1] (put′ər), keep busy in a rather useless way; potter. *v. 18.*
putt er[2] (put′ər), 1. person who putts. 2. golf club used in putting. *n.*
put ty (put′i), 1. a soft mixture of whiting and linseed oil, used for fastening panes of glass, etc. 2. stop up or cover with putty. He puttied the holes in the woodwork before painting it. *n., v., puttied, puttying. 11.*
puz zle (puz′əl), 1. hard problem. How to get all my things into one trunk is a puzzle. 2. a problem or task to be done for fun. A famous Chinese puzzle has seven pieces of wood to fit together. 3. perplex. How the cat got out puzzled us. 4. be perplexed; exercise (one's mind) on something hard. They puzzled over their arithmetic for an hour. *n., v. 4.*
pyg my (pig′mi), 1. a dwarf. The pygmies living in Africa and Asia are less than five feet high. 2. very small; as, a pygmy mind. *n., pl. pygmies, adj. 11.* Also spelled **pigmy.**
py ja mas (pi jä′məz), pajamas. *n. pl.*
py lon (pī′lon), 1. post or tower for guiding aviators. 2. tall steel framework used to carry high-tension wires across country. 3. a gateway, particularly of an Egyptian temple. See the picture in the last column. *n.*
py or rhe a or **py or rhoe a** (pī′ə rē′ə), a disease of the gums, in which pockets of pus form about the teeth, the gums shrink, and the teeth become loose. *n. 19.*

Egyptian pyramid

pyr a mid (pir′ə mid), 1. a solid having triangular sides meeting in a point; especially, the huge stone pyramids in Egypt. 2. raise or increase (costs, wages, etc.). 3. make larger and larger additions. *n., v. 7.*

Figures shaped like pyramids

py ram i dal (pi ram′i dəl), shaped like a pyramid; as, a pyramidal tree. *adj. 12.*
pyre (pīr), a pile of wood for burning a dead body. *n. 19.*
Pyr e nees (pir′i nēz), mountain range between Spain and France. *n. 17.*
py ri tes (pī rī′tēz). Iron pyrites is fool's gold, a mineral which has a yellow color and glitters so that it suggests gold. *n. 19.*
py ro tech nic (pī′rō tek′nik), 1. of or pertaining to fireworks; as, a pyrotechnic display. 2. resembling fireworks; brilliant; sensational. *adj.*
py ro tech nics (pī′rō tek′niks), 1. the making of fireworks. 2. the use of fireworks. 3. a display of fireworks. *n.*
Pyr rhic (pir′ik), of Pyrrhus. A **Pyrrhic victory** is one obtained at too great cost, so named after Pyrrhus who won a battle, but with an enormous loss of life. *adj.*
Pyr rhus (pir′əs), a brave, cruel king in Greece (318?-272 B.C.). *n. 14.*
Py thag o ras (pi thag′ə rəs), a famous Greek philosopher, religious teacher, and mathematician (582?-500? B.C.). *n. 16.*
Pyth i as (pith′i əs), one of a famous pair of friends. Damon was the other. *n. 16.*

Python

py thon (pī′thon), a large snake that crushes its prey. Pythons usually live in trees near water. See the picture just above. *n. 19.*

hat, āge, cãre, fär; let, ēqual, tėrm; it, īce; hot, ōpen, ôrder; oil, out; cup, pu̇t, rüle, ūse; th, thin; ᴛʜ, then; ə represents *a* in about, *e* in taken, *i* in pencil, *o* in lemon, *u* in circus.

Q

Q, q (kū), the 17th letter of the alphabet. Q comes after n, o, p. *n., pl. Q's, q's.*

qt., quart; quarts. *5.*

quack[1] (kwak), 1. the sound a duck makes. 2. make such a sound. *n., v. 5.*

quack[2] (kwak), 1. a dishonest person who pretends to be a doctor. 2. an ignorant pretender to knowledge or skill of any sort. 3. used by quacks. 4. not genuine. *n., adj.*

quack er y (kwak′ər i), the practices or methods of a quack. *n., pl. quackeries.*

quad ran gle (kwod′rang′gəl), 1. four-sided space or court wholly or nearly surrounded by buildings. 2. the buildings around a quadrangle. 3. a quadrilateral. *n. 16.*

quad ran gu lar (kwod rang′gū lər), like a quadrangle; having four corners or angles. *adj. 14.*

quad rant (kwod′rənt), 1. a quarter of a circle or of its circumference. 2. an instrument used in astronomy, navigation, etc., for measuring altitudes. *n. 14.*

Quadrants

quad ri lat er al (kwod′ri lat′ər əl), 1. having four sides. 2. a plane figure or surface having four sides and four angles. *adj., n. 19.*

Quadrilateral figures

qua drille (kwə dril′), 1. a square dance for four couples. 2. music for it. *n. 16.*

quad ru ped (kwod′rů ped), an animal that has four feet. *n. 13.*

quad ru ple (kwod′rů pəl), 1. fourfold; consisting of four parts; including four parts or parties. 2. four times; four times as great. 3. a number or amount four times as great as another. 80 is the quadruple of 20. 4. make or become four times as great. *adj., adv., n., v. 14.*

quad ru plet (kwod′rů plet), 1. one of four children born at the same time from the same mother. 2. a group of four. *n.*

quaff (kwäf or kwaf), drink in large drafts; drink freely. *v. 10.*

quag mire (kwag′mīr′), soft, muddy ground; a boggy or miry place. *n. 16.*

quail[1] (kwāl), a game bird about ten inches long, especially the bobwhite. See the picture. *n., pl. quails or quail. 6.*

Quail or bobwhite

quail[2] (kwāl), be afraid; lose courage; shrink back with fear. The slave quailed at his master's look. *v.*

quaint (kwānt), strange or odd in an interesting, pleasing, or amusing way. Old photographs seem quaint to us today. *adj. 5.*

quake (kwāk), 1. shake; tremble. She quaked with fear. 2. a shaking; a trembling. 3. an earthquake. *v., n. 5.*

Quak er (kwāk′ər), member of a Christian group called the Society of Friends. Quakers are opposed to war and favor simple clothes and manners. *n. 8.*

quali fi ca tion (kwol′i fi kā′shən), 1. that which makes a person fit for a job, task, office, etc. To know the way is one qualification for a guide. 2. that which limits or changes, and makes less free and full. His pleasure had one qualification: his friends could not enjoy it, too. *n. 8.*

quali fied (kwol′i fīd), 1. fitted; competent. 2. limited; modified. *adj.*

quali fy (kwol′i fī), 1. make fit or competent. 2. become fit; show oneself fit. Can you qualify for the Boy Scouts? 3. limit; make less strong; change somewhat. Qualify your statement that dogs are loyal by adding "usually." *v., qualified, qualifying. 8.*

quali ta tive (kwol′i tā′tiv), concerned with quality or qualities. Both the qualitative and the quantitative facts about foods are important. *adj.*

quali ty (kwol′i ti), 1. the kind that anything is. That is a poor quality of cloth. 2. something special about an object that makes it what it is. One quality of iron is hardness; one quality of sugar is sweetness. 3. fineness; merit; excellence. Look for quality rather than quantity. *n., pl. qualities. 2.*

qualm (kwäm), 1. sudden disturbing feeling in the mind; uneasiness; a misgiving or doubt. I tried the test with some qualms. 2. disturbance or scruple of conscience. Kate felt some qualms at staying away from church. 3. feeling of faintness or sickness, especially of nausea, that lasts for just a moment. *n. 13.*

quan da ry (kwon′də ri), state of perplexity or uncertainty; dilemma. *n., pl. quandaries. 19.*

quan ti ta tive (kwon′ti tā′tiv), 1. concerned with quantity. 2. that can be measured. 3. In chemistry, **quantitative analysis** means the testing of something to find out not only what substances are in it, but also just how much there is of each substance. *adj. 13.*

quan ti ty (kwon′ti ti), 1. amount. Use equal quantities of nuts and raisins in the cake. 2. large amount; large number. The baker buys flour in quantity. She owns quantities of books. 3. the length of a vowel sound or a note of music. *n., pl. quantities. 2.*

quar an tine (kwor′ən tēn), 1. keep (a person, etc., having an infectious disease) away from others. James was quarantined for three weeks when he had scarlet fever. 2. state of being quarantined. Our house was in quarantine for three weeks when James was ill with scarlet fever. 3. time during which ships coming into large ports are held until doctors have made sure that there is no infectious disease on board. *v., n. 10.*

quar rel (kwor′əl), 1. an angry dispute; a fight with words. The children had a quarrel over the division of the candy. 2. fight with words; dispute; disagree. 3. cause for dispute. An honest man has no quarrel with the laws. A bully likes to pick quarrels. The knight took up the poor man's quarrel and fought his oppressor. 4. breaking off of friendship. Ruth and May have had a quarrel and don't speak to each other. 5. stop being friends. 6. find fault. It is useless to quarrel with fate. *n., v., quarreled, quarreling. 2.*

quar rel some (kwor′əl səm), too ready to quarrel; fond of fighting and disputing. A quarrelsome child has few friends. *adj. 8.*

quar ry[1] (kwor′i), 1. place where stone is dug, cut, or blasted out for use in building. 2. obtain from a quarry. We watched the workmen quarry out a huge block of stone. *n., pl. quarries, v., quarried, quarrying. 5.*

quar ry[2] (kwor′i), animal chased in a hunt; game; prey. The fox hunters chased their quarry for hours. *n., pl. quarries.*

quart (kwôrt), 1. a measure for liquids, equal to one fourth of a gallon. 2. a measure for dry things, equal to one eighth of a peck. *n. 3.*

quar ter (kwôr′tər), 1. one of four equal parts; half of a half; one fourth; as, a quarter of an apple, a quarter of lamb. A quarter of an hour is 15 minutes. A quarter of a dollar is 25 cents. 2. divide into fourths. She quartered the apple. 3. direction. Each of the four points of the compass is called a quarter. From what quarter does the wind blow? 4. region; section; place. The Mexican quarter is near the railroad. 5. **At close quarters** means very close together; almost touching. 6. **Quarters** sometimes means a place to live or stay in. The baseball team has winter quarters in the South. The servants have quarters in a cottage. 7. give a place to live. Troops were quartered in the conquered town. 8. mercy to an enemy. The Indians gave no quarter. 9. The quarters of the moon are four periods of seven days each. *n., adj., v. 1.*

One quarter of this circle is shaded.

quar ter deck (kwôr′tər dek′), the part of the upper deck between the mainmast and the stern. The quarterdeck is for the use of the officers of a ship. *n.*

quar ter ly (kwôr′tər li), 1. happening or done four times a year; as, to make quarterly payments on one's insurance. 2. once each quarter of a year; as, to pay one's insurance premiums quarterly. 3. a magazine published every three months. *adj., adv., n., pl. quarterlies. 15.*

quar ter mas ter (kwôr′tər mas′tər), 1. in the army, the officer who has charge of providing quarters, clothing, fuel, transportation, etc., for troops. 2. an officer on a ship who has charge of the steering, the compasses, signals, etc. *n. 15.*

quarter note, musical note equal to one fourth of a whole note.

Quarter note

quarter section, piece of land, usually square, containing 160 acres.

quar ter staff (kwôr′tər staf′), old English weapon consisting of a stout pole 6 to 8 feet long, tipped with iron. *n., pl. quarterstaves* (-stāvz′).

quar tet or **quar tette** (kwôr tet′), 1. four singers or players. 2. piece of music for four voices or instruments. 3. any group of four. *n. 13.*

quar to (kwôr′tō), 1. the page size of a book in which each leaf is one fourth of a whole sheet of paper. 2. having this size. 3. a book having this size, usually about 9 by 12 inches. *n., pl. quartos, adj. 15.*

quartz (kwôrts), a very hard mineral composed of silica. Agate, amethyst, jasper, and many other stones are quartz. *n. 13.*

quash (kwosh), 1. put down completely; crush; as, to quash a revolt. 2. make void;

annul. The judge quashed the charges against the prisoner and set him free. *v.*

qua si or **qua si-** (kwā′sī), 1. as if; as if it were. 2. seeming; not real; halfway; almost; as, quasi humor. 3. seemingly; not really; half; as, a quasi-official statement. *conj., adj., adv., prefix. 16.*

qua ver (kwā′vər), 1. shake; tremble. The old man's voice quavered. 2. sing or say in trembling tones. 3. a trembling of the voice. 4. use trills in singing. 5. sing with trills. 6. a trill in singing. *v., n. 11.*

quay (kē), solid landing place for ships, often built of stone. *n. 11.*

Quay

quea sy (kwē′zi), 1. tending to unsettle the stomach. 2. inclined to nausea; easily upset; as, a queasy stomach. 3. uneasy; uncomfortable. 4. squeamish; fastidious. *adj.*

Que bec (kwi bek′), 1. a province in eastern Canada. 2. its capital, a city on the St. Lawrence River. *n. 9.*

queen (kwēn), 1. wife of a king. 2. woman ruler. 3. the most important woman or girl; as, the queen of society, the queen of the May. 4. act like a queen. 5. a playing card with the picture of a queen on it. 6. the most important piece in the game of chess. *n., v. 1.*

queen ly (kwēn′li), 1. of a queen; fit for a queen. 2. like a queen; like a queen's. 3. in a queenly manner; as a queen does. *adj., queenlier, queenliest, adv. 17.*

Queens land (kwēnz′lənd), a State in eastern Australia. *n. 20.*

queer (kwēr), 1. strange; odd; peculiar. 2. not well; faint; giddy. 3. to spoil. *Slang. adj., v. 3.*

quell (kwel), put down; overcome; subdue. *v. 6.*

quench (kwench), 1. drown out; put out. Water will quench a fire. 2. put an end to; stop; as, to quench a thirst. *v. 3.*

quench less (kwench′lis), that cannot be quenched. *adj. 15.*

quer u lous (kwer′ů ləs), complaining; fretful; peevish. *adj. 11.*

que ry (kwēr′i), 1. a question. 2. the sign (?) put after a question. 3. ask; ask about; inquire into. 4. express doubt about. *n., pl. queries, v., queried, querying. 10.*

quest (kwest), 1. a search; a hunt. Mary went to the library in quest of something to read. 2. to search; to seek. 3. expedition of knights. There are many stories about the quest of the Holy Grail. *n., v. 5.*

ques tion (kwes′chən), 1. ask in order to find out. 2. the thing asked. 3. a matter to be talked over. What is the question you have raised? 4. matter to be voted upon. The president asked if the club members were ready for the question. 5. to doubt; to dispute. I question the truth of many fish stories. 6. A matter is **out of the question** when it is not to be considered. It is **beyond question** or **without question** when there is no doubt about it. *v., n. 1.*

ques tion a ble (kwes′chən ə bəl), open to question or dispute; doubtful; uncertain. Whether your statement is true or not is questionable. *adj. 9.*

question mark, mark (?) put after a question in writing or printing.

ques tion naire (kwes′chən ãr′), list of questions, usually a written or printed list. *n.*

Chinese queue

queue (kū), 1. braid of hair hanging down the back. 2. line of persons, automobiles, etc. *n.*

quib ble (kwib′əl), 1. an unfair and petty evasion of the point or truth by using words with a double meaning; as, a legal quibble. 2. evade the point or the truth by twisting words. *n., v. 13.*

quick (kwik), 1. fast and sudden. The cat made a quick jump. Many weeds have a quick growth. 2. lively; ready; active; as, a quick wit, a quick ear. 3. coming soon; prompt; as, a quick reply. 4. not patient; hasty; as, a quick temper. 5. living; as, the quick and the dead. 6. the tender, sensitive part. The child bit his nails down to the quick. The boy's pride was cut to the quick by the words of blame. 7. quickly. *adj., adv., n. 1.*

quick en (kwik′ən), 1. move more quickly; hasten. Quicken your pace. 2. stir up; make alive. He quickened the hot ashes into flames. 3. become more active or alive. *v. 4.*

quick lime (kwik′līm′), a white substance that comes in a powder or hard lumps, got by burning limestone, and used for making mortar. It is also called lime, or unslaked lime. *n.*

quick ly (kwik′li), with haste; very soon. *adv.*

quick ness (kwik′nis), 1. speed. 2. the quality of understanding things easily. *n. 12.*

quick sand (kwik′sand′), soft wet sand, very deep, that will not hold up one's weight. A quicksand may swallow up men, animals, etc. *n. 14.*

quick sil ver (kwik′sil′vər), the metal mercury. *n. 15.*

quick-wit ted (kwik′wit′id), having a ready wit; clever. *adj.*

quid (kwid), 1. piece to be chewed. 2. bite of chewing tobacco. *n.*

qui es cence (kwī es′əns), quietness; stillness; motionlessness; absence of activity. *n. 16.*

qui es cent (kwī es′ənt), quiet; still; motionless; inactive. *adj. 16.*

qui et (kwī′ət), 1. making no sound; without noise; as, quiet footsteps, a quiet room. 2. still; moving very little; as, a quiet river. 3. at rest; not busy; as, a quiet evening at home. 4. peaceful; with nothing to fear; as, a quiet mind. 5. gentle; not offending others; as, a quiet girl. 6. not loud; not showy and bright. Gray is a quiet color. 7. make quiet. Mother quieted the frightened child. 8. become quiet. The wind quieted down. 9. state of rest; stillness; no noise; peace; as, to read in quiet. *adj., v., n. 1.*

qui et ness (kwī′ət nis), quiet condition; stillness; rest; calmness. *n. 9.*

qui e tude (kwī′ə tūd or kwī′ə tüd), stillness; calmness; quietness. *n. 13.*

qui e tus (kwī ē′təs), a final getting rid of anything; finishing stroke; anything that ends or settles. The arrival of the militia gave the riot its quietus. *n. 17.*

quill (kwil), 1. large stiff feather. 2. pen made from a feather. 3. a stiff sharp hair or spine like the end of a feather. A porcupine has quills. *n. 9.*

Quill (def. 1)

quilt (kwilt), 1. a bedcover; a bedcover made of two pieces of cloth with a soft pad between, held in place by lines of stitching. 2. to make quilts. 3. to stitch as in a quilt. She made a quilted bathrobe. *n., v. 5.*

quilt ing (kwil′ting), 1. quilted work. 2. material for making quilts. *n.*

quince (kwins), 1. a hard, yellowish fruit, used for preserves. 2. the tree it grows on. *n. 14.*

Quince

quin in (kwin′in), quinine. *n.*

qui nine (kwī′nīn), a bitter medicine used for colds and malaria. *n. 8.*

quin sy (kwin′zi), tonsillitis with pus; a very sore throat with an abscess in the tonsils. *n.*

quint (kwint), familiar abbreviation of quintuplet. *n.*

quin tes sence (kwin tes′əns), 1. pure essence; purest form. 2. the most perfect example of something. Her costume was the quintessence of good taste and style. *n. 14.*

quin tet or **quin tette** (kwin tet′), 1. five singers or players. 2. piece of music for five voices or instruments. 3. any group of five. *n.*

quin tu plet (kwin′tū plet or kwin′tü plet), 1. one of five children born at a birth. Many people go to see the Dionne quintuplets in Canada. 2. any group or combination of five. *n.*

quip (kwip), 1. a clever or witty saying. 2. a sharp, cutting remark. 3. something odd or strange. *n. 12.*

quire (kwīr), 24 or 25 sheets of paper of the same sort and size. *n. 10.*

quirk (kwėrk), 1. a peculiar way of acting. 2. a clever or witty saying. 3. a sudden twist or turn. 4. a flourish in writing. *n. 12.*

quirt (kwėrt), riding whip with a short, stout handle and a lash of braided leather. *n.*

quit (kwit), 1. stop. The men quit work when the whistle blew. 2. leave. If he doesn't pay his rent, he will receive notice to quit. 3. pay; pay off (a debt). 4. free; clear. I gave him money to be quit of him. 5. behave. "Quit yourselves like brave men" means act bravely. *Old use. v., quit* or *quitted, quitting, adj. 2.*

quit claim (kwit′klām′), 1. giving up a claim. 2. a document stating that somebody gives up a claim. 3. give up claim to (a possession, etc.). *n., v.*

quite (kwīt), 1. completely; entirely; altogether. I am quite alone. The ground was quite wet. 2. in fact; really; truly. 3. very; rather; somewhat. It is quite hot. *Used in common talk. adv. 1.*

quits (kwits), even or on equal terms by having given or paid back something. "I'll be quits with you yet for breaking my bicycle," called Fred to Jack. *adj.*

quit tance (kwit′əns), 1. release from debt

or obligation. 2. the paper certifying this; receipt. 3. getting back at somebody. *n. 20.*

quit ter (kwit′ər), one who shirks or gives up easily. *n.*

quiv er[1] (kwiv′ər), shake; shiver; tremble. The dog quivered with excitement. *v., n. 4.*

quiv er[2] (kwiv′ər), case to hold arrows. *n.*

Quiver

Quix ote (kwik′sət), Don, a famous character in a book, who was chivalrous and idealistic, but extremely impractical. *n.*

quix ot ic (kwiks ot′ik), 1. resembling Don Quixote; extravagantly chivalrous or romantic. 2. visionary; not practical. *adj.*

quiz (kwiz), 1. examine by questions; test the knowledge of. 2. a test; an informal examination; as, to have a quiz in history. 3. make fun of. 4. person who makes fun of others. *v., quizzed, quizzing, n., pl. quizzes.*

quiz zi cal (kwiz′i kəl), 1. odd; queer; comical. 2. that suggests making fun of others; teasing; as, a quizzical smile. *adj.*

Quoit

quoit (kwoit), 1. a heavy flattish iron or rope ring thrown to encircle a peg stuck in the ground or to come as close to it as possible. 2. **Quoits** is the game so played. The game of quoits is often played with horseshoes. *n. 12.*

quon dam (kwon′dam), that once was; former. The quondam servant is now the master. *adj. 16.*

quo rum (kwō′rəm), the number of members of any society or assembly that must be present if the business done is to be legal or binding. *n. 17.*

quo ta (kwō′tə), the share of a total due from or to a particular district, State, person, etc. Each State in the United States was assigned its quota of soldiers during the World War. *n. 14.*

quot a ble (kwōt′ə bəl), that can be quoted; suitable for quoting. *adj.*

quo ta tion (kwō tā′shən), 1. somebody's words repeated exactly by another person; passage quoted from a book, speech, etc. From what author does this quotation come? **Quotation marks** (" ") are put at the beginning and end of any matter that is quoted. 2. a price. What was today's market quotation on wheat? *n., adj. 7.*

quote (kwōt), 1. repeat exactly the words of another or a passage from a book. She often quotes her husband. The minister quoted from the Bible. 2. a quotation. 3. a quotation mark. 4. give the price of. *v., n. 5.*

quoth (kwōth), said. "Come hither," quoth the prince. *v.* [*Old use*] *5.*

quo tient (kwō′shənt), a number obtained by dividing one number by another. If you divide 26 by 2, the quotient is 13. *n. 9.*

R

R, r (är), the 18th letter of the alphabet, coming after o, p, q. There are two r's in carry. **The three R's** are reading, writing, and arithmetic. *n., pl. R's, r's.*

Ra (rä), Egyptian sun god and supreme deity, typically represented as a hawk-headed man bearing the sun on his head. *n.*

Ra, radium.

R.A., 1. Rear Admiral. 2. Royal Academy. 3. member of the Royal Academy. 4. Royal Artillery.

rab bi (rab′ī), teacher of the Jewish law; pastor of a Jewish congregation. *n., pl. rabbis* or *rabbies. 14.*

Rabbit

rab bit (rab′it), an animal about as big as a cat, with soft fur and long ears. A rabbit can make long jumps. *n. 2.*

rab ble (rab′əl), 1. a disorderly crowd; a mob. 2. the rude lower class of persons. The nobles scorned the rabble. *n. 8.*

rab id (rab′id), 1. furious; violently intense or severe; unreasonably extreme. 2. mad; as, a rabid dog. *adj. 16.*

ra bies (rā′bēz), the disease a mad dog has; hydrophobia. If bitten by a mad dog you may get the disease. *n. 11.*

rac coon (ra kün′), 1. a small, grayish animal with a bushy ringed tail, that eats flesh, lives mostly in trees, and is active at night. 2. its fur. *n. 17.*

Raccoon (about 22 in. long, without the tail)

race[1] (rās), 1. a run. 2. a run to see who will do best. 3. run; move fast. 4. make go fast. 5. run a race with. 6. a strong or rapid current of water. *n., v. 1.*

race[2] (rās), 1. a group of persons, animals, or plants having the same ancestry; as, the white race, the race of fishes. 2. a group of people of the same kind; as, the brave race of seamen. *n.*

race course, race track.

ra ceme (ra sēm′), simple flower cluster having its flowers on short stalks at equal distances along a stem, as in the lily of the valley. *n. 19.*

Raceme

rac er (rās′ər), 1. person, animal, ship, or machine that takes part in races. 2. a kind of American blacksnake. *n. 13.*

race track, ground laid out for racing.

Ra chel (rā′chəl), wife of Jacob. *n. 12.*

ra cial (rā′shəl), pertaining to a race; characteristic of a race; as, racial traits, racial dislikes. *adj. 10.*

rac i ness (rās′i nis), vigor; liveliness. *n.*

rack[1] (rak), 1. frame with bars, shelves, or pegs to hold, arrange, or keep things on, such as a hat rack, tool rack, or baggage rack. 2. a frame of bars to hold hay and other food for cattle. 3. a framework set on a wagon for carrying hay, straw, etc. 4. an instrument once used for torturing people by stretching them. 5. hurt very much; as, racked with grief, a racking earache. 6. stretch; strain. 7. a bar with pegs or teeth on one edge, into which teeth on the rim of a wheel may fit. Many kinds of machines use a rack. *n., v. 3.*

Rack for holding hay

Towel rack

WHEEL
RACK
Rack (def. 7)

rack[2] (rak), wreck; destruction. *n.*

rack et[1] (rak′it), 1. loud noise; din; loud talk. Don't make a racket when others are reading. 2. a time of gay parties and social excitement. She is tired after all the racket. 3. a trick; a scheme; a dishonest scheme for extorting money. *Slang. n. 12.*

rack et[2] (rak′it), a light wide bat made of network stretched on a frame, used for games like tennis. *n.*

Tennis racket

rack et eer (rak′i tēr′), 1. person who extorts money from a business by threatening violence or damage. 2. extort money by threatening violence or damage. *n., v.*

ra coon (ra kün′), raccoon. *n.*

rac quet (rak′it), racket used in tennis and similar games. *n.*

rac y (rās′i), 1. having an agreeably peculiar taste or flavor; as, a racy apple. 2. vigorous; lively (said of speech or writing). *adj., racier, raciest.*

ra di al (rā′di əl), 1. of or like radii or rays. 2. arranged like or in radii or rays. *adj. 17.*

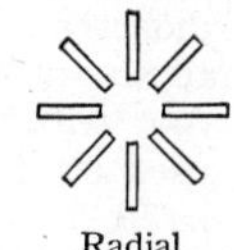
Radial arrangement

ra di ance (rā′di əns), brightness; as, the radiance of the sun, of electric lights, or of a person's smile. *n. 8.*

ra di an cy (rā′di ən si), radiance. *n.*

ra di ant (rā′di ənt), 1. shining; bright; beaming; as, radiant sunshine, a radiant smile. 2. sent off in rays from some source; radiated. We get radiant energy from the sun. *adj. 5.*

ra di ate (rā′di āt), 1. give out rays of. The sun radiates light and heat. 2. issue in rays. Heat radiates from hot steam pipes. 3. spread out from a center. Roads radiate from the city in every direction. 4. give out; send forth. His face radiates joy. 5. having rays. A daisy is a radiate flower. 6. radiating from a center. *v., adj. 11.*

ra di a tion (rā′di ā′shən), 1. giving out light, heat, etc. The steam pipes do not afford sufficient radiation for so large a room. 2. a ray or rays. *n. 16.*

ra di a tor (rā′di ā′tər), set of pipes that give off heat. The radiator of an automobile gives off heat very fast and so cools the water inside it. *n. 6.*

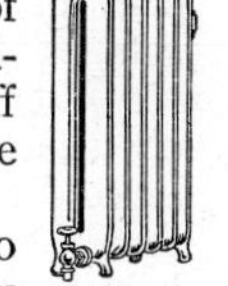
Radiator

rad i cal (rad′i kəl), 1. going to the root; fundamental. Cruelty is a radical fault. If she wants to grow thin, she must make a radical change in her diet. 2. extreme; favoring extreme changes or reforms. 3. person with extreme opinions. 4. an atom or group of atoms acting as a unit in chemical reactions. *adj., n. 7.*

rad i cal ism (rad′i kəl izm), principles or practices of radicals; extreme views. *n. 16.*

ra di i (rā′di ī), more than one radius. *n. pl. 20.*

ra di o (rā′di ō), 1. wireless telegraph or telephone; a way of sending and receiving words, music, etc., by electric waves without wires. We can listen to music broadcast by radio. 2. of, pertaining to, used in, or sent by radio; as, a radio set, radio speeches. 3. transmit or send out by radio. *n., pl. radios, adj., v., radioed, radioing. 11.*

ra di o ac tive (rā′di ō ak′tiv), giving off rays that pass through opaque matter. Radium is radioactive. *adj.*

rad ish (rad′ish), a small crisp root with a red or white skin, used as a relish and in salads. *n. 10.*

Radish

ra di um (rā′di əm), a radioactive metallic element, discovered in 1898. Radium is used in treating cancer. *n. 13.*

ra di us (rā′di əs), 1. any line going straight from the center to the outside of a circle or a sphere. Any spoke of a wheel is a radius. 2. circular area measured by the length of its radius. The explosion could be heard within a radius of ten miles. *n., pl. radii* (-di ī) or *radiuses. 8.*

Each line from C (center) is a radius.

raf fi a (raf′i ə), fiber from the leafstalks of a palm tree, used in making baskets, mats, etc. *n.*

raf fle (raf′əl), 1. a sale in which many people each pay a small sum for a chance of getting an article. 2. sell chances of winning (an article) to a number of people, one of whom gets it. *n., v.*

raft (raft), logs or boards fastened together to make a floating platform. Having no boat we had to cross the stream on a raft. *n. 8.*

Raft

raft er (raf′tər), slanting beam of a roof. *n. 6.*

RAFTER RAFTER

rag[1] (rag), 1. a small cloth. A washrag is a washcloth. 2. a torn or waste piece of cloth. Use clean rags to rub this mirror bright. His clothes were in rags. 3. small piece of anything of no value. The meat was boiled to rags. 4. made from rags; as, a rag doll, a rag rug. *n., adj. 3.*

rag[2] (rag), 1. scold. 2. tease. 3. play jokes on. *v., ragged, ragging.* [*Slang*]

rag a muf fin (rag′ə muf′in), 1. ragged, disreputable fellow. 2. ragged child. *n. 18.*

rage (rāj), 1. violent anger; passion. Mad with rage, Dick dashed into the fight. 2. talk or act violently; storm. Keep your temper; don't rage. The wind rages wildly. 3. what everybody wants for a short time; the fashion. Red ties are all the rage this season. *n., v. 3.*

rag ged (rag′id), 1. worn or torn into rags; as, ragged clothing. 2. wearing ragged clothes. 3. rough; not smooth and tidy; as, an Airedale's ragged coat, a ragged garden. 4. having loose shreds or bits; as, a ragged wound. *adj. 4.*

ra gout (ra gü′), a highly seasoned stew of meat and vegetables. *n. 20.*

rag time (rag′tīm′), 1. musical rhythm with accents falling at unusual places. 2. music with accents falling at unusual places; jazz. *n.*

rag weed (rag′wēd′), a common weed whose pollen is one cause of hay fever. *n.*

Ragweed

raid (rād), 1. an attack; a sudden attack. 2. attack suddenly. 3. entering and seizing what is inside. 4. force a way into; enter and seize what is in. The police raided the gambling house. *n., v. 8.*

raid er (rād′ər), person, ship, etc., that raids. *n. 19.*

rail[1] (rāl), 1. bar of wood or of metal. There are stair rails, fence rails, rails protecting monuments, etc. Bars laid along the ground for a car or railroad track are called rails. 2. a railroad. We travel by rail and by boat. 3. **Rail in** means shut in with bars. **Rail off** means shut off or separate with bars. They railed off a space for the horses. *n., v. 2.*

Rail fence

rail[2] (rāl), complain bitterly; use violent and reproachful language. He railed at his hard luck. *v.*

rail[3] (rāl), a bird like a crane but smaller. It lives in marshes and swamps. *n., pl. rails* or *rail.*

Rail (10 in. long)

rail er (rāl′ər), person who utters violent complaints or reproaches. *n. 14.*

rail ing[1] (rāl′ing), 1. a fence of rails. 2. material for rails. 3. rails. *n. 18.*

rail ing[2] (rāl′ing), violent complaints or reproaches; jeers. *n.*

rail ler y (rāl′ər i), good-humored ridicule or joking. *n., pl. railleries. 14.*

rail road (rāl′rōd′), 1. road or track with parallel steel rails on which the wheels of cars may go. Engines pull trains on the railroad. 2. the tracks, stations, trains, and the people who manage them. 3. to work on a railroad. 4. send along quickly or too quickly to be fair. *Used in common talk. n., v. 2.*

rail road ing (rāl′rōd′ing), railroad business. *n.*

rail way (rāl′wā′), 1. railroad. 2. track made of rails. *n. 3.*

rai ment (rā′mənt), clothes. *n. 7.*

rain (rān), 1. water falling in drops from the clouds. The rain wet the windows. 2. the fall of such drops. 3. a thick, fast fall of anything; as, a rain of bullets. 4. to fall in drops of water. It rained all day. 5. to fall like rain. Sparks rained down from the burning building. 6. send like rain. The children rained flowers on the May queen. *n., v. 1.*

rain bow (rān′bō′), 1. a bow or arch of seven colors seen sometimes in the sky, or in mist or spray, when the sun shines on it from behind one. The colors of the rainbow are violet, indigo, blue, green, yellow, orange, and red. 2. having many colors like a rainbow. *n., adj. 3.*

rain coat (rān′kōt′), coat for protection from rain. *n.*

rain drop (rān′drop′), drop of rain. *n. 7.*

rain fall (rān′fôl′), 1. shower of rain. 2. the amount of water falling in a given time. The yearly rainfall in New York is much greater than that in Arizona. *n. 6.*

rain storm (rān′stôrm′), a storm with much rain. *n. 20.*

rain y (rān′i), 1. having rain; having much rain. 2. bringing rain. April is a rainy month. 3. wet with rain. *adj., rainier, rainiest. 4.*

raise (rāz), 1. lift up; put up. The soldiers raised a white flag. Children in school raise their hands to answer. 2. build; build up; set up. People raise monuments to soldiers who have died for their country. 3. cause to rise. The automobiles raise a dust. Bread is raised by yeast. 4. make higher or larger; increase in degree, amount, etc.; as, to raise prices, to raise the rent, to raise one's courage. 5. rouse; stir up. The dogs had raised a rabbit and were chasing it. 6. bring up; make grow; help to grow. The farmer raises chickens and corn. 7. cause; bring about. The child's remark raised a smile. 8. bring together; get together; gather. The leader raised an army. 9. lift up in mind, morals, rank, position, etc. The boy raised himself by hard study to be a great lawyer. 10. utter in a loud voice; cause to be heard. The boys raised a shout. 11. end; as, to raise a blockade, to raise a siege. 12. an increase in amount; as, a raise in pay. 13. **Raise the dead** means bring them to life. *v., n. 1.*

rais er (rāz′ər), person who grows or raises things; as, a raiser of fine vegetables, a cattle raiser. *n. 9.*

rai sin (rā′zən), a sweet dried grape. *n. 5.*

ra jah or **ra ja** (rä′jə), ruler or chief in India, Java, etc. *n. 12.*

rake[1] (rāk), 1. a long-handled tool having a bar at one end with teeth in it. A rake is used for smoothing the soil or gathering together loose leaves, hay, straw, etc. 2. move with a rake. Rake the leaves off the grass. 3. use a rake. 4. gather; gather together. 5. search carefully. He raked the newspapers for descriptions of the accident. 6. fire guns along the length of (a ship or a line of soldiers). *n., v. 4.*

Rake

rake[2] (rāk), dissolute person. That young rake gambles and gets drunk all the time. *n.*

rake[3] (rāk), the slope of a ship's mast and smokestacks. *n.*

rak ish (rāk′ish), 1. smart; jaunty; dashing; as, a hat set at a rakish angle. 2. suggesting dash and speed. He owns a rakish boat. 3. like a rake; immoral; dissolute. *adj.*

Ra leigh (rô′li), 1. Sir Walter Raleigh was an English soldier, explorer, and statesman (1552?-1618). 2. the capital of North Carolina. *n. 8.*

ral ly[1] (ral′i), 1. bring together; bring together again; get in order again. The commander was able to rally the fleeing troops. 2. come together for a common purpose. 3. come to help. Bob rallied to the side of his frightened sister. 4. recover health and strength. The sick man may rally now. 5. coming together; mass meeting; as, a political rally. *v., rallied, rallying, n., pl. rallies. 8.*

ral ly[2] (ral′i), tease; make fun of. The boys rallied John on his short haircut. *v., rallied, rallying.*

Ram

ram (ram), 1. male sheep. 2. butt against; strike head on; strike violently. One ship rammed the other ship. I rammed my head against the door in the dark. 3. push hard: drive down or in by heavy blows. 4. a machine or part of a machine that strikes heavy blows. A battering ram knocks walls down. See the picture under **battering ram.** *n., v., rammed, ramming. 4.*

ram ble (ram′bəl), 1. wander about. We rambled here and there through the woods. 2. a walk for pleasure, not to go to any special place. 3. talk about first one thing and then another with no useful connections. *v., n. 8.*

ram bling (ram′bling), 1. wandering about. 2. going from one thing to another with no useful connections; as, a rambling speech. 3. climbing; as, rambling roses. 4. extending irregularly in various directions; not planned in an orderly way; as, a rambling old farmhouse. *adj.*

Ram e ses (ram′i sēz), Ramses. *n.*

ram i fi ca tion (ram′i fi kā′shən), 1. dividing or spreading out into branches or parts. 2. branch; part. *n. 17.*

ram i fy (ram′i fī), divide or spread out into branches or branchlike parts. *v., ramified, ramifying.*

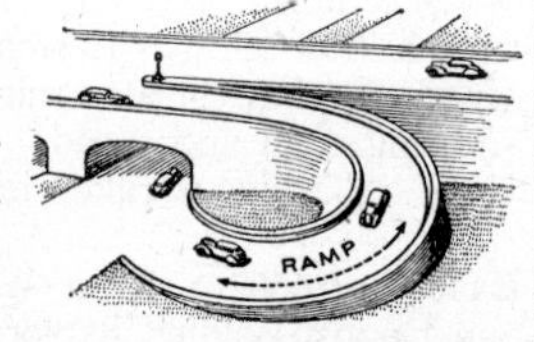

ramp[1] (ramp), sloping way connecting two different levels of a building, road, etc.; slope. *n. 15.*

ramp[2] (ramp), 1. rush wildly about. 2. jump or rush with fury. *v.*

ram page (ram′pāj for 1, ram pāj′ for 2), 1. rushing wildly about; violent behavior; wild outbreak. The mad elephant went on a rampage and killed its keeper. 2. rush wildly about; rage; behave violently. *n., v.*

Lion rampant (def. 3)

ramp ant (ram′pənt), 1. unchecked; growing without any check. The vines were rampant over the fence. 2. angry; excited; violent. 3. springing up on the hind legs. *adj. 11.*

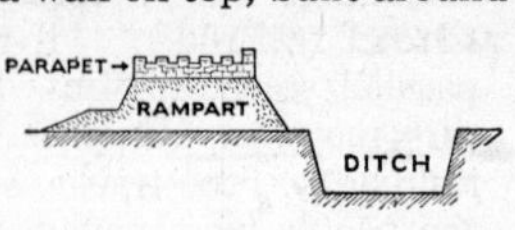

ram part (ram′pärt), 1. a wide bank of earth, often with a wall on top, built around a fort to help defend it. 2. anything that defends; defense; protection. *n. 9.*

ram rod (ram′rod′), 1. a rod for ramming down the charge in a gun that is loaded from the muzzle. 2. rod for cleaning the barrel of a gun. *n. 20.*

Ram ses (ram′sēz), the name of several kings of ancient Egypt. *n. 19.*

ram shack le (ram′shak′əl), loose and shaky; likely to come apart. *adj. 19.*

ran (ran). See **run.** The dog ran after the cat. *pt. of run. 1.*

ranch (ranch), 1. a very large farm. Many ranches are used for raising cattle. 2. a farm; as, a chicken ranch, a fruit ranch. 3. to work on a ranch; manage a ranch. *n., v. 7.*

ranch er (ran′chər), person who owns, manages, or works on a ranch. *n.*

ranch man (ranch′mən), rancher. *n., pl. ranchmen. 20.*

ran cid (ran′sid), 1. stale; spoiled; as, rancid fat. 2. tasting or smelling like stale fat or butter. *adj. 17.*

ran cor (rang′kər), bitter resentment or ill will; extreme hatred or spite. *n. 15.*

ran cor ous (rang′kər əs), spiteful; bitterly malicious. *adj. 19.*

ran dom (ran′dəm), by chance; with no plan. John was not listening and made a random answer when called upon to recite. **At random** means by chance. Alice took a book at random from the shelf. *adj., n. 5.*

rang (rang). See **ring**[2]. The telephone rang. *a pt. of ring*[2]. *4.*

range (rānj), 1. a row or line; as, a range of mountains. 2. put in a row or rows. Range the books by size. 3. put in groups or classes. 4. put in line on someone's side. Loyal citizens ranged themselves with the king. 5. land for grazing. 6. district in which certain plants or animals live. 7. distance between any limits; extent; as, a range of colors to choose from, a range of prices from 5 cents to 25 dollars, the range of hearing. 8. distance a gun can shoot. 9. place to practice shooting; as, a rifle range. 10. wander; rove; roam. Buffaloes ranged the plains. Our talk ranged over all that had happened on vacation. 11. extend; be found; occur; as, a boundary ranging east and west, a plant ranging from

Canada to Mexico. 12. a stove for cooking. *n., v. 2.*

rang er (rān′jər), 1. person employed to guard a tract of forest. 2. one of a body of armed men employed in ranging over a region to police it. 3. one that ranges; rover. *n. 14.*

rang y (rān′ji), 1. suitable for ranging or moving about. 2. slender and long-limbed; as, a rangy horse. *adj. 20.*

rank[1] (rangk), 1. a row or line, usually of soldiers, placed side by side. 2. Common soldiers or ordinary people are said to be in **the ranks** or to be **the rank and file.** 3. position; grade; class. New York is a city of first rank. 4. high position. A duke is a man of rank. 5. arrange in a row or line. 6. put in some special order in a list. Rank the states for area. 7. have a certain rank. John ranked low. 8. be more important than; be higher in grade than. A general ranks, that is, outranks, a major in the army. *n., v. 2.*

rank[2] (rangk), 1. large and coarse; as, rank grass. 2. growing richly. 3. producing a dense but coarse growth; as, rank swamp land. 4. having a bad, strong taste or smell; as, rank meat, rank tobacco. 5. strongly marked; extreme; as, rank ingratitude, rank nonsense. *adj.*

ran kle (rang′kəl), be sore; cause soreness; give pain. The memory of the insult rankled in his mind. *v. 10.*

ran sack (ran′sak), 1. search thoroughly through. The thief ransacked the house for jewelry. 2. rob; plunder. *v. 13.*

ran som (ran′səm), 1. price paid or demanded before a captive is set free. The robber chief held the travelers in hope of a ransom. 2. obtain the release of (captives) by paying a price. 3. redeem. *n., v. 5.*

rant (rant), 1. speak wildly, extravagantly, violently, or noisily. 2. extravagant or violent speech. *v., n. 17.*

rap (rap), 1. a quick light blow; a light sharp knock; as, a rap on the door. 2. knock sharply; tap. The chairman rapped on the table for order. 3. say sharply; as, to rap out an answer. 4. an old coin worth almost nothing. So we say, "I don't care a rap." *n., v., rapped, rapping. 5.*

ra pa cious (rə pā′shəs), 1. plundering; seizing by force; as, rapacious pirates. 2. grasping; greedy; as, a rapacious miser. *adj. 14.*

ra pac i ty (rə pas′i ti), rapacious spirit, action, or practice; greed. *n. 14.*

rape[1] (rāp), a seizing and carrying off by force. *n. 9.*

rape[2] (rāp), a small plant whose leaves are used as food for sheep and hogs. Rape seeds yield an oil. *n.*

Raph a el (raf′i əl), 1. a famous Italian painter (1483-1520). 2. one of the chief angels. *n. 10.*

rap id (rap′id), 1. very quick; swift; as, a rapid walk. 2. **Rapids** are a part of a river where the water rushes very swiftly. *adj., n. 1.*

ra pid i ty (rə pid′i ti), quickness; swiftness; speed. *n. 7.*

ra pi er (rā′pi ər), a light sword used for thrusting. *n. 14.*

Rapier

rap ine (rap′in), robbing by force and carrying off; plundering. The soldiers in the enemy's land got their food by rapine. *n. 7.*

rap scal lion (rap skal′yən), rascal; rogue; scamp. *n.*

rapt (rapt), 1. lost in delight. 2. so busy thinking of or enjoying one thing that one does not know what else is happening. The children listened to the story with rapt minds. 3. showing a rapt condition; caused by a rapt condition; as, a rapt smile. *adj. 6.*

rap ture (rap′chər), strong feeling that absorbs the mind; very great joy. The mother gazed with rapture at her long-lost son. *n. 4.*

rap tur ous (rap′chər əs), full of rapture; feeling rapture; expressing rapture. *adj. 12.*

rare[1] (rãr), 1. not usually found; few; not happening often. Storks and peacocks are rare birds in the United States. 2. unusually good. Edison had rare powers as an inventor. 3. thin; not dense. The higher we go above the earth, the rarer the air is. *adj. 2.*

rare[2] (rãr), not cooked much; as, a rare piece of steak. *adj.*

rare bit (rãr′bit or rab′it), melted cheese poured over toast. Welsh rabbit is the correct name for it. *n.*

rar e fy (rãr′i fī), 1. make less dense. The air on high mountains is rarefied. 2. become less dense. 3. refine; purify. *v., rarefied, rarefying.*

rare ly (rãr′li), 1. seldom; not often. 2. unusually; unusually well. *adv.*

rar i ty (rãr′iti), 1. something rare. A man over a hundred years old is a rarity. 2. fewness; scarcity. 3. thinness. The rarity of the air in the mountains is bad for people with weak hearts. *n., pl. rarities. 10.*

ras cal (ras′kəl), bad, dishonest person. Sometimes *rascal* is used jokingly, as when one calls a child a little rascal. *n. 5.*

ras cal i ty (ras kal′i ti), rascally character, conduct, or act. *n., pl. rascalities. 19.*

ras cal ly (ras′kəl i), mean; dishonest; bad. To steal the poor boy's lunch was a rascally trick. *adj. 14.*

rash[1] (rash), too hasty; careless; taking too much risk. It is rash to cross the street without looking both ways. *adj. 4.*

rash[2] (rash), a breaking out with many small red spots on the skin. Scarlet fever causes a rash. *n.*

rash er (rash′ər), thin slice of bacon or ham for frying or broiling. *n.*

rash ness (rash′nis), unwise boldness; recklessness. *n. 12.*

rasp (rasp), 1. make a harsh, grating sound. The file rasped as he worked. 2. a harsh, grating sound; as, the rasp of crickets, a rasp in a person's voice. 3. grate on; affect harshly; irritate. Her rasped feelings exploded into anger. 4. scrape with a rough instrument. 5. a coarse file with pointlike teeth. *v., n. 11.*

Rasp (def. 5)

rasp ber ry (raz′ber′i), 1. a small fruit that grows on bushes. It is usually red or black, but some kinds are white or yellow. 2. the bush it grows on. *n., pl. raspberries. 11.*

Raspberries and leaves

rat (rat), a gnawing animal like a mouse, but larger. Rats are gray, black, brown, or white. *n. 2.*

ra tan (ra tan′), rattan. *n.*

ratch et (rach′it), 1. a wheel or bar with teeth that come against a catch so that motion is permitted in one direction but not in the other. Jacks by which automobile wheels are raised from the ground have a ratchet. 2. the catch. 3. the entire device, wheel and catch, or bar and catch. *n. 15.*

RATCHET
CATCH

rate[1] (rāt), 1. quantity, amount, or degree, measured in proportion to something else. The rate of interest is 6 cents on the dollar. The railroad rate is 3 cents a mile. The parcel-post rate is 10 cents for the first pound. The car was going at the rate of 40 miles an hour. 2. price. We pay the regular rate. 3. put a value on. We rated the house as worth $10,000. 4. rank; estimate. He was rated one of the richest men in town. 5. class; grade; as, first rate, second rate. 6. **At any rate** means anyway; in any case. **At that rate** means in that case. *n., v. 2.*

rate[2] (rāt), scold. *v.*

rathe (rāᴛʜ), early. *adj., adv. [Old use] 17.*

rath er (raᴛʜ′ər), 1. more willingly. I would rather go today than tomorrow. **Had rather** means would prefer to. Mary had rather play than rest. 2. more truly; with better reason. This is rather for father to decide than for you. 3. somewhat; to some extent. After working so long he was rather tired. 4. "Rather!" means "Yes, indeed!" or "Very much." *Used in common talk. adv., interj. 1.*

rat i fi ca tion (rat′i fi kā′shən), confirmation; approval; as, the ratification of a treaty by the Senate. *n. 12.*

rat i fy (rat′i fī), confirm; approve. The two countries will ratify the agreement made by their representatives. *v., ratified, ratifying. 8.*

rat ing (rāt′ing), 1. class or grade. 2. position in a class or grade; as, the rating of a seaman, the rating of a ship according to tonnage. 3. an amount fixed as a rate; as, a rating of 80% in English. *n.*

ra tio (rā′shō), the relation between two numbers or quantities meant when we say *times as many, times as much,* etc. "He has sheep and cows in the ratio of 10 to 3" means that he has ten sheep for every three cows, or 3⅓ times as many sheep as cows. The ratio between two quantities is the number of times one contains the other. The ratios 3 to 5, 30 to 50, and 6 to 10 are the same. *n., pl. ratios. 7.*

ra tion (rā′shən or rash′ən), 1. a fixed allowance of food; the daily allowance of a soldier, sailor, or a horse. 2. portion of anything dealt out; as, rations of sugar, of coal, etc. 3. supply with rations; as, to ration an army. 4. allow only certain amounts to; as, to ration citizens when supplies are scarce. 5. distribute in limited amounts; as, to ration food to the public in wartime. *n., v. 7.*

ra tion al (rash′ən əl), 1. sensible; reasonable; reasoned out. When very angry, people seldom act in a rational way. 2. able to think and reason clearly. As children grow older, they become more rational. 3. of reason; based on reasoning. *adj. 9.*

ra tion al i ty (rash′ən al′i ti), the possession of reason; reasonableness. Mr. Smith is queer, but no one doubts his rationality. *n.*

ra tion al ly (rash′ən əl i), reasonably; sensibly. *adv.*

rat line or **rat lin** (rat′lin), one of the small ropes that cross the shrouds of a ship, used as steps for going aloft. *n.*

R, ratlines.

rat tan (ra tan′), 1. a kind of palm with a very long stem. 2. the stems of such palm trees, used for wickerwork, canes, etc. 3. a cane or switch made from a piece of such a stem. *n. 19.*

rat tle (rat′əl), 1. make a number of short sharp sounds. The window rattled in the wind. 2. cause to rattle. She rattled the dishes. 3. a number of short sharp sounds. We hear the rattle of the milk bottles in the morning. 4. a toy or instrument that makes a noise when it is shaken. The baby shakes his rattle. 5. talk or say quickly, on and on. 6. confuse. *Used in common talk. v., n. 3.*

Rattlesnake (from 2 to 8 ft. long, according to the kind)

rat tler (rat′lər), rattlesnake. *n.*

rat tle snake (rat′əl snāk′), a poisonous snake that makes a rattling noise with its tail. *n. 13.*

rau cous (rô′kəs), hoarse; harsh-sounding; as, the raucous caw of a crow. *adj.*

Rattlesnake's tail

rav age (rav′ij), 1. destroy; lay waste; damage greatly. The forest fire ravaged many miles of country. 2. violence; destruction; great damage. War causes ravage. *v., n. 8.*

rave (rāv), 1. talk wildly. An excited, angry person raves; so does a madman. 2. talk with too much enthusiasm. She raved about her food. 3. howl; roar; rage. The wind raved about the lighthouse. *v. 5.*

rav el (rav′əl), 1. fray out; separate into threads. The sweater has raveled at the elbow. Ravel a bit of the leftover cloth to mend the tear in your dress. 2. tangle; involve; confuse. *v., raveled, raveling.*

rav el ing or **rav el ling** (rav′əl ing), something raveled out; a thread drawn from a woven or knitted fabric. *n.*

ra ven (rā′vən), 1. a large black bird like a crow. 2. deep glossy black. *n., adj. 3.*

Raven (about 2 ft. long)

rav en ing (rav′ən ing), greedy and hungry. *adj.*

rav en ous (rav′ən əs), 1. very hungry. 2. greedy. *adj. 9.*

rav in (rav′in), rapine. *n. 16.*

ra vine (rə vēn′), a long, deep, narrow valley. The river had worn a ravine between the two hills. *n. 11.*

rav ish (rav′ish), 1. fill with delight. The prince was ravished by Cinderella's beauty. 2. carry off by force. The wolf ravished the lamb from the flock. *v. 7.*

rav ish ing (rav′ish ing), very delightful; enchanting; as, jewels of ravishing beauty. *adj.*

raw (rô), 1. not cooked; as, raw meat. 2. in the natural state; not manufactured, treated, or prepared; as, raw materials, raw hides. 3. not experienced; not trained; as, a raw soldier in the army. 4. damp and cold; as, a raw wind. 5. with the skin off; sore; as, a raw spot on a horse where the harness rubbed. 6. harsh; unfair. *Slang. adj. 3.*

raw-boned (rô′bōnd′), having little flesh on the bones; gaunt. *adj.*

raw hide (rô′hīd′), 1. the untanned skin of cattle. 2. a rope or whip made of this. 3. whip with a rawhide. *n., v. 17.*

ray[1] (rā), 1. a line or beam of light; as, rays of the sun. 2. a line or stream of heat or electricity or energy; as, X rays. 3. a thin line like a ray coming out from a center. 4. something bright or light; a gleam; as, a ray of hope, a ray of intelligence. 5. send out rays. *n., v. 2.*

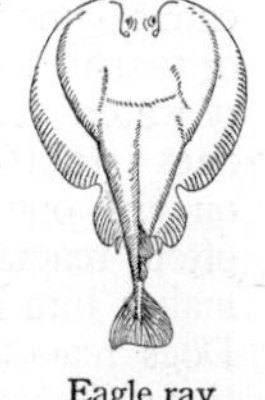

Eagle ray (about 5 ft. long)

ray[2] (rā), a kind of broad flat fish. See the picture. *n.*

ray on (rā′on), a fiber stiffer than silk but not so strong; artificial silk. *n.*

raze (rāz), tear down; destroy completely. The old school was razed to the ground, and a new one was built. *v. 9.*

ra zor (rā′zər), a tool with a sharp blade to shave with. See the picture below. *n. 6.*

rd., 1. road. 2. rod; rods. *20.*

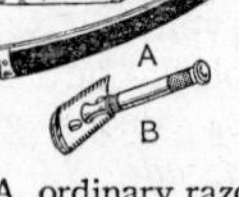

A, ordinary razor used by barbers; B, safety razor.

re (rā), in music, the second tone of the scale. Do, re, mi, fa, sol, la, ti, do are the names of the tones of the scale. *n.*

re-, a prefix meaning:—
1. again; as in reopen, reappear.
2. back; as, in rebound, recall.

There are many words made by putting **re** with another word in which **re** means again. To find the meaning of any word beginning with **re** that is not given in this dictionary, take the word from which it is made and put "again" after the word. For example, if you are looking for **refasten** and do not find it, think "fasten again" and look for **fasten.**

reach (rēch), 1. get to; arrive at; come to. Your letter reached me yesterday. 2. stretch out; hold out. A hand reached from the dark and seized Jack. 3. hold out to be taken; give or pass by handing. 4. move to touch or seize something; try to get. The man reached for his gun. 5. stretch; extend. The United States reaches from ocean to ocean. 6. touch; put a hand on. 7. get at; influence. Men are reached by flattery. The speaker reached the hearts of his hearers. 8. amount to; be equal to. The cost of the war reached billions. 9. reaching; stretching out. By a long reach the drowning man grasped the rope. 10. the extent or distance of reaching. Food and water were left within reach of the sick dog. 11. range; power; capacity. Philosophy is beyond a child's reach; he cannot understand it. 12. a long stretch or extent; as, a reach of woodland, a reach of water. *v., n. 1.*

re act (ri akt′), 1. act back; have an effect on the one that is acting. Unkindness often reacts on the unkind person and makes him unhappy. 2. act in response. Dogs react to kindness by showing affection. 3. act chemically. Acids react on metals. 4. **React against** means act unfavorably toward or take an unfavorable attitude toward. *v. 10.*

re-act (rē akt′), act over again. *v.*

re ac tion (ri ak′shən), 1. action in response to some influence. Our reaction to a joke is to laugh. 2. chemical action of two substances when put together. Putting an acid and a metal together causes a reaction. 3. action in the opposite direction. *n. 9.*

re ac tion ar y (ri ak′shən ãr′i), 1. pertaining to, marked by, or favoring action in the opposite direction. The bad results of the revolution brought about a reactionary feeling. 2. person who favors reaction, especially in politics. *adj., n., pl. reactionaries. 11.*

read[1] (rēd), 1. get the meaning of writing or print. We read books. 2. speak out loud the words of writing or print. Please read it to me. 3. get the meaning of other things; understand. God reads men's hearts. The prophet reads the future. 4. get the meaning of by the use of the finger tips. The blind girl reads special raised print by touching it. 5. study. John is reading law. 6. learn from writing or print. We read of heroes of other days. 7. show by figures, letters, signs, etc. The thermometer reads 70 degrees. The ticket reads "From New York to Boston." 8. give the meaning of; interpret. Silence is not always to be read as consent. **Read between the lines** means find a meaning not actually expressed in the writing or print. *v., read* (red), *reading. 1.*

read[2] (red), 1. having knowledge gained by reading; informed; as, a well-read man. 2. See **read.** *adj., pt. and pp. of read.*

read a ble (rēd′ə bəl), 1. easy to read; interesting. 2. capable of being read. *adj. 18.*

read er (rēd′ər), 1. person who reads. 2. a book for learning to read. *n. 4.*

read i ly (red′i li), 1. quickly. A bright boy answers readily when called on. 2. easily. 3. willingly. *adv. 4.*

read i ness (red′i nis), 1. being ready; preparedness. 2. quickness; promptness. 3. ease. 4. willingness. *n. 7.*

read ing[1] (rēd′ing), 1. getting the meaning of written or printed words. 2. speaking out loud written or printed words; public recital. 3. study of books. 4. written or printed matter read or to be read. 5. the amount shown on the scale of an instrument. The reading of the thermometer was 96 degrees. 6. the form of a given word or passage in a particular edition of a book. No two editions have the same reading for that passage. 7. interpretation. Each actor gave the lines a different reading. *n.*

Read ing[2] (red′ing), a city in southeastern Pennsylvania. *n.*

re ad just (rē′ə just′), adjust again; arrange again. *v. 15.*

re ad just ment (rē′ə just′mənt), an adjustment made again. *n. 14.*

read y (red′i), 1. prepared for action or use at once; prepared. The soldiers are ready for battle. Dinner is ready. We were ready to start at nine. 2. willing. The soldiers were ready to die for their country. Mary is ready to forgive. 3. likely; liable. Kate is too ready to find fault. 4. quick; prompt. The speaker has a ready wit. A kind man gave ready help to the children. 5. easy to get at; easy to reach; as, ready money. *adj., readier, readiest. 1.*

read y-made (red′i mād′), ready for immediate use; made for anybody who will buy; not made to order. Department stores sell ready-made clothes. *adj. 19.*

re a gent (ri ā′jənt), a substance used to detect the presence of other substances by the chemical reactions it causes. *n. 17.*

re al[1] (rē′əl), actual; existing as a fact; true; not imagined; not made up; as, the real thing, real diamonds, real pleasure, the real reason. *adj. 1.*

re al[2] (rē′əl), a former small Spanish silver coin. *n.*

real estate, land together with the buildings, fences, trees, water, and minerals which belong with it.

re al ism (rē′əl izm), 1. in literature and art, picturing life as it actually is. 2. the belief that material objects have a real existence independent of our consciousness of them. *n. 18.*

re al ist (rē′əl ist), 1. a writer or artist who represents things as they are in real life. 2. person interested in what is real and practical rather than what is imaginary or theoretical. 3. person who believes that material objects have a real existence. *n. 12.*

re al is tic (rē′əl is′tik), 1. like the real thing; lifelike. 2. representing things as they really are. 3. interested in what is real or practical. 4. pertaining to realists or realism. *adj. 14.*

re al i ty (ri al′i ti), 1. actual existence; the true state of affairs. I doubted the reality of what he had seen, and thought he must have dreamed it. 2. **In reality** means really; in fact. We thought he was serious, but in reality he was joking. 3. real thing or fact. Slaughter and destruction are the terrible realities of war. *n., pl. realities. 5.*

re al i za tion (rē′əl i zā′shən), 1. a making real or the being made real of something imagined or planned. The realization of her hope to be an actress made her happy. 2. understanding. The explorers had a full realization of the dangers they would face. 3. act of realizing or changing (property) into money. *n. 9.*

re al ize (rē′əl īz), 1. understand. The teacher realizes now how hard you worked. 2. make real. Her uncle's present made it possible for her to realize the dream of going to college. 3. change (property) into money. Before going to England to live, he realized all his property in this country. 4. obtain as a return or profit. He realized $118 from his work. 5. bring as a return or profit. *v. 3.*

re al ly (rē′əl i), 1. actually; truly; in fact. 2. indeed. *adv. 2.*

realm (relm), 1. kingdom. 2. region. *n. 3.*

re al ty (rē′əl ti), land; buildings. *n. 19.*

ream[1] (rēm), 480 sheets of paper, now often 500 sheets. *n. 19.*

ream[2] (rēm), enlarge or shape (a hole). *v.*

ream er (rēm′ər), tool for enlarging or shaping a hole. *n. 19.*

re an i mate (rē an′i māt), restore to life; give fresh spirit, vigor, activity, etc., to; as, to reanimate discouraged troops, to reanimate trade. *v.*

reap (rēp), 1. cut (grain). 2. gather (a crop). 3. cut grain or gather a crop from. 4. get as a return or reward. Kind acts reap happy smiles. *v. 3.*

reap er (rēp′ər), person or machine that cuts grain. *n. 8.*

re ap pear (rē′ə pēr′), come into sight again. *v. 8.*

rear[1] (rēr), 1. back part; the back. The kitchen is in the rear of the house. **In the rear** often means behind. 2. back; at the back. Leave by the rear door of the car. 3. the last part of an army, fleet, etc. *n., adj. 2.*

rear[2] (rēr), 1. make grow; help to grow; bring up. The mother was very careful in rearing her children. 2. set up; build. The men reared altars to the gods. 3. raise; lift up. 4. rise on the hind legs. The horse reared as the fire engine dashed past. *v.*

rear admiral, naval officer next in rank above a captain.

rear guard, part of an army that protects the rear.

re ar range (rē′ə rānj′), 1. arrange in a new way. 2. arrange again. *v. 13.*

re ar range ment (rē′ə rānj′mənt), new or different arrangement. *n. 17.*

rear ward (rēr′wərd), toward the rear; in the rear. *adv., adj. 19.*

re as cend (rē′ə send′), go up again. *v. 14.*

rea son (rē′zən), 1. cause; motive; explanation. Sickness is the reason for Mary's absence. Tell me your reasons for not liking him. 2. think things out; solve new problems. An idiot cannot reason. 3. power to think. That poor old man has lost his reason. 4. right thinking; common sense. The stubborn child was at last brought to reason. **It stands to reason** means it is reasonable and sensible. 5. argue. Reason with Helen and try to make her change her mind. *n., v. 1.*

rea son a ble (rē′zən ə bəl), 1. according to reason; sensible; not foolish. 2. able to reason. 3. moderate; fair; as, a reasonable price. *adj. 4.*

rea son a bly (rē′zən ə bli), in a reasonable manner; with reason. *adv.*

rea son ing (rē′zən ing), 1. the process of drawing conclusions from facts. 2. reasons; arguments. *n.*

re as sem ble (rē′ə sem′bəl), come together again; bring together again. *v. 15.*

re as sert (rē′ə sėrt′), assert again. *v. 19.*

re as sume (rē′ə süm′), assume again or anew; resume. *v. 19.*

re as sur ance (rē′ə shür′əns), 1. a new or fresh assurance. 2. restoration of courage or confidence. *n. 19.*

re as sure (rē′ə shür′), 1. assure again or anew. 2. restore to confidence. The teacher's calmness during the storm reassured the children. *v. 8.*

re a wak en (rē′ə wāk′ən), awaken again or anew. *v. 17.*

re bate (rē′bāt), 1. a discount; something paid back. 2. give as a discount. *n., v. 15.*

reb el (reb′əl for 1 and 2, ri bel′ for 3 and 4), 1. person who resists or fights against authority instead of obeying. The rebels armed themselves against the government. 2. defying law or authority; as, the rebel army. 3. resist or fight against law or authority. 4. feel a great dislike or opposition. We rebelled at having to stay in on so fine a day. *n., adj., v., rebelled, rebelling. 3.*

re bel lion (ri bel′yən), a fight against government; revolt; rebelling. The nobles rose in rebellion against the king. *n. 5.*

re bel lious (ri bel′yəs), defying authority; acting like a rebel. The rebellious boy would not obey the school rules. *adj. 6.*

re bind (rē bīnd′), bind again or anew. This book with the broken back needs rebinding. *v., rebound, rebinding.*

re birth (rē′bėrth′), new birth; being born again. *n.*

re born (rē bôrn′), born again. *adj. 20.*

re bound[1] (ri bound′ for 1, rē′bound′ for 2), 1. spring back. 2. springing back. You hit the ball on the rebound in handball. *v., n. 12.*

re bound[2] (rē bound′). See **rebind.** Send this book to be rebound. *pt. and pp. of rebind.*

re buff (ri buf′), 1. a blunt or sudden check to a person who makes advances, offers help, makes a request, etc. We tried to be friendly, but his rebuff made us think he wanted to be left alone. 2. give a rebuff to. The friendly dog was rebuffed by a kick. *n., v. 8.*

re build (rē bild′), build again or anew. *v., rebuilt, rebuilding. 7.*

re built (rē bilt′), built again. *pt. and pp. of* **rebuild.** *20.*

re buke (ri būk′), 1. find fault with; reprove. The teacher rebuked the child for throwing paper on the floor. 2. finding fault; scolding. The child feared the teacher's rebuke. *v., n. 5.*

re bus (rē′bəs), the representation of a word or phrase by pictures suggesting the syllables or words. A picture of a cat on a log is a rebus for catalog. *n. 18.*

re but (ri but′), oppose by evidence on the other side or by argument; try to disprove; as, to rebut the argument of the other team in a debate. *v., rebutted, rebutting.*

re cal ci trant (ri kal′si trənt), resisting authority or control; disobedient. The recalcitrant patient would not take his medicine. *adj. 20.*

re call (ri kôl′), 1. call back to mind; remember. I can recall stories that my mother told me years ago. 2. call back; order back. The captain was recalled from the front line. 3. take back; withdraw. I shall recall my order for a new coat because I have had one given me. 4. recalling. The people voted for the recall of the governor because they did not think him fit for his office. *v., n. 3.*

re cant (ri kant′), take back (an opinion); withdraw or renounce (a statement, opinion, purpose, etc.). Tortures failed to make the prisoner recant his religion. *v. 15.*

re can ta tion (rē′kan tā′shən), recanting; a formal or public renouncing. *n. 14.*

re ca pit u late (rē′kə pich′ů lāt), repeat or recite the main points of; tell briefly; sum up. *v. 15.*

re ca pit u la tion (rē′kə pich′ů lā′shən), summary; a brief statement of the main points. *n. 20.*

re cap ture (rē kap′chər), capture again. *v., n. 13.*

re cast (rē kast′), 1. cast again or anew; as, to recast a bell. 2. remodel; make over; as, to recast a sentence. *v., recast, recasting. 17.*

recd., received.

re cede (ri sēd′), 1. go back; move back. Houses and trees seem to recede as you ride past in a train. 2. slope backward. This boy has a receding chin. 3. withdraw. He receded from the agreement. *v. 10.*

re ceipt (ri sēt′), 1. written statement that money, a package, a letter, etc., has been received. Sign the receipt for this parcel. 2. write on (a bill, etc.) that something has been received or paid for. Pay the bill and ask the grocer to receipt it. 3. **Receipts** means money received. Our expenses were less than our receipts. 4. receiving; being received. On receipt of the news he went home. 5. directions for preparing something to eat; recipe. Please give me your receipt for cookies. *n., v. 3.*

re ceiv a ble (ri sēv′ə bəl), 1. fit for acceptance. Gold is receivable all over the world. 2. which is to be received. 3. on which payment is to be received. He will get $100 soon from bills receivable. Bills receivable is the opposite of bills payable. *adj.*

re ceive (ri sēv′), 1. take (something offered or sent); as, to receive presents. 2. take or let into the mind; accept; as, to receive new ideas, news, an education. 3. let into one's house, society, etc. The ladies of the town would not receive Mrs. Loud. 4. be at home to friends. Mrs. Rich receives on Tuesdays. 5. be given; experience; suffer; as, to receive blows, insult, or punishment. 6. take in; support; bear; hold. The boat received a heavy load. A basin receives the water from the fountain. *v. 1.*

re ceiv er (ri sēv′ər), 1. person who receives. The receiver of a gift should thank the giver. 2. person appointed by law to take charge of the property of others. Mr. Jones will act as receiver for the firm that has failed in business. 3. thing that receives; as, an ash receiver, a telephone receiver. *n. 7.*

re ceiv er ship (ri sēv′ər ship), 1. position of a receiver in charge of the property of others. 2. condition of being in the control of a receiver. *n.*

re cent (rē′sənt), done or made not long ago. *adj. 3.*

re cent ly (rē′sənt li), lately; not long ago. *adv.*

re cep ta cle (ri sep′tə kəl), any container or place used to put things in to keep them conveniently. Bags, baskets, and vaults are all receptacles. *n. 7.*

re cep tion (ri sep′shən), 1. act of receiving. Her calm reception of the bad news surprised us. 2. being received. 3. manner of receiving. We were given a warm reception on returning home. 4. party; entertainment. Our school gave a reception to our new principal. *n. 5.*

re cep tive (ri sep′tiv), able, quick, or ready to receive ideas, suggestions, impressions, etc.; as, a receptive mind. *adj. 17.*

re cess (ri ses′), 1. time during which work stops. Our school has an hour's recess at noon. 2. take a recess. 3. a part in a wall, set back from the rest. This long seat will fit nicely in that recess. 4. inner place or part; as, the recesses of a cave, the recesses of one's secret thoughts. 5. to place in a recess. *n., v. 3.*

re ces sion (ri sesh′ən), receding; becoming more distant; withdrawal; departure; as, the recession of objects as seen from a moving train. *n.*

re ces sion al (ri sesh′ən əl), 1. sung or played while the clergy and the choir retire from the church at the end of a service. 2. recessional hymn or piece of music. *adj., n.*

re ces sive (ri ses′iv), receding; likely to go back. *adj. 11.*

Re ci fe (rä sē′fə), official name of Pernambuco. *n.*

rec i pe (res′i pi), 1. directions for preparing something to eat. Give me your recipe for cookies. 2. directions for preparing any thing or result. *n. 9.*

re cip i ent (ri sip′i ənt), 1. person who receives something. The recipients of the prizes had their names printed in the paper. 2. receiving; willing to receive. *n., adj. 12.*

re ci pro cal (ri sip′rə kəl), 1. in return; mutual; as, reciprocal liking, reciprocal visits, reciprocal distrust. Although I gave him many presents, I had no reciprocal gifts from him. 2. in grammar, expressing mutual action or relation. In "The children like each other," *each other* is a reciprocal pronoun. 3. a number so related to another that when multiplied together they give 1. 3 is the reciprocal of ⅓, and ⅓ is the reciprocal of 3. 100 is the reciprocal of .01. *adj., n. 9.*

re cip ro cal ly (ri sip′rə kəl i), in a reciprocal way; each to the other; mutually. *adv.*

re cip ro cate (ri sip′rə kāt), 1. give or feel in return. She loves me and I reciprocate her affection. 2. interchange; as, to reciprocate favors. 3. move or cause to move with an alternating backward and forward motion. A reciprocating engine is one in which the piston moves back and forth in a straight line. *v. 12.*

re cip ro ca tion (ri sip′rə kā′shən), reciprocating; return; as, a reciprocation of a favor received. *n. 20.*

rec i proc i ty (res′i pros′i ti), 1. reciprocal state; mutual action. 2. mutual exchange; especially, an exchange of special privileges in regard to trade between two countries. *n. 16.*

re cit al (ri sīt′əl), 1. reciting; telling facts in detail. Her recital of her experiences in the hospital bored her hearers. 2. story; account. 3. musical entertainment. My music teacher will give a recital Tuesday afternoon. *n. 12.*

rec i ta tion (res′i tā′shən), 1. reciting; reciting a prepared lesson by pupils before a teacher. 2. repeating something from memory before an audience. 3. piece repeated in this way. *n. 13.*

rec i ta tive (res′i tə tēv′), 1. a style of music half way between speaking and singing. Operas often contain long passages of recitative. 2. a passage or part in this style. *n. 20.*

re cite (ri sīt′), 1. say over; repeat. Pupils recite their lessons. He can recite that poem from memory. 2. tell one by one. Will you recite the names of the pupils who have not been absent this term? *v. 4.*

reck (rek), 1. care; heed. The brave soldier recked little of danger. 2. matter. What recks it whether we win or lose? *v.* [*Old use*] *10.*

reck less (rek′lis), rash; heedless; careless. Reckless of consequences, the boy played truant. Reckless driving causes many automobile accidents. *adj. 8.*

reck less ness (rek′lis nis), carelessness; heedlessness; excessive boldness. *n. 16.*

reck on (rek′ən), 1. count; find the number or value of. Reckon the cost before you decide. 2. consider; judge. He is reckoned the best speller in the class. 3. think; suppose. *Used in common talk.* 4. depend; rely. Can we reckon on your help? 5. settle; settle accounts. *v. 4.*

reck on ing (rek′ən ing), 1. count; calculation. By my reckoning we are miles from home. 2. rendering or settling an account; as, a day of reckoning. 3. a bill, especially at an inn or tavern. 4. the calculation of the position of a ship. *n.*

re claim (ri klām′), 1. bring back to a useful, good condition. They reclaim waste land. The church reclaims a bad man by helping him to be good. 2. demand the return of. He had no right to take your book away; so reclaim it. *v. 7.*

rec la ma tion (rek′lə mā′shən), restoration to a useful, good condition; as, the reclamation of deserts by irrigation. *n. 13.*

re cline (ri klīn′), lean back; lie down. The tired woman reclined on the couch. *v. 7.*

re cluse (ri klüs′), 1. person who lives shut up or withdrawn from the world. 2. shut up or apart from the world. A hermit lives a recluse life. *n., adj. 14.*

rec og ni tion (rek′əg nish′ən), 1. knowing again; recognizing. 2. being recognized. By a good disguise he escaped recognition. 3. acknowledgment. We insisted on complete recognition of our rights. 4. attention; favorable notice. The actor soon won recognition from the public. *n. 8.*

re cog ni zance (ri kog′ni zəns), 1. in law, a bond binding a person to do some particular act. 2. the sum of money to be forfeited if the act is not performed. *n. 17.*

rec og nize (rek′əg nīz), 1. know again. You have grown so that I scarcely recognized you. 2. acknowledge; accept; admit. I recognize your right to ask that question. 3. take notice of. Anyone who wishes to speak in a public meeting should stand up and wait till the chairman recognizes him. 4. show appreciation of. 5. acknowledge and agree to deal with. For some years other nations did not recognize the new government. *v. 3.*

re coil (ri koil′), 1. draw back; shrink back. Most people would recoil at seeing a snake in the path. 2. spring back. A gun recoils after being fired. 3. springing back. *v., n. 6.*

rec ol lect (rek′ə lekt′), remember; call back to mind. *v. 6.*

re-col lect (rē′kə lekt′), 1. collect again. 2. **Re-collect oneself** means recover self-control. *v.*

rec ol lec tion (rek′ə lek′shən), 1. act or power of recalling to mind. 2. memory; remembrance. This has been the hottest summer within my recollection. 3. thing remembered. *n. 7.*

re com bine (rē′kəm bīn′), combine again or anew. *v.*

re com mence (rē′kə mens′), begin again or anew. *v. 13.*

rec om mend (rek′ə mend′), 1. speak in favor of; suggest favorably. Can you recommend a good story of adventure? 2. advise. 3. make pleasing or attractive. The position of the camp recommends it as a summer home. 4. hand over for safekeeping. He recommended his soul to God. *v. 3.*

rec om men da tion (rek′ə men dā′shən), 1. a recommending. 2. anything that recommends a person or thing. 3. words of advice or praise. *n. 5.*

re com mit (rē′kə mit′), 1. commit again. 2. refer again to a committee. *v., recommitted, recommitting.*

rec om pense (rek′əm pens), 1. to reward; pay back. The travelers recompensed the man who so carefully directed them. 2. make a fair return for (anything lost, damage done, hurt received, etc.). 3. payment; reward; return. *v., n. 4.*

rec on cile (rek′ən sīl), 1. make friends again. The children had quarreled but were soon reconciled. 2. settle (quarrels or differences). The teacher had to reconcile disputes among her pupils. 3. make satisfied. It is hard to reconcile oneself to being sick a long time. 4. make agree; bring into harmony. It is impossible to reconcile his story with the facts. *v. 4.*

rec on cile ment (rek′ən sīl′mənt), reconciliation. *n. 13.*

rec on cil i a tion (rek′ən sil′i ā′shən), 1. bringing together again in friendship. 2. settlement or adjustment of disagreements, differences, etc. *n. 9.*

rec on dite (rek′ən dīt), 1. profound; hard to understand. 2. little known; obscure. *adj. 20.*

re con nais sance (ri kon′i səns), examination or survey, especially for military purposes. *n.*

rec on noi ter or **rec on noi tre** (rek′ə noi′tər), 1. approach and examine or observe in order to learn something; make a survey of (the enemy, the enemy's strength or position, a region, etc.), in order to gain information for military purposes. 2. approach a place and make a first survey of it. It seemed wise to reconnoiter before entering the town. *v. 16 for -ter, 17 for -tre.*

re con quer (rē kong′kər), conquer again. *v. 19.*

re con sid er (rē′kən sid′ər), consider again. The assembly voted to reconsider the bill. *v. 17.*

re con sti tute (rē kon′sti tūt or rē kon′sti-tüt), constitute anew; reconstruct. *v. 20.*

re con struct (rē′kən strukt′), construct again; make over. *v. 11.*

re con struc tion (rē′kən struk′shən), 1. building again or anew; making over. 2. thing made by reconstructing. 3. The **Reconstruction** was the process by which the Southern States were reorganized as parts of the United States after the Civil War. *n. 9.*

re cord (ri kôrd′ for 1 and 2, rek′ərd for 3-8), 1. set down in writing so as to keep for future use. Listen to the speaker and record what he says. 2. put in some permanent form; keep for remembrance. We record music on a phonograph; we record history in books. 3. the thing written or kept. 4. an official account. A secretary keeps a record of what is done at a meeting. **Off the record** means not to be recorded. 5. a disk or cylinder used on a phonograph. 6. the known facts about what a person, animal, ship, etc., has done. John has a fine record at school. 7. the best yet done; the best amount, rate, speed, etc., yet attained. Who holds the record for the high jump? **Break a record** means make a better record. 8. making or affording a record; as, a record wheat crop. *v., n., adj. 2.*

re cord er (ri kôr′dər), 1. person whose business is to make and keep records. 2. part of a machine that records. The recorder of a cash register adds up and prints the amount of sales made. 3. the title given to certain judges in some cities. *n. 13.*

re count[1] (ri kount′), tell; give an account of. He recounted the events of the day. *v. 6.*

re count[2] or **re-count** (rē kount′ for 1, rē′-kount′ for 2), 1. count again. 2. a second count. A recount of the votes was made. *v., n.*

re coup (ri küp′), 1. make up for. He recouped his losses. 2. repay. I will recoup you for any money you spend. *v.*

re course (ri kōrs′), 1. an appealing; a turning for help or protection. Our recourse in illness is to a doctor. **Have recourse to** means turn to for help. When we do not know what a word means, we have recourse to a dictionary. 2. person or thing resorted to for help or protection. A child's great recourse in trouble is its mother. *n. 9.*

re cov er (ri kuv′ər), 1. get back (something lost, taken away, or stolen); as, to recover one's temper or health, to recover a purse. 2. make up for (something lost or damaged); as, to recover lost time. 3. get well; get back to a normal condition. Amy is recovering from scarlet fever. 4. **Recover oneself** means get back to a proper position or condition. *v. 2.*

re-cov er (rē kuv′ər), put a new cover on. *v.*

re cov er y (ri kuv′ər i), 1. coming back to health or normal condition. We heard of your recovery from fever. 2. getting back something that was lost, taken away, or stolen. 3. getting back to a proper position or condition. He started to fall, but made a good recovery. *n., pl. recoveries. 8.*

rec re ant (rek′ri ənt), 1. cowardly. 2. coward. 3. unfaithful; false. 4. traitor. *adj., n. 11.*

rec re ate (rek′ri āt), 1. refresh with games, pastimes, exercises, etc. 2. take recreation. *v. 17.*

re-cre ate (rē′krē āt′), create anew. *v.*

rec re a tion (rek′ri ā′shən), play; amusement. Walking, gardening, and reading are quiet forms of recreation. *n. 7.*

re crim i na tion (ri krim′i nā′shən), accusing in return; counter accusation. The quarreling children indulged in many recriminations. *n. 16.*

re cross (rē krôs′), cross again. *v. 16.*

re cruit (ri krüt′), 1. a newly enlisted soldier or sailor. 2. get (men) to join an army or navy. 3. new member of any group or class. The Nature Club needs recruits. 4. get (people) to join. 5. increase the number of. 6. renew; get a sufficient number or amount of; replenish. Before sailing, we recruited our provisions. 7. renew health, strength, or spirits; refresh. *n., v. 7.*

rec tan gle (rek′tang′gəl), a four-sided figure with four right angles. *n. 5.*

rec tan gu lar (rek tang′gū lər), shaped like a rectangle. *adj. 8.*

Rectangles

rec ti fy (rek′ti fī), 1. make right; put right; adjust; remedy. The storekeeper admitted his mistake and was willing to rectify it. 2. purify or refine; as, to rectify a liquor by distilling it several times. 3. change (an alternating current) into a direct current. *v., rectified, rectifying. 10.*

rec ti tude (rek′ti tūd or rek′ti tüd), upright conduct; honesty; righteousness. *n. 12.*

rec tor (rek′tər), 1. clergyman in the Protestant Episcopal Church who has charge of a parish. 2. a priest in the Roman Catholic Church who has charge of a congregation or religious house. 3. the head of a school or university. *n. 9.*

rec tor y (rek′tər i), 1. a rector's house. 2. the church living with all its rights, tithes, and lands held by a rector. *n., pl. rectories. 14.*

rec tum (rek′təm), the lowest part of the large intestine. See the diagram under **intestine.** *n. 17.*

re cum bent (ri kum′bənt), lying down; reclining; leaning. *adj. 13.*

re cu per ate (ri kū′pər āt), restore to health, strength, etc.; be restored; recover. The men paused to recuperate their horses. It takes weeks to recuperate after a severe illness. *v. 18.*

re cu per a tion (ri kū′pər ā′shən), recovery from sickness, exhaustion, etc. *n. 20.*

re cur (ri kėr′), 1. come up again; occur again; be repeated. Leap year recurs every four years. 2. return in thought or speech. He recurred to the matter of cost. Old memories constantly recurred to him. *v., recurred, recurring. 9.*

re cur rence (ri kėr′əns), recurring; return; repetition. More care in the future will prevent recurrence of the mistake. *n. 14.*

re cur rent (ri kėr′ənt), 1. occurring again; repeated. 2. turned back so as to run in the opposite direction. *adj. 15.*

red (red), 1. the color of blood or of the lips. 2. having the color of blood or of the lips. 3. being like or suggesting the color of blood; as, red hair, a red cent, red fox, red clover. 4. violent; favoring revolution. The **Reds** are (1) Communists, anarchists, and extreme socialists. (2) the Russians. The **red flag** is a symbol of revolution. 5. **See red** means become very angry. *n., adj., redder, reddest. 1.*

red bird (red′bėrd′), 1. cardinal bird. 2. scarlet tanager. 3. European bullfinch. *n.*

red breast (red′brest′), robin. *n. 7.*

red coat (red′kōt′), a British soldier. *n.*

Red Cross, an international organization to care for the sick and wounded in war, and to relieve suffering caused by floods, fire, diseases, and other calamities. Its badge is a red cross on a white background.

red deer, 1. a deer native to the forests of Europe and Asia, and formerly very abundant in England. 2. the common American deer in its summer coat.

red den (red′ən), 1. make red. 2. become red. 3. blush. *v. 7.*

red dish (red′ish), somewhat red. *adj. 9.*

re deem (ri dēm′), 1. buy back. Property on which money has been lent is redeemed when the loan is paid back. 2. pay off. He redeemed the mortgage. 3. make up for; as, a redeeming feature. 4. fulfill; carry out; make good. We redeem a promise by doing what we said we would. 5. set free; rescue; save; as, redeemed from sin. *v. 4.*

re deem er (ri dēm′ər), person who redeems. **The Redeemer** means Jesus Christ, the Saviour of the world. *n. 11.*

re demp tion (ri demp′shən), 1. buying back; paying off. 2. ransom. 3. deliverance; rescue. 4. salvation. *n. 9.*

red-hand ed (red′han′did), 1. having hands red with blood. 2. in the very act of crime; as, a man caught red-handed. *adj.*

red-hot (red′hot′), 1. red with heat; very hot; as, red-hot iron. 2. very enthusiastic; excited; violent; as, a red-hot radical. *adj.*

re dis cov er (rē′dis kuv′ər), discover again or anew. *v. 20.*

red-let ter (red′let′ər), 1. marked by red letters. 2. memorable; especially happy. *adj.*

red ness (red′nis), quality of being red; red color. *n. 16.*

red o lent (red′ə lənt), 1. having a pleasant smell; fragrant. 2. smelling strongly; giving off an odor; as, a house redolent of fresh paint. 3. suggesting thoughts or feelings. Ivanhoe is a name redolent of romance. *adj. 20.*

re dou ble (rē dub′əl), 1. double again. 2. double; increase greatly. When he saw land ahead, the swimmer redoubled his speed. *v. 9.*

re doubt (ri dout′), small fort standing alone. *n. 13.*

re doubt a ble (ri dout′ə bəl), that should be feared or dreaded; as, a redoubtable warrior, a redoubtable debater. *adj. 15.*

re dound (ri dound′), come back as a result; contribute. The noble deeds of women redound to the glory of womanhood. *v. 15.*

red pepper, cayenne pepper.

re dress (ri dres′), 1. set right; repair; remedy. King Arthur tried to redress wrongs in his kingdom. 2. reparation; setting right. Any man deserves redress if he has been injured unfairly. *v., n. 6.*

Red Sea, a narrow sea between Arabia and Africa. It is part of the Indian Ocean and is connected with the Mediterranean Sea by the Suez Canal.

red skin (red′skin′), a North American Indian. *n.*

red start (red′stärt′), 1. a fly-catching warbler of America. 2. a small European bird with a reddish tail. *n.*

Redstart (def. 1) (about 5½ in. long)

red tape, too much attention to details and forms. There is much red tape in some school systems.

re duce (ri dūs′ or ri düs′), 1. decrease; make less; make smaller. We have reduced expenses this year. She is trying to reduce her weight. 2. bring down; lower. That poor woman is reduced to begging. She was reduced to tears by the cruel words. 3. change to another form. The chalk was reduced to powder. Reduce that statement to writing. If you reduce 3 lbs. 7 oz. to ounces, you have 55 ounces. 4. bring to a different condition; change. The teacher soon reduced the noisy class to order. 5. conquer. *v. 3.*

re duc i ble (ri dūs′i bəl or ri düs′i bəl), that can be reduced. *adj.*

re duc tion (ri duk′shən), 1. a reducing or being reduced. 2. change of form or condition. 3. amount by which a thing is reduced. The reduction in cost was $5. 4. copy of something on a smaller scale. *n. 5.*

re dun dance (ri dun′dəns), redundancy. *n.*

re dun dan cy (ri dun′dən si), 1. more than is needed. 2. the use of too many words for the same idea. 3. a redundant thing, part, or amount. *n., pl. redundancies. 17.*

re dun dant (ri dun′dənt), 1. extra; not needed. 2. that says the same thing again; using too many words for the same idea. "We two both had an apple each" is a redundant sentence. *adj. 11.*

re du pli cate (ri dū′pli kāt or ri dü′pli kāt), to double; repeat. *v.*

re du pli ca tion (ri dū′pli kā′shən or ri dü′-pli kā′shən), 1. doubling; repetition. 2. something resulting from repeating; duplicate; copy. To the prisoner each day seemed a reduplication of the preceding day. *n.*

red wing (red′wing′), 1. an American blackbird. The male has a scarlet patch on each wing. 2. a European thrush with reddish color on the under side of the wings. *n. 17.*

red wood (red′wu̇d′), 1. a California evergreen tree. Redwoods sometimes grow to a height of 300 feet. 2. the brownish-red wood of this tree. *n. 14.*

Redwood

re ëch o (rē ek′ō), 1. to echo back. The house reëchoes children's laughter. 2. an echo; an echo of an echo. *v., n., pl. reëchoes. 13.*

reed (rēd), 1. a kind of tall grass with a hollow stalk that grows in wet places. 2. anything made from the stalk of a reed, such as a pipe to blow on or an arrow. 3. thin piece of wood or metal in a musical instrument that produces sound when a current of air moves it. *n. 3.*

reed organ, musical instrument producing tones by small metal reeds.

reed y (rēd′i), 1. full of reeds; as, a reedy pond. 2. made of a reed or reeds. 3. like a reed or reeds; as, reedy grass. 4. sounding like a reed instrument; as, a thin, reedy voice. *adj. 11.*

reef[1] (rēf), a narrow ridge of rocks or sand at or near the surface of the water. The ship was wrecked on the hidden reef. *n. 7.*

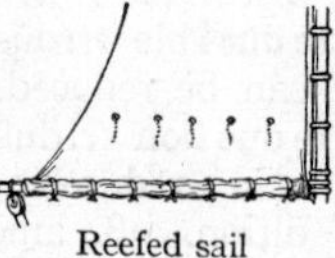

Reefed sail

reef[2] (rēf), 1. the part of a sail that is taken in or let out. 2. reduce the size of (a sail) by rolling or folding up a part of it. *n., v.*

reef er (rēf′ər), 1. one who reefs. 2. a short coat of thick cloth, worn especially by sailors and fishermen. *n. 20.*

reek (rēk), 1. vapor; unpleasant smell. We noticed the reek of cooking cabbage as we entered the hall. 2. send out vapor or an unpleasant smell. She reeked with cheap perfume. 3. be wet with sweat or blood. *n., v. 9.*

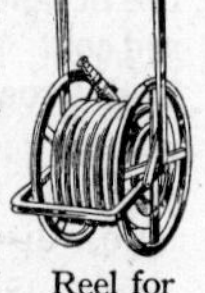

Reel for a hose

reel[1] (rēl), 1. a frame turning on an axis, for winding thread, yarn, a fish line, rope, wire, etc. 2. spool; roller. 3. something wound on a reel; as, two reels of moving-picture film. 4. to wind on a reel. 5. draw with a reel or by winding. He reels in a fish. 6. **Reel off** means say, write, or make in a quick, easy way. He can reel off stories by the hour. *n., v. 3.*

reel[2] (rēl), 1. be in a whirl; be dizzy. 2. sway, swing, or rock under a blow or shock. 3. sway in standing or walking. *v.*

reel[3] (rēl), 1. a lively dance. Two kinds are the Highland reel and the Virginia reel. 2. music for it. *n.*

re ë lect (rē′i lekt′), elect again. *v. 14.*

re ë lec tion (rē′i lek′shən), election again; election for a second time. *n. 13.*

re ëm bark (rē′em bärk′), embark again. *v. 18.*

re ën force (rē′en fōrs′), 1. strengthen with new force or materials; as, to reënforce an army or a fleet, to reënforce a garment with an extra thickness of cloth, to reënforce a wall or a bridge. 2. strengthen; as, to reenforce an argument, a plea, an effect, a supply, etc. *v. 20.* Also spelled **reinforce.**

re ën force ment (rē′en fōrs′mənt), 1. strengthening; being strengthened. 2. something that strengthens. **Reënforcements** means extra soldiers or warships. Reënforcements were sent to the battle front. *n.* Also spelled **reinforcement.**

re ën ter (rē en′tər), enter again; go in again. *v. 9.*

re ën try (rē en′tri), new entry; second entry. *n.*

re ës tab lish (rē′es tab′lish), establish again; restore. *v. 10.*

re ës tab lish ment (rē′es tab′lish mənt), an establishing again; restoration. *n.*

re fec tion (ri fek′shən), 1. refreshment by food or drink. 2. meal; repast. The hostess served a light refection to her guests. *n. 16.*

re fec to ry (ri fek′tə ri), a room for meals, especially in a monastery, convent, or school. *n., pl. refectories. 14.*

re fer (ri fėr′), 1. hand over; send or direct for information or help or action. Let's refer our disputes to Mother. Our teacher refers us to many good books. 2. turn for information or help. A person refers to a dictionary to find the meaning of words. 3. **Refer to** may mean (1) direct attention to or speak about. The preacher often referred to the Bible. (2) assign to or think of as caused by. Some people refer all their troubles to bad luck instead of to lack of ability. *v., referred, referring. 3.*

ref er ee (ref′ər ē′), 1. a judge of play in games and sports; as, the referee in a football game. 2. person to whom something is referred for decision or settlement. 3. to act as a referee. *n., v. 17.*

ref er ence (ref′ər əns), 1. direction of the attention. This history contains many references to larger histories. 2. statement referred to. You will find that reference on page 16. 3. use for information or help. A dictionary is a book of reference. 4. mention. Do not make any reference to his lameness. 5. person who can give information about another person's character or ability. Tom gave his principal as a reference. 6. a statement about someone's character or ability. The boy had excellent references from men for whom he had worked. 7. relation; respect; regard. This test is to be taken by all pupils without reference to age or grade. *n. 5.*

ref er en dum (ref′ər en′dəm), 1. submitting a bill already passed by the lawmaking body to the direct vote of the citizens for approval or rejection. 2. submitting any matter to a direct vote. *n., pl. referendums, referenda* (-də). *11.*

re fill (rē fil′ for 1, rē′fil for 2), 1. fill again. 2. something to refill a thing. *v., n. 17.*

re fine (ri fīn′), 1. make pure; become pure. Sugar, oil, and metals are refined before being used. 2. make or become fine, polished, or cultivated. Reading good books helps to refine one's speech. *v. 3.*

re fined (ri fīnd′), 1. freed from impurities; as, refined sugar. 2. free from coarseness, vulgarity, etc.; well-bred; as, refined tastes, refined manners, a refined voice. *adj.*

re fine ment (ri fīn′mənt), 1. fineness of feeling, taste, manners, or language. Good manners and correct speech are marks of refinement. 2. act or result of refining. *n. 7.*

re fin er y (ri fīn′ər i), a building and machinery for purifying metal, sugar, petroleum, or other things. *n., pl. refineries. 10.*

re fit (rē fit′), fit, prepare, or equip for use again; as, to refit a ship for a voyage. *v., refitted, refitting. 15.*

re flect (ri flekt′), 1. throw back (light, heat, sound, etc.). The sidewalks reflect heat on a hot day. 2. give back an image of. The mirror reflects my face. The stage reflects the customs of the time. 3. cast blame, reproach, or discredit. That child's bad behavior reflects on his home training. 4. think carefully. Take time to reflect on important things. *v. 4.*

re flec tion (ri flek′shən), 1. act of reflecting. 2. something reflected; image. See the reflection of the tree in this still water. 3. thinking; careful thinking. On reflection, the plan seemed too dangerous. 4. thought; idea. 5. expression of unfavorable opinion; blame. *n. 5.*

re flec tive (ri flek′tiv), 1. reflecting; as, the reflective surface of polished metal. 2. thoughtful. The judge had a reflective look. *adj. 17.*

re flec tor (ri flek′tər), 1. any thing, surface, or device that reflects light, heat, sound, etc.; especially, a piece of glass or metal, usually concave, for reflecting light in a required direction. 2. a telescope with a concave mirror. *n.*

re flex (rē′fleks), 1. not voluntary; not controlled by the will; coming as a direct response to a stimulation of some sensory nerve cells. Sneezing is a reflex act. 2. action in direct response to a stimulation of some nerve cells. Sneezing, vomiting, and shivering are reflexes. 3. something reflected; image; reflection. A law should be a reflex of the will of the people. 4. bent back; turned back. The reflex effect of anger is its effect on the person who gets angry. *adj., n. 9.*

re flex ive (ri flek′siv), 1. in grammar, meaning an action that turns back upon the subject. 2. a reflexive verb or pronoun. In "The boy hurt himself," *hurt* and *himself* are reflexives. *adj., n. 13.*

re flux (rē′fluks), flowing back; the ebb of a tide. *n. 15.*

re for est (rē for′ist), plant again with trees. *v.*

re for est a tion (rē'for is tā′shən), replanting with trees. *n.*

re form (ri fôrm′), 1. make better. Prisons should try to reform wrongdoers. 2. become better. The boy promised to reform if given another chance. 3. improvement. The new government made some needed reforms. *v., n. 4.*

re-form (rē fôrm′), form again; take a new shape. *v.*

ref or ma tion (ref'ər mā′shən), change for the better, improvement. *n. 8.*

Ref or ma tion (ref'ər mā′shən), the great religious movement in the 16th century that tried to reform the Roman Catholic Church and that led to the establishment of Protestant churches. *n.*

re form a to ry (ri fôr′mə tō'ri), 1. serving to reform; intended to reform. 2. an institution for reforming young offenders against the laws; a prison for young criminals. *adj., n., pl. reformatories. 17.*

re form er (ri fôr′mər), person who reforms, or tries to reform, some state of affairs, custom, etc.; supporter of reforms. *n. 11.*

re fract (ri frakt′), bend (a ray of light, etc.) from a straight course. Water refracts light. *v. 19.*

re frac tion (ri frak′shən), the turning or bending of a ray of light when it passes obliquely from one medium into another of different density. The ray of light *SP* in passing into the water is refracted from its original direction *SPL* to *SPR*. *n. 18.*

re frac to ry (ri frak′tə ri), 1. hard to manage; stubborn; disobedient. Mules are refractory. 2. not yielding readily to treatment. She had a very refractory cough. 3. hard to melt or work. Some ores are more refractory than others. *adj. 14.*

re frain[1] (ri frān′), hold back. Refrain from wrongdoing. *v. 5.*

re frain[2] (ri frān′), a phrase or verse repeated regularly in a song or poem. In "The Star-Spangled Banner" the refrain is "O'er the land of the free and the home of the brave." *n.*

re fresh (ri fresh′), 1. make fresh again; renew. His bath refreshed him. Cool drinks are refreshing on a warm day. She refreshed herself with a cup of tea. He refreshed his memory by a glance at the book. 2. become fresh again. *v. 5.*

re fresh ing (ri fresh′ing), 1. that refreshes. 2. welcome as a pleasing change. *adj.*

re fresh ment (ri fresh′mənt), 1. refreshing; being refreshed. 2. thing that refreshes. 3. food or drink. Cake and lemonade were the refreshments at our party. *n. 5.*

re frig er ate (ri frij′ər āt), make or keep cool or cold. *v. 19.*

re frig er a tion (ri frij'ər ā′shən), act or process of cooling or keeping cold. *n. 14.*

re frig er a tor (ri frij′ər ā'tər), something that keeps things cool. An electric refrigerator keeps things cool without ice. *n. 9.*

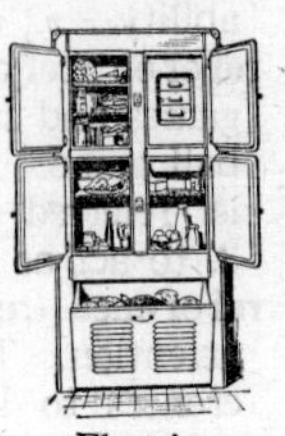
Electric refrigerator

reft (reft), stripped; robbed. The king reft the barons of their power. *v. 14.*

ref uge (ref′ūj), shelter; protection. The cat took refuge in a tree. *n. 3.*

ref u gee (ref'ū jē′), person who flees for refuge or safety. During the first World War, England cared for many Belgian refugees. *n. 9.*

re ful gent (ri ful′jənt), shining brightly; splendid; as, a refulgent sunrise. *adj. 14.*

re fund (ri fund′ for 1, rē′fund for 2), 1. pay back. If these shoes do not wear well, the shop will refund your money. 2. return of money paid. *v., n. 12.*

re fus al (ri fūz′əl), 1. act of refusing. His refusal to play the game provoked the other boys. 2. the right to refuse or take a thing before it is offered to others. Give me the refusal of the car till tomorrow. *n. 8.*

re fuse[1] (ri fūz′), 1. say "no." 2. say "no" to. He refuses the offer. She refused him when he begged her to marry him. 3. say one will not do it, give it, etc. He refuses to obey. *v. 2.*

ref use[2] (ref′ūs), useless stuff; waste; rubbish. The street-cleaning department takes away all refuse from the streets. *n.*

ref u ta tion (ref'ū tā′shən), disproof of a claim, opinion, or argument. *n. 17.*

re fute (ri fūt′), prove (a claim, opinion, or argument) to be false or incorrect. How would you refute the statement that the cow jumped over the moon? *v. 7.*

re gain (ri gān′), 1. get again; as, to regain health. 2. get back to; reach again. *v. 4.*

re gal (rē′gəl), 1. belonging to a king; royal. The regal power descends from father to son. 2. kinglike; fit for a king. It was a regal banquet. *adj. 5.*

re gale (ri gāl′), 1. entertain agreeably; delight with something pleasing. The old sailor regaled the boys with sea stories. 2. entertain with a choice repast; feast. The rabbits regaled themselves with the young lettuce. *v. 14.*

re ga li a (ri gā′li ə), 1. the emblems of royalty. Crowns and scepters are regalia. 2. the emblems or decorations of any society or order. *n. pl.*

re gard (ri gärd′), 1. look at; look closely at; watch. The cat regarded me anxiously when I picked up her kittens. 2. a look; a steady look. The man's regard seemed fixed upon some distant object. 3. consider; think of. He is regarded as the best doctor in town. 4. care for; respect. She always regards her parents' wishes. 5. consideration; thought; care. Have regard for the feelings of others. 6. esteem; favor; good opinion. The teacher has high regard for John's ability. 7. **Regards** means good wishes or an expression of esteem. He sends his regards. 8. to concern; relate to. As regards money, I have enough. 9. **In regard to** or **with regard to** means concerning or about. The teacher wishes to speak to you in regard to being late. *v., n. 2.*

re gard ful (ri gärd′fəl), heedful; observant; mindful. *adj.*

re gard ing (ri gär′ding), concerning; about. A letter regarding the boy's rudeness was sent to his father. *prep. 9.*

re gard less (ri gärd′lis), with no heed; careless. Regardless of grammar, he said, "Him and I have went." *adj., adv. 7.*

re gat ta (ri gat′ə), boat race; series of boat races; as, the annual regatta of the yacht club. *n.*

re gen cy (rē′jən si), 1. the position, office, or function of a regent. The Queen Mother held the regency till the young king became of age. 2. a body of regents; a government consisting of regents. 3. the time during which there is a regency. *n., pl. regencies. 14.*

re gen er ate (ri jen′ər āt for 1, 3, and 5, ri jen′ər it for 2 and 4), 1. give a new and better spiritual life to. Being converted sometimes regenerates a man. 2. born again spiritually. 3. improve the moral condition of; put new life and spirit in. 4. made over in better form; formed anew morally. 5. grow again; bring or come into new existence. If a crab loses a claw, it will often regenerate a new one. *v., adj. 13.*

re gen er a tion (ri jen′ər ā′shən), 1. regenerating; being regenerated. 2. spiritual rebirth; making over. 3. growing again. *n. 12.*

re gen er a tive (ri jen′ər ā′tiv), regenerating; tending to regenerate. *adj. 20.*

re gent (rē′jənt), 1. person who rules when the regular ruler is absent or unfit. The queen will be the regent till her son grows up. 2. member of a governing board. Mr. Lee is one of the regents of our State university. *n. 8.*

reg i cide (rej′i sīd), 1. person who kills a king. 2. the crime of killing a king. *n. 17.*

re gime or **ré gime** (rā zhēm′), 1. system of government or rule. Under the old regime women could not vote. 2. system of living. Baby's regime includes two naps a day. *n. 11.*

reg i men (rej′i men), a set of rules or habits of diet, exercise, or manner of living, intended to improve health, reduce weight, etc. *n. 13.*

reg i ment (rej′i mənt for 1 and 2, rej′i ment for 3), 1. several companies of soldiers organized into one large group, commanded by a colonel. 2. large number. 3. form into a regiment or organized group. *n., v. 6.*

reg i men tal (rej′i men′təl), of a regiment; pertaining to a regiment. **Regimentals** means a military uniform. *adj., n. 17.*

re gion (rē′jən), 1. space; place; part of the world; as, the region of the equator, an unhealthful region. 2. part of the body; as, the region of the heart. *n. 2.*

re gion al (rē′jən əl), of or in a particular region; as, a regional storm. *adj.*

reg is ter (rej′is tər), 1. a list; record. A register of attendance is kept in our school. 2. a book in which a list is kept. Look up Tom's record in the register. 3. write in a list. Register the names of the new pupils. 4. have one's name written in a list. You must register if you intend to vote. 5. thing that records. A cash register shows the amount of money taken in. 6. indicate; record. The thermometer registers 90 degrees. 7. have recorded in the post office. Register this letter. 8. show (surprise, joy, anger, etc.) by the expression on one's face or by actions. 9. the range of a voice or an instrument. 10. an opening with an arrangement to regulate the amount of air or heat that passes through. *n., v. 3.*

reg is trar (rej′is trär), an official who keeps a register; official recorder. *n. 20.*

reg is tra tion (rej′is trā′shən), 1. registering. 2. an entry in a register. 3. number of people registered. *n. 9.*

reg is try (rej′is tri), 1. registration. 2. a book in which a list is kept; register. 3. place where a register is kept. *n., pl. registries. 17.*

re gress (ri gres′), go backward. *v. 20.*

re gret (ri gret′), 1. the feeling of being sorry; sorrow; sense of loss. 2. feel sorry for; mourn. 3. **Regrets** sometimes means a polite reply declining an invitation. She could not come but sent regrets. *n., v., regretted, regretting. 3.*

re gret ful (ri gret′fəl), sorry; sorrowful; expressing regret. *adj. 19.*

re gret ta ble (ri gret′ə bəl), that should be regretted. *adj.*

reg u lar (reg′ū lər), 1. usual; fixed by custom or rule. Our regular sleeping place is in a bedroom. 2. coming again and again at the same time. Saturday is a regular holiday. 3. well-balanced; even in size, spacing, or speed; as, regular teeth, regular breathing. 4. following some rule or principle; according to rule. A period is the regular ending for a sentence. 5. orderly; methodical. He leads a regular life. 6. properly fitted or trained. 7. person belonging to a religious order bound by certain rules. 8. member of a regularly paid group of any kind. The army was made up of regulars and volunteers. *adj., n. 2.*

reg u lar i ty (reg′ū lar′i ti), order; system; steadiness; being regular. *n. 10.*

reg u lar ly (reg′ū lər li), 1. in a regular manner. 2. at regular times. *adv.*

reg u late (reg′ū lāt), 1. control by rule, principle, or system. Accidents happen even in the best regulated families. 2. keep at some standard. This instrument regulates the temperature of the room. *v. 5.*

reg u la tion (reg′ū lā′shən), 1. control by rule, principle, or system. 2. law; rule; as, traffic regulations. 3. regular; required by some regulation. Soldiers wear a regulation uniform. 4. usual; ordinary. *n., adj. 6.*

reg u la tor (reg′ū lā′tər), 1. person or thing that regulates. 2. a device in a clock or watch for causing it to go faster or slower. 3. a very accurate clock used as a standard of time. *n.*

re ha bil i tate (rē′hə bil′i tāt), 1. restore to a good condition; make over in a new form. The old house is to be rehabilitated. 2. restore to former standing, rank, rights, privileges, reputation, etc. The former criminal completely rehabilitated himself and was trusted and respected by all. *v. 19.*

re ha bil i ta tion (rē′hə bil′i tā′shən), restoration to former standing, rank, etc., or to good condition. *n. 17.*

re hash (rē hash′ for 1, rē′hash for 2), 1. deal with again; work up (old material) in a new form. The question had been rehashed again and again. 2. rehashing; something old put in a different form. This boy's composition is simply a rehash of an article in the encyclopedia. *v., n.*

re hears al (ri hėr′səl), rehearsing; performance beforehand for practice or drill. *n. 12.*

re hearse (ri hėrs′), 1. practice for a public performance. We rehearsed our parts for the school play. 2. repeat. The child rehearsed the happenings of the day to his father in the evening. *v. 6.*

Reich (rīk), Germany; German nation. *n.*

reign (rān), 1. act of ruling; royal power. 2. the period of power of a ruler. Queen Victoria's reign lasted sixty-four years. 3. to rule. A king reigns over his kingdom. 4. prevail. On a still night silence reigns. *n., v. 2.*

re im burse (rē′im bėrs′), pay back. You reimburse a person for expenses made for you. *v. 16.*

Reims (rēmz), city in northern France. *n.*

rein (rān), 1. a long, narrow strap or line fastened to a bridle, by which to guide and control an animal. A driver or rider of a horse holds the reins in his hands. See the diagram under **harness.** 2. a means of control and direction; as, taking the reins of government. 3. to guide and control. He reined his horse well. Rein your tongue. 4. **Give rein to** anything means leave it free to go without guiding. *n., v. 3.*

re in car nate (rē′in kär′nāt), give a new body to (a soul). *v.*

re in car na tion (rē′in kär nā′shən), rebirth of the soul in a new body. *n.*

rein deer (rān′dēr′), a kind of large deer, with branching horns, found in the north. Santa Claus's sleigh is drawn by reindeer. *n., pl. reindeer. 5.*

Reindeer (about 4½ ft. high at the shoulder)

re in force (rē′in fōrs′), 1. strengthen with new force or materials; as, to reinforce an army or a fleet, to reinforce a garment with an extra thickness of cloth, to reinforce a wall or a bridge. 2. strengthen; as, to reinforce an argument, a plea, an effect, a stock, a supply, etc. *v. 8.* Also spelled **reënforce.**

re in force ment (rē′in fōrs′mənt), 1. strengthening; being strengthened. 2. something that strengthens. **Reinforcements** means extra soldiers or warships. Reinforcements were sent to the battle front. *n. 12.* Also spelled **reënforcement.**

re in state (rē′in stāt′), put back in a former position or condition; establish again. *v. 15.*

re it er ate (rē it′ər āt), repeat again; say or do several times. The boy did not move though the teacher reiterated her command. *v. 8.*

re it er a tion (rē it′ər ā′shən), repetition; saying again. *n.*

re ject (ri jekt′), 1. refuse to take. He rejected our help. He tried to join the army but was rejected. 2. throw away. Reject all spotted apples. *v. 4.*

re jec tion (ri jek′shən), 1. rejecting. 2. being rejected. 3. thing rejected. *n. 13.*

re joice (ri jois′), 1. be glad. Mother rejoiced at our success. 2. make glad. *v. 2.*

re join (rē join′ for 1, ri join′ for 2), 1. join again; unite again. 2. answer; reply. *v. 11.*

re join der (ri join′dər), an answer to a reply; response. The debater's rejoinder was not convincing. *n.*

re ju ve nate (ri jü′vi nat), make young again; give youthful qualities to. The long rest and new clothes have rejuvenated Mrs. Brown. *v. 17.*

re kin dle (rē kin′dəl), set on fire again; kindle anew. *v. 15.*

re lapse (ri laps′), 1. fall or slip back into a former state or way of acting. After one cry of surprise she relapsed into silence. 2. falling or slipping back. He seemed to be getting over his illness but had a relapse. *v., n. 11.*

re late (ri lāt′), 1. tell; give an account of. The traveler related his adventures. 2. connect in thought or meaning. *Better* and *best* are related to *good.* 3. **Relate to** means have to do with. John's coming home early relates to the fact that all the cookies disappeared. 4. **Be related** sometimes means belong to the same family. Cousins are related. *v. 3.*

re la tion (ri lā′shən), 1. act of telling; account. We were interested by his relation of his adventures. 2. connection. The relation between master and servant has changed greatly during the last century. Our firm has business relations with his firm. Part of your answer has no relation to the question. The relation of mother and child is the closest in the world. 3. reference; regard. We must plan with relation to the future. 4. father, brother, aunt, nephew, cousin, etc. *n. 3.*

re la tion ship (ri lā′shən ship), connection. What is the relationship of clouds to rain? *n. 8.*

rel a tive (rel′ə tiv), 1. father, brother, aunt, nephew, cousin, etc. 2. having relation or connection with each other. Before ordering our dinner, we considered the relative merits of chicken and roast beef. 3. depending for meaning on a relation to something else. East is a relative term; for example, Chicago is east of California but west of New York. 4. referring to a person or thing mentioned; as, a relative pronoun. 5. a relative pronoun. *Who, which, what,* and *that* are relatives. 6. **Relative to** means (1) about; concerning. (2) in proportion to. *n., adj., adv. 3.*

rel a tive ly (rel′ə tiv li), 1. with respect to some relation or relationship. 2. comparatively. One inch is a relatively small difference in a man's height. 3. in proportion (to). *adv.*

re lax (ri laks′), 1. loosen up; become less stiff or firm. Relax your muscles to rest them. Relax when you dance. 2. make or become less strict or severe. Discipline is relaxed on the last day of school. 3. weaken. Don't relax your efforts because the examinations are over. *v. 7.*

re lax a tion (rē′lak sā′shən), 1. loosening; as, the relaxation of the muscles. 2. lessening of strictness, severity, force, etc.; as, the relaxation of discipline. 3. recreation; amusement. Walking and reading were the only relaxations permitted on Sunday. *n. 10.*

re lay[1] (rē′lā for 1, ri lā′ for 2), 1. a fresh supply. New relays of men were sent to the battle front. 2. take and carry farther. Messengers will relay your message. *n., v., relayed, relaying. 11.*

re lay[2] (rē lā′), lay again. That floor must be relaid. *v., relaid, relaying.*

re lease (ri lēs′), 1. let go. Release the catch and the box will open. 2. let loose; set free. She released him from his promise. 3. free; relieve. The nurse is released from duty at seven o'clock. 4. setting free. Lincoln proclaimed the release of the slaves. 5. freedom; relief. This medicine will give you a release from pain. *v., n. 3.*

rel e gate (rel′i gāt), 1. send away, usually to a lower position or condition; as, to relegate a dress to the rag bag. 2. send into exile; banish. 3. hand over (a matter, task, etc.). *v.*

re lent (ri lent′), become less harsh; be more tender and merciful. After hours of cruel treatment of the prisoners, the soldiers relented. *v. 7.*

re lent less (ri lent′lis), unyielding; harsh; without pity. The storm raged with relentless fury. *adj. 11.*

rel e vance (rel′i vəns), relevancy. *n.*

rel e van cy (rel′i vən si), bearing upon or having connection with the matter in hand; being to the point. *n. 18.*

rel e vant (rel′i vənt), bearing upon or connected with the matter in hand; to the point; as, relevant questions. *adj. 17.*

re li a bil i ty (ri lī′ə bil′i ti), quality of being reliable; trustworthiness; dependability. A machine has reliability when it can be counted on always to do what is expected of it. *n. 12.*

re li a ble (ri lī′ə bəl), worthy of trust; that can be depended on. Send Joe to the bank for the money; he is a reliable boy. *adj. 6.*

re li ance (ri lī′əns), 1. trust; dependence. A child has reliance on his mother. 2. confidence. 3. thing on which one depends. *n. 10.*

re li ant (ri lī′ənt), 1. trusting; depending. 2. confident. 3. relying on oneself. *adj.*

rel ic (rel′ik), 1. thing or piece left from the past. This ruined bridge is a relic that reminds us of the war. 2. something belonging to a holy person, kept as a sacred memorial. *n. 5.*

re lief (ri lēf′), 1. the lessening of, or freeing from, a pain, burden, difficulty, etc. 2. aid; help; something that lessens or frees from pain, burden, difficulty, etc. Relief was quickly sent to the sufferers from the great fire. 3. **On relief** sometimes means receiving a dole from public funds. 4. freedom from a post of duty. This nurse is on duty from seven in the morning until seven at night, with only two hours' relief. 5. change of persons on duty. 6. persons who relieve others from duty. 7. projection of figures and designs from a surface in sculpture, etc. 8. design standing out from the surface from which it is cut, shaped, or stamped. *n. 3.*

Relief (def. 7)

re lieve (ri lēv′), 1. make less; make easier; reduce the pain or trouble of. What will relieve a headache? We telephoned to relieve our mother's uneasiness. 2. set free. Your coming relieves me of the bother of writing a long letter. 3. free (a person on duty) by taking his place. 4. bring aid to; help. Soldiers were sent to relieve the fort. 5. give variety to. The black dress was relieved by red trimming. *v. 3.*

re li gion (ri lij′ən), 1. belief in God or gods. 2. worship of God or gods. *n. 3.*

re li gious (ri lij′əs), 1. of religion; connected with religion; as, religious meetings, religious books, religious differences. 2. much interested in religion; devoted to the worship of God or gods. She is very religious and goes to church every day. 3. strict; done with care. 4. monk or nun; member of a religious order. *adj., n. 3.*

re lin quish (ri ling′kwish), give up; let go. The small dog relinquished his bone to the big dog. She has relinquished all hope of going to Europe this year. *v. 9.*

rel ique (rel′ik), an old way of spelling relic. *n. 20.*

rel ish (rel′ish), 1. pleasant taste; good flavor. Hunger gives relish to simple food. 2. something to add flavor to food. Olives and pickles are relishes. 3. liking; appetite. The hungry boy ate with a great relish. The teacher has no relish for John's jokes. 4. like the taste of; like. A cat relishes cream. Dick did not relish the prospect of staying after school. *n., v. 6.*

re load (rē lōd′), load again. *v. 17.*

re luc tance (ri luk′təns), unwillingness; slowness in action because of unwillingness. She agreed with reluctance to take part in the game. *n. 11.*

re luc tant (ri luk′tənt), unwilling; slow to act because unwilling. The policeman led the reluctant boy to the principal. I am reluctant to see the summer end. *adj. 7.*

re ly (ri lī′), depend; trust. Rely on your own efforts. I rely upon your word absolutely. *v., relied, relying. 6.*

re main (ri mān′), 1. stay. We shall remain at the seashore till October. 2. continue; last; keep on. The town remains the same year after year. 3. be left. A few apples remain on the tree. If you take 2 from 5, 3 remains. *v. 1.*

re main der (ri mān′dər), the part left over; the rest. If you take 2 from 9, the remainder is 7. After studying an hour, Alice spent the remainder of the afternoon in play. *n. 3.*

re mains (ri mānz′), 1. what is left. The remains of the meal were fed to the dog. 2. dead body. Washington's remains are buried at Mount Vernon. *n. pl.*

re make (rē māk′), make anew; make over. *v., remade, remaking.*

re mand (ri mand′), 1. send back. 2. send back (a prisoner or an accused person) to prison. 3. remanding. *v., n. 18.*

re mark (ri märk′), 1. say; speak; comment. Mother remarked that Bill's hands would be better for a wash. 2. something said in a few words; short statement. The president made a few remarks. 3. to notice; observe. Did you remark that queer cloud? *v., n. 3.*

re mark a ble (ri mär′kə bəl), worthy of notice; unusual. He has a remarkable memory. *adj. 3.*

re mark a bly (ri mär′kə bli), notably; unusually. *adv.*

re mar ry (rē mar′i), marry again. *v., remarried, remarrying. 20.*

Rem brandt (rem′brant), a Dutch painter and etcher (1606-1669). *n.*

re me di al (ri mē′di əl), remedying; curing; helping; relieving. *adj. 17.*

rem e dy (rem′i di), 1. a cure; a means of removing or relieving diseases or any bad condition. 2. to cure; put right; make right. *n., pl. remedies, v., remedied, remedying. 3.*

re mem ber (ri mem′bər), 1. call back to mind. I can't remember that man's name. 2. keep in mind; take care not to forget. Remember me when I am gone. 3. have (something) return to the mind. 4. keep in mind as deserving a reward, gift, etc. My dead uncle remembered me in his will. 5. mention as sending greetings. Ruth asked to be remembered to Ann's sister. *v. 1.*

re mem brance (ri mem′brəns), 1. memory; act of remembering. It comes to my remembrance. 2. keepsake; any thing or action that makes one remember a person. 3. **Remembrances** means greetings. Give my remembrances to your sister when you write to her. *n. 4.*

re mind (ri mīnd′), make (one) think or remember. This picture reminds me of a story I heard. *v. 4.*

re mind er (ri mīn′dər), something to help one remember. *n. 11.*

rem i nis cence (rem′i nis′əns), 1. remembering; recalling past happenings, etc. 2. recollection; an account of something remembered; as, an old man's reminiscences, reminiscences of the war. *n. 13.*

rem i nis cent (rem′i nis′ənt), 1. recalling past events, etc.; as, reminiscent talk. 2. awakening memories of something else; suggestive; as, a manner reminiscent of a statelier age. *adj. 18.*

re miss (ri mis′), careless; slack; neglectful; negligent. A policeman who lets a thief escape is remiss in his duties. *adj. 15.*

re mis sion (ri mish′ən), 1. pardon; forgiveness. Remission of sins is promised to those who repent. 2. letting off (from debt, punishment, etc.). A bankrupt seeks remission of his debts. 3. lessening (of pain, force, labor, etc.). The slave rejoiced at any remission of his work. *n. 10.*

re miss ness (ri mis′nis), carelessness; slackness; negligence. *n. 18.*

re mit (ri mit′), 1. send money to a person or place. Enclosed is our bill; please remit. 2. refrain from carrying out. The king remitted the prisoner's punishment. 3. pardon; forgive. Christ gave His disciples power to remit sins. 4. decrease; make less. After we had rowed the boat into calm water, we remitted our efforts. *v., remitted, remitting. 5.*

re mit tance (ri mit′əns), 1. sending money to someone at a distance. 2. the money that is sent. *n. 9.*

rem nant (rem′nənt), small part left. She bought a remnant of silk at a bargain. This town has only a remnant of its former population. *n. 4.*

re mod el (rē mod′əl), 1. model again. 2. make over. The old barn was remodeled into a house. *v., remodeled, remodeling. 8.*

re mon strance (ri mon′strəns), protest; complaint. *n. 10.*

re mon strate (ri mon′strāt), object; protest. The teacher remonstrated with the boy about the poor quality of his work. *v. 11.*

re morse (ri môrs′), deep, painful regret for having done wrong. The thief felt remorse for his crime and confessed. *n. 6.*

re morse ful (ri môrs′fəl), feeling remorse. *adj. 18.*

re morse less (ri môrs′lis), 1. without remorse. 2. pitiless; cruel. *adj. 12.*

re mote (ri mōt′), 1. far away; far off. The North Pole is a remote part of the world. Those queer animals, the dinosaurs, lived in remote ages. This remote village is so out of the way that mail comes only once a week. 2. distant. He is a remote relative. 3. slight. I haven't the remotest idea what you mean. *adj. 4.*

re mote ly (ri mōt′li), in a remote manner; distantly; slightly. *adv.*

re mount (rē mount′), 1. mount again. The fallen rider remounts his horse. The troops remounted the hill. 2. furnish with fresh horses. 3. a fresh horse, or a supply of fresh horses, for use. *v., n. 19.*

re mov al (ri müv′əl), 1. taking away. After the removal of the soup, fish was served. 2. change of place. The store announces its removal to larger quarters. 3. dismissal from an office or position. *n. 8.*

re move (ri müv′), 1. move from a place or position; take off; take away. People remove their hats in a theater. The governor removed the mayor for failing to do his duty. 2. get rid of; put an end to. 3. go away; move away. 4. moving away. 5. step or degree of distance. At every remove the mountain seemed smaller. *v., n. 2.*

re mov er (ri müv′ər), person or thing that removes. I want a bottle of ink remover. *n. 12.*

re mu ner ate (ri mū′nər āt), reward; pay for work, services, trouble, etc. The boy who returned the lost jewels was remunerated. The harvest will remunerate the laborers for their toil. *v.*

re mu ner a tion (ri mū′nər ā′shən), reward; pay. *n. 13.*

re mu ner a tive (ri mū′nər ā′tiv), paying; profitable. *adj. 17.*

Re mus (rē′məs), 1. the twin brother of Romulus. 2. **Uncle Remus** is a character who relates Negro folklore. *n.*

Ren ais sance (ren′ə säns′), 1. the great revival of art and learning in Europe during the 14th, 15th, and 16th centuries. 2. the period of time when this revival occurred. 3. the style of art, architecture, etc., of this period. 4. of or pertaining to the Renaissance; as, Renaissance sculpture. 5. Any similar revival or new birth may be called a **renaissance.** *n., adj. 11.*

re name (rē nām′), give a new name to; name again. *v. 14.*

re nas cence (ri nas′əns), 1. revival; new birth; renewal; as, a renascence of religion. 2. the Renaissance. *n.*

ren coun ter (ren koun′tər), 1. hostile meeting; conflict; battle; duel. 2. chance meeting. *n.*

rend (rend), 1. tear; pull apart violently; split. Wolves will rend a lamb in pieces. 2. split. Lightning rent the tree. 3. disturb violently. John was rent by a wish to keep the money he found and the knowledge that he ought to return it. *v., rent, rending. 4.*

ren der (ren′dər), 1. cause to become; make. An accident has rendered him helpless. 2. give; do. Can I render any aid? What service has he rendered to the school? 3. hand in; report. The committee rendered an account of all the money spent. 4. give in return. Render thanks for your blessings. 5. pay as due. The conquered rendered tribute to the conqueror. 6. represent; bring out the meaning of. The actor rendered the part of Hamlet well. 7. play or sing (music). 8. change from one language to another. Render that Latin proverb in English. 9. give up. 10. melt (fat, etc.); get or make clear by melting. Fat from hogs is rendered for lard. *v. 2.*

ren dez vous (rän′də vü), 1. an appointment or engagement to meet at a fixed place or time; meeting by agreement. 2. meeting place; gathering place. The family had two favorite rendezvous, the library and the garden. 3. place agreed on for a meeting at a certain time, especially of troops or ships. 4. meet at a rendezvous. *n., pl. rendezvous* (-vüz), *v. 11.*

ren di tion (ren dish′ən), the rendering of a dramatic part, music, etc., so as to bring out the meaning; translation. *n.*

ren e gade (ren′i gād), 1. deserter from a religious faith, a political party, etc.; traitor. 2. deserting; disloyal; like a traitor. *n., adj. 16.*

re new (ri nū′ or ri nü′), 1. make new again; make like new; restore. 2. begin again. He renewed his efforts to open the window. 3. replace by new material or a new thing of the same sort; fill again. She renewed the sleeves of her dress. The well renews itself no matter how much water is taken away. 4. give or get for a new period. We renewed the lease for another year. *v. 3.*

re new al (ri nū′əl or ri nü′əl), renewing; being renewed. Next summer there will be a renewal of swimming. *n. 9.*

Re no (rē′nō), city in southwestern Nevada. *n.*

re nounce (ri nouns′), 1. give up; give up entirely; declare that one gives up. He renounces his claim to the money. 2. cast off; refuse to recognize as one's own. He renounced his wicked son. *v. 5.*

ren o vate (ren′ō vāt), make new again; make like new; restore to good condition; as, to renovate a garment or a house. *v. 13.*

ren o va tion (ren′ō vā′shən), restoration to good condition; renewal. *n. 17.*

re nown (ri noun′), fame. A hero in war wins renown. *n. 3.*

re nowned (ri nound′), famous. *adj.*

rent[1] (rent), 1. a regular payment for the use of property. 2. to pay for the use of (property). We rent a house from Mr. Smith. 3. take pay for the use of (property). He rents several other houses. 4. be rented. This farm rents for $500 a year. *n., v. 2.*

rent[2] (rent), 1. a tear; a torn place; a split. 2. See **rend.** The tree was rent by the wind. *n., pt. and pp. of rend.*

rent al (ren′təl), amount received or paid as rent. *n. 15.*

rent er (ren′tər), person who pays rent for using another's things. A renter of a piano pays money to the owner. *n. 13.*

re nun ci a tion (ri nun′si ā′shən), renouncing; giving up a right, title, possession, etc. *n. 15.*

re o pen (rē ō′pən), open again. School will reopen in September. *v. 10.*

re or gan i za tion (rē′ôr gən i zā′shən), reorganizing; being reorganized. *n. 14.*

re or gan ize (rē ôr′gən īz), organize anew; form again; arrange in a new way. Classes will be reorganized after the first four weeks. *v. 11.*

re paid (ri pād′). See **repay.** He repaid the money he had borrowed. All debts should be repaid. *pt. and pp. of repay. 11.*

re pair[1] (ri pãr′), 1. mend; put in good condition again. He repairs shoes. 2. act or work of repairing. Repairs on the school building are made during the summer. 3. condition fit to be used. The State keeps the roads in repair. 4. condition for use. They used to be in very bad repair. 5. make up for. How can I repair the harm done? *v., n. 2.*

re pair[2] (ri pãr′), go (to a place). After dinner we repaired to the porch. *v.*

re pair a ble (ri pãr′ə bəl), that can be repaired. *adj.*

re pair er (ri pãr′ər), person who mends or repairs. I sent the broken chair to an excellent repairer. *n. 11.*

rep a ra ble (rep′ə rə bəl), that can be repaired or remedied. *adj.*

rep a ra tion (rep′ə rā′shən), 1. repairing or being repaired; restoration to good condition. 2. giving satisfaction or compensation for wrong or injury done. 3. compensation for wrong or injury. *n. 13.*

rep ar tee (rep′är tē′), 1. witty reply or replies. 2. making witty replies or retorts. 3. wit and skill shown in replies. *n. 15.*

re pass (rē pas′), 1. pass back. 2. pass again. *v. 13.*

re past (ri past′), meal; food. Breakfast at our house is a light repast. *n. 8.*

re pay (ri pā′), 1. pay back. He repaid the money he had borrowed. 2. make return for. No thanks can repay such kindness. 3. make return to. The boy's success repaid the teacher for her efforts. *v., repaid, repaying. 4.*

re pay ment (ri pā′mənt), payment in return for something. *n.*

re peal (ri pēl′), 1. take back; withdraw; do away with. The Stamp Act was finally repealed. 2. act of repealing; withdrawal; abolition. He voted for the repeal of that law. *v., n. 7.*

re peat (ri pēt′), 1. do again. 2. say again. 3. say over; recite. Mary can repeat many poems from memory. *v., n. 2.*

re peat ed (ri pēt′id), said, done, or made more than once. Her repeated efforts at last won success. *adj.*

re peat ed ly (ri pēt′id li), again and again; more than once. *adv. 12.*

re pel (ri pel′), 1. force back; drive back; drive away. They repelled the enemy. We can repel bad thoughts. 2. be displeasing to; cause dislike in. Spiders and worms repel me. *v., repelled, repelling. 7.*

re pel lent (ri pel′ənt), 1. unattractive; disagreeable. Mr. Stern has a cold, repellent manner. Cheating is repellent to an honest boy. 2. repelling; driving back. *adj. 20.*

re pent (ri pent′), 1. feel sorry for sin and seek forgiveness. He had done wrong, but repented. 2. feel sorry for; regret. She bought the red hat and has repented her choice. *v. 3.*

re pent ance (ri pen′təns), sorrow for wrongdoing; regret. *n. 6.*

re pent ant (ri pen′tənt), repenting; feeling repentance or regret; sorry for wrongdoing. *adj. 10.*

re per cus sion (rē′pər kush′ən), 1. rebound; springing back; recoil; as, the repercussion of a cannon. 2. a sound flung back; echo. *n.*

rep er toire (rep′ər twär), the list of plays, operas, parts, pieces, etc., which a company, an actor, or a singer is prepared to perform. *n. 18.*

rep er to ry (rep′ər tō′ri), 1. catalogue or list of things; repertoire. 2. a store or stock of things ready for use. *n., pl. repertories.*

rep e ti tion (rep′i tish′ən), 1. repeating; doing again; saying again. Repetition helps learning. Any repetition of the offense will be punished. 2. repeated occurrence; thing repeated. *n. 7.*

rep e ti tious (rep′i tish′əs), full of repetitions; repeating in a tiresome way. *adj.*

re pine (ri pīn′), be discontented; fret; complain. It does no good to repine at one's lot. *v. 7.*

re place (ri plās′), 1. fill or take the place of. Tom replaced Will as captain. 2. get another in place of. I will replace the cup I broke. 3. put back; put in place again. Replace the books on the shelves. *v. 5.*

re place ment (ri plās′mənt), 1. replacing; being replaced. The law required the replacement of all wooden cars by steel cars. 2. something that replaces. *n. 15.*

re plant (rē plant′), plant again. *v. 20.*

re plen ish (ri plen′ish), fill again; provide a new supply for. Her wardrobe needs replenishing. You had better replenish the fire. *v. 7.*

re plete (ri plēt′), filled; abundantly supplied. *adj. 11.*

re ple tion (ri plē′shən), fullness; excessive fullness. *n.*

rep li ca (rep′li kə), copy; reproduction. The artist made a replica of his picture. *n. 19.*

re ply (ri plī′), answer. *v., replied, replying, n., pl. replies. 1.*

re port (ri pōrt′), 1. an account of something seen, heard, or read about. 2. anything formally expressed, generally in writing; as, a school report. 3. give or bring an account of; make a report of; state formally. Our treasurer reports that all dues are paid up. 4. describe; tell. 5. present oneself. Report for work at eight o'clock. 6. the sound of an explosion; as, the report of a gun. 7. rumor; common talk. Report has it that the Smiths are leaving town. 8. reputation. *n., v. 1.*

re port er (ri pōr′tər), 1. person who reports. 2. person who gathers news for a newspaper. *n. 9.*

re pose[1] (ri pōz′), 1. rest; sleep. Do not disturb her repose. 2. lie at rest. The cat reposed upon the cushion. 3. lay to rest. Repose yourself in the hammock. 4. quietness; ease. She has repose of manner. *n., v. 3.*

re pose[2] (ri pōz′), put; place. We repose entire confidence in his honesty. *v.*

re pos i to ry (ri poz′i tō′ri), a place or container where things are stored or kept. The box was a repository for old magazines. A library is a repository of information. *n., pl. repositories. 15.*

re pos sess (rē′pə zes′), possess again; get possession of again. *v. 19.*

rep re hend (rep′ri hend′), reprove; rebuke; blame. *v. 14.*

rep re hen si ble (rep′ri hen′si bəl), deserving reproof, rebuke, or blame. *adj. 16.*

rep re sent (rep′ri zent′), 1. stand for; be a sign of. The stars in our flag represent the States. A policeman represents the power of the law. 2. act in place of; speak and act for. We chose a committee to represent us. 3. act the part of. Each child will represent an animal at the party. 4. describe; show. He represented the plan as safe, but it was not. 5. bring before the mind; make one think of. Images in the mind represent real objects. *v. 2.*

rep re sen ta tion (rep′ri zen tā′shən), 1. act of representing. 2. condition or fact of being represented. "Taxation without representation is tyranny." 3. picture, model, play, etc.; presentation. A representation of the story of Rip Van Winkle will be given in the school assembly today. 4. account; statement. *n. 5.*

rep re sent a tive (rep′ri zen′tə tiv), 1. person appointed to act or speak for others. Who is your Representative in Congress? 2. having its citizens represented by chosen persons; as, a representative government. 3. representing. Images representative of animals were made by the children. 4. example; type. The tiger is a common representative of the cat family. 5. enough like all those of its kind to stand for all the rest. Balls, blocks, and trains are representative toys. *n., adj. 3.*

re press (ri pres′), 1. prevent from acting; check. She repressed an impulse to cough. 2. keep down; put down. The government repressed a revolt. *v. 9.*

re pres sion (ri presh′ən), 1. repressing. 2. being repressed. *n. 10.*

re pres sive (ri pres′iv), tending to repress; having power to repress. *adj.*

re prieve (ri prēv′), 1. delay the execution of (a person condemned to death). At the last moment the prisoner was reprieved for three weeks. 2. a delay in carrying out a punishment, especially of the death penalty. 3. the order giving authority for such delay. 4. temporary relief from any evil or trouble. 5. give such relief to. *v., n. 11.*

rep ri mand (rep′ri mand), 1. a severe or formal reproof. 2. reprove severely or formally. The principal reprimanded the boys for smoking. *n., v. 11.*

re print (rē print′ for 1, rē′print′ for 2), 1. print again; print a new impression of. 2. a second print; a new impression of printed work. *v., n. 16.*

re pris al (ri prīz′əl), injury done in return for injury, especially by one nation to another. *n. 14.*

re proach (ri prōch′), 1. blame. Bad people bring reproach on their families. Father reproached me for being late. 2. a cause of blame or disgrace. A coward is a reproach to an army. *v., n. 3.*

re proach ful (ri prōch′fəl), full of reproach; expressing reproach. *adj. 11.*

rep ro bate (rep′rō bāt), 1. very wicked person. 2. very wicked. 3. disapprove; condemn; censure. *n., adj., v. 11.*

rep ro ba tion (rep′rō bā′shən), disapproval; condemnation; censure. *n. 14.*

re pro duce (rē′prə dūs′ or rē′prə düs′), 1. produce again. A radio reproduces sounds. 2. make a copy of. A camera will reproduce a picture. 3. produce offspring. Most plants reproduce by seeds. *v. 7.*

re pro duc tion (rē′prə duk′shən), 1. reproducing; being reproduced. 2. copy. 3. the production of offspring. *n. 7.*

re pro duc tive (rē′prə duk′tiv), 1. that reproduces. 2. concerned with reproduction. *adj. 13.*

re proof (ri prüf′), blame; words of blame or disapproval. *n. 6.*

re prov al (ri prüv′əl), reproving; reproof. *n.*

re prove (ri prüv′), find fault with; blame; disapprove. Reprove the boy for teasing the cat. *v. 6.*

rep tile (rep′til), 1. a cold-blooded animal that creeps or crawls. Snakes, lizards, turtles, alligators, and crocodiles are reptiles. 2. crawling; creeping. 3. a low, mean person. What reptile tripped up the blind boy? *n., adj. 8.*

re pub lic (ri pub′lik), nation or state in which the citizens elect representatives to manage the government. *n. 3.*

re pub li can (ri pub′li kən), 1. of a republic; like that of a republic. Many countries have a republican form of government. 2. person who favors a republic. The republicans fought with the royalists. 3. The **Republican Party** is one of the two main political parties in the United States. 4. Its members are called **Republicans.** 5. of the Republican Party. *adj., n. 4.*

re pu di ate (ri pū′di āt), 1. cast off; disown; as, to repudiate a son. 2. refuse to accept; reject; as, to repudiate a doctrine. 3. refuse to acknowledge or pay; as, to repudiate a debt. *v. 13.*

re pu di a tion (ri pū′di ā′shən), 1. a casting off. 2. a being cast off. 3. refusal to accept; rejection. 4. refusal to acknowledge. *n. 19.*

re pug nance (ri pug′nəns), strong dislike, distaste, or aversion. Some people feel a strong repugnance for snakes. *n. 12.*

re pug nant (ri pug′nənt), 1. distasteful; disagreeable; offensive. Work is repugnant to some people. 2. objecting; averse; opposed. We are repugnant to every sort of dishonesty. *adj. 12.*

re pulse (ri puls′), 1. drive back; repel. Our soldiers repulsed the enemy. 2. driving back; being driven back. After the second repulse, the enemy surrendered. 3. refuse to accept; reject. She coldly repulsed him. 4. refusal; rejection. *v., n. 8.*

re pul sion (ri pul′shən), 1. strong dislike or aversion. 2. repulse; repelling or being repelled. *n. 19.*

re pul sive (ri pul′siv), 1. causing strong dislike or aversion; as, a repulsive snake. 2. tending to drive back or repel. *adj. 15.*

rep u ta ble (rep′ū tə bəl), having a good reputation; well thought of; in good repute. *adj. 10.*

rep u ta tion (rep′ū tā′shən), 1. what people think and say the character of a person or thing is; character in the opinion of others. This store has an excellent reputation for fair dealing. 2. good name; good reputation. 3. fame. *n. 4.*

re pute (ri pūt′), 1. reputation. This is a district of bad repute on account of many robberies. 2. consider; suppose; suppose to be. He is reputed the richest man in the State. *n., v. 6.*

re put ed (ri pūt′id), supposed. *adj.*

re quest (ri kwest′), 1. ask for; ask; ask as a favor. He requested a loan from the bank. 2. act of asking. Your request for a ticket was made too late. 3. what is asked for. The king granted his request. 4. state of being desired or sought after. She is such a good dancer that she is in great request. *v., n. 2.*

Re qui em or **re qui em** (rē′kwi em), 1. Mass for the dead; musical church service for the dead. 2. music for it. *n. 12.*

re quire (ri kwīr′), 1. need. We shall require more spoons at our party. 2. demand; order; command. The rules require us all to be present. *v. 1.*

re quire ment (ri kwīr′mənt), 1. a need; thing needed. Patience is a requirement in teaching. 2. a demand; thing demanded; as, requirements for graduation. *n. 7.*

req ui site (rek′wi zit), 1. required by circumstances; needed; necessary; as, the qualities requisite for a leader, the number of votes requisite for election. 2. requirement; thing needed. Food and air are requisites for life. *adj., n. 7.*

req ui si tion (rek′wi zish′ən), 1. act of requiring. 2. a demand made, especially a formal written demand; as, the requisition of supplies for troops. 3. demand or take by authority; as, to requisition supplies, horses, or labor. 4. make demands upon. The army requisitioned the village for food. 5. state of being required for use or called into service. The car was in constant requisition for errands. *n., v. 14.*

re quit al (ri kwīt′əl), repayment; payment; return. What requital can we make for all his kindness to us? *n. 15.*

re quite (ri kwīt′), 1. pay back; make return for. The Bible says to requite evil with good. 2. make return to. The knight requited the boy for his warning. *v. 7.*

re scind (ri sind′), deprive of force; repeal; cancel; as, to rescind a law or a treaty. *v. 16.*

res cue (res′kū), 1. save from danger or harm; free; deliver. The dog rescued the child from drowning. 2. saving or freeing from harm or danger. The fireman was praised for his brave rescue of the children in the burning house. A dog was chasing our cat when Mary came to the rescue. *v., n. 3.*

res cu er (res′kū ər), one that rescues. *n. 17.*

re search (ri sėrch′), a careful hunting for facts or truth; inquiry; investigation. The researches of men of science have done much to lessen disease. *n. 9.*

re sem blance (ri zem′bləns), likeness; similar appearance. Twins often show great resemblance. *n. 8.*

re sem ble (ri zem′bəl), be like. An orange resembles a grapefruit. *v. 4.*

re sent (ri zent′), feel injured and angry at; feel indignation at. Grace resented being called a baby. Our cat resents having anyone sit in its chair. *v. 7.*

re sent ful (ri zent′fəl), feeling resentment; injured and angry; showing resentment. *adj. 17.*

re sent ment (ri zent′mənt), the feeling that one has at being injured or insulted; indignation. Everyone feels resentment at being treated unfairly. *n. 8.*

res er va tion (rez′ər vā′shən), 1. keeping back; hiding in part; something not expressed. She outwardly approved of the plan with the mental reservation of changing things to suit herself. 2. limiting condition. The United States accepted the plan with reservations plainly stated. 3. land set aside for a special purpose. The government has set apart Indian reservations. 4. arrangement to keep a thing for a person; the securing of accommodations, etc. We make reservations of rooms at a hotel, seats in a parlor car, and passage on a steamship. *n. 7.*

re serve (ri zėrv′), 1. keep back; hold back; set apart; save for use later. Reserve enough money for your fare home. 2. something kept back for future use; store. Banks must keep a reserve of money. Reserves will be sent to help the men fighting at the front. 3. public land set apart for a special purpose; as, a forest reserve. 4. keeping back; holding back; setting apart. You may speak before her without reserve. 5. self-restraint in action or speech.

6. a silent manner that keeps people from making friends easily. *v., n. 3.*

re served (ri zėrvd′), 1. kept in reserve. 2. set apart. 3. self-restrained in action or speech. 4. disposed to keep to one's self. A reserved boy does not make friends easily. *adj.*

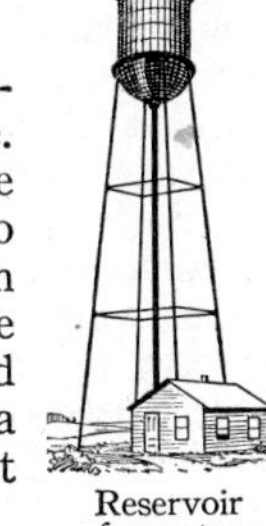
Reservoir for water

res er voir (rez′ər vwär), 1. place where water is collected and stored for use. This reservoir supplies the entire city. 2. anything to hold a liquid. A fountain pen has an ink reservoir. 3. place where anything is collected and stored. His mind was a reservoir of facts. 4. a great supply. *n. 8.*

re set (rē set′), set again. The diamonds were reset in platinum. John's broken arm had to be reset. *v., reset, resetting.*

re side (ri zīd′), 1. dwell; live (in or at) for a long time. This family has resided in Richmond for 100 years. 2. be (in); exist (in). Her charm resides in her happy smile. *v. 4.*

res i dence (rez′i dəns), 1. house; home; abode. 2. residing; living; dwelling. *n. 3.*

res i dent (rez′i dənt), 1. person living in a place, not a visitor. The residents of the town are proud of its new library. 2. staying; dwelling in a place. Grandmother wants a resident companion. Dr. Jones is a resident physician at the hospital. 3. an official sent to live in a foreign land to represent his country. *n., adj. 5.*

res i den tial (rez′i den′shəl), of, pertaining to, or fitted for homes or residences. They live in a good residential district. *adj. 15.*

re sid u al (ri zij′ü əl), remaining; left over. *adj. 19.*

res i due (rez′i dū or rez′i dü), remainder; what remains after a part is taken. Mr. Smith's will directed that, after the payment of all debts, and $10,000 to his brother, the residue of his property should go to his son. The syrup had dried up, leaving a sticky residue. *n. 10.*

re sign (ri zīn′), 1. give up; give up a job, office, etc. John resigned his position on the school paper. The manager of the football team resigned. 2. yield; submit. Jim had to resign himself to a week in bed when he hurt his back. *v. 3.*

res ig na tion (rez′ig nā′shən), 1. act of resigning. There have been so many resignations from the committee that a new one must be formed. 2. written statement giving notice that one resigns. 3. patient acceptance; quiet submission. She bore the pain with resignation. *n. 8.*

re signed (ri zīnd′), accepting what comes without complaint. *adj.*

re sil i ence (ri zil′i əns), 1. power of springing back; elasticity; resilient quality or nature. Rubber has resilience. 2. buoyancy; cheerfulness. *n.*

re sil i ent (ri zil′i ənt), 1. springing back; as, resilient steel, resilient turf. 2. buoyant; cheerful; as, a resilient nature that throws off trouble. *adj.*

res in (rez′in), sticky substance that flows from some trees. Resin is used in medicine, varnishes, etc. Pine resin is much used and is often called rosin. *n. 10.*

res in ous (rez′i nəs), 1. of resin. 2. like resin. 3. containing resin; full of resin. *adj.*

re sist (ri zist′), 1. act against; strive against; oppose. The window resisted his efforts to open it. 2. strive successfully against; keep from; withstand. I could not resist laughing. *v. 4.*

re sist ance (ri zis′təns), 1. act of resisting. The bank clerk made no resistance to the robbers. 2. power to resist. She has little resistance to germs and so is often ill. 3. opposition; opposing force; thing or act that resists. An airplane can overcome the resistance of the air and go in the desired direction, but an ordinary balloon simply drifts. *n. 7.*

re sist ant (ri zis′tənt), resisting. *adj. 16.*

re sist less (ri zist′lis), that cannot be resisted. A resistless impulse made him wander over the earth. *adj. 13.*

res o lute (rez′ə lüt), determined; firm; bold. He was resolute in his attempt to climb to the top of the mountain. A soldier must be resolute in battle. The captain's resolute words cheered the team. *adj. 4.*

res o lu tion (rez′ə lü′shən), 1. thing decided on; thing determined. He made a resolution to get up early. 2. power of holding firmly to a purpose. 3. a formal expression of opinion. The club passed a resolution thanking Mr. Kay for his help throughout the year. 4. breaking into parts. 5. act or result of solving; solution. *n. 5.*

re solve (ri zolv′), 1. make up one's mind; determine; decide. He resolved to do better work in the future. 2. thing determined on; thing decided. He kept his resolve to do better. 3. firmness in carrying out a purpose; determination. Washington was a man of great resolve. 4. decide by vote. It was resolved that our school have a lunchroom. 5. break into parts. 6. solve; answer and explain. His letter resolved all our doubts. *v., n. 3.*

re solved (ri zolvd′), determined; firm; resolute. *adj.*

res o nance (rez′ə nəns), 1. resounding quality; being resonant; as, the resonance of an organ. 2. a reinforcing and prolonging of sound by reflection or by the vibration of other objects. The sounding board of a piano gives it resonance. *n. 17.*

res o nant (rez′ə nənt), 1. resounding; continuing to sound. 2. tending to increase or prolong sounds. *adj. 16.*

re sort (ri zôrt′), 1. go; go often. Many people resort to the beaches in hot weather. 2. place people go to. There are many summer resorts in the mountains. 3. **Resort to** sometimes means seek help from or make use of. The mother resorted to punishment to make the child obey. 4. act of turning to for help. The resort to force is forbidden in this school. 5. person or thing turned to for help. Books are her resort when she is lonely. Friends are the best resort in trouble. *v., n. 3.*

re sound (ri zound′), 1. echo; give back sound. The hills resounded when we shouted. 2. sound loudly. Radios resound from every house. 3. be filled with sound. The room resounded with the children's shouts. 4. be much talked about. The fame of the first flight across the Atlantic resounded all over the world. *v. 5.*

re source (ri sōrs′), 1. any supply that will meet a need. We have resources of money, of quick wit, of strength, etc. 2. any means of getting success or getting out of trouble. Climbing a tree is a cat's resource when chased by a dog. 3. skill in meeting difficulties, getting out of trouble, etc. *n. 6.*

re source ful (ri sōrs′fəl), good at thinking of ways to do things; quick-witted. *adj. 20.*

re spect (ri spekt′), 1. honor; esteem. Children should show respect to those who are older and wiser. 2. feel or show honor or esteem for. We respect an honest person. 3. **Respects** means expressions of respect; regards. Give her my respects. We must pay our respects to the governor. 4. care; consideration. We should show respect for school buildings, parks, and other public property. 5. to care for; show consideration for. Respect the ideas of others. 6. relation; reference. We must plan with respect to the future. 7. feature; point; matter; detail. Giving to beggars is unwise in many respects. *n., v. 2.*

re spect a bil i ty (ri spek′tə bil′i ti), 1. quality or condition of being respectable. 2. respectable social standing. *n., pl. respectabilities. 15.*

re spect a ble (ri spek′tə bəl), 1. worthy of respect; having a good reputation. Respectable citizens obey the laws. 2. fairly good; moderate in size or quality. John's record in school was always respectable, if never brilliant. 3. good enough to use; fit to be seen. *adj. 7.*

re spect ful (ri spekt′fəl), showing respect; polite. He was always respectful to older people. *adj. 5.*

re spect ing (ri spek′ting), regarding; about; concerning. A discussion arose respecting the merits of different automobiles. *prep. 17.*

re spec tive (ri spek′tiv), belonging to each; particular; individual. The classes went to their respective rooms. *adj. 5.*

re spec tive ly (ri spek′tiv li), as regards each one in his turn or in the order mentioned. Bob, Dick, and Tom are 6, 8, and 10 years old, respectively. *adv.*

res pi ra tion (res′pi rā′shən), breathing. A bad cold hinders respiration. *n. 7.*

re spir a to ry (ri spīr′ə tō′ri), pertaining to breathing. The lungs are respiratory organs. *adj. 14.*

re spire (ri spīr′), breathe; inhale and exhale. *v. 14.*

res pite (res′pit), 1. time of relief and rest; lull. A big cloud brought a respite from the glare of the sun. 2. putting off; delay, especially in carrying out a sentence of death; reprieve. 3. give a respite to. *n., v. 7.*

re splend ent (ri splen′dənt), very bright; shining; splendid. The queen was resplendent with jewels. *adj. 7.*

re spond (ri spond′), 1. answer; reply. He responded briefly to the question. 2. act in answer; react. A dog responds to kind treatment by loving its master. Mary responded quickly to the medicine and was well in a few days. *v. 5.*

re sponse (ri spons′), 1. an answer by word or act. Her response to my letter was prompt. Mary stuck out her tongue in response to Tom's teasing. 2. words said or sung by the congregation or choir in answer to the minister. *n. 5.*

re spon si bil i ty (ri spon′si bil′i ti), 1. being responsible; obligation. A little child does not feel much responsibility. 2. thing for which one is responsible. A task, a debt, and little children to care for are all responsibilities. *n., pl. responsibilities. 8.*

re spon si ble (ri spon′si bəl), 1. obliged or expected to account (for). Each pupil is responsible for the care of the books given him. 2. deserving credit or blame. The bad weather is responsible for the small attendance. 3. trustworthy; reliable. The class should choose a responsible pupil to take care of its money. 4. involving obligation or duties. The presidency is a very responsible position. *adj. 6.*

re spon sive (ri spon′siv), 1. making answer; responding; as, a responsive glance. 2. easily moved; responding readily; as, to have a responsive nature, to be responsive to kindness. 3. using or containing responses; as, responsive reading in church in which minister and congregation read in turn. *adj. 11.*

rest[1] (rest), 1. sleep. The children had a good night's rest. 2. quiet; freedom from anything that tires, troubles, disturbs, or pains. The medicine gave the sick man a short rest from pain. 3. ease after work or effort. The workmen were allowed an hour for rest. 4. absence of motion; stillness. The driver brought the car to rest. The lake was at rest. 5. in music or reading, a pause. 6. a mark to show such a pause. 7. be still or quiet. My mother rests for an hour every afternoon. 8. be free from work, effort, care, trouble, etc. Schoolteachers can rest in the summer. 9. be at ease. Don't let Mrs. White rest till she promises to visit us. 10. lie in death or the grave. The old man rests with his forefathers. 11. give rest to; refresh by rest. Stop and rest your horse. It rests one's feet to take off one's shoes. 12. to look; be fixed. Our eyes rested on the open book. 13. a support; something to lean on; as, a footrest. 14. lean; lie; be supported. The ladder rested against the walls. The roof rests on columns. 15. depend. Our hope rests on you. 16. lie; be found; be present. In a democracy, government rests with the people. A smile rested on the girl's lips. 17. place for resting. 18. **Lay to rest** means bury. Lay his bones to rest. *n., v. 1.*

Rests: W, whole; H, half; Q, quarter; E, eighth; S, sixteenth; T, thirty-second.

rest[2] (rest), 1. what is left; those that are left. 2. continue to be; remain. The final control rests with the owner. *n., v.*

re state (rē stāt′), 1. state again or anew. 2. state in a new way. *v.*

re state ment (rē stāt′mənt), 1. act of stating again. 2. statement made again. 3. new statement. *n.*

res tau rant (res′tə rənt), place to buy and eat a meal. *n. 4.*

rest ful (rest′fəl), 1. full of rest; giving rest. She had a restful nap. 2. quiet; peaceful. *adj. 12.*

res ti tu tion (res′ti tū′shən or res′ti tü′shən), 1. the giving back of what has been lost or taken away. 2. act of making good any loss, damage, or injury. It is only fair that those who do the damage should make restitution. *n. 11.*

res tive (res′tiv), 1. restless; uneasy. 2. hard to manage. 3. balky; refusing to go ahead. *adj.*

rest less (rest′lis), 1. unable to rest; uneasy. The dog seemed restless, as if he sensed some danger. 2. without rest or sleep; not restful. The sick child passed a restless night. 3. never still or quiet. That nervous boy is very restless. *adj. 3.*

rest less ness (rest′lis nis), the quality or state of being restless. *n. 13.*

res to ra tion (res′tə rā′shən), 1. restoring or being restored; bringing back to a former condition; as, the restoration of health, the restoration of a king. 2. something restored; as, the restoration of a Roman temple. *n. 7.*

re stor a tive (ri stōr′ə tiv), 1. capable of restoring; tending to restore health or strength. 2. something that does so. Ammonia is used as a restorative when a person has fainted. *adj., n. 13.*

re store (ri stōr′), 1. bring back; establish again. 2. bring back to a former condition or to a normal condition. The old house has been restored. He is completely restored to health. 3. give back; put back. He was obliged to restore the money to its owner. *v. 2.*

re stor er (ri stōr′ər), person or thing that restores. *n. 12.*

re strain (ri strān′), hold back; keep down; keep in check; keep within limits. She could not restrain her curiosity to see what was in the box. *v. 3.*

re straint (ri strānt′), 1. restraining or being restrained. That poor man is not right in his mind and requires restraint. 2. a means of restraining. 3. tendency to restrain natural feeling; reserve. *n. 5.*

re strict (ri strikt′), keep within limits; confine. Our club membership is restricted to twelve. *v. 10.*

re strict ed (ri strik′tid), 1. limited; kept within limits. She is on a very restricted diet, and can have no sweets. 2. having restrictions or limiting rules. Factories may not be built in this restricted residential section. *adj.*

re stric tion (ri strik′shən), 1. something that restricts; a limiting condition or rule. The restrictions on the use of the playground are: No fighting. No damaging property. 2. a restricting or being restricted. This park is open to the public without restriction. *n. 8.*

re stric tive (ri strik′tiv), restricting; limiting. Some laws are prohibitive; some are only restrictive. *adj.*

re sult (ri zult′), 1. that which happens because of something; what is caused. The result of his fall was a broken leg. 2. good or useful result. We want results, not talk. 3. be a result; follow as a consequence. Sickness often results from eating too much. 4. end. **Result in** means have as a result. Eating too much often results in sickness. *n., v. 2.*

re sult ant (ri zul′tənt), 1. resulting. 2. a result. *adj., n. 15.*

re sume (ri züm′), 1. begin again; go on. Resume reading where we left off. 2. take again. Those standing may resume their seats. *v. 4.*

ré su mé (rā′zü mā′), summary. *n. 19.*

re sump tion (ri zump′shən), resuming; as, the resumption of duties after absence. *n. 16.*

res ur rect (rez′ə rekt′), 1. raise from the dead; bring back to life. 2. bring back to sight, use, etc.; as, to resurrect an old law or an old custom. *v.*

res ur rec tion (rez′ə rek′shən), 1. coming to life again; rising from the dead. **The Resurrection** is the rising again of Christ after His death and burial. 2. being alive again after death. 3. revival; restoration from decay, disuse, etc. *n. 9.*

re sus ci tate (ri sus′i tāt), bring back to life or consciousness; revive. *v. 19.*

re tail (rē′tāl), 1. sale of goods in small quantities at a time. He buys at wholesale and sells at retail. 2. in small lots or quantities. The wholesale price of this coat is $20; the retail price is $30. 3. selling in small quantities; as, a retail merchant, the retail trade. 4. sell in small quantities. 5. tell over again. She retails everything she hears about her acquaintances. *n., adj., adv., v. 6.*

re tail er (rē′tāl ər), retail merchant or dealer. *n. 12.*

re tain (ri tān′), 1. keep. China dishes retain heat longer than metal pans do. The old lady has retained all her interest in life. 2. keep in mind; remember. She retained the tune but not the words of the song. 3. employ by payment of a fee. He retained the best lawyer in the State. *v. 3.*

re tain er (ri tān′ər), 1. one who serves a person of rank; vassal; attendant; follower. 2. a fee paid to secure services. This lawyer receives a retainer before he begins work on a case. *n. 12.*

re take (rē tāk′ for 1 and 2, rē′tāk′ for 3), 1. take again. 2. take back. 3. a retaking; as, a retake of a scene in a moving picture. *v., retook, retaken, retaking, n. 18.*

re tal i ate (ri tal′i āt), pay back wrong, injury, etc.; return like for like, usually to return evil for evil. If we insult them, they will retaliate. *v. 13.*

re tal i a tion (ri tal′i ā′shən), paying back evil with evil; return of evil for evil. *n. 15.*

re tard (ri tärd′), make slow; delay the progress of; keep back; hinder. Lack of education retards progress. Bad roads retard the car. *v. 11.*

re tar da tion (rē′tär dā′shən), 1. act of retarding. 2. that which retards; hindrance. *n.*

retch (rech), make efforts to vomit; make movements like those of vomiting. *v.*

re tell (rē tel′), tell again. *v., retold, retelling.*

re ten tion (ri ten′shən), 1. retaining. 2. being retained. 3. power to retain. 4. ability to remember. *n. 13.*

re ten tive (ri ten′tiv), 1. able to hold or keep. 2. able to remember. *adj. 16.*

ret i cence (ret′i səns), tendency to be silent or say little; reserve in speech. *n. 15.*

ret i cent (ret′i sənt), disposed to keep silent or say little; not speaking freely; reserved in speech. *adj.*

ret i na (ret′i nə), the layer of cells at the back of the eyeball that is sensitive to light and receives the images of things looked at. See the diagram of **eye.** *n. 11.*

ret i nue (ret′i nū or ret′i nü), a group of attendants or retainers; a following. The King's retinue accompanied him on the journey. *n. 10.*

re tire (ri tīr′), 1. withdraw; draw back; send back. The government retires worn or torn dollar bills from use. 2. go back; retreat. 3. go away to be quiet. She retired to a convent. 4. give up an office, occupation, etc. Our teachers retire at 70. 5. remove from an office, occupation, etc. 6. go to bed. We retire early. 7. take up and pay off (bonds, loans, etc.). *v. 2.*

re tired (ri tīrd′), 1. withdrawn from one's occupation; as, a retired sea captain, a retired teacher. 2. reserved; retiring. She has a shy, retired nature. 3. secluded; shut off; hidden; as, a retired spot. *adj.*

re tire ment (ri tīr′mənt), 1. withdrawing or being withdrawn. The teacher's retirement from service was regretted by the school. 2. a quiet way or place of living. She lives in retirement, neither making nor receiving visits. *n. 8.*

re tir ing (ri tīr′ing), shrinking from society or publicity; reserved; shy. *adj.*

re told (rē tōld′), told over again. *pt. and pp. of* **retell.** *17.*

re tort[1] (ri tôrt′), 1. reply quickly or sharply. "It's none of your business," he retorted. 2. a sharp or witty reply. "Why are your teeth so sharp?" asked Red Ridinghood. "The better to eat you with" was the wolf's retort. *v., n. 9.*

re tort[2] (ri tôrt′), container used for distilling or decomposing substances by heat. *n.*

A, retort; B, receiver; C, flame to heat retort; D, water to keep receiver cool.

re touch (rē tuch′), improve by new touches or slight changes. The photograph should be retouched. *v. 13.*

re trace (ri trās′), go back over. We retraced our steps to where we started. *v. 9.*

re-trace (rē trās′), go over again; as, retraced lines in a drawing. *v.*

re tract (ri trakt′), 1. draw back or in. The dog snarled and retracted his lips. 2. withdraw; take back; as, to retract an offer or an opinion. *v. 13.*

re trac tion (ri trak′shən), 1. drawing back or in. 2. being drawn back or in. 3. taking back; a withdrawal of a promise, statement, etc. The boy who accused Fred of cheating made a retraction of the charge. *n.*

re treat (ri trēt′), 1. go back; withdraw. The enemy retreated before the advance of our soldiers. Seeing the big dog, the tramp retreated rapidly. 2. act of going back or withdrawing. The army's retreat was orderly. 3. signal for retreat. The drums beat a retreat. 4. a safe, quiet place; place of rest or refuge. *v., n. 3.*

re trench (ri trench′), cut down; reduce (expenses, etc.). *v. 11.*

re trench ment (ri trench′mənt), 1. reduction of expenses. 2. cutting down; cutting off. *n. 20.*

re tri al (rē trī′əl), second trial; new trial. *n.*

ret ri bu tion (ret′ri bū′shən), a deserved punishment; a return for evil done, or sometimes for good done. *n. 13.*

re trib u tive (ri trib′ū tiv), paying back; bringing or inflicting punishment in return for some evil, wrong, etc. *adj.*

re trieve (ri trēv′), 1. get again; recover; as, to retrieve a lost pocketbook. 2. restore; bring back to a former or better condition; as, to retrieve one's fortunes. 3. make good; repair; as, to retrieve a mistake, to retrieve a loss or defeat. 4. find and bring to a person. A dog can be trained to retrieve game. *v. 11.*

re triev er (ri trēv′ər), a dog trained to find killed or wounded game and bring it to a hunter. *n.*

Labrador retriever (about 2 ft. high at the shoulder)

ret ro ac tive (ret′rō ak′tiv), acting upon what is past. A retroactive law applies to events which occurred before the law was passed. *adj.*

ret ro grade (ret′rō grād), 1. moving backward; retreating. 2. move or go backward. 3. becoming worse. 4. fall back toward a worse condition; decline; grow worse. *adj., v. 15.*

ret ro gres sion (ret′rō gresh′ən), 1. backward movement. 2. becoming worse; falling off; decline. *n.*

ret ro spect (ret′rō spekt), a survey of past time, events, etc.; thinking of the past.

In retrospect means when looking back. *n. 14.*

ret ro spec tion (ret′rō spek′shən), act of looking back on things past; survey of past events or experiences. Old people often enjoy retrospection. *n. 19.*

ret ro spec tive (ret′rō spek′tiv), 1. looking back on things past. 2. applying to the past. *adj. 15.*

re try (rē trī′), try again. The murder case was retried in a higher court. *v., retried, retrying.*

re turn (ri tėrn′), 1. bring back; give back; send back; put back; pay back. Return that book to the library. You took his cap; return it at once. Return good for evil. She admired my dress, and I returned the compliment. 2. bringing back; giving back; sending back; putting back; paying back. Dick's bad behavior was a poor return for his uncle's kindness. 3. go back; come back. Return home for your report card. Your mother will return in a moment. We'll return to this hard example after doing the easy ones. 4. going back; coming back. We look forward all winter to our return to the country. We wish you many happy returns of your birthday. 5. reply; answer. "Not I," he returned crossly. 6. report; account. I must make my income-tax return. The election returns are all in. 7. profit. The returns from the sale were more than a hundred dollars. 8. pertaining to a return; as, a return ticket to the point of starting. 9. sent, given, or done in return; as, a return game. *v., n., adj. 1.*

re un ion (rē ūn′yən), coming together again. We have a family reunion every Thanksgiving Day. *n. 13.*

re u nite (rē′ū nīt′), bring together again; come together again. Mother and child were reunited after years of separation. *v. 10.*

Rev., Reverend. *9.*

re vamp (rē vamp′), patch up; repair. *v.*

re veal (ri vēl′), 1. make known. Promise never to reveal my secret. 2. display; show. Her laugh revealed her even teeth. *v. 3.*

rev eil le (rev′ə li), a signal on a bugle or drum to waken soldiers or sailors in the morning. The bugler blows reveille. *n.*

rev el (rev′əl), 1. take great pleasure. The children revel in country life. 2. a merry-making; a noisy good time. Christmas revels with feasting and dancing were common in England. 3. make merry. *v., reveled, reveling, n. 5.*

rev e la tion (rev′ə lā′shən), 1. act of making known. The revelation of the thieves' hiding place caused their capture. 2. the thing made known. Her true nature was a revelation to me. 3. **Revelation** is the last book of the New Testament. It is often called **Revelations.** *n. 7.*

rev el er or **rev el ler** (rev′əl ər), person who revels. *n. 16.*

rev el ry (rev′əl ri), boisterous reveling or festivity; wild merrymaking. *n., pl. revelries. 8.*

re venge (ri venj′), 1. harm done in return for a wrong; vengeance; returning evil for evil; as, a blow struck in revenge. 2. desire for vengeance. 3. to do harm in return for. I will revenge that insult. 4. **Revenge oneself on** a person means pay back the injury that person did to one. The cat revenged herself on John by scratching him. 5. **Be revenged** means have the person who hurt you get hurt in return. *n., v. 3.*

re venge ful (ri venj′fəl), feeling or showing a strong desire for revenge. *adj. 12.*

rev e nue (rev′ə nū or rev′ə nü), money coming in; income. The government gets revenue from taxes. *n. 5.*

re ver ber ate (ri vėr′bər āt), 1. echo back. His voice reverberates from the high ceiling. 2. cast back or reflect (light or heat). *v. 14.*

re ver ber a tion (ri vėr′bər ā′shən), 1. an echoing back of sound; echo. 2. reflection of light or heat. *n. 14.*

re vere[1] (ri vēr′), love and respect deeply; honor greatly; show reverence for. We revere sacred things. *v. 7.*

Re vere[2] (ri vēr′), Paul, an American patriot (1735-1818) noted for his ride to give warning of the coming of the British troops. *n.*

rev er ence (rev′ər əns), 1. a feeling of deep respect, mixed with wonder, fear, and love. 2. revere; regard with reverence. We reverence men of noble lives. 3. a deep bow. 4. **Your Reverence** or **His Reverence** is a title applied to a clergyman. *n., v. 4.*

rev er end (rev′ər ənd), 1. worthy of great respect. 2. a title for clergymen; as, the Reverend Thomas A. Johnson. *adj., n. 4.*

rev er ent (rev′ər ənt), feeling reverence; showing reverence. He gave reverent attention to the sermon. *adj. 7.*

rev er en tial (rev′ər en′shəl), reverent. *adj. 15.*

rev er ie or **rev er y** (rev′ər i), dreamy

thoughts; dreamy thinking of pleasant things. She was so lost in reverie that she did not hear the doorbell ring. He loved to indulge in reveries about his future. *n., pl. reveries. 9.*

re ver sal (ri vėr′səl), change to the opposite; reversing or being reversed. *n. 18.*

re verse (ri vėrs′), 1. turned backward; opposite or contrary in position or direction. Play the reverse side of that record. 2. the opposite or contrary. She did the reverse of what I ordered. 3. the back. His name is on the reverse of the medal. 4. a change to bad fortune; check or defeat. He used to be rich, but he met with reverses. 5. to turn the other way; turn inside out; turn upside down. Reverse that gun; don't point it at me. 6. to change to the opposite; repeal. The court reversed its decree of imprisonment, and the man went free. *adj., n., v. 4.*

re vers i ble (ri vėr′si bəl), 1. that can be reversed. 2. that can reverse. 3. finished on both sides so that either can be used as the right side. *adj.*

re ver sion (ri vėr′zhən), 1. return; return to a former condition. 2. return of property to the person who makes the grant or to his heirs. 3. right to possess a certain property under certain conditions. *n. 11.*

re vert (ri vėrt′), go back; return. If a man dies without heirs, his property reverts to the State. After the settlers left, the natives reverted to their savage customs. My thoughts reverted to the last time that I had seen her. *v. 8.*

re view (ri vū′), 1. study again; look at again. Review today's lesson for tomorrow. 2. studying again. Before the examinations we have a review of the term's work. 3. look back on. Before falling asleep, Helen reviewed the day's happenings. 4. looking back on; survey. 5. look at with care; examine. A superior court may review decisions of a lower court. 6. examination; inspection. A review of the troops will be held during the general's visit to camp. 7. inspect formally. The President reviewed the fleet. 8. examine to give an account of. Mr. Brown reviews books for a living. 9. an account of a book giving its merits and faults. *v., n. 2.*

re view er (ri vū′ər), person who reviews; especially, one who writes articles discussing books, plays, etc. *n. 19.*

re vile (ri vīl′), call bad names; abuse with words. The tramp reviled the man who drove him off. *v. 7.*

re vise (ri vīz′), read carefully in order to correct; look over and change; examine and improve. *v. 7.*

re vi sion (ri vizh′ən), 1. the act or work of revising. 2. revised form. A revision of this book will be published in June. *n. 10.*

re vis it (rē viz′it), visit again; return to. *v. 16.*

re viv al (ri vīv′əl), 1. bringing or coming back to life or consciousness. 2. restoration to vigor or health. 3. bringing or coming back to style or use; as, the revival of a play of years ago. 4. an awakening or increase of interest in religion. 5. special services or efforts made to awaken or increase interest in religion. *n. 9.*

re vive (ri vīv′), 1. bring back or come back to life or consciousness; as, to revive a half-drowned person. 2. come back to a fresh, lively condition. Flowers revive in water. 3. restore; make fresh. Hot coffee revives a cold tired man. 4. bring back or come back to notice, use, fashion, memory, activity, etc. *v. 4.*

rev o ca ble (rev′ə kə bəl), that may be repealed, canceled, or withdrawn. *adj.*

rev o ca tion (rev′ə kā′shən), repeal; canceling; withdrawal; as, the revocation of a law. *n. 20.*

re voke (ri vōk′), 1. take back; repeal; cancel; withdraw. The dictator revoked his decree. 2. in cards, a failure to follow suit when one can and should. 3. make a revoke. *v., n. 9.*

re volt (ri vōlt′), 1. turn away from and fight against a leader; rise against the government's authority. The people revolted against the king. 2. act or state of rebelling. The town is in revolt. 3. turn away with disgust; as, to revolt at a bad smell. 4. to cause to feel disgust. *v., n. 4.*

re volt ing (ri vōl′ting), disgusting; repulsive. *adj. 18.*

rev o lu tion (rev′ə lü′shən), 1. a complete change in government. The American Revolution (1775-1783) gave independence to the colonies. 2. complete change. The automobile caused a revolution in ways of traveling. 3. a moving round some point in a circle or curve. One revolution of the earth around the sun takes a year. 4. turning round. The revolution of the earth causes day and night. 5. the time or distance of one revolution. *n. 4.*

rev o lu tion ar y (rev′ə lü′shən ãr′i), 1. of a revolution; connected with a revolution. 2. bringing or causing great changes. 3. revolutionist. *adj., n., pl. revolutionaries. 7.*

Revolutionary War, the war from 1775 to 1783 by which the thirteen American colonies won independence from England.

rev o lu tion ist (rev′ə lü′shən ist), person who advocates, or takes part in, a revolution. *n. 12.*

rev o lu tion ize (rev′ə lü′shən īz), change completely; produce a very great change in. The automobile and radio have revolutionized country life. The new chief has revolutionized the fire department. *v. 12.*

re volve (ri volv′), 1. move in a circle; move in a curve round a point. The moon revolves around the earth. 2. turn round. The wheels of a moving car revolve. 3. turn over in the mind; consider from many points of view. He wishes to revolve the problem before giving an answer. *v. 5.*

re volv er (ri vol′vər), a pistol that can be fired several times without loading it again. *n. 9.*

Revolver

re vul sion (ri vul′shən), a sudden, violent change or reaction. My feeling toward my new friend underwent a revulsion when I realized his cruelty and dishonesty. *n. 15.*

re ward (ri wôrd′), 1. return made for something done. 2. money payment given or offered. Rewards are given for the capture of criminals, the return of lost property, etc. 3. give a reward to. 4. give a reward for. *n., v. 3.*

re word (rē wėrd′), put into other words; state again. *v.*

re write (rē rīt′), write again; write in a different form. *v., rewrote, rewritten, rewriting. 14.*

Reyn ard (ren′ərd), name for the fox in stories and poems. *n. 7.*

Reyn olds (ren′əldz), Sir Joshua, a famous English portrait painter (1723-1792). *n.*

R.F.D., Rural Free Delivery.

rhap so dy (rap′sə di), 1. an utterance or writing marked by extravagant enthusiasm. May went into rhapsodies over the dress. 2. in music, an instrumental composition irregular in form. *n., pl. rhapsodies. 15.*

Rheims (rēmz), Reims. *n.*

Rhen ish (ren′ish), 1. of the river Rhine or the regions near it. 2. Rhine wine. *adj., n.*

rhe o stat (rē′ō stat), an instrument for regulating the strength of an electric current by introducing different amounts of resistance into the circuit. *n. 17.*

rhet o ric (ret′ə rik), 1. art of using words in speaking or writing. 2. book about this art. 3. mere display in language. *n. 8.*

rhe tor i cal (ri tor′i kəl), 1. of rhetoric. 2. using rhetoric. 3. making a display of words. 4. A **rhetorical question** is a question asked only for effect, not for information. 5. oratorical. *adj. 16.*

rhet o ri cian (ret′ə rish′ən), 1. person skilled in rhetoric. 2. person given to display in language. *n. 15.*

rheum (rüm), 1. a watery discharge, such as mucus, tears, or saliva. 2. catarrh; a cold. *n. 15.*

rheu mat ic (rü mat′ik), 1. of rheumatism. 2. having rheumatism; liable to have rheumatism. 3. causing rheumatism. 4. caused by rheumatism. Rheumatic fever is a fever that accompanies inflamed and painful joints. 5. person who has rheumatism. *adj., n. 15.*

rheu ma tism (rü′mə tizm), a disease with inflammation, swelling, and stiffness of the joints. *n. 7.*

Rhine (rīn), a river flowing from Switzerland through Germany and the Netherlands into the North Sea. The Rhine is famous in songs, stories, and history. *n. 5.*

rhine stone (rīn′stōn′), an imitation diamond made of glass. *n.*

rhi no (rī′nō), rhinoceros. *n., pl. rhinos.*

rhi noc er os (rī nos′ər əs), large, thick-skinned animal of Africa and Asia with one or two upright horns on the snout. *n., pl. rhinoceroses* or *rhinoceros. 8.*

Rhinoceros
(5 ft. high; 10 ft. long)

Rhode Is land (rōd′ ī′lənd), a New England State of the United States. Rhode Island is the smallest State. *9.*

Rhodes (rōdz), 1. an island in the Aegean Sea. A huge statue of Apollo called the "Colossus of Rhodes" stood over the harbor entrance. 2. Cecil John Rhodes was an English statesman and administrator in South Africa (1853-1902). *n. 14.*

rho do den dron (rō′də den′drən), an evergreen shrub somewhat like an azalea.

Rhododendrons have beautiful pink, purple, or white flowers. *n. 17.*

Rhone or **Rhône** (rōn), river flowing from Switzerland into the Mediterranean Sea, mostly through France. *n. 11.*

rhu barb (rü′bärb), 1. a garden plant with very large leaves, whose sour stalks are used for making sauce, pies, etc. 2. the stalks. 3. sauce made of them. *n. 13.*

Rhubarb

rhyme (rīm), 1. sound alike in the last part. *Long* and *song* rhyme. *Go to bed* rhymes with *sleepy head.* 2. a word or line having the same last sound as another. *Cat* is a rhyme for *mat.* "Hey! diddle, diddle" and "The cat and the fiddle" are rhymes. 3. verses or poetry with a regular return of similar sounds. 4. agreement in the final sounds of words or lines. 5. make rhymes. *v., n. 3.* Also spelled **rime.**

rhythm (riTHm), 1. movement with a regular repetition of a beat, accent, rise and fall, or the like; as, the rhythm of dancing, skating, swimming, the rhythm of the tides, the rhythm of one's heartbeats. 2. the repetition of an accent; the arrangement of beats in a line of poetry. The rhythms of the *Lord's Prayer, The Night before Christmas,* and *America* are different. 3. grouping by accents or beats; as, triple rhythm. *n. 10.*

rhyth mic (riTH′mik), rhythmical. *adj. 17.*

rhyth mi cal (riTH′mi kəl), having rhythm; of rhythm; pertaining to rhythm. *adj. 17.*

R.I., Rhode Island.

rib (rib), 1. one of the curved bones extending round the chest from the backbone to the front of the body. 2. something like a rib. The curved timbers in a ship's frame are called ribs. The thick vein of a leaf is also called a rib. 3. furnish or strengthen with ribs; mark with riblike ridges. *n., v., ribbed, ribbing. 3.*

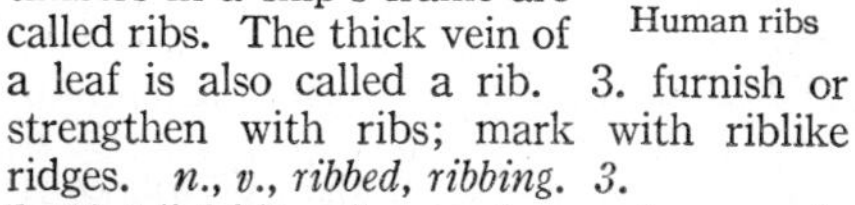
Human ribs

rib ald (rib′əld), offensive in speech; coarsely mocking; irreverent; indecent. *adj. 15.*

rib ald ry (rib′əld ri), ribald language. *n. 16.*

rib and (rib′ənd), ribbon. *n.* [*Old use*] *15.*

rib band (rib′ənd), ribbon. *n.* [*Old use*] *10.*

ribbed (ribd), having ribs or ridges; as, ribbed cloth. *adj.*

rib bon (rib′ən), 1. a strip or band of silk, satin, velvet, etc. Bows for the hair, belts, and badges are often made of ribbon. 2. anything like such a strip; as, a typewriter ribbon. Her dress was torn to ribbons by the thorns and briers she had come through. *n. 2.*

rice (rīs), 1. the starchy seeds or grain of a plant grown in warm climates. Rice is an important food in India, China, and Japan. 2. the plant itself. *n. 3.*

Rice

rice bird (rīs′bėrd′), 1. a name for the bobolink in the southern United States. 2. a songbird like a finch. *n.*

rich (rich), 1. having much money, land, goods, etc. 2. rich people. 3. abounding; well supplied. The United States is rich in oil and coal. 4. fertile; producing much; as, a rich soil, a rich mine. 5. valuable; worthy; as, a rich harvest, a rich suggestion. 6. costly; elegant; as, rich dresses, jewels, carpets, etc. 7. containing plenty of butter, eggs, flavoring, etc.; as, a rich fruit cake. 8. deep; full; as, a rich red, a rich tone. *adj., n. pl. 1.*

Rich ard (rich′ərd). Richard I was king of England from 1189 to 1199. He was called "Richard the Lion-Hearted" (1157-1199). *n.*

Rich e lieu (rish′ə lü), a famous French cardinal and statesman (1585-1642). *n. 17.*

rich es (rich′iz), wealth; abundance of property; much money, land, goods, etc. *n. pl. 4.*

rich ly (rich′li), 1. in a rich manner. 2. fully; abundantly. *adv.*

Rich mond (rich′mənd), the capital of Virginia. *n. 5.*

rich ness (rich′nis), rich condition or quality. The richness of the soil favored the growth of crops. *n. 12.*

rick (rik), a stack of hay, straw, etc., especially, one made so that the rain will run off it. *n. 18.*

rick ets (rik′its), a disease of childhood, caused by improper feeding and lack of sunshine. It results in softening, and sometimes bending, of the bones. *n. 13.*

rick et y (rik′i ti), 1. weak; liable to fall or break down; shaky; as, a rickety chair. 2. feeble in the joints. 3. having rickets; suffering from rickets. *adj. 17.*

rick shaw or **rick sha** (rik′shô), small, two-wheeled, hooded carriage drawn by one or more men, used in Japan; a jinrikisha. *n.*

ric o chet (rik′ə shā′ or rik′ə shet′), 1. the skipping or jumping motion of an object as it goes along a flat surface; as, the ricochet of a cannon ball along the ground, the ricochet of a stone thrown along the surface of water. 2. to move in this way. *n., v., ricocheted* (-shād′), *ricocheting* (-shā′ing) or *ricochetted* (-shet′id), *ricochetting* (-shet′ing).

rid[1] (rid), make free. What will rid a house of rats? **Get rid of** means get free from. I can't get rid of this cold. *v., rid* or *ridded, ridding. 3.*

rid[2] (rid), 1. rode. 2. ridden. *v., pt. and pp. of* **ride.** [*Old use*]

rid dance (rid′əns), clearing away or out; removal. **Good riddance** is an exclamation expressing relief that something or somebody has been removed. *n. 12.*

rid den (rid′ən). See **ride.** The horseman had ridden all day. *pp. of ride. 10.*

rid dle[1] (rid′əl), 1. a puzzling question, statement, problem, etc. *Example:* When is a door not a door? *Answer:* When it is ajar. 2. speak in riddles. *n., v. 4.*

rid dle[2] (rid′əl), 1. make many holes in. The door of the fort was riddled with shot. 2. a coarse sieve. 3. sift; as, to riddle gravel. *v., n.*

ride (rīd), 1. sit on a horse and make it go. 2. sit on something and make it go; as, to ride a camel, to ride a bicycle. 3. manage; control. 4. be carried along; as, to ride on a train, to ride in a car. 5. move or float on the water. The ship rides at anchor. 6. a trip on horseback, in an automobile, on a train, etc. *v., rode, ridden, riding, n. 1.*

rid er (rīd′ər), 1. person who rides. The West is famous for its riders. 2. anything added to a record, document, or statement after it was supposed to be complete. *n. 4.*

ridge (rij), 1. the long and narrow upper part of something; as, the ridge of an animal's back. 2. the line where two sloping surfaces meet; as, the ridge of a roof. 3. a long narrow chain of hills or mountains; as, the Blue Ridge of the Appalachian Mountains. 4. any raised narrow strip; as, the ridges in plowed ground, the ridges on corduroy cloth. 5. make into ridges; form into ridges. 6. cover with ridges. *n., v. 3.*

ridge pole (rij′pōl′), the horizontal timber along the top of a roof or tent. *n.*

rid i cule (rid′i kūl), 1. laugh at; make fun of. 2. laughter in mockery; words or actions that make fun of somebody or something. Percy's curls made him an object of ridicule. *v., n. 8.*

ri dic u lous (ri dik′ū ləs), deserving ridicule; absurd; laughable. It would be ridiculous to walk backward all the time. *adj. 6.*

rife (rīf), 1. happening often; common; numerous. 2. full; well supplied. The land was rife with rumors of war. *adj. 11.*

riff raff (rif′raf′), 1. worthless people. 2. trash. 3. worthless. *n., adj.*

ri fle[1] (rī′fəl), 1. gun with spiral grooves in its barrel which spin or twist the bullet as it is shot. 2. cut such grooves in. *n., v. 5.*

ri fle[2] (rī′fəl), 1. search and rob; ransack and rob. 2. steal; take away. 3. strip bare. The bad boys rifled the apple tree. *v.*

ri fle man (rī′fəl mən), 1. soldier armed with a rifle. 2. man skilled in the use of the rifle. *n., pl. riflemen.*

rift (rift), split; cleft; break; crack. There's a rift in the clouds; perhaps the sun will come out soon. *n., v. 9.*

rig (rig), 1. fit (a ship) with masts and sails; fit out. The sailor rigged a toy boat for the little boy. 2. the arrangement of masts, sails, etc., on a ship. A schooner has a fore-and-aft rig; that is, the sails are set lengthwise on a ship. 3. dress. On Halloween the children rig themselves up in queer clothes. John's rig consisted of a silk hat and overalls. *Used in common talk. v., rigged, rigging, n. 6.*

Ri ga (rē′gə), 1. a gulf of the Baltic Sea. 2. the capital of Latvia, a seaport city on this gulf. *n. 17.*

rig ging (rig′ing), 1. the ropes, chains, etc., used to support and work the masts, yards, sails, etc., on a ship. 2. tackle; equipment. *n.*

right (rīt), 1. good; just; lawful. Jack did the right thing when he told the truth. 2. in a way that is good, just, or lawful. 3. correct; true; as, the right answer. 4. that which is right, just, good, true. Do right, not wrong. 5. a just claim; something that is due to a person. Each member of the club has a right to vote. He demanded his rights. A **right of way** is the right to pass over another's land. 6. correctly. I guessed right. **By rights** or **by right** means rightly; properly; correctly. 7. fitting; suitable; proper. Learn to say the right thing at the right time. 8. properly; well. It serves you right to lose if you cheat. 9. well; healthy; in good condition. Tommy was thin and pale, but he looks all right now. 10. meant to be seen;

most important; as, the right side of cloth. 11. make correct; set right; as, to right a wrong. 12. to put right; get into the proper position. The boys righted the boat. The ship righted after the big wave passed. 13. You have a right hand and a left hand. Your right side is toward the east when you face north. Most people eat, write, and work with their right hands. 14. the right-hand side; as, turn to your right, the school on the right. 15. to the right hand; as, turn right. 16. exactly. Your cap is right where you left it. 17. at once; immediately. Stop playing right now. 18. very; as, right honorable. 19. in a straight line; directly. Dick looked the man right in the eye. 20. straight. *adj., adv., n., v. 1.*

right angle, an angle that is formed by a line perpendicular to another line, as shown in the diagram; an angle of 90 degrees. The angles in a square or in the capital letters **F**, **L**, and **T** are right angles.

right eous (rī′chəs), 1. doing right; virtuous; behaving justly. 2. proper; just; right; as, righteous anger. *adj. 5.*

right eous ness (rī′chəs nis), upright conduct; virtue; being right and just. *n. 6.*

right ful (rīt′fəl), 1. according to law; by rights; as, the rightful owner of this dog. 2. just and right; proper. *adj. 8.*

right ful ly (rīt′fəl i), 1. according to right, law, or justice. 2. properly; fittingly. 3. in a righteous manner. *adv.*

right-hand (rīt′hand′), 1. situated on the right. 2. of, for, or with the right hand. 3. most helpful or useful; as, one's right-hand man. *adj.*

right-hand ed (rīt′han′did), 1. using the right hand more easily and readily than the left. 2. done with the right hand. 3. made to be used with the right hand. 4. turning from left to right; as, a right-handed screw. *adj.*

right ly (rīt′li), 1. justly; fairly. 2. correctly. He rightly guessed that I was safe. 3. properly; suitably. *adv.*

rig id (rij′id), 1. stiff; firm; not bending. Hold your arm rigid. 2. strict; not changing. In our home, it is a rigid rule to wash one's hands before eating. *adj. 7.*

ri gid i ty (ri jid′i ti), 1. stiffness; firmness. 2. strictness; severity. *n. 14.*

rig ma role (rig′mə rōl), foolish talk; words without meaning; nonsense. *n. 19.*

rig or (rig′ər), strictness; severity; harshness; as, the rigor of a long, cold winter. *n. 6.*

rig or ous (rig′ər əs), 1. very severe; harsh; strict; as, the rigorous discipline in a prison. 2. exact; thoroughly logical and scientific. *adj. 13.*

rig or ous ly (rig′ər əs li), with rigor; severely; strictly. *adv.*

rile (rīl), 1. make (water, etc.) muddy by stirring up sediment; roil. 2. disturb; irritate; vex. *v.* [*Used in common talk*]

Ri ley (rī′li), James Whitcomb, an American poet (1853-1916). *n.*

rill (ril), tiny stream; little brook. *n. 4.*

rim (rim), 1. an edge, border, or margin on or around anything; as, the rim of a wheel, the rim of a cup. 2. form a rim around. Wild flowers and grasses rimmed the little pool. *n., v., rimmed, rimming. 5.*

rime[1] (rīm), rhyme. *v., n. 11.*

rime[2] (rīm), white frost; hoarfrost. *n.*

rind (rīnd), firm outer covering. We do not eat the rind of oranges, melons, and cheese. The bark of a tree or plant may be called the rind. *n. 8.*

ring[1] (ring), 1. circle. The fairies danced in a ring. You can tell the age of a tree by the number of rings in the wood. 2. thin circle of metal, etc.; as, a wedding ring, a key ring, a napkin ring. 3. put a ring around; enclose; form a circle around. 4. enclosed space (for races or games); as, a circus ring, a ring for a prize fight. 5. put a ring in the nose of (an animal). 6. group of men combined for a selfish or bad purpose. A ring of corrupt politicians controlled the city. *n., v., ringed, ringing. 1.*

Finger rings

ring[2] (ring), 1. sound or cause to sound. Did the telephone ring? Ring for a servant. His words ring true. Ring the coin on the counter to find out if it is good money. 2. echo; give back sound. The woods rang with their shouts. 3. sound of a bell. Did you hear a ring? 4. a sound like that of a bell. On a cold night we can hear the ring of the skates on ice. *v., rang, rung, ringing, n.*

ring er (ring′ər), person or thing that rings. *n. 12.*

ring lead er (ring′lēd′ər), person who leads others in opposition to authority or law; as, the ringleaders of the mutiny. *n. 16.*

ring let (ring′lit), 1. little ring. 2. curl. She wears her hair in ringlets. *n. 9.*

ring worm (ring′wėrm′), a contagious skin disease that causes ring-shaped patches. *n.*

rink (ringk), 1. a sheet of ice for skating. 2. a smooth floor for roller skating. *n.*

rinse (rins), 1. wash with clean water. Rinse all the soap out of your hair after you wash it. Give it a last rinse in cold water. 2. wash lightly. Rinse your mouth with water and soda. 3. a rinsing. *v., n. 11.*

Rio de Janeiro (rē′ō dā zhə nār′ō), the capital of Brazil, an important seaport city in South America. *17.*

Rio Grande (rē′ō grän′dā), river forming part of the boundary between the United States and Mexico.

ri ot (rī′ət), 1. disturbance; confusion; disorder; a wild, violent public disturbance. The police stopped several riots on election night. **Run riot** means (1) act without restraint. (2) grow wildly or luxuriantly. (3) run wild. 2. behave in a wild, disorderly way. 3. revel. 4. bright display. The garden was a riot of color. *n., v. 4.*

ri ot er (rī′ət ər), person who riots. *n. 14.*

ri ot ous (rī′ət əs), taking part in a riot; boisterous; disorderly. He was expelled from college for riotous conduct. Sounds of riotous glee came from the playhouse. *adj. 9.*

rip[1] (rip), 1. cut roughly; tear apart; tear off. Rip the cover off this box. 2. cut or pull out (the threads in the seams of a garment). 3. torn place; a seam burst in a garment. Please sew up this rip in my sleeve. 4. saw (wood) along the grain, not across the grain. *v., ripped, ripping, n. 3.*

rip[2] (rip), 1. a stretch of rough water made by cross currents meeting. Between these islands there is a rip. 2. a swift current made by the tide. *n.*

ripe (rīp), 1. full-grown and ready to be gathered and eaten; as, ripe fruit, ripe grain, ripe vegetables. 2. fully developed and fit to use; as, ripe knowledge. 3. ready; as, ripe for mischief. *adj. 2.*

rip en (rīp′ən), become ripe; make ripe. *v. 4.*

ripe ness (rīp′nis), the quality or state of being ripe; full development. *n. 12.*

rip ple (rip′əl), 1. a very little wave. Throw a stone into still water and watch the ripples spread in rings. 2. anything that seems like a tiny wave; as, ripples in hair. 3. a sound that reminds one of little waves; as, a ripple of laughter in the crowd. 4. make little ripples on. A breeze rippled the quiet waters. *n., v. 5.*

rip saw (rip′sô′), saw for cutting wood along the grain, not across the grain. *n.*

rise (rīz), 1. stand up; get up. Rise when you recite. The slaves rose in rebellion against their masters. 2. go up; come up. The kite rises in the air. Bread rises. Mercury rises in a thermometer on a hot day. Fish rise to the surface. 3. go higher; increase. The wind rose rapidly. His anger rose at that remark. Butter rose five cents in price. 4. going up; increase. We watched the rise of the balloon. There had been a great rise in prices since the war. 5. slope upward. Hills rise in the distance. 6. start; begin. The river rises from a spring. Quarrels often rise from trifles. 7. origin; start; beginning. The circumstances of his death gave rise to a suspicion of murder. 8. upward slope. The rise of the hill is gradual. The house is situated on a rise. *v., rose, risen, rising, n. 1.*

ris en (riz′ən). See **rise.** The sun had risen long before I woke up. *pp. of rise. 8.*

ris i bil i ty (riz′i bil′i ti), ability or disposition to laugh. **Risibilities** means desire to laugh; sense of humor. A man chasing his hat arouses the risibilities of many people. *n., pl. risibilities.*

ris ing (rīz′ing), 1. act of that which rises; as, the rising of the sun. Seven o'clock is my hour for rising. 2. a fight against the government; revolt. 3. that rises; advancing in power, influence, etc.; growing. *n., adj.*

risk (risk), 1. chance of harm or loss; danger. He rescued the dog at the risk of his own life. If you drive carefully, there is no risk of being fined. 2. expose to the chance of harm or loss. Don't risk any money in oil stock. You risk your neck trying to climb that tree. 3. take the risk of. They risked defeat in fighting the larger army. *n., v. 4.*

risk y (ris′ki), full of risk; dangerous. *adj., riskier, riskiest. 19.*

rite (rīt), solemn ceremony. The church has rites for baptism, marriage, and burial. Secret societies have their special rites. *n. 5.*

rit u al (rich′ü əl), 1. a form or system of rites. The rites of baptism, marriage, and burial are parts of the ritual of the church. Secret societies have rituals for initiating new members. 2. a book containing rites or ceremonies. 3. of or pertaining to rites;

done as a rite; as, ritual laws, a ritual dance. 4. the carrying out of ritual acts. *n., adj. 12.*

ri val (rī′vəl), 1. person who wants the same thing as another; one who tries to equal or do better than another. The two boys were rivals for the same class office. They were also rivals in sports. 2. wanting the same thing as another; being a rival. The rival store tried to get the other's trade. 3. try to equal or outdo. The stores rival each other in beautiful window displays. 4. equal; match. The sunset rivaled the sunrise in beauty. *n., adj., v., rivaled, rivaling. 3.*

ri val ry (rī′vəl ri), competition; effort to obtain something another person wants. There is rivalry among business firms for trade. *n., pl. rivalries. 9.*

riv en (riv′ən), torn apart; split. *adj. 15.*

riv er (riv′ər), large stream of water. *n. 1.*

riv er side (riv′ər sīd′), 1. the bank of a river. We walked along the riverside. 2. beside a river. The riverside path is much used. *n., adj. 7.*

riv et (riv′it), 1. metal bolt with each end hammered into a head. Rivets fasten heavy steel beams together. 2. fasten with rivets. 3. fasten firmly; fix firmly. Their eyes were riveted on the speaker. *n., v. 8.*

Riv i er a (riv′i ãr′ə), a section of France and Italy along the Mediterranean Sea, famous as a resort. *n.*

riv u let (riv′ū lit), very small stream. *n. 7.*

rm., room.

roach[1] (rōch), an insect often found in kitchens, around water pipes, etc. See the picture under **cockroach.** *n. 14.*

roach[2] (rōch), a small fresh-water fish resembling a carp. *n., pl. roaches* or *roach.*

Roach[2]

road (rōd), 1. a way between places; as, the road from New York to Boston. Our road went through the woods. 2. a way; as, the road to ruin, a road to peace. 3. a place near the shore where ships may anchor. *n. 1.*

road bed (rōd′bed′), foundation of a road or of a railroad. *n.*

road side (rōd′sīd′), 1. the side of a road. Flowers grew along the roadside. 2. beside a road; as, a roadside inn. *n., adj. 7.*

road stead (rōd′sted), a place near the shore where ships may anchor. *n. 17.*

road ster (rōd′stər), 1. an open automobile with only one seat. 2. horse for riding or driving on the roads. *n. 14.*

road way (rōd′wā′), 1. road. 2. the part of a road used by wheeled vehicles. Walk on the path, not in the roadway. *n. 11.*

roam (rōm), wander; go about with no special plan or aim; as, to roam through the fields. *v. 3.*

roan (rōn), 1. yellowish or reddish brown sprinkled with gray or white. 2. a roan horse. *adj., n.*

Ro a noke (rō′ə nōk), a city in southwestern Virginia. *n. 17.*

roar (rōr), 1. make a loud deep sound; make a loud noise. The bull roared with anger. The wind roared at the windows. 2. a loud deep sound; loud noise; as, the roar of the cannon, a roar of laughter. *v., n. 2.*

roast (rōst), 1. bake; cook by dry heat. We roasted meat and potatoes. 2. piece of baked meat; piece of meat to be roasted. 3. roasted; as, roast beef, roast pork. 4. prepare by heating; as, to roast coffee, to roast a metal ore. 5. make or become very hot. *v., n., adj. 2.*

roast er (rōs′tər), 1. pan used in roasting. 2. something fit to be roasted. 3. one that roasts. *n. 17.*

rob (rob), take away from by force; steal. Thieves robbed the bank of thousands of dollars. The boys robbed the orchard. They said they would not rob again. *v., robbed, robbing. 2.*

rob ber (rob′ər), person who robs; thief. *n. 3.*

rob ber y (rob′ər i), robbing; theft; stealing. *n., pl. robberies. 6.*

robe (rōb), 1. long, loose, outer garment. The Arabs wear robes. John has a bathrobe. 2. garment that shows rank, office, etc.; as, a judge's robe, the king's robes of state. 3. covering or wrap. Put a robe over you if you go for a ride on a cold day. 4. put a robe on; dress. *n., v. 3.*

rob in (rob′in), 1. a large American thrush with a reddish breast. 2. a small European bird with a yellowish-red breast. *n. 2.*

American robin

Rob in Hood (rob′in hu̇d′), in English legend, an outlaw who robbed the rich but gave money to the poor.

ro bot (rō′bot), 1. a machine-made man. 2. person who acts or works in a dull, mechanical way. *n.*

ro bust (rō bust′), strong and healthy; sturdy. *adj. 11.*

roc (rok), a bird having enormous size and strength, famous in Arabian tales. *n.*

Roch es ter (roch′es tər), a city in western New York. *n. 8.*

rock[1] (rok), 1. large mass of stone. The ship was wrecked on the rocks. 2. stone. The earth's crust is made up of rock under a layer of soil. 3. made of rock. 4. something firm like a rock; support; defense. Christ is called the Rock of Ages. 5. anything that suggests a rock. The division of the money was the rock on which the thieves split. 6. **Go on the rocks** or **run on the rocks** means be wrecked or ruined or in very serious trouble. *n., adj. 1.*

rock[2] (rok), 1. move backward and forward, or from side to side. My chair rocks. The waves rocked the ship. The earthquake rocked the houses. Mother rocked the baby to sleep. 2. rocking. *v., n.*

rock er (rok′ər), 1. one of the curved pieces on which a cradle, rocking chair, etc., rocks. 2. rocking chair. *n. 16.*

ROCKERS

rock et (rok′it), 1. a firework that shoots up high in the air and bursts into a shower of sparks or stars. Rockets are used by ships as signals of distress. 2. go like a rocket. *n., v. 9.*

Rock ies (rok′iz), the Rocky Mountains. *n. pl.*

rocking chair, chair mounted on rockers, or on springs, so that it can rock back and forth.

rock salt, common salt got from mines; salt in large crystals.

Rocket

rock y[1] (rok′i), 1. full of rocks. 2. made of rock. 3. like rock; hard; firm. *adj., rockier, rockiest. 4.*

rock y[2] (rok′i), shaky; likely to rock. That table is a bit rocky; put a piece of wood under the short leg. *adj.*

Rocky Mountains, a group of mountain ranges in western North America. They extend from Alaska to northern Mexico.

ro co co (rō kō′kō), 1. a style of architecture and decoration with elaborate ornamentation, combining shellwork, scrolls, foliage, etc., much used in the first half of the 18th century. 2. of or pertaining to this style. *n., adj.*

Rococo architecture

rod (rod), 1. a thin straight bar of metal or wood. 2. a thin straight stick, either growing or cut off. 3. a stick used to beat or punish; punishment. 4. a long light pole; a fishing pole. 5. a measure, $5\frac{1}{2}$ yards or $16\frac{1}{2}$ feet. A square rod is $30\frac{1}{4}$ square yards or $272\frac{1}{4}$ square feet. *n. 2.*

rode (rōd). See **ride.** We rode ten miles yesterday. *pt. of ride. 2.*

ro dent (rō′dənt), 1. an animal that gnaws. Rats, mice, squirrels, hares, and rabbits are rodents. 2. gnawing. *n., adj. 14.*

ro de o (rō dā′ō or rō′di ō), 1. a contest or exhibition of skill in roping cattle, riding horses, etc. 2. the driving of cattle together. *n., pl. rodeos.*

roe[1] (rō), fish eggs. *n. 6.*

roe[2] (rō), a small deer of Europe and Asia. *n., pl. roes* or *roe.*

roe buck (rō′buk′), a male roe. *n. 13.*

Roent gen rays (rent′gən rāz′), X rays. Roentgen rays are used to locate breaks in the bones or bullets lodged in the body and to treat certain diseases.

Roebuck

rogue (rōg), 1. tricky, dishonest, or worthless person; rascal. The **rogues' gallery** is a collection of photographs of known criminals. 2. Rogue is used playfully to mean a mischievous person. The little rogue has his grandpa's glasses on. 3. an animal with a savage nature that lives apart from the herd. A rogue elephant is very dangerous. *n. 5.*

ro guer y (rō′gər i), 1. conduct of rogues. 2. playful mischief. *n., pl. rogueries.*

ro guish (rō′gish), 1. dishonest; rascally; pertaining to rogues. 2. playfully mischievous. *adj. 16.*

roil (roil), 1. make (water, etc.) muddy by stirring up sediment. 2. disturb; irritate; vex. *v.*

rois ter (rois′tər), swagger; be boisterous; revel noisily. *v.*

rois ter er (rois′tər ər), a noisy reveler; a swaggering or riotous fellow. *n.*

Ro land (rō′lənd), the most famous of Charlemagne's knights. *n.*

rôle or **role** (rōl), 1. an actor's part in a play. Helen wished to play the leading rôle. 2. a part played in real life. A mother's rôle is to comfort and console. *n. 9.*

roll (rōl), 1. move along by turning over and over. Wheels roll. A ball rolls. The child rolls a hoop. 2. turn round and round on itself or on something else; wrap; be wrapped round. She rolled the string into a ball. The boy rolled himself up in a blanket. 3. move on wheels. The nurse rolls the baby carriage. The automobile rolls along. 4. move smoothly; sweep along. Waves roll in on the beach. The years roll on. 5. make flat or smooth with a roller; spread out with a rolling pin, etc. Rolling the grass makes a smooth lawn. Mother rolls the dough for cookies. 6. move with a side-to-side motion. The ship rolls in the waves. The girl rolled her eyes. 7. the act of rolling; motion from side to side. The ship's roll made many people sick. 8. rise and fall again and again; as, rolling country, rolling waves. 9. trill; as, to roll your r's. 10. make deep, loud sounds. Thunder rolls. 11. a deep, loud sound. 12. pile (up); increase. Bills roll up fast. 13. anything rolled up; as, a roll of carpet, a roll of paper. 14. a list of names; list. I will call the roll to find out who are absent. 15. roller. 16. a rounded or rolled up mass; as, a roll of butter. 17. a kind of bread or cake; as, a sweet roll. *v., n. 1.*

roll call, the calling of a list of names, as of soldiers, pupils, etc., to find out who are present.

roll er (rōl′ər), 1. thing that rolls; cylinder on which something is rolled along or rolled up. 2. a cylinder of metal, stone, wood, etc., used for smoothing, pressing, crushing, etc. A steam roller is used in making and repairing roads. A wet garment is put between the rollers of a clothes wringer to squeeze out the water in it. 3. a long, swelling wave. Huge rollers broke on the rocky shore. 4. person who rolls something. *n. 5.*

Steam roller

roller skate, a skate with small wheels instead of a runner, for use on a floor or sidewalk.

Roller skate

roll er-skate (rōl′ər skāt′), skate on roller skates. *v.*

rol lick (rol′ik), frolic; be merry; enjoy oneself in a free, hearty way. *v. 19.*

rolling mill, 1. factory where metal is rolled into sheets and bars. 2. machine for doing this.

rolling pin, a cylinder of wood or glass about a foot long for rolling out dough.

Rolling pin

rolling stock, the locomotives and cars of a railroad.

ro ly-po ly (rō′li pō′li), 1. short and plump; as, a roly-poly child. 2. a short, plump person or animal. 3. a pudding made of jam or fruit spread on a rich dough, rolled up and cooked. *adj., n., pl. roly-polies.*

Ro man (rō′mən), 1. of Rome; pertaining to Rome. 2. a native, inhabitant, or citizen of Rome. 3. of or pertaining to the Roman Catholic Church. 4. **Romans** is a book of the New Testament. 5. the style of printing type commonly used. This sentence is in roman type. 6. A **Roman nose** is a hooked nose curved somewhat like an eagle's beak. *adj., n. 2.*

Roman Catholic, 1. of, pertaining to, or belonging to the Christian church that recognizes the Pope as the supreme head. 2. member of this church.

ro mance (rō mans′), 1. a story or poem telling of heroes. Have you read the romances about King Arthur and his knights? 2. a story of adventure. *The Arabian Nights* and *Treasure Island* are romances. 3. a love story; a love affair. 4. interest in adventure and love. 5. a made-up story. Nobody believes her romances about the wonderful things that have happened to her. 6. make up romances; think or talk in a romantic way. Some children romance because of their lively imaginations. *n., v. 6.*

Ro mance (rō mans′). The Romance languages are French, Italian, Spanish, Portuguese, and others which come from Latin, the language of the Romans. *adj.*

ro manc er (rō man′sər), 1. writer of romances. 2. person who makes up false or extravagant stories. *n. 17.*

Roman Empire, the empire of ancient Rome lasting from 27 B.C. to 395 A.D. It was divided into the **Eastern Roman Empire** (395-1453) and the **Western Roman Empire** (395-476 A.D.). See the map just below.

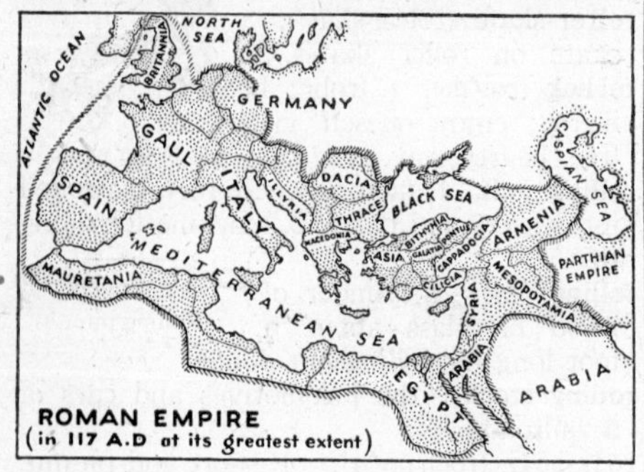

Ro man esque (rō′mən esk′), 1. a style of architecture developed in Europe during the early Middle Ages before the Gothic period. Romanesque architecture used round arches and vaults. 2. of, in, or having to do with this style of architecture. *n., adj.*

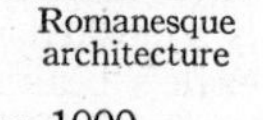
Romanesque architecture

Roman numerals, numerals like XXIII, LVI, and MDCCLX, in which I = 1, V = 5, X = 10, L = 50, C = 100, D = 500, and M = 1000.

Ro ma ni a (rō mā′ni ə), a country in southeastern Europe.

ro man tic (rō man′tik), 1. characteristic of romances or romance; appealing to fancy and the imagination. She likes romantic tales of love and war. The poet Shelley had a romantic face, lived a romantic life, and wrote romantic poetry. May thinks it would be romantic to be an actress. 2. having ideas or feelings suited to romance. The romantic schoolgirl's mind was full of handsome heroes, jewels, balls, and fine clothes. 3. suited to a romance. What a romantic wood! Fairies might live here! 4. of or pertaining to a style of literature and art (opposed to the classical, and also to the realistic). The romantic writer pictures life as he pleases, usually in its unusual and adventurous aspects. *adj. 6.*

ro man ti cism (rō man′ti sizm), the romantic tendency in literature and art (contrasted with classicism or with realism). *n. 19.*

Rome (rōm), 1. the capital of Italy. The headquarters of the Pope and the Roman Catholic Church are in Rome. 2. capital of the Roman Empire. It was captured by the barbarians in 410 A.D. 3. ancient Roman republic. Rome once ruled the world. *n. 2.*

Ro me o (rō′mi ō), the hero of Shakespeare's *Romeo and Juliet,* who died for love. *n. 8.*

romp (romp), 1. to play in a rough, boisterous way; rush, tumble, and punch in play. 2. rough, lively play or frolic. A pillow fight is a romp. 3. a girl or boy who likes to romp. *v., n. 10.*

romp ers (romp′ərz), a loose outer garment, worn by young children at play. *n. pl. 14.*

Baby wearing rompers

Rom u lus (rom′ū ləs), the mythical founder and first king of Rome, who, together with his brother Remus, was nourished by a wolf. *n.*

rood (rüd), 1. the cross on which Christ died. 2. a representation of it; a crucifix. 3. forty square rods, or one fourth of an acre. *n. 12.*

roof (rüf), 1. the top covering of a building. 2. something like it; as, the roof of a cave, the roof of a car, the roof of the mouth. 3. to cover with a roof; form a roof over. The trees roofed the glade where we camped. *n., v. 1.*

roof ing (rüf′ing), material used for roofs. Shingles are a common roofing for houses. *n. 11.*

roof less (rüf′lis), 1. having no roof. 2. having no shelter. *adj. 17.*

roof tree (rüf′trē′), the horizontal timber along the top of the roof. *n.*

rook[1] (rủk), 1. a European crow that nests in trees near buildings. 2. a person who cheats at cards or dice. 3. to cheat. *n., v. 7.*

Rook (about 19 in. long)

rook[2] (rủk), one of the pieces with which the game of chess is played, also called a castle. *n.*

rook er y (rủk′ər i), 1. a breeding place of rooks; a colony of rooks. 2. a breeding place or colony where other birds or animals are crowded together. 3. a crowded, mean, and poor tenement house or group of such houses. *n., pl. rookeries.*

room (rüm), 1. a part of a house, or other building, with walls of its own; as, a dining room, a schoolroom. 2. people in a room. The whole room laughed. 3. space.

The street was so crowded that the cars did not have room to move. There is room for one more in the automobile. 4. opportunity. There is room for improvement in John's work. 5. occupy a room; live in a room. Mr. Smith rooms in the gray house. Ethel rooms with Edith at boarding school. *n., v. 1.*

room er (rüm′ər), person who lives in a rented room or rooms in another's house; lodger. *n.*

room ful (rüm′fu̇l), 1. enough to fill a room. 2. people or things in a room. *n., pl. roomfuls.*

room i ness (rüm′i nis), ample space; abundance of room. *n.*

room mate (rüm′māt′), person who shares a room with another. *n.*

room y (rüm′i), large; spacious; having plenty of room. *adj., roomier, roomiest. 14.*

Roo se velt (rō′zə velt), 1. Franklin D. Roosevelt (born 1882) became president in 1933. 2. Theodore Roosevelt (1858-1919) was a famous writer and statesman who was president of the United States from 1901 to 1909. *n. 9.*

roost (rüst), 1. a bar, pole, or perch on which birds rest or sleep. 2. sit as birds do on a roost; settle for the night. 3. place for birds to roost in. 4. a place to rest or stay in; as, a robber's roost in the mountains. *n., v. 11.*

Rooster

roost er (rüs′tər), male domestic fowl. *n. 5.*

root[1] (rüt), 1. the part of a plant that grows down into the soil, holds it in place, and feeds it. 2. any underground part of a plant. 3. something like a root in shape, position, use, etc.; as, the root of a tooth, the roots of the hair. 4. a part from which other things grow and develop; a cause; source. The love of money is the root of all evil.

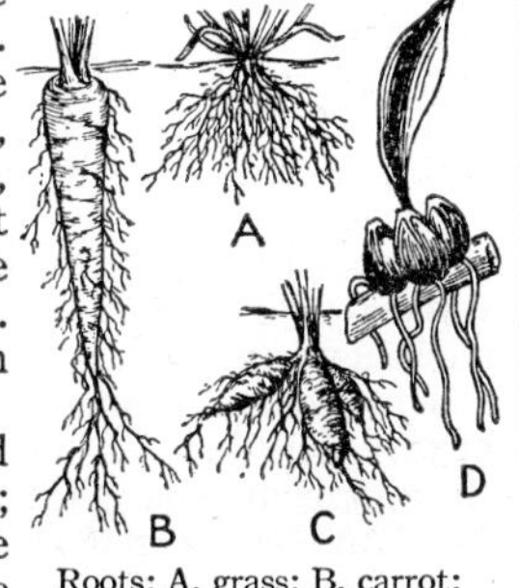

Roots: A, grass; B, carrot; C, sweet potato; D, orchid.

5. become fixed in the ground; send out roots and begin to grow. Some plants root more quickly than others. 6. fix firmly. He was rooted to the spot by surprise. 7. pull, tear, or dig (up, out, etc.) by the roots; get completely rid of. 8. a term used in mathematics. 2 is the square root of 4, and the cube root of 8. In the equation $x^2+2x-3=0$, 1 and —3 are the roots. 9. word from which others are derived. *Room* is the root of *roominess, roomer, roommate,* and *roomy. n., v. 2.*

root[2] (rüt), 1. dig with the snout. The pigs rooted up the garden. 2. cheer. *Slang. v.*

root let (rüt′lit), little root; small branch of a root. *n.*

rope (rōp), 1. a strong thick line or cord made by twisting smaller cords together. 2. a number of things twisted or strung together; as, a rope of onions, a rope of pearls. 3. to tie, bind, or fasten with rope. 4. enclose or mark off with a rope. 5. catch with a lasso. 6. a sticky, stringy mass; as, a rope of molasses candy. 7. form a rope; become ropy. Cook the syrup until it ropes when you lift it with a spoon. 8. **Know the ropes** means (1) know the various ropes of a ship. (2) know about a business or activity. *n., v. 2.*

Rope (def. 1)

rop y (rōp′i), 1. forming sticky threads; stringy. 2. like a rope. *adj.*

ro sa ry (rō′zə ri), 1. a series of prayers. 2. a string of beads for keeping count in saying these prayers. 3. rose garden; rose bed. *n., pl. rosaries. 12.*

rose[1] (rōz), 1. a flower that grows on a bush with thorny stems. Roses are red, pink, white, or yellow. They usually smell very sweet. 2. pinkish red; rose-pink. Her dress was rose. 3. something shaped like a rose, or suggesting a rose. *n., adj. 1.*

Red rose

rose[2] (rōz). See **rise.** The cat rose and stretched itself. *pt. of rise.*

ro se ate (rō′zi āt), rose-colored; rosy. *adj. 16.*

rose bud (rōz′bud′), the bud of a rose. *n. 7.*

rose bush (rōz′bu̇sh′), shrub or vine bearing roses. *n.*

rose leaf, petal of a rose.

rose mar y (rōz′mãr′i), an evergreen shrub whose leaves yield a fragrant oil used in making perfume. Rosemary is a symbol or emblem of remembrance. *n. 17.*

ro sette (rō zet′), an ornament shaped like a rose. Rosettes are often made of ribbon. *n. 13.*

rose water, water made fragrant with oil of roses.

rose wood (rōz′wůd′), a beautiful reddish wood that grows in the tropics. Rosewood is used in fine furniture. *n. 14.*

ros i ly (rōz′i li), with a rosy color. *adv.*

ros in (roz′in), 1. pine resin, a hard, yellow substance made from turpentine gum. Rosin is rubbed on violin bows, and on the shoes of circus performers to keep them from slipping. 2. cover or rub with rosin. *n., v. 12.*

ros i ness (rōz′i nis), rosy color. *n.*

ros ter (ros′tər), 1. a list giving each person's name and duties. 2. any list. *n.*

ros trum (ros′trəm), platform for public speaking. *n. 13.*

ros y (rōz′i), 1. like a rose; rose-red; pinkish-red. 2. bright; cheerful; as, a rosy future. *adj., rosier, rosiest. 4.*

rot (rot), 1. decay; spoil. So much rain will make the fruit rot. 2. process of rotting; decay. 3. a disease of plants and animals, especially sheep. *v., rotted, rotting, n. 6.*

ro ta ry (rō′tə ri), 1. turning like a top or a wheel; rotating. 2. having parts that rotate. 3. a circle with several roads leading off from it. 4. a system of signals to direct traffic at a place where roads cross. *adj., n. 7.*

ro tate (rō′tāt), 1. move around a center or axis; turn in a circle; revolve. Wheels, tops, and the earth rotate. 2. change in a fixed order; cause to take turns; as, to rotate men in office, to rotate crops in a field. *v. 9.*

ro ta tion (rō tā′shən), 1. a turning round; as, the rotation of a top. The earth's rotation causes night and day. 2. **In rotation** means in turn; in regular succession. 3. **Rotation of crops** means varying the crops grown in the same field. *n. 7.*

ro ta to ry (rō′tə tō′ri), 1. rotating; rotary. 2. causing rotation; as, a rotatory muscle. 3. passing or following from one to another in succession; as, a rotatory office in a club. *adj. 7.*

R.O.T.C., Reserve Officers' Training Corps.

rote (rōt). **By rote** means by memory without thought of the meaning. *n. 13.*

rot ten (rot′ən), 1. decayed; spoiled. 2. foul; bad-smelling; as, rotten air. 3. not in good condition; unsound; weak. The rotten ice gave way, letting the skater fall into the water. 4. corrupt; dishonest. 5. bad; nasty. *Slang. adj. 5.*

rot ten ness (rot′ən nis), 1. rotten condition; decay. The rottenness of the wood made it useless for building purposes. 2. very bad condition; corruption. *n. 13.*

Rot ter dam (rot′ər dam′), an important seaport city in the Netherlands. *n.*

ro tund (rō tund′), 1. round; plump; as, a rotund face. 2. full-toned; sounding rich and full; as, a rotund voice. *adj.*

ro tun da (rō tun′də), a round building or room, especially one with a dome. The Capitol at Washington has a large rotunda. *n.*

ro tun di ty (rō tun′di ti), 1. roundness; plumpness. 2. something round. 3. rounded fullness of tone. *n., pl. rotundities. 18.*

rou ble (rü′bəl), ruble. *n.*

Rou en (rü än′), city in northern France, famous for its cathedral and for being the place where Joan of Arc was burned at the stake. *n. 17.*

rouge (rüzh), 1. a red powder or paste for coloring the cheeks or lips. 2. to color with rouge. *n., v. 11.*

rough (ruf), 1. not smooth; not level; as, a rough rocky hill. 2. stormy. 3. harsh; rude; not gentle; likely to hurt others; as, rough manners. 4. without luxury and ease; as, rough life in camp. **Rough it** means live without comforts and conveniences. 5. without polish or fine finish; as, rough diamonds. 6. not completed; done as a first try; without details; as, a rough drawing, a rough idea. 7. coarse and tangled; as, rough fur, a rough coat of hair. 8. a coarse, violent person. 9. make rough; roughen. 10. shape (out) roughly. 11. roughly. *adj., v., n., adv. 2.*

rough age (ruf′ij), 1. rough or coarse material. 2. the coarser parts or kinds of food. Bran, fruit skins, and straw are roughage. *n. 18.*

rough en (ruf′ən), 1. make rough. 2. become rough. *v. 15.*

rough-hew (ruf′hū′), hew roughly; shape roughly without smoothing or finishing. *v.*

rough ly (ruf′li), 1. in a rough manner. 2. approximately. From New York to Los Angeles is roughly three thousand miles. *adv.*

rough ness (ruf′nis), 1. the state or quality of being rough. 2. a rough part or place. *n. 13.*

rough shod (ruf′shod′), having horseshoes with pointed projections to prevent slipping. **Ride roughshod over** (others) means follow one's own way without regard to (others). *adj.*

rou lette (rü let′), 1. a gambling game in which people bet on the turn of a wheel. 2. a small wheel with sharp teeth for making lines of marks, dots, or perforations; as, a roulette for perforating sheets of stamps. *n. 18.*

Rou ma ni a (rü mā′ni ə), Romania. *n. 10.*

round (round), 1. shaped like a ball. 2. shaped like a ring or circle. 3. shaped like the trunk of a tree. 4. full; complete; large; as, a round dozen, a good round sum of money. 5. plain-spoken; frank; plainly expressed. Dan's father scolded him in good round terms. 6. with a full tone; as, a mellow, round voice. 7. vigorous; brisk; quick; as, a round trot. 8. spoken with the lips curved. *O* is a round vowel. 9. anything shaped like a ball or circle or tree trunk; as, the rounds of a ladder. 10. a fixed course ending where it begins. The watchman makes his rounds every hour. 11. movement in a circle or about an axis; as, the earth's yearly round. 12. a cut of beef just above the leg. See the diagram under **beef.** 13. The round is a form of sculpture in which figures are apart from any background. 14. a dance in which the dancers move in a circle. 15. a series (of duties, events, etc.); routine; as, a round of pleasures, a round of duties. 16. a section of a game or sport; as, a round in a fight, a round of cards. 17. the distance between any limits; range; circuit; as, the round of human knowledge. 18. an act which a number of people do together; as, a round of applause, a round of cheers. 19. a short song sung by several persons or groups beginning one after another. "Three Blind Mice" is a round. 20. a discharge of guns by a group of soldiers all together. 21. powder, bullets, etc., for one such discharge. Only three rounds of ammunition were left. 22. make or become round. We round our lips to say *oo.* 23. go round; make a turn to the other side of; as, to round a corner, to round Cape Horn. 24. to fill (out); complete; as, to round out a paragraph, to round out a career. 25. **Round up** means drive or bring (cattle, etc.) together. 26. on all sides; around. The travelers were compassed round by dangers. 27. in a circle; with a whirling motion. Wheels go round. 28. in circumference; the distance around. The pumpkin measures 50 inches round. 29. from one to another. A report is going round that the schools will close. 30. through a round of time. Summer will soon come round again. In the tropics it is warm all the year round. 31. by a longer road or way. 32. on all sides of; so as to make a turn to the other side of. 33. about; around. 34. in all directions from; to all parts of. *adj., n., v., adv., prep. 1.*

round a bout (round′ə bout′), 1. indirect; as, a roundabout route, to hear in a roundabout way. 2. a short tight jacket for men or boys. *adj., n. 12.*

roun de lay (roun′də lā), 1. song in which a phrase or a line is repeated again and again. 2. dance in which the dancers move in a circle. *n. 16.*

round house (round′hous′), 1. a building for locomotives built about a platform that turns around. 2. a cabin on the after part of a ship's deck. *n.*

round ish (roun′dish), somewhat round. *adj. 17.*

round ly (round′li), 1. in a round manner; in a circle. 2. plainly; bluntly; severely; as, to refuse roundly, to scold roundly. 3. fully; completely. *adv.*

round number, 1. a whole number. 2. a number like 40, 200, 500, 1000, 3000, sixty million. 3874 in round numbers would be 3900 or 4000.

round-shoul dered (round′shōl′dərd), having the shoulders bent forward. *adj.*

Round Table, 1. a table about which King Arthur and his knights sat. 2. King Arthur and his knights.

round trip, a trip to a place and back again.

round up (round′up′), 1. act of driving or bringing cattle together from long distances. 2. the men and horses who round up cattle. 3. any similar gathering; as, a roundup of old friends. *n.*

rouse (rouz), wake up; stir up; excite. I was roused by the telephone bell. The dogs roused a deer from the bushes. He was roused to anger by the insult. *v. 4.*

Rous seau (rü sō′), Jean Jacques (1712-1778), French philosopher who wrote about government and education. *n. 17.*

roust a bout (roust′ə bout′), an unskilled laborer on wharves or ships. *n.*

rout[1] (rout), 1. flight of a defeated army in disorder. 2. put to flight. Our soldiers routed the enemy. 3. complete defeat. 4. defeat completely. *n., v. 6.*

rout[2] (rout), 1. dig (out); get by searching. 2. put (out); force (out). The farmer routed his sons out of bed at five o'clock. 3. dig with the snout. *v.*

route (rüt or rout), 1. way to go; road. Shall you go to California by the northern route? 2. arrange the way for. 3. send by a certain route. *n., v. 3.*

rou tine (rü tēn′), 1. a fixed, regular method of doing things; habitual doing of the same things in the same way. Getting up and going to bed are parts of your daily routine. 2. using routine; as, routine methods, routine workers. *n., adj. 8.*

rove (rōv), wander; wander about; roam. He roved over the fields and woods. *v. 4.*

rov er (rōv′ər), 1. wanderer. 2. pirate. 3. pirate ship. *n. 5.*

row[1] (rō), line; rank. The children stood in a row in front of the row of chairs. Corn is planted in rows. *n. 1.*

row[2] (rō), 1. use oars. 2. move by oars. Row us to the island. 3. trip in a rowboat. It's only a short row. *v., n.*

Boy rowing

row[3] (rou), noisy quarrel; noise. The children had a row over the bicycle. What's all this row about? *n.* [*Used in common talk*]

row boat (rō′bōt′), boat moved by oars. See the picture under **row**[2]. *n. 16.*

row dy (rou′di), 1. a rough, disorderly person. 2. rough; disorderly. *n., pl. rowdies, adj., rowdier, rowdiest. 20.*

row dy ism (rou′di izm), disorderly conduct; rough, noisy behavior. *n.*

Rowel

row el (rou′əl), a small wheel with sharp points at the end of a spur. See the picture just above. *n. 17.*

row er (rō′ər), person who rows a boat. *n. 13.*

row lock (rō′lok), a notch in which the oar rests in rowing; oarlock. See the picture. *n.*

Rowlock

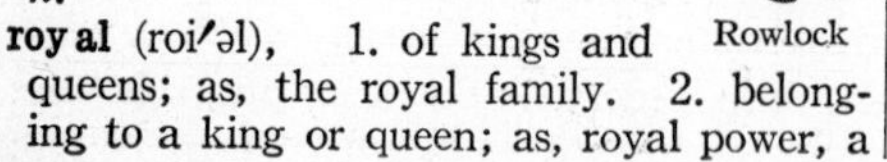

roy al (roi′əl), 1. of kings and queens; as, the royal family. 2. belonging to a king or queen; as, royal power, a royal palace. 3. from or by a king or queen; as, a royal command. 4. of a kingdom. 5. appropriate for a king; splendid; as, a royal welcome, a royal feast. 6. like a king. The lion is a royal beast. 7. a small mast or sail set above the topgallant. *adj., n. 2.*

roy al ist (roi′əl ist), 1. a supporter of a king or of a royal government. The Royalists supported Charles I of England while the Puritans opposed him. 2. of or pertaining to royalists; as, royalist principles. *n., adj. 15.*

roy al ly (roi′əl i), in a royal manner; grandly; richly. *adv.*

roy al ty (roi′əl ti), 1. a royal person; royal persons. Kings, queens, princes, and princesses are royalty. A box in the theater was reserved for royalty. 2. the rank or dignity of a king or queen; royal power. The crown is the symbol of royalty. 3. kingliness; royal quality; nobility. 4. a share of the profits paid to an owner of a patent, copyright, etc. An author receives royalties from the publishers of his books. *n., pl. royalties. 7.*

R.R., railroad.

R.S.V.P., please answer.

rub (rub), 1. move one thing back and forth against another. He rubbed his hands with soap. 2. to clean, smooth, or polish by moving one thing firmly against another. Rub out your work with an eraser and do it over again. 3. push and press along the surface of. The nurse rubbed Dick's lame back. That door rubs on the floor. 4. act of rubbing. Give the silver a rub with the polish. 5. thing that rubs or hurts the feelings. He didn't like her mean rub at his slowness. 6. difficulty. The rub came when both boys wanted to sit with the driver. *v., rubbed, rubbing, n. 2.*

rub ber (rub′ər), 1. person or thing that rubs. 2. an elastic substance made from the juice of various tropical plants. Rubber will not let water through. 3. made of rubber. 4. something made from this substance. I need a strong rubber to hold these papers together. We wear rubbers on our feet when it rains. Pencils often have rubbers for erasing pencil marks. 5. two games out of three or three out of five won by the same side. 6. the deciding game. If each side has won two games, the fifth game will be the rubber. *n., adj. 3.*

rub ber ized (rub′ər īzd), coated or treated with rubber; as, rubberized cloth. *adj. 19.*

rub bish (rub′ish), 1. waste stuff of no use; trash. Pick up the rubbish and burn it. 2. nonsense; silly words and thoughts. *n. 7.*

rub ble (rub′əl), 1. rough broken stone or bricks. 2. masonry made of this. The house was built of rubble and plaster. *n. 17.*

Ru bens (rü′bənz), a Flemish painter (1577-1640). *n.*

Ru bi con (rü′bi kon), small river forming the northern boundary of ancient Italy. By crossing the Rubicon, Caesar began a civil war. So, the phrase **crossing the Rubicon** has come to mean a decisive act. *n. 14.*

ru bi cund (rü′bi kund), reddish; ruddy. The jolly captain had a rubicund face. *adj.*

ru ble (rü′bəl), a Russian silver coin, formerly worth about 50 cents. *n. 17.*

ru bric (rü′brik), 1. a title or heading of a chapter, a law, etc.; a title or heading printed in red or in special lettering. 2. a direction for the conducting of divine services inserted in a prayer book, ritual, etc. *n. 15.*

ru by (rü′bi), 1. a precious stone, red in color, clear, and hard. Real rubies are very rare. 2. red; as, ruby lips, ruby wine. *n., pl. rubies, adj. 5.*

rud der (rud′ər), 1. a movable flat piece at the rear end of a boat or ship by which it is steered. See the picture. 2. a similar piece in an airplane. See the diagram of **airplane.** *n. 9.*

RUDDER

Rudder of a boat

rud di ness (rud′i nis), healthy redness of skin; redness. *n.*

rud dy (rud′i), 1. red. 2. healthy red; as, ruddy cheeks. *adj., ruddier, ruddiest. 6.*

rude (rüd), 1. coarse; rough; without finish or polish. He made a rude bed from the branches of evergreen trees. The savage made rude ornaments from shells and pebbles. 2. rough in manners or behavior; violent. Rude hands seized the child and threw him into the car. John was given a rude shock when the other boys poured a pail of water on him. 3. impolite; not courteous. It is rude to stare at people or to point. 4. not having learned much; rather wild; barbarous. *adj. 2.*

rude ness (rüd′nis), roughness; coarseness; bad manners; violence. His rudeness is inexcusable. *n. 12.*

ru di ment (rü′di mənt), 1. part to be learned first; beginning; as, the rudiments of grammar. 2. something in an early stage; as, the rudiments of wings on a baby chick. *n. 8.*

ru di men ta ry (rü′di men′təri), 1. to be learned or studied first; elementary. 2. in an early stage of development; undeveloped. *adj. 12.*

rue[1] (rü), be sorry for; repent; regret. She will rue the day she insulted your mother. *v. 6.*

rue[2] (rü), plant with yellow flowers and leaves that have a strong smell and a bitter taste. *n.*

rue ful (rü′fəl), 1. sorrowful; unhappy; mournful; as, a rueful expression. 2. causing sorrow or pity; as, a rueful sight. *adj. 10.*

ruff (ruf), 1. a deep frill stiff enough to stand out, worn around the neck by men and women in the 16th century. 2. a collar of specially marked feathers or hairs on the neck of a bird or an animal. *n. 13.*

Ruff

ruffed grouse (ruft′ grous′), North American game bird with a tuft of feathers on each side of the neck. It is sometimes called a partridge or pheasant.

Ruffed grouse (about 1½ ft. long)

ruf fi an (ruf′i ən), 1. a rough, brutal, or cruel fellow. 2. rough; cruel. *n., adj. 6.*

ruf fle (ruf′əl), 1. to wrinkle; make rough or uneven. A breeze ruffled the lake. The hen ruffled her feathers at the sight of the dog. 2. a strip of cloth, ribbon, or lace gathered along one edge and used for trimming. Ruffles used to be much worn; even men had ruffled shirts. 3. gather into a ruffle. 4. disturb; annoy. Nothing can ruffle her calm temper. 5. disorder; confusion; disturbance. *v., n. 5.*

Dress with four ruffles

rug (rug), 1. a heavy floor covering. We have Turkish rugs, rag rugs, a fur rug, and a grass rug. 2. a thick warm cloth used as covering. He wrapped his woolen rug around him. *n. 3.*

Rug by (rug′bi), 1. a famous school for

boys in England. 2. a variety of football. *n.*

rug ged (rug′id), 1. rough; wrinkled. 2. harsh; stern; severe. 3. strong; vigorous. 4. rude. 5. stormy. *adj. 5.*

ru in (rü′in), 1. a building, wall, etc., that has fallen to pieces. 2. destruction; very great damage; overthrow. The ruin of property caused by the earthquake was enormous. They planned the duke's ruin. 3. a fallen or decayed condition. The house had gone to ruin from neglect. 4. cause of destruction, decay, or downfall. Gambling was his ruin. 5. destroy; spoil; bring to ruin. The rain has ruined my new dress. *n., v. 2.*

ru in a tion (rü′i nā′shən), ruin; destruction; downfall. *n.*

ru in ous (rü′i nəs), 1. bringing ruin; causing destruction. 2. fallen into ruins. *adj. 9.*

rule (rül), 1. a principle governing conduct, action, etc.; statement of what to do and what not to do. Learn the rules of the game. 2. set of rules. 3. decide; make a rule. **Rule a thing out** means decide that it does not belong in. 4. to control; govern. The majority rules in a democracy. 5. control; government. Democracy means the rule of the people. 6. regular method; thing that usually happens; what is usually true. Fair weather is the rule in Arizona. **As a rule** means usually. 7. straight strip of wood, metal, etc., used to measure or as

Rule or ruler

a guide in drawing. 8. to mark with lines. He used a ruler to rule the paper. 9. mark off. *n., v. 1.*

rul er (rül′ər), 1. person who rules. 2. a straight strip of wood, metal, etc., used in drawing lines. *n. 3.*

rul ing (rül′ing), 1. a decision of a judge or court. 2. controlling; chief. *n., adj.*

rum[1] (rum), 1. alcoholic liquor made from sugar cane, molasses, etc. 2. alcoholic liquor. *n. 10.*

rum[2] (rum), odd; queer. *adj.* [*Slang*]

Ru ma ni a (rü mā′ni ə), Romania, a country in southeastern Europe. *n. 20.*

rum ble (rum′bəl), 1. make a deep, heavy, continuous sound. 2. a deep, heavy, continuous sound. We hear the far-off rumble of thunder. 3. move with such a sound. 4. the rear part of an automobile or carriage containing an extra seat or place for baggage. *v., n. 7.*

ru mi nant (rü′mi nənt), 1. animal that chews the cud. Cows, sheep, and camels are ruminants. 2. belonging to the group of ruminants. 3. much given to thought; engaged in thought. *n., adj. 18.*

ru mi nate (rü′mi nāt), 1. chew the cud. 2. chew again. A cow ruminates its food. 3. keep thinking about; ponder; meditate. He ruminated on the strange events of the past week. *v. 9.*

ru mi na tion (rü′mi nā′shən), 1. chewing the cud. 2. meditation; reflection. *n. 19.*

rum mage (rum′ij), 1. search thoroughly by moving things about. I rummaged three drawers before I found my gloves. 2. search in a disorderly way. I rummaged in my drawer for a pair of gloves. 3. pull from among other things. 4. a rummaging search. 5. A **rummage sale** is a sale of odds and ends, old clothing, etc., usually held to raise money for charity. *v., n., adj. 12.*

rum my (rum′i), a kind of card game. *n.*

ru mor (rü′mər), 1. a story or statement talked of as news without any proof that it is true. The rumor spread that a new school would be built here. 2. vague, general talk. Rumor said that Italy would quarrel with France. 3. tell or spread by rumor. *n., v. 4.*

rump (rump), the hind part of the body of an animal, where the legs join the back. A rump steak is a cut of beef from this part. See the diagram under **beef.** *n. 7.*

rum ple (rum′pəl), crumple; crush; wrinkle. Don't play in your best dress; you'll rumple it. *v., n. 11.*

rum pus (rum′pəs), a noisy quarrel; noise; disturbance; uproar. *n.* [*Used in common talk*]

run (run), 1. move the legs quickly; go faster than walking. A horse can run faster than a man. 2. go; move; keep going. This train runs from Kansas City to St. Louis. Does your watch run well? 3. creep; grow; climb. Vines run along the sides of the road. 4. flow. Blood runs from a cut. The child's nose runs. The boy has a running sore. 5. spread. The color of the dress ran when it was washed. 6. extend; stretch. Shelves ran around the walls. The man ran a fence across the lot. 7. get; become. The well ran dry in summer. Never run into debt. 8. occur; be in action. A thought ran through my mind. 9. sew by passing a needle in and out with even stitches in a line. 10. get past or through; as, to run a blockade. 11. expose oneself to; as, to run a risk of taking cold. 12. be a candidate for election. Mr. Smith will run for president. 13. make run; as, to run a horse. 14. make go; force; thrust. Tom ran his nose against a post. He ran a splinter into his hand. 15. shape by melting; as, to run bullets in a mold. 16. act of running. The dog came on the run. 17. course; direction; trend; as, the run of events. 18. free use; as, to give a person the run of a house. 19. a trip. The train makes a run of one hundred miles in two hours. 20. drop stitches; ravel. Silk stockings often run. 21. place where stitches have slipped out or become undone; as, a run in a stocking. 22. time; period; spell; as, a run of good luck, a run of wet weather. 23. a sudden demand or call; as, a run on a bank to draw out money. 24. series of performances. This play had a run of 200 nights. 25. kind; class; as, the common run of mankind. 26. number of fish moving together; as, a run of salmon. 27. a stretch of ground or an enclosed place for animals; as, a cattle run, a chicken run. 28. a unit of score in baseball or cricket. 29. Some special meanings are:

in the long run, on the whole; in the end.

run down, 1. stop going or working. The clock has run down. 2. chase till caught. 3. speak evil against. 4. make tired or ill. She is run down from working too hard.

run out, come to an end.

run out of, use up; have no more.

run through, 1. spend rapidly and foolishly. 2. pierce.

v., ran, run, running, n. 1.

run a bout (run′ə bout′), 1. a light automobile or carriage with a single seat. 2. a small motorboat. 3. person who runs about from place to place. *n. 14.*

run a gate (run′ə gāt), 1. runaway. 2. vagabond; wanderer. *n. [Old use] 17.*

run a way (run′ə wā′), 1. person, horse, etc., that runs away. 2. running away. 3. running with nobody to guide or stop it; out of control; as, a runaway horse, a runaway car. 4. done by runaways; as, a runaway marriage. *n., adj. 8.*

run-down (run′doun′), 1. tired; sick. 2. falling to pieces; partly ruined. 3. that has stopped going or working. *adj.*

rune (rün), 1. any letter of an ancient Teutonic alphabet. 2. a mark that looks like a rune and has some mysterious, magic meaning. 3. an old Scandinavian poem or song. *n.*

rung[1] (rung). See **ring**[2]. *pp. or pt. of ring*[2]. *6.*

rung[2] (rung), 1. round rod or bar used as a step of a ladder. 2. crosspiece set between the legs of a chair or as part of the back or arm of a chair. 3. spoke of a wheel. 4. bar of wood having a similar shape and use. *n.*

R, rungs.

R, rungs.

run nel (run′əl), small stream. *n. 19.*

run ner (run′ər), 1. one that runs; messenger; racer. A runner arrived out of breath. 2. either of the narrow pieces on which a sleigh or sled slides; the blade of a skate. 3. a slender stem that takes root along the ground, thus producing new plants. 4. a ship that tries to evade somebody; smuggler; as, a blockade runner. 5. a long narrow strip. We have a runner of carpet in our hall, and runners of linen and lace on bureaus. *n. 5.*

Runner of a strawberry plant

run ning (run′ing), 1. act of one that runs. 2. flow of liquids; as, a running of the nose in a cold. 3. that runs. Running handwriting joins all letters of a word together. A running sore discharges pus. A person keeps a running commentary on a movie when he talks about is as it is shown. For three nights running is for three nights in succession. A running jump is one made with a run first. 4. Some special meanings are:

be out of the running, have no chance to win.

running board of an automobile, the board along the side near the ground.

running gear, the wheels and axles of an automobile, locomotive, or other vehicle.

running knot, a knot so made as to slide along the rope.

running noose, a noose with a slip knot.

n., adj.

runt (runt), a stunted animal, person, or plant. *n.*

run way (run′wā′), 1. a way, track, groove,

trough, or the like, along which something moves, slides, etc. 2. the beaten track of deer or other animals. 3. enclosed place for animals to run in. *n. 17.*

ru pee (rü pē'), 1. a unit of money of British India, worth about 62 cents in normal times. 2. a silver coin of British India, worth about 32 cents. *n.*

rup ture (rup'chər), 1. a break; breaking. 2. the sticking out of some tissue or organ of the body through the wall of the cavity which should hold it in. 3. to break; burst; break off. *n., v. 13.*

ru ral (rür'əl), in the country; belonging to the country; like that of the country. Rural life is healthful and quiet. *adj. 3.*

rural free delivery, delivery of mail in country districts by regular carriers.

ruse (rüz), trick; stratagem. *n. 18.*

rush[1] (rush), 1. move, go, or send with speed and force. The river rushed past. Rush this order, please. 2. go or act with great haste. He rushes into things without knowing anything about them. 3. to attack with much speed and force. The soldiers rushed the enemy's trenches. 4. act of rushing; dash. The rush of the flood swept everything before it. 5. hurry. What is your rush? Wait a minute. 6. pressure; eager demand; effort of many people to go somewhere or get something. The Christmas rush is hard for clerks. *v., n. 1.*

rush[2] (rush), a plant with a hollow stem that grows in wet soil or marshy places. The seats of chairs are sometimes made of rushes. *n.*

rush y (rush'i), 1. abounding with rushes; covered with rushes. 2. made of rushes. *adj.*

rusk (rusk), 1. piece of bread or cake toasted in the oven. 2. a kind of light, soft, sweet biscuit. *n.*

Rus kin (rus'kin), John, an English author, art critic, and social reformer (1819-1900). *n. 18.*

rus set (rus'it), 1. yellowish brown; reddish brown. The leaves in the fall are scarlet, yellow, and russet. 2. a coarse, russet-colored cloth. The peasants used to make and wear russet. 3. a kind of apple with a rough brownish skin. *adj., n. 8.*

Rus sia (rush'ə), country in eastern Europe and northwestern Asia. Before the revolution in 1917, it was an empire ruled by a czar, with its capital at St. Petersburg. It is now a large part of the Union of Soviet Socialist Republics. *n. 3.*

rus sia (rush'ə), Russia leather. *n.*

Russia leather, fine smooth leather, often dark red, produced by careful tanning and dyeing.

Rus sian (rush'ən), 1. of or pertaining to Russia, its people, or their language. 2. a native or inhabitant of Russia. 3. the language of Russia. *adj., n.*

rust (rust), 1. the reddish-brown or orange coating that forms on iron or steel when exposed to air or moisture. 2. become covered with this. 3. become spoiled by not being used. Don't let your mind rust during the vacation. 4. a plant disease that spots leaves and stems. *n., v. 3.*

rus tic (rus'tik), 1. belonging to the country; rural; suitable for the country. 2. simple; countrylike. His rustic speech and ways made him uncomfortable in the city school. 3. rough; awkward. 4. country person. The rustics had gathered at the county fair. *adj., n. 4.*

rus tic i ty (rus tis'i ti), 1. rustic quality, characteristic, or peculiarity. 2. rural life. 3. awkwardness; ignorance. *n., pl. rusticities. 19.*

rust i ness (rus'ti nis), rusty condition. *n.*

rus tle (rus'əl), 1. sound that leaves make when moved by the wind; sound like this. 2. move so as to make such a sound. 3. move or stir (something) so that it makes such a sound; as, to rustle the papers. 4. steal (cattle, etc.). *n., v. 4.*

rus tler (rus'lər), 1. active, energetic person. *Slang.* 2. cattle thief. *n.*

rust y (rus'ti), 1. rusted; covered with rust; as, a rusty knife. 2. made by rust. 3. colored like rust. 4. faded; as, a rusty black. 5. damaged by lack of use. *adj., rustier, rustiest. 5.*

rut (rut), 1. a track made in the ground by wheels. 2. make ruts in. 3. fixed or established way of acting; groove. *n., v., rutted, rutting. 13.*

ru ta ba ga (rü'tə bā'gə), a large, yellow turnip. *n.*

Ruth (rüth), a book of the Old Testament that tells about a heroine having this name. *n. 3.*

ruth less (rüth'lis), cruel; having no pity; showing no mercy. *adj. 8.*

Rye

Rut land (rut'lənd), a city in western Vermont. *n. 20.*

Ry., railway.

-ry, suffix meaning:—

1. occupation or work of a———; as in dentistry, chemistry.

2. act of a———; as in mimicry.

3. state or condition of a——; as in rivalry.
4. group of ——s; as in jewelry.

rye (rī), 1. a grain that is made into a kind of flour. Peasants in Germany and Russia eat a great deal of almost black rye bread. 2. the plant rye grows on. See the picture on page 704. *n. 4.*

S

S, s (es), 1. the 19th letter of the alphabet. There are two s's in sister. S comes after p, q, r. 2. anything shaped like an S. 3. shaped like an S. *n., pl. S's, s's, adj.*

S. or **s.**, south.

Sab bath (sab′əth), 1. the day of the week used for rest and worship. Sunday is the Christian Sabbath. Saturday is the Jewish Sabbath. 2. of or belonging to the Sabbath. *n., adj. 4.*

sa ber or **sa bre** (sā′bər), a heavy, curved sword with a sharp edge, used by cavalry. *n. 10.*

Saber

Sa bine (sā′bīn), member of a tribe in central Italy which was conquered by the Romans in about the third century B.C. *n. 13.*

sa ble (sā′bəl), 1. a small animal valued for its dark, glossy fur. 2. its fur. Sable is one of the most costly furs. 3. black. The widow's sable garments showed that she was in mourning. *n., adj. 6.*

Sable (about 1½ ft. long, without the tail)

sab ot (sab′ō), 1. wooden shoe hollowed out of a single piece of wood. French peasants wear sabots. 2. leather shoe with a thick wooden sole. *n.*

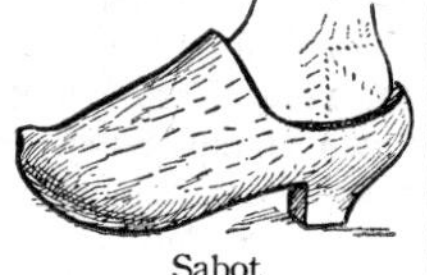
Sabot

sac (sak), a baglike part in an animal or plant, often one containing liquids; as, the sac of a honeybee. *n. 11.*

sac cha rine (sak′ərin), sugary; very sweet; as, a saccharine smile. *adj.*

sac er do tal (sas′ər dō′təl), of priests or the priesthood; priestly. *adj. 15.*

sa chem (sā′chəm), the chief of an American Indian tribe. *n. 16.*

sa chet (sa shā′ or sash′ā), 1. small bag or pad containing perfumed powder. 2. perfumed powder. *n. 13.*

sack[1] (sak), 1. large bag made of coarse cloth. Sacks are used for holding grain, flour, potatoes, and coal. 2. such a bag with what is in it. He bought two sacks of corn. 3. any bag with what is in it; as, a sack of candy. 4. put into a sack. 5. loose coat; as, a knitted sack for a baby. *n., v. 2.*

sack[2] (sak), 1. plunder (a captured city). The soldiers sacked the town. 2. plundering (of a captured city). *v., n.*

sack[3] (sak), sherry or similar wines. *n.*

sack cloth (sak′klôth′), 1. coarse cloth for making sacks. 2. coarse cloth like this worn as a sign of mourning. *n. 11.*

sack ing (sak′ing), coarse cloth for making sacks, etc. *n.*

sacque (sak), loose jacket for a woman, girl, or baby. *n.*

sac ra ment (sak′rə mənt), 1. a solemn religious ceremony of the Christian church. Baptism is a sacrament. The Lord's Supper is often called the Sacrament. 2. something especially sacred. *n. 10.*

sac ra men tal (sak′rə men′təl), 1. of or pertaining to a sacrament; used in a sacrament; as, sacramental wine. 2. especially sacred. *adj. 17.*

Sac ra men to (sak′rə men′tō), the capital of California. *n. 13.*

sa cred (sā′krid), 1. belonging to God; holy. 2. connected with religion; religious. 3. worthy of reverence. 4. that must not be injured. *adj. 3.*

sac ri fice (sak′ri fīs), 1. act of offering to a god; thing offered. The ancient Hebrews killed animals on the altars as sacrifices to God. 2. give or offer to a god. They sacrificed oxen, sheep, and doves. 3. giving up one thing for another. Our teacher does not approve of any sacrifice of studies to sports. 4. give up. A mother will sacrifice her life for her children. 5. loss. He will sell his house at a sacrifice because he needs money. 6. sell at a loss. *n., v. 2.*

sac ri fi cial (sak′ri fish′əl), 1. having to do with sacrifice. 2. used in a sacrifice. *adj. 18.*

sac ri lege (sak′ri lij), intentional injury to anything sacred; disrespectful treatment of anyone or anything sacred. Robbing a church is a sacrilege. *n. 18.*

sac ri le gious (sak′ri lij′əs), injurious or insulting to sacred things. *adj. 13.*

sac ris ty (sak′ris ti), a place where the sacred vessels, robes, etc., of a church are kept. *n., pl. sacristies.*

sac ro sanct (sak′rō sangkt), 1. very holy; very sacred. 2. consecrated; set apart as sacred. *adj.*

sad (sad), 1. You feel sad if your best friend goes away. Mary was sad because she lost her money. 2. causing sorrow. The death of a pet is a sad loss. 3. dark; dull in color. *adj., sadder, saddest. 1.*

sad den (sad′ən), make sad; become sad. *v. 9.*

Saddle on a horse

sad dle (sad′əl), 1. seat for a rider on a horse's back, on a bicycle, etc. **In the saddle** sometimes means in a position of control. 2. thing shaped like a saddle. A ridge between two mountain peaks is called a saddle. 3. put a saddle on. Saddle the horse. 4. to burden. Mr. Brown is saddled with a big house which he does not need or want. *n., v. 2.*

sad dle bag (sad′əl bag′), one of a pair of bags laid over a horse's back behind the saddle. *n.*

sad dle bow (sad′əl bō′), the front part of a saddle, which sticks up. *n.*

sad dler (sad′lər), person who makes or sells saddles and harness. *n. 20.*

sad ness (sad′nis), sorrow; grief. *n. 4.*

safe (sāf), 1. free from harm or danger. The package came safe and sound. The cat in the tree is safe from the dog. Keep money in a safe place. 2. not causing harm or danger. Is it safe to leave the house unlocked? A soft rubber ball is a safe plaything. 3. careful; as, a safe guess, a safe move. 4. that can be depended on; as, a safe guide. 5. a place or container for keeping things safe. *adj., n. 1.*

Safe (def. 5)

safe-con duct (sāf′kon′dukt), 1. the privilege of passing safely through a region, especially in time of war. The nurse was given safe-conduct through the enemy's camp. 2. a paper granting this privilege. *n. 17.*

safe guard (sāf′gärd′), 1. keep safe; guard against hurt or danger; protect. Pure food laws safeguard our health. 2. protection; defense. Keeping clean is a safeguard against disease. *v., n. 8.*

safe keep ing (sāf′kēp′ing), protection; keeping safe; care. *n.*

safe ty (sāf′ti), 1. freedom from harm or danger. A bank affords safety for your money. You can cross the street in safety when the policeman holds up his hand. 2. bringing no harm or danger; making harm unlikely; as, a safety pin, a safety match, a safety razor. *n., adj. 2.*

safety valve, 1. valve that lets off steam when there is too much pressure. 2. something that helps a person get rid of anger, nervousness, etc., in a harmless way.

saf fron (saf′rən), 1. an orange-yellow coloring matter obtained from a kind of crocus. Saffron is used to color and flavor candy, drinks, etc. 2. orange yellow. *n., adj. 10.*

sag (sag), 1. sink under weight or pressure; bend down in the middle. 2. hang down unevenly. Your dress sags in the back. 3. become less firm or elastic; droop; sink. Our courage sagged. 4. a sagging. *v., sagged, sagging, n. 12.*

sa ga (sä′gə), 1. an old Norse story of heroic deeds. 2. any story of heroic deeds. *n. 17.*

sa ga cious (sə gā′shəs), shrewd; wise in a keen, practical way. *adj. 10.*

sa gac i ty (sə gas′i ti), shrewdness; keen, sound judgment; mental acuteness. *n. 8.*

sag a more (sag′ə mōr), the chief of an American Indian tribe. *n. 20.*

sage[1] (sāj), 1. wise. 2. wise-looking. Owls are sage birds. 3. wise man. The sage gave sage advice to his followers. *adj., n. 4.*

sage[2] (sāj), 1. a plant whose leaves are used in cooking and in medicine. The turkey stuffing is seasoned with sage. 2. sagebrush. *n.*

Sagebrush (2 to 12 ft. high)

sage brush (sāj′brush′), a grayish-green, bushy plant, common on the dry plains of the western United States. *n.*

sa go (sā′gō), 1. a starchy food used in making puddings, etc. 2. a palm tree from which this starchy food is made. *n., pl.* *sagos. 19.*

Sa har a (sə hãr′ə), the great desert in northern Africa. *n. 12.*

sa hib (sä′ib), sir; master. Natives in India call a European "sahib" when speaking to or of him. *n.*

said (sed), 1. See **say.** He said he would come. She had said "No" every time. 2. named before; as, the said witness, the said sum of money. *pt. and pp. of say, adj. 1.*

sail (sāl), 1. piece of cloth spread to the wind to make a ship move through the water. 2. something like a sail. 3. a ship; ships; as, a fleet numbering 30 sail. 4. a trip on a boat with sails. 5. travel on water by the action of wind on sails. 6. travel on a steamboat. 7. travel through the air. 8. move smoothly like a ship with sails. The swans sail along the lake. The eagle sailed by. Mrs. Grand sailed into the room. 9. sail upon, over, or through; as, to sail the seas. 10. manage a ship. The boys are learning to sail. 11. begin a trip by water. 12. Some special meanings are:

make sail, 1. spread out the sails of a ship. 2. begin a trip by water.

set sail, begin a trip by water.

under sail, with the sails spread out.

n., v. 1.

sail boat (sāl′bōt′), boat that is moved by sails. See the pictures of **schooner** and **sloop.** *n. 16.*

sail or (sāl′ər), 1. person whose work is sailing. In these days most sailors are on steamships. The men in our navy are called sailors if they are not officers. 2. A **good sailor** sometimes means a person who does not get seasick. 3. like a sailor's. Little boys wear sailor suits and sailor caps. Her middy blouse has a sailor collar. 4. The flat-brimmed hat that we call a sailor today is modeled after the kind of hat sailors used to wear years ago. *n., adj. 2.*

Sailor collar on a middy blouse

Sailor (def. 4)

saint (sānt), 1. very holy person; true Christian. 2. person who has gone to heaven. 3. person declared a saint by the Roman Catholic Church. *n. 2.*

For places beginning with **Saint** look under the **St.** words.

Saint Ber nard (sānt bər närd′), a big tan-and-white dog with a large head. These intelligent dogs are kept by the monks on the St. Bernard passes to rescue travelers lost in the snow.

Saint Bernard (about 2½ ft. high at the shoulder)

saint ed (sān′tid), 1. declared to be a saint. 2. thought of as a saint; gone to heaven. 3. sacred; very holy. *adj.*

saint hood (sānt′hůd), character or status of a saint. *n.*

saint li ness (sānt′li nis), piety; holiness; godliness. *n.*

saint ly (sānt′li), like a saint; very holy; very good. *adj., saintlier, saintliest. 11.*

Saint Valentine's Day, February 14.

Saint Vi tus's dance (sānt vī′təs iz dans′), a nervous disease that causes an involuntary twitching of the muscles.

saith (seth), old form meaning **says.** *v. 7.*

sake (sāk). Sake is used with *for.* **For the sake of** means (1) because of; on account of. (2) to help; to please. **For your own sake** means on your own account; to help yourself. *n. 2.*

sa laam (sə läm′), 1. a greeting in the Orient that means "Peace." 2. a very low bow, with the palm of the right hand placed on the forehead. 3. greet with a salaam. 4. make a salaam. *n., v.*

sal a ble (sāl′ə bəl), that can be sold; fit to be sold; easily sold. *adj.*

sa la cious (sə lā′shəs), lustful; lewd; obscene; indecent. *adj.*

sal ad (sal′əd), raw green vegetables, such as lettuce and celery, served with a dressing. Often cold meat, fish, eggs, cooked vegetables, or fruits are used along with, or instead of, the raw green vegetables. *n. 5.*

sal a man der (sal′ə man′dər), 1. a kind of lizard supposed to live in fire. 2. person who likes or can stand a great deal of heat. 3. a spirit or imaginary being that lives in fire. 4. an animal shaped like a lizard, but belonging to the same group as frogs and toads. Salamanders live in damp places. *n. 8.*

Salamander (def. 4)

sal a ried (sal′ə rid), receiving a salary. *adj.*

sal a ry (sal′ə ri), fixed pay for regular work.

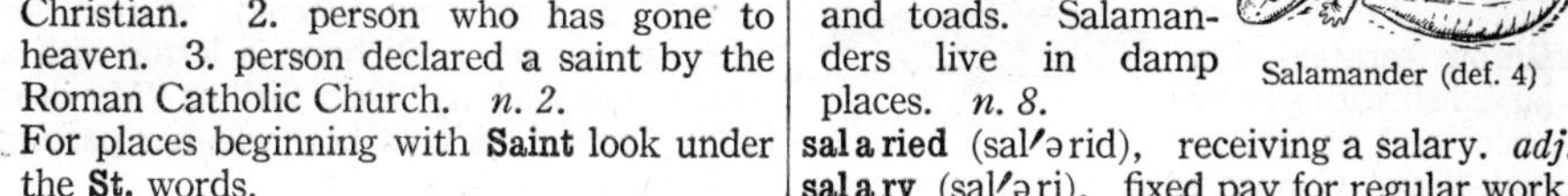

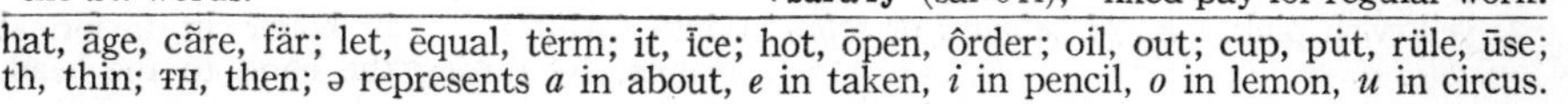

Teachers and clerks receive salaries. *n., pl. salaries. 3.*

sale (sāl), 1. act of selling; exchange of goods for money. The sale of his old home made him sad. **For sale** or **on sale** means to be sold. That car is for sale. 2. amount sold. Today's sales were larger than yesterday's. 3. chance to sell. There is almost no sale for carriages in these days. 4. selling at lower prices than usual. This store is having a sale on suits. *n. 2.*

sale a ble (sāl′ə bəl), salable. *adj.*

Sa lem (sā′ləm), 1. one of the oldest towns in Massachusetts. 2. capital of Oregon. *n. 10.*

sales man (sālz′mən), person whose work is selling. The salesman showed her nearly all the hats in the shop. *n., pl. salesmen. 6.*

sales man ship (sālz′mən ship), 1. business of a salesman. 2. ability at selling. *n. 19.*

sales tax, tax based on the amount received for articles sold. Her coat cost 14 dollars plus 35 cents sales tax.

sales wom an (sālz′wu̇m′ən), woman whose work is selling. *n., pl. saleswomen. 20.*

sa li ent (sā′li ənt), standing out; easily seen or noticed; prominent; striking; as, the salient features in a landscape, the salient points in a speech. *adj. 13.*

sa line (sā′līn), 1. of salt; like salt; salty. 2. containing common salt or any other salts. 3. a salt spring, well, or marsh. 4. substance containing common salt or any other salts. *adj., n. 18.*

Salis bur y (sôlz′ber′i), city in southern England. A famous cathedral is located there. *n. 9.*

sa li va (sə lī′və), the liquid produced by glands in the mouth. *n. 8.*

sali var y (sal′i vãr′i), producing saliva; as, the salivary glands. *adj. 13.*

sal low (sal′ō), having a sickly, yellowish color or complexion. *adj. 10.*

sal ly (sal′i), 1. sudden rushing forth. The men in the fort made a brave sally and returned with many prisoners. 2. rush forth suddenly; go out; set out briskly. We sallied forth at dawn. 3. witty remark. She continued her story undisturbed by the merry sallies of her hearers. *n., pl. sallies, v., sallied, sallying. 5.*

salm on (sam′ən), 1. a large fish with silvery scales and yellowish-pink flesh. Canned salmon is a good food. 2. yellowish pink. *n., pl. salmons* or *salmon, adj. 6.*

Salmon

sa lon (sa lon′), 1. large room for receiving or entertaining guests. 2. assembly of guests in such a room. 3. place used to exhibit works of art. 4. exhibition of works of art. *n. 13.*

sa loon (sə lün′), 1. place where alcoholic drinks are sold and drunk. 2. large room for general or public use. Concerts were often held in the saloon of the steamship. The ship's passengers ate in the dining saloon. *n. 13.*

sal si fy (sal′si fi), a parsniplike vegetable whose root is good to eat. *n. 20.*

sal so da (sal′ sō′də), the kind of soda used for washing.

salt (sôlt), 1. a white substance found in the earth and in sea water. Salt is used to season and preserve food. 2. containing salt. 3. tasting like salt. 4. mix or sprinkle with salt. 5. preserve with salt. 6. seasoning. **The salt of the earth** means the best people. 7. **Take a statement with a grain of salt** means season one's belief in the statement with a little doubt. 8. a chemical compound of a metal and an acid. Baking soda is a salt. 9. sailor. *Used in common talk.* 10. **Salts** is a medicine that causes movements of the bowels. *n., adj., v. 1.*

salt cel lar (sôlt′sel′ər), dish or shaker for holding salt, used on the table. *n.*

Salt Lake City, the capital of Utah.

salt lick, place where natural salt is found on the surface of the ground and where animals go to lick it up.

salt pe ter or **salt pe tre** (sôlt′pē′tər), 1. a salty, white mineral, used in making gunpowder, in preserving meat, and in medicine. 2. a kind of fertilizer. *n. 11.*

salt-wa ter (sôlt′wô′tər), 1. consisting of or containing salt water. 2. living in the sea or in water like sea water. *adj.*

salt y (sôl′ti), containing salt; tasting of salt. *adj., saltier, saltiest.*

sa lu bri ous (sə lü′bri əs), healthful. *adj. 15.*

sal u tar y (sal′ū tãr′i), 1. good for the health; wholesome. Walking is a salutary exercise. 2. beneficial. The teacher gave the boy salutary advice. *adj. 12.*

sal u ta tion (sal′ū tā′shən), 1. greeting; saluting. A man raises his hat in salutation. 2. something uttered, written, or done to salute. You begin a letter with a salutation, such as "Dear Sir" or "My dear Mrs. Jones." A cold bow was her parting salutation. *n. 7.*

sa lute (sə lüt′), 1. honor in a formal manner by raising the hand to the head, by firing guns, or by dipping flags. We salute the flag every day at school. Soldiers salute their officers. 2. meet with kind words, a bow, a kiss, etc.; greet. The old gentleman walked along the avenue saluting his friends and receiving their salutes. 3. a saluting; sign of welcome or honor. 4. position of the hand, gun, etc., in saluting. *v., n. 4.*

Soldier saluting

Sal va dor (sal′və dôr), El Salvador, a country in Central America. *n. 17.*

sal vage (sal′vij), 1. saving a ship or its cargo from wreck or capture. 2. payment for saving it. 3. rescue of property from fire, etc. 4. save from fire, shipwreck, etc. 5. property salvaged; as, the salvage from a shipwreck or a fire. *n., v. 15.*

sal va tion (sal vā′shən), 1. saving; being saved. 2. saving the soul; deliverance from sin and from punishment for sin. 3. person or thing that saves. Christians believe that Christ is the salvation of the world. *n. 5.*

Salvation Army, organization to spread religion and help the poor, founded in England in 1865.

salve[1] (sav), 1. a soft, greasy substance put on wounds and sores; a healing ointment; as, a salve good for burns. 2. put salve on. 3. something soothing. The kind words were salve to his hurt feelings. 4. soothe; smooth over. He salved his conscience by the thought that his lie harmed no one. *n., v. 10.*

salve[2] (salv), save from loss or destruction; salvage. *v.*

sal ver (sal′vər), tray. *n. 18.*

Salver

sal vo (sal′vō), 1. the discharge of several guns at once as a salute. 2. a round of cheers or applause. *n., pl. salvos* or *salvoes.*

Sa mar i a (sə mãr′i ə), 1. district in ancient Palestine. 2. its chief city. *n. 12.*

Sa mar i tan (sə mar′i tən), 1. native or inhabitant of Samaria. 2. person who helps another in trouble or distress. The **good Samaritan** rescued the Jewish traveler who had been attacked by robbers. Luke 10:30-37. *n. 11.*

same (sām), 1. not another. We came back the same way we went. 2. just alike; not different. Her name and mine are the same. 3. just spoken of. The boys were talking about a queer man. This same man wore his hair very long and always dressed in white. 4. same person or thing. *adj., pron. 1.*

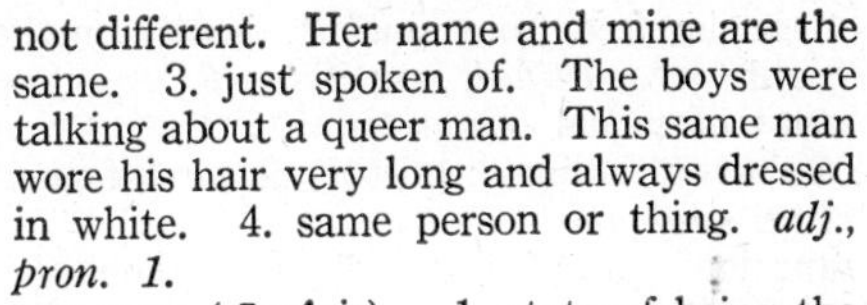

same ness (sām′nis), 1. state of being the same; exact likeness. 2. lack of variety; tiresomeness. *n. 18.*

sam ite (sam′īt), a heavy, rich, silk fabric, sometimes interwoven with gold, worn in the Middle Ages. *n.*

Sa mo a (sə mō′ə), group of islands in the southern Pacific. Several of these islands belong to the United States. *n. 17.*

sam o var (sam′ə vär), a metal urn used for heating water for tea. *n.*

Samovar

samp (samp), coarsely ground corn. *n.*

sam pan (sam′pan), any of various small boats of China, etc. A sampan is sculled by one or more oars at the stern; it usually has a single sail. *n.*

Sampan

sam ple (sam′pəl), 1. a part to show what the rest is like; one thing to show what the others are like. Get samples of blue silk for a new dress. The salesman showed samples. 2. take a part of; test a part of. We sampled the cake and found it very good. *n., v. 4.*

sam pler (sam′plər), 1. person who samples. 2. piece of cloth embroidered to show a beginner's skill in needlework. *n. 18.*

Sam son (sam′sən), 1. a man in the Bible story who was unusually strong. 2. any very strong man. *n. 7.*

Sam u el (sam′ū əl), either of two books in the Bible, the first of which is about the prophet Samuel. *n. 5.*

San An to ni o (san an tō′ni ō), city in southern Texas.

san a to ri um (san′ə tō′ri əm), sanitarium. *n.*

sanc ti fi ca tion (sangk′ti fi kā′shən), 1. making holy. 2. consecration; a setting apart as holy. 3. purification from sin. *n. 17.*

sanc ti fy (sangk′ti fī), 1. make holy. A life of sacrifice had sanctified her. 2. set apart as sacred; observe as holy. "Lord, sanctify this our offering to Thy use."

3. make free from sin. 4. justify; make right. *v., sanctified, sanctifying. 6.*

sanc ti mo ni ous (sangk′ti mō′ni əs), making a show of holiness; putting on airs of sanctity. *adj. 19.*

sanc tion (sangk′shən), 1. permission with authority; support; approval. We have the sanction of the law to play ball in this park. 2. approve; authorize; allow. Her conscience does not sanction stealing. 3. penalty or reward. 4. consideration that leads one to obey a rule of conduct. *n., v. 7.*

sanc ti ty (sangk′ti ti), 1. holiness; saintliness; godliness; as, the sanctity of a saint. 2. sacredness; holy character; as, the sanctity of a temple, the sanctity of the home. *n., pl. sanctities. 8.*

sanc tu ar y (sangk′chü ãr′i), 1. sacred place. A church is a sanctuary. 2. the part of a church about the altar. 3. place to which people can go for refuge or protection. 4. refuge or protection. The escaped prisoner found sanctuary in the temple. *n., pl. sanctuaries. 5.*

sanc tum (sangk′təm), 1. sacred place. 2. private room or office where a person can be undisturbed. *n. 17.*

sand (sand), 1. tiny grains of worn-down rocks. We have all heard of the sands of the seashore, the sands of the desert, sandbanks, and sandstorms. Sand is used for scraping and cleaning, and so are sandpaper and sand soap. 2. sprinkle with sand. People used to sand the kitchen floor; they also sanded letters to dry the ink. *n., v. 1.*

san dal (san′dəl), 1. a kind of shoe made of a sole fastened to the foot by straps. 2. a kind of slipper. 3. a light, low, rubber overshoe that has no heel. *n. 7.*

A B

Sandals: A (def. 1); B (def. 2).

san daled (san′dəld), wearing sandals. *adj.*

san dal wood (san′dəl wu̇d′), 1. a fragrant wood used for making boxes, fans, etc., and burned as incense. 2. the tree that it comes from. *n.*

sand bag (sand′bag′), 1. bag filled with sand. Sandbags are used to protect trenches and as ballast on balloons. 2. small bag of sand used as a club. 3. hit or stun with a sandbag. *n., v., sandbagged, sandbagging.*

sand bank (sand′bangk′), ridge of sand. *n.*

San Die go (san di ā′gō), a seaport city in southern California. *13.*

sand man (sand′man′). When children rub their sleepy eyes, they are told that the sandman has come to put them to sleep. *n. 14.*

sand pa per (sand′pā′pər), 1. strong paper with a layer of sand glued on it. Sandpaper is used for smoothing, cleaning, or polishing. 2. to smooth, clean, or polish with this. *n., v. 18.*

sand pip er (sand′pīp′ər), a small bird with a long bill, living on sandy shores. *n. 12.*

Sandpiper (about 7 in. long)

sand stone (sand′stōn′), a kind of rock formed mostly of sand. *n. 8.*

sand wich (sand′wich), 1. two slices of bread with meat, jelly, cheese, or some other filling between them. 2. put in (between). John was sandwiched between two fat women. *n., v. 5.*

sand y (san′di), 1. containing sand; consisting of sand. 2. covered with sand. Most of the shore is rocky, but there is a sandy beach. 3. yellowish-red. Alec has sandy hair. *adj., sandier, sandiest. 3.*

sane (sān), 1. having a healthy mind. 2. having good sense; sensible. *adj. 8.*

San Fran cis co (san frən sis′kō), 1. large seaport city in California. 2. **San Francisco Bay** is an inlet of the Pacific Ocean on which San Francisco is located. *5.*

sang (sang). See **sing.** The bird sang for us yesterday. *pt. of sing. 2.*

san gui nar y (sang′gwi nãr′i), 1. with much blood or bloodshed; bloody; as, a sanguinary battle. 2. bloodthirsty; delighting in bloodshed. *adj. 15.*

san guine (sang′gwin), 1. naturally cheerful and hopeful; as, a sanguine disposition. 2. confident; hopeful; as, sanguine of success. 3. having a healthy red color; ruddy; as, a sanguine complexion. *adj. 8.*

san i tar i um (san′i tãr′i əm), 1. place, especially in a good climate, for treatment of the sick. Sick people who are getting better, or who are suffering from a long, slow disease like tuberculosis, often go to a sanitarium. 2. health resort. *n. 15.*

san i tar y (san′i tãr′i), 1. of or pertaining to health; favorable to health; preventing disease. 2. free from dirt and filth. *adj. 6.*

san i ta tion (san′i tā′shən), working out ways to improve health conditions; practical application of sanitary measures. *n. 8.*

san i ty (san′i ti), 1. soundness of mind; mental health. 2. soundness of judgment. *n. 16.*

San Juan (san hwän′), 1. a hill in Cuba captured by the United States troops, July 1, 1898, during the Spanish-American War. 2. the capital of Puerto Rico. *19.*

sank (sangk). See **sink.** The ship sank before help reached her. *pt. of sink. 4.*

sans (sanz, *French* sän), a French word meaning without. *prep. 19.*

San Sal va dor (san sal′və dôr), 1. an island of the eastern Bahamas, the first land seen by Columbus. 2. the capital of El Salvador. *19.*

San ta (san′tə for 1, san′tə or sän′tä for 2), 1. Santa Claus. 2. a Spanish or an Italian word meaning holy or saint, used in such combinations as Santa Maria. *n., adj. 16.*

San ta Claus (san′tə klôz′), Saint Nicholas, the saint of Christmas giving. On Christmas father dresses up as Santa Claus. *4.*

San ta Fé or **San ta Fe** (san′tə fā′), the capital of New Mexico. *13.*

San ti a go (sän′ti ä′gō), the capital of Chile. *n. 13.*

San ti a go de Cu ba (sän′ti ä′gō dā kü′bä), a seaport city in southeastern Cuba.

San to Do min go (san′tō dō ming′gō), 1. former name of the capital of the Dominican Republic on the east end of the island of Haiti. 2. former name of the Dominican Republic.

sap¹ (sap), the life-giving juice of a plant. Sap does for trees what blood does for us. Maple sugar is made from the sap of some maple trees. *n. 4.*

sap² (sap), 1. dig under or wear away the foundation of. The walls of the boathouse had been sapped by the waves. 2. weaken; use up. The extreme heat sapped her strength. *v., sapped, sapping.*

sa pi ence (sā′pi əns), wisdom. *n. 19.*

sa pi ent (sā′pi ənt), wise. *adj. 17.*

sap less (sap′lis), without sap; withered; without energy or vigor. *adj. 15.*

sap ling (sap′ling), young tree. *n. 8.*

sap per (sap′ər), a soldier employed in the construction of trenches, fortifications, etc. *n.*

sap phire (saf′īr), 1. a bright-blue precious stone. A sapphire is hard and clear like a diamond. 2. bright blue; as, a sapphire sky. *n., adj. 7.*

sap py (sap′i), 1. full of sap. 2. vigorous; energetic. 3. silly; foolish. *Used in common talk. adj. 17.*

sap suck er (sap′suk′ər), a small American woodpecker that feeds on the sap of trees. *n. 19.*

Sapsucker (about 8 in. long)

Sar a cen (sar′ə sən), 1. an Arab. 2. a Mohammedan at the time of the Crusades. 3. of or pertaining to the Saracens. *n., adj. 8.*

Sar ah (sãr′ə), in the Bible, the wife of Abraham and the mother of Isaac. *n.*

sar casm (sär′kazm), 1. a sneering or cutting remark. 2. act of making fun of a person to hurt his feelings; harsh or bitter irony. "How unselfish you are!" said Ellen in sarcasm as Mary took the biggest piece of cake. *n. 12.*

sar cas tic (sär kas′tik), using sarcasm; sneering; bitterly cutting. "Don't hurry!" was his father's sarcastic comment as Dick began to dress at his usual slow rate. *adj. 9.*

sar cas ti cal ly (sär kas′ti kəl i), in a sarcastic manner; with sarcasm. *adv.*

sar coph a gus (sär kof′ə gəs), stone coffin, especially an ornamental one. *n. 17.*

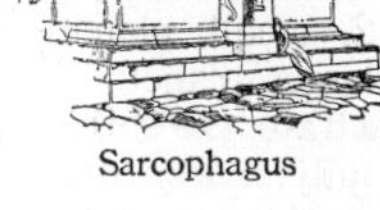

Sarcophagus

sar dine (sär dēn′), a kind of small fish preserved in oil for food. *n. 10.*

Sar din i a (sär din′i ə), large Italian island in the Mediterranean Sea, west of Italy. *n. 16.*

sar don ic (sär don′ik), bitterly sarcastic; scornful; mocking; as, a fiend's sardonic laugh. *adj. 16.*

sar sa pa ril la (sär′sə pə ril′ə), 1. a tropical American plant or its root. See the picture. 2. a medicine or a cooling drink made from the root. *n. 17.*

Sarsaparilla

sar to ri al (sär tō′ri əl), of tailors or their work. His clothes were a sartorial triumph. *adj.*

sash¹ (sash), a long broad strip of cloth or ribbon, worn as an ornament around the waist or over one shoulder. She wore a white dress with a blue sash around her waist. *n. 4.*

sash[2] (sash), frame for the glass of a window or door. The sash in the picture has four panes of glass. *n.*

Window sash

Sas katch e wan (sas kach′i-won), a province in southern Canada. *n.*

sas sa fras (sas′ə fras), 1. a slender American tree that has fragrant yellow flowers and bluish-black fruit. 2. the aromatic bark of its root, used in medicine and to flavor candy, soft drinks, etc. 3. the flavor. *n. 17.*

sat (sat). See **sit.** Yesterday I sat in a train all day. The cat has sat at that mouse hole for hours. *pt. and pp. of sit. 1.*

Sat., Saturday. *14.*

Sa tan (sā′tən), the evil spirit; the enemy of goodness; the Devil. *n. 4.*

sa tan ic or **Sa tan ic** (sā tan′ik), of Satan; like Satan; like that of Satan; very wicked. *adj.*

satch el (sach′əl), small bag for carrying clothes, books, etc.; handbag. *n. 13.*

sate (sāt), 1. satisfy fully (any appetite or desire). 2. supply with more than enough. *v. 9.*

sa teen (sa tēn′), cotton or woolen cloth made to imitate satin. Sateen is often used for lining sleeves. *n. 12.*

sat el lite (sat′ə līt), 1. a follower or attendant upon a person of importance. 2. small planet that revolves around a larger planet. *n. 12.*

sa ti ate (sā′shi āt), 1. feed fully; satisfy fully. For once John's appetite for ice cream was satiated. 2. supply with too much. **Be satiated** means have so much of a thing that one feels sick of it. *v. 10.*

sa ti e ty (sə tī′ə ti), the feeling of having had too much; disgust caused by excess; satiated condition. *n. 15.*

sat in (sat′ən), 1. silk or rayon cloth with one very smooth glossy side. 2. of satin; like satin; smooth and glossy. *n., adj. 4.*

sat in wood (sat′ən wu̇d′), 1. the beautiful smooth wood of an East Indian tree, used to ornament furniture, etc. 2. the tree itself. *n. 20.*

sat in y (sat′ən i), like satin in smoothness and gloss. *adj.*

sat ire (sat′īr), 1. the use of sarcasm or irony to attack or ridicule a habit, idea, custom, etc. 2. poem, essay, story, etc., that attacks or ridicules in this way. Some of Aesop's *Fables* are satires. *n. 7.*

sa tir ic (sə tir′ik), satirical. *adj.*

sa tir i cal (sə tir′i kəl), of satire; containing satire; fond of using satire. *adj. 15.*

sat i rist (sat′i rist), writer of satires; person who uses satire. The follies and vices of their own times are the chief subjects of satirists. *n. 16.*

sat i rize (sat′i rīz), attack with satire; criticize with mockery; seek to improve by ridicule. *v. 17.*

sat is fac tion (sat′is fak′shən), 1. condition of being satisfied, or pleased and contented. 2. anything that makes us feel pleased or contented. It is a great satisfaction to have things turn out just the way you want. 3. fulfillment; satisfying. 4. payment of debt; discharge of obligation; a making up for wrong or injury done. *n. 3.*

sat is fac to ri ly (sat′is fak′tə ri li), in a satisfactory manner. *adv.*

sat is fac to ry (sat′is fak′tə ri), satisfying; good enough to satisfy. *adj. 5.*

sat is fy (sat′is fī), 1. give enough to; fulfill (desires, hopes, demands, etc.); put an end to (needs, wants, etc.). He satisfied his hunger with bread and milk. 2. make contented; please. Are you satisfied now? 3. pay; make right. After the accident he satisfied all claims for the damage he had caused. 4. convince. The teacher is satisfied that Jack's lateness was an accident. *v., satisfied, satisfying. 2.*

sa trap (sā′trap), 1. ruler who is subordinate to a higher ruler. 2. the governor of a province under the ancient Persian monarchy. *n. 15.*

sat u rate (sach′u̇ rāt), 1. soak thoroughly; fill full. During a fog, the air is saturated with moisture. Saturate the moss with water before planting the bulbs in it. 2. cause (a substance) to unite with the greatest possible amount of another substance. A saturated solution (of sugar, salt, etc.) is one that cannot dissolve any more (sugar, salt, etc.). *v. 11.*

sat u ra tion (sach′u̇ rā′shən), 1. act or process of saturating. 2. fact of being saturated; saturated condition. The saturation of a color increases as the amount of white in it is decreased. *n. 13.*

Sat ur day (sat′ər di), the seventh day of the week. *n. 2.*

Saturn and its rings

Sat urn (sat′ərn), 1. the Roman god of agriculture. 2. the large planet that has rings around it. *n. 10.*

sat ur na li a (sat′ər nā′li ə), period of unrestrained revelry and license. In ancient Rome, the **Saturnalia** was the festival of Saturn, celebrated in December with feasting and merrymaking. *n. pl. or sing. 20.*

sat ur nine (sat′ər nīn), gloomy; grave. *adj. 16.*

sat yr (sat′ər), 1. a merry creature of the woods, part man and part beast. The satyrs were followers of Bacchus, the god of wine. 2. a man who is beastly in thought and action. *n. 8.*

Satyr

sauce (sôs), 1. something, usually a liquid, served with a food to make it taste better. We have cranberry sauce with turkey, mint sauce with lamb, egg sauce with fish, and many different sauces with puddings. 2. stewed fruit; as, applesauce. 3. give interest or flavor to. 4. sauciness. 5. be saucy to. *Used in common talk. n., v. 4.*

sauce pan (sôs′pan′), a metal dish with a handle, used for stewing, boiling, etc. *n. 7.*

Saucepan

sau cer (sô′sər), 1. shallow dish to set a cup on. 2. a small round dish with its edge curved up. 3. something round and shallow like a saucer. *n. 6.*

sau ci ness (sô′si nis), pertness; impudence. *n.*

sau cy (sô′si), 1. rude; showing lack of respect. 2. pert; smart. She wore a saucy hat with a saucy smile. *adj., saucier, sauciest. 6.*

sauer kraut (sour′krout′), cabbage cut fine, salted, and allowed to sour. *n. 18.*

Saul (sôl), the first king of Israel. *n. 6.*

saun ter (sôn′tər), stroll; walk along slowly and happily. People saunter through the park on summer evenings. *v., n. 11.*

sau sage (sô′sij), chopped pork, beef, or other meats, seasoned and usually stuffed into a thin tube. *n. 5.*

sau té (sō tā′), 1. cooked or browned in a little fat. 2. dish of food cooked in this way. *adj., n. 18.*

sav age (sav′ij), 1. wild. He likes savage mountain scenery. 2. not civilized; barbarous. Gaudy colors please a savage taste. 3. person living somewhat as wild animals do. 4. fierce; cruel; ready to fight. The savage lion attacked the hunter. 5. a fierce, brutal, or cruel person. *adj., n. 2.*

sav age ness (sav′ij nis), 1. wildness; as, the savageness of a jungle scene. 2. savage or uncivilized condition; as, the savageness of some African tribes. 3. cruelty; fierceness. *n. 20.*

sav age ry (sav′ij ri), wildness; savage state; cruelty. *n., pl. savageries. 15.*

sa van na (sə van′ə), a treeless plain. *n.*

Sa van nah (sə van′ə), 1. seaport in eastern Georgia. 2. river between South Carolina and Georgia. *n. 11.*

sav ant (sav′ənt), man of learning. *n. 16.*

save[1] (sāv), 1. make safe; keep or rescue from harm, danger, hurt, loss, etc. The dog saved the boy's life. The woman saved her jewels from the fire. 2. set free from sin and its results. Christ came to save the world. 3. lay aside; as, to save money. She saves pieces of string. 4. keep from spending or wasting. Save your strength. 5. avoid expense or waste. She saves in every way she can. 6. prevent; make less; as, to save work, to save trouble, to save expense. 7. treat carefully to lessen wear, weariness, etc. Large print saves one's eyes. *v. 1.*

save[2] (sāv), except. He works every day save Sundays. *prep., conj.*

sav er (sāv′ər), person or thing that saves. The Scotch are noted as savers of money. A washing machine is a saver of time and strength. *n. 12.*

sav ing (sāv′ing), 1. that saves. 2. economical; avoiding waste; tending to save up money. 3. way of saving money, time, etc. It will be a saving to take this short cut. 4. except; with the exception of. 5. **Saving your presence** means with an apology for doing or saying this in your presence. *adj., n., prep., conj.*

sav ings (sāv′ingz), money saved. *n. pl.*

sav ior or **sav iour** (sāv′yər), one who saves or rescues. *n. 5.*

Sav iour or **Sav ior** (sāv′yər), Jesus Christ. *n.*

sa vor (sā′vər), 1. taste or smell; flavor. The soup has a savor of onion. 2. to taste; to smell. He savored the soup with pleasure. 3. have the quality or nature (of). The plot savored of treason. 4. give flavor to; season. *n., v. 6.*

sa vor y[1] (sā′vər i), pleasing in taste or smell. The savory smell of roasting turkey greeted us as we entered the house. *adj. 7.*

sa vor y[2] (sā′vər i), a fragrant herb used for seasoning food. *n.*

Sa voy (sə voi′), region in eastern France. *n. 17.*

saw[1] (sô), 1. a tool for cutting, made of a thin blade with sharp teeth on the edge. 2. cut with a saw. The man saws wood. 3. make with a saw. 4. use a saw. 5. be sawed. Softwood saws more easily than hardwood. 6. **Saw the air** means make motions in the air with the hands as if using a saw. *n., v., sawed, sawed* or *sawn, sawing. 1.*

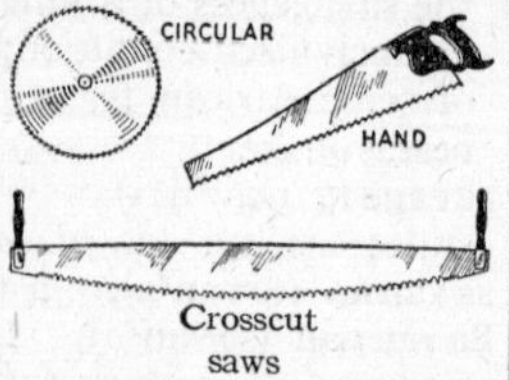

Crosscut saws

saw[2] (sô). See **see**[1]. I saw a robin yesterday. *pt. of* **see**[1].

saw[3] (sô), wise saying; proverb. "A stitch in time saves nine" is a familiar saw. *n.*

saw buck (sô′buk′), sawhorse. *n.*

saw dust (sô′dust′), particles of wood made by sawing. *n. 13.*

saw horse (sô′hôrs′), frame for holding wood that is being sawed. *n.*

BUCKSAW
SAWHORSE

saw mill (sô′mil′), building where machines saw timber into planks, boards, etc. *n. 10.*

sawn (sôn), sawed. *pp. of* **saw**[1].

saw yer (sô′yər), man whose work is sawing timber. *n. 19.*

sax i frage (sak′si frij), a plant with white, yellow, or red flowers, that grows in rocky places. *n.*

Sax on (sak′sən), 1. member of a German tribe in northwestern Germany; Anglo-Saxon. Some of the Saxons conquered England in the 5th and 6th centuries. 2. language of the Saxons. 3. native of Saxony in modern Germany. 4. of or pertaining to the Saxons. *n., adj. 8.*

Sax o ny (sak′sə ni), 1. a State in central Germany. 2. province in northwestern Germany. *n. 11.*

Saxophone

sax o phone (sak′sə fōn), a brass musical instrument with keys and a reed mouthpiece. See the picture. *n. 20.*

say (sā). Say "Please" and "Thank you." Say your prayers. The Bible says to do good unto all men. It is hard to say which dress is prettier. You can learn to dance in, say, ten lessons. James said his say and sat down. *v., said, saying, n. 1.*

say est (sā′ist), an old form meaning **say.** "Thou sayest" means "you say." *v.*

say ing (sā′ing), 1. something said; a statement. 2. a proverb. "Haste makes waste" is a saying. *n.*

says (sez). See **say.** He says "No" to everything. *v.*

sayst (sāst), an old form meaning **say.** "Thou sayst" means "you say." *v.*

S.C., South Carolina.

scab (skab), 1. the crust that forms over a sore during healing. The scab from his vaccination has just dropped off. 2. become covered with a scab. 3. a skin disease in animals, especially sheep. *n., v., scabbed, scabbing. 12.*

scab bard (skab′ərd), a sheath or case for the blade of a sword, dagger, etc. *n. 9.*

SWORD
SCABBARD

scaf fold (skaf′əld), 1. temporary structure for holding workmen and materials. 2. raised platform on which criminals are put to death. 3. any raised framework. *n. 7.*

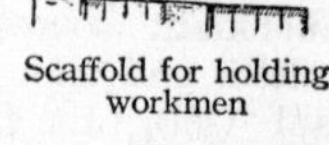
Scaffold for holding workmen

scaf fold ing (skaf′əl ding), 1. scaffold. 2. materials for scaffolds. *n.*

scald (skôld), 1. pour boiling liquid over. Scald the dishes before drying them. 2. burn with hot liquid or steam. She scalded herself with hot grease. 3. heat almost to boiling, but not quite. Scald the milk. 4. a burn caused by hot liquid or steam. The scald on her hand came from lifting a pot cover carelessly. *v., n. 8.*

scale[1] (skāl), 1. one of the thin, flat hard plates forming the outer covering of some fishes, snakes, and lizards. 2. thin layer like a scale. Scales of skin peel off after scarlet fever. 3. remove scales from. He scaled the fish with a sharp knife. 4. come off in scales. The paint is scaling off the house. 5. an insect that has a large shieldlike covering under which it hides and feeds. *n., v. 2.*

scale[2] (skāl), 1. the dish or pan of a balance. 2. a balance; an instrument for weighing. She weighed some meat on the scales. **Turn the scales** means decide. 3. weigh. He scales 180 pounds. *n., v.*

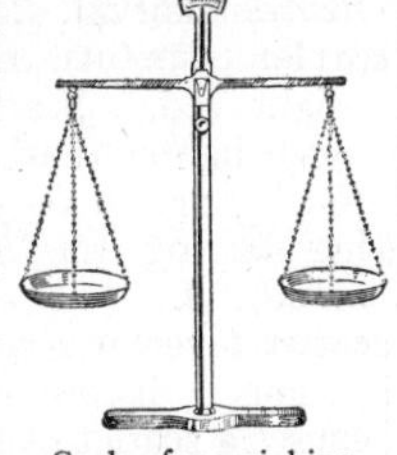
Scales for weighing

scale[3] (skāl), 1. series of steps or degrees; scheme of graded amounts. The scale of wages in this factory ranges from three dollars to twelve dollars a day. 2. series of marks made along a line at regular distances to use in measuring. A thermometer has a scale. 3. an instrument marked in this way, used for measuring. 4. the size of a plan or map compared with what it represents. This map is drawn to the scale of one inch for each 100 miles. 5. system of numbering. The decimal scale counts by tens, as in cents, dimes, dollars. 6. in music, a series of tones ascending or descending in pitch. She practices scales on the piano. 7. climb. They scaled the wall by ladders. 8. relative size or extent; as, to entertain on a large scale. 9. make according to a scale. 10. reduce by a certain proportion. All prices were scaled down 10 per cent. *n., v.*

scal lion (skal′yən), a kind of onion that has no large, distinct bulb. *n.*

scal lop (skol′əp), 1. a shellfish somewhat like a clam. He ate scallops and bacon. 2. curve on the edge of anything. This cuff has scallops. See the picture below. 3. make with such curves. She scallops the edge of the paper with which she covers shelves. 4. bake with sauce and bread crumbs in a dish; as, scalloped oysters, scalloped tomatoes. *n., v. 10.*

Scallop (def. 1)

Scallops on a cuff

scalp (skalp), 1. the skin and hair on the top and back of the head. 2. part of this skin and hair cut off as a token of victory. Indians used to collect the scalps of their enemies. 3. cut or tear the scalp from. *n., v. 5.*

scal pel (skal′pəl), small, straight knife used by surgeons. *n.*

scal y (skāl′i), 1. covered with scales; having scales like a fish. This iron pipe is scaly with rust. 2. suggesting scales. *adj., scalier, scaliest. 12.*

scamp[1] (skamp), rascal; rogue; worthless person. *n.*

scamp[2] (skamp), do (work, etc.) in a hasty, careless manner. *v.*

scam per (skam′pər), 1. run quickly. The mice scampered when the cat came. 2. a quick run. Let the dog out for a scamper. *v., n. 7.*

scan (skan), 1. look at closely; examine with care. His mother scanned his face to see if he were telling the truth. 2. mark off (lines of poetry) into feet. *Example:* Sing′a | song′of | six′pence. *v., scanned, scanning. 6.*

scan dal (skan′dəl), 1. shameful action that brings disgrace or offends public opinion. It is a scandal for a city official to take tax money for his own use. 2. disgrace; damage to reputation. 3. public talk about a person which will hurt his reputation; evil gossip. *n. 6.*

scan dal ize (skan′dəl īz), offend by something wrong or improper; shock. Amy scandalized her grandmother by smoking cigarettes. *v. 12.*

scan dal mon ger (skan′dəl mung′gər), person who spreads gossip and scandal. *n. 20.*

scan dal ous (skan′dəl əs), 1. disgraceful; shocking. 2. spreading scandal or slander; slandering. *adj. 9.*

Scan di na vi a (skan′di nā′vi ə), 1. Norway, Sweden, and Denmark. 2. the peninsula on which Norway and Sweden are located. *n. 10.*

Scan di na vi an (skan′di nā′vi ən), 1. of or pertaining to Scandinavia, its people, or their languages. 2. a native or inhabitant of Scandinavia. 3. the languages of Scandinavia. *adj., n.*

scant (skant), 1. not enough in size or quantity. Her coat was short and scant. **Scant of** means having not enough. She was scant of breath. 2. barely enough. Use a scant cup of butter in the cake. You have a scant hour in which to pack. 3. make scant; cut down; limit. Don't scant the butter if you want a rich cake. *adj., v. 6.*

scant i ly (skan′ti li), in a scanty manner; insufficiently. *adv.*

scant i ness (skan′ti nis), too small an amount; quality or state of being scanty. *n.*

scant ling (skant′ling), 1. small beam or piece of timber. 2. small beams or timbers. *n. 18.*

scant y (skan′ti), 1. not enough. His scanty clothing did not keep out the cold. 2. barely enough. *adj., scantier, scantiest. 5.*

'scape or **scape** (skāp), escape. *n., v.* [*Old use*] *13.*

scape goat (skāp′gōt′), one made to bear the blame for the mistakes or sins of others. The ancient Jewish high priests used to lay the sins of the people upon a goat (called the scapegoat) which was driven out into the wilderness. *n. 18.*

scape grace (skāp′grās′), scamp; a reckless, good-for-nothing person. *n.*

scar (skär), 1. the mark left by a healed cut, wound, burn, or sore. My vaccination scar is small. 2. any mark like this. See the scars your shoes have made on the chair. 3. mark with a scar. 4. form a scar; heal. *n., v., scarred, scarring. 4.*

scar ab (skar′əb), 1. a beetle, especially the sacred beetle of the ancient Egyptians. 2. an image of this beetle. Scarabs were much used in Egypt as charms or ornaments. *n.*

A

B

Scarab (def. 2): A, side; B, top.

scarce (skãrs), 1. hard to get; rare. Good cooks are scarce. Very old stamps are scarce. 2. scarcely. *adj., adv. 2.*

scarce ly (skãrs′li), not quite; barely. We could scarcely see through the thick fog. *adv. 7.*

scar ci ty (skãr′si ti), too small a supply; lack; rarity. *n., pl. scarcities. 8.*

scare (skãr), 1. frighten. 2. a fright. 3. frightened condition. *v., n. 3.*

scare crow (skãr′krō′), 1. the figure of a man dressed in old clothes, set in a field to frighten birds away from growing crops. 2. person dressed in ragged clothes. 3. anything that fools people into being frightened. *n. 11.*

Scarecrow

scarf (skärf), 1. a long broad strip of silk, lace, etc., worn about the neck, shoulders, or head. See the picture in the next column. 2. necktie with hanging ends. 3. long strip of linen, etc., used as a cover for a bureau, table, piano, etc. *n., pl. scarfs, scarves* (skärvz). *4.*

scar let (skär′lit), 1. very bright red. Scarlet is much lighter than crimson. 2. cloth or clothing having this color. *n., adj. 3.*

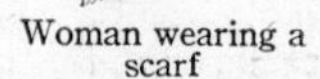

Woman wearing a scarf

scarlet fever, a very contagious disease that causes a scarlet rash, sore throat, and fever.

scarlet tanager, common tanager of North America. The male has black wings and tail and a scarlet body.

scar y (skãr′i), 1. causing fright or alarm. 2. easily frightened. *adj., scarier, scariest.* [*Used in common talk*]

scathe (skāᴛʜ), hurt; harm. *n., v.* [*Old use*] *13.*

scath ing (skāᴛʜ′ing), bitterly severe. *adj.*

scat ter (skat′ər), 1. throw here and there; sprinkle. The farmer scatters seed over the fields. Scatter ashes on the icy sidewalk. 2. separate and drive off in different directions. The police scattered the disorderly crowd. 3. separate and go in different directions. The hens scattered when they saw the hawk. *v. 2.*

scat ter brained (skat′ər brānd′), heedless; thoughtless; not able to think steadily. *adj.*

scat ter ing (skat′ər ing), widely separated; occurring here and there. *adj.*

scav en ger (skav′in jər), 1. person who cleans streets, taking away the dirt and filth. 2. animal that feeds on decaying matter. Vultures are scavengers. *n. 12.*

sce nar i o (si nãr′i ō), the outline of a moving picture, giving the main facts about the scenes, persons, and acting; the outline of any play. *n., pl. scenarios. 20.*

scene (sēn), 1. the time, place, circumstances, etc., of a play or story. The scene is laid in Virginia during the Civil War. 2. the painted screens, hangings, etc., used in a theater to represent places. The scene represents a city street. 3. part of an act of a play. The king comes to the castle in Act I, Scene 2. 4. a particular incident of a play. The trial scene is the most exciting one in *The Merchant of Venice.* 5. action, incident, situation, etc., represented in literature or art. He has painted a series of pictures called *Scenes of My Boyhood.* 6. view; picture. The white sailboats in the blue water made a pretty scene. 7. show

sconce (skons), a bracket projecting from a wall to hold a candle or other light. *n. 14.*

Sconce

scone (skōn), a thick, flat round cake cooked on a griddle. Some scones taste much like bread; some are like buns. *n. 20.*

scoop (sküp), 1. a tool like a shovel. 2. the part of a dredge, steam shovel, etc., that holds coal, sand, etc. 3. a large ladle. 4. a kitchen utensil to take out flour, sugar, etc. 5. amount taken up at one time by a scoop. She used two scoops of flour and one of sugar. 6. take up or out with a scoop. The children scooped up the snow with their hands to build a snow man. Scoop up that spilled grain from the barn floor. 7. act of scooping. 8. hollow out; dig out; make by scooping. The children scooped holes in the sand. 9. place hollowed out. The rabbit hid in the scoop it had made in the earth. *n., v. 6.*

Scoop (def. 4)

scoot (sküt), 1. go quickly; dart. 2. act of scooting. *v., n.* [*Used in common talk*]

scope (skōp), 1. distance the mind can reach; extent of view. Very hard words are not within the scope of a child's understanding. 2. space; opportunity. Football gives scope for courage and quick thinking. *n. 7.*

scorch (skôrch), 1. burn slightly; burn on the outside. The cake tastes scorched. The maid scorched the shirt in ironing it. 2. a slight burn. 3. dry up; wither. The grass is scorched by so much hot sunshine. *v., n. 5.*

score (skōr), 1. the record of points made in a game or contest. The score was 9 to 2 in favor of our school. 2. make as points in a game or contest. 3. keep a record of the number of points in a game or contest. The teacher will appoint some pupil to score for both sides. 4. make as an addition to the score; gain; win. James scored five runs for our team. 5. amount owed; debt; account. He paid his score at the inn. **Settle a score** means get even for an injury or wrong. She had many old scores to settle with her enemies. **On the score of** means because of; on account of. She was excused on the score of illness. 6. to record; mark; set down. The innkeeper scored on a slate the number of meals each person had. 7. written or printed piece of music. He was trying over the score of a musical comedy on the piano. 8. twenty; set of twenty. A score or more were present at the party. 9. cut or scratch; stroke; mark; line. The slave's back showed scores made by the whip. Moving the furniture across the floor scores the polish. Mistakes are scored in red ink. *n., v. 2.*

scorn (skôrn), 1. look down upon; think of as mean or low; despise. Honest boys scorn sneaks and liars. 2. reject or refuse as low or wrong. The judge scorned to take a bribe. 3. a feeling that a person or act is mean or low; contempt. The big dog walked past the little dog with scorn. Most pupils feel scorn for those who cheat. 4. person, animal, or thing that is scorned or despised. That coward is the scorn of the school. *v., n. 3.*

scorn ful (skôrn′fəl), showing contempt; mocking; full of scorn. He spoke of our old car in a scornful voice. *adj. 6.*

scorn ful ly (skôrn′fəl i), with scorn; in a scornful manner. *adv.*

scor pi on (skôr′pi ən), 1. a small animal belonging to the same group as the spider and having a poisonous sting in its tail. 2. a whip or scourge. *n. 9.*

Scorpion (1 to 8 in. long)

Scot (skot), person born in or living in Scotland. *n. 5.*

Scotch[1] (skoch), 1. of or pertaining to Scotland, its people, or their language; as, Scotch lakes, Scotch words, Scotch cake. 2. the people of Scotland. 3. English as spoken by Scotch people. *adj., n. 4.*

scotch[2] (skoch), 1. stamp on; make harmless; as, to scotch a snake without killing it. 2. cut or gash. *v., n.*

Scotch man (skoch′mən), person living in Scotland, born there, or having Scotch parents. *n., pl. Scotchmen. 20.*

scot-free (skot′frē′), free from injury, punishment, etc.; unharmed. *adj.*

Sco tia (skō′shə), Scotland. *n.* [*Used in poetry*] *17.*

Scot land (skot′lənd), the division of Great Britain north of England; the land of the Scotch. *n. 4.*

Scots (skots), 1. Scottish. 2. people of Scotland. *adj., n. pl.*

Scots man (skots′mən), Scotchman; Scot. *n., pl. Scotsmen.*

Scott (skot), Sir Walter, a famous Scotch novelist and poet (1771-1832). *n. 8.*

Scot tish (skot′ish), 1. of or having to do with Scotland, its people, or their language. 2. the people of Scotland. 3. the dialect of English spoken by the people of Scotland. *adj., n. 9.*

scoun drel (skoun′drəl), bad person without honor or good principles. The scoundrels who set fire to the barn have been caught. *n. 8.*

scour[1] (skour), 1. clean or polish by hard rubbing. The maid scours the knives with sand soap, and the floor with a brush and soapsuds. 2. remove dirt and grease from (anything) by rubbing. 3. make clear by flowing through or over. The stream had scoured a channel. 4. clean; cleanse. 5. act of scouring. *v., n. 5.*

scour[2] (skour), 1. move quickly over. Men scoured the country for the lost child. 2. go swiftly in search or pursuit. *v.*

scourge (skėrj), 1. whip. 2. any means of punishment. 3. punish. 4. some thing or person that causes great trouble or misfortune. In olden times, an outbreak of disease was called a scourge. 5. trouble very much; afflict. *n., v. 4.*

scout[1] (skout), 1. person sent to find out what the enemy is doing. A scout wears a uniform; a spy does not. 2. act as a scout; hunt around to find something. Go and scout for firewood for the picnic. 3. one that acts as a scout. Some ships and airplanes are scouts. 4. A person belonging to the Boy Scouts or Girl Scouts is a Scout. *n., v. 4.*

Scow

scout[2] (skout), refuse to believe in; reject with scorn. He scouted the idea of a dog with two tails. *v.*

scout mas ter (skout′mas′tər), the leader in charge of a troop or band of scouts. *n.*

scow (skou), a large, flat-bottomed boat used to carry freight, sand, etc. See the picture above. *n. 20.*

scowl (skoul), 1. look angry or sullen by lowering the eyebrows; to frown. 2. an angry, sullen look; a frown. *v., n. 8.*

Man scowling

scrab ble (skrab′əl), 1. scratch or scrape about with hands, claws, etc.; scramble. 2. scrawl; scribble. 3. a scraping; a scramble. *v., n.*

scrag (skrag), 1. a lean, skinny person or animal. An old bony horse is a scrag. 2. lean, bony part. A scrag of mutton is the lean end of a neck of mutton. 3. neck. *Slang.* 4. wring the neck of. *Slang. n., v., scragged, scragging.*

scrag gly (skrag′li), rough or irregular; ragged. *adj., scragglier, scraggliest.*

scrag gy (skrag′i), 1. lean; thin. 2. scraggly. *adj., scraggier, scraggiest.*

scram ble (skram′bəl), 1. make one's way by climbing, crawling, etc. The boys scrambled up the steep, rocky hill. 2. a climb or walk over rough ground. It was a long scramble through bushes and over rocks to the top of the hill. 3. struggle with others for something. The boys scrambled to get the football. 4. a struggle to possess; as, the scramble for wealth and power. 5. scrambling; any disorderly struggle or activity. The pile of boys on the football seemed a wild scramble of arms and legs. 6. cook (eggs), mixing the whites and yolks together. *v., n. 6.*

Scran ton (skran′tən), city in northeastern Pennsylvania. *n. 20.*

scrap (skrap), 1. small piece; little bit; small part left over. The cook gave some scraps of meat to the dog. Put the scraps of paper in the waste basket. 2. make into scraps; break up. 3. throw aside as useless or worn out. *n., v., scrapped, scrapping. 4.*

scrap book (skrap′bu̇k′), book in which pictures or clippings are pasted and kept. *n. 20.*

scrape (skrāp), 1. rub with something sharp or rough so as to remove; remove in this way. Scrape your muddy shoes with this old knife. The man scraped some paint off the table when he pushed it through the doorway. 2. act of scraping. 3. scraped place. 4. rub with a harsh sound. Don't scrape your feet on the floor. The branch of the tree scraped against the window. 5. give a harsh sound; grate. 6. a harsh, grating sound; as, the scrape of the bow of a violin. 7. dig. The child scraped a hole in the sand. 8. collect by scraping or with difficulty. The hungry boy scraped up the last crumbs from his plate. John has scraped together enough money for his first year at college. 9. **Scrape through** means get through with difficulty. Jack barely scraped through the examination. 10. a difficulty; position hard to get out of. Boys often get into scrapes. 11. **Scrape acquaintance** means take the trouble to get acquainted. *v., n. 3.*

scrap er (skrāp′ər), tool for scraping. Wipe your shoes on the scraper. *n. 9.*

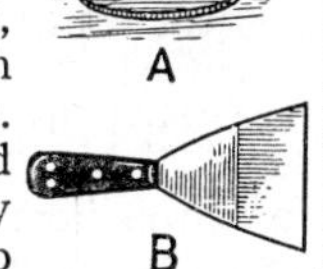

Scrapers: A, for shoes; B, for walls.

scratch (skrach), 1. break, mark, or cut slightly with something sharp or rough. Your feet have scratched the chair. 2. mark made by scratching. There are deep scratches on this desk. 3. tear or dig with the nails or claws. The cat scratched him. 4. very slight cut. That scratch on your hand will soon be well. 5. rub or scrape to relieve itching Don't scratch your mosquito bites. 6. rub; rub with a harsh noise. He scratched a match on the wall. 7. sound of scratching; as, the scratch of a pen. 8. write in a hurry and carelessly. 9. scrape out; strike out; draw a line through. 10. withdraw (a horse, candidate, etc.) from competition. 11. the starting place of a race. **From scratch** means with no advantages. *v., n. 3.*

scrawl (skrôl), 1. write or draw poorly or carelessly. 2. poor, careless handwriting. *v., n. 10.*

scraw ny (skrô′ni), lean; thin; skinny. Turkeys have scrawny necks. *adj., scrawnier, scrawniest.*

scream (skrēm), 1. make a loud, sharp, piercing cry. People scream in fright, in anger, and in sudden pain. 2. a loud, sharp, piercing cry. *v., n. 3.*

screech (skrēch), 1. cry out sharply in a high voice; shriek. "Help! help!" she screeched. 2. a shrill harsh scream. The woman's screeches brought the police. *v., n. 8.*

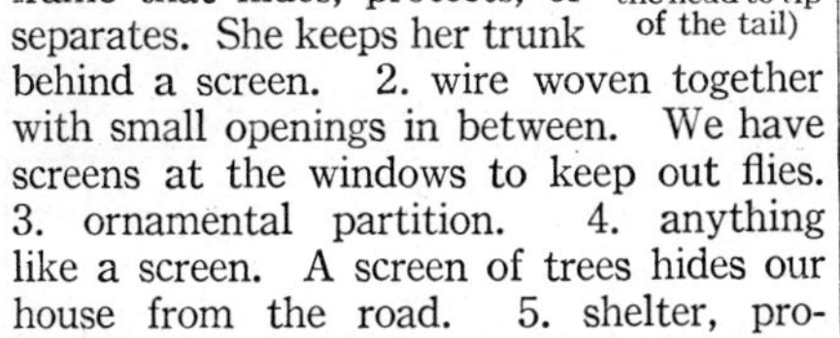
Screech owl (about 9 in. from top of the head to tip of the tail)

screech owl, an owl that screeches, but does not hoot.

screen (skrēn), 1. covered frame that hides, protects, or separates. She keeps her trunk behind a screen. 2. wire woven together with small openings in between. We have screens at the windows to keep out flies. 3. ornamental partition. 4. anything like a screen. A screen of trees hides our house from the road. 5. shelter, protect, or hide with a screen. We have screened our porch to keep out flies. She screened her face from the fire with a fan. The mother tried to screen her guilty son. 6. surface on which moving pictures, etc., are shown. 7. show (a moving picture) on a screen. 8. photograph with a moving-picture camera. 9. sieve for sifting sand, gravel, coal, seed, etc. 10. sift by using a sieve of screen. *n., v. 4.*

Screen door

screw (skrü), 1. a kind of nail, with a ridge twisted evenly round its length. Turn the screw to the right to tighten it. 2. cylinder with a ridge winding around it. See the picture. 3. anything that turns like a screw or looks like one. 4. turn as a screw does; twist. Screw the lid on the jar. 5. fasten with a screw or screws. The carpenter screwed the hinges to the door. 6. force, press, or stretch tight by using screws. 7. force (prices) down; force (people) to tell or to give up. 8. propeller that moves a boat. 9. very stingy person; miser. *n., v. 5.*

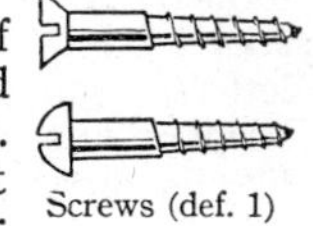
Screws (def. 1)

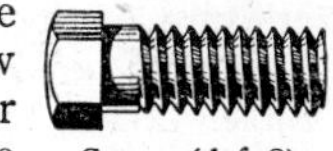
Screw (def. 2)

screw driv er (skrü′drīv′ər), tool for putting in or taking out screws by turning them. *n.*

screw propeller, revolving hub with radiating blades for propelling a steamship, airship, etc.

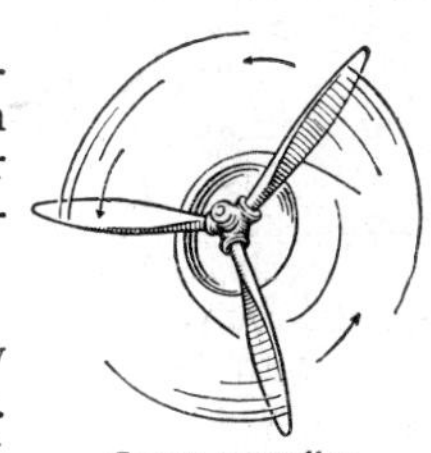
Screw propeller

scrib ble (skrib′əl), 1. write or draw carelessly or hastily. 2. make marks that do not mean anything. 3. something scribbled. *v., n. 9.*

scrib bler (skrib′lər), 1. person who scribbles. 2. author who has little or no importance. *n. 20.*

scribe (skrīb), 1. person whose occupation is writing. Before printing was invented, there were many scribes. 2. teacher of the Jewish law. *n. 9.*

scrim (skrim), a loosely woven cotton or linen material, much used for window curtains. *n. 13.*

scrim mage (skrim′ij), 1. rough fight or struggle. 2. take part in a rough fight or struggle. 3. the play in football that takes place when the two teams are lined up and the ball is snapped back. *n., v.*

scrimp (skrimp), 1. be sparing of; stint; skimp; be very economical. Many parents have to scrimp to keep their children in school. 2. treat stingily or very economically. *v.*

scrip (skrip), 1. a writing. 2. receipt showing a right to something. 3. paper money in denominations of less than a dollar, formerly issued in the United States. *n. 13.*

script (skript), 1. handwriting; written letters, figures, signs, etc.; as, German script. 2. a style of printing that looks like handwriting. 3. manuscript of a play or actor's part. *n. 14.*

scrip tur al or **Scrip tur al** (skrip′chər əl), of the Scriptures; according to the Scriptures; based on the Scriptures. *adj. 13.*

Scrip ture (skrip′chər), 1. the Bible. **The Scriptures** or **Holy Scripture** means the Bible. 2. Any sacred writing may be called a scripture. *n. 5.*

scrive ner (skriv′nər), public writer of letters or documents for others; clerk; notary. *n.* [*Old use*] *19.*

scrof u la (skrof′ū lə), a disease like tuberculosis that causes a swelling of the lymphatic glands, inflammation of the joints, etc. *n.*

Scroll (def. 1)

scroll (skrōl), 1. roll of parchment or paper, especially one with writing on it. He slowly unrolled the scroll as he read from it. 2. ornament resembling a partly unrolled sheet of paper, or having a spiral or coiled form. *n. 6.*

Three scrolls in a border

Scrooge (skrüj), the old miser in Dickens's story *A Christmas Carol.* *n. 11.*

scrub[1] (skrub), 1. rub hard; wash or clean by rubbing. She scrubbed the floor with a brush and soapsuds. 2. scrubbing. Give your face and hands a good scrub. *v., scrubbed, scrubbing, n. 5.*

scrub[2] (skrub), 1. low, stunted trees or shrubs. Scrub pine was coming up in the pasture. 2. anything small or below the usual size. He is a little scrub of a man. 3. small; poor; inferior. A scrub ball team is made up of inferior, substitute, or untrained players. *n., adj.*

scrub by (skrub′i), 1. low; stunted; as, scrubby trees. 2. covered with scrub; as, scrubby land. 3. shabby; mean. *adj., scrubbier, scrubbiest.*

scruff (skruf), the skin at the back of the neck; the back of the neck. *n.*

scru ple[1] (skrü′pəl), 1. a feeling of doubt about what one ought to do. No scruple ever holds him back from having his own way. 2. a feeling of uneasiness that keeps a person from doing something. She has scruples about playing cards for money. 3. hesitate or be unwilling (to do something). A dishonest man does not scruple to deceive others. 4. have scruples. *n., v. 6.*

scru ple[2] (skrü′pəl), 1. a weight of 20 grains. 3 scruples make 1 dram. 2. very small amount. *n.*

scru pu lous (skrü′pū ləs), 1. having or showing a strict regard for what is right. 2. attending thoroughly to details; very careful. A soldier must pay scrupulous attention to orders. *adj. 7.*

scru ti nize (skrü′ti nīz), examine closely; inspect carefully. The jeweler scrutinized the diamond for flaws. *v. 13.*

scru ti ny (skrü′ti ni), close examination; careful inspection. His work looks all right, but it will not bear scrutiny. *n., pl. scrutinies. 12.*

scud (skud), 1. run or move swiftly. Clouds scud across the sky when there is a high wind. 2. scudding. 3. clouds or spray driven by the wind. *v., scudded, scudding, n. 12.*

scuff (skuf), 1. walk without lifting the feet; shuffle. 2. wear or injure the surface of by hard use; as, to scuff one's shoes. 3. act of scuffing. *v., n.*

scuf fle (skuf′əl), 1. struggle or fight in a confused manner. 2. such a fight or struggle. 3. shuffle. *v., n. 10.*

scull (skul), 1. an oar worked with a side twist over the end of a boat to make it go. 2. one of a pair of oars used, one on each side, by a single rower. 3. propel (a boat) by a scull or by sculls. 4. act of propelling by sculls. *n., v. 17.*

Man sculling

scul ler y (skul′ər i), small room where the dirty, rough work of a kitchen is done. *n., pl. sculleries. 17.*

scul lion (skul′yən), servant who does the dirty, rough work in a kitchen. In the castle kitchen, the scullions made the fires, cleaned the floors, and washed the dishes. *n. 14.*

sculp tor (skulp′tər), person who carves or models figures. Sculptors make statues of marble and bronze. *n. 8.*

sculp ture (skulp′chər), 1. the art of carving or modeling figures. Sculpture includes the cutting of statues from blocks of marble or stone, casting in bronze, and modeling in clay or wax. 2. carve or model. 3. sculptured work; a piece of such work. There are many famous sculptures in Italy. 4. cover or ornament with sculpture. **Sculptured** means carved or ornamented with sculpture. *n., v. 7.*

scum (skum), 1. thin layer that rises to the top of a liquid. When she makes jelly, she skims off the scum. Green scum rises to the top of the pond. 2. low, worthless people. The saloon was filled with the scum of the town. *n. 10.*

scup per (skup′ər), an opening in the side of a ship to let water run off the deck. *n. 20.*

scurf (skėrf), 1. small scales of dead skin; dandruff. 2. any scaly matter on a surface. *n. 19.*

scur ri lous (skėr′i ləs), coarsely joking; abusive in an indecent way. *adj. 16.*

scur ry (skėr′i), 1. run quickly; scamper; hurry. We could hear the mice scurry about in the walls. 2. hasty running; hurrying. With much fuss and scurry, Aunt Martha at last got started. *v., scurried, scurrying, n. 10.*

scur vi ly (skėr′vi li), in a manner deserving contempt; meanly. *adv.*

scur vy (skėr′vi), 1. a disease caused by a lack of vegetables and fruits. It causes swollen and bleeding gums, extreme weakness, and livid spots on the skin. Scurvy used to be common among sailors when they had little to eat except salt meat and bread. 2. mean; contemptible; base; as, a scurvy fellow, a scurvy trick. *n., adj., scurvier, scurviest. 11.*

scutch eon (skuch′ən), escutcheon, a shield with a coat of arms on it. *n. 16.*

scut tle[1] (skut′əl), a kind of bucket for holding or carrying coal. See the picture. *n. 8.*

Scuttle

scut tle[2] (skut′əl), 1. an opening in the deck of a ship with a lid or cover; such an opening in the side of a ship or in a wall or roof. 2. the lid or cover. 3. cut holes through the bottom or sides of (a ship) to sink it. After the pirates captured the ship, they scuttled it. *n., v.*

scut tle[3] (skut′əl), scamper; scurry. The dogs scuttled off into the woods. *v., n.*

Scyl la (sil′ə), a dangerous rock opposite the whirlpool Charybdis. **Between Scylla and Charybdis** means between two dangers, one of which must be met. *n. 10.*

scythe (sīᴛʜ), a long, curved blade on a long handle, for cutting grass, etc. *n. 8.*

Farmer using a scythe

Scythi a (sith′i ə), an ancient region that extended over parts of Europe and Asia. Scythia was north and east of the Black and Caspian seas. *n. 20.*

S. Dak. or **S.D.,** South Dakota.

SE or **S. E.** or **s.e.** southeast.

sea (sē), 1. the great body of salt water that covers almost three fourths of the earth's surface; the ocean. 2. any large body of salt water, smaller than an ocean; as, the North Sea, the Mediterranean Sea, the Black Sea. 3. a large, heavy wave; the swell of the ocean. A high sea swept away the ship's masts. 4. Some special meanings are:

at sea, 1. out on the sea. We were at sea out of sight of land for ten days. 2. puzzled; confused. I can't understand this problem; I'm all at sea.

follow the sea, be a sailor.

go to sea, 1. become a sailor. 2. begin a voyage.

put to sea, begin a voyage.

n. 1.

sea anemone, a flowerlike polyp, a rather simple form of water animal.

Sea anemone (3 in. wide is a common size)

sea board (sē′bōrd′), the land near the sea; seacoast; seashore; as, the Atlantic seaboard. *n. 13.*

sea coast (sē′kōst′), land along the sea; as, the seacoast of North America. *n. 7.*

sea cow, a large, fishlike mammal living in the sea.

sea dog, 1. sailor; sailor with long experience. 2. the common seal. 3. the dogfish, a small shark.

sea far er (sē′fãr′ər), 1. traveler on the sea. 2. sailor. *n. 20.*

sea far ing (sē′fãr′ing), that goes, travels, works, or lives on the sea. Sailors are seafaring men. *adj. 11.*

sea girt (sē′gėrt′), surrounded by the sea. *adj.*

sea go ing (sē′gō′ing), 1. going by sea; seafaring. 2. fit for going to sea. *adj. 20.*

Sea gull (about 1½ ft. long)

sea green, light bluish green.

sea gull, gull, a sea bird with long wings and webbed feet.

sea horse, 1. a kind of small fish (2 to 10 inches long) with a head suggesting that of a horse. 2. walrus. 3. in old stories, a sea animal supposed to be half horse and half fish.

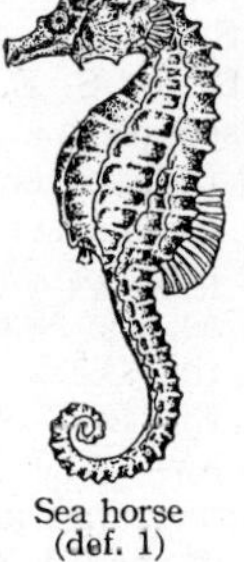
Sea horse (def. 1)

seal[1] (sēl), 1. design stamped on a piece of wax, etc., to show ownership or authority; a paper, circle, mark, etc., representing it. The seal of the United States is attached to important government papers. 2. stamp for marking things with such a design. Mabel has a seal with her initials M.B. on it, with which she stamps sealing wax to fasten her letters securely. 3. piece of wax, etc., on which the design is stamped. Letters that have seals, or the door of a room that is fastened by a metal seal, cannot be opened without breaking the seal. 4. mark with a seal. The treaty was signed and sealed by both governments. 5. close tightly; shut; fasten. She sealed the letter. We seal jars of fruit. His eyes were sealed with sleep. Her promise sealed her lips. 6. something for keeping a thing secret; as, a seal of secrecy. 7. something that settles or determines; as, the seal of authority. 8. settle; determine. The judge's words sealed the prisoner's fate. 9. give a sign that (a thing) is true; as, to seal a promise with a kiss. 10. **Set one's seal to** sometimes means approve. *n., v. 2.*

Seal of the United States

seal[2] (sēl), 1. a kind of sea animal with flippers. See the picture. Some kinds are hunted for their valuable fur. 2. the fur. 3. leather made from the skin of a seal. 4. hunt seals. *n., v.*

Fur seal (6 ft. long)

sea legs, legs that are accustomed to walking steadily on a rolling or pitching ship.

sea level, the surface of the sea. Heights of mountains, etc., are measured as so many feet above sea level. *20.*

sealing wax, a kind of wax, soft when heated, used for sealing letters, packages, etc.

sea lion, a large seal of the Pacific Coast.

seal skin (sēl′skin′), 1. skin of the fur seal, prepared for use. 2. a garment made of this fur. *n.*

Sea lion (about 7 ft. long)

seam (sēm), 1. the line formed by sewing two pieces of cloth, canvas, leather, etc., together; as, the seams of a coat, seams of a sail. 2. any line where the edges join. The seams of the boat must be filled in if they leak. 3. sew the seam of; join with a seam. 4. any mark or line like a seam. The old sword cut had left a seam in his face. 5. mark (the face, etc.) with wrinkles, scars, etc. 6. a layer; as, a seam of coal. *n., v. 4.*

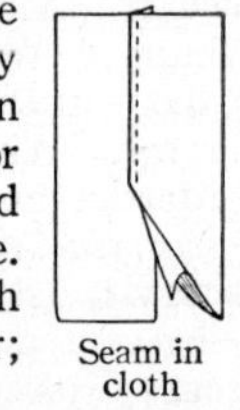
Seam in cloth

sea man (sē′mən), 1. sailor. 2. sailor who is not an officer. *n., pl. seamen. 8.*

sea man ship (sē′mən ship), skill in managing a ship. *n. 20.*

sea men (sē′mən), sailors. *n. pl. 5.*

sea mew, sea gull. *11.*

seam stress (sēm′stris), woman who earns her living by sewing; a sewing woman. *n. 18.*

seam y (sēm′i), 1. showing seams; as, the seamy side of a garment. 2. The **seamy side** sometimes means the worst side. A policeman sees much of the seamy side of life. *adj., seamier, seamiest.*

sé ance (sā′äns), 1. sitting; session. 2. meeting of people seeking to communicate with spirits of the dead by the help of a medium. *n.*

sea plane (sē′plān′), airplane that can rise from and alight on water; hydroplane. *n.*

sea port (sē′pōrt′), a port or harbor on the seacoast; a city or town with a harbor that ships can reach from the sea. San Francisco and New Orleans are seaports. *n. 6.*

sear (sēr), 1. burn the surface of. The hot iron seared his flesh. 2. make hard or unfeeling. That cruel man must have a seared conscience. 3. dry up; wither. 4. dried up; withered. Also spelled **sere.** *v., adj. 10.*

search (sėrch), 1. try to find by looking; seek; look for (something); look through; go over carefully; examine. We searched all day for the lost kitten. The police searched the prisoner to see if he had a gun. The doctor searched the wound for the bullet. 2. searching; examination. John found his book after a long search. **In search of** means trying to find; looking for. *v., n. 2.*

search ing (sėr′ching), 1. examining carefully; thorough; as, a searching gaze, a searching examination. 2. piercing; sharp; as, a searching wind. *adj.*

search light (sėrch′līt′), 1. powerful light that can throw a beam in any direction. 2. the beam of light so thrown. *n. 14.*

search warrant, paper authorizing the searching of a house or building for stolen goods, etc.

sea rover, 1. pirate. 2. pirate ship.

sea shell, shell of any sea mollusk.

Sea shells

sea shore (sē′shōr′), land along the sea. *n. 8.*

sea sick (sē′sik′), sick because of a ship's motion. *adj. 13.*

sea sick ness (sē′sik′nis), sickness caused by the motion of a ship. *n.*

sea side (sē′sīd′), 1. land along the sea; seacoast. 2. of or at the seaside; as, a seaside hotel. *n., adj. 8.*

sea son (sē′zən), 1. The four seasons of the year are spring, summer, autumn, and winter. 2. any period of time marked by something special; as, the Christmas season, the harvest season. 3. suitable or fit time. **In season** means at the right time. 4. improve the flavor of. Season your egg with salt. 5. make or become fit for use by a period of keeping or treatment. Wood is seasoned for building by drying and hardening it. 6. make less severe; soften. Season justice with mercy. *n., v. 1.*

sea son a ble (sē′zən ə bəl), 1. suitable to the season. Hot weather is seasonable in July. 2. coming at the right or proper time. The second expedition brought seasonable aid to the men who had survived the first. *adj. 13.*

sea son al (sē′zən əl), having to do with the seasons; depending on a season; happening at regular intervals. *adj. 16.*

sea son ing (sē′zən ing), something that gives a better flavor. Salt, pepper, and spices are seasonings. We like conversation with a seasoning of humor. *n.*

seat (sēt), 1. thing to sit on. Chairs, benches, and stools are seats. Take a seat, please. 2. place in which one has the right to sit. Our seats are in the fifth row of the balcony. If a man has a seat in Congress or a seat in the stock exchange, it means that he is a member. 3. that part of a chair, bench, stool, etc., on which one sits. This bench has a broken seat. 4. that part of the body on which one sits, or the clothing covering it. The seat of his trousers was patched. 5. manner of sitting on horseback. That rider has a good seat. 6. established place or center. 7. residence; home. The family seat of the Howards is Kent. A university is a seat of learning. The seat of our government is in Washington, D.C. 8. to set or place on a seat. He seated himself in the most comfortable chair. 9. have seats for. Our school assembly seats one thousand pupils. 10. put a seat on. *n., v. 1.*

Se at tle (sē at′əl), a seaport city in Washington, on Puget Sound. *n. 14.*

sea urchin, a small round sea animal with a spiny shell.

Sea urchin (2 to 6 inches in diameter)

sea ward (sē′wərd), 1. toward the sea. Our house faces seaward. 2. direction toward the sea. The island lies a mile to seaward. *adv., adj., n. 8.*

sea wards (sē′wərdz), seaward. *adv.*

sea weed (sē′wēd′), any plant or plants growing in the sea. *n. 13.*

sea wor thy (sē′wėr′ᴛʜi), fit for sailing on the sea; able to stand storms at sea; as, a seaworthy ship. *adj. 20.*

se ba ceous (si bā′shəs), pertaining to fat; fatty; greasy. The sebaceous glands and ducts supply oil to the skin and hair. *adj. 20.*

sec., 1. secretary. 2. second; seconds. 3. section.

se cede (si sēd′), withdraw formally from an organization. *v. 11.*

se ces sion (si sesh′ən), formal withdrawing from an organization. *n. 13.*

se clude (si klüd′), keep apart from company; shut off from others. He secludes himself and sees only his close friends. *v. 11.*

se clu sion (si klü′zhən), 1. a secluding or being secluded; retirement. She lives in seclusion apart from her friends. 2. secluded place. *n. 13.*

sec ond[1] (sek′ənd), 1. next after the first; as, the second seat from the front, the second prize. 2. below the first; inferior; as, the second officer on a ship, cloth of second quality. 3. another; other. Napoleon has been called a second Caesar. Ella says her friend Amy is her second self. 4. person or thing that is second. 5. goods below first quality. These stockings are seconds and have some slight defects. 6. person who supports or aids another. The prize fighter had a second. 7. support; back up; assist. A man seconded the motion to adjourn. *adj., adv., n., v. 1.*

sec ond[2] (sek′ənd). Sixty seconds make one minute. *n.*

sec ond ar y (sek′ən dãr′i), 1. next after the first in order, place, time, etc. A high school is a secondary school; it comes after the elementary school. 2. having less importance. *adj. 7.*

secondary accent, weaker accent. In *second-class* there is a secondary accent on *class.*

sec ond-class (sek′ənd klas′), 1. of or belonging to the class next after the first. We traveled in second-class cars in Europe. 2. of inferior grade or quality. *adj.*

sec ond-hand (sek′ənd hand′), 1. not original; obtained from another; as, second-hand information. 2. not new; used already by someone else; as, second-hand clothes. 3. dealing in used goods; as, a second-hand bookshop. *adj. 18.*

sec ond ly (sek′ənd li), in the second place. *adv.*

sec ond-rate (sek′ənd rāt′), 1. rated as second-class. 2. inferior. *adj.*

se cre cy (sē′krə si), 1. condition of being secret or being kept secret. 2. ability to keep things secret. *n., pl. secrecies. 8.*

se cret (sē′krit), 1. kept from sight; hidden, as, a secret room, a secret drawer, a secret spring. 2. kept from knowledge of others; as, a secret errand, a secret marriage. 3. known only to a few; as, a secret sign. 4. something secret or hidden. 5. hidden cause or reason. *adj., n. 2.*

sec re tar i al (sek′ri tãr′i əl), of a secretary; having to do with a secretary. She learned to do stenography, typewriting, and other secretarial work. *adj.*

sec re tar y (sek′ri tãr′i), 1. person who writes letters, keeps records, etc., for a person, company, club, etc. Our club has a secretary who keeps the minutes of the meetings. 2. person who has charge of a department of a government. The Secretary of the Treasury is the head of the Treasury Department. 3. a writing desk with a set of drawers and often with shelves for books. *n., pl. secretaries. 3.*

se crete (si krēt′), 1. hide; keep secret. 2. make; prepare; produce. Glands in the mouth secrete saliva. *v. 10.*

se cre tion (si krē′shən), 1. substance that is secreted by some part of an animal or plant. Bile is the secretion of the liver. 2. secreting or production of such a substance. *n. 8.*

se cre tive (si krē′tiv), 1. having the habit of secrecy; not frank and open. 2. causing or aiding secretion. *adj.*

secret service, 1. the branch of a government that makes secret investigations. In war, the secret service tries to learn the enemy's plans. 2. official service that is secret.

sect (sekt), group of people holding certain principles, beliefs, or opinions. There are many religious sects or denominations. *n. 6.*

sec tar i an (sek tãr′i ən), 1. of or pertaining to a sect; denominational. 2. devoted member of a sect, especially a narrow-minded or strongly prejudiced member. *adj., n. 18.*

sec tion (sek′shən), 1. part cut off; part; division; slice. His section of the family estate was larger than his brother's. Mother cut the pie into eight equal sections. Anna divided the orange into sections. 2. division of a book. Study sections 10 to 16 of

Chapter V of your grammar for tomorrow's lesson. 3. region; part of a country, city, etc. A town has a business section, residential sections, etc. 4. act of cutting. 5. cut into sections. 6. a representation of a thing as it would appear if cut straight through. 7. a district one mile square. A township contains 36 sections. *n., v. 2.*

Section of an apple (def. 6)

sec tion al (sek′shən əl), 1. pertaining to a particular section; local. 2. made of sections; as, a sectional bookcase. *adj. 13.*

sec tion al ism (sek′shən əl izm), too great regard for local interests; sectional prejudice or hatred. *n.*

sec tor (sek′tər), 1. the part of a circle between two radii and the included arc. 2. one of the districts into which an area is divided for military purposes. *n. 16.*

sec u lar (sek′ū lər), 1. worldly; not religious or sacred; as, secular music, a secular education. 2. living in the world, not shut up in monasteries; as, the secular clergy, a secular priest. *adj. 8.*

se cure (si kūr′), 1. free from care or fear. The old couple lived a quiet, secure life. 2. safe against loss, attack, escape, etc. Keep the prisoner secure within the dungeon. This is a secure hiding place. Land in a growing city is a secure investment. 3. firmly fastened; not liable to give way. Are the prisoner's bonds secure? The boards of this bridge do not look secure. 4. sure; certain; that can be counted on. We know in advance that our victory is secure. He felt secure of salvation. 5. make firm or fast. Secure the locks on doors and windows. 6. make safe. You cannot secure yourself against all risks and dangers. 7. get; obtain. We have secured our tickets for the school play. *adj., v. 2.*

se cu ri ty (si kūr′i ti), 1. freedom from danger, care, or fear; feeling or condition of being safe. You may cross the street in security when a policeman holds up his hand. 2. something that secures or makes safe. A watchdog is a security against burglars. 3. something given as a pledge that a person will fulfill some duty, promise, etc. A life-insurance policy may serve as security for a loan. 4. bond or stock certificate. These railroad securities can be sold for $5000. *n., pl. securities. 5.*

se dan (si dan′), 1. a closed automobile seating four or more persons. 2. a covered chair carried on poles by two men. Sedan chairs were much used during the 17th and 18th centuries. *n. 11.*

Sedan chair

Se dan (si dan′), town in France. Prussia defeated France there in 1870. *n. 11.*

se date (si dāt′), quiet; calm; serious. She is very sedate for a child and would rather read or sew than play. *adj. 13.*

sed a tive (sed′ə tiv), 1. medicine that lessens pain or excitement. 2. soothing; calming. *n., adj. 17.*

sed en tar y (sed′ən tãr′i), 1. used to sitting still much of the time. Sedentary people get little physical exercise. 2. that keeps one sitting still much of the time. Bookkeeping is a sedentary occupation. *adj. 9.*

sedge (sej), a grasslike plant that grows in wet places. *n. 8.*

sed i ment (sed′i mənt), matter that settles to the bottom of a liquid. When the river Nile overflows, it leaves sediment on the surrounding fields. *n. 10.*

sed i men ta ry (sed′i men′tə ri), 1. of sediment; having to do with sediment. 2. formed from sediment. Slate is a sedimentary rock. *adj. 20.*

se di tion (si dish′ən), speech or action causing discontent or rebellion against the government; incitement to discontent or rebellion. *n. 11.*

se di tious (si dish′əs), 1. stirring up discontent or rebellion. 2. taking part in sedition; guilty of sedition. 3. pertaining to sedition. *adj. 15.*

se duce (si dūs′ or si düs′), 1. tempt to wrongdoing; persuade to do wrong. General Arnold was seduced by the offer of great wealth, and betrayed his country to the enemy. 2. lead away; lead astray; beguile. *v. 6.*

se duc tion (si duk′shən), 1. act of seducing; condition of being seduced. 2. something that seduces; a temptation; an attraction. *n.*

se duc tive (si duk′tiv), alluring; captivating; charming. *adj. 14.*

sed u lous (sej′ů ləs), hard-working; diligent; taking pains. *adj. 15.*

see[1] (sē), 1. look at; be aware of by using the eyes. See that black cloud. 2. have the power of sight. The blind do not see. 3. understand. I see what you mean. 4. find out. See what you can do for him. 5. take care; make sure. See that the work is done properly. See that you come home early. 6. have knowledge or experience of. That coat has seen hard wear. 7. go with; attend; as, to see a girl home. 8. call on. I went to see a friend. 9. receive a call from. Mrs. Brown is too ill to see anyone. *v., saw, seen, seeing. 1.*

see[2] (sē), 1. the position or authority of a bishop. 2. the district under a bishop's authority; diocese. *n.*

seed (sēd), 1. thing from which anything grows. We plant seeds in the garden. Part of every crop is saved for seed. 2. thing grown; children; descendants. The Jews are the seed of Abraham. 3. sow with seeds; scatter seeds over. The farmer seeded the field with corn. Dandelions seed themselves. 4. remove seeds from. Mary seeded the raisins for the cake. 5. produce seeds; shed seeds. 6. **Go to seed** means (1) come to the time of yielding seed. (2) come to the end of vigor, usefulness, prosperity, etc. *n., pl. seeds* or *seed, v. 1.*

Seeds

seed case (sēd′kās′), any pod, capsule, or other dry, hollow fruit that contains seeds. *n.*

seed corn, corn saved for seed.

seed er (sēd′ər), 1. one that seeds. 2. machine or device for planting seeds. 3. machine or device for removing seeds. *n. 18.*

seed i ness (sēd′i nis), seedy condition. *n.*

seed ling (sēd′ling), 1. young plant grown from a seed. 2. small young tree less than three feet high. *n. 8.*

seeds man (sēdz′mən), 1. sower of seed. 2. dealer in seed. *n., pl. seedsmen. 17.*

seed y (sēd′i), 1. full of seed. 2. gone to seed. 3. shabby; no longer fresh or new; as, seedy clothes. *adj., seedier, seediest.*

see ing (sē′ing), in view of the fact. Seeing that it is ten o'clock, we will not wait for Mary any longer. *conj.*

seek (sēk), 1. try to find; look for; hunt. The boys are seeking a good camping place. 2. try to get. Most men seek wealth; all men seek happiness. He seeks your advice. 3. try; attempt. We sought to make peace between Fred and Tom. *v., sought, seeking. 1.*

seem (sēm). This apple seemed good but was rotten inside. Does this room seem hot to you? The dog seems to like that bone. Men far off seem small; they look as if they were dots. *v. 1.*

seem ing (sēm′ing), 1. apparent; that appears to be. 2. appearance. It was worse in its seeming than in reality. *adj., n.*

seem ing ly (sēm′ing li), apparently; as far as appearances go. This hill is, seemingly, the highest around here. *adv. 11.*

seem li ness (sēm′li nis), fitness; suitability; propriety; decorum. *n.*

seem ly (sēm′li), fitting; suitable; proper. Grandmother does not consider modern dances seemly. *adj., seemlier, seemliest. 13.*

seen (sēn). See **see**[1]. Have you seen William? *pp. of see*[1]. *1.*

seep (sēp), ooze; trickle; percolate. Water seeps through sand. *v. 17.*

seep age (sēp′ij), trickling; oozing; leakage; slow passing through. *n. 20.*

seer (sēr), prophet; person who foresees or foretells future events. *n. 8.*

seer suck er (sēr′suk′ər), cloth with alternate stripes of plain and crinkled material. *n.*

see saw (sē′sô′), 1. plank resting on a support near its middle so that the ends can move up and down. 2. move up and down on such a plank. 3. a moving up and down on such a plank. See the picture. 4. moving up and down or back and forth. 5. move up and down or back and forth. *n., v., adj. 17.*

Children seesawing

seethe (sēᴛʜ), 1. boil. The cook seethed the mutton. 2. bubble and foam. The seething waters carried the light boat down over the falls. 3. be excited; be disturbed. The pirate crew was seething with discontent and ready for open rebellion. *v. 8.*

seg ment (seg′mənt), piece or part cut off, marked off, or broken off; division; section. An orange is easily pulled apart into its segments. *n. 7.*

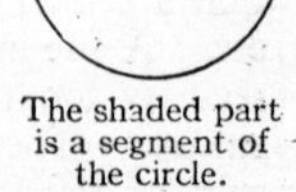
The shaded part is a segment of the circle.

seg re gate (seg′ri gāt), 1. separate from others; set apart; isolate. The doctor segregated the child sick with scarlet fever to protect the other patients. 2. go apart; separate. *v. 19.*

seg re ga tion (seg′ri gā′shən), separation from others; setting apart; as, the segregation of lepers. *n. 14.*

sei gneur (sen yėr′), feudal lord or landowner. A grand seigneur was a person of high rank or one who behaved as a person of high rank should. *n. 19.*

Seine[1] (sān), a river in northern France. Paris is on the Seine. *n. 9.*

seine[2] (sān), 1. a fishing net that hangs straight down in the water. A seine has floats at the upper edge and sinkers at the lower. 2. fish with a seine. 3. catch with a seine. *n., v.*

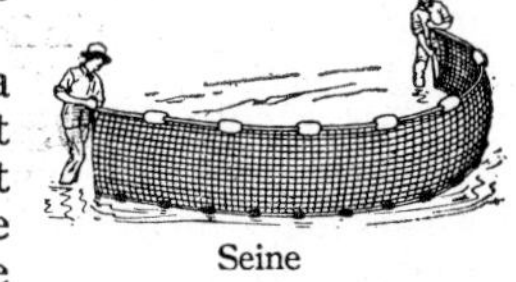
Seine

seis mo graph (sīz′mə graf), an instrument for recording the direction, intensity, and duration of earthquakes. *n.*

seize (sēz), 1. take hold of suddenly; grasp. In fright she seized his arm. 2. take possession of. The soldiers seized the city. *v. 1.*

sei zure (sē′zhər), 1. act of seizing. 2. condition of being seized. 3. sudden attack of disease. *n. 9.*

sel dom (sel′dəm), rarely; not often. He is seldom ill. *adv. 2.*

se lect (si lekt′), 1. choose; pick out. John's uncle let him select his own Christmas present. 2. picked as best; chosen specially. The captain needs a select crew for this dangerous job. 3. careful in choosing; particular as to friends, company, etc. She belongs to a very select club. *v., adj. 2.*

se lec tion (si lek′shən), choice. Her selection of a hat took a long time. The shop offered a very good selection of hats. The plain blue hat was her sister's selection. *n. 6.*

se lec tive (si lek′tiv), selecting; having the power to select. *adj. 15.*

se lect man (si lekt′mən), one of a board of town officers in New England, chosen each year to manage certain public affairs. *n., pl. selectmen.*

Se le ne (se lē′nē), Greek goddess of the moon. *n.*

self (self), 1. Your self is you. My self is I. Jane does not seem like her former self. It is a good thing to think more of others and less of self. 2. *Self* is used with other words to mean (1) of self; as, self-assertion. (2) in self; as, self-confidence. (3) by self; as, self-evident. 3. *Self* is also used in special meanings; as, self-important. *pron., n., pl. selves, prefix. 1.*

self-a buse (self′ə būs′), 1. abuse of one's body or mind. 2. wrong use of the sex organs. *n.*

self-ad dressed (self′ə drest′), addressed to oneself. *adj.*

self-as ser tion (self′ə sėr′shən), insistence on one's own wishes, opinions, claims, etc. *n.*

self-as ser tive (self′ə sėr′tiv), putting oneself forward; insisting on one's own wishes, opinions, etc. *adj.*

self-cen tered (self′sen′tərd), 1. occupied with one's own interests and affairs. 2. selfish. *adj.*

self-com mand (self′kə mand′), control of oneself. *n.*

self-com pla cent (self′kəm plā′sənt), pleased with oneself; self-satisfied. *adj.*

self-con ceit (self′kən sēt′), conceit; too much pride in oneself or one's ability. *n.*

self-con fi dence (self′kon′fi dəns), belief in one's own ability, power, judgment, etc.; confidence in oneself. *n.*

self-con fi dent (self′kon′fi dənt), believing in one's own ability, power, judgment, etc. *adj.*

self-con scious (self′kon′shəs), made conscious of how one is appearing to others; embarrassed, especially by the presence or the thought of other people and their attitude toward one; shy. *adj.*

self-con scious ness (self′kon′shəs nis), being self-conscious; embarrassed or shy feeling. *n. 20.*

self-con tained (self′kən tānd′), 1. independent of others; containing in oneself all that is necessary. 2. saying little; reserved. *adj.*

self-con trol (self′kən trōl′), control of one's actions, feelings, etc. *n. 20.*

self-de fense or **self-de fence** (self′di fens′), defending one's own person, property, reputation, etc. *n.*

self-de ni al (self′di nī′əl), sacrifice of one's own desires and interests; going without things one wants. *n. 19.*

self-de ny ing (self′di nī′ing), unselfish; sacrificing one's own wishes and interests. *adj.*

self-de ter mi na tion (self′di tėr′mi nā′shən), 1. direction from within only, without influence or force from without. 2. the deciding by the people of a nation what form of government they shall have, without reference to the wishes of any other nation. *n. 18.*

self-de vo tion (self′di vō′shən), self-sacrifice. *n.*

self-es teem (self′es tēm′), 1. thinking well of oneself. 2. thinking too well of oneself; conceit. *n.*

self-ev i dent (self′ev′i dənt), evident by itself; needing no proof. *adj.*

self-ex pres sion (self′eks presh′ən), expression of one's personality. *n.*

self-gov ern ing (self′guv′ər ning), that governs itself. *adj.*

self-gov ern ment (self′guv′ərn mənt), 1. government of a group by its own members. 2. self-control. *n. 18.*

self-im por tant (self′im pôr′tənt), having or showing too great an opinion of one's own importance. *adj.*

self-im posed (self′im pōzd′), imposed on oneself by oneself. *adj.*

self-in ter est (self′in′tər est), 1. interest in one's own welfare with too little care for the welfare of others; selfishness. 2. personal advantage. *n.*

self ish (sel′fish), caring too much for oneself; caring too little for others. A selfish person puts his own interests first. *adj. 4.*

self ish ness (sel′fish nis), too great care for oneself; too little care for others. *n. 9.*

self-love (self′luv′), 1. love of oneself; selfishness. 2. conceit. *n.*

self-made (self′mād′), 1. made by oneself. 2. successful through one's own efforts. *adj.*

self-pos sessed (self′pə zest′), calm; having or showing control of one's feelings and acts; not excited, embarrassed, or confused. *adj.*

self-pos ses sion (self′pə zesh′ən), control of one's feelings and actions; composure; calmness. *n.*

self-pres er va tion (self′prez′ər vā′shən), preservation of oneself from harm or destruction. *n.*

self-re li ance (self′ri lī′əns), reliance on one's own abilities, powers, etc. *n.*

self-re li ant (self′ri lī′ənt), having or showing self-reliance. *adj.*

self-re spect (self′ri spekt′), respect for one's self; proper pride. *n. 18.*

self-re spect ing (self′ri spek′ting), having self-respect; properly proud. *adj.*

self-re straint (self′ri strānt′), self-control. *n.*

self-right eous (self′rī′chəs), thinking that you are more moral than others; thinking that you are very good and pleasing to God. *adj.*

self-sac ri fice (self′sak′ri fīs), sacrifice of one's own interests and desires. *n. 17.*

self same (self′sām′), very same. We study the selfsame books that you do. *adj. 5.*

self-sat is fac tion (self′sat′is fak′shən), satisfaction with oneself. *n.*

self-sat is fied (self′sat′is fīd), pleased with oneself. *adj.*

self-seek er (self′sēk′ər), person who seeks his own interests too much. *n.*

self-seek ing (self′sēk′ing), 1. selfish. 2. selfishness. *adj., n.*

self-styled (self′stīld′), called by oneself; as, a self-styled leader whom no one follows. *adj.*

self-suf fi cien cy (self′sə fish′ən si), 1. ability to supply one's own needs. 2. conceit; self-assurance. *n.*

self-suf fi cient (self′sə fish′ənt), 1. asking no help; independent. 2. too ready to go ahead without help or advice. *adj.*

self-sup port ing (self′sə pōr′ting), earning one's expenses; getting along without help. *adj.*

self-willed (self′wild′), insisting on having one's own way; objecting to doing what others ask or command. *adj. 18.*

sell (sel), 1. give up for money or other payment. Mr. Jones has sold his house. The butcher sells meat. The traitor sold his country for money. 2. be on sale; be sold. Strawberries sell at a high price in January. *v., sold, selling. 1.*

sell er (sel′ər), 1. person who sells. A druggist is a seller of drugs. 2. a thing considered with reference to its sale. This book is a best seller. *n. 8.*

sel vage or **sel vedge** (sel′vij), the edge of a fabric finished off to prevent raveling; border; edge. *n. 20.*

selves (selvz), more than one self. He had two selves—a good self and a bad self. *n. pl. 13.*

sem a phore (sem′ə fōr), 1. apparatus for signaling; upright post or structure with movable arms, an arrangement of lanterns, flags, etc., used in railroad signaling. 2. signal by semaphore. *n., v.*

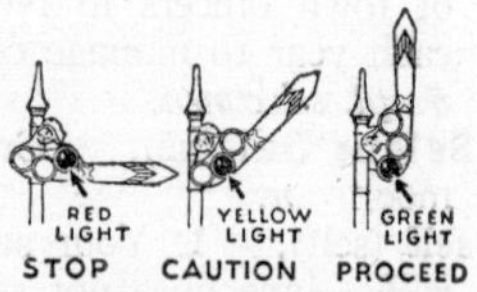

RED LIGHT STOP — YELLOW LIGHT CAUTION — GREEN LIGHT PROCEED

Railroad semaphores

sem blance (sem′bləns), likeness; appearance. These clouds have the semblance of a huge head. His story had the semblance of truth, but was really false. *n. 7.*

se mes ter (si mes′tər), half of a school year. *n. 17.*

semi-, prefix meaning:—
1. half. semicircle = half circle.
2. partly; incompletely. semicivilized = partly civilized. *20.*

semi an nu al (sem′i an′ū əl), 1. occurring every half year. 2. lasting a half year. *adj.*

semi cir cle (sem′i sėr′kəl), a half circle. We sat in a semicircle about the fire. *n. 13.*

semi cir cu lar (sem′i sėr′kū lər), having the form of half of a circle. *adj. 13.*

semi co lon (sem′i kō′lən), a mark of punctuation (;) that shows a separation not so complete as that shown by a period. *n.*

semi nar y (sem′i nãr′i), 1. school, especially one beyond high school. 2. academy or boarding school, especially for young women. 3. school to educate men for the ministry or priesthood. *n., pl. seminaries. 14.*

semi pre cious (sem′i presh′əs), having value but not great value. Amethysts and garnets are semiprecious stones; diamonds and rubies are precious stones. *adj.*

Sem ite (sem′īt), member of the race that includes the Hebrews, Arabs, Syrians, Phoenicians, and Assyrians. *n. 19.*

Se mit ic (si mit′ik), 1. of or pertaining to the Semites or their languages; as, a Semitic nation. 2. a group of languages including Hebrew, Arabic, Phoenician, and Assyrian. *adj., n. 18.*

sen ate (sen′it), 1. a governing or lawmaking assembly. The highest council of state in ancient Rome was called the senate. 2. the upper and smaller branch of an assembly that makes laws. The Congress of the United States is made up of the Senate and the House of Representatives. *n. 3.*

sen a tor (sen′ə tər), member of a senate. *n. 4.*

sen a to ri al (sen′ə tō′ri əl), 1. of or befitting a senator or senators. 2. consisting of senators. 3. entitled to elect a senator; as, a senatorial district. *adj. 15.*

send (send), 1. cause to go. Mother sends Harold on errands. Send a messenger. 2. cause to be carried; as, to send letters, news, etc. 3. cause to come. Send help at once! *v., sent, sending. 1.*

Sen e ca (sen′i kə), a famous Roman Stoic philosopher and author (4? B.C.-65 A.D.). *n. 13.*

sen es chal (sen′i shəl), steward of a prince or great noble in the Middle Ages. Seneschals often had the powers of judges or generals. *n. 14.*

se nile (sē′nīl), 1. of old age. 2. showing the weakness of old age. 3. caused by old age. *adj. 20.*

se nil i ty (si nil′i ti), 1. old age. 2. the weakness of old age. *n.*

sen ior (sēn′yər), 1. older. 2. the older; a father whose son has the same given name; as, John Parker, Senior. 3. an older person. Paul is his brother's senior by two years. 4. higher in rank or longer in service. Mr. Jones is the senior member of the firm. 5. person of higher rank or longer service. 6. member of the graduating class of a high school or college. 7. of or pertaining to the graduating class. *adj., n. 6.*

sen ior i ty (sēn yor′i ti), superiority in age or standing; state or fact of being older. Harry felt that two years' seniority gave him the right to advise his brother. *n. 16.*

sen na (sen′ə), 1. a laxative made from the dried leaves of a cassia plant. 2. the dried leaves. 3. cassia plant; any of various similar plants. *n.*

Sen nach er ib (se nak′ər ib), a king of Assyria (died 681 B.C.). *n. 19.*

se ñor (sā nyôr′), a Spanish word meaning Mr. or sir or a gentleman. *n.*

se ño ra (sā nyō′rä), a Spanish word meaning Mrs. or madame or a lady. *n.*

se ño ri ta (sān′yō rē′tä), a Spanish word meaning Miss or a young lady. *n.*

sen sa tion (sen sā′shən), 1. action of the senses; power to see, hear, feel, taste, smell, etc. Blindness is the loss of the sensation of sight. 2. feeling. Ice gives a sensation of coldness; polished wood, of smoothness; sugar, of sweetness. Tom has a sensation of dizziness when he walks along cliffs. 3. strong or excited feeling. The announcement of war caused a sensation throughout the nation. 4. cause of such feeling. The sudden conquest of France was the great sensation of 1940. *n. 7.*

sen sa tion al (sen sā′shən əl), 1. exciting; startling; trying to cause excitement. There were sensational developments in the murder case. 2. of the senses; having to do with sensation. *adj. 12.*

sense (sens), 1. Sight, smell, taste, hearing, and touch are the five senses. A dog has a keen sense of smell. 2. feeling. Duty well done brings a sense of pleasure. He seems to have no sense of shame. 3. understanding; appreciation. She has a poor sense of duty. Everyone thinks he has a sense of humor. 4. a clear or sound state of mind. He must be out of his senses to act so. 5. judgment; intelligence. He is a man of sense. He hasn't sense enough to come in when it rains. Common sense would have prevented the accident. 6. meaning. Mr. Trent is a gentleman in the true sense of the word. **Make sense** means be understandable; be reasonable. The sentence James wrote on the board didn't make sense. 7. feel; understand. Mother sensed that Father was tired. *n., v. 2.*

sense less (sens′lis), 1. unconscious. A hard blow knocked him senseless. 2. stupid; foolish. *adj. 7.*

sense organ, an eye, ear, or other part of the body by which a person or an animal feels heat, cold, color, pain, etc.

sen si bil i ty (sen′si bil′i ti), 1. ability to feel or perceive. Some drugs lessen a person's sensibilities. 2. fineness of feeling. She has an unusual sensibility for colors. 3. tendency to feel hurt or offended too easily, to cry at nothing, etc. *n., pl. sensibilities. 9.*

sen si ble (sen′si bəl), 1. having good sense; showing good judgment; wise. 2. aware; conscious. I am sensible of your kindness. 3. that can be noticed. There is a sensible difference between yellow and orange. *adj. 4.*

sen si bly (sen′si bli), 1. in a sensible manner; with good sense. 2. so as to be felt. *adv.*

sen si tive (sen′si tiv), 1. receiving impressions readily. The eye is sensitive to light. 2. easily affected or influenced. The mercury in the thermometer is sensitive to changes in temperature. 3. easily hurt or offended. Alice is sensitive when scolded. *adj. 7.*

sen si tive ness (sen′si tiv nis), sensitive quality or state; keenness of feeling. *n. 16.*

sen so ry (sen′sə ri), of or pertaining to sensation. The eyes and ears are sensory organs. *adj. 14.*

sen su al (sen′shü əl), 1. pertaining to the bodily senses rather than to the mind or soul. 2. caring too much for the pleasures of the senses. 3. lustful; lewd. *adj. 9.*

sen su al i ty (sen′shü al′i ti), 1. sensual nature. 2. excessive indulgence in the pleasures of the senses. 3. lewdness. *n., pl. sensualities. 15.*

sen su ous (sen′shü əs), 1. of or derived from the senses; having an effect on the senses; perceived by the senses; as, the sensuous thrill of a cold bath, a sensuous love of color. 2. enjoying the pleasures of the senses. *adj. 14.*

sent (sent). See **send.** They sent the trunks last week. Nan was sent on an errand. *pt. and pp. of send. 1.*

sen tence (sen′təns), 1. group of words that expresses a complete thought. "Boys and girls" is not a sentence. "The boys are here" is a sentence. 2. decision. 3. decision by a judge on the punishment of a criminal. 4. the punishment itself. 5. pronounce punishment on. The judge sentenced the thief to five years in prison. *n., v. 3.*

sen ten tious (sen ten′shəs), 1. full of meaning; saying much in few words. 2. speaking as if one were a judge settling a question. *adj. 13.*

sen tient (sen′shənt), that can feel. *adj. 20.*

sen ti ment (sen′ti mənt), 1. mixture of thought and feeling. Admiration, patriotism, and loyalty are sentiments. 2. feeling, especially refined or tender feeling. Ann thinks clearly, but Kate is full of sentiment. 3. a thought or saying that expresses feeling. 4. mental attitude. 5. personal opinion. *n. 5.*

sen ti men tal (sen′ti men′təl), 1. having or showing much tender feeling; as, sentimental poetry. 2. likely to act from feelings rather than from logical thinking; having too much sentiment. 3. of sentiment; dependent on sentiment. She values her mother's gift for sentimental reasons. *adj. 8.*

sen ti men tal ist (sen′ti men′təl ist), a sentimental person; one who indulges in sentimentality. *n. 17.*

sen ti men tal i ty (sen′ti men tal′i ti), 1. tendency to be influenced by sentiment rather than reason. 2. excessive indulgence in sentiment. 3. feeling expressed too openly or sentimentally. *n., pl. sentimentalities. 19.*

sen ti nel (sen′ti nəl), one stationed to keep watch and guard against surprises. *n. 10.*

sen try (sen′tri), soldier stationed at a place to keep watch and guard against surprises. *n., pl. sentries. 12.*

se pal (sē′pəl), one of the leaflike divisions of the calyx, or outer covering, of a flower. In a carnation, the sepals make a green cup at the base of the flower. In a tulip, the sepals are bright, just like the petals. *n. 10.*

PETAL
SEPAL

sep a ra ble (sep′ə rə bəl), that can be separated. *adj. 19.*

sep a rate (sep′ə rāt for 1, 2, and 3, sep′ə-rit for 4), 1. be between; keep apart; divide. The Atlantic Ocean separates America from Europe. 2. go apart. After school the children separated in all directions. 3. put apart; take away. Separate your things from mine. 4. apart from others; divided; not joined. Our teeth are separate. *v., adj. 1.*

sep a rate ly (sep′ə rit li), in a separate manner; one by one; one at a time. *adv.*

sep a ra tion (sep′ə rā′shən), 1. act of separating; dividing; taking apart. 2. condition of being apart; being separated. The friends were glad to meet after so long a separation. *n. 5.*

sep a ra tist (sep′ə rā′tist), member of a group which separates or withdraws from a larger group. *n. 18.*

sep a ra tor (sep′ə rā′tər), thing that separates, especially a machine for separating the cream from milk, wheat from chaff or dirt, etc. *n. 12.*

se pi a (sē′pi ə), 1. a brown paint or ink prepared from the inky fluid of cuttlefish. 2. dark brown. 3. done in sepia. *n., adj.*

se poy (sē′poi), a native of India who is a soldier in the British army. *n.*

Sept., September. *11.*

Sep tem ber (sep tem′bər), the ninth month. It has 30 days. *n. 2.*

sep tic (sep′tik), 1. causing infection. 2. caused by infection. *adj. 19.*

Sep tu a gint (sep′chü ə jint), a Greek translation of the Old Testament that was made before the time of Christ. *n. 17.*

sep ul cher or **sep ul chre** (sep′əl kər), 1. tomb; grave; place for putting the bodies of persons who have died. 2. bury (a dead body) in a sepulcher. *n., v. 7.*

se pul chral (si pul′krəl), 1. of sepulchers or tombs. 2. of burial; as, sepulchral ceremonies. 3. deep and gloomy; dismal; suggesting a tomb. *adj. 9.*

sep ul ture (sep′əl chər), burial. *n. 19.*

seq., the following. **Et seq.** means "and the following." *20.*

se quel (sē′kwəl), 1. something that follows as a result of some earlier happening; a result of something. Among the sequels of the party were many stomach aches. 2. complete story continuing an earlier one about the same people. *n. 9.*

se quence (sē′kwəns), 1. succession; the coming of one thing after another; order of succession. Arrange the names in alphabetical sequence. 2. connected series; as, a sequence of lessons on one subject. 3. something that follows; result. Crime has its sequence of misery. *n. 8.*

se quent (sē′kwənt), following. *adj. 14.*

se ques ter (si kwes′tər), 1. remove or withdraw from public use or from public view. In this sequestered, retired place we shall not be disturbed. 2. take away (property) for a time from an owner until a debt is paid or some claim is satisfied. 3. seize by authority; take and keep. The soldiers sequestered horses and food from the people they conquered. *v. 7.*

se ques tra tion (sē′kwes trā′shən), 1. confiscation; seizing and holding property till legal claims are satisfied. 2. removal; withdrawal; retirement; seclusion. *n. 19.*

se quin (sē′kwin), 1. small spangle used to ornament dresses, scarfs, etc. 2. a former Italian gold coin worth about $2.25. *n. 20.*

se quoi a (si kwoi′ə), a very tall evergreen tree of California. *n. 18.*

se ra glio (se ral′yō), the women's quarters of a Mohammedan house or palace; harem. *n., pl. seraglios. 15.*

ser aph (ser′əf), one of the highest order of angels. *n., pl. seraphs, seraphim* (-ə fim). *10.*

se raph ic (si raf′ik), 1. of seraphs. 2. like a seraph; angelic. *adj. 15.*

ser a phim (ser′ə fim), more than one seraph. *n. pl. 12.*

Serb (sėrb), native or inhabitant of Serbia. *n.*

Ser bi a (sėr′bi ə), a mountainous country in southeastern Europe, now a division of southeastern Yugoslavia. *n. 10.*

Ser bi an (sėr′bi ən), 1. native or inhabitant of Serbia. 2. of or pertaining to Serbia, its people, or their language. *n., adj.*

sere (sēr), dried up; withered. *adj. 11.* Also spelled **sear.**

ser e nade (ser′ə nād′), 1. music played or sung outdoors at night, especially by a lover under his lady's window. 2. piece of music suitable for such performance. 3. sing or play to in this way. 4. sing or play a serenade. *n., v. 12.*

se rene (si rēn′), 1. peaceful; calm; as, serene happiness, a serene smile. 2. clear; bright; not cloudy. *adj. 5.*

se ren i ty (si ren′i ti), 1. calmness; peacefulness. 2. clearness; quietness. *n. 15.*

serf (sėrf), 1. a slave who cannot be sold off the land but passes from one owner to another with the land. 2. person treated almost like a slave. *n. 8.*

serf dom (sėrf′dəm), 1. the condition of a serf. 2. the custom of having serfs. Serfdom existed all over Europe in the Middle Ages and lasted in Russia till the middle of the 19th century. *n. 18.*

serge (sėrj), a kind of cloth woven with slanting ridges in it. *n. 8.*

ser geant (sär′jənt), 1. army officer ranking next above a corporal. Sergeants and corporals are noncommissioned officers. The sergeant drilled his men. 2. a police officer ranking next above a common policeman. *n. 8.*

ser geant-at-arms (sär′jənt ət ärmz′), officer who keeps order in a legislature, law court, etc. *n., pl. sergeants-at-arms.*

se ri al (sēr′i əl), 1. story published one part at a time in a magazine or newspaper. 2. of a series; arranged in a series; making a series; as, in serial order. *n., adj. 12.*

se ries (sēr′iz), 1. things alike in a row. A series of rooms opened off the hall. 2. things placed one after another. 3. things happening one after the other. A series of rainy days spoiled our vacation. *n., pl. series. 4.*

se ri ous (sēr′i əs), 1. thoughtful; grave; as, a serious face. 2. in earnest; not fooling. Are you joking or serious? 3. important; needing thought. Raising money for our club is a serious matter. 4. important because it may do much harm; dangerous. *adj. 2.*

se ri ous ness (sēr′i əs nis), state or quality of being serious; earnestness; importance. *n. 11.*

ser mon (sėr′mən), 1. a public talk on religion or something connected with religion. Ministers preach sermons in church. 2. a serious talk; a moral lecture; a warning. The teacher gave us a sermon on cheating. *n. 5.*

ser pent (sėr′pənt), 1. snake; big snake. 2. a sly, treacherous person. 3. the devil; Satan. *n. 4.*

ser pen tine (sėr′pən tēn), 1. of or like a serpent. 2. winding; twisting; as, the serpentine course of a creek. 3. cunning; sly; treacherous; as, a serpentine suggestion. 4. a mineral, usually green and sometimes spotted like a serpent's skin. *adj., n. 14.*

ser rate (ser′āt), toothed; notched like the edge of a saw. *adj.*

Serrate leaf

ser ried (ser′id), crowded closely together. *adj. 20.*

se rum (sēr′əm), 1. the clear, pale-yellow liquid of the blood, which separates from the clot when blood coagulates. 2. a liquid used to prevent or cure a disease, obtained from the blood of an animal that has been made immune to the disease. Diphtheria antitoxin is a serum. 3. any watery animal liquid. Lymph is a serum. *n. 11.*

serv ant (sėr′vənt), 1. person employed in a household. Cooks and nursemaids are servants. 2. person employed by another. Policemen and firemen are public servants. 3. person devoted to any service. Ministers are called the servants of God. *n. 2.*

serve (sėrv), 1. work for; be a servant; work. A slave serves his master. Good citizens serve their country. The soldier served three years in the army. 2. be useful; be what is needed; be used. A flat stone served as a table. 3. be favorable or suitable; satisfy. The ship will sail when wind and tide serve. 4. wait on at table; bring food to. 5. put (food or drink) on the table. The waiter served the soup. Dinner is served. 6. supply; furnish. The dairy serves us with milk. The men were served with a round of ammunition. 7. deliver; present. Mr. White was served with a summons to appear in court. 8. treat; act toward. The punishment serves George right. 9. pass; spend. The thief served a term in prison. 10. put (the ball) in play by hitting it in tennis and similar games. 11. act or way of doing this. *v., n. 1.*

serv er (sėr′vər), 1. person who serves. 2. tray for dishes. *n. 10.*

serv ice (sėr′vis), 1. helpful act or acts; aid; being useful to others. "Service" is the motto of our school. 2. supply; arrangements for supplying. The train service was good. 3. occupation or employment as a servant. Mary is in service with Mrs. Brown. 4. work for others; work; performance of duties. Mrs. Brown no longer needs the services of a doctor. He was in active service during the war. 5. advantage; benefit; use. Would this coat be of service to you? 6. department of government or public employment; the persons working in it. **The service** often means the army or the navy. The air service was very important in the war. The **Civil Service** is a name for the departments of the government not connected with the army or navy. 7. religious meeting, religious ceremony. We attend church services twice a week. The marriage service was performed at the home of the bride. 8. manner of serving food; the food served. The service in this restaurant is excellent. 9. set of dishes, etc. She has a silver tea service. 10. act or manner of putting a tennis ball in play. 11. make fit for service. The mechanic serviced our automobile. *n., v. 1.*

serv ice a ble (sėr′vis ə bəl), 1. useful; capable of giving good service. 2. useful for a long time; able to stand much use. *adj. 11.*

ser vile (sėr′vil), 1. of slaves; pertaining to slaves; as, a servile revolt, servile work. 2. like that of slaves; fit for a slave; mean; base; as, servile flattery. *adj. 6.*

ser vil i ty (sər vil′i ti), attitude or behavior fit for a slave. *n. 15.*

ser vi tor (sėr′vi tər), servant; attendant. *n. 13.*

ser vi tude (sėr′vi tūd or sėr′vi tüd), 1. slavery; bondage. 2. forced labor as a punishment. The criminal was sentenced to five years' servitude. *n. 7.*

ses a me (ses′ə mi), a password at which doors and barriers fly open. *n. 19.*

ses sion (sesh′ən), 1. a sitting or meeting of a court, council, legislature, etc. **In session** means meeting. Congress is now in session. 2. a series of such sittings. 3. the term or period of such sittings. This year's session of Congress was unusually long. 4. a single, continuous course or period of lessons. Our school has two sessions, one in the morning and one in the afternoon. *n. 6.*

set (set), 1. put in some place; put; place. Set the box on its end. 2. put in the right place, position, or condition for use; arrange; put in proper order. The hunter sets his traps. Set the table for dinner. Set the clock. The doctor will set Dan's broken leg. 3. put in some condition or relation. A spark set the woods on fire. The slaves were set free. 4. fix. If he sets his mind on it, he will do it. 5. become fixed; become firm or hard. Jelly sets as it cools. 6. form; shape; the way a thing is put or placed. There was a stubborn set to his jaw. 7. direction; tendency; course; drift. The set of opinion was toward building a new bridge. 8. tend; have a certain direction. The current sets to the south. 9. group; things or people belonging together; as, a set of dishes. 10. go down; sink. The sun sets in the west. 11. begin to move; start. He set out to cross the river. 12. young plant. 13. that has been set; fixed; arranged; formal; as, a set smile, a set speech. 14. Some special meanings are:

set about, begin; start work upon.

set back, stop; hinder; check.

set forth, 1. make known; express; declare. 2. start to go.

set in, 1. begin. 2. blow or flow toward the shore.

set off, 1. explode. He will set off the firecrackers. 2. start to go. 3. increase by contrast.

setting hen, a hen sitting on eggs to hatch them.

set up, 1. build. 2. begin; start. 3. put up; raise in place, position, power, pride, etc. 4. claim; pretend.

v., set, setting, n., adj. 1.

set back (set′bak′), check to progress; reverse. *n.*

Settee

set tee (se tē′), a sofa or long bench with a back. See the picture just above. *n. 12.*

set ter (set′ər), 1. person who sets; as, a setter of type or of jewels. 2. a long-haired hunting dog, trained to stand motionless and point his nose toward the game that he scents. *n. 17.*

English setter (about 2 ft. high at the shoulder)

set ting (set′ing), 1. frame or other thing in which something is set. The mounting of a jewel is a setting. 2. scenery of a play. 3. place, time, etc., of a play or story. 4. surroundings; background. 5. music composed to go with certain words. 6. the eggs that a hen sits on for hatching. *n. 18.*

set tle[1] (set′əl), 1. set or be set in a fairly permanent position, place, or way of life. At last we are settled in our new home. Our cousin intends to settle in California. 2. place in a desired or comfortable position. The cat settled herself down in the chair for a nap. 3. put in order; arrange. I must settle all my affairs before going away for the winter. 4. make quiet; become quiet. A vacation will settle your nerves. After the excitement over the Christmas presents had settled down, the children went out to play. 5. clear (a liquid). A beaten egg or cold water will settle coffee. 6. determine; decide; agree upon. Children bring their disputes to mother to settle. Have you settled on a day for the picnic? 7. pay. He settled all his bills before leaving town. Let us settle up our expenses for the trip. 8. establish colonies in; take up residence in (a new country or place) as colonists. The English settled New England. 9. sink. Our house has settled several inches since it was built. 10. come to rest in a particular place; become set or fixed. His cold settled in his lungs. 11. **Settle upon** or **on** means give (property, etc.) to (a person) by law. He settled one thousand dollars a year upon his old servant. *v. 1.*

set tle[2] (set′əl), a long bench. See the picture. *n.*

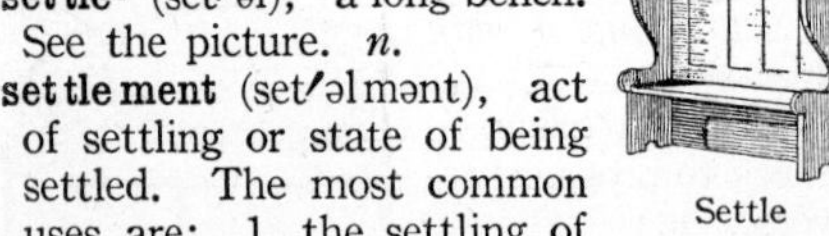
Settle

set tle ment (set′əl mənt), act of settling or state of being settled. The most common uses are: 1. the settling of property upon some one. She was given $20,000 by her marriage settlement. 2. putting in order; arrangement. No settlement of the dispute is possible unless each side yields some point. 3. payment. Settlement of all claims against the firm will be made shortly. 4. the settling of persons in a new country. The settlements by the English along the Atlantic Coast assured that section to England. 5. a group of buildings and the people living in them. Indians often attacked the little settlements of the colonists. 6. place in a poor, neglected neighborhood where work for its improvement is carried on. Hull House is a famous settlement on the west side of Chicago. *n. 3.*

set tler (set′lər), 1. one who settles. 2. person who settles in a new country. The early settlers in America had to fight the Indians. *n. 4.*

sev en (sev′ən), one more than six; 7. *n., adj. 1.*

sev en fold (sev′ən fōld′), 1. seven times as much or as many. 2. having seven parts. 3. seven times as much or as often. *adv., adj. 19.*

sev en teen (sev′ən tēn′), seven more than ten; 17. *n., adj. 4.*

sev en teenth (sev′ən tēnth′), 1. next after the 16th. 2. one of 17 equal parts. *adj., n. 10.*

sev enth (sev′ənth), 1. next after the sixth. Saturday is the seventh day of the week. 2. one of seven equal parts. A day is one seventh of a week. *adj., n. 3.*

sev enth ly (sev′ənth li), in the seventh place. *adv.*

sev en ti eth (sev′ən ti ith), 1. next after the 69th. 2. one of 70 equal parts. *adj., n. 20.*

sev en ty (sev′ən ti), seven times ten; 70. *n., pl. seventies, adj. 2.*

sev er (sev′ər), 1. cut apart; separate. The sailor severed the rope with a knife. The rope severed, and the swing fell down. 2. break off. The two countries severed friendly relations. *v. 5.*

sev er al (sev′ər əl), 1. some; a few; more than two or three but not many. 2. different; individual. The boys went their several ways, each minding his own business. *adj., n. 1.*

sev er ance (sev′ər əns), 1. severing or being severed; separation; division. 2. breaking off; as, the severance of diplomatic relations between two countries. *n. 19.*

se vere (si vēr′), 1. very strict; stern; harsh. The teacher was severe with the children and used severe punishment. 2. serious; grave; as, a severe illness. 3. very plain or simple; without ornament She has a severe haircut like a boy's. 4. sharp; violent. I have a severe headache. That was a severe storm. 5. difficult. The new gun had to pass a series of severe tests. *adj. 2.*

se ver i ty (si ver′i ti), 1. strictness; sternness; harshness. The children feared their father because of his severity. 2. simplicity of style or taste; plainness. The severity of a nun's dress is often becoming. 3. violence; sharpness; as, the severity of storms, pain, disease, grief, etc. 4. seriousness. *n., pl. severities. 7.*

Se ville (sə vil′), a city in southwestern Spain. *n. 16.*
sew (sō), 1. work with a needle and thread; fasten with stitches. You can sew by hand or with a machine. 2. close with stitches. The doctor sewed up the wound. *v., sewed, sewed* or *sewn, sewing. 2.*
sew age (sü′ij), the waste matter which passes through sewers. *n. 11.*
sew er (sü′ər), a drain to carry off waste water and refuse. *n. 7.*
sew er age (sü′ər ij), 1. removal of waste matter by sewers. 2. system of sewers. 3. the waste matter that passes through sewers; sewage. *n. 19.*
sew ing (sō′ing), work done with a needle and thread; something to be sewed. *n.*
sewn (sōn), sewed. *pp. of* **sew.**
sex (seks), the character of being male or female. A boy is of the male sex; a girl is of the female sex. *n. 4.*
sex tant (seks′tənt), an instrument used in measuring angles. In determining latitude and longitude at sea, a navigator uses a sextant to measure the altitude of the sun. *n.*

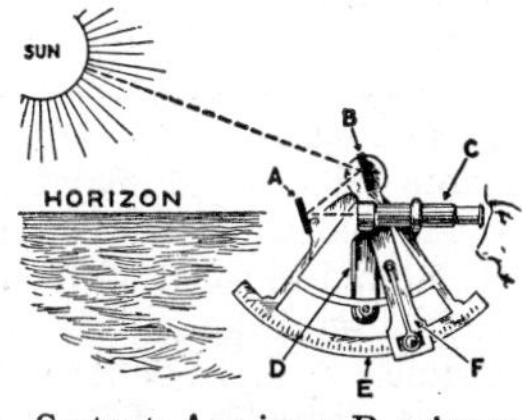

Sextant: A, mirror; B, mirror; C, telescope; D, handle; E, graduated arm; F, arm.

sex tet or **sex tette** (seks tet′), 1. piece of music for six voices or instruments. 2. six singers or players. 3. any group of six. *n.*
sex ton (seks′tən), man who takes care of a church. The sexton keeps the church clean and warm. *n. 10.*
sex u al (sek′shü əl), of or pertaining to sex or the sexes. *adj. 8.*
shab by (shab′i), 1. much worn. His old suit looks shabby. 2. wearing old or much worn clothes. She is always shabby. 3. mean; not generous; unfair. It is shabby not to speak to an old friend because he is poor. *adj., shabbier, shabbiest. 9.*
shack (shak), roughly built hut; house in bad condition. *n. 13.*
shack le (shak′əl), 1. metal band fastened around the ankles or wrists of a prisoner, slave, etc. Shackles are usually fastened to each other, the wall, floor, etc., by chains. **Shackles** means fetters or chains. 2. link fastening together the two rings for the ankles and wrists of a prisoner. 3. put shackles on. 4. anything that prevents freedom of action, thought, etc. 5. restrain; hamper. 6. thing for fastening or coupling. *n., v. 9.*

Shackles

shad (shad), food fish of the North Atlantic Coast of America. Shad have many small loose bones. *n., pl. shad* or *shads. 12.*
shade (shād), 1. partly dark place, not in the sunshine. He sat in the shade of a big tree. 2. something that shuts out light. Pull down the shades of the windows. 3. keep light from. A big hat shades the eyes. 4. depth of color; lightness or darkness of color. I want to see silks in all shades of blue. 5. make darker than the rest; darken. A person shades one side of a dish when he draws or paints it. 6. very small difference; little bit. Your coat is a shade longer than your dress. 7. show very small differences; change little by little. This scarf shades from deep rose to pale pink. *n., v. 1.*
shad i ness (shād′i nis), quality or state of being shady. *n.*
shad ing (shād′ing), 1. covering from the light. 2. use of black or color to give the effect of shade in a picture. 3. slight variation or difference of color, character, etc. *n.*
shad ow (shad′ō), 1. shade made by some person or thing. Sometimes a person's shadow is much longer than he is, and sometimes much shorter. 2. darkness; partial shade. Don't turn on the light; we like to sit in the shadow. 3. little bit; small degree; slight suggestion. There's not a shadow of a doubt about his guilt. 4. ghost; faint image. You look worn to a shadow. 5. protect from light; shade. The grass is shadowed by huge oaks. 6. follow closely. *n., v. 2.*
shad ow y (shad′ō i), 1. having much shadow or shade; shady. We are glad to leave the hot sunshine and come into the cool shadowy room. 2. like a shadow; dim. He saw a shadowy outline on the window curtain. *adj. 6.*
shad y (shād′i), 1. in the shade. 2. giving shade. 3. of doubtful honesty, character, etc. He has engaged in rather shady occupations. *Used in common talk. adj., shadier, shadiest. 4.*

shaft[1] (shaft). A shaft is always a long, slender part or piece. It may be: 1. the long, slender stem of an arrow, spear, etc. 2. arrow; spear. 3. one of the two wooden poles between which a horse is harnessed to a carriage, etc. 4. the main part of a column. See the picture under **column.** 5. a bar to support parts of a machine that turn, or to help move parts. *n. 4.*

shaft[2] (shaft), 1. deep passage sunk in the earth. The entrance to a mine is called a shaft. 2. a well-like passage; a long, narrow space; as, an elevator shaft. *n.*

S, shaft in a mine; T, tunnel.

shag (shag), 1. rough, matted hair, wool, etc. 2. the long, rough nap of cloth. 3. cloth having such a nap. *n. 14.*

shag bark (shag′bärk′), a hickory tree whose rough bark peels off in long strips. *n.*

shag gy (shag′i), 1. covered with a thick rough mass of hair, wool, etc.; as, a shaggy dog. 2. long, thick, and rough; as, shaggy eyebrows. *adj., shaggier, shaggiest. 7.*

Shah (shä), a title of the ruler of Persia. *n.*

shake (shāk), 1. move quickly backwards and forwards, up and down, or from side to side. The woman shook her little boy. John shook his fist in Tom's face. 2. tremble or make tremble. He is shaking with cold. 3. disturb; make less firm. His lie shook my faith in his honesty. 4. act of shaking. A shake of the head was her answer. *v., shook, shaken, shaking, n. 1.*

shak er (shāk′ər), 1. person who shakes something. 2. a machine or utensil used in shaking. *n. 12.*

Shak er (shāk′ər), member of an American religious sect, so called from movements of the body that formed part of their worship. Shakers owned all property in common. *n.*

Shake speare (shāk′spēr), William, England's greatest poet and dramatist (1564-1616). *n. 6.*

Shake spear i an or **Shake sper i an** (shāk-spēr′i ən), of or pertaining to Shakespeare or his works. *adj.*

shak y (shāk′i), 1. shaking; as, a shaky voice. 2. liable to break down; weak; as, a shaky porch. 3. not reliable; not to be depended on. *adj., shakier, shakiest. 18.*

shale (shāl), rock formed from hardened clay, etc., that splits easily into thin layers. *n. 10.*

shall (shal). We shall come soon. You shall go to the party, I promise you. She shall drink her milk, even if I have to pour it down her throat. Shall is used to express future time, command, obligation, and necessity. *v., pt. should. 1.*

shal lop (shal′əp), a small, light boat. *n. 20.*

shal low (shal′ō), 1. not deep; as, shallow water, a shallow dish, a shallow mind. 2. shallow place. The boys splashed in the shallows of the pond. *adj., n. 3.*

shalt (shalt), old form meaning **shall.** *v. 3.*

sham (sham), 1. fraud; pretense. His goodness is all a sham. 2. false; pretended; imitation. The soldiers had a sham battle. 3. pretend. John is not really sick but only shamming. *n., adj., v., shammed, shamming. 9.*

sham ble (sham′bəl), 1. walk awkwardly or unsteadily. The tired old man shambles. 2. shambling walk. *v., n. 11.*

sham bles (sham′bəlz), 1. slaughter house. 2. place of butchery or great bloodshed. *n. pl. or sing.*

shame (shām), 1. painful feeling of having done something wrong, improper, or silly. The child blushed with shame when he was caught stealing candy. 2. cause to feel shame. 3. drive or force by shame. 4. disgrace; dishonor. That young man's arrest has brought shame to a fine family. 5. bring disgrace upon. He has shamed his parents. 6. a fact to be sorry about; a pity. It is a shame to be so wasteful. What a shame you can't come to the party! *n., v. 2.*

shame faced (shām′fāst′), 1. bashful; shy. 2. showing shame and embarrassment. *adj. 17.*

shame ful (shām′fəl), causing shame; bringing disgrace. *adj. 5.*

shame less (shām′lis), 1. without shame. 2. not modest. *adj. 9.*

sham poo (sham pü′), 1. wash (the hair). 2. washing the hair. 3. preparation used for shampooing. *v., n. 16.*

sham rock (sham′rok), a three-leaved plant like clover. The shamrock is the national emblem of Ireland. *n.*

Shamrock

Shang hai (shang′hī′), large seaport in eastern China. *n. 16.*

shang hai (shang′hī), make unconscious by drugs, liquor, etc., and put on a ship needing sailors. *v., shanghaied, shanghaiing.*

shank (shangk), 1. the part of the leg between the knee and the ankle. 2. the corresponding part in animals. 3. the whole leg. 4. any part like a leg, stem, or shaft. *n. 10.*

shan't (shant), shall not. *11.*

Shan tung (shan'tung'), a peninsula and province in northeastern China. *n. 17.*

shan ty (shan'ti), roughly built hut or cabin. *n., pl. shanties. 18.*

shape (shāp), 1. form; figure; appearance. An apple is different in shape from a banana. A witch could take the shape of a cat or a bat. A white shape stood at his bedside. 2. condition; order. Take time to get your thoughts into shape. 3. to form. The child shapes clay into balls. The hat is shaped to fit her head. 4. **Take shape** means have or take on a definite form. 5. develop; take shape. His plan is shaping well. *n., v. 1.*

shape less (shāp'lis), 1. without definite shape. 2. having an unattractive shape. He wore a shapeless old hat. *adj. 6.*

shape ly (shāp'li), having a pleasing shape; well-formed. *adj., shapelier, shapeliest. 16.*

shard (shärd), 1. piece of broken earthenware. 2. the hard case that covers a beetle's wing. *n. 17.*

share[1] (shãr), 1. part; portion; part belonging to one individual. The father left each child an equal share of his property. John does more than his share of the work and does not always get his share of the praise. 2. each of the parts into which the ownership of a company or corporation is divided. The ownership of this railroad is divided into several million shares. 3. divide into parts, each taking a part. The knight shared his bread with the beggar. 4. use together; enjoy together; have in common. The sisters share the same room. 5. have a share; take part. Everyone shared in making the picnic a success. *n., v. 2.*

share[2] (shãr), part of a plow that cuts through the soil; plowshare. *n.*

share hold er (shãr'hōl'dər), person owning shares of stock; part owner. This railroad has many thousands of shareholders. *n. 20.*

shark (shärk), 1. a large fish that eats other fish and is said to attack people. 2. a dishonest person who preys on others. *n. 9.*

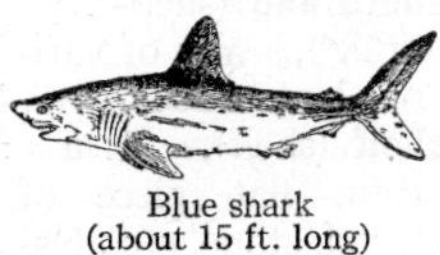

Blue shark (about 15 ft. long)

Shar on (shãr'ən), a plain in western Palestine, noted for its fertility in Bible times. Isaiah 65:10. *n. 18.*

sharp (shärp), 1. having a thin cutting edge or a fine point; as, a sharp knife, a sharp pin. 2. having a point; not rounded; as, a sharp nose, a sharp corner on a box. 3. with a sudden change of direction; as, a sharp turn. 4. very cold; as, sharp weather, a sharp morning. 5. severe; biting; as, sharp words. 6. feeling somewhat like a cut or prick; affecting the senses keenly; as, a sharp taste, a sharp noise, a sharp pain. 7. clear; distinct; as, the sharp contrast between black and white. 8. quick; brisk; as, a sharp walk or run. 9. fierce; violent; as, a sharp struggle. 10. keen; eager; as, a sharp desire, a sharp appetite. 11. being aware of things quickly; as, a sharp eye, sharp ears. 12. watchful; wide-awake. 13. quick in mind; shrewd; clever; as, a sharp boy, a sharp lawyer, sharp at a bargain. 14. promptly; exactly. Come at one o'clock sharp. 15. in music, above the true pitch; as, to sing sharp. 16. a tone one half step above a given tone. 17. the sign (♯) that shows this. 18. in a sharp manner; keenly; suddenly. *adj., adv., n. 2.*

sharp en (shär'pən), 1. make sharp. Sharpen the pencil. Sharpen your wits. 2. become sharp. *v. 4.*

sharp en er (shär'pən ər), person or thing that sharpens; as, a pencil sharpener. *n.*

sharp ness (shärp'nis), quality or condition of being sharp. *n. 11.*

sharp shoot er (shärp'shüt'ər), 1. person who shoots very well. 2. soldier chosen to do accurate shooting. *n.*

shat ter (shat'ər), 1. break into pieces. A stone shattered the window. 2. destroy; disturb greatly; as, shattered hopes, a shattered mind. *v. 4.*

shave (shāv), 1. cut hair from (the face, chin, etc.) with a razor. 2. cutting off hair with a razor. 3. cut off (hair) with a razor. 4. cut off in thin slices. She shaved the chocolate. 5. come very close to; graze. The car shaved the corner. 6. narrow miss or escape. The shot missed him, but it was a close shave. *v., shaved, shaved* or *shaven, shaving, n. 4.*

shav ing (shāv'ing), 1. very thin piece or slice. Shavings of wood are cut off by a plane. 2. act or process of cutting hair from the face, chin, etc., with a razor. *n. 17.*

shawl (shôl), square or oblong piece of material worn about the shoulders or head. *n. 7.*

shay (shā), a chaise, a light carriage with two wheels and one seat. *n.* [*Used in common talk*] *17.*

she (shē), 1. the girl, woman, or female animal spoken about. My sister says she likes to read and her reading helps her in school. 2. female. *pron., pl. they, n., pl. shes. 1.*

sheaf (shēf), bundle of things of the same sort; as, a sheaf of wheat, a sheaf of arrows. *n., pl. sheaves* (shēvz). *6.*

shear (shēr), 1. cut with shears or scissors. 2. cut the wool or fleece from. The farmer sheared his sheep. 3. cut close; cut off. *v., sheared, sheared* or *shorn, shearing. 4.*

shears (shērz), 1. large scissors. 2. any cutting instrument resembling scissors. *n. pl.*

Shears

sheath (shēth), 1. a case or covering for the blade of a sword or knife. 2. any similar covering. *n., pl. sheaths* (shēᴛʜz). *6.*

sheathe (shēᴛʜ), 1. put (a sword, etc.) into a sheath. 2. enclose in a case or covering; as, a mummy sheathed in linen, doors sheathed in metal. *v. 11.*

sheath ing (shēᴛʜ′ing), casing; covering. The first covering of boards on a house is sheathing. *n.*

sheave (shēv), gather into a sheaf or sheaves, and tie. *v.*

sheaves (shēvz), more than one sheaf. *n. pl. 7.*

She ba (shē′bə), an ancient country in southern Arabia. *n. 11.*

shed[1] (shed), a building used for shelter, storage, etc., usually having only one story; as, a train shed, a woodshed. *n. 2.*

shed[2] (shed), 1. pour out; let fall. He shed his blood for his country. The girl shed tears. 2. throw off. A snake sheds its skin. An umbrella sheds water. 3. cause to flow. He shed his enemy's blood. 4. scatter abroad; give forth. The sun sheds light. Flowers shed perfume. *v., shed, shedding.*

Sheep

sheen (shēn), brightness; luster. Satin and polished silver have a sheen. *n. 10.*

sheep (shēp), 1. an animal raised for wool and mutton. See the picture in the last column. 2. person who is weak, timid, or stupid. 3. leather made from the skin of a sheep. 4. **Make sheep's eyes** means give a longing, loving look. *n., pl. sheep. 1.*

sheep cote (shēp′kōt′), shelter for sheep. *n. 19.*

sheep fold (shēp′fōld′), a pen for sheep. *n. 16.*

sheep ish (shēp′ish), 1. awkwardly bashful or embarrassed; as, a sheepish smile. 2. like a sheep; timid; weak; stupid. *adj. 18.*

sheep skin (shēp′skin′), 1. the skin of a sheep, especially with the wool on it. 2. leather or parchment made from it. 3. diploma. *Used in common talk. n. 17.*

sheer[1] (shēr), 1. very thin; almost transparent. She wore a sheer white dress. 2. unmixed; complete. She fainted from sheer weariness. 3. straight up and down; steep. From the top of the wall was a sheer drop of 100 feet to the water below. 4. completely; quite. *adj., adv. 8.*

sheer[2] (shēr), 1. swerve; turn aside; turn from a course. 2. a turning of a ship from its course. *v., n.*

sheet[1] (shēt), 1. large piece of linen or cotton cloth used to sleep on or under. 2. a broad thin piece of anything; as, a sheet of paper, a sheet of glass. 3. single piece of paper. 4. newspaper. 5. a broad flat surface; as, a sheet of water. 6. furnish or cover with a sheet. *n., v. 2.*

sheet[2] (shēt), a rope that controls the angle at which a sail is set. *n.*

sheet iron, iron in sheets or thin plates.

Shef field (shef′ēld), 1. a manufacturing city in central England. 2. **Sheffield plate** is an especially durable silver plate made by rolling out sheets of copper and silver fused together. *n., adj. 15.*

sheik or **sheikh** (shēk), 1. Arab chief or head of a family, village, or tribe. 2. a Mohammedan religious leader. 3. a title of respect used by Mohammedans. *n. 19.*

shek el (shek′əl), an ancient silver coin of the Hebrews. *n. 11.*

shel drake (shel′drāk′), any of various large ducks. *n.*

shelf (shelf), 1. a thin, flat piece of wood, stone, etc., fastened to a wall or frame to hold things, such as books, dishes, etc. 2. anything like a shelf. *n., pl. shelves. 4.*

Shelf

shell (shel), 1. hard outside covering. Nuts, eggs, oysters, turtles, and beetles, all have shells. 2. something like a shell. The framework of a house, a very light racing boat, the pods or husks of some vegetables, and a case filled with gunpowder to be fired from a cannon are all called shells. 3. take out of a shell. The cook is shelling peas. 4. separate (grains of corn) from the cob. 5. fire cannon at. The enemy shelled the town. *n., v. 2.*

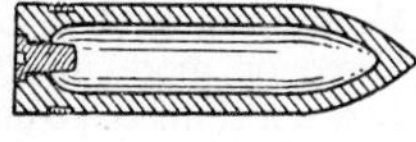

Shell for firing from a cannon

she'll (shēl), 1. she shall. 2. she will. *20.*

shel lac (shə lak′), 1. a varnish made with alcohol. 2. put shellac on. *n., v., shellacked, shellacking. 13.*

Shel ley (shel′i), a famous English poet (1792-1822). *n. 20.*

shell fish (shel′fish′), a water animal with a shell. Oysters, clams, crabs, and lobsters are shellfish. Shellfish are not fish at all. *n., pl. shellfishes* or *shellfish. 17.*

shell shock, a nervous or mental disorder resulting from the strain of war.

shell y (shel′i), 1. abounding in shells. 2. consisting of a shell or shells. 3. shell-like. *adj. 20.*

shel ter (shel′tər), 1. something that covers or protects from weather, danger, or attack. Trees are a shelter from the sun. 2. protection; refuge. We took shelter from the storm in a barn. 3. protect; shield; as, to shelter runaway slaves. 4. find shelter. *n., v. 2.*

shelve[1] (shelv), 1. put on a shelf. 2. lay aside. Let us shelve that argument. 3. furnish with shelves. *v. 7.*

shelve[2] (shelv), slope gradually. *v.*

shelves (shelvz), more than one shelf. *n. pl.*

She ol (shē′ōl), Hebrew name for the abode of the dead. *n.*

shep herd (shep′ərd), 1. man who takes care of sheep. 2. take care of. He will shepherd his flock. 3. guide; direct. The teacher shepherded the children safely out of the burning building. 4. person who cares for and protects. The **Good Shepherd** means Jesus Christ. *n., v. 2.*

shep herd ess (shep′ər dis), woman who takes care of sheep. *n. 12.*

sher bet (shėr′bət), 1. frozen mixture of fruit juice, sugar, and water or milk. 2. a drink of fruit juice, sugar, and water, popular in the Orient. *n. 14.*

sher iff (sher′if), the most important law-enforcing officer of a county. The sheriff pursued the thieves. *n. 6.*

sher ry (sher′i), 1. a strong, light-colored wine of southern Spain. 2. any similar wine. *n., pl. sherries. 14.*

Sher wood (shėr′wůd), a forest in England where Robin Hood and his men lived. *n. 20.*

she's (shēz), 1. she is. 2. she has. *10.*

Shet land (shet′lənd), 1. The **Shetland Islands** are a group of islands northeast of Scotland. 2. A **Shetland pony** is a small, sturdy, rough-coated pony. *adj., n. 14.*

Shetland pony (3 ft. high at the shoulder)

shew (shō), show. *v., n. 7.*

shib bo leth (shib′ə leth), any test word, watchword, or pet phrase of a political party, a class, sect, etc. *n. 20.*

shied (shīd). See **shy.** *pt. and pp. of shy.*

shield (shēld), 1. piece of armor carried on the arm to protect the body in battle. 2. anything used to protect. A windshield on a car keeps off the wind. 3. something shaped like a shield. 4. protect; defend. His mother shielded him from punishment. *n., v. 3.*

Knight holding a shield

shift (shift), 1. change from one place, position, person, etc., to another; to change. He shifted the suitcase from one hand to the other. He always tries to shift the blame to someone else. The wind has shifted to the southeast. 2. a change; substituting in the place of another person or thing. There are two shifts of work in the factory. 3. group of workmen; a group. This man is on the night shift. 4. manage to get along. **Shift for oneself** means get along by one's own efforts. 5. way of getting on; scheme; trick. Lazy Tom used many shifts to avoid doing his work. *v., n. 3.*

shift less (shift′lis), lazy; inefficient. *adj. 15.*

shift y (shif′ti), 1. full of shifts; quick-witted; inventive. 2. tricky; not straightforward. *adj., shiftier, shiftiest.*

shil ling (shil′ing), a British silver coin. In ordinary times it was worth about 24 cents in United States money. *n. 7.*

shil ly-shal ly (shil′i shal′i), 1. vacillating; wavering; hesitating; undecided. 2. in a vacillating or hesitating manner. 3. vacillate; be undecided; hesitate. *adj., adv., v., shilly-shallied, shilly-shallying.*

Shi loh (shī′lō), town in ancient Palestine. *n. 12.*

shim mer (shim′ər), 1. gleam faintly. The satin shimmers. 2. faint gleam or shine. Pearls have a beautiful shimmer. *v., n. 15.*

shim mer y (shim′ər i), shimmering; gleaming softly. *adj.*

shin (shin), 1. the front part of the leg from the knee to the ankle. 2. climb. Tom shinned up the tree. *n., v., shinned, shinning. 9.*

KNEE THIGH SHIN CALF ANKLE

shine (shīn), 1. send out light; be bright with light. The sun shines. John's face shines with soap and water. 2. light; brightness; as, the shine of a lamp. 3. sunshine; fair weather. He goes to school rain or shine. 4. luster; polish. Silk has a shine. 5. do very well; be bright. Mary shines in school. Fred is a shining athlete. 6. make bright or light; polish. *v., shone* or *shined, shining, n. 1.*

shin gle[1] (shing′gəl), 1. a thin piece of wood, etc., used to cover roofs, etc. 2. cover with such pieces. 3. small signboard. *Used in common talk.* 4. cut (the hair) short. She has had her hair shingled. *n., v. 8.*

Shingles on a roof

shin gle[2] (shing′gəl), loose stones or pebbles such as lie on the seashore; coarse gravel. *n.*

shin gles (shing′gəlz), a painful skin disease. The spots which itch often form a band round the body. *n. sing. or pl.*

shin gly (shing′gli), consisting of or covered with small loose stones. *adj.*

shin ing (shīn′ing), that shines; brilliant; distinguished. *adj.*

shin ny (shin′i), 1. a simple kind of hockey. 2. play shinny. *n., v., shinnied, shinnying.*

shin y (shīn′i), bright; shining; as, a shiny new penny, a coat shiny from hard wear. *adj., shinier, shiniest. 12.*

ship (ship), 1. a large, seagoing vessel with masts and sails. 2. any large vessel for use on water or in air; as, a steamship, a battleship, an airship. 3. a sailing vessel with three or more masts. 4. put or take on board a ship. 5. go on board a ship. 6. travel on a ship; sail. 7. send or carry from one place to another by a ship, train, truck, etc. Did he ship it by express or by freight? 8. engage for service on a ship; as, to ship a new crew. 9. take a job on a ship. He shipped as cook. 10. take in (water) over the side. A boat ships water when waves break over it. 11. fix in a ship or boat in its proper place for use; as, to ship a rudder. *n., v., shipped, shipping. 1.*

-ship, suffix meaning:—

1. office or rank of ———; as in lordship, governorship.
2. quality, state, or condition of ———; as in kinship.
3. act, acts, power, or skill of ———; as in horsemanship, dictatorship.
4. relation between ———s; as in fellowship.
5. special meanings; as in authorship, membership.

ship board (ship′bōrd′), ship. **On shipboard** means on a ship. *n. 19.*

ship build ing (ship′bil′ding), 1. the building of ships. 2. the art of building ships. *n. 18.*

ship load (ship′lōd′), a full load for a ship. *n.*

ship mas ter (ship′mas′tər), the master, commander, or captain of a ship. *n.*

ship mate (ship′māt′), fellow sailor on a ship. *n. 20.*

ship ment (ship′mənt), 1. act of shipping goods. 2. goods sent. The shipment of boxes from the factory has not reached us. *n. 5.*

ship own er (ship′ōn′ər), a person who owns a ship or ships. *n. 20.*

ship per (ship′ər), one who ships goods. *n. 12.*

ship ping (ship′ing), 1. the sending of goods by water, rail, etc. 2. ships. 3. the ships of a nation, city, or business. *n.*

ship shape (ship′shāp′), 1. trim; in good order. 2. in a trim, neat manner. *adj., adv. 19.*

ship worm (ship′wėrm′), any of various mollusks that burrow into the timbers of ships, etc. *n.*

ship wreck (ship′rek′), 1. destruction or loss of a ship. Only two people were saved from the shipwreck. 2. wrecked ship. 3. destruction; ruin. The shipwreck of his plans discouraged him. 4. wreck, ruin, or destroy. 5. suffer shipwreck. *n., v. 7.*

ship yard (ship′yärd′), place near the water where ships are built or repaired. *n. 13.*

shire (shīr), one of the counties into which Great Britain is divided, especially one whose name ends in *shire;* as, Yorkshire. *n. 11.*

shirk (shėrk), 1. avoid or get out of doing (work, a duty, etc.). Tom lost his job because he shirked his work. 2. person who shirks or does not do his share. *v., n. 18.*

shirr (shėr), 1. draw up or gather (cloth) on parallel threads. 2. shirred arrangement of cloth, etc. 3. bake (eggs) in a shallow dish with butter, etc. *v., n. 19.*

Shirring

shirt (shėrt), 1. a garment for the upper part of a man's body. 2. an undergarment for the upper part of the body. *n. 2.*

shirt ing (shėr′ting), cloth for shirts. *n. 17.*

shirt waist (shėrt′wāst′), woman's loose waist or blouse, worn with a separate skirt. *n.*

shiv er[1] (shiv′ər), 1. shake with cold, fear, etc. 2. shaking from cold, fear, etc. *v., n. 3.*

shiv er[2] (shiv′ər), 1. break into small pieces. He shivered the mirror with a hammer. 2. small piece; splinter. *v., n.*

shiv er y (shiv′ər i), 1. quivering from cold, fear, etc.; shivering. 2. inclined to shiver from cold. 3. chilly. 4. causing shivers. *adj.*

shoal[1] (shōl), 1. shallow. 2. place where the water is shallow. 3. a sandbank or sand bar which makes the water shallow. The ship was wrecked on the shoals. 4. become shallow. *adj., n., v. 8.*

shoal[2] (shōl), 1. large number; crowd. We saw a shoal of fish in the water. 2. form into a shoal; crowd together. *n., v.*

shoat (shōt), young pig able to feed itself. *n.* Also spelled **shote.**

shock[1] (shok), 1. a sudden, violent shake. Earthquake shocks are often felt in Japan. The two trains collided with a terrible shock. 2. a sudden, violent disturbance. His death was a great shock to his family. 3. disturbance produced by an electric current passing through the body. 4. sudden attack of illness that makes a person senseless or takes away the power to move or speak. 5. give a shock to; cause to feel surprise, horror, or disgust. That child's bad language shocks everyone. *n., v. 2.*

shock[2] (shok), 1. group of cornstalks or bundles of grain set up on end together. 2. make into shocks. *n., v.*

shock[3] (shok), a thick bushy mass. He has a shock of red hair. *n.*

shock ing (shok′ing), 1. causing intense and painful surprise. 2. offensive; disgusting; revolting. *adj.*

shod (shod). See **shoe.** The blacksmith shod the horses. *pt. and pp. of shoe. 9.*

shod dy (shod′i), 1. inferior kind of wool made of woolen waste, old rags, yarn, etc. 2. made of woolen waste. 3. cloth made of woolen waste. 4. anything inferior made to look like what is better. *n., adj., shoddier, shoddiest.*

shoe (shü), 1. an outer covering for a person's foot. 2. something used like a shoe; as, a horseshoe. 3. furnish with shoes. A blacksmith shoes horses. *n., v., shod, shoeing. 1.*

A, lady's shoe; B, child's shoe.

shoe lace (shü′lās′), cord, braid, or leather strip for fastening a shoe. *n.*

shoe mak er (shü′māk′ər), man who makes or mends shoes. *n. 4.*

shoe string (shü′string′), 1. shoelace. 2. very small amount of money. They started in business on a shoestring. *n.*

sho gun (shō′gün), hereditary commander in chief of the Japanese army. The shoguns were the real rulers of Japan for hundreds of years until 1867. *n.*

shone (shōn). See **shine.** The sun shone all last week. It has not shone since. *pt. and pp. of shine. 3.*

shoo (shü), 1. an exclamation used to scare away hens, birds, etc. 2. scare or drive away by calling "Shoo!" *interj., v. 20.*

shook (shu̇k). See **shake.** They shook hands. *pt. of shake. 2.*

shoon (shün), shoes. *n. pl.* [*Old use*] *18.*

shoot (shüt), 1. hit with a bullet, arrow, etc. John shot a rabbit. 2. fire (a gun, etc.). The boys shot at the mark. 3. send swiftly. A bow shoots an arrow. He shot question after question at us. 4. move suddenly and swiftly. A car shot by us. Flames shoot up from a burning house.

Pain shot up his arm from his hurt finger. 5. come forth from the ground; grow; grow rapidly. Buds shoot forth in the spring. The corn is shooting up during the warm weather. 6. new part growing out; young branch. The rosebush is putting out new shoots. 7. take (a picture) with a camera; photograph. 8. project sharply. 9. sloping trough for conveying coal, grain, water, etc., to a lower level. 10. vary with some different color, etc. Her dress was shot with threads of gold. *v., shot, shooting, n. 2.*

shooting star, star or other luminous body seen falling or darting through the sky; meteor.

shop (shop), 1. place where things are sold; a store. 2. visit stores to look at or to buy things. We shopped all morning for new coats. 3. place where things are made or repaired. He works in a carpenter's shop. 4. **Talk shop** means talk about one's own occupation. 5. place where a certain kind of work is done; as, a barber shop. 6. **Set up shop** means start work or business. *n., v., shopped, shopping. 1.*

shop keep er (shop′kēp′ər), person who carries on business in a shop or store. *n. 12.*

shop lift er (shop′lif′tər), person who steals goods from a shop while pretending to be a customer. *n.*

shop lift ing (shop′lif′ting), stealing goods from a shop or store while pretending to be a customer. *n.*

shop man (shop′mən), 1. salesman in a shop. 2. shopkeeper. *n., pl. shopmen. 18.*

shop per (shop′ər), person who visits stores to look at or buy things. *n.*

shop worn (shop′wōrn′), soiled by being displayed or handled in a store. *adj.*

shore[1] (shōr), 1. land at the edge of a sea, lake, etc. **Off shore** means in or on the water, not far from the shore. 2. land near a sea. 3. land. *n. 1.*

shore[2] (shōr), prop; support. *n., v.*

shore less (shōr′lis), 1. having no shore. 2. boundless. *adj. 20.*

shore line (shōr′līn′), line where shore and water meet. *n.*

Frame of a ship supported by shores

shore ward (shōr′wərd), toward the shore. *adv., adj. 16.*

shorn (shōrn), sheared. The sheep was shorn of his wool. *pp. of* **shear.** *8.*

short (shôrt), 1. not long; as, a short time, a short life, a short street. 2. not tall; as, a short man, short grass. 3. not coming up to the right amount, measure, standard, etc. The cashier is short in his accounts. The prisoners were kept on short allowance of food. 4. so brief as to be rude. He was so short with me that I felt hurt. 5. breaking or crumbling easily. Pastry is made short with butter and lard. 6. in a short manner; suddenly. He stopped short. 7. Some special meanings are:

cut short, end suddenly.

fall short, 1. fail to reach. 2. be insufficient.

for short, to make shorter.

in short, briefly.

run short, 1. not have enough. 2. not be enough.

short of, 1. not up to; less than. Nothing short of your best work will satisfy me. 2. not having enough of. 3. on the near side of.

adj., adv., n. 1.

short age (shôr′tij), lack; too small an amount. There is a shortage of grain because of poor crops. *n. 13.*

short cake (shôrt′kāk′), a cake made of rich biscuit dough, covered or filled with berries or other fruit. *n. 19.*

short circuit, side circuit of electricity of relatively low resistance, connecting two points of a larger electric circuit so as to carry most of the current.

short-cir cuit (shôrt′sėr′kit), make a short circuit in. *v.*

short com ing (shôrt′kum′ing), fault; defect. *n. 16.*

short en (shôr′tən), 1. make shorter; cut off; take in. She has had all her dresses shortened. 2. become shorter. The days shorten in November. 3. make rich with butter, lard, etc. She used butter to shorten her cakes. *v. 6.*

short en ing (shôr′tən ing), butter, lard, etc., used to make pastry, cake, etc., crumbly. *n.*

short hand (shôrt′hand′), 1. method of rapid writing which uses symbols in place of letters, sounds, words, etc.; stenography. For example, the symbols in the picture mean "Your letter was received today." 2. writing in such symbols. 3. using shorthand. 4. written in shorthand. *n., adj. 18.*

A sample of shorthand

short-hand ed (shôrt′han′did), not having enough workmen or helpers. *adj.*

short horn (shôrt′hôrn′), a breed of cattle with short horns, raised for beef. *n. 18.*

short-lived (shôrt′līvd′), living only a short time; lasting only a short time. *adj. 15.*
shortly (shôrt′li), 1. soon; in a short time. 2. in few words; briefly. *adv.*
shorts (shôrts), 1. knee breeches. 2. short loose trousers worn by men in sports; trunks. 3. baby's short clothes. 4. mixture of bran and coarse meal. *n. pl.*
short-sighted (shôrt′sīt′id), 1. near-sighted; not able to see far. 2. lacking in foresight; not prudent. *adj. 15.*
shortstop (shôrt′stop′), baseball player between second and third base. *n.*
short wave, radio wave having a sixty-meter wave length or less.
short-winded (shôrt′win′did), getting out of breath too quickly; having difficulty in breathing. *adj.*
shot[1] (shot), 1. act of shooting. 2. tiny balls of lead; bullets; single ball of lead for a gun or cannon. 3. discharge of a gun or cannon. He heard two shots. 4. an attempt to hit by shooting. That was a good shot, and it hit the mark. 5. the distance a weapon can shoot. We were within rifle shot of the fort. 6. person who shoots. Mr. Smith is a good shot. 7. something like a shot. An aimed stroke or throw in a game is sometimes called a shot. 8. a remark aimed at some person or thing. 9. a heavy metal ball. **Put the shot** means throw a heavy ball of metal as far as possible. *n., pl. shots* or for defs. 2 and 9 *shot. 2.*
shot[2] (shot), 1. See **shoot.** Many years ago he shot a rival and was himself shot in revenge. 2. woven so as to show a play of colors; as, silk shot with gold. *pt. and pp. of shoot, adj.*
shote (shōt), young pig able to feed itself. *n.* Also spelled **shoat.**
shotgun (shot′gun′), a gun for firing cartridges filled with very small shot. *n. 14.*
should (shůd), 1. See **shall.** "I said that I should come next week" means that I said, "I shall come next week." 2. ought to. You should try to make fewer mistakes. 3. **Should** is used to express uncertainty. If it should rain, I should not go. 4. **Should** is used in speaking of something which might have happened but did not. I should have gone if you had asked me. *pt. of shall. 1.*
shoulder (shōl′dər), 1. the part of the body to which an arm or foreleg is attached. 2. **Shoulders** often means the two shoulders and the upper part of the back. The man carried a trunk on his shoulders. 3. take on the shoulders; bear (a burden, blame, etc.). 4. push with the shoulders. He shouldered his way through the crowd. 5. something that sticks out like a shoulder. 6. side or edge of a road, especially a part supporting the road itself. 7. Some special meanings are:
shoulder to shoulder, 1. side by side; together. 2. with united effort.
straight from the shoulder, frankly; directly.
turn or **give a cold shoulder to,** shun; avoid; show dislike for.
n., v. 1.
shoulder blade, flat bone of the shoulder.
shoulder strap, 1. strap worn over the shoulder to hold a garment up. 2. ornamental strip fastened on the shoulders of an officer's uniform to show his rank.

Shoulder strap for a captain's uniform

shouldn't (shůd′ənt), should not.
shouldst (shůdst), an old form meaning **should.** "Thou shouldst" means "You should." *v. 10.*
shout (shout), 1. call or cry loudly and vigorously. The drowning boy shouted for help. We shouted, "Fire!" The crowd shouted with laughter. 2. a loud, vigorous call or cry. Shouts of joy rang through the halls. 3. talk or laugh very loudly. *v., n. 1.*
shove (shuv), push. The people shoved to get on the crowded car. Fred gave the boat a shove which sent it far out into the water. **Shove off** sometimes means (1) push away from the shore; row away. (2) leave; start. *Slang. v., n. 5.*
shovel (shuv′əl), 1. tool for lifting and throwing loose matter; as, a snow shovel, a coal shovel. A steam shovel is worked by steam. 2. lift and throw with a shovel. The men shoveled the sand into a cart. 3. make with a shovel. They shoveled a path through the snow. *n., v., shoveled, shoveling. 4.*

Coal shovel

show (shō), 1. let be seen; put in sight. The little girl showed us her dolls. The dog showed his teeth. 2. be in sight. The hole in Jack's stocking shows above his shoe. 3. point out; direct; guide. A boy showed us the way to town. 4. make clear; explain. The teacher showed the children how to do the problem. 5. grant; give; as, to show mercy, to show favor. 6. showing. The club voted by a show of hands. 7. **Show off** means display; as, to show off fine clothes. 8. display. The jewels made a fine show. 9. display for effect. **For show** means to attract attention; to make a good appearance. The Smith's house is furnished for show, not for comfort. 10. appearance. There is some show of truth in Joe's argument. 11. false appearance. The boy made a show of interest. 12. any kind of public exhibition or display. We are going to the flower show and to the automobile show. *v., showed, shown* or *showed, showing, n. 1.*

show case (shō′kās′), glass case to display and protect articles in stores, museums, etc. *n.*

show er (shou′ər), 1. short fall of rain. 2. anything like a fall of rain; as, a shower of hail, a shower of tears, a shower of sparks from an engine. 3. come in a shower. 4. send in a shower; pour down. *n., v. 2.*

show er y (shou′ər i), 1. raining in showers. 2. having many showers. 3. like a shower. *adj. 19.*

show i ly (shō′i li), in a way that attracts attention. *adv.*

show i ness (shō′i nis), display; quality of being showy. *n.*

show man (shō′mən), man who manages a show. *n., pl. showmen. 19.*

show man ship (shō′mən ship), management of shows; skill in managing shows. *n.*

shown (shōn). See **show.** The clerk has shown the lady many hats. *pp. of show.*

show y (shō′i), 1. making a display; striking; conspicuous. A peony is a showy flower. 2. too bright and gay to be in good taste. *adj., showier, showiest. 15.*

shrank (shrangk). See **shrink.** That shirt shrank in the wash. *pt. of shrink. 9.*

shrap nel (shrap′nəl), a shell filled with bullets and powder, arranged to explode in a shower. *n. 17.*

Shrapnel

shred (shred), 1. very small piece torn off or cut off; very narrow strip; scrap. The wind tore the sail to shreds. 2. fragment; particle; bit. There's not a shred of evidence that he took the money. 3. tear or cut into small pieces. *n., v., shredded* or *shred, shredding. 8.*

Shreve port (shrēv′pōrt), a city in northwestern Louisiana. *n.*

shrew (shrü), 1. a bad-tempered, quarrelsome woman. 2. a small animal like a mouse, that has a long snout and eats insects. *n. 8.*

Shrew (about 5 in. long, including the tail)

shrewd (shrüd), sharp; keen; clever. He is a shrewd businessman. *adj. 5.*

shrewd ness (shrüd′nis), sharpness; keenness; cleverness. *n. 15.*

shrew ish (shrü′ish), scolding; bad-tempered. *adj. 19.*

shriek (shrēk), 1. a loud, sharp, shrill sound. We heard the shriek of the engine's whistle. 2. make such a sound. People sometimes shriek because of terror, anger, or pain. *n., v. 3.*

shrift (shrift), 1. shriving. *Old use.* 2. confession to a priest, followed by the imposing of penance and the granting of absolution. *Old use.* 3. **Short shrift** means little time between fixing a punishment and carrying it out. *n.*

shrike (shrīk), a bird with a strong, hooked bill that sometimes feeds on other birds. *n.*

shrill (shril), 1. having a high pitch; high and sharp in sound; piercing. Crickets, locusts, and katydids make shrill noises. 2. make a shrill sound; sound sharply. *adj., v. 4.*

shril ly (shril′li), in shrill tones. *adv.*

shrimp (shrimp), 1. a small shellfish, used for food. 2. a small or insignificant person. *n., pl. shrimps* or *shrimp. 14.*

Shrimp (2 in. long)

shrine (shrīn), 1. sacred place; place where sacred things are kept. A shrine may be the tomb of a saint, an altar in a church, or a box holding a holy object. 2. any place or object sacred because of its history; something sacred because of memories connected with it. America sometimes is called freedom's shrine. Shakespeare's birthplace is visited as a shrine. *n. 4.*

Shrine

shrink (shringk), 1. become smaller; make smaller. Wool shrinks in washing. 2. draw back. The dog shrank from the whip. She shrinks from making new acquaintances. *v., shrank* or *shrunk, shrunk* or *shrunken, shrinking. 5.*

shrink age (shringk′ij), 1. act or process of shrinking. 2. the amount or degree of shrinking; as, a shrinkage of two inches in the length of a skirt. *n. 17.*

shrive (shrīv), 1. hear the confession of, impose penance on, and grant absolution to. 2. **Shrive oneself** means confess to a priest and do penance. *v., shrove* or *shrived, shriven* or *shrived, shriving.* [*Old use*] *18.*

shriv el (shriv′əl), dry up; wither; wrinkle. The hot sunshine shriveled the grass. *v., shriveled, shriveling. 10.*

shriv en (shriv′ən). See **shrive.** The penitent was shriven by the priest. *pp. of shrive.*

Shrop shire (shrop′shir), county in western England. *n. 18.*

shroud[1] (shroud), 1. cloth or garment in which a dead person is wrapped for burial. 2. wrap for burial. 3. something that covers, conceals, or veils. 4. cover; conceal; veil. The earth is shrouded in darkness. *n., v. 5.*

shroud[2] (shroud), a rope from a mast to the side of a ship. Shrouds help support the mast. *n.*

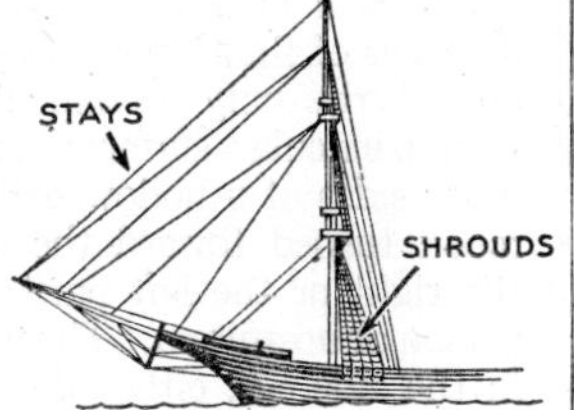

shrove (shrōv). See **shrive.** The priest shrove the penitent. *pt. of shrive.*

shrub (shrub), a bush; a woody plant smaller than a tree, with many separate stems starting from or near the ground. A lilac bush is a shrub. *n. 4.*

shrub ber y (shrub′ər i), 1. shrubs. 2. place planted with shrubs. *n., pl. shrubberies. 12.*

shrub by (shrub′i), 1. like shrubs. 2. covered with shrubs. 3. consisting of shrubs. *adj.*

shrug (shrug), 1. raise (the shoulders) as an expression of dislike, doubt, indifference, impatience, etc. He merely shrugged his shoulders in answer to our request for help. 2. raising the shoulders in this way. *v., shrugged, shrugging, n. 8.*

shrunk (shrungk). See **shrink.** His wool stockings have shrunk so that he can't get them on. *pp. and pt. of shrink. 9.*

shrunk en (shrungk′ən), grown smaller; shriveled. *adj., pp. of* **shrink.**

shuck (shuk), 1. husk; pod. 2. remove the shucks from. *n., v.*

shud der (shud′ər), 1. tremble with horror, fear, cold, etc. She shudders at the sight of a snake. 2. trembling; quivering. *v., n. 6.*

shuf fle (shuf′əl), 1. walk without lifting the feet; scrape or drag the feet. The old man shuffles feebly along. 2. a scraping or dragging movement of the feet. 3. mix; jumble together. He shuffled the pack of cards. 4. a shuffling of cards. 5. the right or turn to shuffle (cards). 6. push about. 7. move this way and that; as, to shuffle into your clothes. 8. movement this way and that. After a hasty shuffle through his papers, the speaker began to talk. 9. put or bring in a tricky way. 10. trick; unfair act; evasion. Through some legal shuffle he secured a new trial. *v., n. 8.*

shuf fle board (shuf′əl bōrd′), a game played by pushing disks along a surface to certain spots. *n.*

shun (shun), keep away from; avoid. She was lazy and shunned work. *v., shunned, shunning. 3.*

shunt (shunt), 1. turn aside; move out of the way. 2. sidetrack; put aside; get rid of. *v. 15.*

shut (shut), 1. close. Shut your eyes. You can shut a door, window, book, knife, etc. 2. keep (from coming in). The curtains shut out the light. Shut the dog out of this room. 3. close tight; close securely. When we shut up our house for the summer, we lock all doors and windows. 4. enclose; confine; keep (from going out). Shut the kitten in the basket. 5. check; turn off. Shut off the radio. 6. be closed; become closed. *v., shut, shutting. 1.*

shut ter (shut′ər), 1. a movable cover for a window. When we shut up our cottage for the winter, we put shutters on all the windows. 2. device that opens and closes in front of the lens of a camera. 3. any movable cover, slide, etc., for closing an opening. 4. person or thing that shuts. *n. 6.*

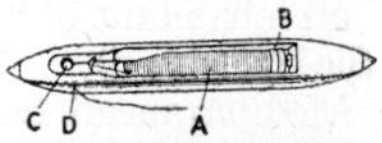

shut tle (shut′əl), 1. an instrument that carries the thread from one side of the web to the

Shuttle for weaving: A, yarn; B, bobbin; C, eye through which the yarn is led; D, yarn.

other in weaving. 2. an instrument on which thread is wound. Shuttles are used in tatting (a kind of lacemaking). 3. something that goes back and forth. 4. move quickly to and fro. *n., v. 11.*

shut tle cock (shut′əl kok′), a cork with feathers stuck in one end, which is hit back and forth by a small racket, or battledore, in the game of battledore and shuttlecock. *n.*

Children playing battledore and shuttlecock

shy[1] (shī), 1. bashful; uncomfortable in company. John is shy and dislikes parties. 2. easily frightened away. A deer is a shy animal. 3. start back or aside suddenly. A horse will often shy at a newspaper blowing along the ground. *adj., shyer, shyest* or *shier, shiest, v., shied, shying. 4.*

shy[2] (shī), throw. The boy shied a stone at the tree. *v., shied, shying, n., pl. shies.*

Shy lock (shī′lok), 1. the relentless and revengeful Jewish moneylender in Shakespeare's play *The Merchant of Venice.* 2. greedy moneylender. *n. 18.*

shy ly (shī′li), in a shy manner. *adv.*

shy ness (shī′nis), quality or state of being shy. *n. 13.*

si (sē), in music, the seventh tone of the scale. Do, re, mi, fa, so, la, ti (si), do are the names of the tones of the scale. *n. 20.*

Si am (sī am′), a country in southeastern Asia. *n. 17.* Also called **Thailand.**

Si a mese (sī′ə mēz′), 1. of or pertaining to Siam, its people, or their language. 2. a native of Siam. 3. the language of Siam. *adj., n., pl. Siamese.*

Si be ri a (sī bēr′i ə), region in northern Asia, extending from the Ural Mountains to the Pacific. It is part of the Soviet Union. *n. 10.*

sib yl (sib′il), woman who foretells future events; prophetess; witch. *n. 11.*

Si cil ian (si sil′yən), 1. of or having to do with Sicily or its people. 2. a native or an inhabitant of Sicily. *adj., n. 7.*

Sic i ly (sis′i li), the largest island in the Mediterranean Sea. It is a part of the kingdom of Italy. *n. 9.*

sick (sik), 1. in poor health; having some disease; ill. 2. vomiting; inclined to vomit; feeling nausea. 3. for a sick person. 4. sick people. The sick need special care. 5. weary; tired. He is sick of school. 6. affected with sorrow or longing. She is sick at heart. *adj., n. 1.*

sick en (sik′ən), 1. become sick. The bird sickened when kept in the cage. 2. make sick. The sight of blood sickened him. *v. 6.*

sick en ing (sik′ən ing), 1. making sick; causing nausea, faintness, disgust, or loathing. 2. becoming sick. *adj.*

sick ish (sik′ish), 1. somewhat sick. 2. somewhat sickening. *adj.*

sick le (sik′əl), tool consisting of a short, curved blade on a short handle, for cutting grass, etc. *n. 6.*

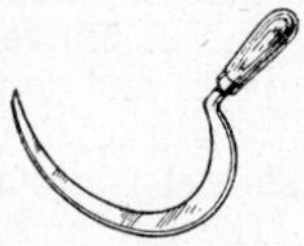

Sickle

sick ly (sik′li), 1. often sick; not strong; not healthy. 2. of or pertaining to sickness. Her skin is a sickly yellow. 3. causing sickness; as, a sickly climate. 4. faint; weak; pale. *adj., sicklier, sickliest. 6.*

sick ness (sik′nis), 1. illness; poor health; disease. 2. nausea; vomiting. *n. 3.*

side (sīd), 1. a surface or line bounding a thing; as, the sides of a square, a side of a box. 2. one of the two surfaces of an object that is not the front, back, top, or bottom. There is a door at the side of the house. 3. either of the two surfaces of paper, cloth, etc. Write only on one side of the paper. 4. a particular surface; as, the outer and inner sides of a hollow ball, the side of the moon turned toward the earth. 5. either the right or the left part of the body of a person or an animal. The man was wounded in the side. 6. either the right or the left part of a thing; either part or region beyond a central line; as, the east side of a city, our side of the street, to turn to one side. 7. the slope of a hill or bank. 8. group of persons who stand up for their beliefs, opinions, ways of doing things, etc., against another group. 9. the position, course, or part of one person or party against another. It is pleasant to be on the winning side. 10. part of a family; a line of descent. The man is English on his mother's side. 11. at one side; on one side; as, a side door, a side aisle. 12. from one side; as, a side view. 13. toward one side; as, a side glance. 14. less important; as, a side issue. 15. take sides; place oneself with a side or group. The sisters always side with each other when the children quarrel. *n., adj., v. 1.*

side board (sīd′bōrd′), piece of dining-room furniture. A sideboard has drawers and shelves for holding silver and linen, and space on top for dishes. *n. 9.*

-sided, suffix meaning:—having a side or sides; as, three-sided.

side long (sīd′lông′), to one side; toward the side. *adj., adv. 11.*

si de re al (sī dēr′i əl), 1. of or pertaining to the stars. 2. measured by the apparent daily motion of the stars; as, sidereal time. *adj.*

side track (sīd′trak′), 1. short railroad track to which a train may be switched from a main track. 2. switch (a train, etc.) to a sidetrack. 3. put aside; turn aside. The teacher refused to be sidetracked by questions on other subjects. *n., v.*

side walk (sīd′wôk′), place to walk at the side of a street. *n. 4.*

side ways (sīd′wāz′), 1. to one side; toward one side. 2. from one side. 3. with one side toward the front. *adv., adj. 13.*

side wise (sīd′wīz′), sideways. *adv., adj. 18.*

sid ing (sīd′ing), a short railroad track to which cars can be switched from a main track. *n.*

si dle (sī′dəl), move sideways. Tom shyly sidled up to the visitor. *v. 12.*

Sid ney (sid′ni), Sir Philip (1554-1586), an English soldier, poet, and writer of romances. *n. 11.*

siege (sēj), 1. the surrounding of a fortified place by an army trying to capture it. **Lay siege to** means (1) besiege. The Greeks laid siege to Troy for ten years. (2) attempt to win or get by long and persistent effort. 2. any long or persistent effort to overcome resistance. *n. 5.*

Sieg fried (sēg′frēd), hero who killed a dragon, won a treasure, and rescued a maiden from an enchanted sleep. *n.*

si er ra (si er′ə), chain of hills or mountains whose peaks suggest the teeth of a saw. *n. 14.*

Sierra Nevada, mountain range in eastern California.

si es ta (si es′tə), a nap or rest taken at noon or in the afternoon. *n.*

sieve (siv), a utensil used to separate large pieces from small, or solids from liquids. See the picture. We shake flour through a sieve and pour soup through a sieve. *n. 6.*

Sieve

sift (sift), 1. separate large pieces from small by shaking in a sieve. Sift the ashes. 2. put through a sieve. Sift sugar on the top of the cake. 3. use a sieve. 4. fall through, or as if through, a sieve. The snow sifted softly down. 5. examine very carefully. The teacher will sift the evidence and decide which boy copied from the other. *v. 4.*

sigh (sī), 1. let out a very long deep breath because one is sad, tired, relieved, etc. We heard Mary sigh. 2. wish very much; long. She sighed for home and friends. 3. make a sound like a sigh. The wind sighed in the treetops. 4. act or sound of sighing. *v., n. 2.*

sight (sīt), 1. power of seeing. Birds have better sight than dogs. 2. act of seeing. **At sight** or **on sight** means as soon as seen. She reads music at sight. 3. range of seeing; view. We live in sight of the school. 4. thing seen. 5. something worth seeing. Niagara Falls is one of the sights of the world. 6. something that looks queer. Jane is a sight in that ugly dress. 7. see. At last Columbus sighted land. 8. device to guide the eye; as, the sights on a rifle. 9. the aim or observation taken by such devices. 10. look at through sights; point to; aim at. 11. way of looking or thinking; regard. Dolls are precious in a little girl's sight. *n., v. 1.*

sight less (sīt′lis), 1. blind. 2. invisible; not in sight. *adj. 17.*

sight ly (sīt′li), 1. pleasing to the sight. 2. affording a fine view. *adj. 20.*

sight see ing (sīt′sē′ing), going around to see objects or places of interest. *n., adj. 17.*

sign (sīn), 1. any mark, thing, or motion used to mean, represent, or point out something. See the sign over the door. The sign reads, "Keep off the grass." The signs for add, subtract, multiply, and divide are +, −, ×, ÷. The robin is a sign of spring. There are no signs of life about the house. The hunters found no signs of deer. The Star in the East was the sign of Christ's coming. She made the sign of the cross. A nod is a sign of agreement. The deaf and dumb talk by signs. He gave the sign of the secret society. A thing or act that stands for something else is a sign of it. 2. put one's name on; write one's name. A man signs a letter, a deed, a lease, a note promising to pay a debt, a check, his will, etc. We sign for telegrams, parcels, etc. A man **signs up** for a job. 3. **Sign off** means stop broadcasting. 4. give a sign to. The teacher signed me to enter. *n., v. 1.*

sig nal (sig′nəl), 1. sign giving notice of something. A red light is a signal of danger. 2. make a signal or signals (to). He signaled the car to stop by raising his hand. 3. make known by a signal or signals. A bell signals the end of a school period. 4. used as a signal or in signaling. 5. remarkable; striking. *n., v., signaled, signaling, adj. 4.*

sig nal ize (sig′nəl īz), make stand out; make notable. We signalized her birthday by giving her a party. *v. 15.*

sig nal ly (sig′nəl i), remarkably. *adv.*

sig na ture (sig′nə chər), 1. person's name written by himself. 2. signs printed at the beginning of a staff to show the pitch, key, and time of a piece of music. *n. 5.*

sign board (sīn′bōrd′), board having a sign, notice, advertisement, inscription, etc., on it. *n.20.*

sig net (sig′nit), a seal. The order was sealed with the king's signet. *n. 8.*

sig nif i cance (sig nif′i kəns), 1. meaning. She did not understand the significance of my nod. 2. importance; consequence. The President wanted to see him on a matter of significance. 3. expressiveness; significant quality; as, the significance of her smile. *n. 7.*

sig nif i cant (sig nif′i kənt), 1. full of meaning; important; of consequence. July 4, 1776, is a significant date for Americans. 2. having a meaning; expressive. Smiles are significant of pleasure. 3. having or expressing a hidden meaning. A significant nod from his friend warned him to stop talking. *adj. 8.*

sig ni fi ca tion (sig′ni fi kā′shən), meaning; sense. *n. 19.*

sig ni fy (sig′ni fī), 1. mean; be a sign of. "Oh!" signifies surprise. 2. make known by signs, words, or actions. He signified his consent with a nod. 3. be important; have importance. What a fool says does not signify. *v., signified, signifying. 5.*

si gnior (sē′nyōr), signor. *n.*

si gnor (sē′nyōr), an Italian word meaning Mr., or gentleman. *n. 13.*

si gno ra (sē nyō′rä), an Italian word meaning Mrs., or lady. *n. 15.*

si gno ri na (sē′nyō rē′nä), an Italian word meaning Miss, or young lady. *n.*

sign post (sīn′pōst′), post having signs, notices, or directions on it; guidepost. *n. 18.*

Sig urd (sig′ėrd), Siegfried. *n.*

Sikh (sēk), member of a religious sect of northern India, famous as fighters. *n. 20.*

si lage (sī′lij), green food for farm animals, preserved in a silo. *n.16.*

si lence (sī′ləns), 1. absence of sound or noise. The teacher asked for silence. 2. keeping still; not talking; not mentioning. Silence gives consent. Mother passed over Tom's foolish remarks in silence. 3. stop the noise of; make silent; to quiet. The nurse silenced the baby's crying. 4. "Silence!" means "Keep still!" or "Be still!" *n., v., interj. 2.*

si lenc er (sī′lən sər), 1. device for silencing a gun. 2. any person or thing that silences. *n.*

si lent (sī′lənt), 1. not speaking; saying little or nothing. He was silent about his early life. Pupils must be silent during the study hour. 2. quiet; still; noiseless; as, a silent house. 3. not spoken; not said out loud; as, a silent prayer. The *e* in *time* is a silent letter. 4. taking no open or active part. A silent partner has no share in managing a business. *adj. 2.*

Si le nus (sī lē′nəs), the leader of the satyrs. He is represented as a short, stout, drunken old man. *n. 19.*

Si le sia (si lē′shə), a region in central Europe formerly divided between Germany, Poland, and Czecho-Slovakia. *n. 17.*

sil hou ette (sil′ü et′), 1. outline portrait cut out of black paper or filled in with some single color. 2. dark image outlined against a lighter background. 3. **In silhouette** means shown in outline, or in black against a white background. 4. show in outline. The mountain was silhouetted against the sky. *n., v. 12.*

Silhouette

sil i ca (sil′i kə), a hard, white or colorless substance, silicon dioxide. Flint, quartz, and sand are forms of silica. *n. 15.*

sil i cate (sil′i kāt), a compound containing silicon with oxygen and an alkali. Mica, soapstone, asbestos, and feldspar are silicates. *n. 15.*

sil i con (sil′i kon), a nonmetallic element found only combined with other substances. Silicon combines with oxygen to form silica. *n. 19.*

silk (silk), 1. a fine soft thread spun by silk worms. 2. cloth made from it. She sewed the silk dress with silk thread. 3. thread or cloth like silk, made artificially. 4. anything like silk; as, artificial silk, corn silk. 5. of silk; like silk. *n., adj. 1.*

silk en (sil′kən), 1. made of silk. The king wore silken robes. 2. like silk; smooth, soft, and glossy. She has silken hair. *adj. 6.*

silk i ness (sil′ki nis), smoothness; softness; luster; silky quality. *n.*

silk worm (silk′wėrm′), a caterpillar that spins silk to form a cocoon. *n. 12.*

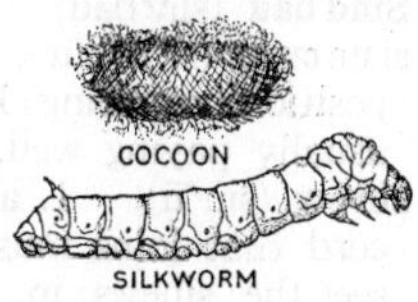

silk y (sil′ki), like silk; smooth, soft, and glossy. A kitten has a silky fur. *adj., silkier, silkiest. 13.*

sill (sil), piece of wood or stone across the bottom of a door, window, or house frame. *n. 7.*

sil li ness (sil′i nis), 1. foolishness; being silly. 2. a silly act, thing, etc. *n.*

sil ly (sil′i), foolish; without sense or reason. *adj., sillier, silliest. 4.*

si lo (sī′lō), an airtight building or pit in which green food for farm animals is preserved. *n., pl. silos. 18.*

Silo

silt (silt), 1. earth, sand, etc., carried by moving water and deposited as sediment. The harbor is being choked up with silt. 2. to fill or choke up with silt. *n., v. 19.*

sil van (sil′vən), sylvan. *adj. 17.*

sil ver (sil′vər), 1. a shining white precious metal. Silver is used for making coins, jewelry, spoons, knives, forks, dishes, etc. 2. coins made from silver; as, a pocketful of silver. 3. utensils or dishes made from silver; as, table silver. 4. made of silver; as, a silver spoon. 5. to cover or coat with silver. 6. the color of silver. 7. having the color of silver; as, a silver slipper. 8. make the color of silver. 9. become the color of silver. The old lady's hair had silvered. 10. having a clear ringing sound. *n., adj., v. 1.*

sil ver smith (sil′vər smith′), person who makes articles of silver. *n. 17.*

sil ver ware (sil′vər wãr′), silver things; utensils or dishes made from silver. Her silverware consisted of knives, forks, spoons, a water pitcher, and candlesticks. *n. 10.*

sil ver y (sil′vər i), like silver; like that of silver. Moonbeams are silvery. The bell has a silvery sound. *adj. 6.*

sim i an (sim′i ən), 1. apelike; monkeylike. 2. an ape; a monkey. *adj., n.*

sim i lar (sim′i lər), 1. alike; like; much the same. A river and a brook are similar. A gas stove is similar to an oil stove. 2. having the same shape. *adj. 3.*

sim i lar i ty (sim′i lar′i ti), likeness; resemblance. *n., pl. similarities. 12.*

sim i le (sim′i li), a statement that one thing is like another. *Examples:* a face like marble, as brave as a lion. *n. 8.*

si mil i tude (si mil′i tūd or si mil′i tüd), 1. likeness; resemblance. 2. comparison. She could think of no similitude to describe the sunset. 3. copy; image. *n. 10.*

sim mer (sim′ər), 1. make a murmuring sound while boiling gently. The kettle simmered on the stove. 2. boil gently; keep at or just below the boiling point. 3. process of cooking at or just below the boiling point. Do not let the soup cook faster than a simmer. 4. be on the point of breaking out; as, simmering anger, simmering rebellion. *v., n. 11.*

Si mon (sī′mən). **Simon Peter** was one of the twelve disciples of Jesus. *n. 5.*

sim o ny (sim′ə ni), act of buying and selling sacred things, especially positions or promotion in the church. *n. 16.*

si moom (si müm′), a hot, suffocating, sand-laden wind of the deserts of Arabia, Syria, and northern Africa. *n.*

si moon (si mün′), simoom. *n.*

sim per (sim′pər), 1. smile in a silly, affected way. 2. a silly, affected smile. *v., n. 12.*

sim ple (sim′pəl), 1. easy to do or understand. This book is in simple language. 2. not divided into parts; single; not compound. An oak leaf is a simple leaf. "John called his dog" is a simple sentence. 3. bare; mere; with nothing added. My answer is the simple truth. 4. plain; without ornament; not rich or showy. He eats simple food and wears simple clothing. 5. natural; not affected; not showing off. She has a pleasant, simple manner. 6. common; ordinary. His parents were simple people. 7. dull; weak in mind. *adj. 1.*

sim ple-heart ed (sim′pəl här′tid), 1. having or showing a simple unaffected nature. 2. sincere. *adj.*

sim ple-mind ed (sim′pəl mīn′did), 1. artless; inexperienced. 2. ignorant; foolish; stupid. 3. feeble-minded. *adj.*

sim ple ton (sim′pəl tən), silly person; fool. *n. 15.*

sim plic i ty (sim plis′i ti), 1. being simple. 2. clearness; freedom from difficulty. The simplicity of the book makes it suitable for children. 3. plainness. A room in a hospital should be furnished with simplicity. 4. absence of show or pretense; sincerity. 5. lack of shrewdness; dullness. His simplicity made him easily fooled. *n., pl. simplicities. 4.*

sim pli fi ca tion (sim′pli fi kā′shən), 1. making simpler. 2. being made simpler. 3. change to a simpler form. *n.*

sim pli fy (sim′pli fī), make simple or more simple; make plainer or easier. *v., simplified, simplifying. 9.*

sim ply (sim′pli), 1. in a simple manner. 2. plainly; without much ornament; without pretense or affectation; as, simply dressed. 3. merely; only. The baby did not simply cry; he yelled. 4. foolishly. He acted as simply as an idiot. 5. absolutely; as, simply perfect. *adv.*

sim u late (sim′ū lāt), 1. pretend; feign. Ann simulated interest to please her friend. 2. act like; look like; imitate. Certain insects simulate flowers or leaves. *v. 16.*

si mul ta ne ous (sī′məl tā′ni əs), existing, done, or happening at the same time. All the people in the audience burst into simultaneous applause. *adj. 9.*

si mul ta ne ous ly (sī′məl tā′ni əs li), at once; at the same time; together. *adv.*

sin (sin), 1. breaking the law of God. 2. break the law of God. 3. wrongdoing of any kind; immoral act. Lying, stealing, dishonesty, and cruelty are sins. 4. do wrong. *n., v., sinned, sinning. 2.*

Si nai (sī′nī), mountain where God gave the Ten Commandments to Moses. *n. 11.*

Sin bad (sin′bad), sailor in *The Arabian Nights* who had seven extraordinary voyages. *n. 20.*

since (sins), 1. from then till now. John caught cold Saturday and has been in bed ever since. 2. at some time between then and now. Mr. Cole at first refused the position, but since has accepted it. 3. ago; before now. Old Rover died long since. 4. from (a past time) till now. We have been up since five. 5. after. Charles has worked hard since he left school. 6. after the time that; from the time when. He has been home only once since he went to New York. 7. because. Since you feel tired, you should rest. *adv., prep., conj. 1.*

sin cere (sin sēr′), free from pretense or deceit; genuine; real; honest. *adj. 3.*

sin cer i ty (sin ser′i ti), freedom from pretense or deceit; honesty. No one doubts the sincerity of Abraham Lincoln. *n., pl. sincerities. 6.*

Sind bad (sin′bad), Sinbad. *n.*

si ne cure (sī′ni kūr), extremely easy job; position requiring little or no work and usually paying well. *n. 16.*

sin ew (sin′ū), 1. a tough, strong band or cord that joins muscle to bone. You can see the sinews in a cooked chicken leg. 2. strength; energy. 3. means of strength; source of power. Men and money are the sinews of war. *n. 5.*

sin ew y (sin′ū i), 1. having strong sinews; strong. A blacksmith has sinewy arms. 2. vigorous; forcible. *adj. 9.*

sin ful (sin′fəl), full of sin; wicked; wrong. The sinful man repented. *adj. 6.*

sing (sing), 1. make music with the voice. People sing in church. 2. make pleasant, musical sounds. Birds sing. 3. bring, send, or put by singing. Sing the baby to sleep. 4. tell in poetry. Homer sang of Troy. 5. make a ringing, whistling, humming, or buzzing sound. The teakettle sang. *v., sang or sung, sung, singing. 1.*

sing., singular.

Sin ga pore (sing′gə pōr′), important seaport city on an island off southeastern Asia. Great Britain's chief naval base in eastern Asia is there. *n. 20.*

singe (sinj), 1. burn a little. The cook singes a chicken to remove the pinfeathers. 2. slight burn. 3. burn the ends or edges of. The barber singed my hair after he cut it. *v., singed, singeing, n. 12.*

sing er (sing′ər), 1. person who sings. Caruso was a famous singer. 2. bird that sings. Our canary is a fine singer. *n. 4.*

sing ing (sing′ing), 1. sound made by one that sings. 2. ringing in the ears. 3. that sings. *n., adj.*

sin gle (sing′gəl), 1. only one; one and no more. The spider hung by a single thread. Each child spoke a single line of the poem. 2. for only one; individual. The sisters share one room with two single beds in it. 3. not married. They rent rooms to single men. 4. having only one on each side. The knights engaged in single combat. 5. having only one set of petals. Most cultivated roses have double flowers with many petals; wild roses have single flowers with five petals. 6. sincere; honest; genuine. She showed single devotion to her religion. 7. pick from others. The teacher singled Harry out. 8. something single. *adj., v., n. 1.*

single file, a line of persons or things arranged one behind another.

sin gle-hand ed (sing′gəl han′did), without help from others; working alone. *adj.*

sin gle-heart ed (sing′gəl här′tid), 1. sincere; free from deceit. 2. having only one purpose. *adj.*

sin gle-mind ed (sing′gəl mīn′did), 1. having only one purpose in mind. 2. sincere; straightforward. *adj.*

sin gle ness (sing′gəl nis), 1. oneness; state or quality of being single. 2. the unmarried state. 3. sincerity; honesty; freedom from deceit. *n. 13.*

sin gle tree (sing′gəl trē′), the swinging bar of a carriage or wagon, to which the traces are fastened. *n. 19.*

sin gly (sing′gli), 1. by itself; separately. Let us consider each point singly. 2. one by one; one at a time. Misfortunes never come singly. 3. by one's own efforts; without help. *adv.*

sing song (sing′sông′), 1. monotonous up-and-down rhythm. 2. a monotonous tone or sound in speaking. 3. monotonous in rhythm; as, a singsong recitation of the multiplication table. 4. recite or speak in a singsong way. *n., adj., v.*

sin gu lar (sing′gū lər), 1. extraordinary; unusual. *Treasure Island* is a story of singular interest to boys. 2. strange; queer; peculiar. 3. being the only one of its kind. 4. one in number. *Boy* is singular; *boys* is plural. 5. the singular number in grammar. *adj., n. 5.*

sin gu lar i ty (sing′gū lar′i ti), 1. peculiarity; oddness; strangeness; unusualness. The singularity of the dwarf's appearance attracted much attention in the village. 2. something singular; a peculiarity; an oddity. One of the singularities of this strange beast is that its horn grows out of its nose. *n., pl. singularities. 15.*

sin gu lar ly (sing′gū lər li), unusually; extraordinarily; peculiarly. *adv.*

sin is ter (sin′is tər), 1. threatening; showing ill will; as, a sinister rumor, a sinister look. 2. bad; evil. *adj. 9.*

sink (singk), 1. go down; fall slowly; go lower and lower; go under. She sank to the floor in a faint. The sun is sinking in the west. The swimmer is sinking. 2. make go down; make fall; make go under. The enemy has sunk our ships. 3. become lower or weaker. The wind has sunk down. 4. make lower. Sink your voice to a whisper. 5. go deeply. Let the lessons sink into your mind. 6. make go deep; dig. The men are sinking a well. 7. a shallow basin or tub with a drainpipe. The dishpan is in the kitchen sink. 8. place where dirty water or any filth collects. *v., sank or sunk, sunk, sinking, n. 2.*

sink er (singk′ər), 1. one that sinks. 2. a lead weight for sinking a fishing line or net. *n. 18.*

sin less (sin′lis), without sin. *adj. 15.*

sin ner (sin′ər), person who sins or does wrong. The sinner who repented was forgiven. *n. 5.*

sin u os i ty (sin′ū os′i ti), 1. curve; bend; turn. 2. sinuous form or character; winding. A snake has sinuosity. *n., pl. sinuosities.*

sin u ous (sin′ū əs), 1. having many curves or turns; winding. The motion of a snake is sinuous. 2. indirect; morally crooked. *adj. 11.*

si nus (sī′nəs), 1. cavity in a bone. 2. a long narrow abscess with a small opening. 3. curve; bend. *n. 15.*

Si on (sī′ən), 1. hill on which the old city of Jerusalem was built. 2. heaven. 3. the church of God. *n. 11.* Also spelled **Zion.**

Sioux (sü), 1. member of a tribe of American Indians. 2. of this tribe. *n., pl. Sioux, adj. 14.*

Sioux City, city in western Iowa, on the Missouri River.

sip (sip), 1. drink little by little. She sipped her tea. 2. a very small drink. *v., sipped, sipping, n. 5.*

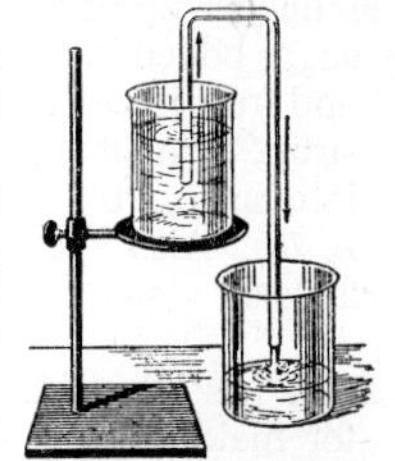

Siphon. The arrows show the direction of the liquid.

si phon (sī′fən), 1. bent tube through which liquid can be drawn over the edge of one container into another at a lower level by air pressure. 2. draw off or pass through a siphon. The farmer siphoned water from the cellar into the ditch. 3. bottle for soda water with a tube through which the liquid is forced out by the pressure of the gas in the bottle. *n., v. 11.*

sir (sėr), 1. a title of respect or honor. A boy calls an older man "Sir." We begin business letters with "Dear Sir." 2. the title of a knight or baronet; as, Sir Walter Scott. 3. Mr. or Master. You, sir, do not belong here. *n. 1.*

sire (sīr), 1. father; male ancestor. "Fight for the green graves of your sires!" 2. male parent. Lightning was the sire of the race horse Danger. 3. be the father of. Lightning sired Danger. 4. a title of respect used formerly to a great noble, and now to a king. "I'm killed, Sire!" said the messenger to Napoleon. *n., v. 3.*

si ren (sī′rən), 1. a nymph who lured sailors to destruction upon the rocks by her sweet singing. 2. woman who lures, tempts, or entices. 3. of a siren; tempting; charming. 4. a kind of whistle that makes a loud piercing sound. We heard the sirens of the fire engines. *n., adj. 8.*

Sir i us (sir′i əs), the brightest star in the sky. *n. 20.*

sir loin (sėr′loin), the cut of beef from the part of the loin in front of the rump; as, a sirloin steak. *n., adj. 11.*

RIBS LOIN RUMP

The shaded part is the sirloin.

si roc co (si rok′ō), 1. hot, dry, dustladen wind blowing from northern Africa across the Mediterranean Sea and southern Europe. 2. any hot, unpleasant wind. *n., pl. siroccos. 16.*

sir rah (sir′ə), fellow. "Silence, sirrah!" said the prince to the stable boy. *n. [Old use] 15.*

sir up (sir′əp or sėr′əp), a sweet thick liquid; sugar boiled in water; a liquid made of sugar and fruit juices. We have sugar sirup, maple sirup, corn sirup, etc. Vanilla sirup, chocolate sirup, etc., are used at soda fountains. *n. 10.* Also spelled **syrup.**

sis (sis), sister. *n. [Used in common talk] 14.*

sis al (sis′əl), 1. strong, white fiber, used for making rope, twine, etc. 2. plant that it comes from. *n.*

sis sy (sis′i), 1. sister. 2. a boy or man who behaves too much like a girl. *n., pl. sissies. [Used in common talk]*

sis ter (sis′tər), 1. A girl or woman is sister to the other children of her parents. 2. close friend. 3. members of the same church are often called sisters. 4. nun; as, Sisters of Charity. *n. 1.*

sis ter hood (sis′tər hůd), 1. the bond between sisters; the feeling of sister for sister. 2. persons joined as sisters; an association of women with some common aim or characteristic. Nuns form a sisterhood. *n. 13.*

sis ter-in-law (sis′tər in lô′), 1. the sister of one's husband or wife. 2. the wife of one's brother. *n., pl. sisters-in-law. 18.*

sis ter ly (sis′tər li), suitable for a sister; like a sister; very kindly. *adj. 16.*

Sis y phus (sis′i fəs), a king condemned forever to roll a heavy stone up a steep hill in Hades, only to have it always roll down again. *n. 20.*

sit (sit), 1. I sit in a chair. My cat sits on the rug. 2. seat; cause to sit. The woman sat the little boy down hard. 3. sit on. He sat his horse well. 4. "Still sits the schoolhouse by the road." The clock has sat on that shelf for years. 5. have a seat in an assembly; be a member of a council; as, to sit in Congress. 6. hold a session. The court sits next month. 7. place oneself in a position for having one's picture made; pose; as, to sit for a portrait. 8. press or weigh. Care sat heavy on his brow. 9. perch. The birds were sitting on the fence rail. 10. cover eggs so that they will hatch; brood. 11. fit. The coat sits well. *v., sat, sitting. 1.*

site (sīt), position or place (of anything). This house has one of the best sites in town. A new school is to be built on the site of the old town hall. *n. 4.*

sit ting (sit′ing), 1. a meeting or session of a legislature, court, etc. 2. a time of remaining seated. He read five chapters at one sitting. 3. the number of eggs on which a bird sits. *n.*

sitting room, a room to sit in, as distinguished from a bedroom, kitchen, etc.; a parlor.

sit u at ed (sich′ü āt′id), placed; located. The school is so situated that it can be easily reached from all parts of town. The city is situated by a river. *adj. 3.*

sit u a tion (sich′ü ā′shən), 1. position; location. Our house has a beautiful situation on a hill. 2. circumstances; case; condition. It is a very disagreeable situation to be alone and without money in a strange city. 3. place to work; job. She is trying to find a situation. *n. 4.*

six (siks). Six is one more than five. Six means 6. *n., adj. 1.*

six fold (siks′fōld′), 1. six times as much or as many. 2. having six parts. *adj., adv.*

six pence (siks′pəns), 1. six pence; six British pennies. Sixpence equals about 12 cents in American money. 2. a silver coin worth six pence. *n. 8.*

six teen (siks′tēn′), six more than ten; 16. *n., adj. 3.*

six teenth (siks′tēnth′), 1. next after the 15th. 2. one of 16 equal parts. An ounce is one sixteenth of a pound. *adj., n. 8.*

sixth (siksth), 1. next after the 5th. 2. one of 6 equal parts. *adj., n. 2.*

six ti eth (siks′ti ith), 1. next after the 59th. 2. one of 60 equal parts. *adj., n. 18.*

six ty (siks′ti), six times ten; 60. *n., pl. sixties, adj. 3.*

siz a ble (sīz′ə bəl), fairly large. *adj. 17.*

size[1] (sīz), 1. amount of space a thing takes up. The two boys are of the same size. The library contains books of all sizes, big and little. We need a house of larger size. 2. one of a series of measures. The size of card I want is 3 by 5 inches. His collar size is fourteen. 3. arrange according to size. Will you size these nails? 4. **Size up** means form an opinion of. *Used in common talk. n., v. 1.*

size[2] (sīz), 1. sticky substance used to glaze paper, cover plastered walls, stiffen cloth, etc. 2. coat or treat with size. *n., v.*

size a ble (sīz′ə bəl), fairly large. *adj.*

Ice skate

siz zle (siz′əl), 1. make a hissing sound, as when fat is frying or burning. 2. such a sound. *v., n.*

skald (skôld), a Scandinavian poet and singer of long ago. *n.*

Roller skate

skate[1] (skāt), 1. a frame with a blade that can be fastened to a shoe so that a person can glide over ice. 2. a similar frame with small wheels for use on any smooth, hard surface. 3. glide or move along on skates. *n., v. 3.*

skate[2] (skāt), a kind of broad, flat fish. *n.*

Barn-door skate (about 4 ft. long)

skat er (skāt′ər), person who skates. *n. 15.*

skein (skān), a small bundle of yarn or thread. *n. 10.*

skel e tal (skel′i təl), of a skeleton; attached to a skeleton. *adj. 18.*

skel e ton (skel′i tən), 1. the bones of a body, fitted together in their natural places. See the picture. 2. frame; as, the steel skeleton of a building. *n. 7.*

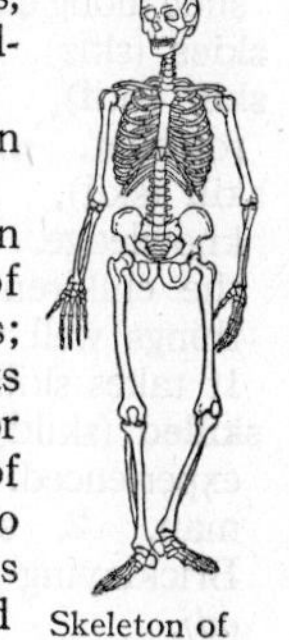

Skeleton of a man

skeleton key, key made to open many locks.

skep tic (skep′tik), 1. person who questions the truth of theories or apparent facts; doubter. 2. person who doubts or questions the possibility or certainty of our knowledge of anything. 3. person who doubts the truth of religious doctrines. *n.* Also spelled **sceptic.**

skep ti cal (skep′ti kəl), inclined to doubt; questioning the truth of theories and apparent facts; not believing easily. *adj. 11.* Also spelled **sceptical.**

skep ti cism (skep′ti sizm), skeptical attitude, doubt; unbelief. *n.* Also spelled **scepticism.**

sketch (skech), 1. a rough drawing or design; an outline; a plan. 2. a short description, story, or play. 3. make a sketch of; draw roughly; outline. *n., v. 5.*

sketch y (skech′i), 1. like a sketch; having or giving only outlines or main features. 2. incomplete; done very roughly; as, a sketchy meal. *adj., sketchier, sketchiest.*

skew (skū), 1. slanting; twisted to one side. 2. slant; twist. *adj., n., v.*

skew er (skū′ər), 1. a long pin of wood or metal stuck through meat to hold it together while it is cooking. 2. fasten with skewers. *n., v. 18.*

ski (skē), 1. one of a pair of long, slender pieces of hard wood fastened to the shoes to enable a person to walk or glide over snow. 2. glide over the snow on skis. *n., pl. skis* or *ski, v., skied, skiing. 17.*

Boys on skis

skid (skid), 1. slip or slide sideways while moving. Automobiles sometimes skid on a slippery road. 2. piece of wood or metal to prevent a wheel from going round. 3. hold from turning by means of a skid. 4. slide along without going round, as a wheel does when held by a skid. 5. a timber or frame on which something rests, or on which something heavy may slide. 6. to slide along skids. *v., skidded, skidding, n. 16.*

skies (skīz). See **sky.** *n. pl. 14.*

skiff (skif), 1. small light boat. 2. light rowboat. *n. 11.*

skill (skil), 1. ability gained by practice or knowledge. The trained teacher managed the children with skill. 2. ability to do things well with one's body or with tools. It takes skill to tune a piano. *n. 3.*

skilled (skild), 1. having skill; trained; experienced. A carpenter is a skilled workman. 2. showing skill; requiring skill. Bricklaying is skilled labor. *adj.*

skil let (skil′it), 1. a shallow pan with a handle, used for frying. 2. long-handled saucepan. *n. 14.*

Skillet for frying

skill ful or **skil ful** (skil′fəl), 1. having skill; expert. He is a very skillful carpenter. 2. showing skill. That is a skillful piece of bricklaying. *adj. 4.*

skill ful ly or **skil ful ly** (skil′fəl i), with skill. *adv.*

skim (skim), 1. remove from the top. The cook skims the cream from the milk and the fat from the soup. 2. take something from the top of. She skims the milk to get cream. 3. move lightly over. The skaters were skimming over the ice. 4. glide along. The swallows went skimming by. 5. read hastily or carelessly; read with omissions. I skimmed the book. 6. act of skimming. *v., skimmed, skimming, n. 4.*

skim mer (skim′ər), 1. one that skims. 2. a long-handled shallow ladle, full of holes, used in skimming liquids. 3. a kind of sea bird that skims along the surface of water to get food. *n. 19.*

Skimmer (def. 2)

skim milk, milk from which the cream has been removed.

skimp (skimp), 1. supply in too small an amount; as, to skimp the butter in making a cake. 2. be very saving or economical. She had to skimp to send her son to college. 3. do imperfectly. *v.*

skimp y (skimp′i), 1. scanty; not enough. 2. too economical; too saving. *adj., skimpier, skimpiest.*

skin (skin), 1. the covering of the body in persons, animals, and plants. Cows have thick skins. He slipped on the banana skin. 2. hide; pelt. 3. take the skin off. Jack skinned his knees when he fell. The hunter skinned the deer. 4. container made of skin for holding liquids. *n., v., skinned, skinning. 1.*

skin flint (skin′flint′), a mean, stingy person. *n.*

skin ny (skin′i), 1. very thin; very lean. 2. like skin. *adj., skinnier, skinniest. 13.*

skip (skip), 1. leap lightly; spring; jump. Lambs skip in the fields. 2. a light spring, jump, or leap. The child gave a skip of joy. 3. leap lightly over. Girls skip rope. 4. send bounding along a surface. Boys like to skip stones on the lake. 5. pass over; fail to notice. She skips the hard words when she reads. Answer the questions in order without skipping. 6. change quickly from one task, pleasure, subject, etc., to another. *v., skipped, skipping, n. 3.*

skip per (skip′ər), 1. the captain of a ship, especially of a small trading or fishing boat. 2. any captain or leader. *n. 12.*

skir mish (skėr′mish), 1. slight fight between small groups of soldiers. 2. any slight conflict. 3. take part in a skirmish. *n., v. 7.*

skirt (skėrt), 1. the part of a dress that hangs from the waist. 2. woman's or girl's garment that hangs from the waist. 3. border; edge. 4. outer part of a place, group of people, etc. 5. pass along the border or edge of. The boys skirted the forest instead of going through it. *n., v. 2.*

skit (skit), short sketch that contains humor or satire. When we graduated, the school paper had skits about each one of us. *n.*

skit tish (skit′ish), 1. easily frightened; apt to start, jump, or run; as, a skittish horse. 2. fickle; changeable. 3. coy. *adj. 19.*

skit tles (skit′əlz), game in which the players try to knock down nine wooden pins by rolling wooden disks at them. *n.*

skulk (skulk), 1. sneak; lurk; hide from fear; hide for a bad purpose. 2. move in a stealthy, sneaking way. The wolf was skulking in the woods near the sheep. *v. 9.*

skull (skul), 1. the bones of the head. 2. the bones around the brain. *n. 5.*

Skunk (length about 2 ft., including the tail)

skull cap (skul′kap′), close-fitting cap without a brim. *n.*

skunk (skungk), 1. a bushy-tailed animal of North America about the size of a cat, black with white stripes along the back. Skunks give off a very strong smell when frightened or attacked. 2. fur of this animal, used on coats, etc. 3. a mean, contemptible person. *Used in common talk. n. 14.*

sky (skī), 1. the covering over the world; the region of the clouds or the upper air; the heavens; as, a blue sky, a cloudy sky. 2. heaven; place where God and His angels live. *n., pl. skies. 1.*

sky blue, clear soft blue.

sky ey (skī′i), 1. of or from the sky. 2. very high. 3. sky-blue. *adj. 17.*

sky lark (skī′lärk′), 1. the common European lark, a small bird that sings very sweetly as it flies toward the sky. 2. play pranks; frolic. *n., v. 19.*

English skylark (about 7 in. long)

sky light (skī′līt′), window in a roof or ceiling. *n.*

sky line (skī′līn′), 1. the line at which earth and sky seem to meet; the horizon. 2. outline of mountains, trees, buildings, etc., as seen against the sky. The tall buildings and towers of New York make a remarkable skyline. *n. 19.*

sky rock et (skī′rok′it), 1. rocket; a firework that goes up high in the air and bursts into a shower of stars, sparks, etc. 2. act like a skyrocket; rise suddenly, make a brilliant show, and disappear. 3. rise much and quickly. *n., v.*

sky scrap er (skī′skrāp′ər), a very tall building. New York is famous for its skyscrapers. *n. 11.*

sky ward (skī′wərd), toward the sky. *adj., adv.*

sky wards (skī′wərdz), skyward. *adv.*

slab (slab), 1. a broad, flat, thick piece (of stone, wood, meat, etc.). Some sidewalks are made of slabs of stone. He ate a slab of cheese as big as my hand. 2. rough outside piece cut from a log. *n. 6.*

slack (slak), 1. loose. The rope hung slack. 2. part that hangs loose. He pulled in the slack of the rope. 3. careless. She is a slack housekeeper. 4. slow. The horse was moving at a slack pace. **Slack water** is the time when the least tide is felt. 5. not active; not brisk; dull. Business is slack at this season. 6. make slack; let up on. 7. be or become slack; let up; slacken. 8. slake (lime). 9. in a slack manner. *adj., n., v., adv. 6.*

slack en (slak′ən), 1. make slower. Don't slacken your efforts till the work is done. 2. become slower. Work slackens on a hot day. 3. make looser. Slacken the rope. 4. become loose. The rope slackened as the wave sent the boat toward the pier. *v. 7.*

slack er (slak′ər), person who shirks work or evades his duty. *n. 19.*

slack ness (slak′nis), sluggishness; carelessness; negligence; looseness; slack quality or state. *n. 17.*

slacks (slaks), loose trousers. *n. pl.*

slag (slag), 1. the rough hard waste left after metal is taken from ore by melting it. 2. form slag. 3. light, spongy lava. *n., v., slagged, slagging. 12.*

slain (slān). See **slay.** The sheep were slain by the wolves. *pp. of slay. 3.*

slake (slāk), 1. satisfy (thirst, revenge, wrath, etc.). 2. put out (a fire). 3. change (lime) by leaving it in the air or putting water on it. Plaster contains slaked lime and sand. *v. 10.*

slam (slam), 1. shut with force and noise; bang. He slammed the window down. The door slammed. 2. throw hard with force. 3. violent and noisy closing; bang. John threw his books down with a slam. 4. taking 12 or 13 tricks in the game of bridge. *v., slammed, slamming, n. 7.*

slan der (slan′dər), 1. false statement meant to do harm. 2. talk falsely about. 3. speak or spread slander. 4. the spreading of false reports. *n., v. 6.*

slan der ous (slan′dər əs), 1. containing a slander. 2. speaking or spreading slanders. *adj. 11.*

slang (slang), 1. words, phrases, etc., not accepted as good English. Slang is mostly made up of new words or meanings that are popular for only a short time. *Cop* and *highbrow* are slang. 2. special talk of a particular class of people. *Crib* often means *cheat* in students' slang. *n. 10.*

slang y (slang′i), 1. containing slang; full of slang. 2. using much slang. *adj.*

slant (slant), 1. slope. Most handwriting slants to the right. Has your roof a sharp slant? 2. sloping. *v., n., adj. 4.*

slant wise (slant′wīz′), 1. in a slanting manner; obliquely. 2. slanting; oblique. *adv., adj.*

slap (slap), 1. a blow with the open hand or with something flat. 2. strike with the open hand or with something flat. He slapped at the fly with a folded newspaper. 3. put with force. She slapped the book down on the table. *n., v., slapped, slapping. 6.*

slash (slash), 1. cut with a sweeping stroke of a sword, knife, whip, etc.; gash; lash. He slashed the bark off the tree with his sword. 2. make a slashing stroke. 3. a sweeping, slashing stroke. 4. a cut or wound made by such a stroke. 5. make slits in (a garment) to let a different material or color show through. 6. criticize sharply, severely, or unkindly. 7. cut down severely; reduce a great deal. His salary was slashed when business became bad. *v., n. 8.*

slat (slat), a long, thin, narrow piece of wood or metal. *n. 17.*

slate (slāt), 1. a bluish-gray rock that splits easily into thin smooth layers. Slate is used to cover roofs and for blackboards. 2. thin piece of this rock. Children used to write on slates, but now they use paper. The roof was covered with slates. 3. cover with slate. 4. dark, bluish gray. 5. list of candidates, officers, etc., to be considered for appointment, nomination, etc. 6. put on such a list. He is slated for the office of club president. *n., v., adj. 5.*

slat tern (slat′ərn), woman who is dirty, careless, or untidy in her dress, her ways, her housekeeping, etc. *n.*

slat tern ly (slat′ərn li), untidy; slovenly. *adj.*

slat y (slāt′i), 1. of slate; like slate. 2. slate-colored. *adj.*

slaugh ter (slô′tər), 1. killing; butchering. The battle resulted in a frightful slaughter. 2. kill; butcher. Millions of cattle are slaughtered in Chicago every year. *n., v. 4.*

slaughter house, place where animals are killed for food. *17.*

slaugh ter ous (slô′tər əs), murderous; destructive. *adj.*

Slav (släv), 1. one of a race of peoples including the Russians, Poles, Czechs, Bulgarians, Slovaks, and Yugoslavs, widely spread over eastern Europe. 2. of the Slavs. *n., adj. 8.*

slave (slāv), 1. person who is the property of another. Slaves could be bought and sold like horses. 2. person who works like a slave. 3. work like a slave. 4. of slaves; done by slaves; as, slave labor. 5. person who is controlled or ruled by some desire, habit, or influence. He is a slave of drink. *n., v., adj. 2.*

slave hold er (slāv′hōl′dər), owner of slaves. *n. 19.*

slav er[1] (slāv′ər), 1. dealer in slaves. 2. ship used in the slave trade. *n. 19.*

slav er[2] (slav′ər), 1. let saliva run from the mouth. 2. wet with saliva. 3. saliva running from the mouth. *v., n.*

slav er y (slāv′ər i), 1. condition of being a slave. Many African Negroes were captured and sold into slavery. 2. the custom of keeping slaves. Where slavery is permitted, certain men own others. 3. condition like that of a slave. 4. hard work like that of a slave. *n. 5.*

slave trade, the business of getting and selling slaves.

Slav ic (släv′ik), 1. of or pertaining to the Slavs or their languages. 2. the language or group of languages spoken by Slavs. *adj., n. 19.*

slav ish (slāv′ish), 1. of a slave or slaves. 2. like a slave; mean; base; weakly submitting. 3. like that of slaves; fit for slaves. 4. lacking originality and independence. *adj. 10.*

slaw (slô), finely sliced or chopped cabbage, raw or cooked, served with dressing. *n.*

slay (slā), kill with violence. A hunter slays wild animals. *v., slew, slain, slaying. 4.*

slay er (slā′ər), killer. *n. 11.*

slea zy (slē′zi), flimsy and poor (said of cloth). *adj.*

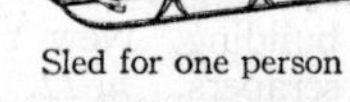

Sled for one person

sled (sled), 1. framework of boards mounted on runners for use on snow or ice. 2. ride on a sled. 3. carry on a sled. *n., v., sledded, sledding. 5.*

sledge[1] (slej), 1. sled; sleigh. 2. carry on a sledge. 3. ride in a sledge. *n., v. 5.*

sledge[2] (slej), a large, heavy hammer; sledge hammer. *n.*

sledge hammer, a large, heavy hammer.

Sledge hammer

sleek (slēk), 1. smooth; soft and glossy; as, sleek hair. 2. having smooth, soft skin, hair, fur, etc.; as, a sleek cat. 3. smooth of speech, manners, etc.; as, a sleek salesman. 4. to smooth. He sleeked down his hair. *adj., v. 6.*

sleep (slēp), 1. rest body and mind; be without ordinary thought or movement.

We sleep at night. All animals sleep. 2. rest of body and mind occurring naturally and regularly. Most people need eight hours of sleep a day. 3. be in a condition like sleep. The seeds sleep in the ground all winter. 4. state or condition like sleep. The **last sleep** means death. 5. spend in sleeping. **Sleep away** means pass or spend in sleeping. Sarah slept away the whole morning. **Sleep off** means get rid of by sleeping. She was sleeping off a headache. *v., slept, sleeping, n. 1.*

sleep er (slēp′ər), 1. one that sleeps. The noise woke the sleepers. 2. a railroad car that has berths for passengers to sleep in. 3. horizontal beam. Sleepers support the rails of a railroad track. *n. 8.*

sleep i ly (slēp′i li), in a sleepy manner. *adv.*

sleep i ness (slēp′i nis), sleepy condition; drowsiness. *n. 20.*

sleeping car, railroad car with berths for passengers to sleep in.

sleeping sickness, a disease, usually causing death, carried by a kind of fly.

sleep less (slēp′lis), without sleep; not sleeping; restless. *adj. 15.*

sleep walk er (slēp′wôk′ər), person who walks while asleep. *n.*

sleep walk ing (slēp′wôk′ing), walking in one's sleep. *n.*

sleep y (slēp′i), 1. ready to go to sleep; inclined to sleep. 2. quiet; not active. *adj., sleepier, sleepiest. 3.*

sleet (slēt), 1. half-frozen rain; snow or hail mixed with rain. 2. to rain and snow or hail at the same time. *n., v. 7.*

sleet y (slēt′i), of sleet; like sleet; with sleet; having much sleet. *adj., sleetier, sleetiest.*

sleeve (slēv), 1. the part of a garment that covers the arm. **Laugh in one's sleeve** means be amused but not show it. 2. tube into which a rod or another tube fits. *n. 3.*

sleeve less (slēv′lis), without sleeves; as, a sleeveless dress. *adj. 13.*

sleigh (slā), 1. a carriage or cart mounted on runners for use on snow or ice. In northern countries people use sleighs in the winter. 2. travel or ride in a sleigh. *n., v. 5.*

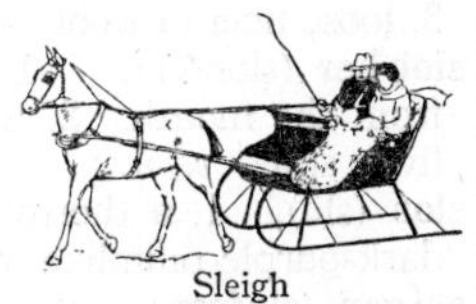
Sleigh

sleigh ing (slā′ing), 1. a riding in a sleigh. 2. the going for sleighs. Snow packed hard makes good sleighing. *n.*

sleight (slīt), skill; dexterity; clever trick. *n. 20.*

sleight of hand, skill and quickness in moving the hands; the tricks or skill of a modern magician; juggling.

slen der (slen′dər), 1. long and thin; not big around. A boy 6 feet tall and weighing only 130 pounds is very slender. A pencil is a slender piece of wood. 2. slight; small; as, a slender meal, a slender income, a slender hope. *adj. 3.*

slept (slept). See **sleep.** The child slept soundly. *pt. and pp. of sleep. 3.*

sleuth (slüth), 1. bloodhound. 2. detective. *n.*

slew[1] (slü). See **slay.** Jack slew the giant. *pt. of slay. 5.*

slew[2] (slü), turn; swing; twist. *v., n.* Also spelled **slue.**

slice (slīs), 1. a thin, flat, broad piece cut from something; as, a slice of bread, a slice of meat. 2. cut into slices. Slice the bread. We ate sliced peaches. 3. cut (off). *n., v. 4.*

slick (slik), 1. sleek; smooth; as, slick hair. 2. smooth of speech, manners, etc. 3. sly; tricky. 4. make sleek or smooth. 5. smoothly; slyly; cleverly. 6. directly. *adj., v., adv. 18.*

slick er (slik′ər), a long, loose waterproof coat. *n.*

Slickers

slid (slid). See **slide.** The minutes slid rapidly by. *pt. and pp. of slide. 9.*

slide (slīd), 1. move smoothly as a sled moves on snow or ice. The bureau drawers slide in and out. 2. move easily and quietly. The thief quickly slid behind the curtains. 3. slip. He slid a pistol into his pocket. 4. act of sliding. The children each take a slide in turn. 5. smooth surface for sliding on. The frozen brook makes a good slide. 6. track, rail, etc., on which something slides. 7. mass of earth, snow, etc., sliding down. **Let things slide** means let things take their own course. 8. a small thin sheet of glass. Slides with pictures on them are used in magic lanterns. *v., slid, slid or slidden, sliding, n. 3.*

slight (slīt), 1. slender; not big around. She is a slight girl. 2. small; not much;

not important. One slice of bread is a very slight lunch. I have a slight headache. 3. pay too little attention to. This maid slights her work. She felt slighted because she was not asked to the party. 4. slighting treatment; an act of neglect. *adj., v., n. 2.*

slight ly (slīt′li), 1. in a slight manner. 2. to a slight degree; somewhat; a little. I knew him slightly. *adv.*

slim (slim), 1. slender; thin. He was very slim, being 6 feet tall and weighing only 130 pounds. 2. small; slight; weak. We had a slim attendance because of the rain. *adj., slimmer, slimmest. 10.*

slime (slīm), 1. soft, sticky mud or something like it. His shoes were covered with slime from the swamp. 2. a sticky substance given off by snails, snakes, fish, etc. *n. 8.*

slim y (slīm′i), 1. of slime; like slime. 2. covered with slime. *adj., slimier, slimiest. 10.*

sling (sling), 1. strip of leather with a string fastened to each end, for throwing stones. 2. throw with a sling; throw; cast; hurl. John slung stones at the poor cat. 3. a rope, band, or chain by which heavy objects are lifted, carried, or held. The men lowered the boxes into the cellar by a sling. 4. hanging loop of cloth fastened around the neck to support a hurt arm. 5. hang in a sling; hang so as to swing loosely. The soldier's gun was slung over his shoulder. *n., v., slung, slinging. 5.*

A, sling for lifting; B, sling lifting a barrel.

sling shot (sling′shot′), Y-shaped stick with a rubber band fastened to its prongs, used to shoot pebbles, etc. *n.*

slink (slingk), move in a secret, guilty manner; sneak. After stealing the meat, the dog slunk away. *v., slunk, slinking. 11.*

slip (slip), 1. go or move smoothly and easily. The ship slips through the waves. The drawer slips into place. He slipped back the bolt. She slipped the ring from her finger. 2. slide; move out of place. The knife slipped and cut him. 3. slide suddenly without wanting to. He slipped on the icy sidewalk. 4. go or move quietly, easily, or quickly; escape. She slipped out of the room. Time slips by. Don't let this opportunity slip. Your name has slipped my mind. 5. put quietly or secretly. Slip the note into Mary's hand. 6. **Slip on** or **off** means put on or take off (something) easily or quickly. Slip on your coat and come with us. 7. slipping. His broken leg was caused by a slip on a banana peel. 8. make a mistake or error. **Let slip** means tell without meaning to. 9. mistake; an error in conduct. He makes slips in grammar. That remark was a slip of the tongue. 10. thing that can be slipped on or off; covering. During the summer many people put slips on furniture. We put white slips on pillows. Some garments are called slips. 11. narrow strip of paper, wood, etc. 12. a small branch or twig cut from a plant to grow a new plant. She has promised us slips from her rosebushes. *v., slipped, slipping, n. 2.*

slip knot, 1. knot that slips along the cord around which it is made. 2. knot which can be undone by a pull.

Slip knot

slip per (slip′ər), a light shoe. She has pretty dancing slippers and comfortable bedroom slippers. *n. 3.*

slip pered (slip′ərd), wearing slippers. *adj.*

slip per i ness (slip′ər i nis), slippery condition or quality. *n.*

slip per y (slip′ər i), 1. causing slipping. A wet street is slippery. The steps are slippery with ice. 2. slipping away easily. Wet soap is slippery. 3. not to be depended on; tricky. *adj., slipperier, slipperiest. 4.*

slip shod (slip′shod′), 1. untidy; careless in dress, habits, speech, etc. 2. shuffling; as, a slipshod gait. 3. wearing shoes worn down at the heel. *adj. 19.*

slit (slit), 1. cut or tear along a line; make a long cut in; as, to slit cloth into strips, to slit a skirt to make a pocket. 2. a straight, narrow cut or opening; as, a slit in a bag, the slit in the letter box. *v., slit, slitting, n. 9.*

sliv er (sliv′ər), 1. a long, thin piece that has been split off, broken off, or cut off; a splinter. 2. split or break into slivers. 3. loose fiber of wool, cotton, etc. *n., v. 19.*

slob ber (slob′ər), 1. let liquid run out from the mouth. 2. wet with spit. 3. saliva; spit. *v., n.*

sloe (slō), 1. a thorny shrub with a small, dark-purple plumlike fruit. 2. the fruit. *n.*

slo gan (slō′gən), 1. a word or phrase used like a war cry by any group, party, class, or business. "Safety First" is our slogan. 2. war cry; battle cry. *n. 15.*

sloop (slüp), a sailboat having one mast, a mainsail, a jib, and sometimes other sails. *n. 18.*

Sloop

slop (slop), 1. spill; splash. 2. liquid carelessly spilled or splashed about. 3. dirty water; liquid garbage; as, the kitchen slops. 4. weak liquid food, such as gruel. *v., slopped, slopping, n. 12.*

slope (slōp), 1. go up or down as shown in the picture. The land slopes toward the sea. The house has a sloping roof. 2. any line, surface, or land that goes up or down from a level. If you roll a ball up a slope, it will roll down again. 3. amount of slope. The floor of the theater has a slope of four feet from the back seats to the front. *v., n. 2.*

Slope

slop py (slop′i), 1. very wet; slushy; as, sloppy ground, sloppy weather. 2. splashed with liquid; as, a sloppy table. 3. careless; slovenly; as, to use sloppy English, to do sloppy work. 4. weak; silly. *Used in common talk. adj., sloppier, sloppiest.*

slot (slot), 1. a small, narrow opening. Put a penny in the slot to get a stick of gum from this machine. 2. make a slot or slots in. *n., v., slotted, slotting. 13.*

Sloth (about 2 ft. long)

sloth (slōth), 1. slowness; laziness; idleness. His sloth keeps him from engaging in sports. 2. a very slow-moving animal of South America that lives in trees. Sloths hang upside down from tree branches. *n. 8.*

sloth ful (slōth′fəl), lazy; sluggish. *adj. 11.*

slouch (slouch), 1. to stand, sit, walk, or move in an awkward, drooping manner. The weary beggar slouched. 2. droop or bend downward. 3. bending forward of head and shoulders; an awkward, drooping way of standing, sitting, or walking. 4. slouchy person. *v., n. 11.*

slouch y (slouch′i), slouching; careless; slovenly. *adj., slouchier, slouchiest.*

slough[1] (slou or slü), piece of soft, muddy ground; mud hole; marsh; bog. *n. 12.* Also spelled **slue.**

slough[2] (sluf), 1. old skin shed or cast off by a snake. 2. anything that has been shed or cast off. 3. shed; cast off; throw off. *n., v.*

Slo vak (slō′vak), 1. one of a Slavic people living in Slovakia. The Slovaks are closely related to the Bohemians and the Moravians. 2. their language. *n.*

Slo va ki a (slō vä′ki ə), country in central Europe under the control of Germany. From 1919 to 1939 it was a province in eastern Czecho-Slovakia. *n.*

slov en (sluv′ən), person who is untidy, dirty, or careless in dress, appearance, habits, work, etc. *n.*

slov en li ness (sluv′ən li nis), lack of neatness; dirtiness; carelessness in appearance, dress, habits, work, etc. *n.*

slov en ly (sluv′ən li), 1. untidy, dirty, or careless in dress, appearance, habits, work, etc. 2. in a slovenly manner. *adj., slovenlier, slovenliest, adv. 13.*

slow (slō), 1. taking a long time. 2. behind time. 3. dull; stupid; not interesting. 4. make slow; become slow; go slower. 5. slowly. *adj., v., adv. 1.*

slow match, a match or fuse that burns very slowly, used for setting fire to gunpowder, dynamite, etc.

sludge (sluj), 1. soft mud; mire; slush. 2. broken ice. In winter there is sludge on the sea near the shore. *n. 16.*

slue[1] (slü), turn; swing; twist. *v., slued, sluing, n.*

slue[2] (slü), swampy place; marshy inlet. *n.* Also spelled **slough.**

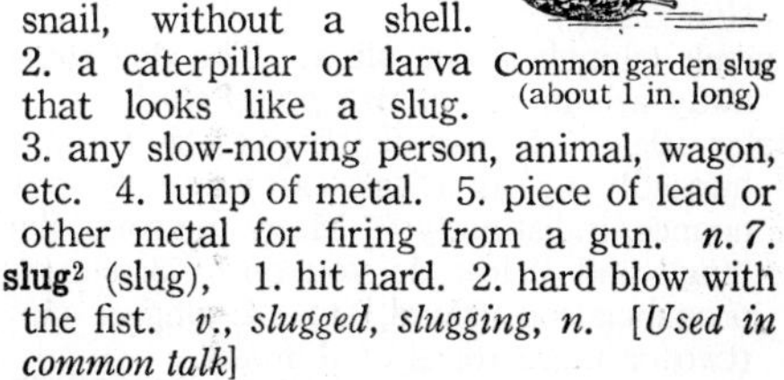
Common garden slug (about 1 in. long)

slug[1] (slug), 1. a slow-moving creature like a snail, without a shell. 2. a caterpillar or larva that looks like a slug. 3. any slow-moving person, animal, wagon, etc. 4. lump of metal. 5. piece of lead or other metal for firing from a gun. *n. 7.*

slug[2] (slug), 1. hit hard. 2. hard blow with the fist. *v., slugged, slugging, n.* [*Used in common talk*]

slug gard (slug′ərd), a lazy, sluggish person. *n. 11.*

slug gish (slug′ish), slow; lazy; not active. The stream was so sluggish that I could hardly tell which way it flowed. He has a sluggish mind and shows little interest in anything. *adj. 9.*

slug gish ness (slug′ish nis), slowness; laziness; lack of energy, action, or vigor. *n. 17.*

sluice (slüs), 1. structure with a gate for holding back or controlling the water of a canal, river, or lake. 2. gate that holds back or controls the flow of water. When the water behind a dam gets too high, the sluices are opened. 3. let out or draw off (water) by opening a sluice; rush out. 4. flush or cleanse with a rush of water; pour or throw water over. 5. channel for carrying off water. 6. a long, sloping trough through which water flows, used to wash gold from sand or gravel. 7. wash (gold) from sand, dirt, or gravel in a sluice. *n., v. 10.*

Sluice for washing gold

slum (slum), 1. a crowded, dirty part of a city or town. Poverty, disease, and crime are common in slums. 2. go into or visit slums. *n., v., slummed, slumming. 12.*

slum ber (slum′bər), 1. sleep. He awoke from his slumber. 2. light sleep. 3. pass in sleep. Baby slumbers away for hours. 4. be like a person asleep. The volcano had slumbered for years. *n., v. 3.*

slum ber ous (slum′bər əs), 1. sleepy. 2. causing sleep. *adj. 14.*

slum brous (slum′brəs), slumberous. *adj.*

slump (slump), 1. drop heavily; fall suddenly. The boy's feet slumped repeatedly through the rotting ice. 2. a heavy or sudden fall; as, a slump in prices. *v., n. 18.*

slung (slung). See **sling.** The boy slung his books over his shoulder. *pt. and pp. of sling. 13.*

slunk (slungk). See **slink.** The dog slunk away ashamed. *pt. and pp. of slink. 11.*

slur (slėr), 1. pass lightly over; go through hurriedly or in a careless way. 2. pronounce indistinctly. Many persons slur "ing" and "How do you do." 3. slurred pronunciation, sound, etc. 4. sing or play (two or more tones of different pitch) without a break. 5. slurring of tones. 6. curved mark (⌢) (⌣) indicating this. 7. mark with a slur. 8. a blot or stain (upon reputation), an insulting or slighting remark. 9. harm the reputation

A slur in music

of; insult; slight. *v., slurred, slurring, n. 16.*

slush (slush), partly melted snow; snow and water mixed. *n. 18.*

slush y (slush′i), 1. having much slush. 2. of or like slush. *adj., slushier, slushiest.*

slut (slut), 1. a dirty, careless woman. 2. female dog. *n. 17.*

sly (slī), 1. able to do things without letting others know; acting secretly. That girl is as sly as a fox. The sly cat stole the meat while the cook's back was turned. 2. such as a sly person would use. She asked sly questions. 3. playfully mischievous or knowing. The week before Christmas the children exchanged many sly looks and smiles. 4. **On the sly** means secretly. *adj., slyer, slyest or slier, sliest, n. 4.*

sly ly (slī′li), in a sly manner; secretly. *adv.*

smack[1] (smak), 1. slight taste or flavor. This sauce has a smack of nutmeg. 2. trace; touch. The old sailor still had a smack of the sea about him. 3. have a taste, trace, or touch (of). His speech smacked of the old country. *n., v. 6.*

smack[2] (smak), 1. pull (the lips) apart quickly so as to make a sharp sound. 2. such a movement. 3. sharp sound made in this way. 4. kiss loudly. 5. loud kiss. 6. slap. 7. crack (a whip, etc.). *v., n.*

smack[3] (smak), a small sailboat with one mast. *n.*

Smack

smack ing (smak′-ing), 1. making a quick, sharp sound; as, a smacking kiss, a smacking blow. 2. lively, brisk, or strong; as, a smacking breeze. *adj.*

small (smôl), 1. not large; little. A cent is a small amount of money. 2. not important. A man who keeps a little shop is a small dealer. 3. having little strength; as, the still small voice of conscience. 4. mean. A boy with a small nature is not generous. 5. Some special meanings are:

feel small, be ashamed or humiliated. Mrs. Smith's kindness to Jack after he had broken her window made him feel small.

small hours, early hours of the morning.

small letters, ordinary letters, not capitals.

small talk, talk about matters having little importance; chat.

the small of the back, the narrowest part of the back.

adj., n. 1.

small pox (smôl′poks′), a very contagious disease characterized by fever and eruptions on the skin that often leave permanent scars shaped like little pits. Vaccination prevents smallpox. *n. 9.*

smart (smärt), 1. feel sharp pain. He smarted from the scolding. 2. cause sharp pain. The cut smarts. 3. sharp pain. The smart of the hurt kept him awake. 4. sharp; severe. He gave the horse a smart blow. 5. keen; active; lively. They walked at a smart pace. 6. clever; bright. Jack is a smart boy. 7. fresh and neat; in good order. 8. stylish; fashionable. 9. smartly. *v., n., adj., adv. 3.*

smart ly (smärt′li), in a smart manner; cleverly; in style. *adv.*

smart ness (smärt′nis), quality or condition of being smart; cleverness; stylishness. *n. 20.*

smash (smash), 1. break into pieces with violence and noise. The boy smashed a window with a stone. 2. destroy; shatter. 3. be broken to pieces. The dishes smashed as the tray upset. 4. become ruined. 5. rush violently; crash. The car smashed into the store window. 6. a smashing or the sound made by it; a crash. We heard a smash as the other automobile hit ours. 7. crushing defeat; disaster; destruction. *v., n. 9.*

smat ter ing (smat′ər ing), slight knowledge. *n. 17.*

smear (smēr), 1. cover with anything sticky, greasy, or dirty. Mary smeared her fingers with jam. 2. rub or spread (oil, grease, paint, etc.). 3. a mark or stain left by smearing. There are smears of paint on the wallpaper. *v., n. 8.*

smell (smel), 1. Can you smell the smoke? We smell with our noses. 2. She picked a rose and smelled it. The dog smelled the tramp's legs. 3. The hall smelled of onions. Roses smell sweet. 4. Smell is keener in dogs than in men. 5. The smell of burning cloth is not pleasant. 6. Have a smell of this rose. *v., smelled* or *smelt, smelling, n. 2.*

smelling salts, a form of ammonia used to relieve faintness, headaches, etc.

smell y (smel′i), having or giving out a strong or unpleasant smell. Rotten fish are smelly. *adj., smellier, smelliest.*

smelt[1] (smelt), 1. melt (ore) in order to get metal out of it. 2. obtain (metal) from ore. 3. refine (impure metal) by melting. *v. 6.*

smelt[2] (smelt), smelled. *pt. and pp. of* **smell.**

smelt[3] (smelt), a small food fish with silvery scales. *n.*

smelt er (smel′tər), 1. furnace for smelting ores. 2. place where ores are smelted. *n. 14.*

smile (smīl), 1. look pleased or amused; show pleasure, favor, kindness, amusement, etc., by an upward curve of the mouth. 2. show scorn or disdain by a curve of the mouth. She smiled bitterly. 3. bring, put, drive, etc., by smiling. Smile your tears away. 4. act of smiling. *v., n. 1.*

smirch (smėrch), 1. make dirty; soil with soot, dirt, dust, dishonor, disgrace, etc. 2. dirty mark; blot; stain. *v., n.*

smirk (smėrk), 1. smile in an affected, silly, self-satisfied way. 2. an affected, silly, self-satisfied smile. *v., n. 15.*

smit (smit), 1. smitten. 2. smote. *Not used now. pp. and pt. of* **smite.** *17.*

smite (smīt), strike; strike hard; hit hard. The hero smote the giant with his sword. His conscience smote him. She was smitten with curiosity about the forbidden room. *v., smote, smitten* or *smit, smiting. 4.*

smith (smith), 1. man who makes or shapes things out of metal; as, a goldsmith, a tinsmith. 2. blacksmith. *n. 3.*

Smith (smith), 1. Captain John Smith was an English explorer and early settler in Virginia (1580-1631). 2. Joseph Smith was the founder of the Mormon Church (1805-1844). *n.*

smith y (smith′i), workshop of a smith, especially a blacksmith. "Under a spreading chestnut tree the village smithy stands." *n., pl. smithies. 12.*

smit ten (smit′ən), 1. struck; hard hit. 2. See **smite.** The giant was smitten with the sword of the knight. *adj., pp. of smite. 6.*

smock (smok), 1. loose outer garment worn to protect clothing. 2. draw (cloth) into a honeycomb pattern by stitches. *n., v. 7.*

Smock

smoke (smōk), 1. cloud from anything burning, or something like it. 2. give off smoke or steam, or something like it. The fireplace smokes. The turkey was brought smoking hot to the table. 3. draw the smoke from (a pipe, cigar, etc.) into the mouth and puff it out again. 4. act of smoking tobacco. 5. expose to smoke. People smoke fish to preserve them. 6. drive (out) by smoke. *n., v. 1.*

smoke less (smōk′lis), making no smoke; having very little smoke. *adj. 13.*

smok er (smōk′ər), 1. person who smokes tobacco. 2. a car or a part of a car where smoking is allowed. 3. informal gathering of men for smoking and entertainment. *n. 9.*

smoke stack (smōk′stak′), tall chimney. *n.*

smok y (smōk′i), 1. sending out much smoke; as, a smoky fire. 2. full of smoke. 3. darkened or stained with smoke. 4. like smoke or suggesting smoke; as, a smoky gray, a smoky taste. *adj., smokier, smokiest. 11.*

smol der (smōl′dər), 1. burn and smoke without flame; as, the smoldering ashes of a cigar. 2. slow, smoky burning without flame; smoldering fire. 3. exist or continue in a suppressed condition; as, smoldering anger or rebellion. *v., n. 18.*

smooth (smüᴛʜ), 1. even, like glass, silk, or still water. 2. free from unevenness or roughness; as, smooth sailing, a smooth voyage. 3. without lumps; as, smooth sauce. 4. easy; flowing; polished; pleasant; polite. That salesman is a smooth talker. 5. make smooth; make flat. Smooth this dress with a hot iron. He smoothed out the ball of crushed paper and read it. 6. cure or get rid of (roughness, difficulties, troubles, etc.); make easy. He smoothed away all objections to the plan. She smoothed down her father's temper. 7. in a smooth manner. *adj., v., adv. 2.*

smooth bore (smüᴛʜ′bōr′), not rifled. A smoothbore gun has no grooves in its barrel. *adj.*

smooth-faced (smüᴛʜ′fāst′), 1. having a smooth face; beardless; clean-shaven. 2. having a smooth surface. 3. agreeable in speech and manner; as, a smooth-faced hypocrite. *adj.*

smooth ness (smüᴛʜ′nis), smooth quality or condition. The smoothness of the cat's fur pleased the baby. *n. 9.*

smote (smōt). See **smite.** God smote the wicked city with fire from heaven. *pt. of smite. 4.*

smoth er (smuᴛʜ′ər), 1. make unable to get air; kill by depriving of air. The wicked king smothered the two little princes. The fire is smothered by ashes. 2. be unable to breathe freely; suffocate. We are smothering in this stuffy room. 3. cover thickly. In the fall the grass is smothered with leaves. 4. keep back; check; suppress. He smothered a sharp reply. His smothered anger suddenly broke out. 5. cloud of dust or smoke. *v., n. 7.*

smoul der (smōl′dər), smolder. *v., n. 12.*

smudge[1] (smuj), 1. dirty mark; smear. 2. mark with dirty streaks; smear. The child's drawing was smudged. *n., v. 18.*

smudge[2] (smuj), smoky fire made to drive away mosquitoes, flies, or other insects. *n.*

smug (smug), 1. self-satisfied; too pleased with one's own goodness, cleverness, etc. 2. sleek. *adj., smugger, smuggest. 18.*

smug gle (smug′əl), 1. bring in or take out of a country secretly and against the law; as, to smuggle opium into the United States. 2. bring, take, put, etc., secretly. Robert tried to smuggle his puppy into the house. *v. 9.*

smug gler (smug′lər), 1. one who smuggles. 2. ship used in smuggling. *n. 16.*

smut (smut), 1. soil with a black or dirty substance; as, to smut one's hands with coal. 2. a black or dirty mark; a bit of soot or dirt. 3. a plant disease in which the ears of grain are changed to a black dust. 4. of plants, to give or get the disease called smut. 5. dirty, indecent talk. *v., smutted, smutting, n. 12.*

smutch (smuch), smudge. *v., n.*

smut ty (smut′i), 1. soiled with smut, soot, etc.; dirty. 2. indecent; nasty. 3. having the plant disease called smut. *adj., smuttier, smuttiest. 20.*

Smyr na (smėr′nə), important seaport in western Turkey, on the Aegean Sea. *n. 18.*

snack (snak), 1. light meal. He eats a snack before going to bed. 2. share. *n. 13.*

snaf fle (snaf′əl), 1. a slender, jointed bit used on a bridle. 2. control or manage by a snaffle. *n., v. 19.*

Snaffle

snag (snag), 1. a tree or branch held fast in a river or lake. Snags are dangerous to boats. 2. any sharp or rough projecting point, such as the broken end of a branch. 3. run or catch on a snag. 4. hinder. 5. to clear of snags. 6. stump of a tooth; projecting tooth. *n., v., snagged, snagging.*

snail (snāl), 1. a small soft animal that crawls very slowly. Most snails have shells on their backs. See the picture. 2. a lazy, slow-moving person. *n. 6.*

Snail

snake (snāk), 1. a long, slender, crawling reptile without limbs. 2. a sly, treacherous person. 3. to move, wind, or curve like a snake. *n., v. 3.*

Snake

snak y (snāk′i), 1. of a snake or snakes. 2. like a snake; twisting; winding. 3. having many snakes. *adj., snakier, snakiest. 15.*

snap (snap), 1. make a sudden, quick bite or snatch; seize suddenly. The dog snapped at the child's hand. The dog snapped up the meat. She snapped at the chance to go to college. 2. a quick, sudden bite or snatch. The dog made a snap at a fly. 3. speak quickly and sharply. "Silence!" snapped the captain. 4. make or cause to make a sudden, sharp sound. This wood snaps as it burns. 5. a quick, sharp sound. 6. break suddenly. The violin string snapped. 7. sudden breaking. One snap made the knife useless. 8. a quick, sharp way. She moves with snap and energy. 9. short spell of weather; as, a cold snap. 10. fastener; a clasp. One of the snaps of your dress is unfastened. 11. a thin crisp cooky; as, a gingersnap. 12. made or done suddenly. 13. take a snapshot of. *v., snapped, snapping, n., adj. 3.*

snap drag on (snap′drag′ən), a garden plant with showy flowers of crimson, purple, white, etc. *n. 19.*

Snapdragon

snap pish (snap′ish), 1. apt to snap. 2. impatient; sharp in speech or manner. *adj. 17.*

snap py (snap′i), 1. snappish. 2. quick. 3. lively. *Used in common talk. adj., snappier, snappiest.*

snap shot (snap′shot′), 1. photograph taken in an instant. 2. quick shot taken without time for careful aim. *n. 17.*

snare (snãr), 1. noose for catching small animals and birds; a trap. The boys made snares to catch rabbits. 2. catch with a snare; to trap. One day they snared a skunk. *n., v. 4.*

Snare

snare drum, a small drum with strings stretched across the bottom to make a rattling sound.

Bottom of snare drum

snarl[1] (snärl), 1. growl sharply and show one's teeth. The dog snarled at the stranger. 2. speak in a sharp, angry tone; say with a snarl. 3. sharp growl; angry words. A snarl was his only reply. *v., n. 6.*

snarl[2] (snärl), tangle. My sewing silks are all in a snarl. *n., v.*

snatch (snach), 1. seize suddenly. The hawk snatched the chicken and flew away. 2. grasp (at). He snatched at the rail. 3. act of snatching. The boy made a snatch at the ball. 4. short time. He had a snatch of sleep sitting in his chair. 5. small amount; bit; scrap. We heard snatches of their conversation. *v., n. 3.*

sneak (snēk), 1. move in a stealthy way. The man sneaked about the barn watching for a chance to steal the cow. 2. act like a thief or a person who is ashamed to be seen. 3. person who sneaks; a sneaking, cowardly person. *v., n. 8.*

sneak ing (snēk′ing), 1. cowardly; underhand; concealed. 2. that one cannot justify or does not like to confess. *adj.*

sneak y (snēk′i), cowardly; mean. *adj., sneakier, sneakiest.*

Man sneering

sneer (snēr), 1. show scorn or contempt by looks or words. The mean girls sneered at poor Dora's clothes. "Bah!" he sneered with a curl of his lip. 2. a look or words expressing scorn or contempt. He feared sneers more than blows. *v., n. 7.*

sneeze (snēz), 1. expel air suddenly and violently through the nose and mouth. A person sneezes when he has a cold. Pepper makes you sneeze. 2. sneezing. *v., n. 7.*

snick er (snik′ər), 1. half-suppressed laugh; a giggle; a sly or silly laugh. 2. to laugh in this way. *n., v.*

sniff (snif), 1. draw air through the nose in short breaths that can be heard. A person with a cold sniffs. She sniffed at the present to show her contempt. 2. draw in through the nose with the breath. He sniffed the medicine. 3. smell; try the smell of. The dog sniffed suspiciously at the stranger. 4. act or sound of sniffing. He cleared his nose with a loud sniff. 5. a single breathing in of something; a breath. *v., n. 10.*

snif fle (snif′əl), 1. sniff again and again as one does from a cold in the head or in trying to stop crying. 2. a sniffling; a moist sniff. 3. The **sniffles** means a cold in the head. *v., n.*

snip (snip), 1. cut with a small, quick stroke with scissors. She snipped the thread. 2. act of snipping. With a few snips she cut out a paper doll. 3. small piece cut off. Pick up the snips of cloth and thread from the floor. *v., snipped, snipping, n. 10.*

snipe (snīp), 1. a marsh bird with a long bill. 2. hunt snipe. 3. shoot at soldiers as a sportsman shoots at game; shoot from under cover. *n., v. 9.*

Snipe (about 11 in. long from tip of beak to tip of tail)

sniv el (sniv′əl), 1. run at the nose; sniffle. 2. running from the nose; sniffling. 3. cry with sniffling. 4. whine; put on a show of grief. 5. whining; pretended grief or crying. *v., sniveled, sniveling, n. 17.*

snob (snob), person who cares too much for rank, wealth, position, etc., and too little for real merit; person who tries too hard to please those above him and too little to please those below him. *n. 19.*

snob ber y (snob′ər i), snobbishness. *n., pl. snobberies.*

snob bish (snob′ish), of or like a snob; looking down on those in a lower position. *adj.*

snob bish ness (snob′ish nis), character or conduct of a snob; being a snob. *n.*

snood (snüd), 1. a band or ribbon formerly worn around the hair by young, unmarried women. 2. bind up (hair) with a snood. *n., v.*

Snood

snoop (snüp), go about in a sneaking, prying way; prowl; pry. *v. [Used in common talk]*

snooze (snüz), 1. sleep; doze; take a nap. 2. a doze; a nap. *v., n. [Used in common talk]*

snore (snōr), 1. breathe during sleep with a harsh, rough sound. 2. the sound so made. *v., n. 6.*

snort (snôrt), 1. force the breath violently through the nose with a loud harsh sound. The horse snorted. 2. make a sound like this. The engine snorted. 3. act of snorting; the sound made. 4. say with a snort. "Indeed!" snorted my aunt. *v., n. 7.*

snout (snout), 1. the long nose of an animal; the nose and mouth of an animal; as, the snout of a pig. 2. anything like an animal's snout. *n. 7.*

snow (snō), 1. frozen water in soft white flakes. Rain falls in summer; snow falls in winter. 2. a fall of snow. 3. fall as snow; as, to snow all day. 4. **Snowed in** means shut in by snow. *n., v. 1.*

snow ball (snō′bôl′), 1. ball made of snow. 2. throw balls of snow at. They snowballed each other. 3. a shrub with white flowers in large clusters like balls. *n., v. 13.*

snow bird (snō′bėrd′), 1. a small, slate-gray bird seen in flocks during the winter. 2. a kind of bunting that lives in cold regions. *n. 20.*

Snowbird (def. 2) (about 7 in. long)

snow-bound (snō′bound′), shut in by snow. *adj.*

snow-capped (snō′kapt′), having its top covered with snow. *adj.*

snow drift (snō′drift′), 1. bank of snow piled up by the wind. 2. snow driven before the wind. *n.*

snow drop (snō′drop′), a small plant with white flowers that blooms early in the spring. *n. 14.*

snow fall (snō′fôl′), 1. a fall of snow. 2. amount of snow falling in a given time. The snowfall in that one storm was 16 inches. *n.*

snow flake (snō′flāk′), a small, feathery piece of snow. *n. 9.*

snow plow (snō′plou′), a machine for clearing away snow from streets, railroad tracks, etc. *n.*

snow shoe (snō′shü′), a light wooden frame with strips of leather stretched across it. Trappers in the far north wear snowshoes on their feet to keep from sinking in deep, soft snow. *n. 16.*

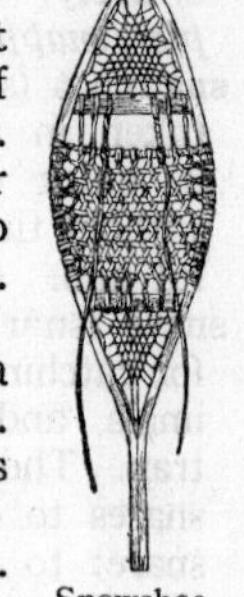
Snowshoe

snow storm (snō′stôrm′), a storm with much snow. *n. 18.*

snow-white (snō′hwīt′), white as snow. *adj.*

snow y (snō′i), 1. having snow. 2. covered with snow. 3. like snow; snow-white. The old lady has snowy hair. *adj., snowier, snowiest. 6.*

snub (snub), 1. treat coldly, scornfully, or with contempt. 2. cold, scornful, or disdainful treatment. 3. check or stop (a boat or a horse) suddenly. 4. sudden check or stop. 5. short and turned up at the tip; as, a snub nose. *v., snubbed, snubbing, n., adj. 15.*

snuff[1] (snuf), 1. draw in through the nose; draw up into the nose. He snuffs up salt and water to cure a cold. 2. sniff; smell. The dog snuffed at the track of the fox. 3. powdered tobacco to be taken into the nose. *v., n. 5.*

snuff[2] (snuf), 1. cut or pinch off the burned part of a candlewick. 2. **Snuff out** means put an end to suddenly and completely. *v.*

snuff box (snuf′boks′), very small box for holding snuff. *n. 19.*

snuff ers (snuf′ərz), little tongs for taking off the burned wick or putting out the light of a candle. *n. pl. 19.*

Snuffers

snuf fle (snuf′əl), 1. breathe noisily through the nose like a person with a cold in the head; speak through the nose. 2. act or sound of snuffling. 3. the tone of voice of a person who snuffles. 4. The **snuffles** means a cold in the head. *v., n. 14.*

snug (snug), 1. comfortable; warm; sheltered. The cat has found a snug corner behind the stove. 2. neat; trim; compact. The cabins on the boat are snug. 3. fitting closely. That coat is a little too snug. 4. in a snug manner. *adj., snugger, snuggest, adv. 4.*

snug gle (snug′əl), nestle; cuddle. *v.*

so[1] (sō), 1. in that way; in the same way or degree; as stated; as shown. Hold your pen so. The chair is broken and has been so for a long time. Do not walk so fast. Jack is not so tall as his brother. Grace is sick. Is that so? 2. very. You are so kind. 3. very much. My head aches so! 4. therefore; accordingly; on this account. The dog seemed hungry; so we fed him. 5. **So** is sometimes used alone to ask a question or to exclaim. So! late again! The train is late. So? 6. Some special meanings are:

and so, 1. likewise; also. Dick is here, and so is John. 2. accordingly. I said I would go, and so I shall.

or so, more or less. It happened a day or so ago.

so as, with the result or purpose. Jack goes to bed early so as to get plenty of sleep.

so that, 1. with the result that. The boy studies so that he will do well. He studies so hard that he gets high marks. 2. with the purpose that.

adv., interj., conj., 1.

so[2] (sō), in music, the fifth tone of the scale; sol. *n.*

soak (sōk), 1. make very wet; become very wet. Soak the clothes all night before you wash them. 2. take up; suck. A sponge soaks up water. 3. soaking. Give the clothes a long soak. 4. go; enter; make its way. Water will soak through the earth. *v., n. 5.*

so-and-so (sō′ənd sō′), some person or thing not named. *n.*

soap (sōp), 1. a substance used for washing, made of a fat and caustic soda or potash. 2. rub with soap. *n., v. 3.*

soap stone (sōp′stōn′), a kind of stone that feels somewhat like soap, used for griddles, hearths, etc. *n. 19.*

soap suds (sōp′sudz′), soap and water mixed and foaming. *n. pl.*

soap y (sōp′i), 1. covered with soap or soapsuds. 2. full of soap or soapsuds. 3. of or like soap. *adj., soapier, soapiest.*

soar (sōr), 1. fly upward; fly at a great height. An eagle soars. 2. aspire; rise beyond what is common and ordinary. His ambition soared to the throne. *v. 5.*

sob (sob), 1. cry or sigh with short quick breaths. Jane sobbed herself to sleep. "I have lost my penny," the child sobbed. 2. make a sound like a sob. The wind sobbed. 3. catching the breath from grief, etc. *v., sobbed, sobbing, n. 5.*

so ber (sō′bər), 1. not drunk. 2. temperate; moderate. The Puritans led sober, hard-working lives. 3. quiet; serious; solemn. John looked sober at the thought of missing the picnic. 4. calm; sensible; free from exaggeration. The judge's sober opinion was not influenced by prejudice or strong feeling. 5. make sober; become sober. The class sobered down as the teacher came into the room. *adj., v. 3.*

so bri e ty (sō brī′ə ti), 1. soberness. 2. temperance in the use of strong drink. 3. moderation. 4. quietness; seriousness. *n. 12.*

so bri quet (sō′bri kā), nickname. *n.*

so-called (sō′kôld′), 1. called thus. 2. called thus improperly or untruthfully. Her so-called friend hasn't even written to her. *adj.*

soc cer (sok′ər), a game played between two teams of eleven men each, using a round ball. The ball may be struck with any part of the body except the hands and arms. *n.*

Boys playing soccer

so cia bil i ty (sō′shə bil′i ti), sociable disposition; friendly behavior. *n. 20.*

so cia ble (sō′shə bəl), 1. liking company. The Smiths are a sociable family and entertain a great deal. 2. marked by conversation and companionship. We had a sociable afternoon together. 3. an informal social gathering. *adj., n. 13.*

so cial (sō′shəl), 1. for companionship or friendliness; pertaining to companionship or friendliness. Ten of us girls have formed a social club. 2. liking company. She has a social nature. 3. connected with fashionable society. Mrs. Walker is the social leader in our town. 4. a social gathering or party. 5. living or liking to live with others. Man is a social being. 6. concerned with human beings as a group. She does social work in a poor section of the city. History and geography are social studies. *adj., n. 3.*

so cial ism (sō′shəl izm), the principle that the interests of the community should prevail over the interests of individuals; any of various plans for greater public control of property, business, and industry. *n. 12.*

so cial ist (sō′shəl ist), 1. person who favors and supports socialism. 2. socialistic. *n., adj. 9.*

so cial is tic (sō′shəl is′tik), 1. pertaining to socialism or socialists. 2. advocating or supporting socialism. *adj. 17.*

so cial ize (sō′shəl īz), 1. make fit for living with others; make social. 2. establish or regulate in accordance with socialism. *v. 20.*

so cial ly (sō′shəl i), 1. in a social way or manner. 2. as a member of society or of a social group. He is an able man, but socially he is a failure. *adv.*

so ci e ty (sə sī′ə ti), 1. company; companionship. I enjoy your society. 2. all the people; the people of any particular time or place; their customs. The good of society demands that wrongdoing be punished. 3. a group of persons united by a common purpose or interest. A club, a fraternity, a lodge, or an association may be called a society. 4. the fashionable class; its doings. She shines in society. *n., pl. societies. 2.*

so ci o log i cal (sō′si ə loj′i kəl), 1. of or pertaining to human society or problems relating to it. The care of the poor is a sociological problem. 2. of sociology. *adj. 16.*

so ci ol o gy (sō′si ol′ə ji), the study of the nature, origin, and development of human society and community life; the science of social facts. Sociology deals with the facts of crime, poverty, marriage, divorce, the church, the school, etc. *n. 20.*

sock (sok), short stocking. *n. 5.*

sock et (sok′it), a hollow part or piece for receiving and holding something. A candlestick has a socket in which to set a candle. Your eyes are set in sockets. *n. 6.*

Soc ra tes (sok′rə tēz), famous Athenian philosopher (469-399 B.C.) whose teachings were written down by his disciple Plato. *n. 10.*

sod (sod), 1. ground covered with grass. 2. piece or layer of this containing the grass and its roots. 3. cover with sods. We must have the bare spots of our lawn sodded. *n., v., sodded, sodding. 5.*

so da (sō′də), 1. a chemical substance that has many uses. Soda is used in the manufacture of soap and glass. Washing soda, or sal soda, is used in cleaning. Baking soda is used in cooking and as a medicine. 2. soda water flavored with fruit juice or syrup. *n. 6.*

so dal i ty (sō dal′i ti), 1. fellowship; friendship. 2. in the Roman Catholic Church, a society with religious or charitable purposes. *n., pl. sodalities.*

soda water, water charged with carbon dioxide to make it bubble and fizz.

sod den (sod′ən), 1. soaked through. His clothing was sodden with rain. 2. heavy and moist. This bread is sodden because it was not baked well. 3. stupid; dull-looking. *adj. 10.*

so di um (sō′di əm), a soft, silver-white metallic element occurring in nature only in compounds. Salt and soda contain sodium. *n. 11.*

Sod om (sod′əm), a wicked city destroyed by fire from heaven. *n. 11.*

so ev er (sō ev′ər), at all; in any case; of any kind; in any way. *Soever* is usually added to words such as *who, what, when,* and *how* to give an indefinite meaning.

I will fight any man howsoever bold he may be. *adv. 7.*

so fa (sō′fə), long, upholstered seat or couch having a back and arms. *n. 5.*

So fi a (sō fē′ə), the capital of Bulgaria. *n.*

soft (sôft), 1. Feathers, cotton, and wool are soft, not hard. 2. Pine wood is softer than oak. Copper and lead are softer than steel. 3. Silk is soft, not rough or coarse. A kitten's fur is soft and pleasant to touch. 4. quietly pleasant; mild; as, a soft spring morning, soft air, soft words, the soft light of candles. 5. gentle; kind; tender; as, soft voice, soft eyes, soft heart. 6. weak. The army had become soft from idleness and luxury. 7. in pronunciation, having a more or less hissing sound. For example: *c* is soft in *city* and hard in *corn; g* is soft in *gentle* and hard in *get.* 8. made with the vocal cords. *B* and *d* are soft, while *p* and *t* are hard. 9. softly; quietly; gently. 10. Some special meanings are:

soft coal, coal that burns with a yellow, smoky flame; bituminous coal.

soft drinks, drinks that do not contain alcohol.

soft water, water that is easy to wash with.

adj., adv. 1.

soft en (sôf′ən), make softer; become softer. *v. 4.*

soft ness (sôft′nis), being soft; ease; comfort; mildness; gentleness; weakness. *n. 9.*

soft wood (sôft′wu̇d′), any wood that is easily cut. Pine is a softwood; oak is a hardwood. *n.*

sog gy (sog′i), 1. soaked; thoroughly wet. 2. damp and heavy; as, soggy bread. *adj., soggier, soggiest. 18.*

soil[1] (soil), ground; earth; dirt; land. Most plants grow best in rich soil. *n. 1.*

soil[2] (soil), 1. make dirty; become dirty. Mary soiled her dress. White gloves soil easily. 2. disgrace. His actions have soiled the family name. 3. spot; stain; soiling. *v., n.*

soi ree or **soi rée** (swä rā′), an evening party. *n. 20.*

so journ (sō′jėrn), 1. stay for a time. The Israelites sojourned in the land of Egypt. 2. brief stay. During his sojourn in Africa the missionary learned much about the native customs. *v., n. 5.*

so journ er (sō′jėr nər), person who stays for a time. *n. 10.*

Sol[1] (sol), the sun. *n. 14.*

sol[2] (sōl), in music, the fifth tone of the scale. Do, re, mi, fa, sol, la, ti, do are the names of the tones of the scale. *n.*

sol ace (sol′is), 1. comfort; relief. She found solace from her troubles in music. 2. to comfort; cheer; relieve. She solaced herself with a book. *n., v. 6.*

so lar (sō′lər), 1. of the sun; as, a solar eclipse. 2. having to do with the sun. The **solar system** is the sun and all the planets, etc., that revolve around it. 3. determined by the sun; as, solar time. 4. The **solar plexus** is a collection of nerves behind the stomach. *adj. 9.*

sold (sōld). See **sell.** He sold his car. *pt. and pp. of sell. 1.*

sol der (sod′ər), 1. metal that can be melted and used for joining or mending. 2. fasten with solder; mend with solder. He soldered four small holes in the kettle. *n., v. 9.*

sol dier (sōl′jər), 1. man who serves in an army. 2. enlisted man in the army, not a commissioned officer. 3. man having skill or experience in war. 4. one who serves in any cause; as, Christian soldiers. 5. act or serve as a soldier. 6. pretend to work but do very little. 7. A **soldier of fortune** is a man ready to serve as a soldier under any government for money, adventure, or pleasure. *n., v. 1.*

sol dier ly (sōl′jər li), like a soldier; like that of a soldier. *adj.*

sol dier y (sōl′jər i), 1. soldiers. 2. military training or knowledge. *n. 13.*

sole[1] (sōl), 1. one and only; single. 2. only. We three were the sole survivors. *adj. 2.*

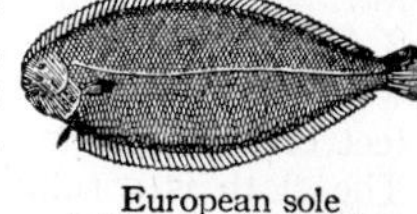
European sole (about 1 ft. long)

sole[2] (sōl), 1. the bottom or under surface of the foot. 2. the bottom of a shoe, slipper, boot, etc. 3. piece cut in the same shape. 4. put a sole on. I must have my shoes soled. *n., v.*

sole[3] (sōl), a kind of flatfish. *n.*

sol e cism (sol′i sizm), 1. a mistake in using words. "I done it" is a solecism. 2. a mistake in social behavior; a breach of good manners or etiquette. *n. 19.*

sole ly (sōl′li), 1. alone. I am solely responsible. 2. only. Bananas grow outdoors solely in the tropics. *adv.*

sol emn (sol′əm), 1. serious; grave; earnest. He gave his solemn promise never to return. That minister speaks in a solemn voice. 2. causing serious or grave thoughts. 3. done with form and ceremony. 4. connected with religion; sacred. *adj. 3.*

so lem ni ty (sə lem′ni ti), 1. solemn feeling; seriousness; impressiveness. The solemnity of the church service was felt even by the children. 2. solemn, formal ceremony. Easter is observed with solemnity. *n., pl. solemnities. 7.*

sol em nize (sol′əm nīz), 1. observe with ceremonies. Christian churches solemnize Easter. 2. hold or perform (a ceremony or service). The marriage was solemnized in the cathedral. 3. make serious or grave. *v. 14.*

so lic it (sə lis′it), ask earnestly; make appeals. The tailor has sent around cards soliciting trade. *v. 5.*

so lic i ta tion (sə lis′i tā′shən), soliciting; urging; earnest request. *n. 10.*

so lic i tor (sə lis′i tər), 1. person who entreats or requests. 2. person who seeks trade or business. 3. lawyer. In England a solicitor prepares a case, and a barrister pleads it. 4. lawyer for a town, city, State, etc. *n. 8.*

so lic i tous (sə lis′i təs), 1. showing care or concern; anxious; concerned. Parents are solicitous for their children's progress. 2. desirous; eager; as, solicitous to please. *adj. 13.*

so lic i tude (sə lis′i tūd or sə lis′i tüd), anxiety; concern; anxious care. *n. 10.*

solid (sol′id), 1. not a liquid or a gas. Iron, wood, and ice are solids. 2. not hollow. A bar of iron is solid; a pipe is hollow. 3. hard; firm; strongly put together. They were glad to leave the boat and put their feet on solid ground. 4. alike throughout. The cloth is a solid blue. 5. sound; real. He studied solid subjects, such as algebra, chemistry, and physics. 6. that can be depended on. He is a solid citizen. 7. firmly united. The country was solid for defending itself. 8. whole; undivided; continuous. He spent a solid hour on his arithmetic. 9. having length, breadth, and thickness. 10. a body that has length, breadth, and thickness. A cube is a solid. *n., adj. 3.*

sol i dar i ty (sol′i dar′i ti), unity or fellowship arising from common responsibilities and interests. *n. 16.*

so lid i fy (sə lid′i fī), make solid; become solid; harden. Extreme cold will solidify water. Jelly solidifies as it gets cold. *v., solidified, solidifying. 13.*

so lid i ty (sə lid′i ti), state or quality of being solid; firmness or hardness; density. *n., pl. solidities. 15.*

so lil o quize (sə lil′ə kwīz), talk to oneself. *v.*

so lil o quy (sə lil′ə kwi), 1. talking to oneself. 2. speech made by an actor to himself when alone on the stage. It reveals his thoughts and feelings to the audience, but not to the other characters in the play. *n., pl. soliloquies. 16.*

sol i taire (sol′i tãr), 1. a game of cards played by one person. 2. a diamond set by itself. *n. 19.*

sol i tar y (sol′i tãr′i), 1. alone; single; only. A solitary rider was seen in the distance. 2. without companions; lonely; away from people. He leads a solitary life in his hut in the mountains. The house is in a solitary spot miles from a town. *adj. 4.*

sol i tude (sol′i tūd or sol′i tüd), 1. being alone. He likes company and hates solitude. 2. lonely place. *n. 4.*

so lo (sō′lō), piece of music for one voice or instrument. *n., pl. solos. 18.*

so lo ist (sō′lō ist), person who sings or plays a solo. *n.*

Sol o mon (sol′ə mən), a king of Israel, who was a son of David. Solomon built a great temple in Jerusalem. He was famous for his wisdom. *n. 5.*

So lon (sō′lon), 1. wise Athenian lawgiver (638?-558? B.C.). 2. a wise man; a sage. *n. 15.*

sol stice (sol′stis), either of the two times in the year when the sun is at its greatest distance from the equator. June 21 or 22, the summer solstice, is the longest day of the year; December 21 or 22, the winter solstice, is the shortest. *n. 15.*

sol u bil i ty (sol′ū bil′i ti), 1. the quality that some substances have of dissolving or being dissolved easily. Anyone can see the great solubility of sugar in water. 2. the quality that problems, difficulties, questions, etc., have of being solved or explained. *n., pl. solubilities.*

sol u ble (sol′ū bəl), 1. that can be dissolved. Salt is soluble in water. 2. that can be solved; as, soluble puzzles. *adj 8.*

so lu tion (sə lü′shən), 1. solving a problem. That problem was hard; its solution required many hours. 2. explanation. The police are seeking a solution of the crime. 3. separating into parts; dissolving; changing a solid or gas to a liquid by treatment with a liquid. 4. being dissolved. Sugar and salt can be held in solution in water.

5. a liquid or mixture formed by dissolving. *n. 5.*

solve (solv), clear up; explain; find the answer to. The detective solved the mystery. He has solved all the problems in the lesson. *v. 3.*

sol ven cy (sol′vən si), ability to pay all one owes. *n.*

sol vent (sol′vənt), 1. able to pay all one owes. That firm is solvent. 2. able to dissolve. Gasoline is a solvent liquid that removes grease spots. 3. a substance, usually a liquid, that can dissolve other substances. Water is a solvent of sugar and salt. *adj., n. 13.*

So ma li land (sō mä′li land′), region in eastern Africa divided into British, French, and Italian colonies. *n.*

som ber or **som bre** (som′bər), 1. dark; gloomy. It was a somber room with dark furniture and heavy black hangings. A cloudy winter day is somber. 2. melancholy; dismal. His losses made him very somber. *adj. 7.*

som brer o (som brãr′ō), a broad-brimmed hat worn in the southwestern United States, Mexico, and Spain. *n., pl. sombreros.*

Sombrero

some (sum), 1. a; any. Ask some girl to come here. 2. a number of. Ask some boys to help you. 3. a quantity of. Drink some milk. 4. particular, but not known or named. Some dogs are large; some are small. 5. about. Some twenty men asked for work. 6. a certain number or quantity. Jack ate some, and threw the rest away. *adj., pron. 1.*

-some[1], suffix meaning:—
1. tending to; as in frolicsome, meddlesome.
2. causing; as in awesome, troublesome.
3. to a considerable degree; as in lonesome.

-some[2], suffix meaning:—group of; as in twosome, foursome.

some bod y (sum′bod i), 1. person not known or named; some person. Somebody has taken my pen. 2. person of importance. She acts as if she were somebody since she won the prize. *pron., n., pl. somebodies. 3.*

some how (sum′hou), in a way not known or not stated; in one way or another. I'll finish this work somehow. *adv. 8.*

some one (sum′wun), some person; somebody. Someone has to lock up the house. *pron. 3.*

som er sault (sum′ər sôlt), turn heels over head. *n., v. 13.*

Som er set[1] (sum′ər set), a county in southwestern England. *n. 13.*

som er set[2] (sum′ər set), somersault. *n., v.*

Som er ville (sum′ər vil), city in eastern Massachusetts, near Boston. *n.*

some thing (sum′thing), 1. some thing; a particular thing not named or known. I'm sure I've forgotten something. 2. a part; a certain amount; a little. 3. somewhat; to some extent. 4. thing of importance. *n., adv. 1.*

some time (sum′tīm), 1. at one time or another. Come to see us sometime. 2. former. Alice Brown, a sometime pupil of our school, is now a teacher there. *adv., adj. 1.*

some times (sum′tīmz), now and then; at times. *adv.*

some what (sum′hwot), 1. in some degree; slightly. My hat is somewhat like yours. 2. some part; some amount. A joke loses somewhat of its fun when you hear it the second time. *adv., n. 2.*

some where (sum′hwãr), 1. in some place; in one place or another. John is somewhere about the house. 2. at some time. It happened somewhere in the last century. *adv. 3.*

some while (sum′hwīl), 1. at times. 2. sometime. 3. formerly. *adv.*

som no lent (som′nə lənt), sleepy; drowsy. *adj.*

son (sun), 1. A boy is the son of his father and mother. 2. male descendant. 3. a boy or man attached to a country, cause, etc., as a child is to its parents; as, sons of America, sons of liberty. 4. **The Son** is a name for Jesus. *n. 1.*

so na ta (sə nä′tə), piece of music, usually for the piano, having three or four movements in contrasted rhythms but related keys. *n. 18.*

song (sông), 1. something to sing; a short poem set to music. 2. singing. The canary burst into song. 3. poetry that has a musical sound. 4. **For a song** sometimes means very cheap. *n. 1.*

song bird (sông′bėrd′), bird that sings. *n.*

song ster (sông′stər), 1. singer. 2. writer of songs or poems. 3. songbird. *n. 10.*

song stress (sông′stris), 1. female singer. 2. poetess. 3. female songbird. *n.*

son-in-law (sun′in lô′), the husband of one's daughter. *n., pl. sons-in-law. 20.*

son net (son′it), a poem having fourteen lines with a fixed measure and a formal arrangement of rhymes. *n. 7.*

son ny (sun′i), little son. *Sonny* is used as a pet name, or as a way of speaking to a little boy. *n. 17.*

so no rous (sə nō′rəs), 1. giving out a deep, loud sound. 2. full and rich in sound. *adj. 10.*

soon (sün), 1. in a short time; before long. 2. early. Why have you come so soon? 3. promptly; quickly. As soon as I hear, I will let you know. 4. readily; willingly. The brave soldier would sooner die than yield. *adv. 1.*

soot (sůt), black substance in the smoke from burning coal, wood, oil, etc. Soot makes smoke dark and collects on the inside of chimneys. *n. 9.*

sooth (süth), truth. He speaks sooth. Are you in sooth Lancelot? *n.* [*Old use*] *6.*

soothe (süᴛʜ), 1. quiet; calm; comfort. The mother soothed the crying child. 2. make less painful. *v. 5.*

sooth say er (süth′sā′ər), person who claims to tell what will happen. *n. 12.*

soot y (sůt′i), covered with soot; black with soot; black. *adj.*

sop (sop), 1. piece of food dipped or soaked in milk, broth, etc. 2. something given to soothe or quiet. 3. dip or soak; as, to sop bread in milk. 4. take up (water, etc.). Please sop up that water with a cloth. 5. **Sopping wet** means thoroughly wet, or drenched. *n., v., sopped, sopping. 11.*

soph ist (sof′ist), a clever but misleading reasoner. *n. 15.*

so phis ti cat ed (sə fis′ti kāt′id), experienced in worldly ways; changed from natural simplicity; artificial. *adj. 12.*

so phis ti ca tion (sə fis′ti kā′shən), lessening or loss of naturalness, simplicity, or frankness; worldly experience or ideas; artificial ways. *n. 15.*

soph ist ry (sof′is tri), 1. unsound reasoning. 2. a clever but misleading argument. *n., pl. sophistries. 15.*

Soph o cles (sof′ə klēz), a famous Greek tragic poet (495?-406? B.C.). *n. 15.*

soph o more (sof′ə mōr), student in the second year of a high-school or college course. *n. 19.*

soph o mor ic (sof′ə mor′ik), 1. of a sophomore. 2. crude but complacent; satisfied with oneself though ignorant. *adj.*

sop py (sop′i), soaked; very wet; rainy; as, soppy ground, soppy weather. *adj.*

so pran o (sə pran′ō), 1. the highest singing voice in women and boys. 2. part to be sung by such a voice. 3. singer with such a voice. 4. of, for, or pertaining to the soprano. *n., pl. sopranos, adj. 14.*

sor cer er (sôr′sər ər), magician; person who practices magic with the aid of evil spirits. *n. 8.*

sor cer ess (sôr′sər is), woman who practices magic with the aid of evil spirits; witch. *n. 13.*

sor cer y (sôr′sər i), magic by the aid of evil spirits; witchcraft. The prince had been changed into a lion by sorcery. *n., pl. sorceries. 8.*

sor did (sôr′did), 1. dirty; filthy. The poor family lived in a sordid hut. 2. mean; low; base; caring too much for money; meanly selfish. *adj. 8.*

sore (sōr), 1. painful. The suffering of the poor makes her heart sore. 2. causing pain; causing great pain; severe. Mary has a bad cold and a sore throat. 3. causing sorrow. Their defeat is a sore subject with the members of the team. 4. hurt; offended. He is sore at missing the game. 5. painful place on the body where the skin or flesh is broken or bruised. 6. a hurt to the feelings. *adj., n. 2.*

sor ghum (sôr′gəm), 1. a kind of molasses or thick syrup. 2. a tall plant grown for its sweet juice. Other kinds of sorghum are grown for fodder or grain, and for making brooms or brushes. *n. 19.*

Sorghum

so ror i ty (sə ror′i ti), 1. sisterhood. 2. a club or society of women or girls. *n., pl. sororities.*

sor rel[1] (sor′əl), 1. reddish brown; as, a sorrel horse. 2. horse having this color. *adj., n. 15.*

sor rel[2] (sor′əl), a plant with sour leaves. *n.*

sor row (sor′ō), 1. grief; sadness; regret. Mary felt sorrow at the loss of her kitten. She expressed sorrow at her mistake. 2. cause of grief; trouble. Her sorrows have aged her. 3. be sad; feel sorry; feel or show grief, sadness, or regret. She sorrowed over the lost money. *n., v. 2.*

sor row ful (sor′ō fəl), sad; full of sorrow; feeling sorrow; causing sorrow. A funeral is a sorrowful occasion. *adj. 5.*

sor row ful ly (sor′ō fəl i), with sorrow; sadly. *adv.*

sor ry (sor′i), 1. I am sorry that you are sick. We are sorry that we cannot come to the party. Everyone is sorry for a blind man. 2. wretched; poor; pitiful. The blind beggar in his ragged clothes was a sorry sight. *adj., sorrier, sorriest. 2.*

sort (sôrt), 1. kind; class. What sort of work does he do? I like this sort of candy best. 2. arrange by kinds or classes; arrange in order. Sort these cards according to their colors. 3. put; separate from others. The farmer sorted out the best apples for eating. 4. **Out of sorts** means uncomfortable, ill, or cross. *n., v. 1.*

sor tie (sôr′ti), sudden rushing forth of troops from a besieged castle, fort, town, etc., to attack the besiegers. *n. 19.*

S O S (es′ō′es′), call for help.

so-so (sō′sō′), neither very good nor very bad; fairly good. *adj., adv.*

sot (sot), drunkard; person whose mind has been dulled by drinking too much alcohol. *n. 14.*

sot tish (sot′ish), 1. drunken; stupid and foolish from drinking too much alcohol. 2. of a sot; like a sot. *adj. 15.*

sou (sü), a former French coin worth 5 centimes, or $\frac{1}{20}$ of a franc. *n.*

sou bri quet (sü′bri kā), sobriquet. *n.*

sough (suf), 1. make a rustling or murmuring sound. The pines soughed when the wind blew. 2. such a sound. *v., n.*

sought (sôt). See **seek.** For days he sought a safe hiding place. *pt. and pp. of seek. 2.*

soul (sōl), 1. the part of the human being that thinks, feels, and makes the body act; the spiritual part of man. Death separates soul and body. Christians believe that the soul lives forever. 2. energy of mind or feelings; spirit. She puts her whole soul into her work. 3. cause of inspiration and energy. Florence Nightingale was the soul of the movement to reform nursing. 4. person. Don't tell a soul. *n. 1.*

soul ful (sōl′fəl), 1. full of feeling; deeply emotional. 2. expressing or suggesting deep feeling. *adj.*

soul less (sōl′lis), having no soul; without spirit or noble feelings. *adj. 19.*

sound[1] (sound), 1. what can be heard; as, the sound of music, the sound of thunder. 2. make a sound or noise. The trumpet sounds for battle. The wind sounds like an animal howling. 3. cause to sound. 4. utter; call. 5. make known. The trumpets sounded the call to battle. 6. seem. That excuse sounds queer. 7. **Within sound of** means near enough to hear. *n., v. 1.*

sound[2] (sound), 1. healthy; free from disease; as, a sound body, a sound mind. 2. free from injury, decay, or defect; as, sound walls, a sound ship, sound fruit. 3. strong; safe; secure; as, a sound business firm. 4. correct; right; reasonable; reliable; as, sound advice, sound religious teaching. 5. thorough; hearty; as, a sound whipping, a sound sleep. 6. deeply; thoroughly. *adj., adv.*

sound[3] (sound), 1. measure the depth of (water) by letting down a weight fastened on the end of a line. 2. examine or test by a line arranged to bring up a sample. 3. try to find out the views of; test; examine. 4. go toward the bottom; dive. The whale sounded. *v.*

sound[4] (sound), 1. long, narrow strip of water joining two larger bodies of water; as, Long Island Sound. 2. an inlet or arm of the sea; as, Puget Sound. *n.*

sound er[1] (soun′dər), 1. person or thing that makes a sound. 2. a receiving instrument by whose sounds a telegraph message is read. *n. 13.*

sound er[2] (soun′dər), person or thing that measures the depth of water. *n.*

sound ing (soun′ding), 1. measuring the depth of water with a weight on the end of a line. 2. the depth of water learned by this means. **Soundings** often means water not more than 600 feet deep. *n.*

sound less[1] (sound′lis), without sound; making no sound; still. *adj.*

sound less[2] (sound′lis), so deep that the bottom cannot be reached. *adj.*

sound ly (sound′li), 1. in a sound manner; without weakness or defect. 2. with unbroken, deep sleep. 3. vigorously; heartily; thoroughly. 4. with good judgment. *adv.*

sound ness (sound′nis), 1. good health; as, soundness of body and mind. 2. freedom from weakness or defect. 3. good judgment; correctness and reliability. We have confidence in the doctor's soundness. *n. 12.*

soup (süp), liquid food made by boiling meat, vegetables, fish, etc. *n. 3.*

sour (sour), 1. having a taste like vinegar or lemon juice. Green fruit is sour. 2. fermented; spoiled. Sour milk is healthful, but most foods are not good to eat when they have become sour. 3. disagreeable; bad-tempered; peevish; as, a sour face, a sour remark. 4. become sour; make sour; turn sour. 5. make or become peevish, bad-tempered, or disagreeable. 6. in a sour manner. *adj., adv., v. 4.*

source (sōrs), 1. fountain; spring; beginning of a brook or river. 2. place from which anything comes or is obtained. A newspaper gets news from many sources. Mines are the chief source of diamonds. *n. 3.*

souse (sous), 1. plunge into liquid; throw liquid over; soak in a liquid. 2. plunging into a liquid; drenching. 3. soak in vinegar, brine, etc. 4. something soaked or kept in pickle, especially the head, ears, and feet of a pig. 5. liquid used for pickling. *v., n. 16.*

south (south), 1. the direction to your right as you face the rising sun; away from the North Pole. 2. toward the south; farther toward the south. Drive south forty miles. 3. **South of** means farther south than. New York is south of Boston. 4. from the south; as, a south wind. 5. in the south; living in the south. 6. the part of any country toward the south. In the United States, **the South** means the States south of Pennsylvania and the Ohio River. *n., adj., adv. 1.*

NORTH
WEST EAST
SOUTH

South Africa. The Union of South Africa is a British dominion in southern Africa.

South America, the continent of the western world southeast of North America.

South amp ton (south amp′tən), seaport in southern England. *n. 17.*

South Bend, a city in northern Indiana.

South Carolina, a Southern State of the United States.

South Da ko ta (south′ də kō′tə), a Middle Western State of the United States.

south east (south′ēst′), 1. halfway between south and east. 2. a southeast direction. 3. place that is in the southeast part or direction. 4. toward the southeast. 5. from the southeast; as, a southeast wind. *adj., n., adv. 7.*

south east er (south′ēs′tər), a wind or storm from the southeast. *n.*

south east er ly (south′ēs′tər li), 1. toward the southeast. 2. from the southeast. *adj., adv.*

south east ern (south′ēs′tərn), 1. toward the southeast. 2. from the southeast. 3. of the southeast. *adj. 9.*

south er ly (suтн′ər li), 1. toward the south. The windows face southerly. 2. from the south. 3. of the south. *adj., adv. 20.*

south ern (suтн′ərn), 1. toward the south; as, the southern side of a building. 2. from the south; as, a southern breeze. 3. of the south. He has traveled in southern countries. 4. of the South of the United States; as, a Southern city. *adj. 2.*

South ern er (suтн′ər nər), person born or living in one of the Southern States. *n.*

Southern Hemisphere, the half of the world that is south of the equator.

south ern most (suтн′ərn mōst), farthest south. *adj.*

South Pole, southern end of the earth's axis. It was first reached in 1911 by Amundsen.

South Sea Islands, islands in the South Pacific.

south ward (south′wərd), toward the south; south. He walked southward. The orchard is on the southward slope of the hill. **To the southward** means south. *adv., adj., n. 5.*

south wards (south′wərdz), southward. *adv.*

south west (south′west′), 1. halfway between south and west. 2. a southwest direction. 3. place that is in the southwest part or direction. 4. toward the southwest. 5. from the southwest; as, a southwest wind. *adj., n., adv. 5.*

south west er (south′wes′tər), 1. wind or storm from the southwest. 2. a waterproof hat having a broad brim behind to protect the neck, worn especially by seamen. *n.*

Southwester

south west er ly (south′wes′tər li), 1. toward the southwest. 2. from the southwest. *adj., adv.*

south west ern (south′wes′tərn), 1. toward the southwest. 2. from the southwest. 3. of the southwest. *adj. 9.*

sou ve nir (sü′və nēr′), something given or kept for remembrance; a remembrance. *n. 17.*

sou′ west er (sou′wes′tər), southwester. *n. 20.*

sov er eign (sov′rin), 1. above all others; supreme; greatest. Character is of sovereign importance. 2. greatest in rank or power. 3. supreme ruler; king; queen; monarch. King George VI is the sovereign of England. 4. independent of the control of other governments. 5. a British gold coin worth 20 shillings, or one pound. *adj., n. 4.*

sov er eign ty (sov′rin ti), supreme power or authority. State sovereignty was the doctrine that each State was superior to and independent of the United States in power over its own territory. *n., pl. sovereignties. 7.*

so vi et (sō′vi et), 1. a Russian word meaning council or assembly. 2. any of the councils or assemblies which have been parts of the government of Russia since 1917. 3. of or pertaining to soviets. 4. communistic; socialistic. *n., adj. 19.*

Soviet Russia, largest republic in the Union of Soviet Socialist Republics, approximately the same size as the former empire of Russia.

Soviet Union, Union of Soviet Socialist Republics.

sov ran (sov′rən), sovereign. *adj., n.* [*Used in poetry*] *19.*

sow[1] (sō), 1. scatter (seed) on the ground; plant (seed); plant seed in. He sows more wheat than oats. The farmer sowed the field with oats. 2. scatter (anything); spread abroad. *v., sowed, sown* or *sowed, sowing. 2.*

sow[2] (sou), fully grown female pig. *n.*

sown (sōn). See **sow**[1]. *a pp. of sow*[1].

soy (soi), 1. a Chinese and Japanese sauce for fish made from soybeans. 2. soybean. *n. 19.*

soy bean (soi′bēn′), 1. a bean widely grown in China, Japan, and the United States. Soybeans are used in making an oil and as cattle food. 2. the plant it grows on. *n.*

spa (spä), 1. a mineral spring. 2. place where there is a mineral spring. *n. 19.*

space (spās), 1. unlimited room or place extending in all directions. Our earth moves through space. 2. limited place or room. This brick will fill a space 2½ by 4 by 8 inches. Is there space in the car for another person? 3. distance. The road is bad for a space of two miles. The trees are set at equal spaces apart. 4. length of time. He has not seen his brother for the space of ten years. Many changes occur within the space of one man's life. 5. fix the space of; separate by spaces; divide into spaces. Space your words evenly when you write. *n., v. 1.*

spa cious (spā′shəs), containing much space; with plenty of room; vast. The rooms of the palace were spacious. *adj. 5.*

spade (spād), 1. a tool for digging; a kind of shovel. 2. dig with a spade. Spade up the garden. *n., v. 3.*

Spade

spa ghet ti (spə get′i), the same mixture of flour and water as macaroni, but made up in long, slender, solid sticks. *n.*

Spain (spān), a country in southwestern Europe. *n. 2.*

spake (spāk), spoke. *old pt. of* **speak.** *3.*

span[1] (span), 1. the distance between the tip of a man's thumb and the tip of his little finger when the hand is spread out; 9 inches. 2. measure by the hand spread out. This post can be spanned by one's two hands. 3. short space of time. His span of life is nearly over. 4. part between two supports. The bridge crossed the river in a single span. 5. extend over. A bridge spanned the railroad tracks. *n., v., spanned, spanning. 5.*

span[2] (span), pair of horses or other animals harnessed and driven together. *n.*

span gle (spang′gəl), 1. small piece of glittering metal used for decoration. The dress was covered with spangles. 2. any small bright bit. This rock shows spangles of gold. 3. decorate with spangles. The dress was spangled with gold. 4. sprinkle with small bright bits. The sky is spangled with stars. *n., v. 5.*

Span iard (span′yərd), person living in Spain, born there, or having Spanish parents. *n. 4.*

Cocker spaniel

span iel (span′yəl), a dog of small or medium size with long, silky hair and drooping ears. Spaniels are very gentle and affectionate. A person who yields too much to others is sometimes called a spaniel. *n. 10.*

Irish water spaniel

Span ish (span′ish), 1. of Spain; pertaining to Spain, its people, or their language. 2. the people of Spain. 3. the language of Spain. *adj., n. 2.*

Spanish America, countries and islands south and southeast of the United States, in which the principal language is Spanish.

Spanish-American War, war between Spain and the United States in 1898 over Spain's rule of Cuba.

Spanish Main, 1. the northwestern coast of South America. 2. the Caribbean Sea, a sea near Central America.

spank (spangk), 1. strike with the open

hand, a slipper, etc. The nurse spanked the naughty child. 2. a slap. *v., n. 5.*

spank ing (spangk′ing), 1. blowing briskly; as, a spanking breeze. 2. quick and vigorous. 3. unusually fine, great, large, etc.; as, a spanking team of horses. *adj.* [*Used in common talk*]

spar[1] (spär), 1. stout pole used to support or extend the sails of a ship; mast, yard, gaff, boom, etc., of a ship. 2. provide (a ship) with spars. *n., v., sparred, sparring. 14.*

spar[2] (spär), 1. make motions of attack and defense with the arms and fists; to box. 2. a boxing match. 3. dispute. *v., sparred, sparring, n.*

spar[3] (spär), a shiny mineral that splits into flakes easily. *n.*

spare (spãr), 1. use in small quantities or not at all; be saving of. "Spare the rod and spoil the child." 2. small in quantity. Fat people should live on a spare diet. 3. do without; omit; get along without. Father couldn't spare the car; so John had to walk. 4. show mercy to. He spared his enemy. Her cruel tongue spares nobody. 5. extra; in reserve; as, a spare tire. 6. thin; lean. Lincoln was a tall, spare man. *v., adj. 2.*

spare rib (spãr′rib′), rib of pork having less meat than those near the loins. *n.*

spar ing (spãr′ing), economical; frugal; as, a sparing use of sugar. *adj. 17.*

spar ing ly (spãr′ing li), economically; frugally. *adv. 17.*

spark[1] (spärk), 1. small bit of fire. Burning wood throws off sparks. 2. flash given off when electricity jumps across an open space. An electric spark explodes the gas in the engine of an automobile. 3. flash; gleam. 4. small amount. I haven't a spark of interest in the plan. The doctor tried to keep a spark of life alive in the sick child. 5. glittering bit. 6. send out small bits of fire; produce sparks. *n., v. 3.*

spark[2] (spärk), 1. a gay and showy young man. 2. beau; lover. *n.*

spar kle (spär′kəl), 1. send out little sparks. The fireworks sparkled. 2. little spark. 3. shine; glitter; flash. Diamonds sparkle. A sparkling drink bubbles. I like the sparkle of her eyes. He has a sparkling wit. *v., n. 3.*

spark plug, a device in the cylinder of a gasoline engine by which the mixture of gasoline and air is exploded by an electric spark.

spar row (spar′ō), a small, brownish-gray bird. English sparrows have driven away many of our native American birds. *n. 3.*

sparrow hawk, a small hawk which feeds on sparrows and other small animals.

English sparrow (about 6 in. long)

sparse (spärs), thinly scattered; occurring here and there; as, a sparse population, sparse hair. *adj. 10.*

Spar ta (spär′tə), one of the most important cities in ancient Greece, famous for its soldiers. *n. 9.*

Spar tan (spär′tən), 1. of Sparta or its people. 2. native or inhabitant of Sparta. The Spartans were noted for their simplicity of life, severity, courage, and brevity of speech. 3. like the Spartans; simple, frugal, severe, sternly disciplined, brave, brief, and concise. 4. person who is like the Spartans. *adj., n.*

spasm (spazm), 1. a sudden, abnormal, involuntary contraction of a muscle or muscles. The child in a spasm kept twitching his arms and legs. 2. any sudden, brief fit or spell of unusual energy or activity; as, a spasm of temper, a spasm of industry. *n. 10.*

spas mod ic (spaz mod′ik), 1. pertaining to spasms; resembling a spasm; as, a spasmodic cough. 2. sudden and violent, but brief; occurring very irregularly. *adj. 16.*

spas mod i cal ly (spaz mod′i kəl i), in a spasmodic manner; by fits and starts. *adv.*

spat[1] (spat), 1. slight quarrel. 2. quarrel slightly. 3. light blow; slap. 4. slap lightly. *n., v., spatted, spatting. 9.*

spat[2] (spat). See **spit**[1]. The cat spat at the dog. *pt. and pp. of spit*[1].

spat[3] (spat), a short gaiter covering the ankle. *n.*

Spats

spat[4] (spat), 1. the spawn of oysters; young oyster. 2. of oysters, to spawn. *n., v., spatted, spatting.*

spa tial (spā′shəl), 1. of or pertaining to space. 2. existing in space. *adj.*

spat ter (spat′ər), 1. scatter or dash in drops; as, to spatter mud. 2. fall in drops. Rain spatters on the sidewalk. 3. strike in a shower. Bullets spattered the wall. 4. spattering; as, a spatter of bullets. 5. sound of spattering. 6. splash or spot with mud, slander, disgrace, etc. 7. splash or spot. *v., n. 10.*

spat u la (spach′ů lə), tool with a broad, flat, flexible blade, used for mixing drugs, spreading plasters and paints, etc. *n.*

Spatulas. A, cake knife, B, palette knife.

spav in (spav′in), a disease of horses in which a bony swelling forms at the hock, causing lameness. *n. 14.*

spawn (spôn), 1. the eggs of fish, frogs, shellfish, etc.; the young newly hatched. 2. produce eggs. 3. bring forth; give birth to. 4. offspring; a swarming brood. *n., v. 7.*

speak (spēk), 1. say words; talk. A cat cannot speak. Speak distinctly. 2. make a speech. John spoke for the group that wanted a picnic. 3. say; tell; express; make known. Speak the truth. 4. use (a language). Do you speak French? 5. **Speak out** or **speak up** means speak loudly, clearly, or freely. 6. **So to speak** means to speak in such a manner. 7. make sounds. The cannon spoke. *v., spoke, spoken, speaking. 1.*

speak er (spēk′ər), 1. person who speaks. 2. the presiding officer. *n. 3.*

spear[1] (spēr), 1. weapon with a long shaft and a sharp-pointed head. 2. pierce with a spear. The Indians speared the fish. *n., v. 3.*

spear[2] (spēr), a sprout or shoot of a plant; as, a spear of grass. *n.*

spear man (spēr′mən), man armed with a spear. *n., pl. spearmen. 19.*

spear mint (spēr′mint′), common mint, a fragrant herb much used for flavoring. *n.*

Spear

spe cial (spesh′əl), 1. of a particular kind; distinct from others; not general. This desk has a special lock. Have you any special color in mind for your new coat? 2. for a particular person, thing, purpose, etc. The railroad ran special trains on holidays. Send the letter by a special messenger. 3. unusual; exceptional; more than ordinary. Today's topic is of special interest. 4. special train, car, bus, etc. *adj., n. 2.*

spe cial ist (spesh′əl ist), person who devotes himself to one particular branch of study, business, etc. Dr. White is a specialist in diseases of the nose and throat. *n. 10.*

spe cial i za tion (spesh′əl i zā′shən), 1. specializing. 2. being specialized. *n. 14.*

spe cial ize (spesh′əl īz), 1. pursue some special branch of study, work, etc. Many college students specialize in English. 2. adapt to special conditions; develop in a special way. Animals and plants are specialized to fit their surroundings. *v. 8.*

spe cial ly (spesh′əl i), in a special manner or degree; particularly; unusually. *adv. 6.*

spe cial ty (spesh′əl ti), 1. special study; special line of work, profession, trade, etc. American history is Professor Wood's specialty. 2. thing to which special attention is given. This store makes a specialty of children's clothes. 3. special character; special quality. 4. a special or particular characteristic; a peculiarity. 5. a special point or item; a particular; a detail. *n., pl. specialties. 12.*

spe cie (spē′shi), money in the form of coins. Silver dollars are specie. *n. 20.*

spe cies (spē′shiz), group of animals or plants that have certain permanent characteristics in common; distinct sort or kind. All kinds of apples belong to the same species. Wheat is a species of grass. *n., pl. species. 7.*

spe cif ic (spi sif′ik), 1. definite; precise; particular. There was no specific reason for the quarrel. 2. characteristic (of); peculiar (to). A scaly skin is a specific feature of snakes. 3. produced by some special cause. 4. a cure for some particular disease. Quinine is a specific for malaria. 5. of or pertaining to a species. *adj., n. 7.*

spe cif i cal ly (spi sif′i kəl i), in a specific manner; definitely; particularly. The doctor told Kate specifically not to eat eggs. *adv. 13.*

spec i fi ca tion (spes′i fi kā′shən), 1. act of specifying; definite mention; detailed statement of particulars. Mary made careful specification as to the kinds of cake and candy for her party. 2. a detailed description of the dimensions, materials, etc., for a building, road, dam, sewer, etc. 3. something specified; a particular item, article, etc. *n. 12.*

specific gravity, the ratio of the weight of a given volume of any substance to that of the same volume of some other substance taken as a standard, water being used for solids and liquids, and hydrogen or air for gases.

spec i fy (spes′i fī), mention or name definitely. Did you specify any particular time for us to call? *v., specified, specifying. 12.*

spec i men (spes′i mən), part taken to show the kind or quality of the whole; sample. Arthur collects specimens of all kinds of rocks and minerals. *n. 6.*

spe cious (spē′shəs), making a good appearance; seeming desirable, reasonable, or probable, but not really so; apparently good or right, but without real merit. The teacher saw through John's specious excuse. *adj. 11.*

speck (spek), 1. small spot; stain. Can you clean the specks off this wallpaper? 2. tiny bit. I have a speck in my eye. 3. mark with specks. This fruit is badly specked. *n., v. 6.*

speck le (spek′əl), 1. small spot or mark. This hen is gray with white speckles. 2. mark with speckles. The boy is speckled with freckles. *n., v. 5.*

spec ta cle (spek′tə kəl), 1. thing to look at; sight. The children at play among the flowers made a charming spectacle. A quarrel is an unpleasant spectacle. 2. public show or display. A big army parade is a fine spectacle. *n. 4.*

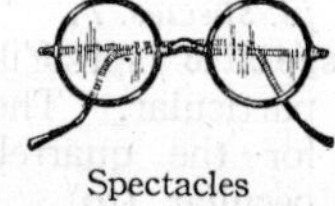
Spectacles

spec ta cles (spek′tə kəlz), pair of glasses to help a person's sight or to protect his eyes. *n. pl.*

spec tac u lar (spek tak′ū lər), 1. making a great display. Moving pictures present spectacular scenes like battles, processions, storms, or races. 2. pertaining to a spectacle or show. *adj. 12.*

spec ta tor (spek′tā tər), person who looks on. There were many spectators at the game. *n. 7.*

spec ter or **spec tre** (spek′tər), ghost. *n. 7.*

spec tral (spek′trəl), of or like a specter; ghostly. He saw the spectral form of the headless horseman. *adj. 11.*

spec tro scope (spek′trə skōp), an instrument for obtaining and examining the spectrum of a ray from any source. *n. 17.*

spec trum (spek′trəm), the band of colors formed when a beam of light is broken up by being passed through a prism or by some other means. A rainbow has all the colors of the spectrum: red, orange, yellow, green, blue, indigo, and violet. *n. 12.*

spec u late (spek′ū lāt), 1. reflect; meditate; consider; conjecture. The philosopher speculated about time and space. 2. buy or sell when there is a large risk. *v. 11.*

spec u la tion (spek′ū lā′shən), 1. thought; reflection; conjecture. Former speculations about electricity were often mere guesses. 2. buying or selling at a large risk. His speculations in stocks made him poor. *n. 8.*

spec u la tive (spek′ū lā′tiv), 1. thoughtful; reflective. 2. theoretical rather than practical. 3. of or involving buying or selling at a large risk. *adj. 8.*

spec u la tor (spek′ū lā′tər), person who speculates, usually in business. A ticket speculator buys tickets for shows, games, etc., in advance, hoping to sell them later at a higher price. *n. 17.*

sped (sped). See **speed.** The dog sped away. *pt. and pp. of speed. 5.*

speech (spēch), 1. act of speaking; talk. 2. power of speaking. Animals lack speech. 3. manner of speaking. His speech showed that he was Southern. 4. what is said; the words spoken. We made the usual farewell speeches. 5. a public talk. The President gave an excellent speech. 6. language. *n. 2.*

speech less (spēch′lis), 1. not able to speak. Animals are speechless. George was speechless with anger. 2. silent. Her frown gave a speechless message. *adj. 8.*

speed (spēd), 1. swift or rapid movement. 2. go fast. He was arrested for speeding. 3. make go fast. Speed up the work. 4. rate of movement. The boys ran at full speed. 5. success; good luck. *Old use.* 6. succeed. *Old use.* 7. give success to. God speed you. *Old use.* *n., v., sped* or *speeded, speeding. 2.*

speed er (spēd′ər), person or thing that speeds; especially, a person who drives an automobile at a higher speed than is legal or safe. *n.*

speed i ly (spēd′i li), quickly; with speed; soon. *adv. 17.*

speed om e ter (spēd om′i tər), an instrument to indicate speed. Automobiles have speedometers. *n. 18.*

speed way (spēd′wā′), a road or track for fast driving. *n. 20.*

speed well (spēd′wel), a plant with blue flowers. *n. 14.*

speed y (spēd′i), fast; rapid; quick; swift. *adj., speedier, speediest. 4.*

spell[1] (spel), 1. write or say the letters of (a word) in order. We learn to spell in school. 2. mean. Delay spells danger. *v., spelled* or *spelt, spelling. 2.*

spell[2] (spel), 1. word or words having magic power. 2. fascination; charm. *n.*

spell[3] (spel), 1. period of work or duty. The sailor's spell at the wheel was four hours. 2. a period or time of anything. The child has spells of coughing. 3. work in place of (another person) for a while. I'll spell you at turning the ice-cream freezer. 4. relief of one person by another in doing something. *n., v., spelled, spelling.*

spell bound (spel′bound′), too interested to move; fascinated; enchanted. *adj. 19.*

spell er (spel′ər), 1. person who spells words. 2. book for teaching spelling. *n.*

spell ing (spel′ing), 1. writing or saying the letters of a word in order. John is poor at spelling. 2. the way in which a word is spelled. Ax has two spellings. *n.*

spelling bee, spelling contest.

spelt[1] (spelt), spelled. *pt. and pp. of* **spell**[1]. *17.*

spelt[2] (spelt), a kind of wheat. *n.*

spend (spend), 1. pay out. She spent ten dollars today. 2. pay out money. 3. use; use up. Don't spend any more time on that lesson. The storm has spent its force. *v., spent, spending. 1.*

spend thrift (spend′thrift′), 1. person who wastes money. 2. extravagant with money; wasteful. *n., adj.*

spent (spent), 1. tired; used up; as, a spent swimmer, a spent horse. 2. See **spend.** Saturday was spent in playing. *adj., pt. and pp. of spend. 2.*

sperm (spėrm), 1. the fluid of a male animal that fertilizes the eggs of the female. 2. one of the male germ cells which are in it. *n. 9.*

sperm whale, a large, square-headed whale, valuable for its oil. See the picture.

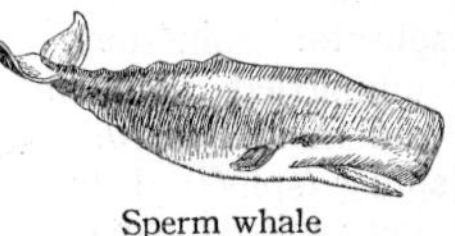
Sperm whale (about 60 ft. long)

spew (spū), vomit; throw out; cast forth. *v.*

sphere (sfēr), 1. round body whose surface is at all points equally distant from the center. 2. ball; globe. The sun, moon, earth, and stars are spheres. A baseball is a sphere. 3. place or surroundings in which a person or thing exists, acts, works, etc. The waitress changed to a higher social sphere after she married the rich man. 4. range; extent; region; as, England's sphere of influence. *n. 3.*

spher i cal (sfer′i kəl), 1. shaped like a sphere. 2. of or pertaining to a sphere or spheres. *adj. 11.*

sphe roid (sfēr′oid), a body shaped somewhat like a sphere. *n. 19.*

sphinx (sfingks), 1. statue of a lion's body with the head of a man, ram, or hawk. There are many sphinxes in Egypt. 2. **The Sphinx** was a huge statue with a man's head and a lion's body near Cairo, Egypt. 3. puzzling or mysterious person. *n. 11.*

Sphinx (def. 1)

Sphinx (sfingks), a mythical monster with the head of a woman, the body of a lion, and wings. The Sphinx proposed a riddle to every passer-by and killed those unable to guess it. *n.*

spice (spīs), 1. seasoning. Pepper, cinnamon, cloves, ginger, and nutmeg are common spices. 2. put spice in; season; as, spiced peaches, spiced pickles. 3. something that adds flavor or interest. 4. add flavor or interest to. *n., v. 3.*

spic i ness (spīs′i nis), spicy flavor or smell. *n.*

spick-and-span (spik′ənd span′), new; fresh; spruce or smart; neat and clean; as, a spick-and-span apron, uniform, or room. *adj.*

spic y (spīs′i), 1. flavored with spice. The cookies were rich and spicy. 2. like that of spice. Some apples have a spicy smell and taste. 3. like spice; lively; keen; as, spicy conversation. *adj., spicier, spiciest. 13.*

spi der (spī′dər), 1. a small animal with eight legs and no wings. Spiders spin webs to catch insects for food. 2. something like or suggesting a spider. A kind of frying pan is called a spider. *n. 4.*

Garden spider. Line shows actual length.

spied (spīd). See **spy.** The hunter spied the stag in the distance. *pt. and pp. of spy.*

spig ot (spig′ət), 1. a peg or plug used to stop the small hole of a cask or barrel. 2. faucet. *n. 16.*

spike[1] (spīk), 1. a large, strong nail. 2. fasten with spikes. The men spiked the rails to the ties when laying the track. 3. sharp-pointed piece or part. Ballplayers wear shoes with spikes. 4. provide with spikes. Runners wear spiked shoes to keep from slipping. 5. pierce or injure with a spike.

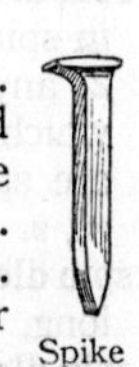
Spike (def. 1)

6. make (a cannon) useless by driving a spike into the opening where the powder is set off. 7. make useless; as, to spike an attempt. *n., v. 9.*

spike[2] (spīk), 1. ear of grain. 2. long, pointed flower cluster. *n.*

spike nard (spīk′nərd), 1. a sweet-smelling ointment used by the ancients. 2. the fragrant East Indian plant from which it was probably obtained. *n.*

A B
Spike: A, of grain; B, of flower.

spik y (spīk′i), 1. having spikes; set with sharp, projecting points. 2. having the shape of a spike. *adj. 17.*

spill (spil), 1. let (liquid or any matter in loose pieces) run or fall; as, to spill milk or salt. 2. fall or flow out. Water spilled from the pail. 3. cause to fall from a horse, carriage, car, boat, etc. The boat upset and spilled the boys into the water. 4. such a fall. John got a bad spill trying to ride. *v., spilled* or *spilt, spilling, n. 5.*

spill way (spil′wā′), channel or passage for the escape of surplus water from a dam, river, etc. *n.*

spilt (spilt), spilled. *pt. and pp. of* **spill.** *12.*

spin (spin), 1. draw out and twist (cotton, flax, wool, etc.) into thread. A spider spins a web. 2. produce; draw out; tell. The old sailor used to spin yarns about his adventures at sea. 3. make turn around rapidly. The boy spins his top. 4. turn around rapidly. The wheel spun round. 5. feel as if one were whirling around. 6. spinning. 7. rapid run, ride, drive, etc. *v., spun, spinning, n. 3.*

spin ach (spin′ich), a plant whose green leaves are boiled and eaten. *n. 11.*

spi nal (spī′nəl), of the spine or backbone; pertaining to the backbone. The **spinal column** means the backbone. The **spinal cord** is a cord of nervous tissue in the spinal column. *adj. 8.*

spin dle (spin′dəl), 1. the rod or pin used in spinning to twist, wind, and hold thread. 2. any rod or pin that turns around or on which something turns. Axles and shafts are spindles. 3. grow very long and thin. *n., v. 5.*

spin dle-legged (spin′dəl legd′), having long, thin legs. *adj.*

spin dle shanks (spin′dəl shangks′), 1. long, thin legs. 2. person with thin legs. *n.*

spin dling (spin′dling), very long and slender; too tall and thin. *adj.*

spin drift (spin′drift′), spray blown or dashed up from the waves. *n.*

spine (spīn), 1. the backbone. See the picture. 2. a thorn or something like it. A cactus has spines; so has a porcupine. See the pictures under **cactus** and **porcupine.** *n. 8.*

Human spine

spine less (spīn′lis), 1. having no spine or backbone. 2. without courage; weak. 3. having no spines. *adj.*

spin et (spin′it), an old-fashioned musical instrument like a small harpsichord. See the picture just below. *n. 18.*

spin na ker (spin′ə kər), a large triangular sail carried by yachts on the side opposite the mainsail when running before the wind. *n.*

spin ner (spin′ər), person, animal, or thing that spins. *n. 15.*

spin ner et (spin′ər et), organ by which spiders, silkworms, etc., spin their threads. *n.*

Spinet

spinning jenny, an early type of spinning machine having more than one spindle, whereby one person could spin a number of threads at the same time.

spinning wheel, a wheel arranged for spinning wool, cotton, or flax into thread or yarn.

spin ster (spin′stər), unmarried woman; old maid. *n. 10.*

spin y (spīn′i), 1. having spines; covered with spines; thorny; as, a spiny cactus, a spiny porcupine. 2. spinelike. *adj. 20.*

Spinning wheel

spi ra cle (spī′rə kəl), small opening for breathing. Insects take in air through spiracles. The whale breathes through a spiracle in the top of its head. *n.*

spi ral (spī′rəl), 1. a coil. A watch spring is a spiral. The thread of a screw is a spiral. 2. coiled. A snail's shell has a spiral shape. *n., adj. 9.*

Spirals

spire (spīr), 1. the top part of a tower or steeple that narrows to a point. See the picture on the next page. 2. anything tapering and pointed. A blade of grass is sometimes called a spire of grass. The sunset shone on the rocky spires of the mountains. *n. 4.*

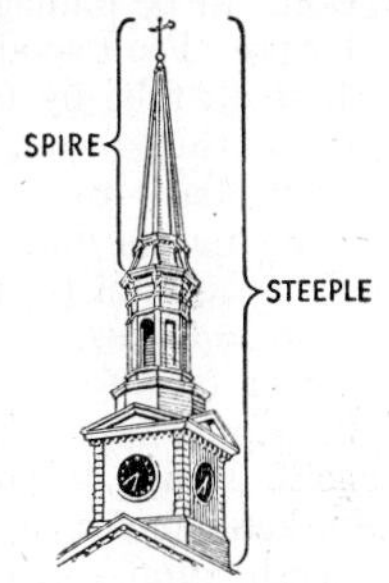

spir it (spir′it), 1. soul. He is present in spirit, though absent in body. 2. supernatural being. God is a spirit. Ghosts and fairies are spirits. 3. man's moral, religious, or emotional nature. 4. courage; vigor; liveliness. A race horse must have spirit. 5. state of mind; disposition; temper. He is in good spirits. **Out of spirits** means sad; gloomy. 6. person; personality. He is a brave spirit. He was one of the leading spirits of the revolution. 7. influence that stirs up and rouses. A spirit of progress marked the nineteenth century. 8. what is really meant as opposed to what is said or written. The spirit of a law is more important than its words. 9. strong alcoholic liquor. Whiskey or brandy is called spirits. 10. solution in alcohol; as, spirits of camphor. 11. carry (away or off) secretly. The child has been spirited away. *n., v. 1.*

spir it ed (spir′i tid), lively; dashing; brave. *adj. 19.*

spir it less (spir′it lis), without spirit or courage; tame; depressed. *adj. 18.*

spir i tu al (spir′i chü əl), 1. of or pertaining to the spirit or spirits. 2. caring much for things of the soul or spirit. 3. sacred; religious. 4. a religious song; as, a Negro spiritual. *adj., n. 4.*

spir i tu al ism (spir′i chü əl izm), 1. the belief that spirits of the dead communicate with the living, especially through persons called mediums. 2. spiritual quality. *n.*

spir i tu al ist (spir′i chü əl ist), person who believes that the dead communicate with the living. *n.*

spir i tu al i ty (spir′i chü al′i ti), devotion to spiritual things; spiritual quality. *n., pl. spiritualities. 15.*

spir i tu al ize (spir′i chü əl īz), make spiritual. *v. 20.*

spir i tu ous (spir′i chü əs), 1. containing alcohol. 2. distilled, not fermented. *adj. 20.*

spirt (spėrt), spurt. *v., n.*

spit[1] (spit), 1. throw out saliva from the mouth. The cat spits when angry. 2. throw out. The gun spits fire. He spat curses. 3. the liquid produced in the mouth; saliva. *v., spat or spit, spitting, n. 4.*

Spits for roasting

spit[2] (spit), 1. a sharp-pointed, slender rod or bar on which meat is roasted. 2. run a spit through; pierce; stab. 3. narrow point of land running into the water. *n., v., spitted, spitting.*

spite (spīt), 1. ill will; grudge. Joan stayed away from May's party out of spite. 2. annoy; show ill will toward. He left his yard dirty to spite the people who lived next door. 3. **In spite of** means not prevented by; notwithstanding. The children went to school in spite of the rain. *n., v. 2.*

spite ful (spīt′fəl), full of spite; eager to annoy; malicious; behaving with ill will and malice. *adj. 10.*

spit fire (spit′fīr′), person who has a quick and fiery temper. *n.*

Spittoon

spit tle (spit′əl), saliva; spit. *n.*

spit toon (spi tün′), a container to spit into. See the picture just above. *n. 19.*

spitz (spits), a kind of small dog with long hair and a pointed nose. *n.*

Spitz (about 20 in. high at the shoulder)

splash (splash), 1. dash liquid about. The baby likes to splash in his tub. The waves splashed on the beach. 2. to wet, spatter, or soil. Our car is all splashed with mud. 3. splashing; sound of splashing. The splash of the wave knocked him over. The boat upset with a loud splash. 4. spot of liquid splashed upon a thing. Jane has splashes of grease on her dress. 5. spot; patch. The dog is white with brown splashes. *v., n. 5.*

splat ter (splat′ər), splash; spatter. *v., n.*

splay (splā), 1. spread out. 2. wide and flat. 3. slanting surface; surface which makes an oblique angle with another. 4. make slanting. *v., adj., n. 19.*

spleen (splēn), 1. a ductless gland at the left of the stomach. See the diagram under **intestine.** People used to think that the spleen caused low spirits, bad temper, and spite. 2. low spirits; bad temper; spite; anger. *n. 6.*

splen did (splen′did), brilliant; glorious; magnificent; grand; as, a splendid sunset, a splendid palace, a splendid victory. *adj. 2.*

splen dor (splen′dər), 1. great brightness; brilliant light. 2. magnificent show; pomp; glory. *n. 4.*

sple net ic (spli net′ik), 1. pertaining to the spleen. 2. bad-tempered; irritable; peevish. *adj. 16.*

splice (splīs), 1. join together (ropes) by weaving together ends which have been untwisted. 2. join together (two pieces of timber) by overlapping. 3. joining of ropes or timbers by splicing. *v., n. 13.*

Splicing

splint (splint), thin strip of wood. The man's broken arm was set in splints to hold it in position. My basket is woven from splints. *n. 13.*

splin ter (splin′tər), 1. a thin, sharp piece of wood, bone, glass, etc. John got a splinter in his hand. The mirror broke into splinters. 2. split or break into splinters. *n., v. 7.*

splin ter y (splin′tər i), 1. apt to splinter; as, splintery wood. 2. rough and jagged. 3. full of splinters. *adj.*

split (split), 1. break or cut from end to end or in layers. The man is splitting wood. She split the cake and filled it with jelly. 2. separate into parts; divide. The old farm has been split up into house lots. The two men split the cost of the dinner between them. He split his vote by voting for some Republicans and some Democrats. 3. splitting; break; crack. Frost caused the split in the rock. 4. division in a group, party, etc. There was a split in the Republican Party. 5. **Split hairs** means make too fine distinctions. 6. Her **head is splitting** means that it aches very badly. *v., split, splitting, n. 3.*

splotch (sploch), 1. a large, irregular spot; splash. 2. make splotches on. *n., v.*

splurge (splėrj), 1. showing off. 2. show off. *n., v.* [*Used in common talk*] *20.*

splut ter (splut′ər), 1. talk in a hasty, confused way. People sometimes splutter when they are excited. 2. sputter; make spitting or popping noises. The baked apples are spluttering in the oven. 3. spluttering. *v., n.*

spoil (spoil), 1. damage; injure; destroy. He spoils a dozen pieces of paper before he writes a letter. The rain spoiled the picnic. That child is spoiled by too much attention. 2. be damaged; become bad or unfit for use. Fruit spoils if kept too long. 3. rob. 4. steal; take by force. 5. things taken by force; things won. The soldiers carried the spoils back to their own land. 6. **Spoils** often means offices and positions filled by the successful political party. *v., spoiled or spoilt, spoiling, n. 2.*

spoil er (spoil′ər), 1. one that spoils. 2. person who takes spoils. *n. 13.*

spoilt (spoilt), spoiled. *pt. and pp. of* **spoil.**

Spo kane (spō kan′), a city in eastern Washington. *n. 18.*

spoke[1] (spōk). See **speak.** She spoke about that yesterday. *pt. and old pp. of speak. 1.*

spoke[2] (spōk), one of the bars from the center of a wheel to the rim. *n.*

spo ken (spō′kən), 1. uttered; told; expressed with the mouth. A child understands a spoken direction better than a written one. 2. See **speak.** They have spoken about having a picnic. *adj., pp. of speak. 4.*

spoke shave (spōk′shāv′), a cutting tool having a blade with a handle at each end. *n.*

spokes man (spōks′mən), person who speaks for another or others. Mr. Smith was the spokesman for the factory workers. *n., pl. spokesmen. 10.*

spo li a tion (spō′li ā′shən), 1. robbery; plundering. 2. the plundering of neutrals at sea in time of war. *n.*

sponge (spunj), 1. a kind of sea animal. 2. its light framework used for soaking up water in bathing or cleaning. 3. something like a sponge, such as bread dough, a kind of cake, a pudding, etc. 4. wipe or rub with a wet sponge. Sponge the mud spots off the car. Sponge up the spilled water. 5. clean in this way; make damp. 6. live or profit at the expense of another in a mean way. That big boy won't work, but sponges on his mother. *n., v. 5.*

spon gy (spun′ji), 1. like a sponge; soft, light, and full of holes; as, spongy moss, spongy dough. 2. hard and full of holes; as, a spongy rock. *adj., spongier, spongiest. 9.*

spon sor (spon′sər), 1. person who is responsible for a person or thing; as, the sponsor of a law. 2. person who takes vows for an infant at baptism; a godfather or godmother. 3. act as sponsor for. *n., v. 18.*

spon ta ne i ty (spon′tə nē′i ti), state or quality of being spontaneous. *n., pl. spontaneities. 15.*

spon ta ne ous (spon tā′ni əs), of one's own free will; natural; of itself. Both sides burst into spontaneous cheers at the skillful play. A pile of oily rags will sometimes break into a spontaneous flame. Spontaneous combustion occurs when something sets itself on fire. *adj. 8.*

spook (spük), ghost; specter. *n.*

spook y (spük′i), like a spook; suited to spooks; suggesting spooks. *adj., spookier, spookiest.* [*Used in common talk*]

Spool of thread

spool (spül), small cylinder of wood or metal on which thread or wire is wound. *n. 7.*

spoon (spün), 1. See the pictures. 2. take up in a spoon. *n., v. 2.*

spoon drift (spün′drift′), spindrift. *n.*

spoon ful (spün′fůl), as much as a spoon can hold. *n., pl. spoonfuls.*

spoor (spür), track; trail of a wild animal. *n.*

Spoons

spo rad ic (spə rad′ik), occurring in scattered cases; here and there; now and then; separate. *adj. 19.*

spo rad i cal ly (spə rad′i kəl i), here and there; now and then; separately. *adv.*

spore (spōr), 1. a single cell capable of growing into a new plant or animal. Ferns produce spores. 2. germ; seed. *n. 9.*

spor ran (spor′ən), in a Scottish Highland costume, a large purse, commonly of fur, hanging from the belt in front. *n.*

SPORRAN

sport (spōrt), 1. a game; outdoor play. Baseball, golf, tennis, swimming, racing, hunting, and fishing are familiar sports. 2. fun; play; amusement. 3. to play. Lambs sport in the fields. The kitten sports with its tail. 4. joking. The man teased the child in sport. 5. ridicule. **Make sport of** means laugh at. Don't make sport of the lame boy. 6. the object of jokes and ridicule. A very fat boy is the sport of other boys. 7. display. *Used in common talk.* 8. sportsman. *n., v. 2.*

sport ing (spōr′ting), 1. of or interested in sports. 2. playing fair. 3. willing to take a chance. 4. involving risk; uncertain. *adj.*

spor tive (spōr′tiv), playful; merry. The old dog seemed as sportive as the puppy. *adj. 11.*

sports (spōrts), of sports; suitable for sports; as, sports clothes. *adj.*

sports man (spōrts′mən), 1. person who takes part in sports, especially hunting, fishing, or racing. 2. person who likes sports. 3. person who plays fair. *n., pl. sportsmen. 11.*

sports man like (spōrts′mən līk′), like a sportsman; like a sportsman's; fair and honorable. *adj.*

sports man ship (spōrts′mən ship), 1. ability in sports. 2. fair play. *n.*

spot (spot), 1. mark; stain; speck. You have grease spots on your suit. That spot on her cheek is a bruise. His character is without spot. 2. small part unlike the rest. His tie is blue with white spots. 3. make spots on; become spotted; have spots. He has spotted the tablecloth. This silk spots from rain. 4. place. From this spot you can see the ocean. **On the spot** means (1) at that very place. (2) at once. 5. ready; on hand. He paid spot cash for the horse. *n., v., spotted, spotting, adj. 1.*

spot less (spot′lis), without a spot. She wore a spotless white apron. *adj. 9.*

spot light (spot′līt′), 1. strong light thrown upon a particular spot or person. 2. the lamp that gives the light; as, a spotlight in a theater. *n.*

spot ted (spot′id), 1. stained with spots; as, a spotted reputation. 2. marked with spots; as, a spotted dog. *adj.*

spot ty (spot′i), 1. having spots; spotted. 2. not of uniform quality. His work was spotty. *adj., spottier, spottiest.*

spouse (spouz), husband or wife. Mr. Smith is Mrs. Smith's spouse, and she is his spouse. *n. 5.*

spout (spout), 1. throw out a liquid in a stream or spray. The fountain spouted up high. A whale spouts water. 2. flow out with force. Water spouted from the break in the pipe. 3. stream; jet. A spout of water shot up from the hole in the pipe. 4. a pipe for carrying off water. Rain runs down a spout from our roof to the ground. 5. a tube or lip by which liquid is poured. A teakettle, a coffee pot, and a syrup jug have spouts. 6. speak in loud tones with affected emotion. The old-fashioned actor used to spout his lines. *v., n. 6.*

sprain (sprān), 1. injure (a joint or muscle) by a sudden twist or wrench; as, to sprain your ankle. 2. injury caused in this way. *v., n. 13.*

sprang (sprang). See **spring.** The tiger sprang at the man. *pt. of spring. 3.*

sprat (sprat), a small sea fish like a herring. *n., pl. sprats* or *sprat. 16.*

sprawl (sprôl), 1. toss or spread the limbs about. 2. lie or sit with the limbs spread out. The people sprawled on the beach in their bathing suits. 3. spread out in an irregular or awkward manner. 4. act or position of sprawling. *v., n. 10.*

spray[1] (sprā), 1. liquid going through the air in fine drops. We were wet with the sea spray. 2. something like this. A spray of bullets hit the tree behind which he was hiding. 3. an instrument that sends a liquid out as spray. 4. sprinkle; scatter spray on. Spray this liquid on your throat. Spray the apple tree. *n., v. 3.*

spray[2] (sprā), a small branch or piece of some plant with its leaves, flowers, or fruit; as, a spray of ivy, a spray of lilacs, a spray of fern, a spray of berries. *n.*

spray er (sprā′ər), one that sprays; apparatus for spraying. *n. 17.*

spread (spred), 1. stretch out; open out. The bird spread its wings. 2. extend; lie. Fields of corn spread out before us. 3. cover with a thin layer. He ate bread spread with butter. 4. put as a thin layer. Spread the paint evenly. 5. scatter; distribute. The Jewish race is spread all over the world. 6. push farther apart. Spread out your fingers. 7. width; extent; amount of spreading. 8. covering for a bed or table. 9. food put on the table; a feast. *Used in common talk.* 10. put food on (a table). *v., spread, spreading, n. 1.*

spread er (spred′ər), 1. person who spreads; as, a spreader of good news. 2. thing that spreads. *n. 13.*

spree (sprē), 1. lively frolic. 2. a spell of drinking intoxicating liquor. *n. 10.*

sprig (sprig), a shoot, twig, or small branch. He wore a sprig of lilac in his buttonhole. *n 7.*

spright ly (sprīt′li), lively; gay. A kitten is sprightly. *adj., sprightlier, sprightliest. 6.*

spring (spring), 1. a leap or jump. 2. to leap or jump; rise or move suddenly and lightly. The dog sprang at the thief. The boy sprang to his feet. 3. elastic quality. There is no spring left in these old rubber bands. The old man's knees have lost their spring. 4. fly back or away. A bent branch will spring back into place. 5. elastic device that returns to its original shape after being pulled or held out of shape. Beds have wire springs. The spring in a clock makes it go. See the picture. 6. cause to spring; as, to spring a trap. 7. bring out, produce, or make suddenly; as, to spring a surprise on someone. 8. To **spring a mine** is to cause the gunpowder or other explosive in it to explode. 9. the season after winter when plants begin to grow. 10. small stream of water coming from the earth. 11. source; beginning; cause. 12. come from some source; arise; grow. A wind sprang up. Plants spring from seeds. 13. split; crack; break; bend; strain. To **spring a leak** means to crack and begin to let water through. 14. of or pertaining to spring or springs. *n., v., sprang* or *sprung, sprung, springing, adj. 1.*

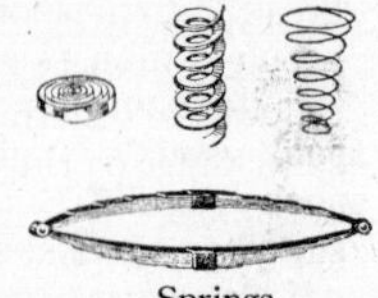

Springs

Springboard for diving

spring board (spring′bōrd′), board used to give added spring in diving, jumping, or vaulting. *n.*

spring bok (spring′bok′), a gazelle or small antelope of South Africa. *n.*

Springbok (about 2½ ft. high at the shoulder)

Spring field (spring′fēld), 1. the capital of Illinois. 2. a city in southern Massachusetts. *n. 12.*

spring tide (spring′tīd′), springtime. *n.*

spring tide, 1. the exceptionally high tide coming at the time of the new moon or the full moon. 2. any great flood, swell, or rush.

spring time (spring′tīm′), the season of spring. Flowers bloom in the springtime. *n. 6.*

spring y (spring′i), 1. elastic. His step was springy. 2. having many springs of water. *adj., springier, springiest.*

sprin kle (spring′kəl), 1. scatter in drops or tiny bits. He sprinkled ashes on the icy sidewalk. 2. spray or cover with small drops. Helen sprinkled the flowers with water. 3. sprinkling; small quantity. The cook put a sprinkle of nuts on the cake. 4. rain a little. 5. light rain. *v., n. 3.*

sprin kler (spring′klər), 1. person who sprinkles. 2. thing that sprinkles. *n.*

sprin kling (spring′kling), small quantity or number. *n.*

sprint (sprint), 1. run at full speed for a short distance. 2. short race at full speed. *v., n.*

SPRIT

sprit (sprit), a small pole that supports and stretches a sail. *n.*

sprite (sprīt), elf; fairy; goblin. Puck was a mischief-loving sprite. *n. 6.*

sprit sail (sprit′səl or sprit′sāl′), sail supported and stretched by a sprit. *n.*

sprock et (sprok′it), 1. one of a set of projections on the rim of a wheel, arranged so as to engage the links of a chain. 2. a wheel made with sprockets. *n. 16.*

Sprocket wheel

sprout (sprout), 1. begin to grow; shoot forth. Seeds sprout. Buds sprout in the spring. Weeds have sprouted in the garden. 2. cause to grow. The rain has sprouted the corn. 3. a shoot of a plant. The gardener was setting out sprouts. *v., n. 6.*

spruce[1] (sprüs), 1. a kind of evergreen tree. 2. its wood. *n. 10.*

Branch of spruce with cones

spruce[2] (sprüs), 1. neat; trim. John looked very spruce in his new suit. 2. make spruce; make oneself spruce; become spruce. John spruced up for dinner. *adj., v.*

sprung (sprung). See **spring.** The trap was sprung. *pp. and pt. of spring. 4.*

spry (sprī), active; lively; nimble. A mouse is a spry animal. *adj., spryer, spryest* or *sprier, spriest. 17.*

spud (spud), 1. a tool with a narrow blade for digging up or cutting the roots of weeds. 2. a tool like a chisel for removing bark. 3. a potato. *Used in common talk. n. 20.*

spume (spūm), foam; froth. *n., v. 14.*

spun (spun), 1. See **spin.** She spun all day yesterday. The thread was spun from silk. 2. **Spun silk** is silk waste spun into yarn. *pt. and pp. of spin, adj. 5.*

spunk (spungk), courage; pluck; spirit; mettle. *n.* [*Used in common talk*]

spunk y (spungk′i), courageous; plucky; spirited. *adj., spunkier, spunkiest.* [*Used in common talk*]

spur (spėr), 1. a pricking instrument worn on a horseman's heel for urging a horse on. 2. prick with spurs. The rider spurred his horse on. 3. ride quickly. 4. something like a spur; a point sticking out. A cock has spurs on his legs. A spur of rock stuck out from the mountain. 5. anything that urges on. Ambition was the spur that made him work. 6. urge on. Pride spurred the man to fight. *n., v., spurred, spurring. 4.*

Horseman's spur

spu ri ous (spūr′i əs), not genuine; not coming from the right source; false; sham; as, a spurious document. *adj. 12.*

spurn (spėrn), 1. strike with the foot; kick away. The king spurned the kneeling slave. 2. scorn; refuse with scorn. The judge spurned the bribe. *v. 5.*

spurred (spėrd), having spurs or a spur. *adj.*

spurt (spėrt), 1. flow suddenly in a stream or jet; gush out; squirt. Blood spurted from the wound. 2. sudden rushing forth; jet. Spurts of flame broke out all over the building. 3. a great increase of effort or activity for a short time. 4. put forth great energy for a short time; show great activity for a short time. The swimmers spurted near the end of the race. *v., n. 12.*

sput ter (sput′ər), 1. make spitting or popping noises; as, sputtering firecrackers, fat sputtering in the frying pan. 2. throw out drops of spit, bits of food, etc., in excitement or in talking too fast. 3. say words or sounds in haste and confusion. 4. sputtering. 5. confused talk. *v., n. 15.*

spu tum (spū′təm), 1. saliva; spit. 2. what is coughed up from the lungs and spat out. *n. 20.*

spy (spī), 1. person who keeps secret watch on the actions of others. 2. person who, in time of war, tries to get information about the enemy, usually by visiting the enemy's territory in disguise. 3. find out or try to find out by careful observation. She spies out everything that goes on in the neighborhood. 4. keep secret watch. Mr. Smith saw two men spying on him from behind a tree. 5. catch sight of; see. He was the first to spy the rescue party in the distance. *n., pl. spies, v., spied, spying. 2.*

spy glass (spī′glas′), small telescope. *n. 19.*

sq., square. *6.*

squab (skwob), very young bird, especially a young pigeon. *n.*

squab ble (skwob′əl), 1. a petty, noisy quarrel. Children's squabbles annoy their parents. 2. take part in a petty, noisy quarrel. *n., v. 15.*

squad (skwod), 1. small number of soldiers grouped for drill, inspection, or work. 2. any small group of persons. *n. 11.*

squad ron (skwod′rən), 1. a part of a naval fleet used for special service; as, the Atlantic squadron of the navy. 2. a body of cavalry usually having from 120 to 200 men. 3. a number of airplanes that fly or fight together. 4. group. *n. 6.*

squal id (skwol′id), filthy; degraded; wretched. *adj. 15.*

squall[1] (skwôl), sudden, violent gust of wind, often with rain, snow, or sleet. *n. 9.*

squall[2] (skwôl), 1. cry out loudly; scream violently. The baby squalled. 2. loud, harsh cry. The parrot's squall was heard all over the house. *v., n.*

squall y (skwôl′i), having many sudden, violent gusts of wind. *adj.*

squal or (skwol′ər), filth; misery and dirt. *n.*

squan der (skwon′dər), spend foolishly; waste. He squandered his time and money in gambling. *v. 10.*

square (skwãr), 1. a figure with four equal sides and four right angles; having this shape □; anything having this shape, or nearly this shape. The troops were drawn up in a square. 2. space in a city or town, bounded by streets on four sides. This square is full of stores. 3. distance along one side of such a space; a block. We live three squares from the school. 4. open space in a city or town bounded by streets on four sides, often planted with grass, trees, etc. The soldiers' monument is in the square opposite the city hall. 5. any similar open space, as at the meeting of streets. 6. instrument for drawing right angles and testing the squareness of anything. See the picture in the next column. 7. the product obtained when a number is multiplied by itself. 16 is the square of 4. 8. multiply (a number) by itself. 25 squared makes 625. 9. just; fair; honest. You will get a square deal at this shop. 10. settle. Let us square our accounts. 11. satisfying; as, a square meal. 12. make square in shape. 13. mark in squares. The children squared off the sidewalk to play hopscotch. 14. bring to the form of a right angle. 15. forming a right angle; as, a square corner. 16. make straight or level. 17. straight; level; even. 18. agree; conform. His acts do not square with his promises. 19. A **square dance** is a dance performed by a series of couples arranged about a square space or in some set form. *n., v., adj. 1.*

Square (def. 6)

square-rigged (skwãr′rigd′), having the principal sails set square across the masts. *adj.*

A ship with the sails on its foremast square-rigged

squash[1] (skwosh), 1. crush; press until soft or flat. The boy squashed the bug. This package was squashed in the mail. 2. something squashed; a crushed mass. The grapes are just a squash and not fit to eat. 3. a game somewhat like handball and tennis. *v., n. 8.*

squash[2] (skwosh), a vegetable that grows on a vine. We eat squash as a vegetable or make it into pie. *n.*

Summer squash

squash y (skwosh′i), 1. easily squashed; as, squashy cream puffs. 2. soft and wet; as, squashy ground. *adj.*

Winter squash

squat (skwot), 1. crouch on the heels. 2. sit on the ground or floor with the legs drawn up closely beneath or in front of the body. 3. settle on another's land without title or right. 4. settle on public land to acquire ownership of it. 5. crouching. A squat figure sat in front of the fire. 6. short and thick; low and broad. The Italian was a squat dark man. That is a squat teapot. 7. act of squatting. *v., squatted* or *squat, squatting, adj., n. 10.*

squat ter (skwot′ər), 1. person who settles on another's land without right. 2. person who settles on public land to acquire ownership of it. *n. 14.*

squat ty (skwot′i), short and thick; low and broad. *adj., squattier, squattiest.*

squaw (skwô), an American Indian woman or wife. *n. 12.*

squawk (skwôk), 1. make a loud, harsh sound. Hens and ducks squawk when frightened. 2. a loud, harsh sound. *v., n. 20.*

squeak (skwēk), 1. make a short, sharp, shrill sound. A mouse squeaks. 2. such a sound. We heard the squeak of the rocking chair. *v., n. 5.*

squeak y (skwēk′i), squeaking. *adj.*

squeal (skwēl), 1. make a long, sharp, shrill cry. A pig squeals when it is hurt. 2. such a cry. *v., n. 13.*

squeam ish (skwēm′ish), 1. easily shocked; too particular; too proper, modest, etc. 2. slightly sick at one's stomach; sickish. 3. easily turned sick. *adj. 16.*

squeeze (skwēz), 1. press hard. Don't squeeze the kitten; you will hurt it. 2. force by pressing. I can't squeeze another thing into my trunk. 3. a tight pressure. She gave her sister's arm a squeeze. 4. hug. 5. crush; crowd. It's a tight squeeze to get five people in that little car. 6. force a way. He squeezed through the crowd. 7. yield to pressure. Sponges squeeze easily. *v., n. 5.*

squeez er (skwēz′ər), thing that squeezes; as, a lemon squeezer. *n. 16.*

squelch (skwelch), crush; silence. Helen squelched her little sister with a look of contempt. *v.*

squib (skwib), 1. a broken firecracker. 2. a small firework which burns with a hissing noise and finally explodes. 3. a short, witty attack in speech or writing; a sharp sarcasm. *n. 14.*

squid (skwid), a sea animal like a cuttlefish. See the picture. Small squids are much used as bait. *n., pl. squids* or *squid. 18.*

Squid

squint (skwint), 1. look with the eyes partly closed. 2. sidelong look; hasty look; look. 3. look sideways. 4. tendency to look sideways. 5. looking sideways. 6. be cross-eyed. 7. cross-eyed. **Squint-eyed** means cross-eyed. *v., n., adj. 10.*

squire (skwīr), 1. in England, a country gentleman, especially the chief landowner in a district. 2. in the United States a justice of the peace or a local judge. 3. young man of noble family who attended a knight till he himself was made a knight. 4. woman's escort. 5. to escort (a lady). *n., v. 4.*

squirm (skwėrm), wriggle; writhe; twist. The boy squirmed in his seat. *v., n. 13.*

Common gray squirrel (about 1½ ft. long, including the tail)

squir rel (skwėr′əl), 1. a small, bushy-tailed animal that lives in trees. Some kinds live mostly on the ground. 2. its gray, reddish, or dark-brown fur. *n. 3.*

squirt (skwėrt), 1. force out (liquid) through a narrow opening; as, to squirt water through a tube. 2. come out in a jet or stream; as, water squirting from a hose. 3. act of squirting. 4. jet. *v., n. 14.*

Sr., Senior; the older.

S.S., steamship. *20.*

St., 1. Street. 2. Saint. *3.*

stab (stab), 1. pierce or wound with a pointed weapon. 2. a thrust or blow made with a pointed weapon. 3. wound made by stabbing. 4. wound sharply or deeply in the feelings. The mother was stabbed to the heart by her son's lack of gratitude. *v., stabbed, stabbing, n. 5.*

sta bil i ty (stə bil′i ti), 1. firmness; being fixed in position. A concrete wall has more stability than a light wooden fence. 2. permanence. 3. steadfastness of character, purpose, etc. *n., pl. stabilities. 8.*

sta bi li za tion (stā′bi li zā′shən), stabilizing; being stabilized. *n. 18.*

sta bi lize (stā′bi līz), 1. make stable or firm. 2. hold steady; prevent changes in. 3. keep well-balanced. *v. 14.*

sta bi liz er (stā′bi līz′ər), 1. person or thing that makes something stable. 2. device for keeping an airplane, ship, etc., steady. *n.*

sta ble[1] (stā′bəl), 1. a building where horses or cattle are kept and fed. 2. group of animals housed in such a building. The black race horse is one of Mr. King's stable. 3. put or keep in a stable. *n., v. 2.*

sta ble[2] (stā′bəl), firm; steady; not likely to move or change. Concrete reinforced with steel is stable. *adj.*

stac ca to (stə kä′tō), disconnected; abrupt; with breaks between the successive tones. *adj.*

stack (stak), 1. large pile of hay, straw, etc. Haystacks are often round and arranged to shed water. 2. pile of anything; as, a stack of wood. 3. number of rifles arranged to form a cone or pyramid. 4. pile or arrange in a stack; as, to stack hay, to stack firewood, to stack guns. 5. arrange (playing cards) unfairly. 6. chimney. *n., v. 6.*

Stack of rifles

sta di um (stā′di əm), structure for athletic games, consisting of tiers of seats about an open field. *n., pl. stadiums, stadia* (stā′di ə). *16.*

staff (staf), 1. stick; pole; rod. The old man leaned on his staff. The flag hangs on a staff. 2. something that supports or sustains. Bread is called the staff of life because it will support life. 3. group assisting a chief; group of employees. 4. group of officers that makes plans for an army but does no fighting. 5. provide with officers or employees. 6. the five lines and the spaces between them on which music is written. *n., pl. staves* (stāvz) or *staffs* for 1 and 2, *staffs* for 3 and 4, *v. 3.*

Musical staff

stag (stag), 1. a full-grown male deer. 2. a male. A stag dinner is attended by men only. *n., adj. 6.*

Stag (about 4 ft. high at the shoulder)

stage (stāj), 1. a platform; flooring. 2. the raised flooring in a theater on which the actors perform. 3. the theater; the drama; actor's profession. He writes for the stage. She is **on the stage** means she is an actress. 4. scene of action. Bunker Hill was the stage of a famous battle. 5. arrange. The play was excellently staged. Mother had staged a surprise for the children's party by hiring a magician to perform. 6. place of rest on a journey; a regular stopping place. 7. the distance between two places on a journey. We climbed the mountain **by easy stages** means we often stopped to rest. 8. one step or degree in a process; a period of development. 9. stagecoach; bus. *n., v. 3.*

stage coach (stāj′kōch′), a coach carrying passengers and parcels over a regular route. *n. 17.*

Stagecoach

stag ger (stag′ər), 1. sway or reel (from weakness, a heavy load, or drunkenness). 2. make sway or reel. The blow staggered him for the moment. 3. swaying or reeling. 4. become unsteady; waver. The troops staggered under the severe gunfire. 5. hesitate. 6. cause to hesitate or become confused. The difficulty of the examination staggered him. 7. make helpless. 8. arrange in a zigzag order or way. *v., n. 4.*

stag nant (stag′nənt), 1. not running or flowing; foul from standing still. The water in a stagnant pool is not good to drink. 2. not active; sluggish; dull. *adj. 7.*

stag nate (stag′nāt), 1. be stagnant; become stagnant. 2. make stagnant. *v. 17.*

stag na tion (stag nā′shən), becoming or making stagnant; stagnant condition. *n. 14.*

stag y (stāj′i), artificial; pompous; affected. *adj.*

staid (stād), 1. having a settled, quiet character. Quakers are staid people. 2. old form of **stayed.** *adj., pt. and pp. of stay. 8.*

stain (stān), 1. soil; spot. He has ink stains on his shirt. The tablecloth is stained where food has been spilled. 2. spot by wrongdoing or disgrace. His character is without stain. His crimes stained the family honor. 3. color. She stained the chair with a green stain. *n., v. 3.*

stain less (stān′lis), without stain; spotless. *adj. 13.*

stair (stãr), 1. one of a series of steps for going from one level or floor to another. A broken stair may make someone fall. 2. a set of such steps. We climbed the winding stair to the tower. *n. 2.*

stair case (stãr′kās′), stairs; a flight of stairs. *n. 11.*

stair way (stãr′wā′), stairs; a way up and down by stairs. The servants use the back stairway. *n. 11.*

stake[1] (stāk), 1. a stick or post pointed at one end for driving into the ground. Joan of Arc was fastened to a stake and burned. Such a punishment was called **the stake.** 2. fasten to a stake or with a stake. 3. mark with stakes; mark the boundaries of. The miner staked off his claims. *n., v. 3.*

stake[2] (stāk), 1. risk (money or something valuable) on the result of a game or on any chance. He staked all his money on the black horse. 2. the money risked; what is staked. The men played for high stakes. He has much **at stake** means he has much to win or lose. 3. the prize in a race or contest. The stakes were divided up among the winners. 4. something to gain or lose; an interest; a share in a property. Each of us has a stake in the future of our country. *v., n.*

Stalactites and stalagmites

sta lac tite (stə lak′-tīt), a formation of lime, shaped like an icicle, hanging from the roof of a cave. Stalactites and stalagmites are formed by dripping water that contains lime. *n. 18.*

sta lag mite (stə lag′mīt), 1. a formation of lime, shaped like a cone, built up on the floor of a cave. *n.*

stale (stāl), 1. not fresh; as, stale bread, a stale joke. 2. out of condition. The horse has gone stale from too much running. *adj. 4.*

stale mate (stāl′māt′), 1. position of the pieces at chess when no move can be made without putting the king in check. 2. any position in which no action can be taken. 3. put in such a position; bring to a standstill. *n., v.*

Sta lin (stä′lin), Joseph (born 1879), Russian Bolshevik leader, head of the Soviet government. *n.*

stalk[1] (stôk), 1. the stem of a plant. 2. any stemlike part. A flower or leaf blade may have a stalk. *n. 4.*

stalk[2] (stôk), 1. approach wild animals without being seen by them. The hunters stalked the lion. 2. pursue an animal or a person without being seen. 3. spread silently and steadily. Disease stalked through the land. 4. walk with slow, stiff, or haughty strides. 5. stalking. *v., n.*

stalk ing-horse (stôk′ing hôrs′), 1. a horse, or a dummy of a horse, behind which a hunter conceals himself in stalking game. 2. anything used to hide plans or acts; a pretext. *n.*

Stalls for animals

stall (stôl), 1. place in a stable for one animal. 2. small place for selling things. At the public market different things are sold in different stalls under one big roof. 3. seat in the choir of a church. 4. seat in the front part of a theater. 5. put or keep in a stall. The horses were safely stalled. 6. stop against one's wish. He had stalled the engine of his automobile. We were stalled in the mud. *n., v. 3.*

stal lion (stal′yən), a male horse useful for breeding purposes. *n. 18.*

stal wart (stôl′wərt), 1. strongly built. 2. strong and brave. 3. firm; steadfast. *adj. 17.*

S

S, stamen.

sta men (stā′mən), the part of a flower that contains the pollen. *n. 9.*

stam i na (stam′i nə), strength; endurance. *n. 15.*

stam mer (stam′ər), 1. repeat the same sound in an effort to speak; hesitate in speaking. *Example:* I s-s-see a d-d-dog. 2. stammering; stuttering. John has a nervous stammer. *v., n. 6.*

stamp (stamp), 1. bring down one's foot with force. Jack stamped on the spider. 2. act of stamping. 3. pound; crush. She stamped out the fire. 4. mill or machine that crushes rock, etc. 5. make a mark on; the mark made; the thing making it. She stamped the papers with a stamp that had her name on it. 6. show to be of a certain quality or character. His speech stamps him as a man of education. 7. impression; marks. Her face bore the stamp of suffering. 8. small piece of paper with a sticky back which is put on letters, papers, parcels, etc., to show that a charge has been paid; as, a postage stamp. 9. put a stamp on. *v., n. 2.*

stam pede (stam pēd′), 1. a sudden scattering or headlong flight of a frightened herd of cattle or horses. 2. any headlong flight of a large group; as, a stampede of a panic-stricken crowd from a burning building. 3. scatter or flee in a stampede. 4. general rush; as, a stampede to newly discovered gold fields. 5. make a general rush. 6. cause to stampede. *n., v. 14.*

stance (stans), the position of the feet of a golf player when making a stroke. *n.*

stanch[1] (stänch), 1. stop or check the flow of (blood, etc). 2. stop the flow of blood from (a wound). *v. 8.* Also spelled **staunch.**

stanch[2] (stänch), 1. strong; firm; as, stanch walls, a stanch defense, stanch friends, a stanch supporter of the law. 2. watertight; as, a stanch boat. *adj.* Also spelled **staunch.**

stan chion (stan′shən), an upright bar, post, or support (in a window, in a stall for cattle, on a ship, etc.). *n. 15.*

stand (stand), 1. be on one's feet. Don't stand if you are tired, but sit down. 2. rise to one's feet. The children stand to salute the flag. 3. set upright. Stand the box here. 4. be set upright. 5. be in a certain place, rank, scale, etc. Pillars stand on each side of the door. John stood first in his class for service to the school. 6. be in a special condition. He stands innocent of any wrong. The poor man stands in need of food and clothing. 7. take a certain position. "Stand back!" called the policeman to the crowd. 8. stay in place; last. The old house has stood for a hundred years. 9. bear; endure. Many plants cannot stand cold, and die in the winter. 10. be unchanged; hold good; remain the same. The rule against lateness will stand. 11. stop moving; halt; stop. 12. a halt; a stop; a stop for defense. We made a last stand against the enemy. 13. place where a person stands; position. The policeman took his stand at the street corner. 14. place or fixtures for a small business; as, a newsstand. 15. something to put things on or in. Leave your wet umbrella in the stand in the hall. 16. raised place where people may stand or sit. 17. Some special meanings are:

stand by, 1. be near. 2. side with; help. 3. make ready to use.

stand for, 1. represent; mean. 2. be on the side of; take the part of; uphold. Our school stands for fair play.

stand out, 1. project. 2. be noticeable or prominent. 3. refuse to yield.

It can **stand over** means it can wait until another time.

stand up for, take the part of; defend; support.

v, stood, standing, n. 1.

stand ard (stan′dərd), 1. anything taken as a basis of comparison; model; rule. Choose good standards of living. Your work is not up to the class standard. 2. used as a standard; according to rule. **Standard time** is the time officially adopted for a region or country. 3. having recognized excellence or authority. Scott and Dickens are standard authors. 4. flag, emblem, or symbol. The dragon was the standard of China. 5. upright support. The floor lamp has a long standard. *n., adj. 2.*

stand ard i za tion (stan′dər di zā′shən), standardizing. *n.*

stand ard ize (stan′dər dīz), 1. make standard in size, shape, weight, quality, strength, etc. The parts of an automobile are standardized. 2. regulate by a standard. 3. test by a standard. *v. 13.*

stand ing (stan′ding), 1. position; reputation; as, men of good standing. 2. duration; as, a feud of long standing between two families. 3. erect; straight up. 4. done from an erect position; as, a standing jump. 5. not flowing; stagnant; as, standing water. 6. established; permanent; as, a standing army. *n., adj.*

Stan dish (stan′dish), Miles, the military leader of the colony at Plymouth, Massachusetts (1584?-1656). *n. 17.*

stand pipe (stand′pīp′), big vertical pipe or tower to hold water. *n.*

stand point (stand′point′), the point at which one stands to view something; point of view; mental attitude. *n. 13.*

stand still (stand′stil′), stop; halt; pause. *n. 12.*

stank (stangk). See **stink.** The dead fish stank. *pt. of stink.*

Stan ley (stan′li), Sir Henry M., a British explorer of Africa (1841-1904). *n.*

stan za (stan′zə), verse of a poem; group of lines of poetry. They sang the first and last stanzas of "America." *n. 9.*

sta ple[1] (stā′pəl), 1. piece of metal with pointed ends bent into a U shape. Staples are driven into doors, etc., to hold hooks, pins, or bolts. 2. bent piece of wire used to hold together papers, parts of a book, etc. 3. fasten with staples. *n., v. 7.*

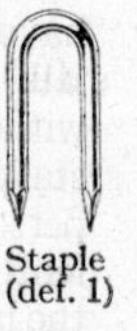
Staple (def. 1)

sta ple[2] (stā′pəl), 1. the most important or principal article grown or manufactured in a place. Cotton is the staple in many Southern States. 2. most important; principal. The weather was their staple subject of conversation. 3. raw material. 4. fiber of cotton or wool. *n., adj.*

star (stär), 1. any of the bright points seen in the sky at night. 2. a heavenly body that is not a planet, comet, or meteor. 3. person having brilliant qualities; a famous actor, singer, etc; as, a movie star. 4. be a leading performer. She has starred in many pictures. 5. a figure having usually five points, sometimes six, like these: ☆ ✡. 6. thing having this shape. 7. a sign like this (*). Smith's name was starred twice means that it was printed like this: Smith**. 8. ornament with stars. Nan's card was starred for perfect attendance. *n., v., starred, starring. 1.*

star board (stär′bərd), 1. the right side of a ship. 2. on the right side of a ship. 3. turn (the helm) to the right side. *n., adj., v. 14.*

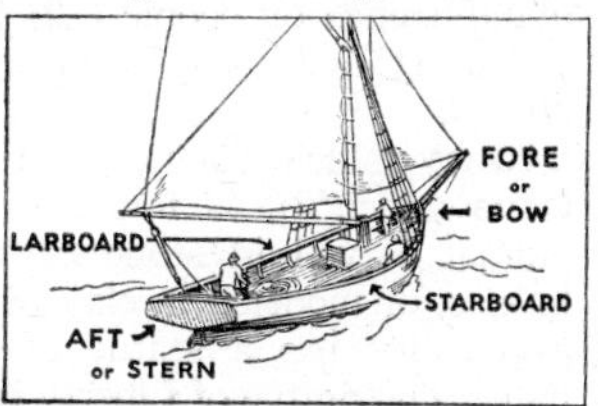

starch (stärch), 1. a white, tasteless food substance. Potatoes, wheat, rice, and corn contain much starch. 2. preparation of it used to stiffen clothes. 3. stiffen (clothes) with it. Men's collars are often starched. 4. stiffness; a stiff, formal manner. *n., v. 8.*

starch y (stär′chi), 1. like starch; containing starch. 2. stiff with starch. 3. stiff in manner; formal. *adj.*

stare (stãr), 1. look directly with the eyes wide open. A person stares in wonder, surprise, stupidity, curiosity, or from mere rudeness. The little girl stared at the toys in the window. 2. fixed look with the eyes wide open. The doll's eyes were set in an unwinking stare. 3. be very striking or glaring. *v., n. 3.*

star fish (stär′fish′), a star-shaped sea animal. It is not a fish. *n., pl. starfishes* or *starfish. 12.*

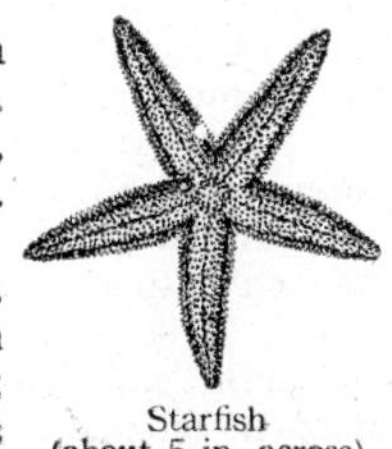

Starfish
(about 5 in. across)

stark (stärk), 1. stiff. The dog lay stark in death. 2. downright; complete. That fool is talking stark nonsense. 3. entirely; completely. The boys went swimming stark naked. *adj., adv. 9.*

star light (stär′līt′), 1. light from the stars. 2. lighted by the stars. *n., adj. 13.*

star like (stär′līk′), 1. shaped like a star. 2. shining like a star. *adj. 19.*

star ling (stär′ling), 1. a common European bird which nests about buildings and is easily tamed. 2. a kind of American blackbird. *n. 16.*

star lit (stär′lit′), lighted by the stars. *adj.*

star ry (stär′i), 1. lighted by stars; containing many stars; as, a starry sky. 2. shining like stars; as, starry eyes. *adj. 7.*

Stars and Stripes, the flag of the United States.

star-span gled (stär′spang′gəld), spangled with stars. The Star-Spangled Banner is the flag of the United States. *adj.*

start (stärt), 1. begin to move, go, or act; set going; put in action. The train started on time. I started a fire. 2. setting in motion. 3. begin. 4. beginning to move, go, or act. 5. move suddenly. Mrs. Jones started in surprise. 6. a sudden, jerking movement. I awoke with a start. 7. come or rise suddenly; spring suddenly. Tears started from her eyes. 8. a sudden, springing movement. On seeing the snake, the man sprang up with a start. 9. become loose; make loose. The huge waves had started some of the ship's bolts. 10. rouse; as, to start a rabbit. *v., n. 1.*

start er (stär′tər), 1. person or thing that starts. 2. person who gives the signal for starting. *n. 18.*

star tle (stär′təl), 1. surprise; frighten. 2. cause to make a sudden movement. *v. 4.*

star va tion (stär vā′shən), 1. starving. The starvation of prisoners of war is barbarous. 2. being starved; suffering from extreme hunger. Starvation caused his death. *n. 8.*

starve (stärv), 1. die because of hunger; suffer severely because of hunger. 2. weaken or kill with hunger. That cruel man half starves his horses. The enemy starved the men in the fort into surrendering. 3. **Starve for** sometimes means suffer from the lack of. That child is starving for affection. *v. 3.*

starve ling (stärv′ling), 1. starving; hungry. 2. one that is suffering from lack of food. *adj., n. 16.*

state (stāt), 1. condition of a person or thing. He is in a poor state of health. The house is in a bad state of repair. 2. nation. 3. one of several organized political groups of people which together form a nation. The State of Texas is one of the United States. 4. rank; person's position in life. 5. dignity; pomp; high style of living. Kings live in great state. 6. tell in speech or writing. State your opinion of the new school rules. 7. with ceremony; of ceremony. *n., v., adj. 1.*

stat ed (stāt′id), fixed; settled; set; as, stated times, for a stated fee. *adj.*

State house (stāt′hous′), the capitol of a State; the building in which the legislature of a State meets. *n.*

state li ness (stāt′li nis), dignity; stately appearance or behavior. *n. 18.*

state ly (stāt′li), having dignity; imposing; majestic. The Capitol at Washington is a stately building. *adj., statelier, stateliest. 4.*

state ment (stāt′mənt), 1. something stated; account; report. His statement was correct. 2. stating; manner of stating something. The statement of an idea helps me to remember it. *n. 4.*

state room (stāt′rüm′), 1. private room on a ship or railroad train. 2. a room for ceremonies in a palace. *n. 18.*

states man (stāts′mən), man skilled in the management of public or national affairs. Abraham Lincoln was a famous American statesman. *n., pl. statesmen. 3.*

states man like (stāts′mən līk′), having the qualities of a statesman. *adj. 20.*

states man ship (stāts′mən ship), the qualities of a statesman; skill in the management of public affairs. *n. 13.*

stat ic (stat′ik), 1. at rest; standing still. Civilization does not remain static, but changes constantly. 2. acting by weight without producing motion; as, static pressure. 3. pertaining to bodies at rest or to forces that balance each other. ‖4. electrical disturbances in the air. Static interferes with radiobroadcasting. *adj., n. 14.*

sta tion (stā′shən), 1. place to stand in. The policeman took his station at the corner. 2. a building or place used for a definite purpose. A place where soldiers live, a harbor for ships, and the police headquarters of a district are all called stations. 3. place or equipment for sending out or receiving programs, messages, etc., by radio. 4. regular stopping place. She met her at the railroad station. 5. social position; rank. A street cleaner is a man of humble station in life. 6. place. He stationed himself just outside the main doorway of the hotel. *n., v. 1.*

sta tion ar y (stā′shən ãr′i), 1. having a fixed station or place; standing still; not movable. A factory engine is stationary. 2. not changing in size, number, activity, etc. The population of this town has been stationary for ten years at about 5000 people. *adj. 7.*

sta tion er (stā′shən ər), person who sells paper, pens, pencils, ink, etc. *n. 16.*

sta tion er y (stā′shən ãr′i), writing materials; paper, cards, and envelopes. *n. 9.*

sta tis ti cal (stə tis′ti kəl), dealing with facts and figures. *adj. 15.*

stat is ti cian (stat′is tish′ən), person skilled in statistics; person who prepares statistics. *n.*

sta tis tics (stə tis′tiks), 1. numerical facts about things or people. 2. the science of collecting and using such facts. *n. pl. or sing. 9.*

stat u ar y (stach′ü ãr′i), statues. *n. 10.*

stat ue (stach′ü), image of a person or animal carved in stone or wood, cast in bronze, or modeled in clay or wax. Nearly every city has a statue of some famous man. The Statue of Liberty is in New York Bay. *n. 3.*

stat u esque (stach′ü esk′), like a statue in dignity, formal grace, or classic beauty. *adj.*

stat u ette (stach′ü et′), small statue. *n. 16.*

stat ure (stach′ər), height. A man 6 feet tall is above average stature. *n. 5.*

sta tus (stā′təs), 1. state; condition; position. The status of the world in 1940 was discouraging to lovers of peace. 2. social or professional standing. *n. 11.*

sta tus quo (stā′təs kwō′), the way things were or are; the existing state of affairs.

stat ute (stach′üt), a law. The statutes for the United States are made by Congress. *n. 6.*

stat u to ry (stach′ü tō′ri), 1. pertaining to a statute. 2. fixed by statute. 3. punishable by statute. *adj. 17.*

St. Au gus tine (sānt ô′gəs tēn), a seacoast town in northeastern Florida. It was founded in 1565 and is the oldest town in the United States.

staunch[1] (stônch), 1. stop the flow of (blood, etc.). 2. stop the flow of blood from (a wound). *v. 9.* Also spelled **stanch.**

staunch[2] (stônch), 1. strong; firm; as, staunch walls, a staunch defense, staunch friends, a staunch supporter of the law. 2. watertight. *adj.* Also spelled **stanch.**

stave (stāv), 1. one of the curved pieces of wood which form the sides of a barrel, tub, etc. 2. stick or staff. 3. break a hole in (a barrel, boat, etc.). 4. become smashed or broken in. 5. keep (off); put (off). The lost campers ate birds' eggs to stave off starvation. 6. a verse or stanza of a poem or song. 7. the musical staff. 8. furnish with staves. *n., v., staved* or *stove, staving. 6.*

staves (stāvz), 1. more than one staff. 2. more than one stave. *n. pl.*

stay[1] (stā), 1. Stay here till I tell you to move. The cat stayed out all night. Shall I go or stay? 2. live for a while; dwell. Alice is staying with her aunt while her mother is ill. 3. put an end to for a while; stop; satisfy. Jim ate some bread and butter to stay his hunger till time for dinner. 4. put off; hold back; delay. The teacher stayed judgment till she could hear both sides. 5. endure. 6. staying; stop; time spent; as, a pleasant stay at the seashore. 7. delay in carrying out the order of a court. The judge granted the condemned man a stay for an appeal. *v., n. 1.*

stay[2] (stā), 1. a strong rope, often made of wire, which supports the mast of a ship. 2. any rope or chain attached to something to steady it. *n.*

stay[3] (stā), support; prop; brace. The oldest son was the family's stay. *n., v.*

stay sail (stā′səl or stā′sāl′), a sail fastened on a stay or rope. *n.*

stead (sted), 1. place. Our laundress could not come, but sent her sister in her stead. 2. **Stand** (a person) **in good stead** means be an advantage to him. His ability to swim stood him in good stead when the boat upset. *n. 5.*

stead fast (sted′fast), firmly fixed; constant; not moving or changing. Benjamin Franklin was a steadfast servant of his country. *adj. 5.*

stead ily (sted′ili), in a steady manner; firmly; uniformly. *adv. 8.*

stead iness (sted′inis), being steady. *n. 13.*

stead y (sted′i), 1. firmly fixed; firm; not swaying or shaking. This post is steady as a rock. 2. changing little; uniform; regular. John is making steady progress at school. 3. reliable; having good habits. Fred is a steady young man. 4. make steady; keep steady. Steady the stepladder while I take down the dishes from the shelves. 5. become steady. The wind steadied. *adj., steadier, steadiest, v., steadied, steadying. 3.*

steak (stāk), slice of meat or fish for broiling or frying. Steak often means beefsteak. *n. 5.*

steal (stēl), 1. take something that does not belong to one; take dishonestly. 2. take, get, or do secretly. Jane stole time from her lessons to read a story. 3. move secretly or quietly. She stole softly out of the room. 4. act of stealing. *Used in common talk. v., stole, stolen, stealing, n. 2.*

stealth (stelth), secret action. He obtained the letter by stealth, taking it while his sister was out of the room. *n. 8.*

stealth ily (stel′thili), in a stealthy manner; by stealth. *adv.*

stealth y (stel′thi), done in a secret manner; secret; sly. The cat crept in a stealthy way toward the bird. *adj., stealthier, stealthiest. 12.*

steam (stēm), 1. water in the form of vapor or gas. Boiling water gives off steam. Steam is used to heat houses, run engines, etc. 2. give off steam; as, a cup of steaming coffee. 3. move by steam. The ship steamed off. 4. cook, soften, or freshen by steam. She steamed the plum pudding. 5. power; energy; force. *Used in common talk. n., v. 2.*

steam boat (stēm′bōt′), boat moved by steam. *n. 6.*

steam engine, engine worked by steam.

steam er (stēm′ər), 1. steamboat; steamship. 2. engine or car run by steam. 3. container in which something is steamed. *n. 3.*

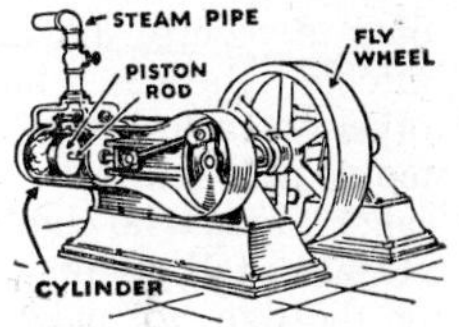

Steam engine

steam fitter, man who installs and repairs steam pipes. *20.*

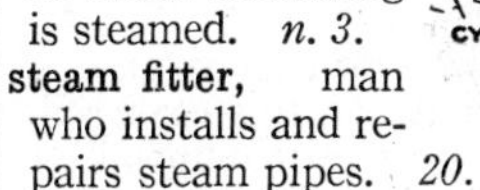

steam roller, 1. heavy roller moved by steam, used to crush and level materials in making roads. 2. means of crushing opposition. *Used in common talk.*

steam ship (stēm′ship′), ship moved by steam. *n. 6.*

steam shovel, machine for digging, operated by steam.

steam y (stēm′i), 1. of steam; like steam. 2. full of steam; giving off steam. *adj.*

steed (stēd), horse; high-spirited horse; war horse; riding horse. *n. 4.*

steel (stēl), 1. iron mixed with carbon so that it is very hard, strong, and tough.

Most tools are made from steel. 2. something made from steel. A sword or a piece of steel for making sparks can be called a steel. 3. made of steel. 4. make hard or strong like steel. He steeled his heart against the sufferings of the poor. *n., adj., v. 2.*

steel y (stēl′i), 1. made of steel. 2. like steel in color, strength, or hardness. *adj. 18.*

steel yard (stēl′-yärd), a scale for weighing. A steelyard has unequal arms, the longer one having a movable weight, and the shorter a hook for holding the object to be weighed. *n. 20.*

Steelyard

steep[1] (stēp), having a sharp slope; almost straight up and down. The hill is steep. *adj. 2.*

steep[2] (stēp), soak. She steeped the tea in boiling water. His sword was steeped in blood. Professor Jones steeps himself in Latin. *v.*

stee ple (stē′pəl), high tower on a church. Steeples usually have spires. *n. 4.*

stee ple chase (stē′pəl-chās′), a horse race over a course having ditches, hedges, and other obstacles. *n.*

stee ple jack (stē′pəl-jak′), man who climbs steeples, tall chimneys, or the like, to make repairs, etc. *n.*

steer[1] (stēr), 1. guide; as, to steer a ship, to steer a sled, to steer an automobile, to steer an airplane. The pilot steered for the harbor. 2. be guided. This car steers easily. 3. direct one's way or course. *v. 3.*

steer[2] (stēr), 1. young ox, usually two to four years old. 2. any male of beef cattle. *n.*

steer age (stēr′ij), the part of a passenger ship occupied by passengers traveling at the cheapest rate. *n. 16.*

steering wheel, wheel that is turned to steer an automobile, ship, etc.

steers man (stērz′mən), man who steers a boat or ship. *n., pl. steersmen. 16.*

stein (stīn), beer mug. *n. 19.*

stel lar (stel′ər), of or pertaining to the stars; of a star; like a star. *adj. 19.*

stem[1] (stem), 1. the main part of a plant above the ground, which supports the other parts. The trunk of a tree and the stalks of corn are stems. 2. the part of a flower, a fruit, or a leaf that joins it to the plant or tree. 3. remove the stem from (a leaf, fruit, etc.). 4. anything like the stem of a plant; as, the stem of a goblet, the stem of a pipe, etc. 5. line of descent of a family. 6. the part of a word to which endings are added and in which changes are made. *Run* is the stem of *runner, ran,* etc. 7. bow or front end of a boat. *n., v., stemmed, stemming. 3.*

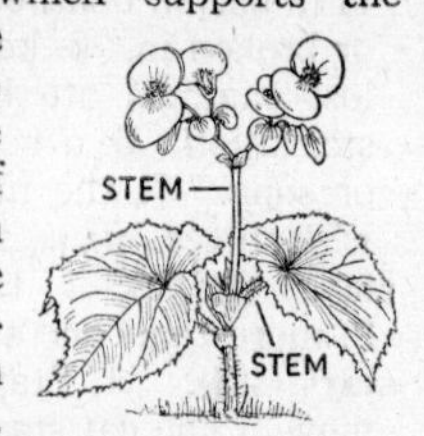

stem[2] (stem), 1. stop; check; dam up. 2. make progress against. *v., stemmed, stemming.*

stench (stench), very bad smell; as, the stench of a pigpen, the stench of gas. *n. 12.*

sten cil (sten′səl), 1. thin sheet of metal, paper, etc., having letters or designs cut through it. When it is laid on a surface and ink or color is spread on, these letters or designs are made on the surface. 2. the letters or designs so made. 3. mark or paint with a stencil. The curtains have a stenciled border. *n., v., stenciled, stenciling. 17.*

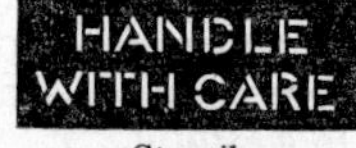

Stencil

ste nog ra pher (stə nog′rə fər), person whose work is stenography and typewriting. *n. 10.*

sten o graph ic (sten′ə graf′ik), 1. of stenography. 2. made by stenography. *adj.*

ste nog ra phy (stə nog′rə fi), 1. method of rapid writing which uses symbols in place of letters, sounds, and words. For example, the symbols in the picture mean "Your letter was received today." 2. act of writing in such symbols. *n. 18.*

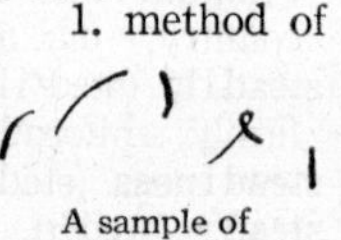
A sample of stenography

sten to ri an (sten tō′ri ən), very loud or powerful in sound. *adj. 19.*

step (step), 1. one motion of the leg in walking, running, dancing, etc. 2. distance covered by one such motion. 3. move the legs as in walking, running, dancing, etc. Step lively! 4. short distance; little way. 5. walk a short distance. Step this way. 6. way of stepping; as, a quick step, a dance with fancy steps. 7. **Keep step** means move the same leg at the same time that another person does. **In step** means making one's steps fit those of some other person. **Out of step** means not in step. 8. measure (off) by taking steps. Step off the distance from the door to the window. 9. place for the foot in going up or coming down. A stair or a rung of a ladder is a step. 10. sound made by putting the foot down. 11. footprint. 12. an action. The principal took steps to stop needless absence from school. 13. a degree in a scale; a grade in rank. *n., v., stepped, stepping. 1.*

step broth er (step′bruᴛʜ′ər), a stepfather's or stepmother's son by a former marriage. If John's father marries a widow with a little boy, this boy will be John's stepbrother. *n.*

step child (step′chīld′), child of one's husband or wife by a former marriage. *n., pl. stepchildren.*

step daugh ter (step′dô′tər), daughter of one's husband or wife by a former marriage. *n.*

step fa ther (step′fä′ᴛʜər), man who has married one's mother after the death or divorce of one's real father. *n. 15.*

step lad der (step′lad′ər), ladder with flat steps instead of rungs. *n.*

Stepladder

step moth er (step′muᴛʜ′ər), woman who has married one's father after the death or divorce of one's real mother. *n. 9.*

steppe (step), 1. one of the vast treeless plains in southeastern Europe and Siberia. 2. a vast treeless plain. *n. 10.*

stepping stone, 1. a stone or one of a line of stones in shallow water, a marshy place, or the like, used in crossing. 2. a stone for use in mounting or ascending; anything serving as a means of advancing or rising.

step sis ter (step′sis′tər), a stepfather's or stepmother's daughter by a former marriage. *n.*

step son (step′sun′), son of one's husband or wife by a former marriage. *n. 20.*

ster e op ti con (ster′i op′ti kən), a kind of magic lantern having a powerful light that projects pictures upon a screen. *n.*

ster e o scope (ster′i ə skōp′), an instrument through which two pictures of the same object or scene are viewed, one by each eye. The object or scene thus viewed appears as it would if really seen. See the picture just below. *n.*

Stereoscope

ster e o typed (ster′i ə tīpt′), fixed or settled in form; conventional. "It gives me great pleasure to be with you tonight" is a stereotyped beginning for a speech. *adj. 15.*

ster ile (ster′il), 1. barren; not fertile. Sterile land does not produce good crops. 2. free from living germs. A doctor's instruments must be kept sterile. *adj. 10.*

ste ril i ty (stə ril′i ti), barrenness; sterile condition or character. *n. 18.*

ster i li za tion (ster′i li zā′shən), a sterilizing or being sterilized; as, the sterilization of dishes by boiling them. *n. 20.*

ster i lize (ster′i līz), make sterile; free from living germs. The water had to be sterilized by boiling to make it fit to drink. *v. 9.*

ster ling (stėr′ling), 1. British money. 2. of British money; payable in British money. 3. of standard quality; containing 92.5% pure silver. *Sterling* is stamped on solid silver knives, forks, etc. 4. sterling silver. 5. made of sterling silver. 6. genuine; excellent; dependable. *n., adj. 8.*

sterling silver, solid silver; silver 92.5% pure.

stern[1] (stėrn), 1. severe; strict; harsh. His father was a stern man. His stern frown frightened the children. 2. hard; not yielding; firm. *adj. 3.*

stern[2] (stėrn), the hind part of a ship or boat. *n.*

ster num (stėr′nəm), the breastbone, a thin, flat bone in the front of the chest to which the ribs are attached. *n. 20.*

ste ve dore (stē′və dōr), man who loads and unloads ships. *n. 20.*

Ste ven son (stē′vən sən), Robert Louis, a famous author (1850-1894). *n. 11.*

stew (stū or stü), 1. cook by slow boiling. The cook stewed the chicken for a long time. 2. food cooked by slow boiling; as, beef stew. 3. worry. She is all in a stew over her lost trunk. *v., n. 7.*

stew ard (stū′ərd or stü′ərd), 1. man who manages another's property. He is the steward of that great estate. 2. man who takes charge of the food and table service for a club, a ship, etc. 3. servant on a ship; as, a dining-room steward, a deck steward, a cabin steward. *n. 7.*

stew ard ess (stū′ər dis or stü′ər dis), 1. a woman steward. 2. woman servant who waits upon women and children on a ship. *n.*

stew ard ship (stū′ərd ship or stü′ərd ship), position or work of a steward. *n. 17.*

St. He le na (sānt he lē′nə), a British island in the southern Atlantic Ocean where Napoleon lived in exile.

stick[1] (stik), 1. a long, thin piece of wood. Put some sticks on the fire. 2. such a piece of wood shaped for a special use; as, a walking stick or a golf stick. 3. something like a stick in shape; as, a stick of candy, a drumstick. 4. a stiff, awkward, or stupid person. *Used in common talk. n. 1.*

stick[2] (stik), 1. stab; pierce with a pointed instrument. He stuck his fork into the potato. 2. fasten by thrusting the point or end into or through something. He stuck a flower in his buttonhole. 3. put into a position. Don't stick your head out of the train window. 4. fasten; attach; be fastened. Stick a stamp on the letter. Two pages of the book stuck together. 5. keep on; hold fast. John sticks to a task until he finishes it. He sticks to his friends in trouble. 6. puzzle. That problem in arithmetic stuck me. *Used in common talk.* 7. be puzzled; hesitate. He sticks at nothing to get his own way. 8. bring to a stop; become fixed; be at a standstill. The car was stuck in the mud. 9. **Stick up** means (1) stand up. (2) hold up; rob. *Slang.* 10. **Stick up for** means support; defend. *Used in common talk. v., stuck, sticking.*

stick i ness (stik′i nis), a being sticky. *n.*

stick le (stik′əl), 1. make objections about trifles; insist stubbornly. 2. have objections; feel difficulties about trifles; scruple. *v.*

stick ler (stik′lər), person who contends stubbornly or insists on trifles. *n.*

stick y (stik′i), that sticks; as, sticky flypaper. *adj., stickier, stickiest. 12.*

stiff (stif), 1. not easily bent; hard to move. He wore a stiff collar. The old man's joints were stiff. 2. firm. The jelly is stiff enough to stand alone. 3. not easy in manner; formal. He made a stiff bow. He writes in a stiff style. 4. hard to deal with; hard. A stiff breeze was blowing. It was a stiff examination. 5. more than seems suitable. He asks a stiff price for his house. *adj. 2.*

stiff en (stif′ən), 1. make stiff. She stiffened the shirt with starch. 2. become stiff. The jelly will stiffen as it cools. He stiffened with anger. *v. 8.*

stiff-necked (stif′nekt′), 1. having a stiff neck. 2. stubborn; obstinate. *adj.*

sti fle (stī′fəl), 1. stop the breath of; smother. The smoke stifled the firemen. 2. be unable to breathe freely. I am stifling in this close room. 3. stop; suppress; keep back; as, to stifle a cry, to stifle a yawn. *v. 6.*

←STIGMA

stig ma (stig′mə), 1. mark of disgrace; a stain or reproach on one's reputation. 2. small spot or mark; spot in the skin which bleeds or turns red. 3. the part of the pistil of a plant which receives the pollen. *n. 8.*

stig ma tize (stig′mə tīz), brand; set some mark of disgrace upon; reproach. *v. 15.*

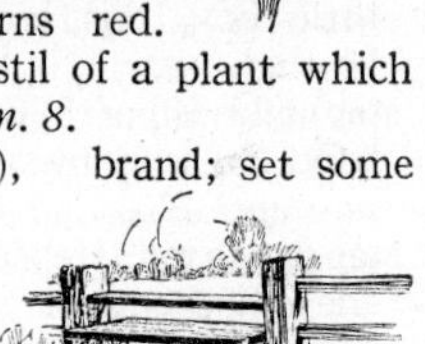

Stile

stile (stīl), 1. step or steps for getting over a fence or wall. 2. turnstile. *n. 8.*

sti let to (sti let′ō), 1. a dagger with a narrow blade. 2. a small sharp-pointed instrument for making eyelet holes in embroidery. *n., pl. stilettos.*

Stiletto

still[1] (stil), 1. without motion; without noise; quiet. Sit still. The lake is still today. The room was so still that you could have heard a pin drop. 2. to quiet. The mother stilled the crying baby. The people prayed that the storm might be stilled. 3. even to this time; even to that time. Was the store still open? 4. and yet; but yet; nevertheless. He was hungry; still he would not eat. Though she has new dolls, still Mary loves her old one best. 5. even; yet. You can read still better if you try. 6. always; ever. *Used in poetry. adj., adv., v., conj. 1.*

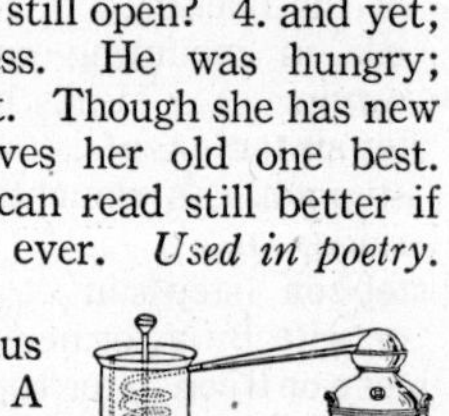

Still

still[2] (stil), apparatus for distilling liquids. A still is used in making alcohol. *n.*

still born (stil′bôrn′), dead when born. *adj.*

still ness (stil′nis), 1. quiet; silence. 2. absence of motion; calm. *n. 5.*

still y (stil′i), quiet; still. *adj. 20.*

stilt (stilt), one of a pair of poles, each with a support for the foot at some distance above the ground. Stilts are used in walking through shallow water, or by children for amusement. *n. 10.*

stilt ed (stil′tid), stiffly dignified or formal. *adj.*

stim u lant (stim′ū lənt), 1. something that excites or stirs or stimulates. Tea, coffee, and alcohol are stimulants. 2. stimulating. *n., adj. 10.*

stim u late (stim′ū lāt), excite; spur on; rouse to action. Praise stimulated Mary to work hard. *v. 7.*

stim u la tion (stim′ū lā′shən), stimulating; being stimulated. Lazy children need some stimulation to make them work. *n. 12.*

stim u lus (stim′ū ləs), 1. something that stirs to action or effort. Ambition is a great stimulus. 2. something that excites some part of the body to activity. The stimulus of a loud sound, carried by nerves to the brain, made the baby cry. *n., pl. stimuli* (-lī). *8.*

sting (sting), 1. prick; wound. Bees, wasps, and hornets sting. A bee stung John. John put mud on the sting to take away the pain. 2. sharp-pointed part of an animal that pricks or wounds and often poisons. 3. pain sharply. Jim was stung by the mockings of the other children. 4. sharp pain. The ball team felt the sting of defeat. 5. cause a feeling like that of a prick. Mustard stings. *v., stung, stinging, n. 3.*

stin gi ly (stin′ji li), in a stingy manner. *adv.*

stin gi ness (stin′ji nis), meanness about spending or giving money. *n.*

sting ray, a broad flat fish that can inflict severe wounds with its sharp spines.

Sting ray (may reach a length of 10 to 12 ft., including the tail)

stin gy (stin′ji), mean about spending or giving money. *adj., stingier, stingiest. 18.*

stink (stingk), 1. very bad smell. 2. have a bad smell. Decaying fish stink. *n., v., stank* or *stunk, stunk, stinking. 7.*

stint (stint), 1. to limit; keep on short allowance; be saving or careful in using or spending. The parents stinted themselves of food to give it to the children. 2. limit; limitation. That generous man gives without stint. 3. task assigned. Mary had to wash the supper dishes as her daily stint. *v., n. 9.*

sti pend (stī′pend), salary; fixed or regular pay. A postman receives a stipend. *n. 15.*

stip u late (stip′ū lāt), arrange definitely; demand as a condition of agreement. He stipulated that he should receive a month's vacation every year if he took the job. *v. 13.*

stip u la tion (stip′ū lā′shən), agreement; definite arrangement; a condition in an agreement or bargain. We rented the house with the stipulation that certain rooms should be papered and painted. *n. 13.*

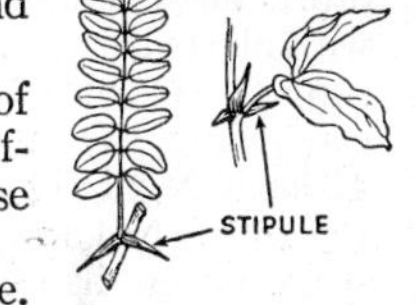

stip ule (stip′ūl), one of the pair of little leaflike parts at the base of a leaf stem. *n. 18.*

stir (stėr), 1. move. The wind stirs the leaves. No one was stirring in the house. 2. mix by moving around with a spoon, fork, stick, etc. He stirs the sugar in his tea with his spoon. 3. set going; excite; affect strongly. John stirs up the other children to mischief. 4. movement; excitement. The coming of the queen caused a great stir. 5. act of stirring. *v., stirred, stirring, n. 2.*

stir rup (stėr′əp), a support for the rider's foot, hung from a saddle. *n. 6.*

Stirrups

stitch (stich), 1. one complete movement of a threaded needle through cloth in sewing. Take short stitches. 2. one complete movement in knitting, crocheting, embroidering, etc. 3. result of such a movement. Rip out these long stitches. The doctor will take the stitches out of the wound tomorrow. 4. particular methods of taking stitches; as, buttonhole stitch, etc. 5. make stitches in; fasten with stitches; sew. 6. a sudden, sharp pain. *n., v. 4.*

sti ver (stī′vər), anything having small value. *n.*

St. John, 1. a seaport city in southeastern Canada. 2. the disciple whom Jesus loved. *18.*

St. John's, capital of Newfoundland.

St. Joseph, 1. a city in northwestern Missouri, on the Missouri River. 2. the husband of Mary, the mother of Jesus.

St. Lawrence, 1. a river in North America flowing into the Atlantic Ocean. 2. a gulf in eastern Canada. *11.*

St. Lou is (sānt lü′is or sānt lü′i), city in eastern Missouri, on the Mississippi River. *12.*

St. Nich o las (sānt nik′ə ləs), 1. the patron saint of young people, travelers, and sailors. 2. Santa Claus.

stoat (stōt), 1. the ermine in its summer coat of brown. 2. the weasel. *n. 20.*

stock (stok), 1. things for use or for sale; supply used as it is needed. This store keeps a large stock of toys. 2. cattle or other farm animals. The farm was sold with all its livestock. 3. lay in a supply of; supply. Our camp is well stocked with everything we need for a short stay. 4. keep regularly for use or for sale. A toy store stocks toys. 5. kept regularly in stock or on hand; as, stock sizes. 6. in common use; commonplace; everyday. The weather is a stock subject of conversation. 7. shares in a company. Father owns some stock in that railroad. 8. family; race. She is of old New England stock. 9. part used as a support or handle; as, the wooden stock of a rifle. 10. an old-fashioned stiff necktie. 11. lifeless and stupid thing. "You stocks and stones!" 12. trunk of a tree. 13. **The stocks** was a framework with holes for the feet, and sometimes for the hands, used as a punishment. *n., v., adj. 1.*

Man in the stocks

stock ade (stok ād′), 1. a defense or pen made of strong posts fixed upright in the ground. 2. protect, fortify, or surround with a stockade. *n., v. 10.*

Stockade

stock bro ker (stok′brō′kər), person who buys and sells stocks and bonds for others for a commission. *n.*

stock exchange, 1. place where stocks are bought and sold. 2. association of brokers and dealers in stocks and bonds.

stock hold er (stok′hōl′dər), owner of stocks or shares in a company. *n. 14.*

Stock holm (stok′hōlm), the capital of Sweden. *n. 20.*

stock ing (stok′ing), close-fitting knitted covering for the foot and leg. *n. 2.*

stock market, 1. place where stocks are bought and sold. 2. the buying and selling in such a place. 3. prices of stocks and bonds.

stock-still (stok′stil′), motionless. *adj.*

stock y (stok′i), having a solid or sturdy form or build; thick for its height. *adj., stockier, stockiest.*

stock yard (stok′yärd′), pens and sheds for cattle, sheep, hogs, and horses. A stockyard is usually connected with a slaughter house, railroad, or market. *n. 19.*

stodg y (stoj′i), 1. heavy. 2. dull. *adj., stodgier, stodgiest.*

sto gie or **sto gy** (stō′gi), a long, slender, cheap cigar. *n., pl. stogies.*

sto ic (stō′ik), 1. person who remains calm, represses his feelings, and is indifferent to pleasure and pain. 2. stoical. *n., adj. 10.*

sto i cal (stō′i kəl), like a stoic; self-controlled; indifferent to pleasure and pain. *adj. 15.*

sto i cism (stō′i sizm), patient endurance; caring little about pleasure and pain. *n. 17.*

stoke (stōk), poke, stir up, and feed (a fire); tend the fire of (a furnace). *v. 18.*

stoke hold (stōk′hōld′), place in a steamship where the furnaces and boilers are. *n.*

stoke hole (stōk′hōl′), 1. hole through which fuel is put into a furnace. 2. space in front of furnaces where men shovel in coal and take out ashes. *n.*

stok er (stōk′ər), 1. man who tends the fires of a furnace or boiler. 2. mechanical device for tending and feeding a furnace. *n. 19.*

stole[1] (stōl). See **steal.** He stole the money years ago. *pt. of steal. 3.*

stole[2] (stōl), a narrow strip of silk or other material worn over the shoulders by a clergyman. *n.*

sto len (stō′lən). See **steal.** The money was stolen by a thief. *pp. of steal. 4.*

stol id (stol′id), hard to arouse; not easily excited; seeming dull. *adj. 14.*

stom ach (stum′ək), 1. the most important part of the body for receiving and digesting food. See the diagram under **intestine.** 2. the part of the body containing the stomach. Dick hit Bill in the stomach. 3. appetite. 4. bear; endure; put up with. He could not stomach such an insult. *n., v. 4.*

Lady wearing a stomacher

stom ach er (stum′ək ər), a part of a woman's dress covering the stomach and chest. *n. 17.*

stone (stōn), 1. hard mineral matter which is not a metal; rock; piece of rock. Stone is much used in building. 2. made of stone; as, a stone wall, a stone house. 3. pertaining to stone. The **Stone Age** means the period when tools and weapons were made of stone. 4. put stone on; line with stone. 5. gem; jewel. The queen's diamonds were very fine stones. 6. something hard and rounded like a stone, which sometimes forms in the kidneys or gall bladder, causing sickness and pain. 7. throw stones at; kill by throwing stones. The cruel boys stoned the dog. Stephen was stoned. 8. hard seed; as, peach stones, plum stones. 9. take stones or seeds out of; as, to stone cherries or plums. 10. made of stoneware or coarse clay. 11. A **stone's throw** means a short distance. 12. 14 pounds. *British use. n., adj., v. 1.*

stone cut ter (stōn′kut′ər), person who cuts or carves stones. *n.*

stone ware (stōn′wãr′), coarse, hard, glazed pottery. *n.*

stone work (stōn′wėrk′), work in stone; the part of a building made of stone or brick and mortar. *n.*

ston y (stōn′i), 1. having many stones. The beach is stony. 2. hard like stone. He has a stony heart. *adj. 5.*

stood (stu̇d). See **stand.** Tom stood in the corner for five minutes. *pt. and pp. of stand. 1.*

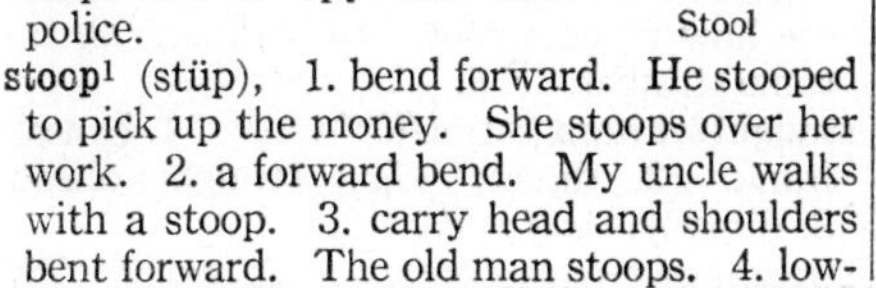
Stool

stool (stül), seat without back or arms. *n. 4.*

stool pigeon, 1. pigeon used to lead other pigeons into a trap. 2. a spy for the police.

stoop[1] (stüp), 1. bend forward. He stooped to pick up the money. She stoops over her work. 2. a forward bend. My uncle walks with a stoop. 3. carry head and shoulders bent forward. The old man stoops. 4. lower oneself; descend. He stooped to cheating. *v., n. 3.*

stoop[2] (stüp), a porch or platform at the entrance of a house. *n.*

stop (stop), 1. close (a hole or opening) by filling (it). The boy stopped up the rat-holes. 2. block (a way). A big box stops up the doorway. 3. keep (from moving, doing, being, working, etc.). The men stopped the boys from teasing the cat. I stopped the clock. 4. put an end to; as, to stop a noise. 5. come to an end; cease: leave off (moving, acting, doing, being, etc.). The baby stopped crying. 6. stay. Mrs. Blank stopped at the bank for a few minutes. 7. any act of stopping; a closing; a filling up; a blocking; a hindering; a checking. 8. thing that stops, such as a block, a plug, etc. 9. punctuation mark. The most used stops are ? ! . , ; : —. 10. a device that controls the pitch of a musical instrument. *v., stopped, stopping, n. 1.*

stop gap (stop′gap′), thing that fills the place of something lacking. *n.*

stop page (stop′ij), 1. stopping. 2. being stopped. 3. block; obstruction. *n. 18.*

stop per (stop′ər), a plug or cork for closing a bottle, tube, etc. *n. 17.*

stop ple (stop′əl), 1. stopper for a bottle, etc. 2. close or fit with a stopper. *n., v.*

stop watch, a watch which has a hand that can be stopped or started at any instant. A stop watch indicates fractions of a second and is used for timing races and contests.

stor age (stōr′ij), 1. place for storing. She has put her furniture in storage. 2. price for storing. She paid $30 storage on her furniture. 3. act or fact of storing goods. 4. condition of being stored. Cold storage is used to keep eggs and meat from spoiling. *n. 7.*

storage battery, a battery for storing electrical energy. A storage battery consists of one or more cells that can be charged with electricity.

store (stōr), 1. place where goods are kept for sale; as, a clothing store. 2. supply; stock; something put away for use later. She puts up stores of preserves and jellies every year. **In store** means on hand; saved for the future. 3. put away for use later; lay up. The squirrel stores away nuts. We stored our furs during the summer. 4. place where supplies are kept for future use; a storehouse. *n., v. 1.*

store house (stōr′hous′), place where things are stored. The factory has many storehouses for its products. A library is a storehouse of information. *n. 8.*

store keep er (stōr′kēp′ər), person who has charge of a store or stores. *n. 10.*

store room (stōr′rüm′), room where things are stored. *n.*

sto ried[1] (stō′rid), celebrated in story or history; as, "the storied Rhine." *adj.*

sto ried[2] (stō′rid), having stories or floors; as, a two-storied house. *adj.*

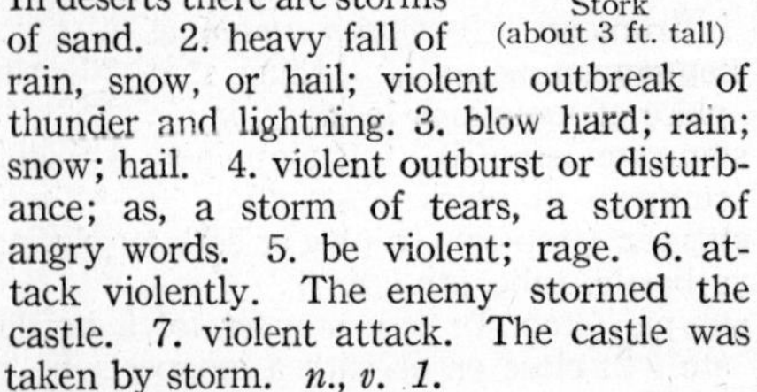

Stork (about 3 ft. tall)

stork (stôrk), a large, long-legged bird with a long neck and a long bill. *n. 5.*

storm (stôrm), 1. strong wind with rain, snow, hail, or thunder and lightning. In deserts there are storms of sand. 2. heavy fall of rain, snow, or hail; violent outbreak of thunder and lightning. 3. blow hard; rain; snow; hail. 4. violent outburst or disturbance; as, a storm of tears, a storm of angry words. 5. be violent; rage. 6. attack violently. The enemy stormed the castle. 7. violent attack. The castle was taken by storm. *n., v. 1.*

storm y (stôr′mi), 1. having storms; likely to have storms; troubled by storms; as, a stormy sea, stormy weather, a stormy night. 2. violent; rough and disturbed. They had stormy quarrels. *adj., stormier, stormiest. 3.*

sto ry[1] (stō′ri), 1. an account of some happening or group of happenings. The man told the story of his life. 2. such an account, either true or made-up, intended to interest the reader or hearer; as, fairy stories, ghost stories, stories of adventure, funny stories. 3. falsehood. That boy is a liar; he tells stories. *n., pl. stories. 1.*

sto ry[2] (stō′ri), the set of rooms on the same level or floor of a building. The house has two stories. *n., pl. stories.*

stoup (stüp), 1. drinking vessel of various sizes, such as a cup, flagon, or tankard. 2. amount it holds. 3. basin for holy water. *n.*

stout (stout), 1. fat and large. 2. firm; strong; strongly built. The fort has stout walls. 3. brave; bold. 4. a dark-brown beer. *adj., n. 3.*

stout ness (stout′nis), 1. bravery. 2. firmness; strength. 3. fatness. *n. 17.*

stove[1] (stōv), apparatus for cooking and heating. See the pictures. There are coal, gas, oil, and electric stoves. *n. 3.*

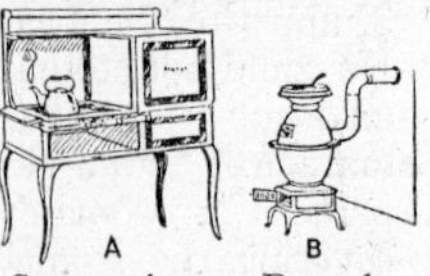

Stoves: A, gas; B, coal.

stove[2] (stōv), staved. That barrel was stove in when it dropped off the truck. *pt. and pp. of* **stave.**

stow (stō), 1. pack. The cargo was stowed in the ship's hold. 2. fill by packing; pack things closely in. The boys stowed the little cabin with supplies for the trip. 3. **Stow away** means hide on a ship, airplane, etc., to get a free ride. *v. 13.*

stow a way (stō′ə wā′), person who hides on a ship, train, etc., to get a free passage or to escape secretly. *n. 18.*

St. Paul, the capital of Minnesota, on the Mississippi River.

St. Pe ters burg (sānt pē′tərz bėrg), former capital of Russia, now called Leningrad.

strad dle (strad′əl), 1. walk, stand, or sit with the legs wide apart. 2. spread (the legs) wide apart. 3. have a leg on each side of (a horse, bicycle, chair, ditch, etc.). 4. avoid taking sides. 5. a straddling. *v., n. 15.*

strag gle (strag′əl), 1. wander in a scattered fashion. Cows straggled along the road. 2. spread in an irregular, rambling manner. Vines straggled over the yard. It was a straggling little town. *v. 10.*

straight (strāt), 1. without a bend or curve; as, a straight line, a straight stick, a straight path, straight hair. 2. directly. Harry went straight home. 3. frank; honest; upright. 4. frankly; honestly. 5. in the proper order or condition. Set the room straight. Our accounts are straight. He kept a straight face, though he wanted to laugh. 6. **Straight away** or **straight off** means at once. *adj., adv. 1.*

straight en (strāt′ən), 1. make straight. He straightened the bent pin. Straighten your shoulders. 2. put in the proper order or condition. Straighten up your room. We must straighten out our accounts and see how much we owe each other. 3. become straight. *v. 6.*

straight for ward (strāt′fôr′wərd), 1. honest; frank. 2. direct; going straight ahead. 3. directly. *adj., adv. 12.*

straight way (strāt′wā′), at once. The captain read the letter and burned it straightway. *adv. 5.*

strain[1] (strān), 1. draw tight; stretch. The weight strained the rope. 2. stretch as much as possible. She strained the truth in telling that story. 3. use to the utmost. He strained every muscle to lift the rock. 4. injure by too much effort or by stretching. The runner strained his heart. 5. injury caused by too much effort or by stretching; a sprain. The doctor said the injury to John's ankle was only a slight strain. 6. press closely; squeeze; hug. She strained her child to her breast. 7. press or pour through a strainer. Strain the soup before serving it. 8. force; compel. *Not used now.* 9. force or weight that stretches. The strain on the rope made it break. 10. any severe, trying, or wearing effort; its effect on the body or mind. The strain of sleepless nights made her ill. 11. a part of a piece of music; melody; song. 12. manner or style (of doing or speaking). *v., n. 3.*

strain[2] (strān), 1. line of descent; race; stock. The Irish strain in him makes him like jokes. 2. inherited quality. There is a strain of madness in that family. 3. trace or streak. That horse has a mean strain. *n.*

strained (strānd), forced; not natural. Her greeting was cold and strained. *adj.*

strain er (strān′ər), thing that strains. A filter, a sieve, and a colander are strainers. *n. 11.*

Strainer or colander

strait (strāt), 1. narrow. *Old use.* 2. strict. The nun took strait vows. *Old use.* 3. narrow channel connecting two larger bodies of water. The Strait of Gibraltar connects the Mediterranean Sea and the Atlantic Ocean. 4. difficulty. He was in desperate straits for money. *adj., n. 3.*

strait en (strāt′ən), limit by the lack of something; restrict. **In straitened circumstances** means needing money badly. *v. 11.*

strait jacket, a strong coat that holds the arms close to the sides. A strait jacket is used to keep a violent person from harming himself or others.

strait-laced (strāt′lāst′), very strict in matters of conduct. *adj.*

strait ness (strāt′nis), 1. narrowness. 2. strictness. *n.*

strand[1] (strand), 1. shore; land bordering a sea, lake, or river. 2. run aground; drive on the shore. The ship was stranded on the rocks. 3. bring into a helpless position. He was stranded a thousand miles from home with no money. *n., v. 5.*

strand[2] (strand), 1. one of the threads, strings, or wires that are twisted together to make a rope. This is a rope of three strands. 2. thread or string; as, a strand of hair, a strand of pearls. *n.*

strange (strānj), 1. not known, seen, or heard of before. She is moving to a strange place. A strange cat is on our steps. 2. unusual; queer; peculiar. What a strange experience! She wore strange, old-fashioned clothing. 3. out of place; not at home. The poor child felt strange in the palace. *adj. 1.*

stran ger (strān′jər), 1. person not known, seen, or heard of before. She is a stranger to us. 2. person or thing new to a place. He is a stranger in New York. 3. person from another country. The king received the strangers with kindness. *n. 2.*

stran gle (strang′gəl), 1. kill by squeezing the throat to stop the breath; choke. Hercules strangled a snake with each hand. His high collar seemed to be strangling him. 2. choke down; suppress; keep back. *v. 6.*

strap (strap), 1. narrow strip of leather or other material that bends easily. He has a strap around his books. Put a strap around the trunk. 2. a narrow band or strip of cloth. The general wore shoulder straps. 3. narrow strip for fastening things, holding things together, etc. The box was strengthened by straps of steel. 4. fasten with a strap. 5. beat with a strap. 6. narrow strip of leather to sharpen razors on. 7. sharpen on a strap. *n., v., strapped, strapping. 4.*

strap ping (strap′ing), tall, strong, and healthy; as, a fine strapping girl. *adj.*

Stras bourg (stras′bėrg), a city in northeastern France. *n. 17.*

stra ta (strā′tə), layers. *n. pl. 13.* See **stratum.**

strat a gem (strat′ə jəm), a scheme or trick for deceiving the enemy; trick. The stratagem of having a soldier enter the castle in the clothes of a beggar was successful. *n. 7.*

stra te gic (strə tē′jik), 1. of strategy; based on strategy; useful in strategy. 2. important in strategy. The Panama Canal is a strategic link in our national defense. *adj. 14.*

stra te gi cal ly (strə tē′ji kəl i), in a strategic manner; by strategy. *adv.*

strat e gist (strat′i jist), person trained or skilled in strategy. *n.*

strat e gy (strat′i ji), 1. the science or art of war; the planning and directing of military movements and operations. 2. skillful planning and management of anything. *n., pl. strategies. 12.*

Strat ford-on-A von (strat′fərd on ā′vən), the town in England where Shakespeare was born. *n. 17.*

strat i fi ca tion (strat′i fi kā′shən), arrangement in layers. *n.*

strat i fy (strat′i fī), arrange in layers; form into layers. *v., stratified, stratifying. 18.*

strat o sphere (strat′ə sfēr), the upper region of the atmosphere, which begins about seven miles above the earth. In the stratosphere, temperature varies little with changes in altitude, and the winds are chiefly horizontal. *n.*

stra tum (strā′təm), a layer of material; especially, one of several parallel layers or strata placed one upon another. In digging the well, the men struck first a stratum of sand, then several strata of rock. Tramps are from the lowest stratum of society. *n., pl. strata* (strā′tə) or *stratums. 13.*

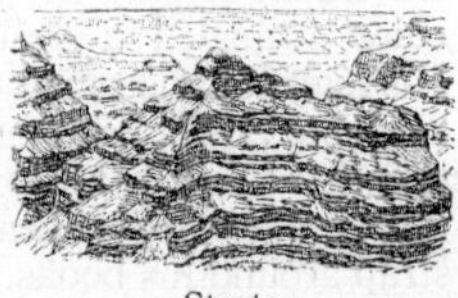

Strata

Strauss (strous), 1. Johann, Austrian composer of dance music (1804-1849). 2. his son, Johann, Austrian composer of dance music and light operas (1825-1899). 3. Richard, German musical composer and conductor. He was born in 1864. *n.*

straw (strô), 1. the stalks or stems of grain after drying and threshing. Straw is used for bedding for horses and cows, for making hats, and for many other purposes. 2. hollow stem or stalk; something like it. Straws made of waxed paper are used for sucking up drinks. 3. made of straw; as, a straw hat. 4. a bit; a trifle. He doesn't care a straw. *n., adj. 2.*

straw ber ry (strô′ber′i), 1. a small, juicy, red fruit. 2. the plant it grows on. *n., pl. strawberries. 3.*

Strawberry

straw board (strô′bōrd′), coarse cardboard made of straw, used for boxes, etc. *n.*

straw vote, unofficial vote taken to find out general opinion.

stray (strā), 1. wander; roam; lose one's way. Our dog has strayed off somewhere. 2. wandering; lost. A stray cat is crying at the door. 3. wanderer; lost animal. 4. scattered; here and there. There were a few stray fishermen's huts along the beach. *v., adj., n. 3.*

streak (strēk), 1. a long thin mark or line. He has a streak of dirt on his face. We saw the streaks of lightning. 2. layer. Bacon has streaks of fat and streaks of lean. 3. vein; strain; element. He has a streak of humor, though he looks very serious. 4. put long thin marks or lines on. The Indians used to streak their faces with paint. *n., v. 6.*

streak y (strēk′i), 1. marked with streaks. 2. occurring in streaks. 3. varying; uneven. The dress has faded so much that the color is streaky. *adj., streakier, streakiest.*

stream (strēm), 1. running water; flow of liquid. Small rivers and large brooks are both called streams. **Up stream** means against the current of the water; **down stream** means with the current. 2. any steady flow; as, a stream of lava, a stream of light, a stream of words. 3. flow or pour out in a stream. Tears streamed from her eyes. 4. wave. The flags streamed in the wind. *n., v. 1.*

stream er (strēm′ər), 1. any long, flowing thing. Streamers of ribbon hung from her hat. 2. a long, narrow flag. *n. 7.*

stream let (strēm′lit), small stream. *n. 15.*

stream line (strēm′līn′), 1. having a shape that offers the least possible resistance to air or water. The fastest automobiles, airplanes, and trains have streamline bodies. 2. give a streamline shape to. *adj., v.*

street (strēt), 1. road in a city or town, usually with buildings on both sides. 2. place or way for automobiles, wagons, etc., to go. 3. people who live in the buildings on a street. *n. 1.*

street car (strēt′kär′), passenger car that runs on rails in the streets. *n. 19.*

street lamp, lamp that lights a street.

strength (strength), being strong; power; force; vigor. Because of his strength he could lift great weights. He did not have enough strength of mind to refuse. The strength of the dog's love for his master had often been tested. Flavorings lose their strength in cooking. **On the strength of** means relying or depending on. Father bought the dog on the strength of Tom's promise to take care of it. *n. 1.*

strength en (streng′thən), 1. make stronger. The people in the town strengthened their defenses. 2. grow stronger. *v. 4.*

stren u ous (stren′ū əs), very active; full of energy. We had a strenuous day moving into our new house. Theodore Roosevelt was a strenuous man. *adj. 7.*

stress (stres), 1. pressure; force; strain. Under the stress of hunger the man stole some food. 2. emphasis; importance. That school lays stress on arithmetic and reading. 3. accent. In *hero*, the stress is on the first syllable. 4. lay stress on; emphasize. Stress the important words of a sentence. *n., v. 9.*

stretch (strech), 1. draw out; extend; extend one's body or limbs. The bird stretched its wings. The blow stretched him out on the ground. 2. reach out; hold out. He stretched out a hand for the money. 3. draw tight; strain. He stretched the violin string until it broke. 4. draw out to greater length or size. Rubber stretches. 5. continue over a distance; extend from one place to another; fill space; spread. The forest stretches for miles to the westward. 6. stretching; being stretched. With a sudden stretch, John took Tom's cap. 7. unbroken length; extent. A stretch of sand hills lay between the road and the ocean. *v., n. 2.*

stretch er (strech′ər), 1. person or thing that stretches. A glove stretcher makes gloves larger. 2. canvas stretched on a frame for carrying the sick, wounded, or dead. *n. 10.*

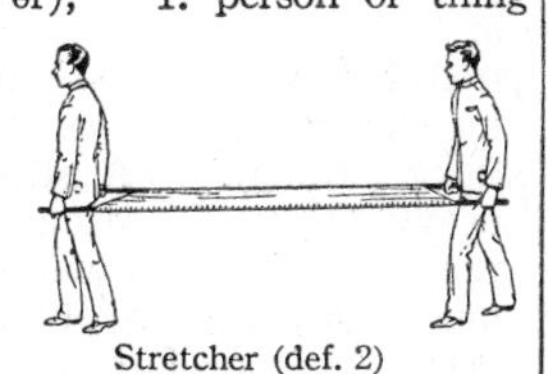
Stretcher (def. 2)

strew (strü), 1. scatter; sprinkle. She strewed seeds in her garden. 2. cover with something scattered or sprinkled. *v., strewed, strewed* or *strewn, strewing. 6.*

strewn (strün), strewed. *pp. of* **strew**. *10.*

strick en (strik′ən), 1. affected by (wounds, diseases, trouble, sorrows, etc.). Help was rushed to the fire-stricken city. 2. **Stricken in years** means old. 3. struck. *adj., pp. of* **strike.** *5.*

strict (strikt), 1. very careful in following a rule or in making others follow it. The Puritans were very strict. 2. harsh; severe. 3. exact; precise; accurate. He told the strict truth. 4. perfect; complete; absolute. The secret was told him in strict confidence. *adj. 4.*

strict ness (strikt′nis), 1. exactness. 2. severity; harshness. *n. 19.*

stric ture (strik′chər), 1. unfavorable criticism; critical remark. 2. unhealthy narrowing of some duct or tube of the body. *n. 16.*

stride (strīd), 1. walk with long steps. The tall man strides rapidly down the street. 2. pass with one long step. He strode over the brook. 3. sit or stand with one leg on each side of; as, to stride a fence. 4. long step. The child could not keep up with his father's stride. *v., strode, stridden, striding, n. 4.*

stri dent (strī′dənt), harsh-sounding; creaking; shrill. *adj. 20.*

strife (strīf), struggle; quarreling; fighting. *n. 3.*

strike (strīk), 1. hit. Jim struck his enemy. The ship struck a rock. 2. set on fire by hitting or rubbing. Strike a match. 3. make by stamping, printing, etc. A medal was struck in memory of the great victory. 4. influence; overcome (by death, disease, suffering, terror, fear, etc.). All were struck with terror at her wild cry. 5. occur to. She smiled as an amusing thought struck her. 6. sound. The clock strikes twelve times at noon. 7. **Strike up** means begin. Dick and Bob struck up a friendship. 8. **Strike out** means (1) cross out; rub out. (2) fail to hit three times. 9. lower or take down (a sail, flag, tent, etc.). The ship struck her flag as a sign of surrender. 10. go; advance. We walked along the road a mile, then struck out across the fields. 11. go (into); cause to go (into); send roots. 12. stop work to get better pay, shorter hours, etc. The coal miners struck. 13. stopping work in this way. 14. make; decide; enter upon. The employer and the workmen have struck an agreement. 15. find or come upon (ore, oil, water, etc.). 16. finding rich ore in mining, oil in boring, etc.; sudden success. *v., struck, struck* or *stricken, striking, n. 1.*

strik er (strīk′ər), 1. person or thing that strikes. 2. worker who is on a strike. *n. 15.*

strik ing (strīk′ing), 1. attracting attention; very noticeable. 2. on a strike. *adj.*

strik ing ly (strīk′ing li), in a way that attracts attention. *adv. 17.*

string (string), 1. thick thread; small cord or wire; very thin rope. The package is tied with red string. 2. such a thread with things on it. She wore a string of beads around her neck. 3. put on a string. The child is stringing beads. 4. special cord for musical instruments, bows, etc.; as, the strings of a violin. **Strings** sometimes means violins, cellos, and other stringed instruments. 5. furnish with strings. He had his tennis racket strung. 6. anything used for tying; as, shoestrings, apron strings. 7. tie with string; hang with a string or rope. 8. cordlike part of plants. String beans have little strings in them. 9. remove strings from. String the beans. 10. form into strings. 11. number of things in a line or row. A string of cars came down the street. 12. stretch; extend. The program was strung out too long. *n., v., strung, stringing. 2.*

string bean, 1. unripe pod of a bean plant. 2. the plant itself.

stringed (stringd), having strings. A harp is a stringed instrument. *adj.*

strin gen cy (strin′jən si), 1. strictness; severity. 2. tightness. *n.*

strin gent (strin′jənt), 1. strict; severe; as, stringent laws against speeding. 2. tight. A stringent money market is one where money is scarce and hard to borrow. *adj. 13.*

string y (string′i), 1. like a string or strings. 2. forming strings; as, a stringy syrup. 3. having tough fibers; as, stringy meat. *adj., stringier, stringiest.*

strip[1] (strip), 1. make bare or naked; undress. 2. take off the covering of. The boy stripped the skin from a banana. 3. take away. The boys stripped the fruit from the trees. 4. rob. Thieves stripped the house of everything valuable. *v., stripped, stripping. 2.*

strip[2] (strip), a long, narrow, flat piece (of cloth, paper, bark, etc.). *n.*

stripe[1] (strīp), 1. a long, narrow band. A tiger has stripes. The American flag has thirteen stripes. Stripes on an army officer's sleeve show his rank. 2. mark with stripes. The stick of candy was striped with red. *n., v. 4.*

stripe[2] (strīp), a stroke or lash with a whip. *n.*

striped (strīpt or strīp′id), having stripes. Zebras are striped. *adj.*

strip ling (strip′ling), a youth; lad; boy just coming into manhood. *n. 10.*

strive (strīv), 1. try hard; work hard. Strive to succeed. 2. struggle; fight. The swimmer strove with the tide. *v., strove, striven, striving. 3.*

striv en (striv′ən). See **strive.** She has striven hard to make the party a success. *pp. of strive.*

strode (strōd). See **stride.** He strode over the ditch. *pt. of stride. 8.*

stroke[1] (strōk), 1. act of striking; a blow. He drove in the nail with one stroke of the hammer. The house was hit by a stroke of lightning. 2. sound made by striking. We arrived at the stroke of three. 3. single complete movement to be made again and again. He rowed with a strong stroke of the oars. He swims a fast stroke. 4. a movement or mark made by a pen, pencil, brush, etc. He writes with a heavy down stroke. 5. single effort; very successful effort; as, a stroke of work. 6. sudden attack (of disease); as, sunstroke, a stroke of paralysis. 7. the rower who sets the time for the other oarsmen. 8. be the stroke of. *n., v. 2.*

stroke[2] (strōk), 1. move the hand gently along. She likes to stroke her kitten. 2. such a movement; as, to brush away the crumbs with one stroke. *v., n.*

stroll (strōl), 1. walk; take a quiet walk for pleasure. 2. leisurely walk. 3. go from place to place; as, strolling gypsies. *v., n. 6.*

stroll er (strōl′ər), 1. wanderer. 2. strolling player or actor. *n. 19.*

strong (strông). A strong man can lift heavy things. A strong wind blew down the trees. A strong nation is one that has much power because of its wealth and numbers. A strong fort is one that cannot be easily captured. A strong acid is one that contains much acid and little water. Strong tea has more flavor than weak tea. Anything that has much force or power may be called strong. *adj. 1.*

strong hold (strông′hōld′), strong place; safe place; fort. The robbers have a stronghold in the mountains. *n. 10.*

strop (strop), 1. leather strap used for sharpening razors. 2. sharpen on a strop. *n., v., stropped, stropping. 14.*

stro phe (strō′fi), stanza; group of lines of poetry. *n. 17.*

strove (strōv). See **strive.** They strove to win the game. *pt. of strive. 5.*

struck (struk). See **strike.** The clock struck four. *pt. and pp. of strike. 2.*

struc tur al (struk′chər əl), pertaining to structure; used in building; of a structure. Structural steel is steel made into beams, girders, etc. *adj. 10.*

struc tur al ly (struk′chər əl i), with regard to structure. The new church is structurally perfect, but it is not beautiful. *adv.*

struc ture (struk′chər), 1. manner of building; way parts are put together; construction. The structure of the schoolhouse was excellent. 2. a building; something built. The city hall is a large stone structure. 3. anything composed of parts arranged together. The human body is a wonderful structure. *n. 7.*

strug gle (strug′əl), 1. make great efforts with the body; try hard; work hard against difficulties. The swimmer struggled against the tide. The poor have to struggle for a living. 2. great effort; hard work. 3. fighting. *v., n. 2.*

strum (strum), 1. play on (a stringed musical instrument) unskillfully or carelessly; as, to strum a guitar, to strum on the piano. 2. act of strumming. 3. sound of strumming. *v., strummed, strumming, n.*

strum pet (strum′pit), immoral woman; prostitute. *n. 14.*

strung (strung). See **string.** The children strung along after the teacher. *pt. and pp. of string. 10.*

strut[1] (strut), 1. walk in a vain, important manner. The rooster struts about the barnyard. 2. a strutting walk. *v., strutted, strutting, n. 6.*

strut[2] (strut), brace; supporting piece. *n.*

STRUT

strych nine (strik′nin or strik′nīn), poisonous drug used in medicine in small doses as a tonic. *n. 13.*

Stu art (stū′ərt or stü′ərt), the name of the royal family that ruled Scotland from 1371 to 1603 and England and Scotland from 1603 to 1714. *n. 10.*

stub (stub), 1. the stump of a tree, a broken tooth, etc. 2. short piece that is left; as, the stub of a pencil. 3. short piece of each leaf in a checkbook, etc., kept as a record. 4. pen having a short blunt point. 5. strike (one's toe) against something. *n., v., stubbed, stubbing. 11.*

stub ble (stub′əl), 1. the lower ends of stalks of grain left in the ground after the grain is cut. The stubble hurt the boy's bare feet. 2. any short rough growth. He had three days' stubble on his unshaven face. *n. 7.*

stub born (stub′ərn), 1. fixed in purpose or opinion; not giving in to argument or requests. 2. hard to deal with. *adj. 4.*

stub by (stub′i), 1. short and thick; as, stubby fingers. 2. short, thick, and stiff; as, a stubby beard. 3. having many stubs or stumps. *adj., stubbier, stubbiest.*

stuc co (stuk′ō), 1. plaster for covering walls. 2. cover with stucco. *n., v. 11.*

stuck (stuk). See **stick**[2]. She stuck out her tongue. *pt. and pp. of stick*[2]. *3.*

stuck-up (stuk′up′), too proud; conceited; haughty. *adj.* [*Used in common talk*]

stud[1] (stud), 1. a nailhead, knob, etc., sticking out from a surface. The belt was ornamented with silver studs. 2. a kind of small button used in men's shirts. 3. set with studs or something like studs. He plans to stud the sword hilt with jewels. 4. be set or scattered over. Little islands stud the harbor. *n., v., studded, studding. 8.*

stud[2] (stud), collection of horses kept for breeding, hunting, racing, etc. *n.*

stu dent (stū′dənt or stü′dənt), person who studies. Mrs. Smith is a student of birds. *n. 2.*

stud ied (stud′id), carefully planned; done on purpose; resulting from deliberate effort; as, a studied insult. *adj. 7.*

stu di o (stū′di ō or stü′di ō), 1. workroom of a painter, sculptor, photographer, etc. 2. place where moving pictures are made. 3. place where a radio program is given. *n., pl. studios. 11.*

stu di ous (stū′di əs or stü′di əs), 1. fond of study. He is a studious boy and likes school. 2. careful; thoughtful; zealous; showing careful consideration. The clerk made a studious effort to please customers. Mary is always studious of her mother's comfort. *adj. 6.*

stud y (stud′i), 1. effort to learn by reading or thinking. After an hour's hard study he knew his lesson. 2. make an effort to learn. Helen studied her spelling lesson for half an hour. James is studying to be a doctor. 3. subject that is studied; branch of learning. History, music, and law are studies. 4. room to study in. The preacher was reading in his study. 5. earnest effort. Her constant study is to please her parents. 6. think (out); plan; consider with care.

The prisoner studied ways to escape. 7. give care and thought to; try hard. The grocer studies to please his customers. 8. examine carefully. We studied the map to find the shortest road home. 9. investigation; careful examination. 10. sketch for a picture, story, etc. 11. piece of music for practice or testing. *n., pl. studies, v., studied, studying. 1.*

stuff (stuf), 1. material; what a thing is made of. She bought some white stuff for curtains. That boy has good stuff in him. 2. worthless material; useless things. Their attic is full of old stuff. 3. fill; pack full. She stuffed the pillow with feathers. 4. fill (a chicken, turkey, etc.) with seasoned bread crumbs, etc. 5. fill the skin of (a dead animal) to make it look as it did when alive. 6. stop (up); block; choke (up). 7. eat too much. *n., v. 2.*

stuff ing (stuf′ing), 1. material used to fill or pack something. 2. seasoned bread crumbs, etc., used to stuff a chicken, turkey, etc., before cooking. *n.*

stuff y (stuf′i), 1. lacking fresh air; as, a stuffy room. 2. lacking freshness or interest; dull. 3. stopped up. A cold makes my head feel stuffy. *adj., stuffier, stuffiest.*

stul ti fy (stul′ti fī), make foolish; cause to appear foolish. *v., stultified, stultifying.*

stum ble (stum′bəl), 1. trip by striking the foot against something. The horse stumbled on a stone and fell. 2. walk unsteadily. The tired old man stumbled along. 3. speak, act, etc., in a clumsy or hesitating way. The boy made many blunders as he stumbled through his recitation. 4. make a mistake; do wrong. 5. mistake; wrong act. 6. come by accident or chance. While in the country, she stumbled upon some fine old pieces of linen. 7. stumbling. *v., n. 4.*

stumbling block, something that makes a person stumble. *12.*

stump (stump), 1. the lower end of a tree or plant left after the main part is cut off. We sat on top of a stump. 2. anything left after the main or important part is removed. The dog wagged his stump of a tail. 3. make political speeches in. The candidates for governor will stump the State. 4. walk in a stiff, clumsy way. The lame man stumped along. 5. make unable to answer, do, etc. *Used in common talk. n., v. 3.*

stump y (stump′i), 1. short and thick. 2. having many stumps. *adj.*

stun (stun), make senseless; bewilder; shock; overwhelm. He was stunned by the fall. The sound of the cannon stunned the new soldier. *v., stunned, stunning. 8.*

stung (stung). See **sting.** A wasp stung John. *pt. and pp. of sting. 6.*

stunk (stungk), smelled nasty. *pp. and a pt. of* **stink.**

stun ning (stun′ing), having striking excellence, beauty, etc.; very attractive; good-looking; pretty. She has a stunning new hat. *adj.* [*Used in common talk*]

stunt[1] (stunt), check in growth. Lack of proper food stunts a child. *v., n. 9.*

stunt[2] (stunt), feat; performance. The members of the circus did all sorts of riding stunts. *n.* [*Used in common talk*]

stu pe fac tion (stū′pi fak′shən or stü′pi fak′shən), stupor; dazed or senseless condition; overwhelming amazement. *n. 17.*

stu pe fy (stū′pi fī or stü′pi fī), make stupid, dull, or senseless. *v., stupefied, stupefying. 11.*

stu pen dous (stū pen′dəs or stü pen′dəs), amazing; marvelous; immense. Niagara Falls is a stupendous sight. *adj. 8.*

stu pid (stū′pid or stü′pid), dull; not intelligent; not interesting. *adj. 4.*

stu pid i ty (stū pid′i ti or stü pid′i ti), 1. dullness; lack of intelligence. 2. a stupid act, idea, etc. *n., pl. stupidities. 12.*

stu por (stū′pər or stü′pər), dazed condition; loss or lessening of the power to feel. The man lay in a stupor, unable to tell what had happened to him. *n. 13.*

stur di ness (stėr′di nis), 1. strength. 2. firmness. *n. 20.*

stur dy (stėr′di), 1. strong; stout. 2. firm; not yielding. *adj., sturdier, sturdiest. 5.*

stur geon (stėr′jən), large food fish whose long body has a tough skin with rows of bony plates. Caviar and isinglass are obtained from sturgeons. *n., pl. sturgeons or sturgeon. 16.*

Sturgeon (about 6 ft. long)

stut ter (stut′ər), 1. repeat the same sound in an effort to speak. *Example:* C-c-c-c-can't th-th-th-they c-c-c-come? 2. act or habit of stuttering. *v., n.*

St. Vi tus's dance (sānt vī′təs iz dans′), a nervous disease that causes involuntary twitching of the muscles.

sty[1] (stī), 1. pen for pigs. 2. any filthy place. *n., pl. sties. 13.*

sty[2] (stī), a small, sore swelling on the edge of the eyelid. A sty is like a small boil. *n., pl. sties.*

Styg i an (stij′i ən), 1. pertaining to the river Styx or the lower world; infernal. 2. dark; gloomy. *adj. 15.*

style (stīl), 1. fashion. Paris set the style in dress for the world. Her dress is out of style. 2. manner, method, or way of speaking, writing, doing, building, etc. Books for children should have a clear, easy style. 3. name; call. Joan of Arc was styled "the Maid of Orléans." 4. stemlike part of the pistil of a flower. *n., v. 2.*

styl ish (stīl′ish), having style; fashionable. She wears stylish clothes. *adj. 11.*

sty lus (stī′ləs), a pointed instrument for writing on wax. *n.*

styp tic (stip′tik), 1. able to stop or check bleeding; astringent. 2. something that stops or checks bleeding by contracting the tissue. Alum is a styptic. *adj., n.*

Styx (stiks), in Greek mythology, a river in the lower world. The souls of the dead were ferried across it into Hades. *n. 8.*

sua sion (swā′zhən), persuasion; advising or urging. *n.*

suave (swäv), smoothly agreeable or polite. *adj. 19.*

suav i ty (swav′i ti), smoothly agreeable quality of behavior; blandness; smooth politeness. *n., pl. suavities.*

sub-, a prefix that means:—
1. under; below; as in subway, submarine.
2. near; as in subconscious.
3. slightly; somewhat; as in subacid.

sub., 1. subscription. 2. substitute. *17.*

sub al tern (səb ôl′tərn), 1. commissioned officer in the army, ranking below a captain. 2. ranking below a captain. 3. subordinate; having lower rank. *n., adj. 16.*

sub con scious (sub kon′shəs), not wholly conscious; existing but not felt. Her sore tooth caused Alice a subconscious irritation that made her cross. *adj. 20.*

sub di vide (sub′di vīd′), divide again; divide into smaller parts. A real estate dealer bought the farm and subdivided it into building lots. *v. 13.*

sub di vi sion (sub′di vizh′ən), 1. division into smaller parts. 2. part of a part. 3. tract of land divided into building lots. *n. 12.*

sub due (səb dū′ or səb dü′), 1. conquer; overcome. The Spaniards subdued the Indian tribes in Mexico. We subdued a desire to laugh. 2. soften; tone down. The window curtains give the room a subdued light. *v. 3.*

sub ject (sub′jikt for 1, 2, 4, 5, 6, and 8, səb jekt′ for 3 and 7), 1. person who is under the power, control, or influence of another. The people are the subjects of the king. 2. under some power or influence. We are subject to our country's laws. 3. bring under some power or influence. Rome subjected all Italy to her rule. 4. something thought about, discussed, studied, etc. The subject for our composition was "An Exciting Moment." 5. the word or words that perform or receive the action of the verb. I is the subject of the following sentences: I see the cat. I am seen by the cat. I can see. 6. **Subject to** means (1) likely to have. I am subject to colds. Japan is subject to earthquakes. (2) depending on; on the condition of. I bought the car subject to your approval. 7. To **subject to** sometimes means to cause to undergo or experience something. The savages subjected their captives to torture. 8. person or thing that undergoes or experiences something. *n., adj., v. 1.*

sub jec tion (səb jek′shən), 1. conquering; bringing under some power or influence. The subjection of the rebels took a long time. 2. condition of being under some power or influence. Women used to live in subjection to men. *n. 8.*

sub jec tive (səb jek′tiv), 1. existing in the mind; belonging to the person thinking rather than to the object thought of. 2. about the thoughts and feelings of the speaker, writer, painter, etc.; personal. Lyric poetry is subjective, expressing the feelings of the author; narrative poetry is objective, telling a story. *adj. 20.*

subject matter, 1. something thought about, discussed, studied, or written about. 2. the meaning of a talk, book, etc., as distinguished from its form or style. *18.*

sub ju gate (sub′jü gāt), subdue; conquer. *v. 15.*

sub ju ga tion (sub′jü gā′shən), conquest; subjection. *n. 18.*

sub junc tive (səb jungk′tiv), the mood of a verb which expresses a state, act, or event as possible, conditional, or dependent, rather than as actual. The subjunctive is going out of use in English. *n. 11.*

sub lease (sub′lēs′ for 1, sub lēs′ for 2), 1. lease granted by a person who rents the property himself. 2. grant or take a sublease of. *n., v.*

sub let (sub let′), 1. rent to another (something which has been rented to oneself). We sublet our house for the summer. 2. give part of (a contract) to another. The contractor for the whole building sublet the contract for the plumbing. *v., sublet, subletting.*

sub li mate (sub′li māt), 1. purify; refine. 2. **Corrosive sublimate,** a compound of mercury, is a powerful and very poisonous disinfectant. *v., n. 15.*

sub lime (səb līm′), 1. lofty; noble; majestic; grand. Mountain scenery is often sublime. 2. purify; refine. *adj., v. 5.*

sub lim i ty (səb lim′i ti), lofty excellence; grandeur; majesty. *n., pl. sublimities. 14.*

sub ma rine (sub′mə rēn′), 1. a boat that can go under water. 2. under the surface of the sea; under water; as, submarine plants, submarine warfare. *n., adj. 9.*

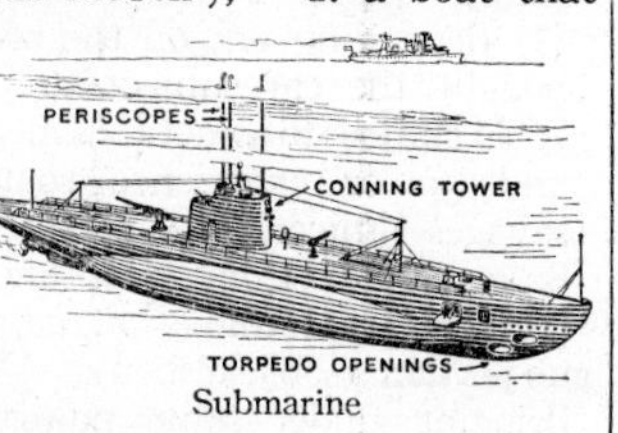

Submarine

sub merge (səb mėrj′), put under water; cover with water; sink under water. *v. 7.*

sub mer gence (səb mėr′jəns), submerging; being submerged. *n.*

sub mer sion (səb mėr′zhən), submerging; being submerged. *n.*

sub mis sion (səb mish′ən), 1. submitting; yielding to power, control, or authority. The defeated general showed his submission by giving up his sword. 2. obedience; humbleness. He bowed in submission to the king's order. *n. 7.*

sub mis sive (səb mis′iv), yielding to power, control, or authority; obedient; humble. *adj. 9.*

sub mit (səb mit′), 1. yield to the power, control, or authority of some person or group; surrender; yield. The thief submitted to arrest by the police. 2. refer to the consideration or judgment of others. The secretary submitted a report of the last meeting. *v., submitted, submitting. 3.*

sub nor mal (sub nôr′məl), below normal; inferior to the normal. *adj.*

sub or di nate (sə bôr′di nit for 1, 2, and 3, sə bôr′di nāt for 4), 1. in a lower order or rank; having less importance; secondary; dependent. 2. under the authority of a superior. 3. subordinate person or thing. 4. place in a lower order or rank; make subject to or dependent on. *adj., n., v. 9.*

sub or di na tion (sə bôr′di nā′shən), 1. a subordinating or being subordinated. 2. subordinate position or importance. 3. submission to authority; willingness to obey. *n. 15.*

sub orn (sə bôrn′), 1. get by bribery or other unlawful means. 2. persuade or cause (a witness) to tell a lie in court. 3. persuade or cause (a person) to do an evil deed. *v. 13.*

sub poe na or **sub pe na** (sub pē′nə), 1. an official written order commanding a person to appear in a law court. 2. summon with such an order. *n., v.*

sub scribe (səb skrīb′), 1. write underneath; sign (one's name). The men who subscribed to the Declaration of Independence are now famous. 2. agree. He could not subscribe to their unfair plan. 3. promise to give or pay. He subscribed $5 to the hospital fund. 4. promise to take. We subscribe for several magazines. *v. 7.*

sub scrib er (səb skrīb′ər), person who subscribes. The magazines make a special offer to new subscribers. *n. 8.*

sub scrip tion (səb skrip′shən), 1. subscribing. 2. money subscribed. His subscription to the Fresh Air Fund was $5. 3. the right obtained for the money. His subscription to the newspaper expires next week. 4. sum of money raised by a number of persons. We are raising a subscription for the family of the workman who was killed. *n. 7.*

sub se quent (sub′si kwənt), later; following; coming after Subsequent events proved the truth of his prophecy. The story will be continued in subsequent chapters. *adj. 6.*

sub se quent ly (sub′si kwənt li), later; afterward. *adv.*

sub serve (səb sėrv′), be useful in helping (a purpose, an action, etc.). Chewing food subserves digestion. *v. 16.*

sub ser vi ence (səb sėr′vi əns), tame submission; slavish politeness and obedience; servility. *n. 16.*

sub ser vi ent (səb sėr′vi ənt), 1. tamely submissive; slavishly polite and obedient; servile. 2. useful as a means to help a purpose or end; serviceable. *adj. 14.*

sub side (səb sīd′), 1. sink to a lower level. After the rain stopped, the flood waters subsided. 2. grow less; die down; become less active. 3. fall to the bottom; settle. *v. 8.*

sub sid ence (səb sīd′əns), subsiding; as, the subsidence of a flood. *n. 19.*

sub sid i ar y (səb sid′i ãr′i), 1. useful to assist or supplement; auxiliary; supplementary. The teacher sold books as a subsidiary occupation. 2. thing or person that assists or supplements. 3. maintained by a subsidy. *adj., n., pl. subsidiaries. 16.*

sub si dize (sub′si dīz), help or assist with a contribution of money. The government subsidizes steamship and air lines that carry mail. *v. 14.*

sub si dy (sub′si di), a grant or contribution of money. *n., pl. subsidies. 13.*

sub sist (səb sist′), 1. exist; continue to be. A club cannot subsist without members. 2. live; keep alive. People in the far north subsist on fish and meat. *v. 8.*

sub sist ence (səb sis′təns), 1. existence. 2. keeping alive; living. Selling papers was the cripple's only means of subsistence. 3. means of keeping alive; food and clothing. The sea provides a subsistence for fishermen. *n. 15.*

sub soil (sub′soil′), the layer of earth that lies just under the surface soil. *n. 16.*

sub stance (sub′stəns), 1. the real, main, or important part of anything. The substance of an education is its effect on your life, not just learning lessons. 2. real meaning. Give the substance of the speech in your own words. 3. what a thing consists of; matter; material. Ice and water are the same substance in different forms. 4. wealth; property. *n. 3.*

sub stan tial (səb stan′shəl), 1. real; actual. People and things are substantial; dreams and ghosts are not. 2. strong; firm; solid. That house is substantial enough to last a hundred years. 3. large; important; ample. John has made a substantial improvement in arithmetic. 4. well-to-do; wealthy. 5. in the main; in substance. The stories told by the two boys were in substantial agreement. *adj. 4.*

sub stan tial ly (səb stan′shəl i), 1. essentially; mainly. 2. really; actually. 3. strongly; solidly. *adv.*

sub stan ti ate (səb stan′shi āt), 1. prove; establish by evidence; as, to substantiate a rumor, a claim, or a theory. 2. give concrete or substantial form to. *v. 17.*

sub stan tive (sub′stən tiv), 1. a noun; the name of a person or thing. 2. used as a noun. 3. showing existence. The verb *to be* is the substantive verb. 4. independent. 5. real; actual. *n., adj. 11.*

sub sti tute (sub′sti tūt or sub′sti tüt), 1. thing used instead of another; person taking the place of another. A substitute taught us at school today. 2. put in the place of another. We substituted brown sugar for molasses in these cookies. 3. take the place of another. She substituted for Miss Brown who is ill. *n., v., adj. 4.*

sub sti tu tion (sub′sti tū′shən or sub′sti tü′shən), the use of one thing for another; putting (one person or thing) in the place of another; taking the place of another. *n. 16.*

sub stra tum (sub strā′təm), 1. a layer lying under another. Beneath the sandy soil there was a substratum of clay ten feet thick. 2. something that underlies or serves as a basis. The story has a substratum of truth. *n., pl. substrata* (sub strā′tə) or *substratums. 12.*

sub ter fuge (sub′tər fūj), a trick, excuse, or expedient used to escape something unpleasant. The girl's headache was only a subterfuge to avoid taking the examination. *n. 15.*

sub ter ra ne an (sub′tə rā′ni ən), underground. A subterranean passage led from the castle to a cave. *adj. 11.*

sub tle (sut′əl), 1. thin; delicate; fine. Some subtle odors are hard to recognize. Subtle humor is hard to understand. 2. faint; mysterious; as, a subtle smile. 3. having a keen, quick mind; discerning; acute. She is a subtle observer of slight differences in things. 4. sly; crafty; tricky; as, a subtle scheme to get some money. 5. skillful; clever; expert. *adj. 5.*

sub tle ty (sut′əl ti), 1. subtle quality. 2. something subtle. *n., pl. subtleties. 8.*

sub tly (sut′li), in a subtle manner. *adv.*

sub tract (səb trakt′), take away. Subtract 2 from 10 and you have 8. *v. 6.*

sub trac tion (səb trak′shən), taking one number or quantity from another; finding the difference between two quantities. 10—2=8 is a simple subtraction. *n. 12.*

sub tra hend (sub′trə hend), a number or quantity to be subtracted from another. In 10—2=8, the subtrahend is 2. *n. 19.*

sub trop i cal (sub trop′i kəl), bordering on the tropics; nearly tropical. *adj. 20.*

sub urb (sub′ėrb), district lying outside a city or town. Many people who work in the city live in the suburbs. *n. 5.*

sub ur ban (səbėr′bən), 1. pertaining to a suburb; in a suburb. We have excellent suburban train service. 2. characteristic of a suburb or its inhabitants. *adj. 8.*

sub ver sion (sub vėr′zhən), overthrow; destruction; ruin. *n. 16.*

sub ver sive (sub vėr′siv), tending to overthrow; destructive; causing ruin. *adj.*

sub vert (sub vėrt′), overturn; overthrow; destroy; ruin. *v. 12.*

sub way (sub′wā′), 1. underground passage. 2. underground electric railroad. *n. 10.*

suc ceed (sək sēd′), 1. turn out well; do well; have success. Washington's plans succeeded. 2. come next after; follow; take the place of. John Adams succeeded Washington as President. In England the oldest son succeeds to his father's estate. *v. 2.*

suc cess (sək ses′), 1. favorable result; wished-for ending; good fortune. Success in school comes from intelligence and work. What success did you have in finding a new cook? 2. person or thing that succeeds. The circus was a great success. *n. 2.*

suc cess ful (sək ses′fəl), having success; ending in success; prosperous; fortunate. *adj. 3.*

suc ces sion (sək sesh′ən), 1. the coming of one person or thing after another. **In succession** means one after another. 2. things happening one after another; a series. A succession of accidents spoiled our automobile trip. 3. the right of succeeding to an office, property, or rank. There was a dispute about the rightful succession to the throne. 4. a set or arrangement of persons having the right of succeeding. The Prince of Wales is usually the next in succession to the English throne. *n. 5.*

suc ces sive (sək ses′iv), following in order. It has rained for three successive days. *adj. 5.*

suc ces sive ly (sək ses′iv li), one after another; in order. *adv.*

suc ces sor (sək ses′ər), one who follows or succeeds another in office, position, or ownership of property; thing that comes after another in a series. *n. 6.*

suc cinct (sək singkt′), expressed briefly and clearly; concise. *adj. 16.*

suc cor (suk′ər), help; aid. *n., v. 7.*

suc co tash (suk′ə tash), corn and beans cooked together. *n.*

suc cu lence (suk′ū ləns), juiciness. *n. 14.*

suc cu lent (suk′ū lənt), juicy. *adj. 15.*

suc cumb (sə kum′), 1. give way; yield. He succumbed to the temptation and stole the money. 2. die. *v. 14.*

such (such), 1. of that kind; of the same kind or degree. Such men as Washington and Lincoln are rare. The child had such a fever that he nearly died. The food, such as it was, was plentiful. 2. of the kind already spoken of or suggested. The ladies took only tea and coffee and such drinks. 3. so great, so bad, so good, etc. Dan is such a liar! 4. some; certain. The bank was robbed at such a time in such and such a town by such and such persons. 5. such a person or thing. Take from the blankets such as you need. *adj., pron. 1.*

suck (suk), 1. draw into the mouth. Lemonade can be sucked through a straw. 2. draw something from with the mouth; as, to suck oranges. 3. drink; take; absorb. Plants suck up moisture from the earth. A sponge sucks in water. 4. act of sucking. The baby took one suck at the empty bottle and pushed it away. *v., n. 4.*

Sucker (about 2 ft. long)

suck er (suk′ər), 1. an animal or thing that sucks. 2. a fish that sucks in food or has a mouth that suggests sucking. 3. a shoot from an underground stem or root. 4. a lump of hard candy. *n. 9.*

suck le (suk′əl), 1. nurse at the breast. The cat suckles her kittens. 2. suck at the breast. *v. 8.*

suck ling (suk′ling), 1. a very young animal or child. 2. very young. 3. not yet weaned; sucking. *n., adj. 13.*

suc tion (suk′shən), 1. process of drawing in liquids or gases by sucking out the air. We draw lemonade through a straw by suction. Some pumps work by suction. 2. making one thing stick to another by removing the air between them. *n. 10.*

Su dan (sü dan′), a grassy region in Africa, between the Sahara desert and the jungle. *n. 13.*

sud den (sud′ən), 1. not expected. Our army made a sudden attack on the fort. 2. quick; rapid. The cat made a sudden jump at the mouse. 3. **All of a sudden** means unexpectedly or quickly. *adj., n. 1.*

suds (sudz), 1. soapy water. 2. bubbles and foam on soapy water. *n. pl. 15.*

sue (sü), 1. beg or ask (for). Messengers came suing for peace. 2. start a lawsuit against. He sued the railroad because his cow was killed by the engine. *v. 6.*

suede (swād), 1. soft leather that has a velvety nap on one or both sides. 2. a kind of cloth that has a similar appearance. 3. made of suede. *n., adj. 20.*

su et (sü′it), the hard fat of cattle or sheep. Beef suet is used in cooking and for making tallow. *n. 12.*

Su ez (sü ez′), the isthmus between Asia and Africa. *n. 13.*

Suez Canal, canal across the Isthmus of Suez, connecting the Mediterranean and Red seas. It is controlled by Great Britain.

suf fer (suf′ər), 1. have or feel pain, grief, etc.; experience harm, loss, etc.; endure. She suffers from headache. He suffered harm from being out in the storm. His business suffered greatly during the war. 2. allow; permit. "Suffer the little children to come unto me." *v. 1.*

suf fer ance (suf′ər əns), permission; consent; lack of objection. **On sufferance** means allowed or tolerated but not really wanted. *n. 7.*

suf fer ing (suf′ər ing), pain. Hunger causes suffering. *n. 6.*

suf fice (sə fīs′), be enough; satisfy. Fifty dollars a month sufficed for the old lady's needs. *v. 3.*

suf fi cien cy (sə fish′ən si), sufficient amount; large enough supply. The ship had a sufficiency of provisions for the voyage. *n. 12.*

suf fi cient (sə fish′ənt), 1. enough; as much as is needed. The poor child did not have sufficient clothing for such a cold day. 2. competent; able. *Old use. adj. 3.*

suf fi cient ly (sə fish′ənt li), enough; as much as is needed. *adv.*

suf fix (suf′iks), 1. an addition made to the end of a word to change the meaning or to make a new word, such as rust*y*, bad*ly*, good*ness*, act*ion*, spoon*ful*, and amaze*ment*. 2. put after; add at the end. *n., v. 18.*

suf fo cate (suf′ə kāt), 1. choke. 2. kill by stopping the breath. 3. keep from breathing; hinder in breathing. *v. 11.*

suf fo ca tion (suf′ə kā′shən), 1. suffocating. 2. being suffocated. *n. 13.*

Suf folk (suf′ək), former county in southeastern England, now divided into Suffolk East and Suffolk West. *n. 11.*

suf fra gan (suf′rə gən), 1. assisting. 2. a bishop assisting another bishop. *adj., n. 20.*

suf frage (suf′rij), 1. vote; vote for some person or thing. The voters gave their suffrage to Roosevelt. 2. right to vote. The United States granted the suffrage to women in 1920. *n. 7.*

suf fuse (sə fūz′), overspread; as, eyes suffused with tears. *v. 16.*

suf fu sion (sə fū′zhən), 1. suffusing. 2. being suffused. 3. that with which anything is overspread. 4. flush of color. *n. 16.*

sug ar (shu̇g′ər), 1. a sweet substance made from sugar cane or sugar beets. Other kinds of sugar made from cornstarch, grapes, etc. 2. sweeten with sugar. She sugared her tea. 3. cover with sugar; sprinkle with sugar. 4. form sugar. Maple syrup will sugar if cooked. *n., v. 1.*

sugar beet, a large beet with a white root used in making sugar.

sugar cane, a tall plant with a strong, jointed stem and flat leaves, growing in warm regions. Sugar cane is the chief source of sugar.

Sugar cane

sugar maple, a maple tree yielding a sweet sap from which maple sugar is made.

sug ar plum (shu̇g′ər plum′), piece of candy; bonbon. *n.*

sug ar y (shu̇g′ər i), consisting of sugar; like sugar; sweet. *adj.*

sug gest (səg jest′), 1. bring (a thought, plan, etc.) to a person's mind. John suggested a game of tag. 2. show in an indirect way; hint. Joe's bad manners suggest a lack of proper home training. *v. 3.*

sug ges tion (səg jes′chən), 1. suggesting. The suggestion of a walk made the dog jump with joy. 2. thing suggested. The picnic was Jane's suggestion. *n. 6.*

sug ges tive (səg jes′tiv), 1. tending to suggest ideas, acts, or feelings. The teacher gave an interesting and suggestive list of composition subjects. 2. tending to suggest something improper or indecent. *adj. 10.*

su i cid al (sü′i sīd′əl), 1. pertaining to suicide; leading to suicide; causing suicide. 2. ruinous to one's own interests; disastrous to oneself. It would be suicidal for a store to sell many things below cost. *adj.*

su i cide (sü′i sīd), 1. killing oneself on purpose. **Commit suicide** means kill oneself. 2. person who kills himself on purpose. 3. destruction of one's own interests. *n. 13.*

suit (süt), 1. set of clothes or armor. A man's suit consists of coat, vest, and trousers. 2. case in a law court. Mr. Morton won his suit for damages against the railroad. 3. make fit; make suitable. The teacher suited the punishment to the fault by making Dick sweep the room after he threw bits of paper on the floor. 4. agree with; agree. A cold climate suits apples and wheat, but not oranges and tea. 5. be becoming to. Her blue hat suits her fair skin. 6. please; be convenient for; satisfy. It is hard to suit everybody. 7. one of the four sets of cards (hearts, diamonds, spades, clubs), or a similar set in any other game. 8. request; asking; wooing. King Arthur's suit was successful, and Guinevere married him. *n., v. 1.*

suit a bil i ty (süt′ə bil′i ti), fitness; appropriateness. *n.*

suit a ble (süt′ə bəl), fitting; right for the occasion. A simple dress is suitable for school wear. The park gives the children a suitable playground. *adj. 4.*

suit a bly (süt′ə bli), in a suitable manner; fitly; appropriately. *adv.*

suit case (süt′kās′), a flat, rectangular traveling bag. *n. 13.*

Man carrying a suitcase

suite (swēt), 1. group of attendants. The queen traveled with a suite of twelve. 2. number of things forming a series or set. She has a suite of rooms at the hotel—a living room, bedroom, and bath. *n. 9.*

suit or (süt′ər), 1. man courting a woman. The princess had many suitors. 2. person bringing suit in a law court. *n. 7.*

sul fur (sul′fər), sulphur. *n.*

sulk (sulk), 1. be sulky. 2. ill humor shown by sullen silence; sulky mood. Mary has a fit of the sulks. *v., n. 16.*

sulk i ness (sul′ki nis), sulky behavior; sullenness. *n.*

sulk y (sul′ki), 1. sullen; silent because of bad humor. Peter gets sulky and won't play if he can't be leader. 2. a light carriage with two wheels, for one person. *adj., sulkier, sulkiest, n., pl. sulkies. 11.*

Sulky racing

sul len (sul′ən), 1. silent because of ill humor. Harry becomes sullen if he is punished. 2. gloomy; dismal. The sullen skies threatened rain. *adj. 4.*

sul ly (sul′i), soil; stain; tarnish. *v., sullied, sullying. 11.*

sul phate (sul′fāt), any salt of sulphuric acid. *n. 9.*

sul phide (sul′fīd), any compound of sulphur with another element or radical. *n.*

sul phur (sul′fər), a light-yellow substance that burns with a blue flame and a stifling odor. Sulphur is used in making matches and gunpowder. *n. 6.*

sul phu re ous (sul fūr′i əs), 1. consisting of or containing sulphur; pertaining to sulphur. 2. like sulphur. *adj. 20.*

sul phu ric (sul fūr′ik), 1. of or pertaining to sulphur. 2. containing sulphur. 3. **Sulphuric acid** is a heavy, colorless, oily, very strong acid. *adj. 17.*

sul phu rous (sul′fū rəs), 1. of or pertaining to sulphur. 2. containing sulphur. 3. like sulphur; like burning sulphur. 4. of or like the fires of hell; hellish. *adj. 12.*

sul tan (sul′tən), the ruler of a Mohammedan country. Turkey was ruled by a sultan until 1922. *n. 8.*

sul tan a (sul tan′ə), 1. wife of a sultan. 2. the mother, sister, or daughter of a sultan. *n. 16.*

sul tan ate (sul′tən āt), 1. position, authority, or period of rule of a sultan. 2. territory ruled over by a sultan. *n.*

sul tri ness (sul′tri nis), sultry heat; moist hotness. *n.*

sul try (sul′tri), 1. hot, close, and moist. We expect some sultry weather during July. 2. hot. *adj., sultrier, sultriest. 9.*

sum (sum), 1. the total of two or more numbers or things taken together; the whole. The sum of 2 and 3 and 4 is 9. Tom reached the sum of his happiness when he became captain of the football team. 2. problem in arithmetic. 3. amount of money. He paid the sum of $7 for a new hat. 4. **Sum up** often means express or tell briefly. Sum up the main points of the lesson in three sentences. The judge summed up the evidence. *n., v., summed, summing. 2.*

su mac or **su mach** (shü′mak), a shrub or small tree which has divided leaves that turn scarlet in the autumn and cone-shaped clusters of red fruit. *n. 17.*

Sumac

Su ma tra (sü mä′trə), large Dutch island in the East Indies. *n.*

sum ma ri ly (sum′ə ri li), in a summary manner; briefly; without delay. *adv.*

sum ma rize (sum′ə rīz), make a summary of; express briefly. *v. 12.*

sum ma ry (sum′ə ri), 1. brief statement giving the main points. This history has a summary at the end of each chapter. 2. brief; short. 3. direct and prompt; without delay. The Indian took summary vengeance by killing both his enemies. *n., pl. summaries, adj. 10.*

sum mer (sum′ər), 1. the warmest season of the year. 2. spend the summer; as, to summer at the seashore. 3. of summer; pertaining to summer; as, summer heat. *n., v., adj. 1.*

sum mer house (sum′ər hous′), a building in a park or garden in which to sit in warm weather. Summerhouses often have no walls. *n.*

sum mit (sum′it), highest point; top. We could see the summit of the mountain twenty miles away. The summit of her ambition was to be an actress. *n. 5.*

sum mon (sum′ən), 1. call; send for. The church bells summon people to worship. A telegram summoned him home. 2. stir to action; rouse. Jack summoned his courage and entered the deserted house. *v. 3.*

sum mons (sum′ənz), 1. an order to appear at a certain place. Mr. Black received a summons to be at the police court at 10 A.M., October 5. 2. a command. *n., pl. summonses.*

sump ter (sump′tər), a horse or mule for carrying baggage. *n. 17.*

sump tu ar y (sump′chü ãr′i), having to do with the spending of money; regulating expenses. Laws forbidding women to wear jewelry would be sumptuary laws. *adj.*

sump tu ous (sump′chü əs), costly; magnificent; rich. The king gave a sumptuous banquet. *adj. 6.*

sun (sun), 1. the brightest object in the sky. The sun lights and warms the earth. 2. the light and warmth of the sun. The cat likes to sit in the sun. 3. put in the light and warmth of the sun. 4. any heavenly body like the sun. Many stars are suns and have their worlds that travel around them. 5. something bright like the sun. *n., v., sunned, sunning. 1.*

Sun., Sunday.

sun beam (sun′bēm′), ray of sunlight. A sunbeam brightened the child's hair to gold. *n. 4.*

sun bon net (sun′bon′it), large bonnet that shades the face and neck. *n.*

Sunbonnet

sun burn (sun′bėrn′), 1. a burning of the skin by the sun's rays. His sunburn was red and painful. 2. burn the skin by the sun's rays. He is sunburned from a day on the beach. *n., v., sunburned* or *sunburnt, sunburning. 13.*

sun dae (sun′di), individual portion of ice cream with syrup, crushed fruit, nuts, etc., over it. *n.*

Sun day (sun′di), the first day of the week; the day of rest and worship among Christians. *n. 2.*

sun der (sun′dər), 1. separate; part; divide. Time often sunders friends. 2. **In sunder** means apart. *v., n. 7.*

sun dew (sun′dū′), a bog plant that captures and absorbs insects with its hairy, sticky leaves. *n. 20.*

sun di al (sun′dī′əl), an instrument for telling the time of day by the position of a shadow cast by the sun. *n. 16.*

Sundial

sun down (sun′doun′), sunset. We'll be home by sundown. *n. 14.*

sun dries (sun′driz), sundry things; items not named, odds and ends. We spent almost two dollars for sundries. *n. pl.*

sun dry (sun′dri), various; several. From sundry hints, Jack guessed he was to have a bicycle and a new book on his birthday. *adj. 8.*

sun fish (sun′fish′), 1. a large sea fish. 2. a small fresh-water fish. Sunfish are like perch. *n. 20.*

sun flow er (sun′flou′ər), a tall plant having large yellow flowers with brown centers. *n. 10.*

Sunflower

sung (sung). See **sing.** *pp. and pt. of sing. 3.*

sun god, god of the sun. Many different tribes have worshiped sun gods. *20.*

sunk (sungk). See **sink.** The ship had sunk to the bottom. *pp. and pt. of sink. 4.*

sunk en (sungk′ən), 1. sunk; as, a sunken ship. 2. submerged; under water; as, a sunken rock. 3. situated below the general level; as, a sunken garden. 4. fallen in; hollow; as, sunken eyes. *adj. 12.*

sun less (sun′lis), without sun; without sunlight; dark. Most flowers will not grow in a sunless place. *adj. 13.*

sun light (sun′līt′), the light of the sun. *n. 4.*

sun lit (sun′lit′), lighted by the sun. *adj.*

sun ny (sun′i), 1. having much sunshine. 2. like the sun. 3. bright; cheerful. The baby gave a sunny smile. *adj., sunnier, sunniest. 3.*

sun rise (sun′rīz′), the rising of the sun; the first appearance of the sun in the morning. *n. 5.*

sun set (sun′set′), the going down of the sun; the last appearance of the sun in the evening. *n. 3.*

sun shine (sun′shīn′), 1. the shining of the sun; the light of the sun. 2. brightness; cheerfulness. *n. 2.*

sun shin y (sun′shīn′i), 1. having much sunshine. 2. bright; cheerful; happy. *adj. 20.*

sun spot (sun′spot′), one of the dark spots that appear at intervals on the sun. *n.*

sun stroke (sun′strōk′), a sudden illness caused by the sun's rays or by too much heat. *n. 18.*

sup[1] (sup), eat the evening meal. He supped alone on bread and milk. *v., supped, supping. 6.*

sup[2] (sup), 1. sip; take (liquid) into the mouth a little at a time. He supped his soup from the spoon. 2. mouthful; spoonful. *v., supped, supping, n.*

super-, a prefix meaning:—
1. over; above; as in superimpose, superstructure.
2. besides; as in superadd, supertax.
3. exceedingly; in high proportion; to excess; as in superabundant; superfine.
4. surpassing; as in superman, supernatural. *20.*

su per a bun dance (sü′pər ə bun′dəns), 1. very great abundance; as, a superabundance of rain. 2. greater amount than is needed. *n.*

su per a bun dant (sü′pər ə bun′dənt), 1. very abundant. 2. more than enough. *adj.*

su per add (sü′pər ad′), add besides. A toothache was superadded to her other troubles. *v. 16.*

su per an nu ate (sü′pər an′ū āt), allow to retire from service or office on a pension, because of age or infirmity. *v. 17.*

su perb (sü pėrb′), 1. grand; stately; majestic. Mountain scenery is superb. The queen's jewels are superb. 2. very fine; excellent. The actor gave a superb performance. *adj. 9.*

su per car go (sü′pər kär′gō), person on a merchant ship who represents the owner and has charge of the cargo and the business affairs of the voyage. *n., pl. supercargoes* or *supercargos. 18.*

su per cil i ous (sü′pər sil′i əs), haughty, proud, and contemptuous; disdainful; showing scorn or indifference because of a feeling of superiority. The duchess looked down at the workman with a supercilious stare. *adj. 14.*

su per em i nent (sü′pər em′i nənt), having higher rank or dignity; distinguished or conspicuous above others. *adj. 19.*

su per e rog a to ry (sü′pər i rog′ə tō′ri), doing more than duty requires; unnecessary; superfluous. *adj.*

su per fi cial (sü′pər fish′əl), 1. of the surface; on the surface; at the surface. His burns were superficial and soon got well. 2. shallow; not thorough; concerned with or understanding only what is on the surface. Girls used to receive only a superficial education. *adj. 9.*

su per fine (sü′pər fīn′), 1. very fine; extra fine. 2. too refined; too nice. *adj.*

su per flu i ty (sü′pər flü′i ti), 1. greater amount than is needed. Our tree gives us a superfluity of apples. 2. something not needed. Luxuries are superfluities. *n., pl. superfluities. 11.*

su per flu ous (sü pėr′flü əs), needless; more than is needed. That author uses superfluous words. *adj. 6.*

su per hu man (sü′pər hū′mən), 1. above or beyond what is human. Angels are superhuman beings. 2. above or beyond ordinary human power. By a superhuman effort, the hunter choked the lion to death. *adj. 13.*

su per im pose (sü′pər im pōz′), put on top of something else. *v. 16.*

su per in tend (sü′pər in tend′), oversee and direct (work or workers); manage (a place, institution, etc.). *v. 9.*

su per in tend ence (sü′pər in ten′dəns), direction; management. *n. 17.*

su per in tend en cy (sü′pər in ten′dən si), the position, office, or work of a superintendent. *n., pl. superintendencies. 20.*

su per in tend ent (sü′pər in ten′dənt), person who oversees, directs, or manages; as, a superintendent of schools, a superintendent of a factory. *n. 5.*

su pe ri or (sə pēr′i ər), 1. above the average. Bert has a superior mind. This hotel serves a superior grade of coffee. 2. better; higher; greater. A lion is superior to a wolf. Our army had to fight off a superior force. 3. higher in position, rank, etc. A captain is superior to a lieutenant. 4. person who is superior. As a violin player, he has no superior. A captain is a lieutenant's superior. 5. showing a feeling of being above others; proud. The other girls disliked Ann's superior manner. 6. not giving in; above yielding (to). **Superior to** means above. A wise man is superior to flattery. 7. the head of a monastery or convent. *adj., n. 2.*

Su pe ri or (sə pēr′i ər), the largest of the Great Lakes, between the United States and Canada. *n.*

su pe ri or i ty (sə pēr′i or′i ti), superior state or quality. No one doubts the superiority of modern ways of traveling over those of olden times. *n. 11.*

su per la tive (sü pėr′lə tiv), 1. of the highest kind; above all others. Solomon is said to have been a man of superlative wisdom. 2. highest degree of comparison of an adjective or adverb. *Fairest, fastest,* and *best* are the superlatives of *fair, fast,* and *good.* *adj., n. 11.*

su per la tive ly (sü pėr′lə tiv li), to the highest degree; above all others; supremely. *adv.*

su per man (sü′pər man′), man having more than human powers. *n., pl. supermen.*

su per nal (sü pėr′nəl), 1. heavenly; divine. 2. lofty; exalted. *adj. 18.*

su per nat u ral (sü′pər nach′ə rəl), above or beyond what is natural. Angels and devils are supernatural beings. *adj. 11.*

su per nu mer ar y (sü′pər nū′mər ãr′i or sü′pər nü′mər ãr′i), 1. extra; more than the usual or necessary number. 2. extra person or thing. *adj., n., pl. supernumeraries. 15.*

su per pose (sü′pər pōz′), place above or on something else. *v. 20.*

su per scrip tion (sü′pər skrip′shən), 1. act of writing above, on, or outside of something. 2. something written above or on the outside; address on a letter or parcel. *n. 14.*

su per sede (sü′pər sēd′), 1. take the place of; replace. A new governor superseded the old. 2. displace; set aside. Gaslight has been superseded by electric light in most cities. *v. 14.*

su per sti tion (sü′pər stish′ən), 1. unreasoning fear of what is unknown or mysterious; unreasoning expectation. As knowledge increases, superstition decreases. 2. a belief or practice founded on ignorant fear or mistaken reverence. A common superstition considered it bad luck to sleep in a room numbered 13. *n. 5.*

su per sti tious (sü′pər stish′əs), full of superstition; likely to believe superstitions; caused by superstition; pertaining to superstition. *adj. 7.*

su per struc ture (sü′pər struk′chər), 1. structure built on something else. 2. all of a building above the foundation. *n. 14.*

su per tax (sü′pər taks′), tax in addition to a normal tax. *n.*

su per vene (sü′pər vēn′), come as something additional or interrupting. *v. 20.*

su per vise (sü′pər vīz), look after and direct (work or workers, a process, etc.); oversee; superintend; manage. Study halls are supervised by teachers. *v. 11.*

su per vi sion (sü′pər vizh′ən), management; direction; oversight. The house was built under the careful supervision of the architect. *n. 9.*

su per vi sor (sü′pər vī′zər), person who supervises. The music supervisor has charge of the school band, chorus, and orchestra. *n. 9.*

su per vi so ry (sü′pər vī′zə ri), 1. of a supervisor; having to do with supervision. 2. supervising. *adj.*

su pine (sü pīn′), 1. lying flat on the back. 2. lazily inactive; listless. *adj. 15.*

sup per (sup′ər), the evening meal; a meal often eaten early in the evening if dinner is near noon, or late in the evening if dinner is at six or later. *n. 2.*

sup plant (sə plant′), 1. take the place of. Machinery has supplanted hand labor in making shoes. 2. take the place of by unfair methods. The prince plotted to supplant the king. *v. 8.*

sup ple (sup′əl), 1. bending easily; as, a supple birch tree, supple leather. 2. bending readily to different ideas, circumstances, people, etc.; yielding. Jane gets along well with people because of her supple nature. *adj. 9.*

sup ple ment (sup′li mənt for 1, sup′li ment for 2), 1. something added to complete a thing, or to make it larger or better. This history has a supplement containing an account of what has happened since 1930. 2. add to; complete. *n., v. 9.*

sup ple men tal (sup′li men′təl), supplementary. *adj. 17.*

sup ple men ta ry (sup′li-men′tə ri), 1. additional. 2. added to supply what is lacking. The new members of the class received supplementary instruction. 3. Two angles are supplementary when their sum is 180 degrees. *adj. 12.*

A
C B D
Angle ABC is supplementary to angle ABD.

sup pli ance (sup′li əns), supplication. *n. 18.*

sup pli ant (sup′li ənt), 1. asking humbly and earnestly. He sent a suppliant message for help. 2. person who asks humbly and earnestly. She knelt as a suppliant at the altar. *adj., n. 9.*

sup pli cant (sup′li kənt), suppliant. *n., adj. 19.*

sup pli cate (sup′li kāt), beg humbly and earnestly. The mother supplicated the judge to spare her son. *v. 10.*

sup pli ca tion (sup′li kā′shən), a humble, earnest request. Supplications to God arose from all the churches. *n. 8.*

sup ply (sə plī′), 1. furnish; provide. The school supplies books for the children. Joe supplies us with ice. 2. quantity ready for use; stock; store. Our school gets its supplies of books, paper, pencils, chalk, etc., from the city. The United States has very large supplies of coal and oil. 3. make up for; fill. Rocks and stumps supplied the place of chairs at the picnic. 4. act of supplying. *v., supplied, supplying, n., pl. supplies. 1.*

sup port (sə pōrt′), 1. hold up; keep from falling. Walls support the roof. 2. keep up; help; give strength or courage to. Hope supports us in trouble. 3. provide for. A man supports his family. 4. be in favor of; back; second. He supports the President. 5. help prove; bear out. The facts support his claim. 6. bear; endure. She couldn't support life without friends. 7. act of supporting; condition of being supported; help; aid. He needs our support. 8. person or thing that supports; prop. The neck is the support of the head. *v., n. 2.*

sup port er (sə pōr′tər), person or thing that supports. He is a firm supporter of justice. *n. 8.*

sup pose (sə pōz′), 1. consider as possible. Let's suppose we have three wishes. Suppose we are late, what will the teacher say? 2. believe; think; imagine. I suppose Helen will come as usual. 3. imply; involve as necessary. An invention supposes an inventor. *v. 1.*

sup posed (sə pōzd′), accepted as true; assumed; considered as possible or probable. *adj.*

sup pos ed ly (sə pōz′id li), according to what is supposed or was supposed. *adv.*

sup pos ing (sə pōz′ing), supposing that; if. Supposing it rains, shall we go? *conj.*

sup po si tion (sup′ə zish′ən), 1. act of supposing. 2. thing supposed; belief; opinion. The speaker planned his talk on the supposition that his hearers would be school children. *n. 10.*

sup press (sə pres′), 1. put an end to; put down; stop by force. The troops suppressed the rebellion by firing on the mob. 2. keep in; hold back; keep from appearing. She suppressed a yawn. Each nation suppressed news that was not favorable to it. *v. 5.*

sup pres sion (sə presh′ən), 1. putting down by force or authority; putting an end to. Troops were used in the suppression of the revolt. 2. keeping in; holding back; as, the suppression of a childish fear. *n. 11.*

sup pu rate (sup′ū rāt), form pus; discharge pus; fester. *v.*

su prem a cy (sə prem′ə si), supreme authority or power. *n. 9.*

su preme (sə prēm′), 1. highest in rank or authority; as, a supreme ruler, a supreme court. 2. highest in degree; greatest; utmost; extreme. Soldiers who die for their country make the supreme sacrifice. *adj. 4.*

Supreme Being, God.

Supreme Court, 1. highest court in the United States, which meets at Washington, D.C. It consists of a chief justice and eight associate justices. 2. highest court in some States. 3. similar court in other countries.

Supt., Superintendent.

sur cease (sėr sēs′), end; stop. *n.* [*Old use*] *17.*

sur charge (sėr′chärj′ for 1, sėr chärj′ for 2), 1. an additional or excessive charge, load, or burden. A surcharge was made by the express company for delivering trunks outside the city limits. 2. charge extra; overcharge; overload; overburden. The widow's heart was surcharged with grief. *n., v. 16.*

sur cin gle (sėr′sing′gəl), a strap or belt around a horse's body to keep a saddle, blanket, or pack in place. *n. 19.*

sur coat (sėr′kōt′), outer coat; especially, such a garment worn by knights over their armor. *n.*

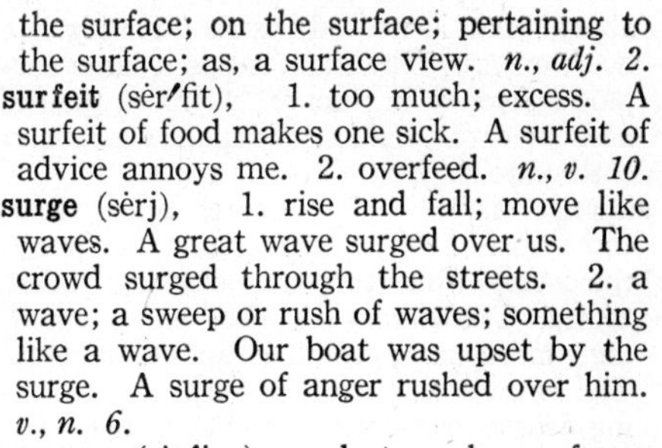
Surcoat

sure (shür), 1. I know it; I am sure of it. Are you sure you locked the door? 2. You can trust John; he is a sure messenger. Air mail is not quite so sure as ordinary mail. 3. firm; as, to stand on sure ground. 4. surely. *Used in common talk. adj., adv. 1.*

sure-foot ed (shür′fu̇t′id), not liable to stumble, slip, or fall. *adj.*

sure ly (shür′li), 1. certainly. Half a loaf is surely better than none at all. 2. firmly; without mistake; without missing, slipping, etc. The goat leaped surely from rock to rock. *adv.*

sure ty (shür′ti), 1. security against loss or damage. An insurance company gives surety against loss by fire. 2. person who agrees to be responsible for another. Mr. White was surety for his brother's appearance in court on the day set. 3. a sure thing; certainty. Of a surety he will come. *Old use. n., pl. sureties. 7.*

surf (sėrf), the waves or swell of the sea breaking on the shore. The surf is high just after a storm. *n. 9.*

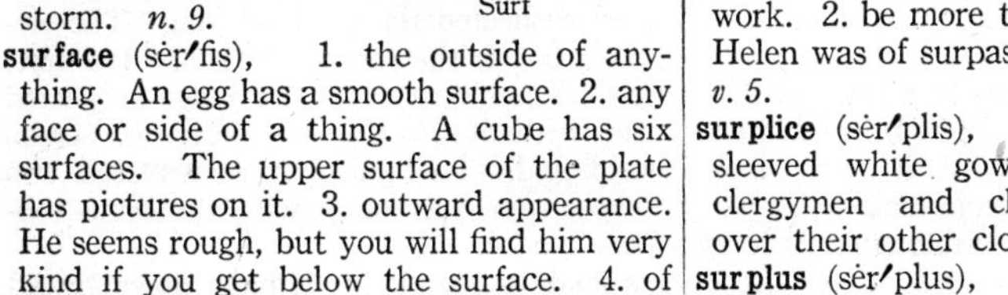
Surf

sur face (sėr′fis), 1. the outside of anything. An egg has a smooth surface. 2. any face or side of a thing. A cube has six surfaces. The upper surface of the plate has pictures on it. 3. outward appearance. He seems rough, but you will find him very kind if you get below the surface. 4. of the surface; on the surface; pertaining to the surface; as, a surface view. *n., adj. 2.*

sur feit (sėr′fit), 1. too much; excess. A surfeit of food makes one sick. A surfeit of advice annoys me. 2. overfeed. *n., v. 10.*

surge (sėrj), 1. rise and fall; move like waves. A great wave surged over us. The crowd surged through the streets. 2. a wave; a sweep or rush of waves; something like a wave. Our boat was upset by the surge. A surge of anger rushed over him. *v., n. 6.*

sur geon (sėr′jən), doctor who performs operations. A surgeon took out Fred's tonsils. *n. 7.*

sur gery (sėr′jər i), the art and science of treating diseases, injuries, etc., by operations and instruments. Malaria can be cured by medicine, but cancer usually requires surgery. *n. 8.*

sur gi cal (sėr′ji kəl), 1. of surgery; having to do with surgery. 2. used in surgery. *adj. 11.*

sur ly (sėr′li), ill-tempered and unfriendly; rude. The surly dog growled at the child. The impolite servant grumbled a surly reply. *adj., surlier, surliest. 9.*

sur mise (sėr mīz′), guess. His guilt was a matter of surmise; there was no proof. We surmised that the delay was caused by some accident. *n., v. 8.*

sur mount (sər mount′), 1. rise above. 2. be on top of. A statue surmounts the column. 3. overcome. Lincoln surmounted many difficulties before he rose to be President. *v. 7.*

sur name (sėr′nām′), 1. a last name; a family name. Smith is the surname of John Smith. 2. name added to a person's real name. William II of England received the surname of Rufus, meaning red. 3. give an added name to. Simon was surnamed Peter. *n., v. 7.*

sur pass (sər pas′), 1. do better than; be better than. Anna surpasses her sister in schoolwork. 2. be more than; exceed. Helen was of surpassing beauty. *v. 5.*

sur plice (sėr′plis), a broad-sleeved white gown worn by clergymen and choir singers over their other clothes. *n. 14.*

Surplice

sur plus (sėr′plus), 1. amount over and

above what is needed; extra quantity left over; excess. The bank keeps a large surplus of money in reserve. 2. more than is needed; extra; excess. Surplus wheat and cotton are shipped abroad. *n., adj. 7.*

sur prise (sər prīz′), 1. catch unprepared; come upon suddenly. Our army surprised the enemy while they were sleeping. 2. astonish. The victory surprised us. 3. catching unprepared; coming upon suddenly. The fort was captured by surprise. 4. feeling caused by something unexpected. His face showed surprise at the news. 5. something unexpected. Mother always has a surprise for the children on holidays. 6. surprising; that is not expected; as, a surprise party, a surprise visit. *v., n., adj. 1.*

sur pris ing (sər prīz′ing), causing surprise or wonder. *adj.*

sur ren der (sə ren′dər), 1. give up; give oneself up; yield. The captain had to surrender his ship to the enemy. As the storm increased, the men on the raft surrendered all hope. 2. act of surrendering. *v., n. 4.*

sur rep ti tious (sėr′ep tish′əs), stealthy; secret. *adj. 17.*

sur rey (sėr′i), a light, four-wheeled carriage having two seats. *n., pl. surreys. 10.*

Surrey

sur ro gate (sėr′ə gāt), 1. a substitute; a deputy, especially the deputy of a bishop. 2. a judge having charge of the probate of wills, the administration of estates, etc. *n. 18.*

sur round (sə round′), be around; shut in on all sides. Mountains surrounded the little valley. The surrounding country is flat and sandy. *v. 3.*

sur round ings (sə roun′dingz), surrounding things, conditions, etc. The poor child had never had cheerful surroundings. *n. pl. 8.*

sur tax (sėr′taks′), an additional or extra tax. *n. 13.*

sur veil lance (sər vāl′əns), 1. watch kept over a person. The police kept the criminal under strict surveillance. 2. supervision. *n. 14.*

sur vey (sər vā′ for 1 and 3, sėr′vā for 2, 4, and 5), 1. look over; view; examine. Grandma surveyed Mary with a stern look. 2. general look; view; examination; inspection. We were pleased with our first survey of the house. 3. measure for size, shape, position, boundaries, etc. Men are surveying the land before it is divided into house lots. 4. careful measurement. A survey showed that the northern boundary was not correct. 5. plan or description of such a measurement. He pointed out the route of the railroad on the government survey. *v., n., surveys. 4.*

sur vey ing (sər vā′ing), 1. the business or act of making surveys of land. 2. mathematical instruction in the principles and art of making surveys. *n.*

sur vey or (sər vā′ər), person who surveys. The surveyor set up his instruments and began to make a survey of the road. *n. 13.*

sur viv al (sər vīv′əl), 1. surviving; continuance of life; living or lasting longer than others. 2. a person, thing, custom, belief, etc., that has lasted from an earlier time. Belief in the evil eye is a survival of ancient magic. *n. 10.*

sur vive (sər vīv′), 1. live longer than; remain alive after. Only ten of the crew survived the shipwreck. 2. continue to exist; remain. Books have survived from the time of the Egyptians. *v. 5.*

sur vi vor (sər vī′vər), person, animal, or plant that remains alive; thing that continues to exist. *n. 7.*

sus cep ti bil i ty (sə sep′ti bil′i ti), 1. quality or state of being susceptible; readiness to receive impressions; sensitiveness. 2. **Susceptibilities** often means sensitive feelings. *n., pl. susceptibilities. 14.*

sus cep ti ble (sə sep′ti bəl), 1. easily influenced by feelings or emotions; very sensitive. Poetry appealed to his susceptible nature. 2. **Susceptible of** means (1) capable of receiving or undergoing. Oak is susceptible of a high polish. (2) sensitive to. 3. **Susceptible to** means easily affected by; especially liable to; open to. Vain people are susceptible to flattery. *adj. 8.*

sus pect (səs pekt′ for 1, 2, and 3, sus′pekt for 4), 1. imagine to be so; think likely. The mouse suspected danger and did not touch the trap. I suspect that some accident has delayed him. 2. believe guilty, false, bad, etc., without proof. The policeman suspected the thief of lying. The elevator boy is the suspected thief. 3. doubt; feel no confidence in. The judge suspected the truth of the thief's excuse. 4. person suspected. The police have arrested two suspects in connection with the bank robbery. *v., n. 4.*

sus pend (səs pend′), 1. hang down by attaching to something above. The lamp was suspended from the ceiling. 2. hold in place as if by hanging. We saw the smoke suspended in the still air. 3. stop for a while. We suspended building operations during the winter. 4. remove or exclude for a while from some privilege or job. Fred is suspended from school for a week for bad conduct. 5. keep undecided; put off. The court has suspended judgment till next Monday. *v. 5.*

sus pend ers (səs pen′dərz), straps worn over the shoulders to hold up the trousers. *n. pl. 12.*

sus pense (səs pens′), 1. condition of being uncertain. This detective story keeps you in suspense till the last chapter. 2. anxious uncertainty; anxiety. Mothers feel suspense when their children are sick. *n. 9.*

sus pen sion (səs pen′shən), a suspending or being suspended; as, the suspension of a boy from school for bad conduct. *n. 9.*

suspension bridge, bridge hung on cables or chains between towers.

Suspension bridge

sus pi cion (səs pish′ən), 1. suspecting; the state of mind of one who suspects. The real thief tried to turn suspicion toward others. 2. being suspected. Our old servants are all above suspicion. 3. very small amount; a suggestion. She spoke with a suspicion of spite. *n. 5.*

sus pi cious (səs pish′əs), 1. causing one to suspect. A man was hanging about the house in a suspicious manner. 2. suspecting; feeling suspicion. The dog is suspicious of strangers. 3. showing suspicion. He gives suspicious sniffs at their legs. *adj. 6.*

Sus que han na (sus′kwi han′ə), a river flowing through Pennsylvania and Maryland into Chesapeake Bay. *n. 15.*

Sus sex (sus′iks), a former county in southeastern England. *n. 12.*

sus tain (səs tān′), 1. hold up; support. Arches sustain the weight of the roof. 2. keep up; keep going. Hope sustains him in his misery. 3. bear; endure. The sea wall sustains the shock of the waves. 4. suffer; experience. She sustained a great loss in the death of her husband. 5. allow; admit; favor. The court sustained his suit. 6. agree with; confirm. The facts sustain his theory. *v. 4.*

sus te nance (sus′ti nəns), 1. food. He has gone for a week without sustenance. 2. support. He gave money for the sustenance of a poor family. *n. 10.*

su ture (sü′chər), 1. seam formed in sewing up a wound. 2. the method of doing this. 3. one of the stitches or fastenings used. 4. line where two bones, especially of the skull, join. *n. 18.*

su ze rain (sü′zə rān), 1. feudal lord. 2. state or government exercising political control over a dependent state. *n. 20.*

su ze rain ty (sü′zə rān ti), position or authority of a suzerain. *n. 20.*

SW or **S.W.** or **s.w.,** southwest. *14.*

swab (swob), 1. a mop for cleaning decks, floors, etc. 2. a bit of sponge, cloth, or cotton for cleansing some part of the body or for applying medicine to it. 3. a cleaner for a tube. 4. clean with a swab; apply a swab to; as, to swab a person's throat. *n., v., swabbed, swabbing. 18.*

swad dle (swod′əl), bind (a baby) with long, narrow strips of cloth; wrap tightly with clothes, bandages, etc. The picture shows a baby wrapped in swaddling clothes. *v. 17.*

Baby wrapped in swaddling clothes

swag (swag), things stolen; booty; plunder. *n.* [*Slang*]

swag ger (swag′ər), 1. walk with a bold, rude, or superior air; strut about or show off in a vain or insolent way. The bully swaggered into the schoolyard. 2. boast or brag noisily. 3. swaggering way of walking or acting. *v., n. 11.*

swain (swān), 1. young man who lives in the country. *Old use.* 2. lover. *n. 5.*

swale (swāl), low, wet piece of land; low place. *n.*

swal low[1] (swol′ō), 1. take into the stomach through the throat. We swallow all our food and drink. 2. take in; absorb. The waves swallowed up the swimmer. 3. believe too easily; accept without question or suspicion. He will swallow any story. 4. put up with; take meekly; accept without opposing or resisting. He swallowed the insults of the bully without saying anything. 5. take back; as, to swallow words said in anger. 6. keep back; keep from expressing. She swallowed her displeasure and smiled. 7. swallowing. He took the medicine at one swallow. 8. amount swallowed at one time. *v., n. 2.*

swal low[2] (swol′ō), a small, swift-flying bird with a deeply forked tail. *n.*

Barn swallow (about 7 in. long)

swam (swam). See **swim.** When the boat sank, we swam to shore. *pt. of swim. 6.*

swamp (swomp), 1. wet, soft land. The farmer will drain the swamp so that he can plant crops there. 2. plunge or sink in a swamp or in water. The horses were swamped in the stream. 3. fill with water and sink. Their boat swamped. 4. overwhelm as a flood would; make helpless. *n., v. 4.*

swamp y (swomp′i), 1. like a swamp; soft and wet. 2. containing swamps. *adj. 11.*

swan (swon), 1. a large, graceful water bird with a long, slender, curving neck. 2. a sweet singer; poet. *n. 3.*

Swan (nearly 5 ft. long, including the head and neck)

swan's-down (swonz′doun′), 1. the soft fine feathers of a swan, used for trimming, powder puffs, etc. 2. a fine, thick, soft cloth made from wool or cotton, used for babies' coats, bathrobes, etc. *n.*

swan song, 1. the song which a dying swan is supposed to sing. 2. a person's last piece of work.

swap (swop), exchange; barter; trade. *v., swapped, swapping, n.* [*Used in common talk*] *18.*

sward (swôrd), grassy surface; turf. *n. 15.*

sware (swãr), swore. *old pt. of* **swear.** *11.*

swarm (swôrm), 1. group of bees that leave a hive and fly off together to start a new colony. 2. group of bees settled together in a hive. 3. large group of insects flying or moving about together. 4. crowd; great number. Swarms of children were playing in the park. 5. fly off together to start a new colony. 6. fly or move about in a swarm; move about in great numbers; be in very great numbers. The mosquitoes swarmed about us. 7. be crowded. The swamp swarms with mosquitoes and other insects. *n., v. 3.*

swart (swôrt), dark; swarthy. *adj. 17.*

swarth y (swôr′ᴛʜi), having a dark skin. A swarthy Italian kept the fruit store. *adj., swarthier, swarthiest. 9.*

swash (swosh), 1. dash (water, etc.) about; splash. 2. such action or sound; as, the swash of waves against a boat. *v., n. 20.*

swash buck ler (swosh′buk′lər), swaggering swordsman, bully, or boaster. *n.*

swas ti ka (swos′ti kə), a symbol or ornament supposed to bring good luck. See the picture. Swastikas have been used in many parts of the world from very early times. *n.*

Swastikas

swat (swot), 1. hit with a smart or violent blow; as, to swat a fly. 2. a smart or violent blow. *v., swatted, swatting, n. 20.*

swath (swôth), 1. the space covered by a single cut of a scythe; one cut of a mowing machine. 2. row of grass, grain, etc., cut by a scythe or mowing machine. 3. a strip. *n. 20.*

swathe (swāᴛʜ), 1. wrap up closely or fully; as, swathed in a blanket. 2. bind; wrap; bandage. 3. a wrapping; a bandage. *v., n. 16.*

sway (swā), 1. swing back and forth; swing from side to side, or to one side. She swayed and fell in a faint. The pail swayed in Jack's hands as he ran. 2. a swinging back and forth or from side to side. The sway of the pail caused some milk to spill out. 3. make move; cause to sway. The wind sways the grass. 4. move to one side; turn aside. Nothing could sway him after he had made up his mind. 5. influence; control; rule. A mob is swayed by its feelings. Few countries are now under the sway of kings. *v., n. 3.*

swear (swãr), 1. make a solemn statement, appealing to God or some other sacred being or object. A witness at a trial has to swear, "I promise to tell the truth, the whole truth, and nothing but the truth, so help me God." 2. promise; vow. 3. bind by an oath; require to promise. Members of the club were sworn to secrecy. 4. curse; use profane language. *v., swore, sworn, swearing. 3.*

sweat (swet), 1. give out moisture through the pores of the skin. We sweat when it is very hot. 2. cause to sweat. He sweated his horse by riding him too hard. 3. moisture coming through the skin. He wiped the sweat from his face. 4. a fit or condition of sweating. He was in a cold sweat from fear. 5. cause to work hard and under bad conditions. That employer sweats his workers. 6. a fit of anxiety, impatience, or anything that might make a person sweat. 7. give out moisture; collect moisture from the air. A pitcher of ice water sweats on a hot day. 8. moisture given out by something or gathered on its surface. *v., sweat* or *sweated, sweating, n. 4.*

sweat er (swet′ər), a knitted jacket, usually of wool. *n. 6.*

Sweater

sweat shop (swet′shop′), place where workers are employed under very bad conditions of work and wages. *n.*

sweat y (swet′i), 1. sweating; covered or moist with sweat. 2. causing sweat. 3. laborious. *adj.*

Swede (swēd), person born in Sweden; person living in Sweden. *n. 9.*

Swe den (swē′dən), country in northern Europe, east and south of Norway. *n. 9.*

Swed ish (swēd′ish), 1. of or pertaining to Sweden, its people, or their language. 2. the people of Sweden. 3. the language of Sweden. *adj., n. 9.*

sweep (swēp), 1. to clean or clear (a floor, etc.) with a broom; to brush. The maid sweeps the floor. 2. move, drive, or take away with a broom; remove with a sweeping motion; carry along. The maid sweeps the dust into a pan. A flood swept away the bridge. 3. act of sweeping; clearing away; removing. He made a clean sweep of all his debts. 4. pass over with a steady movement. Her fingers swept the harp strings. His eye swept the sky, searching for signs of rain. 5. move swiftly; pass swiftly. Pirates swept down on the town. The wind swept over the valley. 6. move with dignity. The lady swept out of the room. 7. a steady, driving motion or swift onward course of something. The sweep of the wind kept trees from growing tall. 8. move or extend in a long course or curve. The shore sweeps to the south for miles. 9. swinging or curving motion. He cut the grass with strong sweeps of his scythe. 10. reach; range; extent. The mountain is beyond the sweep of your eye. 11. stretch; continuous extent. The house looks upon a wide sweep of farming country. 12. curve; bend. 13. person who sweeps chimneys, streets, etc. 14. long oar. 15. long pole used to raise or lower a bucket from a well. *v., swept, sweeping, n. 2.*

sweep er (swēp′ər), person or thing that sweeps; as, a carpet sweeper. *n. 8.*

sweep ing (swēp′ing), 1. passing over a wide space; as, a sweeping glance. 2. having wide range; as, a sweeping victory, a sweeping statement. *adj.*

sweep ings (swēp′ingz), dust, rubbish, scraps, etc., swept out or up. *n. pl.*

sweep stake (swēp′stāk′), sweepstakes. *n.*

sweep stakes (swēp′stāks′), 1. a scheme for gambling on horse races, etc. People buy tickets, and all the money they pay goes to the holder or holders of winning tickets. 2. a race or contest. 3. a prize in such a race or contest. *n.*

sweet (swēt), 1. having a taste like sugar or honey. 2. having a pleasant taste or smell. 3. pleasant; as, a sweet child, a sweet smile, sweet music. 4. fresh; not sour, salt, bitter, or spoiled. John drinks sweet milk and likes sweet butter better than salted. Ice helps to keep food sweet. 5. something sweet. **Sweets** often means candy. 6. dear; darling. 7. sweetly. *adj., n., adv. 1.*

sweet bread (swēt′bred′), a gland of a calf or lamb, used for food. Neck sweetbread is the thymus gland; stomach sweetbread is the pancreas. *n. 16.*

sweet bri er or **sweet bri ar** (swēt′brī′ər), a rose with a tall, prickly stem and single pink flowers; the eglantine. *n.*

sweet cider, unfermented cider.

sweet corn, a kind of corn which is eaten when it is soft, and which is canned for food. Sweet corn is sometimes called green corn.

sweet en (swēt′ən), 1. make sweet. He sweetened his coffee with two lumps of sugar. 2. become sweet. *v. 7.*

sweet en ing (swēt′ning), something that sweetens. Sugar is the most common sweetening. *n.*

sweet heart (swēt′härt′), loved one; lover. *n. 6.*

sweet ish (swēt′ish), somewhat sweet. *adj.*

sweet meats (swēt′mēts′), candy; candied fruits; sugar-covered nuts; bonbons. *n. pl. 15.*

sweet ness (swēt′nis), sweet quality. The sweetness of her manners made everyone like her. *n. 4.*

sweet pea, 1. climbing plant with delicate fragrant flowers of various colors. 2. the flower.

sweet potato, a yellow root with a sweetish taste, used as a vegetable.

sweet wil liam or **sweet Wil liam** (swēt′ wil′yəm), a plant with small flowers in dense clusters.

Sweet william

swell (swel), 1. grow bigger; make bigger. The river is swollen by rain. Bread dough swells as it rises. His head is swollen where he bumped it. 2. stick out; be larger or thicker in a particular place. A barrel swells in the middle. 3. increase in amount, degree, force, etc. His fortune had swollen during the war. 4. act of swelling; increase in amount, degree, force, etc. 5. condition of being swollen. 6. rise above the level. Rounded hills swell gradually from the village plain. 7. part that swells out. 8. piece of higher ground; rounded hill. 9. long, unbroken wave or waves. 10. grow louder; make louder. The sound swelled from a murmur to a roar. All joined in to swell the chorus. 11. swelling tone or sound. 12. fashionable person. *Used in common talk.* 13. stylish; grand. *Used in common talk. v., swelled, swelled* or *swollen, swelling, n., adj. 2.*

swell ing (swel′ing), an increase in size; swollen part. There is a swelling on Dick's head where he bumped it. *n.*

swel ter (swel′tər), 1. suffer from heat. 2. perspire freely; sweat. 3. sweltering condition. *v., n. 20.*

swept (swept). See **sweep.** The wind swept across the fields. *pt. and pp. of sweep. 3.*

swerve (swėrv), 1. turn aside. The car swerved and hit a tree. 2. a swerving. *v., n. 7.*

swift (swift), 1. moving very fast; coming quickly; quick; rapid. 2. swiftly. 3. a small bird with long wings. A swift looks somewhat like a swallow. *adj., adv., n. 2.*

Chimney swift (about 5 in. long)

swift ness (swift′nis), speed; rapid motion; quickness. He turned with the swiftness of a cat. *n. 9.*

swig (swig), 1. a big drink. 2. drink heartily or greedily. *n., v., swigged, swigging.* [*Used in common talk*]

swill (swil), 1. kitchen refuse; garbage; slop. 2. drink greedily; drink too much. 3. deep drink. *n., v. 14.*

swim[1] (swim), 1. move along on or in the water by using arms, legs, fins, etc. Fish swim. Most boys like to swim. 2. swim across. He swam the river. 3. make swim. He swam his horse across the stream. 4. float. The ham was swimming in gravy. 5. overflow. Her eyes were swimming with tears. 6. act, time, motion, or distance of swimming. May's swim had tired her. 7. **The swim** means the current of affairs. An active and sociable person likes to be in the swim. *v., swam, swum, swimming, n. 2.*

swim[2] (swim), be dizzy. The close air and noise made my head swim. *v., swam, swum, swimming.*

swim mer (swim′ər), person or animal that swims. *n. 11.*

swin dle (swin′dəl), 1. cheat; defraud. Honest merchants will not swindle you. 2. an act of swindling; a cheat or fraud. *v., n. 15.*

swin dler (swin′dlər), person who cheats or defrauds. *n. 13.*

swine (swīn), 1. hogs. 2. a hog. 3. coarse or beastly person. *n. pl. or sing. 5.*

swine herd (swīn′hėrd′), person who tends pigs or hogs. *n. 17.*

swing (swing), 1. move back and forth. The hammock swings. He swings his arms as he walks. 2. move in a curve. He swings the club twice around his head. He swung the automobile around the corner. 3. move with a free, swaying motion. The soldiers came swinging down the street. 4. act or manner of swinging. He brought the hammer down with a swing. 5. a swinging gait or movement; steady, marked rhythm. "Dixie" has a swing. 6. movement; activity. 7. seat hung from ropes in which one may sit and swing. *v., swung, swinging, n. 2.*

swin ish (swīn′ish), like swine; beastly; dirty; greedy; hoggish. *adj. 15.*

swirl (swėrl), 1. move or drive along with a twisting motion; whirl; as, dust swirling in the air, a stream swirling over rocks. 2. a whirl; eddy; swirling movement. 3. twist. Her hat had a swirl of lace around it. *v., n. 11.*

swish (swish), 1. move with a hissing sound; make a hissing sound. The whip swished through the air. 2. such a movement or sound; as, the swish of little waves on the shore. *v., n. 15.*

Swiss (swis), 1. of or having to do with Switzerland or its people. 2. person born in Switzerland; person living in Switzerland. 3. the people of Switzerland. *adj., n. sing. or pl. 5.*

switch (swich), 1. slender stick used in whipping. 2. whip; strike. He switched the boys with a birch switch. 3. stroke; lash. The big dog knocked a vase off the table with a switch of his tail. 4. move or swing like a switch. The horse switched his tail to drive off the flies. 5. bunch of long hair worn by a woman in addition to her own hair. 6. device for changing the direction of something, or for making or breaking a connection. A railroad switch shifts a train from one track to another. An electric switch turns the current off or on. 7. change, turn, or shift by using a switch. 8. change; turn; shift. *n., v. 5.*

switch board (swich′bōrd′), apparatus containing a number of plugs by which numerous electrical circuits are made, broken, or combined; as, the switchboard of a telephone system. *n.*

switch man (swich′mən), man in charge of a switch or switches on a railroad. *n., pl. switchmen.*

Switz er land (swit′sər lənd), a small country in Europe, north of Italy. *n. 6.*

swiv el (swiv′əl), 1. a fastening that allows the thing fastened to turn round freely upon it. 2. a support on which a chair can revolve. 3. support on which a gun can turn round. 4. in a chain, a link having two parts, one of which turns freely in the other. 5. turn on a swivel. *n., v., swiveled, swiveling. 12.*

A, swivel; B, hook turning freely in swivel; C, chain.

swob (swob), swab. *n., v., swobbed, swobbing.*

swol len (swōl′ən), swelled; as, a swollen ankle. *adj., pp. of* **swell.** *6.*

swoln (swōln), swollen. *adj. 18.* [*Old use*]

swoon (swün), faint. She swoons at the sight of blood. Cold water will bring her out of the swoon. *v., n. 7.*

swoop (swüp), 1. come down with a rush, as a hawk does; sweep rapidly down upon. The pirates swooped down on the towns. 2. a rapid downward sweep of a bird of prey upon its victim; a sudden, swift descent or attack. **At one swoop** means at a single blow or stroke. *v., n. 11.*

sword (sōrd), a weapon with a long, sharp blade. The sword has come to stand for fighting in general or for military power. "Those that live by the sword shall perish by the sword." "The pen is mightier than the sword." *n. 2.*

Sword

sword fish (sōrd′fish′), a very large sea fish that has a sword of bone sticking out from its head. *n.*

Atlantic swordfish (about 7 ft. long)

swords man (sōrdz′mən), 1. person skilled in using a sword. 2. person using a sword. *n., pl. swordsmen.*

swore (swōr). See **swear.** He swore to be a loyal American when he became a citizen. *pt. of swear. 5.*

sworn (swōrn), 1. bound by an oath. There were ten sworn witnesses. 2. declared, promised, etc., with an oath. 3. See **swear.** A solemn oath of loyalty was sworn by all the knights. *adj., pp. of swear. 4.*

swum (swum). See **swim.** He had never swum before. *pp. and old pt. of swim. 17.*

swung (swung). See **swing.** The door swung open. *pt. and pp. of swing. 9.*

syc a more (sik′ə mōr), a kind of shade tree. In the United States, a sycamore is a buttonwood; in England, a kind of maple; in Egypt and Syria, a kind of fig tree. *n. 8.*

syc o phant (sik′ə fənt), selfish flatterer. Great men are likely to be surrounded by sycophants who want favors. *n. 15.*

Syd ney (sid′ni), the largest city in Australia. *n. 18.*

syl lab ic (si lab′ik), of or pertaining to syllables; consisting of syllables. *adj.*

syl lab i cate (si lab′i kāt), divide into syllables. *v.*

syl lab i ca tion (si lab′i kā′shən), division into syllables. *n.*

syl lab i fy (si lab′i fī), divide into syllables. *v., syllabified, syllabifying.*

syl la ble (sil′ə bəl), part of a word pronounced as a unit, consisting of a vowel alone or with one or more consonants. *A mer i can* and *Al a ba ma* are words of four syllables. *Do, this,* and *stretch* are words of one syllable. *n. 5.*

syl la bus (sil′ə bəs), a brief statement of the main points of a speech, a book, a course of study, etc. *n., pl. syllabuses, syllabi* (-bī).

syl lo gism (sil′ə jizm), a form of argument or reasoning, consisting of two statements and a conclusion drawn from them. *Example:* All trees have roots; an oak is a tree; therefore, an oak has roots. *n. 14.*

sylph (silf), 1. a slender, graceful girl or woman. 2. a spirit of the air. *n. 14.*

syl van (sil′vən), of the woods; in the woods; consisting of woods; having woods. They lived in a sylvan retreat. *adj. 9.*

sym bol (sim′bəl), something that stands for or represents something else. The lion is the symbol of courage; the lamb, of meekness; the olive branch, of peace; the cross, of Christianity. The marks +, −, ×, and ÷ are symbols for add, subtract, multiply, and divide. *n. 4.*

sym bol ic (sim bol′ik), 1. used as a symbol. A lily is symbolic of purity. 2. of a symbol; expressed by a symbol; using symbols. *adj. 18.*

sym bol i cal (sim bol′i kəl), symbolic. *adj. 13.*

sym bol ism (sim′bəl izm), 1. use of symbols; representation by symbols. 2. system of symbols. The cross, the crown, the lamb, and the lily are parts of Christian symbolism. *n.*

sym bol ize (sim′bəl īz), 1. be a symbol of; stand for; represent. 2. represent by a symbol or symbols. 3. use symbols. *v. 12.*

sym met ri cal (si met′ri kəl), having symmetry; well-proportioned. *adj. 9.*

sym me try (sim′i tri), 1. regular form or arrangement. A swollen cheek spoiled the symmetry of his face. 2. well-balanced arrangement of parts; harmony. *n. 11.*

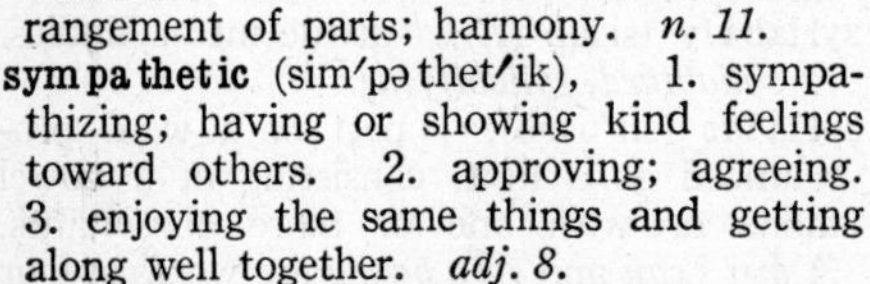
Five symmetrical figures

sym pa thet ic (sim′pə thet′ik), 1. sympathizing; having or showing kind feelings toward others. 2. approving; agreeing. 3. enjoying the same things and getting along well together. *adj. 8.*

sym pa thize (sim′pə thīz), 1. feel or show sympathy; as, to sympathize with a child who has hurt himself. 2. share in or agree with a feeling or opinion. My mother sympathizes with my plan to be a doctor. *v. 7.*

sym pa thiz er (sim′pə thīz′ər), person who sympathizes; person who is favorably inclined toward some belief or person. *n. 17.*

sym pa thy (sim′pə thi), 1. having the same feeling. The sympathy between the twins was so great that they always smiled or cried at the same things. 2. sharing another's sorrow or trouble. 3. agreement; approval; favor. Mother is in sympathy with my plan. *n., pl. sympathies. 3.*

sym pho ny (sim′fə ni), 1. harmony of colors. "She was a symphony in brown" means that she was dressed in shades of brown. 2. an elaborate musical composition for an orchestra. 3. harmony of sounds. *Old use. n., pl. symphonies. 10.*

sym po si um (sim pō′zi əm), 1. a collection of the opinions of several persons on some subject. This magazine contains a symposium on sports. 2. a meeting for the discussion of some subject. *n. 18.*

symp tom (simp′təm), sign; indication. Fever is a symptom of illness. *n. 8.*

symp to mat ic (simp′tə mat′ik), being a sign; signifying; indicative; as, headaches symptomatic of eyestrain. *adj.*

syn a gogue (sin′ə gog), 1. assembly of Jews for religious instruction and worship. 2. place used by Jews for instruction and worship. *n. 10.*

syn chro nize (sing′krə nīz), 1. occur at the same time; agree in time. 2. move or take place at the same rate and exactly together. 3. make agree in time; as, to synchronize all the clocks in a building. *v.*

syn chro nous (sing′krə nəs), 1. occurring at the same time; simultaneous. 2. going on at the same rate and exactly together. The movements of the two dancers were synchronous. *adj. 20.*

syn co pate (sing′kə pāt), 1. shorten (a word) by taking letters from the middle, as in syncopating *Gloucester* to *Gloster.* 2. in music, to begin (a tone) on an unaccented beat and hold it into an accented one. *v. 20.*

syn co pa tion (sing′kə pā′shən), syncopating; being syncopated. Jazz and ragtime are forms of syncopation in music. *n.*

syn di cate (sin′di kāt), 1. a combination of persons or companies to carry out some undertaking. This syndicate supplies stories to a hundred newspapers. 2. combine into a syndicate. 3. manage by a syndicate. 4. publish through a syndicate. *n., v. 13.*

syn od (sin′əd), 1. assembly called together under authority to discuss and decide church affairs; church council. 2. court of the Presbyterian Church ranking next above the presbytery. 3. assembly; convention; council. *n. 14.*

syn o nym (sin′ə nim), word that means the same or nearly the same as another word. *Keen* is a synonym of *sharp*. *n. 11.*

syn on y mous (si non′i məs), having the same or nearly the same meaning; expressing the same idea. *adj. 16.*

syn op sis (si nop′sis), brief statement giving a general view of some subject, book, play, etc.; a summary. Write a synopsis of *Treasure Island* in 200 words or less. *n., pl. synopses* (-sēz). *18.*

syn tax (sin′taks), sentence structure; arrangement of the words of a sentence in their proper forms and relations. *n. 16.*

syn the sis (sin′thi sis), the combination of parts or elements into a whole. Synthesis is the opposite of analysis. *n., pl. syntheses* (-sēz). *11.*

syn thet ic (sin thet′ik), 1. pertaining to synthesis; as, synthetic chemistry. 2. made artificially; as, synthetic rubies. *adj. 11.*

syph i lis (sif′i lis), an infectious disease with very harmful consequences. *n. 19.*

sy phon (sī′fən), siphon. *n., v.*

Syr a cuse (sir′ə kūs), 1. a city in central New York. 2. an ancient city in Sicily. *n. 9.*

Syr i a (sir′i ə), a country in western Asia between Palestine and Turkey. *n. 5.*

Syr i an (sir′i ən), 1. of or pertaining to Syria or its people. 2. a native or inhabitant of Syria. *adj., n.*

sy rin ga (si ring′gə), a shrub with fragrant white flowers blooming in early summer. *n.*

syr inge (sir′inj or si rinj′), 1. device for drawing in a quantity of fluid and then forcing it out in a stream. Syringes are used for cleaning wounds, injecting fluids into the body, etc. 2. clean, wash, inject, etc., by means of a syringe. *n., v. 19.*

Syringe

syr up (sir′əp or sėr′əp), a sweet, thick liquid; sugar boiled in water; a liquid made of sugar and fruit juices. *n. 6.* Also spelled **sirup.**

sys tem (sis′təm), 1. set of things or parts forming a whole; as, a mountain system, a railroad system, the digestive system, etc. 2. ordered group of facts, principles, beliefs, etc.; as, a system of government, system of education, etc. 3. plan; scheme; method. 4. orderly way of getting things done. 5. the body as a whole. *n. 2.*

sys tem at ic (sis′təm at′ik), 1. according to a system; having a system, method, or plan. 2. orderly in arranging things or in getting things done. *adj. 10.*

sys tem at i cal ly (sis′təm at′i kəl i), with system; according to some plan or method. *adv.*

sys tem a tize (sis′təm ə tīz), arrange according to a system; make into a system; make more systematic. *v. 19.*

T

T, t (tē), the 20th letter of the alphabet. There are two t's in tablet. **To a T** means exactly or perfectly. *n., pl. T's, t's.*

tab (tab), 1. a small flap, strap, loop, or piece. He wore a fur cap with tabs over the ears. 2. check; account; as, to keep tab. *Used in common talk. n. 13.*

tab ard (tab′ərd), 1. short, loose coat worn by heralds. 2. mantle worn over armor by knights. *n.*

tab by (tab′i), 1. brown or gray cat that has dark stripes. 2. female cat. 3. a spiteful female gossip. *n., pl. tabbies. 12.*

tab er nac le (tab′ər nak əl), 1. temporary dwelling. 2. place of worship for a large audience. 3. tomb, shrine, etc., with a canopy. 4. Jewish temple. 5. container for something holy or precious. The human body is called the tabernacle of the soul. *n. 6.*

Tab er nac le (tab′ər nak əl), the covered wooden framework used by the Jews as a place of worship during their journey from Egypt to Palestine. *n.*

ta ble (tā′bəl), 1. piece of furniture having a smooth flat top on legs. 2. food put on a table to be eaten. Mrs. Brown sets a good table. 3. the persons seated at a table. **King Arthur and his Round Table** means King Arthur and his knights. 4. put on a table. 5. a list; very condensed information; as, a table of contents in the front of a book, the multiplication table, a timetable. 6. make a list or condensed statement. 7. a thin flat piece of wood, stone, metal, etc. The Ten Commandments were written on tables of stone. 8. To **table a bill** or **motion** means to put off discussing it. 9. To **turn the tables** means to reverse conditions. *n., v. 1.*

tab leau (tab′lō), 1. picture; striking scene. 2. representation of a picture, statue, scene, etc., by persons. Our school is going to present several tableaux from American history. *n., pl. tableaux* (-lōz) or *tableaus. 17.*

ta ble cloth (tā′bəl klôth′), cloth for covering a table. Spread the tablecloth and set the table for dinner. *n. 12.*

ta ble land (tā′bəl land′), high plain; plateau. *n. 17.*

ta ble spoon (tā′bəl spün′), large spoon used to serve vegetables, etc. *n. 12.*

ta ble spoon ful (tā′bəl spün′fu̇l), as much as a tablespoon holds. *n., pl. tablespoonfuls. 11.*

tab let (tab′lit), 1. a small flat surface with an inscription. The Hall of Fame is a building that has many tablets in memory of famous people. 2. a small flat sheet of stone, wood, ivory, etc., used to write or draw on. The ancient Romans used tablets as we use pads of paper. 3. number of sheets of paper fastened together at the edge. 4. a small flat piece of medicine or candy; as, aspirin tablets. *n. 4.*

Tablet with inscription

ta ble ware (tā′bəl wãr′), dishes, knives, forks, spoons, etc., used at meals. *n. 14.*

tab loid (tab′loid), 1. a newspaper that has many pictures and gives the news in short articles. 2. condensed. *n., adj.*

ta boo or **ta bu** (tə bü′), 1. forbidden. Eating human flesh is taboo in all civilized countries. 2. forbid. 3. the system or act of setting things apart as forbidden; a prohibition. *adj., v., n., pl. taboos, tabus. 11.*

ta bor (tā′bər), small drum. *n. 7.*

Tabor

tab u lar (tab′ū lər), 1. of tables or lists; arranged in lists; written or printed in columns. *Example:*

Book	*Author*	*Type*
Ivanhoe	Scott	Romantic novel
Evangeline	Longfellow	Narrative poem
Tales	Andersen	Fairy stories

2. flat like a table; as, a tabular rock. *adj. 14.*

tab u late (tab′ū lāt), arrange (facts, figures, etc.) in tables or lists. *v. 10.*

tab u la tion (tab′ū lā′shən), arrangement in tables or lists. *n. 17.*

tac it (tas′it), 1. silent. 2. implied or understood without being expressed. His eating the food was a tacit confession that he liked it. *adj. 13.*

tac i turn (tas′i tərn), speaking very little; not fond of talking. *adj. 19.*

tack (tak), 1. a short, sharp-pointed nail or pin having a broad flat head; as, carpet tacks, thumbtacks. 2. fasten with tacks. She tacked mosquito netting over the windows. 3. stitch used as a temporary fastening. 4. sew with such stitches. 5. attach; add. He tacked a postscript to the end of the letter. 6. sail in a zigzag course against the wind. The ship was tacking, trying to make the harbor. 7. zigzag course against the wind. 8. course of action or conduct. He took the wrong tack to get what he wanted. *n., v. 6.*

tack le (tak′əl), 1. equipment; apparatus; gear. Ropes and pulleys for lifting furniture through windows are called tackle; so are the ropes that work the sails of a ship. **Fishing tackle** means the rod, line, hooks, etc. 2. try to deal with. Everyone has his own problems to tackle. 3. seize; lay hold of. John tackled the boy with the football and threw him. 4. act of tackling. 5. player between the guard and the end on either side of the line in football. *n., v. 7.*

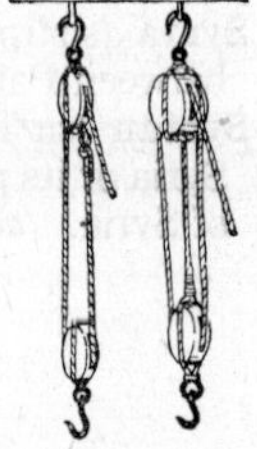
Tackles for lifting

Ta co ma (tə kō′mə), a seaport city in Washington, on Puget Sound. *n.*

tact (takt), ability to say and do the right thing; skill in dealing with people or handling difficult situations. Mother's tact kept her from talking about things likely to be unpleasant to her guests. *n. 8.*

tact ful (takt′fəl), 1. having tact. 2. showing tact. *adj. 20.*

tac ti cal (tak′ti kəl), 1. of tactics; concerning tactics. 2. pertaining to the disposal of military or naval forces in action against an enemy. 3. characterized by adroit procedure and skillful expedients. *adj.*

tac ti cian (tak tish′ən), person skilled or trained in tactics. *n.*

tac tics (tak′tiks), 1. the art or science of disposing military or naval forces in action; the operations themselves. 2. procedures to gain advantage or success; methods. When coaxing failed, Helen changed her tactics and began to cry. *n. sing. and pl. 10.*

tact less (takt′lis), 1. without tact; as, a tactless person. 2. showing no tact; as a tactless reply. *adj.*

tad pole (tad′pōl′), very young frog or toad. See the pictures. *n. 10.*

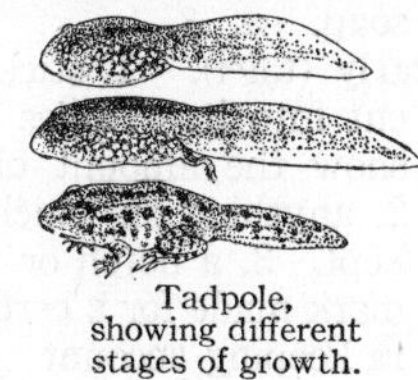
Tadpole, showing different stages of growth.

taf fe ta (taf′i tə), 1. rather stiff silk cloth with a smooth, glossy surface. 2. similar cloth of linen, rayon, etc. *n. 11.*

taff rail (taf′rāl), a rail around a ship's stern. *n.*

taf fy (taf′i), 1. a kind of chewy candy; as, salt-water taffy. 2. flattery. *Used in common talk. n.*

Taft (taft), William Howard (1857-1930), president of the United States from 1909 to 1913 and chief justice of the Supreme Court from 1921 to 1930. *n. 13.*

tag[1] (tag), 1. piece of card, paper, leather, etc., to be tied or fastened to something. Each coat in the store has a tag with the price mark on it. 2. a small, hanging piece; a loosely attached piece; a loose end. 3. a metal point at the end of a string. A shoelace has a tag on each end. 4. furnish with a tag or tags. All his trunks and suitcases are tagged with his name and address. 5. follow closely. The baby tagged after Helen. *n., v., tagged, tagging. 6.*

tag[2] (tag), 1. a children's game in which one child chases the rest of the children until he touches one of them. 2. touch or tap with the hand. *n., v., tagged, tagging.*

Ta hi ti (tä hē′ti), a small island in the southern part of the Pacific Ocean. *n.*

tail (tāl), 1. Mice have long tails. 2. something like an animal's tail; as, the tail of a kite. 3. hind part of anything; back; rear. Boys fastened their sleds to the tail of the cart. A crowd of small boys formed the tail of the procession. 4. follow close behind. 5. coming from behind; as, a tail wind. *n., v., adj. 1.*

tai lor (tā′lər), 1. man whose business is making clothes. 2. make by tailor's work. The suit was well tailored. *n., v. 2.*

tail spin, downward movement of an airplane with the nose first and the tail spinning in a circle above.

taint (tānt), 1. stain or spot; trace of decay, corruption, or disgrace. No taint of dishonor ever touched George Washington. 2. give a taint to; spoil. Flies sometimes taint what they touch. His mind was tainted from reading bad books. 3. decay; become tainted. *n., v. 6.*

take (tāk), 1. lay hold of. A little child takes its mother's hand in walking. 2. seize; capture. Wild animals are taken in traps. 3. catch hold; lay hold. 4. accept. The man won't take a cent less for the car. 5. receive. George took first prize. 6. win. 7. get; have. Mr. Jones took a holiday. 8. use; make use of. Dick hates to take medicine. Take care not to fall. We took a train to go to Boston. 9. need; require. It takes time and patience to learn how to drive an automobile. 10. choose; select. Take the shortest way home. 11. remove. Please take the waste basket away and empty it. If you take 2 from 7, you have 5. 12. go with. Harry likes to take his dog out for a walk. 13. carry. We take flowers to sick friends. 14. do; make. Take a walk. Please take my photograph. 15. feel. Mary takes pride in her schoolwork. 16. act; have effect. The vaccination did not take. 17. suppose. I take it you won't go to school since you feel sick. 18. regard; consider. Let us take an example. 19. engage; hire; as, to take a cottage for the summer. 20. become affected by. Marble takes a high polish. I take cold easily. 21. please; attract. The song took the fancy of the public. 22. amount taken; as, a great take of fish. 23. Some special meanings are:

take after, be like; resemble. Mary takes after her mother.

take down, 1. write down. 2. lower the pride of.

take in, 1. receive. 2. make smaller. 3. understand. 4. deceive; cheat.

take off, 1. leave the ground or the water. Three airplanes took off at the same time. 2. give a funny imitation of. *Used in common talk.*

take on, 1. engage; hire. 2. undertake to deal with. 3. show great excitement, grief, etc. *Used in common talk.*

take to, 1. form a liking for. 2. go to. The cat took to the woods and became wild.

take up, 1. soak up; absorb. 2. make smaller. 3. begin; undertake. 4. pay off. 5. lift.

v., took, taken, taking, n. 1.

tak en (tāk′ən). See **take.** I have taken this toy from the shelf. *pp. of take.*

take-off (tāk′ôf′), 1. an amusing imitation; mimicking. *Used in common talk.* 2. a taking off; the leaving of the ground in leaping or in beginning a flight in an airplane. 3. the place or point at which one takes off. *n.*

tak est (tāk′ist), take. "Thou takest" means "you take." *v.* [*Old use*] *18.*

tak eth (tāk′ith), takes. *v.* [*Old use*]

tak ing (tāk′ing), 1. attractive. 2. infectious or contagious. *Used in common talk.* 3. act of one that takes. 4. what is taken; receipts. *adj., n.*

talc (talk), a soft smooth mineral, used in making face powder. *n. 20.*

tal cum (tal′kəm), powder made from talc. *n. 10.*

tale (tāl), 1. story. Grandfather told the children tales of his boyhood. 2. falsehood; lie. To **tell tales** often means to tell something about a person to get him into trouble. 3. number; count. His tale of sheep amounted to three hundred. *n. 2.*

tal ent (tal′ənt), 1. special natural ability; ability. She has a talent for music. 2. people who have talent. 3. an ancient weight. A talent of silver was worth about $2000. *n. 4.*

tal ent ed (tal′ən tid), having natural ability; gifted; as, a talented musician. *adj.*

tal is man (tal′is mən), a stone, ring, etc., engraved with figures or characters supposed to have magic power; a charm. *n., pl. talismans. 13.*

talk (tôk), 1. use words; speak. A very small baby cannot talk. 2. the use of words; spoken words; speech; conversation. The old friends met for a good talk. 3. informal speech. 4. discuss. The men talked politics. 5. consult; confer. 6. spread ideas by other means than speech; as, to talk by signs. 7. gossip; report; rumor. *v., n. 1.*

talk a tive (tôk′ə tiv), having the habit of talking a great deal; fond of talking. *adj. 15.*

talk er (tôk′ər), 1. person who talks. 2. talkative person. *n. 7.*

talking picture, moving picture with sound.

tall (tôl). The man is 5 feet 8 inches tall. The tree is a hundred feet tall. A giant is a very tall man. *adj. 1.*

Tal la has see (tal′ə has′i), the capital of Florida. *n.*

tal low (tal′ō), hard fat from sheep, cows, etc. Tallow is used for making candles and soap. *n. 8.*

tal ly (tal′i), 1. stick of wood with notches cut into it. Tallies were formerly used to show the amount of a debt or payment. 2. anything on which a score or account is kept. 3. a notch or mark made on a tally; mark made for a certain number of objects in keeping account. 4. to mark on a tally; count up. 5. account; reckoning; score. 6. agree; correspond. Your account tallies with mine. *n., pl. tallies, v., tallied, tallying. 10.*

tal ly ho (tal′i hō′), 1. a coach drawn by four horses. 2. a hunter's cry on catching sight of the fox. *n., pl. tallyhos, interj.*

Tal mud (tal′mud), a collection of Jewish laws not in the Old Testament. *n.*

tal on (tal′ən), claw of a bird of prey; claw. The eagle seized a chicken with its talons. *n. 11.*

ta ma le (tə mä′li), a Mexican food made of corn meal and small pieces of meat, seasoned with red peppers, wrapped in corn husks, and roasted or steamed. *n.*

tam a rack (tam′ə rak), an American larch tree. *n.*

tam a rind (tam′ə rind), 1. a tropical tree grown for its wood and fruit. 2. the fruit of this tree, used in foods, drinks, and medicine. *n. 16.*

tam bou rine (tam′bə rēn′), a small drum with metal disks, played by striking it with the knuckles or by shaking it. *n. 15.*

Tambourine

tame (tām), 1. taken from the wild state and made obedient. The man has a tame bear. 2. gentle; without fear. The birds are so tame that they will eat from our hands. 3. make tame; break in. The lion was tamed for the circus. 4. become tame. 5. subdue; deprive of courage; tone down. Severe discipline in childhood had tamed him and broken his will. 6. without spirit; dull. The party was tame because all the people were sleepy. *adj., v. 3.*

Tam-o'-shanter

tam-o'-shan ter (tam′ə shan′tər), a Scotch cap. See the picture just above. *n. 12.*

tamp (tamp), 1. in blasting, to fill (the hole containing explosive) with dirt, etc. 2. pack down; as, to tamp the earth about a newly planted tree. *v.*

Tam pa (tam′pə), city in western Florida. *n.*

tam per (tam′pər), meddle; meddle improperly. Do not tamper with the lock. *v. 9.*

tan (tan), 1. make (a hide) into leather by soaking in a special liquid. 2. bark used in tanning hides, and also for covering riding tracks and circus rings. 3. yellowish brown. He wore tan shoes. 4. make or become brown by exposure to sun and air. 5. the change in a person's skin caused by being in the sun and air. *v., tanned, tanning, n., adj. 5.*

tan a ger (tan′ə jər), a small American bird. The male is brilliantly colored. *n.*

tan bark (tan′bärk′), crushed bark used in tanning hides. Riding tracks and circus rings are often covered with used tanbark. *n.*

tan dem (tan′dəm), 1. one behind the other; as, to drive horses tandem. 2. two horses so harnessed. 3. a carriage drawn by two horses so harnessed. 4. a bicycle with two seats, one behind the other. *adv., adj., n.*

Tandem

tang (tang), 1. strong taste or flavor. 2. a long, slender projecting point, strip, or prong forming the part of a chisel, file, etc., that fits into the handle. *n. 16.*

tan gent (tan′jənt), 1. touching. 2. in geometry, touching at one point only and not cutting. These circles are tangent ○○. 3. **Fly off at a tangent** or **go off at a tangent** means go suddenly from one course of action or thought to another. *adj., n. 16.*

tan ge rine (tan′jə rēn′), a small, deep-colored orange with a very loose peel. *n.*

tan gi ble (tan′ji bəl), 1. capable of being touched or felt by touch. Ghosts are visible but not tangible. 2. real; actual; definite. The good will of a business is not so tangible as its buildings and stock. *adj. 13.*

Tan gier (tan jēr′), seaport in northwestern Africa, on the Strait of Gibraltar. *n. 18.*

tan gle (tang′gəl), 1. twist and twine together in a confused mass. The kitten tangled the ball of yarn. 2. such a confused mass. The climbing vines are all one tangle and need to be pruned and tied up. *v., n. 8.*

tank (tangk), 1. large container for liquid or gas. Our school has a swimming tank. He always kept plenty of gasoline in the tank of his automobile. 2. put or store in a tank. 3. a small, self-moving steel fort used to attack in war. Tanks are mounted on caterpillar wheels so they can travel over rough ground, fallen trees, etc. *n., v. 4.*

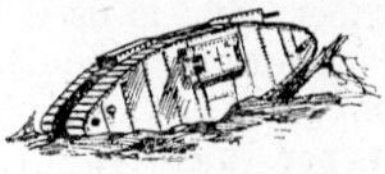

Tank used in war

tank ard (tangk′ərd), a large drinking mug with a handle and hinged cover. *n. 17.*

tank er (tangk′ər), ship with tanks for carrying oil or other liquid freight. *n.*

Tankard

tan ner (tan′ər), person whose work is tanning hides. *n. 14.*

tan ner y (tan′ər i), place where hides are tanned. *n., pl. tanneries. 18.*

tan nic (tan′ik), of or obtained from tanbark or tannin. **Tannic acid** is obtained from bark or from the nutlike balls found on oak trees. It is used in tanning, dyeing, and making ink. *adj. 19.*

tan nin (tan′in), an acid obtained from oak bark, used in tanning, dyeing, making ink, and in medicine. *n. 15.*

tan sy (tan′zi), a coarse, strong-smelling weed with yellow flowers, formerly used in cooking and medicine. *n., pl. tansies.*

tan ta lize (tan′tə līz), torment or tease by keeping something desired in sight but out of reach, or by holding out hopes that are repeatedly disappointed. *v. 16.*

tan ta mount (tan′tə mount′), equivalent. *adj. 19.*

tan trum (tan′trəm), fit of bad temper or ill humor. *n.*

tap[1] (tap), 1. strike lightly. He tapped on the floor with his foot. 2. light blow. There was a tap at the door. *v., tapped, tapping, n. 3.*

tap[2] (tap), 1. a stopper or plug to close a hole in a cask containing liquid. 2. a means of turning on or off a flow of liquid; faucet. 3. make a hole in to let out liquid. Sugar maples are tapped when the sap begins to flow. *n., v., tapped, tapping.*

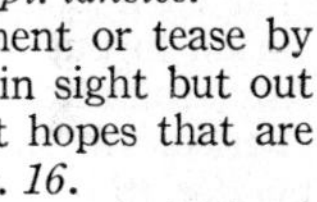

Tap (def. 1)

tape (tāp), 1. a long, narrow strip of cloth, paper, etc. That candy store uses fancy tape to tie all packages. 2. something like such a strip. The strip stretched across the finish line in a race is called the tape. A tape of cloth or steel, marked in inches, feet, etc., is used for measuring. 3. fasten with tape. The doctor taped up the wound. *n., v. 6.*

ta per (tā′pər), 1. become gradually smaller toward one end; make gradually smaller toward one end. A church spire tapers off to a point. 2. becoming smaller toward one end. She has taper fingers. 3. very slender candle; long wick coated with wax. The maid used one taper to light all the candles. *v., adj., n. 4.*

tap es try (tap′is tri), fabric with pictures or designs woven in it, used to hang on walls, cover furniture, etc. *n., pl. tapestries. 6.*

tape worm (tāp′wėrm′), a long flat worm that lives in the intestines of people and animals. *n. 11.*

tap i o ca (tap′i ō′kə), a starchy food obtained from the root of a tropical plant, used for puddings. *n. 18.*

ta pir (tā′pər), a large piglike animal of tropical America that has a flexible snout. *n. 20.*

Tapir (about 3 ft. high at the shoulder)

tap root (tap′rüt′), main root growing downward. *n. 19.*

taps (taps), a signal on a bugle or drum to put out lights at night. Taps are also sounded when a soldier or sailor is buried. *n. pl.*

tap ster (tap′stər), person who draws beer, wine, etc., from barrels, kegs, casks, etc. *n. 20.*

tar[1] (tär), 1. a black, sticky substance obtained from wood or coal. The rope was coated with tar. 2. cover or smear with tar; soak in tar. Tarred paper is used on sheds to keep out water. To **tar and feather** is to pour heated tar on and cover with feathers as a punishment. *n., v., tarred, tarring. 4.*

tar[2] (tär), sailor. *n.*

ta ran tu la (tə ran′chü lə), a large, hairy spider whose bite is painful, if not dangerous. People used to think that its bite caused an insane desire to dance. *n.*

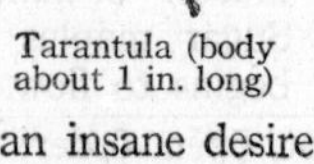

Tarantula (body about 1 in. long)

tar di ly (tär′di li), slowly; late; with delay. *adv.*

tar di ness (tär′di nis), slowness; lateness. *n. 17.*

tar dy (tär′di), 1. late; behind time. Tom was tardy for school four times last year. 2. slow. *adj., tardier, tardiest. 4.*

tare[1] (tãr), a weed. Tares killed the wheat. *n. 11.*

tare[2] (tãr), weight of the wrapper, box, conveyance, etc. The tare is subtracted from the total weight to give the weight of the things themselves. *n.*

tar get (tär′git), 1. mark for shooting at; thing aimed at. Anything may be used as a target. The poor boy was made the target of his stepfather's anger and scorn. 2. small shield. *n. 8.*

Target for shooting

tar iff (tar′if), 1. list of duties or taxes on imports or exports. 2. system of duties or taxes on imports or exports. The United States has a tariff on imports. 3. any duty or tax in such a list or system. There is a very high tariff on jewelry. 4. any table or scale of prices. The tariff at the Grand Hotel ranges from $3 to $5 a day for rooms. *n. 7.*

tarn (tärn), a small lake or pool in the mountains. *n. 16.*

tar nish (tär′nish), 1. dull the luster or brightness of. Salt will tarnish silver. 2. lose luster or brightness. Brass will tarnish. 3. loss of luster or brightness. *v., n. 13.*

ta ro (tä′rō), a starchy root grown for food in the Pacific islands. *n., pl. taros. 19.*

tar pau lin (tär pô′lin), 1. canvas, or other coarse strong cloth, made waterproof. 2. sheet of this used as a covering. *n. 14.*

tar pon (tär′pon), a large fish found in the warmer parts of the Atlantic Ocean. *n., pl. tarpons* or *tarpon.*

Tar quin (tär′kwin), one of a family of kings of early Rome. *n. 14.*

tar ry[1] (tar′i), 1. remain; stay. He tarried at the inn till he felt strong enough to travel. 2. wait; delay. Why do you tarry so long? *v., tarried, tarrying. 5.*

tar ry[2] (tär′i), 1. of tar; like tar. 2. covered with tar. *adj.*

Tar ry town (tar′i toun), a town near New York City, mentioned often in the stories of Washington Irving. *n. 14.*

Tar sus (tär′səs), a city in southeastern Asia Minor, the home of Saint Paul. *n. 11.*

tart[1] (tärt), 1. sour; having a sharp taste. Some apples are tart. 2. sharp. Her reply was too tart to be polite. *adj. 6.*

tart[2] (tärt), pastry filled with cooked fruit, jam, etc. In the United States, a tart is small and the fruit shows; in England, any fruit pie is a tart. *n.*

tar tan (tär′tən), 1. plaid woolen cloth. Each Scotch Highland clan has its own pattern of tartan. 2. made of tartan. 3. like tartan; of tartan. *n., adj.*

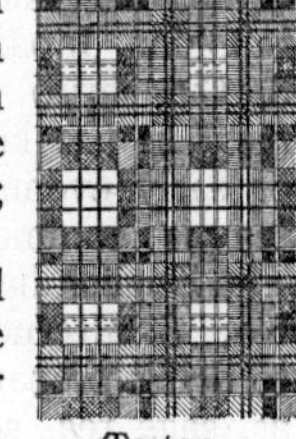
Tartan

tar tar[1] (tär′tər), 1. an acid substance deposited on the inside of wine casks. After it is purified, this substance is called cream of tartar and is used with baking soda to make baking powder. 2. a hard substance deposited on the teeth. *n. 10.*

Tar tar[2] (tär′tər), 1. member of a mixed horde of Mongols and Turks who overran Asia and eastern Europe during the Middle Ages. Tartars now live in parts of Russia and central and western Asia. 2. of or pertaining to a Tartar or Tartars. 3. A **tartar** is a person who has a bad temper. 4. **Catch a tartar** means attack someone who is too strong. *n., adj.*

Tar ta rus (tär′tə rəs), 1. place of punishment below Hades. 2. underworld; Hades. *n.*

task (task), 1. work to be done; piece of work. Mary's task is to set the table. 2. put work on; force to work. 3. burden. The master tasked his slaves beyond their strength. 4. **Take to task** means blame or reprove. The teacher took John to task for not studying. *n., v. 2.*

task mas ter (task′mas′tər), person who sets tasks for others to do. *n. 16.*

Tas ma ni a (taz mā′ni ə), a large island south of Australia. *n. 18.*

tas sel (tas′əl), 1. a hanging bunch of threads, small cords, beads, etc. See the picture. 2. something like this. Corn has tassels. 3. put tassels on. 4. take tassels from. 5. grow tassels. *n., v., tasseled, tasseling. 6.*

Tas so (tas′ō), a famous Italian poet (1544-1595). *n. 18.*

taste (tāst), 1. flavor. Sweet, sour, salt, and bitter are the four most important tastes. 2. try the flavor of (something) by taking a little into the mouth. The cook tastes everything to see if it is right. 3. the sense by which the flavor of things is perceived. Her taste is unusually keen. 4. get the flavor of by the sense of taste. I taste almond in this cake. When I have a cold, I can taste nothing. 5. have a particular flavor. The soup tastes of onion. 6. eat or drink a little bit of. The children barely tasted their breakfast Christmas morning. 7. little bit. Give me just a taste of the pudding. The snowstorm will give you a taste of northern winter. 8. to experience; have. Having tasted freedom, the bird would not return to its cage. 9. liking. Every one to his taste. 10. ability to perceive and enjoy what is beautiful and excellent. Good books and pictures appeal to people of taste. 11. a manner or style that shows such ability. Her house is furnished in excellent taste. *n., v. 1.*

taste ful (tāst′fəl), 1. having good taste. 2. showing or done in good taste. *adj.*

taste less (tāst′lis), 1. without taste. 2. without good taste; in poor taste. *adj. 19.*

tast y (tās′ti), 1. tasting good; pleasing to the taste. 2. having or showing good taste. *adj., tastier, tastiest.* [*Used in common talk*]

tat ter (tat′ər), 1. torn piece; rag. After the storm the flag hung in tatters upon the mast. 2. wear or tear to tatters. *n., v. 6.*

tat tered (tat′ərd), 1. torn; ragged. 2. wearing torn or ragged clothes. *adj.*

tat ting (tat′ing), 1. process or work of making a kind of lace by looping and knotting cotton or linen thread with a shuttle. 2. lace made in this way. *n.*

tat tle (tat′əl), 1. tell tales or secrets. 2. talk foolishly; gossip. 3. idle or foolish talk; gossip; telling tales or secrets. *v., n.*

tat too[1] (ta tü′), 1. a signal on a drum or bugle calling soldiers or sailors to their quarters at night. 2. series of raps, taps, etc. The hail beat a loud tattoo on the windowpane. *n., pl. tattoos. 11.*

tat too[2] (ta tü′), mark (the skin) in patterns by pricking it and putting in colors. The sailor had a ship tattooed on his arm. *v., tattooed, tattooing.*

Tattooed face

taught (tôt). See **teach.** Miss Jones taught my mother. She has taught arithmetic for many years. *pt. and pp. of teach. 2.*

taunt (tônt), 1. jeer at; mock; reproach. Some mean girls taunted Jane with being poor. 2. a bitter or insulting remark; mocking; jeering. *v., n. 9.*

taupe (tōp), dark, brownish gray. *n., adj. 20.*

taut (tôt), 1. tightly drawn; tense; as, a taut rope. 2. tidy; neat. *adj. 18.*

tau tol o gy (tô tol′ə ji), saying a thing over again in other words without adding clearness or force; useless repetition. *n., pl. tautologies.*

tav ern (tav′ərn), 1. place where alcoholic drinks are sold and drunk; saloon. 2. inn. Hotels have taken the place of the old taverns. *n. 4.*

taw (tô), 1. fancy marble. 2. game of marbles. 3. the line from which the players shoot their marbles. *n.*

taw dry (tô′dri), gaudy; showy and cheap. *adj. 18.*

taw ny (tô′ni), brownish yellow. A lion has a tawny skin. *adj., n. 8.*

tax (taks), 1. money paid by people for the support of the government; money taken from people by their rulers. Mr. Jones pays taxes to the city and to the State. 2. put a tax on. People who own property are taxed in order to provide clean streets, good roads, protection against crime, and free education. 3. a burden, duty, or demand that oppresses; strain. Climbing stairs is a tax on a weak heart. 4. lay a heavy burden on; be hard for. The work taxed her strength. Reading in a poor light taxes the eyes. 5. reprove; accuse. The teacher taxed Tom with having neglected his work. *n., v. 2.*

tax a tion (taks ā′shən), 1. taxing. Taxation is necessary to provide roads, schools, and police. 2. amount people pay for the support of the government; taxes. *n. 7.*

tax i (tak′si), 1. taxicab; automobile with a meter for recording the fare. 2. ride in a taxi. 3. move over the surface of the ground or water. An airplane or a seaplane taxis to get into a position for rising. *n., pl. taxis, v., taxied, taxiing. 12.*

tax i cab (tak′si kab′), automobile for hire with a meter to record the amount to be paid. *n. 14.*

tax i der my (tak′si dėr′mi), art of preparing the skins of animals and stuffing and mounting them so that they look like living animals. *n.*

tax pay er (taks′pā′ər), person who pays a tax or may have to do so. *n. 16.*

Tay lor (tā′lər), Zachary (1784-1850), the 12th president of the United States, from 1849 to 1850. *n. 10.*

tea (tē), 1. a common drink. 2. the dried and prepared leaves of a shrub from which this drink is made. Tea is raised chiefly in China, Japan, and India. 3. the shrub itself. 4. a meal in the late afternoon or early evening, at which tea is commonly served. The English have afternoon tea. 5. afternoon reception. 6. something to drink prepared from some thing named; as, sage tea, senna tea, pepper tea. Beef tea is a strong broth made from beef. *n. 2.*

Tea leaves and flowers

teach (tēch), 1. help to learn; show how to do; make understand. John taught his dog to shake hands. 2. give lessons in; as, to teach arithmetic, music, or swimming. 3. give lessons; act as teacher. *v., taught, teaching. 1.*

teach a ble (tēch′ə bəl), capable of being taught. *adj. 19.*

teach er (tēch′ər), person who teaches. Our school has fifty teachers. *n. 1.*

teach ing (tēch′ing), 1. work or profession of a teacher. 2. what is taught. *n.*

tea cup (tē′kup′), cup for drinking tea. *n. 17.*

teak (tēk), 1. a large tree of the East Indies with a hard, durable, yellowish-brown wood. 2. the wood. *n.*

tea ket tle (tē′ket′əl), rather small kettle with a spout, for heating water. *n. 16.*

teal (tēl), small fresh-water duck. *n., pl. teals or teal. 20.*

team (tēm), 1. number of people working or acting together; as, a football team, a debating team. 2. two or more horses or other animals harnessed together to work. 3. join together in a team. 4. drive a team. *n., v. 2.*

team ster (tēm′stər), man whose work is driving a team of horses. *n. 18.*

team work (tēm′wėrk′), the acting together of a number of people to make the work of the group successful and effective. Football requires teamwork even more than individual skill. *n.*

tea pot (tē′pot′), a container with a handle and a spout for making and serving tea. *n. 11.*

tear[1] (tãr), 1. pull apart by force. Don't tear up paper, but put it in the waste basket. 2. make by pulling apart. He tore a hole in his coat. 3. pull hard; pull violently. He tore down the enemy's flag. 4. scratch badly; wound. He tore his hand on a nail. 5. make miserable; distress. His heart was torn by sorrow. 6. become torn. Lace tears easily. 7. torn place. She has a tear in her dress. 8. move with great force or haste. An automobile came tearing down the road. *v., tore, torn, tearing, n. 1.*

tear[2] (tēr), drop of salty water coming from the eye. *n.*

tear ful (tēr′fəl), weeping. *adj. 12.*

tease (tēz), 1. annoy; vex or worry by jokes, questions, requests, etc. The other boys teased Jim about his curly hair. 2. beg. That child teases for everything he sees. 3. person who teases. 4. comb out; shred (wool, etc.). *v., n. 6.*

tea spoon (tē′spün′), small spoon commonly used to stir tea or coffee. *n. 6.*

tea spoon ful (tē′spün fu̇l), as much as a teaspoon holds. *n., pl. teaspoonfuls. 17.*

teat (tēt), a part of the breast or udder from which the young suck milk. A person milks a cow by pressing or squeezing her teats. *n. 10.*

tech nic (tek′nik), 1. technique. 2. technical. *n., adj.*

tech ni cal (tek′ni kəl), 1. of or pertaining to a mechanical or industrial art or applied science. This technical school trains engineers, chemists, and architects. 2. of or pertaining to the special facts of a science or art. *Electrolysis, enzyme,* and *proteid* are technical words. 3. of or pertaining to any art or science. May had technical skill in singing, but her voice was weak. 4. by the rules of a certain science, art, game, etc. *adj. 7.*

tech ni cal i ty (tek′ni kal′i ti), 1. a technical matter, point, detail, term, expression, etc. Books on engineering contain many technicalities which the ordinary reader does not understand. 2. technical quality; technical character. *n., pl. technicalities. 19.*

tech nique (tek nēk′), 1. the method of performance in any art; technical skill in art. This musician has perfect technique but little expression. Technique must be gained by practice. 2. special method or system used to accomplish something. *n. 10.* Also spelled **technic.**

tech nol o gy (tek nol′ə ji), the science of the industrial arts. Engineering is studied at a school of technology. *n. 19.*

Te De um (tē dē′əm), 1. a hymn of praise and thanksgiving sung in Roman Catholic and Anglican churches at morning service, and also on special occasions. 2. music for this hymn.

te di ous (tē′di əs or tē′jəs), long and tiring. A long talk that you cannot understand is tedious. *adj. 5.*

te di um (tē′di əm), tiresomeness; tediousness. *n. 18.*

tee (tē), 1. the mark aimed at in quoits and other games. 2. a mark or place from which a player starts in playing each hole in golf. 3. little mound of sand or dirt on which a golf ball is placed when a player drives; piece of wood or rubber used instead of the sand or dirt. 4. put (a golf ball) on a tee. 5. **Tee off** means drive (a golf ball) from a tee. *n., v., teed, teeing. 18.*

teem (tēm), be full; abound; swarm. The swamp teemed with mosquitos. *v. 7.*

teens (tēnz), the years of life from 13 to 19 inclusive. *n. pl.*

tee pee (tē′pē), tent of the American Indians; wigwam. See the picture under the usual spelling, **tepee.** *n.*

tee ter (tē′tər), seesaw. *v., n.*

teeth (tēth), 1. more than one tooth. You often show your teeth when you smile. 2. **By the skin of one's teeth** means by a very narrow margin. 3. **In the teeth of** means straight against. He advanced in the teeth of the wind. *n. pl. 2.*

Teeth: I, incisor; C, canine; B, bicuspid; M, molar.

teethe (tēᴛʜ), grow teeth; cut teeth. Baby is teething. *v., teethed, teething.*

teg u ment (teg′ū mənt), natural covering of an animal body, or of any part of it. A turtle's shell is a tegument. *n.*

Te heran or **Te hran** (te rän′), capital of Persia, in the northern part. *n.*

tel e gram (tel′i gram), message sent by telegraph. Mother sent a telegram telling us what train to take. *n. 4.*

tel e graph (tel′i graf), 1. a means for sending messages by electricity. 2. send (a message) by telegraph. When you want to telegraph, you give the message to an operator who telegraphs it to the distant city. *n., v. 4.*

te lep a thy (ti lep′ə thi), communication of one mind with another by some means beyond what is normal. *n. 19.*

tel e phone (tel′i fōn), 1. a means for transmitting sound by electricity. A man in New York can talk to a man in Chicago by using a telephone. 2. talk through a telephone; send (a message) by telephone. *n., v. 3.*

tel e scope (tel′i skōp), 1. an instrument for making distant objects appear nearer and larger. The stars are studied by means of telescopes. 2. force together, one inside another, like the sliding tubes of some telescopes. When two railroad trains crash into each other, the cars are sometimes telescoped. 3. be forced together in this way. *n., v. 8.*

Man using a telescope

tel e scop ic (tel′i skop′ik), 1. of or having to do with a telescope. 2. obtained or seen by means of a telescope; as, a telescopic view of the moon. 3. visible only through a telescope. 4. far-seeing. 5. consisting of parts which slide one inside another like the tubes of some telescopes. *adj.*

tel e vi sion (tel′i vizh′ən), a means for seeing objects at a distance by electricity. We can see things or people in another city by television. *n.*

tell (tel), 1. put in words; say. Tell us a story. Tell the truth. 2. inform; tell to. Tell us about it. Tell him the story. 3. make known. Don't tell where the candy is. 4. know. Can you tell them apart? 5. order; command. Do as I tell you. 6. count; count one by one. The officer told off ten men for special duty. The nun tells her beads. 7. have effect or force. Every blow told. The strain was telling on the man's health. 8. **Tell time** means know what time it is by the clock. *v., told, telling. 1.*

tell er (tel′ər), 1. person who tells. Our teacher is a good teller of stories. 2. person who counts. A teller in a bank takes in, gives out, and counts money. *n. 6.*

tell ing (tel′ing), having effect or force; striking; as, a telling blow. *adj.*

tell tale (tel′tāl′), 1. person who tells tales on others; person who reveals private or secret matters from malice. 2. telling what is not supposed to be told; revealing. *n., adj. 19.*

te mer i ty (ti mer′i ti), rashness; reckless boldness. *n. 17.*

tem per (tem′pər), 1. bring to a proper or desired condition by mixing or preparing. A painter tempers his colors by mixing them with oil. Steel is tempered by heating it and working it till it has the proper degree of hardness and toughness. Temper justice with mercy. 2. the hardness or toughness of the mixture. The temper of the clay was right for shaping. 3. state of mind; disposition; condition. She has a sweet temper. She was in no temper to be kept waiting. 4. angry state of mind. He flies into a temper at trifles. *v., n. 3.*

tem per a ment (tem′pər ə mənt), a person's nature; make-up; disposition. She has a nervous temperament. *n. 9.*

tem per a men tal (tem′pər ə men′təl), 1. constitutional; due to temperament. Cats have a temperamental dislike for water. 2. showing a strongly marked individual temperament. 3. sensitive; easily irritated; subject to moods and whims. *adj. 19.*

tem per ance (tem′pər əns), 1. being moderate in action, speech, habits, etc.; self-control. Temperance should be applied, not only to food and drink, but to work and play. 2. being moderate in the use of alcoholic drinks. 3. the principle and practice of not using alcoholic drinks at all. *n. 5.*

tem per ate (tem′pər it), 1. not very hot, and not very cold. The United States is mostly in the north temperate zone. 2. moderate; self-restrained. He spoke in a temperate manner, not favoring either side especially. Mr. Gray is a temperate man, and never eats or drinks too much. 3. moderate in using alcoholic drinks. *adj. 3.*

tem per a ture (tem′pər ə chər), degree of heat or cold. The temperature of freezing water is 32 degrees. The temperature of a person with fever is over 98½ degrees. *n. 3.*

tem pest (tem′pist), 1. violent storm with much wind. The tempest drove the ship on the rocks. 2. violent disturbance. She burst into a tempest of anger. *n. 4.*

tem pes tu ous (tem pes′chü əs), 1. stormy. It was a tempestuous night. 2. violent. She was in a tempestuous mood. *adj. 6.*

Tem plar (tem′plər), member of a religious and military order called Knights Templars, founded among the Crusaders for the protection of the Holy Sepulcher and of pilgrims to the Holy Land. *n. 17.*

tem ple[1] (tem′pəl), 1. a building used for the service or worship of a god or gods. Greek temples were beautifully built. 2. any of three temples in ancient Jerusalem built at different times by the Jews. 3. a building set apart for Christian worship; church. *n. 2.*

tem ple[2] (tem′pəl), the flattened part on either side of the forehead. *n.*

tem po (tem′pō), in music, the time or rate of movement; the proper or characteristic speed of movement; as, the correct tempo for a dance tune. *n., pl. tempos. 14.*

tem po ral[1] (tem′pə rəl), 1. of time. 2. lasting for a time only. 3. of this life only. 4. worldly; not religious or sacred. *adj. 8.*

tem po ral[2] (tem′pə rəl), of the temples, or sides of the forehead. *adj.*

tem po rar i ly (tem′pə rãr′i li), for a short time; for the present. The work is postponed temporarily. *adv. 19.*

tem po rar y (tem′pə rãr′i), lasting for a short time only. The hunter made a temporary shelter out of branches. *adj. 5.*

tem po rize (tem′pə rīz), 1. evade immediate action or decision; act so as to gain time or avoid trouble. 2. fit one's acts to the time or occasion. *v. 16.*

tempt (tempt), 1. make, or try to make, (a person) do something. The sight of the food tempted the hungry man to steal. The serpent tempted Eve to pick the forbidden fruit. 2. attract; appeal strongly to. That candy tempts me. 3. test. God tempted Abraham by asking him to sacrifice his son. *Old use.* 4. provoke. It is tempting Providence to go in that old boat. *v. 3.*

temp ta tion (temp tā′shən), 1. tempting. No temptation could make him false to a friend. 2. being tempted. "Lead us not into temptation." 3. thing that tempts. Money left carelessly about is a temptation. *n. 4.*

tempt er (temp′tər), person who tempts. **The Tempter** means the Devil. *n. 9.*

tempt ress (temp′tris), woman who tempts. *n.*

ten (ten). Ten is one more than nine. Ten means 10. Five and five make ten. *n., adj. 1.*

ten a ble (ten′ə bəl), capable of being held or defended; as, a tenable position, a tenable theory. *adj. 17.*

te na cious (ti nā′shəs), 1. holding fast; as, the tenacious jaws of a bulldog, a person tenacious of his rights, a tenacious memory. 2. holding fast together; not easily pulled apart. 3. sticky. *adj. 13.*

te nac i ty (ti nas′i ti), 1. firmness in holding fast. 2. firmness in holding together. 3. stickiness. *n. 13.*

ten an cy (ten′ən si), 1. state of being a tenant; occupying and paying rent for land or buildings. 2. property so held. 3. length of time a tenant occupies a property. *n., pl. tenancies. 20.*

ten ant (ten′ənt), 1. person paying rent for the use of land or buildings. That building has apartments for one hundred tenants. 2. one that occupies. Birds are tenants of the trees. 3. hold or occupy as a tenant. *n., v. 5.*

ten ant less (ten′ənt lis), without a tenant; vacant. *adj. 16.*

ten ant ry (ten′ənt ri), all the tenants on an estate. *n. 16.*

tend[1] (tend), 1. be apt; incline (to). Fruit tends to decay. Homes tend to use more machinery now. 2. move (toward); be directed. The coast line tends to the south here. *v. 3.*

tend[2] (tend), take care of; look after; attend to. He tends shop for his father. A shepherd tends his flock. A nurse tends the sick. *v.*

tend ance (ten′dəns), attention; care. *n. 14.*

tend en cy (ten′dən si), inclination; leaning. Boys have a stronger tendency to fight than girls. Wood has a tendency to swell if it gets wet. *n., pl. tendencies. 6.*

ten der[1] (ten′dər), 1. soft; not hard or tough. The meat is tender. 2. delicate; not strong and hardy. The leaves in spring are green and tender. 3. kind; affectionate; loving. She sent tender messages to her friends. 4. gentle; not rough or crude. 5. young. Two years old is a tender age. 6. sensitive; painful; sore. Automobiles are a tender subject with John since he wrecked his. The elbow joint is a tender spot. 7. feeling pain or grief easily. She has a tender heart and would never hurt anyone. *adj. 2.*

ten der[2] (ten′dər), 1. offer formally. He tendered his thanks. 2. offer. She refused his tender of marriage. 3. thing offered. Money which must be accepted as payment for a debt is called **legal tender.** *v., n.*

tend er[3] (ten′dər), 1. person or thing that tends another. Dick did not like his job as baby tender. 2. a small boat carried or towed by a big one and used for landing passengers. 3. a small ship used for carrying supplies and passengers to and from larger ships. 4. the car attached behind a locomotive and used for carrying coal, oil, and water. *n.*

ten der foot (ten′dər fůt′), 1. newcomer to the pioneer life of the western United States. 2. person not used to rough living and hardships. 3. beginner; inexperienced person. *n., pl. tenderfoots* or *tenderfeet.*

ten der-heart ed (ten′dər här′tid), kindly; sympathetic. *adj. 19.*

ten der loin (ten′dər loin′), a tender part of the loin of beef or pork. *n.*

ten der ness (ten′dər nis), 1. being tender. A steak is judged by its flavor and tenderness. 2. tender feeling. She has a tenderness for cats. *n. 5.*

ten don (ten′dən), a tough, strong band or cord that joins a muscle to a bone; a sinew. *n. 10.*

ten dril (ten′dril), 1. a threadlike part of a climbing plant, that attaches itself to something and supports the plant. 2. something similar; as, tendrils of hair curling about a child's face. *n. 9.*

Tendrils on a grape vine

ten e ment (ten′i mənt), 1. a dwelling house, or part of a dwelling house, occupied by a tenant. A two-family house has two tenements. 2. a building divided into cheap apartments. The tenements are in a poor section of the city. *n. 7.*

ten et (ten′it), opinion, belief, principle, or doctrine held as true. *n. 14.*

ten fold (ten′fōld′), ten times as much or as many. *adj., adv., n. 11.*

Tenn., Tennessee.

Ten nes see (ten′ə sē′), 1. a Southern State of the United States. 2. a river flowing from eastern Tennessee into the Ohio River. *n. 5.*

ten nis (ten′is), a game played by two or four players, in which a ball is driven back and forth over a net with rackets. *n. 6.*

Ten ny son (ten′i sən), a famous English poet (1809-1892). *n. 12.*

ten on (ten′ən), 1. the end of a piece of wood cut so as to fit into a hole (the mortise) in another piece and so form a joint. See the picture just below. 2. cut so as to form a tenon. 3. fit together with tenon and mortise. *n., v. 17.*

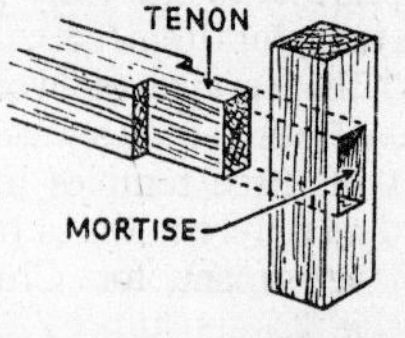

ten or (ten′ər), 1. course; general tendency. The calm tenor of her life has never been disturbed by excitement or trouble. 2. general meaning. I understand French well enough to get the tenor of his speech. 3. the highest adult male voice. Bass and tenor are two parts for men's voices. 4. part sung by, or written for, such a voice. 5. man who sings this part. *n. 6.*

ten pins (ten′pinz′), a game in which the players try to knock down ten wooden pins by rolling balls at them. *n.*

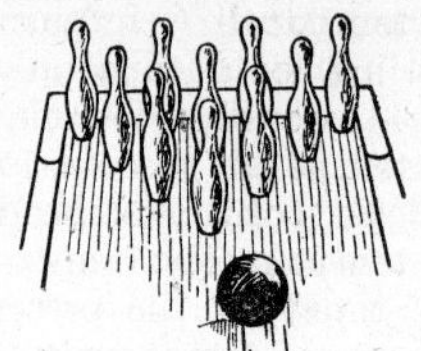
Tenpins

tense[1] (tens), stretched tight; strained; as, a tense rope, tense nerves, a tense moment. *adj. 17.*

tense[2] (tens), 1. a form of a verb to show the time of the action or state shown.
He obeys is in the present tense.
He obeyed is in the past tense.
He will obey is in the future tense.
2. set of such forms for the various persons. The present tense of *obey* is: I obey, thou obeyest, he obeys, we obey, you obey, they obey. *n.*

ten sile (ten′sil), 1. of or having to do with tension. 2. capable of being stretched or drawn out. *adj.*

ten sion (ten′shən), 1. stretching. 2. stretched condition. The tension of the spring is caused by the weight. 3. strain. A mother feels tension when her baby is sick. *n. 12.*

tent (tent), 1. movable shelter made of cloth or skins supported by a pole or poles. 2. live in a tent. "We are tenting tonight on the old campground." *n., v. 2.*

Tents

ten ta cle (ten′tə kəl), 1. a feeler; a long, slender, flexible growth on the head or around the mouth of an animal, used to touch, hold, or move. 2. a sensitive, hairlike growth on a plant. *n. 12.*

ten ta tive (ten′tə tiv), done as a trial or experiment; experimental; as, a tentative plan. *adj. 15.*

tenth (tenth), 1. next after the ninth. 2. one of 10 equal parts. *adj., n. 3.*

ten u ous (ten′ū əs), 1. thin; slender; as, the tenuous thread of a spider's web. 2. not dense. The air ten miles above the earth is very tenuous. 3. not substantial; having slight importance; as, a tenuous argument. *adj.*

ten ure (ten′yər), 1. holding; possessing. 2. length of time of holding or possessing. The President's tenure of office ends January 20. 3. manner of holding or possessing. *n. 12.*

te pee (tē′pē), tent of the American Indians; wigwam. *n.* Also spelled **teepee.**

Tepees

tep id (tep′id), slightly warm; lukewarm. *adj. 12.*

term (tėrm), 1. word or group of words used in connection with some special subject; as, medical terms, terms about radio. She praised his book in flattering terms. 2. name; call. John might be termed handsome. 3. a set time; length of time. The President's term of office is four years. Most schools have a fall term and a spring term. 4. boundary; end; limit. 5. **Terms** means (1) conditions. The terms of the peace were very hard for the defeated nation. (2) personal relations. 6. **Not on speaking terms** means not speaking to one another. *n., v. 2.*

ter ma gant (tėr′mə gənt), 1. a violent, quarreling, scolding woman. 2. violent; quarreling; scolding. *n., adj. 19.*

ter mi na ble (tėr′mi nə bəl), 1. that can be ended. This contract is terminable by either party. 2. coming to an end after a certain time. *adj.*

ter mi nal (tėr′mi nəl), 1. at the end; forming the end. Terminal buds grow at the end of stems. 2. the end. A railroad terminal is the station, sheds, tracks, etc., at either end of the line. *adj., n. 13.*

ter mi nate (tėr′mi nāt), 1. bring to an end; put an end to; end. 2. come to an end. 3. form the end of; bound; limit. *v. 7.*

ter mi na tion (tėr′mi nā′shən), ending; end. *n. 8.*

ter mi nol o gy (tėr′mi nol′ə ji), the special words or terms used in a science, art, business, etc.; as, medical terminology, the terminology of engineering. *n., pl. terminologies. 17.*

ter mi nus (tėr′mi nəs), 1. either end of a railroad line, bus line, etc. 2. boundary; goal; end. *n., pl. termini* (-nī) or *terminuses. 17.*

ter mite (tėr′mīt), white ant. Termites are very destructive to buildings, furniture, provisions, etc. *n.*

tern (tėrn), sea bird like a gull but with a more slender body and bill and a long, forked tail. *n.*

ter race (ter′əs), 1. a flat, raised piece of land; raised level. 2. form into a terrace or terraces; furnish with terraces. They made a terraced garden. 3. a row of houses or a short street running along the side or top of a slope. She lives at 7 Oak Terrace. *n., v. 6.*

Terraces

ter ra cot ta (ter′ə kot′ə), 1. a kind of hard, unglazed, brownish-red earthenware. It is used for vases, statuettes, decorations on buildings, etc. 2. dull brownish red. *13.*

ter ra fir ma (ter′ə fėr′mə), solid earth; dry land.

ter ra pin (ter′ə pin), a North American turtle used for food. It lives in fresh water or tidewater. *n.*

ter res tri al (tə res′tri əl), 1. of the earth; not of the heavens; as, this terrestrial globe. 2. of land, not water. 3. living on the ground, not in the air or water or in trees. A cow is a terrestrial animal. *adj. 11.*

ter ri ble (ter′i bəl), causing great fear; dreadful; awful. The terrible storm destroyed many lives. *adj. 2.*

ter ri bly (ter′i bli), in a terrible manner; dreadfully. *adv.*

ter ri er (ter′i ər), a kind of small, active, intelligent, and courageous dog that pursues prey into its burrow. The best known kinds are fox terriers, Irish terriers, and Scotch terriers. *n. 10.*

Wire-haired terrier (about 15 in. high at the shoulder)

ter rif ic (tə rif′ik), causing great fear; terrifying; very severe. A terrific earthquake shook Japan. *adj. 10.*

ter ri fy (ter′i fī), fill with great fear; frighten very much. Terrified by the sight of the lion, Bill climbed a tree. *v., terrified, terrifying. 6.*

ter ri to ri al (ter′i tō′ri əl), 1. of territory. The purchase of Louisiana made a territorial increase for the United States. 2. of a particular territory. Alaska has its own Territorial laws. *adj. 12.*

ter ri to ry (ter′i tō′ri), 1. land; region. Much territory in Africa is desert. 2. land belonging to a government; land under the rule of a distant government. Gibraltar is British territory. 3. a district not admitted as a State but having its own assembly. Alaska and Hawaii are Territories of the United States. *n., pl. territories. 3.*

ter ror (ter′ər), 1. great fear. The child has a terror of thunder. 2. cause of great fear. Pirates were once the terror of the sea. *n. 2.*

ter ror ism (ter′ər izm), 1. terrorizing; use of terror. 2. condition of fear and submission produced by frightening people. *n.*

ter ror ize (ter′ər īz), 1. fill with terror. 2. rule or subdue by terror. *v. 20.*

terse (tėrs), brief and to the point (said of writing, speaking, writers, or speakers). *adj. 19.*

ter tian (tėr′shən), 1. fever or ague with a bad spell recurring every other day. 2. recurring every other day. *n., adj. 17.*

ter ti ar y (tėr′shi ãr′i), of the third order, rank, formation, etc.; third. *adj. 19.*

test (test), 1. examination; trial. The teacher gave the children a test in arithmetic. People who want to drive an automobile must pass a test. 2. means of trial. Trouble is a test of character. 3. examination of a substance to see what it is or what it contains. A test showed that the water from our well was pure. 4. put to a test of any kind; try out. He tested the boy's honesty by leaving money about. That food was tested for poison. *n., v. 2.*

tes ta ment (tes′tə mənt), written instructions telling what to do with a person's property after his death; a will. *n. 7.*

Tes ta ment (tes′tə mənt). The Bible consists of two parts, the Old Testament and the New Testament. Testament used alone means the New Testament. *n.*

tes ta men ta ry (tes′tə men′tə ri), 1. of or having to do with a testament or will. 2. given, done, or appointed by a testament or will. Mr. Jones made testamentary provision that all his paintings be given to the Museum. 3. in a testament or will. *adj. 18.*

tes ta tor (tes tā′tər), person who makes a will; person who has died leaving a valid will. *n. 16.*

test er (tes′tər), one that tests. *n. 12.*

tes ti fy (tes′ti fī), give evidence; bear witness; declare. The witness testified that the larger car had crowded the smaller one into the ditch. He hated to testify against a friend. *v., testified, testifying. 5.*

tes ti mo ni al (tes′ti mō′ni əl), 1. certificate of character, conduct, qualifications, value, etc.; recommendation. The boy looking for a job has testimonials from his teachers and a former employer. Advertisements of patent medicines often contain testimonials from people who have used them. 2. something given or done to show esteem, admiration, gratitude, etc. The members of the church collected money for a testimonial to their retiring pastor. 3. given or done as a testimonial. *n., adj. 17.*

tes ti mo ny (tes′ti mō′ni), 1. statement used for evidence or proof. A witness gave testimony that Mr. Doe was at home from 9 to 11 P.M. 2. evidence. The pupils presented their teacher with a watch in testimony of their respect and affection. 3. **Testimonies** sometimes means the laws of God. *n., pl. testimonies. 4.*

tes ty (tes′ti), easily irritated; impatient. *adj., testier, testiest. 14.*

tet a nus (tet′ə nəs), a disease that causes violent spasms, stiffness of many muscles, and even death. Tetanus of the lower jaw is called lockjaw. *n. 13.*

tête-à-tête (tāt′ə tāt′), 1. two together in private. They dined tête-à-tête. 2. of or for two people in private; as, a tête-à-tête conversation. 3. a private conversation between two people. *adv., adj., n. 15.*

teth er (teᴛʜ′ər), 1. rope or chain by which an animal is fastened. The cow had broken her tether and was in the cornfield. 2. fasten with a tether. The horse is tethered to a stake. 3. **At the end of one's tether** means at the end of one's resources or endurance. *n., v. 10.*

Teu ton (tū′tən or tü′tən), 1. German. 2. member of a group of northern Europeans that includes Germans, Dutch, and Scandinavians. *n., adj. 13.*

Teu ton ic (tū ton′ik or tü ton′ik), 1. German. 2. of or having to do with the Teutons. 3. their languages. *adj., n. 11.*

Tex., Texas.

Tex as (tek′səs), a Southern State, the largest of the United States. *n. 4*

text (tekst), 1. the main body of reading matter in a book. This history contains 300 pages of text, and about 50 pages of notes, explanations, and questions for study. 2. the original words of a writer. A text is often changed here and there when it is copied. 3. a short passage in the Bible used as the subject of a sermon, or as proof of some belief. The minister preached on the text "Judge not, that ye be not judged." 4. topic; subject. Town improvement was the speaker's text. 5. textbook. *n. 3.*

text book (tekst′bük′), book for regular study by pupils. Most arithmetics and geographies are textbooks. *n. 14.*

tex tile (teks′til), 1. woven. Cloth is a textile fabric. 2. woven fabric. Beautiful textiles were sold in Paris. 3. material that can be woven. 4. suitable for weaving. Linen, cotton, silk, and wool are common textile materials. 5. of or having to do with weaving; as, the textile art. *adj., n. 10.*

tex ture (teks′chər), 1. arrangement of threads woven together. Homespun is cloth which has a loose texture. This linen tablecloth has a fine texture. 2. arrangement of the parts of anything; structure; constitution; make-up. Her skin has a fine texture. *n. 9.*

Thai land (tī′lənd), name of Siam since 1940. *n.*

tha ler (tä′lər), a former German silver coin worth about 71½ cents. *n., pl. thaler.*

thal lus (thal′əs), a plant not divided into leaves, stem, and root. Mushrooms, toadstools, and lichens are thalli. *n., pl. thalli* (-ī) or *thalluses. 19.*

Thames (temz), a river in England. London is on the Thames. *n. 6.*

than (ᴛʜan). John is taller than his sister. Ruth would rather read than play. Than shows comparison. You know better than I do. How else can we come than by train? *conj. 1.*

thane (thān), man who ranked between an earl and an ordinary freeman in early England. Thanes held lands of the king or lord and gave military service in return. *n. 13.*

thank (thangk). Say "thank you" when someone does you a favor. Helen thanked her teacher for helping her. **Have oneself to thank** means be to blame. You have yourself to thank if you eat too much. *v. 1.*

thank ful (thangk′fəl), feeling thanks; grateful. He is thankful for good health. *adj. 4.*

thank less (thangk′lis), 1. ungrateful. 2. not likely to get thanks. Giving advice is usually a thankless act. *adj. 9.*

thanks (thangks), 1. I thank you. 2. act of thanking; expression of pleasure and gratitude. 3. feeling of kindness received; gratitude. 4. **Thanks to** sometimes means owing to or because of. Thanks to John's efforts, the garden is a great success. *n. pl.*

thanks giv ing (thangks giv′ing), 1. giving thanks. 2. expression of thanks. They offered thanksgiving to God for their escape. 3. In the United States, **Thanksgiving** is usually the last Thursday in November, a day set apart every year to acknowledge God's favor. Many people forget the original purpose of Thanksgiving and think only of the good dinner. *n. 3.*

that (ᴛʜat), 1. *That* is used to point out some one person or thing or idea. We use *this* for the thing nearer us, and *that* for the thing farther away from us. Do you know that boy? Shall we buy this book or that one? I like that better. 2. who; whom. Is he the man that sells dogs? She is the girl that you saw in school. 3. which. Bring the box that will hold most. 4. *That* is also used to connect a group of words. I know that 6 and 4 are 10. 5. *That* is used to show purpose. He ran fast that he might not be late to school. 6. *That* is used to show result. He ran so fast that he was five minutes early. 7. to that extent; to such a degree; so. The baby cannot stay up that long. 8. when; as, the day that school began. 9. **In that** means because. *adj., pron., pl. those, conj., adv. 1.*

thatch (thach), 1. straw, rushes, or the like, used to cover roofs or stacks. 2. cover with thatch. *n., v. 8.*

Thatched roof

that's (ᴛʜats), that is. *13.*

thaw (thô), 1. melt (ice, snow, or anything frozen); free from frost. The sun at noon thaws the ice on the streets. It thawed early last spring. 2. weather above the freezing point (32 degrees); time of melting. In January we usually have a thaw. 3. become less cold, less formal, or less reserved. His shyness thawed under her kindness. *v., n. 5.*

the[1] (ᴛʜə or ᴛʜi, *stressed* ᴛʜē). The dog I saw had no tail. The boys on the horses are my brothers. *definite article. 1.*

the[2] (ᴛʜə or ᴛʜi), in that degree; to that degree. The longer you work, the more you get. The later I sit up, the sleepier I become. *adv.*

the a ter or **the a tre** (thē′ə tər), 1. place where plays are acted; place where moving pictures are shown. 2. place that looks like a theater in its arrangement of seats. The surgeon performed an operation before the medical students in the operating theater. 3. place of action. Belgium and France were the theater of the first World War. 4. plays; writing and producing plays; the drama. *n. 2.*

the at ric (thi at′rik), theatrical. *adj. 20.*

the at ri cal (thi at′ri kəl), 1. of or pertaining to the theater or actors; as, theatrical performances, a theatrical company. 2. suggesting a theater or acting; artificial; for display or effect. 3. **Theatricals** are dramatic performances given by amateurs. *adj., n. pl. 10.*

The ban (thē′bən), 1. of or pertaining to Thebes in ancient Greece or Thebes in ancient Egypt. 2. a native or an inhabitant of Thebes in Greece. *adj., n. 14.*

Thebes (thēbz), 1. an important city in ancient Greece. 2. an ancient city on the Nile, formerly a center of Egyptian civilization. *n. 10.*

thee (ᴛʜē), you. "The Lord bless thee and keep thee." *pron. 1.*

theft (theft), stealing. The theft of the jewels caused much excitement. People are put in prison for theft. *n. 7.*

their (ᴛʜãr), of them; belonging to them. They like their school and do their lessons well. *pron. 1.*

theirs (ᴛʜãrz), 1. of them; belonging to them. Those books are theirs, not mine. 2. the one or ones belonging to them. Our house is white; theirs is brown. *pron. 5.*

them (ᴛʜem). The books are new; take care of them. *They* and *them* mean the persons, animals, or things spoken about. *pron. pl. 1.*

theme (thēm), 1. subject; topic. Patriotism was the speaker's theme. 2. short written composition. Our school themes must be written in ink and on white paper. 3. principal melody in a piece of music; short melody repeated in different forms. *n. 5.*

The mis to cles (thi mis′tə klēz), an Athenian leader and statesman (527?-460? B.C.). Under his leadership, the Athenians defeated the Persians in a great naval battle. *n. 16.*

them selves (ᴛʜem selvz′), 1. *Themselves* is used to make a statement stronger. The teachers themselves said the test was too hard. 2. *Themselves* is used instead of *they* or *them* to refer back to the subject of a verb. The boys hurt themselves sliding down hill. *pron. pl. 1.*

then (ᴛʜen), 1. at that time. 2. that time. By then we shall know the result of the election. 3. soon afterward. The noise stopped and then began again. 4. next in time or place. First comes spring, then summer. 5. at another time. Now one boy does best and then another. 6. also; besides. The dress seems too good to throw away, and then it is so becoming. 7. in that case; therefore. If Harry broke the window, then he should pay for it. *adv., n. 1.*

thence (ᴛʜens), 1. from that place. He went to Italy; thence he went to France. 2. for that reason. 3. from that time. *adv. 3.*

thence forth (ᴛʜens′fōrth′), from then on; from that time forward. Women were given the same rights as men. Thenceforth they could vote. *adv. 9.*

thence for ward (ᴛʜens′fôr′wərd), from that time forward. *adv. 16.*

the oc ra cy (thē ok′rə si), 1. a government in which God is recognized as the supreme civil ruler and His laws are taken as the laws of the state. 2. a country or state having such a government. *n., pl. theocracies.*

the o lo gian (thē′ə lō′jən), person skilled or trained in theology. *n. 14.*

the o log i cal (thē′ə loj′i kəl), of theology; pertaining to theology. A theological school trains young men for the ministry. *adj. 9.*

the ol o gy (thē ol′ə ji), doctrines concerning God and His relations to the universe; the study of divine things or religious truth. *n., pl. theologies. 8.*

the o rem (thē′ə rəm), 1. statement in mathematics to be proved. 2. statement or rule that can be proved to be true. *n. 15.*

the o ret ic (thē′ə ret′ik), theoretical. *adj. 20.*

the o ret i cal (thē′ə ret′i kəl), 1. limited to theory; planned or worked out in the mind, not from experience; based on theory, not on fact. 2. dealing with theory only; not practical. *adj. 10.*

the o ret i cal ly (thē′ə ret′i kəl i), in theory; according to theory; in a theoretical manner. *adv.*

the o rist (thē′ə rist), person who theorizes. *n. 16.*

the o rize (thē′ə rīz), form a theory or theories. *v. 19.*

the o ry (thē′ə ri), 1. explanation; explanation based on thought; explanation based on observation and reasoning. There were several theories about the way in which the fire started. According to the theory of evolution, the more complicated forms of life developed from the simple ones. 2. the principles or methods of a science or art rather than its practice; as, the theory of music. 3. idea or opinion about something. *n., pl. theories. 5.*

ther a peu tic (ther′ə pū′tik), having to do with the treating or curing of diseases. *adj. 18.*

there (ᴛʜãr), 1. in that place; at that place; at that point. Sit there. Finish reading the page and stop there. 2. to that place. Have you seen the new house? We are going there tomorrow. 3. that place. We go to New York first and from there to Boston. 4. in that matter. You are mistaken there. 5. *There* is also used in sentences in which the verb comes before its subject. There are three new houses on our street. Is there a drug store near here? 6. *There* is used to call attention to something. There goes the bell. 7. *There* is also used to express some feeling. There, there! **don't cry.** *adv., n., interj. 1.*

there a bout (ᴛʜãr′ə bout′), thereabouts. *adv. 11.*

there a bouts (ᴛʜãr′ə bouts′), 1. near that place. 2. near that time. 3. near that number or amount. *adv.*

there af ter (ᴛʜãr af′tər), after that; afterward. He was very ill as a child and was considered delicate thereafter. *adv. 8.*

there at (ᴛʜãr at′), 1. when that happened; at that time. 2. because of that; because of it. 3. at that place; there. *adv.* [*Old use*] *11.*

there by (ᴛʜãr bī′), 1. by means of that; in that way. He wished to travel and thereby study the customs of other countries. 2. in connection with that. George won the game, and thereby hangs a tale. 3. near there. *adv. 4.*

there for (ᴛʜãr fôr′), for that; for this; for it. He promised to give a building for a hospital and as much land as should be necessary therefor. *adv. 6.*

there fore (ᴛʜãr′fōr), for that reason; as a result of that. Louise went to a party and therefore did not study her lessons. *adv. 1.*

there from (ᴛʜãr from′), from that; from this; from it. He opened his bag and took therefrom an apple. *adv. 16.*

there in (ᴛʜãr in′), 1. in that place; in it. God created the sea and all that is therein. 2. in that matter; in that way. The captain thought all danger was past. Therein he made a mistake. *adv. 6.*

there of (ᴛʜãr ov′), 1. of that; of it. 2. from it; from that source. *adv. 3.*

there on (ᴛʜãr on′), 1. on that; on it. Before the window was a table. A huge book lay thereon. 2. immediately after that. Jesus touched the sick man. Thereon he was healed and arose from his bed. *adv. 4.*

there's (ᴛʜãrz), there is. *5.*

there to (ᴛʜãr tü′), 1. to that; to it. The castle stands on the hill. The road thereto is steep and rough. 2. in addition to that. The king gave his faithful servant rich garments and added thereto a bag of gold. *adv. 9.*

there un to (ᴛʜãr un′tü), to that; to it. *adv. 20.*

there up on (ᴛʜãr′ə pon′), 1. immediately after that. The speaker sat down. Thereupon the people clapped. 2. because of that; therefore. The stolen jewels were found in his room; thereupon he was put in jail. 3. upon that; upon it. The knight carried a shield with a cross painted thereupon. *adv. 4.*

there with (ᴛʜãr wiᴛʜ′), 1. with that; with it. The lady gave him a rose and a smile therewith. 2. then; immediately after that. "Avenge me!" said the ghost and therewith disappeared. *adv. 7.*

there with al (ᴛʜãr′wiᴛʜ ôl′), 1. with that; with this; with it. 2. in addition to that; also. *adv. 17.*

ther mal (thėr′məl), 1. of or pertaining to heat. 2. warm; hot. *adj. 15.*

ther mom e ter (thər mom′i tər), instrument for measuring temperature. On the thermometer shown in the picture 0° is the freezing point of water and 100° is the boiling point of water. *n. 5.*

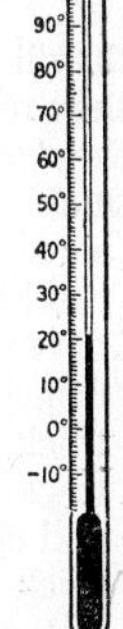

Thermometer

Ther mop y lae (thər mop′i lē), a mountain pass in Greece. In 480 B.C. a few Spartan soldiers defended it against a great army of Persians until every Spartan was killed. *n. 18.*

ther mos bot tle (thėr′məs bot′əl). A thermos bottle or jug will keep its contents at about the same temperature for hours. It will keep hot coffee hot or cold milk cold. It has a case or jacket that heat cannot pass through easily. [*Trade name*] *17.*

ther mo stat (thėr′mə stat), automatic device for regulating temperature. *n.*

these (ᴛʜēz). *These* is used to point out persons, things, etc. These days are cold. These two problems are hard. These are my books. *adj., pron. pl. of* **this.** *1.*

The seus (thē′süs), a Greek hero who had many adventures. *n.*

the sis (thē′sis), 1. a proposition or statement to be maintained against objections. 2. essay; essay presented by a candidate for a diploma or degree. *n., pl. theses* (-sēz). *12.*

Thes pi an (thes′pi ən), 1. actor or actress. 2. pertaining to the theater. *n., adj.*

Thes sa lo ni ans (thes′ə lō′ni ənz), either of two books of the New Testament written by Saint Paul. *n.*

Thes sa ly (thes′ə li), a district in eastern Greece. *n. 20.*

The tis (thē′tis), a sea nymph, the mother of Achilles. *n. 20.*

thews (thüz), 1. muscles. 2. sinews. *n. pl. 18.*

they (ᴛʜā), 1. the persons, animals, things, or ideas spoken about. 2. people; persons. They say we should have a new school. *pron. pl. 1.*

they'd (ᴛʜād), 1. they had. 2. they would. *20.*

they'll (ᴛʜāl), 1. they will. 2. they shall. *6.*

they're (ᴛʜār), they are. *10.*

they've (ᴛʜāv), they have. *13.*

thick (thik), 1. with much space from one side to the opposite side; not thin. The castle has thick stone walls. 2. measuring between two opposite sides. This brick is 8 inches long, 4 inches wide, and 2½ inches thick. 3. set close together; dense. She has thick hair. It is a thick forest. 4. many and close together; abundant. Bullets came thick as hail. 5. like glue or syrup; not like water. Thick liquids pour much more slowly than thin liquids. 6. not clear; foggy. The weather was thick. 7. not clear in sound; hoarse; as, a thick voice. 8. stupid; dull. He has a thick head. 9. thickly. 10. thickest part. King Arthur was in the thick of the fight. 11. very friendly; intimate. *Used in common talk.* 12. **Through thick and thin** means through plenty and poverty. A true friend sticks through thick and thin. *adj., adv., n. 1.*

thick en (thik′ən), make thick; become thick. The cook thickens the sauce with flour. The pudding will thicken as it cools. *v. 7.*

thick et (thik′it), shrubs, bushes, or small trees growing close together. We crawled into the thicket and hid. *n. 4.*

thick-head ed (thik′hed′id), stupid, dull. *adj.*

thick ly (thik′li), 1. in a thick manner; closely; densely; as, a thickly settled region. 2. in great numbers. 3. frequently. 4. hoarsely. *adv.*

thick ness (thik′nis), 1. being thick. The thickness of the walls shuts out all sound. 2. the distance between opposite surfaces; the third measurement of a solid, not length nor breadth. The length of the board is 10 feet, the width 6 inches, the thickness 2 inches. 3. thick part. 4. layer. The pad was made up of three thicknesses of blotting paper. *n. 4.*

thick-set (thik′set′), 1. thickly set; as, a thick-set hedge. 2. thick in form or build; as, a thick-set man. *adj.*

thick-skinned (thik′skind′), 1. having a thick skin. 2. not sensitive to criticism, reproach, rebuff, or the like. *adj.*

thief (thēf), person who steals. Thieves steal secretly and usually without using force. *n., pl. thieves. 3.*

thieve (thēv), steal. Tom saw a boy thieving in the coatroom. *v. 5.*

thiev er y (thēv′ər i), stealing; theft. *n., pl. thieveries.*

thieves (thēvz), more than one thief. *n. pl.*

thiev ish (thēv′ish), 1. having the habit of stealing; likely to steal. 2. like a thief; sly. That cat has a thievish look. *adj. 12.*

thigh (thī), the part of the leg between the hip and the knee. *n. 4.*

thim ble (thim′bəl), a small metal cap worn on the finger to protect it when pushing the needle in sewing. *n. 6.*

Thimble

thin (thin), 1. with little space from one side to the opposite side; not thick. The ice on the pond is too thin for skating. 2. having little flesh; as, a thin man. 3. not set close together; scanty. He has thin hair. 4. not dense. The air on the tops of high mountains is thin. 5. few and far apart; not abundant. The actors played to a thin audience. 6. like water; not like glue or syrup. This gravy is too thin. 7. not deep or strong; having little depth, fullness, or intensity. She speaks in a shrill thin voice. 8. easily seen through. It was a thin excuse that satisfied no one. 9. make thin; become thin. *adj., thinner, thinnest, v., thinned, thinning. 1.*

thine (ᴛʜīn), 1. yours; your; thy. "My daughter shall be thine," said the king to the knight. 2. the one or ones belonging to you; yours. Thine is the swiftest steed. 3. your; thy (used only before a vowel or *h*); as, thine eyes. *pron., adj. 3.*

thing (thing). All the things in the house were burned. Put these things away. If you can see or hear or touch or taste or smell it, you can call it a thing. A strange thing happened. It was a good thing to do. **Things** sometimes means (1) personal belongings. (2) clothes. I packed my things and took the train. *n. 1.*

think (thingk), 1. have ideas; use the mind. I want to think about that question before I answer it. 2. have an opinion; believe. Do you think it will rain? 3. consider; have in mind. Think of me when I am away. *v., thought, thinking. 1.*

third (thėrd), 1. next after the second. C is the third letter of the alphabet. 2. one of three equal parts. Mother divided the cake into thirds. *adj., n. 1.*

third ly (thėrd′li), in the third place. *adv.*

thirst (thėrst), 1. a painful feeling caused by having nothing to drink. The traveler in the desert suffered from thirst. 2. desire for something to drink. He satisfied his thirst at the spring. 3. feel thirst. 4. strong desire. Many boys have a thirst for adventure. 5. have a strong desire. *n., v. 3.*

thirst y (thėrs′ti), 1. feeling thirst; having thirst. The dog is thirsty; please give him some water. 2. without water or moisture; dry. *adj., thirstier, thirstiest. 4.*

thir teen (thėr′tēn′), three more than ten; 13. Some people think thirteen is an unlucky number. *n., adj. 3.*

thir teenth (thėr′tēnth′), 1. next after the 12th. 2. one of 13 equal parts. *adj., n. 7.*

thir ti eth (thėr′ti ith), 1. next after the 29th. 2. one of 30 equal parts. *adj., n. 8.*

thir ty (thėr′ti), three times ten; 30. *n., pl. thirties, adj. 2.*

this (ᴛʜis). *This* is used to point out some one person, thing, or idea as present, or near, or spoken of before. School begins at eight this year. This is my brother. Shall we buy this or that? **This much** means as much as this. *adj., pron., pl. these, adv. 1.*

this tle (this′əl), a plant with a prickly stalk and leaves. The purple thistle is the national flower of Scotland. *n. 4.*

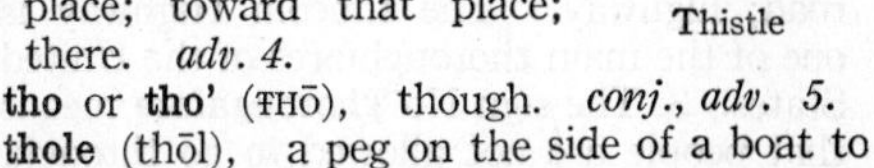
Thistle

this tle down (this′əl doun′), the down or fluff of a thistle. *n. 14.*

thith er (ᴛʜiᴛʜ′ər), to that place; toward that place; there. *adv. 4.*

tho or **tho'** (ᴛʜō), though. *conj., adv. 5.*

thole (thōl), a peg on the side of a boat to hold an oar in rowing. *n.*

thole pin (thōl′pin′), thole. *n.*

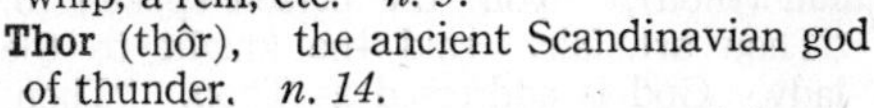

Tholes: A, single; B, double.

Thom as (tom′əs), one of the twelve disciples chosen by Jesus as his apostles. He at first doubted the resurrection. John 20: 24-29. *n.*

thong (thông), 1. narrow strip of leather, used as a fastening. 2. the lash of a whip, a rein, etc. *n. 9.*

Thor (thôr), the ancient Scandinavian god of thunder. *n. 14.*

tho rac ic (thō ras′ik), of or pertaining to the thorax. The thoracic cavity contains the heart and lungs. *adj. 17.*

tho rax (thō′raks), 1. the part of the body between the neck and the abdomen. A man's chest is his thorax. 2. the second division of an insect's body, between the head and the abdomen. *n. 11.*

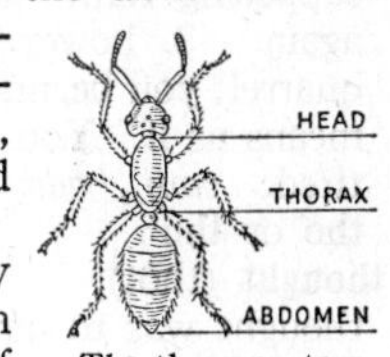

The three parts of an insect

Tho reau (thō′rō), Henry David, an American author and lover of nature (1817-1862). *n.*

thorn (thôrn), 1. sharp point on a plant. Roses have thorns. 2. a plant that has thorns on it. Thorns sprang up and choked the wheat. 3. a **thorn in the flesh** often means a trouble or annoyance. *n. 3.*

thorn y (thôr′ni), 1. full of thorns. He scratched his hands on the thorny rosebush. He tried to make his way through the thorny thicket. 2. troublesome. The boys argued over the thorny points in the lesson. *adj., thornier, thorniest. 8.*

thor o (thėr′ō), thorough. *adj.*

thor ough (thėr′ō), complete; being all that is needed; doing all that should be done. Please make a thorough search for the lost money. He is a thorough gentleman. This school gives thorough instruction. *adj. 2.*

thor ough bred (thėr′ō bred′), 1. of pure breed or stock. 2. a thoroughbred animal, especially a horse. 3. well-bred; thoroughly trained. 4. a well-bred or thoroughly trained person. *adj., n. 19.*

thor ough fare (thėr′ō fãr′), 1. a passage, road, or street open at both ends. 2. main road; highway. The Lincoln Highway is one of the main thoroughfares of the United States. 3. The sign **No Thoroughfare** means that people are not allowed to go through. *n. 10.*

thor ough go ing (thėr′ō gō′ing), thorough; complete. *adj. 18.*

thor ough ness (thėr′ō nis), completeness. *n. 16.*

those (ŦHōz). *Those* is used to point out several persons or things. She owns that dog; the boys own those dogs. That is his book; those are my books. *adj., pron., pl. of* **that.** *1.*

thou (ŦHou), you; the person spoken to. "Thou art fair," said the knight to the lady. God is addressed as Thou. "Thou, God, seest me." *pron. 1.*

though (ŦHō), 1. We take our medicine, though we do not like it. Though it was pouring, the girls went to school. 2. even supposing that. Though I fail, I shall try again. 3. however. I am sorry for our quarrel; you began it, though. 4. **As though** means as if. You look as though you were tired. *conj., adv. 1.* Sometimes written **tho** or **tho'.**

thought (thôt), 1. idea; notion. Her thought was to have a picnic. 2. thinking. Thought helps us solve problems. 3. care; attention; regard. Show some thought for others than yourself. 4. See **think.** We thought it would snow yesterday. *n., pt. and pp. of think. 1.*

thought ful (thôt′fəl), 1. thinking; full of thought. George was thoughtful for a while and then replied, "No." 2. careful; heedful; careful of others; considerate. She is always thoughtful of her mother. *adj. 5.*

thought less (thôt′lis), 1. without thought; doing things without thinking; careless. He is a thoughtless boy and is always making blunders. 2. showing little or no care or regard for others. It is thoughtless of her to keep us waiting so long. *adj. 6.*

thou sand (thou′zənd), ten hundred; 1000. *n., adj. 1.*

thou sandth (thou′zəndth), 1. last in a series of a thousand. 2. one of a thousand equal parts; .001. *adj., n. 14.*

Thrace (thrās), region in the eastern part of the Balkan Peninsula. See the map of **Roman Empire.** *n.*

thrall (thrôl), 1. person in bondage; slave. The thralls did the work of the castle. 2. bondage; slavery. An enchantress had the prince in thrall. *n. 7.*

thrall dom or **thral dom** (thrôl′dəm), bondage; slavery. A sorcerer held the knight in thralldom. *n. 16.*

thrash (thrash), 1. beat the grain or seeds from (wheat, etc.); thresh. 2. beat. The man thrashed the boy for stealing apples. *v. 5.*

thrash er (thrash′ər), 1. person or thing that thrashes. 2. large shark with a long tail. 3. bird somewhat like a thrush. *n.*

thread (thred), 1. cotton, silk, flax, etc., spun out into a fine cord. You sew with thread. 2. pass a thread through. She threaded her needle. Mary threaded a hundred beads. 3. something long and slender like a thread. The spider hung by a thread. 4. main thought that connects the parts of a story or speech. 5. make one's way through; make (one's way) carefully; go in a winding course. He threaded the forest. The cat threaded its way among the dishes on the shelf. 6. the winding, sloping ridge of a screw. See the picture. 7. form a thread on (a screw, etc.). *n., v. 2.*

Screws showing threads

thread bare (thred′bãr′), 1. having the nap worn off; worn so much that the threads show; as, a threadbare coat. 2. wearing clothes worn to the threads; shabby; as, a threadbare beggar. 3. old and worn; as, a threadbare excuse. *adj. 12.*

thread like (thred′līk′), like a thread; long and very slender. *adj. 20.*

threat (thret), 1. statement of what will be done to hurt or punish someone. The boys stopped playing ball in the street because of the policeman's threats to arrest them. 2. a sign or cause of possible evil or harm. Those black clouds are a threat of rain. *n. 5.*

threat en (thret′ən), 1. make a threat against; say what will be done to punish or harm. The teacher threatened to keep after school those pupils who had not done their lessons.

She threatens and scolds too much. 2. give warning of (coming trouble). The clouds threaten rain. 3. be a cause of possible evil or harm to. A flood threatened the city. *v. 2.*

three (thrē). Three is one more than two. Three means 3. Three feet make one yard. *n., adj. 1.*

three fold (thrē′fōld′), 1. three times as much or as many. 2. having three parts. *adj., adv., n. 9.*

three score (thrē′skōr′), three times twenty; sixty. *adj. 7.*

thresh (thresh), 1. separate the grain or seeds from (wheat, etc.); thrash. Nowadays most farmers use a machine to thresh their wheat. 2. toss about; move violently. *v.*

thresh er (thresh′ər), 1. person or thing that threshes. 2. threshing machine. *n. 17.*

thresh old (thresh′ōld), 1. piece of wood or stone under a door. 2. doorway. 3. point of entering; beginning point. He was on the threshold of an important discovery. *n. 5.*

threw (thrü). See **throw**. He threw a stone and ran away. *pt. of throw. 2.*

thrice (thrīs), three times. He knocked thrice. Bob is thrice as strong as his little brother. *adv. 4.*

thrid (thrid), thread. *v., thridded, thridding.* [*Old use*] *17.*

thrift (thrift), absence of waste; saving; economical management; habit of saving. By thrift she managed to get along on her small salary. A bank account encourages thrift. *n. 9.*

thrift i ly (thrif′ti li), in a thrifty manner; with thrift; economically. *adv.*

thrift less (thrift′lis), without thrift; wasteful. A thriftless person can earn much but save little. *adj. 14.*

thrift y (thrif′ti), 1. saving; careful in spending; economical. 2. thriving; prosperous; as, a thrifty plant. *adj., thriftier, thriftiest. 6.*

thrill (thril), 1. a shivering, exciting feeling. She gets thrills from the movies. 2. give a shivering, exciting feeling. Stories of adventure thrilled him. 3. have a shivering, exciting feeling. The children thrilled with joy at the sight of the Christmas tree. 4. tremble; quiver. Her voice thrilled with terror. *n., v. 4.*

thrive (thrīv), prosper; be successful; grow rich; grow strong. Flowers will not thrive without sunshine. *v., throve* or *thrived, thriven* or *thrived, thriving. 4.*

thro′ or **thro** (thrü), through. *prep., adv., adj. 5.*

throat (thrōt), 1. the front of the neck. 2. the passage from the mouth to the stomach or the lungs. A bone stuck in his throat. 3. any narrow passage. The throat of the valley was blocked by fallen rocks. *n. 2.*

throat y (thrōt′i), produced in the throat; guttural; as, a throaty sound. *adj., throatier, throatiest.*

throb (throb), 1. beat rapidly or strongly. Climbing stairs makes her heart throb. His wounded arm throbbed with pain. 2. a rapid or strong beat. A throb of pain shot through his head. *v., throbbed, throbbing, n. 9.*

throe (thrō), a violent pain or pang; anguish; agony. *n. 15.*

throne (thrōn), 1. the chair on which a king, queen, bishop, or other person of high rank sits during ceremonies. 2. the power or authority of a king, queen, etc. *n. 2.*

Throne for a king

throng (thrông), 1. a crowd; a multitude. 2. to crowd; fill with a crowd. People thronged the theater to see the famous actress. 3. come together in a crowd; go or press in large numbers. The people thronged to see the king. *n., v. 3.*

thros tle (thros′əl), a thrush. *n. 17.*

throt tle (throt′əl), 1. choke; strangle. The thief throttled the dog to keep it from barking. 2. a valve or lever for regulating the supply of steam or gasoline to an engine. 3. stop or check by closing a valve; as, to throttle a steam engine. *v., n. 11.*

through (thrü), 1. from end to end of; from side to side of; between the parts of. The soldiers marched through the town. The man went through a doorway. Fish swim through the water. The carpenter bored holes through a board. We look through windows. 2. from beginning to end. Elizabeth read the book through. 3. here and there in; over. We traveled through New England visiting many old towns. 4. because of; by reason of; by means of. The woman refused help through pride. He became rich through hard work and ability. 5. going all the way without change; as, a through train from New York to Chicago. 6. having reached the end of; finished with. We are through school at three o'clock. *prep., adv., adj. 1.* Sometimes written **thru** or **thro'.**

through out (thrü out′), 1. all the way through; through all; in every part of. The Fourth of July is celebrated throughout the United States. 2. in every part. The house is well built throughout. *prep., adv. 2.*

throve (thrōv). See **thrive.** *pt. of thrive.*

throw (thrō), 1. the boy is throwing a ball to his brother. The fire hose threw water on the burning house. He was thrown from his horse. The tree throws a shadow on the grass. He was thrown into prison. He lost two dollars on a throw of dice. 2. Some special meanings are:

throw cold water on, discourage.

throw in, add as a gift.

throw over, give up; discard; abandon.

throw up, vomit.

v., threw, thrown, throwing, n. 1.

thrown (thrōn). See **throw.** Mary has thrown her old toys away. *pp. of throw. 6.*

thru (thrü), through. *prep., adv., adj.*

thrum (thrum), 1. play on a stringed instrument by plucking the strings; as, to thrum a guitar. 2. drum or tap idly with the fingers; as, to thrum on a table. 3. the sound made by such playing or tapping. *v., thrummed, thrumming, n. 14.*

thrush (thrush), a common songbird. A robin is a kind of thrush. *n. 6.*

Song thrush (about 9 in. long)

thrust (thrust), 1. push with force. Jack thrust his hands into his pockets. Frances thrust past me into the room. A soldier thrusts himself into danger. 2. a push with force. She hid the book behind the pillow with a quick thrust. 3. stab; pierce. He thrust the villain through with his sword. 4. a stab. A thrust with the sword killed him. *v., thrust, thrusting, n. 3.*

thud (thud), a dull sound. A heavy blow or fall may cause a thud. *n. 15.*

thug (thug), ruffian; cutthroat. *n.*

thumb (thum), 1. the short thick finger. 2. part that covers the thumb. There was a hole in the thumb of his mitten. 3. soil or wear by handling with the thumbs. The schoolbooks were badly thumbed. 4. handle awkwardly. 5. **Under the thumb of** means under the power or influence of. *n., v. 3.*

thumb screw (thum′skrü′), 1. a screw so made that its head may be turned easily with the thumb and a finger. 2. an old instrument of torture which squeezed the thumbs. *n. 16.*

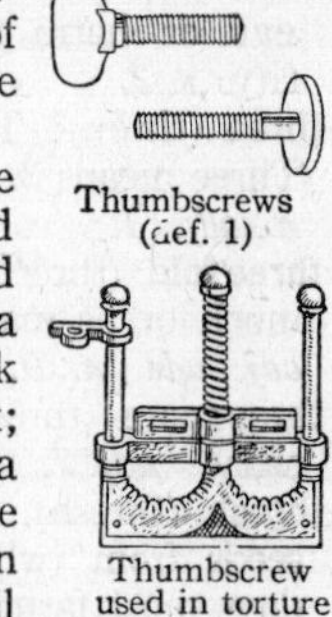

Thumbscrews (def. 1)

Thumbscrew used in torture

thump (thump), 1. strike with something thick and heavy; pound. He thumped the table with his fist. 2. a blow with something thick and heavy; heavy knock; the dull sound made by a blow, knock, or fall. The thief hit him a thump on the head. 3. make a dull sound. His heart thumped as he walked past the graveyard at night. *v., n. 5.*

thun der (thun′dər), 1. the loud noise which often follows a flash of lightning. 2. give forth thunder. It thundered, but no rain fell. 3. any noise like thunder; as, the thunder of Niagara Falls, a thunder of applause. 4. make a noise like thunder. The cannon thundered. *n., v. 2.*

thun der bolt (thun′dər bōlt′), 1. a flash of lightning and the thunder that follows it. 2. something sudden, startling, and terrible. *n. 6.*

thun der clap (thun′dər klap′), 1. loud crash of thunder. 2. something sudden or startling. *n.*

thun der cloud (thun′dər kloud′), dark cloud that brings thunder and lightning. *n. 17.*

thun der ous (thun′dər əs), 1. producing thunder. 2. making a noise like thunder. *adj. 18.*

thun der show er (thun′dər shou′ər), shower with thunder and lightning. *n.*

thun der storm (thun′dər stôrm′), storm with thunder and lightning. *n. 13.*

thun der struck (thun′dər struk′), astonished; amazed; overcome as if hit by a thunderbolt. *adj. 18.*

Thur. or **Thurs.,** Thursday.

Thurs day (thėrz′di), the fifth day of the week. Thanksgiving always comes on Thursday. *n. 2.*

thus (ᴛʜus), 1. in this way. He spoke thus: "Friends, Romans, Countrymen." 2. therefore. He studied hard; thus he got high marks. 3. to this extent; to this degree. Thus far may you go and no farther. *adv. 1.*

thwack (thwak), 1. strike vigorously with a stick or something flat. 2. sharp blow with a stick or something flat. *v., n. 18.*

thwart (thwôrt), 1. oppose and defeat; keep from doing something. The boy's family thwarted his plans for college. 2. a seat across a boat, on which a rower sits. 3. a brace in a canoe. 4. lying across; across. *v., n., adj., adv. 6.*

Canoe with thwarts

thy (ᴛʜī), your. "Thy kingdom come, Thy will be done." *pron. 2.*

thyme (tīm), a low shrub. Its sweet-smelling leaves are used for seasoning. *n. 11.*

thy mus (thī′məs), a small gland, near the base of the neck. The thymus of calves is used for food and called sweetbread. *n. 19.*

thy roid (thī′roid), 1. a ductless gland of the throat that is very important to health. 2. of this gland. 3. the principal cartilage of the throat, forming the lump known as Adam's apple. *n., adj. 14.*

Thyme

thy self (ᴛʜī self′), yourself. 1. *Thyself* is used to make a statement stronger. "Thou, thyself, must choose between us," said the knight to the lady. 2. *Thyself* is used instead of thee or thou when thee or thou has already been used in the sentence. *pron. 3.*

ti (tē), in music, the seventh tone of the scale. Do, re, mi, fa, sol, la, ti, do are the names of the tones of the scale. *n.*

ti ar a (tī är′ə), 1. a band of gold, jewels, or flowers worn around the head as an ornament. 2. the triple crown of the Pope. *n. 13.*

Tiara (def. 1)

Ti ber (tī′bər), a river in Italy. Rome is on the Tiber. *n. 9.*

Ti bet (ti bet′), a country north of India, on a lofty plateau in southern Asia. *n.*

tib i a (tib′i ə), inner and thicker of the two bones of the lower leg. *n., pl. tibiae* (-ē) or *tibias. 16.*

tic (tik), twitching of the muscles. *n.*

tick[1] (tik), 1. a sound made by a clock or watch. 2. make such a sound. The clock ticked. 3. a sound like it. 4. small mark. We use √ or / as a tick. 5. mark with a tick; check. He ticked off the items one by one. *n., v. 3.*

tick[2] (tik), a tiny insect or spider that lives on animals and sucks their blood. See the picture just below. *n.*

Tick. Line shows actual length.

tick[3] (tik), the cloth covering of a mattress or pillow. *n.*

tick et (tik′it), 1. a card or piece of paper which gives its holder a right or privilege. In his pocket he has a railroad ticket for his trip home, a ticket to the theater, and a ticket to the ball game. 2. a card or piece of paper attached to something to show its price, etc. 3. put a ticket on; mark with a ticket. All articles in the store are ticketed with the price. 4. the list of candidates to be voted on belonging to one political party. *n., v. 3.*

tick le (tik′əl), 1. touch lightly causing little thrills, shivers, or wriggles. John tickled the baby's feet and made her laugh. 2. have a feeling like this. My nose tickles. 3. tingling or itching feeling. 4. amuse; excite pleasantly. The story tickled him. The child was tickled with his new toys. 5. a tickling. *v., n. 5.*

tick lish (tik′lish), 1. sensitive to tickling. 2. requiring careful handling; delicate; risky. 3. easily upset; unstable. 4. easily offended. *adj. 19.*

tid al (tīd′əl), of tides; having tides; caused by tides. A tidal river is affected by the ocean's tide. *adj. 11.*

tidal wave, 1. large destructive ocean wave produced by an earthquake, strong wind, etc. 2. any great movement or manifestation of feeling, opinion, or the like; as, a tidal wave of popular indignation.

tid bit (tid′bit′), very pleasing bit of food, news, etc. *n. 20.* Also spelled **titbit.**

tide (tīd), 1. the rise and fall of the ocean about every twelve hours, caused by the attraction of the moon and the sun. We go swimming at high tide; at low tide we dig clams. 2. anything that rises and falls like the tide. 3. stream; current; flood. 4. season; time; as, Christmastide. 5. **Tide over** means help along. This money will tide him over his illness. *n., v. 2.*

tide wa ter (tīd′wô′tər), 1. water having tides. 2. seacoast. Tidewater country is land along the seacoast. *n., adj. 18.*

ti di ness (tī′di nis), neatness. *n.*

ti dings (tī′dingz), news; information. The

messenger brought tidings from the battle front. *n. pl. 5.*

ti dy (tī′di), 1. neat and in order. 2. make tidy; put in order. She tidied the room. 3. considerable; as, a tidy sum of money. *Used in common talk.* 4. a small cover to keep the back of a chair, etc., from becoming dirty or worn. *adj., tidier, tidiest, v., tidied, tidying, n., pl. tidies. 10.*

tie (tī), 1. fasten; bind. Please tie this bundle with string. Tie up your shoes. He tied the horse to a tree. Tie the ribbon in a pretty bow. He refused to be tied down to a steady position. He left the money tied up, so that his family could use only the interest on it. 2. thing that ties; fastening; bond; connection. Family ties have kept him from success. 3. necktie. 4. equality in points. The game ended in a tie, 3 to 3. 5. make the same score; be equal in points. The two teams tied. **Be tied** means be alike in scores. 6. heavy piece of timber or iron. The rails rest on ties about a foot apart. 7. a curved line joining two notes of the same pitch. *v., tied, tying, n. 1.*

Musical tie

Tien tsin (tyen′tsin′), city in northeastern China. *n.*

tier (tēr), one of a series of rows arranged one above another; as, tiers of seats at a baseball game. *n. 12.*

Tier ra del Fue go (tyer′ə del fwā′gō), group of islands at the southern end of South America. Part belongs to Argentina, part to Chile.

tiff (tif), little quarrel. *n.*

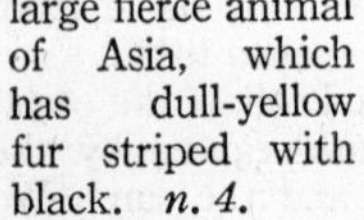

Bengal tiger (about 10 ft. long, including the tail)

ti ger (tī′gər), a large fierce animal of Asia, which has dull-yellow fur striped with black. *n. 4.*

tiger beetle, beetle whose larvae live in burrows in sandy soil and catch insects that come near.

tiger lily, a lily with dull-orange flowers spotted with black.

tight (tīt), 1. firm; held firmly; packed or put together firmly. The sailor made a tight knot. 2. firmly. 3. stretched. He performed on the tight rope. 4. fitting closely; fitting too closely; close; closely. This hat is tight. 5. not letting water, air, or gas in or out. A boat should be watertight. 6. scarce; hard to get. Money is tight just now. 7. stingy. *Used in common talk. adj., adv. 2.*

tight en (tīt′ən), 1. make tight. He tightened his belt. 2. become tight. The rope tightened when I pulled on it. *v. 9.*

tight rope (tīt′rōp′), rope stretched tight on which acrobats perform. *n.*

tights (tīts), close-fitting garment worn by acrobats, dancers, etc. *n. pl.*

ti gress (tī′gris), a female tiger. *n. 17.*

Ti gris (tī′gris), river flowing from southeastern Turkey through Iraq, where it joins the Euphrates River and empties into the Persian Gulf. *n. 13.*

tike (tīk), 1. dog. 2. child. *n.*

til de (til′də), 1. mark (~) used to show a special sound. **Cañon** is pronounced kanyon. 2. In this dictionary such a mark is also used over *a* to show that it is pronounced as in **fare** (fãr). *n.*

tile (tīl), 1. thin piece of baked clay, stone, etc. Tiles are used for covering roofs, paving floors, and ornamenting. 2. pipe for draining land. 3. put tiles on or in. *n., v. 4.*

till[1] (til), until; up to the time of; to the time when. The child played till eight. Walk till you come to a white house. *prep., conj. 1.*

till[2] (til), cultivate (land); plow. Farmers till the land. *v.*

till[3] (til), a small drawer for money. The till is under or behind the counter. *n.*

till age (til′ij), cultivation of land. *n. 10.*

till er[1] (til′ər), bar or handle used to turn the rudder in steering a boat. *n. 10.*

till er[2] (til′ər), farmer. *n.*

tilt (tilt), 1. slope; slant; lean; tip. You tilt your head forward when you bow. You tilt your cup when you drink. This table tilts. 2. a slope; a slant. 3. rush, charge, or fight with lances. Knights used to tilt on horseback. 4. a fight on horseback with lances. 5. **At full tilt** means at full speed; with full force. *v., n. 6.*

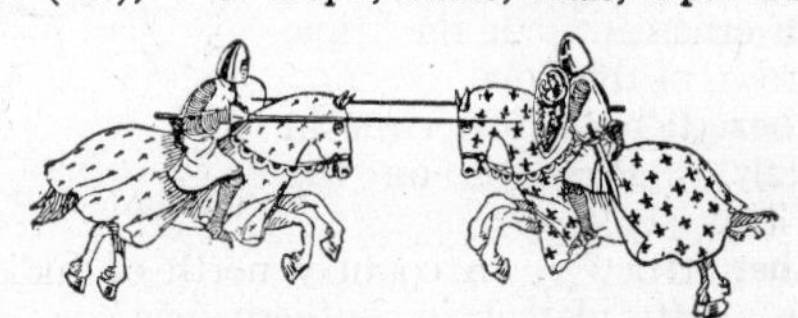

Tilt (def. 4)

tilth (tilth), 1. cultivation of land. 2. tilled land. *n. 18.*

tim ber (tim′bər), 1. wood for building and making things. Houses, ships, and furniture are made from timber. 2. large piece of wood used in building. Beams and rafters are timbers. 3. growing trees; forests. *n. 4.*

tim bered (tim′bərd), 1. made of timber. 2. covered with growing trees. *adj.*

tim bre (tim′bər), quality in sounds that distinguishes a certain voice or instrument from other voices or instruments. Notes of the same pitch and loudness are told apart by differences in their timbre. *n. 17.*

tim brel (tim′brəl), small drum with metal disks; a tambourine. *n. 13.*

time (tīm), 1. all the days there have been or ever will be; the past, present, and future. 2. a part of time. A minute is a short time. A long time ago people lived in caves. 3. a long time. What a time it took you! 4. some point in time. The time the game begins is two o'clock, November 8. 5. the right part or point of time. It is time to go to bed. 6. occasion. Ann got the right answer every time. Do it five times. 7. way of reckoning time; as, standard time, daylight-saving time. 8. condition of life. War brings hard times. 9. rate of movement in music; rhythm; as, march time, waltz time. 10. measure the time of. He timed the racers for each half mile. 11. do at regular times; set the time of. The dancers time their steps to the music. 12. choose the moment or occasion for. The lady timed her entrance so that she went in when the prince did. 13. In arithmetic, **times** means multiply by or multiplied by. 14. Some special meanings are:

at times, now and then; once in a while.

from time to time, now and then; once in a while.

in time, 1. after a while. 2. soon enough. 3. in the right rate of movement in music, dancing, marching, etc.

on time, at the right time; punctual.

n., v. 1.

time-hon ored (tīm′on′ərd), honored because old and established; as, a time-honored custom. *adj.*

time keep er (tīm′kēp′ər), a measurer of time; person or thing that keeps time. *n.*

time less (tīm′lis), 1. eternal; never ending. 2. referring to no special time. *adj. 19.*

time ly (tīm′li), at the right time. The timely arrival of the police stopped the riot. *adj., timelier, timeliest. 9.*

time piece (tīm′pēs′), clock or watch. *n. 18.*

time ta ble (tīm′tā′bəl), a schedule showing the times when trains, boats, busses, or airplanes come and go. *n.*

tim id (tim′id), easily frightened; shy. The timid child was afraid of the dark. Deer are timid animals. *adj. 4.*

ti mid i ty (ti mid′i ti), timid behavior; shyness. *n. 12.*

tim ing (tīm′ing), 1. arrangement of the time or speed of an event; as, the timing of a stroke in tennis. 2. arrangement of the times and speeds of a series of events; as, the timing of a play, a movie, or a circus. 3. measurement of time; as, the timing of a runner. *n.*

tim or ous (tim′ər əs), easily frightened; timid. The timorous rabbit ran away. *adj. 10.*

tim o thy (tim′ə thi), a kind of coarse grass grown for hay. *n. 6.*

Tim o thy (tim′ə thi), 1. a disciple of the Apostle Paul. 2. either of the two books of the New Testament, written as letters by Paul to Timothy. *n.*

tin (tin), 1. a metal that shines like silver but is softer and cheaper. 2. thin sheets of iron or steel coated with tin. 3. made of tin. 4. cover with tin. 5. any can, box, pan, or pot made of tin. *n., adj., v., tinned, tinning. 3.*

tinct (tingkt), 1. tinged. 2. tint; tinge. *adj., n.* [*Used now only in poetry*] *17.*

tinc ture (tingk′chər), 1. solution of medicine in alcohol; as, tincture of iodine. 2. trace; tinge. His stern face showed for a moment a slight tincture of amusement. There is a tincture of clove in this gingerbread. Her usually pale cheeks showed a faint tincture of pink. 3. give a trace or tinge to. Everything he says is tinctured with conceit. *n., v. 10.*

tin der (tin′dər), 1. anything that catches fire easily. 2. material used to catch fire from a spark. *n. 11.*

tin der box (tin′dər boks′), a box for holding tinder, flint, and steel for making a fire. *n.*

tine (tīn), a sharp projecting point or prong; as, the tines of a fork. *n.*

tin foil, very thin sheet of tin used as a wrapping for candy, tobacco, etc. *19.*

ting (ting), 1. make a clear, ringing sound. 2. such a sound. *v., n. 19.*

tinge (tinj), 1. color slightly. A drop of

ink will tinge a glass of water. 2. slight coloring. There is a tinge of red in her cheeks. 3. give a slight taste or smell to; change a very little. 4. trace; very small amount. *v., tinged, tingeing* or *tinging, n. 8.*

tin gle (ting′gəl), 1. have a feeling of thrills or a pricking, stinging feeling. He tingled with excitement on his first train trip. 2. such a feeling. *v., n. 8.*

tink er (tingk′ər), 1. man who mends pots, pans, etc. 2. mend; patch. 3. work or repair in an unskilled or clumsy way. *n., v. 16.*

tin kle (ting′kəl), 1. make sounds like a little bell. 2. cause to tinkle. 3. series of short, light, ringing sounds; as, the tinkle of sleigh bells. *v., n. 5.*

tin ny (tin′i), 1. of tin; containing tin; like tin. 2. sounding like tin. *adj.*

tin sel (tin′səl), 1. glittering copper, brass, etc., in thin sheets, strips, threads, etc. Tinsel is used to trim Christmas trees. 2. anything showy but having little value. 3. showy but not worth much. 4. trim with tinsel. 5. thin cloth woven with threads of gold, silver, or copper. *n., adj., v., tinseled, tinseling. 9.*

tin smith (tin′smith′), person who works with tin; maker of tinware. *n.*

tint (tint), 1. variety of a color. The picture was painted in several tints of blue. 2. delicate or pale color. 3. put a tint on; color slightly. *n., v. 6.*

tin ware (tin′wãr′), articles made of tin. *n.*

ti ny (tī′ni), very small; wee. *adj., tinier, tiniest. 2.*

-tion, suffix meaning:—

1. act or state of ——ing; as in addition, opposition.

2. condition or state of being ——ed; as in exhaustion.

tip[1] (tip), 1. end, point; as, the tips of the fingers. 2. small piece put on the end of something. 3. put a tip on; furnish with a tip. *n., v., tipped, tipping. 2.*

tip[2] (tip), 1. slope; slant. She tipped the table toward her. 2. upset; overturn. 3. empty out; dump. She tipped all the money in her purse on to the table. *v., tipped, tipping, n.*

tip[3] (tip), 1. small present of money. He gave the waiter a tip. 2. give a small present of money to. Did you tip the porter? 3. piece of secret information. Fred had a tip that the black horse would win the race. 4. **To tip a person off** means (1) to give him secret information. (2) to warn him. 5 hit lightly and sharply; tap. 6. a light, sharp blow; a tap. *n., v., tipped, tipping.*

tip pet (tip′it), 1. scarf for the neck and shoulders with ends hanging down in front. 2. long, narrow, hanging part of a hood, sleeve, or scarf. *n.*

tip ple (tip′əl), 1. drink (alcoholic liquor) often. 2. alcoholic liquor. *v., n. 16.*

tip sy (tip′si), 1. unsteady; tipping easily. 2. intoxicated; drunk. *adj. 11.*

tip toe (tip′tō′), 1. the tips of the toes. **On tiptoe** sometimes means (1) in a secret manner. (2) eager. 2. walk on the tips of the toes. *n., v. 10.*

tip top (tip′top′), 1. the very top; the highest point. 2. first-rate; excellent. *n., adj.*

ti rade (tī′rād), 1. a long, vehement speech. 2 a long, scolding speech. *n. 18.*

tire[1] (tīr), 1. make weary. The long walk tired her. 2. become weary. *v. 1.*

tire[2] (tīr), 1. a band of rubber or metal around a wheel. Put more air in all four tires. 2. furnish with a tire. *n., v. 6.*

tired (tīrd), weary; wearied; exhausted. *adj.*

tire less (tīr′lis), 1. never becoming tired; requiring little rest; as, a tireless worker. 2. never stopping; as, tireless efforts. *adj. 17.*

tire some (tīr′səm), tiring; uninteresting. *adj. 6.*

'tis (tiz), it is. *3.*

tis sue (tish′ü), 1. substance forming the parts of animals and plants; a mass of cells; as, brain tissue, skin tissue. 2. a fine, light cloth. 3. web; network. Her whole story was a tissue of lies. 4. tissue paper. *n. 8.*

tissue paper, very thin soft paper used for wrapping or covering things.

tit (tit), a small bird; a titmouse or a titlark. *n. 7.*

Ti tan (tī′tən), 1. one of a family of giants who ruled the world. Prometheus and Atlas were Titans. 2. A **titan** is a person or thing having enormous size, strength, power, etc.; a giant. 3. gigantic; huge; very powerful. *n., adj. 10.*

Ti ta ni a (ti tā′ni ə), queen of the fairies. *n.*

ti tan ic (tī tan′ik), having great size, strength, or power; gigantic; huge; as, titanic energy. *adj. 18.*

tit bit (tit′bit′), very pleasing bit of food, news, etc. *n. 20.* Also spelled **tidbit.**

tithe (tīᴛʜ), 1. one tenth. 2. tax of one tenth of the yearly produce of land, animals, and personal work, paid for the support of the church. 3. put a tax of a tenth on. 4. pay a tithe on. *n., v. 9.*

Ti tian (tish′ən), a famous Italian painter (1477?-1576). *n. 13.*

tit il late (tit′i lāt), tickle; excite agreeably. *v.*

tit lark (tit′lärk′), small bird like a lark. *n.*

ti tle (tī′təl), 1. the name of a book, poem, picture, song, etc. 2. name showing rank, occupation, or condition in life. King, duke, lord, countess, captain, doctor, professor, Madame, and Miss are titles. 3. championship; first-place position; as, the tennis title. 4. legal right to the possession of property; the evidence showing such a right. When a house is sold, the seller gives title to the buyer. 5. claim; right. *n. 2.*

ti tled (tī′təld), having a title. She married a titled nobleman. *adj.*

tit mouse (tit′mous′), a small bird. A chickadee is one kind of titmouse. *n., pl. titmice. 20.*

tit ter (tit′ər), laugh in a half-restrained manner; giggle. *v., n. 15.*

tit tle (tit′əl), 1. very little bit. 2. a small stroke or mark over a letter in writing or printing. The dot over an *i* is a tittle. *n. 14.*

tit tle-tat tle (tit′əl tat′əl), gossip. *n., v.*

tit u lar (tich′u̇ lər), 1. in title or name only. He is a titular prince without any power. 2. having a title. 3. pertaining to a title. *adj. 15.*

Ti tus (tī′təs), 1. a Roman emperor (40?-81 A.D.). 2. a companion of the Apostle Paul. *n. 9.*

TNT or **T.N.T.,** a colorless solid used as an explosive in hand grenades, torpedoes, etc.

to (tü, *unstressed* tu̇ or tə), 1. in the direction of. Go to the right. 2. as far as. This apple is rotten to the core. 3. for the purpose of; for. Mother came to the rescue. 4. compared with. 2 is to 6 as 3 is to 9. 5. *To* is also used (1) to show action toward. Give the book to me. (2) with verbs. John likes to read. (3) to show result. He tore it to pieces. (4) to show addition or to mean with. He hummed to the music. 6. **To and fro** means first one way and then back again; back and forth. *prep., adv. 1.*

Toad (about 3 in. long)

toad (tōd), a small animal somewhat like a frog, which lives on land. *n. 5.*

toad stool (tōd′stül′), poisonous mushroom. See the picture below. *n. 9.*

toad y (tōd′i), 1. fawning flatterer. 2. act like a toady. 3. fawn upon; flatter. *n., pl. toadies, v., toadied, toadying.*

Toadstools

toast (tōst), 1. brown by heat. We toast bread. 2. slices of bread browned by heat. 3. heat thoroughly. 4. person or thing whose health is proposed and drunk. "The King" was the first toast drunk by the officers. 5. act of drinking to the health of a person or thing. 6. propose as a toast; drink to the health of. The men toasted the general. *v., n. 4.*

toast er (tōs′tər), thing or person that toasts; as, an electric toaster. *n. 20.*

toast mas ter (tōst′mas′tər), person who presides at a dinner and introduces the speakers. *n.*

to bac co (tə bak′ō), a plant whose leaves are used for smoking or chewing or as snuff. *n., pl. tobaccos. 3.*

to bog gan (tə bog′ən), 1. a long, narrow, flat sled without runners. 2. slide downhill on such a sled. *n., v. 12.*

Toboggan

toc sin (tok′sin), 1. alarm sounded on a bell; a warning signal. 2. bell used to sound an alarm. *n. 16.*

to day or **to-day** (tu̇ dā′), 1. this day. What are you doing today? 2. the present time; now. Many girls wear their hair short today. *n., adv. 1.*

tod dle (tod′əl), walk with short, unsteady steps, as a baby does. *v., n. 19.*

tod dy (tod′i), 1. fermented palm sap. 2. drink made of whiskey, brandy, etc., with hot water and sugar. *n., pl. toddies.*

toe (tō), 1. one of the five end parts of the foot. 2. the part of a stocking, shoe, etc., that covers the toes. 3. anything like a toe. 4. touch or reach with the toes. *n., v. 3.*

to ga (tō′gə), 1. a loose outer garment worn by men of ancient Rome. 2. robe of office. *n. 19.*

to geth er (tu̇ geTH′ər), 1. with each other; in company. The girls were walking together. 2. into one gathering, company, mass, or body. The pastor called the people together. The woman will sew these pieces together and make a dress. 3. at the same time. You cannot have day and night together. 4. without a stop or break; continuously. He reads for hours together. *adv. 1.*

toil[1] (toil), 1. hard work. 2. work hard. 3. move with difficulty, pain, or weariness. *n., v. 2.*

toil[2] (toil), net; snare. A lion was caught in the toils. The thief was caught in the toils of the law. *n.*

toil er (toil′ər), hard worker; laborer. *n. 20.*

toi let (toi′lit), 1. process of dressing. She made a hurried toilet. Combs and brushes are toilet articles. 2. person's dress; costume. 3. bathroom or water closet. *n. 5.*

toil some (toil′səm), requiring hard work; laborious; as, a long, toilsome climb up the mountain. *adj. 11.*

to ken (tō′kən), 1. a mark or sign (of something). Black is a token of mourning. 2. sign of friendship. She received many birthday tokens. 3. piece of metal stamped for a higher value than the metal is worth. Tokens are used for some purposes instead of money. 4. piece of metal indicating a right or privilege. *n. 4.*

To kyo or **To kio** (tō′kyō), the capital of Japan. *n.*

told (tōld). See **tell.** You told me that last week. *pt. and pp. of tell. 1.*

To le do (tə lē′dō), 1. a city in northwestern Ohio. 2. a city in central Spain. *n.*

tol er a ble (tol′ər ə bəl), 1. bearable. The pain has become tolerable. 2. fairly good. She is in tolerable health. *adj. 8.*

tol er a bly (tol′ər ə bli), 1. in a tolerable manner. 2. moderately. *adv.*

tol er ance (tol′ər əns), 1. willingness to be tolerant and patient toward people whose opinions or ways differ from one's own. 2. the power of enduring or resisting the action of a drug, poison, etc. 3. action of tolerating. *n. 13.*

tol er ant (tol′ər ənt), 1. willing to let other people do as they think best; willing to endure beliefs and actions of which one does not approve. The United States government is tolerant toward all religious beliefs. 2. able to endure or resist the action of a drug, poison, etc. *adj. 11.*

tol er ate (tol′ər āt), 1. put up with; allow; permit. The teacher won't tolerate any disorder. 2. bear; endure. 3. resist the action of (a poison, etc.). *v. 11.*

tol er a tion (tol′ər ā′shən), tolerance; willingness to put up with beliefs and actions of which one does not approve; willingness to let other people do as they think best. Complete religious toleration exists in the United States. *n. 9.*

toll[1] (tōl), 1. sound with single strokes slowly and regularly repeated. Bells were tolled all over the country at the President's death. 2. such a stroke or sound of a bell. *v., n. 7.*

toll[2] (tōl), a tax or fee paid for some right or privilege. We pay a toll when we use that bridge. *n.*

toll gate (tōl′gāt′), gate where toll is collected. *n.*

tom a hawk (tom′ə hôk), 1. light ax used by North American Indians as a weapon and a tool. 2. strike or kill with a tomahawk. *n., v. 13.*

Tomahawk

to ma to (tə mā′tō or tə mä′tō), 1. a juicy fruit used as a vegetable. Tomatoes are usually red, but are sometimes yellow. 2. the plant it grows on. *n., pl. tomatoes. 5.*

tomb (tüm), place for a dead body. *n. 3.*

tom boy (tom′boi′), girl who likes to play boys' games. *n.*

tomb stone (tüm′stōn′), stone that marks a tomb or grave. *n. 10.*

tom cat (tom′kat′), male cat. *n.*

tome (tōm), large heavy book; book. *n. 14.*

tom fool er y (tom′fül′ər i), silly behavior; nonsense. *n., pl. tomfooleries.*

to mor row (tü mor′ō), 1. the day after today. 2. the near future. 3. very soon. *n., adv. 1.*

tom-tom (tom′tom′), a kind of drum used by savages. *n.*

ton (tun), measure of weight, 2000 pounds in the United States and Canada, 2240 pounds in England. A **long ton** is 2240 pounds; a **short ton** is 2000 pounds. A **metric ton** is 1000 kilograms. *n. 3.*

ton al (tōn′əl), of or pertaining to tones or tone. *adj.*

tone (tōn), 1. sound; quality of sound; as, low, angry, or gentle tones, the deep tone of the organ. 2. musical sound. 3. difference in pitch between two notes. F is three tones higher than C. 4. manner of speaking or writing. 5. spirit; character; style. A tone of quiet elegance prevails in her home. 6. vigor; normal healthy condition. 7. effect of color and of light and shade in a picture. I like the soft green tone of that painting. 8. shade of color. The room is furnished in tones of brown. 9. harmonize. This rug tones in well with the wallpaper and furniture. 10. give a tone to. 11. **Tone down** means soften. Tone down your voice. Tone down the colors in that painting. 12. **Tone up** means to give more sound, color, or vigor to. Bright curtains would tone up this dull room. *n., v. 2.*

tong (tông), a secret Chinese club. *n.*

tongs (tôngz), tool for seizing, holding, or lifting. He changed the position of the burning log with the tongs. *n. pl. 5.*

Lifting log with fire tongs

tongue (tung), 1. the movable piece of flesh in the mouth. The tongue is used in tasting and, by people, for talking. We eat the tongues of some animals. 2. power of speech. Have you lost your tongue? 3. way of speaking. 4. the language of a people; as, the English tongue. 5. something shaped or used like a tongue. The tongue of a shoe is the strip of leather under the laces. Tongues of flame leaped from the fire. 6. To **hold one's tongue** is to keep still. *n. 1.*

tongue less (tung′lis), 1. having no tongue. 2. unable to speak. *adj. 19.*

tongue-tied (tung′tīd′), 1. having the motion of the tongue hindered. 2. unable to speak because of shyness, embarrassment, etc. *adj.*

ton ic (ton′ik), 1. anything that gives strength; medicine to give strength. Cod-liver oil is a tonic. 2. giving strength; bracing. The mountain air is tonic. 3. the keynote of a musical scale. 4. pertaining to a tone or tones. *n., adj. 9.*

to night or **to-night** (tů nīt′), 1. this night; the night of this day. I am going to bed early tonight. 2. on or during this night. *n., adv. 2.*

ton nage (tun′ij), 1. carrying capacity of a ship. A ship of 50,000 cubic feet of space for freight has a tonnage of 500 tons. 2. total amount of shipping in tons. 3. duty or tax on ships at so much a ton. *n. 6.*

ton sil (ton′səl), either of the two small oval masses at the back of the mouth. *n. 15.*

ton sil li tis (ton′si lī′tis), inflammation of the tonsils. *n. 19.*

ton sure (ton′shər), 1. shaving the head or clipping the hair of a person entering the priesthood or an order of monks. 2. the bare part of the head of a priest or monk. 3. shave the head of. *n., v.*

too (tü), 1. also; besides. The dog is hungry, and thirsty too. We, too, are going away. 2. more than enough. My dress is too long for you. Jack ate too much. The summer passed too quickly. 3. very. I am only too glad to help you. *adv. 1.*

took (tůk). See **take.** She took the car an hour ago. *pt. of take. 1.*

tool (tül), 1. a knife, hammer, saw, shovel, or any instrument used in doing work. 2. person or thing used like a tool. He is a tool of the party boss. Books are a scholar's tools. 3. use a tool on. 4. work with a tool. *n., v. 2.*

toot (tüt), 1. sound of a horn, whistle, etc. 2. sound (a horn, whistle, etc.). *n., v. 11.*

tooth (tüth), 1. one of the hard bonelike parts in the mouth, used for biting and chewing. 2. something like a tooth. Each one of the projecting parts of a comb, rake, or saw is a tooth. 3. put teeth on; cut teeth on. 4. **To fight tooth and nail** means to fight fiercely, with all one's force. *n., pl. teeth, v. 2.*

tooth ache (tüth′āk′), pain in a tooth or the teeth. *n. 12.*

tooth brush (tüth′brush′), small brush for cleaning the teeth. *n.*

toothed (tütht), 1. having teeth. 2. notched. *adj.*

tooth less (tüth′lis), without teeth. *adj.*

tooth pick (tüth′pik′), small pointed piece of wood or sharpened quill for removing bits of food from between the teeth. *n. 9.*

tooth some (tüth′səm), pleasing to the taste; tasting good. *adj.*

top[1] (top), 1. highest point or part; upper part; as, the top of a mountain. Henry is at the top of his class. The boys were yelling at the top of their voices. 2. the part of a plant above ground. 3. head. The girl was dressed in brown from top to toe. 4. the cover of an automobile, carriage, etc. 5. the upper part of a shoe or boot. 6. pertaining to the top; highest; greatest. The runners set off at top speed. 7. put a top on. 8. be on top of; be the top of. A church tops the hill. 9. reach the top of; rise above. 10. be higher or greater than; do better than. Frank's story topped all the rest. 11. remove the top of. 12. a platform around the upper part of a lower mast on a ship. *n., adj., v., topped, topping. 1.*

top[2] (top), toy that spins on a point. *n.*

Spinning top

to paz (tō′paz), a precious stone. Topazes are usually yellow. *n. 10.*

top coat (top′kōt′), overcoat. *n.*

To pe ka (tə pē′kə), capital of Kansas. *n. 14.*

top er (tōp′ər), person who drinks a great deal of alcoholic liquor. *n.*

top gal lant (tə gal′ənt or top′gal′ənt), 1. the mast or sail next above the topmast; the third section of a mast above the deck. 2. next above the topmast. *n., adj.*

top ic (top′ik), subject that people think, write, or talk about. *n. 5.*

top i cal (top′i kəl), 1. about something having local or current interest. 2. of or pertaining to a topic. Some books have topical outlines for each chapter. *adj. 20.*

top knot (top′not′), a knot of hair or a tuft of feathers on the top of the head. *n.*

top mast (top′məst or top′mast′), second section of a mast above the deck. *n. 18.*

top most (top′mōst), highest. The best cherries always seem to grow on the topmost branches. *adj. 9.*

top o graph i cal (top′ə graf′i kəl), of or pertaining to topography. A topographical map shows mountains, rivers, etc. *adj. 18.*

to pog ra phy (tə pog′rə fi), 1. the accurate and detailed description of places. 2. the features of a place or region. You should know the topography of your town or city; that is, the plan of its streets, the car and bus lines, the location of parks, museums, important buildings, etc. *n., pl. topographies. 14.*

top ple (top′əl), 1. fall forward; tumble down. The chimney toppled over on the roof. 2. throw down; overturn. *v. 10.*

top sail (top′səl or top′sāl′), the second sail above the deck on a mast. *n. 20.*

top sy-tur vy (top′si tėr′vi), 1. upside down. 2. in confusion or disorder. 3. confusion; disorder. *adv., adj., n. 9.*

Toque

toque (tōk), hat without a brim; small hat with very little brim. *n.*

torch (tôrch), light to be carried about or stuck in a holder on a wall. A piece of pine wood or anything that burns easily makes a good torch. "Liberty" is represented as holding up a torch. Torches with very hot flames are used to burn off paint, to solder metal, and to melt metal. *n. 4.*

torch light (tôrch′līt′), light of a torch or torches. *n. 18.*

tore (tōr). See **tear**[1]. Mabel tore her dress on a nail. *pt. of tear*[1]. *4.*

tor e a dor (tôr′i ə dôr), Spanish bullfighter. *n.*

tor ment (tôr ment′ for 1 and 4, tôr′ment for 2 and 3), 1. cause very great pain to. Rheumatism tormented him. 2. cause of very great pain. Instruments of torture were torments. 3. very great pain. He suffered torments from his aching teeth. 4. worry or annoy very much. Tom torments everyone with silly questions. *v., n. 3.*

tor men tor or **tor ment er** (tôr men′tər), person or thing that torments. *n. 14.*

torn (tōrn). See **tear**[1]. He has torn up the plant by the roots. His coat was old and torn. *pp. of tear*[1]. *3.*

tor na do (tôr nā′dō), violent whirlwind; a violent, destructive wind. *n., pl. tornadoes* or *tornados. 11.*

To ron to (tə ron′tō), city in Canada, on Lake Ontario. *n. 13.*

tor pe do (tôr pē′dō), 1. a large cigar-shaped shell that contains explosives and travels by its own power. Torpedoes are sent under water to blow up enemy ships. 2. a shell containing explosives. 3. attack or destroy with a torpedo. 4. explosive and gravel wrapped in tissue paper, which makes a bang when it is thrown against something hard. 5. an explosive put on a railroad track, which makes a loud noise for a signal when a wheel of the engine runs over it. *n., pl. torpedoes, v., torpedoed, torpedoing. 10.*

Torpedo (def. 1)

torpedo boat, a small, fast warship used for attacking with torpedoes.

tor pid (tôr′pid), 1. inactive; sluggish. 2. not moving or feeling. *adj. 11.*

tor por (tôr′pər), torpid condition. *n. 18.*

tor rent (tor′ənt), 1. a violent, rushing stream of water. The mountain torrent dashed over the rocks. 2. any violent, rushing stream; a flood. *n. 5.*

tor ren tial (to ren′shəl), of or caused by a torrent; like a torrent. *adj.*

tor rid (tor′id), very hot. Brazil is in the torrid zone. July is a torrid month. *adj. 8.*

tor so (tôr′sō), 1. trunk or body of a statue without any head, arms, or legs. 2. trunk of the human body. *n., pl. torsos.*

tor toise (tôr′təs), 1. turtle. 2. turtle living on land. *n., pl. tortoises* or *tortoise. 5.*

Tortoise (def. 2)

tortoise shell, the yellow-and-brown shell of a turtle or tortoise. Tortoise shell is much used for combs and ornaments.

tor toise-shell (tôr′təs shel′), 1. made of tortoise shell. 2. having the colors of a tortoise shell. *adj.*

tor tu ous (tôr′chü əs), full of twists, turns, or bends; twisting; winding; crooked; as, a tortuous path. *adj. 11.*

tor ture (tôr′chər), 1. act of inflicting very severe pain. Torture was formerly used to make people give evidence about crimes, or to make them confess. 2. very severe pain. She suffered tortures from rheumatism. 3. cause very severe pain to. That cruel boy tortures animals. 4. twist the meaning of. 5. twist or force out of its natural form. *n., v. 4.*

To ry (tō′ri), 1. member of a political party in Great Britain favoring royal power and the established church, and opposed to change. 2. an American who favored England at the time of the Revolutionary War. 3. of or pertaining to Tories. *n., pl. Tories, adj. 10.*

toss (tôs), 1. throw; cast; fling. Mary tossed the ball to the baby. 2. throw about; pitch about. The ship is tossed by the waves. 3. throw upward. She tossed her head. He was tossed by the bull. 4. **Toss off** means (1) do quickly. (2) drink all at once. 5. a throw; a tossing. *v., n. 2.*

tot (tot), little child. *n. 18.*

to tal (tō′təl), 1. whole; entire. The total cost of the house and land will be $25,000. 2. the whole amount. His expenses reached a total of $100. Add the different sums to get the total. 3. find the sum of; add. Total that column of figures. 4. reach an amount of; amount to. The money spent yearly on chewing gum totals millions of dollars. 5. complete. He is a total failure. We were in total darkness. *adj., n., v., totaled, totaling. 2.*

to tal i tar i an (tō tal′i tãr′i ən), of or having to do with a government controlled by one political group that permits no other political groups. *adj.*

to tal i ty (tō tal′i ti), total amount; entirety. *n., pl. totalities. 20.*

to tal ly (tō′təl i), wholly; entirely; completely. *adv.*

to tem (tō′təm), 1. a natural object, often an animal, taken as the emblem of a tribe, clan, or family. 2. image of such an object. Totems are often carved and painted on poles. *n.*

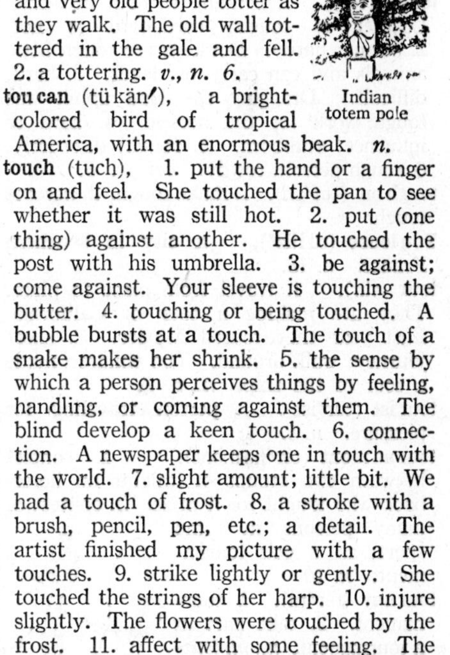
Indian totem pole

tot ter (tot′ər), 1. be unsteady; walk with shaky, unsteady steps; shake; tremble. Babies and very old people totter as they walk. The old wall tottered in the gale and fell. 2. a tottering. *v., n. 6.*

tou can (tü kän′), a bright-colored bird of tropical America, with an enormous beak. *n.*

touch (tuch), 1. put the hand or a finger on and feel. She touched the pan to see whether it was still hot. 2. put (one thing) against another. He touched the post with his umbrella. 3. be against; come against. Your sleeve is touching the butter. 4. touching or being touched. A bubble bursts at a touch. The touch of a snake makes her shrink. 5. the sense by which a person perceives things by feeling, handling, or coming against them. The blind develop a keen touch. 6. connection. A newspaper keeps one in touch with the world. 7. slight amount; little bit. We had a touch of frost. 8. a stroke with a brush, pencil, pen, etc.; a detail. The artist finished my picture with a few touches. 9. strike lightly or gently. She touched the strings of her harp. 10. injure slightly. The flowers were touched by the frost. 11. affect with some feeling. The poor woman's story touched our hearts. 12. have to do with; concern. The matter touches your interests. 13. speak of; treat lightly. Our conversation touched on Mrs. Brown. 14. reach; come up to. 15. act or manner of playing a musical instrument. The girl playing the piano has an excellent touch. 16. **Touch up** means change a little; improve. *v., n. 1.*

touch down (tuch′doun′), 1. act of a player in putting the football on the ground behind the opponents' goal line. 2. the score made in this way. *n.*

touch ing (tuch′ing), 1. arousing tender feeling. *A Christmas Carol* is a touching story. 2. concerning; about. He asked many questions touching my home, parents, and school life. *adj., prep.*

touch stone (tuch′stōn′), 1. a black stone used to test the purity of gold or silver by the color of the streak made on it by rubbing it with the metal. 2. any means of testing; a test. Adversity is the touchstone of friendship. *n. 15.*

touch y (tuch′i), apt to take offense at trifles; too sensitive. *adj., touchier, touchiest.*

tough (tuf), 1. bending without breaking. Leather is tough; cardboard is not. 2. strong; hardy. Donkeys are tough little animals and can carry big loads. 3. hard; difficult. Dragging the load uphill was tough work for the horses. 4. hard to influence; stubborn. 5. rough; disorderly. 6. rough person; rowdy. *adj., n. 6.*

tough en (tuf′ən), 1. make tough. 2. become tough. *v.*

Tou louse (tü lüz′), a city in southern France. *n. 18.*

tour (tür), 1. travel from place to place. They are making a tour of California. Last year they toured Mexico. 2. short journey; walk around. The children made a tour of the ship. *n., v. 7.*

tour ist (tür′ist), person traveling for pleasure. *n. 8.*

tour na ment (tėr′nə mənt), 1. contest between two groups of knights on horseback who fought for a prize. 2. contest of many persons in some sport; as, a golf tournament. *n. 10.*

tour ney (tėr′ni), 1. tournament. 2. take part in a tournament. *n., pl. tourneys, v. 14.*

tour ni quet (tėr′ni kā), device for stopping bleeding by compressing a blood vessel, such as a bandage tightened by twisting with a stick, or a pad pressed down by a screw. *n. 19.*

Tourniquet: A. blood vessel.

tou sle (tou′zəl), muss; put into disorder; as, tousled hair. *v.*

tow[1] (tō), 1. pull by a rope. The tug is towing three barges. 2. act of towing. 3. condition of being pulled along in this way. The launch had the sailboat in tow. 4. what is towed. 5. the rope used. *v., n. 6.*

tow[2] (tō), the coarse and broken parts of flax or hemp. This string is made of tow. *n.*

to ward (tōrd or tü wôrd′), 1. in the direction of. He walked toward the north. 2. with respect to; regarding. What is his attitude toward war? 3. near. It must be toward four o'clock. 4. for. Will you give something toward our new hospital? *prep. 1.*

to wards (tōrdz or tü wôrdz′), toward. *prep.*

tow el (tou′əl), a piece of cloth or paper for wiping and drying something wet. *n. 4.*

tow er (tou′ər), 1. a high structure. See the picture. A tower may stand alone or form part of a church, castle, or other building. 2. defense; a protection. 3. rise high up. *n., v. 2.*

Tower

tow er ing (tou′ər ing), 1. very high. 2. very great. 3. very violent. *adj.*

tow er y (tou′ər i), 1. having towers. 2. towering; lofty. *adj. 20.*

town (toun), 1. large group of houses and buildings, smaller than a city. 2. any large place with many people living in it. 3. the people of a town. The whole town was having a holiday. *n. 1.*

town hall, a building used for a town's business.

towns folk (tounz′fōk′), the people of a town. *n. pl. 20.*

town ship (toun′ship), 1. part of a county having certain powers of government. 2. district six miles square in United States surveys of land. *n. 8.*

towns man (tounz′mən), 1. person who lives in a town. 2. person who lives in one's own town. *n., pl. townsmen. 10.*

towns peo ple (tounz′pē′pəl), the people of a town. *n. pl.*

tox ic (tok′sik), poisonous; of poison; caused by poison. *adj. 20.*

tox in (tok′sin), poison produced in animals or plants. Diphtheria is caused by a toxin. *n. 10.*

toy (toi), 1. something for a child to play with; plaything. 2. thing that has little value or importance. 3. of, made as, or like a toy. 4. play; amuse oneself; trifle. She toyed with her string of beads. *n., adj., v. 2.*

trace[1] (trās), 1. mark left. We saw traces of rabbits and squirrels on the snow. 2. follow by means of marks, tracks, or signs. The dog traced the fox to its den. 3. follow the course of. He traced the river to its source. The Aldens trace their family back to John Alden, one of the Pilgrims. 4. mark out. The spy traced a plan of the fort. 5. copy. By putting thin paper over the map, John traced it. 6. very small amount. There was not a trace of color in her cheeks. *n., v. 2.*

trace[2] (trās), either of the two straps, ropes, or chains by which an animal pulls a wagon or carriage. *n.*

trac er y (trās′ər i), ornamental work or designs consisting of lines. Stonework, carving, and embroidery often have tracery. *n., pl. traceries. 14.*

Tracery

tra che a (trā′ki ə), the windpipe. *n. 11.*

trac ing (trās′ing), a copy. *n.*

track (trak), 1. a line of metal rails for cars to run on; as, a railroad track. 2. mark left. The dirt road showed many automobile tracks. 3. footprint. We saw wild animals' tracks near the camp. 4. follow by means of marks, footprints, smell, etc. The hunter tracked the bear and killed it. 5. To **keep track of** is to keep within one's sight, knowledge, or attention. 6. make tracks on. 7. path; road. A track runs through the woods to the farmhouse. 8. course for running or racing. *n., v. 2.*

track less (trak′lis), 1. without a track. 2. without paths or trails. *adj. 18.*

tract[1] (trakt), stretch of land, water, etc.; area; as, a wild mountain tract. *n. 4.*

tract[2] (trakt), 1. little book or pamphlet on a religious topic. 2. any little book or pamphlet. *n.*

trac ta ble (trak′tə bəl), 1. easily managed or controlled; easy to deal with; docile. Dogs are more tractable than mules. 2. easily worked. Copper and gold are tractable. *adj. 14.*

trac tion (trak′shən), 1. drawing or pulling; being drawn. 2. the drawing or pulling of loads along a road, track, etc. 3. kind of power used for this. Electric traction is used on parts of some railroads. 4. friction. Wheels slip on ice because there is too little traction. *n. 14.*

trac tor (trak′tər), 1. something used for pulling. 2. engine on wheels for pulling wagons, trucks, plows, etc. A tractor can do the work of many horses on a farm. *n. 9.*

trade (trād), 1. buying and selling; commerce; exchange of goods. The United States has much trade with foreign countries. 2. buy and sell. The settlers traded with the savages. 3. exchange. 4. bargain; deal. English ships trade all over the world. He made a good trade. 5. kind of work; business. He is learning the carpenter's trade. 6. people in the same kind of work or business. 7. **Trade on** sometimes means take advantage of. 8. **The trades** are the trade winds. *n., v. 1.*

trade mark (trād′märk′), a mark, picture, name, or letters used by a manufacturer or merchant to distinguish his goods. *n. 14.*

trade name, 1. the name chosen by a firm for some article which it sells. 2. a special name used for any thing by those who buy and sell it.

trad er (trād′ər), 1. person who trades. The trappers sold furs to traders. 2. ship used in trading. *n. 5.*

trades man (trādz′mən), storekeeper; shopkeeper. *n., pl. tradesmen. 7.*

trade union, association of workers in any trade to protect and promote their interests. *17.*

trade wind, a wind blowing steadily toward the equator. *20.*

tra di tion (trə dish′ən), 1. the handing down of beliefs, opinions, customs, stories, etc., from parents to children. 2. what is handed down in this way. According to the old tradition, the founder of Rome was the son of the god of war. *n. 4.*

tra di tion al (trə dish′ən əl), 1. of tradition. 2. handed down by tradition. 3. according to tradition. 4. customary. *adj. 12.*

tra di tion ar y (trə dish′ən ãr′i), traditional. *adj. 17.*

tra duce (trə dūs′ or trə düs′), speak evil of (a person) falsely; slander. *v. 16.*

traf fic (traf′ik), 1. people, automobiles, wagons, ships, etc., coming and going along a way of travel. Police control the traffic in large cities. 2. buying and selling; commerce; trade. 3. buy; sell; exchange; carry on trade. The men trafficked with the natives for ivory. 4. business done by a railroad line or steamship line; number of passengers or amount of freight carried. *n., v., trafficked, trafficking. 4.*

traf fick er (traf′ik ər), person who buys and sells; trader; as, a trafficker in opium. *n. 20.*

tra ge di an (trə jē′di ən), 1. actor in tragedies. 2. writer of tragedies. *n. 14.*

trag e dy (traj′i di), 1. serious play having an unhappy ending. Shakespeare's play *Hamlet* is a tragedy. 2. very sad or terrible happening. The father's sudden death was a tragedy to his family. *n., pl. tragedies. 4.*

trag ic (traj′ik), 1. of tragedy; having to do with tragedy; as, a tragic actor, a tragic poet. 2. very sad; dreadful; as, a tragic death, a tragic event. *adj. 7.*

trag i cal (traj′i kəl), tragic. *adj. 13.*

trag i cal ly (traj′i kəl i), in a tragic manner; dreadfully. *adv.*

trail (trāl), 1. pull or drag along behind. The child trailed a toy horse after him. 2. grow along. Poison ivy trailed by the road. 3. anything that follows along behind. The car left a trail of dust behind it. 4. track or smell. The dogs found the trail of the rabbit. 5. hunt by track or smell; follow along behind. The dogs trailed the rabbit. 6. path across a wild region. The men had followed desert trails for days. *v., n. 3.*

trail er (trāl′ər), 1. person or animal that follows a trail. 2. vine that grows along the ground. 3. wagon or cart pulled by an automobile, truck, etc. *n. 20.*

trailing arbutus, plant with fragrant pink and white flowers; Mayflower.

train (trān), 1. line of cars; as, a railroad train. 2. part that hangs down and drags along; as, the train of a lady's gown. 3. group of followers; as, the king and his train. 4. series; succession. A train of misfortunes overcame the hero. 5. bring up. "Train up a child in the way he should go." 6. teach; make skillful by teaching and practice. Saint Bernard dogs were trained to hunt for travelers lost in the snow. 7. make or become fit by exercise and diet. Runners train for races. 8. point; aim; as, to train guns upon a fort. 9. bring into a particular position. We trained the vines around the post. 10. line of gunpowder that acts as a fuse. *n., v. 1.*

train ing (trān′ing), 1. practical education in some art, profession, etc.; as, training for teachers. 2. developing strength and endurance. 3. good condition maintained by exercise and care. *n. 7.*

train oil, oil obtained from the blubber of whales, seals, fishes, etc.

trait (trāt), feature; quality; characteristic. Courage, love of fair play, and common sense are desirable traits. *n. 14.*

trai tor (trā′tər), person who betrays a friend, a duty, his country, etc. *n. 4.*

trai tor ous (trā′tər əs), like a traitor; treacherous; faithless. *adj. 13.*

trai tress (trā′tris), woman traitor. *n. 19.*

tra jec to ry (trə jek′tə ri), the path of a projectile in its flight through the air. *n., pl. trajectories. 18.*

tram (tram), 1. streetcar. *In British use.* 2. a truck or car on which loads are carried in coal mines. *n. 15.*

tram mel (tram′əl), 1. anything that hinders or restrains. 2. hinder; restrain. 3. net to catch fish, birds, etc. 4. hook in a fireplace to hold pots and kettles over the fire. *n., v., trammeled, trammeling. 15.*

tramp (tramp), 1. walk heavily. We heard soldiers tramping by. 2. step heavily (on). He tramped on the dog's foot. 3. sound of a heavy step; as, the tramp of marching feet. 4. walk; go on foot. We tramped a hundred miles. 5. a long, steady walk. The boys took a tramp together over the hills. 6. man who wanders about and begs. A tramp came to the door and asked for food. 7. freight ship which takes a cargo when and where it can. *v., n. 4.*

tram ple (tram′pəl), 1. tread heavily; tread on; crush. The man was trampled to death by the herd of wild cattle. 2. **Trample on** sometimes means treat with scorn or cruelty. 3. act or sound of trampling. We heard the trample of many feet. *v., n. 4.*

tram way (tram′wā′), track for streetcars. *n. [In British use] 19.*

trance (trans), 1. state or condition somewhat like sleep, in which the mind seems to have left the body. A person may be in a trance from illness, from the influence of some other person, or from his own will. 2. dreamy or absorbed condition which is like a trance. The old man sat before the fire in a trance, thinking of his past life. *n. 7.*

tran quil (trang′kwil), calm; peaceful; quiet. *adj. 6.*

tran quil li ty (trang kwil′i ti), calmness; peacefulness; quiet. *n. 6.*

trans-, a prefix meaning across, over, through, beyond, or on the other side of, as in transcontinental. *18.*

trans act (tran zakt′), do; manage; attend to; carry on (business). He transacts business with stores all over the country. A lawyer will transact many affairs connected with the purchase of a home. *v. 8.*

trans ac tion (tran zak′shən), 1. carrying on (of business). Mr. Smith attends to the transaction of important matters himself. 2. piece of business. A record is kept of all the firm's transactions. *n. 9.*

trans at lan tic (trans′ət lan′tik), 1. crossing the Atlantic; as, a transatlantic liner, a transatlantic cable. 2. on the other side of the Atlantic. *adj. 16.*

tran scend (tran send′), 1. go beyond; be above. The grandeur of Niagara Falls transcends words. 2. be higher or greater than. The speed of airplanes transcends that of any previous form of transportation. *v. 11.*

tran scend ent (tran sen′dənt), surpassing; superior; extraordinary. *adj. 12.*

tran scen den tal (tran′sen den′təl), 1. transcendent. 2. supernatural. 3. explaining matter and objective things as products of the mind that is thinking about them; idealistic. *adj. 19.*

trans con ti nen tal (trans′kon ti nen′təl), 1. crossing a continent; as, a transcontinental railroad. 2. on the other side of a continent. *adj. 14.*

tran scribe (tran skrīb′), to copy in writing or in typewriting. *v. 12.*

tran script (tran′skript), a copy; a written copy. *n. 13.*

tran scrip tion (tran skrip′shən), 1. copying. 2. a copy. *n. 20.*

tran sept (tran′sept), 1. the shorter part of a cross-shaped church. See diagram I. 2. either end of this part. See diagram II. *n. 19.*

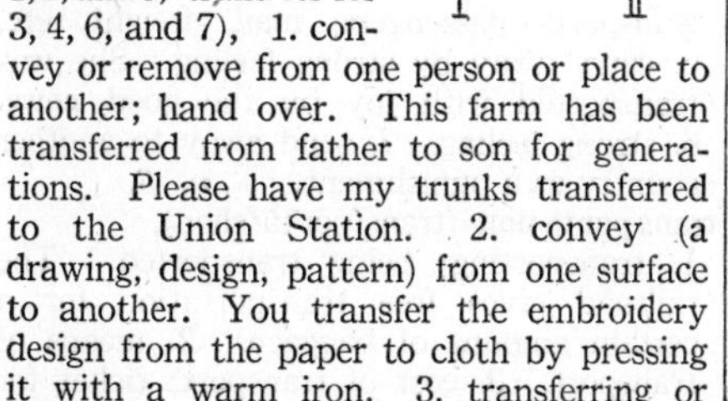

trans fer (trans fėr′ for 1, 2, and 5, trans′fər for 3, 4, 6, and 7), 1. convey or remove from one person or place to another; hand over. This farm has been transferred from father to son for generations. Please have my trunks transferred to the Union Station. 2. convey (a drawing, design, pattern) from one surface to another. You transfer the embroidery design from the paper to cloth by pressing it with a warm iron. 3. transferring or being transferred. 4. thing transferred. 5. change from one streetcar, bus, or train to another. 6. ticket allowing a passenger to continue his journey on another streetcar, bus, or train. 7. a point or place for transferring. *v., transferred, transferring, n. 4.*

trans fer a ble (trans fėr′ə bəl), capable of being transferred. *adj.*

trans fer ence (trans fėr′əns), transferring or being transferred. *n. 20.*

trans fig u ra tion (trans fig′ū rā′shən), 1. change in form or appearance. 2. the change in the appearance of Christ on the mountain. Matthew 17; Mark 9. *n. 19.*

trans fig ure (trans fig′yər), 1. change in form or appearance. New paint and furnishings had transfigured the old house. 2. change so as to glorify; exalt. *v. 12.*

trans fix (trans fiks′), 1. pierce through. The hunter transfixed the lion with a spear. 2. make motionless (with amazement, terror, etc.). *v. 11.*

trans form (trans fôrm′), 1. change in form or appearance. 2. change in condition, nature, or character. The witch transformed men into pigs. A tadpole becomes transformed into a frog. *v. 5.*

trans for ma tion (trans′fər mā′shən), transforming; as, the transformation of a caterpillar into a butterfly. *n. 8.*

trans form er (trans fôr′mər), thing or person that transforms. *n. 13.*

trans fuse (trans fūz′), 1. pour from one container into another. 2. transfer (blood) from one person or animal to another. *v. 16.*

trans fu sion (trans fū′zhən), 1. causing to pass from one container or holder to another. 2. transferring blood from one person or animal to another. *n. 16.*

trans gress (trans gres′), 1. go beyond (a limit or bound). Her manners transgressed the bounds of good taste. 2. break (a law or command); sin. *v. 6.*

trans gres sion (trans gresh′ən), transgressing; breaking a law; sin. *n. 9.*

trans gres sor (trans gres′ər), sinner; person who transgresses. *n. 12.*

tran sient (tran′shənt), 1. passing soon; fleeting; not lasting. Joy and sorrow are often transient. 2. a visitor or boarder who stays for a short time. *adj., n. 6.*

tran sit (tran′sit), 1. passing across or through. 2. carrying across or through. The goods were damaged in transit. 3. an instrument used in surveying to measure angles. *n. 8.*

tran si tion (tran zish′ən), a change or passing from one condition, place, or thing to another. The life of Lincoln illustrates a transition from poverty to power. Abrupt transitions in a book confuse the reader. In music, a transition is a change of key. *n. 7.*

tran si tion al (tran zish′ən əl), of transition; of change from one more or less fixed condition to another. *adj.*

tran si tive (tran′si tiv), 1. taking a direct object. *Hit, bring,* and *tie* are transitive verbs. 2. a transitive verb. *adj., n.*

tran si to ry (tran′si tō′ri), passing soon; lasting only a short time. We hope this hot weather will be transitory. *adj. 11.*

Trans-Jor dan (trans jôr′dən), country east of Palestine, across the Jordan River. It is under British supervision. *n.*

trans late (trans lāt′), 1. change from one language into another. 2. change into other words. 3. change from one place, position, or condition to another. She was translated to the fairy palace in a second. *v. 4.*

trans la tion (trans lā′shən), 1. act of translating; change into another language; change from one position or condition to another. 2. result of translating; version. *n. 8.*

trans la tor (trans lā′tər), person who translates. *n. 16.*

trans lu cent (trans lü′sənt), letting light through, but not transparent. Frosted glass is translucent. *adj. 9.*

trans mi gra tion (trans′mī grā′shən), 1. going from one country to another to settle there. 2. the passing of a soul at death into another body. Many people in India believe in the transmigration of souls. *n. 15.*

trans mis sion (trans mish′ən), 1. sending over; passing on; passing along; letting through. Mosquitoes are the only means of transmission of malaria. 2. the part of an automobile which transmits power from the engine to the rear axle. 3. passing through space of radio waves. When transmission is good, foreign stations can be received. *n. 11.*

trans mit (trans mit′), 1. send over; pass on; pass along; let through. I will transmit the money by special messenger. Rats transmit disease. 2. send out (signals, voice, music, etc.) by radio. *v., transmitted, transmitting. 9.*

trans mit ter (trans mit′ər), 1. person or thing that transmits something. 2. that part of a telegraph or telephone by which messages are sent. 3. apparatus for sending out signals, voice, music, etc., by radio. *n. 16.*

trans mu ta tion (trans′mū tā′shən), a change from one nature, substance, or form into another. *n. 16.*

trans mute (trans mūt′), change from one nature, substance, or form into another. We can transmute water power into electrical power. *v. 15.*

tran som (tran′səm), 1. window over a door or other window. 2. horizontal bar across a window; crossbar separating a door from the window over it. *n. 19.*

trans par en cy (trans păr′ən si), transparent quality or condition. *n. 16.*

trans par ent (trans păr′ənt), easily seen through. Window glass is transparent. *adj. 7.*

tran spi ra tion (tran′spi rā′shən), transpiring. *n. 11.*

tran spire (tran spīr′), 1. pass off or send off in the form of vapor through a wall or surface, as from the human body or from leaves. 2. leak out; become known. 3. happen; take place. *Used in common talk. v. 17.*

trans plant (trans plant′), 1. plant again in a different place. We start the flowers indoors and then transplant them to the garden. 2. remove from one place to another. All the people in the village were transplanted from Canada to Louisiana. *v. 10.*

trans plan ta tion (trans′plan tā′shən), 1. transplanting. 2. something that has been transplanted. *n. 20.*

trans port (trans pōrt′ for 1, 5, and 7, trans′pōrt for 2, 3, 4, and 6), 1. carry from one place to another. Wheat is transported from the farms to the mills. 2. carrying from one place to another. Trucks are much used for transport. 3. ship used to carry men and supplies. 4. airplane that transports passengers, mail, freight, etc. 5. carry away by strong feeling. She was transported with joy by the good news. 6. strong feeling. 7. send away to another country as a punishment. *v., n. 3.*

trans por ta tion (trans′pōr tā′shən), 1. transporting; being transported. The railroad gives free transportation for a certain amount of baggage. 2. means of transport. 3. cost of transport; ticket for transport. 4. sending away to another country as a punishment. *n. 4.*

trans pose (trans pōz′), 1. change the position or order of; interchange. 2. change the usual order of (letters or words). *Example:* Then *comes he* with *horses many* the *road along.* 3. in music, to change the key of. *v. 11.*

tran sub stan ti a tion (tran′səb stan′shi ā′shən), 1. changing of one substance into another. 2. the changing of the substance of the bread and wine of the Eucharist into the substance of the body and blood of Christ. The Roman Catholic Church believes in transubstantiation. *n. 17.*

trans verse (trans vėrs′), 1. lying across; placed crosswise; crossing from side to side; as, transverse beams. 2. something transverse. *adj., n. 11.*

Tran syl va ni a (tran′sil vā′ni ə), a province in Rumania. Transylvania was formerly a part of Hungary. *n. 14.*

trap (trap), 1. thing or means for catching animals. 2. trick or other means for catching someone off guard. The police set traps to make the thief tell where the money was. 3. catch in a trap. The bear was trapped. 4. set traps for animals. 5. door in a floor or roof. 6. a U-shaped bend in a pipe to prevent the escape of air or gas. 7. a light, two-wheeled carriage. 8. a device to throw things into the air to be shot at. *n., v., trapped, trapping. 2.*

trap door, door in a floor or roof. *19.*

tra peze (trə pēz′), a short, horizontal bar hung by ropes like a swing, used in gymnasiums and circuses. See the picture. *n.*

Trapeze

trap e zoid (trap′i zoid), four-sided plane figure having two sides parallel and two sides not parallel. *n. 19.*

Trapezoid

trap per (trap′ər), one who traps; especially, a man who traps wild animals for their furs. *n. 11.*

trap pings (trap′ingz), 1. ornamental coverings for a horse. 2. ornaments; things worn; as, trappings of a king and his court. *n. pl. 17.*

trash (trash), 1. worthless stuff; rubbish. That magazine is simply trash. 2. broken or torn bits. Rake up the trash in the yard and burn it. 3. worthless people. *n. 11.*

trav ail (trav′āl), 1. toil; labor. 2. trouble; hardship. 3. the pains of childbirth. 4. suffer the pains of childbirth. *n., v. 9.*

trav el (trav′əl), 1. go from one place to another; journey. She travels in Europe every summer. 2. going from one place to another. She loves travel. *v., traveled, traveling, n. 1.*

trav eled (trav′əld), 1. that has made many journeys; as, a traveled man. 2. much used by travelers. *adj.*

trav el er or **trav el ler** (trav′əl ər), 1. one who travels. 2. a traveling salesman. *n. 2.*

trav erse (trav′ərs or trə vėrs′), 1. pass across; go across. We traversed the desert. 2. something put or lying across. A traverse was laid across the trench to protect it from the gunfire from the side. 3. oppose; hinder; thwart. *v., n. 5.*

trav es ty (trav′is ti), 1. ridiculous treatment of a serious literary work or subject. 2. any treatment or imitation that makes a serious thing seem ridiculous. The trial was a travesty of justice, since the judge and jury were prejudiced. 3. make (a serious subject or matter) ridiculous; imitate in an absurd or grotesque way. *n., pl. travesties, v., travestied, travestying. 16.*

trawl (trôl), 1. a strong net dragged along the bottom of the sea. 2. to fish with a net by dragging it along the bottom of the sea. 3. a line supported by buoys and having many short lines with baited hooks attached to it. 4. to fish with lines supported by buoys. *n., v. 20.*

trawl er (trôl′ər), boat used in trawling. *n.*

tray (trā), a flat, shallow holder with a rim around it. The waiter carries the dishes on a tray. She keeps her brush and comb in one tray, and her hairpins in another. *n. 6.*

treach er ous (trech′ər əs), 1. not to be trusted; not faithful. The treacherous soldier carried reports to the enemy. 2. deceiving; not reliable; having a false appearance of strength, security, etc. Thin ice is treacherous. *adj. 5.*

treach er y (trech′ər i), 1. deceit; breaking faith; treacherous behavior. 2. treason. *n., pl. treacheries. 6.*

trea cle (trē′kəl), molasses. *n.*

tread (tred), 1. walk; step; set the foot down. Don't tread on the flower beds. 2. press under the feet; trample; trample on; crush. Tread out the fire before you go away. 3. make or form by walking.

Cattle had trodden a path to the pond. 4. way of walking; step. He walks with a heavy tread. 5. the part of stairs or a ladder that a person steps on. The stair treads were covered with rubber to prevent slipping. 6. the part of a wheel or tire that touches the ground. *v., trod, trodden* or *trod, treading, n. 2.*

trea dle (tred′əl), 1. lever worked by the foot to impart motion to a machine; as, the treadle of a sewing machine. 2. work a treadle. *n., v. 20.*

T, treadle.

tread mill (tred′mil′), 1. apparatus for producing a turning motion by having a person or animal walk on the moving steps of a wheel or of a sloping, endless belt. 2. any wearisome or monotonous round of work or of life. *n.*

trea son (trē′zən), 1. falseness to one's country or to one's king. Helping the enemies of one's country is treason. 2. betraying a trust; treachery. *n. 4.*

trea son a ble (trē′zən ə bəl), of treason; involving treason; traitorous. *adj. 13.*

trea son ous (trē′zən əs), treasonable. *adj. 17.*

treas ure (trezh′ər), 1. wealth or riches stored up; valuable things. The pirates buried treasure along the coast. The palace contains treasures. 2. anything that is much valued; person loved. The silver teapot was the old lady's chief treasure. 3. value highly. She treasures that doll more than all her other toys. 4. put away for future use; store up. *n., v. 2.*

treas ur er (trezh′ər ər), person in charge of money. The treasurer of a club pays its bills. *n. 6.*

treas ur y (trezh′ər i), 1. place where money is kept. The national treasury is in Washington, D.C. 2. funds; money owned. We voted to pay for the party out of the club treasury. 3. department which has charge of the income and expenses of a country. The Secretary of the Treasury is a member of the President's cabinet. 4. place where treasure is kept. *n., pl. treasuries. 4.*

treat (trēt), 1. act toward. The driver treats his horses well. 2. deal with to relieve or cure. The dentist is treating my tooth. 3. deal with; discuss; express in literature or art. *The Medical Journal* treats of the progress of medicine. 4. discuss terms; arrange terms. Messengers came to treat for peace. 5. give food, drink, or amusement. He treated his friends to ice cream. 6. gift of food, drink, or amusement. 7. anything that gives pleasure. *v., n. 2.*

trea tise (trē′tis), a book or other writing treating of some subject. A treatise is more formal and systematic than most books. *n. 8.*

treat ment (trēt′mənt), 1. act or process of treating. My cold won't yield to treatment. 2. way of treating. This cat has suffered from bad treatment. 3. thing done or used to treat something else. *n. 3.*

trea ty (trē′ti), an agreement between nations. The peace treaty was signed in Paris. *n., pl. treaties. 5.*

tre ble (treb′əl), 1. three times. 2. make or become three times as much. He trebled his money by buying a dog for $5 and selling it for $15. 3. the highest part in music; soprano. The treble and the bass sang a duet. *adj., v., n. 8.*

tre bly (treb′li), three times. *adv.*

tree (trē), 1. a large plant with a woody trunk, branches, and leaves. 2. a piece of wood used as a part of something. 3. anything like a tree. A **family tree** is a diagram with branches showing how the members of a family are related. 4. drive up a tree. The cat was treed by a dog. *n., v., treed, treeing. 1.*

trek (trek), 1. travel by ox wagon. 2. travel slowly by any means; travel. 3. journey; stage of a journey between one stopping place and the next. *v., trekked, trekking, n.*

trel lis (trel′is), frame of light strips of wood or metal crossing one another with open spaces in between; lattice. *n. 13.*

Trellis

trem ble (trem′bəl), 1. shake because of fear, excitement, weakness, cold, etc. The old woman's hands trembled. Her voice trembled with fear. 2. move gently. The leaves trembled in the breeze. 3. a trembling. There was a tremble in her voice as she began to recite. *v., n. 2.*

tre men dous (tri men′dəs), 1. dreadful; very severe. The army suffered a tremendous defeat. 2. very great. 3. extraordinary. *Used in common talk. adj. 5.*

trem or (trem′ər), 1. a shaking or trembling; as, a nervous tremor in the voice. 2. thrill of emotion or excitement. *n. 14.*

trem u lous (trem′ū ləs), 1. trembling; quivering. The child's voice was tremulous with sobs. 2. timid; feeling fear. *adj. 7.*

trench (trench), 1. a long, narrow ditch with earth thrown up in front to protect soldiers. 2. ditch. 3. dig a trench in. *n., v. 5.*

trench ant (tren′chənt), 1. sharp; keen; cutting; as, trenchant wit. 2. vigorous; effective. *adj. 13.*

trench er (tren′chər), wooden platter on which meat was formerly served and carved. *n. 14.*

trend (trend), 1. general direction; course; tendency. The hills have a western trend. The trend of modern living is away from many old customs. 2. have a general direction; tend; run. The road trends to the north. *n., v. 9.*

Trent (trent), a city in northern Italy. A famous church council was held there from 1545 to 1563. *n. 14.*

Tren ton (tren′tən), the capital of New Jersey. *n. 14.*

trep i da tion (trep′i dā′shən), 1. fear; fright. 2. trembling. *n. 13.*

tres pass (tres′pəs), 1. go on somebody's property without any right. The farmer put up "No Trespassing" signs to keep people off his farm. 2. go beyond the limits of what is right. I won't trespass on your time any longer. 3. a trespassing. 4. do wrong; sin. 5. a wrong; a sin. *v., n. 6.*

tress (tres), a lock, curl, or braid of hair; as, golden tresses. *n. 10.*

tres tle (tres′əl), frame used as a support. *n.*

Trestle

tri ad (trī′ad), group of three, especially of three closely related persons or things. *n. 16.*

tri al (trī′əl), 1. process of trying or testing. He gave the machine another trial to see if it would work. 2. for a try or test; as, a trial trip. 3. examining and deciding a case in court. 4. trouble; hardship. Her life has been full of trials—sickness, poverty, and loss of loved ones. *n., adj. 2.*

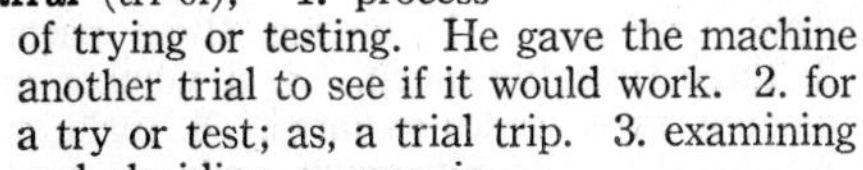

Triangles

tri an gle (trī′ang′gəl), 1. a figure having three sides and three angles. 2. a musical instrument made of a triangle of steel that is struck with a steel rod. *n. 6.*

tri an gu lar (trī ang′gū lər), shaped like a triangle; three-cornered. *adj. 10.*

trib al (trīb′əl), of a tribe. *adj. 16.*

tribe (trīb), 1. group of people united by race and customs under the same leaders. America was once the home of savage tribes of Indians. 2. class or set of people; as, the tribe of artists, the whole tribe of gossips. 3. class, kind, or sort of animals, plants, or other things. *n. 2.*

trib u la tion (trib′ū lā′shən), affliction; great trouble; severe trial. The early Christians suffered many tribulations. *n. 10.*

tri bu nal (tri bū′nəl), court of justice; place of judgment. He was brought before the tribunal for trial. *n. 8.*

trib une[1] (trib′ūn), 1. an official in ancient Rome who protected the plebeians from the patricians. 2. defender of the people. *n. 19.*

trib une[2] (trib′ūn), raised platform. *n.*

trib u tar y (trib′ū tãr′i), 1. stream that flows into a larger stream or body of water. The Ohio River is a tributary of the Mississippi River. 2. flowing into a larger stream or body of water. 3. paying tribute; required to pay tribute. 4. one that pays tribute. *n., pl. tributaries, adj. 4.*

trib ute (trib′ūt), 1. money paid by one nation to another for peace or protection or because of some agreement. 2. any forced payment. 3. an acknowledgment of thanks or respect; compliment. Memorial Day is a tribute to our dead soldiers. *n. 4.*

trice[1] (trīs), haul up and tie with a rope; as, to trice up a sail. *v. 11.*

trice[2] (trīs), very short time; an instant. *n.*

trick (trik), 1. something done to deceive or cheat. The false message was a trick to get him to leave the house. 2. deceive; cheat. We were tricked into buying a poor car. 3. clever act; feat of skill. We enjoyed the tricks of the trained animals. 4. piece of mischief. Stealing John's lunch was a mean trick. 5. play tricks. 6. a peculiar habit or way of acting. He has a trick of pulling at his collar. 7. the cards played in one round. 8. a turn at steering a ship. 9. dress. *n., v. 2.*

trick er y (trik′ər i), use of tricks; deception; cheating. *n., pl. trickeries. 17.*

trick le (trik′əl), 1. flow or fall in drops or in a small stream. Tears trickled down her cheeks. The brook trickled through the valley. 2. small flow or stream. *v., n. 8.*

trick ster (trik′stər), a cheat; deceiver. *n. 19.*

trick y (trik′i), 1. full of tricks; deceiving. 2. not doing what is expected. *adj., trickier, trickiest.*

tri col or (trī′kul′ər), 1. having three colors. 2. flag having three colors. *adj., n.*

tri cy cle (trī′si kəl), three-wheeled vehicle worked by pedals or handles. Sometimes tricycles are used by lame people. *n. 15.*

tri dent (trī′dənt), 1. three-pronged spear. 2. three-pronged. *n., adj. 13.*

tried (trīd), 1. tested; proved. 2. See **try.** *adj., pt. and pp. of try. 2.*

tri en ni al (trī en′i əl), 1. lasting three years. 2. occurring every three years. 3. event that occurs every three years. *adj., n. 19.*

Tri este (tri est′), a seaport city in northeastern Italy. *n. 14.*

tri fle (trī′fəl), 1. thing having little value or importance. 2. small amount; little bit. 3. small amount of money. 4. talk or act lightly, not seriously. Don't trifle with serious matters. 5. play (with); handle. He trifled with his pencil and pen. 6. spend (time, effort, money, etc.) on things having little value. She had trifled away the whole morning. *n., v. 3.*

tri fler (trī′flər), person who trifles. *n. 15.*

tri fling (trī′fling), 1. having little value; not important; small. 2. frivolous; shallow. *adj.*

trig ger (trig′ər), 1. the lever pulled back by the finger in firing a gun. 2. a lever which releases a spring when pulled or pressed. *n. 12.*

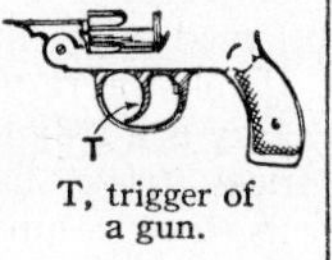

T, trigger of a gun.

trig o nom e try (trig′ə nom′i tri), the branch of mathematics that deals with the relations between the sides and angles of triangles. *n.*

trill (tril), 1. sing, play, sound, or speak with a tremulous, vibrating sound. The Spanish trill the letter *r.* 2. act or sound of trilling. *v., n. 10.*

tril lion (tril′yən), 1. in the United States and France, 1,000,000,000,000. 2. in Great Britain, 1,000,000,000,000,000,000. *n., adj. 19.*

tril li um (tril′i əm), a plant with three leaves around a single flower. *n.*

tril o gy (tril′ə ji), three plays, operas, novels, etc., which fit together to make a related series. *n., pl. trilogies. 19.*

trim (trim), 1. put in good order; make neat by cutting away parts. The gardener trims the hedge. The barber trimmed Father's hair and beard. 2. neat; in good condition or order. A trim maid appeared. 3. good condition or order. 4. decorate. The children trimmed the Christmas tree. 5. balance (a boat) by arranging the load carried. 6. arrange (the sails) to fit wind and direction. 7. change (opinions, etc.) to suit circumstances. 8. defeat; beat. *Used in common talk. v., trimmed, trimming, adj., trimmer, trimmest, n. 2.*

trim ming (trim′ing), 1. ornament; anything used to trim or decorate; as, the trimmings of a Christmas tree, trimming for a dress. 2. **Trimmings** means (1) parts cut away in trimming. (2) additions to simple dishes; as, a turkey with all the trimmings. *Used in common talk. n.*

Trin i dad (trin′i dad), British island in the West Indies, near Venezuela. *n. 18.*

trin i ty (trin′i ti), being three. *n. 10.*

Trin i ty (trin′i ti), the union of Father, Son, and Holy Ghost in one divine nature. *n.*

trin ket (tring′kit), 1. any small fancy article, bit of jewelry, or the like. 2. a trifle. *n. 10.*

tri o (trē′ō), 1. piece of music for three voices or instruments. 2. three singers or players. 3. any group of three. *n., pl. trios. 16.*

trip (trip), 1. journey; as, a trip to Europe. 2. stumble. He tripped on a tree root. 3. cause to stumble. 4. catching a person's foot to throw him down. 5. make a mistake; commit a fault. 6. cause to make a mistake. 7. loss of footing; stumble; blunder. 8. take light quick steps. The children came tripping down the path to meet us. 9. light quick step. *n., v., tripped, tripping. 1.*

tri par tite (trī pär′tīt), 1. divided into three parts. 2. having three corresponding parts or copies. 3. made or shared by three parties; as, a tripartite treaty between Germany, Italy, and Japan. *adj. 20.*

tripe (trīp), the stomach of an ox, etc., used for food. *n. 17.*

tri ple (trip′əl), 1. having three parts. 2. three times as much. 3. a number or amount three times as large. 4. make or become three times as much. *adj., n., v. 8.*

tri plet (trip′lit), 1. one of three children born at the same time from the same mother. 2. group of three. *n.*

trip li cate (trip′li kāt for 1, trip′li kit for 2 and 3), 1. to triple; make threefold. 2. triple; threefold. 3. one of three things exactly alike. *v., adj., n. 19.*

tri pod (trī′pod), a stool, frame, or stand with three legs. A camera is sometimes supported on a tripod. *n. 13.*

Trip o li (trip′ə li), 1. a district in northern Africa. Tripoli was formerly Turkish, but now belongs to Italy. 2. its capital. *n. 17.*

trip ping (trip′ing), light and quick. *adj.*

tri reme (trī′rēm), ancient ship with three rows of oars, one above the other, on each side. *n.*

Trireme. Diagram shows position of rowers.

trite (trīt), worn; commonplace; stale. Such expressions as "like sardines in a box" and "cheeks like roses" have become trite. *adj. 16.*

Tri ton (trī′tən), a Greek sea god having the head and body of a man and the tail of a fish. *n. 11.*

tri umph (trī′umf), 1. victory; success. 2. gain victory; win success. Our team triumphed over theirs. 3. joy because of victory or success. John brought home the prize in triumph. 4. rejoice because of victory or success. 5. Roman procession in honor of a victorious general. *n., v. 3.*

tri um phal (trī um′fəl), of or for a triumph; celebrating a victory. *adj. 8.*

tri um phant (trī um′fənt), 1. victorious; successful. 2. rejoicing because of victory or success. The winner spoke in triumphant tones to his defeated rival. *adj. 6.*

tri um vir (trī um′vər), one of three men who shared the same public office or job in ancient Rome. *n. 16.*

tri um vi rate (trī um′vi rit), 1. government by three men together. 2. any association of three in office or authority. 3. any group of three. *n. 18.*

triv et (triv′it), a stand or support with three legs or feet. Trivets are used over fires and under platters. *n. 11.*

Trivet for a platter

triv i al (triv′i əl), not important; trifling. Your composition has only a few trivial mistakes. *adj. 6.*

triv i al i ty (triv′i al′i ti), 1. trivial quality. 2. something trivial; a trifle. *n., pl. trivialities. 18.*

trod (trod), 1. See **tread**. He trod on a tack. 2. trodden. *pt. and a pp. of tread. 4.*

trod den (trod′ən). See **tread**. The cattle had trodden down the corn. *pp. of tread. 11.*

Troi lus (trō′i ləs or troi′ləs), a son of Priam, king of Troy. Troilus loved Cressida. *n. 13.*

Tro jan (trō′jən), 1. of Troy; pertaining to Troy or its people. The Trojan War lasted ten years. 2. a native or inhabitant of Troy. 3. person who shows courage or energy. They all worked like Trojans. *adj., n. 10.*

troll[1] (trōl), 1. sing in a full, rolling voice. 2. sing in succession. When three people troll a song or catch, the soprano sings one line, the alto comes in next with the same line, and then the bass sings it, and so on, while the others keep on singing. 3. song whose parts are sung in succession. "Three Blind Mice" is a well-known troll. 4. to fish with a moving line. He trolled for bass. In trolling, a man usually trails the line behind his boat near the surface. *v., n. 6.*

troll[2] (trōl), ugly giant or dwarf living in caves or underground. *n.*

Troll

trol ley (trol′i), 1. pulley moving against a wire to carry electricity to a streetcar, electric engine, etc. 2. electric streetcar. 3. pulley running on an overhead track, used to support and move a load. *n., pl. trolleys. 5.*

trom bone (trom′bōn), a large brass musical instrument, usually with a sliding piece for varying the length of the tube. A trombone usually has a long U-shaped sliding piece. *n. 17.*

Boy playing a trombone

troop (trüp), 1. a company; a group; as, a troop of boys, a troop of deer. 2. **Troops** often means soldiers. 3. cavalry unit having 60 to 100 men commanded by a captain. 4. unit of 16 or 32 Boy Scouts. 5. gather in troops or bands; move together. The children trooped around the teacher. 6. walk; go; go away. The young boys trooped off after the older ones. *n., v. 2.*

troop er (trüp′ər), 1. soldier in a troop of cavalry. 2. mounted policeman. *n. 16.*

troop ship (trüp′ship′), ship used to carry soldiers; transport. *n.*

trope (trōp), the use of a word or phrase in a sense different from its ordinary meaning. *Example:*

"All in a hot and *copper* sky,
The *bloody* sun at noon . . ." *n. 14.*

tro phy (trō′fi), memorial of victory. The hunter kept the lion's skin and head as trophies. *n., pl. trophies. 5.*

trop ic (trop′ik), 1. either of the two circles around the earth, one 23.45 degrees north and one 23.45 degrees south of the equator. The tropic of Cancer is the northern circle, and the tropic of Capricorn is the southern circle. 2. **The tropics** often means the regions between these circles. It is hot in the tropics. 3. of the tropics. *n., adj. 6.*

trop i cal (trop′i kəl), of the tropics. Bananas are tropical fruit. *adj. 7.*

trot (trot), 1. go by lifting the right forefoot and the left hind foot at about the same time. Horses trot. 2. the motion of a trotting horse. 3. ride at a trot. 4. make (a horse) trot. 5. run, but not fast. The child trotted along after his mother. *v., trotted, trotting, n. 3.*

troth (trôth), 1. faithfulness; fidelity; loyalty. "I plight my troth" means "I promise to be faithful." 2. promise. 3. truth. *n., v. 9.*

trou ba dour (trü′bə dōr), one of the lyric poets of southern France and northern Italy from the 11th to the 13th centuries. The troubadours wrote mainly about love and chivalry. *n. 14.*

trou ble (trub′əl), 1. disturb; cause distress or worry to. We sailed on troubled waters. She is troubled by headaches. Don't let what George says trouble you. 2. disturbance; distress; worry; difficulty. That boy makes trouble for his teachers. Jim has stomach trouble. 3. extra work; bother; effort. We have gone to a great deal of trouble for her. If she won't take the trouble to answer our letters, we shall stop writing. 4. cause extra work or effort to. May I trouble you to pass the sugar? 5. cause oneself inconvenience. Don't trouble to come to the door. *v., n. 1.*

trou ble some (trub′əl səm), causing trouble; annoying; full of trouble. *adj. 6.*

trou blous (trub′ləs), 1. disturbed; restless. 2. troublesome. *adj. 13.*

trough (trôf), 1. a long, narrow container for holding food or water. He led the horses to the watering trough. 2. something shaped like this. The baker uses a trough for kneading dough. 3. channel for carrying water; gutter. A wooden trough under the eaves of the house carries off rain water. 4. a long hollow between two ridges; as, the trough between two waves. *n. 6.*

trounce (trouns), beat; thrash. *v.*

troupe (trüp), troop; band; company; especially, a group of actors, singers, or acrobats. *n.*

trou sers (trou′zərz), a two-legged outer garment reaching from the waist to the ankles or knees. *n. pl. 4.*

trous seau (trü sō′), bride's outfit of clothes, linen, etc. *n., pl. trousseaux* (-sōz′) or *trousseaus. 19.*

trout (trout), a fresh-water food fish. *n., pl. trout* or *trouts. 5.*

trow (trō), believe; think. *v. [Old use] 13.*

trow el (trou′əl), 1. a tool for spreading or smoothing plaster or mortar. 2. a tool for taking up plants, loosening dirt, etc. *n. 16.*

Trowels: A, for plaster; B, for plants.

Troy[1] (troi), 1. ancient city in Asia Minor. The Greeks laid siege to Troy for ten years. 2. city in eastern New York State. *n. 6.*

troy[2] (troi). One pound troy equals a little over four fifths of an ordinary pound. 12 troy ounces = 1 troy pound. Troy weight is used for gems and precious metals. *adj.*

tru ant (trü′ənt), 1. child who stays away from school without permission. 2. person who neglects duty. 3. neglecting duty. 4. lazy. 5. wandering. That truant dog won't stay at home. *n., adj. 7.*

truce (trüs), 1. a stop in fighting; peace for a short time. A truce was declared between the two armies. 2. a rest from trouble or pain. The hot weather gave the old man a truce from rheumatism. *n. 11.*

truck[1] (truk), 1. an automobile, big cart, or wagon for carrying heavy loads. 2. carry on a truck. 3. frame with two or more pairs of wheels for supporting the end of a railroad car, locomotive, etc. 4. small wheel. *n., v. 5.*

truck[2] (truk), 1. vegetables raised for market. 2. rubbish; trash. *Used in common talk. n.*

truck le (truk′əl), give up tamely; be servile. That man got his position by truckling to his superiors and flattering them. *v. 17.*

truc u lence (truk′ū ləns), fierceness; savageness; cruelty. *n.*

truc u lent (truk′ū lənt), fierce; savage; cruel. *adj. 16.*

trudge (truj), 1. walk. 2. walk wearily or with effort. 3. a hard or weary walk. It was a long trudge up the hill. *v., n. 7.*

true (trü), 1. agreeing with fact; not false. It is true that 6 and 4 are 10. 2. real; genuine; as, true gold, true kindness. 3. faithful; loyal. 4. agreeing with a standard; correct; exact. This is a true copy of my letter. 5. rightful; lawful; as, the true heir to the property. 6. in a true manner: truly; exactly. His words ring true. *adj., adv. 1.*

truf fle (truf′əl), a fungus that grows underground, valued as a food. *n. 18.*

tru ism (trü′izm), statement that almost everybody knows is true, such as "Health is a blessing." *n. 15.*

tru ly (trü′li), 1. in a true manner; exactly; rightly; faithfully. 2. really; in fact. *adv. 5.*

trump[1] (trump), 1. any playing card of a suit that for the time ranks higher than the other suits. 2. the suit itself. 3. play a card of this suit. *n., v. 9.*

trump[2] (trump), make (up) to deceive. *v.*

trump[3] (trump), a trumpet or its sound. *n.* [*Old use*].

trump er y (trump′ər i), 1. something showy but without value; worthless ornaments; useless stuff; rubbish; nonsense. 2. showy but useless; trifling; worthless. *n., pl. trumperies, adj. 13.*

trum pet (trum′pit), 1. a musical wind instrument that has a powerful tone. 2. thing shaped like a trumpet. The deaf old lady has an ear trumpet to help her hearing. 3. blow a trumpet. 4. a sound like that of a trumpet. 5. make a sound like a trumpet. The elephant trumpeted. 6. proclaim loudly or widely. She'll trumpet that story all over town. *n., v. 3.*

Man playing a trumpet

trum pet er (trum′pit ər), person who blows a trumpet. *n. 12.*

trun cheon (trun′chən), 1. stick; club; as, a policeman's truncheon. 2. staff of office or authority; as, a herald's truncheon. *n. 13.*

trun dle (trun′dəl), roll along; push along. The workman trundled a wheelbarrow hour after hour. *v. 10.*

trunk (trungk), 1. the main stem of a tree. 2. the main part of anything; as, the trunk of a column. 3. main; chief; as, the trunk line of a railroad. 4. big box for holding clothes, etc., when traveling. 5. a body without the head, arms, and legs. 6. elephant's snout. 7. **Trunks** sometimes means very short trousers or breeches worn by athletes, swimmers, acrobats, etc. *n., adj. 2.*

Trunk for clothes

truss (trus), 1. tie; fasten. The cook trussed up the chicken before roasting it. 2. beams or other supports connected to support a roof, bridge, etc. 3. bandage or pad used for support. 4. bundle of hay or straw. *v., n. 12.*

trust (trust), 1. faith; firm belief in someone's honesty, truth, justice, or power. A child puts trust in his mother. 2. believe firmly in the honesty, truth, justice, or power of another; have faith in. "In God we trust." 3. rely on; depend on. A forgetful man should not trust his memory, but should write things down in a notebook. 4. person or thing believed in. God is our trust. 5. property managed for another. Mr. Adams does not own the house. It is a trust which he holds for his dead brother's children. 6. managing for an owner. A trust company undertakes to manage property for anyone. 7. obligation assumed by a person who takes charge of another's property. Mr. Adams will be faithful to his trust. 8. commit to the care of; let be with. Can I trust the keys to Jack? 9. hope; believe. I trust you will soon feel better. 10. a group of men or companies that controls much of a certain kind of business. 11. business credit. When you buy anything and do not pay for it until later, you are getting it on trust. 12. give business credit to. The butcher will trust us for the meat. *n., v., adj. 1.*

trus tee (trus tē′), person responsible for the property or affairs of another person, a company, or an institution. A trustee will manage the children's property until they grow up. *n. 8.*

trust ful (trust′fəl), trusting; believing; ready to confide; ready to have faith. *adj. 18.*

trust ing (trus′ting), that trusts; trustful. *adj.*

trust wor thy (trust′wėr′ᴛʜi), that can be depended on; reliable. The class chose a trustworthy boy for treasurer. *adj. 11.*

trust y (trus′ti), 1. that can be depended on; reliable. The master left his money with a trusty servant. 2. a convict who is given special privileges because of his good behavior. *adj., trustier, trustiest, n., pl. trusties. 6.*

truth (trüth), 1. that which is true. Tell the truth. 2. true, exact, honest, sincere, or loyal quality or nature. *n., pl. truths* (trüᴛʜz or trüths). *1.*

truth ful (trüth′fəl), telling the truth. George is a truthful boy and will tell what really happened. *adj. 9.*

truth ful ness (trüth′fəl nis), truthful nature or quality. *n. 18.*

try (trī), 1. attempt; make an effort. If at first you don't succeed, try, try again. 2. an attempt. 3. experiment on; make trial. Try this candy and see if you like it. 4. test; find out about. We try each car before we sell it. 5. **Try on** means put on to test the fit, etc. Helen tried on her new dress. 6. investigate in a law court. The man was tried and found guilty of murder. 7. strain. Don't try your eyes by reading in a poor light. Her mistakes try my patience. 8. make pure by melting or boiling. *v., tried, trying, n., pl. tries. 1.*

try ing (trī′ing), hard to endure; annoying; distressing; as, a trying day. *adj.*

tryst (trist), 1. appointment to meet at a certain time and place. 2. place of meeting. *n. 16.*

Tsetse fly. Lines show actual size.

tsar (tsär), czar. *n.*

tsa ri na (tsä rē′nə), czarina. *n.*

tset se (tset′si), tsetse fly. *n.*

tsetse fly, bloodsucking fly of Africa. One kind of tsetse fly spreads sleeping sickness. See the picture just above.

tub (tub), 1. open container for washing or bathing. 2. a round wooden container for holding butter, lard, etc. 3. as much as a tub can hold. 4. bathtub. 5. bath. He takes a cold tub every morning. 6. wash or bathe in a tub. *n., v., tubbed, tubbing. 4.*

Tubs for washing

tu ba (tū′bə or tü′bə), a very large horn, low in pitch. *n.*

Boy playing a tuba

tube (tūb or tüb), 1. long pipe of metal, glass, rubber, etc. Tubes are mostly used to hold or carry liquids or gases. 2. small cylinder of thin, easily bent metal with a cap that screws on the open end, used for holding tooth paste, cold cream, paint, etc. 3. a pipe or tunnel through which something is sent. The railroad runs under the river in a tube. 4. thing like a tube; as, a radio tube. *n. 4.*

tu ber (tū′bər or tü′bər), thick part of an underground stem. A potato is a tuber. *n. 10.*

tu ber cle (tū′bər kəl or tü′bər kəl), 1. a small rounded swelling or knob. 2. a swelling caused by tuberculosis. *n. 14.*

tu ber cu lar (tū bėr′kū lər or tü bėr′kū lər), 1. having tubercles. 2. pertaining to tubercles. 3. having tuberculosis. 4. pertaining to tuberculosis. *adj. 18.*

tu ber cu lo sis (tū bėr′kū lō′sis or tü bėr′kū-lō′sis), a disease affecting various tissues of the body, but most often the lungs. Tuberculosis of the lungs is often called consumption. *n. 11.*

tu ber ous (tū′bər əs or tü′bər əs), 1. bearing tubers. 2. of or like tubers. 3. covered with rounded knobs or swellings. *adj.*

tub ing (tūb′ing or tüb′ing), 1. material in the form of a tube; as, rubber tubing. 2. tubes. 3. a piece of tube. *n.*

tu bu lar (tū′bū lər or tü′bū lər), 1. shaped like a tube; round and hollow. 2. of or pertaining to a tube or tubes. *adj. 11.*

tu bule (tū′būl or tü′būl), small tube. *n. 20.*

tuck (tuk), 1. thrust into some narrow space or into some retired place. She tucked her purse under her arm. He tucked the letter in his pocket. The little cottage is tucked away under the hill. 2. thrust the edge or end of (a garment or covering) closely into place. Jack tucked a napkin under his chin. Mother comes every night to tuck in the bedclothes. 3. draw close together; fold. A bird tucks his head under his wing when he sleeps. **Tuck up** means draw together and up. He tucked up his sleeves before washing his hands. 4. a fold sewed in a garment. 5. sew a fold in a garment for trimming or to make it shorter. The baby's dress was beautifully tucked with tiny stitches. *v., n. 4.*

T, tucker.

tuck er (tuk′ər), piece of muslin, lace, etc., worn about the neck or over the chest. *n. 12.*

Tuc son (tü son′), a city in southern Arizona. *n.*

Tu dor (tū′dər or tü′dər), the family name of the kings and queens of England who ruled from 1485 to 1603. *n.*

Tues., Tuesday. *16.*

Tues day (tūz′di or tüz′di), the third day of the week. *n. 2.*

tuft (tuft), 1. bunch of feathers, hair, grass, etc., held together at one end. A goat has a tuft of hair on its chin. 2. clump of bushes, trees, etc. 3. put tufts on; furnish with tufts. 4. grow in tufts. *n., v. 6.*

tug (tug), 1. pull with force or effort; pull hard. We tugged the boat in to shore. The child tugged at his mother's hand. 2. hard pull. The baby gave a tug at Mary's hair. 3. a small and powerful steamboat used to tow other boats. 4. tow by a tug. 5. one of a pair of long leather straps by which a horse pulls a wagon, cart, etc. See the diagram under **harness.** *v., tugged, tugging, n. 4.*

Tug

Tui ler ies (twē′lər iz), former royal palace in Paris. It was burned in 1871. *n. 19.*

tu i tion (tū ish′ən or tü ish′ən), 1. teaching; instruction. 2. money paid for instruction. *n. 13.*

tu lip (tū′lip or tü′lip), a spring flower having various colors. Tulips are grown from bulbs. *n. 9.*

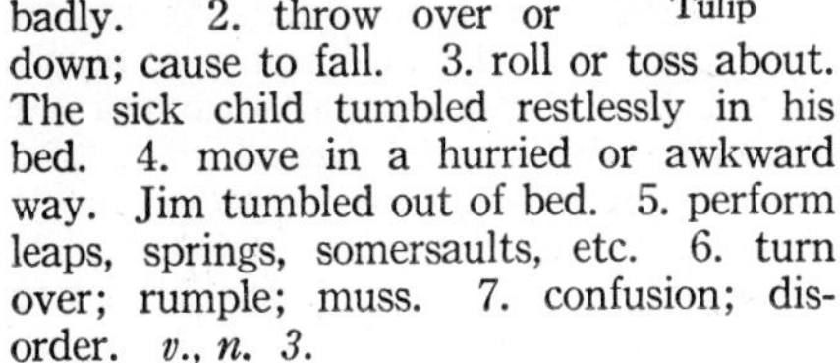

Tulip

Tul sa (tul′sə), a city in northeastern Oklahoma. *n.*

tum ble (tum′bəl), 1. fall. The child tumbled down the stairs. The tumble hurt him badly. 2. throw over or down; cause to fall. 3. roll or toss about. The sick child tumbled restlessly in his bed. 4. move in a hurried or awkward way. Jim tumbled out of bed. 5. perform leaps, springs, somersaults, etc. 6. turn over; rumple; muss. 7. confusion; disorder. *v., n. 3.*

tum bler (tum′blər), 1. person who performs leaps or springs; acrobat. 2. a drinking glass. *n. 9.*

tum brel or **tum bril** (tum′brəl), cart; cart that carried prisoners to be executed. *n. 20.*

tu mid (tū′mid or tü′mid), 1. swollen. 2. swollen with big words; pompous. *adj. 20.*

tu mor (tū′mər or tü′mər), 1. a swelling. 2. a growth in any part of the body caused by disease. *n. 11.*

tu mult (tū′mult or tü′mult), 1. noise; uproar. The sailors' voices could not be heard above the tumult of the storm. 2. violent disturbance or disorder. The cry of "Fire! Fire!" caused a tumult in the theater. *n. 5.*

tu mul tu ous (tū mul′chü əs or tü mul′chü əs), 1. violent; very noisy or disorderly. The football team celebrated its victory in a tumultuous fashion. 2. greatly disturbed. 3. rough; stormy. *adj. 9.*

tun (tun), 1. a large cask for holding liquids. 2. a measure of capacity for liquor, equal to 252 gallons. *n.*

tu na (tü′nə), large sea fish used for food; the tunny. It sometimes grows to a length of ten feet or more. *n., pl. tuna* or *tunas.*

tun dra (tun′drə), a vast, level, treeless plain in the arctic regions. The ground beneath the surface of the tundras is frozen even in summer. *n. 20.*

tune (tūn or tün), 1. piece of music; an air or melody; as, hymn tunes. 2. the proper pitch. The piano is out of tune. He can't sing in tune. 3. agreement; harmony. A person out of tune with his surroundings is unhappy. 4. put in tune. A man is tuning the piano. 5. **Tune in** means adjust a radio to hear (what is wanted). **Tune out** means adjust a radio to get rid of (what is unwanted). *n., v. 3.*

tune ful (tūn′fəl or tün′fəl), musical; melodious. A robin has a tuneful song. *adj. 12.*

tune less (tūn′lis), without tune; not musical. *adj. 19.*

tung sten (tung′stən), a rare metal used in making steel and for electric lamp filaments. *n. 14.*

tu nic (tū′nik or tü′nik), 1. garment like a shirt or gown, worn by the ancient Greeks and Romans; any garment like it. 2. woman's dress, coat, or blouse extending below the waist. 3. soldier's coat. *n. 10.*

tuning fork, a small steel instrument that makes a musical tone of a certain pitch when it is struck.

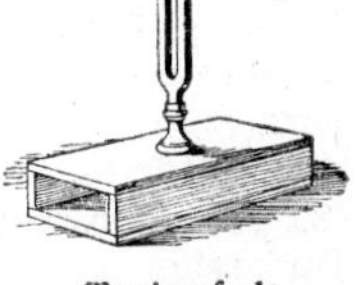

Tuning fork

Tu nis (tū′nis or tü′nis), a seaport city in northern Africa. *n. 9.*

Tu ni si a (tū nish′i ə or tü nish′i ə), country in northern Africa, under French control. *n.*

tun nel (tun′əl), 1. underground passage. The railroad passes under the mountain through a tunnel. 2. make a tunnel. A mole tunnels in the ground. The workmen are tunneling under the river. *n., v., tunneled, tunneling. 5.*

tun ny (tun′i), a large sea fish used for food; the tuna. *n., pl. tunnies. 20.*

tu pe lo (tü′pi lō), a large North American tree with strong, tough wood. *n., pl. tupelos.*

tup pence (tup′əns), two pence; two British pennies. Tuppence equals about four cents. *n. 20.*

tur ban (tėr′bən), 1. a scarf wound around the head or around a cap, worn by men in Oriental countries. 2. a headdress like this. The Negro woman wore a bright-colored turban. 3. small hat with little or no brim, worn by women and children. *n. 7.*

Oriental turban

tur bid (tėr′bid), muddy; thick; not clear; as, a turbid river. *adj. 14.*

tur bine (tėr′bin), an engine or motor in which a wheel with vanes is made to revolve by the force of water, steam, or air. *n. 19.*

tur bot (tėr′bət), 1. a large European flatfish, much valued as food. 2. a similar fish. Some flounders are called turbot. *n., pl. turbots* or *turbot. 20.*

tur bu lence (tėr′bū ləns), disorder; tumult; commotion. *n. 11.*

tur bu lent (tėr′bū lənt), 1. disorderly; unruly; violent. 2. greatly disturbed. *adj. 7.*

tu reen (tü rēn′), a deep, covered dish for serving soup, etc. *n.*

turf (tėrf), 1. grass with its matted roots; sod. 2. piece of this. 3. cover with turf. 4. peat. 5. race track for horses. 6. horse racing. *n., v. 5.*

tur gid (tėr′jid), 1. swollen; bloated. 2. inflated; pompous; using big words and elaborate comparisons; bombastic. *adj. 16.*

Turk (tėrk), 1. person born in Turkey, living there, or having Turkish parents. 2. Mohammedan living in Turkey. *n. 5.*

Tur ke stan (tėr′kə stan′), region in western and central Asia. Part of Turkestan belongs to China, part to Russia, and part to Afghanistan. *n. 18.*

tur key (tėr′ki), 1. a large American bird. 2. the flesh of the turkey, used for food. See the picture in the next column. *n., pl. turkeys. 3.*

Tur key (tėr′ki), a country in western Asia and southeastern Europe. Many countries in southeastern Europe were formerly part of Turkey. *n.*

turkey buzzard, a vulture having a bare, reddish head and dark plumage. Turkey buzzards are common in the southern United States and in Central and South America.

Turk ish (tėr′kish), 1. of Turkey or the Turks; made in Turkey. 2. the language of the Turks. *adj., n. 5.*

tur moil (tėr′moil), commotion; disturbance; trouble. Six robberies in one night put our village in a turmoil. *n. 11.*

turn (tėrn), 1. move round as a wheel does. 2. cause to move round as a wheel does. I turned the crank three times. 3. motion like that of a wheel. At each turn the screw goes in further. 4. move part way round. Turn over on your back. 5. take a new direction. The road turns to the north here. 6. give a new direction to. Turn your thoughts to work. 7. change of direction. A turn to the left brought him in front of us. 8. change; change and become. She turned pale. 9. change. The sick man has taken a turn for the better. 10. spoil; sour. 11. become sour or spoiled. 12. make. He can turn pretty compliments. 13. change from one language into another. 14. form; style. He has a serious turn of mind. 15. unsettle; put out of order. Too much praise turned his head. 16. depend. The success of the picnic turns on the weather. 17. twist. 18. opportunity; occasion. It is Bob's turn to read. 19. deed; act. One good turn deserves another. 20. a walk, drive, or ride. 21. make sick. 22. become dizzy. 23. Some special meanings are:

by turns, one after another.

in turn, in proper order.

to a turn, to just the right degree.

turn off, 1. discharge. 2. do. 3. shut off. 4. turn aside. 5. put out (light).

turn on, 1. let come; let flow. 2. attack; resist; oppose.

turn out, 1. put out. 2. drive out. 3. come out; go out. 4. make; produce. 5. result. 6. be found or known.

Turkey (2 to 4 ft. long)

turn over, 1. think about. 2. give. *v., n. 1.*

turn coat (tėrn′kōt′), person who changes his party or principles; renegade. *n. 19.*

tur ner (tėr′nər), 1. person or thing that turns. 2. person who makes things with a lathe. *n. 12.*

tur nip (tėr′nip), 1. a plant with a large roundish root that is used as a vegetable. 2. this root. *n. 5.*

Turnip (def. 2)

turn key (tėrn′kē′), person in charge of the keys of a prison; a keeper of a prison. *n., pl. turnkeys. 19.*

turn out (tėrn′out′), 1. wide place in the road where vehicles may pass. 2. gathering of people. 3. equipment; way in which somebody or something is equipped. 4. output. *n.*

turn o ver (tėrn′ō′vər), 1. a turning over; an upset. 2. the amount of changing from one job to another. Employers wish to reduce labor turnover. 3. paying out and getting back the money involved in a business transaction. The store reduced prices to make a quick turnover. 4. the total amount of business done in a given time. He made a profit of $6000 on a turnover of $90,000. 5. small pie made by folding half the crust over the filling and upon the other half. 6. having a part that turns over; as, a turnover collar. *n., adj. 16.*

turn pike (tėrn′pīk′), 1. gate where toll is paid. 2. road that has, or used to have, a gate where toll is paid. *n. 13.*

turn spit (tėrn′spit′), one that turns a roast of meat on a spit. *n. 19.*

turn stile (tėrn′stīl′), post with two crossed bars that turn, set in an entrance. *n.*

tur pen tine (tėr′pən tīn), an oil obtained from various cone-bearing trees. Turpentine is used in mixing paints and varnishes, and in medicine. *n. 7.*

tur pi tude (tėr′pi tūd or tėr′pi tüd), shameful wickedness; baseness. *n. 16.*

tur quoise (tėr′koiz), 1. a sky-blue or greenish-blue precious stone. 2. sky blue; greenish blue. *n., adj. 12.*

tur ret (tėr′it), 1. small tower, often on the corner of a building. 2. a low armored structure which revolves and within which guns are mounted. *n. 6.*

Turrets of a building

tur ret ed (tėr′it id), having a turret or turrets. *adj.*

tur tle (tėr′təl), an animal having a hard shell and a soft body. All turtles are reptiles. To **turn turtle** is to turn bottom side up. *n. 4.*

Turtle

tur tle dove (tėr′təl-duv′), a kind of dove noted for the affection that mates have for each other. *n. 20.*

Tus can (tus′kən), 1. pertaining to Tuscany. 2. a native or inhabitant of Tuscany. 3. the form of Italian spoken in Tuscany. Tuscan is regarded as standard Italian. *adj., n. 11.*

Tus ca ny (tus′kə ni), a region in central Italy. Florence is its chief city. *n.*

tusk (tusk), a very long, pointed, projecting tooth. Elephants, walruses, and wild boars have tusks. *n. 14.*

tus sah (tus′ə), 1. a coarse Asiatic silk. 2. the silkworm that makes it. *n. 20.*

Tusks of a walrus

tus sle (tus′əl), struggle; wrestle; scuffle. *v., n. 14.*

tut (tut), an exclamation of impatience, contempt, or rebuke. *interj., n. 13.*

tu te lage (tū′ti lij or tü′ti lij), 1. guardianship; protection. 2. instruction. *n. 20.*

tu te lar (tū′ti lər or tü′ti lər), tutelary. *adj. 15.*

tu te lar y (tū′ti lãr′i or tü′ti lãr′i), 1. protecting. 2. of a guardian. *adj. 20.*

tu tor (tū′tər or tü′tər), 1. private teacher. Rich children sometimes have tutors instead of going to school. 2. instructor at a college or university. 3. teach; instruct. In some schools, the bright pupils tutor the dull ones. *n., v. 5.*

tu to ri al (tū tō′ri əl or tü tō′ri əl), 1. of a tutor. 2. using tutors. *adj.*

tux e do (tuk sē′dō), man's coat for evening wear, made without tails. *n., pl. tuxedos. 18.*

twad dle (twod′əl), 1. silly, feeble, tiresome talk or writing. 2. talk or write in such a way. *n., v.*

twain (twān), an old or poetic word for two. *n., adj. 6.*

Twain (twān), Mark, author of *Tom Sawyer* and *Huckleberry Finn.* His real name was Clemens (1835-1910). *n.*

twang (twang), 1. a sharp ringing sound. The bow made a twang when I shot the arrow. 2. make a sharp ringing sound. The banjos twanged. 3. a sharp nasal tone; as, the twang of a Yankee farmer. 4. speak with a sharp nasal tone. *n., v. 11.*

'twas (twoz), it was. *3.*

tweak (twēk), 1. seize and pull with a sharp jerk and twist. The parrot tweaked Fred's ear and cried, "Ha! Ha!" 2. a sharp pull and twist. *v., n.*

tweed (twēd), 1. a woolen cloth with a rough surface. Tweed is sometimes made of wool and cotton, and usually has two or more colors. 2. **Tweeds** are clothes made of tweed. *n. 8.*

tweet (twēt), the note of a young bird. We heard the "tweet, tweet" from a nest in the tree. *n., interj. 17.*

tweez ers (twēz′ərz), small pincers for pulling out hairs, picking up very small objects, etc. *n. pl. 13.*

Tweezers

twelfth (twelfth), 1. next after the 11th. Lincoln's birthday comes on February twelfth. 2. one of 12 equal parts. *adj., n. 4.*

twelve (twelv), one more than 11; 12. A year has twelve months. *n., adj. 1.*

twelve month (twelv′munth′), 12 months; a year. *n. 13.*

twen ti eth (twen′ti ith), 1. next after the 19th. 2. one of 20 equal parts. *adj., n. 6.*

twen ty (twen′ti), two times ten; 20. *n., pl. twenties, adj. 1.*

'twere (twėr), it were. *4.*

twice (twīs), 1. two times. Twice two is four. 2. doubly. *adv. 2.*

twid dle (twid′əl), 1. twirl; as, to twiddle one's thumbs. 2. play with idly. *v.*

twig (twig), slender shoot of a tree or other plant; very small branch. Dry twigs are good to start a fire with. *n. 3.*

twi light (twī′līt′), 1. the faint light reflected from the sky before the sun rises and after it sets. 2. of twilight; as, the twilight hour. 3. like that of twilight. *n., adj. 3.*

twill (twil), 1. cloth woven in raised diagonal lines. Serge is a twill. 2. weave (cloth) in this way. *n., v. 12.*

'twill (twil), it will. *4.*

twin (twin), 1. one of two children or animals born at the same time from the same mother. Twins sometimes look just alike. 2. being one of two things very much alike. 3. having two like parts. *n., adj. 3.*

twine (twīn), 1. a strong thread or string made of two or more strands twisted together. 2. twist together. She twined holly into wreaths. 3. wind. The vine twines around the tree. 4. a twist; twisted thing. *n., v. 4.*

twinge (twinj), 1. a sudden sharp pain; as, a twinge of rheumatism, a twinge of remorse. 2. feel such pain. 3. cause such pain in. *n., v. 12.*

twin kle (twing′kəl), 1. shine with quick little gleams. Stars twinkle. Jack's eyes twinkled when he laughed. 2. a twinkling; sparkle. 3. move quickly. The dancer's feet twinkled. *v., n. 3.*

twin kling (twing′kling), 1. a quick little gleam. 2. an instant. *n.*

twirl (twėrl), 1. revolve rapidly; spin; whirl. 2. turn round and round idly. 3. twirling; spin; whirl; turn; as, a twirl in a dance. *v., n. 11.*

twist (twist), 1. turn; wind. She twisted her ring on her finger. 2. wind together. This rope is twisted from many threads. Mary twisted flowers into a wreath. 3. have a winding shape; curve or bend in any way. The path twists in and out among the rocks. 4. curve; crook; bend. 5. force out of shape or place. His face was twisted with pain. The lawyer confused the witness by twisting his words into different meanings. 6. twisting; being twisted. 7. anything made by twisting; as, a twist of bread. 8. a thread, cord, or rope made of two or more strands twisted together. *v., n. 3.*

twit (twit), 1. reproach; taunt; jeer at; tease. 2. a reproach; a taunt. *v., twitted, twitting, n. 14.*

twitch (twich), 1. move with a quick jerk. The child's mouth twitched as if she were about to cry. 2. a quick jerky movement of some part of the body. 3. pull with a sudden tug or jerk; pull (at). She twitched the curtain aside. 4. a short sudden pull or jerk. *v., n. 7.*

twit ter (twit′ər), 1. sound made by birds; chirping. 2. make such a sound. 3. excited condition. My nerves are in a twitter when I have to sing in public. 4. tremble with excitement. *n., v. 6.*

two (tü). We count one, two, three, four. Two means 2. *n., pl. twos, adj. 1.*

two fold (tü′fōld′), 1. two times as much or as many; double. 2. having two parts. *adj., adv., n. 10.*

two pence (tup′əns), two pence; two British pennies. Twopence equals about four cents. *n.*

two pen ny (tup′ən i), 1. worth twopence. 2. trifling; worthless. *adj.*

two-step (tü′step′), 1. a dance in march time. 2. music for it. *n.*

'twould (twůd), it would. *13.*

-ty[1], suffix meaning:—tens; as in sixty, seventy, eighty.

-ty[2], suffix meaning:—fact, quality, state, condition, etc., of being ———; as in safety, sovereignty, surety. *-ity* is often used instead of *-ty;* as in artificiality, complexity, humidity.

ty ing (tī′ing). See **tie.** He is tying his shoes. *ppr. of tie.*

Ty ler (tī′lər), John (1790-1862), tenth president of the United States, from 1841 to 1845. *n. 14.*

tym pan ic (tim pan′ik), of the eardrum or the middle ear. The **tympanic membrane** separates the middle ear from the external ear and is called the eardrum. *adj. 18.*

tym pa num (tim′pə nəm), 1. the eardrum. 2. the middle ear. *n. 14.*

Tyne (tīn), a river in northern England, flowing into the North Sea. *n. 14.*

type (tīp), 1. a kind, class, or group having common characteristics. Some men prefer women of the blonde type. 2. person or thing having the characteristics of a kind, class, or group; representative; symbol. John is a fine type of schoolboy. 3. the general form, style, or character of some kind, class, or group. Mary is above the ordinary type of servant. 4. piece of metal or wood having on its upper surface a letter for use in printing. 5. collection of such pieces. 6. typewrite. *n., v. 3.*

Four sizes of type

school	5 point
school	8 point
school	10 point
school	14 point

Some kinds of type

school	*italic*
school	**boldface**
school	roman
School	Old English

type write (tīp′rīt′), write with a typewriter. *v., typewrote, typewritten, typewriting.*

type writ er (tīp′rīt′ər), 1. machine for making letters on paper. 2. typist. *n. 5.*

type writ ing (tīp′rīt′ing), 1. act or art of using a typewriter. Our school teaches typewriting. 2. work done on a typewriter. His typewriting is very clear and accurate. *n. 13.*

type writ ten (tīp′rit′ən), 1. done with a typewriter; as, a typewritten letter. 2. See **typewrite.** *adj., pp. of typewrite. 18.*

ty phoid (tī′foid), 1. **Typhoid fever** is an infectious, often fatal, fever, with intestinal inflammation, caused by a germ taken into the body with food or drink. People can be inoculated against typhoid. 2. of typhoid fever. 3. like typhus. *adj., n. 7.*

ty phoon (tī fün′), violent storm; hurricane. *n. 16.*

ty phus (tī′fəs), an acute, infectious disease caused by germs carried by fleas, lice, etc. *n. 18.*

typ i cal (tip′i kəl), being a type; representative. The typical Thanksgiving dinner consists of turkey, cranberry sauce, several vegetables, and mince pie or pumpkin pie. *adj. 12.*

typ i cal ly (tip′i kəl i), 1. in a typical manner. 2. to a typical degree. 3. ordinarily. *adv.*

typ i fy (tip′i fī), 1. be a symbol of. The lamb typifies Christ's sacrifice. 2. have the common characteristics of. Daniel Boone typifies the pioneer. *v., typified, typifying. 11.*

typ ist (tīp′ist), person operating a typewriter; person who does typewriting as a regular occupation. *n. 16.*

ty ran nic (ti ran′ik), tyrannical. *adj. 16.*

ty ran ni cal (ti ran′i kəl), of a tyrant; like a tyrant; arbitrary; cruel or unjust. Charles I of England was a tyrannical king. *adj. 10.*

tyr an nize (tir′ə nīz), 1. rule as a tyrant. 2. rule cruelly; oppress. *v. 15.*

tyr an nous (tir′ə nəs), acting like a tyrant; arbitrary; cruel or unjust. The Stamp Act seemed tyrannous to the colonists. *adj. 11.*

tyr an ny (tir′ə ni), 1. cruel or unjust use of power. The boy ran away to sea to escape his father's tyranny. 2. tyrannical act. The colonists rebelled against the king's tyrannies. 3. government by an absolute ruler. *n., pl. tyrannies. 4.*

ty rant (tī′rənt), 1. cruel or unjust ruler; cruel master. 2. absolute ruler. Some tyrants of Greek cities were mild and just rulers. *n. 4.*

Tyre (tīr), an ancient city in Phoenicia, noted for its wealth and wickedness. *n. 9.*

Tyr i an (tir′i ən), 1. of or pertaining to Tyre. **Tyrian purple** was a famous dye. 2. a native of Tyre. *adj., n. 16.*

ty ro (tī′rō), beginner in learning anything; novice. Much practice changed the tyro into an expert. *n., pl. tyros. 18.*

Ty rol (ti rōl′), region in the Alps, formerly a part of Austria. Part of it is now in Germany, part in Italy. *n. 16.*

tzar (tsär), czar. *n.*

tza ri na (tsä rē′nə), czarina. *n.*

U

U, u (ū), the 21st letter of the alphabet. There are two u's in usual. *n., pl. U's, u's.*

u biq ui tous (ū bik′wi təs), being everywhere at the same time; present everywhere. *adj. 20.*

U-boat (ū′bōt′), German submarine. *n.*

ud der (ud′ər), the bag of a cow or goat from which the milk comes. *n. 9.*

ugh (ůh or u), an exclamation expressing disgust or horror. *interj.*

ug li ness (ug′li nis), ugly appearance; being ugly. *n. 15.*

ug ly (ug′li), 1. bad to look at; as, an ugly house, an ugly face. 2. disagreeable; unpleasant; bad; offensive; as, an ugly task, an ugly story, ugly language. 3. threatening; dangerous. 4. ill-natured; bad-tempered, quarrelsome. *Used in common talk. adj., uglier, ugliest. 2.*

u kase (ū kās′), 1. an order of the ruler or government of Russia. 2. any official proclamation or order. *n.*

U kraine (ū′krān), a Soviet republic in southwestern Russia. *n. 18.*

u ku le le (ū′kə lā′li), a small guitar having four strings. *n. 12.*

Boy playing a ukulele

ul cer (ul′sər), 1. open sore that discharges pus. 2. moral sore spot; corrupting influence. *n. 10.*

ul cer ate (ul′sər āt), affect or be affected with an ulcer; form an ulcer. An ulcerated tooth is very painful. *v. 20.*

ul ster (ul′stər), a long, loose, heavy overcoat. *n. 14.*

Ul ster (ul′stər), former province of Ireland, now divided between Eire and Northern Ireland. *n.*

ult., in the past month; as, your order of the 14th ult.

ul te ri or (ul tēr′i ər), 1. beyond what is seen or expressed; hidden. 2. more distant; on the farther side. 3. further; later. *adj. 18.*

ul ti mate (ul′ti mit), 1. last; final. 2. underlying; basic; elemental. The ultimate cause of life has not been discovered. *adj. 7.*

ul ti mate ly (ul′ti mit li), finally; in the end. *adv.*

ul ti ma tum (ul′ti mā′təm), a final proposal or statement of conditions. *n.*

ul tra (ul′trə), excessive; extreme; beyond what is usual. *adj. 18.*

ultra-, prefix meaning:—
1. beyond; as in ultraviolet rays.
2. very; excessively; extremely; beyond what is usual; as in ultraexclusive, ultramodern.

ul tra ma rine (ul′trə mə rēn′), 1. deep blue. 2. blue paint made from powdered lapis lazuli; artificial imitation of this which is sometimes green or purple. 3. beyond the sea. *n., adj.*

ul tra vi o let (ul′trə vī′ə lit), beyond the violet. The invisible rays of the spectrum beyond the violet end are called the **ultraviolet rays.** They are important in promoting growth and preventing disease. *adj. 20.*

U lys ses (ū lis′ēz), the shrewdest Greek leader in the Trojan War; Odysseus. Ulysses is the hero of the *Odyssey*, which tells about his adventures. *n. 6.*

um bel (um′bəl), flower cluster in which stalks nearly equal in length spring from a common center. *n.*

Umbel

um ber (um′bər), 1. a brown paint. 2. a reddish-brown paint. 3. brown or reddish brown. *n., adj. 18.*

um brage (um′brij), 1. resentment; suspicion that one has been slighted or injured; feeling offended. 2. shade. *n. 14.*

um bra geous (um brā′jəs), 1. shady. 2. apt to take offense. *adj. 16.*

um brel la (um brel′ə), a light, folding frame covered with cloth, used as a protection against rain or sun. *n. 4.*

um pire (um′pīr), 1. person who rules on the plays in a game. The umpire called the ball a foul. 2. person chosen to settle a dispute. 3. act as umpire in (a game, dispute, etc.). *n., v. 9.*

un-, 1. a prefix used before adjectives and nouns meaning not; the opposite of. 2. a prefix used before verbs meaning the opposite of the action of the verb, as in unbend, undress, unfasten.

un a bashed (un′ə basht′), not embarrassed, ashamed, or awed. *adj. 19.*

un a ble (un ā′bəl), not able. A little baby is unable to walk or talk. *adj. 5.*

un a bridged (un′ə brijd′), complete; not shortened. *adj.*

un ac com pa nied (un′ə kum′pə nid), 1. alone. 2. in music, without an accompaniment. *adj.*

un ac count a ble (un′ə koun′tə bəl), 1. that cannot be accounted for or explained. 2. not responsible. *adj. 15.*

un ac count a bly (un′ə koun′tə bli), in a way that cannot be explained; without reason; strangely. *adv.*

un ac cus tomed (un′ə kus′təmd), 1. not accustomed. 2. unusual. *adj. 12.*

un ac quaint ed (un′ə kwān′tid), not acquainted. *adj. 11.*

un a dul ter at ed (un′ə dul′tər āt′id), not adulterated; pure. *adj. 18.*

un ad vis ed ly (un′əd vīz′id li), in an indiscreet manner; rashly. *adv. 13.*

un af fect ed[1] (un′ə fek′tid), not affected; not influenced. *adj. 10.*

un af fect ed[2] (un′ə fek′tid), 1. sincere. 2. simple and natural. *adj.*

un aid ed (un ād′id), not aided; without help. *adj. 16.*

un al ter a ble (un ôl′tər ə bəl), that cannot be altered; not changeable. *adj. 11.*

un al tered (un ôl′tərd), unchanged. *adj. 13.*

u na nim i ty (ū′nə nim′i ti), complete accord or agreement. *n. 13.*

u nan i mous (ū nan′i məs), in complete accord or agreement; agreed. George was elected president of his class by a unanimous vote. *adj. 7.*

u nan i mous ly (ū nan′i məs li), with complete agreement; without a single opposing vote. *adv.*

un an swer a ble (un an′sər ə bəl), 1. that cannot be answered. 2. that cannot be disproved. *adj. 16.*

un ap proach a ble (un′ə prōch′ə bəl), 1. very hard to approach; distant. 2. unrivaled; without an equal. *adj. 18.*

un arm (un ärm′), 1. take weapons or armor from; disarm. 2. take off (one's) armor. *v. 7.*

un armed (un ärmd′), without weapons; without armor. *adj.*

un as sum ing (un′ə süm′ing), modest; not putting on airs. *adj. 16.*

un at tend ed (un′ə ten′did), 1. without attendants; alone. 2. not accompanied. 3. not taken care of; not attended to. *adj.*

un a vail ing (un′ə vāl′ing), not successful; useless. *adj. 13.*

un a void a ble (un′ə void′ə bəl), that cannot be avoided. *adj. 13.*

un a ware (un′ə wãr′), 1. not aware; unconscious. The child was unaware of any danger from the snake. 2. without thought; unawares. *adj., adv. 5.*

un a wares (un′ə wãrz′), 1. without knowing; as, "to entertain angels unawares." 2. without being expected; by surprise. The police caught the burglar unawares. *adv.*

un bal anced (un bal′ənst), 1. not balanced. 2. not entirely sane; as, an unbalanced mind. *adj. 12.*

un bar (un bär′), unlock; remove the bars from. *v., unbarred, unbarring. 18.*

un be com ing (un′bi kum′ing), 1. not suiting; not appropriate. 2. not fitting; not proper. *adj. 11.*

un be lief (un′bi lēf′), lack of belief; lack of faith. *n. 10.*

un be liev er (un′bi lēv′ər), 1. one who does not believe. 2. one who does not believe in a particular religion. *n. 15.*

In each of the words below **un** *means* not; *the pronunciation of the main part of the word is not changed, but the syllable* **un** *has a slight secondary accent.*

unabated *16.*	unaccredited	unambiguous	unapproved	unauthorized *15.*
unabetted	unacknowledged	unambitious *17.*	unarrested	unavailable
unabsolved	unadaptable	unamiable	unartistic	unavenged
unacademic	unadjustable	unanimated	unashamed	unavowed
unaccented	unadjusted	unannounced	unasked *16.*	unbaptized
unacceptable	unadorned	unappeased	unassisted *16.*	unbarbed
unacclimated	unafraid	unappetizing	unattainable	unbearable *12.*
unacclimatized	unallied	unappreciated	unattempted	unbefitting
unaccommodating	unallowable	unappreciative	unattractive	unbeholden
unaccomplished	unalloyed *20.*	unapproached	unauthentic	
unaccounted-for *20.*	unaltering	unappropriated	unauthenticated	

un be liev ing (un′bi lēv′ing), not believing; doubting. *adj. 13.*

un bend (un bend′), 1. make or become straight. 2. release from strain. 3. unfasten. 4. relax. The judge unbent and behaved like a boy. *v., unbent* or *unbended, unbending.*

un bend ing (un ben′ding), 1. not bending or curving; rigid. 2. firm; not yielding. 3. relaxation. *adj., n.*

un bi ased or **un bi assed** (un bī′əst), not prejudiced; impartial; fair. *adj. 11.*

un bid den (un bid′ən), 1. not bidden; not invited. 2. not commanded. *adj. 13.*

un bind (un bīnd′), untie; unfasten; let loose; release from bonds or restraint. *v., unbound, unbinding. 15.*

un blem ished (un blem′isht), spotless; flawless. *adj. 13.*

un blessed or **un blest** (un blest′), 1. not blessed. 2. evil. 3. unhappy. *adj. 15.*

un blush ing (un blush′ing), not blushing; shameless. *adj. 19.*

un bolt (un bōlt′), draw back the bolts of (a door, etc.). *v.*

un born (un bôrn′), not yet born; still to come; of the future. *adj. 9.*

un bos om (un bu̇z′əm), disclose; reveal. **Unbosom oneself** means tell one's feelings, thoughts, or secrets. *v. 18.*

un bound (un bound′), not bound. Unbound sheets of music were scattered about the room. *adj., pt. and pp. of* **unbind.** *6.*

un bound ed (un boun′did), 1. not limited; boundless; very great. 2. not kept within limits; not controlled. *adj.*

un bri dled (un brī′dəld), 1. not having a bridle on. 2. not controlled. *adj. 13.*

un bro ken (un brō′kən), 1. not broken; whole. 2. continuous; not interrupted. He had eight hours of unbroken sleep. 3. not tamed. *adj. 8.*

un buck le (un buk′əl), 1. unfasten the buckle or buckles of. 2. unfasten. *v. 17.*

un but ton (un but′ən), unfasten the button or buttons of. *v. 20.*

un called-for (un kôld′fôr′), 1. not called for. 2. unnecessary and improper; as, an uncalled-for remark. *adj. 17.*

un can ny (un kan′i), strange and mysterious; weird. The trees took uncanny shapes in the half darkness. *adj.*

un ceas ing (un sēs′ing), continual. *adj. 14.*

un cer tain (un sėr′tən), 1. not certain; doubtful. Alice came so late that she was uncertain of her welcome. 2. likely to change; not to be depended on. This dog has an uncertain temper. *adj. 4.*

un cer tain ty (un sėr′tən ti), 1. uncertain state or condition; doubt. 2. something uncertain. *n., pl. uncertainties. 9.*

un chain (un chān′), free from chains; let loose; set free. *v. 15.*

un change a ble (un chān′jə bəl), that cannot be changed. *adj. 12.*

un changed (un chāngd′), not changed; the same. *adj. 8.*

un char i ta ble (un char′i tə bəl), severe; harsh; not generous; not charitable. *adj. 20.*

un chart ed (un chär′tid), not mapped; not marked on a chart. *adj. 19.*

un chaste (un chāst′), not chaste; not virtuous. *adj. 20.*

un checked (un chekt′), not checked; not restrained. *adj. 11.*

un chris tian (un kris′chən), 1. not Christian. 2. unworthy of Christians. *adj. 15.*

un civ il (un siv′il), not civil; rude; impolite. *adj. 16.*

un civ i lized (un siv′i līzd), not civilized; barbarous; savage. *adj.*

un clasp (un klasp′), 1. unfasten. 2. release from a clasp or grasp. *v. 19.*

un cle (ung′kəl), 1. brother of one's father or mother. 2. husband of one's aunt. *n. 1.*

un clean (un klēn′), 1. dirty; not clean. 2. not pure morally; evil. *adj. 6.*

un clean ly (un klen′li), dirty; filthy; impure. *adj.*

Uncle Sam, the government or people of the United States.

un close (un klōz′), to open. *v. 16.*

un clothed (un klōᴛʜd′), uncovered; undressed; naked. *adj.*

un coil (un koil′), unwind. *v.*

un com fort a ble (un kum′fər tə bəl), 1. not comfortable. 2. uneasy. 3. disagreeable; causing discomfort. *adj. 5.*

In each of the words below **un** *means* not; *the pronunciation of the main part of the word is not changed, but the syllable* **un** *has a slight secondary accent.*

unbeseeming
unbetrothed
unbewailed
unblamable
unblamed *16.*
unbought
unbraced
unbranched
unbranded
unbrotherly
unbruised
unburied *16.*
unburned *17.*
unburnt
uncanceled
uncared-for
uncaught
uncensored
uncensured
unchained
unchallenged
unchanging
unchaperoned
uncharged
unchastened
unchastised
unchivalrous
unchristened
unclaimed *20.*
unclassified
uncleaned
uncleared
unclosed
unclouded *13.*
uncoated
uncocked
uncoerced
uncollected
uncolored
uncombined
uncomely
uncomforted

un com mon (un kom′ən), 1. rare; unusual. 2. remarkable. *adj. 8.*
un com mon ly (un kom′ən li), 1. rarely; unusually. 2. especially. *adv.*
un com pro mis ing (un kom′prə mīz′ing), unyielding; firm. *adj. 19.*
un con cern (un′kən sėrn′), lack of concern; lack of interest; freedom from care or anxiety; indifference. *n. 8.*
un con cerned (un′kən sėrnd′), not concerned; not interested; free from care or anxiety; indifferent. *adj.*
un con di tion al (un′kən dish′ən əl), without conditions; absolute. *adj. 15.*
un con di tion al ly (un′kən dish′ən əl i), without any conditions. *adv.*
un con nect ed (un′kə nek′tid), separated; disconnected. *adj. 16.*
un con quer a ble (un kong′kər ə bəl), that cannot be conquered. *adj. 11.*
un con scious (un kon′shəs), 1. not conscious. 2. not aware. 3. not meant; not intended; as, unconscious neglect. *adj. 4.*
un con scious ness (un kon′shəs nis), unconscious condition; insensibility. *n. 15.*
un con sti tu tion al (un′kon sti tū′shən əl or un′kon sti tü′shən əl), contrary to the constitution; not constitutional. *adj. 13.*
un con trolled (un′kən trōld′), not controlled; not restrained. *adj. 13.*
un cork (un kôrk′), pull the cork from. *v. 20.*
un count ed (un koun′tid), 1. not counted; not reckoned. 2. very many; innumerable. *adj.*
un cou ple (un kup′əl), disconnect; unfasten. *v. 20.*
un cour te ous (un kėr′ti əs), discourteous; impolite; rude. *adj. 18.*
un couth (un küth′), 1. awkward; clumsy; crude; as, uncouth manners. 2. unusual and unpleasant; strange. *adj. 7.*
un cov er (un kuv′ər), 1. remove the cover from. 2. reveal; expose; make known. 3. remove one's hat or cap. *v. 5.*
unc tion (ungk′shən), 1. anointing with oil, ointment, or the like, for medical purposes or as a religious rite. The priest gave the dying man Extreme Unction. 2. the oil, ointment, or the like, used for anointing. 3. something soothing or comforting; as, the unction of flattery. 4. a soothing, sympathetic, and persuasive quality in speaking. 5. fervor; earnestness; affected earnestness. *n. 15.*
unc tu ous (ungk′chü əs), 1. like an oil or ointment; oily; greasy; soapy. 2. soothing, sympathetic, and persuasive. 3. too smooth and oily; as, the salesman's unctuous manner. *adj. 10.*
un cul ti vat ed (un kul′ti vāt′id), not cultivated; wild; undeveloped. *adj. 16.*
un curl (un kėrl′), straighten out. *v.*
un daunt ed (un dôn′tid), not afraid; not discouraged; fearless. The captain was an undaunted leader. *adj. 9.*
un de ceive (un′di sēv′), free from error, mistake, or deception. *v. 20.*
un de cid ed (un′di sīd′id), 1. not decided or settled. 2. having one's mind not made up. *adj. 13.*
un de filed (un′di fīld′), pure; not defiled. *adj. 11.*
un de fined (un′di fīnd′), 1. not defined or explained. 2. indefinite. *adj. 20.*
un de ni a ble (un′di nī′ə bəl), 1. not to be denied. 2. unquestionably good; excellent. *adj.*
un de ni a bly (un′di nī′ə bli), beyond denial or dispute; certainly. *adv. 13.*
un der (un′dər), 1. below; beneath. The book fell under the table. 2. less than. The coat will cost under ten dollars. 3. lower; as, the under lip. 4. *Under* is used for many relations that suggest the idea of being below or beneath. Some are: The witness spoke under oath. The soldiers acted under orders. We learned a great deal under her teaching. *prep., adv., adj. 1.*

In each of the words below **un** *means* not; *the pronunciation of the main part of the word is not changed, but the syllable* **un** *has a slight secondary accent.*

uncompanionable
uncomplaining
uncomplaisant
uncompleted
uncomplimentary
uncompounded
uncomprehending
uncompromised
unconcealed
unconcerted
unconfined
unconfirmed
uncongealed
uncongenial
unconquered *11.*
unconsecrated
unconsidered
unconstrained
unconsumed
uncontaminated
uncontested
uncontradicted
unconverted
unconvinced
unconvincing
uncooked *20.*
uncorked
uncorrected
uncorroborated
uncorrupted *16.*
uncreated *16.*
uncritical
uncultured
uncurbed
uncured *19.*
uncurrent
uncurtained
uncut *15.*
undamaged
undamped
undated
undaughterly
undazzled
undecayed
undeceived
undeciphered
undeclared
undecorated
undefeated
undefended *20.*
undefensible
undelayed
undelivered
undemocratic
undemonstrable
undemonstrative
undependable
undepreciated

under-, prefix meaning:—
1. below; beneath; as in underline.
2. lower in rank; subordinate; as in undersheriff.
3. lower than; as in undersell.
4. not sufficiently; as in underfed.
5. below normal; as in undersized.
6. being beneath; worn beneath; as in underclothes.

un der bid (un′dər bid′), make a lower bid than (another). *v., underbid, underbidding.*

un der brush (un′dər brush′), bushes, small trees, etc., growing under large trees in woods or forests. *n. 10.*

un der clothes (un′dər klōz′), clothes worn under a suit or dress. *n. pl. 19.*

un der cur rent (un′dər kėr′ənt), 1. current below the upper currents, or below the surface, of a body of water, air, etc. 2. underlying tendency. There was an undercurrent of melancholy beneath Lincoln's jokes. *n. 19.*

un der done (un′dər dun′), not cooked enough; cooked very little. *adj.*

un der es ti mate (un′dər es′ti māt for 1, un′dər es′ti mit for 2), 1. to estimate at too low a value, amount, rate, or the like. 2. an estimate that is too low. *v., n.*

un der fed (un′dər fed′), fed too little; not well nourished. *adj.*

un der foot (un′dər fůt′), 1. under one's feet; on the ground. 2. in the way. *adv. 17.*

un der gar ment (un′dər gär′mənt), garment worn under a dress or suit. *n.*

un der go (un′dər gō′), 1. go through; pass through; be subjected to. The town has undergone a great change during the last five years. 2. endure; suffer. Soldiers undergo many hardships. *v., underwent, undergone, undergoing. 5.*

un der gone (un′dər gôn′). See **undergo.** *pp. of undergo. 12.*

un der grad u ate (un′dər graj′ü it), student in a school, college, or university who has not completed his course of study. *n. 18.*

un der ground (un′dər ground′ for 1 and 4, un′dər ground′ for 2, 3, and 5), 1. beneath the surface of the ground. 2. being, working, or used beneath the surface of the ground. 3. place or space beneath the surface of the ground. 4. secretly. 5. secret. *adv., adj., n. 5.*

un der growth (un′dər grōth′), bushes, small trees, etc., growing under large trees in woods or forests. *n. 15.*

un der hand (un′dər hand′), 1. secret; sly; not open or honest. 2. secretly; slyly. 3. with the hand below the shoulder; as, to pitch underhand. *adj., adv. 18.*

un der hand ed (un′dər han′did), underhand; secret; sly; not open or honest. *adj.*

un der lie (un′dər lī′), 1. lie under; be beneath. 2. be at the basis of; form the foundation of. *v., underlay, underlain, underlying. 18.*

un der line (un′dər līn′), draw a line under. In writing, we underline titles of books. *v. 9.*

un der ling (un′dər ling), an inferior; person of lower rank or position. *n. 16.*

un der ly ing (un′dər lī′ing), 1. lying under or beneath. 2. fundamental; basic; essential. 3. See **underlie.** *adj., ppr. of underlie.*

un der mine (un′dər mīn′), 1. dig under; make a passage or hole under. The soldiers undermined the wall. 2. wear away the foundations of. The cliff was undermined by the waves. 3. weaken by secret or unfair means; as, to undermine a man's reputation by scandal. 4. weaken or destroy gradually. Many severe colds had undermined Jane's health. *v. 12.*

un der most (un′dər mōst), lowest. *adj., adv.*

un der neath (un′dər nēth′), beneath; below; under. *prep., adv. 3.*

un der nour ished (un′dər nėr′isht), not sufficiently nourished. *adj.*

un der rate (un′dər rāt′), rate or estimate too low; put too low a value on. *v. 20.*

un der score (un′dər skōr′), underline. *v. 20.*

un der sell (un′dər sel′), sell things at a lower price than. This store can undersell other stores because it sells for cash. *v., undersold, underselling. 17.*

un der shirt (un′dər shėrt′), shirt worn next the skin under other clothing. *n. 13.*

un der shot (un′dər shot′), 1. having the lower jaw projecting beyond the upper. 2. driven by water passing beneath; as, an undershot water wheel. *adj.*

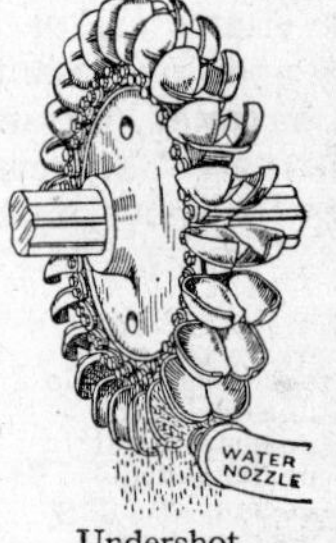

Undershot wheel

un der side (un′dər sīd′), surface lying underneath; bottom side. *n.*

un der sign (un′dər sīn′), sign one's name at the end of (a letter or document). **The undersigned** means the person or persons who have undersigned a letter or document. *v.*

un der stand (un′dər stand′), 1. get the meaning. 2. get the meaning of. He does not understand the question. 3. know well; know how to deal with. A good teacher should understand children. 4. be informed; learn. I understand that Mr. Jones is leaving town. 5. take as a fact; believe. It is understood that you will come. 6. supply in the mind. In "He hit the tree harder than I," the word *did* is understood after *I*. *v., understood, understanding. 1.*

un der stand ing (un′dər stan′ding), 1. comprehension; knowledge; as, a clear understanding of the problem. 2. intelligence; ability to learn and know. Edison was a man of understanding. 3. knowledge of each other's meaning and wishes; agreement. You and I must come to an understanding. 4. that understands; intelligent. *n., adj.*

un der state (un′dər stāt′), state too weakly; say less than the full truth about. *v.*

un der stood (un′dər stu̇d′). See **understand.** Have all of you understood today's lesson? *pt. and pp. of understand. 3.*

un der stud y (un′dər stud′i), 1. learn (a part) in order to replace the regular performer when necessary. 2. a person who can act as a substitute for another. *v., n., pl. understudies.*

un der take (un′dər tāk′), 1. try; attempt. 2. agree to do; promise. *v., undertook, undertaken, undertaking. 3.*

un der tak er (un′dər tāk′ər for 1, un′dər-tāk′ər for 2), 1. person who undertakes something. 2. person who prepares the dead for burial and takes charge of funerals. *n. 13.*

un der tak ing (un′dər tāk′ing for 1 and 2, un′dər tāk′ing for 3), 1. a task; an enterprise. 2. a promise; a pledge. 3. the work of an undertaker. *n.*

un der tone (un′dər tōn′), 1. low tone; as, to talk in undertones. 2. a subdued color; a color seen through other colors. There was an undertone of brown beneath all the gold and crimson of autumn. 3. underlying quality or element; as, an undertone of sadness in her gaiety. *n. 19.*

un der took (un′dər tu̇k′). See **undertake.** John undertook more than he could do. *pt. of undertake. 9.*

un der tow (un′dər tō′), 1. any strong current below the surface, moving in a direction different from that of the surface current. 2. the backward flow from waves breaking on a beach. *n.*

un der val ue (un′dər val′ū), put too low a value on. *v.*

un der waist (un′dər wāst′), waist worn under another waist. *n. 17.*

un der wa ter (un′dər wô′tər), 1. below the surface of the water. 2. made for use under the water. A submarine is an underwater ship. *adj.*

un der wear (un′dər wãr′), clothing worn under one's outer clothes. *n. 7.*

un der weight (un′dər wāt′), having too little weight. *adj.*

un der went (un′dər went′). See **undergo.** *pt. of undergo. 15.*

un der wood (un′dər wu̇d′), shrubs or small trees growing under larger trees; underbrush. *n. 11.*

un der world (un′dər wėrld′), 1. the lower world; Hades. 2. the lower, degraded, or criminal part of human society. *n. 17.*

un der write (un′dər rīt′), 1. insure (property) against loss. 2. write under (other written matter); sign one's name to (a document, etc.). 3. agree to buy (all stock or bonds of a certain sort that are not bought by the public). The British loan was underwritten by American bankers. *v., underwrote, underwritten, underwriting.*

un de sir a ble (un′di zīr′ə bəl), objectionable; disagreeable. *adj. 12.*

un de vel oped (un′di vel′əpt), not fully grown; not put to full use. *adj. 11.*

un did (un did′). See **undo.** *pt. of undo.*

un dis ci plined (un dis′i plind), not disciplined; untrained; without proper control. *adj. 19.*

un dis guised (un′dis gīzd′), not disguised; frank; plain. *adj. 17.*

un dis mayed (un′dis mād′), not dismayed; not discouraged or afraid. *adj. 16.*

In each of the words below **un** *means* not; *the pronunciation of the main part of the word is not changed, but the syllable* **un** *has a slight secondary accent.*

undeserved *11.*
undeserving
undesignated
undesigned
undesired
undespairing
undetachable
undetected
undetermined
undeterred
undeviating
undevout *19.*
undifferentiated
undigested
undignified
undiluted
undiminished *14.*
undimmed
undiplomatic
undiscernible
undiscerning
undischarged
undisclosed
undiscovered *12.*
undiscriminating
undisheartened

un dis put ed (un′dis pūt′id), not disputed; not doubted. *adj. 10.*

un dis tin guish a ble (un′dis ting′gwish ə bəl), that cannot be distinguished. *adj. 19.*

un dis tin guished (un′dis ting′gwisht), not distinguished; commonplace. *adj. 14.*

un dis turbed (un′dis tėrbd′), not disturbed; not troubled; calm. *adj. 6.*

un di vid ed (un′di vīd′id), not divided; not shared; not distributed. *adj. 14.*

un do (un dü′), 1. unfasten; untie. Please undo the package. I undid the string. 2. do away with; spoil; destroy. 3. bring to ruin. *v., undid, undone, undoing. 5.*

un do ing (un dü′ing), 1. doing away with; spoiling; destroying. 2. cause of destruction or ruin. *n.*

un done (un dun′), 1. not done; not finished. 2. ruined. 3. See **undo.** *adj., pp. of undo. 6.*

un doubt ed (un dout′id), not doubted; accepted as true. *adj. 8.*

un doubt ed ly (un dout′id li), beyond doubt; surely; certainly. *adv.*

un draw (un drô′), draw back or away. She undrew the curtain. *v., undrew, undrawn, undrawing. 18.*

un dress[1] (un dres′), take the clothes off; strip. *v. 8.*

un dress[2] (un′dres′), informal dress; ordinary clothes. *n.*

un due (un dū′ or un dü′), 1. not fitting; improper; not right. 2. too great; too much. *adj. 10.*

un du late (un′jù lāt), 1. move in waves; as, undulating water. 2. have a wavy form or surface. *v. 10.*

un du la tion (un′jù lā′shən), 1. waving motion. 2. wavy form. 3. one of a series of wavelike bends, curves, swellings, etc. *n. 11.*

un du ly (un dū′li or un dü′li), 1. improperly. 2. excessively. *adv. 17.*

un dy ing (un dī′ing), deathless; immortal; eternal. *adj. 13.*

un earned (un ėrnd′), 1. not earned. 2. not deserved. *adj.*

un earth (un ėrth′), 1. dig up; as, to unearth a buried city. 2. discover; find out; as, to unearth a plot. *v. 15.*

un earth ly (un ėrth′li), 1. not of this world; supernatural. 2. strange; wild; weird; ghostly. *adj. 12.*

un eas i ly (un ēz′i li), in an uneasy manner; restlessly. *adv.*

un eas i ness (un ēz′i nis), lack of ease or comfort; restlessness; anxiety. *n. 8.*

un eas y (un ēz′i), 1. not comfortable. 2. restless; disturbed; anxious. 3. not easy in manner; awkward. *adj. 5.*

un em ployed (un′em ploid′), 1. not employed; not in use; having no work. 2. people out of work. *adj., n. pl. 9.*

un em ploy ment (un′em ploi′mənt), lack of employment; being out of work. *n.*

un e qual (un ē′kwəl), 1. not the same in amount, size, number, or value. 2. not fair; one-sided. 3. not enough. 4. not regular. *adj. 6.*

un e quiv o cal (un′i kwiv′ə kəl), clear; plain. *adj. 16.*

un err ing (un ėr′ing), making no mistakes; exactly right. *adj. 10.*

un e ven (un ē′vən), 1. not level; as, uneven ground. 2. not equal. 3. that cannot be divided by 2 without a remainder. 27 and 9 are uneven numbers. *adj. 6.*

un e vent ful (un′i vent′fəl), without important or striking occurrences. *adj.*

un ex am pled (un′eg zam′pəld), having no equal or like; without precedent or parallel; without anything like it. This man's run of 100 yards in 9$\frac{1}{5}$ seconds is unexampled. *adj. 15.*

un ex cep tion a ble (un′ek sep′shən ə bəl), beyond criticism; wholly admirable. *adj. 18.*

un ex pect ed (un′eks pek′tid), not expected. *adj. 4.*

un ex pect ed ly (un′eks pek′tid li), without being expected; in a way or to a degree that is not expected. *adv.*

un ex pe ri enced (un′eks pēr′i ənst), without experience or practice. *adj. 15.*

In each of the words below **un** *means* not; *the pronunciation of the main part of the word is not changed, but the syllable* **un** *has a slight secondary accent.*

undissociated
undissolved *19.*
undistinguishing
undistributed
undivulged
undomestic
undomesticated
undoubled
undoubting
undrained
undramatic
undraped
undreamed
undreamt
undressed
undrilled
undutiful
undyed
uneatable
uneaten
uneclipsed
uneconomical
unedifying
uneducated
uneffaced
uneliminated
unembarrassed
unembellished
unemotional
unemphatic
unenclosed
unencumbered
unendangered
unendorsed
unendurable
unenduring
unenforceable
unenforced
unengaged
unenjoyable
unenlightened
unenterprising
unenthusiastic
unenviable
unenvied *16.*
unenvious
unequipped
unestimated
unethical
unexaggerated
unexcelled
unexciting
unexecuted
unexhausted
unexpended
unexpired
unexplained
unexploded
unexplored
unexpressed
unexpressive
unexpurgated
unextinguished *15*
unfaded *17.*
unfading

un fail ing (un fāl′ing), never failing; always ready when needed. *adj. 13.*

un fair (un fãr′), unjust; not honest. *adj. 10.*

un faith ful (un fāth′fəl), not faithful; not true to duty or one's promises; faithless. *adj. 9.*

un fal ter ing (un fôl′tər ing), firm; steadfast; not hesitating. *adj. 19.*

un fa mil iar (un′fə mil′yər), 1. not well known; unusual; strange. That face is unfamiliar to me. 2. not acquainted. He is unfamiliar with the Greek language. *adj. 12.*

un fas ten (un fas′ən), undo; untie; loosen; open. *v. 16.*

un fath om a ble (un faᴛʜ′əm ə bəl), so deep that the bottom cannot be reached; too mysterious to be understood. *adj. 20.*

un fath omed (un faᴛʜ′əmd), not measured; not understood. *adj. 16.*

un fa vor a ble (un fā′vər ə bəl), not favorable; adverse; harmful. *adj. 10.*

un feel ing (un fēl′ing), 1. hard-hearted; cruel. 2. not able to feel. *adj. 13.*

un feigned (un fānd′), sincere; real. *adj. 13.*

un fet tered (un fet′ərd), without chains; free; without restraint. *adj. 15.*

un fin ished (un fin′isht), 1. not finished; not complete. 2. without some special finish; rough; not polished. *adj. 8.*

un fit (un fit′), 1. not fit; not suitable; not good enough. 2. make unfit; spoil. *adj., v., unfitted, unfitting. 5.*

un flinch ing (un flin′ching), not drawing back from difficulty, danger, or pain; firm; resolute. *adj. 13.*

un fold (un fōld′), 1. open the folds of; spread out; as, to unfold a napkin, to unfold your arms. 2. reveal; show; explain. *v. 5.*

un forced (un fōrst′), 1. not forced; not compelled; willing. 2. natural; spontaneous. *adj. 18.*

un fore seen (un′fōr sēn′), unexpected; not known beforehand. *adj. 15.*

un for get ta ble (un′fər get′ə bəl), that can never be forgotten. *adj. 17.*

un for tu nate (un fôr′chə nit), 1. not lucky; having bad luck. 2. not suitable; not fitting. 3. an unfortunate person. *adj., n. 3.*

un found ed (un foun′did), without foundation; baseless; as, an unfounded complaint. *adj. 14.*

un fre quent ed (un′fri kwen′tid), seldom visited; rarely used. *adj.*

un friend ly (un frend′li), 1. not friendly. 2. not favorable. *adj. 9.*

un fruit ful (un früt′fəl), not fruitful; barren; not productive. *adj. 10.*

un furl (un fėrl′), spread out; shake out; unfold. Unfurl the sail. *v. 9.*

un fur nished (un fėr′nisht), not furnished; without furniture. *adj. 13.*

un gain ly (un gān′li), awkward; clumsy. *adj. 15.*

un gen er ous (un jen′ər əs), mean. *adj. 13.*

un gen tle (un jen′təl), harsh; rough. *adj. 11.*

un god ly (un god′li), not religious; wicked; sinful. *adj. 12.*

un gov ern a ble (un guv′ər nə bəl), impossible to control; very hard to control or rule; unruly. *adj. 13.*

un gra cious (un grā′shəs), 1. rude; not polite. 2. unpleasant; disagreeable. *adj. 12.*

un grate ful (un grāt′fəl), 1. not grateful; not thankful. 2. unpleasant; disagreeable. *adj. 5.*

un ground ed (un groun′did), without foundation; without reasons. *adj.*

un guard ed (un gär′did), 1. not protected. 2. careless. *adj. 8.*

un guent (ung′gwənt), salve; ointment for sores, burns, etc. *n. 19.*

un hal lowed (un hal′ōd), 1. not made holy; not sacred. 2. wicked. *adj. 11.*

un hand (un hand′), let go; take the hands from. *v. 16.*

un hap pi ly (un hap′i li), 1. not happily. 2. unfortunately. 3. unsuitably. *adv.*

un hap pi ness (un hap′i nis), 1. sadness; sorrow; being unhappy. 2. bad luck; ill fortune. *n. 16.*

In each of the words below **un** *means* not; *the pronunciation of the main part of the word is not changed, but the syllable* **un** *has a slight secondary accent.*

unfashionable
unfastened
unfeasible
unfeathered
unfed
unfederated
unfelt *13.*
unfeminine
unfenced *20.*
unfermented
unfertilized
unfilial
unfilled
unfiltered
unfitting
unfixed
unflattering
unflavored
unforested
unforgetting
unforgivable
unforgiven
unforgiving
unforgotten
unformulated
unfortified
unframed
unfree
unfrequent *10.*
unfulfilled
ungallant
ungarnished
ungathered
ungentlemanly
ungifted
ungloved
ungoverned *19.*
ungraded
ungrammatical
unguided
unhampered
unhandicapped
unhandsome
unhanged

un hap py (un hap′i), 1. sad; sorrowful. 2. unlucky. 3. not suitable. *adj. 2.*

un har ness (un här′nis), take harness off from (a horse, etc.). *v.*

un health ful (un helth′fəl), bad for the health. *adj. 13.*

un health y (un hel′thi), 1. not possessing good health; not well; as, an unhealthy child. 2. hurtful to health; unwholesome; as, an unhealthy climate. 3. morally harmful. *adj. 9.*

un heard (un hėrd′), 1. not listened to. 2. not heard of; unknown. *adj. 6.*

un heard-of (un hėrd′ov′), never heard of; not known before. *adj. 20.*

un heed ed (un hēd′id), not heeded; disregarded; unnoticed. *adj. 8.*

un hinge (un hinj′), 1. take (a door, etc.) off its hinges. 2. remove the hinges from. 3. detach; separate from something. 4. unsettle; upset. Trouble has unhinged this poor man's mind. *v.*

un hitch (un hich′), free from being hitched; unfasten. *v.*

un ho ly (un hō′li), not holy; wicked; sinful. *adj. 13.*

un hook (un hu̇k′), 1. loosen from a hook. 2. undo by loosening a hook or hooks. 3. become loosed from hooks; become undone. *v.*

un horse (un hôrs′), throw from a horse's back; cause to fall from a horse. *v.*

un hurt (un hėrt′), not hurt; not harmed. *adj. 10.*

u ni corn (ū′ni kôrn), imaginary animal like a horse, but having a single long horn in the middle of its forehead. *n. 20.*

Unicorn

u ni fi ca tion (ū′ni fi kā′shən), 1. formation into one unit; union; as, the unification of many states into one nation. 2. making or being made more alike. The traffic laws of the different States need unification. *n. 14.*

u ni form (ū′ni fôrm), 1. always the same; not changing. The earth turns around at a uniform rate. 2. all alike; not varying. All the bricks have a uniform size. 3. clothes that are uniform in style, etc. Soldiers, policemen, and nurses wear uniforms. 4. clothe or furnish with a uniform. *adj., n., v. 3.*

u ni form i ty (ū′ni fôr′mi ti), uniform condition or character; sameness throughout. *n., pl. uniformities. 12.*

u ni fy (ū′ni fī), unite; make or form into one. *v., unified, unifying. 13.*

un i mag i na ble (un′i maj′i nə bəl), that cannot be imagined or thought of. *adj. 15.*

un im paired (un′im pãrd′), not impaired; not harmed or weakened. *adj. 15.*

un im peach a ble (un′im pēch′ə bəl), blameless; free from fault. *adj.*

un im por tant (un′im pôr′tənt), not important; insignificant; trifling. *adj. 8.*

un in hab it ed (un′in hab′i tid), not lived in; without inhabitants. *adj. 11.*

un in jured (un in′jərd), not hurt; not damaged. *adj. 12.*

un in tel li gi ble (un′in tel′i ji bəl), that cannot be understood. *adj. 13.*

un in ter rupt ed (un′in tə rup′tid), without interruption; continuous. *adj. 10.*

un in vit ed (un′in vīt′id), not invited; without an invitation. *adj. 14.*

un ion (ūn′yən), 1. joining of two or more persons or things into one. The United States was formed by the union of thirteen States. 2. number of persons, groups, states, etc., joined for some common purpose; a combination. The American colonies formed a union against England. **The Union** often means the United States. 3. group of workers joined together to protect and promote their interests. *n. 2.*

un ion ist (ūn′yən ist), 1. person who promotes or advocates union. 2. A **Unionist** was a supporter of the federal government of the United States in the Civil War. 3. member of a labor union. *n. 17.*

Union Jack, the British national flag.

Union of South Africa, British dominion in southern Africa.

In each of the words below **un** *means* not; *the pronunciation of the main part of the word is not changed, but the syllable* **un** *has a slight secondary accent.*

unharassed
unhardened
unharmed *19.*
unharmonious
unharnessed
unhatched
unheedful
unheeding
unheralded
unheroic
unhindered
unhonored
unhoped-for
unhoused
unhurried
unhurtful
unhygienic
unideal
unidentified
unidiomatic
unilluminated
unimaginative
unimpassioned
unimpeded
unimposing
unimpressionable
unimpressive
unimproved
uninclosed
unincorporated
unincumbered
uninfected
uninflammable
uninflected
uninfluenced
uninformed
uninhabitable
uninitiated
uninstructed
uninstructive
uninsured
unintelligent
unintended
unintentional
uninterested
uninteresting
unintermitted
unintermitting
uninventive
uninviting

Union of Soviet Socialist Republics, union of eleven Soviet republics in eastern Europe and western and northern Asia, the largest of which is Soviet Russia.

u nique (ū nēk′), 1. having no like or equal; being the only one of its kind. 2. rare; unusual. *adj. 9.*

u ni son (ū′ni sən), 1. agreement. The feet of marching soldiers move in unison. 2. agreement in pitch of two or more tones, voices, etc.; a sounding together at the same pitch. *n. 8.*

u nit (ū′nit), 1. a single thing or person. 2. any group of things or persons considered as one. The family is a social unit. 3. a standard quantity or amount. A foot is a unit of length; a pound is a unit of weight. 4. smallest whole number; 1. *n. 6.*

U ni tar i an (ū′ni tãr′i ən), 1. person who accepts the moral teachings of Jesus, but does not believe that he was divine. 2. of or pertaining to Unitarians. *n., adj.*

u nite (ū nīt′), join together; make one; become one. Several firms united to form one company. The class united in singing "America." *v. 1.*

United Kingdom, 1. Great Britain and Northern Ireland. 2. Great Britain and Ireland from 1801 to 1922.

United States, country in North America, extending from the Atlantic to the Pacific and from the Gulf of Mexico to Canada; United States of America. *13.*

United States of America, United States.

u ni ty (ū′ni ti), 1. oneness; being united. A circle has more unity than a row of dots. A nation has more unity than a group of tribes. 2. harmony. Brothers and sisters should live together in unity. 3. the number one (1). *n., pl. unities. 5.*

u ni ver sal (ū′ni vėr′səl), 1. of all; belonging to all; concerning all; done by all; general. Food, fire, and shelter are universal needs. 2. moving in all directions; as, a universal joint. *adj. 3.*

U ni ver sal ist (ū′ni vėr′səl ist), a member of a Protestant church holding the belief that all people will finally be saved. *n.*

u ni ver sal i ty (ū′ni vėr sal′i ti), being universal; existence everywhere. *n. 17.*

u ni ver sal ly (ū′ni vėr′səl i), 1. in every instance; without exception. 2. everywhere. *adv.*

u ni verse (ū′ni vėrs), all things; everything there is. Our world is but a small part of the universe. *n. 6.*

u ni ver si ty (ū′ni vėr′si ti), institution of learning of the highest grade. A university usually has schools of law, medicine, teaching, business, etc., as well as colleges for general instruction. *n., pl. universities. 3.*

un just (un just′), not just; not fair. *adj. 3.*

un kempt (un kempt′), 1. not combed. 2. neglected; untidy. *adj. 19.*

un kind (un kīnd′), harsh; cruel. *adj. 5.*

un kind ness (un kīnd′nis), 1. harshness; cruelty. 2. an unkind act. *n. 11.*

un known (un nōn′), not known; not familiar; strange. *adj. 2.*

un lace (un lās′), undo the laces of. *v. 18.*

un law ful (un lô′fəl), contrary to the law; against the law; forbidden. *adj. 9.*

un learn ed (un lėr′nid for 1, un lėrnd′ for 2), 1. not educated; ignorant. 2. not learned; known without being learned. *adj. 9.*

un leav ened (un lev′ənd), not leavened. Unleavened bread is made without yeast. *adj. 16.*

un less (un les′), if not. We shall go unless it rains. *conj. 2.*

un let tered (un let′ərd), 1. not educated. 2. not able to read or write. *adj. 11.*

un like (un līk′), 1. not like; different. 2. different from. *adj., prep. 4.*

un like ly (un līk′li), 1. not likely; not probable. 2. not likely to succeed. *adj. 14.*

un like ness (un līk′nis), being unlike; difference. *n.*

un lim it ed (un lim′i tid), 1. without limits; boundless. 2. indefinite. *adj. 8.*

un load (un lōd′), 1. remove (a load). 2. take the load from. 3. get rid of. 4. remove powder, shot, etc., from (gun). 5. discharge a cargo. The ship is unloading. *v. 8.*

un lock (un lok′), open the lock of; open (anything firmly closed). *v. 6.*

un looked-for (un lu̇kt′fôr′), unexpected; unforeseen. *adj. 10.*

un loose (un lüs′), let loose; set free; release. *v. 14.*

In each of the words below **un** *means* not; *the pronunciation of the main part of the word is not changed, but the syllable* **un** *has a slight secondary accent.*

unissued	unknowing *16.*	unladylike	unlighted	unliquidated
unjustifiable	unlabeled	unlaid	unlikeable	unlit
unkept	unlabelled	unlamented *19.*	unlined	
unknightly	unladen	unlicensed	unliquefied	

un loos en (un lüs′ən), unloose; loosen. *v.*
un love ly (un luv′li), without beauty or charm; unpleasing in appearance; unpleasant; objectionable; disagreeable. *adj.*
un luck y (un luk′i), not lucky; unfortunate; bringing bad luck. *adj. 7.*
un man (un man′), 1. deprive of the qualities of a man; weaken or break down the spirit of. 2. deprive of men; as, to unman a ship. *v., unmanned, unmanning. 13.*
un man ly (un man′li), not manly; weak; cowardly. *adj. 12.*
un man ner ly (un man′ər li), 1. having bad manners; discourteous. 2. with bad manners; rudely. *adj., adv. 18.*
un mask (un mask′), 1. remove a mask or disguise. The guests unmasked at midnight. 2. take off a mask or disguise from. 3. show the real nature of; expose. *v. 15.*
un match a ble (un mach′ə bəl), that cannot be matched or equaled. *adj. 17.*
un mean ing (un mēn′ing), without meaning; meaningless. *adj. 18.*
un meas ured (un mezh′ərd), 1. not measured or limited. 2. not restrained; excessive. *adj. 15.*
un meet (un mēt′), not fit; not proper; unsuitable. *adj. 13.*
un mer ci ful (un mėr′si fəl), having no mercy; showing no mercy; cruel. *adj. 13.*
un mind ful (un mīnd′fəl), regardless; heedless; careless. *adj. 16.*
un mis tak a ble (un′mis tāk′ə bəl), that cannot be mistaken or misunderstood; clear; plain; evident. *adj. 11.*
un mit i gat ed (un mit′i gāt′id), not made milder or softened. *adj.*
un mixed (un mikst′), not mixed; pure. *adj. 12.*
un mo lest ed (un′mō les′tid), not molested; undisturbed. *adj. 11.*
un mor al (un mor′əl), neither moral nor immoral; not perceiving or involving right and wrong. *adj.*
un moved (un müvd′), 1. not moved; firm. 2. not disturbed; indifferent. *adj. 8.*
un named (un nāmd′), 1. having no name. 2. not mentioned by name. *adj. 18.*
un nat u ral (un nach′ə rəl), not natural; not normal. *adj. 7.*
un nec es sar y (un nes′ə sãr′i), not necessary; needless. *adj. 5.*
un nerve (un nėrv′), deprive of nerve, firmness, self-control, etc. *v. 19.*
un no ticed (un nō′tist), 1. not observed. 2. not receiving any attention. *adj. 11.*
un num bered (un num′bərd), 1. not numbered; not counted. 2. too many to count. *adj. 12.*
un ob served (un′əb zėrvd′), not observed; not noticed; disregarded. *adj. 9.*
un ob tru sive (un′əb trü′siv), modest; inconspicuous. *adj. 20.*
un oc cu pied (un ok′ū pīd), not occupied; vacant; idle. *adj. 7.*
un of fend ing (un′ə fen′ding), inoffensive; harmless; innocent. *adj. 20.*
un pack (un pak′), 1. take out (things packed in a box, trunk, etc.). 2. take things out of. *v. 11.*
un paid (un pād′), not paid. His unpaid bills amounted to $20. *adj. 10.*
un par al leled (un par′ə leld), having no parallel; unequaled; matchless. *adj. 13.*
un peo ple (un pē′pəl), deprive of people. *v. 12.*
un pin (un pin′), take out a pin or pins from; unfasten. *v., unpinned, unpinning.*
un pit ied (un pit′id), not pitied. *adj. 11.*
un pleas ant (un plez′ənt), not pleasant; disagreeable. *adj. 5.*
un pleas ant ness (un plez′ənt nis), 1. unpleasant quality. 2. something unpleasant. 3. quarrel. *n. 19.*

In each of the words below **un** *means* not; *the pronunciation of the main part of the word is no changed, but the syllable* **un** *has a slight secondary accent.*

unlovable
unloved
unloving
unmaidenly
unmalleable
unmanageable
unmanned
unmanufactured
unmarked
unmarketable
unmarriageable
unmarried *8.*
unmastered
unmatched *19.*
unmechanical
unmelted
unmentioned
unmerited
unmethodical
unmilitary
unmingled
unmirthful
unmistaken
unmodified
unmodulated
unmotivated
unmounted
unmourned
unmovable *19.*
unmusical
unmuzzled
unnaturalized
unnavigable
unneedful
unnegotiable
unneighborly
unneighbourly
unnoted
unnoticeable
unobjectionable
unobliging
unobscured
unobservant
unobserving
unobstructed
unobtainable
unoccasioned
unoffered
unofficial
unopened *16.*
unopposed
unordained
unoriginal
unorthodox
unostentatious
unowned
unpaired
unpardonable
unpardoned
unpasteurized
unpatriotic
unpaved
unpeaceable
unperceived *15.*
unperceiving
unperplexed *19.*
unpersuaded
unpersuasive
unperturbed
unperused
unphilosophic
unphilosophical
unphonetic
unpicked
unpierced
unpitying
unplaced
unplagued
unplanned
unplanted
unplayed
unpleased *15.*
unpleasing
unpledged
unpliant
unplowed
unpoetic
unpoetical
unpoised
unpolished *20*
unpolluted

un pop u lar (un pop′ū lər), not popular; not generally liked. *adj. 9.*

un pop u lar i ty (un′pop ū lar′i ti), lack of popularity; being unpopular. *n.*

un prac ticed or **un prac tised** (un prak′tist), 1. not skilled; not expert. 2. not put into practice; not used. *adj. 14.*

un prec e dent ed (un pres′i den′tid), having no precedent; never done before; never known before. *adj. 10.*

un prej u diced (un prej′ů dist), without prejudice; fair; impartial. *adj. 20.*

un pre med i tat ed (un′prē med′i tāt′id), not planned in advance. *adj. 17.*

un pre pared (un′pri pãrd′), not made ready; not ready. *adj. 14.*

un pre tend ing (un′pri ten′ding), 1. not pretending. 2. modest. *adj. 16.*

un pre ten tious (un′pri ten′shəs), modest. *adj. 18.*

un prin ci pled (un prin′si pəld), lacking good moral principles; bad. *adj. 16.*

un prof it a ble (un prof′it ə bəl), producing no gain or advantage. *adj. 8.*

un pro nounce a ble (un′prə noun′sə bəl), that cannot be pronounced. *adj. 20.*

un pro voked (un′prə vōkt′), without provocation. *adj.*

un qual i fied (un kwol′i fīd), 1. not qualified; not fitted. 2. not modified, limited, or restricted in any way; as, unqualified praise. 3. complete; absolute. *adj.*

un quench a ble (un kwench′ə bəl), that cannot be extinguished. *adj. 15.*

un ques tion a ble (un kwes′chən ə bəl), beyond dispute or doubt; certain. *adj. 12.*

un ques tion a bly (un kwes′chən ə bli), beyond dispute or doubt; certainly. *adv.*

un ques tioned (un kwes′chənd), not questioned; not disputed. *adj. 15.*

un qui et (un kwī′ət), restless; disturbed; uneasy. *adj. 9.*

un rav el (un rav′əl), 1 separate the threads of; pull apart. The kitten unraveled grandma's knitting. 2. come apart. 3. bring out of a tangled state; as, to unravel a mystery. *v., unraveled, unraveling. 12.*

un read y (un red′i), 1. not ready; not prepared. 2. not prompt or quick. *adj.*

un re al (un rē′əl), imaginary. *adj. 10.*

un rea son a ble (un rē′zən ə bəl), 1. not reasonable. 2. not moderate. *adj. 6.*

un rea son a bly (un rē′zən ə bli), 1. in a way that is not reasonable; contrary to reason; foolishly. 2. extremely; immoderately. *adv.*

un re flect ing (un′ri flek′ting), not thinking; thoughtless. *adj. 20.*

un re gard ed (un′ri gär′did), disregarded; not heeded. *adj. 15.*

un re gen er ate (un′ri jen′ər it), 1. not born again spiritually; not turned to the love of God. 2. wicked; bad. *adj. 18.*

un re lent ing (un′ri len′ting), hard-hearted; merciless; cruel. *adj. 14.*

un re li a ble (un′ri lī′ə bəl), not reliable; not to be depended on. *adj.*

un re mit ting (un′ri mit′ing), never stopping; not slackening; maintained steadily. *adj. 14.*

un re served (un′ri zėrvd′), 1. frank; open. 2. not restricted; without reservation. *adj. 15.*

un re serv ed ly (un′ri zėr′vid li), 1. frankly; openly; 2. without reservation or restriction. *adv.*

un rest (un rest′), restlessness; lack of ease and quiet; a disturbed condition. *n. 13.*

un re strained (un′ri strānd′), not held back; not checked. *adj. 13.*

In each of the words below **un** *means* not; *the pronunciation of the main part of the word is not changed, but the syllable* **un** *has a slight secondary accent.*

unpreparedness
unprepossessing
unpressed
unprevailing
unpreventable
unprinted
unprivileged
unprized
unprocurable
unproductive *20.*
unprofaned
unprogressive
unpromising
unprompted
unpronounced
unpropitious
unproportioned
unprotected *15.*
unproved
unproven
unprovided
unprovoking
unpruned
unpublished
unpunctual
unpunished *13.*
unpurchasable
unpurposed
unpursuing
unquailing
unqualifying
unquenched
unquestioning
unquotable
unraised
unransomed
unratified
unreadable
unrealized
unreasoned
unrebuked
unreceived
unreclaimed
unrecognized *19.*
unrecompensed
unreconciled
unrecorded
unredeemed
unrefined
unreformed
unregistered
unregulated
unrelated
unrelaxed
unrelaxing
unrelieved
unremembered *15.*
unremitted
unremoved
unremunerated
unremunerative
unrenowned
unrented
unrepaid
unrepaired
unrepealed
unrepentant
unrepenting
unreported
unrepresentative
unrepresented
unrepressed
unreproved *20.*
unrequited
unresigned
unresistant
unresisted
unresisting
unresponsive
unrestraint
unrestricted
unretentive
unretrieved
unrevealed
unrevenged
unrevoked
unrewarded
unrhymed

un right eous (un rī′chəs), wicked; sinful; unjust. *adj. 12.*

un right eous ness (un rī′chəs nis), wickedness; sin; injustice. *n. 16.*

un ri valed or **un ri valled** (un rī′vəld), having no rival; without an equal. *adj. 11.*

un roll (un rōl′), 1. open or spread out (something rolled). 2. lay open; display. *v.*

un ruf fled (un ruf′əld), 1. smooth; not ruffled. 2. calm; not disturbed. *adj. 17.*

un ru ly (un rü′li), hard to rule or control; lawless; as, an unruly horse, a disobedient and unruly boy, an unruly section of a country. *adj. 8.*

un sad dle (un sad′əl), 1. take the saddle off (a horse). 2. cause to fall from a horse. *v.*

un safe (un sāf′), dangerous. *adj. 8.*

un san i tar y (un san′i tãr′i), bad for health; not sanitary. *adj. 17.*

un sat is fac to ry (un′sat is fak′tə ri), not good enough to satisfy. *adj. 10.*

un sat is fied (un sat′is fīd), not satisfied; not contented. *adj. 14.*

un sa vor y (un sā′vər i), 1. tasteless. 2. unpleasant in taste or smell. 3. morally unpleasant; offensive. *adj. 12.*

un say (un sā′), take back (something said). *v., unsaid, unsaying. 18.*

un screw (un skrü′), 1. take out the screw or screws from. 2. loosen or take off by turning; untwist. *v.*

un scru pu lous (un skrü′pū ləs), not careful about right or wrong; without principles or conscience. The unscrupulous boy cheated. *adj. 10.*

un seal (un sēl′), 1. break or remove the seal of; as, to unseal a letter. 2. open. The threat unsealed her lips. *v.*

un search a ble (un sėr′chə bəl), not to be searched into; that cannot be understood by searching; mysterious. *adj. 18.*

un sea son a ble (un sē′zən ə bəl), 1. not suitable to the season. 2. coming at the wrong time. *adj. 11.*

un seat (un sēt′), 1. displace from a seat. 2. throw (a rider) from a saddle. 3. remove from office. *v.*

un seem ly (un sēm′li), 1. not seemly; not suitable. 2. improperly. *adj., adv. 12.*

un seen (un sēn′), 1. not seen. 2. not visible. *adj. 4.*

un self ish (un sel′fish), caring for others; generous. *adj. 12.*

un set tle (un set′əl), disturb; make unstable; shake; weaken. *v.*

un set tled (un set′əld), 1. disordered; not in proper condition or order. Our house is still unsettled. 2. not inhabited. Some parts of the world are still unsettled. 3. not fixed or stable. 4. liable to change; uncertain. The weather is unsettled. 5. not adjusted or disposed of; as, an unsettled estate, an unsettled bill. 6. not determined or decided. *adj. 6.*

un shak en (un shāk′ən), not shaken; firm; as, an unshaken faith in democracy. *adj. 11.*

un sheathe (un shēᴛʜ′), draw (a sword, knife, or the like) from a sheath. *v. 15.*

un shod (un shod′), without shoes. *adj. 19.*

un sight ly (un sīt′li), ugly or unpleasant to look at. *adj. 11.*

un skilled (un skild′), not trained; not expert. *adj. 14.*

un skill ful or **un skil ful** (un skil′fəl), awkward; clumsy. *adj. 11.*

un so cia ble (un sō′shə bəl), not sociable; not associating easily with others; as, unsociable behavior, an unsociable hermit. *adj. 18.*

un so phis ti cat ed (un′sə fis′ti kāt′id), simple; natural; artless. *adj.*

un sought (un sôt′), not sought; not looked for; not asked for. *adj. 11.*

un sound (un sound′), not in good condition; not sound. An unsound mind or body is diseased. Unsound walls are not firm. An unsound business is not reliable. *adj. 12.*

un spar ing (un spãr′ing), 1. very generous; liberal. 2. not merciful; severe. *adj. 16.*

un speak a ble (un spēk′ə bəl), 1. that cannot be expressed in words; as, unspeakable joy, an unspeakable loss. 2. extremely bad; so bad that it is not spoken of. *adj. 6.*

In each of the words below **un** *means* not; *the pronunciation of the main part of the word is not changed, but the syllable* **un** *has a slight secondary accent.*

unrightful
unrimed
unripened
unromantic
unruled
unsaid
unsaintly
unsalable
unsaleable
unsalted
unsanctified
unsanctioned
unsatiated
unsatisfying
unsaturated
unscaled
unscared *19.*
unscarred
unscented
unscholarly
unscorched
unscoured
unscreened
unscriptural
unsculptured
unseasoned
unseaworthy
unseconded
unsecured
unseeing
unseized
unselective
unsentimental
unserviceable
unset
unshaded
unshaped
unshapely
unshaven
unshed
unsheltered
unshorn
unshrinking
unsifted
unsighted
unsigned
unsisterly
unsized
unslacked
unslaked
unsocial
unsoiled
unsold
unsoldierly
unsolicited
unsolved
unsorted
unsounded
unsowed
unsown

un speak a bly (un spēk′ə bli), beyond words; extremely. *adv.*

un spot ted (un spot′id), without spot or stain; pure. *adj. 14.*

un sta ble (un stā′bəl), not firmly fixed; easily moved, shaken, or overthrown. *adj. 11.*

un stained (un stānd′), without stain or spot. *adj. 10.*

un stead y (un sted′i), not steady; shaky; likely to change; not reliable. *adj. 9.*

un strung (un strung′), weakened in the nerves; nervous. *adj.*

un sub stan tial (un′səb stan′shəl), not substantial; flimsy; slight; unreal. *adj. 18.*

un suit a ble (un süt′ə bəl), not suitable; unfit. *adj. 10.*

un suit ed (un süt′id), not suited; unfit. *adj. 15.*

un sul lied (un sul′id), without spot or stain; pure. *adj. 16.*

un sung (un sung′), 1. not sung. 2. not honored in song or poetry. *adj. 17.*

un sus pect ed (un′səs pek′tid), 1. not suspected. 2. not thought of. *adj. 11.*

un tan gle (un tang′gəl), 1. disentangle. 2. straighten out or clear up (anything confused or perplexing). *v.*

un taught (un tôt′), 1. not taught; not educated. 2. known without being taught; learned naturally. *adj. 12.*

un thank ful (un thangk′fəl), 1. ungrateful. 2. thankless; not appreciated. *adj. 19.*

un think a ble (un thingk′ə bəl), that cannot be imagined. *adj. 17.*

un think ing (un thingk′ing), thoughtless; heedless; careless. *adj. 14.*

un thought-of (un thôt′ov′), not imagined or considered. *adj. 15.*

un ti dy (un tī′di), not neat; not in order. *adj. 13.*

un tie (un tī′), unfasten; undo. *v., untied, untying. 7.*

un til (un til′), 1. up to the time of. It was cold from Christmas until April. 2. up to the time when. He waited until the sun had set. 3. before. She did not leave until morning. 4. to the degree or place that. He worked until he was too tired to do more. *prep., conj. 1.*

un time ly (un tīm′li), 1. at a wrong time or season. Snow in May is untimely. 2. too early; too soon. *adj., adv. 8.*

un tir ing (un tīr′ing), tireless; unwearying. *adj. 10.*

un to (un′tü), to. The soldier was faithful unto death. *prep. 2.*

un told (un tōld′), 1. not told; not revealed. 2. too many to be counted; very great. *adj. 9.*

un touched (un tucht′), not touched. The cat left the milk untouched. The miser was untouched by the poor man's story. The last topic was left untouched. *adj. 9.*

un to ward (un tōrd′), 1. unfavorable; unfortunate; as, an untoward wind, an untoward accident. 2. perverse; stubborn; willful. *adj. 13.*

un trained (un trānd′), not trained; without education. *adj. 10.*

un tried (un trīd′), not tried; not tested. *adj. 13.*

un trod (un trod′), not trodden. *adj. 10.*

un true (un trü′), 1. false; incorrect. 2. not faithful. 3. not true to a standard or rule. *adj. 7.*

un truth (un trüth′), 1. lack of truth; falsity. 2. a lie; a falsehood. *n. 19.*

un truth ful (un trüth′fəl), not truthful; contrary to the truth. *adj.*

un tu tored (un tū′tərd or un tü′tərd), not educated. *adj. 11.*

un used (un ūzd′), 1. not used; as, an unused room. 2. not accustomed; as, hands unused to labor. *adj. 9.*

In each of the words below **un** *means* not; *the pronunciation of the main part of the word is not changed, but the syllable* **un** *has a slight secondary accent.*

unspecialized
unspecified
unspeculative
unspent
unspiritual
unspoiled
unspoilt
unspoken
unsportsmanlike
unstamped
unstandardized
unstatesmanlike
unstigmatized
unstinted
unstitched
unstopped
unstrained
unstratified
unstressed
unsubdued *16.*
unsubmissive
unsubstantiated
unsuccessful *8.*
unsuggestive
unsupported *15.*
unsuppressed
unsure
unsurpassed *15.*
unsuspecting
unsuspicious *15.*
unsustained
unswayed
unsweetened
unswept *17.*
unswerving
unsymmetrical
unsympathetic
unsympathizing
unsystematic
untactful
untainted *16.*
untalented
untamed *16.*
untanned
untarnished
untaxed
unteachable
untechnical
untempered
untenable
untenanted
untended
unterrified
untested
unthanked
unthought
unthoughtful
unthrifty
untilled
untired
untraced
untracked
untractable
untransferable
untranslated
untransmitted
untraveled
untravelled
untraversed
untrimmed
untrodden
untroubled *14.*
untrustworthy
untwisted

un u su al (un ū′zhü əl), not in common use; not common; rare; beyond the ordinary. *adj. 4.*

un u su al ly (un ū′zhü əl i), uncommonly; rarely; exceptionally; extremely. *adv.*

un ut ter a ble (un ut′ər ə bəl), unspeakable; that cannot be expressed. *adj. 14.*

un var y ing (un vãr′i ing), steady; constant; not changing. *adj. 15.*

un veil (un vāl′), remove a veil from; uncover; disclose; reveal. The statue was unveiled the day the graduating class presented it to the school. The sun broke through the mist and unveiled the mountains. *v. 11.*

un vexed (un vekst′), not troubled; not disturbed. *adj. 17.*

un war rant a ble (un wor′ən tə bəl), not justifiable; illegal; improper. *adj.*

un war y (un wãr′i), not cautious; unguarded; not careful. *adj. 13.*

un wea ried (un wēr′id), 1. not weary; not tired. 2. never growing weary. *adj. 9.*

un wel come (un wel′kəm), not welcome; not wanted. *adj. 6.*

un well (un wel′), ill; sick. *adj.*

un wept (un wept′), not wept for; not mourned. *adj. 14.*

un whole some (un hōl′səm), not wholesome; unhealthy; bad for the body or the mind. *adj. 8.*

un wield y (un wēl′di), hard to handle or manage; not easy to use or control because of size, shape, or weight; clumsy. The armor worn by knights seems unwieldy to us today. *adj. 11.*

un will ing (un wil′ing), not willing; not consenting. *adj. 5.*

un wind (un wīnd′), 1. wind off; take from a spool, ball, etc. 2. become unwound. *v., unwound, unwinding.*

un wise (un wīz′), not wise; foolish; not showing good judgment. *adj. 7.*

un wit ting (un wit′ing), not knowing; unaware; unconscious; unintentional. *adj.*

un wit ting ly (un wit′ing li), not knowingly; unconsciously; not intentionally. *adv. 13.*

un wont ed (un wun′tid), 1. not customary; not usual. 2. not accustomed. *adj. 12.*

un world ly (un wėrld′li), not caring much for the things of this world, such as money, pleasure, and power. *adj.*

un wor thi ness (un wėr′ᴛʜi nis), lack of merit. *n. 12.*

un wor thy (un wėr′ᴛʜi), not worthy; not deserving. Such a silly story is unworthy of belief. *adj. 5.*

un wrap (un rap′), 1. take a wrapping off from; open. 2. become opened. *v., unwrapped, unwrapping.*

un writ ten (un rit′ən), 1. not written. 2. understood or customary, but not actually expressed; as, an unwritten law. *adj. 12.*

un yoke (un yōk′), 1. free from a yoke; separate; disconnect. 2. remove a yoke. *v.*

up (up), 1. to a higher place; in a higher place. The bird flew up. 2. in an erect position. Stand up. Get up. 3. to the top of; near the top of; at the top of. He went up the hill to get a good view. 4. not back of. Keep up with the times. 5. completely. The house burned up. 6. at an end. His time is up now. 7. **Up to** sometimes means doing; about to do. 8. in action. 9. into storage or a safe place; aside; by. *adv., prep., adj. 1.*

up borne (up bōrn′), borne up; carried up; held up; supported. *adj. 20.*

up braid (up brād′), blame; reprove; find fault with. The captain upbraided his men for falling asleep. *v. 7.*

up bring ing (up′bring′ing), bringing up; care and training given to a child while growing up. *n.*

up heav al (up hēv′əl), heaving up; being heaved up. *n.*

up heave (up hēv′), heave up; lift up. *v. 15.*

up held (up held′), held up; supported. See **uphold.** *pt. and pp. of uphold. 9.*

up hill (up′hil′ for 1 and 2, up′hil′ for 3), 1. up the slope of a hill; upward. It is an uphill road all the way. 2. difficult. 3. upward. We walked a mile uphill. *adj., adv. 10.*

up hold (up hōld′), 1. hold up; raise; keep from falling; support. Walls uphold the roof. 2. confirm. The principal upheld the teacher's decision. *v., upheld, upholding. 5.*

up hold er (up hōl′dər), supporter; as, upholders of the law. *n. 19.*

In each of the words below **un** *means* not; *the pronunciation of the main part of the word is not changed, but the syllable* **un** *has a slight secondary accent.*

unuttered
unvaccinated
unvalued
unvaried
unveiled
unventilated
unverified
unversed
unvisited *19.*
unwanted
unwarlike
unwarranted
unwashed
unwatched
unwavering *18.*
unweaned
unwearying
unwed
unwedded
unweeded
unwifely
unwinking
unwitnessed
unwomanly
unworkable
unworkmanlike
unwounded
unwoven
unwrinkled
unwrought
unyielding

up hol ster (up hōl′stər), 1. provide (furniture) with coverings, cushions, springs, stuffing, etc. 2. furnish (a room) with curtains, rugs, etc. *v. 11.*

up hol ster er (up hōl′stər ər), person whose business is to cover furniture and to furnish and put in place curtains, cushions, carpets, and hangings. *n. 13.*

up hol ster y (up hōl′stər i), 1. coverings for furniture; curtains, cushions, carpets, and hangings. 2. the business of upholstering. *n., pl. upholsteries. 17.*

up keep (up′kēp′), 1. maintenance. 2. cost of operating and repair. The upkeep of a big automobile is expensive. *n. 15.*

up land (up′lənd), 1. high land. 2. of high land. *n., adj. 8.*

up lift (up lift′ for 1, up′lift′ for 2), 1. lift up; raise; elevate. The reformer wanted to uplift the stage and make it better. 2. elevation; movement toward improvement. *v., n. 6.*

up most (up′mōst), uppermost. *adj. 18.*

up on (ə pon′), on. *prep. 1.*

up per (up′ər), 1. higher; as, the upper lip, the upper floor, the upper notes of a singer's voice. 2. The **upper hand** means control. 3. the part of a shoe or boot above the sole. *adj., n. 2.*

up per most (up′ər mōst), 1. highest. 2. most prominent; having the most force or influence. 3. in the highest place. 4. first. *adj., adv. 10.*

up raise (up rāz′), raise up; lift. *v. 17.*

up rear (up rēr′), lift up; raise. *v. 13.*

up right (up′rīt′), 1. standing up straight; erect. Hold yourself upright. 2. good; honest; just; as, an upright man. 3. something standing erect; a vertical piece of timber. *adv., adj., n. 3.*

up right ness (up′rīt′nis), 1. honesty; righteousness. 2. erect position. *n. 11.*

up rise (up rīz′), 1. rise up; get up. 2. slope upward. *v., uprose, uprisen, uprising. 7.*

up ris ing (up rīz′ing), 1. rising up. 2. revolt; as, an uprising of the savage tribes. 3. ascent; upward slope. *n.*

up roar (up′rōr′), 1. noisy disturbance. Main Street was in an uproar when the lion escaped during the circus parade. 2. loud or confused noise. *n. 5.*

up root (up rüt′), tear up by the roots. The storm uprooted many trees. *v. 7.*

up rose (up rōz′), 1. rose up; got up. 2. sloped upward. *pt. of* **uprise.** *11.*

up set (up set′ for 1, 4, and 7, up′set′ for 2, 3, 5, and 6), 1. tip over; overturn. 2. a tipping over; overturn. 3. tipped over; overturned. 4. disturb greatly; disorder. Rain upset our plans for a picnic. The shock upset her nerves. 5. great disturbance; disorder. 6. greatly disturbed; disordered; as, an upset stomach. 7. overthrow; defeat. *v., upset, upsetting, n., adj. 5.*

up shot (up′shot′), 1. conclusion; result. 2. the essential facts. *n. 14.*

up side (up′sīd′), the upper side. *n. 11.*

upside down, 1. having what should be on top at the bottom. The slice of bread and butter fell upside down on the floor. 2. in complete disorder. The children turned the house upside down.

up stairs (up′stãrz′ for 1, up′stãrz′ for 2 and 3), 1. up the stairs. 2. on an upper floor. 3. upper story. *adv., adj., n. 6.*

up start (up′stärt′), 1. person who has suddenly risen from a humble position to wealth, power, or importance. 2. an unpleasant, conceited, and self-assertive person. *n. 12.*

up stream (up′strēm′), against the current of a stream; up a stream. *adv., adj. 18.*

up-to-date (up′tü dāt′), 1. extending to the present time. 2. keeping up with the times in style, ideas, etc. *adj. 15.*

up town (up′toun′ for *adv.*, up′toun′ for *adj.*), to or in the upper part of a town; as, an uptown store. *adv., adj.*

up turn (up tėrn′ for 1, up′tėrn′ for 2), 1. turn up. 2. upward turn. *v., n. 10.*

up ward (up′wərd), 1. toward a higher place. Jack climbed upward till he reached the apple. 2. toward a higher or greater rank, amount, age, etc. From ten years of age upward, Jane had studied French. 3. above; more. Children of five years and upward must pay carfare. 4. **Upward of** means more than. *adv., adj. 3.*

up wards (up′wərdz), upward. *adv.*

Ur (ėr), city in ancient Babylonia, on the Euphrates River. *n. 18.*

U ral (ūr′əl), 1. The **Ural Mountains** are between Russia and Siberia. 2. The **Ural River** flows south from these mountains into the Caspian Sea. *adj. 18.*

u ra ni um (ū rā′ni əm), a heavy, white, radioactive metallic element. *n.*

U ra nus (ūr′ə nəs), 1. Greek god, the father of the Titans and the Cyclopes. 2. one of the larger planets. *n.*

ur ban (ėr′bən), 1. of or pertaining to cities or towns. 2. living in cities. 3. characteristic of cities. 4. accustomed to cities. *adj. 14.*

ur bane (ėr bān′), 1. courteous; refined; elegant. 2. smoothly polite. *adj.*

ur ban i ty (ėr ban′i ti), 1. courtesy; refinement; elegance. 2. smooth politeness. *n., pl. urbanities. 18.*

ur chin (ėr′chin), 1. small boy. 2. mischievous boy. 3. a poor, ragged child. Urchins played in the street. *n. 7.*

-ure, suffix meaning:—
1. act or fact of ———ing; as in failure.
2. state of being ———ed; as in pleasure.
3. result of ———ing; as in enclosure.
4. thing that ———es; as in legislature.
5. thing that is ———ed; as in disclosure.
6. other special meanings; as in procedure, sculpture.

u re a (ū rē′ə), substance in the urine of mammals. *n. 12.*

urge (ėrj), 1. push; force; drive. The driver urged on the horses. Hunger urged him to steal. 2. ask earnestly; plead with; recommend strongly. Mrs. Jones urged us to stay longer. Mr. Smith's doctor urges a change of climate. The lawyer urged the boy's youth as an excuse for his crime. *v., n. 2.*

ur gen cy (ėr′jən si), urgent character; need for immediate action or attention. A house on fire is a matter of great urgency. *n., pl. urgencies. 18.*

ur gent (ėr′jənt), demanding immediate action or attention; pressing; as, an urgent duty, an urgent message. *adj. 6.*

Urn for ornament

u ri nal (ūr′i nəl), 1. container for urine. 2. place to discharge urine. *n. 19.*

u ri nate (ūr′i nāt), discharge urine from the body. *v.*

u rine (ūr′in), the fluid that is secreted by the kidneys, goes to the bladder, and is then discharged from the body. *n. 10.*

Urn for hot drinks

urn (ėrn), 1. a kind of vase with a foot. Urns were used in Greece and Rome to hold the ashes of the dead. 2. a coffee pot or teapot with a faucet, used for making coffee or tea at the table. *n. 4.*

U ru guay (ūr′ů gwā), 1. a country in southeastern South America. 2. a river in southeastern South America, flowing into the Plata River. *n. 11.*

us (us). We learn. The teacher helps us. Mother went with us. *We* and *us* mean the persons speaking. *pron. 1.*

U.S., United States. *6.*

U.S.A., 1. United States of America. 2. United States Army. *16.*

us a ble (ūz′ə bəl), that can be used; fit for use. *adj.*

us age (ūs′ij or ūz′ij), 1. way or manner of using; treatment. This car has had rough usage. 2. custom; habit; customary use; long-continued practice. Strangers living in a country should learn many of its usages. Usage determines what is good English. *n. 8.*

use (ūz for 1 and 2, ūs for 4-7), 1. We use our legs in walking. We use a knife to cut meat. 2. Use others as you would have them use you. 3. **Used to** (ūst′tü′) means (1) accustomed to. Eskimos are used to cold weather. (2) formerly did. You used to come at ten o'clock. 4. He had the use of his friend's books. 5. Use forms habits. 6. A hunter often has use for a gun. 7. There is no use in crying. *v., n. 1.*

use ful (ūs′fəl), of use; giving service; helpful. A handkerchief is a useful present. A good guide makes himself useful. *adj. 2.*

use ful ness (ūs′fəl nis), condition of being useful; practical value. *n. 12.*

use less (ūs′lis), of no use; worthless. *adj. 3.*

us er (ūz′ər), one that uses. *n. 11.*

ush er (ush′ər), 1. person who shows people to their seats in a church, theater, etc. 2. to conduct; bring in. The footman ushered the visitors to the door. 3. an assistant teacher in an English school. *n., v. 7.*

U.S.N., United States Navy.

U.S.S.R. or **USSR,** Union of Soviet Socialist Republics.

u su al (ū′zhü əl), in common use; common; ordinary. *adj. 1.*

u su al ly (ū′zhü əl i), according to what is usual; commonly; ordinarily; customarily. *adv.*

u su rer (ū′zhů rər), person who lends money at an extremely high or unlawful rate of interest. *n. 15.*

u su ri ous (ū zhůr′i əs), 1. taking extremely high or unlawful interest for the use of money. 2. having to do with usury. *adj. 20.*

u surp (ū zėrp′), seize and hold (power, position, or authority) by force or without right. The king's brother tried to usurp the throne. *v. 6.*

u surp a tion (ū′zėr pā′shən), seizing and holding power, position, or authority by force or without right. *n. 12.*

u surp er (ū zėr′pər), one who usurps. *n. 9.*

u su ry (ū′zhů ri), 1. lending money at an extremely high or unlawful rate of interest. 2. extremely high or unlawful interest. *n. 10.*

U tah (ū′tô), a Western State of the United States. *n. 10.*

u ten sil (ū ten′səl), 1. container, implement, or tool used for practical purposes. Pots, pans, kettles, and mops are kitchen utensils. 2. implement or tool used for some special purpose. Pens and pencils are writing utensils. *n. 7.*

u ter us (ū′tər əs), the womb; the part of the body that holds and nourishes the young till birth. *n. 18.*

U ti ca (ū′ti kə), a city in central New York State. *n. 16.*

u til i tar i an (ū til′i tãr′i ən), 1. having to do with utility. 2. aiming at usefulness rather than beauty, style, etc. *adj. 13.*

u til i ty (ū til′i ti), 1. usefulness. 2. useful thing. 3. a public service. Railroads, streetcar and bus lines, and gas and electric companies are public utilities. *n., pl. utilities. 7.*

u ti li za tion (ū′ti li zā′shən), putting to use; being put to use. *n. 18.*

u ti lize (ū′ti līz), use; put to use; as, to utilize leftovers in cooking. *v. 8.*

ut most (ut′mōst), 1. farthest; extreme. He walked to the utmost edge of the cliff. 2. greatest; highest. Sunshine is of the utmost importance to health. 3. the extreme limit; the most that is possible. Dick enjoyed himself to the utmost at the circus. *adj., n. 4.*

U to pi a or **u to pi a** (ū tō′pi ə), 1. an ideal place or state with perfect laws. 2. a visionary, impractical system of political or social perfection. *n. 11.*

U to pi an or **u to pi an** (ū tō′pi ən), 1. of or like a Utopia. 2. visionary; impractical. 3. an idealist; an ardent but impractical reformer. *adj., n.*

U trecht (ū′trekt), city in the Netherlands. *n. 19.*

ut ter[1] (ut′ər), complete; total; absolute; as, utter surprise. *adj. 2.*

ut ter[2] (ut′ər), speak; make known; express. He uttered a cry of pain. *v.*

ut ter ance (ut′ər əns), 1. uttering; expressing in words or sounds. The child gave utterance to his grief. 2. way of speaking. 3. something uttered; a spoken word or words. *n. 5.*

ut ter ly (ut′ər li), completely; totally; absolutely. *adv.*

ut ter most (ut′ər mōst), utmost. *adj., n. 7.*

V

V, v (vē), 1. the 22nd letter of the alphabet. There are two v's in vivid. 2. Roman numeral for 5. *n., pl. V's, v's.*

v., 1. verb. 2. versus.

Va., the State of Virginia. *20.*

va can cy (vā′kən si), 1. being vacant; emptiness. 2. unoccupied position. Mr. Smith's death made a vacancy in the business. 3. a room, space, or apartment for rent; empty space. 4. idleness; emptiness of mind. *n., pl. vacancies. 6.*

va cant (vā′kənt), 1. empty; not filled; not occupied; as, a vacant chair, a vacant house. 2. empty of thought or intelligence; as, a vacant smile. *adj. 3.*

va cate (vā′kāt), go away from and leave empty; make vacant. They will vacate the house at the end of the month. *v. 14.*

va ca tion (vā kā′shən), freedom from school, business, or other duties. There is a vacation from schoolwork every year at Christmas time. *n. 3.*

vac ci nate (vak′si nāt), 1. inoculate with vaccine as a protection against smallpox. 2. take similar measures against other diseases. *v. 12.*

vac ci na tion (vak′si nā′shən), vaccinating. Vaccination has made smallpox a very rare disease. *n. 9.*

vac cine (vak′sēn), 1. poison of a very mild form of smallpox, used for the protection of people against the real smallpox. 2. any preparation of disease germs, or the like, that is used for preventive inoculation. *n. 15.*

vac il late (vas′i lāt), 1. move first one way and then another; waver. 2. waver in mind or opinion. A vacillating person finds it hard to make up his mind. *v. 13.*

vac il la tion (vas′i lā′shən), 1. a vacillating; wavering; unsteadiness. 2. a wavering in mind or opinion. *n. 17.*

va cu i ty (va kū′i ti), 1. emptiness. 2. an empty space. 3. emptiness of mind; lack of ideas or intelligence. *n., pl. vacuities. 13.*

vac u ous (vak′ū əs), 1. showing no intelligence; stupid. 2. empty. *adj.*

vac u um (vak′ū əm), empty space without even air in it. *n. 12.*

vacuum bottle, bottle surrounded by a container, with a vacuum between.

vacuum cleaner, apparatus for cleaning carpets, curtains, floors, etc., by suction.

vacuum tube, a sealed tube or bulb from which almost all the air has been removed. It is used in radio sets to control the flow of electric currents.

vag a bond (vag′ə bond), 1. wanderer; idle wanderer; tramp. 2. wandering. The gypsies lead a vagabond life. 3. rascal; good-for-nothing person. *n., adj. 8.*

va gar y (və gãr′i), extravagant or fanciful notion; as, the vagaries of a dream. *n., pl. vagaries. 11.*

va grant (vā′grənt), 1. wanderer. 2. wandering. 3. idle wanderer; tramp. 4. wandering without proper means of earning a living. *n., adj. 7.*

vague (vāg), not definite; not clear; not distinct. In a fog everything looks vague. Nobody can be sure just what a vague statement means. *adj. 6.*

vain (vān), 1. having too much pride in one's looks, ability, etc. She is vain of her beauty. 2. of no use; unsuccessful. I made vain attempts to reach her by telephone. 3. **In vain** means without effect or without success The drowning man shouted in vain, for no one could hear him. *adj. 2.*

vain glo ri ous (vān′glō′ri əs), excessively proud or boastful; extremely vain. *adj. 16.*

vain glo ry (vān′glō′ri), 1. extreme pride in oneself; boastful vanity. 2. worthless pomp or show. *n. 12.*

vain ly (vān′li), 1. in vain. 2. with conceit. *adv.*

val ance (val′əns), 1. short curtain; as, the valance over the top of a window. 2. short curtain hanging around a bed from the frame to the floor. *n. 20.*

Bed with a canopy and a valance (def. 2)

vale (vāl), valley. *n. 3.*

val e dic to ry (val′i dik′tə ri), 1. a farewell address, especially at the graduating exercises of a school or college. 2. bidding farewell. *n., pl. valedictories, adj.*

Val en ci ennes (val′ən si enz′), a fine lace in which the pattern and background are made together of the same threads. *n. 18.*

Valenciennes

val en tine (val′ən tīn), 1. a card or small gift sent on Saint Valentine's Day, February 14. 2. a sweetheart chosen on this day. *n. 6.*

va le ri an (və lēr′i ən), 1. a strong-smelling drug used to quiet the nerves. 2. the plant from whose root it is made. *n. 20.*

val et (val′it or val′ā), 1. servant who takes care of a man's clothes and gives him personal service. 2. servant in a hotel who cleans or presses clothes. 3. serve as a valet. *n., v. 11.*

Val hal la (val hal′ə), 1. in Norse mythology, paradise where the souls of heroes slain in battle feast with the gods. 2. hall of the god Odin where he receives the souls of the slain warrior heroes. *n.*

val iant (val′yənt), brave; as, a valiant soldier, a valiant deed. *adj. 4.*

val id (val′id), 1. true; supported by facts or authority. 2. having force; holding good; effective. A contract made by an insane man is not valid. *adj. 10.*

val i date (val′i dāt), 1. make valid; give legal force to. 2. confirm; support by facts or authority. *v.*

va lid i ty (və lid′i ti), 1. truth; soundness; as, the validity of an argument. 2. holding good; force; as, the validity of a pledge. *n., pl. validities. 13.*

va lise (və lēs′), a traveling bag to hold clothes, etc. *n. 16.*

Val kyr ie (val kēr′i or val′ki ri), one of the handmaidens of Odin, who ride through the air and hover over battlefields, choosing the heroes who are to die in battle and afterward leading them to Valhalla. *n.*

val ley (val′i), 1. low land between hills or mountains. Most large valleys have rivers running through them. 2. wide region drained by a great river system; as, the Mississippi valley. *n., pl. valleys. 1.*

val or (val′ər), bravery; courage. *n. 5.*

val or ous (val′ər əs), valiant; brave; courageous. *adj. 13.*

Val pa rai so (val′pə rī′zō), chief seaport of Chile. *n. 19.*

val u a ble (val′ū ə bəl), 1. having value; being worth something; as, a valuable ring, valuable information, a valuable friend. 2. an article of value. She keeps her jewelry and other valuables in a safe. *adj., n. 2.*

val u a tion (val′ū ā′shən), 1. act of valuing. 2. the value fixed or estimated. The jeweler's valuation of the necklace was $10,000. *n. 13.*

val ue (val′ū), 1. worth; excellence; usefulness; importance; as, the value of education, the value of milk as a food. 2. real worth; proper price. He bought the house for less than its value. 3. power to buy. The value of the dollar lessened from 1900 to 1920. 4. rate at a certain value or price; estimate the value of. The land is valued at $5000. 5. think highly of; regard highly. John values Tom's friendship. 6. meaning; effect; force. *n., v. 1.*

val ue less (val′ū lis), without value; worthless. *adj. 16.*

valve (valv), 1. movable part that controls the flow of a liquid or gas through a pipe by opening and closing the passage. A faucet is one kind of valve. 2. something that works similarly. The valves of the heart control the flow of blood. 3. one of the parts of hinged shells like those of oysters and clams. *n. 6.*

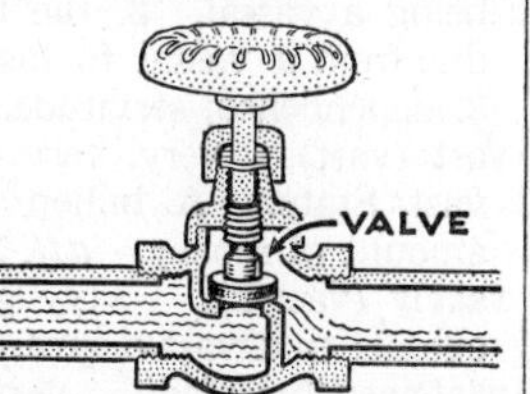

vamp (vamp), 1. the upper front part of a shoe or boot. 2. piece or patch added to an old thing to make it look new. 3. patch up; make (an old thing) look new. *n., v. 13.*

vam pire (vam′pīr), 1. a corpse supposed to come to life at night and suck the blood of people while they sleep. 2. person who preys ruthlessly on others. 3. woman who flirts with men to get money or to please her vanity. 4. a kind of bat. Some vampires suck the blood of people and animals. *n. 16.*

van[1] (van), the front part of an army, fleet, or other advancing group. *n. 4.*

van[2] (van), a covered truck or wagon for moving furniture, etc. *n.*

va na di um (və nā′di əm), a rare metallic element, used in making certain kinds of steel. *n.*

Van Bu ren (van būr′ən), Martin (1782-1862), the eighth president of the United States, from 1837 to 1841.

Van cou ver (van kü′vər), 1. a seaport city in southwestern Canada. 2. an island off the Pacific Coast, that is part of British Columbia. *n.*

Van dal (van′dəl), 1. member of a Germanic tribe that ravaged Gaul, Spain, northern Africa, and Rome during the fifth century A.D. 2. of Vandals. *n., adj. 17.*

van dal (van′dəl), person who willfully or ignorantly destroys or damages beautiful things. *n.*

van dal ism (van′dəl izm), willful or ignorant destruction or damaging of beautiful things. *n.*

vane (vān), 1. movable device to show which way the wind is blowing. 2. blade of a windmill, a ship's propeller, etc. *n. 8.*

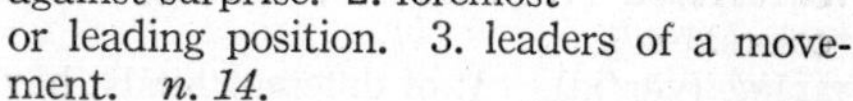

Vane (def. 1)

van guard (van′gärd′), 1. the front part of an army; soldiers marching in front to clear the way and guard against surprise. 2. foremost or leading position. 3. leaders of a movement. *n. 14.*

va nil la (və nil′ə), 1. a flavoring extract used in candy, ice cream, perfume, etc. 2. the tropical plant which yields the beans used in making this flavoring. 3. the bean itself. *n. 12.*

van ish (van′ish), 1. disappear; disappear suddenly. The sun vanished behind a cloud. 2. pass away; cease to be. Many kinds of animals have vanished from the earth. *v. 3.*

van i ty (van′i ti), 1. too much pride in one's looks, ability, etc. Louise's vanity made her look in the mirror often. 2. lack of real value; worthlessness. 3. worthless pleasure or display. *n., pl. vanities. 3.*

van quish (vang′kwish), conquer; defeat. *v. 6.*

van tage (van′tij), advantage; better position or condition. *n. 8.*

vap id (vap′id), without much life or flavor; tasteless; dull. *adj. 17.*

va por (vā′pər), 1. steam from boiling water; moisture in the air that can be seen; fog; mist. 2. a gas formed from a substance that is usually a liquid or a solid. *n. 3.*

va por ize (vā′pər īz), change into vapor. *v. 17.*

va por ous (vā′pər əs), 1. full of vapor; misty. 2. like vapor. 3. unsubstantial; useless. *adj. 18.*

va por y (vā′pər i), full of vapor; like vapor. *adj. 19.*

va que ro (vä kãr′ō), cowboy; herdsman. *n., pl. vaqueros.*

var i a bil i ty (vãr′i ə bil′i ti), 1. changeableness. 2. tendency to vary. *n.*

var i a ble (vãr′i ə bəl), 1. apt to change; changeable; uncertain. The weather is more variable in New York than it is in California. 2. a thing or quantity that varies. *adj., n. 8.*

var i ance (vãr′i əns), 1. difference; disagreement. 2. a varying; a change. *n. 10.*

var i ant (vãr′i ənt), 1. varying; different. *Rime* is a variant spelling of *rhyme.* 2. a different form; a different spelling of the same word. *adj., n.*

var i a tion (vãr′i ā′shən), 1. a varying; a change. 2. amount of change. There was a variation of 30 degrees in the temperature yesterday. *n. 10.*

var i col ored (vãr′i kul′ərd), having various colors. *adj.*

var ied (vãr′id), 1. of different kinds; having variety; as, a varied assortment of candies. 2. changed; altered. *adj.*

var i e gat ed (vãr′i ə gāt′id), varied in appearance; of different colors. Pansies are usually variegated. *adj. 12.*

va ri e ty (və rī′ə ti), 1. lack of sameness. 2. number of different kinds. This shop has a variety of toys. 3. kind or sort. Which variety of cake do you prefer? 4. a division of a species. *n., pl. varieties. 3.*

var i ous (vãr′i əs), 1. different; differing from one another. 2. several; many. *adj. 2.*

var let (vär′lit), low fellow; rascal. *n. 15.*

var nish (vär′nish), 1. a liquid that gives a smooth, glossy appearance to wood, metal, etc. Varnish is often made from substances like resin dissolved in oil or alcohol. 2. the smooth hard surface made when this liquid dries. The varnish on the car has been scratched. 3. put varnish on. 4. glossy appearance. 5. favorable appearance; pretense. She covers her selfishness with a varnish of good manners. 6. give a false or deceiving appearance. *n., v. 6.*

var si ty (vär′si ti), university. *Varsity* is often used when speaking of sports. *n.*

var y (vãr′i), 1. change; make different. The driver can vary the speed of an automobile. 2. be different; differ. Stars vary in brightness. *v., varied, varying. 3.*

vas cu lar (vas′kū lər), pertaining to, made of, or provided with vessels that carry blood, sap, etc. *adj. 13.*

vase (vās), a holder or container used for ornament or for holding flowers. *n. 6.*

Ancient Roman vase

vas e line (vas′ə lēn), a yellow or whitish salve made from petroleum. *n.* [*Trade name*] *13.*

vas sal (vas′əl), 1. person who held land from a lord or superior, to whom in return he gave help in war or some other service. A great noble could be a vassal of the king and have many other men as his vassals. 2. like a vassal; like that of a vassal. 3. servant. *n., adj. 6.*

vas sal age (vas′əl ij), 1. the condition of being a vassal. 2. the homage or service due from a vassal to his lord or superior. 3. dependence; servitude. *n. 12.*

vast (vast), very, very large. Texas is a vast State. A billion dollars is a vast amount of money. *adj. 2.*

vast ly (vast′li), very greatly; to a vast extent; to a vast degree. *adv.*

vast ness (vast′nis), very great size; being vast; hugeness. *n. 11.*

vat (vat), tank; large container for liquids; as, a vat of dye. *n. 9.*

Vat i can (vat′i kən), 1. collection of buildings grouped about the palace of the Pope in Rome. 2. the government, office, or authority of the Pope. *n. 12.*

Vatican City, independent State inside the city of Rome. It is ruled by the Pope.

vaude ville (vōd′vil), theatrical entertainment consisting of a variety of acts. It consists of songs, dances, acrobatic feats, short plays, trained animals, etc. *n. 17.*

vault[1] (vôlt), 1. arched roof or ceiling; series of arches. 2. arched space or passage. 3. something like an arched roof. The vault of heaven means the sky. 4. make in the form of a vault. 5. cover with a vault. 6. underground cellar or storehouse. 7. place for storing valuable things and keeping them safe. Vaults are often made of steel. 8. place for burial. *n., v. 4.*

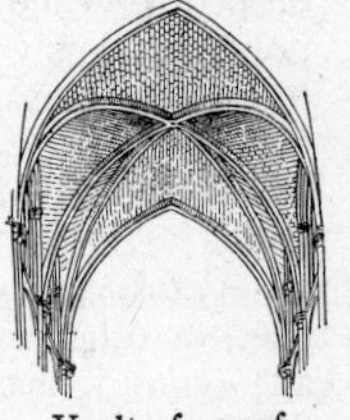
Vault of a roof

vault[2] (vôlt), 1. to jump or leap over by using the hands or a pole. He vaulted the fence. 2. such a jump or leap. 3. to jump; to leap. He vaulted over the wall. *v., n.*

vaunt (vônt), boast. *v., n. 8.*

veal (vēl), meat from a calf. *n. 9.*

veer (vēr), 1. change direction; shift; turn. The wind veered to the south. The talk veered to ghosts. 2. shift; turn. *v., n. 10.*

veg e ta ble (vej′i tə bəl), 1. plant grown for food. Peas, corn, lettuce, tomatoes, and beets are vegetables. 2. any plant. 3. of plants; like plants; pertaining to plants; as, the vegetable kingdom, vegetable life, vegetable oils, a vegetable dinner. *n., adj. 2.*

veg e tar i an (vej′i tãr′i ən), 1. person who eats vegetables but no meat. 2. eating vegetables but no meat. 3. containing no meat. *n., adj. 18.*

veg e tate (vej′i tāt), 1. grow as plants do. 2. live with very little action, thought, or feeling. *v. 17.*

veg e ta tion (vej′i tā′shən), plant life; growing plants; growth of plants. There is not much vegetation in deserts. *n. 7.*

veg e ta tive (vej′i tā′tiv), 1. growing as plants do. 2. of plants or plant life. 3. with very little action, thought, or feeling. *adj. 16.*

ve he mence (vē′i məns), forcefulness; violence; strong feeling. *n. 8.*

ve he ment (vē′i mənt), 1. showing strong feeling; caused by strong feeling; eager. 2. forceful; violent. *adj. 7.*

ve hi cle (vē′i kəl), 1. carriage, cart, wagon, automobile, sled, or any other conveyance used on land. 2. a means of carrying or conveying. Language is the vehicle of thought. Linseed oil is a vehicle for paint. *n. 7.*

veil (vāl), 1. piece of very thin material worn to protect or hide the face, or as an ornament. 2. piece of material worn so as to fall over the head and shoulders. **Take the veil** means become a nun. 3. cover with a veil. 4. anything that screens or hides. A veil of clouds hid the sun. 5. cover; hide; as, a veiled threat. *n., v. 3.*

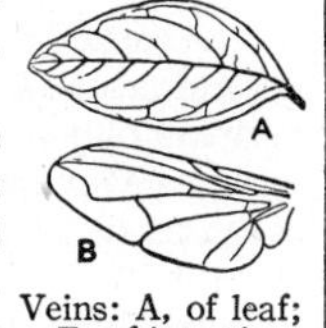

Veins: A, of leaf; B, of insect's wing.

vein (vān), 1. one of the blood vessels or tubes that carry blood to the heart from all parts of the body. 2. rib of a leaf or of an insect's wing. 3. a crack or seam in rock filled with a different mineral; as, a vein of copper. 4. any streak or marking of a different shade or color in wood, marble, etc. 5. special character or disposition; state of mind; mood; as, a vein of cruelty, a joking vein. 6. cover with veins; mark with veins. *n., v. 3.*

veld or **veldt** (velt), open country in South Africa, having grass or bushes but few trees. *n.*

vel lum (vel′əm), 1. the finest kind of parchment, used for writing and binding books. 2. paper or cloth imitating this. *n. 14.*

ve loc i pede (vi los′i pēd), 1. child's tricycle. 2. an early kind of bicycle or tricycle. *n. 15.*

Child's velocipede

ve loc i ty (vi los′i ti), 1. speed; swiftness; quickness. 2. rate of motion. A bullet goes from this gun with a velocity of 3000 feet a second. *n., pl.* *velocities. 9.*

ve lours or **ve lour** (və lür′), a fabric like velvet, made of silk, wool, or cotton. Velours is used for clothing, draperies, upholstery, etc. *n. 15.*

vel vet (vel′vit), 1. cloth with a thick, soft pile. Velvet may be made of silk, rayon, cotton, or some combination of these. 2. made of velvet. 3. like velvet; as, a cat's velvet paws. *n., adj. 3.*

vel vet een (vel′vi tēn′), velvet made of cotton or of silk and cotton. *n.*

vel vet y (vel′vi ti), smooth and soft like velvet. *adj. 12.*

ve nal (vē′nəl), 1. willing to sell one's services or influence basely; open to bribes; corrupt. Venal judges are a disgrace to a country. 2. influenced or obtained by bribery; as, venal conduct. *adj. 15.*

vend (vend), sell; peddle. He vends fruit from a cart. *v.*

vend er (ven′dər), seller; peddler. *n.*

ven det ta (ven det′ə), feud in which a murdered man's relatives try to kill the slayer or his relatives. *n.*

ven dor (ven′dər), seller; peddler. *n. 14.*

ve neer (və nēr′), 1. cover (wood) with a thin layer of finer wood or other material. The pine desk is veneered with mahogany. 2. thin layer of wood or other material used in veneering. The panel had a veneer of gold and ivory. 3. cover (anything) with a layer of something else to give an appearance of superior quality. 4. surface appearance or show. A veneer of piety hid his real meanness. *v., n. 11.*

ven er a ble (ven′ər ə bəl), worthy of reverence; as, a venerable priest, venerable customs. *adj. 7.*

ven er ate (ven′ər āt), regard with reverence; revere. He venerates his father's memory. *v. 13.*

ven er a tion (ven′ər ā′shən), reverence. *n. 14.*

ve ne re al (vi nēr′i əl), 1. pertaining to sexual acts. 2. caused by sexual intercourse. 3. pertaining to diseases caused by sexual intercourse. *adj. 19.*

Ve ne tian (vi nē′shən), 1. of Venice; pertaining to Venice. 2. a native or an inhabitant of Venice. *adj., n. 9.*

Ven e zue la (ven′i zwē′lə), country in the northern part of South America. *n. 10.*

venge ance (ven′jəns), 1. revenge; punishment in return for a wrong. The Indian swore vengeance against the men who murdered his father. 2. **With a vengeance** means (1) with great force or violence. (2) extremely. (3) much more than expected. By six o'clock it was raining with a vengeance. *n. 4.*

venge ful (venj′fəl), feeling or showing a strong desire for vengeance. *adj. 14.*

ve ni al (vē′ni əl), that can be forgiven; pardonable. *adj. 13.*

Ven ice (ven′is), city on the northeastern coast of Italy. Venice has many canals in place of streets. *n. 6.*

ven i son (ven′i zən), deer meat; the flesh of a deer, used for food. *n. 7.*

ven om (ven′əm), 1. the poison of snakes, spiders, etc. 2. spite; malice. She hated the rich and spoke of them with venom. *n. 8.*

ven om ous (ven′əm əs), 1. poisonous. Rattlesnakes are venomous. 2. spiteful; malicious. *adj. 10.*

vent (vent), 1. hole; opening. 2. outlet; way out. Her grief found vent in tears. 3. let out; express freely. He vented his anger on the dog. *n., v. 6.*

ven ti late (ven′ti lāt), 1. change the air in. We ventilate a room by opening windows. 2. purify by fresh air. The lungs ventilate the blood. 3. make known publicly; discuss openly. *v. 9.*

ven ti la tion (ven′ti lā′shən), 1. change of air; act or process of supplying with fresh air. 2. means of supplying fresh air. 3. free discussion. *n. 8.*

ven ti la tor (ven′ti lā′tər), any apparatus or means for changing or improving the air. *n.*

ven tral (ven′trəl), abdominal. We call the side of any animal where its belly is the ventral side. *adj. 13.*

ven tri cle (ven′tri kəl), one of the two lower chambers of the heart that receive blood and force it into the arteries. *n. 9.*

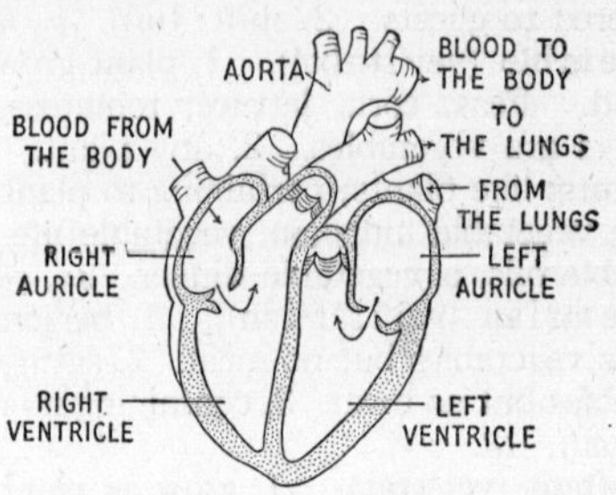

Heart showing ventricles

ven tril o quist (ven tril′ə kwist), person who can make his voice seem to come from some other source. A ventriloquist can talk without any movement of his lips that you can see. *n. 19.*

ven ture (ven′chər), 1. a risky or daring undertaking. A lucky venture in oil stock made his fortune. His courage was equal to any venture. 2. expose to risk or danger. Men venture their lives in war. 3. dare. No one ventured to interrupt the speaker. 4. dare to say or make. He ventured an objection. 5. **At a venture** means at random; by chance. *n., v. 3.*

ven ture some (ven′chər səm), inclined to take risks; rash; daring. *adj. 15.*

ven tur ous (ven′chər əs), 1. bold; daring; adventurous. 2. risky. *adj. 11.*

Ve nus (vē′nəs), 1. the Roman goddess of love and beauty. The Greeks called her Aphrodite. 2. the most brilliant planet. 3. very beautiful woman. *n. 7.*

ve ra cious (vi rā′shəs), 1. truthful. 2. true. *adj.*

ve rac i ty (vi ras′i ti), 1. truthfulness. 2. truth. 3. correctness; accuracy. *n., pl. veracities. 15.*

Ver a cruz or **Ver a Cruz** (ver′ə krüz′), a seaport city in southeastern Mexico. *n. 12.*

ve ran da or **ve ran dah** (və ran′də), large porch along one or more sides of a house. *n. 12.*

Veranda

verb (vėrb), a word that tells what is or

what is done; the part of speech that expresses action or being. *Do, go, come, be, sit, think, know,* and *eat* are verbs. *n. 6.*

ver bal (vėr′bəl), 1. in words; of words. A description is a verbal picture. 2. expressed in spoken words; oral; as, a verbal message, a verbal promise. 3. word for word; literal; as, a verbal translation from the French. 4. pertaining to a verb. Two common verbal endings are *-ed* and *-ing.* 5. derived from a verb. 6. a noun or adjective derived from a verb. *adj., n. 10.*

ver bal ly (vėr′bəl i), 1. in words. 2. in spoken words; orally. The dumb boy could not reply verbally but used signs. 3. word for word. The child reported the conversation verbally. 4. in regard to words only. 5. as a verb. *Breast* is used verbally in "A boat breasts the wave." *adv.*

ver ba tim (vėr bā′tim), word for word; in exactly the same words. His speech was printed verbatim in the newspaper. *adv., adj.*

ver be na (vər bē′nə), low-growing garden plant with flowers having various colors. *n.*

Verbena

ver bi age (vėr′bi ij), use of too many words; abundance of useless words. *n. 20.*

ver bose (vėr bōs′), using too many words. *adj. 18.*

ver bos i ty (vėr bos′i ti), use of too many words; wordiness. *n. 18.*

ver dant (vėr′dənt), 1. green. The fields are covered with verdant grass. 2. inexperienced. *adj. 11.*

Verde (vėrd). **Cape Verde** is the most western point of Africa. *n.*

ver dict (vėr′dikt), 1. the decision of a jury. The jury returned a verdict of "Not Guilty." 2. decision; judgment. *n. 8.*

ver di gris (vėr′di grēs), 1. green or bluish coating that forms on brass, copper, or bronze. 2. green or bluish-green poisonous compound used in paints and as a drug. *n.*

ver dure (vėr′jər), greenness; fresh growth of green grass, plants, or leaves. *n. 8.*

verge (vėrj), 1. edge; rim; brink. His business is on the verge of ruin. 2. be on the verge; border. 3. tend; incline. She was plump, verging toward fat. *n., v. 6.*

Ver gil (vėr′jil), Virgil. *n.*

ver i fi ca tion (ver′i fi kā′shən), proof by evidence or testimony; confirmation. *n.*

ver i fy (ver′i fī), 1. prove to be true; confirm. The driver's report of the accident was verified by eyewitnesses. 2. find out the truth of; test the correctness of. *v., verified, verifying. 8.*

ver i ly (ver′i li), in truth; truly; really. *adv. 6.*

ver i ta ble (ver′i tə bəl), true; real; actual. *adj. 11.*

ver i ty (ver′i ti), 1. truth. 2. true statement or fact. 3. reality. *n., pl. verities. 14.*

ver meil (vėr′mil), 1. vermilion. 2. metal coated with gilt. *n., adj. 18.*

ver mi form (vėr′mi fôrm), shaped like a worm. The **vermiform appendix** is a slender tube, closed at one end, growing out of the large intestine in the lower right-hand part of the abdomen. Appendicitis is inflammation of the vermiform appendix. *adj. 14.*

ver mil ion (vər mil′yən), 1. bright red. 2. bright-red coloring matter. *n., adj. 15.*

ver min (vėr′min), small, troublesome, or destructive animals. Fleas, lice, bedbugs, rats, and mice are vermin. People who are very unpleasant and troublesome are sometimes called vermin. *n. 16.*

Ver mont (vər mont′), a New England State of the United States. *n. 9.*

ver nac u lar (vər nak′ū lər), 1. native language; the language of the country or place where a person was born. 2. of or in the native language. 3. everyday language. 4. the language of a class or a profession. There are many strange words in the vernacular of the lawyers. *n., adj. 14.*

ver nal (vėr′nəl), 1. of spring; pertaining to spring; as, vernal green, vernal flowers, vernal months. 2. belonging to youth. There was a vernal freshness about her. *adj. 11.*

Ver sailles (vär sī′), 1. city in northern France, near Paris. The treaty ending the first World War was signed there on June 28, 1919. 2. a large palace there. *n. 12.*

ver sa tile (vėr′sə til), able to do many things well. Theodore Roosevelt was a versatile man; he was successful as a statesman, soldier, sportsman, explorer, and author. *adj. 17.*

ver sa til i ty (vėr′sə til′i ti), ability to do many things well. *n. 16.*

verse (vėrs), 1. lines of words with a regularly repeated accent; poetry. 2. a single line of poetry. 3. a group of lines of poetry.

Sing the first verse of "America." 4. a short division of a chapter in the Bible. *n. 3.*

versed (vėrst), experienced; practiced; skilled. A doctor should be well versed in medicine. *adj.*

ver si fi ca tion (vėr′si fi kā′shən), 1. the making of verses. 2. art or theory of making verses. 3. form or style of poetry; metrical structure. *n. 16.*

ver si fi er (vėr′si fī′ər), person who makes verses. *n. 20.*

ver si fy (vėr′si fī), 1. write verses. 2. tell in verse. 3. turn (prose) into poetry. *v.*

ver sion (vėr′zhən), 1. a translation from one language to another; as, a version of the Bible. 2. one particular statement, account, or description. Each of the three boys gave his own version of the quarrel. *n. 11.*

ver sus (vėr′səs), against. The most exciting game was Harvard versus Yale. *prep. 20.*

ver te bra (vėr′ti brə), one of the bones of the backbone. *n., pl. vertebrae* (-brē), *vertebras. 14.*

ver te bral (vėr′ti brəl), of or pertaining to a vertebra or the vertebrae. *adj. 18.*

Three vertebrae

ver te brate (vėr′ti brāt), 1. animal that has a backbone. Fishes, amphibians, reptiles, birds, and mammals are vertebrates. 2. having a backbone. *n., adj. 10.*

ver tex (vėr′teks), the highest point; the top. *n., pl. vertexes, vertices* (-ti sēz). *17.*

ver ti cal (vėr′ti kəl), 1. straight up and down; perpendicular to the surface of still water. A person standing up straight is in a vertical position. 2. vertical line, circle, position, part, etc. *adj., n. 6.*

ver ti go (vėr′ti gō), dizziness; giddiness. *n., pl. vertigos* or *vertigoes. 18.*

verve (vėrv), enthusiasm; energy; vigor; spirit; liveliness. *n.*

ver y (ver′i), 1. much; greatly; extremely. The sun is very hot. 2. real; true; genuine. She cries from very shame. 3. actual. He was caught in the very act of stealing. 4. same. The very people who used to love her hate her now. 5. even; mere. The very thought of blood makes her sick. 6. absolutely; exactly. He stood in the very same place for an hour. *adv., adj., verier, veriest. 1.*

ves i cle (ves′i kəl), a small bladder, cavity, sac, or cyst. A blister is a vesicle in the skin. *n.*

Ves per (ves′pər), the evening star. *n.*

ves per (ves′pər), 1. evening. 2. of evening. 3. evening prayer, hymn, or service; evening bell. 4. of or pertaining to vespers. *n., adj.*

ves pers or **Ves pers** (ves′pərz), a church service held in the late afternoon or evening. *n. pl. 9.*

Ves puc ci (ves pü′chi), Amerigo, Italian merchant, adventurer, and explorer (1451-1512). America is named for him. *n.*

ves sel (ves′əl), 1. hollow holder or container. Cups, bowls, pitchers, bottles, barrels, tubs, etc., are vessels. 2. ship; large boat. 3. tube carrying blood or other fluid. Veins and arteries are blood vessels. *n. 2.*

vest (vest), 1. a short, sleeveless garment worn by men under the coat. 2. garment like this worn by women. 3. undershirt. 4. clothe or robe. The vested priest stood before the altar. 5. furnish with powers, authority, rights, etc. Congress is vested with the power to declare war. 6. put in the possession or control of a person or persons. The management of the hospital is vested in a board of trustees. *n., v. 3.*

Ves ta (ves′tə), the Roman goddess of the hearth. A sacred fire was always kept burning in the temple of Vesta. *n.*

ves tal (ves′təl), 1. one of the maidens who tended the sacred fire of the goddess Vesta in ancient Rome. 2. virgin; pure; chaste. 3. of a vestal; suitable for a vestal. *n., adj. 12.*

vest ed (ves′tid), 1. clothed or robed, especially in church garments; as, a vested choir. 2. placed in the possession or control of a person or persons; fixed; as, vested rights. *adj.*

vest ee (ves tē′), a little vest, such as is used for ornament on women's dresses. *n. 18.*

ves ti bule (ves′ti būl), 1. passage or hall between the outer door and the inside of a building. 2. the enclosed space at the end of a railroad passenger car. *n. 11.*

Vestee

ves tige (ves′tij), trace; mark. A blackened, charred stump was a vestige of the fire. Ghost stories are vestiges of a widespread belief in ghosts. *n. 8.*

vest ment (vest′mənt), garment; especially, a garment worn by a clergyman in performing sacred duties. *n. 12.*

ves try (ves′tri), 1. room in a church, where vestments are kept. 2. room in a church or an attached building, used for

Sunday school, prayer meetings, etc. 3. a meeting of parishioners on church business. 4. committee that helps manage church business. *n., pl. vestries. 18.*

ves ture (ves′chər), clothing; garments. *n. 11.*

Ve su vi us (vi sü′vi əs), a volcano near Naples, Italy. *n. 14.*

vetch (vech), a plant often grown as food for animals. *n. 17.*

vet er an (vet′ər ən), 1. grown old in service; experienced; having had much experience in war. Veteran troops fought side by side with the young soldiers. 2. person who has been in the army or navy a long time. *adj., n. 6.*

vet er i nar i an (vet′ər i nãr′i ən), doctor who treats animals. *n.*

vet er i nar y (vet′ər i nãr′i), 1. pertaining to the medical or surgical treatment of animals. 2. doctor who treats animals. *adj., n., pl. veterinaries. 15.*

ve to (vē′tō), 1. the power or right to forbid or prevent. The President has the power of veto over most bills passed in Congress. 2. use the power of veto against; refuse to consent to. Father vetoed our plan to buy a big snake. 3. a prohibition; refusal of consent. *n., pl. vetoes, v. 10.*

vex (veks), 1. annoy; anger by trifles; provoke. It is vexing to have to wait for anyone. 2. disturb. Cape Hatteras is much vexed by storms. 3. A **vexed question** means a question about which people disagree and which is much discussed. *v. 3.*

vex a tion (veks ā′shən), 1. vexing; being vexed. His face showed his vexation at the delay. 2. thing that vexes. These three vexations had annoyed mother: the milk had not come, the cat had upset a lamp, and the cake had burned. *n. 6.*

vex a tious (veks ā′shəs), vexing; annoying. *adj. 15.*

vi a (vī′ə), by way of. He is going from New York to California via the Panama Canal. *prep. 10.*

vi a duct (vī′ə dukt), bridge for carrying a road or railroad over a valley, a part of a city, etc. *n. 13.*

vi al (vī′əl), small glass bottle for holding medicines or the like; bottle. *n. 10.*

vi and (vī′ənd), article of food. **Viands** usually means choice food. *n. 11.*

vi brant (vī′brənt), 1. vibrating. 2. resounding; resonant. *adj. 14.*

vi brate (vī′brāt), 1. move rapidly to and fro. A piano string vibrates and makes a sound when a key is struck. 2. quiver; be moved. 3. thrill. *v. 8.*

vi bra tion (vī brā′shən), rapid movement to and fro; quivering motion; vibrating. The busses shake the house so much that we feel the vibration. *n. 9.*

vi bra tor (vī′brā tər), 1. thing that vibrates. 2. instrument causing vibration. Electric vibrators are used on the scalp. *n. 14.*

vic ar (vik′ər), 1. the minister of an English parish who is paid a salary by the man to whom the tithes are paid. 2. a Roman Catholic clergyman who represents the Pope or a bishop. 3. person acting in place of another. *n. 10.*

vic ar age (vik′ər ij), 1. the residence of a vicar. 2. his position or duties. 3. his salary. *n. 19.*

vi car i ous (vī kãr′i əs), 1. taking the place of another. 2. done or suffered for another. *adj.*

vice[1] (vīs), 1. evil habit or tendency. Lying and cruelty are vices. 2. evil; wickedness. 3. fault; bad habit. Mr. Jones recommended the horse as having no vices. *n. 3.*

vice[2] (vīs), vise. *n.*

vice-, prefix meaning:—substitute; deputy; subordinate; as in vice-president, vice-admiral.

vice-ad mi ral (vīs′ad′mi rəl), a naval officer ranking next below an admiral and next above a rear admiral. *n.*

vice-pres i dent (vīs′prez′i dənt), officer next in rank to the president, who takes the president's place when necessary. If the President of the United States dies, the Vice-President becomes President. *n. 17.*

vice roy (vīs′roi), person ruling a country or province as the deputy of the sovereign. *n. 11.*

vi ce ver sa (vī′si vėr′sə), the other way round; conversely. John blamed Harry, and vice versa (Harry blamed John). *14.*

vi cin i ty (vi sin′i ti), 1. region near or about a place; neighborhood. There are no houses for sale in this vicinity. 2. nearness in place; closeness. *n., pl. vicinities. 6.*

vi cious (vish′əs), 1. evil; wicked. The drunkard led a vicious life. 2. having bad habits or a bad disposition; as, a vicious horse. 3. not correct; having faults. This argument contains vicious reasoning. 4. spiteful; malicious. *adj. 5.*

vi cis si tude (vi sis′i tūd or vi sis′i tüd), change in circumstances; a great variation. The vicissitudes of life may suddenly make a rich man very poor. *n. 8.*

vic tim (vik′tim), 1. person or animal sacrificed, injured, or destroyed; as, victims of war, victims of a swindle, victims of an accident. 2. person or animal killed as a sacrifice to a god. *n. 4.*

vic tim ize (vik′tim īz), 1. make a victim of; cause to suffer. 2. cheat; swindle. *v.*

vic tor (vik′tər), 1. winner; conqueror. 2. victorious. *n., adj. 4.*

Vic to ri a (vik tō′ri ə), 1. queen of England from 1837 to 1901. 2. the capital of British Columbia. 3. a State in southeastern Australia. 4. lake in eastern Africa. *n. 8.*

vic to ri a (vik tō′ri ə), low, four-wheeled carriage with a folding top and a seat for two passengers. A victoria has a raised seat in front for the driver. *n.*

Victoria

Vic to ri an (vik tō′ri ən), 1. of or pertaining to the time of Queen Victoria. 2. person, especially an author, who lived during the reign of Queen Victoria. *adj., n.*

vic to ri ous (vik tō′ri əs), 1. conquering; having won a victory; as, a victorious army. 2. having to do with victory; as, a victorious war. *adj. 4.*

vic to ry (vik′tə ri), defeat of an enemy; success in a contest. The game ended in a victory for our school. *n., pl. victories. 2.*

Vic tro la or **vic tro la** (vik trō′lə), phonograph. *n.* [*Trade name*]

vict ual (vit′əl), supply with food. The captain victualed his ship for the voyage. *v., victualed, victualing. 7.*

vict uals (vit′əlz), food. *n. pl.*

vi cu ña (vi kün′yə), 1. a South American animal somewhat like a camel, having a soft, delicate wool. 2. cloth made from this wool, or from some substitute. *n.*

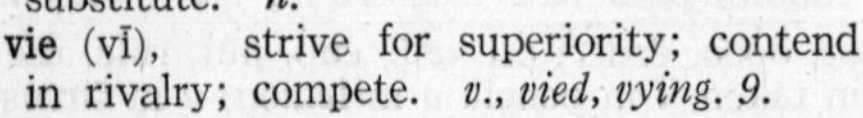

Vicuña (about 2½ ft. high at the shoulder)

vie (vī), strive for superiority; contend in rivalry; compete. *v., vied, vying. 9.*

Vi en na (vi en′ə), capital of Austria, on the Danube River. It is now under German control. *n. 7.*

Vi en nese (vē′ə nēz′), 1. of or pertaining to Vienna or its people. 2. native or inhabitant of Vienna. *adj., n., pl. Viennese.*

view (vū), 1. act of seeing; sight. It was our first view of the ocean. 2. power of seeing; range of the eye. A ship came into view. 3. see; look at. 4. thing seen; a scene. The view from our house is beautiful. 5. picture of some scene. Various views of the coast hung on the walls. 6. a mental picture; an idea. This book will give you a general view of the World War. 7. way of looking at or considering a matter; opinion. Children take a different view of school from that of their teachers. 8. consider; regard. The plan of putting the schools on part time was not viewed favorably by the teachers. 9. Some special meanings are:

in view, 1. in sight. 2. under consideration. 3. as a purpose or intention. 4. as a hope; as an expectation.

in view of, considering; because.

on view, to be seen; open for people to see.

with a view to, with the purpose or intention of; with a hope of; expecting.

n., v. 1.

view less (vū′lis), 1. that cannot be seen. 2. without views or opinions. *adj. 11.*

view point (vū′point′), 1. place from which one looks at something. 2. attitude of mind. *n. 14.*

vig il (vij′əl), 1. keeping awake during the usual hours of sleep; act of watching. All night the mother kept vigil over the sick child. 2. **Vigils** sometimes means devotions, prayers, services, etc., on the night before a religious festival. 3. the day and night before a solemn religious festival. *n. 7.*

vig i lance (vij′i ləns), watchfulness; alertness; caution. The cat watched the mousehole with vigilance. *n. 9.*

vig i lant (vij′i lənt), watchful; alert; wide awake. The dog kept a vigilant guard over the house. *adj. 10.*

vig or (vig′ər), active strength or force; healthy energy or power. A man's vigor lessens as he grows old. *n. 3.*

vig or ous (vig′ər əs), full of vigor; strong and active; energetic; forcible. He keeps himself vigorous by taking exercise. Let us wage a vigorous war against disease. *adj. 7.*

Vi king or **vi king** (vī′king), one of the daring Scandinavian pirates that raided the coasts of Europe during the eighth, ninth, and tenth centuries A.D. *n. 15.*

vile (vīl), 1. very bad; foul; disgusting; as, vile weather, a vile smell. 2. evil; immoral. The criminal used vile language. 3. poor; mean; lowly. The king's son stooped to the vile tasks of the kitchen. *adj. 4.*

vil i fy (vil′i fī), speak evil of. *v., vilified, vilifying. 19.*

vil la (vil′ə), a house in the country or suburbs. A villa is usually a large or elegant residence. *n. 9.*

vil lage (vil′ij), 1. group of houses, smaller than a town. 2. the people of a village. *n. 1.*

vil lag er (vil′ij ər), person who lives in a village. *n. 8.*

vil lain (vil′ən), 1. wicked person. The villain stole the money and cast the blame on his friend. 2. villein. *n. 5.*

vil lain ous (vil′ən əs), extremely bad; very wicked; vile. *adj. 11.*

vil lain y (vil′ən i), 1. great wickedness. 2. very wicked act; a crime. *n., pl. villainies. 8.*

vil lein (vil′ən), one of a class of half-free peasants in the Middle Ages. A villein was under the control of his lord, but otherwise had the rights of a freeman. *n.*

vim (vim), force; energy; vigor. *n.*

vin di cate (vin′di kāt), 1. clear from suspicion, dishonor, hint, or charge of wrongdoing, etc. The verdict of "Not guilty" vindicated him. 2. defend successfully against opposition; uphold; justify. The heir vindicated his claim to the fortune. *v. 11.*

vin di ca tion (vin′di kā′shən), defense; justification. *n. 15.*

vin dic tive (vin dik′tiv), feeling or showing a strong tendency toward revenge; bearing a grudge. *adj. 10.*

vine (vīn), 1. a plant that grows along the ground or that climbs by attaching itself to a wall, tree, or other support. Melons and pumpkins grow on vines. Ivy is a vine. 2. a grapevine. *n. 2.*

vin e gar (vin′i gər), a sour liquid made from cider, wine, etc. Vinegar is used in salad dressing, in flavoring food, and in preserving food. *n. 5.*

vine yard (vin′yərd), place planted with grapevines. *n. 6.*

vi nous (vī′nəs), of wine; like wine; having to do with wine. *adj. 18.*

vin tage (vin′tij), 1. the wine from a certain crop of grapes. The finest vintages cost much more than others. 2. a year's crop of grapes. 3. the season of gathering grapes and making wine. *n. 9.*

vint ner (vint′nər), dealer in wine. *n.*

vi ol (vī′əl), a stringed musical instrument played with a bow. The largest kind of viol is called the double bass. The player usually stands while he plays. *n. 11.*

Man playing a large viol

vi o la (vī ō′lə), a musical instrument shaped like a violin, but slightly larger; a tenor or alto violin. *n. 20.*

vi o late (vī′ə lāt), 1. use force against. 2. break (a law, rule, agreement, promise, etc.); act contrary to; fail to perform. 3. break in upon; disturb. The sound of guns violated the usual calm of Sunday morning. 4. treat with disrespect or contempt. The soldiers violated the church by using it as a stable. *v. 4.*

vi o la tion (vī′ə lā′shən), 1. use of force; violence. 2. breaking a law, rule, agreement, promise, etc. 3. treatment of a holy thing with contempt. *n. 10.*

vi o la tor (vī′ə lā′tər), one who violates. *n.*

vi o lence (vī′ə ləns), 1. rough force in action. Tom slammed the door with violence. 2. rough or harmful action or treatment. 3. injury. It would do violence to her principles to work on Sunday. *n. 3.*

vi o lent (vī′ə lənt), 1. acting or done with strong rough force; as, a violent blow. 2. caused by strong rough force; as, a violent death. 3. showing or caused by very strong feeling, action, etc.; as, violent language. 4. severe; extreme; very great; as, a violent pain, violent heat. *adj. 3.*

vi o let (vī′ə lit), 1. a plant with purple, blue, yellow, or white flowers. 2. bluish purple. Violet is red and blue mixed. *n., adj. 3.*

vi o lin (vī′ə lin′), the commonest musical instrument with four strings played with a bow. See the picture. *n. 5.*

Man playing a violin

vi o lin ist (vī′ə lin′ist), violin player. *n. 15.*

vi o lon cel lo (vī′ə lən chel′ō), a musical instrument like a violin, but very much larger; a bass violin. A violoncello is held between the knees while being played. It is commonly called a cello. *n., pl. violoncellos. 17.*

Man playing a violoncello

vi per (vī′pər), 1. a poisonous snake. 2. a spiteful, treacherous person. *n. 7.*

vi ra go (vi rā′gō), violent, bad-tempered, or scolding woman. *n., pl. viragoes* or *viragos.*

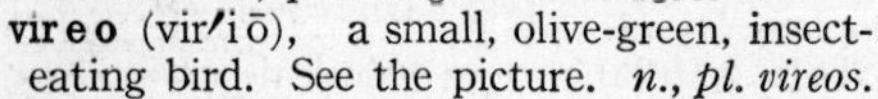

vir e o (vir′i ō), a small, olive-green, insect-eating bird. See the picture. *n., pl. vireos.*

Vir gil (vėr′jil), Roman poet (70-19 B.C.), author of the *Aeneid. n. 11.*

Vireo (about 6 in. long)

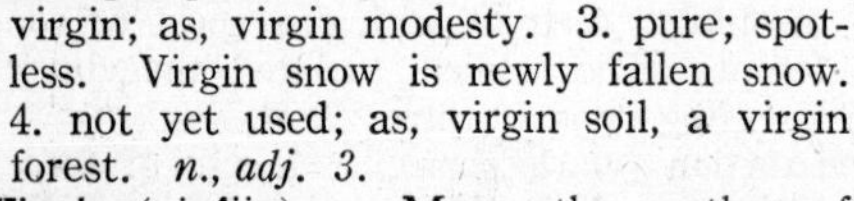

vir gin (vėr′jin), 1. a maiden; a pure, unmarried woman. 2. of a virgin; pertaining to a virgin; as, virgin modesty. 3. pure; spotless. Virgin snow is newly fallen snow. 4. not yet used; as, virgin soil, a virgin forest. *n., adj. 3.*

Vir gin (vėr′jin), Mary, the mother of Jesus. *n.*

vir gin al (vėr′jin əl), maidenly; pure; of or befitting a virgin. *adj. 12.*

Vir gin ia (vər jin′yə), a Southern State of the United States. *n. 3.*

Virgin Islands, group of three islands in the West Indies that belong to the United States.

vir gin i ty (vər jin′i ti), virgin condition; maidenhood. *n. 10.*

Virgin Mary, the mother of Jesus.

vir ile (vir′il), manly; having masculine strength; showing vigor. *adj. 18.*

vi ril i ty (vi ril′i ti), 1. manly strength; masculine vigor. 2. manhood. 3. vigor; forcefulness. *n., pl. virilities.*

vir tu al (vėr′chü əl), real; being something in effect, though not so in name. Mr. Smith is the virtual president, though his title is secretary. The battle was won with so great a loss of soldiers that it was a virtual defeat. *adj. 9.*

vir tu al ly (vėr′chü əl i), actually; really; in effect, though not in name. *adv.*

vir tue (vėr′chü), 1. goodness; moral excellence; purity. 2. a particular moral excellence. Justice and kindness are virtues. 3. a good quality. Jack praised the virtues of his car. 4. power to produce effects. There is little virtue in that medicine. 5. **By virtue of** and **in virtue of** mean because of; on account of. *n. 2.*

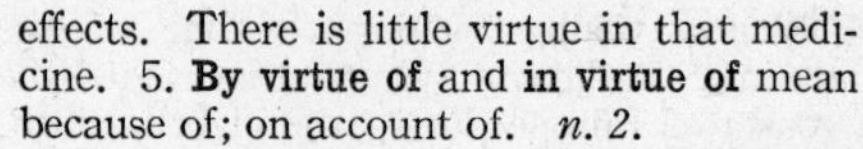

vir tu o so (vėr′chü ō′sō), 1. person skilled in the methods of an art, especially in playing music. 2. person who has a cultivated appreciation of artistic excellence. 3. a student or collector of objects of art, curios, antiquities, etc. *n., pl. virtuosos. 19.*

vir tu ous (vėr′chü əs), good; moral; righteous; pure. *adj. 4.*

vir u lence (vir′ů ləns), 1. quality of being very poisonous; as, the virulence of a rattlesnake's bite. 2. violent hostility; intense bitterness or spite. *n. 20.*

vir u lent (vir′ů lənt), 1. very poisonous; very harmful; as, a virulent form of a disease. 2. violently hostile; intensely bitter or spiteful. *adj. 15.*

vi rus (vī′rəs), 1. a poison produced in a person or animal suffering from an infectious disease; as, smallpox virus. 2. a poison to morals or mind. *n. 17.*

vi sa (vē′zə), an official signature upon a passport or document, showing that it has been examined and approved. *n.*

vis age (viz′ij), face. *n. 7.*

vis cer a (vis′ər ə), the soft inside parts of the body. The heart, stomach, liver, kidneys, and intestines are viscera. *n. pl. 17.*

vis cid (vis′id), sticky; thick like thick syrup or glue. *adj.*

vis cos i ty (vis kos′i ti), being viscous. *n.*

vis count (vī′kount), a nobleman ranking next below an earl or count and next above a baron. *n. 11.*

vis count ess (vī′koun tis), 1. wife or widow of a viscount. 2. woman holding in her own right a rank equivalent to that of a viscount. *n.*

vis cous (vis′kəs), sticky; thick like syrup or glue. *adj. 18.*

vise (vīs), a tool having two jaws moved by a screw, used to hold an object firmly while work is being done on it. *n. 14.*

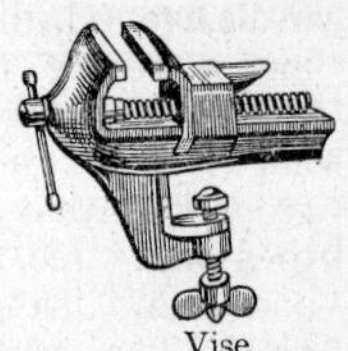

Vise

vi sé (vē′zā), 1. a visa. 2. examine and sign. If you are going abroad, your passport should be viséed by the consul of each country that you intend to visit. *n., v., viséed, viséing.*

vis i bil i ty (viz′i bil′i ti), 1. condition or quality of being visible. In a fog visibility is very poor. 2. distance at which things are visible. *n.*

vis i ble (viz′ibəl), that can be seen. The shore was barely visible through the fog. The tramp had no visible means of support. *adj. 4.*

vis i bly (viz′ibli), so as to be visible; plainly; evidently. *adv.*

vi sion (vizh′ən), 1. power of seeing; sense of sight. The old man wears glasses because his vision is poor. 2. power of perceiving by the imagination or by clear thinking; as, the vision of a prophet, a man of great vision. 3. something seen in the imagination, in a dream, etc. The beggar had visions of great wealth. *n. 3.*

vi sion ar y (vizh′ən ãr′i), 1. not practical; dreamy. Most plans for bringing about world peace are visionary. Ruth is a visionary girl; she spends her time daydreaming. 2. person who is not practical; dreamer. 3. belonging to a vision; seen in a vision. The visionary scene faded, and John awoke. 4. person who sees visions. *adj., n., pl. visionaries. 9.*

vis it (viz′it), 1. go to see; come to see. 2. make a call; stay with; make a stay; be a guest. I shall visit my aunt next week. 3. act of visiting; short stay. 4. go to; come to; come upon. The poor old man was visited by many troubles. *v., n. 1.*

vis it ant (viz′i tənt), visitor; guest. *n. 14.*

vis it a tion (viz′i tā′shən), 1. act of visiting. 2. a visit for the purpose of making an official inspection or examination. A nation at war has the right of visitation of neutral ships; that is, the right to inspect their cargoes. 3. a punishment or reward sent by God. *n. 6.*

vis i tor (viz′i tər), person who visits; person who is visiting; guest. *n. 4.*

VISOR

vi sor (vī′zər), 1. the movable front part of a helmet, covering the face. 2. the brim of a cap, projecting in front. *n. 20.*

vis ta (vis′tə), 1. view seen through a narrow opening or passage. The opening between the two rows of trees afforded a vista of the lake. 2. such an opening or passage itself; as, a shady vista of elms. 3. mental view. Education should open up new vistas. *n. 13.*

Vis tu la (vis′chů lə), river flowing from southeastern Germany into the Baltic Sea. *n.*

vis u al (vizh′ü əl), 1. of sight; having to do with sight. 2. visible; that can be seen. *adj. 10.*

vis u al ize (vizh′ü əl īz), 1. form a mental picture of; as, to visualize a friend's face when he is away. 2. make visible. *v. 16.*

vi tal (vī′təl), 1. of life; having to do with life. 2. necessary to life. Eating is a vital function. The heart is a vital organ. 3. very necessary; essential; very important. 4. causing death, failure, or ruin; as, a vital wound, a vital blow to an industry. 5. full of life and spirit; lively. *adj. 5.*

vi tal i ty (vī tal′i ti), 1. vital force; power to live; strength. Her vitality was lessened by illness. 2. power to endure and act. *n. 9.*

vi tal ize (vī′təl īz), 1. give life to. 2. put vitality into. *v.*

vi tals (vī′təlz), 1. parts or organs necessary to life. The brain, heart, lungs, and stomach are vitals. 2. essential parts or features. *n. pl.*

vi ta min or **vi ta mine** (vī′tə min), any of certain special substances necessary for the proper nourishment of the body, found especially in milk, butter, raw fruits and vegetables, cod-liver oil, and the outside part of wheat and other grains. Lack of vitamins in food causes such diseases as rickets and scurvy. *n. 11.*

vi ti ate (vish′i āt), 1. impair or injure the quality of; spoil. Running an automobile in a closed garage vitiates the air. 2. destroy the legal force or authority of. The contract was vitiated because one person signed under compulsion. *v. 15.*

vit re ous (vit′ri əs), 1. glassy; like glass; as, vitreous china. 2. made from glass. 3. pertaining to glass. *adj. 17.*

vitreous humor, transparent, jellylike substance that fills the eyeball in back of the lens. See the diagram of **eye.**

vit ri fy (vit′ri fī), change into glass or something like glass. *v., vitrified, vitrifying.*

vit ri ol (vit′ri əl), 1. sulphuric acid. Vitriol burns deeply and leaves very bad scars. 2. any of several salts of sulphuric acid. Blue vitriol is copper sulphate. *n. 12.*

vi tu per ate (vī tū′pər āt or vī tü′pər āt), find fault with in abusive words; scold very severely; revile. *v.*

vi tu per a tion (vī tū′pər ā′shən or vī tü′pər-ā′shən), bitter abuse in words; very severe scolding. *n.*

vi va cious (vi vā′shəs), lively; sprightly; animated; gay. *adj. 14.*

vi vac i ty (vi vas′i ti), liveliness; sprightliness; animation; gaiety. *n., pl. vivacities. 13.*

viv id (viv′id), 1. bright; strong and clear. Dandelions are a vivid yellow. 2. lively; full of life. Her description of the party was so vivid that I almost felt I had been there. *adj. 5.*

viv i fy (viv′i fī), give life to; enliven; animate. *v., vivified, vivifying. 15.*

viv i sec tion (viv′i sek′shən), cutting into or experimenting on living animals for scientific study. *n.*

vix en (vik′sən), 1. female fox. 2. bad-tempered or quarrelsome woman. *n. 18.*

viz., namely. He had four sisters, viz., Ella, Alice, Mary, and Jane. *15.*

vi zier or **vi zir** (vi zēr′), a high official in Mohammedan countries; a minister of state. *n. 19.*

vi zor (vī′zər), visor. *n.*

Vla di vos tok (vlä′di vos tok′), seaport in southeastern Siberia. *n. 16.*

vo cab u lar y (vō kab′ū lãr′i), 1. the stock of words used by a people, class, or person. Reading will increase your vocabulary. 2. a list of words with their meanings. *n., pl. vocabularies. 7.*

vo cal (vō′kəl), 1. of the voice; having to do with the voice; made with the voice; as, vocal organs, vocal music. 2. having a voice; giving forth sound. Men are vocal beings. The gorge was vocal with the roar of the cataract. 3. aroused to speech; inclined to talk freely. He became vocal with indignation. *adj. 6.*

vocal cords, two pairs of membranes in the throat, the lower pair of which can be pulled tight or let loose to help make the sounds of the voice.

vo cal ist (vō′kəl ist), singer. *n.*

vo cal ly (vō′kəl i), with the voice; orally; out loud. *adv.*

vo ca tion (vō kā′shən), 1. a particular occupation, business, profession, or trade. She chose teaching as her vocation. 2. an inner call or summons. *n. 10.*

vo ca tion al (vō kā′shən əl), having to do with some occupation, trade, etc. Vocational schools train boys and girls for various occupations. *adj. 15.*

vo cif er ate (vō sif′ər āt), cry out loudly or noisily; shout. *v.*

vo cif er ous (vō sif′ər əs), loud and noisy; shouting; clamoring; as, a vociferous person, vociferous cheers. *adj. 17.*

vod ka (vod′kə), a Russian intoxicating liquor. *n.*

vogue (vōg), 1. the fashion. Hoop skirts were in vogue many years ago. 2. popularity. That song had a great vogue at one time. *n. 10.*

voice (vois), 1. sound made through the mouth. 2. power to make sounds through the mouth. 3. anything like speech or song; as, the voice of the wind. 4. express; utter. They voiced their approval of the plan. 5. expression. They gave voice to their joy. 6. expressed opinion or choice. His voice was for compromise. 7. the right to express an opinion or choice. 8. utter with a sound made by motion of the vocal cords. *Z* and *v* are voiced; *s* and *f* are not. 9. a form of the verb that shows whether the subject is active or passive. *n., v. 1.*

voice less (vois′lis), 1. having no voice; dumb; silent. 2. not voiced. The consonants *p*, *t*, and *k* are voiceless. *adj. 18.*

void (void), 1. empty; vacant; as, a void space. 2. an empty space. The death of his dog left an aching void in Bob's heart. 3. empty out. 4. without force; not binding in law. A contract made by a boy under legal age is void. 5. make of no force or effect in law. *adj., n., v. 4.*

voile (voil), a very thin cloth with an open weave. *n. 10.*

vol., volume.

vol a tile (vol′ə til), 1. evaporating rapidly; passing off readily in the form of vapor. Gasoline is volatile. 2. light and changeable in spirits. Pat has a volatile disposition. *adj. 10.*

Volcano

vol can ic (vol kan′ik), 1. of or caused by a volcano; having to do with volcanoes; as, a volcanic eruption. 2. like a volcano; liable to break out violently. *adj. 9.*

vol ca no (vol kā′nō), mountain having an opening through which steam, ashes, and lava are expelled. *n., pl. volcanoes* or *volcanos. 7.*

Vole (about 5 in. long)

vole (vōl), harmful rodent belonging to the same family as rats and mice. *n.*

Vol ga (vol′gə), great river in western Russia, flowing into the Caspian Sea. *n. 14.*

vo li tion (vō lish′ən), 1. act of willing. The man went away by his own volition.

2. power of willing. The use of drugs has weakened his volition. *n. 16.*

vol ley (vol′i), 1. shower of stones, bullets, arrows, words, oaths, etc. 2. the discharge of a number of guns at once. 3. discharge or be discharged in a volley. Cannon volleyed on all sides. *n., pl. volleys, v. 8.*

vol ley ball (vol′i bôl′), 1. game played with a large ball and a high net. The ball is hit with the hands back and forth over the net without letting it touch the ground. 2. the ball. *n.*

volt (vōlt), the unit of electromotive force. One volt causes a current of one ampere to flow through a resistance of one ohm. *n. 12.*

volt age (vōl′tij), electromotive force expressed in volts. A current of high voltage is used in transmitting electric power over long distances. *n. 16.*

Vol taire (vol tãr′), a famous French writer (1694-1778). *n. 12.*

volt me ter (vōlt′mē′tər), an instrument for measuring the number of volts of an electric circuit. *n. 19.*

vol u bil i ty (vol′ū bil′i ti), 1. readiness to talk much; the habit of talking much. 2. great flow of words. *n. 15.*

vol u ble (vol′ū bəl), ready to talk much; having the habit of talking much; having a great flow of words. *adj. 9.*

vol ume (vol′ūm), 1. book. We own a library of five hundred volumes. 2. a book forming part of a set or series. 3. space occupied. The storeroom has a volume of 400 cubic feet. 4. amount; quantity. Volumes of smoke poured from the chimneys of the factory. 5. amount of sound; fullness of tone. *n. 3.*

vo lu mi nous (və lü′mi nəs), 1. forming, filling, or writing a large book or many books. The Department of Commerce publishes voluminous reports. 2. of great size; very bulky. A voluminous cloak covered him from top to toe. *adj. 13.*

vol un tar i ly (vol′ən tãr′i li), of one's own free will; without force or compulsion. *adv.*

vol un tar y (vol′ən tãr′i), 1. acting of one's own free will. 2. not forced; not compelled. The thief's confession was voluntary. 3. intended; done on purpose. 4. controlled by the will; as, voluntary muscles. Speaking is voluntary; breathing is only partly so. *adj. 6.*

vol un teer (vol′ən tēr′), 1. person who enters any service of his own free will. 2. offer one's services. As soon as war was declared, many men volunteered. 3. offer freely. Jack volunteered to carry the water. 4. of volunteers. Our village has a volunteer fire department. *n., v., adj. 7.*

vo lup tu ar y (və lup′chü ãr′i), person who cares much for luxurious or sensual pleasures. *n., pl. voluptuaries. 17.*

vo lup tu ous (və lup′chü əs), 1. caring much for the pleasures of the senses. 2. giving pleasure to the senses; as, voluptuous music or beauty. *adj. 12.*

vo lup tu ous ness (və lup′chü əs nis), luxury; sensual pleasure. *n. 16.*

vom it (vom′it), 1. throw up what has been eaten. 2. the substance thrown up from the stomach. 3. throw out with force. The chimneys vomited forth smoke. *v., n. 8.*

voo doo (vü′dü), 1. Negro magic. Voodoo probably came from Africa; belief in it still prevails among some Negroes of the West Indies and southern United States. 2. person who practices such magic. *n., pl. voodoos.*

vo ra cious (vō rā′shəs), eating much; greedy in eating; ravenous. *adj. 14.*

vo rac i ty (vō ras′i ti), voracious nature; voracious behavior. *n.*

vor tex (vôr′teks), whirlpool; whirlwind; a whirling mass or movement that sucks in everything near it. *n., pl. vortexes, vortices* (-ti sēz). *15.*

vo ta ress (vō′tə ris), 1. woman bound by a vow; nun. 2. woman devoted to something; devotee. Alice was a votaress of poetry, reading it or writing it in every spare minute. *n. 17.*

vo ta rist (vō′tə rist), votary. *n. 19.*

vo ta ry (vō′tə ri), 1. person bound by a vow; monk or nun. 2. person devoted to something; devotee. Mr. Travis was a votary of golf. *n., pl. votaries. 11.*

vote (vōt), 1. a formal expression of a wish or choice. The person receiving the most votes is elected. 2. the right to give such an expression. Not everybody has the vote. 3. votes considered together; as, the labor vote, the women's vote. 4. give a vote. He voted for the Democrats. 5. pass, determine, or grant by a vote. Money for a new school was voted by the board. 6. ballot. More than a million votes were cast. 7. declare. The children all voted the trip a great success. *n., v. 2.*

vot er (vōt′ər), 1. person who votes. 2. person who has the right to vote. *n. 6.*

vo tive (vō′tiv), promised by a vow; given, done, etc., because of a vow. *adj. 13.*

vouch (vouch), be responsible; give a guarantee. I can vouch for the truth of the story. The principal vouched for Bill's honesty. *v. 9.*

vouch er (vouch′ər), 1. person or thing that vouches for something. 2. written evidence of payment; receipt. Canceled checks returned to a person from his bank are vouchers. *n.*

vouch safe (vouch sāf′), be willing to grant or give; deign (to do or give). Proud Tom vouchsafed no reply. *v. 6.*

vow (vou), 1. solemn promise; as, a vow of secrecy, marriage vows. 2. promise made to God; as, a nun's vows. 3. make a vow. 4. declare earnestly or emphatically. She vowed never to leave home again. *n., v. 3.*

vow el (vou′əl), 1. an open sound produced by the voice. A vowel can form a syllable by itself. 2. a letter representing such a sound. *A, e, i, o,* and *u* are vowels. 3. of or pertaining to a vowel. *n., adj. 7.*

voy age (voi′ij), 1. journey by water; travel by water. 2. journey or travel through the air. *n., v. 3.*

voy ag er (voi′ij ər), person who makes a voyage; traveler. *n. 14.*

vo ya geur (vwä yä zhėr′), French Canadian or half-breed accustomed to travel on foot or by canoe through unsettled regions. *n.*

vs., versus; against.

Vt., Vermont.

Vul can (vul′kən), the Roman god of fire and metalworking. *n. 10.*

vul can ize (vul′kən īz), 1. treat (rubber) with sulphur and heat to make it more elastic and durable. 2. repair (a rubber tire, etc.) by using heat and chemicals to fuse the patch. *v. 18.*

vul gar (vul′gər), 1. not refined; coarse. The tramp used vulgar words. 2. of the common people. The vulgar language differs from the language used by lawyers and preachers. *adj. 5.*

vul gar ism (vul′gər izm), word, phrase, or expression used only by ignorant or careless persons. In "I disremember his name," *disremember* is a vulgarism. *n.*

vul gar i ty (vul gar′i ti), coarseness; lack of fineness of feeling; lack of good breeding, manners, taste, etc. Talking loudly in a streetcar and chewing gum at a dance are signs of vulgarity. *n., pl. vulgarities. 13.*

vul gar ize (vul′gər īz), make vulgar; degrade. *v. 18.*

Vul gate (vul′gāt), the Latin translation of the Bible used by the Roman Catholic Church. The Vulgate was made in the fourth century A.D. *n.*

vul ner a ble (vul′nər ə bəl), 1. capable of being wounded or injured; open to attack. Achilles was vulnerable only in his heel. 2. sensitive to criticism, temptations, influences, etc. Most people are vulnerable to ridicule. *adj. 13.*

Vulture (about 2½ ft. long)

vul ture (vul′chər), 1. a large bird of prey that eats the flesh of dead animals. 2. a greedy, ruthless person. *n. 9.*

vy ing (vī′ing). See **vie.** *ppr. of vie.*

W

W, w (dub′əl ū), the 23rd letter of the alphabet. There are two w's in window. *n., pl. W's, w's.*

W. or **w.,** 1. west. 2. western.

wab ble (wob′əl), 1. move unsteadily from side to side; shake; tremble. 2. waver; be uncertain, unsteady, or inconstant. 3. wabbling motion. *v., n. 19.* Also spelled **wobble.**

wad (wod), 1. a little piece or mass. A wad is used to hold the powder and shot in place in a gun or cartridge. 2. a small, soft mass. 3. make into a wad. 4. stuff with a wad. 5. hold in place by a wad. 6. pad. *n., v., wadded, wadding. 13.*

wad dle (wod′əl), 1. walk with short steps and a swaying motion, as a duck or a short-legged, fat person does. 2. act of waddling. *v., n. 11.*

wade (wād), 1. walk through water, snow, sand, mud, or anything that hinders free motion. 2. make one's way with difficulty; as, to wade through an uninteresting book. 3. go across by wading. *v. 6.*

wa fer (wā′fər), 1. very thin cake or biscuit. 2. the thin round piece of bread used in the Roman Catholic Mass and Communion service. 3. piece of sticky paper, dried paste, etc., used as a seal. *n. 8.*

waf fle (wof′əl), a batter cake cooked in a special griddle that makes the cakes very thin in places. *n. 20.*

waft (waft), 1. carry over water or through air. The waves wafted the boat to shore. 2. a breath or puff of air, etc. 3. waving movement. A waft of the hand was her only farewell. *v., n. 6.*

wag (wag), 1. move from side to side or up and down. A dog wags his tail. 2. wagging motion. 3. person who is fond of making jokes. *v., wagged, wagging, n. 4.*

wage (wāj), 1. amount paid for work. His wages are $25 a week. 2. something given in return. "The wages of sin is death." 3. carry on. Doctors wage war against disease. *n., v. 2.*

wa ger (wā′jər), bet. The wager of $10 was promptly paid. I'll wager the black horse will win the race. *n., v. 9.*

wage work er (wāj′wėr′kər), person who works for wages. *n. 19.*

wag ger y (wag′ər i), joking; a joke. *n., pl. waggeries.*

wag gish (wag′ish), 1. fond of making jokes. 2. funny. *adj. 16.*

wag gle (wag′əl), 1. move quickly and repeatedly from side to side; wag. 2. waggling motion. *v., n.*

Wag ner (väg′nər), Richard (1813-1883), a German musical composer, famous for his operas. *n. 18.*

wag on (wag′ən), four-wheeled vehicle for carrying loads; as, a milk wagon. *n. 2.*

Wagon

wag on er (wag′ən ər), person who drives a wagon. *n. 9.*

waif (wāf), 1. person without home or friends; homeless or neglected child. 2. anything without an owner; stray thing, animal, etc. *n. 16.*

wail (wāl), 1. cry loud and long because of grief or pain. The baby wailed. 2. long cry of grief or pain. 3. a sound like such a cry. 4. make such a sound. 5. lament; mourn. *v., n. 4.*

wain (wān), wagon. *n.* [*Old use*] *11.*

wain scot (wān′skət), 1. lining of wood on the walls of a room. A wainscot usually has panels. 2. line with wood; as, a room wainscoted in oak. *n., v., wainscoted, wainscoting. 12.*

waist (wāst), 1. the part of the body between the ribs and the hips. 2. waistline. 3. a garment or part of a garment covering the body from the neck or shoulders to the waistline. 4. the middle part; as, the waist of a ship. *n. 2.*

waist band (wāst′band′), a band around the waist; as, the waistband of a skirt or of a pair of trousers. *n.*

waist coat (wāst′kōt′), man's vest. *n. 9.*

waist line (wāst′līn′), the line around the body between the ribs and hips. *n. 14.*

wait (wāt), 1. stay till someone comes or something happens. 2. delay or put off. Mother waited dinner for us. *Used in common talk.* 3. be ready; look forward. The children wait impatiently for vacation. 4. act as a servant; change plates, pass food, etc., at table. 5. act or time of waiting. John had a long wait at the doctor's office. 6. Some special meanings are:

lie in wait, stay hidden ready to attack. Robbers lay in wait for the travelers.

The waits, singers and musicians who go about the streets singing and playing at Christmas time.

wait on or **wait upon,** 1. be a servant to. 2. call upon or visit (a superior). The general waited upon the emperor at the palace.

v., n. 1.

wait er (wāt′ər), 1. one who waits. 2. man who waits on table in a hotel or restaurant. 3. tray for carrying dishes. *n. 7.*

wait ing (wāt′ing), 1. that waits. 2. used to wait in. 3. time that one waits. **In waiting** means in attendance on a king, queen, prince, princess, etc. *adj., n.*

waiting room, room at a railroad station, doctor's office, etc., for people to wait in.

wait ress (wāt′ris), woman who waits on table in a hotel or restaurant. *n. 15.*

waive (wāv), 1. give up (a right, claim, etc.); relinquish; refrain from claiming or pressing; do without. The lawyer waived the privilege of cross-examining the witness. 2. put aside; defer. *v. 14.*

waiv er (wāv′ər), 1. a giving up of a right, claim, etc. 2. written statement of this. For $100, the injured man signed a waiver of all claims against the railroad. *n.*

wake[1] (wāk), 1. stop sleeping. She wakes at seven every morning. 2. cause to stop sleeping. The noise will wake the baby. 3. be awake; stay awake. 4. become alive or active. Flowers wake in the spring.

5. make alive or active. John needs some interest to wake him up. 6. keep watch. 7. watching; all-night watch kept beside the body of a dead person. *v., waked* or *woke, waking, n. 2.*

wake² (wāk), 1. track left behind a moving ship; trace or trail. 2. **In the wake of** means following; behind; after. *n.*

wake ful (wāk′fəl), 1. not able to sleep. 2. without sleep. 3. watchful. *adj. 10.*

wake ful ness (wāk′fəlnis), inability to sleep; wakeful condition. *n. 17.*

Wake Island, small island about 2000 miles west of Hawaii, belonging to the United States.

wak en (wāk′ən), wake. *v. 4.*

wale (wāl), 1. a streak or ridge made on the skin by a stick or whip; a welt. 2. to mark with wales; to raise wales on. 3. a ridge in the weave of cloth. *n., v.*

Wales (wālz), the division of Great Britain west of England; land of the Welsh. *n. 6.*

walk (wôk), 1. go on foot. In walking, a person always has one foot on the ground. 2. go over, on, or through. The man walked the floor in pain from toothache. 3. make go slowly. The rider walked his horse up the hill. 4. act of going on foot. The children went for a walk. 5. distance to walk. It is a mile walk from our house to the school. 6. way of walking. We knew the man was a sailor from his rolling walk. 7. place for walking. There are many pretty walks in the park. 8. way of living. A doctor and a street cleaner are in different walks of life. *v., n. 1.*

walking stick, 1. cane. 2. any of various insects having a long round body like a stick.

walk out (wôk′out′), strike of workers. *n.* [*Used in common talk*]

wall (wôl), 1. the side of a house, room, or other hollow thing. 2. stone, brick, or other material built up to enclose, divide, support, or protect. Cities used to be surrounded by high walls to keep out enemies. 3. anything like a wall in looks or use. The flood came in a wall of water twelve feet high. The soldiers kept their ranks a solid wall. 4. enclose, divide, protect, or fill with a wall. The garden is walled. Workmen walled up the doorway. 5. **Drive to the wall** means make desperate or helpless. 6. **Go to the wall** means give way; be defeated. *n., v. 1.*

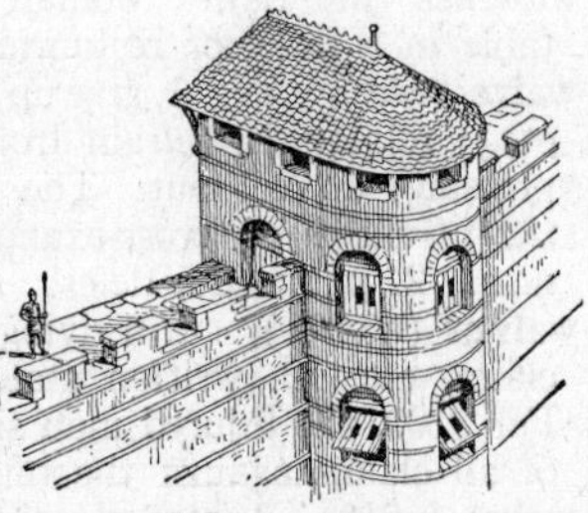
Wall with tower

wal la by (wol′əbi), a kangaroo of the smaller sorts. Some wallabies are no larger than rabbits. *n., pl. wallabies.*

Wallaby

Wal lace (wol′is), Sir William, a famous Scottish leader (1272?-1305). *n. 10.*

wal let (wol′it), 1. folding pocketbook for paper money, papers, etc.; flat leather case. 2. bag for carrying things when on a journey. *n. 7.*

Wallet (def. 1)

wall eyed (wôl′īd′), 1. having eyes that show much white and little color. 2. having both eyes turned away from the nose. 3. having large staring eyes. The pike is a walleyed fish. *adj.*

wall flow er (wôl′flou′ər), 1. a plant with sweet-smelling yellow, orange, or red flowers. 2. person who sits by the wall at a dance instead of dancing. *Used in common talk. n. 18.*

wal lop (wol′əp), 1. beat soundly; thrash. 2. hit very hard. 3. very hard blow. 4. power to hit very hard blows. *v., n.* [*Used in common talk*] *18.*

wal low (wol′ō), 1. roll about. The pigs wallowed in the mud. The boat wallowed helplessly in the stormy sea. 2. live in filth and wickedness like a beast. 3. act of wallowing. 4. place where an animal wallows. *v., n. 8.*

wall pa per (wôl′pā′pər), 1. paper for covering walls. 2. put wallpaper on. *n., v.*

wal nut (wôl′nut), 1. a nut that is good to eat. 2. the tree it grows on. 3. the wood of this tree. Black walnut is used in making furniture. *n. 5.*

wal rus (wôl′rəs), a large sea animal of the Arctic regions, resembling a seal but having long tusks. See the picture. Walrus hide is made into leather for suitcases, bags, etc. *n. 14.*

Walrus
(about 10 ft. long)

waltz (wôlts), 1. a smooth, even, gliding dance. 2. music for it. 3. dance a waltz. *n., v. 15.*

wam pum (wom′pəm), beads made from shells, formerly used by North American Indians as money and for ornament. *n. 10.*

A string of seven pieces of wampum

wan (won), 1. pale. 2. faint; weak; looking worn or tired. The sick boy gave the doctor a wan smile. *adj., wanner, wannest. 6.*

wand (wond), slender stick or rod. The magician waved his wand. *n. 3.*

wan der (won′dər), 1. move about without any special purpose. 2. go from the right way; stray. The dog wandered off and got lost. Mrs. White wanders away from her subject when she talks. A person's mind wanders during very high fever. *v. 2.*

wan der er (won′dər ər), person or animal that wanders. *n. 8.*

wan der lust (won′dər lust′), strong desire to wander. *n.*

wane (wān), 1. lose size, strength, power, importance, etc. The moon wanes after it has become full. Many great empires have waned. 2. a decrease; a decline. **On the wane** means growing less; waning. *v., n. 7.*

want (wont), 1. to wish for; wish. The child wants his dinner. 2. thing desired or needed. Mr. Jones is a man of few wants and is happy with simple pleasures. 3. lack; be without. The fund for a new church wants only a few hundred dollars of the sum needed. 4. condition of being without something desired or needed; lack; need. The plant died from want of water. 5. to need. That plant wants water. 6. great poverty. The old soldier is now in want. 7. be in need of food, clothing, and shelter; be very poor. *v., n. 1.*

want ing (won′ting), 1. lacking; missing; as, a machine with some of the parts wanting. 2. without; less; minus; as, a year wanting three days. 3. not coming up to a standard or need. *adj., prep.*

wan ton (won′tən), 1. reckless; heartless. That bad boy hurts animals from wanton cruelty. 2. not moral; not chaste. 3. playful; not restrained; as, a wanton child, a wanton breeze, a wanton mood. 4. wanton person. 5. act in a wanton manner. The wind wantoned with the leaves. *adj., n., v. 4.*

wan ton ness (won′tən nis), wanton nature or behavior. The boy made trouble in school from mere wantonness. *n. 9.*

wap i ti (wop′i ti), a North American deer with long slender antlers: the American elk. *n., pl. wapiti.*

war (wôr), 1. a fight carried on by force between nations or parts of a nation. 2. fighting; strife; conflict. Doctors carry on war against disease. 3. the occupation or art of fighting with weapons. Soldiers are trained for war. 4. fight; make war. The Greeks warred against Troy. 5. used in war; having to do with war; caused by war. *n., v., warred, warring, adj. 1.*

War between the States, American Civil War, from 1861 to 1865.

war ble (wôr′bəl), 1. sing like a bird; as, the warbling brook. 2. a bird's song or a sound like it. *v., n. 5.*

war bler (wôr′blər), 1. one that warbles. 2. any of several kinds of songbirds. *n. 10.*

ward (wôrd), 1. person under the care of a guardian or of a court. 2. a district of a city or town. 3. a division of a hospital or prison. 4. guard. The soldiers kept watch and ward over the castle. 5. keep watch over. *Old use.* 6. **Ward off** means keep away or turn aside. He warded off the blow with his arm. The habit of saving wards off poverty. *n., v. 3.*

-ward, suffix meaning:—toward; in the direction of; that is, moves, or faces toward; as in backward, heavenward, seaward.

ward en (wôr′dən), 1. keeper; guard. The man in charge of a prison is called the warden. 2. the head of certain colleges, schools, etc. *n. 11.*

ward er (wôr′dər), 1. guard; watchman. 2. warden; jailer. *n. 14.*

ward robe (wôrd′rōb′), 1. a room, closet, or piece of furniture for holding clothes. 2. stock of clothes. She is shopping for her spring wardrobe. *n. 6.*

-wards, suffix meaning:—in the direction of; as in backwards, upwards.

ware[1] (wãr), 1. manufactured thing; article for sale. The peddler sold his wares cheap. 2. kind of manufactured thing or article for sale; goods; as, silverware and tinware. 3. pottery. Delft is a blue and white ware. *n. 4.*

ware[2] (wãr), 1. aware. *Old use.* 2. beware. *Used in common talk.* Jack called, "Ware heads!" as the boat approached the low bridge. *adj., v.*

ware house (wãr′hous′), place where goods are kept; storehouse. *n. 7.*

war fare (wôr′fãr′), war; fighting. *n. 6.*

war horse, 1. horse used in war. 2. person who has taken part in many battles, struggles, etc. *Used in common talk.*

war ily (wãr′ili), in a wary manner; cautiously. *adv.*

wari ness (wãr′inis), caution. *n. 19.*

war like (wôr′līk′), 1. fit for war; ready for war; fond of war; as, warlike tribes. 2. threatening war; as, a warlike speech. 3. of war; having to do with war. *adj. 6.*

warm (wôrm), 1. Sunshine is warm. A fire is warm. 2. We wear warm clothes in winter. 3. easily excited; exciting; lively; as, a warm temper, a warm dispute. 4. having or showing lively feelings; zealous; enthusiastic; as, a warm welcome, a warm friend, a warm heart. 5. suggesting heat. Red and yellow are warm colors. 6. make warm. 7. become warm. The speaker warmed to his subject. *adj., v. 1.*

warm-blood ed (wôrm′blud′id), 1. having warm blood. The temperature of warm-blooded animals is from 98 degrees to 112 degrees. Cats are warm-blooded; snakes are cold-blooded. 2. with much feeling; eager; ardent. *adj.*

Warming pan

warming pan, covered pan for holding hot coals, formerly used to warm beds.

warmth (wôrmth), a being warm. We enjoyed both the warmth of the open fire and the warmth of our host's welcome. *n. 4.*

warn (wôrn), give notice to; put on guard against danger, evil, harm, etc. The clouds warned us that a storm was coming up. He warned the king of the plot against his life. *v. 2.*

warn ing (wôr′ning), something that warns; notice given in advance. *n.*

War of 1812, war between the United States and Great Britain. It lasted from 1812 to 1815.

War of Independence, war between the American colonies and Great Britain, from 1775 to 1783; the American Revolution; Revolutionary War.

warp (wôrp), 1. bend or twist out of shape. This floor has warped so that it is not level. Prejudice warps our judgment. 2. a bend or twist. 3. move (a ship, etc.) by ropes fastened to something fixed. 4. rope used in moving a ship. 5. the threads running lengthwise in a fabric. The warp is crossed by the woof. *v., n. 5.*

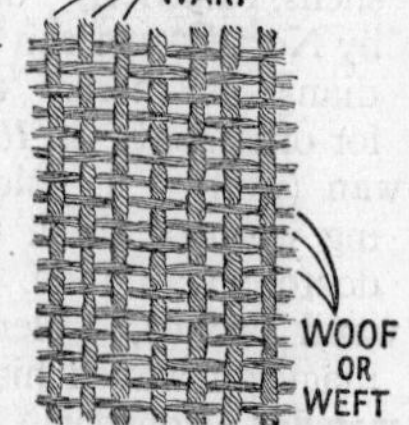

war rant (wor′ənt), 1. that which gives a right; authority. He had no warrant for his action. 2. a written order giving authority for something; as, a warrant to search the house, a warrant for a man's arrest, a warrant for the payment of money. 3. guarantee; promise; good and sufficient reason. He had no warrant for his hopes. 4. justify. Nothing can warrant such rudeness. 5. give one's word for; guarantee; promise. The storekeeper warranted the quality of the coffee. "I'll warrant Dick will behave," said Mr. Black. *n., v. 4.*

warrant officer, 1. an army or navy officer who has received a certificate of appointment, but not a commission. 2. in the United States navy, any of various subordinate officers. A boatswain or a gunner is a warrant officer.

war ren (wor′ən), piece of land where rabbits breed or are plentiful. *n. 11.*

war ri or (wor′iər), fighting man; experienced soldier. *n. 3.*

War saw (wôr′sô), the capital of Poland. It is now under German control. *n. 14.*

war ship (wôr′ship′), ship used in fighting. *n. 11.*

wart (wôrt), 1. a small hard lump on the skin. 2. a similar lump on a plant. *n. 11.*

Wart hog (3 ft. high at the shoulder)

wart hog, wild hog of Africa that has two large tusks and two large wartlike growths on each side of its face.

war y (wãr′i), 1. on one's guard against danger or deception; as, a wary fox. 2. cautious; careful. He gave wary answers to all of the stranger's questions. **Wary of** means cautious about; careful about. Be wary of giving offense. *adj., warier, wariest. 8.*

was (woz). Once there was a king. I was late to school yesterday. The candy was eaten. *a pt. of* **be**. *1.*

wash (wosh), 1. clean with water; as, wash one's face, wash dishes, wash clothes. 2. wash oneself. 3. wash clothes; cleanse anything with water. 4. a washing. 5. quantity of clothes washed or to be washed. She hung the wash on the line. 6. undergo washing without damage. Some silks wash perfectly. 7. that can be washed without damage. 8. carry (by a liquid). Wood is washed up by the sea. 9. material carried and then dropped by water. A delta is formed by the wash of a river. 10. wear by water. The cliffs are being slowly washed away by the waves. 11. motion or rush of water. We listened to the wash of the waves against the boat. 12. make wet. The rose is washed with dew. 13. liquid for special use; as, a mouthwash, a hairwash. 14. waste liquid matter; liquid garbage. The kitchen wash is given to the pigs. 15. thin coating of color or metal. 16. cover with a thin coating of color or of metal. The walls were washed with blue. *v., n., adj. 1.*

Wash., Washington, a Northwestern State of the United States.

wash a ble (wosh′ə bəl), that can be washed without damage; as, washable silk. *adj.*

wash board (wosh′bōrd′), a board having ridges on it, used for rubbing the dirt out of clothes. *n. 12.*

wash er (wosh′ər), 1. person who washes. 2. machine that washes. 3. a flat ring of metal, rubber, leather, etc. Washers are used with bolts or nuts, or to make joints tight. *n. 9.*

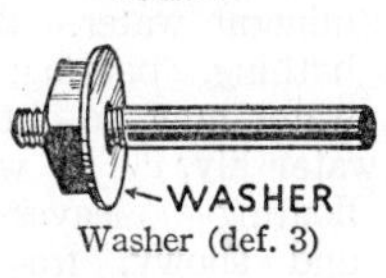

Washer (def. 3)

wash er wom an (wosh′ər wům′ən), woman whose work is washing clothes. *n., pl. washerwomen. 20.*

wash ing (wosh′ing), 1. cleaning with water. 2. clothes, etc., washed or to be washed. 3. liquid that has been used to wash something. 4. matter removed in washing something; as, washings of gold obtained from earth. *n.*

Wash ing ton (wosh′ing tən), 1. George Washington (1732-1799) was commander in chief of the American army in the Revolutionary War, and the first president of the United States, from 1789 to 1797. 2. the capital of the United States. 3. a Northwestern State of the United States on the Pacific coast. *n. 2.*

wash out (wosh′out′), 1. washing away of earth, a road, etc., by water. 2. the hole or break made by it. 3. failure; disappointment. *Slang. n.*

wash stand (wosh′stand′), 1. bowl with pipes and faucets for running water to wash one's hands and face. 2. stand for holding a basin, pitcher, etc., for washing. *n.*

was n't (woz′ənt), was not. *5.*

wasp (wosp), a kind of insect that has a slender body and a powerful sting. See the picture. *n. 6.*

Wasp (about life size)

wasp ish (wos′pish), 1. like a wasp. 2. bad-tempered; irritable. *adj. 20.*

was sail (wos′əl), 1. drinking party. 2. liquor drunk at such a party, usually spiced ale. 3. a salutation meaning "Your health!" *n., interj. 14.*

was sail er (wos′əl ər), 1. reveler. 2. drinker of healths. *n. 20.*

wast (wost), an old form meaning **was.** "Thou wast" means "you were." *v. 4.*

waste (wāst), 1. make poor use of; throw away. Don't waste food. 2. failure to use well. 3. not used. 4. useless. 5. something not used; useless stuff. 6. waste material; stuff that is left over; refuse. Bunches of cotton waste are used to clean machinery. 7. bare; wild. **Lay waste** means destroy; damage greatly. 8. desert; wilderness. We traveled through treeless wastes. Before us stretched a waste of snow and ice. 9. spoil; ruin; destroy. The soldiers wasted the fields of the enemy. 10. wearing down little by little; gradual destruction or decay. Both waste and repair are constantly going on in our bodies. 11. wear away. The man was wasted by disease. *v., n., adj. 1.*

waste ful (wāst′fəl), using or spending too much. *adj. 11.*

watch (woch), 1. look. 2. look at. We watched the kittens play. 3. look or wait with care and attention; be very careful. The boy watched for a chance to cross the street. 4. careful looking; attitude of attention. Be on the watch for automobiles when you cross the street. 5. keep guard. The dog watches over his master's house. 6. protecting; guarding. A man keeps watch over the bank at night. 7. person or persons kept to guard. The man's cry aroused the town watch who came running to his aid. 8. period of time for guarding; as, a watch in the night. 9. stay awake for some purpose. The nurse watches with the sick. 10. staying awake for some purpose. 11. thing for telling time, small enough to be carried in a pocket or worn on the wrist. 12. the time of duty of one part of a ship's crew. A watch usually lasts four hours. 13. the part of a ship's crew on duty at the same time. *v., n. 1.*

watch dog (woch′dôg′), dog kept to guard property. *n. 20.*

watch er (woch′ər), one that watches. *n. 11.*

watch ful (woch′fəl), on the lookout; wide-awake; watching carefully. "Watchful waiting catches mice," said the cat. *adj. 4.*

watch mak er (woch′māk′ər), man who makes and repairs watches. *n. 20.*

watch man (woch′mən), man set to keep watch. A watchman guards the bank at night. *n., pl. watchmen. 6.*

watch tow er (woch′tou′ər), tower from which a man watches for enemies, fires, ships, etc. *n. 17.*

watch word (woch′wėrd′), 1. secret word that allows a person to pass a guard. We gave the watchword, and the sentinel let us pass. 2. motto; slogan. "Forward" is our watchword. *n. 11.*

wa ter (wô′tər), 1. the ocean, rivers, lakes, ponds, and rain are water. We use water for drinking and washing. 2. a liquid like water. When you cry, water runs from your eyes. 3. sprinkle or wet with water; as, to water a street, to water grass. 4. supply with water. New England is well watered by rivers and brooks. 5. weaken by adding water. It is against the law to sell watered milk. 6. fill with water; discharge water. Strong sunlight will make your eyes water. The cake made the boy's mouth water. 7. take a supply of water. A ship waters before sailing. 8. the clearness and brilliance of a precious stone. A diamond of the first water is a very clear and brilliant one. 9. wavy marking on silk, metal, etc. 10. make a wavy marking on. Grandmother had a dress of watered silk. *n., v. 1.*

water bird, bird that swims or wades in water.

wa ter buck (wô′tər buk′), large African antelope. See the picture just below. *n.*

Waterbuck (about 3 ft. high at the shoulder)

Wa ter bur y (wô′tər ber′i), city in western Connecticut. *n.*

water clock, instrument for measuring time by the flow of water.

water color, 1. paint to be mixed with water instead of oil. 2. painting with water colors. 3. picture made with water colors.

wa ter-col or (wô′tər kul′ər), made with water colors. *adj.*

wa ter course (wô′tər kōrs′), 1. stream of water; river; brook. 2. channel for water; as, dried-up watercourses. *n. 15.*

water cress, a plant that grows in water, used for salad and as a garnish. *19.*

wa ter fall (wô′tər fôl′), fall of water from a high place. *n. 5.*

wa ter fowl (wô′tər foul′), 1. water bird. 2. water birds; especially, birds that swim. *n., pl. waterfowls or waterfowl. 16.*

water front, land at the water's edge; especially, the part of a city beside a river, lake, or harbor.

watering place, 1. resort with springs of mineral water. 2. resort where there is bathing, boating, etc. 3. place where water may be obtained.

water lily, a water plant having flat, floating leaves and showy, fragrant flowers. The flowers of the common American water lily are white, or sometimes pink.

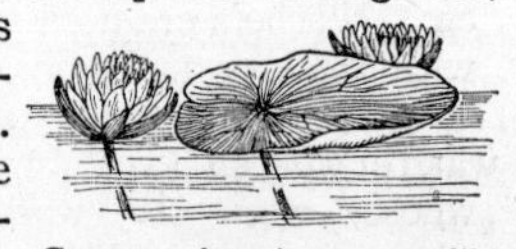
Common American water lily

water line, line where the surface of the water touches the side of a ship or boat.

wa ter-logged (wô′tər lôgd′), so full of water that it will barely float. *adj.*

Wa ter loo (wô′tər lü), 1. the battle in which Napoleon was finally defeated in 1815. 2. decisive or crushing defeat. *n. 13.*

wa ter man (wô′tər mən), 1. boatman; man who works on a boat. 2. oarsman. *n., pl. watermen. 13.*

wa ter mel on (wô′tər mel′ən), a large juicy melon with red or pink pulp and hard green rind. *n. 13.*

water power, the power from flowing or falling water.

wa ter proof (wô′tər prüf′), 1. that will not let water through. 2. waterproof material. 3. waterproof coat; raincoat. 4. make waterproof. *adj., n., v. 8.*

water rat, 1. large European field mouse that lives in the banks of streams or lakes. 2. muskrat.

wa ter shed (wô′tər shed′), 1. ridge between the regions drained by two different river systems. 2. the region drained by one river system. *n. 16.*

wa ter side (wô′tər sīd′), land along the sea, a lake, a river, etc. *n.*

wa ter spout (wô′tər spout′), 1. water pipe. 2. whirlwind over the ocean or a large lake. A waterspout looks like a column of water reaching upward to the clouds. *n. 18.*

wa ter tight (wô′tər tīt′), 1. so tight that no water can get in or out. Steamboats are often divided into watertight compartments by watertight partitions. 2. leaving no opening for misunderstanding, criticism, etc.; perfect. *adj.*

wa ter way (wô′tər wā′), 1. a river, canal, or other body of water that ships can go on. 2. channel for water. *n. 10.*

water wheel, wheel turned by water and used to do work.

wa ter works (wô′tər wėrks′), 1. pipes, reservoir, water towers, pumps, etc., for supplying a city or town with water. 2. building containing engines and pumps for pumping water; pumping station. *n. sing. or pl. 19.*

wa ter y (wô′tər i), 1. of water. 2. wet; full of water. 3. containing too much water. 4. like water. 5. indicating rain; as, a watery sky. *adj. 6.*

watt (wot), a unit of electric power. My lamp uses 60 watts; my toaster uses 660 watts. *n. 10.*

Watt (wot), James, a British engineer and inventor (1736-1819). Watt perfected the steam engine. *n.*

wat tle (wot′əl), 1. sticks interwoven with twigs or branches; framework of wicker; as, a hut built of wattle. 2. make (a fence, wall, roof, hut, etc.) of wattle. 3. twist or weave together (twigs, branches, etc.). 4. the red flesh hanging down from the throat of a chicken, turkey, etc. *n., v. 10.*

Wattle of a turkey

wave (wāv), 1. a moving ridge or swell of water. 2. any movement like this. Light, heat, and sound move in waves. A cold wave is sweeping over the country. 3. move as waves do; sway. The tall grass waved in the breeze. Mary waved to Alice as she passed. 4. move back and forth. Wave your hand. 5. signal by waving. 6. waving; as, a wave of the hand. 7. curve or series of curves; as, waves in a girl's hair. 8. give a wavelike form to. Girls wave their hair. *n., v. 1.*

wa ver (wā′vər), 1. move to and fro. Helen's choice wavered between the blue dress and the green one. 2. become unsteady; begin to give way. The battle line wavered and broke. 3. a wavering. *v., n. 4.*

wav y (wāv′i), having waves; having many waves; as, a wavy line, wavy hair. *adj., wavier, waviest. 14.*

Wavy line

wax[1] (waks), 1. a yellowish substance made by bees. Wax is hard when cold, but can be easily shaped when warm. 2. any substance like this. Most of the wax used for candles, for keeping air from jelly, etc., is really paraffin. Sealing wax and shoemaker's wax are other common waxes. 3. rub, stiffen, polish, etc., with wax. We wax that floor once a month. 4. a person is said to be **wax in someone's hands** when he is very easily influenced and managed. *n., v. 3.*

wax[2] (waks), 1. grow; increase. The moon waxes till it becomes full, and then wanes. 2. become. The party waxed merry. *v.*

wax en (wak′sən), 1. made of wax. 2. like wax. Her skin was waxen. *adj. 9.*

wax wing (waks′wing′), small bird with a showy crest and red markings at the tips of the wings. *n.*

Cedar waxwing (7 in. long)

wax y (wak′si), like wax. *adj., waxier, waxiest. 20.*

way (wā), 1. manner; style. Mary is wearing her hair in a new way. 2. means; method. Men of science are trying to find ways to prevent disease. 3. respect; particular. The plan is bad in several ways. 4. direction. Look this way. 5. coming or going; progress. The beggar made his way from door to door. 6. distance. The moon is a long way off. 7. path; road. The hunter found a way through the forest. 8. space for passing or going ahead. Automobiles must make way for a fire engine. 9. habit; custom. Don't mind Joe's teasing; it's only his way. 10. one's wish; will. A spoiled child wants his own way all the time. 11. condition; state. *Used in common talk.* That sick man is in a bad way. 12. movement of a ship through water; as, head*way*, lee*way*. The boat slowly gathered way as it slid through the water. 13. Some special meanings are:

by the way, 1. while coming or going. 2. in that connection; incidentally.

by way of, 1. by the route of; through. 2. as; for.

give way, 1. retreat; make way; yield. 2. break down or fail. 3. abandon oneself to emotion.

under way, going on; in motion; in progress.

ways, timbers on which a ship is built and launched.

n. 1.

way bill (wā′bil′), list of goods with a statement of where they are to go and how they are to get there. *n.*

way far er (wā′fãr′ər), traveler. *n. 20.*

way far ing (wā′fãr′ing), traveling. *adj. 20.*

way lay (wā′lā′), 1. lie in wait for; attack on the way. Robin Hood waylaid travelers and robbed them. 2. stop (a person) on his way. Newspaper reporters waylaid the famous English author to get his impressions of America. *v., waylaid, waylaying. 12.*

-ways, suffix forming adverbs showing direction or position; as in edgeways, sideways; also adverbs showing manner; as in anyways, noways.

way side (wā′sīd′), 1. edge of a road or path. We ate lunch on the wayside. 2. along the edge of a road or path. We slept in a wayside inn. *n., adj. 7.*

way ward (wā′wərd), 1. turning from the right way; disobedient; willful. In a wayward mood, Bill ran away from home. 2. irregular; unsteady. *adj. 7.*

we (wē), 1. the persons speaking. We are glad to see you. 2. an author, a king, or a judge sometimes uses *we* when he means *I*. *pron. pl. 1.*

weak (wēk). A weak old man totters as he walks. A person with weak eyes cannot see far. A weak mind is a feeble one. A weak fort can be easily captured. A weak nation has very little power because it is poor and small. Weak tea has less flavor than strong tea. A weak acid contains much water and little acid. *adj. 1.*

weak en (wēk′ən), 1. make weaker. You can weaken the tea by adding water. 2. become weaker. *v. 6.*

weak ling (wēk′ling), 1. weak person or animal. 2. weak. *n., adj. 12.*

weak ly (wēk′li), 1. weak; feeble; sickly. 2. in a weak manner. *adj., adv.*

weak ness (wēk′nis), 1. being weak; lack of power, force, or vigor. Weakness kept Mr. Smith in bed. 2. weak point; slight fault. Putting things off is her weakness. 3. fondness; a liking that one is a little ashamed of. Grace has a weakness for sweets. *n. 3.*

weal[1] (wēl), well-being; prosperity; happiness. Good citizens act for the public weal. A loyal man stands by his friends in weal or woe. *n. 9.*

weal[2] (wēl), mark on the skin made by a stick or whip; welt. *n.*

wealth (welth), 1. riches; many valuable possessions; property; as, a man of wealth, the wealth of a city. 2. abundance; large quantity; as, a wealth of hair, a wealth of words. *n. 2.*

wealth y (wel′thi), having wealth; rich. *adj., wealthier, wealthiest. 3.*

wean (wēn), 1. accustom (a child or young animal) to food other than its mother's milk. 2. accustom (a person) to do without something; cause to turn away. Tom was sent away to school to wean him from bad companions. *v. 8.*

weap on (wep′ən), thing used in fighting. Swords, spears, arrows, clubs, guns, cannon, shields, claws, horns, teeth, and stings are weapons. *n. 3.*

wear (wãr), 1. have on the body. Men wear coats, hats, collars, watches, beards. She wears black since her husband died. 2. have; show. The house wore an air of sadness. 3. wearing; being worn. Clothing for summer wear is being shown in the shops. This suit has been in constant wear for two years. 4. clothing; as, underwear, neckwear, footwear. Children's wear is sold in this store. 5. last long; give good service. This coat has worn well. A person wears well if you like him better the longer you know him. 6. lasting quality; service. There is still much wear in these shoes. 7. use up; be used up. The pencil is worn to a stub. The paint wears off the house.

8. damage from use. The rug shows wear. 9. make by rubbing, scraping, or washing away. Walking wore a hole in my shoe. 10. tire. She is worn out by too much work. Teaching is wearing work. *v., wore, worn, wearing, n. 1.*

wear er (wãr′ər), person or thing that wears. *n. 9.*

wea ri ly (wēr′i li), in a weary manner. *adv.*

wea ri ness (wēr′i nis), weary condition; tired feeling. *n. 5.*

wea ri some (wēr′i səm), wearying; tiring; tiresome. *adj. 10.*

wea ry (wēr′i), 1. tired; as, weary feet, a weary brain. 2. tiring; as, a weary wait. 3. make weary; tire. *adj., wearier, weariest, v., wearied, wearying. 2.*

Weasel (6 to 8 in. long, without the tail)

wea sel (wē′zəl), a small animal with a long slender body, that feeds on rats, mice, birds and their eggs, etc. Weasels are quick and sly. *n. 9.*

weath er (weᴛʜ′ər), 1. condition of the air; as, hot weather, windy weather. 2. expose to the weather. Wood turns gray if weathered for a long time. 3. go or come through safely. The ship weathered the storm. 4. sail to the windward of. The ship weathered the cape. 5. toward the wind. *n., v., adj. 1.*

weath er-beat en (weᴛʜ′ər-bēt′ən), worn by the wind, rain, and other forces of the weather. *adj. 16.*

weath er cock (weᴛʜ′ər-kok′), device to show which way the wind is blowing. *n. 7.*

Weathercock

weath er glass (weᴛʜ′ər glas′), instrument to show the weather. A barometer is a weatherglass. *n.*

weather vane, weathercock.

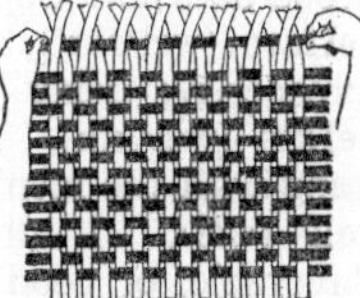
Weaving

weave (wēv), 1. form (threads or strips) into a thing or fabric; make (cloth, etc.) out of thread, etc. People weave thread into cloth, straw into hats, and reeds into baskets. A spider weaves a web. 2. combine into a whole. The author wove three plots together into one story. 3. make by combining parts. 4. method or pattern of weaving. Homespun is a cloth of coarse weave. *v., wove, woven* or *wove, weaving, n. 3.*

weav er (wēv′ər), 1. person who weaves. 2. person who weaves as a regular occupation. *n. 6.*

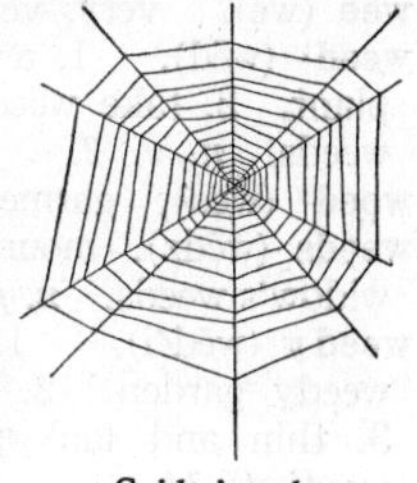
Spider's web

web (web), 1. something woven. A spider spins a web. 2. whole piece of cloth made at one time. 3. anything like a web. His story was a web of lies. 4. the skin joining the toes of ducks, geese, and other swimming birds. *n. 3.*

webbed (webd), 1. formed like a web or with a web. 2. having the toes joined by a web. Ducks have webbed feet. *adj.*

Webbed foot of a duck

web-foot ed (web′fu̇t′id), having the toes joined by a web. *adj.*

Web ster (web′stər), 1. Daniel Webster was a famous American statesman and orator (1782-1852). 2. Noah Webster wrote a famous spelling book and a dictionary (1758-1843). *n. 11.*

wed (wed), marry. *v., wedded, wedded* or *wed, wedding. 3.*

we'd (wēd), 1. we had. 2. we should; we would. *14.*

Wed., Wednesday.

wed ded (wed′id), 1. married. 2. united. 3. devoted. *adj.*

wed ding (wed′ing), 1. marriage ceremony. 2. an anniversary of it. A golden wedding is the fiftieth anniversary of a marriage. *n. 4.*

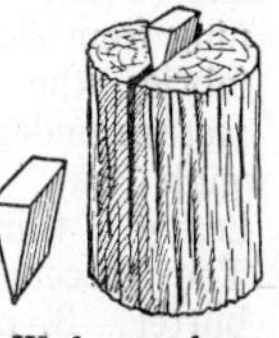
Wedge; wedge splitting a log.

wedge (wej), 1. piece of wood or metal with a thin edge used in splitting, separating, etc. See the picture. 2. something shaped like a wedge or used like a wedge. Her grand party was an entering wedge into society. 3. split or separate with a wedge. 4. fasten with a wedge. 5. thrust or pack in tightly. He wedged himself through the narrow window. The man's foot was wedged between the rocks, so that he could not get away. *n., v. 5.*

wed lock (wed′lok), married life; marriage. *n. 10.*

Wednes day (wenz′di), the fourth day of the week. *n. 2.*

wee (wē), very, very small; tiny. *adj. 3.*

weed[1] (wēd), 1. a useless or troublesome plant. 2. take weeds out of. 3. take out weeds. *n., v. 2.*

weed[2] (wēd), garment. *n.* [*Old use*]

weeds (wēdz), mourning garments; as, a widow's weeds. *n. pl.*

weed y (wēd′i), 1. full of weeds; as, a weedy garden. 2. of weeds; like weeds. 3. thin and lanky; weak. *adj., weedier, weediest. 11.*

week (wēk), 1. seven days, one after another. 2. the six working days. He is away all the week but comes home for Sundays. *n. 1.*

week day (wēk′dā′), any day of the week except Sunday. *n.*

week end (wēk′end′), Saturday and Sunday as a time for recreation, visiting, etc.; as, a weekend in the country. *n.*

week ly (wēk′li), 1. of a week; for a week; lasting a week. His weekly wage is $30. 2. once each week; every week. Mary writes a weekly letter to her grandmother. The *Saturday Evening Post* comes weekly. 3. a newspaper or magazine published once a week. *adj., adv., n., pl. weeklies. 5.*

ween (wēn), think; suppose; believe; expect. *v.* [*Old use*] *15.*

weep (wēp), 1. cry; shed tears. 2. shed tears for; mourn. *v., wept, weeping. 2.*

wee vil (wē′vəl), a small beetle whose larvae eat grain, nuts, fruits, etc. Weevils do much damage to the corn and cotton crops. *n. 11.*

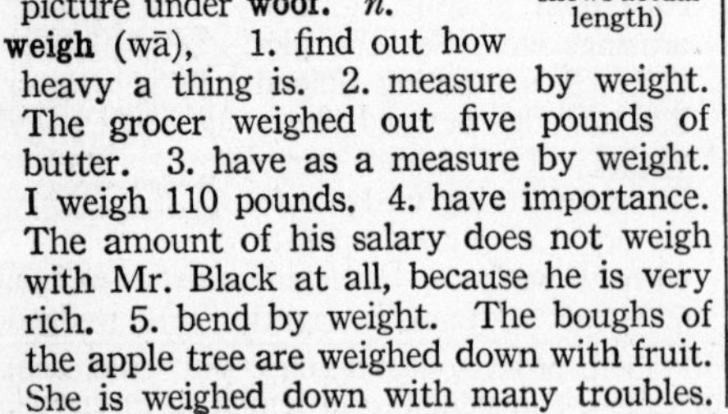
Weevil (line shows actual length)

weft (weft), the threads running from side to side across a fabric; the woof. See the picture under **woof.** *n.*

weigh (wā), 1. find out how heavy a thing is. 2. measure by weight. The grocer weighed out five pounds of butter. 3. have as a measure by weight. I weigh 110 pounds. 4. have importance. The amount of his salary does not weigh with Mr. Black at all, because he is very rich. 5. bend by weight. The boughs of the apple tree are weighed down with fruit. She is weighed down with many troubles. 6. balance in the mind; consider carefully. Mr. Jones weighs his words before speaking. 7. lift up (an anchor). The ship weighed anchor and sailed away. *v. 2.*

weight (wāt), 1. how heavy a thing is; the amount a thing weighs. The dog's weight is 50 pounds. 2. heaviness; the quality which makes all things tend toward the center of the earth. 3. system of units for expressing weight; as, avoirdupois weight, troy weight. 4. piece of metal used in weighing things; as, a pound weight. 5. heavy thing or mass. A weight keeps the papers in place. 6. load; burden. The pillars support the weight of the roof. She sank under the weight of troubles. 7. influence; importance; value. 8. add weight to; put too much weight on; burden. The elevator is weighted too heavily. Job was weighted with troubles. *n., v. 1.*

weight y (wāt′i), 1. heavy. 2. burdensome. 3. important; influential. *adj., weightier, weightiest. 11.*

weir (wēr), 1. dam in a river. 2. fence of stakes or broken branches put in a stream or channel to catch fish. *n. 18.*

weird (wērd), unearthly; mysterious; wild; strange. The shadows made weird figures on the wall. The witches moved in a weird dance. *adj. 8.*

wel come (wel′kəm), 1. kindly greeting. Welcome home! 2. greet kindly. 3. kind reception. You will always have a welcome here. 4. receive gladly. 5. gladly received; as, a welcome visitor, a welcome letter, a welcome rest. 6. gladly or freely permitted. You are welcome to pick the flowers. You say "You are welcome" when someone thanks you. *interj., n., v., adj. 2.*

weld (weld), 1. join together by hammering or pressing while soft and hot. He welded the broken rod. 2. a welded joint. 3. unite closely. Working together for a month welded them into a strong team. 4. be capable of being welded. Iron welds; wood does not. Copper welds easily. *v., n. 8.*

wel fare (wel′fãr′), health, happiness, and prosperity; being well; doing well. *n. 4.*

wel kin (wel′kin), the sky. The welkin rang with the men's shouts. *n. 11.*

well[1] (wel), 1. all right; in a satisfactory, favorable, or good manner. Is everything going well at school? Boston is well supplied with parks. 2. fairly; reasonably. Jim's brother can't well refuse to help him. 3. thoroughly. Shake the medicine well before taking it. 4. much; to a considerable degree. The fair brought in well over a hundred dollars. 5. in good health. Dick is well. 6. satisfactory; good; right. It is well you came along. 7. *Well* is sometimes used to show mild surprise or merely to fill in. Well! well! here's Jack. Well, I'm not sure. 8. **Well off** means (1) in a good condition. (2) fairly rich. *adv., better, best, adj., interj. 1.*

well[2] (wel), 1. hole dug or bored in the ground to get water, oil, gas, etc. The farmer pumped all his water from a well. 2. spring; fountain. 3. something like a well in shape or use. 4. spring; rise; gush. Water wells from a spring beneath the rock. Tears welled up in her eyes. *n., v.*

we'll (wēl), we shall; we will. *3.*

well a day (wel′ə dā′), alas! *interj.* [*Old use*]

well a way (wel′ə wā′), alas! *interj.* [*Old use*]

well-be ing (wel′bē′ing), welfare; health and happiness. *n.*

well born (wel′bôrn′), belonging to a good family. *adj.*

well-bred (wel′bred′), well brought up; having or showing good manners. *adj.*

well-groomed (wel′grümd′), well cared for; neat and trim. *adj.*

Wel ling ton (wel′ing tən). The first Duke of Wellington (1769-1852) was a famous British general who defeated Napoleon at Waterloo in 1815. *n. 15.*

well-known (wel′nōn′), 1. clearly or fully known. 2. familiar. 3. generally or widely known. *adj. 14.*

well-mean ing (wel′mēn′ing), 1. having good intentions. 2. caused by good intentions. *adj.*

well-nigh (wel′nī′), very nearly; almost. *adv. 16.*

well spring (wel′spring′), source; source of a supply that never fails. *n.*

well-to-do (wel′tə dü′), having enough money to live well; prosperous. *adj.*

Welsh (welsh), 1. of or pertaining to Wales, its people, or their language. 2. the people of Wales. 3. their language. *adj., n. 9.*

Welsh man (welsh′mən), a native of Wales. *n., pl. Welshmen. 13.*

Welsh rabbit, a mixture containing cheese cooked and poured over toast.

welt (welt), 1. a strip of leather between the upper part and the sole of a shoe. 2. a streak or ridge made on the skin by a stick or whip. 3. beat severely. *n., v. 13.*

wel ter (wel′tər), 1. roll or tumble about; wallow. 2. a rolling or tumbling about. 3. commotion; confusion. *v., n. 11.*

wen (wen), a harmless tumor of the skin. See the picture. *n.*

Man with a wen on his forehead

wench (wench), 1. girl or young woman. 2. woman servant. *n. 7.*

wend (wend), direct (one's way); go. We wended our way home. *v. 11.*

went (went). See **go.** I went home. *pt. of go. 1.*

wept (wept). See **weep.** She wept for hours. *pt. and pp. of weep. 3.*

were (wėr). The officers were obeyed by the soldiers. If I were rich, I would help the poor. *a pt. of* **be.** *1.*

we're (wēr), we are. *11.*

weren't (wėrnt), were not. *17.*

were wolf (wēr′wu̇lf′), person who has been changed into a wolf; person who can change himself into a wolf. *n., pl. werewolves* (wēr′wu̇lvz′). *20.*

wert (wėrt), an old form meaning **were.** "Thou wert" means "you were." *v. 4.*

wer wolf (wėr′wu̇lf′), werewolf. *n., pl. werwolves* (wēr′wu̇lvz′).

Wes ley (wes′li), 1. John (1703-1791), an English clergyman who founded the Methodist Church. 2. Charles (1707-1788), brother and helper of John, wrote many hymns. *n.*

west (west), 1. the direction of the sunset. 2. toward the west; farther toward the west. Walk west three blocks. 3. **West of** means farther west than. Kansas is west of Pennsylvania. 4. from the west; as, a west wind. 5. in the west; living in the west. 6. the part of any country toward the west. 7. **The West** sometimes means the states or countries in the west. *n., adj., adv. 1.*

west er ly (wes′tər li), 1. toward the west. 2. from the west. *adj., adv. 18.*

west ern (wes′tərn), 1. toward the west. 2. from the west. 3. of the west. 4. of the west of the United States. *adj. 2.*

West ern er (wes′tər nər), person who lives in one of the Western States. *n.*

Western Hemisphere, the half of the world that includes North and South America.

west ern most (wes′tərn mōst), farthest west. *adj.*

West Indies, islands in the Atlantic Ocean between Florida and South America.

West min ster (west′min′stər), a part of London. **Westminster Abbey** is a church there, in which many famous men are buried. *n. 8.*

West Point, the training school for officers of the United States Army. It is located on the Hudson River at West Point, New York.

West Virginia, an Eastern State of the United States. *15.*

west ward (west′wərd), toward the west; west. He walked westward. The orchard is on the westward slope of the hill. Rocks lay westward of the ship's course. *adv., adj. 4.*

west ward ly (west′wərd li), 1. toward the west. 2. from the west. *adj., adv.*

west wards (west′wərdz), westward. *adv.*

wet (wet), 1. covered or soaked with water or other liquid; watery. Don't touch wet paint. Her eyes were wet with tears. 2. make wet. Have you wet your feet? 3. water. 4. rainy; as, wet weather. 5. wetness; rain. Come in out of the wet. *adj., wetter, wettest, v., wet* or *wetted, wetting, n. 2.*

weth er (weᴛʜ′ər), a castrated male sheep. *n. 12.*

we've (wēv), we have. *7.*

whack (hwak), 1. a sharp, resounding blow. 2. strike with a sharp, resounding blow. *n., v.* [*Used in common talk*] *17.*

Greenland whale (about 60 ft. long)

whale (hwāl), 1. an animal shaped like a huge fish and living in the sea. Men get oil and whalebone from whales. 2. hunt and catch whales. *n., v. 6.*

whale boat (hwāl′bōt′), a long, narrow rowboat, pointed at both ends. *n.*

whale bone (hwāl′bōn′), an elastic, horny substance growing in place of teeth in the upper jaw of certain whales, and forming a series of thin, parallel plates. *n. 16.*

whal er (hwāl′ər), 1. hunter of whales. 2. ship used for hunting whales. *n. 20.*

Wharf

wharf (hwôrf), platform built on the shore or out from the shore, beside which ships can load and unload. *n., pl. wharves* or *wharfs. 8.*

wharves (hwôrvz), more than one wharf. *n. pl. 7.*

what (hwot), 1. *What* is used in asking questions about persons or things. What is your name? What is the matter? What time is it? 2. that which; anything that; any that. I don't know what you mean. Do what you please. Give me what paper you don't use. 3. *What* is often used to show surprise, liking, dislike, or other feeling. What a mistake! What a pity! What a good time we had! What! are you late again? 4. partly. What with the wind and what with the rain, our walk was spoiled. *pron., adj., adv., interj. 1.*

what e'er (hwot ãr′), whatever. *pron., adj. 5.*

what ev er (hwot ev′ər), 1. anything that; any that. Do whatever you like. Ask whatever girls you like to the party. 2. no matter what; no matter who. Do it, whatever happens. Any person whatever can tell you the way. 3. *Whatever* is used for emphasis. Whatever do you mean? *Used in common talk. pron., adj. 2.*

Wheat: A, bearded; B, beardless.

what not (hwot′not′), stand with several shelves for books, ornaments, etc. *n.*

what's (hwots), what is. *20.*

what so ev er (hwot′sō ev′ər), whatever. *pron., adj. 3.*

wheat (hwēt), 1. the grain from which flour is made. See the picture. 2. the plant which the grain grows on. *n. 1.*

wheat en (hwēt′ən), made of wheat; as, wheaten flour. *adj. 18.*

whee dle (hwē′dəl), 1. coax; persuade by flattery, smooth words, caresses, etc. The children wheedled their mother into letting them go to the picnic. 2. get by wheedling. They finally wheedled the secret out of him. *v. 11.*

wheel (hwēl), 1. round frame that turns on its center. See the picture. 2. anything round like a wheel or moving like one. A bicycle is often called a wheel. Clay is shaped into dishes, etc., on a potter's wheel. 3. turn. The rider wheeled his horse about. He wheeled around suddenly. 4. move on wheels. The workman was wheeling a load of bricks on a wheelbarrow. 5. **At the wheel** means (1) at the steering wheel. (2) in control. 6. **Wheels** means machinery. *n., v. 1.*

SPOKE
HUB
AXLE
FELLOE OR FELLY
Wagon wheel

wheel bar row (hwēl′-bar′ō), a small vehicle which has one wheel and two handles. See the picture. A wheelbarrow holds a small load which one man can push. *n. 10.*

Man pushing a wheelbarrow

wheel wright (hwēl′rīt′), man whose work is making or repairing wheels, carriages, and wagons. *n.*

wheeze (hwēz), 1. breathe with difficulty and a whistling sound. 2. whistling sound caused by difficult breathing. 3. make a sound like this. The old engine wheezed. 4. funny saying or story. *Slang. v., n. 16.*

wheez y (hwēz′i), wheezing. The dog was old and fat and wheezy. *adj. 20.*

whelk (hwelk), a small animal with a spiral shell, used for food in Europe. *n. 19.*

Whelk (shell 2 to 3 in. long)

whelm (hwelm), overwhelm. A wave whelmed him. She was whelmed with grief when her mother died. *v. 14.*

whelp (hwelp), 1. cub; young dog, wolf, bear, lion, tiger, etc. 2. give birth to whelps. *n., v. 10.*

when (hwen), 1. at what time. When does school close? 2. at the time that; at any time that. The dog comes when he is called. 3. at which time; and then. The dog growled till his master spoke, when he gave a joyful bark. 4. although. We have only three books when we need five. 5. what time; which time. Since when have the Browns had a car? 6. the time or occasion; as, the when and where of an act. *adv., conj., pron., n. 1.*

whence (hwens), 1. from what place; from where. 2. from what source or cause; from what. 3. from which. Let him return to that land whence he came. *adv., conj. 2.*

whence so ev er (hwens′sō ev′ər), from whatever place, source, or cause. *conj.*

when e'er (hwen ãr′), whenever. *conj., adv. 4.*

when ev er (hwen ev′ər), when; at whatever time; at any time that. *conj., adv. 2.*

when so ev er (hwen′sō ev′ər), whenever; at whatever time. *conj., adv.*

where (hwãr), 1. in what place; at what place. Where do you live? 2. to what place. Where are you going? 3. from what place. Where did you get that story? 4. in what way; in what respect. Where is the harm in trying? 5. what place. Where did he come from? 6. in which; at which. 7. to which. 8. in the place in which; at the place at which. *adv., n., conj. 1.*

where a bouts (hwãr′ə bouts′), 1. where; near what place. Whereabouts are my books? 2. place where a person or thing is. Do you know the whereabouts of the Jones cottage? *adv., conj., n. 11.*

where as (hwãr az′), 1. but; while; on the contrary. Some children like school, whereas others do not. 2. considering that; since. *Whereas* is used especially at the opening of a speech or document. "Whereas the people of the colonies have been grieved and burdened with taxes, etc." *conj. 7.*

where at (hwãr at′), at what; at which. *adv., conj. 5.*

where by (hwãr bī′), by what; by which. There is no other way whereby he can be saved. *adv., conj. 4.*

where fore (hwãr′fōr), 1. for what reason; why. 2. for which reason; therefore; so. 3. reason. *adv., conj., n. 4.*

where in (hwãr in′), in what; in which; how. *adv., conj. 4.*

where of (hwãr ov′), of what; of which; of whom. *adv., conj. 6.*

where on (hwãr on′), on which; on what. Summer cottages occupy the land whereon the old farmhouse stood. *adv., conj. 6.*

where so ev er (hwãr′sō ev′ər), wherever. *conj., adv. 9.*

where to (hwãr tü′), 1. to what; to which; where. He went to that place whereto he had been sent. 2. for what purpose; why. Whereto do you lay up riches? *adv., conj. 13.*

where un to (hwãr un′tü), whereto. *adv., conj.* [*Old use*] *12.*

where up on (hwãr′ə pon′), 1. upon what; upon which. 2. at which; after which. *adv., conj. 7.*

wher ev er (hwãr ev′ər), where; to whatever place; in whatever place. He goes wherever he wishes. *conj., adv. 3.*

where with (hwãr wiᴛʜ′), with what; with which. *adv., conj. 7.*

where with al (hwãr′wiᴛʜ ôl for 1, hwãr′-wiᴛʜ ôl′ for 2), 1. means or supplies or money needed. Has she the wherewithal to pay for the trip? 2. with what; with which. Wherewithal shall we be fed? *Old use. n., adv., conj. 11.*

wher ry (hwer′i), 1. a light rowboat. 2. a large fishing boat or barge. *n., pl. wherries. 20.*

whet (hwet), 1. sharpen by rubbing; as, to whet a knife. 2. make keen or eager. The smell of food whetted my appetite. An exciting story whets your interest. 3. a whetting. *v., whetted, whetting, n. 9.*

wheth er (hweᴛʜ′ər). Whether we go or whether we stay matters very little. He does not know whether to go or not. I doubt whether we can find a prettier hat elsewhere. Whether sick or well, she is always cheerful. He asked whether he should finish the work. *Whether* is used in expressing choices. *conj. 1.*

whet stone (hwet′stōn′), a stone for sharpening knives or tools. *n. 14.*

whew (hwū), a word expressing surprise, dismay, etc. *interj., n. 9.*

whey (hwā), the watery part of milk that separates from the curd when milk sours or when cheese is made. *n. 10.*

which (hwich), 1. *Which* is used in asking questions about persons or things. Which boy won the prize? Which books are yours? Which seems the best plan? 2. *Which* is also used in connecting a group of words with some word in the sentence. Read the book which you have. Tom now has the dog which used to belong to his cousin. 3. the one that; any that. Here are three boxes. Choose which you like best. *pron., adj. 1.*

which ev er (hwich ev′ər), 1. any one; any that. Buy whichever hat you like. Whichever you take will be becoming. 2. no matter which. Whichever side wins, I shall be satisfied. *pron., adj. 8.*

which so ev er (hwich′sō ev′ər), whichever. *pron., adj.*

whiff (hwif), 1. slight puff of air, smoke, odor, etc. 2. blow; puff. *n., v. 11.*

whif fle tree (hwif′əl trē′), whippletree. *n.*

Whig (hwig), 1. member of a great political party in Great Britain that favored reforms and progress. The Whig Party became the Liberal Party. 2. an American who favored the Revolution against England. 3. member of a political party in the United States that was formed about 1834 in opposition to the Democratic Party. *n. 9.*

while (hwīl), 1. time. He kept us waiting a long while. The postman came a while ago. 2. during the time that; in the time that. While I was speaking, he said nothing. Summer is pleasant while it lasts. 3. although. While I like the color of the hat, I do not like its shape. 4. pass in some easy or pleasant manner; spend. The children while away many afternoons on the beach. 5. **Worth while** means worth time, attention, or effort. *n., conj., v. 1.*

whiles (hwīlz), 1. sometimes. 2. while. *conj.* [*Old use*]

whilst (hwīlst), while. *conj. 7.*

whim (hwim), sudden fancy or notion. She has a whim for gardening, but it won't last. *n. 10.*

whim per (hwim′pər), 1. cry with low, broken sounds, in the way that a sick child or dog does; complain feebly. 2. whimpering cry. *v., n. 11.*

whim sey (hwim′zi), whimsy. *n., pl. whimseys.*

whim si cal (hwim′zi kəl), 1. having many odd notions or fancies; fanciful; odd. 2. full of whims. *adj. 10.*

whim sy (hwim′zi), 1. odd or fanciful notion. 2. quaintness; odd or fanciful humor. His books are full of whimsy. *n., pl. whimsies. 19.*

whine (hwīn), 1. make a low, complaining cry or sound. The dog whined to go out with us. 2. low, complaining cry or sound. 3. say with a whine. 4. complain in a peevish, childish way. Some people are always whining about trifles. *v., n. 7.*

whin ny (hwin′i), 1. the sound that a horse makes. 2. make such a sound. *n., pl. whinnies, v., whinnied, whinnying. 20.*

whip (hwip), 1. strike; beat. 2. thing to whip with. 3. beat (cream, eggs, etc.) to a froth. 4. move quickly and suddenly. He whipped off his coat and whipped out his knife. *v., whipped* or *whipt, whipping, n. 2.*

whip hand, 1. the hand that holds the whip in driving. 2. position of control; advantage; as, to get the whip hand of a person.

Whippet (about 1½ ft. high at the shoulder)

whip pet (hwip′it), a dog somewhat like a greyhound but smaller. Whippets are very swift and are often used in racing. *n.*

whip ple tree (hwip′əl trē′), the swinging bar of a carriage or wagon, to which the traces of a harness are fastened. *n.*

whip poor will (hwip′pər wil′), American bird whose call sounds somewhat like its name. It is active at night or twilight. *n. 16.*

Whippoorwill (9 to 10 in. long)

whir or **whirr** (hwėr), 1. a noise that sounds like *whir-r-r;* as, the whir of machinery. 2. move quickly with such a noise. The motor whirs. *n., v., whirred, whirring. 11.*

whirl (hwėrl), 1. turn around and around; spin. The leaves whirled in the wind. 2. move around and around. We whirled about the room. He whirled the club. 3. move or carry quickly. We were whirled away in an airplane. 4. whirling movement. We saw whirls of smoke. 5. confused condition. His thoughts are in a whirl. *v., n. 3.*

whirl i gig (hwėr′li gig′), 1. toy that whirls or spins. 2. merry-go-round. 3. thing that whirls around and around. *n. 12.*

whirl pool (hwėrl′pül′), water whirling around and around rapidly and violently. *n. 10.*

whirl wind (hwėrl′wind′), air whirling violently around and around; whirling windstorm. *n. 5.*

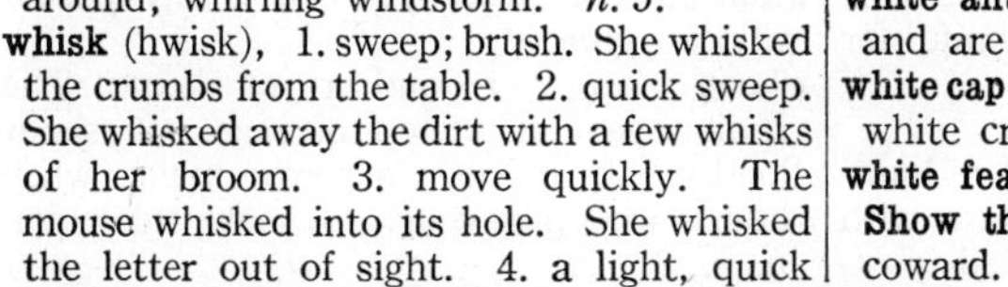

Whirligig

whisk (hwisk), 1. sweep; brush. She whisked the crumbs from the table. 2. quick sweep. She whisked away the dirt with a few whisks of her broom. 3. move quickly. The mouse whisked into its hole. She whisked the letter out of sight. 4. a light, quick movement. 5. a small brush or broom. 6. beat or whip to a froth. *v., n. 6.*

whisk broom, small broom for brushing clothes, etc.

Whisk broom

whisk er (hwis′kər), 1. hair growing on a man's face. 2. long stiff hair growing near the mouth of a cat, rat, etc. *n. 8.*

whis key (hwis′ki), strong intoxicating liquor made from grain. Whiskey is about half alcohol. *n., pl. whiskeys. 9.*

whis ky (hwis′ki), whiskey. *n., pl. whiskies.*

whis per (hwis′pər), 1. speak very softly and low. 2. very soft, low spoken sound. 3. speak to in a whisper. 4. tell secretly or privately. It is whispered that Mr. Smith's business is failing. 5. something told secretly or privately. No whisper about having a new teacher has come to our ears. 6. make a soft, rustling sound. The wind whispered in the pines. 7. a soft, rustling sound. *v., n. 2.*

whist[1] (hwist), 1. hush! silence! 2. hushed; silent. *Old use. interj., adj. 13.*

whist[2] (hwist), a card game for two pairs of players. *n.*

whis tle (hwis′əl), 1. make a clear, shrill sound. The policeman whistled for the automobile to stop. The engine whistled before it started off. A blackbird whistles. 2. the sound made by whistling. 3. an instrument for making whistling sounds. See the picture. 4. blow a whistle. 5. move with a shrill sound. The wind whistled around the house. *v., n. 2.*

Steam whistle

whit (hwit), very small bit. The sick man is not a whit better. *n. 7.*

white (hwīt), 1. the color of snow. 2. having this color. She turned white with fear. 3. white clothing. 4. something white. Take the whites of four eggs. 5. having a light-colored skin. 6. white person. 7. spotless; pure; innocent. *n., adj. 1.*

white ant, termite. White ants eat wood and are very destructive to buildings.

white cap (hwīt′kap′), wave with a foaming white crest. *n.*

white feather, a symbol of cowardice. **Show the white feather** means act like a coward.

hat, āge, cãre, fär; let, ēqual, tėrm; it, īce; hot, ōpen, ôrder; oil, out; cup, pu̇t, rüle, ūse; th, thin; ᴛʜ, then; ə represents *a* in about, *e* in taken, *i* in pencil, *o* in lemon, *u* in circus.

white fish (hwīt′fish′), food fish with white or silvery sides, found in lakes and streams. *n.*

white flag, a flag that means "We want a truce" or "We surrender."

White hall (hwīt′hôl′), important street in London, where many government offices are located. *n. 14.*

White House, 1. the official residence of the President of the United States, in Washington, D.C. 2. office, authority, opinion, etc., of the President of the United States.

white lie, a lie about some small matter; a polite or harmless lie.

whit en (hwīt′ən), make white; become white. *v. 7.*

white wash (hwīt′wosh′), 1. liquid for whitening walls, woodwork, etc. Whitewash is usually made of lime and water. 2. whiten with whitewash. 3. cover up the faults or mistakes of. *n., v. 10.*

whith er (hwiтн′ər), where; to what place; to which place. *adv., conj. 3.*

whith er so ev er (hwiтн′ər sō ev′ər), anywhere at all; wherever. *conj., adv. 15.*

whit ing[1] (hwīt′ing), a common sea fish used for food. *n., pl. whitings* or *whiting.*

whit ing[2] (hwīt′ing), powdered white chalk. Whiting is used in making putty, whitewash, and silver polish. *n.*

whit ish (hwīt′ish), somewhat white. *adj.*

Whit ney (hwit′ni), 1. Eli, American who invented the cotton gin (1765-1825). 2. mountain peak in eastern California. It is the highest mountain in the United States. 14,501 ft. *n.*

Whit sun day (hwit′sun′di), seventh Sunday after Easter. *n.* Also called **Pentecost.**

Whit sun tide (hwit′sən tīd′), the week beginning with Whitsunday, especially the first three days. *n. 18.*

Whit ti er (hwit′i ər), John Greenleaf, an American poet (1807-1892). *n.*

Whit ting ton (hwit′ing tən), Dick, a poor boy who became mayor of London, according to the old story. *n. 10.*

whit tle (hwit′əl), 1. cut or shape (wood) with a knife. The old sailor whittled a boat for Jim. 2. cut with a knife for fun. *v. 14.*

whit y (hwīt′i), whitish. *adj.*

whiz or **whizz** (hwiz), 1. make a humming or hissing sound; move or rush with such a sound. An arrow whizzed past. 2. humming or hissing sound. *v., whizzed, whizzing, n. 9.*

who (hü), 1. *Who* is used in asking questions about persons. Who goes there? Who is your friend? Who told you? 2. *Who* is also used in connecting a group of words with some word in the sentence. The girl who spoke is my best friend. We saw men who were working in the fields. 3. the person that; any person that; one that. Who is not for us is against us. *pron. 1.*

whoa (hwō), stop! *interj. 18.*

who ev er (hü ev′ər), 1. who; any person that. Whoever wants the book may have it. 2. no matter who. Whoever else goes hungry, he won't. *pron. 4.*

whole (hōl), 1. having all its parts; complete. He gave her a whole set of dishes. 2. all of a thing; the total. Four quarters make a whole. 3. thing complete in itself; a system. 4. not broken; in one piece. 5. well; healthy. *Old use. adj., n. 1.*

whole heart ed (hōl′här′tid), earnest; sincere; hearty; cordial. *adj.*

whole number, integer. 1, 2, 3, 15, 106, etc., are whole numbers; $\frac{1}{2}$, $\frac{3}{4}$, and $\frac{7}{8}$ are fractions; $1\frac{3}{8}$, $2\frac{1}{2}$, and $12\frac{2}{3}$ are mixed numbers.

whole sale (hōl′sāl′), 1. sale of goods in large quantities at a time. He buys at wholesale and sells at retail. 2. in large lots or quantities. The wholesale price of this coat is $20; the retail price is $30. 3. selling in large quantities; as, a wholesale fruit business. 4. sell in large quantities. *n., adj., adv., v. 7.*

whole some (hōl′səm), 1. healthful; good for the health. Milk is a wholesome food. 2. healthy-looking; suggesting health. *adj. 4.*

whole-wheat (hōl′hwēt′), made of the entire wheat kernel. *adj.*

who'll (hül), who will; who shall.

whol ly (hōl′i), completely; entirely; totally. The sick boy is wholly cured. *adv. 4.*

whom (hüm), what person; which person. *Whom* is made from *who,* just as *him* is made from *he.* Whom do you like best? He does not know whom to believe. The girl to whom I spoke is my cousin. *pron. 1.*

whom so ev er (hüm′sō ev′ər), any person whom. *pron.*

whoop (hüp), 1. loud cry or shout. The Indian gave a whoop of rage. 2. shout loudly. 3. the noise a person makes when he has whooping cough. 4. make this noise. *n., v. 7.*

whoop ing cough (hüp′ing kôf′), an infectious disease of children, characterized by fits of coughing that end with a loud, gasping sound.

whore (hōr), woman who sells herself for money. *n. 7.*

whorl (hwėrl), 1. circle of leaves or flowers around a stem of a plant. 2. one of the turns of a spiral shell. *n. 15.*

Whorl of leaves

whose (hüz), of whom; of which. The girl whose work got the prize is the youngest in her class. Whose book is this? *pron. 1.*

whose so ev er (hüz′sō ev′ər), whose. *pron. 12.*

who so (hü′sō), whoever. Whoso seeks may find. *pron.* [*Old use*] *11.*

who so ev er (hü′sō ev′ər), whoever; anybody who. *pron. 11.*

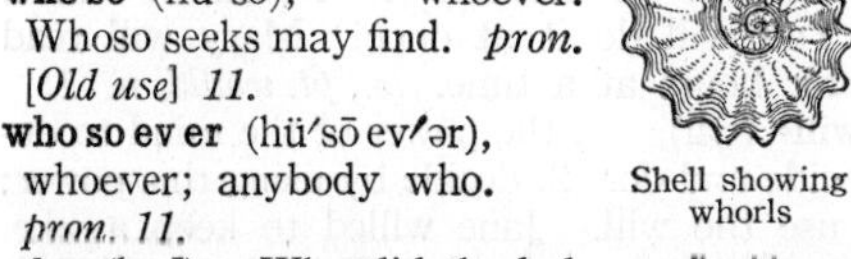

Shell showing whorls

why (hwī). Why did the baby cry? Harry does not know why he failed. The reason why Harry failed was his laziness. Why! Why! the cage is empty! Why, yes, I will if you wish. Tell me all the whys and wherefores. *adv., conj., interj., n., pl. whys. 1.*

Wich i ta (wich′i tô), a city in southern Kansas. *n.*

wick (wik), the part of an oil lamp or candle that is lighted. The oil or melted wax is drawn up the wick and burned. *n. 11.*

Candle cut to show the wick

wick ed (wik′id), 1. bad; evil; sinful. 2. mischievous. *adj. 2.*

wick ed ness (wik′id nis), 1. sin; being wicked. 2. wicked thing or act. *n. 5.*

wick er (wik′ər), 1. a slender, easily bent branch or twig. 2. twigs or branches woven together. Wicker is used in making baskets and furniture. 3. made of wicker. 4. covered with wicker. *n., adj. 13.*

wick er work (wik′ər-wėrk′), 1. twigs or branches woven together. 2. things made of wicker. *n.*

A B

Wickets: A, for croquet; B, for cricket.

wick et (wik′it), 1. small door or gate. The big door has a wicket in it. 2. small window. Buy your tickets at this wicket. 3. in croquet, a hoop or arch. 4. in cricket, either of the two sets of sticks that one side tries to hit with the ball. See the picture in the last column. *n. 11.*

wide (wīd), 1. Broadway is a wide street. They sail on the wide ocean. The door is three feet wide. They went forth into the wide world. A trip around the world gives wide experience. Wide reading gives wide culture. 2. far open. The child stared with wide eyes. 3. far from a named point or object; as, a guess wide of the truth, a shot wide of the mark. 4. to the full extent. Open your mouth wide. The gates stand wide open. *adj., adv. 1.*

wide-a wake (wīd′ə wāk′), 1. fully awake; with the eyes wide open. 2. alert; keen; knowing. *adj.*

wide-eyed (wīd′īd′), with the eyes wide open. *adj.*

wide ly (wīd′li), to a wide extent; as, a widely distributed plant, a man who is widely known, to be widely read, widely opened eyes. Tom and Jim gave two widely different accounts of the quarrel. *adv. 10.*

wid en (wīd′ən), make wide or wider; become wide or wider. He widened the path through the forest. The river widens as it flows. *v. 8.*

wide spread (wīd′spred′), 1. spread widely; as, widespread wings. 2. spread over a wide space; as, a widespread flood. 3. occurring in many places far apart; as, a widespread belief. *adj. 10.*

widg eon (wij′ən), a kind of fresh-water duck. *n., pl. widgeons* or *widgeon.*

wid ow (wid′ō), 1. woman whose husband is dead and who has not married again. 2. make a widow of. She has been widowed three times. *n., v. 3.*

wid ow er (wid′ō ər), man whose wife is dead and who has not married again. *n. 16.*

wid ow hood (wid′ō hu̇d), condition or time of being a widow. *n. 17.*

width (width), 1. how wide a thing is; distance across; breadth; wideness. The room is 12 feet in width. 2. piece of a certain width. It will take two widths of cloth to make the curtains. *n. 3.*

wield (wēld), hold and use; manage; control. A soldier wields the sword. A writer wields the pen. The people wield the power in a democracy. *v. 6.*

wife (wīf), married woman. *n., pl. wives* (wīvz). *1.*

wife ly (wīf′li), of a wife; like a wife; suitable for a wife. *adj.*

wig (wig), covering of hair for the head. Dolls have wigs. The bald man wore a wig. *n. 5.*

Judge's wig

wig gle (wig′əl), 1. wriggle; move with short quick movements from side to side. The restless child wiggled in his chair. 2. such a movement. *v., n.*

wight (wīt), person; human being. *n.* [*Old use*] *7.*

wig wag (wig′wag′), 1. move to and fro. 2. signal by movements of arms, flags, or lights, according to a code. 3. such signaling. *v., wigwagged, wigwagging, n.*

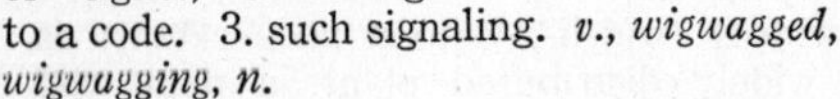

Scout wigwagging

wig wam (wig′wom), a hut of poles covered with bark, mats, or skins, made by American Indians. *n. 4.*

Wigwam

wild (wīld), 1. living or growing in the forests or fields; not tamed; not cultivated. The tiger is a wild animal. The daisy is a wild flower. 2. with no people living in it. 3. waste; desert. Much of northern Canada is wild land. **The wilds** means wild country. 4. not civilized; savage. 5. not checked; not restrained; as, a wild rush for the ball. 6. violent; as, a wild storm. 7. rash; crazy. 8. wildly. *adj., n., adv. 1.*

wild cat (wīld′kat′), 1. a wild animal like a common cat, but larger. A lynx is one kind of wildcat. 2. wild; reckless; not safe. *n., adj. 13.*

Lynx (about 3 ft. long, including the tail)

wil der ness (wil′dər-nis), wild place; region with no people living in it. *n. 3.*

wild fire (wīld′fīr′), fire hard to put out, formerly used in warfare. **Like wildfire** means very rapidly. The news spread like wildfire. *n. 13.*

wild fowl, birds ordinarily hunted, such as wild ducks or geese, partridges, quail, and pheasants.

wile (wīl), 1. a trick to deceive; cunning way. The serpent by his wiles persuaded Eve to eat the apple. 2. coax; lure; entice. The sunshine wiled me from my work. 3. **Wile away** means pass (time, etc.) pleasantly. *n., v. 8.*

wi li ness (wīl′i nis), wily quality; craftiness; slyness. *n.*

Wilkes-Bar re (wilks′bar′i), a city in eastern Pennsylvania. *n.*

will[1] (wil). We cannot always do as we will. Most men feel good will toward their friends and ill will toward their enemies. He will go tomorrow. I will be there. You will do it at once! Mary will read for hours at a time. *v., pt. would, n. 1.*

will[2] (wil), 1. the power of the mind to decide and do. 2. decide by using this power; use the will. Jane willed to keep awake. 3. determine; decide. Fate has willed it otherwise. 4. a legal statement of a person's wishes about what shall be done with his property after he is dead. 5. give by such a statement. *n., v., willed, willing.*

will ful or **wil ful** (wil′fəl), 1. wanting or taking one's own way; stubborn. The willful child would not eat his supper. 2. intended; done on purpose; as, willful murder, willful waste. *adj. 6.*

will ful ly or **wil ful ly** (wil′fəl i), 1. by choice; voluntarily. 2. by design; intentionally. 3. selfishly; perversely; obstinately; stubbornly. *adv.*

will ful ness or **wil ful ness** (wil′fəl nis), willful character or behavior; insistence on one's own way. *n. 17.*

Wil liam I (wil′yəm). William the Conqueror (1027?-1087) was a duke of Normandy who conquered England and became its king. *n. 2.*

Wil liams (wil′yəmz), Roger (1604?-1683), English clergyman who founded Rhode Island. *n.*

will ing (wil′ing), 1. ready; consenting. He is willing to wait. 2. cheerfully ready; as, willing obedience. *adj. 2.*

will ing ly (wil′ing li), readily; gladly. *adv.*

will ing ness (wil′ing nis), being willing; readiness. *n. 12.*

will-o'-the-wisp (wil′ə ᴛʜə wisp′), 1. a moving light appearing at night over marshy places. 2. thing that deceives or misleads. Any scheme to get rich quickly is likely to be a will-o'-the-wisp. *n. 19.*

wil low (wil′ō), 1. a kind of tree or shrub. See the picture. The branches of most willows bend easily and are used to make furniture, baskets, etc. 2. its wood. *n. 3.*

Weeping willow

wil low y (wil′ō i), 1. like a willow; slender; supple; graceful. 2. having many willows. *adj. 18.*

wil ly-nil ly (wil′i nil′i), willingly or not; with or against one's wishes. *adv.*

Wil ming ton (wil′ming tən), a city in northeastern Delaware. *n.*

Wil son (wil′sən), Woodrow (1856-1924), the 28th president of the United States, from 1913 to 1921. *n. 7.*

wilt[1] (wilt), become limp and drooping; wither; lose strength and vigor. *v. 4.*

wilt[2] (wilt), an old form meaning **will.** "Thou wilt" means "you will." *v.*

Wil ton (wil′tən), a kind of velvety carpet. *n. 18.*

wi ly (wī′li), tricky; cunning; crafty; sly. The wily fox got away. *adj., wilier, wiliest. 11.*

wim ble (wim′bəl), tool for boring. *n. 14.*

wim ple (wim′pəl), 1. a cloth formerly worn by women about the head and neck. Nuns still wear wimples. 2. cover with a wimple. 3. ripple. *n., v.*

Wimple

win (win), 1. We win fame, a victory, a prize, sympathy, favor, or a bet. 2. be successful over others. 3. get to; reach; as, to win the summit of a mountain. 4. gain the favor of; persuade. The speaker soon won his audience. Mary won her mother over to her side. *v., won, winning. 1.*

wince (wins), 1. draw back suddenly; shrink. It is hard to keep from wincing when the doctor cleans a cut. 2. act of wincing. *v., n. 8.*

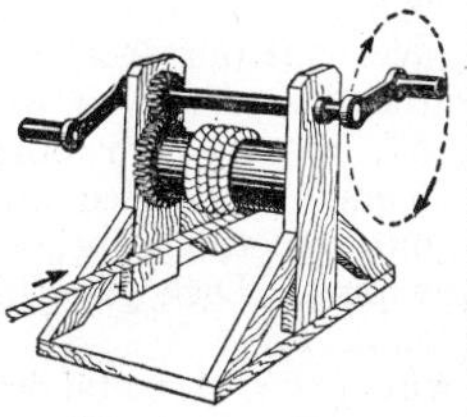
Winch. Arrows show direction.

winch (winch), machine for lifting or pulling, turned by a crank. *n. 17.*

wind[1] (wind, *poetic* wīnd), 1. air in motion. The wind bends the branches. 2. air filled with some smell. The deer got wind of the hunter and ran off. 3. **Get wind of** sometimes means find out about. 4. smell; follow by scent. 5. breath; power of breathing. A runner needs good wind. 6. put out of breath; cause difficulty in breathing. The fat man was winded by walking up the steep hill. 7. **Take the wind out of one's sails** means take away one's advantage, argument, etc., suddenly or unexpectedly. 8. **Winds** sometimes means wind instruments. *n., v., winded, winding. 1.*

wind[2] (wīnd), 1. move this way and that; go in a crooked way; change direction; turn. A brook winds through the woods. We wound our way through the narrow streets. 2. twist or turn around something. The vine winds around a pole. 3. roll into a ball or on a spool. Grandma was winding yarn. Thread comes wound on spools. 4. fold, wrap, or place about something. The mother wound her arms about the child. The man's arm is wound with bandages. 5. make (some machine) go by turning some part of it; as, to wind a clock. 6. a bend; a turn; a twist. 7. **Wind up** sometimes means to end; settle; conclude. *v., wound, winding, n.*

wind[3] (wīnd), blow. The hunter winds his horn. *v., winded* or *wound, winding.*

wind bag (wind′bag′), 1. bag full of wind. 2. person who talks too much. *Informal. n.*

wind break (wind′brāk′), protection from the wind. *n.*

wind fall (wind′fôl′), 1. fruit blown down by the wind. 2. unexpected piece of good luck. *n. 17.*

wind flow er (wind′flou′ər), anemone. *n.*

wind instrument, musical instrument sounded by blowing air into it. Horns, flutes, and trombones are wind instruments.

wind lass (wind′ləs), a machine for pulling or lifting things; a winch. See the picture of **winch.** *n. 19.*

wind mill (wind′mil′), a mill or machine worked by the wind. Windmills are mostly used to pump water. *n. 4.*

Windmill for pumping water

win dow (win′dō), 1. an opening in a wall or roof to let in light or air. 2. such an opening with its frame and glass. *n. 1.*

win dow pane (win′dō pān′), piece of glass in a window. *n.*

window sill, piece of wood or stone across the bottom of a window.

wind pipe (wind′pīp′), the passage from the throat to the lungs. *n. 12.*

wind row (wind′rō′), row of hay raked together to dry before being made into heaps. *n.*

wind shield (wind′shēld′), a sheet of glass, etc., to keep off the wind. Automobiles have windshields. *n. 17.*

Wind sor (win′zər), 1. The Duke of Windsor is the title of King Edward VIII of England after his abdication in December, 1936. 2. **Windsor Castle** is a residence of the King of England. 3. family name of the royal house of Great Britain since 1917. *n., adj. 7.*

wind ward (wind′wərd), 1. toward the wind. 2. the side toward the wind. 3. on the side toward the wind. 4. in the direction from which the wind is blowing. 5. direction from which the wind is blowing. *adv., n., adj. 13.*

Wind ward Is lands (wind′wərd ī′ləndz), southern part of the Lesser Antilles in the West Indies. They extend southwest from Martinique.

wind y (win′di), 1. having much wind; as, a windy street, windy weather. 2. made of wind; empty; as, windy talk. *adj., windier, windiest. 6.*

wine (wīn), 1. the juice of grapes which has fermented and contains alcohol. 2. the fermented juice of other fruits or plants; as, currant wine, dandelion wine. 3. entertain with wine. *n., v. 2.*

wine press, 1. machine for pressing the juice from grapes. 2. vat in which grapes are trodden in making wine.

wing (wing), 1. the part of a bird or insect used in flying. 2. anything like a wing in shape or use; as, the wings of an airplane. 3. part that sticks out from the main thing or body. The house has a wing at each side. Either of the side portions of an army or fleet ready for battle is called a wing. The spaces to the right or left of the stage in a theater are called wings. 4. fly. The bird wings its way to the south. 5. flying; flight. 6. give wings to; make able to fly. Terror winged Tom's steps as the bear drew nearer. 7. wound in the wing. The bullet winged the bird but did not kill it. *n., v. 1.*

wing case, either of the hardened front wings of certain insects.

winged (wingd or wing′id), 1. having wings. 2. swift; rapid. *adj.*

wing less (wing′lis), without wings. *adj. 16.*

wink (wingk), 1. close the eyes and open them again quickly. The bright light made him wink. 2. close and open one eye on purpose as a hint or signal. Father winked at Dick as a sign for him to keep still. 3. **Wink at** sometimes means pretend not to see. The boss winked at a good deal of dishonesty among his men. 4. twinkle. The stars winked. 5. winking. 6. a hint or signal given by winking. 7. very short time. I didn't sleep a wink. *v., n. 3.*

win ner (win′ər), person or thing that wins. The winner got a prize. *n. 6.*

win ning (win′ing), 1. that wins; as, a winning team. 2. charming; attractive. 3. **Winnings** means what is won; money won. He pocketed his winnings. *adj., n.*

Win ni peg (win′i peg), 1. city in southern Canada. 2. lake in southern Canada. *n. 18.*

win now (win′ō), 1. blow off the chaff from (grain); drive or blow away (chaff). 2. separate; sift; sort out; as, to winnow truth from falsehood. *v. 11.*

win some (win′səm), charming; attractive; pleasing. *adj. 13.*

win ter (win′tər), 1. the coldest of the four seasons. 2. of the winter. 3. keep during the winter. We wintered our cattle in the warm valley. 4. pass the winter. Robins winter in the South. *n., adj., v. 1.*

win ter green (win′tər grēn′), 1. a small evergreen plant with bright-red berries. An oil made from its leaves is used in medicine and candy. 2. this oil. 3. its flavor. *n.*

win try (win′tri), of winter; like winter; as, wintry weather, a wintry sky, a wintry manner. *adj., wintrier, wintriest. 6.*

wipe (wīp), 1. rub in order to clean or dry. We wipe our shoes on the mat. We wipe the dishes with a towel. 2. take (away, off, or out) by rubbing. Wipe away your tears. She wiped off the dust. 3. **Wipe out** sometimes means destroy. 4. act of wiping. Dick gave his face a hasty wipe. *v., n. 2.*

wire (wīr), 1. metal drawn out into a thread; as, a telephone wire. 2. made of wire; as, wire netting. 3. furnish with wire; as, to wire a house for electricity. 4. fasten with wire. He wired the two pieces together. 5. telegraph. He sent a message by wire.

Wire your answer at once. 6. telegram. 7. **Pull wires** means use secret influence. Mr. Smith pulled wires to get his son a good job. *n., adj., v. 2.*

wire less (wīr′lis), 1. having no wire. 2. radio. 3. message sent by radio. 4. send by radio. *adj., n., v. 6.*

wir y (wīr′i), 1. made of wire. 2. like wire. 3. lean, strong, and tough. *adj., wirier, wiriest. 8.*

Wis. or **Wisc.,** Wisconsin.

Wis con sin (wis kon′sin), a Middle Western State of the United States. *n. 5.*

wis dom (wiz′dəm), 1. being wise; knowledge and good judgment based on experience. 2. wise conduct; wise words. *n. 2.*

wisdom tooth, the back tooth on either side of each jaw, ordinarily appearing between the ages of 17 and 25.

wise[1] (wīz), 1. having or showing knowledge and good judgment; as, a wise judge, wise advice, wise plans. 2. having knowledge or information. We are none the wiser for his explanations. 3. The **Three Wise Men** came from the East to honor the infant Jesus. *adj. 1.*

wise[2] (wīz), way; manner. John is in no wise an artist; he prefers sports and machinery. *n.*

-wise, suffix meaning:—

1. in —— manner, as in anywise and likewise.
2. in an —— ing manner, as in slantwise.
3. in the characteristic way of a ——. Clockwise means in the way the hands of a clock go.
4. in the direction of the ——, as in lengthwise.
5. special meanings, as in sidewise.

wise a cre (wīz′ā′kər), person who thinks he knows everything. *n.*

wish (wish). I wish I had more money. His wish is for Christmas to come. Kitty's wish is for more milk. Mary sends you best wishes for a Happy New Year. The girl got her wish. *v., n. 1.*

wish bone (wish′bōn′), the forked bone in the front of the breastbone in poultry and other birds. *n.*

Wishbone

wish ful (wish′fəl), having or expressing a wish; desiring; desirous. *adj.*

wish y-wash y (wish′i wosh′i), 1. thin and weak; as, wishy-washy soup with no flavor. 2. feeble; weak; poor; as, a wishy-washy story. *adj.*

wisp (wisp), small bundle; small bunch; bit; as, a wisp of hair, a wisp of hay, a wisp of smoke. *n. 9.*

wist (wist), knew. He wist not who had spoken. *pt. and pp. of* **wit.** [*Old use*] *12.*

wis tar i a (wis tãr′i ə), a climbing shrub with large clusters of purple flowers. *n.*

wis te ri a (wis tēr′i ə), wistaria. *n.*

wist ful (wist′fəl), 1. longing; yearning. A child stood looking with wistful eyes at the toys in the window. 2. pensive. *adj. 8.*

wit (wit), 1. understanding; mind; sense. People with quick wits learn easily. The child was out of his wits with fright. That poor man hasn't wit enough to earn a living. 2. the power to perceive quickly and express cleverly ideas that are unusual, striking, and amusing. His wit made even troubles seem amusing. 3. person with such power. Mark Twain and Oliver Wendell Holmes were wits. 4. know. *Old use.* 5. **To wit** means that is to say; namely. To my son I leave all I own—to wit: my house, what is in it, and the land on which it stands. *n., v., witting. 2.*

witch (wich), 1. woman supposed to have magic power. Witches generally used their power to do evil. 2. an ugly old woman. 3. use the power of a witch on. 4. a charming or fascinating girl or woman. *n., v. 3.*

witch craft (wich′kraft′), what a witch does or can do; magic power. *n. 7.*

witch er y (wich′ər i), 1. witchcraft; magic. 2. charm; fascination. *n., pl. witcheries. 15.*

witch hazel, 1. a shrub that has yellow flowers in the fall or winter after the leaves have fallen. 2. lotion for cooling and soothing the skin, made from the bark and leaves of this shrub. *17.*

witch ing (wich′ing), bewitching; magical; enchanting. *adj.*

with (wiᴛʜ or with). *With* shows that persons or things are taken together in some way. 1. in the company of. Come with me. Do you wish sugar with your tea? 2. among. They will mix with the crowd. 3. having. Mr. Wise is a man with brains. 4. in the keeping or service of. Leave the dog with me. 5. in proportion to. The army's power increases with its size. 6. in regard to. We are pleased with the house. 7. using; showing. Work with care. 8. by means of. The man cut the meat with a knife. 9. because of. The man almost died with thirst. The child is shaking with cold. 10. from. I hate to part with my favorite things. 11. against. The English fought with the Germans. *prep. 1.*

with al (wiᴛʜ ôl′), 1. with it all; also; as well; besides. The lady is rich and fair and wise withal. 2. with. *adv., prep.* [*Old use*] *5.*

with draw (wiᴛʜ drô′), 1. draw back; draw away. The child quickly withdrew his hand from the hot stove. 2. take back; remove. Mr. Green agreed to withdraw the charge of theft if they returned the money. Worn-out paper money is withdrawn from use by the government. Will's parents withdrew him from school. 3. go away. She withdrew from the room. *v., withdrew, withdrawn, withdrawing. 3.*

with draw al (wiᴛʜ drô′əl), withdrawing. *n. 17.*

with drew (wiᴛʜ drü′). See **withdraw.** Bill withdrew from the game because he was hurt. *pt. of withdraw. 5.*

withe (with or wīᴛʜ), willow twig; any tough, easily bent twig suitable for binding things together. *n. 17.*

with er (wiᴛʜ′ər), 1. make or become dry and lifeless; fade; shrivel; blight. The hot sun withers the grass. Flowers wither after they are cut. Age had withered the old lady's face. 2. cause to feel ashamed or confused. Mary blushed under her aunt's withering look. *v. 3.*

with ers (wiᴛʜ′ərz), the highest part of a horse's or other animal's back, behind the neck. *n. pl.*

with held (with held′), held back. See **withhold.** *pt. and pp. of withhold. 7.*

with hold (with hōld′), 1. refuse to give. There was no school play because the principal withheld his consent. 2. hold back; keep back. The captain withholds his men from attack. *v., withheld, withholding. 6.*

with in (wiᴛʜ in′), 1. not beyond; not more than. The task was within the man's powers. He guessed my weight within five pounds. 2. inside of; in the inner part of. By the X ray, doctors can see what is within the body. 3. inside; in the inner part. The house has been painted within and without. The curtains were white without and green within. *prep., adv. 1.*

with out (wiᴛʜ out′), 1. with no; lacking; free from. A cat walks without noise. I drink tea without sugar. 2. not having. Eat what is on the table or go without. 3. outside; on the outside. The house is painted without and within. 4. outside of; beyond. Soldiers are camped within and without the city walls. *prep., adv. 1.*

with stand (with stand′), stand against; hold out against; resist; oppose; endure. Soldiers have to withstand hardships. These shoes will withstand hard wear. *v., withstood, withstanding. 5.*

with stood (with stu̇d′). See **withstand.** The soldiers withstood the attack for hours. *pt. and pp. of withstand. 8.*

wit less (wit′lis), lacking sense; stupid; foolish. *adj. 16.*

wit ness (wit′nis), 1. person or thing able to give evidence; person who saw something happen. 2. see. He witnessed the accident. 3. person who takes an oath to tell the truth in a court of law. 4. evidence; testimony. The man's fingerprints bore witness to his guilt. 5. bear witness; give evidence of. Her whole manner witnessed her surprise. 6. person writing his name on a document to show that he saw the maker sign it. 7. sign (a document) as witness. The two servants witnessed Mr. Smith's will. *n., v. 2.*

wit ti cism (wit′i sizm), witty remark. *n. 16.*

wit ti ly (wit′i li), in a witty manner; with wit. *adv.*

wit ting ly (wit′ing li), knowingly; intentionally. *adv.*

wit ty (wit′i), full of wit; clever and amusing. A witty person makes witty remarks. *adj., wittier, wittiest. 5.*

wive (wīv), 1. marry a woman. 2. take as a wife. *v.*

wives (wīvz), more than one wife. *n. pl. 3.*

wiz ard (wiz′ərd), man supposed to have magic power. *n. 5.*

wiz ened (wiz′ənd), withered; shriveled; dried up; as, a wizened apple, a wizened face. *adj.*

wk., week. *pl. wks. 12.*

wks., 1. weeks. 2. works.

wo (wō), woe. *n., interj.*

wob ble (wob′əl), 1. move unsteadily from side to side; shake; tremble. 2. waver; be uncertain, unsteady, or inconstant. 3. wobbling motion. *v., n. 17.* Also spelled **wabble.**

wob bly (wob′li), unsteady; shaky. *adj.*

Wo den (wō′dən), the most important Anglo-Saxon god, called Odin by the Scandinavians. *n. 19.*

woe (wō), 1. great grief, trouble, or distress. Sickness and poverty are common woes.

2. an exclamation of grief, trouble, or distress. "Woe! woe is me!" the miserable beggar cried. *n., interj. 3.*

woe be gone or **wo be gone** (wō′bi gôn′), woeful; looking sad; sorrowful; wretched. *adj.*

woe ful (wō′fəl), 1. full of woe; sad; sorrowful; wretched. 2. pitiful. *adj. 6.*

wo ful (wō′fəl), woeful. *adj. 20.*

woke (wōk). See **wake.** John woke before we did. *pt. and pp. of wake. 4.*

Timber wolf (2 ft. high at the shoulder)

wold (wōld), high, rolling country, bare of woods. *n. 15.*

wolf (wu̇lf), 1. a wild animal somewhat like a dog. Wolves kill sheep and sometimes even attack men. 2. a cruel, greedy person. 3. **Keep the wolf from the door** means keep safe from hunger or want. *n., pl. wolves* (wu̇lvz). *2.*

wolf hound (wu̇lf′hound′), a large dog of any of various breeds once used in hunting wolves. *n.*

Wolfhound (about 2½ ft. high at the shoulder)

wolf ish (wu̇l′fish), like a wolf; savage; as, a wolfish-looking dog, wolfish cruelty. *adj. 17.*

wolf like (wu̇lf′līk′), like a wolf; like a wolf's. *adj.*

wol ver ine or **wol ver ene** (wu̇l′vər ēn′), 1. clumsy, heavily built, meat-eating animal of northern regions. 2. its fur. *n.*

Wolverine (2 to 3 ft. long, without the tail)

wolves (wu̇lvz), more than one wolf. *n. pl. 5.*

wom an (wu̇m′ən), 1. female human being. A woman is a girl grown up. 2. women as a group. 3. female servant. *n., pl. women* (wim′in). *1.*

wom an hood (wu̇m′ən hu̇d), 1. condition or time of being a woman. 2. character or qualities of a woman. 3. women as a group. Joan of Arc was an honor to womanhood. *n. 11.*

wom an ish (wu̇m′ən ish), like a woman; suitable for women rather than for men; weak. *adj. 20.*

wom an kind (wu̇m′ən kīnd′), women; the female sex. *n. 11.*

wom an like (wu̇m′ən līk′), 1. like a woman. 2. suitable for a woman. *adj.*

wom an li ness (wu̇m′ən li nis), womanly nature. *n.*

wom an ly (wu̇m′ən li), 1. like a woman. 2. like a woman's. 3. proper or becoming for a woman; as, womanly sympathy. *adj. 15.*

womb (wüm), the part of the body that holds and nourishes the young till birth. *n. 6.*

Wombat (about 2½ ft. long)

wom bat (wom′bat), an Australian animal that looks like a small bear. A female wombat has a pouch for carrying her young. *n.*

wom en (wim′in), more than one woman. *n. pl. 2.*

wom en folk (wim′in fōk′), women. *n. pl.*

won (wun). See **win.** Which side won yesterday? We have won four games. *pt. and pp. of win. 2.*

won der (wun′dər), 1. strange and surprising thing or event. The pyramids are one of the wonders of the world. It is a wonder that he refused such a good offer. No wonder that child is sick; he eats too much candy. 2. the feeling caused by what is strange and surprising. The baby looked with wonder at the Christmas tree. 3. feel wonder. We wonder at the splendor of the stars. I shouldn't wonder if it rained before night. 4. be surprised. I wonder that you came at all. 5. be curious about; wish to know. I wonder what time it is. I wonder where Nell bought her new hat. *n., v. 1.*

won der ful (wun′dər fəl), causing wonder; marvelous; remarkable. The works of God are wonderful. The explorer had wonderful experiences. *adj. 1.*

won der land (wun′dər land′), a land full of wonders. *n. 20.*

won der ment (wun′dər mənt), wonder; surprise. *n.*

won drous (wun′drəs), wonderful. *adj. 4.*

wont (wunt), 1. accustomed. He was wont to read the paper at breakfast. 2. custom; habit. He rose early, as was his wont. *adj., n. 3.*

won't (wōnt), will not. *2.*

wont ed (wun′tid), accustomed; customary; usual. *adj.*

woo (wü), 1. make love to; seek to marry. 2. seek to win; try to get; as, to woo fame. 3. seek to persuade; urge. *v. 4.*

wood (wu̇d), 1. the hard substance beneath the bark of trees. Wood is used for making houses, boats, boxes, and furniture. 2. trees cut up for use. The carpenter brought wood to build a playhouse. Put some wood on the fire. 3. made of wood. 4. a large number of growing trees. The children go to the wood for wild flowers and for nuts. *n., adj. 1.*

Honeysuckle woodbine

wood alcohol, a poisonous liquid used for fuel and by painters.

wood bine (wu̇d′bīn′), 1. honeysuckle. 2. the Virginia creeper, a climbing vine with bluish-black berries. *n. 7.*

wood chuck (wu̇d′chuk′), a bushy-tailed thick-set animal, somewhat like rats and rabbits. See the picture. Woodchucks grow fat in summer and sleep in their holes in the ground all winter. *n. 13.*

Woodchuck (1¼ to 1½ ft. long, without the tail)

wood cock (wu̇d′kok′), a small game bird with a long bill and short legs. *n. 13.*

wood craft (wu̇d′-kraft′), knowledge about how to obtain food and shelter in the woods; skill in hunting, trapping, finding one's way, etc. *n.*

American woodcock (nearly 1 ft. long, including the long bill). The European woodcock is longer.

wood cut (wu̇d′kut′), 1. engraved block of wood to print from. 2. a print from such a block. *n.*

wood cut ter (wu̇d′kut′ər), man who cuts down trees or chops wood. *n. 12.*

wood ed (wu̇d′id), covered with trees. *adj. 17.*

wood en (wu̇d′ən), 1. made of wood. 2. stiff as wood; awkward. 3. dull; stupid. *adj. 2.*

wood land (wu̇d′lənd), 1. land covered with trees. 2. of the woods; pertaining to woods. *n., adj. 4.*

wood man (wu̇d′mən), 1. man who cuts down trees. 2. person who lives in the woods. 3. person who takes care of forests. *n., pl. woodmen. 6.*

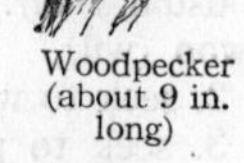
Woodpecker (about 9 in. long)

wood peck er (wu̇d′pek′ər), a bird with a hard, pointed bill for pecking holes in trees to get insects. *n. 6.*

woods (wu̇dz), a large number of growing trees; a forest. *n. pl.*

wood shed (wu̇d′shed′), shed for storing wood. *n.*

woods man (wu̇dz′mən), 1. man used to life in the woods and skilled in hunting, fishing, trapping, etc. 2. man whose work is cutting down trees; lumberman. *n., pl. woodsmen. 17.*

wood thrush, thrush common in the thickets and woods of eastern North America.

wood work (wu̇d′wėrk′), things made of wood; wooden parts inside of a house, especially doors, stairs, moldings, etc. *n. 12.*

wood y (wu̇d′i), 1. having many trees; covered with trees; as, a woody hillside. 2. consisting of wood; as, the woody parts of a shrub. 3. like wood. *adj., woodier, woodiest. 10.*

woo er (wü′ər), man who makes love to a woman; suitor. *n. 19.*

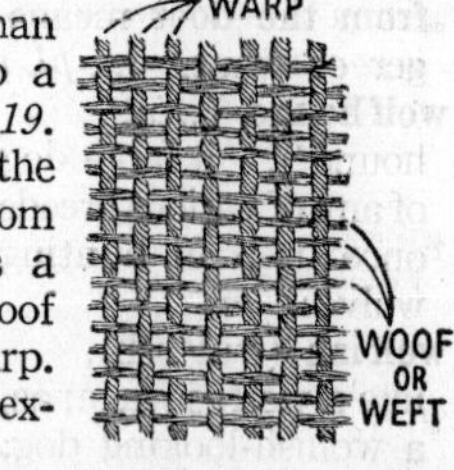

woof (wüf), 1. the threads running from side to side across a fabric. The woof crosses the warp. 2. fabric; cloth; texture. *n. 13.*

wool (wu̇l), 1. the soft hair or fur of sheep and some other animals. 2. short, thick, curly hair. 3. something like wool. 4. yarn, cloth, or garments made of wool. He wears wool in winter. *n. 2.*

wool en or **wool len** (wu̇l′ən), 1. made of wool. 2. cloth made of wool. **Woolens** means cloth or clothing made of wool. 3. of or having to do with wool; as, a woolen mill. *adj., n. 4.*

wool gath er ing (wu̇l′gaᴛʜ′ər ing), 1. inattentive; absent-minded; dreamy. 2. absent-mindedness; absorption in thinking or daydreaming. *adj., n.*

wool ly or **wool y** (wu̇l′i), 1. consisting of wool; as the woolly coat of a sheep. 2. like wool. 3. covered with wool or something like it. *adj., woollier, woolliest* or *woolier, wooliest. 14.*

Worces ter (wu̇s′tər), 1. a city in central Massachusetts. 2. a city in western England. *n. 13.*

word (wėrd), 1. a sound or a group of sounds that has meaning. We speak words when we talk. 2. the writing or printing that stands for a word. This page is filled with words. 3. **Words** sometimes means angry talk. 4. short talk. I want a word with you. 5. brief expression. The teacher gave us a word of advice. 6. command; order. Father's word is law. 7. promise. The boy kept his word. A **man of his word** is a man who keeps his promise. 8. news. No word has come from the battle front. 9. put into words; as, a well-worded letter. *n., v. 1.*

word i ness (wėr′di nis), the use of too many words. *n.*

word ing (wėr′ding), way of saying a thing; choice of words; use of words. Careful wording aids clearness. *n. 14.*

word less (wėrd′lis), without words; speechless. *adj. 20.*

Words worth (wėrdz′wėrth), William, an English poet who wrote mostly about nature (1770-1850). *n. 18.*

word y (wėr′di), using too many words. *adj., wordier, wordiest. 20.*

wore (wōr). See **wear.** He wore out his shoes in two months. *pt. of wear. 3.*

work (wėrk), 1. effort in doing or making something. Few people like hard work. 2. something to do; occupation; employment. The man is out of work. 3. that on which effort is put. The dressmaker took her work out on the porch. 4. something made or done. A picture is a work of art. 5. do work; labor; be employed. Most people must work to live. Henry works in a bank. 6. put effort on. He worked on his farm with success. 7. cause to do work. He works his men long hours. 8. act; operate. This pump will not work. The plan worked well. 9. make or get by effort. 10. bring about; cause; do. The plan worked harm. 11. go slowly or with effort. The ship worked to windward. 12. become (up, round, loose, etc.). The window catch has worked loose. 13. ferment. Yeast makes beer work. *n., v., worked* or *wrought, working. 1.*

work a ble (wėr′kə bəl), that can be worked. *adj. 18.*

work a day (wėr′kə dā′), of working days; practical; commonplace; ordinary. *adj.*

work day (wėrk′dā′), 1. day for work; day that is not Sunday or a holiday. 2. part of a day during which work is done. 3. workaday. *n., adj.*

work er (wėr′kər), one that works. *n. 3.*

work house (wėrk′hous′), 1. place where petty criminals are kept and made to work. 2. in England, a house where poor people are lodged and set to work. *n. 16.*

work ing (wėr′king), 1. operation; action; method of work. Do you understand the working of this machine? 2. that works. 3. used in working. *n., adj.*

work ing man (wėr′king man′), 1. man who works. 2. man who works with his hands or with machines. *n., pl. workingmen. 12.*

work man (wėrk′mən), 1. worker. 2. man who works with his hands or with machines. *n., pl. workmen. 4.*

work man like (wėrk′mən līk′), skillful; well-done. *adj.*

work man ship (wėrk′mən ship), 1. the art or skill in a worker or his work. 2. quality or manner of work. 3. the work done. *n. 6.*

work men (wėrk′mən), more than one workman. *n. pl.*

work room (wėrk′rüm′), a room where work is done. *n.*

works (wėrks), 1. factory; place for doing some kind of work. 2. acting or moving parts of a machine; as, the works of a clock. 3. buildings, bridges, docks, etc. *n. pl.*

work shop (wėrk′shop′), shop where work is done. *n. 9.*

world (wėrld), 1. the earth. Ships can sail around the world. 2. all of certain things or parts of the earth; as, the insect world, woman's world, the world of fashion. The **Old World** is Europe, Asia, and Africa. The **New World** is North America and South America. The **lower world** is another name for Hades, the home of the dead, which the Greeks thought was below the earth. 3. all people; the public. The whole world knows it. 4. the things of this life and the people devoted to them. Monks and nuns live apart from the world. 5. star; planet. 6. all created things; everything; the universe. 7. great deal; very much. Sunshine does children a world of good. 8. **For all the world** means (1) for any reason, no matter how great. (2) in every respect; exactly. *n. 1.*

world li ness (wėrld′li nis), worldly ideas, ways, or conduct. *n.*

world ly (wėrld′li), 1. of this world; not of heaven; as, worldly wealth. 2. caring much for the interests and pleasures of this world. *adj., worldlier, worldliest. 5.*

World War, 1. The first World War was the war in which many nations fought, lasting from 1914 to 1918. The United States, Great Britain, France, Russia, and their allies were on one side; Germany, Austria-Hungary, and their allies were on the other side. 2. The second World War began in 1939. The United States, Great Britain, Russia, and their allies are on one side; Germany, Italy, Japan, and their allies are on the other side.

world-wide (wėrld′wīd′), spread throughout the world. Gasoline has now an almost world-wide use. *adj. 18.*

worm (wėrm), 1. a small, slender, crawling or creeping animal. 2. a small crawling animal without legs. 3. something like a worm in shape or movement, such as the thread of a screw. 4. move like a worm; crawl or creep like a worm. The soldier wormed his way toward the enemy's lines. He wormed himself into our confidence. 5. get by persistent and secret means. John tried to worm the secret out of me. 6. person who deserves contempt or pity. *n., v. 2.*

Worm

worms (wėrmz), disease caused by worms in the body. *n. pl.*

worm wood (wėrm′wu̇d′), 1. a bitter plant used in medicine and in certain liquors. 2. something bitter or extremely unpleasant. *n. 13.*

worm y (wėr′mi), 1. having worms; containing many worms. 2. damaged by worms. *adj., wormier, wormiest. 20.*

Wormwood

worn (wōrn), 1. damaged by use; as, worn rugs. 2. tired; wearied; as, a worn face. 3. See **wear.** He has worn that suit for two years. *adj., pp. of wear. 2.*

worn-out (wōrn′out′), used until no longer fit for use. *adj.*

wor ry (wėr′i), 1. feel anxious; be uneasy. She worries about little things. 2. bother; annoy; vex; trouble. Don't worry your father with so many questions. 3. care; anxiety; trouble. 4. seize and shake with the teeth; bite at; snap at. *v., worried, worrying, n., pl. worries. 3.*

worse (wėrs). Bill is a bad boy, but his brother is worse. We say bad, worse, worst. It is raining worse than ever. Job thought the loss of his property bad enough, but worse followed. *adj., adv., n. 2.*

wor ship (wėr′ship), 1. great honor and respect; as, the worship of God, hero worship. 2. pay great honor and respect to. People go to church to worship God. 3. ceremonies or services in honor of God. 4. take part in a religious service. 5. consider extremely precious; hold very dear. A miser worships money. Helen worships her mother. 6. in England, a title used in addressing certain magistrates. "Yes, your worship," said Sam to the judge. *n., v., worshiped, worshiping* or *worshipped, worshipping. 3.*

wor ship er or **wor ship per** (wėr′ship ər), person who worships. The church was filled with worshipers. *n. 7.*

wor ship ful (wėr′ship fəl), honorable. *adj. 12.*

worst (wėrst), 1. Fred is the worst boy in school. This is the worst cold I ever had. This child acts worst when there is company about. The mean boy kept the best of the fruit for himself and gave the worst to his friends. At the worst, you will only have to do the work over again. If worst comes to worst, Mary will quit school and go to work. 2. beat; defeat. The hero worsted his enemies. *adj., adv., n., v. 2.*

wor sted (wu̇s′tid), 1. firmly twisted woolen thread or yarn. 2. cloth made from such thread or yarn. 3. woolen yarn for knitting, crocheting, and needlework. *n. 10.*

worth (wėrth), 1. good or important enough for; deserving of. New York is a city worth visiting. 2. merit; usefulness; importance. We should read books of real worth. 3. value; power to buy. Jane got her money's worth out of that coat. He bought a dollar's worth of stamps. 4. equal in value to. This book is worth two dollars. That toy is worth little. 5. having property that amounts to. Mr. Rockefeller was worth many millions of dollars. *adj., n. 1.*

wor thi ly (wėr′ᴛʜi li), in a worthy manner. The good man lived worthily. *adv. 13.*

wor thi ness (wėr′ᴛʜi nis), worth; merit. *n. 16.*

worth less (wėrth′lis), without worth; good-for-nothing; useless. Throw those worthless, broken toys away. Don't read that worthless book. *adj. 4.*

worth-while (wėrth′hwīl′), worth time, attention, or trouble; having real merit. *adj. 19.*

wor thy (wėr′ᴛʜi), 1. having worth or merit. She helps the worthy poor. 2. deserving; meriting. His courage was worthy of high praise. Bad acts are worthy of punishment. 3. person of great merit; admirable person. Abraham Lincoln stands high among American worthies. *adj., worthier, worthiest, n., pl. worthies. 2.*

wot (wot), an old form meaning **know.** "I wot" means "I know." *v. 7.*

would (wu̇d), 1. was willing to; wished to; was determined to. He said that he would come. He would go in spite of our warning. 2. *Would* is also used (1) to express action done again and again. The children would play for hours on the beach. (2) to express a wish. I would I were dead. (3) to make a statement or question sound more polite. Would you help us, please? (4) to express condition. If he would only try, he could do it. *pt. of* **will**[1]. *1.*

would n't (wu̇d′ənt), would not. *4.*

wouldst (wu̇dst), an old form meaning **would.** "Thou wouldst" means "you would." *v. 7.*

wound[1] (wünd), 1. a hurt or injury caused by cutting, stabbing, shooting, etc. The man has a knife wound in his arm. 2. injure by cutting, stabbing, shooting, etc.; hurt. The hunter wounded the deer. Unkind words wound. 3. any hurt or injury to feelings, reputation, etc. The loss of his job was a wound to Mr. Black's pride. *n., v. 2.*

wound[2] (wound). See **wind**[2] and **wind**[3]. She wound the string into a ball some time ago. It is tightly wound. *pt. and pp. of wind*[2] *and wind*[3].

wove (wōv). See **weave.** The spider wove a new web after the first was destroyed. *pt. and a pp. of weave. 5.*

wo ven (wō′vən). See **weave.** This cloth is closely woven. *pp. of weave. 4.*

wrack (rak), 1. wreckage. 2. ruin; destruction. 3. seaweed cast ashore. *n. 13.*

wraith (rāth), 1. specter; ghost. 2. ghost of a person seen before or soon after his death. *n. 19.*

wran gle (rang′gəl), 1. argue or dispute in a noisy or angry way; quarrel. The children wrangled about who should sit on the front seat. 2. a noisy or angry dispute; a quarrel. *v., n. 8.*

wrap (rap), 1. cover by winding or folding something around. She wrapped herself in a shawl. The mountain peak is wrapped in clouds. 2. **Wrapped up in** sometimes means devoted to; thinking chiefly of. Mrs. Jones is wrapped up in her children. 3. an outer covering. Shawls, scarfs, coats, and furs are wraps. *v., wrapped* or *wrapt, wrapping, n. 2.*

wrap per (rap′ər), 1. person or thing that wraps. 2. a covering or cover. Magazines are mailed in paper wrappers. 3. a woman's loose garment to wear in the house. *n. 10.*

wrapt (rapt), wrapped. *pt. and pp. of* **wrap.** *18.*

wrath (rath), very great anger; rage. *n. 3.*

wrath ful (rath′fəl), very angry; showing wrath. The wrathful lion turned on the hunters. His wrathful eyes flashed. *adj. 9.*

wreak (rēk), 1. give expression to; work off (feelings, desires, etc.). The cruel boy wreaked his bad temper on his dog. 2. inflict (vengeance, punishment, etc.). *v. 12.*

Girl wearing a wreath

wreath (rēth), 1. a ring of flowers or leaves twisted together. We hang wreaths in the windows at Christmas. 2. something suggesting a wreath; as, a wreath of smoke. *n., pl. wreaths* (rēᴛʜz). *3.*

wreathe (rēᴛʜ), 1. make into a wreath. The children wreathed flowers to put on the soldiers' graves. 2. decorate or adorn with wreaths. The inside of the schoolhouse was wreathed with Christmas greens. 3. make a ring around; encircle. The hills are wreathed in mist. **Wreathed in smiles** means smiling greatly. *v. 6.*

wreck (rek), 1. destruction of a ship. The storm caused many wrecks. 2. destruction or ruin of a building, train, automobile, or airship. 3. destruction or serious injury. The war caused the wreck of many fortunes. 4. what is left of anything that has been destroyed or much injured. The wrecks of six ships were cast upon the shore by the waves. 5. cause the wreck of; destroy; ruin. Robbers wrecked the mail train. *n., v. 3.*

wreck age (rek′ij), 1. a wrecking; a being wrecked. She wept at the wreckage of her hopes. 2. remains of a wreck. The shore was covered with the wreckage of a ship. *n. 19.*

wreck er (rek′ər), 1. one that causes wrecks; person who causes shipwrecks by false lights on shore so as to plunder the wrecks. 2. person or ship that recovers wrecked or disabled vessels or their cargoes. 3. person, car, train, or machine that removes wrecks. *n.*

wren (ren), a small songbird. Wrens often build their nests near houses. *n. 5.*

House wren (about 5 in. long, including the tail)

wrench (rench), 1. a violent twist or twisting pull. He gave his ankle a wrench when he jumped off the car. It was a wrench to leave the old home. 2. twist or pull violently. He wrenched the knob off when he was trying to open the door. The policeman wrenched the gun out of the man's hand. 3. tool to hold and turn nuts, bolts, etc. *n., v. 5.*

Wrench

wrest (rest), 1. twist, pull, or tear away with force; wrench away. The nurse bravely wrested the knife from the insane patient. 2. take by force. The usurper wrested the power from the king. 3. twist; turn. You wrest my words from their real meanings. *v., n. 7.*

wres tle (res′əl), 1. try to throw or force an opponent to the ground. The rules for wrestling do not allow using the fists or certain holds on the body. 2. wrestling match. 3. struggle. We wrestle with temptation. *v., n. 6.*

wres tler (res′lər), one who wrestles. *n. 13.*

wretch (rech), 1. a very unfortunate or unhappy person. 2. very bad person. *n. 4.*

wretch ed (rech′id), 1. very unfortunate or unhappy. 2. very unsatisfactory; miserable; as, a wretched hut. 3. very bad; as, a wretched traitor. *adj. 3.*

wretch ed ness (rech′id nis), wretched condition or quality. *n. 8.*

wrig gle (rig′əl), 1. turn and twist. Children wriggle when they are restless. 2. move by twisting and turning, as a worm does. 3. make one's way by shifts and tricks. That boy can wriggle out of any difficulty. 4. a wriggling. *v., n. 11.*

wright (rīt), maker of something. A wheelwright makes wheels. A playwright makes plays for the theater. *n. 20.*

Wright (rīt), Orville (born 1871) and Wilbur (1867-1912), brothers who invented the airplane in 1903. *n.*

wring (ring), 1. twist with force; squeeze hard. Wring out your wet bathing suit. His soul was wrung with grief. 2. get by twisting or squeezing; force out. The laundress wrings water from the clothes. 3. get by force, effort, or persuasion. The old beggar could wring money from anyone by his sad story. 4. a twist; a squeeze. *v., wrung, wringing, n. 5.*

wring er (ring′ər), machine for squeezing water from clothes. See the picture in the next column. *n. 14.*

wrin kle (ring′kəl), 1. ridge; fold. An old man's face has wrinkles. I must press out the wrinkles in this dress. 2. make a wrinkle or wrinkles in. He wrinkled his forehead. 3. have wrinkles; acquire wrinkles. The sleeves wrinkle. 4. useful hint or idea; clever trick. She knows all the latest wrinkles in style. *Not used in formal writing. n., v. 4.*

wrist (rist), the joint connecting hand and arm. *n. 6.*

wrist band (rist′band′), the band of a sleeve fitting around the wrist. *n.*

writ (rit), 1. something written; a writing. The Bible is Holy Writ. 2. a formal order directing a person to do or avoid something. A subpoena is a writ. 3. wrote. He writ to his father. *Old use.* 4. written. Their names are writ in gold. *Old use. n., old pt. and old pp. of* **write.** *4.*

write (rīt), 1. make letters or words with pen, pencil, or chalk. 2. mark with words. Please write on both sides of the paper. 3. put down the words of. Write your name. 4. make up stories, books, etc.; compose. Mr. Blank writes for the magazines. 5. be a writer. Her ambition was to write. 6. write a letter. Mary writes to her mother every week. 7. Some special meanings are:

write down, 1. put into writing. 2. put a lower value on.

write off, cancel.

write out, 1. put into writing. 2. write in full.

write up, 1. write a description or account of. 2. write in detail. 3. bring up to date in writing. 4. put a higher value on.

v., wrote, written, writing. 1.

writ er (rīt′ər), 1. person who writes. 2. person whose occupation is writing; author. *n. 3.*

writhe (rīTH), twist; twist out of shape; twist about. The wounded man writhed with pain. Tom's soul writhed in agony. *v. 9.*

writ ing (rīt′ing), 1. act of making letters or words with pen, pencil, chalk, etc. 2. written form. Put your ideas in writing. 3. handwriting. 4. something written; a letter, paper, document, etc. 5. literary work; a book or other literary production; as, the writings of Benjamin Franklin. *n.*

Tub with wringer

writ ten (rit′ən). See **write.** He has written a letter. *pp. of write. 2.*

wrong (rông), 1. not right; wicked. Stealing is wrong. 2. not true; not correct. John gave a wrong answer. 3. not proper; not fit. That is the wrong way to throw a ball. 4. not meant to be seen; least important; as, the wrong side of cloth. 5. out of order. Something is wrong with the car. 6. anything not right. Two wrongs do not make a right. 7. injury; harm. Mrs. Brown is doing her child a wrong by spoiling him so. 8. in a wrong manner; ill; badly. Everything went wrong today. 9. do wrong to; treat unfairly; harm. He forgave those who had wronged him. *adj., n., adv., v. 1.*

wrong do ing (rông′dü′ing), doing wrong; evil; wrong. *n.*

wrong ful (rông′fəl), wrong. *adj. 11.*

wrong-head ed (rông′hed′id), 1. wrong in judgment or opinion. 2. stubborn even when wrong. *adj.*

wrote (rōt). See **write.** He wrote his mother a long letter last week. *pt. of write. 2.*

wroth (rôth), angry. *adj. 6.*

wrought (rôt), 1. made. The gate was wrought with great skill. 2. worked. *adj., a pt. and pp. of* **work.** *3.*

wrought iron, a tough form of iron with little carbon in it. Wrought iron will not crack as easily as cast iron.

wrung (rung). See **wring.** The maid wrung out the dishcloth after having washed the dishes. Her heart is wrung with pity for the poor. *pt. and pp. of wring. 9.*

wry (rī), twisted; turned to one side. She made a wry face to show her disgust. *adj., wrier, wriest. 12.*

wt., weight.

Würt tem berg (vir′təm berk), a district in southwestern Germany. *n. 17.*

W.Va., West Virginia.

Wyo., Wyoming.

Wy o ming (wī ō′ming), a Western State of the United States. *n. 10.*

X

X, x (eks), 1. the 24th letter in the alphabet. 2. an unknown quantity. 3. thing shaped like an X. 4. Roman numeral for 10. *n., pl. X's, x's.*

Xan thip pe (zan tip′i), 1. the wife of Socrates, famous as a scold. 2. scolding woman; shrew. *n.*

Xavi er (zav′i ər), Saint Francis, Spanish Jesuit missionary in the Far East (1506-1552). *n.*

xe bec (zē′bek), small three-masted vessel of the Mediterranean. *n.*

X ray of a foot

Xen o phon (zen′ə fən), Greek writer (430?-355? B.C.). *n.*

Xerx es (zėrk′sēz), king of Persia from about 486 to 465 B.C. He tried to conquer Greece, but was defeated. *n. 14.*

Xmas (kris′məs), Christmas. *n. 10.*

X ray, 1. a ray which penetrates substances that ordinary lights cannot. X rays are used to locate breaks in bones, bullets lodged in the body, and to treat certain diseases. 2. a picture made by means of X rays. See the picture in the last column. *19.*

X-ray (eks′rā′), 1. of, by, or pertaining to X rays; as, an X-ray examination of one's teeth. 2. examine, photograph, or treat with X rays. *adj., v.*

xy lem (zī′lem), woody part of plants. *n. 20.*

xy lo phone (zī′lə fōn), a musical instrument consisting of a row of wooden bars, sounded by striking with wooden hammers. *n. 20.*

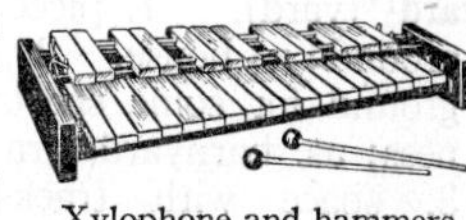

Xylophone and hammers

Y

Y, y (wī), 1. the 25th letter of the alphabet. 2. something shaped like the letter Y. *n., pl. Y's, y's.*

y., 1. yard or yards. 2. year.

-y[1], adjective suffix meaning:— 1. full of, composed of, containing, having, or characterized by; as in airy, cloudy, dewy, icy, juicy, watery.

2. somewhat; as in chilly, salty, whity.
3. inclined to; as in chatty, fidgety.
4. resembling; suggesting; as in messy, sloppy, sugary, willowy.
5. In certain words, such as stilly, vasty, the addition of *y* does not change the meaning.

-y², noun suffix meaning:—small; as in dolly, and used also to show kind feeling or intimacy; as in aunty, Dicky.

-y³, suffix meaning:—1. state or quality; as in jealousy, victory. 2. activity; as in delivery, entreaty.

yacht (yot), 1. boat for pleasure trips or for racing. 2. to sail or race on a yacht. *n., v. 11.*

yacht ing (yot′ing), 1. sport or pastime of sailing a yacht. 2. sailing on a yacht. *n.*

Yak (about 5 ft. tall)

yak (yak), the long-haired ox of Tibet and central Asia. *n.*

Yale (yāl), a university at New Haven, Connecticut. *n. 13.*

yam (yam), 1. the starchy root of a vine grown for food in warm countries. 2. the vine itself. 3. a kind of sweet potato. *n. 20.*

Yang tze (yäng′tse′), river flowing from Tibet through China. It is the longest river in China. 3100 mi. *n.*

yank (yangk), jerk. *v., n.* [*Used in common talk*]

Yan kee (yang′ki), 1. a native of New England. 2. a native of any of the Northern States. 3. a native of the United States. 4. of or having to do with Yankees; as, Yankee shrewdness. *n., adj. 9.*

yap (yap), 1. snappish bark; a yelp. 2. bark snappishly; yelp. *n., v., yapped, yapping.*

yard¹ (yärd), 1. piece of ground near or around a house. 2. piece of enclosed ground for some special purpose or business; as, barnyard, graveyard, navy yard. 3. space with tracks where railroad cars are stored, shifted around, etc. *n. 1.*

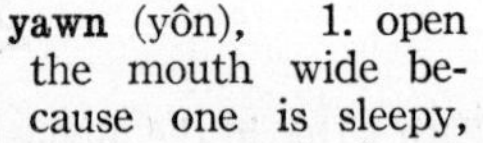

yard² (yärd), 1. 36 inches; 3 feet. 2. a beam or pole fastened across a mast, used to support a sail. *n.*

yard arm (yärd′ärm′), either end of the beam or pole which supports a square sail. *n.*

yard stick (yärd′stik′), 1. a stick one yard long, used for measuring. 2. standard of judgment or comparison. *n.*

yarn (yärn), 1. any spun thread, especially that prepared for weaving or knitting. The woman knits stockings from yarn. 2. tale; story. The old sailor made up his yarns as he told them. *n. 5.*

Yarrow

Yar row¹ (yar′ō), river in Scotland. *n. 18.*

yar row² (yar′ō), a common plant with finely divided leaves and flat clusters of white or pink flowers. *n.*

yaw (yô), 1. turn from the straight course. 2. such a movement. *v., n. 20.*

Yawl (def. 1)

yawl (yôl), 1. a boat with a large mast near the bow and a small mast near the stern. 2. a ship's boat rowed by four or six oars. *n. 19.*

yawn (yôn), 1. open the mouth wide because one is sleepy, tired, or bored. 2. act of doing so. 3. open wide. A wild gorge yawned beneath our feet. *v., n. 4.*

y cleped or **y clept** (i klept′), called; named. *adj.* [*Old use*]

yd., yard; yards. 6 yd. = 18 ft. *5.*

yds., yards.

ye¹ (yē), you. If ye are thirsty, drink. *pron. pl.* [*Old use*] *2.*

ye² (ᴛʜē, *wrongly* yē), an old way of spelling **the.** *definite article.*

yea (yā), 1. yes. 2. indeed. 3. affirmative vote or voter. *adv., n. 3.*

year (yēr), 12 months or 365 days. Leap year has 366 days. *n. 1.*

year book (yēr′bu̇k′), a book or report published every year. Yearbooks often report facts of the year. *n. 17.*

year ling (yēr′ling), 1. an animal one year old. 2. one year old; as, a yearling colt. *n., adj. 13.*

year ly (yēr′li), 1. once a year; in every year. Mr. Davis takes a yearly trip to Europe. 2. lasting a year. The earth makes a yearly revolution around the sun. 3. for a year. He is paid $300 a month, or $3600 yearly. *adj., adv. 5.*

yearn (yėrn), 1. feel a longing or desire; desire earnestly. He yearns for home.

2. feel pity; have tender feelings. Her heart yearned for the starving children. *v. 5.*

yearn ing (yėr′ning), strong desire; longing. *n.*

yeast (yēst), 1. the substance used in raising bread and in making beer. Yeast consists of very small plants or cells that grow quickly in a liquid containing sugar. 2. flour or meal mixed with this substance and pressed into small cakes. *n. 7.*

yell (yel), 1. cry out with a strong, loud sound. He yelled with pain. 2. a strong, loud cry. 3. say with a yell. 4. special shout or cheer used by a school or college. *v., n. 4.*

yel low (yel′ō), 1. the color of gold, butter, or lemons. 2. having this color. 3. having a yellowish skin. The Chinese and Japanese belong to the yellow race. 4. make yellow. Buttercups yellowed the field. 5. become yellow. 6. cowardly; mean. *Used in common talk. n., adj., v. 1.*

yellow fever, a dangerous infectious disease of warm climates, transmitted by the bite of a certain kind of mosquito.

yel low ish (yel′ō ish), somewhat yellow. *adj. 17.*

yellow jacket, wasp or hornet marked with bright yellow.

Yel low stone (yel′ō stōn′), a national park mostly in Wyoming, famous for its scenery, hot springs, and geysers. *n. 14.*

yelp (yelp), 1. the quick sharp bark or cry of a dog, fox, etc. 2. make such a bark or cry. *n., v. 8.*

yen (yen), unit of money of Japan, worth about 84 cents in 1940. *n., pl. yen.*

yeo man (yō′mən), 1. a servant or attendant of a lord or king. *Old use.* 2. in England, a person who owns land, but not a large amount. 3. in the United States navy, a petty officer who has charge of supplies, accounts, etc. *n., pl. yeomen. 9.*

yeo man ry (yō′mən ri), yeomen. *n. 15.*

yes (yes). "Yes, I do," said Tom. "Yes, five and two are seven," said sister. "Your work is good, yes, very good," said the teacher. *adv., n. 1.*

yes ter day (yes′tər di), 1. the day before today. 2. on the day before today. 3. the near past; as, fashions of yesterday. *n., adv. 1.*

yes ter eve (yes′tər ēv′), yesterday evening. *n., adv.*

yes ter night (yes′tər nīt′), last night; the night before today. *n., adv. 13.*

yet (yet), 1. Don't go yet. It was not yet dark. The thief will be caught yet. She is talking yet. 2. also; again. Yet once more I forbid you to go. 3. moreover. He won't do it for you nor yet for me. 4. even. The king spoke yet more harshly. 5. but; nevertheless; however. The work is good, yet it could be better. *adv., conj. 1.*

yew (ū), 1. an evergreen tree of Europe and Asia. 2. the wood of this tree. Bows used to be made of yew. *n. 6.*

CONE

Branch of yew

Yid dish (yid′ish), a dialect of German used by Jews. Yiddish contains many Hebrew expressions. *n.*

yield (yēld), 1. produce. This land yields good crops. Mines yield ore. 2. amount yielded; product. This year's yield from the silver mine was very large. 3. give; grant. Mary's mother yielded her consent to the plan. 4. give up; surrender. The enemy yielded to our soldiers. 5. give way. The door yielded to his touch. 6. give place. We yield to nobody in love of freedom. *v., n. 2.*

yield ing (yēl′ding), submissive; not resisting. *adj.*

Y.M.C.A., Young Men's Christian Association. *17.*

yo del (yō′dəl), 1. sing with frequent changes from the ordinary voice to a forced shrill voice and back again. 2. act or sound of yodeling. *v., yodeled, yodeling, n.*

yo dle (yō′dəl), yodel. *v., yodled, yodling, n.*

Yoke on a pair of oxen

yoke (yōk), 1. a wooden frame to fasten two work animals together. See the picture. 2. A **yoke of oxen** means two oxen. 3. any frame connecting two other parts. The man carried two buckets on a yoke, one at each end. 4. put a yoke on. 5. harness or fasten a work animal (to). 6. part of a garment fitting the neck and shoulders closely. 7. top piece to a skirt, fitting the

Yoke of a dress

hips. 8. something that binds together. 9. join. 10. something that holds people in slavery or submission. Throw off your yoke and be free. 11. rule; dominion. Slaves are under the yoke of their masters. *n., v. 3.*

yoke fel low (yōk′fel′ō), 1. one associated with another in a task; partner. 2. husband or wife. *n. 16.*

yo kel (yō′kəl), a country fellow. *n.*

Yo ko ha ma (yō′kō hä′mə), the chief seaport city in Japan. *n. 18.*

yolk (yōk), the yellow part of an egg. *n. 10.*

yon (yon), yonder. *adj., adv. 4.*

yond (yond), yonder. *adv., adj. 18.*

yon der (yon′dər), over there; within sight, but not near. Look at that wild duck yonder! The sky is getting black yonder in the west. On yonder hill stands a ruined castle. *adv., adj. 3.*

Yon kers (yong′kərz), a city just north of New York City. *n. 20.*

yore (yōr), long ago; years ago. Knights wore armor in days of yore. *adv., n. 8.*

York (yôrk), 1. a city in northern England. 2. a county in northern England. Also called **Yorkshire.** 3. the English royal house from 1461 to 1485. 4. The second son of the King of England is called the Duke of York. *n. 6.*

York shire (yôrk′shir), a county in northern England. *n. 9.*

Yorkshire pudding, a batter cake often served with roast beef.

York town (yôrk′toun), town in southeastern Virginia, where Lord Cornwallis surrendered to George Washington in 1781. *n.*

Yo sem i te (yō sem′i ti), 1. a national park in California. 2. a very deep valley in this park, famous for its lofty, beautiful waterfalls. *n.*

you (ū), 1. the person or persons spoken to. Are you ready? Then you may go. 2. one; anybody. You never can tell. You push this button to get a light. *pron. pl. or sing. 1.*

you'd (ūd), 1. you had. 2. you would. *5.*

you'll (ūl), 1. you will. 2. you shall. *4.*

young (yung), 1. in the early part of life; not old. A puppy is a young dog. 2. young ones. An animal will fight to protect its young. 3. having the looks or qualities of youth or of a young person. Mrs. Jones is young for her age. 4. not so old as another. Young Mr. Jones worked for his father. *adj., younger* (yung′gər), *youngest* (yung′gist), *n. 1.*

young ling (yung′ling), a young person, animal, or plant. *n. 16.*

young ster (yung′stər), 1. child. Jack is a lively youngster. 2. young person. *n. 11.*

Youngs town (yungz′toun), a city in northeastern Ohio. *n.*

youn ker (yung′kər), young fellow. *n. 18.*

your (ūr), 1. belonging to you. Wash your hands. 2. having to do with you. We enjoyed your visit. 3. that you know; well-known; that you speak of; that is spoken of; as, your real lover of music. 4. part of a title; as in Your Highness, Your Lordship, Your Honor, Mayor Jones. *pron. pl. or sing., adj. 1.*

you're (ūr), you are. *4.*

yours (ūrz), 1. of you; belonging to you. The red book is yours. 2. the one or ones belonging to you. My hands are clean; yours are dirty. I like ours better than yours. 3. *Yours* is used at the end of a letter with some other word; as, Yours truly, Sincerely yours. *pron. sing. and pl. 3.*

your self (ūr self′), 1. *Yourself* is used to make a statement stronger. You yourself know the story is not true. 2. *Yourself* is used instead of *you* when *you* has already been used in the sentence. Did you hurt yourself? *pron., pl. yourselves. 2.*

your selves (ūr selvz′). You can all see for yourselves that the room is empty. *pl. pron. 4.*

youth (ūth), 1. being young. He has the vigor of youth. She keeps her youth well. 2. the time between childhood and manhood or womanhood. 3. young man. 4. young people. *n., pl. youths* (yōᴛʜz). *2.*

youth ful (ūth′fəl), 1. young. 2. having the looks or qualities of youth; fresh; lively. 3. of youth. *adj. 4.*

you've (ūv), you have. *7.*

yowl (youl), 1. long, distressful, or dismal cry; a howl. 2. to howl. *n., v.*

yr., year; years. *11.*

yrs., years.

Yu ca tan (ū′kə tan′), 1. peninsula of southeastern Mexico and part of Central America. 2. a State in southeastern Mexico. *n.*

yuc ca (yuk′ə), a plant having large white flowers. *n.*

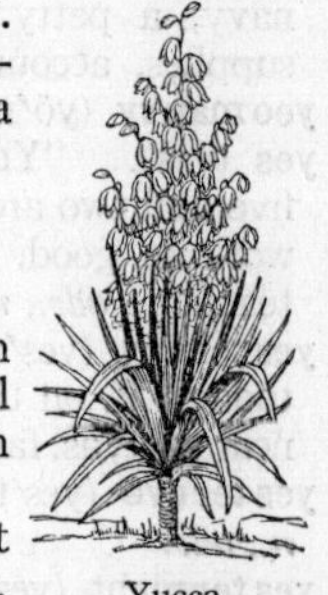
Yucca

Yu go slav (ū′gō släv′), 1. native or inhabitant of Yugoslavia. 2. of or having to do with Yugoslavia or its people. *n., adj.* Also spelled **Jugoslav.**

Yu go sla vi a (ū′gō slä′vi ə), a country in southeastern Europe. *n.* Also spelled **Jugoslavia.**

Yu kon (ū′kon), 1. river in Canada and Alaska, flowing into the Pacific Ocean. 2. a territory in northwestern Canada. *n. 17.*

Yule (ūl), 1. Christmas. 2. Yuletide. *n. 20.*

Yule log, a large log that is burned at Christmas.

Yule tide (ūl′tīd′), Christmas time; the Christmas season. *n.*

Y.W.C.A., Young Women's Christian Association.

Z

Z, z (zē), the 26th and last letter of the alphabet. *n., pl. Z's, z's.*

Zam be zi (zam bē′zi), river flowing 2200 miles through southern Africa into the Indian Ocean. *n. 19.*

za ny (zā′ni), 1. a clown. *Old use.* 2. a fool. *n., pl. zanies. 17.*

zeal (zēl), eager desire or effort. A good citizen feels zeal for his country's interests. Joseph worked with zeal at his business. *n. 3.*

Zea land (zē′lənd), largest island in Denmark, in the eastern part. *n.*

zeal ot (zel′ət), person who shows too much zeal; fanatic. *n. 11.*

zeal ous (zel′əs), full of zeal; eager; earnest. The new cook seems zealous to please. The children made zealous efforts to clean up the house for the party. *adj. 5.*

Zeb e dee (zeb′i dē), in the Bible, the father of the apostles James and John. *n. 17.*

ze bra (zē′brə), a wild animal like a horse but striped with dark bands on white. *n. 13.*

Zebra (4 to 4½ ft. high at the shoulder)

ze bu (zē′bū), an animal like an ox but with a large hump. The zebu is a domestic animal in Asia and eastern Africa. *n.*

Zebu (4 ft. high at the shoulder)

Zech a ri ah (zek′ə rī′ə), 1. a Hebrew prophet. 2. a book of the Old Testament. *n. 17.*

ze nith (zē′nith), 1. the point in the heavens directly overhead; the point where a vertical line would pierce the sky. 2. the highest point. At the zenith of its power Rome ruled all of civilized Europe. *n. 8.*

zeph yr (zef′ər), 1. the west wind. 2. any soft, gentle wind. 3. a fine, soft yarn. *n. 9.*

zep pe lin (zep′ə lin), large dirigible balloon shaped like a cigar with pointed ends. It has compartments for gas, engines, passengers, etc. *n.*

Zeppelin

ze ro (zēr′ō), 1. naught; 0. There are three zeros in 40,006. 2. point marked as 0 on the scale of a thermometer, etc. 3. of or at zero. 4. nothing. 5. not any; none at all. 6. a very low point. The team's spirit sank to zero after its third defeat. *n., pl. zeros* or *zeroes, adj. 5.*

zest (zest), keen enjoyment; relish. The hungry man ate with zest. *n. 11.*

Zeus (züs), the chief god of the ancient Greeks, the ruler of gods and men. The Romans called him Jupiter. *n. 18.*

zig zag (zig′zag′), 1. with short, sharp turns from one side to the other. The path ran zigzag up the hill. 2. move in a zigzag way. Lightning zigzagged across the sky. 3. zigzag line or course. 4. one of the short, sharp turns of a zigzag. *adj., adv., v., zigzagged, zigzagging, n. 6.*

Zigzag design

zinc (zingk), a bluish-white metal very little affected by air and moisture. Zinc is used as a coating for iron, in mixture with other metals, as a roofing material, in electric batteries, in paint, and in medicine. *n. 7.*

zin ni a (zin′i ə), a garden plant grown for its showy flowers of many colors. *n.*

Zi on (zī′ən), 1. hill in Jerusalem on which the royal palace and the temple were built. 2. Israel; the people of Israel. 3. heaven; the heavenly city. 4. the church of God. *n. 7.*

Zi on ism (zī′ən izm), a plan or modern movement to make Palestine a Jewish homeland. *n.*

zip (zip), 1. a sudden brief hissing sound, as of a flying bullet. 2. make such a sound. 3. energy or vim. *Used in common talk.* 4. proceed with energy. *Used in common talk. n., v., zipped, zipping.*

zip per (zip′ər), sliding fastener for clothing, shoes, etc. *n.* [*Trade name*]

Zither

zith er (zith′ər), a musical instrument having 30 to 40 strings, played with the fingers. *n. 20.*

zo di ac (zō′di ak), a belt of the heavens extending on both sides of the apparent yearly path of the sun. The zodiac is divided into 12 equal parts called signs, named after 12 groups of stars. *n. 8.*

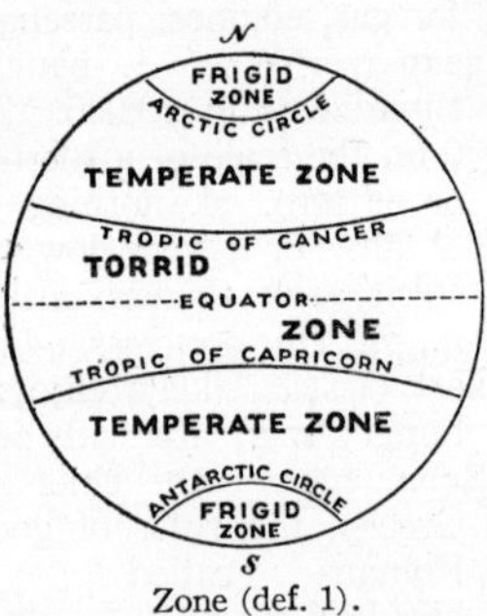

Zone (def. 1).

zone (zōn), 1. any of the five great divisions of the earth's surface, bounded by lines parallel to the equator. See the diagram. 2. any region or area especially considered or set off. A war zone is a district where fighting is going on. 3. in the United States parcel-post system, an area to all points within which the same rate of postage prevails for parcel-post shipments from a place. 4. divide into zones. 5. be formed into zones. 6. belt; girdle. The maiden wore a jeweled zone. 7. surround like a belt. *n., v. 3.*

zoo (zü), place where wild animals are kept and shown. *n. 20.*

zo ö log i cal (zō′ə loj′i kəl), 1. of animals and animal life. 2. having to do with zoölogy. *adj. 6.*

zoölogical garden, place where wild animals are kept and shown; zoo. We saw lions and tigers in the zoölogical garden.

zo öl o gist (zō ol′ə jist), person skilled or trained in zoölogy. *n. 17.*

zo öl o gy (zō ol′ə ji), the science of animals; the study of animals and animal life. *n. 11.*

zoom (züm), 1. move suddenly upward. The airplane zoomed. 2. sudden upward flight. *v., n.*

Zo ro as ter (zō′rō as′tər), famous Persian religious teacher who lived about 1000 B.C. *n.*

zounds (zoundz), an oath expressing surprise or anger. *interj.* [*Old use*]

Zui der Zee or **Zuy der Zee** (zī′dər zē′), shallow gulf in central Netherlands. It is now closed from the North Sea by a dike.

Zu lu (zü′lü), 1. member of a warlike tribe in southeastern Africa. 2. of this tribe. *n., pl. Zulus, adj. 20.*

Zu lu land (zü′lü land′), a part of Natal, an eastern province of the Union of South Africa. *n. 19.*

Zu rich (zür′ik), city in northern Switzerland. *n. 13.*

zwie back (zwē′bäk′), a kind of bread or cake cut into slices and toasted in an oven. *n.*

WORDS MADE FROM OTHER WORDS

You can see what words with **ly, ness, er, est, less, like, ing,** and **ed** added to them mean by these:

ly:

bad badly. John acted badly.
beautiful beautifully. The rose bloomed beautifully.
soft softly. The cat purred softly.

ness:

fresh freshness. The freshness of fish makes it taste better.
big bigness. The bigness of a desk makes it hard to carry.
red redness. The redness of an apple makes it pretty.

er and **est:**

long longer longest.
rich richer richest.
warm warmer warmest.

er meaning a person or thing that does:

A fighter fights. A leader leads. A painter paints.

less:

hairless means having no hair, or without any hair.
motherless means having no mother, or without any mother.
treeless means having no trees, or without any trees.

like:

doglike means like a dog or like a dog's.
A wolf is a doglike animal.
Tom followed his big brother with doglike devotion.
fairylike means like a fairy or like a fairy's.
Lily was a fairylike girl.
She danced with fairylike steps.

ing and **ed:**

He is laughing now. He laughed at the joke.
Laughing is better than crying.
I am buttering my bread. His has been buttered.
The buttering of a hundred sandwiches kept Mother busy.
Buttered toast is good.
Do you like hunting? The hunted fox ran into his hole.
A forested hill is a hill with a forest on it.
Painting is fun if you can do it well.
A painted face is a face that has paint on it or a face that has been painted.
A curtained window is one that has curtains.
A frosted window is one that has frost or has been frosted.

WORDS M[illegible]S

You can see what words with **ly, ness, er, est, less, like, ing,** and **ed** added to them mean by these:

ly:

bad badly. John acted badly.
beautiful beautifully. The rose bloomed beautifully.
soft softly. The cat purred softly.

ness:

fresh freshness. The freshness of fish makes it taste better.
big bigness. The bigness of a desk makes it hard to carry.
red redness. The redness of an apple makes it pretty.

er and **est:**

long longer longest.
rich richer richest.
warm warmer warmest.

er meaning a person or thing that does:

A fighter fights. A leader leads. A painter paints.

less:

hairless means having no hair, or without any hair.
motherless means having no mother, or without any mother.
treeless means having no trees, or without any trees.

like:

doglike means like a dog or like a dog's.
A wolf is a doglike animal.
Tom followed his big brother with doglike devotion.
fairylike means like a fairy or like a fairy's.
Lily was a fairylike girl.
She danced with fairylike steps.

ing and **ed:**

He is laughing now. He laughed at the joke.
Laughing is better than crying.
I am buttering my bread. His has been buttered.
The buttering of a hundred sandwiches kept Mother busy.
Buttered toast is good.
Do you like hunting? The hunted fox ran into his hole.
A forested hill is a hill with a forest on it.
Painting is fun if you can do it well.
A painted face is a face that has paint on it or a face that has been painted.
A curtained window is one that has curtains.
A frosted window is one that has frost or has been frosted.